C0-AEW-588

DICTIONARY OF AMERICAN BIOGRAPHY

The *Dictionary of American Biography* was published originally in twenty volumes. Supplementary volumes were added in 1944 and 1958. This edition of the work combines all twenty-two volumes.

The present Volume I (Abbe–Brazer) contains Volumes I and II of the original edition, but these are now denominated "Part 1" and "Part 2" of the Volume. Volumes II through XI are arranged similarly, the Second Part in each instance representing a volume of the original series. For ease in reference, although the articles follow one another in strict alphabetical order, each Second Part is preceded by a half-title page which relates that Part to its place in the original numbering of the volumes.

The Errata list at the head of Volume I contains corrections of fact and additional data which have come to the attention of the Editors from the first publication of the work up to the present. Minor typographical corrections have been made in many instances directly on the plates.

PUBLISHED UNDER THE AUSPICES OF
THE AMERICAN COUNCIL OF LEARNED SOCIETIES

The American Council of Learned Societies, organized in 1919 for the purpose of advancing the study of the humanities and of the humanistic aspects of the social sciences, is a nonprofit federation comprising forty-five national scholarly groups. The Council represents the humanities in the United States in the International Union of Academies, provides fellowships and grants-in-aid, supports research-and-planning conferences and symposia, and sponsors special projects and scholarly publications.

MEMBER ORGANIZATIONS

AMERICAN PHILOSOPHICAL SOCIETY, 1743
AMERICAN ACADEMY OF ARTS AND SCIENCES, 1780
AMERICAN ANTIQUARIAN SOCIETY, 1812
AMERICAN ORIENTAL SOCIETY, 1842
AMERICAN NUMISMATIC SOCIETY, 1858
AMERICAN PHILOLOGICAL ASSOCIATION, 1869
ARCHAEOLOGICAL INSTITUTE OF AMERICA, 1879
SOCIETY OF BIBLICAL LITERATURE, 1880
MODERN LANGUAGE ASSOCIATION OF AMERICA, 1883
AMERICAN HISTORICAL ASSOCIATION, 1884
AMERICAN ECONOMIC ASSOCIATION, 1885
AMERICAN FOLKLORE SOCIETY, 1888
AMERICAN DIALECT SOCIETY, 1889
AMERICAN PSYCHOLOGICAL ASSOCIATION, 1892
ASSOCIATION OF AMERICAN LAW SCHOOLS, 1900
AMERICAN PHILOSOPHICAL ASSOCIATION, 1901
AMERICAN ANTHROPOLOGICAL ASSOCIATION, 1902
AMERICAN POLITICAL SCIENCE ASSOCIATION, 1903
BIBLIOGRAPHICAL SOCIETY OF AMERICA, 1904
ASSOCIATION OF AMERICAN GEOGRAPHERS, 1904
HISPANIC SOCIETY OF AMERICA, 1904
AMERICAN SOCIOLOGICAL ASSOCIATION, 1905
AMERICAN SOCIETY OF INTERNATIONAL LAW, 1906
ORGANIZATION OF AMERICAN HISTORIANS, 1907
AMERICAN ACADEMY OF RELIGION, 1909
COLLEGE ART ASSOCIATION OF AMERICA, 1912
HISTORY OF SCIENCE SOCIETY, 1924
LINGUISTIC SOCIETY OF AMERICA, 1924
MEDIAEVAL ACADEMY OF AMERICA, 1925
AMERICAN MUSICOLOGICAL SOCIETY, 1934
SOCIETY OF ARCHITECTURAL HISTORIANS, 1940
ECONOMIC HISTORY ASSOCIATION, 1940
ASSOCIATION FOR ASIAN STUDIES, 1941
AMERICAN SOCIETY FOR AESTHETICS, 1942
AMERICAN ASSOCIATION FOR THE ADVANCEMENT OF SLAVIC STUDIES, 1948
METAPHYSICAL SOCIETY OF AMERICA, 1950
AMERICAN STUDIES ASSOCIATION, 1950
RENAISSANCE SOCIETY OF AMERICA, 1954
SOCIETY FOR ETHNOMUSICOLOGY, 1955
AMERICAN SOCIETY FOR LEGAL HISTORY, 1956
AMERICAN SOCIETY FOR THEATRE RESEARCH, 1956
SOCIETY FOR THE HISTORY OF TECHNOLOGY, 1958
AMERICAN COMPARATIVE LITERATURE ASSOCIATION, 1960
AMERICAN SOCIETY FOR EIGHTEENTH-CENTURY STUDIES, 1969
ASSOCIATION FOR JEWISH STUDIES, 1969

DICTIONARY
OF
American Biography

VOLUME III

CUSHMAN-FRASER

Edited by

ALLEN JOHNSON

AND DUMAS MALONE

Charles Scribner's Sons *New York*

Prompted solely by a desire for public service the New York Times Company and its President, Mr. Adolph S. Ochs, have made possible the preparation of the manuscript of the Dictionary of American Biography through a subvention of more than $500,000 and with the understanding that the entire responsibility for the contents of the volumes rests with the American Council of Learned Societies.

Printed in the United States of America

B/C 20

VOLUME III, PART 1

CUSHMAN - EBERLE

(*VOLUME V OF THE ORIGINAL EDITION*)

CROSS REFERENCES FROM THIS VOLUME ARE MADE TO THE VOLUME NUMBERS OF THE ORIGINAL EDITION.

CONTRIBUTORS
VOLUME III, PART 1

Thomas P. Abernethy . . . T. P. A.
LeRoy Abrams . . . . L. R. A.
Adeline Adams . . . . A. A.
James Truslow Adams . . . J. T. A.
Cyrus Adler . . . . C. A.
Carroll S. Alden . . . . . C. S. A.
William H. Allison . . . . W. H. A.
Katharine H. Amend . . . . K. H. A.
John C. Archer . . . . . . J. C. A.
Percy M. Ashburn . . . . . P. M. A.
Frederick W. Ashley . . . F. W. A.
Christina H. Baker . . . . C. H. B.
Charles M. Bakewell . . . C. M. B.
Thomas S. Barclay . . . . . T. S. B.
Howard Barnes . . . . . . H. B.
Claribel R. Barnett . . . . C. R. B.
Ernest Sutherland Bates . E. S. B—s.
William A. Beardsley . . . W. A. B.
Marcus Benjamin . . . . . M. B.
Elbert J. Benton . . . . . E. J. B.
Arthur R. Blessing . . . . A. R. B.
Herbert E. Bolton . . . . H. E. B.
Laetitia Todd Bolton . . . L. T. B.
Milledge L. Bonham, Jr. . . M. L. B., Jr.
Archibald L. Bouton . . . . A. L. B.
Witt Bowden . . . . W. B.
Sarah G. Bowerman . . . . S. G. B.
Claude G. Bowers . . . . . C. G. B.
Benjamin Brawley . . . . . B. B.
Robert P. Brooks . . . . . R. P. B.
Everett S. Brown . . . . . E. S. B—n.
Roberta B. Burnet . . . . R. B. B.
Guy H. Burnham . . . . . . G. H. B.
Isabel M. Calder . . . . . I. M. C.
James M. Callahan . . . . J. M. C.
Robert C. Canby . . . . . R. C. C—y.
Charles F. Carey . . . . . C. F. C—y.
Frank T. Carlton . . . . . F. T. C.
William Glasgow Bruce Carson . . . . W. G. B. C.
Wayland J. Chase . . . . . W. J. C.
Russell H. Chittenden . . . R. H. C.
Robert C. Clark . . . . . . R. C. C—k.
Rudolf A. Clemen . . . . . R. A. C.
Katherine W. Clendinning . K. W. C.
Oral S. Coad . . . . O. S. C.
Charles F. Coan . . . . . . C. F. C—n.
Frederick W. Coburn . . . F. W. C.
R. S. Cotterill . . . . . . R. S. C.
E. Merton Coulter . . . . E. M. C.
Isaac J. Cox . . . . I. J. C.
Edward E. Curtis . . . . . E. E. C.
Robert E. Cushman . . . . R. E. C.
Marion Dargan . . . . . . M. D.
Irwin H. DeLong . . . . . I. H. DeL.
Davis R. Dewey . . . . . . D. R. D.
Charles A. Dinsmore . . . . C. A. D.
Eleanor Robinette Dobson . E. R. D.
William E. Dodd . . . . . . W. E. D.
Charles Wright Dodge . . C. W. D.
Mary Danforth Dodge . . . M. D. D.
Elizabeth Donnan . . . . . E. D.
William Howe Downes . . . W. H. D.
Stella M. Drumm . . . . . S. M. D.
W. E. Burghardt DuBois . . W. E. B. D
Raymond S. Dugan . . . . . R. S. D.
W. F. Durand . . . . W. F. D.
Lionel C. Durel . . . . . . L. C. D.
James H. Easterby . . . . . J. H. E—y.
Walter Prichard Eaton . . W. P. E.
Edwin F. Edgett . . . . . . E. F. E.
J. Harold Ennis . . . . . . J. H. E—s.
Charles R. Erdman, Jr. . . C. R. E., Jr
Marjory Erskine . . . . . M. E.
Ethel Webb Faulkner . . . E. W. F.
Harold U. Faulkner . . . . H. U. F.
Albert B. Faust . . . . . A. B. F.
G. J. Fiebeger . . . . G. J. F.
Byron A. Finney . . . . . . B. A. F.
Harold N. Fowler . . . . . H. N. F.
Early Lee Fox . . . . . . E. L. F.
John H. Frederick . . . . . J. H. F.
Claude M. Fuess . . . . . C. M. F.
George W. Fuller . . . . . G. W. F.
John F. Fulton . . . . . . J. F. F.
Ralph Henry Gabriel . . . R. H. G.
Katharine Jeanne Gallagher . . . . K. J. G.
George Harvey Genzmer . . G. H. G.
W. J. Ghent . . . . W. J. G.
Armistead Churchill Gordon, Jr. . . . . A. C. G., Jr.
Gladys Graham . . . . . . G. G.
Charles B. Gulick . . . . . C. B. G.
J. G. deR. Hamilton . . . . J. G. deR. H.
Talbot Faulkner Hamlin . . T. F. H.
William A. Hamor . . . . . W. A. H.
Ralph V. Harlow . . . . . R. V. H.
Thomas L. Harris . . . . . T. L. H.
Mary Bronson Hartt . . . M. B. H.
George E. Hastings . . . . G. E. H.
Paul L. Haworth . . . . . P. L. H.

Contributors

Fred E. Haynes	F. E. H.
Ellwood Hendrick	E. H.
Frank I. Herriott	F. I. H.
J. D. Hicks	J. D. H.
Homer Carey Hockett	H. C. H.
Jean MacKinnon Holt	J. M. H.
Walter Hough	W. H.
L. O. Howard	L. O. H.
Edgar Erskine Hume	E. E. H.
Asher Isaacs	A. I.
Joseph Jackson	J. J.
Edward H. Jenkins	E. H. J.
Allen Johnson	A. J.
Cecil M. Johnson	C. M. J.
Henry Johnson	H. J.
Herbert Anthony Kellar	H. A. K.
Louise Phelps Kellogg	L. P. K.
Allen Marshall Kline	A. M. K.
James O. Knauss	J. O. K.
Rhea Mansfield Knittle	R. M. K.
H. W. Howard Knott	H. W. H. K.
Ralph S. Kuykendall	R. S. K.
Leonard W. Labaree	L. W. L.
James Melvin Lee	J. M. L.
Frank Grant Lewis	F. G. L.
Charles R. Lingley	C. R. L.
Ella Lonn	E. L.
Lawrence T. Lowrey	L. T. L.
Alexander McAdie	A. M.
Thomas Denton McCormick	T. D. M.
Thomas McCrae	T. M.
P. B. McDonald	P. B. M.
S. S. McKay	S. S. M.
Donald L. McMurry	D. L. M.
Bruce E. Mahan	B. E. M.
Dumas Malone	D. M.
Helen Jo Scott Mann	H. J. S. M.
Frederick H. Martens	F. H. M.
Frank Jewett Mather, Jr.	F. J. M., Jr.
Albert P. Mathews	A. P. M.
David M. Matteson	D. M. M.
William R. Maxon	W. R. M.
Bernard Mayo	B. M—o.
Lawrence S. Mayo	L. S. M.
Newton D. Mereness	N. D. M.
George P. Merrill	G. P. M.
Douglass W. Miller	D. W. M.
Louie M. Miner	L. M. M.
Broadus Mitchell	B. M—l.
Carl W. Mitman	C. W. M.
Frank Monaghan	F. M.
Herbert R. Moody	H. R. M.
Robert E. Moody	R. E. M.
Albert B. Moore	A. B. M.
Samuel E. Morison	S. E. M.
Jarvis M. Morse	J. M. M.
William Bennett Munro	W. B. M.
Charles E. Munroe	C. E. M.
George B. Myers	G. B. M.
Edwin G. Nash	E. G. N.
Allan Nevins	A. N.
Lyman C. Newell	L. C. N.
Jeannette P. Nichols	J. P. N.
Robert Hastings Nichols	R. H. N.
Roy F. Nichols	R. F. N.
Harold J. Noble	H. J. N.
John F. Noll	J. F. N.
Walter B. Norris	W. B. N.
Clara D. Noyes	C. D. N.
Grace Lee Nute	G. L. N.
Frank M. O'Brien	F. M. O'B.
Mildred B. Palmer	M. B. P.
Victor H. Paltsits	V. H. P.
John C. Parish	J. C. P.
Fred Lewis Pattee	F. L. P—e.
Charles O. Paullin	C. O. P.
Frederic Logan Paxson	F. L. P—n.
Robert E. Peabody	R. E. P.
C. C. Pearson	C. C. P.
Donald C. Peattie	D. C. P.
Epaphroditus Peck	E. P—k.
Frederick T. Persons	F. T. P.
A. Everett Peterson	A. E. P.
James M. Phalen	J. M. P.
Francis S. Philbrick	F. S. P.
David Philipson	D. P.
Paul Chrisler Phillips	P. C. P.
John E. Pomfret	J. E. P.
Julius W. Pratt	J. W. P.
Edward Preble	E. P—e.
Walter Prichard	W. P.
Herbert I. Priestley	H. I. P.
Richard J. Purcell	R. J. P.
Arthur H. Quinn	A. H. Q.
James G. Randall	J. G. R.
Belle Rankin	B. R.
P. O. Ray	P. O. R.
Ruth Redfield	R. R.
Thomas C. Richards	T. C. R.
Franklin L. Riley	F. L. R.
Henry Morton Robinson	H. M. R.
William A. Robinson	W. A. R.
J. Magnus Rohne	J. M. R.
J. J. Rolbiecki	J. J. R.
Carl P. Rollins	C. P. R.
Frank Edward Ross	F. E. R.
Edwin Ryan	E. R.
Joseph Schafer	J. S—r.
Jay Frank Schamberg	J. F. S.
Herbert W. Schneider	H. W. S.
Don C. Seitz	D. C. S.
Benjamin F. Shambaugh	B. F. S.
Muriel Shaver	M. S.
William B. Shaw	W. B. S.
Lester Burrell Shippee	L. B. S.
George N. Shuster	G. N. S.

Contributors

Wilbur H. Siebert . . . . . W. H. S.
Sarah H. J. Simpson . . . . S. H. J. S.
David Eugene Smith . . . . D. E. S.
Edgar Fahs Smith . . . . . E. F. S.
Walter M. Smith . . . . . W. M. S.
Charles L. Souvay . . . . . C. L. S.
Thomas M. Spaulding . . . T. M. S.
Charles Worthen Spencer . C. W. S.
Harris Elwood Starr . . . H. E. S.
Martha T. Stephenson . . . M. T. S.
Nathaniel Wright Stephenson . . . . N. W. S.
Wayne E. Stevens . . . . . W. E. S.
George R. Stewart, Jr. . . G. R. S., Jr.
Anson Phelps Stokes . . . A. P. S.
James Sullivan . . . . . . J. S—n.
Alfred H. Sweet . . . . . A. H. S.
William Warren Sweet . . W. W. S.
Fletcher Harper Swift . . F. H. S.
Henry P. Talbot . . . . . H. P. T.
Edwin P. Tanner . . . . . E. P. T.
Frank A. Taylor . . . . . F. A. T.
David Y. Thomas . . . . . D. Y. T.
Holland Thompson . . . . H. T.
Harrison A. Trexler . . . H. A. T.
Roland G. Usher . . . . . R. G. U.
William T. Utter . . . . . W. T. U—r.
Mark Van Doren . . . . . M. V-D.
Arnold J. F. van Laer . . . A. J. F. v-L.
Henry R. Viets . . . . . . H. R. V.
John D. Wade . . . . J. D. W.
W. Randall Waterman . . . W. R. W.
Walter A. Wells . . . . . W. A. W.
Abdel Ross Wentz . . . . . A. R. W.
Thomas Jefferson Wertenbaker . . . . T. J. W.
Allan Westcott . . . . . . A. W.
George F. Whicher . . . . G. F. W.
W. L. Whittlesey . . . . . W. L. W—y.
James F. Willard . . . . . J. F. W.
Paul Wilstach . . . . . . P. W.
John Garrett Winter . . . J. G. W.
Thomas Woody . . . . . . T. W.
Ernest H. Wright . . . . . E. H. W.
Herbert Francis Wright . . H. F. W.
Walter L. Wright, Jr. . . . W. L. W—t., Jr.
James Ingersoll Wyer . . . J. I. W.
Edna Yost . . . . E. Y.

DICTIONARY OF
AMERICAN BIOGRAPHY

Cushman — Eberle

CUSHMAN, CHARLOTTE SAUNDERS (July 23, 1816–Feb. 17, 1876), actress, was born in Boston. Her father, Elkanah Cushman, merchant, was a direct descendant of Robert Cushman [*q.v.*] of the Leyden congregation, agent of the Pilgrims in their negotiations with the Adventurers. Her mother was Mary Eliza Babbitt of Sturbridge (now Southbridge), Mass. The Babbitts were gifted musically. Forced by her father's death to earn a living, Charlotte studied for the operatic stage, and joined the company of Clara Fisher (Mrs. Maeder) in Boston and made her début on Apr. 8, 1835, at the Tremont Theatre, Boston, as Countess Almaviva in *The Marriage of Figaro.* She then secured an engagement to sing in New Orleans. Here her voice, a natural contralto, is said to have broken down by being forced by Mr. Maeder into the soprano register, but Mrs. Maeder denied this, saying Charlotte disliked the toil of vocal practise and was "stage struck." At any rate, in New Orleans she switched from the operatic to the dramatic stage, received some instruction from J. H. Barton, a visiting English actor, and on the night of his benefit, at the age of nineteen, appeared as Lady Macbeth. Encouraged by a local success she came North and secured an engagement at the Bowery Theatre, which promptly burned down, destroying her wardrobe. As she had brought her mother and young sister and brother from Boston, she went to Albany to find work while the theatre was being rebuilt, and there was described as "tall, thin and lanky." But she was socially as well as artistically successful, and prospered. Here she acted Romeo for the first time, and many other parts, including the eternal Belvidera in *Venice Preserved.* On May 8, 1837, under the management of James H. Hackett in New York, she first appeared in one of her most famous impersonations, Meg Merrilies, in *Guy Mannering* (Winter, *The Wallet of Time,* I, 163). It was not at first greatly acclaimed. She joined the Park Company in New York in the fall of 1837, where she made a hit as Nancy Sykes in *Oliver Twist,* another of her famous rôles. From 1842 to 1844 she was stage manager of the Walnut Street Theatre, Philadelphia. Here George Vandenhoff acted with her and records (*Leaves from an Actor's Note-Book,* 1860, pp. 194 ff.) that she then displayed "a rude, strong, uncultivated talent; it was not till after she had seen and acted with Macready,—which she did the next season,—that she really brought artistic study and finish to her performances. . . . Her greatest part, fearfully natural, dreadfully intense, horribly real, was Nancy Sykes; it was too true; it was painful. . . ."

The engagement with Macready, at his request, not only brought her quick mind in contact with a person from whom she could learn, but filled her with an ambition to act in London. Accordingly she made the plunge—the second American actress to do so—and on Feb. 14, 1845, acted Bianca in *Fazio* at the Princess Theatre, London, in support of Edwin Forrest. Her success was decisive. She added, among other rôles, Lady Macbeth and Rosalind. In December 1845, with her sister Susan [*q.v.*] as Juliet, she acted Romeo. Sheridan Knowles likened her Romeo to Kean's Othello, and described the scene with the Friar as one "of topmost passion; not simulated passion—no such thing; real, palpably real . . . my blood ran hot and cold." She remained in England till 1849, and added during this time perhaps her greatest rôle, Queen Katherine. From 1849 to 1852 she toured America, and, with the prestige of her London success and her added skill, was proclaimed without dispute the leading actress of our stage. Then, and later, she acted not only female rôles, but those of Romeo, Wolsey, Hamlet, and Claude Melnotte. By 1852 she had achieved not only fame but a fortune, and announced her retirement from the stage. Till 1857 she lived in England, acting however more or less frequently. In 1857 she returned to America and appeared as Cardinal Wolsey at Burton's Theatre, New York, and in 1858 gave a series of "farewell performances." She then retired to Rome to live. Two years later she was back. Another year, and she gave a farewell performance in New Haven, and returned to Rome, where she remained for the greater part of the next decade, only returning to America in 1865 to give a series of performances which netted $8,267 for the United States Sanitary Commission. In 1870 she came back to America, and devoted the rest of her life chiefly to public readings of famous plays. She made a good many stage appearances, however, a famous engagement being that at Booth's Theatre in October and November 1874, when she acted Queen Katherine, Lady Macbeth, and Meg Merrilies, three of her greatest parts. This was actually her farewell, so far as New York was concerned, and after the concluding performance of *Macbeth* Richard Henry Stoddard read an ode, and William Cullen Bryant made a speech and presented her with a laurel crown. Her farewell appearance in her native Boston was on May 15, 1875, and her last on any stage at Easton, Pa., June 2, 1875. She died in Boston, Feb. 17, 1876. The immediate cause was pneumonia, but her constitution had long been undermined by cancer. She was buried in Mount Auburn Cemetery, Cambridge.

There can be little doubt that Charlotte Cushman was the most powerful actress America has produced. The contemporary records, over a long period of years, pay almost unvarying tribute to the vividness and moving quality of her effects. She was tall, strong-framed, deep-voiced, almost masculine in some respects, without feminine beauty certainly, and totally unable to conquer audiences by "sex appeal." She had to conquer by the keenness of her intellect in shaping a part, the depth of the feeling expressed, and the vividness and power of execution. That she did so conquer, over a period of forty years, is attested by numerous records. Among the most vivid is William Winter's description of her Queen Katherine (*Other Days*, pp. 155 ff.), when he actually shrank back to the rear of the box from the blaze of her eyes. "Whenever," he says, "the occasion arrived for liberated power, passionate feeling, poetic significance, dramatic effect, she rose to that occasion and made it superb." Again he speaks of her Meg Merrilies, and says: "Her voice . . . had in it an unearthly music that made the nerves thrill and the brain tremble." As cool an Englishman as Henry Morley (*Journal of a London Playgoer*, 1866, p. 80) says: "Miss Cushman's melodramatic Meg Merrilies has quite as indisputably the attributes of genius about it as any piece of poetry or tragedy could have. Such is her power over the intention and feeling of the part that the mere words of it become a secondary matter." Dissenting voices were largely confined to those who (like Vandenhoff) objected to her male impersonations, chiefly on the ground that even she could not make them quite convincing. She never married. Her celibate life, her long suffering from cancer, and the energy with which she attacked the great melodramatic or tragic rôles in which she excelled, all conspired, probably, to bring about periods of depression when she felt she could act no more. This accounts for her frequent farewells and reappearances, for which she was much blamed. Like a good many other energetic and keen-minded spinsters of her New England heritage, she was somewhat masculine in appearance and dominating in personality, but deeply fond of children and full of kind deeds. The Cushman School in Boston was named after her, greatly to her delight. Her style of acting was formed, of course, on the great tradition of Garrick and Kean; it belonged to the age of huge auditoriums, rhetorical drama, and large sweeping effects. She was not a pioneer in modern naturalism like Charles Matthews in England, and Jefferson in America. Nor did she seek to develop a native drama. She belonged to the royal line. She brought to our stage, however, not only striking genius, but strong, irreproachable character, a certain social prestige belonging to her ancestry, and a powerful stimulant to all of her sex who sought a wider chance for expression in the arts and in life. She was one of the great American women of the mid-nineteenth century, and so recognized in her own lifetime. The fact that she left behind a fortune of over half a million dollars did nothing in American eyes to lessen her prestige. Such another dominating figure on our stage is hardly likely to arise until the reign of naturalistic drama is ended.

[Emma Stebbins, *Charlotte Cushman; Her Letters and Memories of her Life* (1878); Wm. Winter, *Other Days* (1908) and *The Wallet of Time* (1909–13); H. P. Phelps, *Players of a Century* (1880); B. Matthews and L. Hutton, *Actors and Actresses of Gt. Brit. and the U. S.* (1886); H. W. Cushman, *A Hist. and Biog. Geneal. of the Cushmans* (1855).] W.P.E.

CUSHMAN, GEORGE HEWITT (June 5, 1814–Aug. 3, 1876), miniature painter and engraver, was a native of Windham, Conn., the son of John H. Cushman and Pamela Webb. Early in his life he desired to be a soldier, but was prevented from entering West Point by a change in family fortunes, and turned his attention to cultivating his natural talent for drawing and painting. After studying drawing under Washington Allston (Baker, *post*), he learned line-engraving with Asaph Willard of Hartford, Conn. He also studied with Seth and John Cheney [*qq.v.*], the latter the distinguished line-engraver with whom he later shared a studio in Boston. In 1843 his name first appeared in the Philadelphia Directory, and for the next two decades he was a resident of that city, being described in the Directory as miniature painter and subsequently as portrait painter. Although regarded as one of the best miniature painters in America in his time, and second only to Malbone, Cushman preferred to follow his art without making any bid for fame, painting chiefly for his friends. He never exhibited his charming miniatures although he did sign his engravings, which were "executed with much taste and ability" (*Ibid.*). He engraved, after designs by F. O. C. Darley [*q.v.*], many of the plates for the thirty-four volume edition of Cooper's novels (1859–61) and for the Household Edition of Dickens (1861); plates for Frances S. Osgood's *Poems* (1850), and the portraits of Forrest in Alger's *Life of Edwin Forrest* (1877). He also engraved, *inter alia*, a portrait of Lord Byron, after Phillips, and "Young America in the Alps," after G. P. A. Healy. But though he made many plates for books, as an engraver he was concerned chiefly with notes for the state banks. The passage of the National Banking Act and the opening of the Bureau of Engraving and Printing at Washington caused him to retire from this work. In 1862 he removed to New York City, and resided there until his death, devoting most of his time after leaving Philadelphia to miniature painting. His miniatures have a delicacy and charm that would have won for him great fame, but he never would exhibit his work in public shows. His general reticence so far as his art was concerned is accounted for by one who knew him (French, *post*, p. 87) as having been due to a sense of modesty which "was so extreme that it became a defect." He underestimated his own genius, which was genuine, and which, pursued with ambition and determination, would have placed him at the head of American miniature painters of his period. Mrs. Lippincott (Grace Greenwood), quoted by French (*Ibid.*, p. 86), remarked of Cushman's miniatures that they "were always remarkable for purity and simplicity of character as well as tone." His portrait of himself is reproduced in Anne Hollingsworth Wharton's *Heirlooms in Miniatures* (1898, p. 212). During the latter years of his life he suffered from a painful malady which curbed his ambition as well as his physical energy. He died at a water cure at Jersey City Heights, N. J., and was buried in South Laurel Hill Cemetery, Philadelphia. In 1849 he had married Susan Wetherill, granddaughter of Samuel Wetherill, the "Free Quaker" introduced into S. Weir Mitchell's romance, *Hugh Wynne*, and his funeral was held at the old Wetherill mansion, "Chalkley Hall," Frankford, Philadelphia. The only time his miniatures were publicly exhibited was in 1893 when in the Retrospective Exhibit at the Columbian Exposition in Chicago, a group of them was given the central position. Several examples of his engraving were shown in the exhibition of the works of one hundred notable American engravers, held in the New York Public Library in 1928.

[For many of the dates and particulars, Miss Ida Cushman, a daughter of the artist, has been the authority. See also H. W. French, *Art and Artists in Conn.* (1879), pp. 85–87; W. S. Baker, *Am. Engravers and Their Works* (1875); D. M. Stauffer, *Am. Engravers upon Copper and Steel* (1907). Baker and Stauffer give different birthplaces, and neither notes any work by Cushman.] J. J.

CUSHMAN, JOSHUA (Apr. 11, 1761–Jan. 27, 1834), Congregational clergyman, congressman from Massachusetts and Maine, was the son of Abner and Mary (Tillson) Cushman of Halifax, Mass., and a descendant in the sixth generation of Robert Cushman [*q.v.*], agent of the Pilgrims in England. Nothing is known of his own early life until the time of his enlistment in the 9th Regiment of the Massachusetts line, Apr. 1, 1777. He saw service at Fort Stanwix and Saratoga, wintered at Valley Forge, and later accompanied Washington's army through the Jerseys to White Plains, N. Y. His honorable discharge came in March 1780, after he had served under Gen. Gates at Fishkill and near West Point. He entered Harvard in 1783, but, owing to his inability to meet the bills of his final quarter, he did not receive the degree of A.B. until 1791. Meanwhile he had studied theology under Rev. Ephraim Briggs, and was approved as a candidate for the ministry by the Worcester Association in January 1789. He was ordained religious teacher of Winslow in the District of Maine in 1795. The liberal covenant which Cushman drew up for the church at Winslow is notable for its lack of insistence upon the sacrament of the Lord's Supper. In 1814, by reason of reduced numbers and financial difficulties brought on by the war, his agreement with the town was terminated. It seems entirely probable that his liberal ideas had also caused some discontent. He represented Kennebec County in the Massachusetts Senate in 1810, and the Town of Winslow in the House in 1811 and 1812. He was elected to the national House of Representatives in the fall of 1818. Though an earnest advocate of the separation of Maine from Massachusetts, he, with three other representatives from Maine, hostile to slavery, voted against Clay's compromise, which admitted Missouri and Maine to the Union at the same time. Later, with them, he defended his action in a pamphlet (M. Kingsley and others, *An Address to the People of Maine,* 1820). After the organization of the state of Maine, he served in the Seventeenth and the Eighteenth Congresses as one of its representatives. He was a state senator in 1828, and representative in 1833. As the senior member of the House he presided over its organization early in January 1834. Later in the same month he died at Augusta, where he lies buried in the state tomb. His sermons show him to have been devout and very liberal in his religious views. A clear thinker and an accomplished speaker, he was much in demand as an orator on public occasions; his printed and manuscript orations are good examples of the grandiloquent oratory of the times. In politics he was a supporter of Jefferson, and later of Jackson. His sympathies with struggling debtors, numerous in his own state, led him to speak in Congress in March 1822 in favor of the Bankrupt Bill. He was a strong advocate of Revolutionary pensions, the benefits of which he himself shared in the last years of his life. He married Lucy, the daughter of Peter and Aurah (Tufts) Jones of Medford, Mass., Sept. 13, 1802.

[H. W. Cushman, *A Hist. and Biog. Geneal. of the Cushmans* (1855), pp. 184–99. *Centennial Hist. of Waterville* (1902), pp. 556–61; the Cushman MSS. in the possession of Mr. F. H. Cushman of Winslow. The date of Cushman's birth is taken from the manuscript Harvard College Faculty Records, V, 124. A brief list of his printed sermons and orations is in Jos. Williamson, *A Bibliography of the State of Me.* (2 vols., 1896), I, 336.] R. E. M.

CUSHMAN, PAULINE (June 10, 1833–Dec. 2, 1893), Union spy, actress, the daughter of a Spanish political refugee and a Frenchwoman, was born in New Orleans. In time her father took his large family to Grand Rapids, Mich., where he became a trader. The education of his only daughter was necessarily scanty but it gave her the hardiness to travel to New York in her eighteenth year to earn her own living. She was recruited there by the manager of the New Orleans *Varieties* for his show and soon after her arrival in the South was married to Charles Dickinson, another stage performer. Dickinson enlisted as a musician in the Northern army during the Civil War, and died in the winter of 1862 of dysentery. In March of the following year, she was playing in *The Seven Sisters* at Wood's Theatre in Louisville. At a certain point in the performance she was called on to drink a toast and was urged by certain Southern sympathizers to toast the Southern cause. Making this public avowal of sympathy on the advice of the provost-marshal, she was dismissed from the theatre. She then took an oath of allegiance to the Federal government and was commissioned as secret agent. A supposed rebel, she was subsequently expelled from Nashville, with instructions to penetrate as far South as possible, and to collect all the military information she could, but under no condition to carry notes or plans. Unfortunately, her opportunities to obtain military maps were so great that she violated her instructions. Her uneasy knowledge of the possession of these materials caused her to make an incriminating effort to escape when detained not far from Bragg's headquarters at Tullahoma, Tenn. The papers being discovered, she was tried by a military court and sentenced to be hanged in ten days. Anxiety over her position, added to the strain of her hard journeys, brought on a temporary physical collapse. Removed from the military jail to more comfortable quarters at Shelbyville, Tenn., she was left behind when the Confederates hastily retreated from that place in June 1863. She was able to give the advancing army of Rosecrans much valuable information, but had become so well-known that further spying was impossible.

Sent North, she was treated with great acclaim, fêted as "the spy of the Cumberland," and commended by Lincoln for her services. She returned to the stage, and traveled far and wide, lecturing in a Federal uniform. Her last years were not happy. She was married in 1872 to August Fichtner, who died before many years. Her unhappy marriage to Jerry Fryer in 1879 ended in separation. Her children all died in early childhood, and as she grew older her efforts to make a living by lecturing and sewing were ineffectual. She committed suicide in San Francisco, where the G. A. R., in acknowledgment of her services, gave her a semi-military funeral and burial in their plot.

[F. L. Sarmiento, *Life of Pauline Cushman* (1865), which has some marks of the work of a press-agent, was evidently copied by Frank Moore, *Women of the War* (1866). The War Dept. records, however, and those in the Pension Office, filed as W. C. 362644, bear out the story. See also *San Francisco Call,* Dec. 3, 4,

5, 6, 7, 1893, and *San Francisco Chronicle,* Dec. 3, 4, 5, 7, 1893.] K. H. A.

CUSHMAN, ROBERT (*c.* 1579–1625), one of the organizers of the Pilgrim emigration to America, was born at Canterbury. He married in England, where in 1608 his son Thomas was born, went to Holland about 1609, and at once joined the Pilgrim church at Leyden. He seems to have had some means for, though he earned his living as a wool-comber, he bought two houses there. His wife, Sarah, died in 1616 and he married in June 1617, Mary, widow of Thomas Singleton, herself from Sandwich. In 1617 he went to England with John Carver to seek a patent for the prospective emigrants, and was again in England with Elder Brewster when the first patent was obtained. He and Carver made the financial arrangements with the English merchants which were accepted by the Pilgrims at Leyden in 1620, and organized the group which sailed direct from England on the *Mayflower.* Probably he was responsible for the proposed alterations in the agreement which were rejected by the Pilgrims at Southampton. The resultant quarrel is perhaps the real explanation of Cushman's failure to emigrate to America. Sailing as commander of the *Speedwell,* he and his family remained ashore after that ship put back, though he served as agent of the Pilgrims in England for the rest of his life. On the return of the *Mayflower* in the summer of 1621, Cushman published a pamphlet entitled, *Of the State of the Colony* [of New Plymouth] *and the need of the Public Spirit in the Colonists.* He was instrumental in sending out the *Fortune* with a second contingent of colonists in July 1621, sailing on it himself with his only son, Thomas. He brought with him the agreement with the merchants which the Pilgrims had rejected at Southampton and to which they now consented, an act which they ever after regretted with all their hearts. At Plymouth, though not a minister, he delivered a sermon which was published in London in 1622, the first American religious discourse published anywhere. Leaving his son behind with Bradford, he returned to England on the *Fortune,* Dec. 13, having been in this country only three weeks. He never returned. In 1622 he published a tract entitled, *Reasons and Considerations Touching the Lawfulness of Removing out of England into the Parts of America.* In 1623, he obtained with Edward Winslow a grant of land on Cape Ann, which the Pilgrims long used as a fishing station and which was of great consequence in establishing the economic independence of Plymouth. Cushman died in England in 1625. His son lived his life at Plymouth, dying there in 1691.

[The chief authority is Wm. Bradford, *Hist. of Plimmoth Plantation* (2 vols., 1912). See also H. M. and M. Dexter, *England and Holland of the Pilgrims* (1905); W. H. Burgess, *The Pastor of the Pilgrims: A Biog. of John Robinson* (1920); R. G. Usher, *The Pilgrims and their Hist.* (1918); and H. W. Cushman, *A Hist. and Biog. Genealogy of the Cushmans* (1855). Robert Cushman's tracts are reprinted in Alexander Young, *Chronicles of the Pilgrim Fathers* (1841), and in various facsimile editions.] R. G. U.

CUSHMAN, SUSAN WEBB (Mar. 17, 1822–May 10, 1859), actress, was born in Boston, the daughter of Elkanah Cushman and Mary Eliza Babbitt, and a younger sister of Charlotte Cushman [*q.v.*]. She remained a younger sister all her professional life, under the protection, and the shadow, of the maternal but mighty Charlotte. She and her mother accompanied the elder sister to New York and Albany in 1836, when Charlotte was getting her feet on the professional ladder, and a year later she made her own début as Laura in Epes Sargent's play, *The Genoese.* She was then only fifteen, but in those days the child actor was more admired than at present and her success was considerable. It is recorded (H. W. Cushman, *A Historical and Biographical Genealogy of the Cushmans,* 1855, p. 511), that she was married, Mar. 14, 1836, to Nelson M. Meriman, in Boston, and that she was left destitute by him, with an infant, and took up acting at her sister's advice, as a means of livelihood. Later she acted Grace Harkaway to Charlotte's Lady Gay Spanker, both in New York and Philadelphia, probably in 1841 or 1842, was acclaimed in *Satan in Paris,* and appeared as Desdemona to the Othello of George Vandenhoff, a man of culture and not apparently much given to over-heated eulogies. He later wrote an autobiographical book, called *Leaves from an Actor's Note-Book,* which contains many criticisms of elder players, valuable to-day for their evident cool-headedness and penetration. Among others is one of Susan Cushman, as well as many of her greater sister. In 1842 Charlotte was stage manager of the Walnut Street Theatre, Philadelphia, and Susan was also a member of the company. Vandenhoff gave six performances with them, receiving $180 as his share for the six nights. "Susan," he wrote, "was a pretty creature, but had not a spark of Charlotte's genius; she pleased 'the fellows,' however, and was the best walking-lady on the American stage. (Walking-ladies, madam, are not pedestrians, necessarily; it is the English term for what they call on the French stage, *ingénues;* young ladies of no particular strength of character, whose business is to look pretty, to dress prettily, and to speak prettily; charmingly innocent, and deliciously insipid.)"

In 1845, Charlotte went to England to seek acclaim there, hoping thus to better her position at home, and took Susan with her. She had already played Romeo in America, and now studied the play again with Susan as Juliet, and the two sisters presented this tragedy to London, at the Haymarket, Dec. 30, 1845. They insisted on using the original version, not the theatre prompt copy, and for so doing the vexed company called them "American Indians." The play ran eighty nights in London, and was then taken on a tour of England, with success. Miss Stebbins says that Charlotte chose this play, to effect her sister's début, so that her sister could have the right support, but the statement is a trifle naïve. Charlotte was a good showman, and she also enjoyed assuming masculine rôles. In the numerous reviews of this production, most of the comment is concerned with Charlotte's Romeo, but several critics spoke pleasantly of "the grace and delicacy" of Susan's acting, and Sheridan Knowles, amid his raptures over Charlotte's Romeo, found breath to speak of the first scene as "admirably personated by her beautiful sister." The sisters also played *Twelfth Night* together. A further record of Susan's theatrical career in England is found in the *Autobiography* of Anna Cora Mowatt (pp. 273 ff.). In 1848 Mrs. Mowatt was to appear in London in *The Lady of Lyons,* and Susan Cushman was engaged for Helen. She did not appear at the first rehearsal, and the manager was furious. He persuaded another actress to try the role, but as the next rehearsal was about to begin, in walked Susan. It was now her turn to be furious. "An angry scene ensued," wrote Mrs. Mowatt, "such as I never before, and I rejoice to say never after, witnessed in a theatre." But Susan lost in the encounter, and was forced to leave the house. Her sister would have surely remained. Later that same year, Susan married Dr. James Sheridan Muspratt, "a distinguished chemist and author" of Liverpool, and retired from the stage. She died in Liverpool, May 10, 1859.

[Emma Stebbins, *Charlotte Cushman: Her Letters and Memories of her Life* (1878); Geo. Vandenhoff, *Leaves from an Actor's Note-Book* (1860); Anna Cora Mowatt, *Autobiography of an Actress* (1859).]

W. P. E.

CUSHNY, ARTHUR ROBERTSON (Mar. 6, 1866–Feb. 25, 1926), physician, the son of the Rev. John Cushny of Speymouth, Scotland, by his wife, Catherine Ogilvie Brown, was born at Fochabers (Morayshire). After attending a rural school there he went to the University of Aberdeen, where he received the degree of M.A. in 1886. He then took up the study of medicine at Marischal College, Aberdeen, from which he graduated in 1889 with highest honors, taking the degrees of M.B. and C.M., and M.D. in 1892. While Cushny was at Aberdeen, J. T. Cash, the physiologist, aroused his interest in the physiological action of drugs, and in order to enlarge his experience in this field, he went to study on the Continent, spending a year in the laboratory of Oswald Schmiedeberg at Strassburg, and several months with Hugo Kronecker, the physiologist of Berne, from whom he learned the elements of physiological technique. He remained abroad until 1893 when, at the instigation of Prof. J. J. Abel, he accepted the chair of pharmacology which the latter had just resigned at the University of Michigan. Though only twenty-seven years of age, he rapidly made a place for himself at Michigan. In addition to bearing heavy responsibilities as a teacher, he was active in research and also found time in 1899 to prepare his *Text-Book of Pharmacology and Therapeutics,* a well-written work which has held the field in English almost without a rival for thirty years, a posthumous edition (the ninth) having been brought out in 1928.

Cushny's contributions to pharmacology were outstanding. He carried out, with modern technique, the first experimental analysis of the action of digitalis on warm-blooded animals, and was thus able to explain its effects and to increase considerably the therapeutic uses of this valuable drug. His first paper appeared in 1897 (*Journal of Experimental Medicine*), and his later observations were summarized in 1925 in a monograph, *The Action and Uses in Medicine of Digitalis and Its Allies.* Cushny was the first to recognize the similarity between clinical and experimental auricular fibrillation. His interest in the physiological action of optical isomers, which extended over many years, also culminated in a monograph, which was published posthumously, *The Biological Relation of Optically Isometric Substances* (1926). He took up the subject of the mechanism of kidney secretion about 1900, and between 1901 and 1904 contributed to it a series of three important papers published in the *Journal of Physiology.* In 1917 he advanced what was termed the "modern theory" of kidney-secretion in a separate monograph, *The Secretion of Urine,* a second edition of which prepared by himself was brought out a few months after his death. In this work he put aside the theories which assigned to the kidneys special vital activities inexplicable in physical terms, and added support to the view, now widely accepted, that the chief structures of the kidney, the glomeruli, are in reality simple filters, and that substances useful to the body are re-absorbed during the passage of the filtrate through the urinary tubules, the waste products being thus allowed to escape.

Cushney stayed at Ann Arbor until 1905, when he accepted the chair of pharmacology at University College, London. There he remained until 1918 when he received a call from Edinburgh to succeed Sir Thomas Fraser. To each of the three chairs which he occupied he brought prestige and dignity. On his removal to Scotland he secured an historic manor house near Edinburgh, the "Dumbiedykes" of the *Heart of Midlothian,* where he was able to withdraw somewhat from public life and to entertain the many students and physicians which an international reputation and a kindly disposition had brought to him in increasing numbers. He was an ardent horticulturist, and his pleasure in his garden grew with advancing years. He died suddenly of an apoplectic stroke at his home. In 1896 he had married Sarah Firbank, an Englishwoman whom he had met abroad.

[H. H. Dale, in *Proc. Royal Soc. of London* (1926), 100B, pp. xix–xxvii; *The Times* (London), Feb. 26, 1926; *Nature,* 1926, pp. 117, 387; *Lancet* (London), 1926, I, 519–20; *Brit. Med. Jour.,* 1926, I, 455–57; *Glasgow Herald,* Feb. 26, 1926; *Edinburgh Weekly Scotsman,* Mar. 6, 1926; private information.]

J. F. F.

CUSTER, GEORGE ARMSTRONG (Dec. 5, 1839–June 25, 1876), soldier, was born in New Rumley, Harrison County, Ohio, the son of Emmanuel H. and Maria (Ward) Custer. His paternal great-grandfather was a Hessian officer named Küster, who after surrendering with Burgoyne settled in Pennsylvania, later moving to Maryland. His father was a farmer and blacksmith. Both parents are praised by Custer, in a letter written in after years, as noble, devoted, and self-sacrificing. The boy attended the local schools until he was about ten, and after that until his seventeenth year divided his time between his parents' home and that of his married half-sister, Lydia Reed, at Monroe, Mich. His ambition from early childhood was to be a soldier. From New Rumley, in the summer of 1857, appointed by the local representative in Congress, he went to West Point. Though a rapid reader, with a quick apprehension and good memory, he was a negligent student; he was, moreover, mischievous and given to pranks—a "big jolly boy," as Gen. Morris Schaff characterized him—and he graduated (June 24, 1861) at the foot of a class of thirty-four. A few days later, on the charge of failing, while officer of the guard, to stop a fist-fight between two cadets, he was court-martialed and found guilty. At Washington, however, the proceedings were pigeon-holed, and he was ordered to report for duty.

As a second lieutenant assigned to the 2nd Cavalry, he reached Bull Run on the morning of the battle. Afterward he served in the defense movements about Washington until October, when he was sent home on sick leave. Returning in February 1862, he was transferred to the 5th Cavalry. He came to the notice of McClellan in the Peninsular campaign, and on June 5 was appointed one of his aides, with the rank of captain of volunteers, but with McClellan's retirement his rank lapsed to that of first lieutenant of the regular army, to which he had been promoted on July 17. Pleasanton, head of Hooker's newly formed Cavalry Corps, saw in him the makings of a cavalry leader, and for gallant conduct at Aldie, June 16, 1863, recommended him for a brigadier-generalship and organized for him a brigade of Michigan regiments. Appointed on June 29, Custer served with distinction through the Gettysburg and Virginia campaigns. Conspicuous in figure and attire and noted for the energy and dash of his operations and their almost unvarying success, he became by the end of the year one of the most celebrated commanders at the front. During the winter he returned to Monroe, where on Feb. 9, 1864, he married his boyhood sweetheart, Elizabeth, the daughter of Judge Daniel S. Bacon. He found favor with Sheridan on the opening of the campaigns of 1864 and became in time his most trusted lieutenant. On May 8 he was made a captain in the regular service; the fight at Yellow Tavern, May 11, brought him the brevet of lieutenant-colonel, and Winchester, Sept. 19, that of colonel. The Shenandoah campaign added greatly to his laurels. On Oct. 2 he was placed at the head of the 3rd Division of the Cavalry Corps, and on Oct. 19 was brevetted major-general of volunteers. But it was in the pursuit of Lee's army from Richmond in April 1865 that he won his greatest glory. His division held the van, and day and night, with little pause for rest or food, it kept relentlessly at its task, striking here and there, crumpling up the lines of defense and capturing prisoners, wagons, and guns until on the morning of Apr. 9 it threw itself across Gordon's front and made further resistance useless. It was to Custer that the Confederate flag of truce, a crash towel, was brought, and it was to him that it afterward came as a present from Sheridan, along with the present to his wife of the small table on which Grant had written the terms of surrender. "I know of no one," wrote Sheridan,

Custer

"whose efforts have contributed more to this happy result than those of Custer." Two more honorary promotions were to come to Custer—brevets of brigadier-general and of major-general of the regular army, both dated back to Mar. 13. On Apr. 15 he was made a major-general of volunteers.

After the Grand Review he was sent to the Southwest, where Sheridan had preceded him, and on Feb. 1, 1866, he was mustered out of the volunteer service. The disbandment of the volunteer army stripped him of his honorary rank and left him a mere captain in the 5th Cavalry. He applied for a year's leave of absence and with a strong recommendation from Grant offered his services to the Mexican Army of Liberation. President Johnson, however, refused the request for a leave and instead ordered him to accompany the presidential party in its famous "swing around the circle." On July 28 the organization of the 7th Cavalry was authorized, and Custer was assigned to it with the rank of lieutenant-colonel. Early in the following year he joined his regiment at Fort Riley, Kan., and as its first colonel never joined it, and its second did not assume command until after the battle of the Little Big Horn, he remained its active commander until his death. He took an active part in the muddled Indian campaign of 1867 under Hancock and for its failure was made a scapegoat. On charges of deliberate absence from duty he was court-martialed and sentenced to a year's suspension from the army. Sheridan, who succeeded Hancock, recalled Custer to his regiment in the fall of 1868, and on Nov. 27 he won a brilliant victory over Black Kettle's band of Cheyennes, in the battle of the Washita. After two years more of campaigning on the plains the regiment was broken up and scattered at various garrison points, but early in 1873 was reunited at Fort Rice, in the present North Dakota. He took part in Stanley's Yellowstone expedition of that year and on its return was assigned to the command of the newly established Fort Abraham Lincoln, across the river from Bismarck. In the following summer on orders from the War Department, he led through the Black Hills an exploring expedition of 1,200 men—an event which resulted in the discovery of gold and contributed in some measure to the Sioux War a year and a half later.

He was to have commanded the expedition ordered to set out early in 1876 to cooperate with the columns of Crook and Gibbon in rounding up the hostile Sioux and Cheyennes. In the middle of March, however, he was summonsed to Washington to testify before a Congressional committee regarding frauds in the Indian service. His testimony, unfavorable to Belknap, the former secretary of war, gave great offense to President Grant, who not only deprived him of his command, substituting Terry, the district commander, but ordered that he should not even be permitted to accompany the expedition. A storm of popular disapproval, joined with the earnest plea of Terry, caused Grant to relent so far as to restore Custer to the command of his regiment. Leaving the Missouri on May 17, the expedition under Terry reached the Powder on June 7, and later moved on to the mouth of the Rosebud. At noon of June 22, Custer and his regiment, a total force of about 655 men, set out directly for the Little Big Horn, while Terry, with Gibbon, who had joined him from the west, started up the Yellowstone to reach the field by way of the Big Horn. Custer arrived in the vicinity of the village on the 25th, intending to attack early the following morning. Learning, however, that his presence had been discovered, he decided on an immediate attack. Shortly after noon he divided his force into three battalions, sending Benteen to the left, Reno straight ahead across the river into the valley and taking his own five troops on a detour to the right in order to strike the village further down stream. An overwhelming force, variously reckoned at from 2,500 to 4,000 well-armed warriors, was encountered. Reno was soon driven in flight from the valley, taking refuge on the bluffs on the north of the river, where shortly afterward he was joined by Benteen and where a valiant defense was maintained until the departure of the Indians on the afternoon of the 26th. Custer, on reaching the slope of what has since been known as Custer Hill, was surrounded and with every one of his immediate command was killed. Lieut. Bradley, scouting in advance of Terry and Gibbon on the morning of the 27th, found the bodies, most of them stripped and scalped and many otherwise mutilated. The body of Custer, pierced by a bullet in the left temple and in the left side, though stripped, was unmutilated.

The controversy that began immediately thereafter has continued intermittently ever since, with no signs that it will ever be ended. Custer has been charged with disobedience of orders, with having made his attack before the time agreed upon, with a reckless determination to risk the lives of his command in a vain effort to regain the prestige alleged to have been lost through Grant's disfavor and with much else. His defenders have replied that the only orders known to exist gave him full discretion, that there is no evidence of an agreement as to the time of attack, that if his main motive were personal glory he must have known that recklessness was the one thing sure to defeat his aim, and that had his subordinate, Reno, borne a more courageous part the result might have been different. Sherman, in his official report for the year, admitted that the "campaign had been planned on wrong premises" and that until Custer's death there was nothing to indicate that any detachment would encounter more than 500 or 800 Indians. The cause of Custer's defeat was the dispatch of a force inferior in armament and vastly inferior in numbers to the force it encountered.

Custer was tall, slender, and lithe, with a strong physique and an exceptional capacity for endurance. He had blue eyes, and his hair (which he wore long until his last campaign) and mustache were of a golden tint. His dress in the early days of the Civil War had been slouchy and unkempt; but on attaining the rank of general he donned a conspicuous costume of olive-gray corduroy or velveteen, lavishly tinseled with gold braid and set off with a cavalier hat and a long scarlet necktie. On the plains he usually wore buckskin. His manner on the field was brusque and aggressive and his voice sharp and at times rasping; but in hours of relaxation he was genial and companionable. Lawrence Barrett, the actor, who knew him intimately, says that his voice was "earnest, soft, tender and appealing" and that his personality was one of rare charm. In personal habits he was abstemious; except in the peace-pipe ceremony with Indians he did not use tobacco, and there is no evidence, despite malicious stories to the contrary, that save for a brief period during the Civil War he ever drank liquor. He became, in his later days, an avid student, particularly of military science and of belles-lettres, and he spent much of his leisure time in writing. In 1874 he published in book form his fascinating narrative, *My Life on the Plains* (later re-titled *Wild Life on the Plains*), the text of which had appeared serially in the *Galaxy*. His "War Memoirs"—recollections of the Civil War to the time of the battle of Williamsburg—were published in the *Galaxy* in 1876, after his death. He had a high sense of integrity, and he strove earnestly, with results disastrous to himself, to check the then prevalent corruption in the Indian Bureau. His character was positive, and though he won devoted friends he made vindictive enemies, particularly in the army. He may well be likened, in his last days, to the central figure in a Greek tragedy, hemmed in by a closing net of adverse circumstances, while his every movement to extricate himself served only to hasten the inevitable end.

[See G. W. Cullum, *Biog. Reg.* (3rd ed., 1891); Frederick Whittaker, *A Complete Life of Gen. Geo. A. Custer* (1876); F. S. Dellenbaugh, *Geo. Armstrong Custer* (1917); Elizabeth Bacon Custer, *The Boy General* (1901), ed. by Mary E. Burt. The literature of the Little Big Horn battle is voluminous. Especially noteworthy contributions are: E. S. Godfrey, "Custer's Last Battle," *Century Mag.*, Jan. 1892; J. M. Hanson, *The Conquest of the Missouri* (1909); Jas. McLaughlin, *My Friend the Indian* (1910); W. A. Graham, *The Story of the Little Big Horn* (1926); C. F. Bates and Fairfax Downey, *Fifty Years After the Little Big Horn Battle* (pamph., 1926); Edward J. McClernand, "The Indian and the Buffalo in Montana," *Cavalry Jour.*, Jan. 1927; and the appendices to Cyrus Townsend Brady, *Indian Fights and Fighters* (1904) and *Northwestern Fights and Fighters* (1907). See also the impressionistic biography, *Custer, the Last of the Cavaliers* (1928), by Frazier Hunt.] W. J. G.

CUSTIS, GEORGE WASHINGTON PARKE (Apr. 30, 1781–Oct. 10, 1857), playwright, inherited the traditions of a Southern landholder through his father, John Parke Custis, the stepson of George Washington, and also through his mother Eleanor Calvert, a descendant of Lord Baltimore. Owing to the early death of his father, he grew up under the charge of Washington at Mount Vernon, Va., where he lived until the death of Mrs. Washington, when he made his home at Arlington, Va. After a time spent at Princeton College, he was commissioned in 1799 a cornet of horse in the United States army, and became aide-de-camp to Gen. Charles C. Pinckney, with the rank of colonel. He was not, however, called into active service at this time. In 1804 he married Mary Lee Fitzhugh, and went to live upon his large estate. His daughter, Mary Custis, married Robert E. Lee, thus linking the two great generals in a family connection. In 1803 he inaugurated an annual convention for the promotion of agriculture and especially for the encouragement of the wool industry. During the War of 1812 he served as a volunteer in the defense of the city of Washington. When Lafayette visited the United States in 1824, Custis naturally took an active part in his welcome and was prompted to write his entertaining "Conversations with Lafayette," published in the *Alexandria Gazette*. In 1826 he began in the *United States Gazette* his recollections of Washington, which were continued in the *National Intelligencer*, and were published in 1860. An incident in which Washington was the chief actor became the central motive of Custis's first play, *The Indian Prophecy*, performed at the Chestnut Street Theatre, Philadelphia, July 4, 1827, and published in 1828. His most successful play, *Pocahontas, or the Settlers of Virginia*, produced at the Walnut Street Theatre, Philadelphia, Jan. 16, 1830, and published in the same year, showed his sense of the dramatic, as he violated chronology in the career of Pocahontas in order to make her salvation of Capt. John Smith the climax of the drama. His other plays are known only by contemporary description, for, with the instinct of a Southern gentleman, he published little. *The Railroad,* a "national drama," which was performed at the Walnut Street Theatre, Philadelphia, May 16, 1830, seems to have brought on the stage for the first time a real "locomotive steam carriage." Custis's attitude toward the stage is revealed in a letter to his wife, in which he says, "I had promised the poor rogues of actors, a play for the 12th Sept., the anniversary of the battle of North Point; but finding myself not in the vein, I wrote them to defer it." *North Point,* or *Baltimore Defended,* was, however, finished in nine hours and produced Sept. 12, 1833, in Baltimore (*Recollections,* p. 59). Custis's *Eighth of January* was played Jan. 8, 1834, at the Park Theatre, New York, and there are unconfirmed statements that he wrote another play, *The Pawnee Chief.* He was of medium height, of a fair and somewhat florid complexion, and of great personal charm. He died at Arlington, the last male representative of his family.

[The best source of information concerning Custis is the memoir by his daughter, Mary Custis Lee, published in the *Recollections and Private Memoirs of Washington by his Adopted Son* (1860). For accounts and criticisms of the plays, see Chas. Durang, "Hist. of the Phila. Stage," in the Phila. *Sunday Dispatch,* ser. 2, beginning June 29, 1856, chs. LI and LIII; J. N. Ireland, *Records of the N. Y. Stage* (1866–67), I, 644 and II, 77; A. H. Quinn, *Hist. of the Am. Drama from the Beginning to the Civil War* (1923), pp. 270–73.]

A. H. Q.

CUTBUSH, JAMES (1788–Dec. 15, 1823), chemist, was the son of Edward Cutbush, an English stonecutter in Philadelphia, and his wife Anne Marriat; and younger brother of Edward, a naval surgeon, and of William, a West Point graduate who became a prominent engineer. Where and how he obtained his education is a matter of conjecture. His career is traced chiefly through his publications. In his twentieth year, he wrote a series of fifteen articles which appeared in the Philadelphia *Aurora* (beginning in July 1808), on the "Application of Chemistry to Arts and Manufactures." His purpose was to educate the public in the application of science to practical affairs and to arouse interest in science in general. There is a boyish ardor in his appeal to "you enlightened citizens, men of science and improvement, artists and manufacturers" to seize the auspicious time to develop natural resources by the aid of arts and sciences. In the same year (1808) he published a little volume entitled *A Useful Cabinet*; and an article in the Philadelphia *Medical Museum* on mercury fulminate. To the same journal he contributed in 1809 an article describing a method of purifying ether and the production of ethylene; also an article (1811) on the value of the hop to brewers. To the *Freemason's Magazine* he contributed (1811) an article on "Subjects and Importance of Chemistry" and a short historical sketch of the science. In this same year was founded the Columbian Chemical Society of which he was the first president. Cutbush was also vice-president of the Linnean Society and a member of the Society for the Promotion of a Rational System of Education, before which in 1811 he delivered an oration advocating the introduction of instruction in the physical sciences in schools (*An Oration on Education,* published in 1812). For a time he gave popular lectures on chemistry, and was professor of chemistry, mineralogy and natural philosophy in "St. John's College" of Philadelphia. In 1813 he published a *Philosophy of Experimental Chemistry* in two volumes, one of the first chemical textbooks published by a native American. In 1814 he was appointed assistant apothecary-general of the United States army. In 1820 he became chief medical officer at West Point, and then acting professor of chemistry and mineralogy. He continued to contribute to various journals: to the *American Journal of Science,* among others, articles on the improvement of the Voltaic electrical lamp (1820) and on the composition and properties of Greek fire (1823) and Chinese fire (1824). In 1821 he published *A Synopsis of Chemistry* and after his death his widow published *A System of Pyrotechny* (1825) in two volumes, a notable contribution based on careful experimental study. He died at the early age of thirty-five and was buried at West Point.

[All that has been ascertained about this pioneer in chemical science is contained in *James Cutbush: an American Chemist* (1919), by Dr. Edgar F. Smith, whose death prevented the revision of this article by his own hand.—Editor.]

E. F. S.

CUTLER, CARROLL (Jan. 31, 1829–Jan. 24, 1894), Congregational clergyman, college president, was born in Windham, N. H., the son of Calvin and Rhoda Bartlett (Little) Cutler. As his father had a large family to rear on the meager salary of a rural Presbyterian clergyman, Carroll was obliged to earn his education. He worked on a farm and taught district school, attended Phillips Andover Academy, and graduated from Yale College in 1854. A year of teaching at Bloomfield, N. J., provided him with sufficient money to carry him through the following year at Union Theological Seminary in New York; he continued his reading of divinity while a tutor at Yale 1856–58, and in January of 1858 was licensed to preach by the Congregational West Association of New Haven. Having attained his professional ambition, he returned to Bloomfield, N. J., to be married on Aug. 10 of that year to Frances, daughter of the Rev. Joseph S. Gallagher, who was secretary and treasurer of Union Seminary. The next year he spent in travel and study abroad, especially in Germany, and in the spring of 1860 he was appointed professor of intellectual philosophy and rhetoric in Western Reserve College at Hudson, Ohio. The college was then a representative "freshwater" institution, nourished chiefly on hopes for the future, but its half-dozen scrimped professors included several men of uncommon ability. Cutler soon proved to be one of them, making his mark as a teacher rather than as an administrator or a productive scholar. For four months of 1862 he was a tall, stalwart first lieutenant of Company B of the 85th Ohio Volunteer Infantry, engaged in escorting prisoners to Vicksburg for exchange. In 1871 he assumed the presidency of the college after assuring himself that his new duties need not interfere with his work in the classroom. In 1876 he published *A History of Western Reserve College during its First Half Century 1826–76.* Cutler's learning, his good sense, his command of English style, and his moral fervor are pleasantly revealed in *The Beginnings of Ethics* (1889), which, appearing in the year before James's *Principles of Psychology,* belongs to the era when philosophy, in American colleges, was still dominated by theology. In 1882 Western Reserve College was raised to comparative affluence by endowments made by Amasa Stone and others, was removed from Hudson to Cleveland, and changed its name to Adelbert College of Western Reserve University. Cutler resigned the presidency in 1886, retaining his professorship, but continued to occupy the office until 1888, when his successor was installed. He soon found himself hopelessly at variance with the new president and in 1889 severed all connection with the college. His last years were spent in the South as a teacher in two negro schools, Biddle University at Charlotte, N. C., and Talladega College at Talladega, Ala. He taught until within a week of his death.

[*Records and Statistics of the Academic Class of '54, Yale Univ., 1854–96* (1896); *Obit. Record Grads. Yale Univ.*, 1894; *One Hundred Years of Western Reserve* (Hudson, Ohio, 1926).] G.H.G.

CUTLER, JAMES GOOLD (Apr. 24, 1848–Apr. 21, 1927), architect, inventor, banker, son of John Nathan and Mary E. (Goold) Cutler, of English-Dutch descent. was born in Albany, N. Y., where his father and grandfather had a carriage manufactory. He attended the local city schools and completed his education in Albany Academy. Upon graduation he began work in his grandfather's carriage factory but soon took up the study of architecture with a local firm of architects in Albany. On Sept. 27, 1871, he married Anna K. Abbey of Kingston, N. Y. The next year he and his young bride settled in Rochester, N. Y., where he went to work as a draftsman for a local architect. His progress was rapid and in a few years he became a partner of his first employer. He continued to practise his profession for a total of twenty-two years, his architectural work including residences, office and bank buildings, and factories. During this time he devised and patented the familiar mail chutes observed in modern office buildings and extending from the highest to the first floor. His invention was known as a "letter box connection," for which Patent Number 284,951 was granted him on Sept. 11, 1883. The year after he obtained his patent, Cutler, with his brother J. Warren Cutler, formed the Cutler Manufacturing Company, to build and install letter-chutes. The business grew at a prodigious rate and its products were sold throughout the world. In 1908 the company built its own factory and continued, with Cutler as president, until 1915 when the firm was reorganized and he resigned the presidency. He was interested in municipal and civic affairs and as early as 1895 was appointed a member of the White Charter Commission of New York State to draft a uniform charter for second-class cities. He was a presidential elector in 1896 and in 1916. In 1897 he served as consulting architect for the New York state capitol, in 1900 he was commissioner of public safety for Rochester, and in 1903 he was elected mayor, being reëlected two years later. For more than thirty years prior to his death he was prominently connected with several banks in Rochester. He was one of the first presidents of the Rochester Chamber of Commerce, and a member of the Rochester City Planning Advisory Board from the time of its organization until his resignation two years before his death. He was an honorary member of the American Institute of Architects and served three terms as president of the Western New York State Association of Architects. He was a trustee of the University of Rochester and of the Municipal Art Commission and a member of many clubs.

[Direct correspondence with Rochester Chamber of Commerce; Patent Office records; *Who's Who in America, 1926–27*; *Democrat and Chronicle* (Rochester), Apr. 22, 1927; N. S. Cutler, *Cutler Memorial and Geneal. Hist.* (1889).] C.W.M.

CUTLER, LIZZIE PETIT (1831–Jan. 16, 1902), author, was born in Milton and died in Richmond, Va. Her father's people were "respectable farmers," and her mother was descended from distinguished Anglo-French Virginia landowners. Left motherless as an infant, she was entrusted first to an aunt, a widow much engrossed in social affairs, and later to a grand-aunt, who soon removed from her estate near Charlottesville to Charlottesville itself. The child's education had been irregular, and in her new residence it was made more so by the constant necessity of meeting the social obligations of life in a university environment. In 1855 she published, with half-hearted anonymity, *Light and Darkness, a Story of Fashionable Life*. She chose as her scene places which she had not had the fortune to visit—New York, New Haven, and the expanse of Europe, and she professed "to veil a moral in every scene," but in one essential regard she defied the canons of romance. "I have endeavored," she said, "to portray the bad not as wholly bad nor the good as immaculate, since of human nature either is rarely or never true." The heresy of this view-point was widely and vigorously denounced, and the *Southern Literary Messenger* of October 1855, while admitting the interest of the book, calls it "a story of guilty love," and judges that "it had far better never been published." The author fled to New York. Society there did not blench at receiving her, but the late furore proved so disciplinary that in her next book, *Household Mysteries, a Romance of Southern Life* (1856), she maintained a more seemly attitude. In 1858, she published *The Stars of the Crowd, or Men and Women of the Day*. Soon afterward, a misunderstanding with her publishers made it necessary for her to earn money. She undertook a series of public readings and so won the popular favor that she determined to become an actress. This resolution was defeated by her marriage to Peter G. Cutler, a prominent New York lawyer. During her married life, social activities absorbed most of the energy which she had formerly devoted to writing. When her husband died in 1870 he left her an ample livelihood, but it soon disappeared and she was forced to return to Charlottesville to ask help of friends whom she had long before estranged by the "latitude" of her writings. She sincerely attempted atonement by returning to the stricter ideals of her very young womanhood, and by writing industriously, though not with great success, for any publication that would accept her work. She spoke tenderly of the Confederacy, and people remembered that "during the war, though she was in New York, powerless to aid her people, she had given them her sympathy and tears." But from 1865 to 1902 is a long while, and the Richmond newspapers, when occasion came, gave brief notice of her sudden, solitary death as that of "an aged, dependent old woman, in a cheap boarding house." She had friends, the reporter added, in South Carolina and in Tennessee.

[In addition to sources already mentioned see J. D. Freeman ("Mary Forrest"), *Women of the South* (1861); J. G. Johnson, *Southern Fiction Prior to 1860* (1909); *Richmond Times*, Jan. 17, 1902; O. F. Adams, *Dict. Am. Authors* (1901); S. A. B. Putnam, *Things and Thoughts* (Mar.–Apr. 1902); I. Raymond, *Southland Writers* (1870).] J. D. W.

CUTLER, MANASSEH (May 13, 1742–July 28, 1823), Congregational clergyman, botanist, colonizer, was born in Killingly, Windham County, Conn., and was a direct descendant of John Cutler, who settled in Watertown, Mass., in 1634. He was the third child and oldest son of Hezekiah and Susanna (Clark) Cutler, who had a farm on the borderline between Rhode Island and Connecticut. After some preparatory instruction under Rev. Aaron Brown, he entered Yale College, where he graduated in 1765. Although he showed some aptitude for mathematics and natural science, he won no important collegiate distinctions. During the following winter he taught school in Dedham, Mass. On Sept. 7, 1766, he married Mary, eldest daughter of Rev. Thomas Balch of Dedham, and settled on Martha's Vineyard, where as agent for his wife's aunt, Mrs. Hannah Newman, he opened a store. While residing there, he was admitted to practise as an attorney in the court of common pleas and was employed in several court-room cases. At the Yale Commencement in 1768 he received the degree of A.M. Determining in October 1768 to study divinity, he moved with his family back to Dedham, where he spent the next two years reading theology under the direction of his father-in-law, meanwhile securing a license to preach (1770) and delivering sermons in various towns in the vicinity. On Sept. 11, 1771, he was ordained as pastor of the Congregational church in Ipswich Hamlet (now Hamilton), Mass., and was soon established in that parish, where he was to remain, with frequent absences on business, for the rest of his long life.

Being in sympathy with the Revolution, he was eager to promote the cause of the Patriots. After the battle of Lexington, he addressed the Minute Men of Ipswich Hamlet and then rode with them on horseback to Cambridge. He frequently visited the encampments of Massachusetts militia, and in September 1776 went to Dorchester, on leave from his parish, as chaplain in Col. Ebenezer Francis's 11th Massachusetts Regiment. When that organization broke up in January 1777, Cutler resumed his clerical duties, but in August 1778 he set out with Gen. Titcomb as chaplain in his brigade on its expedition to Rhode Island. When the troops came back in September, Cutler, who needed to add to his meager income, took up the study of medicine under his friend and parishioner, Dr. Elisha Whitney, and soon developed sufficient skill to practise as a physician. In May and June 1779, he had more than forty smallpox patients under his care at Wenham. Meanwhile, his restlessness found outlet in many scientific investigations. He measured the distances of some of the stars with a sextant and telescope; he entered the positions of Jupiter's moons in his journal; he observed hairs and other objects through a microscope; he described a remarkable aurora borealis; he performed experiments with an electrical machine; and he inoculated people for smallpox. One of his preferred avocations was botany, and he was the first to prepare a systematic account of the flora of New England. He examined 350 separate species, classifying them according to the Linnean method. In quest of information, he made an expedition, with six companions, to Mt. Washington in 1784, and was one of those to reach the summit. By means of the crude instruments which he carried, he computed that the top was 9,000 feet above the sea, an error of approximately 2,600 feet. He was elected in 1791 a member of the American Academy of Arts and Sciences and was punctilious in attendance at the meetings, contributing some valuable papers to its *Proceedings*. Among these are descriptions of the transit of Mercury over the sun, Nov. 12, 1782, of the eclipse of the moon, Mar. 29, 1782, and of the sun in the following April, as well as an article called "An Account of Some of the Vegetable Productions Naturally Growing in This Part of America," in which he summarized his conclusions regarding New England flora. He was a member of the American Philosophical Society (1784), the Philadelphia Linnæan Society (1809), the American Antiquarian Society (1813), and the New England Linnæan Society (1815), as well as an honorary fellow of the Massachusetts Medical Society. Yale gave him in 1789 the degree of LL.D. He frequently had pupils under instruction in his house, and in 1782 he opened a private boarding-school, which was continued for more than a quarter of a century. There were years when he had as many as twenty boys, most of them from well-known families in Essex County. One of those whom he prepared for college was Nathaniel Silsbee, later United States senator from Massachusetts.

Up to the age of forty-five, Cutler had played many parts as teacher, storekeeper, clergyman, physician, soldier, explorer, and scientist. He was now, however, to enter upon a series of adventures of an entirely new kind, which were to give him a little-understood but important place in the history of American expansion. At the close of the Revolutionary War, a group of veterans, headed by Gen. Rufus Putnam, Winthrop Sargent, and others, became interested in a colonization scheme in the Ohio Valley; and on Mar. 1, 1786, in Boston, Cutler joined in forming the Ohio Company and was one of the five men who drafted its original articles of agreement. The company desired particularly to secure from Congress the grant of a choice tract at the junction of the Ohio and Muskingum rivers, which could be settled by "the most robust and industrious people in America." After one agent, Samuel H. Parsons, had failed, Cutler was sent by the company to New York in the summer of 1787 to conduct the negotiations. While the proposals of the Ohio Company were being considered by the Continental Congress, plans were also outlined for the administration of the vast territory involved. The draft of the Ordinance of 1787, which contained elements drawn from many sources, was submitted by Nathan Dane [*q.v.*] to Cutler, who made several suggestions, all but one of which he says were adopted. There has been much debate as to Cutler's share in this noted document, and his precise contribution to it has never been exactly determined.

The Ordinance was adopted July 13, 1787. Cutler, who had arrived in New York July 5 with letters of introduction to many influential people, at once began work with Congress. By means of active lobbying and skilful maneuvering he succeeded in winning over a hostile minority and, on Oct. 27, 1787, signed a contract with the Treasury Board giving the Ohio Company the right to take up one and a half million acres at approximately eight cents specie an acre. Colonization in the territory thus acquired began immediately. In December 1787, Putnam with sixty pioneers set out on the journey West, reaching the junction of the Ohio and Muskingum rivers in the following April. They there established the town of Marietta and began the settlement of Ohio. Cutler himself set out on July 21, 1788, driving in a sulky, and covered a distance of 750 miles in twenty-nine days. During his stay in Ohio he examined various mounds and fortifications in the vicinity of Marietta, and concluded that these were the work of ancient tribes. He returned to Massachusetts in 1789, having seen his colony well established. In 1795 he was offered a commission as judge of the supreme court of Ohio Territory, but declined it.

In 1800 Cutler represented his town in the Massachusetts General Court, and in the autumn was elected to Congress as a Federalist from the Essex District. He served two terms, but declined a renomination in 1804, the strain of congressional activities having proved too much for his health. He returned to Hamilton, where he was still pastor of the church, and on Oct. 27, 1814, delivered a "Century Discourse." His wife died, Nov. 2, 1815, but he, in spite of frequent attacks of asthma, continued to preach until his death nearly eight years later. Cutler's journal, carefully kept over a series of years, is an amazing personal record, revealing his eagerness to get authentic information on all sorts of subjects. One of his favorite extracts from Virgil gives the key to his character, *Felix, qui potuit rerum cognoscere causas.* He had an unbounded curiosity which led him to carry on a tremendous correspondence with authorities in many fields. Neatness was his passion, and everything in his library and about his place was in perfect order. In his prime he was a tall and portly figure, usually attired in a black velvet suit, with black silk stockings and silver knee- and shoe-buckles. His manners were courtly, and he entertained most graciously the many guests who came to his house in Hamilton.

[The basis for any biography of Cutler is necessarily Wm. P. and Julia P. Cutler, *Life, Journals, and Correspondence of Rev. Manasseh Cutler* (2 vols., 1888). For discussions of his part in the Ordinance of 1787, see E. Channing, *Hist. of the U. S.*, vol. III (1912), ch. xvii; Jay A. Barrett, *The Evolution of the Ordinance of 1787* (1891); and F. B. Stone, in *Pa. Mag. of Hist. and Biog.*, Oct. 1889. Manasseh Cutler, *An Explanation of the Map which Delineates that Part of the Federal Lands, Comprehended between Pa. West Line, the Rivers Ohio and Scioto, and Lake Erie, etc.*, published anonymously (1787), published in French (1789), has been reprinted many times because it is an early description of Ohio. See also, Wm. B. Sprague, *Annals Am. Pulpit*, vol. II (1857); *Literary Diary of Ezra Stiles* (1901); N. S. Cutler, *Cutler Memorial and Geneal. Hist.* (1889); Jos. B. Felt, *Hist. of Ipswich, Essex and Hamilton* (1834); E. D. Larned, *Hist. of Windham County, Conn.* (1874–80); *New-Eng. Hist. and Geneal. Reg.*, Oct. 1853, Apr. 1873; *North Am. Rev.*, Apr. 1876; *Mag. of Am. Hist.*, Apr. 1881, Dec. 1889; F. B. Dexter, *Biog. Sketches Grads. Yale Coll.*, vol. III (1903).]

C. M. F.

CUTLER, TIMOTHY (May 31, 1684–Aug. 17, 1765), rector of Yale College, Episcopal clergyman, was born in Charlestown, Mass., a descendant of Robert Cutler who settled in that town prior to Oct. 28, 1636. His father was Maj. John Cutler, an anchorsmith, and his mother, Martha Wiswall. The fact that both his father and grandfather opposed the government formed after the overthrow of Andros in 1689, and although severely penalized, refused to subscribe to it until it had received royal sanction, suggests a family tendency to conform to the established order at home, which may have had something to do with Timothy's subsequent conversion to the Church of England. When seventeen years old he graduated from Harvard College, and on Jan. 11, 1709/10, having come from Massachusetts to Connecticut with the recommendation of being "one of the best preachers both colonies afforded," he was ordained pastor of the Congregational church in Stratford. On Mar. 21, 1710/11, he married Elizabeth, daughter of Rev. Samuel Andrew [*q.v.*] of Milford, Conn., then acting rector of Yale College. He served his parish acceptably until March 1718/19 when, conditions at Yale calling imperatively for a resident rector, he undertook that office at the request of the trustees, his appointment being formally approved in September. Although his father-in-law was doubtless instrumental in securing his appointment, Cutler was in general well fitted for the position, being "an excellent Linguist," a "good Logician, Geographer, and Rhetorician," while "in the Philosophy & Metaphysics & Ethics of his Day or juvenile Education he was great. ... He was of an high, lofty, & despotic mien. He made a grand Figure as the Head of a College" (*The Literary Diary of Ezra Stiles,* 1901, II, 339–40).

The new rectorship opened auspiciously and an era of prosperity seemed at hand when, on Sept. 13, 1722, the rector, with Tutor Daniel Browne and several Congregational clergymen, met with the trustees, declared themselves doubtful of the validity of their ordination, and asked advice with regard to entering the Church of England. Upon request they made a written statement of their position, and the meeting was adjourned for a month. In the meantime Gov. Saltonstall arranged a public debate on the matter, held Oct. 16, as a result of which, on the following day, at a special meeting of the trustees, it was voted to "excuse the Rev. Mr. Cutler from all further services as Rector of Yale College," and it was provided that all future rectors and tutors should declare to the trustees their assent to the Saybrook Confession of Faith, and give satisfaction as to their opposition to "Arminian and prelatical corruptions."

Contemporary evidence indicates that Cutler was never whole-heartedly a Dissenter, that he had been converted to Episcopalianism when at Stratford by John Checkley [*q.v.*], and that in spite of this fact had accepted the rectorship of a Congregational college, publicly declaring what he had privately believed only when a desirable place in the Established Church was assured him (*Collections of the Massachusetts Historical Society*, ser. 2, IV, 299; Josiah Quincy, *History of Harvard University*, 1840, I, 365; F. B. Dexter, *Biographical Sketches of the Graduates of Yale College, with Annals of the College History*, vol. I, 1885, p. 271).

After a visit to London where he was ordained by the Bishop of Norwich in March 1723, and received the degree of D.D. from both Oxford and Cambridge, Cutler became rector of the newly formed Christ Church, Boston. Here he remained until his death, one of the leading Episcopal clergymen of New England, full of polemic spirit, venerated for his learning, but too haughty in manner to be popular. He founded the church at Dedham and took care of Christ Church, Braintree. He was a high Tory, intolerant of Dissenters, and a militant defender of the rights of his fellow believers. With Rev. Samuel Myles of King's Chapel he laid claim to a seat on the Board of Overseers of Harvard, as a minister of the Episcopal church in Boston, maintaining that he was a "teaching elder" as required by the college charter. Both the Overseers and General Court decided against him (Quincy, *supra*, pp. 365–76). He never ceased to urge the appointment of a bishop for the American colonies. With the exception of four sermons, two preached before the Connecticut General Assembly, May 9, 1717, and Oct. 18, 1719, he left no published works.

[W. S. Perry, *Hist. Colls. Relating to the Am. Colonial Ch.* (1870) and John Nichols, *Illustrations of the Lit. Hist. of the Eighteenth Century* (1822) contain Cutler letters; Henry W. Foote, *Annals of King's Chapel* (1882–96) is rich in references. See also Nahum S. Cutler, *A Cutler Memorial and Geneal. Hist.* (1889); Richard Frothingham, *Hist. of Charlestown, Mass.*, no. 5 (1847); Edwin Oviatt, *The Beginnings of Yale* (1916); Samuel Orcutt, *Hist. of the Old Town of Stratford and the City of Bridgeport, Conn.* (1886); Justin Winsor, *Memorial Hist. of Boston*, vol. II (1881); E. E. Beardsley, *Hist. of the Episc. Ch. in Conn.* (1866); Wm. S. Perry, *Hist. of the Am. Episc. Ch.* (1885); Wm. B. Sprague, *Annals of the Am. Pulpit*, vol. V (1859); Henry Burroughs, *An Hist. Account of Christ Church, Boston* (1874); Asa Eaton, *Hist. Account of Christ Church, Boston* (1824).] H. E. S.

CUTTER, CHARLES AMMI (Mar. 14, 1837–Sept. 6, 1903), librarian, the third son of Charles Champney and Hannah (Biglow) Cutter, was descended on both sides from ancestors who for eight generations had lived and died within a few miles of Boston. Among them were farmers, housewrights, traders, millers, innholders, but no scholars. Cutter was born in Boston, and spent his boyhood in Charlestown and Cambridge. From the Hopkins Grammar School he entered Harvard College at fourteen, graduating third among the eighty-two members of the class of 1855. While in the Harvard Divinity School (1858–59), where he was librarian as well as student, he became so attracted toward librarianship that after preaching a few months he went into the Harvard library, where he served as an assistant from 1860 to 1868. On May 21, 1863, he was married to Sarah Fayerweather Appleton, daughter of Charles John and Sophia (Haven) Appleton of Portsmouth, N. H. In December 1868 he was elected librarian of the Boston Athenæum, the most famous of American proprietary libraries. It is clear evidence of his quality that he held this prized position under such directors as the first and second Charles Francis Adams, Brooks Adams, Oliver Wendell Holmes, Francis Parkman, and Henry Cabot Lodge, and gave satisfaction to such readers as Emerson, Bronson Alcott, Whipple, Palfrey, Bancroft, Charles Sumner, and many other New England "Brahmins" to whom the Athenæum was a literary sanctuary. In such congenial surroundings it would have been easy to let the demands of the hour absorb one's days; but Cutter devoted twelve years of incessant labor to the production of his monumental *Catalogue of the Library of the Boston Athenæum* (5 vols., 1874–82), which Justin Winsor said was "the best catalogue extant." For years it stood almost alone in American bibliographic undertakings in magnitude and thoroughness. As an aid to other libraries there was at that time nothing remotely comparable to it. Out of the difficulties met in compiling this catalogue grew a work of wide usefulness and more permanent value, his *Rules for a Printed Dictionary Catalogue* (1875), intended for the guidance of himself and his associates but recognized at once as so valuable a tool that it was reprinted by the national Bureau of Education in 1876. It immediately became the world's leading text-book in systematic dictionary cataloguing and has not yet been superseded.

Cutter was now reckoned among the half-dozen foremost American librarians, so that in the great library movement which began with the organization of the American Library Association he had a large part. From its first meeting in Philadelphia in October 1876, until his death, he attended more of its annual conferences than any other person. He helped to establish the *Library Journal* (September 1876); was from the beginning in charge of its bibliographic department; and was its general editor from 1881 to 1893. His *Expansive Classification* (1891–1904), "the most logical and scholarly of modern bibliographic schemes," is his best but not his most famous work. In much wider use are his *Rules* and his alphabetic-order tables on which are based the author name-marks now commonly seen on books in American libraries. Declining reëlection at the Athenæum in 1893, he spent the next year and a half in European travel and study. In October 1894 he began to develop the newly founded Forbes Library in Northampton, Mass. His plans for cultivating literary and artistic taste in his younger readers involved the lending of pictures and musical scores as well as books. He aimed, as he said in the last year of his life, to develop "a new type of public library, which, speaking broadly, will lend everything to anybody in any desired quantity for any desired time." While on a driving trip with his wife, he died suddenly at Walpole, N. H., Sept. 6, 1903, having never fully recovered from a severe illness of the preceding spring.

His books disclose unusual power of analysis, exceptionally accurate scholarship, great knowledge. Evidences of his wide culture are to be found in the files of the *Nation* to which he was a contributor for thirty-five years. He was an ardent lover of nature, was keenly interested in music, art, the drama, and dancing, was devoted to rowing, bicycling, mountain-climbing; a man of spontaneous and unconquerable humor, a delightful companion, and of an incorrigible industry that made him eminent in his profession.

[W. E. Foster and Thorvald Solberg in *Lib. Jour.*, Oct., Nov. 1903; Benj. Cutter, *A Hist. of the Cutter Family of New Eng.* (1871); *Forbes Lib. Reports*, 1894–1903; W. C. Berwick Sayers, *A Manual of Classification for Librarians and Bibliographers* (1926); W. E. Foster, in *Bull. of the Am. Lib. Asso.*, Oct. 1926; *Nation* (N. Y.), Sept. 17, 1903; *Springfield Daily Republican*, Sept. 8, 1903.] F.W.A.

CUTTER, EPHRAIM (Sept. 1, 1832–Apr. 25, 1917), physician, was born at Woburn, Mass., the son of Benjamin and Mary (Whittemore) Cutter. He came of fairly distinguished ancestry, his father being a practitioner at Woburn, and his grandfather, Amos Whittemore, having achieved reputation as an inventor. After preparation at Warren Academy, he entered Yale where he graduated in 1852. Apparently he had a *penchant* for acquiring college degrees, obtaining, from Yale, A.B. (1852), M.D. (1855); from Harvard, M.D. (1856); from the University of Pennsylvania, M.D. (1857). His professional career may be divided into three periods: (1856–74) when he was engaged in practise at Woburn in association with his father; (1875–80) when he practised in Cambridge; (1881–1901) when he practised in New York City. He possessed great ability in medical research and in the invention of medical appliances. His earliest efforts were given to solving some of the problems connected with the examination and photography of the vocal organs. In 1859 an apparatus for viewing the larynx was constructed from his design, and in 1866 he made photographs of the larynx which, it is claimed, went a little further than any of those previously produced, in that they showed the thyroid insertion. Soon after this he published his *Veratrum Viride as a Therapeutical Agent* (1860, 1862). General surgery and gynecology early engaged his attention, and he devised, almost every year, one or more new instruments or new operative procedures. In 1869 he was using a new kind of metallic suture; in 1870 he described an écraseur for removing growths from deep cavities; in 1871 he brought out a new eustachian catheter; in 1873 an invalid chair; in 1874 an inhaler for nascent ammonia chloride; in 1875 a galvanocaustic holder. In 1871 he devoted especial attention to the therapeutic effects of electricity, being one of the first to demonstrate that galvanic currents penetrate the human body. On his removal in 1875 to Cambridge, he returned to his morphological studies, making frequent examinations of the blood and sputum with special reference to their clinical significance. At this time gynecological subjects also claimed his renewed interest, and he wrote *A Contribution to the Treatment of the Versions and Flexions of the Unimpregnated Uterus* (1871–76).

The last period of his life, dating from the beginning of his residence in New York, was largely devoted to the investigation of cancer, tuberculosis, diseases of the heart and blood vessels, and disorders of nutrition. Among his more important contributions of this period were *Partial Syllabic Lists of the Clinical Morphologies of the Blood, Feces, Skin,* etc. (1888, 1892), *Fatty Ills and their Masquerades* (1898), *Fatty and Fibroid Degeneration, Bright's Disease, Apoplexy, Fatty Heart, Puerperal Convulsions,* etc. (1892). He became intensely interested in the subject of food and did much to arouse the public mind against the decorticated and denatured wheat and wheat flours, especially stressing their effect in bringing about an early decay of the teeth. He delved also into the cancer problem and referred to cancer tissue as "being under mob law and rioting in the body systemic," forecasting one of the most prominent theories of the present day as to the origin of malignant growths. On his retirement from practise in 1901, he took up his residence in West Falmouth, Mass., where he died at the age of eighty-four as the result of a cerebral hemorrhage. He was twice married: first, Oct. 7, 1856, to Rebecca Smith Sullivan, and two years after her death in 1899, to Mrs. Anna L. Davidson. There were two sons of his first marriage: Benjamin, and Dr. John Ashburton Cutter who was associated with him in practise and in the writing of some of his later works.

Cutter's writings lacked literary grace and were rather full of arbitrary statements which his arguments failed to support and which subsequent experience has failed to confirm. By virtue of his forceful, positive manner, however, he exercised great influence over the medical opinion of his day, and some of his observations have proved to be strikingly prophetic.

[Jos. M. Toner, *Address before the Rocky Mt. Medic. Asso., June 6, 1877* (1877), with biographies of the members; *Record of the Class of 1852, Yale Coll., for the Quarter Century after Graduation* (1878); Cutter's *Partial Syllabic Lists of the Clinical Morphologies of the Blood, Feces, Skin*, etc. (2 ed. 1892), containing a biographical sketch, and bibliography of his writings; *Trans. Am. Laryngol. Ass.*, 1917; *Boston Medic. and Surgic. Jour.*, CLXXVI, 684; *Va. Medic. Semi-Monthly*, XXII, 128–30; *Obit. Record Grads. Yale Univ.*, 1917; Benj. Cutter, *Hist. of the Cutter Family of New Eng.* (1871); J. W. Leonard, *Men of America* (1908); *Who's Who in America*, 1916–17.] W. A. W.

CUTTER, GEORGE WASHINGTON (1801–Dec. 25, 1865), poet, was born in Quebec, Canada, of a family which had come there from Massachusetts. His education was not extensive but for a time he studied law and, after a residence at Terre Haute, Ind., during which he served in the lower house of the Indiana legislature, 1838–39 (*Complete List of Members*, etc., 1903), he practised in Covington, Ky., until the beginning of the Mexican War stirred his imagination with visions of conquest for his country and of military glory for himself. In 1847 he helped to raise a company of volunteers, which became a part of the 2nd Kentucky Regiment. He was made its captain and joined Taylor's army on the Rio Grande, where he served with distinction until the close of the war. He took part in the battle of Buena Vista during which he helped to carry Col. Clay from a position of danger under the enemy's fire and remained with him until his death. The victory inspired one of his best-known poems, written on the battle-field. At the close of the war he went into politics as a zealous Whig and later became a more or less popular orator in the cause of Know-Nothingism. He was also at one time an earnest advocate and speaker for the temperance cause. Under Taylor's administration he received a clerkship in the Treasury Department at Washington which he held until the close of Fillmore's administration, when he lost it through political changes and left Washington. Early in life he had married Mrs. Frances Ann Drake of Cincinnati, an actress in tragic parts, from whom he was divorced. Later he married again in the West. He published three volumes of verse, *Buena Vista and Other Poems* (1848), *The Song of Steam and Other Poems* (1857), and *Poems, National and Patriotic* (1857)—all vigorous and unconventional in thought, if conventional in metre. *The Song of Steam*, his best work, is suggestive of Kipling's later poetic apotheosis of machinery. A few years before his death Cutter returned to Washington but found no employment. When stricken with paralysis, he was admitted to Providence Hospital on an order from the Commissioner of Public Buildings, and there he died alone. His funeral was conducted by the St. John's Masonic Lodge and he was buried in the lot owned by the Lodge in the Congressional Cemetery.

[Wm. T. Coggeshall, *Poets and Poetry of the West* (1860); J. W. Townsend, *Ky. in Am. Letters, 1784–1912* (1913); Rufus W. Griswold, *Poets and Poetry of America* (rev. ed. 1874); *Lib. of Southern Literature*, vol. XV (1909); Benj. Cutter, *Hist. of the Cutter Family of New Eng.* (1871); *New-Eng. Hist. and Geneal. Reg.*, Apr. 1866; *Evening Star* (Washington, D. C.), Dec. 27, 1865; *Daily Morning Chronicle* (Washington D. C.), Dec. 28, 1865.] S. G. B.

CUTTING, JAMES AMBROSE (1814–Aug. 6, 1867), inventor, son of Abijah Cutting, a descendant of a seventeenth-century English immigrant who settled in the central portion of what is now the state of New Hampshire, was born in the village of Hanover, on the western border of the state. Shortly after his birth his parents moved to Haverhill, N.H., where the family lived in straitened circumstances for a great many years, presumably as farmers. It would seem that young Cutting was interested in bee-keeping to the extent of consistently trying to improve the type of hive then in use. He eventually succeeded and on June 24, 1844, received United States Patent No. 3,638 for a beehive. Armed with his patent, Cutting proceeded to engage in the manufacture of his hive and apparently experienced partial financial success during the succeeding decade. It is said, however, that before the end of this period he was again made destitute through poor investments. He next became interested in photography, the daguerreotype then being in vogue. He is first heard of in this connection in April 1854 through correspondence with the Commissioner of Patents in Washington relative to his application for patents on improvements in the collodion process of photography. The broad claims made by him in the original application were rejected because the process was not new, but for certain details of the process, patents numbered 11,213, 11,266, and 11,267 were eventually granted in July 1854. In one of these he styled his process "ambrotype," from the Greek word *ambrotos*, meaning immortal, his claim being that by his process greater permanency of picture was secured than otherwise. The same month a British patent was granted him. Although Cutting is said to have enjoyed considerable prosperity for a time, it seems probable that these patents were of very little value to him, for the commercial photographers of the day were universally of the feeling that he was not entitled to the inventions, and accordingly paid very little regard to them. Cutting continued to reside in Boston engaging in photographic work and apparently experimenting in several allied directions, for on Mar. 16, 1858, he, with L. H. Bradford of Boston, received Patent No. 19,626 for a photolithographic process. This invention seems to have had some merit, for five years after Cutting's death his administrator, A. O. Butman, and Bradford obtained from the Patent Office an extension of the original patent. Cutting's name appears in the Boston city directories until 1862, when, because of his weakened mental state, he was committed to a lunatic asylum at Worcester, Mass., where he died five years later.

[M. H. Ellis, *The Ambrotype and Photographic Instructor* (1856); *Humphrey's Daguerrian Jour.*, 1854–56; *Ann. Cyc.*, 1867; *Worcester Daily Spy*, Aug. 12, 1867; correspondence with the Am. Antiquarian Soc., Worcester, Mass.; U. S. Patent Office records.]

C. W. M.

CUYLER, THEODORE (Sept. 14, 1819–Apr. 5, 1876), lawyer, was descended from Hendrick Cuyler, a native of Hassett, Overyssel, Netherlands, who emigrated to New Netherland some time prior to 1660, and settled at Albany. Fourth in direct line of descent was Cornelis Cuyler, a prominent pastor of the Reformed Dutch Church at Poughkeepsie, N. Y. He married Eleanor, daughter of Isaac de Graaff of Schenectady, and their eldest son, Theodore, was born at Poughkeepsie. His early education was obtained at the public school there, but, on the family removing in 1834 to Philadelphia, he entered the University of Pennsylvania and graduated in 1838, third in his class. After studying in the office of Charles Chauncey he was admitted to the bar, Oct. 7, 1841, and commenced practise in Philadelphia. Developing unusual legal talent, he was retained in many important causes at an early stage of his career. His brilliant advocacy in the celebrated Christiana treason case in the United States circuit court in November 1851, involving a charge against a number of persons for affording assistance to fugitive slaves from Maryland, placed him in the front rank of contemporary trial counsel. Interested in all local matters of public importance he found time to act as director of public schools in Philadelphia, and in 1856 became a member of the Select Council, a position which he retained for six years, during four of which he was chairman. In April 1857 he was appointed solicitor at Philadelphia for the Pennsylvania Railroad Company, and when, twelve years later, a departmental reorganization took place he became its general counsel. For a number of years the company was involved in heavy litigation, which he conducted with remarkable success, establishing his reputation as the greatest corporation lawyer of the period. He was exceptional in that he was equally effective before a jury or on appeal, and for nearly twenty years he was retained on one side or the other in almost every corporation case of importance in Pennsylvania and the neighboring states. He "was prone to take cases too easily in the initial and middle stages, with the result that, to save the day he was often forced at the end to make herculean efforts. . . . Driven to the last ditch he was most dangerous, and more than once snatched victory out of the very jaws of destruction" (Eastman, *post*). In 1872 he was elected a delegate-at-large from Philadelphia to the Pennsylvania state constitutional convention, and took a prominent part in its discussions. He died in Philadelphia, Apr. 5, 1876. He was married, on Dec. 21, 1853, to Mary Elizabeth, eldest daughter of Rev. Thomas de Witt of New York.

[Maud Churchill Nicoll, *The Earliest Cuylers in Holland and America* (1912); J. T. Scharf and T. Westcott, *Hist. of Phila.* (1884), II, 1546; P. M. Eastman, *Courts and Lawyers of Pa.* (1922), III, 830; *Legal Intelligencer*, Apr. 7, 14, 1876.]

H. W. H. K.

CUYLER, THEODORE LEDYARD (Jan. 10, 1822–Feb. 26, 1909), Presbyterian clergyman, writer, son of Benjamin Ledyard and Louisa (Morrell) Cuyler, was born in Aurora, N. Y., of which town his great-grandfather, Gen. Benjamin Ledyard of New London, Conn., whose daughter Mary married Glen Cuyler, was one of the first settlers. The Cuylers were of Dutch origin, descendants of Hendrick, who came to Albany about 1664 (Maud C. Nicoll, *The Earliest Cuylers in Holland and America and Some of their Descendants*, 1912). Theodore's father died when his son was but four and a half years old, and the latter was brought up on his grandfather Morrell's farm by a deeply religious mother who early determined that he should enter the ministry. Prepared for college by private tutorship and at the Hill Top School, Mendham, N. J., he graduated from Princeton in 1841 at the age of nineteen. The following year he made a trip to Europe where he visited Wordsworth, Dickens, and Carlyle, an interesting description of whom is given in his *Recollections of a Long Life*. In 1846 he graduated from the Princeton Theological Seminary, was licensed by the Second Presbytery of Philadelphia, Apr. 22 of the same year, and ordained by the Presbytery of West Jersey, May 4, 1848. From 1846 to 1849 he supplied the Presbyterian Church at Burlington, N. J., and from 1849 to 1853 he was pastor of the Third Church, Trenton. While here, Mar. 17, 1853, he married Annie E. Mathiot, daughter of Joshua Mathiot of Newark, Ohio. In November of this year he became pastor of the Market Street Dutch Reformed Church of New York, where he remained until 1860 when he began a thirty years' pastorate at the Lafayette Avenue Presbyterian Church, Brooklyn. In April 1890 he became pastor emeritus, continuing to reside in Brooklyn, preaching, lecturing, and writing.

During his long service in Brooklyn, he became one of the most popular preachers of that city and known throughout the country as a public speaker and writer. His sermons were pungent, evangelical in tone, enforced with striking illustrations, and delivered with great earnestness. Preaching he regarded as "spiritual gunnery," and said that his hearers would testify that he had never spared his lungs or their ears. Theologically, he was a conservative, declaring that he had found that "the true things were not new, and most of the new things were not true." In the great revival of 1858 which began in New York he was one of the early leaders. Vigorous in body and abounding in energy, he gave himself to a variety of activities. He was especially interested in the temperance movement, and made his first public address at a welcome to Father Mathew in the City Hall, Glasgow, in 1842. He prepared the constitution for the National Temperance Society and Publication House, founded in 1865, and later was for some years its president. In theory he was a "legal suppressionist," but declared that the only real remedy for the liquor evil lies in removing the desire to use liquor. Without a stiff public sentiment back of legal suppression, he contended, "it may become a delusion and a farce." He wrote for the religious press incessantly, and before his death boasted four thousand articles, many of which were translated into foreign languages. He also published some twenty-two books, several of them widely popular. For the most part they are informally devotional in character, but include two volumes of sermons, *Stirring the Eagle's Nest and other Practical Discourses* (1892) and *A Model Christian* (1903), a volume of foreign travel, *From the Nile to Norway* (1882), and his *Recollections of a Long Life* (1902). The last named has much charm and contains sketches of many famous people at home and abroad whom the author had known.

[In addition to his *Recollections* see, *Necrological Report, Princeton Theol. Sem.* (1909); *Who's Who in America*, 1908–09; *Lafayette Ave. Ch., its Hist. and Commemorative Services* (1885); obituary in *N. Y. Times*, Feb. 27, 1909, editorial, Feb. 28, 1909.]

H. E. S.

DABLON, CLAUDE (Jan. 21, 1619, or Feb. 1618–May 3, or Sept. 20, 1697), Jesuit missionary from Dieppe, began his novitiate at Paris in 1639. From the beginning of his career he had a great desire to enter the foreign field. Sent to Canada in 1655, he was almost immediately designated for the Iroquois mission, the most difficult and dangerous in North America. Dablon was at this time in early middle life, with vigorous intellect and keen powers of observation, and withal physically fit and the possessor of unsurpassed endurance. He left Montreal in the autumn of 1655 together with Father Chaumonot and a party of Iroquois. His diary expresses his delight in the wilderness and in the beauties of nature. "I sleep," he wrote en route, "as well on the ground as I did on a mattress or as I would in a feather bed" (*Jesuit Relations*, XLI, 227). The winter was passed among the Onondaga at the present Liverpool, N. Y. In the spring, it being necessary to consult the authorities in Canada, Dablon went thither on foot, Mar. 2–30, a terrible journey over melting ice and softening snow-fields. At Quebec it was determined to accede to the request of the Iroquois for a French settlement in their midst, and Dablon became leader of a colony of fifty Frenchmen, who for months lived among these Indians in central New York. Then, having learned that the Indians meditated treachery and massacre, the entire group succeeded in escaping in March 1658, and reached Canada in safety.

Dablon remained three years thereafter at Quebec in civilized surroundings. He was, however, always eager for distant explorations and in May 1661, with Father Druillettes, undertook an excursion up the Saguenay and across to Lake St. John on a mission to the Cree tribe. In 1669 he was sent to the Northwest as superior of the Ottawa mission, where Allouez and Marquette were already laboring. He made headquarters at Sault Ste. Marie, and thence he sent Allouez late in the same year to explore the region around Green Bay and begin missions among the tribes there. The next autumn Dablon himself accompanied Allouez on a visit to central Wisconsin. His descriptions of his journey are full of enthusiasm; he likened the passage of the rapids of the lower Fox River to the steps up to Paradise. Into that river the missionaries threw a stone idol, worshipped by the neighboring Indians. Dablon also gave a detailed description of the Lake Superior copper mines, and of the pageant whereby France in June 1671 took possession of the region of the upper Great Lakes. Chosen Superior of all the Canadian missions while still in the Northwest, Dablon returned to Quebec to take office July 12, 1671. It was he who appointed Marquette to accompany Joliet on his voyage of discovery to the Mississippi and who reported that discovery to the authorities in France. Dablon never again left Quebec; his first term as Superior ended in 1680, but he served again in that office 1686–93. He was one of the most energetic, able and conscientious of the Canadian missionaries; his zeal and endurance were notable, and his judgment was excellent; his delight in nature and in the conquering of obstacles distinguished him; and his writings are a source of information about natural phenomena and the habits and customs of the natives. He was a contributor to the *Relations* of 1669–70, reviser of those of 1672–73, 1679, editor of the published *Relations* of 1670–71, 1671–72, and compiler of those from 1673 to 1678. He also edited Marquette's narratives, aided Chaumonot in arranging his autobiography and wrote several diaries of his travels and letters which have been preserved.

[Dablon's writings are in *The Jesuit Relations and Allied Documents* (1896–1901), ed. by R. G. Thwaites, *passim.* See sketch in *The Jesuit Relations,* vol. XLI, p. 257; T. J. Campbell, *Pioneer Priests of North America 1642–1710* (1908), I, 101–24; L. P. Kellogg, *French Régime in Wis. and the Northwest* (1925), 158–63, 169, 188, 191.] L. P. K.

DABNEY, RICHARD (1787–Nov. 25, 1825), poet, was born in Louisa County, Va., a son of Samuel Dabney and his wife Jane Meriwether (aunt of the explorer Meriwether Lewis). His father, member of an old Virginia family of distinguished descent, was a small planter, able to provide his twelve children with only meager educational advantages. Richard, however, when about sixteen entered a classical school where he made astonishing progress with Greek and Latin, and shortly won a position as assistant teacher in a Richmond academy. In 1812 he published at Richmond a small volume of *Poems, Original and Translated,* but, disappointed at the indifference shown it, soon sought its suppression. Seeking a literary career, he moved to Philadelphia, where he remained for a few years in the employ of Mathew Carey [*q.v.*], the publisher, and is supposed to have written a large part of the latter's powerful plea for party unity in war-time, *The Olive Branch; or Faults on Both Sides, Federal and Democratic* (1814). In 1815 a revised and augmented edition of the *Poems,* likewise a losing venture, was issued by Carey. The original poems consist of "Illustrations of the Simple Moral Emotions" and miscellaneous patriotic or love lyrics; two-fifths of the volume is composed of translations or adaptations from the Greek, Latin, and Italian, with one piece from the French. Of the original compositions with their naïve prefaces and notes, shadowy abstractions, and amateurish refrains, little needs to be said; many are didactic and funereal, others echo recent English poets. The translations, the work of a scholar rather than a poet, are better, although undistinguished. His rendering of Greek and Latin lacks the simple lucidity of the classics; his sonnets from the Italian show a prosodical concern unusual in his writings, save in his blank verse, yet similarly fail to "touch the magic string." Intellectual range and vigor are more noticeable in his verse than metrical talent; too often his product is marred by unnatural syntax, limping rhythms, or impossible rhymes. His claim to poetic attainment seemingly lies in the mere fact that his book was twice printed; it is incredible that any one should examine the poems thoughtfully and yet overestimate them so grossly as has customarily been done. From Philadelphia Dabney returned to Louisa County, where he read extensively, enjoyed freely the convivial social life of the region, and, at the instigation of neighbors, taught a small school. To him was erroneously attributed, in 1818, over his disclaimer, the authorship of a widely admired classical poem, *Rhododaphne.* His increased dependence upon opium, first prescribed in consequence of painful injuries contracted at the burning of the Richmond Theatre, Dec. 26, 1811, and his lifelong fondness for drink rendered his last years creatively barren. He died, unmarried, at his birthplace, after considerable bodily suffering, fruit of his infirmities and indulgence, and a no less acute mental anguish born of disappointed hopes and the consciousness of abilities squandered.

[*Dabneys of Va.* (1888), by W. H. Dabney, gives the genealogy of the family. The single authoritative notice of Richard Dabney is the sketch contributed by Lucian Minor of Louisa County, Va., thirty years after the poet's death, to E. A. and G. L. Duyckinck, *Cyclopædia of Am. Lit.* (1856), II, 98–100. On this all subsequent notices have been modeled, without any effort to reveal facts omitted by Minor, or any attempt to corroborate his critical opinions. When it is recalled that Minor was a zealous temperance advocate, it is reasonable to assume that, in his eagerness to point a stronger moral, he may have been led unconsciously to enlarge upon both the poet's intemperance and talents.] A. C. G., Jr.

DABNEY, ROBERT LEWIS (Mar. 5, 1820–Jan. 3, 1898), Presbyterian theologian, teacher, author, son of Charles and Elizabeth R. (Price) Dabney, was born in Louisa County, Va., and died in Victoria, Tex. The Dabneys are believed to have descended from Cornelius Dabney, or d'Aubigné, a French Protestant who came to Virginia in the early eighteenth century, after a considerable residence in England. Robert Dabney's father was a planter in moderate circumstances, and the boy, one of eight children, was educated at such schools as the community afforded. He attended Hampden-Sidney College (1836–37), and after teaching school (1838–39), completed his college work at the University of Virginia (1840–42). He studied at the (Virginia) Union Theological Seminary (1844–46) and, becoming a minister, served first as a rural missionary and later as pastor of the Tinkling Spring Church. He was married on Mar. 28, 1848 to Lavinia Morrison, daughter of the Rev. James Morrison of Rockbridge County. From 1853 to 1883, he taught at the Union Theological Seminary, preached at the local chapel, and from time to time conducted courses at the adjacent Hampden-Sidney College. His prowess as a commentator in church publications made him generally known among Presbyterians, and in 1860 he was twice given opportunity to identify himself with important institutions in the North—as professor at Princeton and as minister of the Fifth Avenue Presbyterian Church in New York. He became a Confederate army chaplain in 1861, and in 1862 he was a major on the staff of his friend and idol, Stonewall Jackson. In 1883, the condition of his health demanding a warmer climate, he became professor of philosophy in the University of Texas, where he remained till 1894. During the late eighties he was instrumental in establishing the Austin School of Theology. He wrote many philosophic books and essays. The most important of these, *Practical Philosophy* (1897), written first as a series of lectures for college students, is Calvinistic in theology and reactionary in politics, based on an assumption that virtue had its origin by divine fiat—literally, as accounted for in the Bible, and that it is for that reason immutable and deserving of all fealty. His best-known work is his *Life and Campaigns of Lieutenant-General Thomas J. Jackson (Stonewall Jackson)*, published in 1866, and his most vivid one, *A Defense of Virginia and the South* (1867). Others were: *The Christian Soldier* (1863); *A Memorial of Lieut.-Col. John T. Thornton* (1864); *Sacred Rhetoric* (1870); *Syllabus and Notes of the Course of Systematic and Polemic Theology* (1871); *Parental Obligation* (1880); *The New South* (1883). Before the Civil War he opposed secession, but once battles were under way he vouched with a progressive assurance for the wickedness of the North and for the purely Christian nature of the conflict as seen from the standpoint of the South. Defeated, he believed these doctrines still, and was unable to think that the mere event of one day at Appomattox could affect principles which he held absolute. He thought that the only way for Southerners to save the true spiritual South, which alone seemed of interest to him, was for them to abandon the conquered geographic South forthwith and completely, and until about 1870 he concerned himself with projects for a grand-scale migration to Australia or perhaps Brazil. The opposition even of Gen. Lee to these plans was to him negligible, the result of military training rather than of a just apprehension of history and human nature. From 1890 till his death he was infirm and totally blind, but he continued active, delivering in the Carolinas as late as the fall of 1897 the two courses of lectures which later appeared in the volume, *Christ Our Penal Substitute* (1898). At these lectures he was a figure not to be observed dispassionately—he was a blind, groping old man, championing with dogmatism a waning creed; but he was none the less majestic—and those who listened to him felt that he embodied learning and benevolence and romantic honor.

[T. C. Johnson, *Life and Letters of Robt. Lewis Dabney* (1903); *In Memoriam, Robt. Lewis Dabney* (1899); W. H. Dabney, *Dabneys of Va.* (1888); J. C. McAllister, "Robt. Lewis Dabney," *Lib. of Southern Lit.* (1907).]

J. D. W.

DABNEY, THOMAS SMITH GREGORY (Jan. 4, 1798–Feb. 28, 1885), planter, was born at "Bellevue," King and Queen County, Va., of well-to-do Huguenot stock, son of Benjamin and Sarah (Smith) Dabney. His father dying early, the boy grew up in New York at the home of his uncle, Dr. John Augustine Smith. After several sessions of boarding-school in New Jersey he entered the College of William and Mary, but soon withdrew to manage the family estate, "Elmington," in Gloucester County, where for fifteen years he raised wheat and tobacco and followed the agreeable existence of the antebellum Virginia gentleman. He married, June 6, 1820, Mary Adelaide, daughter of Samuel Tyler of Williamsburg, who died three years later, and on June 26, 1826, he married Sophia Hill of King and Queen County.

In 1835, to provide more adequately for his growing family and his numerous slaves, he moved to Hinds County, Miss., and turned cotton planter. A diligent and skilled executive, he was successful from the first. Much of his prosperity proceeded from the sense of responsibility which, out of compassion rather than self-interest, he felt toward his negroes: his consideration and affection, and even firmness, they repaid with unvarying devotion. At the same time he managed—more carefully than his own, it was said—four other plantations; was an eager, although personally disinterested, student of public affairs; fished, hunted, and played whist; entertained so open-handedly as to win reputation as an "incomparable host"; and devoted himself to his large family. His Whig principles helped to make him a strong Unionist, and when secession threatened he would have moved to England save for his inability to provide comfortably for his slaves; yet, when war came, he gave unreservedly to the South his crops, his money, and his sons, and fretted because he himself was not in the field.

Peace found him in straitened circumstances. To cap his losses of over a half-million dollars in slaves, livestock, and household goods, the defalcation of a friend caused the sacrifice of his remaining property and saddled him with a debt which took fourteen years of bitterest self-denial to pay. He could have avoided this by declaring himself bankrupt: instead, the hands that had never performed manual labor learned to garden, saw wood, and even—to save his daughters—do the washing. Adversity chastened him, made him tender, more patient, but did not bend him: to his death he remained the patrician, guileless, generous, high-hearted, courageous, tolerant of all save dishonesty or littleness. His actual achievement was slight; his significance was that he symbolized a class, a section, an era. "I never could forget that I was born a gentleman, and incapable, consequently, of a mean action," he wrote, and in living out this creed he embodied the finest traditions of Southern manhood under the institution of slavery. Without aspiring to drive "the horses of the sun," nevertheless he lived greatly, so naturally and unostentatiously filling a long life with honorable deeds that Gladstone, upon reading his biography, was moved to pronounce him "one of the very noblest of human characters."

[The foregoing sketch is based almost entirely on Susan Dabney Smedes, *Memorials of a Southern Planter* (1887), which besides setting forth Dabney's strongly marked individuality is an interesting, though perhaps idealistic, picture of the old régime in the South. There are other biographical touches in the romantic novel, *The Story of Don Miff* (1886), by his son, Virginius Dabney (*q.v.*).] A. C. G., Jr.

DABNEY, VIRGINIUS (Feb. 15, 1835–June 2, 1894), teacher, author, son of Thomas Smith Gregory and Sophia (Hill) Dabney, was born at his father's plantation, "Elmington," in Gloucester County, Va., and died in New York City. His father [*q.v.*], an exemplar as near as might be of the legendary Southern gentleman, removed in 1835 from Virginia to Mississippi, to a plantation in Hinds County, named "Burleigh." Virginius was educated at home by tutors and was later sent to school in Richmond. From eighteen to twenty-three, with the exception of the fourth of these years, when he was traveling in Europe, he studied at the University of Virginia. Then he married Ellen Maria Heath and went to Memphis to practise law. The death of his wife in April 1860 brought him back to Virginia, and the outbreak of the Civil War interrupted his at best half-hearted intention of returning to his office. He entered the Confederate army immediately upon its organization and continued with it till it was disbanded, having the rank of captain when he was mustered out. After the war he established the Loudoun School in Middleburg, Va., and in February 1867 he married Anna Wilson Noland. During 1873–74 he was in charge of a preparatory school at Princeton, and afterward he conducted the New York Latin School in New York City. He was on the editorial staff of the New York *Commercial Advertiser* and he acted as literary adviser to several prominent publishers. In 1886, he published his novel, *The Story of Don Miff,* the proper name being a lisper's version of John Smith. This book, written, according to the title-page, by John Bouche Whacker, and edited by Virginius Dabney, is a record of Virginia from about 1860 to 1865 addressed by one still a bachelor to his supposititious descendant of the year 2200. Regarded at the time of its appearance as exceedingly profound, it in some degree justifies such an estimate. It is conventional at base, but in many important matters its author is revealed as a whimsical, shrewd, and wise critic of the social order he saw making itself paramount in America. He abandoned his school in 1887, and till the fall of 1893, when he became an official in the New York Custom House, devoted himself entirely to literature. His second novel, *Gold that did not Glitter* (1889), omitting the philosophic elements of *Don Miff,* attained neither popularity nor distinction. Circumstance forbade that in its externals his life should be identical with the romantically feudal lives of his father and his grandfather, and he was more sophisticated than they, more tolerant and humorous—but in the essential matter of his high if often unpractical attitude toward life he was never far removed from them.

[V. Dabney, "A Mighty Hunter Before the Lord," in C. King, *Rancho del Muerto* (1894); S. D. Smedes, *Memorials of a Southern Planter* (1887); W. H. Dabney, *Dabneys of Va.* (1888); P. A. Bruce, *Hist. of the Univ. of Va.* (1922); *Richmond Times,* June 3, 1894.] J. D. W.

DABOLL, NATHAN (Apr. 24, 1750–Mar. 9, 1818), philomath, maker of almanacs, teacher of navigation, was born in Groton, Conn., the son of Nathan and Anna (Lynn) Daboll. The former, as witness to the will of the Rev. Jonathan Owen, spelled his name "Dibbell." Although he received some instruction in the local school and under the village parson, Rev. Jonathan Barber, young Nathan was for the most part self-taught. His tutor thought him dull, probably because he showed little interest in anything but mathematics. For this science, however, he had great natural aptitude, and while, through force of necessity, he worked as a cooper, he mastered the intricacies of its higher branches. In 1770 Timothy Green of New London was publishing a series of almanacs prepared by Clark Elliott. An error in the calculations for that year, perhaps discovered by Daboll, so mortified Elliott that he withdrew his name from subsequent issues, substituting the *nom de plume* of "Edmund Freebetter," and Daboll was employed to revise the calculations. In 1773 Green also published the *New England Almanack by Nathan Daboll, Philomath,* the first of a series which, continued by son, grandson, and great-grandson, has endured to the present time. For some years, however, Daboll's name was not on the title-page. According to James H. Trumbull (*List of Books Printed in Connecticut 1709-1800,* 1904). "Mr. Daboll's name appeared first on the Almanac of 1773, and was continued on those of 1774 and 1775. It was then dropped for that of 'Edmund Freebetter,' whose almanacs had gained a degree of popularity hardly inferior to those published with the name of Ames. In 1793 the New England Almanack, &c., 'by Nathan Daboll' was published, and in announcing it (Oct. 18, 1792) Green states that 'to Mr. Daboll the public have for many years been indebted for the correct calculation of Freebetter's Almanack.'"

Living in a maritime town, and proficient in navigation and nautical astronomy, he also devoted much time to the instruction of seamen. In 1783 he was persuaded to become teacher of mathematics and astronomy in Plainfield (Conn.) Academy, but returned to Groton in 1788, and resumed his work as a nautical instructor. In 1799 he published *Daboll's Complete Schoolmaster's Assistant,* an early and extensively used school arithmetic. Members both of the merchant marine and of the navy were his pupils. In 1811, on the invitation of Commodore Rodgers, he taught a large class in the cabin of the frigate *President.* He also prepared *Daboll's Practical Navigator: Being a concise, easy, and comprehensive system of Navigation, calculated for the daily use of seamen, and also for an Assistant to the Teacher.... Also a New, Scientific and very short method of Correcting the Dead Reckoning; with rules for keeping a complete Reckoning at Sea applied to Practice, and exemplified in three separate JOURNALS, in which may be seen all the varieties which can possibly happen in a Ship's Reckoning* (1820). It was printed and sold by Samuel Green of New London, who states that the sickness and death of the author is responsible for delay in publication. He is described as of medium height, stoutly built, inclining somewhat to corpulency in later life, with massive head, high, broad forehead, and heavy overarching eyebrows. Taciturn and reserved, he mingled little in society. He was twice married: first to a cousin, Elizabeth, daughter of John Daboll 2nd; and after her death to "Widow Elizabeth Brown" of Noank, Conn.

[*The New England Almanac* for 1894; Chas. R. Stark, *Groton, Conn.* (1922); F. M. Caulkins, *Hist. of New London, Conn.* (1852); *Conn. as a Colony and as a State* (1904), vols. II and IV, ed. by Forrest Morgan; Hugh A. Morrison, *Preliminary Check List of Am. Almanacs, 1639-1800* (1907); letters from Ernest C. Daboll, publisher of the *New England Almanac.*]

H. E. S.

DĄBROWSKI, JOSEPH (Jan. 19, 1842–Feb. 15, 1903), Roman Catholic priest, founder of SS. Cyril and Methodius Seminary in Detroit, Mich., was born at Żółtańce in Russian Poland. He received his elementary education from his mother. After graduation from the gymnasium of Lublin he matriculated at the University of Warsaw, where he specialized in mathematics and the natural sciences. When the Polish uprising of 1863 broke out, Dąbrowski promptly joined a regiment of teachers and students and fought under Mierosławski. Among the many engagements in which he took part was that of Krzywosącz from which he barely escaped with his life. After the collapse of the insurrection he returned to Warsaw, but, since the Russian spies were searching for those who bore arms in the revolt, he left Poland rather hurriedly for Dresden. Afterward he went to Lucerne and then to Berne, where he studied mathematics and technology. Subsequently going to Rome, he entered the Polish College conducted by the Fathers of the Congregation of the Resurrection. On the completion of his theological studies, he was ordained a priest on Aug. 1, 1869. Landing in America on Dec. 31, 1869, he resided for a short time at St. Francis Seminary, near Milwaukee. In 1870 he took charge of the Polish congregation at Polonia, Portage County, Wis. Perceiving the need of schools and teachers for the children of the Polish immigrants he persuaded the Felician Sisters of Cracow to come to America. Five of these arrived in Polonia in the autumn of 1874. He had built a home for them here and he aided them in establishing a Mother-house and an orphanage in Detroit. Mich. Ill health obliging him to leave Polonia in 1883, he then became chaplain to the Felician Sisters in Detroit. Since the number of immigrants had increased, American bishops frequently wrote to Cardinal Ledochowski, Prefect of the Propaganda, to send them Polish priests. Being unable to do this, he proposed the founding of a Polish seminary in America. Father Leopold Moczygemba, sent here to gather funds, collected about eight thousand dollars, but felt that owing to his advanced age he could not complete the undertaking. He therefore turned it over to Dąbrowski, who purchased a tract of land on Forest and St. Aubin Avenues in Detroit. A building was begun in 1884, but owing to lack of funds it was not completed until 1887. Dąbrowksi himself labored as a carpenter on the building, assisted by some of the first students, who worked as carpenters and bricklayers for their board and lodging. The school opened on Dec. 15, 1887 with only six students, but at the close of the term had twenty-six. In 1891 Dąbrowski established a weekly paper, *Niedziela,* published by the Seminary. In January 1903, when he was preparing to build an extension, he was obliged to dismiss twenty-nine students for insubordination. This unfortunate incident preyed on his mind and affected his health, already enfeebled by years of privation, worry, and intensive work. Suffering a heart attack on Feb. 9, he died as the result of another six days later. A kindly and self-sacrificing priest, he was deeply mourned by the Poles in America.

[*Historya Seminaryum Polskiego* (Detroit, 1910); Wenceslaus Kruszka, *Historya Polska w Ameryce* (6 vols., Milwaukee, 1905); *Sodalis Maryański* (Orchard Lake, Mich.), Feb. 1928, pp. 242–46; *Nasze Pisemko* (Felician Sisters, Detroit, 1928), vol. V; *Detroit Free Press,* Feb. 16, 1903; *Detroit Tribune,* Feb. 19, 1903; *Cath. Encyc.,* App.] J. J. R.

DA COSTA, JACOB MENDEZ (Feb. 7, 1833–Sept. 11, 1900), physician, the son of John Mendez Da Costa, was born on the island of St. Thomas in the West Indies. The Da Costa family was of Spanish and Portuguese extraction; some of the members went to England and from this branch Jacob Da Costa was descended. When he was four years of age the family moved to Europe, where he received his early education, largely in Dresden. He acquired a sound knowledge of the classics, learned to speak French and German fluently, and acquired a reading knowledge of four other languages. His family having suffered financial reverses, he had to give up his plans to follows politics or diplomacy and decided to study medicine, entering the Jefferson Medical College in Philadelphia in 1849 and having Prof. Mütter as a preceptor. He graduated in 1852 and soon after went to Paris for post-graduate study. Of those under whom he studied, Trousseau, whose clinical lectures are among the classics of medicine, probably had the greatest influence on him. This influence is seen in Da Costa's descriptions of disease, the careful choice of words, the orderly arrangement, and the graceful diction of his later productions. From Paris he went to Prague and Vienna, coming under the influence of many of those who were breaking new paths in medicine, among them Oppolzer, Skoda, Rokitansky, and Hebra. He worked particularly in pathology and clinical medicine, and there is much to suggest that he was following out a well-thought plan looking to a career as a teacher and a practitioner of what to-day is termed internal medicine.

In 1853 he returned to Philadelphia and at once became active in teaching. He also gave private classes in his office which became very popular. Probably his special knowledge of the newer methods in physical diagnosis had much to do with the success of these courses. He evidently attracted the attention of the elder Gross, for in 1857 he assisted Gross in the revision of his work on *Elements of Pathological Anatomy.* He was active in the foundation of the Pathological Society of Philadelphia in 1857, serving as its first secretary. In 1865 he was appointed to the staff of the Pennsylvania Hospital, to which he gave freely of his time and energy until his death. In 1872 he was elected professor of medicine in the Jefferson Medical College, and this position he held until 1891. Here his main work was done, with such colleagues as the elder Gross and Pancoast, and here his reputation as a great teacher and clinician was made. A wealth of tradition remains in Philadelphia as to his great ability in both spheres. He was regarded as having an almost uncanny power of diagnosis, which usually means keen powers of observation and an alert mind.

His medical writings were not voluminous, but all were of value and some of outstanding merit. He insisted on the importance of learning and of clear statement and especially on the evil of publishing crude theories and unproved statements. Of his publications, first place belongs to the work on *Medical Diagnosis* (1864). This work may be said to have opened a new era and its influence was wide-spread on teaching and clinical methods. It went through nine editions and was translated into several other languages. In it the problems of the recognition of disease were discussed in a systematic fashion which altered markedly the conception of medical diagnosis and brought order out of what had been too often haphazard guessing. Of his studies on various diseases, that which is best known is his description of the irritable heart in soldiers, in which from his study of soldiers in the Civil War he described a new clinical syndrome (see *Contributions Relating to the Causation and Prevention of Disease, and to Camp Diseases,* edited by Austin Flint and published by the United States Sanitary Commission, 1867). This malady was an important cause of disability in the World War. He also wrote extensively on typhoid fever. His medical papers were of a high standard and he strove for quality rather than quantity in his writings.

Many honors came to him both in an academic way and in medical societies. He was twice president of the College of Physicians of Philadelphia (1884–86 and 1895–98) and took a deep interest in its welfare. He was an original member of the Association of American Physicians and its president in 1897. He was a member of many medical societies and received honorary degrees from several universities. In addition to being physician to the Jefferson and Pennsylvania Hospitals, he held the same position in the Episcopal and Philadelphia General Hospitals. In 1899 he was made a trustee of the University of Pennsylvania. In 1860, he married Sarah Frederica Brinton, the sister of one of his colleagues, Dr. John H. Brinton [*q.v.*]. She died in 1889, leaving one child. For some years Da Costa suffered from angina pectoris, dying in an attack at Villanova, Pa., on Sept. 11, 1900. Admiration for his character seems to have been as great as for his intellectual and professional gifts. He may be regarded as having lived an ideal life for a physician, devoted to the care of the sick, the teaching of students, and the study of disease. Throughout his life the welfare of members of his own profession was always his concern and he has been called "the physician's physician."

[Memoirs by J. C. Wilson, in *Trans. of the Coll. of Physicians of Phila.*, 3 ser., vol. XXIV (1902); and Mary A. Clarke, in *Am. Jour. Medic. Sci.*, CXXV, 318 (1903).]

T. M.

DAFT, LEO (Nov. 13, 1843–Mar. 28, 1922), electrical engineer, inventor, was born in Birmingham, England, the son of Thomas B. and Emma Matilda (Sturges) Daft. His father was a consulting civil engineer specializing in bridge and iron-ship construction. Daft attended the public schools and Liverpool Collegiate until he was fifteen and then entered his father's office as a draftsman. Among his father's friends were Varley and Siemens, pioneers in electricity, and through them young Daft became interested in this subject, devoting much of his spare time for eight years to study and experimental work. In 1866, believing that his best opportunity lay in America, he sailed for New York. For the next five years he was engaged in a variety of occupations while looking for a suitable opportunity in electricity. Finding none, he started a photographic studio in Troy, N. Y., in 1871. Successful in this, he continued it until 1879 when, upon the death of his father, he began his electrical career in earnest. His first connection was with the New York Electric Light Company, which was soon merged into the Daft Electric Company, developing electric-power machinery and building several electric-power plants in Boston, New York, Worcester, and elsewhere. In 1883 Daft began electric-railroad experiments, built an electric locomotive, named "The Ampere," for the Saratoga and Mt. McGregor Railroad, and in the following year installed a short line at Coney Island, N. Y. In 1884 his company supplied the machinery for the New York Power Company's first distributing station of electric power in Gold St., and also manufactured all the electrical apparatus for the Massachusetts Electric Power Company. This was the first instance of a complete central station for the generation and distribution of electricity for power purposes on a commercial scale. In 1885 the company installed its electric railway system in Baltimore on a branch of the Baltimore Union Passenger Railway. This was the first commercially operated electric road in the United States. The Daft system was subsequently used in a number of cities and a Daft locomotive was tried out on the elevated railroad of New York City. Daft's ability not only in electric construction but in distribution attracted universal attention and gave a direct and lasting impulse to the electric motor industry. Until 1890 he was the only inventor who had taken up the problem of the distribution of electric power and worked it out in the same manner as current for electric lighting, perfecting and providing the necessary apparatus throughout. After this, he directed his attention to the electro-chemical field, his chief invention being a process of vulcanizing rubber onto metal, now generally used. Daft was a charter member of the American Institute of Electrical Engineers; a member of the American

Association for the Advancement of Science; and of the Electro-Chemical Society. He never became a citizen of the United States, but married an American woman, Katherine Anna Flansburgh, on Mar. 11, 1871, at Albany, N. Y. With four children she survived him.

[Records Am. Inst. Electrical Engineers; *Cassier's Mag.*, July 1901; *Electrical World*, Mar. 30, 1889; *Jour. Am. Inst. Electrical Engineers*, May 1922; U. S. Nat. Museum correspondence with the Daft family.]
C. W. M.

DAGG, JOHN LEADLEY (Feb. 13, 1794–June 11, 1884), Baptist clergyman, educator, author, was born in a log cabin near Middleburg, Va., eldest of the eight children of Robert and Sarah (Davis) Dagg. His mother was a daughter of Samuel Davis of Pennsylvania and his wife, Sarah Leadley of New Jersey. His paternal grandfather was Thomas, son of John Dagg, who came to Virginia from Bristol, England, soon after 1700. From his youth John Dagg had two controlling and fortunately parallel ambitions, service in the Christian ministry and the promotion of thorough education. Partly because of poverty, however, he had only six or seven years of formal schooling, and this often interrupted, but he began to teach at the age of fourteen, an invitation to take charge of a school having come to him. Entering the Baptist ministry in 1817, he served as pastor, or supply, at Dumfries and other places in Virginia, and for nine years (1825–34) was pastor of the Fifth Baptist Church in Philadelphia. Forced by an affection of the throat to abandon preaching, he became head of the Haddington Institution, near Philadelphia. Chosen principal of the Alabama Female Athenæum in 1836, he became professor of theology at Mercer University, then at Penfield, Ga., in 1843, and president the following year. Finding an institution of a low grade, he left it in 1856 greatly enhanced in prestige. In all this educational work his prime desire was to influence young men to prepare for Christian work.

He left Mercer with the definite idea of still serving in the field of religious leadership by writing books which would aid young men in the service of the Christian ministry. Thus he prepared first a *Manual of Theology* (1857), which was of such significance that it has continued to be published until recently. His *Treatise on Church Order* (1858) has been equally useful. His *Elements of Moral Science* (1859) and his *Evidences of Christianity* (1868), while not popular for so long a period, were widely influential in their respective fields. All this he accomplished in spite of continuous ill health and a defect of eyesight which for many years rendered him nearly blind. When he could no longer see to use a pen he devised a special board which enabled him to write legibly. He was twice married: on Dec. 18, 1817, to Fannie H. Thornton, who died in September, 1823; and in 1831 to Mrs. Mary (Young) Davis, the mother of Noah Knowles Davis [*q.v.*]. He died at Hayneville, Ala.

[See Dagg's very rare *Autobiography* (Rome, Ga., 1886); Hillyer Hawthorne Straton, "John Leadley Dagg" (MS.); *Baptist Argus*, May 7, 1903; Philadelphia *Christian Gazette*, II (1834), 32, and Philadelphia *Nat. Baptist*, 1884, p. 457; all in the library of the Am. Baptist Hist. Soc., Chester, Pa. See also H. Holcombe, *A Hist. of the Rise and Progress of the Baptists in Ala.* (1840); B. F. Riley, *A Memorial Hist. of the Baptists of Ala.* (1923); *Hist. of the Baptist Denomination in Ga.* (1881), compiled for the *Christian Index*; S. G. Hillyer, *Reminiscences of Ga. Baptists* (1902).]
F. G. L.

DAGGETT, DAVID (Dec. 31, 1764–Apr. 12, 1851), lawyer, politician, jurist, born at Attleboro, Mass., was of Puritan descent, the son of Thomas and Sibulah (Stanley) Daggett. After graduating at Yale in 1783, he began the study of law in New Haven, where he maintained his residence throughout the remainder of a long life. Admitted to the bar in 1786, he was recognized from the start as a young man of great promise. An address delivered by him in New Haven as official orator, July 4, 1787, shows that he had already acquired many of the political principles which later made him prominent in the Federalist party, including a generous allowance of that pessimism regarding the future of American institutions which characterized so many of its leaders. Elected in 1791 to the lower branch of the legislature, he served there continuously, the last three years as speaker, until 1797, when he was elected to the Council. This body, under the old charter government prior to 1818, had many of the characteristics of an upper house, and at the same time a share in executive functions, including the patronage, which made its members exceedingly powerful in party affairs. He served here until 1804, when he resigned. He was elected to another term in the lower house in 1805, and in 1809 reëntered the Council where he remained until sent to the United States Senate in 1813.

He had in the meantime acquired a considerable practise and was active in a variety of local business and social affairs. The Jeffersonian Republicans, who became active in Connecticut about 1800, found in him one of their most active opponents. Early in the contest he clashed with Abraham Bishop [*q.v.*], and the two champions belabored each other in a series of pamphlets and newspaper articles. Various pamphlets of Daggett's published in these years, all of considerable literary merit, show his intensely conservative character. In *Count the Cost* (1804) he made an effective presentation of his views on state affairs, defending the church establishment and the retention of the old charter government, and denouncing democracy and universal suffrage. In the Senate he pursued much the same course as the other New England Federalists, who in the space of a dozen years had been transformed by the exigencies of party politics into defenders of state rights. The debates for this period were scantily reported but both of Daggett's recorded speeches, one against the militia bill, Nov. 16, 1814 (*Annals of Congress,* 13 Cong., 3 Sess., pp. 70 ff.), and the other on internal improvements, Feb. 26, 1817 (*Ibid.,* 14 Cong., 2 Sess., p. 165 ff.), are strict-constructionist expositions of the Constitution.

At the close of his term in 1819, he resumed practise in New Haven. In 1826 he began a service of twenty-two years at Yale as Kent Professor of Law, and in the same year was appointed an associate justice of the superior court. He was also mayor of New Haven, 1828–30. In 1832 he became chief justice of the supreme court of errors, serving until Dec. 31, 1834, when he was obliged to retire under the established age limitation. The noted case of Prudence Crandall [*q.v.*] arose (October 1833) during his term as chief justice. This was a prosecution under a Connecticut statute prohibiting the instruction of non-resident colored persons except by permission of the selectmen of the town. Judge Daggett's instructions to the jury, on the basis of which Miss Crandall was convicted, were to the effect that free negroes were not citizens of the United States within the terms of Art. IV, Sec. 2, of the Constitution and that the statute was therefore within the competence of the legislature. This pronouncement has a recognized place in the history of the constitutional status of the American negro. It is less well known, however, than it would have been had the supreme court not reversed the judgment on technical grounds, the chief justice dissenting, and thereby avoided adjudication of the main issue (10 *Conn.* 339). Daggett continued active in the practise and teaching of law for many years after his retirement from the bench. He married, Sept. 10, 1786, Wealthy Ann, daughter of Dr. Eneas Munson of New Haven. Following her death on July 9, 1839, he married, May 4, 1840, Mary, daughter of Capt. Major and Susanna (Mansfield) Lines, who survived him.

[F. B. Dexter, *Biog. Sketches Grads. Yale Coll.,* IV (1907), 260–64, gives a summary of Daggett's career with a bibliography and list of his publications. Dwight Loomis and J. Gilbert Calhoun in *Judicial and Civil Hist. of Conn.* (1895) give a brief sketch. The Yale library has a considerable collection of his papers. An obituary appeared in the *New Haven Jour.,* Apr. 14, 1851.]

W. A. R.

DAGGETT, ELLSWORTH (May 24, 1845–Jan. 5, 1923), metallurgist and mining engineer, was the son of Rev. Oliver and Elizabeth (Watson) Daggett and the grandson of David Daggett [*q.v.*]. Born in Canandaigua, N. Y., where his father happened to be holding a pastorate, he was sent to school in New Haven, Conn. Here he attended Gen. Russell's Military School and graduated in 1864 from the Sheffield Scientific School, thus conforming to the Yale tradition of his family. After he had done postgraduate work at Yale and attained his majority he went to the Gould and Curry mill, at Virginia City, Nev. Here he obtained practical training in mining and formed acquaintanceship with those influential men for whom, in after years, he did large consulting practise from his office in Salt Lake City. In 1870 he entered the United States Geological Survey of the Fortieth Parallel. The plates in volume III of the Survey's report (James D. Hague, *Mining Industry,* 1870) were made from Daggett's field-drawings. In 1872 he became manager of the Winnamuck smelting plant, Bingham Canyon, Utah. The financial organization of this enterprise he himself largely effected through prominent New Haven men. His masterful article, "Economical Results of Smelting in Utah" (*Transactions of the American Institute of Mining Engineers,* vol. II), based on the operations of the Winnamuck smelter, together with his monumental paper, "The Russell Process in its Practical Application and Economic Results" (*Ibid.,* vol. XVI), describing the use of this method of hyposulphite lixiviation of silver ores at Cusihuiriachic, Mexico, are evidence of Daggett's metallurgical ability. He was practically the first manager of an American lead-smelter to appreciate adequately and apply properly a system of metallurgical accounting to smelting operations, while his work with the Russell process ranks him among the earliest of American hydrometallurgists. He spent the year 1874–75 abroad, attending mining lectures at the Bergakademie, Berlin. Later, in his practise as consulting engineer and in his technical contributions for publication he became more identified with mining than metallurgy. He became largely occupied with examination and reports upon mining properties for prospective purchasers, and with testimony as an expert in mining litigation cases. Appointed in 1888 the first United States surveyor-general of Utah, he required that the mineral surveys be referred to true meridian and otherwise improved the accuracy and reliability of the survey. His effective activities in the development of irrigation projects in Utah eventually won for him the distinction of having a county named in his honor. On June 28, 1874, he married June Spencer of Salt Lake City. Their two sons died in childhood.

[*Trans. Am. Inst. Mining & Metallurgical Engineers*, vol. LXIX (1923); *Yale Univ. Obit. Record* (1923); New Haven *Jour.-Courier*, Jan 6, 1923; personal information from relatives.] R. C. C—y.

DAGGETT, NAPHTALI (Sept. 8, 1727–Nov. 25, 1780), Congregational clergyman, first incumbent of the first professorship in Yale College, and for more than ten years acting president, was born at Attleboro, Mass., the son of Ebenezer and Mary (Blackington) Daggett. He prepared for college with Rev. Solomon Reed of Abington, Mass., and with Rev. James Cogswell, of Plainfield, Conn. Graduating from Yale in 1748, having gained the Berkeley Scholarship, he studied theology, and on Sept. 18, 1751, was ordained first pastor of the Presbyterian Church at Smithtown, Long Island. On Dec. 19, 1753, he married Sarah, daughter of Richard and Anna Smith, of that town. In 1755, although he was but twenty-eight years old, he was nominated by President Clap [*q.v.*] for the professorship of divinity which had been established at Yale, and on Mar. 4, 1756 he was installed. Previous to his installation, in order, if possible, to get back the college congregation, which President Clap had removed, the First Church of New Haven invited Daggett to become colleague-pastor with Rev. Joseph Noyes, but acting no doubt under the president's advice, he declined. It was then proposed that he preach there for at least half the time, and the students were invited to attend without payment for sittings. After six months' trial, the arrangement was abandoned, and when in 1757 the Church of Christ in Yale College was established, he became its pastor. Upon the resignation of President Clap in 1766 he was appointed acting president, and served in that capacity until March 1777. The unsettled state in which President Clap left the college, and the pre-war conditions, made the period one of difficulty and little growth, but according to President Dwight, who was a tutor under him, "he had very just conceptions of the manner in which a College should be governed." The college prospered under him, but he was not always "happy in the mode of administering its discipline." (See Sprague, *post*, p. 483.) In 1776 the students petitioned the corporation for his removal. After his resignation he continued to serve as professor until his death. He is described as of "middle height, strong framed, inclining to be corpulent, slow in his gait and somewhat clumsy in his movements" (*Ibid.*, p. 480). He was orthodox, uncontroversial, and as a preacher had a drawling, unanimated delivery. He was an ardent supporter of the Revolution and is credited with the authorship of the "Cato Letters" in the *Connecticut Gazette*, which in 1765 inaugurated the attack on Tax-collector Jared Ingersoll (Lawrence H. Gipson, *Jared Ingersoll*, 1920, p. 158). When in 1779 the British invaded New Haven, he went out with those who resisted them, riding on an old black mare, and carrying a long fowling piece. He was captured and subjected to harsh treatment which, it is supposed, hastened his death.

His publications include *The Faithful Serving of God and Our Generation, the Only Way to a Peaceful and Happy Death, A Sermon Occasioned by the Death of Rev. Thomas Clap* (1767); *The Great Importance of Speaking in the Most Intelligible Manner in Christian Churches* (1768), *The Excellency of a Good Name* (1768), *The Great and Tender Concern of Faithful Ministers for the Souls of their People, Should Powerfully Excite Them Also to Labour After Their Own Salvation* (1770); *The Testimony of Conscience, a Most Solid Foundation of Rejoicing* (1773).

[T. Clap, *The Annals or Hist. of Yale Coll.* (1776); E. Baldwin, *Annals of Yale College* (1831); *The Literary Diary of Ezra Stiles* (1902); F. B. Dexter, *Biog. Sketches Grads. Yale College with Annals of the College Hist.*, vol. II (1896), III (1903), IV (1907); Wm. B. Sprague, *Annals Am. Pulpit*, vol. I (1857).] H. E. S.

DAHL, THEODOR HALVORSON (Apr. 2, 1845–Jan. 18, 1923), Lutheran clergyman, was born at Baastad, Mellem Borgesyssel, Norway, son of Halvor Thoreson Smaadal and his wife Anne Maastad. After attending Gjertsen's Latin School at Christiania for three years, he emigrated to America, where after two years of study at the (Scandinavian) Augustana Theological Seminary, Paxton, Ill., he was ordained a Norwegian Lutheran minister in 1867. Conspicuously successful as a home missionary among the scattered Norwegians in America, he was rapidly transferred from New London, Minn. (1867–68), to a post near Litchfield, Minn. (1868–73), and then to Green Bay, Wis. (1873–81). Eight congregations sprang up in the two latter places. His last pastoral charge was at Stoughton, Wis., where he served (1881–1903) until he was elevated to the full-time presidency of his synod. As a pastor he showed untiring zeal, an unfailingly affable and considerate spirit, and a devout sincerity. As a preacher he had marked mannerisms of voice and gesture, but never failed to draw large and attentive audiences.

His crowning achievement was his active participation in four successful church unions. When he was ordained in 1867 the synod was called the Scandinavian Augustana Synod. In 1870 the Norwegians and Swedes of this body effected an amicable separation into the Swedish and the Norwegian-Danish Augustana Synods. The majority of the latter body in 1870 joined a small group of other pastors and formed the Norwegian Danish Conference. That young Dahl entered actively into these union movements is amply proved by the fact that he was made a visitor of the Conference, 1873–76, and again, 1890–94. In 1876 he became secretary of the Conference and in 1881 its president, serving in the latter capacity until 1886. In 1887 the so-called Anti-Missouri Brotherhood withdrew from the Norwegian Synod, and after due negotiations entered into a union in 1890 with the conference and the latter's twin sister of 1870, the Augustana Synod, thus forming the United Norwegian Lutheran Church of America. In this work of union Dahl was conspicuously active, writing a brochure, *Fred og Strid* (Peace and Strife), in 1894 in defense of the union. From 1894 to 1902 he served as vice-president of the U. C., as it was familiarly called, and from 1902 to 1917 he served as its president. It is fitting that his presidency terminated with the existence of the U. C., this body uniting with the Norwegian Synod and the Hauge Synod to form the Norwegian Lutheran Church of America in 1917. His declining years were spent as rector of the Fairview Lutheran Hospital, Minneapolis, Minn.

Dahl was too busy to write a great deal. He translated *Lys fra Katakomberne* (Light from the Catacombs) in 1876, and in 1890 wrote a brochure, *Saloonforretningen* (The Saloon Business). He also wrote numerous reports as president and secretary. In all his work he was ably seconded by his devoted wife, Rebekka Oline (Gjertsen) whom he married in 1867 and survived.

[Scattered references are found in J. A. Bergh, *Den Norsk Lutherske Kirkes Historie in Amerika* (Minneapolis, 1914); biographies in Jens C. Jenssen (Roseland), *Am. Lutheran Biogs.* (Milwaukee, 1890); O. M. Norlie, *Norsk Lutherske Prester i Amerika 1843–1913* (Minneapolis, 1914), translated and revised by Rasmus Malmin, O. M. Norlie and O. A. Tingelstad as *Who's Who Among Pastors in All the Norwegian Lutheran Synods of America, 1843–1927* (Minneapolis, 1928).]

J. M. R.

DAHLGREN, JOHN ADOLPHUS BERNARD (Nov. 13, 1809–July 12, 1870), naval officer, inventor of ordnance, was born in Philadelphia, Pa. His father, Bernard Ulric Dahlgren, was a graduate of Upsala, a successful merchant well known for his ability and integrity. He was a man of great stature and strength, being over six feet four inches in height, and otherwise of majestic proportions. In 1804 he became involved in an attempt to disseminate republican principles at Gefle, and was obliged to flee from Sweden, and his property was confiscated by the Crown. After extended travel he landed in New York in 1806. The home government having withdrawn its persecution, he was appointed Swedish consul at Philadelphia, which post he held until his death in 1824. John Dahlgren's mother was Martha Rowan, daughter of James Rowan, who had served as an officer in the American Revolution. Dahlgren received his early schooling in a Quaker school in Philadelphia, and was also instructed by his father. When only fifteen years of age he was a good Latin, Spanish, and mathematical scholar. He was continually occupied in study and was particularly interested in the history of ancient Greece and Rome. Born and reared within sight of the river and shipping, the great object of his early ambition was to enter the United States navy. His first application was refused, notwithstanding the fact that he was recommended by many men of influence, including a judge, and members of the state legislature. He then shipped before the mast in the brig *Mary Beckett* bound for Trinidad de Cuba, in order that he might obtain a knowledge of his intended profession. On his return from this cruise, and before he was sixteen years of age, he wrote his first article, entitled "The Fragment," for the *Saturday Evening Post,* in which he described incidents of the voyage.

Appointed acting midshipman in the navy on Feb. 1, 1826, he made his first cruise in the frigate *Macedonian* under the command of Capt. James Barron (1826–28). He was assigned to the brig *Ontario* of the Mediterranean Squadron from 1829 to 1831, and in 1832 was appointed passed midshipman. The following year he was assigned to the United States Naval Station at Philadelphia, and during his leisure time studied law. His health failing, he was granted a leave of absence of several months, and in February 1834, due to his well-known proficiency in mathematics, he was ordered to duty with the Coast Survey, under F. R. Hassler, who was considered one of the foremost mathematicians of his time. Dahlgren was selected to serve in the triangulation of the survey and assist in the astronomical observations, as well as in the measurement of the base on Long Island, the first base line in the United States ever measured scientifically. He was chosen by Hassler to make the counter calculations of the base, to compare with and verify his own, and remained on this duty until 1836 when he was selected to make observations of the solar eclipses of that year. He was detailed from the second triangulation to assist in the first trials of the great theodolite of Houghton, which had just been completed for Hassler, and was made second assistant in the survey and given charge of a party of triangulation. About the time he was ordered to report to the survey for duty, Dahlgren published a series of remarkable papers on naval topics, in the form of open letters, signed "Blue Jacket," in the *National Gazette* of Philadelphia. These letters were addressed to Mr. Southard, chairman of the Naval Committee of the United States Senate, and excited much comment, as they boldly attacked the new regulations for the navy. Efforts were made to find the author, but even the editor of the *Gazette* never discovered the name of his contributor. Dahlgren was promoted lieutenant on Mar. 8, 1837. Due to his work in the Coast Survey, his eyesight became impaired to such an extent that he was threatened with total blindness and was compelled to relinquish work and enter the Naval Hospital. Finding no relief, he was granted leave of absence with permission to visit Paris for the purpose of placing himself under the care of Sichel, the celebrated oculist. After his return to the United States, he was married, Jan. 8, 1839, to Mary C. Bunker, of Philadelphia, and, on the advice of his physician, went to live in the country, where he remained until 1843 when he returned to duty at the Philadelphia Navy Yard, his eyesight fully restored. Later in the same year, he joined the *Cumberland* for a cruise in the Mediterranean, returning to the United States in 1845. While on this cruise he tried out a percussion lock which he had designed in 1835, but which he did not patent until 1847. In the latter year he was ordered to Washington for ordnance duty, and began labors as an ordnance officer which for sixteen years demanded the most extraordinary energy, and which finally made him chief of the Bureau of Ordnance, and gave him world recognition as a man of science and inventive genius.

Dahlgren's initial task was to investigate and introduce into the navy the Hale system of rockets. Coldly received at first by the Commandant, Commodore Warrington, he soon gained the confidence of that distinguished officer, and in August of the same year was placed in charge of all ordnance matter in the Washington Navy Yard. In addition he was professor of gunnery at Annapolis. At this time there was no ordnance establishment; the fuse stocks, cannon locks, and shells, were made and fitted in the plumber's shop. The only sign of ordnance at the Navy Yard was the laboratory. Dahlgren suggested a plan for an ordnance workshop which was accepted by the Bureau and directed to be carried into effect. This was the beginning of the ordnance establishment which was to become of such importance to the country at the outbreak of the Civil War. Under the sole direction of Dahlgren, the ordnance department at the Washington Yard acquired the most extensive additions, including a foundry for cannon, gun-carriage shops, an experimental battery, and other equipment of various kinds. In 1848 he proposed equipping the Navy with "Boat Howitzers," a type of gun suited to both field and naval service, combining both lightness and accuracy. After much opposition they were adopted by the navy in 1850, and later by many European and South American countries. In 1850 he published a book, *32 Pounder Practise for Ranges,* and also proposed to the Bureau of Ordnance two guns after his own designs, one a 50 pounder and the other a 9-inch shell gun, the former of 8,000, the latter of about 9,000 pounds. The following year he submitted the design of an 11-inch gun which was approved and ordered cast. All these were smoothbores. Called "Dahlgrens," they were of iron, cast solid, and cooled from the exterior. They were distinguished by great thickness at the breech, rapidly diminishing from the trunnions to the muzzle, and were the practical application of results obtained by experimental determination of pressures at different points along the bore. During the year 1851 Dahlgren prepared for publication *The System of Boat Armament in the United States Navy,* published in 1852. In 1853 he was elected a member of the American Association for the Advancement of Science, and that year his book *Naval Percussion Locks and Primers* was published. He was promoted to commander, Oct. 11, 1855. In 1856 the second edition of his *Boat Howitzers* was published, a model of a rifle musket and a knife bayonet submitted, and a book entitled *Shells and Shell Guns* prepared for publication. This work was considered by many students of ordnance as the best ever written on the subject. In order to introduce innovations which completely revolutionized the armament of the navy, and to remove objections to his 11-inch gun, which was then considered too heavy for use at sea, Dahlgren was permitted to arm the sloop-of-war *Plymouth* entirely as he wished, and to take her on a six months' experimental cruise. On his return, he reported the 11-inch gun perfectly manageable at sea. The last vestige of opposition to his system then finally disappeared, and it was soon after adopted in the arming of the national vessels.

Dahlgren was on ordnance duty in 1861 when Franklin Buchanan, captain in command of the Washington Navy Yard, resigned to enter the Confederate service, and while the law required that the command of the Washington Navy Yard be restricted to the command of a captain, President Lincoln refused to place any officer over him, though some of the captains asked for the assignment on the ground that it was not legal for Dahlgren to hold it. The Washington Navy Yard was of the utmost importance to the North, not only because of its naval resources, but also as the key to the defenses of Washington on the left. In July 1862, Dahlgren was appointed chief of the Bureau of Ordnance in addition to his other duties as commandant of the Yard, though holding only the rank of commander. On Aug. 5, 1862, he was promoted captain, his commission being ante-dated to July 16, and in February of the following year was promoted to rear admiral. At the same time he received the thanks of Congress, and ten years additional on the active list of the navy, which, however, he did not live to enjoy. On his request for active service, he was ordered to sea and relieved Du Pont in command of the South Atlantic Blockading Squadron. In the following months he cooperated with the land forces under Gen. Gilmore in a number of attacks on the land defenses of Charleston, and succeeded in silencing the batteries on Morris Island and at Sumter, and in securing a safe anchorage for the monitors inside the bar, which put a stop to blockade-running at that port. His failure to take Charleston provoked some hostile criticism, but his operations had the approval of the Navy Department. He led a successful expedition up the St. John's River in February 1864, to aid in throwing a military force into Florida, cooperated with Gen. Sherman in the capture of Savannah on Dec. 23, and entered Charleston with Gen. Schimmelfennig on its evacuation in February 1865. On July 12, 1865, he relinquished command of the South Atlantic Blockading Squadron and returned to Washington, where, some weeks later (Aug. 2, 1865), he married Mrs. Madeleine Vinton Goddard, daughter of the Hon. S. F. Vinton of Ohio. In 1866 he was assigned to the command of the South Pacific Squadron where he remained until 1868, when he returned to the United States and was again appointed chief of the Bureau of Ordnance. At his own request he was relieved as chief of the Bureau on Aug. 10, 1869, and assigned to the command of the Washington Navy Yard where he died July 12, 1870. Dahlgren had seven children by his first marriage and three by his second. After his death, his *Notes on Maritime and International Law* (1877) appeared with a preface by his widow, indicating the plan of an uncompleted work.

[L. R. Hamersly, *Records of Living Officers of the U. S. Navy and Marine Corps* (1870); J. T. Headley, *Our Navy in the Great Rebellion, Heroes and Battles of the War 1861–65* (1891); M. V. Dahlgren, *Memoir of John A. Dahlgren* (1882); Washington *Star*, July 12, 1870.]

C. F. C—y.

DAHLGREN, SARAH MADELEINE VINTON (July 13, 1825–May 28, 1898), author, was born at Gallipolis, Ohio, the daughter of Samuel Finley Vinton, more than twenty years congressman from the district. Her mother was Romaine Madeleine Bureau, daughter of French émigrés settled at Gallipolis. The first American ancestor of the Vintons, who also claimed French descent, was John Vinton, whose name appeared in records of Lynn, Mass., in 1648. When Madeleine was six, her mother died and soon afterward her brother, the only other child. Her father made her his companion and, as soon as she was old enough, his hostess in Washington. She was educated at Monsieur Picot's boarding school in Philadelphia and the Convent of the Visitation, Georgetown, D. C. In June 1846, she was married to Daniel C. Goddard, an Ohio lawyer and an assistant secretary of the newly formed Interior Department. After his death five years later Mrs. Goddard, with her two children, made her home with her father until he died in 1862. On Aug. 2, 1865, she became the second wife of Rear Admiral John Adolphus Dahlgren [*q.v.*], of the United States Navy, and accompanied him on a South American cruise. In 1870, again left a widow, with three small children, she continued to live in her father's Washington home.

Mrs. Dahlgren began to write in 1859 under the pen names "Corinne" and "Cornelia." Her works include: *Idealities* (1859); *Pius IX and France* (1861), translated from Montalembert; *An Essay on Catholicism, Authority and Order* (1862), translated from the Spanish of Don Juan Donoso Cortés; *Thoughts on Female Suffrage* (1871); *Memoir of Ulric Dahlgren* (1872), edited from the work of Admiral Dahlgren; *Etiquette of Social Life in Washington* (1873); *The Executive Power in the United States* (1874), translated from Adolphe de Chambrun; *South Sea Sketches* (1881); *South Mountain Magic* (1882); *Memoir of John A. Dahlgren* (1882); *A Washington Winter* (1883); *The Lost Name* (1886); *Lights and Shadows of a*

Life (1887); *Divorced* (1887); *Chim: his Washington Winter* (1892); *Samuel Finley Vinton* (1895); *The Secret Directory* (1896); *The Woodley Lane Ghost and Other Stories* (1899). Her writings show versatility, the student's aptitude for detail, knowledge of languages, familiarity with Washington life, and certain political and religious prepossessions. Imagination and charm of style are not marked, but in some of her books, for example, *South Mountain Magic,* love of place inspired literary treatment. Mrs. Dahlgren's later life in Washington was concerned with literary and religious activities. She did not believe in women's participation in politics and her pamphlet against woman suffrage was used before committees of Congress by opponents of the cause. She was identified with Catholic missionary work and built near her summer home, "Dahlgren," on South Mountain, Md., a Gothic chapel dedicated to St. Joseph of the Sacred Heart of Jesus. After the death of her eldest son, Vinton Goddard, in 1877, she led a retired life, but her home was something of a salon for a large circle of literary friends. She was a founder of the Washington Literary Society in 1873, and was a vice-president, a frequent hostess, and a contributor of papers and poetry to the programs. She died at her Massachusetts Avenue home in Washington and was buried on South Mountain, Md.

[John Adams Vinton, *The Vinton Memorial, comprising a Genealogy of the Descendants of John Vinton of Lynn, 1648,* etc. (1858); Minutes of the Washington Literary Soc.; obituaries in *Washington Post,* May 29, 1898, and *Evening Star* (Washington), May 30, 1898.]

S. G. B.

DALCHO, FREDERICK (1770–Nov. 24, 1836), physician, Episcopal clergyman, was born in London, England, where his father, a Prussian officer under Frederick the Great, had taken up residence after having been incapacitated by wounds. On the death of his father, Frederick came to live in Baltimore with an uncle who had himself been in America only a few years. There he availed himself of the general education current in his day, studied medicine, and inquired zealously into botany. In April 1792 he became a surgeon's mate in the United States army, and in May 1794 a lieutenant. In June 1799, while stationed at Fort Johnston, he left the army and became a citizen of nearby Charleston (S. C.). Here he followed the practise of medicine, permitting himself for a while no distractions more grave than the organizing of a public botanical garden and the normal votive activities of an enthusiastic Mason. In 1807 he published *Ahiman Rezon,* a handbook for his fellow craftsmen in Masonry, an earnest, solemn production which has been the foundation for similar efforts dating as late as 1901. The title-page of this book proclaims its author a member not only of the medical societies of South Carolina and of Philadelphia, but also of the Academy of Arts, Sciences, and Belles-Lettres of Marseilles. In 1807 he became one of the two editors of the Federalist *Charleston Courier.* In 1808, or thereabout, he was married to Mary E. Threadcraft. Two or three years later his attention began fixing itself more and more on theology, and after a while he became a lay-reader of the Episcopal Church in St. Paul's Parish, Colleton. In 1814 he was made deacon; in 1818, priest; and in 1819, assistant minister of St. Michael's, Charleston. In addition to publishing his sermons and editing the ecclesiastical *Gospel Messenger,* he wrote *A Letter on Public Baptism* (1817), *An Historical Account of the Protestant Episcopal Church in South Carolina* (1820), and *Evidences of the Divinity of Jesus Christ* (1820). Conventional and decorous, the *Historical Account* serves still as a dependable source-book of history. As a pastor in daily contact with his congregation he was respected and loved. He died in Charleston. His gravestone in St. Michael's Church attests that "Fidelity, industry, and Prudence were the characteristics of his ministry," that he was "Steadfast and uniform in his own peculiar convictions and action," and that "he lived and died 'in perfect charity with all men.'"

[W. B. Sprague, *Annals Am. Pulpit,* vol. V (1859); G. S. Holmes, *A Hist. Sketch of the Parish Church of St. Michael* (1887); C. Jervey, *Inscriptions on the Tablets and Gravestones in St. Michael's Church and Churchyard* (1906); F. B. Heitman, *Hist. Reg. and Dict. of the U. S. Army* (1903); A. G. Mackey, *Ahiman Rezon* (1901); *Charleston Courier,* Nov. 25, 1836.]

J. D. W.

DALE, RICHARD (Nov. 6, 1756–Feb. 26, 1826), naval officer, was born in Norfolk County, Va., of an old and highly respected family. He was the son of Winfield, a shipwright of the parish of Portsmouth, and Ann (Sutherland) Dale. Thrown upon his own resources at an early age, in 1768 he shipped on board a merchantman commanded by an uncle and made a voyage to Liverpool. Two years later he was regularly apprenticed to a Norfolk ship-owner, for whom he made several voyages to the West Indies. By 1775 he had risen to the station of chief mate. His first naval service, early in 1776 as a lieutenant on board one of the light cruisers fitted out by Virginia, was terminated by his capture and confinement on a prison ship. Wavering in his allegiance, the young adventurer joined a

Loyalist schoolmate who commanded a British tender and in an engagement with the Patriots received a severe wound. Still under the influence of the Loyalists, he next sailed for Bermuda and on the return voyage his ship was captured by the American naval brig *Lexington*. On the day of his capture he entered the Continental navy as a midshipman. In later life he was wont to confess the error of his service with his Loyalist friends.

After a voyage to the West Indies in the *Lexington,* he sailed on this ship in February 1777 for France, now being rated as master's mate. The *Lexington* made a successful cruise in European waters, but shortly thereafter was compelled to surrender to a superior force. Her officers and crew were committed to Mill Prison, Plymouth, charged with high treason. Escaping with his captain in February 1778, Dale after a variety of adventures was retaken and again confined in Mill Prison, this time for a period of forty days in the dungeon, familiarly known as the "black hole." A year later he again escaped and succeeded in reaching L'Orient where he joined the *Bon Homme Richard,* then being fitted for sea by Capt. John Paul Jones [*q.v.*]. Selected by that discerning commander as first lieutenant, he took part in the memorable cruise that culminated in the brilliant sea fight off Flamborough Head. Being in charge of the gun-deck and second in command on the *Richard,* he was the first to board the *Serapis* when she struck her flag, and not until after he had taken possession of her did he discover that he had been severely wounded. In 1779–80 he cruised with Jones in the frigate *Alliance* and later returned to America with his commander on the *Ariel,* arriving early in 1781. Again going to sea, this time as the first lieutenant of the frigate *Trumbull,* he was wounded in that ship's engagement with the British naval vessel *Iris.* His last sea service during the Revolution was in 1782–83 on the privateer *Queen of France,* first as mate and afterward as captain.

From 1783 to 1794 he was lucratively employed in the merchant service, chiefly in command of East Indiamen. In the latter year this employment was brought to an end by his appointment by Washington as one of the six captains of the new navy. His first naval duty was the superintending of the construction of a frigate at Norfolk. In 1795 he obtained a furlough from the navy and returned to his former occupation, sailing for Canton, China, in command of the *Ganges.* Three years later, when war with France was threatening, this ship was purchased by the government and Dale made in her the first cruise undertaken by a vessel of the new navy. Differences with Commodore Truxtun over rank caused Dale to leave the naval service and take command of a privateer, in which he sailed for China in 1799. On the settlement of this dispute in his favor, he again returned to the navy and in 1801 was appointed to the command of a fleet of five vessels, of which the frigate *President* flew the broad pennant of the commodore. This squadron of observation was dispatched to the Mediterranean in anticipation of trouble with the Barbary Corsairs. After effectively protecting American commerce in that sea, Dale sailed for home, and in December 1802, as the result of a dispute with the Navy Department, he retired from the navy, ranking then as the third officer in the service.

Having accumulated a comfortable fortune, he established himself permanently in Philadelphia, where on Sept. 15, 1791 he had been married to Dorothea (or Dorothy) Crathorne (1767–1832). For upward of a quarter of a century he enjoyed in that city the tranquil life of a private citizen. Highly esteemed by the Philadelphians, he interested himself in their welfare and was often called upon to take the lead in public enterprises. For several years he was president of the Washington Benevolent Society of Pennsylvania, and during the War of 1812 he served on the general committee charged with the protection of the city. Two of his sons entered the navy, Richard, who was killed in action, and John M., who died in the service.

[*Port Folio,* June 1814; J. F. Cooper, *Lives of Distinguished Am. Naval Officers,* II (1846), 233–64; *Jours. of the Cont. Cong.,* July 7, 17, 20, 1781; C. W. Goldsborough, *The U. S. Naval Chronicle* (1824); G. W. Allen, *Our Naval War with France* (1909), and *Our Navy and the Barbary Corsairs* (1905); *Pa. Mag. of Hist. and Biog.,* IV (1880), 494–500.] C. O. P.

DALE, SAMUEL (1772–May 24, 1841), pioneer, soldier, was born in Rockbridge County, Va., and died in Lauderdale County, Miss. His parents, of Scotch-Irish descent, were natives of Pennsylvania, but came to the Virginia frontier soon after their marriage. They kept to the border during all of Samuel's boyhood, moving always as it moved, once in 1775, and again in 1783, when they settled in Greene County, Ga. They both died in December 1792, leaving Samuel with the responsibility of their eight younger children. Having the fixed outlook of a frontiersman, he became a government scout in 1793 and served in that capacity till his company was disbanded in 1796. He then became a trader between Savannah and the border settlements to the west, and in 1808, having acquired some land by state lottery, he set up a mill. These activities were remunerative but not exciting, and he soon abandoned them for the business of guiding immigrants through the Indian lands to Mississippi. He was present in October 1812 when Tecumseh, at the instigation of British agents in Detroit, came to Alabama to enlist the Indians against the Americans. During the hostilities which followed, Dale was engaged in countless stirring adventures with the Indians—now friendly, now hostile. Some of these occurred in December 1814, while he was carrying important dispatches from Georgia to Andrew Jackson in New Orleans, a feat accomplished in the phenomenally short time of eight days. He was elected in 1817 to the first General Assembly of Alabama, and he continued in that body with fair regularity till 1829. His position as legislator and distinguished veteran accounted for his appointment as one of five men to receive Lafayette when he visited Alabama in 1821. Ten years later he was charged with the duty of transporting the expelled Choctaw Indians to the territories which had been assigned to them west of the Mississippi. An accidental injury sustained during the early days of the pilgrimage prevented his going the full distance. He remained in Lauderdale County, Miss., and soon, as the first representative of that county, began anew his career as legislator. Some time after the Choctaw expedition he visited Washington, D. C., seeking compensation for corn and other supplies furnished the troops. Alabama had been pleased to name a county for him and to create him brigadier-general of militia. It seemed reasonable to hope that Washington would give him recognition also—less glittering, perhaps, but more substantial. It was a vain hope. Many prominent men were cordial to him, but the "third auditor," to whom his claim was finally referred, proved, as Dale said, "impracticable. . . . I would rather encounter half a dozen Indians . . . he worried me much and I left the matter unsettled" (Claiborne, *Dale,* p. 212).

[The chief source of this article is J. F. H. Claiborne, *Life and Times of Gen. Sam. Dale* (1860). Here Claiborne serves chiefly as editor, reproducing from memory Dale's own reminiscences as imparted to him some years before the book was written. The form is autobiographical, Dale being represented as speaking in the first person. Other contemporary accounts are in A. B. Meek, *Romantic Passages in S. W. Hist.* (1857); A. J. Pickett, *Hist. of Ala.* (1851); Sketches occur in T. M. Owen, *Hist. of Ala. and Dict. of Ala. Biog.* (1921); D. Rowland, *Mississippi* (1907).] J. D. W.

DALE, Sir THOMAS (d. Aug. 9, 1619), soldier, colonizer, naval commander, enlisted when a youth, about 1588, as a soldier in the service of the Netherlands. Later we find him in Scotland, in the retinue of Prince Henry, to whom he became deeply attached. He returned about 1603 to the Netherlands, where his bravery and the favor of King James won him advancement to a captaincy. On June 19, 1606, he was knighted at Richmond, as Sir Thomas Dale of Surrey, after which he returned to his company. His reputation as a disciplinarian influenced the London Company to appoint him marshal of Virginia, since the disorders and misfortunes of the colony convinced them that stern repression was needed. In January 1611, the States General granted him leave for three years. Before departing for Virginia he married Elizabeth, daughter of Sir Thomas Throckmorton. On Mar. 27, 1611, he set sail with the *Starr, Prosperous,* and *Elizabeth,* carrying settlers, stores, and live stock, and eight weeks later cast anchor off Point Comfort. In the absence of the governor, Lord De la Warr, Dale ruled the colony until August, when he was relieved by Sir Thomas Gates. Gates left in March 1614, and Dale again assumed control. Finding the colony suffering from insubordination, epidemics, Indian attacks, and famines, he was instrumental in surmounting all these evils. Publishing certain martial laws, he enforced them with great severity. This won him the approbation of the London Company, for it restored order to the colony, but brought upon him the execration of the settlers. The Assembly of 1624 said that in defiance of their charter rights he had subjected the people to a cruel tyranny. Men had been hanged, tortured, broken upon the wheel. "One for stealing two or three pints of oatmeal had a bodkin thrust through his tongue and was tied with a chain to a tree until he starved" (Tragical Relation of Virginia Assembly, 1624, Library of Congress). By founding a new settlement near the falls of the James, Dale checked the epidemics of malaria. In a sweeping bend of the river, far from the mosquito-infested marshes of Jamestown, he built Henrico, enclosed a large tract of land with palisades, and laid out fields of corn. Peace with the Indians came when he sanctioned the marriage of John Rolfe with Pocahontas, the captive daughter of the chieftain Powhatan. When Dale returned to England in 1616 he could boast that he had left the colony tranquil and prosperous. On Nov. 28, 1617, he was appointed commander of a London East India Company fleet, and on Feb. 26, 1618, sailed for the East Indies. At this time the rivalry between the English and the Dutch for the eastern trade was intense, and on Dec. 23, Dale fought with a Dutch fleet "a cruel, bloody fight," which ended in a draw. On July 19, 1619, his fleet arrived at Masulipatam, India, and there he died "after twenty days of languishing sickness." "His body was enclosed and housed in the form of a tomb," and brought to England for burial.

[Ralph Hamor, *True Discourse of the Present Estate of Va.* (1615); *Abstract of the Proc. of the Va. Co. of London* (2 vols., 1888); *Va. Hist. Soc. Pubs.*; Alexander Brown, *The Genesis of the United States* (2 vols., 1891), *The First Republic in Am.* (1898); John Rolfe, "Virginia," *Va. Hist. Reg.*, vol. I, no. 3 (1848); *Calendar of State Papers*, East Indies; Edward D. Neill, *The Va. Co. of London* (1869); *Dict. of Nat. Biog.*] T. J. W.

DALL, CAROLINE WELLS HEALEY (June 22, 1822–Dec. 17, 1912), reformer, writer, was born in Boston, Mass., the daughter of Mark and Caroline (Foster) Healey. Her father was a well-to-do merchant and banker. His daughter grew up in an atmosphere of substantial comfort and of genuine though somewhat provincial culture, received her education from tutors and in small private schools, and early showed an inclination toward authorship. When her father's investments in railroads turned out badly, she became a teacher and in 1840 went to Georgetown, D. C., as vice-principal of Miss English's School for Young Ladies. In 1844 she married Charles Henry Appleton Dall, a Unitarian clergyman. She bore him a daughter, Sarah, and a son, William Healey Dall [*q.v.*]. After serving several charges, including one in Toronto, Canada, her husband went to Calcutta in 1855 as the first foreign missionary of the Unitarian Church. He returned to visit his family once every five years and died in Calcutta on July 18, 1886. Reform of every kind was dear to Mrs. Dall's heart, but the cause to which she was especially devoted, and which made her career significant, was the extension of equal educational and economic opportunities to women. On this subject she lectured, preached from such pulpits as were open to her, and wrote indefatigably. She seems to have modeled her life consciously on that of Margaret Fuller, but she lacked Miss Fuller's intellectual keenness and critical sense. Her bias and intellectual immaturity are amusingly revealed in a lecture on *Transcendentalism in New England* (1897), in which she asserts with complete confidence that the movement took its origin in Anne Hutchinson and reached its height in Margaret Fuller. In spite of obvious shortcomings Mrs. Dall did render valuable service to the woman's rights movement in the sixties and seventies. Her publications dealing directly or indirectly with the subject are: *Historical Pictures Retouched* (1860); *Woman's Right to Labor* (1860); *Life of Dr. Marie Zakrzewska* (1860); *Woman's Rights under the Law* (1861); *The College, the Market, and the Court, or Woman's Relation to Education, Labor, and Law* (1867); and *Life of Dr. Anandabai Joshee* (1888). For a time she was editor in Boston of *Una*, a woman's rights magazine. Her later writings are chiefly on literary subjects but are of little importance. *My First Holiday, or Letters Home from Colorado, Utah, and California* (1881) is valuable as a traveler's unvarnished record and is rendered almost comic by its querulous recital of the innumerable discomforts, annoyances, and impositions of western travel. A more gracious mood is exhibited in *Alongside* (privately printed, 1900), a memoir of her early years in Boston and of her father. Some of her other books are: *Patty Gray's Journey to the Cotton Islands* (1869–70), a heavily didactic juvenile in three volumes; *The Romance of the Association, or, One Last Glimpse of Charlotte Temple and Eliza Wharton* (1875), a study of Mrs. Rowson's long-lived novel; *What We Really Know about Shakespeare* (1885); *Sordello—a History and a Poem* (1886); and *Barbara Fritchie—a Study* (1892). During the latter part of her life she made her home in Washington, D. C., where, having outlived her reputation as a publicist, she died in her ninetieth year.

[*Who's Who in America*, 1908–09; *The Evening Star* (Washington, D. C.), Dec. 18, 1912; F. C. Pierce, *Foster Genealogy* (1899).] G. H. G.

DALL, WILLIAM HEALEY (Aug. 21, 1845–Mar. 27, 1927), naturalist, was the son of Charles Henry Appleton Dall, a Unitarian minister, and of Caroline Wells (Healey) Dall [*q.v.*] who for a time had some distinction as a publicist. He was born in Boston, Mass., and there he was educated in public schools and the Boston Latin School. An early fondness for natural history led to his meeting Louis Agassiz under whom he studied zoology. He also followed courses in anatomy—under Jeffries Wyman—and other medical subjects in the medical department of Harvard, although he never graduated. The earning of his livelihood being necessary, he found employment in commercial pursuits in Chicago, Ill., where he was able to continue his studies in natural history at night in the Chicago Academy of Sciences under the direction of William Stimpson and Robert Kennicott [*qq.v.*], both of whom became his warm friends. In 1865 the Western Union International Telegraph Expedition was organized to ascertain the possibility of quick communication with Europe by way of Alaska and Bering Strait. Kennicott, who was made leader, invited Dall to become his lieutenant, charged with collecting the scientific data of that territory. On the death of Kennicott, Dall was unanimously chosen to succeed him in command of the expedition and for three years, until 1868, he continued in Alaska, accumulating valuable collections in natural history, chiefly of mollusks in which he had already begun to specialize. With the success of the Atlantic cable came the abandonment of the expedition, but Dall, appreciating the value of the information he had acquired, promptly gave to the world in 1870 his famous volume, *Alaska and its Resources,* of which several editions were published, one bearing the date of 1897. For many years it was the accepted authority on Alaska.

In 1871, through the influence of Spencer F. Baird [*q.v.*], he was appointed to the United States Coast Survey, with which service he continued until 1884. During these years he was in charge of a scientific survey of the Aleutian Islands and adjacent coasts, the results of which were published in his useful volumes, *Pacific Coast Pilot: Coast and Islands of Alaska; Appendix I, Meteorology* (1879) and *Pacific Coast Pilot: Alaska* (1883), issued by the Coast Survey. In 1880 he was made honorary curator of mollusks in the United States National Museum, and in 1884 love of his specialty led him to accept a transfer from the Coast Survey to the Geological Survey, in which he was given the rank of paleontologist. Working facilities and a room in which to store his collections were found for him in the north tower of the Smithsonian Institution, and there, surrounded by his private library (which he later gave to the Museum), he prepared hundreds of papers and monographs on mollusks, chiefly of the West Coast. In 1909 the Division of Mollusks was moved to the new Natural History Building and he was assigned larger quarters. Although retired in 1923, he persisted in his work and almost daily was in his office.

In addition to his services for the government he also held the chair of invertebrate paleontology in the Wagner Institute of Science in Philadelphia and periodically delivered a course of lectures, receiving in 1889 the gold medal of the Institute. During 1899–1915 he was an honorary curator of the Bishop Museum in Hawaii. In the latter year he published *Spencer Fullerton Baird: A Biography.* He was honored at home and abroad by elections to scientific societies; in the United States he was a fellow of the American Academy of Arts and Sciences, and in 1897 was elected to the National Academy of Sciences. In recognition of the character of the man and of the value of his work authors in various branches of botany and zoology have conferred his name on varied organisms. In this way a monument to his memory has been raised in the literature of science. He was survived by his widow, Annette Whitney, whom he had married on Mar. 3, 1880, by two sons and one daughter.

[C. Hart Merriam, "Wm. Healey Dall," in *Science,* Apr. 8, 1927; data furnished by Dall himself for articles published during his lifetime; G. H. Parker, in *Proc. Am. Acad. Arts and Sci.,* 1926–27; *Annual Report, Board of Regents Smithsonian Inst.,* 1927; *Who's Who in America,* 1926-27; personal acquaintance of forty years.] M. B.

DALLAS, ALEXANDER JAMES (June 21, 1759–Jan. 16, 1817), lawyer, secretary of the treasury, was born on the Island of Jamaica, the third son of Robert Dallas and his second wife Sarah (Cormack) Hewett Dallas. His father, son of James and Barbara (Cockburn) Dallas of St. Martin's, Scotland, emigrated from that country and practised medicine with considerable success in the West Indies. After a few years the family returned to the British Isles where Alexander James attended Kensington School and Edinburgh University; at the former place his scholastic merit attracted the attention of two visitors of the school, Benjamin Franklin and Dr. Samuel Johnson. After financial reverses, his father died, and shortly afterward his mother married Capt. Sutherland of the British navy. As the children were encouraged to look to other sources for support, Alexander in his fifteenth year determined to study law, but postponed this ambition to become a merchant clerk and accountant for his uncle, Mr. Gray. After two years in the latter's business house he returned to Devonshire and resumed academic studies, applying himself under the guidance of a tutor to ancient and modern literature.

On Sept. 4, 1780, he married Arabella Maria Smith, daughter of Maj. George Smith of the British army, who was stationed in Jamaica. The young couple soon quitted England and joined their families in the West Indies. Dallas was there admitted to the bar and appointed a Master in Chancery by Gov. Dalling. Promotion seemed imminent, but his wife's health necessitated a different climate. While contemplating a return to England, and inclined to devote his life to the church, he met the actor, Lewis Hallam, Jr., who had lived several years in the American colonies prior to the Revolution and during their struggle for independence. His description of conditions in the United States influenced Dallas to seek citizenship there. Resolutely he and his wife assembled their meager possessions, secured letters of introduction to William Bingham and Robert Morris, and on Apr. 10, 1783, embarked for the new country. Arriving in New York City on June 7, they proceeded to Philadelphia where Dallas signed citizenship papers ten days later.

A serious and annoying obstacle developed when Dallas found that a newly established requirement of two years' residence in the state must be met before he could satisfy his cherished desire to practise law. By chance he had taken lodgings near the offices of Jonathan Burrall, commissioner for settling the accounts of the commissary and quartermaster's departments of the Revolutionary army. Acquaintance was established, and Dallas was invited to a desk in Burrall's office, where he remained until he opened his own office before the end of 1783. On July 13, 1785, he was admitted as counselor in the supreme court of Pennsylvania. On the return of Hallam from Jamaica in the spring of 1784, he and Dallas attempted the introduction of the regular drama into Philadelphia. Not only did Dallas draw up a memorial to the local legislature in an attempt to allay the common prejudice against the theatre, but even turned his pen to dramatic plots. He also contributed to local papers many articles on pressing political questions and items of literary interest, and in 1787 he served as editor of the *Columbian Magazine,* a monthly miscellany. It was during this period that he edited the first reports of the United States Supreme Court.

Dallas's first political appointment came on Jan. 19, 1791, when he was chosen secretary of the Commonwealth of Pennsylvania by Gov. Thomas Mifflin. He remained with Mifflin through two reappointments, and received one appointment from Gov. McKean. He was a member of the committee of correspondence that organized, on July 4, 1793, the first Democratic society in the United States. Early in March 1805 he aided in the establishment of the Constitutional Republican party, which supported the judiciary of Pennsylvania against the assaults of the extreme Democratic faction, and at various other times devoted himself to political activity. In 1794, at the time of the Whiskey Rebellion, he was appointed aide-decamp to the governor and as paymaster-general with the military forces he was brought into personal contact with Washington and Alexander Hamilton. His second public appointment came on Mar. 10, 1801, when he was commissioned United States district attorney for the Eastern District of Pennsylvania by President Jefferson. During Dallas's thirteen years in this office he handled many cases with ability and skill, including the Olmstead case in 1809, which, due to the ill-defined and conflicting jurisdiction of local and national authorities, aroused considerable controversy. While holding the office he was maligned by political enemies, and from one editor, John Ward Fenno, recovered $2,500 for libel.

Albert Gallatin, a close personal friend of Dallas, left the United States Treasury in May 1813 to promote the mediation of Russia in the War of 1812. President Madison had wished to appoint Dallas to succeed him, but the opposition of the radical Pennsylvania senators, Michael Leib and Abner Lacock, precluded that choice. George W. Campbell was appointed, but his efforts to prevent the suspension of specie payments and provide suitable funds to prosecute the war were weak and fruitless. When he resigned in despair on Sept. 26, 1814, the situation was so desperate that, on Oct. 6, almost as a last resort, Dallas was commissioned secretary of the treasury. He entered office with a bankrupt treasury; the official stoppage of interest payments on the debt was announced in a letter of Nov. 17. His first formal act was an immediate message on Oct. 17 to the Committee on Ways and Means in which he insisted upon a permanent annual revenue of twenty-one million dollars from taxes and duties, a yearly war revenue of like amount to be raised by doubling the direct tax and rate of postage, and a national bank to provide a circulating medium and facilitate exchange (George M. Dallas, *post,* pp. 236–37). This report had a far-reaching psychological effect, and did much to restore confidence. Interest-bearing treasury notes of small denomination were issued in discreet quantities to furnish momentary relief. After some scattered opposition in Congress, his measures for the heaviest taxation hitherto levied by the national government were adopted. The charter of the Bank of the United States had expired in 1811, but Dallas recognized that a national banking institution was the only efficient remedy for the disordered condition of the circulating medium. But after his plan for a bank emerged from the opposition and wrangling of Congress it was so altered that, upon his advice, Madison vetoed the bill. This blighting of prospects was somewhat alleviated by the cessation of war toward the end of 1814. The lack of regulation of state banks and the general financial confusion having forced the Republican leaders to revise their former stand, Calhoun, on Jan. 8, 1816, introduced a bank bill modeled closely on a plan recommended by Dallas. On Apr. 10 it became law. American shipping had been ruined by the war, and manufacturing industries developed with the advent of peace. In his report of Feb. 12, 1816, Dallas made recommendations in regard to a protective tariff that were largely adopted, and thus furnished the basis of a system for the following thirty years. The illness of Monroe caused Dallas to take upon himself, in addition, the duties of acting secretary of war on Mar. 14, 1815. Carrying them until Aug. 8, he organized the army upon a peace establishment of ten thousand men. Although he gave notice in April 1816 of his intended resignation, he was persuaded to remain until the new bank was organized and definite provision made for the resumption of specie payments. On Oct. 20, 1816, these conditions practically accomplished, he formally quit the treasury, leaving with Madison a highly creditable report. Treasury receipts had far exceeded the estimates.

Dallas returned to the practise of law in Philadelphia in an effort to recoup his private fortunes, but scarcely three months later while attending a case in Trenton, N. J., he was seized with what doctors pronounced to be "gout in the stomach." He was immediately taken home, and a few hours later he died. One of his sons, George Mifflin Dallas [*q.v.*], became vice-president. In physical appearance Alexander James Dallas was commanding. In dress he was meticulous, and his powdered hair, the wearing of which was a rapidly disappearing custom, added a formal touch not inconsistent with his highly polished manners. A prodigious worker, he had the faculty of unbending readily from toil to ease and vivacity, and specially excelled in conversation.

Included among his publications were: *Features of Mr. Jay's Treaty* (1795); *Laws of the Commonwealth of Pa.* (4 vols., 1793–1801); *Address of the Society of Constitutional Republicans* (1805); *Reports of Cases Ruled and Adjudged in the Several Courts of the United States and of Pennsylvania, etc.* (4 vols., 1790–1807); *Treasury Reports; An Exposition of the Causes and Character of the War* (1815). He left incomplete and unpublished a history of Pennsylvania.

[Geo. M. Dallas, *The Life and Writings of A. J. Dallas* (1871); Jas. Dallas, *The Hist. of the Family of Dallas* (1921); Madison Papers, Lib. of Cong.; Dallas Letters, and Simon Gratz Coll., Hist. Soc. of Pa.]

J. H. E—s.

DALLAS, GEORGE MIFFLIN (July 10, 1792–Dec. 31, 1864), vice-president, diplomat, was born in Philadelphia and bore the indelible stamp of his social environment. The city took its tone in the early days of the republic from a prosperous group, shrewd in business, conservative in politics, and manifesting a genteel interest in culture and the refinements of life. His father, Alexander James Dallas [*q.v.*], was a successful man of affairs, and his mother, Arabella Maria Smith, was an Englishwoman, with a tradition of gentility. Under the tutelage of local masters such as Robert Andrews, the boy was prepared for Princeton, from which he graduated in 1810. In his father's law office the Princetonian began his legal preparation. Shortly came the War of 1812 but, though he joined a military company, a career of arms was not to be his. In 1813 he was made secretary to Albert Gallatin [*q.v.*], then about to set out for Russia on a peace mission. Though not quite of age, Dallas was admitted to the bar and set out for Europe. After visiting Russia, he proceeded to Belgium and England and was about to go to Italy when the peace commissioners received the British terms. They quickly decided to send these to America by Dallas, and in October 1814 he arrived at home. Shortly thereafter he joined his father, who was then secretary of the treasury, as a clerk in his department. The year 1816 found him back in Philadelphia, where he tried his first case in April and on May 23 married Sophia Nicklin. He had planned to practise law with his father but the latter, just retired, died in 1817. Alexander Dallas had been one of the chief sponsors of the newly formed second Bank of the United States, and soon his son became one of its counsel. But politics was in his blood. He was an active Republican, and when the new partisanship of the twenties began to take shape he became a follower of Calhoun and supported his candidacy for the presidency in 1824. Jackson, however, was to be the man of the hour, and Dallas entered his camp. He held numerous offices, deputy attorney-general for the city and county of Philadelphia, mayor, and, when Jackson became president, district attorney, 1829–31. Then came an appointment to fill out a term in the Senate.

In Washington he spent two active years (1831–33), while the Bank and the tariff were the leading political issues. As a close friend of the Bank he was in a difficult position when Jackson made war on it. He presented a memorial for the re-chartering of the Bank and, instructed by the legislature, supported it, though not actively. Protectionist in his views upon the tariff, he supported Jackson in his controversy with South Carolina. As he could not afford further absence from his profession, he retired at the end of his term. Appointed attorney-general of Pennsylvania by Gov. Wolf in the fall of 1833, he held the office until his party lost power in 1835. President Van Buren appointed him minister to Russia in 1837 but there were few questions save trade in the Pacific to occupy his attention. After two years of social gayety, he was recalled at his own request.

The next few years were spent in law and politics. As a lawyer he prospered but as a politician he was barely able to hold his own against James Buchanan. With him, Dallas had an early misunderstanding and, though they patched it up in 1837, they were never very friendly. When Buchanan refused the federal attorney-generalship in 1840, it was offered to Dallas, who in turn declined it. The rivalry between these two men pursued its uneven way through the mazes of Pennsylvania politics until the national convention of 1844. Here Van Buren, Cass, and Buchanan were outdistanced by Polk, and after Silas Wright had declined the vice-presidential nomination it was given to Dallas. The ticket was successful and the new vice-president presided over the Senate through the troubled days of the Mexican War and the debate on the Wilmot Proviso. The question, however, that troubled him most was the tariff. A Pennsylvanian, he was alive to the needs of the protected interests, while his party was pledged to revision downward. In 1846 he labored strenuously for a compromise which would provide more protection than the Walker Bill offered, but when the vote on the latter measure resulted in a tie he voted for it, making it law, on the ground that as a national officer he must obey the national platform of his party. He retired with Polk, and though occasionally talked of for president by the opponents of Buchanan he did not again figure conspicuously in public life until Pierce appointed him minister to Great Britain, upon the resignation of Buchanan from that post in 1856.

He arrived at London at a critical moment. President Pierce had demanded the recall of Crampton, the British minister at Washington, for violating American neutrality by his activities in enlisting men in the United States for the British army. Great Britain refused to comply with the demand and Crampton was dismissed in May 1856. Would the dismissal of Dallas follow? Fortunately the British ministry refrained from that step, and Dallas could turn his attention to the vexatious dispute over the Clayton-Bulwer Treaty. The United States had demanded that Great Britain abandon the so-called protectorate over the Mosquito Indians in Nicaragua, cease interference in a dispute between Nicaragua and Costa Rica, and withdraw from the Bay Islands off the coast of Honduras—all, it was alleged, in violation of the Clayton-Bulwer Treaty. Buchanan had been unable to obtain much satisfaction from the British ministry, but Dallas and Lord Clarendon after a summer's work signed the Dallas-Clarendon convention, Oct. 17, 1856. The independence of the Mosquito Indians was recognized but they were to be permitted to become a part of Nicaragua by treaty. The boundary dispute between the latter country and Costa Rica was to be arbitrated by the United States and Great Britain. The Bay Islands were to be recognized as a free territory belonging to Honduras in accordance with a treaty just negotiated between that country and Great Britain. Indorsement of the latter treaty was stricken out by the Senate and the Dallas-Clarendon Treaty was then ratified by a close vote. When the British refused to accept it in this form, claiming that it would tempt Honduras to reject the British treaty, Dallas and Clarendon tried an alternative wording, but Buchanan felt that this restored the objectionable feature and did not send the treaty to the Senate. President Buchanan kept Dallas in London during his entire term but conducted the further Central-American negotiations at Washington. The two other matters of diplomatic importance were the right of search in connection with the joint agreement for suppressing the slave-trade, and the clash on San Juan Island over the northwest boundary of the United States. In regard to the latter, Buchanan conducted the negotiations in Washington but Dallas, to his great satisfaction, succeeded in obtaining from the foreign secretary, Lord Malmesbury, a disavowal of the long-disputed right of search. This he felt to be his great diplomatic achievement.

The Civil War closed his career as it did those of so many Democrats. Succeeded by Charles Francis Adams in May 1861, he came home to a distracted country. He had hated abolition and secession both, as he hated all extremes, and though he condemned the South for seceding, he voted the Democratic ticket throughout the war, the end of which he failed to see. He was a striking figure with his shock of prematurely white hair, his strong face, and his distinguished manners. Conservative and cosmopolitan, precise and dignified, he may well be characterized as the gentleman in politics.

[*A Series of Letters from London Written During the Years 1856, '57, '58, '59, and '60* (1869), ed. by Julia Dallas; *Diary of George Mifflin Dallas while U. S. Minister to Russia, 1837–39, and to England, 1856–61* (1892), ed. by Susan Dallas; Chas. J. Biddle, *A Eulogy upon the Hon. George Mifflin Dallas* (1865); letters of Dallas scattered through *Pa. Hist. Soc. Colls.*; Mary W. Williams, *Anglo-Am. Isthmian Diplomacy, 1815–1915* (1916); H. B. Learned, "William L. Marcy," and Lewis Einstein, "Lewis Cass," in *The Am. Secretaries of State and their Diplomacy*, ed. by S. F. Bemis, vol. VI (1928).]

R. F. N.

D'ALOES, CLAUDE JEAN [See ALLOUEZ, CLAUDE JEAN, 1622–1689.]

DALTON, JOHN CALL (Feb. 2, 1825–Feb. 12, 1889), physiologist, was born in Chelmsford, Mass. The son of Dr. John Call Dalton and Julia Ann (Spalding), the former a representative of a notable medical ancestry, he was apparently predestined for the medical profession. Graduating from Harvard College in 1844 and from the Harvard Medical School in 1847, he went to Paris where he came under the influence of the renowned physiologist, Claude Bernard, and was at once impressed with the great value of experimental work in medicine, particularly in physiology. This is significant, because Dalton was the first physician in the United States to devote his life to the pursuit of experimental physiology and the sciences related thereto. He put aside all thought of medical practise, and began his work as a teacher, opening a new era in the teaching of physiology in America. Before his time the didactic lecture and the textbook were the sole methods of instruction; he introduced the experimental method, illustrating the processes of life with living animals, which the action of ether, just then discovered, made it possible to do without pain. From 1851 to 1854 he was professor of physiology at the University of Buffalo; 1854–56 at the University of Vermont; 1855–83 at the College of Physicians and Surgeons, New York. From 1859 to 1861 he was also connected with the Long Island College Hospital. During the period of the Civil War he served as surgeon in the medical corps of the volunteer army, with the rank of brigadier-general. Such work, however, was not congenial to him; he was better fitted for the experimentation of the laboratory, where, with his logical mind and skilful manipulation, he made clear the functioning of the vital mechanisms of the body. His writings were notable because what he wrote was based largely upon what he had actually seen experimentally. They included a *Treatise on Human Physiology* issued in 1859, which in 1882 had reached the seventh edition; *A Treatise on Physiology and Hygiene* (1868); *Experimentation on Animals as a Means of Knowledge in Physiology, Pathology, and Practical Medicine* (1875); *The Experimental Method in Medical Science* (1882); *Doctrines of the Circulation* (1884). Especially noteworthy was his morphological work, *Topographical Anatomy of the Brain* (1885), for which it is said he prepared with his own hands all the specimens, photographs of which made up a large part of the book. His most important physiological research was on the subject, "Sugar Formation in the Liver" (*Transactions of the New York Academy of Medicine*, 1871); it confirmed the results and views of Claude Bernard which had been discredited by several English physiologists. For years he had to fight against interference by individuals and societies of anti-vivisectionists, who with misdirected zeal sought by legislative action to prevent all experimentation upon living animals, but with his firm conviction of the value to humanity of the knowledge to be gained by such methods of experimentation he used all his powers to contest these efforts and to lead the public to a better understanding of the matter. During the later years of his life he served (1884–89) as president of the College of Physicians and Surgeons, bringing to that office his great breadth of knowledge and critical judgment, combined with administrative powers of a high order which were freely used for the advancement of the college. He lived a simple, unpretentious life, a bachelor, a quiet scholar, devoted to his studies; a deep thinker whose greatest happiness was found in his study and in the laboratory. In the last year of his life he wrote down for his family some reminiscences of his Civil War service. These, still uncompleted, were privately printed in 1892 under the title, *John Call Dalton, M.D., U. S. V.* He was a member of many national and European societies and in 1864 was elected a member of the National Academy of Sciences. He died unmarried.

[Memoir by S. Weir Mitchell published in the *Biog. Memoirs Nat. Acad. Sci.*, III (1895), 177–85; S. J. Spalding, *Spalding Memorial* (1872), p. 84; *The Coll. of Physicians and Surgeons, N. Y.* (n.d.), ed. by John Schrady; for dates of professorships, *Harvard Quinquennial Cat.*, 1915.] R. H. C.

DALTON, ROBERT (1867–Oct. 5, 1892), desperado, was born probably in Cass County, Mo. His father, Louis Dalton, was of Irish stock, and his mother, Adaline Lee (Younger) Dalton, is said to have been a half-sister of Col. H. W. Younger, the father of the noted bandits. The family, then consisting of the parents, seven boys and one girl, moved to the Indian Territory and about 1882 to Coffeyville, Kan. In the fall of 1888 Robert was appointed a deputy United States marshal, for service in the Indian Territory, but after a short time gave up the place or was discharged. His criminal career began with the killing of a rival in a love affair. With his brothers Grattan and Emmet he soon afterward organized a band of horse-thieves, which operated around Baxter Springs, Kan. Toward the end of 1890 the three brothers went to California, where in the following February they held up a train on the Southern Pacific railroad at Alila, Tulare County. Grattan was captured and sentenced to twenty years' confinement, but on the way to the penitentiary jumped from a moving train and escaped.

Back in their old range, now Oklahoma Territory, Robert, Emmet, and a recruit, Charley Bryant, robbed a train at Wharton, in May 1891. This daring exploit by three men brought to the authorities the realization that an exceptionally capable bandit leader was in the field, and a relentless pursuit was ordered. Bryant was captured and in an attempted escape was killed. The Daltons, however, could not be found, and for more than a year thereafter remained inactive. In June 1892, Robert, Grattan, and Emmet Dalton, "Bill" Doolin (later to be the leader of a band of his own), and two others robbed a train at Red Rock, Okla. Terr., only twenty-six miles from the scene of the Wharton crime, and six weeks later a train at Adair, Okla. Terr. Prompted partly by vainglory, in the hope of outdoing the record of the James brothers, and partly by the hope of a haul which would enable the band to disperse with a competence for each, Robert now directed a raid on the two banks at Coffeyville. The attempt was made by five men on the morning of Oct. 5. In a pitched battle with the townfolk Robert and Grattan Dalton and two others were killed and Emmet Dalton severely wounded and captured. The last-named served a long term in the penitentiary, and on his release became a law-abiding citizen. Like most of the noted Western outlaws, Robert was of fair complexion, with blue eyes. He is described as "romantic looking" and much given to big boots and revolvers prominently displayed. In personal habits he was temperate. He was an outlaw of desperate and reckless will, who knew no fear and never hesitated to shoot, and the record of his band for daring criminality in so short a time is perhaps unequaled.

[E. de Valcour-Vermont, *The Dalton Brothers* (pamph., 1892); *Kan. City Star*, Oct. 5–8, 1892; L. W. Duncan, pub., *Hist. of Montgomery County, Kan.* (1903); incidental references in A. B. Macdonald, *Hands Up!* (1927).]

W. J. G.

DALY, ARNOLD [See DALY, PETER CHRISTOPHER ARNOLD, 1875–1927.]

DALY, AUGUSTIN [See DALY, JOHN AUGUSTIN, 1838–99.]

DALY, CHARLES PATRICK (Oct. 31, 1816–Sept. 19, 1899), jurist, author, was of pure Irish descent, his parents having emigrated from Galway in 1814 and settled in New York City, where he was born. They were poor, his early education was scanty, and when his father died he had to leave school and earn his own living. He obtained a clerkship in Savannah, Ga., but ran away and shipped as cabin boy on a trading vessel. He spent three years at sea before the mast, being present at Algiers in 1830 when the French captured that town. He then returned to New York City and was apprenticed to a master carpenter. Studying at night in an effort to make good his deficiencies in education, he also joined a literary society, where his abilities attracted attention and subsequently led to his entering a law office in 1836. In 1839 he was admitted to the bar, the seven-year term of studentship being waived in his case on account of his brilliant showing, and he at once commenced practise in New York City. He had already interested himself in politics as an adherent of the Democratic party, was known as an effective platform speaker, and in a short time acquired a reputation as a successful advocate and sound lawyer. In 1843 he was elected to the New York Assembly and here distinguished himself by his able handling of the legislation dealing with the escheat of the Leake and Watts asylum trust. He was then offered the party nomination for Congress but declined, preferring law to politics. Immediately afterward, he was appointed a judge of the court of common pleas of the City of New York, and took his seat on the bench May 4, 1844, being then twenty-eight years old. Though his appointment did not please Tammany Hall, he remained a member of the court for nearly forty-two years, being chosen for four consecutive terms after the position was made elective. For the last twenty-seven years of this period he was chief justice. From the outset he displayed a high conception of the responsibilities of his office, and an implacable determination to follow the course which his instinct convinced him was dictated by principle, totally regardless of public opinion or party sympathies. A notable instance of these characteristics occurred in 1849, after the Astor Place Riots, when seven persons were indicted for complicity in the rioting. Public sentiment was strong in their favor, the prevailing opinion being that occasional riots were safety valves and that a conviction for rioting was impossible. Daly presided at the trial, laid down the law applicable to riots in firm, unmistakable language, and upon the jury rendering a verdict of guilty, imposed heavy sentences, totally oblivious to popular clamor and hostile demonstrations.

During the Civil War, though a Democrat, he supported the administration whole-heartedly, and was consulted on a number of occasions by

President Lincoln and his cabinet. Two important decisions taken in the course of the war were directly due to his advice. In 1861, when members of the crew of the Confederate privateer *Jefferson Davis* were tried, convicted and sentenced to be hanged as pirates, he pointed out the inadvisability of such a course in view of inevitable retaliation, and urged that they be treated as prisoners of war—which was subsequently done. His intervention in the case of Mason and Slidell was, from the international standpoint, of outstanding importance. He advised Secretary Seward that in view of a decision of Chief Justice Marshall's, the seizure of the Confederate envoys could not possibly be justified, and recommended their surrender. William M. Evarts did not agree with him, but the government followed his advice. He exhibited the same sanity and detachment from predilection or prejudice throughout his judicial career, his opinions were invariably developed with the utmost care and based upon exhaustive study of the ultimate sources of the law and displayed an erudition which was astonishing in view of his early lack of education. An example of this occurred in *Re John Snook* (2 *Hilt.* 566) where he had occasion to consider the origin of proper names and exhaustively examined the law and usage respecting them. His opinions are contained in *Reports of Cases Argued and Determined in the Court of Common Pleas for the City and County of New York* (16 vols., 1866–92), covering the period 1859–91, which were prepared by him and are generally known as "Daly's Cases." As a judge he was distinguished by one peculiar failing. When presiding at trials or hearing motions he was a most patient and attentive listener, saying little, but in the appellate branch of the court it was impossible to make a continuous and connected argument before him because of his talkativeness. On appeal he apparently believed "that the colloquial style of argument was the most effective" (*post,* p. 134). He retired from the bench by reason of the age limitation, on Dec. 31, 1885, and though he subsequently opened a law office in New York City, did little afterward except in the capacity of advising counsel. His last years were spent principally in study and writing. He died at North Haven, Sag Harbor, L. I., Sept. 19, 1899. In 1856 he married Maria Lydig of New York City.

After his elevation to the bench he seldom participated in public affairs, the principal exception being in 1867 when he was a delegate to the New York constitutional convention of that year. However, he did not take a very prominent part in the discussions. From his seafaring days he had evinced intense interest in the science of geography and for more than thirty-five years was president of the American Geographical Society, contributing to its Proceedings valuable papers of which the following were published: "On the Early History of Cartography . . . before the time of Mercator" (*Journal,* vol. II, 1869, p. 1), "Recent Geographical Work of the World" (*Bulletin,* vol. XX, 1888, p. 1), and "On the History of Physical Geography" (*Ibid.,* vol. XXII, 1890, p. 1). In addition, he was an enthusiastic student of the drama, and his library contained a remarkable collection of works on Shakespeare and other dramatic literature.

He wrote voluminously, more particularly on the historical aspects of law and judicial institutions, wherein his extensive research and powers of exposition were displayed to great advantage. He was the author of, *inter alia,* "A History of the Court of Common Pleas," etc. (1855), prefixed to vol. I of E. D. Smith's Common Pleas Reports; *The Nature, Extent and History of the Jurisdiction of the Surrogates' Courts of the State of New York* (1863); *Gulian C. Verplanck; His Ancestry, Life, and Character* (1870); *Life and Services of Dr. David Livingstone* (1871); *Barratry: its Origin, History and Meaning in the Maritime Laws* (1872); *In Memory of Henry Peters Gray* (1878); *The Settlement of Jews in North America* (1893); *The Common Law, its Origin, Sources, Nature and Development and what the State of New York has done to Improve it* (1894); *First Theatre in America: When was the Drama first Introduced in America?* (1896); *Is the Monroe Doctrine Involved in the Controversy between Venezuela and Great Britain?* (1896); and *Birthday Verses* (1897). He also wrote the article on Naturalization in the *New American Cyclopædia.*

[*Legal and Judicial Hist. of N. Y.* (1911), ed. by Alden Chester, I, 395; Theron G. Strong, *Landmarks of a Lawyer's Lifetime* (1914), p. 133; Max J. Kohler, *Chas. P. Daly; a Tribute to his Memory* (1899); *Green Bag,* Nov. 1894; *Am. Law Rev.,* XXXIII (1899), 907; *N. Y. Times,* Nov. 15, 1885; obituaries in *Bull. Am. Geog. Soc.,* XXXI (1899), 398; *N. Y. Times,* Sept. 20, 1899.]

H. W. H. K.

DALY, JOHN AUGUSTIN (July 20, 1838–June 7, 1899), playwright and producer, was born in Plymouth, N. C., the son of Capt. Denis Daly, a ship-owner, and Elizabeth (Duffey) Daly, the daughter of a lieutenant in the British army. Early left a widow with two boys, his mother came to New York City, where Augustin grew up with a passion for the theatre. He belonged to amateur organizations like the Murdoch and Burton Associations, corresponding to the Little Theatre groups of a later time, and he

Daly

caught the inspiration of the great romantic actors and the sterling romantic plays which were America's contribution to the mid-century theatre and drama. He rarely acted, for his interest lay from the first in the construction and direction of plays. As early as 1856, he rented a hall in Brooklyn and produced without a cent of capital an entertainment, varying from *Toodles* to *Macbeth.* The details of this performance, related in the biography of Daly by his brother, who was his constant companion, are an epitome of his later career of alternate success and failure, met with courage, resourcefulness, and unquenchable confidence. Ten years spent as a dramatic critic on the weekly *Sunday Courier,* during which time he also wrote for the *Sun,* the *Times,* the *Express* and the *Citizen,* gave him a valuable experience, and he began his play-writing while his critical work was in progress.

After the usual rejections, came his first success, *Leah the Forsaken,* a free adaptation from the German play, *Deborah,* by S. H. von Mosenthal. *Leah* was first played at the Howard Athenæum in Boston, Dec. 8, 1862, and Kate Bateman [*q.v.*] carried the leading rôle into favor at home and abroad. During the sixties, Daly experimented in adaptations from the French and German and in dramatizations of novels like *Griffith Gaunt* and *Pickwick Papers. Under the Gaslight,* his first surviving original play, which was also the occasion of his first independent production, was performed at the New York Theatre, Aug. 12, 1867. A melodrama of New York life, with realistic settings in the police courts and on the wharves of the North River, it introduced to the American stage the rescue, by the heroine, of a person bound to a railroad track in the path of an onrushing train. It proved to be one of the most popular of melodramas, and when played in London in 1868, inspired Dion Boucicault to his imitation of this sensation, in *After Dark.* Subsequent litigation established the exclusive right of Daly to this theatrical property in the United States. Another vigorous melodrama, *A Flash of Lightning,* produced at the Broadway Theatre, June 10, 1868, revealed in its burning of a Hudson River steamboat a source of danger in the construction of real boats. *The Red Scarf,* played first at Conway's Park Theatre in Brooklyn, in 1869, contained the same element of suspense as *Under the Gaslight,* the hero in this case being bound on a log about to be sawed in two.

On Jan. 9, 1869, Daly married Mary Duff, daughter of John A. Duff, owner of the Olympic Theatre. In August of that year, having leased the Fifth Avenue Theatre, he began to establish his own company, including Fanny Davenport [*q.v.*], Mrs. Gilbert, and James Lewis. Here he produced the best of the older English comedies of manners and laid the foundations for his superb productions of Shakespeare. Of even more significance, Daly gave Bronson Howard [*q.v.*] his first opportunity and produced *Saratoga* in 1870, thus aiding the establishment of the profession of play-writing in America, at a time when managers were looking almost exclusively to foreign sources for their plays. It was not at his own theatre, however, but at the Olympic that his best play, *Horizon,* was performed, Mar. 21, 1871. In this drama of Western American life, with its clear-cut characters and natural language, Daly may justly be regarded as the first of the realists, in the modern sense, among American playwrights. He next attacked a growing social problem in *Divorce,* one of the great successes of the Fifth Avenue Theatre, where it began its run of two hundred nights on Sept. 5, 1871. Here Daly adapted certain ideas from an English novel, Trollope's *He Knew He Was Right,* while changing them so as to apply to native conditions.

On Jan. 1, 1873 the Fifth Avenue Theatre burned. Daly, undaunted, leased the old New York Theatre, and in three weeks opened it as Daly's Fifth Avenue Theatre. In the same year he formed the first organization among the producing managers of New York, to avoid cutthroat competition and to provide for the loaning of players to each other. Booth, Wallack, Fechter, Palmer, and Jarrett were members with him. For a time Daly conducted the Grand Opera House and when the New Fifth Avenue Theatre was built for him on Twenty-eighth St. near Broadway, and opened on Dec. 3, 1873, he found the burden of three theatres too great. He therefore confined his efforts to the new house, which he conducted until 1877. *Roughing It,* an amusing travesty on the life described by Bret Harte and Mark Twain, was put on at the Grand Opera House, Feb. 18, 1873, and *Pique,* one of his most successful plays, was produced at the New Fifth Avenue Theatre, Dec. 14, 1875. To a theme derived from Florence Maryatt's novel, *Her Lord and Master,* that of a woman marrying out of pique because her lover is faithless, Daly added that of the search among the purlieus of the city for a stolen child, probably based upon the famous abduction of Charley Ross. The last of his original plays, *The Dark City,* produced Sept. 10, 1877, a melodrama from which he hoped great results, failed, and the consequent financial loss forced him to give up his theatre. After his visit to England in 1878–79, where he established relations with managers and actors that laid the foundations of his future successes, he turned the Old Broadway Theatre into Daly's Theatre. This was long to be the home of the remarkable company he assembled, including John Drew, Ada Rehan [*qq.v.*], and Otis Skinner. With the opening of the new theatre on Sept. 18, 1879 Daly ceased writing original plays and devoted his talents to the adaptation of French and German drama. His energies were spent largely, too, in the direction of the numerous plays with which he sought to give variety to his audiences. His correspondence reveals his efforts to procure the works of native playwrights like Bronson Howard, whose adaptation from Molière, under the title of *Wives,* was one of the first successes of the theatre. But more and more he grew to depend upon his own adaptations, many of which were radical alterations of the originals. Among the French playwrights, Sardou and Dumas were his favorites and with one exception, *Delmonico's; or Larks up the Hudson* (1871), he preserved the French scene when he dealt with the works of these two dramatists. About 1880 he began to transfer the scenes and characters to American conditions, perhaps because he was dealing with the work of less well-known playwrights. Probably his greatest successes were *Hazardous Ground* (1867) from Sardou's *Nos Bons Villageois; Monsieur Alphonse* (1874) from Dumas (*fils*); *Frou Frou* (1870) from Henri Meilhac and Ludovic Halévy; and *The Lottery of Love* (1888) from *Les Surprises du Divorce* by Alexandre Bisson and Antony Mars. In his adaptations from the German, Daly usually changed the scene to America. In *The Passing Regiment* (1881) hardly a trace of the German flavor of *Krieg im Frieden,* by Von Moser and Franz Von Schönthan, is noticeable, and when Daly adapted the latter's sequel, *Reif von Reiflingen,* it became *Our English Friend,* with an Englishman for a hero. His adaptations of German comedy were almost invariably successful, among the most popular being *Seven-Twenty-Eight; or, Casting the Boomerang* (1883), from *Der Schwabenstreich,* of Franz Von Schönthan; *A Night Off* (1885), from *Der Raub der Sabinerrinnen,* by the Von Schönthan brothers; *The Countess Gucki* (1896) by F. Von Schönthan, which was written for Ada Rehan and is unique among the comedies from the German in that it preserves the foreign atmosphere.

Daly took his company to London in 1884, playing at Toole's Theatre and being especially successful with his representation of Colley Cibber's *She Would and She Would Not.* In 1886, after again visiting London, he invaded the Continent, taking to Germany the first English-speaking company of any importance for nearly three hundred years. His reception in Berlin and Paris was only moderately enthusiastic. On a third foreign trip, in 1888, the most significant event was the production of *The Taming of the Shrew,* probably the first time a comedy of Shakespeare had been produced in Europe by an American company. Paris was not captured by this performance, but in 1891 *As You Like It* and *The School for Scandal* were received there with greater enthusiasm. The position which Daly had achieved by 1891 is evidenced by Tennyson's choice of him to adapt his dramatic poem, *The Foresters,* for the stage. It was a thing of beauty when produced at Daly's Theatre, Mar. 17, 1892, especially noteworthy being the performance of Ada Rehan as Maid Marian. On June 27, 1893, Daly opened his own theatre in London and, after varying fortunes, produced *Twelfth Night* for one hundred nights. He continued his productions of Shakespeare after his return to America, *The Tempest* in 1897 being especially effective. Difficulties arising with the lessor of his theatre in London, he made a business trip abroad in the course of which he died in Paris on June 7, 1899.

Daly was tall, handsome, and his flashing eyes and dominating personality reflected his seafaring and military ancestry. A martinet in his theatre, he demanded of his company the loyalty he gave them. Discriminating in his judgments of actors, he developed many who in their opinion outgrew the position he allowed them and passed from his control. Of those who remained he made probably the finest and most complete interpretative instrument for the drama that America has seen. He built up a clientele which was confident that at Daly's Theatre there would be a play worth seeing, and he achieved an identification of manager, playwright, director, company, and theatre, unique in our stage history. The result was a standard which helped to raise the general level of taste, and his productions of Shakespeare alone would render his position secure. But he was more than an interpreter, he was a creative artist. His place in American dramatic history has suffered from his unwillingness to publish his plays. He wrote, altered, or adapted about ninety plays that were produced on the stage. Many of them were privately printed, but those which were published, *Under the Gaslight* (1867), *Griffith Gaunt* (1868), *Frou Frou* (1870), *Seven-Twenty-Eight* (1897), and *A Night Off* (1897), do not represent him at his best. In *Horizon, Divorce, Pique,* and in his more delicate interpretations of foreign comedy, he proved himself a skilled dramatist. How hard he worked on his adaptations is attested by Otis Skinner (*Footlights and Spotlights,* 1924, p. 146) who tells us that when Pinero's *Lords and Commons* was failing, Daly spent his nights adapting *Love on Crutches,* from Heinrich Stobitzer's *Ihre Ideale,* in order to save the season. Daly's biography, *Woffington, A Tribute to the Actress and the Woman* (1888), reveals him in another aspect of his writing. How thoroughly he knew the dramatic past of America and how he scorned the critical stupidity which demands that American drama shall limit itself to the parochial, is revealed in his article "The American Dramatist" (*North American Review,* May 1886, pp. 485–92).

[The authoritative biography is Jos. F. Daly, *The Life of Augustin Daly* (1917). Of some value are two articles under the general heading, "An American School of Dramatic Art," J. R. Towse, "A Critical Review of Daly's Theatre," and G. P. Lathrop, "The Inside Working of the Theatre," *Century,* June 1898; E. A. Dithmar, *Memories of One Theatre with Passing Recollections of Many Others* (1891), and an informal *Diary of a Daly Débutante* (1910), published anonymously but known to be by Dora Knowlton, one of Daly's company. For criticism of the plays, see A. H. Quinn, *Hist. of the Am. Drama from the Civil War to the Present Day* (1927), I, 1–38, with play list, II, 278–84. The prompt-books of several of Daly's plays and a large collection of his scrap-books are in the N. Y. Pub. Lib. The MSS. are in possession of Samuel French.]

A. H. Q.

DALY, MARCUS (Dec. 5, 1841–Nov. 12, 1900), miner and capitalist, was born in Ireland. His parents, Luke and Mary Daly, were very poor and he grew up with little opportunity for education. At the age of fifteen he came to America. He worked for a while around New York, then went to California where he became a miner. Employed as a pick and shovel man, he soon became an expert on mining. After a time he entered the service of Fair and Mackay in Nevada where he displayed ability enough to attract the attention of Walker Brothers, and in 1876 they sent him to Butte, Mont. There he purchased the Alice Silver Mine in partnership with them, but soon sold his interest for $30,000. Geologists had declared the Butte mines to be of little value. Daly, however, believed that the unusual formation of the country concealed rich beds of ore. He went to California to seek aid from some old friends there. He persuaded George Hearst and others to share his convictions and they bought the Anaconda Silver Mine. It was not long before the silver gave out, but beneath it was a rich vein of copper. Daly closed the mine and quietly bought up others in the neighborhood and then started the great copper-mining operations that were to make Butte and the Anaconda Copper Mining Company famous. He mined the coal for his furnaces and acquired huge tracts of timber where he cut the wood for his mines. He built a railway from Butte to Anaconda. He established banks, built power plants and irrigation systems, and encouraged other enterprises. In twenty years he built up a fortune of many million dollars.

His feud with William A. Clark [*q.v.*] dominated Montana society and politics from 1888 to 1900. Daly and Clark had been friends, but their struggle for control of the copper mines of Butte had made them bitter enemies. Clark had control of the Butte reduction plants and Daly built Anaconda with its huge smelter a few miles away. Both men had business and political interest in Missoula, but when Clark gained an advantage, Daly built Hamilton, fifty miles up the Bitter Root, and projected a railroad from Butte and Anaconda, through this town, to the Pacific, with the idea of making it the commercial center of western Montana. He established the *Anaconda Standard* and made it the best paper in the state. Both men were Democrats, and both built up machines of their employees and of business men who were dependent upon them. Daly's genial and generous disposition, combined with a reputation for courage and loyalty, gave him popular favor over the reserved and elegant Clark, who was accused of timidity and a willingness to throw over his friends when they were no longer useful. Daly would never seek office for himself, but he loved to exert influence in politics and for ten years he endeavored to thwart Clark's ambition. In 1888 his followers brought about Clark's defeat as candidate for territorial delegate; in 1893 they prevented his election as senator; and when Clark finally secured his election as senator in 1899, Daly gave $25,000 to carry the fight to the Senate Committee on Elections whose adverse report forced Clark's resignation.

Daly gave lavishly for any cause he favored. He started the first state Democratic campaign with a donation of $40,000, and followed this with more. He apparently spent more than a half million dollars to make Anaconda the state capital. In 1896 he gave $50,000 to the Bryan Campaign fund, out of a total of $350,000 from all sources (statement of J. M. Dixon of a conversation with Senator J. K. Jones, Bryan's campaign manager).

Daly was married in 1872 to Margaret Evans. He built a house in the upper Bitter Root Valley, where he developed one of the finest ranches in the West. There he planted orchards and gave a start to fruit-growing in the valley. His pet extravagance was fast horses. Some of these were among the fastest in the world and he showed great pride in their triumphs on the track. He kept in close touch with the men with whom he had worked as a miner, and brought many of them to Butte and gave them a start to wealth. He was interested in his employees and gave higher wages than were current. His last achievement was the combination of a number of mining and lumber companies into the Amalgamated Copper Company with a capitalization of $75,000,000.

[The sources for the life of Daly are very unsatisfactory. There is a laudatory sketch of him in *Progressive Men of Mont.* (1901), and C. P. Connolly, "Story of Mont.," *McClure's Mag.*, Aug.–Dec. 1906, is partisan in his behalf. S. E. Moffett, "Marcus Daly, Empire Builder," *Rev. of Revs.* (N. Y.), Dec. 1900, is of little value. The files of the *Anaconda Standard*, especially Nov. 3, 1895, express Daly's views and reflect his character; there is a good obituary, *Ibid.*, Nov. 13, 1900. There is also a sketch of Daly in *Harper's Weekly*, Nov. 24, 1900.] P. C. P.

DALY, PETER CHRISTOPHER ARNOLD (Oct. 22, 1875–Jan. 13, 1927), actor, was born in Brooklyn, N. Y., the son of Joseph J. and Mary (Arnold) Daly, both natives of Ireland. He was christened Peter Christopher, but later took his mother's maiden name and dropped the others. He was educated in parochial schools, after being ejected, so he later declared, from four public schools for opposing rules which he considered "an insult to his intelligence." He became a call boy at the Lyceum Theatre, New York, and his first successful impersonation was that of Chambers, in Frank Mayo's production of *Puddn'head Wilson* in the early nineties. In the next few years he had considerable experience there and in London, acting especially well the crazed lover in Miss Marlowe's production of Clyde Fitch's *Barbara Frietchie* and Imp in the London production of *When We Were Twenty-one.* It was while he was with Miss Marlowe that he first conceived the idea of producing G. B. Shaw's *Candida,* a play which Richard Mansfield had put in rehearsal but abandoned. He could not secure, however, the needed support. After Mansfield's tour in 1897–98 with Shaw's *The Devil's Disciple,* no Shaw play had been seen in America. At last, on Dec. 9, 1903, Daly succeeded in making a single matinée production of *Candida,* at the Princess Theatre, New York, with Dorothy Donnelly in the title part and himself as Marchbanks. It was so successful that in partnership with Winchell Smith he rented the Berkeley Lyceum and played *Candida* for 150 performances. This was the real start of the Shaw vogue in America. Thereafter Daly mounted several other Shaw plays—*How He Lied to Her Husband* (written for him), *The Man of Destiny, You Never Can Tell* (Garrick Theatre, New York, January 1905), *John Bull's Other Island* (Garrick, Oct. 10, 1905), and finally *Mrs. Warren's Profession* (Garrick, Oct. 30, 1905). Before the New York opening of this last play, Anthony Comstock sounded a warning, and after one try-out performance in New Haven the police stopped it there. At the New York première, seats were selling on the sidewalk for $25, and Police Commissioner McAdoo was in the audience. The next morning McAdoo announced that further performances would be a violation of the law. None was given, but Daly and his leading lady, Mary Shaw, were arrested, tried in Special Sessions, and acquitted. Except for John Corbin of the *Sun,* all the newspaper critics called the play indecent, and Shaw was provoked to write a now highly prized pamphlet on the subject. The outbreak of Comstockery cost Daly much money and a quarrel with his managers. After reviving *Arms and the Man* at the Lyric Theatre, he again rented the Berkeley Lyceum, and attempted to conduct that tiny house as "a theatre of ideas," during the season of 1907–08. He gave several bills of one-act plays, revived several Shaw successes, refused to advertise in the newspapers, and denied free seats to their critics. But the venture was not successful. He found himself in serious financial difficulties. The Shaw plays passed into other hands, and he never regained the place he had briefly held as a fighting leader of modernism on the American stage. He thereafter alternated engagements in vaudeville with such parts as he could secure, his better known later appearances being with Madame Simone in *The Return from Jerusalem,* in the title rôle of *General John Regan,* in *The Tavern* (produced by G. M. Cohan), in the title rôle of *Voltaire,* and in the Theatre Guild's production of *Juarez and Maximilian,* in October 1926. On the morning of Jan. 12, 1927, he perished in a fire which swept the house in New York where he had an apartment. His body was found seated in a chair, as if he had been caught asleep. Daly was married, on July 1, 1900, to Mary Blythe, an actress. They had one child, Blythe Daly, who eventually went on the stage. They were divorced in 1903 and were later reunited, only to separate again, Mrs. Daly becoming Mrs. Frank Craven.

Arnold Daly was a victim of tempermental excesses, which manifested themselves in violent quarrels, egotistical outbursts, and lack of cooperative spirit. But he had a genuine appreciation of modernism in drama before most of his fellows, he was ready to fight for it and to sacrifice for it, and as an actor he possessed a nervous sensibility which made him, when willing to submit to a director's control, an extremely vivid and effective player, particularly in such parts as Marchbanks. There can be no question but that his production of *Candida* and other Shaw plays, from 1903 through 1905, marked an important step forward in our theatre, and had it not been for the disastrous interference of Comstockery and his subsequent bankruptcy and intensified truculence, his later influence might have equaled that of his early years. He was a double victim of himself and Mrs. Grundy.

[B. H. Goldsmith, *Arnold Daly* (1927); *Who's Who on the Stage* (1906); Arnold Daly Scrap-Book, Locke Collection, N. Y. Pub. Lib.] W. P. E.

DALZELL, JOHN (Apr. 19, 1845–Oct. 2, 1927), congressman, parliamentarian, was born in New York City, of Scotch-Irish parents. Samuel Dalzell, a shoemaker, and his wife Mary (McDonnell) had come from County Down in 1840. When John was two, their pioneer urge pushed them farther across the mountains to Pittsburgh. At sixteen, John became discontented with the educational opportunities offered him at the Western University of Pennsylvania, and found his way to Yale. Entering heartily into the social, athletic, literary, and debating activities there, he succeeded in developing leadership and securing recognition. Upon graduation (A.B., 1865), he was desirous of following his natural bent, the law, in his home community. Two years of study there under John H. Hampton led to a partnership with him.

Twenty years of arduous, successful work as a corporation attorney ensued. The firm became counsel for all the western lines of the Pennsylvania Railroad from the time of their amalgamation, for the Westinghouse industries, and for others of more local significance. After the death of Hampton in 1887 the name of the firm was changed to Dalzell, Scott & Gordon, and Dalzell worked actively in it until 1895. In the midst of his labors in behalf of industrial amalgamation and railroad expansion, his friends persuaded him, somewhat against his will, to go to Congress. In this project they were aided and abetted by his wife. Mary Louise Duff, to whom he was married Sept. 26, 1867, was exceptionally well-fitted to be the helpmate of a congressman. Relieving her husband of many of the burdens which constituents place upon their representatives, she also unobtrusively engineered campaign contacts, quietly supervising that meticulous reëlection detail which is the bane of a congressman's existence, a work which Dalzell abhorred and in which he practically refused to engage. Under such favorable auspices, there began a congressional career which was to last through twenty-six consecutive years.

From 1887 to 1889 and from 1891 to 1895 Dalzell was a member of the minority. He proved himself unwaveringly loyal to Pittsburgh's industries, and although a railroad attorney contributed powerfully to the development of Pittsburgh's waterways. His period of national significance commenced in 1895, when the Republicans gained control of the House; then began a sequence of fourteen years of House leadership, jointly exercised with Reed, Dingley, Payne, and Cannon. From their councils emanated highly developed forms of the special rule, devised to expedite legislation. Already a member of the Ways and Means Committee, Dalzell now went on the Rules Committee, of which he ultimately became ranking member. In this key-position he reported an immense number of the special rules by which much of the important legislation has been since enacted in the House of Representatives. One of the most important of these was that of Mar. 1, 1901, providing for consideration of a conference report without reference to the usual committee, and providing in detail for the previous question thereon.

Dalzell being a thoroughgoing conservative, the La Follette insurgents had him to reckon with from the start. He cornered them many times; as on Mar. 1, 1909, when he proposed Calendar Wednesday in such manner as to put them on record against it; and Apr. 10 and July 31 of that year, when special rules sent the tariff to conference without debate on separate amendments, and provided that the conference report should not be subject to a point of order. Dalzell failed to defeat the Norris resolution abolishing the old Rules Committee; but when the Republicans, debarring from their caucus the insurgents, came to nominate for the new committee, he was named for the ranking position; and when the committee organized he was named chairman. From this new-old vantage, Dalzell reported, June 17, 1910, the first discharge rule of the House, that rule which James R. Mann murdered six months later.

The Senate remained out of Dalzell's reach, Matthew S. Quay [*q.v.*] defeating him in 1899, and again in 1901. For the speakership, he lost in 1902 to Joseph G. Cannon [*q.v.*], the more picturesque Mid-Western candidate. The death of Mrs. Dalzell in 1909 broke the mainspring of his political existence. In 1912 he suffered defeat with Taft, and thereafter steadfastly refused to reënter politics. He chose to remain in retirement in Washington until, two years before his death, he removed to Altadena, Cal.

[*Cong. Record,* Mar. 18, 1906; A. C. McCown, *The Cong. Conference Committee* (1927); P. D. Hasbrouck, *Party Government in the House of Representatives* (1927); G. R. Brown, *The Leadership of Congress* (1922); C. R. Atkinson, *The Committee on Rules and the Overthrow of Speaker Cannon* (1911); W. C. Duyckinck, *Summary of Class Meetings and the Biog. Record of the Class of 1865, Yale Coll.* (1910); *Yale Univ. Obit. Record* (1928); *Pittsburgh Post-Gazette,* Oct. 4, 1927; Dalzell MSS., Lib. of Cong.] J. P. N.

DALZELL, ROBERT M. (1793–Jan. 19, 1873), millwright, inventor, was born in County Down, near Belfast, Ireland. He was the son of John Dalzell, the last of an old family of Scotch Covenanters that had established itself in Ireland and become a family of influence and character, with large property. When Robert was five years old the Rebellion of 1798 began and his father, one of the recognized leaders, was sought for by British soldiers. He escaped to sea in an open boat and was picked up by the crew of a passing ship and carried to New York. Three years later his wife and children came to New York as immigrants to join him. They established themselves on a small farm at Vernon, Oneida County, N. Y., and began life anew under the most adverse, poverty-stricken conditions. Young Dalzell was given all of the educational advantages that the local country school afforded, after which he was apprenticed to a millwright from whom he learned his trade. Following his apprenticeship he worked locally as a millwright until he was thirty-three years of age, when he moved to Rochester to engage in his chosen occupation. It was about this time that the potential water power of the Genesee River and its falls at Rochester began to be recognized. Among the first enterprises utilizing this power were flour-mills, and in their construction Dalzell, as a millwright, found immediate employment. His mechanical ingenuity combined with his skill in mill construction was quickly recognized and for the succeeding twenty-five years or more his services were in great demand. In fact, practically all of the flour-mills in Rochester, which came to be known as the "Flour City," were designed by him and built under his supervision. In the course of this work he perfected and introduced the elevator system for storing grain and meal which is now universally used in all large ocean and inland ports, but he never patented the system. His refusal to do so was probably due to his conscientious scruples against the accumulation of wealth by an individual; it is said that in all of his private transactions, both when he was in active work and after his retirement, he could never under any form or guise be persuaded to take more than seven per cent interest or discount. For the last twenty-five years of his life he lived more or less in retirement, his activities centering about his church. He died in Rochester, N. Y., being survived by his widow, Lucy S. Dalzell, and two children.

[*Ann. Cyc.,* 1873; W. F. Peck, *Semi-Centennial Hist. of the City of Rochester* (1884); obituary in Rochester *Democrat and Chronicle,* Jan. 20, 1873; correspondence with N. Y. State Lib. and Rochester Pub. Lib., Division of Local History.] C. W. M.

DAMROSCH, LEOPOLD (Oct. 22, 1832–Feb. 15, 1885), conductor, composer, violinist, was born in Posen. Like many other musically gifted persons, he encountered paternal opposition as soon as he took steps to follow professionally the art to which he had been inclined since childhood. After graduating from the Breslau Gymnasium, he matriculated as a student of medicine at the University of Berlin in 1854. This, however, was his last concession to his parents' wishes regarding his career; for, once his degree of doctor of medicine was acquired, he abandoned medicine in favor of music, continued his study of the violin with Ries, Dehn, and Böhmer, and soon as a solo artist, and later as a conductor, appeared with success in various minor German towns and cities. In 1857 "he became concert master at the Grand Ducal Opera at Weimar under the direction of Franz Liszt whom he adored and whose music, together with that of Wagner and Berlioz, he promulgated during the rest of his life" (letter from Walter Damrosch). At Weimar he married the talented German ***Lieder*** singer, Helena von Heimburg, with whom he returned to Breslau in 1858, immediately after his marriage. There he took the position of conductor of the Breslau Philharmonic Orchestra, only to resign it in order to accompany the pianists Von Bülow and Tausig on various concert tours. In 1862, again in Breslau, he organized the Breslau Orchestra Society, a choral society, and a string quartet; and for two years conducted the concerts of the Society for Classical Music and the orchestra of the Breslau Stadttheater, besides appearing as a solo violinist.

With his musical reputation now firmly established, though his financial status was far from good, it was natural that Damrosch, in 1871, should have accepted with pleasure an invitation to come to America, as the conductor of the Arion Society of New York. As his son declared: "My father had become more and more discontented with musical, social and political conditions in Breslau. He was really a republican at heart and the Prussian bureaucracy, which had become more and more accentuated by the war (1870–71) irked and angered him. With the greatest difficulty he could make a bare living for his family, and he found the population of Breslau, except a small band of devoted followers, steeped in materialism and not particularly sympathetic toward art, especially the modern German composers."

On May 6, 1871 Damrosch made his New York *début* in the triple capacity of conductor, composer, and violinist, and found little difficulty in soon winning appreciation for the newer German school of composition represented by Wagner, Liszt, and Schumann. His executive capacity was shown by bringing the Arion Society to the highest point of musical efficiency, by the foundation of the New York Oratorio Society in 1873, and, in 1878, of the New York Symphony Society, which succeeded the Thomas Orchestra at the Steinway Hall concerts. In 1880, Columbia University made the German doctor of medicine an American doctor of music, and the following year he conducted New York's first great music festival. In the old Seventh Regiment Armory, with an audience of ten thousand people for each performance, Berlioz's *Requiem,* with the four orchestras and sixteen kettle-drums in the *Tuba Mirum,* Rubinstein's *Tower of Babel,* Händel's *Messiah,* and Beethoven's *Ninth Symphony* were presented by 250 musicians and 1,200 singers. In 1883 Damrosch made a successful tour with his orchestra in the West. His greatest triumph was his last. In 1884–85, the directors of the Metropolitan Opera House, at the suggestion of James Roosevelt, gave a season of German opera, at which he conducted *Tannhäuser, Lohengrin, Die Walküre,* and other noted operas. In achieving this "final triumph of Wagner's art in the new world," at a time when Italian opera still claimed supremacy, the veteran conductor who was attending rehearsals of the Symphony and Oratorio Societies in the meantime, so overworked himself that he fell an easy victim to pneumonia. Leopold Damrosch exerted a great influence in raising the standard of musical taste and appreciation in America during the past half-century; and in infusing the mechanistic excellence of orchestra and oratorio performance which he found on his arrival in the United States with musical soul and spirit. His own compositions include seven cantatas, orchestral numbers, songs, choruses, and three violin concertos.

[Walter Damrosch, *My Musical Life* (1923); H. C. Colles, ed., *Grove's Dict. of Music and Musicians,* vol. II (1927); J. G. Huneker, *Steeplejack* (1920), II, 36; Alfred Remy, ed., *Baker's Biog. Dict. of Musicians* (3rd ed., 1919).]

F. H. M.

DANA, CHARLES ANDERSON (Aug. 8, 1819–Oct. 17, 1897), newspaper editor, was born at Hinsdale, N. H., a descendant of Jacob, eldest son of Richard Dana who in 1640 was a resident of Cambridge, Mass. He had few early advantages beyond the good blood of Puritan ancestors. His father, Anderson Dana, a country storekeeper, failed in business and removed to upper New York, where he became a farmer; his mother, Ann Denison, died when he was nine. Sent to Buffalo at the age of twelve to clerk in the general store of an uncle, he was thrown entirely upon his own resources at eighteen, when the panic of 1837 ruined his employer. While a boy on the farm he had studied Latin on his own initiative; he used his evenings in Buffalo to read widely, become familiar with the Latin classics, and begin the study of Greek. He joined a literary society there called the Coffee Club, and delivered before it a youthful lecture on early English poetry which was much admired. Thus prepared by his own efforts, he was able to matriculate at Harvard without conditions in the fall of 1839, and took high rank in his first college term. Despite one long absence for teaching school he had begun his junior year in 1841, when his eyesight became impaired by overstudy and he returned to Buffalo. Twenty years later he received from Harvard an honorary A.B., as of the class of 1843. About the time he left college, George Ripley [*q.v.*] was launching the Brook Farm enterprise, which Dana, with an idealistic enthusiasm then characteristic of him, hastened to join. He was engaged to teach German, Greek, or anything else, and to work on the Farm, while in view of his storekeeping experience he was made one of the managing trustees. For the next five years he remained at Brook Farm, placing in it what slender capital he could, and proselytizing earnestly for it. With characteristic energy he taught, sang bass in the choir, wrote essays and poems for the *Dial* and the *Harbinger,* and delivered lectures. According to T. W. Higginson, he was the best all-round man at the Farm. He opposed its conversion into a "Phalanx" as demanded by Fourierist ideas, but after this was effected he remained stanchly loyal to the organization (Lindsay Swift, *Brook Farm,* 1900). In a lecture of 1895 at the University of Michigan he paid a warm tribute to the charm of life at the Farm, and the value of his association there with Ripley, Hawthorne, George W. Curtis, Margaret Fuller, and others.

Dana's writings for the *Harbinger* had so fixed his attention upon journalism that when a disastrous fire terminated the Brook Farm experiment in 1846 he naturally turned to that field. A slight previous connection with the Boston *Daily Chronotype* enabled him at once to become its assistant editor. The paper was too poor to pay much, and its strong Congregationalism repelled Dana, who had now progressed far in Unitarian liberalism. In the absence of the editor he made the *Chronotype* come out "mighty strong against hell," so that his superior later had to write a letter of explanation to every Congregational minister in the state. Within the year Dana used his acquaintance with Greeley to obtain the city editorship of the *New York Tribune,* at the munificent wage of first ten and later fourteen dollars a week. For the next fifteen years he devoted himself to the paper, and soon stood second in its office to Greeley alone. Outwardly this period of subeditorship was uneventful. Its first years were broken by a long trip (1848–9) to Europe, where Dana supported himself by contributing no fewer than five letters a week to as many journals in New York, Boston, and Philadelphia. He could not have gone abroad at a more instructive moment, for he witnessed the uprisings in Paris and Berlin at close range. His experiences did more than acquaint him with European affairs. They swept away many of his idealistic illusions, gave him an insight into the selfishness and chicanery of politicians, and helped lay the foundation for his subsequent cynicism. Later, as managing editor, he had little time for travel, but found leisure to edit an American edition of H. J. Meyer's *Universum* (1852), and to compile *The Household Book of Poetry* (1857), which in successive editions commanded an enormous sale. A trip which Dana made with W. H. Appleton to the opening of the Chicago & Rock Island Railroad resulted in plans for an American Cyclopædia in sixteen volumes under the editorship of himself and George Ripley. The first volume appeared in 1858, and despite the interruption of the war, the work was completed in six years. Two editions of it sold more than three million copies (Grant Overton, *Portrait of a Publisher,* 1925, p. 45).

Dana's years on the *Tribune* gave him experience in two directions. As a writer he became the master of a compressed, sententious style, sometimes epigrammatic, and increasingly tinged by cynicism. His principles were largely, though by no means completely, liberal. He took up Kossuth's cause with ardor, advocated a railway to the Pacific, and ably seconded Greeley's opposition to the expansion of slavery, though he had little use for the Abolitionists. He believed in a high protective tariff, and opposed labor unions formed to conduct strikes, arguing that the workers' true remedy for unfair industrial conditions lay in a cooperative industrial effort. His hostility to militant labor persisted throughout his life, and gave many of his utterances on industrial questions an illiberal and even reactionary tendency. In editorial management Dana soon made himself an expert. Frequently, as during Greeley's European trips in 1851 and 1855–56, he was in sole charge. He then decided the entire contents of the paper; edited everything, even Greeley's contributions, with iron hand; and took the initiative in important business changes.

In the events leading up to the Civil War Dana and Greeley acted with substantial harmony, and there is no question that Dana acquiesced in Greeley's willingness to let the erring sisters depart in peace. But, though the words were written by a subordinate, Dana was responsible for the *Tribune's* disastrous war-cry, "Forward to Richmond!" which Greeley opposed. This was the first serious token of a divergence in views and temper which rapidly became intolerable. Dana was too aggressive and positive in dealing with both civil and military policy to suit Greeley. The result was that, after Greeley had acted rather shiftily, Dana's resignation was demanded and accepted (Mar. 28, 1862), with a promise of six months' salary. This virtual dismissal was a blessing in disguise. After declining the suggestion that he take a diplomatic post or a place with the Treasury (Wilson, pp. 182–83), he at once entered the service of the War Department, where Secretary Stanton was eager to repay him for editorial support.

The best part of Dana's war service was performed as a special commissioner at Grant's headquarters, nominally to investigate the pay-service, but actually to report daily on military operations and thus enable the Administration to measure accurately Grant's capacities. During the Vicksburg campaign his observations were equally valuable to the Washington officials and to Grant himself. Dana instantly perceived the general's high qualities, he increased Lincoln's faith in him, set Stanton right regarding the jealous McClernand, and by his daily dispatches relieved Grant of much irksome letter-writing. Of Sherman's military genius Dana also formed a high opinion. Made assistant secretary of war after the fall of Vicksburg, he was sent to report upon the movements of Rosecrans against Bragg. His judgment was not in all regards unerring, but he was right in urging the removal of Rosecrans. Later with

Dana

Grant and Sherman at Chattanooga, Lookout Mountain, and Missionary Ridge, he again proved an excellent advocate for these men. During 1864 he alternated desk service in Washington with field service in Virginia, and formed impressions of Lincoln, the cabinet members, and some leading congressmen which enabled him long afterward to give pungent sketches of them in his *Recollections of the Civil War* (1898). On July 1, 1865, he resigned and immediately left the capital.

Dana's acquisition of the New York *Sun,* which marked the opening of the most significant part of his career, occurred at the close of 1867. It was preceded by an abortive journalistic venture in Chicago, where he became editor of an unsuccessful paper called the *Republican* (*Recollections,* p. 290). When this sheet began to fail, he secured capital for the founding of a newspaper in New York, his associates including W. M. Evarts, Roscoe Conkling, Alonzo Cornell, Cyrus W. Field and A. A. Low. A fortunate chance enabling him to purchase the *Sun* for $175,000, he assumed its editorship on Jan. 25, 1868, with an announcement of policy which has become a journalistic classic. After declaring that the *Sun* would be independent of party, would advocate the speedy restoration of the South, and would support Grant for the presidency, he summed up its new spirit in a single sentence: "It will study condensation, clearness, point, and will endeavor to present its daily photograph of the whole world's doings in the most luminous and lively manner." Imbued with this spirit, the *Sun* at once achieved a new success.

In his capacity as leader of public opinion, Dana was frequently perverse, cynical, and reactionary, and more than once affected by personal resentments. He broke sharply with Grant, and after 1869 attacked his administration more fiercely than did any other New York daily. Yet in 1872, while making the cry "Turn the rascals out" ring through the country and assailing Grant almost scurrilously, he gave only a cynical quasi-support to the Liberal Republican party, whose candidate he contemptuously called "Dr. Greeley." In 1876 the *Sun* opposed Hayes, whom it later branded as a receiver of stolen goods and a fraudulent president. Four years later it relentlessly attacked Garfield, whom it described as a participant in the Crédit Mobilier frauds, the Boss Shepherd thefts, and the back-pay grab; yet at the same time it treated Hancock with ill-veiled condescension, speaking of him as "a good man, weighing two hundred and fifty pounds." The most remarkable exhibition of Dana's political perversity was his unremitting enmity to Cleveland, which grew out of an unworthy bit of personal pique, the failure of Cleveland to keep a supposed promise to appoint Franklin Bartlett, son of Dana's friend W. O. Bartlett, to a post connected with the state judiciary. Dana at the same time declared that sooner than join in making Blaine president, he would quit work and burn his pen. The consequence was that in 1884 he had to support B. F. Butler and his Greenback ticket, which polled a farcically small vote in New York. In his social and economic opinions of these years Dana showed the same perversity, accompanied sometimes by an impudent levity. He denounced the reformed civil service as "a German bureaucratic system," advocated the annexation of Cuba, Santo Domingo, and if possible Canada, and abused Cleveland for his conciliatory foreign policy, demanding the resignation of Secretary Bayard for negotiating the fisheries treaty with England. He declared that the McKinley Act was the most scientific and valuable tariff the country ever had. Dana's hostility toward labor unions cropped out in the great railway strike of 1878; and later he urged that labor organizations be placed under precisely as stringent governmental regulation as affected the trusts. In New York City the *Sun* supported some of the worst figures in Tammany, and opposed some of the best reform movements.

As a news editor, however, Dana at once took a very high place. The Civil War had tended to exalt news at the expense of editorials. Dana approved of this, declaring that "if the newspaper has not the news, it may have everything else, yet it will be comparatively unsuccessful." Under him the *Sun's* news-pages were characterized by conciseness, cleverness, and sparkle of style. Discarding conventional standards of news importance and emphasizing human interest, he taught the staff that a good story on the Sunday crowd at Coney Island might be worth more space than a column on the Carlist War or a lecture by Huxley. The *Sun* gave prominence to crime in its "daily photograph," and specialized in eye-catching headlines. The enterprise of the reporters obtained many scoops, and the foreign and domestic correspondence of the paper attained such excellence that when in 1897 a long-standing quarrel with the Associated Press came to a head, Dana's managing editor, Chester S. Lord, was able to organize over-night a comprehensive news service of his own. Though sternly excluding fine writing, the *Sun* insisted upon vividness, and made generous room for clever brief essays. The paper was at all costs bright, witty, and enjoyable. As a result it became the "newspaper man's newspaper," and attracted to its staff a singularly brilliant roster of writers. Indeed, one of Dana's titles to fame as an editor is that he gave opportunity and advancement to such editorial writers as E. P. Mitchell, and such news writers as Julian Ralph, David Graham Phillips, Jacob Riis, and Richard Harding Davis. He mingled constantly with the staff, encouraging, suggesting, and praising frequently, while chiding rarely and gently.

Dana was a man of wide intellectual and esthetic interests, which in later life he had leisure and money to indulge. He took quiet pride in learning the chief European tongues, living and dead, his last two trips abroad being for the purpose of perfecting his Russian. He liked to conduct private classes in Dante or Icelandic; he had a valuable collection of Chinese porcelains; and at his home on Dosoris Island in Long Island Sound he grew a remarkable variety of foreign trees, shrubs, and flowers. He prided himself on being a connoisseur of wines, though he seldom did more than taste them. Though much interested in politics, he preferred to make his friends among literary people, musicians, and artists. Married, Mar. 2, 1846, to Eunice Macdaniel, he was devoted to wife and children. He had the faculty of endearing himself to close newspaper associates, but he never forgave a grudge or a slight.

[Jas. H. Wilson, *Life of Chas. A. Dana* (1907), is uncritically eulogistic and emphasizes his war services. Chas. A. Dana, *Recollections of the Civil War* (1898), a graphic and honest work, throwing some light on his years upon the *Tribune*, should be supplemented by *The Art of Newspaper Making* (1895), and *Eastern Journeys* (1898). See also Frank M. O'Brien, *The Story of the Sun* (1918); Edw. P. Mitchell, *Memoirs of an Editor* (1924); Chester S. Lord, *The Young Men and Journalism* (1922); Willard G. Bleyer, *Main Currents in the Hist. of Am. Journalism* (1927); Henry Watterson, *Marse Henry: An Autobiography* (1919); Oswald G. Villard, *Some Newspapers and Newspapermen* (1923); J. J. Dana, *Memoranda of Some of the Descendants of Richard Dana* (1865); and biographies of Greeley. The *Sun* published no obituary. Magazine material is voluminous, but must be used with care.]

A. N.

DANA, FRANCIS (June 13, 1743–Apr. 25, 1811), diplomat, jurist, was born in Charlestown, Mass., the son of Richard [*q.v.*] and Lydia (Trowbridge) Dana. Graduating from Harvard in 1762, he received the degree of A.M. in 1765. After studying law for five years under the direction of his mother's brother, Judge Edmund Trowbridge [*q.v.*], one of the ablest lawyers in the colony, he was admitted to the bar in 1767. Six years later he married Elizabeth Ellery of Newport, R. I., daughter of William Ellery [*q.v.*]. One of their sons was Richard Henry Dana [*q.v.*], and a daughter, Martha, became the wife of Washington Allston [*q.v.*]. From his father he acquired an interest in politics, as well as the means to indulge it. His fortune, described as competent by one of his descendants, was invested largely in land. Although not a radical by temperament, he found fault with the colonial policy of the British government, and became identified with the Sons of Liberty. In spite of this connection, however, he held no public office during the early years of the Revolutionary movement, but devoted himself primarily to his law practise.

In the fall and winter of 1774–75, while Samuel Adams and his followers wanted independence, another group, including Dana and some other Sons of Liberty, urged reconciliation with Great Britain. Although chosen in September 1774 as one of the Cambridge delegates to the first provincial Congress of Massachusetts, Dana did not take his seat in that body. Instead he undertook an interesting diplomatic venture, half private and half public in character, in the interests of Anglo-American harmony. Carrying letters from Quincy, Warren, and other leaders, he went to England to represent the patriot cause among the English friends of the colonies, and to discover what the situation actually was in that country. His brother Edmund had gone to live in England, and had married there a daughter of Lord Kinnaird; through her relatives Dana had access to numerous political leaders. Remaining in England for a year and a half, he returned to his home in Cambridge in April 1776 convinced that reconciliation was out of the question and that independence alone would put an end to the controversy over colonial rights and British power. Prepared to devote his whole efforts to the American cause, he was at first undecided whether to take a political or a military part in the war. His constituents may have settled the matter for him; at all events they elected him a member of the Massachusetts Council in 1776, and regularly thereafter until 1780. In December 1776 the legislature made him one of the delegates to the Continental Congress, which apparently he did not attend until Nov. 17, 1777. Four days later he was nominated, though not elected, to succeed Silas Deane as commissioner to France. In 1778 as chairman of a congressional committee on the army he went to Valley Forge to cooperate with Washington in making plans for a general reorganization of the American forces. This work, which took five months, met with the approval of Congress.

In the same year Dana was one of a committee of three appointed to examine the conciliatory proposals of Lord North, the rejection of which was recommended by the committee and unanimously agreed to by Congress. In 1779, when John Adams was appointed minister plenipotentiary to negotiate peace with England, Dana was sent to France with him as secretary of the legation. The two men, who had formerly been associated in their legal work in Boston, reached Paris in February 1780. Finding little opportunity there even to talk peace, Adams went to Holland for the purpose of negotiating a loan, and if possible a treaty. In June, Congress sent Dana a supplementary commission, authorizing him, in the event of the possible disability of Adams, to continue negotiations for loans.

At this time, under the guidance of the Empress Catherine of Russia, the neutral maritime governments of northern Europe joined forces in what was known as the armed neutrality, to prevent the British navy from interfering with their shipping. In order to transform this feeling into actual help for the American cause if possible, Congress determined to send a regularly accredited minister to Russia, and chose Dana for this diplomatic venture. His commission, approved by Congress on Dec. 19, 1780, authorized him to accede to any regulations in harmony with the original declaration which might be adopted by the powers of the armed neutrality, and to sign any treaty embodying the principles of that declaration and at the same time consistent with the dignity and sovereignty of the United States as a free and independent nation. He was also instructed to propose a treaty of amity and commerce between the United States and Russia, "on principles of equality and reciprocity, and for the mutual advantage of both nations."

Before setting out for St. Petersburg, he consulted his American friends in Europe, particularly John Adams, whose youthful son, John Quincy, he took with him as secretary, and also Vergennes, the French minister for foreign affairs, with reference to his proper course in Russia. It was generally agreed that it would be unwise for him to inform the Russian representatives in western Europe of his mission, as Catherine, unwilling openly to offend Great Britain, evidently would not give official consent to the coming of a minister from the United States. It seemed best for him to go to Russia as a private citizen, interested in the country merely out of curiosity. It was apparent that his coming and his real status would be reported to Catherine by her representatives abroad, and probably by Vergennes himself. This situation freed both parties from embarrassment, and at the same time left the way open at any moment for the establishment of official relations.

Dana's stay in St. Petersburg, lasting from August 1781 to September 1783, was by all odds the most dramatic and colorful episode in his whole life, and at the same time probably the least satisfactory to him. For a year and a half after his arrival he found no opportunity whatever to present his credentials and ask for an official interview. By indirect means, however, he did succeed in laying before the Russian foreign office certain arguments in favor of a commercial alliance with his government. Late in December 1782, when he learned of the signing of the preliminary treaty of peace between Great Britain and the United States, he felt that the time had at last come to ask that he be accorded an interview as minister. After receiving unofficial assurance, which seemed dependable, that it would be proper to do so he presented his credentials on Mar. 7, 1783. But the Russian government had not the slightest intention of recognizing him or his country. On Apr. 25 this information was imparted to him orally by Ostermann, the vice-chancellor in charge of foreign relations, not in so many words, but in the form of subterfuges and evasions. Dana asked Ostermann to put his explanations in writing so that he could transmit them to Congress as a reply to his advances. This the wily Russian refused to do. Peace with England, however, had made recognition of the United States by Russia a matter of little importance. Dana was consequently instructed to go no farther with his negotiations, unless they were on the verge of completion. Since they had not really begun and he was anxious to return home, he left for the United States at the earliest opportunity, arriving in Boston in December 1783.

In 1784 Dana was again sent to Congress, but his service with that body was comparatively short. In 1785 Gov. Hancock appointed him one of the associate justices of the supreme court of Massachusetts; from that time until his retirement from public life his career was primarily that of a jurist. In 1787 he was chosen a delegate to the Federal Convention, but poor health prevented him from attending its sessions. In the Massachusetts convention of 1788, however, he was one of the conspicuous advocates of ratification of the Constitution. In 1797 he was asked by his old friend, President John Adams, to serve with Pinckney and Marshall as envoy to France, but again because of ill health was compelled to decline the mission. From 1791 to his resignation in 1806 he was chief justice of the supreme court of Massachusetts. Like many who had been associated with him in the Revolution, he became in his later years a thoroughgoing conservative. His state of mind was shown particularly in his charges to grand juries. A true Federalist, he was seriously disturbed by the growing tendency to find fault with public officials, and looked upon the outspoken Jeffersonians as a menace to the nation. In 1798, not long after the adoption of the Alien and Sedition Acts, the supreme court opened at Salem. Dana, giving the grand jury a longer charge than usual, defined treason and misprision of treason, passed "to a vindication of the Sedition and Alien Bills and then to the negotiation of the United States with France. The necessity of the Sedition Bill he argued from a Liberty Poll [pole] & Inscription at Dedham." He also found an opportunity on this occasion to castigate Talleyrand (*The Diary of William Bentley,* Nov. 13, 1798, II, 289). On Feb. 18, 1799, the Boston *Independent Chronicle,* a Republican newspaper, published a brief commentary on the position of the state, as defined in its constitution. After Dana had laid the matter before the grand jury the next day, the editors of the paper were indicted for the commission of an offense against the peace and dignity of the state. Again in 1800, in another charge to the grand jury, Dana "took notice . . . of the restless aliens who are spreading their disorganizing principles." His views were those of the great majority of the substantial citizens of his community, whose respect and admiration he retained to the end of his life. He was also one of the few leaders of his day looked upon with real affection by John and John Quincy Adams.

[There are two short sketches of Dana's life by R. H. Dana: one, an address published on the occasion of the one hundredth anniversary of Dana, Mass. (1901); the other an address delivered before the Cambridge Hist. Soc., printed in its *Pubs.,* III (1908), 57–78. For his diplomatic career, see Francis Wharton, *The Revolutionary Diplomatic Correspondence of the U. S.* (6 vols., 1884); and F. P. Renaut, *Les Relations Diplomatiques entre la Russie et les États Unis: La Mission Dana* (1923). W. P. Cresson has in preparation a study, "Francis Dana at the Court of Catherine the Great."]

R. V. H.

DANA, JAMES (1735–Aug. 18, 1812), Congregational clergyman, third in descent from Richard Dana who came from England to America about 1640, and son of Caleb, a tanner, and Phœbe (Chandler) Dana, was born in Cambridge, Mass. His father was a brother of Richard Dana [*q.v.*], leader of the Boston bar. The vital records of the town state that James was baptized May 18, 1735, but the date of his birth is not given. At the age of eighteen he graduated from Harvard; then for some time continued his studies there. In 1758 he was called to the church in Wallingford, Conn., which had been without a pastor since the death of Rev. Samuel Whittelsey in 1752, and a council was summoned to ordain him. There followed the "Wallingford Controversy," a noted incident in the ecclesiastical history of the state. Coming from Massachusetts, Dana was suspected of unorthodoxy, and known to be of the "Old Light" party. Some of the church, instigated, it is said, by "New Light" ministers, determined to prevent his ordination by bringing complaint before the consociation of the county. Ordaining council and consociation met on the same day. Haled before the latter, Dana and his church protested its jurisdiction over them in such a case, and the council, though forbidden by the consociation, proceeded to ordain. Later that body, augmented by the Hartford consociation, declared the pastoral relation between Dana and the church dissolved, and since both ignored the action, it finally passed sentence of non-communion upon them and those who sat in the ordaining council. (For list of pamphlets evoked by the controversy, see Leonard Bacon, *Thirteen Historical Discourses,* 1839, pp. 268 f.) On May 8, 1759 he married Catherine Whittelsey, the daughter of his predecessor at Wallingford, and a granddaughter of President Chauncy of Harvard.

Despite its inauspicious opening, Dana's career in Connecticut was long and distinguished. His learning, sturdy conscientiousness, and good judgment came to be generally respected among the clergy. He won favor with many, also, by taking an early and decided stand for national independence, and whenever the General Assembly met in New Haven, its members expected the pastor of the First Church, Dana's brother-in-law, Chauncey Whittelsey, to exchange with him. Of this church he himself was installed pastor, Apr. 29, 1789, the council being made memorable by a theological tilt between Dana and Jonathan Edwards, the younger. In the controversy between the "Old Divinity" and the "New" he became a strong defender of the former as against the opinions of Drs. Bellamy, Hopkins, West, and Edwards. (For doctrines he assailed, see Bacon's *Discourses,* p. 273.) In 1770 he published anonymously *An Examination of the Late Reverend President Edwards's 'Enquiry on Freedom of Will,'* and in 1773, under his name, *The "Examination . . ." Continued.* Captivated by the preaching of Moses Stuart who supplied the church during the pastor's illness, the Society voted in 1805 that "Dr. Dana retire from his pastoral labors." In December he was dismissed by council, but continued to reside in New Haven until his death. Among his published sermons are *The Intent of Capital Punishment, a Discourse Delivered in the City of New Haven, Oct. 20, 1790. Being the Day of the Execution of Joseph Mountain for a Rape* (1790); *The African Slave Trade* (1791); *The Heavenly Mansions, a Sermon Preached . . . at the Interment of the Reverend Ezra Stiles, D. D., President of Yale-College* (1795); *Two Discourses, I. On the Commencement of a New Year; II. On the Completion of the Eighteenth Century* (1801). Physically he was the mere shadow of a man, tall, slender, and with a sharp, thin face. He is described by those who knew him as kindly and companionable, an interesting conversationalist, and everywhere at ease. The University of Edinburgh honored him with the degree of D.D. in 1768. His first wife died Aug. 18, 1795, and on July 10 of the following year he married Mrs. Abigail (Porter) Belden, daughter of Dr. Ezekiel Porter. She died Mar. 17, 1798, and on Sept. 14, he married Mrs. Mary (Miles) Rice. Samuel Whittelsey Dana [*q.v.*], lawyer, and United States senator, was his son.

[Besides authorities cited, see references in *The Literary Diary of Ezra Stiles* (1901), and *Extracts From the Itineraries and Other Miscellanies of Ezra Stiles* (1916), both edited by F. B. Dexter; Benj. Trumbull, *A Complete Hist. of Conn.* (1818); C. H. S. Davis, *Hist. of Wallingford, Conn.* (1870); W. B. Sprague, *Annals of the Am. Pulpit*, vol. I (1857); John J. Dana, *Memoranda of Some of the Descendants of Richard Dana* (1865); *Vital Records of Cambridge, Mass., to the Year 1850* (1914), vol. I.] H. E. S.

DANA, JAMES DWIGHT (Feb. 12, 1813–Apr. 14, 1895), geologist, zoologist, the eldest of ten children of James and Harriet (Dwight) Dana was born and passed his boyhood in Utica, N. Y. His father was of New England stock, a nephew of Rev. James Dana [*q.v.*], and a descendant of Richard Dana who came from England in 1640 and settled in Cambridge, Mass. The boy's early training was acquired in Charles Bartlett's academy at Utica where he displayed a markedly studious disposition with strong tendencies toward the sciences. He entered Yale College as a sophomore in 1830, but left it in 1833 in advance of graduation to avail himself of an appointment as instructor in the navy, which involved, incidentally, a cruise in the Mediterranean, on the ship *Delaware*. Returning in 1836, he was for a short period an assistant to Prof. Benjamin Silliman. When the United States exploring expedition to the South Seas under Capt. Wilkes was organized in 1837, he was appointed geologist and mineralogist. The expedition sailed from New York in August 1838. Off the coast of Oregon his vessel, the *Peacock*, was wrecked near the mouth of the Columbia River, and he and his party made their way overland to San Francisco where they were taken aboard one of the companion ships, the *Vincennes*, and returned home by way of the Cape of Good Hope, reaching New York June 10, 1842. For thirteen years following his return Dana was engaged in writing up his reports in Washington. In 1840 he had been made editor of the *American Journal of Science*, or "Silliman's Journal" as it was commonly known, and on the retirement of Silliman in 1849 was appointed professor of natural history in Yale College, though he did not take up his duties until six years later. In 1864 the title of the professorship was changed to that of geology and mineralogy. This position he retained until he resigned from active duties in 1890.

Dana's industry and productivity under conditions of health that to a less virile man would have been insurmountable were without counterpart in American geological history. His first geological paper was in the form of a letter to Prof. Silliman, descriptive of a visit to the volcano of Vesuvius. This appeared in the *American Journal of Science* for 1835. The first of his reports from the Wilkes Expedition was a quarto volume of 741 pages on *Zoophytes*, with folio atlas of sixty-one plates (1846); the second, on *Geology*, a quarto volume of 756 pages, with atlas of twenty-one plates (1849), and the third, two quarto volumes on *Crustacea*, aggregating 1,620 pages (1852–54), followed by an atlas of ninety-six plates.

While assistant to Prof. Silliman, Dana wrote his *System of Mineralogy*, published in 1837. A *Manual of Geology* followed in 1862 and two years later his smaller *Textbook of Geology*. All these were standard works and passed through several editions, the fourth and the last of the *Manuals* being completed after he had reached his eighty-second year. In 1872 appeared his work on *Corals and Coral Islands* and in 1890, after a second visit to the Hawaiian Islands, a companion volume on *Characteristics of Volcanoes*. In 1859 Dana suffered a serious nervous breakdown, from which he never completely recovered, and through the remainder of his life it was only by husbanding his strength in the most careful manner that he was able to carry on his work. It was during the period of his convalescence that he made his single trip to Europe, barring the one to the Mediterranean in 1833. Another illness followed in 1880 and in 1890 the most serious of all. Thenceforth his periods of labor were limited to but three hours a day at the most. Notwithstanding these difficulties, Dana throughout the entire active period stood head and shoulders above his contemporaries. He had a mental capacity for large problems, though their solution involved the marshaling of infinite details. His interest never flagged; no problem was too large for him to grasp; no detail too small for his consideration.

As a teacher, Dana won the respect and regard of all with whom he came in contact, and left on the minds of his students a lasting and favorable impression. Though he was an attractive lecturer, he was in no sense a popular writer or speaker. In 1872 he was awarded the Wollaston medal by the Geological Society of London, and in 1877 the Copley medal by the Royal Society of the same city. In 1892, the Boston Society of Natural History conferred upon him the Walker prize of $1,000. In 1854 he was made president of the American Association for the Advancement of Science. He received many honorary degrees. He was a member of many scientific societies, including the Royal Society of London, the Royal Academies of Berlin, Vienna, and St. Petersburg, and an original member of the National Academy of Sciences. On June 5, 1844 he married Henrietta Frances Silliman, third daughter of Benjamin Silliman. Four children were born to them, one of whom, Edward S. Dana, became America's leading mineralogist.

[D. C. Gilman, *The Life of James Dwight Dana* (1899); "James Dwight Dana," by his son, E. S. Dana, *Am. Jour. Sci.*, vol. XLIX (1895), containing full bibliography; C. E. Beecher, "James Dwight Dana," in *Am. Geologist*, vol. XVII (1896); addresses at the Dana Centenary, Dec. 29, 1912, by A. T. Hadley, Wm. N. Rice, E. O. Hovey and Geo. P. Merrill (*Bull. Geol. Soc. Am.*, XXIV, 1913).] G. P. M.

DANA, JAMES FREEMAN (Sept. 23, 1793–Apr. 14, 1827), chemist, was descended in the fourth generation from Benjamin, son of Richard Dana who settled at Cambridge, Mass., in 1640. He was born at Amherst, N. H., the son of Luther and Lucy (Giddings) Dana, and the brother of Samuel Luther Dana [*q.v.*]. First named Jonathan, he became James in 1820 by a legislative act. In 1804 the family moved to Exeter, N. H., where the sons attended Phillips Exeter Academy. Both entered Harvard College in 1809 and graduated in 1813 with the A.B. degree. In college both spent their leisure time in studying natural science. James organized among the students the Hermetic Society, for informal scientific study. He took all the courses in chemistry offered by Prof. John Gorham, and toward the close of the college course took care of the chemical lecture-room and prepared lecture experiments. While an undergraduate he received the Boylston prize for a paper on "Tests for Arsenic." After graduation he continued his work in chemistry and geology, though most of his time was devoted to medical studies, in which he was assisted personally by Prof. Gorham. Selected by the Corporation of Harvard in 1815 to go to England and purchase new equipment for the chemical department, he took lessons in London from Friedrich Accum, the best teacher of experimental chemistry in Europe. On the return voyage he wrote a paper on the "Composition of Oxymuriatic Acid" for which he received in 1817 the Boylston prize a second time. He supervised the installation of the new equipment in both laboratory and lecture-room. Soon appointed assistant to the professor of chemistry, he was really the instructor in experimental chemistry, and at the same time he pursued his medical studies. In 1817 he received the M.D. degree, and immediately began to practise in Cambridge. In the fall he was appointed lecturer on chemistry to medical students at Dartmouth College. Since Cambridge did not offer him much opportunity as a surgeon, he resigned from the faculty of Harvard in 1820, giving up his practise, and moved to Hanover, N. H., where as professor of chemistry and mineralogy at Dartmouth he remained till 1826. He retained his interest in geology and medicine, and in 1818 with his brother Samuel published *Outlines of Mineralogy and Geology of Boston and its Vicinity,* which was one of the first scientific interpretations of this complicated area. He also published the following papers: "On a New Form of Electric Battery," "On the Effect of Vapor on Flame," "On the Theory of the Action of Nitrous Gas in Eudiometry," "Preparation of Euchlorine Gas." In 1825 he published *Epitome of Chymical Philosophy,* which was a summary of his lectures on general chemistry, though some space in it was devoted to chemical theory. His connection with Dartmouth College ended in 1826, when he was appointed professor of chemistry in the College of Physicians and Surgeons at New York. His work was suddenly terminated by his death in the following year. He married in 1818 Matilda, daughter of Rev. Samuel Webber, president of Harvard.

[*N. H. Hist. Soc. Colls.*, vol. II; a short account of his work in *American Chemist*, vol. V, nos. 2, 3, 6, reprinted in Benj. Silliman, *Am. Contributions to Chemistry* (1875); J. J. Dana, *Memoranda of Some of the Descendants of Richard Dana* (1865).] L. C. N.

DANA, JOHN COTTON (Aug. 19, 1856–July 21, 1929), librarian, museum director, au-

Dana

thor, printer, was born in Woodstock, Vt., the fourth of the six children of Charles and Charitie Scott (Loomis) Dana. He was of New England English lineage, sixth in descent from Richard Dana, who settled at Cambridge, Mass., in 1640, eighth from Joseph Loomis, who settled at Windsor, Conn., in 1639. His father was a first cousin of James Dwight Dana [*q.v.*]. John Cotton Dana and his immediate forebears were rooted in the soil of Woodstock: he returned there summer after summer to rest and there he was buried. It was eleven years after his graduation from Dartmouth College in 1878 before he found his work. He studied law in Woodstock 1878–80, shattered his health by too sedulous application and was compelled to seek a higher altitude and a drier air, became a surveyor in Colorado and was a member of a party that discovered ruins of the cliff dwellers on the Mesa River in 1881. He resumed the study of law in New York in the office of Bristow, Peet, and Opdyke and was admitted to the New York bar in 1883, but was again threatened with tuberculosis. He engaged in newspaper work for a short time at Ashby, Minn., found a position with a coal and coke company at Glenwood Springs, Colo., in 1884, worked for a year as a civil engineer, was married Nov. 15, 1888, to Adine Rowena Wagener of Russellville, Ky., and in 1889 was appointed librarian of the Denver Public Library and secretary of the board of education. He had had no specific training for librarianship and needed none. During the eight years of his administration the Library grew from 2,000 to 40,000 volumes, readers were given access to the stacks, and a children's department was organized. In 1898 he went to Springfield, Mass., as librarian of the City Library, which had an excellent collection of 100,000 volumes. "The worth of a book is in its use" was one of Dana's favorite precepts, and he proceeded to make the books in the City Library useful. In four years' time its home circulation increased forty-five per cent. On Jan. 15, 1902, Dana became librarian of the Public Library of Newark, N. J.

In Newark he made the Public Library the most effective institution of its kind in the United States. During his administration the number of its books increased from 79,000 to 392,000, the number of its borrowers from 19,000 to 75,000, the yearly home circulation from 314,000 to nearly 2,000,000—figures far in excess of the proportionate growth of the city. Branch libraries were opened in various parts of the city, including a school library in the Barringer High School and, in 1904, the famous Business Branch, located in the heart of the financial and commercial district, which was soon rendering service to users throughout the United States and even abroad. The popularity of the Library was due chiefly to Dana's skilful use of publicity and to his revolutionary changes in library management and policy. He helped to found the Newark Museum Association in 1909 (see article on William Stephen Disbrow) and was director of its museum until his death. He made the Newark Museum in its sphere as popular as the Library; by changing exhibits frequently he coaxed the public into visiting it often; by stressing the industrial arts and the work of contemporary artists he tried to show that art is something living and attainable. "Beauty has no relation to price, rarity, or age" was a legend that met the eye of every visitor to the Museum and that many of the exhibits strikingly exemplified. Dana himself was especially interested in printing; he and his brother had their own Elm Tree Press at Woodstock and produced work of unusual beauty and character. He contributed frequently to magazines and periodicals and published numerous pamphlets and broadsides. His *Library Primer* (1896; numerous later editions) has been a standard text-book since its first appearance. As an author he is best represented, however, by *Libraries: Addresses and Essays* (1916). His style is spare and pungent; he had a knack for aphorism and for making old truths sound startling and portentous. He took delight in deflating sentimental altruisms and in "stirring up the animals," as in his presidential address, "Hear the Other Side," to the American Library Association in 1896. On everything he touched he left the stamp of a unique personality.

Though known as the "first citizen of Newark" he shunned publicity, declined honorary degrees from Dartmouth, Rutgers, and Princeton, and cultivated few close friendships. The honors that he seemed to prize most were a directorship in the Deutscher Werkbund and honorary membership in the Chinese Library Association. For the last five years of his life he was in precarious health. He died in St. Vincent's Hospital in New York. His death was the occasion for editorial comment throughout the United States. Though it is still too early to measure his influence on American culture, it is already clear that he was one of the significant men of his generation.

[J. J. Dana, *Memoranda of Some of the Descendants of Richard Dana* (privately printed, 1865); Elias Loomis and Elisha S. Loomis, *Descendants of Joseph Loomis in America* (privately printed, 1908), p. 320; H. S. Dana, *Hist. of Woodstock, Vt.* (1889); *Gen. Cat. Dartmouth Coll. 1769–1910* (1910–11); *Who's Who in America*, 1928–29; *Libraries*, Oct. 1929; *Nation* (N.

Y.), July 31, 1929 (editorial); N. Y. *World*, July 23, 1929 (editorial); *Newark Evening News*, July 22, 23, 24, 29, Aug. 1, 1929.] G. H. G.

DANA, NAPOLEON JACKSON TECUMSEH (Apr. 15, 1822–July 15, 1905), soldier and business executive, was born at the military post of Fort Sullivan, Eastport, Me. His father, Nathaniel Giddings Dana, brother of James Freeman and Samuel Luther Dana [*qq.v.*], was an army officer, and his grandfather, Luther Dana, had been an officer in the navy during the Revolution. On the side of his mother, Mary Langdon Harris, he was descended from Woodbury Langdon, a member of the Continental Congress and brother of John Langdon. Graduating from West Point in 1842, he was commissioned in the 7th Infantry. In 1844 he married Sue Lewis Martin Sandford, at St. Louis. He served in the military occupation of Texas and in the Mexican War, taking part in the defense of Fort Brown, the battle of Monterey, the siege of Vera Cruz, and the battle of Cerro Gordo, where he was severely wounded at the storming of Telegraph Hill, and left on the field as dead until picked up by a burying party thirty-six hours later. He had been promoted to first lieutenant early in 1847, and in 1848 was appointed a captain and assistant quartermaster. He was stationed in Minnesota, became familiar with business conditions there, and in 1855 resigned from the army, establishing a banking business in St. Paul, as a member of the firm of Dana & Borup. He was brigadier-general in the Minnesota militia from 1857 to 1861. He entered the volunteer army as colonel of the 1st Minnesota Infantry, Oct. 2, 1861, and within a few days took it into action at Ball's Bluff. The regiment, composed in large part of lumbermen, was called upon after the battle to bring off the defeated troops to the Maryland shore of the Potomac, a task reminiscent of Glover's, with his Marblehead men, after the battle of Long Island. Dana was appointed brigadier-general of volunteers, Feb. 3, 1862, and commanded a brigade of the II Corps in the Peninsular campaign and at Antietam, where he was again badly wounded. He was disabled for many months, but was meanwhile appointed major-general of volunteers, Nov. 29, 1862. After his return to duty he had no considerable field service, but commanded successively the defenses of Philadelphia, the expedition which secured a lodgment on the Texas coast late in 1863, and districts along the Mississippi River, no longer the theatre of active operations. He resigned from the army, May 27, 1865. For five years he was general agent of the American-Russia Commercial Company of Alaska, and thereafter an executive officer of several railroads, notably the Chicago, Burlington & Quincy. Under authority of a special act of Congress passed in 1894, he was appointed captain—the rank he had formerly held in the regular army—and placed on the retired list. He was deputy commissioner of pensions from 1895 to 1897. He died at Portsmouth, N. H.

[J. J. Dana, *Memoranda of Some of the Descendants of Richard Dana* (1865); G. W. Cullum, *Biog. Reg.* (3rd ed., 1891), II, 135–36, IV, 59, V, 56; *Bull Asso. Grads. U. S. Mil. Acad.*, 1907, pp. 30–36; *Official Records*, ser. I, vols. V, XI (pts. 1, 2), XIX (pt. 1), XXVI (pt. 1), XXVII (pt. 3), XXXIV (pt. 2), XXXIX (pts. 1, 2, 3), XLI (pts. 3, 4), XLV (pt. 2), XLVIII (pts. 1, 2).] T. M. S.

DANA, RICHARD (June 26, 1700–May 17, 1772), lawyer, was of the third generation of Danas in America. The European origins of the family are involved in uncertainty but in 1640 Richard Dana was a well-to-do resident of Cambridge, Mass. His son, Daniel Dana, who also lived at Cambridge and was tithingman and selectman, married Naomi Croswell of Charlestown, Mass., and their third son, Richard Dana, was born at Cambridge. No details of his boyhood or early education have survived, but he entered Harvard College and graduated there in 1718. On leaving college he taught school for a time but subsequently studied law at Marblehead and was admitted to the Suffolk County bar. He then commenced practise at Marblehead, but moved to Charlestown, and shortly afterward settled in Boston, with which city he thereafter became permanently associated. Though little or no information is available as to his professional work, contemporary sources testify to his early attainment of a prominent position at the Boston bar, of which in his later years he was described as the leader. He was retained as counsel on behalf of the city in much of its litigation, and acquired great influence in public affairs, though he steadfastly declined all offers of political or municipal office. In the early stages of the growing controversy between the province of Massachusetts and Great Britain he unhesitatingly identified himself with the Colonial cause, and was a prominent figure in all the popular movements in opposition to the various steps taken by the administration to enforce the authority of the home government. From 1763 onward he took a leading part in the town meetings at the Old South Church and Faneuil Hall, frequently acting as chairman, and as a member of the numerous committees through which the wishes of the townspeople were expressed during the preliminary steps of the Revolution, his advice on legal and constitutional points was invaluable. An original member of the Sons of Liberty, he instigated the measures which were taken in 1765 to defeat the enforcement of the Stamp Act, and it was before him as a magistrate that Andrew Oliver, the commissioner, was dragged Dec. 17, 1765 and compelled to swear that he would take no further steps to carry out the provisions of the Act. He was a member of the committee which investigated the circumstances of the Boston Massacre in 1770, and almost the last occasion upon which he appeared in public was the meeting in Faneuil Hall, Mar. 5, 1772 in commemoration of that event, at which he officiated as moderator. His death in Boston some two months later, was at the time regarded as a severe if not irreparable loss to the Colonial cause.

Of unimpeachable integrity, unswerving principles and a fanatic in his devotion to duty as he saw it, his was a strong and impressive but unattractive personality. Austere to the point of parsimony, "he was exemplary in Carefulness, Diligence, and Frugality, whereby he has left to his Widow . . . and to his Children . . . a handsome Fortune. . . . A very steady and strenuous, and it must be confessed, many Times a passionate Opposer of all those . . . who, in his Judgment were Enemies to the Civil and Religious Rights of his Country; and he very well understood what those Rights were" (*Boston Gazette,* June 1, 1772). On May 31, 1737, Dana married Lydia, daughter of Thomas Trowbridge and sister of Judge Edmund Trowbridge; Francis Dana [*q.v.*] was their son.

[*Hist. Families of America* (1907), ed. by W. W. Spooner, p. 47; R. Frothingham, *Life and Times of Jos. Warren* (1865), p. 195; *Proc. Mass. Hist. Soc.,* 1 ser. XII (1873), 246 f.; Alden Bradford, *Biog. Notices of Distinguished Men in New England* (1842).]

H.W.H.K.

DANA, RICHARD HENRY (Nov. 15, 1787–Feb. 2, 1879), poet, essayist, came of distinguished ancestry. His father was Francis Dana [*q.v.*], Revolutionary patriot, and his mother was Elizabeth Ellery, daughter of William Ellery [*q.v.*], a signer of the Declaration of Independence. There were seven children of this marriage, an elder sister becoming the wife of Washington Allston. Richard Henry Dana was born in Cambridge, and almost all his life was passed within the borders of his native Massachusetts. Entering Harvard College in 1804, he was not graduated in regular course, being implicated in the "rotten cabbage" rebellion of the classes in 1807. Many years later he received his degree as of 1808. His studies of law in Boston, Newport, and Baltimore were interspersed with wide readings in English literature, and on returning to Boston he was admitted to the bar in 1811 and later represented Cambridge in the Massachusetts legislature. Neither the law, nor politics, nor any form of public affairs, attracted him permanently, and before he was twenty-five years of age he had abandoned them wholly for literature, thus forsaking the profession which so many of his forebears had adorned. For some years after the establishment of the *North American Review* in 1815, he was associated with its editorial direction and contributed to it reviews and essays on literary subjects. In 1821 he began the publication of a periodical called *The Idle Man,* modeled upon Washington Irving's *Salmagundi,* continued it for about six months with no financial success, and wrote some of his earliest fiction, including two novels, "Tom Thornton" and "Paul Felton," for its pages. He also wrote for and contributed some of his first poetry to the *New York Review*—edited by his warm friend William Cullen Bryant—the *American Quarterly Observer, The Biblical Repository, The Literary and Theological Review,* and other periodical publications. In 1827 his first book of poetry, *The Buccaneer and Other Poems,* was published, followed in 1833 by his *Poems and Prose Writings,* which seventeen years later was brought out in a new and extended edition. A reviewer in *Blackwood's Magazine* described "The Buccaneer" as "by far the most powerful and original of American poetical compositions," and added that, although Dana was "no servile follower of those great masters," his style showed the influence of Crabbe, Wordsworth, and Coleridge. The supernatural is one of its dominant elements, and for it he may have derived some inspiration from "The Ancient Mariner." Some of his poems appear in anthologies and school books on literature. During the great controversy in 1825–35 which resulted in the schism between the Trinitarians and the Unitarians in the Congregational Church, he took active part with the former, and later in life became affiliated with the Protestant Episcopal Church. Although his reputation survived through his entire lifetime, his active career practically ended by the time he was forty. He had acquired no popularity, none of his writings appealing to the general public, and he did not seek it. As a writer he had little sympathy with or interest in the affairs of the world, or with social and personal progress in politics, art, science, or literature, tendencies which were foremost in the son who bore his name. His view was academic, and he looked upon mankind and the world from the library and the scholar's cloister. The influence of Dana on the literary development of the country came from the vigorous thought, simplicity, and directness of expression which marked his work, in contrast to the sentimental and florid style which characterized most writings of his time. Perhaps his most conspicuous appearance in public was in 1839–40, when he delivered a course of eight lectures on Shakespeare, in Boston, New York, Philadelphia, and other cities, contending that Shakespeare was the greatest poet of the English language, and not Pope, as was then claimed by many authorities. During more than half his years he lived in a quiet and dignified retirement, writing, studying, reading, in Cambridge in early life, later in Boston, and during the summer on the shores of Cape Ann, where his son Richard Henry [*q.v.*] bought an estate for him in 1845. Although he had been a delicate child, he lived to reach his ninety-second year, during which he died at his home in Boston. He was a notable personality and a man of physical and mental distinction. He married Ruth Charlotte, daughter of John Wilson Smith, of Taunton, Mass., in 1813, and they had four children.

[S. A. Allibone, *Critical Dict. of Eng. Literature and British and Am. Authors* (1858); article by Richard Henry Stoddard, *Harper's Mag.*, Apr. 1879; sketch in *The Later Years of the Saturday Club* (1927), ed. by M. A. De Wolfe Howe; obituaries in *Boston Transcript, Boston Post*, Feb. 3, 1879, and *Boston Herald*, Feb. 4, 1879; Chas. Francis Adams, *Richard Henry Dana, a Biography* (2 vols., 1890); valuable information from members of the family.] E. F. F.

DANA, RICHARD HENRY (Aug. 1, 1815–Jan. 6, 1882), author, lawyer, the son of Richard Henry Dana [*q.v.*] and Ruth Charlotte (Smith) Dana, was born in Cambridge, Mass. Solely as the writer of a remarkable first-hand account of sea adventure he has a permanent place in American literature; he was also one of the most active and influential lawyers of his day. Entering Harvard College in 1831, he gave up his studies two years later because of eye trouble resulting from measles, and on Aug. 14, 1834 set sail on a voyage around Cape Horn to California as a common sailor on the brig *Pilgrim*. Two years later, a robust young man of twenty-one, he reached Boston on the ship *Alert*. Joining the senior class at Harvard in December 1836, he was graduated the following June, ranking at the head of his class for that year. He became instructor in elocution at Harvard in 1839–40, under Edward T. Channing, and in 1866–68 he was a lecturer in the Harvard Law School. His *Two Years Before the Mast* (1840), published the year of his admission to the bar, was written from notes made during his voyage, and is a lively, fresh, and unconventional narrative. His definite and successful purpose in it was to give an account of sea life from the point of view of the forecastle, and to secure justice for the sailor. "In it," he wrote, "I have adhered closely to fact in every particular, and endeavored to give everything its true character." The book immediately became popular both in this country and in England, and has since been reprinted in many editions, including one in French attributed to James Fenimore Cooper.

His youthful taste of the salt of the sea had given him a liking for the law of the sea, and he immediately began to specialize in admiralty cases. His manual, *The Seaman's Friend* (1841), became at once a standard work on maritime law, being reprinted in England as *The Seaman's Manual*. Early becoming interested in both the political and social aspects of slavery, he was one of the founders of the Free-Soil party, was a delegate to the convention at Buffalo in 1848, and took personal part in its campaigns, as he did also in the later campaigns of the Republican party. In 1853 he was a member of the convention for the revision of the constitution of Massachusetts, taking a leading part in the debates. Although he did not become an Abolitionist, his political and legal activities involved him deeply in the anti-slavery movement. He was attorney for the defense of the persons involved in the rescue of the negro Shadrach in Boston in 1851, and in the Anthony Burns rendition case in 1854. Serving for five years, from April 1861 to September 1866, as United States attorney for the district of Massachusetts, he succeeded in persuading the Democratic Supreme Court of the United States to sustain the power of blockade and the taking of neutral vessels as prizes during the blockade by the Federal government. In 1867–68, with William M. Evarts, he was counsel for the United States in the proceedings against Jefferson Davis for treason. In 1877 he was senior counsel for the United States before the Fisheries Commission at Halifax. In his many years of practise he was always the advocate, working mainly in the courts and paying little attention to the business of the office, which he disliked and left largely to his partner. He laboriously prepared all his cases himself with indefatigable zeal.

Possibly because of Dana's inability to mingle with the throng and his unwillingness to descend to machine politics, he did not realize upon his political ambitions. Among the disappointments he suffered were his defeat by Benjamin F. Butler in a contest for a seat in Congress in 1868, and his failure to be confirmed by the Senate when he was appointed minister to England in 1876 by President Grant, who had named him without consulting the leaders of his party. Failing to attain high public office, he determined to give his later years to the intensive study of his favorite subject, international law, and to the preparation of an authoritative work upon it. As early as 1866, his edition of Henry Wheaton's *Elements of International Law* was accepted as an authority. An enthusiastic traveler, he visited England in 1856 and 1866, and met the great political and social leaders of the kingdom. The literary result of one of his trips was a book entitled *To Cuba and Back* (1859). He made a journey round the world in 1859–60, and in 1878 he went to Europe for rest, pleasure, and further study of the problems of international law. While in Rome, before he had written his projected work, he died suddenly of pneumonia, and was buried in the Protestant Cemetery, where lie the remains of Keats and Shelley. He married Sarah Watson of Hartford, Conn., Aug. 25, 1841, and was survived by her and their six children, in whose religious and literary education he had taken great interest. He was a man of distinguished and dignified manner, with a certain formality that did not encourage intimacy.

[Chas. Francis Adams, *Richard Henry Dana, A Biography*, 2 vols. (1890); E. W. Emerson. *The Early Years of the Saturday Club* (1918); tribute of the bar, *Am. Law Rev.*, XVI (1882), 253; remarks by Rt. Rev. Wm. Lawrence, Bliss Perry, Moorfield Storey, and Joseph H. Choate, *Cambridge Hist. Soc. Pubs.*, no. X (1917); valuable information from the family.] E. F. E.

DANA, SAMUEL LUTHER (July 11, 1795–Mar. 11, 1868), chemist, born at Amherst, N. H., was the son of Luther and Lucy (Giddings) Dana and the brother of James Freeman Dana [*q.v.*]. Entering Harvard College in 1809, he graduated in 1813. Immediately after graduation, he joined the army and served till the end of the War of 1812. He then resumed his studies, specializing in medicine, and received the M.D. degree in 1818. He at once began to practise at Waltham, Mass., and continued there until 1826. Realizing the need of solving the chemical problems of the manufacturers of cotton goods in Massachusetts, he gave up medicine and devoted his time to applied chemistry. In 1826 he built a small plant in Waltham for the manufacture of sulphuric acid and bleaching substances. This was soon merged with the Newton Chemical Company, of which he was the superintendent and chemist till 1833. On his return from a professional visit to Europe, he became chemist at the Merrimac Print Works, Lowell, Mass., where he remained till his death. The results of one of his early investigations concerning the bleaching of cotton cloth led to the adoption throughout the United States of what became known as the "American system of bleaching." Another investigation, concerning calico-printing, resulted in the improvement in the minor details which gave the goods printed in Lowell a high reputation. A special result related to the use of cow-dung in calico printing. Dana showed that the action of this animal material was largely due to the sodium phosphate in it. Immediate improvements in calico-printing were made in the United States by the substitution of sodium phosphate, made from bones, for the bulky, undesirable animal excrement. This work naturally led Dana to study the nature of manures. In 1842 he published *A Muck Manual for Farmers*, a work dealing with the chemistry of soils and manures and one of the first scientific treatises on agriculture written by an American and published in the United States. It attracted immediate attention and went through several editions. Later he wrote *An Essay on Manures* (1850), which was widely used as a rural handbook and for which the author was awarded a prize by the Massachusetts Society for Promoting Agriculture. About 1848 he investigated the cause of the bright inner surface of lead service-pipes in Lowell, and found the corrosion was due to the chemical action of gases in the water obtained from driven wells. He presented to the local authorities a report in which he pronounced the water unfit for drinking owing to the danger of lead-poisoning. This report was soon followed by his translation from the French of L. Tanquerel Des Planches, of a work which he published under the title, *Lead Diseases* (1848). In 1851 he became interested in the manufacture of oil from rosin and within the next few years he made many improvements in this industry. Much of his time in latter years was spent on a farm, where his views on agriculture were tested. He was twice married, first, on June 5, 1820, to Ann Theodora, daughter of Joseph Willard, a president of Harvard, and subsequently to Augusta, her older sister.

[Obituary notice in *Am. Jour. of Sci.*, May 1868, pp. 424–25; short account of his work in *Am. Chemist*, vol. V, nos. 2, 3, 6, reprinted in Benjamin Silliman, *Am. Contributions to Chemistry* (1875); W. J. Youmans, *Pioneers of Science in America* (1896); J. J. Dana, *Memoranda of Some of the Descendants of Richard Dana* (1865).] L. C. N.

DANA, SAMUEL WHITTELSEY (Feb. 13, 1760–July 21, 1830), lawyer, statesman, was born in Wallingford, Conn., the elder son of James Dana [*q.v.*], Congregational minister at Wallingford, by his first wife, Catherine Whittelsey. He graduated from Yale in the class of 1775 with high honors. Three years later he was appointed to deliver a congratulatory oration in Latin on behalf of the student body upon the occasion of the inauguration of President Ezra Stiles. He studied law at Middletown, Conn., under Judge J. T. Hosmer and was admitted to the bar in 1778. He interested himself in the Connecticut militia and in 1790 was commissioned brigadier-general. From 1789 to 1796 he served as member of the General Assembly of Connecticut. In January 1797 he took his seat in the lower house of Congress and held this office until he was transferred to the Senate in May 1810, upon the resignation of James Hillhouse. His career in national politics ended with the expiration of his term on Mar. 3, 1821, his defeat being due to the political overturn in Connecticut in 1818. Returning from Washington to Middletown he resumed the practise of law. In 1822, however, he returned to public life as the mayor of Middletown, and held this post almost to the time of his death. From 1825 until his death he was also chief judge of the Middlesex country court. He died as the result of a cerebral hemorrhage. His estate was insolvent, but his contemporaries were agreed that he could have amassed a considerable fortune had he devoted himself continuously to the practise of his profession.

In Congress he belonged to the Federalist group, although he was not a leader. He voted for the Sedition Act of 1798, and in the same year introduced a resolution to abrogate the treaty of 1778 with France. He opposed the acquisition of Louisiana, the Embargo and Non-Intercourse Acts, and also the impeachment of Justice Chase. He consistently supported a navy of frigates and expressed his contempt for those "aquatico-terrene vehicles denominated gun boats." He favored the bill of 1816 increasing congressional salaries and opposed the measure of the same year chartering the second Bank of the United States. He opposed slavery and objected to the Missouri Compromise on the ground that the admission of a state should be considered on its individual merits. In his actions, Dana followed his own judgment and convictions rather than the lead of his party. His speeches were for the most part arguments on legal points raised by pending legislation. His best effort was inspired by a proposed resolution of censure of the actions of the British minister, Francis J. Jackson (*Annals of Congress,* 11 Cong., 2 Sess., pp. 762–83). Dana made clear his complete disapproval of Jackson and of British policy with respect to the United States and then proceeded to discuss in an impressive manner the problems of international law which were involved not only in the pending resolution but in the policy of the Madison administration toward Jackson. The speech was the work of a careful student of political science who was familiar not only with Grotius, but with Martens, Vattel, and Wicquefort.

Dana followed John Adams in distinguishing between the interests of the aristocratic "few" and the "many," and his belief that the system of checks and balances in a republican government was the proper means for the protection of both classes. He broke with Adams on the supreme necessity for the protection of property and did not share in the distrust of the masses which characterized the thinking of Hamilton and Fisher Ames. In his system Dana combined the best thought of the Federalists and the Jeffersonians. His philosophy explains why he shared in neither the plots of Harrison Gray Otis nor the despair of Fisher Ames at the growth of democracy. Two years after the revolution of 1818 in Connecticut had doomed his party in that state, Dana exclaimed: "Look at the young empire in the New World! See the American States advancing in the ascent of glory" (*Observations on Public Principles and Characters,* pamphlet, November 1820). He married on July 13, 1821, Mary Wyllys Pomeroy, widow of Richard Alsop, the poet.

[F. B. Dexter, *Biog. Sketches Grads. Yale Coll.,* III (1903), 558; MSS. (a few letters and an unpublished essay on government) in Yale Library; D. D. Field, *Centennial Address with Hist. Sketches of Cromwell, Portland, Chatham, Middle-Haddam, Middletown and its Parishes* (1853); A. A. Pomeroy, *Hist. and Geneal. of the Pomeroy Family* (1912), I, 352; *Biog. Dir. of the Am. Congress, 1774–1927* (1928); *Middletown Gazette,* July 28, 1830.] R. H. G.

DANCEL, CHRISTIAN (Feb. 14, 1847–Oct. 13, 1898), inventor, was born in Cassel, Germany. He was educated in the graded and polytechnic schools there and completed the mechanical engineering course, after which he learned the machinist's trade. When a little over eighteen years of age, he emigrated to the United States and settled in New York City. Working for the next two years as a practical machinist in different shops about New York, Dancel during this time devised a machine for sewing shoes. Soon after this, Charles Goodyear, Jr., who was engaged in the manufacture of shoe-machinery in New York, bought Dancel's device and engaged him as superintendent of his factory. The latter first undertook improve-

Dane

ments on his own and other inventions and built the first practical machines for sewing turned shoes. About 1870, he turned his attention to making machines for sewing shoe-welts and stitching the out-soles. Using one of the turned-shoe machines as a foundation, he first altered it into a "stitcher," fifty models of which were made and sold to different manufacturers. He then devised and patented a welt-guide, and by adding it to the same machine, produced in 1874 one which would sew both turns and welts. This machine, which Goodyear began manufacturing in 1875, is still used, with minor improvements, in shoe manufacture. In 1876 Dancel opened a machine-shop of his own and patented a number of small machines used in the finishing of shoes, which because of their value to the trade he had no difficulty in selling. While so engaged, he was again called upon by the Goodyear Company to undertake the perfection of a machine to sew the outer sole and the upper of a shoe while the shoe was on the last. He worked constantly on this problem for almost eight years and delivered in 1885 a complete machine, which used a curved needle and sewed a lock-stitch. This was followed by a straight-needle machine, patented Sept. 8, 1891 and delivered in 1892. About 1895 he organized the Dancel Machine Company in Brooklyn, and before he died built a curved-needle machine to sew welts on the shoe with a lock-stitch while the shoe was on the last, the welt, upper, and in-sole being caught by one stroke of the needle. It was Dancel's solution of the stitch-forming problems that made the Goodyear Welt System, now so widely used, a success. Incorporated in each one of his finished products were many devices for which patents were granted to him. Besides his shoe-machine inventions, Dancel was co-patentee in machines for making barbed-wire fence, for skiving leather, for gaging and marking leather, for making leather buttonholes, for rubbing type, and for removing bristles from sealskins. He died in Brooklyn, as a result of a fall, at the age of fifty-two, survived by his widow and two children.

[W. T. Davis, *Professional and Indust. Hist. of Suffolk County, Mass.* (3 vols., 1894); *Shoe and Leather Reporter*, 1898, vol. LXVI, no. 16; Waldemar Kaempffert, *A Popular Hist. of Am. Invention* (1924); obituary in *Brooklyn Daily Eagle*, Oct. 14, 1898; Patent Office records.]
C. W. M.

DANE, NATHAN (Dec. 29, 1752–Feb. 15, 1835), lawyer, statesman, was a descendant of John Dane of Berkhamstead and Bishop's Stortford, Hertfordshire, England, who settled at Ipswich, Mass., in 1638 and subsequently became a freeman of Roxbury. Fourth in the direct line from him, Daniel Dane, a farmer, married Abigail Burnham and resided at Ipswich, where their son, Nathan, was born. His life, until he was twenty, was spent on the farm, his education being obtained at the common schools. In 1772, however, he determined to attempt a college course, and having prepared himself privately in eight months, entered Harvard College in 1774, where he graduated in 1778 with high honors. He then read law in the office of Judge William Wetmore of Salem, at the same time teaching school at Beverly, Mass. In November 1779 he was married to Mrs. Mary Brown. On his admission to the bar in 1782 he commenced practise at Beverly, being in the same year elected a representative of that town in the General Court of Massachusetts. His ability was early recognized; he was reëlected in three successive years, and in 1785 was elected a delegate from Massachusetts to the Continental Congress. In the proceedings of this body he took an active part, serving on important committees and displaying great assiduity in the performance of his duties. He was reëlected in 1786 and 1787. In the latter year the chief subject for consideration before the Congress was the organization and government of the territory lying northwest of the Ohio River, respecting which he took a memorable part. He assisted in drafting the Ordinance for the Government of the Northwest Territory, and, after reporting it to Congress, on his own initiative prepared and moved the addition of an article reading "There shall be neither slavery nor involuntary servitude in the said territory" (*Indiana Historical Society Publications*, no. 1, 1897, p. 69). The Ordinance as thus amended was adopted without further change. He opposed the new Federal Constitution as finally drafted, and at the ensuing election for the state convention to consider its ratification, was an unsuccessful candidate. On retiring from Congress he resumed his law practise at Beverly, but in 1790 was elected to the Massachusetts Senate. He was reëlected in 1793, being the same year appointed a judge of the court of common pleas for Essex County, which position he resigned without taking his seat on the bench. In 1795 he was appointed a commissioner to revise the laws of the Commonwealth. He was reëlected annually to the Massachusetts Senate from 1793 to 1798 (*Fleet's Register and Pocket Almanac*, 1794–99), but the last mentioned year was the last occasion upon which he was a member of the legislature, an increasing deafness rendering it difficult for him to participate in public assemblages. He continued, however, to assist in the work of statute revision and, in 1812, with Prescott and Story, composed the commission appointed to revise and publish the Massachusetts Colonial and Provincial laws. He was also in that year presidential elector, and in 1814 made his last public appearance, at the Hartford Convention, though subsequently he was chosen as delegate from Beverly to the constitutional convention of 1820, it being known at the time that he would be unable to attend. He had now become almost entirely deaf, and, withdrawing from practise, devoted his time to completing two works upon which he had been engaged continuously for upward of thirty years. One of these, "A Moral and Political Survey of America," composed of a lengthy series of essays, was never published. The other, a *General Abridgment and Digest of American Law, with Occasional Notes and Comments,* was published in eight volumes in 1823, a supplementary volume appearing in 1829. This work was important as being the first comprehensive compendium of law to be prepared and printed on this continent, and displayed not only his great legal attainments but a meticulous attention to detail and a methodical labor which was characteristic of everything which he undertook. His outstanding characteristics were industry, directness and simplicity. "He was uniformly prompt, punctual and systematic. He had a particular time and a particular way for doing everything." Always a student, during the last twenty years of his life he never spent less than twelve and often fourteen hours a day in his library. He possessed a singularly well-balanced judgment, a great forethought, and was totally devoid of temperament. Of his powers as a speaker, there is little information, but it may be confidently surmised that his extraordinary influence with his contemporaries was due more to the matter than the manner of his utterances, and that his intellectual endowments more than compensated for his lack of popular attributes. He was a benefactor of Harvard Law School, to which he gave in his lifetime $15,000, the fruits of which were the establishment of the Dane Professorship of Law and the founding of Dane Hall. He died at Beverly, in his eighty-third year.

[Details of Dane's ancestry are contained in J. W. Dean, "A Pedigree of the Dane Family," published in John Dane, *A Declaration of Remarkable Providences in the Course of My Life* (1854). Much the best review of his life and achievements appeared in *Green Bag,* III, 548. See also A. P. Peabody, *Harvard Grads. Whom I Have Known* (1890), p. 12; E. M. Stone, *Hist. of Beverly* (1843), p. 135; *Proc. Mass. Hist. Soc., X* (1869), 475; *Pa. Mag. of Hist. and Biog.,* XIII (1889), 309; J. A. Barrett, *Evolution of the Ordinance of 1787* (1891). Date of birth given in tombstone inscription published in Stone's *Hist. of Beverly* is Dec. 27, 1752; most accounts, however, including that by Stone, give Dec. 29.] H. W. H. K.

DANENHOWER, JOHN WILSON (Sept. 30, 1849–Apr. 20, 1887), Arctic explorer, was born in Chicago, Ill., the son of William W. Danenhower. He attended the public schools of his native city until he was seventeen when he secured an appointment to the United States Naval Academy. Upon his graduation in 1870, he was ordered to the European Squadron where he served on both the *Plymouth* and the *Juniata.* His next assignment was with the Portsmouth surveying party in the North Pacific; and in 1875, he was sent to the Naval Observatory for signal duty. He attained the rank of master in 1873 and was commissioned a lieutenant in 1879. In 1878, he showed signs of an unbalanced mind and was confined to an insane asylum for two months. At the end of this period, he had recovered sufficiently to return to active duty and was assigned to the *Vandalia* which was sent to the Mediterranean with Gen. Grant's cruise. While at Smyrna, he heard of the proposed *Jeannette* Arctic expedition and at once offered his services. He was accepted and joined Capt. G. W. De Long [*q.v.*] at Havre, France, just before the *Jeannette* sailed for San Francisco. On this voyage, he acted as executive officer. Upon the arrival at the Mare Island Navy Yard, the *Jeannette* was made ready for the northward voyage. These preparations, which were in charge of Danenhower and Lieut. Chipp, were finally completed and the trip to the Arctic via Bering Strait began on July 8, 1879. On the voyage north De Long studied his crew, and of Danenhower he wrote, in a letter to Mrs. De Long, "He is a hard worker, always writing the log or figuring over his navigation or provision account" (Emma De Long, *Voyage of the Jeannette,* I, 91). A little later, when the ship became wedged in the ice pack, this desire to be always busy led him to start a school of navigation for the crew; but on Dec. 22, 1879, he was rendered unfit for duty by an inflammation in his left eye, which constantly grew worse in spite of dark room treatments and many operations. Throughout the weary months of waiting Danenhower, practically lost to the expedition, bore his troubles bravely.

On June 12, 1881 the *Jeannette* was crushed in the ice in latitude 77°15′ north, longitude 155° east; and from this point the party, dragging its boats and provisions over the ice, retreated toward the Asia mainland. On this stage of the journey, which lasted over two months, Danenhower, although handicapped by having one eye bandaged and the other covered with a dark goggle, trudged along resolutely. At last open water was reached and the party set out for the Lena Delta in three boats which on Sept 12 became separated in a gale. The boat to which Danenhower was assigned under the command of Engineer George W. Melville [*q.v.*] weathered the storm and reached the eastern Lena Delta five days later (G. W. Melville, *In the Lena Delta,* 1885). Here its crew was rescued by friendly natives and Danenhower started for the United States, where he arrived May 28, 1882. His book, *Lieutenant Danenhower's Narrative of the Jeannette,* which gives a graphic account of his experiences, was published this same year.

For the next few years, although in bad health, he acted as assistant commander of cadets at Annapolis. On Apr. 11, 1887 he went to Norfolk to assume command of the *Constellation;* but the vessel grounded in going out of harbor; and Danenhower, much disturbed, returned to the Academy. There on Apr. 20, while brooding over this mishap, he committed suicide. His widow and two children survived him.

[Besides the authorities cited above, the following are important: R. W. Bliss, *Our Lost Explorers: the Narrative of the Jeannette Arctic Expedition* (1882); H. L. Williams, *Hist. of the Adventurous Voyage and Terrible Shipwreck of the U. S. Steamer Jeannette in the Polar Seas* (1882); Record of the proceedings of a Court of Inquiry to investigate the loss of the steamer *Jeannette, House Exec. Doc. 108,* 47 Cong., 2 Sess.; *Jeannette Inquiry, House Miscel. Doc. 66,* 48 Cong., 1 Sess. Obituary notices appeared in the Washington *Evening Star,* in the *Washington Post,* and in the *N. Y. Times* for Apr. 21, 1887.] G. H. B.

DANFORTH, CHARLES (Aug. 30, 1797–Mar. 22, 1876), inventor, manufacturer, was born at Norton, Mass., the fifth child of Thomas and Betsey (Haskins) Danforth. He was a descendant in the seventh generation from Nicholas and Elizabeth Danforth of Framlingham, England, who came to America in 1634 and settled in Cambridge, Mass. Charles's father was a farmer and clothier as his father and grandfather had been before him; he served in the Revolution as fife-major, and was with Washington on Long Island and at New York. From early boyhood young Danforth showed a decided inclination to the mechanical arts, and after attending school until he was fourteen years old he entered a cotton-mill at Norton as a throttle-piercer. With the outbreak of the War of 1812, he joined the army, first as a substitute and later on his own account, and after the war went to sea for several voyages as a common sailor. Then taking up school-teaching, he was given charge of a district school near Rochester, N. Y., but he soon returned to the cotton-manufacturing business, this time as foreman of a factory in Matteawan, N. Y. When twenty-eight years old he moved with his family to Sloatsburg, N. Y., on the Ramapo River, where he worked in a cotton factory as a carder and setter-up of machinery. While engaged in this latter occupation he designed and patented, on Sept 2, 1828, an important improvement in spinning frames known as the cap spinner. This contrivance, which improved the spinning of weft before the self-acting mule was devised, was immediately in great demand. The idea was appropriated by others, with the result that Danforth received very little profit from it. Armed with his patent, however, he moved to Paterson, N. J., obtained a machinist's job with the firm of Godwin, Rogers & Clark, and after explaining his patent, prevailed upon them to manufacture his spinner. Within a comparatively short time he was offered and accepted Rogers's place in the firm, but continued in the machine-shop and designed and patented at least five definite improvements on the original cap spinner. In 1840 he purchased the machine-shop branch of the company's operations and two years later bought the cotton-mill as well, and immediately undertook the expansion of the business to include the making of machine tools. Remarkably successful in this, and wishing to add a locomotive shop to his works, in 1852 he prevailed upon John Cooke, a foreman in the Rogers Locomotive Works, to join him. Within two years the company, then known as Danforth, Cooke & Company, received a large order for locomotives from the Delaware, Lackawanna & Western Railroad which brought them so much celebrity that their good name was firmly established and their locomotives were sold throughout the world. In 1865 the Danforth Locomotive and Machine Company was incorporated, Danforth retaining the presidency until 1871 when he retired and was succeeded by John Cooke. Cooke died in 1882, but his sons carried on the business until 1901 when the works were sold to the International Power Company, who in turn sold them to the American Locomotive Company. Danforth married Mary, daughter of Thomas and Sarah Willett of Matteawan, N. Y., on Oct. 18, 1823. Although averse to public life, he accepted the presidency of the Paterson City Council for one term. He died in Paterson, at the age of seventy-nine. survived by his wife and daughters.

[Wm. Nelson and C. A. Shriner, *Hist. of Paterson and Its Environs*, vol. I (1920); John Joseph May, *Danforth Genealogy* (1902); *N. Y. Tribune*, Mar. 23, 1876; Patent Office records.] C. W. M.

DANFORTH, MOSELEY ISAAC (Dec. 11, 1800–Jan. 19, 1862), engraver, painter, was born in Hartford, Conn., the son of Edward and Jerusha (Moseley) Danforth. In 1818 he began the study of engraving under Asaph Willard of the Hartford Graphic Company, and in 1821 established himself in New Haven, where his work soon gained him a wide reputation. Later he moved to New York and became one of the founders of the National Academy of Design. In 1827 he went to London to study at the Royal Academy; there he found that he was already favorably known for his full-length portrait of Lafayette. For ten years he remained in London, associating with Sir Thomas Lawrence, Gilbert Stuart Newton, Washington Irving, and other men of note, and upholding an excellent reputation as an engraver and water-colorist. Perhaps his best-known work was his engraving of Leslie's painting, "The Sentry Box"; but his original water-colors were very popular and brought high prices, and his copies of Titian and Veronese were much admired. His drawings from the Elgin Marbles are to-day considered remarkable. Danforth returned to New York in 1837. In 1843 he married Mrs. Hannah B. Duryee Kennedy, daughter of Abraham Duryee of Harlem, and after a few years in Hartford, made his permanent home in New York. During these years he became interested in the engraving of banknotes, and his work in this department was characterized by great finish and delicacy. About 1850 he formed the firm of Danforth, Underwood & Company, which about 1858 was merged with the American Bank Note Company, of which he was vice-president at the time of his death. Judged by his few paintings now in this country, Danforth had great ability in portraiture. The following are some of his best-known engravings: "Don Quixote"; "Sir Walter Scott," of which 14,000 prints were sold; "Lord Holland's Daughter"; "Washington Irving"; "Andrew Jackson"; "Alexander Pope"; "Landing of Columbus"; "Landing at Jamestown"; "Chaldean Shepherd"; "Forsaken"; "Lady Arabella Johnson"; "The Token"; "Red Jacket"; and portraits of many early preachers. Danforth was fond of music and played the flute. His was a lovable personality, deeply religious, loyal in friendship, and of great modesty; he was "a man whose good qualities cannot be too highly estimated, an honor to art and society" (French, p. 65).

[W. Dunlap, *Hist. of the Rise and Progress of the Arts of Design in the United States* (1918), III, 164; H. W. French, *Art and Artists in Conn.* (1879); D. M. Stauffer, *Am. Engravers upon Copper and Steel* (1907), pt. I, p. 58 and pt. II, p. 75; W. S. Baker, *Am. Engravers and their Works* (1875), p. 37; Manuscript genealogy, letters, and papers in possession of family. Collections of Danforth's work are in the Nat. Acad. of Design, the Metropolitan Museum of Art, and the Pub. Lib. in N. Y. City; the Wadsworth Atheneum and Morgan Memorial in Hartford, Conn.; the U. S. Nat. Museum in Washington, D. C.; and the Pub. Lib. in Newark, N. J.] M. D. D.

DANFORTH, THOMAS (November 1623–Nov. 5, 1699), deputy-governor of Massachusetts, was born at Framlingham, Suffolk, England, and baptized there Nov. 20, 1623. He was the eldest son of Nicholas and Elizabeth Danforth, whose family name was spelled in eleven different ways in the parish registers. The father was evidently a man of considerable property, and after the death of his wife emigrated to Massachusetts (*c.* 1634), taking his children with him. He was elected to various political offices in the colony, and his son Thomas was admitted as a freeman May 10, 1643, soon becoming a man of note. In 1650 he was named as treasurer of Harvard College in the charter granted to the institution in May of that year, although he does not appear to have assumed the duties of office until 1654, from which time he performed them until 1669. In that year he became steward, serving until 1682. He was also chosen clerk of the Overseers in 1654. His interest in the college was deep and continuing, and its historian, Josiah Quincy, speaks of him as among "the earliest, most steadfast, and faithful of its friends."

He was also distinguished on the small stage of the colony's political life. With the organization of Middlesex County he was elected recorder of deeds (1652) and held the office until 1686. He represented Cambridge, in which town he lived, as deputy in the General Court in 1657 and 1658 and was chosen an Assistant for twenty successive years beginning with 1659. From May 28, 1679 until the dissolution of the government in May 1686, he was associated with Simon Bradstreet [*q.v.*] as deputy-governor. He was appointed president of the Province of Maine, Feb. 4, 1680, and held that office until dropped by the Dudley administration, May 29, 1686. He also for many years served his town in the offices of selectman and town clerk, and at times was head of the Commissioners of the United Colonies. He was an acknowledged leader of the popular as opposed to the prerogative party, was an enemy of Joseph Dudley [*q.v.*], and in 1682 was one of the committee entrusted with the task of drawing up instructions for the colony's agents. Owing to his political opinions, he was naturally not in office during the Andros régime. On Apr. 18, 1689, he was one of those who signed the demand upon Andros [*q.v.*] to surrender the government and after the fall of the governor, he was again annually elected to his former offices until the grant of the new charter in 1692. In December of that year, however, he was chosen an associate judge of the superior court and held that office until his death.

He was a man of strong character and, although willing to go to almost any length in opposing the Laws of Trade and the demands of the British government, he was far from being as narrow-minded as most of his party. In the public excitement attending the Indian war of 1675 he joined Daniel Gookin and John Eliot [*qq.v.*] in defending the "Praying Indians," incurring so much obloquy by so doing that his life was threatened. Again he showed his ability to rise above the mob by his condemnation of the witchcraft trials in 1692. He appears to have had ample means and lived on what is now Kirkland St., Cambridge, owning, besides other property, ten thousand acres at Framingham, in which town he bequeathed three valuable leases to Harvard. In February 1644 he married Mary, daughter of Henry Withington of Dorchester, by whom he had twelve children. She died Mar. 26, 1697.

[J. J. May, *Danforth Geneal.* (1902); Wm. Thaddeus Harris, "Notes on the Danforth Family," *New Eng.-Hist. and Geneal. Reg.*, VII (1853), 315–21; Josiah Quincy, *Hist. of Harvard Univ.* (2 vols., 1840); *Me. Hist. Soc. Colls.*, all three series, *passim.*]

J. T. A.

DANFORTH, THOMAS (May 22, 1703–*c.* 1786), pewterer, was born in Taunton, Mass., the ninth of fourteen children of Samuel Danforth, who was born in 1666, graduated from Harvard in 1683, and entered the ministry. His grandfather, Samuel, a graduate of Harvard in 1643, was ordained in 1650, and became a coworker with John Eliot, missionary to the Indians. Nicholas, the first colonial Danforth, left England in 1634 and settled in Cambridge, Mass. Thomas learned the pewterer's and brazier's trade, and became the ancestor of the two largest pewtering families in America, the Danforths and the Boardmans. Moving to Norwich in 1733 he there opened a pewter and copper shop. In 1730 he had married Sarah Leonard, who bore him five children; four months after her death in 1742 he wed Hannah Hall, who became the mother of nine. Thomas engaged actively in the pewterer's trade until 1773, and from then on intermittently until his death. His output of pewter was large and diverse, the metal was of good quality, the workmanship conscientious, and the feeling for form sympathetic and intelligent. He was what is known as an "eight inch plate man," and was one of six contemporaries who adhered to the English style of marks. His products included plates, platters, trenchers, porringers, flagons, mugs, basins, salts, spoons, buttons, alphabet stamps, and various molds. Two sons, Thomas and John, learned the pewterer's trade. The latter was the only native craftsman who used a date in his touch mark. A grandson —also a Thomas—opened a branch in Philadelphia, 1807–13, and his son Thomas fashioned pewter in Philadelphia and Augusta, Ga. Sarah, probably the grand-daughter of the first Thomas, married Oliver Boardman of Hartford, Conn., in 1781, and their son, Thomas Danforth Boardman, was the first pewterer of the Danforth-Boardman group.

[J. B. Kerfoot, *American Pewter* (1924); Louis G. Myers, *Some Notes on American Pewterers* (1926); J. J. May, *Danforth Genealogy* (1902).] R. M. K.

DANIEL, JOHN MONCURE (Oct. 24, 1825–Mar. 30, 1865), journalist, diplomat, son of John Moncure and Elizabeth (Mitchell) Daniel, was born in Stafford County and died in Richmond, Va. His rearing as well as his actual schooling was conducted almost exclusively by his father, a country doctor. At fifteen, he went to Richmond to live with his father's uncle, Judge Peter V. Daniel [*q.v.*]. After several years he went to Fredericksburg to study law in the office of an attorney held in esteem by his family, but in 1845 the death of his father and his own indifference to law resulted in his coming back to Richmond. At a salary of $100 a year he became librarian of the Patrick Henry Society, a body of aspiring young gentlemen interested in reading and debating. Soon he became editor of the *Southern Planter,* and a little later (1847) of the new *Richmond Examiner.* His quick, sharp intelligence and his slashing literary style were both dominated by a superb journalistic instinct, practical enough to earn him wealth. His paper was irresistibly interesting, and its name and power soon went far beyond Virginia. In 1853, in recognition of certain political exertions, President Franklin Pierce made him representative of the United States at the Court of Sardinia. As a diplomat his independent conduct and frank speech often involved him in difficulties with the magnificos of Turin, but he was sufficiently discreet to refuse a request made of him by Garibaldi that he take over Nice as an American protectorate. On learning of the secession of South Carolina, he hurried home and reassumed the editorship of the *Examiner.* Still under middle age, handsome, dark, slight of build, his body padded with luxurious clothing, he was a romantic figure and conscious of the fact. His likes and dislikes among men were fast and furious. He entertained frequently in his rooms, amusing his guests at times by provoking battle between his two dogs, by displaying his books, or, mounted on a kind of throne, by discoursing endlessly with recurrent gusts of dogmatism. As for women, he was contemptuous of them: he had loved one only—her he would not name—and he would love no other, for there were no others worthy. Solitary, misanthropic, cloudy in his opinions as to the deity, he was none the less severe in his demand for the most punctilious niceties of social convention. His political opinions were unmistakable. He thought that secession was the only course left open to the Southern states, and he fiercely urged in his editorials that that inescapable action be taken promptly. He advocated the adoption of military conscription, over the protest of Jefferson Davis, and, as the war advanced, he became almost frantic in his distrust of the Davis administration. He served two brief terms in the army, once in 1861 and again in 1862. The military life was, he admitted, indeed horrible, but he softened his own excursions into it as best he could by taking with him two slaves and other elaborate provisions for his comfort, and he was anxious for an honorable scar to show (Bagby, *post,* p. 10). Wounded in his right arm in the summer of 1862, he usually thereafter thought of himself as incapacitated for further service at the front. In 1864, he was wounded again, this time in a duel with the Confederate secretary of the treasury. For many months before the war ended he favored peace by negotiation. The dream he had for the future was to buy the family estate in Stafford County, retire thither, and, as soon as he could provide all the feudal equipment which he held necessary, set himself up as a pattern for Virginians. Then, he confided to a friend, "I shall teach these people what they never knew—how to live like a gentleman" (*Ibid.,* p. 36). But disease laid hold of him, and then he died, and a few days afterward, in the great fire which marked the Confederate abandonment of Richmond, the plant of the *Examiner* perished utterly.

[*Richmond Examiner During the War: or Writings of John M. Daniel with Memoir of his Life by his Brother, Frederick S. Daniel* (1868); G. W. Bagby, *John M. Daniel's Latch-key* (1868); R. W. Hughes, *Editors of the Past* (1897); *Richmond Examiner,* Mar. 31, 1865; *The South in the Building of the Nation,* vol. XI (1909); L. G. Tyler, *Encyc. of Va. Biog.,* vol III (1915).] J. D. W.

DANIEL, JOHN WARWICK (Sept. 5, 1842–June 29, 1910), senator from Virginia, was born in Lynchburg, Va., the only son of William and Sarah Anne (Warwick) Daniel. From Gessner Harrison's classical school the handsome, high-minded, and ambitious lad went into the Confederate army as a private in May 1861. At twenty he was major and chief of Early's staff, but a wound in the battle of the Wilderness (May 1864) ended his military career and put him on crutches for life. After a year at the University of Virginia (1865–66) the young major began the practise of law with his father in Lynchburg. In 1869 he married his neighbor, Julia E. Munnell. Slowly, against keen competition, he won a remunerative practise. He was peculiarly good at oral argument before the state supreme court. Slowly and laboriously, too, he brought to publication *A Treatise on the Law of Negotiable Instruments* (1876). Meanwhile he had entered politics. In the House of Delegates he spoke out boldly against the passage of the debt-funding act in 1871; but as state senator (1875–79), believing that the honor of Virginia was involved, he worked for its support through measures of Spartan economy. On this issue he stumped the state in 1879 against the Readjusters. Meanwhile he had twice unavailingly sought the Democratic nomination for Congress and once (1877) for governor. When, in 1881, he gained the gubernatorial nomination, he was decisively defeated by a coalition of Readjusters and Republicans. Elected to Congress, however, in 1884, and a year later to the United States Senate for the term beginning Mar. 4, 1887, he represented his state continuously, and was a member of every Democratic national convention, until his death.

As a party leader his chief concern was the solidarity of the whites. "I am a Democrat," he said in 1881, "because I am a white man"; and in 1902 he forced through the constitutional convention of Virginia suffrage provisions which still substantially secure his great objective (*Report of the Proceedings and Debates,* 1906, pp. 2943 ff.; W. A. Watson, *Notes on Southside Virginia,* 1925). His political method was direct appeal to the masses. His Roman face, his lameness converted into grace and ever recalling his war service, his courtliness of manner, his sonorous voice and solemn rolling phrases, all combined to hypnotize them. To them he was the "Lame Lion," and though he was no special pleader for the "forgotten man," he doubtless deemed himself their tribune. Hence, though associated with the Democratic machine, he was never a part of it (*Richmond Times*, December 1893, *passim*); and he virtually spurned the powerful and politically inclined Anti-Saloon League (*Civic Sentinel*, January 1905). In 1896, as temporary chairman, he organized the Democratic convention for Free Silver and delivered the key-note address; in 1900 and in 1904, as a faithful friend of Bryan, he headed the convention's Committee on Resolutions (*Review of Reviews*, New York, August 1896, August 1900, August 1904). In the Senate, despite his excellent committee assignments, he initiated no important legislation. His colleagues, however, noted that he was dignified, courteous, sincere, that he spoke infrequently but showed that "he had thought much and independently." As an occasional orator he was much sought after. His style was "copious, ornate, solemn, touched always with emotion, appealing at once to the head and to the heart." He felt that fighting the Civil War to the last ditch not only "gave finality to its results and well-nigh extinguished its embers with its flames" but also preserved to Southerners "their title to respect . . . and their incentive to noble and unselfish deeds." To his personal friends alone, however, were known his open-heartedness, his loyalty, and his brave fight against unceasing pain.

[See Lyon G. Tyler, *Men of Mark in Va.* (1906); *Memorial Addresses of Cong., "Senator Daniel"* (1911); Wm. M. Thornton, *John Warwick Daniel* (1915); E. M. Daniel, ed., *Speeches and Orations of John Warwick Daniel* (1911). C. C. Pearson, *The Readjuster Movement in Va.* (1927), gives the setting down to 1888.]

C. C. P.

DANIEL, PETER VIVIAN (Apr. 24, 1784–May 31, 1860), jurist, was a member of a family whose connection with Virginia dated from the early days of the colony. His grandfather, Peter Daniel, was one of the pioneer settlers in Stafford County and a justice of the peace. His father, Travers Daniel, married Frances, daughter of Rev. John Moncure, and resided at "Crows Nest," Stafford County, where he owned an extensive estate. Peter Vivian Daniel was born at "Crows Nest." Receiving his early education at home from private tutors, he subsequently proceeded to the College of New Jersey (Princeton), but did not complete his academic course. He took up the study of law in the Richmond office of Edmund Randolph, attorney-general and later secretary of state in Washington's cabinet, and was admitted to the Virginia bar in 1808. The same year he fought a duel with Capt. John Seddon, father of J. A. Seddon, Confederate secretary of war, in which he wounded his adversary. Following the traditions of his family, the members of which had always taken a prominent share in provincial affairs, he entered the Virginia legislature in 1809, when only twenty-five years of age. In 1812 he was elected a member of the Privy Council of Virginia, and on the adoption of the new constitution, whereby the membership of that body was reduced from eight to three, he was again elected, continuing as such until 1835. He was lieutenant-governor of the state and *ex officio* chairman of the Council during the latter years of his tenure of office. In 1834 President Jackson had tendered him the position of attorney-general of the United States in succession to Roger B. Taney, but he declined. In 1836, on the elevation of Judge P. P. Barbour to the Supreme Court bench, he was appointed by President Jackson judge of the United States district court of Virginia. Four years later, following the death of Judge Barbour, he was nominated by President Van Buren associate justice of the Supreme Court of the United States. The appointment was confirmed Mar. 3, 1841, and he continued a member of the Court until his death at Richmond, Va., May 31, 1860. As a judge he was neither learned nor profound, but he displayed great care and industry in the study of all causes which came before him, overlooking nothing and weighing the arguments with the utmost solicitude and detachment. A man of wide culture and considerable scholarship, his opinions were distinguished by their fine literary style as well as by their clarity.

The year after his admission to the bar he had married Lucy Nelson, daughter of his legal mentor, Edmund Randolph. Late in life (1853) he married, as his second wife, Mary, daughter of Dr. Thomas Harris. In politics a steadfast Democrat, his absolute rectitude of character, unswerving adherence to his principles and code of conduct, and conscientious dedication to the calls of public duty, rendered him a much respected figure in Washington and Richmond.

[A good account of Daniel's life and career appeared in H. E. Hayden, *Va. Genealogies* (1891), p. 309, which also contains a careful survey of his ancestry. See also 24 *Howard*, iii; and obituary in *Richmond Enquirer*, June 1, 1860.]

H. W. H. K.

DANIELS, FRED HARRIS (June 16, 1853–Aug. 30, 1913), engineer, metallurgist, inventor, born in Hanover Center, N. H., was one of the five children of William Pomeroy and H. Ann (Stark) Daniels. He was a lineal descendant of Robert Daniel who came from England in 1636 and settled in Watertown, Mass., and of Thomas Harris who accompanied Roger Williams to

America from Bristol, England. When he was a year old his parents moved to Worcester, Mass., where he lived for the rest of his life. At the age of twenty, immediately after receiving the degree of M.E. from Worcester Polytechnic Institute, he entered the employ of the Washburn & Moen Manufacturing Company at Worcester, makers of steel rod and wire products, where he continued for a little over a year. Upon the opening of the college term of 1874, he entered Lafayette College at Easton, Pa., as an assistant in chemistry, and also took a special course in chemistry under the head of the department, Dr. Thomas M. Drown. Employed for a summer at the close of the school term by the Glendon Iron Works at Easton, completing the plans of their blast furnaces, he then returned to Worcester to resume his connection with the Washburn & Moen Manufacturing Company as mechanical engineer and chemist. His greatest pleasure was derived from experimental work in the laboratory, and as early as 1878, when but twenty-five years of age, he had made some remarkable inventions relating principally to the manufacture of steel rods and wire. These earlier inventions were patented jointly with Charles H. Morgan who was his senior by twenty-one years and an engineer of wide reputation. In Daniels, however, Morgan found a worthy associate, and for years worked with him on rolling-mill problems. As his special abilities in iron and steel working developed, Daniels was sent several times to Europe in the interests of his company for the particular purpose of studying methods, especially in Sweden. Between 1880 and 1909, upwards of one hundred patents were granted to him, all relating to the manufacture of steel rods and wire. Twenty-five of these were of the greatest economic importance inasmuch as they greatly improved the quality of the finished product, tremendously increased the speed of production, and materially lowered the cost of production of the finished rods. During this period, too, Daniels advanced through the position of chief engineer and when but thirty-six years of age was made general superintendent and chief engineer of all of the company's properties. Ten years later (1899), when the Washburn & Moen Manufacturing Company was purchased by the American Steel & Wire Company, he was made chief engineer of the thirty-two wire plants which came into the ownership of that corporation, and in 1902 he became a director of the company. Finally, when the American Steel & Wire Company became the property of the United States Steel Corporation, he was appointed chairman of the board of engineers of the latter, and for the last six years of his life he served as president of the Worcester plants of the American Steel & Wire Company.

Daniels was an honored member of the American Institute of Mining and Metallurgical Engineers, the American Society of Mechanical Engineers; the American Society for Testing Materials, and the British Iron and Steel Institute. The Paris Exposition of 1900 awarded him the Grand Prize and gold medal for his meritorious achievements in the development of the steel rod and wire industry, and William Garrett, famous as the inventor and builder of rolling-mills, said of him in 1901: "No one has done more than he to perfect wire drawing in all its phases." Daniels was an ardent sportsman, particularly in the hunting of big game, and a prominent clubman. He was married on May 17, 1883, to Sarah Lydia White, of Worcester, Mass.

[Ellery B. Crane, *Geneal. and Personal Memoirs of Worcester County* (1907), vol. II; *Who's Who in America*, 1914–15; Chas. G. Washburn, *Industrial Worcester* (1917); Correspondence with secretary, Industrial Museum Committee, Am. Steel and Wire Co., Worcester; Patent Office records.] C. W. M.

DANNREUTHER, GUSTAV (July 21, 1853–Dec. 19, 1923), violinist, conductor, teacher, was the son of Abraham and Sophie (Fishbacher) Dannreuther, who came from Strasbourg to Cincinnati in 1849. There Gustav was born four years later. After studying the violin with Henry Eich, of Cincinnati, he was sent, in 1871, to the Berlin Hochschule, which had been reorganized by Joseph Joachim only a few years before, and there he studied the violin with Heinrich De Ahna, the eminent solo violinist and quartet player, who had joined the faculty of the Hochschule, and with Joachim himself; besides taking theory courses with Heitel. Leaving the Hochschule in 1874, he spent six months in Paris, and then passed to London, where he taught and played in public until 1877. He then returned to the United States and became a member of the Mendelssohn Quintet Club of Boston, with which he traveled through the United States, as well as in Canada and Newfoundland, until 1880. It was a period favorable toward a string organization devoted to high ideals. The severe industrial depression of 1873 had abated; the South was emerging from the era of the carpet baggers with Reconstruction well under way; in the West the age of the mining camp was merging in that of the railroad town. Musicians of merit devoted to the ensemble could win an appreciation once only accorded to the virtuoso; and the services of

Gustav Dannreuther and his associates in this field played their part in laying a foundation for the present widespread cult of chamber music in the United States. In 1880, the year of Garfield's election to the presidency, Dannreuther established himself in Boston; and the year following he became a member of the Boston Symphony Orchestra called into existence by the liberality of Col. Henry Lee Higginson, and played in its first concert in the old Music Hall, Oct. 22, 1881. As soon as a favorable opportunity offered, however, he felt himself unable to refuse a call to return to the chamber music ensemble, and from 1882 to 1884 was active as the conductor of the Buffalo Philharmonic Society, an organization which gave some sixty concerts of chamber music during the time he had it in charge. In 1882, in Buffalo, he married Nellie M. Taylor of that city. In 1884 he realized a long-cherished ambition and formed a string quartet of his own, which antedated by two years the founding of the Kneisel Quartet. The Beethoven String Quartet, renamed the Dannreuther Quartet on the tenth anniversary of its existence, was composed of Dannreuther himself (first violin), E. Schenck ('cello), O. Schill and later F. L. Smith (second violin), and I. Kovarik (viola). For a time it was the oldest in the United States, and its cultural achievement during its more than thirty years of existence under the direction of its founder represents the latter's greatest contribution to the cause of better music in America. While prior to 1899 he was for three years the leader of the New York Symphony and Oratorio Societies under Walter Damrosch, after that date he devoted himself altogether to chamber music and to teaching, in which he was notably successful. He became an instructor in music at Vassar College in 1907. His activities as a teacher (in which connection he wrote a set of *Chord and Scale Studies for Young Players*) are cast in the shade, however, by his service in arousing appreciation for the classic literature of the string quartet, presented with meticulous beauty and reverence by the organization which bore his name. For years the three concerts given annually in New York by the quartet, assisted by distinguished artists, were regarded by the cognoscenti as events of the musical season, and while at the time the Dannreuther Quartet played, composers such as Debussy, Stravinsky, Goossens, Bloch, Malipiero and others had not yet introduced new harmonic factors of color and atmosphere in string quartet literature, the Quartet established, for the older literature, the standard the Kneisels maintained.

[*The Dannreuther Quartet; A Sketch of Its Hist.* (1904), issued in commemoration of the organization's twentieth anniversary, gives a survey of its work. See also "The Dannreuther Quartet" in *Musical America*, Dec. 9, 1905. An obituary notice of Dannreuther may be found in *Musical America*, Jan. 5, 1924; and a reliable sketch of his life in *The Metronome*, Nov. 1903.]

F. H. M.

DA PONTE, LORENZO (Mar. 10, 1749–Aug. 17, 1838), poet, librettist, and founder of Italian culture in America, was born in the Ghetto at Ceneda, near Venice. The son of a Jewish tanner named Geremia Conegliano and his wife Rachele Pinerchele, Lorenzo was originally named Emanuele. At the age of fourteen, together with his father and two brothers, he turned to the Christian faith and was baptized by Monsignor Lorenzo Da Ponte, bishop of Ceneda; and following the custom of the time he took the distinguished name of his spiritual father. Placed through the bishop's influence in the seminary of Ceneda and later in that of Portogruaro, Lorenzo acquitted himself so well that in 1770 he was made tutor in the latter school and in 1771 became its vice-rector, having meanwhile taken ecclesiastical orders. In 1773, however, under the delusion of persecution that was to torment his entire life, he resigned this office and went to Venice, where he spent a year in idleness and dissipation. Then followed two years of teaching in the seminary at Treviso, a pleasant post in which his stay was cut short by certain ill-considered utterances in verse, the *Accademia Poetica*, which led to his expulsion. Returning to his former profligacy in Venice, he was by 1779 so variously involved in personal delinquencies and public scandals that he was banished from Venetian territory for fifteen years and threatened with imprisonment for seven in case of his return. He escaped into Austria.

Circumstances now forced him to seek a living by his pen. After drifting from Gorizia to Dresden and thence to Vienna, he was fortunate enough to secure appointment in the Austrian capital as "Poet to the Italian Theatre." This stroke of fortune converted him overnight from a struggling adventurer into a man of letters and of fashion, whose librettos were sought by the foremost operatic composers of Europe. It was at this time that he wrote *Il Ricco d'un Giorno, Il Burbero di Buon Cuore,* and *Il Finto Cieco;* but only after his collaboration with Mozart was he recognized as the foremost living librettist. Their first opera, *Le Nozze di Figaro,* was successfully produced in 1786, and was followed by *Don Giovanni* (1787) and *Cosi Fan Tutte* (1790). Meanwhile he continued to write for the score of Salieri, Martini, Righini, and Storace, and to this period belong such pieces as *Gli Equivoci, Una Cosa Rara, Il Filosofo Punito, Bertoldo, L'Arbore di Diana, Il Pastor Fido, La Cifra,* and *Axur, Re d'Ormus.* After the death of Joseph II in 1790 the poet's customary indiscretions led to another disgrace, and he was ordered to quit Vienna. For a year he lived in Trieste, where he married Ann Celestine Ernestine ("Nancy") Grahl, the English daughter of a German merchant in the city; and after another year or so of travel, during which he visited Prague and his old friend Casanova, settled in London late in 1793.

The rest of his long career is mainly a story of disappointment and misfortune ameliorated by the loyalty and sound sense of his wife. Continuing his career as librettist he wrote, among other things, *La Capricciosa Corretta, L'Isola del Piacere,* and *La Scuola de Maritati* for production at Drury Lane. But his genius for falling out with his associates led to his discharge from the theatre about the end of 1799. He had previously set up a small printing-shop and after his dismissal opened a bookstore. In 1803 he was recalled to the theatre for a time and wrote *Castore e Polluce* and *Il Ratto di Proserpina*; but ill-advised speculation brought him to bankruptcy and in 1805 he set sail for America. Faced in late middle life with the task of providing for a family of small children in a strange land, he opened a grocery business in New York, and later, in Elizabethtown, N. J., following this by a variety of similar ventures at Sunbury, Pa. All ended in failure. He was more successful, however, with a class of pupils in Italian in New York, where he gathered so large and aristocratic a following that in 1825 he was appointed professor of Italian literature in Columbia College. Charm of personality and an extensive learning enabled him to give the initial impetus to the spread of Italian culture in this country, and particularly to the study of Dante. Though now advanced in years he established a business for importing Italian books and undertook the furthering of Italian opera in America. By 1833 he had raised sufficient capital to build an Italian opera house. But this venture also failed. He died a poor man five years later. In 1823 he had published his *Memorie* in Italian, an interesting but unreliable autobiography.

[J. L. Russo, *Lorenzo Da Ponte, Poet and Adventurer* (1922), gives a full account and exhaustive bibliography; a revised and enlarged edition of the *Memorie* was published 1829–30, and two English translations in 1929, one by L. A. Sheppard, with an introduction and notes, and one by Elisabeth Abbott edited and annotated by Arthur Livingston.] E. H. W.

DARBY, JOHN (Sept 27, 1804–Sept. 1, 1877), educator, author, was born at North Adams, Mass. One of several children of poor parents, Joseph and Farrand Darby, he was left fatherless at ten years of age and had to bear his share of the support of the family. Apprenticed to a fuller, he had few opportunities for schooling but worked at his books while at his machine in the mill. Thus learning the subjects required for entrance to college, he entered Williams when he was twenty-three. Following graduation in 1831 he taught in the Williamstown Academy but, forced to leave New England for the sake of his health, he accepted a position in the Barhamville Seminary for young ladies near Columbia, S. C. Devoted to the study of science, he published in 1841 *A Botany of the Southern States* as a text-book for the schools of the South. This, improved and enlarged in subsequent editions, became the authoritative manual for the flora of this part of the country. In 1842 he was made professor of natural science in Wesleyan Female College, Macon, Ga. His health failing after several years of teaching here, he returned to Williamstown, where he was appointed professor of mathematics in Williams College. After a year, however, the state of his health again compelled him to go to a warmer climate and for two years he taught again at Barhamville Seminary. Assuming then the direction of Sigourney Institute at Culloden, Ga., he continued at that school for six years and he is credited with having contributed largely to the renown it gained (Knight, *post*). In 1855 he accepted the headship of Auburn (Ala.) Masonic Female College which he relinquished after a year to become professor of natural science in the East Alabama Male College, also located at Auburn and just established under the auspices of the Methodist church. Of this he was one of the trustees whose names appear in the Act of Incorporation. Here he remained till the Civil War caused a suspension of college activities. In 1860 he published a text-book on chemistry which was widely used thereafter. Accepting in 1869 the professorship of science in Kentucky Wesleyan College at Millersburg, he remained there as professor and president till his resignation in 1876. On Aug. 20, 1833, he married a fellow teacher of his in the Barhamville Seminary, Julia P. Sheldon, daughter of Calvin Sheldon of Manchester, Vt. She died in 1875. There were several children, with whom in New York City the last few years of his life were spent. He was active and prominent in the Methodist church and a frequent contributor to the religious press. He won from his students both high respect for his scholarship and their regard because of his character as a man and inspirational power as a teacher.

[The chief source of information about John Darby is the *Obituary Record of Grads. of Williams Coll. deceased during the Academical Year ending June 15, 1878*, ser. 2, no. 3. See also L. I. Knight, *Georgia's Landmarks, Memorials and Legends* (1913–14). A sketch of his life appeared in the *N. Y. Tribune*, Sept. 21, 1877.] W. J. C.

DARBY, WILLIAM (Aug. 14, 1775–Oct. 9, 1854), geographer, was born in Hanover Township, Lancaster (now Dauphin) County, Pa., the eldest son of Patrick and Mary (Rice) Darby. Both parents were Irish, and settled in Pennsylvania a few years prior to the Revolution. In 1781 they migrated to the Ohio country, where William's youth was spent. Without means of securing an education, he read assiduously, and at the age of eighteen began teaching school. After the death of his father in June 1799 he went to Natchez, where he became a cotton-planter. He suffered heavy losses by fire in 1804 and during the next five years was deputy surveyor for the United States. Conceiving the plan of a map and statistical account of Louisiana, he found government surveys inadequate and began a series of extensive explorations at his own expense. Interrupted by the British invasion, he acted as one of Jackson's topographical staff in the campaign of 1814–15. He returned to Pennsylvania in 1815, after having failed to secure aid from Louisiana officials in publishing his surveys. In Philadelphia, John Melish [*q.v.*] agreed to publish Darby's *A Geographical Description of the State of Louisiana . . . Being an Accompaniment to the Map of Louisiana* (1816, 2nd edition, 1817). Using Darby's statistical account and map, which Jackson and members of his staff considered accurate and valuable, the publisher compiled the Melish map of the United States, which was used as the basis for boundary delineation in the treaty of 1819 between the United States and Spain. This map, which brought profit and prestige to Melish, left the explorer "to mourn for non-requited toil and mis-directed credit" until Congress appropriated (Aug. 1, 1854) $1,500 as partial compensation (*U. S. Statutes at Large*, 33 Cong., 1 Sess., ch. 170). In 1818 Darby was one of the surveyors engaged in running the boundary between the United States and Canada, made the trip to the Michigan territory described in *A Tour from the City of New-York to Detroit* (1819) and wrote, for Kirk & Mercein, *The Emigrant's Guide to the Western and Southwestern States and Territories* (1818), valuable for its information upon French and Spanish land titles. During the next thirty-five years he lived in Harrisburg, Pa., on a farm near Sandy Spring, Montgomery County, Md., and in Washington, D. C., where he was for some years a government clerk. He lectured widely, wrote and compiled much, and for a quarter of a century was one of the leading American geographers. He compiled three editions (1823, 1827 and 1843) of Richard Brookes's ever popular *General Gazetteer or Compendious Geographical Dictionary* (London, 1762). Brookes's work he found defective and he substituted his own so freely that *Darby's Edition* bears little resemblance to the original. He wrote most of the geographical articles in Vols. XIII to XVIII of the first American edition (Philadelphia, 1832) of Sir David Brewster's *Edinburgh Encyclopædia.* In 1833 he and Theodore Dwight, Jr., prepared *A New Gazetteer of the United States of America* (2nd edition 1835). He contributed a long series of border tales under the signature of Mark Bancroft to Samuel C. Atkinson's *The Casket,* a Philadelphia monthly magazine, and wrote upon public affairs under the pseudonym Tacitus for the *Daily National Intelligencer* (Washington, D. C.). He also published a *Plan of Pittsburgh and Vicinity* (1817), *Memoir on the Geography and Natural and Civil History of Florida, Attended by a Map of that Country* (1821), *Lectures on the Discovery of America and Colonization of North America by the English* (1828), *View of the United States, Historical, Geographical and Statistical* (1828), *Mnemonika, or, the Tablet of Memory* (1829), and *The Northern Nations of Europe, Russia and Poland* (1841). He was twice married: first, at Natchez, to Mrs. Boardman, a widow with a family of children "and quite handsome property"; she died Oct. 23, 1814, and in February 1816 he married Elizabeth Tanner, sister of Benjamin and Henry S. Tanner [*qq.v.*].

[Autobiographical letters written by Darby in 1834 to Dr. M. L. Dixon, of Winchester, Tenn., printed in Wm. H. Egle's *Dixons of Dixon's Ford* (pub. in 1878 by the Dauphin County Hist. Soc.) and in *Notes and Queries* (Harrisburg, 1894); *Senate Report No. 236*, 30 Cong., 1 Sess.; *Senate Report No. 222*, 33 Cong., 1 Sess.; *Hist. Mag.*, Oct. 1867; C. D. Harris and A. C. Veatch, *A Preliminary Report on the Geology of La.* (1899); *Daily Globe* and *Daily National Intelligencer* (both Washington, D. C.), Oct. 10, 1854.] F. E. R.

DARE, VIRGINIA (b. Aug. 18, 1587) was the first English child born in America. On July 22, 1587, Gov. John White with 150 householders landed at Hatteras, on his way to plant a colony on the Chesapeake. It was decided to remain and settle at Roanoke. That summer, on Aug. 18, Gov. White's daughter, Ellinor, or Elyoner, wife of Ananias Dare, gave birth to a daughter, who was christened Virginia. On Aug. 27, Gov. White sailed to England to obtain help and supplies for the colony, but the Spanish War interfered and it was not until 1591 that help came. No trace could be found of the colonists and their fate has remained a complete mystery. Unless absorbed by some Indian tribes, they must all have perished. Virginia's known life is thus limited to nine days, and she is perhaps the youngest person to appear in any biographical dictionary as the subject of a separate article.

[For the history of the colony, see Alexander Brown, *The Genesis of the U. S.* (1891), I, 14–21. Virginia is mentioned in the few contemporary accounts of the settlement, *e.g.*, John Smith's *Travels and Works* (Arber, ed. 1910), I, 328, but there is no information beyond that noted above.] J. T. A.

DARGAN, EDMUND STROTHER (Apr. 15, 1805–Nov. 24, 1879), jurist, the son of a Baptist minister of Irish descent who married a Miss Lilly, of English parentage, was born in Montgomery County, N. C. His father died when he was young, and he was compelled to earn his living by farm labor. Though practically self-educated, he acquired a fair knowledge of the classics and in 1828 entered a law office at Wadesboro, N. C. The following year he went to Alabama, walking the entire distance to Washington, Autauga County, where he was admitted to the bar and commenced practise, at the same time teaching school. He was elected a justice of the peace, but there was little scope for a lawyer in that district and in 1833 he moved to Montgomery, opened a law office, and in a short time, despite certain peculiarities of habit and temperament, obtained a good connection. Defeated for the state legislature in 1840, he was the following year elected by the General Assembly judge of the circuit court for the district of Mobile and took up his residence in that town, but resigned in 1842 in order to resume practise. He had now commenced to take an active interest in public affairs, and in 1844 became mayor of Mobile, in the same year serving as a member of the state Senate. In 1845 he went to the Twenty-ninth Congress as a Democrat, and took a prominent part in the House discussions on the Oregon question. It was he who, in the course of debate, suggested the compromise settlement which was ultimately adopted. Declining a renomination at the end of his term, he was elected by the General Assembly a judge of the supreme court of Alabama, Dec. 16, 1847, becoming chief justice on July 1, 1849. On the bench he displayed a judicial ability which his somewhat erratic temperament had ill prepared the public to expect. His opinions were characterized by an originality which did not detract from their soundness, and his resignation, Dec. 6, 1852, deprived the court of the most picturesque figure in its history. He resumed practise in Mobile, abstaining from active politics until the crisis which induced the constitutional convention of 1861, in which, as a delegate from Mobile, he voted for the ordinance of secession. His district also elected him to the Confederate Congress of 1862, but he declined reëlection in 1864, and thereafter took no part in public affairs. He died at Mobile. His wife was Roxana Brack of Montgomery.

"In person, Judge Dargan has a dull and unattractive look, as if he was always drowsy, and dissatisfied with things about him. His conversation is sluggish, and he appears to be in a reverie most of his time, when he is without a law-book in his hand, and when not engaged in Court. *There,* he wakes up . . . a transformation comes over him and the purest logic and the boldest grasp of thought comes to his aid as if by intuition . . . his face is luminous with intellectual life until he closes his argument, and then he looks sleepy again." (W. Garrett, *post.*) His eccentricity in dress and habits was a source of many anecdotes, and his general views upon current events indicated a train of thought that was independent of environment or precedent.

[Vivid contemporary appreciations appeared in Wm. Garrett, *Reminiscences of Public Men in Ala.* (1872), p. 385, and in W. Brewer, *Alabama: Her Hist., Resources, War Record and Public Men* (1872), p. 411. See also *Memorial Record of Ala.* (1893), II, 152; B. F. Riley, *Makers and Romance of Ala. Hist.* (n.d.), p. 176; and *Southern Law Jour. and Reporter,* I, 64 (Dec. 1879).] H. W. H. K.

DARKE, WILLIAM (May 6, 1736–Nov. 26, 1801), soldier, son of Joseph Darke, was descended through his paternal grandmother from John Rush, one of Cromwell's commanders who became a Quaker and emigrated in 1683 to Pennsylvania. When William was only a few years old, his parents moved to Virginia, settling near Shepherdstown (now W. Va.). His military career began when he served as corporal in the Rutherford Rangers for a brief period (1758–59) during the French and Indian War. There appears to be no proof of the assertion that he shared in Braddock's defeat. After about fifteen years on the Virginia frontier, as soldier-farmer, he received at the outbreak of the Revolution a commission as captain of a company raised among his neighbors and friends. Captured at the battle of Germantown in October 1777, he was confined on board a prison-ship at New York until November 1780, when he was exchanged. In the spring of 1781 he recruited the Berkeley and Hampshire regiment, which rendered effective service at the siege of Yorktown. Some of these troops were discharged a few days before the surrender of Cornwallis, but there is evidence which suggests Darke's presence on that historic occasion. He retired from the Revolution with the rank of lieutenant-colonel as the reward of distinguished service.

Darke was one of a distinguished group of officers sent to the Virginia convention of 1788 to ratify the Federal Constitution. Though he served on no committees and made no speeches, the records show that he voted for ratification. He was a member of the Virginia legislature in the session of 1791–92, but apparently served only three days (*Journal of the House of Delegates,* 1791, p. 6), resigning to accept a military commission from the United States in order to fight the Indians under General St. Clair. He commanded the left wing of the army at the defeat of Nov. 4, 1791, on a branch of the Wabash, where he saw his youngest son, Capt. Joseph Darke, fall mortally wounded and he himself sustained a severe wound. He was rewarded for his services by being given the rank of brigadier-general and a generous grant of nearly 8,000 acres of public land (L. A. Burgess, *Virginia Soldiers of 1776,* 1927, I, 79). He spent the last decade of his life on his estate near Charles Town (now in West Virginia), serving at one time as justice of the peace. Darke, with his herculean frame, was a striking figure; his manners were rough; his disposition was frank and fearless. Notwithstanding a fiery temper, he was loved as well as respected by his officers and neighbors. His wife was a widow named Sarah Delayea. She bore him three sons, all of whom died in early manhood, and a daughter who has left descendants.

[F. V. Aler, *Aler's Hist. of Martinsburg and Berkeley County, W. Va.* (1888); Danske Dandridge, *Historic Shepherdstown* (1910); F. B. Heitman, *Hist. Reg. of Officers of the Continental Army during the War of the Revolution* (1914); V. A. Lewis, *Hist. of W. Va.* (1889); J. E. Norris, *Hist. of the Lower Shenandoah Valley* (1890); L. G. Tyler, *Encyc. of Virginian Biog.,* vol. II (1915); *Pa. Mag. of Hist. and Biog.,* XVII (1893), 330.]

E. L.

DARLEY, FELIX OCTAVIUS CARR (June 23, 1822–Mar. 27, 1888), illustrator, was the son of John Darley, a comedian, and his wife, Eleonora Westray, at one time a popular actress. Though both were natives of England they were married in the United States in 1800, while John Darley was serving as lieutenant of United States marines (*Polyanthos,* October 1806). Of their children, older than Felix, one became a teacher of music and another a portrait-painter. Felix was born in Philadelphia, where his parents had settled, and at fourteen was an apprentice in a mercantile house there. In 1842 some of his sketches of Philadelphia street characters were brought to the attention of Thomas Dunn English [*q.v.*] and shortly reached the editor of the *Saturday Museum,* who published them. Others appeared in *Godey's Magazine* and the *Democratic Review.* In 1843 J. R. Colon published in six monthly numbers a series, *Scenes in Indian Life,* by Darley, in outline, etched on stone. About the same time the young artist was commissioned by Carey & Hart to make illustrations for their series, the Library of American Humorous Works. His facility in caricature lent itself readily to the interpretation of the American humor of the forties. There was in him, however, a more serious vein, already suggested by the *Scenes in Indian Life,* which showed itself in sketches made for his own pleasure to illustrate Sylvester Judd's *Margaret.* These drawings, not published until later, were shown to the managers of the American Art Union and so pleased them that after Darley's removal to New York in 1848 they commissioned him to illustrate Irving's *Rip Van Winkle* and *Legend of Sleepy Hollow.* The illustrations of these two tales appeared in 1849 and 1850 respectively. He also illustrated several of Irving's works for G. P. Putnam with considerable success, Irving later saying to his nephew, "Jarvis tried, but failed to embody my conception of Diedrich Knickerbocker, Leslie also. Darley hit it in the illustrated History of New York" (P. M. Irving, *Life and Letters of Washington Irving,* vol. IV, 1864, p. 242; the edition referred to was published in 1850). Elected to the National Academy of Design in 1852, Darley was thenceforth regularly represented at its annual exhibitions. "Illustrated by Darley" became a potent phrase in new-book advertisements. His notable productions during the early fifties include illustrations for "Ik Marvel's" *Lorgnette* (1851) and the title-page of a comic periodical, *The Lantern* (1852). The thirty *Compositions in Outline from Judd's Margaret,* etched on stone like the *Scenes in Indian Life, Rip Van Winkle,* and *Sleepy Hollow,* were published in 1856. In these he "invited comparison with Moritz Retzsch, master of outline. He showed much of the grace of that German artist and vigor of characterization to which the other one does not quite attain" (Weitenkampf, "Illustrated by Darley," *International Studio,* March 1925, p. 49). In the same year he was commissioned to illustrate Cooper's works for James G. Gregory. The illustrations, reproduced on steel by bank-note engravers, were also published as *The Cooper Vignettes* (1862), in a large folio volume of India proofs. After his marriage, in 1859, to Jane, daughter of Warren Colburn the arithmetician, he established his home at Claymont, Del. He drew regularly for *Appletons'* and *Harper's,* continued his book illustrations, made vignettes for bank-notes, and drawings for large framing prints. Among these, "On the March to the Sea," engraved by A. H. Ritchie, was perhaps the best known. In 1868, after a visit to Europe, he published *Sketches Abroad With Pen and Pencil.* Other outstanding work included illustrations of Longfellow, notably *Evangeline,* Dickens, and Shakespeare, the latter with Alonzo Chappell (1886). Perhaps the most distinguished product of his later years was the series, *Compositions in Outline from Hawthorne's Scarlet Letter* (1879), which he dedicated to Longfellow.

Prolific and versatile as he was, he apparently did not permit the quantity of his production to mar its quality. He was always a good draftsman, and had a keen appreciation of the picturesque and the dramatic. His genius was essentially American; he was at his best in the reflection of American humor, the characterization of American types, the illustration of American scenes. His work attracted favorable attention at the Paris Exhibition of 1867 and at the Centennial Exhibition in Philadelphia in 1876.

[The best recent criticisms of Darley are those by Frank Weitenkampf, in *American Graphic Art* (1912), *passim,* and "Illustrated by Darley," *International Studio,* Mar. 1925, pp. 445–49. See also R. H. Stoddard in *Nat. Mag.,* Sept. 1856; H. T. Tuckerman, *Book of the Artists* (1867), pp. 471–76; obituary in Phil. *Telegraph,* repr. in *Am. Architect and Building News,* Apr. 14, 1888; Appletons' *Ann. Cyc.,* 1888; *N. Y. Times, N. Y. Tribune,* and *Evening Post* (N. Y.), Mar. 28, 1888.] E. R. D.

DARLING, FLORA ADAMS (July 25, 1840–Jan. 6, 1910), author, founder of patriotic organizations, descendant in the seventh generation of Henry Adams who settled in Braintree, Mass., in 1636, was born in Lancaster, N. H., the daughter of Harvey and Nancy (Rowell) Adams. Her father, to whom she was devoted, was a Democrat and she shared his views of history and politics, subjects in which she was interested from childhood. On Mar. 12, 1860, she was married to Col. Edward Irving Darling, twenty-two years older than herself, and went with him to his Louisiana home just before the outbreak of the Civil War. Throughout that struggle her sympathies were divided between North and South, and as a Yankee Protestant her life was not altogether easy in a family of Southern Catholics. Going to England with her husband in January 1861, she tried to keep him there when the Civil War began, but he hastened home and joined the Confederate army. Before the birth of her son in October 1862, she returned to her father's New England home, intending to remain there until the war was over, but her husband's serious illness from a wound caused her to join him at Richmond in February 1863, after much difficulty in securing permission to cross the lines. Her husband, wounded at Franklin, Tenn., died Dec. 2, 1863. Under suspicion because she had taken the oath of allegiance to the Confederacy, she was arrested in New Orleans by Union officials and on her release found that her securities and jewelry had been stolen from her trunks. This loss occasioned a prolonged claim case before Congress. Illnesses from malarial and typhoid fever in the South injured her health, and a recurrence of malaria in 1876 resulted in the loss of her hearing and the impairment of her sight. After the war, she was for a time employed in a government department in Washington, where most of her remaining life was passed.

In September 1890, Mrs. Darling asked Mrs. Mary S. Lockwood to join her in organizing a patriotic society, which became the Daughters of the American Revolution, formally founded Oct. 11, 1890. She was the second signer, was elected vice-president in charge of the organization of chapters, and became editor of the official organ, the *Adams Magazine.* Friction shortly arose between her and the National Board of the D. A. R. because she opposed eligibility to membership through the maternal side and because of her alleged refusal to recognize the authority of the Board. By a resolution of the Board, July 1, 1891, she was removed from office and on Aug. 7, 1891, she resigned her life membership and severed all connection with the organization. The Darling Chapter of New York, named for her, also withdrew and became the parent of the Daughters of the Revolution, founded by Mrs. Darling Aug. 20, 1891, on the basis of lineal descent only. On Jan. 8, 1892, she founded the Daughters of the United States of the War of 1812, of which she became the first president-general. Mrs. Darling was the author of several books, most of them autobiographical: *Mrs. Darling's Letters, or Memories of the Civil War* (1883); *A Winning, Wayward Woman* (1889); *A Social Diplomat* (1889); *Was It a Just Verdict?* (1890); *Memories of Virginia* (1907); *The Senator's Daughter* (1907). Her writing is emotional, very personal in point of view, and reveals her as opinionated and given to controversy. Late in life she organized the Edward Irving Darling Musical Society in memory of her son, a composer. She died at the home of her brother, John Quincy Adams, in New York City.

[Flora Adams Darling, *Founding and Organization of the D. A. R. and D. R., with an App., The Adams Ancestry in Europe and America* (1901); Mrs. Adlai E. Stevenson, *A Brief History of the D. A. R.* (1913); Mary S. Lockwood and Emily Lee Sherwood, *Story of the Records, D. A. R.* (1906); *Who's Who in America,* 1908–09; obituary in Washington *Evening Star,* Jan 6, 1910, and *Washington Post,* Jan. 7, 1910.] S. G. B.

DARLING, HENRY (Dec. 27, 1823–Apr. 20, 1891), Presbyterian clergyman, eighth president of Hamilton College, was born at Reading, Pa., the son of Judge William Darling, a native of Maine, and Margaretta Vaughn Smith. Graduating at nineteen from Amherst College, he declined an appointment as instructor to take training for the ministry. Since his religious connections were with the New School Presbyterian Church, he entered Union Theological Seminary. Desire for preparation for missionary work in the West led him a year later to Auburn Seminary, where he graduated in 1845. After a year in charge of the Presbyterian Church at Vernon, N. Y., near Utica, he became pastor of the Presbyterian Church of Hudson. Thence in 1853 he went to the Clinton Street Church of Philadelphia, succeeding Joel Parker. During his eight successful years in this pastorate he began his long activity in general ecclesiastical affairs. For nine years from 1854 he was permanent clerk of the General Assembly, and he served in the church's missionary and educational organizations. Compelled by illness in 1861 to resign his pastorate, he lived for three years in Germantown. During this time he wrote: *The Closer Walk* (1862), a devotional book which attained considerable fame, being republished in England and translated for use in India; "Worship as an Element of Sanctuary Service" (*Presbyterian Quarterly Review,* April 1862), an article which marked him as a pioneer in the movement among non-liturgical churches for betterment of worship; and *Slavery and the War* (1863), which was widely circulated as a pamphlet.

His best years were the seventeen spent in the pastorate of the Fourth Presbyterian Church of Albany, N. Y., beginning in 1864. The church, which had had conspicuous ministers, flourished more than ever under his leadership, and exerted a powerful influence in the city. Competent in all phases of church work, he was preeminently a pastor, and was warmly regarded for constant personal ministry. He was active in the reunion of the New School and Old School Presbyterian churches in 1869, and in efforts for the union of the Presbyterian Church in the United States of America with the Reformed (Dutch) Church and the Presbyterian Church in the United States (Southern). In 1881 he was elected moderator of the General Assembly. The same year he became president of Hamilton College, being also professor of Christian evidences and pastor of the college church. While his ten years of service saw a measure of advance in teaching and in buildings and funds, his chief contribution to the life of the college lay in the strengthening of religious influences and in friendly relations with students. He was remembered for establishing a "more wholesome confidence and sympathy" between students and faculty. He died in the midst of his work at Hamilton.

Darling was married in 1846 to Julia Strong of Fayetteville, N. Y., who died in 1851, and in 1853 to Ophelia Wells of Hudson. His publications, besides the book mentioned, were contributions to the *Presbyterian Quarterly Review* and other periodicals, and sermons.

[Richard W. Darling, *Memorial of Pres. Henry Darling* (1893), containing valuable address by A. S. Hoyt, newspaper articles at time of death, resolutions of ecclesiastical bodies, etc.; Minutes Gen. Assembly Presbyt. Ch. New School and Presbyt. Ch. reunited, *passim*; H. C. Stanton, *Origin and Growth of Presbyterianism in Albany* (1886); C. E. Allison, *Hist. Sketch of Hamilton Coll.* (1889); *Biog. Record of Alumni of Amherst Coll., 1821–71* (1883); general biographical catalogues of Union and Auburn seminaries; *Hamilton Coll. Alumni Reg., 1812–1922* (1922).] R. H. N.

DARLING, SAMUEL TAYLOR (Apr. 6, 1872–May 20, 1925), pathologist and authority on tropical medicine, the son of Edmund Adams Darling by his wife, Sarah Ann Patterson, was born in Harrison, N. J. He passed his early life at Pawtucket, R. I., where he attended public schools and later became a druggist. His interest was thus aroused in medicine, the study of which he began rather late in life at the College of Physicians and Surgeons in Baltimore. He received the M.D. degree from that institution in 1903 and served there during the next two years as instructor in histology and pathology, being at the same time pathologist to the Baltimore City Hospital. In 1906 he joined the Isthmian Canal Commission under Gen. W. C. Gorgas [*q.v.*], and held the post of chief of laboratories at the Panama Canal Zone until 1915. During 1913–14, however, he went in company with Gorgas to investigate the sanitary conditions of the Rand Mines in Rhodesia. He received appointment in 1915 to the staff of the International Health Board, and during the next three years carried out investigations on the cause of anemia common among the people of Fiji, Java, and Malaya. Having completed this work, he accepted in 1918 the post of professor of hygiene and director of laboratories of hygiene at the medical school of Sao Paulo, Brazil. He returned to the School of Public Health at Baltimore in 1921, and in the following year became director of the field laboratory for research in malaria under the International Health Board of the Rockefeller Foundation. He went accordingly to Leesburg, Ga., where the chief laboratory was located, and continued to work there until his death.

Through his study of sanitation, Darling was one of those who made possible the construction of the Panama Canal. During his stay in the Canal Zone he identified the organism, *trypanosoma hippicum* (Darling), which was responsible for a fatal epidemic among mules and work horses, discovered its mode of transmission, and checked the epidemic which threatened to delay operations. While at Leesburg he made valuable additions to the knowledge of malaria, his emphasis upon the diagnostic value of splenic enlargement in early and in chronic cases being of particular value since it often disclosed unsuspected carriers ("The Spleen Index in Malaria," *Southern Medical Journal*, 1924, XVII, 590–6). His last published work was an article entitled "Comparative Helminthology as an Aid in the Solution of Ethnological Problems" (*American Journal of Tropical Medicine*, 1925, V, 323–37). He was a leading authority on the bionomics of the hookworm, introducing important measures for control of hookworm disease. He shared with Gorgas the distinction of being elected an honorary fellow of the Royal Society of Tropical Medicine and Hygiene in London, no other Americans being so honored. In March 1925, he left America to join the Malaria Commission of the Health Section of the League of Nations, of which he had recently been appointed corresponding member, to assist in a survey of the malaria conditions of Syria, Palestine, and Sicily. On May 20, he and another member of the commission were killed near Beirut, Syria, in a motor accident. He was married on Feb. 18, 1905, to Nannyrle Llewellyn.

[*Amer. Jour. Tropical Medicine*, 1925, V, 319–21; *Lancet*, London, 1925, I, 320–21; M. C. D. Gorgas and B. J. Hendrick, *William Crawford Gorgas, His Life and Work* (1924); *Who's Who in America*, 1924–25.] J. F. F.

DARLINGTON, WILLIAM (Apr. 28, 1782–Apr. 23, 1863), botanist, the son of Edward and Hannah (Townsend) Darlington, was born at Dilworthtown, Chester County, Pa. His early life was that of the hardy farm boy, and like John Bartram, his great neighbor of an earlier generation, he was observant at his plow of every weed and sapling. His early education was obtained under John Forsythe, one of the best teachers in the locality, and later he studied medicine under Dr. John Vaughan of Wilmington, Del. In 1804 he received the degree of M.D. from the University of Pennsylvania where he received splendid training in medical botany from Dr. B. S. Barton. In 1806 he was appointed surgeon on a ship clearing for Calcutta, and soon after his return, in June 1808, he married Catherine, daughter of Gen. John Lacey of New Jersey. When the War of 1812 sounded the call to arms, Darlington was appointed a major in the "American Grays," a unit of state volunteers, but did not see active service. During the remainder of his life he practised medicine, engaged in politics and finance, and gave himself to the avocation of botany, the one field in which his name will be long commemorated. His political services were of a minor sort; he was elected representative from his district to the Fourteenth, Sixteenth, and Seventeenth Congresses, and spoke against the extension of slave territory when the admission of Missouri was under discussion. In 1830 he was elected president of the Bank of Chester County, and for some years he was prothonotary and clerk of the courts. He served on the Canal Commission with Gallatin, being also a trustee of the Westchester Academy and an organizer of the Chester County Cabinet of Natural Sciences and of the Medical Society of Chester County. He enjoyed membership in forty learned societies.

Darlington's contributions to science were perhaps more highly esteemed in his day than the same works would be if produced at present. His *Florula Cestrica* (1826) and *Flora Cestrica* (1837) were models of careful natural history studies of a local nature, and were received with marked respect. More important at the present time are reckoned his *Reliquiae Baldwinianae* (1843), an excellent biography and collection of the works of William Baldwin the naturalist, and his *Memorials of John Bartram and Humphry Marshall* (1849), which, though the biographies are imperfect, constitute valuable collections of historical material relating to early botany in America. His *Agricultural Botany* (1847) was useful in its day and still, from an historical point of view, makes interesting reading. In 1859 he published *American Weeds and Useful Plants*. The impress which he made upon his science is not clearly seen in his works, and is only implied in the writings of his contemporaries. His fresh enthusiasm for his subject, his wide correspondence and friendship with naturalists throughout the country, made him a personal force and inspiration in his day. In his old age he was called by Asa Gray, "the Nestor of American botany," and there is no doubt that if he was not precisely the leader of American botany at any time, he enjoyed a position of unusual respect and affection. The inscription upon his tomb, composed by himself, conveys rather poignantly his love of the placid charm of the flora of his native county: *Plantae Cestrienses quas dilexit atque illustravit super tumulum eius semper floreant.*

[Washington Townsend, *Memorial of Wm. Darlington* (privately printed, Chester, Pa., 1863); T. P. James in *Proc. Am. Phil. Soc.*, IX, 330–43 (1863–64); *Bull. Chester County Hist. Soc.*, Sept. 1913; J. W. Harshberger, *Botanists of Phila.* (1899).] D. C. P.

DAVEIS, CHARLES STEWART (May 10, 1788–Mar. 29, 1865), lawyer, was born in Portland, Me. Ebenezer Davis of Haverhill, Mass., probably a descendant of an Amesbury family, had fought throughout the Revolutionary War and at its close settled in Portland, marrying Mehitabel, daughter of Deacon Ebenezer Griffin of Bradford, Mass. Charles, their only child, received his early education at the common schools in Portland. When his father died in 1799 the family was left in straitened circumstances, but his mother, a woman of strong character, was able to send him in 1802 to Phillips Academy at Andover, and in 1803 he entered Bowdoin College, which had been founded only the previous year. While there he read extensively and was known as "Grecian Daveis." He graduated in 1807 at the head of his class, and in the same year took up the study of law with Nicholas Emory of Portland. On his admission to the bar in 1810 he commenced practise in Portland, with which city he remained associated throughout his life. Though possessing no local influence he was energetic, of untiring industry, and a close student; and gradually acquired a good practise, specializing in Admiralty law, a department wherein it was said later that he had no equal in the state. His legal reading had been of wide scope, embracing both common law and the English equity jurisprudence, and when in 1821 the state legislature extended the equitable jurisdiction of the supreme court he secured a large proportion of the new Chancery business. In 1827 the long-drawn-out dispute with Great Britain over the northeastern boundary of Maine as delimited in the Treaty of 1783 came to a head, a United States citizen being arrested on his own land within the disputed area by the New Brunswick authorities, and Daveis was retained by the governor of Maine—a personal friend of his—to proceed to Fredericton, N. B., with instructions to demand the release of the prisoner and at the same time to procure all information possible as to the British encroachments. His mission failed, since the lieutenant-governor of New Brunswick refused to treat officially with an agent of the State of Maine, but on his return in January 1828 he presented to the Executive a long report embodying the information he had collected (*Maine Legislature, Jan. Sess., 1828, Document No. 18*). Shortly afterward the controversy was submitted to the arbitration of the King of the Netherlands, and, at the request of the United States minister to The Hague, Daveis was appointed special agent of the United States government to receive the evidence and present it to the arbitrator. He left New York, Jan. 11, 1830, and proceeded to The Hague, where he remained for a month, after which he traveled through England and Scotland, returning to Boston, Aug. 26, 1830. He at once resumed practise at Portland, declining a professorship at the Harvard Law School which was tendered him a short time afterward. In 1838 he was again retained by the State of Maine in connection with the boundary question. The award under the submission to arbitration had been unsatisfactory; nothing had been done by either government to adjust the controversy; and he was sent by the governor of Maine to Washington to urge the claims of the state. For two months he was engaged at the Capital, but only partially accomplished his objects. The following year, however, he was called to Washington by the federal secretary of state for a conference on the subject. In 1840 he was elected to the state Senate from Cumberland County, having been defeated the previous year, and as chairman of the joint special committee on the northeastern boundary prepared the able and exhaustive report of Mar. 30, 1841, embodying the claims of Maine (*Senate Report 19,* 21

Leg.). In 1842 the Ashburton Treaty finally terminated the controversy to which he had practically devoted fifteen years of his life. The ability which he had displayed throughout was warmly recognized by both state and federal authorities. He retired from active practise in 1850, and died at Portland, Mar. 29, 1865. On June 1, 1815, he had married Elizabeth Taylor, daughter of John Taylor Gilman, governor of New Hampshire.

In politics a Whig, Daveis had no desire for public office, and was never a partisan, though in 1848 he actively supported Taylor for the presidency. He frequently wrote for the current magazines on various subjects, but his only permanent contributions to literature were his extremely able reports on the boundary question.

[The chief authority on Daveis's life and career is the excellent biography by D. G. Haskins in *New-Eng. Hist. and Geneal. Reg.*, LI (1897), 141. See also W. Willis, *Hist. of the Law, the Courts and the Lawyers of Maine* (1863), p. 577; N. Cleaveland, *Hist. of Bowdoin Coll.* (1882), p. 153; *The Letters of John Fairfield* (1922), ed. by A. G. Staples, App. 1; and H. S. Burrage, *Maine in the Northeastern Boundary Controversy* (1919).] H. W. H. K.

DAVEISS, JOSEPH HAMILTON (Mar. 4, 1774–Nov. 8, 1811), lawyer, was the son of Joseph Daveiss, of Irish descent, and Jean (Hamilton) Daveiss, of Scotch ancestry. His parents were both born in Virginia and resided in Bedford County, from which they removed in 1779 and settled near Danville, Ky. Young Daveiss had no formal instruction until his twelfth year, when for some time he attended private schools in the vicinity of Harrodsburg. Here he made rapid progress in the classics and in natural science, largely impelled, it seems, by an ambition for distinction rather than a zeal for scholarship. Already skilful in fighting Indians, he took part in a campaign north of the Ohio at the age of eighteen. On his return he studied law under George Nicholas, and at twenty-one began at Danville the practise of his profession. In the winter of 1801–02 he argued the celebrated land case of *Mason* vs. *Wilson* before the Supreme Court of the United States (1 *Cranch*, 45). His associates were at first inclined to sneer at the uncouth backwoods lawyer, but he presented his argument so as to gain their respect and win the admiration of Chief Justice Marshall. His marriage in 1803 to the latter's sister, Ann, confirmed him in his Federalist leanings. In 1800 Adams had made him district attorney for Kentucky.

Early in 1806, shortly after Aaron Burr [*q.v.*] made his first visit to the western country, Daveiss called Jefferson's attention to his movements. Daveiss claimed that those who formerly had been concerned in the "Spanish Conspiracy," including Gen. James Wilkinson [*q.v.*], were reviving that project, and that Burr's activities had some relation to their machinations. His first warning was followed by other reports, and he became increasingly bitter in his charges against contemporary officials. Failing to arouse the administration to take the action which he regarded as necessary, he attempted to organize public opinion against the supposed peril by joining Humphrey Marshall and others in publishing the *Western World,* a sheet that bitterly attacked the alleged conspirators. Moreover, when Burr crossed the mountains a second time and visited Kentucky, Daveiss made complaint against him in the federal district court and tried to procure his indictment by a grand jury. In the course of two hearings Daveiss failed to establish the charge of conspiracy against the United States to separate the western states from the Union, or to lead an expedition against Mexico. Removed from office by President Jefferson after this failure, he vented his resentment in a pamphlet (*post*), which bitterly criticized the latter's conduct. If he and his associates had hoped to discredit the administration and build up a Federalist following in the West, their attempt was an utter failure. Shortly after this, he removed to Lexington, where he continued the practise of law. In the campaign against the Indians under Gen. Harrison he served as volunteer with the rank of major, was wounded in the battle of Tippecanoe, and died the next day. In addition to the pamphlet to which reference has been made, he also prepared an *Address to Congress* describing a proposed system for organizing the militia of the country.

[The pamphlet of Daveiss, *View of the President's Conduct Concerning the Conspiracy of 1806* (Frankfort, 1807), is a biased narrative of the events described, but affords an insight into the temper of the author. It may be supplemented by the manuscript autobiography of Jas. Taylor, Durrett Papers, Univ. of Chicago; and the letters of Taylor to Madison and Jefferson, in Madison MSS. and Jefferson MSS., Lib. of Cong. See also Maria T. Daveiss, *A Hist. of Mercer and Boyle Counties* (1885); Mann Butler, *A Hist. of the Commonwealth of Ky.* (1834), ch. 18; Chas. Warren, *The Supreme Court in U. S. Hist.*, vol. I (1922); *Quart. Publication Hist. and Philos. Soc. of Ohio,* vol. XI (1917); L. J. Bigelow, *Bench and Bar* (1857); *Harper's Weekly,* Apr. 27, 1867; Alfred Pirtle, "The Battle of Tippecanoe," Filson Club *Pubs.*, no. 15 (1900). The name is also spelled "Daviess" and occasionally appears in contemporary print as "Davis."] I. J. C.

DAVENPORT, EDWARD LOOMIS (Nov. 15, 1815–Sept. 1, 1877), actor, was born in Boston, the son of an inn-keeper, Asher Davenport, and his wife, Demis Loomis. In his youth he

Davenport

drifted from one commercial position to another, nursing an increasing desire to go on the stage. In spite of his father's aversion to such a career, he made his theatrical début, under the transparent name of "Mr. Dee" (Davenport), at the old Lion Theatre, or Brick Circus, in Providence, playing Parson Willdo in *A New Way to Pay Old Debts* to Junius Brutus Booth's Sir Giles Overreach. His first ten years in the theatre were devoted to playing every variety of character in the exhaustive and exhausting routine of the stock companies, and at the end of that decade he emerged a finished actor, in a position among the foremost young leading men of his time. He had headed companies in Boston, Philadelphia, and New York, and had toured with success throughout the country. His versatility was such that he had as yet made no particular rôle or type of rôle his own. In 1847 he went to England as leading man for Anna Cora Mowatt, with whom he played Claude Melnotte in *The Lady of Lyons,* Clifford in *The Hunchback,* Benedick in *Much Ado About Nothing,* and other standard rôles. When Gustavus Brooke joined the company, Shakespeare's *Othello* was revived, and Davenport and Brooke alternated in the rôles of Othello and Iago. Brooke, whose style was somewhat robust, had two years before made something of a sensation for himself as Othello, yet one critic, in writing of Mrs. Mowatt's revival, said that "when he [Davenport] plays Iago to Mr. Brooke's Othello, Iago is the ruling spirit of the piece; but when the cast is reversed Iago sinks to the level of a truculent ruffian, and Othello rises into the dignity of a brave, honorable and injured man." There were other comments in favor of "the American actor's superior discrimination, intelligence and good taste" (Edgett, *post,* p. 25). During his six years in England, Davenport added Shylock, Virginius, Hamlet, Richelieu, Wolsey, Brutus, Ingomar, and King Lear to his English repertoire, and, in spite of his many comedy and romantic characters, he became known as "the American tragedian." One of his successful comedy impersonations was William, in Douglas Jerrold's *Black Eyed Susan,* sacred in London's esteem to their popular comedian, T. P. Cooke. In this rôle he followed Macready's season at the Haymarket Theatre, with a first night's audience which included Charles Dickens, William M. Thackeray, Mark Lemon, and the author, Douglas Jerrold, himself. The performance was acclaimed with the same enthusiasm as London had already shown for his tragic characterizations. Davenport returned to America in 1854 and for twenty years thereafter sustained his position as one of America's leading contemporary actors. His health began to fail about 1874, and during the ensuing three years he acted infrequently, spending most of his time at his home in Canton, Pa., where he died. He was buried in Forest Hills Cemetery, Boston. Temperamentally Davenport had a natural dignity without austere reserve and was known for a genial, courteous disposition. Though his early education was limited he later in life became distinguished as "a scholarly actor." His wide versatility made it difficult to define his manner of acting, but he was acclaimed for his penetration and force in tragedy, his vigorous impulsive style in romantic rôles, and his intelligence in acting every character that he attempted. From the long list of rôles associated with his career those which emerged finally as the favorites were Shakespeare's Brutus and Sir Giles Overreach in Massinger's *A New Way to Pay Old Debts.*

While in England, in 1849, Davenport married Fanny Elisabeth Vining (Mrs. Charles Gill), a popular English actress. She was the daughter of Frederick Vining who, at the time of her birth (in July 1829), was the manager of the Haymarket Theatre, London. Her mother was the daughter of the Irish comedian, John Johnstone, and was a first cousin to Lester Wallack. Fanny Vining was carried on the stage as a baby in arms; she made her début at the Haymarket Theatre in 1847, as Juliet to the Romeo of Gustavus Brooke. After her marriage to E. L. Davenport, she acted with her husband as long as he acted, always in America after her début in New York, Mar. 2, 1855. Her last appearance was made at the Globe Theatre, Boston, Apr. 7, 1890, as Lady Macbeth. She died at her home, Canton, Pa., July 20, 1891 (see obituary in *New York Times,* July 22, 1891). The Davenports had nine children, seven of whom lived to grow up and adopt the stage as a profession. Of these, Fanny Lily Gypsy Davenport [*q.v.*] was the eldest and became the most celebrated.

[*Edward Loomis Davenport,* ed. by E. F. Edgett (Dunlap Soc., 1901); Anna Cora Mowatt, *The Autobiography of an Actress* (1854); *Actors and Actresses of Gt. Britain and the U. S.* (1886), ed. by Brander Matthews and Laurence Hutton; Lewis Strang, *Players and Plays of the Last Quarter Century* (1902); Montrose J. Moses, *Famous Actor-Families in America* (1906), which contains a Davenport bibliography; Eugene Tompkins, *Hist. of the Boston Theatre* (1908); Mary Caroline Crawford, *The Romance of the Am. Theatre* (1913); John Ranken Towse, *Sixty Years of the Theatre* (1916), esp. ch. XVI; Arthur Hornblow, *Hist. of the Theatre in America* (1919); H. P. Goddard, "Recollections of E. L. Davenport," in *Lippincott's Mag.,* Apr. 1878; E. S. Loomis, *Descendants of Joseph Loomis in America* (1908).]

P. W.

DAVENPORT, FANNY LILY GYPSY (Apr. 10, 1850–Sept. 26, 1898), actress, was a real child of the theatre. She was the daughter of E. L. Davenport [*q.v.*], one of America's leading actors during the nineteenth century, and Fanny (Vining) Davenport, daughter of an English actor and manager and herself an actress all her life. The eldest of seven brothers and sisters who all adopted the theatre as a profession, Fanny Davenport was born in London, in a house opposite the British Museum, while her father was in the midst of six years in the English theatre. Her parents brought her with them to America in 1854, and she went to school in Boston where the family made their home. "I cannot remember when I did not love the theatre," she wrote in *Lippincott's Magazine,* in October 1888; "and a passion for acting seemed born in me. When but ten years old I was constantly engaged in writing scenes (which my younger sisters would never study, much to my annoyance), arranging climaxes for acts, and planning all sorts of things to perform." She made her first public appearance as the child in *Metamora,* with her father's company at the Howard Athenæum, Boston, and thereafter she accompanied her parents on tour, whenever a child was needed being chosen to play the part. She spoke her first lines on the stage of Burton's Theatre, in New York City, Feb. 23, 1857. In these earlier appearances she was billed as "Miss Fanny." Always rather robust than petite, she was often cast for boy parts and actually made her début in an adult rôle as King Charles of Spain, in *Faint Heart Never Won Fair Lady,* with her parents, at Niblo's Garden, New York City, Feb. 14, 1862. Soon after this she left her father's company and began an independent career, acting first in the Louisville Theatre company as Carline in *The Black Crook,* and later in Mrs. Drew's company at the Arch Street Theatre, Philadelphia, where she attracted the attention of Augustin Daly [*q.v.*], who engaged her for his old Fifth Avenue Theatre in West Twenty-fourth St. She made her first appearance there as Lady Gay Spanker, in *London Assurance,* and met with immediate success. So began the second phase of her career. Here, and later at Daly's Globe and new Fifth Avenue theatres, she acted a wide variety of leading rôles in revivals of Shakespearian and other old English comedies as well as in new comedies. As she matured in this experience she developed a capacity for more emotional and dramatic rôles. Her success in W. S. Gilbert's *Charity* induced Daly to write *Pique,* in which she created the part of Mabel Renfrew, Dec. 14, 1876. The play ran for 238 consecutive performances. After this run she entered upon the third phase of her career by purchasing *Pique* and in it beginning a tour at the head of her own company. Gradually she accumulated a repertoire of Shakespearian and modern French works covering a wide range, though eventually she forsook her earlier comedy rôles for more emotional and tragic parts. In 1882 she attempted to establish herself on the English stage, and chose *Pique* for her London début, but met with little success. At that moment Sarah Bernhardt's performance of Sardou's *Fédora* had carried both actress and playwright to the zenith of their careers. With the American rights to this play, Fanny Davenport returned to New York, where she produced it with such success that she continued to act it profitably for five consecutive seasons. Thereafter, as long as she acted (with the exception of a brief ill-fated effort in a play on Joan of Arc), she played only Sardou's *La Tosca, Cleopatra,* and *Gismonda.* On July 30, 1879, she married Edwin H. Price, an actor in her company. They were divorced in 1888, and on May 19, 1889, she married Melbourne MacDowell, also an actor in her company, who became her leading man. He survived her. She was of a full-blown, buxom type, and strikingly handsome. There is no question of her wide popularity or of the eminence of the position she reached and maintained in her profession. Of her acting there is a variety of opinions, though all seem to agree in choosing Nancy Sykes in *Oliver Twist,* Fédora, and La Tosca as her best rôles. She died at her summer home at South Duxbury, Mass.

[Jay B. Benton in F. E. McKay and C. E. L. Wingate, *Famous Am. Actors of To-day* (1896); M. J. Moses, *Famous Actor-Families in America* (1906); M. C. Crawford, *Romance of the Am. Theatre* (1913); Arthur Hornblow, *A Hist. of the Theatre in America* (1919); obituaries in *N. Y. Clipper* and *N. Y. Dramatic Mirror* for Oct. 8, 1898. Fanny Davenport is best studied in the dramatic criticisms of the daily papers of her time. References are made to her in the published reminiscences of contemporary players, especially in those of Clara Morris, Mrs. Gilbert, John Drew, and Otis Skinner. There is an extended, but discursive and verbose, sketch of her in Lillie W. Brown ("Amy Leslie"), *Some Players* (1899). Some account of her childhood, over her own signature, appeared in *Lippincott's Mag.,* Oct. 1888.] P. W.

DAVENPORT, GEORGE (1783–July 4, 1845), soldier, trader, one of the founders of Davenport, Iowa, was born in Lincolnshire, England. As a boy he followed the sea, and came as a member of a ship's crew to New York in 1804. While his vessel lay in the harbor, he broke his leg in attempting to save a fellow sailor from drowning. This accident rendered him unfit for duty, and he was left at that city in the hospital. Soon after his recovery he enlisted in the United

States army, receiving an appointment as a sergeant. In the spring of 1806 his regiment was ordered to New Orleans where it was placed under the command of Gen. James Wilkinson. Davenport served as a soldier in the regular army for ten years, participating with distinction in expeditions into the Indian country and in the War of 1812. After his discharge from the army he was employed by Col. William Morrison of Kentucky, a government contractor, as his agent to supply troops with provisions. In the spring of 1816 he accompanied a body of troops from St. Louis to Rock Island, where Fort Armstrong was erected. Soon after his arrival at Rock Island he began trading with the Indians both in that part of Illinois and in the Iowa country, and in a short time built up an extensive and profitable business. In 1825 a post office was established at Rock Island and Davenport received the appointment as postmaster. In the fall of 1826 he quit independent trading with the Indians and became a member of the American Fur Company, having charge of the trade from the mouth of the Iowa River north to the Turkey River. He took an active part in the Black Hawk War, receiving an appointment from Gov. John Reynolds of Illinois as acting quartermaster-general with the rank of colonel. In 1833 he built the fine residence on Rock Island which is still preserved as one of the historic spots in this part of the Mississippi Valley. In 1835, he and a company of associates purchased a tract of land in Iowa opposite Rock Island. The new owners laid out a town which was called Davenport out of respect for their friend and associate. His influence with the Indians, particularly the Sauk and Foxes, was great. In 1837, he accompanied a delegation of Sauk and Fox chiefs to Washington and assisted in negotiating the second Black Hawk Purchase. Again in 1842 he was of considerable assistance to Gov. John Chambers in shaping the treaty by which the Sauk and Foxes surrendered the remainder of their land in Iowa. On the fourth of July 1845, while his family was absent attending a celebration, he was brutally murdered by a band of ruffians who planned to rob him. He was a man of a free, generous, and open-hearted disposition, pleasing in conversation, and full of wit and humor. He delighted to recount anecdotes connected with his wild and adventurous life.

[Franc B. Wilkie, *Davenport Past and Present* (1858), pp. 145–66; *Annals of Iowa*, 1 ser., VIII, 305–09; A. P. Richter, *Geschichte der Stadt Davenport und des County Scott* (1917); Davenport Collection, in Historical, Memorial and Art Building at Des Moines, containing valuable records of his activities as a fur-trader.]

B. E. M.

DAVENPORT, HOMER CALVIN (Mar. 8, 1867–May 2, 1912), cartoonist, was born at Silverton, Marion County, Ore., the son of Timothy Woodbridge Davenport, a politically minded farmer, and his wife Florinda Geer, daughter of R. C. Geer of Waldo Hills, Ore. Homer's mother died when he was but three and a half years old. The farm home was the scene of his early childhood. After various unsuccessful attempts to enter the business world, he finally obtained a position on the Portland *Oregonian* and, in 1892, on the San Francisco *Examiner*. In 1895, after three very successful years on the latter paper, he was brought by William Randolph Hearst to New York where his cartoons for the *New York Evening Journal* won for him an international reputation and caused him to become one of the highest-salaried men in the profession. As a cartoonist for the *Journal* he greatly influenced public opinion during the free-silver campaign of 1896, the Spanish-American War, and the second McKinley campaign of 1900. With the *New York Evening Mail* during the Roosevelt campaign of 1904, Davenport drew the noted "He's Good Enough for Me" cartoon, of which millions of copies were printed. His work was responsible for the attempt to pass an anti-cartoon bill in the New York legislature.

Certain of his creations, notably Mark Hanna's dollar-marked suit of clothes and the Trust figure—brutal, unintelligent, lawless, relentless—have been accepted as permanent contributions to the symbolism of his craft. His Uncle Sam also was one of the best conceived by any cartoonist. Despite the lack of formal education and technical training in art, Davenport made steady progress because of his ability to express his ideas with clarity and force, and to use the satirical touch skilfully. His first work of wide significance was the creation of C. P. Huntington as a comic character. He excelled as an advocate of municipal reform and is said to have done for San Francisco what Thomas Nast did for New York during the Tweed scandal. His picture, "The Boss" (Sam Rainey), duplicated the success of Nast's famous "What Are You Going To Do About It?" When Admiral Dewey was being criticized for presenting to his wife the house given him by admiring friends, Davenport's cartoon depiciting his victory in Manila Bay and bearing the significant caption "Lest We Forget," brought about a change of public sentiment which earned for Davenport the Admiral's lasting gratitude. Davenport attended the Dreyfus trial, making studies of the principal characters connected with it. He also caricatured prominent English statesmen. Returning to the

Hearst press, he joined the staff of the *New York American,* occasionally lecturing on the influence and work of the cartoonist. In 1898 he published *Cartoons,* with an introduction by John J. Ingalls. Other published works include: *The Bell of Silverton* (1899); *Other Stories of Oregon* (1900); *The Dollar or the Man?* (1900); *My Quest of the Arab Horse* (1909); *The Country Boy* (1910). As an avocation he raised horses, and he longed for an Arabian steed. Through a letter from Theodore Roosevelt to the Sultan of Turkey, he finally obtained twenty-seven Arabian horses for his farm at Morristown, N. J. On Sept. 7, 1893, he married in Chicago, Daisy, daughter of Robert A. Moore of San Francisco.

[*Overland Monthly,* Aug. 1912; *Who's Who in America,* 1910–11; *Rev. of Revs.* (N. Y.), June 1912; *Chicago Tribune,* Sept. 6, 1893 (marriage license recorded); *N. Y. Tribune,* May 4, 1912; Walter Geer, *The Geer Geneal.* (1923).] J. M. H.

DAVENPORT, IRA ERASTUS (Sept. 17, 1839–July 8, 1911), medium, was the son of Ira and Virtue (Honeysett) Davenport, and was the elder brother of William Henry Harrison Davenport, who was born Feb. 1, 1841. During the excitement caused in 1848 by the so-called "spirit rappings" of Margaret [*q.v.*] and Kate Fox, a number of children became the flattered objects of attention of parents alert for supernatural phenomena. Among these were the Davenport boys, in Buffalo. While tied with heavy sash-ropes in intricate knots—known later as the "Davenport ties"—they could produce sounds from musical instruments hung near them in a darkened room. Their reputation spread and they were brought to New York in 1855 but were soon exposed as mere sleight-of-hand performers and sent home. They then worked out a more elaborate program in which they were tied hand and foot at opposite ends of a large boxlike affair with doors. When the doors were closed, instruments hung in the cabinet were played, bells sounded, and "spirit hands" appeared in the small opening in one of the doors. The brothers were immediately successful in attracting public interest and in 1864 went to Europe where they became the center of excited controversy in which many prominent people took part. William M. Fay acted as their manager and sometimes substituted for William whose health was poor. J. B. Fergeson joined them as a lecturer, and later his place was taken by T. L. Nichols, both firm believers in the supernatural character of the Davenports' performance. At one time Harry Kellar traveled with them. During their stay in Paris, apparently in the spring of 1866, Ira married his second wife, Louise Toulet, having previously been married in February 1862 to Augusta Green who died soon after. The next year William was married, according to his father, to Matilda May in Königsberg, and, according to Houdini, to Adah Isaacs Menken, "the Bengal Tiger Woman," in Paris. The first tour abroad lasted four years. The brothers then toured America until 1874 when they started on a world tour that ended with the death of William in Australia, July 1, 1877. Ira was much broken by the death of his brother and retired to a farm near Mayville, N. Y. He made one brief attempt to "come back" with Fay in 1895, but it was without success and he returned to Mayville, where he died July 8, 1911.

The brothers, who looked much alike, were handsome men of medium height, with mustaches and goatees. Their cabinets and rope-ties were the fathers of many vaudeville acts thereafter. In a letter to Houdini in 1909 Ira wrote, "We never in public affirmed our belief in spiritualism, that we regarded as no business of the public, nor did we offer our entertainments as the results of sleight of hand, nor on the other hand as spiritualism, we let our friends and foes settle that as best they could between themselves." No such statements, however, have shaken the faith of certain groups who still consider the Davenports to have been possessed of supernatural powers.

[The fullest and most accurate account of the career of the Davenports is found in the letters written by the older brother to Harry Houdini, which are now in the possession of Mrs. Houdini. A brief account of the brothers and the Houdini-Davenport relationship can be found in Houdini's *A Magician Among the Spirits* (1924). See also *The Davenport Brothers* (1869), by Ira Davenport, father of the brothers, an amusing but not always accurate account; *A Biography of the Brothers Davenport* (London, 1864), by Thos. L. Nichols; *Spiritual Experiences, Including Seven Months With the Brothers Davenport* (1867), by Robt. Cooper.] K. H. A.

DAVENPORT, JAMES (1716–1757), clergyman, was born in Stamford, Conn., the son of Rev. John Davenport, great-grandson of the celebrated minister of New Haven, and Elizabeth (Morris) Maltby Davenport. He graduated from Yale College in 1732, one of the youngest men who ever took her degree. Remaining in New Haven to study theology, he was licensed to preach on Oct. 8, 1735, and three years later was ordained minister of the church in Southold, Long Island. Coming under the powerful influence of George Whitefield, he resolved to become an itinerant preacher. Calling his people together, he addressed them for twenty-four hours, and as a result was confined to his room for several days. He journeyed through New York and New Jersey, traveling part of the time with the great evangelist himself. The latter afterward said of him, "that he never knew one keep so close a walk with God." In 1741 Davenport conducted vigorous revivals in Connecticut in the settlements between Stonington and New Haven. Immersed in the spirit of the Great Awakening, he embodied the zeal, many of the virtues, and most of the unsafe extravagances of that revival. A man of considerable eloquence, he was a leader of those who claimed a special illumination of the Spirit and who trusted to impulses and impressions to guide their conduct. He denounced as unconverted the ministers who were opposed to emotional extravagances and urged their parishioners to withdraw from their unregenerating ministrations. In New Haven his influence was such that many members left the historic First Church and formed a new organization known as the North Church.

So intense was the excitement and so pronounced were the abuses connected with this revival that the General Assembly of Connecticut in 1742 passed an "Act for regulating Abuses and correcting Disorders in Ecclesiastical Affairs," treating as vagrants those who preached in a parish without the consent of the minister, or a majority of the church. A month later two inhabitants of Stratford entered a complaint against Davenport for disturbing the peace of that town. Brought before the Assembly at Hartford, he was judged not fully sane and sent back to Southold. Before the end of the month he was once more on his travels. On his arrival in Boston the ministers of that town interviewed him, and, being dissatisfied with his answers, declared against him. Davenport preached in the streets with such violent condemnation of the clergy that he was imprisoned by the authorities, adjudged insane, and sent back to his home. At the call of his church in Southold, a council of ministers met to consider his frequent absences from his church and his unusual behavior, and passed a vote of censure, but not of dismission. In March 1743 he went to New London, Conn., to organize a company of his converts into a church. To cure them of idolatrous pride in the things of this world he compelled them to bring their ornaments and fine clothes to be burned. Books whose teachings did not meet with his approval, by such men as Increase Mather, Colman, and Sewall, were also cast into the flames, the smoke reminding Davenport of the eternal torment which their authors must suffer in hell. This fanaticism led to earnest expostulations on the part of his friends, which, aided by a protracted illness, so sobered him that he wrote his *Confession and Retractions* (1744). In this he humbly confessed that he was led by a "false spirit" in severely judging his fellow ministers, in advising separations, in following "impulses," in encouraging private persons to exhort, and in his practise of singing in the streets. Dismissed from his church in Southold in 1743, he served various churches in the presbyteries of New Brunswick and New York, and was finally installed as pastor in Hopewell, N. J. This relationship being not altogether satisfactory, a petition was presented to the presbytery in 1757 for his removal. Before action was taken his stormy career came to a close.

[F. B. Dexter, *Biog. Sketches Grads. Yale Coll., 1701–45* (1885); A. B. Davenport, *A Supp. to the Hist. and Geneal. of the Davenport Family* (1876); A. E. Dunning, *Congregationalists in America* (1894); Leonard Bacon, *Thirteen Hist. Discourses on the Completion of Two Hundred Years*, etc. (1839); letters in Yale Lib.]

C. A. D.

DAVENPORT, JOHN (1597–March 1669/70), clergyman, author, was born at Coventry, England, and was baptized there in the Church of the Holy Trinity, Apr. 9, 1597, presumably a few days after his birth, the exact date of which is unknown. He was the fifth son of Henry Davenport who was mayor of Coventry, Warwickshire, in 1613, after having been chamberlain and sheriff, and who had married, as his first wife, Winifred, daughter of Richard Barnabit. The American compiler of the Davenport genealogy traces the family back in the direct line to Ormus de Dauneporte who was born in 1086. In any case the line was an ancient and honorable one.

As a boy Davenport attended the Free Grammar School of Coventry, at the age of sixteen going up to Oxford, where he apparently became a member of Merton College in 1613. (Mather says Brazenose in 1611 and there is some doubt.) After two years he transferred to Magdalen but left without taking his degree because he did not have sufficient money to continue. In 1615 he was preaching in the private chapel of Hilton Castle, near Durham, probably as chaplain to the Hilton family. He was there until at least March 1616 but after that the record is blank until June 1619 when we find him chosen curate of the Church of St. Lawrence Jewry in London. Here he became acquainted with members of the growing Puritan party and with some noble families, notably the Veres. In 1624 he was elected to the vicarage of St. Stephen's in Coleman Street, the adjoining parish, and one of the rare ones in which the parishioners had the right of electing their own vicar. The election met with much ecclesiastical opposition, and in a series of letters Davenport disclaimed any Puritan leanings and professed complete conformity. He was finally allowed to enter upon his work and in 1625 returned to Magdalen for a short time where he took his degree as Bachelor of Divinity. He appears to have been a faithful vicar to his flock, rendering particularly notable service when he remained at his post in London throughout the great plague of 1625.

It is impossible to say how early Davenport may have turned to the Puritan wing of the church but about this time we find him becoming closely associated with it. He appears to have become the spiritual adviser of that stanch Puritan, Lady Mary Vere, and in 1629 he was deeply interested in the procuring of the charter for the Massachusetts Company. Although not named as an incorporator, he contributed £50 and attended several meetings of the corporation. He became an object of suspicion to Laud from having been one of a group who had formed a plan of buying up certain lay impropriations in order to elect and provide ministers for such parts of England as most needed them. Innocent and even admirable as the plan was, its possibilities of erecting a sort of minor ecclesiastical organization within the larger one of the Church of England were obvious and it was impossible that it should escape the condemnation of the higher powers. The leaders were proceeded against, and the considerable amount of money already spent in the purchase of the impropriations was confiscated to the Crown, although personal criminal proceedings were dropped.

By 1632 Davenport seems to have definitely become a non-conformist, though still hoping that he might continue within the Church. He entertained John Cotton while in London on his flight to America, and talked over the problems of the times with him, but it was not until it was definitely known that Laud was to become archbishop that Davenport himself decided to flee the country. He resigned his cure and on Aug. 5, 1633 escaped from London into the country, crossing to Holland about three months later. Arrived at Haarlem he was invited to become the assistant in the Rev. John Paget's English church; but he objected to the baptism of children whose parents were not themselves leading Christian lives, came into conflict with the Dutch Classis, and was obliged to stop preaching within six months of his arrival. As usual, a printed controversy started, and Davenport, who had entered the lists before leaving England, published several pamphlets. Since he was unable to preach either in England or Holland, his thoughts now naturally turned to New England. His friend John Cotton had written to him of conditions there. Moreover the closest friend of his entire life from boyhood on, Theophilus Eaton the London merchant, had also been much interested in the founding of the Massachusetts colony. Davenport therefore returned to England, probably early in 1637, for the purpose of emigrating to America. Eaton decided to go also and as joint leaders of a new expedition the two set sail with their company, arriving at Boston in the *Hector* and another vessel, June 26, 1637. Meanwhile Davenport had married Elizabeth Wolley and had had a son John, born, it is said without proof, in London in 1635. The child was left in England and did not arrive at New Haven until 1639.

On arrival, the party remained in Boston about nine months, having reached the little town in the midst of the exciting Antinomian controversy, in which Davenport took part. For a number of reasons, they decided not to remain but to establish an independent colony, and in April 1638 settled at the present New Haven in Connecticut. Eaton became governor and Davenport pastor of the church in the new colony. Church and state were closely united and a New England clergyman was almost of necessity a politician, but, although never shirking his duties in that regard, Davenport seems to have been rather less aggressively political than most of the cloth. Throughout his life his biography is largely that of the colony, but he found time also to publish many tracts and small volumes on religious topics.

In 1661 the somewhat even tenor of his life was punctuated by a dramatic incident—the coming to the colony of the regicide judges Whalley and Goffe. Pursued by the vengeance of the returned Stuarts, the two proscribed men had landed at Boston and after a time, deeming it safer, had retreated farther into the wilderness. Davenport had generously paved the way for them at New Haven by a series of sermons and there they found refuge temporarily while the royal officers searched for them. It is said that for a month they remained hid in Davenport's own house. He, however, disclaimed all knowledge of their whereabouts in a letter which one of his Connecticut biographers says he wishes "for his sake were blotted out." About this time he also took part in the controversy which was rending New England and which resulted in the adoption of the "Half Way Covenant" to which he was strenuously opposed.

When Connecticut was applying for a new charter and it became evident that New Haven might be absorbed by its largest neighbor, Davenport began to take a more active and leading part in politics. On Oct. 17, 1662, he was one of the ten signers of a letter to the General Court of Connecticut asking for delay and that New Haven might remain a distinct colony until more definite news came from Winthrop. He spoke a number of times in meetings of the New Haven Freemen, strongly denouncing the proposed union, denying that they could be legally annexed or that they should ever voluntarily give up their independence. With Nicholas Street he was appointed to draw up the pamphlet called *New Haven's Case Stated.* [Reprinted as Appendix VII in Atwater's *History of New Haven,* 1881, pp. 566–95.] When the union was finally consummated he felt that Christ's interest was "miserably lost."

This failure of his life's work, as he felt it, was perhaps influential in his acceptance of a call which came to him, in 1667, to the pastorate of the First Church in Boston, following the death of John Wilson. The church in New Haven was opposed to his dismission. According to the prevailing ideas of the times, a church had almost a vested interest in its pastor, and without proper dismission officially from one church, he could not accept a call to another. Whatever his reasons may have been, Davenport evidently wished to go to Boston. The church there was divided on the question of the call, a considerable body opposing it, in part because of Davenport's position on the Half Way Covenant. Certain of the elders in favor of Davenport felt that the two letters sent him by his former congregation would not be considered adequate as dismission in Boston, and, with his knowledge, these were suppressed and a portion only of the second one was read to the Boston church. The true state of affairs was finally revealed and resulted in a great scandal. Davenport claimed, incorrectly, a certain amount of ignorance but defended the three elders and his own son, who he said had written the abstract of the letter. This episode was the most disastrous in Davenport's life, which it probably shortened. It had, as all religious matters then had, its political repercussions and, combined with the feeling over the Half Way Covenant, resulted in a split in the First Church and the founding of the Third. It was an example, and not the first, in Davenport's life, of his acceptance of the doctrine that the end justifies the means. The letters, however, from the New Haven church indicated a deep love and reverence for their pastor. He lived in Boston only a few months, dying on Mar. 11, 15 or 16, according to varying accounts, in the year 1669/70. He was buried in King's Chapel Burying Ground.

[There is no full biography of Davenport. There is a sketch of his life by Cotton Mather in his *Magnalia Christi Americana* (ed. 1853), I, 321–31. Leonard Bacon in his *Thirteen Historical Discourses* (1839) devotes considerable space to him in the naturally laudatory fashion of a fellow Congregational divine. A somewhat more scholarly account, with a bibliography, is given by Franklin B. Dexter in his "Life and Writings of John Davenport" in the *New Haven Colony Hist. Soc. Papers,* vol. II (1877). Many of the earlier accounts are conflicting, and Wood's life in *Athenæ Oxonienses* (ed. 1817) is inaccurate, as is also the genealogy in the *New-Eng. Hist. and Geneal. Reg.,* vol. IX. The descent of the family has been worked out by A. B. Davenport in *Hist. and Geneal. of the Davenport Family* (1851) and *Supplement to the History* (1876) which include a number of documents and letters. The letter written by Davenport and Eaton relative to planting the colony in New Haven, addressed to the Mass. General Court, has been reprinted many times, e. g., see *Mass. Hist. Soc. Colls.,* 3 ser. III, 165–67. For the incident of the suppressed letters and the call to the Boston church see H. A. Hill, *Hist. of the Old South Church* (1890), I, 12 ff., and *Proc. Am. Antiquarian Soc.,* n. s., VIII, 9–13. See also the general histories of New Haven.] J. T. A.

DAVENPORT, THOMAS (July 9, 1802–July 6, 1851), inventor of the electric motor, was born on his father's farm in Williamstown, Orange County, Vt., the eighth in the family of eleven children of Daniel and Hannah (Rice) Davenport. He had attended school but a few years when his father died, and he was forced to assist in the support of the family. When fourteen years old he was apprenticed to the local blacksmith with whom he remained for seven years. Immediately after the close of his apprenticeship, in 1823, he moved to Brandon, Vt., where he opened a blacksmith shop and prospered, as indicated by the fact that shortly after his marriage to Emily Goss of Brandon on Feb. 14, 1827, he "built a commodious brick house." The topic of conversation around Brandon in 1831 was a mysterious magnet (a Henry electro-magnet) used at the Penfield Iron Works at Crown Point, N. Y. When Davenport saw the magnet, he was overcome with the desire to possess one like it. Trading his brother's horse for a poorer one (without his brother's knowledge) to gain the necessary cash, he purchased an extra magnet which the iron works had for sale instead of the iron for which he had gone to Crown Point. He afterward made a larger one, his wife sharing his enthusiasm to the point of tearing up her silk wedding dress to insulate the wires. For some unaccountable reason he saw in the device a possible source of power, and with the help of a friend "handy with tools," by July 1834 he had built a little machine composed of four electro-magnets, two arranged as opposite spokes in a horizontally revolving wheel and two fixed, and the four connected up through a crude commutator to an electric battery. When current was applied the wheel revolved at a high rate of speed. This machine unquestionably constituted a complete embodiment of the principles of the modern electric motor. Upon the advice of a college professor of Middlebury, Vt., Davenport, with the financial assistance of friends, for he had totally abandoned his regular business during the preceding two years, went to Washington in 1835 to have his machine patented. By the time he reached there, having stopped at various cities to show his device to prominent individuals, his money was gone, and he made his way back to Brandon totally discouraged. Amos Eaton [*q.v.*] of Rensselaer Polytechnic Institute prevailed upon him, however, to demonstrate his motor at Troy, N. Y., that autumn, and as a result he secured some additional financial assistance. In the hope of obtaining sufficient funds to patent the motor and go into manufacture, Davenport spent the year of 1836 building and exhibiting a number of miniature machines, including one which is now recognized as the embyro of the electric trolley car. With the money thus raised, he applied for a patent, sending in a model, but all was lost in the Patent Office fire on Dec. 15, 1836. A second application and model were immediately submitted and Davenport received letters patent on Feb. 25, 1837. For the next six years he endeavored in various ways to establish a market, but never succeeded. He organized a workshop and laboratory in New York City where he was constantly engaged in improving and enlarging his machine, but one after another of his supporters deserted him. He undertook to publish a technical journal called the *Electro-Magnet and Mechanics Intelligencer,* for which an electric motor of his own design operated the printing press, but after a few issues this was abandoned. Finally, about 1843, he broke down physically, returned to Brandon, and three years later retired to a small farm in Salisbury, Vt. Here in the last year of his life he undertook successful experiments with an electro-magnetic player piano, but his death at the early age of forty-nine brought an end to this work. He was survived by two sons.

[F. L. Pope in *The Electrical Engineer,* Jan. 7 to Feb. 4, 1891; Waldemar Kaempffert, *A Popular Hist. of Am. Invention* (1924); D. B. E. Kent in *Proc. Vt. Hist. Soc.,* 1926–27–28; Patent Office records; U. S. Nat. Museum records.] C. W. M.

DAVENPORT, WILLIAM H. (1841–1877) [See Davenport, Ira Erastus 1839–1911.]

DAVEY, JOHN (June 6, 1846–Nov. 8, 1923), known as "the father of tree surgery in America," was born in Somersetshire, England, the son of Samuel and Ann (Shopland) Davey. From his father, who had charge of a large farm, he learned much in his boyhood days about elementary agriculture. Indeed, the farm was his school, for no formal educational opportunities were offered him. At eight years of age he began working ten hours a day, but instead of permitting his tasks to become drudgery he made them aids to learning and to physical and mental discipline. At eighteen a foreman superintending an estate, he could neither read nor write, but his own application soon remedied the lack. In 1866 he went to Torquay to make himself more proficient in horticulture and landscape gardening. After serving an apprenticeship of six years in those branches, he emigrated to the United States. Friends having preceded him to Warren, Ohio, he made that place his destination. For several years after his arrival there the country was in a period of financial depression. Davey's attempt to conduct a greenhouse and landscape-gardening business was unsuccessful, but after his removal to Kent, Ohio, he enjoyed steady prosperity for many years.

Davey was past fifty before he really struck his stride. His unusual knowledge of the vegetable world, acquired as a youth in England and continually broadened and amplified after he came to America, was gradually brought to the notice of estate-owners and others who needed his counsel. In regard to shade and ornamental trees, especially, he possessed a stock of information that seemed almost uncanny. It was the result of years of research and experiment. Once having grasped the importance of a better understanding of the care and culture of trees in America, he set out on a one-man campaign to advance the cause. In his early efforts to spread the gospel of tree surgery, he expended thousands of dollars. Bringing out his first book, *The Tree Doctor* (1902), put him in debt, and years elapsed before the practise of his new profession was in itself remunerative. After his service came widely into demand it was necessary to start at Kent an institute for the training of helpers. Later a research department was organized. This was intended to test proposed improvements in tree surgery and to furnish free information about the care of trees. Although two-thirds of Davey's lifetime was spent in preparation for his actual career, the progress made in the last twenty years was significant. At his death in 1923, he left a business of $750,000 a year. His methods of tree surgery were everywhere in use and his researches were regarded by scientists with respect. In addition to *The Tree Doctor* he published: *A New Era in Tree Growing* (1905),

Davey's Primer on Trees and Birds (1905), *Instruction Books on Tree Surgery and Fruit Growing* (1914), and various magazine articles on the subject of tree surgery.

On Sept. 21, 1879, he was married to Bertha A. Reeves, of Salem, Ohio. He left two sons, Martin Luther Davey, member of Congress, and Paul H. Davey, who carried on their father's work from the headquarters at Kent.

[Lester S. Ivins and A. E. Winship, *Fifty Famous Farmers* (1924), pp. 199–209; *Who's Who in America, 1922–23*; Mary B. Mullett in *Am. Mag.*, Aug. 1922; *Literary Digest*, Dec. 29, 1923.] W. B. S.

D'AVEZAC, AUGUSTE GENEVIEVE VALENTIN (May 1780–Feb. 15, 1851), lawyer, diplomat, was born in Santo Domingo, where his father, Jean Pierre Valentin Joseph D'Avezac de Castera, of French parentage, owned an extensive plantation. His mother, her husband's kinswoman, was Marie Rose Valentine de Maragon D'Avezac de Castera. The family being wealthy, Auguste was sent to Europe for his education and attended the College of La Flèche, France. In 1791 his two older brothers were killed in the Santo Domingo insurrection of that year, his father fled to Virginia, where he died of yellow fever, and the other members of the family escaped to Louisiana. On returning to America Auguste joined his mother and sister Louise in New Orleans, where the latter became, June 3, 1805, the second wife of Edward Livingston [*q.v.*]. He studied law in his brother-in-law's office and on admission to the Lousiana bar commenced practise in New Orleans. His knowledge of law was not profound, but he possessed an intuitive appreciation of the mental processes of the mixed Spanish and French population from whose ranks the average Lousiana juries were drawn, and he soon became known as an exceptionally successful advocate. Following the declaration of war against Great Britain in 1812 he joined the local Committee of Defense organized by Livingston and in December 1814 when Jackson assumed command of the forces in New Orleans he became the latter's personal aide, being also appointed judge advocate. In the subsequent operations his topographical knowledge was of inestimable service to Jackson, who twice specially commended him in dispatches. On the termination of hostilities he resumed practise in New Orleans, serving an extensive if not first class clientele, and was recognized as without a rival in the criminal courts, to which his work was mainly confined. He was constantly retained in homicide cases, where his Gallic eloquence had full scope, and it has been said that no client of his ever suffered capital punishment. During this period he retained the friendship of Jackson who, on becoming president, appointed him secretary of legation at The Hague, Aug. 11, 1829. Promoted chargé d'affaires to the Netherlands Oct. 15, 1831, he was, Jan. 30, 1833, appointed special diplomatic agent of the Two Sicilies and empowered to negotiate a treaty of general commerce, upon which mission he spent a year in Naples. Upon his retirement from the Netherlands legation, July 15, 1839, he settled in New York City and, becoming actively affiliated with Tammany Hall, was elected to the state legislature in 1843. On the nomination of President Polk he again became chargé d'affaires to the Netherlands, Apr. 19, 1845. Leaving the service Sept. 28, 1850, he returned to New York City, where he died a few months later.

Of outstanding natural ability and charm, enjoying the esteem and confidence of Jackson, and for thirty years closely associated with Livingston, who was his constant mentor and during his early diplomatic career his anxious adviser, he was a striking and distinguished figure in contemporary Lousiana affairs. Yet his career presents somewhat of an enigma. Perhaps because of too volatile a nature, an inconstance of purpose, or lack of high ideals, he never attained the eminence which his intellectual endowments should have assured. He was the author of the anonymous "Fragments of Unpublished Reminiscences of Edward Livingston," which appeared in *The United States Magazine and Democratic Review,* VIII (1840), 366.

[See C. H. Hunt, *Life of Edward Livingston* (1864), *passim;* Louise Livingston Hunt, *Memoir of Mrs. Edward Livingston* (1886); H. S. Foote, *The Bench and Bar of the South and South West* (1876), p. 194; *Louisiana* (1909), ed. by A. Fortier, I, 336; files of Dept. of State, Washington, D. C.; *U. S. Mag. and Democratic Rev.*, Feb. 1845; *N. Y. Herald*, Feb. 16, 1851.] H. W. H. K.

DAVID, JOHN BAPTIST MARY (June 4, 1761–July 12, 1841), Catholic missionary, theologian, and bishop, was born in Couëron, Brittany, the son of Jean and Jeanne (Audrain) David, humble tillers of the soil. Intended for the church, he was trained by an uncle, a nearby pastor, and entered the College of Nantes conducted by the Oratorians. On receiving his master's degree, he enrolled in the Seminary of Nantes where the notorious Fouché was a fellow student. Serving as a tutor on completion of his training, he joined the Sulpicians and was ordained in 1785. Thereupon, he was appointed lecturer in theology and Scripture in the petit seminary of Angers under Father Benedict Joseph Flaget. His quiet, studious life ended when the seminary was seized by the French Revolutionists. The faculty and students escaped with their lives, David finding a refuge with a courageous family of his acquaintance.

Father David besought Superior-General Emery to send him with the heroic Sulpicians who were embarking for the United States, and Emery gave his consent. David, Flaget, Stephen Badin, and Guy Chabrat arrived in Philadelphia (1792) after a stormy voyage of three months. Proceeding to Baltimore, David was assigned to the missions of Charles County, Md., where his spirituality and untiring labors won the recognition of his charges and also episcopal favor. Within four months, he was preaching in acceptable English. A strongly built man of middle height, full of vigor, active of mind, he made an ideal missionary, able to stand fatigue and buffeting. In 1804, he was called to teach philosophy at Georgetown College. Soon he was transferred to the Sulpician Seminary at Baltimore, from which he attended Charles Carroll's chapel on Doughoregan Manor. In 1806, the bishop wished to send this tried servant to take charge of ecclesiastical affairs in schism-torn New Orleans, but David was without episcopal ambitions and declined the doubtful honor. For a short interval he acted as superior of the spiritual and temporal affairs of Mother Seton's Sisters of Charity who had recently commenced their mother house and St. Joseph's College for girls at Emmitsburg, Md.

In 1811 he accompanied the recently appointed Bishop Flaget to his primitive See of Bardstown, Ky. It was a tortuous journey across the mountains to Pittsburgh and thence by flat-boat to Louisville and over the trail to Bardstown, especially as the missionaries were burdened by vestments, religious articles, a library, and a slave-boy. Only men of Gallic blood could visualize a bishop's palace and cathedral in the two-room log cabin. In Kentucky, there were only ten log-chapels, eight priests, and a few hundred communicants of doubtful practise. Growth was relatively rapid as Maryland colonists appeared and as public works brought Irish laborers. David proved a tower of strength to Flaget, as the business head of the diocese. On a donated farm near Bardstown, he and his Sulpician associates erected with their own hands a frame building which served as his seminary. In time this little Seminary of St. Thomas prospered and David's students became ardent frontier missionaries and in several instances renowned bishops. The older students were soon removed to the major seminary at Bardstown where in 1816 the corner stone of the cathedral was laid. A primitive school, nurtured by David, became the College of St. Joseph. He also aided in the foundation of St. Mary's College in Marion County. In the meantime, seeing the need of a teaching order of women he founded the Sisters of Charity of Nazareth with Mother Catherine Spalding as superioress. To the end of his life, he was their guide and benefactor, and it was with pride that he saw their mother house at Nazareth grow strong enough to establish several academies and send out hundreds of nuns as teachers and nurses.

For the diocese of Bardstown, it is well that Father David had successfully plead to Rome and Archbishop Carroll against an appointment to the See of Philadelphia. In 1819, lest he be removed, Flaget had him named coadjutor-bishop. David still continued as an active missionary braving all hardships, even heated religious debates with challenging exhorters. For them the spirited French scholar was a dangerous opponent, since the untutored auditors had a mysterious respect for his erudition and linguistic powers. He won the countryside and the town of Louisville by his sacrifices during the cholera days of 1831 when his priests and nurses aided the stricken, and cared for their orphans in the newly established St. Vincent's Asylum in Louisville. He was more than a missionary and builder, however; he was a writer of religious books and brochures in a region devoid of literary men. He contributed original articles and French translations on theological and philosophical subjects to the Cincinnati *Catholic Telegraph* and to the *Metropolitan.* Some of the writings of Bellarmine and St. Alphonsus Liguori are said to have been first rendered into English by his pen. His *True Piety* (1814) was long used as a prayer book; his compiled *Catechism of Christian Doctrine* (1825) served for a generation; his *Spiritual Retreat for Eight Days* was edited (1864) by his scholarly student Bishop M. J. Spalding: and his *Manual of the Religious Life* outlined the guide of conduct for the Sisters of Nazareth. In addition, he wrote several respectable brochures of a purely controversial and tractarian character. A student of church music, he issued in 1815 *Compilation of Church Music and Hymns.* He humbly resigned his bishopric in 1833, a year after he had succeeded Flaget, and thereafter had more time for study and missionary visitations. He was named representative to the Second Provincial Council of Baltimore (1833) where his views on church administration won general attention. Full of vigor, he continued active until his death.

[Sister Columba Fox, *The Life of the Rt. Rev. J. B. M. David* (U. S. Cath. Hist. Soc. Monographs, IX, 1925); W. J. Howlett, *Hist. Tribute to St. Thomas Seminary* (1906); A. B. McGill, *The Sisters of Charity of Nazareth* (1917); M. J. Spalding, *Sketches of Early Cath. Missions in Ky.* (1844), and *Sketches of the Life, Times and Character of the Rt. Rev. Benedict Joseph Flaget* (1852); P. K. Guilday, *Life and Times of John Carroll* (1922); C. G. Herbermann, *The Sulpicians in the U. S.* (1916); Ben J. Webb, *Centenary of Catholicity in Ky.* (1884); R. H. Clarke, *Lives of the Deceased Bishops of the Cath. Ch. in U. S.* (1872); *Cath. Encyc.*, IX, 387; *Cath. Herald* (Phila.), July 29, 1841.] R. J. P.

DAVIDGE, JOHN BEALE (1768–Aug. 23, 1829), anatomist and surgeon, founder of the University of Maryland, was born at Annapolis, the son of Capt. Davidge of the British army and Honor Howard of Anne Arundel County, Md. When he was a small boy his father died, and his mother resolved to apprentice him to a cabinetmaker, but his ambition to study medicine was gratified by aid afforded by friends and by the legacy of some slaves on the death of a relative. He entered St. John's College, where he received his M.A. degree in 1789, and shortly afterward began the study of medicine with Drs. James and William Murray of Annapolis. Continuing his education in Edinburgh, he specialized in anatomy, and received the degree of M.D. at Glasgow in 1793. About this time he married Wilhelmina Stuart of the Firth of Solway, several years his senior. For a short time he practised medicine in Birmingham, England, but soon removed to Baltimore. He played a prominent rôle in fighting the great epidemic of yellow fever in Baltimore (1797) and his views and work have been widely quoted (*Transactions of the International Medical Congress*, 1876). At the foundation of the Baltimore General Dispensary (1801) he was one of the attending physicians. From 1802 to 1807 he delivered private courses of medical lectures, and in the latter year he was associated with Drs. James Cocke and John Shaw in obtaining a charter for a medical school, known as the College of Medicine of Maryland. When the charter for the University of Maryland was issued (1813), this school became the medical department, and Davidge occupied the chairs of anatomy and surgery until his death. For a part of this time he was also dean. His first wife dying, he married Mrs. Rebecca Troup Polk, widow of Josiah Polk of Harford County, Md. He died in Baltimore of malignant disease.

His most important writings are his *Treatise on Yellow Fever* (1798), *Nosologia Methodica*, in Latin (1812, 2nd edition 1813); two volumes of *Physical Sketches* (1814 and 1816), *Treatise on Amputation* (1818), and an edition of *Bancroft on Fevers* (1821). He edited the *Baltimore Philosophical Journal and Review*, a quarterly journal of which but a single issue appeared (1823). His name is associated with a number of operations for which he was well known, including shoulder joint amputation (1792), ligation of the gluteal artery for aneurysm (he was the first to ligate this vessel), ligation of the carotid artery for fungus of the antrum, and total extirpation of the parotid gland (1823). His method of amputation became known as the "American." His lectures, said Prof. Lunsford P. Yandell, "were models of simple elegance," but "the moment he took his pen in hand he seemed to forget the English idiom," his style being obscure, stiff, and full of obsolete spellings and expressions (*Ibid.*, 234).

[The foregoing account is based on the several articles contributed to the *Hist. Sketch of the Univ. of Md.* (1891), *Medic. Annals of Md.* (1903), and H. A. Kelly and W. L. Burrage, *Am. Medic. Biogs.* (1920) by Eugene F. Cordell.] E. E. H.

DAVIDGE, WILLIAM PLEATER (Apr. 17, 1814–Aug. 7, 1888), actor, was born in London, at Ludgate Hill, the son of a merchant. When he was only nine or ten years of age he loitered about the stage doors of theatres in order to catch a glimpse of the actors and actresses, whom he considered more than mortal. When he was about fourteen, some one discovered that he could sing and he was immediately given vocal lessons. He made his stage début in June 1836, at Nottingham, playing Adam Winterton in *The Iron Chest.* Following this he filled engagements at the Queens, Victoria, Olympic, and Drury Lane theatres. In 1845 he gave an entertainment based on the works of Dickens, in whom he was intensely interested. Through mutual friends he later met the author and spent several happy evenings with him. He came to America in 1850 and made his first appearance as Sir Peter Teazle at the Old Broadway Theatre in New York City. During the next five years he supported many of the stage favorites of that time, then went on the road with stock companies and appeared in the leading American cities. From 1860 to 1868 he played again in New York City, appearing at various theatres. He was happiest when playing Shakespearian comedy. He joined Augustin Daly's company in 1869 and remained with him until 1877. Probably his most noted and important rôle was that of Dick Deadeye in the first American presentation of *H. M. S. Pinafore*, at the Standard Theatre in New York. In 1885 he joined the Madison Square Theatre Company and was traveling with them in Wyoming at the time of his death. In addition to playing eleven hundred different rôles during his career, he wrote a play, *The Family Party* (which Daly promised to produce but never did), articles for newspapers, and an autobiographical book, *Footlight Flashes* (1866), which possesses no literary value and contains little information. In 1859 he attracted some attention by a paper, *The Drama Defended,* written in reply to an article by the Rev. Dr. Cuyler attacking theatricals and theatre folk. Davidge was one of the original members of the American Dramatic Fund Association. On Sept. 30, 1842, he was married to Elizabeth Clark. For her and their three children he maintained as a home in Brooklyn a house he had won in a lottery in 1858.

[W. D. Adams, *A Dict. of the Drama* (1904), vol. I; *The Theatre,* Sept. 1888; obituaries in *N. Y. Tribune, Sun* (N. Y.), Aug. 8, *Cheyenne Weekly Leader,* Aug. 9, *N. Y. Clipper,* Aug. 25, 1888.] M. S.

DAVIDSON, GEORGE (May 9, 1825–Dec. 2, 1911), geodesist, geographer, astronomer, was born in Nottingham, England, the son of Thomas Davidson and Janet Drummond. In 1832 he came to America with his parents, who settled in Pennsylvania. He graduated first in his class, from the Central High School, Philadelphia, and in 1843 was appointed magnetic observer at Girard College, through the influence of Alexander D. Bache [*q.v.*], who had been a member of the High School faculty. His service in the United States Coast Survey began in 1845, when he went to Washington as secretary to Superintendent Bache, and ended with his retirement in 1895. He was sent to California in 1850, at the head of a party entrusted with the task of making an accurate survey of the Pacific Coast to meet the needs of navigation. The rest of his life, with the exception of the years 1860–66, which he spent in the Atlantic Coast service, was passed in the West. The first requirements of the survey were the determination of the latitudes and longitudes of prominent coast features, and the survey of harbors and harbor surroundings. Longitudes of principal stations were determined from observations of the moon's place among the stars and from occultations of stars by the moon; those of secondary stations by the transport of chronometers. Telegraphic communication was at that time not available. Data were so quickly and thoroughly assembled that soon he was able to issue his first "Directory for the Pacific Coast of the United States" for the use of mariners. (Published first as App. 44 of *Senate Executive Document No. 14,* 35 Cong., 2 Sess., it went through many later editions under the title, *Coast Pilot of California, Oregon and Washington Territory.*) Its great value came from the fact that the compiler had become intimately acquainted with all the natural dangers and possibilities of the coast. His experience enabled him to devise a much improved form of meridian instrument which was generally adopted for use by the Coast Survey. In 1866 he was ordered to make a survey of the coast of Alaska. His official report, first published as an appendix to the report of the superintendent of the Coast Survey (App. 18, *House Executive Document No. 275,* 40 Cong., 2 Sess.), was republished in revised and enlarged form as the *Coast Pilot of Alaska* (1869). In 1869 telegraphic signals were exchanged between Harvard College Observatory and a temporary observatory in San Francisco and the longitudes of Pacific Coast points placed on an accurate basis.

Davidson's work in applied astronomy gave him the incentive to contribute also to pure astronomy, and his reports and writings show that he always had this broader aspect of his work in mind. At various stations he observed several partial eclipses of the sun and, more elaborately, two total eclipses and a transit of Mercury. He was appointed to direct the observations of the transit of Venus, once in Japan (1874) and once in New Mexico (1882). From time to time he published catalogues of star positions. At the San Buena Ventura station, he observed 556 meteors in 1870. At a station in the Sierra Nevada Mountains he tested astronomical conditions and was much impressed by the advantages of a high altitude. This investigation bore important fruit when Davidson adroitly guided and defined the somewhat vague intention of James Lick [*q.v.*] to leave money for a great telescope, although the final selection of the site, on Mount Hamilton instead of in the high Sierras, was somewhat of a disappointment to the former. Before the Lick Observatory was built, Davidson had his own private observatory in LaFayette Park, San Francisco. Erected in 1879 and containing a 6.4-inch Clark telescope, this was the first observatory in California. Here, in 1891–92, he made a long series of observations of latitude pairs as a contribution to the puzzling question of the variation of latitude, and confirmed the results found elsewhere ("On the Variation of Latitude in San Francisco, Cal.," App. 11, *Senate Executive Document No. 19,* pt. 2, 53 Cong., 2 Sess.).

While his chief studies were in astronomy, his help and interest were always available in other departments of science. He was president of the California Academy of Sciences for many years and of the Geographical Society of the Pacific. He was an authority on the early history of the Pacific Coast. He was appointed a member of the Irrigation Commission of California in 1873, and the following year was sent by the federal government to China, India, Egypt, and Europe to examine and report upon irrigation and reclamation work. He served on the Advisory Harbor Improvement Commission for San Francisco, 1873–76, the Mississippi River Commission, 1888, and the United States Assay Commissions of 1872 and 1884. He was elected a Regent of the University of California, serving in 1877–84, and later was appointed honorary professor of geodesy and astronomy in the University. It is said that for sixty years his name was more familiar to the scientifically inclined on the Pacific Coast than that of any other resident. His interest in the concerns of his community was active and his personal charm brought him many friends. In October 1858 he was married to Ellinor Fountleroy of Virginia.

[*Reports Supt. U. S. Coast and Geodetic Survey; Univ. of Cal. Biennial Report of the President,* 1896–98 and 1898–1900; biographical sketches of Davidson by J. J. Gilbert and Wm. Churchill in *Bull. Am. Geog. Soc.*, Jan. 1912; R. S. Holway in *Univ. of Cal. Chronicle and Official Record,* Jan. 1912, and in *Science,* Feb. 16, 1912; Geo. W. Dickie, Ralph Harrison, and Samuel B. Christy in *Proc. Cal. Acad. Sci.*, 1914; W. W. Campbell, in *Pubs. Astronomical Soc. of the Pacific,* Feb. 1914; *San Francisco Chronicle,* Dec. 3, 1911.]

R. S. D.

DAVIDSON, JAMES WOOD (Mar. 9, 1829–c. June 15, 1905), author, journalist, was born in Newberry County, S. C., the son of Alexander and Sarah Davidson. His parents were in hard circumstances, but he early developed such a regard for education that he determined to pursue it even though he knew it would be necessary for him to work his way through college. Graduated from the South Carolina College in 1852, he taught Greek in one village or another, in Winnsboro for five years, till 1859, when he went to teach in Columbia. During the Civil War he was adjutant of the 13th Regiment of South Carolina Volunteers, serving in Virginia with the army corps of Stonewall Jackson. After the war he returned to teach in Columbia and to work as a graduate student at his alma mater. As late as 1868 he was still so impoverished that he was wearing his old army uniforms. Later he worked with newspapers, first for two years in Washington and afterward for ten years in New York, where he was on the staff of the *Evening Post.* In 1869 he published *A School History of South Carolina* and *Living Writers of the South.* In the former, while clearly holding orthodox Southern views, he succeeded admirably in the desire expressed in the preface, to be "as little as possible tinged with sectional feelings." *The Living Writers* is made up of specimen pieces from many Southern writers, accompanied by biographical and critical notices. It has been justly characterized as "incondite and curious, but interesting" (Wauchope, *post*), and it is certain that it is highly informative about important matters not to be learned of elsewhere. In 1884 he married Josephine Allen, a widow, and moved from New York to a home near Lake Worth, Fla. Two years later he was a member of the Florida constitutional convention, and in 1887 he was in the state legislature. In 1886 he published *The Correspondent,* a handbook for persons wishing to write conventional letters. Soon after this, he went to live in Washington where for a long time he was a clerk in the Treasury Department. In 1888 he published *The Poetry of the Future,* a critical volume which is undoubtedly his most urbane memorial. Learned without being pedantic, it exhibits remarkable perspicacity in its maintenance of rhythm as perhaps the only technical requirement of verse. His *Florida of Today,* the handbook of a sincere enthusiast, appeared in 1889. From the time of his preparation of the *Living Writers* to the date of his death, he was engaged upon a dictionary of Southern authors which comprised at last, it is said, 4,000 names. This has never been published. He also wrote a long but undistinguished poem, "The Bell of Doom."

[*Who's Who in America,* 1906–07, 1908–09; G. A. Wauchope, *Writers of S. C.* (1910); E. A. Alderman and J. C. Harris, *Lib. of Southern Lit.* (1909), vol. XV; J. C. Yonge, letter, Mar. 2, 1928; E. L. Green, letter, May 24, 1928; Columbia *State,* July 25, 1897, and July 3, 1905.]

J. D. W.

DAVIDSON, JOHN WYNN (Aug. 18, 1823–June 26, 1881), soldier, was born in Fairfax County, Va. His grandfather was a general in the Revolution, and his father, William Benjamin Davidson, served in the Florida wars and died in the service in 1840. After graduating from West Point in 1845, Davidson did frontier duty in Kansas and Wisconsin. Assigned to the Army of the West at the outbreak of the Mexican War, he participated in the battles of San Pasqual, Passage of the San Gabriel River, and the Plains of Mesa. After the war, again on the frontier, he took part in the Indian fights at Clear Lake, Russian River, and Sacramento River. In 1854 he defeated the Jicarilla Apaches at Cieneguilla, N. Mex., where he himself was wounded. In this hard-fought engagement, the American troops surrounded and captured the Indian camp, but while plundering it were in turn surprised by the Indians, who had escaped. Davidson was taken at such a disadvantage that his command narrowly escaped annihilation. He was promoted captain in 1855. At the beginning of the Civil War he was offered a commission in the Confederate service, but, though a Virginian by birth, family ties, and education, remained loyal to the Union. In February 1862 he was appointed brigadier-general, United States Volunteers, and commanded a brigade in the Peninsular campaign, participated in the battles of Gaines's Mill and Golding's Farm, and won the brevets of lieutenant-colonel and colonel for gallant conduct. He took part in the actions at Lee's Mills, Mechanicsville, Savage Station, and Glendale, commanded the St. Louis District in 1862, the Army of Southeast Missouri the following year, the Army of Arkansas in 1863–64, and was chief of cavalry, Division of the West Mississippi, in 1865. He participated in the Little Rock expedition, directed the movement of troops against Pilot Knob, Fredericktown, and Cape Girardeau, drove Marmaduke out of Missouri, commanded in the actions of Bayou Metre and Ashley's Mills, Ark., and received the brevets of brigadier-general and major-general for his services in the capture of Little Rock. On Jan. 15, 1866, he was mustered out of the volunteers and assigned to the 2nd Cavalry. He served in the Inspector-General's Department (1866), was professor of military science and tactics at the Kansas Agricultural College (1868–71), and held various commands in Indian Territory and Texas during the next seven years. On Mar. 20, 1879, he was promoted colonel, 2nd Cavalry, and served in the District of the Yellowstone and at Fort Custer, Mont. At the latter station he received an injury when his horse fell upon him, from the effects of which he died four months later while on sick leave at St. Paul, Minn. Though a strict disciplinarian Davidson was thoughtful and considerate of his men, and a popular commander. He married the daughter of George K. McGunnegle of St. Louis.

[*Asso. Grads. U. S. Mil. Acad., Ann. Reunion, June 12, 1882* (1882); G. W. Cullum, *Biog. Reg.* (3rd ed., 1891); *Battles and Leaders of the Civil War*, II (1887), 206; *Official Records (Army)*, ser. 1, vols. I, V, IX, XI, XIII; obituaries in St. Paul *Pioneer Press*, St. Louis *Missouri Republican*, June 27, 1881, and *St. Louis Globe Democrat*, June 30, 1881.] C. F. C—y.

DAVIDSON, LUCRETIA MARIA (Sept. 27, 1808–Aug. 27, 1825) and **MARGARET MILLER** (Mar. 26, 1823–Nov. 25, 1838), poets, were born at Plattsburg, N. Y., the daughters of Oliver and Margaret (Miller) Davidson. Their father, a doctor with cultivated tastes, was barely able to support his family; their mother, who had received the showy, superficial instruction in music, drawing, and belles-lettres then usual among girls of good family, was always in delicate health and was frequently confined to her bed for several months at a time. Seven of her nine children died before her. Lucretia Maria, an intelligent, affectionate, docile child. began to draw and to scribble rhymes in a chirography of her own before she had properly been taught to write. She was covered with shame when her papers were discovered and exclaimed over as evidences of unfolding genius. Her mother encouraged the child to write more and bestowed great pains on her moral, religious, and literary instruction at home. When the mother became seriously ill, Lucretia would act as housekeeper; at other times she read avidly and wrote rapidly, occasionally producing four or five copies of verses in a single day and standing, sometimes, rather than take time to sit down to her work. Finding the child's fondness for versifying was developing into an obsession, Mrs. Davidson forbade her to write altogether. Her daughter quickly grew depressed and nervous, and was allowed to resume her writing. She enjoyed several trips to friends and relatives in Canada; and through the generosity of a family friend, Moss Kent, a brother of James Kent the jurist, she was sent in November 1824 to Mrs. Willard's School at Troy. There she studied feverishly, but was already hopelessly consumptive and neurotic. The school physician attempted to restore her health with emetics and bleeding, and the ordeal of a public examination took what vitality was left. She was taken home sick, but her father, with the advice of another doctor, sent her to a school in Albany, thinking that she would benefit by the "change of air." She died of tuberculosis a month before her seventeenth birthday, her last words being an expression of gratitude to her benefactor, Moss Kent.

Margaret Miller Davidson was brought up to revere the memory of her gifted sister and early began, with her mother's encouragement, to emulate her. Her career closely paralleled Lucretia's, except that she was never sent away to school and that on an extended sojourn in New York she had—what her sister had never experienced—an evening at a theatre. Like her sister she read constantly and almost as constantly wrote verse that is indistinguishable from Lucretia's. She died of tuberculosis at Saratoga in her sixteenth year. The poetical remains of the two children and, even more, the story of their pitiable, exemplary lives made a strong appeal to the religious and moral sentiments of their generation. Distinguished writers were easily induced to furnish biographical introductions to their poems, and critical eyes suffused with sympathetic tears quite naturally mistook precocity for poetic merit. One reader, Caroline Southey, the wife of the Poet Laureate, even went so far as to address Mrs. Davidson in a sonnet that compared the grief of the mother over her two children to the anguish of the Virgin Mary at the crucifixion of the Saviour. As a matter of fact, the work of the Davidson sisters was what precocious verse is almost inevitably—an echo of the conventional poetic language and sentiment of its time. To the social and literary historian their writings and the full accounts preserved of their lives are of considerable value.

[Samuel F. B. Morse, "Biog. Sketch" in L. M. Davidson, *Amir Khan and Other Poems* (1829); Catharine Maria Sedgwick, "A Memoir of L. M. Davidson" in Jared Sparks, ed., *Library of Am. Biog.*, vol. VII (1837) and in various eds. of the *Poetical Remains* (1841, and subsequent eds.); Robt. Southey in *Quart. Rev.*, XLI, 289–301; Washington Irving, *Biog. and Poetical Remains of the Late M. M. Davidson* (1841, 1849, new ed., rev., 1852); *Selections from the Writings of Mrs. Margaret M. Davidson, the Mother of Lucretia Maria and Margaret M. Davidson* (1843); Edgar Allan Poe in *Complete Works of E. A. Poe* (Va. Ed., ed. by J. A. Harrison), X, 174–78 and 221–26 (original reviews in *Graham's Mag.*, Aug. and Dec. 1841); Caroline May, *The American Female Poets with Biog. and Critical Notices* (1848); R. W. Griswold, *The Female Poets of America* (1848, and subsequent eds.); *The Davidson Family* (a pamphlet of unknown source in the Library of Congress).] G. H. G.

DAVIDSON, ROBERT (1750–Dec. 13, 1812), Presbyterian clergyman, was born at Elkton, Md., and graduated from the University of Pennsylvania in 1771. While a student of divinity he was taken dangerously ill at a farmhouse and was kept alive only by the assiduous care and kind nursing of the farmer's daughter. On his recovery he ascertained that there was only one way to repay his benefactress. "Although she was older than himself, had not the slightest pretension to beauty, and moved in a humble sphere of life," wrote his son by a second marriage, "she made him for upward of thirty years an excellent and devoted wife." In his twenty-third year he was ordained by the Second Presbytery of Philadelphia. Until 1784 he lived in that city, teaching history in the University of Pennsylvania and acting as assistant to Dr. Ewing of the First Presbyterian Church. At the outbreak of the Revolution he spoke so frequently and vigorously in behalf of the revolting patriots that when the British occupied Philadelphia he found it prudent to retire unobtrusively into Delaware. In 1784 first appeared his *Geography Epitomized; or, a Tour round the World: Being a short but comprehensive Description of the Terraqueous Globe attempted in Verse for the Sake of the Memory: And principally designed for the Use of Schools.* Other editions of the pamphlet, with its ingenious rhymes, were published in London in 1787 and at Burlington, N. J., in 1791. In November 1784 he was called to Carlisle, Pa., in the double capacity of professor of history, geography, chronology, rhetoric, and belles-lettres in Dickinson College and of pastor of the Presbyterian Church. There for twenty-eight years he served church, state, and school with his extensive learning and his sterling private character. Acquainted with eight languages, well read in theology and in the sciences he had studied at Franklin's college, he was particularly fond of astronomy. In 1794 with mingled tact and resolution he upheld law and order against the Whiskey Insurrectionists. In 1796 he was chosen moderator of the General Assembly of the Presbyterian Church. From Dr. Nisbet's death in 1804 until 1809 he was president of Dickinson College, resigning to devote his time to his ministerial duties. His second wife, Margaret Montgomery of Carlisle, died in 1809, and on Apr. 17, 1810, he married Jane Harris, who survived him. In 1811 he published *The Christian's A. B. C., or the 119th psalm in metre, each octave commencing with the appropriate letter of the alphabet, with the exception of Q, X, and Z.* In the year of his death appeared a *New Metrical Version of the Psalms,* which his son rates above Sternhold and Hopkins but below Watts. He left behind him twenty manuscript volumes of sermons and scientific lectures, for, strangely diffident of his powers, he always entered pulpit or classroom with his discourse completely written out.

[Article by Davidson's son in W. B. Sprague, *Annals of the Am. Pulpit*, vol. III (1858); *The Centennial Memorial of the Presbytery of Carlisle* (2 vols., 1889); A. Nevin, *Churches of the Valley or an Hist. Sketch of the Old Presbyt. Congregations of Cumberland and Franklin Counties in Pa.* (1852) and *Men of Mark of Cumberland Valley, Pa., 1776–1876* (1876); incidental mention in S. Miller, *Memoir of the Rev. Charles Nisbet, D.D.* (1840), pp. 158, 228, 288–96; *Gen. Alumni Cat. of the Univ. of Pa.* (1917); R. Davidson, *A Sermon on the Freedom and Happiness of the U. S. A., preached in Carlisle on the 5th Oct. 1794 before President Washington, Gov. Mifflin, etc.* (1794); J. C. Fitzpatrick, *The Diaries of Geo. Washington, 1748–99* (1925), IV, 212.] G. H. G.

DAVIDSON, THOMAS (Oct. 25, 1840–Sept. 14, 1900), philosopher and wandering scholar, was born in the parish of Old Deer in Aberdeenshire, Scotland. He came of very humble antecedents, his father, Thomas Davidson, being a small farmer, and his mother, Mary Warrender, of sturdy peasant stock. She was a stern disciplinarian, and a woman of deep piety and resolute will, qualities which were but intensified in her son Thomas. He was from the first avid of learning and eagerly devoured all the books he could lay hands upon. Games and sports played no part in his life, but Baxter's *Saints' Rest* was his delight. The reading of this book marked an epoch in his life. It gave him a sense of religious exaltation and illumination that transformed his world, and left an indelible impression of the sublimity of human life and its infinite possibilities for weal or woe. At the same time his never-failing and contagious good humor made him a general favorite with his companions, old and young. He was prepared for college by Robert Wilson, the parish schoolmaster of Old Deer, who, discovering the making of a scholar in him, took him into his home and treated him as a son, helping him in his studies every evening in return for his assistance during the day in teaching the junior classes in school. At the age of sixteen he entered King's College, Aberdeen, having won a four-year scholarship in the Bursary Competition. Here he acquired, as a second nature, the habit of exact and thorough scholarship. He distinguished himself especially in the classics, carrying off the highest honors in Greek, the Simpson prize, on his graduation in 1860. After serving for three years as rector of the Old Aberdeen Grammar School, he went to England and taught Latin and Greek, first at Tunbridge Wells and later at Wimbledon. In 1866 he moved to Canada where he taught for a year in the Collegiate Institute of London, Ontario. He then came to the United States, and, after a short stay in Boston, where he fell among the radicals, with whom he cordially sympathized, he accepted a position in the public schools of St. Louis, where he was soon promoted to the principalship of a branch high school. Here he made the acquaintance of that famous group of enthusiastic Hegelian philosophers whose leader, W. T. Harris [*q.v.*], became his intimate and life-long friend. The influence of this group was profound and lasting, although Davidson himself could never find anything in Hegel. They convinced him of the shallowness of positivism, which had all but caught him in the stormy years of doubt that had followed his college career; sent him back to the study of German thought, and through that to the deeper study of Plato and especially of Aristotle who remained for him to the end "the master of those who know"; and they gave him a better appreciation of the educational value of art and literature when interpreted philosophically.

But Davidson was a radical individualist and a born dissenter, and could not and would not fit into any niche. He chafed under all restraint, and was not entirely contented until, after removing to Boston in 1875, he found his liberty in the life of a free lance and wandering scholar, gaining a modest livelihood by teaching private classes, tutoring, lecturing, writing, while holding himself responsible to himself alone. His mode of life gave him six months of every year for leisurely study and frequent opportunities for long visits to Europe. He took extended walking tours through Greece where he gained a vivid appreciation and a thorough and intimate knowledge of ancient Hellenic art and culture. From 1878 to 1884 most of his time was spent in Domo d' Ossola, Italy, in close contact with the members of the Rosminian order. Here he lived the life of a hermit, devoting himself to the study of the writings of Rosmini, in which he felt that he had at last found the philosophy that all his life he had been seeking, one that justified the claims of the intellect and provided an adequate ground for a spiritual, religious interpretation of life. At the same time he carried further his researches into the whole period of scholastic philosophy. His own philosophy underwent further development in later years, but never wholly lost the Rosminian stamp. If it must be described in a word it might be said to be a form of pluralistic idealism (apeirotheism, he sometimes called it), coupled with a stern ethical rigorism,—but all labels are misleading.

While studying in Italy he seriously contemplated joining the Catholic Church, but he could not bring himself to accept the dogmas. Nevertheless the practical activities of his later life were given direction by this experience. Their common purpose was the organization of the spiritual life, but on the basis of philosophical insight rather than of dogma. During a brief sojourn in London in 1883, he founded the Fellowship of the New Life, of which the Fabian Society was an offshoot. Later he established a branch of the Fellowship in New York, and a Summer School for the Culture Sciences, held first at St. Cloud, N. J., then at Farmington, Conn., and finally on a farm that he had bought in the Adirondacks near the village of Keene, N. Y. None of these undertakings proved entirely satisfactory and it was only toward the end of his life that he stumbled, almost by chance, upon the opportunity to carry out his ideal in a way that seemed to him altogether encouraging. In association with the People's Institute and the Educational Alliance of New York he gathered together a group of eager, earnest young men and women from the lower East Side and organized a Bread-Winners' College inspired by the idea of helping the wage-earners to share in the best culture of the ages and to rise to a higher level of mental and spiritual power.

Davidson had a prodigious memory; he seemed never to forget anything he had ever read. He spoke nearly all the languages of Europe except Slavic with fluency, including Latin and modern Greek. The range of his learning was vast, and his scholarship accurate and thorough. Yet he carried this load lightly, and with all modesty, and prized it only for its value in pointing the way to a nobler life for himself and for others, to whom he was ever ready to give himself without stint. It is perhaps chiefly as a great personal force that his influence has been manifest. He had a vivid and exuberant personality and a genius for friendship, and he carried with him an air of elevation which came from his constant association with the saints and seers of all times.

Davidson was a frequent contributor to philosophical periodicals, especially the *Journal of Speculative Philosophy,* and also wrote for the *Radical* (Boston), the *Round Table* (New York), and the *Western Educational Review* (St. Louis), of which for a time he was editor. His published works include: *The Philosophical System of Antonio Rosmini-Serbati,* with a sketch of Rosmini's life (1882); *The Parthenon Frieze and Other Essays* (1882); *Scartazzini's Handbook to Dante,* with notes and additions (1887); *Prolegomena to In Memoriam* (1889); *Aristotle and Ancient Educational Ideals* (1892); *Education of the Greek People, and its Influence on Civilization* (1894); *Rousseau and Education According to Nature* (1898); *A History of Education* (1900); translation of Rosmini's *Psychology* (1883).

[Wm. A. Knight, *Some Nineteenth Century Scotsmen; Being Personal Recollections* (1902), and *Memorials of Thos. Davidson* (1907); Wm. James, art. on Davidson in *Memories and Studies* (1911); Morris R. Cohen, in *A Cyc. of Education,* vol. II (1911); personal recollections, and unpublished letters and MSS.]

C. M. B.

DAVIDSON, WILLIAM LEE (1746–Feb. 1, 1781), Revolutionary soldier, was born in Lancaster County, Pa., the son of George Davidson, who, in 1750, settled in Rowan (now Iredell) County, N. C. He was educated in the rural schools and then attended Queen's Museum College in Charlotte. He married in early life Mary Brevard, the sister of Dr. Ephraim Brevard, reputed author of the Mecklenburg Declaration of 1775. After serving on the Rowan County Committee of Safety, he was appointed major of the 4th North Carolina Regiment (1776) and marched north under Gen. Francis Nash to join Washington's army in New Jersey. For gallant conduct in the battle of Germantown he was promoted to lieutenant-colonel (1777). In November 1779 the North Carolina line was detached and ordered to reinforce the southern army. Davidson stopped in North Carolina to visit his family and upon his arrival at Charleston found the city so closely invested that he was unable to rejoin his regiment. After the surrender of Gen. Lincoln he returned to Mecklenburg, where he commanded the local militia in its efforts to subdue uprisings of the Loyalists, who were much encouraged by the success of the British in the South. While proceeding vigorously in this service he was severely wounded in an engagement at Coulson's Mill on the Yadkin in the summer of 1780. He was then promoted to brigadier-general of militia, in command of the Salisbury district. After defeating Tarleton at the battle of Cowpens, Gen. Morgan began retreating northward with great celerity, pursued by Cornwallis. Davidson, commanding the hastily assembled local militia, called by Cornwallis "Gang of Plunderers," was ordered by Greene to guard the fords of the Catawba, after Morgan's passage. Early on the morning of Feb. 1, 1781, Cornwallis crossed the river at Cowan's (or McCowan's) Ford, in spite of a "galling and constant fire" from the Americans. Davidson, with the majority of his forces, was some distance away, and arrived too late to prevent the passage of the British. He was killed and his troops were dispersed. Gen. Henry Lee wrote that the loss of Davidson was "particularly detrimental" at that time, "as he was the chief instrument relied upon by Greene for the assemblage of the militia" (*Memoirs,* I, 398). A monument to his memory was voted by the Continental Congress (Sept. 20, 1781) but the money was not appropriated by Congress until 1903. The monument has since been erected on the Guilford Court House battle-field. His name is also perpetuated in Davidson College in his adopted state, and in counties in North Carolina and Tennessee.

[*Jours. of the Continental Cong.,* Sept. 20, 1781; *N. C. State Records* (1895); Banastre Tarleton, *Hist. of the Campaigns of 1780 and 1781 in the Southern Provinces of North America* (1787); Chas. Stedman, *Hist. of the Origin, Progress and Termination of the Am. War* (1794); Henry Lee, *Memoirs of the War in the Southern Dept. of the U. S.* (1812); Wm. Johnson, *Sketches of the Life and Correspondence of Nathanael Greene* (1822); J. H. Wheeler, *Hist. Sketches of N. C.* (1851); Jas. Graham, *Life of Gen. Daniel Morgan of the Va. Line* (1856); C. L. Hunter, *Sketches of Western N. C., Hist. and Biog.* (1877); Robt. Henry, *Narrative of the Battle of Cowan's Ford* (1891); F. B. Heitman, *Hist. Reg. of Officers of the*

Continental Army (1893); Wm. A. Graham, *Gen. Jos. Graham and His Papers on N. C. Revolutionary Hist.* (1904); S. A. Ashe, *Biog. Hist. of N. C.*, vol. IV (1906).]

F. E. R.

DAVIE, WILLIAM RICHARDSON (June 20, 1756–Nov. 29, 1820), Revolutionary soldier, governor of North Carolina, was born at Egremont, Cumberlandshire, England. Taken by his father, Archibald Davie, to the Waxhaw settlement, S. C., in 1763, he was there adopted by his maternal uncle, William Richardson, a Presbyterian clergyman. He attended Queen's Museum College, Charlotte, N. C., and Princeton, where, after about four years of study and a bit of military service in New York, he graduated with first honors in 1776. Though he at once began to study law at Salisbury, N. C., and was licensed to practise in 1780, he chiefly pursued war during the next seven years. After three months' service under Gen. Allen Jones in the Camden region during 1777–78, he helped raise a troop of cavalry near Salisbury and received successive commissions as lieutenant, captain, and major. Joining Pulaski's division, he was seriously wounded on June 20, 1779, while leading a charge at Stono, near Charleston. After a slow recovery he raised another troop early in the next year, equipping it partly from a bequest from his uncle. Operating north of Waxhaw Creek, independently or with Sumter, he kept the Patriot cause alive in western North Carolina despite Tarleton and the numerous Loyalists. When Gates fled from Camden, Davie, now a colonel, acting contrary to that general's orders, thrust his little command to the rear, saved valuable equipment, fought a reckless but brilliant rear-guard action at Charlotte on Sept. 26, 1780, and continued to harass Cornwallis until the latter retreated into South Carolina in October. Having in these glorious six months proved himself not only a daring and skilful individual fighter but also an alert and resourceful commander, Davie was seeking a separate command when Gen. Greene enlisted him as commissary-general for the Carolina campaign and procured his appointment in a similar capacity by the North Carolina Board of War on Jan. 16, 1781. Though almost without funds, he succeeded in feeding Greene's army and the state militia to the satisfaction of that general, who liked him and kept him with him from Guilford Court House to Ninety-six (March–May 1781). Davie detested his work and resented bitterly the inevitable criticism, but persisted in the office until it was discontinued and his voluminous accounts were fully made up.

Settling at Halifax, N. C., in 1782, he married Sarah Jones, daughter of his old commander and niece of Willie Jones, who brought him a fine farm and eventually bore him six children. For the next fifteen years he rode the circuits of the state, save the westernmost, as a lawyer. Soon he was appearing in all the important civil cases, and for the defense in every capital case. Men ranked him with Alfred Moore as first of an able bar. Since he liked to argue broad principles rather than precedents, he was helpful in the necessary adjustment of the old law to the new situation. With the instinct of a military man he found the strong points in the case, and brought to bear on them a studied oratory. Tall, elegant, and commanding, he had a mellow and flexible voice and a "lofty and flowing" style which became him well and "astounded and enraptured" his audiences (Hubbard, *post*, p. 83). Representing the borough of Halifax in the legislature of North Carolina almost continuously from 1786 to 1798, he more than any one else was responsible for the action of that body in ordering the revision and codification of the laws, the sending of representatives to the constitutional conventions at Annapolis and Philadelphia, the cession of Tennessee to the Union, and endeavoring to fix disputed state boundaries. He was chiefly responsible for the establishment, location, building, and endowment of the University of North Carolina, selected its instructors and planned for it an elastic curriculum that included literary and social studies as well as the familiar mathematics and classics. As Grand Master of the Masons he laid the cornerstone of its first two buildings. The University, in turn, awarded him its first honorary degree and dubbed him "father," years before Jefferson's intellectual child, the University of Virginia, was born. The state made him commander of its troops in 1797, chairman of its boundary commissions, and governor in 1798.

These honors and achievements can by no means be ascribed to politics; for North Carolina was thoroughly Democratic and Davis was not. In the Federal Convention, though he represented a large state, he swung his delegation to the "Connecticut Compromise," lest the movement for stronger government fail. He there favored election of senators and later of presidential electors by the legislature, and strenuously insisted on representation for slave property. In the fight for ratification in North Carolina he was second only to Iredell. While governor he denounced the Virginia and Kentucky Resolutions and accepted appointment from President Adams, first as brigadier-general for the French War, and in 1799 as peace commissioner to France. Returning after an enjoyable year, he advised against Federalist support of Burr as bad policy, but urged the appointment of popular and active men as federal judges since the cause of Federalism depended on their exertions. Under presidential appointment, he negotiated the Tuscarora treaty in 1802 but otherwise waved aside overtures from "that man" Jefferson. His political attitude seems to have been grounded originally on contempt for the war boards, the judges, and the legislators whom democracy thrust up; it was confirmed by the subservience of politicians to Virginia leadership. Refusing either to modify his aristocratic habits or to solicit votes personally, he was eliminated from politics by the Jefferson-Macon machine in the important congressional election of 1803. Disgusted with politics and saddened by the loss of his wife, he retired in 1805 to his plantation, "Tivoli," in Lancaster County, S. C., where he could enjoy farming, friends, horses, and books, and give an occasional bit of advice to his university or make a biting remark about North Carolina politicians. He was the first president of the South Carolina Agricultural Society. Though long an admirer of Madison, he declined appointment as major-general in 1813 and defended the conduct of the New England Federalists during the War of 1812.

[F. W. Hubbard, "Life of W. R. Davie," in Jared Sparks, *The Lib. of Am. Biog.*, ser. 2, vol. XV (1848), an uncritical work but based on papers now lost; sketch by J. G. de R. Hamilton, and letters with notes by Kemp P. Battle in *Jas. Sprunt Hist. Monographs*, No. 7 (1907); Walter Clark in W. J. Peele, *Lives of Distinguished North Carolinians* (1898), for Davie's career as soldier and lawyer; Wm. K. Boyd, *Hist. of N. C., 1783–1860*, vol. II (1919), for his services in the Federal Convention; H. M. Wagstaff, in *Proc. N. C. Lit. and Hist. Asso.*, 1920, for his Federalism; S. A. Ashe, *Biog. Hist. of N. C.*, vol. VI (1905), which should be read in connection with Wm. E. Dodd's sketch of Willis Alston in same work.] C. C. P.

DAVIES, ARTHUR BOWEN (Sept. 26, 1862–Oct. 24, 1928), painter, was born in Utica, N. Y. His father was a Welsh immigrant, David Thomas Davies, who brought his English wife, Phœbe Loakes, to America, set up a tailor's shop, and interested himself in the Welsh church, and especially in its choir. The marriage was blessed with five children of which Arthur was the fourth. He passed a free and happy boyhood, roving the rich meadows and river terraces of the Mohawk, observing its trees, its windswept vast skies, and the distant rim of its blue hills. He began to draw early, and his parents sympathetically encouraged his bent, putting him under the tutelage of a local painter, Dwight Williams, who, with prophetic intuition of Davies's genius, confined his teaching to sharpening the boy's naturally keen and accurate vision and inculcating broad principles of composition. Soon the family moved to Chicago, and the youth found casual employment in business with the Board of Trade, working also for a time with an engineering expedition in Mexico. Returning to Chicago after two years in the West, Davies with three young painters undertook and achieved the copying of Munkacsy's gigantic painting of "Christ before Pilate," in the hope that the group might raise money for European study through its exhibition in circuit. The plan failed, but at least it demonstrated that tenacity and athleticism which were no small part of Davies's artistic endowment.

Before and after his two years in Mexico and the West, Davies had studied with Charles Corwin at the Chicago Art Institute. In 1887 he sought new fortunes at New York, pursuing his studies with the Gotham Art Students and at the Art Student's League. Davies's cronies at this time were Robert Henri and George Luks. Falling under the attention of that most open-minded of art editors, Alexander W. Drake of the Century Company, Davies began to draw for *Saint Nicholas.* To the volumes for 1888 and 1889 he was a steady contributor, and thereafter occasionally until 1891. This work, influenced perhaps by the English Pre-Raphaelites, is charming, but it gives little hint of what was to come. Davies was refractory even to the gentlest editorial supervision, and within three years he had abandoned illustration, and a relatively sure success, for poverty and painting. In 1890 he exhibited two small paintings at the National Academy without attracting attention. Marrying Dr. Virginia Merriweather Davis, like himself of Welsh extraction, he retreated to a little farm near the Hudson at Congers, N. Y., where he alternated between tilling the soil and filling his portfolio with sketches of romantic scenery. The Academy continued to accept his small landscapes, and a few were sold. He competed for the decoration of the Appellate Court of New York, and the merits of his design were recognized, but it was feared that a painter barely thirty could not execute the sketch creditably, and the commissions fell to such veterans as Cox, Mowbray, and Simmons.

About 1894 the far-sighted and sympathetic Scotch dealer, William Macbeth, took Davies up, soon gave him a studio over the shop in lower Fifth Avenue, and with the aid of the merchant prince and art collector, Benjamin Altman, sent Davies to Europe. There ensued a sudden and beautiful flowering of his genius. The few canvases of his early days, such as "Along the Erie Canal," in the Phillips Memorial Gallery of

Washington, are notable for their simple composition and fragile harmonies. The pictures were small and invariably idyls. Women and children played, brooded, or merely lived blissfully amid flowers in green paradises embowered with great trees. The pastorals recalled the pensiveness of a Giorgione or a Watteau, but were also oddly near to our common experience. Every posture and gesture had been observed and lived. These denizens of an Arcadia were after all akin to real women and children. One felt that the Arcadia itself was real, and that a sufficiently searching eye might find it round the corner. In short, Davies had created his illusion without much departing from the look of things. One of the richest of these early pictures is the "Fantasy of the Vine," a lovely arrangement of nudes in landscape. There is a hint of Puvis in it, though it is far richer in color. In general it is idle to try to trace influences in Davies. Being of a curious and scholarly disposition, he drew from many sources, but from none overtly or constantly. For the little idyls of the nineties the moment was unpropitious. Conservative taste still favored the artificial polish of the French Institute; radical taste was attached to the various naturalisms of Courbet, Manet, and the Impressionists. In the nineties in New York one could buy the idyls of Monticelli, akin to Davies's, though more flimsy and fantastic, for a matter of twenty-five dollars. Still, under Mr. Macbeth's tactful and convincing championship, Davies became the idol of a cult, whose spokesman in criticism was soon to be the brilliant and enthusiastic James G. Huneker. There ensued a modest prosperity, more frequent trips to Europe, the beginnings of what was to be a notable art collection. To many art-lovers the idyls which Davies produced between his thirtieth and fortieth years are still his best work. They early passed into the hands of discriminating amateurs, and for the most part are now in private collections.

About the turn of the century his style changed. The canvases are somewhat larger, the color is cooler and more limited in range, the scene is vaster, and its denizens are no longer women and children one might see, but abstract figures, frequently nude, symbolizing poetical ideas. The forms are now moderately distorted for the sake of greater compositional coherence. If in the early idyls one thought of Giorgione and Schiavone, now one divined Blake of the prophetic books. The material is less rich, the meaning more various, recondite, and profound. Some of his best pictures are transitional; such as "Four O'Clock Ladies," in the Phillips Memorial Gallery, in which the old idyllic theme of girls at play is treated in the new technique and with the new breadth. The pictures in this second manner have passed into the public galleries. The Phillips Memorial Gallery, which is rich in every phase of Davies's work, has five or six; the Metropolitan has "The Girdle of Ares"; and the Chicago Art Institute, "Leda and the Dioscuri"; but many of the best pictures are in private collections. In this adventure in symbolism and mythology, Davies's work kept its actuality. The forms, whether human figures or the architecture of trees and earth, had been justly observed before their ultimate pictorial transformation. Nothing was flimsy or improvised. He drew incessantly in every medium, and he kept and classified his drawings. They were of every sort, but most were of the nude in every posture and in every scale. Many of the drawings were complete and elaborate compositions. There must be thousands of these studies. No artist of our day has made such rich and intense preparation. It is this element of probity that keeps the sanity and soundness of Davies's art even in its most sublimated flights and even through its not infrequent preciosities. In his last fifteen years he occasionally perpetuated these exercises in admirable lithographs and etchings which are quintessential for his talent and accessible to those who cannot own or see his pictures.

It was inevitable that a man of Davies's mobile yet strenuous intelligence should respond to those modernists who sought a new basis for the arts in an unlimited emotionalism or in an equally unlimited intellectualization. And it was as inevitable that he should find his affinities, not with the Expressionist Left, but with the Intellectualist Right which found expression in that Cubism which in turn stemmed from Cézanne. His own experiments in this direction, dating from about 1914, were moderate enough. In the main he employed geometrical surface patterns, and sought to create a sense of space without evoking a specific place. A large frieze of dancing figures and the decoration of a private music room in New York are the more permanent products of this adventure, which was also very variously pursued in his lithographs and etchings. These experiments may be taken at best as a mere episode in a varied career, or at worst as an interesting aberration of a versatile and distinguished mind.

Davies's single public gesture was made in connection with the modernistic movement. Accepting the presidency of the Society of Independent Artists, he arranged the memorable Armory Show of 1913, in which, beside a full representation of the so-called Post-Impressionists and Cubists and Futurists, was hung a series of fine pictures from a century back. It was an informing and liberating effort, bringing into the art atmosphere of New York, and for that matter of America, which had gone very stale, a salutary whiff of contention and ideas. It was the single public act of a habitual recluse, and a notable one. Davies fought for his privacy, and his personal dignity and reticence served him as a good defense. Of middle stature, black-haired, slight and alert, with gray eyes that would have been sharp except that his gaze seemed directed inward, Davies to a superficial observer might readily have seemed an efficient university professor or an intellectual West Pointer. He never saw you first, but if you addressed him he responded charmingly and with tact. When people began to find and visit his studio, he took a new one. But his seclusion was enriched by strong family ties, by a few firm friendships, by much reading and speculation, and by an incredible amount of work.

It may be doubted whether, following precedent, one should speak of a third manner for Davies. After a trip to California, in 1905, his landscapes inspired by the Sierras are larger; and in his later years the figure composition in his mythologies and abstractions are more dense and elaborate, more closely knit with the lines and forms of the landscape, and tend to assume the form of a frieze. Perhaps the most instructive picture of the latest phase is "Movement of Waters," in a private collection. Here the group of nudes in the foreground surges and sinks with the rhythm of the waves behind. It would be easy to find the accord too conscious and far-fetched, and difficult to deny its ingenuity and distinction.

Always a devout admirer of Greek art, Davies sought to discover its principles. Thus a few years before his death he worked out the theory that the peculiar vitality of Greek art, its sense of aspiration, lay in its use of the act of inhalation. The figure is caught as it inhales, the stroke is drawn while the artist inhales. The act centralizes, informs, and energizes the posture and the stroke. The theory is developed at length by Davies's friend the archeologist, Dr. Gustavus Eisen (in *Phillips Publications* no. 3). Perhaps this conscious control of the breathing while working may have contributed to that weakness of heart from which Davies died. The warning came in 1923. After a seizure, he lay alone and helpless for many hours in his studio. Travel and apparent convalescence led to even more relentless activity. He practised small sculpture, prepared for new mural decorations, made tapestry designs which were executed by the Gobelins, did admirable mural decorations, now free from Cubist mannerism, in International House, New York. His fame grew rapidly, and brought unavoidable interruptions. He decided to spend half of every year in Europe. As he was passing from Paris to Florence, amid the mountains of Italy, the fatal attack came. He died in Florence unknown, on Oct. 24, 1928, having just entered his sixty-seventh year. The news did not reach his family in America for six weeks. It was a characteristic end for a spirit which had ever courted solitude. He received few official honors, for the reason that he did not value them, and rarely exhibited where they were awarded. Among them were the silver medal of the Pan-American Exposition, Buffalo, 1901, an honorable mention at the Carnegie Institute, Pittsburgh, and the W. A. Clark Prize and Corcoran gold medal, Washington, 1916.

[Appreciations and some biographical material may be found in "Arthur B. Davies: Essays on the Man and his Art" in *Phillips Pubs.* no. 3 (1924), and in F. Newlin Price, *Etchings and Lithographs by Arthur B. Davies* (1929). The earliest substantial critical recognition of Davies was that by Samuel Isham in his *Hist. of Am. Painting* (1905). Jas. G. Huneker was thereafter Davies's constant champion in the N. Y. *Sun.* See also Huneker's *The Pathos of Distance* (1913); *Art in America,* Oct. 1918, Aug. 1929; *Art Digest,* Jan. 1929; *Am. Mag. of Art,* Feb. 1929; *Art News,* Apr. 27, 1929; *Art and Archæology,* Sept. 1916; *International Studio,* Feb. 1921, June 1922, June 1923.] F. J. M., Jr.

DAVIES, HENRY EUGENE (July 2, 1836–Sept. 6, 1894), Union soldier, was born in New York City, the son of Henry Ebenezer and Rebecca Waldo (Tappan) Davies. His original immigrant ancestor was John Davies, who came from Herefordshire to Litchfield, Conn., in 1735. After spending a year at Harvard and a year at Williams, Henry graduated at Columbia in 1857, studied law, was admitted to the bar, and began to practise. On Aug. 10, 1858, he married Julia daughter of John T. Rich. His first military service was as captain in the 5th New York Infantry (mustered in May 9, 1861), but he was appointed major, Aug. 1, 1861, in the 2nd New York Cavalry (called the Harris Light Cavalry), and remained in the mounted service for the rest of the war. As it was a part of McDowell's corps, his regiment remained near Washington when the army moved in the spring of 1862, and so did not participate in the Peninsular campaign. Under Judson Kilpatrick, who was its lieutenant-colonel and later its colonel, it had some experience in skirmishes, and saw its first hard fighting at the second battle of Bull Run. From that time it served with the Army of the Potomac, but took no part in the battle of Gettysburg, being at Westminster, Md., with the

Davies

rest of the brigade. Until he was advanced to higher command, Davies served with it constantly, being promoted lieutenant-colonel, Dec. 6, 1862, and colonel, June 16, 1863. He was appointed brigadier-general of volunteers, Sept. 16, 1863, and commanded brigades in the second and third divisions of the Cavalry Corps until after Appomattox, occasionally holding temporary command of a division. He took part in the great raids toward Richmond in 1864, and in the cavalry operations which immediately preceded Lee's surrender. He was appointed major-general of volunteers, May 4, 1865, and resigned from the army, Jan. 1, 1866. After the war he returned to the practise of law in New York, was for a time public administrator for the city, and was later assistant district-attorney for the southern district of New York. In the latter part of his life he made his home at Fishkill. He published *Ten Days on the Plains* (1871); a genealogical work, the *Davies Memoir* (1895); and a biography, *General Sheridan* (1895). He died at Middleboro, Mass. Though without early military training, he was a cavalryman by instinct, and quickly learned his trade. His rise was steady and was well earned. Gen. Rodenbough describes him as "unpolished, genial, gallant" (*Battles and Leaders of the Civil War,* 1887–88, IV, 188.)

[*Davies Memoir* (1895); F. B. Heitman, *Hist. Reg. and Dict. U. S. Army* (1903), I, 356; *Official Records (Army)*, ser. 1, vols. XII (pt. 1), XXIX (pt. 1), XXXIII, XXXVI (pt. 1), XL (pt. 1), XLII (pts. 1, 2, 3), XLVI (pts. 1, 2, 3).] T. M. S.

DAVIES, SAMUEL (Nov. 3, 1723–Feb. 4, 1761), fourth president of the College of New Jersey, now Princeton, was born in New Castle County, Del. He was the son of David and Martha (Thomas) Davies, both of Welsh extraction. His mother early determined that the boy should be trained for the ministry, and with that end in view he was enrolled in the famous school of Samuel Blair at Fagg's Manor, Pa. He was licensed to preach by the Presbytery of New Castle on July 30, 1746, and on Oct. 23 of that year married Sarah Kirkpatrick. Ordained as an evangelist on Feb. 19, 1747, he was forthwith sent to Virginia on evangelical service. His first wife having died, on Oct. 4, 1748, he was married to Jean, daughter of John Holt of Hanover County, Va.

In Virginia dissenters were frowned upon, and the activities of their preachers were made the subject of strict surveillance. When Davies settled in Hanover County there were many suits in court against Presbyterians for holding forbidden assemblies and preaching without license from the General Court. He made the cause of the non-conformists his own, and was soon regarded as the advocate and defender of their civil rights and liberties. Though always in feeble health he spared neither his body nor his time in his proselytizing efforts. Almost single-handed he built up a strong Presbyterian membership in Virginia. He conducted services in seven houses of worship scattered through five counties; and in addition traveled over the whole state organizing revival meetings. He was "the animating soul of the whole dissenting interest in Virginia and North Carolina" (Collins, *post,* 59).

In 1753, with Gilbert Tennant, he was commissioned by the Synod of New York to go to the British Isles and endeavor to raise funds for the College of New Jersey, which since its inception in 1747 had been in straitened circumstances. The envoys were eminently successful. Over £3,000 were raised; the larger portion among loyal Presbyterians of Scotland. To Davies, despite his youth, for he was but thirty, came renown. In England and Scotland he delivered some sixty sermons, many of which were distributed and widely read. As a result of his work for the college he became intimately associated with Jonathan Edwards, Aaron Burr, Sr., and others of its supporters. Immediately after his journey he returned to Virginia, where in the latter part of 1755, largely through his instrumentality, the Presbytery of Hanover, the first presbytery in Viginia, was founded.

Two years later occurred the death of President Burr of the College of New Jersey, and within a few weeks that of his successor, Jonathan Edwards. The trustees, after a considerable delay, elected Samuel Davies to the presidency. He felt constrained for a time to reject the offer, since faction was rife among the trustees, but finally, yielding to their importunities, he took office on July 26, 1759. On Feb. 4, 1761, he died of pneumonia. During his brief régime, however, he inaugurated several important changes. The standard for the bachelor's degree was raised and the requirements for admission were strengthened. Plans for a more suitable library were made, but these were interrupted by his death. Although his career was short, Davies left behind an enviable record. Lacking the educational background of his predecessors, he had attained the presidency of the College of New Jersey. He had also achieved the reputation of being the greatest pulpit orator of his generation. For fifty years after his death, his sermons were more widely read than those of any of his contemporaries.

[See John Maclean, *Hist. of the Coll. of N. J.* (1877); V. L. Collins, *Princeton* (1914); J. DeWitt,

Planting of Princeton Coll. (1897); J. F. Hageman, *Hist. of Princeton and its Institutions* (1879); J. W. Wilson, *An Hist. Sketch of the Coll. of N. J.* (1859); W. B. Sprague, *Annals Am. Pulpit*, vol. III (1858); H. A. Davis, *The Davis Family* (1927). Davies's writings, largely addresses and sermons, are listed in Maclean, vol. I, 245. A complete collection is in the Princeton Univ. Library.] J. E. P.

DAVIESS, JOSEPH HAMILTON [See DAVEISS, JOSEPH HAMILTON, 1774–1811.]

DAVIESS, MARIA THOMPSON (Nov. 25, 1872–Sept. 3, 1924), painter, author, daughter of John Burton Thompson and Leonora (Hamilton) Daviess, was born in Harrodsburg, Ky., and died in New York City. Her father belonged to a family long prominent in Kentucky, and his mother, whose full name he gave to his daughter, was a woman of considerable literary interests and performance. He died early and his widow with her children took up residence at her family home, Nashville, Tenn. There, except for long visits to her father's relatives in Kentucky, Maria spent all of her childhood. After attending the Nashville Young Ladies' College and the Hill School in Shelbyville, Ky., she entered Wellesley, where she remained (1891–92) until her mother's ill health necessitated her being at home. She studied in the (Nashville) Peabody Art School, and, after her mother's death, spent two years (1902–04) in various schools of art in Paris. In 1904–05 specimens of her painting were exhibited in the Paris Salon. Returning to Nashville in the summer of 1904, she taught art, and during the next few years maintained a studio of photography, miniature painting, jewelry design—and general discussion for the local illuminati. Almost by accident she discovered that she could write stories acceptable to the juvenile readers of Sunday-school magazines, and in 1909 her *Miss Selina Lue and the Soapbox Babies* made it evident that she could please also many persons of more advanced years. By 1920 she had published thirteen other books, romances for the most part, all thin and sentimental, but all popular, inspired by a quick, ebullient, amiably disposed mind. Her best-known work, *The Melting of Molly* (1912), attained the distinction of being rendered into drama and motion picture. Some of her other books had distinct and aggressive aims: *The Tinderbox* (1913), to advance the cause of woman suffrage; *Over Paradise Ridge* (1915), to check the flow of population from farm to city; *The Heart's Kingdom* (1917), to solve religious difficulties; and *The Matrix* (1920), to emphasize the extent of the nation's indebtedness to Lincoln's mother. Most of these purposes were restated along with many convictions of hers in her autobiography, *Seven Times Seven*, presented in seven "reels," as she named her chapters, during 1924. As soon as the income from her books warranted her doing so she bought a farm near Nashville and lived on it when she was not more attracted to New York. During the World War in 1917–18 she was commissioned by the government to go about making speeches to show the importance of food conservation. For the last five years of her life she suffered pitiably from articular rheumatism.

[Sources not already mentioned: *Who's Who in America*, 1924–25; *N. Y. Times*, Sept. 4, 1924; *Nashville Banner*, Sept. 4, 1924.] J. D. W.

DAVIS, ALEXANDER JACKSON (July 24, 1803–Jan. 14, 1892), architect, was born in New York City, the son of Cornelius Davis, editor of the *New York Theological Magazine*, bookseller and publisher of religious books, and of Julia Jackson, his second wife. As a boy he showed marked talent for drawing, and at the age of seventeen he was, according to Dunlap (*post*), a compositor in a printer's shop in Florida, N. Y. When twenty years old, he was again in New York City and a member of the "Antique School" which met in the rooms of the Philosophical Society. He early began a series of views of important buildings in New York and was soon busy with other illustration work in the course of which he made two trips to New England, in 1827 and 1828. These produced a famous view of the State House in Boston, drawn directly on stone, the best example of architectural lithography produced up to that time in America. During his early twenties Davis was also working, probably as an apprentice, with J. C. Brady, an architect in New York City, under whom he made an intensive study of Greek detail. He was later employed as draftsman by Ithiel Town [*q.v.*], who had just come to New York from New Haven, for whom Davis made such a beautiful elevation of his Connecticut capitol design at New Haven, that Town took him in as an associate and on Feb. 1, 1829, they opened an office together. Their first important work was the New York Customs House in 1832 (still standing on the northeast corner of Wall and Nassau streets, although the interior was never completed according to their wishes). From this time on, the firm of Town & Davis was continuously busy with a large amount of work, some of it of great importance. After 1843 Davis practised by himself for over thirty years. The complete list of the buildings designed by him, and by the firm of Town & Davis, includes outstanding examples of every style fashionable in America from 1820 to 1880.

The high reputation of the firm is witnessed by the four state capitols entrusted to it: Indiana (1832–35); North Carolina (1831), in association with David Paton; Illinois (1837, altered and enlarged from Davis's designs, 1866–67); and Ohio (1839), where Davis acted as expert and produced a design in association with Thomas U. Walter, Martin E. Thompson, and Thomas Cole. In addition, Davis was the designer of the Patent Office, Washington, D. C. (1832); the Pauper Lunatic Asylum, Blackwell's Island, New York City (1834); the Wadsworth Atheneum, Hartford (1842); the assembly hall of the University of North Carolina (1844); buildings for the Virginia Military Institute (1852, 1859); Alumni Hall at Yale (1852), destroyed to make way for Wright Hall; the North Carolina Hospital for the Insane (1852); and Davidson College, North Carolina (1858). Besides all this public work, Davis designed many churches, commercial buildings, and private houses in New York and in the country, and after his retirement, he claimed to have designed more buildings than any other living American architect. In addition, he made many studies for buildings executed by others, *e.g.*, Haviland's Egyptian design for the Tombs, New York City, which Davis maintained was adapted from one of his unexecuted sketches, this claim being borne out by a drawing in the Metropolitan Museum.

The chief characteristic of Davis as designer and draftsman is his meticulous care. This appears even in drawings of his student days, which are frequently rendered with painstaking beauty and exquisite finish. It is this quality which sets his lithographs of the America of 1820 apart from so many of the engravings and drawings of the time. Their accuracy is unimpeachable, and by their quality they give perfectly the atmosphere of the place and period. It is this same quality which gives such soundness to his Greek Revival work, as in the New York Customs House and the Patent Office at Washington. Alert to the intellectual movement of the day, he frequently anticipated popular taste. His Gilmer house in Baltimore (1832) and the buildings for the University of Michigan (1838) are remarkably advanced examples of Gothic for their period. Yet he was not tied to any current style, for the Stevens "palace" in New York (1845), perhaps his finest work, returns to the Greek Revival for its details, although it is freely composed. Davis's drawings (preserved in the Metropolitan Museum and the New York Historical Society) comprise dozens of schemes for museums, libraries, and public buildings of all kinds, which show not only a consistent feeling for logical planning, but also an inventive mind, continually irked by the limitations of his period. Despite Davis's training in the strict use of Greek forms, and later in the romanticism of the Victorian Gothic, he was not blind to the architectural possibilities of metal. Town & Davis were responsible for the first iron shop-front in New York (for the Lyceum of Natural History in 1835), and in an undated drawing for a building at 751 Broadway (New York Historical Society) there is an amazingly modern expression of vertical lines, the front consisting merely of slim vertical marble shafts, the spaces between entirely filled with glass and bronze. One of many sketches for the New York Post Office (1867–68, Metropolitan Museum) shows a huge circular building with a central circular tower, running up several stories, whose windows are treated in the same way, with metal panels between them, so that the masonry piers run through unbroken.

From the beginning of his professional career, Davis was in the center of the artistic life of New York. Dunlap remarks that the great architectural library of Ithiel Town was a center of interest in his day, and Davis's wide acquaintance among those interested in the arts is evidenced by his membership in numerous societies. He was one of a committee of three appointed by a group of architects who had met in New York to arrange and issue the call for the first meeting of the American Institute of Architects in Philadelphia, in May 1837. Although thus a founder of the A. I. A., he fell out of sympathy with it in his later life, and, despite many efforts on its part to renew his membership, he consistently refused to return. He was the author of *Views of the Public Buildings in the City of New York* (published without date, probably prior to 1830); and *Rural Residences, Consisting of Designs Original and Selected for Cottages, Farm-houses, Villas and Village Churches* (1837). On July 14, 1853, he married Margaret Beale, at Florida, N. Y. Instrumental in 1857 in the founding of Llewellyn Park, West Orange, N. J., he spent his later years near there, at his home, "Wildmont," where he died.

[Wm. Dunlap, *Hist. of the Rise and Progress of the Arts of Design in the U. S.* (new ed., 1918, III, 210) has an account of Davis's work up to the date of its first edition, 1834. S. A. Ashe, in an address reprinted in the N. C. Hist. Commission Pubs. (*Bull. No. 4*, Mar. 12, 1909) gives almost entire credit for the N. C. capitol to Paton, but this is not borne out by original drawings in the Metropolitan Museum and the N. Y. Hist. Soc. See also: manuscript papers of the A. A. F. A. in the N. Y. Hist. Soc.; "An Architect of the Romantic Era," by Richard H. Platt in *House and Garden*, Oct. 1927 (LII, 122); *N. Y. Herald* and *N. Y. Tribune*, Jan. 17, 1892; *Appletons' Annual Cyc.*, 1892, p. 543.] T. F. H.

DAVIS, ANDREW JACKSON (Aug. 11, 1826–Jan. 13, 1910), spiritualist, the son of Samuel Davis, was born in Blooming Grove, Orange County, N. Y. His father, a stern, poverty-stricken shoemaker, given to drink, was totally uneducated, as was also his mother, a woman with a weak body but with strong visionary powers. They moved frequently from one small New York town to another without seeming to better themselves. Some time prior to 1842 they finally settled in Poughkeepsie, N. Y., whence Davis later received his name of "the Poughkeepsie Seer." His academic education consisted of a total of five months' schooling acquired at different periods of a few weeks each. He declares in his autobiography (written about 1857) that he had read only one book, but this statement was probably not literally true. At the age of fifteen he was apprenticed to a shoemaker and when he seemed incapable of learning the trade was employed by a merchant in a general store; but he was a failure at this latter occupation as well. In 1843 at the age of seventeen, he allowed a Professor Grimes, who visited Poughkeepsie and performed mesmeric miracles at the town hall, to attempt to hypnotize him. The attempt was unsuccessful, but a few weeks later William Levingston, a local tailor and amateur mesmeric philosopher, succeeded in "magnetizing" him. The result was such a "rare clairvoyance" that Levingston gave up his own business and devoted his whole time to Davis and to using his "clairvoyant" powers for the cure of disease. After two years during which Davis was subject to the will and hypnotism of Levingston, he had his first "psychic flight through space" in January 1844. Davis supposed himself influenced while in the trance state by a number of persons and particularly by Swedenborg whom he believed to have guided his steps personally from the time he was twenty-one. A "clairvoyant clinic" which he opened at Poughkeepsie and which extended to Bridgeport had but indifferent success. By 1845 he felt the urge to turn from healing to writing. He selected as magnetizer, Dr. S. S. Lyon, a Bridgeport physician, and as reporter and scribe, the Rev. William Fishbough. From Nov. 28, 1845, to Jan. 25, 1847, he delivered in Manhattan, while in a state of trance, one hundred and fifty-seven lectures. These, copied down verbatim by the Rev. Fishbough, constituted his *Principles of Nature, Her Divine Revelations, and a Voice to Mankind,* published in 1847. In this strange mélange of occult history, mysticism, philosophy, and science, critics have discerned likenesses to the works of Swedenborg and Brisbane. Next came *The Great Harmonia* (1850–52) and from 1851 to 1885 a long succession of twenty-six works in all, of which perhaps the most important, aside from two autobiographical works, were *The Philosophy of Spiritual Intercourse* (1856), *The Penetralia* (1856), *A Stellar Key to the Summer Land* (1867), *Views of our Heavenly Home* (1878), and *The Children's Progressive Lyceum* (1893). *The Great Harmonia* and all subsequent publications were written without the assistance of magnetism; thus marking Davis's transition from mesmerism to spiritualism. Davis was best known for his "clairvoyant" prescriptions for disease and for his idea of the Children's Lyceum or Spiritualist Sunday School. He was twice married. His first wife died Nov. 2, 1853. Two years later he married Mrs. Mary (Robinson) Love, who, like his first wife, was a divorcée.

Davis belongs to the interregnum between mesmerism and spiritualism; he practised both but was wholly identified with neither. In common with transcendentalism and the idealistic socialism of his day, he preached social reconstruction as going hand in hand with spiritual regeneration. He gave modern spiritualism much of its phraseology and first formulated its underlying principles.

[*The Magic Staff* (1857), an autobiography of Davis, and its sequel, *Beyond the Valley* (1885); E. C. Hartmann, *Who's Who in Occultism* (1927); G. B. Butt in the *Occult Rev.*, Mar. 1925; W. B. Pickens and W. H. Evans, articles on Davis in *Light* for 1925 and 1926; Frank Podmore, *Modern Spiritualism,* vol. I (1902).]

H. W. S.
R. R.

DAVIS, ANDREW McFARLAND (Dec. 30, 1833–Mar. 29, 1920), author, antiquarian, was born at Worcester, Mass., youngest son of John Davis, governor of Massachusetts, and a descendant of Dolor Davis, who came to America in 1634. His mother was Eliza Bancroft, sister of George Bancroft [*q.v.*], the historian. He was educated at the public schools of Worcester, with the intention of entering Harvard College; but his uncle secured for him an appointment to the Naval Academy at Annapolis, and for three years he remained in service, being attached to the Mediterranean Squadron. He then entered the Lawrence Scientific School of Harvard College, receiving the degree of B.S. in 1854. For a brief period he was employed on railroads in the Southern and Middle states. Within a few years he returned to Worcester, studied law, and was admitted to the bar in 1859. He entered the office of his brother, John C. B. Davis [*q.v.*], in New York, counsel of the Erie Railroad, and was employed by that company as general freight agent. When Gould and Fisk obtained control of the Erie, he resigned and moved with his family to San Francisco, where he joined his brother Horace [*q.v.*], already engaged in flour milling. For a time he served as president of the board of education of San Francisco. In 1882 he returned to Cambridge, Mass., where he henceforth made his home. He abandoned active business pursuits, and devoted his leisure time to research, particularly in the field of American colonial history. Among his earliest contributions, in 1887, were chapters in Justin Winsor's *Narrative and Critical History of America:* "Canada and Louisiana" (vol. V, pp. 1–63) and "The Indians and the Border Warfare in the Revolution" (vol. VI, pp. 605–47). His antiquarian interest soon centered upon the history of currency and banking experiments in the colony of Massachusetts; on these topics he wrote many papers and monographs which showed exhaustive research in original documents, diaries, and account books. He was a member of the American Antiquarian Society, Massachusetts Historical Society, Colonial Society of Massachusetts, New-England Historic Genealogical Society, and Fellow of the American Academy of Arts and Sciences. The results of his studies were first presented before these societies, and in printed form are to be found scattered in their proceedings. The studies dealing with colonial currency were incorporated into an extended treatise, "Currency and Banking in the Province of the Massachusetts Bay," which appeared in *Publications of the American Economic Association* (Pt. I, "Currency," ser. 3, vol. I, December 1900, pp. 692–1173; Pt. II, "Banking," ser. 3, vol. II, May 1901, pp. 293–632). He performed a useful and lasting service in editing reprints of pamphlets which appeared in the early eighteenth century in Massachusetts in connection with the currency controversy. These appeared as: *Tracts Relating to the Currency of the Massachusetts Bay, 1682–1720* (1902); and *The Colonial Currency Reprints, 1682–1751,* four volumes in Publications of the Prince Society (Boston, 1910–11). In this latter collection there are fifty-eight reprints, to which Davis added many notes. He also prepared a monograph for the National Monetary Commission on "The Origin of the National Banking System" (published as *Senate Document No. 582,* 61 Cong. 2 Sess., 1910), and "Certain Old Chinese Notes or Chinese Paper Money" (*Proceedings of the American Academy of Arts and Sciences* for June 1915, vol. L, pp. 245–86).

Davis had a strong, alert personality, and impressed some as brusque. His friends, however, found him sympathetic and warm-hearted. The brief tribute of the Council of the Colonial Society of Massachusetts summed up his characteristics as: "Blunt, witty, sagacious, generous, tender-hearted, and dependable." He married Henrietta Parker Whitney Oct. 23, 1862, and had four children.

[H. H. Edes in *Proc. Mass. Hist. Soc.,* LIII (1920), 141–45, and "Memoir" by Wm. Roscoe Thayer, in *Proc. Mass. Hist. Soc.,* LIV (1922), 204–11.]

D. R. D.

DAVIS, CHARLES HENRY (Jan. 16, 1807–Feb. 18, 1877), naval officer, born in Boston, youngest of the thirteen children of Daniel Davis, solicitor general of Massachusetts, and Lois (Freeman) Davis, came of pure New England stock. He was accurately described by his friend, Admiral Samuel F. Du Pont, as "a man of science and a practical officer, keeping the love of science subordinate to the regular duties of his profession." After preparation in the Boston Latin School and two years at Harvard, he was appointed midshipman, and sailed in January 1824 in the frigate *United States* for the west coast of South America. There transferred to the schooner *Dolphin,* he had the novel experience of a year's cruise in the South Seas. After his return in 1827 he took his examination for lieutenant, standing sixth of the thirty-nine who passed, and was then in the Mediterranean in the *Ontario,* 1829–32, flag lieutenant in the *Vincennes,* 1833–35, and in the *Independence* on a voyage to Russia and thence to Brazil, 1837–41. Between cruises he studied mathematics at Harvard, and after this last cruise took his degree. He was married in 1842 to Harriette Blake Mills, daughter of Elijah Hunt Mills, and maintained his home at Cambridge, Mass., until after the Civil War.

The next fifteen years were taken up with scientific work connected with the navy. In charge of the coast survey from Rhode Island north, Davis made the first thorough study of the dangerous waters around Nantucket; served on numerous harbor commissions; and published two notable scientific articles, "A Memoir upon the Geological Action of the Tidal and Other Currents of the Ocean" (*Memoirs American Academy,* vol. IV, n.s. 1849), and "The Law of Deposit of the Flood Tide" (*Smithsonian Contributions to Knowledge,* vol. III, 1852). He was a prime mover in establishing the *American Ephemeris and Nautical Almanac* in 1849, and supervised its publication at Cambridge until 1855 and again 1859–62. Enlisting the aid of scientific leaders in this work, he brought the navy into profitable cooperation with scientific progress. He was one of the founders of the National Academy of Sciences in 1863. Promoted to commander in 1854, he resumed sea duty in command of the *St. Mary's* in the Pacific, 1856–59, during which service he secured the release of the filibuster William Walker and his followers besieged at Rivas, Nicaragua.

At the outbreak of the Civil War he became practically executive head of the new Bureau of Detail for selecting and assigning officers; and his alert mind, facility in writing, and great capacity for work led to his appointment on several important commissions engaged in planning and organizing the naval war. The active board for consideration of measures for effectually blockading the South Atlantic Coast, of which he was a member and secretary, planned the expeditions against Hatteras Inlet and Port Royal and was in no small measure responsible for the earlier naval strategy of the war. Appointed Du Pont's fleet captain in the latter expedition, Davis organized the immense flotilla, took charge of sounding and buoying Port Royal Channel, and, with Du Pont, should be given considerable credit for the admirable plan of attack (Nov. 7, 1861), which was later imitated by Dewey at Manila. Recalled to Washington in February 1862, Davis in May assumed command of the Upper Mississippi gunboat flotilla above Fort Pillow. His position was singularly difficult and required generosity and tact as well as leadership, for Foote, on sick leave, was left in titular command until June 17, and the rams under Ellet, though operating with Davis, were under the War Department and outside his control. On May 10, the day after his arrival, the Confederate flotilla delivered a sharp attack which was repulsed, several vessels on both sides being disabled. When the Confederate army evacuated Fort Pillow, Davis moved down to Memphis, where on June 6 his five gunboats, with Ellet's rams, destroyed or captured seven of the eight Confederate vessels. He now joined Farragut before Vicksburg. In discussing plans for destroying the ram *Arkansas,* which had run through the whole Union fleet and taken refuge under the guns of Vicksburg, Davis's judgment came in sharp though friendly conflict with the impetuosity of Farragut. This spirit of discretion, remarked upon by Secretary Welles (*Diary of Gideon Welles,* 1911, I, 158) as a reason for the later appointment of Porter to the flotilla, was perhaps a weakness in Davis since recklessness was warranted by the Northern superiority of means; and, rightly or wrongly, it operated against his selection for high sea-command later in the war. Commissioned chief of the Bureau of Navigation in July 1862, Davis did not turn over his command until September. In his Washington post, which included the old Bureau of Detail and supervision of all scientific activities of the navy, he did important administrative work until 1865. Thereafter he was superintendent of the Naval Observatory for two years, and following command on the Brazilian station, 1867–69, and at the Norfolk Navy Yard, 1870–73, was again at the Observatory until his death. Of his three sons, Charles Henry [*q.v.*] became a rear admiral, the others dying young; of his three daughters, one married Brooks Adams and another, Henry Cabot Lodge. Senator Lodge (*Early Memories,* 1913, p. 195) describes his father-in-law as a most charming and lovable man, "handsome and distinguished looking," with perfect manners. This glowing tribute is borne out by the admiral's popularity in the service. A lover of literature as well as science, he combined intellectual distinction with well-proved capacity for active administration and command.

[In addition to the excellent *Life of Chas. Henry Davis, Rear Admiral, 1807–1877* (1899), by Chas. H. Davis, there is a brief sketch by the same author in *Biog. Memoirs, Nat. Acad. Sci.,* vol. IV. See also Hiram Paulding, *Jour. of a Cruise of the U. S. Schooner Dolphin,* etc. (1831), and the various Civil War records.]

A. W.

DAVIS, CHARLES HENRY (Aug. 28, 1845–Dec. 27, 1921), naval officer, son of Charles Henry Davis [*q.v.*] and Harriette Blake (Mills) Davis, was born and brought up in Cambridge, Mass. Though without similar opportunities for wartime distinction, his career followed closely that of his father, whom he resembled in scientific bent and versatility of mind. At sixteen he entered the Naval Academy, then at Newport, graduating in November 1864. The following winter he was in the receiving ship at New York, and during the next two years, when he was attached to the *Colorado* in European waters, we catch glimpses of him at Paris with his elder brother, an art student, and his future brother-in-law, Henry Cabot Lodge (Lodge, *Early Memories,* p. 159). After ten years of routine assignments, Davis spent two years in astronomical and geodetic work at the Naval Observatory. He then engaged in a series of expeditions (1877–85) in the North Atlantic, Far East, and on the west coast of South America, for fixing exact longitude by use of submarine cables, the results of which he published in three volumes, each prepared in collaboration with another officer, on *Telegraphic Determination of Longitudes* (1880, 1883, 1885). He also published in 1877 a treatise, *Chronometer Rates as Affected by Changes of Tempera-*

ture and Other Causes (*Navy Scientific Papers,* no. 6). He was promoted to commander in 1885, and his special qualifications were recognized by his appointment, in intervals between sea commands, as chief intelligence officer (1889–92), and superintendent of the Naval Observatory (1897–1902). This last duty was interrupted by the Spanish-American War, during which he commanded the auxiliary cruiser *Dixie* in Cuban waters and was in charge of the division which, on July 27, 1898, forced the surrender of Ponce, Porto Rico, preparatory to its occupation by the army. He was made a rear admiral in August 1904, and thereafter commanded a division and then a squadron of the Atlantic Fleet.

Davis's range of interests and attractive personal qualities led to his selection for various special duties, notably as representative of the president at the reception of the Infanta Eulalie on her visit to the United States in 1893, as a member of the joint army and navy board that reported favorably on the Langley flying machine in 1898, of the international commission that met in Paris in 1904–05 to investigate the Dogger Bank dispute between England and Russia, and of the Perry's Victory Centennial Committee in 1912. On Mar. 31, 1875, he married Louisa, daughter of Dr. John Quackenbush of Albany, N. Y. His elder son, Charles Henry Davis, entered the navy prior to his father's retirement, so that in 1928 there had been one of that name in the navy continuously for 105 years. In later years Davis found his chief recreation in water-color painting, to which he devoted himself with notable success, selling many pictures and giving exhibitions in Newport, Boston, and Washington. Nervous, irritable, and whimsical at times—his barred cabin had to be entered once through a port-hole to apprise him of an admiral's call—he was enthusiastic in his pleasures, a delightful companion, thoroughly democratic, and had an extraordinary store of general information. On shipboard he was a strict but just disciplinarian, and drew his men to him by personal affection.

[Some information regarding his early life may be drawn from his *Life of Chas. Henry Davis, Rear Admiral, 1807–1877* (1899). See also *Army and Navy Reg.,* Dec. 31, 1921; *Science,* Feb. 24, 1922; *Boston Transcript,* Dec. 28, 1921; *Who's Who in America,* 1920–21.] A. W.

DAVIS, CHARLES HENRY STANLEY Mar. 2, 1840–Nov. 7, 1917), physician, philologist, Orientalist, was born at Goshen, Conn., the son of Timothy Fisher Davis, also a physician, and Moriva (Hatch) Davis. He was educated in the public school of Meriden, Conn., and then by a private tutor. Beginning the study of medicine at the University of Maryland about 1864, he took his medical degree at the University of the City of New York in 1866. He then did some post-graduate work at Boston and began the publication of the *Boston Medical Register* which he conducted for its first year. He pursued further medical study at New York, London, and Paris; married Caroline Elizabeth Harris, Sept. 23, 1869; and settled in Meriden, Conn., where he was to remain for the rest of his life. In addition to his professional activities he took a lively interest in local history and politics. In 1870 his *History of Wallingford, Conn., . . . including Meriden* appeared, and in 1873 he was elected to the legislature, serving again in 1885 and 1886. His first effort in philology was in 1878, when he published his *Grammar of the Old Persian Language.* In the same year he began an *Index of Periodical Literature* which was maintained for the period 1878–81. He was active professionally in, and from 1870 until 1917 was clerk of, the local medical society. Among the subjects of his interest was child welfare: in 1879 he published an account of the epidemic of diphtheria which had prevailed in Meriden during 1875–76, while in 1883 appeared his booklet *Classification, Education and Training of Feeble-Minded, Imbecile and Idiotic Children.* In 1886 he was appointed physician to the Curtis Home for Orphans, which position he retained until 1898; in 1895 he began to serve as physician to the State School for Boys, resigning in 1900. During 1887–88 he was mayor of Meriden and from 1898 to 1908 he was president of its board of education. In addition to the medical publications already mentioned he was the author of *The Voice as a Musical Instrument* (1879, reprinted 1907); *The Self-Cure of Consumption without Medicine* (1904), and *How To Be Successful as a Physician* (1905).

His career as an antiquarian appears to have begun in earnest in 1887 when he took over the editorship of *Biblia,* a journal of Oriental archeology, which in 1906 was merged in the *American Antiquarian and Oriental Journal.* He published two volumes on Egypt, the *History of Egypt in the Light of Modern Discoveries* (1896) and *The Egyptian Book of the Dead* (1894). In 1909 he returned to philology in the publication of his *Grammar of the Modern Irish Language.* Finally he was the author of two philosophical works, *Greek and Roman Stoicism* (1903) and *Some of Life's Problems* (1914), his last literary effort. His death took place at the Connecticut State Hospital from a perforated duodenal ulcer.

[Wm. B. Atkinson, *The Physicians and Surgeons of the U. S.* (1878); *Commemorative Biog. Record of New Haven County, Conn.* (1902); *Jour. Am. Medic. Asso.*, Nov. 24, 1917; *Who's Who in America*, 1916–17.] E. P–e.

DAVIS, CUSHMAN KELLOGG (June 16, 1838–Nov. 27, 1900), lawyer, governor of Minnesota, United States senator, was born at Henderson, N. Y., the eldest of eight children. His father, Maj. Horatio Davis, a pioneer settler there, was of Puritan stock, while his mother, Clarissa F. (Cushman) Davis, was a direct descendant of Thomas and Mary (Allerton) Cushman, both of whom came early to Plymouth. Visiting New England only late in life, Davis "took great delight in his descent from the early settlers of Plymouth, and valued exceedingly the good-will of the people of Massachusetts" (Hoar, *post*). He received his formal education at Carroll College, an academy at Waukesha, Wis., and the University of Michigan, from which he was graduated in 1857. He was admitted to the bar and practised in Waukesha until he enlisted in 1862 as first lieutenant of Company B, 28th Wisconsin Infantry. Frequently serving as judge-advocate, he was for a time adjutant-general on the staff of Gen. Gorman. He resigned his commission in 1864 and returned to Waukesha, where he married Laura Bowman. Subsequently a divorce by agreement was obtained, and in 1880 he married Anna Malcolm Agnew of St. Paul, Minn. Moving to St. Paul, he joined his former commanding officer in the legal firm of Gorman & Davis. Adding politics to law, he was elected to the legislature in 1867, and was United States district attorney from 1868 to 1873. He was interested in the Granger Movement and his speech on "Modern Feudalism," an attack on railroads, was delivered before many audiences and even, by invitation, before the state legislature. Made available by his anti-railroad stand, and brought forward as a result of internal faction in the Republican party, Davis was nominated for governor in 1873 and elected by a narrow majority. By preventing a bolt of Granger Republicans to the Anti-Monopoly-Democratic fusion ticket, he had accomplished the purpose of his backers (William W. Folwell, *A History of Minnesota*, 1926, III, 81–85). "But the anti-monopolists were inevitably disappointed. They did not realize that the rhetoric of a lecturer could never be the policy of a governor" (St. Paul *Pioneer Press*, Nov. 28, 1900). He did not seek a renomination in 1875, but was brought forward to contest the senatorial seat of the veteran Alexander Ramsey; the ensuing deadlock resulted in the choice of a third man. For eleven years Davis, inactive in politics, devoted himself to his profession. His firm, Davis, [F. B.] Kellogg & [C. A.] Severance, was one of the strongest in the Northwest, while Davis himself was regarded as a particularly outstanding member of the bar in his state. The ex-governor found an avocation in the study of Shakespeare, publishing a volume on *The Law in Shakespeare* (1884), and on the life of Napoleon. He had not forsaken his political career, but awaited a favorable time for resuming it. Elected United States senator in 1887, he was reëlected in 1893 by a close vote, and again in 1899 with no serious opposition.

As senator, Davis rarely participated in formal debates on the floor, but concentrated his efforts on committee work, especially in the Committee on Pensions, of which he was chairman from 1887 to 1893. He was particularly instrumental in pushing through the Dependent Pension Bill in 1890. Whatever interest he had in the tariff, trust legislation, monetary questions, and the like, was manifested only by a rare remark, or by his vote. He supported Cleveland in sending federal troops to Chicago in 1894, in the face of considerable Minnesota sentiment against this action, and thus strengthened his position with the upholders of law and order. In 1891 he became a member of the Committee on Foreign Relations and here, throughout the remainder of his life, he found the most congenial part of his public work. He strenuously opposed President Cleveland's foreign policy ("Two Years of Democratic Diplomacy," *North American Review*, March 1895); advocated the annexation of the Hawaiian Islands (speech of Jan. 10, 11, 1894, *Congressional Record*, 53 Cong., 2 Sess., 621–28, 694–702); and opposed the Chinese Exclusion Act of 1892 which he characterized as "flagitious and ferocious legislation" (*Ibid.*, 53 Cong., 1 Sess., 1893, pp. 3080–85). In bringing before the Senate the joint resolution evoked by Cleveland's Venezuelan message, he reaffirmed adherence to the Monroe Doctrine but maintained that throughout the controversy there had been no danger of war between Great Britain and the United States, for interests of both countries "in the great and common cause of civilization" were "too enormous and too vital to each of them to bring about such a consummation" (*Ibid.*, 54 Cong., 1 Sess., pp. 1786–92). Nevertheless he was "among the first senators clearly to perceive and to explain the hidden pitfalls of the proposed arbitration treaty between Great Britain and the United States" (St. Paul *Pioneer Press*, Nov. 28, 1900).

In 1897, when Sherman became secretary of

state, Davis as chairman of the Committee on Foreign Relations was brought into intimate contact with the renewed project of Hawaiian annexation, advocated the ratification of the treaty of 1897, and, when that failed, led the fight to push through the joint resolution in the face of a determined filibuster (*Congressional Record,* 55 Cong., 2 Sess., pp. 6140–6403 *passim*). On the Cuban issue, Davis was in close touch with the administration throughout. He introduced in the Senate the joint resolution authorizing the President to intervene in Cuba and led in opposing a minority which would recognize the independence of Cuba, maintaining that such action would infringe upon executive prerogative (*Ibid.,* 55 Cong., 2 Sess., pp. 3827 ff.). He was convinced that the "Spanish war was a just and necessary war" (speech before the Union Club of Chicago, Feb. 2, 1899). As one of the Paris peace commissioners, he joined with Reid and Frye in believing that some of the Philippines should be retained by the United States, but, according to Reid, was not at first insistent on retaining all (Royal Cortissoz, *The Life of Whitelaw Reid,* 1921, II, 247). Once committed to the idea of retention, he even objected to paying the twenty millions to Spain (letters quoted in Folwell, *History of Minnesota,* III, 238 n.). The Philippines and Hawaii, he believed, would protect the western coast of the United States from an inundation of Chinese (Union League Club speech, Feb. 2, 1899). He was, however, opposed to tariff barriers between the United States and the new dependencies (*Congressional Record,* 56 Cong., 1 Sess., 1900, p. 2648). The situation arising from the Boxer Rebellion in China filled him with alarm lest it might lead to a general war (Cortissoz, *Reid,* II, 258). His career, which some thought might bring him to the presidency, was suddenly terminated while he was participating in the campaign of 1900. His *Treatise on International Law, including American Diplomacy* (1901), was published posthumously.

[Biographical sketches of Davis by Geo. F. Hoar in *Proc. Am. Antiq. Soc.,* n.s., XIV (1901), reprinted in Hoar, *Autobiog. of Seventy Years* (1903); Samuel G. Smith in *Rev. of Revs.* (N. Y.), Jan. 1901; Samuel H. Church in the *Century Mag.,* May 1901; Jas. H. Baker in *Minn. Hist. Soc. Colls.,* vol. XIII (1908); *Western Mag.,* Aug. 1918; *Outlook,* Dec. 8, 1900; memorial addresses in both Houses of Congress reprinted from the *Cong. Record* as *Sen. Doc. No. 230,* 56 Cong., 2 Sess.]

L. B. S.

DAVIS, DAVID (Mar. 9, 1815–June 26, 1886), jurist, born in Cecil County, Md., the son of Dr. David Davis, came of Welsh ancestry. He was the cousin of Henry Winter Davis. At seventeen he had completed an academic course at Kenyon College, Gambier, Ohio, after which he studied law in the office of Judge Henry W. Bishop of Lenox, Mass., and later in the Yale Law School, from which he graduated in 1835. In the same year he settled as a practising lawyer at Pekin, Ill., but finding the river town unhealthful he moved in 1836 to Bloomington, Ill., which remained thereafter his home. From the commonplace activities of a struggling lawyer in a pioneer town he turned to politics and was elected as a Whig to the state legislature in 1844. He was an active member of the state constitutional convention of 1847, devoting special attention to the judiciary. Despite the heavy circuit duties and traveling expenses of the state judges, he urged for the judicial office the low salary of $600, which was not adopted; and he advocated popular election of judges, contending that he would rather see them become "the weather-cocks of public sentiment" than the tools of the legislature or the governor.

For fourteen picturesque years (1848–62) he presided over the noted eighth judicial circuit in Illinois, his popularity being demonstrated in three elections as judge. Many lawyers of distinction, including Lincoln, Orville H. Browning, Douglas, Leonard Swett, S. T. Logan, and Lyman Trumbull, practised before him. An intimate friendship with Lincoln was formed during this period; Davis has even been referred to as "Lincoln's closest friend" (*Chicago Tribune,* June 27, 1886). Lincoln at times presided over Davis's court when the Judge was pressed with private business. In the Republican convention at Chicago in 1860, Davis was the acknowledged leader of the Lincoln forces. "To Judge Davis," wrote a contemporary, "more than to any other man, . . . is the American people indebted for . . . the nomination . . . of Abraham Lincoln" (letter of Jesse W. Fell, quoted in *Chicago Tribune,* June 27, 1886, p. 11). Having assisted in opening the Lincoln headquarters at the Tremont House prior to the convention, he labored tirelessly for his friend's success; and after the nomination he was active in promoting the Lincoln campaign. In February 1861 he accompanied Lincoln from Springfield to Washington, his great bulk and white hat being no less conspicuous than the rugged form of the president-elect. Lincoln further showed his confidence by appointing him in 1861 to investigate claims in Frémont's Missouri department. By request of the family he became administrator of Lincoln's estate.

Davis's eagerness for an appointment to the supreme bench was no secret to his friends; and one of them, Leonard Swett, claims the credit for persuading Lincoln to name him at a time when many regarded the choice of Orville H. Browning as a foregone conclusion. Swett is not inclined as others are to attribute Lincoln's action to the motive of rewarding a friend for having promoted his nomination; and it should be noted that Lincoln had appointed two supreme justices, Swayne and Miller, before choosing Davis. Davis remained a member of the Supreme Court for over fourteen years (1862–77), during which time he supported the prevailing nationalistic tendency in judicial interpretation. He delivered the opinion in the Milligan case (4 *Wallace,* 107), holding the trial of citizens by military commission in areas not within the theatre of military operations to be unlawful, though conducted in war time. For this he was abused by the Republican press but commended by Democratic papers; and his fondness for the Democratic party now becomes increasingly noticeable. When the constitutionality of the Legal Tender Act of 1862 was denied in *Hepburn* vs. *Griswold* (8 *Wallace,* 603), he dissented; and he stood with the majority of the Court when this decision was reversed (Legal Tender Cases, 12 *Wallace,* 457). While he was a member of the Supreme Court his circuit covered Illinois, Indiana, and Wisconsin; and he is said to have remarked that his heavy judicial duties shortened his life.

His judicial office had not caused him to avoid politics; and in 1872 his friends made a vigorous effort to obtain for him the Liberal Republican nomination. Having become known for certain "radical" views, he was nominated for the presidency by the Labor Reform Convention at Columbus, Ohio, in February 1872. This convention denounced monopolies and advocated paper-money legislation, the payment of the national debt in paper, a low tariff, general amnesty, and the collection of the cost of future wars from the wealth of the country. The wealthy Davis, however, was far from the typical labor reformer; and it was generally supposed that he associated himself with the movement not for itself, but as a preliminary to the coming Liberal Republican and Democratic nominations. When the Republican liberals met in convention at Cincinnati in 1872, Davis was reckoned one of the foremost contenders for the nomination. He was widely indorsed by Democratic conventions in the Middle West; and, despite the vigorous candidacy of Trumbull, he commanded great strength among the Liberal Republicans of Illinois. A number of factors, however, worked against him: his monetary policies, his judicial office, his alliance with Labor, division within the Illinois forces, influential newspaper opposition, and, perhaps chiefly, the overactivity of his friends. Though he received 92½ votes on the first ballot, Davis's strength soon dwindled; and the net result of his candidacy was the diminution of the chances of such men as Trumbull or Charles Francis Adams whom many earnest liberals regarded as preferable to Greeley, the convention's choice. The inference that his place on the Columbus ticket had been intended as a stepping-stone to the Cincinnati nomination was strengthened when, after failing at Cincinnati, he withdrew as Labor nominee.

In 1877 Davis passed from the Supreme Court to the United States Senate under circumstances that produced wide-spread comment. In the presidential contest between Hayes and Tilden the Democrats in Congress would probably never have supported the Electoral Commission Bill, had they not expected that Davis would serve as the fifth justice—the all-important "fifteenth member"—whose vote they hoped would turn the scale for Tilden. With a strange fatuity, however, the Democrats of the Illinois legislature, after a protracted contest, joined with the Independents to elect Davis to the United States Senate. His acceptance of the office, affecting as it did the presidential controversy, brought down on his head a storm of abusive epithets. As the wits remarked, he was transferred "from the bench to the fence," for in an evenly divided Senate his wavering vote turned the scale now to the Republicans and now to the Democrats. When Vice-President Arthur became president, Davis, as presiding officer of the Senate, still wielded the balance of power; and as he came more and more to support the Republican administration, he was denounced as a betrayer of the Democrats to whom he owed his senatorship. As a member of the Judiciary Committee of the Senate he made certain proposals in regard to federal appellate jurisdiction which were later adopted. His support of Hancock in 1880 and of Blaine in 1884 emphasized his lack of party regularity.

Davis was twice married. His first wife, Sarah Woodruff, daughter of Judge William Walker of Lenox, Mass., whom he married Oct. 30, 1838, when a young lawyer at Bloomington, died in 1879; and on Mar. 14, 1883, he married Adeline Burr of Fayetteville, N. C. Two children of the first marriage survived him. A man of great physical bulk who, as some wit remarked, had to be "surveyed" for a pair of trousers, he was practical rather than brilliant in his mental operations. He had a talent for party organization and combined in his person the dissimilar qualities of jurist and politician. His peculiar aptitude seems to have been for the work of circuit judge in pioneer Illinois, where he commanded such confidence that many cases were submitted to him without a jury. His decisions in this period were rarely appealed and seldom reversed. By making systematic investments in real estate, buying in farms at tax sales, foreclosing mortgages, and the like, he accumulated immense wealth, which he guarded with rigid economy and augmented by the vigorous collection of all claims due him. It was estimated that his estate at the time of his death was worth two million dollars. After his retirement from the Senate in March 1883, he spent his remaining years at Bloomington, where he died.

[H. E. Pratt, "David Davis" (MS. dissertation, Univ of Ill., 1930); J. M. Palmer, ed., *The Bench and Bar of Ill.* (1899), I, 154, 541–49; H. C. Whitney, *Life on the Circuit with Lincoln* (1892), ch. iii; *Memoirs of Gustave Koerner, 1809–1896* (1909), II, 539 ff.; *Chicago Times*, Mar. 20, 1880; *Chicago Tribune*, June 27, 1886; Thomas Dent, "David Davis of Illinois: A Sketch," *Am. Law Rev.*, July–Aug., 1919; Leonard Swett, "Memorial Address," etc., *Proc. Ill. State Bar Asso.*, 1887.] J. G. R.

DAVIS, EDMUND JACKSON (Oct. 2, 1827–Feb. 7, 1883), governor of Texas, was born in St. Augustine, Fla., but moved to Texas with his widowed mother in 1838, settling at Galveston. He studied law in Corpus Christi and practised his profession in Brownsville, Laredo, and Corpus Christi. He was deputy collector of customs under the Fillmore administration, was elected district attorney for the Rio Grande Valley district in 1853, and became judge of that district in 1854, serving until 1861. Alienated from the Confederate cause by his defeat in the race for delegate to the Secession Convention, he organized a regiment of Texas Unionists in Mexico. While recruiting near Matamoras he was captured by Confederates and narrowly escaped hanging. He led the unsuccessful Union attack on Laredo in 1864, but his regiment spent most of the war period in Louisiana. Davis was made a brigadier-general after the battle of Mansfield. He declined Gen. Sheridan's appointment as chief justice of the Texas state supreme court in 1865.

As a delegate to the constitutional convention of 1866 and as president of the Reconstruction convention of 1868–69 he advocated disfranchisement of ex-Confederates, unrestricted negro suffrage, and other radical measures of his party; in the latter convention he advocated dividing Texas into three states. In an election held by the military commander in 1869 he was elected governor of Texas over A. J. Hamilton, Democrat and Union army officer. His majority was less than one thousand, but he was the state's dictator for the next four years. He supported measures which, passed by the subservient Radical legislature, gave unusual power into the hands of the governor and alienated all but his own political partisans. The governor was empowered to appoint more than eight thousand state, county, and local officials, leaving a very small percentage of the state's employees to be elected by the voters.

The verdict of the people was that almost all of the Davis appointees were either incapable or dishonest. Although Richard Coke [*q.v.*] polled a majority of more than 40,000 in the election for governor in 1873, Davis declared the election law unconstitutional and refused to give up his office. He appealed to President Grant to order troops to Austin to sustain him in his claim. While Gov. Coke and the Democratic legislature organized the new administration on the second floor of the Capitol, Davis and the old legislature continued to maintain their positions on the first floor, guarded by a company of negro troops. After several days of dual government, during which time an armed clash was constantly expected, President Grant wired Davis that he declined to intervene, and Davis retired from office.

He continued to make his home in Austin, practised law, and was the Republican leader in the state until his death. He ran for governor against O. M. Roberts in 1880, but was defeated by a hundred thousand votes. He was warmly supported by a strong faction for a place in the cabinet of President Arthur, and was defeated for Congress in the Austin district in 1882. Even his most bitter opponents believed that he was personally honest (*Dallas Herald*, Feb. 8, 1883). He was the "ablest and most influential" Texas Republican of the Reconstruction period, and had the power of a czar within his own party. His domestic and social life was above reproach, and he was a man of unusual culture and refinement. At Corpus Christi in 1858 he had married Anne Britton, daughter of Maj. Forbes Britton, Texas officer in the Mexican War. Although her twin brother and other relatives were Confederates and Democrats, Mrs. Davis remained loyal to her husband throughout the period of the war and Reconstruction.

[Newspaper files in the Univ. of Texas Lib.; *Senate and House Jours.*, 1866–74; *Constitutional Convention Jours.*, 1866, 1869, and 1875; Executive Correspondence, Davis, File Boxes 206–20, in Secretary of State's office, Austin, Texas; S. S. McKay, "Texas During the E. J. Davis Régime" (MS., Austin, 1919); S. S. McKay, *Making the Texas Constitution of 1876* (1924); C. W. Ramsdell, *Reconstruction in Texas* (1910); F. W. Johnson, *A Hist. of Texas and Texans* (1914), I, 563; *Daily Statesman* (Austin), and *Galveston News*, of Feb. 8, 1883; *Weekly Democrat Statesman* (Austin), Feb. 15, 1883. Date of birth from tombstone erected by Davis's brother in the State Cemetery, Austin.]

S. S. M.

DAVIS, EDWIN HAMILTON (Jan. 22, 1811–May 15, 1888), archeologist, physician, a son of Henry Davis and Avis (Slocum) Davis, was born at Hillsboro in southern Ohio. This locality is celebrated for the number of circular, square, and octagonal earthworks of the Mound Builders, and as a youth Davis became attracted to the question of their origin. Archeology at that time being a science offering little sustenance to its followers, the young man was bent toward medicine, yet he kept up the exploration of the mounds while studying at Kenyon College where he graduated in 1833. His address on the subject at the college commencement interested Daniel Webster, then traveling in the West, and the latter's encouragement stimulated Davis in his determination to continue the researches at the first opportunity. Graduating at Cincinnati Medical College in 1837 or 1838, he began to practise in Chillicothe, Ohio, where he was to remain until 1850. His profession keeping him occupied, he joined hands with E. G. Squier, an ambitious archeologist, talented but without means, and thus at his own expense prosecuted the survey of one hundred mounds. The results of this collaboration were published as the first work issued by the newly founded Smithsonian Institution: *Ancient Monuments of the Mississippi Valley* (Smithsonian Contributions to Knowledge, no. 1, 1847, by E. G. Squier and E. H. Davis). This large memoir, well presented and illustrated, and embodying the surveys and descriptions of the more important works of the Mound Builders, being based on facts, has lost none of its value to archeologists. As a historical record of the ancient works of the Indians, especially since many of the monuments have disappeared under the plow and the encroachment of habitations, it is of summary value. A. Morlot, the Swiss archeologist, declared it to be as "glorious a monument of American science, as Bunker's Hill is of American bravery" (*American Philosophical Society Proceedings,* November 1862). During his stay in Ohio, Davis gathered a collection of cultural objects of the Mound Builders which was remarkable in revealing the surprising advance these Indians had made in art. The larger collection was acquired by the Blackmore Museum at Salisbury, England, where it has been for many decades an object of pilgrimage of American archeologists. A smaller collection by Davis is in the American Museum of Natural History of New York City.

Called to the chair of materia medica and therapeutics in the New York Medical College in 1850, Davis taught there till 1860. As might be suspected, he managed to interest some members of his classes in his hobby, for he refers to specimens "sent by my former students from Central and South America" (*Smithsonian Report,* 1866, p. 370). Addressing Prof. Joseph Henry, secretary of the Smithsonian, in 1866, he broached a project for correlating specimens with tribes on which he had been engaged, using the ethnological map of Waitz and taking in the results of Gallatin, Ludwig, Gibbs, and Morgan. In making this map, which did not become a reality for many years, he suggested the use of physical measurements on the skeleton and sent Prof. Henry the scheme of Scherzer and Schwarz for use of the Institution (*Smithsonian Report,* 1866, p. 371). In 1854 he delivered a course of lectures on archeology before the Lowell Institute of Boston and later repeated these lectures to societies in New York City and Brooklyn. He was tall, and distinguished by a highly refined, intellectual countenance. Kindly, a gentleman in temperament, he was learned in medical science, but easily imposed upon with regard to fees. He was married on Nov. 9, 1841, to Lucy Woodbridge who bore him nine children, among them John Woodbridge Davis, a well-known civil engineer.

[*N. Y. Times, N. Y. Tribune,* May 16, 1888; *Appletons' Annual Cyc.,* 1888; John Woodbridge, *The Woodbridge Record* (1883); information from Dr. Marcus Benjamin.]

W. H.

DAVIS, GARRET (Sept. 10, 1801–Sept. 22, 1872), lawyer, congressman and senator from Kentucky, was born in Mount Sterling, Ky., the son of Jeremiah Davis and his wife, a Miss Garret before marriage, who were both natives of Maryland. His father, though a blacksmith, was a leader in his community, serving for a time in the Kentucky legislature. Garret's brother, Amos, was a member of Congress from 1833 until his death in 1835. After attending the common schools, Garret studied Latin, Greek, and history without help. He was early led to an interest in law through his services as a deputy in the office of the clerk of the circuit court, first in Mount Sterling and then in Paris, to which town his family had moved. Admitted to the bar in the latter place in 1823, he there began the practise of his profession. Elected to the legislature in 1833, he served three consecutive terms in this body (1833–35). As political disputations were pleasing to him and he desired to continue in the service of his state, he ran for Congress and was elected. Here he served four consecutive terms (1839–47), representing for the last six years

Henry Clay's noted Ashland district, to which Bourbon County had been transferred from the Maysville district. He was an enthusiastic Whig and a close friend of Clay. He refused to break a promise not to run again for Congress in 1847 and declined the nomination for the lieutenant-governorship the next year. Elected to the state constitutional convention in 1849 he participated with great zeal in its debates, but quit the sessions and returned home when his fight against the elective judiciary failed and, in common with the Whigs, opposed the new constitution. Following the trend of a growing opposition to Roman Catholics, he made a bitter speech against them in the convention and shortly went over to the Know-Nothing party. In 1855 he declined the nomination for the governorship, and the following year the Know-Nothing nomination for the presidency.

The approach of the Civil War awakened him to great activity. When most Kentuckians were undecided in their course of action he came out for unswerving and complete adherence to the Union. In April 1861 he talked with Lincoln about Kentucky affairs, and in May supervised the distribution of Federal rifles to Kentucky Unionists throughout the central and eastern parts of the state. As a reward he was elected in December to the United States Senate to the seat vacated by John C. Breckinridge, and now became one of the most radical of the senators in his support of the Union, proposing among other things the confiscation of the property of all who aided the "rebellion" in any way. But it took only three years of war to work a complete revolution in him. In January 1864 he introduced a set of resolutions so astonishingly critical of Lincoln's war policy that he himself escaped expulsion only by explaining them away, and he ever afterward fought with all his powers of oratory and sarcasm against the war party and the radical reconstructionists. He was reëlected in 1867 by the Democrats, whom he had by this time solidly embraced. Davis was regarded as an effective debater and a learned man. He developed a large estate and became a close student of agriculture. He was married in 1825 to a daughter of Robert Trimble, later a justice of the United States Supreme Court. Three years after her death in 1843, he married the widow of Thomas Elliott, a lawyer of Paris, Ky. He successfully lived down his war record and died highly respected by his fellow Kentuckians, whose sympathies were now strongly Southern.

[Sketches of Davis may be found in L. and R. H. Collins, *Hist. of Ky.* (1882), II, 82–83; *Biog. Cyc. of the Commonwealth of Ky.* (1896), pp. 385–86; and *Biog. Encyc. of Ky.* (1878), pp. 413–14. See also: W. H. Perrin, ed., *Hist. of Bourbon, Scott, Harrison and Nicholas Counties, Ky.* (1882). His speeches in Congress are in the *Cong. Globe.* Much concerning his war record may be found in the *Official Records (Army)*, ser. 1, vols. II, IV, XVI, XXXVI, LI, LII.] E. M. C.

DAVIS, GEORGE (Mar. 1, 1820–Feb. 23, 1896), lawyer, attorney-general of the Confederacy, was born at Porter's Neck, New Hanover (now Pender) County, N. C., at the home of his parents, Thomas Frederick and Sarah Isabella (Eagles) Davis. Among his ancestors were Sir John Yeamans and Gen. James Moore of South Carolina and the Lillington and Swann families of the Albemarle Sound region. For nearly a century the Davis family had been living in the Cape Fear district. Graduating from the state university in 1838 at the head of his class, he was admitted to the Wilmington bar and soon gained a flattering reputation as a lawyer and an orator. A sincere and active Whig, he was very nearly named for governor in 1848, though he never sought office and never carried his home county for his party. A strong Union man in 1860, he was sent to the Peace Conference of February 1861; but in a "masterly" address in Wilmington, Mar. 2, he repudiated as dishonorable the recommendations of that body. In the Provisional Congress of the Confederacy he was the lawyer and the literary man, careful of the interests of property and critical of verbosity, as well as the conscientious representative, presenting many petitions. He served in the Confederate Senate from 1862 until he became attorney-general, Jan. 4, 1864 (*Journal of the Congress of the Confederate States of America,* 1904, III, 517). Jefferson Davis found him congenial and valuable, not always agreeing with the president but generally "right at last." On the collapse of the Confederacy, Apr. 26, 1865, having correctly ended his work as attorney-general, he fled the country, desperate but cool, only to meet imprisonment at Fort Hamilton for several months.

Back at the law in Wilmington, he met marked success, notably as leading counsel of the Atlantic Coast Line system during its formative period. Judges listened to him because he was careful, honest, and learned. To the public, however, he was known mainly through the occasional addresses in which for forty years he voiced the opinions of cultured and propertied Wilmingtonians. His "Early Men and Times of the Lower Cape Fear" (*Address before the Literary Societies of the University of North Carolina, Raleigh,* 1855), which is no longer accepted as final, had "brought the most romantic section of North Carolina permanently into history" (Smith, *post,* III, 1229). Fittingly, his last public address was in eulogy of Jefferson Davis (1889). Short, heavy-set, dark, without striking advantage of voice, he was an effective speaker because of his careful preparation, interpretative imagination, and a style "clear, strong, flexible." For his service "in shaping and toning the political ethics of our society" Gov. Vance tendered him in 1878 the chief justiceship, which he declined for pecuniary reasons. The next year Gov. Jarvis, wishing through the sale of the Western North Carolina Railroad to reverse the state's historic policy as to railroads, sought his legal skill and political influence; these he gave, in company with Thomas Ruffin, refusing compensation. He was buried with military honors from St. James's Church, Wilmington. He was twice married: on Nov. 17, 1842, to Mary A. Polk, who died in 1863; and on May 9, 1866, to Monimia Fairfax of Richmond.

[S. A. Ashe, *Geo. Davis, Attorney-General of the Confed. States* (1916); H. G. Connor, *Geo. Davis* (1911); Jas. Sprunt, *Chronicles of the Cape Fear River* (2nd ed., 1916). Selections from Davis's addresses appear in *A Memorial of the Hon. Geo. Davis* (1896) and in E. A. Alderman and J. C. Harris, *Lib. of Southern Lit.*, vol. III (1909), which also contains a sketch by C. Alphonso Smith. The Davis eulogy was published in *Wilmington's Tribute . . . Jefferson Davis* (1890). The *Wilmington Morning Star*, Feb. 25, 1896, and the *Wilmington Weekly Tribune*, Feb. 28, 1896, carried obituaries.]

C. C. P.

DAVIS, GEORGE BRECKENRIDGE (Feb. 13, 1847–Dec. 15, 1914), soldier and judge advocate general, was born at Ware, Mass., where his parents, Solomon B. and Sarah (Dunbar) Davis resided. His education was received at the public schools at Ware and Springfield, immediately upon leaving which in 1863 he enlisted in the 1st Massachusetts Volunteer Cavalry, and served with that regiment till the close of the Civil War, attaining the rank of lieutenant. He then, with a view to a permanent career in the army, entered the Military Academy at West Point as a cadet, July 1, 1867, and graduated June 12, 1871, being assigned to the 5th Cavalry as second lieutenant. On July 6, 1871, he married Ella I. Prince of West Springfield, Mass. For the next two years he saw service in Wyoming and Arizona, but returned to West Point Aug. 30, 1873, as assistant professor of Spanish, later giving instruction also in French, chemistry, mineralogy and geology. Promoted first lieutenant, May 9, 1878, he spent the next five years on service in the West. He was appointed principal assistant professor of history, geography and ethics, and assistant professor of law at West Point on Aug. 28, 1883, and during his tenure of office wrote *Outlines of International Law with an Account of its Origin and Sources and of its Historical Development* (1887), a work which became popular and passed through several editions. On his promotion to captain, Aug. 21, 1888, he returned to frontier duty, being stationed in Indian Territory. Four months later, however, he was appointed judge advocate with the rank of major, being at first detailed on special duty in the office of the secretary of war, Washington, D. C., and subsequently assuming charge of the publication of the *War of the Rebellion: Official Records of the Union and Confederate Armies*. He began the study of law at Columbian (now George Washington) Law School and graduated in 1891. He was appointed deputy judge advocate general and promoted lieutenant-colonel, Aug. 3, 1896, becoming in addition professor of law and history at West Point. In 1897 he published *The Elements of Law: An Introduction to the Study of the Constitutional and Military Law of the United States,* and under direction of the secretary of war prepared a manual of *The Military Laws of the United States* (War Department Document no. 64, 1897). This was followed by *A Treatise on the Military Law of the United States, Together with the Practice and Procedure of Courts-Martial and other Military Tribunals* (1898), which became the standard work on the subject. At the close of the Spanish-American War he was engaged in the investigation and trial of the so-called "canned beef cases." He relinquished his professorship on appointment as judge advocate general with the rank of brigadier-general and occupied this position for nearly ten years. In 1906 he was United States delegate to the Red Cross Conference at Geneva. In 1907 as United States delegate he attended the second Peace Conference at The Hague. He retired with the rank of major-general, Feb. 13, 1911, and died at Washington, D. C., Dec. 15, 1914.

He contributed a number of articles to military and historical publications, among them being "The Operations of the Cavalry in the Gettysburg Campaign" in *Cavalry Studies from Two Great Wars* (1896), and "The Antietam Campaign," "The Strategy of the Gettysburg Campaign," "From Gettysburg to Williamsport" and "The Bristoe and Mine Run Campaigns" in *Papers of the Military Historical Society of Massachusetts,* vol. III (1903).

[G. W. Cullum, *Biog. Reg.* (3rd ed., 1891); F. B. Heitman, *Hist. Reg. and Dict. of the U. S. Army* (1903), I, 358; obituary in *N. Y. Times,* Dec. 17, 1914; *Who's Who in America,* 1912–13.]

H. W. H. K.

DAVIS, GEORGE WHITEFIELD (July 26, 1839–July 12, 1918), soldier, engineer, was born in Thompson, Windham County, Conn., the son of George and Elizabeth (Grow) Davis, whose ancestors were early settlers in Massachusetts and Rhode Island. He attended district school in his native village and an academy in a neighboring town, and then divided his time between working on his father's farm and teaching school. In 1860 he secured a place as tutor in the family of a Georgian, but the outbreak of the war cut short this employment. In September 1861 he made his escape to the North. His long and difficult journey was interrupted by his arrest in Atlanta, and in its last stages was through the theatre of active operations in Kentucky. Enlisting in the 11th Connecticut Infantry, Nov. 27, 1861, he accompanied his regiment on the North Carolina expedition and after its first engagement, at New Berne, was appointed first lieutenant, Apr. 5, 1862. The regiment was with the Army of the Potomac at South Mountain, Antietam, and Fredericksburg, and was then sent to southeastern Virginia, where it eventually became a part of the Army of the James and participated with it in the final campaign against Richmond. As captain and major, Davis then served as a quartermaster in the XXV Army Corps, which was stationed in Texas in preparation for possible war in Mexico against Maximilian and the French.

He was mustered out of the volunteer service, Apr. 20, 1866, and appointed a captain of infantry in the regular army, Jan. 22, 1867. He served for some years with his regiment in the Southwest, was in charge of building operations at Fort Douglas, Utah, and San Antonio, Tex., and was then selected as assistant engineer on the construction of the Washington Mounment. After the completion of this work he was aide to Gen. Sheridan and later an instructor at the service school at Fort Leavenworth. Though a self-trained engineer, he had acquired so high a reputation that the Nicaragua Canal Construction Company sought his services, and by joint resolution of Congress he was granted indefinite leave of absence without pay that he might accept their offer. He was vice-president and general manager of the company from 1890 to 1893, when financial difficulties caused the suspension of work and his return to military duty. He was promoted major in 1894. In 1895 he became president of the board in charge of the publication of the *Official Records* (of the Civil War), succeeding Maj. George B. Davis, with whom he is constantly confused, and carried on the work until the outbreak of the Spanish-American War. He became lieutenant-colonel on Apr. 26, 1898, and on May 4 he was appointed brigadier-general of volunteers. He organized and commanded a division of the II Corps, stationed at Camp Alger, Va., and then commanded the department of Pinar del Rio, in Cuba, until recalled to serve on the court of inquiry convened to investigate Gen. Miles's allegations as to the quality of the beef furnished to the troops in the field. He thus played a part in the "embalmed beef" controversy. From April 1899 until December 1900 he held the military governorship of Porto Rico. He was promoted colonel in the regular army in October 1899, retaining his brigadier-generalcy of volunteers until appointed brigadier-general in the regular army, Feb. 2, 1901. From Porto Rico he was sent to the Philippines, where he served as provost-marshal general in Manila for a short time, as commander of the department of Mindanao for fourteen months, and, after his appointment as major-general in July 1902, as commander of the entire Philippine division. He was retired from active service on July 26, 1903, and returned to the United States. In 1904 President Roosevelt appointed him a member of the Isthmian Canal Commission, according to an intention which he had confidentially expressed shortly before Davis's retirement. The latter was also designated as governor of the Canal Zone, where he organized the new government before retiring from office in 1905. He served as chairman of the board of engineers convened to recommend the type of canal to be constructed, his vote being cast in favor of a sea-level canal. His opinion was shared by all the foreign members of the board, but by a minority of the Americans. He resided in Washington for the remainder of his life, but twice went on special diplomatic missions to Guatemala. On Apr. 30, 1870, he married Maria Carmen, daughter of Alexander J. Atocha.

[Brief autobiography filed in the War Dept.; F. B. Heitman, *Hist. Reg. and Dict. of the U. S. Army* (1903), I, 358; G. W. Davis, *John Grow of Ipswich* (1913); *Puerto Rico, embracing the Reports of Brig. Gen. Geo. W. Davis, Mil. Gov.* (War Dept., 1899); G. W. Davis, *Report on the Mil. Govt. of the City of Manila, P. I., from 1898 to 1901;* Jos. B. Bishop, *The Panama Gateway* (1913, 1915). The sketch in *Who's Who in America* is incorrect as to several dates.]

T. M. S.

DAVIS, HENRY (Sept. 15, 1771–Mar. 8, 1852), clergyman, president of two colleges in their formative periods, was born at East Hampton, L. I., the son of John and Mary (Conkling) Davis, who were of Connecticut stock. Graduating from Yale in 1796, he was for a time tutor at Williams and then, from 1798 to 1803, at Yale. During the latter period he studied theology with Rev. Charles Backus of Somers,

Conn. In 1801 he was elected protessor of divinity at Yale, but while he was preparing to assume this position the failure of his health caused him to decline it. He was married on Sept. 22, 1801, to Hannah Phoenix, daughter of Thomas Treadwell of Smithtown, L. I., a member of the Continental Congress. Leaving Yale, Davis spent some time in travel for his health, and in 1806 became professor of Greek at Union College. Three years later he became president of Middlebury College, which had been established in 1800. His administration was such that after eight years he was offered in 1817 the presidency of Hamilton College and that of Yale, in succession to Timothy Dwight, both of which he declined. Later in the year, however, he was again elected president of Hamilton and took office. The college was only five years old, and his task in many ways was that of a first president, not a second. Under his direction Hamilton at first prospered, the number of students rising to about a hundred. Before long, however, he and the leading trustees were in disagreement. The country was booming, and the trustees wished the college to boom likewise. They were unacquainted with college management, as they showed by interference in discipline, and were overconfident in their use of funds. Davis was conservative in opinions and temper, and steeped in New England college traditions. While very kindly in spirit and manner, he was undiplomatic, humorless, and unyielding in what he thought his duty. His disapproval of Finney's methods in revivals in neighboring towns increased opposition to him among the trustees. In this discord the college lost most of its faculty, and in 1829 had only nine students. Davis held on in almost impossible circumstances and was ultimately victorious. Having seen the board of trustees and faculty reconstituted and the student body restored, he resigned the presidency in 1832. The rest of his life was spent at the college, in much bodily feebleness. By his character, teaching, and preaching Davis exercised a strong influence over his students. His earnest religious life moved many to enter the ministry, especially through Auburn Theological Seminary, in the establishment and early life of which he took an important part. He published several sermons and addresses and *A Narrative of the Embarrassments and Decline of Hamilton College* (1833), recounting the college troubles in excessive detail.

[Davis's papers and letters in the lib. of Hamilton Coll.; his sermons and addresses; F. B. Dexter, *Biog. Sketches Grads. Yale Coll. 1792–1805* (1911); G. G. Bush, *Hist. of Education in Vt.* (1900); *Documentary Hist. of Hamilton Coll.* (1922); *A Memorial of the Semi-Centennial Celebration of the Founding of Hamilton Coll.* (1862); J. Q. Adams, *A Hist. of Auburn Theol. Sem., 1818–1918* (1918).] R. H. N.

DAVIS, HENRY GASSAWAY (Nov. 16, 1823–Mar. 11, 1916), United States senator, railroad builder, the son of Caleb and Louise Warfield (Brown) Davis, was descended from old Maryland families. The third of six children, he was born at Woodstock, Md. From his father's shoulder he witnessed in 1828 the exercises marking the beginning of the construction of America's first railroad, the Baltimore and Ohio, on which his father was later a construction contractor, and of which he himself became a trusted employee. His early schooling was begun by his mother who, after her husband's financial reverses which were soon followed by his death, opened a school for girls to contribute to the support of the family. Entering the service of the Baltimore and Ohio Railroad as a brakeman in 1842, he rose to the position of conductor, and in 1847 became supervisor of the line to Cumberland. He personally installed the first night trains. On Feb. 22, 1853, at Frederick, Md., he married Katharine Anne, daughter of Gideon Bantz. Following his marriage he sought a wider field of action. Accepting the position of station agent at Piedmont, Va. (now W. Va.), he really assumed the duties of a division superintendent because of his responsibility for directing the movement of trains up the long incline to the summit, and over the Appalachian Divide. During the first year he lived in a box car while building a home to which he brought his wife a year later.

A general store which he started at Piedmont in 1854 marked the beginning of his enterprises, which came to include trading with the interior and the opening of timber and coal fields. In 1858 he resigned his railroad position to devote his entire time to his growing business. With profits accumulated during the Civil War from the sale of supplies to the government and of equipment to railroads, he pursued larger plans based on his confidence in the resources of the upper Potomac region and the country beyond on the Cheat River. In 1867 he bought several thousand acres of timber-land on the crest of the Alleghanies, built a home in the woods, began lumbering on a large scale, and soon thereafter laid out the village of Deer Park. By 1870 he was regarded as a man of large wealth. In 1881 he began the construction of the West Virginia Central and Pittsburgh Railway, which was completed through primeval woods to Elkins in 1889, and with a branch extension to Durbin on the Greenbrier in 1904. At Elkins he built a large residence which became his home in 1892. In 1902 he sold the West Virginia Central and began the construction of an important outlet from the upper Monongahela region of Tygart's Valley via the Elk to Charleston, the Coal and Coke Railway which was completed in 1906 and the management of which he supervised until 1912. His success was largely due to business foresight, tenacity and determination, incessant industry, and inflexible and economical business rules, but also in part to social qualities.

In politics he attained prominence. In 1861 he voted against the secession of Virginia, and throughout the Civil War he was a strong Union man. At the close of the war his sympathies were with the Republicans on the questions of a protective tariff and industrial development, but his advocacy of a conciliatory policy toward the Confederates and his opposition to test-oaths and negro suffrage determined his later cooperation with the Democrats. In 1865 he was elected to the West Virginia House of Delegates as a Union-Conservative candidate. In 1868 he was elected, and two years later was reëlected, to the state Senate. For two decades after 1868 he represented his state in the Democratic national conventions. Elected to the United States Senate in January 1871, he was reëlected in 1877, but declined to be a candidate for a third term, chiefly because of the desire to devote himself to his railroad projects. In the Senate he was a useful member of the special committee on transportation routes to the seaboard, and for two years was chairman of the Committee on Appropriations. He was a delegate to the first two International American (Pan-American) Congresses. He was also appointed a member of the Intercontinental Railway Survey Commission which held sessions from 1890 to 1894. In 1904, at the age of eighty-one, he was the Democratic candidate for vice-president. He died in Washington at the home of his daughter, Mrs. Stephen B. Elkins.

[Chas. M. Pepper, *The Life and Times of Henry Gassaway Davis* (1920); Geo. W. Atkinson and Alvaro F. Gibbens, *Prominent Men of W. Va.* (1890); J. M. Callahan, *Hist. of W. Va., Old and New* (1923).]

J. M. C.

DAVIS, HENRY GASSETT (Nov. 4, 1807–Nov. 18, 1896), pioneer orthopedic surgeon, born at Trenton, Me., was the son of Isaac Davis, manufacturer and mechanic, by his wife, Polly Rice, and grandson of Deacon Isaac Davis of Northboro, Mass., who was descended from Dolor Davis, an early settler at Cape Cod (1634). Henry Davis intended to follow his father's trade and was on his way South to set up an establishment for the manufacture of cotton-bagging when, en route, he stopped to visit a sister who was under treatment for scoliosis. The treatment appeared to him completely to ignore certain elementary mechanical principles, and he forthwith gave up his intended career to begin the study of medicine. He received his M.D. in March 1839 from the Yale Medical School, having obtained the greater part of his clinical training at Bellevue Hospital. He spent the first fifteen years of his medical career practising at Worcester and Millbury, Mass., after which he settled in New York. He gained wide experience as a general practitioner and surgeon, and it was not until his removal to New York that he directed his attention more exclusively to the problems of orthopedics. In so doing he became the founder of the so-called "traction school" of orthopedic surgery. While still in Millbury his interest had been aroused in the treatment of fractures and deformities, and he advocated energetically the use of continuous traction for the correction of deformity and for relief of joint irritation. His first use of weights and pulleys and of other traction devices for treatment of fracture (*American Medical Monthly,* May 1856) preceded those introduced in 1860 by Gurdon Buck [*q.v.*] and met with equal success. His practise eventually grew so large that he opened a private hospital at Thirty-seventh St. and Madison Ave., chiefly to receive patients from abroad. Davis's beliefs, new in their day, concerning the nature and treatment of club foot, congenital dislocation of the hip, chronic diseases of the joints, and the deformities resulting from poliomyelitis, formed the basis for the modern approach to these problems. It is interesting that in dealing with abscesses he recommended opening and evacuation, and subsequent lavage with warm water and a French preparation of chlorine, thus anticipating the Carrel-Dakin therapy used at the present time. He was the first to devise a splint for traction and the protection of the hip joint (Nutt). Davis was also a physician in the broad sense of the term, for in treating the part he did not neglect the whole, and constitutional treatment is not more wisely taught to-day than by him in the middle of the nineteenth century. He influenced younger men who were about him, notably Lewis A. Sayre [*q.v.*], Charles Fayette Taylor [*q.v.*], and, though less directly, Edward Hickling Bradford [*q.v.*], and it was through these followers that the specialty of orthopedic surgery in this country was rapidly developed. His most important work, *Conservative Surgery, as Exhibited in*

Davis

Remedying some of the Mechanical Causes that Operate Injuriously both in Health and Disease (1867), is a volume of unusual clarity and literary excellence, and was the first notable textbook in the history of American orthopedic surgery. Several other contributions were important: "On the Effect of Pressure upon Ulcerated Vertebrae" (*New York Journal of Medicine,* 1859), "On the Pathological Basis of the Treatment of Joint Disease" (*American Medical Monthly,* 1862), "The American Method of Treating Joint Diseases and Deformities" (*Transactions of the American Medical Association,* 1863). He was a member of local medical societies in New York and in 1895 was elected an honorary member of the newly formed American Orthopedic Association. At the age of eighty-nine he died at his home in Everett, Mass. He was survived by his widow, Ellen W. Deering, whom he had married in 1856, and by a son and two daughters. He is said to have been the first to suggest to railroad engineers the advantage of elevating the outer rail of the track at curves.

[Two excellent accounts of Davis are available by J. J. Nutt, *Medic. Record,* N. Y., 1905, LXVIII, 298–302; *Ibid.,* 868–69. See also *Trans. Am. Orthop. Asso.,* 1889, II, 7; *Ibid.,* 1897, X, 4; *Bull. N. Y. Acad. Med.,* ser. I, vol. I, 1861; J. D. Estabrook, *Three Generations of Northern Davises 1781–1894* (1908).] J. F. F.

DAVIS, HENRY WINTER (Aug. 16, 1817–Dec. 30, 1865), politician, statesman, was the son of Rev. Henry Lyon Davis, president of St. John's College (Md.), an ardent Federalist and Episcopalian, and Jane (Brown) Winter, a cultured woman with aristocratic connections in the town of Annapolis. During the campaign of 1828 Davis's father was removed from his position by the partisans of Jackson on the board of trustees of the college, and set adrift under circumstances which greatly influenced the career of Henry Winter Davis. After a strenuous course at Kenyon College (Ohio), young Davis procured, after much delay and difficulty, the meager funds necessary to enable him to study law at the University of Virginia. He left the University in June 1840 with some knowledge of law, mainly *Coke on Littleton,* and began his career at Alexandria, Va., a handsome man of twenty-three, six feet tall, and of aristocratic bearing and manner. Here he quickly won an enviable reputation, obtained a good income from his profession, and on Oct. 30, 1845, married Constance C. Gardiner, daughter of a prominent citizen of the town. After her death, he married, on Jan. 26, 1857, Nancy Morris of Baltimore, whither he had moved in 1849.

Attaching himself to the Whig party, Davis appeared on the platform as a speaker with Robert Winthrop and Horace Greeley in the unhappy campaign of Gen. Winfield Scott for the presidency in 1852. In 1855 he was chosen to a seat in Congress where he immediately took a prominent place among the leaders of the Know-Nothing party. The hot disputes about Kansas left him unmoved, nor did the ardent campaign of 1856 budge him from his steady conservatism. He supported Fillmore, and endeavored to hold his neutral position from 1856 to 1860. But the decline of the Know-Nothing party and the break between Douglas and Buchanan compelled him to take sides. On the last day of January 1860, after a deadlock of seven weeks, he cast his vote for William Pennington, Republican candidate for speaker. This enabled the new party to organize the House and to prepare more effectively for the presidential campaign already opened. The decision made Davis a national character, but the legislature of Maryland repudiated his action by a vote of 62 to 1. From that day to his death every public act of Davis was a matter of immediate concern to the country. He was for a moment candidate for the Republican nomination for the vice-presidency, and thought of himself from that time forward as a suitable candidate for the presidency. He was guided by an overweening ambition, but his abilities as a statesman and an orator were acknowledged to be extraordinary. In his district he was both hated and loved beyond all other public men and his campaigns for reëlection were violent and bloody. Notwithstanding his vote for the Republicans in January 1860, he was the guiding spirit of the Bell and Everett party in Maryland; and he procured the nomination of Thomas H. Hicks [*q.v.*], Unionist, for governor. His purpose was not to defeat the Republican party in Maryland, but the regular Democrats, with Breckinridge as their candidate. Bell and Everett won; Hicks likewise was successful.

Davis, serving the balance of his term in the House of Representatives during the critical winter of 1860–61, keenly desired to sit in the new cabinet. But Montgomery Blair, a member of perhaps the most influential family in the country and the leader of a forlorn hope of Republicans in Maryland, was chosen. Davis was alone and without a party, for the Union party was rapidly disintegrating. On Feb. 7, when the Confederacy was just raising its head in Montgomery and the leading Republicans of the North were acquiescing in the secession movement, Davis in one of the important speeches of his life asserted that in Maryland they did not recognize the right of secession and that they would not be dragged from the Union (*Congressional Globe, Appendix,* 36 Cong., 2 Sess.). But Gov. Hicks and the people of Maryland did recognize the right of Southerners to secede and they seemed about to take legislative action in that direction. Davis said later that but for his activity Lincoln would have been inaugurated in some Pennsylvania village. He wrote a public letter to the *New York Tribune* urging that the Federal forts in Maryland be placed in the hands of Union men. Then he simply announced himself as a candidate for a seat in the House of Representatives. It was the 15th of April. Four days later the 6th Massachusetts Regiment was attacked in Baltimore. One of the most spectacular and bitter of political contests ensued, with Davis everywhere the militant leader of the Unionists. On June 13 his opponent, Henry May, a Southern sympathizer, was elected by a vote of 8,335 to 6,287.

It was a decisive defeat, but Davis became even better known to the country, traveled widely, and spoke often for the Union. However, either his chagrin at the presence of Montgomery Blair in Lincoln's cabinet or the President's open violation of many of the sacred traditions of the country led him into opposition. He could hardly contain himself when he thought of the procedure in the many courts martial of the day, or of the thousands of men in prison without proved offense. To him the *habeas corpus* was sacred beyond a question. Before a very hostile Brooklyn audience, early in November, he bitterly arraigned the President and all about him. There are few instances of a speaker's attaining such complete mastery over his audience as Davis did on that occasion. Nor did he ever cease to oppose most of the President's policies. He was not arrested or imprisoned, however, and in the hotly contested election of 1863 he was returned to the House, where he was at once made chairman of the Committee on Foreign Relations. He then became and remained a close friend and ally of Thaddeus Stevens, chairman of the Committee of Ways and Means. It was at the moment when Lincoln sent to Congress his program of reconstruction, known as the Louisiana Plan. Davis ranged himself at once on the side of the opposition, attacking upon every possible occasion the "usurpations" of the President, and ridiculing unmercifully the foreign policy of Seward, the management of the navy by Gideon Welles, the conduct of Gen. Frank P. Blair as an army commander, and the unrelenting campaign of Montgomery Blair against himself in Maryland. In a little while the great majority of the House hung upon his words and followed him implicitly. He was more the master of that body than Thaddeus Stevens himself.

The most important of Davis's campaigns in the House of Representatives began early in the session and culminated in a victory over the President in spite of all that Seward, Welles, and the Blairs could do. Instead of reporting a reconstruction bill such as Lincoln suggested, Davis wrote and substituted a measure of his own. The President would leave the reconstructed states to abolish slavery themselves; Davis would compel immediate emancipation. The President would allow ten per cent of the voters to set up a new state government; Davis would require a majority. The President would proscribe only a few of the leading Confederates; Davis would proscribe a vast number. The President said nothing about repudiating Southern debts; Davis would compel repudiation of all Southern war debts, state and Confederate. His was a policy of "thorough," like that of the Cromwellians in England. Davis's principal speech in support of his drastic plan was made on Mar. 22, 1864, when the supporters of the President and the rising radical opposition were engaged in the bitterest warfare. He denied the right of the President to reconstruct a state and considered the Emancipation Proclamation as invalid until approved by Congress. He claimed all power for Congress and wished so to reconstruct the Southern states, when they were completely beaten and utterly helpless, that no court could ever undo the work. The Davis bill passed the House and the Senate by large majorities. When at last, after his renomination and the adjournment of Congress, Lincoln pocket-vetoed the measure, Davis was beside himself with rage. He took the extreme risk of a violent attack upon the nominee of his party at a moment when few thoughtful men had any real hope of complete success in the war. In July, conferences of leading Republicans were held in New York. Davis took part. In the spirit of these troubled men, Davis wrote the famous Wade-Davis manifesto which appeared in the leading papers on Aug. 8, 1864. In this document he reviewed the history of the congressional plan of reconstruction and ridiculed the President's plan in unmerciful language (*Speeches and Addresses of Henry Winter Davis,* pp. 415–426).

It is said that Davis never entered the White House during Lincoln's incumbency and that this manifesto brought the relations of the two men, as well as of the opposing groups in the Republican party, to the necessity of some understanding. The presidential election was pending and the people of the North had plainly lost heart. Davis was in Baltimore waging his campaign for reëlection, while Seward, Weed, Welles, and the rest were fighting in Washington and elsewhere for the success of their chief. On July 1, Chase resigned and gave up his open fight on the President. On Sept. 4, the news of victory at Atlanta reached Washington. Early in September, Montgomery Blair ceased his war upon Davis and offered his resignation. Before the end of September, Davis called at the White House and henceforth made speeches on behalf of the President. Lincoln was reëlected and Chase took his seat as chief justice, but the ambitious chairman of the Committee on Foreign Relations was defeated in his district.

When Congress met, however, in December 1864, Davis, now a "lame duck," was the most popular man in it. He fought through the short session, saw Andrew Johnson inaugurated with more than wonted pleasure, and, after the death of Lincoln, went to Chicago to make another of his great speeches: He attacked Johnson as he had attacked Lincoln, and outlined once more the program of congressional reconstruction which was indorsed by Charles Sumner at Worcester on Sept. 14 and readopted by Congress the next year. Davis, still only forty-eight years old, looked forward to the day when he might sit in the coveted White House, meanwhile impeaching Andrew Johnson, as he must have sought the impeachment of Lincoln if the latter had lived. A private citizen of extraordinary prestige, he returned to Washington in December 1865, and with his mere presence at the door of the House of Representatives broke up the session. Exposed to inclement weather during the holidays, he took cold. This developed into pneumonia and on Dec. 30 he died.

[There has never been an adequate study of Davis's career, though Bernard C. Steiner, *The Life of Henry Winter Davis* (1916), offers a brief review of the main facts and incidents. J. A. J. Creswell's sketch of Davis's life is published as an introduction to *The Speeches and Addresses Delivered in the Cong. of the U. S. and on Several Public Occasions, by Henry Winter Davis* (1867). Gideon Welles and Adam Gurowski make frequent mention of him in their diaries.]

W. E. D.

DAVIS, HORACE (Mar. 16, 1831–July 12, 1916), manufacturer, congressman, was born in Worcester, Mass., the son of "Honest John" Davis [*q.v.*] and Eliza (Bancroft) Davis, sister of George Bancroft, the historian. His brothers were J. C. Bancroft Davis and Andrew McFarland Davis [*qq.v.*]. Upon his graduation from Harvard College in 1849, he entered the Law School, but because of failing eyesight soon withdrew. He thereupon sailed for San Francisco, via Cape Horn. Upon his arrival in California, he started for the gold-mines and for a short time ran, unsuccessfully, a store at Shaw's Flat. Returning to San Francisco, he successively found employment as lumber-surveyor on the water-front, as supercargo on a coasting steamer owned by his cousin, Isaac Davis, and as a purser in the Pacific Mail Steamship Company. In 1852 he was one of a small group who organized the Mercantile Library Association, the oldest public library in California. Since the enterprise was suffering from lack of financial support, he was persuaded to assume the duties of librarian in February 1854. Under his administration popular interest was revived, and the library was soon operating upon a substantial foundation. His duties, however, especially in compiling the first catalogue, strained his eyes and so undermined his health that he resigned in December 1855. He and his brother Andrew had loaned their savings to a miller, and in satisfaction of the unpaid debt were obliged to take over the milling property; in 1860 he established the Golden Gate Flouring Mills, which proved to be highly profitable. He became an accepted authority on wheat and the production of flour; and at his death, was president of the Sperry Flour Company. At the beginning of the Civil War, he was active in the "Home Guard," a secret league formed in San Francisco to insure the loyalty of California to the Lincoln administration. The league helped elect Leland Stanford governor by keeping peace around the polls on election day, and then dissolved. Later Davis was an active member of the Sanitary Commission.

Elected to Congress in 1876, he served two terms there. His most important activity as a member of the House was in connection with the Chinese question. In January 1878, he introduced a bill to restrict immigration from China, and he made his only lengthy speech in Congress, June 8, 1878, in support of it (*Congressional Record,* 45 Cong., 2 Sess., pp. 4328–32). He was president of the Produce Exchange in San Francisco for ten years previous to his election to Congress. After his retirement from that body, he became president of the San Francisco Chamber of Commerce (1883–84), president of the Savings and Loan Society (1885), and member of the Republican National Committee (1880–88). In February 1888 he was elected president of the University of California, but resigned in April 1890. He was also closely associated with Stanford University, having been named by its founder as one of the original trustees, and in his last years served as president of the board. One of his chief interests was the School of Mechanic Arts in San Francisco, established by James Lick [*q.v.*]. He served as president of its board of trustees, and was instrumental in effecting its consolidation with the Wilmerding and Lux schools. A devoted Unitarian, he was deeply interested in the Pacific Unitarian School for the Ministry, to which he contributed generously.

Davis found time to take an active interest in historical and literary studies, and to publish a number of essays. The most important of these was his monograph, "American Constitutions," in which he traced the changes in the relations of the three departments of government "which have been silently going on in the United States for the past century" (*Johns Hopkins University Studies in Historical and Political Science,* I, 1885). He was twice married. His first wife, the daughter of Capt. Macondray, died in 1872 after years of invalidism. Three years later, he married Edith, the daughter of Rev. Thomas Starr King [*q.v.*]. He died at San Francisco at the age of eighty-five, following an operation for appendicitis.

[Newspaper clippings pertaining to Horace Davis's political life, 1876–80, pamphlets on Cal., and "How I Got into the Library Business" (MS. 1916), in the Univ. of Cal. Lib.; "The 'Home Guard' of 1861," reprinted from H. Morse Stephens and H. E. Bolton, *The Pacific Ocean in Hist.* (1917); W. C. Jones, *Illustrated Hist. of the Univ. of Cal.* (1901), pp. 140 ff.; *San Francisco Chronicle,* July 13, 1916; C. A. Murdock, *A Backward Glance at Eighty* (1921), pp. 219–24; *Who's Who in America,* 1916–17.] P. O. R.

DAVIS, JEFF (May 6, 1862–Jan. 3, 1913), governor of Arkansas, United States senator, son of Lewis W. and Elizabeth (Phillips) Davis, was born in Little River County, Ark. He attended the common schools, the preparatory department of the University of Arkansas, and the law school of Vanderbilt University, and received a degree in law from Cumberland University. Admitted to the bar at nineteen, he began practising with his father at Russellville, Ark. Entering public life in 1890, he remained in it most of the time until his death. Prosecuting attorney of the fifth judicial district for four years (1890–94), he became attorney-general of Arkansas in 1899. Shortly after assuming the latter office, he attracted considerable attention by his interpretation of the state anti-trust law, which provided that no corporation belonging to an association for the fixing of prices should be allowed to do business in Arkansas. Davis, holding this to mean any association outside as well as inside the state, secured indictments against numerous corporations, but was overruled by the supreme court. This decision and the building of a new state capitol became the issues on which he was elected governor for three terms (1901–07), breaking all records in the state. His first and second legislatures refused to amend the law, but the third (1905) changed it to meet his wishes. The result was that the insurance companies quit the state. The law soon became a dead letter and part of it was repealed in 1907. He supported the bill to repeal the fellow-servants rule, which it took several years of agitation to enact; and he favored the abolition of the suicide clause in life-insurance policies, more liberal Confederate pensions, and larger appropriations for state charitable institutions. At the close of his last term he juggled the financial statement so as to make it appear that the state was out of debt and had a surplus, and induced the legislature to reduce the taxes,—a policy which caused a deficit and a later bond issue. Following his governorship, he served a term in the United States Senate (1907–13). Two days after being sworn in he introduced a bill to apply his anti-trust law to the nation, and kept it on the calendar for five years. He denounced "gambling in agricultural products" and introduced a bill prohibiting dealing in futures. Another bill proposed to prohibit the sale or gift of intoxicating liquors in prohibition territory. Although he supported the repeal of the fellow-servants rule in Arkansas, he opposed, in Congress, the employers' liability and workmen's compensation bill in 1912. He made little effort to push his own bills, but "occupied himself with looking after the wants of his constituents, answering their letters, . . . sent out all the seeds allotted to him and all he could borrow . . . and kept himself in political condition for the next campaign."

Davis revolutionized Arkansas politics. He was largely instrumental in bringing about the substitution of the general primary for the convention system in nominating officers. Most of those who opposed him he treated as personal as well as political enemies, but he became completely reconciled when they returned to his camp. His unalterable purpose was self-advancement and every one who stood in the way had to pay the penalty. Most of the newspapers opposed him, but Davis capitalized this, telling his "hill-billies" and "red necks" that the newspapers said no one would vote for him "except the fellow who wears patched breeches and one gallus and lives up the forks of the creek, and don't pay anything except his poll tax." He set the country against the town. He never scrupled to repeat stories proved to be false. No one in his day in Arkansas excelled him in ability to appeal to the passions and prejudices of the people. He was fond of fishing, hunting, and baseball. He rarely wore black, his favorite suit being a Prince Albert of Confederate gray. He was a member of the Baptist church, but was turned out for drinking. Thereafter he referred to those who turned him out as "quart" Baptists, himself as a "pint" Baptist. His first wife, Ina McKenzie, whom he married in 1882, bore him twelve children. Of her Senator J. P. Clarke said that she was the only person who could influence Davis against his own convictions. In October 1911 he married Leila Carter.

[Chas. Jacobson, *The Life Story of Jeff Davis* (1925), a well-written, unbiased account by his private secretary, who might have told more; L. S. Dunaway, *Jeff Davis, Governor and U. S. Senator: His Life and Speeches* (1913), made up almost wholly of speeches and Memorial Addresses; *Arkansas Gazette*, Mar. 31, 1912, and Jan. 3, 1913; *Arkansas Democrat*, Jan. 3, 1913; Davis's messages to the legislature, in *House Jour.*, 1901, pp. 42 ff.; 1903, pp. 35 ff.; 1905, pp. 28 ff.; 1907, pp. 43 ff.; *Cong. Record*, 60 Cong., 1 Sess., pp. 136, 634; 2 Sess., pp. 65, 361; 61 Cong., 2 Sess., pp. 76, 5542, 8455–57; 62 Cong., 2 Sess., pp. 616, 617, 5810–11; Memorial Addresses in *Cong. Record*, 62 Cong., 3 Sess., pp. 4389–93.]

D. Y. T.

DAVIS, JEFFERSON (June 3, 1808–Dec. 6, 1889), president of the Confederate States of America, was born in Christian (now Todd) County, Ky., the tenth child of Samuel and Jane (Cook) Davis, who had moved westward from Georgia. Samuel Davis commanded a troop of irregular horse in the Revolutionary War. His father, Evan Davis, was a Welsh emigrant who had entered America through Philadelphia and had followed the drift of emigration southward into the new lands of Georgia. In Kentucky, the Davis family do not appear to have thriven. When Jefferson was a mere child they wandered on to Mississippi, where they found their anchorage on a small plantation near Woodville, Wilkinson County. Though Samuel Davis does not appear to have done much by way of lifting his middle-class family in the social scale, that result was achieved by his eldest son, Joseph Emory Davis, who rapidly acquired a fortune, an education, and a prominent position in the new community of the Southwest. While Samuel Davis lapses into the background of the picture, Joseph becomes the real head of the family and the patron of his younger brother, many years his junior. Eventually Joseph Davis was considered one of the wealthiest men in the South.

Jefferson Davis was an extremely sensitive, a highly imaginative child and boy. At the age of seven he rode northward, nearly a thousand miles, to become a pupil of the Roman Catholic Seminary, St. Thomas's College, in Washington County, Ky. What induced his Baptist parents to place him there is not known. They very nearly had a reward that doubtless would have appalled them. The impressionable lad became so fond of the priests who were his teachers that he wished for a time to adopt their religion (Davis, *Memoir, post,* I, 13–14). The incident in its fullness has a reminder of Henry Esmond and Father Holt. Indeed, one may find a sort of clue to Davis, to his strength and his weakness, his loftiness, his sensibility, his egoism and his illusions, in Thackeray's famous character. Nothing came of the juvenile Roman enthusiasm, and at nine he was back in Mississippi. After several years in local schools he was entered at Transylvania University, in 1821. Very little is known of his college life. The early records of Transylvania have been destroyed and the traditions are few. Davis himself has said, "There I completed my studies in Greek and Latin, and learned a little of algebra, geometry, trigonometry, surveying, profane and sacred history, and natural philosophy" (*Memoir,* I, 27). He did not finish the course at Transylvania. A Mississippi congressman nominated him to West Point. It is safe to attribute this to the growing influence, social and political, of his brother Joseph. On Sept. 1, 1824, Jefferson Davis matriculated at West Point. In 1828 he was graduated and became a second lieutenant in the United States army. Among the other distinguished Southerners who were cadets when he was, and who were destined to have fateful relations with him in after time, were both the Johnstons and Robert E. Lee. Of the youth of Davis anecdote has preserved a good deal and if most of it may be trusted, we may think of him as a very engaging young man, fearless, generous, modest, with personal charm, and in friendship rashly loyal.

His military apprenticeship of nearly seven years was spent in Wisconsin and in the unsettled portions of Illinois, in little, remote posts, garrisoned by mere handfuls of men, in as lonely regions as the world possessed. The Black Hawk Indian war in 1832 was like a brief interlude of relieving storm that blew across this dreary period. Nobody did anything distinguished in that war. But both Jefferson Davis, as a minor officer of the regular army, and Abraham Lincoln, as an inconspicuous officer of volunteers, took part in it. They did not meet. In 1833 Lieut. Davis was stationed much of the time at Fort Crawford, Wis., where the commandant was Col. Zachary Taylor. He had a daughter, Sarah Knox. The young people fell in love. Col. Taylor disapproved. But they would have their way. Davis resigned June 30, 1835; Miss Taylor sought a friendly aunt in Kentucky; Davis followed; they were speedily married and set out for Mississippi.

During the next ten years, 1835–45, from the age of twenty-seven to the age of thirty-seven, he was a planter, absorbing the mental atmosphere of the distinctive new state, which had been peopled by emigrants from so many regions and where his family was now entering the upper rank. The outward story of these years was lacking in drama except for one event. His early romance closed suddenly, tragically within three months of his marriage. Mrs. Davis died of malarial fever Sept. 15, 1835. Except for a little travel in Cuba while convalescing from the same malady that had killed his wife, followed by a brief visit to New York and Washington, where he made a short sojourn among important politicians at a senatorial boarding-house, the remainder of the ten years was spent quietly on his plantation or at near-by cities. The period closed with two events which took place close together, his election to the national House of Representatives and his second marriage. Varina Howell, who on Feb. 26, 1845, became the second Mrs. Davis [*q.v.*] was a local beauty, a member of the upmost social rank, a high-spirited and accomplished woman. This marriage identified him conclusively with the local aristocracy.

It was during these long quiet years as a country gentleman that Davis's mind was formed politically. His father who had died several years before had bequeathed him a little money. His brother Joseph added to it. Not far from Joseph's plantation, "Hurricane," the plantation "Brierfield" became the seat of the younger brother. It was rough new land overlooking the Mississippi. Much of it was "cleared" for the first time by its new owner. He was a hard worker, taking the most intense interest in his estate, and often sharing field work with his slaves. Nevertheless, he now became an extensive, even omnivorous, reader especially in the fields of politics and history. Joseph was also a natural student. He had been bred to the law and never lost his delight in close argument. Frequently the brothers would spend the night at the same plantation and there would be long evenings of discussion of books and politics. Hitherto the younger Davis had lived since childhood away from home; he had been a student or a soldier in distant lands; he had lacked the sense of soil. This he now acquired. He was permeated by that peculiar atmosphere which belonged to the Mississippi environment. Like those others whom it had drawn to itself from such great distances he became devoted to its social system.

The quietude of life at Brierfield in the late thirties was a sharp contrast with the stormy life of the nation at large. The Abolitionists had begun their crusade. The country rang with their denunciation of the Southern social system. As was often pointed out, they made no distinction between slavery and slaveholders, cursing both in the same breath. The relation of Davis to his slaves was peculiarly gentle and patriarchal. He resented bitterly the Abolitionist attack, and, like practically all the members of the planter class, met it with state-rights arguments. These were destined to be turned against him when he was chief executive of the Confederacy.

It is more than likely that a temperamental influence throughout these quiet years was his deep-seated love of the army and of the military life. He had renounced it for sentimental reasons; he was destined to renounce it twice again for other reasons; but he never lost his zeal for it. Nor did he ever lose his faith in himself as a soldier. A rooted egoism was thus revealed. Though he never did anything of first importance in a military way he was capable, in the heat of the Civil War, of regarding himself as the equal of the greatest generals of the time. Another quality of his mind, his lack of humor, was brought out eventually by this invincible delusion. Mrs. Davis, with Olympian indiscretion, has preserved one of the most unfortunate of the slips in speech that have been made by men of genius. In the darkest hour of the Confederacy, Davis said to his wife, "If I could take one wing and Lee the other, I think we could between us wrest a victory from those people" (*Memoir,* II, 392).

This extraordinary self-confidence rested on nothing but a brief, creditable service in the year 1846, and on one very gallant action in the year 1847. He had gone to Congress as a Democrat in December 1845; the outbreak of the Mexican War was the cause of his resignation the following June. He accepted command of a volunteer regiment known as the "Mississippi Rifles," swiftly whipped it into shape, and joined Gen. Taylor [*q.v.*] in time to participate in the attack upon Monterey. What had passed between himself and his former father-in-law since the death of his first wife is not known, but apparently they were again friends. Taylor appointed him one of the commissioners to negotiate the surrender of Monterey. The next year, in the strangely jumbled battle of Buena Vista, Davis won his reputation as a soldier. Very probably the stand made by the Mississippi Rifles at a crucial moment saved Taylor from defeat. The action was praised extravagantly, far and wide. There came a time when the effect of its applause upon Davis's mind formed the basis of sneers. Long afterward, a Confederate newspaper, bitter against Davis's military policy, alluded to the form in which he disposed his men at Buena Vista, and said "If the Confederacy perishes, it will have died of a V."

The course of the authorities at Washington caused Davis's second renunciation of the military life. Taylor was side-tracked in favor of Scott, and the Mississippi Rifles were left with the minor force that plainly was to have no more chances. The "Rifles" had enlisted for a short period. At its expiration in the summer of 1847 Davis withdrew from the army. Mississippi made him a national senator. He took his seat in December 1847. He was a conspicuous figure; in the popular eye, he was a "hero" of Buena Vista. But popular heroes are not always the heroes of the Senate. His first period as a senator, closing with his resignation in the autumn of 1851, lasted nearly three years, and while it gave him for the first time a national reputation politically, it ended without his having attained a commanding position in his party. In 1848 he steadily supported President Polk and opposed Calhoun, approving the great seizure of Mexican territory on which the President had set his heart. He went so far as to advocate the occupation of Yucatan by the United States, expressing the fear that otherwise it might be taken by Great Britain (*Congressional Globe,* 30 Cong., 1 Sess., p. 729, May 5, 1848). When it was proposed to organize the territory of Oregon without provision for slavery he "denied that there was any power in Congress or in the people of the Territory to interrupt the slave system" by forbidding a slaveholder to take his slaves thither (*Ibid.,* 30 Cong., 1 Sess., p. 927, July 12, 1848). In the debate over the admission of California he reiterated this position but was willing to compromise on the extension of the line of the Missouri Compromise to the Pacific (*Ibid.,* 31 Cong., 1 Sess., App., p. 286, Mar. 8, 1850). He was one of ten senators who opposed to the last the admission of California and who signed a "Protest against the California Bill."

In his course with regard to California, Davis was opposed by his colleague from Mississippi, Senator Henry S. Foote [*q.v.*], a politician of great boldness. Though the legislature of Mississippi passed resolutions instructing their senators to resist the admission of California "by all honorable and constitutional means," Foote refused to be bound by them. It turned out that he had gauged the conditions at home with deep shrewdness. He was nominated for governor on a "Union" ticket, supported by Whigs and dissatisfied Democrats, and in September 1851, seemed about to carry the election. The political situation in the South in 1851 was extremely complex and Davis's relation to it is not altogether clear. The struggle against the admission of California and the failure to extend the Missouri Compromise line had produced a general movement for secession. A convention of the whole South which held two meetings at Nashville, one in June 1850, the other in November, had secession in view. The desire to secede was practically universal, but there were two policies on the subject. Extreme state-rights men such as R. B. Rhett [*q.v.*] of South Carolina and W. L. Yancey [*q.v.*] of Alabama wanted their states to rush ahead irrespective of what other states might do. The course followed by another group revealed a point of view that may be labeled Southern nationalism. Between the first and second meetings of the Nashville convention these others concluded that it was impossible to effect an immediate secession of the whole South. Thereupon they threw themselves into an attempt to arrest the secession movement, to postpone it until the whole South could be persuaded to leave the Union together. Rhett, who refused to accept this view, was eventually defeated in a popular campaign, on the issue of secession, by the South Carolina "cooperationists."

A third Southern party was for accepting the compromise measures of 1850 as the start of a satisfactory new chapter in the history of the Union. With this group Foote was associated. His opponent was Gen. John A. Quitman [*q.v.*], who was in Mississippi pretty much what Rhett was in South Carolina. By September 1851 it was plain that the tide had turned. The genuine Unionists and the "cooperationists" between them were going to prevent an immediate movement for secession. The Democratic leaders in Mississippi appear to have concluded that the game was up. They looked around for a way out. Quitman was persuaded to resign; Davis was persuaded to leave the Senate and take his place. Though there is no positive evidence upon his motives a safe guess would fix upon two. He was instinctively a party man; all his military predisposition, his *esprit de corps,* tended that way. The desire to save the party, to perform a strategic retreat with as much credit as possible, must have influenced him. But it is fair to assume a deeper motive. In him, even more thoroughly than in the anti-Rhett men of South Carolina, the vision of the South as a nation was a real thing. We may conclude that Davis took the place of the secessionist Quitman with a view to relieving his party of its hasty commitment to immediate secession and for the purpose of aligning it, tacitly at least, with "cooperation." His strategic retreat was a success. A vote for a convention that was to decide the issue of secession or "submission" had given Foote a majority of 8,000, but when the vote was cast for governor, his majority was less than 1,000.

Davis resumed his life as a planter, only to reënter politics on Mar. 7, 1853, when he became secretary of war in the cabinet of his friend Franklin Pierce. His tenure of the war office was perhaps the peak of his career; certainly no chapter of his life was more to his taste. His health, which both before and after was delicate, was during most of this period robust. The Davises were the center of a delightful coterie in Washington; Mrs. Davis, witty and charming, drew all sorts of people into her drawing-room. Despite political differences, men as unlike her husband as Seward were his close personal friends. The most brilliant portrait of him is contained in a passage from Carl Schurz: "I had in my imagination formed a high idea of what a grand personage the War Minister of this great Republic must be. I was not disappointed. He received me graciously. His slender, tall, and erect figure, his spare face, keen eyes, and fine forehead, not broad, but high and well-shaped, presented the well-known strong American type. There was in his bearing a dignity which seemed entirely natural and unaffected—that kind of dignity which does not invite familiar approach, but will not render one uneasy by lofty assumption. His courtesy was without any condescending air. . . . His conversation ran in easy . . . well-chosen and sometimes even elegant phrase, and the timbre of his voice had something peculiarly agreeable. . . . I heard him deliver a speech in the Senate, and again I was struck by the dignity of his bearing, the grace of his diction, and the rare charm of his voice—things which greatly distinguished him from many of his colleagues" (*The Reminiscences of Carl Schurz,* II, 1907, p. 21).

Apparently, the idea of secession was allowed to lapse in Davis's mind during several years. But the idea of the South as a social and economic unit, a nation within the Union, was constant. His policies were governed by the steadfast hope of so enlarging the South territorially and of so developing it economically that it would prove the equal in political power of the opposite section. Consequently he was eager for expansion southward, and was frequently in opposition to the secretary of state, William L. Marcy [*q.v.*], whose eyes were on the Northern, not the Southern, wing of the party. In their general attitudes toward Spain and Mexico, Davis may be described as belligerent, Marcy as conciliatory. In the case of the ship *Black Warrior* seized by the Spanish authorities at Havana on a legal technicality, and in connection with the Ostend Manifesto issued by three American ambassadors as a statement of our Spanish policy Davis failed to control the foreign policy of the administration. With all the more zeal he turned to the advancement of Southern economic interests at home. Asia had become of first importance in the minds of most Americans who thought about trade. To obtain a window upon the Pacific was a great part of the inspiration of the Southern nationalists in 1850. Davis, still hoping for Southern expansion to the Pacific, took the liveliest interest in promoting a great scheme for a transcontinental railway that should be close to the Mexican border and terminate in that part of California which the Southerners in 1850 had attempted to obtain. To make such a railroad possible he induced Pierce and Marcy to acquire from Mexico the region now known as the Gadsden Purchase. To demonstrate the practicability of such a road he dispatched an expedition comprising engineers, artists, and scientists who prepared a monumental report on the Southwest which the government published in ten large volumes.

The close of his term as secretary of war (1857) was followed immediately by his reëntry into the Senate. During the period in which he had been withdrawn from obvious participation in congressional politics one main chapter in American history had closed, and another had opened. He had had a part in the conclave of party leaders that met at the White House on Sunday, Jan. 22, 1854, from which emerged the Kansas-Nebraska Bill. Just how much he contributed to this epoch-making bill must remain a matter of conjecture. Promptly after his return to the Senate he became again a conspicuous defender of the South. During the three years and more of his second period as senator his arguments are much the same as in the first period; but they are presented with more heat. He defends slavery because it "bears to capital as kind a relation as can exist between them anywhere" and assures the South that the election of an Abolitionist as president "would be a species of revolution by which the purposes of the Government would be destroyed and the observance of its mere forms entitled to no respect" (Speech before the Mississippi Legislature, Nov. 16, 1858; Rowland, *post*, III, 356). It seems probable that he had already passed the summit of his career both mentally and physically. The splendid manifestation of energy that so impressed Schurz is now pathetically absent from the picture. Ill health returned. He suffered intensely from neuralgia, from nervous indigestion, and from a very painful disease of the eyes that came near wrecking his sight. The frequency of the heated tone in his speeches may be a significant symptom. Intellectually, he does not stand forth from the group of Southerners who opposed a firm but desperate front to the growing power of the North. He had a place in their first rank and in all their councils but his contribution to their battle was mainly oratorical and emotional. He was still a brilliant figure in the public eye, and the intensity of his convictions, the patent honesty of his purpose, gave great weight to all his utterances.

In the bitterly furious internal history of the Democratic party from the day of the Dred Scott decision of 1857, to the breakup of the Charleston convention in 1860, Davis and Douglas fought each other to the death. Ostensibly the issue was between "popular sovereignty" defended by Douglas, and the doctrine of the Dred Scott decision which affirmed Davis's constant position that neither Congress nor local law could interfere with slavery in a territory. Behind this ostensible issue was something else that is not quite apparent. Davis joined with Yancey and Rhett in their successful effort to prevent the nomination of Douglas at Charleston, and therefore it has been assumed rashly that he shared their hope for secession as a result of the events of 1860. On the other hand, when the party had been split in two and both Douglas and Breckinridge were "Democratic" nominees, Davis, though a supporter of Breckinridge, wrote to Rhett discouraging secession and reviving exactly the "cooperationist" reasoning of 1851. Perhaps one may assume that what Davis really wanted was a confessed duality within the Union —the South to have substantially what was afterward known as "dominion status," like that of Canada or Ireland in the British Empire today—and that he did not share Rhett's enthusiasm for secession in itself.

He was relatively passive during the anxious weeks that followed the election of Lincoln. The one issue of the moment which seemed to him vital was whether the South was to continue to have an open frontier with the possibility to expand. Lincoln settled this by his declaration that while he would concede almost every other point at issue between the sections, there should be no more slave states. Thereafter Davis's course was predestined. When Mississippi seceded he acquiesced. In one of his most noted speeches he announced to the Senate the secession of his state and himself formally withdrew, Jan. 21, 1861.

Unlike most of the Southern leaders, Davis expected war. There can be no doubt that he hoped to be the chief commander of the Southern armies. Mississippi promptly appointed him major-general of the state troops. Meanwhile, a general convention of the seceding states had made one of those compromise choices so common in American conventions, and had agreed upon a provisional President of the Confederacy who was nobody's first choice. It was Davis. "The messenger with the notification . . . found him in our garden [at Brierfield] assisting to make rose cuttings; when reading the telegram he looked so grieved that I feared some evil had befallen our family" (*Memoir*, II, 18). It was the summons of circumstance to make the third, the final renunciation of his own unconquerable ambition, the desire for military fame. He accepted his destiny. On Feb. 18, 1861, at Montgomery, he was inaugurated president.

A tired man in very delicate health attempted an almost impossible task. The South was unprepared for war, and based its hopes of independence mainly upon the idea that "Cotton was King." Foreign affairs at once became the master key to the situation. But neither Davis nor his successive secretaries of state were able to exert much influence upon the policies of Europe. Those were determined by circumstances beyond their control which are part of Federal rather than Confederate history. The successful blockade of the Confederate coast quickly shut off the outflow of cotton and also prevented the inflow of munitions.

Davis found himself unable to control the course of events except in two respects, both of which brought into clear view convictions and qualities of mind that had been taking form during many years. First of all he kept a close hand upon the management of the army. In doing so he gave rein to his delusion that he was the equal of any one as a strategist. To Lee, alone, does he appear to have conceded preëminence. With other generals, he permitted his egoism and his irritability frequently to assert themselves. He was not always wise in his choice of men to trust. He would not listen to any one who belittled either Gen. Braxton Bragg [*q.v.*] or that brilliant but unpopular Jew who served both as secretary of war and as secretary of state, Judah P. Benjamin [*q.v.*]. He did not hesitate to set public opinion at defiance. When Congress was about to vote a condemnation of Benjamin because of the disaster of Roanoke Island in 1862, Davis showed his haughty contempt for it by promoting Benjamin from the War Department to the State Department. His animosities were as uncompromising as his friendships. He had a relentless quarrel with Joseph Johnston [*q.v.*], whom he removed from command in Georgia at a critical moment in 1864. When Congress compelled the reinstatement of Johnston in high command Davis evaded making the necessary appointment and contrived to have it made by Lee. Another assertion of his autocratic will was the letter he wrote to J. A. Seddon [*q.v.*], secretary of war, deploring the resignation that had been wrung from him by the hostility of Congress.

His imperious temper aggravated by ill health —his wife speaks of his coming home from his office, "fasting, a mere mass of throbbing nerves" —did not help him in the difficult political problems which rapidly developed. As soon as it became apparent that Davis's loyalty was given to the South as a whole, that he would sacrifice the interest of any Southern state if thus he could create a Southern nation committed to the preservation of the Southern social order, excessively theoretical advocates of state rights like Rhett and Yancey became his bitter political enemies. An anti-Davis party was quickly formed which was rallied, ostensibly at least, around the central idea of state sovereignty. Gov. Brown of Georgia and such powerful politicians as Robert Toombs [*q.v.*] and Alexander H. Stephens [*q.v.*] were drawn into the opposition. It controlled some of the most influential Southern newspapers including the most influential of all, the *Richmond Examiner*. The *Charleston Mercury*, owned by the Rhett family, was Davis's uncompromising enemy throughout the war (see Owsley, *post*).

The active beginning of opposition to his government very nearly coincided with his formal inauguration as regular president. He had been elected in October 1861, and was inaugurated Feb. 22, 1862. Even before this he had stirred antagonism by his veto of a bill that would have permitted the officering of a Texas regiment by the governor of the state. The *Mercury* was very sharp in its comments on this veto. Within a month of the inauguration he had defied Congress by transferring Benjamin to the State Department. About the same time he proposed a general conscription law which, though enacted, was at once taken up by the state-rights apologists and denounced as unconstitutional. This was the beginning of a desultory quarrel between state and Confederate authorities over control of enlistments that did not cease until the Confederacy collapsed (see Moore, *post*). Incidental to this controversy were the repeated attempts of the administration party to vest in the President large powers through the suspension of the writ of *habeas corpus*. Though, of course, the usual complex of political interests informed the two parties, it is fair to impute to them a real antagonism over ideas—centralization upon the one hand, local autonomy upon the other. The controversy was quieted briefly by the brilliant military events of 1862, but broke out with renewed vigor after the failure of the great triple offensive—in Maryland, in Kentucky, in Mississippi—of the autumn of that year.

Among the tremendous military events of the following year the political issues seem almost to escape from view, but, in fact, the hostility of the two parties raged with increasing violence. Confederate money had ceased to have value worth talking about. Financial taxation was an unreality. To meet this difficult situation the government revived the ancient system of tithes through a statute known as the Tax in Kind. Being all but unable to support itself, the government was also empowered, by means of an Impressment Act, to seize supplies and to pay for them at prices fixed by official commissioners. A third measure inspired the *Mercury* to publish an attack upon the government entitled "A Despotism over the Confederate States Proposed in Congress." It referred to a renewed attempt to suspend the writ of *habeas corpus*. The argument in favor of suspension was chiefly the flagrant obstruction of the conscription acts, connived at, if not encouraged, by many state officials, especially in North Carolina and Georgia. The leader of the opposition in Congress was the same Henry S. Foote who had defeated Davis for governor in 1851. His furious denunciations of the administration ended in the defeat of the bill.

Despite a great deal of spasmodic opposition, the administration had been able on most questions to obtain adequate support hitherto in Congress. The general elections of the autumn of 1863 made a change. The resulting Congress was composed very largely of men who were new to legislation; and it contained a majority hostile to Davis. The constitutional issue had melted into a less definite but even more dangerous one. There was a real though vague belief widely spread that the President was a despot, that some sort of *coup d'état* might be expected at any moment. An atmosphere of dread, created by unlimited denunciation of Davis's motives, was darkened by a series of difficulties with regard to labor. Early in the war it was tacitly agreed that the government should not be allowed to own slaves. The imaginary vision of a government owning an army of obedient barbarians—a hundred thousand, two hundred thousand—gave point to the cries against despotism and a *coup d'état.* The government had to rent slaves from their owners and used them as army laborers. At the same time it exempted one white man for every plantation of fifteen slaves or more to serve as overseer. This "Fifteen Slave Law" produced envy in men of small property. They were further embittered by a law which permitted the hiring of substitutes by men drafted for the army. They vented their anger in the saying that the Confederacy was waging "a rich man's war and a poor man's fight." There was no end of complaint against impressment commissioners; also charges of profiteering by government officials, some of which seem to have been justified.

Against this background of discontent three passages in Davis's annual message, November 1864, took on, in the popular mind, menacing significance. He urged Congress to authorize the government to purchase outright 40,000 slaves. He suggested that when the government was through with them these slaves should be set free. He recognized the existence of a disturbing popular controversy by saying that he dissented "from those who advise a general levy and arming of the slaves for the duty of soldiers" (*Journal, post,* IV, 258; Rowland, *post,* VI, 396). This was the beginning of the last important controversy of Confederate history. The army, worn and wasted by three and a half years of dreary valor, had to be reinforced. Negroes were the only remaining source of supply. The message was doubtless a "feeler" to take the sense of the country upon a policy which originated probably with Secretary Benjamin. Incidentally it carried with it the policy of emancipation. The administration party at once introduced both subjects into Congressional debate. During the terrible winter of 1864–65, while the military power of the Confederacy was visibly crumbling on every hand, the fanatical slaveholders in Congress kept the discussion in suspense. Eventually a bill was passed permitting a fresh levy of 300,000 men, but making no mention of emancipation, and providing that these new troops were "to be raised from such classes of the population irrespective of color, in each State as the proper authorities thereof may determine" (*Journal,* VII, 611–12). Virtually, it was a defeat for the administration. But Davis refused to admit that it was a defeat. He had become infatuated with the idea of emancipation as the last trump in his hand. He believed that by means of it he could yet win over the British government, induce it to enter the war, and at the eleventh hour save the Confederacy. A secret agent, Duncan F. Kenner, was sent to London only to be told that the offer came too late.

The frame of mind of Davis this concluding winter was strangely deluded. He appears to have had no doubt of a successful outcome of the war. In the preceding autumn with Sherman entrenched at Atlanta he had gone South on a tour of inspiration. His aim was to stir up a "people's war" by giving to popular audiences a true picture of the soldier's task. But he was not happy in his way of doing it. In describing Gen. Beauregard whom he had placed in command in Georgia, he attempted to give an impression of soldierly self-effacement. He said that this brave general would do whatever the President told him to do. His enemies seized upon the words. Here was further evidence that he was planning a *coup d'état.* Davis's last effective reinforcement of the army was accomplished by a general order this autumn revoking all exemptions, stripping the plantations of the overseers, and calling to the colors all soldiers furloughed or in hospital "except those unable to travel." Davis returned to Richmond, and Sherman began his march to the sea. While a wide swath of desolation was sweeping over the lower South, Davis confronted a crisis, the seriousness of which he did not in the least appreciate. There were "peace movements" agitating the South, and here and there something like a clamor for negotiations with Washington. The advocates of these movements had no clear notion of what they were trying to do, and had they not inspired overtures from the North would have little historical significance. They contributed indirectly to bring about a series of attempts to negotiate. In the summer of 1864 two Northerners came to Richmond unofficially for the purpose of catching Davis in a trap. They believed that he would refuse to treat for peace on any terms except the recognition of Southern independence, and they wanted to use the fact to hearten the North for the reëlection of Lincoln. As they had no official credentials Davis refused to discuss public affairs with them (Rowland, X, 32). A notable, but informal attempt to induce Davis to consent to reunion was made by Francis P. Blair [*q.v.*] in January 1865. Napoleon III, defying the Monroe Doctrine, had recently established Maximilian as Emperor

Davis

of Mexico. Blair proposed to Davis a plan of reconciliation involving the complete abandonment of slavery, the reunion of all the states, and an expedition against Mexico in which Davis was to play the leading rôle. Davis cautiously refrained from committing himself, though he gave Blair a letter in which he expressed his willingness to enter into negotiations for peace between "the two countries." The visit of Blair gave new impetus to the peace movements. The Committee on Foreign Affairs of the Confederate House reported resolutions favoring an attempt to negotiate with the United States so as to "bring into view" the possibility of cooperation between the United States and the Confederacy to maintain the Monroe Doctrine. Before the end of the month Davis appointed commissioners to confer with the Northern authorities with regard to peace. There followed the famous Hampton Roads Conference, Feb. 3, 1865, at which Lincoln was present and Stephens was the chief spokesman for the Confederacy. Whether it is true, as tradition has it, that Lincoln told Stephens to write Union at the top of a page and anything he pleased under it, there is no doubt that the tradition fairly represents the situation of the moment. But Davis, though now committed in his own mind to emancipation, was determined to accept nothing short of independence. His delusion of power could not be shaken. Three days after the conference he made his last public oration as President of the Confederacy. He spoke in the precincts of the African Church in Richmond. Snow lay thick on the ground. A man in a dream, he talked with the passion of a seer and for the moment swept his audience before him. "Let us then unite our hands and our hearts, lock our shields together, and we may well believe that before another summer solstice falls upon us, it will be the enemy who will be asking us for conferences and occasions in which to make known our demands" (see Dodd, *post*, p. 353). Two months later Richmond had fallen and Davis was a fugitive.

The President's party left the city on Apr. 3. The next day he was at Danville where he waited five days. On Apr. 4 he issued his last proclamation calling on his people to resist to the last and promising them that Richmond would soon be recovered. The news of Lee's surrender caused him to turn southward. At Greensboro, Apr. 12, a cabinet council was held which Johnston and Beauregard attended. Reluctantly, Davis gave Johnston permission to negotiate for the surrender of his army to Sherman. Twelve days later, at Charlotte, Davis held his last council with his cabinet, approved Johnston's surrender, and finally admitted that the Confederacy had been overthrown. The party broke up. Davis continued southward hoping to escape out of the country. At Irwinville, Ga., he was captured by Federal cavalry, May 10.

During two years he was a state prisoner in Fortress Monroe. The commandant, Gen. Nelson A. Miles [*q.v.*], acting upon instructions from Gen. Halleck and Assistant Secretary of War Charles A. Dana, ordered him put in irons (*A Statement of the Facts concerning the Imprisonment and Treatment of Jefferson Davis,* etc., 1902). He was later accorded different treatment. His health failed. At length he was assigned comfortable quarters which his family were permitted to share. He was never brought to trial. The lawyers of the government saw technical danger in every charge that was suggested. He was released on bond, May 13, 1867 (Nichols, *post*). Greeley and Gerrit Smith [*qq.v.*], once the bitter enemies of everything Southern, were among his bondsmen.

He was not yet an old man, and twenty-two years of life remained to him. They were valiant but sad years. His fortune was wrecked, his home a ruin, and his health impaired. Though these years, with the exception of three, contain no remarkable achievement they have a moral distinction second to nothing in his career. Health was recovered gradually, partly through European travel but more through sheer resolution and strength of will. In his seventieth year Davis was probably a more vigorous man than at any time since the great days when he was secretary of war. He embarked in a succession of business ventures but as he had no predilection for business and no business experience, they were all unsuccessful. Though a portion of the Brierfield estate was saved he was in his later years a poor man. A home was provided for his old age through the bequest of Mrs. Sarah A. Dorsey, a friend of Mrs. Davis. This was "Beauvoir" on the Gulf of Mexico. There he prepared his own version of his stormy career by writing *The Rise and Fall of the Confederate Government,* devoting to it the three years, 1878–81. Though Mississippi would have sent him to the Senate, he refused to ask for the Federal pardon without which it was impossible for him to take his seat. He died at New Orleans in his eighty-second year.

[The most important biography is Wm. E. Dodd, *Jefferson Davis* (1907). *Jefferson Davis, Ex-President of the Confederate States of America: a Memoir,* by his wife (2 vols., 1890), is an invaluable but rambling and fragmentary collection of details. *Jefferson Davis, Constitutionalist, His Letters, Papers, and Speeches* (10 vols., 1923), ed. by Dunbar Rowland, though voluminous, does not contain all the known private letters, omits all the dispatches in the *Official Records,* and is not complete in its selections from the *Cong. Globe.* For the mind of Davis, previous to secession, the *Globe,* after all, is the true record. His own apologia is *The Rise and Fall of the Confed. Govt.* (2 vols., 1881). J. P. Richardson, *A Compilation of the Messages and Papers of the Confederacy* (2 vols., 1905), contains some of the state papers; others are embedded in *Jour. of the Cong. of the Confed. States of America* (7 vols., 1904–05), being *Sen. Doc. No. 234,* 58 Cong., 2 Sess., and in the Fourth Series of the *Official Records.* Three newspapers may be regarded as government organs: the *Richmond Enquirer,* the Richmond *Sentinel* and the *Charleston Courier.* The official gazette of the government abroad was the *Index* published in London. As Davis was engaged in many controversies, all the writings of Confederate leaders contain Davis matter, but as a rule it is sharply partisan. Important recent studies are: A. B. Moore, *Conscription and Conflict in the Confederacy* (1924); F. L. Owsley, *State Rights in the Confederacy* (1925); R. F. Nichols, "United States vs. Jefferson Davis," *Am. Hist. Rev.,* XXXI, 266–84 (Jan. 1926). A number of excellent essays on Davis have been written by Walter L. Fleming, but have not been collected. For his military career, see G. W. Cullum, *Biog. Reg. Officers and Grads. U. S. Mil. Acad.* (3rd ed., 1891), I, 416.]

N. W. S.

DAVIS, JEFFERSON COLUMBUS (Mar. 2, 1828–Nov. 30, 1879), soldier, the son of William and Mary (Drummond) Davis, was born on a farm in Clark County, Ind., whither his family had come from Kentucky. He had a year's service in the Mexican War as an enlisted man in the 3rd Indiana Regiment, and fought at Buena Vista. Appointed a second lieutenant in the 1st Artillery in 1848, he was promoted first lieutenant in 1852 and captain in 1861. He was in garrison at Fort Sumter at the time of the bombardment. In August 1861 he was appointed colonel of the 22nd Indiana Infantry, and in December was made brigadier-general of volunteers. He commanded a division at the battle of Pea Ridge and at the siege of Corinth. He seemed to have a brilliant future before him when he stained his reputation with a crime which is often remembered when his military services are forgotten. Brooding over a severe rebuke received some days before from Gen. William Nelson, his commanding officer, he sought out Nelson (Sept. 29, 1862) in the lobby of a Louisville hotel with the evident purpose of forcing a quarrel upon him. After high words, Davis crumpled up a card and threw it in Nelson's face, and Nelson retaliated with a slap. Davis then left him, but returning a few minutes later with a revolver shot him as he passed through the hall, inflicting a mortal wound. Partly on account of his military abilities, but more, it is surmised, because of the exertion of strong political influence—especially through his friend, Gov. Oliver P. Morton, who accompanied him when he quarreled with Nelson—Davis went wholly unpunished and after a short time was restored to duty. He commanded a division at Murfreesboro and Chickamauga and in the Atlantic campaign, and a corps on the march to the sea and in the campaign of the Carolinas. He received, however, no further promotion, although Rosecrans, and later Grant, recommended that he be made a major-general. Perhaps the administration felt about him as Dr. Johnson did about the American colonists, that he "ought to be thankful for anything . . . short of hanging." He was mustered out of the volunteer service in 1866, and appointed colonel of the 23rd Infantry. He served for a considerable time in Alaska, and took part in the Modoc War which followed the murder of Gen. Canby in 1873. He died in Chicago. Gen. Fry describes him as "brave, quiet, obliging, humorous in disposition and full of ambition, daring, endurance and self-confidence." It is said that he never regretted killing Nelson, but that he bitterly resented his failure to receive a major-generalcy of volunteers and a brigadier-generalcy in the regular army. He was married to Mariette Woodson Athon of Indianapolis.

[Jas. B. Fry, *Mil. Miscellanies* (1889), pp. 486–505, gives a full account of the murder of Nelson, which is also described in *Battles and Leaders of the Civil War* (1887), III, 43–44, 60–61. See also: F. B. Heitman, *Hist. Reg. and Dict. of the U. S. Army* (1903), I, pp. 358–59; Jacob B. Dunn, *Ind. and Indianans* (1919), IV, pp. 1563–64; *Official Records (Army),* ser. 1, I, III, VIII, XVI (pt. 2), XX (pts. 1, 2), XXIII (pts. 1, 2), XXX (pts. 1, 3, 4), XXXI (pts. 2, 3), XXXII (pt. 1), XXXVIII (pts. 1, 2, 3, 4, 5), XXXIX (pts. 1, 3), XLIV, XLVII (pts. 1, 2, 3), LII (pt. 1).]

T. M. S.

DAVIS, JEROME DEAN (Jan. 17, 1838–Nov. 4, 1910), Congregational clergyman and missionary, was born in Groton, N. Y., one of the seven children of Hope and Brooksy (Woodbury) Davis. The ancestors of both his parents came from England to Massachusetts, John Woodbury to Salem about 1623, and Isaac Davis to Cape Cod about 1690. When Jerome was fourteen or so, his father, a rigid, righteous combination of farmer and country school-teacher, took his family with him to live at Dundee, Ill. Shortly before, the boy had been converted, and when he was sixteen he took part as church clerk in the trial of a minister suspected of Unitarianism. With little or no encouragement from any one, he studied what books he could lay hold of, and by the time he was twenty was head teacher in a school at Carpentersville. As soon as he was twenty-one and was no longer bound to help his father, he began to follow definitely his plans for an education. He attended Lawrence University at Appleton, Wis., decided to become a minister, and during 1860 and 1861 was a sophomore and junior in Beloit College. He entered the Union army as a private in September 1861, and rose in rank till at the close of the war he was a lieutenant-colonel. Among the soldiers he was drastic in his attacks on liquor—rearing empty whiskey bottles on poles with the legend "Death to the Bottle"—and whenever possible he went about distributing Bibles. He was severely wounded at the battle of Shiloh and he conducted himself with bravery and shrewdness on his long march with Sherman to the sea. During 1865–66 he completed his course at Beloit College; and in 1869, he was graduated from the Chicago Theological Seminary, married to Sophia D. Strong, and sent by the Congregational Home Missionary Society to Cheyenne, Wyo. Financial support of his activities was not liberal, and other considerations persuaded him that his true work was in Japan. He left San Francisco in November 1871 as a missionary of the American Board. Arriving at Kobe several weeks afterward, he settled there, and by his teaching formed the nucleus of what became Kobe College. Later, in association with his friend, the American-educated Joseph Hardy Neesima, he helped found and in the most intimate fashion helped shape the Doshisha University in Kyoto. His wife died in 1886 and two years later he was married in Kyoto to Frances Hooper. Practically throughout the nineties, there was controversy both in America and Japan between persons who wished the Doshisha to be Christian pervadingly and by constant implication, and those who wished it to be so pointedly and aggressively. The former of these positions seeming to Davis to be spineless pacifism, he became chief, in a sense, of those who agreed with him, and in the end had the satisfaction of seeing his view adopted in the official policy of the school. He was a prolific writer on subjects of a theological and historical nature. In English, his most important work is perhaps his biography of his friend, *A Maker of New Japan: Rev. Joseph Hardy Neesima* (1890), and in Japanese, the thousand-page *Great Principles of Theology* (1893). For all his virility and the glamour of his Civil War recollections, he counseled his student son at the time of the Spanish-American War to keep out of the army; leave soldiering, he said, in so far as you can, to others —"War is hell on earth—keep out of it" (J. M. Davis, *post*, p. 331). He was a delegate to the World Missionary Conference in Edinburgh in the summer of 1910, and on his way back to Japan he stopped at Oberlin, Ohio. Illness overtook him and it became apparent that he was dying. Some one asked him if he would leave a message to his children. "My life," he said. He had three daughters and one son, all of whom were foreign missionaries.

[J. M. Davis, *Davis: Soldier Missionary* (1916); Beloit Coll. Cat. 1860–62, 1865–66; *Congreg. and Christian World*, Nov. 12, 1910; letter from Beloit Alumni League, Apr. 13, 1928.] J. D. W.

DAVIS, JOHN (Jan. 25, 1761–Jan. 14, 1847), jurist, was born at Plymouth, Mass. He was the fourth child of Thomas Davis, a native of England who came to Plymouth in 1737, became a prosperous merchant of that town, and married in 1753 Mercy, daughter of Barnabas Hedge, a descendant of Gov. William Bradford. Being a delicate child, John received his early education privately, and was prepared for college by Rev. Ezra Sampson of Plympton. He entered Harvard College in 1777, where he distinguished himself in science as well as the classics, and attended Prof. Samuel Williams on the latter's journey in October 1780 to Penobscot Bay, to take observation of a solar eclipse. After graduating in 1781, he conducted a private school in Plymouth, becoming later tutor in the family of Gen. Otis at Barnstable. He then studied law in the office of Oakes Angier, at Bridgewater, and on being admitted to the bar in 1786, commenced practise at Plymouth. He rapidly came to the front and two years later was chosen delegate from Plymouth to the state convention which was called to consider the adoption of the Federal Constitution—being the youngest member thereof. Taking an active part in public matters, he was three times elected to the state House of Representatives, and in 1795 became state senator for Plymouth County, but in the same year was tendered by Washington the office of comptroller of the treasury of the United States, which he accepted. He held the position for only a year, however, his resignation being prompted by the inadequacy of his salary, and on retiring was appointed by Washington United States attorney for the district of Massachusetts. He thereupon removed to Boston, which became his permanent home. In 1801 he was appointed by President Adams judge of the United States district court for the district of Massachusetts—a position which he occupied for forty years. His judicial career was characterized by patience, urbanity, and sound discretion, and his exploration of the then almost untrodden paths of admiralty and maritime jurisdiction laid the legal profession under lasting obligations to him. Perhaps his outstanding achievement was his wise and firm attitude during the period of commercial embarrassment in New England caused by the Embargo and the War of 1812, when, unaffected by the ill-concealed hostility of the exasperated mercantile interests, he steadily maintained the supremacy of the law, and by so doing ultimately acquired the respect and confidence of the community. He resigned from the bench July 9, 1841, in his eighty-first year, upon which occasion the bar paid him a remarkable tribute. The remainder of his days were spent in retirement in Boston, where he died. In June 1786 he married Ellen, daughter of W. Watson of Plymouth.

Throughout his life he maintained his interest in scientific phenomena, and was deeply versed in the history and antiquities of New England, being president of the Massachusetts Historical Society from 1818 to 1835. He is said to have been the first to use the word "pilgrim" as applicable to the Plymouth colonists, in his ode written for the anniversary celebration in 1794. In addition to a number of addresses and papers contributed to learned societies he edited *Two Lectures on Comets by Professor Winthrop, Also an Essay on Comets by A. Oliver, Jr. Esq.* (1811), with biographies and supplementary matter, and a fifth edition of Morton's *New England's Memorial* (1826), with large additions in marginal notes and an appendix. He was a fellow of the American Academy of Arts and Sciences. A devoted supporter of Harvard, he actively shared in its administration, being successively Fellow in 1803, treasurer in 1810, and member of the board of overseers in 1827, which latter office he retained for ten years.

[Davis's ancestry is traced in W. T. Davis, *Ancient Landmarks of Plymouth* (2nd ed. 1899), pt. II, p. 82. A detailed and authoritative account of his career entitled "Memoir of Hon. John Davis, LL.D.," by Convers Francis appeared in *Mass. Hist. Soc. Colls.*, ser. 3, vol. X, and was subsequently published in pamphlet form in 1848. See also W. T. Davis, *Professional and Industrial Hist. of Suffolk County, Mass.* (1894), I, 149; *Law Reporter*, IV, 159 and IX, 521.]
H. W. H. K.

DAVIS, JOHN (*c.* 1780–*c.* 1838), operatic and theatrical manager, despite his English name was a French refugee from Santo Domingo. He is said to have come to New Orleans in 1811, though it is possible that he may have appeared some years before, with that "company . . . of half a dozen actors and actresses, formerly attached to the theatre of Cape Français in the isle of San Domingo," mentioned by Berquin-Duvallon (*Vue de la colonie espagnole du Mississippi*, etc., Paris, 1803, p. 30). In 1813 he erected in New Orleans the first Théâtre d'Orléans, where opera was given three evenings a week, and comedy, drama, and vaudeville on the remaining nights. When it was burned to the ground four years later, he rebuilt it with, for that day, unexampled magnificence; so that when it entered upon its first season (Nov. 20, 1819), it deserved its reputation of being "the grandest" opera-house then existing on the continent. Under Davis's management (he was its owner as well as manager) the Théâtre d'Orléans, provided with all the scenic and mechanical appliances then known to the best European houses, was the musical focus of cultured Creole society, and its winter seasons were a magnet for the wealthy planters along the Mississippi, who came to town with their wives and families to attend the opera. To the theatre proper its owner later added a great separate dancing hall, where the famous New Orleans Quadroon Balls were given and which, when the parquette floor of the opera was boarded over, constituted together with it one immense ballroom. To the dancing hall he adjoined a gambling house and a restaurant, which was a favorite haunt of the gilded youth of New Orleans; and the fortune derived from his gaming-tables, his restaurant, and his dance hall supplied John Davis with the capital for his theatrical ventures. The operas and ballets given in Paris found their way to the Théâtre d'Orléans, where French grand opera was given in the best style by French opera singers, and French actors and dancers appeared in comedy and ballet.

In spite of Davis's local prominence in New Orleans during the first quarter of the nineteenth century, we catch only occasional glimpses of him in the records of his day. It would seem that he enjoyed general respect, however, for we find that when, during Count de Roffignac's mayoralty, the famous old State House was burned, the ballroom of the Théâtre d'Orléans was offered for temporary use "by that good citizen . . . John Davis" (G. King, *Creole Families of New Orleans*, 1912, p. 438). And when Gen. Lafayette was entertained in New Orleans in 1825, and had spent an evening at the Théâtre d'Orléans, he extended his thanks to John Davis and the actors (J. G. de Baroncelli, *Le Théâtre-Français à la Nlle. Orleans, Essai Historique*, 1906, p. 34). It was largely due to Davis that New Orleans became the first American city to have an annual opera season. In his musical and dramatic activities he stressed the French cultural note which still lends a distinctly Latin tone to the modern city.

[The best account of Davis is that given in H. Rightor's *Standard Hist. of New Orleans* (1900), p. 467. See also F. L. Ritter, *Music in America* (1890); H. C. Lahee, *Grand Opera in America* (1902), p. 27; W. D. Darby, *Music in America* (1916), p. 115.] F. H. M.

DAVIS, JOHN (Jan. 13, 1787–Apr. 19, 1854), lawyer, statesman, was born in Northboro, Worcester County, Mass., the fifth and youngest son of Isaac and Anna (Brigham) Davis. Preparing at Leicester Academy, he graduated from Yale College in 1812 with high honors, studied law with Francis Blake of Worcester, was admitted to the bar in 1815, and after practising at Spencer, Mass., settled in Worcester. There he rapidly made a reputation as a forceful advocate in the court-room, being recognized as a redoubtable antagonist by even such lawyers as Choate, Mason, and Webster. Elected to Congress in 1824 as a supporter of John Quincy Adams for the presidency, he served four consecutive terms. In 1833, he was the National Republican candidate for governor of Massachusetts, and received a plurality of votes over Adams (Anti-Mason) and Morton (Democrat). Because the law required a majority, the election was thrown into the legislature, where, after Adams had withdrawn, Davis was chosen over Morton. A year later he again defeated Morton, this time by a popular majority of 8,000.

Elected by the General Court as United States senator to succeed Nathaniel Silsbee, Davis took his seat, Dec. 7, 1835, as a member of the newly formed Whig party. At the insistence of the state Whig organization, he resigned in 1840 in order to run for governor against his old rival, Marcus Morton, over whom he was again victorious by a considerable majority. In 1841, he once more won over Morton, but in 1842 the election was thrown into the legislature, where Davis was beaten. He then returned to his law practise, but when Isaac C. Bates, who had succeeded him in the Senate, died (Mar. 16, 1845), Davis was again sent to the Senate, and in 1847 was elected for the full term. He retired on Mar. 3, 1853, after more than twenty-five years of public service in state and nation.

In Congress, first as a Federalist and later as a National Republican and a Whig, he held conservative views on most controversial questions. He became a spokesman for those New England interests which demanded a protective tariff, and consequently opposed Clay's compromise tariff act of 1833. He made some widely circulated replies to the free-trade arguments of Southern statesmen. A consistent opponent of President Jackson and all his works, he protested when, in 1837, the Senate expunged from its records the well-known resolution censuring the Executive. He was against any further spread of slavery in the states or territories, and was one of two senators to vote against the declaration of war with Mexico. It seemed for a time that he would be Clay's running mate on the Whig ticket in 1844, but his uncompromising position with regard to slavery prevented his nomination. It is probable that if Clay had been elected Davis would have been appointed secretary of the treasury. His speech of Aug. 12, 1846, caused the Senate session to end without a vote on the Wilmot Proviso and led to criticism of his "unseasonable loquacity." He was opposed to the compromise measures of 1850, and exerted all his influence in the campaign of 1852 for the success of the Whig candidate, Gen. Scott.

Although he had little grace of manner and, because of his shaggy locks, reminded people of "a great white bear," Davis possessed a kind of awkward dignity which was impressive. Without being showy or brilliant, he was convincing because of his sincerity and earned the nickname of "Honest John." Though temperamentally cautious, he did not lack courage in a crisis. A man of judgment rather than of imagination, he enjoyed the respect and confidence of his constituents. He married, on Mar. 28, 1822, Eliza Bancroft, daughter of Rev. Aaron Bancroft and sister of George Bancroft. Three of their sons, John Chandler Bancroft, Horace, and Andrew McFarland [*qq.v.*], had distinguished careers. Davis was president of the American Antiquarian Society and received many honors. He died in Worcester at the age of sixty-seven.

[*Proc. Am. Antiq. Soc.*, Apr. 1854, Oct. 1893; *Trans. and Colls. Am. Antiq. Soc.*, vols. III (1857), VIII (1901); *Memorial Biogs. of the New-Eng. Hist. Geneal. Soc.*, vol. II (1881); F. B. Dexter, *Biog. Sketches Grads. Yale Coll.*, vol. VI (1912); Geo. Watterston, *Gallery of Am. Portraits* (1830); *Memoirs of John Quincy Adams*, vol. IX (1876); *Reminiscences of the Rev. Geo. Allen of Worcester* (1883); *The Diary of Jas. K. Polk* (1910); Wm. Lincoln, *Hist. of Worcester, Mass.* (1837); H. Davis, *Ancestry of John Davis* (1897); J. D. Estabrook, *Three Generations of Northboro Davises* (1908); Geo. F. Hoar, *Autobiog. of Seventy Years* (1903).]
C. M. F.

DAVIS, JOHN CHANDLER BANCROFT (Dec. 29, 1822–Dec. 27, 1907), diplomatist, was born in Worcester, Mass., the son of John Davis [*q.v.*] and Eliza (Bancroft) Davis, a sister of George Bancroft. He was usually known as Bancroft Davis. After attending the Worcester public schools, he entered Harvard College with the class of 1840. Unjustly suspended in his senior year, he did not return, but was given the A.B. degree in 1847. He studied law, was admitted to the Massachusetts bar in 1844, and then opened an office in New York City. On Aug. 31, 1849, he succeeded John R. Brodhead as secretary of the American legation in Great Britain, acting as chargé d'affaires for several months during the absence of the newly appointed minister, Abbott Lawrence. Resigning on Nov. 30, 1852, he returned to his profession in New York, entering the firm of Kent, Eaton & Kent, which afterward became Kent, Eaton & Davis. From 1854 to 1861 he was American correspondent of the London *Times*. He married (Nov. 19, 1857) Frederica Gore, daughter of James Gore King and grand-daughter of Rufus King. They had no children. Because of ill health he retired from practise in 1862, and after two years abroad settled on a farm in Orange County, N. Y.

Having regained his vigor, Davis was elected to the New York legislature in 1868, and on Mar. 25, 1869, accepted an appointment as assistant secretary of state, a post for which he had exceptional qualifications. He was an arbitrator in a dispute between Portugal and Great Britain regarding their African possessions. When, in 1871, a Joint High Commission was appointed to arrange a settlement of the dispute between the United States and Great Britain arising out of the depredations of the *Alabama* and other cruisers during the Civil War, he was made secretary of the commission on the part of the United States. After the signing of the Treaty of Washington (May 8, 1871) providing for a Tribunal of Arbitration to meet at Geneva, Davis, who had the full confidence of Secretary Fish and was familiar with all the details of the prolonged controversy, was designated as American agent.

He personally prepared "The Case of the United States" (*Senate Executive Document No. 31,* 42 Cong., 2 Sess.; Moore, *post,* I, 591 n.), an imposing book of nearly 500 pages in which American grievances were fully stated. The sixth chapter, which contained the formal statement of claims, was not submitted in advance by Davis for American criticism, as the other chapters had been. In it compensation was demanded not only for losses directly due to the activities of the Confederate cruisers, but also for general injuries to United States commerce, for enhanced insurance rates, and for the expenditures necessitated by the prolongation of the war. Opinions differ as to the merits of Davis's presentation, and particularly as to the wisdom of incorporating the latter claims, termed "national" or "indirect," which aroused bitter British protests (Rhodes, *post,* VI, 364 ff.; Cushing, *post,* p. 31; Moore, *post,* I, 628 ff.). Whether or not his advocacy of American claims was marked by undue assertiveness, it was at least spirited. The case was presented to the Tribunal on Dec. 16, 1871. Meanwhile Davis had sailed for Europe, reaching Havre in November and proceeding to Geneva. Here he set to work preparing the "Counter Case of the United States" (*Senate Executive Document No. 67,* 42 Cong., 2 Sess.), which was delivered on Apr. 15. When the matter of the indirect claims seemed likely to disrupt the Tribunal, Davis's friendly relations with the British agent, Lord Tenterden, enabled him, with the assistance of Caleb Cushing, to devise a plan by which the arbitrators declared themselves in an extra-judicial announcement as not favoring the American demands. After the award, giving the United States a lump sum of $15,500,000 in gold for direct damages, had been announced (Sept. 14, 1872), Davis sailed for home and made a formal report to the Department of State. On Jan. 24, 1873, he was reappointed assistant secretary of state, but resigned in July 1874, to become minister to Germany, in succession to his uncle, George Bancroft. He spent the next three years in Berlin, with occasional intervals of travel in the Mediterranean countries.

After the inauguration of President Hayes, Davis resigned, only to be appointed judge of the United States Court of Claims, on which he served from January 1878 until December 1881. Then, at President Arthur's request, he accepted an assignment as assistant secretary of state, on special duty. At the expiration of six months, he was reappointed to the Court of Claims. Retaining this position until Nov. 5, 1883, he then accepted an appointment as reporter of the United States Supreme Court, editing in this capacity Volumes 108–186 of the *United States Reports.* He retired after nineteen years and spent his last days in Washington. Among his publications were: *The Massachusetts Justice* (1847); a revision of "Treaties and Conventions Concluded between the United States of America and other Powers," etc. (*Senate Executive Document No. 36,* 41 Cong., 3 Sess.); *Mr. Fish and the Alabama Claims* (1893), and a pamphlet on the *Origin of the Book of Common Prayer of the Protestant Episcopal Church in the United States of America* (1897). He was recognized as an authority on historical data relating to the judicial functions of the United States government.

[While at Geneva, Davis kept a diary, which is now preserved in the archives of the Dept. of State. See also H. Davis, *Ancestry of John Davis* (1897); *Harvard Grads. Mag.,* Mar. 1908; *Proc. Am. Antiq. Soc.,* Apr. 1908; *Proc. upon the Occasion of Presenting to the Court of Claims of the U. S. a Portr. of John Chandler Bancroft Davis* (1912); John Bassett Moore, *Hist. and Digest of the International Arbitrations to which the U. S. has been a Party,* I (1898, 495–678); F. W. Hackett, *Reminiscences of the Geneva Tribunal of Arbitration* (1911); Caleb Cushing, *The Treaty of Washington: Its Negotiation, Execution and the Discussions Relating Thereto* (1873); J. F. Rhodes, *Hist. of the U. S.,* vol. VI (1906); *Nation* (N. Y.), Jan. 31,

1907; *Evening Post* (N. Y.), *N. Y. Tribune*, and *Washington Post*, all Dec. 28, 1907.] C. M. F.

DAVIS, JOHN LEE (Sept. 3, 1825–Mar. 12, 1889), naval officer, was the first child of the young physician—later prominent Democratic political leader—John Wesley Davis [*q.v.*] and Ann Hoover, born shortly after their removal from southeastern Pennsylvania to Carlisle, Sullivan County, Ind. He went to school in Carlisle, and through his father, then a congressman, was appointed a midshipman, Jan. 9, 1841. From then until the Civil War, except for a year at the new Naval Academy, 1846–47, and two tours of duty in the Coast Survey, 1851–52, 1855–57, he was almost constantly in sea service, in the Far East, on the African Coast, in the Pacific, and elsewhere. He had blockade duty in the Mexican War; and in November 1849, while acting lieutenant in the *Preble*, he led a boat party of seventeen which captured a Chinese junk engaged in piracy off Macao, killing three of the crew and wounding many others. In the Civil War he was among the younger ship commanders who won distinction for energy and reliability. As executive officer of the *Water Witch* he was in the sharp engagement with the *Manassas* and other Confederate vessels in the mouth of the Mississippi, Oct. 12, 1861. Declining command of the *Water Witch* in deference to officers senior to him, he was promoted in July following to lieutenant commander. In command of the gunboat *Wissahickon* he took part in an attack on enemy batteries below Fort McAllister, Nov. 19, 1862, in which his vessel was pierced below the waterline, but was run aground and successfully patched at low tide. The *Wissahickon* was in subsequent attacks on the fort on Jan. 27 and Feb. 1 and 28. On Mar. 19, 1863, his vessel sank the valuable blockade-runner *Georgiana* entering Charleston harbor. Transferred in August to command of the monitor *Montauk*, he took active part in the bombardments of the Charleston forts, September–November 1863. In the *Sassacus*, 1864–65, he was engaged in the attacks on Fort Fisher in December 1864, and January 1865, and in subsequent operations in the Cape Fear River. Admiral Du Pont (*Official Records of the Union and Confederate Navies*, XIII, 697) commended Davis's "extreme vigilance and spirit" in blockade work, and the latter was among the officers recommended by Porter for promotion after the capture of Fort Fisher. Advanced to commander, 1866, to captain, 1873, to commodore, 1882, and to rear admiral, 1885, he had shore duty at various times on the Lighthouse, Retirement, and Inspection Boards; commanded the *Trenton*, flagship of the European Squadron, 1877–78; and was in command of the Asiatic Squadron, 1883–86. He was retired Sept. 3, 1887.

Davis was of erect, handsome figure, with curly reddish brown hair, moustache, and goatee, which turned white in later years. He was strict and sharp in discipline—a "sun-downer" in the naval phrase—but withal respected as a brave, upright officer and expert seaman, the last borne out by the anecdote of the old tar of the eighties who said there were only three sailors left in the Navy, "me, and John Lee Davis, and Stephen B. Luce" (Albert Gleaves, *Life and Letters of Rear Admiral Stephen B. Luce*, 1925, p. 307). Somewhat enteebled by his Asiatic service, he died of pneumonia at the Ebbitt House, Washington, where he had made his home after the war, and was buried in Rock Creek Cemetery. He was survived by his wife, Frances Latta Robinson, whom he married Dec. 12, 1855, and by one daughter.

[Lewis R. Hamersly, *Records of Living Officers of the U. S. Navy and Marine Corps* (3rd ed., 1878) gives Davis's complete service record to that date. Some comment on his character and his last cruise appears in Rear Admiral A. S. Barker, *Everyday Life in the Navy* (1928), pp. 147–83. See also *Washington Post*, Mar. 13, 1889, and *Army and Navy Jour.*, Mar. 16, 1889.] A. W.

DAVIS, JOHN WESLEY (Apr. 16, 1799–Aug. 22, 1859), congressman, the son of Rev. John Davis and ——— (Jones) Davis, was born at New Holland, Lancaster County, Pa. He studied medicine at the University of Maryland, graduating in 1821. Two years later, with his wife, Ann Hoover, he moved to Carlisle, Ind., traveling in a cart and arriving, as he afterward related, with three cents in his pocket. He practised his profession for some years, but yielding to the lure of politics he ran for the state Senate in 1828 and was beaten. His magnanimous opponent, however, aided him to secure the appointment as sergeant-at-arms of that body. In 1829 he was elected probate judge of Sullivan County and soon passed from that post into the state House of Representatives, of which he was six times a member in the course of his career, being three times elected speaker. In politics he was so ardent a Democrat that in a speech made near the close of his career he declared, in reply to a heckler: "I will say now that I endorse everything the Democratic party ever has done, and everything that it ever will do" (Wolfe, *post*, pp. 48–9). Elected in 1835 to the Twenty-fourth Congress, he subsequently served in the Twenty-sixth, Twenty-eighth, and Twenty-ninth. Though not an orator, he wielded much influence and in 1845 was elevated to the speakership, presiding over the House during the first part of the Mexican War. Sent early in 1848 as commissioner to China, he returned home in 1850. He was repeatedly a delegate to Democratic national conventions and presided over the convention of 1852 that nominated Pierce. Upon the return of his party to power in 1853 he was appointed governor of Oregon Territory but resigned the next year. In 1856 he was again elected to the state legislature. Three years later he died at his home in Carlisle. Though he was a strong partisan, no one ever questioned his integrity, and he died a poor man. His oldest son, John Lee Davis [*q.v.*], rendered distinguished service as a naval officer.

[Thos. J. Wolfe, *A Hist. of Sullivan County, Ind.* (2 vols., 1909); W. W. Woolen, *Biog. and Hist. Sketches of Early Ind.* (1883), containing an account of Davis based mainly on an autobiographical sketch by him near the end of his life; a master's thesis on Davis's career by Hope Bedford, Butler Univ. Lib.] P. L. H.

DAVIS, JOSEPH ROBERT (Jan. 12, 1825–Sept. 15, 1896), Confederate soldier, was a son of Isaac Davis, and a nephew of Jefferson Davis [*q.v.*]. Isaac Davis, after serving in the War of 1812 as a private and later as an officer in the regiment of Lieut.-Col. Thomas Hinds in the army led by Andrew Jackson, married in 1822 Susan Garthy, a native Mississippian of Irish parentage. Joseph, their second child, was born at Woodville, Wilkinson County, Miss. Educational advantages were meager about his father's plantations in Wilkinson and Warren counties, so as a boy Joseph was sent to Nashville, Tenn., for his preliminary training. The law seemed to afford the best opportunity for the advancement of an aspiring youth, and Joseph's father accordingly sent him to Miami University, Oxford, Ohio, where he was graduated. After thoroughly fitting himself for the profession of law, he entered upon its practise, which he continued in Madison County, Miss., until 1860. In that year he was elected to the Mississippi state Senate, but after his state's ordinance of secession he resigned from the legislature and enthusiastically entered the service of the Confederacy. He was quickly elected captain of a company from the county where he had recently made his home, Madison. In April 1861 he was made lieutenant-colonel in the 10th Mississippi Regiment at Pensacola, Fla. Some four months later, his uncle, the president of the Confederacy, offered "Joe," as Jefferson Davis called his nephew, a commission as colonel on the president's staff. The colonel performed inspection duty in various parts of the South until 1862, when he was assigned to the command of a brigade of Mississippi troops, in the Army of Northern Virginia, with rank of brigadier-general. His brigade was engaged in some of the most bitter battles of the Civil War, including the Wilderness, Cold Harbor, and the siege of Petersburg. At the very beginning of the battle of Gettysburg, the brigade of Davis clashed with Buford's dismounted cavalry, and was much engaged until the third day of the battle, when the entire brigade was in Pickett's charge, conducting itself most gallantly. After Davis had surrendered with Lee at Appomattox, he returned to Mississippi and resumed the practise of law, spending most of the remainder of his life at Biloxi. He was married twice: in 1848 to a Miss Peyton, and in 1879 to Margaret Cary Green, who was the mother of his two daughters and one son, Jefferson. According to Goodspeed's *Biographical and Historical Memoirs of Mississippi* (1891) he was a "logical reasoner, decisive in statement, and possessed of sufficient eloquence to render his declamation vigorous and of the most convincing order."

[Dunbar Rowland in his *Jefferson Davis, Constitutionalist* (1923) refers in several volumes to Jos. R. Davis, prints a number of letters between him and the members of his family, and gives a short biography (V, 346). *The Davis Family in Wales and America* (1927), by Harry A. Davis, is perhaps the best reference for genealogy. *Miss. Hist. Soc. Pubs.*, vol. IX, refers to Davis repeatedly. A short sketch of his life appears in Dunbar Rowland's *Mississippi* (1907), I, 632, and his military career is treated somewhat fully in the same author's *Miss. the Heart of the South* (1925), II, 53–78.] L. T. L.

DAVIS, MARY EVELYN MOORE (Apr. 12, 1852–Jan. 1, 1909), author, was born in Talladega, Ala., and died in New Orleans. Her mother, Marian Lucy Crutchfield, whose family had migrated from Virginia to Chattanooga, had two brothers who were colonels in the Civil War, one Unionist, the other Confederate. Her father, John Moore, was born and educated as a physician in Massachusetts. He went to Alabama to practise medicine, but as early as 1848 he was interesting himself there in the commercial possibilities of iron deposits. A few years before the Civil War he removed with his family to "La Rose Blanche," a cotton plantation in Texas. Here Mary—Mollie she was called—grew up, educated by private tutors. She was a precocious child, and many of her fervent war poems appeared in Southern newspapers in 1861–65. A collected edition of her verse, *Minding the Gap*, was published in Houston in 1867. She was married on Oct. 20, 1874, to Thomas Edward Davis, who, after serving during the Civil War as major in the Virginia cavalry, had become editor of the *Houston Telegraph*. He was called to New Orleans in 1879 to become associated with the *Daily Picayune*, and he and his wife took up residence in the old French quarter in a house once occupied by Edward Livingston and visited by Andrew Jackson. In this house Mrs. Davis developed and maintained for many years a gathering place for those about her who prized subtlety of talk and thought. She was gentle, humorous, and wise, and many competent witnesses bore testimony to the spell of her presence. This presence and the just scale of values which by direction and indirection she helped to establish constitute her chief claim upon enduring memory. She was among the first to exploit negro dialect for literary purposes, but her writings do not keep their vitality. *Under Six Flags, the Story of Texas* (1897) is of slight permanent value; *In War Times at La Rose Blanche* (1888) and *Jaconetta* (1901) have some autobiographical interest. The little plays in *A Bunch of Roses* (1903)—the poems in *A Christmas Masque* (1896)—the stories in *An Elephant's Track* (1897)—and the novel, *The Little Chevalier* (1903)—though all conscientiously executed, often thrust her into comparison with either Uncle Remus or Dr. Sevier, and the result is not flattering to her. Even local patriotism recognized at the time of her death the discrepancy between the force of her actual self, and the rating which it already seemed would at last be given to her work. She had no children, but she adopted a niece whom she reared as her own daughter. The last years of her life were spent in pain which she bore with fortitude.

[There is a biographical note in the posthumous *Selected Poems* (1927). See also W. B. Smith, "Mary Evelyn Moore Davis," *Lib. of Southern Lit.*, vol. III (1909); J. W. Davidson, *Living Writers of the South* (1869); T. McA. Owen, *Hist. of Ala. and Dict. of Ala. Biog.* (1921), vol. III; *Who's Who in America*, 1908–09; *Daily Picayune* (New Orleans), Jan. 2, 1909.]

J. D. W.

DAVIS, MATTHEW LIVINGSTON (Oct. 28, 1773–June 21, 1850), politician, journalist, born presumably in New York, the son of Matthew and Phebe (Wells) Davis, is remembered for his forty years' association with Aaron Burr, of whom he was an adoring friend, a zealous henchman, and an unwise biographer. His life was passed amid the rough-and-tumble of partisan politics and partisan journalism. Starting as a printer, he edited the short-lived *Evening Post* in 1794, collaborated with Philip Freneau on the *Time Piece and Literary Companion*, 1797–98, and was Burr's indefatigable lieutenant in the New York political campaign of 1800. How much he then contributed to the vote-getting technique of the Tammany Society is a matter of conjecture, but tirelessly active and enthusiastic in the cause he certainly was. By way of reward Burr, with Gallatin's support, tried to have Davis made naval officer of the port; Jefferson hesitated, and Davis bolted down to Monticello in a tactless, futile effort to secure action. Jefferson's refusal to give Davis an office was a serious affront to the Vice-President, and had its consequences. On July 11, 1804, Davis accompanied his chief across the Hudson to the dueling ground at Weehawken, and subsequently went to jail rather than give incriminating testimony against his friend. Sometime before the War of 1812 he was a member of the trading firm of Davis & Strong, which prospered in South-American ventures, Davis' own profits, later lost, amounting to about $50,000. He was accused of smuggling flour out of the country during the Embargo, which officially he was supporting. In 1814 and 1815 he was Grand Sachem of the Tammany Society, and was a Sachem for some years thereafter. While Grand Sachem he is said, by Myers, to have cleared $80,000 on a government contract. On Sept. 15, 1826, with several others he was indicted for swindles aggregating several million dollars. The first jury disagreeing, they were convicted on a second trial; a third trial was procured for Davis, who was at last acquitted. To Burr he was faithful to the end; he inherited Burr's papers, and after his death (Sept. 14, 1836) published *Memoirs of Aaron Burr* (1836–37) and *The Private Journal of Aaron Burr during his Residence of Four Years in Europe* (1838). For Davis as biographer and as custodian of Burr's papers scholars have shown a good deal of scorn. He destroyed the greater part of Burr's correspondence, gave away letters for their autographs, and displayed scant knowledge of historical methods. In his later years he was Washington correspondent of the London *Times* ("The Genevese Traveller") and of the *Morning Courier and New York Enquirer* ("The Spy in Washington"). In the capital he was known as "the Old Boy in Specs," was reputed to have been a duelist, and was esteemed for his fund of anecdote and reminiscence. After a paralytic stroke in 1848 he gave up writing. Holding a minor political sinecure, he died at his son's home at Manhattanville, N. Y., and was laid to rest in Trinity Cemetery.

[H. Adams, *Hist. of the U. S.*, vol. I (1889, 1898); H. Adams, *Life of Albert Gallatin* (1879); H. Adams, ed., *Writings of Albert Gallatin*, vol. I (1879); W. C. Ford, *Some Papers of Aaron Burr* (1920); F. Hudson, *Journalism in the U. S. from 1690 to 1872* (1873); G. Myers, *Hist. of Tammany Hall* (1901); M. R. Werner, *Tammany Hall* (1928); S. H. Wandell and M. Minnigerode, *Aaron Burr* (1925), portrait of Davis, after original in possession of N. Y. Hist. Soc., in vol. I; obituaries in *Littell's Liv. Age*, Aug. 3, 1850, and in N. Y. newspapers, June 24, 1850; E. A. and G. L.

Duyckinck, *Cyc. of Am. Lit.* (1875); F. L. Pattee, ed., *The Poems of Philip Freneau* (1902), vol. I, p. lxxv; J. Parton, *Life and Times of Aaron Burr* (1892); H. S. Randall, *Life of Thos. Jefferson* (1857).]

G. H. G.

DAVIS, NATHAN SMITH (Jan. 9, 1817–June 16, 1904), "father of the American Medical Association," was born to Dow Davis and Eleanor Smith, both of English descent, in a farmhouse at Greene, Chenango County, N. Y. Here he spent his first sixteen years, attending district school in the winters with one six months' session at Cazenovia Seminary, in Madison County. In 1834 he commenced the study of medicine under Dr. Daniel Clark in the near-by village of Smithville Flats. After three courses of medical lectures at the College of Physicians and Surgeons of the Western District of New York at Fairfield, he was graduated in January 1837. He began practise in Vienna, N. Y., where he married Anna Maria Parker on Mar. 5, 1838, but during the latter year he moved to Binghamton, N. Y., where he remained nine years. There he soon became prominent in medical affairs. He was secretary of the Broome County Medical Society from 1841 to 1843, and from 1843 to 1846 he represented the county society at meetings of the Medical Society of the State of New York. At the session of 1843 he presented a resolution upon the elevation of standards of medical education, which led to the organization of the American Medical Association.

He moved to New York City in 1847, where he took charge of the dissecting room of the College of Physicians and Surgeons, lectured on medical jurisprudence, and assumed editorial charge of the *Annalist,* a semi-monthly medical journal. In 1849 he went to Chicago to fill the professorship of physiology and pathology at Rush Medical College, and in 1850 was given the chair of principles and practise of medicine and of clinical medicine. During the latter year he headed a movement for the introduction of a sewage system and an adequate water supply for the city, then of 27,000 inhabitants, and for the establishment of a public hospital. Through his efforts, funds were raised to furnish twelve beds, the nucleus for Mercy Hospital, the oldest and now one of the largest hospitals in Chicago. In 1859, a group from the faculty of Rush Medical College, including Davis, founded the medical department of Lind University, which later became the Chicago Medical College and still later the medical department of Northwestern University. Upon this faculty Davis was professor of principles and practise of medicine and later emeritus professor until his death. He was dean of the faculty during his entire active association with the school, and was able to put into practise his advanced ideas on medical education.

Davis was among the small group that organized the Illinois Medical Society and the Chicago Medical Society. He was one of the founders of Northwestern University, of the Chicago Academy of Science, the Chicago Historical Society, the Union College of Law and the Washingtonian Home. He was honorary member of many medical and scientific societies in this country and abroad, and held official positions in most of the societies to which he belonged. He was editor of the *Chicago Medical Journal* from 1855 to 1859. In 1860 he founded the *Chicago Medical Examiner,* which he edited until its merger with the *Chicago Medical Journal* in 1873. He was editor of the *Journal of the American Medical Association* for the first six years after its establishment in 1883. At different times he was also editor of the *Northwestern Medical and Surgical Journal,* of the *Eclectic Journal of Education and Literary Review,* and of the *American Medical Temperance Quarterly.* Besides editorials and journal articles he wrote: *A Text Book on Agriculture* (1848); *History of Medical Education and Institutions in the United States* (1851); *History of the American Medical Association* (1855); *Clinical Lectures on Various Important Diseases* (1873), which went through two editions; *Lectures on the Principles and Practice of Medicine* (1884); and *History of Medicine, with the Code of Medical Ethics* (1903). One of his chief interests was the temperance cause, which he supported actively with tongue and pen. Possessed of a dynamic presence and a fiery eloquence, as a lecturer he has had few equals in American medicine. To his apparently frail body was united a tireless energy and an intense intellectuality. His head was disproportionately large, with a high and broad forehead. His portrait taken in his later years shows the face of a zealot, long, thin, and smooth shaven, with flaming eyes and a ruff of neck whiskers.

[I. N. Danforth, *Life of Nathan Smith Davis* (1907) and a memoir in the *Quart. Bull. of Northwestern Univ. Medic. School,* Dec. 1908; R. O. Beard, in the *Bull. Asso. Am. Medic. Colleges,* I (1892), 32; J. H. Hollister, in the *Ill. Medic. Jour.,* July 1904; F. S. Johnson, in *Science,* Aug. 19, 1904; E. C. Dudley, in the *St. Paul Medic. Jour.,* May 1905; V. Robinson, in the *Medic. Rev. of Revs.,* Aug. 1917; H. O. Marcy, in *Am. Medicine,* July 1919; *N. J. Medic. Reporter,* VIII (1855), 248; *New Eng. Medic. Monthly,* II (1882–83), 421; *Jour. Am. Medic. Asso.,* June 3, 1899, June 25, 1904; *Medic. Record* and *N. Y. Medic. Jour.,* both June 25, 1904; *Medic. Standard* and *Chicago Medic. Recorder,* both July 1904; *Boston Medic. and Surgic. Jour.,* June 30, 1904, and a memoir by H. T. Byford in the same magazine for June 19, 1919, reprinted in H. A. Kelly and W. L. Burrage, *Am. Medic. Biogs.* (1920).]

J. M. P.

DAVIS, NOAH (Sept. 10, 1818–Mar. 20, 1902), jurist, was born at Haverhill, N. H., but the greater part of his youth was spent at Albion, N. Y., to which place his parents moved in 1825. They were poor, and his only education was obtained at the public schools. Later, by copying deeds in the evening for the deputy clerk, S. E. Church, he earned money which enabled him to attend Lima Seminary in the daytime. Subsequently he studied law at Lewiston, Niagara County, and was admitted to the bar in 1841. Practising first at Gaines, and then at Buffalo, N. Y., he met with no success and returned in 1844 to Albion, where the deputy clerk—now a lawyer—took him into partnership. Under the firm name of Church & Davis they rapidly acquired an extensive practise and became one of the best-known firms in western New York. In March 1857 he was appointed a justice for the 8th division of the supreme court of New York, to fill a vacancy, and when his term expired, November 1857, was elected for the succeeding term. He had always taken an active interest in political affairs, being a strong Republican, and in 1868 he was elected to Congress from Orleans and Monroe counties and resigned from the bench. He did not complete his term, however, as President Grant in July 1870 appointed him United States district attorney for southern New York. It was a critical period in the history of New York City, the contest between the Reform party and the adherents of William M. Tweed being at its bitterest, but his firm and vigorous administration of the duties of his office defeated the endeavors of the "Tweed Ring" to influence the municipal elections, and the Reform party triumphed over bribery and intimidation. The judiciary also needed to be delivered from the Tweed influence, so in 1872 he was nominated by the Republican party, indorsed by the Reform "Committee of Seventy," and elected a justice of the supreme court for the 1st judicial district. The first trial of Tweed took place before Davis in January 1873 and was abortive, owing to disagreement of the jury. A retrial was held in November, its opening being signalized by a unique incident, all the defense counsel signing and presenting to Davis a written protest against his again officiating as trial judge, on the ground that he was prejudiced and had expressed unfavorable opinions respecting the defendant. The second trial resulted in a conviction on twelve counts, and, feeling that to treat the verdict as if rendered upon a single misdemeanor would result in an entirely inadequate punishment, Davis imposed a cumulative sentence upon Tweed of twelve years' imprisonment and $3,000 fine. He also treated as a contempt of court the protest of the defense counsel, fining three of them $250 each. Subsequently the court of appeals set aside the cumulative sentence on purely legal grounds. In 1874 he was appointed presiding justice of the General Term, and retained this position until his retirement Dec. 31, 1886, thus completing a service of more than twenty-five years upon the bench. Among other celebrated trials over which he presided were those of Edward S. Stokes for the murder of "Jim" Fisk, Jr., and of Chancellor Wallworth's son for the murder of his father. A great deal of the litigation in which the City of New York was involved through the operations of the Tweed Ring also came before him. On leaving the bench he resumed practise in New York City, and for a time was active in local political circles, but retired from public life in 1901, and died in New York City, Mar. 20, 1902.

As a judge he was an outstanding figure. He "brought to the bench wide experience, broad and comprehensive knowledge of the law, and a dignified and forceful personality which made him the strongest and most eminent of our judges during his entire term of service" (Theron G. Strong, *post*, p. 78). By nature a man of strong convictions and prejudices, he found it difficult to conceal his feelings on all occasions, and his austere demeanor procured for him a reputation for severity which his scrupulous fairness, patient attention, and the care which he bestowed upon all matters before him, did not always dispel. His attitude in the Tweed case, though subjected to strong criticism from some quarters, met with emphatic popular approval. As a public speaker he was in the front rank and his jury charges were masterpieces of exposition. Throughout his life he was a close student of public affairs. An intimate friend of Gen. Grant, he often acted as his personal counsel. His only contribution to literature was a small book, *Intemperance and Crime* (1883).

[An extended sketch of Davis's career appeared in the *Albany Law Jour.*, Nov. 1904, and Theron G. Strong in *Landmarks of a Lawyer's Lifetime* (1914), p. 78, makes a valuable contribution from personal knowledge to an appreciation of his character and services. See also *Hist. of the Bench and Bar of N. Y.*, ed. by D. McAdam and others, II (1899), 123; *Hist. Album of Orleans County, N. Y.* (1879), p. 116; *Green Bag*, Jan. 1897, *N. Y. Times*, Mar. 21, 1902.]

H. W. H. K.

DAVIS, NOAH KNOWLES (May 15, 1830–May 3, 1910), teacher, author, was the son of Noah Davis of Maryland and Mary (Young) Davis of Alexandria, Va. He was born in Philadelphia, where his father, a minister still under thirty, was in charge of the recently formed

Baptist Tract Society. In July 1830, his father died, and a few years later his mother was married to John L. Dagg [*q.v.*], like herself a Virginian, and like her former husband a Baptist ecclesiastic. The Dagg family removed to the far south, and in 1849, during his step-father's term as its president, Noah Davis was graduated from the sectarian Mercer College, then located in Penfield, Ga. Soon afterward he went to Philadelphia and studied chemistry, and later he was for about twenty years connected with the faculties of various Baptist colleges. From 1852 to 1865 he was in Alabama, for seven years as teacher of natural science in Howard College, and for the remaining six as head of the Judson Female Institute. From 1868 to 1873 he was president of Bethel College, in Kentucky. He was married in 1856 (or 1857) to Ella Hunt of Albany, Ga. From 1873 to 1906 he was professor of moral philosophy in the University of Virginia. He was an effective teacher, learned, diligent, and sincere. His writings were largely of the kind used as text-books. His *Theory of Thought* (1880) was followed by his series: *Elements of Psychology* (1892), *Elements of Deductive Logic* (1893), *Elements of Inductive Logic* (1895), and *Elements of Ethics* (1900) —a group employed, it is said, in more than fifty schools and colleges, and so highly regarded as to be "analyzed" in a volume specially devoted to the purpose by his one-time student, the Methodist bishop, Collins Denny. These books, gracefully written and cogently built up, did not neglect the uses and even claims of deterministic scrutiny, but their author kept himself free to abandon all these uses and claims when he believed that more valid considerations presented themselves. He did not hesitate, for example, to condemn a speculation as in essence illusory if, put into practise, it would befog what he considered the ideal goal of mankind, nor did he hesitate to assume the existence of a thing if its existence had been wished for by many good men for many generations. He adhered, in short, to the age-old concepts of virtue by which he was dominated, and by which he was exalted into something approaching greatness. For if he was a metaphysician pondering on Reality in the abstract, he was as well a conforming Baptist whose experience on the Southern frontier had made plain for him other realities which he could never quite disregard. In the early eighties he inaugurated his custom of delivering a religious discourse every Sunday. These lectures were popular in the university community, and the substance of them was made available to a wider audience in his three religious volumes, *Juda's Jewels, a Study of the Hebrew Lyrics* (1895), *Synopsis of Events in the Life of Jesus of Nazareth* (1900), and *The Story of the Nazarene in Annotated Paraphrase* (1903). He was a large man, stooped, bearded, deliberate, garbed in baggy black, crowned with a high silk hat—eccentric to look upon, eccentric too, in many of his opinions—openly, a little boisterously, irreverent of much knowledge usually held sacrosanct. The last four years of his life were spent in retirement in Charlottesville.

[C. Denny, *Analysis of Noah K. Davis's Elements of Deductive Logic and of his Elements of Psychology* (1916); "Noah Knowles Davis," *Lib. of Southern Lit.*, vol. III (1909); W. B. Sprague, *Annals Am. Pulpit*, vol. VI (1860); *Who's Who in America*, 1910–11; P. A. Bruce, *Hist. of the Univ. of Va.* (1921); L. G. Tyler, *Men of Mark in Va.*, vol. V (1909); *The South in the Building of the Nation*, vol. XI (1909); Catalogues of Howard Coll. 1918, Bethel Coll. 1917–18, Mercer Univ. 1902–03; *Richmond Times Despatch*, May 4, 1910.]

J.D.W.

DAVIS, PAULINA KELLOGG WRIGHT (Aug. 7, 1813–Aug. 24, 1876), editor, suffragist, was born in Bloomfield, N. Y., daughter of Capt. Ebenezer and Polly (Saxton) Kellogg. Both parents were very conservative in their views and their associates. When Paulina was seven years old she was left an orphan and was subsequently adopted by an aunt in Le Roy, N. Y., where she received her education. Her aunt was an unyielding Puritan and the child was under constant restraint, which probably accounts for her later advocacy of freedom and personal rights. Religion was part of her daily routine, and upon leaving school she decided to become a missionary to the Sandwich Islands. This idea was abandoned in 1833 when she married Francis Wright, a merchant of wealth and position in Utica, N. Y. The Wrights took an active part in the anti-slavery convention held in Utica in 1835. Mr. Wright died during that year. Mrs. Wright had spent much of her leisure time in studying anatomy and physiology, and in 1844 she began lecturing on the subject to groups of women. She imported from Paris the first known *femme modèle* in this country. Its use in her lectures brought much unfavorable comment. Her early efforts, however, helped to open the medical profession to women. She contributed many articles to the *Woman's Advocate* and *McDowell's Journal*. In 1849 she married Thomas Davis of Providence, R. I. When he was elected to Congress in 1853, she went with him to Washington. There she was badly received by the women, who considered her knowledge and work unbecoming to her sex. In February 1853, she established the *Una*, the first distinctively woman's rights paper published in this country, which she continued for nearly three years at her own expense. The paper expressed the broadest view of individual freedom. In 1859 she visited Europe and spent a year in travel, giving her leisure time to picture galleries and the study of art. On her return she continued her activities in behalf of woman suffrage. She took charge of the arrangements for the meeting of the National Woman Suffrage Movement held in New York in 1870. At the opening session she gave a report of the history and progress of the movement during the preceding twenty years (published as *A History of the National Woman's Rights Movement,* 1871). In 1871, with her niece and an adopted daughter, she visited Europe, where she took up seriously the study of art, under the direction of Carl Marko, of Florence, Italy. In 1874 her health failed and she returned to the United States. Most of her remaining time was spent as an invalid at her home in Providence, R. I., where she died in 1876.

[An obituary of Paulina Davis appears in the *Woman's Jour.,* Sept. 2, 1876. See also Elizabeth Cady Stanton and others, *Hist. of Woman Suffrage* (1881), I, 283–89; Timothy Hopkins, *The Kelloggs in the Old World and the New* (1903).] M.S.

DAVIS, PHINEAS (1800–Sept. 27, 1835), inventor, the son of Nathan and Mary Davis, was born on his father's farm in Grafton County, N. H. He attended the common schools near his home during the winter months and displayed at an early age an unusual amount of mechanical ingenuity. The farm yielded few opportunities in this field and at the age of fifteen Davis left home. Some months later he arrived in York, Pa., alone and unknown. He soon found employment, however, with the local clock- and watch-maker, Jonathan Jessup, with whom he remained for six years, gaining a local reputation for his inventive skill, reliability, and ambition. In 1821 he met and formed a partnership with Israel Gardner, the proprietor of an iron foundry and machine-shop for the manufacture of steam-engines. After making a few stationary engines of Davis's design the partners began work on an iron-clad steamboat. In this undertaking they called in to assist them a local boat-builder and a fourth helper. Several years were required to complete the boat, but on Nov. 22, 1825, the *Codorus* was launched at York on the Susquehanna River and made one or two voyages to its headwaters. Small as was its draft, the boat, which was sixty feet long and sheathed with sheet iron, was unsuited at certain seasons for the shallows of the river and was abandoned. The engine, designed by Davis, was of the high-pressure type, working under a pressure of one hundred pounds per square inch. In January 1831 when the Baltimore & Ohio Railroad Company issued an advertisement offering $4,000 for the best locomotive delivered on or before June 1, 1831, Davis entered the competition. The requirements were that the locomotive must burn coal or coke, consume its own smoke, and draw fifteen tons' weight at fifteen miles an hour. Davis delivered his locomotive, "York," on time, transporting it by wagon to Baltimore, and won the prize against four competitors. Shortly thereafter the railroad company offered him, and he accepted, the managership of its mechanical shops. Moving to Baltimore with his family early in 1832, he continued to design locomotives and locomotive parts. Under his superintendence the first steel springs were installed on the "York" in 1832, and that year he and Gardner placed in service the "Atlantic," first of the "Grasshopper" engines which were the standard type for many years on the railroad. Davis made a close study of all improvements through actual trial on the company's road between Baltimore and Washington. When he was returning to Baltimore on one of these trial trips, a misplaced rail threw the engine off the track and Davis, who was on the tender, was crushed to death between the engine and the trailing cars, though no one else on board was injured. He had married Hannah Taylor of York on Nov. 15, 1826.

[John C. Jordan, *An Hist. Citizen, Career of Phineas Davis* (1904); Angus Sinclair, *Development of the Locomotive Engine* (1907); W. Kaempffert, *A Popular Hist. of Am. Invention* (1924); Edw. Hungerford, *The Story of the B. & O. R. R.* (1928); *Baltimore American,* Jan. 4, July 13, 1831.] C.W.M.

DAVIS, RAYMOND CAZALLIS (June 23, 1836–June 10, 1919), librarian, was born in Cushing, Knox County, Me., the son of George and Katharine (Young) Davis, of English and Welsh descent through his father, and Scotch and Irish on his mother's side. His father had had long experience on the sea, and eked out the meager returns from his sea-coast farm by commanding tramp sailing vessels. In September 1849, after the death of his wife, he started for California as captain of the ship *Hampton,* taking with him his two sons, the younger of whom, Raymond, although but little over thirteen years of age, was already nearly six feet in height. This trip was continued for two years till the circuit of the globe had been completed, and Raymond had become a proficient sailor. On his return to America he prepared for college, and in 1855 entered the University of Michigan at Ann Arbor. In 1857 he was obliged to give up his studies on account of ill health, and for some years he engaged in the coasting trade. But his heart clung to schools and schooling, and in 1868 he secured the position of assistant librarian in the University of Michigan. This work with the books was suited to his ideals and ambitions, and he retained the position for four years, during which time he published *Reminiscences of a Voyage Around the World* (1869). Without prospect of advancement, except by displacement of the incumbent librarian, he resigned in 1872, and returned to follow the sea for five years.

In 1877, the office of librarian of the University of Michigan having become vacant, Davis was appointed to that position, which he retained with marked success for twenty-eight years. During his administration, from 1877 to 1905, the library grew from 23,909 volumes to 194,672, becoming one of the important libraries of the country. To help freshmen in the use of books and in the library, he started, in 1879, a short course of lectures, to which was added in 1881 a course in bibliography, for which university credit was allowed. This course he described in a paper read at the Milwaukee Conference of the American Library Association in 1886 (*Papers and Proceedings,* 1886, pp. 91–96). In 1887 he was called to give lectures on bibliography in the newly established Library School in Columbia University. These courses were probably the beginning of the instruction in library economy and the use of books which is now becoming common in many educational institutions. On July 6, 1880, he was married to Ellen Regal, daughter of the Rev. Eli Regal, a minister of the Disciples of Christ. In the following year the Regents of the University of Michigan conferred upon him the honorary degree of A.M. Davis had a keen sense of humor, which induced him to write some short stories and sea-yarns which delighted his friends. Several of these appeared in *Fore and Aft* and other magazines. After his retirement as librarian in 1905 he continued his lectures on bibliography until 1914, when he dropped the lectureship, and was made beneficiary of the Williams Emeritus Professorship Fund. He died in Ann Arbor in 1919, survived by his wife and leaving his impress as one of the pioneers of the library movement in America.

[In addition to the references above, see *Who's Who in America,* 1918–19; Davis's own comments on "The Function of a Librarian" in the *Mich. Alumnus,* Mar. 1906; his annual reports, 1878–1905; W. W. Bishop, "In Memoriam, Raymond C. Davis" (with portr.) in *Mich. Alumnus,* Oct. 1919; C. B. Grant, *Ibid.,* Dec., 1919; Memorial adopted by the University Senate, *Ibid.,* June 1920; B. A. Finney, "As it Was in the Beginning: Raymond C. Davis" (with portr.) in *Public Libraries* (Chicago), Oct. 1924; Elizabeth M. Farrand, *Hist of the Univ. of Mich.* (1885); B. A. Hinsdale, *Hist. of the Univ. of Mich.* (1906); Wilfred B. Shaw, *The Univ. of Mich.* (1920).]

B.A.F.

DAVIS, REBECCA BLAINE HARDING (June 24, 1831–Sept. 29, 1910), novelist, daughter of Richard Harding and Rachel Leet Wilson who was of old Virginia descent, was born in Washington, Pa. In her early childhood her parents removed to Alabama and shortly afterward to Wheeling, then in Virginia, where she lived until her marriage. She was very largely self-educated. Attracted to literature by the phenomenal success of the feminine writers of the fifties—Mrs. Stowe, the Warner sisters, Maria Cummins, and others—but without guidance or knowledge of literary art save as she had gained it from voluminous reading, she began early to write fiction, some of which was accepted by the periodicals of the day. She was thirty, however, before she gained anything like real recognition. In April 1861, Lowell published in the *Atlantic,* at the time the leading magazine in America, her short story "Life in the Iron Mills," following it in October with the beginning of her serial "A Short Story of To-day," later issued as *Margaret Howth* (1862). She quickly found herself famous. Though often crude and amateurish in workmanship, these stories were nevertheless remarkable productions, distinct landmarks in the evolution of American fiction. Written when the American novel was in all its areas ultra-romantic and over-sentimental, they are Russian-like in their grim and sordid realism. That she was doing pioneer work she seems fully to have realized. "You want something," she said, "to lift you out of this crowded, tobacco-stained commonplace; to kindle and chafe and glow in you. I want you to dig into this commonplace, this vulgar life, and see what is in it. Sometimes I think it has a new and awful significance that we do not see."

On Mar. 4, 1863, she was married to L. Clarke Davis, later a prominent figure in Pennsylvania journalism, and for the rest of her life made her home in Philadelphia. With a growing family she did not cease from literary activity. In 1869 she became a member of the editorial staff of the *New York Tribune* retaining the position for several years. She was a constant contributor to the magazines and until late in life continued to produce popular fiction. Her leading titles are, *Dallas Galbraith* (1868); *Waiting for the Verdict* (1868); *Berrytown* (1872); *John Andross* (1874); *A Law unto Herself* (1878); *Natasqua* (1886); *Silhouettes of American Life* (1892); *Kent Hampden* (1892); *Doctor Warrick's Daughters* (1896); *Frances Waldeaux*

(1897). None of her later works, however, fulfilled the promise of her first *Atlantic* stories. With achieved reputation she allowed herself to drift into the prevailing fictional conventions and sentimentality. Practically none of her work has been republished. She died at Mount Kisco, N. Y., Sept. 29, 1910. Two sons, Richard Harding Davis [*q.v.*] and Charles Belmont Davis, both writers of distinction, survived her.

[In 1904 Mrs. Davis published an autobiographical volume entitled *Bits of Gossip*. See also a biographical sketch by Dalton Dorr in the *American*, III, 328, Mar. 4, 1882; *N. Y. Times*, Sept. 30, 1910; *Who's Who in America*, 1910–11.] F. L. P—e.

DAVIS, REUBEN (Jan. 18, 1813–Oct. 14, 1890), lawyer, was the youngest of the twelve children of the Rev. John Davis, a Baptist minister who had gone to Tennessee, settling near Winchester. About five years after the birth of Reuben the family removed to northern Alabama. Here Reuben spent much time with the Indians, though he attended the public school about three months each year. Disregarding the boy's early inclination to the law, his father, who thought that "lawyers were wholly given up to the Devil even in this world" and that "it was impossible for any one of them ever to enter the kingdom of heaven," persuaded Reuben, then about sixteen years old, to "read medicine" with his brother-in-law, Dr. George Higgason, in Monroe County, Miss. But a brief experience of the medical profession was sufficient to confirm Davis's original preference for the law (*Recollections*, pp. 2–9). Meanwhile, in 1831, he was married to Mary Halbert. In 1832 he opened a law office in Athens, Monroe County, but later moved to Aberdeen. From the beginning, his success as a lawyer was remarkable. At the age of twenty-two, he was elected district attorney of the 6th Mississippi judicial district. At twenty-six, he had saved $20,000 from his earnings. Defeated for Congress on the Whig ticket in 1838, he was, in 1842, appointed judge of the Mississippi high court of appeals, but resigned after four months on the bench. When the Mexican War broke out, he was elected colonel of the 2nd Mississippi Volunteers. This organization reached the mouth of the Rio Grande the day of the battle of Buena Vista; but Davis, whose health was poor, saw no actual fighting, returning home in June of the same year. After serving a term as a member of the state legislature (1855–57), he was elected to Congress, as a Democrat, and served two terms (1857–61). He believed that war between the North and the South was inevitable, and so strongly defended the Southern position that his opponents called him a fire-eater. After his resignation from the Federal Congress in 1861, he became major-general of Mississippi troops, commanding a brigade for a short time; but was soon elected to the Confederate Congress, and was present at the Richmond inauguration of President Davis. He served in the Confederate legislative body till 1864, when he resigned because of his inability to work harmoniously with President Davis, to whom, incidentally, he was not related. His criticism of the Confederate war policy probably caused his defeat by Gen. Charles Clark for the governorship of Mississippi in 1863. During the Reconstruction period, Davis belonged to the group who believed in controlling the negro by threats of force. (See G. J. Leftwich, "Reconstruction in Monroe County," *Publications of the Mississippi Historical Society,* IX, 76.) He was defeated for Congress in 1878 as a candidate of the Greenback party. During most of the last quarter-century of his life he devoted his energies to the practise of criminal law. He defended more than two hundred clients accused of murder, not one of whom went to the gallows. His principal literary work is his book, *Recollections of Mississippi and Mississippians,* published in 1889. He died the following year in Huntsville, Ala.

[Reuben Davis's *Recollections of Mississippi and Mississippians* (1889) is virtually his autobiography. The *Miss. Hist. Soc. Pubs.* refer to him frequently, especially volumes II, V, IX, X, and XIV. The Goodspeed Publishing Company's *Biog. and Hist. Memoirs of Mississippi* (1891), I, 632–34, contains a considerable sketch of his life. Dunbar Rowland's *Mississippi* (1907), I, 632, tells of the career of Davis, and the same author's *Hist. of Mississippi: the Heart of the South* (1925), vols. I and II, refers to him many times. See also obituary in the *Daily Picayune* (New Orleans), Oct. 15, 1890.] L. T. L.

DAVIS, RICHARD HARDING (Apr. 18, 1864–Apr. 11, 1916), journalist, author, was born in Philadelphia, the son of L. Clarke and Rebecca (Harding) Davis [*q.v.*]. His surroundings were literary from his childhood. His father was editor of the Philadelphia *Public Ledger,* and his mother was one of the prominent feminine novelists of her generation. Reared in the city of his birth, he attended the Episcopal Academy at Swarthmore, Pa., Ulrich's Preparatory School at Bethlehem, Pa., Lehigh University, where he spent three years, and finally Johns Hopkins. In 1886 he entered actively upon the newspaper career that was to make him the most widely known reporter of his generation. After employment by the *Philadelphia Record* for a brief time, he went to the *Press,* for which he reported the Johnstown flood disaster. Later he was sent by the *Telegraph* to England with the cricket team, and in

September 1889 he joined the staff of the New York *Sun*. His stories and "specials" in this paper and his articles in *Scribner's Magazine* attracted wide attention. Leaving the *Sun* in 1890, he became managing editor of *Harper's Weekly* and for this journal made a tour of the West, the literary result of which appeared in 1892 under the title, *The West from a Car Window.* During the next year he spent several months making a comprehensive tour of the Mediterranean for *Harper's Weekly,* his letters appearing in book form in 1894 with the title, *The Rulers of the Mediterranean.* Other journalistic tours during this period he recorded in *Our English Cousins* (1894), and *About Paris* (1895). Next sent to report on conditions in the regions bordering the Canal Zone, he wrote *Three Gringos in Venezuela and Central America* (1896). In a single year he witnessed the coronation of the Czar, the millennial celebration at Budapest, and the Queen's Jubilee in London. It was his fortune to report for prominent New York and London papers six notable wars: the Spanish War in Cuba, the Greco-Turkish, the Spanish-American, the Boer War, the Russo-Japanese, and finally the World War. Seven volumes record his observations: *Cuba in War Time* (1897); *A Year from a Reporter's Note Book* (1898); *The Cuban and Porto Rican Campaigns* (1898); *With Both Armies in South Africa* (1900); *Notes of a War Correspondent* (1910); *With the Allies* (1914); *With the French in France and Salonika* (1916). Only one other of his many assignments need be recorded, his trip to Central Africa in 1907 for *Collier's Weekly* to investigate the reported atrocities, the resulting book being *The Congo and the Coasts of Africa* (1907). As a correspondent Davis was quick to see the picturesque, and unerring in his selection of the features having news value. A tendency, however, to the sensational and startlingly dramatic is to be found in all his journalistic work.

Davis was equally successful in the field of popular fiction. His short story "Gallegher," first published in *Scribner's Magazine* in August 1890, and used a year later as the title number of a collection of tales, attracted wide attention. Following it at varied intervals came eleven other collections aggregating upward of eighty stories with widely varied backgrounds and technique: *Van Bibber and Others* (1892); *The Exiles and Other Stories* (1892); *The Lion and the Unicorn* (1899); *Ranson's Folly* (1902); *The Scarlet Car* (1907); *Once Upon a Time* (1910); *The Man Who Could Not Lose* (1911); *The Red Cross Girl* (1912); *The Lost Road* (1913); *The Boy Scout* (1917). In addition, he produced no less than seven popular novels, some of them among the best sellers of their period: *Soldiers of Fortune* (1897); *The King's Jackal* (1898); *Captain Macklin* (1902); *The Bar Sinister* (1903); *Vera the Medium* (1908); *The White Mice* (1909). In all his fiction Davis was essentially a journalist, quick to sense the demands of the larger public and working in the fashions of the hour. Most of his critics agree that while he was always vivid in his descriptive passages, often picturesque, and easily readable, he dealt mainly with the surface of life, and that even his best work will not long endure. He was too facile, too headlong, too obsessed with contemporaneousness, and he unquestionably published too much.

It was but natural that the lure of dramatic composition should have worked its spell upon him. From his pen came first and last no less than twenty-five dramatic pieces, some of them highly successful on the stage. *Ranson's Folly* had a long run at the Hudson Theatre in 1904; *The Dictator* was presented by Charles Frohman at the Criterion Theatre the same year; *Miss Civilization,* with Ethel Barrymore, as star, was the attraction of the Broadway Theatre in 1906; *The Seventh Daughter* ran for a month at the Cort Theatre in Chicago in 1910; and *The Girl from Home,* a musical comedy, was an attraction in New York as late as 1920. He added, however, nothing permanent to American drama. He was twice married: first, on May 4, 1899, to Cecil Clark of Chicago, who divorced him in 1910; second, on July 8, 1912, to Elizabeth G. McEvoy (Bessie McCoy), who survived him. He died suddenly at his home at Mount Kisco, N. Y.

[Four sets of his writings have been published: first collected edition (8 vols., 1898); second collected edition (6 vols., 1899); third collected edition (6 vols., 1903); and the Cross Roads edition (12 vols., 1916). See also Chas. Belmont Davis, ed., *Adventures and Letters of Richard Harding Davis* (1917); Henry C. Quimby, *Richard Harding Davis, a Bibliography* (1924); and, for criticism of his fiction, Blanche C. Williams, *Our Short Story Writers* (1920).]

F. L. P—e.

DAVIS, VARINA ANNE JEFFERSON (June 27, 1864–Sept. 18, 1898), daughter of Jefferson and Varina (Howell) Davis [*qq.v.*] was born at Richmond during the darkest days of the Confederacy. With her mother she spent some time in Fortress Monroe while her father was a prisoner there. At an early age she showed a remarkable love for books, and at twelve could repeat many passages from Shakespeare. At the age of thirteen she was taken abroad by her parents, and left in a boarding-school at Karlsruhe, Germany, where she remained five years. In 1882 she went to Paris, and on her return spoke French and German more fluently than she did English. At "Beauvoir," now the family home, she was her father's constant companion, and she frequently accompanied him on his trips through the South. On one of these occasions Gov. Gordon of Georgia presented "Winnie" Davis to an enthusiastic crowd as the "Daughter of the Confederacy," a title which she valued and by which she has ever since been known. Adopted, idolized, idealized by the veterans, she became one of the cherished symbols of the "Lost Cause." Beginning her writing before her father's death, she continued it as a means of support when she and her mother went to New York to live. Her published works include: *An Irish Knight of the Nineteenth Century: Sketch of the Life of Robert Emmet* (1888); *The Veiled Doctor; A Novel* (1895); *A Romance of Summer Seas; A Novel* (1899). She died at Narragansett Pier and was buried in Richmond.

[An essay by C. C. Ferrell, " 'The Daughter of the Confederacy,'—her Life, Character and Writings," *Miss. Hist. Soc. Pubs.*, II (1899), 69–84; articles in *N. Y. Times*, New Orleans *Picayune*, *Atlanta Jour.*, Sept. 19, 1898, and in other newspapers; incidental references in the writings of her mother.] M. T. S.

DAVIS, VARINA HOWELL (May 7, 1826–Oct. 16, 1906), wife of Jefferson Davis [*q.v.*], president of the Confederacy, was born at "The Briers," near Natchez, Miss. Her father was William Burr, son of Richard Howell, Revolutionary governor of New Jersey; her mother was Margaret Louisa, daughter of James Kempe, a Virginian of Irish descent. Her girlhood was spent chiefly on the plantation or at Natchez. Much of her early education was received from a devoted tutor, a friend of her father's, Judge George Winchester, whom she affectionately called "Great Heart." Later she spent two years at Madame Greenland's school at Philadelphia. On Feb. 26, 1845 she married Jefferson Davis who that year entered Congress. Mrs. Davis lived in close intellectual companionship with her husband. Though brought up a Whig, she eventually accepted his politics, became jealously watchful of his reputation, and was keenly sensitive to any criticism of his political theories. While her husband was at the front in the Mexican War, she took sole charge of their plantation, "Brierfield." In 1847 he was sent to the Senate. Though Mrs. Davis felt regret at leaving "Brierfield," this was overcome by her pride in her husband's elevation. Being of an ambitious nature, she was gratified by her social success at Washington. While her husband was a senator, and later when he was secretary of war, the drawing room of their house was the scene of many distinguished gatherings. The hostess was a brilliant and vivacious talker, often witty.

Very different was her life a few years later as the wife of the president of the Confederacy. Conditions at Richmond were hard and there was much captious criticism. If she entertained, there was an outcry that the "White House" was indifferent to the sufferings of the people; if she lived simply, her critics complained that she was not keeping up the dignity of her position. Her Northern antecedents made her an object of suspicion, but there was no doubt of her sympathy with the Southern cause. With her husband she had great influence, which her enemies believed to be far from beneficial, especially in the matter of appointments.

The whole of her later life was filled with bitter trials in which she was sustained by her deeply religious nature. The flight from Richmond with her husband and four children was followed by his capture and imprisonment, which for a time she was allowed to share. She made long and untiring efforts for his release, and was at last successful. At "Beauvoir," which they purchased soon after, she was his amanuensis while he wrote *The Rise and Fall of the Confederate Government* (1881). Here, after his death, she wrote her one important literary work: *Jefferson Davis, Ex-President of the Confederate States of America: A Memoir* (2 vols., 1890). Giving "Beauvoir" to the state of Mississippi as a home for Confederate soldiers, Mrs. Davis with her daughter "Winnie" (see article on Varina Anne Jefferson Davis) went to New York, where she wrote articles for periodicals and magazines as a means of support. She survived all but one of her six children.

[The only biography is Eron (Mrs. Dunbar) Rowland, *Varina Howell, Wife of Jefferson Davis* (1927), which contains many reminiscences. The *Memoir* of her husband contains a tolerably full narrative of their personal life. A sympathetic character study is in Gamaliel Bradford, *Wives* (1925). There is a large amount of disjointed information about her seattered through the Southern newspapers of the war period.] M. T. S.

DAVIS, WILLIAM AUGUSTINE (Sept. 21, 1809–Jan. 15, 1875), postmaster, inventor, was born in Barren County, Ky., the son of Hardin and Elizabeth (Wynne) Davis and a descendant of Nathaniel Davis who came from England about 1690 and settled in Virginia. He attended the district schools in winter and helped with the farm work until he was fourteen, and was then sent alone on horseback over the mountains to Charlottesville, Va., to live with a relative and attend private school there. His uncle was postmaster at Charlottesville and in his spare time while at school, and later while at the University of Virginia, young Davis helped in the post-office and became thoroughly acquainted with mail distribution methods. At the age of twenty-one and before completing his University work he accepted a position in the Richmond, Va., post-office. Here he remained for twenty-five years, serving several terms as postmaster. In the spring of 1855 he resigned his position and moved with his family to St. Joseph, Mo., where on Oct. 19, 1855 he was commissioned postmaster. Within a year this position was made a presidential one and he was recommissioned, serving until 1861, when a Republican was appointed, and after that continuing as assistant. The St. Joseph post-office was at that time the point where all western mails were transferred from railroad cars to overland stage-coaches. To make their journeys the stage-coaches had to leave promptly and although there was a three-hour interval in which to sort the mail between the scheduled train arrival and stage-coach departure, the irregularity in arrival of the former rarely permitted sufficient time for this work to be completed, so that the stage-coaches often departed without their consignment of mail. To alleviate this condition, Davis, in the spring of 1862, suggested that the distribution of mail for the West be made on the railroad cars before they reached St. Joseph. With his recommendation he submitted drawings and sketches of his proposed arrangement of cars for the purpose. As a result and with the approval of the Post Office Department, in July 1862 a railroad post-office was successfully inaugurated on the Hannibal & Saint Joseph Railroad (Quincy, Ill., to St. Joseph, Mo.) with Davis in charge of the undertaking. In the *History of the Railway Mail Service,* published by order of Congress in 1885, appears the following: "There seems to be no doubt that Mr. Davis was the first to distribute through mails in the United States, and the first to have cars prepared for that purpose, as was done by the Hannibal and Saint Joseph Railroad for the transportation of the over-land mails" (p. 81). He operated the system until by the extension of railroads westward to connect with the Union Pacific Railroad, the distribution of overland mails was changed. On June 25, 1843, he married Anne Hopkins of Richmond, Va., by whom he had four sons and four daughters, all of whom with his wife survived him at the time of his death in St. Joseph.

[*Hist. of Eminent Men,* pub. by Jas. T. White; *Ry. Postoffice,* n.s., vol. VII, no. 12; *Hist. of the Railway Mail Service,* cited above; original correspondence and documents.]

C. W. M.

DAVIS, WILLIAM THOMAS (Mar. 3, 1822–Dec. 3, 1907), lawyer, author, was descended from Thomas Davis who, settling in Plymouth, Mass., in 1737, engaged in the shipping business and foreign trade. The latter's grandson, William Davis, also of Plymouth, married Joanna, daughter of Capt. Gideon White, and their youngest son, William Thomas Davis, was born there. His early education having been received in private schools, he entered the high school in Plymouth in 1832, proceeding thence to Harvard College, graduating in 1842. He then studied medicine for a short time and in 1846 went to Europe, spending some months in Paris and London. Returning to the United States in 1847, he entered his brother's law office in Boston, and was called to the Suffolk County bar on Nov. 9, 1849. Ten days later he married Abby Burr, daughter of Thomas Hedge of Plymouth. He practised his profession in Boston for four years, but had no great inclination for law, and in 1853 returned to Plymouth, where he entered into business, and remained closely identified with that town during the remainder of his life. He devoted much of his time to investigating the pioneer records of the Plymouth settlement and until 1892—a period of thirty-eight years—there was not a year when he did not hold municipal office. In 1858 and 1859 he represented his district in the state Senate, and in 1876 served as a delegate to the Republican National Convention at Cincinnati. He was also prominent in the Pilgrim Society of which he became president. He embodied the results of his researches into the early history of his neighborhood in two authoritative volumes, *Ancient Landmarks of Plymouth* (1883) and *History of the Town of Plymouth* (1885), which were distinguished for their erudition and attractive style, and also contributed a number of historical articles to the *History of Plymouth County, Mass.* (1884), edited by D. H. Hurd. Thereafter he was constantly engaged in literary production, much of which maintained the high standard attained by his first works. He edited *Records of the Town of Plymouth,* volumes I to III (1889–1903), *The Professional and Industrial History of Suffolk County, Massachusetts* (1894), and *The New England States* (1897), a history in four volumes, contributing himself a number of the articles which appeared in the two last named. He wrote a *History of the Judiciary of Massachusetts* (1900), and in 1906 published *Plymouth Memories of an Octogenarian,* containing much autobiographical material. His last undertaking was the editing of *Bradford's History of Plymouth Plantation 1606–1646* for Scribner's series, Original Narratives of Early American History, to which he contributed a valuable introduction. He died at Plymouth Dec. 3, 1907, while the volume was in the press.

[Davis's ancesty is traced in his *Ancient Landmarks of Plymouth,* pt. 2, pp. 82–83, and a biographical sketch appears in the *Professional and Industrial Hist. of Suffolk County,* vol. I, p. 150. His *Plymouth Memories* contains much personal matter not to be found elsewhere. There is an obituary notice in the *Boston Transcript,* Dec. 4, 1907.] H. W. H. K.

DAVIS, WINNIE [See DAVIS, VARINA ANNE JEFFERSON, 1864–1898.]

DAVISON, HENRY POMEROY (June 13, 1867–May 6, 1922), banker, head of the Red Cross War Council 1917–19, the son of George B. and Henrietta (Pomeroy) Davison, was born at Troy, Bradford County, Pa., where he received his schooling up to his fifteenth year. During the ensuing five years he attended Greylock Institute at South Williamstown, Mass. He began teaching in the Troy school in which he had been a pupil, as early as his seventeenth year, and returned to it at intervals for three years. His first work after leaving the academy was in the bank at Troy owned by brothers of his mother. There he began at the bottom and as he worked up became restless and eager to find a wider horizon than the Pennsylvania town afforded. At twenty-one he applied for a job in a New York City bank, but failed to get it. For the next three years he was employed by a bank at Bridgeport, Conn., rising step by step to a receiving tellership. In 1891 a new bank, the Astor Place (later absorbed by the Corn Exchange), opened its doors in New York. Davison obtained personal interviews with the cashier, was twice told that his application would have to be declined because of his limited city acquaintance, but at the third interview was given the position. He quickly made friends and easily held them. Near the end of the third year of his service there as paying teller a mentally deranged man approached the teller's window, pointed a revolver at Davison, and presented a check calling for the payment of $1,000,000 "to the Almighty." Davison was alone in the teller's cage. As calmly as if the demand were an every-day business detail he remarked, in a slightly raised voice so as to attract the attention of his associates, "A million dollars for the Almighty—how will you have it?" and proceeded to count out bills of small denomination. The bank detective heard the words, sensed the situation, and quickly seized and disarmed the would-be payee. The afternoon papers of that day, carrying the story, reached the board-room of a downtown New York bank at the moment when the directors were planning to fill the post of assistant cashier. Davison was already known to one of them, who soon convinced his colleagues that the courage, resourcefulness, and steadiness of nerve displayed in the Astor Place incident would be useful in the position under consideration. Davison thus became assistant cashier of the Liberty National Bank in 1894, and within five years he was president of the institution. It was then that he conceived the plan which resulted in the formation of the Bankers' Trust Company, intended to serve as a depository for the funds of national banks and insurance companies. In 1902 George F. Baker and Francis L. Hine of the First National Bank invited him to become vice-president and director. There he soon won recognition from J. Pierpont Morgan, Sr., who frequently consulted him, especially in the monetary crisis of 1907, when Davison had an important part in determining the action of New York banks. During the next year he joined the Monetary Commission headed by Senator Aldrich and in the capacity of banking expert with that commission he visited France, Germany, and England. He then acquainted himself with the prevailing European idea of a flexible national currency. In association with Senator Aldrich, Paul M. Warburg, Frank A. Vanderlip, and A. Piatt Andrew, he took part in drawing up the "Jekyl Island" report that led to the crystallization of sentiment resulting in the creation of the Federal Reserve System. Having become a partner in J. P. Morgan & Company, he served with distinction in 1910 as chairman of the Six-Power Chinese Loan Conference at Paris. He was now one of the small group of Americans whose names were recognized at the counsel board of international finance.

When the United States entered the World War it was clearly foreseen that great responsibilities would devolve upon the head of the Red Cross War Council. The appointment of Davison by President Wilson as Chairman of the Council was hailed as one of the most important steps taken by the government at Washington in the first stages of the war. He accepted the appointment on the condition that the proposed solicitation of a $15,000,000 fund for the American Red Cross be abandoned and that plans be made at once for a national drive to raise $100,000,000. In the outcome $115,000,000 was secured at a time when the war demands in every city and village of the country were exceeding anything ever before dreamed of; but the second drive, in 1918, had even greater results, reaching the unparalleled total of $170,000,000 for the Red Cross war chest. The handling of these great sums in time of war called for administrative talent of the highest order. Having the vision and the knowledge of war-time conditions that enabled him to understand more clearly than most of his contemporaries in America the true magnitude of the war effort required of the United States, he saw that only the most generous support of the Red Cross could make that effort successful. He refused to think of the organization as merely incidental to military and naval operations, insisting that it was a vital and essential part of the government's war machinery. He impressed this conception upon his aides, chosen with fine discrimination, many of whom, like himself, were men of wealth giving their services without pay and in not a few instances meeting their own expenses. After the Armistice in 1918, Davison, in cooperation with the Red Cross officers of the Allied nations, planned an International League of Red Cross Societies intended to function somewhat as the League of Nations. In 1922 he died as the result of an operation for tumor on the brain. He had married Kate Trubee, of Bridgeport, Conn., on Apr. 13, 1893. She, with two sons and two daughters, survived him. In the last year of the war he received decorations and honors from all the Allied nations.

[In 1919 Davison published *The Am. Red Cross in the Great War*. See also *Who's Who in America*, 1922–23; articles in the *N. Y. Times* for May 7, 8, 9, 10, 15, and 29, 1922; article in *Everybody's Mag.*, Nov. 1917.]

W. B. S.

DAWES, HENRY LAURENS (Oct. 30, 1816–Feb. 5, 1903), congressman, senator, was born in Cummington, Hampshire County, Mass., the son of Mitchell and Mercy (Burgess) Dawes. After graduating from Yale College in 1839, he taught school for a few months, gaining meanwhile some newspaper experience writing editorials for the Greenfield *Gazette and Courier* and the North Adams *Transcript*. Admitted to the bar in 1842, he opened an office in North Adams, but moved later to Pittsfield, where, in 1848, he began his long political career by being chosen to the Massachusetts lower house, of which he was a member in 1848, 1849, and 1852. He sat for one term (1850) in the state Senate, and he was an active participant in the Massachusetts constitutional convention of 1853. For some years (1853–57) he was United States attorney for the western district of Massachusetts. He married, on May 1, 1844, Electa Allen Sanderson (1822–1901), daughter of Chester Sanderson, of Ashfield, Mass.

Dawes came into national prominence in 1857, when he was elected to the Thirty-fifth Congress from the Berkshire district of Massachusetts; and he sat in the House of Representatives term after term until 1875, growing steadily in influence until he was recognized as perhaps its most useful and reliable member. His colleague, George F. Hoar, wrote of Dawes, "There has never been, within my experience, a greater power than his on the floor of the House" (*Autobiography*, I, 203). At first appointed only to the Committee on Revolutionary Claims, he became chairman in succession of the two most important House committees, Appropriations (1869) and Ways and Means (1871). He was also for ten years chairman of the Committee on Elections. There was very little law-making of this period in which he was not consulted. He was a consistent advocate of a protectionist policy and was himself the author of important tariff measures, including the wool and woolen tariff of 1868 which he wrote conjointly with Bingham of Ohio. Manufacturers of textiles in New England depended upon him as their champion when legislation affecting them was introduced. He was responsible for the establishment of the Fish Commission, and, in 1869, at the suggestion of Prof. Cleveland Abbe [*q.v.*], he initiated a plan for a daily weather bulletin, which was to collect and compare weather reports from all sections of the country, and which soon became the United States Weather Bureau. He was chairman, in 1872, of a House committee for investigating the so-called "Sanborn Contracts." In 1869 he was a candidate for speaker, but was defeated by James G. Blaine.

In 1875 Dawes was elected to succeed William B. Washburn as United States senator from Massachusetts and served three consecutive terms, retiring in 1892. As a member of the Committee on Buildings and Grounds, he proposed and carried through a bill under which the Washington Monument, left unfinished since 1856 because of lack of funds, was finally completed and dedicated in 1885. His most enduring work, however, was accomplished as chairman of the Committee on Indian Affairs. A faithful and intelligent friend of the red men, he did his utmost to make their lot a happy one, and Edward Everett Hale said of him, "While he held the reins, nobody talked of dishonor in our dealings with the Indians." He was the author of the Dawes Act of 1887, which opened the way for granting land within the reservations to individual Indians, and citizenship to those competent to manage their own affairs. It was his influence which created a system of Indian education and placed the Indians under the protection of the federal criminal laws. After his retirement from the Senate, he visited Indian Territory in 1895, as the head of the Commission to the Five Civilized Tribes, designated by Congress to secure the voluntary consent of the Indians to the abandonment of tribal relations. His report was widely discussed.

Senator Hoar once declared that Dawes had "proved himself fit for every position in our Republican army except that of trumpeter." In appearance, he was a shrewd-looking Yankee, with high cheek-bones and a gray beard. He was a man of simple tastes, without any showy qualities, and he never sought popular applause. Without any gift of eloquent speech, he confined himself always to a dignified and lucid presentation of his case; but he worked more often in the committee rooms than on the floor of the House or the Senate. Although he influenced legislation upon which millions of dollars depended, he never accumulated a fortune, and his probity was unquestioned. During his last months in the Senate, Dawes was troubled by an increasing deafness, which prevented him from seeking another term. Upon his formal retirement, after thirty-six years of continuous service in Congress, he was tendered a farewell banquet by his associates. In his old age, he became the "Sage of Pittsfield," where he died in his eighty-seventh year.

[There is no extended biography of Dawes, but ample material upon him is to be found in newspapers and magazines of the period. See G. F. Hoar, *Autobiog. of Seventy Years* (2 vols., 1903); *Biog. Dir. Am. Congress, 1774–1927* (1928); *Obit. Record Grads. Yale Univ.* (1910); *Outlook*, Feb. 14, 1903; *Boston Transcript*, Feb. 5, 1903.] C. M. F.

DAWES, WILLIAM (Apr. 6, 1745–Feb. 25, 1799), one of the "warners" of the 18th of April 1775, the descendant of a William Dawes who was born in Sudbury, England, in 1620 and emigrated to Massachusetts in 1635, was the second of the nine children of William and Lydia (Boone) Dawes of Boston. His father was tailor, grocer, and goldsmith by turns, and owing to the fact that he survived his son the latter was always referred to as "Junior." He learned the tanner's trade and had a tan-yard for some years. On May 3, 1768, he married Mehitable May, by whom he had seven children. Tradesmen had been active in the Revolutionary movement and in some way he had been brought to the attention of its leaders. He was one of the two men chosen to spread the alarm if the British troops should attempt a raid on the countryside. Such an occasion occurred on Apr. 18, 1775. It had been thought possible that a messenger might not be able to get out of Boston, so Paul Revere was staying on the mainland side of the Charles River and the well-known signal displayed from the North Church tower was for him. As soon as it became necessary to arouse the country, however, Joseph Warren sent for Dawes and started him by way of Brighton Bridge and the Cambridge Road. He slipped through the British lines and met Revere at Parson Clark's at Lexington where Hancock and Samuel Adams were staying. Having warned the two leaders and made a short stop for refreshments, Revere, Dawes, and a new recruit, Dr. Prescott, went on toward Concord, rousing the men at all the houses on the way. Revere was captured and never reached Concord but either Prescott or Dawes, it is not known which, got through and gave the alarm. After the siege of Boston began, Dawes joined the Continental Army and is thought to have fought at Bunker Hill. Before long, however, he moved his family to Worcester, where he was appointed by Congress a commissary to the army. While there he became a partner of his brother-in-law Coolidge in the grocery business, and when he returned to Boston after the war, he continued in the same business. His first wife died on Oct. 28, 1793, and on Nov. 18, 1795, he was married to Lydia Gendall.

[The best account is H. W. Holland, *Wm. Dawes and his Ride with Paul Revere* (privately printed 1878). See also E. H. Goss, *The Life of Col. Paul Revere* (2 vols., 1891); R. Frothingham, *The Alarm on the Night of April 18, 1775* (pamphlet, 1876), and *Hist. of the Siege of Boston* (1851).] J. T. A.

DAWKINS, HENRY (fl. 1753–1780), was one of the earliest engravers to work upon copper in America, and although even the years of his birth and death are unknown, much apocryphal information has been printed about him. He learned to engrave upon metals in London, and about the year 1753 settled in New York City. He is said by Dunlap to have been originally an engraver of buttons and shop bills, but after coming to this country he became a general practitioner of the art, finding the field open. His book plates, of which about twenty have been identified, are poor copies of the Chippendale style. The earliest example of his work in America is the book plate for John Burnet of New York, which bears the date 1754. In 1757 he was in Philadelphia as assistant to James Turner, engraver, and in the following year he began business for himself. In the *Pennsylvania Journal*, July 19, 1758, in an advertisement, he described himself as engraver from London, who lately wrought with Mr. James Turner," and stated that "he engraves all sort of maps, shopkeepers bills, bills of parcel, coats of arms for gentlemen's books, coats of arms, cyphers, and other devices on plate; likewise seals, and mourning rings cut after the neatest manner and at the most reasonable rates." He married Priscilla Wood, Oct. 2, 1757, in Philadelphia, and there his seven children were born. Two of them were buried in that city, the second being Capt. John Dawkins, a mariner, who died in 1804. Dawkins was notorious for his poor equipment for the higher forms of engraving which he essayed. He cut caricatures, notably one picturing an incident in Philadelphia in 1764, at the time of the Paxton Boys excitement. While in Philadelphia he became a member of the Grand Lodge of Masons, and in 1764 was elected junior warden of his lodge. Two of his engravings illustrate the first volume of the *Transactions of the American Philosophical Society,* 1771; one of these is a plate to illustrate the paper by Rittenhouse on the Transit of Venus, 1769. During the Revolution (May 1776) he was arrested in New York on suspicion of counterfeiting Continental and Provincial currency. In October 1776, he petitioned the New York Committee of Safety "for a termination of his sorrows by a death." The history of the Grand Lodge of Pennsylvania (*Philadelphia Devizes Lodge No. 1, Pennsylvania,* vol. II, 1899) states that Dawkins was probably hanged for counterfeiting. That this view is erroneous is proved by the *Journals of the Continental Congress* (XVIII, 922), where it is recorded that on Oct. 13, 1780, a warrant to Henry Dawkins was issued on the treasurer for fifteen hundred dollars "on account for engraving and altering the border and back pieces for striking the bills of credit of the United States." After this date he disappears from view.

[Records of Christ Church, Phila. (MS.); *Jours. of the Provincial Cong. . . . of the State of N. Y.* (2 vols., 1842); Wm. Dunlap, *Hist. of the Rise and Progress of the Arts of Design in the U. S.* (1834); *Am. Archives,* ser. 5, vol. III; D. M. Stauffer, *Am. Engravers upon Copper and Steel* (1907); Chas. Dexter Allen, *Am. Book Plates* (1905); *Jours. of the Continental Cong.,* vol. XVIII.]

J. J.

DAWSON, FRANCIS WARRINGTON (May 17, 1840–Mar. 12, 1889), journalist, who, on coming to manhood, changed his name from Reeks, was born and educated in London. His parents were Austin and Mary Perkins Reeks. After completing his schooling, he promptly began literary work; four or five comedies from his pen were acted at the city theatres. As a result of his studies and because of his romantic nature, he became an ardent partisan of the Southern States, and when Fort Sumter fell determined to enlist in their armed service. The Confederate cruiser *Nashville* having run the blockade from Charleston and arrived at Southampton Nov. 21, 1861, he hastened from London to present himself to its commander, Capt. Pegram, but this officer in view of Dawson's youth refused to take him on board. A few days before the ship sailed, however, Dawson, this time dressed as a sailor, succeeded in enlisting on her in Pegram's absence. For his service on the voyage home he was made master's mate in the Confederate navy. After serving at Norfolk and in the James River, wishing more action he resigned his commission in the navy and enlisted as a private in Purcell's battery, Hill's division, Army of Northern Virginia, in June 1862. He was promoted for valiant action at Mechanicsville, and after serving as ordnance officer with Longstreet's Corps received his captaincy in April 1864, becoming ordnance officer of Fitzhugh Lee's division. He fought in a dozen battles, was three times wounded, and suffered imprisonment at Fort Delaware. After the surrender, he had only a three-cent postage stamp in the pocket of his uniform. Going to Richmond in July 1865, he planned to start a small weekly newspaper with a friend. The plant was seized by the military forces before the first issue appeared, and, after brief service as a bookkeeper in Petersburg, Dawson worked on the *Richmond Examiner* and later the *Richmond Dispatch* until September of the next year. He then became route agent for the National Express and Transportation Company, but this project soon failed. Through B. R. Riordan, whom he had known on the *Examiner* and who had gone to the *Charleston Courier,* Dawson was engaged for the *Charleston Mercury,* where he began work Nov. 10, 1866. A year later, with Riordan and Henry Evans he purchased the *Charleston News.* Acquiring the much older *Courier* in April 1873, they combined the two papers as the *News and Courier,* of which Dawson became editor.

Dawson was quick of perception, sudden to anger and as sudden in forgiveness. He was thoroughly democratic and made loyal friends, but his imperiousness and persistence in his decisions made him bitter enemies. He was an accurate observer, had an unusual memory for scenes and conversations, and wrote with ease, interest, and vigor. At a time when it was dangerous in South Carolina to counsel moderation and advocate compromise, he favored the placing of negroes on the Democratic ticket for municipal office in Charleston. When Chamberlain, the Radical governor whom he at first opposed, proved a good executive, he supported him against the popular idol, Wade Hampton. His most important service was in advocating economic measures for the rebuilding of the state and section after the war. In this work he was original, resourceful, successful. He is the first conspicuous figure in the post-bellum movement to "bring the cotton mills to the cotton fields." He urged agricultural diversification, particularly through the introduction of tobacco culture in South Carolina. He wanted Southern farmers to grow their own meat instead of depending so heavily upon the West. Immigration of European farmers and artisans and of workers from the North was constantly espoused by Dawson. He was largely responsible for the South Carolina statute against dueling, and for this service was made a Knight of the Order of St. Gregory the Great by Pope Leo XIII in 1888. He was a devoted Catholic. He first married Virginia Fourgeaud of Charleston, daughter of a French family, in 1867. In January 1874 he married Sarah, daughter of Judge Thomas Gibbes Morgan of Louisiana, who with two children survived him. Dawson was shot and killed by Dr. T. B. McDow in the latter's office whither he had gone resentful of an affront to the Swiss governess of his children. McDow was acquitted, many believed through corrupt means, but some years later died under circumstances pointing to suicide.

[Dawson's partial but spirited autobiography, *Reminiscences of Confed. Service* (Charleston, 1882; only a few copies distributed); *Centennial Edition, The News and Courier* (1903); sketch in Abbeville, S. C., *Medium*, Feb. 9, 1876, and a brief paraphrase of this in J. T. Scharf, *Hist. of the Confed. States Navy* (1887), p. 712; files of the *Charleston News* 1867–73, and of the *News and Courier* 1873–89; Sarah Morgan Dawson, *A Confed. Girl's Diary* (1913), ed. by Warrington Dawson, a lively recital of the early life of his second wife; private information.] B. M—l.

DAWSON, HENRY BARTON (June 8, 1821–May 23, 1889), editor, historian, came with his parents, Abraham and Mary (Barton) Dawson, from his birthplace at Gosberton, Lincolnshire, to New York City in 1834. His formal education, begun in England and continued in the public schools of New York, ended in March 1836. His natural interest in books was undoubtedly enhanced by a short but agreeable term of service in a publishing and book-selling house in Ithaca, N. Y., whither the family had moved in 1837. From 1839 to 1856 he was engaged in business in New York City. For a few months in 1847, he was the editor and proprietor of the financially unsuccessful *Crystal Fount and Rechabite Recorder*, a temperance paper. He was associated with several pre-Republican party movements (*Historical Magazine*, ser. 3, II, 329–33), including the Free-Soil party, for whose first New York City meeting he issued the call, and of which he was elected secretary. Later, thinking that he had discovered in the Republican party a tendency to a centralization which he considered unconstitutional, he retired from politics.

The publication of Dawson's article, "The Park and its Vicinity" (in Valentine's *Manual of the Corporation of the City of New York*, 1855), and several valuable historical papers which followed, established his reputation and enlarged his circle of friends. He gained wide recognition from his *Battles of the United States by Sea and Land* (2 vols., 1858). His strictures therein on the military conduct of Gen. Israel Putnam led to bitter controversy in the columns of the *Hartford Daily Post* (reprinted as *Gleanings from the Harvest-field of American History*, Part VI, 1860). His excellent edition of *The Fœderalist* (1863), of which but one volume appeared, resulted in controversy with James A. Hamilton and with John Jay (*Current Fictions Tested by Uncurrent Facts, No. I*, 1864). After a year as editor of the *Yonkers Gazette*, he purchased the *Historical Magazine*, which he edited from July 1866 to its discontinuance for financial reasons in April 1876. His frequent contributions to this magazine, including hundreds of book-notices, show, as do his other writings, critical ability, accuracy, keen analysis, great industry, and trenchancy of style. These characteristics, combined with his "revisionist" tendencies, were bound to provoke controversy and hostility among local patriots and filio-pietistic zealots. His natural pugnacity was undoubtedly increased by his ill health, which, proceeding from an attack of malaria in 1868, prostrated him completely from 1876 to 1884. He recovered sufficiently to write what is perhaps his ablest work, "Westchester County, New York, during the American Revolution" (in J. T. Scharf, *History of Westchester County*, 1886). During his life many historical societies honored him with membership. He died at Tarrytown, leaving his wife, Catherine (Martling) Dawson, whom he had married May 28, 1845, and several children.

[See C. C. Dawson, *A Collection of Family Records with Biog. Sketches* (1874); a memoir of Dawson by John A. Todd in the *New-England Hist. and Geneal. Reg.*, XLIV (1890), 233–48; and a nearly complete bibliography in the sale catalogue, *The Lib. of the Late Henry B. Dawson, LL.D.* (1890), pt. I, pp. 33–37, 77–78; pt. III, pp. 26–27.] R. E. M.

DAWSON, JOHN (1762–Mar. 30, 1814), statesman, was a son of the Rev. Musgrave Dawson and nephew of the Revs. William and Thomas Dawson, both of whom were presidents of William and Mary College. Musgrave Dawson was a bachelor of arts of Queen's College, Oxford (1747), who later came to Virginia where he served Raleigh parish, Amelia County, and St. Mary's parish, Caroline County. In 1757 he married Mary Waugh, who became the mother of John Dawson. The latter, "Beau" as he was called because of his immaculate dress and courtly manners (H. A. Garland, *Life of John Randolph,* 1851, II, 92; *William and Mary College Quarterly,* XVII, 141, 251), graduated from Harvard at the age of twenty, and four years later was already representing Spotsylvania County in the House of Delegates (1786–87, 1787–88, and 1789). He also represented, with James Monroe, the same county in the Virginia convention on ratification of the Federal Constitution. Here he was considered by Madison one of the leading opponents of the Federal Constitution (*Letters and Other Writings of James Madison,* congressional edition, 1865, I, 387). He made only one speech, in which he admitted serious defects in the Articles of Confederation and likewise the high motives of the members of the Philadelphia convention, but agreed that "by the adoption . . . [of the Constitution] as it now stands, the liberties of America in general, the property of Virginia in particular, would be endangered." He believed in a "firm, federal, energetic government," but feared a "consolidated" government. He further feared a union of executive and legislative departments, the probable high cost of running the government, the extent of the president's treaty-making power, and the absence of a declaration of rights. Finally he feared the establishment of an army "whose only occupation would be idleness; whose only effort the introduction of vice and dissipation; and who would, at some future day, deprive us of our liberties . . . by the introduction of some military despot" (J. Elliott, *Debates in the Several State Conventions on the Adoption of the Federal Constitution,* 1854, III, 604–13). Nevertheless, he later referred to the Constitution as "the greatest of all good," and to the wilful violator of it, as "the greatest of all traitors." Dawson was also a member of the Executive Council of Virginia (*National Intelligencer,* Apr. 2, 1814), presidential elector in 1793 (C. C. Dawson, *A Collection of Family Records,* 1874, p. 315), and bearer of the ratified convention of 1800 to France (*Annual Report of the American Historical Association,* 1912, pp. 697–99). He was a member of Congress continuously from 1797 to 1814. As a Jeffersonian he opposed the Alien and Sedition Acts (*Annals of Congress,* 6 Cong., pp. 1048–49), favored the amendment of the Federalist Judiciary Act of 1801 (*Ibid.,* 7 Cong., 1 Sess., pp. 762–67), proposed an amendment providing for the separate election of the president and vice-president (*Ibid.,* 8 Cong., 1 Sess., p. 374), and for several years before the War of 1812 advocated "the adoption of every measure, the object of which was to place our country in a complete state of defence" (T. H. Benton, *Abridgment of the Debates of Congress,* 1860, IV, 452–53). During the war, as a voluntary aide to Gen. Jacob Brown, he made a trip to the Great Lakes that led to an illness developing into tuberculosis, from which he died on Mar. 30, 1814. He was a bachelor and owned a home in Fredericksburg. The personal property and land-tax books of Spotsylvania County (manuscript in the Virginia State Library) indicate that in 1810 he owned no slaves. His total tax bill on personalty and real estate was $2.07.

[In addition to the references above, see *Wm. and Mary College Quart.,* II, 51–52, V, 211; *Biog. Dir. Am. Cong.* (1928); S. J. Quinn, *Hist. of the City of Fredericksburg, Va.* (1908).] E. L. F.

DAWSON, THOMAS CLELAND (July 30, 1865–May 1, 1912), diplomat, was born in Hudson, Wis., the son of Allan and Anna (Cleland) Dawson. He graduated at Hanover College, Indiana, in 1883, studied at Harvard during 1884 and 1885 and received the degree of LL.B. from the Cincinnati Law School in 1886. He practised law in Des Moines, 1886–89 and in Council Bluffs, Iowa, 1891–97; was assistant attorney-general of Iowa, 1891–94; and during these years was active in state and national politics in connection with the Republican party. After 1897 he was in the diplomatic service beginning his career as secretary of the United States legation in Brazil. He remained at that post for nearly seven years and it was during this period that he wrote his two-volume history, *The South American Republics,* published in 1903–04. During this period also he was married to Luiza Guerra Duval, of Porto Alegre, Brazil, the ceremony taking place in London, Apr. 5, 1900. In 1904 he became minister resident and consul general to the Dominican Republic. He entered upon his duties at the time when the government was practically bankrupt and European creditors were pressing for payment. On Dec. 30 Dawson was directed to suggest to the Dominican government that it request the United States to take charge of its customs. He negotiated a convention, signed early in 1905, providing that the United States should conduct the custom houses of the Republic, administer its finances, and settle its financial obligations. The Senate failed to ratify the agreement, but under a *modus vivendi* a receiver of customs was appointed who administered affairs under the protection of the United States navy. Later the Senate decided to give a legal status to the collection of revenue and ratified a new convention negotiated by Dawson. During the entire time he was in Santo Domingo the internal political conditions were in a very turbulent state and foreign affairs were scarcely less disturbed. The situation made the work of the American representative very difficult.

Late in 1907 Dawson became envoy extraordinary and minister plenipotentiary to Colombia, where he remained until April 1909, when he was transferred to Chile. His service in that country was brief, for with the establishment of divisions in the State Department he was, on Aug. 31, 1909, appointed chief of the division of Latin-American affairs—the first to hold the position. In 1910 he was appointed to represent the United States in Panama. He had scarcely entered upon his duties, when he was instructed to go to Nicaragua, where there had been a successful revolution, to arrange a settlement of the differences between the United States and the new government. An agreement was signed early in November 1910. On June 27, 1911, Dawson was appointed resident diplomatic officer in the Department of State, an office which he held until his death on May 1, 1912.

At the time of his death he was referred to as "the foremost Latin-American diplomat of the government." He was personally familiar with every Latin-American country and had served in many of them. In this service he injured his health and his early death was primarily due to this cause. The New York *Evening Post* declared that "the fairness, the fearlessness and the plain American sense of this diplomat made him a traveling specialist who triumphed wherever he was sent." He was famous for his skill in handling difficult problems. Many times his work was done at the risk of his life. He knew how it felt to look into the muzzle of a revolver in the hands of a fanatic whose pet project he was thwarting. He had sat quietly in his home when it was besieged by furious mobs. He had addressed hostile crowds in Santo Domingo and Colombia when he fully expected that the reply to his arguments would be a shower of bullets. But he was no boaster and he was seldom willing to describe his adventures.

[J. E. Briggs, "Iowa and the Diplomatic Service," *Iowa Jour. of Hist. and Politics*, XIX, 360–65 (July 1921); *Rev. of Revs.* (N. Y.), May 1905 (portr.); *Bull. Pan American Union*, XXXIV, 579 (portr.); *Register and Leader* (Des Moines), May 2, 5, 1912; John H. Latané, *America as a World Power* (1907), pp. 278–81; N. Y. *Evening Post*, May 1, 1912; *Washington Post*, May 2, 1912; Washington *Evening Star*, May 1, 1912; *Who's Who in America*, 1912–13.]

F. E. H.

DAWSON, WILLIAM CROSBY (Jan. 4, 1798–May 5, 1856), senator, a son of George and Ruth (Skidmore) Dawson, was born in Greene County, Ga., where his father was a farmer. Greene County was then on the extreme western frontier of Georgia and the Dawsons were among the earliest settlers. The future senator was not a member of one of the aristocratic families that controled state politics, though his associations in after life were largely with that group. He received the best educational advantages available, in the academy of Greensboro, at the University of Georgia, graduating in 1816, and at the Litchfield Law School in Connecticut. Returning to Georgia after completing his law course, he set up as a lawyer in Greensboro and was soon regarded as an able advocate. In 1828 he was appointed by the legislature to compile the statutes of Georgia, and the well-known *Compilation of the Laws of the State of Georgia* (1831) was the result of his labors. After serving a political apprenticeship in the Georgia House of Representatives and Senate, he was elected to Congress in 1836 as a Whig. In his first election he was the only Whig who defeated his Democratic opponent. After three years in the House, he resigned and resumed the practise of law at Greensboro. Four years later he was appointed judge of the Ocmulgee circuit. As a judge he made an excellent record, though he remained on the bench less than a year, and then went back to the practise of his profession.

His reputation as a politician was made in the United States Senate. He took his seat in 1849, having defeated a strong Democratic opponent, Walter T. Colquitt [*q.v.*]. His senatorial colleague in the Thirty-first and Thirty-second Congresses was John MacPherson Berrien, and in the Thirty-third, Robert Toombs, both Whigs. In the House in the same period were Alexander H. Stephens, Howell Cobb, and Alfred H. Colquitt. Dawson was on intimate terms with Webster and Clay. With Toombs, Stephens, and Cobb he championed Clay's compromise measures in 1850 and is said to have been instrumental in bringing Webster to their support (Cole, *post*, p. 165 n.). He was a leading member of the Georgia convention in 1850 which adopted the "Georgia Platform," committing the state to the compromise measures, and he was one of the originators of the Union party which supported Howell Cobb for governor on a compromise platform (1851). He also supported the Kansas-Nebraska Act of 1854.

At the close of the Thirty-third Congress, Dawson did not offer for reëlection. He retired to his home in Greensboro, where he died suddenly the following year. He was married, first, in 1819, to Henrietta Wingfield, by whom he had seven children, and who died in 1850, and, second, in 1854, to Mrs. Eliza M. Williams. He is described as above medium height, well knit and strong; his voice powerful, his walk elastic and his carriage erect; his gray eyes "quick, vigilant and hilarious."

[S. F. Miller, *Bench and Bar of Ga.* (1858), vol. I, containing a long account of Dawson's career, the last part of which is a sketch prepared by Judge Eugenius A. Nisbet immediately after Dawson's death; G. C. Cole, *The Whig Party in the South* (1913); R. H. Shryock, *Ga. and the Union of 1850* (1926); C. C. Dawson, *A Collection of Family Records* (1874).]

R. P. B.

DAY, BENJAMIN HENRY (Apr. 10, 1810–Dec. 21, 1889), printer, journalist, was sixth in descent from Robert Day, who came from England with his wife Mary in the *Elizabeth* in 1634 and settled at Cambridge, Mass., to become, two years later, one of the original settlers of Hartford, Conn. Robert's son Thomas established himself in West Springfield, Mass., where this branch of the family lived for two centuries. Benjamin H. Day was the son of Henry Day and Mary Ely, his mother being a descendant of Elder William Brewster, fourth signer of the *Mayflower* compact. He entered the office of the *Springfield Republican* as an apprentice soon after it was founded by Samuel Bowles [*q.v.*] in 1824. When he was twenty years old and a first-class compositor, he went to New York City and worked at the case in the offices of the *Evening Post*, the *Commercial Advertiser* and the *Journal of Commerce*. On Sept. 13, 1831, he married Eveline Shepard and a year later, with savings from his wages, set up as a job printer. In 1833 the business depression, caused by the faulty banking system and the visitation of cholera on the city, made Day's business so poor that in desperation he started a newspaper. It was based on the obsession of Dave Ramsey, a compositor with whom he worked on the *Journal of Commerce* in 1830, that a one-cent daily, to be called the *Sun*, would be successful. The "penny paper" was not a new idea. The *Cent* in Philadelphia, the *Bostonian* in Boston, and the *Morning Post* in New York City had tried and failed. The solemn "six-penny" papers held the New York field. Day got out the first number of the *Sun* on Sept. 3, 1833, practically single-handed, in a 12 x 16 room at 222 William St., setting the type, rewriting news from other papers, and "lifting" advertisements to make a show of prosperity. There were four pages, each 11¼ x 8 inches. The *Sun* announced that its object was "to lay before the public, at a price within the means of everyone, all the news of the day." Day engaged a reporter, George W. Wisner, at four dollars a week and hired newsboys to hawk the *Sun*—an innovation in journalism. In four months the paper had a circulation of 4,000, almost equaling that of the *Morning Courier and New York Enquirer*. In April 1834, the *Sun* sold 8,000 copies daily. In the summer of 1835 Wisner left the *Sun*, and his place was taken by Richard Adams Locke [*q.v.*], who wrote for the *Sun* the Moon Hoax, a fabrication which made the circulation (*Sun*, Aug. 28, 1835) the highest in the world. Day boasted that with 19,360 copies daily he had surpassed the 17,000 circulation of the London *Times*. In that year he used steam power for printing—its first trial in America. "From the epoch of the hoax," wrote Edgar Allan Poe (*The Literati*, 1850, p. 126) " 'The Sun' shone with unmitigated splendor. The start thus given the paper insured it a triumph. . . . Its success firmly established 'the penny system' throughout the country." On New Year's Day 1836, when the size of the *Sun's* page was increased to 14 x 20 inches, Day boasted that his paper had a circulation "double that of all the six-penny respectables combined." Of all his rivals who had rushed in to compete with the *Sun* in the popular field, only James Gordon Bennett's *Herald* had survived; Horace Greeley's *Tribune* was not founded until 1841.

Day sold the *Sun* to his brother-in-law and mechanical superintendent, Moses Yale Beach [*q.v.*], in 1838, for $40,000. The price was low, considering that Day had made in some years $20,000 profit. "The silliest thing I ever did in my life," he said in his old age, "was to sell that paper" (interview with Day written by Edward Page Mitchell and printed in the *Sun* on Sept. 3, 1883). In 1840 Day established another penny paper called the *True Sun*, which he sold after a few months. In 1842, with James Wilson, he founded *Brother Jonathan*, a monthly which republished English novels. This afterward became the first American illustrated weekly, with Nathaniel P. Willis [*q.v.*] as one of its editors. Day retired from business in 1862, when the Civil War caused a paper famine, and he spent the remainder of his life at ease. He died in New York City. He was a man of industry and determination. His portraits show an intellectual forehead and an aggressive jaw.

He was inclined to be professionally belligerent, as is indicated by his journalistic assaults on J. Watson Webb of the *Courier and Enquirer* and Bennett of the *Herald.* He was not a great editor, but he proved that newspapers at a popular price could be successful. "More by accident than design," as he said at a dinner to Robert Hoe in 1851, he "remade American journalism."

[The important facts are taken from the files of the *Sun* and particularly from the issue of Sept. 3, 1883. See also F. M. O'Brien, *The Story of the Sun* (1918); G. E. Day, *A Geneal. Reg. of the Descendants . . . of Robert Day, of Hartford, Conn.* (2nd ed., 1913); *Am. Year Book,* 1889, which gives Apr. 11 as day of birth.] F. M. O'B.

DAY, DAVID ALEXANDER (Feb. 17, 1851–Dec. 17, 1897), Lutheran missionary to West Africa, was born out of wedlock in Adams County, Pa., on a farm near Dillsburg. His childhood was one of poverty and hardship. His early schooling was meager. At the age of twelve he became a hostler in the government stables at Harrisburg, and he relates that in his sense of utter loneliness he often cried himself to sleep on his bed of straw. When not yet fourteen he enlisted in Company D, 78th Pennsylvania Volunteers, and served for eight months. Returning to the farm in Pennsylvania, he professed conversion the next year at a revival meeting held in the school-house near his home. He became an ardent and active Christian and his thought soon turned to the gospel ministry. He had shown much aptitude in study, and after teaching one winter term in the country school, in the fall of 1869 he entered Missionary Institute (now Susquehanna University) at Selinsgrove, Pa., to prepare for the Lutheran ministry. After a year and a half in the classical department and three years in the theological department of the Institute, he was ordained as a minister (May 1874) and sent as a missionary to the Muhlenberg Mission in Liberia, Africa. In this field he spent the remaining twenty-three and a half years of his life with the exception of two short furloughs, one in 1883 and the other in 1893. The inroads of the African fever upon his robust frame finally compelled him to leave the Mission for America, but he died on board the Cunard liner *Lucania,* the day before landing in New York. He was buried at Selinsgrove.

Those who knew Day were impressed with his manliness, his strong will, his great courage, his sound judgment, his child-like faith, and his utter unselfishness. All these varied talents were devoted without reserve to the cause that was single and supreme in his affections, the Christian Mission in Liberia. Flattering offers from Church and State failed to tempt him away from that work. His many-sided nature led him to expand his work of the Mission so that it included not only the preaching of the gospel but also the founding of schools and the organizing of industrial operations such as farming, carpentering, and blacksmithing. This enlargement of program, together with Day's tenacity of purpose and his ability to interest the people at home, assured the permanence of the missionary undertaking that the Lutheran Church had begun in Liberia in 1860.

Day was married twice. In May 1874, before sailing for Africa, he married Emily V. Winegarden of Selinsgrove. Their three children all died in Africa, two in infancy, the third at the age of nine. Mrs. Day died in America in 1895. On Dec. 6, 1896, Day married Anna E. Whitfield of Dundas, Ontario, who also was a missionary on the west coast of Africa.

[L. B. Wolf, *Missionary Heroes of the Lutheran Ch.* (1911), ch. ix, by Geo. Scholl; *Lutheran Observer,* Jan. 21, 1898; *Reports of Lutheran Foreign Mission Board,* 1875–98.] A. R. W.

DAY, DAVID TALBOT (Sept. 10, 1859–Apr. 15, 1925), chemist, statistician, geologist, was born in East Rockport (Lakewood), Ohio, near Cleveland, son of Willard Gibson and Caroline (Cathcart) Day. In 1881 he received the degree of A.B. from Johns Hopkins University, and in 1884 that of Ph.D. He served for a year as demonstrator in chemistry at the University of Maryland, and made a connection with the United States Geological Survey. In 1886, when he was twenty-seven, he married Elizabeth Eliot Keeler of Mayport, Fla., and in the same year became chief of the Mineral Resources Division of the Geological Survey, a position which he held until 1907 when he undertook petroleum investigations for the Survey. As chief of the Division of Mineral Resources he instituted the direct collection of data from the producers of minerals and advocated personal contact between them and members of the Survey. Previously such statistics had been obtained from secondary sources and were of doubtful value. He was called the father of the Mineral Resources Division. From September 1901 to October 1902 he edited the *Engineering & Mining Journal,* a task for which he was not particularly well-fitted. While making petroleum investigations for the Survey from 1907 to 1914, he joined with others in recommending the creation of reserves of western lands containing petroleum and oil shales, and out of these reserves the present Naval Reserves eventually grew. The problem of the oil shales interested him in particular and it was largely through his interest and enthusiasm that the modern researches that have led to such wide-spread recognition of the potential value of this resource were inaugurated. For several years he continued his oil-shale studies and investigated cracking processes for increasing the yield of light distillates from petroleum. Several patents for such processes were granted to him and to him and his nephew, Roland B. Day, in conjunction. In 1914 he became consulting chemist for the Bureau of Mines, continuing in that capacity until 1920 and at the same time carrying on private practise as a petroleum chemist. Upon his retirement to private work he moved to Santa Maria, Cal., in order to be near the oil fields and the shale lands, and there he made extensive experiments on the treatment of oil shale in a special plant. Perhaps his most widely known work was the voluminous *Handbook of the Petroleum Industry,* compiled by himself as editor and published in 1922, a book of timely interest at that period. During his long official career in government work in Washington, he served in many temporary and honorary capacities, such as director of mining and oil exhibits at national and international expositions, commissioner on petroleum tests, and member of committees of adjudication. He gave much time to the Geological Society of America, but he was really a chemist rather than a geologist, although he figured in the public eye as a geological authority. Day was essentially one of the types of scientist that have built up the government's technical bureaus at Washington, and the period when he was there was a formative one in the history of those bureaus. He died in Washington, in his sixty-sixth year.

[*Who's Who in America,* 1924–25; obituaries in *Engineering & Mining Jour.-Press,* Apr. 25, 1925; *Mining & Metallurgy,* June 1925 (by M. R. Campbell); *Trans. Am. Inst. Mining and Metallurgical Engineers,* LXXI (1925), 1371; *Evening Star* (Washington), Apr. 16, 1925.]

P. B. M.

DAY, FRANK MILES (Apr. 5, 1861–June 15, 1918), architect, was born in Philadelphia. His father, Charles, came from Kent, England, in 1842; his mother, Anna R. Miles, was a member of one of the earliest Welsh families to settle in Pennsylvania and was also a descendant of early Swedish settlers on Tinicum Island in the Delaware. Day was educated at Rittenhouse Academy and at the department of architecture of the University of Pennsylvania where he graduated as valedictorian in 1883. He traveled extensively in France, Italy, and England, residing abroad for three years and continuing his studies at the Royal Academy, the South Kensington Museum, and in the office of the London architect, Basil Champneys. Returning to Philadelphia in 1886, he opened his own office on Oct. 10, 1887, with the Philadelphia Art Club as his first large commission. This building, begun in that year, was a most original composition in the then fashionable Francis I style. On Feb. 1, 1892, he formed a partnership with his brother, H. Kent Day, as Frank Miles Day & Brother, and on Jan. 1, 1911, Charles Z. Klauder was added to the partnership, then known as Day Brothers & Klauder. H. Kent Day retired at the end of 1912 and the firm name continued as Day & Klauder until Frank Miles Day's death.

Day established practise at a period of popular bad taste, but to it he never succumbed. Although some of his initial work is obviously of that period, all of it is refined, careful, and inventive. As time went on he showed increasing mastery of form. His early work was of a varied character, comprising the office building of the American Baptist Publishing Society in Philadelphia, an interesting tower-like treatment of a building of great height (twelve stories) for its date; residences in New York and Philadelphia; and hospital buildings in Philadelphia and Washington. Of these, a residence on Locust St., Philadelphia, is the most interesting. The sureness of the design shows how fitted was its Tudor style to express those special qualities of good taste, quietness, and freedom which characterized Day's work.

But it was in educational architecture that he found his most creative and congenial expression. His Gymnasium at the University of Pennsylvania is a quiet but forceful composition in a free collegiate Gothic; its plan is direct and simple. He was supervising architect at Yale, Johns Hopkins, Delaware College, New York University, Pennsylvania State College, and the University of Colorado; he also supervised portions of the Wellesley College group. Besides buildings designed for these colleges, the firm did much educational work elsewhere. Prudence Risley Hall at Cornell shows immense skill in adapting the informality of the collegiate style to hilly sites, and in producing groups full of charm and picturesque character derived absolutely from the demands of the problem. The greatest work of the firm is undoubtedly the freshman dormitory and dining hall group at Princeton, known as "Holder and the Halls" (1909). Here with a more ample site, units are larger, lower, simpler; the plan economical, and with that simplicity which only painstaking study can give; the details in the great tower and dining halls, both inside and out, of exquisite richness and delicacy.

Day was never a stylist, though so much of his work was in the collegiate Gothic. Sensitive to the colonial tradition so strong in Philadelphia, his firm aimed to adapt local materials and traditions to the work in hand. This accounts for the direct forcefulness of the colonial designs for the dormitory group at Delaware College and the much simplified southern renaissance of the Liberal Arts building and women's dormitory at the University of Colorado. It also shows in the Gothic of the Liberal Arts building at Wellesley, which differs greatly in character from much of Day's other collegiate work. Constant familiarity with the use of brick and stone in the Philadelphia colonial work also accounted for much of his skill in holding true the balance between brick and stone, or between rubble walling and cut stone in his own designs. Even his collegiate Gothic work is never strictly archeological, but shows a continually growing creative freedom and inventiveness. Day's interests outside of his office were wide; he was a lecturer at Harvard and the University of Pennsylvania and a professor of perspective at the Pennsylvania Academy of the Fine Arts. He was deeply interested in the legal and professional aspects of architecture and at the time of his death was engaged in work on a book on professional practise.

He was the author of *Suggestions in Brickwork* (1895); *The Existing and Proposed Outer Park Systems of American Cities* (1905), with A. W. Crawford; and the preface of *American Country Houses of To-day* (1912). He died of apoplexy at his home, Mount Airy, Philadelphia. He was married on Nov. 5, 1896, to Anna Blanchard Blakiston, daughter of Presley Blakiston, a publisher.

[Sketch in *Brickbuilder,* Dec. 1915; tribute by Dean West of Princeton and an extended obituary in the *Jour. Am. Inst. Architects,* Aug. 1918; the *Architectural Record,* May 1904, containing an enlightening critical study by Ralph Adams Cram.] T. F. H.

DAY, HENRY NOBLE (Aug. 4, 1808–Jan. 12, 1890), Congregational clergyman, educator, was born in New Preston, Conn., the son of Noble and Elizabeth (Jones) Day. Almost from the cradle to the grave his life lay within the influence of Yale College. After obtaining his first instruction in the local academy and in a family school, he was sent for three years to the Hopkins Grammar School at Hartford, where he had Solomon Stoddard (Yale 1820) and Edward Beecher (Yale 1822) for preceptors. He proceeded as by a law of nature to Yale College, where during both undergraduate and postgraduate days he lived with his uncle, President Jeremiah Day [*q.v.*], whose second wife was a sister of Henry's mother. Following his graduation in 1828 he taught for one year in John Gummere's seminary at Burlington, N. J., studied law in Philadelphia with Charles Chauncey (Yale 1792), was tutor at Yale 1831–34, traveled for a year in Europe, and on Apr. 27, 1836, married Jane Louisa Marble of New Haven, who outlived him. On Nov. 9 of the same year he was ordained and installed as pastor of the First Church of Waterbury, Conn. In 1840 he went to Hudson, Ohio, as one of the professors of theology in Western Reserve College, where he remained till 1858, laboring with his colleagues to make the institution even in matters of architecture an exact duplicate of Yale. After 1852, however, his connection with the institution was nominal, the theological department having disappeared during the troubles that beset the administration of President George E. Pierce. For a while Day edited the *Ohio Observer* and dabbled in railroading as a director of the former Cleveland & Pittsburgh Railroad, and as president for a few months of a branch road connecting Hudson with Akron. He is also said to have conceived grandiose plans for an East and West trunk system. From 1858 till 1864 he was president of Ohio Female College at College Hill, on the outskirts of Cincinnati. The college did not prosper and at last its trustees transformed it into a sanitarium. Day returned to New Haven, where he remained for the rest of his life, and devoted himself to writing text-books, of which he produced almost twenty in all. He began with bookkeeping, grammar, and rhetoric but later turned to the group of subjects then known as the "mental sciences." In rhetoric he claimed some originality in emphasizing content more than expression; his books on esthetics, ethics, psychology, and philosophy all belong to the period when these subjects, in American education, were still the handmaidens of theology; and since his style lacks animation his books are now of interest only to historians of education. In their generation, however, they filled a worthy place. The most important of them are: *Elements of the Art of Rhetoric* (1850); *The Systematic Accountant: the Art of Book-Keeping Methodically Unfolded* (1861); *Rhetorical Praxis* (1861); *Elements of Logic* (1867); *The Art of Discourse* (1867); *Grammatical Synthesis: the Art of English Composition* (1867); *An Introduction to the Study of English Literature* (1869); *The Science of Æsthetics* (1872)

The Science of Ethics (1876); *Logical Praxis* (1876); *Elements of Psychology* (1876); *Outlines of Ontological Science* (1878); *Elements of Mental Science* (1886); *The Science of Thought* (1886); and *The Science of Education* (1889).

[*Biog. Sketches of the Class of 1828 in Yale Coll.* (1898); *A Geneal. Reg. of the Descendants in the Male Line of Robert Day* (2nd ed., Northampton, Mass., 1848); *The Family of the Rev. Jeremiah Day of New Preston* (1900); E. L. Clarke, *Remarks at the Funeral Services of H. N. Day* (n.d.); C. Cutler, *Hist. of Western Reserve Coll.* (1876), pp. 36, 51, and 58.] G. H. G.

DAY, HORACE H. (July 10, 1813–Aug. 23, 1878), manufacturer of rubber fabrics, was born at Great Barrington, Mass. He was a son of William and Mary (Pixley) Day, in the seventh generation of the family in America. As a lad he went to live with an uncle, Samuel H. Day, at New Brunswick, N. J. When only fourteen or fifteen years old he experimented in processes for manufacturing India rubber, but it is not known that he achieved any practical results until 1839, in which year, with the financial aid of friends and neighbors of his uncle, he opened a small factory at New Brunswick for the production of rubber fabrics. At that time all rubber manufacturers were seeking a process that would enable the fabric to retain its texture when subjected to heat. Charles Goodyear and Nathaniel Hayward [*qq.v.*] had introduced sulphur in the treatment of molten rubber, at first without complete success. Goodyear, by accident, hit on the practical process of vulcanization, but it was not until 1844 that he could secure a patent. In the meantime Day, through several of his employees, had obtained patents on different branches of rubber manufacture. The personal interests of Day and Goodyear soon clashed. Each claimed violation of his rights and brought suit in the United States circuit court. In the manufacture of shirred goods Day's process and machinery were generally preferred and adopted by other manufacturers, several of whom combined to resist his monopoly. After jury disagreements in the first cases, Goodyear pressed new suits against Day and his agents and customers in Massachusetts, Pennsylvania, New Jersey, Maryland, and New York. There is no question that Day's processes in making shirred goods were being used by the men who were combining to fight him, under Goodyear's banner, but how far there was actual infringement of patents is still a matter of doubt. At any rate there was enough merit in his claims to cause Goodyear to sign an agreement with Day in 1846 by the terms of which the latter was to discontinue the manufacture of all but shirred goods, while the former was to put an end to violations of the Day patents. Almost immediately there were complaints of the breaking of this contract by the "Shoe Associates," a group of manufacturers allied with the Goodyear interests. Day charged that these men were still using his processes for shirred goods. In 1848, he repudiated his agreement with Goodyear and began making all kinds of rubber fabrics. About the same time he bought the rights, for the United States, under an English patent for making car springs. His New Brunswick factory yielded a profit of $50,000 a year, but this was practically all spent in litigation which came to a climax in March 1852 in equity suits brought in the federal circuit court at Trenton, N. J., by Goodyear to obtain a permanent injunction against Day. In point of money interests involved the case was one of the most important ever brought, up to that time, in an American court. Daniel Webster was retained by Goodyear and Rufus Choate by Day. Thus two of the ablest lawyers in the country were pitted against each other. The arguments on both sides were highly praised by members of the bar, but only that of Webster has been preserved. He upheld Goodyear's claims as a pioneer in the vulcanizing process, and his reasoning convinced the court. The injunction was issued, and Day was never able to reinstate his business. In 1860 he took over the completion of the power canal at Niagara Falls, but several years passed before any use was made of this canal by factories, and he seems never to have been repaid for his investment. In 1870 he planned the utilization of the power in the form of compressed air, promising to deliver 6,000 horse-power at Buffalo, twenty miles distant. His experiments in that direction were approved by competent engineering authority, but the project failed to command sufficient capital and was not carried through. On Apr. 25, 1838, Day married Sarah Wykoff from whom he was divorced six years later (*Divorce Case: Mrs. Sarah Day and Horace H. Day*, 1844); and on Sept. 14, 1844, he married Catherine Alice Day, his cousin. He died at Manchester, N. H.

[Geo. E. Day, *A Geneal. Reg. of the Descendants in the Male Line of Robert Day of Hartford* (1848); *Decision in the Great India Rubber Case of Charles Goodyear vs. Horace H. Day* (1852); *Speech of Daniel Webster in the Great India Rubber Suit at Trenton, N. J., March 1852 . . . Goodyear vs. Day*, reported by Arthur Cannon; J. W. Wallace, reporter, *Cases in the Circuit Court of the U. S. for the Third Circuit*, vol. II (1854); "The Great India-Rubber Litigation" in *Hunt's Merchant's Mag.*, Mar. 1856; obituaries in *N. Y. Tribune*, *N. Y. Times*, *N. Y. Herald*, Aug. 27, 1878.] W. B. S.

DAY, JAMES GAMBLE (June 28, 1832–May 1, 1898), jurist, was of English descent. His father, George Day, was a farmer in Jefferson County, Ohio; his mother, Sarah (Gamble), was a sister of Judge John A. Gamble of the Pennsylvania court of common pleas. His youth was spent upon his father's farm, his early education being obtained in the public schools. In 1850 he entered Richmond College, Ohio, and after spending two years there became a school-teacher, reading law in his spare hours. Three years later he entered the Cincinnati Law School where he graduated in 1857. That same year he went West, and opened a law office in Afton, Union County, Iowa, becoming prosecuting attorney. In 1860 he removed to Sidney, Fremont County, which continued to be his home for the ensuing twenty-three years. On the outbreak of the Civil War he enlisted in the 15th Iowa Infantry which was organized at Keokuk, November 1861. Commissioned first lieutenant, he took part in much heavy fighting in the West, was promoted captain, and at the battle of Shiloh, Apr. 6, 1862, was so severely wounded as to be incapacitated for further service. While yet with the army he had been nominated by the Republican judicial convention for judge of the 3rd judicial district of Iowa, and elected. He took his seat on the bench Jan. 1, 1863, and was reëlected in 1867. In August 1870 he was appointed by Gov. Merrill a judge of the supreme court of Iowa to fill a vacancy. By subsequent election and reëlection he retained this position till Jan. 1, 1884, being chief justice in 1871, 1877, and 1883. As supreme court judge he enhanced his already considerable judicial reputation. "He was . . . one of the very best judges that ever sat upon that bench. His learning was mature, his judicial temperament perfect, his opinions models of good reasoning, clearness and force" (Stiles, *post*). In addition he displayed a boldness and independence of thought which ultimately brought him into collision with public sentiment. In 1882 an amendment to the Iowa constitution prohibiting the manufacture and sale of intoxicating liquors within the state had been adopted by a large majority, but in the opinion of the state supreme court the procedure had not complied with constitutional requirements. The public displeasure at this decision prompted a petition for a rehearing, and the case was reargued; but the court, ignoring the popular feeling, adhered to its previous holding. Day, who was at the time chief justice, embodied his reasons in a masterly opinion, in the course of which he said: "If courts could be coerced by popular majorities into a disregard of their provisions [*i. e.,* of constitutions], constitutions would become mere 'ropes of sand,' and there would be an end of social security and of constitutional freedom. The cause of temperance can sustain no injury from the loss of this amendment, which would be at all comparable to the injury to republican institutions which a violation of the constitution would inflict" (*Koehler et al.* vs. *Hill,* 60 *Iowa,* 543 at p. 646). Although a candidate for reëlection in the following year, he was refused the Republican nomination on account of his stand, as were also his three concurring colleagues. Speaking later of his decision in this case he said that it was "one which I could not have refused to make without a surrender of manhood." On relinquishing office he removed to Des Moines, where he resumed practise, but abstained from further participation in public life. He died at Des Moines. On Dec. 1, 1857, he had married Minerva C. Manley of Steubenville, Ohio. He was of powerful physique, nearly six feet in height, and broad in proportion. In disposition singularly equable, with his feelings invariably under control, and his natural dignity never ruffled, he was extremely popular with all classes, and quickly lived down the unreasoning resentment which his opinion on the prohibition amendment had provoked.

[An excellent account of Day's career appeared in E. H. Stiles, *Recollections and Sketches of Notable Lawyers and Public Men of Early Iowa* (1916), p. 595, the author being a contemporary court reporter. See also *Am. Bar Asso. Report,* 1898, p. 661; *Hist. of Fremont County, Iowa* (1881); obituary in *Iowa State Register,* May 2, 1898.] H. W. H. K.

DAY, JAMES ROSCOE (Oct. 17, 1845–Mar. 13, 1923), Methodist clergyman, educator, was born in Whitneyville, Me., the son of Thomas and Mary Plummer (Hillman) Day. His mother was a daughter of Samuel Hillman, a Vineyardman six feet six inches tall, who got religion in the depths of the Maine woods and became an old-time Methodist preacher, earnest, untaught, bold of speech, and unabashed in his habit of mixing politics with religion. In mind and body Day closely resembled this burly grandfather. With his father, who was a lumberman, he went by sea in 1860 to the Pacific Northwest, where for about five years he worked as a steamboat roustabout, stage-driver, and cattle herder. "I have been through the whole gamut of the workingman," he wrote late in life, "omitting the saloon and its kindred precincts." Somewhere in the course of his rovings he acquired a glass eye that added not a little to his picturesqueness of figure and deportment. On his return to Maine he went through the experience known as conversion and determined to be a minister. After studying for a while at Kent's Hill Seminary he was assigned to a charge in Auburn. While in

Auburn, 1871–72, he attended the scientific course in Bowdoin College, being rated as a sophomore, presumably because of his earlier studies for the ministry. His college course did not extend beyond this single year. In 1872 he was ordained and on July 14, 1873, married Anna E. Richards of Auburn, who survived him. He quickly became the most popular Methodist preacher in the state. His pastorates were: Bath, 1872–74; Biddeford, 1874–76; Portland, 1876–79; Nashua, N. H., 1879–81; First Church, Boston, 1881–82; St. Paul's, New York City, 1883–85; Trinity, Newburgh, N. Y., 1885–89; and Calvary, New York City, 1889–94. Even after leaving the active ministry he continued to be one of the dominating forces in the Methodist Church. At the General Conference of 1900 he got 199 votes for bishop, and in 1904 he was actually elected after a hot fight during which he himself took the floor and denied that he had ever knocked down a brother clergyman for impugning his attitude toward the higher criticism. Two days later he resigned the episcopal office, explaining that he felt that his real work lay in education. Such was indeed the fact. While pastor of the wealthy St. Paul's congregation in New York he had had John D. Archbold [*q.v.*] as one of his pewholders, the two men became friends, and when Syracuse University needed a new chancellor Archbold, as chairman of the board of trustees, secured Day's election to the vacancy. Under Day's energetic, optimistic, paternalistic management Syracuse grew like corn under an August sun. In 1894 it was a drooping denominational institution with three departments, some 750 students, and property worth about $1,780,000. In 1922, when he became chancellor emeritus, it was a flourishing university with eight colleges, eight schools, a stadium officially described as "somewhat larger than the Colosseum at Rome," and an enrolment of more than five thousand students. Approximately ten million dollars had flowed into the treasury. But although Syracuse was rich in grounds and buildings it had no adequate budget system nor provision for the future, its teachers were overworked and underpaid, the yearly deficit was dangerously large, and murmurs against some of Day's mannerisms and policies at times became distinctly audible. The chancellor resigned soon after an attempt to raise an endowment fund had been abandoned for lack of support. To a public that cared little about his other activities Day was known as a publicist. From the time when, in 1907, he engaged in a personal controversy with President Roosevelt over the merits of large corporate enterprises in general and of the Standard Oil Company in particular, his frequent, and often picturesque, utterances on questions of politics, economics, and morals were regarded by the newspapers as good copy. He published two books: *The Raid on Prosperity* (1907) and *My Neighbor the Workingman* (1920). The second is a remarkable revelation of the after-war state of mind. He died while on a vacation at Atlantic City.

[*Gen. Cat. Bowdoin Coll. 1794–1912* (1912); letter from G. G. Wilder, librarian of Bowdoin Coll., to editor, Jan. 28, 1928; *The Golden Jubilee of Syracuse Univ. 1870–1920* (n.d.); obituaries in *Christian Advocate*, Mar. 22, 1923, in *Zion's Herald*, Mar. 21, 1923, and in various newspapers, Mar. 14 and 15, 1923; R. F. Dibble, "The Hammer of Heretics" in *Am. Mercury*, Nov. 1924; S. Allen and W. H. Pillsbury, *Methodism in Maine* (1887). Numerous references to Day may be located through the *N. Y. Times Index* from June 1914 till his death.]

G. H. G.

DAY, JEREMIAH (Aug. 3, 1773–Aug. 22, 1867), educator, for twenty-nine years president of Yale College, was the son of Rev. Jeremiah and Abigail (Noble) Osborn Day, and a descendant of Robert Day who came from Ipswich, England, in 1634, settled in Newtown (Cambridge), Mass., and later became one of the original proprietors of Hartford, Conn. He was born in the parish of New Preston, Conn., then a part of New Milford, but since 1779, of Washington, where his father was pastor of the Congregational church. (For biography of Jeremiah Day, Sr., see W. B. Sprague's *Annals of the American Pulpit*, 1857, I, 688.) One of the latter's theological pupils, David Hale, brother of Nathan, first instructed him, and later he continued his preparation for college under John Kingsbury of Waterbury, Conn. He entered Yale in 1789, left because of pulmonary trouble in 1791, reëntered in 1793, having taught school in the meantime, and graduated in 1795. He then succeeded Timothy Dwight [*q.v.*], as principal of the academy which the latter had established at Greenfield Hill, Conn., but soon left there to become tutor at Williams College. Two years later he accepted a similar position at Yale. On June 3, 1800, he was licensed to preach by the New Haven West Association of Ministers. During all this time he had been suffering from tuberculosis, and in July 1801 a hemorrhage brought on by the exertion of preaching caused him to go to Bermuda where he spent nearly a year. Upon his return he went to his father's home with little expectation of recovery, but life among the Connecticut hills arrested the disease, and in the summer of 1803 he undertook the duties of the professorship of mathematics and natural philosophy at Yale to which he had been elected shortly after his departure for Bermuda. On Jan. 14, 1805, he married Martha, daughter of the

Hon. Roger Sherman and Rebecca Prescott, who died in 1806; and on Sept. 24, 1811, Olivia, daughter of Major Daniel and Olive (Tinker) Jones of Hartford, Conn.

For sixty-nine years he was officially connected with Yale College. On Apr. 22, 1817, he was appointed president, succeeding Timothy Dwight, and was both installed and ordained to the ministry on July 23. In his seventy-fourth year he insisted on resigning, but was immediately elected a member of the Corporation, in which office he served until a month before his death, which occurred just after the completion of his ninety-fourth year. In 1835 he had been urged to become head of Andover Theological Seminary, but had declined. Never strong, and after 1836 subject to attacks of angina pectoris, he prolonged his life by self-knowledge and moderation in all things. He was a man of dignity and extreme reserve. Although, as described by Timothy Dwight, the younger (*post*, p. 42), "he was a wise disciplinarian, a judicious governor, a thorough and accurate scholar, a valuable teacher, and a man of intelligent and penetrative mind," his influence was due chiefly to his goodness and his reputation for deep wisdom. He combined serenity, self-control, modesty, and unselfishness in such a degree that all of the 2,500 students who had been under him, according to President Woolsey, would have unquestionably declared him the best man they had ever known. As president he built slowly on the foundation laid by his predecessor. Stability, conservatism, and great caution were his conspicuous characteristics. Improvements that were made were generally suggested by others. Outside of Connecticut he was known principally through his text-books. In 1814 he published *An Introduction to Algebra,* which went through many editions. This was followed by works on trigonometry, geometry, and the mathematical principles of navigation and surveying. After 1820 he taught mental and moral philosophy, and in 1838 published *An Inquiry Respecting the Self-determining Power of the Will*; and in 1841 *An Examination of President Edwards's Inquiry on the Freedom of the Will.* He also contributed numerous articles to periodicals, and published a few sermons.

[Full and discriminating accounts of Day's character and work are given in the funeral address by President T. D. Woolsey, printed in the *New Englander,* Oct. 1867; and by Timothy Dwight in *Memories of Yale Life and Men* (1903). See also Geo. E. Day, *A Geneal. Reg. of the Descendants in the Male Line of Robt. Day of Hartford, Conn.* (1848); Thos. Day Seymour, *The Family of the Rev. Jeremiah Day of New Preston* (1900); Ellen D. Putnam, *Some Chronicles of the Day Family* (1893); F. B. Dexter, *Biog. Sketches Grads. Yale Coll. with Annals of the Coll. Hist.,* vol. V (1911). A portrait painted by S. F. B. Morse is the property of Yale Univ.]

H. E. S.

DAY, LUTHER (July 9, 1813–Mar. 8, 1885), jurist, was born at Granville, Washington County, N. Y., the son of David and Rhoda (Wheelock) Day. His father was a farmer and sawmill proprietor in a small way, and he barely obtained the rudiments of an education, being required to assist on the farm at the age of twelve years. In 1826 his father was accidentally killed and he was compelled to devote himself entirely to the task of operating the farm and mill in order to save a home for his mother. This he had accomplished by 1833, when he proceeded to remedy his educational deficiencies and in 1835 entered Middlebury Academy, Vt., where he was able to spend two years by teaching and doing other odd work in his spare time. In 1838 he went to Ravenna, Portage County, Ohio, and entered the law office of R. P. Spalding, defraying his expenses by undertaking clerical work for the clerk of the common pleas of Portage County. On his admission to the bar he rapidly acquired a reputation for competence and reliability. In 1843 he was elected prosecuting attorney for Portage County and, with an intermission of one year which he spent at Akron, held that position till 1851. In the election of 1850 he was unsuccessful Democratic candidate for the representation of the district in Congress, but in 1851 he was elected judge of the common pleas for the united counties of Portage, Trumbull, and Mahoning, and remained on the bench for six years. He was a stanch supporter of the Lincoln administration in the pre-war period and on the outbreak of the conflict left the Democratic party. For a short time in 1862 he acted as judge advocate general on Gov. Tod's staff, with the rank of colonel. The following year he was elected as a Republican to the state Senate, but resigned on being elected a judge of the supreme court of Ohio in 1864. On the supreme court bench, if not brilliant, he was efficient. A sound lawyer, familiar with Western customs of life and business, and exercising great care in the consideration of all cases which were brought before him, he procured the confidence of the bar and the public alike. Reëlected in 1869, he was for four years acting chief justice, but in the elections of 1874 he met defeat, the Democratic ticket sweeping the state. On his retirement in 1875 he was appointed by Gov. Allen a member of the commission to revise and codify the state statutes, but resigned in February 1876, having been appointed by Gov. Hayes to the first supreme court commission, a position which he occupied for three years, during one of which he was chief justice. He died at Ravenna, Ohio. He was married on July 24, 1845, to Emily Spalding, daughter of his old principal, R. P. Spalding, and after her death, was married in April 1854 to Ellen Barnes. William Rufus Day [*q.v.*] was his son by his first wife.

["In Memoriam Luther Day," 42 *Ohio*, xi; *Bench and Bar of Ohio* (1897), ed. by G. I. Reed, I, 29; *Green Bag*, VII, 278; *Hist. of Portage County, Ohio* (1885), p. 818; obituary in *Cincinnati Enquirer*, Mar. 9, 1885.] H. W. H. K.

DAY, STEPHEN (*c.* 1594–Dec. 22, 1668), first printer in British America, was born in England about 1594. He was a locksmith in Cambridge, England, in 1618, when he married Rebecca, widow of Andrew Bordman, a baker of that town. In the summer of 1638, with his wife, two boys, and stepson, he emigrated to New England in the ship *John* of London, under contract to work two years for the Rev. Josse Glover of Sutton, Surrey. Glover brought with him a printing-press which cost £20, a font of type, and £60 worth of paper, but died on the voyage to Boston. Mrs. Glover settled in Cambridge, and purchased a house for the Days, on the present Holyoke St. There the press was probably set up. The first imprint, a single sheet reproducing the Freeman's Oath of the colony, was issued within six months. There are known to have been twenty-two imprints made by the Cambridge press before 1649, when Samuel Green became the printer: the Freeman's Oath; ten annual almanacs; five Harvard commencement broadsides; the Capital Laws, 1642; *The Book of General the Lawes and Libertyes,* 1648; the Bay Psalm Book, 1640; a spelling book, 1643; Winthrop's *Declaration of . . . the Narrowgansets,* 1645; and Norris's Catechism, 1648. Copies of only nine of the twenty-two are known to be extant.

Stephen Day's relationship to the Cambridge press during this period is a matter of conjecture. The General Court made him a land grant on Dec. 10, 1641, as "the first that set upon printing" (*Records of the Governor and Company of the Massachusetts Bay in New England,* 1853–54, I, 344), but his name does not appear on any existing imprint. There is no evidence that he knew anything about printing before coming to America; and his letters are those of an uneducated, almost illiterate, man. As a locksmith he undoubtedly set up the press, and managed it for Mrs. Glover. She married, on June 21, 1641, Henry Dunster [*q.v.*], to whose house, on the site of Massachusetts Hall, the press was soon removed. When Mrs. Dunster died in 1643, Stephen Day, who disliked President Dunster, may then have left the management of the press to his son Matthew, who had probably been apprenticed to the printing trade in England, and whose name appears on the title-page of the Almanac for 1647. Mr. Wilberforce Eames, however, believes that the press remained under the nominal if not actual management of Stephen until 1649, and that he should be credited with all previous imprints. Stephen Day had acquired considerable land by 1642, when he became active as a mining prospector in the wilderness for the Winthrops and as a promoter of ironworks at the plantation of Nashaway (Lancaster), of which he was an "undertaker." Committed by a local court "for his defrauding several men" in 1643, he was released two days later by the General Court (*Ibid.,* II, 47). About 1655 Day forfeited his rights in Nashaway for non-residence, settled down to his old trade in Cambridge, joined the church, married a second time in 1664, and died Dec. 22, 1668, leaving a small property, including gunsmith's and locksmith's tools. His name is spelled *Day* in most contemporary documents, and in the greater part of his surviving signatures; in the others it is spelled *Daye.*

[Samuel A. Green, *Ten Fac-Simile Reproductions Relating to New England* (Boston, 1902); George E. Littlefield, *The Early Massachusetts Press* (Boston, Club of Odd Volumes, 1907, vol. I), a work to be used with caution; A. McF. Davis, "The Cambridge Press," *Proc. Am. Antiq. Soc.,* n.s., V, 295–302 (1888); Dunster MSS., Harvard University Archives. The above list of imprints of the Cambridge Press, 1639–48, represents Mr. Eames's opinion of what actually was printed; other conjectural items are in Evans's *American Bibliography.*] S. E. M.

DAY, WILLIAM RUFUS (Apr. 17, 1849–July 9, 1923), secretary of state, justice of the Supreme Court, was born at Ravenna, Ohio, the son of Luther and Emily (Spalding) Day. His ancestry ran back to sound New England stock. In his maternal line was found the name of Zephaniah Swift, at one time chief justice of Connecticut, while both his father, Luther Day, and his maternal grandfather, Rufus P. Spalding, had been judges of the Ohio supreme court. He was educated at the University of Michigan, where he graduated in 1870. He then read law for a time at Ravenna, spent another year at the University, and was admitted to the bar in 1872. He began practise at Canton, where he soon made the acquaintance of William McKinley, who was at that time county prosecutor.

Successful at the bar, Day won the respect and esteem of the people of his county to such a degree that he was elected judge of the court of common pleas in 1886 upon the nomination of both political parties. In 1889 he was appointed, by President Harrison, United States district judge for the northern district of Ohio, but because of ill health resigned before taking office.

The intimacy already formed with McKinley made him the latter's legal and political adviser during McKinley's service as member of Congress and governor of Ohio. Once more Day refused high office when McKinley as president offered him the attorney-generalship. It was only when Secretary of State Sherman's physical condition made the choice of an able lieutenant a matter of necessity that the President, in March 1897, was successful in persuading Day to accept the post of first assistant, on the plea of personal loyalty. Acceptance, it is said, cost Day the sacrifice of a $15,000 income as practitioner for a salary of $4,500 (H. H. Kohlsaat, *From McKinley to Harding,* 1923, p. 65). In April 1898, a serious lapse of memory on Sherman's part, during a conversation with the Austrian minister, led to Day's appointment as secretary of state; but he did not desire the appointment, and it is probable that the President was already turning his thoughts toward John Hay. On Aug. 13, he notified Hay of his desire to have him assume the secretaryship not later than Sept. 1, as Day would resign to serve with the United States Commission appointed to make peace with Spain.

Soon after the completion of the last-named task, Day was appointed (1899) to succeed William H. Taft as judge of the United States court of appeals for the sixth circuit. In January 1903, as chairman of a memorial meeting at Canton, held on the anniversary of McKinley's birth, he introduced President Roosevelt as the speaker of the day; and Roosevelt, by addressing him as "Mr. Justice Day," announced his intention of elevating him to the Supreme Bench, an intention carried out in the ensuing month. Day served nearly twenty years as associate justice of the Supreme Court, resigning late in 1922 to become umpire in the Mixed Claims Commission chosen to pass upon the claims of American citizens against Germany. In spite of a winter in Georgia, however, failing health compelled him, in May 1923, to resign this position also. In June he went, as had been his custom for forty years, to his summer home on Mackinac Island, where death overtook him a few weeks later. An attack of pneumonia in 1920 had left his left lung seriously impaired, and as his physician said, he had "lived on his nerve," during his last years. His wife, who died in 1912, was Mary Elizabeth Schaefer, whom he had married in 1875. She came of an old Southern family, members of which had fought under Marion during the Revolution.

In the State Department, on the Paris Commission, and as associate justice, Day rendered signal service. In diplomacy he had had no training, but he was acquainted with international law, and his tact, discretion, and ability to make use of trained subordinates enabled him to perform his duties as secretary with more than ordinary success. During the period of negotiation with Spain over Cuba he secured the recall of Weyler and the promise of reforms; and when war came, after the blowing up of the *Maine,* he succeeded in the difficult task of securing the neutrality, if not the good will, of the powers of western Europe. "Judge Day made one of the greatest reputations of the Spanish-American War," wrote the editor of the *World's Work* (September 1923). "Day," said President McKinley, "never made a single mistake."

When in the summer of 1898 M. Cambon proposed a cessation of hostilities between Spain and the United States, the protocol was prepared under Day's direction. On the question of the Philippines cabinet opinion was divided, Day desiring to relinquish everything except a naval station—which called forth McKinley's humorous comment, "Judge Day wants only a hitching-post." It was in relation to the Philippine problem that Day made his chief contribution to the work of the United States Commission. His associates, Reid (former ambassador to France), Davis, and Frye (Republican senators), desired to require the cession of the entire archipelago, while Gray (Democratic senator) opposed the acquisition of any portion of it. Day took an intermediate position. In the spirit of fairness which characterized him, he urged that the United States had made no conquest which justified a demand for the cession, and questioned the ethics of acquisition of territory by conquest. Writing to the President on Nov. 2, he said that, since there had been no conquest which could give ground for demanding the cession, it was unnecessary to "consider how far the United States, as the leading Christian nation of the world, in a war unselfishly waged in the interest of humanity, would permit itself to stand upon the ancient practise of holding territory taken from an enemy in course of war, without compensation or other reason for permanent acquisition than military occupation" (Olcott, *post,* II, 115). Thus he paved the way for the treaty provision under which the United States paid Spain $20,000,000 for the islands.

Despite some differences of opinion, the members of the Commission esteemed Day highly. Writing to McKinley near the end of the negotiations, Reid said: "Judge Day, in particular, has shown great clearness, precision of view, and well-balanced judgment" (*Ibid.,* 127). Gray, although of the opposite party faith, declared:

"No State in this Union could have contributed to that function . . . a mind and a character more equipoised, settled, clear and strong than was contributed by Ohio when she sent that quiet, sensible, strong statesman, William R. Day, to Paris to conclude the treaty of peace" (quoted in *New York Times,* editorial, July 10, 1923).

As a lawyer, Day had won a reputation for fluent and effective oratory. As associate justice he was highly regarded for his learning, and was chosen by the Court to deliver some important decisions. These concerned chiefly questions affecting interstate commerce, bankruptcy, patents, corporate rights, contracts, and court procedure. The following may be noted: *Dorr* vs. *U. S.* (1903), 195 *U. S.* 138; *Hammer* vs. *Dagenhart* (1917), 247 *U. S.* 251; *U. S.* vs. *Doremus* (1918), 249 *U. S.* 86; *Hawke* vs. *Smith* (1919), 253 *U. S.* 221; *Green* vs. *Frazier* (1919), 253 *U. S.* 233. He also concurred in the dissenting opinion of Justice Harlan in the famous case of *Lochner* vs. *New York* (1905), 198 *U. S.* 45. His language was always chaste and elegant, and his opinions are models of concise judicial expression.

Judge Day was a slight man, who through life was hampered by ill health. He never participated in sports of any kind, although he was an ardent baseball "fan." Highly endowed with intellect and purpose, he was singularly modest, and never sought office. Reserved and dignified, he nevertheless was the soul of tact and courtesy, and was much beloved by those who knew him. He was never more happy than when in private life in his unostentatious Canton home, amid his books and friends. As the *Ohio State Journal* commented at the time of his death, "He represented the type of American citizen, contented at home, but ready for high service if the call came."

[Some data concerning Judge Day's ancestry may be found in *Biog. Cyc. and Portrait Gallery, with an Hist. Sketch of the State of Ohio* (1895), VI, 1359; also in the *Hist. of Portage County* (1885), p. 818. The main facts relating to his service in the State Department and on the Peace Commission are given in T. E. Burton, *John Sherman* (1906), C. S. Olcott, *The Life of William McKinley* (1916), and W. R. Thayer, *The Life and Letters of John Hay* (1915). See also F. E. Chadwick, *Relations of the U. S. and Spain* (1911), and J. F. Rhodes, *McKinley and Roosevelt Administrations* (1922). The chief available source of biographical information, however, consists of the sketches and notices which appeared in newspapers and other periodicals at the time of Day's death. See *Outlook,* July 18; *World's Work,* September; *N. Y. Times,* July 10, 11; *Ohio State Jour.,* July 10, 13; *Evening Repository* (Canton), July 9–12, 1923.]

H. C. H.

DAYTON, ELIAS (May 1, 1737–Oct. 22, 1807), soldier, was the son of Jonathan Dayton, a militia captain, Presbyterian church trustee, and leading citizen of Elizabeth-Town (now Elizabeth), N. J. He was descended from Ralph Dayton who left England for Boston, Mass., about 1638, later founding East Hampton, L. I. Apprenticed as a mechanic, Elias became lieutenant of militia Mar. 19, 1756, and captain Mar. 19, 1760, serving under Wolfe at Quebec and against Pontiac near Detroit. Later opening a general store on the town square across from church and court-house, he acquired an independent competency and was chosen alderman before the Revolution. He was a member of the local committee of thirty-one, appointed Dec. 6, 1774, to enforce measures recommended by the Continental Congress, and on Oct. 26, 1775, became one of the four Essex County muster-masters. He was commissioned colonel of the 3rd Battalion, New Jersey Line, on Jan. 10, 1776, and on the 22nd of that month led seventy-seven volunteers in three shallops to capture the British supply-ship *Blue Mountain Valley,* for which exploit Lord Stirling got the credit (*American Archives,* ser. 4, IV, 987–89). His son Jonathan [*q.v.*] served under him from Feb. 9, 1776, first as paymaster and later as captain. His regiment was at Albany in May 1776; it built Fort Schuyler, and Fort Dayton (at Herkimer), and warded off Indian raids from Johnstown and German Flats, returning to Morristown, N. J., in March 1777.

Dayton saw service at Bound Brook, Staten Island, and Brandywine, and spent the winter of 1777–78 at Valley Forge. He had horses shot under him at Germantown, Springfield, and Crosswicks. After harassing Clinton's march and fighting at Monmouth, his regiment guarded New Jersey against British raids from Staten Island until ordered on Sullivan's campaign of reprisals against the Indians of northern New York (May 11–Oct. 9, 1779). Dayton destroyed Runonvea, near Big Flats (Stryker, *post,* p. 25), but neither Dayton nor his son signed the semi-political indorsement which Sullivan secured from his officers (Botta, *post,* II, 196).

Declining election to Congress, Dayton led in foiling Knyphausen's and Clinton's sallies against the Continental Army at Morristown, for this service winning the comment "Colonel Dayton merits particular thanks" (Washington's General Orders, June 1780; Maj.-Gen. Greene's orders also; see *New Jersey Archives,* ser. 2, IV, 460). Leading his brigade of 1,328 men to Yorktown, he was in active service until the discharge of the New Jersey Line on Nov. 3, 1783. On Jan. 8, 1783, in response to Washington's insistence, he had been promoted brigadier-general, the resolution being in Hamilton's handwriting (*Journals of the Continental Congress,* XXIV, 38).

After the war he returned to Elizabeth and to the general store of Elias Dayton & Son. A leading citizen of his town and state, he served as major-general of militia; trustee of the Presbyterian church; member of Congress, 1787–88; recorder of Elizabeth, 1789; member of the New Jersey Assembly 1791–92 and 1794–96; and president of the New Jersey Society of the Cincinnati. He died of "gout in the stomach" in his seventy-first year. By his wife, a Miss Rolfe, he left eight children. He is described as open, generous, and sincere, ardent in friendship, scrupulously upright; and in appearance is said to have resembled Washington.

[N. Murray, *Notes, Hist. and Biog. Concerning Elizabeth-Town* (1844); E. F. Hatfield, *Hist. of Elizabeth, N. J.* (1868); *Revolutionary Hist. of Elizabeth, N. J.* (1926), prepared by the Sesquicentennial Committee; W. W. Clayton, *Hist. of Union and Middlesex Counties, N. J.* (1882); W. S. Stryker, *Gen. Maxwell's Brigade of the N. J. Continental Line in the Expedition against the Indians in the Year 1779* (1885); Chas. Botta, *Hist. of the War of the Independence of the U. S. A.* (3rd ed., 1834).] W. L. W—y.

DAYTON, JONATHAN (Oct. 16, 1760–Oct. 9, 1824), soldier, congressman, son of Elias Dayton [*q.v.*], was born in Elizabeth-Town, N. J. He graduated from the College of New Jersey in 1776, served with his father through much of the Revolution, and was a captain at Yorktown. After the war he studied law and was admitted to the bar. He sat in the New Jersey Assembly 1786–87, and at the age of twenty-seven in the Federal Convention, his father having declined an appointment in his favor. He was the youngest member of the Convention. William Pierce, an army comrade, described him as "of Talents, with ambition to exert them. . . . There is an impetuosity in his temper that is injurious to him, but there is an honest rectitude about him that makes him a valuable Member of Society" (Farrand, *post,* III, 90). Dayton attended the convention from June 21 to the end, spoke frequently, and while opposing some features finally signed the Constitution.

On Nov. 25, 1788, he was chosen to the First Congress under the Constitution, but declined to serve. He served, however, in the New Jersey Council in 1789, and in the following year in the Assembly, of which he was speaker. He was chosen for the Second, Third, and Fourth Congresses, and served as speaker in the Fifth Congress. He argued in favor of having the secretaries of the treasury and of war appear in the House, and for a larger regular army, rather than militia. With Elias Boudinot he voted five times (Mar. 1, 1793) to uphold Hamilton's financial policy against the Giles-Madison assaults. His first speech was on his own motion to sequester British debts. He took a leading part in the debate of Nov. 24, 1794, supporting the administration in its report on the Whiskey Insurrection. As speaker of the House he is described as of ordinary ability, "of commanding mediocrity" (H. B. Fuller, *The Speakers of the House,* 1909, p. 30), yet his "personal popularity" is said to have been of "vast importance to the nation . . . in tempering the bellicose attitude of the House" toward the Jay Treaty (*Ibid.,* pp. 26–27). Dayton served also as a member of the Senate for one term (1799–1805). Here he voted against the repeal of the Judiciary Act of 1801. After a visit to New Orleans in July 1803, he favored the purchase of Louisiana. He opposed the Twelfth Amendment, but his remarks did not prevent its adoption. In the impeachment of Justice Chase his vote on all eight counts was "not guilty."

Dayton was interested in the projected canal around the Ohio Falls and held title to some 250,000 acres between the Big and Little Miami rivers. Dayton, Ohio, was subsequently named for him. He played some part in his friend Burr's adventure, but probably from ill health he did not accompany Burr's expedition down the Ohio. He was indicted for high treason and misdemeanor June 25, 1807, but a *nolle prosequi* was entered Sept. 1, 1807 (David Robertson, *Aaron Burr. Trial for Treason,* etc., 1808, I, 330, II, 448). His political career was now ended, though he held local office and served two terms in the New Jersey Assembly (1814–15). He was visited by Lafayette at Elizabeth in 1824, and "such were his exertions to honor his guest and gratify the numbers of people to see him that he . . . expired a few days later" (D. L. Pierson, *Narratives of Newark,* 1917, p. 261).

[References occur in *The Records of the Federal Convention of 1787* (3 vols., 1927), ed. by Max Farrand; T. H. Benton's *Abridgment of the Debates of Congress* (1861), and in local histories, especially E. F. Hatfield, *Hist. of Elizabeth, N. J.* (1868); W. W. Clayton, *Hist. of Union and Middlesex Counties, N. J.* (1882). W. F. McCaleb, *The Aaron Burr Conspiracy* (1903), and Henry Adams, *Hist. of the U. S.,* vol. III (1890), have minor references. These authorities, Channing, and McMaster also, are not exempt from mistakes of fact as to Dayton. The usual historical treatments of him entirely divorce his career prior to Mar. 4, 1805, from what took place later.] W. L. W—y.

DAYTON, WILLIAM LEWIS (Feb. 17, 1807–Dec. 1, 1864), lawyer, politician, diplomat, great-grandson of Elias Dayton [*q.v.*], was born at Baskingridge, N. J., his father, Joel, being a mechanic who educated two sons to law and one to medicine. His mother, Nancy, daughter of Edward and Nancy (Crowell) Lewis, was a grand-daughter of Edward Lewis, a commissary of Washington's army. After finishing at the local academy under Dr. Brownlee, he was graduated from Princeton in 1825, taught school at Pluckemin, and read law with Peter D. Vroom at Somerville, being admitted to the bar in May term 1830. Despite feeble health and slowly maturing powers, his "large mind and strong common sense" (J. P. Bradley, *post,* 75) made Dayton a master of common law. Settling at Freehold, N. J., he attracted attention in November 1833 by persuading the court to quash certain indictments (L. Q. C. Elmer, *post,* 375), and became the leading lawyer there. Elected to the legislative council in 1837, as a Whig, he was chosen one of two new associate justices of the state supreme court on Feb. 28, 1838. He decided the important case of *Freeholders* vs. *Strader* (3 *Harrison,* 110) but resigned in 1841, against friendly protests, to practise law in Trenton, the salary of a justice ($2,000) being too small to support his growing family. On July 2, 1842, Gov. William Pennington appointed him United States senator for the unexpired term of S. L. Southard, and the legislature chose him for the full term to Mar. 4, 1851. He resolutely defended his right to independence of action in the face of legislative instructions, insisting (December 1843) that, "if the legislature of New Jersey go further than to advise me of their wishes . . . they usurp a power which does not belong to them" (Bradley, *post,* p. 85).

An independent Whig, he urged protection for home markets and industrial independence (speech of April 1844), and opposed the tariff of 1846. Favoring arbitration of the Northwestern claims, he thought statehood for Oregon undesirable and improbable. He voted against the treaty for the annexation of Texas (June 8, 1844), warning his Newark constituents that the annexation would mean the repeal of a protective tariff and four more slave states (speech of Feb. 24, 1845). Although he protested against the Mexican War, "he invariably voted the necessary measures to sustain the executive in its prosecution" (Bradley, p. 99). He opposed the extension of slavery but voted for the ratification of the Mexican Treaty.

Following the policy of the new administration he opposed the compromise measures of 1850, especially the Fugitive-Slave Act, and lost his seat in the Senate to Commodore Robert Field Stockton, Democrat. Resuming law practise at Trenton, he was "almost invariably employed on one side or the other of every important cause" (Bradley, *post,* 114). With Chancellor Green, S. G. Potts, and P. D. Vroom he had compiled the New Jersey revised statutes of 1847. He served as attorney-general of New Jersey 1857–61, and as such acted as prosecutor in the famous Donnelly murder case (2 *Dutcher,* 463, 601). His speech at the "Fusion Convention" in Trenton, May 28, 1856, resulted in his being nominated for vice-president on the ticket with Frémont, though many of his friends desired him to have first place, and in the Republican convention of 1860 his state supported him, on the first three ballots, for the presidential nomination (C. M. Knapp, *New Jersey Politics During the Period of the Civil War and Reconstruction,* 1924). In 1861 he was appointed minister to France. Not knowing French, quite unversed in diplomacy, he yet established the best of relations with Louis Napoleon's government, with diplomatic colleagues, and with the press. He wore court dress since "he had not come to France to make a point with the government about buttons" (Elmer, *post,* p. 391) and gained the entire confidence of the Emperor whom he had "frequently met during his residence in New Jersey" (Galignani's *Messenger,* Paris, Dec. 5, 1864). Keeping both governments advised on innumerable topics, he was able to avert French intervention, to stop Confederate use of French ports, to prevent construction of six Southern war vessels, to intern the *Rappahannock,* and to force the *Alabama* out to meet the *Kearsarge.* His long letter on the war, Nov. 16, 1862, to Drouyn de l'Huys, produced gratifying results (Seward to Dayton, Jan. 9, 1863, see *Executive Document No. 38,* 37 Cong., 3 Sess.). Seward came to have much confidence in him, and referred to his "approved discretion" (Seward to Dayton, Feb. 8, 1864). Dayton died abruptly at 9 p. m., Dec. 1, 1864, of apoplexy, leaving an estate of over $100,000. His wife, Margaret Elmendorf Van Der Veer, whom he married May 22, 1833, bore him five sons and two daughters. Their married life was entirely happy. He had no enemies. At his funeral John Bigelow said of Dayton, "He could not act falsely."

[J. P. Bradley, "A Memoir of the Life and Character of Hon. Wm. L. Dayton," in *Proc. N. J. Hist. Soc.,* ser. 23, IV, 69–118; L. Q. C. Elmer, *The Constitution and Govt. of the Province and State of N. J. . . . with Reminiscences of the Bench and Bar* (1872), pp. 372–96; genealogy in *Lewis Letter* (Lisle, N. Y.), Nov.–Dec. 1889, pp. 135, 138; obituaries in many newspapers.]

W. L. W—y.

DEADY, MATTHEW PAUL (May 12, 1824–Mar. 24, 1893), jurist, son of Daniel and Mary Ann (McSweeney) Deady, was born near

Easton, Talbot County, Md. His father and his mother's father came from County Cork, Ireland. Matthew acquired a taste for good literature by access to his father's well-stocked library, where as a boy he read such books as Pope's *Iliad* and *Odyssey* and Hume's *History of England.* He attended schools taught by his father until he was twelve years of age, spent four years on the latter's farm in Ohio, and left home at the age of sixteen to attend the Barnesville (Ohio) Academy. At the same time he was apprenticed to the blacksmith's trade for four years. He then taught school and studied law until admitted to the Ohio bar in 1847. Two years later he worked his way to Oregon, taught school at Lafayette during the winter that followed, and began the practise of law at the same place the next spring. He was elected to the territorial House of Representatives in 1850, and in 1851 was elected a member of the Council, over which he presided during the session of 1852–53. On June 24, 1852, he was married to Lucy A. Henderson. In 1853 he was appointed an associate justice of the territorial supreme court. As his circuit was made up of the five southern counties, he made the Umpqua Valley his home until 1860. He presided over the convention assembled in 1857 to form a state constitution and exercised a conservative influence over that body. He suggested the provision prescribing six-year terms for judges, and supported those providing biennial sessions of the legislature and four-year terms for state officers, all of which were incorporated in the fundamental law. He favored the *viva voce* method of voting, unsuccessfully opposed a provision giving married women exclusive control of their own property, and succeeded in having struck out a provision for a state university on the ground that "experience had demonstrated it to be of little use to anybody." Elected a justice of the state supreme court, he accepted, instead, in 1859, appointment as United States district judge for Oregon. Portland, the seat of his court, thenceforth became his home until his death.

Some three hundred and fifty of Judge Deady's decisions, prepared by him for publication, show that he gave most exhaustive study to every issue that came before his court. While generally reverential toward the common law and established precedent, he dared at times, when moved by a strong common sense, a spirit of justice, or conceptions of a sound morality, to make new rules of interpretation. He was lawgiver as well as judge. He drew up codes of civil and criminal procedure, a penal code, and a code of procedure and practise for justices of the peace which were enacted into law by the state legislature, and which, but slightly amended, are still in force. He twice, 1864 and 1872, codified all the general laws of the state. He often acted, in his own words, as "judge and advocate" for the judicial committees of both houses of the legislature and drafted much important legislation; such as the corporation act of 1862 and the Portland charter act of 1864, a measure that became the model for other city charters. His salary as judge, paid in paper currency and at times worth as little as $800 in coin and never much in excess of $3,000, proved inadequate to the needs of a growing family. He wrote weekly letters for the *San Francisco Bulletin,* accepted fees for drawing legal papers or for opinions given clients, received pay from the state for making codes and compilations ($2,500 for the four years ending with 1864), and in other ways supplemented a meager salary.

Deady contributed much to the cultural progress of his community and the state. He was founder of the Multnomah County Library and long its managing director, raising its endowment and selecting its books; he wrote editorials for the *Oregonian*; he was much in demand as a public speaker and delivered lectures on a variety of subjects that show study and erudition; he was a devoted churchman; and, having modified his earlier opinion, for twenty years as president of the board of regents of the State University (during its formative period, 1873–93), he dominated its policies, secured for it necessary financial support, and was the most important single influence in assuring its survival and progress. He was Oregon's "first citizen" in his day and, probably, more than any other single individual gave form to its political, cultural, and legal institutions.

[Deady's diaries and letters, in possession of the Ore. Hist. Soc., are the best source of information. The life in H. H. Bancroft, *Chronicles of the Builders of the Commonwealth,* II (1892), 465–515, is an autobiography. *Great Am. Lawyers,* ed. by W. D. Lewis, VII (1909), 357–92, contains an appreciative sketch by H. G. Platt.] R. C. C—k.

DEAN, AMOS (Jan. 16, 1803–Jan. 26, 1868), lawyer, educator, the son of Nathaniel and Rhoda (Hammond) Dean, was born at Barnard, Vt., where his father, originally from Hardwick, Mass., had a farm. He attended public school during the winters, working on the farm in the summers, and saved sufficient money to enable him to enter the academy at Randolph, Vt., whence he proceeded to Union College, Schenectady where he graduated with honors in 1826. He then studied law with his maternal uncle, J. D. Hammond, at Albany, N. Y., and in May

1829 was admitted to the bar. He commenced practise by himself at Albany but in 1833 entered into partnership with Azor Taber, who was at the time one of the leading lawyers in that part of the state. Having no aptitude for court work he confined himself to consultation and the preparation of documents, and was frequently employed as a referee. He took a keen interest in the well-being of the youth of the city, and in December 1833 organized "The Young Men's Association of Albany" for the purpose of mutual improvement and education—the first of its kind. So successful was the venture that it was taken as a model for similar associations which were gradually established throughout the country. In 1838 he was active in the organization of the Albany Medical College, and became, as professor of medical jurisprudence, a member of its original faculty—a position which he held for over twenty years. On Sept. 14, 1842, he married Eliza Joanna Davis of Uxbridge, Mass. In 1851 he procured the establishment of the Department of Law (unofficially known as the "Albany Law School") of the University of Albany, joined its faculty, and became its active manager. Lecturing regularly, he set a high standard for the students and laid the foundation for the ultimate complete success of the undertaking. He retired from active practise in 1854. When the University of Iowa was chartered in 1855 he was elected its chancellor and professor of history and for three summers resided in Iowa City, devoting his energies to establishing the university upon a firm and broad basis, but he did not enter on the more special duties of his office (A. H. Dean, *post*). In 1860 he resigned, and returned to Albany. Resuming his position on the faculty of the Law School, he thenceforth devoted himself to his professorial duties and literary pursuits. He died at Albany, Jan. 26, 1868.

A man of wide sympathies, high ideals, and great driving force, he was yet never in the front rank as a lawyer. As a professor, he was more a source of inspiration than of knowledge, though his lectures were clear, accurate, and interesting. As a promoter of educational interests, however, he was in advance of his times, and his uniform success in this connection is his chief claim upon posterity. He shunned public life and was not interested in politics, though his sympathies were with the Whigs. He was a wide reader, not only in law but in history, medicine, and general literature, as is evidenced by the catalogue of his library containing 1,893 items, which was printed for the sale which took place after his death.

He was a voluminous writer on many subjects, and left a large mass of manuscripts, a great portion of which was in a completed state. During his lifetime he published: *Lectures on Phrenology* (1834); *A Manual of Law for the Use of Business Men* (1838); *The Philosophy of Human Life* (1839); *Eulogy on the Life and Character of the Late Judge Jesse Buel* (1840); *Principles of Medical Jurisprudence, a Course of Lectures* (1850), and *Bryant & Stratton's Commercial Law for Business Men* (1863). After his death the following selections from his unpublished works were printed: *The History of Civilization* (1868–69) in seven volumes; *History of European Art* (1876); *History of Religion and Government in Europe* (1876); *The British Constitution* (1883). He was also the author of numerous addresses on social and historical subjects.

[A well-balanced review of Dean's career appeared in the *Am. Law Reg.*, Mar. 1868, and a long biographical sketch in vol. I (1868), of his *Hist. of Civilization.* For details of his academic life and activities, see Andrew V. Raymond, *Union University* (1907), and A. H. Dean, "Amos Dean" in *Iowa Hist. Record*, Apr. 1895. See also Joel Munsell, *The Annals of Albany*, vols. IX (1858), X (1859), and *Colls. on the Hist. of Albany*, vol. II (1867); *Albany Evening Jour.*, Jan. 27, 1868; *New-Eng. Hist. and Geneal. Reg.*, July 1868; Roland Hammond, *A Hist. and Geneal. of the Descendants of Wm. Hammond* (1894).] H. W. H. K.

DEAN, BASHFORD (Oct. 28, 1867–Dec. 6, 1928), zoologist, armor expert, was the son of a wealthy New York lawyer of a Tarrytown family, William Dean, and of Emma (Bashford) Dean of Yonkers. His ancestry was Puritan with Dutch and Huguenot strains. The major interests of his life—ichthyology and armor—rooted themselves in childhood. At five he was fascinated by a Gothic helmet; he bid in his first piece of ancient arms before he was ten. Prof. Edward Morse, of Salem, introduced him at the age of seven to the charms of fishes. Apparently so diverse, these interests were made to dovetail harmoniously throughout his career. His education was scientific. At nineteen he graduated from the College of the City of New York, where he began his teaching as tutor in natural history. Meanwhile he attended Columbia College where he won his A.M. in 1889, his doctorate in 1890, studying American paleozoic fishes under John S. Newberry. After study in Munich and Naples, he joined the Columbia faculty as instructor in 1891, becoming full professor of vertebrate zoology in 1904, a post which he held until his death. As early as 1889 he was elected fellow of the New York Academy of Sciences on the strength of his published researches. His summers he devoted to investigating oyster-culture in England, France, Belgium, Spain, Portugal, Italy, and later Japan, for the United States Fish Commission. At twenty-three he was made director of the Biological Laboratory at Cold Spring Harbor, L. I. He married in 1893 Mary Alice Dyckman, of an old Manhattan family. He edited Newberry's memoirs on Devonian fishes and undertook a remarkable series of restorations based on Newberry's collection which, according to Osborn, established his fame as an ichthyologist (*post,* p. 102). In search of early developmental stages of hag-fish and sharks he made explorations in Japan, California, and Puget Sound. Between 1891 and 1909 he published a long series of important papers on paleichthyology and the embryology of fishes. "A thorough fusion of zoological and paleontological concepts . . . characterized all his work" (Gregory, *post,* p. 635).

Always an avid collector and student of ancient arms and armor, Dean seized opportunities offered by his scientific quests to study foreign museum and private collections and to explore remote castles where armor could be studied in its original setting. Pursuit of primitive fish-forms in Oriental waters led to his acquiring a notable collection of Japanese armor. His interest in both subjects was developmental. A student of Devonian armored-fishes he was, wrote one of his students, "quick to perceive the striking analogies in the evolution of human armor," the study of which "was to him almost a branch of zoology" (*Ibid.,* p. 637).

In 1903 he became curator of reptiles and fishes at the American Museum of Natural History. Here during seven years of active service, he planned and directed the installation of the synoptic exhibit of fishes, a series of habitat groups, and the collection of fossil fishes. He outlined plans for a new Hall of Fishes which, after years of disappointment and delay, was dedicated shortly before his death. In 1906 he began his curatorship of arms and armor at the Metropolitan Museum of Art, where, before his retirement in 1927 he had built up a collection ranking easily first in America and perhaps fourth among armor-museums of the world. Himself a large donor, he secured important gifts and made important discoveries during arduous armor-hunts abroad. "Not a nook or corner of Europe or Asia escaped his search. He even excavated wells in Crusaders' castles in Palestine. He probably knew the location of every potentially purchasable piece of armor in existence" (*Bulletin of the Metropolitan Museum,* January 1929, p. 5). His growing absorption in this work caused him in 1910 to resign his post at the American Museum where he was made honorary curator. During the World War, as major of ordnance, he used his technical knowledge in designing special helmets and body-armor for trench and aerial warfare.

He had considerable skill as an artist, and illustrated his work with minutely finished drawings and lithographic engravings. Of his many publications over two hundred are on fishes, and a hundred or more on ancient and modern armor. The monumental *Bibliography of Fishes* (3 vols., 1916–23), one of the great enterprises of his life, catalogues details relating to fishes from remote classical times to the present, indexing 50,000 titles. For this he was awarded in 1923 the Elliot medal of the National Academy of Sciences. A similar bibliography of armor, completed before his death, awaits publication by the Metropolitan Museum. He carried on these multiform activities, together with the organization of his private armor-collection at his home at Riverdale, despite physical handicaps which would have quenched a lesser man. On his retirement from the curatorship of arms and armor in the Metropolitan Museum he was made a trustee of that institution. His death occurred in Battle Creek, Mich.

[W. K. Gregory in *Science,* Dec. 28, 1928; H. F. Osborn in *Natural Hist.,* Jan.–Feb. 1929; *Nature* (London), Jan. 19, 1929; *N. Y. Times,* Dec. 8, 1928; *N. Y. Herald-Tribune,* Jan. 26, 1929; L. Hussakof, *Bibliog. of Bashford Dean, 1887–1910* (1910).]
M. B. H.

DEAN, JULIA (July 22, 1830–Mar. 6, 1868), one of the most beloved actresses in the theatrical annals of the country, was the daughter of an actor named Edwin Dean and Julia Drake, the second daughter of "Old Sam" Drake, the pioneer Kentucky theatre-manager. She was born in Pleasant Valley, N. Y., and after her mother's death two years later, was brought up there by her father's Quaker parents. When she was about eleven, Dean took her from her grandparents and carried her about with him, using her as a drudge in a boarding-house kept by him and his wife and in small rôles in the various theatres with which he was connected. In 1844–45 the three Deans were members of the Ludlow and Smith company in Mobile, and there Julia served a rather trying apprenticeship. In 1845, she went North with her father and, the following year, appearing on short notice as Lady Ellen in *The Lady of the Lake,* scored her first success. Dean promptly took her to New York, where on May 18, 1846, she played Julia in *The Hunchback* at the Bowery Theatre. So great was her success that for a time she made this favorite tragic rôle almost her own. She was, according to Laurence Hutton, "the *Julia* of *Julias,*" for "quiet effect and subdued intensity" excelling in his opinion all others. The next few years saw her rise to the highest place in her profession and to a popularity which few, if any, have since achieved. Her success was short-lived, however. In 1855 she married Dr. Arthur Hayne, son of Senator Robert Hayne of South Carolina, and from that day her fortunes declined. The marriage proved wretchedly unhappy, and the public for some reason turned away from its favorite. The next year, the Haynes went to California, with which state the greater part of her subsequent career was identified. In San Francisco she became again a popular idol, and she traveled about the state playing in small towns and even acting as joint proprietress of a theatre in Sacramento. In 1865 she toured the Rocky Mountain states, ending up at Salt Lake City late in July. She remained in the Mormon capital till the following June when she returned to San Francisco. There she at last divorced her husband, and set out once more for New York, which she had not visited for several years and where she tried again, but in vain, to win back her former place. Hardship and distress had broken her, and her acting had lost the simple naturalness which had constituted its charm. In 1867 she married James G. Cooper, but died suddenly in childbirth, on Mar. 6, 1868, five months after her last appearance on the stage. That Julia Dean was a great actress is certainly to be questioned, but she was undoubtedly a talented one, and the beauty of her gentle personality as well as the loveliness of her face won her way to the hearts of the public, who saw in her their ideal of American girlhood.

[See J. N. Ireland, *Records of the N. Y. Stage* (2 vols., 1866–67); N. M. Ludlow, *Dramatic Life as I Found It* (1880); *The Autobiog. of Joseph Jefferson* (1889); Francis Wilson, *Joseph Jefferson* (1906); Constance Rourke, *Troupers of the Gold Coast* (1928); Geo. D. Pyper, *The Romance of an Old Playhouse* (1928); Laurence Hutton, *Plays and Players* (1875). The many biographical sketches published in the various New York papers after Julia Dean's death, should be read with caution.]

W. G. B. C.

DEAN, SIDNEY (Nov. 16, 1818–Oct. 29, 1901), Methodist clergyman, Congressman, author, was the second of seven sons of Amos Dean, a silk and woolen manufacturer of Glastonbury, Conn., and his wife, Nancy Robinson Kempton. His father was descended from Walter Dean of Taunton, a colonel of the Massachusetts train bands, and his mother from Manasseh Kempton who came to Plymouth in the ship *Anne* in 1623. Sidney learned his trade in his father's mill at Glastonbury and at twenty entered the employ of the Du Ponts in Delaware. Deciding to enter the ministry he studied at the academies at Wilbraham, Mass., and Suffield, Conn., and began preaching in the latter state in 1843. His first charge was the Lyme, Saybrook and Haddam circuit. This was followed by an appointment at Woodstock and next at Putnam where ill health compelled him to abandon the ministry for business. His strong anti-slavery interest which was aroused by his experience in Delaware, led him into politics. He was a member of the Connecticut legislature from Putnam in 1854, and in 1855 was elected to Congress on the American ticket. Two years later he was reëlected as a Republican. During both terms he served on important committees and was the Washington correspondent of the New York *Independent.* He was an outspoken Abolitionist, a member of the Underground Railroad, and had a price set on his head in two Southern states.

Declining renomination, he spent a year in travel and then resumed the work of the ministry. He served in Pawtucket, R. I., from 1859 to 1861, at the Mathewson Street Church in Providence from 1861 to 1863, and at Warren, R. I., from 1863 to 1865. From 1865 to 1880 he was editor and publishing manager of the *Providence Evening Press,* the *Providence Morning Star,* and a weekly, the *Rhode Island Press.* In addition to his editorial work he preached and lectured extensively during this period. In 1870 he was a member of the Rhode Island Senate. Retiring from journalism in 1880 but continuing to live in Warren, he devoted himself to writing and published *A History of Banking and Banks from the Bank of Venice to the Year 1883* (1884). The last ten years of his life were spent in retirement in Brookline, Mass., where he died.

Dean was of robust stature, and had the orator's power of winning a hostile audience. He was a man of strong convictions, a strenuous opponent of slavery and the liquor traffic, and a militant upholder of public morals. In the early days of the Prohibition party in Rhode Island he was prominent in its councils and was once its candidate for the United States Senate. In 1884 he became a Cleveland Democrat and remained such till 1896 when he returned to the Republican party. He was prominent in Masonry and Odd Fellowship. His tastes were refined and his home contained a valuable collection of books and art treasures. In 1839 he married Martha A. Hollister of South Glastonbury, Conn., who died in 1841. In 1865 he married Annie Eddy of Warren. His children were a son and a daughter by the first marriage and three sons by the second.

[*Boston Transcript, Providence Jour.,* Oct. 30, 1901; *Biog. Dir. Am. Cong., 1774–1927* (1928); information from Dean's son concerning his father's career and personal characteristics.]

F. T. P.

DEANE, CHARLES (Nov. 10, 1813–Nov. 13, 1889), merchant, historian, was the son of

Deane

Dr. Ezra Deane of Connecticut who settled at Biddeford, Me., where he engaged in the practise of medicine and there married his second wife, a daughter of the Rev. Silas Moody of Kennebunkport, the mother of Charles. The boy went to the public school at Biddeford, then to the Academy at Saco, and a private school. It was intended that he should enter Bowdoin, but the death of a brother prevented and at fifteen he went to work in a store at Kennebunkport where he remained a year and a half. After spending a couple of years in a store at Saco he went to Boston and found a position with the well-known dry-goods house of Waterston, Pray & Company. In 1840 he became a partner; a year later married Helen, the eldest daughter of Mr. Waterston; and in 1864 retired with an ample fortune. After that he devoted himself almost wholly to research work in American colonial history. Even while still in business it had been his avocation and in recognition of his work he had been made a member of the Massachusetts Historical Society in 1849, of the American Antiquarian Society in 1851, and had received the honorary degree of A.M. from Harvard in 1856. Eleven volumes of the *Proceedings* of the Massachusetts Historical Society were issued under his supervision, to all of which he contributed important articles. He had secured a copy of the supposedly long-lost *History of Plymouth Plantation* by Gov. Bradford from England, and in 1856 edited it with copious and scholarly notes. This is the most important single piece of work which he did. In 1865 he gave standing to the newly started series of publications of the Prince Society by editing the first of them, Wood's *New England Prospect.* The following year he was one of the three delegates elected to represent the American Antiquarian Society at the Archeological Congress to be held at Antwerp. In 1878 he was elected a member of the London Society of Antiquaries. Deane in the opinion of such contemporaries as Justin Winsor was "almost peerless" as an American historical scholar although he had no long-sustained historical work to his credit as author. His special field was early Virginia and New England including certain earlier special topics such as the Cabot voyages and the Cabot *mappe-monde* of 1544. He was unbiased, judicial, tireless in minute research. He was friend and counselor of most of the leading historians of his time. So much of his work was devoted to the correction and elucidation of minor points that, invaluable as it was, he is considered rather an antiquarian than a historian. He set a most useful and scholarly standard in the editing of documents.

[The best account of Deane is the memorial by Justin Winsor in the *Proc. Mass. Hist. Soc.*, ser. 2, VII (1892), 45–89. There are also appreciations of him at the time of his death in the same series vol. V (1890), pp. 116–41, and a fairly complete bibliography of his writings in vol. VI (1891), pp. 224–28.] J. T. A.

DEANE, SAMUEL (July 10, 1733–Nov. 12, 1814), Congregational clergyman and agricultural writer, was a descendant of Walter Deane of Chard, England, who emigrated to Boston in 1636. The son of Samuel and Rachel (Dwight) Deane, he was born in Dedham, Mass., where from 1732 to 1745 his father was a blacksmith and keeper of the inn. The younger Samuel was educated at Harvard College, graduating in 1760. He was an excellent scholar, fond of the classics, and had some ability as a poet. He contributed an English poem of twelve six-line verses to a collection of congratulatory addresses to George III on his accession to the throne, included with thirty others in a small volume, *Pietas et Gratulatio Collegii Cantabrigiensis apud Novanglos, Bostoni, Massachusettsium* (1761). From the time of his graduation till 1763 he was tutor and librarian at the College. In 1764 he was called to the first parish in Portland (Me.), then included in the Town of Falmouth, as a colleague of its pastor, Rev. Thomas Smith, and was ordained Oct. 17, 1764. He remained connected with the church as colleague and pastor for fifty years. In October 1775 a British fleet bombarded and burned the larger part of the village of Portland. The church was hit though not seriously damaged, but its members became scattered, poverty-stricken, and discontented as a result of the war. In November Deane moved to a farm in Gorham, built a house at "Pitchwood Hill," and lived there some six years. During this period, though he went frequently to Portland to preach, he was much engaged in farming operations and experiments, and probably in the preparation of his best-known work, announced in 1787 and published in 1790 with the title, *The New England Farmer or Georgical Dictionary, Containing a Compendious Account of the Ways and Methods in which the Most Important Art of Husbandry in all its Various Branches is or may be Practiced to the Greatest Advantage in this Country. By a Fellow of the American Academy of Arts and Sciences.* A second edition was printed at Worcester in 1797 and a revised edition was printed much later (1822) by Fessenden. This encyclopedic work, the first of the kind in this country, contains the results of his own experience and reveals wide acquaintance with the observations and experimental work of other American authors. Deane also published an oration, July 4, 1793, several sermons, short verses in periodicals, and a long poem, "Pitchwood Hill," written in hexameters and published without his consent in the *Cumberland Gazette,* Mar. 5, 1795, and later in pamphlet form. Returning to Portland, in March 1782, he remained there till his death; until 1795 as the colleague of the Rev. Thomas Smith who died in that year, and then as pastor of the church. In 1809 the Rev. Mr. Nichols was chosen his colleague. In the sharp religious controversies of that day Deane occupied a middle ground betwen the strict Calvinists and the Unitarians. He denied Calvin's views of the Trinity and the Atonement, nor did he fully accord with the views of the Unitarians. His catholicity of spirit is indicated by the fact that while firm in his own convictions he was in friendly relation with the representatives of both factions. He was vice-president and a trustee of Bowdoin College from 1794 to 1813. From Harvard College he received the degree of M.A. and from Brown University the degree of D.D. in 1790.

On Apr. 3, 1776, he married Eunice Pearson, who died Oct. 14, 1812, aged eighty-five. They had no children. Deane was of commanding presence, tall, erect, and portly, with grave and dignified carriage and deportment and keen wit. His ministry began in a time of controversy and church factions, his church was demoralized by the war, but he brought strength to it and lived to see his parish on a firm foundation. He died in the eighty-second year of his age and the fifty-first of his ministry.

[*Jours. of the Rev. Thomas Smith and the Rev. Samuel Deane, Pastors of the First Church in Portland* (2nd ed., 1849), ed. by Wm. Willis; B. W. Dwight, *Hist. of the Descendants of John Dwight of Dedham, Mass.* (1874); Wm. Willis, *The Hist. of Portland, 1632–1864* (1865); Wm. Goold, *Portland in the Past* (1886); H. D. McLellan, *Hist. of Gorham, Me.* (1903); *Gen. Cat. Bowdoin Coll., 1794–1902.*] E. H. J.

DEANE, SILAS (Dec. 24, 1737–Sept. 23, 1789), member of the Continental Congress, diplomat, was born in Groton, Conn., the son of Silas Deane, blacksmith, and his wife, Sarah Barker of Marshfield, Mass. After his graduation from Yale in 1758 (A.M. 1763) he taught school and studied law. In 1761 he was admitted to the bar, and in the following year he opened a law office in the thriving town of Wethersfield, Conn. His first wife, Mehitabel Webb, whom he married in 1763, was possessed of such resources as to give her husband a substantial start toward worldly success. A widow, she brought him, along with six children, a prosperous store. After her death in 1767, Deane married Elizabeth Saltonstall of Norwich, grand-daughter of a former governor of the colony; by this step he strengthened his connections with the Connecticut aristocracy. These highly satisfactory alliances made it unnecessary for him to undergo the training in adversity which often comes to a young man in his profession. On the contrary, he rose almost at once to a position of comparative affluence, as well as of social prestige, and for eleven years after his first marriage he lived as a prosperous lawyer and merchant in Wethersfield.

Even had he desired to do so, a man of his prominence and connections would have found it difficult to keep clear of politics, and Deane had no such desire. In 1769 his fellow townsmen made him chairman of a local committee to enforce a non-consumption agreement, to help defeat the Townshend Acts. Three years later he became a member of the General Assembly. In May 1773 he held the post of secretary of the newly appointed legislative committee of correspondence. During these years he became one of the recognized leaders of the Revolutionary movement in his colony, not in the capacity of mere agitator, but rather as a substantial man of affairs, prepared to sacrifice his own comfort and well-being in behalf of a cause he believed to be right. In 1774 the Connecticut Committee of Correspondence, under the authorization of the legislature, sent him as one of the three delegates to represent the colony in the first Continental Congress; the next year he was appointed to the second Congress. Just before leaving for Philadelphia in 1775 Deane, with S. H. Parsons and S. Wyllys, assumed the responsibility of sending the force which resulted in the capture of Fort Ticonderoga. As a member of the second Congress, he of necessity had an active connection with the various preparations for war. He served on committees appointed to formulate rules for the new Continental navy, to purchase ships for the service, and to secure arms and ammunition. For some reason which is not entirely clear, the Connecticut Assembly refused to give him an appointment for a third year in Congress, and in January 1776 he withdrew from that body.

If Deane's talents and services to the American cause were lost upon his constituents in Connecticut, they were fully apparent to his colleagues in Congress; these men had no intention of allowing him to resume his former comfortable place in private life. In March 1776 he was selected to go to France—the first American to represent the united colonies abroad. Marking as it did the climax of his life and the end of his official career—of his private fortune, health, and peace of mind too, for that matter—this mission deserves special notice. He derived his authority from two separate committees of Congress, both secret, one commercial, the other diplomatic in character. The commercial committee, on behalf of Congress, entered into a formal contract with five merchants, of whom Deane was one. These merchants were authorized to buy colonial produce, with money furnished by Congress; to ship commodities so purchased abroad, sell them there, and invest the proceeds in supplies needed by the colonies. Deane was specifically named to handle the European end of these commercial transactions, for a consideration named in the contract. The other committee, the "Committee of Secret Correspondence" instructed Deane to go to France for the purpose of buying clothing and arms for 25,000 men, also munitions and artillery. These he was to secure on credit if possible, otherwise by direct purchase. In addition to this, he was ordered to sound the French foreign office on the subject of American independence, and to find out whether an American ambassador would be received and whether the French government would be willing to enter into treaties of alliance and commerce with the colonies. According to the instructions, Holland and even England were included within the scope of his activities. With the help of one of those extraordinary characters who sometimes appear in public life, Caron de Beaumarchais, Deane succeeded in securing eight shiploads of military supplies. These reached the colonies in time to be of material, perhaps decisive, help in the Saratoga campaign in 1777. Besides sending these supplies Deane commissioned and sent over a large number of European military officers, some of whom, especially Lafayette, De Kalb, Steuben, and Pulaski, gave valuable help to the American cause. Along with these he sent many more of the merest soldiers of fortune, whose coming proved an embarrassment to Congress and a liability to the country.

In September 1776 Congress decided to strengthen its connection with France, and for that purpose it appointed a commission of three: Deane, Benjamin Franklin, and Arthur Lee. The work originally undertaken by Deane alone was continued so successfully that in February 1778, the commissioners signed two treaties with the French government, one of commerce, the other providing for an offensive and defensive alliance. This was Deane's last work as diplomatic representative. Shortly after the treaties were signed he learned that Congress had ordered him home, ostensibly to give information concerning the state of affairs in Europe. The real reason for his recall, as he himself suspected, lay in certain insinuations made against him by Arthur Lee. This erratic personage professed to believe that all the supplies which Deane had secured in France were intended as gifts by the French government to the Americans, and that Deane and Beaumarchais, in asking Congress to pay for them, were planning merely to line their own pockets. Some members of Congress found it easy to believe these libels on Deane's character; others found fault with him because he had shown poor judgment in sending over so many military adventurers.

Deane had responded so promptly to the order for his recall that before he left Europe he could not secure proper vouchers covering his financial transactions. Without these it was impossible to effect a settlement with Congress. After waiting for two years, he returned to Europe, of course as a private citizen, hoping to speed up the auditing of his accounts there. Still finding it impossible to secure a settlement, smarting under a sense of injustice, and worn down by ill health, he lost confidence in the American cause. In 1781 he was so indiscreet as to embody his pessimistic views in letters to friends in America, advising them to drop the war for independence, and to work for a reconciliation with England. These were private letters, but unfortunately for Deane they were intercepted by the British, and published by a Loyalist press in New York. This evidence seemed to prove that he was a traitor, as well as a rascal. After the war he lived as an exile, financially bankrupt and broken in health, for a short time in Ghent, and for a few years in England. He died on shipboard, just outside Deal, England, as he was starting on a voyage to Canada.

Deane's services to the American cause were substantial, and his own losses were heavy. For all this he was rewarded with suspicion, calumny, and ill will. In 1842 Congress made partial restitution to his heirs, voting them the sum of $37,000. At this time the original audit of his accounts, the one made under Lee's direction, was characterized as *"ex parte,* erroneous, and a gross injustice to Silas Deane."

[The best biography of Silas Deane is G. L. Clark, *Silas Deane* (1913). His papers have been published in the *N. Y. Hist. Soc. Coll.*, vols. XIX–XXIII. *Paris Papers; or Mr. Silas Deane's Late Intercepted Letters* was published in New York in 1782. Additional material is contained in Francis Wharton, *The Revolutionary Diplomatic Correspondence of the U. S.* (1889). See also F. B. Dexter, *Biog. Sketches Grads. Yale Coll.*, vol. II (1896).] R. V. H.

DEARBORN, HENRY (Feb. 23, 1751–June 6, 1829), soldier, secretary of war, and congressman from Massachusetts, was born at Hampton, N. H., the son of Simon Dearborn and his wife

Sarah Marston. He was descended from Godfrey Dearborn, a native of Exeter, England, who in 1639 came to America, settling first at Exeter, N. H., and subsequently at Hampton, with which place four successive generations of his descendants were connected. Henry attended the local district school and studied medicine under Dr. Hall Jackson of Portsmouth. In 1772 he began practise as a physician at Nottingham Square, N. H. As trouble with England approached, young Dearborn undertook the organization of a militia company and was elected captain. Upon receiving the news of the fighting at Lexington and Concord, he led his sixty men with celerity to Cambridge. His company was incorporated in the regiment of Col. John Stark and took part in the battle of Bunker Hill, June 17, 1775. In September 1775 Dearborn volunteered for service in Benedict Arnold's expedition to Quebec. In that trying and hazardous march through the Maine woods, in which he commanded one of the companies of musketmen, he kept a journal which is an important source of information for the campaign. On the latter part of the march he became seriously ill and had to be left behind in a cottage on the Chaudiere River, but rejoined the army in time to take part in the assault on Quebec by the combined forces of Arnold and Gen. Richard Montgomery, Dec. 31, 1775. In the battle, in which Montgomery was killed and Arnold seriously wounded, Dearborn was taken prisoner and confined for a time at Quebec. In May 1776, he was released on parole, but was not exchanged until March 1777. He was then (Mar. 19) appointed major of the 3rd New Hampshire Regiment, commanded by Col. Alexander Scammell. In September 1777 he was transferred to the 1st New Hampshire Regiment, Col. Joseph Cilley. He took part in the campaign against Burgoyne, being in the fighting at Ticonderoga and Freeman's Farm. He passed the winter of 1777–78 at Valley Forge, and at the battle of Monmouth in the following June the conduct of his regiment won commendation from Gen. Washington. In the summer of 1779 his regiment formed a part of Gen. John Sullivan's army in the campaign from the Wyoming Valley against the Six Nations, which laid waste the Genesee Valley and the region of the Finger Lakes in central New York. He later joined Washington's staff and served at the siege of Yorktown. In June 1783 he received his discharge from the army and settled in Kennebec County, Me., then a district of Massachusetts. He became a brigadier-general and later a major-general of militia, and in 1790 was appointed United States marshal for the District of Maine. He represented this district of Massachusetts as a Republican in the Third and Fourth Congresses (1793–97) but was not prominent there. When Jefferson became president, Dearborn was appointed secretary of war, and in this position he served through Jefferson's eight years of office. As secretary of war he helped form the plan for the removal of the Indians beyond the Mississippi (*Annual Report of the American Historical Association,* 1906, I, 253–54). In March 1809 he resigned his position in the cabinet and became collector for the port of Boston. In January 1812, President Madison made him the senior major-general in the United States army and placed him in command of what was expected to be the most important theatre of war—the northeast sector from the Niagara River to the New England coast. Dearborn, like William Hull [*q.v.*], had exhibited excellent military qualities as a young officer in the Revolution, but, as with Hull, those qualities appeared to have evaporated with age and long disuse. Dearborn prepared a plan of campaign which called for simultaneous attacks upon the British at Montreal, Kingston, Niagara, and Detroit, but showed neither energy nor speed in preparing for its execution. After establishing headquarters at Albany he went to Boston to superintend recruiting and coast-defense. His stay here was prolonged for weeks beyond the declaration of war, with the result that no preparations were made for attacking the British at any point east of Detroit. Consequently, Gen. Brock was enabled to throw his whole force against Hull at Detroit and compel his surrender. The year ended with another American defeat at Queenston on the Niagara River and a futile march to the Canadian border and back again by the troops at Plattsburgh under Dearborn's direct command. The campaign of the following spring (1813) gave further proof of Dearborn's incompetence. John Armstrong [*q.v.*], now secretary of war, gave orders for an attack on Kingston at the eastern end of Lake Ontario. Dearborn, greatly overestimating the British strength at Kingston, secured Armstrong's consent for an attack upon the western end instead. He captured York (Toronto), Apr. 27, 1813, but with heavy losses and no corresponding advantage. He also took Fort George at the mouth of Niagara River (May 27), but the British army escaped and inflicted severe defeats upon two detachments sent in pursuit. Dearborn was taken ill, and the active command devolved upon Gen. Morgan Lewis. Meanwhile Sackett's Harbor, the American base at the east end of the lake, had been left exposed to the

British fleet and army at Kingston, which in a surprise attack, May 28, barely failed in their effort to capture it, and retired only after inflicting considerable damage. The entire campaign had been so seriously mismanaged that the demand for Dearborn's removal was imperative. A letter from Armstrong, July 6, 1813, relieved him of command on the frontier. Dearborn's request for a court of inquiry went unheeded, but he was given command of New York City and was later appointed president of the court martial which tried and condemned Gen. Hull—a most improper appointment, since Dearborn's negligence had contributed to bring about Hull's defeat. Dearborn was honorably discharged from the army on June 15, 1815. Madison had nominated him in March for secretary of war, but the nomination called forth such strong remonstrance that Madison withdrew it. The Senate had meanwhile rejected his name, but consented to erase the record from its journal. In 1822 Monroe sent him as minister to Portugal, a post which he held two years. He returned at his own request and retired to Roxbury, Mass. Dearborn was thrice married: to Mary Bartlett in 1771; to Dorcas (Osgood) Marble in 1780; and to Sarah Bowdoin, widow of James Bowdoin, in 1813. Henry Alexander Scammell Dearborn [*q.v.*] was his son by his second wife.

[Dearborn's "Journal while on Arnold's Expedition to Quebec" mentioned above, journals which he kept at various times from July 1776 to March 1783, are published in *Proc. Mass. Hist. Soc.*, ser. 2, vol. III (1886–87). Another portion of his journals is included in *Jours. of the Military Expedition of Maj.-Gen. John Sullivan against the Six Nations of Indians in 1779* (1887), ed. by Frederick Cook, pp. 62–80. For other accounts of the march to Quebec consult Justin H. Smith, *Arnold's March from Cambridge to Quebec* (1903) and *The Struggle for the Fourteenth Colony* (2 vols., 1907). Of Dearborn's performances in the War of 1812 the best account is in Henry Adams, *Hist. of the U. S.*, vols. VI and VII (1890–91). Dearborn's side of the case was presented by his son, Gen. H. A. S. Dearborn, in *Defence of Gen. Henry Dearborn against the Attack of Gen. William Hull* (1824). See also Jos. Dow, "The Dearborns of Hampton, N. H.," in *The Hist. of Hampton, N. H.* (1893).] J. W. P.

DEARBORN, HENRY ALEXANDER SCAMMELL (Mar. 3, 1783–July 29, 1851), politician, author, was the son of Henry Dearborn [*q.v.*] and his second wife Dorcas, daughter of Col. John Osgood of Andover, Mass., and widow of Isaac Marble. He was born at Exeter, N. H. After a boyhood spent on a farm in Maine, he attended Williams College, Mass., but, on his father becoming secretary of war and moving to Washington, D. C., in 1801, he entered the College of William and Mary, Williamsburg, Va., where he graduated in 1803. For a time he studied law in the office of William Wirt, at Washington, D. C., then completed his course with Judge Story at Salem, Mass., and was admitted to the Massachusetts bar. Having conceived a distaste for law he then applied for a foreign diplomatic station, but, under the advice of President Jefferson, relinquished the idea and commenced to practise at Salem. In 1806, however, he was appointed to superintend the erection of the new forts in Portland harbor. On the completion of these works, he became an officer in the custom-house at Boston, of which port his father had been appointed collector. In 1812, on Gen. Dearborn's assumption of the command of the Northern army, he was appointed collector in his father's stead, becoming also brigadier-general of militia in charge of the defenses of the port. He resided at Roxbury, Mass., and on the termination of the war, took an active interest in local affairs. At the same time he devoted a portion of his leisure to literary pursuits, writing a *Memoir on the Commerce and Navigation of the Black Sea and the Trade and Maritime Geography of Turkey and Egypt* (1819), in two volumes with an additional volume of charts. Retaining his position as collector throughout the administrations of Madison, Monroe, and John Quincy Adams, he was removed by President Jackson in 1829. In that year he was elected representative for Roxbury in the Massachusetts legislature, becoming shortly afterward a member of the Governor's Council. In 1830 he was a delegate to the state constitutional convention, being also elected state senator for Norfolk County. The following year he was elected representative from Roxbury in the federal House, but served only one term. In 1835 he received the appointment of adjutant-general of Massachusetts, and held this position for eight years. He was Massachusetts commissioner, or "Superintendent of Massachusetts" for the sale of the Seneca Indian lands in 1838–39. In 1843, in the absence of the governor, he loaned the state arms to the government of Rhode Island for the purpose of suppressing the "Dorr Rebellion" then in progress, and was dismissed from office in consequence. In 1847 he was elected mayor of Roxbury, and continued to hold that position until his death which occurred at Portland, Me., July 29, 1851.

In addition to his work on the Black Sea he was the author of: *Defence of Gen. Henry Dearborn against the Attack of Gen. William Hull* (1824); a translation from the French of *Monography of the Genus Camellia* (1838), by the Abbé Lorenzo Berlese; *Letters on the Internal Improvements and Commerce of the West*

(1839); *A Sketch of the Life of the Apostle Eliot* (1850), and a large number of papers and addresses on various subjects, particularly horticulture, in which he was deeply interested. Many of his writings, left in manuscript at the time of his death, have never been published.

His career was one of ceaseless activity and his interests were very diverse. As a public officer he was efficient without being brilliant, and his integrity and devotion to duty were unquestioned. He was keenly alive to the necessity of public improvements, particularly lines of internal communication, and vigorously supported the project of the Hoosac Tunnel. The Massachusetts Horticultural Society largely owed its success to his efforts in its behalf. His personality was attractive. Tall and of fine physique, the essence of dignity, at the same time he kept in touch with all classes of the community, and was extremely hospitable, maintaining open house at Roxbury. When Collector he "usually drove to the Custom House in a stately carriage drawn by a double span of horses with postillions, and his elegant turnout was the envy of all" (F. S. Drake, *post*).

[Daniel Goodwin, Jr., *The Dearborns* (1884); Geo. Putnam, *Address Delivered Before the City Government and Citizens of Roxbury on The Life and Character of the Late Henry A. S. Dearborn* (1851), containing intimate details of Dearborn's life by a close associate; Francis S. Drake, *The Town of Roxbury* (1878); H. A. Homes, *An Account of the MSS. of Gen. Dearborn as Mass. Commissioner in 1838 and 1839* (1881); Dearborn's Journals, 1838–39, printed in *Buffalo Hist. Soc. Pubs.*, vol. VII (1904), which also contains a sketch of Dearborn by F. H. Severance; *Salem Register*, July 31, 1851, reprinted in the *Portland Daily Advertiser*, Aug. 2, 1851; *Boston Daily Advertiser*, July 31, 1851; *Norfolk County Jour.* (Roxbury), Aug. 9, 1851.] H. W. H. K.

DEARING, JOHN LINCOLN (Dec. 10, 1858–Dec. 20, 1916), missionary, for twenty-eight years associated with the Christian movement in Japan, was born in Webster, Me., the son of Joseph Henry and Susan Vinton (Adams) Dearing. A farmer's boy, eager for an education, he prepared for Colby College from which, having supported himself throughout his course, he graduated in 1884. For the next two years he was superintendent of schools in Deep River, Conn. He then entered Newton Theological Institution, graduating in 1889. The call to missionary service had come to him in 1888 at a Student Volunteer Convention, and, soon after his graduation, having first been ordained to the Baptist ministry, he sailed for Japan under appointment by the American Baptist Missionary Union. Returning in 1891, he married, July 27, Mary Lyon Hinckley of Lynn, Mass., daughter of Rev. Henry L. Hinckley.

During his entire missionary career his home was at Yokohama. The first years were spent in acquiring the language and in general evangelical work. He was essentially an administrator, however, and in 1894 he became president of Yokohama Baptist Theological Seminary, and professor of theology and ethics. This office he held for fourteen years, during which time the institution improved greatly in both buildings and equipment as well as in the character of its instruction. He also prepared and published in Japanese, *Outline of Theology* (1895). His advanced ideas regarding missionary organization and administration, moreover, had a marked influence on Baptist activities throughout the empire. From 1908 to 1911 he was general missionary superintendent of the American Baptist Missionary Union for Japan, China, and the Philippines. When this plan of field administration was discontinued he instituted at Yokohama a work for Japanese business and professional men, centering in a night school and dormitory combined. During the last years of his life he was prominent in the advancement of union missionary enterprises, serving them in various capacities, notably as secretary of Federated Missions in Japan and as editor of its annual publication, *The Christian Movement in the Japanese Empire,* both of which offices he held at his death. Returning to America on a furlough in May 1916, he was conducting the annual course of lectures on Missions at Colgate Theological Seminary when, in November, he suffered an attack of spinal meningitis from which he died at the Clifton Springs Sanitarium on the 20th of the following month.

[*Third General Catalogue of Colby College, . . . 1820–1908* (1909); *Who's Who in America,* 1916–17; Jas. H. Franklin, "John Lincoln Dearing," in the *Watchman-Examiner,* Jan. 4, 1917; Shailer Mathews, "John L. Dearing: An Appreciation," in the *Standard,* Jan. 20, 1917; *One-Hundred-Third Ann. Report, Am. Baptist Foreign Mission Soc.* (1917); *The Christian Movement in the Japanese Empire,* 1917.] H. E. S.

DEARTH, HENRY GOLDEN (Apr. 22, 1864–Mar. 27, 1918), painter, was born at Bristol, R. I., the son of John Willis and Ruth (Marshall) Dearth. His early instruction was received from Horace Johnson, a portrait-painter of Providence, with whom he began work on the figure. Later, at the École des Beaux-Arts, in Paris, he studied under Hébert and Aimé Morot. The charm of the Normandy coast turned his attention to landscapes and in 1893 he was awarded the Webb Landscape Prize by the Society of American Artists, of which he was a member.

His earlier work reflected the influence of

picturesque France. He was a fine draftsman and a colorist of unusual ability; his work is characterized by a directness and simplicity indicating close sympathy with his theme, and by an appreciation of values—a skilful subordination of mass and group and tones to achieve their proper relations. By a hint here and there, a graceful suggestion of thought that the imagination may carry further at will, he used detail to complete his idea. This characteristic is especially noticeable in "A Sunset in Normandy," with its delightful arrangement of trees, earth, and sky, and a few brush strokes indicating the cattle which complete the scene. About 1912, a distinct change was apparent in his technique, and his paintings, including both portraits and genre subjects, became brilliant interpretations in broken colors, the pigment being thickly applied. Noteworthy canvases of this period included pictures of the rock pools of Brittany, done with a fine, imaginative touch. Entirely different characteristics marked the later period of his art. Many of his still-life groups were from treasures in his own remarkable collection; frequently there is an Oriental touch in the backgrounds of Chinese carving and similar details. A high note of estheticism and idealism is apparent in all these later paintings.

Dearth received a bronze medal at the Paris Exposition of 1900, a silver medal at Buffalo in 1901, a medal at Charleston in 1902, and one at St. Louis; was made an associate of the National Academy of Design in 1902 and an academician in 1906.

He spent his winters in New York, his summers in Normandy, and a few months of each year in his studio at Montreuil-sur-Mer in the Pas-de-Calais by the English Channel. On Feb. 26, 1896, he married Cornelia Van Rensselaer Vail of New York. At the age of fifty-four, he died of heart disease, survived by his wife and their daughter. He was a member of the Fencers', Lotos, and Century clubs.

[*Century Mag.*, May 1905, p. 157; *Who's Who in America,* 1916–17; sketch by Cornelia B. Sage-Quinton, Art Director, Albright Art Gallery, Buffalo Fine Arts Academy, in the *Catalogue,* 1918–19, no. 7; obituary in *N. Y. Times,* Mar. 28, 1918.] J. M. H.

DEAS, ZACHARIAH CANTEY (Oct. 25, 1819–Mar. 6, 1882), commission merchant, Confederate soldier, was the son of Col. James Sutherland Deas and Margaret Chesnut of Camden, S. C. His mother was a sister of James Chesnut, Jr. [*q.v.*], United States senator from S. C. He was educated in Columbia, S. C., and at Caudebec, France. He moved with his parents from Charleston to Mobile, Ala., in 1835 when the "flush times" spirit in the state was rife. Great developments were in prospect and with certain transportation improvements Mobilians expected to see Mobile become the commercial exchange for a vast hinterland, including all of Alabama and portions of Mississippi, Tennessee, Georgia, North Carolina, and Virginia. Thus Mobile seemed an ideal place for one who was interested in commercial pursuits. Deas became a cotton broker and acquired considerable wealth. He married on May 16, 1853, Helen Gaines Lyon, the daughter of Francis Strother Lyon [*q.v.*], one of the state's most favorably known citizens who had distinguished himself by saving the state from financial bankruptcy and discredit after the collapse of the state bank.

Deas had seen service in the Mexican War, and when the Civil War began he promptly enlisted with the Alabama volunteers. He fought in some of the most stubborn engagements of the war and was wounded several times. His first duty was that of aide-de-camp to Gen. J. E. Johnston. In the fall of 1861 he was commissioned colonel and with the assistance of Maj. Robert B. Armistead recruited the 22nd Alabama Infantry which he equipped with Enfield rifles at a cost to himself of $28,000 in gold. He was reimbursed by the government in Confederate bonds. At Shiloh (Apr. 6–7, 1862) he commanded his brigade after his superior officers had fallen, was badly wounded himself, but recovered in time to lead his regiment through Kentucky with Gen. Bragg. Commissioned brigadier-general on Dec. 13, 1862, in the battle of Murfreesboro (Dec. 31, 1862–Jan. 3, 1863), he superseded Gen. Gardner. He led his brigade in the battles of Chickamauga (Sept. 19–20, 1863) and Missionary Ridge (Nov. 25, 1863), and in the battles and skirmishes against Gen. Sherman from Dalton to Atlanta and Jonesboro. He returned to Nashville with Gen. Hood and took a conspicuous part in the battles of Franklin and Nashville (Nov. 30 and Dec. 15–16, 1864). After the latter engagement he was transferred to the East to assist in the opposition to Sherman's march through the Carolinas. At Raleigh he became ill and turned his command over to Col. H. T. Toulmin. After the war he removed to New York City and reëntered the cotton trade. He became a cotton broker again and a prominent member of the stock exchange, but in New York, as formerly in Mobile, he lived the life of "a quiet and modest citizen."

[W. Brewer, *Alabama* (1872); T. M. Owen, *Hist. of Ala. and Dict. of Ala. Biog.*, vol. III (1921); *Confed. Mil. Hist.*, VII (1899), 401 ff.; *Daily Reg.* (Mobile, Ala.), *N. Y. Tribune,* Mar. 7, 1882.] A. B. M.

DE BARDELEBEN, HENRY FAIRCHILD (July 22, 1840–Dec. 6, 1910), Alabama industrialist, was the descendant of a Hessian captain who landed in South Carolina during the Revolution to serve against the colonies. De Bardeleben's father, Henry, had migrated to Alabama where he married Jennie Fairchild of New York. He died when his son was ten years of age. The mother subsequently moved to Montgomery where the boy secured work in a grocery. When he was sixteen he became the ward of Daniel Pratt [*q.v.*], the first great industrial magnate of Alabama, whose plants were at Prattville, a few miles from Montgomery. Young De Bardeleben lived in the Pratt mansion and attended school. He was made "boss" of the teamsters and foreman of the lumber-yard, and later superintendent of the gin factory. Upon the outbreak of the Civil War he joined the Prattville Dragoons in the Confederate service, serving at Pensacola and in the Shiloh campaign. On Feb. 4, 1863, he married Pratt's second daughter, Ellen.

In 1872, when Pratt, the wealthiest man in the state, turned his attention toward the district surrounding Birmingham—which town had been founded in the previous year—bought a controlling interest in the Red Mountain Iron & Coal Company, and undertook the reconstruction of the Oxmoor furnaces and the development of the Helena mines, he made De Bardeleben manager, although the latter stated frankly that he knew nothing of making iron. The panic of 1873 temporarily closed the works. This same year Pratt died, leaving his son-in-law the richest man in the district. In 1877 J. W. Sloss [*q.v.*] and T. H. Aldrich interested him in the great Browne seam of coal west of Birmingham. He joined them in the Eureka Coal Company, doubling the capital. The name of the seam was changed to that of "Pratt" in honor of Daniel Pratt. "De Bardeleben," said his partner, T. H. Aldrich, "put the whole power of his fortune, his credit, and his tremendous vitality into the advancement of the company." A year later the company was reorganized as the Pratt Coal & Coke Company, with De Bardeleben as president. With T. T. Hillman [*q.v.*] he built the Alice furnaces in 1879–81, naming them in honor of his eldest daughter.

Fearing that he was developing tuberculosis, in 1881 he sold his holdings and went to Mexico, but was sufficiently recovered to return to Birmingham the next year, when, with W. T. Underwood, he built the Mary Pratt furnace and named it for his second daughter. Illness again attacked him and he went to Texas. Whenever he traveled away from home his personality attracted men of means and enterprise who followed him to Birmingham. Thus David Roberts joined him in 1886, and together they formed the De Bardeleben Coal & Iron Company. He also organized the Pinckard & De Bardeleben Land Company. These interests, with a capital of $2,500,000, founded the town of Bessemer, ten miles west of Birmingham, and near the great Red Mountain iron seam. Here four furnaces and an iron mill were erected. The firm held 150,000 acres of mineral lands. The venture was the greatest up to that time in the South. All of this property in 1887 was formed into the De Bardeleben Coal & Iron Company, capitalized at $13,000,000. In 1891 it was taken over by the Tennessee Coal, Iron & Railroad Company, of which De Bardeleben was made vice-president. After three years of virtual retirement his restlessness tempted him to go to New York and make the attempt to obtain control of the company. In this effort he failed, however, losing, it is said, his entire fortune save a forgotten bank deposit of $75,000. Indomitable in the face of ill fortune, with his sons Henry and Charles De Bardeleben, he explored new fields and started mining at Margaret in St. Claire County, Ala., and in the Acton Basin southeast of Birmingham.

De Bardeleben's Red Mountain seam, with his Pratt coal seam, was the basis for the development of industrial Birmingham. He was the first to succeed in making pig iron in Birmingham cheaper than it could be made elsewhere. He built the first coal road in Alabama, and aided T. H. Aldrich in exploring and in exploiting the Montevallo coal fields. He contributed to the development of his region not only through the enterprises with which he was directly connected but also by attracting to Birmingham moneyed men of ambition who established others. President M. H. Smith of the Louisville & Nashville stated that De Bardeleben persuaded him to build the Mineral Railroad and invest in all thirty millions of the company's funds in the district. He was "always talking steel"; in fact he talked of it long before it was made in the Birmingham district. Through him the Caldwell interests were led to build the first rolling-mill in Birmingham. He induced J. W. Sloss to build furnaces and joined T. T. Hillman in building others. "The King of the Southern Iron World" as he was called, he was the most spectacular figure in Alabama's industrial growth. After the death of his first wife, De Bardeleben married a sister of Judge W. P. McCroffin.

[De Bardeleben's early life is mentioned by Mrs. S. F. H. Tarrant in *The Honorable Daniel Pratt* (1894). There are many references to him in Ethel Armes, *The Story of Coal and Iron in Ala.* (1910), B. F. Riley, *Makers and Romance of Ala. Hist.* (1914), and G. W. Cruikshank, *Hist. of Birmingham and Its Environs* (1920). See also the obituary in *Birmingham Age Herald,* Dec. 7, 1910. Valuable scrapbooks on his career are in the possession of his son Chas. F. De Bardeleben of Birmingham.] H. A. T.

DE BERDT, DENNYS (*c.* 1694–Apr. 11, 1770), colonial agent, was a member of a family which emigrated from Ypres in Flanders to England to escape religious persecution under the Duke of Alva. They had a good estate on the continent but took with them only money and jewels. After reaching England some of the family left off the "De" and others spelled the name Bert. At first they settled at Colchester but John De Berdt, the father of Dennys, was apprenticed to a cousin who was a merchant in London. Dennys was born in or about 1694 and the *Gentleman's Magazine,* August 1731, records the death of a John De Berdt "of Battersea, Esq.; Grandson to the late Sir John Fleet," who was probably his father. Dennys was of a very devout religious temper and a pronounced Dissenter. Of his earlier interest in America or his connections with the Massachusetts leaders we know almost nothing. In 1758 the Rev. Samuel Davies preached a sermon in Virginia called "The Curse of Cowardice" and sent a manuscript copy to De Berdt who, the same year, published it in London with a dedication, favorable to the colonies, to the Earl of Halifax. Again in 1766, in one of the numerous pamphlets relating to the founding of the Rev. Eleazar Wheelock's Indian School, the forerunner of Dartmouth College, it was stated that English donations might be left with Dennys De Berdt, "Merchant, in Artillery-Court, Chiswell-street." On Nov. 5, 1765, the lower house of the General Court at Boston, considering the nomination of an agent for the colony in London, agreed on the name of De Berdt, who was then seventy years old. The house, in their notification of his election, said that since they were informed of his "Ability and Inclination to serve the Province" his election had been soon determined by a very large majority. The first letter from Samuel Dexter to De Berdt in his official capacity says that for some years De Berdt had been known as a "sincere friend of the American colonies."

It has been stated that he was agent for New York also but this is an error. He was, however, agent for Delaware as well as Massachusetts, and the former colony sent him a piece of silver plate for his services in securing the repeal of the Stamp Act. Massachusetts frugally contented herself with a vote of thanks on the same occasion, and finally settled the arrears of salary due him with his son Dennis after his death. Years afterward the state accepted the gift from his friend, Richard Cary, of his portrait which now hangs in the State House. He left a considerable estate and his will mentions his wife Martha as residuary legatee. Besides the son, Dennis, he had a daughter, Esther, who married the American Joseph Reed [*q.v.*] in London. As agent he seems to have been assiduous and faithful in a very trying period in spite of his advanced age.

[There is no biography of De Berdt and the contemporary references to him are scanty except for the official votes and letters in connection with his agencies. The only account of him, drawn upon for this article, is that by Albert Mathews in the *Mass. Colonial Soc. Pubs.,* XIII (1912), 294–307, forming an introduction to the reprint of his Letter-Book, the original of which is in the Lib. of Cong. A few other letters not in that are appended.] J. T. A.

DEBOW, JAMES DUNWOODY BROWNSON (July 10, 1820–Feb. 27, 1867), editor, statistician, was born in Charleston, S. C. His father was Garret De Bow, a native of New Jersey, once a prosperous merchant, but ruined shortly before his death. His mother was a Miss Norton. De Bow was left an orphan when still a lad, and used his tiny patrimony to enter a mercantile house in Charleston. Here he saved his money with Spartan self-denial for seven years in order to attend the Cokesbury Institute, Abbeville District. He entered the College of Charleston, and resorted to many shifts to maintain himself. In his last year he was in particularly desperate straits, his friends scarcely knowing how he lived. He graduated in 1843 at the head of his class, and, still existing on a crust, devoted an arduous year to the reading of law, after which he was admitted to the bar. He soon saw that he would not succeed in this profession; he was a poor speaker, and his emaciated appearance was against him. The *Southern Quarterly Review,* published in Charleston, offered an escape. He began contributing philosophical and political essays to its columns, and soon became its editor. His most notable article, "Oregon and the Oregon Question," appeared in July 1845; in this he discountenanced the claims of France to the northwest country, but saw much in those of Britain, toward which country he counseled, against the popular clamor, moderation and a spirit of compromise. This article attracted notice abroad, being debated in the French Chamber of Deputies. At the Memphis Convention, held the same year, De Bow was one of the secretaries. The convention considered principally projects of internal improvement in the South, and the extent to which the federal government should be expected to aid in their construction. This discussion of economic questions decided young De Bow to found a monthly magazine devoted to social and business matters, so, after Calhoun, Poinsett, and others had encouraged the venture, he left Charleston with "a diminutive capital and a very slender baggage" for New Orleans as a more bustling commercial center. The South had supported literary journals poorly, and economic ones not at all, but De Bow believed he could succeed because the interests of the southern frontier were practical. Accordingly he issued, in January 1846, the first number of the *Commercial Review of the South and Southwest.* He had difficulty in getting contributors, there were almost no subscribers, and in a few months his capital was exhausted and the *Review* suspended (August 1847). Then matters began to mend. He came to the notice of Maunsel White, who, from a poor Irish immigrant, had risen in sugar planting and merchandise to wealth. He admired the young editor and loaned him money to resume publication, promising more should it be needed. For a time De Bow and his assistant endured a struggle which only youth could have survived. After working till far into the night, they slept on a mattress on the floor of a room given them by J. C. Morgan, the bookseller. De Bow said afterward that they rarely spent more than ten cents each for a day's food. Within two years, however, they had the largest circulation of any magazine published in the South; De Bow had paid his debts, moved his office to better quarters, and was able to eat steak and chops for the first time in his life. He soon had money enough to make a trip through New England, which resulted in added information for the *Review.*

When the University of Louisiana was organized at New Orleans, he advocated inclusion of a comprehensive course of economic and commercial instruction in its curriculum, outlined the subjects to be treated (recommending the works of Henry C. Carey [*q.v.*] with those of the English classical school) and persuaded his friend Maunsel White to subsidize the professorship of political economy. De Bow was promptly appointed (1848) to the chair (probably the first of its kind in this country), but it was an empty honor, for he had no students and few listeners at his public lectures. Soon afterward he was made head of the new Louisiana Bureau of Statistics, and within a year compiled and presented to the legislature a report made up from returns to a brave questionnaire. The bureau went out of existence when the legislature failed to make further appropriation. De Bow, bound to have the South systematic, was one of the founders of the Louisiana Historical Society, which dragged out a sickly life until merged with the Academy of Sciences. Greater opportunity opened to him when he was appointed by President Pierce superintendent of the United States Census. He issued the seventh census, of 1850, and in 1854 the Senate printed his *Statistical View of the United States,* a compendium of the larger work. De Bow in an introductory essay made important suggestions for the improvement of the census, particularly through appointment of a permanent superintendent who should maintain a staff between decennial periods. While bringing out the report of the census he continued to publish his *Review,* and when he quitted his government post in 1855 took to public lecturing. He presided at the commercial convention at Knoxville in 1857, and wrote on American subjects for the *Encyclopædia Britannica.*

He will be longest remembered for *De Bow's Review,* which occupied in the South and Southwest a place similar to that of *Hunt's Merchants' Magazine* in the country at large. The journal was always influential, and had a part in bringing on the Civil War. His own articles appeared regularly, and were marked by serious, if somewhat lengthy, deliberation. Beginning with the resolve not to engage in debate on the matters threatening to divide North and South ("We have the broadest notions of our country; we cherish Maine and Louisiana as sisters; we have no jealousies of the North") he became, little by little, an outspoken and violent partisan. This was a natural consequence of his abiding admiration for Calhoun. More interested than Calhoun in economic prosperity, however, he retained a measure of the nationalism which his preceptor abandoned. He was influenced by the writings of the Careys, felt that protective tariffs were often desirable, and did not wish to contract the field of federal operation in internal improvements. He believed that "the negro was created essentially to be a slave, and finds his highest development and destiny in that condition." He worked for industry in the South, but expected to see agriculture remain predominant in that section. He contributed importantly to the policies of the series of commercial conventions held in the South prior to the Civil War, particularly with respect to a transcontinental railroad through the South, direct trade between the South and Europe, and a canal through Central America. His economic advocacies, where practical and untinged with political pique, had little constructive issue. In the main he was a very vocal drifter with the tide which set toward secession.

During the Civil War the Confederate government made him its chief agent for the purchase and sale of cotton. In the false flush of prosperity that came to the Southern commercial cities immediately after the war, he revived the *Review*, and at the same time was president of the Tennessee Pacific Railroad Company, a paper project which seemed to embody his old ambition of a transcontinental line through the South. He died of pleurisy, at Elizabeth, N. J., after a short illness contracted on a journey to the bedside of his dying brother and co-worker, B. F. De Bow. De Bow was ugly, with a great shock of hair standing in every direction, and a heavy moustache and beard. His nose was prominent, he had a long lower lip and an obstinate chin. Though in his writings he took himself very seriously, he was genial in personal contacts. He married in 1854 Caroline Poe, of Georgetown, D. C., and in 1860 Martha E. Johns, who with three children survived him.

[For biographical sketches see *De Bow's Review*, post-war series, Apr. and May 1867, pp. 480–81; June 1867, pp. 497–506 (with a rare portrait); July and Aug. 1867, pp. 1–10. *De Bow's Review*, with differing titles, was published in New Orleans, Columbia, or Nashville, with longer or shorter suspensions, from Jan. 1846 to June 1880. De Bow's *Industrial Resources of the Southern and Western States* (3 vols., 1853), contains the more important articles published in the *Review* up to that time.] B. M—l.

DE BRAHM, WILLIAM GERARD (1717–*c.* 1799), surveyor general of the Southern District, first used the given name of John Gerar William. A Dutch Protestant who had received competent training as a military engineer, he was also the founder of a prosperous colony in Georgia, a surveyor of that province, surveyor general for the Southern District, a geographer, climatologist, naturalist, meteorologist, navigator, and the author of navigation tables, pilot guides, and treatises on barometric hypsometry, the apparition of eternity, and the everlasting Gospel. He prefaced his reports on his surveys of South Carolina, Georgia, and East Florida with summaries of the early history of those provinces. His reports fill four folio volumes, are copiously illustrated with local and general maps, and contain his observations on practicable inlets and rivers, their surroundings, his directions for mariners, his notes on soils, useful trees and shrubs, game, fish, Indians, Spaniards, etc. These volumes show an excellent command of the English language, some classical knowledge, and much special and technical information.

De Brahm's young manhood fell in the period of the scientific renaissance in Europe, when science began to be applied to the affairs of life. It was also a time of political readjustment and colonial expansion. After serving in the army of Emperor Charles VI as a captain of engineers, De Brahm proceeded in 1751 with 160 Protestant Salzburgers by way of England to Georgia, where he founded Bethany. Before the end of another year the town's population was increased by about thirteen hundred relatives and acquaintances of the first settlers. Their progress during the next two decades in agriculture and horticulture was notable among the many German communities of the Georgian coast and Savannah River. When, in August 1754, the king appointed the officials of Georgia, De Brahm was made a surveyor at a salary of £50 per annum. Three years later he planned the town of Ebenezer on the Savannah, erected its fort, and took up lands there on both sides of the river. At that time also he drew the first map of Georgia and South Carolina. In 1755 he rebuilt the curtain line around the battery at Charleston, extending it to Vanderhorst Creek. Six years later he constructed Fort George on Cockspur Island in the Savannah, and in 1762 fortified the town of Savannah against the Indians. After ten years of valuable service, in June 1764, he was appointed by the king surveyor general for the Southern District, at a salary of £150, and was given £30 more for his deputy, Bernard Romans [*q.v.*]. Early in January 1765 he set out from Savannah in the schooner *Augustine* with three boats and other equipment for an eighteen weeks' cruise to survey the coast from St. Augustine to the Cape of Florida. Meantime, he had been named one of the commissioners to mark the northern boundary of New Jersey from the Hudson to the Delaware. Besides sounding and mapping the inlets along the Florida coast, he platted the land along the rivers flowing into them. He also conducted inland surveys, marking out lands for settlement and locating town sites with their church and school lands. In November 1766 he announced in the *South Carolina Gazette*, of Charleston, the building of a galley on St. John's River with which to continue his survey down to the promontory and his wish to employ a master acquainted with the Keys and qualified in theoretical and practical navigation, also a geometrician versed in navigation. During this period his residence was at St. Augustine and he acquired a grant of 10,000 acres in the province of Florida.

On Oct. 4, 1770, Gov. James Grant suspended De Brahm from the provincial surveyorship for incivilities, overcharges, and obstructing applicants for lands. He appointed De Brahm's son-in-law, Capt. Frederick George Mulcaster, as his successor; but the Surveyor General continued to perform his duties until he sailed for England. There he produced a map of the Atlantic Ocean for his mariners' guide, *The Atlantic Pilot,* published in London in 1772. He also delivered his general map of East Florida to the plantation office, submitted his elaborate report, and sought reinstatement, presenting a memorial to that end in 1774. In the same year he published two volumes, *The Levelling Balance and Counter-Balance; or, The Method of Observing, by the Weight and Height of Mercury* and *De Brahm's Zonical Tables for the Twenty-Five Northern and Southern Climates.* Early in July he sailed with Mrs. De Brahm for Charleston in an armed vessel placed at his disposal by the Privy Council. They arrived on Sept. 7, and the next day Mrs. De Brahm died. Nearly two months later the Lords of the Treasury wrote to the Council of East Florida that in their opinion the Surveyor should be reinstated. Thereafter De Brahm seems to have divided his time between St. Augustine and Charleston. On Feb. 18, 1776, he was married to Mary, daughter of Thomas Drayton and widow of Edward Fenwick. Late in the course of the Revolution he wrote to London begging not to be superseded. He was left unprovided for from 1783 to the end of his life, except that he was awarded £1,138 6*s* 8*d* for his property losses in Florida by the British commissioners on East Florida claims. During this period he lived in Philadelphia, where he published several small works, including *Time an Apparition of Eternity* (1791) and *Apocalyptic Gnomon Points Out Eternity's Divisibility,* etc. (1795). His will, dated July 11, 1796, was proved July 3, 1799.

[De Brahm's Report to the King as surveyor general for the Southern District of North America, 4 vols. (MS.) in Brit. Museum; copies of Vols. I and II in Harvard Coll. Lib.; part of Report in P. C. J. Weston, *Docs. Connected with the Hist. of S. C.* (London, 1856); also in De Brahm, *Hist. of the Province of Ga.* (1849), ed. by G. Wymberly-Jones; *Acts of the Privy Council, Colonial Ser., 1745–1766,* p. 647; *Ibid., 1766–1783,* pp. 394, 592; Colonial Office 5/571, Minutes of Council of E. Florida, Apr. 6 and Oct. 4, 1770; *Am. Archives,* ser. 4, III, 835, 837; W. H. Siebert, *Loyalists in E. Florida, 1774–85,* being *Fla. State Hist. Soc. Pubs.,* No. 9 (2 vols., 1929), II, 337–38; P. L. Phillips, *Notes on the Life and Works of Bernard Romans,* pp. 16, 29, being No. 2 of the same series; *S. C. Hist. and Geneal. Mag.,* XI (1910), 160, and XIV (1918), 7–9; C. C. Jones, *Hist. of Ga.* (1883), I, 212, 374, 460–62, 505; information from Ernest Spofford, Esq., librarian of the Hist. Soc. of Pa.]

W. H. S.

DEBS, EUGENE VICTOR (Nov. 5, 1855–Oct. 20, 1926), Socialist advocate, was one of the ten children of Jean Daniel and Marguerite Marie (Bettrich) Debs and was born in Terre Haute, Ind. The parents, who were married in New York City on Sept. 13, 1849, were both natives of Colmar, Alsace, and had come to America in that year. After some wandering they settled in Terre Haute in the fall of 1854. Young Debs attended school until the middle of his fifteenth year, when he went to work in the shops of the Terre Haute and Indianapolis Railway, later becoming a locomotive fireman. Four years later (1874) he quit his fireman's job and took a clerkship in a wholesale grocery house. In February of the following year he participated in the organization in his city of a lodge of the Brotherhood of Locomotive Firemen, of which he was made secretary, and in 1878 he was appointed associate editor of the *Firemen's Magazine.* He continued with the grocery firm (doing his work for the labor-union at night) until September 1879, when he was elected city clerk. In 1880 he was appointed (and later in the year elected) national secretary and treasurer of the Brotherhood and editor of its magazine. By working incredibly long hours he contrived to fill all three offices until the close of his term as city clerk in 1883, thereafter for ten years giving most of his time to his union. On June 9, 1885, he was married to Katherine Metzel of Pittsburgh, and in the fall of the year was elected to the lower house of the Indiana legislature. In 1892 he resigned his offices in the union, but against his protest was unanimously reëlected.

From an early day he was an opponent of the organization of labor by crafts and an advocate of organization by industries. In June 1893, he took part in the formation of a labor society of the "industrial" type, the American Railway Union, of which he was chosen president. In several minor contests with employers the new union won considerable prestige, and it came into nation-wide prominence through the strike for higher wages (Apr. 13, 1894) against the Great Northern Railroad. Eighteen days later the employees returned to work with most of their demands granted. In June the employees of the Pullman Company, at South Chicago, went out, and an appeal was made to the A. R. U. to aid them by a sympathetic strike. Debs opposed the move as inexpedient, but at a hastily called convention of the union a boycott on the moving of Pullman cars was ordered, and he at once took energetic charge of the campaign. Against the protest of Gov. Altgeld, President Cleveland ordered federal troops to Chicago; Judges Grosscup and Woods issued a sweeping injunction against the strikers, and on July 10 a federal grand jury, charging conspiracy to obstruct the mails, indicted Debs and three others, who were immediately arrested, and were again arrested

Debs

on July 17 for contempt of court in violating the injunction. The trial before Judge Grosscup, Feb. 6–12, 1895, resulted in a discontinuance because of the illness of a juror, but on the charge of contempt Debs and six others were sentenced by Judge Woods to six months in the McHenry County jail at Woodstock. Here Debs spent much of his time in reading, with the result that he avowed himself a convert to Socialism. Released on Nov. 22, he returned to Chicago, where he was accorded one of the most remarkable demonstrations in the history of the city, and thence to Terre Haute.

In 1896 he campaigned for Bryan, but, in June 1897, brought about the transformation of what was left of the A. R. U. into the Social Democratic Party of America. Three years later a tentative combination was made with the faction of the Socialist Labor party that had seceded in 1899, and Debs, as the fusion candidate for president, polled 96,116 votes. In the following year the two wings were formally united under the name of the Socialist Party of America, and in 1904 Debs was again nominated for president, polling 402,321 votes. About this time he became associate editor of the Socialist weekly, the *Appeal to Reason,* of Girard, Kan., and for five or six years gave his time to editorial work and to lecture tours in behalf of the *Appeal* and the Socialist party. At Chicago, June 27–July 8, 1905, he aided in founding the Industrial Workers of the World, but after a time became dissatisfied with the organization and withdrew, though frequently thereafter defending its members from charges he deemed unjust. In 1908 he was again the Socialist candidate, and in a train known as the "Red Special" made a speaking canvass of the entire country; but though he drew large crowds, his vote (420,973) showed only a slight gain over that of 1904. In 1912 he was nominated for the fourth time, and he again made a general canvass. The year was one of an unparalleled social ferment; and though the liberal platform of Wilson and the specifically progressive platform of Roosevelt were expected to diminish the Socialist vote, it increased to 901,062, or nearly six per cent of the total. In 1916 Debs declined to be a candidate.

The manifesto of the St. Louis convention of the party (April 1917), denouncing the war and counseling party members to oppose it by all means in their power, was warmly approved by Debs, though later in the year he favored some modification of the language and of the party's policy. But in the following year, stirred no doubt by resentment over the many convictions for sedition, he took more extreme ground. At the Socialist state convention in Canton, Ohio, June 16, 1918, he delivered a speech in which he bitterly assailed the administration for its prosecution of persons charged with sedition. Four days later, at Cleveland, he was indicted by a federal grand jury for a violation of the Espionage Act, and on Sept. 14, after a four-days trial, was sentenced to ten years' imprisonment on each of two accounts, the sentences to run concurrently. Appeal was taken to the federal Supreme Court, which on Mar. 10, 1919, upheld the verdict. On Apr. 13 Debs was taken to the penitentiary at Moundsville, W. Va., and on June 13–14 was transferred to the penitentiary at Atlanta. In the following year, while still a prisoner, he was nominated for the fifth time as his party's candidate for president, and polled 919,799 votes, a figure exceeding that of 1912 though representing but little more than half its proportion of the total. On Christmas Day, 1921, by order of President Harding, he was released, though without restoration of his citizenship.

He returned to his home, but in the following year spent several months in the Lindlahr Sanitarium, at Elmhurst, near Chicago. During this period he prepared for a newspaper syndicate a series of articles on prison conditions, which, in 1927, with additions, were published in book form with the title *Walls and Bars.* In 1924 the Socialist party, with Debs's approval, joined with the La Follette forces. In the following year it established in Chicago a national weekly organ, the *American Appeal,* of which Debs was made editor. His health declining, early in 1926 he went to Bermuda. In April he returned home, but in September again became an inmate of the sanitarium at Lindlahr, where a month later he died. Funeral services, attended by 10,000 persons, were held in his home city on Oct. 23. The body was cremated at Indianapolis, and the ashes were buried in Terre Haute.

Though the standard-bearer of his party, Debs was at no time its intellectual leader. He was not a student or a reasoner, but a passionate advocate, and his words and acts were impulsive. He initiated none of the policies of the party, and he formulated none of its programs. Even his place as standard-bearer was anomalous; for though the fundamental tactic of the party was to seek a close affiliation with the trade-unions, Debs was their steadfast opponent, and in his prime there was perhaps no man in the labor movement whom the union leaders regarded as a greater menace. He had promoted the organization of two rival bodies (the A. R. U. and the I. W. W.), and he might at any time, it was feared, break bounds and join in some further action deemed disruptive. This anomaly was not unrecognized by thoughtful members of the party; but the sterling character of the man, his moral earnestness, his personal popularity, and his energy as a campaigner combined to override all opposition within the ranks.

Everywhere he drew large and responsive audiences. His manner as an orator was impressive; and his diction, if not always eloquent, was fluent and forceful. Tall, lean, and supple, his eager countenance aflame, he bent far forward over the edge of the platform and with right arm extended and long forefinger pointing from place to place at his audience, he thundered out his invectives against the capitalist system and sought to bring home to each of his hearers a guilty sense of responsibility for its continuance. Each of his addresses was, from the standpoint of its immediate influence over his hearers, a personal triumph, and he was greeted with every demonstration of approval. But though the common people heard him gladly, most of them voted against him. They learned to respect and love the man, but his message did not convert them.

His language, both of denunciation and of praise, was often extreme. His social philosophy was naïve and all-embracing; capitalism, with all its works, was an unqualified evil, and Socialism, with all its promises, a panacea. He had neither time nor thought for any modification of this simple creed; what was not white was black, and he spoke his convictions with a positiveness that revealed a mind untroubled with doubts. He was often inconsistent. Though he opposed repression and violence, he could find palliation for either provided it was employed in behalf of "the cause." To a friendly interviewer who talked with him in the Atlanta penitentiary he asserted (*Appeal to Reason,* Apr. 17, 1920) that because the Russian revolution was "a forward step" it was right for the Soviet Government to suppress free speech and a free press, whereas it was wrong to deny free speech in his own case because American participation in the war was "a reactionary step." He denounced the assassination of the Czar and his family, and on July 26, 1922, protested to Lenin by cable against the probable execution of twenty-two Social Revolutionists then on trial; but in a long manifesto issued on the following Oct. 8 indulged in a sweeping defense of the Soviet Government in spite of its imprisonment and execution of dissentients.

His personal character won tributes from all who knew him. His home life was happy; not often is there revealed to the world a family such as his, so closely bound by affection and community of interest and belief, and to one of its members, his brother Theodore, for many years his constant companion and auxiliary, must be credited no small part of his achievement. Debs's rectitude, his genial and unaffected friendliness, his sympathy and his open-handed generosity were widely recognized, and nowhere was he held in greater regard than in his home city. "While the overwhelming majority of the people here are opposed to the social and economic theories of Mr. Debs," wrote Mayor James Lyons in 1907 to an inquirer, "there is not perhaps a single man in this city who enjoys to a greater degree than Mr. Debs the affection, love and profound respect of the entire community."

[*Debs: His Life, Writings and Speeches, with a Department of Appreciations* (1908), ed. by Stephen Marion Reynolds; David Karsner, *Debs: His Authorized Life and Letters* (1919), and *Talks with Debs in Terre Haute* (1922); E. V. Debs, *Walls and Bars* (1927); *Speeches of Eugene V. Debs* (1929), ed. with a critical introduction by Alexander Trachtenberg; *Debs and the Poets* (1920), ed. by Ruth Le Prade; files of the *Firemen's Mag.*, later the *Brotherhood of Locomotive Firemen's Mag.*, and still later *The Brotherhood of Locomotive Firemen and Enginemen's Mag.*; Grover Cleveland, "The Government in the Chicago Strikes of 1894," *McClure's Mag.*, July 1904; Debs's reply in the *Appeal to Reason,* Aug. 27, 1904; *N. Y. Times,* Oct. 21–25, Nov. 7, and Dec. 22, 1926; information as to specific facts from Theodore Debs; notes and recollections of the writer.]

W. J. G.

DE CAMP, JOSEPH RODEFER (Nov. 5, 1858–Feb. 11, 1923), painter, was born at Cincinnati, Ohio, the son of Lambert and Lydia (Garwood) De Camp. He received his early training in the Cincinnati School of Design, under Frank Duveneck [*q.v.*], and continued his studies later in the Royal Academy at Munich. He was a member of the group of art students who accompanied Duveneck to Munich, Florence, and Venice, in 1878. In the company were Alexander, Twachtman, Chase, Vinton, MacEwen, Rolshoven, Currier, Grover, Bacher, and others. This band of students attained a certain celebrity; they figured in fiction as "the Inglehart boys" in William Dean Howells's *Indian Summer* (1885). There can be no doubt as to the marked influence of Duveneck's personality and principles on all the young men. Though few of them remained as consistent adherents of the Munich methods as their leader, none of them failed to make his mark in his own way. De Camp returned to America in 1880 and settled in Boston, where he was soon recognized as a sound and capable portrait-painter and an efficient teacher. He was for many years instructor in the Massachusetts Normal Art School. He held to the fundamental essentials of his art, especially good drawing and firm construction. In September 1891 he married Edith F. Baker, daughter of Joseph E. Baker, lithographer, a colleague of Winslow Homer in Bufford's shop, Boston, 1855–57. De Camp's home was in Medford, and his studio was in Boston. His vacations were spent on an island in Penobscot Bay, where his occupations included designing and building boats, piers, cottages; gardening, fishing, golfing. His friend George R. Agassiz spoke of his courage, honesty, and humanity; "under a somewhat rugged exterior lay the simplicity and tender-heartedness of a child." His death occurred at Bocagrande, Fla.

Many of De Camp's best paintings were first shown at the St. Botolph Club, of which he was a member. In 1911 he exhibited seventeen pictures there, including his full-length portrait of Theodore Roosevelt, presented by his classmates to the Harvard Union; a portrait of Frank Duveneck; a self-portrait; and likenesses of Sally and Polly, the artist's daughters. He was also a regular exhibitor at the Guild of Boston Artists, the annual exhibitions of the Ten Americans, and the Pennsylvania Academy. His best-known figure pieces are: "The Pink Feather," "The Guitar Player," "The Fur Jacket," "The New Gown," "The Blue Cup," "The Window," "La Penserosa." Ten of his works were in the retrospective exhibition of the Ten Americans, 1908. His works may be seen in the permanent collections of the Cincinnati Museum, the Boston Art Museum, the Worcester Art Museum, the Pennsylvania Academy of the Fine Arts, the Wilstach collection, Memorial Hall, Philadelphia, and the Boston Art Club. Among his last works were his portraits of Prime Minister Borden of Canada and Gen. Currie, commander of the Canadian forces in France (1919); also a noteworthy picture of the elderly negro chef of the Porcellian Club, Harvard University, in the act of bringing to the table a roast suckling pig.

De Camp was a member of the National Institute of Arts and Letters, the Portrait Painters, the Ten Americans, associate member of the National Academy of Design, member of the Philadelphia Art Club, the St. Botolph Club, and the Guild of Boston Artists. Among the honors conferred on him were three prizes from the Pennsylvania Academy of the Fine Arts, viz.: the Temple gold medal, the Beck medal, and the Lippincott prize; the gold medal of the Louisiana Purchase exposition; the gold medal of the Philadelphia Art Club; the second Clark prize of the Corcoran Gallery, Washington; and the first prize in the Philadelphia City Hall decorative competition.

[*Jos. De Camp: an Appreciation* (1924), edited by Lee W. Court, and published by the Student Asso. of the Mass. Normal Art School, contains tributes and reminiscences by Geo. R. Agassiz, Geo. H. Bartlett, and Rose V. S. Berry; a portrait of the artist, and reproductions of seven of his pictures. See also Wm. H. Downes, "Jos. De Camp and His Work," *Art and Progress,* Apr. 1913; Arthur Hoeber, "De Camp, a Master of Technique," *Arts and Decoration,* Apr. 1911; *Am. Mag. of Art,* Apr. 1923; *Art News,* Feb. 17, 1923; *Boston Herald* and *Boston Transcript,* Feb. 12, 1923.]

W. H. D.

DECATUR, STEPHEN (1752–Nov. 14, 1808), naval officer, was the son of a French seaman of the same name, who according to family tradition was a lieutenant in the French navy. Of a seafaring family originally Dutch (de Kater) but settled for a century in La Rochelle, France, the father came to Newport, R. I., about 1750 and was married there in Trinity Church, Sept. 26, 1751, to Priscilla Hill. According to the records of this church their son Stephen was baptized June 7, 1752. The family soon moved to Philadelphia, where the father died in straitened circumstances. The boy Stephen followed his father's calling and in 1774 was master of the sloop *Peggy.* He was married, Dec. 20, 1774, at the home of Capt. Moore, her guardian, to Ann Pine, of Scotch-Irish descent, daughter of John and Nancy Pine (daughter of James Bruce of Edinburgh). During the Revolution he engaged in privateering, commanding in succession, 1779–81, the galley *Retaliation,* sloop *Comet,* brig *Fair American,* and ships *Royal Louis* and *Rising Sun.* All these were Pennsylvania vessels (*Naval Records of the American Revolution,* 1906). In 1781, before his cruise to Teneriffe in the last-named vessel, he was for some months imprisoned in New York (Scharf and Westcott, *History of Philadelphia,* 1884, I, 423). Later, with the Philadelphia merchants Gurney & Smith, he was commander and part owner of the ships *Pennsylvania* and *Ariel,* taking his son Stephen, aged eight, on one voyage to Bordeaux. Commissioned captain in the United States navy, May 11, 1798, at the outbreak of hostilities with France, he put to sea in the *Delaware,* and in July captured the French privateer *Le Croyable,* renamed *Retaliation,* the first prize of the war and of the new American navy. In the *Delaware,* with two smaller vessels, he was senior officer during the winter of 1798–99 off northern Cuba. In May 1800, he arrived on the Guadeloupe station in the new frigate *Philadelphia,* and was senior officer of the squadron there until August. The *Philadelphia* captured five prizes, returning home in March 1801. Honorably discharged at the close of hostilities, and after some further connection with Gurney & Smith in Philadelphia, Decatur purchased an estate, "Millsdale," near Frankford, Pa., where he established a gunpowder works. His portrait, an apparently excellent likeness of this later period by St. Memin, pictures a frank, open-faced seaman, rougher and heavier of feature than his famous son. Four children lived to maturity: Ann, who married Lieut. James McKnight of the Marine Corps; Stephen [*q.v.*]; James, killed before Tripoli; and John Pine, who retired after three years' naval service in 1810. At a dinner in Philadelphia in honor of his son Stephen after the Tripolitan War, the father with mingled pride and grief responded to a toast with the words, "Our children are the property of their country." He died at "Millsdale," and, with his wife, who died four years later, lies buried in St. Peter's churchyard, Philadelphia.

[In addition to references cited, see A. S. Mackenzie, *Life of Stephen Decatur* (1846); Wm. Decatur Parsons, *The Decatur Geneal.* (1921); G. W. Allen, *Our Naval War with France* (1909).] A. W.

DECATUR, STEPHEN (Jan. 5, 1779–Mar. 22, 1820), naval officer, came of seafaring stock, his father Stephen [*q.v.*] having risen to prosperity by commerce and privateering. Stephen, Jr., was born in a log cabin at Sinepuxent on the Eastern Shore of Maryland, where his mother had gone during the British occupation of Philadelphia. Brought soon afterward to the family home on South Front St., he grew up in the pleasant companionship of his elder sister Ann and his younger brothers. From childhood he was daring and a bit belligerent, if we accept stories of his dives from the tips of jib-booms and defense of his mother against a drunken ruffian at fourteen. He attended the Episcopal Academy and was for over a year at the University of Pennsylvania. Impatient of studies, he entered the employ of Gurney & Smith, a shipping firm in Philadelphia. At the outbreak of the naval war with France he was commissioned midshipman, Apr. 30, 1798, and sailed in July in the *United States,* Commodore Barry, for the West Indies, and on a second cruise in November. Aptitude and advanced age gained him quick promotion on this cruise to acting lieutenant, his commission dating May 21, 1799. Five feet ten, erect and athletic, with handsome aquiline features, large eyes, and waving brown hair, he is described by a younger officer as even then a man "more highly endowed than any other I ever knew" (Mackenzie, *post,* p. 35). During the summer of 1799, in a quarrel arising from recruiting duty in Philadelphia, he fought with the mate of a merchant vessel the first of the two duels in which he was a principal, wounding his opponent in the hip. In the winter he sailed in the *United States* with the peace commissioners for France: then, after a short cruise in the *Norfolk,* he was again in the *United States* on the Guadeloupe station until the close of hostilities. There is general testimony that in these early years Decatur won the hearts of his men and maintained excellent discipline. After but three years' service, he was appointed first lieutenant of the *Essex* in Commodore Dale's squadron to Tripoli (May 1801–July 1802), and, in August 1802, to the same responsible position in the *New York,* Capt. James Barron, in the second squadron which sailed in September. On this last cruise, acting as second for Midshipman Joseph Bainbridge in a duel with the secretary to the governor of Malta, Decatur protected his principal against an expert opponent by insisting on a distance of but four paces. The secretary was killed, and the American participants were sent home (March 1803). In November 1803, Decatur was again in the Mediterranean in his first command, the *Argus.* shifting at Gibraltar to the schooner *Enterprise* (12 guns).

This was the year of action in the Tripolitan War under Commodore Preble, and of Decatur's rise to fame. Off Tripoli he captured the ketch *Mastico* (4 guns), renamed *Intrepid,* and proposed to Preble her use for destruction of the frigate *Philadelphia,* which had stranded and fallen into the hands of the Tripolitans. This exploit, in words ascribed to Nelson "the most bold and daring act of the age," was carried out on the evening of Feb. 16, 1804. With her Mediterranean rig, the ketch approached within 200 yards of the *Philadelphia* before she was hailed. A request from the Maltese pilot Catalano to moor alongside was granted, and in a moment the Americans, eighty-one all told (G. R. Clark, and others, *A Short History of the United States Navy,* 1911, p. 76), were leaping aboard the frigate. Completely surprised, the Tripolitan crew were for the most part swept overboard. Combustibles were placed and fired, and in twenty minutes the boarders, with but one man wounded, were back in the *Intrepid* and leaving the harbor, lighted by the burning frigate and under fire from shore batteries. For this daring and effective blow Decatur was promoted to post captain, his commission arriving six months later. Meantime, in the first bombardment of Tripoli on Aug. 3, 1804, with six gunboats procured from Naples, he commanded one of the two divisions. In this hard-fought action Decatur with twenty-three men boarded and cleared the decks of an enemy craft with a crew estimated at thirty-six. Learning, as he towed out his prize, that his younger brother James, in command of another boat, had been treacherously killed, he reëntered the enemy line and with but ten followers leaped aboard a second vessel. In the fierce fight that followed, Decatur, armed with a cutlass, attacked the Tripolitan leader, a huge man wielding a boarding pike. The two grappled and fell. A blow directed at Decatur by another Tripolitan was foiled by a devoted sailor, Daniel Frazier (for identity see "Reuben James or Daniel Frazier," by C. L. Lewis, *Maryland Historical Magazine,* March 1924), who received the blow on his own head and was severely wounded. Decatur finally killed his opponent with a pistol, fired from his pocket, just as the Tripolitan, who was uppermost, was aiming a blow with his knife.

These feats of dashing leadership and personal prowess made Decatur the most striking figure of the war. He commanded a division in the second bombardment on Aug. 7, 1804, and in subsequent attacks. In September, after receipt of his captain's commission, he was given command of the *Constitution,* then overhauling at Malta, but in November was shifted to the *Congress.* After peace with Tripoli in the next spring, the *Congress* was stationed for a time off Tunis, Decatur going ashore to negotiate with the Bey, and then, in September 1805, returning to America with the Tunisian envoy. Upon his arrival at Norfolk he first met his future wife, Susan, daughter of Luke Wheeler, a wealthy merchant and mayor of the city, to whom he was married Mar. 8, 1806. At this time he commanded the gunboat flotilla in the Chesapeake, and during the next winter he was head of the Norfolk Navy Yard. In 1808 he was given charge of naval forces on the southeastern coast, hoisting his flag in the *Chesapeake* and later (1810) in the *United States.* He was a member of the court martial that suspended Capt. James Barron [*q.v.*] in 1808 after the *Chesapeake-Leopard* encounter, and president of the court of inquiry in 1811 after the *President–Little Belt* affair.

Still in the United States at the outbreak of the War of 1812, Decatur joined his squadron of three vessels with those of his senior Rodgers in New York, sailing thence on June 21 for a cruise which netted only seven prizes. Again with Rodgers he left Boston Oct. 8, but this time separated from the other vessels, following his preference for independent cruising, and on the 25th, near Madeira, fought the *Macedonian,* gaining the second of the three famous frigate victories in the first year of the war. Having a slower ship but fifty per cent superiority in artillery, Decatur maneuvered with wariness and great skill, using his longer-range guns when the *Macedonian* held off to windward, and upon her final approach shooting away all three of her topmasts, with but slight injuries to his own vessel. The casualties were 104 British to 12 American. The *United States* with her prize entered New London Dec. 4, and thence proceeded to New York, where a series of festivities celebrated the victory. Attempting to get to sea through the Sound at the close of the following May, the two ships were driven by the blockading force into New London, remaining there till the close of the war. In May 1814, Decatur, taking along his devoted ship's company, was transferred to the *President* in New York, where during the summer and autumn he had charge also of the naval defenses of the port. In a heavy northeaster, on the night of Jan. 14, 1815, the *President* attempted escape to sea, but grounded for two hours on the bar with injuries which cut down her speed, and next morning off Long Island ran into the British blockading force—the razee *Majestic* (56 guns) and frigates *Endymion* (40), *Pomone* (38), and *Tenedos* (38). The chase continued till nightfall, when all the pursuers had been thrown off save the *Endymion.* With four to three superiority of broadside (Mahan, *post,* II, 401), Decatur now turned on the *Endymion* and in two hours left her stripped of sails, though meantime the *President's* crew had suffered severely from the enemy fire directed at her decks. Unfortunately at eleven P.M. the *President* again came in contact with the pursuers, and now surrendered without further firing, "with one-fifth of my crew killed and wounded, my ship crippled, and a more than four-fold force opposed to me" (Decatur's report). Only the *Pomone* seems to have been in actual range at the time, and Mahan (*post,* p. 403) remarks truly that the defense should not be called "desperate" or "heroic." Decatur himself was painfully though not seriously wounded, and the constant strain of the preceding twenty-four hours, together perhaps with a recognition that the war was virtually over (the treaty had been signed at Ghent Dec. 24), influenced his decision to avoid further bloodshed. After weathering a severe gale the prize was taken to Bermuda. Efforts to attribute the victory to the *Endymion* alone were hotly resented by the Americans, who found comfort however in Admiral Cochrane's comment, "She [the *President*] was completely mobbed." Decatur was soon paroled, landing in New London on Feb. 22. The court of inquiry ascribed his capture to injuries in crossing the bar, credited him with a victory over the *Endymion,* and gave him the highest praise.

Offered by the secretary almost his own choice of future duties, he selected command of the first squadron of nine ships which sailed from New York, May 20, 1815, to settle with Algiers for injuries which had persisted since 1812. After an extraordinarily fast passage, the squadron reached Gibraltar June 15. On the 17th it captured the Algerian flagship *Mashuda,* on the 19th drove another enemy vessel ashore, and on the 28th was off the port of Algiers. Decatur sent officers ashore giving the Dey choice of war or peace on American terms. Two days later, aboard the flagship *Guerrière,* a treaty was negotiated, ending tribute and requiring full payment for injuries to Americans. This was sent ashore for the Dey's signature. No truce was granted, and when in the interval an Algerian vessel approached the harbor Decatur was prevented from attack only by the hasty appearance of a boat with a white flag, the pre-arranged signal that the treaty was signed. On this occasion the Commodore wore full uniform, his "splendid figure" enhanced by "laced coat and hat, tight cassimere pantaloons, and long boots . . . bound at the top with gold lace and having tassels of gold in front" (Mackenzie, p. 267). This is the costume of the Sully portrait in the New York City Hall. The squadron proceeded to Tunis and then to Tripoli, exacting payment for injuries suffered during the British war. When Bainbridge arrived with a second squadron the work was already done, a result in large measure due to Decatur's energy and prestige with the Barbary powers. Fêtes and dinners again greeted his return. It was to a toast at one of these dinners in Norfolk that Decatur made his familiar response: "Our country! In her intercourse with foreign nations may she always be in the right; but our country, right or wrong."

From November 1815 until his death Decatur served with Rodgers and Porter on the Board of Navy Commissioners. In this administrative work, Porter (*Memoir,* p. 277) declares he was "arbitrary" and "interfering," but he could ably defend his views, as evidenced by his well-argued report favoring Norfolk as chief base in the Chesapeake (Mackenzie, Appendix, p. 386). On Oct. 10, 1818, he was second to his close friend Perry in a duel with a marine officer at Weehawken. Prize money had brought him considerable wealth, which he invested largely in Washington realty (*Records of the Columbia Historical Society,* XXVIII, 4), building his own home on President's (now Lafayette) Square. The Decaturs were prominent in Washington society. Childless themselves, they were devoted to the daughters of Decatur's widowed sister, Mrs. McKnight. Decatur's death was an aftermath of the suspension of Capt. Barron. As Navy Commissioner he vigorously opposed Barron's efforts to secure reinstatement, on the ground that Barron had not made proper efforts to reënter the service in 1812. A heated correspondence, in which Decatur was correct though not conciliatory, led to Barron's challenge. The meeting was at Bladensburg, near Washington. Decatur in deference to his opponent's faulty eyesight selected the shortest distance, eight paces, and stated privately that he would aim low to avoid mortal injury. At the first exchange both fell, Barron wounded in the thigh and Decatur shot through the body. The intense feeling of the time was expressed in the words of the *National Intelligencer,* "Mourn Columbia! for one of thy brightest stars has set, a son without fear and without reproach." All official Washington attended the stately funeral on Mar. 24. The body was placed in a vault on the Joel Barlow estate near Washington, but in 1846 was removed to St. Peter's churchyard, Philadelphia, and placed beside the bodies of Decatur's parents.

Decatur's attractive personal qualities are best seen in the devotion of his crews, and in his genial relations with fellow officers. Not a student or reader, he had a mechanical bent, shown in experiments with shells and in the invention of a device for making horseshoes, and a lively, intelligent mind in conversation, as suggested by the poet Coleridge's citation of a remark of Decatur's—on the danger to national unity in the rapid expansion of his country—made years before in Malta. A stickler for honor, passionate for glory, he was neither braggart nor bully. Commanding only in single-ship actions, he attained not quite the first rank among American naval leaders, but has remained a popular favorite through his stainless character, winning personality, and the brilliant exploits of Tripolitan days.

[The biographies by Benj. Folsom (*A Compilation of Biog. Sketches of Distinguished Officers of the Am. Navy,* 1814), and S. Putnam Waldo (*The Life and Character of Stephen Decatur,* 1821) were superseded by Capt. A. S. Mackenzie's *Life of Stephen Decatur* (1846), which has remained standard, more trustworthy than the shorter life, *Stephen Decatur* (1900), by C. T. Brady. Aside from naval histories, especially G. W. Allen, *Our Navy and the Barbary Corsairs* (1905), A. T. Mahan, *Sea Power in its Relations to the War of 1812* (1905), and Theodore Roosevelt, *The Naval War of 1812* (1882) and sources there cited, material on special points may be found in *Correspondence between . . . Decatur and . . . Barron* (Washington, 1820), *Docs. Relative to the Claims of Mrs. Decatur* (for *Philadelphia* prize money) (Georgetown, 1826); *Memoir of Commodore D. Porter* (Albany, 1875), pp. 416–18 (on Decatur-Barron duel); and "Decatur and Coleridge," by C. G. Calkins, *Proc. U. S. Naval Inst.*, XXXIV (1908), 917.] A.W.

DE COPPET, EDWARD J. (May 28, 1855–Apr. 30, 1916), banker, patron of music, was the son of Louis de Coppet, a Swiss who came to America in 1828, and married Juliet Minerva Weston of Connecticut. Edward was educated in Switzerland, and on his return to America as a young man succeeded his father as a banker in New York, eventually founding the Stock Exchange house of De Coppet & Doremus. So passionately was he devoted to the art of tone in one of its noblest manifestations, the chamber ensemble, that finance might be called his avocation and music his profession. A cultivated Mæcenas in the highest sense of the word, his devotion to music was shared by his wife, an excellent pianist; and it was in the sympathetic atmosphere of a home where the cult of the string ensemble (as of the piano trio, quartet, and quintet) was supreme, that the central interest of his life took form, which always will be associated with his name. His fine impersonal desire to advance the art he loved raised his efforts above the status of a mere personal amusement. It is only just to regard him as an artist whose masterpiece was the Flonzaley Quartet. As Daniel Gregory Mason has said, "He never supposed that, as do those who aspire to be patrons of art less for the sake of the art than for that of patronage, that he could create what he was after by the simple process of signing checks. His method was that of all genuine art: indefatigable experiment . . . extending through a long series of years." The books in which are recorded the programs, participants, and guests of all his musical gatherings for thirty years, from Oct. 21, 1886, to Apr. 21, 1916, record one thousand and fifty-four meetings for chamber music in his home. The Flonzaley Quartet which, though long self-supporting, was Edward de Coppet's great achievement, was founded in 1904. It represented an attempt to weld four artists of superior merit into a homogeneous artistic whole, by making it financially possible for them to devote their entire time and effort to the development of a perfect string ensemble. The members of the original Quartet (Messrs. Betti, Pochon, Ara, and Archambeau) entered with zeal into the spirit of the esthetic adventure. It took the name of the "Flonzaley Quartet" from the Villa Flonzaley, near Vevey, on Lake Geneva, the De Coppet summer home in Switzerland; and passed in time from playing for the private entertainment of its patron and guests, and in public concerts made possible by his generosity, to independent existence as a self-supporting musical organization whose primacy in its particular field was still generally acknowledged after a quarter of a century. To thousands of American music-lovers it has revealed at their best the choicest works of ancient and modern string quartet literature. Edward de Coppet died a few hours after listening to the ensemble he had created play one of the later Beethoven quartets. In an "Appreciation" written by his friend Ara, the latter said: "Sustained by Beethoven's sublime thought, whose beauties he had lucidly analyzed an hour before his death, he passed suddenly and painlessly away . . . and this death, so serene and simple, seemed the inevitable epilogue of a life like his, altogether expended in the pursuit of goodness and the love of beauty."

[Of modest and retiring disposition Edward de Coppet was averse to publicity. The best idea of the man and his work is given by Daniel Gregory Mason, "Edward J. de Coppet," *Musical Quart.*, Oct. 1916; *Musical America*, May 6, 1916, the *Bull. of New Music*, Oct. 1916, and the *N. Y. Times*, May 2, 1916, contain obituaries.] F. H. M.

DE COSTA, BENJAMIN FRANKLIN (July 10, 1831–Nov. 4, 1904), clergyman and writer, was born in Charlestown, Mass. The surname was brought to Boston from England in 1699 by Isaac De Costa, a Huguenot of Portuguese ancestry who had been driven from France by the revocation of the Edict of Nantes. Beginning with Isaac, the Massachusetts line found wives in New England families of English descent. Ezekiel Carver De Costa, fourth generation from Isaac, married Elizabeth Jackson, and Benjamin Franklin De Costa was the fifth of their six children. In 1856 he graduated from the Biblical Institute at Concord, N. H. In 1857 he entered the Episcopal ministry and served for three years as rector in Massachusetts, one year in North Adams, and two years in Newton Lower Falls. From 1861 to 1863 he was chaplain of Massachusetts troops in the Civil War, and special correspondent of the Charlestown *Advertiser*. He also wrote some letters for other newspapers. Leaving the army, he settled in New York and engaged in editorial and historical work. The *Christian Times* (New York) carried his name as editor from Dec. 22, 1864, to Mar. 29, 1866, and he seems to have served for about nine months afterward its continuator, the *Episcopalian* (New York and Philadelphia). Fruits of historical research began to appear in 1864, and eventually reached about fifty titles. He was married in 1866 to Harriet Cooper Spencer, and with her traveled extensively (especially after 1873), lingering with special interest in places where he might collect historical material and crossing the ocean twenty-two times (*New York Tribune*, Aug. 24, 1899).

His historical publications relate chiefly to early American discovery and exploration, including cartology, and most of them are brief, ranging from eight to twenty-five pages. A considerable number consist of documents with editorial introductions and notes. His *Pre-Columbian Discovery of America by the Northmen* (1868, revised in 1890 and again in 1901) presented in this way the case for the Northmen and brought together the largest collection of sagas available in English before the appearance of Reeves's *Finding of Wineland the Good* (1890). A better piece of editing, however, is found in his edition of Bishop William White's *Memoirs of the Protestant Episcopal Church* (1880). Several of his works show an amiable weakness for rescuing characters and events from the neglect or disparagement of historians. The service performed for the Northmen was extended to Verrazano, Champdoré, John Walker, and others, and to Welsh and Irish discoverers of America.

In 1881 De Costa became rector of the Church of St. John the Evangelist in New York City. The duties of his office were arduous and were made more so by his activity in social-uplift movements. He organized the first American branch of the White Cross and wrote a history of the movement (*The White Cross: Its Origin and Progress*, 1887). He frequently addressed working men, and was a member of the Knights of Labor. He was one of the charter members and first president of a church association for the advancement of labor. He was one of the organizers, and for years secretary, of the Church Temperance Society. He still, however, found time for historical work; in 1881 he went as a delegate to the International Congress of Americanists at Madrid; he was for a time (1882–83) editor of the *Magazine of American History*; he contributed to Justin Winsor's *Narrative and Critical History of America* two chapters, including the critical essays on the sources—the chapter on "Norumbega and its English Explorers" in vol. III (1885), and the chapter on "Jacques Cartier and his Successors" in vol. IV (1885). In 1899 he became involved in the controversy over the ordination of Prof. C. A. Briggs [*q.v.*], late of Union Theological Seminary, as a priest in the Episcopal Church. De Costa, taking strong ground against the higher criticism of the Bible, led the opposition. Briggs was ordained in May. In August De Costa offered his resignation as rector. In October he withdrew from the Episcopal ministry and was deposed by Bishop Potter. In December he became a member of the Roman Catholic Church. The death of his wife in 1901 invited a further step; he prepared for the priesthood, and in November 1903 was ordained in Italy by the Bishop of Fiesole.

[For genealogy see *De Costa Family Chart* (1876), and references in De Costa's memorial sketches of Wm. Hickling De Costa (1878), Elizabeth De Costa (1880), and Mary Rebecca De Costa (1896). For his travels, see his memorial sketch, *In Memoriam: Harriet Cooper Spencer De Costa* (1901); for activities after 1864, the files of the *New-Eng. Hist. and Geneal. Reg.*; for his change of faith, the *N. Y. Tribune*, May 22, Aug. 24, Oct. 10–23, 1899, and Nov. 30, 1903; further clues are found in his article, "The Bible in the Life, Thought, and Homes of the People," *Catholic World*, Sept. 1900, and in his *Whither Goest Thou?* (1902). In 1899 he published a bibliography of his writings, *The Titles of 55 Separately Printed Works, with some other Matters, Covering a Half Century.*]

H. J.

DEEMER, HORACE EMERSON (Sept. 24, 1858–Feb. 26, 1917), Iowa jurist, was born in Bourbon, Ind., the eldest son of John A. and Elizabeth (Erwin) Deemer. His paternal ancestors emigrated from Holland to Pennsylvania after the Thirty Years' War, and his mother's family were Scotch-Irish. On both sides his ancestors were opponents of slavery. His early church associations were with the Friends and Baptists. The family moved from Indiana to a farm near West Liberty, Iowa in 1866. The son attended the public schools and was a member of the first class graduating from the local high school. Later he entered the State University and graduated from the law school in June 1879. He is said to have been the first college baseball pitcher to use the curved ball, having developed the method from reading accounts of big league players. During all the time that he was getting his education, he paid his own way. Then, for a while, he worked with his father in the lumber business, and, incidentally, learned the carpenter's trade.

After his admission to the bar, he entered a law office in Lincoln, Nebr. He remained there only a few months and, on his return to Iowa, he formed a partnership with a classmate, Joseph M. Junkin of Red Oak. The firm was successful from the beginning and it continued until his elevation to the bench in 1886, when he was still only twenty-eight years old. Four years earlier he had married Jeannette Gibson of Red Oak, July 12, 1882. He served very successfully as district judge for more than seven years, until he was appointed to the supreme court in 1894. He remained on the bench of the highest state court up to the time of his death in 1917. His service of twenty-three years constituted the longest continuous tenure of any judge in that court. By rotation he was chief justice in 1898, 1904, 1910, and 1915. His opinions numbered about two thousand. Many of them were in cases involving the construction of anti-trust statutes; others involved problems of constitutionality, such as the constitutionality of the mulct law, of the party-wall statute, of damages in delayed death messages, of the anti-cigarette act, and of various police measures, including the regulation of the use of oleomargarine. His decisions gave ample evidence of his legal knowledge, his sense of justice, and his ability as a writer. He was twice considered for appointment to the Supreme Court of the United States, and he received the indorsement of the lawyers of his own state and of the whole country.

Besides his legal decisions, which comprise his most important work, Deemer probably gave most time and thought to his duties as trustee of the State Library, of the governing board of which he was *ex officio* a member. For many years he was chairman of the book committee, and under his guidance a great reference library was developed. With Judge Kinne he had an important part in the establishment of traveling libraries. From 1895 to 1904 he was a lecturer in the law department of the state university. His work on *Iowa Pleading and Practice, Law and Equity with Forms* was published in three volumes in 1914, and a revised edition in two volumes was issued in 1927. In 1911 he received votes as a successor to Jonathan P. Dolliver in the United States Senate. He consented to be a candidate only on the understanding that it would help to "adjust serious differences within the Republican party." Johnson Brigham, librarian of the Iowa State Library, in a tribute to Deemer after his death, described him as "a man of rare capacity and unbounded desire for service. He had a genius for friendship and yet was wholly free from the petty arts of a 'jollier.' Absolutely honest himself, he could brook no dishonesty in others."

[*Proc. Iowa State Bar Asso.* (1917), XXIII, 116–22; *Iowa Jour. of Hist. and Politics,* XV, 319–20; E. H. Stiles, *Recollections and Sketches of Notable Lawyers and Public Men of Early Iowa* (1916), pp. 953–54; *Des Moines Reg.,* Feb. 27, 28, 1917; B. F. Gue, *Hist. of Iowa* (1903), IV, 70 (portrait).]

F. E. H.

DEEMS, CHARLES FORCE (Dec. 4, 1820–Nov. 18, 1893), clergyman, author, son of George W. and Mary (Roberts) Deems, was born in Baltimore and died in New York City. His father, whose ancestral name was De Heems, was of Dutch extraction; his mother was the daughter of Zachary Roberts, a Methodist minister. Both were extremely pious. Their son, a melancholy boy, oppressed by the sinful state of man, was at about thirteen soundly converted—not, however, without striving, for he had made "temperance" lectures repeatedly to that end, and had prayed out of doors before spectators in front of a little altar improvised of stones. His mother died in 1834, and he was sent under the suzerainty of a maiden aunt to the Methodist Dickinson College, to study law. He soon determined to enter the ministry. Following his graduation in 1839, he preached in New York, at some of "the most aristocratic worshiping places of Methodism" (Deems, *Autobiography,* p. 61), but he was soon "located" in Asbury, N. J. Here he renewed his acquaintance with Annie Disosway, whom he had met in New York, and whom, on June 20, 1843, he married. In 1840 he went to North Carolina as an agent for the American Bible Society. From 1842 to 1848 he was professor of humanistic studies in the University of North Carolina, and during 1849 of natural sciences in Randolph-Macon College, Va. During 1850–54 he was president of the Greensboro (N. C.) Woman's College. From 1854 to 1859 he was actively engaged in the ministry, busying himself—after his life-long habit—not only with the routine duties of his profession but with the editing of many theological and semi-theological pronouncements. During 1859–60 he was in charge of a boarding-school at Wilson, N. C. He believed that secession was inexpedient, but once the Civil War began, he conducted himself as a loyal Carolinian—to the point of losing his eldest son in battle on the Southern side. Late in 1865 he changed his residence to New York, at first to edit a paper which he called *The Watchman,* but soon to begin preaching—independently—in an auditorium hired by himself. As late as 1866 he was mentioned in connection with a bishopric in the Southern Methodist Church, but in spite of his own persistent orthodoxy, the ecclesiastical body of which he was head—The Church of the Strangers—had no ties with any recognized religious denomination. His reputation as a preacher and author, reënforced by his intimacy with people of wealth and influence, soon made him one of the conspicuous men of his environment. Among his many books, the ponderous biography, *Jesus* (1872), was perhaps the one to cost him most effort in the writing, but the *Scotch Verdict in re Evolution* (1885) was probably most widely read. It was for him that Cornelius Vanderbilt first violated his resolve against philanthropy by presenting him with a church (1870) and it seems that it was somewhat through his influence that a group of Southerners—with whom he always retained a kind of sentimental identity—procured the million dollars which enabled them (1873) to establish Vanderbilt University. In 1880 he visited Europe and Palestine. On his way home, at a meeting of the Victoria Institute in London, he conceived the idea of organizing an American Institute of Christian Philosophy. This was accomplished in 1881, and the Institute continued in operation till two years after the death of the founder. Then its resources were combined to create the Deems Lectureship of Philosophy in the University of the City of New York. Except for his final year, when he was incapacitated by illness, he spent the last part of his life in the zealous pursuit of his ministry.

[Sources not already mentioned: C. F. Deems, *Autobiog. and Memoir by his Sons* (1897); *Dr. Deems' Sermons* (1885); K. P. Battle, *Hist. of the Univ. of N. C.* (1907); R. Irby, *Hist. of Randolph-Macon Coll.* (1898); C. F. Himes, *Dickinson Coll.* (1879); *Cat. Officers and Students Dickinson Coll.*, 1840; *Appletons' Annual Cyc.* (1893); *N. Y. Times*, Nov. 19, 1893; A. D. H. Smith, *Commodore Vanderbilt* (1927).]

J. D. W.

DEERE, JOHN (Feb. 7, 1804–May 17, 1886), manufacturer, was born at Rutland, Vt., the third son of William Rinold and Sarah (Yates) Deere. His father was a native of England, while his mother was born in Connecticut, the daughter of a British army officer who served through the entire Revolutionary War and subsequently settled in Connecticut. John had the usual country boy's experiences, attending the common schools of his native town and acquiring an ordinary education. At the age of seventeen he started to learn the blacksmith's trade, beginning as an apprentice to Capt. Benjamin Lawrence of Middlebury, Vt. This apprenticeship required four full years but at the end of that time Deere had fully mastered his trade, proving it during the succeeding twelve years by the admirable work which he did in various towns of his native state. In 1837, when thirty-three years old, he went West, taking his tool kit with him. He headed for Illinois and eventually settled at Grand Detour in that state, where he immediately opened a blacksmith shop, sending back for his wife and children in the following year. His skill was quickly recognized and the pioneer farmers about him kept him and his forge busy hammering out lap rings for chains, welding clevises, and laying their plowshares. His contacts with the farmers early revealed the fact that the plow brought from the East was most unsatisfactory for working the prairie soil of the new West, and Deere immediately began experimenting on plow improvements. Within a year three new plows were made by Deere and his partner, Maj. Andrus. These plows had a wrought-iron landside and standard, and for the former wooden mouldboard there were substituted a mouldboard and share of sheet steel cut from an old sawmill saw and bent to shape over a log shaped for the purpose, and with the beam and handles of white oak rails. While the excellent work which these three plows did aroused considerable interest and they were readily sold by Andrus and Deere, the latter continued experimenting, particularly in an effort to determine the curvature of the steel mouldboard that would be most efficacious for scouring not only new land but old and sticky bottom land as well. Ten improved plows were made in 1839, and in 1840 a second anvil was added to the shop and forty plows were produced. The business continued to develop until, in 1846, the annual output had been increased to approximately a thousand plows. About this time Deere became convinced that Grand Detour was poorly situated in regard to transportation and sources of power and raw materials, so he sold out his interest to Andrus and moved to Moline, Ill., where he organized a new company. He had concluded, too, that the greatest obstacle to further plow improvements was the quality of the steel plates then available. He knew the kind of steel he needed, but found that it could be obtained only in England. Accordingly he ordered a quantity of English steel sufficient for fifty plows which he made in his new plant in 1847 and distributed throughout the country in order to test out his theories. The experiment proved entirely successful, whereupon he opened negotiations in Pittsburgh for the manufacture of steel plate and brought about the first manufacture of plow steel in the United States. In J. M. Swank's *History of the Manufacture of Iron in All Ages* (1884, p. 297) is written, "The first slab of cast plow steel ever rolled in the United States was rolled by William Woods, at the steel works of Jones & Quigg, in 1846, and shipped to John Deere of Moline, Ill." There is some question about Swank's date, but the event undoubtedly occurred *circa* 1846 or 1847, and by 1857 Deere's annual output of plows had risen to 10,000. In 1858 he took his son Charles into partnership, and five years later, his son-in-law Stephen H. Velie, and in 1868 the firm was incorporated under the name of Deere & Company, with John Deere president; his son, vice-president and general manager; and Velie, secretary, the business having by that time expanded to include the manufacture of cultivators and other allied products known as "plow goods." Deere continued as active president until his last illness, when his son succeeded him. He was twice married: first, on Jan. 28, 1827, to Damaris Lamb of Granville, Vt., who died at Moline Feb. 17, 1865; and second, in 1867, to Lucinda Lamb, a younger sister of his first wife.

[R. L. Ardrey, *Am. Ag. Implements* (1894); Newton Bateman and Paul Selby, *Hist. Encyc. of Ill. and Hist. of Rock Island County* (2 vols., 1914); U. S. Nat. Museum correspondence with Deere & Co.] C. W. M.

DEERFOOT (1828–Jan. 18, 1897), Indian runner, was born on the Cattaragus Reservation, Erie County, N. Y., and died on the same reservation. A Seneca of the Snipe Clan, his real Indian name was Ha-ga-sa-do-ni, and his English name, Lewis Bennett. The name "Deerfoot" was assumed for professional purposes. Under the old Indian system of training, he early developed extraordinary ability as a distance runner. He competed successfully in many races in western New York and Pennsylvania, but he was most remarkable for his endurance. According to the testimony of several old Indians he could run so long a time that he frequently exhausted horses, and it is tradition that one of them died after having followed him for thirty or forty miles. Attracting the attention of promoters of pedestrianism, Bennett was taken to England in the summer of 1861 and matched, under the name "Deerfoot" against the leading English distance runners. Among these were such famous champions as John White, "the Gateshead Clipper," Edward Mills of East London, and W. Lang of Middlesbrough. By sporting experts the Indian was conceded little chance. But though Deerfoot lost his first race, he soon turned the tables and in a series of stirring contests, defeated practically every notable British distance runner (*The Times,* London, Sept. 24, 1861, p. 10; Oct. 3, 1861, p. 7; Oct. 15, 1861, p. 12 and *passim*). His strongest rival was Mills, with whom in an eight-mile match for £200 at Hackney-Wick, he ran a dead heat (*Ibid.,* Dec. 17, 1861, p. 4). During 1862–63 he continued his English career. His greatest single achievement was the record for twelve miles, made in a race at the Crystal Palace on Apr. 3, 1863, when he ran the distance in one hour, two minutes, and two and a half seconds, though he lost the race by a half yard to Lang who had a handicap of 100 yards (*New York Clipper Almanac,* 1876, p. 53). He made other records of ten miles in fifty-one minutes, twenty-nine seconds; of twelve miles in one hour, five minutes, and six seconds; and of eleven and a half miles in one hour less six seconds. Considering the relatively crude condition of tracks in his day these were unusual performances, but the Senecas have always insisted that Deerfoot while at home, under the strict conditions of Indian training, had far surpassed these exploits. He was a remarkably handsome Indian, standing five feet, eleven and a half inches and weighing 160 pounds. He usually appeared on the track clad in a wolfskin with feathers in his head-band and tinkling bells around his waist (*The Times,* London, Oct. 3, 1861, p. 7). English critics were astonished at the curious loping stride of the Indian runner in contrast with the fine track "style" of their own distance men, but Deerfoot finished most of his races quite fresh. He enjoyed unbounded popularity in the British Isles, being greeted by great crowds at railway stations and receiving ovations on the track. After one of his races the Prince of Wales shook hands with him and gave him a purse. He sometimes capitalized the fact that he was an Indian by curious actions like giving two huge leaps in the air after winning a ten-mile race at Portsmouth and uttering a war-whoop to frighten from the track Irish spectators who had invaded the course before the finish. His career would no doubt have attracted more attention in the United States had it not come at the time of the Civil War.

[Printed sources of information are scanty. Deerfoot's races in England can be followed in the London *Times.* Comment is also given in the contemporary New York sporting paper, *Wilkes' Spirit of the Times.* The recollection of Deerfoot among the Seneca Indians has been furnished the writer by Arthur C. Parker, Director of the Rochester Municipal Museum, himself a Seneca.] E. P. T.

DEERING, NATHANIEL (June 25, 1791–Mar. 25, 1881), author, editor, and dramatist, was the son of James Deering (1766–1850), and the grandson of Nathaniel Deering (1737–1795), an influential merchant, shipbuilder, landowner, and man of affairs during the formative days of Portland, Me., where the younger Nathaniel was born. He was a descendant in the eighth generation from George Deering, who emigrated from England to Maine in the early part of the seventeenth century. His mother was Almira, daughter of Enoch Ilsley, at one time a selectman and town treasurer of Portland. After studying first at a private school in Portland, and following a course at Phillips Academy in Exeter, N. H., he went to Harvard College, from which he was graduated in 1810, the fourteenth in a class of sixty-three. Upon his graduation he entered a counting-house in Portland with the intention of becoming a merchant, but after a short experience in business, and in compliance with the wish of his father, he studied law and was admitted to the bar in 1815. For a time he practised his profession in Skowhegan. Returning to Portland, where his beginnings in authorship and journalism were made as a member of a literary club and as editor of a manuscript paper, he gradually turned his professional interests toward books and writing, eventually becoming editor of the *Independent Statesman,* a political paper which supported the candidacy of Henry Clay for the presidency. At one time he was in popular demand as a Fourth of July orator. During the greater part of his life he was an assiduous contributor of prose and verse, usually unsigned, to newspapers and other publications in Portland and elsewhere. Attracting the attention of William Cullen Bryant, he was offered a position on the staff of the New York *Evening Post,* but declined it. He wrote several plays, among them, *Carabasset, or the Last of the Norridgewocks,* a tragedy in five acts dealing with the incidents of the massacre of the Rasle and the Norridgewock Indians by the British in 1720; *The Clairvoyant,* a comedy which was acted in Boston and Portland; and *Bozzaris,* another tragedy, which was published in 1851. He had a little musical talent; wrote ballads and political songs, and composed some church music. In October 1824 he married Anna Margaret Holwell, a daughter of Maj. John Z. Holwell of the British Army. They had nine children, four sons and five daughters. Deering's last years were spent in retirement on the family estate of two hundred acres on the outskirts of Portland. He was the last survivor of a large family of brothers and sisters, the youngest of the latter being the wife of William Pitt Fessenden [*q.v.*].

[H. C. Williams, *Biog. Encyc. of Me.* (1885); *Biog. Rev. Cumberland County, Me.* (1896); brief obituary in *Daily Eastern Argus* (Portland, Me.), Mar. 26, 1881.]

E. F. E.

DEERING, WILLIAM (Apr. 25, 1826–Dec. 9, 1913), manufacturer, the son of James and Eliza (Moore) Deering, both of Puritan descent, was born in South Paris, Me., where his father was engaged in woolen cloth manufacture. He was educated in the public schools and later attended Readfield Seminary, from which he graduated in 1844. He then began the study of medicine with Dr. Barrows of Fryeburg, Me., but his father persuaded him to enter his manufacturing company in which for several years he acted as manager. On Oct. 31, 1849, he was married to Abby Reed Barbour, daughter of Charles and Joanna (Cobb) Barbour. During the next few years he was interested in western farming lands, but, on the death of his wife in 1856, he returned to South Paris, where he opened a dry-goods store. He was married to Clara Hamilton, on Dec. 15, 1856. After a number of years he organized a wholesale commission dry-goods house under the firm name of Deering, Milliken & Company in 1865 with headquarters at Portland, Me., and offices in New York City. He continued as its directing head for five years acquiring in the interval the executive ability and foresight which enabled him subsequently to take a leading part in the development of America's agricultural machinery business. In the meantime one of his old Maine friends, a Methodist preacher named Elijah H. Gammon, who had been for many years in Illinois, became interested in the manufacture of agricultural machinery, particularly in the hand-binding harvester of the brothers Charles W. and William W. Marsh. Gammon purchased the rights to manufacture the Marsh harvester and aroused Deering's interest in the project to such an extent that he gave up his wholesale business and went to Plano, Ill., to join Gammon as a partner. Deering invested $40,000 in the company, and, owing to his persistent and tireless management, the harvester trade was pushed out into channels that it had hitherto been unable to reach. A year later the manufacture of the Gordon wire binder was undertaken much against the advice of his partner, but Deering seemed to see more clearly than any one else the demand for a harvesting machine with automatic binding. Again, in 1879, when he became sole owner of the business, Deering made another bold move by beginning the manufacture of a twine binder after the invention of John F. Appleby, and with the jeers of his competitors ringing in his ears he built and moved to a new and larger establishment at Chicago. The venture almost failed, because of the difficulty of finding a twine adapted for use on the binder. Deering at last persuaded Edwin H. Fitler, a large Philadelphia rope manufacturer, to undertake experiments for him, and Fitler eventually produced a single strand manila twine that made the binder successful. From 1880 the business progressed steadily. Year after year the shops were enlarged and new departments added until it became the largest agricultural-implement factory in the world, employing in the neighborhood of 9,000 operatives. Deering had the business incorporated in 1883 under the name William Deering & Company, having taken into the organization in 1880 his two sons, Charles W. and James E., and, subsequently, his son-in-law, Richard F. Howe. Later the name was changed to the Deering Manfacturing Company. In 1901 Deering retired and in 1902 the corporation was merged with the International Harvester Company of Chicago.

Although his knowledge of public affairs was recognized, Deering's only public service was in the councils of Governors Chamberlain and Perham of Maine in 1870–73. He was a director of the Metropolitan National Bank of Chicago and president of the board of trustees of Northwestern University at the time of his death. His gifts to educational and charitable institutions were many, especially to Northwestern University, the Garrett Biblical Institute, and Wesley Hospital, all of Chicago. He also built and endowed the Deering School at Lake Bluff, near Chicago, for the accommodation of the orphanage there. He died at his winter home at Cocoanut Grove, Fla., survived by his wife and two sons.

[*Wm. Deering* (Chicago, privately printed, 1914); *Wm. Deering* (n.d.); E. L. Barker, *Creeds of Great Business Men* (1913); Robt. L. Ardrey, *Am. Agric. Implements* (1894); *Chicago Evening Post, Chicago American*, and the *Portland Evening Express and Daily Advertiser*, all Dec. 10, 1913; *Chicago Daily Tribune, Daily Inter Ocean* (Chicago), and *Farm Implement News* (Chicago), all Dec. 11, 1913; *Implement Age* (Springfield, Ohio), Dec. 20, 1913; *Custer County Chief* (Broken Bow, Nebr.), Dec. 26, 1913.] C. W. M.

DE FONTAINE, FELIX GREGORY (1834–Dec. 11, 1896), journalist, author, was born in Boston, Mass., and died in Columbia, S. C. His father, Louis Antoine De Fontaine, a French nobleman attached to the court of Charles X, accompanied that monarch into exile in Edinburgh. In the latter part of 1830 he came to America, and about two years later he was married to a woman whose surname was Allen, said to have been of the family of Ethan Allen. Their son Felix was educated by private tutors. He was in Washington in 1859, acting as reporter in the notorious trial of a congressman for shooting a district attorney. About 1860, he married Georgia Vigneron Moore, daughter of the Rev. George W. Moore of Charleston, S. C. At about this time he founded in Columbia the *Daily South Carolinian*. In February 1861, the *New York Herald* published his discussion of anti-slavery agitation and of conditions then obtaining in the South. These articles, completely Southern in view-point, soon appeared in a booklet, *A History of American Abolitionism together with a History of the Southern Confederacy* (1861). At the bombardment of Fort Sumter, his friendship with Gen. Beauregard resulted in his being able to send out to the *Herald* the first account of that event to appear in the Northern press. In May 1861, as a military correspondent with the rank of major, he went to the front with the first South Carolina regiment. He continued in this capacity throughout the war, signing all that he wrote, "Personne." In 1864, he published under this name his *Marginalia*, a reprint of newspaper clippings selected from various sources, with the one fervent purpose of exalting the South and debasing the North. His press was burned in the fire that occurred when Sherman entered Columbia. In November 1867 he was secretary of a convention in Columbia, held to consider the abuses of carpet-bag rule. Soon afterward he went to live in New York. For three years he was managing editor of the *Telegram*, and for the remainder of his active life he was the financial editor and later the dramatic and art editor of the *Herald*. He did a considerable amount of writing aside from his routine work for his paper. "Shoulder to Shoulder, Reminiscences of Confederate Camps and Fields" appeared in the (Charleston) *XIX Century*, June 1869–January 1870. In 1873 he published his ponderous *Cyclopedia of the Best Thoughts of Charles Dickens*. A second edition, called *The Fireside Dickens*, appeared in 1883. In 1886 he published *De Fontaine's Condensed Long-Hand and Rapid-Writer's Companion*. At the time of his death, he was preparing from documents which fell into his hands early in 1865 a book on the missing records of the Confederate cabinet.

[F. G. De Fontaine, *Trial of the Hon. Daniel E. Sickles* (1859); W. H. De Fontaine, letter to the writer, Jan. 30, 1928; Y. Snowden, *Hist. of S. C.* (1920), II, 884; *Appletons' Annual Cyc.*, 1896; Charleston *News and Courier*, Dec. 12, 1896.] J. D. W.

DE FOREST, DAVID CURTIS (Jan. 10, 1774–Feb. 22, 1825), merchant and Argentine consul, was born at Huntington, Conn., the eldest son of Benjamin and Mehitable (Curtis) De Forest. His father, a prosperous farmer, came of a Walloon Protestant family, whose founder in this country, Isaac, emigrated from Amsterdam to New York in 1636. David was a robust and adventurous boy who ran away from home and followed the sea until 1795, when he invested his small patrimony in business at Bridgeport. In the following year his store was robbed and the firm failed. From March 1799 to June 1800 he was a lieutenant in the army which the United States raised when war with France impended. He then returned to the sea as officer on a vessel which he quitted on the coast of Patagonia late in 1801. Thence he went to Brazil, and by land back to the La Plata River, studying carefully commercial possibilities and languages. Settling at Buenos Aires, he established there the first permanent American commercial house. Despite British attacks and generally unsettled political conditions, his business so prospered that by 1809 he was wealthy. A change of viceroys in that year drove him into an exile which he improved by returning to Huntington and marrying on Oct. 6, 1811, Julia Wooster, a blonde beauty less than sixteen years of age. Permitted in 1812 to return to Buenos Aires, he had hardly reopened his establishment when the war with England forced him to close it again. By the autumn of 1814 he was once more extremely active in commerce. Dispensing open-handed hospitality, he played the part of merchant prince and through a friend who was secretary of the treasury he obtained much government business. When Buenos Aires revolted against Spain in 1815, he received letters of marque for privateers from the revolutionary authorities. These he gave to American shipowners in return for a commission on prizes and cleared over one hundred thousand dollars. In April 1817 he sent his family home and a year later followed them, after presenting his large ranch to the new republic. With him he brought a fortune and a commission as consul general to the United States from the nascent Argentine Republic. Building a large mansion at New Haven, he lived on a generous scale and devoted his time to the interests of his adopted country. On May 7, 1818, he interviewed Secretary of State John Quincy Adams, asking for an exequatur as consul general. This was refused, as it implied official recognition of Argentine independence at a time when Adams was negotiating with Spain for the cession of Florida. Undismayed by the secretary's frigid attitude, De Forest continued to importune both Adams and President Monroe for recognition, presenting "cunning and deceptive" (Adams, *Memoirs,* IV, 223) notes which provided Henry Clay with ammunition against the administration when referred to Congress in January 1819. His activities in Washington earned him a reputation as "one of the most troublesome of the South American agents" (Adams, *Ibid.,* IV, 472), while his lavish annual celebration in New Haven of the Argentine Independence Day kept his mission well advertised. Though the recognition of the new South American nations was decided in March 1822, he was refused an exequatur a month later on the ground that a new commission was necessary, while his claim to be received as diplomatic representative was denied because he was an American citizen. But his task was over, and he resigned his official position. In 1823 he endowed at Yale College the De Forest scholarships and a prize in English. During the following year he was much annoyed by suits for damages arising out of the illegal activities of privateers which had operated under his guarantee, but he died before the cases were decided. A man of swarthy complexion, powerful physique, and haughty manner, his generosity was almost unlimited, while in business and diplomacy he was enterprising to the point of temerity.

[J. W. De Forest, *The De Forests of Avesnes* (1900); C. F. Adams, ed., *Memoirs of John Quincy Adams* (1875), vols. IV and V; Henry Hill, *Recollections of an Octogenarian* (1884); *Am. State Papers, Foreign Relations,* IV, 412–18.] W. L. W—t., Jr.

DE FOREST, ERASTUS LYMAN (June 27, 1834–June 6, 1888), mathematician, was descended from an old Walloon family, and was the only son of Dr. John and Lucy Starr (Lyman) De Forest, and the last of the male line of Benjamin De Forest of Watertown, Conn. Entering Yale at the age of sixteen, he was graduated in 1854 with the degree of B.A. He then pursued his scholastic work in the engineering department of the Sheffield Scientific School (Yale), where he was graduated two years later with the degree of Ph.B. In 1867 he received the degree of M.A. Although he inherited sufficient means from his grandfather to provide for his modest needs, he determined to show his independence of such assistance. The gold fever of 1849 had not yet subsided when he left Sheffield, and a year later he went to California where for a time he worked in the mines. Inspired no doubt by the love of travel, he next went to Australia and became a tutor in the University of Melbourne. After this venture he traveled in the East and in Europe, finally returning to America to the enjoyment of a more quiet life, devoting the rest of his years to mathematical research in a field at that time but little cultivated in the United States. In 1886 he gave $4,000 to Yale to increase the fund established by his father in 1855—still the source of the De Forest Mathematical Prizes. Just before his death (1888) he gave $10,000 toward the endowment of a chair of mathematics in that university. He was never married.

His scientific work related chiefly to the theory of probability and errors and has come to be looked upon in late years as showing unusual ability. His first paper appeared in the *American Journal of Science* (XLI, 371–79) in 1866, and from that time until his death he published on an average approximately a paper a year, all in the same general field. Most of these papers appeared in the journal mentioned, in *The Analyst,* or in the Smithsonian *Reports.* Being of a technical nature, they failed to attract popular attention and, indeed, were hardly appreciated during his lifetime by scientists in his particular line of interest. Hugh H. Wolfenden, however, called the attention of a mathematical congress at Toronto, in 1924, to the notable work done by De Forest. In the paper there presented it was shown that his contribution to the development of formulas for graduation by linear compounding (a subject of great importance in actuarial work), "in a most invaluable series of papers which appeared in the Smithsonian *Reports* of 1871 and 1873, a pamphlet, *Interpolation and Adjustment of Series* (1876), and *The Analyst* (Des Moines), 1877–80," was one of the most important of its kind ever made by an American scholar.

[For a complete list of De Forest's papers and for a study of his scientific work, see the article by Hugh H. Wolfenden in the *Trans. Actuarial Soc. of America,* May 1925, XXVI, 81–121. There is a brief biographical sketch on p. 121 of the same article, together with a bibliography relating to the De Forest family.] D. E. S.

DE FOREST, JOHN KINNE HYDE (June 25, 1844–May 8, 1911), missionary to Japan, was the son of the Rev. William Albert and Martha (Sackett) Hyde, being the fifth of their eight children. He was born at Westbrook, Conn. When he was ten years of age, his father moved to a parish in Greenwich, Conn. John's earliest education was obtained in the public schools of Westbrook and Greenwich. He afterward spent a year and a half in Phillips Academy, Andover, Mass., and graduated in 1862, ranking fifth in a class of forty-five. He served in the Civil War for nine months during 1862–63 in Company B, 28th Connecticut Volunteers, and entered Yale College in the fall of 1863. For want of funds he had to withdraw shortly and take a position as teacher in a boys' school at Irvington-on-Hudson, N. Y. After a few months at Irvington he learned that the income from a De Forest Fund at Yale would be available to him on condition that he assume the name of De Forest. With this aid and other sums loaned by friends, he spent the years 1864–68 in Yale, graduating with honors in 1868. The next three years were spent in Yale Divinity School from which he received the degree of B.D., in 1871. In the same year he was ordained to the ministry, assumed the pastorate of the Congregational church in Mt. Carmel, Conn., and married, on June 5, 1871, Sarah C. Conklin of New Haven. The death of his wife and their baby the following spring was so great a shock to him that he was given leave from his parish for several months for recovery. On Sept. 23, 1874, he married Sarah Elizabeth Starr of Guilford, Conn., and almost immediately sailed with her from San Francisco to Yokohama for service in Japan under the American Board. The edicts against Christianity had been removed the previous year by the Japanese Emperor. After a brief stay in Yokohama, the De Forests went on to Kobe, and thence to Osaka, spending the winter with Dr. and Mrs. M. L. Gordon of that station. On the arrival of their possessions, they went to a home of their own. For twelve years De Forest was officially stationed at Osaka. He devoted himself seriously to a mastery of the spoken Japanese and in due time gave his earnest attention to the written language, attaining ultimately a remarkable command of Japanese. He preached frequently and gave much time to translation. In September 1886 with Mrs. De Forest and their four children he removed to Sendai, where, in the following March a church—one of the first Kumi-ai or independent churches—was organized. In June 1887 he opened there the Tokwa School for boys. After 1889 the Sendai station suffered much opposition from Japanese nationalists, and the Tokwa School was closed in 1892. The church continued and from 1897 had its own Japanese pastor. De Forest was from the first among those who advocated Japanese responsibility and independence in Christian affairs in Japan, and he proved an acceptable co-worker toward these ends. He made five trips to America. On his return to Japan from his furlough in 1895 he left his children in America. He traveled in Manchuria in 1905, spent the summer of 1909 in China, and in 1910 made a tour of Korea on behalf of Japanese Christians there. On his return from Korea he fell ill from heart disease to which, after five months, pneumonia was added. He was taken to St. Luke's Hospital in Tokyo, and died there. He was buried in Sendai, where the De Forest Memorial Church now stands. In November 1908, the Emperor of Japan had conferred upon him the Fourth Order of the Rising Sun in recognition of his work among Japanese troops in the Russo-Japanese War, and for his part in famine relief in the Sendai area in 1905–06. De Forest wrote often for the *Missionary Herald,* the *Religious Herald,* the *Congregationalist,* and the Japanese press, and for many years was a regular correspondent of the *Independent.* He was the author of "The Ethics of Confucius as Seen in Japan" (*Andover Review,* May 1893, reprinted in Tokyo); *Mixed Residence* (Yokohama, 1898); *Sunrise in the Sunrise Kingdom* (1904, revised in 1908); *Sketch of the Japan Mission of the American Board, 1869–1904* (1904); and the article on Shintoism in *Religions of Mission Fields* (1905).

[*Annual Reports, Am. Board of Commissioners for Foreign Missions,* 1875–1911; *Missionary Herald,* 1875–

1911; C. B. De Forest, *The Evolution of a Missionary: A Biog. of John Hyde De Forest* (1914); S. L. Gulick, *John Hyde De Forest* (1914); *Outlook*, May 27, 1911; *Congregationalist*, May 20, 1911; *Japan Evangelist*, June 1911; H. P. Wright, *Hist. of the Class of 1868, Yale Coll., 1864–1914* (1914); *Obit. Record Grads. Yale Univ.* (1911).]

J. C. A.

DE FOREST, JOHN WILLIAM (May 31, 1826–July 17, 1906), author, was born in Humphreysville, now Seymour, Conn., the son of John Hancock De Forest, a successful merchant and cotton manufacturer, and Dotha Woodward, daughter of Elijah Woodward of Watertown, Conn. The De Forests came from Avesnes in French Hainaut, the first to settle in this country being Isaac, son of Jesse, who sailed for New Netherland in the fall of 1636, on a ship owned jointly by the De Forest and Van Rensselaer families. Here he became a great burgher, a schepen, and a member of the Nine Men. His son, David, settled in Stratford, Conn. The parents of John expected to send him to Yale, but the death of his father when the boy was thirteen years old, and a serious illness, deprived him of a college education, although in 1859 Amherst College awarded him an honorary A.M. He had a decided taste for study and writing, however, and as early as 1851, after a careful investigation of available sources, he published under the patronage of the Connecticut Historical Society a *History of the Indians of Connecticut*. He spent several years abroad, chiefly in Syria, where at Beirut his brother, Rev. Dr. Henry A. De Forest, conducted a girls' school, and in Florence and Paris. Returning to this country, he married in New Haven, Conn., June 5, 1856, Harriet Silliman Shepard, daughter of Charles Upham Shepard [*q.v.*], considered in her day an exceptional classical scholar, and the center of a brilliant group of university people. The literary fruits of his life abroad were *Oriental Acquaintance* (1856), and *European Acquaintance* (1858), pleasantly written books descriptive of persons and scenes encountered in his travels. In *Witching Times* (1856), and *Seacliff* (1859) he also made a successful beginning as a novelist. He was again in Europe when the Civil War broke out, but hastening back he recruited a company in New Haven which was mustered into the service as Company I, 12th Connecticut Volunteers, of which he became captain. He served under Generals Weitzel and Banks in the Southwestern states, and under Gen. Sheridan in the Shenandoah Valley. He also acted as inspector general of the 1st Division of the XIX Corps, and as aide on the staff of that corps. He was brevetted major, Mar. 13, 1865. After the war he was commissioned as captain in the Veteran Reserve Corps, detailed as captain of Company I, 14th Regiment, and assigned to duty as acting assistant adjutant-general. For a period he was in command of a district of the Freedman's Bureau, with headquarters at Greenville, S. C. He was mustered out of the service Jan. 1, 1868.

The rest of his life was spent for the most part in New Haven. His military service had not altogether interrupted his literary work, for he had written for *Harper's Monthly* some vivid descriptions of battle scenes, and in 1867 he published a novel dealing with the war and its results, *Miss Ravenel's Conversion from Secession to Loyalty*. Another novel, *Kate Beaumont*, a notable portrayal of certain aspects of Southern life, appeared in 1872. Other short stories and novels followed, among the latter: *The Wetherel Affair* (1873), *Honest John Vane* (1875), *Justine's Lovers* (1875), *Playing the Mischief* (1876), *Irene the Missionary* (1879), *The Bloody Chasm or Oddest of Courtships* (1881), *A Lover's Revolt* (1898). Critics agree that these novels with their vigorous realism and skilful character portrayal deserve more appreciation than they have received. Their excellences and limitations have been pointed out by W. D. Howells (*Harper's Bazar*, XXXV, 538–44, October 1901), who attributes their failure to achieve a longer popularity to a "sort of disdainful honesty to the effects of art," and to "a certain scornful bluntness in dealing with the disguises in which women's natures reveal themselves," because of which they failed to gain feminine approval. In his later years De Forest published two volumes of verse, *The Downing Legends* (1901) and *Poems: Medley and Palestina* (1902). He was also the author of *The De Forests of Avesnes (and of New Netherland) a Huguenot Thread in American Colonial History* (1900).

[Main facts of career furnished by a grandson, L. Effingham de Forest. See *Who's Who in America*, 1906–07; *New Haven Evening Register*, July 18, 1906.]

H. E. S.

DE GRAFFENRIED, CHRISTOPHER [See GRAFFENRIED, CHRISTOPHER, BARON DE, 1661–1743.]

DE HAAS, JOHN PHILIP (*c.* 1735–June 3, 1786), Revolutionary soldier, was born in Holland, the son of John Nicholas De Haas, a descendant of Baron Charles De Haas of Brandenburg, Prussia, and later of Strasbourg, Alsace, who is said to have received the family arms—those of the city of Florence—from Emperor Rudolph as a reward for services in the conquest of Italy. The parents of John Philip emigrated to America about 1737 and settled in

Lancaster County, Pa. Practically nothing is known of his early life prior to his entry into the military service other than that he had married Eleanor Bingham. He was commissioned ensign of the Provincial Battalion of Pennsylvania in December 1757, and was stationed at Fort Augusta on the Susquehanna River. In 1758 he participated in the Forbes expedition against the French at Fort Duquesne, and from then on to the close of the war he served continuously, his last campaign being with Col. Henry Bouquet [*q.v.*] on the western frontier. From 1765 until 1779 he was a local magistrate in Lancaster County and was engaged in the iron industry of that place. On the outbreak of the Revolution, without waiting for a commission, he raised a company of militia on his own responsibility. The Continental Congress appointed him colonel of the 1st Pennsylvania Battalion on Jan. 22, 1776 (*Journals of the Continental Congress,* vol. IV, 1906, p. 78). By that time his regiment was already on its way to join Gen. Benedict Arnold on his ill-fated Canadian expedition. He joined his regiment and rendered valuable service, saving Arnold from possible capture by the British commander Forster at Lachine, by arriving with four companies and forcing Forster to retire to Fort Allen, at the head of Montreal Island. During June 1776 Arnold kept De Haas's detachment "dancing between Sorel and Montreal," and soon thereafter the invading army, defeated and thinned by desertion, fell back on Fort Ticonderoga. The troops of the 1st Pennsylvania Battalion reached their homes in December, and afterward formed the nucleus for the 2nd Pennsylvania Regiment, Continental Line. De Haas was commissioned brigadier-general of the Continental Line, Feb. 21, 1777, but at the close of that year he suddenly resigned his commission and returned to Lancaster County. His resignation has never been fully explained. He seems to have been a strict disciplinarian and hence made enemies in the service; but Washington believed him to be a capable officer and regretted his loss. In 1778 De Haas offered his services to the board of war to lead an expedition against the Indians who had raided the Wyoming Valley. He collected some local militia and marched to the scene, but Gen. Arnold sent Col. Hartley with a detachment of regular troops and orders to take command. The next year De Haas moved to Philadelphia where he remained until his death.

[Abram Hess, "The Life and Services of Gen. John Philip de Haas," in *Lebanon Hist. Soc. Papers,* vol. VII, no. 2 (1916); Washington Papers (Lib. of Cong.), Correspondence with the Military, BII, pt. 2, 257; *Pa. Archives,* ser. 1 and 2, *passim*; *Pa. Mag. Hist. and Biog.,* vols. II (1878) and V (1881).] T.D.M.

DE HAVEN, EDWIN JESSE (May 7, 1816–May 1, 1865), naval officer, was the son of William and Maria (McKeever) De Haven of Philadelphia. He was a descendant of Evert in den Hofen who in 1690 emigrated to Philadelphia (now Montgomery) County, Pa., from Mülheim on the Ruhr, Germany (H. D. H. Ross, *History of the De Haven Family,* 1st ed., 1894, App.). Entering the navy on Oct. 2, 1829, as a midshipman, he made his first cruise on the *Natchez* in the West Indies. In 1832–35 he was with the Brazil Squadron, first on the *Lexington* and later on the *Natchez,* being advanced in the latter year to the grade of passed midshipman. In 1837 he went to sea on the *Falmouth* and saw service in the Pacific. Two years later at Callao he joined the *Vincennes,* the flagship of the Wilkes exploring expedition, receiving the rating of acting master, and during the next three years visited the Antarctic continent, many of the islands of the Pacific, and the west coast of North America. When the sloop *Peacock,* one of the vessels of this expedition, was wrecked at the mouth of the Columbia River, De Haven saved the lives of a boat's crew and received the thanks of the Navy Department for his bravery. He was commissioned lieutenant on Sept. 21, 1841, taking rank from Sept. 8. After serving on several vessels of the Home Squadron, in 1847–48 he was attached to the steamer *Mississippi* and took part in the Mexican War. He next was employed at the Naval Observatory in Washington under Lieut. Matthew F. Maury [*q.v.*], the noted meteorologist.

Early in 1850 the federal government, in coöperation with Henry Grinnell, a wealthy New York merchant, decided to send an expedition in search of Sir John Franklin and his companions who disappeared in the Arctic region in 1845 while on a voyage of discovery. Having had experience in polar exploration and having acquired a reputation as a scientific officer, De Haven was chosen to command the expedition. Most of the month of April 1850 he spent in New York preparing his fleet for sea. It consisted of two small brigs, the *Advance* and the *Rescue,* with a complement of thirty-three officers and seamen. According to his instructions, the chief object of the expedition was to search for Franklin and his companions and relieve them if found, and the secondary object was to acquire scientific information. On May 22 he sailed from New York and two months later to the westward of Greenland began his search for the missing Englishmen. In September the vessels were caught and frozen in the ice and for nine months were confined in this perilous situation, drifting to and fro more than a thousand miles. De Haven discovered and named Grinnell Land, but failed to find Franklin. He arrived at New York on Sept. 30, 1851.

In 1853–57 he was employed with the Coast Survey in making deep-sea soundings off the Southern coast and in other work of that service. He never went to sea after 1857, as his eyesight was affected and his health impaired by his Arctic experiences. In 1862 he was placed on the retired list, the first in the grade of lieutenant. He is buried in Old Christ Church graveyard, Philadelphia. On May 7, 1844, he was married to Mary Norris Da Costa.

[Record of Officers, Bureau of Navigation, 1830–66; Letters to Officers Ships of War, vol. XLIV, and Officers' Letters, Apr. and May 1850, and Oct. 1851, Navy Dept.; U. S. Navy Registers, 1830–66; *Report of Sec. of Navy*, 1850 and 1851; E. K. Kane, *The U. S. Grinnell Expedition* (1854); A. Gleaves, "The De Haven Arctic Expedition" (*U. S. Naval Inst. Proc.*, LIV, 1928, 579–91); Letters of Mrs. Kate DaC. (De Haven) Rolfe to the writer, Jan. 1929; note of death in *Pub. Ledger* (Phila.), May 3, 1865.] C. O. P.

DEINDÖRFER, JOHANNES (July 28, 1828–May 14, 1907), Lutheran clergyman, was born in Bavaria at Ross-stall near Nürnberg, the son of Georg Heinrich and Anna Eva (Leupold) Deindörfer. His father was a farmer and basket maker. In pursuance of his desire to become a minister Deindörfer studied theology 1847–51 in Nürnberg and Neuendettelsau under Friedrich Bauer and Wilhelm Löhe. In those years Löhe was giving much of his time to preparing missionaries for work among the German Lutherans in the western United States and recently had founded three Lutheran colonies—Frankenmuth, Frankentrost, Frankenlust—in Saginaw County, Mich. At Löhe's suggestion Deindörfer accepted the pastorship of a fourth colony, Frankenhilf, which was to be comprised chiefly of young couples who were unable to obtain legal permission to marry in Bavaria because of their poverty. He was ordained at Hamburg Sept. 14, 1851, by the Rev. J. Meinel and preached his first sermon at Frankenhilf on the second Sunday in Advent. On Oct. 18, 1852, he married Katharina Elisabeth Weege, by whom he had nine children. The other German Lutheran pastors in the country round about were members of the Missouri Synod, with the exception of his friend Georg Martin Grossmann [*q.v.*]; and when the rupture over the doctrine of the ministry came between Löhe and the Synod, Grossmann and Deindörfer, for failing to agree with the Missourians, found themselves in a serious position. It was soon clear that they must either move further west to territory unoccupied by the Missouri Synod or else prepare to endure ceaseless petty persecution. In July and August 1853, therefore, Deindörfer and the one man of property among his parishioners, Gottlob Amman, visited northeastern Iowa on a tour of inspection, and that autumn they and Grossmann with their families settled there. Grossmann took up his work in Dubuque, while Deindörfer made his headquarters in Clayton County at a spot that he piously named St. Sebald, in honor of the saint who first brought the evangel to the vicinity of Nürnberg. The hardships of pioneer life told heavily on Deindörfer: during the first winter he and his family suffered severely from cold and were compelled to take refuge at last in Amman's log cabin; a little later Deindörfer almost succumbed to typhoid fever. On Aug. 24, 1854, in Deindörfer's cabin at St. Sebald, he, Grossmann, Conrad Sigmund Fritschel [*q.v.*], and Michael Schüller organized the German Lutheran Synod of Iowa. Deindörfer was vice-president of the Synod 1854–93, meanwhile serving as pastor at St. Sebald 1853–56; Madison, Wis., 1856–60; West Union and Waucoma, Iowa, 1860–65; Toledo, Ohio, 1865–70; Defiance, Ohio, 1870–89; and Ripon, Wis., 1889–93. For sixteen years he was president of the Eastern District. He was president of the Synod from 1893 to 1904 and editor of its *Kirchenblatt*, with a few interruptions, from 1878 to 1904. It was characteristic of him that when he accepted the presidency he stipulated that his salary should be but $800 a year, since he had found that he could live sufficiently on that sum. He was a good student and had a distinct literary gift. He published *Denkschriften* commemorating the tenth, twenty-fifth, and fiftieth anniversaries of the founding of the Synod and in 1897 an excellent *Geschichte der Evangel.-Luth. Synode von Iowa*. His simplicity, kindliness, and strength of character made him generally beloved. He died at Waverly, Iowa.

[G. J. Fritschel, ed., *Quellen und Dokumente zur Geschichte und Lehrstellung der ev.-luth. Synode von Iowa* (Chicago, n.d.); obituary notice in *Dubuque Times-Jour.*, May 15, 1907; additional information, derived from Deindörfer's MS. autobiography and other papers, through the courtesy of Prof. Geo. J. Fritschel of Wartburg Theological Seminary.] G. H. G.

DEITZLER, GEORGE WASHINGTON (Nov. 30, 1826–Apr. 10, 1884), anti-slavery leader in Kansas, the son of Jacob and Maria Deitzler, was born at Pine Grove, Pa. There he grew to manhood with only a common-school education—"very common" he once said. While still a young man he emigrated to the new West. After a short residence in Illinois and in California he went in March 1855 to Lawrence, Kan., where he engaged in farming and real-estate dealing. He soon took an active part in politics, so that when the plan to organize a free-state government, in opposition to the pro-slavery territorial government, was set on foot he was sent to Boston to see Amos Lawrence and other friends of the cause. He at once received an order for one hundred Sharps rifles which were very soon on their way to Kansas in boxes marked "books." Other shipments of "books" followed. Military companies armed with these new weapons were formed among the free-state men. In the so-called Wakarusa War in November 1855, Deitzler was aide-de-camp to the commander of the free-state forces and during part of the time was in full command. A few months later, when the territorial judiciary began to function, Chief Justice Lecompte instructed a grand jury sitting at Lecompton that levying war on the authorities of the territory was treason against the federal government. Deitzler and several other free-state leaders were promptly indicted on a charge of treason. They were immediately arrested and kept in a prison tent at Lecompton for about four months. In September 1856 they were freed on bail. Later their cases were nolle-prossed.

Deitzler's activities in behalf of the free-state cause were incessant. He served on committees, attended meetings and conventions, of which there were many, counseled with other leaders, and wrote for the press. He was elected a member of the free-state territorial legislature of 1857–58 and was chosen speaker of the House of Representatives. He was also a member of the Kansas Senate under the Topeka constitution. In 1860 he became mayor of Lawrence and in 1866 treasurer of the University of Kansas. When the Civil War began he was active in organizing the first regiment of Kansas Volunteer Infantry and was appointed its colonel. In August 1861 his regiment took a prominent part in the battle of Wilson's Creek where he was severely wounded. Promoted to the rank of brigadier-general in November 1862, he served under Grant until October 1863 and then resigned on account of impaired health caused by his former wound. During all of these years he had remained a bachelor. His home was at the Eldridge House in Lawrence. In September 1864 he was married to Anna McNeil of Lexington, Mo. A month later Gen. Price led an invading Confederate army into Missouri and eastern Kansas. The entire militia of the latter state were called out—about 20,000 in number—and Deitzler was placed in chief command with the rank of major-general. He directed the movements against the Confederates in the successful campaign that followed. Various enterprises engaged his attention after the return of peace. He promoted the Emporia Town Company and was a director in the new Leavenworth, Lawrence & Fort Gibson Railroad Company. In 1872 he removed with his family to California. While in southern Arizona in the spring of 1884 he was thrown from a buggy and killed.

[The main facts of Deitzler's career are presented in his brief autobiography, now in the archives of the Kan. State Hist. Soc. Secondary sources are: D. W. Wilder, *Annals of Kan.* (1875); G. T. Andreas, *Hist. of the State of Kan.* (1883); L. W. Spring, *Kansas* (1885); F. W. Blackmar, *Life of Chas. Robinson* (1902); *Trans. Kan. Hist. Soc.*, IV (1886–88); V (1891–96); VI (1897–1900); VIII (1903–04); X (1907–08); XIII (1913–14). The date of his death is sometimes given as Apr. 11, although the Leavenworth *Evening Standard*, Apr. 11, 1884, states that he died Apr. 10.] T. L. H.

DE KAY, GEORGE COLMAN (Mar. 5, 1802–Jan. 31, 1849), sea fighter in the service of the Argentine Republic, was born in or near New York City, the second son of George and Catherine (Colman) De Kay, and younger brother of James E. De Kay [*q.v.*]. During George's infancy his father died. The lad was placed for a time in a private school in Connecticut, but eluded his guardian and shipped before the mast on a merchantman. At twenty he was captain of a ship and at home in many foreign ports. Arriving at Buenos Aires in 1826, while Brazil was blockading the port as an incident to the dispute with the Argentine Republic over the province that later became the Republic of Uruguay, he offered his services to the Argentine navy, and was intrusted by Admiral Brown with the command of the *Brandzen*, a brig of eight guns with a motley crew of Americans, Irish, Scotch, and a few South Americans. Having run the blockade of the Rio de la Plata, he engaged two Brazilian men-of-war and captured one of them. In the following summer (1827) he took three Brazilian ships and fought the *Cacique* (18 guns) off Pernambuco, boarding her and accepting surrender from Capt. Manson, in spite of the fact that his crew was outnumbered three to one by that of the *Cacique*. His success was attributed to his skill in maneuvering his ship rather than to any superiority in gunnery. The Brazilian fleet, with which he had to contend, was manned and commanded, for the most part, by Englishmen. Taking command of the *Cacique* and hoisting the Argentine colors, De Kay sailed past Rio de Janeiro, northward through the Carribbean Sea, and as far up the North American coast as New York. He had been made a captain and after his victories was made a lieutenant-colonel—a rank that nearly corresponded with the then existing naval grade of commodore in the United States navy. From the date of this promotion he was known in the United States as Commodore De Kay. In the following year while returning to Buenos Aires, the *Brandzen* was surrounded and overpowered in the Rio de la Plata by Brazilian ships. De Kay scuttled her and, taking off the crew, proceeded by land to Buenos Aires. Peace was declared and, shortly, relieved of active duty, he returned to the United States, promising to rejoin Argentine service whenever he should be recalled. After his return to New York he was associated, as he had been earlier, with Henry Eckford [*q.v.*], the ship-builder. In 1831 he sailed a corvette, or sloop-of-war, built by Eckford for the Sultan of Turkey, to Constantinople. With him on the voyage went his brother, James E. De Kay, and Eckford himself. While in Turkey during the following year Eckford died and De Kay returned to America with the body. His marriage in 1833 to Janet Halleck Drake, a grand-daughter of Henry Eckford, and the only child of the poet, Joseph Rodman Drake, continued and cemented his early alliance with the ship-builder's family and the group of writers with whom he had been associated from boyhood days. His placid life as a family man in the Palisades region of New Jersey for several years was in sharp contrast with the adventurings of his youth. From this peaceful existence he was summoned during the Irish famine of 1847 to take leadership in an international enterprise of succor and good will which was a forerunner of the great Red Cross and other emergency relief efforts of the present century. He prevailed upon Congress to grant the use of the federal war-ship *Macedonian* for transporting goods from New York to Ireland. Although the United States was engaged in war with Mexico at the time, the appeal in behalf of the Irish famine-sufferers met with a quick response. A cargo of corn meal, Indian meal, rice, beans, and clothing, valued at over $60,000, was promptly secured and the cost of the expedition (amounting to $15,000) was voted by public meetings. De Kay took the responsibility of sailing the ship to Cork. This novel use of a war vessel on an errand of mercy caught the British imagination for the moment, but the well-intentioned enterprise suffered disastrously from lack of organization. The pledges made in public meetings remained unfulfilled. De Kay was compelled to advance from his own pocket the principal cost of the voyage and to look to Congress for reimbursement (R. B. Forbes, *Personal Reminiscences*, 1876). He died suddenly at Washington, where he had just purchased a house, survived by his wife and seven children.

[Chas. De Kay, the youngest son of Geo. Colman De Kay, published in the *National Marine* for Apr. 1918 extracts from the log of the *Brandzen* in 1827 and in the same article he supplied information about his father's early life. See also J. E. De Kay, "The Book of the Children of De Kay" (MS.) in Lib. of Cong.; obituary notice in *Nat. Intelligencer* (Washington), Feb. 3, 1849.]

W. B. S.

DE KAY, JAMES ELLSWORTH (Oct. 12, 1792–Nov. 21, 1851), naturalist, author, was the eldest son of George and Catherine (Colman) De Kay and brother of Commodore George Colman De Kay [*q.v.*]. His birthplace was probably Lisbon, Portugal, where his father, an American sea captain, had lived for many years, and had married a girl of Irish parentage. George De Kay took his family to New York in 1794, died when James was ten years old, and was survived only four years by his widow. The senior member of an orphaned family, the boy grew up in and near New York City. Most of his formal schooling was obtained in Connecticut, but the name and location of the school have not been preserved. De Kay early showed bookish proclivities and was also a keen observer and student of nature. At nineteen he was a medical student, spending at least one summer at Guilford, Conn., in reading to fit himself for that profession. Botany and zoology attracted him more than medicine, however, while in his early twenties he became closely associated with a group of young writers in New York. Throughout his life his relationships with literary men seem to have been more intimate than those with physicians or scientists. It was he who brought together Fitz-Greene Halleck and Joseph Rodman Drake. He was one of the five men to whom was entrusted the secret of the Drake-Halleck authorship of the papers of "Croaker & Co." in the *Evening Post*. He stood with Halleck at Drake's death-bed and was probably among the first to read, in manuscript, the lines beginning, "Green be the turf above thee"—long regarded as one of the most exquisite epitaphs in the language. De Kay went to Europe in the spring of 1818 and for a year was in attendance as a student of medicine at the University of Edinburgh, where he received the degree of M.D. in 1819. Returning to New York, he interested himself in the activities of the Lyceum of Natural History, which had been recently organized by Samuel Latham Mitchill and others and was known as the fourth institution of its kind to be founded in the United States. De Kay served the Lyceum in various capacities. He edited the first two volumes of its transactions, acted as librarian, building up a collection of scientific works that was remarkable for its day, and helped in assembling a museum.

While thus employed De Kay was married, on July 31, 1821, to Janet Eckford, one of the daughters of Henry Eckford [*q.v.*] and sister of the widow of Joseph Rodman Drake [*q.v.*]. For several years he seems to have toyed with the thought of a writer's career. Henry Eckford at one time had a controlling interest in a New York political journal, the *National Advocate,* and proposed to install De Kay as editor, but nothing came of the suggestion. Later De Kay himself offered to start a literary magazine, with Halleck as editor. This dream also failed to materialize. After his father-in-law had sustained severe business losses and had been commissioned by the Sultan of Turkey to take charge of the Turkish navy yard, De Kay sailed with him to Constantinople in a corvette built by Eckford for the Sultan and temporarily commanded by Commodore George C. De Kay. The group remained in Turkey for several months in 1831–32. Eckford died there. On returning to the United States, De Kay published anonymously *Sketches of Turkey by an American* (1833), his impressions of Turkey and the Turks. So far as these were favorable to the Turkish people, they were displeasing to the strong pro-Greek partisans who had sympathized with the recent revolution; but they undoubtedly were in accord with the matured opinions of such American observers as Dr. William Goodell, the missionary, and Commodore David Porter, then serving as United States Minister to the Porte, with both of whom De Kay had conversed.

While in Turkey De Kay had made a special study of the Asiatic cholera, about which little was known in America. After his return to New York the research was continued and in epidemics that later swept large regions in this country De Kay did what he could as a physician to stem their ravages. But, like several of his contemporaries among the scientific men of New York who had been educated in medicine, much of the time he took only a secondary interest in his profession. There was pioneer work to be done in natural science and he was always eager to have a part in it. An unexampled opportunity came to him in the form of a commission from the State of New York to prepare the zoological section of the elaborate Natural History Survey to be published by that state. This undertaking occupied him for nearly eight years, and resulted in the *Zoology of New York* (6 pts. in 5 vols., 1842–44). He described 1,600 species of animal life, including mammals, birds, reptiles, amphibians, fishes, molluscans, and crustaceans. As the work was intended for popular use, he introduced the common names of species so far as possible. His researches demanded much travel and personal investigation. The remainder of his life was passed at Oyster Bay, Long Island, where he died on Nov. 21, 1851, about two months after the death of James Fenimore Cooper, his friend of many years' standing.

[A typewritten copy of a manuscript entitled "The Book of the Children of De Kay" prepared by Jas. E. De Kay, and annotated by Gen. A. W. Greely, is in the Lib. of Cong. This traces the De Kay genealogy to Holland and, ultimately, Franche-Comté. Letters to and from De Kay are to be found in *Correspondence of Jas. Fenimore Cooper* (1922); these are dated, for the most part, in the decade of the forties; the intimacy of the two men seems to have antedated Cooper's long residence in Europe. See also H. L. Fairchild, *Hist. N. Y. Acad. Sci.* (1877); Jas. Grant Wilson, *Life and Letters of Fitz-Greene Halleck* (1869); E. D. G. Prime, *Forty Years in the Turkish Empire; or Memoirs of Rev. Wm. Goodell* (1876), pp. 120–21; *Am. Jour. Sci.*, 2 ser., XIII (1852), 300–01; *N. Y. Herald,* Nov. 23, 1851.] W. B. S.

DE KOVEN, HENRY LOUIS REGINALD (Apr. 3, 1859–Jan. 16, 1920), composer, was the son of Dr. Henry de Koven of Middletown, Conn., who was a brother of the Rev. James de Koven [*q.v.*]. His mother was Charlotte Le Roy of New York. Reginald de Koven was born in Middletown, but at the age of eleven accompanied his father to England where he remained until he took his degree at St. John's College, Oxford, in 1879, with intermittent periods at Stuttgart, where he studied the piano with Speidel. After his graduation he spent a year in Stuttgart, studying piano with Lebert and harmony with Pruckner. These studies were supplemented by a six months' course in composition with Hauff (Frankfort), by a vocal course with Vannuccini (Florence), and the study of operatic composition under Genée (Vienna, 1888) and Delibes (Paris, 1889). On May 1, 1884, he married Anna Farwell of Chicago. During the winter of 1887 his first comic opera, *The Begum,* was produced. It was followed by *Don Quixote* (Boston, 1889). On June 9, 1890, in Chicago, his one outstanding score, the romantic comic opera *Robin Hood,* was first heard; it was produced in London on Jan. 5 of the following year under the title *Maid Marian.* In *Robin Hood* he achieved a score to Harry Smith's libretto which "is analogous in its melodic fertility to Sullivan." It had more than 3,000 successive performances after its initial success in Chicago. As his wife has said in her memoirs, "in the forty-one productions which succeeded this opera he wrote music quite as melodic, and often more mature, but for freshness and gayety, and for uninterrupted flow of happy inspiration, 'Robin Hood' is unquestionably preëminent" (*A Musician and his Wife,* p. 134). Similarly, the composer's best-known and most popular song remains his "O Promise Me," interpolated in this score, and which for a number of years has been widely used as an organ number at weddings. *Robin Hood* at once established De Koven's reputation, and in rapid succession a number of light, melodious comic opera scores flowed from his facile pen. They included: *The Fencing Master* (Boston, 1892), *The Algerian* (Philadelphia, 1893), *Rob Roy* (Detroit, 1894), *The Tzigane* (New York, 1895), *The Mandarin* (Cleveland, 1896), *The Paris Doll* (Hartford, 1897), *The Highwayman* (New Haven, 1897), and *The Three Dragoons* (New York, 1899). In addition he was music-critic for the *Chicago Evening Post* from 1889 to 1890, and for the New York *World* from 1892 to 1897. In the latter year the De Koven family transferred its residence from New York to Washington, D. C., and there, in 1902, the composer organized the Washington Philharmonic Orchestra, which he conducted for three seasons. During this time De Koven was the music-critic for the *New York Journal* (1898–1900). After his return to New York, he again became the music-critic of the New York *World* (1907–12), and produced *Red Feather* (New York, 1903), *Happy Land* (New York, 1905), *Student King* (New York, 1906), *The Golden Butterfly* (New York, 1907), *The Beauty Spot* (New York, 1909), *The Wedding Trip* (New York, 1911), and *Her Little Highness* (New York, 1913). His grand opera, *The Canterbury Pilgrims* (New York, Mar. 7, 1917), with book by Percy Mackaye, was composed in Switzerland, in the first year of the World War. At the time, his wife wrote later, "we sometimes even heard the echo of the guns over the Lake of Geneva." It was a departure from his accustomed field, and achieved a *succès d'estime.* His last opera, *Rip Van Winkle,* which he wrote with the same librettist, was an essay in what he termed "folk-opera," developing an American subject. It was given for the first time in Chicago, Jan. 2, 1920, and was favorably received. On the evening of Jan. 16, the day on which he had received word that the house had been "sold out" for the third performance of *Rip Van Winkle,* De Koven was stricken with apoplexy at a supper party given in his honor, and died in ten minutes without regaining consciousness. Aside from his twenty comic operas (his "grand" and his "folk" operas may be regarded as endeavors to adapt his natural gifts in the field of light music to types alien to them), he wrote some 120 songs and a number of piano pieces of the salon variety. Among the individual songs, the setting of Kipling's "Recessional" is probably the best-known. The originality of his melodies, in various instances, has been questioned; but though he did not create a distinctive type of operetta, like Sullivan, his *Robin Hood* is regarded as a classic of its kind; and his service in a legitimate musical cause will make him long remembered. As a critic and writer on musical subjects, he was consistently committed to a recognition of American composers and artists equaling that accorded foreigners.

[Summary biographies are found in *Grove's Dict. of Music and Musicians* (3rd ed., 1919), rev. by Alfred Remy; A. Eaglefield-Hull, *A Dict. of Music and Musicians* (1924); *Who's Who in America,* 1920–21; Helen Beach, *The Descendants of Jacob Sebor, 1709–93, of Middletown, Conn.* (1923). An obituary sketch and a good editorial summary of achievement will be found in *Musical America* (Jan. 24, 1920). The most detailed account of his life and work, however, is contained in *A Musician and his Wife* (1926), by Mrs. Reginald de Koven.]

F. H. M.

DE KOVEN, JAMES (Sept. 19, 1831–Mar. 19, 1879), Episcopal clergyman, became the leader of the so-called "ritualistic group" in the Protestant Episcopal Church during the factious period following the Civil War. He was born in Middletown, Conn., and was the son of Henry Louis and Margaret (Sebor) de Koven. Graduating from Columbia College in 1851, second in his class, he attended the General Theological Seminary, was graduated in 1854, and was immediately ordained deacon. The Protestant Episcopal Church in America had reflected the Oxford disputes during the forties and the Home-Mission group had associated itself at that time with the high-church party, toward which De Koven was inclined. Quite naturally, therefore, he chose the Home Mission field for his labors. In 1855 Bishop Kemper, who was still missionary bishop of the Northwest, ordained him to the priesthood.

His life in the West began strenuously. During his first year he became assistant rector of a church at Delafield, Wis., and professor of ecclesiastical history at Nashotah Theological Seminary, and was also placed in charge of St. John's Hall, a preparatory school for Nashotah. Bishop Kemper transferred him in 1859 to Racine College where he was made rector, or warden. Racine developed greatly under his charge—not in size only, but in definiteness of policy as well. It was but natural that a man of his convictions should feel that the greatest problem in education lay in the misguiding influence of science and the weakening of faith. He discussed this problem in 1874 in a general report on the educational needs of the times. Inevitably, the strict ceremonial observed at Racine aroused adverse criticism, and many disquieting rumors—mostly false—in regard to the "papal abominations" encouraged at that institution disturbed the bosoms of low churchmen.

From 1868 to the end of his life, De Koven represented his diocese in the General Convention. His gifts as a debater, his incisive wit, and his thorough knowledge of ecclesiastical history made him feared as well as admired in the lower house. His greatest contribution to the Church was, perhaps, his opposition to the low-church effort to dictate ritualistic uniformity. From 1871 to 1874 he fought this attempt with ardor and ability, and he won his cause. The great speech of his life was delivered upon this subject in 1874. In it he movingly explained the attitude of the sincere ritualist and refuted all charges of Romanism.

Church partisanship was particularly acrimonious in the seventies. De Koven was attacked in religious papers and in the secular press. In 1871 Rev. James Craik of Louisville, Ky., even accused the rector of Racine of idolatrous views and practises. De Koven was not the man to sit silent under such an onslaught, and replied in the *Church Journal and Gospel Messenger* (see correspondence beginning Nov. 21, 1871). His published works are mostly sermons, tracts, and letters regarding religious controversies. Some of his papers were included in an undated collection, covering the years 1870–75, which was published under the title, *Tracts by Dr. De Koven and Others.* The year after his death *Sermons Preached on Various Occasions* was published, with a preface by Morgan Dix.

The diocese of Massachusetts failed to elect him bishop in 1873 by a few votes only. On the death of Bishop Kemper in 1874, he lost the election of Wisconsin by his failure to command the lay vote. On this occasion a series of garbled and misleading allegations concerning candles on the altar, incense during ceremonies, and auricular confession assumed great importance. In 1875 he was elected Bishop of Illinois but the Standing Committee of the General Convention refused to accept his election because of his opinions on the Eucharist, and he withdrew his acceptance. Trinity Church of New York City and St. Mark's in Philadelphia both called him to their parishes, but he declined these invitations and remained at Racine, where he died in March 1879. He left his property, including his library and all his papers, to Racine College.

[The preface by Morgan Dix in De Koven's *Sermons Preached on Various Occasions* (1880) is almost a memoir. See also: *Hist. of Racine and Kenosha Counties, Wis.* (1879), pp. 404–14; Helen Beach, *The Descendants of Jacob Sebor, 1709–93, of Middletown, Conn.* (1923), pp. 21–22; *Jours. of the P. E. Ch. in Wis.*, 1854–79; *Jours. of the Gen. Convention of the P. E. Ch. in America*; catalogues of Racine Coll.] K. J. G.

DE LACY, WALTER WASHINGTON (Feb. 22, 1819–May 13, 1892), soldier, engineer, was born at Petersburg, Va. His father, William De Lacy, was of distinguished Irish family, claiming descent from Hugh de Lacy, one of the conquerors of Ireland in the twelfth century. His mother, Eliza, was the daughter of William Charles Lee, long British vice-consul at Oporto, Portugal. Walter De Lacy's parents died when he was quite young and he was brought up and given his early education by two maiden aunts. In 1834 they sent him to St. Mary's Catholic College in northern Maryland where he remained four years, engaged chiefly in the study of mathematics and languages. During this time he secured the promise of an appointment at West Point, but in some way the promise failed of fulfilment. There was at West Point an eminent mathematician and engineer, Prof. Mahan, who felt under obligations to De Lacy's family, and he offered to give Walter private lessons in mathematics and engineering free of charge. After a year there, De Lacy began work as a construction engineer for the Illinois Central and Iron Mountain railways. In 1840 he became assistant professor of French at West Point and later taught foreign languages to midshipmen in the navy. In 1846 he was employed by a syndicate to search for abandoned mines in Texas. While he was there the Mexican War broke out, and he volunteered and served throughout the war. Afterward, he was engaged in railroad work, helping survey the thirty-second parallel from San Antonio to San Diego. In 1855 he was in the Puget Sound country and served with distinction in the Nez Percé War.

In 1858 De Lacy joined the party of Lieut. John Mullan, who was building the "Mullan Road" from Fort Benton to Walla Walla. He was placed in charge of construction from Sohon Pass to the Bitterroot River. He was also directed to make a map and report of the Bitterroot country. In 1860 he had finished this task and in 1861 became a prospector for gold in what is now Montana. He did not have much success and engaged for a time in packing from Walla Walla to the gold-mines. In 1863 he led a gold-seeking party into the Snake River country and discovered Shoshone Lake and the Lower Geyser Basin of the Yellowstone Park. The first legislature of Montana (1864–65) employed him to make the first map of Montana; and it long remained the best. From then on, he was engaged in surveying. He located the initial point for public surveys in Montana and did much work in surveying and locating the line of the Northern Pacific. The last few years of his life he was employed in the surveyor general's office in Helena, Mont.

"Col. De Lacy," as he was popularly called, always remained a bachelor. He was regarded as a genial and charming companion and had many friends. He was a brilliant talker and a noted teller of humorous stories and tales of adventure. He was one of the founders of the Montana Society of Engineers and of the Montana Historical Society.

[There are brief sketches of De Lacy in: *Contribs. Hist. Soc. Mont.*, vol. II (1896); *Quart. Jour. Mont. Soc. Engineers* (Jan. 1916); *Jour. Asso. Engineering Socs.* (June 1897). His own account, *A Trip up the South Snake River in 1863* is in *Contribs. Hist. Soc. Mont.*, vol. I (1876).] P. C. P.

DELAFIELD, EDWARD (May 7, 1794–Feb. 13, 1875), ophthalmologist and surgeon, third son among the eleven children of John Delafield [*q.v.*], an English merchant who had emigrated to America, by his wife, Ann Hallett of New York. He received his primary education first under a tutor named Adam Smith, and later at the Union Hall Academy under L. E. A. Eigenbrodt who gave him a good foundation in mathematics and the languages. He graduated from Yale with the degree of A.B. in 1812, after which he became a pupil to Dr. Samuel Borrowe of New York, under whose tutelage he obtained, in 1816, the degree of Doctor of Medicine from the College of Physicians and Surgeons, New York, for which he wrote *An Inaugural Dissertation on Pulmonary Consumption* (1816). After receiving his degree, Delafield went to Europe with John Kearny Rodgers where he had a year (1817) in the clinics of England, Scotland, Holland, and France. On returning to New York, though he continued in general surgery and obstetrics, his attention was directed chiefly to the diseases of the eye. He edited in 1825 an American edition (based on the third London edition) of Benjamin Travers's *Synopsis of the Diseases of the Eye, and Their Treatment,* with notes and additions, and he later made important contributions to ophthalmological journals. He was thus one of the first in the United States to devote himself to ophthalmology. In 1818 he formulated a plan for establishing the New York Eye Infirmary modeled after the London Infirmary in which he had studied, and succeeded in carrying it out in association with Kearny Rodgers in 1820; two rooms were opened (No. 45 Chatham St.), and during the first seven months 436 patients were treated. Later, largely through Delafield's influence, more ample accommodations were secured. Between 1820 and 1906 over a million patients were treated. In 1824 the Massachusetts Charitable Eye and Ear Infirmary was founded in Boston by Edward Reynolds and John Jeffries [*q.v.*], who had received their stimulus from New York. Delafield was one of the founders and the first president of the American Ophthalmological Society (1864), an organization which immediately flourished and is still in existence. He was also largely responsible for founding a society in 1842 for the relief of the widows and orphans of medical men, which also was based upon a similar society then existing in London. In addition to his labors at the Eye and Ear Infirmary, he occupied from 1825 until 1838 the chair of obstetrics and diseases of women and children at the College of Physicians and Surgeons of New York, and from 1858 to 1875 he was president of the College. As a practitioner he was unusually successful and is said to have possessed to a remarkable degree the power of inspiring the confidence of his patients. He was a genial and kindly man, and owing to his long gray beard and sideburns was rather striking in personal appearance. In October 1821 he married Elina E. Langdon Elwyn, grand-daughter of John Langdon, governor of New Hampshire and president *pro tempore* of the Senate in the First Congress of the United States. There were six children, all of whom died before their father. In January 1839 he married his second wife, Julia Floyd, grand-daughter of William Floyd, signer of the Declaration of Independence; she became the mother of Francis Delafield [*q.v.*], the pathologist.

[S. W. Francis, *Medic. and Surgic. Reporter,* XV (1866), 509–15; *Medic. Record,* N. Y., X (1875), 135; *Trans. Am. Ophthalm. Soc.,* II (1876), 275, 339–41; A. A. Hubbell, *The Development of Ophthalmology in America 1800–1870* (1908).] J. F. F.

DELAFIELD, FRANCIS (Aug. 3, 1841–July 17, 1915), pathologist and physician, was the son of Edward Delafield [*q.v.*] and his wife, Julia Floyd. After receiving the degree of A.B. from Yale in 1860 he entered the College of Physicians and Surgeons in New York and there received his medical degree in 1863. On graduation he went immediately to Europe where he continued his medical work in London, Berlin, and Paris, taking full advantage of the opportunities then being offered for detailed post-mortem study. The influence of Rudolf Virchow was at that time beginning to be felt strongly in medical science, and Delafield became an ardent follower. He returned to America firmly convinced that pathological anatomy was the *sine qua non* of scientific medicine, and he accordingly passed the greater part of his time during the next thirty years in the post-mortem room making detailed studies of pathological tissues, meticulously correlating his findings with clinical features observed before death. He was soon recognized as a leading authority in pathology and clinical diagnosis. In 1866 he became curator at Bellevue Hospital, in 1871 pathologist at the Roosevelt Hospital, and in 1875 visiting physician in the Bellevue Hospital. In the following year he was made adjunct professor of pathology and the practise of medicine at the College of Physicians and Surgeons, New York, and in 1882 was made full professor in the place of Alonzo Clark [*q.v.*]. In 1886, in company with William Osler, James Tyson [*qq.v.*], James E. Graham, and William Pepper [*q.v.*], he founded and became president of the Association of American Physicians, which was to have a profound influence upon the development of medicine. The first meeting of this organization was picturesquely referred to by Osler as "the coming-of-age party of internal medicine in America" (*International Clinics,* Philadelphia, 1915, IV, 1).

Delafield was a remarkably effective teacher. It is said that his lectures were particularly attractive because of his simple, forceful delivery and the fact that the information which they contained was based wholly on first-hand experience. By nature he was somewhat austere and little given to amusements or levity, but to his students he was stimulating and always sympathetic. In accordance with a decision made early in life, he retired from professional and hospital duties at the age of sixty, though he was then at the height of his physical and mental vigor. He continued in practise as a consultant until shortly before his death, which resulted from apoplexy, at Noroton, near Stamford, Conn.

Delafield made contributions of first importance to pathology, especially of nephritis and of the diseases of the colon. He was also among the first to insist upon the difference between acute lobar pneumonia and bronchopneumonia (1882). His scientific papers number nearly a hundred, and his influence and teachings were widely felt through an unusually successful textbook, *A Handbook of Post Mortem Examinations and of Morbid Anatomy,* first published in 1872, and revised and enlarged, in collaboration with T. Mitchell Prudden, in 1885. The twelfth edition appeared in 1922. In 1878 Delafield issued with Charles F. Stillman a *Manual of Physical Diagnosis.* His fame as a pathologist was greatly enhanced through the publication of his *Studies in Pathological Anatomy,* an elaborately illustrated pathological atlas which appeared in parts between 1878 and 1891. He also contributed chapters to many medical and surgical treatises, such as his "Pyæmia and Allied Conditions" in *The International Encyclopedia of Surgery* (1881) and his "Diseases of the Kidneys" in *Twentieth Century Practice* (1895). On Jan. 17, 1870, Delafield married Katherine Van Rensselaer of New York.

[T. C. Janeway, *Medic. Record,* 1915, LXXXVIII, 929; *N. Y. Medic. Jour.,* 1915, CII, 202; *Am. Medicine,* 1915, X, 522; *Boston Medic. and Surgic. Jour.,* 1915, CLXXIII, 186; *Jour. Am. Medic. Asso.,* 1915, LXV, 349; *Who's Who in America,* 1914–15.] J. F. F.

DELAFIELD, JOHN (Mar. 16, 1748–July 3, 1824), merchant, son of John and Martha (Dell) Delafield, was among the first men of English birth to establish themselves in America after the close of the Revolution. His family had lived in England since the Norman Conquest, having been, as the name suggests, of French origin. His father was a prosperous dealer in cheese. One of his sisters married William Arnold, customs collector on the Isle of Wight, and was the mother of Dr. Thomas Arnold of Rugby, while another sister became the teacher of the six-year-old boy Thomas after the death of his father. John Delafield as a young man had accumulated property and at thirty-five was prepared to emigrate to the United States and cast his lot with the new Republic. The manner of his coming had in it something of the spice of adventure. He took passage on a British ship that carried letters of marque; during the voyage a French merchantman was seized and Delafield received £100 as his share of the prize money. He arrived at New York, which was still held by British troops, in the spring of 1783, bringing with him the first copy of the provisional treaty of peace between the United States and Great Britain to reach America. Shortly after the British evacuation of New York, Delafield went into trade and conducted his affairs so shrewdly that within fifteen years he became one of the wealthiest men in the city. He married Ann, the daughter of Joseph Hallett, a Revolutionary officer. They had eleven children. His home on Long Island, just across the East River from New York, was among the best-known mansions of its period. He was one of the original directors of the Mutual Assurance Company of New York, organized in 1787 by Alexander Hamilton and others. In 1798 he retired from mercantile business, but later became president of the United Insurance Company. During the War of 1812, when American merchantmen were at the mercy of both British and French war vessels he shared the fate of all American underwriters who had offered marine insurance; to meet the losses he was compelled to sacrifice his property. Stripped of his wealth, Delafield found himself far less favorably situated than when he landed at New York thirty years before. At this time his oldest son John Delafield [*q.v.*], while technically a prisoner in London because of his American citizenship, was permitted to engage in banking. Thus in a few years the family fortunes were measurably retrieved. Delafield was the founder of a line that was notable in New York to the second and third generation, in commerce, in finance, in the army, and in the medical profession. His personal example in assuming obligations that were not legally his as to the payment of losses to policy-holders in his insurance companies was of great value in the early days of American underwriting practise. It was the irony of fate that he, a man of English birth and antecedents, should suffer in America from British depredations on American shipping, although he retained strong family ties and associations with the mother country.

[*The Pedigree of Delafield* (Extract from the Records of the College of Arms, London); *Matthews American Armory and Blue Book* (1901), ed. by John Matthews; M. A. Hamm, *Famous Families of N. Y.* (1902), I, 79; S. H. Weston, *Memorial Sermon on the Brothers Delafield* (1875).] W. B. S.

DELAFIELD, JOHN (Jan. 22, 1786–Oct. 22, 1853), banker and farmer, was the eldest son of John [*q.v.*] and Ann (Hallett) Delafield. He was born in New York City three years after his father's arrival from England. The elder Delafield had become a citizen of a country that as yet had no established national government. He soon prospered in business and gave his son as good a schooling as the New York of that period afforded. The boy was graduated from Columbia College at sixteen. Then going as supercargo on merchant ships he made several voyages from the port of New York and after a few years became himself the owner of vessels. It was in the course of a voyage on one of his own ships that he witnessed the siege of Corunna, Spain, by the French. When the shipping in the harbor was fired he escaped, with several members of the Spanish nobility who took refuge on his ship and sailed to England. In London he engaged in banking and for some years prospered in that undertaking. During the War of 1812 his American citizenship caused him to be technically held as a prisoner of war, but influential family friends obtained for him unusual liberties, including permission to continue his business unmolested, so long as he kept within the limits of a certain area, having its center in London. After the war he continued for a time to accumulate wealth, but serious reverses came in 1819 through the failure of some of his investments. It was then that Washington Irving, who had become his intimate friend, wrote for the *Sketch Book* the story of Delafield's experiences in the chapter entitled "The Wife" (Delafield had married his English cousin, Mary Roberts of Whitechurch, Buckshire), alluding to the courageous and sweet-tempered spirit in which the bride faced the loss of home and comforts. In the following year Delafield returned to America after a twelve years' absence, taking the cashiership and later the presidency of one of the New York banks, which he held for eighteen years, in the meantime becoming interested in various enterprises outside his business. He was a prominent member of the New York Philharmonic Society, was active in raising funds for the University of the City of New York at the time of its founding, and took part in the revival of the New York Historical Society. In 1838 he became president of the New York Banking Company, which had only a brief career, suffering heavy losses through the failure of Western institutions. For the second time Delafield's fortune was wiped out. He left the city and engaged in farming in Seneca County, N. Y. Within a few years his had become one of the model farms of the state (*Transactions of the New York State Agricultural Society,* 1847, p. 200). He gave his attention to the practical problems of drainage, soil analysis, and rotation of crops. In these matters he was far in advance of his times. Chosen president of the State Agricultural Society, he exerted much influence in his later years in behalf of progressive and scientific farming. Two books seem to have been erroneously attributed to him—*A Brief Topographical Description of the County of Washington, Ohio* (1834), and *Inquiry into the Origin of the Antiquities of America* (Cincinnati, 1839). There is evidence that both were written by his son, John Delafield, Jr., a graduate of Columbia College, who lived in Ohio in 1831 and for many years thereafter (Wilson Waters, *The History of Saint Luke's Church, Marietta, Ohio,* Marietta, 1884, pp. 39–40). His second wife was Harriet Wadsworth Tallmadge. He died at Geneva, N. Y.

[*The Pedigree of Delafield* (Extract from the Records of the College of Arms, London); John Matthews, ed., *Matthews Am. Armory and Blue Book* (1901); M. A. Hamm, *Famous Families of N. Y.* (1902), I, 790; *N. Y. Times,* Oct. 25, 1853; *N. Y. Herald,* Oct. 26, 1853.] W.B.S.

DELAFIELD, RICHARD (Sept. 1, 1798–Nov. 5, 1873), military engineer, was the son of John Delafield [*q.v.*] of London, who came to America in 1783, married Ann, the daughter of Joseph Hallett, and founded one of the well-known families of New York. The Delafield family (of noble French descent) held rich possessions in Alsace, and John brought wealth with him to the New World. He became one of the richest merchants of New York City and has often been called "one of the fathers of Wall Street." His son Richard was born in New York City and entered West Point Military Academy at the age of sixteen. He was graduated and commissioned a second lieutenant in July 1818. He was twice married: first, to Helen Summers and, after her death, to Harriet, the daughter of Gen. E. M. Covington.

In forty-eight years of continuous service in the United States army, Richard Delafield rose from a second lieutenancy to the rank of major-general. He served twice—from 1838 to 1845, and again from 1856 to 1861—as superintendent of the United States Military Academy at West Point. At the outbreak of the Civil War, at the age of sixty-three, he was appointed to the staff of Gen. Morgan, in which position he helped to organize and equip New York state forces for the field, and to supply ordnance stores for the Atlantic and Lake defenses. Part of this time he was superintending engineer of the defenses for The Narrows in New York harbor, of the fortifications of Governors Island, and of the fort at Sandy Hook. Then, on Apr. 22, 1864, he was made brigadier-general and chief of engineers, United States army, and until his retirement in August 1866 was in command of the Corps of Engineers and in charge of the Engineer Bureau in Washington. In 1865 he was brevetted major-general "for faithful, meritorious and distinguished services in the Engineer Department during the Rebellion."

In his earlier years of service Delafield was engineer on the construction of fortifications and defenses at Hampton Roads, Va., 1819–24; at the Plaquemine Bend on the Mississippi River, 1824–32; and on the Atlantic Coast defenses, 1845–55. Many of his plans, drawings, and studies were preserved and treasured because they so admirably combined an artistic value with a strict scientific accuracy. He was appointed in 1855 to act as a member of the Military Commission to the Crimea and the theatre of the war in Europe, and his report and observations, entitled "Report on the Art of War in Europe in 1854–56" was published by order of Congress in 1860. He lived for seven years after his retirement from active army service and during part of that time served as a member of a commission for the improvement of the Boston harbor and as a regent for the Smithsonian Institution.

[Material for this sketch has been found in *Professional Memoirs, Corps of Engineers, and Engineer Dept. at Large, U. S. Army* (1911), III, p. 416; Richard Delafield, *The Pedigree of Delafield* (1925); "Famous N. Y. Families—The Delafields," in *N. Y. Evening Post,* June 1, 1901.] E. Y.

DE LAMAR, JOSEPH RAPHAEL (Sept. 2, 1843–Dec. 1, 1918), capitalist, son of Maximilian and Johanna (Teune) De Lamar, was born in Amsterdam, Holland, and died in New York City. He was privately educated. While he was still young he went to sea. Once when he was on a voyage, the captain of the ship died, and he—though only twenty-three years old—was put into control. Soon after this he came to America and settled at Vineyard Haven, Mass., as a ship-contractor. Perhaps his most notable achievement in this connection occurred in 1872 when he raised the submerged transatlantic liner, *Charlotte.* The excitement over gold discoveries in Colorado tempted him West in the late seventies. He secured certain tracts of land near Leadville, and then returned to Chicago where he studied chemistry and metallurgy. After about two years he sold his mining property to a London organization for two million dollars. In 1884 he was a member of the territorial Senate of Idaho, but he soon abandoned politics, and though his mining interests in the West were in a sense personally maintained till 1891, he spent most of his time after 1888 in New York

City. He married Nellie Sands, the daughter of a New York druggist, and the two went to live in Paris. They were later divorced. He was back in New York by 1902. He became a director in many rich corporations, and for a long time he was vice-president of the International Nickel Company. In his business relationships he was extremely taciturn and aloof, but he belonged to numerous clubs and he entertained lavishly at his expensive residences in the city and at Glen Cove, L. I. He was an accomplished organist. When he died, half of his estate of twenty million dollars was left to his daughter, Alice Antoinette, and the other half was divided between the medical schools of Columbia, Harvard, and Johns Hopkins Universities.

[Who's Who in America, 1916–17; H. T. French, *Hist. of Idaho* (1914); *N. Y. Times*, Dec. 2, 10, 1918.]

J. D. W.

DELAMATER, CORNELIUS HENRY (Aug. 30, 1821–Feb. 7, 1889), mechanical engineer, was born at Rhinebeck, Dutchess County, N. Y., the only child of William and Eliza (Douglass) Delamater. When he was three years of age his parents took him to New York City and there he received a common-school education. He had neither profession nor trade, but being studious and very fond of reading, he acquired more than most boys who had only his advantages. At the age of fourteen he left school to become an errand boy in the hardware store of Schuyler & Swords, where he remained for two years. At sixteen he entered the office of James Cunningham who had established the Phœnix Foundry on West St., New York City, and who had as his associates Peter Hogg, an engineer and draftsman, and Cornelius's father, William Delamater, as cashier and confidential adviser. Cornelius started as a clerk but he made himself so useful and gained such an insight into the work that Cunningham, desiring to retire, offered the business to him and his cousin, Peter Hogg. The offer was very promptly accepted and the two young men found themselves at the head of a fairly prosperous business, doing repair work and building boilers and engines for side-wheel steamers. Their capital was small but their friends were many and warm and they prospered.

When in 1839 John Ericsson [*q.v.*] settled in New York he was persuaded by Samuel Risley of Greenwich Village to give his work to the Phœnix Foundry. There he met Cornelius Delamater and a friendship was formed which was to be life-long. Rarely thereafter did either of them enter upon a business venture without consulting the other. Delamater's foundry built, after designs developed by Ericsson, the first iron boats and the first steam fire-engines used here. The 36-inch cast-iron pipe used for the Croton Aqueduct was made at the Phœnix Foundry and before the end of 1840 over fifty propeller steamers were also constructed. At the end of eight years when the lease on the foundry expired, Hogg and Delamater bought property at the foot of West Thirteenth St., on the North River, and in 1850 they built the large establishment in which they conducted their business until 1856, when Hogg retired from the firm. Delamater continued alone with the business for many years, the firm thereafter being known as the Delamater Iron Works.

Upon the outbreak of the Civil War, the firm entered upon a new and interesting chapter of its history. When in August 1861 the government, in response to the news that the Confederates were building the *Merrimac,* advertised for proposals to build iron-clad vessels, Delamater at once called upon Ericsson to determine a method of approaching the government with the latter's plans for an armed iron-clad turreted steamer. The contract on the basis of Ericsson's plans was received in October 1861, the keel of the *Monitor* was laid the same day at the Continental Iron Works in Greenpoint, L. I. (now Brooklyn, N. Y.), and the engines were built at the Delamater Iron Works. The *Monitor* left New York harbor on Mar. 6, 1862, and three days later engaged in the famous battle with the *Merrimac.* The men who actually operated the boilers and engines of the *Monitor* on that occasion were workmen from the Delamater Iron Works.

In 1869 the Delamater Works constructed thirty gunboats, each armed with a 100-pound bow-chaser, for the Spanish government. The firm was notable too for its propellers; for the manufacture of air compressors; and for constructing in 1881 John P. Holland's first successful submarine torpedo-boat. In fact a complete enumeration of the important productions at these Works would prove that they were a veritable school of invention, contributing greatly to the history of the country. Delamater, the guiding genius, was a man of deep, kindly, tolerant sympathies, well-known for his genial disposition, and his warm and lasting friendships. He believed in human nature and as an employer invested in it. At one time in his career he became bankrupt through no fault of his own, but his creditors had such faith in him that they helped him to continue the Works. In later years he invited them all to a banquet at which each of them found under his plate a check with compound interest for what was owed him. He was one of the original members of the American Society of Mechanical Engineers. Early in life he was married to Ruth O. Caller of Poughkeepsie, N. Y., who with five daughters and one son survived him. He died suddenly of pneumonia after an illness of eight days, and was buried in Woodlawn Cemetery.

[Files of the Am. Soc. Mech. Engineers, and *Trans. Soc. Mech. Engineers,* X (1889), 836–38; account of the Delamater-Ericsson Commemoration in New York City (privately printed, 1920); H. F. J. Porter, "The Delamater Iron Works—The Cradle of the Modern Navy," *Trans. Soc. Naval Architects and Marine Engineers,* vol. XXVI (1919); Wm. C. Church, *The Life of John Ericsson* (2 vols., 1890), *passim*; obituary notices in *Engineering News,* Feb. 16, 1889; and *Am. Machinist,* Feb. 14, 1889, as well as in many other trade and technical papers and in all of the leading newspapers of New York City.] K. W. C.

DE LANCEY, JAMES (Nov. 27, 1703–July 30, 1760), chief justice and lieutenant-governor of colonial New York, political leader, was the eldest son of Stephen De Lancey and Anne van Cortlandt. His father, a refugee from France after the revocation of the Edict of Nantes, came to New York in 1686, having first obtained letters of denization in England. By virtue of his success in business, his marriage into the Van Cortlandt family, and the vigorous part which he took in the politics of the city and province, he came to occupy a place in the provincial aristocracy. James, his eldest son, was sent to England for his education, and was a fellow commoner at Corpus Christi College, Cambridge, later reading law in the Inner Temple. During his period of residence in England he made personal acquaintances and connections which were of great importance in his subsequent career. Returning to New York in 1725, he was shortly afterward admitted to the bar, was called to the Council on Jan. 26, 1729, and not long before this was married to Anne, elder daughter of Hon. Caleb Heathcote, receiver general of customs of North America, who brought him additional wealth. With advantages afforded by social position enhanced by his considerable gifts he began his career in New York politics.

At first he threw in his fortunes with the group who supported the governor and the official class, and in June 1731 received an appointment as second judge of the supreme court. During the administration of William Cosby [*q.v.*], from 1732 to 1736, a period when the violence of factional passion and popular excitement reached dangerous heights, De Lancey was promoted to be chief justice (1733), the governor thus brusquely dismissing the veteran Lewis Morris [*q.v.*] from that office. De Lancey now engaged without reserve in the defense of Cosby and the supreme court against their opponents who, through the use of the press, a weapon then first becoming effective in provincial politics, were making dangerous headway. In the government prosecution of Peter Zenger [*q.v.*] for libel, the passionate boldness of both sides led the youthful chief justice to disbar James Alexander and William Smith [*qq.v.*], the two leaders of his profession in the province, for a plea which in his judgment called in question the very existence of his court. From his part in the Zenger trial, which the eloquence of Andrew Hamilton [*q.v.*] turned into a triumph for the freedom of the press, De Lancey reaped much unpopularity. But, considering the circumstances and standards of the time, his conduct professionally seems to have been altogether reputable and what would naturally be expected from his training.

During the administration of George Clarke, [*q.v.*], from 1736 to 1743, he figured less conspicuously, though he was an active and increasingly influential member of the Council. It was at this period that the Assembly became the dominant element of the provincial government, attaining at last the key position of complete financial control. With the accession of George Clinton [*q.v.*] to the governorship, however, especially after his grant (Sept. 14, 1744) to the Chief Justice of a commission for his office for good behavior instead of during pleasure, De Lancey completely reversed his political rôle. Undeterred by any scruples touching the nonpartisanship of the judicial office, he developed with great energy and success a system of control of both Council and Assembly which effectually blocked all the governor's efforts to lead New York's participation in the third intercolonial war with the vigor desired by other colonies and by the Home Government. Clinton's "interest" at Whitehall proved inferior in effectiveness to that of De Lancey, reinforced as the latter was by the prestige of his brother-in-law, Sir Peter Warren. At Clinton's departure in 1753 he was obliged to deliver to De Lancey a commission for the lieutenant-governorship which he had kept suppressed for six years.

The immediate exercise of this commission came unexpectedly as a result of the suicide of the new governor, Sir Danvers Osborne. De Lancey was thus put in an extremely delicate position, for Gov. Osborne's instructions required an enforcement upon the Assembly of a complete surrender of those features of legislative "encroachment" upon prerogative which had been developed out of their financial control under the leadership of De Lancey himself. By the exercise of great political dexterity, and undoubtedly favored by the emergency conditions imposed by the fourth intercolonial war, he succeeded in keeping both of his great offices and at the same time in preserving for the Assembly the essential features of the position of dominance in the provincial government which were retained until the Revolutionary period. In 1754 he presided over the Albany convention and in the following year attended the conference of governors with Gen. Braddock at Alexandria, Va. He signed the charter for King's College in 1754, thus helping to fix the charge of "Episcopalianism" upon "the De Lancey party," and raising a Presbyterian opposition under William Livingston which soon came to be known as "the Livingston party." These issues, groupings, and names survived for long after De Lancey's death. He remained the leading figure in New York during the term of Gov. Hardy, 1755–57, and again, as lieutenant-governor, administered the affairs of the province in 1757–60. He died suddenly on July 30 of the latter year, being succeeded in the lieutenant-governorship by his political opponent, Cadwallader Colden [*q.v.*], president of the Council.

[The most accessible sources are to be found in the *Docs. Relative to the Colonial Hist. of the State of N. Y.*, vols. VI and VII (1855–56). There is a memoir by E. F. De Lancey in E. B. O'Callaghan, *Doc. Hist. of the State of N. Y.*, vol. IV, quarto ed. (1851). William Smith, *Hist. of N. Y.* (Albany, 1814), covers the whole period. For the Zenger trial see Livingston Rutherfurd: *John Peter Zenger* (1904); H. L. Osgood, *Hist. of the American Colonies in the Eighteenth Century*, vol. II (1924), ch. v; and J. G. Wilson, *Memorial Hist. of the City of N. Y.* (1892–93), vol. II, ch. vii. On the Clinton administration, see Osgood, vol. IV, ch. x, and Wilson, vol. II, ch. viii. For date of birth see Thos. Jones, *Hist. of N. Y. during the Revolutionary War* (1879), I, 650.] C. W. S.

DE LANCEY, JAMES (1732–1800), colonial politician, turfman, was the eldest son of Lieutenant-Governor James De Lancey [*q.v.*] and Anne Heathcote. Born in New York City, in a house built by his grandfather, Stephen De Lancey, which later became famous as Fraunce's Tavern, he was educated at Eton and Cambridge, and on leaving the University entered the army, reaching the rank of captain. He is said to have served as aide to Abercrombie in the Lake George campaign of 1758, and was certainly with Prideaux and Johnson at the capture of Fort Niagara in 1759. His military activities, however, were brought to a close by the sudden death of his father, in 1760, which left him, before his thirtieth year, with the responsibilities of the headship of one of the wealthiest and most powerful families of the provincial aristocracy. During his young manhood in England he had acquired the sporting tastes of the period. Soon after he came into his great property he imported what are believed to have been the first English race-horses, or thoroughbreds, ever brought to New York, and in a few years assembled the largest and most select stud and stable of running horses in the Colony if not in the whole country. Cadwallader R. Colden, historian of the early racing, called him "the Father of the New York Turf." His chief opponent in racing and in politics was Lewis Morris, Jr., later a signer of the Declaration of Independence. From Wildair, Lath, and the Cub Mare, imported by De Lancey, were descended most of the great race-horses of America prior to the Civil War period, while True Briton, another of his horses, was, according to the Morgan Horse Register, the progenitor of that famous breed of early American road and carriage horses.

His responsibilities as head of the family comprehended not only the development of the extensive De Lancey estates and the conduct of the family mercantile business, but also the continuation of the political influence of the "De Lancey interest." At first, under the leadership of the son, who lacked his father's dominant official position in the province, and his powerful influence in London, the political fortunes of the family suffered a decline. At the Assembly elections in 1761 held in consequence of the demise of the Crown, the Livingston party scored a triumph. But the next seven years offered abundant opportunity for the younger De Lancey to exercise a gift for dexterous management which came to be recognized as not inferior to that of his father. Provincial resistance to the policies of the British government in these exciting days was a matter in which the aristocratic De Lancey faction and the Livingston "Whigs" could and did combine with great effect. Into this contest, however, an element new to the political life of the province, the unfranchised classes, ready for radical and dangerous extremes of action, had begun to force its way. Taking advantage of the reaction against this encroachment of the masses, the De Lancey merchant ticket won the city delegation in the elections of 1768 over the "Whig lawyers," and again in 1769 the Tory-Episcopalian De Lancey combination obtained control of the Assembly. At this time "Captain James" was offered and refused a seat at the Council. In the proceedings of this last Assembly of New York's provincial period, which were in line with its traditional policy of over half a century, he took a leading part. At its last session, beginning in

January 1775, his hand is to be traced in the papers addressed to King, Lords and Commons, strongly resisting the ministerial policy but as carefully refraining from commitments to revolutionary activity. His was one of the eleven negative votes—to ten in favor—upon the resolution to approve the proceedings of the First Continental Congress. Shortly thereafter he sold out his stud and racing stable and, taking his family with him, retired to England. He was included with his uncle Oliver and his cousin James [*qq.v.*] in the Confiscation Act of 1777 and the Act of Attainder of 1779, and thus the famous "De Lancey interest" became a casualty of the American Revolution.

On the conclusion of peace De Lancey became very active in proceedings for compensating the Loyalists. He and his uncle Oliver were among those who suffered the heaviest losses by the American success. In dealing with the commissioners appointed by Parliament the claimants acted through a board of Agents, and in this organization James De Lancey represented New York, served as vice-president of the Board, and, next to Sir William Pepperell, was the most active member. He claimed a loss of $284,000 and was allowed $160,000, an amount of grant in this connection exceeded only by those to Frederick Phillipse and Sir John Johnson. His holdings of New York City real estate, situated on what is now the lower East Side, brought at the sale of forfeited estates shortly after 1783 something over $234,000, a figure which bears a quaint ratio to its present-day valuation. De Lancey's death at Bath, England, is recorded in the *Gentleman's Magazine* for April 1800. As his children died without issue the eldest male De Lancey line became extinct. His wife, whom he had married in 1771, was Margaret Allen of Philadelphia, daughter of William Allen [*q.v.*], chief justice of Pennsylvania, and grand-daughter of Andrew Hamilton [*q.v.*], of Zenger trial fame.

[C. L. Becker, *The Hist. of Political Parties in the Province of N. Y. 1760–76* (1909); A. C. Flick, *Loyalism in N. Y.* (1901); J. H. Wallace, *The Am. Horse* (1897); information as to his sporting interest from Gurney C. Gue, Esq., Merrick, N. Y. See also bibliographies of others of the De Lancey family.]

C. W. S.

DE LANCEY, JAMES (1746–May 2, 1804), Loyalist, leader of partisan troops, was the fourth son of Peter De Lancey and Elizabeth, eldest daughter of Cadwallader Colden [*q.v.*], lieutenant-governor of New York just before the Revolution. Peter De Lancey, "Peter of the Mills," was a brother of James De Lancey [*q.v.*], chief justice and lieutenant-governor of the province, and was the second son of Stephen, the founder of the family in America. Presumably he bore his share in the family politics, though his alliance with the Colden family must have created awkward personal situations. He represented the Borough of Westchester in the Assembly from 1750 to 1768. His son, "Colonel James," held the office of sheriff of Westchester from 1770 to 1776. From the occupation of New York City by Howe in the autumn of the latter year to the close of hostilities, "The Neutral Ground," a belt some twenty miles in width between the northern end of Manhattan Island and a line from the mouth of the Croton River to the Sound, was the scene of irregular partisan warfare, full of exciting incidents of the most destructive and demoralizing character, pictured later by J. Fenimore Cooper in his story of *The Spy.* Amid these activities "De Lancey's Horse" became a household word of terror, for in 1777 he had become captain of a troop of fifty men, selected from the Westchester militia by Gov. Tryon. They had soon gained the nickname of "Cowboys" from their success as cattle-raiders. In 1781 their leader signed himself as "Colonel, Westchester Refugees." "The Outlaw of the Bronx" was one of his soubriquets.

He was proscribed by the New York Act of Attainder of 1779, and in 1782 removed with his family to Nova Scotia, where he settled at Annapolis on a farm a part of which is still held by his descendants. He became a member of the Assembly of the province and in 1794 was appointed to the Council. His wife, by whom he had six sons and four daughters, was Martha Tippetts, of the family which until the Revolution held Tippetts' Hill, immediately north of Spuyten Duyvil Creek.

[T. Jones, *The Hist. of N. Y. During the Revolutionary War* (N. Y. Hist. Soc., 1879); Carl L. Becker, *The Hist. of Political Parties in the Province of N. Y. 1760–76* (1909); A. C. Flick, *Loyalism in N. Y.* (1901), in Columbia Univ. Studies in Hist., etc.; R. Bolton, *The Hist. of the Several Towns . . . of the County of Westchester* (1881); J. T. Scharf, *Hist. of Westchester County, N. Y.* (1886); O. Hufeland, "Westchester County During the Am. Rev.," *Westchester Hist. Soc. Pubs.*, 1926.]

C. W. S.

DE LANCEY, OLIVER (Sept. 16, 1718–Oct. 27, 1785), colonial politician, Loyalist soldier, was the youngest son of Stephen De Lancey and Anne van Cortlandt. Like the other members of his family he was a successful merchant. For a time he was associated in business with his brother-in-law, John Watts. It was Oliver De Lancey's fate to cooperate with his brother James [*q.v.*], the chief justice and lieutenant-governor, in erecting the De Lancey party into a powerful position in New York provincial politics, to survive his brother into a period of entirely new conditions in contest with which the family "interest" was utterly wrecked, and finally himself to die in exile. He lacked entirely the far-sighted astuteness, the capacity for persistent pursuit of objects by indirect methods, and the urbanity of demeanor which characterized his leader-brother. His contribution was made by vigor in action and in exploiting the prestige and formidable power of the family interest. The violence of his language and conduct in behalf of the faction opposed to Gov. Clinton was frequently referred to in the latter's dispatches to England, with particular emphasis laid on the difficulty in finding lawyers willing to appear in court to prosecute for his words a person so nearly related to the chief justice of the province. These circumstances were mentioned in the famous Representation by the Lords of Trade to the Privy Council in the affairs of New York in 1751. Oliver De Lancey was prominent in New York's participation in the fourth intercolonial war, raising troops and commanding the provincial contingent in the Ticonderoga campaign of 1758. For such services he twice received votes of thanks from the Assembly of the province. He served as an alderman for the Out Ward from 1754 to 1757 and was a member of the city delegation to the Assembly elected in 1759. At the close of 1760 he took his seat in the Council by virtue of a *mandamus* dated two years earlier, and was a member of that body until the end of the provincial period. He was appointed receiver general in 1763, and in 1773 was colonel-in-chief of the Southern Military District. The notable contribution of his military career was in raising a brigade of fifteen hundred Loyalists "for the defense of Long Island and for other exigencies." Of these "De Lancey's Battalions," two afterward took a brilliant part in the British campaigns in the south, while the third remained in Queens County during the whole period of hostilities. De Lancey himself, in chief command of this force as brigadier-general, remained in New York, and was the senior Loyalist officer in the British army in America. Patriot notice of his zeal was effectively shown by the sacking of his mansion at Bloomingdale in 1777 and by his inclusion in the New York Act of Attainder of 1779, by which his property was confiscated. On the other hand, Lord George Germain in a dispatch in 1780 commented on the satisfaction it must afford De Lancey "to know that his services are approved by His Majesty" (*Documents,* VIII, 790).

After the war, in the proceedings in England for the benefit of the Loyalists, he received $125,000 on a claim of $390,000 loss. Two years after leaving New York he died, in 1785, at Beverley, England, and was buried in the cathedral church of that town. His wife was Phila, daughter of Jacob Franks of Philadelphia. Of their children, two sons attained high office, one as chief justice of the Bahamas and governor of Tobago, and the other as adjutant general of the British army.

[*Orderly Book of the Three Battalions of Loyalists Commanded by Brig. Gen. Oliver De Lancey 1776–78* (N. Y. Hist. Soc., 1917); Thos. Jones, *Hist. of N. Y. During the Revolutionary War* (1879), ed. by E. F. De Lancey; A. C. Flick, *Loyalism in N. Y.* (1901); *Docs. Relative to the Colonial Hist. of the State of N. Y.*, esp. vol. VIII (1857); references in bibliographies of other members of the family.] C. W. S.

DE LANCEY, WILLIAM HEATHCOTE (Oct. 8, 1797–Apr. 5, 1865), Episcopal bishop, was the third son of John Peter De Lancey of Mamaroneck, N. Y., and Elizabeth Floyd of Mastic, N. Y. His father was the fourth son of Lieutenant-Governor James De Lancey [*q.v.*]. In spite of his service in the British army and as major in a Pennsylvania corps of Loyalists, John Peter De Lancey seems to have succeeded in escaping the vengeful notice of New York politicians, and in 1789 settled on the Heathcote property in Mamaroneck. His son William was graduated at Yale in 1817, and until Mar. 6, 1822, when he received priest's orders in the Protestant Episcopal Church, was occupied in studies with Bishop Hobart and with services in Trinity and Grace churches in New York City and at St. Thomas's in Mamaroneck. The next fifteen years constituted a period of apprenticeship which, as it turned out, was of especial serviceability for his later episcopal career. His position as one of the assistant ministers of the united parishes of Christ's, St. Peter's, and St. James's in Philadelphia brought him into close intimacy with Bishop White of Pennsylvania. He served as secretary of that diocese for seven years, and as secretary of the House of Bishops of the General Convention in 1823 and in 1826. From 1828 to 1833 he was Provost of the University of Pennsylvania and had very considerable success in checking a decline into which that institution had fallen.

By 1838 a division of the original diocese of New York had become imperative. The territory west of Utica was set off as the diocese of western New York and De Lancey was elected as its first bishop, being consecrated at Auburn, May 9, 1839, and thereafter making Geneva his residence. Of decided opinions, expressed with moderation and unfailing courtesy of demeanor, he carried much before him by sheer weight of personality. "He was the most *impressive* man I have ever seen," wrote Andrew D. White. "I have stood in the presence of many prelates in my day, from Pope Pius IX down; but no one of them has ever so awed me as this Bishop of western New York. His entry into a church chancel was an event; no music could be finer than his reading of the service; his confirmation prayer still dwells in my memory as the most perfect petition I have ever heard, and his simple, earnest sermons took strong hold of me" (*Autobiography,* 1905, II, 524). In the administration of his extensive charge De Lancey succeeded in laying foundations of orderly management and steady ecclesiastical progress which earned for it the reputation of "the model diocese." Regarded at the time of his election as a "High Church" man, he was able in the reverberations in America of the controversy over the Oxford Movement to preserve a remarkable degree of unity in the affairs of his diocese. He took great interest in denominational institutions of education, and the continuation of Hobart College and the founding of De Veaux College at Niagara Falls have been ascribed to his exertions. In respect to church affairs on a national scale, he was the first to suggest officially a plan of provincial organization, though the proposal did not bear fruit till a much later date. His appointment by the General Convention to represent the American Church in 1852 at London, at the third jubilee of the Society for the Propagation of the Gospel was peculiarly appropriate in view of the substantial labors in behalf of the work of the Venerable Society in America accomplished by one of his great-grandfathers, Caleb Heathcote [*q.v.*]. Upon this visit to England the Bishop received the degree of D.C.L. from Oxford; he had already received that of D.D. from Yale in 1827. He was married, Nov. 22, 1820, to Frances, second daughter of Peter Jay Munro of Mamaroneck. Of their eight children, Edward Floyd De Lancey is especially remembered as the editor of Judge Thomas Jones's *History of New York During the Revolutionary War* (1879), the manuscript of which had been confided to the Bishop in 1835.

[C. W. Hayes, *The Diocese of Western N. Y.* (1904); *Jour. Proc. Twenty-eighth Ann. Convention Protestant Episc. Ch. in the Diocese of Western N. Y.* (1865); H. G. Batterson, *A Sketch-Book of the Am. Episcopate* (1878); W. S. Perry, *The Episcopate in America* (1895); J. V. Van Ingen, *An Address . . . at the Funeral of the Rt. Rev. Wm. H. De Lancey* (1865); *Am. Ann. Cyc.*, 1865; J. T. Scharf, *Hist. of Westchester County, N. Y.* (1886).] C.W.S.

DE LANGLADE, CHARLES MICHEL (May 1729–*c.* 1801), was a remarkable French half-breed of the West. His father, Augustin Mouet de Langlade, was a scion of nobility from Guienne, and his mother (baptized Domitelle) was an Ottawa Indian, daughter and sister of the chiefs Nis-so-wa-quet or La Fourche. Charles, born at Mackinac, was their only child, but by his mother's previous marriage to a trader named Villeneuve, he had several half brothers and sisters. He was educated by the Jesuit priests of the post where he lived, wrote a good hand, and was everywhere received as a gentleman. The first event of his career occurred when at the age of ten he accompanied his Indian uncles on a war expedition down the Mississippi. Thither a considerable French army came from New Orleans, and built a post near Memphis and there passed a winter preparing for a campaign against the rebellious Chickasaw. Young De Langlade became enamored of military life and learned much of its details from French officers. Before 1750 he had been enrolled as a cadet in the colonial troops, in 1755 was ensign, and in 1760 lieutenant. His first expedition was that of 1752, when he drove the British traders from the post of Pickawillany and killed the Miami chief "Old Britain."

During all the French and Indian War De Langlade was actively employed as a leader of Indian auxiliaries; he was credited by his contemporaries with the victory over Braddock; he defeated Rogers's Rangers in 1757 on Lake Champlain; he aided in the attack on Fort William Henry; and served in the Quebec campaign of 1759. The next year he left Montreal before its capitulation to Amherst, and brought to Mackinac the news of the French downfall. Upon the desertion of that post by the commandant, De Langlade as second in command delivered it to the English, and soon thereafter transferred his allegiance and became a loyal British subject. In Pontiac's conspiracy he was instrumental in saving the lives of several British soldiers; soon thereafter he removed his home to Green Bay, where he and his father had long had a trading-post. There as the chief settler he became known as the "Father of Wisconsin." His services for the British during the American Revolution were considerable; he had the rank of captain in the Indian department and sent Indian auxiliaries to Carleton and Burgoyne. In the West he parried the efforts of George Rogers Clark, and opposed both American and Spanish partisans. The King granted him lands in Canada for his services. In 1754 he was married at Mackinac to Charlotte Bourassa, and left numerous descendants chiefly in the Grignon line. He lived at Green Bay in patriarchal fashion and there died in the midst of his descendants and retainers.

Essentially military in his characteristics,

known to the western tribesmen as Akewaugeketauso, a soldier chief, he was in his home a kind and devoted father and master, was deeply loved by the Indians, and maintained under three flags his integrity and honor.

[De Langlade's life is narrated by his grandson in *Wis. Hist. Soc. Colls.*, III (1857), 195–295; a sketch by Tassé is translated in *Ibid.*, VII (1876), 123–88. Documentary evidence corrected these earlier sketches and is the basis of a sketch in *Ibid.* (1908), XVIII, 130–32. See also Jos. Tassé, *Les Canadiens de l'Ouest* (Montreal, 1878); *Ontario Hist. Soc. Papers and Records*, III (1901), 147–49; "Langlade Papers, 1737–1800" in *Wis. Hist. Soc. Colls.*, VIII (1879), 209–23.]

L. P. K.

DELANO, AMASSA (Feb. 21, 1763–Apr. 21, 1823), ship-captain, author, son of Samuel and Abigail (Drew) Delano, was born in Duxbury and died in Boston, Mass. The founder of the Delano family in America, Philippe de La Noye, was a Huguenot who affiliated himself with the English Puritans while they were in Holland, and came with them to America in 1621. Samuel Delano, after serving in the French and Indian War, returned to his work of ship-building in Duxbury, and with the exception of two years spent in Braintree continued there till the time of the Revolution. Amassa was a vigorous youngster too absorbed in sports to give much time to books. In later life he recognized his "want of an early and academic education," but added, "I have always seized every possible opportunity during my whole life for the improvement of my mind in the knowledge of useful literature and those sciences that are immediately concerned with the pursuits to which I have been professionally devoted" (Delano, *Narrative of Voyages*, p. 17). Upon the outbreak of the Revolution, Amassa's father entered the Colonial army, but he was soon taken prisoner and confined on the British ship *Rainbow*. Amassa, aged fourteen, also went into the army, and remained in it intermittently till 1779, when he was for some months on board the privateer *Mars*. Afterward he was engaged off and on in shipping between various American ports and the West Indies. This was a stirring life, involving for some years ceaseless vigilance in the direction of the British, and sometimes actual fighting. In the spring of 1787, he took command of a ship bound for Portugal. In returning he was wrecked off Cape Cod, and he came home to find himself in a tangle of difficulties. Notes which he had been obliged to draw on the ship's owner had not been honored, and he was out of acceptable work. His financial state was acute, and he seized as a kind of bonanza an opportunity to become second officer of the *Massachusetts*, a 900-ton ship newly built in Quincy, expressly for the Canton trade. The years of his life from 1790 to 1810 were spent almost wholly at sea, first in one trading-ship, then in another, the most notable of them being perhaps *The Perseverance* and *The Pilgrim*. His experiences during this time, and his meticulous, sometimes naïve, observations are set forth in his book, *Narrative of Voyages and Travels in the Northern and Southern Hemispheres, Comprising Three Voyages Round the World* (1817). In general he writes without digression, but sometimes he turns philosopher—"virtue and vice, happiness and misery," he once pronounces, "are much more equally distributed to nations than those are permitted to suppose who have never been from home, and who believe, like the Chinese, that their residence is the center of the world, of light, of privilege, and of enjoyment" (*Ibid., Voyages*, p. 256). The last years of his life were spent in obscurity. A contemporary account refers to "his recent misfortunes and embarrassments," and the assurance felt by his friends that though he had sometimes erred in judgment, he was "not capable of designing to do wrong to others" (*Ibid.*, p. 593). He was married in Boston to a widow, Hannah Appleton. They had no children.

[J. A. Delano, *Geneal. Hist. and Alliances of the Am. House of Delano 1621 to 1899* (1899); D. H. Hurd, *Hist. of Plymouth County* (1884); L. V. Briggs, *Hist. of Shipbuilding on North River* (1889); S. E. Morison, *Maritime Hist. of Mass.* (1921); F. S. Drake, *Dict. Am. Biog.* (1879); H. H. Scudder, "Melville's Benito Cereno and Capt. Delano's Voyages" in *Mod. Lang. Asso. Pubs.*, XLIII (1928), 502–32, with portrait.]

J. D. W.

DELANO, COLUMBUS (June 5, 1809–Oct. 23, 1896), congressman from Ohio, secretary of the interior, was born at Shoreham, Vt. He was the son of James and Elizabeth (Bateman) Delano, and was descended from a French Huguenot, baptized at Leyden, Holland, as Philippe de la Noye, who came to America on the ship *Fortune*, arriving in Plymouth Harbor in November 1621 (Joel A. Delano, *The Genealogy, History and Alliances of the American House of Delano*, 1899, p. 311). His father died when Columbus was six years old, and two years later, in 1817, the boy's mother moved with him to Mount Vernon, Ohio. His education was the meager schooling of a poor boy in a frontier village. After the manner of the time he read law for a year in a law office and in 1831 secured his license to practise. Three years later, on July 13, 1834, he married Elizabeth Leavenworth of Mount Vernon. For several years, he was prosecuting attorney of Knox County. In 1844 he was elected to Congress, serving one term, 1845–47. He was a Whig and like the other members of his party regarded the Mexican War as a

Southern conspiracy for the extension of slave territory, an offensive war of the United States, with a wicked purpose (*Congressional Globe,* 29 Cong., 2 Sess., App., pp. 278–82). On the Oregon question he supported Polk's boundary compromise at the 49th parallel. In 1847 he tried without success to be the nominee of his party for governor of Ohio. Soon after retiring from Congress he moved to New York City, where he became a member of the banking firm of Delano, Dunlevy & Company (1850–55). He has left no account of this chapter in his life. On his return to Ohio he established his home on the outskirts of Mount Vernon, and gave his attention chiefly to agriculture, sheep raising in particular, but he retained an active interest in party politics. In 1860 and again in 1864 he was delegate to the Republican National Convention. During the Civil War he was for a short time commissary general of Ohio, and for one term a member of the state House of Representatives. From 1865 to 1869 he again represented his district in the national House of Representatives. Though at first inclined to the support of the presidential reconstruction policy, he was among the radical congressmen in 1867, convinced that the South required military government. He was one of the most effective advocates of protective duties for wool and a supporter of the Wool and Woolens Act of 1867 (Delano's speech, July 10, 1866, *Congressional Globe,* 39 Cong., 1 Sess., App., p. 258). In debate, according to Rutherford B. Hayes, one of his associates in Congress (see *Diary and Letters,* vol. III, 1924, pp. 7, 10), Delano was "clear and correct . . . a good specimen of the lively, earnest style of Western talkers." In 1869 President Grant appointed him commissioner of Internal Revenue. Under his administration the whiskey revenue frauds, already notorious when he took office, continued to blacken the record of the national government. In 1870 he succeeded Gen. J. D. Cox as secretary of the interior, and during his five-year tenure serious charges of frauds in the Bureau of Indian Affairs came to a head. Congressional committees of investigation and a special commission appointed by the President, partisan bodies, found evidence of neglect and incompetency within the Indian Bureau, but refused to throw the blame upon the officials at the head (*House Report No. 98,* 42 Cong., 3 Sess., *No. 778,* 43 Cong., 1 Sess.). In order to escape the persecution that newspaper critics visited upon his conduct of public affairs, Delano resigned. It is impossible to avoid the conclusion that though he was probably personally honest he was woefully lacking in high ideals of public service or an appreciation of the responsibility of a department chief (J. F. Rhodes, *History of the United States,* vol. VII, 1906, p. 182 n.; E. P. Oberholtzer, *A History of the United States Since the Civil War,* vol. III, 1926, p. 168; *Report of the Special Commission Appointed to Investigate the Affairs of the Red Cloud Indian Agency,* 1875; *House Miscellaneous Document No. 167,* 44 Cong., 1 Sess.). The care of his country place, the presidency of the National Wool Growers' Association, and duties as a trustee of Kenyon College were the interests of his latter years. He gave liberally to the endowment of the college and built for it Delano Hall.

[*Biog. Record of Knox County* (1902), pp. 184–90 (portrait); public documents cited in text. See list in Oberholtzer, III, 167–70; *Cincinnati Commercial Tribune, Cincinnati Enquirer,* and *Cleveland Plain Dealer,* all Oct. 24, 1896; *Nation* (N. Y.), Apr. 29, Aug. 5, 19, Sept. 18, 30, Oct. 14, 28, 1875 and Mar. 16, 1876.]

E. J. B.

DELANO, JANE ARMINDA (Mar. 12, 1862–Apr. 15, 1919), teacher, nurse, descended from New England stock, was born at Townsend, N. Y., the second child of George and Mary Ann (Wright) Delano. After a brief period of teaching she entered the Bellevue Hospital School of Nursing, New York City, in 1884. Those associated with her during this period speak of her as a well-poised, earnest student, so unobtrusive in her work that to few, if any, of her classmates did it occur that she possessed the force and character that would later bring her name and accomplishment before the eyes of the world. In 1887, the year after her graduation, she was superintendent of nurses at a hospital in Jacksonville, Fla., during an epidemic of yellow fever. The following year she gave to pioneer service as a visiting-nurse in a mining camp at Bisbee, Ariz. After a period of private practise she was appointed superintendent of nurses at the University of Pennsylvania Hospital School of Nursing, serving 1891–96. In 1898 she took a course at the New York School of Civics and Philanthropy. She was Director of the Girls' Department, House of Refuge, Randall's Island, New York, in 1900–02; and from May 1902 to October 1906 was Director of the School of Nursing at her alma mater, resigning to take care of her aged mother whose death two years later released her for work destined to be the most important in her career.

During the Spanish-American War she had joined the New York Branch of the American Red Cross and become interested in securing nurses for enrolment in the Red Cross Nursing Service. After the reorganization of the American Red Cross in 1905, the National Nursing Associations secured an affiliation with that organization which placed the enrolment of nurses in the hands of state and local committees of Red Cross nurses supervised by a National Committee, of which, in 1909, Miss Delano, just appointed superintendent of the newly authorized Army Nurse Corps, was made chairman. While occupying this dual position she developed the plan for making the Red Cross Nursing Service the reserve of the Army Nurse Corps. From 1908 to 1911 she was president of the board of directors of the *American Journal of Nursing,* and from 1909 to 1912 she was president of the American Nurses' Association.

She resigned from the Army Nurse Corps in 1911 to devote her entire time to Red Cross organization. A Bureau of Nursing Service was created in 1916 under which was placed the selection and assignment of nurses and organization of all military and other nursing units. The writer, then superintendent of the Bellevue and Allied Hospital Schools of Nursing, was selected for this office, Miss Delano retaining her connection with the service as chairman of the National Committee. The declaration of war in 1917 was quickly followed by a speeding up of all Red Cross activities. The demand for nurses made by the Army, the Navy, and the United States Public Health Service in its work in the extra cantonment zones, as well as for the use of the Red Cross brought such heavy burdens upon both the chairman of the National Committee and the director of the Bureau of Nursing Service that a Department of Nursing was created in 1918 with Miss Delano as director. When the Armistice was signed the Red Cross Nursing Service had assigned 17,931 nurses to the Army; 1,058 to the Navy; 284 to the United States Public Health Service, while 604 were working under the Red Cross with the civilian population in the countries of the Allies. The Nursing Service also supplied 553 Red Cross aides for special work in France, and to the influenza epidemic in 1918, especially to war industries, over 15,000 graduate and practical nurses and volunteer aides.

The war over and the influenza epidemic allayed, Miss Delano sailed on Jan. 2, 1919, for France, on her last tour of inspection. Developing a mastoid, from which she never recovered, she died at Savenay Hospital Center, Apr. 15, 1919. It was characteristic of her devotion to the Red Cross that her last words were, "What about my work? I must get back to my work." It was also characteristic of her that, as a memorial to her mother and father, she should leave a legacy, together with the royalties from the *American Red Cross Textbook on Elementary Hygiene and Home Care of the Sick* (1913), which with Isabel McIsaacs she found time to prepare during her busy Red Cross days, and to support one or more visiting nurses in communities where none existed. Many decorations were bestowed upon her by foreign countries; the Distinguished Service Medal of the United States and that of the American Red Cross were posthumously awarded.

[*Hist. of Am. Red Cross Nursing* (1922); *Am. Nat. Red Cross, Ann. Report,* June 30, 1919; H. P. Davison, *The Am. Red Cross in the Great War* (1919); *Red Cross Bulletin,* Apr. 21, May 12, 1919; *N. Y. Times,* Apr. 17, 20, 1919; J. A. and M. Delano, *The Hist. and Geneal. of Delano and Launoy* (1899), p. 522; personal acquaintance.]
C. D. N.

DELANY, MARTIN ROBINSON (May 6, 1812–Jan. 24, 1885), first negro major in the United States army, was born in Charles Town, Va. (now in W. Va.), the son of free negroes, Samuel and Pati Delany. His paternal grandfather, a member of the Golah tribe, once fled to Toronto with his wife and two sons, but was brought back and later lost his life in an encounter with a slaveholder. His maternal grandfather, a prince of the Mandingo tribe, had been captured in the Niger Valley, sold, and brought to America along with his betrothed. As a boy of six Delany received his first instruction from peddlers of books. Because of persecution his people were forced to remove to Chambersburg, Pa., in 1822. In 1831 he went to Pittsburgh, where he found better opportunity for study under Rev. Louis Woodson, who was employed by a society of negroes interested in education. By 1834 he was already showing his interest in organizations for the welfare of the poor people of the city; and within the next two years he began the study of medicine under Dr. Andrew N. McDowell, though his work in this field was soon interrupted. On Mar. 15, 1843, he was married to Kate A. Richards of Pittsburgh, and he became the father of eleven children. In 1843 also he began in Pittsburgh the publication of the *Mystery,* a small paper that somehow attracted a good deal of attention to itself, as when it gave a notable description of the fire in the city in 1844. Sued for libel by a negro who was said to be assisting slave-catchers, he was once fined $200 and costs; but several citizens came to his assistance and the fine was later remitted. During the years 1847–49 he was associated with Frederick Douglass in bringing out the *North Star,* published by that orator at Rochester, N. Y. In July 1848 he was mobbed in northern Ohio. The next year he resumed his studies, being received in the medical department of Harvard College after he had been refused entrance at institutions in Pennsylvania and New York. After leaving Harvard he lectured in the West and served with great efficiency in the cholera epidemic in Pittsburgh in 1854. His little book, *The Condition, Elevation, Emigration, and Destiny of the Colored People of the United States, Politically Considered,* issued in Philadelphia in 1852, was earnest and thoughtful, and anticipated Booker T. Washington in its emphasis on practical education. In 1854 he issued a call for a National Emigration Convention, which met in Cleveland in August. The convention established a permanent board of commissioners, of which Delany was made president. A second convention was held in Cleveland in August 1856, and in this year he removed to Chatham, Ontario, where he engaged in the practise of medicine. Two years later a third convention, held at Chatham, chose Delany as chief commissioner to explore the Valley of the Niger, making inquiries "for the purpose of science and for general information and without any reference to, and with the Board being entirely opposed to, any Emigration there as such" (see *Official Report of the Niger Valley Exploring Party,* 1861, by Delany himself). Accordingly, in May 1859 he sailed from New York in the bark *Mendi,* owned by three African merchants. The next year he visited Liverpool and London. On his return to the United States he assisted Charles L. Remond and Charles H. Langston in recruiting negro soldiers, and he was an acting examining surgeon in Chicago. On Feb. 8, 1865, he received his commission as major and on Apr. 5 was ordered to Charleston. After the war he served for three years in the Freedmen's Bureau, was for several years custom-house inspector in Charleston, also for four years a trial justice in the city. He was a severe critic of the corruption of the Reconstruction period in South Carolina and, with Richard H. Cain [*q.v.*] and Joseph H. Rainey, was a leader of the Honest Government League. He was nominated for lieutenant-governor on the Independent Republican ticket, in 1874, but was defeated. In 1879 he published *Principia of Ethnology: the Origin of Races and Color,* etc. In 1884 he was employed to act as agent for a Boston firm in Central America; but by this time his health was failing. He died the following year at Xenia, Ohio.

[In addition to references given above see A. Rollin, *Life and Public Services of Martin R. Delany* (1868); sketch in Wm. J. Simmons, *Men of Mark* (1887); W. P. and F. J. Garrison, *Wm. Lloyd Garrison* (4 vols., 1885–89); A. A. Taylor, *The Negro in S. C. during the Reconstruction* (1924); *Daily Morning Post* (Pittsburgh), Oct. 18, 1854; *News and Courier* (Charleston, S. C.), Feb. 13, Sept. 2, 15, Oct. 2, 3, 1874; Jas. T. Holly, "In Memoriam," *A. M. E. Church Rev.,* Oct. 1886.]

B. B.

DELANY, PATRICK BERNARD (Jan. 28, 1845–Oct. 19, 1924), electrical engineer, inventor, was born in Killavilla, Kings County, Ireland, the son of James and Margaret Delany. Until he was nine years of age he lived in Ireland and attended private school there, but in 1854 his parents came to the United States with their children and settled in Hartford, Conn. Here Delany continued his education, attending parochial schools for the next five years. He then went to work as an office boy in a telegraph office in Hartford. He had always been greatly interested in electricity and took every opportunity to learn telegraphy. By the time he was sixteen years old he had the reputation of being a good telegraph operator. Making this his chosen profession he progressed rapidly and at eighteen was appointed press telegraph operator at Worcester, Mass. Two years later he was given the position of night telegraph circuit manager at Albany, N. Y., for all wires between New York and Buffalo, and three years later became chief operator of the Franklin Telegraph Company at Philadelphia. About 1870 he left Philadelphia to become assistant general superintendent of the newly organized Southern & Atlantic Telegraph Company at Washington, D. C., whose wires began there and spread out through the Southern states to New Orleans, Memphis, and Louisville. About five years later he resigned this position to accept one of superintendent of the Automatic Telegraph Company, also of Washington. His association during these years with George H. Grace, to whom the success of the Southern & Atlantic Telegraph Company was largely due and who was one of the originators of the American Press Association, influenced Delany to abandon telegraphy about 1876 and become a newspaper correspondent. Subsequently, but only for a short time, he was editor of the *Old Commonwealth,* a newspaper at Harrisonburg, Va., but in 1880 he gave up this work to devote his whole time to electrical invention, particularly telegraphy. In that year he moved North with his family and settled in South Orange, N. J., where he became a neighbor and close friend of Thomas Edison for the rest of his life. All told, in the course of his inventive career Delany received a hundred and fifty or two hundred patents. Of these inventions the most prominent were the anti-Page relay; anti-induction cables; a synchronous, multiplex telegraph by which six messages could be sent simultaneously over a single wire and which was subsequently adopted by the British Post Office Department; a perforator for telegraphic transmitting tapes; telegraphic keyboard apparatus; a sound-reproducing machine; a talking-machine recorder and reproducer; as well as the method for manufacture of a talking-machine, known commercially as Vox Humana. He devoted years to improving cable telegraphy, the reward of which was that his automatic system for cables when put in service showed an increase of thirty per cent in speed over hand signaling. During the World War Delany's experimental work in his laboratory at Nantucket, Mass., was concerned principally with the invention of devices for submarine detection and the general location of submerged metallic objects. With these latter inventions, for which he received patents between 1916 and 1918, and with apparatus based on them, it is said that a valuable shipment of gold bullion sunk with the liner *Laurentic* off the coast of Ireland during the war was recovered for the British government. Credit is also given Delany for the recovery in 1923 of a large quantity of copper buried in nine feet of mud on the floor of New York Harbor. He received the Elliott Cresson gold medal on two separate occasions and also the John Scott legacy medal, both awarded by the Franklin Institute. At both the Buffalo and St. Louis expositions he was awarded gold medals for his inventions. He was charter member of the American Institute of Electrical Engineers, founded in 1884, and was one of its vice-presidents, and was also a member of the American Association for the Advancement of Science. He married Annie M. Ovenshine of Philadelphia on Mar. 31, 1869. He died at South Orange and was buried at Nantucket, Mass. An only son survived him.

[*Jour. Am. Inst. Electrical Engineers,* Nov. 11, 1924; *Telegraph and Telephone Age,* Nov. 1, 1924; Jas. D. Reid, *The Telegraph in America* (1879); *Who's Who in America,* 1922–23; obituary in *N. Y. Times,* Oct. 20, 1924; Patent Office records; U. S. National Museum correspondence.] C. W. M.

DELAVAN, EDWARD CORNELIUS (1793–Jan. 15, 1871), reformer, publisher, was born in Westchester County, N. Y. Although named Edward Cornelius, he rarely used the "Edward." His father having died, at the age of eight he went to Albany with his mother, a brother, and two sisters. He entered a printing-office in that place at the age of thirteen, worked there for several years, then went into his older brother's hardware store. While in the hardware store he also engaged in selling wine, which proved very successful financially. In 1814 he formed a partnership with his brother and shortly after went to Europe as purchasing agent for the firm. Returning to America in 1816 he settled in New York City where he lived until 1825. He then returned to Albany and dealt in real estate for the next five years. His speculations in that field added greatly to his already ample fortune. By the time he had reached middle age he was convinced of the evils of alcohol and during the remainder of his life spent a considerable fortune for the temperance cause. With Dr. Eliphalet Nott [*q.v.*] he organized the New York State Temperance Society in 1829. The *American Temperance Intelligencer,* and the *Temperance Recorder,* both published at Albany, were virtually under his control, and with his own money he secured a large circulation, thus enabling his two papers to exert more influence than all other temperance journals then published. In 1835 he engaged in a public discussion of the undesirability of alcoholic wines for use in church communion, and his arguments attracted wide attention. In the same year he published an article in the *Albany Evening Journal* stating that the Albany brewers were using filthy water for brewing. He was sued for libel, and other persons, gaining courage from the brewers, sued for contended damage in times past. Delavan won the first case and the others dropped their suits. He had the entire proceedings of the trial printed for use as propaganda. When the American Temperance Union was organized in 1836 he became chairman of the executive committee and donated $10,000 to its funds. In 1840 he secured a collection of drawings of the human stomach showing the evil effects of alcohol. At a personal expense of $7,000 he circulated in the state of New York 150,000 of these colored and engraved plates. In 1841 he began to publish the *Enquirer,* a small temperance journal. In 1843 he collected and edited a group of documents which had appeared in the public papers in relation to the drawings which he had published. In 1858 he presented to Union College, Schenectady, a deed of trust to a collection of shells and minerals valued at $10,000. Later publications of Delavan's include a pamphlet, *Temperance of Wine Countries* (1860), and a collection of articles, published in book form under the title, *Temperance Essays* (1865). Delavan was twice married: first, to Abby Smith of Lyme, Conn., and second, to Harriet Schuyler, daughter of Cornelius Schuyler of Albany. He died at his home in Schenectady, N. Y.

[*Nat. Temperance Advocate,* Feb. 1871; *Standard Encyc. of the Alcohol Problem,* vol. II (1924); G. W. Schuyler, *Colonial N. Y.* (1885), II, 154.] M. S.

DE LA WARR, THOMAS WEST, Baron (July 9, 1577–June 7, 1618), first governor and captain general of the colony of Virginia, was the son of Thomas West, second or eleventh Baron De La Warr, and Anne, the daughter of Sir Francis Knollys. He was born probably at Wherwell, Hampshire, where he was baptized. He matriculated at Queen's College, Oxford, Mar. 9, 1591/2, but left without having taken a degree. After traveling in Italy, he returned to England in 1596 and on Nov. 25 of that year married Cecilia, the daughter of Sir Thomas Shirley, at St. Dunstan's in the West, London. In the following year he was elected to Parliament for Lymington. After serving with distinction in the army in the Low Countries, he was with his cousin, the Earl of Essex, in Ireland in 1599, and was there knighted by Essex on July 12 (W. A. Shaw, *The Knights of England,* 1906, II, 96). He was implicated in the Essex rebellion, imprisoned in the Counter in Wood St., London, in February 1600/1, and subsequently fined 1,000 marks. West's father died Mar. 24, 1601/2, and he succeeded to the peerage and was named a member of the Privy Council. He was created M.A. of Oxford on Aug. 30, 1605.

De La Warr was named as a grantee in the second charter to the Virginia Company of London. He was a member of the Council of the Company in 1609 and it was planned that he should head a mammoth expedition to Virginia. As an initial step the Company appointed Sir Thomas Gates [*q.v.*] lieutenant-general and Sir George Somers admiral. They sailed from England with eight ships and a pinnace, carrying five hundred colonists, in June 1609. The vessel upon which Gates and Somers embarked was wrecked at Bermuda and they were forced to remain there until two pinnaces had been built to carry them to the mainland. It was not until May 1610 that they reached Virginia, where they found the colonists in a deplorable condition and decided to abandon the colony and take them back to England.

Meanwhile, on Feb. 28, 1609/10, the Company had appointed De La Warr first governor and captain general for life of the Colony of Virginia. He sailed from England at the head of an expedition of three ships and 150 colonists on Apr. 1, 1610, arriving at Cape Henry on June 5, at Point Comfort on the following day, and at Jamestown on June 10 just in time to save the colony, the inhabitants of which Gates had already embarked on vessels for the return voyage to England. De La Warr dispatched Somers to Bermuda for supplies and Gates to England for help. He caused Fort Henry and Fort Charles at the mouth of the river and a third fort at the falls to be erected.

De La Warr had arrived in Virginia in the summer season. The company he brought with him suffered severely from the effects of the heat and he himself became ill. He appointed Capt. George Percy as deputy governor, until Sir Thomas Dale should arrive in the colony, and on Mar. 28, 1611, sailed for the island of "Mevis" [Nevis?] in the West Indies to recuperate, but was driven from his course to the Western Islands, whence, upon his recovery, he returned to England, arriving in June 1611. There he published *The Relation of the Right Honourable the Lord De-la-Warre, Lord Governour and Captaine Generall of the Colonie, planted in Virginea* (London, 1611), and worked to win support for the colony. He was planning a second voyage to Virginia as early as December 1616, but it was not until March 1617/18, that he sailed from England with 200 men. The vessel touched at Terceira in the Azores where De La Warr and his crew were feasted. Immediately afterward they became ill, and it was suspected that they had been poisoned. De La Warr died on June 7, 1618.

Lady De La Warr survived her husband and was named executrix of his will. To provide for her five daughters, she petitioned for and was granted on Sept. 13, 1619, a pension of £500 per annum to be paid by the farmers of the customs of Virginia for thirty-one years. This was renewed in 1634 but lapsed during the period of the Civil Wars, the Commonwealth, and the Protectorate. A new grant of £200 per annum was made to Jane West, a daughter, in 1662. De La Warr left seven children, of whom Henry, born Oct. 3, 1603, succeeded to the title.

[*Calendar of State Papers, Domestic Ser.*; *Calendar of State Papers, Colonial Ser.*; *Acts of the Privy Council*; *Acts of the Privy Council, Colonial Ser.*; Alexander Brown, *The Genesis of the U. S.* (2 vols., 1890); *The Records of the Va. Company of London* (2 vols., 1906), ed. by Susan Myra Kingsbury; E. S. Neill, "Va. Governors under the London Company," in *Macalester College Contribs., Dept of Hist., Lit., and Pol. Sci.*, 1 ser., no. 1 (1889). There is an article in the *Dict. of Nat. Biog.* with further references.]

I. M. C.

DE LEON, DANIEL (Dec. 14, 1852–May 11, 1914), Socialist advocate, was of Jewish stock, the son of Salomon and Sara (Jesurun) De Leon, and was born on the island of Curaçao. His early education was received at home, but was interrupted by the death of his father, a surgeon in the Dutch colonial army, when the boy was twelve years old. In 1866 he was sent to a gymnasium at Hildesheim, Germany, and he afterward studied at Amsterdam. The belief that he was a graduate of the University of Leyden is not borne out by the records of the institution, which do not reveal his name. About 1874 he came to the United States, making his home in New York City, where later his mother rejoined him. For a time he was associate editor of a Spanish paper advocating Cuban liberation and later taught school in Westchester County, N. Y. While thus employed he attended classes in law and political science at Columbia College, in 1878 receiving the degree of LL.B. After practising law for a time in Texas, he returned to New York City and in 1883 won a prize lectureship at Columbia in Latin-American diplomacy, which he retained for two three-year terms, thereafter retiring from the college.

In the meantime he had become deeply interested in social questions. He actively supported the candidacy of Henry George for mayor in 1886; in 1888 he joined the Knights of Labor; about a year later he became affiliated with the Nationalist movement, founded by Edward Bellamy, and in October 1890, he joined the Socialist Labor party. His partisans have always asserted that his retirement from the college was forced by his radical activities, but the statement has been denied by competent authority, and it is evident that his lectureship expired by self-limitation. In 1891 he was appointed national lecturer of the party and later in the year was chosen as its candidate for governor of New York. About the beginning of 1892 he became the editor of its organ, *The People,* a weekly, to which a daily edition was added in 1900 but discontinued in February, 1914. He was again a candidate for governor in 1902 and several times conducted spirited but unsuccessful campaigns for the state Assembly and for Congress.

He early assumed a dominant position in the party, and despite repeated attempts to dislodge him maintained his leadership to the end. He took a strongly antagonistic attitude toward the existing trade-unions, characterizing their leaders as "labor fakers," and demanding the reorganization of the unions on a frankly Socialist basis. In 1895 he led a seceding faction from the Knights of Labor and founded the Socialist Trade and Labor Alliance, and in the following year obtained its indorsement by the national convention of the party. An opposing faction, friendly to the old unions, now began to make headway, and charging De Leon with being a "doctrinaire" and a "dictator," gradually won to its side the greater part of the membership. In July 1899, failing to oust De Leon from his place, this faction withdrew and formed a new organization, which ultimately became the Socialist Party of America. From this loss of members and prestige his own party never recovered. At Chicago, in June 1905, De Leon took part in the formation of the Industrial Workers of the World, the Socialist Trade and Labor Alliance being immediately merged with it. The new organization, however, soon came under the control of the extreme "direct actionists," who rejected all political effort, and in the convention of 1908 De Leon was refused a seat. A few weeks later, at Paterson, N. J., his partisans organized a rival I. W. W., which subsequently changed its name to that of the Workers' International Industrial Union. To a greatly diminished following he continued during the next six years to expound his conception of Socialism and Socialist tactics and to excoriate those who disagreed with him. In 1913 he moved from New York City to Pleasantville, in Westchester County. He died in a hospital in New York City.

De Leon was twice married—on Aug. 2, 1882, to Sara Lobo (who died in April 1887), and on June 10, 1892, to Bertha Canary, who survived him. His character has been the subject of the most contradictory estimates. His opponents have assailed him as a disruptive fanatic, avid of power and an adept in dissimulation and intrigue. It is certain that in at least one matter he was uncandid, for despite the known facts regarding his ancestry, he professed among his intimates to be a "Venezuelan Catholic," of a wealthy and aristocratic family. His partisans have portrayed him as a man friendly in disposition, genial in temperament, and of incorruptible integrity, content in his single-minded devotion to the cause of the workers to live and die poor. The value of his contribution to social politics is also a matter of dispute. By his opponents he is held to have brought to the social movement nothing but turmoil and dissension. His followers, on the other hand, declare that his concept of a revolutionary working-class organization, formed by industries instead of by crafts, determined to "take and hold" and operate the means of production and distribution, is a prescient foreshadowing of the means by which society is some day to be reconstructed. Lenin, who became acquainted with his writings after the Bolshevik revolution, admired them greatly and declared that they incorporated the germ of the Soviet system. His literary product was mostly propaganda pamphlets such as *Two Pages from Roman History* (1903), *What Means This Strike?* (1898), *Socialist Reconstruction of Society* (1905), but he also translated Marx's *The Eighteenth Brumaire of Louis Napoleon* and seventeen of the nineteen historical romances in Eugène Sue's series, *The*

Mysteries of the People; or History of a Proletarian Family Across the Ages.

[*Who's Who in America,* 1914–15; *Daniel De Leon, The Man and His Work. A Symposium* (1919); Olive M. Johnson, *Daniel De Leon* (pamphlet, 1923); *Annual Registers of Columbia College* (1883–89); records of the University of Leyden; recollections of the writer; information as to certain details from Sol. J. Delvalle of the Congregation Mikve Israel of Curaçao, Solon De Leon (the son of Daniel) and Arnold Petersen of New York City, J. M. L. Maduro of The Hague, and others.]

W. J. G.

DE LEON, THOMAS COOPER (May 21, 1839–Mar. 19, 1914), author, son of Mardici Heinrich and Rebecca (Lopez-y-Nunez) De Leon, was born in Columbia, S. C., and died in Mobile, Ala. The ancestors of both his parents came to this country from the Spanish West Indies before the Revolution. His father was a physician, an intimate friend of Thomas Cooper, president of the University of South Carolina, for whom he named the youngest of his three sons. Of the older sons, David Camden became surgeon-general of the Confederacy, and Edwin, an author and a diplomat in Egypt. Thomas Cooper was educated primarily in Washington at Rugby Academy and at Georgetown University; at the first, he was a fellow student of Henry Watterson, and at the second, of James Ryder Randall. From 1858 to 1861 he was in Washington as a clerk in the bureau of topographical engineers. He was in the Confederate army (1861–65), apparently always on duty at the capital, whether Montgomery or Richmond. His experiences and observations during this period—social as well as political—were recorded later in his graphic and judicious if somewhat journalistic books, *Four Years in Rebel Capitals* (1890) and *Belles Beaux and Brains of the 60's* (1907). He was in Baltimore (1865–66) as editor of the *Cosmopolite Magazine,* and in New York (1866–67) as writer for various newspapers and magazines, and—to the scandal of his friends—as translator of French novels. His anthology, *South Songs* (1866), and his political writings under the name Dunne Browne recommended him favorably to Southern publicists, and in 1868, on the summons of John Forsyth, he removed to Mobile as managing editor, and after 1877 as editor, of the *Mobile Register.* He remained there for the rest of his life, incredibly tireless and versatile—as editor, printer, advocate of free-silver, theatre-manager, director of carnivals both North and South, and society-man agreeably tinged with Bohemianism. In addition, he was a poet, essayist, parodist, novelist, and playwright—in whatever capacity, always keenly sensitive to the shifts of popular taste. Aside from his important books of war reminiscence, the most notable of his writings were perhaps his burlesque play, *Hamlet ye Dismal Prince,* produced in New York in 1870, and said to have been the first American play to run for 100 nights—his two "travesties," *The Rock or the Rye* (1888) parodying Amélie Rives, and *Society as I have Foundered It* (1890) parodying Ward McAllister—and his two local-color novels *Creole and Puritan* (1889) and *Crag-Nest* (1897). Although he was blind for the last eleven years of his life, he remained ceaselessly active. He never married.

[T. McA. Owen, *Hist. of Ala. and Dict. of Ala. Biog.,* III (1921); L. DeV. Chaudron, "Sketch of the Author of Four Years in Rebel Capitals," in T. C. De Leon, *Four Years in Rebel Capitals* (ed. 1892); *Who's Who in America,* 1912–13; *Mobile Reg.,* Mar. 20, 1914.]

J. D. W.

DELÉRY, FRANÇOIS CHARLES (Jan. 28, 1815–June 12, 1880), physician, writer, was a typical Louisiana Creole, born in the Parish of St. Charles, La., of French-Canadian ancestry. His father was Louis Boisclair Deléry; his mother, Marie Corbin Babin. In 1829 he was sent to Paris to complete his classical education and to prepare himself for medicine. His studies successfully ended, his thesis, *Questions sur diverses branches des sciences médicales,* published in Paris in 1842, he returned to Louisiana to exercise his chosen profession and to take an active part in civic affairs. He was for seven years city physician of New Orleans, and president of the board of health for two; he founded *l'Union Médicale* to which he contributed frequently; in 1858 he represented his adopted city at the Quarantine Congress held in Philadelphia. He opposed secession, but when it had occurred his love for Louisiana caused him to espouse the Southern cause and he was one of the first to leave New Orleans after the arrival of Federal troops. He went to Havana, where he wrote in support of the Confederacy. On his return to New Orleans, after the war, he became city coroner.

His chief claims to fame are his writings on the problems of yellow fever: *Précis historique de la fièvre jaune de 1858* (1859), *Réplique au mémoire du Dr. Faget* (1860), *Mémoire sur l'épidémie de fièvre jaune qui a régné à la Nouvelle-Orléans et dans les campagnes* (1867), *Quarantaine* (1878). These reveal sound scientific training, skilful treatment, and a sincere passion for investigation. He studied his subject carefully and thoroughly. He fought quarantine as a preventive of yellow fever, although he attributed the cause of the disease to a germ. With the exception of an unpublished collection of poems written under the influence of the French poet Delavigne, his non-medical writings were educational, philosophical, and patriotic. They include: *Essai sur la liberté* (1847), *Études sur les passions, suivies d'un aperçu sur l'éducation qu'il convient de donner au peuple* (1849), *Quelques mots sur le Nativisme* (1854), *Confédérés et Fédéraux* (1864), *Le dernier chant du guerrier orateur, à la mémoire du lieutenant-colonel C. D. Dreux* (1861), *Le spectre noir ou le radicalisme aux États-Unis* (1868), and a comedy in one act, *l'École du peuple* (1877). All were published in New Orleans and in French; *Black Ghost* was also published in English. Deléry was a man of ideals, devoted to his profession and his state. He had the courage of his convictions and he worked consistently and persistently for what he felt to be right. His last years were spent in the practise of his profession at Bay St. Louis, where he died, survived by his wife Odile, who was also a Deléry.

[Chas. Testut in his *Portraits littéraires* (1850), and J. W. Davidson in *Living Writers of the South* (1869) have both contributed interesting sketches of Deléry. C. P. Dimitry in the *Times-Democrat* (New Orleans), Oct. 9, 16, 1892, and Grace King in *Creole Families of New Orleans* (1921), see "Lafreniere," have given the family background. A good obituary notice is to be found in the *New Orleans Medic. & Surgic. Jour.* for Dec. 1880. See also Bussière Rouen, "Les Poètes Louisianais" in the *Comptes Rendus* of the Athenée Louisianais, Jan.–April 1921, and Ruby Caulfeild, *The French Literature of Louisiana* (1929), pub. by the Inst. of French Studies, Columbia Univ.] L. C. D.

DEL MAR, ALEXANDER (Aug. 9, 1836–July 1, 1926), mining engineer, economist, historian, was born in New York, the eldest son of Jacques and Belle (Alexander) Del Mar. The former was descended from a Spanish family which settled in Pennsylvania in the seventeenth century and the latter was of British stock. Jacques Del Mar, for many years an official in the Treasury Department, maintained an active interest in his Spanish connections, and his son, receiving his early education in private schools in New York, spent several of his boyhood years in England and Spain. In the latter country he attended the Madrid School of Mines. In London he came under the guidance of his uncle, Manuel Del Mar, an author, and also Sir Arthur Helps. These associations stimulated his interest in history and political economy. Returning to New York in 1854, he found no opening for the active practise of his profession. By nature a student and investigator, at an early age he undertook to prepare a book on the history of precious metals published much later. He also formed editorial connections with *Hunt's Merchants' Magazine*, *DeBow's Review*, the *Commercial and Financial Chronicle*, and the *Social Science Review*, and contributed to these journals essays dealing for the most part with public finance and monetary problems.

From 1866 to 1869 he was director of the Bureau of Statistics, a new bureau designed to concentrate statistical work previously undertaken by officers in the Treasury and State departments. Unfortunately, he undertook to develop these statistical inquiries on a scale far too extended, and became involved in administrative difficulties with his superiors. In 1871 he moved to Brooklyn, where for a brief period he was engaged in promoting municipal reform and in 1872 joined the Liberal Republican party in support of Greeley. During the same period he rendered a signal service to life insurance companies in predicting, contrary to prevailing opinion, that interest rates would fall and that consequently it would be necessary for these companies to face decreasing earnings (*Proceedings of the Second Session of the National Insurance Convention*, 1872, pp. 188–216). In 1872 also he accepted an invitation from the Russian government to attend the sessions of the International Statistical Congress in St. Petersburg and in 1876 he served as mining engineer of the United States Monetary Commission. After a period in California studying the history of mining in the Western states, in 1878 he returned to the East to serve for a short while as clerk to the committee on naval expenditures of the House of Representatives.

Two years later he published in London *A History of the Precious Metals from the Earliest Times to the Present* (1880; second edition, thoroughly revised, New York, 1901). This supplements William Jacob's *Historical Inquiry into the Production and Consumption of the Precious Metals*, published in 1831. Del Mar's volume contains a series of tables showing the stocks of gold and silver coin in each country over a long series of dates. The influence of new supplies of gold and silver in the progress of civilization had early absorbed his attention; in this book he noted particularly that the search for gold had extended the area and prolonged the establishment of slavery. The cost of production theory as applied to the precious metals in his opinion had no significance. Moreover, he held, the changes in price, due to new supplies of metallic money, were not synchronous, or uniform for all commodities, and speculators were thus enabled to reap large rewards. The *History of the Precious Metals* was followed by a long series of monographs and pamphlets dealing with metallic money, coinage, and the mints, including: *The Science of Money* (1885); *Money and Civilization* (1886); *The History of Money in America from the Earliest Times to the Establishment of the Constitution* (1899). He also published historical and archeological studies, in which he assembled much curious information in regard to the interrelations of the religions of ancient peoples with their economic life. Among these were: *The Worship of Augustus Cæsar* (1900), based upon a study of coins, money, calendars, astronomical and astrological cycles; *The Middle Ages Revisited; or, The Roman Government and Religion and Their Relations to Britain* (1900); *Ancient Britain in the Light of Modern Archeological Discoveries* (1900); and *The Messiah* (1907), developing the history of the Messianic cult. Between 1899 and 1902 he edited the *Cambridge Encyclopædia* of esoteric subjects. In his contributions to the study of money, he accumulated much curious data, but for students of monetary theory his volumes have but a limited value. He was married in 1861, to Emilia José (Emily Joseph), and after her death in 1912, to Alice Demorest who survived him. He died at the home of his daughter, in Little Falls, N. J.

[Most of Del Mar's volumes contain in appendices the long list of the various pamphlets which he issued. See also Hamilton Willcox, *The Life of the Honorable Alexander Del Mar* (1898); *Who's Who in America*, 1924–25; obituary in *N. Y. Times*, July 3, 1926.]

D. R. D.

DELMAS, DELPHIN MICHAEL (Apr. 14, 1844–Aug. 1, 1928), lawyer, the son of Antoine and Coralie Delmas, was born in France, but his father joined the gold rush in 1849, and the family followed to California in 1854, settling at San José in the Santa Clara Valley. The boy's early education was received at home, and in 1858 he entered Santa Clara College, where he graduated with a brilliant record (A.B., 1862, A.M. 1863), and was awarded a gold medal for proficiency in the classics. After a few months in a law office in San Francisco, he entered the Yale Law School (LL.B., 1865), and was admitted to the California bar in February 1866. Opening an office in San José, he made slow progress, and was compelled to add to his means by teaching school. In 1867, however, an eloquent Fourth-of-July address attracted the attention of the local Democrats, who elected him district attorney for Santa Clara County, in which office he displayed marked efficiency. Among his early cases was a series of successful damage suits against the Southern Pacific Railroad in which he exhibited such ability that he was soon enjoying a large and lucrative practise. In February 1883 he removed to San Francisco where he quickly became one of the leaders of the California bar. For the next twenty years, not confining himself to any special field, he was associated with every outstanding case before the state courts, including *Colton* vs. *Leland Stanford et al.* (82 *Cal.*, 351), by reason of the vast financial interest involved the most important private litigation ever conducted in California; and the spectacular claim of Nettie R. Craven to the Fair estate. A delegate to the Democratic National Convention in 1904, he there nominated William Randolph Hearst for the presidency.

In 1907 he achieved nation-wide notoriety through his conduct of the defense of Harry K. Thaw on the latter's first trial for the murder of Stanford White in New York City. His invocation on Thaw's behalf of a higher and "unwritten" law and a type of insantity which he designated "*dementia Americana*"—stigmatized as "brain storm, the paranoia of the millionaire," by the district attorney, W. T. Jerome—was a contribution of doubtful value to criminal jurisprudence. For a short period thereafter he was engaged professionally in New York City, but ultimately returned to California, practising in San Francisco and later in Los Angeles, up to within a few months of his death, which occurred at Santa Monica. He married, Apr. 7, 1869, Pauline, daughter of Col. J. P. Hoge of San Francisco.

Known as the "Napoleon of the California bar" from his strong facial resemblance to the Emperor, he also possessed the latter's trait of rapid decision and faculty of instinctively finding his opponent's weak spots. An accomplished lawyer, a master of the art of cross-examination, an astute tactician of keen intellect and wide vision, he prepared his briefs with infinite care, leaving no contingency unprovided for. Endowed with unusual fluency and a wide vocabulary, which, aided by his classical education, he assiduously cultivated, he earned the title of the "silver-tongued spell-binder of the Pacific Coast," though he never sacrificed lucidity to mere phrase-making. A book entitled *Speeches and Addresses,* published in 1901 in San Francisco, embodies his outstanding achievements.

[*Who's Who in America*, 1928–29; Santa Clara College catalogues, 1858–63; *Hist. of the Bench and Bar of Cal.* (1901), ed. by Oscar T. Shuck, p. 625; *The Trial of Harry Thaw* (London, 1928), ed. by F. A. Mackenzie; *Hist. of Santa Clara County, Cal.* (1881), p. 707; *The Bay of San Francisco* (1892), II, 453; *Santa Clara County and its Resources* (1895), p. 268. Obituary notices appeared in the San Francisco, Los Angeles, and New York City press of Aug. 2, 1928.]

H. W. H. K.

DELMONICO, LORENZO (Mar. 13, 1813–Sept. 3, 1881), restaurateur, was born at Marengo, at the eastern base of Mount St. Gothard, in the canton of Ticino, Switzerland. His father was a small farmer and Lorenzo's schooling advantages were slight—a deficiency that he sought to remedy in after years. At nineteen he left his native village and migrated to America, landing at New York, whither two uncles, John and Peter Delmonico, had preceded him. John, the elder, had been master of a sailing vessel trading between Cuba and the United States, but in 1825 he had given up the sailor's calling, settled in New York City, and become a dealer in wines. With his brother Peter he had started a small confectionery and catering business. After some hesitation, they took their nephew into partnership, and he soon suggested a departure in their modest business which was destined to make the name Delmonico famous throughout the United States and in every European capital. His idea was that the firm open a restaurant in downtown New York which should provide foods cooked and served in the European manner of the day. As a people Americans had neglected the science of the table. The value of salads was practically unknown. In a land of abundance only the most imperfect use was made of vegetables, many of which could have been provided at a minimum of cost. Lorenzo Delmonico became a teacher of gastronomy, and in a surprisingly short time he won national recognition. Without capital and at first without influential friends, within twenty years he made New York known the world over as a center of good living. From materials that could be had almost for the asking he prepared dishes such as few native New Yorkers had ever tasted. The variety of American game, fish, and meats that appeared on his menus astonished all visitors from the Old World. Yet he was merely making obvious use of what had been largely overlooked by the Americans themselves. He seems to have been guided by his own shrewd divination of New York's culinary needs and the practical means of supplying them. His fame spread so quickly that within a few years experienced cooks from Parisian kitchens were coming to New York and offering Delmonico their services. He was never at a loss for competent help nor for information of the latest developments in European cuisine. The first Delmonico restaurant, on William St., was destroyed in the great fire of 1835. It was succeeded by restaurants at 76 Broad St., and at Beaver and William Sts. About the same time the Delmonicos bought more than 200 acres of land within the limits of what later became the Borough of Brooklyn and began farming operations modeled on those with which they had been familiar in Switzerland. Among their guests during that period were Louis Napoleon and the Prince de Joinville.

John Delmonico having died in 1842, Lorenzo continued the business with Peter, and in 1848 succeeded to the chief proprietorship of the business. From 1846 to 1856 a Delmonico hotel was conducted at 21–25 Broadway and from 1855 to 1875 the principal restaurant was at Broadway and Chambers St., but one was opened at Fourteenth St. and Fifth Ave., the first year of the Civil War, and in 1876 began the career of the famous Delmonico restaurant at Broadway and Twenty-sixth St. Lorenzo's brother Siro and other members of the family came from Switzerland and took places in the organization, which grew to be one of the greatest of its kind in existence. In 1861, through unfortunate investments in oil stocks, Delmonico lost $500,000, which was made up within a few years from the profits of the restaurants. In 1856 he had married a widow, Mme. Miège. He founded a public school in his native village and was for years a liberal giver to the Catholic Church in New York. Together with his noteworthy part in bringing about changes in American diet, he was largely responsible, through his success in entertaining the public, for the growth of the restaurant as an institution in American cities. Before his time New York had no restaurants where extensive bills of fare were served, save at particular hours. His restaurants at once sprang into favor. It was said at the time of his death, in 1881, that every president of the United States from Jackson to Garfield had been his guest, while New York, next to Paris, was believed to be better supplied with restaurants than any other city in the world. Delmonico was a quiet, methodical man of business, noted for his thrift; he was an inveterate smoker, often consuming thirty strong Havana cigars in a day. For many years after his restaurant business had become the largest in the city he personally attended to the marketing.

[*N. Y. Times*, Sept. 4, Dec. 20, 1881; Geo. S. Chappell, *Restaurants of N. Y.* (1925), pp. 16–18; Leopold Rimmer, *Hist. of Old N. Y. Life and the House of the Delmonicos* (1898), an employee's recollections.]

W. B. S.

DE LONG, GEORGE WASHINGTON (Aug. 22, 1844–Oct. 30, 1881), Arctic explorer, was born in New York City, the son of Levi and Catherine Greames De Long. His parents moved to Brooklyn when the boy was four years old and there he spent his boyhood, which, because of parental fear of the dangers of the outside world, was one of great seclusion. He attended the public schools of Brooklyn and "was a hard student, thorough in his application to books, and faithful to his school work" (Emma De Long, *post,* I, 2). His ambition was kindled by reading some tales of exploits in the War of 1812, and he resolved to become a naval officer. When he was selected for an appointment to the Naval Academy in 1857, however, his parents refused their permission as they were desirous of having him enter a profession. He finally yielded to his parents' wishes and began the study of law in the office of John Oakey. With the outbreak of the Civil War, Oakey entered the service and De Long begged hard to accompany him but without success. Having been denied a place in the army, the young man again turned his thoughts toward the Naval Academy. After considerable persuasion, he secured the consent of his parents and by sheer determination won an appointment. He applied himself vigorously to his work and was graduated with distinction in 1865.

His first sea duty was a three-year cruise on the *Canandaigua* to the western shores of Europe and Africa and in the Mediterranean. Then followed assignments to several vessels, a period at Washington for signal practise, and work in the equipment division in New York. In 1869 he was commissioned a lieutenant and in 1879 a lieutenant-commander. Early in 1871, he obtained a leave of absence to journey to Havre, France, where, on Mar. 1, he married Emma J. Wotton. One daughter was born to this union.

In 1873, De Long was assigned to the *Juniata* which was soon afterward sent to the Arctic in search of the missing steamer *Polaris.* The adventures of this trip fired his enthusiasm for further Arctic research; and upon his return to New York, he interested James Gordon Bennett in the project. After several years of planning, they secured the Arctic steamer *Pandora,* rechristened her the *Jeannette,* and fitted her out for the dash through Bering Strait to the Pole. With a crew of thirty-three officers and men, the *Jeannette* sailed from San Francisco, July 8, 1879. On Sept. 5, while about twenty-five miles east of Herald Island, the vessel was caught in an ice pack and drifted to the northwest for over twenty-one months, finally reaching latitude 77° 15′ north and longitude 155° east, where on June 12, 1881, she was crushed by the heavy ice floes and sank at four in the morning of the next day. De Long was prepared for this emergency, however, and abandoned the ship in an orderly fashion, salvaging most of the provisions and equipment. The retreat southward toward the Siberian coast commenced on June 18 and for over two months De Long and his men, hampered by their provisions and boats, fought their way over a frozen sea. At last open water was reached and the party embarked in three boats for the Lena Delta.

During a heavy gale on Sept. 12, the boats became separated; and while the two commanded respectively by De Long and Engineer Melville managed to weather the storm, Lieutenant Chipp's craft was never heard from again. The two surviving boats reached widely separated portions of the delta; Melville's party landed in one of the eastern outlets and was rescued by natives; while De Long's group reached a northern arm of the river and landed in an uninhabited country. With only a few days' provisions, De Long, ever hopeful of rescue, led his men southward, until thoroughly exhausted they could go no farther. Two of the strongest—Nindemann and Noros—were sent ahead to bring assistance but without avail. Finally toward the end of October, the entire command succumbed one by one to starvation and exposure. Their bodies were found the next spring by Melville and were subsequently brought to New York and buried with honors. Melville also recovered the records of the expedition including De Long's journal, which was later published by his widow under the title, *The Voyage of the Jeannette.* Although the *Jeannette* expedition failed in its original purpose, it established the existence of a northwestward polar drift and at the same time changed the map of the Arctic by delimiting the size of Wrangel Island and by discovering the small group of islands now named for its courageous commander.

[*Lieut. Danenhower's Narrative of the Jeannette* (1882); Emma De Long, ed., *The Voyage of the Jeannette* (1883); I. H. De Long, *The Lineage of Malcolm Metzger Parker from Johannes De Lang* (1926); Wm. H. Gilder, *Ice-Pack and Tundra* (1883); G. W. Melville, *In the Lena Delta* (1885); R. W. Bliss, *Our Lost Explorers* (1882); H. M. Prentiss, "The *Jeannette* Search and the Polar Current" in his *Great Polar Current* (1897); Record of the Proceedings of a Court of Inquiry, to investigate the loss of the steamer *Jeannette, House Exec. Doc. No. 108,* 47 Cong., 2 Sess.; *Jeannette Inquiry, House Miscel. Doc. No. 66,* 48 Cong., 1 Sess.]

G. H. B.

DE MÉZIÈRES Y CLUGNY, ATHANASE (*c.* 1715–Nov. 2, 1779), soldier, explorer, Indian agent, was born in Paris, St. Sulpice Parish, the son of Louis Christophe de Mézières and Marie Antoinette Clugny. His was a distinguished family. One of his sisters, the Marchioness de Montessons, married the Duke of Orleans; two uncles were generals in the French army; a cousin, Minard de Clugny, was minister of state; a nephew, the Marquis de Genlis, was inspector of infantry; a niece was lady-in-waiting to the Duchess of Chartres. De Mézières came to Louisiana about 1733. Ten years later he was a soldier at Natchitoches, where most of his career was spent thereafter. He rose through the ranks of ensign, lieutenant, and captain to that of lieutenant-colonel. On Apr. 18, 1746, he married Marie Petronille Feliciane de St. Denis, daughter of the famous Luis Juchereau de St. Denis. She died in 1748 and some time later he married Dame Pélagie Fazende. In 1756 he was appointed by Gov. Kerlérec on a commission to determine the Texas-Louisiana boundary at the Gulf of Mexico. Besides being a soldier he was a trader and a planter. He was prosperous, and in 1766 he possessed thirty-five slaves and ten thousand pounds of tobacco.

When Louisiana was transferred to Spain he entered the Spanish service, and for ten years he was ruler of Red River Valley. The governor of Texas declared that he had "such knowledge of these provinces of Texas and Louisiana as is possessed by no one else, and likewise of the tribes which surround them." This reputation he sustained until his death.

His most signal service was to supervise the Indian trade, and to win to Spanish allegiance the tribes of Louisiana, Texas, Arkansas, and Oklahoma. To install the new system he held an assembly of chiefs at Natchitoches (Apr. 21, 1770). He issued licenses to traders, cut off illicit traffic, and induced the Indians to deliver up vagabonds or intruding Englishmen. To hold conferences with distant tribes he made extensive explorations, and his well-written diaries and reports give us our first definite information regarding a large part of northern Texas. In 1770 he went to Cadodachos and held a council with several tribes, making eloquent speeches. The fruit of this meeting was a treaty made at Natchitoches in 1771. In the next year he made a long tour to the northwest, visiting Quitseis, Yscanes, Tawakoni, and Wichita villages on the Trinity and Brazos rivers, and conducting seventy chiefs and headmen to San Antonio to see the governor of Texas. On this expedition he had spent eighty-seven days. His report of the journey is a classic. By his persistent efforts of three years having won to Spanish allegiance the "Nations of the North," he now went to France and Spain, "to recuperate his health and settle various matters of private business which he had pending in those realms." While abroad he was promoted by the King of Spain to the rank of lieutenant-colonel (Nov. 8, 1772), and was made a knight of the Order of St. Louis. Back at Natchitoches, he devoted the next five years to extending trade and influence among the new allies. By his energetic fostering of the Louisiana trade he aroused opposition from ambitious San Antonio merchants, but he was vigorously defended by the Baron de Ripperdá, governor of Texas. The reorganization of the northern provinces of New Spain by Teodoro de Croix [*q.v.*] after 1776 brought De Mézières and his work into greater prominence. Croix made a tour of the frontier, and held councils at Monclova and San Antonio. After long deliberations it was decided to cement the alliance with the Nations of the North and lead them in a grand campaign against the Apaches, farther West. The advice of De Mézières was needed and he was called to San Antonio. The plan which he presented there is a most illuminating document. While Croix and others were considering the proposals, De Mézières made a tour up the Brazos, and to the Taovayas on Red River (1778). On the way he wrote sixteen reports which constitute another historical treasure. At the end of this tour he returned to Natchitoches, but in further preparation for the great war, at the request of Croix he was permanently released from his Louisiana post. On his way to San Antonio he made still another tour among the northern tribes (1779). While en route he received from the King of Spain a letter of thanks for his distinguished services. In September he reported at San Antonio for duty, only to be told, a few days later, that he had been appointed governor of Texas in the place of Cabello. He never entered upon his new office, however, for he died on Nov. 2 from the effects of an accident during his last journey. He was buried at the parish church, now the Cathedral of San Fernando, in San Antonio, where his remains still rest.

De Mézières was cultured and versatile. He wrote letters in French, Spanish, and Latin, and we are told that he was a mathematician of ability. In his day he was a prominent figure on the frontier, and with propriety he can be compared with his contemporaries, Juan Bautista de Anza, Bernardo de Gálvez, and George Rogers Clark [*qq.v.*].

[The principal sources of information regarding De Mézières are his own letters and reports. These were translated and edited by H. E. Bolton in *Athanase De Mézières and the Louisiana-Texas Frontier, 1768–80* (2 vols., 1914). A summary of his work is contained in H. E. Bolton, *Texas in the Middle Eighteenth Century* (1915).] H. E. B.

DE MILLE, HENRY CHURCHILL (Sept. 17, 1853–Feb. 10, 1893), playwright, the son of William Edward and Margaret Blount (Hoyt) De Mille, both of Washington, N. C., was born in that place and spent his boyhood on a farm. Going to New York, he became a student in Columbia College, being graduated in 1875 and receiving the degrees of A.B. and A.M. His first intention was to become a clergyman, but he soon changed his mind, and, after teaching at the Columbia Grammar School in New York, he became permanently associated with the theatre, successively as an actor for a short time under A. M. Palmer's management, as an instructor in the American Academy of Dramatic Arts, as a reader of plays at the Madison Square Theatre, and as a writer of plays. A thorough knowledge and understanding of the technique of the stage enabled him to do skilful work in the revising and reshaping of plays by other hands for production at the Madison Square, where he was closely associated with Steele MacKaye and David Belasco. His first original play, *John Delmer's Daughters or Duty,* was produced there on Dec. 10, 1883, but it attracted the public for only one week. After the production, at the Lyceum Theatre, on Sept. 18, 1886, of *The Main Line or Rawson's Y,* a melodrama of Western scenes and incidents written in collaboration with Charles Barnard, he began the partnership with Belasco which resulted in a series of plays that reflected more of the glare of the footlights than of the actual light of day. These were *The Wife,* produced Nov. 1, 1887; *Lord Chumley,* produced Aug. 21, 1888, written especially for E. H. Sothern to give that actor a character somewhat like the Lord Dundreary his father had made famous; and *The Charity Ball,* produced Nov. 19, 1889. They were among the most popular plays of the period and, acted for several successive seasons throughout the country under the management of Daniel Frohman at whose Lyceum Theatre they had first been produced, gave De Mille a national reputation. Since he saw life mainly in terms of the theatre, his plays were artificial in structure, written in the conventional manner of the society drama of the day, with alternate layers of intrigue, drama, farce, and comedy, their only appeal being in their entertaining qualities and in the opportunity they gave for skilful acting by groups of expert players. Except for occasional performances by local stock companies, their popularity did not continue beyond the early years of the twentieth century. Another Belasco–De Mille play, *Men and Women,* produced at Proctor's Twenty-third Street Theatre in New York on Oct. 21, 1890, dealt with the sensations of American business and political life. De Mille's last play, also produced at Proctor's, was *The Lost Paradise,* an English version of the German dramatist Ludwig Fulda's *Das Verlorene Paradies.* He died suddenly of pneumonia at his home in Pompton, N. J. In 1876 he married Mathilde Beatrice Samuel; of their three children a daughter died in childhood, and two sons, William C. and Cecil B. De Mille, have reached positions of prominence in the motion-picture world.

[M. J. Moses, *The Am. Dramatist* (1917), pp. 237–40; T. A. Brown, *A Hist. of the N. Y. Stage,* III (1903), 421; Wm. Winter, *The Life of David Belasco* (1918); A. H. Quinn, *A Hist. of the Am. Drama from the Civil War to the Present Day* (1923); C. M. S. McLellan in *The Theatre,* Nov. 24, 1888; contemporary articles and newspaper reviews; information from William C. De Mille and Miss Agnes De Mille.] E. F. E.

DEMING, HENRY CHAMPION (May 23, 1815–Oct. 9, 1872), lawyer, politician, was a member of a family identified throughout with Connecticut. John Deming recorded his homestead at Wethersfield, Conn., in 1641. His descendants settled at Lyme and later at Colchester, and one of them, David Deming, was a prominent merchant of the latter place and a member of the legislature. He married Abigail, daughter of Henry Champion, and their youngest child, Henry Champion Deming, was born at Colchester. His parents were well-to-do, and his early education was of the best, being completed at Yale, where he graduated in 1836. He then entered the law school at Harvard (LL.B., 1839), and on being admitted to the Massachusetts bar moved to New York City, where he opened a law office. His inclinations however were toward literature rather than law, and for a time he was on the editorial staff of the *New World,* a literary monthly. In 1847 he returned to Connecticut and practised law at Hartford for a short time. Possessed of unusual gifts as a public speaker and debater, he entered into local politics. A Democrat of the old school, he was elected as representative of Hartford in the state legislature in 1849, and from that time forward practically relinquished law and devoted himself to public affairs. In 1851 he became a member of the state Senate and in 1854 was elected mayor of Hartford, which office he held for five successive years. In 1859 he became again the city representative in the state legislature, and in 1860 was once more elected mayor. When the Southern states threatened secession he was strongly opposed to the adoption of coercive methods, and after the outbreak of the Civil War, announced that, though he adhered to the Federal government, he would not support a war of aggression or invasion of the seceded states. The subsequent advance of the Confederate forces upon the Federal capital, however, induced him to become a strong Unionist, and the Republican majority elected him speaker *pro tempore* of the state legislature. Late in 1861 the 12th ("Charter-Oak") Connecticut Regiment was raised, in order to participate in the New Orleans expedition, and he was appointed lieutenant-colonel. He took part in all the subsequent operations under Gen. Butler and the regiment under his command was the first body of Federal troops to enter New Orleans. In October 1862 he was detached and appointed provisional mayor of New Orleans, performing his difficult duties with great tact and efficiency. He resigned however in February 1863, returned to Hartford, and was at once elected to the Thirty-eighth Congress by the Republicans. He served two terms in Congress, being placed on the committees on military affairs and on expenditures in the War Department, of which latter he was chairman. In the national House, his oratorical powers, strong character, and practical experience of war conditions combined to assure him an outstanding position. In 1866 he was a delegate to the Loyalists convention at Philadelphia, and in 1869 was appointed United States collector of Internal Revenue for his home district. This latter position he continued to hold till his death, which occurred at Hartford, Oct. 9, 1872. He was married twice: in 1850 to Sarah, daughter of Laurent Clerc of Hartford, and in 1871 to Annie Putnam, daughter of Myron W. Wilson and widow of Sherman L. Jittson.

Holding public office almost uninterruptedly for twenty-three years, prominent alike in federal, state, and municipal politics, his reputation rested principally upon his unusual oratorical powers, though he possessed great administrative ability. Of cultured tastes and widely read, he published translations of Eugène Sue's *Mysteries of Paris* and *The Wandering Jew* (1840), and, in collaboration with G. C. Hebbe, *The Smugglers of the Swedish Coast, or The Rose of Thistle Island* (1844), from the original Swedish of Mrs. E. S. F. Carlén. He also wrote *The Life of Ulysses S. Grant, General, United States Army* (1868).

[J. K. Deming, *Geneal. of the descendants of John Deming of Wethersfield, Conn.* (1904), traces his ancestry and contains a sketch of his life. See also *Annual Cyc.*, 1872, p. 630; *Obit. Record Grads. Yale Coll.*, 1873; *Hist. and Biog. Record of the Class of 1836 in Yale Coll.* (1882); *Hartford Daily Courant*, Oct. 10, 1872.]

H. W. H. K.

DEMING, PHILANDER (Feb. 6, 1829–Feb. 9, 1915), pioneer court stenographer, lawyer, author, was born in Carlisle, Schoharie County, N. Y., the third son of Rev. Rufus Romeo Deming, a minister in Champlain Presbytery, and Julia Ann, daughter of Norman Porter, M.D., of Oneida County. He was descended from Thomas Deming, one of the early settlers of Wethersfield. The Deming family moved from one charge to another; they lived for a time in Huntingdon, Quebec. From there they moved to Burke, Franklin County, N. Y., where during 1852–54 Philander Deming taught school. In Burke, also, for a number of years he and two of his brothers operated a sawmill which they had built, machinery and all, with their own hands. He prepared for college at Whitestown Seminary, Whitesboro, N. Y.; he was graduated from the University of Vermont in 1861 with the rank of Phi Beta Kappa. In 1864 the University conferred upon him the A.M. degree; in 1881 he gave the oration before the associate alumni, and was president of that body 1891–92 (*General Catalogue of the University of Vermont and State Agricultural College, 1791–1900*, p. 117). In 1872 he was graduated from the Albany Law School, and was admitted to the bar at May sessions the same year.

As a boy he had taught himself shorthand; at the close of his college course he obtained a file of Albany newspapers, and in two months' time he had mastered the technique of legislative reporting. He was legislative reporter for the *Albany Evening Journal* in 1862 and in 1864–65 for the *New York Times*. In 1863–64 he was assistant editor of the *Burlington Free Press*. In November 1865, he demonstrated in an Albany court-room the value of verbatim reporting. Thereafter he was so overwhelmed with court work that he was forced to give up his legislative and newspaper reporting. He was made official stenographer of the supreme court, 3rd Judicial District, New York, and continued in that position until his retirement about 1882. In 1878–79 he was president of the New York Law Stenographers' Association. His handbook, *The Court Stenographer*, was published in 1879.

The *Atlantic Monthly* in 1873 contained the first of Deming's series of short stories or sketches depicting scenes and the life of the people in the Adirondacks and in the Valley of the Hudson. In consequence of this "the reporter learned the pleasant road to Boston, and trod the pathway to the famous banquets to meet the great names he (and all America) had so long honored in the realm of letters" (*Story of a Pathfinder*, p. 55). These sketches were later published in *Adirondack Stories* (1880), followed by *Tompkins and Other Folks* (1885), and *The Story of a Pathfinder* (1907). One and all these grew directly out of Deming's own life and observation, so it is not surprising that they were self-revealing to a marked degree. They give us the reticence, the quiet tastes, the mellowness of a man at once self-possessed, reflective, and shy. One understands why his fellows at college dubbed him "the philosopher," why the people of Burke considered him "odd," even why the pastor of the Albany Congregational Church, of which he had been a member since 1880, found it as difficult as it was rewarding to draw him into conversation. Long before it was customary to take long walks for the fun of it, Deming roamed the country side. He enjoyed fishing, although he outgrew his early zest for hunting because of his distaste for the wantonness of killing. He had a distinct bent for things mechanical, but refused to patent his inventions. In later life he was a striking figure on the streets of Albany, because of his abundant white hair and his deeply lined face. He resembled portraits of Franz Liszt. He was highly esteemed, yet few knew him intimately. He never married. He died at his rooms, 12 Jay St., Albany, and was buried at Burke.

[Pages 3–55 in *The Story of a Pathfinder* are autobiographical; besides these Philander Deming wrote "Growing Old" for *Scribner's Mag.*, Mar. 1915. See also "The Curious Origin of the Court Reporter," by W. H. Brainerd in *Leslie's Weekly*, May 24, 1906. Deming appears in *Who's Who in America*, 1899–1915, and in the *Cat. Alumni Albany Law School*, 1851–1908, pp. 42, 99. The reference librarian of the New York State Library, the minister of the First Congregational Church, Albany, and the town clerk of Burke have furnished data for this sketch compiled from their own knowledge or from that of relatives and friends of Deming. For a critical estimate of Deming's writings see F. L. Pattee, *History of Am. Lit. since 1870* (1915), p. 24; and W. D. Howells, "Recollections of an Atlantic Editorship," *Atlantic Monthly*, Nov. 1907, p. 600.]

L. M. M.

DEMING, WILLIAM [See DENNING, WILLIAM 1736–1830.]

DEMME, CHARLES RUDOLPH (Apr. 10, 1795–Sept. 1, 1863), Lutheran clergyman, was born at Mühlhausen in Thüringen, Germany, the son of Hermann Gottfried and Frederika (König) Demme. His father was an eminent Lutheran divine, Superintendent in Mühlhausen and later General Superintendent in Altenburg. Demme studied at the Gymnasium in Altenburg and at the Universities of Göttingen and Halle. He was wounded in the battle of Waterloo, and a scar across nose and cheek served as a lesser, although life-long, reminder of that 18th of June. His friends in the United States believed that it was his experiences as a soldier that turned his thoughts from the law to the ministry and made him decide to leave Germany for America. Whatever his inner life may have been, the young man who came to Philadelphia in 1818 and sought ordination from the Lutheran Ministerium of Pennsylvania proved to be a sound scholar, a devoted pastor, and a born leader of men. After ministering for three years to several congregations in Hummelstown, Pa., and its vicinity, he was called in 1822 to the historic St. Michael's and Zion's Church in Philadelphia as assistant to Frederick David Schaeffer [*q.v.*]. On Oct. 7, 1828, he married Schaeffer's only daughter, Mariana. Of their eleven children only five survived him. After his father-in-law's retirement in 1834 Demme was sole pastor until 1850, when William Julius Mann [*q.v.*], who in turn was to succeed him, became his assistant. By virtue of his scholarship but still more by virtue of his personality Demme became the most influential man in the Ministerium, and his influence continued even after his own career had ended. His one independent book was *Die Werke des Flavius Josephus* (Phila., 1839), a revision of the German translation by J. F. Cotta and A. F. Gfrörer with variorum notes drawn from many sources, but this was less important than his editorial work on the Lutheran *Liturgie und Kirchenagende* (1842; 2nd ed., 1855) and the *Deutsches Gesangbuch* (1849). The conservative Lutheranism of his theological position did much to arrest the Methodistic tendencies of many Pennsylvania Lutherans, for beginning in 1846 he gave formal instruction in theology to candidates for the ministry. He was a member of the American Philosophical Society, did much work for the American Tract Society, and was untiringly active in his efforts to reclaim criminals in the penitentiaries. He was one of the greatest masters of sacred rhetoric that the United States has ever heard, but since he preached in German, and allowed only a few of his sermons to be printed, his fame is incommensurate with his achievement. His sermons were primarily logical in their appeal, but so charged with emotion was the preacher that at times tears would roll down his cheeks, though his voice never faltered or quavered. He was a close student of Reinhard in German, Bourdaloue in French, and South in English. Overwork brought on a mental breakdown from which he never recovered; he was made pastor emeritus in 1859; and his last years passed in all but complete darkness. To the end he prayed and read in the Bible and would cry softly when he heard the bell of his church on Sunday mornings.

[M. L. Stoever, "Chas. Rudolph Demme, D.D.," in the *Evangelical Quart. Rev.*, XV, 428–48 (1864); W. J. Mann, *Rede über Dr. Demme* (1863); J. G. Morris, *Fifty Years in the Lutheran Ministry* (Baltimore, 1878); *Documentary Hist. of the Ev. Luth. Ministerium of Pa.* (1898); A. Spaeth, "Hist. of the Liturgical Development of the Ministerium of Pa.," in *Luth. Ch. Rev.*, XVII, 93–119 (1898); personal information. A number of Demme's sermons, together with some letters to

Chas. Philip Krauth, are in the library of the Luth. Hist. Soc. at Gettysburg, Pa.] G. H. G.

DEMPSTER, JOHN (Jan. 2, 1794–Nov. 28, 1863), theologian, pioneer founder of Methodist theological seminaries, was born in Florida, Montgomery County, N. Y. His father, the Rev. James Dempster, a Scotch Presbyterian and a graduate of the University of Edinburgh, came under Methodist influence and was sent by Wesley to America, where he served as a missionary in New York City. Severing his Methodist connection, he became pastor of the Presbyterian church in Florida, N. Y., where he died in 1803. John, the second son of his second wife, grew up after the death of his father a frivolous young man with scarcely the rudiments of a common-school education. At the age of eighteen, while employed as a tin-peddler, he received at a Methodist camp meeting a powerful religious impulse which transformed his life. He at once began a rigorous course of self-education which continued as long as he lived. Almost without instruction he became a proficient scholar in the classics, mathematics, Hebrew, theology, and philosophy, at the same time preaching constantly. In 1816 he began a regular conference ministry and served various charges in New York State with growing power and influence till 1836, when on account of impaired health he went to Buenos Aires where he built a Methodist church, established day and Sunday-schools and had an active ministry among the Protestant population of the city and the surrounding region. Returning to the United States in 1842, he spent the next three years in two Methodist pastorates in New York City.

Early in his ministry he became convinced of the need of theological training for Methodist ministers and zealously advocated it, often in the face of stubborn opposition. Largely as the result of his efforts which were continued by correspondence from South America, the Wesley Theological Institute was founded at Newbury, Vt., in 1845, the first Methodist theological seminary in the United States. It was removed to Concord, N. H., in 1847 and to Boston in 1867, later becoming the Theological School of Boston University. At the close of his New York ministry, Dempster spent several months in the British Isles, making friends and collecting funds for the school, after which he passed seven years as professor of theology at Concord, exerting a strong influence on his pupils and throughout the region. In 1854 he resigned and became one of the founders of the Garrett Biblical Institute in Chicago, taking, when its permanent faculty was formed in 1855, the office of senior professor, which he held till the close of his life. He died while on a leave of absence for the purpose of founding a theological seminary on the Pacific Coast.

Dempster was of medium size, pale, with bright eyes, deep and penetrating voice, courtly manners and impressive presence. He had a strong will, great originality and an alert and philosophical mind. He was widely read and inspired his pupils with enthusiasm. The only book that bears his name is, *Lectures and Addresses . . . with an Appendix, containing the Funeral Sermon and Memorial Services occasioned by the Death of the Author* (1864), edited by the Rev. Davis W. Clark. He was survived by his wife, one son and three daughters.

[In addition to biographical material already referred to, see *Methodist Quart. Rev.*, July 1864; *Minutes of the Annual Conferences of the M. E. Ch.*, 1864; *Zion's Herald*, Dec. 9, 1863, and Aug. 26, 1896. The latter contains a portrait.] F. T. P.

DENBY, CHARLES (June 16, 1830–Jan. 13, 1904), lawyer, diplomat, was born at Mount Joy, Botetourt County, Va. His grandfather emigrated from England and settled in Virginia, where his father, Nathaniel Denby, a merchant at Richmond, was born. His mother was Jane Harvey, daughter of Matthew and Magdalen (Hawkins) Harvey, and descendant of Benjamin Burden, an Englishman who brought with him to Virginia a grant of many acres on the Shenandoah and James rivers, known as Burden's Grant. His mother's father served in Lee's legion in the Revolution. From the Tom Fox Academy in Hanover County, Va., he proceeded to Georgetown College, D. C., where he spent three years, taking in 1842 "three medals, more than had ever before been received by any one boy" (*Georgetown College Journal,* vol. XIII, no. 8, p. 93). Among his classmates was Thomas J. Semmes, later a member of the Confederate Senate. While still a youth Denby accompanied his father to Marseilles, France, and attended the Collège Royal in that city, where his father was United States naval agent. On returning to the United States, he entered the Virginia Military Institute at Lexington, Va., from which he was graduated with high honors in 1850. After three years as professor of tactics at the Masonic University, Selma, Ala., he moved to Evansville, Ind., where he was employed by John B. Hall as editor of the Democratic newspaper, *Daily Enquirer,* learning to set type and frequently setting up editorials, while at the same time he studied law in the office of Baker & Garvin. Admitted to the bar in 1855, he began the practise of law the following year in Evansville, in partnership

Denby

with Judge James Lockhart, and in the same year was elected to represent Vanderburg County in the state legislature. The day after Fort Sumter fell, he abandoned his law practise to raise a regiment for border service. In September 1861 he was appointed by Gov. Morton as lieutenant-colonel of the 42nd Indiana Volunteers, serving in southern Kentucky, first with Crittenden's division from Fort Donelson to Nashville, and thence to Huntsville, Ala., under Gen. Mitchel. Returning with Gen. Buell in the summer of 1862 in pursuit of Bragg, he engaged in the battle of Perryville, Ky., on Oct. 8, 1862, and was severely wounded, his horse being killed under him. Some days later (Oct. 21, 1862) he was appointed colonel of the 80th Indiana Volunteers, but in January 1863 he resigned on a surgeon's certificate of disability, returned to the practise of law in Evansville, and became interested in politics again. In 1876 he was a delegate to the St. Louis Democratic Convention which nominated Tilden and Hendricks and in 1884 to the Chicago Convention which nominated Cleveland and Hendricks. His consistent support of Hendricks of Indiana resulted in his appointment on May 29, 1885, by President Cleveland as minister to China to succeed John Russell Young, and in this position he continued during Harrison's administration and Cleveland's second administration. On July 11, 1898, President McKinley yielded to political pressure and appointed Edwin H. Conger in his place. In his thirteen years in China, Denby came very close to the Chinese statesmen and his efforts in aid of peace with Japan at the time of the Sino-Japanese War put him in high favor in China. His prestige was enhanced by the fact that the Japanese government had entrusted its interests in China to his care. Upon his retirement he received many complimentary resolutions from various missionary boards in the United States and China. In September 1898 President McKinley appointed him a member of the committee which investigated the conduct of the war with Spain, and in the next year appointed him a member of the Philippine Commission. On Apr. 4, 1898, he participated with the other members of the Commission (Jacob Gould Schurman, Dean C. Worcester, Admiral George Dewey, and Gen. Elwell S. Otis) in issuing a proclamation to the effect that, while the supremacy of the United States would be enforced, the Government had in view the welfare and advancement of the people. The *Report of the Philippine Commission to the President* (four volumes) was published in 1900–01, while Denby's "observations, reminiscences and conclusions" as an American diplomat, entitled *China and Her People* (two volumes profusely illustrated with reproductions of photographs collected by the author, with a biographical sketch by the editor), appeared in Boston posthumously in 1906. In September 1858 he had married Martha, elder daughter of Senator Graham Newell Fitch and Harriet S. Fitch of Logansport, Ind. There were eight children born of this union. On Jan. 13, 1904, he was stricken with heart trouble at Jamestown, N. Y., where he had been lecturing, and where he died.

[*Who's Who in America*, 1903–05; *N. Y. Times*, Jan. 14, 1904; *Georgetown Coll. Jour.*, XLVII, 195.]

H.F.W.

DENBY, EDWIN (Feb. 18, 1870–Feb. 8, 1929), secretary of the navy, was born in Evansville, Ind., a son of Charles and Martha (Fitch) Denby, both of whom were of old American stock. After an education in the local schools, he was taken by his parents to China, where his father was minister from the United States. Here he was for ten years employed in the Chinese customs service. Returning to the United States he entered the University of Michigan, acquiring fame as a football player, and a degree of LL.B. in 1896. In the war with Spain he volunteered as a common seaman, and ended as a gunner's mate aboard the *Yosemite*. When the World War came he was overweight and unqualified for active duty, but he accomplished his enlistment in the Marine Corps as a private, and was used in building up the morale of that service. He rose through the non-commissioned grades, and was discharged as a major, with which rank he entered the Officers' Reserve Corps. In the years between the two wars he practised law in Detroit and undertook various enterprises in connection with the automobile trade. In 1903 he was in the Michigan legislature, and two years later he became representative from the first Michigan district in the Fifty-ninth Congress. He was twice reëlected to Congress. The announcement that President Harding had selected him to be secretary of the navy came without warning to the public, and with little to Denby himself.

As secretary of the navy he appears to have had little influence upon naval organization, or upon national naval policy. It has not been shown that his decisions were important in connection with the Washington Conference on Limitation of Armaments, or with the treaties that arose from it. His administration was terminated by a scandal in the handling of the naval oil reserves.

In the autumn of 1923 the Senate Committee on Public Lands and Surveys, engaged in the investigation of the oil reserves, came upon a series of events that endangered the safety of naval reserve No. 1 at Elk Hills, and No. 3 at Teapot Dome. By act of June 25, 1910, various withdrawals of oil lands from public entry, made by President Roosevelt with perhaps incomplete authority, were legalized by Congress; and after long discussion an oil-land leasing act, to be administered by the secretary of the interior, was passed Feb. 25, 1920. By the naval act of June 4, 1920, the reserves that had been set aside for navy use, under the act of 1910, were placed under jurisdiction of the secretary of the navy. They were already coveted by the oil-producing interests, and there was a suggestion that they were in some danger of losing their oil by drainage into adjacent basins not controlled by the government. The administration of the naval oil reserves was transferred to the Department of the Interior by executive order of President Harding, May 31, 1921, upon the theory that the Department of the Interior, having the machinery for controlling leases of other oil lands under the act of 1920, could administer the reserves to better advantage than could the Navy Department. Almost instantly the secretary of the interior, Albert B. Fall, entered into negotiations with the oil interests represented by Edward L. Doheny and Harry Sinclair, and into contracts for taking the oil from the ground, which the lessees insisted must bear the signature of Denby as well as that of Fall. These leases the Supreme Court later declared to have been "consummated by conspiracy, corruption and fraud" (*Pan American Petroleum and Transport Company et al.* vs. *United States,* 273 *U. S.*, 509). While executing these contracts Fall was at the same time accepting favors and financial assistance from both Doheny and Sinclair. The testimony as to this sinister relationship became public in the winter of 1923–24. Fall had retired from the cabinet and was beyond reach of impeachment. Denby took "no active part in the negotiations" (273 *U. S.*, 498), and was not seriously charged with corruption. "Stupidity is the high crime and misdemeanor of which the Senate accuses Mr. Denby, and the only one," said the *New York Tribune* (Feb. 12, 1924). The Senate on Feb. 11, 1924, by resolution requested President Coolidge to dismiss Denby from the cabinet. It had already joined the House in asserting a belief that the leases were "executed under circumstances indicating fraud and corruption," and in setting in motion suits for cancellation that resulted in the restoration of the lands to the government. Coolidge declined to dismiss Denby, and the latter continued to insist that the leases were both legal and expedient (*Leases upon Naval Oil Reserves. Hearing before the Committee on Public Lands and Surveys, United States Senate, on S. Res. 282 and S. Res. 294,* Washington 1923–24, pp. 283, 363, 1283). Denby resigned on Feb. 18, 1924, believing that a further continuance in the cabinet of President Coolidge "would increase your embarrassment" (*New York Tribune,* Feb. 19, 1924); but he made the resignation effective only on Mar. 10, and defied the House of Representatives to initiate impeachment proceedings against him. He returned to Detroit where he enjoyed the personal esteem of his associates until his death. He was survived by his wife, Marion (Thurber) Denby, and two children.

[There is a good obituary in the *New York Times,* Feb. 9, 1929; and a good survey of the Teapot Dome proceedings in the same for Jan. 24, 1927. See also *Who's Who in America,* 1928–29.] F. L. P—n.

DENNIE, JOSEPH (Aug. 30, 1768–Jan. 7, 1812), essayist and editor, was born in Boston, Mass., the only child of Joseph and Mary (Green) Dennie. His father came of a prosperous family of West-India merchants, but he had hardly established himself in business when his career was cut short by recurring periods of insanity. His mother's family, the Greens, had been for several generations engaged in the printing trade.

The first seven years of Dennie's boyhood were spent in Boston. During the siege of 1775 his parents, who numbered many Loyalists among their kin, removed to Lexington, where the boy was sent to dame school and read largely in his father's library. His precocious literary talent was not encouraged, but after two years in commercial school and counting-house had proved his unfitness for a business career, he was allowed to prepare for Harvard under the care of Rev. Samuel West of Needham. He entered college as a sophomore, and though his course was interrupted by illness and during his senior year by a period of rustication, he was permitted to graduate with his class in 1790. Partly because he smarted under college discipline, partly because he considered the course of study arid, Dennie conceived a petulance against Harvard which occasionally found vent in his later writings. He was noted among his classmates for his elegance and for his unusual acquaintance with polite letters.

After six months' hesitation Dennie selected the law as a means of livelihood. He served a not very assiduous clerkship of three years in the office of Benjamin West, brother of his tutor, at Charlestown, N. H., and was admitted to the bar in March 1794. His practise, however, never became extensive and he soon abandoned it. During his clerkship he had made the acquaintance of several young professional men who acted as volunteer writers for local newspapers and who strongly encouraged his bent for letters. With one of them, Royall Tyler, he now formed a partnership for the production of light literary wares under the firm name of "Colon & Spondee." (Dennie was Colon and sometimes signed his contributions with a C). At about the same time he commenced a series of periodical essays called the "Farrago" in which he sought to revive "the Goldsmith vivacity of thought and the Addisonian sweetness of expression." These essays, in part reprinted from New Hampshire journals, formed the main feature of a weekly paper devoted to belles-lettres, the *Tablet* (May 19–Aug. 11, 1795), which Dennie started in Boston but which was discontinued by the publisher after the thirteenth number. Between 1792 and 1802 he wrote twenty-nine numbers of the "Farrago," but the series was never collected in book form.

Failing to find other employment in Boston, Dennie returned to New Hampshire and settled at Walpole. There he soon became the center of a group of "wags, wits, and literati" from all the surrounding country, who, like the Hartford Wits, were fond of holding convivial meetings for the discussion of literature and politics. They were all strong Federalists. Stimulated by this congenial company, Dennie entered upon his most active period of authorship. For the *Farmer's Weekly Museum* of Walpole, one of the best New England papers of its day, he wrote a new series of miscellaneous essays entitled the "Lay Preacher," in which, by heading his lucubrations with a text and posing as a moralist, he was successful in winning the applause of even puritanical and utilitarian readers. The publishers of the *Farmer's Museum* were not slow to perceive the value of his services. In April 1796, he was appointed editor. He enlisted his literary friends as contributors, gave the previously non-partisan sheet a strong Federalist bias, and within a year and a half could boast that his paper was read in nearly every state in the Union. Its literary success, however, did not bring its financial prosperity. In several successive failures of his publishers Dennie was himself a heavy loser. Though he continued to act as editor at a reduced salary, he was convinced that a literary career could not be pursued in a small town. Philadelphia, as the political and literary centre of the nation, naturally attracted him. His services to the Federalist cause secured him an appointment as personal secretary to Timothy Pickering, Adams's secretary of state. He also accepted an editorial position on Fenno's *Gazette of the United States,* a semi-official Federalist organ. And a final inducement was an offer from William Cobbett to publish a handsome edition of the "Lay Preacher" and to pay generously for the copyright. With these bright prospects before him, Dennie left Walpole in September 1799, and journeyed leisurely to Philadelphia.

His reception by Philadelphia society was as cordial as he could have wished, but his affairs did not prosper. Pickering was dismissed from the cabinet in May 1800, and Dennie was not retained by John Marshall, the new secretary. His connection with Fenno's *Gazette* ended in December of the same year, soon after Jefferson's election to the presidency had marked the end of Federalist rule. And Cobbett, having been convicted of libel and heavily fined, was obliged to leave the city before the publication of the "Lay Preacher" could be effected. An attempt to publish the work by subscription failed.

Nothing daunted, Dennie persuaded a bookseller named Asbury Dickins to join him in establishing a new magazine. On Jan. 3, 1801, *The Port Folio,* edited by "Oliver Oldschool, Esq.," commenced publication as a weekly devoted to literature and politics and enjoyed from the first a great success. Dennie rallied to its support the brightest talent of Philadelphia, which he organized in the Tuesday Club. During the period of its greatest popularity, from 1802 to 1805, the magazine had a distinguished list of contributors in all parts of the country and even attained the previously unheard of honor of printing from the original manuscripts poems by such English writers as Campbell, Moore, Leigh Hunt, and "Monk" Lewis. Until the *North American Review* was founded in 1815 it remained without a rival. Dennie's own contributions consisted of a large number of "Lay Preacher" essays reprinted from the *Farmer's Museum,* a few new ones, and a considerable body of literary criticism, including notably some early appreciations of *Lyrical Ballads.* But his activities as an editor and man about town, combined with frail health and temperamental indolence, severely limited his output. He was, moreover, in constant financial difficulties, which were greatly increased by the long illness that preceded his death. He was buried in the churchyard of St. Peter's, Philadelphia. *The Port Folio* continued publication in various forms until 1827.

Dennie's reputation as an original writer rests upon his "Lay Preacher" essays (118 numbers, 1795–1808), which unfortunately have never been collected. About forty of the early numbers were issued in a volume printed at Walpole in 1796, and this book, according to the English traveler John Davis, was in 1803 "the most popular work on the American continent." A second selection, edited by J. E. Hall, appeared in Philadelphia in 1817. As an "American Addison" Dennie was soon superseded by Irving; moreover, his failure to get his books published and the neglect of his early biographers have doomed him to an unmerited obscurity. He should rank with Freneau and Charles Brockden Brown as a pioneer American man of letters.

Two portraits and a full-length silhouette of Dennie are extant. Buckingham has preserved an amusing description of his appearance and habits during his residence in Walpole (*Specimens of Newspaper Literature,* II, 196), and Irving, who met Dennie in 1807, used his whimsicalities as the basis for "Launcelot Langstaff" (*Salmagundi,* no. 8. Dennie was slight of build; fastidious to an extreme in dress and speech, mercurial in disposition. The charm of his conversation was widely attested and his love of sound literature was genuine and infectious. Born of the mercantile aristocracy of Boston and nurtured on the English classics of the eighteenth century, he cherished the past, especially the tradition of British gentility, and loathed democratic innovation in any form. In the course of a life of perpetual disappointment he had perhaps his supreme reward when the rising Irish poet Thomas Moore, after his visit to America in 1804, declared that the few agreeable moments which his tour through the United States afforded him were those passed in the society of Dennie and his friends.

[The most complete account of Dennie is by H. M. Ellis, *Joseph Dennie and His Circle* (1915), with portrait, list of Dennie's essays, and full bibliography. Among earlier sources the following are the most valuable: E. P. Oberholtzer, *Lit. Hist. of Phila.* (1906); *The Port Folio,* Feb. 1812 (memorial article, with silhouette); *New Eng. Galaxy,* July 10 and 24, 1818; J. E. Hall, *Phila. Souvenir* (1826); J. T. Buckingham, *Specimens of Newspaper Lit.* (1850); W. W. Clapp, Jr., *Joseph Dennie* (1880), with portrait; G. Aldrich, *Walpole as It Was and as It Is* (1880); A. H. Smyth, *Phila. Mags. and their Contributors* (1892); A. R. Marble, *Heralds of Am. Lit.* (1907). Smyth's assertion that Dennie was the "first American editor of Shakespeare" has been shown to have little foundation.]

G. F. W.

DENNING, WILLIAM (1736–Dec. 19, 1830), maker of cannon for the Revolutionary army, is said to have made the first successful attempt to manufacture cannon of wrought iron. Nothing is known of him until he became an "artificer" for or in the Revolutionary army. He made two small cannon successfully at Middlesex, Pa., and then attempted to make a larger one at Mount Holly. The latter experiment was a failure, owing, it was said in the obituary written at the time of his death, to the fact that he could get no workmen who could stand the heat which was so great as to melt the lead buttons off their clothes. The cannon were made of wrought-iron staves, hooped with bands of wrought iron, four layers of staves, breaking joints, being finally bound together, and then boxed and breached like other cannon. One of those in use at the battle of Brandywine was captured by the British and placed in the Tower of London where it may still be seen. The British government offered a large sum and an annuity to any one who would instruct them in the manufacture of the cannon, but Denning declined. The United States government, however, gave him no reward until near his death and he passed his later years in poverty. He died in his ninety-fourth year at his home in Mifflin Township, Cumberland County, Pa.

[The main source is the obituary in Samuel Hazard's *Register of Pa.,* Jan 15, 1831. The account in the *Pa. Mag. of Hist. and Biog.,* vol. XXXVIII (1914), p. 459, is wrong in several particulars.]

J. T. A.

DENNIS, GRAHAM BARCLAY (June 1, 1855–Aug. 18, 1923), capitalist, was born in London, England. His father, Mendenhall John Dennis, was a Presbyterian clergyman, educated at Oxford and Heidelberg, and his mother, Sophia (Kiehl) Dennis, was of German ancestry. The family came to America, and Graham lived as a boy in Boston and Cincinnati. He left school at the age of fourteen but took a course four years later at Bethany College (1873–74). He became city editor of the *Dayton Daily Journal,* Dayton, Ohio, in 1875 and, after two years on the city desk, served as business manager for two years. In the next six years, he engaged in various private enterprises in Dayton. He invented an electric postal canceling machine, organized G. B. Dennis & Company, a general brokerage firm, and established and edited an agricultural newspaper, *The Farmer's Home.* Partly on account of poor health, in May 1885 he moved to Spokane, Wash., where he published the *Spokane Miner,* 1885–86, and engaged in real estate and mining operations. The population of Spokane was then only 2,000. The Northern Pacific Railroad had been completed two years before, and the development of the "Inland Empire" was just commencing. The lode mining industry, which was the foundation of the region's prosperity, began in the year Dennis arrived with the discovery of the Old Dominion mine, near Colville. About 1891 or 1892, in association with three Chicago men, Dennis bought the mine. He became its manager, and expended some $550,000 on improvements. One showing of ore which had been picked up seemed so promising that the company was offered $1,000,000 for the property. Dennis wished to sell, but his partners refused, and after a carload or two had been taken from it the new showing was exhausted.

In the nineties Dennis was president or treasurer of eight or ten mines. He organized a company to develop the mica deposits of Idaho, was for many years, from its beginning in 1895, president of the Northwest Mining Association and in 1896 represented it at parliamentary hearings in Victoria, B. C., when the mining interests were successful in opposing a proposed 2 per cent tax on the gross output of the British Columbia mines. In 1897, he assisted in drafting a memorial to Congress regarding revision of the federal mining laws. With his numerous business connections he combined civic interests. He was a member of the Spokane City Council in 1886–88 and was elected to the school board in 1890. In the same year, he organized the Spokane Industrial Exposition and served as its vice-president. He was treasurer of Jenkins University, a pioneer educational experiment. He organized and built the Ross Park Electric Railway, opened in 1889, one of the first electric lines in the West. In 1906, he was the first president of the Pacific Northwest Development League, formed by leading men of the four states.

A nervous breakdown curtailed the activities of his last ten years, and he died of apoplexy on Aug. 18, 1923. He had an attractive personality and was forceful in his business leadership. He won confidence because he believed thoroughly in all his enterprises and put his own money into them. On May 20, 1879, he married Hester L. Bradley of Dayton, Ohio. Besides his widow, living in Spokane, he left three children.

[Jonathan Edwards, *An Illustrated Hist. of Spokane County* (1900), pp. 487–89; N. W. Durham, *Hist. of the City of Spokane and the Spokane Country* (1912), vol. I, ch. xli, and vol. II, p. 5; G. W. Fuller, *The Inland Empire* (1928), III, 67; *Sketches of Washingtonians* (1906); obituary in the *Spokesman-Review* (Spokane), Aug. 19, 1923.] G. W. F.

DENNIS, JAMES SHEPARD (Dec. 15, 1842–Mar. 21, 1914), missionary in Syria, historian, and statistician of missions, was the son of Alfred Lewis Dennis, an important and wealthy business man of Newark, N. J., and Eliza (Shepard) Dennis. His boyhood was surrounded with influences of culture and earnest religion. He graduated with the degree of B.A. from Princeton in 1863, and after a year's study of law at Harvard entered Princeton Theological Seminary, graduating in 1867. Ordained in the following year by the Presbytery of Newark, early in 1869 he arrived in Syria as a missionary of the American Board. A year later, when the mission was taken over by the Presbyterian Board of Foreign Missions, he joined the service of this board, with which he was connected all his life. For four years he was a field missionary in Sidon and Zahleh. It is remembered as characteristic that since the sound of his name has an unpleasant sense in Arabic he dropped its first letter, and was called by the Syrians "Ennis," meaning "courteous." He was married in Newark, June 26, 1872, to Mary Elizabeth, daughter of James B. Pinneo. From 1873 to 1891 he was professor in the Presbyterian Theological Seminary in Beirut. His command of Arabic led him into writing texts for missionary teaching, of which the most important were *Evidences of Christianity* (1877), *Biblical Interpretation* (1880), and *Christian Theology* in two volumes (1882–83). These books attained large use in missionary work among Arabic-speaking peoples. Because of business responsibilities and family circumstances in 1892 he resigned his missionary appointment. He had determined to serve the missionary cause by literary work, the way to which was opened by inherited wealth.

Returning to America he lived in New York City and Montclair, N. J. Soon there came to him, in connection with lectures given in Princeton Seminary (published as *Foreign Missions after a Century*, 1893), the idea of a thorough presentation of the social effects of Protestant missions on non-Christian peoples. He sought information on a large scale from over three hundred missionaries in all parts of the field. An immense correspondence resulted, giving him a unique acquaintance with missionaries and their work, and bringing him a flood of material. The issue was three large abundantly documented volumes on *Christian Missions and Social Progress* (1897, 1899, 1906). While this book has defects natural to work which broke much new ground, as a contribution to the science of missions it has not been surpassed in America. In addition to its great value as a storehouse of knowlege of missionary results, it deeply influenced the thinking of the friends of missions. Beside the older individualistic proselytizing conceptions it established the idea of missions as an enterprise releasing transforming forces into the common life of peoples. While the book was in preparation, portions formed the material for lectures at several theological seminaries.

As a "statistical supplement" to this book, Dennis published his *Centennial Survey of Christian Missions* (1902), reporting all Protestant missionary operations which were being maintained at the close of the nineteenth century and exhibiting with descriptions and statistics their conditions and achievements in all forms of work—"the most comprehensive and authoritative collection of missionary statistics which had ever been made" (R. E. Speer). Some of this material was presented by Dennis to the Ecumenical Missionary Conference in New York in 1900. In the preparations for this and also for the World Missionary Conference at Edinburgh in 1910 he took active part. For the Edinburgh Conference he did important work in improving methods of missionary statistics, and was editor of the statistical section of its *Statistical Atlas of Christian Missions.* In the *World Atlas of Christian Missions* (1911), he provided a directory of missionary societies, enrolling all Protestant missionary organizations in the world.

Dennis wrote many articles for missionary periodicals and papers for missionary meetings, of which some were collected in *The New Horoscope of Missions* (1908) and *The Modern Call of Missions* (1913). He spent much money in preparing and publishing his books, and took no financial returns. After his return from Syria he maintained active connection with missionary work, as honorary secretary of the Presbyterian Board, giving large service, and as a member of the Board from 1904 till his death. Seldom making public appearances, he greatly impressed and attracted those who knew him by a singular grace and loftiness of character. He died at Montclair.

[Records of Presbyterian Board of Foreign Missions, containing biographical data supplied by Dennis himself; records of Presbytery of Newark; his books, especially prefaces; general catalogues of Princeton Univ. and Princeton Theol. Sem.; issues of *Men (and Women) of America* and *Who's Who in America*; H. H. Jessup, *Fifty-three Years in Syria* (1910); article by R. E. Speer, in *Missionary Rev. of the World,* June 1914; *Ecumenical Missionary Conference,* N. Y., 1900, vols. I, II; Report of Commission I, *World Missionary Conf.,* 1910; articles in *N. Y. Times* and *Newark Evening News* at time of his death.] R. H. N.

DENNISON, AARON LUFKIN (Mar. 6, 1812–Jan. 9, 1895), pioneer watch manufacturer, was born at Freeport, Me., the third of ten children of Andrew and Lydia (Lufkin) Dennison. His father, a soldier in the War of 1812 and later a colonel of militia, was a shoemaker by trade who in his later years experimented with the making of paper boxes. At the age of thirteen Aaron was earning his living sawing wood and at fifteen was learning the cobbler's trade in his father's shop at Brunswick, Me. The boy, having a distinct mechanical bent, took little interest in cobbling, and his father, recognizing the fact, apprenticed him in 1830 to James Carey, a Brunswick watchmaker. Three years later Aaron left for Boston to perfect himself as a journeyman, entering first the employment of Currier & Trott, then of Jones, Low & Ball, and finally setting up for himself. As his skill increased and his knowledge of watches widened he was astonished at the imperfections in even the best of the hand-made products and became convinced that watches could be manufactured by machinery under a system of interchangeable parts. He predicted "in the year 1846 that within twenty years the manufacture of watches would be reduced to as much system and perfection and with the same expedition that fire-arms were then made in the Springfield armory. He often visited this armory and took great interest in examining the various processes of finishing fire-arms" (Hazlitt, *post,* p. 11). In 1849 Edward Howard, a clock and scale maker of Boston, tried to interest Dennison in the manufacture of locomotives, but instead he was himself persuaded to embark upon the manufacture of watches. Samuel Curtis of Boston invested $20,000 in the project, and while Dennison was on a tour of investigation in Europe, Howard supervised the construction of a factory in Roxbury. Here Dennison designed the first factory-made watches in the world. The business was conducted first under the name of the American Horologue Company and later under that of the Boston Watch Company. Two or three years' experience convinced the management that the atmosphere in Roxbury was too dusty, and a new location was determined upon at Waltham. The expenses of these early years, however, combined with the effect of the panic of 1857, forced the concern into bankruptcy. It was purchased by New York and Philadelphia interests and was continued after Feb. 8, 1859, as the American Watch Company and finally as the American Waltham Watch Company, which developed into the largest watch company in America. Dennison continued as superintendent under the new management until December 1861, while Howard returned to Roxbury and continued the manufacture of watches there.

In 1864 Dennison interested A. O. Bigelow of Boston in the idea of manufacturing medium-priced watches, certain parts of which were to be made in Switzerland, the whole to be assembled in America. As a result the Tremont Watch Company was organized and Dennison went to

Zurich to oversee production of Swiss parts. The company prospered until 1866 when the management decided to manufacture all of the parts in America. Dennison thereupon withdrew, but remained in Switzerland until 1870, having taken a contract to furnish certain material for the firm. The company soon fell into financial difficulties and Dennison returned to America in the hope of reorganizing it. Failing in this, he succeeded in selling the machinery to an English firm. He himself eventually moved to Birmingham, England, where he successfully manufactured watch-cases. Known during his lifetime as the "Father of American Watchmaking," he is believed to have been the first person to have constructed the entire watch under one roof by machinery manufacturing interchangeable parts. An inventor and not a business man, he saw other men grow rich with the tools that he devised, and in the end was forced to earn a living manufacturing merely the shell to surround the delicate mechanism which he knew so well. On Jan. 15, 1840, he was married to Charlotte W. Foster, by whom he had five children.

[G. M. Rogers, *The Dennison Family* (1906), pp. 50–1; G. H. A. Hazlitt ("H. G. Abbott"), *The Watch Factories of America Past and Present* (1888), chs. i and ix; D. H. Hurd, *Hist. of Middlesex County, Mass.* (1890), III, 738–49; *Daily Evening Transcript* (Boston), Jan. 10, 1895; *Springfield Republican*, Jan. 11, 1895.]
H. U. F.

DENNISON, WALTER (Aug. 9, 1869–Mar. 18, 1917), teacher, scholar, was born at Saline, near Ypsilanti, Mich., the son of James L. and Eliza J. (Flowers) Dennison. He received his early education in public schools, entered the University of Michigan, and was graduated in 1893 as bachelor of arts. While an undergraduate he married, Aug. 5, 1891, Anna L. Green of Ypsilanti. Upon graduation he was appointed to a fellowship for two years, the first of which he spent in the Graduate School of the University of Michigan, receiving the degree of M.A. in 1894. The following year he spent in Europe, first at the University of Bonn, then in Italy. When the American School of Classical Studies in Rome was opened in 1895, Dennison received one of the two fellowships established in connection with the School, and his appointment was renewed for the year 1896–97. One of the four papers which resulted from his studies in Rome, "The Epigraphic Sources of Suetonius," was accepted as a thesis by the University of Michigan, which granted him the degree of Ph.D. in 1897. The paper was published in the *American Journal of Archæology* in 1898. He was instructor in Latin in the University of Michigan, 1897–99; professor of Latin and Roman archeology at Oberlin College, 1899–1902; junior professor of Latin at the University of Michigan, 1902–10; and professor of Greek and Latin at Swarthmore College from 1910 until his death. In the year 1908–09 he was annual professor of Latin in the American School of Classical Studies in Rome. He was a member of the American Philological Association and the Archæological Institute of America. For three years, 1913–16, he was secretary of the Philadelphia Society of the Institute, and he was a member of the council of the Institute from 1916 until his death. He was one of the founders, and first president, of the Philadelphia Society for the Promotion of Liberal Studies, and in 1914–15 was president of the Classical Association of the Atlantic States. He was also (1913–17) associate editor of the *Classical Weekly*.

During his earlier stay in Italy Dennison came upon a collection of Latin inscriptions formed by the parish priest of Pozzuoli, De Criscio, which he published under the title, "Some New Inscriptions from Puteoli, Baiae, Misenum, and Cumae," in the *American Journal of Archæology*, in 1898. Eventually he secured the inscriptions themselves for the University of Michigan. During his year as annual professor in the school in Rome he attended an archeological congress at Cairo, and while there learned of the discovery of a gold treasure of the Roman period. This he recommended to the attention of Charles L. Freer of Detroit, who purchased it for his collection of objects of art. Dennison published, in addition to valuable articles, *A Junior Latin Book* (with John C. Rolfe, 1898), an edition of *Livy, Book I and Selections from Books II–X* (1908), revised editions of F. W. Kelsey's *Topical Outline of Latin Literature* (1899) and H. S. Frieze's *Virgil's Æneid* (1902). At the time of his death the final proofs of his scholarly monograph, *A Gold Treasure of the Late Roman Period*, were awaiting his attention. It was published in 1918 as Part II of Volume XII of the University of Michigan Studies, Humanistic Series.

Dennison was above the average height, well formed and of erect carriage. His hair and moustache were dark brown, with a reddish tinge. His habitual expression was kindly, gentle, and thoughtful. He was a very lovable man. As a teacher he impressed his students by the breadth and soundness of his learning, his high ideals of scholarship, his modesty and sincerity. His classes were cheery and pleasant, yet stimulating and thorough. He did not make his students work, but inspired them with the desire to learn. His interest in his pupils was hearty and unaffected. He knew them well, and they talked with him as with a friend. He had a gentle, kindly humor and refrained from all unkindly criticism. His colleagues found in him a friendly and considerate associate. He was an untiring worker, and organized his life so as to enable him to accomplish the tasks which he set out to accomplish. His death came upon him suddenly, as the result of pneumonia, while he was in the midst of the work which he loved and in which he excelled.

[*Who's Who in America,* 1916–17. A privately printed booklet contains a portrait, an appreciation by Spencer Trotter, the main facts of Dennison's life, minutes and resolutions of the faculty, the Phi Beta Kappa chapter, and the Student Government Associations of Swarthmore College, of the Pa. Soc. of the Archæological Inst. of America, and of the Phila. Soc. for the Promotion of Liberal Studies; also a poem, *"Integer Vitae,"* by John Russell Hayes, and several photographic illustrations. Obituary notices are published in the *Classical Jour.,* June 1917, pp. 587–88; the *Am. Jour. of Archæol.,* XXI (1917), p. 341 (a summary of the preceding); in *A Gold Treasure of the Late Roman Period,* pp. 167–68 (by F. W. Kelsey), and in *The Phœnix* (Swarthmore Coll. paper), Mar. 20, 1917. The *Phœnix,* Apr. 10, 1917, contains an account of the funeral services.] H. N. F.

DENNISON, WILLIAM (Nov. 23, 1815–June 15, 1882), governor of Ohio, was the son of William Dennison, who with his New England wife, Mary Carter, about 1805 removed from New Jersey to Cincinnati, and there became a successful business man. The son attended Miami University, where he proved to be a capable student of political science, history, and literature. Graduating in 1835, he read law in the office of Nathaniel G. Pendleton, father of George H. Pendleton [*q.v.*]. He was admitted to the bar in 1840 and practised until 1848, when he was elected to the state Senate as a Whig. After a hot contest, which prevented organization of the Senate for two weeks, he was defeated as his party's candidate for the position of presiding officer.

In 1844, in his maiden speech before the public, Dennison had opposed the admission of Texas and the extension of the area of slavery. The position then taken foreshadowed his course through the next twenty years. As a member of the state Senate, he had a part in the fight for the repeal of the notorious "Black Laws," and while adhering to the Whig party through 1852 he was one of the first of the Ohio party leaders to join the Republican movement. In February 1856 he attended the preliminary convention at Pittsburgh and served as a member of the Committee on Resolutions; and in June he was acting chairman of the Ohio delegation in the Philadelphia Convention, which nominated Frémont. Three years later, as Republican candidate for governor, he defeated Judge Rufus P. Ranney, who ranked as the leader of the state bar, and thus found himself in the executive chair when the Civil War began. He came to the governor's chair with little experience in public affairs. Although he was well regarded by the business men of the capital city, to whom in large part he owed his nomination, he was but little known to the public, and his nomination was thought to be due to a dearth of able rivals. He campaigned with unexpected brilliance in 1859, but his success did not win for him the full confidence of the people, who decided that he was aristocratic and vain. Thus handicapped, he met the war crisis without adequate support in public opinion. Disposed in advance to be discontented, the people of Ohio were unable for a time to appreciate the energy and wisdom with which he performed his duties. Regarding the Ohio River as an unsafe line of defense for his state, Dennison dispatched McClellan with state troops to aid the loyal citizens of western Virginia in driving out the Confederates. He advocated a similar campaign in Kentucky, but the Federal government preferred to respect the state's neutrality. As a means of preventing the transportation of war supplies and war news without his approval, he practically assumed control of the railways, telegraph lines, and express companies at the outset of hostilities; and against the advice of his attorney-general, he used money refunded by the Federal government on account of state military expenditures without turning it into the treasury for reappropriation. Many complaints thus arose, not without some justification, in spite of the fact that he had with extraordinary promptness succeeded in placing in the field more than the state's quota of the troops called for by the Federal government. As a war governor, Dennison proved unpopular, and the party leaders did not venture to renominate him in 1861. Moreover, they felt the necessity of uniting with the War Democrats, and effected this purpose by supporting David Tod. Dennison accepted the situation without any show of personal feeling, and continued to give loyal support to his party. Gov. Tod, in particular, constantly sought his advice and aid.

In 1864, Dennison acted as chairman of the Republican National Convention, and in the same year was appointed postmaster-general by Lincoln, which office he held until 1866, when he resigned it on account of dissatisfaction with President Johnson's course. In 1872 he was mentioned for the vice-presidential nomination, and in 1880 was defeated by Garfield for the Republican nomination as United States senator. In the same year he was chairman of the Sherman Committee in Ohio, and leader of his forces in the national convention. It is thought that had Grant been nominated, Dennison might have won the vice-presidency.

Notwithstanding his prominence in political affairs, Dennison was primarily a business man. Soon after his admission to the bar he had married the daughter of William Neil of Columbus, a promoter of stage transportation, and had settled in that city. In the early fifties he became president of the Exchange Bank, member of the city council, and organizer of the Franklin County Agricultural Society. In the dawning era of the railway, he was a pioneer promoter of the new type of transportation, leading in the organization, especially, of the Hocking Valley and Columbus & Xenia railroads. An enterprise of another type which he was influential in establishing was the Columbus Rolling Mills. By such ventures, notwithstanding heavy losses in the panic of 1873, he acquired a considerable fortune. To the end of his life, mostly on account of his reserved manner, few knew him well. On the street he spoke only to old and intimate friends. Yet no man knew better how to treat his fellows in parlor or office, and never, intentionally, did he mistreat friend or foe (*Cincinnati Enquirer,* June 16, 1882). He died in Columbus after a period of invalidism lasting about eighteen months.

[Most sketches of Dennison are based on Whitelaw Reid, *Ohio in the War* (1868), I, 1017–22, and index. See also E. O. Randall and D. V. Ryan, *Hist. of Ohio* (1912), IV, *passim*; *Ohio Archæol. and Hist. Soc. Pubs.*, I, 123; IV, 444; IX, 149; *Harper's Weekly,* Jan. 28, 1865; *Ohio State Jour.* and *Cincinnati Enquirer,* June 16, 1882. The best source for the years of Dennison's governorship is his message of Jan. 6, 1862, which includes documents.] H. C. H.

DENT, FREDERICK TRACY (Dec. 17, 1821–Dec. 24, 1892), soldier, was born in St. Louis County, Mo., son of Frederick F. and Ellen (Wrenshall) Dent, and a classmate of Gen. Grant, who married his sister, Julia Dent. He was graduated from the United States Military Academy, July 1, 1843. Promoted brevet second lieutenant of the 6th Infantry, he served on frontier duty at Fort Towson, Indian Territory, at Baton Rouge, La., and through the Mexican War, taking part in the siege of Vera Cruz, the capture of San Antonio, and the battles of Contreras, Churubusco, and Molino del Rey. In the last of these battles he was severely wounded. After the Mexican War he served on the Pacific Railroad Survey, in the removal of the Seminole Indians, and at various frontier posts. He participated in the Yakima Expedition (1856), the Spokane Expedition in Washington Territory, the combats of Four Lakes, Spokane Plain, Spokane River, and the expedition to Snake River, Ore., to rescue the survivors of the massacre of Salmon Falls. During the Civil War he served in command of a regiment in the Army of the Potomac, and as a member of the military commission for the trial of state prisoners. Upon the appointment of Gen. Grant as lieutenant-general, he was selected by his brother-in-law as one of his aides-de-camp, with the rank of lieutenant-colonel. He served on the staff of Gen. Grant during the Richmond campaign, and upon the fall of the city of Richmond he was made its military governor, and later commanded the garrison of Washington. He was appointed brigadier-general, United States Volunteers, Apr. 5, 1865, and was mustered out of the volunteer service Apr. 30, 1866. On May 3, 1866, he was again appointed aide-de-camp to Gen. Grant, with the rank of lieutenant-colonel, and in July of the same year was promoted colonel. When Gen. Grant became president, Dent accompanied him to the White House as military secretary, and remained in this capacity until May 1873 when he was assigned to the command of Fort Trumbull, Conn. He was brevetted first lieutenant and captain at the battles of Contreras, Churubusco, and Molino del Rey in the Mexican War, and in the Civil War received the brevets of lieutenant-colonel, colonel, and brigadier-general, for his services. He was retired from active service as colonel of the 1st Artillery, Dec. 1, 1883, upon his own application, after more than forty years of service. While Dent was not a brilliant soldier, and owed much to his relationship to Gen. Grant, he was a brave and chivalrous man, kindly, and of unfailing courtesy, who did his duty zealously and well. He was of medium size, pleasant address, and amiable manners.

[G. W. Cullum, *Biog. Reg.* (3rd ed., 1891); *Official Records (Army)*, ser. 1, vols. XXXVI and L; *Battles and Leaders of the Civil War,* IV (1889), 736; *Twenty-fourth Annual Reunion Asso. Grads. U. S. Mil. Acad.,* 1893.] C. F. C—y.

DENVER, JAMES WILLIAM (Oct. 23, 1817–Aug. 9, 1892), lawyer, soldier, was of Irish descent, his grandfather, Patrick Denver, a participant in the Rebellion of '98, having fled to the United States and settled in Virginia. He was born at Winchester, Frederick County, Va., and his youth was spent on his father's farm there, and at Wilmington, Clinton County, Ohio, where his parents, Frederick and Jane (Campbell) Denver, moved with their family in 1830. He was educated in the local schools, studied engineering and land surveying, and in 1841 went to Missouri in the hope of procuring some survey work. This he failed to do, and so took up school-teaching, both there and in Kentucky. In 1842 he determined to become a lawyer, removed to Ohio, entered the Cincinnati Law School, and graduated in 1844. Opening an office in Xenia, Ohio, he commenced practise, also editing *The Thomas Jefferson,* a local Democratic paper, but in a few months returned to Missouri, and finally settled at Platte City. After the outbreak of the war with Mexico, in 1847 he raised a company for the 12th United States Volunteer Infantry, was commissioned captain, joined Gen. Scott's army at Pueblo, and served throughout the subsequent campaign, participating in all the fighting, including the battles of Molino del Rey and Chapultepec. At the close of the war he returned to Platte City, resumed practise, and purchased the *Platte Argus,* which he edited. In the spring of 1850, attracted by the gold discoveries in California, he traveled to Sacramento by way of Salt Lake and engaged in trading. Shortly afterward, without his knowledge or consent, he was elected state senator, and served in that capacity during 1852–53. In 1852 Gov. Bigler placed him in command of the supply trains which had been provided by vote of the legislature for the assistance of the overland immigrants who were pouring over the mountains and meeting with great hardships. This duty he performed with complete success. Bitter criticism of the project by Edward Gilbert, editor in chief of the *Daily Alta California,* resulted in a duel between the latter and Denver, Aug. 2, 1852, in which Gilbert was killed. Public opinion was overwhelmingly with Denver, and no action was ever taken against him in the matter. Early in 1853 he became secretary of state for California, and while holding that office was elected as a Democrat to the Thirty-fourth Congress. He took his seat in December 1855, and at once became a prominent figure, being appointed chairman of the Special Committee on Pacific Railroads. He astonished the House by reporting a bill providing for three transcontinental lines, but the members declined to support even one. At the close of his term in 1857 he was appointed Commissioner of Indian Affairs by President Buchanan, and in that capacity went West to negotiate treaties with the Indians. Kansas at that period was experiencing a wave of lawlessness and chronic disorder which successive governors had failed to cope with, and President Buchanan, seeking a strong man to take charge of the situation, in the autumn of 1857 turned to Denver. He reluctantly consented and became secretary of the Territory of Kansas in December 1857, and governor in May 1858. Acting with great decision and impartiality, and impervious to threats, in less than a year he had restored law and confidence, and when he resigned in October 1858 violence and intimidation had ceased and the government was functioning normally. The city of Denver was so named in his honor, he having provided the machinery for the civil organization of Arapahoe County, at the time when the town site was laid out. Returning to Washington, he resumed the commissionership of Indian Affairs, assisting also in the separation of Colorado from Kansas, and suggesting the name for the new Territory. He remained commissioner until March 1859. On his retirement, he returned to California, was unsuccessful candidate for a senatorship and, realizing that he had lost touch with that state, went back to Ohio. On the outbreak of the Civil War he was commissioned brigadier-general of volunteers by President Lincoln, and placed in command of the troops in Kansas. He subsequently joined Halleck at Pittsburg Landing, and commanded a brigade in the Army of the Tennessee, taking part in the advance upon Corinth. He resigned his command, however, in the spring of 1863, and saw no further service. At the termination of the war he opened a law office in Washington, D. C. In 1866 he was a delegate to the Soldiers Convention at Cleveland, and four years later was unsuccessful candidate for Congress from Ohio. He continued active in politics, and in 1876 and 1884 his name was mentioned in connection with the Democratic nomination for the presidency. A distorted version of his duel with Gilbert made its appearance on each occasion, much to his disadvantage. He died in Washington, D. C.

Essentially a product of the frontier, he was a man of fine physique, being six feet two inches in height, and broad in proportion. Remarkable for energy, tenacity and far-sightedness, he was an outstanding figure in the West, where his sincerity of purpose and absolute fearlessness in the discharge of his public duties were appreciated to the full. "Genial, dignified and urbane, he possessed peculiarly winning ways, and the faculty of making men his loyal and enduring friends" (Smiley, *post*). In 1856 he had married Louisa C. Rombach, a native of Ohio. Their son Matthew Rombach Denver was a member of Congress from Ohio.

[An excellent sketch of Denver's career appeared in J. C. Smiley, *Hist. of Denver* (1903), p. 216, which also contains details of his connection with the location of that city and the first organization of Colorado. The article "Jas. W. Denver and Edward Gilbert and their fatal duel in 1852," in O. T. Shuck, *Hist. of the Bench and Bar of Cal.* (1901), p. 227, is informative. See also *A Democratic Nomination for 1884, Jas. W. Denver, of Ohio. His Life, his Services and his Availability*

(1884), a political pamphlet, but interesting; *Hist. of Clinton County, Ohio* (1882), p. 854; *Biog. Dir. of the Am. Congress* (1928).] H. W. H. K.

DE PAUW, WASHINGTON CHARLES (Jan. 4, 1822–May 5, 1887), manufacturer, philanthropist, was born in Salem, Washington County, Ind., the second son of John and Elizabeth (Battiste) De Pauw. The name is derived from Pau, the capital of French Navarre, where the family originated, but from which, owing to its Huguenot sympathies, it migrated in the late sixteenth century to French Flanders and the Walloon provinces where the name was modified to its present spelling. Cornelius De Pauw (1737–99) was the private reader of Frederick the Great. Charles, his son, born at Ghent in 1756, was educated in Paris, became imbued with the principles of the American Revolution and came to America with Lafayette in 1776. At the close of the Revolution he married a Virginia lady and settled in the Blue-Grass region of Kentucky. Here John, the father of Washington Charles, was born. In early manhood he settled in Washington County, Ind., where he was made county surveyor; and in 1814 he laid out the town of Salem (Dunn, *post,* I, 299). Later he was admitted to the bar, was a member of the state constitutional convention of 1816, became a judge, was a general of the state militia, and on four different occasions served as a member of the General Assembly.

Washington De Pauw spent his early life in Salem, Ind. Before the age of twenty-one he entered the county clerk's office and at the age of twenty-two was elected to the clerkship. He invested his first savings in a saw and grist-mill, and on retiring from the clerk's office (1853), started a small bank. He later invested in other banks and became one of the leading bankers in the state. At the opening of the Civil War he was employed for a short time in the army-supply department, but soon withdrew, devoting his entire time to banking. He was a large purchaser of government bonds and securities—as a patriotic duty—but he later profited greatly from these investments. Following the war he became interested in manufacturing, and among other ventures established a plate-glass plant in New Albany, Ind., which became one of the largest and most successful of its kind in the country. In 1882 it was estimated that his manufacturing enterprises in New Albany alone represented an investment of $2,000,000 (*History of the Ohio Falls Cities and their Counties,* 1882, II, 230–31).

From early manhood he was interested in religious and educational activities, but he always declined to participate in politics, refusing the Democratic nomination for lieutenant-governor in 1872. For a number of years he was a trustee of Indiana University, and also of Indiana Asbury University. He was a delegate to the General Conference of the Methodist Episcopal Church in 1872 and 1876, and to the Ecumenical Methodist Council in London in 1881. He gave liberally to schools and churches, but his largest benefaction was made to Indiana Asbury University (established 1837) which became De Pauw University in 1884. In 1881 he provided in his will for the founding and endowment of an institution to be known as De Pauw University. At this time Indiana Asbury University was in financial distress, and when it became known to the trustees that De Pauw contemplated the founding of a new institution, they appealed to him to take over Indiana Asbury, the trustees offering to change the name to De Pauw University. The negotiations were successful and the contract was signed Oct. 16, 1882. The contract between De Pauw and the trustees provided for the raising of $150,000 for the purchase of additional grounds and the erection of buildings, De Pauw agreeing to pay two dollars for every one dollar thus raised. Altogether De Pauw gave, during his lifetime, about $300,000 to the University. His sudden death—from the effects of an apoplectic stroke—left his affairs in confusion, and the terms of his will, which had made liberal provision for carrying on the work of the University and for an endowment, were found impossible of fulfilment.

De Pauw was married three times. His first wife, Sarah Malott, whom he married about 1846, died after the birth of their second child. In 1855 he married Katharine, daughter of Dr. Elijah Newland. She bore him three sons, and died while the youngest was an infant. On Jan. 8, 1867, De Pauw married Frances Marion Leyden, by whom he had four daughters, two dying in infancy. He was a broad, solid, and strong man, slightly below the average in height, with a florid, good-humored face. Deeply religious, and generous to every good cause, he abhorred waste and prodigality. His business ethics were far above the average of his time and no man ever had a more sincere desire to serve his fellow men.

[J. C. Ridpath, in *Meth. Rev.,* May 1890; J. P. Dunn, *Indiana and Indianans,* I (1919), 299; *Asbury Mo.,* 1881–84; *De Pauw Mo.,* 1884–89; manuscript minutes of the Board of Trustees Indiana Asbury-De Pauw University; information from Mrs. Florence De Pauw Seaman, a daughter of W. C. and Frances (Leyden) De Pauw.] W. W. S.

DEPEW, CHAUNCEY MITCHELL (Apr. 23, 1834–Apr. 5, 1928), lawyer, wit, railway president, United States senator, was the son of

Depew

Isaac and Martha (Mitchell) Depew. His father was of French Huguenot descent and a man of enterprise. His mother came from the line of Roger Sherman, Connecticut statesman and signer of the Declaration of Independence, being a grand-daughter of the latter's brother, Rev. Josiah Sherman. To few men has it been given to live so long and well as did Chauncey M. Depew. His path followed the lines of good fortune and least resistance from his birth in the Hudson River town of Peekskill, Westchester County, N. Y., to his death at 27 West 54th St., New York City. Peekskill had been the home of the Depew family ever since the first of the name arrived along with the Palatines imported by Robert Livingston to clear his land grants on the eastern shore of the lordly river. Isaac Depew took to river transportation before the days of railroads and did well with it. From the start his son had advantages. He began his education with five years in a private school kept by Mrs. Westbrook, wife of the Dutch Reformed pastor in Peekskill, to whose faith his father and mother conformed and which was his own through life. The school was adequate; its course classical. A high-school course at the Peekskill Academy fitted him for Yale, which he entered in 1852. Among his classmates in New Haven were David James Brewer and Henry Billings Brown, who were to become justices of the United States Supreme Court. Fellow students of note and lifelong intimacy were Wayne MacVeagh, later attorney-general of the United States, and Andrew D. White, president of Cornell University. Depew was a popular student and a superior scholar. He was one of the Commencement Day orators when graduating in 1856.

Returning to Peekskill he entered the law office of Edward Wells and for two years studied the statutes and the intricacies of justice. In 1858 he was admitted to the bar and began practise in his native village, a risky proceeding which like all else in his lucky life turned out well. The Republican party came into being before young Depew's departure from Yale. Though his family were Democrats the doctrine of free soil appealed to the rising attorney. Upon graduation he joined his fortunes with the new organization locally and made a name for himself when put on the stump by the state committee in the Frémont-Buchanan campaign. He attended the New York Republican state convention in 1858 as a delegate from Peekskill. Won over by Thurlow Weed, he supported for the governorship Edward D. Morgan, a metropolitan merchant, who was nominated, elected, then reëlected for a second term that made him a "war" governor. When the Civil War began in 1861, Depew was prominent in public counsels. He served in the legislature in the sessions of 1862 and 1863, being Republican nominee for the speakership the latter year. The two parties were tied in the House, though the Republicans controlled the Senate and had a sufficient majority in joint-session to insure the election of their candidate for the United States Senate, Gov. Morgan, if only the House could be organized. After a prolonged deadlock, during which Depew's name was withdrawn and again presented, a deal was finally effected whereby a Democrat, T. C. Callicot, was chosen speaker in return for the assurance of Morgan's election to the Senate. Depew refused to take advantage of the offer of a group of Democrats to give him the speakership if he would oppose this scheme, and relates that he was overwhelmed with compliments on his virtue (Depew, *My Memories of Eighty Years,* pp. 24–6). He could hardly have acted otherwise without affronting the powerful Thurlow Weed, who was managing Morgan's candidacy and was party to the arrangement. Owing to legal action instituted against Callicot by injured Democrats, however, Depew acted as speaker a good part of the session. He was also chairman of the ways and means committee, and floor leader for his party. His activities brought him into contact with Lincoln and made him nationally prominent. Political promotion was easy. In 1863 he was elected secretary of state and in the campaign of 1864 he stumped New York, following and answering Gov. Horatio Seymour who was running for reëlection. After Lincoln's assassination Depew, as secretary of state, received his body in New York and escorted it to Buffalo, on the way to Springfield, Ill., where it was interred.

Appointed in 1866 by Andrew Johnson as the first minister from the United States to Japan, he was duly confirmed by the Senate. The salary —$7,500 a year—looked large in Peekskill, but while Depew was contemplating acceptance Commodore Cornelius Vanderbilt, then head of the Hudson River and Harlem railroad lines, offered him the place of attorney for his roads at a much smaller salary. He hesitated. "Railroads are the career for a young man; there is nothing in politics. Don't be a damned fool," the Commodore is said to have remarked. Depew resigned and entered the service of Vanderbilt interests, which did not take him out of politics. He handled the political contacts of his employer with great tact and skill. At the Commodore's behest Depew joined the Independent Republican movement in 1872, took a hand in securing Horace Greeley's nomination for president and himself ran for lieutenant-governor in New York State on the Greeley ticket. He was beaten but made a good race. It was all in the day's work as Vanderbilt's attorney. Legislation had a considerable share in his duties and he smoothed the way for his client at Albany. The consolidation of the several cross-state lines that became the New York Central was full of complexities, legal and legislative. These he straightened out. Securing Chicago connections was a matter of further importance. In 1874 he became a director in the Vanderbilt system; in 1875 its general counsel; in 1877, a director in the Chicago & Northwestern; in 1882 second vice-president of the New York Central & Hudson River, which had become the designation of the combined railroads; and in 1885, its president. During his term of office, which lasted thirteen years, he brought about the absorption of the rival West Shore system and was for a time its president.

In 1881, following the resignation of the New York senators, Conkling and Platt, Depew was a candidate before the legislature. After prolonged balloting during which he was within ten votes of election, he withdrew his name. In 1885 he was offered the Republican nomination for senator from New York, but declined. In 1888 his party in the state indorsed him for president. He attended the convention at Chicago where he received 99 votes. Railroads were unpopular at the moment and he withdrew in favor of Benjamin Harrison, whom he nominated and whose candidacy he actively supported in the campaign that followed. Harrison tendered him a cabinet position of his own choice but he declined. When James G. Blaine retired as secretary of state in 1892 the President invited Depew to fill out the term but he again refused. In the presidential campaign of that year Depew again took the stump for Harrison. In 1896 he nominated Levi P. Morton for president, but the honor went to McKinley. In 1899 he was elected United States senator from New York and retired from the presidency of the New York Central Railroad but became chairman of the board of directors, a position he retained to the end. He was received in a hostile spirit at Washington as a railway man but preserved his personal popularity. In 1905 he was reëlected and served another full term. That year his name came under a cloud through the revelation made by Charles E. Hughes, counsel for the Armstrong legislative committee when investigating the practises of the great New York life insurance companies, that he had been receiving an annual retainer of $20,000 from the Equitable Life Assurance Company. This he at once gave up. The exposé put him in the background for a time, but the spot in the public heart that had grown cold, warmed up in season and Depew resumed his place in general esteem.

He was a favorite after-dinner speaker and raconteur. "I am known as an after-dinner speaker," he said on his eightieth birthday. "I hope I am also known as the man who works. My dinners have never interfered with my business. They have been my recreation. . . . My digestion might have bothered me if I had not been careful. . . . I soon determined to play with everything, but to eat nothing except the roast and game courses. The trouble with the average man is that he cannot restrain his appetite. But a public banquet, if eaten with thought and care, is no more of a strain than a dinner at home." He was fond of quoting President James A. Garfield to the effect that "he might be president if he did not tell funny stories." He would drink nothing but champagne and that in moderation. With his fortunes well guided by the Vanderbilts he escaped worry, and with his rules of health was able to continue active until past ninety. His only office besides those named was that of Regent of the University of the State of New York, which he held from 1877 to 1904. He was a delegate to every Republican national convention from 1888 to 1924. At eighty-two he calmed the convention of 1916 which almost got out of hand. On the appeal of the chairman, Warren G. Harding, Depew took the floor for forty-five minutes and mastered the disorder. He spoke again at the gathering of 1920. For thirty years he attended an annual birthday celebration given by the Montauk Club of Brooklyn. Yale alumni dinners and the choice affairs of the Lotos Club were occasions upon which he shone conspicuously.

He occupied a large place in directorates, holding membership on the boards of many railroads, chiefly the New York Central and its dependencies, the Western Union Telegraph Company, and various bridge companies. He was a member of the Society of the Cincinnati, and, from 1893 to 1906, of the Yale Corporation. At the time of his death he was the oldest graduate of Yale. He was devoted to the interests of the university and to many benefactions during his lifetime he added by will a million dollars. Depew married Elsie A. Hegeman, Nov. 9, 1871. One son, Chauncey M. Depew, Jr., was born to them. Mrs. Depew died May 7, 1893. On Dec. 27, 1901, at Nice, Depew married May Palmer, who survived him.

[Depew's speeches have been published in a succession of volumes, the most extensive collection being

Orations, Addresses and Speeches, ed. by J. D. Chaplin (8 vols., 1910). His *My Memories of Eighty Years* (1922), and *The Depew Story Book* (1898), ed. by W. M. Clemens, are of interest. See also *Century Mag.*, Aug. 1925; *Literary Digest,* Apr. 28, 1928; *Rev. of Revs.* (N. Y.), May 1928; *Nation* (N. Y.) and *Outlook,* both Apr. 18, 1928; *Current Hist.*, Apr. 1926; W. A. D. Eardeley, *Chronology and Ancestry of Chauncey M. Depew* (1918); *F. J. Conkling,* "The Family of Dupuis, De Puy, Depew, etc.," *N. Y. Geneal. and Biog. Rec.*, Jan., Apr., July, Oct. 1901; *Yale Univ. Obit. Rec. of Grads.* (1928); obituaries in *N. Y. Times, N. Y. Herald Tribune,* and *World,* Apr. 6, 1928.] D. C. S.

DE PEYSTER, ABRAHAM (July 8, 1657–Aug. 2, 1728), colonial merchant and public official, was born in New Amsterdam, the son of Johannes and Cornelia (Lubberts) de Peyster. The father was a native of Haarlem and descended from a line of ancestors conspicuous "in goldsmithing industry and in other handicraft arts," of considerable wealth, and for the most part converts to the Protestant faith; he emigrated to New Amsterdam prior to 1649 and was one of the dozen or so most substantial citizens. Abraham enlarged the possessions inherited from his father, became an enterprising merchant, "importing in his own ships," built warehouses near the dock which are mentioned several times in the city records, and acquired a tract of land north of the Wall (the present Wall St.) which was known as the "Great Garden of Col. de Peyster." He built a house near the East River shore in 1695, for years one of the finest residences in the city. In a list of members of the Dutch Church, his name appears as one of six to which the courtesy title "de Heer" is attached, emblematic of influence and wealth. The young city struggling under its financial burdens often looked to him for loans; an entry in the Council Minutes, Apr. 22, 1702, states that "Abr'm de Peyster offers to assist the government in financial difficulties" (*Calendar*). Letters from Gov. Bellomont (in *De Peyster and Watts,* pp. 124–40) reveal the extent to which the Governor relied on De Peyster in connection with supplies of ship timber and wine, and in money matters generally. It is apparent that the latter combined with his affluence and business capacity popularity and good sense, for he was called by his fellow citizens or the provincial authorities to fill almost every public office in municipality or province: alderman (1685), captain of a train band, mayor for four successive terms (1691–94), colonel of the local militia, member of the governor's council (1698–1702, 1709, 1710–22), and as such, in 1701, acting-governor for a short period, deputy auditor-general (1701) and receiver general of the port (1708), justice of the supreme court (1698–1702; he succeeded to the position of chief-justice on Jan. 21, 1701, holding the office until Aug. 4 of that year), and finally, treasurer of the province (1706–21). As mayor he was instrumental in developing a system for the better care of the city poor. He possessed a decided military instinct and was one of six captains of train bands in 1689, at the time of the Leisler rebellion. He was identified with the Leisler faction although he was one of those who signed a petition of protest (May 19, 1690) to William and Mary against being ruled "by the sword at the sole Will of an Insolent Alien" (*Documents,* III, 748–49). During the years of war which followed between English and French colonists De Peyster (now with the rank of colonel) was active on committees for building or repairing fortifications, and on one occasion, at least, when government funds were lacking he shared with another the entire expense of subsisting "the soldiers in his Majesty's Pay" (*Journal of the Votes and Proceedings of the General Assembly,* Apr. 14, 17 and 18, 1701).

De Peyster went to Holland in 1684 and married Catharine de Peyster, a kinswoman, by whom he had eight sons and five daughters. His son Abraham succeeded him as treasurer of the province in 1721.

[Important contemporary sources include: *Minutes of the Common Council of the City of N. Y. 1675–1776* (8 vols., 1905), vols. I, VIII; *Calendar of Council Minutes, 1668–1783* (N. Y. State Lib. Bull. 58, 1902); *Documents Relative to the Colonial Hist. of the State of N. Y.*, vols. III, IV, V (1853–55); De Peyster Papers (MS.) in N. Y. Hist. Soc., some of which are printed in J. Watts de Peyster, *De Peyster and Watts Geneal. Reference* (1854). "The De Peyster Family in Connection with the Colonial Hist. of N. Y." in Valentine's *Manual of the Corporation of the City of N. Y.*, 1861, pp. 556–76, and W. W. Spooner, *Hist. Families in America,* I, 1–40, are secondary accounts which need to be checked for inaccuracies. See also Frank Allaben, *John Watts de Peyster* (1908), I, 17–19; Jas. G. Wilson, *Memorial Hist. of N. Y.*, esp. vol. I (1892).]

A. E. P.

DE PEYSTER, JOHN WATTS (Mar. 9, 1821–May 4, 1907), author, soldier, the son of Frederic de Peyster and Mary Justina Watts, was born in New York City at the home of his maternal grandfather, John Watts. The De Peysters were of "stout Holland ancestry," descendants of Huguenot refugees, Johannes de Peyster being the first of the family in America. John's paternal grandmother was English, a daughter of Gen. Hake of the British army, while his own mother was of Scotch descent. Philanthropic interests, participation in the civic events of their times, and especially a marked devotion to military pursuits were characteristic of many branches of his family, and he rather faithfully reflected this background, adding to it extended activities as a scholar and writer. Inherited fortunes gave him the leisure and means for the pursuit of his various interests.

His mother died soon after his birth and he was reared in the home of his grandfather Watts, of whom he speaks in terms of affection and esteem. His education was largely tutorial, supplemented by wide reading and European travel. His dedication in his *History of the Life of Leonard Torstenson* pays the following tribute to his father: "Throughout my life, nothing has afforded me such unalloyed pleasure as that taste for the study of history, to which you early ministered by furnishing my book-shelves with sound and instructive publications judiciously selected." His early military interests were quickened by association with his cousin Philip Kearny [*q.v.*], later a famous general. Nearly all their leisure time, he says, was spent managing mimic campaigns involving four to six thousand lead soldiers. At the age of eighteen De Peyster, while in service as foreman of a volunteer fire company, became the victim of a troublesome heart affection from which he suffered throughout his life. He entered Columbia College, but ill health prevented his graduation. A lifetime of self-education was however recognized by various collegiate institutions and he received degrees of M.A., Ph.D., Litt.D., and LL.D.

In 1841 he married Estelle Livingston, daughter of John Swift Livingston. Much of their time was spent at the country estate, Rose Hill, in Dutchess County. In 1845 he joined an infantry brigade of New York militia, drawn from the northern districts of the county, as judge-advocate with rank of major, and the next year he was made colonel of the 111th Regiment of New York State Infantry. Although legislated out of office by change of law in 1849, he was later placed by Gov. Fish in command of the 22nd Regiment in spite of the fact that he was the youngest available colonel; two years later he was ranked as brigadier-general. Gov. Clark chose him for his adjutant-general, but he resigned after a few months of service. Circumstances prevented the acceptance by President Lincoln of three regiments which De Peyster offered to raise at the outbreak of the Civil War, nor was the latter physically able to serve on the field. He contributed three sons to the service, however, and used his influence for the cause whenever possible through the press or otherwise. In 1866, by concurrent action of the legislature of New York, the governor was empowered to confer upon him the brevet rank of major-general in the National Guard for meritorious services.

In 1851, a serious bronchitis threatening to develop into consumption caused his doctor to order him to go abroad. He secured an appointment from Gov. Hunt as military agent and spent the next few years in the study of military affairs and the conduct of fire companies in Europe. The results were embodied in a full report and formed the basis for later improvements in the state troops. He also advocated a paid fire department, steam fire-engines, and fire-escapes, and he was interested in the reorganization of the New York City police force.

As a writer he was exceedingly versatile, his works including drama, historical romance, poetry, genealogical and biographical sketches, miscellaneous articles such as "Did our Savior speak Greek?" "Buddhism and Romanism compared," "Michael Angelo," "Gypsies." His principal works dealt with historical events and characters, representative productions being: *The History of the Life of Leonard Torstenson* (1855), *The Ancient, Medieval and Modern Netherlanders* (1859), *Practical Strategy, as Illustrated by the Life and Achievements of a Master of the Art, the Austrian Field Marshal Traun* (1863), *Secession in Switzerland and in the United States Compared* (1863), *Personal and Military History of Philip Kearny* (1869), *An Inquiry into the Career and Character of Mary Stuart* (1883), *Napoleone di Buonaparte* (1896). He rejoiced in overriding conventionalities and often showed strong bias, particularly in defense of a family connection, but his writings show exceptional knowledge of military history and science. His philanthropies and memberships in clubs and other organizations were nearly as varied and numerous as his writings. Family estrangements embittered his later years, which despite physical frailties extended to the advanced age of eighty-six.

[Frank Allaben, *John Watts de Peyster* (2 vols., 1908), carries a portrait as a frontispiece and ends with an exhaustive fifty-page list of his writings. See also obituaries in *N. Y. Times, N. Y. Herald,* and *N. Y. Sun,* issues of May 6, 1907; *Who's Who in America,* 1906–07; J. W. de Peyster, *De Peyster and Watts* (1854).]

A. E. P.

DERBIGNY, PIERRE AUGUSTE CHARLES BOURGUIGNON (1767–Oct. 6, 1829), judge, governor, was born in Laon, France and died in Gretna, La. His parents were Auguste Bourguignon and Louise Angeline Blondel d'Herbigny. As they were of noble family, their son found it expedient, about 1793, to migrate from revolutionary France to Santo Domingo. In the time remaining before 1800, he lived successively in Pennsylvania—where he married Félicité Odile Dehault de Lassus—in

Missouri, in Florida, and in Louisiana, where he soon became a French colonial official. He was secretary of the municipality of New Orleans under French rule, and official interpreter of the American territorial government under Claiborne. In 1804 he delivered in French the first Fourth-of-July oration ever made in New Orleans. In 1805, as one of three commissioners—representing to a degree the longer established elements of the population in Louisiana—he went to Washington to protest against the determination of the federal government to delay the admission of the new territory as a state. The protest was not fruitful. He returned home disgruntled, and after some delay collaborated with others in publishing a statement of grievances. At the organization of the "University of Orleans" in 1805 he was made one of its regents, and later he was clerk of the court of common pleas, secretary of the legislative council, and member of the first state legislature. In 1813 he became a member of the state's first supreme court. As a jurist he was impeccable but not brilliant. It is said that in framing his opinions he labored always under the handicap of being obliged to translate into English, ideas which he had first thought out in a French fashion and in the French tongue. In 1820 he resigned as judge and became a candidate for governor. During the campaign the number of votes cast for him was not so great as the number cast for one of his opponents, T. B. Robertson. The final choice between the two lay with a legislature which, often more Franco-American than Anglo-American in its composition, could with reason be supposed to prefer Derbigny. He repudiated the office in advance, saying that he was too good a democrat to contravene the will of the people, and that he hoped his friends would vote for the majority candidate. As secretary of state (1820–27) he found time, in addition to his other duties and a meticulous devotion to his large family, to interest himself in the operation of the first steam ferry upon the Mississippi River, and also, in company with Edward Livingston and Moreau-Lislet, to revise the Civil Code of Louisiana. Inaugurated governor in 1828, he advocated popular education and did what he could to obliterate the old political cleavage between persons who were in general of French tradition and those who were in general of English tradition. On Oct. 1, 1829, as he was riding near the village of Gretna, his horses, becoming frightened, overturned his carriage, inflicting upon him an injury which proved fatal.

[W. C. C. Claiborne, *Letter Books 1801–1816* (6 vols., 1917); *Louisiana Courier* (New Orleans), Oct. 7, 1829; J. D. B. DeBow, "Louisiana," in *DeBow's Review*, May 1846; C. Gayarré, *Hist. of La.* (4 vols., 1854–66); Marc Villiers du Terrage, *Les Dernières Années de la Louisiane Française* (1904); A. Fortier, *Hist. of La.* (1904), and *Louisiana* (1909); H. P. Dart, "Hist. of the Supreme Court of La.," and W. K. Dart, "Justices of the Supreme Court" in *La. Hist. Quart.*, Jan. 1921; Parish Records of St. Louis Cathedral, New Orleans, examined by Prof. Jas. E. Winston.] J. D. W.

DERBY, ELIAS HASKET (Aug. 16, 1739–Sept. 8, 1799), merchant and ship-owner, was born in Salem, Mass., the son of Richard Derby [*q.v.*] and his first wife, Mary Hodges. His father was a merchant in Salem, who built up a considerable trade with the West Indies and the Spanish Peninsula in the latter part of the Colonial period, and Elias Hasket Derby succeeded to this business at about the outbreak of the Revolution. During the war, in common with other American merchants, he fitted out a number of his ships as privateers and the spoils brought in by these vessels, together with the proceeds of a number of successful trading voyages, made him at the close of the Revolution one of the wealthiest merchants in New England. He did not, however, thereupon retire to a life of ease, but taking advantage of the new circumstances embarked upon an extensive commerce to many parts of the world hitherto unvisited by Americans. In 1784 he dispatched his ship *Light Horse* from Salem to St. Petersburg, Russia, with a cargo of West India sugar. This was the first vessel to display the Stars and Stripes in the Baltic. In 1785 he sent his ship *Grand Turk* on a trading voyage to the Cape of Good Hope and the next year dispatched her to the Isle of France in the Indian Ocean. From there she proceeded to Canton, China, being the first New England ship to reach the Orient. Encouraged by these pioneer voyages, Derby's vessels found their way to such distant ports as Manila, Batavia, Rangoon, Calcutta, Bombay, and Canton. But while he traded with all these ports and with the ports of Europe and the West Indies as well, his most lucrative trade was with the Isle of France, or Mauritius as it is now called, a small island in the Indian Ocean, where he exchanged the humble products of the New England farms for the exotic commodities of the East. Toward the end of his career, he profited greatly through the situation created by the Napoleonic Wars, when neutral ships were in demand for the carrying trade.

His success lay partly in his far-seeing initiative as a trader—he had the courage to embark in new fields of commerce and was ever ready to take advantage of changing conditions—and partly in the superior type of men which he employed as captains and supercargoes of his ships.

As the vessels were often gone a year or more without their owner hearing from them, responsibility for the outcome of the voyage rested largely in the hands of the captain or supercargo. These men were therefore encouraged by Derby with large shares in the profits, and as a result many of them became wealthy. In fact, some of the principal family fortunes of New England were founded by men who sailed in Derby ships. Derby himself never went to sea, but he had, nevertheless, a thorough knowledge of ships and most of his fleet was built under his own supervision. Of all the vessels he dispatched to the ends of the earth, only one was lost.

Although Derby was one of the leading citizens of Salem and took an active interest in the welfare of the town, he never held political office. During the Revolution he gave freely of guns, ammunition, and supplies for the use of the Continental Army, and after the war he took an active interest in the original tariff acts. It was largely through his advice that the bonded warehouse system was adopted by the Government.

He devoted practically his entire time to his business and the little relaxation which he allowed himself was principally of a domestic nature. As he began to prosper he purchased a large farm on the outskirts of Salem where he experimented with many new plants brought by his ships from abroad. Although for the greater part of his life he lived in a house of modest proportions, in 1797 he built a magnificent mansion, the finest in Salem. The plans were drawn by McIntyre, the noted American architect of the period, and many of the elaborate furnishings for the house were brought from Europe and China; it was surrounded by stables and gardens. The owner, however, lived to enjoy it but two years. In September 1799, while still at the height of his career, he died, leaving one of the largest fortunes amassed in America up to that time. On Apr. 23, 1761, he had married Elizabeth Crowninshield, thus uniting two of the leading merchant houses of Salem. Four sons and three daughters survived him. The eldest, Elias Hasket Derby, Jr. [*q.v.*], carried on the great business until the adverse period of the Embargo, when the Derby flag disappeared from the high seas. The trade, however, which the elder Elias Hasket Derby established to China, India, the East Indies, and the Baltic laid the foundations of American commerce with those distant parts of the world.

[Derby business papers, in Essex Inst., Salem, Mass.; E. H. Derby, "Memoir of E. H. Derby," in *Hunt's Merchants' Mag.*, XXXVI (1857), 147–88; Robt. E. Peabody, *Merchant Venturers of Old Salem* (1912); Perley Derby, "Geneal. of the Derby Family," *Essex Inst. Hist. Colls.*, III (1861), 154–67, 201–07.]

R. E. P.

DERBY, ELIAS HASKET (Jan. 10, 1766–Sept. 16, 1826), merchant, was born in Salem, Mass., the third child and eldest son of Elias Hasket Derby [*q.v.*], the famous Salem merchant, by his wife, Elizabeth Crowninshield. A year or two at Harvard was the least part of his education, which in other respects was the counterpart of that given to all the Derby apprentices: several years in the counting-house, thorough instruction in navigation under old Capt. Jonathan Archer, several voyages as captain's clerk, and finally a voyage to the West Indies as supercargo of the brig *Rose*. In November 1787 he sailed in the *Grand Turk* for the Isle of France (Mauritius), which had been opened to American commerce in 1784, and did not get back to Salem until Dec. 31, 1790. During these three years he also visited Bombay, Madras, and Calcutta and established the Derby firm as the dominant American commercial house on the Isle of France. These activities are said to have added $100,000—a large sum for the time—to the Derby fortune. On July 14, 1799, he sailed from Salem in the *Mount Vernon*, a new ship of 355 tons and armed with twenty guns, for the Mediterranean. The Napoleonic Wars made the certain hazards and the possible profits of this voyage triply great. The *Mount Vernon* had several brushes with the French but was able either to outsail or to outshoot them. She captured a large latineer off Algeciras Point but was unable to bring her to port. At Naples Derby was entertained by Lord Nelson and Lady Hamilton. This voyage added another $100,000 to the Derby fortune, but before Elias Hasket Derby, Jr., reached Salem, July 7, 1800, the head of the house was dead.

The rest of his career was an anti-climax. In recognition of his extraordinary services, the elder Derby in his will left his son an equal share in the estate, although he had already received his portion. As a result a family quarrel arose; once Derby and his brother-in-law, Nathaniel West, came to blows on the Derby wharf (Bentley, II, 353); and the once proud family became a subject of gossip and scandal. Derby, too, cut a somewhat ridiculous figure as a brigadier-general of militia; he was embroiled in the violent politics of Salem; and his reduced income did not suffice to maintain the Derby mansion, which had been built to satisfy the extravagance and vanity of his mother. In 1809, in an effort to retrieve his fortune, he made a voyage to Rio de Janeiro and London in the *Mount Hope*, but this venture was a failure. He then moved to Londonderry, N. H. He was the first to bring merino sheep to America in any number. During the War of 1812 he manufactured broadcloth. He died at Londonderry of gout. His wife, Lucy Brown, who had borne him four daughters and five sons, survived him.

[Perley Derby, "Geneal. of the Derby Family," in *Essex Inst. Hist. Colls.*, III (1861), 154–67, 201–07, 283–89; E. H. Derby, "Memoir of E. H. Derby, Merchant of Salem, Mass.," in *Hunt's Merchants' Mag.*, XXXVI (1857), 147–88; *The Diary of Wm. Bentley, D.D.* (Salem, 1905–14); Fiske Kimball, "The E. H. Derby Mansion in Salem," in *Essex Inst. Hist. Colls.*, LX (1924), 273–92; Robt. E. Peabody, *Merchant Venturers of Old Salem* (1912); *Essex Register* (Salem, Mass.), Sept. 18, 21, 1826.] G. H. G.

DERBY, ELIAS HASKET (Sept. 24, 1803–Mar. 31, 1880), lawyer, was born in Salem, Mass., the son of Elias Hasket Derby, second [*q.v.*], and Lucy (Brown) Derby. He was a twin, and the fourth son to be named for the father and grandfather. He received his preparatory schooling at Dr. Stearns's academy in Medford, Pinkerton Academy in Londonderry, N. H., and the Boston Latin School. After graduating in 1824 from Harvard College, he read law in the office of Daniel Webster and was admitted to the bar of the court of common pleas in Suffolk County in October 1827 and of the supreme court in October 1829. He soon won distinction at the bar, especially in railway cases. He acquired an extensive knowledge of railroading, was president for some years of the Old Colony Railroad and a director of several others, worked indefatigably to extend various lines, and was instrumental in securing the completion of the Hoosac Tunnel. Much of his work brought him into close relations with public men and public affairs; he was sometimes consulted by high officers of the government on matters of difficulty and contributed not a little toward shaping their opinions and determining their policy. His most notable services of this nature were his *Preliminary Report on the Treaty of Reciprocity with Great Britain to Regulate the Trade between the United States and the Provinces of British North America* (1866), prepared for Secretary of the Treasury Hugh M'Culloch, and his *Letter to the Hon. William H. Seward . . .* [*on*] *the Relations of the United States with the British Provinces and the Actual Condition of the Question of the Fisheries* (1867). He wrote much for the press on a wide range of business and economic subjects, so that his favorite signature, "Massachusetts," was long familiar to readers in the neighborhood of Boston. He also contributed to the *Atlantic Monthly*, the *Edinburgh Review*, and other periodicals. His few independent publications were of little importance, though they now possess some interest for a curious reader. *Two Months Abroad; or, A Trip to England, France, Baden, Prussia, and Belgium* (1844) and *The Overland Route to the Pacific: A Report on the . . . Union Pacific and Central Pacific Railways* (1869) are fairly well described by their titles. In both of them the serious student of railways and the business man alert for more business are much in evidence. Another side of Derby's character is revealed in *The Catholic: Letters Addressed by a Jurist to a Young Kinsman Proposing to Join the Church of Rome* (1856). The young kinsman, the preface announces with modest pride, was dissuaded. Derby died in Boston at his home on Charles St. He was survived by his wife, Eloise Lloyd Strong, daughter of George W. Strong of St. George's Manor, L. I., whom he had married on Sept. 4, 1834, and by five of his seven children. He had amassed what was for the times a considerable fortune and was known for his generosity to his less fortunate relatives.

[Perley Derby, "Geneal. of the Derby Family" in *Essex Inst. Hist. Colls.*, III (1861), 154–67, 201–07, 283–89; *Mem. Biogs. of the New-Eng. Hist. Geneal. Soc.*, vol. VII (1907); H. F. Jenks, *Cat. of the Boston Public Latin School* (1886); *Harvard Quinquennial Cat. 1636–1915* (1915); W. T. Davis, *Bench and Bar of the Commonwealth of Mass.*, vol. I (1895); Abner Forbes, *Rich Men of Mass.* (2nd ed., 1852); *Boston Transcript*, Apr. 1, 1880.] G. H. G.

DERBY, GEORGE HORATIO (Apr. 3, 1823–May 15, 1861), humorist, although notable for his development of the boisterous "Western" style of humor, was born in Dedham, Mass., the son of John Barton and Mary (Townsend) Derby, and the descendant of a long line of New England ancestors. His father was known for his oddity of character and his literary bent, both of which he transmitted to his son. The latter attended school at Dedham, and then lived for a time at Concord, Mass., working in a store, reading voraciously, and already displaying his eccentric qualities. Entering the United States Military Academy on July 1, 1842, he graduated four years later, standing seventh in a class of fifty-nine. At the Academy he established a reputation as a wit and notorious practical joker which remained with him throughout life. He was first appointed brevet second lieutenant of ordnance, but was almost immediately transferred to the Topographical Engineers, with which corps he served thenceforth.

After a brief period spent in the survey of New Bedford Harbor, the outbreak of the Mexican War gave him a taste of active campaigning. He served at the siege of Vera Cruz, and with distinction at Cerro Gordo, where he was severely wounded. For gallant and meritorious conduct in that battle he was brevetted first lieutenant. After recovering from his wound he served in the Topographical Bureau (1847–48), and on exploring expeditions in Minnesota Territory (1848–49). Early in 1849 he was sent to California. According to a tradition, which has at least the value of illustrating his character, his transfer to the Pacific Coast was a kind of banishment resulting from too great flippancy in a report addressed to the secretary of war. Except for a brief term of duty in Texas (1852), he remained on the Pacific Coast until 1856. He conducted three exploring expeditions in California (in the gold country, in the San Joaquin Valley, along the Colorado River), and wrote the official reports describing them, managing to enliven even such dry-as-dust material with sudden outbursts of his burlesque humor.

Since 1850 he had been writing sketches; in 1853 he was sent to San Diego, and there almost by accident became famous. His friend, J. J. Ames, editor of the *San Diego Herald,* left town temporarily, putting Derby in unofficial charge of the paper. In the course of a few issues the latter transformed a sober, Democratic, small-town weekly into a riotous conglomeration of wit, burlesque, and satire, devoted to the Whig party. All California laughed, and Derby's outbursts were even reprinted in the East. He became immediately the state wit, and humorous stories without number were credited to him. The founders of *The Pioneer; or California Monthly Magazine* (San Francisco, 1854) solicited his aid, and introduced him to their readers as one "whom not to know argues oneself unknown." Much of his best work appeared in this short-lived monthly. In 1855 Ames, with consent of the author, selected some of the sketches, and the next year published *Phœnixiana; or Sketches and Burlesques,* a volume which became immediately, and remained for a generation, immensely popular. The pseudonym, John Phœnix, was in this case an advertisement rather than a disguise, since Derby was commonly known by that appellation or by his nickname, "Squibob."

Derby continued in the army, regarding writing only as an avocation. While in California he married Mary Ann Coons of St. Louis. In 1856 he was transferred to the East, and there wrote other humorous sketches, some of which were published in book form as *The Squibob Papers* (1865). He was promoted to the rank of captain on July 1, 1860. In the previous year, while working as light-house engineer in Florida he had suffered a sunstroke which, reacting upon his already eccentric personality, deranged his mind. After Dec. 20, 1859, he was on sick leave, and a year and a half later he died in New York City.

Derby's writings are important as representing one of the earliest developments of the so-called American, or Western, style of humor. As a master of puns, grotesque exaggeration, ridiculous understatement, pseudo-serious irony, and robustious burlesque, he is scarcely excelled. His influence can be seen in many subsequent writers of whom Mark Twain is the most noteworthy. As a personality he was unusually interesting; his hoaxes, and his ready wit under cover of extreme gravity were for many years the subject of reminiscences in California, and in the army.

[See preface to an edition of *Phœnixiana* edited by John Vance Cheney and published in 1897; G. W. Cullum, *Biog. Reg. U. S. Mil. Acad.* (3rd ed., 1891); C. Johnston, "The First Jester in California," *Harper's Weekly,* May 17, 1913; W. P. Trent, "A Retrospect of Am. Humor" in *Century Mag.,* Nov. 1901. One of Derby's reports is contained in P. T. Tyson, *Geology and Industrial Resources of California* (1851).]

G. R. S., Jr.

DERBY, RICHARD (Sept. 16, 1712–Nov. 9, 1783), was a leading New England ship-owner and merchant of the Colonial and Revolutionary periods. Born in Salem, Mass., the son of Richard and Martha (Hasket) Derby, he went to sea at an early age and when only twenty-four became captain of the sloop *Ranger* trading between Salem and ports in Spain and the West Indies. After sailing for a number of years in the employ of several Salem merchants, he acquired a vessel of his own, and by means of successful trading was enabled at the age of forty-five to retire from the sea and set up for himself as a merchant in Salem. He then began to build up a thriving commerce with Spain, and at the same time he sent his vessels on voyages through the West Indies exchanging New England fish, lumber, and farm products for rum and sugar. In those days England was almost continually at war with France and Spain, but Derby and other New England merchants, in spite of being British Colonials, continued to trade with Spain and the French islands in the West Indies. Derby's ships were, therefore, subject to capture not only by French and Spanish men-of-war as natural enemies, but by British men-of-war on account of trading with the enemy. Under these circumstances it was inevitable that several of his ships should be captured; but so great were the profits made by those which successfully evaded seizure that he began to amass a considerable fortune. To take care of his increasing business, he built Derby Wharf in Salem harbor and soon he became recognized as one of the most substantial men of the community.

In 1735 he married Mary Hodges of Salem. The family, including three sons and three daughters, lived in a fine brick mansion near the head of Derby Wharf. In 1770 Mrs. Derby died and in 1771 Derby married Mrs. Sarah (Langley) Hersey of Hingham.

The various British Acts of Trade and Navigation which gave rise to the Revolution so greatly hampered Derby's business that it was only natural for him to take an active part in the cause of the Colonies. When in February 1775 a detachment of British troops was sent to Salem to seize some cannon and ammunition concealed there, Derby headed the band of determined citizens which met the troops at the entrance to the town. On the commander demanding that the guns be given up, Derby is said to have replied, "Find them if you can, take them if you can, they will never be surrendered." Whereupon the British commander, evidently fearing to provoke an engagement, hastily withdrew. Two months later, however, actual hostilities began with the battles of Lexington and Concord and shortly thereafter, in order to enlist the sympathy of the British people, the Provincial Congress decided to send a fast vessel to England with affidavits showing that the British troops began the affair and that the Colonists acted only in self-defense. Derby immediately placed his schooner, *Quero,* at the disposal of the Congress for this service. The little vessel, commanded by his son John, reached England two weeks ahead of the ship bearing the British general's dispatches, and caused a great sensation in London. By this time Derby had begun to withdraw from the active management of the business, turning his affairs over to his second son, Elias Hasket Derby [*q.v.*], and a few years later, in 1783, the old merchant died.

[Jas. D. Phillips, *The Life and Times of Richard Derby, Merchant of Salem* (1929); Robt. E. Peabody, *Merchant Venturers of Old Salem* (1912); Perley Derby, "Geneal. of the Derby Family," in *Essex Inst. Hist. Colls.,* III (1861), 154–67.] R. E. P.

DE ROSSET, MOSES JOHN (July 4, 1838–May 1, 1881), physician, came from a family of distinguished medical ancestry, François Rosset (1590) having been known as a medical writer. Moses, born at Wilmington, N. C., was the fifth child of Dr. Armand John De Rosset (b. 1807) of that city and Eliza Jane Lord, his wife, and grandson of Dr. Armand John De Rosset (1767–1859). At the age of sixteen he was placed in Diedrich's Academy at Geneva, Switzerland, where he remained as a student for three years, thereafter spending a year at Cologne to acquire German. He returned to America in 1857 and began the study of medicine with Dr. Gunning S. Bedford of New York, and graduated at the Medical Department of the University of the City of New York in 1860. As a result of a competitive examination he was appointed a resident physician at Bellevue Hospital, New York, in the same year, and there remained until the outbreak of the Civil War, when he returned to North Carolina and was commissioned assistant surgeon in the Confederate army (1861). He served as surgeon of Marye's battery of artillery through Gen. Jackson's campaign in the Valley of Virginia. On his promotion to surgeon (1863) he was placed in charge of General Hospital No. 4 (officers' hospital) in Richmond and later was inspector of hospitals for the Department of Henrico. At the close of the war he moved to Baltimore (1865), where he was soon made adjunct professor and later professor of chemistry both at the medical department of the University of Maryland and the Baltimore Dental College. In Baltimore he became interested in diseases of the eye and ear and devoted himself thenceforth to this field. In 1873 he returned to Wilmington, there continuing his specialty until 1878, when he removed to New York where, after three years, his brilliant career was cut short by death. He was buried in the Oakdale Cemetery at Wilmington. He was married, on Oct. 13, 1863, to Adelaide Savage Meares (b. 1839) of Wilmington, N. C., who bore him seven children.

De Rosset was not only skilled in his own branch of medicine but had an extensive knowledge of general science. In addition to many papers on ophthalmology and otology and the physiology of vision and audition, he issued a translation of *Bouchardat's Annuaire* entitled *Annual Abstract of Therapeutics, Materia Medica, Pharmacy and Toxicology for 1867 by A. Bouchardat,* but the work was a financial failure, on account, it was said, of the decline in interest in French therapeutics. He was known as an independent thinker, a teacher and practitioner who accepted no theories without confirmation and demonstration. For a time he was editor of the *North Carolina Medical Jaurnal.*

[*N. C. Medic. Jour.,* VII (1881), 309; *Medic. Record of N. Y.,* XIX (1881), 586 f.; family documents printed in Jas. Sprunt, *Hist. Monograph No. 4* (1904); D. C. Meares, *Annals of the De Rosset Family* (1906); manuscript memoranda of Louis Henry (brother of Moses John) De Rosset, in the possession of the family.] E. E. H.

DE SAUSSURE, HENRY WILLIAM (Aug. 16, 1763–Mar. 29, 1839), lawyer, director of the United States Mint, chancellor of South Carolina, was born at Pocotaligo, Prince William's Parish, S. C., descendant in the eighth generation of Antoine, Sieur de Dommartin in Lorraine, who, having adopted the Protestant religion, emigrated to Switzerland, where he became a citizen of Lausanne in 1556. He was the grandson of Henry (d. 1761), the founder of the De Saussure family in America, who came to South Carolina about the year 1730 and settled near Coosawhatchie, Beaufort District, and the eldest child and only son of Daniel and Mary (McPherson) De Saussure. Daniel (1735–1798), the father, was a successful merchant, first at Beaufort and later at Charleston, who served the state in important civil and military capacities during the Revolution and was for a number of years after the war a member of the state Senate. Henry William's education, promisingly begun in private schools of Beaufort and Charleston, was interrupted when at the age of sixteen he volunteered for service during the siege of the latter place. Being made a prisoner on the fall of the city, he was first paroled, then confined on a prison ship in the harbor, and finally (1781) sent to Philadelphia for exchange. There he was reunited with his father who had been held a prisoner at St. Augustine, and his mother and sisters, who had been forced by the British to leave their home (E. McCrady, *The History of South Carolina in the Revolution 1780–1783*, 1902, p. 378). In Philadelphia he entered the law office of Jared Ingersoll and attended lectures on moral and natural philosophy and mathematics at "the university of the city." He was admitted to the bar of Philadelphia in 1784 and, having returned to Charleston shortly afterward, to that of South Carolina in 1785. In the latter year he married Eliza Ford, daughter of Col. Jacob Ford of Morristown, N. J. His political career began when he sat for his constituency in the state constitutional convention of 1790. From time to time during the next eighteen years he was a member of the lower house of the General Assembly (1790–94, 1796–98, 1800–02, 1807?, and 1808). His chief concern as legislator was the conflict between up-country and low-country over the apportionment of representation in the legislature. He defended the disproportion then apparently existing in favor of the low-country chiefly on the ground that property as well as population was entitled to representation (see his *Letters on the Questions of the Justice and Expediency of Going into Alterations of the Representation in the Legislature of South Carolina. By Phocion*, 1795). Realizing, however, that the low-country could not permanently retain its leadership, he advocated a programme of gradual concessions to the up-country. In 1801 he took an active part in the establishment of the state university at Columbia in order that the up-country might have trained leaders, and in 1808 he supported a reapportionment measure which partially redressed the balance between the two sections. During one of the intervals in his attendance upon the legislature while seeking "the restoration of his health at the North," De Saussure was appointed (1795) director of the United States Mint. His administration, especially his success in bringing about the first coinage of gold, won the approbation of Washington, but, eager to return home, he resigned before the year was out (Washington to De Saussure, MS. in the possession of the De Saussure family). During another interval he served as intendant of the city of Charleston (1797–98). In 1808 he was elected to the chancery bench, a position which he occupied for the next twenty-nine years. In this capacity he performed his principal public service. "To him," says Judge J. B. O'Neall, "the system of equity owes its shape, *form and existence*. He was to South Carolina what Kent was to New York" (*post*, I, 245). This reputation rests not only upon his decrees but also upon his work of compiling and publishing four volumes of Chancery Reports (1817–19) covering the years from the Revolution to 1817.

[Four years before his death De Saussure prepared a "Memoir of the American Branch of the De Saussure Family" in which he gave the main facts of his own career. This was later supplemented by a genealogy compiled by Col. Jas. D. Blanding. Both of these MSS. are now in the possession of descendants living in Charleston, S. C. Other sources of information about him are: Wm. Harper, *Memoir of the Life, Character and Public Services of the Late Hon. Henry Wm. De Saussure* (1841); J. B. O'Neall, *Biog. Sketches of the Bench and Bar of S. C.* (1859), I, 243–52; *Eminent and Representative Men of the Carolinas* (1892), I, 59–60; and obituary in the *Charleston Courier*, Apr. 1, 1839. For a careful study of his part in the reapportionment of representation in 1808 the writer is indebted to Miss Louisa E. Gaillard, a student in his historical seminar in the Coll. of Charleston.] J. H. E—y.

DE SCHWEINITZ, EDMUND ALEXANDER. [See SCHWEINITZ, EDMUND ALEXANDER DE, 1825–1887.]

DESHA, JOSEPH (Dec. 9, 1768–Oct. 12, 1842), congressman, governor of Kentucky, was born in Monroe County, Pa., of French Huguenot ancestry. In 1781 his parents became a part of the great western migration then beginning, and settled in Kentucky, where they remained only a year before going on to the Cumberland district in Tennessee. Here Desha grew into young manhood, spending more time fighting the Indians than seeking an education. In these skirmishes he acquired his first taste for military activities, a taste bred more by his hatred of the Indians for killing his two brothers than by any innate liking for war. When twenty-one years old he married Peggy Bledsoe, a daughter of Col. Jesse Bledsoe, a prominent Tennessee pioneer, and three years later returned to Kentucky, settling in Mason County. In 1794 he joined Gen. Anthony Wayne's forces against the Indians north of the Ohio River and rendered valuable service in the campaign which ended with the Treaty of Greenville in 1795. He soon developed political ambitions, and with the military record he had acquired he found little trouble in winning election to the state House of Representatives five times before 1802, at which time he was elected to the state Senate, where he remained until he was elected to Congress in 1807. He was constantly returned to Congress until 1819, serving in all six consecutive terms.

Desha's congressional career was characterized by rather ornate oratory, and an extreme patriotism. He did not speak, however, as often as did some other congressmen who were less able than he, as he held it to be the part of wisdom "to think much and speak but little." In 1807 he called for an adequate army to protect American territory—especially to prevent any disaffection in New Orleans. He supported Jefferson on the Embargo measures and refused to abandon these laws until a substitute could be found. During this period he showed bitter hatred of England and France, and in January 1810, he was one of the most intensely warlike of all the lesser War Hawks. During the conflict he argued for larger armies and longer terms of service, and in 1813 he left the halls of Congress long enough to accept a major-generalship of Kentucky volunteers and to command a division in the battle of the Thames. With the coming of peace he opposed a large standing army. He was also opposed to re-chartering the United States Bank and to increasing the pay of congressmen. Desha was essentially a man of the people with all the rugged honesty and mistaken zeal that often went with being such a representative. At no time did these qualities show more clearly than in his term as governor of Kentucky. He was elected to this position in 1824 by a majority of more than 8,000 on the issues of relief and replevin laws and hostility to the federal judiciary and to the two Kentucky branches of the second United States Bank. When balked by the Kentucky court of appeals he led the fight for setting up the new court. As governor he stood for internal improvements, for common schools, and against the aristocratic Transylvania University. While governor he brought down upon himself much criticism by pardoning his son Isaac B. Desha, who had been convicted of murder. He retired from the governorship in 1828 to his farm in Harrison County and twelve years later died at Georgetown in Scott County.

[Lewis and Richard H. Collins, *Hist. of Ky.* (Covington, 1882), I, 32, 33, 538, II, 547, 705, 706; W. E. Connelley and E. M. Coulter, *Hist. of Ky.* (1922), vol. II, chs. xlix, l, li; *Biog. Encyc. Ky.* (Cincinnati, 1878), p. 37; *Biog. Cyc. Commonwealth of Ky.* (Cincinnati, 1896), p. 389; *Niles' Reg.*, XXIX, 221; *Proc. Ky. State Bar Asso.*, 1915, pp. 48, 49; *Annals of Congress* from 1807 to 1819.] E. M. C.

DE SMET, PIERRE-JEAN (Jan. 30, 1801–May 23, 1873), Jesuit missionary, was born at Termonde, Belgium, the son of Josse-Arnaud De Smet and Marie-Jeanne Buydens De Smet. He was educated at the seminary of Malines, where he distinguished himself both in his studies and in what was the contemporary equivalent of athletic sports. His physical strength and prowess were remarkable and go far to explain the wonderful endurance with which he bore the almost inconceivable toils incident to his later missionary labors. His youthful friends called him "Samson." In stature he was medium, about five feet six inches, stockily built, muscular, and resilient. His countenance was oval, regular in outline, exceedingly handsome and benignant; the eyes were peculiarly luminous, expressing both shrewdness and spirituality. His weight tended to be excessive, around two hundred and ten pounds, which caused him at times to employ drastic reducing methods in order to keep fit for his taxing physical labors. He once fasted thirty days, thereby losing thirty-five pounds. His appearance and bearing were so friendly, his actions so frank and trust-inspiring, that red men of all tribes and whites of every nationality instinctively confided in him.

De Smet came to America in July 1821 and entered the novitiate of the Jesuit order established near Baltimore (at Whitemarsh) ten years earlier. In 1823 he was chosen for the new novitiate, the second in the United States, which was founded at Florissant near St. Louis and which became the Catholic University of St. Louis. He was ordained in 1827 and after devoting somewhat more than a decade to a round of priestly service, including several years spent in Europe to solicit reinforcements and supplies for his order in America, he entered in 1838 upon his distinctive career as missionary to the Indians. His first mission was St. Joseph at the site of the later Council Bluffs, among the Potawatomi. In 1840 he was commissioned to survey the possibilities for Catholic missions in the Oregon country. From that time the scope of his activities widened to include the Pacific Northwest as well as the great plains; for all of which work he sought support in the eastern cities, in New Orleans, in Ireland, England, Holland, Belgium, France, and Italy. In carrying out his great projects he traveled 180,000 miles. He crossed the Atlantic sixteen times, and once he sailed from Europe around Cape Horn and up the Pacific coast to Oregon. He aided the Catholic mission established in the Willamette Valley by Canadian priests—Fathers Blanchet and Demers; he founded, in September 1841, St. Mary's Mission among the Flatheads; also the Mission of St. Ignatius among the Kalispels; later he planted the Sacred Heart Mission of the Cœur d'Alenes; he touched with his unique regenerative influence nearly all the native populations of the Columbia Valley. This work was accomplished mainly between the years 1840 and 1846.

In his travels to the far West, Father De Smet made the acquaintance also of the Sioux, the Blackfeet, and other tribes east of the Rockies, all of whom held "Blackrobe" in highest esteem. Accordingly, when troubles arose among rival tribes, he was the one man who could hope to bring peace. Also, when the Indians, goaded by ill treatment at the hands of Indian agents or of traders, actually broke bonds and went on the war-path against the whites, Father De Smet was the final resource as mediator. In 1851 he attended the great council held near Fort Laramie, and aided powerfully to bring about a general understanding among the tribes who had become restive under the flood of emigration through their country. He mediated also in the "Mormon War" and in the Yakima Indian War of 1858–59. But his most notable achievement in Indian diplomacy was in June 1868 when he visited in the Bighorn Valley the camp of Sitting Bull's hostiles who had sworn to take the life of the first white man to show himself among them. There, again, as the reverend missionary who always held the scales even between the two races, he succeeded in paving the way for a conference and eventual peace. De Smet's service in this supreme instance was performed quite independently of the government; the Indians, who were intent on attacking the American flag, yielding to the magic of his priestly emblem.

Father De Smet was a zealous churchman, devoted to the promotion of the faith as he understood it. In practical matters he was efficient and business-like; in social intercourse cheerful, of charming address, fond of genial conversation, and full of a simple delightful humor. His kindly tolerance extended to all except religionists of non-Catholic persuasion. He was quite as unable to see the merit of the work done by Protestant missionaries as they were to appreciate the value of Catholic missionary effort. Yet he was the personal friend of all whom he met. And to the Indians of the great West he was the ambassador of Heaven—he was "Blackrobe."

[*Life, Letters and Travels of Father Pierre-Jean De Smet,* ed. by H. M. Chittenden and Alfred Talbot Richardson (1905), is the best source of information. In it are assembled most of the materials published during the missionary's lifetime, some of which were printed in several languages, also his detailed journals and many letters not published previously. English translations are given in all cases. Additional references are E. Laveille, *Life of Father De Smet* (1915); J. D. Shea, *Hist. of the Cath. Missions Among the Indian Tribes of the U. S.* (1855); L. B. Palladino, *Indian and White in the Northwest* (1922).] J. S—r.

DE SOTO, HERNANDO (*c.* 1500–May 21, 1542), discoverer of the Mississippi River, was born at Barcarrota, Spain, of an impoverished but noble family. His education was obtained through the generosity of Pedrarias Dávila, who is said to have sent his protégé to the University of Salamanca. When the youth was about nineteen he followed Pedrarias to Central America, serving as captain in that cruel governor's conquests; and he married his patron's daughter Isabel, thus becoming brother-in-law to Vasco Núñez de Balboa. After earning a reputation for valor in Central America, he sailed in 1532 to serve Francisco Pizarro and Diego Almagro in the conquest of Peru, arriving in time to be the first European to salute the Inca Atahualpa, whom he met at Caxamarca. The Inca admired the doughty conqueror for his horsemanship and soldierly qualities, and Soto was one of the few Spaniards who condemned Pizarro for executing Atahualpa, though Soto himself had led the van in the Inca's capture. Following the sack of Cuzco and the development of the Pizarro-Almagro feud over possession of that city, Soto astutely withdrew from Peru, leaving behind him his mistress, the princess Curicuillar, and their daughter, and carrying to Spain a share of Inca booty amounting to 180,000 *cruzadas.* With this fortune, a pleasing manner and handsome face, and deserved reputation as a vigorous but not needlessly bloodthirsty *conquistador,* he won the favor of Charles V, and at Valladolid on Apr. 20, 1537, obtained from the monarch a contract to conquer Florida. His reward was to be a marquisate and twelve square leagues of land; he was also made governor of Cuba, which island he used as the base of his expedition. His small army was composed of Spanish and Portuguese Estremadurans, and numbered nearly one thousand men. Alvar Núñez Cabeza de Vaca, then returning to Spain after crossing North America with three survivors of the Florida expedition of Pánfilo de Narváez, declined to join

Soto, having hoped for this new commission himself.

Soto's fleet sailed from San Lucar on Apr. 6, 1538, reaching Cuba in May. After replenishing his equipment, he left the island in charge of his wife, and sailed from Havana on May 18, 1539. He landed on the Florida coast on May 30, near the village of Ucita on Charlotte Bay, not at Tampa, as has sometimes been stated.

Here began that warfare with the Indians which continued with brief interludes through three years. Soto's method was to capture the chiefs he visited, compelling each in turn to guide the Spaniards through his territory. For interpreter he had Juan Ortiz, a rescued Spaniard who had been twelve years among the Indians. Leaving four ships under guard, he marched his army north through Florida, entering successively Georgia, North and South Carolina, Tennessee, Alabama, Mississippi, Arkansas, Oklahoma, and Texas; detachments may have entered Missouri and Louisiana. The quest, like those of Coronado in New Mexico and Narváez in Florida, was for another Mexico or Peru; failing to find such a Golden Chersonese, he would tarry nowhere, though his followers were several times ready to plant colonies.

After approaching the Carolina border, he returned south and west to Apalache. Wintering here, the Spaniards discovered on Horse Bay, now called Ocklockonee, remnants of the outfitting of the makeshift ships of the unfortunate Narváez. From here Juan de Añasco, Soto's readiest navigator, went to bring forward the people from Charlotte Harbor, and another subordinate, Francisco Maldonado, sailed west along the Gulf to find a better port. Maldonado located Achusi (Pensacola) sixty leagues away, and then went to Cuba, with orders to return the next season. Breaking camp on Mar. 3, 1540, the gold-hunters crossed the Flint and other rivers, reaching the Savannah at Cutifachiqui, some miles below Silver Bluff. The unnamed queen of this realm graciously presented them with many pearls, and they found relics of the Lucas Vásquez de Ayllón expedition to the near-by Atlantic coast, but there was no gold, and Soto marched north to Xualla province, around the headwaters of Broad River, North Carolina. Crossing the Blue Ridge into northeastern Georgia, the adventurers rested in Guaxule province, where they feasted on "dogs," praising the flavor of what may have been opossum. In near-by Chiaha they heard of gold in Chisca, thirty leagues away, but it proved to be only copper, and the march was resumed from what is now Loudon County, Tenn., southward through Coste, just above Chattanooga, to Cosa in Talladega County, Ala. Here was a chief of sumptuous ménage who urged the strangers to tarry and colonize his opulent land, but Soto, unimpressed, and anxious now for word and supplies from Cuba, hurried along the Alabama to Mauvila, between the Alabama and the Tombigbee. In October the Mauvilians trapped and defeated him, killing many soldiers and horses. Mortified at the reverse, Soto nevertheless concealed the fact that Maldonado was waiting at Achusi, and again led his ragged army north, to winter at Chicaça, in Pontotoc County, Miss., where new Indian attacks added numerous losses to other miseries.

April 1541 found the dogged explorers floundering through swamps to the Mississippi, which the most recent authoritative opinion thinks to have been crossed from Tunica County below Memphis. It was the first conscious discovery of the great river by white men; Narváez had passed the mouth unknowingly, and Cabeza de Vaca had landed to the west of it. Fortune now beckoned Soto's men into St. Francis and Mississippi counties, Ark. At Pacaha, their farthest north, the undaunted treasure-hunters swung west to Quiguate, perhaps in Lee, or St. Francis County, and thence through Woodruff and Cleburne counties into Oklahoma on Grand River. A final bitter winter was spent in "Autiamque" beyond Fort Smith.

Another April arriving, the now disillusioned *conquistadores* turned homeward. Crossing the Arkansas near Pine Bluff, they struggled on to Guachoya, probably near Arkansas City, reaching the Mississippi on Apr. 16; but lack of vessels and Indian hostility rendered futile all efforts to cross. Balked thus, the tireless leader was forced to bed, death at hand. Taking leave of his companions, and naming Luis de Moscoso [*q.v.*] his successor, the warrior died. Buried first within the camp to conceal his death from the enemy, his body was soon disinterred for the same purpose, and ceremoniously consigned to the river.

[The sources on Soto are: *The True Relation* of the Gentleman of Elvas, the Narrative of Luis Hernández de Biedma, an account by Rodrigo Rangel, Soto's secretary, found in Oviedo's *Historia general,* and the memoirs of participants used by Garcilaso de la Vega in *La Florida del Inca.* All are available in English in E. G. Bourne, *Narratives of the Career of Hernando de Soto* (2 vols., 1904). There are also several Soto letters; and in the Archivo de Indias is a map, 148–7–8, reproduced in Henry Harrisse, *The Discovery of America* (1892). It is also reproduced by T. H. Lewis, *Spanish Explorers in the Southern United States* (1907) and the findings of that investigation are followed in this article. J. G. Shea, "Ancient Florida," in Justin Winsor, *Narr. and Crit. Hist. of America,* vol. II (1886), gives ample bibliography, and locates Soto's letters. W. Lowery in *The Spanish Settlements within the Present Limits of the U. S.* (1905), reviews anterior commentators, subordinates itineraries to human interest, but errs in places and distances. R. B. Cunninghame Graham, *Hernando de Soto* (1924), draws largely for story and style from Garcilaso. Dunbar Rowland and A. C. Sanders have "A Symposium on the Place of Discovery of the Mississippi River by Hernando de Soto" in *Miss. Hist. Soc. Special Bulletin No. 1* (1927), which reviews the controversy over the spot of the crossing. See also John Preston Young, *De Soto at Chickasaw Bluffs* (1918).] H. I. P.

DETMOLD, CHRISTIAN EDWARD (Feb. 2, 1810–July 2, 1887), civil engineer, writer, was born in Hanover, Germany, the son of Johann Detmold, a practising physician. He was educated at a military academy in Hanover and at the age of sixteen came to the United States on his way to Brazil to enter the army there. Unsettled conditions in Brazil at that time, however, deterred him, and he remained in the United States. Shortly after his arrival he went to Charleston, S. C., and established himself as a surveyor. His first major work was in making the surveys for the projected railroad of the newly organized Charleston & Hamburg Railroad & Canal Company. Upon completing this in 1830, he competed for and won a five hundred dollar prize offered by the railroad company for the best locomotive operated by horse-power. Detmold's mechanism, consisting of a horse treadmill mounted on a four-wheel car, carried twelve passengers at a speed of twelve miles an hour. After remaining in Charleston a few years longer, Detmold in 1833–34 was in the employ of the United States War Department and superintended the laying of the foundation of Fort Sumter. During the succeeding ten years he was engaged in railroad survey work on various projected roads in the East, after which he became interested in the manufacture of iron and from 1845 to 1852 was engaged in this business in Maryland. The success of the great industrial exposition held in London in 1851 brought about the agitation for a similar exposition to be held in New York. As a result, on Jan. 3, 1852, the municipal authorities of New York granted a site for a building to be erected on Reservoir Square at Sixth Ave., between Forty-first and Forty-second Sts., and two months later the state legislature granted a charter for the "Exhibition of the Industry of All Nations." In granting the lease the authorities stipulated that the building should be constructed of iron and glass. Because of his interest in the project and his reputation as an engineer, Detmold was made supervising architect and engineer and he, in turn, appointed as consulting engineer Horatio Allen, with whom he had been associated on the Charleston Railroad. The opening of the great Crystal Palace of New York City took place on July 14, 1853, the opening address being made by President Pierce. Following this work Detmold spent a number of years traveling in Europe and upon his return to the United States became interested to a considerable extent in various manufactories. Failing health, however, compelled him to return to Europe where he remained, residing in Paris, until a few years before his death when he again returned to New York where he died. Detmold was a lover of literature and art and possessed a fine collection of paintings. He spent a number of his last years in the translation of Machiavelli's writings. These were published in Boston in 1882 in four volumes, under the title, *"The Historical, Political and Diplomatic Writings of Niccolo Machiavelli; Translation from the Italian."* Detmold married Phœbe Crary who with two daughters survived him.

[*First Semi-Annual Reports . . . of the S. C. Canal and Railroad Co.*, 1828–30; *Cat. Mechanical Engineering Coll. in the U. S. Nat. Museum* (1922), by Carl W. Mitman; *N. Y. Tribune*, July 6. 1887; *N. Y. Times*, July 5, 1887.] C. W. M.

DE TROBRIAND, RÉGIS DENIS DE KEREDERN (June 4, 1816–July 15, 1897), soldier, author, son of Joseph, Baron de Trobriand and Rochine Hachin de Courbeville, was born at his father's château near Tours, France, and died in Bayport, L. I. The history of his family has been traced to Irish warriors who settled on the continent of Europe early enough to accompany William on his conquest of England. They returned thereafter to France, and their descendants were in 1426 made French nobles. Joseph de Trobriand, a student in Paris at the outbreak of the French Revolution, became a soldier in Royalist forces outside France, but after 1806 he served as an officer under successive French governments till 1830. Then—relentlessly hostile to Louis Philippe—he resigned his commission as general, and left the army. In 1825 his son Régis was sent to school in Paris, but was driven away for exposing a priest—as he thought—in a betrayal of the confessional (Post, De Trobriand, p. 50). He was graduated in 1834 from the Collège de Tours, and in law (1837) from Poitiers. He engaged in duels, wrote poetry, and published a novel, *Les Gentilshommes de l'Ouest* (1840). In 1841, on something resembling a dare, he came to America. He made the customary tour of the country, wrote a story, "Le Rebelle: Histoire Canadienne" which was published in the *Courrier des États-Unis*, became acquainted with prominent people, and betrothed himself in New York to the heiress, Mary Mason Jones. These two were married in Paris in January 1843. After a year spent in touring Europe, they settled in Venice, where they associated intimately with all the available royalty and nobility—exiled and otherwise. In 1847 they returned to New York. There De Trobriand became a member of the facile literary group adorned by N. P. Willis and George P. Morris. He was a rich man accustomed to making voyages to Europe, he was editor of the *Revue du Nouveau Monde* (1849–50), and he was a regular contributor, commenting with a wealth of allusion on opera and whatnot, to *Le Courrier des États-Unis*. In the summer of 1861, on being elected colonel of the "Gardes Lafayette" of the New York militia, he became an American citizen, and set out to help subdue the Confederacy. He was a valiant and sagacious officer throughout the war, and in April 1865 he was made by brevet a major-general of volunteers. In July 1866 he was commissioned colonel in the regular army, but he was in France when this news reached him, and he continued there on leave till June 1867 in order that he might complete his reminiscent *Quatre Ans de Campagnes à l'Armée du Potomac* (2 vols., 1867–68). This book, highly praised at the time of its publication, and translated, before long, into English, assumes a philosophy of the war which is often not valid. Returning to America, he was on duty with the army—between his numerous trips to France—in Dakota, in Montana, in Utah, and in Wyoming. In 1874, on the death of a cousin, he succeeded to the title of count. In January 1875, as the federal officer charged with upholding an alien government in Louisiana, he performed his work with a tact which won the regard even of his opponents. Upon his retirement from the army in March 1879, he made his residence in New Orleans. He read much, cultivated his roses, visited in France, and spent the summers with his daughter on Long Island. This was his routine until he died.

[M. C. de T. Post, *Post Family* (1905), *Life and Memoirs of Comte Régis de Trobriand* (1910); F. B. Heitman, *Hist. Reg. and Dict. of the U. S. Army* (1903); *New Orleans Daily Picayune*, July 17, 1897.]

J. D. W.

DEUTSCH, GOTTHARD (Jan. 31, 1859–Oct. 14, 1921), educator, son of Bernhard L. and Elise (Wiener) Deutsch, was born in Kanitz, Austria. He received his elementary and secondary education in the schools of his birthplace and of Nikolsburg from whose gymnasium he graduated at the age of seventeen. Shortly thereafter, on Oct. 6, 1876, he entered the famous rabbinical seminary at Breslau, Germany. While pursuing his Jewish studies at this seminary he attended also afternoon classes at the university of that city. Foremost among the professors at the rabbinical seminary was Heinrich Graetz, the famous historian whose *History of the Jews*, has long been recognized as the *magnum opus* in the field of Jewish history. Graetz exerted so decisive an influence on the young student that he was chiefly instrumental in determining the bent of his studies. At the close of a three years' term, the "academic triennium," at Breslau Deutsch went to Vienna with the purpose of matriculating at the university. He began his studies there in the fall of 1879, specializing in the history and literature of the Jews. The two leading Jewish scholars in the Austrian capital at this time were Isaac Hirsch Weiss, an encyclopedic Talmudic scholar, and Adolf Jellinek, famed not only as a great preacher but as an authority in the province of midrashic research. These two men were inspiring influences in the formative student years of young Deutsch. After a stay of two years at the university he received the degree of Ph.D. He also passed the required examination for a teacher's diploma in history. At about the same time he received his rabbinical diploma from Isaac Hirsch Weiss.

His first position after graduation was in the religious school of the Jewish congregation at Brünn, the Moravian capital. In 1882 he was appointed teacher of religion in the German high school of that city. He had chosen the teaching profession rather than the rabbinate but owing to the governmental discrimination against Jewish teachers he was led to change his purpose and in 1887 accepted the call extended to him by the congregation of Brüx to become its rabbi. He served there for four years, resigning in 1891 to accept the position of professor of history and philosophy of religion at the Hebrew Union College, the rabbinical seminary of liberal Judaism at Cincinnati, Ohio, upon which post he entered on Dec. 2 of that year and which he filled with distinction until his death. He served as acting president of the institution for six months from February until October 1903. While still at Brüx he had married Hermine Bacher in 1888.

During his residence of three decades in the United States, Deutsch occupied a distinguished position in the Jewish world. He played an active rôle in many Jewish movements. He wrote extensively, both on historical themes and on subjects of current Jewish interest. He was a constant contributor not only to the well-known Cincinnati Jewish journals, the *American Israelite* and its German supplement, *Die Deborah*, but likewise to Jewish newspapers in Europe and throughout the United States. Shortly after his removal to Cincinnati he contributed to the *Allgemeine Zeitung des Judenthums,* the foremost Jewish newspaper of Germany if not of the European continent, a series of sketches on American-Jewish life that created somewhat of a sensation at the time. As one of the editors of the *Jewish Encyclopedia* and the head of its historical department he contributed many articles to this publication. Possibly the most important of these contributions is his lengthy article on Anti-Semitism in which he traced the origin and history of this movement. He was a very prolific writer. Besides the hundreds of newspaper and magazine articles which flowed from his facile pen he published the following books: *Paradigmen—Tafeln zur hebräischen Grammatik* (Brünn, 1886); *Die Symbolik in Cultus und Dichtung bei den Hebräern* (Brünn, 1886); *Philosophy of Jewish History* (Cincinnati, 1897); *Andere Zeiten, eine Erzählung aus dem jüdischen Leben der jüngsten Vergangenheit* (Berlin, 1898); *Unlösbare Fesseln, eine Erzählung aus dem jüdischen Leben der Gegenwart* (Frankfurt-a.-M., 1903); *Memorable Dates of Jewish History* (1904); *Four Epochs of Jewish History* (1905); *Israel Bruna, An Historical Tragedy* (1908); *The History of the Jews* (1910); *Der Glaube an Hobelspäne* (1915), a survey of modern Judaism; *Scrolls* (2 vols., 1917, 3rd vol., 1919), studies in Jewish history, literature, etc.; *Jew and Gentile* (1920).

[*Year-Book Central Conference Am. Rabbis,* XXXII, 145–50; *Hebrew Union Coll. Mo.,* vol. VIII, no. 5; obituaries in Cincinnati newspapers, Oct. 15, 1921; Adolph S. Oko, *Selected List of the Writings of Gotthard Deutsch* (1916).]

D. P.

DE VARGAS ZAPATA Y LUJAN PONCE DE LEON, DIEGO (*c.* 1650–Apr. 4, 1704), Marqués de la Nava de Braziñas, Spanish governor of New Mexico, was born in Madrid, Spain, the son of the *maestro de campo,* Alonso de Vargas Zapata y Lujan, chevalier of the order of Santiago, and Maria Margarita de Contréras, both of whom were natives of Madrid. De Vargas belonged to the Spanish-born governing class of New Spain. The events of his life prior to his appointment as governor and captain-general of New Mexico (June 18, 1688) are not known. At that time he was holding the office of chief magistrate of the Real de Minas de Talpugajua in Mexico; he had reached his early forties and had had some military training and experience. On Aug. 14, 1690, a power of attorney was executed in Madrid which gave his wife, Juana de Vargas Ponce de Leon, control over extensive property rights in Spain and Mexico. In 1692 he made a military reconquest of the upper Rio Grande Valley, out of which the Spanish settlers had been driven in 1680 by the Pueblo Indians. In the following summer (1693) he led the settlers northward to their former homes. He quelled several uprisings of the Pueblos between 1693 and 1697.

Having succeeded where others had failed, namely, in the reconquest of New Mexico, he was reappointed to his office by the viceroy of New Spain, Feb. 22, 1696, but the king had already selected his successor, Pedro Rodríguez Cubero [*q.v.*], who arrived at the capital, Santa Fé, July 2, 1697. De Vargas was thrown into prison on charges brought against him by the *cabildo* (town council) of Santa Fé. He and his friends made a concerted effort to obtain what they deemed to be justice, and their activities bore fruit. A short time before the close of Cubero's governorship De Vargas was appointed by the king for a second term as governor and captain-general of New Mexico. In recognition of his services to the Crown of Spain in bringing about the reconquest of New Mexico he was made Marqués de la Nava de Braziñas. His second administration was cut short by his death. He assumed office on Nov. 10, 1703, and died Apr. 4, 1704, while conducting a campaign in the Sandia mountains against the Faraon Apache who had been making attacks upon the Indian pueblos and the Spanish haciendas in the Rio Grande Valley between Bernalillo and Belen.

De Vargas was a man of courage, military skill, and administrative ability. His will leads one to believe that he liked fine articles of clothing, silverware, and jewelry; and that he was considerate of his family, servants, and debtors. His successful reconquest of New Mexico in 1693 and the reëstablishment of the Spanish settlements, which were never again destroyed, gives to him a prominent place in the history of the Southwest.

[R. E. Twitchell, *Old Santa Fé* (1925), pp. 87–150, and "The Pueblo Revolt of 1696," in *Old Santa Fé,* III (1916), 27–34; extracts from the journal of De Vargas were published under the titles: "The Last Campaign of Gen. De Vargas," in *Old Santa Fé,* II (1914–15), 66–72, and "The Reconquest of New Mexico, 1692," *Old Santa Fé,* I (1913–14), 288–307, 402–35; C. F. Coan, *A Hist. of New Mexico* (1925), I, 214–28; F. V. Scholes, "Documents from the Archives of Mexico City," in manuscript.]

C. F. C—n.

DEVENS, CHARLES (Apr. 4, 1820–Jan. 7, 1891), soldier, jurist, cabinet officer, was born in Charlestown, Mass., the son of Charles and Mary (Lithgow) Devens, and the grandson of Richard Devens, a Revolutionary patriot. After preparing at the Boston Latin School, he graduated from Harvard in 1838, studied at the Harvard Law School, and was admitted to the bar in 1840. He then established himself as a lawyer, first in Northfield and later in Greenfield, Franklin County, Mass. He sat for two terms in the Massachusetts Senate (1848–49), and held for four years (1849–53) the office of United States marshal for the district of Massachusetts. On Apr. 3, 1851, the Boston police arrested Thomas Sims, a negro slave who had escaped from his Georgia owner. The United States commissioner under the Fugitive-Slave Act heard the case, decided it in favor of the master, and directed Devens, as marshal, to escort the prisoner to the vessel on which he was to be carried back to Savannah. Although this legal duty was repugnant to Devens, he performed it. Later, however, in 1855, he tried to obtain the freedom of Sims, offering to pay whatever sum was necessary for the purpose, but he was unsuccessful. During the Civil War Sims was liberated, and Devens was able eventually to secure for him a government position.

Devens resumed the practise of law in 1854, settling in Worcester, Mass., and forming a partnership with George F. Hoar and J. Henry Hill. He acted as city solicitor for three years (1856–58) and quickly made a reputation as an advocate and a public speaker. Having early displayed a keen interest in military matters, he was steadily promoted in the state militia until he reached the rank of brigadier-general. When the news of Lincoln's call for 75,000 volunteers arrived in Worcester, Devens immediately turned over his affairs to another lawyer, offered his services to the Government, was chosen major of the 3rd Battalion of Massachusetts Rifles, was commissioned on the next day (Apr. 16, 1861), and departed for the front on Apr. 20. He was shortly (July 24, 1861) appointed colonel of the 15th Massachusetts Regiment. At Ball's Bluff (Oct. 21, 1861) he was struck by a musket ball which would have pierced his heart if it had not hit a metallic button. On Apr. 15, 1862, he was made a brigadier-general of volunteers and assigned to Couch's Division of the IV Corps, being in action during the Peninsular campaign. Severely wounded at Fair Oaks (May 31, 1862), he would not leave the field of battle until evening; but he recovered in season to participate at Fredericksburg (Dec. 13, 1862), where he commanded the advance guard. At Chancellorsville (May 3, 1863), he was wounded in the foot early in the day, while leading a division of the XI Corps. He took part in the battle of Cold Harbor (June 3, 1864), while he was so crippled with inflammatory rheumatism that he had to be carried along the line on a stretcher. On Apr. 3, 1865, he led the advance on Richmond and was brevetted a major-general. For a year after hostilities were over, he remained in service, being assigned as second in command to Gen. Sickles in charge of the Southeastern Department. He was mustered out in June 1866, after a military career covering five years and three months.

During his absence in the field, Devens was nominated in 1862 for governor of Massachusetts by the so-called "People's Party." Although he took no part in the campaign, he received the support of the Democrats and of some moderate Republicans. He was defeated by John A. Andrew, the Republican candidate, whose majority was 20,000. After the war he attempted to resume his practise. In April 1867 he was appointed, by Gov. Bullock, as a justice of the superior court, and, in 1873, was named by Gov. Washburn as judge of the supreme court of Massachusetts. President Hayes offered him a place in his cabinet as secretary of war, but he declined it, only to accept a nomination as attorney-general (Mar. 10, 1877). At the expiration of his term in the cabinet, he was appointed by Gov. Long to his former position as judge of the supreme court and held his seat on the bench until his death.

As a lawyer, Devens was distinguished by his thoroughness in research, his fidelity to his clients, and his skill in pleading. He was a handsome man, with a commanding presence, and his native gifts as an orator were great. He delivered several notable addresses, among them a speech at Bunker Hill on the occasion of the Centennial of 1875, an oration before the Army of the Potomac at New Haven in commemoration of Gettysburg, and a eulogy on Gen. Grant spoken at Worcester. He received the degree of Doctor of Laws from Harvard (1877), and, as President of the Harvard Alumni Association, presided in 1886 at the observance of the 250th anniversary of the founding of the college. As a judge, he was distinguished by his perfect impartiality, his abundant learning, and his scrupulous integrity. In his capacity as attorney-general, he was recognized as one of the strongest members of a strong cabinet. He had a wide acquaintance, and his urbane and kindly nature made him a social favorite. He never married.

It was, however, as a soldier that he was best known. He was for years Commander of the Military Order, Loyal Legion, in Massachusetts, and he was elected National Commander of the Grand Army of the Republic in 1874 to succeed Gen. Burnside. When he died in Boston, at the age of seventy-one, he was buried from Trinity Church, with military honors. In 1894 the Massachusetts legislature appropriated $15,000 for a bronze statue of him in uniform by Olin H. Warner, and this was erected on the State House grounds, where it now stands. During the World War, in 1917, the New England army camp, established at Ayer, Mass., was named Camp Devens, in his honor. A volume of *Orations and Addresses,* edited by A. L. Devens, was published in 1891.

[See John C. Ropes, "Memoir of Chas. Devens," in *Procs. Mass. Hist. Soc.,* 2 ser., VII (1891–92), 104; *Biog. Encyc. of Mass.,* vol. II (1883); W. R. Cutter & W. G. Adams, *Genealogical and Personal Memoirs,* vol. IV (1910).] C.M.F.

DE VERE, MAXIMILIAN SCHELE [See Schele De Vere, Maximilian, 1820–1898.]

DEVEREUX, JOHN HENRY (Apr. 5, 1832–Mar. 17, 1886), civil engineer, railroad executive, came from an adventurous stock. A remote ancestor was a Robert d'Evreux of the Norman conquerors of England. Another was among the founders of Marblehead, Mass. (*The Probate Records of Essex County, Mass.,* I, 60). John Henry's father was Capt. John Devereux, a well-known Marblehead and Boston sea captain (B. J. Lindsey, *Old Marblehead Sea Captains, and the Ships in Which They Sailed,* 1915, p. 41). The son's life was that of a pioneer among the builders of the modern American railroad system, an adventurer in capitalism. Only fragments of information of his early life have survived. He attended an academy in Portsmouth, N. H., for a time. At sixteen, the age his father went to sea, young Devereux left his home to begin life in Cleveland, Ohio. His arrival in Cleveland (1848) was at the beginning of its railroad era. Capitalists had been slow to invest in the new means of transportation. Cleveland found the solution in municipal aid, voting to the Cleveland, Columbus & Cincinnati Railway Company $200,000 for a line to Columbus and to the Cleveland & Pittsburgh $100,000 for one to Pittsburgh. Construction work on these lines gave the newcomer his opportunity, and a short apprenticeship in an engineering corps made him a railway engineer. In 1851 he married Antoinette, the daughter of L. A. Kelsey (mayor of Cleveland, 1848). The following year his profession led him to Nashville, Tenn., also a center of western railroad building. On the outbreak of the Civil War he returned to Ohio. When the Federal government took over the operation of the border railroads for military purposes, Devereux offered his services. In 1862 he became superintendent of the railroads centering at Alexandria, Va. The *Official Records* bear frequent testimony to his share in maintaining an efficient railroad service back of the Army of the Potomac (1 ser., vol. XII, pt. 3, pp. 634, 636; vol. XIX, pt. 2, pp. 559, 564).

At the beginning of 1864 Devereux withdrew from government service to become general superintendent and shortly vice-president of the Cleveland & Pittsburgh Railroad (leased in 1871 by the Pennsylvania Railroad). In 1868 he resigned in order to accept a place as vice-president and general manager of the Lake Shore & Michigan Southern. Five years later (1873) he became president of the Big Four (Cleveland, Columbus, Cincinnati, & Indianapolis), an office he held until his death. From 1874 to 1880 he was also receiver of the Atlantic & Great Western (later incorporated in the Erie System), and in 1881 its president. During his connection with the Atlantic & Great Western, entrances into Pittsburgh and Chicago were acquired. During the same period the Big Four was extended to St. Louis. His administration of these railroads fell across the hard times of the seventies and the severe railroad competition of the eighties. He sought to maintain a profitable business through pooling and consolidations. Attempts to combine the Big Four with the Atlantic & Great Western and later with the Cincinnati, Hamilton & Dayton were frustrated by the courts of Ohio. Under Devereux's régime extensions were financed by bond issues. Fierce competition brought down rates. Before the two attacks on profits—increasing fixed charges and declining rates—dividends on Big Four stock vanished. Devereux was ready for government control, that is, government intervention as a protection for railway investments. As a witness before the Cullom Interstate Commerce Committee in St. Louis in June 1885 he advocated the punishment of railway officials giving secret rebates, legalization of pooling, publicity of rates, and, if constitutional, an interstate commerce commission with power to maintain fair rates (*Senate Report,* 49 Cong., 1 Sess., vol. III, no. 46, pt. 2, pp. 816–39). His professional life was also intimately connected with the New York Central. He was William K. Vanderbilt's agent in the negotiations by which the New York Central acquired the New York, Chicago & St. Louis Railroad (the Nickel Plate). On the whole his achievements were to the advantage of his section, as well as to his personal fortunes. He was a man of large physique and great energy. Those who knew him said his most marked characteristic was a genial magnetic personality. His interests reached far beyond his business activities. He was one of the incorporators of the Case School of Applied Science, a member of the Cleveland Humane Society, and a life member of the American Association for the Advancement of Science.

[J. H. Kennedy, "Gen. J. H. Devereux," in *Mag. of Western Hist.*, IV (1886), 217–29; *Cleveland Plain Dealer*, Mar. 18, 1886; *Railroad Gazette*, Mar. 26, 1886.]
E. J. B.

DEVIN, THOMAS CASIMER (Dec. 10, 1822–Apr. 4, 1878), soldier, was born in the city of New York, and except for five years spent in Missouri passed his entire early life there. He was educated in the common schools, and became a painter by trade. Entering the New York militia, he rose to the rank of lieutenant-colonel before the outbreak of the Civil War. Organizing a company of men selected from his militia regiment for the three months' service, he was mustered in, July 19, 1861, as captain in the 1st New York Cavalry, which was stationed in the vicinity of Washington. A month after this organization was mustered out, he returned to the army, Nov. 18, 1861, as colonel of the 6th New York Cavalry (called the 2nd Ira Harris Guards). After some months spent in camps in Pennsylvania and Maryland, the regiment joined the army at Washington, and during Pope's Bull Run campaign of 1862 was employed in observing the country south of the Rapidan. South Mountain was its first real battle, followed immediately by Antietam, and thereafter the regiment was actively employed until Lee's surrender. After the battle of Fredericksburg, Devin succeeded to the command of a brigade, of which the 6th New York was a part, in Pleasanton's cavalry division. Within the next few months Pleasanton repeatedly and unsuccessfully urged his appointment as brigadier-general. Devin's brigade fought at Chancellorsville and Beverly Ford, and as a part of Buford's command, fighting on foot, met the Confederate advance west of Gettysburg at daybreak on July 1, 1863, and helped to hold it back until the infantry arrived on the field. Still with the Army of the Potomac, it went through the Wilderness campaign of 1864, and took part in Sheridan's great raid around Richmond. Early in August it moved to the Shenandoah Valley, for service in Sheridan's campaign against Early. In the action at Crooked Run (Aug. 16) Devin was slightly wounded; he continued in the saddle during the fight, but was absent from the army, recuperating, for the next month. He returned to duty in time to take part in the battles of Winchester, Fisher's Hill, and Cedar Creek, and was at last appointed brigadier-general of volunteers (Mar. 13, 1865, to date from Oct. 19, 1864). He commanded a division of the Cavalry Corps at Five Forks, Sailor's Creek, and Appomattox. After his muster out of the volunteer service he was appointed lieutenant-colonel of the 8th Cavalry, July 28, 1866, and became colonel of the 3rd Cavalry, June 25, 1877. Long service on the frontier, following the strenuous campaigning of the Civil War, undermined his health, and he was absent from his regiment, on account of sickness, for nearly a year in 1873–74. In 1878, following another breakdown in his health, he returned to his home in New York, where he died. Much older than most of the cavalry leaders of the Civil War, many of whom were little more than boys, the "Old War Horse" was one of the best.

[*Hist. of the 6th N. Y. Cavalry* (1908), pp. 417–30; *The Union Army* (Madison, Wis., 1908), VIII, 73–74; *N. Y. Herald* of Apr. 5, 1878; *Official Records (Army)*, ser. I, vols. XXV (pt. 1), XXVII (pts. 1, 3), XXIX (pts. 1, 2), XXXIII, XXXVI (pt. 1), XLIII (pts. 1, 2), XLVI (pts. 1, 2, 3); unpublished records in the War Dept.]
T. M. S.

DE VINNE, THEODORE LOW (Dec. 25, 1828–Feb. 16, 1914), printer, the son of Daniel and Joanna Augusta (Low) De Vinne, was born in Stamford, Conn. Instruction from his father (including Latin), and the village schools of Amenia and White Plains, N. Y., gave him his early education. At fourteen he was apprenticed to the printer's trade in the office of the Newburgh *Gazette*. He went to New York City in 1848, and, after working in various printing-offices, entered the employ of Francis Hart. In the same year, 1850, he married Grace Brockbank of New York City. He soon became foreman of the composing-room, and in 1858 he was made a junior partner. On the death of Hart in 1877, De Vinne became, under the terms of the will, possessed of the business. The firm name was changed to Theo. L. De Vinne & Company, his son Theodore B. becoming associated with his father. In 1908 the business was incorporated as The De Vinne Press, De Vinne retiring from active management but taking the office of president.

As a printer, De Vinne was the most learned man of his time in the history of the art and in its practise. His printing-office became prominent through the work which it did on *Scribner's Monthly, St. Nicholas,* and especially the *Century Magazine*. The publishers of the latter demanded a degree of excellence in its printing which was then unknown, and through cooperation of the publishers with De Vinne, and the latter's installation of heavier presses, the use of hard packing, and the invention of coated paper (by S. D. Warren & Company of Boston, largely at De Vinne's instigation), fine-line wood-engravings and later half-tone plates were printed with a brilliance never before achieved. De Vinne was a meticulous workman in all the technical minutiæ of printing. He printed most of the early books for the Grolier Club (of which he was a founder and president), thereby setting a high standard; the Book of Common Prayer and the "Jade" book are two of his fine productions; while the *Century Dictionary* is considered by many critics as his finest achievement.

As an employer he was active in the affairs of employers' organizations, being one of the founders of the Typothetæ of the City of New York and of the United Typothetæ of America, serving as secretary and president of these organizations. In and out of these groups he worked for years to make printing a profitable craft, and to make the relations of masters and men as harmonious as the changing industrial conditions would allow. In his own office he was a kindly employer whose one insistent demand was first quality work. His almost exclusive devotion to his calling gave him an insight into its problems which was unusual and always at the service of his fellow employers and workmen.

De Vinne's name is likely to live longest in connection with his writings. His major published works include: *The Printers' Price List* (1869); *The Invention of Printing* (1876), the standard work on the subject in English, used as the text for George Bruce's Sons & Company's type specimen books of 1878 and 1882; *Historic Printing Types* (1886); *Christopher Plantin* (1888); *The Practice of Typography* (four volumes, 1900, 1901, 1902, 1904); *Title-Pages as Seen by a Printer* (1901); *Notable Printers of Italy During the Fifteenth Century* (1910). He also contributed prefaces and notes to Moxon's *Mechanick Exercises,* printed by him and issued by the Typothetæ of the City of New York in 1896, and a preface to *A Decree of Star Chamber Concerning Printing,* the first publication of the Grolier Club (1884). The printer's specimen books of the De Vinne Press also contain much historical information from his pen.

De Vinne's contribution to the progress of printing in America consisted in his codification of the practises of the craft as they obtained in his lifetime, of historical writings relating to the history of printing, and more especially, as a master printer, of successful working out of details of composition and presswork as affected by photo-mechanical processes of reproduction and the type-setting machine. The types he used and the way he used them are not now esteemed as highly as in his day, which is to say that his taste in typographic design suffered from the general low state of printing in the nineteenth century; his zeal for perfection, however, set new standards which were a fitting and necessary prelude to the work of present-day American printers.

[*Catalogue of Work of The De Vinne Press* (1929) pub. by the Grolier Club and containing addresses by Ira H. Brainerd and others; *Theodore Low De Vinne, Printer* (privately printed, 1915); *Literary Review of the N. Y. Evening Post,* Jan. 20, 1923; *Century Mag.,* Nov. 1910, Nov. 1911; *Inland Printer,* July 1922, p. 515; *N. Y. Herald, N. Y. Times, N. Y. Tribune,* Feb. 17, 1914.] C. P. R.

DEVOY, JOHN (Sept. 3, 1842–Sept. 29, 1928), journalist and Fenian leader, born at Kill, County Kildare, Ireland, was the son of a farmer, actively interested in the Young Ireland movement and in Catholic Emancipation. His mother was Elizabeth Dunne Devoy. The Devoy household was a small debating club and local political center; here and in the schools of Dublin, whither the family had moved, Devoy received his early education; he later attended evening classes at the Catholic University. In 1861 he joined the Irish Republican Brotherhood and, to obtain military experience, he served a year with the French Foreign Legion in Algeria. Returning to Ireland in 1862, Devoy, a born conspirator, became conspicuous in the Republican movement. Because of his notorious organizing of Fenians within the British army the government attempted to arrest him in September 1865, but it was not until he had assisted in the escape of James Stephens from a Dublin jail, that he was finally apprehended in February 1866. Judged guilty of treason he was sentenced to fifteen years' penal servitude, but was released with four other Fenian prisoners in 1871 on the understanding that they would not return to the United Kingdom until after the expiration of their sentences. They arrived in New York in February 1871, where they were received with honors by the Irish population. Devoy joined the staff of the *New York Herald* as a reporter; he became telegraph editor and later was in charge of the foreign desk. After eight years he was dismissed by James Gordon Bennett [*q.v.*] because of his support of Charles Stewart Parnell, whom Bennett opposed. Before he established his weekly newspaper, the *Irish Nation,* in New York in 1881, he was connected with various newspapers: the *Daily Telegraph* and the *Morning Journal* of New York and the *Herald* and the *Evening Post* of Chicago. From the time of his arrival in New York his efforts toward Irish freedom were more vigorous and fruitful. He organized the famous "Catalpa" rescue of Irish prisoners from Australia in 1875–76; he was later instrumental in securing funds for the submarine experiments of John P. Holland [*q.v.*] that they might aid in the destruction of the British navy. The moral and financial support that Devoy secured from the Clan-na-Gael in America and the Irish Republican Brotherhood contributed greatly to the success of the Land League movement under Parnell. The *Irish Nation* had been forced to cease publication in 1885; in 1903 Devoy founded in New York the weekly *Gaelic American* to combat British propaganda and to disseminate the principles of the Fenians and the Clan-na-Gael, who had withdrawn their support from the Irish parliamentarian movement. He edited the *Gaelic American* until his death in 1928. During the World War he was closely associated with German agents in America and was responsible for much of the financial support given the Irish insurgents in the Dublin Easter Week Rebellion of 1916. He was later conspicuous in organizing Irish opinion in America against the League of Nations and the World Court, which he considered to be entangling alliances dangerous to American freedom. He was associated with De Valera until the latter advocated an English protectorate for Ireland; he supported the treaty under which the Irish Free State was established and aided successfully in floating its first bonds in America. He had completed his *Recollections of an Irish Rebel,* a substantial contribution to the history of Fenianism, when he died in Atlantic City in his eighty-sixth year. Devoy, the last great Fenian leader, was characterized by English opinion as "the most bitter and persistent, as well as the most dangerous enemy of this country which Ireland has produced since Wolfe Tone" (*Times,* London, Oct. 1, 1928), and in that statement Devoy would have found ample satisfaction.

[John Devoy, *Recollections of an Irish Rebel* (1929); *N. Y. Times,* Sept. 30, 1928; *Manchester Guardian* and *Times* (London), Oct. 1, 1928; *Gaelic Am.* (N. Y.), Oct. 6, 13, 20, 27 and Nov. 3, 10, 1928; private information.]

F. M.

DE VRIES, DAVID PIETERSEN (fl. 1618–1655), merchant skipper and colonizer of New Netherland, was born in 1592 or 1593 at La Rochelle, France, where his father, a native of Hoorn, North Holland, had resided at different times since 1584. His mother was of Amsterdam. After his fourth year he lived mostly in Holland, being from his youth well trained in merchandising, both there and in France. In 1618–19, as owner and commander of a new ship of 400 tons burden, mounting eight guns, he made a voyage to the Mediterranean. The next year he sailed to Newfoundland to procure a cargo of codfish, which he sold in Spanish ports. In the course of this voyage he won a notable fight against pirates off Cartagena, and at Toulon was engaged by the Duc de Guise to serve with his ship against the Turks. When shortly afterward the Duke sought to change his contract and to employ him against the Huguenots at La Rochelle, De Vries refused to comply with his request, sold his ship, and returned overland to Holland. In 1624 he made preparations to go to Canada for furs, but his plans were frustrated by the Dutch West India Company and he sailed to La Rochelle instead. In 1627–30 he made a voyage to the Dutch East Indies. Shortly after his return from this voyage he entered into partnership with Samuel Godyn and other directors of the West India Company to plant a colony on the Delaware. An expedition sent out by them in 1631 founded a small settlement, called Swanendael, on the west side of Delaware Bay, near the present town of Lewes, which was soon after destroyed by the Indians. Thereafter De Vries made three voyages to America: May 24, 1632–July 24, 1633, under a contract with his former partners, in command of a ship and a yacht, to Delaware, Virginia, and New Amsterdam; July 10, 1634–October 1636, in the interest of another group of merchants, who wished to plant a colony on the coast of Guiana, to that coast, the West Indies, and New Netherland; and Sept. 25, 1638–June 21, 1644, in partnership with Frederick de Vries, secretary of the city of Amsterdam, to plant a colony on Staten Island. Shortly after his return from his second voyage, on Dec. 8, 1636, he made application to the West India Company to be sent to New Netherland as director, in the place of Wouter van Twiller [*q.v.*], who was about to be recalled, but his petition was rejected with the statement that "a more capable person is needed." In addition to the small settlement on Staten Island established during his last voyage he planted a colony near Tappan, which he called Vriessendael. Both colonies were destroyed in the disastrous Indian war of 1643. Discouraged in his undertakings, he returned to Holland and settled at Hoorn, where some ten years later he wrote an interesting account of his travels, printed at Alckmaer in 1655 under the title: *Korte Historiael, ende Journaels aenteyckeninge Van verscheyden Voyagiens in de vier deelen des Wereldts-Ronde, als Europa, Africa, Asia, ende Amerika gedaen.* Of this little book, which contains a portrait of the author, dated 1653, on which his age is given as sixty years, but a few copies are known to be in existence. Written in a plain but vivid style, the book contains many picturesque descriptions of events in New Netherland that are not known from official documents, so that it forms a valuable source for the history of the colony. On the title-page De Vries is called Artillery Master of the Deputy States of West-Vrieslandt and the Noorder-Quartier, or northern quarter of the province of North Holland. Little is known of his later life, and the date of his death is uncertain.

[The chief source of information about De Vries is his above mentioned *Korte Historiael*. A complete reprint of this book, edited by Dr. H. T. Colenbrander, with portrait, two maps and eighteen plates, was published at 's-Gravenhage in 1911 as volume III of the *Werken* issued by the Linschoten-Vereeniging. All the parts of De Vries's book relating to Newfoundland, New Netherland and Virginia are presented, in translation by Henry C. Murphy, in the *N. Y. Hist. Soc. Colls.*, 2 ser., III, 1–129, and were separately printed in 1853 by James Lenox. A revised translation of the parts relating to New Netherland is included in the *Narratives of New Netherland, 1609–1664* (1909), ed. by J. F. Jameson, pp. 181–234.] A. J. F. v—L.

DEW, THOMAS RODERICK (Dec. 5, 1802–Aug. 6, 1846), economist, was the son of Thomas Dew, who was born in Maryland in 1763 of an old family of that state. The latter moved to King and Queen County, Va., when a young man, and soon, by successful farming and money lending, came to own the plantation called "Dewsville." He married Lucy E. Gatewood, a native of the county, and they had ten children, several of whom came to some distinction. Thomas Dew served for a time in the Revolutionary army, was a captain in the War of 1812, and died the leading figure in his community. His son, Thomas R. Dew, attended the College of William and Mary, probably entering in the grammar school, and graduating with the degree of A.B. in 1820. He traveled two years in Europe, and in 1827 was appointed to one of the six chairs in the College as professor of political law, his assignment including "History, Metaphysics, Natural and National Law, Government and Political Economy." Political economy was probably taught at William and Mary as early as 1798, Smith's *Wealth of Nations* being the text, and it is certain that in 1801 this college gave the earliest instruction in the subject as a science. Political economy was given separate recognition when Dew became professor; indeed, he came very near being described as "Professor of Political Economy." His salary was $1,000, and he probably lived with the other bachelors in the college building. He published his *Lectures on the Restrictive System* ("delivered to the senior political class of William and Mary College"), in 1829, a compact volume of 196 pages. In this he upheld the free-trade argument, relying upon the Physiocrats and Smith and Say. Though he declared his intention "to avoid mingling in the politics of the day," his lectures came squarely into collision with the heated assertions of the protectionist school, then being cemented under the advocacy of Mathew Carey [*q.v.*] and the Philadelphia Society for the Promotion of National Industry. The Virginian, in an economic environment of a staple agriculture, foretold that disunion would follow if protection were pressed by the industrial North, and from his cloister he resented the imputation of men of affairs that sound practise gave the lie to current economic theory. It has been thought by some that his work influenced the subsequent reduction in the tariffs. In 1832 he published in Richmond his *Review of the Debate* [on the Abolition of Slavery] *in the Virginia Legislature of 1831 and 1832.* (This became better known after it was incorporated in a volume of Southern essays under the title *The Pro-Slavery Argument,* 1852, second edition, 1853.) George Wythe and St. George Tucker [*qq.v.*], Dew's predecessors in the faculty of the College, had been anti-slavery men. But now Dew's pro-slavery opinion reflected what appeared to be the economic interest of the dominant tide-water counties. His argument was inclusive, careful and ingenious, but proved too much. The state was still in the custom of looking to the College for guidance, and his pronouncement undoubtedly exercised a wide influence. J. D. B. De Bow [*q.v.*], as might have been expected, said of Dew that his "able essay on the institution of slavery entitles him to the lasting gratitude of the whole South." Dew's *Digest of the Laws, Customs, Manners, and Institutions of the Ancient and Modern Nations,* an outline printed first for the use of his students, and after his death published (1853) in New York, shows, as Herbert B. Adams has said, that Dew's teaching of history exhibited a lively appreciation of human institutions at a time when contemporaries were following dull chronology. While he accepted scriptural authority on antediluvian history without question, he had his own views on after developments. In 1836 he became president of the College, succeeding Rev. Adam P. Empie. Since the Revolution, due largely to the cession of Virginia's claims to public lands, the loss of royal favor, and the removal of the capital to Richmond, the College had declined in wealth and in students, those in attendance sometimes numbering as low as twenty. Dew, by "tact at management, great zeal, and unwearied assiduity," in the words of Bishop Meade, brought the number of students to 140, and made the institution almost as prosperous as ever before. He was a tall, angular man, awkward in movement, but amiable in his manners. He married Natilia Hay, daughter of a physician of Clarke County, Va., in 1845, and died on his wedding trip, in Paris, probably of pleurisy or pneumonia.

[Herbert B. Adams, *The Coll. of Wm. and Mary* (1887), containing an excellent bibliography of the history of the college, useful in connection with Dew's life; Wm. Meade, *Old Churches, Ministers and Families of Va.* (1857), I, 177 f.; E. R. A. Seligman, in *Economic Essays Contributed in Honor of John Bates Clark* (1927), ed. by J. H. Hollander; *Wm. and Mary Coll. Quart.*, VI (1897), 186, XIV (1906), 81 ff., XXVII (1920), 135; *Southern Lit. Messenger*, Oct. 1856.]

B. M—l.

DEWEES, WILLIAM POTTS (May 5, 1768–May 20, 1841), physician, obstetrician, was born near Pottstown, Pa., founded by his maternal grandfather, Thomas Potts. On his father's side he was of Swedish descent. He apparently had only a moderate amount of school education, seems to have made an early decision to study medicine, and was placed in the office of a Dr. Phyle who was a practising apothecary. Later he was placed with Dr. William Smith, a practitioner of medicine, and attended classes at the University of Pennsylvania from 1787 to 1789. There is some doubt as to whether he took the degree of M.B. at that time. In any event it was not until 1806 that he received the degree of Doctor of Medicine from the University of Pennsylvania. His thesis was entitled *An Essay on the Means of Lessening Pain and Facilitating certain cases of Difficult Parturition* (1806). He began practise at Abington, Pa., and in December 1793 he moved to Philadelphia, it is said with the encouragement and patronage of Dr. Benjamin Rush.

At this time the subject of obstetrics received little attention from the profession in general and the great majority of deliveries were in the hands of midwives. There was no proper teaching of the subject and no formal instruction was given in the University of Pennsylvania. There was still a strong prejudice against men engaging in obstetrics. The "man midwife" was an object of derision well exemplified in the character which Laurence Sterne drew of Dr. Slop in *Tristram Shandy*. It must have required a good deal of courage to take up this specialty. Dewees devoted himself not only to the practise of obstetrics but to teaching it and was soon giving instruction to classes in his office. He became a very successful practitioner and it is said that he delivered over ten thousand women.

About this time there was strong pressure brought to bear on the authorities of the University of Pennsylvania to establish a chair of obstetrics and after much pleading this was done in 1810, but with the handicap that attendance on the lectures was not necessary for graduation. There was a keen struggle for the appointment and Dewees saw it given to a rival, Dr. Thomas C. James. Other disappointments came as his health failed and he developed pulmonary tuberculosis. On this account he was compelled to give up the practise of medicine for a time and went to Phillipsburgh, where he took up farming. He lost money in this venture but regained his health so that in 1817 he was able to return to Philadelphia and resume practise. He became associated with the Medical Institute and resumed teaching. Soon afterward he was made a member of the American Philosophical Society. As the health of Dr. James had been such that he was unable to carry on the duties of his chair, Dewees was appointed adjunct professor of obstetrics in the University of Pennsylvania in 1825 and did most of the work of the department for nine years. He succeeded James in 1834 when he was appointed professor of obstetrics. Misfortune continued to follow him, as in 1835 he had what was probably a cerebral hemorrhage and was compelled to resign his professorship. It was a tragedy that when he had reached the height of his ambition, sickness so soon compelled him to give up active work. Afterward he lived in Mobile, Ala., for four years, later returning to Philadelphia where he died in 1841.

Dewees did much to advance the art of obstetrics by his skill but more by his teaching and writings. His chief work was *A Compendious System of Midwifery* (1852), which went through twelve editions. It must be regarded as the first authoritative work in America on the subject. In it Dewees followed the ideas of the French School to a considerable extent but introduced his own ideas and showed much original thought. He also published volumes on the diseases of women and children and went farther afield in a work on the practise of medicine. This last was evidently written hurriedly and did not add to his reputation. He is described as having been a good speaker and teacher but caustic in his criticism. He was married twice: first, to Martha Rogers, a daughter of a Dr. Rogers of New England, and second, to Mary Lorrain of Philadelphia (1802).

[S. W. Williams, *Am. Medic. Biog.* (1845); Jos. Carson, *Hist. of the Medic. Dept. Univ. Pa.* (1869); *Autobiography of S. D. Gross* (1887); F. P. Henry, *Standard Hist. of the Medic. Profession of Phila.* (1897); A. L. Kelly and W. L. Burrage, *Am. Medic. Biogs.* (1920).]

T. M.

DEWEY, CHESTER (Oct. 25, 1784–Dec. 15, 1867), Congregational clergyman, educator, pioneer scientist, was born in Sheffield, Mass., the son of Stephen Dewey and Elizabeth Owen, and a descendant of Thomas Dewey, one of the first settlers of Dorchester, Mass. His boyhood was spent on a farm where he acquired the vigorous constitution and sound health which he enjoyed throughout life. Here, too, was probably awakened that compelling interest in plants, minerals, and the weather which determined the trend of his scientific studies. After a common-school education he prepared to enter Williams College and was admitted at the age of eighteen. Graduating in 1806, he followed a strong religious bent and studied for the ministry. A year later he was licensed to preach by the Berkshire Congregationalist Association. After a brief pastorate at West Stockbridge and Tyringham, Mass., he returned to Williams College as a tutor. From 1810 to 1827 he served as professor of mathematics and natural philosophy during which period he devoted much time to the development of work in physics and chemistry on the laboratory side and to the collection of museum specimens of geology and botany. Most of these he gathered by personal effort, others he obtained by exchange with collectors in this country and abroad, thus making the start for the fine museum now owned by the Institution. In 1823 he organized among the students the first antislavery society in Massachusetts. He served as principal of the Berkshire Gymnasium, at Pittsfield, Mass., 1827–36, and of the High School, afterward known as the Collegiate Institute at Rochester, N. Y., 1836–50. At the founding of the University of Rochester in the latter year he was elected the first professor of chemistry and natural sciences, which position he held until his retirement in 1861 as emeritus professor. From 1837 until within a week of his death, he made daily observations on the weather conditions of Rochester. He also lectured for many years, beginning in 1822, on chemistry and medical botany in the Berkshire Medical Institution, and in the Medical School at Woodstock, Vt., from 1842 to 1849. He was a born teacher and acquired knowledge, seemingly, chiefly for the purpose of communicating it to others. He was a leaven of intellectual activity in whatever community he resided.

His scientific observations covered a wide range. To the first volume (1819) of the *American Journal of Science* he contributed a "Sketch of the Mineralogy and Geology of the Vicinity of Williams' College," and fifty-three later volumes contain papers by him. Between 1824 and 1866 he contributed a long series on the sedges entitled "Caricography." These were never collected into a single volume but were characterized by Asa Gray as an "elaborate monograph patiently prosecuted through more than forty years." He further classed Dewey with Schweinitz and Torrey, two of the foremost students of North American plants, saying that they "laid the foundation and insured the popularity of the study of Sedges in this country." Dewey also prepared a *Report on the Herbaceous Plants and on the Quadrupeds of Massachusetts,* published by the state in 1840, and the section on the *carices* or sedges in Alphonso Wood's *Class-Book of Botany* (1845), the work being dedicated to him. His service to botany has been recognized in the name of the genus *Deweya,* umbelliferous plants of California. In the line of ethnology his writings include two critical reviews of Agassiz's *Essay on Classification* (*Princeton Review,* 1863), and one entitled "Examination of Some Reasonings Against the Unity of Mankind" (*Ibid.,* July 1862). Although familiar with the teachings of Lamarck and Darwin regarding evolution his acceptance of them was apparently prevented by his theological beliefs.

Dewey was married twice: in 1810 to Sarah Dewey, and in 1825 to Olivia Hart Pomeroy of Pittsfield, Mass. There were five children by the first marriage and ten by the second.

[Obituary by Asa Gray in *Am. Jour. Sci.,* 2 ser., XLV (1868); Martin B. Anderson, "Sketch of the Life of Prof. Chester Dewey" in *Smithsonian Inst. Ann. Report,* 1870; Chas. W. Seelye, "A Memorial Sketch of Chester Dewey, M.D., D.D.," in *Proc. Rochester Acad. Sci.,* vol. III; Florence Beckwith, "Early Botanists of Rochester," in *Ibid.,* vol. V (1912); and the sketch in H. A. Kelly and W. L. Burrage, *Am. Medic. Biogs.* (1920); L. W. Spring, *Hist. of Wms. College* (1917); W. F. Peck, *Hist. of Rochester, Monroe County, N. Y.* (1908); family records, including a four-page sketch by Dewey's son, prepared for the Rochester Hist. Soc. Obituaries appeared in newspapers all over the country; see especially *Rochester Express* and *Rochester Daily Democrat* for Dec. 16, 1867.]

C. W. D.

DEWEY, GEORGE (Dec. 26, 1837–Jan. 16, 1917), naval officer, was born at Montpelier, Vt. Among his ancestors were Douai, a Huguenot, who settled in Kent, England, the latter half of the sixteenth century; Thomas Duee of Sandwich, Kent, who emigrated to Dorchester, Mass., in 1634, changing his name to Dewey; Josiah Dewey his son, who had the rank of sergeant in King Philip's War; William Dewey, great-grandfather of the admiral, one of the volunteers at the battle of Lexington. George was the youngest of three sons, children of Dr. Julius Yemans Dewey and Mary Perrin. His mother died when he was five years old, but his father, whom his son characterizes as "a natural leader," with "ideas of right and wrong . . . very fixed, in keeping with his deep religious principles," gave himself without stint to the bringing up of his boys. "To my father's influence in my early training I owe, primarily, all that I have accomplished in the world," Dewey later wrote. When he was between sixteen and seventeen he was appointed a midshipman at the United States Naval Academy at Annapolis. The class numbered sixty on entrance, and the modesty of Dewey's beginning is shown by the fact that out of thirty-five surviving at the end of the first year he stood number thirty-three. At the close of the four-year course in June 1858, fifteen graduated, and Dewey had now risen in standing to five. This he further improved on the final examination after two years at sea. He was third in his class to receive his commission, and plainly had found a serious interest in his profession.

On leaving Annapolis he had been assigned to the steam-frigate *Wabash,* which sailed for the Mediterranean. During the next year he visited such historic cities as Constantinople, Beirut, Jerusalem, and Alexandria. In April 1861, he was commissioned lieutenant, and a few months later in spite of his youthful age, he was made executive officer of the *Mississippi,* a side-wheeler, one of the largest and most heavily armed ships in the Union navy. The *Mississippi* was assigned to Farragut's fleet about to begin operations against New Orleans; and as the Union ships advanced to take that city, passing Forts Jackson and St. Philip in the battle of Apr. 24, 1862, she occupied an important position in the first division. Her commanding officer, Capt. Melancthon Smith, mistrusting his ability to direct the ship in the darkness, assigned that duty to Dewey, with his "younger eyes," while he himself took charge of the battery. Dewey, his post on the hurricane deck, succeeded in passing the forts without running the ship aground, and also had a sharp encounter with the Confederate ram *Manassas,* which in the end was compelled to make for the shore, where she was set on fire. Two years later when Farragut made a similar move against Port Hudson, the *Mississippi* was again in the thick of the fight. Though an experienced river pilot was in charge of the ship, he ran her hard aground, where, being at the mercy of the Confederate batteries, she caught fire. Officers and crew worked desperately to save her, but in vain. Dewey's coolness and efficiency were commended in the official report. Later he was made the executive officer of the *Monongahela,* which Farragut used as his flagship when he supervised operations on the lower Mississippi. This gave opportunity for an intimate acquaintance with the first admiral of the United States navy. "Valuable as the training of Annapolis was, it was poor schooling beside that of serving under Farragut in time of war" (*Autobiography,* p. 50). After a brief period of service on the James River, Dewey was made executive officer of the heavy steam-frigate *Colorado*; he brought an undisciplined crew under control, and his ship was one of Porter's fleet that participated in the attack on Fort Fisher. After nine years at sea, Dewey was ordered to the Naval Academy for his first shore duty. The same year, on Oct. 24, 1867, he was married to Susan Boardman Goodwin, daughter of ex-Governor Goodwin of New Hampshire. She died in 1872, five days after the birth of a son, George Goodwin Dewey.

Dewey's first command was the sloop-of-war *Narragansett.* When the *Virginius* affair was arousing the country, the *Narragansett* was engaged in surveying the Gulf of California. Wardroom officers were gloomy, for if a conflict with Spain were to follow they "would be entirely out of it." In the light of later events Dewey's reply is interesting: "On the contrary, we shall be very much in it. If war with Spain is declared, the *Narragansett* will take Manila." Dewey had read a few books about the Philippines, and saw that they would be a logical point of attack. Further tours of duty, of minor importance, followed: first, as light-house inspector for the Second District, with headquarters in Boston; second, as naval secretary of the Light-house Board, which brought him to Washington, with a round of dinners and the opportunity of meeting prominent officials; and, third, as commanding officer of the sloop *Juniata,* ordered to the Mediterranean. The last duty was cut short by a severe illness, a complication of typhoid fever and abscess of the liver. Dewey was taken to the British naval hospital at Malta, where only the skill and personal care of the head surgeon saved him. At the age of forty-seven he was promoted to the rank of captain. Then followed another cruise in command of the *Pensacola,* of no significance save for the many agreeable meetings with men of distinction in northern and southern Europe. In July 1889, he was made chief of the Bureau of Equipment, Navy Department, Washington. This was a fortunate assignment. Recently authorized cruisers were being completed and the first battleships were being planned. Not less important as leading to his great achievement of 1898 was his assignment in October 1895, as president of the Board of Inspection and Survey. Several battleships were then approaching completion, and it was the Board's duty to pass on them, making sure that construction was sound and conforming to specifications. Presiding at the trials of the *Texas, Maine, Iowa, Indiana,* and *Massachusetts,* and also of several of the cruisers and torpedo-boats, Dewey gained an intimate and detailed knowledge of the "New Navy."

In November 1897, he was ordered to take command of the Asiatic Squadron. Relations with Spain were strained, but conservative Americans did not believe that war was probable. Dewey, however, resolved to take every precaution. Before sailing he began an intensive study of the Philippine Islands. Inquiring into the supply of ammunition in his new command, he learned that the ships had not even a peace allowance; further, that the cruiser which was scheduled to take the ammunition to them was under repair and not likely to be in commission for six months. By insistence and personal application, he succeeded in getting one-half of the necessary stores loaded at once on the little *Concord,* with the assurance that the rest should be expedited to Honolulu where it would be forwarded by the cruiser *Baltimore.* As it happened, the latter ship reached him only forty-eight hours before the message that war had been declared.

He took over his new command in the harbor of Nagasaki, Jan. 3, 1898. For two years he had held the rank of commodore. In February the ships proceeded to Hongkong, nearer to their possible objective, and from then until April there was constant drilling of the crews, as well as docking and overhauling of ships and machinery. Knowing that the British in case of war would, with strict neutrality, grant no harbor facilities, Dewey quietly improvised a base at Mirs Bay, purchased two supply ships, and contracted with the Chinese for the delivery of coal, provisions, and general stores, as needed. In Washington he had applied at the Office of Naval Intelligence for information relating to Manila, but as our warships had not visited the latter for years, none was to be had. While at Hongkong, however, Dewey kept closely in touch with O. F. Williams, the American consul at Manila, who sent valuable reports. It was seemingly hazardous to operate against an enemy fleet in a harbor that had great defensive possibilities, supported by an army with land batteries, an arsenal, and a large city. The British in Hongkong, though friendly to the American forces, were frankly doubtful of the outcome, and at the clubs betting odds heavily favored the Spanish. Dewey, however, had made every preparation, and when, on Apr. 26, he received a cablegram that war had been declared he waited only that Williams might arrive and then set his course for Manila Bay, six hundred miles distant.

When near his destination he reconnoitered Subig Bay, where the Spanish Squadron had made a brief visit a few days before. Finding that they were not there, he steamed on to Manila Bay reducing his speed so that he might not enter until about midnight. He had heard from both the consul-general of Singapore and Williams that Boca Grande (the main entrance) had been mined. Although on the American ships there were fifty-three guns above four-inch caliber to the Spaniards' thirty-one, and 1,743 men to their 1,134, in the Spanish land batteries there were thirty-nine heavy guns, the largest of greater caliber than any in the American Squadron. These, the ships being unarmored, might if properly handled have been the decisive factor. A defeat or even a serious check to the American forces, with the nearest navy-yard 7,000 miles away, would have been fatal. Dewey afterward related that his mind went back to the advance on the forts below New Orleans thirty-six years before. Asking himself the question "What would Farragut do?" he drew strength from the conviction that he was doing precisely what the great leader would have done. The entrance into the bay was executed without a hitch. Not a mine exploded. Only a few shots were fired from the land batteries, and these fell harmlessly as the rear of the column was passing. The squadron then steamed slowly on toward Manila, twenty-five miles distant. When the mist of tropical dawn cleared away, the Spanish ships were discovered at anchor in front of Cavite, "formed in an irregular crescent" protected on the west by Cavite peninsula and the battery at Sangley Point, and on the east by the shoals off Las Pinas. The American column, consisting of the *Olympia* (flagship), the *Baltimore,* the *Raleigh,* the *Petrel,* the *Concord,* and the *Boston,* headed south toward the Spanish Squadron. At 5:30 A.M., May 1, Dewey gave the word to begin firing, and an eight-inch shell from the *Olympia* was the signal to the squadron for battle. They had been approaching on a converging course, and as they reached the five-fathom curve near Cavite they turned westward and ran in the general direction of the Spanish line, using their port broadside. Reaching its extremity, with helm to port, they "countermarched" and brought the opposite batteries to bear. In this way they traversed the course three times to the west and two times to the east, the range varying from 5,000 to 2,000 yards. The fire from the land batteries, as was soon evident, could be for the most part ignored. And though the Spanish ships fought with spirit, the inaccuracy of their fire showed that the rapid shots of the American Squadron and the changing range had proved utterly confusing. At 7:35, when the battle had been in progress about two hours, and the Spanish Squadron, as far as could be seen, was still intact, Dewey withdrew. He had received a disturbing report that ammunition was near to exhaustion. The report proved to be erroneous, but the interruption served to disclose the effectiveness of the American gunnery. Of the Spanish Squadron, the *Castilla* burst into flames and the *Reina Cristina* (flagship) blew up. The smaller vessels fled for refuge behind the arsenal at Cavite, and only the *Don Antonio de Ulloa* kept her ensign flying and held to her original position beside the battery on Sangley Point. At 11:16 Dewey again led his ships into action, and soon the *Ulloa* went down. In the afternoon the little *Petrel* took or destroyed the small ships, tugs, and launches concealed in the harbor of Cavite. The entry in Dewey's diary written that evening reads: "Reached Manila at daylight. Immediately engaged the Spanish ships and batteries at Cavite. Destroyed eight of the former, including the *Reina Cristina* and *Castilla*. Anchored at noon off Manila." (*Autobiography*, p. 223). Rarely has there been such disproportion in losses. The *Olympia* was hulled five times and her rigging cut, the *Baltimore* was hit five times, and the *Boston* and the *Petrel* received some unimportant hits; but the total American casualties amounted to only eight wounded. On the other hand, the Spaniards, besides losing all their ships, had one hundred and sixty-seven killed and two hundred and fourteen wounded (Chadwick, p. 205).

The victory at once made the United States one of the principal powers in the East, and was of influence with the American people for it showed the quality of the "New Navy," in which some had not felt any too great confidence. Following his victory Dewey had a problem to face much like that of Farragut immediately after the battle of New Orleans; he had a large enemy city at his mercy, but no army with which to occupy it. Informing Washington of his victory by cable from Hongkong, he told of his need, and then waited for reënforcements. Meanwhile circumstances developed which caused anxiety. Spain at the beginning of the war had fitted out a fleet for the West Indies, and now giving her attention to the East organized another fleet under Admiral Camara, which in tonnage, type of ship, and guns was superior to Dewey's squadron. When this started for the Orient, going by the short route through Suez, it had a chance of reaching the Philippines before the arrival of additional American ships. Meanwhile Great Britain, France, Germany, and Japan were hurrying certain of their ships already in the East to Manila. Furthermore, Filipino insurgents swarmed about Manila and Cavite in increasing numbers.

The batteries at Manila had been silenced by the threat of a bombardment of the city. Mindful of the Spanish forces there and what they might do with torpedoes, Dewey employed, especially at night, every means to safeguard his ships. He had established a blockade, but permitted warships of neutral powers to enter and leave the bay as they pleased, subject to the commonly recognized rules of blockaded waters. The British, French, and Japanese reported their arrival and asked where they should anchor. But the Germans came in with little or no formality, choosing their own anchorage. Altogether, there appeared five of their warships under Vice-Admiral von Diederichs—a force out of all proportion to the limited German interests in the Islands. Their officers were guilty of visiting Spanish posts and of ignoring the blockade in other particulars. But Dewey, taking a firm stand and receiving the moral support of Capt. Chichester, the senior British officer, maintained control in important affairs and avoided a rupture. Meanwhile the Filipino leader, Aguinaldo, had, with Dewey's encouragement, organized native forces and invested the city on the land side. (It is difficult to determine just how far Dewey may also have encouraged Aguinaldo's aspirations for the independence of the Islands. Dewey's extensive testimony before the Senate Committee in 1902 was exceedingly confused. See *Senate Document No. 311, Pt. III*, 57 Cong., 1 Sess). Finally, Major-General Merritt arrived with the necessary troops. The army and the navy joined in attacking Manila, Aug. 13, and, after a few shots from Dewey's guns, the city surrendered.

Dewey's duty in the East lasted for a year after the battle of Manila Bay. Meanwhile enthusiasm at home knew no bounds, and a grateful Congress had created for him the rank of Admiral of the Navy, with the provision that he should not be placed on the retired list except by his own application. On his return he received an ovation of unprecedented brilliance in New York and elsewhere, and was presented a home in Washington by the American people. He was married on Nov. 9, 1899, to his second wife, Mrs. Mildred McLean Hazen. An unfortunate incident followed when he deeded to her the home that had been the gift of the nation, the incident calling forth much adverse criticism. Yielding to numerous suggestions that he become a candidate for the presidency of the United States, he gave out a public interview on Apr. 4, 1900, in which he said, "If the American people want me for this high office, I shall be only too willing to serve them . . . Since studying this subject I am convinced that the office of President is not such a very difficult one to fill." Popular support of his candidacy failed to develop, however, and his name was not brought up at either of the party conventions. Dewey was made president of the General Board of the Navy Department in 1900 on its inception, and held this office until his death seventeen years later. By his keen interest in its problems and by his prestige he gave power to that body such as otherwise it would not likely have had during the years following the Spanish-American War. His career "ran in full current to the end." He served in the navy, including the period at the Naval Academy, for over sixty-two years. Proud, especially in his old age, of his physical vigor he kept the existence of disease (arteriosclerosis) a secret even from close friends until a week from the end when, on Jan. 16, 1917, he died in Washington.

[*Autobiog. of Geo. Dewey* (1913); French Ensor Chadwick, *Relations of the U. S. and Spain* (1911), vol. I; *Official Records (Navy)*, vol. XVIII (for New Orleans) and vol. XIX (for Port Hudson); "Appendix to the Report of the Chief of the Bureau of Navigation, 1897–98," *House Doc. No. 3*, 55 Cong., 3 Sess. (for Manila Bay); R. F. Dibble, *Strenuous Americans* (1923); Mark Sullivan, *Our Times* (1926), vol. I.]
C. S. A.

DEWEY, ORVILLE (Mar. 28, 1794–Mar. 21, 1882), clergyman, author, was a son of Silas and Polly (Root) Dewey of Sheffield, Berkshire County, Mass. His boyhood was spent on his father's farm and at the district school. At sixteen he began to prepare for college under William H. Maynard and Elisha Lee of Sheffield, entered Williams College in the third term of sophomore year, and graduated with the valedictory in 1814. The next two years were spent in teaching at Sheffield and in business in New York. He graduated from Andover Seminary in 1819, spent eight months as agent for the American Education Society, and a year as pastor of the Congregational church at Gloucester, Mass. While a student at Andover he began to question the doctrine of the Trinity and during his Gloucester pastorate he became a Unitarian. His Unitarian pastorates were as follows: from 1821 to 1823 he was associated with Dr. Channing at the Federal Street Church in Boston; from 1823 to 1833, First Church, New Bedford, Mass.; from 1835 to 1848, Second Congregational Church (later Church of the Messiah), New York; from 1857 to 1861, New South Church, Church Green, Boston. He supplied Unitarian churches two winters each in Washington and in Albany and preached and lectured extensively. After his retirement from his New York pastorate, he lived mostly at his Sheffield home, where he died. He was the fourth president of the American Unitarian Association, serving from 1845 to 1847. Harvard gave him the degree of D.D. in 1839. He made several trips to Europe, and spent nearly two years there with his family, October 1841–August 1843. His Lowell lectures in 1851 on "The Problem of Human Destiny" (published under the same title in 1864) were given in various places and were afterward repeated in Boston at Lowell's request. He gave a second Lowell course in 1855 on the "Education of the Human Race." His publications include: *Discourses on Various Subjects* (1835); *The Old World and the New* (1836), the fruit of his first trip to Europe; *The Works of Orville Dewey* (1844, republished in 3 volumes, 1847) and numerous sermons and addresses. He was the first clerical member of the Artists' Club of New York, was deeply interested in social questions, and was a founder of the Employment Society which first put poor relief in that city on an organized basis. He was an opponent both of slavery and of abolitionism, thus subjecting himself to criticism in both North and South. After an attack of measles while in college, his eyesight was always defective and his work was several times interrupted by ill health.

He had a natural eloquence and preached on the great subjects with extraordinary insight and ability. He was an unusual interpreter of religious life, and has been characterized as "a man of unique power in the pulpit . . . in whom thought was more intimately blended with emotion than in any other great preacher we can bring to mind" (J. H. Allen, *The Unitarians*, American Church History Series, 1894). He retained his youthful spirit to an advanced age, and was a vivacious and charming companion. He was married, Dec. 26, 1820, to Louisa Farnham of Boston.

[*Autobiography and Letters of Orville Dewey*, ed. by his daughter, Mary E. Dewey (1883); J. H. Allen, *Hist. Sketch of the Unitarian Movement Since the Reformation* (Am. Ch. Hist. Ser., vol. X, 1894); W. H. Fowler, *The Am. Pulpit* (1856); Calvin Durfee, *Williams Biographical Annals* (1871).]
F. T. P.

DEWING, FRANCIS (fl. 1716–1722), was the first important engraver on copper in America. He sailed from London in the *Jollif Galley* commanded by Capt. John Aram and arrived in Boston on July 12, 1716. On July 30 he advertised in a local newspaper: "Lately arrived from London, Francis Dewing who Engraveth and Printeth Copper Plates, Likewise Coats of Arms and cyphers in Silver Plate. He Likewise Cuts Neatly in wood and Printeth Callicoes, etc. Lodging at Mrs. Hawksworths against the Bunch of Grapes in King Street." He executed the repeating designs which were cut upon heavy blocks of pear-wood and were used in printing cotton cloth. His engraving coats of arms would imply that he also engraved bookplates. When the Massachusetts Bay Colony first issued a paper currency in 1690 it was counterfeited so quickly and successfully that the treasury officials had difficulty in identifying their own currency: all engravers were suspect. The Town Clerk had carefully noted Dewing's arrival. On July 9, 1718, Gov. Shute issued a warrant for his arrest as Francis Doing, for "being suspected to be concerned in Counterfeiting the Bills of Credit of this Province, and searching his chamber and seizing any tools and materials that probably have been employed." He was probably cleared of the charge and on the following Jan. 7 Sheriff Edward Winslow was paid £4–10–0 for his expenses in making the arrest. Dewing married Katherin Hart on Dec. 8, 1719 (*Boston Marriages,* 1898, p. 98). He engraved Southack's "Sea Coast of English America and the French New Settlements" in 1716, Southack's "Canso Harbour" and his "Casco Bay" in 1720, and possibly the first issue of his "New York to Cape Breton" in the same year. His most important work was Capt. John Bonner's "The Town of Boston," which he engraved on copper in 1722. Authorities have thought that Dewing either died of the smallpox in Boston in 1723 or that he emigrated to St. Lucia in that year. In 1745, however, he was again in England and engraved a view of the East front of the New Organ in Salisbury Cathedral (Thomas Dodd, Memoirs of English Engravers, in British Museum).

[Justin Winsor, *Memorial Hist. of Boston,* vol. II (1881); Wm. Dunlap, *Hist. of the Rise and Progress of the Arts of Design in the U. S.,* vol. III (ed. 1918); David McNeely Stauffer, *Am. Engravers upon Copper and Steel,* vol. I (1907); Brit. Mus. Add. MSS. 33,400; information from A. E. Popham of Brit. Mus. and C. S. Brigham of the Am. Antiquarian Soc.] F. M.

DEWING, MARIA RICHARDS OAKEY (Oct. 27, 1845–Dec. 13, 1927), painter, the daughter of William Francis and Sally (Sullivan) Oakey, was born in New York City. After a period of study at the National Academy of Design and under John La Farge and Dr. Rimmer, in 1876 she went to London, Italy, and France, while in Paris being a pupil of Thomas Couture. Returning to the United States she published *From Attic to Cellar: A Book for Young Housekeepers* (1879), which was followed by *Beauty in Dress* (1881) and *Beauty in the Household* (1882). She also contributed to magazines. On Apr. 18, 1881, she was married to Thomas Wilmer Dewing, an American painter who during the previous year had opened a studio in New York City.

For some years Mrs. Dewing devoted her efforts chiefly to painting flowers out-of-doors, in the garden of her summer home in Cornish, N. H. In later years she painted both figures and portraits in her New York studio. Because of her long residence in New York, she had a wide circle of friends and in her professional contacts met practically all the foremost artists of her time. Her work was delicate and refined, yet vigorous. In referring appreciatively to the salient features of her art, Royal Cortissoz has emphasized her deep feeling for beauty and intensely individual touch; her rare ability to interpret the soul, the genius of a flower, with marked originality of vision. She will be gratefully remembered for her inspiring contribution to the dignity of flower painting in which she was rivaled only by La Farge in America and Fantin-Latour in France (*New York Herald Tribune,* Dec. 18, 1927). Her life-size "Mother and Child" exhibited at the 1927 Winter Academy Exhibit, is full of delicacy, charm and sentiment, strengthened by a fine harmony of color. It represents another phase of her versatility and evoked warm tribute as showing an art of profound distinction (*New York Times,* Dec. 4, 1927). She was awarded a bronze medal at the Columbian Exposition, Chicago, 1893, and also at the Pan-American Exposition, Buffalo, 1901.

Notable flower pictures painted out-of-doors were: "Poppies and Italian Mignonette," "Rose Garden, Roses with Border of White Carnations," "In the Springtime, Persian Lilacs, Narcissus Poeticus, Flowering Almond," "White Mountain Roses," "Iris at Dawn," "Marigold and Ribbon Grass." Among her flower pictures painted in the studio were "The Cabbage Rose," also called "Provence and Centifolia," "Carnations in Japanese Vase," "Carnations in a Satsuma Vase," "Souvenir de Mal Maison Roses," painted in extreme youth, "Roses Against Antique Brocade," "An Oak Wreath," "Marigolds in a Glass," "The Peacock Fan with Roses," "Heliotrope and Daphne Odorata," "Annual Phlox." Figure pictures were "The Mother," "The Prelude," "The Rose," "In Italy," "Child with Doll," "Elizabeth Dewing at the Age of Six Months," "Sketch for Portrait of My Father, William Francis Oakey." Taken together, these pictures enumerated are representative of the work of Maria Dewing in its various phases.

She died in her New York studio, survived by her husband and a daughter.

[Pa. Acad. of the Fine Arts, *An Exhibition of Paintings of Maria Oakey Dewing* (Mar. 1–23, 1907); B. F. Dewing, *Descendants of Andrew Dewing of Dedham, Mass.* (1904), p. 108; Mich. State Lib., *Biog. Sketches of Am. Artists* (1912), p. 96; *Who's Who in America*, 1924–25; *Am. Art Annual*, XXIV (1917), 540; J. D. Champlin, Jr., *Cyc. of Painters and Painting* (1886), I, 401; family data; date of birth verified by Mr. Thomas Wilmer Dewing.] J. M. H.

DEWITT, SIMEON (Dec. 25, 1756–Dec. 3, 1834), surveyor-general of New York, was born at Wawarsing, Ulster County, N. Y., the son of Dr. Andries and Jannetje (Vernooy) DeWitt. After having received such an English education as a colonial rural community could afford, he was placed with the Rev. Dr. Romeyn of Schenectady to prepare for college, and in due time entered Queen's (now Rutgers) College in New Jersey. His course, however, was sadly interrupted by the Revolution, for the British burned the college buildings and dispersed the students. In spite of this break, he was awarded the bachelor's degree in 1776 and twelve years later received from the same institution the master's degree. With the closing of the college, he returned to his home and pursued his studies as he found opportunity; but when the whole state rose in arms to repel Burgoyne's invasion, he joined a battalion being formed in Ulster County and was given the rank of adjutant. Upon reaching the scene of action, this unit was absorbed into another regiment and DeWitt, deprived of his command, became a private, and in this capacity participated in the battles that led up to Burgoyne's surrender. This emergency over, he again went home and continued his mathematical studies, combining with these an attention to the practical business of surveying which served him in good stead when Gen. Washington wrote to his uncle, Gen. James Clinton, inquiring if he knew of any person qualified to act as geographer to the army. DeWitt was immediately recommended and in 1778 was appointed as assistant to Col. Robert Erskine, then geographer-in-chief. Upon the death of Col. Erskine in 1780, DeWitt became the head of the department. Ordered to headquarters by Gen. Washington in December of that year, he remained attached to the main army until the end of the campaign. This led him to Yorktown where he witnessed the surrender of Cornwallis. Besides making the necessary surveys and maps for the conduct of military operations, he prepared an interesting series of maps showing the course of the war. This he tried to induce Congress to publish but the state of the public finances forbade it.

At the close of the Revolution, he planned to go on with his surveying work, and, on May 13, 1784, upon the resignation of Gen. Philip Schuyler as surveyor-general for New York State, he was appointed to the office. For over fifty years he served the state in this capacity. In 1786–87 he was one of the commissioners actively engaged in delineating the boundary between New York and Pennsylvania and during this same period began work upon a map of New York which was finally published in 1802. This map is an index even to this day of what the state was at that time. Offered the position of surveyor-general to the United States by Washington in 1796, he reluctantly declined the honor and remained with his work in New York. When the state adopted its canal policy, the surveyor-general was naturally chosen one of the commissioners for "exploring the whole route, examining the present condition of . . . navigation, and considering what further improvement ought to be made therein" (Whitford, *post*, p. 63).

Although busy with these regular duties, he found time to engage in educational and scientific matters. He served the University of the State of New York from 1798 until his death, first as a regent, then as vice-chancellor, and finally, after 1829, as chancellor. In this latter office, he originated the taking of meteorological observations by every academy under the board. As early as 1790 he was a member of the American Philosophical Society, and he contributed to the sixth volume of its *Transactions* (1809), a communication entitled "Observations on the Eclipse of the Sun, June 16, 1806, at Albany." He was also one of the charter members of the Society for the Promotion of Agriculture, Arts and Manufactures, founded in New York in 1793, and in 1813 became its second president. Upon the establishment of the state Board of Agriculture, the Society was merged with the Lyceum of Natural History as Albany Institute, and for many years DeWitt served this body as vice-president. To the older organization he contributed two papers: one "On a Plan of a Meteorological Chart," and the other on "Establishment of a Meridian Line in the City of Albany," while his writings for the *Transactions* of Albany Institute were "A Table of Variations of the Magnetic Needle," "Observations on the Functions of the Moon, Deduced from the Eclipse of 1806," and "A Description of a New Form of Rain Gauge." In *American Journal of Science* he discussed the theory of meteors; and in 1813 his writings upon drawing and perspective were published in book form under the title, *The Elements of Perspective.*

DeWitt married three times. His first wife

was Elizabeth Lynott, whom he married on Oct. 12, 1789. Her death occurred in 1793 and he later married Jane Varick Hardenberg, by whom he had six children. After the latter's death, he married, on Oct. 29, 1810, Susan Linn, daughter of the Rev. William Linn. DeWitt died at Ithaca, N. Y., on Dec. 3, 1834.

[T. Romeyn Beck, *Eulogium on Life and Services of Simeon DeWitt* (1835); B. J. Lossing, *The Empire State* (1887); Cuyler Reynolds, *Hudson-Mohawk Geneal. and Family Memoirs* (1911), I, 364–66; N. E. Whitford, "Hist. of the Canal System of the State of N. Y.," *Ann. Report of* (N. Y.) *State Engineer and Surveyor*, Supp., 1905; Jas. G. Wilson, *Memorial Hist. of the City of N. Y.*, vols. III and IV, *passim*; Thos. G. Evans, *The DeWitt family of Ulster County, N. Y.* (1886).]
G. H. B.

DE WOLF, JAMES (Mar. 18, 1764–Dec. 21, 1837), slave-trader, manufacturer, senator, was born in Bristol County, R. I., and was the seventh son of Mark A. and Abigail (Potter) De Wolf. Both his father and his uncle Simeon Potter were seafaring men, and had been interested in slave-trading in French Guinea. The family was poor and the boys hoed corn on their father's farm until, throwing down their hoes, they walked to Providence and sailed upon one of Potter's privateers. This was during the Revolutionary War and the sea was infested with private pirates who increased in audacity and lucrative gain after the French Revolution. James De Wolf went through wild experiences. He fought in many naval battles, was captured twice by the enemy, and once was imprisoned. The result of this cruelty and hardship made him a man of force and indomitable energy with no nice ethical distinctions. Before his twentieth birthday he was master of a ship and before he was twenty-five he had accumulated wealth enough to make him independent for the rest of his life.

His earliest voyages were made to Africa where he seized and transported Africans as slaves to the West Indies. Providence merchants of highest commercial and social standing backed him in this trade. Apparently he had no qualms of conscience, and often went to Southern ports personally to supervise the sale of his captives. He was careful to follow the lines of largest profit. As long as the slave-trade was flourishing after the Revolutionary War, his ships were in it. Later some of them turned to the furs of the northwest coast, then to whale-fishing, and finally even went to China. His principal trade, however, was always in the West Indies, and when, in 1804, South Carolina threw open her ports to the importation of slaves because of the threatened national prohibition, De Wolf leaped to aid, and ten of the 202 vessels that entered Charleston between 1804 and 1808 belonged to him.

The attitude of England during the Napoleonic Wars greatly angered and embarrassed De Wolf and he sustained heavy losses through the impressment of seamen. He was a strong advocate of war with England and eleven days after the declaration of the War of 1812, he offered the government at his own expense "an armed Brig (one of the most suitable in this country for a Privateer), of one hundred and sixty tons burthen, mounting eighteen guns and carries one hundred and twenty men, called the *Yankee*, commanded by Oliver Wilson." The *Yankee* was immensely successful. It made six cruises in less than three years and captured more than five million dollars' worth of British property.

After the close of the war, De Wolf sensed the coming development of manufactures in the United States. Gradually he withdrew his capital from shipping and he had already built one of the earliest cotton-mills in the United States, at Coventry, R. I., in 1812. He sensed, too, that the new industry needed political influence. For thirty years he represented the town of Bristol in the Rhode Island legislature, becoming finally speaker of the House. In 1821 he was elected to the United States Senate. Here he was a strong advocate of protection for the new young industries and he opposed the extension of slavery to Missouri and the West. His interest now was no longer in the African slave but in the white mill laborer. He did not like the atmosphere of Washington and resigned his seat in the Senate in 1825 and returned to the legislature of Rhode Island. He made the town of Bristol his especial care. Here on a great estate of one thousand acres, he built himself a stately mansion, and devised many schemes for the advancement of the town and its industries. De Wolf was tall and commanding in person and very careful about his dress. He married Nancy Bradford, a daughter of William Bradford, and died in New York City.

[W. H. Munro, *Hist. of Bristol, R. I.* (1880), and *Tales of an Old Sea Port* (1917); C. B. Perry, *Charles D'Wolf of Guadaloupe, His Ancestors and Descendants* (1902); G. M. Fessenden, *Geneal. Memoir of the Descendants of Wm. Bradford* (1850).] W. E. B. D.

DEXTER, FRANKLIN (Nov. 5, 1793–Aug. 14, 1857), lawyer, the son of Samuel Dexter [*q.v.*] and of his wife Catherine (Gordon) Dexter, was born in Charlestown, Mass. He received his early education in the public schools, and, proceeding to Harvard College, graduated there in 1812. He then read law with Samuel Hubbard and was admitted to practise in the court of common pleas, Suffolk County, September 1815, and in the supreme judicial court, December 1818. On Sept. 28, 1819, he was married to Catherine Elizabeth, daughter of Judge William Prescott of Boston. He commenced practise in Boston and from the first evinced great interest in public affairs. In 1825 he was elected representative from Boston in the Massachusetts House of Representatives, in the same year also becoming a member of the Common Council of Boston. The first occasion upon which he came prominently before the public was the trial of Theodore Lyman for a criminal libel upon Daniel Webster in the *Jackson Republican,* Oct. 29, 1828. He was retained for the defense, which he conducted with great ability, and the jury were unable to agree, a nolle prosequi being subsequently entered on behalf of the Commonwealth (12 *American State Trials,* 327). This case attracted national attention owing to its political attributes. In 1830 as counsel for defense of the two Knapps in connection with the murder of Joseph White at Salem he at once stepped into the foremost rank as an advocate. The Commonwealth had retained Daniel Webster on the trial of John Francis Knapp who was charged with murder, and after a ten days' hearing, the jury disagreed, but at the new trial the accused was found guilty, as was also Joseph Jenkins Knapp, Jr., who was charged as an accessory (7 *American State Trials,* 395). Though both prisoners were hanged, Dexter's conduct of the defense was considered masterly. In 1835 he was elected state senator and in 1836 again became representative from Boston in the legislature, serving on this occasion as a member of the Select Committee on Revision of Statutes. In 1840 he was associated with another Boston *cause célèbre,* the trial of Mrs. Kenney for the murder of her husband, appearing for the defense and securing an acquittal. In 1841 he was appointed by President Harrison United States district attorney for Massachusetts and retained this position for four years exhibiting "the most exact appreciation of the duties of his station and every qualification for their performance" (*Monthly Law Reporter,* X, 316). In 1848–49 he was a lecturer at Harvard Law School. He was reappointed district attorney by President Taylor in 1849, but held office only a short time. He had practically retired from professional work at this period, and devoted the remainder of his life to travel and literary study. He died at Beverly, Mass.

Although he was conspicuous among his contemporaries for his sound legal knowledge, possessing outstanding ability as an advocate and equipped with every qualification for public life, Dexter's achievements fell far short of his intellectual promise. The possession of independent means obviated the necessity of continuous and sustained effort to put forth his best, and posterity can only judge him by his record in the three great cases with which his name is associated.

[See O. P. Dexter, *Dexter Geneal.* (1904), p. 136; W. T. Davis, *Professional and Industrial Hist. of Suffolk County, Mass.* (1894), I, 568; *Proc. Mass. Hist. Soc.,* XIX (1881–82); Jos. Palmer, in *Boston Daily Advertiser,* July 21, 1858, reprinted in Palmer's *Necrology of Alumni of Harvard Coll.* (1864). For the memorial meetings of the supreme judicial court and the Suffolk bar, see the *Boston Daily Advertiser,* Sept. 9, 1857.] H. W. H. K.

DEXTER, FRANKLIN BOWDITCH (Sept. 11, 1842–Aug. 13, 1920), antiquarian and historian, was born in Fairhaven, Mass., where his father, Rodolphus Williams Dexter—a direct descendant of the Puritan Thomas Dexter of Bristol, England, who in 1630 was settled at Lynn, Mass.—was engaged in business. His mother, Mary Hathaway Taber, was also of old New England stock. He prepared for college at a typical New England school, Williston Seminary, and entered Yale with the class of 1861. He proved himself a painstaking and competent, rather than brilliant, scholar, graduating with membership in Phi Beta Kappa. For two years after graduation he taught Greek in Gen. Russell's "Collegiate and Commercial Institute" in New Haven, and then (in 1863) entered the service of Yale University, holding in turn the following positions: librarian of the Linonian Society (1863); tutor in Yale College, first in mathematics, later in Greek (1864–67); assistant in the College Library (1867–68); assistant in the Treasurer's office (1868–69); assistant librarian of the College (1869–1912); registrar of the College Faculty (1869–92); secretary of the Yale Corporation (1869–99); Larned Professor of American History (1877–88); assistant librarian emeritus (1912–20).

His entire life, from 1857, when he entered Yale College, until his death sixty-three years later, was spent in New Haven, and except for the two years of his school-teaching he gave his time almost exclusively to the interests of the University. His gifts were not those of an administrator or of a teacher. His mind was mainly concerned with ascertaining historical facts regarding Yale College, its graduates, and its city, and in publishing them with extraordinary accuracy and completeness. He was happy if he could run down information hitherto not generally known and was content to state it succinctly in volumes that were extremely well arranged, well annotated, and well indexed, and that showed throughout that capacity for meticulous research characteristic of great antiquarians. Of the philosophy of history and of the interpretation of events, there was practically none.

In addition to more or less routine University publications, all of which he greatly improved, and three editions of the new *Acts of the General Assembly of the State of Connecticut with other Permanent Documents respecting Yale College* (1871, 1878, 1889), he published: *Roll of Honor* (1866), a roll of the alumni of Yale in the United States service 1861–65, reprinted with additions in Kingsley's *Yale College, a Sketch of its History* (1879); *The College Hymnal for Divine Service in the Battell Chapel* (1876); *Sketch of the History of Yale University* (1887); *A Catalogue, with Descriptive Notices, of the Portraits, Busts, etc. belonging to Yale University* (1892); *Diary of David McClure, Doctor of Divinity, 1748–1820* (1899); *Literary Diary of Ezra Stiles, D.D., LL.D.* (1901), in three volumes, a work of special value to every student of New England history because of its thorough editing and full notes; *Biographical Notices of Graduates of Yale College, including those graduated in classes later than 1815, who are not Commemorated in the Annual Obituary Records* (Supplement to *Obituary Record*, 1913); *Documentary History of Yale University, 1701–1745* (1916); *Extracts from the Itineraries and other Miscellanies of Ezra Stiles, 1755–1794* (1916); *Jared Ingersoll Papers* (1918). New Haven as the home of Yale College and as the home of his wife's Davenport ancestors also greatly interested him. Among his publications in this congenial field of research were: *The First Public Library in New Haven* (1900); *Historical Catalogue of the Members of the First Church of Christ in New Haven . . . 1639–1914* (1914); and *New Haven Town Records, 1649–1662* and *1662–1684*, two volumes (1917, 1919).

The most important of his literary labors is his *Biographical Sketches of the Graduates of Yale College with Annals of the College History*, commonly referred to by its cover title of *Yale Biographies and Annals*. This includes the classes from 1701 to 1815, after which date competent class records began to be published, and is contained in six volumes published from 1885 to 1912. The work, suggested by Sibley's *Biographical Sketches of Graduates of Harvard University* (1873–85), contains the College Annals for each year, followed by the biographies of all men graduating in that year. It is a monumental work of reference, devoid of any attempt at literary charm, but so accurate and exhaustive that although new editions may be called for, it will never be superseded. Among his other writings two may be mentioned as of specially broad interest and value: *The Influence of the English Universities in the Development of New England* (1880) and *Estimates of Population in the American Colonies* (1887). These are both included in *A Selection from the Miscellaneous Historical Papers of Fifty Years* (1919). For forty years, from 1867 to 1907, he was directly responsible for the catalogue of the University Library, which increased in this period from about 50,000 to nearly 400,000 books, writing in his own hand tens of thousands of library cards. He also prepared and published *A Catalogue of the Linonian and Brothers Library* (1873), and was engaged in his seventy-seventh year, just prior to his death, in preparing an "author list" of the manuscripts in the Library.

His industry was as prodigious as his scholarship was exact, and his loyalty to Yale unbounded. He was over six feet tall, and of slender build, and had a quick, nervous manner and walk. He was shy and reserved, playing no part in public life and little part in social life, except for attending the fortnightly meetings of "The Club"—a dining club made up mostly of older members of the Faculty. He was a member of the Massachusetts Historical Society, and foreign secretary and a member of the Council of the American Antiquarian Society. He was a Congregationalist, attending regularly the College Church Sunday mornings, until late in life when he transferred his membership to the Center Church. His wife, who survived him, was Theodosia Mary Wheeler, daughter of Russell Wheeler of New York City.

[In addition to Dexter's writings, and personal acquaintance over a period of twenty-five years, the principal authorities for the above sketch have been the *Yale Univ. Obit. Record* for 1921–22; the various *Records* of the Class of 1861, Yale College; resolutions of the Yale Corporation, Sept. 11, 1920; and a sketch of his life under the title "The Annalist of Yale" in the *Yale Alumni Weekly*, Oct. 15, 1920. His portrait, painted in 1913 by Paul K. M. Thomas, is in the Yale Library. An earlier picture is reproduced in Kingsley's *Yale College*.] A. P. S.

DEXTER, HENRY (Oct. 11, 1806–June 23, 1876), sculptor, son of Smith and Clarasa (Dexter) Dexter, was born in grim poverty on a wilderness-surrounded farm in Nelson, N. Y., where his parents had settled the year before. He could trace his ancestry through eight generations to the Rev. Gregory Dexter of Olney, England, called the first educated printer in New England, who in London in 1643 printed for Roger Williams a dictionary of the Indian language and in the following year accompanied Williams to Providence. Henry's childish impulse toward art was inborn. Having neither canvas, colors, nor the money with which to buy them, he painted on scraps of cloth with the juice of red and green berries. His efforts met reproof as signs of sinfulness. When he was eleven years old, his father disappeared. His mother was from Connecticut, and returning thither, placed the boy on a Connecticut farm, where he worked industriously three years. He was kindly treated, went to school in winter, and stood at the head of his class. At sixteen, much against his secret hope for an artist's career, he was apprenticed to a blacksmith. In 1828, having mastered his craft, he married Calista Kelley, daughter of Ebenezer Kelley and niece of the enterprising portrait-painter, Francis Alexander [*q.v.*], a man but six years Dexter's senior. Alexander dissuaded him from trying to make likenesses for a living, and induced him to work at his trade seven years longer. At last, in the spring of 1836, Dexter went to Providence, R. I., where he opened a studio, and for some months painted likenesses, first at five, then at ten, then at fifteen, and finally at twenty dollars apiece, Alexander giving him friendly counsel. That autumn, he moved to Boston, where, acting on a chance suggestion to make use of some clay left by the sculptor Greenough, he attempted the modeling of portrait-busts. Having completed in marble (1838) the portrait of Samuel A. Eliot, mayor of Boston, he presently received commissions for busts of other distinguished men. Among his sitters were Longfellow, Agassiz, Henry Wilson, Anson Burlingame, Prof. C. C. Felton of Harvard, and Charles Dickens. While the novelist was sitting, Dexter's studio was a rendezvous for the élite of Boston. Both Dickens and his wife expressed pleasure in the portrait when completed.

Dexter's success in portrait-busts (he is said to have made nearly two hundred) shows what could be done by a self-taught pioneer, inventive, industrious, and agreeable, working in a circle of intelligent and even intellectual persons, at a time when knowledge of the art of sculpture was extremely limited in the United States. Undoubtedly his training as a blacksmith was of service, not only because of the skill of hand gained thereby, but because of the ability it gave him to make and keep in condition the tools necessary in marble cutting. Also, he had a gift for "catching the likeness," and this was mainly what his sitters wanted. In 1857 his wife died, and two years later he married Mrs. Martha Billings of Millbury, Mass. He had just formed an interesting project of making portrait-busts of all the governors in the United States. As a prelude, taking with him a letter from Edward Everett, he went to Washington, where he was favorably received by President Buchanan, whose bust he made. He thereupon began his tour as itinerant sculptor of governors, visiting every state but California and Oregon. In 1860 he returned to Boston with his plaster casts of thirty-one portraits, exhibiting these casts in the State House rotunda, and preparing to immortalize their subjects in marble. Unfortunately the Civil War defeated this ambition; only four of the portraits were made permanent. The collection was largely dispersed, history, if not art, losing thereby. Dexter's eight marble statues, ranging from the "Binney Child," Mt. Auburn Cemetery (1839), to the "Gen. Warren," Charlestown (1857), appear to-day of little importance, however remarkable they may be as the work of a self-taught artist, who before his own attempts had never seen any one model in clay or carve in marble. Dexter's nature was at once sensitive and energetic. He enjoyed music and poetry, and wrote interestingly of his experiences. He died in Boston at the age of seventy, honored and beloved.

[John Albee, *Henry Dexter* (privately printed, 1898); Lorado Taft, *Hist. of Am. Sculpture* (1903); S. C. Newman, *Dexter Genealogy* (1859).] A. A.

DEXTER, HENRY (Mar. 14, 1813–July 11, 1910), business man, the son of Jonathan Marsh and Elizabeth (Balch) Dexter, and a descendant of Richard Dexter, who was admitted freeman of Boston in 1642, was born at West Cambridge, Mass. He was educated in public and private schools. Beginning in his fourteenth year he served a three-year apprenticeship in a Boston printing office. Although he never attended Harvard College as he had desired to do at one time, that institution contributed greatly to his education through opportunities offered him during three years which he spent as second foreman in the printing office of the college. He went to New York in 1836 and six years later bought an interest in the firm of Dexter & Tuttle, dealers in books, periodicals, and daily newspapers, having had, meanwhile, several years of business experience including employment in a hardware store conducted by the Whittemores, inventors of the carding machine. The firm of Dexter & Tuttle later became Dexter & Brother, then Henry Dexter & Company, and still later H. Dexter, Hamilton & Company. Dexter's greatest achievement was a consolidation of leading newspaper dealers which developed into the present American News Company of which he was president for many years until 1896. He organized a similar London corporation, the International News Company.

On Oct. 11, 1853, he was married to Lucretia Marquand Perry. He was greatly interested in civic projects. He gave liberally to the Metropolitan Museum of Art at the time of its founding and contributed approximately $225,000 toward the building of the present home of the New York Historical Society. A dispute arose over this gift. On the day the building was opened Dexter caused pamphlets to be distributed to the guests stating that he had erected it in memory of his only son, Orrando Perry Dexter. Trustees of the society stopped distribution of the pamphlets, claiming that Dexter did not have a right to claim the building as his own since the society had put some $171,000 into its construction in addition to his gift and had supplied the valuable site for the building. One room of the New York Historical Society building is known as Henry Dexter Hall and an ornamental doorway leading into the lecture hall memorializes his son.

The extent of Dexter's interest in reform movements and in philanthropy is indicated by the long list of organizations with which he was connected. He was vice-president of the Protestant Episcopal Church Missionary Society for Seamen, trustee of the Midnight Mission, life director of the American Bible Society and American Tract Society, and member of the New York Society for the Prevention of Cruelty to Children, St. Luke's Hospital Society, the Children's Aid Society, the Home for Incurables, the Charity Organization Society, the New York Association for Improving the Condition of the Poor, and the Home for Aged Married Couples. Not long before his death, he published a collection of his letters written to newspapers on various topics between his nineteenth and ninety-fourth birthdays.

[*Who's Who in New York City and State*, 1907; *N. Y. Times*, July 12, 1910; Orrando Perry Dexter, *Dexter Geneal. 1642–1904* (1904), pp. 160–63; Moses King, *Notable New Yorkers 1896–99* (1899), p. 315.]
D. W. M.

DEXTER, HENRY MARTYN (Aug. 13, 1821–Nov. 13, 1890), Congregational clergyman, was born at Plympton, Plymouth County, Mass. He was the son of the Rev. Elijah and Mary (Morton) Dexter, and sixth in descent from Thomas Dexter, who was a prominent colonist of Lynn by 1630. Elijah Dexter was a graduate of Brown University and for more than forty-two years pastor of the Congregational Church at Plympton. In 1836, at the age of fifteen, Henry entered Brown, changing in his sophomore year to Yale, where he graduated in 1840, having partially supported himself by teaching summers during his college course. On graduation he became principal of the Academy at Rochester, Mass., for a year, after which he attended Andover Theological Seminary, graduating in 1844. On Nov. 6 of that year he was ordained pastor of the newly organized church in Manchester, N. H., where he remained for four and a half years. He was married to Emeline Augusta Palmer, daughter of Simeon Palmer of Boston on Nov. 19, 1844. On Apr. 18, 1849, he became pastor of the Pine Street Church in Boston and continued there for eighteen years in spite of internal troubles in the church which were not of his own making. A few months after his move to Boston he became a special contributor to the newly established *Congregationalist*, and for some years was special correspondent of the New York *Independent*. In October 1851 he became a member of the editorial staff of the *Congregationalist*, a post he retained, with an interval of a year, until his death. From 1856 he was editor-in-chief. In 1854 he took the leadership of the New England clergy in drawing up resolutions opposing the Nebraska Bill, going to Washington to present the protest personally to Congress. In the same year he moved to Roxbury. In 1858 he helped to found the *Congregational Quarterly*. In 1867 he had a call, which had been made previously also, to a church in California, and was about to accept when he was offered the editorship and partial ownership of the combined *Congregationalist* and *Boston Recorder*. He resigned his pastorate and from that time devoted himself to editorial and historical work, from 1873 making his home in New Bedford.

Dexter's passion for the advancement of Congregationalism was life-long. He wrote much on that topic and also on early New England history. Among his more important books may be mentioned: *Congregationalism* (1865); *The Church Policy of the Pilgrims* (1870); *As to Roger Williams* (1876); *The Congregationalism of the Last 300 Years* (1880); *A Handbook of Congregationalism* (1880). His writings for the periodical press were voluminous, and his editorial contribution of considerable value, in the case of such works as *Mourt's Relation* and Church's *King Philip's War*. Much of his writing was special pleading and marred by his strong bias in favor of the Puritans and Congregationalists, but it was accurate in detail. He was a member of many historical societies, including the Massachusetts Historical and the American Antiquarian. He was chairman of the committee appointed to erect in Leyden a memorial to John Robinson. He was an indefatigable worker, a competent scholar, and in constant demand as preacher and lecturer. He took an active part in the ecclesiastical affairs and controversies of his day. In 1890 he was chosen one of the representatives of American Congregationalism at the Conference held in London, but was found dead in his bed on Nov. 13 of that year.

[Wm. A. Warden and Robt. L. Dexter, *Geneal. of the Dexter Family in America* (1905); *Proc. Mass. Hist. Soc.*, 2 ser. VI (1891); sketch by John E. Sanford, *Ibid.*, VII (1892), 90–103, with a bibliography of Dexter's more important writings.] J. T. A.

DEXTER, SAMUEL (Mar. 16, 1726–June 10, 1810), merchant, was descended from Richard Dexter, a native of County Meath, Ireland, who was admitted a townsman of Boston, Mass., in 1642 and settled at Malden. His great-grandson, the Rev. Samuel Dexter, married Catherina Mears, and their eldest son, Samuel, was born at Dedham, Mass., where his father was minister of the First Church. He was apprenticed to a merchant in Boston and later built up a prosperous business of his own in that town. He married Hannah, daughter of Andrew Sigourney, and when thirty-six years of age retired to Dedham with a modest fortune. In the troublous years 1764–68 he represented his native town in the General Court (Herman Mann, *Historical Annals of Dedham*, 1847, p. 106) and from 1768 to 1774 he was a member of the Council (*Monthly Anthology*, IX, 5). In 1774 his election to the Council was negatived by Gov. Gage because of Dexter's political sentiments. In the first Provincial Congress he was one of the delegates from Dedham (*Journals of Each Provincial Congress of Massachusetts*, 1838, p. 7) and was placed on the committee to provide for the public defense; subsequently he was one of the committee for the support of the army besieging Boston. He differed with his associates in regard to the conduct of the war, believing that better results could be accomplished by withdrawing the army from the siege and training it efficiently for a vigorous campaign. In July 1775 he retired to private life. This induced a popular suspicion that he had become a lukewarm patriot. Dexter disdained to justify his action, left Dedham, and established himself in Woodstock, Conn., where he resided about ten years. He appears to have returned to Dedham in or before 1785, for in that year he was a representative from that town in the General Court. In 1786 he moved to Weston, Mass., and made his home there till 1800. The closing years of his life were spent in Mendon, Mass. Samuel Dexter [*q.v.*], born in 1761, was his youngest child.

By his will Dexter bequeathed $5,000 to Harvard College to promote critical study of the Bible. This bequest reflected his profound interest in the Scriptures and his longing for the truth. His benevolence expressed itself throughout his life in unostentatious generosity to the poor and by contributions to educational and charitable institutions. One of the provisions of his will stipulated that he was to be buried in a certain field in Woodstock, Conn., in such manner that his grave might not be visible after the earth had settled; no monument should mark where his body lay. A pamphlet of sixty pages entitled *Thoughts Upon Several Passages of Scripture, Both in the Old and New Testament, Relative to Jacob and Esau with Incidental Excursions* (Worcester, 1791) is probably the only one of his writings which he printed. This he issued under the pseudonym "Philotheorus." In it he defends Esau, expresses doubt as to his eternal damnation, and suggests that a more careful study of the original text would sustain this view. Dexter's belief in a just God was stronger than his belief in orthodox Calvinism.

[The most comprehensive account of Dexter's life is in Clarence Winthrop Bowen's admirable *Hist. of Woodstock, Conn.* (1926), pp. 179–95. It is the result of long, careful study, abounds in helpful references, and includes a portrait by Maj. John Johnston. A sketch by C. A. Staples, *Samuel Dexter*, containing a portrait and other illustrations, was printed in *Dedham Hist. Reg.*, Apr. 1892, and was also published (1892) in pamphlet form. Glimpses of Dexter are given in Sidney Willard, *Memories of Youth and Manhood* (1855), II, 68–72; and in Herman Mann, *Hist. Annals of Dedham* (1847); and the family genealogy in O. P. Dexter, *Dexter Geneal.* (1904). A number of Dexter's letters are preserved in the library of the Mass. Hist. Soc. An excellent obituary by Samuel Dexter, Jr., is in *Monthly Anthology*, IX, 3–7 (July 1810).] L. S. M.

DEXTER, SAMUEL (May 14, 1761–May 4, 1816), lawyer, was born at Boston, Mass., the youngest child of Samuel [*q.v.*] and Hannah (Sigourney) Dexter. Brought up with great care, he received a thorough classical education at the hands of the Rev. Aaron Putnam of Pomfret, and entered Harvard College in 1777 where he graduated in 1781 with highest honors. He then studied law at Worcester, Mass., with Levi Lincoln and was admitted to the Worcester County bar in 1784. He commenced practise in Lunenberg in 1786, but moved to Chelmsford and later to Billerica, finally establishing himself at Charlestown in 1788. He was in the same year elected a member of the state House of Representatives from Charlestown, and during his two years in that body acquired a wide reputation for sound judgment, and exercised great influence over its deliberations. In 1792 he was elected Federalist representative of Middlesex, Mass., in the Third Congress and served as such till Mar. 3, 1795. Four years later he was elected United States senator from Massachusetts, occupying that position from Dec. 2, 1799 till June

1800, when he resigned in order to enter the cabinet of President Adams as secretary of war, to which office he had been appointed on May 13. He remained head of the War Department until Dec. 31 of that year, when he became secretary of the treasury. His temperament and intellectual endowment ill suited him for that minute diligence and attention to intricate details which the departments of War and Finance impose on incumbents of office, but his application was intense and his success undoubted (Story, *post*). For a short period he, in addition, executed the office of secretary of state in order to administer the oath of office to John Marshall on the latter's appointment as chief justice of the United States. Shortly before the termination of the Adams administration the President offered him a foreign embassy but he declined and remained in office till after the accession of Jefferson, when Gallatin succeeded him on Jan. 26, 1802. He then moved to Roxbury, Mass., and resumed the practise of law. Partially withdrawing from political activities, he devoted himself to his profession, and in a short time attained a commanding position at the bar, being constantly retained in the higher state courts and particularly in the Supreme Court of the United States. In 1807 he appeared as leading counsel for the defense of Thomas O. Selfridge, charged with the murder of Charles Austin, a Harvard student. The prominent position of all the participants caused intense interest to be taken in the proceedings, which resulted in a verdict of acquittal (2 *American State Trials,* 544). In his address to the jury Dexter is said to have "combined the closest reasoning with the most finished eloquence" (Davis, *post*). He had always manifested considerable independence of thought, invariably approaching both political and legal problems in his own way, and his attitude in the matter of the War of 1812 was thoroughly characteristic. He believed that the war was a just one and, declining to follow the Federalists, actively supported the policy of the government in that respect, but was vehemently opposed to the Embargo and non-intercourse policy, and unsuccessfully contested its constitutionality. In 1815 he was offered an extraordinary mission to the Court of Spain by President Madison, which he declined. In 1814 and 1815 he was an unsuccessful candidate for governor of Massachusetts, disclaiming all sympathy with Madison's policy apart from his attitude toward Great Britain. He died at Athens, N. Y. On Mar. 7, 1786, he married Catherine, daughter of William Gordon of Charlestown, and Franklin Dexter [*q.v.*] was their son.

Dexter was inclined to be reserved, precise, and formal in manner, and his appearance on public occasions was not impressive. He had a strong dislike for mass meetings at which he never appeared to advantage. Possessed of rare intellectual gifts, however, he enjoyed a prestige both in Congress and the courts of last resort which placed him in the first rank of contemporary public men. At the same time it is doubtful whether he was profoundly learned. One who knew him well says that the impression was that he read few professional books (Sargent, *post*), and Story bears testimony to the fact that he referred to "black lettered law" as "the scholastic refinements of monkish ages." A poem, *The Progress of Science* (1780), and a biographical notice of his father in the *Monthly Anthology and Boston Review,* July 10, 1810, are the most noteworthy of his published writings.

[Dexter's ancestry is traced in O. P. Dexter, *Dexter Genealogy 1642–1904* (1904), which also contains (p. 86) a short biography. Judge Story's "Sketch of the life and character of the Hon. Samuel Dexter" in 1 *Mason,* 523, and *Reminiscences of Samuel Dexter* (1857), by Lucius Manlius Sargent under the pseudonym "Sigma," are authoritative surveys of his life and career. See also C. W. Bowen, *Hist. of Woodstock, Conn.* (1926), pp. 190 ff., and "Samuel Dexter, Councilor, and his son, Hon. Samuel Dexter, Secretary of War, and Secretary of the Treasury," *Proc. Am. Antiq. Soc.,* n.s., XXXV, 23 (Apr. 8, 1825); W. T. Davis, *Hist. of the Bench and Bar of Suffolk County, Mass.* (1894); *Memoir of Theophilus Parsons* (1859), by his son, T. Parsons, p. 180; and Charles Warren, *Hist. of the Am. Bar* (1911), p. 309.]

H. W. H. K.

DEXTER, TIMOTHY (Jan. 22, 1747–Oct. 23, 1806), merchant, was born in Malden, Mass., where his ancestor, Richard Dexter of County Meath, Ireland, had settled some hundred years before. His parents, Nathan and Esther (Brintnall) Dexter, were indigent and inconspicuous. He had little schooling and throughout his life ignored the conventional rules of spelling and punctuation. At the age of nine he was placed on a farm, but, after nearly seven years of service, went to Charlestown, where he "stayed Leven months at Dressin of skins for briches & gloves." Having earned his freedom from apprenticeship, he arrived in Newburyport in 1769, with a "bondel" and "Eight Dolors & 20 sents" in cash.

In May 1770, having set up as a leather dresser, he married Elizabeth (Lord) Frothingham, a widow with four children and a small property. The couple had two children,—Samuel, born in 1772, and Nancy, born in 1776. With his wife's money and what he himself was able to accumulate, he shrewdly bought up depreciated Continental currency during and after the Revolution at a fraction of its face value; and, when Hamilton's policy of funding and assumption was adopted in 1791, he suddenly found himself a wealthy man. With prosperity, he indulged his vanity and a natural inclination toward eccentricity. Although he soon became an inveterate sot, he transacted his business in the morning when he was comparatively sober, and he engaged in enterprises which have become legendary. According to his own statements, he sent 42,000 warming pans to Cuba, where they passed as cooking utensils; he cornered the market in whalebone, disposing of 342 tons at a large profit; and he bought 21,000 Bibles, which he sold in the "west inges" at an advance of one hundred per cent. Some of these wild stories may have a basis of fact. It is certain that he owned two vessels, that he was the largest stockholder in the Deer Island Bridge across the Merrimac (opened in 1793), and that he achieved notoriety as a cunning speculator.

In 1791 he bought the splendid house of Patrick Tracy, one of Newburyport's broken-down merchant princes, furnished it luxuriously, and emerged in the rôle of gentleman. In 1796, annoyed by some practical jokers, he moved to Chester, N. H., but returned in a few months to Newburyport, now styling himself "Lord" Timothy Dexter, with a title "made by the voice of hamsher state," and purchased the mansion of Jonathan Jackson, on High St. He engaged Joseph Wilson, a ship carver, to make more than forty life-sized wooden statues, painted in colors, of great personages, including Presidents Washington, Adams, and Jefferson, three of the apostles,—St. Paul, St. John, and St. Peter,—Adam and Eve, Benjamin Franklin, John Jay, Louis XIV, Lord Nelson, and others. These were arranged on the grounds so that they could easily be seen from the street. Most striking of all was an image of himself on a pedestal near the front fence bearing the inscription, "I am first in the East." He subsidized a laureate, Jonathan Plummer, formerly a fish peddler, who composed odes in his honor, and appeared as an author himself in a pamphlet entitled *A Pickle for the Knowing Ones,* filling twenty-four small pages and privately printed in 1802. The first edition had no marks of punctuation whatever, but at the end of the second Dexter added a whole page of "stops," telling his readers to "peper and solt it as they plese."

In his old age he was a quaint figure in a wide cocked hat and long blue coat, who strolled aimlessly about his estate, carrying a gold-headed cane and followed by a porcine dog. His eccentricity displayed itself in startling ways, as, for instance, when he had his coffin made and kept on exhibition in his parlor and actually held a mock funeral, after which he beat his wife because of her failure to shed tears. With an insatiable mania for publicity, he offered a market house to Newburyport on condition that it be called Dexter Hall and agreed to repave High St. if it could be named after him; but the town refused his proposals. He did, however, make gifts to various institutions, including a bell to the Second Presbyterian Church; and, of the $35,000 which he left at his death, $2,000 was bequeathed to Newburyport, the income of which is still used for the benefit of the poor. Many of his images were blown down in the great tempest of 1815, but the three presidents still kept their places on the entrance arch until 1850. The house is still standing (1930), with Dexter's gilded eagle shining on the roof.

[The best book on Dexter is John P. Marquand's *Lord Timothy Dexter* (1925), which deals with him in a delightfully ironic manner. There are two excellent essays on him by W. C. Todd in his *Biog. and Other Articles* (1901). An early biography was written by S. L. Knapp, a resident of Newburyport (*Life of Timothy Dexter,* 1838), but it is unreliable. Dexter's *A Pickle for the Knowing Ones, or Plain Truths in a Homespun Dress* is printed in full in Marquand's biography. See also *Births, Marriages and Deaths in the Town of Malden, Mass., 1649–1850* (1903), pp. 21, 126, and O. P. Dexter, *Dexter Geneal.* (1904).] C. M. F.

DEXTER, WIRT (Oct. 25, 1832–May 17, 1890), lawyer, was a grandson of Samuel Dexter [1761–1816, *q.v.*], and son of Samuel William Dexter and his third wife Millisent Bond. His father, a native of Boston, and a brother of Franklin Dexter [*q.v.*], moved West, became a county judge in Wisconsin, and subsequently practised law at Dexter, Wis., a town which he had founded and where his son Wirt was born. Having obtained his early education in the local schools, the latter went to Ann Arbor, Mich., where he studied for a time, later attending Cazenovia Seminary in New York State. On his return to Michigan he entered the lumber business, in which his father was largely interested. This involved the management of saw-mills, the marketing of the output, and the organization of logging camps, all the details of which he mastered. The life, however, had no attractions for him, and in 1853 he moved to Chicago, read law, and was admitted to the bar. Opening an office there, he soon obtained a good practise, particularly in commercial cases, his previous experience in business standing him in good stead. His successful defense of Devine, a foundryman, who had shot an employee during a quarrel, first attracted public attention to his abilities. The case was one of more than ordinary local interest and his speech to the jury was remarkable for its force and effect. From that time forward, he was in constant request, and soon became one of the leading counsel in Chicago. He did not specialize, and the wide range of cases in which he was briefed testified as much to his versatility as to his legal attainments. In *Pullman Palace Car Company* vs. *Smith* (73 *Ill.*, 360), appearing on behalf of the company, he successfully established that the liability of his clients for property lost or stolen from passengers while riding in Pullman cars was neither that of an innkeeper nor a common carrier. His argument in *Blatchford et al.* vs. *Newberry et al.* (99 *Ill.*, 11), involving the construction of a will and the application of the doctrine of acceleration of remainders, was masterly, and, though unsuccessful, was concurred in by Judge Dickey, who contributed a dissenting opinion fifty-five pages in length. This case was unique in legal experience, owing to one of the appellate judges' changing his opinion after the decision had been rendered. He was retained in [Northwestern] *University* vs. *People* (99 *U. S.*, 309) on behalf of the University in the Supreme Court of the United States, where he obtained a reversal of the opinion of the Illinois court to the effect that the University was liable for taxes on land owned by it but not in its immediate use. For a number of years prior to his death he was general counsel and member of the executive committee of the Board of Directors of the Chicago, Burlington & Quincy Railroad Company and represented it throughout the "Granger" litigation. He took intense interest in all movements for the advancement of the interests of Chicago, and was one of the founders of the Chicago Relief and Aid Society, being chairman of its executive committee in 1871 when the Chicago fire occurred, and to him was confided the work of administering the $5,000,000 contributed from all over the world for the purposes of relief. He at once gave up all professional work and for a year devoted himself solely to the task of evoking order out of chaos and distributing relief. In this work his services were invaluable and crowned with complete success. He was not interested in political matters, and never held or aspired to public office. Normally a Republican, he declined to follow his party in its nomination of Blaine for the presidency, and in local contests invariably supported whomsoever he considered the better man, irrespective of politics.

For years prior to his death he was admittedly the leader of the bar in Chicago. Both in consultation and in court he was distinguished for an intuitive common sense which dominated all his utterances. A fluent speaker, methodical, always thoroughly prepared, and impressive in his earnestness, he was extremely effective with a jury, and his legal acumen and power of analysis always carried great weight with the bench. He was tall, with an athletic frame, and an air of dignity and refinement, "genial and affable, . . . luxurious in his habits and artistic in his tastes" (F. B. Wilkie, *post*). He was married twice: on June 15, 1858, to Kate Augusta Dusenberry of Marshall, Mich., who died in 1864, and on Dec. 18, 1866, to Josephine Moore. He died suddenly in Chicago in his fifty-eighth year.

[O. P. Dexter, *Dexter Geneal.* (1904), p. 194; F. H. Head in *Great Am. Lawyers*, vol. VIII (1909), ed. by W. D. Lewis; J. M. Palmer, *The Bench and Bar of Ill.* (1899), II, 659; F. B. Wilkie, *Sketches and Notices of the Chicago Bar* (1871), p. 42; *Daily Inter Ocean* (Chicago), May 19, 1890.]

H. W. H. K.

DE YOUNG, MICHEL HARRY (Sept. 30, 1849–Feb. 15, 1925), editor and publisher, was born in St. Louis, Mo., the son of Michel H. and Amelia (Morange) de Young. At the age of five he went with his family to a California mining town and later to San Francisco, then a village. He was educated in the public schools of that town, and spent his life as one of its citizens, taking an active part in its civic and political affairs. When he was a boy in his teens, San Francisco had a theatrical activity equaled in only a few Eastern cities, and his entry into newspaper publishing came via the *Daily Dramatic Chronicle,* which he and his brother Charles founded in January 1865 when M. H. de Young was sixteen and his brother two years older. At first, the paper was little more than a theatre program, filled with advertising and circulated free. It had a crisp, snappy manner of presenting and commenting upon news which attracted readers, and it soon became a full-fledged newspaper, paralleling in its rapid growth the expansion of the city. The position of the new daily surprised and alarmed its competitors as it soon grew to have the largest circulation on the Coast. Among its early contributors, before any of them had achieved fame, were Mark Twain, Bret Harte, Prentice Mulford, and Charles Warren Stoddard. The word "dramatic" was dropped from the title, Sept. 1, 1868, the paper then appearing as the *Daily Morning Chronicle,* and later as the *San Francisco Chronicle.* In 1872, it began an agitation against land monopoly which led to the exposure of several federal officials, bringing about the retirement of a group of politicians. One of the results was the establishment of a bank commission for the state. In 1879 the *Chronicle* successfully fought for a new state constitution.

On the death of his brother Charles in 1880, M. H. de Young became owner and editor-in-chief. Personally and through the paper he exerted a powerful influence on the Pacific Coast. He was thoroughly identified with the Republican party, acting as delegate to three national conventions, those of 1888, 1892, and 1908, and serving on the National Committee for eight years, and as its vice-chairman for four years. In 1892 he was an unsuccessful candidate for the United States Senate to succeed George Hearst, throwing his votes to Charles N. Felton to break a deadlock. He was named commissioner from California to the Paris Exposition in 1889; three years later he was selected as commissioner and as vice-president of the World's Columbian Exposition; in 1898 he was commissioner-general from California to the Trans-Mississippi Exposition at Omaha; he attended the Paris Exposition in 1900 as president of the United States Commission; and in 1915 he was vice-president of the Panama-Pacific Exposition. For twenty-five years he was a director of the Associated Press, and for a short time he served as president of the International League of Press Clubs. Following the San Francisco fire he served on the executive committee of the Red Cross directing relief work. In spite of many political and civic connections and frequent trips to the East and abroad, he never lost close touch with the *Chronicle*. He continued to define its policies and watch their execution carefully. It is said that until his final and extremely brief illness those in his employ regularly awaited the kindly, constructive comments on the handling of news and editorials which it was his practise to make daily.

[Information from Mrs. Marjorie D. Brown, librarian of the *San Francisco Chronicle*; issues of that paper for Feb. 16–19, 1925; *N. Y. Times*, Feb. 16, 1925; *New International Year Book*, 1925; John P. Young, *Journalism in Cal.* (Chronicle Publishing Co., San Francisco, 1915); *Who's Who in America*, 1899–1925. M. H. de Young apparently preferred to use only his initials. His name is sometimes given as Michael Henry, and in *Who's Who in America*, 1924–25, appears as Meichel Harry; the form adopted above is that used in *Who's Who in America* from 1899 till 1923. The date of his birth is given as Oct. 1 in *Who's Who in America*, but as Sept. 30 in a biographical article said to have been dictated by De Young shortly before his death and used in the *Chronicle*, Feb. 16, 1925.]

J. M. L.
H. J. S. M.

DIAZ, ABBY MORTON (1821–Apr. 1, 1904), author, was born in Plymouth, Mass., the only girl among the six children of Ichabod and Patty (Weston) Morton. Her father was described by Emerson as "a plain man who formerly engaged in the fisheries with success" (Swift, *Brook Farm*, p. 120). It was said of him that he was a Puritan divested of all the Puritan's superstition and bigotry (Swift, *Brook Farm*, p. 79), and it seems sure that as concerned organized religion both he and his daughter were at the opposite extreme from dogmatism. Once while he was in Boston he saw by a supernatural light which flooded his room a vision of a world governed by the principles of human brotherhood. He determined to help make this vision a reality, and to that end became a temperance worker and later the pioneer abolitionist of Plymouth. Abby was still a child but she quickly made the slaves' cause her own, and became secretary of a juvenile abolitionist society (see "Anti-slavery Times in Plymouth," *New England Magazine*, April 1899). Later, when her father's interest shifted to the Brook Farm activities—he was a trustee December 1842–April 1843—she and two of her brothers were sent there to live. The entire family joined them in the spring of 1843. After two weeks, persuaded that sentiment rather than sound judgment was ruling the community, Ichabod abandoned the house he had built, and went home. Abby remained longer, a teacher in the infant school. Later she was married to Emanuel Diaz, but after a brief married life which left her with the care of two sons, she began teaching school in Plymouth. It was her habit to write verse for use in local festivities, and in May 1861, the *Atlantic Monthly* published her "Pink and Blue," a prose story of "how I won my wife." Upon this she determined to devote her life to writing, and from then till the close of the century she published books at a rate of considerably more than one every two years. She was most widely known by her humorous and homely stories for children—the series beginning with *The William Henry Letters* (1870) having become within five years so popular that they were turned into drama. In 1878, with N. A. Calkins, she published a natural history series, setting forth in six booklets the family history of creatures ranging from cow to condor. She was also active as an emancipator of women, "slaves," as she expressed it, "of the rolling-pin" (Diaz, *Domestic Problems*, 1884, p. 123). Her concern was to explain "how woman may enjoy the delights of culture and at the same time fulfil her duties to family and household" (*Ibid.*, p. 7). She discussed this subject in four books, the most vigorous, perhaps, *Only a Flock of Women* (1893). As early as 1876 she published *Neighborhood Talks* on arbitration versus war, and as years went on she interested herself in questions of always greater magnitude and vagueness. She contributed articles to the *Metaphysical Magazine* (New York), wrote four papers on the "Science of Human Beings," and from December 1901 to September 1902, published in the magazine *Mind* (New York) a long sequence of articles called "Hindrances to World Betterment." After about 1880, she lived in Belmont, Mass. At the time of her death she was collecting extracts from her past writings with the view of putting them together in a kind of anthology.

[L. Swift, *Brook Farm* (1900); *Who's Who in America*, 1903–05; W. T. Davis, *Plymouth Memories of an Octogenarian* (1906); *Boston Transcript*, Apr. 1–2, 1904.]
J. D. W.

DIBBLE, ROY FLOYD (Mar. 12, 1887–Dec. 3, 1929), author, was born in Portland, Chautauqua County, N. Y., the son of George E. Dibble, a farmer, and Miriam H. (Quilliam) Dibble. His life until he became of age was spent almost entirely in his native county, where he grew up on his father's farm and attended the local schools at Elm Flats and Westfield. Graduating from the Westfield high school in 1906, he was prevented from proceeding directly to college by the necessity of caring for a sick brother. This and farming for his father were his occupations for the next two years, though it was at this time also that the reading he had done in Shakespeare inspired him to write a lengthy and resounding series of sonnets on the themes of love and poetry. In 1908 he entered Allegheny College in Pennsylvania, but at the end of the first term he went on to Clark University, where he graduated in 1912. After a summer's walking tour in France and the British Isles he commenced a career as teacher at the Sanford School for boys, Redding Ridge, Conn.

The reading he had done in college, however, together with his own natural bent determined that he should pursue the study of literature in a larger place, and in 1914 he entered the Graduate School of Columbia University. The next year he was made a University Fellow in English, and in the year following he was given the position of instructor in English in Columbia College. The remainder of his life was to be spent in New York, though an operation he was forced to undergo in the summer of 1916 led him to believe that less life remained for him than actually did. The surgeon who removed a tubercular kidney from his body told him that he had Addison's Disease and had only three years to live. The general effect of this sentence was to dull the edge of his ambition, and to confirm in him a quietism which had always been present in his character but which had been encouraged for a number of years by annual readings of Thoreau's *Walden*, which he often called his "bible." As a teacher at Columbia he made a greater impression upon his students, who found him contagiously enthusiastic about the authors he taught, than upon his colleagues, who found him singularly uninterested in himself. His life proceeded uneventfully; the summers were spent either in Europe or on the farm near Westfield; the winters passed in teaching; his spare time was given to a dissertation for the Ph.D. degree, a life of Albion W. Tourgée, which was published in 1921.

Meanwhile the business of teaching "war aims" at Columbia in 1918 had stirred him to make an examination of his ideas; the result was a sudden access of energy which at first expressed itself in terms of the prevailing radicalism, but which a little later found definite expression in a desire to write iconoclastic biographies in the manner of Lytton Strachey, whose *Eminent Victorians*, appearing in America, created a whole school of "new" biographers. Dibble set to work upon a series of biographical essays which he published in 1923 under the title *Strenuous Americans* and with a dedication, somewhat less cryptic perhaps than he thought it, "To the Greatest Living Biographer." The subjects treated were Jesse James, Admiral Dewey, Brigham Young, Frances E. Willard, James J. Hill, P. T. Barnum, and Mark Hanna; the treatment was remarkable for its gusto, its narrative power, its pervasive though not always subtle irony, and its orotund, decorated, yet rapid style. Encouraged by the success of this book, Dibble resigned his position at Columbia in order that he might devote all of his time to authorship. His next work was *John L. Sullivan: An Intimate Narrative* (1925), a rollicking and rather Rabelaisian life of still another strenuous American. This was followed in 1926 by *Mohammed*, wherein he went far afield in search of picturesque and violent material. His interest thus aroused in religious leaders, he wrote a life of Martin Luther, but this volume failed to find a publisher; and in 1927 he resumed his teaching, becoming associate professor of English at Hunter College, New York City. At the time of his death he had in hand a second collection of biographical essays, which he had contributed to various magazines. For the *Dictionary of American Biography* he wrote the article on Robert Prometheus Fitzsimmons. He died when his disease passed at last into an acute stage, probably in consequence of depression over unfortunate investments. In appearance he was short, stout, fair, and phlegmatic; he always lived alone; and though he had many friends, few of them ever got beyond the well-armed exterior to the sensitive man within.

[*Who's Who in America*, 1928–29; obituary in *N. Y. Times*, Dec. 5, 1929; personal acquaintance 1915–29.]
M. V–D.

DIBRELL, GEORGE GIBBS (Apr. 12, 1822–May 6, 1888), merchant, planter, politician, soldier, industrialist, was descended from Dr. Christopher Du Brey, a French Huguenot, who settled with a colony of refugees on the James River in Virginia fifteen years after the revocation of the Edict of Nantes. His son Charles was a patriot soldier in the American Revolution, and the son of this Charles, whose name was Anthony, migrated from Virginia to Kentucky where he married Mildred Carter, who was also from Virginia. In the meantime, the name Du Brey had been changed to DeBrill and finally to Dibrell. In 1811 Anthony moved his family to White County, Tenn., and settled in the little town of Sparta, where he became successful as a merchant and presently rose to be a man of some political importance. Here his son George Gibbs was born. The boy helped his father on the farm and attended the local school. When he was fifteen years old he drove a herd of cattle to market in Virginia, a difficult and responsible job for a lad of his age. During the next year he went for one term to the East Tennessee College at Knoxville. The following year his father was a candidate for Congress and George managed the farm during his absence. The elder Dibrell about this time lost much of his property by indorsing notes for friends, and it became necessary for his son to shift for himself. His career began in 1840 when, at the age of eighteen, he was elected clerk of the branch of the Bank of Tennessee which had been established at Sparta. He served in this capacity until 1846, and later acted for some years as clerk of the court of White County.

In 1842, at the age of twenty, he married Mary E. Leftwich, whose father also was a merchant of Sparta and a native of Virginia. Four years later, he severed his connection with the Bank of Tennessee and went into business as a merchant. His first venture proved decidedly profitable, and from this time until the outbreak of the Civil War he continued in business on his own account. He followed his father in his loyalty to the Whig party, and followed his party in its opposition to secession. He let it be known, however, that, in case of a conflict, his sympathies were with the South. Accordingly upon the outbreak of hostilities, he volunteered as a private in the Confederate service, and on Aug. 10, 1861, he was elected lieutenant-colonel of his regiment. He served in Tennessee and Kentucky under Gen. Zollicoffer, but when the army was reorganized at Corinth he was not reëlected as lieutenant-colonel. He thereupon repaired to Richmond to obtain authority to raise a body of cavalry. Returning to his home at Sparta, he organized the 8th Tennessee Cavalry Regiment, behind the Federal lines, as a body of independent partisan rangers; but he joined Gen. Forrest at Murfreesboro and his troops were mustered into the service as regular cavalry, with Dibrell as colonel of the regiment. After this time he saw much service under Forrest. On the death of Col. Starnes, he was given command (July 1, 1863) of Forrest's "Old Brigade" and continued in command of that organization until the end of the war, being raised to the rank of brigadier-general in July 1864. After having taken part in the battle of Chickamauga, this brigade was detached from Forrest's command and ordered to join Joseph E. Johnston at Dalton, Ga. It took part in the retreat to Atlanta, and later in the retreat through South and North Carolina. On reaching Raleigh, it was ordered to join Jefferson Davis at Greensboro, from which point it accompanied him to Washington, Ga., where the military force was disbanded. Dibrell's Tennessee regiment marched home in a body. Debts and desolation awaited them, but Dibrell himself soon restored his fortunes. In 1865 he again embarked in the mercantile business. His friends aided him, and he prospered as before the war. In 1870 he took part in the convention which drew up the new constitution of the state, and in 1874 he was elected to Congress. For ten years he served diligently in the House of Representatives, and retired voluntarily in 1884.

In the meantime, he had ceased to be a merchant and had become a financier. In 1866 the legislature revived the charter of the Southwestern Railroad, which was to connect Sparta with the Nashville-Chattanooga road at Tullahoma (*Acts of the State of Tennessee,* 1865–66, p. 295). He was immediately made a director of this company, and in 1869 he became its president. The road was completed under his direction and a branch was built to the Bon Air coal mines, where fifteen thousand acres of his land had served as the nucleus around which he had organized a successful mining company (Scrapbook, clippings on county history, sketch of White County, in Tennessee State Library). His last years were spent in the quiet of his Sparta home, where he died in 1888.

[The best account is that in *Sketches of Prominent Tennesseans* (1888), ed. by W. S. Speer; another is in the Goodspeed Publishing Company's *Hist. of Tenn.,* White County Suppl. (1887). All other sketches appear to be based upon these two. There is a detailed account of the operations of the 8th Tenn. Cavalry written by Dibrell himself and published in J. B. Lindsley, *The Military Annals of Tenn., Confederate* (1886).] T. P. A.

DICK, ELISHA CULLEN (Mar. 15, 1762–Sept. 22, 1825), physician, the son of Archibald and Mary (Barnard) Dick, was born near Marcus Hook, Pa. His father was a Pennsylvania farmer of means, a horse-breeder and a publicist. Elisha was sent to an academy in Philadelphia, then to the "Pequa Academy." He returned to his father's house at the age of sixteen and there continued his studies under Rev. Samuel Armor. In 1780 he began the study of medicine under Dr. Benjamin Rush, but the following year he entered the office of Dr. William Shippen. He graduated from the University of Pennsylvania as bachelor of medicine in March 1782, and settled in Alexandria, Va., where he became successful professionally and prominent socially. In October 1783 he married Hannah Harman of Darby, Pa. He was one of the organizers of the Masonic Lodge at Alexandria and served as its Worshipful Master both before and after George Washington's tenure of the office. In 1794 he commanded a troop of cavalry in the Whiskey Rebellion in Pennsylvania. For years he was colonel of the cavalry regiment in Alexandria, and in 1804 he was chosen mayor of the city.

For many years Washington's friend, he was also one of the two physicians called in consultation by Dr. James Craik [*q.v.*] at the time of Washington's last illness, and with Craik he signed the account of the illness and death which was published in *The Times* of Alexandria on Dec. 19, 1799. He likewise conducted the Masonic services at Washington's funeral. He published in the *Medical Repository* (Second Hexade, vol. I, p. 190, 1804) an article on "Yellow Fever at Alexandria," describing an epidemic of some two hundred cases, which he attributed to the stench of decomposing oysters and shells which were treated in a brick-kiln for the purpose of making quicklime. This is on a par with Benjamin Rush's attribution of the Philadelphia epidemic to decomposing coffee. In 1808 he wrote on "Facts and Observations Relative to the Disease Cynanche Trachealis, or Croup" (*Philadelphia Medical and Physical Journal,* 1806, p. 2). This disease was assigned by Craik and Dick as the cause of Washington's death. Most of such cases are nowadays shown to be diphtheria, and that appears to have been what Dick was discussing, as the term *angina membranosa* is used as a synonym, some cases of tracheotomy are reported, and Washington's case is discussed. The disease was then epidemic in and about Alexandria, and three adults had suffered attacks before Washington became sick. Dick had advocated tracheotomy in Washington's case. The treatment used in the case, repeated blood lettings, administration of calomel and tartar emetic, and application of blisters, was that advocated by medical leaders of the day.

An accomplished musician and in early life a believer in and attendant at duels, Dick later changed his church affiliation from Episcopalian to Presbyterian and then to Quaker, threw his dueling pistols into the river, destroyed as a useless vanity an organ which he had built, and otherwise took a more serious view of life and eternity. He was described as being five feet ten inches tall, weighing 175 pounds, and, before he became a Quaker, addicted to ruffles, wearing his hair in a queue or tied with a ribbon. He had a fine and attractive sickroom presence and courtly manners. He died at Alexandria.

[*Va. Herald,* Sept. 28, 1825; W. A. Wells, "Last Illness and Death of Washington," *Va. Medic. Monthly,* Jan. 1927; J. M. Toner, "A Sketch of the Life of Elisha Cullen Dick," *Trans. Medic. Soc. of Va.,* 1885; date of birth and name of wife from a grand-daughter, Miss Ethelinde Crisfield of Washington, D. C.] P. M. A.

DICK, ROBERT PAINE (Oct. 5, 1823–Sept. 12, 1898), jurist, was born in Greensboro, N. C. His father, John McClintock Dick, was an able and respected judge; his mother, Parthenia P. Williamson, came of a prominent family of Person County. After attending Caldwell Institute, young Dick entered the University of North Carolina and graduated in 1843. He read law, was admitted to the bar in 1845, practised at Wentworth but returned to Greensboro. Immediately after he began practise he married Mary Eloise, the daughter of George Adams of Pittsylvania County, Va. Active in Democratic politics, and a delegate to the Baltimore convention of 1852, he was made federal district attorney in 1853 and served to 1861. In 1860 he supported Douglas, with whom he was on terms of close friendship, in the Charleston convention. Later at Baltimore he was the one North Carolina delegate who refused to secede, and, after voting for Douglas, he returned to North Carolina and, securing the nomination of a Douglas electoral ticket, made a tireless campaign for it; he pleaded for his election as the sole hope of preserving the Union, and was one of the Spartan band of 1,500 who voted for him. With the call for troops he gave up the fight, and was a member of the secession convention where, after voting for the Badger ordinance of revolution, he voted for the ordinance of secession. In 1862 the legislature elected him to the council of state, and in 1864 he supported Holden for governor and was himself elected as a peace candidate to the state Senate. At the close of the war President Johnson summoned him to Washington for advice as to restoration, and, without success, Dick urged him to undertake it on the basis of the Sherman-Johnson agreement and to proclaim a general amnesty. Johnson declined to follow his advice, but appointed him federal judge for North Carolina. In spite of the attorney-general's ruling that he was eligible, Dick felt unable to take the "ironclad" oath, and declined. He was active in the "Johnson" convention of 1865–66, and, conservative, he seemed inclined to part from his late political associates, but in 1866 he advocated the Fourteenth Amendment and, gradually aligning himself with the radicals, supported Congressional Reconstruction and participated in organizing the Republican party in North Carolina. Under the new constitution he was elected an associate justice of the supreme court, serving from 1868 until 1872 when he was appointed federal district judge.

On the supreme bench of the state he took an important part in deciding the many difficult questions growing out of the new constitution and the system of jurisprudence ushered in by the code of civil procedure. His opinions are clear, brief, and direct. He was, perhaps, a better trial than appellate judge. A hard and consistent student, he grew steadily and tempered knowledge with understanding, common sense, and humanity. As the passions of reconstruction cooled, he won a wide and deserved popularity. For many years, with John H. Dillard, he conducted a private law school which won reputation for the legal training it gave.

[B. D. Caldwell, *Founders and Builders of Greensboro* (1925); *Cyc. of Eminent and Representative Men of the Carolinas of the Nineteenth Century* (1892), II, 633; J. Dowd, *Sketches of Prominent Living North Carolinians* (1888); 63–66 *N. C. Reports*; *Who's Who in America*, 1899–1900.] J. G. de R. H.

DICKERSON, EDWARD NICOLL (Feb. 11, 1824–Dec. 12, 1889), lawyer, son of Philemon [*q.v.*] and Sidney (Stotesbury) Dickerson and nephew of Mahlon Dickerson [*q.v.*], was born at Paterson, N. J. Entering the College of New Jersey (Princeton) at an early age, he there met Joseph Henry of the Smithsonian Institution, who induced him to take an interest in science and mechanics which gradually developed into an absorbing study and had a permanent effect upon his professional career. Leaving college without graduating, he read law with his father, and was admitted to the New Jersey bar at Paterson in 1845. For a short time thereafter he officiated as clerk of the federal district court, of which his father was judge, and then commenced practise for himself. By this time he had become an expert mechanical engineer; he ran the first locomotive that was used on the railroad between Paterson and Jersey City. His earliest case of first-class importance was *Colt* vs. *Massachusetts Arms Company* (*Fed. Cas.* no. 3030), a suit brought to establish the validity of Samuel Colt's patent for fire arms. Dickerson represented the plaintiff throughout and at the trial, which took place at Boston and extended over three weeks, won a decisive victory, despite the fact that Rufus Choate was his opponent. In 1852 he moved his office to New York City, and at once assumed a leading position at the bar there, specializing in patent law. During this period his outstanding case was *Goodyear* vs. *Day* (*Fed. Cas.* no. 5569), involving the validity of Charles Goodyear's patent for vulcanized India rubber, in which he was associated with J. T. Brady and Daniel Webster for the plaintiff, Rufus Choate being for the defense. The heavy work in connection with the vital scientific details of the case was all performed by him and resulted in a complete triumph. He was now recognized as the outstanding authority on patent law in the United States. He was an incessant worker and, despite his weighty professional engagements, which of their very nature invariably involved intense technical attention, continued to enlarge the scope of his investigations in the field of mechanical engineering, more particularly as regards marine propulsion. This gave rise eventually to his connection with the "expansion" and "non-expansion" controversy, at the commencement of the Civil War. Acting upon a theory of the chief engineer of the navy that James Watt had made a serious error in maintaining that steam produced more power when worked expansively than otherwise, Secretary Gideon Welles had ordered engines of the non-expansion type for the new naval vessels. Dickerson promptly protested, in letters to the secretary and in communications to Congress which attracted wide attention, and, though his efforts were fruitless at the time, experience subsequently demonstrated the correctness of his views.

At the height of his reputation he retired temporarily from practise in order to undertake an extensive program of foreign travel, in the course of which he spent considerable time in Europe, and also visited Central America. In 1873, however, he returned to the bar, and thenceforth was constantly engaged, the great majority of his retainers being in patent matters. He appeared for the defense in the suits arising out of the disaster to the Staten Island ferry boat *Westfield* involving the loss of many lives, and gained a verdict in each case. The last years of his life were occupied chiefly in the suits involving the electrical patents of Thomas A. Edison, and the rights of the Western Union Telegraph Company and the American Bell Telephone Company. He acted as counsel for the latter company throughout its protracted litigation, and made the final successful argument in the Supreme Court of the United States (126 *U. S. Reports*). As an advocate in his own sphere he was supreme, his profound knowledge of scientific technique combining with a facility of lucid explanation and intense industry in mastering every detail of his cases to make him equally formidable on trial or in appeal. He did not, however, possess a judicial mind, his greatest fault being his inability to see more than one side of a case.

Apart from law and science, his only interest was sailing; he maintained and himself sailed a splendidly equipped yacht. Politically he was "a Democrat of the Jackson school of Democracy" (George Ticknor Curtis, *post*), though he never took a prominent part in public affairs. During the Civil War he was a War Democrat and was outspoken in support of the reëlection of Lincoln. Later he disapproved of the free-trade policy of his party under Cleveland. His appearance was impressive. He was six feet three inches in height, of massive frame, always erect, firm of step and dignified in manner. He died at "Wave Crest" near Far Rockaway, L. I.

[Dickerson's ancestry is traced in C. J. Werner, *Geneals. of Long Island Families* (1919), pp. 1–19. A careful summary of his career appeared in *N. Y. State Bar Asso. Report*, 1890, p. 123; and the authoritative obituary notice by George Ticknor Curtis in the *Sun* (N. Y.), Dec. 13, 1889. See also *N. Y. Times* and *N. Y. Tribune* of same date, and *Ann. Cyc.*, 1889, p. 628.]

H. W. H. K.

DICKERSON, MAHLON (Apr. 17, 1770–Oct. 5, 1853), governor of New Jersey, senator, secretary of the navy, brother of Philemon Dickerson [*q.v.*], was descended from Philemon Dickerson who emigrated from England on the *Mary Anne* of Yarmouth in 1637, became a freeholder of Salem, Mass., in 1638, and later purchased a tract of land at Southold, L. I., where he died. Philemon's grandson, Peter Dickerson, removed in 1741 to Morris County, N. J., becoming an extensive landowner. His son Jonathan married Mary, daughter of Thomas Coe of Queens, L. I., and their son Mahlon was born at Hanover Neck (Morris Plains?), N. J. Graduating at Princeton in 1789, he engaged in the study of law and was licensed as an attorney in 1793. Following a brief military experience in the expedition which suppressed the "Whiskey Rebellion," he settled with two of his brothers in Philadelphia. His active political career began in 1802 with his election to the Philadelphia Common Council. In 1805 Gov. M'Kean appointed him adjutant-general of Pennsylvania, which office he resigned in 1808 to become recorder of the city. His father died two years later, leaving an extensive estate to be settled and a large iron business to be carried on. Mahlon, having purchased the claims of the other heirs, transferred his residence to Succasunna, N. J., and took over the management of the famous iron works of that name. This change from a professional to a business life colored his subsequent political career. Though a Democrat, being a manufacturer he became, for the remainder of his public career, an uncompromising advocate of a protective tariff; his reputation among his contemporaries was summed up by President Van Buren who referred to him as "that ultra-protectionist," and he may rightly be regarded as one of those who established the policy of protection.

In 1811 and 1812 he was elected a member of the Assembly from Morris County, and while serving in that body was chosen a justice of the state supreme court, which position he held until elected governor (and chancellor by virtue of that office) in 1815. Reëlected the following year, he resigned when elected to the United States Senate, serving in that body from 1817 to 1833. His career in the Senate was noteworthy for his able support of two policies, one of which originated with him. Fearing that the treasury surplus expended under the "general welfare" clause would result in a centralization of governmental power, he advocated the division of the surplus each year to the states, prorating it according to the ratio of direct taxation (speech in United States Senate, Feb. 1, 1827, *Register of Debates in Congress*, pp. 209–22); and President Jackson paid him the compliment of adopting this proposal in a message to Congress. The other policy which received his able support was that of a protective tariff. As chairman of the Committee of Manufacturers in the Senate, he was in a strategic position to war against free trade which he denounced as "a system as visionary and impracticable as the everlasting and universal pacification of the world." In 1832 he was a prominent candidate for the vice-presidential nomination after Calhoun's retirement from the Democratic party, but gave way to his friend, Van Buren. In May 1834 he declined the post of minister to Russia, remaining at home to promote Van Buren's aspiration for the presidency. He was soon after appointed secretary of the navy, taking office June 30, and serving until ill health forced his resignation in 1838. Retiring to private life he soon regained his health, rescuing as well his business, threatened by the depression following the panic of 1837.

In 1844 he was a prominent and useful member of the constitutional convention which revised the fundamental law of New Jersey. Meeting at the same time in Baltimore, the Democratic Convention nominated Polk. This was so bitter a disappointment to Dickerson who had supported Gen. Cass, that he took no part in the campaign. He could never excuse the nomination of Polk by that "horrible Democratic Convention" and worked vigorously during the ensuing four years to prevent his renomination and to secure that prize for Cass. In this he was successful, but the disappointment of Gen. Taylor's election was overwhelming to him and marked the end of his active participation in politics. He was then seventy-eight years of age and retired permanently to his estate, "Ferrommonte," where he died five years later. He was unmarried.

[J. C. Pumpelly, "Mahlon Dickerson," in *Proc. N. J. Hist. Soc.*, 2 ser., XI, 133–56; obituary notice in *Daily True American* (Trenton), Oct. 8, 1853; G. B. Lee, ed., *Geneal. and Memorial Hist. of the State of N. J.* (1910), III, 1074; "Autobiography of Martin Van Buren," ed. by J. C. Fitzpatrick in *Ann. Report Am. Hist. Asso. for the Year 1918* (1920); L. Q. C. Elmer in *N. J. Hist. Soc. Colls.*, VII, 168–73; C. G. Bowers, *Party Battles of the Jackson Period* (1922).] C. R. E., Jr.

DICKERSON, PHILEMON (June 26, 1788–Dec. 10, 1862), jurist, was born at Succasunna, N. J., a son of Jonathan and Mary (Coe) Dickerson, and a younger brother of Mahlon Dickerson [*q.v.*]. Much of his youth was passed in Philadelphia, where he attended the public schools, subsequently passing to the University of Pennsylvania and graduating there in 1808. He then took up the study of law and in 1813, on being licensed as an attorney, opened an office in Philadelphia. In 1816 he removed to Paterson, N. J., which thenceforth remained his home. In 1817 he was admitted a counselor-at-law and, devoting himself steadily to his profession, gradually acquired an extensive practise. He was a member of the state Assembly in 1821–22. In 1834 he became a sergeant-at-law, being the last to hold that dignity in New Jersey. A Jacksonian Democrat, he was elected a representative from New Jersey in the Twenty-third Congress, and was reëlected to the Twenty-fourth, serving from 1833 to Nov. 3, 1836, when he resigned, having been elected governor of New Jersey and chancellor by the state legislature. He held this office for only one year, being defeated on seeking reëlection in 1837. In 1839 the "Great Seal War" occurred. He was again the Democratic nominee for Congress, and the election returns showed that he had been elected together with four other Democrats and one Whig. The balance of parties was such that the control of the House depended upon the complexion of the New Jersey delegation. Charges of fraud were made, and the Whig governor, on counting up the votes, rejected returns from two townships, and affixed the Great Seal of the State of New Jersey to certificates of election of the six Whig candidates. This action transferred the dispute to Washington, where a bitter discussion took place, though ultimately by vote, Feb. 28, 1840, the five Democrats were declared to be members of the House. On the expiration of his term in Congress, Dickerson was appointed by President Van Buren United States judge for the district of New Jersey. At that period and for a number of years thereafter, the business of the court was small in volume, and in the performance of his judicial duties, which were not onerous, he gave general satisfaction. The outbreak of the Civil War caused a large accession of work, litigation in all the federal courts becoming heavy, and his health broke down under the sudden strain, but he remained on the bench till his death at Paterson, Dec. 10, 1862.

As judge he had little opportunity of showing his qualifications for judicial office. A few of his opinions delivered during the year in which he was chancellor are reported in Green's *Chancery Reports,* vol. III, but no cases of any major importance came before him when on the district court bench. However, though he had no pretense to being a learned lawyer, he was energetic, impartial, and dignified. For a number of years he was a leader of the Democratic party in the state, and possessed great influence in its counsels. He was instrumental in procuring for Paterson its city charter, Mar. 19, 1851, and was the author of *The City of Paterson, its Past, Present and Future* (1856). His wife was Sidney, the daughter of Col. John Stotesbury of New York. His second son, Edward Nicoll Dickerson [*q.v.*], became a leading member of the New York bar.

[C. J. Werner, *Geneal. of Long Island Families* (1919), p. 11; E. Q. Keasbey, *The Courts and Lawyers of N. J.* (1912), II, 672, 801; F. B. Lee, *N. J. as a Colony and as a State* (1902), III, 327–44; *Biog. Dir. Am. Congress, 1774–1927* (1928).] H. W. H. K.

DICKEY, THEOPHILUS LYLE (Oct. 2, 1811–July 22, 1885), jurist, soldier, was descended from John Dickey, a native of northern Ireland, who, early in the eighteenth century, emigrated to Virginia and settled in North Carolina. John Dickey's grandson, James Henry Dickey, a Presbyterian minister, married Polly De Pew of Halifax County, Va., and their son, Theophilus Lyle Dickey, was born at Paris, Bourbon County, Ky. The family moved to Ohio in 1814, and Dickey's early education was received in the country schools there and in Kentucky. In 1826 he entered Ohio University at

Athens where he spent four years, proceeding thence to Miami University at Oxford, Ohio, and graduating there with honors in 1831. He then taught school in Ohio and Kentucky for two years. In 1834 he removed to Macomb, McDonough County, Ill., and studied law, being admitted to the bar in 1835. For a short time he practised law at Macomb, but in 1836 went to Rushville, where, in addition to his legal work, he edited a newspaper and became largely interested in real estate. The following year, owing to a financial panic, he lost everything, in addition to being saddled with a heavy debt which embarrassed him for many years, but which he finally paid in full. In 1839 he moved to Ottawa, Ill., which became his permanent home. Here he built up a large practise, acquiring a wide reputation as a skilful advocate and sound lawyer. At the outbreak of the war with Mexico he raised a company for the 1st Illinois Infantry, was commissioned captain, and saw service in Mexico, but was compelled to retire on account of ill health, whereupon he resumed practise in Ottawa. In 1848 he was elected judge of the circuit court for his district, and remained on the bench four years, resigning in 1852, and opening an office in Chicago in 1854. In the latter year he was a delegate to the first Republican state convention at Bloomington, and in 1856 was an Independent candidate for Congress, but withdrew. During this period he retained his residence in Ottawa, and resumed practise there in 1858, having finally paid off his old debts. In 1858 and 1860 he was an ardent supporter of Stephen A. Douglas against Lincoln, speaking throughout the state on behalf of the former. In 1861 when the Civil War broke out, he raised the 4th Illinois Cavalry and became its colonel. Joining Grant at Cairo in December, he took part in the capture of Fort Henry, led the advance at Fort Donelson, and was present at Shiloh. In 1862 he became a member of Grant's staff and was placed in command at Memphis, Tenn., subsequently becoming commander of Grant's cavalry division. He suggested and organized Grierson's Raid in 1863, but in the latter part of that year resigned his command and returned to Ottawa. In 1866 he was nominated for congressman-at-large for Illinois against Gen. Logan. In 1868 he became assistant attorney-general of the United States, having the conduct of all suits in the Court of Claims, and in the course of his duties appeared frequently in the United States Supreme Court. In this capacity he displayed great ability and efficiency, but was compelled to resign in 1870 owing to ill health. He thereupon resumed practise at Ottawa but in 1873 moved again to Chicago, where he was in August 1874 appointed corporation counsel. In December 1875 he was elected a judge of the supreme court of Illinois to fill a vacancy and in 1879 was reëlected as an Independent, remaining on the bench till his death, which occurred at Atlantic City, N. J. He was married twice: first, on Dec. 6, 1831, to Juliet Evans of Hillsboro, Ohio, who died on Dec. 31, 1854; and second, in the summer of 1870, to Mrs. Beulah Hirst.

A contemporary describes him as "a man of very superior legal ability, without very great learning, but who is a natural lawyer" (F. B. Wilkie, *Sketches and Notices of the Chicago Bar*, 1871). A brilliant advocate, he achieved his success by means of a singular forcefulness and simplicity of appeal, never attempting oratory. He possessed a remarkably retentive memory and great resource. On the bench he exhibited clearness of perception and an independence of thought which did not detract from the soundness of his opinions—very few of them being reversed on appeal. Possessing great charm of manner, kindly, considerate and generous to a fault, he was extremely popular with all classes.

[See *Proc. Ill. State Bar Asso.*, 1886, p. 62; 121 *Ill.*, p. 9; *Bench and Bar of Chicago* (1883); J. D. Caton, *Early Bench and Bar of Ill.* (1893), p. 147; John M. Palmer, ed., *Bench and Bar of Ill.* (1899), I, 61; *Jour. Ill. State Hist. Soc.*, Jan. 1911; *Daily Inter Ocean* (Chicago), July 23, 1885; *Official Records (Army)*; J. Dickey Templeton, *Dickey Genealogy* (1918).]

H. W. H. K.

DICKIE, GEORGE WILLIAM (July 17, 1844–Aug. 17, 1918), engineer and ship-builder, was born in Arbroath, Scotland, the son of William and Margaret (Watson) Dickie. In earlier years at Perth, Scotland, and subsequently on a strip of land bordering the Tay at Arbroath which is still known as Dickies Beach, at least five generations of Dickies had built wooden ships after the practise of the day. Dickie's education, aside from what he received at home, comprised three years in the parochial school, under an Oxford graduate who not only took care of the stated curriculum but who acted as town clerk and city engineer as well, and held evening classes in navigation. From him the boy acquired a love for study which continued throughout life, and through him he met Dr. Thomas Dick, the author of several works on science and philosophy which had great vogue in the middle decades of the nineteenth century. The latter gave Dickie an opportunity to meet Michael Faraday and Sir David Brewster, a meeting which awakened the youth's ambition and was an inspiration to him in later years. Dick also planted in him his life-long interest in astronomy.

The trend toward the use of iron and steel for shipbuilding, which developed in the late sixties, forced upon many wooden-ship builders a competition difficult to meet, and the Dickie family came to the United States and to San Francisco late in 1869. There Dickie first found employment with the Pacific Gas Company in the design, construction, and erection of a gas plant; then, in the employ of the Risdon Iron Works, he was engaged in other important engineering undertakings of an ever widening scope. He was interested in pioneer enterprises and in new and bold projects. It is claimed that he designed the first successful triple-expansion engine built in the United States, and the first Scotch marine boiler built on the Pacific Coast. He was also a successful designer of marine compound engines for steamers navigating Pacific waters. These achievements in the field of marine design brought him into contact with Irving M. Scott of the Union Iron Works; he became a member of that organization, and was its general manager from 1883 to 1905. During that time he was responsible for the construction of some eleven vessels of the then new steel navy—most notable among them being the battleship *Oregon* which made a name for itself by its record voyage around Cape Horn at the beginning of the Spanish-American War, and the cruiser *Olympia* which served as Dewey's flagship at Manila Bay. He was also responsible for the design and construction of many ships for the merchant marine and for a wide variety of other engineering work carried on by his company, including the dome of the Lick Observatory, designed and built under his direction. With the entrance of the United States into the World War in 1917, he offered his services to the government and was appointed chief inspector at the Moore & Scott Yards in Oakland, Cal., in which position he was active up to the time of his death.

He was a prolific writer on engineering subjects, especially in the field of marine construction. He took an active part in the organization of the American Society of Naval Architects and Marine Engineers and was a frequent contributor to its *Transactions* and a regular attendant at its annual meetings. He was also a member of the American Society of Mechanical Engineers and served a term as vice-president of that organization. His special contribution to his day and age is to be found in the example which he set of high standards of life both professionally and personally and more directly in the pioneer work which he did in many fields of engineering design and construction. Through work of this character carried out to practical and useful application and often discussed and presented in the form of papers before the societies of which he was a member, he made a deep and lasting impression on engineering art and practise, especially on the Pacific Coast. He was a man of wide vision and of many interests outside that of his profession. Most notable perhaps were his interest in astronomy already referred to, and his interest as a bibliophile in the collection of books and of rare and beautiful bindings. One of the tragedies of his life was the loss of his library of rare and precious bindings and of rare first editions in the San Francisco fire of 1906. He was a man of deep and lasting friendships, kindly and sympathetic in his relations to those with whom he came in contact, but not sparing in helpful and searching criticism where he judged such to be called for. On Aug. 5, 1873, he married Anna Jack, born in Denny, Scotland, on her mother's side coming from a long line of Presbyterian preachers. After her death, he was married a second time, in 1901, to Louise Barney. He died as he would have wished, in harness, active to the last, and left an enduring record both as an engineer and as a good citizen and a kind friend.

[*Trans. Am. Soc. Mech. Engineers,* XL (1919), 1152; *Trans. Soc. Naval Architects and Marine Engineers,* vol. XXVI (1918); C. E. Grunsky in *Pacific Marine Rev.,* Sept. 1918, and in *Jour. Am. Soc. Mech. Engineers,* Oct. 1918; *Who's Who in America,* 1918–19; *San Francisco Chronicle,* Aug. 18, 1918; information as to certain facts, including names of Dickie's parents, from a son, A. J. Dickie of San Francisco; personal acquaintance.]
W. F. D.

DICKINS, JOHN (*c.* Aug. 24, 1747–Sept. 27, 1798), clergyman of the Methodist Episcopal Church, and prominent among those who laid its foundations in this country, was born in London, received a good education, and came to America some years before the Revolution. He was converted in 1774, began evangelistic work in Virginia, and was admitted to the itinerant ministry on trial at the Conference of 1777, bringing to the Methodist movement an intellectual equipment, an interest in literature and learning, and an administrative wisdom, which few of his contemporaries possessed. He traveled extensively in North Carolina and Virginia until 1781, when the Conference Minutes list him among those "who desist from travelling." On Apr. 5, 1783, Asbury, then in North Carolina, records: "This day I prevailed with Brother Dickens to go to New-York, where I expect him to be far more useful than in his present station" (*Journal of Rev. Francis Asbury,* 1852, I, 458). Here, with the exception of 1785, he labored until 1789, rehabilitating John Street Church, cradle of Methodism in America. which the removal of Loyalists, and other war conditions, had weakened. He became an intimate friend and counselor of Asbury. They were "like unto Jonathan and David, . . . one in hand, mind, and mutual affection" (Ezekiel Cooper, *A Funeral Discourse, on the Death of that Eminent Man, the Late Reverend John Dickens,* 1799). He was the first to meet and advise with Dr. Coke when the latter arrived as Wesley's emissary in 1784. At the "Christmas Conference" held the same year, he was one of the leading spirits, offering the resolution which constituted the Methodist Episcopal Church in America, the name of which he himself had suggested. At this Conference he was ordained deacon, but was not made elder until Sept. 16, 1786 (Asbury's *Journal,* I, 518). He was one of the few married men in the itinerancy, having married Elizabeth Yancey of North Carolina (John Lednum, *A History of the Rise of Methodism in America,* 1859, p. 198); and the text of Asbury's ordination sermon included the admonition: "Even so must their (the deacons') wives be grave, not slanderers, sober, faithful in all things." With Thomas Morrell he was delegated by the Conference of 1789 to wait on President Washington with a copy of the bishops' congratulatory address. He also accompanied them when the President received them and made his reply.

Perhaps Dickins's most important contribution to Methodism was his work in behalf of education. He was associated with Asbury and Coke in the founding of Cokesbury College, and when the Conference of 1789 established the Methodist Book Concern, he offered the loan of all his savings, £120, about $600, to finance it. He was appointed Book Steward, being then pastor of the church in Philadelphia, St. George's. During the nine years of his management, which included the superintendency of printing, binding, and distribution, he made the Book Concern a permanent and increasingly valuable institution. Besides issuing more than one hundred and fourteen thousand copies of books and pamphlets, he published the *Arminian Magazine* (1789–90) and the *Methodist Magazine* (January 1797–August 1798). Although urged to seek safety, he continued at his work during the yellow fever epidemic of 1798, and died of that disease. "What I have greatly feared for years," Asbury wrote, "hath now taken place. Dickins, the generous, the just, the faithful, skillful Dickins, is dead!"

[Besides references above and general histories of Methodism, see S. A. Seaman, *Annals of N. Y. Methodism* (1892); W. F. Whitlock, *The Story of the Book Concerns* (1903); H. C. Jennings, *The Methodist Book Concern* (1924); W. B. Sprague, *Annals Am. Pulpit,* vol. VII (1859); *Beams of Light on Early Methodism in America* (1887), comp. by G. A. Phoebus; J. B. Wakeley, *Lost Chapters Recovered from the Early Hist. of Am. Methodism* (1858); G. W. Archer, *An Authentic Hist. of Cokesbury Coll.* (1894).] H. E. S.

DICKINSON, ANSON (Apr. 19, 1779–Mar. 9, 1852), portrait-painter in miniature and oils, was born in Milton, Litchfield County, Conn. He was the eldest son of Oliver Dickinson, Jr. (1757–1847), who is known to have painted a few portraits in oils. Oliver's wife was Anna Landon of Long Island. Of their ten children, Anson and his brother Daniel who was born in 1795, seem to have carried on the artistic tradition of the family. Anson was apprenticed to a silversmith and worked at that craft until, toward the turn of the century, he began to interest himself in painting. Of his early work in oils little is known. About 1804 he commenced painting portraits in miniature. At this time he was living in New York City, and had come under the influence of Edward Malbone, to whom he sat for a portrait in 1804. The story is told that during one of the sittings the funeral of Alexander Hamilton passed the house. Dickinson would have gone to the window to look out, but Malbone was too intent on his work to allow his sitter even this respite. In 1805 Dickinson went to Albany, where he remained until 1810. It was during this time that William Dunlap met him and perceived his work to be "indicative of talent." By 1811 Dickinson had returned to New York and was established as a leader in his profession there. In 1818 he visited Canada where he met and married Sarah B——, a woman of French descent. They had no children of their own, but later, while living in New York, adopted two children whose father was an Englishman named Walker. From 1818 to 1840 Dickinson seems to have wandered a good deal, working for a time in Boston. After 1840 he lived first in New Haven and later in Hartford. He died in 1852 at his birthplace, Milton.

Among the most noteworthy of Dickinson's patrons and sitters was Gilbert Stuart, of whom three miniatures by Dickinson are in existence (one in the possession of the New York Historical Society). Other prominent persons who sat to him were Robert Fulton, Archbishop Du Bois, Gov. Oliver Wolcott, Chancellor Livingston, the Seymours of Litchfield, and Gov. Sam Houston of Texas. Other portraits now in existence include those of Robert Dorlon, Dr. Jonathan Hall, J. W. Gale, and Mrs. Robert Watts (the last two now in the Metropolitan Museum of Art in New York City). At its best Dickinson's work is characterized by capable draftsmanship, as in the miniature of Dorlon, which is now in the Dupuy collection. His accomplishment was very uneven, however, and it is chiefly as a colorist, and, especially in this aspect of his work, as a follower and imitator of Malbone, that he is distinguished.

[William Dunlap, *Hist. of the Rise and Progress of the Arts of Design in the U. S.* (1834; new ed., 1918); H. W. French, *Art and Artists in Conn.* (1879); T. Bolton, *Early Am. Portrait Painters in Miniature* (1921); H. B. Wehle and T. Bolton, *Am. Miniature* (1927), containing a colored reproduction of a miniature by Dickinson; A. T. Gesner, *The Dickinson Family of Milton and Litchfield* (1913); *History of the Dickinson Family* (Amherst, 1884); Metropolitan Mus., *Cat. of an Exhibition of Miniatures Painted in America 1720–1850* (1927).] L. T. B.

DICKINSON, CHARLES MONROE (Nov. 15, 1842–July 3, 1924), newspaperman, diplomat, the son of Richard and Bessie (Rea) Dickinson, was born on a farm near Lowville, N. Y. The only educational advantages he had as a youth were afforded by the public schools, Fairfield Seminary, and Lowville Academy. By his fifteenth year he was doing a man's work assisting his father who was a farmer and miller. A tenth of the first year's wages which he earned in this way was invested in a copy of Webster's *Unabridged Dictionary.* His diligent study of this volume was an important factor in preparation for his literary work. For two years after leaving Lowville Academy he taught at Haverstraw-on-the-Hudson, where, in 1863, he composed "The Children," a poem which became widely popular and is included in most collections of American verse.

He began the study of law in the office of the distinguished Daniel S. Dickinson [*q.v.*] at Binghamton, N. Y., in 1864. The following year he was admitted to the bar and practised in Cameron County, Pa. Returning to Binghamton, he began law practise with Giles W. Hotchkiss, whose daughter, Bessie Virginia, he married on Mar. 24, 1867. His advancement in the law was rapid, resulting in the establishment of his office in New York City where he conducted a large practise until 1877 when the great volume of his work broke his health and compelled him to abandon his profession. Retiring to Binghamton, he lived an outdoor life while improving the estate which he purchased there. In 1878 he resumed his public career by acquiring a controlling interest in the *Binghamton Republican,* which continued under his management until 1911. As a newspaperman he took a prominent part in bringing about the organization of the present Associated Press. Appointed consul general to Turkey by President McKinley in 1897, in 1901 he received an additional appointment as diplomatic agent to Bulgaria. In that capacity, he obtained the release of Ellen M. Stone [*q.v.*], American missionary, whose kidnapping by Bulgarian brigands was one of the most widely discussed events of the time. He was appointed consul general at large with jurisdiction over consulates of the entire Middle East in 1906, and in the same year was appointed on the board to draft regulations for the entire consular service. He retired from public service in 1908 because of the illness of his wife, who died in that year. On Feb. 2, 1910, he married Alice Bond Minard of Poughkeepsie. The closing years of his life were spent in Binghamton where he devoted himself to business and literary interests. His literary work includes: *History of the Dickinson Family* (1885); *The Children and Other Verses* (1889); *Political History of New York State—Cleveland to Hughes* (1911); *Political History of New York State—From the Colonial Period* (1914); *The Children After Fifty Years in Little Verses and Big Names* (1915); "The Greatest Miracle," in *Liber Scriptorum* of the Authors Club, 1921.

[The best account of Dickinson's life is to be found in the *Binghamton Press,* June 5, 1920. Additional information is available in accounts of his funeral in the *Binghamton Press and Leader* and *Binghamton Sun,* July 7, 1924. A partial record is included in *Biographical Review . . . of Broome County, N. Y.* (1894). A portrait and complete account of his activities are available in W. F. Seward, ed., *Binghamton and Broome County, N. Y., A History,* vol. III (1924). E. C. Stedman's *Lib. of Am. Lit.* includes a reprint of "The Children" (vol. X, 1889, p. 129) and a brief biographical sketch (vol. XI, 1890, p. 502). See also *Who's Who in America,* 1899–1925.] D. W. M.

DICKINSON, DANIEL STEVENS (Sept. 11, 1800–Apr. 12, 1866), lawyer, politician, was born at Goshen, Conn., the fourth of eight children of Daniel T. and Mary (Caulkins) Dickinson. Both parents were natives of Connecticut and of English descent, the father being a farmer in moderate circumstances. They moved in 1806 to Chenango County, N. Y., settling at the present Guilford. There young Daniel did the usual boy's work on the farm and attended the local public schools. While apprenticed to a clothier he managed to study (alone) Latin, mathematics, and more or less of general science. For five years he taught in public and private schools, studying law and surveying at the same time. Continuing his legal studies in the office of Clark & Clapp, at the county seat, Norwich, he was admitted to the bar in 1828 and began practise at Guilford, where he was postmaster. Three years later he moved to Binghamton, where he soon acquired a good practise and became prominent in the Democratic party. When Binghamton was incorporated (1834) Dickinson was elected its first president. The next year he was a member of the national convention which nominated Van Buren and Johnson. From 1837 to 1841 he was one of the Democratic leaders in the state Senate, taking much interest in such matters as banking reform, railroads, and canals. Defeated for lieutenant-governor in 1840, he declined to be a candidate in 1842 yet was nominated and elected. Besides presiding over the Senate this office entailed the presidency of the court of errors and membership on the canal board, to both of which Dickinson rendered valuable service. By this time he was recognized as one of the leading conservative Democrats of New York, along with Silas Wright, Horatio Seymour, and the like. At the national convention of 1844 he cast the vote of New York for Polk. When the state convention nominated Silas Wright over Gov. W. C. Bouck, Dickinson refused the nomination for lieutenant-governor, despite Wright's urging. Upon the resignation of United States Senator N. P. Tallmadge (December 1844), Gov. Bouck appointed Dickinson for the rest of the term. The legislature promptly confirmed this nomination and elected him for the ensuing term (1845–51). For much of this time he was chairman of the finance committee, being recognized as one of the leading Democrats in the Senate. He spoke upon the annexation of Texas, the occupation of Oregon, the Mexican War, the Wilmot Proviso (which he opposed), and the Clayton-Bulwer Treaty. As a member of the Committee of Thirteen he did such valiant service for the compromise measures of 1850 as to evoke the praises of both Clay and Webster. In December 1847 he introduced some resolutions which practically embodied the doctrine of "squatter sovereignty." He was a member of the national Democratic conventions of 1848 and 1852. After leaving the Senate, he devoted himself to the law, occasionally delivering addresses at fairs, centennials, corner-stone and dedication ceremonies, and before temperance and literary societies. In the campaigns of 1852 and 1856 he took the stump for the Democratic ticket. President Pierce nominated him as collector of the port of New York (1853), and the Senate confirmed him without reference, but he declined the position. He hoped to receive the nomination for president in 1860, but never got over sixteen votes in the convention. After the secession of South Carolina he strove for reconciliation with the South, holding the North responsible for secession, but after the firing on Fort Sumter he vigorously supported the government, making hundreds of speeches in Pennsylvania, New York, and New England and doing much to stimulate enlistment in his own district. Both the 89th New York Infantry and the battery recruited at Binghamton were named for him. His earnest support of the government procured him the nomination and triumphant election as attorney-general on the "Union" ticket in 1861. The next year he sought in vain the Republican nomination for United States senator. Appointed and confirmed on the Northwest Boundary Commission in 1863, he declined this office as well as Gov. Fenton's proffer of a seat on the state court of appeals. He was a delegate to the Union convention of 1864, where, though he would have preferred another candidate to Lincoln, he supported the latter loyally. On the first ballot for vice-president Dickinson received 108 votes. In 1865 he was appointed federal district attorney for the southern district of New York, and served until his death the following year in New York City. He was married in 1822 to Lydia, the daughter of Colby Knapp, a physician of Chenango County. Dickinson was not only an able lawyer—as president of the court of errors he wrote some able opinions—but a skilful debater; clear, forceful, at times scathingly sarcastic.

[*Speeches and Correspondence, etc. of the Late Daniel S. Dickinson of N. Y.* (1867), ed. by his brother, John R. Dickinson, contains a biographical sketch. Besides the newspapers of the period, E. H. Roberts, *New York* (1887), and D. S. Alexander, *A Political Hist. of the State of N. Y.*, vols. II (1906) and III (1909), should be consulted.]

M. L. B., Jr.

DICKINSON, DONALD McDONALD (Jan. 17, 1846–Oct. 15, 1917), lawyer, postmaster-general, was born at Port Ontario, Oswego County, N. Y., the son of Col. Asa C. and Minerva (Holmes) Dickinson. One of his boasts was that his paternal grandfather and great-grandfather and his maternal grandfather and great-grandfather were all natives of American soil. His ancestors had an enviable record of service in the Revolutionary army and in the formation of the federal government. His father, as a young man, explored the shores of Lakes Erie, Huron, and Michigan in a birch-bark canoe and was greatly impressed with the future of the country. In 1848 he moved with his family to Michigan, settling on an island in the St. Clair River. Four years later he removed to Detroit. Don M. Dickinson attended the public schools of Detroit but was prepared for college under the instruction of private tutors. He entered the Law School of the University of Michigan at Ann Arbor and was graduated with the class of 1867. Admitted to the bar in the same year, he entered at once upon a brilliant and successful career. He gained a reputation as one of the leading lawyers of the Middle West and was frequently called upon to argue important cases before the Supreme Court of the United States. Worthy of particular mention in this connection are the Telephone Appeals case, in which his argument for Drawbaugh is printed in full in the stenographic record (126 *U. S.*, 329–73), and the Homestead cases (155 *U. S.*, 356–88). In the latter cases he successfully defended the rights of homesteaders upon lands covered by unearned public grants to railroads, thereby securing to many poor farmers their homes and lands.

He was the second Michigan Democrat—the first being Lewis Cass—to rise to a position of national political importance. His political career began in 1872, when he was chosen to serve as secretary of the Democratic state central committee in the Greeley campaign. Attributing the overwhelming defeat of Greeley to the Democratic party, he wrote to Dr. Foster Pratt, chairman of the state committee, declaring that Greeley's defeat broke any link which might have bound the progressive men of the party to it, that he would never vote or act with the party again, but would await the new party which should carry forward the living principles of the dead leader, Greeley. However, he did not carry his threat into execution. The leadership of Gov. Tilden of New York quickened the party into new life, and the campaign of 1876 found Dickinson in the position of chairman of the Democratic state central committee. In 1880 he was chosen a member of the Democratic national committee for Michigan and served in that capacity until 1885. He had early formed a high opinion of Grover Cleveland, and his support of Cleveland for the presidency marked the definite beginning of a close and enduring political and personal friendship between the two men. After Cleveland's election, there being no Democratic senator from Michigan, the President recognized Dickinson as the titular head of the party in that state and consulted him on all appointments to office affecting Michigan men. Dickinson did not desire a political office for himself, but when William F. Vilas was transferred from the position of postmaster-general to that of secretary of the interior, he accepted the postmaster-generalship upon the urgent request of President Cleveland. He was nominated for the office Dec. 6, 1887, was confirmed and commissioned Jan. 16, 1888, and entered upon his duties the next day (*Executive Register of the United States*, 1903, p. 250). He served until the close of the administration in 1889. In his honor the Democratic legislature of Michigan in 1891 organized a new county in the Upper Peninsula and named it Dickinson County (*Public Acts*, 1891, pp. 98 ff.). In 1892 he took a leading part in the campaign which elected Cleveland to the presidency for the second time. He declined an unsolicited offer of a cabinet position, preferring to devote himself to the profession of law and to private life. During Cleveland's second administration and in his opposition to the free-silver wing of the party, Dickinson gave him unfailing support. He opposed the nomination of Bryan in 1896, and in 1900, when Bryan was again nominated, advocated the reëlection of President McKinley. In 1912 he again showed his independence in politics by sending a telegram to Roosevelt, dated Oct. 16, pledging to him his unqualified support "because of the reactionary teachings of the two old parties" (Fitzgibbon, *post*).

Twice in his later years he was called to the service of the government in his legal capacity. In 1896 he was senior counsel for the United States before the international high commission on the Bering Sea claims (*Bering Sea. Fur Seal Arbitration*, etc., 1897). He was the member for the United States of the court of arbitration formed in 1902 to adjust a controversy between the United States and the Republic of Salvador, arising from a claim against Salvador presented by an American company which had a concession for the collection of port duties at the port of El Triunfo. The majority of the commission, Dickinson and Sir Henry Strong, chief justice of the Dominion of Canada, decided against Salvador. Señor Don José Rosa Pacas, the representative of Salvador, declined to sign the award (see *Papers Relating to the Foreign Relations of the United States, 1902,* pp. 838–73). For several years prior to his death at his home in Trenton, Mich., Dickinson lived in retirement. He was a man of exalted character, loyal to friends or to a cause, and always ready to fight for what he deemed to be right (Reed, *post,* p. 142). On June 15, 1869, he was married to Frances Platt, daughter of Dr. Alonzo Platt of Grand Rapids, Mich.

[See *Who's Who in America*, 1899–1917; *Am. Biog. Hist.* (*Mich. Vol.*, 1878), pp. 42–43; C. M. Burton, *The City of Detroit, Mich.* (1922), IV, 6–9; *Chronography of Notable Events in the Hist. of the Northwest Territory and Wayne County* (1890), comp. by Fred Carlisle, pp. 357–62; Silas Farmer, *Hist. of Detroit and Wayne County* (1890), II, 1114–19; Chas. Moore, *Hist. of Mich.* (1915), II, 668–69; *Bench and Bar of Mich.* (1897), ed. by G. I. Reed, pp. 138–42. The most comprehensive account of Dickinson's political activities is given by John Fitzgibbon. "Don M. Dickinson One of the State's Two Great Democrats," *Detroit News*, Oct. 17, 1917. His papers are in the possession of his family in Detroit. His letters to Cleveland were sent to Princeton for use in R. McElroy's *Grover Cleveland* (1923), and several were printed in the second volume of that work. For his suggestions concerning the P. O.

Dept., see his article, "Progress and the Post," *North Am. Rev.*, Oct. 1889.]

E. S. B—n.

DICKINSON, EMILY ELIZABETH (Dec. 10, 1830–May 15, 1886), poet, was born, lived, and died in Amherst, Mass. Her father, Edward Dickinson, was a leading lawyer of Amherst, a member at various times of the state legislature and of Congress, and treasurer of Amherst College. In this last office he was succeeded by his son, William Austin, who in 1856 married Susan Gilbert and occupied a house built for him next door to his father's. Emily's mother, who was Emily Norcross of Monson, and younger sister, Lavinia, completed the family circle. Edward Dickinson, though austere in his domestic manners, demanded that his children remain about him. Neither daughter married, and the fact that the family circle was not broken until her father's death in 1874 made it possible for Emily to protract her childhood relation to her parents almost to the end of her own life.

She received rather more than the normal education of a New England girl of good family at that time, in the public schools, at Amherst Academy, where the encouragement given her by the young principal, Leonard Humphrey, strongly affected her awakening mind, and for one year, 1847–48, at Mount Holyoke Female Seminary in the neighboring village of South Hadley. Among her schoolmates were several girls of marked individuality, including her life-long friend Helen Fiske, later Helen Hunt Jackson. Emily Dickinson was noted for her wit and love of drollery, which found expression in comic valentines sent to members of her brother's college circle and in humorous squibs contributed to a manuscript magazine circulated at the Academy. She was fond of music, of country walks, and of gardening, joined a Shakespeare club, and attended dancing parties surreptitiously organized by the girls of the village. In her own home and in the homes of various college dignitaries she met preachers, missionaries, men of affairs, and writers. Among these last, Samuel Bowles, the proprietor and editor of the *Springfield Republican,* and his wife, and Dr. and Mrs. Josiah Gilbert Holland were intimate friends of the family. In the social life of the village, then devoid of standardized amusements except for the annual college commencements and the autumn cattle shows, Emily took part freely until her middle twenties. Gradually, however, as her individuality asserted itself, she became increasingly impatient of all formal occasions.

During the spring of 1854, Emily with her mother and sister spent a few weeks in Washington, where her father was attending Congress, and on the return journey stopped to visit a friend in Philadelphia. It is supposed that at this time she met the man to whom her love poems were later addressed, but the circumstances of this episode are still far from clear. According to her niece and biographer, Mme. Bianchi, she fell in love with a young preacher and awakened in him an answering passion that made him reckless of his ties of family and profession. Upon learning that he was a married man, she fled to Amherst and finally refused his proposal to elope (*Life and Letters,* pp. 45 ff.; *Further Poems,* pp. xvi–xx). Miss Josephine Pollitt (*post*), offers the inherently improbable suggestion that Emily's lover was Lieut. Edward Bissell Hunt, the husband of her friend Helen Fiske. Local tradition perpetuates the story that Emily wished to marry an eligible young man, but refused him because of her father's opposition to the match (Clara B. Green, *Bookman,* November 1924).

For the rest of her life she lived quietly at home, never leaving Amherst except to go to Boston for the care of her eyes in 1864 and again in the following year. However important the frustration of her love may be as a background for her poetry, it should not be thought of as wrecking her life or even as the direct cause of her preference for solitude. "She lived in seclusion from no love-disappointment" is the categorical statement of Mrs. Todd, her ablest editor (*Poems,* Second Series, p. 8). Most of her early friends had married and left town. Imperceptibly she drifted into a habit of seclusion, finding her satisfactions in the hills and sunsets, her garden, the companionship of her dog, and "the little toil of love" of her household routine. Her retirement may in part be explained by her increasing preoccupation with poetry, which she says in a letter to her literary mentor, Thomas Wentworth Higginson, began in the winter of 1861–62. Her desire for "polar privacy," indulged by a brother and sister who in their own ways were no respecters of convention, deepened as the years passed. After the shock of her father's death, which was followed a year later by the invalidism of her mother, she immured herself in the house and showed a morbid dread of being seen by strangers. But until she was stricken by illness two years before her death, she continued to perform her part in the exacting duties of her New England housekeeping. She has described herself in a letter to Higginson: "I . . . am small, like the wren; and my hair is bold, like the chestnut burr; and my eyes, like the sherry in the glass that the guest leaves."

Emily Dickinson, like Emerson, belonged to

the generation when the frost was coming out of the Puritan soil. Her intense inner life recognized no law save that of her own nature. Though her days to outward seeming were utterly eventless, her brief, breathless poems, written in the solitude of her room and guarded like a secret journal, show that her mind was filled with events, with tiny ecstasies set in motion by home and garden incidents, with deep and candid intuitions of her own states of consciousness, with speculations on the timeless mysteries of love and death suggested by her reading, by her quick imaginative sympathy, and by her piercing memories.

Only two of her poems were printed during her lifetime, neither with her consent. One was sent to the *Springfield Republican* (Feb. 14, 1866) by her sister-in-law. Mrs. Jackson was responsible for the inclusion of the other, without signature, in G. P. Lathrop's *A Masque of Poets* (1878). After her death her poems were found among her papers and by a fortunate decision of her sister Lavinia were preserved and published in three series: *Poems* (1890), *Poems* (1891), *Poems* (1896). A fourth volume, *The Single Hound* (1914), contains the messages in swift, spontaneous verse that she was in the habit of sending across the lawn to her sister-in-law, and a fifth, *Further Poems* (1929), includes a series of love poems reflecting her frustrated attachment. The first four are reprinted in *Complete Poems of Emily Dickinson* (1924).

[The prefaces to the several volumes of poems listed above contain some biographical information. The *Letters of Emily Dickinson*, published in 1894 by Mrs. Mabel Loomis Todd and preceded by Col. Higginson's "Emily Dickinson's Letters," *Atlantic Monthly*, Oct. 1891, have been supplemented by Mme. Bianchi's "Selections from the Unpublished Letters of Emily Dickinson," *Atlantic Monthly*, Jan. 1915, and M. H. Barney's "Fragments from Emily Dickinson to her Brother's Family," *Atlantic Monthly*, June 1927. Martha Dickinson Bianchi's *Life and Letters of Emily Dickinson* (1924) reprints material given in the earlier collection with some additions and many omissions; the early printings of this book (1924–29) are marred by gross inaccuracies. Josephine Pollitt's *Emily Dickinson: The Human Background of her Poetry* (1930) is fully documented. Manuscript letters and poems of Emily Dickinson, some unpublished, are in the Galatea Collection of the Boston Public Library. Important studies of her character have been written by Gamaliel Bradford, *Portraits of Am. Women* (1919), Conrad Aiken, preface to his *Selected Poems of Emily Dickinson* (1924), and Katherine Bregy, *Catholic World*, Dec. 1924.] G. F. W.

DICKINSON, JACOB McGAVOCK (Jan. 30, 1851–Dec. 13, 1928), lawyer, secretary of war, son of Henry and Anna (McGavock) Dickinson, was born in Columbus, Miss. His father was long a chancery judge (a vice chancellor, 1843–54) of the state; his mother's grandfather was Felix Grundy [*q.v.*]. When only fourteen years of age Dickinson served as a private in the Confederate cavalry. After the war his parents moved to Nashville, Tenn., the home of his mother's family. He took a college course, graduating with distinction, in the University of Nashville (A.B. 1871, A.M. 1872), briefly studied law at Columbia College and then continued his studies abroad—chiefly in law—in Leipzig and in Paris. To the end of his life he retained a fair command of the classics. He spoke German easily, and French and German books were conspicuous in his library. After admission to the Tennessee bar, in 1874, he made his home in Nashville until 1899, when he moved to Chicago. In his profession he attained a standing that was very high, and of stainless repute. His most striking characteristics in the preparation and argument of cases were a strict attention to details and to truth. He scorned resort to a specious argument. Perhaps not unnaturally, therefore, although he was of commanding physique and of distinguished bearing and manners, he was not particularly notable as a jury lawyer. The presidency of the Bar Association of Tennessee (1889–90), four appointments for temporary service as a member of the supreme court of the state (1891, 1892, 1893), and two years of service as an assistant attorney-general of the United States (1895–97), marked the high regard which he enjoyed among his fellows. In the early years of practise he gained as a client the Louisville & Nashville Railroad, of which he ultimately became the general attorney (1897–99); passing from its service to that of the Illinois Central, as general solicitor (1899–1901) and general counsel (1901–09). He was not, however, a mere specialist in railroad law, but a general practitioner of notable all-round ability. In 1907–08 he was president of the American Bar Association. Public life called him briefly in 1903, when he served with distinction as one of counsel (making the closing argument) for the United States before the Alaskan Boundary Tribunal; and his continued interest, thereafter, in international problems was manifested in his participation in the organization, in 1906, of the American Society of International Law, which he served as a member of the Executive Council (1907–10) and as a vice-president (1910 onward). In 1909 he became secretary of war (March 1909–May 1911) in the cabinet of his old-time friend and professional associate, President Taft. This office was abandoned when his family suffered financial reverses. Later, he served the government as a special assistant attorney-general in the prosecution of the United States Steel Corporation (1913), and in im-

Dickinson

portant labor cases (1922); and from 1915 to 1917 was receiver of the Rock Island Lines, and markedly successful. After this he gradually abandoned practise. In 1927–28 he was president of the Izaak Walton League at a critical moment in its history. A life-time devotion to fishing and hunting had made him appreciative of the need, and sympathetic to the conservation purposes, of that organization. His services to it illustrated as well as any task of his life his wisdom, force, and winning personality. He owned and gave much time to a plantation, and a stock farm of national repute.

Dickinson belonged by family tradition in the Democratic party, and long served it actively; but voted, apparently, more often as a Republican than a Democrat after the Bryan campaign of 1896. He was devoted and ever loyal to friends; notably sociable, fond of converse and companionship, though not of conventional sports and amusements; devoted to reading, and widely informed. Rather than compete with friends he rejected what was at least a probability of appointment to the federal bench. High spirits, a keen humor, great stores of anecdotes, and varied knowledge made him a prized companion. Temperance characterized his personal habits; tolerance, his opinions—except of intolerance, as in some forms of social legislation. He was married (on Apr. 20, 1876) to Martha Overton who bore him three sons, two of whom survived him. Before his burial, in Nashville, his body lay in state in the capitol.

[Blewett Lee, "Jacob McGavock Dickinson: 1851–1928," *Jour. Am. Bar. Asso.*, Feb. 1929, pp. 69–71; *N. Y. Times*, Dec. 14, 1928, p. 29; editorial (by C. N. Burch) in *Commercial Appeal* (Memphis), Dec. 15, 1928.]

F. S. P.

DICKINSON, JOHN (Nov. 8, 1732–Feb. 14, 1808), statesman, was the second son of Samuel Dickinson of Talbot County, Md., and his second wife, Mary Cadwalader of Philadelphia. In his boyhood, the family moved to a new estate near Dover, Del. There were a number of children and they were educated at home by a tutor. In 1750 John became a student in the law office of John Moland, one of the leading members of the Philadelphia bar. Three years later he went to London to continue his studies in the Middle Temple, remaining there until 1757 when he returned to Philadelphia and at once began the practise of law. Within five years he had risen to eminence and was arguing cases before the colonial supreme court. His interests, however, were historical and political rather than legal, and after the beginning of the Revolution he left the bar completely. In October 1760 he was elected to the Assembly of the Lower Counties (Delaware), and became speaker. Two years later he was elected representative from Philadelphia to the Pennsylvania legislature. The questions of the proprietary government, taxation, military service, representation, and the frontier were then being discussed with the greatest bitterness, and Dickinson and Franklin were opposing leaders. The former, who was always intensely conservative, adopted the unpopular side. In the great debate of 1764 he admitted all the evils of the proprietary system but feared that any change might bring worse, and that any royal government granted by a British ministry of that day would be still more dangerous. As a result, he lost his seat in the Assembly and was not reelected until 1770.

In 1765 he published a pamphlet, *The Late Regulations Respecting the British Colonies . . . Considered.* He believed that the only way to secure the repeal of the Sugar and Stamp acts was to enlist the English merchants on the American side by economic interest, and his argument was therefore devoted to showing the injury that would be done to the British mercantile interests by attempting to enforce the acts. His opposition to these acts and his knowledge of the subject resulted in his appointment by the legislature, October 1765, as one of the Pennsylvania delegates to the Stamp Act Congress at New York, and he was there called on to draft the resolution (Stillé, *post*, pp. 339–40). Although one of the leaders of the opposition to the Stamp Act, he had also opposed all violent resistance, including even the non-use of stamps by lawyers.

Owing to the continued crisis between England and the colonies, the Non-Importation agreement was proposed in Boston in 1767. In December of that year, Dickinson began publishing anonymously in the *Pennsylvania Chronicle* the series later known in pamphlet form as *Letters from a Farmer in Pennsylvania to the Inhabitants of the British Colonies* (1768). In these he pointed out the evils of the British policy, suggested force as an ultimate remedy, but stated a belief that conciliation was possible. The *Letters*, although very pacific in tone, showed wide knowledge both of the practical economics of the situation and of the broad legal principles underlying English liberty and created a deep impression here and abroad. He was thanked at a public meeting in Boston, given the degree of LL.D. by Princeton, and received other honors. In April 1768 he addressed a great meeting in Philadelphia and strongly urged the adoption of the Non-Importation and Non-Exportation agreement. In 1771, as a member of the legislature, he drafted the Petition to the King which was unanimously adopted. He was opposed, however, to the resort to force and because he condemned the more violent opinions and actions in New England he lost most of his popularity and influence there. In 1774, when Boston asked aid from the other colonies after her actions had precipitated a crisis, Dickinson refused to sanction anything other than friendly expressions of sympathy, as he felt she had destroyed the hope of conciliation. He became, however, chairman of the Philadelphia Committee of Correspondence. At the conference held in July to discuss the situation and consider appointing delegates to a Continental Congress, Dickinson drew up three papers which were unanimously adopted. They consisted of a series of resolutions stating the principles upon which the colonies based their claim to redress; instructions to the Congressional delegates to be chosen by the Assembly; and a treatise on the constitutional power of Great Britain to tax the colonies. These papers expressed the views of the more conservative patriots up to the time when all was thrown over on the adoption of the Declaration of Independence.

In October 1774 Dickinson was a member of the Continental Congress, although for a week only, he believing he had been excluded up to that time by Galloway's influence. It was Dickinson, however, who drew up the Petition to the King, and the address to the people of Canada. On June 23, 1775, he was made chairman of a committee of safety and defense and held the post for a year, and he became colonel of the first battalion raised in Philadelphia. At the second Continental Congress, 1775, he still wished to adopt peaceful methods of settlement if possible and wrote the second Petition to the King, although he was engaged at the same time in strengthening the military resources of the colony. His action in drawing up the petition greatly angered the New England members. He also wrote the great part, if not all, of the "Declaration of the Causes of taking up Arms." In the Assembly, November 1775, he drafted the resolutions instructing the delegates to the Congress to meet in 1776, which asked them to use every possible means to gain redress of grievances but to countenance no measures looking toward separation. The general feeling in the country was changing and by the beginning of 1776 many began to believe separation the only solution of the problem. Dickinson and some of the other leaders still clung to conciliation.

In Congress, desirous of making one more peaceful effort and fearful of the results of a civil war without foreign allies and with no federal government binding the colonies together, he cast his vote against the Declaration of Independence. It should be noted that although he did what he believed to be his duty in this voting, yet when it came to fighting he and McKean were the only two members of Congress who took up arms in defense of the measures they had been advocating. He at once went with his regiment, as ordered, to Elizabethtown, but shortly afterward, when new members of Congress were elected and his name was rejected, he resigned his commission. Soon, for other causes, he resigned from the Assembly. In November he was elected to Congress from Delaware but declined to serve. In December, when the British neared Philadelphia, he retired to his estate in Delaware. Temporarily he appears to have served as a private in a special force raised in that colony which took part in the battle of Brandywine. In 1779 he was again elected to Congress from Delaware and took his seat. In the autumn he resigned but in 1781 was elected president of the Supreme Executive Council of Delaware. Returning to live in Philadelphia he was elected to the same office in Pennsylvania. At this time he was scurrilously attacked in a series of articles signed "Valerius," which he answered in his "Vindication," published in the Philadelphia *Freeman's Journal,* January–February 1783. In 1787 as a delegate from Delaware he became a member of the convention to frame the Federal Constitution, and took an active and useful part in its proceedings. In a series of letters signed "Fabius" he strongly urged the adoption of the new instrument. For the seventeen years which he lived afterward he held no public office, but continued an active interest in public affairs. In 1801 he published two volumes of his writings under the title, *The Political Writings of John Dickinson, Esq., Late President of the State of Delaware and of the Commonwealth of Pennsylvania.* These were republished in 1814. In 1895 P. L. Ford edited the first of what was to be a complete set, in three volumes, and it was published in that year as Vol. XIV of the Memoirs of the Historical Society of Pennsylvania, with the title, *The Writings of John Dickinson, vol. I, Political Writings 1764–74.* The others have not appeared. Dickinson was married on July 19, 1770, to Mary Norris, daughter of Isaac Norris of Philadelphia. He died at Wilmington.

[The standard biography is that by C. J. Stillé, *The Life and Times of John Dickinson* (1891), being vol. XIII of the Memoirs of the Hist. Soc. of Pa. In 1882 G. H. Moore prepared a paper for the N. Y. Hist. Soc. Pubs., as *John Dickinson, the Author of the Declaration on Taking up Arms in 1775* (1890), to prove that Dickinson wrote the whole of that Declaration, a part of which has been attributed to Jefferson.] J. T. A.

DICKINSON, JOHN WOODBRIDGE (Oct. 12, 1825–Feb. 16, 1901), educator, was born to William Dickinson and his wife, Elizabeth (Worthington) Dickinson, in Chester, Mass., the youngest but one of nine children. His boyhood was spent at South Williamstown in the Berkshires where his early scanty schooling consisted of a few weeks each winter at the district school. This he later supplemented by attendance at the Greylock Institute, South Williamstown, and Williston Seminary at East Hampton. In 1848 he entered Williams College, graduating in 1852 with classical honors and local renown as a logician. That year he became instructor in the Westfield (Mass.) State Normal School, and held that position till in 1857 he became its principal. In this office he remained for twenty years, and his leadership gained for the school a national reputation. Memory of his service to it is preserved there by Dickinson Hall, erected in 1903 and named in his honor. In 1869 he spent six months in Germany, making an intensive study of the school systems there. During his principalship at Westfield he was regularly a speaker at the teachers' institutes held annually throughout the state, and came to be recognized as one of the foremost educators of New England. In 1877 he was chosen secretary of the Board of Education of Massachusetts and held this office till his resignation, Dec. 31, 1893. In this position he originated and promoted measures that proved of lasting value to the schools of the state and enhanced his distinction as an educational leader. Among these measures were the abolishing of old district systems and the substitution of town control; the instituting of free text-books and school supplies; the establishing in nearly every county of parental schools for truant children; the expansion of the normal-school system by the addition of four new normal schools; the strengthening and reorganizing of teachers' institutes; and the introduction of the new practise of holding institutes (in sixteen districts) for school committees and superintendents (*Annual Report* of the Board of Education, 1899–1900, p. 253). Probably his chief service in this office was the originating and carrying out of the plan by which the smaller and poorer towns were given improved schools through a co-partnership system of employing school superintendents. Towns unable alone to buy expert supervision thus got it through cooperation. (*Springfield Weekly Republican,* Feb. 22, 1901.) His name appeared frequently in the list of those chosen to address the gatherings of the National Education Association. From 1886 to 1890 he was a trustee of Williams College. During the last years of his life he held an instructorship in the Emerson School of Oratory in Boston. Besides his official reports, public addresses and contributions to the educational magazines, he published the following: *The Limits of Oral Training* (1890), *Brief Descriptive Sketch of the Massachusetts Public School System* (1893), *Principles and Method of Teaching, Derived from a Knowledge of the Mind* (1899), *Rhetoric and Principles of Written Composition* (1901), and in collaboration with M. B. C. True, *Our Republic* (1888).

He was of tall and graceful figure, dignified, quiet, unassuming, scholarly. Yet physical, mental, and moral virility was characteristic of him; his views were positive, clearly defined, effectively expressed. Throughout his adult life he was actively connected with the Congregational Church. In 1857 he was married to Arexene G. Parsons of North Yarmouth, Me. His residence from 1877 was at Newton, Mass., where for several terms he was a member of the city school board. Of a son and daughter, the latter alone survived him.

[The chief sources of information about him are the *Sixty-Fourth Ann. Report of the Board of Educ. of Mass.,* 1899–1900, p. 253; *Education,* Oct. 1901, p. 65; *Springfield* (Mass.) *Weekly Republican,* Feb. 22, 1901; *Sunday Herald* (Boston), Feb. 17, 1901; *Boston Daily Globe,* Feb. 17, 1901; information as to certain facts from Dickinson's daughter.] W. J. C.

DICKINSON, JONATHAN (Apr. 22, 1688–Oct. 7, 1747), first president of the College of New Jersey (now Princeton), was born in Hatfield, Mass. His parents, Hezekiah and Abigail, came of pioneer Connecticut Valley stock. Jonathan was graduated from Yale College in 1706 and forthwith turned to the study of theology. He was ordained pastor of the church at Elizabeth Town, N. J., in September 1709. Shortly before, he had married Joanna Melyen, the sister of his predecessor. The Elizabeth Town charge like many early New Jersey churches was Congregational and did not share its pastor's admiration for the Presbyterian organization. Not until 1717 was Dickinson able to persuade his congregation to join the presbytery of Philadelphia. Though the youngest of the members of the synod, he was soon regarded as one of the ablest. Twice he was elected moderator of that body, in 1721 and 1742. For nearly forty years he labored in behalf of the church, earning the reputation of being "one of the greatest and safest men of his age" (Hatfield, *post,* 354). Within the synod faction was rife; many desired to enforce a rigid and narrow view of Presbyterianism. On several occasions, for example, it was proposed to compel the clergy to subscribe to the Westminster Confessions and Catechisms. Dickinson, in keeping with his Congregational heritage, opposed such measures on the ground that the rights of the clergy would be infringed. For many years by the exercise of rare judgment he was able to compose the differences between the factions. At the same time he defended Presbyterianism with great vigor against external criticism. His pen was active in all the religious controversies of his day, and indeed his ability to define authoritatively such a variety of theological issues led Dr. Erskine of Edinburgh to remark that the British Isles had produced no such critics on Divinity in the eighteenth century as Dickinson and Edwards (Sprague, *post,* p. 17). Particularly bitter were the assaults made upon the actions and sermons of George Whitefield, the evangelist. Dickinson not only defended the revival in the synod but repelled the attacks of those outside the church who dared question the sincerity of the mission. He was impatient of the erratic movements of the day, particularly Deism and Arminianism. "It may be doubted whether, with the exception of the elder Edwards, Calvinism has ever found an abler or more efficient champion in this country, than Jonathan Dickinson" (*Ibid.,* p. 16).

The need of a school to train young men for the ministry had become pressing. At Neshaminy the Rev. William Tennant had founded a school which its opponents had derisively dubbed the "Log College." In 1738, however, the synod decreed that no one without a degree from Harvard, Yale, or a European institution might be ordained without its consent. This ruling outraged the feelings of the Log College adherents and finally led, among other differences, to the "great schism." The dissatisfied presbyteries of New Brunswick and New York met at Elizabeth Town in 1745 and organized the Synod of New York, with Dickinson as moderator. Dickinson clearly realized the need of an institution of higher learning in the Middle Colonies, not only to train men for the ministry but to serve in a broad sense the whole community. He was not satisfied with the Log College. With a larger purpose in view he approached the Anglican Gov. Morris of New Jersey, but his application for a charter was refused. Shortly after, on Oct. 22, 1746, Acting-Governor Hamilton, though also an Anglican, was prevailed upon to grant the first charter of the College of New Jersey. The college was formally opened in May of 1747 at Elizabeth Town and Dickinson was elected its first president. Great must have been his joy when it was learned that the new governor, Jonathan Belcher, not only approved the undertaking but was willing to cooperate in obtaining a more secure charter. Plans were made to remove the college to Princeton, more centrally situated. Before these changes could be consummated Dickinson died suddenly, on Oct. 7, 1747, from an attack of pleurisy. He was survived by his second wife, Mary Crane Dickinson, whom he had married in April 1747.

[A. Alexander, *Biog. Sketches of the Founder . . . of the Log Coll.* (1851); H. C. Cameron, *Jonathan Dickinson and the Coll. of N. J.* (1880); V. L. Collins, *Princeton* (1914); F. B. Dexter, *Biog. Sketches Grads. Yale Coll.*, vol. I (1885), which includes a list of Dickinson's publications; J. DeWitt, *Planting of Princeton Coll.* (1897); J. F. Hageman, *Hist. of Princeton and its Institutions* (1879), vol. II; E. F. Hatfield, *Hist. of Elizabeth, N. J.* (1868); J. Maclean, *Hist. of the Coll. of N. J.* (1877); W. B. Sprague, *Annals Am. Pulpit,* vol. III (1859).]

J. E. P.

DICKINSON, PHILEMON (Apr. 5, 1739–Feb. 4, 1809), Revolutionary soldier, congressman, was the son of Judge Samuel and Mary (Cadwalader) Dickinson, and the brother of John Dickinson [*q.v.*]. His birthplace was probably Croisia-doré, Talbot County, Md., though it is sometimes given as somewhere near Dover, Kent County, Del. His education began under the tutorship of William Killen afterward chancellor of Delaware, at that time a law student in Judge Dickinson's office. He then entered the College of Philadelphia (now the University of Pennsylvania), from which he was graduated in 1759. For some time prior to his father's death in 1760 he managed the latter's enormous estates in Kent County, Del., and in Talbot, Dorchester, and Queen Anne counties, Md. He then settled in Philadelphia, where he read law with his brother John, whom he later joined in signing the non-importation agreement of November 1765. When New Jersey voted to raise ten battalions of infantry in 1775, Philemon, who had an estate near Trenton, was appointed colonel of the Hunterdon County Battalion, and in October was commissioned brigadier-general of New Jersey militia. The following year he was elected to the Provincial Congress of New Jersey, but he was not a member, as is alleged, of the committee that drafted the New Jersey constitution of 1776 (*Journal . . . of the Convention of New Jersey,* 1776). In January 1777 Dickinson, with 400 raw militia, defeated a foraging expedition sent out by Cornwallis to capture flour stored in a mill near Somerset Court House on the Millstone River, and captured forty wagons and a hundred draft horses. In reporting the engagement to the president of Congress Washington warmly commended Dickinson. In June, Gov.

William Livingston appointed him major-general and commander-in-chief of the New Jersey militia. In November Dickinson suggested that he himself descend upon Staten Island while Gates and Putnam attack Long Island and New York. Washington disapproved the proposed attack on Long Island, but thought the general plan "of counteracting the intended reinforcements for Mr. Howe's army, by a demonstration of designs upon New York . . . an exceedingly good one." Dickinson accordingly landed on Staten Island, which was occupied by the Loyalist regiments of Gen. Cortland Skinner and the Waldeckers of Gen. Campbell, both of whom, warned of Dickinson's plans, narrowly escaped. In the spring of 1778 Clinton, having evacuated Philadelphia, began retreating across the Jerseys toward New York. Dickinson and Gen. William Maxwell, having been ordered by Washington to obstruct the roads and harass the British, "destroyed every bridge on the road," as Clinton reported, in a country abounding in small streams and marshes. The delay enabled the Continental Army to come up with the British. Then came the battle of Monmouth, following which victory Washington, in his order to the troops, thanked Dickinson and the New Jersey militia. In July Dickinson acted as second to Gen. John Cadwalader [*q.v.*] in his duel with Thomas Conway [*q.v.*]. He was for a short time chief signal officer of the middle department (1778–79). For his "spirited attack" at the battle of Springfield in June 1780 he received the praise of Gen. Greene.

Defeated for governor by William Livingston [*q.v.*] in 1778, 1779, and 1780, he was appointed in 1781 commissioner of the newly created state loan office, and the following year was elected to Congress from Delaware, where he was a property owner. In Congress he was chairman of the committee that was appointed to consider what powers were to be vested in the secretary at war. Elected to the New Jersey Council, he served two terms as vice-president of that body (1783–84). In 1785 Congress appointed him, Robert Morris, and Philip Schuyler commissioners to select a site for a Federal capital. The question was not settled, however, until the adoption of the Constitution. Defeated for United States senator by William Paterson [*q.v.*], Dickinson was later elected to fill Paterson's unexpired term (1790–93) when the latter succeeded Livingston as governor. Dickinson was married twice: on July 14, 1767, to Mary Cadwalader, daughter of his uncle, Dr. Thomas Cadwalader [*q.v.*], and, after her death, to her sister Rebecca.

[Papers of the Cont. Cong., in the Lib. of Cong.; *Jours. of Cong.*; *Proc. of a Gen. Court Martial, Held . . . for the Trial of Maj. Gen. Lee* (1778); *Docs. Relating to the Revolutionary Hist. of the State of N. J.*; Jared Sparks, ed., *Writings of Geo. Washington* (1834–37) and *Corr. of the Am. Revolution* (1853); biog. sketch by Wharton Dickinson, in the *Mag. of Am. Hist.*, Dec. 1881; *Pa. Mag. of Hist. and Biog.*, vol. V (1881); Chas. P. Keith, *Provincial Councillors of Pa.* (1883); Wm. S. Stryker, *Battle of Monmouth* (1927); W. J. Mills, *Hist. Houses of N. J.* (1902); *Trenton Federalist*, Feb. 6, 1809.] F. E. R.

DICKMAN, JOSEPH THEODORE (Oct. 6, 1857–Oct. 23, 1927), soldier, was born at Dayton, Ohio, the son of Theodore and Mary (Weinmar) Dickman. He graduated from the U. S. Military Academy in 1881, and was commissioned second lieutenant in the 3rd Cavalry. On Sept. 26, 1882, he married Mary Rector of Fort Smith, Ark. Until the war with Spain his service was chiefly in the West, where he participated in the campaign against Geronimo and aided in suppressing disturbances along the Mexican border. He was an honor graduate of the Infantry and Cavalry School at Fort Leavenworth in 1883, and was an instructor there from 1895 to 1898. He was promoted to first lieutenant, Jan. 18, 1886, and to captain, May 27, 1898. As a staff officer of Wheeler's cavalry division, he took part in the Santiago campaign, and as major and lieutenant-colonel of a volunteer infantry regiment, in operations against Filipino insurgents in the island of Panay. He was chief of staff of the American forces in China, after the taking of Peking, and was discharged from his volunteer commission, May 13, 1901. When the General Staff of the army was organized in 1903, he was selected as one of its original members, serving for three years. In due course he was promoted to major in 1906, lieutenant-colonel in 1912, and colonel in 1914, serving meanwhile with his regiment and for a time as an inspector-general. He was appointed brigadier-general in the regular army May 15, 1917, and major-general in the emergency forces, Aug. 5, 1917. He first commanded the 85th Division at Camp Custer, Mich., and later the 3rd Division at Camp Greene, N. C., and in France. With the latter he went into the battle sector on the south bank of the Marne, June 2, 1918, and commanded it in battle on July 15 and 16, in the repulse of the last great German offensive. He commanded the IV Corps from Aug. 18 to Oct. 12, and the I Corps from then until after the Armistice, assisting in the reduction of the Saint Mihiel salient and the Meuse-Argonne operations. On Nov. 15 he was assigned to the command of the III Army, organized it for the occupation of Germany, and remained with it until Apr. 28, 1919. Decorations for his services in the war were conferred on him by the United States, Great Britain, France, Italy, Belgium, and Panama. He was made major-general in the regular army, Jan. 9, 1919, and retired, Oct. 6, 1921. He died at Washington. It is still too early to pass final judgment on the leaders in the World War, but Dickman must be ranked among the ablest of the American generals in France. His somewhat heavy and unexpressive features masked a shrewd and active mind whose qualities had already been tested in duties of widely varying character. His narrative of the World War, *The Great Crusade* (1927), is not such a rhetorical effusion as its title might suggest, but a simple straightforward account of military operations, clearly and entertainingly written.

[Dickman's military record is given in G. W. Cullum, *Biog. Reg.* (3rd ed., 1891), III, 349–50; IV, 345–46; V, 322; VI A, 319–20. *General Orders No. 17, War Dept.*, 1927, summarizes his career. For his services in the World War, consult *The Great Crusade.* See also Washington *Evening Star* and *Washington Post,* Oct. 24, 1927.] T. M. S.

DICKSON, DAVID (July 6, 1809–Feb. 18, 1885), farmer and agricultural writer, was of English descent. His father, Thomas Dickson, was a Virginian who served in the Revolutionary War and soon after moved to Hancock County, Ga., where his son David was born. The latter had limited educational advantages, but his natural mental ability and the best use of all his opportunities for reading, study, and thought equipped him well for his future labors and achievements. With a small patrimony he began as a country trader. In 1835 he entered a partnership and opened a store in Sparta, Ga., which was very successful financially. When he was thirty-seven he closed this business and invested all his capital in land, slaves, live stock, and tools at and near his father's homestead. In his boyhood and youth spent on the farm he had recognized defects in the system of management and now had the desired opportunity to experiment in its improvement. From the first he was successful, and land which he bought for one or two dollars an acre under his management increased to many times its original value. His success in securing abundant crops was due to his skill as an organizer, to his improved methods of tillage, of cultivating and harvesting his crops and of increasing the efficiency of his labor. This last point he emphasizes. "I have, in five minutes, taught a hand to pick 100 pounds more of cotton per day than he had picked on the previous day," so that he would pick three bales a week. He taught his workmen similar efficiency in handling the plow, the hoe, and the axe; "with more ease and less of sweat and muscle." His methods of plowing, planting, and cultivating were quite original and most of his writing on these matters is as valid to-day as it was before the Civil War.

He never had a crop failure even in the driest season, and his crop yields were phenomenal. When the Civil War broke out his property was valued at $500,000. After the first year of the war he abandoned cotton, raising only provisions for the Confederate army, for most of which he received no pay, even in Confederate money. Much of his property was swept away in Sherman's march to the sea, and he lost his 250 slaves, specially trained and valuable laborers. After the war he became prosperous again and at the time of his death he owned a plantation of some 15,000 acres in Hancock and Washington counties and another tract of 13,000 acres in Texas, managing the farm land on the tenant system. He bred a variety of cotton called "Dickson's Select" which, at the time, "outlived every other in productiveness and popularity."

Dickson was the first to introduce the use of Peruvian guano as a fertilizer in the cotton states (1846). He is significant, however, not only because he was the most successful farmer in Georgia and probably in the whole South, but chiefly because his careful study and observation, set forth in voluminous private correspondence and in letters to agricultural journals, led to great improvements in the farm practise of the cotton-growing states. He explained clearly and fully his theory and practise. He gave instruction in seed selection, the management of cattle, and the handling of various crops, indicating that he practised mixed farming, not confining himself to a one-crop system. He emphasized the proper handling of the soil, shallow cultivation, the proper distance of planting, the use of commercial fertilizers, instruction of farm hands in all labor-saving devices, etc. In 1870 his writings were collected in a volume edited by J. Dickson Smith and published under the title, *A Treatise on Agriculture, to which is Added the Author's Published Letters, by David Dickson.* Dickson was above medium height, stout and robust, with a fair ruddy face, in manner serious, thoughtful, and benevolent, with a vein of quiet humor. Quite unpretentious, he nevertheless spoke his mind frankly and with very decided views on matters of general interest as well as on his special business. He died on his plantation on the Little Ogoochee River, in Hancock County, Ga.

[The volume, *A Treatise on Agriculture,* mentioned above, contains a sketch of Dickson; the contents of this volume, considerably abridged, were republished by the Cultivator Publishing Company of Atlanta as *David*

Dickson's System of Farming (1906) and *David Dickson's and Jas. M. Smith's Farming* (1908, 1910). See also the *Rural Carolinian* (Charleston, S. C.), Oct. 1869; the *Atlanta Constitution,* Feb. 19, 1885.]

E. H. J.

DICKSON, ROBERT (*c.* 1765–June 20, 1823), fur-trader, was the son of John Dickson, a merchant of Dumfries, Scotland. As a young man he migrated to Canada about the close of the American Revolution and entered the fur trade. In 1787 he was employed as interpreter and storekeeper of government goods at a great Indian council held at Michilimackinac. As a result of this council he began trading operations among the Sioux. About the year 1797 he took as his wife To-to-win, the sister of an influential Sioux chief. Apparently his position and influence were recognized, for in 1803 the governor of Indiana Territory, which included part of Dickson's trading area, appointed him a justice of the peace for St. Clair County. By 1805 he was one of the chief traders of the region bounded by the upper Mississippi, the James, and the Des Moines rivers. In that year a firm known as Robert Dickson & Company was formed, with headquarters at Michilimackinac. Two years later this firm became a member of the recently organized Michilimackinac Company.

When the War of 1812 broke, Dickson's position became a matter of significance on both sides: the American leaders took steps to prevent him from bringing his Indians to the aid of the British; and Gov. Brock of Upper Canada selected him as his agent to keep the Indians of the Northwest friendly and to lead them to Canada to join the British forces. In the capture of Michilimackinac he and his Indians played a significant rôle and thus aided indirectly, also, in the capture of Detroit. In January 1813 his services and influence were recognized by a commission from Governor-General Prevost making him agent for the Indians west of Lake Huron, with extensive authority. Later he was made superintendent of Indian affairs for these tribes. His power, however, awoke the jealousy of military men in the Northwest and led to his arrest at the close of the war and to his dismissal from the service in 1815. He claimed and secured from the British government a hearing in London which not only cleared his name but recognized his services to the extent of awarding him the title of lieutenant-colonel and a retirement pension of £300 a year. At the close of the war he made arrangements with Lord Selkirk to carry on his business within the supposed limits of the latter's colony on the Red River, close to Dickson's former post. A part of his plan seems to have been an agricultural and industrial settlement of Indians and traders on the site of Grand Forks, N. Dak. In the midst of his plans, however, Lord Selkirk died, and shortly thereafter Dickson himself died suddenly at Drummond Island.

[L. A. Tohill, *Robt. Dickson, British Fur Trader on the Upper Miss.* (1927); Helen D. Weaver, "Life of Robt. Dickson" (M.A. thesis, Iowa, 1924); Selkirk papers in the Canadian archives; papers of John J. Astor, Harvard Univ.; E. A. Cruikshank, "Robt. Dickson, the Indian Trader" in *Wis. State Hist. Soc. Colls.*, vol. XII; manuscript letter-book of Thomas Blackwood, in McGill Univ. Lib.; archives of the War Dept., and Indian Office.]

G. L. N.

DICKSON, SAMUEL HENRY (Sept. 20, 1798–Mar. 31, 1872), physician, second son of Samuel and Mary (Neilson) Dickson, was born in Charleston, S. C. Both parents were Presbyterians of Scottish descent who had emigrated from Belfast, Ireland, before the Revolution. After study with his father, who was a schoolmaster, and with Dr. Mackay of Charleston, he entered the sophomore class at Yale at the age of thirteen, graduating (B.A.) in 1814. He returned to his home and began the study of medicine in the office of Dr. Philip Gendron Prioleau and, under his guidance, practised during the epidemic of yellow fever in 1817. In the two succeeding winters he attended the University of Pennsylvania (M.D., 1819). His practise continued at Charleston where he devoted the greater part of his time to the yellow fever sufferers in the Marine and Yellow Fever Hospitals. Though he was only twenty-one years of age, circumstances gave him entire charge of both institutions. While endeavoring to found a medical school he gave free lectures on physiology, and in 1824 a Medical College came into being as a result of the efforts of Dickson and his colleagues. He was made professor of the institutes and practise of medicine. In 1832 he resigned, in consequence of a controversy with the medical society, and in 1833 founded the Medical College of South Carolina which became entirely successful. He held the new chair until 1847 when he accepted a call to the professorship of the practise of medicine at the University of the City of New York. Here he remained for three years but upon urgent invitation and partly for reasons of health, he returned to his former position at Charleston. In 1858 he accepted a call to fill the chair of practise vacated by the death of his warm personal friend, Dr. John K. Mitchell, at the Jefferson Medical College of Philadelphia, and though suffering from a lingering and painful disease, continued to lecture until within a month of his death, which occurred in Philadelphia. He was thrice married: first, to Elizabeth Brownlee Robertson of Charleston, who died in 1832; second, in 1834, to Jane Robertson Robertson (sister of his first wife), who died in 1842; and third, in 1845, to Marie Seabrook DuPré, also of Charleston, who died in 1873.

Dickson was a versatile man, being not only an "attractive Medical stylist and litterateur" (F. H. Garrison, *An Introduction to the History of Medicine*, 3rd ed., 1921, p. 466), but a public speaker of note. He wrote a large number of articles and monographs on medicine, also papers on philosophy, history, and current events. His most important medical works are: *Manual of Pathology and Practice* (1839 with later editions); *Essays on Pathology and Therapeutics* (2 vols., 1845); *Essays on Life, Sleep, Pain, Intellection, and Hygiene* (1852); *Elements of Medicine* (1855); *Studies in Pathology and Therapeutics* (1867). He claimed to have been one of the first to abandon the heroic treatment of fevers in vogue at the time he began practise, and the first in this country to employ stimulants and anodynes in febrile diseases. He was one of the early writers on racial anthropometry (*Charleston Medical Journal*, 1857, p. 607). He delivered one of the first temperance addresses ever heard in the South and is said to have established the first temperance society, directing his attack against the use of distilled liquors, while approving of wines.

[*Charleston Medic. Jour. and Record*, XII, 3 (with portrait); F. B. Dexter, *Biog. Sketches Grads. Yale Coll.*, VI (1912), 641 (with bibliography); *Phila. Medic. Times*, II (1872), 278, 292; *Press* (Phila.), Apr. 2, 1872.] E. E. H.

DICKSON, THOMAS (Mar. 26, 1824–July 31, 1884), capitalist, the son of James Dickson, a Scottish millwright of Lauder, Berwickshire, and his wife, Elizabeth Linen, was born in Leeds, England, where his parents were living temporarily. When he was eight years old, the family moved to Canada, and two years later to Dundaff in northeastern Pennsylvania. James Dickson, finding little opportunity to follow his trade, attempted farming in what was then a pioneer community. Finding farming distasteful he sought employment elsewhere, leaving the farm and his large family in charge of his wife and Thomas, the oldest son. These early strenuous experiences constituted Dickson's principal preparation for life. Almost immediately after his schooling began it was abruptly ended by a violent quarrel with the village school-teacher. In the meantime his father had secured employment as a millwright with the Delaware & Hudson Canal Company, and the boy's first job after leaving school was with the same company, guiding a mule in drawing coal from the mines. It happened that this company, with which Dickson's fortunes were so closely interwoven, had been organized in 1824, the year of his birth (Logan, *post*, pp. 6–24). In various minor positions he saved a portion of his wages, and characteristically added to his hoard the money sent by his grandfather to defray the cost of a visit to Scotland. At length he accumulated savings enough for a venture of his own, under the firm name of Dickson & Company, a manufacturing enterprise organized in 1856 at Carbondale, but soon established at Scranton. Scranton was the center of a region with immense possibilities and potential needs in the rapidly developing mining, lumbering, manufacturing, and transport industries. The crudest of methods prevailed, but these were being supplanted, and the extensive foundries and machine-shops built by the Dickson firm for the making of locomotives, engines for mills and mines, and machinery of various kinds, played a vital rôle in the industrializing of the region (*Ibid.*, pp. 39–52).

The basic resources of the region were particularly important in their relation to other regions, and the early tapping of these resources was largely the work of the Delaware & Hudson Canal Company. Dickson's ingenuity and enterprise in furnishing the company with needed equipment led to his being offered, in 1859, the post of superintendent. This he accepted, while retaining for about ten years the headship of his own company. The latter was reorganized in 1862 as the Dickson Manufacturing Company. Under his direction the two companies rapidly developed the anthracite coal industry and other enterprises in the Lackawanna and Wyoming valleys. The expansion of business led to his resignation as head of his own company and to his being made president, in 1869, of the Delaware & Hudson Canal Company. In the meantime he had become associated with a number of other enterprises, including the First National Bank of Scranton (1863), and the Moosic Powder Company (1865), the latter merging later with the Du Pont projects. When Dickson first became interested in the development of Scranton, there was little more than the beginning of a town. By means of his foresight and business acumen he became the principal molder of the city's fortunes. His influence extended beyond the Lackawanna and Wyoming valleys, not only in the direction of New York and Philadelphia, but northward as well. He promoted, for instance, the extension of a railway line to Canada (*Ibid.*, 98–100; Hitchcock, *post*, I, 89, and *passim*). Thus he became one of the outstanding figures in the American industrial revolution.

Outside of his business life, he was a man of limited attainments. Aside from his boyhood migration to America, his travels were very slight until shortly before his death, when he spent almost a year in a tour of the world. He had virtually no formal schooling. He nevertheless accumulated a choice library, established a circulating library, read extensively, and even cherished literary ambitions. He acquired a remarkable knowledge of law. His associations, aside from his numerous business connections, were slight. His principal benevolences were connected with conventional religious and social groups. On Aug. 31, 1846, he was married to Mary Augusta Marvine. His daughter, Elizabeth Linen, became the wife of Henry Martyn Boies [*q.v.*], another Scranton capitalist.

[S. C. Logan, *The Life of Thomas Dickson* (1888); *Henry Martyn Boies* (1904), ed. by J. H. Odell; F. L. Hitchcock, *Hist. of Scranton and Its People* (2 vols., 1914); *Geneal. and Family Hist. of the Wyoming and Lackawanna Valleys, Pa.*, vol. II (1906), ed. by H. E. Hayden; *Portr. and Biog. Record of Wyoming and Lackawanna Counties, Pa.* (1899).] W. B.

DIDIER, EUGENE LEMOINE (Dec. 22, 1838–Sept. 8, 1913), author, son of Franklin James and Julia (LeMoine) Didier, was born in Baltimore, where he lived all his life. His father was a physician of literary tastes, who in the early twenties published *Letters from Paris and Other Cities of France, Holland &c.* (1821), and *Franklin's Letters to Kinsfolk* (1822), both written between 1816 and 1820, during a residence abroad. Eugene attended Loyola College, and afterward for a brief time engaged in business. During 1867–68 he was one of the three editors of *Southern Society*, a magazine which published the work of the best-known Southern writers of that time. He was an enthusiastic admirer of Poe—as a young man he cultivated the acquaintance of the aged Maria Clemm; by 1874 he was writing articles about Poe for the magazines, and in 1877 he published *The Life and Poems of Edgar Allan Poe*, a carefully written but sentimental sketch of some 30,000 words. It is said to have gone through nineteen editions (Shepherd, p. 160). In 1879 he published as by "Stylus" (a favorite name with Poe), his *American Publishers and English Authors*. The purpose of this slashing little booklet was to show that only by protecting foreign copyrights could America be independent of England culturally as well as politically. In 1879 he published also *The Life and Letters of Madame Bonaparte*, a frankly curious account of her doings. During the early eighties he was interested in editing a series of *Primers for the People*. Through this channel it was his plan to popularize knowledge of the following subjects, at the rate of ten cents each: Criticism, History, Matrimony, Politeness, Health, Wealth, and Literature. In the first of these *Primers*, written by himself, he essays to reduce to plain chaff the reputation of many of his contemporaries, particularly of Henry James and Howells. In 1884 he issued his mordant *Political Adventures of James G. Blaine*. Throughout his life he seems to have had money to do as he chose. He had an extensive library, and from time to time he traveled through Europe and America, meeting celebrities. His *Poe Cult* (1909) is made up of about twenty articles which appeared over many years in various magazines. It unquestionably contributed some items to the fund of knowledge about Poe, but it is less valuable on that score than it seems to have been considered by the author. False modesty was never one of his vices. Often indeed, and particularly in this last book, he treads so drastically upon nearly everybody except himself and Poe that even the meekest bookworm at last finds himself turning. In 1873 Didier was married to Mary Louisa Innocentia Northrop, daughter of the Confederate general, Lucius Bellinger Northrop. Their only son, J. D'Arcy Didier, died in early manhood.

[A. J. Northrup, *Northrup-Northrop Geneal.* (1908); *Who's Who in America*, 1908–09; H. E. Shepherd, *Representative Authors of Md.* (1911); *Baltimore Evening Sun*, Sept. 9, 1913.] J. D. W.

DIETRICHSON, JOHANNES WILHELM CHRISTIAN (Apr. 4, or Aug. 23, 1815–Nov. 14, 1883), Lutheran clergyman, was born at Fredrikstad, Norway, son of Capt. Fredrik Batington and Karen Sophie Henriette (Radich) Dietrichson. Stirred by the fervent religious instruction of his pastor, the Rev. J. Tandberg, Wilhelm decided to become a minister of the gospel. In 1837 he graduated from the university at Christiania (now Oslo) with high honors. After spending one year as a tutor at the salt works at Tönsberg, he returned to Christiania and spent the years 1839 to 1843 in study and teaching. In 1841 he lost his wife, Jörgine Laurense Broch, after two years of wedded life, and this bereavement greatly intensified his spiritual life. Thus trained and tested, he did what could least be expected of the aristocratic clergy of Norway at that time. He overcame the hostility of his own social class to emigration to America, and volunteered to embark for the new country when urged to do so by a pious dyer, P. Sörenson. Securing ordination on Feb. 26, 1844, at the hands of Bishop C. Sörenson, he set out for America. He delivered sermons in New York and Buffalo, and on Friday, Aug. 30, 1844, in Amund Endresen Hornefjeld's barn on the Koshkonong Prairies in Wisconsin, preached his first sermon in the American West.

From his one-room log parsonage, he immediately undertook to rule and order the vast, though chaotic, virgin church among the Norwegian Lutherans in America. Stressing his prerogatives as the first Lutheran pastor in America who had been ordained in Norway, he scrutinized carefully the ordinations of Elling Eielsen and Claus Lauritz Clausen [*qq.v.*], both of whom had been ordained in America in 1843, and found Eielsen's ordination faulty, but Clausen's at least passable. Thus were sown the seeds of future controversies. With a keen strategic sense which he had inherited from forebears who had been prominent in church and state, Dietrichson drew up a pledge consisting of four points, and on this basis organized various Norwegian Lutheran congregations in Wisconsin. Each of these congregations was given a constitution, these constitutions revealing such a remarkable insight into American Lutheran congregational needs that they have become the foundation for all subsequent organizational development in this field among Norwegian American Lutherans.

In order to secure pastors for his prolific American field in which new congregations could be organized almost at will, Dietrichson went to Norway in 1845, remaining one year. While there he was married again, this time to Charlotte Mueller. By means of sermons, debates, articles in the newspapers, and, finally, a book, the title of which, in translation reads: *Travels Among the Norwegian Emigrants in "The United North American Free States"* (1846), he sought to interest the young clergy in the new field. In this endeavor he was successful, attracting to the American Lutheran church some of the finest young clergymen that Norway has ever produced. In 1850, feeling that his usefulness in America had come to an end, he issued a farewell sermon which was printed, and returned to Norway, where he held two pastorates, and the office of postmaster at Porsgrund from 1876 to 1882. In that year he suffered a stroke of paralysis which in the following year caused his death. *The Travels* have been an invaluable source of Norwegian American history.

[J. Magnus Rohne, *Norwegian American Lutheranism Up to 1872* (1926); Rasmus B. Anderson, *The First Chapter of Norwegian Immigration (1821–40)* (1896); *Who's Who Among Pastors in All the Norwegian Synods of America 1843–1927* (1928); J. Arndt Bergh, *Den Norsk Lutherske Kirkes Historie i Amerika* (1914); Thrond Bothne, "Kort Udsigt over det Lutherske Kirkearbeide Blandt Nordmändene i Amerika" in Knut Takla's edition of Hallvard G. Heggtveit, *Illustreret Kirkehistorie* (1898).] J.M.R.

DIKE, SAMUEL WARREN (Feb. 13, 1839–Dec. 3, 1913), Congregational clergyman, reformer and sociologist, was born in Thompson, Conn. A descendant of Capt. Anthony Dike who came to Plymouth Colony on the ship *Ann* in 1623, he was the son of George Dike, a farmer, and Hannah Waters (Snow) Dike. After preparation at Nichols Academy, he graduated from Williams College with high scholastic honors in 1863. For two years he studied at the Theological Institute of Connecticut, East Windsor Hill (now Hartford Theological Seminary), and for one year at Andover Theological Seminary, from which he graduated in 1866. He was ordained to the Congregational ministry in 1869 at West Randolph, Vt., and served as acting pastor at Pomfret, Conn., 1866–67; as pastor at West Randolph, Vt., 1868–77; and at Royalton, Vt., 1879–82. During his year at Andover Seminary he became interested in the study of social subjects, especially the family. He wrote editorially on this theme in the *Vermont Chronicle* and in 1881 gave one of the Boston Monday Lectures on "Facts as to Divorce in New England." That same day the New England Divorce Reform League was organized. It became the National Divorce Reform League in 1885 and still later the National League for the Protection of the Family. Dike was creator, corresponding secretary, and mainspring of the League from 1881 until his death. He was the pioneer in the study of American family conditions, and the annual reports of the League written by him constitute the history of the movement for the betterment of the family. He brought such pressure to bear on Congress that Carroll D. Wright, United States commissioner of labor, gathered and published a valuable mass of statistics and information in his *Report on Marriage and Divorce in the United Staes, 1867–86* (1889). Dike did an immense amount of research for this publication. Before colleges, theological seminaries, and scientific societies he lectured on the same theme. He wrote extensively for periodicals, including the *Andover Review, Atlantic Monthly, Princeton Review,* and *Political Science Quarterly.* Many of his articles were reissued in pamphlet form. He powerfully influenced legislation for stricter marriage and divorce laws and achieved international reputation as an authority on them. He devised the Home Department of the Sunday-school. With Bishop Potter, Seth Low, Washington Gladden, and others he formed a "Sociological Group" which did much first-hand work in the study of "present-day problems." Dike had a large philosophic grasp of the complicated social problem of the development and changes in the American family. He combined to an unusual degree patience in the quest for facts with a firm grasp of the whole social situation, a combination in which very few of his more distinguished successors have equaled him (Prof. W. F. Willcox). He was clear in his judgments, tenacious of his opinions, firm in his faith, but modest and self-effacing in his disposition and generous in his relations with his colleagues (Francis G. Peabody in *National League for the Protection of the Family, Annual Report for 1913 and 1914,* p. 3). He married Augusta Margaret Smith of Montpelier, Vt., on Oct. 29, 1872. After taking up the work of the League they resided in Royalton, Vt., until 1887 and then in Auburndale, Mass., until his death.

[*Class of Sixty-three, Williams Coll., 40th Year Report* (1903); autobiographical material in *Nat. Reform League Reports* and *Nat. League for the Protection of the Family Ann. Reports*; *Andover Theol. Sem. Necrology, 1911–14* (1914); *Congreg. Year Book,* 1913, and *Who's Who in America,* 1912–13; personal acquaintance of thirty years.]
T. C. R.

DILL, JAMES BROOKS (July 25, 1854–Dec. 2, 1910), jurist, was born in the village of Spencerport, N. Y. He was the eldest son of a Congregational minister, James Horton Dill, a native of Massachusetts, and of Catherine D. Dill, a member of the Brooks family of Connecticut. The Dills moved to Chicago in 1858 and upon the death of the father, killed in battle in 1862, the family moved to New Haven, Conn., where young Dill's schooling was continued. After three years in Oberlin Academy (1868–71) and one year in Oberlin College, he entered Yale in 1872 and, though supporting himself, graduated with honors in 1876. He then taught for a year in a private school in Philadelphia and studied law at night under the direction of a prominent lawyer. He became instructor in Latin and mathematics in Stevens Institute at Hoboken, N. J., and attended the Law School of the University of the City of New York at night where he graduated as salutatorian of the class of 1878. He was admitted to the bar in New York the same year. Entering upon the practise of the law with a capital of forty dollars, he eked out an income by newspaper work on the *Jersey City Evening Journal* and later on the *New York Tribune.* Dill's days of penury were brief, however. In 1879 he won a conspicuous case, largely on a technicality, freeing his client from heavy liability under the New York law as director of an insolvent corporation. This enlarged his practise and directed his interest to the field of corporation law, an interest evidenced by a pamphlet which he wrote on "The Advantages of Business Corporations," which attracted wide attention. He was admitted to the New Jersey bar in 1894. Upon being consulted by the governor of New Jersey as to the best way to increase the financial resources of the state, Dill suggested the liberalizing of the corporation laws. He thereupon drafted the famous New Jersey statute of 1889, legalizing the holding company and allowing incorporation for almost any purpose. It also required a corporation to have an agent in the state upon whom papers could be served, thus excluding the "tramp" corporation, and prescribed "private publicity," or the keeping of adequate records for the protection of stockholders. The rush of business concerns to take advantage of these laws led Dill to organize a corporation to organize other corporations, the Corporation Trust Company of New Jersey. Later he organized other companies to meet similar needs. He aided in the creation of hundreds of corporations, was director of many, and counsel for many more. His practise was lucrative and he amassed a large fortune. He is reputed to have received the largest fee ever paid to an American lawyer ($1,000,000) for his services in healing the breach between Carnegie and Frick in 1900.

Dill wrote extensively and authoritatively on corporation law. His works, *The Statutory and Case Law Applicable to Private Companies Under the General Corporation Act of New Jersey* (1898), *The Laws of New Jersey Relating to Banks and Banking, Trust Companies and Safe Deposit Corporations* (1899), and *Business Corporations* (1910), served as legal guides for the business world, since the author had largely created the law he was expounding. He occasionally gave addresses or wrote articles on subjects relating to business organizations or corporation law ("Trusts: Their Uses and Abuses," an address before the Merchants' Club of Chicago, 1901; "National Incorporation Laws for Trusts," *Yale Law Journal,* XI, 273–95, 1902; "Some Aspects of New Jersey's Corporate Policy," an address before the Pennsylvania Bar Association, *Report of the Ninth Annual Meeting,* 1903, pp. 265–88). In 1899 he served as member of the committee which revised the laws of New Jersey, and later served as counsel to the committee which revised the laws of Canada. In 1905 he was appointed a member of the court of errors and appeals in New Jersey and served in that office until his death. Dill was married in 1880 to Mary W. Hansell of Philadelphia. While he kept his principal office in New York City, he maintained a beautiful home in East Orange,

N. J., where he had a very large private library. He was fond of out-door activity, especially camping and horseback riding. He was a genial and sociable man with a very large circle of friends.

[*National Corporation Reporter,* XXV, 486 (1902); *N. J. Law Jour.,* XXXIII, 382 (1910); *World's Work,* III, 1902, p. 1885; *Banking Law Jour.,* X, 375 (1894); *N. Y. Times,* Dec. 3, 1910; *Who's Who in America,* 1903–05.] R. E. C.

DILLINGHAM, WILLIAM PAUL (Dec. 12, 1843–July 12, 1923), lawyer and statesman, was the son of Paul Dillingham, a lawyer by profession and prominent in the politics of the state, and his second wife, Julia Carpenter. He was born at Waterbury, Vt., whither his grandfather had moved from Massachusetts in 1805, attended the local common schools, Newbury Seminary, and Kimball Union Academy, and then moved to Milwaukee, Wis., where he studied law in the office of his brother-in-law, Matthew H. Carpenter [*q.v.*]. Two years later he returned to Vermont and completed his legal studies under his father, then governor of the state. This circumstance favored young Dillingham's entrance into political life. His first public office was that of secretary of civil and military affairs, to which he was appointed in 1866. In 1872 he was elected state's attorney of Washington County, and was reëlected for a second term. During the period from 1876 to 1884 he served four terms in the state legislature. In 1888 he received the Republican nomination for governor and was elected by the largest plurality ever given to a candidate for that office up to that time. On Oct. 18, 1900, he was elected to the United States Senate to fill the vacancy caused by the death of Justin S. Morrill [*q.v.*], being reëlected by the legislature in 1902 and 1908, and by popular vote in 1914 and 1920.

The phase of Dillingham's career of most historical interest is his long service on the Senate Committee on Immigration and his espousal of the quota principle of immigration restriction. He was elected to this Committee shortly after taking his seat in the Senate, in the place of his colleague, Senator Proctor, who asked to be relieved of his duties on it. At the next session of Congress Dillingham became chairman of the Committee, a position which he held from 1903 to 1911, though he continued to be a member till the time of his death. In 1907 Congress authorized the appointment of a special immigration commission, composed of three members from the Senate, three from the House, and three to be appointed by the President, to make a study of the problem and to submit recommendations concerning it. Dillingham was appointed one of the three members from the Senate, and, when the commission effected its organization, was chosen as its chairman. The commission devoted over two years to a thorough investigation of foreign immigration in all its aspects, and its report extending through forty-one volumes is the most complete and exhaustive survey of the subject ever made.

In June 1913 Dillingham introduced a bill proposing that the annual amount of immigration for each nationality be limited to ten per cent of those of that nationality already in the United States. The adoption of the measure would have marked a departure from the immigration policy of the past. The outbreak of the World War, however, and the almost complete suspension of foreign immigration removed the need of immediate legislation upon the subject. At the end of the war the country was in a mood of intensified nationalism and Congress was more favorably inclined toward the restriction of immigration. A bill introduced by Senator Dillingham in December 1920, embodying the quota principle of restriction, passed Congress but was killed by a pocket veto of President Wilson. At the next session the Senate repassed the bill, but the House, while favoring a policy of immigration restriction, had passed another measure for the total suspension of foreign immigration for one year pending a more thorough study of the problem. The main features of the Dillingham measure were accepted in conference between the two houses, then enacted into law. This act, approved May 19, 1921, and commonly referred to in contemporary discussion as the "Dillingham Bill," limited the amount of annual immigration to three per cent of those of that nationality already in the country. It was avowedly a temporary measure, but its essential features were incorporated into subsequent legislation upon the subject, and it remains the basis of the national immigration policy to the present time (1930). Dillingham was married on Dec. 24, 1874, to Mary Ellen Shipman. He died at Montpelier, Vt., from complications following an operation.

[*The Vermonter* published articles relating to the life and career of Dillingham in the following issues: vol. VI, pp. 51–53 (Nov. 1900), vol. VIII, p. 132 (Nov. 1902), vol. XXIX, pp. 20–23 (Feb. 1924). Considerable material relating to his public career and his candidacy for office is scattered through the files of the *Burlington Free Press,* and the several issues following his death on July 12, 1923, contain considerable biographical material and personal reminiscences. A report of the Senate Committee on Immigration, printed as *Senate Report No. 17,* 67 Cong., 1 Sess., gives a full account of the history of the Dillingham immigration bill and the evolution of the policy of immigration restriction which he championed. A speech of Dillingham's published in the *Cong. Record,* 64 Cong., 1 Sess., pp. 12,769–77 is a good source of information for his views regarding immigration. Some information has been supplied by personal friends.] A. M. K.

DILLON, JOHN FORREST (Dec. 25, 1831–May 6, 1914), jurist, was born in Montgomery County, N. Y., to Thomas and Rosannah (Forrest) Dillon, both of Irish descent. In 1838 the family moved to Davenport, Iowa, where young Dillon spent a boyhood of plenty of hard work and little regular schooling. At seventeen he began the study of medicine in the office of a local practitioner, later attended lectures at the medical school at Keokuk, and took the M.D. degree in 1850 at the college of physicians and surgeons at Davenport, a branch of the University of Iowa.

He practised medicine at Farmington, Iowa, but discovered that a hernia from which he suffered made unsafe the horseback riding necessary to medical practise in a pioneer country and compelled a radical change of plans. His friendship for a young lawyer of the community inclined him toward the law, and returning to Davenport, he supported himself by running a drug-store while he engaged in a Lincoln-like struggle for a legal education. With no teacher, no law-school training, and no law-office apprenticeship, he achieved admission to the bar of Scott County in 1852. A few months later he was elected county prosecuting attorney at a salary of $250. He held this office till his election in 1858 as judge of the seventh judicial district of Iowa, to which office he was reëlected. In 1862 he was elected on the Republican ticket to the supreme court of the state. Here he sat for six years during the last two of which he was chief justice. In 1869 President Grant appointed him United States circuit judge for the newly created 8th judicial circuit. For ten years he sat on the federal bench, holding thirteen terms of court annually, and traveling more than ten thousand miles. During most of this period he lectured each winter on medical jurisprudence at the University of Iowa. In 1879 he resigned from the court to accept a professorship of law at Columbia College, teaching real property and equity, and at the same time he opened a law office in New York City. He resigned his chair in 1882 and from that time until his death he engaged in the active practise of law in New York.

Dillon quickly assumed a place of prominence and distinction at the bar, arguing many cases of importance before the United States Supreme Court. He was primarily a corporation lawyer, but he never bound himself to any one corporation. He was counsel for the Union Pacific Railroad, the Missouri Pacific Railroad, the Texas Pacific Railroad, and the Western Union Telegraph Company. He was counsel for the Goulds in connection with all their railroad interests and also for the estate of Jay Gould. His practise was lucrative, he was a shrewd business man, and he left a substantial estate.

His reputation, however, rests upon his contributions to legal scholarship, a reputation, as one writer puts it, "so monumental that promotion to any coveted judicial office would not have added to his fame." While district judge in Iowa he made a *Digest of the Decisions of the Supreme Court of Iowa 1839–1860* (8 vols., 1860). Upon promotion to the federal bench he published a work on *Removal of Causes from State Courts to Federal Courts* (1876), which ran through five editions. But his name will always be associated with his monumental treatise on *Municipal Corporations* (1872), a work which created municipal corporations as a separate field of the law. This appeared as a single volume of 800 pages. It ran through five editions, all edited by the author, and the last of which, in five volumes, he dedicated in 1911 to the American Bar Association of which he had been president in 1891–92. He founded the *Central Law Journal* in 1874 and edited it for a year. He was a steady contributor to magazines and law journals. In 1876 he published a work on *The Law of Municipal Bonds.* In 1891–92 he delivered the Storrs Lectures at Yale which he published in 1894 under the title *The Laws and Jurisprudence of England and America.* In 1903 he edited the three-volume collection of addresses and papers on John Marshall which had grown out of the Marshall centenary celebrations in 1901. After the death of his wife he published privately a substantial memoir of her. He had married Anna Price in 1853 and they had two children, a son and a daughter. His wife and daughter were drowned at sea in 1898. His office was in New York but he had a beautiful home at Far Hills, N. J. He was a companionable man, placid in temperament, courteous and unhurried, and perhaps a little ponderous in speech. He had an absolute honesty of mind and integrity of character and in spite of his wealthy corporation practise his services were never to be had in aid of sharp or questionable practises. He was a Republican in politics and had been an ardent anti-slavery advocate before the Civil War.

[E. E. Stiles, *Annals of Iowa* in Apr., July 1909, and in *Recollections and Sketches of Notable Lawyers and Public Men of Early Iowa* (1916); G. S. Clay, Dillon's law partner, in *Green Bag*, Sept. 1911; H. Hubbard in *Am. Bar Asso. Jour.*, Jan. 1928; *Who's Who in America,* 1914–15; "Judge Dillon's Law Publications" in *Annals of Iowa,* Jan. 1903; obituary in *N. Y. Times,* May 6, 1914.] R. E. C.

DILLON, SIDNEY (May 7, 1812–June 9, 1892), railroad-builder and financier, was born in Northampton, Montgomery County, N. Y., where the family had resided for several generations. He was the son of Timothy Dillon, a farmer. The family was poor, and Sidney received only a meager education. At the age of seven, tiring of farm life, he began work as a "water boy" on the Mohawk & Hudson Railroad from Albany to Schenectady, and when this road was finished he was employed in a similar capacity on the Rensselaer & Saratoga Railroad. Later he acted as an overseer and then foreman on several other railroad construction projects in New England. Finally he decided to enter into business for himself, and although he had but little capital he made a bid for the construction of a short section of what is now the Boston & Albany Railroad. The bid was accepted and the work was satisfactorily completed in 1840. This was the beginning of a contracting career of unusual extent and success; during the next thirty years he built thousands of miles of railroad in all parts of the country, either individually or in association with other contractors. Among the roads partially constructed by him were the Rutland & Burlington Railroad, the Central Railroad of New Jersey, the Philadelphia & Erie Railroad, the Morris & Essex Railroad, the Pennsylvania Railroad, the New Orleans, Mobile & Chattanooga Railroad, and the Canada Southern Railroad. He also built for Cornelius Vanderbilt the tunnel from the Grand Central Station at Forty-second St., New York City, to the Harlem River.

The greatest enterprise of his life was the construction of the Union Pacific Railroad, with which company he became actively associated in 1865 through stock purchase in the Crédit Mobilier. He was one of the principal contractors and the directing authority for subsidiary contractors. During the next four years he took an active part in the construction of the road, frequently traveling backward and forward along the line and aiding the builders out of his abundant experience. He took part in the ceremony of laying the last rail in 1869, and one of the silver spikes with which the road was completed remained in his possession until his death. In 1892 he published an article on the opening of the Union Pacific, with the title "Historic Moments: Driving the Last Spike of the Union Pacific" (*Scribner's Magazine,* August 1892). He was a director of the Union Pacific Railroad Company for twenty-eight years (1864–92) and its president for nearly twelve years (from Mar. 11, 1874, to June 19, 1884, and again from Nov. 26, 1890, to Apr. 27, 1892). At the time of his death he was chairman of the board of directors, having been the first to be elected to that office.

After 1870 he was chiefly known as a financier. He had by then accumulated a large fortune, principally invested in railroad securities because of the fact that he had early adopted the policy of taking as part payment shares of stock of the companies for which he did construction work. The management of these investments gradually occupied a larger part of his time and he became actively associated with Jay Gould in the management of many of the properties controlled by the latter. He also served as a director in the Western Union Telegraph Company, the Manhattan Elevated Railroad Company, the Missouri Pacific Railroad, and several other transportation organizations. On Mar. 26, 1870, he was elected a Fellow of the American Society of Civil Engineers. Over six feet tall, heavily built yet active, and speaking in a direct, incisive manner, he conveyed the impression of a man who knew what to do and how to do it, and was fully able to command others in carrying out his plans. He was unusually careful in negotiating and entering into contracts and obligations, but, when once undertaken, displayed great energy and perseverance in carrying them out. In 1841 he married Hannah Smith of Amherst, Mass., and they had two daughters. He died at his home in New York City after an illness of three months.

[Jas. Parton and others, *Sketches of Men of Progress* (1870–71), pp. 587–93; *Trans. Am. Soc. Civil Engineers,* XXXVI, 603–04, Dec. 1896; H. K. White, *Hist. of the U. P. Ry.* (1895); E. L. Sabin, *Building the Pacific Ry.* (1919); N. Trottman, *Hist. of the Union Pacific* (1923); obituaries in the N. Y. papers of June 10, 1892, in *Harper's Weekly,* June 18, 1892, and in the *Ry. Age and Northwestern Railroader,* June 17, 1892.]

J.H.F.

DIMAN, JEREMIAH LEWIS (May 1, 1831–Feb. 3, 1881), clergyman, educator, was born in Bristol, R. I., where his ancestors had lived for four generations. His father, Byron, a business man of scholarly tastes, governor of his native state in 1846–47, was a descendant of Thomas Dimont, of French extraction, who settled in East Hampton, L. I., about 1656; his mother, Abby Alden Wight, was seventh in descent from John Alden. After attending the public schools of Bristol, J. Lewis, as from boyhood he chose to be called, prepared for college under Rev. James N. Sykes. Before he was sixteen he had written a history of Bristol based on researches in the town records and conversations with old inhabitants, which was published in a weekly newspaper. At Brown University, from which he graduated in 1851, he added to the work required a large amount of reading in history, philosophy, and literature. After studying German, philosophy, and the classics for a year with Rev. Dr. Thayer of Newport, R. I., he entered Andover Theological Seminary. Two years later he went to Germany and attended lectures at Halle, Heidelberg, and Berlin. Returning to America, he graduated from Andover in 1856.

Important churches at once sought to avail themselves of his training, rare gifts, and attractive personality, but he chose finally to settle in Fall River, Mass., where he was ordained as pastor of the First Congregational Church, Dec. 9, 1856. Three years later, January 1860, he resigned, and shortly afterward became pastor of the Harvard Congregational Church, Brookline, Mass. On May 15, 1861, he married Emily G. Stimson, daughter of John J. Stimson of Providence. A brilliant career in the ministry seemed to be before him. Horace Bushnell long and patiently endeavored to secure him as his successor at Hartford. Churches in New York, Philadelphia, and Charleston, S. C., beckoned to him. In spite of his gifts and deeply devotional nature, however, he had characteristics which interfered with his happiness in his calling. He was essentially a student and teacher, historically minded, frank and fearless in stating his views, unwilling to wear denominational chains. He abhorred revivals and all cheap expedients to attract people, was strongly inclined to the Episcopal Church, and sympathetic toward much in Roman Catholicism, while some of his doctrinal views led orthodox Bostonians to accuse him of Unitarian leanings. Accordingly, when in 1864 he was offered the chair of history and political economy at Brown University he accepted it.

Here his lectures—for he soon discarded textbook instruction—rich, penetrating, polished, and enlivened by wit, made him the idol of the students in spite of his high-bred reserve (W. C. Bronson, *The History of Brown University*, 1914, p. 409). His historical addresses on public occasions and his contributions to periodicals were widely read. On three occasions President Eliot tried to persuade him to leave Providence for Cambridge; he was offered professorships at Princeton and Johns Hopkins, and the presidency of the University of Vermont, and of the University of Wisconsin; but he chose to stay at Brown. He became an editorial writer for the *Providence Journal* when it was under the management of his intimate friend, James B. Angell [*q.v.*], and was regarded as one of its ablest contributors until his death. Of his publications in periodicals, "Religion in America," a survey for the century 1776–1876 (*North American Review*, January 1876), attracted wide notice. From 1877 to 1881 he reviewed historical publications for *The Nation*. In 1879 he delivered a notable course of lectures at Johns Hopkins on the "Thirty Years' War," and in 1880 he gave the Lowell Lectures, Boston. The latter were published in 1881 under the title, *The Theistic Argument as Affected by Recent Theories*. His career was suddenly cut short by an attack of malignant erysipelas when he was in his fiftieth year. In such high regard was he held in the state that the Rhode Island House of Representatives adjourned to attend his funeral. After his death a volume of selections from his writings, *Orations and Essays: with Selected Parish Sermons* (1882), including a commemorative discourse by James O. Murray, was published.

[In addition to references above, see Caroline Hazard, *Memoirs of the Rev. J. Lewis Diman, D.D.* (1887), and *A Precious Heritage* (1929); Louise Diman, *Emily Gardner Stimson Diman, A Memorial Sketch* (privately printed, 1902); E. R. Dimond, *The Geneal. of the Dimond or Dimon Family* . . . (1891); *Proc. Mass. Hist. Soc.*, 1 ser., vol. XVIII (1880–81); *Nation* (N. Y.), Feb. 10, 1881; *Providence Jour.*, Feb. 4, 1881, and following days.] H. E. S.

DIMITRY, ALEXANDER (Feb. 7, 1805–Jan. 30, 1883), educator, public official, son of Andrea and Celeste (Dragon) Dimitry, was born in New Orleans, where he also died. His father, a Greek from the island of Hydrea, came to America in the last quarter of the eighteenth century. His mother's father, also a Greek, came to New Orleans soon after 1760, but his mother's mother was of a family long resident in Louisiana, and one of her remote ancestors had taken for wife an Indian. Alexander was sent to school in New Orleans, and in 1820 to Georgetown College in the District of Columbia. Returning to Louisiana, he taught for two years in the Baton Rouge College before becoming the first English editor of the *New Orleans Bee*, a paper edited theretofore in French. During this time (1830–35) he contributed some short stories to "annuals" published in New York and Philadelphia. From 1834 to 1842 he was in Washington as a clerk in the Post Office Department and as active member, for some of that time, of the Union Literary Society. His *Lecture on the Study of History as Applied to the Progress of Civilization* and *Address on July Fourth*, both delivered before that body in 1839, exhibit in rounded oratory the erudition and patriotism characteristic of their time and title. He was married in 1835 to Mary Powell Mills, daughter of Robert Mills [*q.v.*] of South Carolina, architect of the Washington Monument. Returning to Louisiana in 1842 and establishing a school in St. Charles Parish, he continued as its head till

1847, when he began his three years of valuable service as first superintendent of education in his state. From 1854 to 1859 he was a translator in the State Department in Washington, and from 1859 till he resigned, upon the secession of Louisiana, he was minister to Costa Rica and Nicaragua. During the Civil War he was assistant postmaster-general of the Confederacy. After the war he took up his residence in the vicinity of New York City, to remain there till 1867. From then until his death, with the exception of a brief period spent in teaching at Pass Christian, Miss., he lived in New Orleans. He wrote little but read and talked much. Having as a young man faced and definitely put from him the temptation to write books, he indulged instead throughout his life a taste for buying them—up to the number of 15,000—for his private library, and a taste also for setting forth his conclusions in public discourse, whether upon his literary and philological investigations or upon the state-rights theories which he thought should dominate American politics.

[Alcée Fortier, *Hist. of La.* (1906); *Louisiana* (1909); H. Rightor, *Standard Hist. of New Orleans* (1900); E. W. Fay, *Hist. of Education in La.* (1898); J. G. Shea, *Memorial of the First Centenary of Georgetown Coll.* (1891); *New Orleans Times Democrat*, Jan. 31, 1883.] J. D. W.

DIMITRY, CHARLES PATTON (July 31, 1837–Nov. 10, 1910), journalist, author, was born in Washington, D. C., and died in New Orleans. His father, Alexander Dimitry [*q.v.*], a citizen of New Orleans who spent much of his life in Washington, was a man of considerable literary distinction, and his mother, Mary Powell Mills, was the daughter of Robert Mills, architect of the Washington Monument. As a boy Charles went to school in Louisiana, and in 1856 he entered Georgetown College, but apparently did not graduate, although he was given the degree of A.M. in 1867. At the beginning of the Civil War he was a clerk in New Orleans. He immediately went into the Confederate army, and remained there, in the Army of Tennessee, till 1865. During 1864 he published serially in Richmond a novel, "Guilty or Not Guilty." At the concluson of the war he went to New York, where till 1874 he was connected at one time or another with the *World, Graphic, News, Star,* and *Brooklyn Union*. In 1868 he published *The House in Balfour Street,* a romance with its scenes laid in a Victorian English village. Here he introduced, in dialects which he fancied appropriate to each, a sort of Brontëan hero, a French roué, several shop-keepers and house-servants, and many country ladies and gentlemen. The story is concerned with the struggle of the most important of these characters through love and disaster, both of which for a while seem criminal, to final just deserts of happiness. He wrote also, besides many short stories, three other novels, published in periodicals: "Angela's Christmas," "Gold Dust and Diamonds," and "Two Knaves and a Queen"; and he contributed frequently to a number of newspapers, among them, the Alexandria *Commercial Advertiser,* the *New Orleans Bee* and the *Washington Daily Patriot.* He was employed for short periods in journalistic work in Mobile, Richmond, and Baltimore, and at one time in his life was engrossed in inventing and patenting an ink which would not rust pens. After reaching middle age he settled down in New Orleans, where he was connected for a long time with the editorial staff of the *Picayune.* There, writing sometimes as Tobias Guarnerius, Jr., or as Braddock Field, he prepared for various newspapers a number of articles on local history. His wife, Anne Elizabeth Johnson, whom he married in 1871 in Alexandria, Va., died in 1880, after the death of their only child. His last years were spent in comparative solitude, made heavier by poverty and approaching blindness.

[Alcée Fortier, *Louisiana* (1909); Georgetown Univ., *Gen. Reg.* (1916); *Who's Who in America,* 1910–11; *New Orleans Picayune,* Nov. 11, 1910; letter from Jas. M. Dimitry of New Orleans, July 3, 1928.] J. D. W.

DINGLEY, NELSON (Feb. 15, 1832–Jan. 13, 1899), editor, governor, and congressman from Maine, was born in Durham, Me. The first Dingley came to America from Lynn, England, to settle in Lynn, Mass., as early as 1637, and one of his descendants removed to Maine about 1773. Nelson Dingley, the grandson of this early pioneer, married Jane Lambert, a descendant of Revolutionary stock, whose father had been one of the founders of the first Baptist church in the village of Durham, and Nelson Dingley, Jr., was their son. As a lad he was not brilliant, but industrious, conscientious, careful to read the best books, the sort of boy who would begin a diary at the age of fourteen and continue it to within a month of his death. From his earliest youth he was an advocate of temperance, took a keen interest in debating, attended Sunday-school, taught for two months in a day school at the age of sixteen, joined the church when twenty, and the same year was a delegate to a Whig state convention. He attended Waterville College (now Colby University) for nearly two years, and then transferred to Dartmouth College, from which he graduated sixth in a class of fifty-one in 1855. In college, as before, his interests were serious; books, debating, the temperance cause, religion. His political idol was Daniel Webster.

The turning point in his career came in 1856, when, after being admitted to the bar, he decided not to follow the law but purchased a half interest in the *Lewiston Evening Journal.* From that time on, his main interests were the newspaper, politics, and the advancement of education, religion, and the cause of temperance. Under Dingley's leadership the *Journal* immediately espoused the cause of the newly forming Republican party, and he found himself appointed a member of the Republican committee for the second congressional district. From this time onward his absorption in politics became almost complete. In 1861 he was elected to the state legislature as a Republican; he was reëlected five times, and was twice speaker. At this time he was described as a slight, frail, almost delicate man, industrious, methodical, and painstaking. In January 1874 he became governor of Maine, and served two terms. His first inaugural struck some distinctly modern notes, particularly his care for free public education, his insistence on prohibition and on reform in the taxation of railroads and corporations. "Railroads . . . are public works," he asserted, "no matter by whose capital built" (Dingley, *post,* p. 109).

In 1881 he was elected to the United States House of Representatives, serving there without intermission until his death. During this period of about eighteen years—the climax of his career—he retained his boyhood interests, matured and expanded. Quiet, regular in his attendance upon his duties, an effective debater but not an orator, a repository of facts and figures, he was uninterested in the usual routines of society but gave evidence of his keen interest in temperance, education, and religion by constant addresses at conferences and institutions of learning. His thorough knowledge of finance, especially as related to the controversy over silver coinage, and his enthusiastic championship of a protective tariff gave him prominence on the floor of the House. He was a member of the Committee on Ways and Means in 1889, and in 1895 was made chairman. When the election of 1896 resulted in the triumph of President McKinley and a Republican Congress, with the consequent choice of Thomas B. Reed as speaker of the House, and of Dingley again as chairman of the Committee on Ways and Means, the latter undertook the task of preparing a tariff measure to replace the Democratic Wilson-Gorman Act. While Dingley was at work on the bill, he was offered the position of secretary of the treasury by President McKinley. On the grounds that his strength was not sufficient for the arduous duties of the treasury, and that his inclinations lay in the direction of congressional service, he felt obliged to refuse the offer. The tariff law which finally resulted, commonly known as the Dingley Act, was passed in 1897 and remained in force until 1909. In 1898 Dingley was appointed by President McKinley to serve on the United States and British Joint High Commission for the settlement of points relating to the Alaskan boundary, the Alaskan seal fisheries, and other subjects of dispute, but his death occurred in the following January.

Champ Clark described him as a "pronounced brunette, with a Hebraic cast of features," destitute of humor, but a master of the subjects he discussed, who constituted a constant refutation of the common belief that nobody listens to speeches in Congress, inasmuch as the members always gathered when he took the floor. "Physically, Dingley was small, spare, and frail, with an appearance suggestive of consumption. He had what is called 'the scholar's stoop' in a marked degree. He was a frequent, lucid, and instructive, but not a pleasant speaker; had a weak, rasping voice, a well developed nasal twang, an acquiline nose, and a bald head" (Clark, *My Quarter Century of American Politics,* 1920, II, 11). On June 11, 1857, he was married to Salome McKenney.

[*The Life and Times of Nelson Dingley, Jr.* (1902), by his son E. N. Dingley (Kalamazoo, 1902), in the preparation of which Mr. Dingley's diary was largely used; *Just Maine Folks* (1924), published by the Maine Writers' Research Club; *Lewiston Journal,* immediately following Dingley's death.]

C. R. L.

DINSMOOR, ROBERT (Oct. 7, 1757–Mar. 16, 1836), poet, was the great-grandson of John Dinsmoor, who came from County Antrim, Ireland, in 1723 and settled in Londonderry, N. H., and the son of William and Elizabeth (Cochran) Dinsmoor. He was born in Windham, N. H., grew up on his father's farm, and, whenever he could be spared from work, went to such schools as were available in a frontier town, learning to "read, write and cipher tolerably." In 1775 at the age of eighteen he enlisted with the New Hampshire troops under Gen. John Sullivan and took part in the battle of Saratoga. Thoroughly convinced of the truth of the Longer and Shorter Catechisms, he was chosen deacon of the local Presbyterian church and was clerk of the session. He was twice married: first, to Mary Park, who died leaving him two sons and nine daughters, and afterward to Mary Davidson Anderson. He was of massive build, strong-limbed, broad-shouldered, and about five feet ten inches in height. A man of genial humor, a lover of good food and homely joys, he was widely esteemed for his kindly heart and his unbending integrity. Inheriting a gift of versification from his father, who had written some creditable verses in the Lowland Scotch dialect used in the Londonderry settlement, he cheered his lonely hours by writing about the thoughts and happenings of his daily life in natural, spontaneous melodies. Most of his verses were composed in the Scotch dialect, still spoken among his neighbors, and they won for him much local popularity. An edition of his poems was published in 1828, but it was of unsatisfactory appearance. Seventy years later Leonard Allison Morrison made a new compilation and arrangement in a more creditable form: *Poems of Robert Dinsmoor, the Rustic Bard* (1898). The opening poem is a lengthy narrative of "Jamie Cochran; the Indian Captive." Dinsmoor found his inspiration in the events and traditions of his neighborhood, local genealogists and historians have found much material of value in his writings, but that his name has survived is due largely to Whittier's friendship. The Quaker poet felt that American literature was sadly lacking in the "poetry of home, of nature and the affections," and in this "Rustic Bard" he found one who sensed the poetry of common life and in "home-taught, household melody" gave it genuine, if not very competent, expression. Whittier's essay on "Robert Dinsmore" (thus he spelled the name) in his collection entitled *Old Portraits and Modern Sketches* (1850) is well worth reading as a tribute to a friend, and for its reflections on native American literature.

[Besides the essay by Whittier, above mentioned, see *Poems of Robert Dinsmoor* (1898), which contains introductory recollections by the poet's nephew, Jas. Dinsmoor, letters written by Robert Dinsmoor during his service in the Revolutionary army and afterward, an appendix reprinting a letter establishing what is known of the origin of the Dinsmoor family, a brief genealogy of the McKeen family, and short papers on Gen. John Stark and Gen. John Sullivan under whom the New Hampshire men served.] C. A. D.

DINWIDDIE, ROBERT (1693–July 27, 1770), colonial administrator, the son of Robert Dinwiddie, was born in 1693 at "Germiston," near Glasgow. His mother, a daughter of Matthew Cumming, is called Elizabeth in one place (genealogical sketch, Dinwiddie *Records,* I, xxii) and Sarah in another (p. viii of the same volume). Robert worked in his father's counting house, and later, apparently, became a merchant. On Dec. 1, 1727, he was made collector of customs for Bermuda. In 1730 he was placed upon the regular establishment, at £30 a year. So satisfactory was his work that on Apr. 11, 1738, he was made surveyor-general for the Southern Part of America, with jurisdiction over the Carolinas, Virginia, Maryland, Pennsylvania, Bahama Islands, and Jamaica. In the same year he visited Barbados, where he uncovered many frauds in the revenues. On June 29, 1743, he appeared before the Lords of the Treasury to explain a plan for collecting the duty on colonial sugar. Late in the same year he was back in Barbados, where he found the frauds in the customs more glaring than ever. Charging several of the officials with false entries, fraudulent sales, and embezzlement, he dismissed them. These men complained to the Lords of the Treasury, and it is probable that Dinwiddie had to spend much time in London defending himself. While surveyor-general he took up his residence in Virginia. His commission entitled him to membership in the councils of the southern colonies, and in October 1741 he took his seat in the Council of Virginia.

On July 20, 1751, he was appointed lieutenant-governor of Virginia. On Nov. 20 he landed at York, with his wife, Rebecca Affleck, and two daughters, and was escorted to Williamsburg. Despite his acquaintance with Virginia affairs, he made the mistake of provoking a quarrel with the House of Burgesses. It had long been the practise in the colony for those taking up land to secure an order for a certain number of acres, and to occupy them for years before securing a patent. In this way they escaped the payment of quit-rents. Dinwiddie not only ordered all landholders to take out patents at once, but charged a fee of a pistole for signing the patent and for the use of the seal. To the latter provision the Burgesses objected violently. "The rights of the subjects are so secured by law," they declared, "that they cannot be deprived of the least part of their property but by their own consent." Little dreaming that twenty-two years later the American colonies would rebel against the Crown in support of this principle, Dinwiddie persisted in his course. Thereupon the Burgesses laid the matter before the Board of Trade, through the attorney-general, Peyton Randolph. The Board directed that no fee should be charged for patents on land west of the mountains, or upon lands surveyed before Apr. 22, 1752. This meant victory for the Burgesses, and Dinwiddie reluctantly obeyed. But the dispute was settled only after it had done untold harm by preventing the cooperation of governor and Assembly at a time when the French were threatening the very existence of British America.

Dinwiddie was deeply interested in the Ohio region. Upon his arrival in 1751 he brought with him generous gifts for the Indians, in the hope of binding them to the English interest.

He gave his approval and support to the Ohio Company. With alarm he learned that the French not only claimed the region, but had erected a fort on French Creek. If they succeeded in their designs, the English would be cut off from the entire western country. In 1753 he sent George Washington, then a young officer in the Virginia militia, to warn the French to withdraw. When Washington returned with the report that the French were preparing to descend the Ohio with 220 canoes and 1,500 men, Dinwiddie tried to anticipate them. In February 1754 he sent seventy men to the site of Pittsburgh to erect a fort. A few weeks later he dispatched after them two larger detachments, the more advanced under Washington, at the same time appealing for aid to the neighboring governors and to the Board of Trade. When the French drove away his workmen from the fort, attacked Washington at Fort Necessity, and drove him back over the mountains, the governor made strenuous efforts for a new expedition. But the Assembly failed him, some of his troops deserted, and he was compelled to abandon the plan.

Hope revived when news arrived that two picked regiments under Gen. Edward Braddock had been ordered to Virginia. During the spring of 1755 Dinwiddie was busy gathering stores of food, recruiting the Virginia companies, urging other governors to aid, seeking Indian allies, pleading with the Assembly for funds. When Braddock led his force into the wilderness, Dinwiddie was confident of success. After the crushing defeat at Great Meadows, he criticized the English general for "leaving half his army forty miles behind," and for the "want of scouts to clear the woods." But defeat did not discourage him. The Assembly voted £40,000 and 1,200 men, which with the remnant of Braddock's army under Col. Dunbar he thought sufficient to retrieve the situation. To his dismay, Dunbar marched to Philadelphia, leaving "the fort and frontier to be defended by 400 sick and wounded, and the poor remains of our provincial forces." Hard upon the heels of the British came the Indians, robbing, pillaging, burning, murdering. So Dinwiddie had to face alone the task of defending hundreds of miles of exposed frontier. He sent out companies of rangers, raised a regiment and placed it under Washington, sent for the friendly Indians, and built forts at the points of greatest danger. Despite these efforts it was a time of terror for western Virginia, and more than once Dinwiddie had to order out the militia to meet expected raids. An expedition to the Shawnee country failed because of rain, snow, and swollen rivers. At last, in the spring of 1757, some four hundred Cherokees, Catawbas, Saponies, Tuscaroras, and Nottaways gathered at Winchester, and for the time being the frontier was comparatively safe.

From the outbreak of the war until his return to England Dinwiddie constantly was seeking intercolonial cooperation. Repeatedly he wrote to the governors of Pennsylvania, Maryland, and the Carolinas, urging them to send money and men. In April 1755 he went to Annapolis for a conference of governors, and two years later he met the Earl of Loudoun at Philadelphia, to discuss plans of defense. His discouraging experience with assemblies led him to suggest that Parliament impose upon the colonies a poll tax of a shilling and a land tax of two shillings for each 100 acres, to aid in financing the war. "I know our people will be inflamed if they hear of my making this proposal," he added (Dinwiddie *Records,* II, 341). His constant exertions told upon his health. On Mar. 22, 1757, he wrote Pitt asking for leave of absence to visit Bath. He left Virginia on Jan. 12, 1758, and was succeeded by Francis Fauquier. He died at Clifton, Bristol, on July 27, 1770. His career as colonial administrator was marked by vision, strength, attention to detail, and untiring energy. As the man who precipitated the struggle which brought about the downfall of New France, he is a figure of first importance in the early history of the American continent.

[The chief sources of information are *The Official Records of Robert Dinwiddie* (2 vols., 1883–84), in the Va. Hist. Soc. Colls.; Correspondence of the Board of Trade, in the British Public Record Office; *Calendar of Treasury Books and Papers, 1729–30* (1897), *1735–38* (1900), *1742–45* (1903); *Jours. of the House of Burgesses of Va.* (1909); *Exec. Jours. of the Council of Colonial Va.* (3 vols., 1925–28); and *Va. Mag. of Hist. and Biog.*, Jan. 1906.] T. J. W.

DISBROW, WILLIAM STEPHEN (Mar. 18, 1861–Dec. 26, 1922), physician, collector, was born in Newark, N. J., the son of Henry G. and Catherine Cline (Clickener) Disbrow. His early life was a struggle for education and professional training, but by dint of hard work in factories and drug stores he paid his way through the New York College of Pharmacy (Ph.G., 1880) and the medical department of the University of the City of New York (M.D., 1887). After a year in North Adams, Mass., as a chemist with the Zylonite Company, he returned in 1888 to his native Newark, married Clara E. Valentine of that city, and spent the remaining thirty-four years of his life in the practise of medicine. Over a long period of years he was a staff physician at St. Barnabas's Hospital and at the City Hospital, a professor in the New Jersey College of Pharmacy, and a member of the

Newark board of health, of which he in time became president. His private practise was large, but since his generosity to needy patients was also large it never became especially lucrative. Though his professional career was unusually successful and beneficent, Disbrow's chief claim to remembrance is as a collector. A burly man with great physical and mental powers and a voracious appetite for knowledge, he threw into his hobbies such energy as few men can devote to the main business of their lives. His principal fields were the natural sciences, medical history, and numismatics, but almost anything that interested him and that he thought might interest some one else he gathered in. Whenever an old family was broken up, an old house abandoned, an old cemetery removed, Disbrow was on hand to inquire whether papers, relics, or inscriptions were to be had. He examined every excavation for a new building lest some deposit of sand or clay or some stratum of rock escape him. He ransacked the old bookstores almost daily and kept his eyes open for objects of interest when visiting factories and the homes of his patients. But if he took a freebooter's joy in collecting stamps, coins, medical medals, plants and flowers, weapons, pottery, Indian curios, rocks, minerals, crystals, shells, gums, seeds, fossils, books, pamphlets, maps, pictures, and portraits of physicians, he was generous in bestowing his finds on institutions and on other private collectors; indeed much of his material came to him from men who wished to make some return for the lavish generosity that he had shown them. He was not, as one might suppose, an indiscriminate collector: the range and exactness of his information were amazing. The chief beneficiaries of his collecting were the Smithsonian Institution, the United States National Museum, and the Surgeon-General's Library in Washington, and the Academy of Medicine of Northern New Jersey, the New Jersey Historical Society, and the Newark Museum Association in Newark, to which he gave his largest collection. This consisted of 74,000 science specimens, 5,000 scientific books, 10,000 pamphlets, and 5,000 pictures and maps. Housed during the latter years of Disbrow's life on the fourth floor of the Newark Public Library, where he spent the long hot summer days in classifying and labeling his materials, it became after his death the science collection of the Newark Museum. He died at the height of his powers. He was seized with a cerebral hemorrhage just after finishing Christmas dinner at his son's home in Summit, N. J., and succumbed twleve hours after.

[J. C. Dana, G. P. Merrill, F. Neumann, and others, *A Great Collector: Dr. Wm. S. Disbrow* (Newark Museum Asso., 1925); *Gen. Alumni Cat. of N. Y. Univ.: Medical Alumni* (1908); *Newark Evening News*, Dec. 27, 1922; *Newark Sunday Call*, Jan. 1, 1923.] G. H. G.

DISSTON, HENRY (May 23, 1819–Mar. 16, 1878), manufacturer, was born at Tewkesbury, Gloucestershire, England, son of Thomas and Ann (Harrod) Disston. His father, a mechanic experienced in the manufacture of lace-making machinery, brought him and his sister to America when the boy was fourteen years old. Three days after reaching Philadelphia, the port of destination, the father died. Left to his own resources, the young immigrant became a saw maker's apprentice. In 1840 he started a small business of his won, with a capital of $350. He had to overcome many difficulties. The industry was then in the handicraft stage, was dependent on imported steel, and was confronted with the competition of superior English technology. In addition, Disston was unfortunate in his relations with lessors. In 1846, however, he established his factory at Front and Laurel Sts., Philadelphia, where during the next quarter-century his business rapidly increased.

His significance as a manufacturer was twofold. In the first place, he was an innovator in technology. Secondly, he transformed a small and struggling industry into one that outrivaled foreign competitors and conquered world markets. As early as 1844 he made use of steam power in his saw factory. Another early innovation was the conversion of waste steel into ingots in place of its reshipment to England. Out of these early experiments he evolved formulas for the manufacture of the highest grade of crucible steel demanded by the peculiar strains to which saws are subjected, and thus the industry was at length freed from dependence on imported steel. His adaptability was indicated by his transformation of his plant during the Civil War into an establishment for manufacturing war supplies. For the purpose of making metal plates, the importation of which was interrupted by the Southern cruisers, he built a rolling-mill. An experimental sawmill was established for the purpose of determining the types of saws best adapted to various kinds of timber and to the varying needs of woodworkers. Timber was conserved by reducing the thickness of the saws while at the same time greater speed and driving power were made possible by improvements in the quality of steel and in the models of saws. He was unusually gifted as a mechanic and inventor, and made personally a large number of improvements. He encouraged his employees to observe defects and to suggest improvements. The expansion of the business continued until at length the works produced all types of saws from the largest circular saw of the lumbering industry to the minute keyhole saw, and also a great variety of files, knives, screw-drivers, trowels, molders' tools, etc. By establishing agencies in various places, the company contributed to the significant tendency of modern manufacturers to subordinate the mercantile to the industrial group. In 1871 the widely known Disston factory at Tacony, near Philadelphia, was opened. The establishment came to include a tract of several hundred acres, and a factory town rapidly grew up, the houses of the workers being financed in part by the company. The plant attracted the interest of visitors from various parts of the world.

Henry Disston was not prominently connected with organized activities outside of his own business, nor was he a man of particular intellectual or cultural distinction. He contributed liberally to community enterprises, however, building a school for the promotion of industrial and general education, maintaining a dispensary, and supporting the conventional activities. His participation in politics included membership on the Hayes electoral ticket and support of protective tariffs. His first marriage was to Amanda Mulvina Bickley; his second, to Mary Steelman, the mother of his children, some of whom came to be associated with him in the firm of Henry Disston & Sons.

[The most important source is the "Disston History," a two-volume manuscript history in the company's archives, compiled in 1920, the second volume being a history of the Works. Some additional information is in the *Public Ledger* (Phila.), Mar. 18, 1878; *The Manufactories and Manufacturers of Pa.* (1875); and J. T. Scharf and T. Westcott, *Hist. of Phila.* (3 vols., 1884).]

W. B.

DISTURNELL, JOHN (Oct. 6, 1801–Oct. 1, 1877), compiler of guide-books, was born in Lansingburg, N. Y., and died in New York City. He began work as a printer in Albany, N. Y., but the first available contemporary record of his whereabouts is in the New York Directory of 1830. From then till 1865 he appears in successive issues of the Directory as a book-dealer, and from 1865 to 1870 as librarian of the Cooper Union; he is missing from the Directories of 1870–76, but reappears in 1877. He is in the Philadelphia Directories for the early seventies. In 1836 he published *A Guide to the City of New York*, and in the same year, *The Traveller's Guide through the State of New York*. With the rapid development of means of transportation he became a prolific compiler of railway and steamship guides, one of the earliest being *The Western Traveller; Embracing the Canal and Railroad Routes from Albany to Troy, to Buffalo and Niagara Falls. Also the Steamboat Route, from Buffalo to Detroit and Chicago* (1844). For two or three decades in the middle of the century he issued, in various editions and under various titles, *Disturnell's Railway, Steamship and Telegraph Book*. Quick to anticipate popular demand, in 1849, he published *The Emigrant's Guide to New Mexico, California, and Oregon*. He gave off a constant succession of writings about any region or subject, specific or vague, in America or elsewhere, that interested him or might conceivably interest his "trade." He published handbooks, distance-tables, maps, gazetteers, and censuses too numerous to name, a book on *Springs, Waterfalls, Seabathing Resorts, and Mountain Scenery* (1855), and disquisitions on the *Influence of Climate in a Commercial, Social, Sanitary, and Humanizing Point of View* (1860), and on *Political Economy, or Interest, Usury, and Taxation* (1877). From 1851 to 1877 he compiled yearly *The United States National Register Containing Authentic Political and Statistical Information*. In 1866 he issued *Politician's Manual, The Constitution of the United States of America Together with Amendments and Proposed Amendments*. He was a good salesman—not only industrious and aggressive, but comfortably at one with the opinions and desires of his environment. In 1876 he published *New York as It Was and as It Is*. As late as 1877 he was still promoting travel. He thought that Americans should be thrifty like Europeans, so that they too might patronize the centers of rest and recreation. His *Summer Resorts*, published in that year, deals only with the immediate vicinity of New York; it was not, he said, so full as he had meant it to be—want of time and patronage had persuaded him to issue only a part of what he had planned. He hoped, however, that in 1878 he could "continue this work to completion, hereafter furnishing the public with a complete Guide within a circuit of Fifty Miles around the City of New York."

[Disturnell's own publications; New York and Philadelphia directories; *Appletons' Ann. Cyc.*, 1877; *Evening Post* (N. Y.), Oct. 2, 1877.]

J. D. W.

DITRICHSTEIN, LEO (Jan. 6, 1865–June 28, 1928), actor, dramatist, was one of a considerable number of members of his profession who came to the United States from Europe to make their reputations and to spend the greater part of their lives on the American stage. With him, as with others, English was an acquired tongue, and he always spoke it with a noticeable foreign accent. He was born on the paternal estate at Tamesvar, Hungary, the son of Sigismond Ladislav Ditrichstein, and of Bertha von Eötvös, whose father was the Hungarian novelist, Joseph von Eötvös. His parents had other aims for him, but he insisted upon becoming an actor. After several years' service in the theatres of Vienna, where he had the advantage of training from Adolph Sonnenthal, and in Berlin and other Continental cities, including engagements in light opera, he came to the United States, and at once started upon the career in which he achieved distinction as an actor and as a maker of plays.

His first appearance on the American stage was made at the Amberg Theatre in New York, Mar. 12, 1890, with a company of German actors in a production of Sudermann's play, *Die Ehre.* Not long afterward he had gained sufficient facility in the English language to appear in English-speaking parts, and he soon found himself in demand for the playing of important characters. His first part in English was in a popular farce of that period called *Mr. Wilkinson's Widows,* one of William Gillette's adaptations from the French. When the *Trilby* furore began in 1895, his foreign manner and vocal intonations made him the very actor for the eccentric Zou Zou in the stage version of George Du Maurier's novel made by Paul M. Potter. Thereafter he was continuously active in the American theatre as a writer and adapter of plays, and as an actor. He did little original play-writing, but he had the clever knack, so common with many capable actors, of taking a foreign play and of making it over into other scenes and languages. The greater number of plays that bear his name, nearly forty in all, had their originals in the European drama, and since German was thoroughly familiar to him, he drew them mainly from German dramatists. Occasionally he worked in collaboration with American dramatists, notably with Clyde Fitch, with whom he wrote *Gossip* (1895), *A Superfluous Husband* (1897), and *The Head of the Family* (1898). Two of his most popular farces were *All on Account of Eliza* (1900), and *Are You a Mason?* (1901), one of the most popular plays of its kind for more than twenty years. In 1901 he collaborated with Robert Grant in a dramatization of that author's novel, *Unleavened Bread,* but although it was received with critical favor, it met with scant success from the public. His active service as an actor covered nearly thirty-five years of appearance in plays by many others as well as his own. *The Concert* and *The Phantom Rival,* both from the German, *The King,* from the French, and *The Great Lover,* written in collaboration with Frederic and Fanny Hatton, are especially the plays that brought him deserved fame both as dramatist and actor. He had a liking also for melodrama, and in 1920 he appeared in *The Purple Mask,* turning thereto from the intriguing and passionate lover in chase of the sophisticated woman to the fascinating hero who surmounts all dangers and wins his way by his valor to happiness and love. From the graceful youth of such parts as Zou Zou in *Trilby* the years changed him in physique to a heavier and more imposing type of stage character, but there persisted in all his impersonations the light and airy touch that gave a romantic quality to his entire repertory. He had acted minor parts in Shakespeare's plays during his youth in the European theatres, and during his final years on the stage he had an ambition to make Shakespearian productions and play leading rôles in them, but it was not fulfilled. In 1924, he announced his retirement from all stage work, and went abroad to live in Europe until his death at Auersperg, Jugoslavia. His wife, to whom he was married in 1896, was Josephine Wehrle.

[Interview in the *Christian Science Monitor,* Mar. 16, 1920; *Current Opinion,* Nov. 1917; A. D. Storms, *The Playgoers' Blue Book,* 1901; *Who's Who in America,* 1924–25; John Parker, *Who's Who in the Theatre,* 1925; obituary in *N. Y. Times,* June 30, 1928. The date of Ditrichstein's birth is given variously in the last four sources as Jan. 6, 1864, 1867, and Jan. 6, 1865, respectively, the *N. Y. Times* adopting Parker's date.]

E. F. E.

DITSON, GEORGE LEIGHTON (Aug. 5, 1812–Jan. 29, 1895), author, son of William and Mary (Leighton) Ditson, was born in Westford, Mass., and died in New York City. He went to school at the Westford Academy and later began to study medicine in Boston. Here his health failed, and he was advised to take a sea voyage. He went away and remained for two years, largely in Egypt and India, where he became engrossed in the study of oriental languages. He had scarcely returned home when he set out again, this time with a party intending to make excavations around Carthage. During the forties, under both Tyler and Polk, he was the American consul at Nuevitas, Cuba, and in 1842–43 he taught English in a college in Puerto-Príncipe. By 1847 he was off again for the East, making during that year his seventh crossing of the Atlantic. He had already visited western Europe, and it was at this time, most likely, that he went to Russia and Palestine. In 1850 he published *Circassia, or a Tour of the Caucasus*—loyal to America, to be sure, but suggestive of Cooper in its quarrel with American provincialism, and of Byron in its assumption of a flinty sophistication. *The Para Papers on*

France, Egypt and Ethiopia—"para," it is explained, being one of the smallest of oriental coins—was published in English, and in French. A year later (1859) appeared his voluminous *The Crescent and French Crusaders,* based on a residence in Northern Africa. He wrote two novels, both having to do with love and marriage in Scotland and Italy, *Crimora, or Love's Cross* (1852) and *The Federati of Italy* (1871). In 1860 he married Oralie Bartlett, daughter of a naval officer, Washington Allen Bartlett, and his wife, Ruth Budd Bloom. During 1863 and 1864 he was a student at the University of Vermont, and in the latter year he was given his degree in medicine. During his travels he formed a friendship with Madame Blavatsky [*q.v.*] and became a member of the Adyar branch of the Theosophical Society. His home in Albany, N. Y., which she later visited, was the scene of many psychical investigations, and the meeting-place of any spiritualists, apparently, who were in the neighborhood, or could manage to get there.

[The principal source is a letter from Oralie D. Lodge, Albany, N. Y., Feb. 24, 1928. An obituary of Ditson's wife was published in the *Albany Evening Jour.*, Apr. 9, 1906.]

J. D. W.

DITSON, OLIVER (Oct. 20, 1811–Dec. 21, 1888), music publisher, was descended from Hugh Ditson who settled at Billerica, Mass., in 1685. His father, Joseph Ditson, who married in 1797 Lucy Pierce of Lexington, became a Boston merchant and ship-owner, prosperous for a time but later dependent on Oliver, the fifth of nine children. The boy, born at 74 Prince St., near Copp's Hill, was graduated in 1823 from the Eliot School, leading his class. He entered the store of Col. Samuel H. Parker, bookseller and publisher, a founder of the Handel and Haydn Society, and later apprenticed himself to Isaac Butts, then printer of the *North American Review,* from whom he learned the printing trade thoroughly. His most intimate friend, while he was with Butts, was John Henry Howard Graupner, son of Gottlieb Graupner, the celebrated orchestral conductor. Through the Graupners, Oliver became a competent musician and for a time he was organist at the Bulfinch Street Church. He also saw opportunities in music publishing which induced him in 1835 to start his own business at 107 Washington St. The *Saturday Evening Gazette* said, June 6, 1835: "Mr. Oliver Ditson has just published a new song entitled 'There's not a Leaf within the Bower.'" Thus was initiated a business which became the largest of its kind in North America. Ditson interested his first employer in his venture and in 1836 the co-partnership was announced of "Parker & Ditson, dealers in Piano Fortes and Sheet Music." In 1840 Ditson bought out his partner, and in 1845 he took into his employ John C. Haynes, then fifteen years old, who became his efficient associate and later, under the name of Oliver Ditson & Company, adopted in 1857, his partner. This firm's business, after the Civil War, reached $2,000,000 annually. Its successor, the Oliver Ditson Company, is still (1930) important in the world's music trade.

The success which Ditson achieved as a music publisher was based on sound business methods, understanding of the public capacity to appreciate music, personal sympathy with the aspirations of composers, and sufficient musical ability of his own to professionalize his commercial instincts. He was methodical and industrious. As church organist and as conductor of the Malibran Glee Club he kept in close touch with his fellow musicians. He cherished his friendships, which were many. He was philanthropic and public-spirited. Banks sought his counsel. He was president for twenty years of the Continental Bank, a trustee of the Franklin Savings Bank of which he was an organizer, and a director of other banks. He was a friend and supporter of Father Taylor in his work among seamen. He helped to found the Home for Aged Men on West Springfield St. He was among the subscribers who made it possible for Dr. Eben Tourjée to buy the Franklin Square House as a home for the New England Conservatory of Music.

Ditson was a good trader as well as a humanitarian. He was quick to see a profit where others had met with a loss and made his money largely by publishing popular music at prices low enough to permit large sales. His firm owed much of its expansion to a policy of buying the plates of publishers who were in difficulty. Allied houses were established in several cities. Oliver Ditson performed a service to musical journalism by publishing for John S. Dwight *Dwight's Journal of Music* from 1858 to 1876. He was one of the guarantors who made up the deficit of $100,000 incurred by the Peace Jubilee at Boston in 1872. His personal activities were closely limited to his native city from which he rarely traveled further than to his summer home at Swampscott. In religion he was a Unitarian, though an attendant in his later years upon Episcopal services. In 1888 he suffered a stroke of paralysis which ended his career after a lingering illness. He was buried from Trinity Church, with Phillips Brooks officiating, and with J. C.

D. Parker, a son of his first employer, at the organ. A contemporary said of him, "He was courteous and kindly in manner and, although of a somewhat reserved and retiring disposition, exceedingly amiable, witty and appreciative." He was married, about 1840, to Catherine Delano, by whom he had five children.

[H. A. Hazen, *Hist. of Billerica* (1883); W. A. Fisher, *Notes on Music in Old Boston* (1918); *A Hundred Years of Music in America* (1889), ed. by W. S. B. Mathews; *Boston Musical Review*, Jan. 1889; *Boston Transcript*, Dec. 22, 1888; obituary notices and other biographical data in scrapbook compiled by Allen A. Brown for the collection bearing his name in the Boston Pub. Lib. The date of Ditson's birth is given variously as Oct. 20, 21, and 30, 1811; the authority for the first of these is the sketch in the *Boston Musical Review*, carefully prepared before Ditson's death, and presumably with the aid of his son.] F. W. C.

DIVEN, ALEXANDER SAMUEL (Feb. 10, 1809–June 11, 1896), lawyer, soldier, railroad promoter, was the son of John and Eleanor (Means) Diven of the town of Catharine, Tioga County—now Watkins, Schuyler County, N. Y., where he was born. He obtained his education in the local school and Penn Yan and Ovid academies. He then took up the study of law in the office of Judge Gray at Elmira, Chemung County, N. Y., and was admitted to the bar in 1831. Commencing practise in Elmira, he acquired in a short time an extensive connection and there formed the well-known firm of Diven, Hathaway & Woods, which for years enjoyed the largest practise in that part of the state. He did not confine himself to the legal profession, but, becoming interested in internal communications, turned his attention to the railroad projects affecting his district. In 1844 he became a director of the New York & Erie Railroad, which at that time was built only as far as Binghamton. The company's funds were exhausted and at a meeting of the directors that year it was proposed to abandon the enterprise. Diven, however, successfully opposed this move, procured the adoption of a resolution recommending the prosecution of the work, and as attorney for the road took charge of the steps required to implement this decision. For the next six years he devoted his time to the task of rescue, including the raising of large sums of money for construction purposes. He drafted the necessary legislation in aid of the road, the first issues of bonds, and the mortgages by which they were secured, and acted as commissioner of construction through its building. After its completion he continued as its attorney. In 1849 he was chiefly instrumental in organizing the company which built the Binghamton-Corning line, and the Williamsport & Elmira Railroad, being president of the latter throughout its construction, and at a later period taking an active part in the extension of its system to the west under the name of the Pennsylvania Northern Central Railroad. He also contracted, in conjunction with Gen. Price and J. P. Kirkwood, for the construction of the Missouri Pacific Railroad and engaged in the construction of the Southwestern branch of the road. He had from an early age interested himself in public affairs, and was prominent in organizing the Republican party, but, owing to his professional and railroad engagements, was unable to take an active part in politics till 1858 when he represented Chemung County in the state Senate. In 1859 he was the Free-Soil candidate for governor of New York. In 1860 he was elected to the Thirty-seventh Congress, from the 27th Congressional District of New York, and served 1861–63, being a member of the Judiciary Committee and as a strong Unionist giving the administration unstinted support. When, however, the proposition was made to confiscate the property of the "rebels" he denounced it as barbarous in a powerful speech. As an anti-slavery man he supported the bill abolishing slavery in the District of Columbia. He drafted and introduced the first measure authorizing the employment of colored troops in the field. In July 1862 at the request of Secretary Stanton, he went to Elmira where he raised the 107th Regiment of New York Volunteers from Schuyler, Chemung, Steuben, and Allegany counties, being commissioned lieutenant-colonel. Joining the 5th Brigade of Whipple's division in the Reserve Corps, his regiment received its baptism of fire at Antietam, after which battle he was promoted colonel (Oct. 21, 1862), and as such was in the thick of the fight at Chancellorsville. In May 1863 he was appointed assistant adjutant-general and assumed command of the troop depot at Elmira. Brevetted brigadier-general, Aug. 30, 1864, he acted as assistant provost-marshal-general for the Western District of New York, becoming later commander of the Northern and Western districts, and continuing as such until the close of hostilities, when he returned to Elmira and resumed his law practise. In 1865 he was elected vice-president of the New York & Erie Railroad and held the office for three years. His last public service was as mayor of Elmira, and he retired from active business in 1879. His first wife, Amanda Beers, whom he married in 1835, died in 1875, and in 1876 he married Maria Joy. In character extremely modest and unassuming, he was very methodical in his habits and an incessant worker. As lawyer, soldier, railroad magnate, and politician he was equally successful.

For years he was looked upon as the foremost citizen of Elmira, and his devotion to the city's interests induced the unbounded respect and confidence of his townsfolk.

[H. P. Peirce and D. H. Hurd, *Hist. of Tioga, Chemung, Tompkins and Schuyler Counties, N. Y.* (1879), p. 281; J. L. Sexton, *An Outline Hist. of Tioga and Bradford Counties in Pa., Chemung . . . in N. Y.* (1885), p. 130; F. B. Heitman, *Hist. Reg. and Dict. U. S. Army* (1903); *Biog. Dir. Am. Cong.* (1928).]

H. W. H. K.

DIX, DOROTHEA LYNDE (Apr. 4, 1802–July 17, 1887), humanitarian, of New England ancestry, was born at Hampden, Me. Her parents were Joseph and Mary (Bigelow) Dix. Dorothea (she was christened Dorothy) probably inherited her traits of energy, public-spiritedness, and disregard for popularity from her grandfather, Dr. Elijah Dix, a Boston physician. Her father was a feeble character and religious fanatic. On her own initiative, at ten years old, she left her home, which had been so unhappy that she would never speak of it in detail, to seek with her grandmother, in Boston, stable conditions for an education. "I never knew childhood," she said in later life. At fourteen she was teaching school in Worcester, Mass., and soon after she established in the Dix Mansion in Boston a school for young girls which, with intervals of ill health, she conducted until her thirty-third year. The school mirrored herself. An unusual emphasis was put on the natural sciences, in which she was always keenly interested, but the dominant note was stress on moral character. She taught the children of the Rev. William Ellery Channing [*q.v.*] and traveled to the West Indies with his family. A Unitarian, she was a member of Dr. Channing's congregation. During these years, in addition to her teaching, she produced a number of long-since forgotten books: *Conversations on Common Things* (1824, 60th edition, 1869); *Evening Hours* (1825); *Meditations For Private Hours* (1828, many times reprinted); *The Garland of Flora* (1829); *The Pearl, or Affection's Gift; a Christmas and New Year's Present* (1829); *Ten Short Stories For Children* (1827–28; republished as *American Moral Tales For Young Persons,* 1832); *Hymns for Children, Selected and Altered* (1825; rearranged, 1833). She was, however, nervous, overstrained, and delicate, with incipient lung trouble. Obliged to give up her school, she spent eighteen months with the William Rathbones, friends of Dr. Channing's, at Greenbank, outside Liverpool, England. She returned to Boston in 1838, still an invalid. If she had died then, she would be remembered, if at all, only as one of numberless conscientious, self-sacrificing teachers of youth. But for fifty years she was to be an agent of change, and at her death the attitude of mind toward insanity and the treatment of the insane were to be different over the whole United States because she had lived.

The medieval conception of insanity as a possession by devils had gradually changed to one as cruel in effect, that of nature depraved and fallen to the brute and treated as a beast. In 1840 there were only eight insane asylums in the United States. Devoted and high-principled doctors were there practising the enlightened ideas of Philippe Pinel of France and William Tuke of England, but their efforts made only a flicker of light in the darkness where cruelty, callous indifference, and self-interest created misery unnoticed and unchallenged. An apostle was needed to bring the evil to public attention. On Mar. 28, 1841, Dorothea Dix undertook a Sunday-school class in the East Cambridge (Mass.) House of Correction. Visiting the jail, she found insane persons in an unheated room. After vain protest, she brought the matter to the East Cambridge court, with success. Aroused by the distress she had observed, she spent two years in a quiet, unobserved, thorough investigation of the condition of the insane, in jails, almshouses, and houses of correction, throughout Massachusetts. With incontrovertible evidence in hand, she chose influential men to present a memorial to the state legislature, calling attention to "the *present* state of Insane Persons confined within this Commonwealth, in *cages, closets, cellars, stalls, pens! Chained, naked, beaten with rods,* and *lashed* into obedience!" (*Memorial to the Legislature of Massachusetts,* 1843, p. 4). By letters to the press, she aroused public opinion. Over indignant protest and disbelief, the bill was carried for the enlargement of the Worcester insane asylum. Miss Dix soon saw the inadequacy of demanding intelligence and humanity from the keepers of almshouses and jails, and that asylums, with intelligent personnel, supported by state taxation, were necessary. Her work became national in scope. Five years later, in her first petition to Congress, she could write: "I have myself seen *more than nine thousand idiots, epileptics, and insane in these United States, destitute of appropriate care and protection*; and of this vast and most miserable company, sought out in *jails,* in *poorhouses,* and in *private dwellings,* there have been hundreds, nay, rather thousands,—bound with galling chains, bowed beneath fetters and heavy iron balls attached to drag chains, lacerated with ropes, scourged with rods, and terrified beneath storms of profane execrations and cruel blows; now subject to gibes and scorn and torturing tricks, now abandoned to the most loathsome necessities, or subject to the vilest and most outrageous violations. These are strong terms, but language fails to convey the astonishing truths. I proceed to verify this assertion, beginning with the State of Maine" (*Senate Miscellaneous Documents No. 150,* 30 Cong., 1 Sess.).

She followed her Massachusetts procedure in each state—a thorough, independent research; wise choice of spokesmen; influence of the press. She never appeared in public. A sweet, low voice, a gentle manner, quiet dignity turned aside hostile comment, while her persistence, driven by the white heat of compassion, was always based on self-observed facts. She had prejudice, as well as ignorance and self-interest, to combat. At this time for a woman to undertake public work was considered unfeminine. At times she hesitated. "I am naturally timid and diffident, like all my sex," she wrote to a friend. The force that carried her over all obstacles was due to three characteristics. First: independence of spirit, "The feeling, right or wrong, that aloneness is my proper position"; second, the emotional intensity of her compassion, "I have no particular love for my species, but own to an exhaustless fund of compassion"; third, the profound influence of Dr. Channing, whose insistence on the presence in every human being, however degraded, of the possibility of endless spiritual development was the heart of her religious belief and gave the driving power to her pity.

Travel was by infrequent railroad, steamboat, a few lines of coaches, and small vehicles; over rough roads, through deep mud, by fords; subject to discomfort, accident, and exposure. In 1845 she wrote, "I have travelled over more than ten thousand miles in the last three years. Have visited eighteen state penitentiaries, three hundred county jails and houses of correction, more than five hundred almshouses and other institutions, besides hospitals and houses of refuge" (Tiffany, *post,* p. 132). She was now middle-aged, with persistent lung trouble and susceptible to malaria, but no difficulty could check her.

Between 1841 and 1845, three hospitals for the insane were enlarged or re-founded (Worcester, Mass.; Butler, at Providence, R. I.; Utica, N. Y.) and three new hospitals founded (Trenton, N. J.; Harrisburg, Pa.; Toronto, Canada). Between 1845 and 1852, she carried the legislatures of Indiana, Illinois, Kentucky, Tennessee, Missouri, Mississippi, Louisiana, Alabama, South Carolina, North Carolina and Maryland, for state hospitals and caused the founding of the hospital at Halifax, N. S. But her great effort for the passage of a twelve-million-dollar bill for land, to be set aside for taxation toward the care of the insane, met defeat in 1854 by President Pierce's veto, after the bill had passed the houses of Congress.

Between 1854 and 1857, she traveled in England and on the Continent, investigating the care of the insane. Queen Victoria's order for a Royal Commission to investigate the condition of the insane in Scotland, the founding of a hospital on the Island of Jersey, and that of a hospital in Rome, were results of this journey. From 1857 to 1861 she was constantly active, raising money, advising on hospital buildings, and choosing hospital personnel. Illustrative of her many other activities, outside her main work, is her accomplishment at Sable Island. In 1853, while working for the hospital at St. John's, Newfoundland, she heard of the dangerous shores of Sable Island, where there was only a small life-saving station with inadequate apparatus, and where, for lack of a lighthouse, there was a succession of wrecks. She went to the island, undertaking the risk of the exposed landing, and herself made an examination of conditions. She then applied to merchants of Boston, New York, and Philadelphia for funds and sent four life-saving boats to the station. Within a week of their arrival a ship carrying 168 persons was thereby saved.

On Apr. 19, 1861, three hours after the 6th Massachusetts Regiment had been fired upon in Baltimore, she passed through that city on her way to Washington to offer her services to the surgeon-general. She was appointed, June 10, 1861, "Superintendent of Women Nurses, to select and assign women nurses to general or permanent military hospitals, they not to be employed in such hospitals without her sanction and approval, except in cases of urgent need." On July 14, 1862, Circular Number 7, issued by William Hammond, surgeon-general, repeated the authorization of selection and assignment of women nurses, now specified as one woman to each two men nurses, and gave her oversight, but put "control and direction" under the "medical officer in charge." General Orders No. 357, Oct. 27, 1863, restated this. Behind these orders are visible the autocratic action of a powerful personality, used to independence, in power over the incompetence, venality, and cruelty inevitable in crises impossible to anticipate, and the jealousy, thwarted ambition, and hurt pride of small natures. Miss Dix's biographer, Dr. Tiffany, considers her war work an episode, not equal in quality to her life-work. It is true that it differs in quality. This was not creative pioneer work. Judged, however, by the unfailing support of Stanton, secretary of war, by the comments of nurses under her personal attention, and seen in the light of nursing experience in the World War, it seems probable that these four years of war work deserve more credit than has been given them.

With the coming of peace, she resumed service in behalf of her hospitals, inspecting, advising, and giving them support. Again she traveled, investigated, and created new hospitals. In her eightieth year, she retired to the home gratefully offered her by her "first child," the hospital at Trenton, N. J. Here she died on July 17, 1887. To the last she longed to serve, saying, "I think even lying in my bed I can still do something."

[Francis Tiffany, *Life of Dorothea Lynde Dix* (1890); Alfred S. Roe, *Dorothea Lynde Dix* (1889); L. P. Brockett and Mary C. Vaughan, *Woman's Work in the Civil War* (1867); *Our Army Nurses* (1895), compiled by Mary A. Gardner Holland; Louisa Alcott, *Hospital Sketches* (1863); Harvey E. Brown, *The Medic. Dept. of the U. S. Army, 1775–1873* (1873); J. S. Woolsey, *Hospital Days* (1870); *Women Nurses with the Union Forces during the Civil War*, reprinted from the *Military Surgeon*, Jan.–Feb. 1928.] C. H. B.

DIX, JOHN ADAMS (July 24, 1798–Apr. 21, 1879), soldier in two wars, cabinet officer, and governor, the son of Col. Timothy and Abigail (Wilkins) Dix, began life in New England with a highly unusual training. This was because his father, a merchant and local leader of Boscawen, N. H., was a man of marked individuality and versatile talents. After giving the boy a good elementary education in the classics, English literature, and public speaking, including a year in Phillips Exeter Academy, and helping personally to instruct him in music and drawing, the father sent him to the College of Montreal, a Catholic institution. This was for tuition in French and contact with a different civilization. After fifteen months here the boy was recalled by the outbreak of the War of 1812, and was sent to a distant relative in Boston who saw that he was privately prepared in Spanish, Latin, mathematics, and elocution. But when he chafed to enter military service, his father, who had become a major of infantry in Baltimore, consented, helped the spirited fourteen-year-old lad to obtain a commission, and was proud to see him participate in the battle of Lundy's Lane as an ensign. Young Dix, large for his years, made an ardent soldier, and at Chrysler's Field wept when ordered to go to the rear with a body of prisoners.

The death of his father in the campaign of 1813 ushered in what Dix called "the most trying period of my life" (*Memoirs,* I, 50). His father's large family, nine children in all, were left in straitened circumstances, and the youth had not only to support himself but to contribute aid to his stepmother. During years "full of anxiety and trial" he remained in the army, gradually rising to the rank of major, and serving for a time in Washington, New York, and elsewhere as traveling aide to Maj.-Gen. Jacob Brown. He read much, was a close student, and improved his social opportunities in the capital, meeting Madison, Randolph, and others of note, and becoming intimate with Calhoun. The belief that he could find a better field than the army was strengthened by the advice of friends, who were struck by his forensic talents, industry, and handsome bearing. He studied law, partly under the direction of Attorney-General William Wirt, and was admitted to the bar in the District of Columbia (1824); while he also did much newspaper writing upon political subjects in the last years of Monroe's administration.

His determination to resign from the army was fixed by his marriage in 1826 to Catharine Morgan, adopted daughter of John J. Morgan, a Representative from New York who owned large areas of land up-state and who offered Dix the position of managing agent at Cooperstown. Settling in this town in 1828, Dix practised law for three years, became county leader of the Jacksonian Democracy, and made himself so prominent that at the end of 1830 Gov. Throop appointed him adjutant-general of the state. The salary was only $800, but Dix seized the place because it carried a seat in the powerful "Albany Regency." From this point his rise in political life was rapid, being checked only by occasional defeats of his party at the hands of the Whigs. He made an especial mark as secretary of state (1833–39) of New York; this position carried with it the superintendency of the public schools, and he did much to improve the training of teachers, while he also took the first steps toward organizing a geological survey of the state. Labors of this nature displayed his scholarly bent to advantage. Following the Harrison victory of 1840, he not only practised law, but established in Albany a literary and scientific journal, the *Northern Light,* which endured for a little more than two years (1841–43). It might have lasted longer but for a breakdown in his wife's health, which took him to Madeira and the Mediterranean, and resulted in a small volume of travel sketches.

Embarkation in national politics came immediately after Dix's return home, when he was elected (1845) to the United States Senate for the five unexpired years of Silas Wright's term. Here he manifested an especial interest in international affairs—he spoke for fixing the Oregon boundary at the 49th parallel, and against the withdrawal of the United States diplomatic agent from the Papal States—while he showed the free-soil sentiments that were ultimately to carry him out of the Democratic party. He was consistently aligned during the Mexican War with the anti-slavery or Barnburner Democrats; he supported the Wilmot Proviso; and in 1848 he was in favor of the separate nomination of Van Buren by the free-soil Democrats, though he opposed any alliance with the free-soil Whigs, and acquiesced very reluctantly in the final free-soil nomination of himself for governor (Alexander, *post,* II, 133). Indeed, his son said that to be associated with Whigs in this campaign was a painful and distressing surprise to him. His last speech in the Senate, in 1849, opposed the admission of New Mexico and California unless the enabling act prohibited slavery in these states.

In the next decade Dix should have been accepted as one of the leaders of Democracy. He was a cultivated writer, a fluent, vigorous speaker, a man of great courage, prompt decision, and proved executive ability. The opposition of the slavery wing of the party was, however, a fatal impediment. Franklin Pierce in 1853 intended to make him secretary of state, but party enemies interfered, and when he was offered the post of minister to France, this also was snatched from him by Southern opposition (James Ford Rhodes, *History of the United States From the Compromise of 1850,* vol. I, 1892, pp. 387, 395). The results were a withdrawal from public life, another trip abroad, a term as president of the Chicago & Rock Island, and the Mississippi & Missouri railroads (1854–57), and practise at the New York City bar. In 1860–61, however, public sentiment in New York City forced his promotion in striking fashion. A disastrous defalcation in the post-office caused his appointment as postmaster by Buchanan to straighten out affairs; and this had no sooner been accomplished than the moneyed interests of the East, in the crisis following the secession of South Carolina, demanded that he be made secretary of the treasury. He took office in January 1861, living at the White House till March.

Dix's chief service to the Union was in his brief period at the head of the treasury. Bankers and financiers had complete confidence in him, and though other states were seceding, he quickly obtained five millions at an average rate of slightly over ten per cent (John Jay Knox, *United States Notes,* 1884, p. 76). Moreover, one of his dispatches was as a clarion call to the North. On Jan. 29, 1861, he telegraphed a treasury official in New Orleans to take possession of a revenue cutter there, concluding with the words: "If anyone attempts to haul down the American flag, shoot him on the spot" (*Memoirs,* I, 371). In a dark hour this was a heartening vindication of the national honor. He placed the chaotic department in order and handed it over to Chase in excellent condition. Lincoln rewarded him by commissioning him a major-general, and he was ordered to Washington in June to take charge of the Alexandria and Arlington Department. It was believed, however, that at sixty-three he was too old for active service, and political intrigue resulted in changing this assignment to the Department of Maryland. In Baltimore, at Fortress Monroe, and later in New York as commander of the Department of the East, he did useful but never spectacular service. His authority in New York lasted just two years (July 1863–July 1865); arriving just after the end of the draft riots, he took energetic steps to suppress sympathizers with the Confederacy.

Dix's career after the war was that of a distinguished and honored man well past his prime, chosen to public offices with the expectation that he would occupy them with passive dignity. As minister to France for three years, 1866–69, he was popular with the American colony but played no important rôle in diplomacy. Returning to America, he was the recipient in 1872 of an extraordinary compliment. Though still a Democrat, he was nominated for governor by the New York Republicans as the candidate who could best help defeat Horace Greeley in Greeley's own state, and he was elected by a majority of 53,000. Though then in his seventy-fifth year, he was still vigorous, and discharged the routine duties of his office capably. His was not the hand, however, to carry through the great task of cleansing the state's Augean stables, and in 1874 he was defeated for reëlection by Samuel J. Tilden. His last years were spent in peaceful retirement in New York City, with occasional appearances in behalf of civil service reform and other causes dear to him. He left behind him a reputation for loftiness of purpose, serene purity of life, and an amount of learning remarkable in politics. For a number of years he was a vestryman of Trinity Church, New York, of which, in 1862, his son Morgan Dix [*q.v.*] became the rector.

His published works include: *A Winter in Madeira; and a Summer in Spain and Florence* (1850), a popular book which went through five editions; *Speeches and Occasional Addresses* (2 vols., 1864); translations of *Dies Irae* (1863), and *Stabat Mater* (1868), in which he took especial pride.

[The all-sufficient source upon Dix's life is the *Memoirs of John Adams Dix* (2 vols., 1883) compiled by Morgan Dix. This is supplemented by some of his own works, notably the first two mentioned above. Brief characterizations may be found in the *Atlantic Monthly*, Aug. 1883, in D. S. Alexander, *Political History of the State of New York*, II (1906), 2 ff., and in C. C. Coffin, *The Hist. of Boscawen and Webster* (1878), pp. 348–56, with a genealogy of the Dix family on pp. 518–20. See also obituaries in *N. Y. Times*, Apr. 21, 22, 23, 1879, and *N. Y. Herald*, Apr. 22, 23, 1879.]

A.N.

DIX, JOHN HOMER (Sept. 30, 1811–Aug. 25, 1884), ophthalmologist, was born in Boston, Mass., the son of John Dix, a surgeon in the United States Navy, and his wife, Sarah Jaffery Eddy. He was graduated from Harvard College in 1833 and after attending the Harvard Medical School for two years, transferred to the Jefferson Medical College, Philadelphia, where he obtained the degree of M.D. in 1836. The next year he became a member of the Massachusetts Medical Society and began practise in Boston as a specialist in diseases of the eye and ear. On Sept. 9, 1840, he performed one of the first operations in America for congenital strabismus (Dieffenbach operation), reporting his results in a brief letter to the *Boston Medical and Surgical Journal*, Sept. 24, 1840 (1841, XXIII, 128). Further cases were reported the same year (*Ibid.*, 1841, XXIII, 265, also *Medical Examiner*, Philadelphia, 1840, III, 760) and later, in book form (*Treatise on Strabismus, or Squinting, and the New Mode of Treatment*, 1841). In 1846 he went to Europe and studied for a time under Von Graefe. He was one of the early proponents of ophthalmoscopic investigation of the eye and imported various instruments from Europe, including the first ophthalmoscope developed by Helmholtz in 1851. The results of his work were published in four papers in the *Virginia Medical Journal* (1856, VI, 361, 465; 1856, VII, 19, 389). Other papers are concerned with rare diseases of the eye, such as: "On the Sparkling Eye" (*Virginia Medical and Surgical Journal*, 1853, I, 12) and "Dacryocystitis" (*Ibid.*, 1854, III, 279). He was one of the early members of the American Ophthalmological Society.

Dix practised ophthalmology in Boston for nearly fifty years. He was a laborious student, keen to investigate new ideas, especially those from foreign sources, a pioneer and skilful operator on the eye before the days of modern anesthesia, a man of great self-confidence, strict integrity and genial disposition. Much of his fortune was willed to charitable institutions. Besides his contributions to his science, he has been credited with introducing the apartment house into the United States, when, in 1856–57, impressed by dwellings of that type which he had seen in Europe, he built the Hotel Pelham at the corner of Tremont and Boylston Sts., Boston. His wife, whom he married on June 9, 1859, was Helen Perhan Curtis.

[A. A. Hubbell, *The Development of Ophthalmology in America, 1800–1870* (1908); *Jour. Am. Medic. Asso.*, Mar. 24, 1888; *Boston Transcript*, Aug. 26, 1884; J. L. Sibley's Annotated Catalogue of the Early Harvard Graduates (MS.) in Mass. Hist. Soc.]

H.R.V.

DIX, MORGAN (Nov. 1, 1827–Apr. 29, 1908), Episcopal clergyman, for more than half a century connected with the Parish of Trinity Church, New York, and for almost forty-six years its rector, was born in New York; received his higher education there, graduating from Columbia in 1848, and from the General Theological Seminary in 1852; and, after having been long one of its first clergymen and citizens, died and was buried there. He was notably a child, not only of New York, but of Trinity Parish. In one of its chapels, St. John's, his distinguished father, John A. Dix [*q.v.*], had been married to Catharine Morgan, adopted daughter of John Jordan Morgan. The latter was long a vestryman of the parish, and in this office John Dix succeeded him. In St. John's Chapel, Morgan Dix was ordained deacon in 1852, though he was advanced to the priesthood the following year in St. Mark's Church, Philadelphia. Except for a brief term of service as assistant in the latter church, his entire ministry was spent in association with Trinity Parish. He accepted the office of assistant minister in 1855, and in 1859 was elected assistant rector, being recommended by Dr. Berrian, the rector, in preference to older ministers in the parish, because besides being a man of discretion, judgment, unaffected modesty, well regulated temper, and courteous manners, he combined in a rare degree high intellectual gifts with a practical turn of mind, orderly, methodical, business-like habits, and remarkable minuteness and accuracy in all matters of detail. On the evening of Nov. 10, 1862, Dr. Berrian having been buried that afternoon, he was elected rector. Twelve years later, June 3, 1874, he married Emily Woolsey Soutter, daughter of James T. Soutter.

From youth he had all the advantages of wealth, social position, travel, cultivated parents, and inspiring family traditions. Although his father, having rebelled as a boy against the long sermons, bleak theology, barren worship, and intense cold of a New Hampshire meeting-house, had broken the Congregational descent and become an Episcopalian, Morgan Dix was of old Puritan, New England stock, and of a family of fighters as well. Great-grandfather, grandfather, and father all served in the army. Austerity and soldier-like qualities were conspicuous in his character. "You can see in his face," some one said upon meeting him, "that he is determined to keep the devil down." Although rector of the wealthiest and most fashionable parish in the country, he denounced the vices of fashionable society with startling frankness and directness. Pacifism was a doctrine repugnant to him. While the International Arbitration and Peace Conference was being held in New York in 1907, he preached a sermon before the Loyal Legion in which he spoke of the "ancient, honorable, and necessary art of war," and affirmed the dignity of the military profession, and the necessity of an adequate army and navy (*Outlook,* May 9, 1908). He was an able administrator, and during his rectorship the varied religious, educational, and charitable work of the parish had large and wise extension. For years he presided over the House of Deputies of the General Convention, and was influential in the councils of the church. From 1862 to 1908 he was an active trustee of Columbia College. At his death, however, there was unanimous agreement that he was first and foremost a parish priest, concerned primarily with the moral and spiritual needs of his people. He was an active supporter of the Sisterhood of St. Mary, one of the earliest sisterhoods of the Episcopal Church, and long its pastor, preparing for it the *Book of Hours* (1866), and writing the life of its first Mother Superior, *Harriet Starr Cannon* (1896). His liturgical knowledge was extensive, and he did much for the development of church music, especially the choral service. Theologically he was strongly conservative, deploring the exercise of private judgment in matters of religion and worship, and proclaiming the divine institution of the church, priesthood, and sacraments, and the authority of the ancient creeds. Believing that marriage is not merely a civil contract but a holy ordinance, and ought never to be dissolved, he took strong ground against the "divorce abomination." His old-fashioned attitude on the sphere of women, set forth in *Lectures on the Calling of a Christian Woman* (1883), evoked a spirited reply from Lillie Devereux Blake [*q.v.*], entitled *Woman's Place Today* (1883). He had more than average literary ability and his numerous publications include sermons, manuals of religious instruction, aids to worship, lectures on theological subjects, *An Exposition of the Epistle of St. Paul to the Romans, According to the Analogy of the Catholic Faith* (1862) and a similar study of Galatians and Colossians (1864); *A History of the Parish of Trinity Church in the City of New York* (4 vols., 1898–1906); and an excellent life of his father, *Memoirs of John Adams Dix* (2 vols., 1883). On Apr. 19, 1908, ten days before his death, he preached the Easter sermon at Trinity Church.

[*Year Book and Register of the Parish of Trinity Church,* 1909; *Columbia Univ. Quarterly,* June 1908; *Who's Who in America,* 1906–07; *The Churchman,* May 9, 1908; *N. Y. Tribune, Times,* and *Evening Post* for Apr. 30, 1908.] H. E. S.

DIXON, JAMES (Aug. 5, 1814–Mar. 27, 1873), congressman, was born in Enfield, Conn., the son of William and Mary (Field) Dixon. He prepared for college in the neighboring town of Ellington, and entered Williams at the age of sixteen, graduating with the class of 1834. Soon afterward he began the study of law under his father, and on being admitted to the bar, began practise in his home town, Enfield. In 1839 he moved to Hartford, and was taken into partnership with W. W. Ellsworth. On Oct. 1 of the following year Dixon married Elizabeth, daughter of the Rev. Jonathan Cogswell, professor of ecclesiastical history in the Theological Institute at East Windsor, Conn. His political career began in 1837, when at the age of twenty-three he was sent to the state legislature as a representative from Enfield. He was reëlected the following year. After 1839 he became a leader of the Whig party in Hartford. In 1844 he served another term as state legislator. A year later he was sent to Congress, serving until 1849. In Congress he was a conservative Whig. His speeches in the House followed accepted lines of Whig policy. In 1846 he spoke against the reduction of import duties. The point at issue was, he declared, whether this country should employ its own labor to supply its wants, or give occupation to foreign workmen. The laboring classes, he asserted, desired a protective tariff (*Congressional Globe,* 29 Cong., 1 Sess., App., pp. 1061 ff.). He spoke several times on the important question of the Mexican War. In 1847 he energetically supported the Wilmot Proviso (*Ibid.,* 29 Cong., 2 Sess., App., pp. 332 ff.). Later he upheld the Whig point of view that the war had been unnecessarily and unconstitutionally commenced by the president (*Ibid.,* 30 Cong., 1 Sess., pp. 227 ff.). Returning to Hartford from Congress, he resumed law practise, and was also for some years president of the Hartford Life Insurance Company. In 1854 he served a term as senator in the state legislature. Two years later he was elected to the United States Senate, where he remained until 1869, throughout the trying period of the Civil War, and the early years of Reconstruction. In the Senate, in 1859, he made a strong speech against the proposed acquisition of Cuba, on the ground that the matter was a Democratic party scheme for the purpose of furthering slavery interests (*Ibid.*, 35 Cong., 2 Sess., pp. 1335 ff.). Dixon was, of course, a loyal supporter of the Union cause during the Civil War. After the assassination of Lincoln, he became an ardent supporter of President Johnson, partly because of a desire for lenient treatment of the Southern states, and thus incurred the enmity of the radical Republicans. Having, therefore, no chance of receiving the Republican nomination for a third senatorial term, he stood for election in 1868 as a Democrat, but was defeated. In 1869, declining appointment as minister to Russia, he retired to private life, residing in Hartford, and being in rather feeble health until his death in 1873. Mrs. Dixon had died two years previously.

Outside of his political life, Dixon was something of a literary man, with a taste for poetry. He wrote several sonnets, which were published in the *New England Magazine,* and the *Connecticut Courant.* The poems are rather sweet and musical, although very amateurish. In public affairs, his attitude was thoroughly conservative. His political career was guided by ideals of abstract philosophy rather than by considerations of a purely practical, or temporary character. He was survived in 1873 by four children.

[The best source is *The Harvey Book* (1899), a genealogy. Supplementary details may be found in the *Memorial Hist. of Hartford County* (2 vols., 1886), ed. by J. H. Trumbull; *Commemorative Biog. Record of Hartford County, Conn.* (1901); *Biog. Dir. Am. Congress* (1928); and in an obituary notice in the *Hartford Courant,* Mar. 28, 1873. A few of Dixon's poems were published in *The Poets of Connecticut* (1843), by C. W. Everest.]

J. M. M.

DIXON, JOSEPH (Jan. 18, 1799–June 15, 1869), inventor, manufacturer, was the son of Joseph and Elizabeth (Reed) Dixon and was born at Marblehead, Mass., where his father and grandfather before him were born. His education was meager, but he possessed a restless brain and in his early youth displayed remarkable mechanical ingenuity. Before he was of age he had invented a machine for cutting files. He then took up printing, but not having the money to buy metal type, he made type of wood, incidentally becoming a skilled wood-carver and, in turn, mastering wood-engraving and lithography. The desire to possess metal type brought about his invention of a matrix for casting it, and the further necessity of providing a receptacle in which to melt the type metal caused him to undertake experiments with the mineral graphite. Early in 1820 Dixon was looked upon as a chemist, presumably because of his constant experimental work with crucibles, which he tested with intense fires, and of the then popular conception of an individual so engaged. Besides, he began to study medicine, but he discontinued that because of his lost faith in drugs. He proved to his own satisfaction that graphite was an ideal material to use in crucibles to withstand high temperatures, but he recognized, too, that the market for such a product was extremely limited. In his experiments, however, he had observed a number of other properties of the mineral and he proceeded to devise products for which there was a market, namely, lead pencils and stove-polish. In 1827, therefore, he established at Salem, Mass., a factory for the manufacture of these materials and continued there, it is said, for twenty years. His products were marketed by peddling in which he was helped by Francis Peabody, and supported by the profits, he went on inventing. His interest in lithography led him to devise a photolithographic process; when he found that it afforded a ready means of counterfeiting banknotes, he and Peabody devised and patented, on Apr. 20, 1832, a process in which colored inks could be used to prevent counterfeiting. In the thirties Dixon perfected also a process for making collodion, and as a result of his studies of the work of Daguerre, a camera equipped with a reflector to rectify the position of the image. On Jan. 21, 1845, he was granted a patent for an anti-friction bearing-metal. In the application for this patent, which is a joint one with I. S. Hill of Boston, he gave his address as Taunton, Mass., although his business is supposed to have been at Salem. All this time the pencil and stove-polish business was expanding, and, in order to be nearer the market center, in 1847 Dixon gave up his Salem location and erected a plant in Jersey City, N. J. He apparently decided, too, that the time was ripe to introduce the graphite crucible, and accordingly in March and April 1850, patents No. 7,136 and No. 7,260 were granted him on uses of graphite crucibles in pottery and steel making, respectively. Again, on Nov. 2, 1858, he obtained patent No. 21,948 the title of which is "Improvement in Manufacturing Steel." From this time until his death he was compelled to devote more of his time to the manufacturing end of the business than to research but even so, his mechanical ingenuity was called upon for most of the improvements about the factory. A single instance of this is recorded in patent No. 54,511, granted to him in 1866 for a wood-planing machine for shaping the wood form of pencils. The few spare moments that he had for research were always used to good advantage, evidence of which is his patent of Sept. 2, 1866, No. 57,687, for a galvanic battery. In 1867, realizing that his own strength was failing, he formed the Joseph Dixon Crucible Company, the affairs of which he directed until his death two years later. With his demise the business passed into the hands of men of his own training who retained the original name of the company. Dixon married Hannah Martin of Marblehead on July 28, 1822.

[*Vital Records of Marblehead, Mass.* (1903); *New-Eng. Hist. and Geneal. Reg.*, XXIII (1869), 477; Elbert Hubbard, *Jos. Dixon* (1912); *Am. Ann. Cyc.*, 1869; *Biog. Encyc. of N. J. of the Nineteenth Century* (1877); *N. Y. Times*, *N. Y. Herald*, June 16, 1869; Patent Office records; U. S. Nat. Museum correspondence with Jos. Dixon Crucible Co.] C. W. M.

DIXON, LUTHER SWIFT (June 17, 1825–Dec. 6, 1891), jurist, was born at Underhill, Chittenden County, Vt. He was a descendant of Archibald Dickson of Irvine, Argyleshire, Scotland, who came to Boston in 1719. His father, Col. Luther Dixon, was a Vermont farmer who had commanded a regiment on the northern frontier during the War of 1812. The younger Luther's boyhood was spent on the farm, his early education being obtained at the common schools. He then attended the military academy at Norwich, Vt., for two years, becoming an excellent Latin scholar. Designing to become a lawyer, he taught school for a time in order to defray expenses, studying law at intervals, and was admitted to the Vermont bar in 1850. In the same year he proceeded West, settled in Portage, Columbia County, Wis., and commenced practise there. In 1851 he was elected district attorney for Columbia County, being reëlected in 1853 and holding the office for four years. In August 1858, Gov. Randall appointed him judge of the 9th judicial circuit of Wisconsin, but he occupied this position for only eight months, being appointed chief justice of the supreme court in April 1859. He was comparatively unknown, and the impression was general that he did not possess the necessary experience. He was almost immediately confronted with the most important judicial question that had ever been brought before the court, arising from a conflict between the state and national governments respecting the enforcement of the Fugitive-Slave Law. The supreme court of Wisconsin had held that law to be unconstitutional, and on a writ of error the Supreme Court of the United States had reversed this decision. The case came before Dixon at the June term, 1859, upon a motion to file the remittitur, and, despite the strong personal and political influences at work to bring him in alignment with the predominant state-rights supporters, he rendered an opinion upholding the appellate jurisdiction of the Supreme Court (*Ableman* vs. *Booth* and *The United States* vs. *Booth*, 11 *Wis.*, 498). His opinion in this case was masterly from the juridical standpoint and amply vindicated his appointment, but it provoked a political storm. In 1860, however, he was elected to succeed himself as an Independent, having been repudiated by the state Republican party, and, being reëlected three times subsequently, remained on the supreme court bench till 1874, when he resigned because of the inadequacy of his salary. Opening a law office at Milwaukee, he declined an election to the United States Senate, and, devoting himself to his profession, speedily acquired a large practise. During a period of five years he was continuously engaged in heavy litigation, including the "Granger cases," in which he was retained by the state of Wisconsin and successfully upheld the constitutionality of the questioned railroad legislation (*Attorney General* vs. *Chicago & North Western Railroad Company*; *Attorney General* vs. *Chicago, Milwaukee & St. Paul Railroad Company*, 35 *Wis.*, 425). He was counsel for the Atchison, Topeka & Santa Fé Railway Company in the litigation with the Denver & Rio Grande Railroad Company for the right of way through the Royal Gorge of the Arkansas River. In 1879, asthmatic trouble compelled him to seek a higher altitude, and he moved to Colorado, settling at Denver. Here he appeared constantly in the state and national courts of last resort. He died at Milwaukee on Dec. 6, 1891.

Though not brilliant, he was an exceptionally sound judge. He was not a case lawyer, but founded his opinions on established principles, utilizing precedents merely in illustration. His mental processes, singularly clear and invariably logical, were set out in opinions which were distinguished for felicity of style, simplicity of language, and compelling reasoning. In person over six feet in height, broad and athletic, gifted with much charm of manner, he was unobtrusive and retiring by nature. Public life had no attraction for him, and though in principle a Republican, he never appeared as a political speaker.

[*Am. Bar Asso. Report*, 1892, p. 429; *Green Bag*, IX, 116; *In Memoriam Luther S. Dixon*, 81 *Wis.*, xxxi, 17 *Colo.*, xix; biographical sketch in *Selected Opinions of Luther S. Dixon and Edward G. Ryan* (1907), ed. by G. E. Roe; P. M. Reed, *Bench and Bar of Wis.* (1882); *Rocky Mountain News* (Denver), Dec. 7 1891.] H. W. H. K.

DIXON, WILLIAM (Sept. 25, 1850–Mar. 9, 1913), frontiersman, scout, known as "Billy" Dixon, was born in Ohio County, W. Va. His mother dying when he was ten, and his father two years later, he went to live with an uncle in Ray County, Mo. Determined to be a buffalo-hunter and an Indian-fighter, he left home before he was fourteen, and with a boy companion hunted and trapped along the lower Missouri. Early in 1865, despite his youth, he got employment at Fort Leavenworth as a driver in a government mule train, and in this capacity journeyed to such outlying posts as Fort Lyon and Fort Collins, Colo., and Camp Supply, Okla. In the fall of 1869 he left the government service and engaged with a party of hunters and trappers, who in the following year began the hunting of buffaloes for the hides. He bore a distinguished part in the second battle of Adobe Walls, in the present Hutchinson County, Tex., June 27, 1874, when a company of twenty-eight hunters, in an all-day fight, repelled the determined attacks of a force of about 700 Indians led by the Comanche, Quanah. He was one of the party that carried the news to Fort Dodge, where Gen. Miles appointed him a scout, and he returned to the Walls with Lieut. Baldwin's command. The most desperate experience of his career came on Sept. 12, when he and a fellow scout and four enlisted men were suddenly attacked by a band of about 125 Kiowas and Comanches. All six were wounded (one seriously and one mortally) early in the fight. Four took refuge in a buffalo wallow, to which Dixon, under a rain of bullets, carried one of the two badly wounded men; and by keeping up a steady and effective fire the whites forced the savages to withdraw at nightfall, when Dixon brought in the other men. The five survivors received the Congressional medal of honor. The account of this episode in R. I. Dodge, *Our Wild Indians* (1882), is obviously erroneous, and it is generally recognized that Dixon saved the party from annihilation.

Attached to Fort Elliott, which was established in the spring of 1875, he continued as a scout until 1883, when he homesteaded a claim that included Adobe Walls and started a ranch. He was postmaster at Adobe Walls for nearly twenty years, and at various times served as local land commissioner, justice of the peace, and sheriff. On Oct. 18, 1894, he was married to Olive King of Virginia, later to become well-known as a newspaper woman. In 1902 he sold his ranch and moved to the near-by town of Plemons, and about 1906 homesteaded a new claim in the present Cimarron County, Okla. At the solicitation of his wife he began, in the fall of 1912, to dictate to her his reminiscences, which were published in the year after his death.

Dixon was of medium height, strong and rugged, and capable of great endurance. His skill with the rifle was exceptional. He was characterized by W. B. ("Bat") Masterson, who knew him both as a buffalo-hunter and as a scout, as "a typical frontiersman of the highest order," who, though stoical and uncommunicative, was kind-hearted, generous, and hospitable.

[*Life and Adventures of "Billy" Dixon*, etc. (1914), ed. by F. S. Barde, revised edition by Olive K. Dixon (1927); R. I. Dodge, *Our Wild Indians* (1882); J. B. Thoburn, *A Standard Hist. of Okla.* (1916); E. A. Brininstool, "Billy Dixon, A Frontier Hero," *Hunter-Trader-Trapper* (Mar.–Apr. 1925).] W. J. G.

DIXWELL, JOHN (*c.* 1607–Mar. 18, 1688/9), regicide, was the son of William Dixwell of Coton Hall, near Rugby, Warwickshire, and his wife, Elizabeth Brent. He was the brother of Mark Dixwell of Folkestone, Kent. Upon the death of Mark Dixwell, who had inherited the estates of Sir Basil Dixwell, John Dixwell became the guardian of his brother's children and managed their landed estates in Kent. During the Civil Wars he served on various committees appointed by Parliament to raise forces and to levy assessments in that county. In 1646 he was elected to Parliament from Dover. He was a member of the High Court of Justice erected to try Charles I, was present when sentence was given, and signed the death warrant. On June 27, 1650, he was commissioned colonel of Troop F, in Kent. On Nov. 25, 1651, he was elected a member of the Council of State and served on many committees of the Council. In 1652 he was governor of Dover Castle and, on the outbreak of war with the Dutch, was entrusted to guard the seacoast of Kent. He was a member of Cromwell's Parliaments of 1654 and 1656 (Cobbett, *post*, III, 1429, 1480), and was named a commissioner for Kent in ordinances of Aug. 28, 1654, for ejecting scandalous, ignorant, and indifferent ministers and schoolmasters, and of June 9, 1657, to levy an assessment for three months. On the restoration of the Long Parliament in 1659 Dixwell took his seat for Dover and on May 14 and on Dec. 31, 1659, was again elected a member of the Council of State. Following the Restoration, he was excepted from the Act of Pardon and Oblivion and fled to Hanau, Germany. From Hanau he migrated—just when is not known—to New England. He was first mentioned as being in America in February 1664/5, when he visited his fellow regicides, Edward Whalley and William Goffe [*q.v.*], at Hadley in the Colony of Massachusetts Bay. Soon after this he settled at New Haven, where he assumed the name of

James Davids. He was married twice: to Mrs. Joanna Ling on Nov. 3, 1673, and to Bathsheba Howe on Oct. 23, 1677. From the second marriage there were three children. On Dec. 29, 1685, James Davids, *alias* John Dixwell, was admitted to the church at New Haven (F. B. Dexter, *Historical Catalogue of the Members of the First Church of Christ in New Haven, Conn.*, 1914). On Mar. 18, 1688/9, Dixwell died at New Haven and was there buried. Before his death he had conveyed to his wife and son his estates in Kent, and in September 1693 his widow was taking steps to recover Dixwell's property (James Pierpont to Fitz-John Winthrop, Sept. 6, 1693, in *Massachusetts Historical Society Collections*, 6 ser., III, 266). In 1710 Dixwell's son visited England in an attempt to recover his father's property but was unsuccessful.

["Dixwell Papers," ed. by F. B. Dexter, in *New Haven Colony Hist. Soc. Papers*, VI (1900), 337–74; *Calendar of State Papers, Domestic Series*; *Jours. of the House of Commons*, vols. VII, VIII; *Acts and Ordinances of the Interregnum, 1642–60* (3 vols., 1911), ed. by C. H. Firth and R. S. Rait; W. Cobbett, *Parliamentary Hist. of England* (1808), vol. III; John Nalson, *A True Copy of the Jour. of the High Court of Justice for the Trial of Charles I* (1684); *The Memoirs of Edmund Ludlow* (2 vols., 1894), ed. by C. H. Firth; *Vital Records of New Haven* (2 vols., 1917); David Masson, *The Life of John Milton* (7 vols., 1859–94); Mark Noble, *The Lives of the English Regicides* (2 vols., 1798); Ezra Stiles, *A Hist. of Three of the Judges of King Charles I* (1794); Lemuel Aiken Welles, *The Hist. of the Regicides in New England* (1927).]

I. M. C.

DOAK, SAMUEL (August 1749–Dec. 12, 1830), clergyman, educator, was of Scotch-Irish descent, the third son of Samuel and Jane (Mitchaell) Doak, who, in their youth, came to America from the north of Ireland. They were married in Chester County, Pa., and soon after moved to Augusta County, Va. There Samuel was born. He worked on his father's farm until he was sixteen, when he entered a classical school conducted by Robert Alexander and later by John Brown. In order to obtain funds to continue his studies he relinquished his interest in his father's estate, and later earned additional money as assistant teacher in Brown's school. He entered Princeton in 1773, graduated in 1775, and began the study of theology under the Rev. John Blair Smith, at the same time tutoring for Mr. Smith in Prince Edward Academy (later Hampden-Sidney College). On Oct. 31, 1777, he was licensed to preach by the Presbytery of Hanover. He married Esther H. Montgomery, a sister of Rev. John Montgomery of Virginia, by whom he had two sons and two daughters. She died, July 3, 1807. His second wife was Margaretta H. McEwen of Nashville, Tenn.

He began his preaching on the frontier in what is now Sullivan County, Tenn., but soon moved to another settlement, to what is known as the Fork Church (New Bethel) at the fork of the Holston and Watauga rivers. After a year he moved again to a settlement on the Little Limestone, eight miles southwest of the present town of Jonesboro, Tenn., and founded Salem Church and the school which was to become the first institution of higher learning west of the Alleghanies. The founding of Salem Church is said to have come about in the following way: Riding through the woods, seeking a frontier settlement where his services might be of use, his only baggage a sack full of books, he came upon some men felling trees. When they learned that he was a clergyman they asked him to preach for them and his preaching pleased them so much that they asked him to remain. He is described as a man "of powerful frame, medium stature, with a short, thick neck. His hair was sandy, his complection ruddy and his eyes blue. His demeanor was dignified, his countenance grave. His was a stentorian voice, and he was withal a striking individuality" (S. C. Williams, *post*). His preaching was "original, bold, pungent, and sometimes pathetic." One of the "old side" Presbyterians, he rigidly opposed any innovations in religious tenets. When a schism arose in the Abington Presbytery over the Hopkinsianism taught by one of its members, he was active in the "old side" group opposing the new teaching. His influence in furthering the Presbyterian faith was considerable. In addition to Salem Church, he assisted in organizing churches at New Bethel, Concord, New Providence, and in Carter's Valley (*Pioneer Presbyterianism in Tennessee*).

Active in the affairs of the settlement, he was one of the delegates to the first general convention of representatives from Washington, Sullivan, and Greene counties of North Carolina to consider the formation of a separate state, which movement culminated in the State of Franklin, later a part of Tennessee. Probably his most important work, however, was as an educator. The school which he opened in a log cabin on his farm was, in 1783, chartered by the legislature of North Carolina as Martin Academy, named for the governor of that state. In 1795, when the region had become a territory, it was incorporated as Washington College. "For many years it was the only, and for still more, the principal seat of classical education for the western country" (Ramsey, *post*). Its students were found in all the learned professions in the early days of Tennessee. Especially was it successful in training men for the ministry. Anticipating modern methods, in the early days the pupils were not divided into classes by years, but were allowed to complete the course as swiftly as they could. The nucleus of the college library was a gift of books received by Doak while attending a meeting of the General Assembly in Philadelphia in 1795, and which he had to carry 500 miles on horseback to the settlement. As a teacher his chief interest was philology. Always a student, after he was sixty years old he mastered Hebrew and chemistry sufficiently to teach them. Commencement was his one gala day. "On that occasion he wore his antique wig, his shorts, and his old-fashioned shoes: the muscles of his stern brow were relaxed, and he gave himself up to an unusual urbanity and kindliness of manner" (J. G. M. Ramsey, a former pupil, in Sprague, *post*). In 1818 he resigned the presidency of Washington College and moved to Bethel, Tenn., where he opened Tusculum Academy, later Tusculum College. He died at Bethel in his eighty-first year. Both of his sons were ordained to the ministry, John W. succeeding him in the presidency of Washington College and Samuel W. in that of Tusculum Academy.

[M. L. Morris, *The Irvins, Doaks, Logans and McCampbells of Va. and Ky.* (1916); S. C. Williams, *Hist. of the Lost State of Franklin* (1924); *The Scotch-Irish in America, Proc. and Addresses of the 9th Cong.* (1900); W. B. Sprague, *Annals Am. Pulpit*, vol. III (1858); *Pioneer Presbyterianism in Tenn.* (1898); E. H. Gillett, *Hist. of the Presbyterian Church* (1864); H. A. White, *Southern Presbyterian Leaders* (1911); Alfred Nevin, *Presbyterian Encyc.* (1884); J. Allison, *Dropped Stitches in Tenn. Hist.* (1897); J. T. Moore and A. P. Foster, *Tenn., the Volunteer State 1769–1923* (1923); J. Phelan, *Hist. of Tenn.* (1888); J. G. M. Ramsey, *The Annals of Tenn.* (1853).] B. R.

DOANE, GEORGE WASHINGTON (May 27, 1799–Apr. 27, 1859), second Episcopal bishop of New Jersey, was born in Trenton, N. J., the son of Jonathan and Mary (Higgins) Doane. His father was a contractor and builder. After graduating in 1818 from Union College, Doane read law in the office of Richard Harrison of New York and in 1820 became the sixth student in the General Theological Seminary, which Bishop Hobart was just starting in a room over a saddler's shop. Hobart ordained his pupil a deacon on Apr. 19, 1821, and a priest on Aug. 6, 1823, and kept him as his assistant at Trinity Church until 1825. Doane was professor of rhetoric and belles-lettres in Washington (now Trinity) College at Hartford, Conn., 1825–28, edited for a time the *Episcopal Watchman*, the *Banner of the Church*, and, later, the *Missionary*, was assistant minister and subsequently rector of Trinity Church, Boston, 1828–32. In 1829 he married Eliza Greene (Callahan) Perkins, widow of James Perkins of Boston. On Oct. 31, 1832, in St. Paul's Chapel, New York City, he was consecrated bishop of New Jersey; since there was no special provision for the support of the bishop, he soon after accepted the rectorship of St. Mary's at Burlington, N. J. Doane was one of the notable bishops of the American Episcopal Church. As a thinker, whether on theological or on other subjects, he does not rank very high, and his want of business acumen brought him to the verge of disaster, but he had other talents that stood him in good stead. He was handsome and magnetic and had a resonant voice and great social gifts. His vitality seemed inexhaustible. On his rector's salary of $700 a year, together with his none too abundant perquisites, he conducted himself successfully in the grand manner of an English prelate, thereby making numerous enemies but also many friends, and building up a strong diocese. He was one of the principal promoters of the missionary movement in the Episcopal Church and of Episcopal schools, founding St. Mary's Hall for girls at Burlington in 1837 and Burlington College for men in 1846. When Parliament repealed the act prohibiting American clergymen from preaching in English churches or taking part in the services, Walter Farquhar Hook, vicar of Leeds, invited him to preach at the consecration of the new parish church in Leeds. Doane's visit to England (1841) did much to bring the English Church into closer relations with its American offshoot. One curious by-product of this visit was the intrusion of three sonnets on "Aspects of Christianity in America" into Wordsworth's *Ecclesiastical Sonnets*, Doane and Henry Reed, Wordsworth's American editor, having besought the poet to recognize the filiation of the American Church. He edited the first American edition (Philadelphia, 1834) of Keble's *Christian Year*, and was himself fond of writing verse. He is, indeed, one of the best American hymn-writers, author of "Softly now the light of day," "Thou art the way, to Thee alone," "Lord, should we leave Thy hallowed feet," "Father of mercies, hear, Thy pardon we implore" [*Audi, benigne Conditor*], "Fling out the banner, let it float," and of several other well-known hymns. Most of these appeared in his *Songs by the Way* (1824). He was the leader of the High Church party in America, having no fellowship either with "dissenters" or with the "Roman intrusion." He was a warm friend of the Tractarian Movement, even going so far as to defend the notorious Tract XC that had brought the Movement to a head. Misfortunes fell upon him in the latter part of his life. In his effort to support his educational institutions at Burlington he finally was forced into bankruptcy

(Mar. 26, 1849). His own diocesan convention exonerated him of any culpability, but a persistent effort was made to bring him to trial before the House of Bishops. To a man of Doane's pride the idea of standing trial was even more humiliating than any imputation of guilt, and he announced that he would "make the trial of a bishop hard." By using every resource at his disposal he managed to block proceedings for almost five years, and eventually the case was dismissed. But a heavier blow awaited him. His elder son, George Hobart Doane, turned Catholic, having come to doubt the efficacy of the ordination received at his father's hands. On Sept. 15, 1855, the Bishop went through the ordeal of deposing his own son. Only four more years were allowed him, but he served his Church and his God indefatigably to the end.

[*The Life and Writings of George Washington Doane, with a Memoir by his son, William Croswell Doane* (4 vols., 1860–61); A. A. Doane, *The Doane Family* (1902); J. Julian, *A Dict. of Hymnology* (rev. ed., 1907); C. C. Tiffany, *A Hist. of the P. E. Church in the U. S. A.* (1895); *Cat. of the Officers and Alumni of Union Coll. 1797–1884* (1884); *Gen. Theol. Sem. Cat.;* G. M. Hills, *Hist. of the Church in Burlington, N. J.* (1876); H. G. Batterson, *A Sketch-Book of the Am. Episcopate . . . 1783–1883* (2nd ed., rev. and enl. 1884); F. C. Morehouse, *Some Am. Churchmen* (1892).]

G. H. G.

DOANE, THOMAS (Sept. 20, 1821–Oct. 22, 1897), mechanical engineer, was descended from Deacon John Doane who came to Plymouth, Mass., on the ship *Fortune,* in 1621. Thomas was born in Orleans, Mass., on Cape Cod, the oldest child of John and Polly (Eldredge) Doane. His father was a lawyer and served for a time in the state Senate. Thomas attended an academy on the Cape and when he was nineteen entered the English Academy at Andover, Mass., spending five terms there. At the conclusion of this period he took advantage of an opportunity to enter the employ of Samuel L. Felton of Charlestown, Mass., a well-known civil engineer. Three years later, having thus served his professional apprenticeship, he accepted his first employment with the Windsor White River Division of the Vermont Central Railroad. He served as resident engineer of the Cheshire Railroad at Walpole, N. H., from 1847 to 1849. In the latter year he began in Charlestown an independent practise as civil engineer and surveyor, which he continued until his death. During his professional career he was associated with practically all of the railroads running out of Boston, but he was more especially known for his connection with the Boston & Maine. Appointed in 1863 chief engineer of the Hoosac Tunnel, on which construction had already been begun, he introduced new engineering methods, relocated the line of the tunnel, and achieved great accuracy in the meeting of the borings. He was largely responsible for the development, in the United States, of the advanced system of tunneling with machinery and high explosives. He has also been called a pioneer in the use of compressed-air machinery in this country. In 1869 he became chief engineer of the Burlington & Missouri River Railroad in Nebraska, laying down approximately 241 miles of track in about four years. During this period he became much interested in the establishment of a Congregational college at Crete, Nebr., and was instrumental in obtaining for its location a square mile on the Big Blue River near that town. In gratitude for his aid the college was named in his honor and until his death he was one of its trustees. In 1873 he returned to Charlestown where he was again appointed chief engineer of the Hoosac Tunnel. When the tunnel was formally opened, on Feb. 9, 1875, he ran the first engine through it. For two more years he continued in charge of construction. He was actively interested in professional societies, was for over twenty years a member and for nine years president of the Boston Society of Civil Engineers, and joined the American Society of Civil Engineers in 1882. He was active in numerous civic, charitable, and educational enterprises in and around Boston, and was for many years a deacon in his church, the Winthrop Church, at Charlestown. On Nov. 5, 1850, he married Sophia Dennison Clarke, who died in 1868. Later he married Louisa Amelia Barber of Brattleboro, Vt. While on a visit to relatives at West Townsend, Vt., he died of heart-failure, survived by his second wife and four children of his first marriage.

[*Trans. Am. Soc. Civil Engineers,* XXXIX (1898), 690–94, an account prepared by F. W. D. Holbrook, who at intervals for a number of years was Doane's chief assistant; A. A. Doane, *The Doane Family* (1902), pp. 444–47; *Boston Transcript,* Oct. 23, 1897.]

K. W. C.

DOANE, WILLIAM CROSWELL (Mar. 2, 1832–May 17, 1913), first bishop of the Protestant Episcopal diocese of Albany, was one of the most influential leaders of his own communion and an honored figure in American public life. His parents were Rev. George Washington Doane [*q.v.*], afterward Bishop of New Jersey, and his wife, Eliza Greene (Callahan) Perkins, widow of James Perkins. He was born in Boston where his father was at the time Rector of Trinity Church. He graduated at Burlington College, N. J., in 1850, was ordained deacon in 1853 and priest in 1856. Between 1853 and 1869 he was successively rector of St. Mary's Church, Burlington; St. John's, Hartford, Conn., and St.

Peter's, Albany. During the same period he was for six years adjunct professor of literature at Burlington College and for four years lecturer in the same subject at Trinity College. Consecrated bishop on Feb. 2, 1869, he devoted the rest of his long life to the building up of his diocese. He held that no episcopate was complete without its cathedral which should have free seats, frequent services, schools and houses of mercy of all kinds; and the fruition of this idea, All Saints Cathedral of Albany, having in its connection St. Agnes School, the Child's Hospital, St. Margaret's Home, and the Sisterhood of the Holy Child, has been influential in establishing the American ideal of cathedral administration. He was visitor, trustee, and honorary chancellor of Hobart College, and regent and chancellor of the University of the State of New York. At two Lambeth Conferences he was spokesman for the American Episcopate. Indefatigable in his diocesan activities, he was actively interested in the betterment of social and moral conditions, and fearless in expressing his opinion on public questions. He was a stanch upholder of the cause of missions, vigorous in his opposition to divorce and a leader in his church for its suppression. He did much to advance Episcopal legislation in this matter and his influence was also felt in promoting marriage and divorce reform in the civil law. His principal literary work was the biography of his father entitled, *The Life and Writings of George Washington Doane, with a Memoir* (4 vols., 1860–61). His *Rhymes from Time to Time* (1901) show him to have been more than moderately gifted as a poet, and his hymn, "Ancient of Days," has a permanent place in the hymnals of many communions. He was the recipient of honorary degrees from Trinity, Columbia, Hobart, and Union colleges, and from the universities of Oxford, Cambridge, and Dublin.

Doane was a friend and admirer of Dr. Pusey, and in his earlier ministry was looked upon as a high churchman. He was fond of ceremony, wore the dress of an English bishop, and was frequently regarded as aristocratic. While always a pronounced churchman, however, he was really democratic in spirit, and numbered among his friends all sorts and conditions of people. Broadening and mellowing with the years, at his summer chapel at Northeast Harbor, Me., he ministered to and even gave the Communion to members of all denominations. In November 1853 he married Sarah Katharine Condit of Newark, N. J., whom he survived.

[A. A. Doane, *The Doane Family* (1902); *Who's Who in America*, 1912–13; *Outlook*, May 31, 1913; *Rev. of Revs.* (N. Y.), July 1913; *Churchman*, and *Living Church*, May 24 and 31, 1913; Jas. Hooper, *A Hist. of St. Peter's Ch. in the City of Albany* (1900); *N. Y. Tribune*, May 18, and *N. Y. Times*, May 19–20, 1913.]

F. T. P.

DOBBIN, JAMES COCHRAN (Jan. 17, 1814–Aug. 4, 1857), secretary of the navy, was a native of Fayetteville, N. C., where his father, John Moore Dobbin, was a prosperous merchant. His mother was Anness, the daughter of James Cochran of Person County, a planter and for several terms a member of Congress. Dobbin's early education was received in Fayetteville and at the Bingham School in Hillsboro. In 1828 he entered the University of North Carolina and was graduated in 1832. For three years he read law, and after his admission to the bar, he settled in Fayetteville. Refusing all requests to engage in politics, he devoted himself to his profession. He had a fine intellect, much charm of personality, and was a spirited and graceful speaker. His tastes were simple, and he led a quiet and dignified life, brightened by much personal friendship. He married Louisa Holmes of Sampson County who died in 1848. In 1845 the Democrats of his district, without his knowledge, nominated him for Congress. He accepted with genuine unwillingness, made a rather brilliant campaign, and serving one term with unusual distinction for a new member, refused reëlection. But in 1848 he was elected to the House of Commons where he won reputation by his efforts in behalf of the charter of the North Carolina Railroad and by the eloquent speech by which, in fulfilment of a promise to his dying wife, he converted the legislature and secured the establishment of a hospital for the insane. He was speaker of the House in the legislature of 1850 and by the close of the session was generally regarded as the leader of his party. Heading the North Carolina delegation in the Baltimore convention of 1852, he made the speech which precipitated the stampede for Pierce, and as candidate for elector at large he made an active campaign for him. He was again elected to the Commons, and was the caucus nominee of his party for United States senator. A deadlock ended in failure to elect any one, but in March 1853 Pierce appointed him secretary of the navy and he accepted.

Like most secretaries of the navy, Dobbin knew little or nothing of naval matters when he was appointed, but he directed his keenly analytical mind to the question, and, by the time he wrote his first report, he had formulated the policy which he successfully carried out. The navy was at a low ebb, with few ships and most of those antiquated, with a large body of officers too old or too incompetent for efficiency, with hopelessness and dissatisfaction general among the officers of lower grades, and with no regularly enlisted body of seamen and a practical impossibility of securing the crews, even for the limited number of ships. To remedy the situation, Dobbin recommended a radical increase in the navy, and, enthusiastic for steam, he urged a minimum of six steam propeller frigates, and, by a later recommendation, of five steam sloops. He suggested the creation of a retired list of officers on half pay, with a naval board to have direction of the system, the institution of a merit system for promotion, and a thorough-going reform of the whole plan of handling seamen. He prevented any restoration of flogging, but secured an effective scheme of punishment to replace it. He further recommended the establishment of a naval apprentice system, the enlistment of seamen for a definite term of years, with better treatment, better provision for their health and comfort, increased pay with adequate rewards for long and meritorious service, and honorable discharge at the end. Bold and aggressive in his attacks upon existing abuses, he secured the passage of the act to increase the efficiency of the navy by which many of them were reformed. No secretary of the navy up to that time so completely won the confidence of the service; and at the same time he secured popular indorsement and approval. Under him the navy was largely remade. He won applause by sending the relief expedition to Dr. E. K. Kane [*q.v.*] and, catching a vision of what cable communication would mean to the world, he performed a valuable service by sending Lieut. Berryman on a naval vessel to make a survey of possible submarine telegraph routes. He was not only a man of vision but an able executive as well; clear-headed, practical, tactful, and possessed of magnetism which, combined with his capacities and the discernible fact that personal considerations carried little weight with him, made him easily the most popular of the Pierce cabinet.

During his service, he was heavily overworked. He was offered a seat in the Senate, but he heeded Pierce's request and as a matter of duty remained at his post. His health, which had never been robust, failed, and he went home from Washington, at the close of the Pierce administration, only to die.

[*North Carolina Booklet,* XVI, no. 1 (1916–17); S. A. Ashe, *Biog. Hist. of N. C.,* vol. VI (1907); *N. C. House Journals*; *Exec. Doc.,* Serial nos. 712, 778, 812, 876; New York and Washington newspapers of the dates of his retirement and death.] J. G. de R. H.

DOBBS, ARTHUR (Apr. 2, 1689–Mar. 28, 1765), colonial governor of North Carolina, was born at Castle Dobbs, County Antrim, Ireland. His parents were Richard Dobbs of Castletown and Mary, the daughter of Archibald Stewart of Ballintoy. A younger brother was Francis Dobbs, the well-known writer and statesman. Nothing is known of his early life, but it is clear that he was well educated, for he was a man not only of wealth but of broad attainment. In 1711 he succeeded to his father's estate and in 1720 became high sheriff of Antrim. A few years later he published *An Account of Aurora Borealis, Seen in Ireland . . . 1725, with a Solution of the Problem* (see a discussion in *Philosophical Transactions,* 1726). In 1727 he was returned from Carrickfergus to the House of Commons of the Irish Parliament, and while there he gained considerable reputation by his investigations into the trade, agriculture, and political arithmetic of Ireland, the results of which he published in a series of very valuable tracts of which the *Essay on the Trade and Improvement of Ireland* (1729) is best known. In it he advocated an improved system of land tenure and he later pressed the reform in Parliament, declaring that Ireland was suffering "from the Commonalty's having no fixed property in their land." In 1730 Dr. Boulter, Archbishop of Armagh, introduced him to Robert Walpole as "one of the members of our House of Commons, where he on all occasions endeavors to promote his majesty's service. He . . . has for some time applied his thoughts to the trade of Great Britain and Ireland, and to the making of our colonies in America of more advantage than they have hitherto been" (Hugh Boulter, *Letters,* etc., 1770, quoted in J. R. McCulloch, *The Literature of Political Economy,* 1848, p. 46). Walpole at once appointed him engineer-in-chief and surveyor-general of Ireland. In 1732 Dobbs carried through Parliament a bill to encourage the enclosure of waste land and the planting of trees.

About 1730 he became deeply interested in the discovery of a northwest passage to India and was active in promoting the search for it. In 1731 he made abstracts of all the voyages on this quest and after an effort to interest the South Sea Company, laid the matter before the Hudson's Bay Company and the Admiralty. An expedition was sent out under Christopher Middleton who had been recommended by Dobbs, but after his return Dobbs accused him of falsifying his records, and a controversy, lasting some years, followed which drew from Dobbs his *Remarks upon Captain Middleton's Defence* (1744). In the same year he wrote *An Account of the Countries Adjoining to Hudson's Bay,* full of valuable information and advocating the dissolution of the Hudson's Bay Company. A later expedition justified Middleton, and Dobbs, in his *On Bees and the Mode of Gathering Wax and Honey* (see discussion in *Philosophical Transactions,* 1750), made an allusion taking leave of the question.

In 1745 Dobbs with John Selwyn purchased from the McCulloh estate 400,000 acres of land in North Carolina, lying in the present counties of Mecklenburg and Cabarrus, and was thereafter much interested in the affairs of the colony and increasingly dissatisfied with the administration of Gov. Gabriel Johnston. In 1754 he was selected as Johnston's successor and, sailing at once, was sworn in at New Bern on Oct. 31. He was received with great cordiality, and for a time his administration was peaceful. But he was a fanatical Protestant, obsessed by hatred of the French, a zealous servant of the Crown and an opponent of popular government, and very ignorant of conditions in the colony, and quiet could not last. Bent on carrying out his instructions without reference to the will of the people, he was soon in difficulties from which he was never extricated. He urged support of the French and Indian War far beyond the resources of the colony where, indeed, there was small interest in the struggle. At the heart of his North Carolina problems, however, was the question of how far the prerogatives of the Crown, and the governor as its agent, extended, and this question appears in every dispute between the governor and the assembly. Among these disputes were those concerning the appointment of the agent of the colony in London, the appointment of treasurers, the fixing of fees, control of the purse, regulation of the courts, the apportionment of representation, and the support and maintenance of the Church of England. Yet there is abundant evidence to show that Dobbs was eager for the welfare of the people of the colony. Also, he brought North Carolina into the stream of American affairs by his part in the war. But, while he had a quick and vigorous mind, he was impulsive in speech and action, and positive to the point of obstinacy in his own opinions, and his advancing years served only to emphasize these qualities. In 1762, while preparing to go to England, he suffered a stroke of apoplexy and died three years later at his home on Towncreek in Brunswick. He was twice married. His first wife was Anne Norbury of Drogheda, a widow and the daughter and heir of Capt. Osborne of Timahoe, County Kildare. When he was seventy-three years old he married Justina Davis of North Carolina, a girl still in her teens.

[S. A. Ashe, *Biog. Hist. of N. C.*, III (1905), 80; article by H. M. Chichester in *Dict. of Nat. Biog.*; *South Atlantic Quart.*, XVI (1917), 30; *Colonial Records of N. C.*, vols. V and VI (1887, 1888); *Correspondence of Wm. Pitt* (2 vols., 1906), ed. by Gertrude S. Kimball; S. A. Ashe, *Hist. of N. C.*, vol. I, 1908; Connor, *The Colonial Period* (1919).]

J. G. de R. H.

DOCK, CHRISTOPHER (*c.* 1698–1771), Mennonite schoolmaster, came to Pennsylvania between 1710 and 1714, attracted, doubtless, by the freedom accorded there to those of his faith. Reliable information as to his family, early education, and the place and date of his birth is lacking. Possibly in 1714, certainly as early as 1718, he opened a school among the Mennonites on the Skippack, in Montgomery County. After teaching ten years, he devoted his time chiefly to farming till 1738, when, praying that the Lord might "graciously overlook my neglect of youth" for the time past, he returned to the profession of schoolmaster until his death. Two schools, one at Skippack, the other at Salford, now claimed his attention, three days each in turn.

His fame spread, and Christopher Saur of Germantown sought a description of his methods (1749) as a guide for other less skilful teachers. The latter refused, fearing it would appear as an "unsavory monument" to himself and deserve "before God and all pious, Christian people, not honor but rather ridicule and shame." Finally Saur wrote certain questions to a mutual friend, Dielman Kolb, who drew the answers from Dock, the latter stipulating that they should not be published in his lifetime. These answers make up his famous *Schulordnung,* the earliest treatise in America on schoolkeeping thus far discovered. The manuscript was completed on Aug. 8, 1750. Meantime, at the solicitation of Saur, Dock prepared a few articles, in 1764, for the *Geistliches Magazien* and this probably prepared the way for publication of the *Schulordnung* before its author's death. The first and second editions of the latter appeared in 1770, and a third in 1861. The best known of the articles were "A Hundred Necessary Rules of Conduct for Children" and "A Hundred Christian Rules for Children." These rules give an insight into the early German family life much as the *Schulordnung* pictures Dock's school. He also composed a number of hymns, some of which are used to-day.

The fame of the pious schoolmaster rests not wholly upon the early date of his publication on schoolkeeping but upon the modernity of much of his practise. Constructive writing and composition exercises were secured by an interchange of pupils' letters from one school to the other; use of gentle persuasion superseded harsh discipline; rewards were given for good work, social disapproval for the lazy and disobedient; and investigation sought to find the reason for swearing, lying, stealing and quarreling, punishment being varied to suit the individual case. Understanding love was the chief principle of discipline; and simplicity and directness, the chief virtues of his instruction. Each evening, with the roll before him, he prayed that his injustice or neglect of any be forgiven; that on the morrow he might do the best for each and all. Late in 1771 he failed to return from school. There he was found, on his knees, dead.

[The best sources of information are: "Christopher Dock, the Pious Schoolmaster on the Skippack, and his Works," published in S. W. Pennypacker, *Hist. and Biog. Sketches* (1883), and Martin G. Brumbaugh, *The Life and Works of Christopher Dock* (1908).]

T. W.

DOCKSTADER, LEW (Aug. 7, 1856–Oct. 26, 1924), black-face minstrel, vaudeville actor, was one of the most popular comedians of his generation. His trick shoes, voluminous dress suit, engaging smile, and impromptu whimsicalities provoked hearty laughter alike in metropolitan theatres and in remote "opera houses" of provincial towns; his songs—"Oh Mr. Austin"; "Peter, You're in Luck This Morning"; "Everybody Works but Father"; "He Used to Breakfast with Us Every Morning"—were the hits of the day. A diligent student of humorous effects, he became a master at furbishing up old jokes about the Ark, Jonah, Congress, and Hoboken, at convulsing his audiences with unexpected and ingenious "local gags," at mimicking the voice, stride, and gesture of political figures such as Presidents Harrison, Cleveland, and Roosevelt. About all his clowning there was a simplicity and finish that gave it the dignity of art. Among actors he was admired as one of the most versatile and likable men in the profession, and he became the hero of numerous anecdotes. During his fifty years on the stage he is said to have missed only one performance.

His original name was George Alfred Clapp. He was born in Hartford, Conn., the son of Chester and Harriet Gouge (Miller) Clapp. His father kept the bar of the City Hotel, of which an uncle, Caleb Clapp, was the proprietor. From boyhood Clapp seemed cut out for the stage: he was completely at ease before an audience, could play any musical instrument, apparently, that he picked up, and possessed an inexhaustible fund of drollery. He early became the stage manager and end man of an amateur minstrel company and made his professional début, under the name of Lew Clapp, in Hartford in 1873. A few years later he and Charles Dockstader formed an acting partnership and were billed as the Dockstader Brothers, and Clapp was thereafter known as Lew Dockstader. As a member of various minstrel troupes he played in every state in the Union and always cherished an ambition to have a company of his own. He was too generous with his money, however, to be long successful as a manager. His first venture, in New York 1886–89, left him deep in debt and threatened with bankruptcy, but going into vaudeville he soon repaid his creditors in full. In 1898 he returned to minstreldom in partnership with George H. Primrose; and in 1903 he became sole proprietor of the company; but minstrel shows were no longer in favor, and Dockstader had to betake himself again to vaudeville, in which he was highly paid and free from managerial worries. On Jan. 6, 1920, his wife, Lucin, died. In January 1923, at New Brunswick, N. J., he sustained a fall, as a result of which a bone tumor developed in his left leg. In December he had to quit the stage. He died at his daughter's home in New York and was buried at Kensico. His death, as truly as Garrick's, diminished the public stock of harmless pleasure.

[G. W. Russell, ed., *Additional Contributions to the Hist. of Christ Church, Hartford, Conn.*, II, 95 (Hartford, 1908); Ebenezer Clapp, *Record of the Clapp Family in America* (1876), p. 336; *Geer's Hartford City Directory for 1856–57* and *for 1860–61*; D. Paskman and S. Spaeth, *"Gentlemen, Be Seated"* (1928); Walt McDougall, *This is the Life!* (1926), p. 213; *N. Y. Times*, Jan. 8, 1920, Oct. 27, 29, Nov. 2 (Pt. VIII), 10, 1924; *N. Y. World*, Oct. 28, 1924 (editorial); *Hartford Daily News, Hartford Courant, N. Y. Herald Tribune*, Oct. 27, 1924.]

G. H. G.

DOD, ALBERT BALDWIN (Mar. 24, 1805–Nov. 19, 1845), Presbyterian minister, college professor, was born in Mendham, N. J., the son of Daniel [*q.v.*] and Nancy (Squier) Dod. His father was a builder of engines, was master of several other trades, read widely in Calvinistic theology, and wrote verse. Proficiency in mathematics was a family trait. From early childhood Albert was quiet and studious, quickly assimilating what the schools of Elizabethtown and Bloomfield, N. J., had to teach him, entering the sophomore class in the College of New Jersey in the spring of 1821, and graduating in the autumn of 1822. At Princeton he came under clerical influences and decided to become a minister. Through Samuel Lewis Southard [*q.v.*], who was a friend of his father's, he secured a place as tutor in a family living near Fredericksburg, Va. After three years in the Old Dominion he studied at the Princeton Theological Seminary 1825–26 and in the following year was made tutor in the College. In 1828 he was licensed to preach by the Presbytery of New York, but although he supplied many pulpits in New York, Philadelphia, and elsewhere, he never felt inclined to abandon teaching for the active ministry. In April 1830 he married Caroline, daughter of Samuel Bayard of Princeton, and in the autumn of that year he was promoted to the professorship of mathematics, which he continued to occupy until his death. His love of mathematics, his zeal for imparting instruction, and his remarkable gift for lucid exposition made him an unusually successful teacher. "There was nothing he could not make plain," said his friend Charles Hodge. He introduced written examinations into the College, and at the suggestion of his colleague, Joseph Henry, gave a course of lectures on architecture. He had a taste for literature and the fine arts, was a laborious student of metaphysics, and from 1835 on contributed able articles to the *Biblical Repertory and Princeton Review.* Of his eight contributions the most interesting are, "Beecher's Views in Theology" (1837), "Transcendentalism" (1839), "Capital Punishment" (1842), and "Vestiges of Creation" (1845). In these articles he displays a real gift for argument, a trenchant style, and a reactionary mind. Hegel, Cousin, and Emerson he lumped together as no better than atheists, thereby winning the commendation of Andrews Norton, who republished one of his reviews in *Two Articles . . . Concerning the Transcendental Philosophy* (Cambridge, Mass., 1840). Himself gentle and religiously minded, he believed that God had ordained capital punishment in Genesis IX, 5–6. A committee of the New York legislature agreed with him and adopted his argument as their report. The blunders in Robert Chambers's famous essay, *Vestiges of the Natural History of Creation* (1844), which, though bad science, contained the germ of the Darwinian theory, he exposed scornfully, but failed to appreciate its underlying idea. Among his friends Dod was remembered for his brilliant conversation.

[W. B. Sprague, *Annals Am. Pulpit*, vol. IV (1858); *Gen. Cat. Princeton Univ. 1746–1906* (1908); *Biblical Repertory and Princeton Rev., Index Vol. 1825–68* (1871); J. Maclean, *Sermon Preached in the Chapel of the Coll. of N. J., Mar. 1, 1846* (Princeton, 1846), and *Hist. of the Coll. of N. J.* (1877).] G. H. G.

DOD, DANIEL (Sept. 8, 1778–May 9, 1823), inventor, steam-engine builder, was of the fourth generation descended from Daniel and Mary Dod, natives of England, who emigrated to Branford, Conn., about 1645. His parents were Lebbeus, a brother of Thaddeus Dod [*q.v.*], and Mary (Baldwin) Dod. Daniel was born in northern Virginia whither his father had removed from New Jersey to establish himself as a maker of clocks and watches, but on account of Indian troubles the latter returned north with his family and settled in Mendham, N. J., before the close of the Revolution. Young Dod was trained by his father for the business of clock and watchmaking, mathematical instrument making and surveying. He attended the public schools and also Queen's (now Rutgers) College at New Brunswick. About the time that he became of age, with his two older brothers, he started a manufactory of cotton machinery which developed nicely but failed in the depression following the War of 1812. Just prior to this he had declined the chair of mathematics at Rutgers, and with the collapse of the cotton machinery business he removed with his family to Elizabethtown. For some time he had been interested in steam-engine building, and on Nov. 29, 1811, and May 12, 1812, he was granted United States patents on steam-engines, including boilers and condensers, for use in steamboats as well as mills. These engines operated on the general principle of the Watt engine. In Elizabethtown Dod entered into partnership with the former Governor, Aaron Ogden [*q.v.*], who operated a ferry, to manufacture steam-engines and steamboat machinery. Armed with Dod's patents and the manufacturing rights to John Fitch's steamboat machinery which they had purchased, they began the manufacture of a steam ferryboat and their first product was put in service in 1813. Robert Fulton's steamboat monopoly, which was then in force, prevented, however, Dod and Ogden from continuing to use steam in this ferry service. They continued for five years, making steamboat machinery for boats in other waters: on Lake Ontario; in Philadelphia, Norfolk, Mobile, and New Orleans. Dod's greatest contribution was the machinery for the steamboat *Savannah,* which crossed the Atlantic Ocean in 1819—the first steam-vessel to make this voyage. In 1818 Dod and Ogden dissolved partnership, Dod retaining the manufacturing plant. As a friend he indorsed notes for Ogden who was in need of working capital for his ferry system. Ogden failed, and Dod's works were seized under a mortgage, which loss, together with those on the *Savannah,* forced him in 1819 to pass over all of his property to his creditors. With the help of friends he repurchased all of his tools and in 1820 set up business anew in New York. Three years later, while examining his machinery on board the steamboat *Patent* in the East River, he was so injured by the explosion of the boiler that he died several days later at the age of forty-five. In 1801 he had married Nancy Squier of Caldwell, N. J., who with three daughters and five sons, among them Albert Baldwin Dod [*q.v.*], survived him.

[G. H. Preble, *A Chronological Hist. of the Origin and Development of Steam Navigation* (1883); B. L. Dodd and J. R. Burnet, *Geneals. of the Male Descendants of Daniel Dod* (1864); *Proc. N. J. Hist. Soc.*, vol. IX (1864); H. W. Dickinson, *Robt. Fulton* (1913); *Evening Post* (N. Y.), May 14, 1823.] C. W. M.

DOD, THADDEUS (Mar. 7, 1740 o.s.–May 20, 1793), pioneer Presbyterian clergyman and educator, was born at Newark, N. J., the second son of Stephen and Deborah (Brown) Dod. The family were of New England Puritan stock, descendants of Daniel Dod, who was born in England and settled about 1645 in Branford, Conn. While Thaddeus was still an infant his parents moved to Mendham, Morris County, N. J., where he was brought up. They were in straitened circumstances, which may account for his lateness in entering college. He graduated from the College of New Jersey in 1773, and began his theological studies. About this time he married Phebe Baldwin, whose sister Mary was the wife of his brother Lebbeus. In 1775 he was licensed and two years later, Oct. 15, 1777, he was ordained *sine titulo* by the Presbytery of New York, for work on the western frontier.

To Lindley's Settlement, an outpost newly established by pioneers from New Jersey, on Ten Mile Creek in the present Washington County, Pa., Dod had made his way that summer, and had there found his future field of work. A week after his ordination he again started westward with his wife and two children; but conditions in western Pennsylvania were unfavorable, and for two years he stayed at Patterson's Creek, Va. In September 1779 he moved with his family to Ten Mile, where he acquired a farm, built a log cabin, and started his pastoral work. The Ten Mile church was formally organized on Aug. 15, 1781. In addition to his ministerial duties there, Dod preached at other settlements where there was no resident pastor. He was one of four clergymen whom the Synod of New York and Philadelphia erected into a separate presbytery in 1781. Their first meeting was not held at the designated place, "as the circumstances of some of the members by reason of the incursions of the savages, rendered it impracticable" (*Minutes Presbytery of Redstone,* p. 3).

In the spring of 1782, in a log cabin near his own home, Dod opened, with thirteen pupils, the first classical school west of the Alleghanies. There he taught English, the classics, and mathematics—this last including surveying. His intellectual attainments were rated highly by those who knew him. He was a good classical scholar, he knew Hebrew (in his extant sermon manuscripts the texts are given in the original tongue), he tried his hand at English verse, but his especial interest lay in mathematics. His log cabin academy was closed in the autumn of 1785, when he sold his farm. Two years later he was one of the trustees to whom a charter was granted for Washington Academy; and when the academy was opened on Apr. 1, 1789, Dod was its first principal. He had accepted the position reluctantly and for one year only, though he stayed a few months longer, dividing his time between Washington and Ten Mile. The court-house in which the academy met was burned in the winter of 1790–91, and Dod lost most of his books in the fire. Before the academy reopened, another school was started at Canonsburg, which later became Jefferson College; while Washington Academy became in 1806 Washington College.

As a clergyman, Dod laid his emphasis on personal piety, and he is spoken of as a "son of consolation." Yet he was not superior to the current amenities of theological controversy. "To the witness of Cain," he said in a sermon, "I might add those of Balaam, Saul, Ahab, Judas, Simon the Sorcerer, Julian the Apostate, and John Wesley." He died at Ten Mile on May 20, 1793.

[Jos. Smith, *Old Redstone* (1854), which is the basis of several later accounts; E. C. Wines, *Hist. Discourse* (Pittsburgh, 1859); Jos. Smith, *Hist. of Jefferson Coll.* (1857); *Minutes of the Presbytery of Redstone* (1878); *Centenary Memorial . . . of Presbyterianism in Western Pa.* (1876); B. L. Dodd and J. R. Burnet, *Geneals. of the Male Descendants of Daniel Dod* (1864); "Autobiog. and Memoir of Rev. Thaddeus Dod" in *Presbyterian Mag.*, Aug. and Sept. 1854, with a brief introduction by Dod's son, Cephas Dod; W. B. Sprague, *Annals Am. Pulpit,* III (1858), 356. To Dr. C. T. Dodd of Washington, Pa., and Dr. W. L. Dodd of Amity the writer is indebted for permission to examine MSS. written by Thaddeus Dod.] A. H. S.

DODD, FRANK HOWARD (Apr. 12, 1844–Jan. 10, 1916), publisher, was born at Bloomfield, N. J., the son of Moses Woodruff and Rachel (Hoe) Dodd. His mother was a member of the Hoe family, long active in the manufacture of printing-presses. His father had been associated with John S. Taylor in publishing religious and theological works at Brick Church Chapel, City Hall Square, New York City; in 1840 he bought out his partner in that business. After the son had been graduated from the Bloomfield Academy (at the age of fifteen), he joined his father in the publishing enterprise, served a ten years' apprenticeship, and in 1870 succeeded to the control of the house, later taking as partners Edward S. Mead, who died in 1894, and B. Van Wagenen, who retired in 1909. The new firm entered the field of popular fiction, bringing out several books that reached a high

Dodd

rank among the "best sellers" of their time. The first pronounced success in that capacity was E. P. Roe's *Barriers Burned Away,* a story deriving its chief incidents from the Chicago fire in 1871. Other popular stories by the same author followed. A score of years passed before the firm published anything comparable in financial returns with the Roe books, although its lists contained many titles of superior literary merit. In 1894, *Beside the Bonnie Brier Bush,* by Ian Maclaren (Dr. John Watson), was brought out in America by Dodd, Mead & Company, and at once achieved a remarkably large sale. Another profitable venture of the house was Paul Leicester Ford's *Janice Meredith* (1899). In the late nineties Dodd and his associates were instrumental in founding and maintaining *The Bookman,* a literary monthly of high quality. In this undertaking they were greatly aided by the coöperation of the London *Bookman.* Dodd at that time formed lasting friendships with several British authors and publishers, among others William Robertson Nicoll and Miss Beatrice Harraden. With the opening of the twentieth century he began to make definite plans for a reference book that should provide for American readers what the German public was then getting from the compilations of Brockhaus and Meyer. The result of his carefully developed project was the *New International Encyclopædia* (1902–04), a work that met with favor because of the convenient arrangement of its material and the compact form of its articles. In 1907 the *New International Year Book* was begun. This annual publication supplemented the information given in the *Encyclopædia* and contained much special material in chronicle form. Before his death the founder saw most of the second edition of the *Encyclopædia* (1914–17) and eight successive issues of the *Year Book* off the press. Dodd had served as president of the American Publishers' Association, had strongly advocated net prices in the book trade, and was always active in promoting the general interests of the craft. He was a leader in accelerating the uptown movement of New York's publishing district. His wife, whom he married in 1868, was Martha Bliss Parker, daughter of President Joel Parker of Union Theological Seminary. His brother, Robert H. Dodd, joined the firm in 1889 and his son, Edward H., in 1903.

[Article in the *New International Year Book,* 1916; *Publisher's Weekly,* Jan. 1916; *Who's Who in America,* 1914–15; *Bookman,* Apr. 1916; Wm. Robertson Nicoll in *British Weekly,* Jan. 20, 1916; B. L. Dodd and J. R. Burnet, *Geneals. of the Male Descendants of Daniel Dod* (1864); *N. Y. Tribune, N. Y. Times,* Jan. 11, 1916.]

W. B. S.

DODD, SAMUEL CALVIN TATE (Feb. 20, 1836–Jan. 30, 1907), lawyer, was born in Franklin, Venango County, Pa., one of the ten children of Levi L. and Julia Parker Dodd. His father was a cabinetmaker and carpenter, a respected citizen, and a stanch Presbyterian. Young Dodd had his early education in the schools of Franklin and worked as errand boy and printer's devil to help finance his college education, which he received in Jefferson College (now Washington and Jefferson), at Canonsburg, Pa., graduating in 1857. He studied law in Franklin for two years and was admitted to the bar of Venango County in 1859, the year in which oil was discovered in western Pennsylvania. His whole career was shaped by this event. A vast influx of capital and business came upon the heels of the great discovery and he found himself immediately involved in the complications and competition growing out of the boom. Unlike most of the lawyers of the community he gave his attention mainly to corporation law and equity, foreseeing that the day of big business was at hand and that the cutthroat competition among the oil producers was wasteful and temporary. The seventies found him fighting the battles of the consumers and the independents against the Rockefeller interests, and he acquired considerable reputation as an anti-rebate lawyer. In 1872–73 he served as a delegate to the Pennsylvania constitutional convention, where he fathered the anti-rebate clause which that body wrote into the new constitution. During this period he served as counsel for numerous oil operators and transportation companies, especially the transportation companies from which the United Pipe Lines were later formed. In 1881 he became general solicitor for the Standard Oil Company and moved to New York. This relationship was in one respect an unusual one. He felt that in order to give the best legal advice he should occupy a detached, almost judicial position, uninfluenced by personal financial interests. Accordingly he refused to allow John D. Rockefeller to place to his credit for gradual payment a block of stock which would have made him many times a millionaire; contrary to popular rumor his salary was never more than $25,000, and he left an estate of less than $300,000. His business relations with the Rockefellers and other Standard Oil magnates were always cordial, but otherwise he stood somewhat aloof, never becoming an intimate friend.

His reputation rests upon his organization in 1882 of the Standard Oil Trust. He is sometimes called the inventor of the trust as a form of business combination. There had, however, been a less comprehensive Standard Oil trust agreement in 1879. The state laws of the period did not afford a way for corporations to combine and what Dodd was seeking was a means of creating a "corporation of corporations." Under the trust agreement which he drew up, the voting stocks of some forty companies were placed in the hands of nine trustees. The change effected was, however, more apparent than real. There had been no competition between the companies thus combined for some time and the nine trustees did in fact own a majority of the stock of the component corporations. The trust agreement was kept secret for six years. It fell to Dodd's lot to officiate not only at its birth but also at its death. In 1892 the Supreme Court of Ohio decided that it was an illegal combination in restraint of trade and also that the Standard Oil Company of Ohio, one of the component companies, had exceeded its lawful corporate powers in entering the agreement. Accordingly, in March of that year Dodd presented the resolutions for the dissolution of the trust. This dissolution did not materially alter the actual conditions of the business. For six years the now dissociated corporations conducted their business under a gentlemen's agreement, and under the shrewd legal guardianship of Dodd who steered them, as one writer puts it, "through the stormy seas of anti-trust agitation," and kept them within the law. In 1899 he drew up the plans for the organization of the great holding company, the Standard Oil Company of New Jersey. He continued as legal adviser until 1905 when he retired from active service on a pension, retaining the title of counsel for the Standard Oil Company.

Dodd was a firm believer in big business lawfully conducted and he bitterly resented the idea that combinations are vicious merely because they are large. Accordingly he criticized the early interpretation of the Sherman Act which penalized all combinations in restraint of trade. He held that only unreasonable combinations should be barred, a view later adopted by the Supreme Court in 1911 (*Standard Oil Company of New Jersey et al.* vs. *United States, 221 U. S.,* 1) in dissolving the very holding company which he had organized (see his paper, "Present Legal Status of Trusts," *Harvard Law Review,* Oct. 25, 1893). He was a firm believer in the federal incorporation of business companies and favored a constitutional amendment to make that possible (J. H. Bridge, "Trusts as Their Makers View Them," *World's Work,* November 1902). In politics he was a nominal Democrat, an admirer of Cleveland, but an independent voter. His published writings include, "Ten Years of the Standard Oil Company" (*Forum,* May 1892); the following pamphlets: *Uses and Abuses of Combinations* (1888); *History of the Standard Oil Company* (1888); *Trusts* (1889); *Aggregated Capital* (1889); and *Trusts* (1900), a collection of addresses.

He married, in 1860, Mary E. Geer of Waterford, Pa., who bore him two sons and died in 1872. On Mar. 8, 1877, he married Melvina E. Smith, who died in 1906. From this marriage there were two children. In private life Dodd was genial, friendly, and generous. He shunned publicity and seldom appeared in court. He lived quietly and modestly with his family, a few congenial friends, and his books. He read deeply in history, economics, and philosophy, and Spencer and Huxley were his gods. Deeply religious, he became in later life a reverent freethinker.

[B. L. Dodd and John R. Burnet, *Genealogies of the Male Descendants of Daniel Dod, of Branford, Conn.* (1864); Paul Latzke, "The Trust Builder," *Nat. Corporation Reporter,* Dec. 4, 1902 (reprinted from *Saturday Evening Post*); "The Master Builder of the Standard Oil Company," *Rev. of Revs.* (N. Y.), Mar. 1908; *Who's Who in America,* 1906–07; obituaries in *N. Y. Times,* Feb. 1, 1907, and *N. Y. Journal of Commerce,* Feb. 1907; information as to certain facts from a son, Mr. Lee Wilson Dodd.] R. E. C.

DODDRIDGE, JOSEPH (Oct. 14, 1769–Nov. 9, 1826), clergyman, physician, author, and pioneer, was born at Friend's Cove, near Bedford, Pa., eldest son of John and Mary (Wells) Doddridge of Maryland, and brother of Philip Doddridge [*q.v.*]. Four years later his parents removed to Washington County, Pa., then wilderness, so that from childhood he was thrown into intimate association with the Indians and early settlers of the frontier. His powers of observation and his life-long interest in recording historical incident helped him to capitalize this association in his valuable *Notes on the Settlement and Indian Wars of the Western Parts of Virginia and Pennsylvania, from 1763 to 1783 Inclusive* (1824), an accurate account of the country and the life that prevailed there during the days of its colonization.

The elder Doddridge was a devout man who reared his children along strictly pious and moralistic lines, and it was not strange that Joseph at eighteen, with a background of Bible reading, a few sessions of schooling in Maryland, and several years of labor on his father's farm, should have been received as a circuit preacher of the Wesleyan Methodist connection, traveling through western Pennsylvania. The death of his father in 1791 called him from this itinerant ministry, but enabled him to resume his interrupted education. After a year of diligent study at Jefferson Academy, Canonsburg, Pa., he transferred to the Episcopal ministry, received ordination from Bishop White at Philadelphia, and removed temporarily to western Pennsylvania; soon, however, he settled permanently in Charlestown (now Wellsburg, W. Va.), Brooke County, Va. For the remainder of his life he acted as an advance guard of the Protestant Episcopal Church in northwestern Virginia and eastern Ohio, traveling on horseback over an extensive and sparsely settled territory to render truly apostolic service in his effort to keep the church in the van of western progress. After 1800 he extended his missionary operations chiefly into Ohio, and it was owing in great measure to his unselfish and indefatigable exertions that an episcopate was obtained in that state. His never robust physique was undermined by his frequent exposure and constant toil, and his cheerful and hopeful disposition was depressed and turned irritable by a painful asthmatic disease which made his last years burdensome.

About 1795 he married Jemima, daughter of Capt. John Bukey, and soon found it essential that he augment his meager income. He settled upon medicine as a profession compatible with the ministry, completed a course of preparation under Dr. Benjamin Rush of Philadelphia, and thenceforth successfully nurtured the bodily as well as the spiritual wants of his parishioners, winning popularity with his patients at the same time that he won praise from his fellow physicians for his "abilities and scientific skill." He managed also to do a fair amount of writing but beyond the *Notes,* etc., with its wealth of original material, little of it is important. His *Treatise on the Culture of Bees* (1813) reveals one of his especial interests, and his prose drama *Logan* (1823) won him recognition, but its intention to render justice to the famous Indian leader is more apparent than are its dramatic or literary qualities.

[The fullest account of Joseph Doddridge is the Memoir by his daughter Narcissa Doddridge, included in the second (Albany, 1876) and third (Pittsburgh, 1912) editions of the *Notes on the Settlement and Indian Wars.* The edition of 1876 contains likewise a seven-page sketch of him, written in 1855, by Judge Thomas Scott of Chillicothe, Ohio. The latter sketch is quoted in G. W. Peterkin, *Hist. and Record of the Protestant Episcopal Church in the Diocese of W. Va.* (1902), with occasional other references to Doddridge. The index to Vol. II of Perry's *Hist. of the Am. Epis. Church 1587–1883* (1885) may mislead the reader through its confusion of Joseph Doddridge, who did write some unimportant verse, with the English hymn-writer and divine, Philip Doddridge. Most of the *Notes on the Settlement,* etc., has been reprinted in Samuel Kercheval's *Hist. of the Valley of Va.* (1833). See also S. E. Dodderidge, *The Dodderidges of Devon* (1909).]

A. C. G., Jr.

DODDRIDGE, PHILIP (May 17, 1773–Nov. 19, 1832), lawyer, politician, was the youngest son of John Doddridge, a farmer, and his wife, Mary, daughter of Col. Richard Wells. He was born in Bedford County, Pa., whither his father had removed from Maryland. His youth was spent on the farm and he had little opportunity of acquiring education before he was seventeen, when he went to Charlestown (now Wellsburg, W. Va.), Brooke County, Va., and attended Johnson's private school there. On leaving school he took a trip by flatboat down the Ohio and Mississippi rivers to New Orleans, and upon his return began the study of law. In the spring of 1797 he commenced practise in Wellsburg. Details of his early years at the bar are meager; contemporary testimony agrees, however, that his success was rapid and his powers of speech remarkable. He was appointed state's attorney for Ohio County in 1808, and that his practise was expanding is indicated by the fact that he held briefs in the court of appeals of Virginia and the Supreme Court of the United States. In 1815–16, a period when sectionalism was emerging as a major feature of Virginia politics, he was a member of the House of Delegates, for Brooke County. Under the Virginia constitution of 1776 the basis of representation was such that the legislature was controlled by the "Tidewater" constituencies, despite the rapid settlement of the western counties. Doddridge entered the House as an aggressive western protagonist. His powerful denunciation of existing anomalies made a deep impression, but he could make no progress. He was a member of the legislature again in 1822–23 and 1828, the latter session being of vital importance, inasmuch as a decision had been arrived at to hold a constitutional convention in which any amendments considered should be framed by the legislature. His proposals to make the white population the basis of representation and have a census taken were voted down, but he did not abandon hope. He was delegate from Brooke County to the convention which met at Richmond, Oct. 5, 1829, his eloquence, earnestness, and resource making him the commanding figure there, but again he failed and the amended constitution of 1830 was as unreformed as its predecessor (see J. M. Callahan, *History of West Virginia,* 1923, I, 320–24). His efforts nevertheless paved the way for the creation later of the State of West Virginia.

Doddridge had been an unsuccessful candidate for Congress in 1822 and 1824, but in 1828 was elected and, having been reëlected in 1830, remained a member till his death at Washington, Nov. 19, 1832. On Apr. 30, 1800, he married

Julia Parr Musser of Lancaster, Pa. He was said to have been "not less celebrated on the west side of the Alleghany Mountains for his eloquence and splendid talents, than Patrick Henry was by the men of his day in the eastern portions of Virginia" (*The American Pioneer,* April 1842, p. 135). By the unanimous verdict of his contemporaries he was a lawyer and statesman of the first rank, but since he never became a national figure his brilliant personality was only locally appreciated.

[An excellent review of Doddridge's life and political career appeared in an article, "Hon. Philip Doddridge of Brooke County, Va.," by W. S. Laidley in the *W. Va. Hist. Mag.,* Jan. 1902; see also V. A. Lewis, *Hist. of W. Va.* (1889), p. 685; and W. T. Willey, *A Sketch of the Life of Philip Doddridge* (1875), which though unreliable in the matter of dates gives several of Doddridge's speeches.] H. W. H. K.

DODGE, AUGUSTUS CÆSAR (Jan. 2, 1812–Nov. 20, 1883), United States senator, diplomat, son of Henry Dodge [*q.v.*] and Christina McDonald, was born at Ste. Genevieve, Mo. At the age of fifteen he removed with his parents to the lead-mines in the southwestern part of what is now Wisconsin. Here he worked with his father at mining and served with him in the Winnebago War of 1827 and in the Black Hawk War in 1832. There was little opportunity for schooling, but on Mar. 19, 1837, he made up for this lack in part, perhaps, by marrying Clara Ann Hertich, the daughter of the Ste. Genevieve schoolmaster. From 1838 to 1840 he was registrar of the public land office at Burlington in the Territory of Iowa. In December of the latter year he entered Congress as delegate for the Territory and for six years held this position, occupying himself largely with the questions of appropriations and boundaries. In 1848 he was chosen as Iowa's first United States senator, after the legislature had been deadlocked over the election for two years. He and his father had been together for four years as delegates from the neighboring territories of Wisconsin and Iowa. Now for a period of over six years they were together in the Senate.

Dodge was a Democrat, warmly attached to the West, and with a sympathy for the South that grew out of his early life in Missouri. He voted for all of the provisions of the compromise measures of 1850. He was outspoken in his opposition to abolitionism and in defense of the Fugitive-Slave Law. In December 1853, he introduced a bill to organize the Territory of Nebraska. This was referred to the committee on territories of which Douglas was chairman. In January a substitute measure was presented providing for the creation of two territories instead of one and applying to this region the principle of popular sovereignty. Dodge supported the Kansas-Nebraska Bill with enthusiasm, characterizing it as "the noblest tribute which has ever yet been offered by the Congress of the United States to the sovereignty of the people." A rising tide of anti-Nebraska sentiment developed, however, in his state, and in January 1855 the legislature chose James Harlan to succeed him in the Senate. President Pierce then appointed him to the post of minister to Spain. One of his first duties in Madrid was the final settlement of the *Black Warrior* affair which had threatened the peaceful relations of the two nations. The particular hope of the administration at this time was to acquire the island of Cuba, and Dodge set himself energetically to the task, but without success. In 1859 he resigned and returned to Iowa, where he was defeated by the Republicans in a race for the governorship in 1859 and, again by James Harlan, in a contest for the United States senatorship in 1860. The remainder of his years, nearly a quarter of a century, he spent in private life in Burlington. He was a representative of the ante bellum Democracy and like his party was unable to adjust himself to the change in sentiment on the slavery question. On issues relating to the West, notably the homestead and Pacific railroad problems, he fought vigorously for measures which the Republican party enacted during its first term of office. He was a man of sincere convictions and aggressive force, consistent in his policies but without great flexibility of mind. He faithfully served his state in the early days when the people of Iowa were largely of Southern origin, but with the influx of Northerners and the growth of Republicanism, his supporters became a minority, with the result that retirement from public life overtook him before he reached the age of sixty.

[Most of Dodge's correspondence was unfortunately destroyed. There exist, however, two letter-books embodying his diplomatic correspondence, and a manuscript containing autobiographical notes. Letters of his contemporaries, newspaper files, and the *Congressional Globe* enable one to follow his public career. An adequate biography is found in Louis Pelzer, *Augustus Cæsar Dodge* (1908). See also William Salter, "Augustus C. Dodge," in the *Iowa Hist. Record,* vol. III, Jan. 1887.] J. C. P.

DODGE, DAVID LOW (June 14, 1774–Apr. 23, 1852), merchant, founder of the New York Peace Society, was born on a farm in Brooklyn, originally a part of Pomfret, Conn., in the year before the outbreak of the Revolution. His parents were David and Mary (Stuart) Earl Dodge. His father, David Dodge, was of English and Welsh colonial stock, a descendant of Richard Dodge who came to Salem, Mass., from England about 1638; his mother, Mary Stuart, was said to be the daughter of a Scotch nobleman and at the time of her marriage to David Dodge she was the widow of William Earl. The boyhood of David Low Dodge was not without its privations. He was early inclined to reading, but advantages were meager. At the age of six he attended a school kept by a spiritually minded Irish woman, Mary Moxley. From seven to fourteen, except for two months of district school each winter, he was employed on the farm in Hampton, Conn., to which his father had removed. The only books available were the Bible and the school primer, spelling-book, and arithmetic. After his fifteenth year there was little opportunity for schooling; but at nineteen he was a full-fledged schoolmaster, and in that calling he continued successfully for several years, at first in community schools and later in private ventures. On June 7, 1798, he was married to Sarah, daughter of the Rev. Aaron Cleveland [*q.v.*]. His wife's cousins, the Messrs. Higginson of Boston, who were large importers for that day, helped him to inform himself about the dry-goods trade, and in 1802 he began buying stocks of imported wares at Boston, transporting them by wagon to Connecticut, and selling at a good profit. He established a store at Hartford, with a branch at Litchfield. Prospering in this enterprise, in 1807 he started a jobbing business in New York City in co-partnership with the Higginsons, who within a few years suffered serious reverses in the Napoleonic wars. The New York house of Higginson, Dodge & Company was not involved in these losses, but a dissolution of the firm became necessary. In 1813 Dodge became manager of a cotton-mill near Norwich, Conn.

After his removal to New York, he had taken a more and more active part in religious and philanthropic efforts. In 1809 he wrote a pamphlet entitled, *The Mediator's Kingdom not of This World,* containing an argument against the lawfulness of war waged by Christians. He began a vigorous campaign to enlist the so-called evangelical churches of America in his war against war, entering into an extensive correspondence with such contemporary leaders as Lyman Beecher, John B. Romeyn, Walter King, and Aaron Cleveland. In 1812 appeared his second pamphlet, *War Inconsistent with the Religion of Jesus Christ,* and in the same year a group of men in New York, under his leadership, were ready to form a society to promote pacifist principles. They decided on postponement, however, because it was felt that during the war with England the motives of such propaganda might be misunderstood. On Aug. 16, 1815, after the close of the war, the New York Peace Society was launched, with thirty or forty members, representing various religious denominations. It is said to have been the first organization of its kind in the world. Dodge was the first president of the society and took the leading part in shaping its policies. He does not seem to have tried to interest persons outside the membership of churches. His arguments were based on the Scriptures, in the main, and addressed to Christians. His writings indicate, indeed, that he doubted the wisdom of making a more general appeal for the application of peace principles in human governments. He was a thoroughgoing Calvinist and all his pleas were couched in terms familiar to those versed in the precepts of that faith. So far did he carry his disapproval of every form of militarism that he would neither vote nor hold office. In 1827 he retired from business. In the following year the New York Peace Society united with other similar bodies that had been formed since 1815 in creating the American Peace Society. Dodge presided at the organization meeting of the new society, May 8, 1828, and at its first annual meeting, May 13, 1829, was a member of its board of directors, and later became a life director. He was also active in the founding of the New York Bible Society and the New York Tract Society. His son, William Earl Dodge [*q.v.*], and his grandson, of the same name, followed by great-grandsons, continued these and similar activities to the fourth generation.

[Near the close of his life Dodge prepared, at the request of his children, an autobiography. This, with a few selections from his writings, was published for the family at Boston as *Memorial of Mr. David L. Dodge, Consisting of an Autobiography . . . with a Few Selections from his Writings* (1854). Dodge's pamphlet, *War Inconsistent with the Religion of Jesus Christ,* was republished in 1905, with a biographical introduction by Edwin D. Mead. See also E. L. Whitney, *The Am. Peace Soc.: A Centennial Hist.* (1928); *Geneal. of the Dodge Family of Essex County, Mass.* (1894).]

W. B. S.

DODGE, EBENEZER (Apr. 21, 1819–Jan. 5, 1890), clergyman, theologian, educator, was born at Salem, Mass., the son of a sea captain, whose name he bore, and Joanna (Appleton) Dodge. Little is known of his youth save that his early religious influences came from his mother, while his pastor, Rev. Lucius Bolles of the Baptist Church, gave him a broader world horizon which doubtless had been extended by the maritime associations of his boyhood. At the age of seventeen, he entered Brown University from the Salem Latin School, having the legal profession in view; but a religious revival in the college awakened in him a positive conception of the Christian life, so that what he considered his conversion (see *One Honest Effort,* tract issued by the American Tract Society) was almost identical with his call to the ministry. His native scholarly talent was greatly stimulated by Francis Wayland, president of the University, from which he was graduated in 1840. Before proceeding to his theological studies, he served as principal of the academy at Shelburne Falls for two years and then entered Newton Theological Institution, graduating in 1845. Here the influence of Barnas Sears was especially important upon him. After a somewhat unsatisfactory year as teacher in an embryonic theological school at Covington, Ky., he became pastor of the Baptist Church at New Hampton (1846–49) and at New London, N. H. Both were rural fields with educational interests offering incentives to his mental development. In various ways he participated in the broader interests of the churches; in 1848, he made a penetrating report upon some questions at issue connected with the American and Foreign Bible Society.

In November 1853 he was elected professor of Biblical criticism in the Theological Institution at Hamilton, N. Y., and also professor of the evidences of revealed religion in Madison University (now Colgate), beginning his services the following month. Here his career was to continue, though definite calls came later both to Rochester and to Newton. In 1858–59, he spent more than a year in Europe, where he became especially well acquainted with the eminent theologians, Tholuck and Dorner. In 1861, he was transferred to the chair of doctrinal theology in the Seminary and in 1868 he was elected president of Madison University, retaining the professorships he already held, which had come to include psychology and Christian ethics. His administration of the University was marked by substantial progress in the development of the productive assets and by adjustments in the educational program to meet the changing conditions. The secondary and the theological instruction were both separated from the collegiate, the resultant Academy and the relatively more free Seminary being given his sympathetic and honest support. Long after his death, the traditions of his strength of character, his catholicity of feeling and his unselfish disinterestedness were still current on the campus, with many a striking epigram.

His only published book was *The Evidences of Christianity* (1869), but some of his lectures were privately printed for his students' use in his classes, among them a substantial volume entitled *Lectures in Christian Theology.* Dodge was twice married: first, in 1846, to Sarah Abbot Putnam of Salem, who died in 1861; and in 1863, to Eleanor F. Rogers of Providence, R. I., who survived him.

[Biographical sketches by Sylvester Burnham in the memorial number of the *Madisonensis,* Jan. 18, 1890; by Dodge's pastor and successor in the chair of theology, W. N. Clarke, *Baptist Quart. Rev.,* July 1890; a recent tribute by C. H. Dodd, *Crozer Quart.,* July 1925; and J. T. Dodge, *Geneal. of the Dodge Family of Essex County, Mass.* (1894).] W. H. A.

DODGE, GRACE HOADLEY (May 21, 1856–Dec. 27, 1914), social worker, philanthropist, was born in New York City, eldest of six children of William Earl Dodge, Jr., and Sarah Hoadley. She was a sister of Cleveland H. Dodge and a grand-daughter of William Earl Dodge [*q.v.*]. Her ancestors on both sides for several generations were business men and Grace Dodge had marked business ability. When she was seven, her father built Greyston, in Riverdale, N. J., her much loved summer home throughout life. Her first instruction was from governesses, one of whom taught her the promptness and attention to detail which were always characteristic of her. In 1872 she went to Miss Porter's School in Farmington, Conn., but left in 1874, went abroad with her parents, and on her return became absorbed in social work. Sunday-school and sewing classes and the Children's Aid Society first interested her. Soon she was chairman of the Committee on the Elevation of the Poor in their Homes of the State Charities Aid Association, and helped to initiate the struggle for tenement reform in 1879. Meanwhile she had assisted in the organization of the Kitchen Garden Association, for "the promotion of the Domestic Industrial Arts among the laboring classes" and had founded a working girls' club, from which grew the Associations of Working Girls' Societies. In much of this work she would probably have been more effective had her own education and training been more extended. Perhaps because of a realization of this, she came to believe strongly in education as an all-important social agency. During these early years, her summers at Riverdale were also filled with philanthropic activity. She started a village library, at first housed in her father's greenhouse, a Riverdale woman's club, and a sewing school for girls.

In 1884 the Kitchen Garden Association was dissolved and the Industrial Education Association took its place, with Dr. F. A. P. Barnard [*q.v.*], president of Columbia College, an honorary member. Grace Dodge became vice-president and performed most of the presidential duties. Because of this connection, she was appointed in 1886 a member of the New York City Board of Education. To coordinate home duties with organization business, she equipped an office in the basement of her Madison Avenue home and employed a secretary. She had set herself the task of introducing industrial education into the public schools; the report of a committee of the Board of Education on which she served secured the first experiment in this direction. The Industrial Education Association, with Nicholas Murray Butler as president, was developing in the direction of the training of teachers and in 1889, largely through its influence, the New York College for the Training of Teachers, located at 9 University Place, was provisionally chartered. When, in 1892, a new site was given on Morningside Heights, Grace Dodge became acting treasurer of the College and chairman of the finance committee of the Board of Trustees. In spite of the financial panic of 1893, she succeeded in raising money for completing the main building. Through difficult years, it was, in the words of Dr. James E. Russell, for over twenty-five years dean of Teachers College, "only Miss Dodge's faith that kept Teachers College alive." To her fell the task of raising money for new buildings, mortgage payments, additional professors, and any increases in the budget. Though Teachers College was now her chief interest, her other activities were numerous. In 1896 she resigned the directorship of the Working Girls' Societies, feeling that the movement had developed into an economic struggle, involving legislation and publicity for which she was unsuited. At her home the American Social Hygiene Association was formed, by the merging of five organizations of kindred aims. She was a founder of the New York Travelers Aid Society in 1907, and in her last days was working on plans for a National Travelers Aid Society. She was president of the Board of the Constantinople Woman's College from 1910 and contributed liberally to its needs. The greatest work of her later years was with the Young Women's Christian Associations: first as arbitrator in helping to unite the two overlapping organizations, under the International Board and the American Committee respectively; then, in 1906 as president of the National Board of the united Young Women's Christian Associations of the United States of America. In 1910 she attended the conference of the World's Young Women's Christian Associations in Berlin. She died in New York City, at the height of her many activities.

[Abbie Graham, *Grace H. Dodge; Merchant of Dreams* (1926), is the official biography published by the National Board of the Y. W. C. A. The memorial number of the *Association Monthly* (Y. W. C. A.), Mar. 1915, contains articles by a number of persons associated with her in social work. See also sketch in *Who's Who in America*, 1912–13; obituaries in the *N. Y. Tribune* and *N. Y. Times*, both Dec. 28, 1914.]

S. G. B.

DODGE, GRENVILLE MELLEN (Apr. 12, 1831–Jan. 3, 1916), civil engineer, politician, son of Sylvanus and Julia Theresa (Phillips) Dodge, was born in a farmhouse in Danvers, Mass. He was of English descent—eight generations removed from Richard Dodge who came to Salem, Mass., in 1638, and four generations removed from James Phillips who emigrated to America in 1700. As a boy Grenville M. Dodge was active, robust, and healthy. He drove a butcher's cart, clerked in a store, and worked on Mrs. Edward Lander's celebrated fruit and vegetable farm—where he gained valuable training in business methods—but he was also interested in books, went to school, and prepared for college. During the winter of 1845–46 he attended Durham Academy (N. H.). In 1848 he entered Norwich University (Vt.). He graduated from the scientific department of this institution, and finished at Partridge's private school in July 1851, receiving a diploma as a military and civil engineer. His college days fell in the period of "railroad excitement." Men were dreaming of a transportation system that would stretch from the Atlantic to the Pacific, and even college students were discussing the subject. Dodge became fired with enthusiasm for civil engineering and railroad building, and after graduating he made a beginning in this field at Peru, Ill., where two of his classmates had preceded him. His first job was surveying town lots. Parties, barn-dances, horseback riding, and "girls in flaming calico dresses" interested him. Here he met Anne Brown, and later (May 29, 1854), married her. Together with his classmates, the Ransom boys, he organized an artillery squad, which later saw service in quelling some labor trouble at Vermilionville. In January 1852 he was given a position with an engineering party on the Illinois Central Railroad, and in the autumn of that year he met Peter A. Dey, and was taken into one of his surveying parties. When Dey was selected to make the surveys across Iowa for the Mississippi & Missouri Railroad, he took Dodge with him as his chief assistant and put him in charge of the survey from Davenport to Iowa City (1853). From Iowa City, Dodge pushed on westward with his party and reached the Missouri River near the village of Council Bluffs on Nov. 22, 1853. Here he was to make his permanent home. From 1855 to 1861 he was engaged in railroad construction work in Iowa, and in mercantile business in Council Bluffs, helped to organize a bank, made some reconnaissances and surveys west of the Missouri River under the patronage of Henry Farnham and Thomas C. Durant, traded with the Indians, and did some freighting on the plains between the Missouri River and Denver.

At the outbreak of the Civil War, he tendered his services and the services of the Council Bluffs Guards, a company which he had organized in 1856, to Gov. Kirkwood. Appointed first to a position on the governor's staff, then to the colonelcy of the 4th Iowa Regiment, he saw active service in the field in Missouri, Kentucky, Tennessee, Mississippi, Alabama, and Georgia, and in the end was promoted to the rank of major-general of volunteers. Early in the war he was wounded at the battle of Pea Ridge. On Aug. 19, 1864, in front of Atlanta he was severely wounded in the head and compelled to retire temporarily from active service. He visited Grant's headquarters at City Point upon invitation; and interviewed Lincoln in Washington. Upon his return to the field (Nov. 1, 1864) he saw service in Missouri, and later against the Indians in the country west of the Missouri River. During the war his services both as a soldier and as an engineer were distinguished. In three days he built a bridge 14 feet high and 710 feet long across the Chattahoochee River. For his skill and efficiency in building bridges and reconstructing and equipping railroads for the use of the army, he was highly commended by Gen. Grant.

Relieved of his military command at his own request (May 1866), he immediately entered upon his duties as chief engineer of the Union Pacific Railroad, to which position he had been appointed in January 1866. The first grading on this road had been done in the autumn of 1864; the first rail was laid in July 1865; and the last spike was nailed on May 10, 1869. In one year 568 miles of road were located, built, and equipped. The completion of this stupendous project was the fulfilment of the great ambition of Dodge's life. In January 1870 he resigned as chief engineer. He became chief engineer of the Texas & Pacific Railway in 1871, and upon the failure of that road in the panic of 1873 joined Jay Gould [*q.v.*] in railroad development in the Southwest. During the ten years of this association he assisted in the building and consolidation of nearly nine thousand miles of road (Perkins, *post,* p. 262). Among the roads in the construction of which he was interested in the later eighties were the Denver, Texas & Fort Worth, and the Denver, Texas & Gulf. He was president of the Union Pacific, Denver & Gulf in 1892, but the road went into the hands of receivers in the following year and he resigned his office. After the war with Spain, in association with Sir William Horne, he organized the Cuba Railroad Company and by 1903 had completed the line from Santa Clara to Santiago. This was his last piece of railroad construction.

Dodge's surveys alone totaled approximately 60,000 miles. For half a century he was active as projector, builder, financier and director of railroads in the West and Southwest and was called by some the ablest railroad lobbyist of his time. His record places him high among the railroad builders of the world. In politics he was a Republican; he attended the national party conventions; took an active part in presidential elections; and always, of course, kept a watchful eye on railroad legislation. In 1866 he was elected to Congress from the 5th Congressional District in Iowa. He declined a renomination in 1868 in order to devote all of his energies to the construction of the Union Pacific. In his later years he was much interested in patriotic organizations such as the Society of the Army of the Tennessee and the Military Order of the Loyal Legion.

[Letters (1856–1916) and an incomplete autobiographical MS. are deposited in the rooms of the Historical, Memorial, and Art Building, Des Moines, Iowa. The best published sources of information are: J. R. Perkins, *Trails, Rails and War—The Life of Gen. G. M. Dodge* (1929); *A Brief Biog. Sketch of the Life of Maj. Gen. Grenville M. Dodge* (1893), comp. from official records by his private secretary, J. T. Granger; and "In Memoriam: Grenville Mellen Dodge," in the *Norwich Univ. Record,* Jan. 29, 1916. See also H. H. Field and J. R. Reed, *Hist. of Pottawattamie County, Iowa* (1907), vol. I; *Who's Who in America,* 1914–15; J. T. Dodge, *Geneal. of the Dodge Family of Essex County, Mass.* (1894).]

B. F. S.

DODGE, HENRY (Oct. 12, 1782–June 19, 1867), soldier, governor, United States senator, was born at Post Vincennes (now Vincennes, Ind.), three years after its capture by George Rogers Clark. His father, Israel Dodge, a Revolutionary soldier, had moved west and married Nancy Ann Hunter, a girl of the Kentucky frontier. After a number of years in the Illinois country and Kentucky, the Dodges crossed the Mississippi and settled in the Ste. Genevieve district of Spanish Louisiana. Here Henry Dodge reached maturity, receiving little formal education but assisting his father in the various frontier occupations of lead mining, farming, brewing and distilling. In 1800 he married Christina McDonald. Five years later he succeeded his father as sheriff of the Ste. Genevieve district, and held this office for sixteen years. From 1813 he served as marshal of the Territory of Missouri, and in the Missouri militia he rose to the grade of major-general.

Dodge

After the War of 1812, in which he led troops to the relief of the Boone Lick settlement on the Missouri, he returned to lead mining, but the fame of the mineral fields of the Upper Mississippi River caused him to migrate in 1827, settling finally in the region of the present Dodgeville, Wis., then a part of the Territory of Michigan. He commanded a force of mounted volunteers in the Winnebago War of 1827, and took a distinguished part in the Black Hawk War in 1832. His military success led to his appointment by President Jackson as major of a battalion of mounted rangers, recruited to patrol the frontier in the Upper Mississippi Valley. In 1833 this body was replaced by the first regiment of United States dragoons with Dodge as its colonel. Its range of activity is indicated by the march to the Pawnee villages on the upper waters of the Red River in 1834, and the expedition in 1835 to the Rocky Mountains in Colorado.

When the Territory of Michigan was divided in 1836, Dodge was made governor of the Territory of Wisconsin, which comprised the present states of Wisconsin, Minnesota, and Iowa, and parts of the Dakotas. In 1838 the land west of the Mississippi was separately organized as the Territory of Iowa. Dodge continued as governor of the diminished Territory of Wisconsin until 1841 when he was replaced by a Whig. The people, however, at once elected him as their delegate in Congress and in this capacity he served until a Democratic president in 1845 restored him to the office of governor. Three years later Wisconsin was admitted to statehood and Dodge became one of its first United States senators. In 1857 he retired from the Senate and from public life, and died a decade later in his eighty-fifth year.

He was primarily a soldier and a frontiersman. Over six feet in height, erect, aggressive, and courageous, he commanded the respect of his soldiers and of the Indians with whom he waged war and negotiated treaties. His greatest contribution to public life was his service of eight years as governor of a pioneer territory. His varied experiences on the border prepared him for the duties pertaining to the government of settlers and for the associated duties of superintendent of Indian affairs. As delegate to Congress and senator his record is merely that of a conscientious servant of his constituents, whose instructions he sought faithfully to carry out. An interesting instance is his vote against the Kansas-Nebraska Bill which his son and senatorial colleague from Iowa, Augustus Cæsar Dodge [*q.v.*], was warmly espousing.

[The most important body of original material on Dodge consists of commissions, military order book, and letters in the Hist. Dept. of Iowa at Des Moines. For the history of the dragoons see Louis Pelzer, *The Marches of the Dragoons in the Mississippi Valley* (1917). The best biography of Dodge is Louis Pelzer, *Henry Dodge* (1911). See also William Salter, "Henry Dodge," in the *Iowa Hist. Record*, vols. V and VI (Oct. 1889–Apr. 1890), and Moses M. Strong, *Hist. of the Territory of Wis.* (1885).]

J. C. P.

DODGE, JACOB RICHARDS (Sept. 28, 1823–Oct. 1, 1902), agricultural statistician and journalist, was born at New Boston, N. H., the son of Capt. Jacob D. Dodge and Tryphena (Colburn) Dodge. He was a descendant in the seventh generation of Richard Dodge, who emigrated from Somerset, England, in 1638 and settled in Salem, Mass. At an early age he moved with his family to Nashua, N. H. His education was obtained in common schools and academies. Between 1845 and 1849 he was in charge of an academy in Mississippi. His tastes then led him into journalism. He was editor and publisher of the *Oasis*, Nashua, N. H., from 1850 to 1854, and of the *American Ruralist*, Springfield, Ohio, from 1857 to 1861. He was Senate reporter of the Washington *National Intelligencer* and of the *National Republican* from 1861 to 1862. On the organization of the United States Department of Agriculture in 1862, he entered its employ, becoming editor, and in May 1866, statistician. He continued to serve, however, as editor. The early annual reports of the Department were edited by him as were also the monthly reports of the Division of Statistics. The principal features of the latter were the crop reports, but they also included a large amount of miscellaneous and valuable statistical matter. Dodge soon became eminent among American statisticians and held a foremost place in all statistical matters relating to agriculture. In 1873 he spent the summer in Europe, under a commission from the Department of Agriculture for investigating the statistical methods of European countries, and as one of the commissioners to the Vienna World's Exposition by appointment from the State Department. He resigned his position in the Department of Agriculture in 1878, intending to reënter agricultural journalism, but was induced by the secretary of the treasury to accept a temporary commission for the investigation of commercial agriculture. In 1879 he took charge of the agricultural statistics of the Tenth Census, under Gen. Francis A. Walker, superintendent. Two years later he was recalled to his former position as statistician of the Department of Agriculture. Under a special congressional appropriation he attended the session of the International Statistical Institute in 1887 as a delegate from the Department of Agriculture. He made a more thorough investigation of the statistical bureaus of London, Paris, Rome, Vienna, and Berlin. The Paris Exposition of 1889 awarded him a gold medal for exhibits of graphic illustrations of agricultural statistics. During his more than thirty years of official service he won not only the esteem and confidence of his associates, but recognition by the public at large as a man of rare attainments, broad views, sound judgment, and sterling quality. A study of the history of the Department of Agriculture shows the large part he took in its early development. He finally resigned his position on Mar. 20, 1893, shortly after the change of administration. After his retirement he joined the editorial staff of the *Country Gentleman* as statistical editor, which position he held until his death. Though he was a frequent contributor to magazines, newspapers, and the farm press, and the author of several books, his most voluminous literary work appears in the official monthly, annual, and special reports of the Department of Agriculture from 1862 to 1893. In politics he was a Republican and in his unofficial writings an avowed and ardent protectionist. He was at one time treasurer of the American Protective Association and prepared several brochures on protection for distribution by protectionist organizations. He was married in October 1846, to Frances G. Buxton of Nashua, N. H., by whom he had one child, Charles Richards Dodge. His death occurred in his eightieth year, at Nashua, where he was buried.

[Five scrapbooks of contributions to the agricultural press, in U. S. Dept. of Agric. Library; *Home Market Bull.*, Boston, Apr. 1899; *Country Gentleman*, Oct. 9, 1902; *Experiment Station Record*, Oct. 1902; *Nashua Daily Telegraph*, June 2, 1893, quoted in J. T. Dodge, *Geneal. of the Dodge Family of Essex County, Mass.*, vol. I (1894).] C. R. B.

DODGE, MARY ABIGAIL (Mar. 31, 1833–Aug. 17, 1896), author, under the pseudonym Gail Hamilton, was born in Hamilton, Mass., the seventh and youngest child of James Brown Dodge and Hannah (Stanwood) Dodge. Her ancestors, of pure English stock, had lived in the same New England county for two hundred years. Very early in childhood she showed evidence of the tremendous vitality and activity that were later to be the recognized qualities of "Gail Hamilton." At two years she not only talked but gave recitations from memory; she is reported to have taken up advanced geography when five years old and to have written creditable essays at six. She received her formal education in Ipswich, Mass., graduating from the Ipswich Female Seminary in 1850. At the age of twenty-one she became a teacher of English in a high school in Hartford. This position she held until September 1858 when she went to Washington, D. C., to become the governess of the children of Dr. Gamaliel Bailey, the editor of the anti-slavery organ, the *National Era*. Having already, while at Hartford, begun to write for newspapers, as "Gail Hamilton," she now became a regular contributor to the *National Era*. This early work was marked by the same vigorous and rationalistic approach to her subject and the same ready, effervescent wit which caused her later essays to run into edition after edition. Following her two years with the Baileys, she returned to Hamilton to take care of her invalid mother, and remained there until the latter's death in 1868. During these years, she edited, in 1865–67, together with J. T. Trowbridge and Lucy Larcom, *Our Young Folks,* an illustrated magazine for boys and girls which was later merged with *St. Nicholas,* and published somewhat more than a dozen volumes of essays, of which the most notable were *Country Living and Country Thinking* (1862), *A New Atmosphere* (1865), and *Woman's Wrongs: A Counter-Irritant* (1868). All these books had been brought out by Ticknor & Fields, with whom Miss Dodge's relations had been uniformly cordial, but, in 1868, becoming convinced that she had been defrauded in the matter of royalties, she severed connection with the firm, and, in 1870, brought out in *The Battle of the Books,* a veiled account of the whole transaction, written in her usual sprightly, caustic style, but devoid of malice. In January 1871 she moved to Washington which was henceforth to be the center of her activities, varied, however, by frequent trips to Hamilton, a journey across the Continent in 1873, and a trip to Europe in 1887–88. She edited, with S. S. Wood, *Wood's Household Magazine* (1872–73), and continued to produce numerous volumes. Of these the most important were: *Woman's Worth and Worthlessness* (1872), *Our Common School System* (1880), *A Washington Bible Class* (1891), *Biography of James G. Blaine* (1895), and *X Rays* (1896). Owing to her charm of manner, prestige as a writer, and position in Washington—she was a cousin of the wife of James G. Blaine—she is said to have exerted some influence over American politics, in which she was keenly interested throughout her adult life. Such indirect influence she felt to be woman's only proper function in politics, and during a stanch advocacy of other liberal causes she was thoroughly opposed to woman suffrage.

[There is little biographical information beyond that to be found in the carelessly edited *Gail Hamilton's Life in Letters* (2 vols., 1901), and in scatttered notes, of which see especially Wallace Rice in *Dial*, Sept. 16, 1901; *Independent*, Nov. 14, 1901; *Critic*, Aug. 22, 1896; M. B. Thrasher in *Arena*, Dec. 1896.] G. G.

DODGE, MARY ELIZABETH MAPES (Jan. 26, 1831–Aug. 21, 1905), editor, author, was one of the three daughters of Prof. James Jay Mapes, free-lance scientist and inventor, and Sophia (Furman) Mapes, and a descendant of Gen. Jonas Mapes who served in the War of 1812. The Mapes home in New York City, where Mary was born, was frequented by literary and scientific people, among them William Cullen Bryant and Horace Greeley. The Mapes children were educated at home by tutors, and under their father's guidance became familiar with the best in English literature. In 1851 Mary Mapes married William Dodge, New York lawyer, who died in 1858. Under the necessity of supporting her two sons she went to live in her father's home, now near Newark, N. J., and began writing. In a deserted farmhouse near by she fitted up a workshop, decorated with Florida moss and leaves, furnished with cast-off furniture, and warmed by a Franklin stove. Here she worked for regular hours and after work played with her boys and their friends. She was their companion, and tramped, collected specimens, swam, and skated with them. One of the sons died in 1881; the other became an inventor and manufacturer. Her writing was quickly accepted by magazines. Her first volume of children's stories was *Irvington Stories* (1864). *Hans Brinker; or the Silver Skates* (1865), begun as a serial, grew into a book. The idea came from reading Motley's *Rise of the Dutch Republic*, and for years she collected material on Dutch life, though she had never seen Holland. Dutch friends in New York acted as critics. The book had immediate success and has remained her best work and a leading juvenile classic. It was translated into many foreign languages and received a prize from the French Academy. When she afterward visited Holland, *Hans Brinker* was recommended to her son by a Dutch bookseller as the best juvenile story of Dutch life. Her other books are: *A Few Friends and How They Amused Themselves* (1869); *Rhymes and Jingles* (1874); *Theophilus and Others* (1876); *Along the Way* (1879), verse; *Donald and Dorothy* (1883); *When Life is Young* (1894), verse; and *The Land of Pluck* (1894). She wrote frequently for the *Atlantic Monthly*, the *Century*, and *Harper's Magazine*. In 1870 she became associate editor of *Hearth and Home*. The directors of the Century Company, noticing her work here in 1873 secured her as editor for their new juvenile monthly, which she named *St. Nicholas Magazine*. She continued in this position until her death and her sane policy and personal supervision made *St. Nicholas* a leader in its class. She excluded preachiness, sentimentalism, the morbid, and the inartistic. Her acquaintance with authors helped in securing contributions. Her volumes for little children, *Baby Days* (1876) and *Baby World* (1884), were compiled from her contributions to *St. Nicholas*. During this period her home was an apartment near Central Park, New York. In 1888 she purchased "Yarrow Cottage," at Onteora Park in the Catskills. She later added to the cottage, where she always spent as long a summer as possible. There she went in her last illness, hoping for healing among her loved mountains, and there, at the height of summer, she died. The children of the community, all her friends, formed the procession at her funeral. Mrs. Dodge's personality was adapted to both success and friendship. She was brilliant, original, and possessed of discriminating judgment and executive ability. Her sympathy and love of fun never failed. She was a woman of fine appearance, with a full oval face, soft wavy hair, a small nose, and a pouting, childlike mouth. Years drew character lines in her face but made her only more handsome. Her successor as editor of *St. Nicholas* places her, probably with justice, as "the recognized leader in juvenile literature for almost a third of a century." Her stories, wholesome but not "goody-goody," have suggestive atmosphere and truthful characterization. Her verse has humor, quaint turns of thought, and a quality which does not grow old.

["In Memory of Mary Mapes Dodge," by her successor, William Fayal Clarke, in *St. Nicholas*, Oct. 1905; "Mary Mapes Dodge: an Intimate Tribute," by her friend, Sarah S. McEnery, in *The Critic*, Oct. 1905; *Who's Who in America*, 1903–05; Frances E. Willard and Mary A. Livermore, *Am. Women* (1897), vol. I; Lucia Gilbert Runkle, *Our Famous Women* (1884); obituaries in *N. Y. Tribune*, and *N. Y. Times*, Aug. 22, 1905.] S. G. B.

DODGE, THEODORE AYRAULT (May 28, 1842–Oct. 25, 1909), military historian, son of Nathaniel S. and Emily (Pomeroy) Dodge, was born at Pittsfield, Mass. He was educated abroad, in Berlin, at the University of Heidelberg, and at University College, London. He returned to the United States in July 1861 and at once enlisted in the New York militia. He entered the volunteer army as a first lieutenant, 101st New York Infantry, Feb. 13, 1862, served in the defenses of Washington until May, and then took part in the Peninsular campaign, commanding his company throughout. He was slightly wounded at Chantilly, in the northern Virginia campaign that summer, and immediately after was taken sick with typhoid fever, which kept him from duty until November. He then joined the 119th New York Infantry, to which he had been transferred, and served as its adjutant at Fredericksburg and Chancellorsville. He was wounded on the first day at Gettysburg, and fell into the hands of the Confederates, but was left behind during their retreat after the battle and did not remain a prisoner. His wound required the amputation of his right leg below the knee. Disabled for field service, he was appointed a captain in the Veteran Reserve Corps, Nov. 12, 1863, and assigned to duty in Washington, where he was in charge of the enrolment branch, and later of the deserters' branch, of the Provost Marshal-General's office. He was promoted to major, Aug. 17, 1864, and mustered out of the volunteer service, Dec. 1, 1866. Meanwhile he had taken a bachelor's degree in law at Columbian (now George Washington) University. Appointed captain of infantry in the regular army, July 28, 1866, and later brevetted lieutenant-colonel, he served as superintendent of the War Department buildings until infirmity resulting from his wound caused his retirement from active service, Apr. 28, 1870. He was promoted to major on the retired list in 1904. Upon retirement from military service he made his home at Cambridge, Mass., and entered upon a business career with the purpose of "gathering a fortune which should leave him free for the more congenial pursuit of letters" (Livermore, *post*, p. 211), becoming treasurer and manager of the McKay Sewing Machine Company in 1870. Later, having purchased several patents and become interested in the manufacture of cotton woven hose, he resigned from the McKay Company and in 1880, took the presidency of the Boston Woven Hose Company which became one of the largest manufacturers of rubber, and especially of single-tube tires, in the United States. His business did not absorb all his time, however, some of which he was able to devote to military history. His first studies were concerned with the Civil War, but his books—*The Campaign of Chancellorsville* (1881), and *A Bird's-eye View of Our Civil War* (1883)—were not published until after he had extended his researches to a wider field. In 1877 he went abroad for two years to study European campaigns, and this visit was followed by repeated trips, in the course of which he crossed the ocean over eighty times, until finally, after his retirement from business in 1900, he took up his home in Paris, in order to make use of its library facilities in studying the career of Napoleon. He planned a history of the art of war, as exemplified in the careers of "great captains." The first work, *Alexander*, appeared in 1890, and was followed by *Hannibal* (1891), *Cæsar* (1892), *Gustavus Adolphus* (1895), and *Napoleon* (4 vols., 1904–07). These are careful studies, based not only on examination of written records but also on personal inspection of the actual battle sites in Europe, Asia, and northern Africa, where he made his own topographical sketches. In the United States there was little appreciation of the practical value of the study of early military history, and at the time of their publication his works attracted the interest of classical scholars rather than of soldiers. The World War has brought about some change in this respect. A series of lectures delivered by Dodge before the Lowell Institute was also published (1889) under the title of *Great Captains*, the name he adopted to designate the series of works already referred to. His literary activity was not confined to military subjects. He wrote numerous essays, reviews, and even verses, and published two books inspired by his interest in horsemanship, *Patroclus and Penelope* (1885), and *Riders of Many Lands* (1894). He was a member of the Massachusetts Historical Society, and a visiting lecturer at Harvard University. He was twice married, first, on Oct. 19, 1865, to Jane Marshall Neil of Columbus, and second, on Oct. 8, 1892, to Clara Isabel Bowden of Boston, who survived him. He died at the Château de Rozières, near Nanteuil-le-Haudouin, in the department of the Oise, and was buried in Arlington National Cemetery.

[This account is based largely on unpublished records in the War Department; F. B. Heitman, *Hist. Reg. and Dict. of the U. S. Army* (1903), I, 377; *Who's Who in America*, 1908–09; memoir by T. L. Livermore in *Proc. Mass. Hist. Soc.*, 1909–10; A. H. Pomeroy, *Hist. and Geneal. of the Pomeroy Family* (1912), pp. 469–71. Dodge's report on the work of his office in 1864–66 is in *Official Records (Army)*, 3 ser., V, 750–58.]
T. M. S.

DODGE, WILLIAM EARL (Sept. 4, 1805–Feb. 9, 1883), merchant, was born at Hartford, Conn. His father was David Low Dodge [*q.v.*], a school-teacher who became a business man; his mother, Sarah Cleveland. During his boyhood the family, because of changes in the father's business connections, lived for several years in New York City, and New Jersey. William's schooling was obtained in Norwich, Conn., New York City, and Mendham, N. J. He seems to have inherited from his father a certain literary bent, which, however, was never freely followed. When only thirteen years old he began work in a wholesale dry-goods store in New York City. A year later he was employed as a clerk in the country store connected with his father's factory in Connecticut. After the elder Dodge had entered the New York dry-goods trade, in 1825, the son assisted him in the Beekman St. store; but after reaching his majority he went into the wholesale business on his own account. His marriage on June 24, 1828, to Melissa Phelps connected him with a New York family distinguished for its wealth and enterprise in business. His father-in-law had been successful in the metals trade and in 1833 young Dodge retired from dry-goods merchandizing and joined the firm of Phelps, Dodge & Company, which for two generations held a foremost place as dealers in copper and other metals. The firm had an important part in the development of Lake Superior copper and of Pennsylvania iron. Dodge personally made heavy investments outside the metals trade. He bought pine lands extensively in Pennsylvania, Michigan, Wisconsin, and the South. He was also a large stockholder in railroad enterprises—the Erie, Lackawanna, Jersey Central, and Texas Central. He was early interested in religious and philanthropic effort, was one of the organizers and always a stanch supporter of the Young Men's Christian Association in America, and later had a prominent part in the work of the Evangelical Alliance. His public identification with temperance reforms may be dated from the Washingtonian movement of 1840, although as a boy and young man he had been impressed by the evils of alcoholism, and his father had brought about prohibition of the liquor traffic in his Connecticut factory settlement. William supported the work of John B. Gough and Father Mathew as temperance advocates. In 1854 he was one of the leaders in the political campaign that carried New York State for prohibition by a small plurality. From 1865 to his death in 1883, he was president of the National Temperance Society and was characterized by Dr. Theodore L. Cuyler as "the most catholic representative of the temperance reform in all its phases and activities" (*Our Leader and His Life*, 1883, by T. L. Cuyler). He proposed a national commission of inquiry on the liquor traffic. In politics, he escaped many of the bitter antagonisms to which men of prominence were frequently subjected in his day. He was known as an anti-slavery man and yet seems to have retained the respect and good-will of those Southern communities in which he had extensive business interests. He was a member of the unsuccessful Peace Conference held at Washington in February 1861. After the Civil War had begun he helped to arm and equip Union soldiers in West Virginia and East Tennessee. In 1865 he delivered an address at Baltimore on *The Influence of the War on our National Prosperity*. He was distinctly in advance of his time in pointing out the positive evils and the ultimate futility of war. As a Republican member of Congress from New York City in 1866, he urged moderation in reconstruction measures and maintained an attitude toward the South similar to that which was held ten years later by President Hayes. Dodge was a man of fine physical presence and had a winning manner. He left a son, of the same name, who continued an active interest in the public causes to which his father had been devoted.

[*Memorials of Wm. E. Dodge* (1887), compiled and edited by D. Stuart Dodge; Carlos Martyn, *Wm. E. Dodge: The Christian Merchant* (1890); J. T. Dodge, *Geneal. of the Dodge Family of Essex County, Mass.* (1894).]

W. B. S.

DODS, JOHN BOVEE (1795–Mar. 21, 1872), spiritualist, was born in New York City. He was of a Swiss Huguenot family called Beaufils, but adopted the name Dods from a Dutchman who married his aunt. He preached many years in Levant, Penobscot County, Me., early dabbling in new and strange theories, particularly concerned with psychic phenomena, and continually expounding these theories from the pulpit. In 1836 he moved to Provincetown, Mass., and began to preach universalism. He published a volume entitled *Thirty Short Sermons on Various Important Subjects, Doctrinal and Practical,* in which he defended his universalistic ideas, such as his disbelief in hell, his denial of Christ's divine origin, and his emphasis on the universal Fatherhood of God. He founded a school, called "The Academy," published an English grammar, and devoted much of his time to scholarly pursuits.

His universalism was soon eclipsed by his theories on psychic phenomena. On this subject he published the following works: *Six Lectures on the Philosophy of Mesmerism* (1843); *The Philosophy of Electrical Psychology* (1850); *Immortality Triumphant* (1852); and *Spirit Manifestations Examined and Explained* (1854). Like Dr. Edward Coit Rogers, he at first tried to explain these phenomena neurologically, but whereas Rogers emphasized the action of the cerebrum under the action of a certain "odic force," Dods emphasized the "automatic action of the cerebellum" under some sort of electrical influence. He had vague ideas about the rôle of nerve centers in hypnotism, and several other general theories. The precise mechanisms, however, he failed to understand. Nevertheless he supplemented his philosophical theories and his preaching by continual experiments, demonstrations, and practical lectures.

Hardly had he gotten his cerebellum theory well launched than he abandoned it and joined the spiritualist movement and church. His daughter, Jennie, was a good medium, and with her help Dods soon spread spiritualist practises and teachings. His own interest apparently was chiefly in the medical problems connected with mental disorders. He was commonly called Dr. Dods, though he was merely an amateur physician, practising on his congregations and on his family. He was one of the first to use electricity for therapeutic purposes; he continually carried on experiments in drugs, hypnotism, massage, etc., and gained a sufficient reputation and income from his various devices to enable his widow to build up a practise with them. He was married three times. By his first wife (Mercy Hodgdon), he had three daughters and one son; by his second, one child, and none by the third. He died in Brooklyn, N. Y., Mar. 21, 1872.

[Simeon G. Smith, *Leaves from an Old Church Record Book* (1922); Frank Podmore, *Modern Spiritualism*, vol. I (1902); Emma Hardinge Britten, *Modern Am. Spiritualism* (1870), *Nineteenth Century Minds* (1884).]
H. W. S.
R. R.

DOE, CHARLES (Apr. 11, 1830–Mar. 9, 1896), jurist, was born in Derry, N. H., the youngest child of Joseph Doe, Jr., and Mary Bodwell (Ricker) Doe. He was descended from Nicholas Doe, who, according to family tradition, came from London, England, and who was living at Oyster River, N. H., in 1666. Charles's father, a large landowner and farmer of Somersworth (later Rollinsford), and a member of the legislature, being well off, the boy enjoyed a good education at the academies of South Berwick, Exeter, and Andover, after which he went to Harvard College for a term, and thence to Dartmouth College where he graduated in 1849. He then entered the law office of Daniel M. Christie of Dover, N. H., and subsequently passed some time at the Harvard Law School, but, being offered the post of solicitor for Strafford County, did not complete his course. He accepted the office, was called to the bar in January 1854, and commenced practise at Dover. As county solicitor he had much criminal work, and his family connections assisted him to acquire a good share of the civil business of the neighborhood. He had at an early age taken an active interest in politics on the Democratic side, being assistant clerk of the state Senate in 1853 and 1854 and appearing frequently on the public platform. In 1856 he was, upon an address of the Republican legislature, removed from his office of county solicitor, but three years later he joined the Republican party, being urged thereto by the Democratic attitude toward the growing disaffection in the Southern states and his realization that in this matter there could be no compromise. To the general surprise he was appointed an associate justice of the supreme judicial court of New Hampshire, Sept. 23, 1859. For a considerable time thereafter his position was a difficult one, since politically he was extremely unpopular with a strong element, and in legal circles, owing to his unconventional type of mind and strong reform tendencies, he was unacceptable to the elder generation of judges and practitioners alike. Indifferent however to this under-current of dislike and the more open opposition of personages prominent in public and professional circles, he resolutely adhered to the principles of conduct which he had formulated for himself and declining to modify his views on legal reform, in course of time, earned the respect, if not the assent, of the bar, and impressed the public with his absolute sincerity of purpose. His efficiency and competence were demonstrated from the outset of his judicial career. He never, however, overcame the animosity of his political opponents, and when in 1874 the Democrats obtained control of the legislature, they proceeded to reorganize the state courts, doing away with the supreme judicial court, and substituting a superior court of judicature to which he was not appointed. He did not resume practise, but returned to his home at Rollinsford, and there lived in retirement, declining a proffered nomination for Congress. In 1876, however, the Republican party regained power, created the supreme court of New Hampshire and he was offered and accepted the position of chief justice. Having conceived a distaste for trial work, he made an arrangement with his colleagues in 1878 by which he was relieved of most of the Trial Term business and concentrated his attention on the Law Term. His peculiar genius was afforded full opportunity on the Appeal side of the court, and "for nearly twenty years . . . by the general *concensus* of his contemporaries he was the foremost man of the profession in the state; foremost not merely in name or in official position, but in fact" (Smith, *post*, p. 149). His health now commenced to cause him anxiety, and he experienced recurrent attacks of insomnia. In 1887 he took a vacation in Europe, spending some time in Great Britain and France. On his return he resumed his judicial duties, but never regained his former vigor. His intellect, nevertheless, was unimpaired and he continued to take a dominant part in the administration of justice up to the day of his death, which occurred suddenly at Rollinsford. On Apr. 11, 1865, he married Edith, daughter of George Wallis Haven of Portsmouth, N. H.

The remarkable series of opinions rendered by Doe when chief justice indicate his outstanding legal attainments, and have left an ineffaceable impression upon the law of New Hampshire. Originality marked all his work, and he declined to be bound by precedent, saying, "as there was a time when no precedents existed, everything that can be done with them can be done without them." At the same time, somewhat paradoxically, he delighted in research, frequently investigating legal principles to their foundation, and embodying the result of his labors in opinions which were treatises on the law involved. In *Hale* vs. *Everett* (53 *N. H.*, 8, 133–277), his opinion extended to 144 pages of the report, and it is said that he devoted a whole summer to study of history and theology prior to writing it. His influence was most powerfully exercised, however, in the field of procedure, where he effected a revolution by a radical departure from well-established principles. He held that common law rights existed independently of any particular writ, that a mistake in procedure was formal merely, and not substantive, and therefore that the court had power to effect any necessary amendments independently of the legislature. On this principle, historically untrue, he brought about procedural reforms which were effective, though radical, by means of court decisions and without recourse to legislation. Apart from law his acquaintance with literature was slight, since he never read unless he had some special object in so doing, and it is said that he read only one novel in his life.

In appearance and manner he was plain and unassuming, having a strong aversion to ceremony. He is pictured in middle age as "of medium height, slightly bent, his beard shaggy and grizzled. He might have been a country storekeeper, a farmer, or a lumberman. He wore a sort of brown frock coat, coarse trousers and heavy boots or brogans, which showed no trace of blacking. An old battered straw hat completed the ordinary summer costume of the chief justice of New Hampshire. In winter he frequently wore a dark-blue cloth cap with laps to pull down over the ears; and he wore in court a coarse rug which onlookers insist was a horse-blanket" (Henning, *post*). He was a thorough believer in fresh air and on the coldest days in winter would have all the windows of his courtroom wide open, despite all protest from bar, jury, and public.

[The family antecedents are detailed in *The Descendants of Nicholas Doe* (1918), by Elmer E. Doe. The article "Chas. Doe" by C. D. Henning in *Great Am. Lawyers*, VIII (1909), 241, and "Memoir of Chas. Doe," by Jeremiah Smith in *Proc. Southern N. H. Bar Asso.*, 1897, p. 125, are excellent appreciations of his character and legal achievements. See also *Harvard Law Rev.*, IX, 534; *Am. Law Review*, XXX, 286; *Albany Law Jour.*, LIII, 161, and "Memories of Judge Doe" by Robt. G. Pike in *Proc. of the Bar Asso. of the State of N. H.* (1916).]

H. W. H. K.

DOLAN, THOMAS (Oct. 27, 1834–June 12, 1914), capitalist, was born in Montgomery County, Pa., of obscure ancestry. His formal schooling was limited to a few years in the public schools, his career in business beginning when he became salesman in a store at the age of fifteen. Seven years later his connection with the wholesale knit-goods business began. During the industrial depression of the early Civil War period he successfully reorganized a factory under the firm name of the Keystone Knitting Mills, and maneuvered himself into a position of virtual monopoly in his particular branch of the industry. His business acumen found expression in adaptations not only to war-time conditions but to changes of fashion during the following decades. To meet successive shifts in the demand for fabrics, he reorganized his business for the manufacture, in turn, of knit goods, worsted shawls, and worsted coating goods. His initiative found expression more significantly in important innovations in technology, chiefly the use of electric power in factories. As early as 1882 he became a director of the United Gas Improvement Company of Philadelphia, and he expanded his activities in the fields of public utilities until his interests extended over a large part of the country. In this way he became a national figure in the earlier development of gas and electric lighting and power facilities.

He was made president of the United Gas Improvement Company in 1892, and five years later his company secured a thirty-year lease of the city's gas lighting system, the city retaining the option of resuming operation at the end of ten years. In 1905 the question was reopened. Should the city exercise its option, or continue the existing lease, or negotiate with the company for a new lease? The third course was chosen. The company's operation of the system had been profitable alike to the company and to the city. But on Apr. 20 the Select Council adopted resolutions instructing its finance committee to propose a new lease by which the city would surrender annual payments under the existing lease in return for a cash consideration. The alleged motive was the avoiding of increased taxes and borrowings for needed public improvements. The result was a political storm that attracted nation-wide attention, with Dolan, president of the company, the storm center. It was widely believed that the political organization in control of the city was proposing to mortgage or "rob" the city's future for the sake of ready money for corrupt uses. City officials nevertheless disregarded the storm signals and proceeded to open negotiations for a new lease. As finally adopted in Council, the proposed new lease was to expire in 1980 instead of 1927, and the payments to the city were to amount to $25,000,000 (Philadelphia *Public Ledger,* Apr. 21, 27, May 19, 1905). These actions were accompanied by city-wide organized remonstrances and by threats of violence which went so far as the wearing of buttons bearing a picture of a gallows and the inscription, "No gas steal. The last resort. We mean it" (*Ibid.,* May 3, 1905). Mayor John Weaver was at length induced to veto the Council's bill, and while steps were being taken to pass the bill over the veto, Dolan wrote a letter stating that in view of evidences of opposition his company no longer desired and would not accept the proposed new lease (*Ibid.,* May 28, 1905).

His other business connections were so extensive as to make him a pioneer in the development of modern interlocking directorates. He was one of the organizers and the first president of the Manufacturers' Club of Philadelphia. He was actively connected with many industrial and commercial associations, serving, for instance, as president of the National Association of Manufacturers. Politically, he was prominent in raising funds for a number of presidential campaigns and in bringing personal and group influence to bear on public policies. In 1888 he was organizer and chairman of an advisory committee of the Republican National Committee. He was particularly prominent as an advocate of protective tariffs.

Dolan was often hard and ruthless, and amazing in his display of energy, but he was hardly more than typical of his generation. He was profoundly influenced by the rapid industrial expansion of the North after the Civil War, and by the public and private demoralization of that era. Characteristically, his relations with other business men and with public officials can hardly be described as urbane or even subtle.

[The chief printed sources are the files of the Philadelphia newspapers, particularly the *Public Ledger* and the *North American,* containing extremely detailed accounts especially of the most conspicuous episode in his life (the "gas fight" of April and May 1905). The *Fourth Annual Message* of Mayor Weaver (Phila., 1907) contains numerous letters and annual reports of city officials. Rudolph Blankenburg [*q.v.*], a "reform" mayor of the city, wrote a series of critical articles for the *Arena,* vols. XXXIII and XXXIV (1905, 1906), entitled "Forty Years in the Wilderness," containing illustrations and extracts from documentary sources. The best accounts in local histories are in E. P. Oberholtzer, *Philadelphia* (1912) and J. T. Scharf and T. Westcott, *Hist. of Phila.* (1884); The *N. Y. Times* and the Philadelphia papers contained extensive sketches at the time of his death.]

W. B.

DOLD, JACOB (June 25, 1825–Oct. 25, 1909), meat-packer, was born in Tuttlingen, Würtemberg, Germany, where his family had been for generations in the meat business. At ten years of age he was helping his father, John Jacob Dold, in slaughtering and in sausage making; afterward he became apprenticed to the largest butcher in his native town. At sixteen he was given the duties of stock buying. At nineteen he came to the United States and settled in Buffalo, where for two or three years he worked as a butcher for Joshua Barnes, receiving $15 a month and his board. In 1848 he entered business for himself with his savings, at first making sausages in small quantities and peddling them from house to house with a basket on his arm. His trade soon increased to such an extent that he was obliged to buy a horse. In 1852 he sent for his father, mother, brothers, and sisters—six in number—and shortly after they came he built his first slaughter-house, which had a capacity of ten hogs a day. By energy, enterprise, and economy he acquired an extensive trade. His sausages became well known. In 1860 he started a small beef and pork packing plant at the Elk Street Market, putting up a building combining a meat market, dwelling rooms, and an abattoir. With the Civil War, the food resources of the North were taxed to support the needs of the army. Dold received government contracts which gave his business its first real impetus and from that time on his progress was phenomenal. In 1873 he bought ten acres of ground near the Buffalo stock-yards and erected an abattoir which was the nucleus of the present plant. He erected a plant at Kansas City, Mo., in 1880 and five years later, one at Wichita, Kan. In 1888 he incorporated his business into a stock company of which he continued to be the active head for the rest of his life. By 1909 his three plants were killing a million head of live stock annually.

In 1850, or thereabout, Dold was married to Elizabeth Schiesz, and after her death, which occurred in Buffalo some thirty years later, he was married again, to Bertha Bettock who survived him. He was an unostentatious, kindly man, addicted to anonymous charity. On the day of his funeral his family learned for the first time that he had supplied the funds to build the German Lutheran church which he attended. He was succeeded in his business by his son, Jacob C. Dold, as able a man as his father. The latter was instrumental in the establishment of the Institute of American Meat Packers, and was a counsellor of the United States Chamber of Commerce, and of the International Chamber of Commerce. Under his administration the company's activities spread all over the United States and it established selling agencies in many foreign countries. In its subsequent history the traditions and policies of its founder were adhered to, although on the death of Jacob C. Dold in 1924 the financial control of the company passed from the Dold family.

[R. A. Clemen, *The Am. Livestock and Meat Industry* (1923); obituaries in the *Nat. Provisioner*, Oct. 30, 1909, and *Buffalo Express*, Oct. 26, 1909; obituary of Jacob C. Dold in *Nat. Provisioner*, Sept. 13, 1924; letter from E. C. Andrew, president of the Jacob Dold Packing Co., Buffalo; information as to certain facts from a son, Chas. H. Dold, Esq.] R. A. C.

DOLE, CHARLES FLETCHER (May 17, 1845–Nov. 27, 1927), Congregational clergyman, was seventh in descent from William Dole of Thornbury, Gloucester County, England, whose son Richard settled in Newburyport, Mass., in 1639. He was born at Brewer, Me., the son of the Rev. Nathan and Caroline (Fletcher) Dole. Nathan Haskell Dole, well known as a translator and author, was his brother. After his father's death at Chelsea, Mass., in 1855, his mother, who died in 1914 at the age of ninety-five, returned with her children to the home of her mother, Sally Ware Fletcher, in Norridgewock, Me. There the boy was reared in an atmosphere of sturdy independence, simplicity, and piety. To the theological dogma of the time and place he was, even as a child, impervious but not recalcitrant. Neither at Harvard College, where he graduated second in the class of 1868, nor at Andover Theological Seminary, where he graduated in 1872, did he gain much from his teachers, though Francis James Child returned his themes "with the most suggestive and useful blue pencilings that I ever had. . . . I owe him thanks to this day for the severe and straightforward style of composition that he set for us," and J. Henry Thayer at Andover impressed him by his unswerving intellectual honesty. Dole was acting professor of Greek at the University of Vermont from January 1873 till the end of the academic year. On Mar. 4, 1873, he married Frances, daughter of the Rev. James and Esther (Swett) Drummond, whom he had known since boyhood. He was pastor of the Plymouth Church, Portland, Me., 1874–76, and of the First Congregational (Unitarian) Society, Jamaica Plain, Mass., for the next forty years, becoming pastor emeritus in 1916. In the summer of 1887 he engaged in missionary work in the Northwest, at Duluth, Superior, and Winona. He visited Europe in 1892, 1896, and 1913, made four trips to Honolulu, where his son, James Drummond Dole, was a pineapple magnate, and traveled somewhat extensively in the South and West. For twenty-three years (1893–1916) he was a trustee of Tuskegee Institute, and he was a constant and devoted supporter, likewise, of Hampton Institute. His political views owed much to E. L. Godkin. A lingering Puritanism made him in time a total abstainer. He was an honest pacifist, and during the Spanish-American War and the European War of 1914–18 he remained honest. For some years he was president of the Association to Abolish War. Fanaticism, however, was utterly alien to his character. He was rich in friends.

In all he published at least thirty books and pamphlets, of which the more significant are: *The Citizen and the Neighbor* (1884); *Jesus and the Men About Him* (1888); *The Golden Rule in Business* (1895, 1896); *The Coming People* (1897); *The American Citizen* (1891); *The Religion of a Gentleman* (1900); *The Smoke and the Flame: A Study in the Development of Religion* (1902); *From Agnosticism to Theism* (1903); *The Spirit of Democracy* (1906); *The Hope of Immortality* (1906, 1908—a Harvard Ingersoll Lecture); *What We Know About Jesus* (1908); *The Ethics of Progress* (1909); *The Coming Religion* (1910); *The Burden of Poverty* (1912); *The New American Citizen* (1918); *A Religion for the New Day* (1920); *The Victorious Goodness: An Epic of Spiritual Evolution* (1927); and *My Eighty Years* (1927)—the last a summary of his life and opinions. He also wrote for the *Atlantic Monthly* and other magazines.

Neither a popular preacher and leader nor a thinker of striking originality, Dole made little impression on his time. For half a century his quiet voice pleaded for a dogmaless religion of devotion, unselfishness, disinterestedness. A scattered group of intellectuals in America and England, never large but growing with the years, cherished him as one of their most intelligent and persuasive spokesmen.

[*Who's Who in America*, 1926–27; *Harvard Coll. Class of 1868 Fortieth Anniversary*, *1868–1908* (1909); *Harvard Quinquennial Cat. 1636–1915* (1915); *Gen. Cat. of the Theol. Sem. Andover, Mass., 1808–1908* (1909); *N. Y. Times*, Nov. 28, 1927; editorial in *The Southern Workman* (Hampton, Va.), Mar. 1928; obituary in *Unitarian Year Book*, 1928–29.] G. H. G.

DOLE, SANFORD BALLARD (Apr. 23, 1844–June 9, 1926), judge, president of the Republic of Hawaii, first governor of the Territory of Hawaii, was the son of Daniel and Emily (Ballard) Dole. His father, one of the group of New England missionaries who planted and tended Christianity in the Hawaiian Islands, was the first principal of Punahou School (founded by the missionaries). Sanford Dole was born in Honolulu and there and on the outlying island of Kauai he spent his childhood and youth, acquiring a fine physical development, a love of nature and skill in outdoor sports, and a thorough and sympathetic acquaintance with the native Hawaiian people. The main part of his formal education was received in missionary schools in Hawaii, but he spent two years (1866–68) in the United States, attending Williams College and studying law. He was admitted to the bar in Massachusetts and then returned to Honolulu to take up the practise of law. For the next twenty years he devoted his working time to his profession, but not without taking the interest in public affairs which he conceived to be the duty of a citizen. During these years he established himself in the community and won to a remarkable degree the confidence of those with whom he came in contact.

Although thoroughly American in his ideas of government, Dole was not unfriendly to the Hawaiian monarchy, but rather favored it, as being best suited to the native race, and wished it to continue as long as possible. He and many other thoughtful persons observed with deep regret, however, what he called the "retrogressive tendencies" of the monarchy in its later years and "sought through legislative work, the newspapers and by personal appeal and individual influence . . . to avert the catastrophe that seemed inevitable if such tendencies were not restrained" (Dole to Willis, Dec. 23, 1893). In 1880 he had an active share in the movement which compelled the dismissal of an irresponsible adventurer who had been appointed head of the ministry. In 1884 and 1886 he was elected to the legislature by the reform party. He was one of the leaders of the revolution of 1887, which ended the notorious Gibson régime and forced King Kalakaua to grant a new constitution, reducing him to a status somewhat like that of the British sovereign. It was essentially the failure of Kalakaua and his successor, Liliuokalani, to accept in good faith the results of this revolution of 1887 which led to the more thoroughgoing revolution of 1893.

On Dec. 28, 1887, Dole was appointed associate justice of the supreme court, the appointment being exacted of the king by the reform ministry. He continued in that office until Jan. 17, 1893, when he resigned to become head of the revolutionary Provisional Government. He was not one of the original organizers of the revolution of 1893, and consented to join the movement only after he became satisfied that further continuance of the monarchy was out of the question and that the best interests of all, including the native Hawaiians, demanded its overthrow. He was the more willing to cast in his lot with the revolutionists since their ultimate goal was the annexation of Hawaii to the United States. The immediate object of the revolution—the overthrow of the monarchy—was easily accomplished; but the annexation project was postponed by the opposition of President Cleveland. Dole and his associates believed that Cleveland's Hawaiian policy was originated by Secretary of State Gresham, and that it was based upon a fundamental misapprehension of the facts of the revolution and the character and purpose of the Provisional Government, a misapprehension not removed by the partial and one-sided investigation (so it looked to them) made by Commissioner J. H. Blount [*q.v.*]. When President Cleveland, speaking through Minister Willis in December 1893, asked the Provisional Government to step down and permit the restoration of Liliuokalani, Dole, as minister of foreign affairs, wrote a reply which is considered one of his ablest and most important state papers, denying the right of the president of the United States to interfere in the internal affairs of Hawaii, setting forth the true causes of the overthrow of the monarchy, and firmly refusing to yield to President Cleveland's demand. At the same time he expressed the conviction that sooner or later the political union of the two countries would be accomplished.

It being evident that annexation could not be expected while Cleveland was president of the United States, a constitutional convention was held and a permanent government, the Republic of Hawaii, was brought into existence on July 4, 1894. By article 23 of the constitution Dole was declared to be the president of the republic, to hold office until the end of 1900. His administration as president was beset with difficulties including a royalist attempt at a counter-revolution in January 1895, dissensions within the ranks of the annexationists, a very serious diplomatic controversy with Japan growing out of the efforts of the Hawaiian government to restrict Japanese immigration. Relations with the government of the United States, while friendly in a formal way during the latter part of

Cleveland's administration, required tact and discretion on the part of the Hawaiian executive; after the inauguration of President McKinley relations were very cordial and a new annexation treaty was negotiated. In January 1898 Dole visited Washington in the interest of the treaty. When the United States became involved in war with Spain, while the annexation treaty still lacked ratification by the United States government, President Dole's view was that Hawaii should shape its policy exactly in accordance with the desires of the American government. After the consummation of annexation in the summer of 1898, he was a member of the commission appointed to recommend to Congress legislation for the future government of the islands, meanwhile continuing as executive head of the existing government; and was then (1900) made first governor of the Territory of Hawaii. He resigned from that office in 1903 to become judge of the United States district court for Hawaii, remaining on the bench until 1915, when he retired to private life.

He was married in 1873 to Anna Cate of Castine, Me., who died in 1918. Dole's interests were many and varied. To the end of his life he kept up his membership in a number of public service societies and semi-public organizations. He contributed a few historical articles to the publications of the Hawaiian Historical Society and to periodicals. Characterized by "quiet modesty . . . calm judgment . . . ready cooperation," he was of a mild and conciliatory disposition where principles were not at stake; but in public matters, having once made up his mind as to the proper course, he followed it with inflexible purpose.

[Public and private papers and official correspondence filed in the Archives of Hawaii and in possession of the Historical Commission of Hawaii; *Who's Who in America,* 1926–27; obituary articles in Honolulu newspapers, among them *Honolulu Star-Bulletin* and *Honolulu Advertiser,* June 10, 1926; Dole's judicial decisions are printed in the reports of the courts over which he presided; part of his state papers are printed in U. S. Congressional documents and Hawaiian government documents. *The Hawaiian Crisis: Correspondence Between President Dole and U. S. Minister Willis, Dec. 1893* was published in Honolulu in 1893.]

R. S. K.

DOLLIVER, JONATHAN PRENTISS (Feb. 6, 1858–Oct. 15, 1910), statesman, was born near Kingwood, Va. (now W. Va.). His father, James J. Dolliver, a camp-meeting convert, was then riding the Preston County circuit with untiring zeal, preaching Methodist salvation and the sin of slaveholding. He and his wife, Elizabeth J. Brown, found shelter for their family at the house of Grandfather Brown, an anti-secession Democrat. Life thereabouts was simple, with food in plenty and money scarce. It was a sturdy, ardent environment. When the time came for Jonathan's advanced schooling, his ambitious parents moved to Morgantown, which had lately become the seat of West Virginia's university. Jonathan helped earn his education in the hard panic years; and the academic episode which made the greatest impression upon him was a suit against the University which unloosed upon the campus a flood of stirring oratory.

At seventeen he found himself a graduate with an urge to explore the world. Toward Illinois he started afoot; then took the stage, and then (he related), "I came to Connellsville in Pennsylvania and saw a railroad train for the first time. I attended Barnum's show in the afternoon, in the evening, full of strange thrills, I started on my journey to the west . . . I said to myself 'This, then, is life, real life'" (J. B. Morrow, *post*). But with his temperament, "life" as a winter-time school-teacher at Sandwich, Ill., and as a summer-time law student in a Morgantown office, seemed dull. He managed to attend the Republican convention of 1876 which, as he recalled, sent him home "full of new joy and fresh noise." At twenty he determined to launch his legal career in Iowa. The career did not immediately eventuate, but Dolliver enjoyed the impecunious interlude, for his warm, friendly nature basked in the personal contacts of the Fort Dodge community, which so delighted in his speeches as to stir him to perfect his epigrammatic style. The easy familiarity of this period took him little further than the office of corporation counsel at $200 yearly (1880–87); but the year 1884 brought a political opportunity. His oratorical prowess had attracted Iowa's Republican vote-getters; and they had him strike the key-note for them at the state convention. Albert Beveridge [*q.v.*], selling books in Des Moines, heard in wonder "this amazing address" (*Palimpsest,* V, 40). To Dolliver's astonishment and delight, he was invited to stump with Blaine, "whom I idolized," he said, "as I have idolized no other man" (Morrow, *post*). Iowa's tenth district began considering him for Congress, tentatively in 1886 and decisively (on the 110th ballot) in 1888.

As a congressman, he subscribed to regular Republican doctrine, especially in regard to protection and soldiers' pensions. He won five reelections, besides obtaining membership on the ways and means committee in 1895. This also was the year of his fortunate marriage with Louise Pearsons. He supported Iowa's favorite son, William Boyd Allison [*q.v.*], for president in 1888 and 1896; but his own candidacy for vice-president, taken seriously by Dawes and others in 1900, neither he nor his wife favored. Allison counseled him in his wonted fatherly manner and Dolliver proved a popular and useful adjunct to the conservative organization. He won his reward when that group chose him—rather than Cummins, who had displeased them—to succeed Senator Gear. Life as a senator proved complicated. Dolliver felt the new spirit expressed by George Roberts in Iowa's tariff plank of 1901, yet the ancient conservative loyalties bound him. He tried to meet Allison's wish that he continue to follow him, but the railroad and tariff issues prevented. Clashes with the Senate's parliamentary leader, Nelson W. Aldrich [*q.v.*], began in 1903, and grew increasingly significant as Dolliver aligned himself with La Follette, Clapp, and Beveridge. The emotional orator of forty-five with the mid-Western, agricultural constituency, was pitted against the impersonal, silent parliamentarian of sixty-two with the New England manufacturing constituency. As the former turned insurgent, his chances of advancement in the Senate organization inevitably lessened. The year 1906 was most trying. In that year Aldrich thwarted Dolliver's desire to attach his name to the railroad law and Roosevelt abandoned the position on court review of decisions of the Interstate Commerce Commission which Dolliver thought they had agreed upon, thus leaving the latter high and dry in the midst of the controversy. Late the next year there was a burden to shoulder for Allison—to defeat the attempt of Cummins to take the next primary nomination. Dolliver won the nomination for Allison, but the death of the latter in August of 1908 set Dolliver free to coöperate openly with Cummins thenceforward.

He was powerfully energized by his new sense of liberty. Evidence of the change came when, Aldrich refusing him a place on the finance committee, he turned scathingly upon Aldrich's cotton and woolen schedules. Similarly, when with Cummins he mastered the state convention in 1910, he defied the hootings of his former friends among the conservatives with a threat that he would campaign in every district he pleased. Throughout this, his last summer, though wretchedly undermined in health, he immersed himself in plans for the future. He desired to attack Aldrich further, utilizing the rubber schedule. He was complimented by the party harmonizers, when they brought him and Roosevelt together in a love feast at Sioux City and when they demanded Dolliver's skilled services in disaffected Republican districts. In the midst of these, his days of greatest independence and moral strength, doctors told him his life depended upon complete withdrawal from the political scene, and within a week after their warning he was dead.

[Dolliver gave recollections of his early experiences to Jas. B. Morrow in an interview which the latter copyrighted and syndicated; it can be found entire in the *Dubuque Times-Jour.*, Oct. 16–18, 1910. For Dolliver's political career see *Annals of Iowa* (Iowa State Dept. of Hist., Des Moines), especially 3 ser., vols. IV–VII, IX–X, XIII–XIV; *Palimpsest* (State Hist. Soc. of Iowa, Iowa City), especially Feb. 1924; "Dedication of Dolliver State Park," *Bulletin* (Iowa State Board of Conservation, Des Moines), III, 1–24; Sioux City *Journal*, especially Oct. 16, 1910; *La Follette's Autobiography* (1913); F. E. Haynes, *Third Party Movements* (1916); Champ Clark, *My Quarter Century of Am. Politics* (1920); *Selections from the Correspondence of Theodore Roosevelt and Henry Cabot Lodge 1884–1918* (1925). The best available manuscript collections are W. B. Allison MSS., and G. M. Dodge MSS. (Iowa State Dept. of Hist., Des Moines); W. E. Chandler MSS., and T. Roosevelt MSS. (Lib. of Cong.). For Dolliver's change in attitude toward the tariff, compare his speeches of Mar. 23, 1897, and Aug. 5, 1909 (*Cong. Record*, 55 Cong., 1 Sess., pp. 191–97, and 61 Cong., 1 Sess., pp. 4925–32). For his analysis of the progressive movement, see his "Forward Movement in the Republican Party" (*Outlook*, Sept. 24, 1910). The writer obtained data from many of Dolliver's contemporaries, including the late Senators Beveridge, Clapp, La Follette, ex-Director of the Mint Roberts, and many prominent Iowans.]

J. P. N.

DOLPH, JOSEPH NORTON (Oct. 19, 1835–Mar. 10, 1897), United States senator from Oregon, was born in the village of Dolphsburg, near Watkins, N. Y. He was the son of Chester V. and Eliza (Vanderbilt) Dolph, both of New England ancestry. At sixteen he left the farm to become a lock-tender on the Chemung Canal. Afterward he alternated short terms of attendance at the Genesee Wesleyan Seminary at Lima with the teaching of country schools and the study of law until admitted to the bar at Binghamton in 1861. The next spring he enlisted in a military company bound for Oregon and reached Portland, in October 1862. In October 1864 he was married to Augusta E. Mulkey. Upon settling in Portland he had at once become a law partner of John H. Mitchell, a recent arrival but already a leading attorney of the city and in 1872 elected a United States senator. The commerce and business of Portland were booming at this period as the result of the opening of new mines in the upper Columbia River basin; many business corporations were formed, and the railroad era began. Mitchell & Dolph shared in this prosperity and soon reached a position of leadership in the social, political, and financial life of the city and state. The first great railroad promoter of the state, Ben Holladay [*q.v.*], became their client and they entered the legislature where they could better serve his interests.

Dolph's rise was rapid; he was city attorney for Portland in 1864, United States district attorney, 1865, chairman of the Republican state committee, 1866, and four times state senator, 1866–76. At the same time he had become a director in and the attorney for the transportation companies organized by Henry Villard and was vice-president of the latter's Northern Pacific Railroad when his turn to be elected United States senator came in 1882 at the end of a session of the legislature and after a long deadlock.

In the Senate his career was creditable though his name is not associated with any legislation of lasting importance. He was an ardent supporter of protection and other party measures, yet generally voted with the more liberal wing of the Republican party on bills that involved a concession to the reform spirit of the time. He voted for the Interstate Commerce Act of 1887 and the Sherman Anti-Trust Act of 1890. He defended the woman's suffrage amendment and spoke in favor of a proposed amendment giving Congress control of marriage and divorce. He voted for the Sherman Silver Purchase Act of 1890, though opposed to free silver, and somewhat inconsistently voted against its repeal when that was called for by President Cleveland. He was reëlected without opposition in 1888, but his stand in opposition to free silver so angered the numerous supporters of that cause in Oregon that he failed of reëlection in 1894. Aside from his being "the only member in Congress from the Pacific Coast who stood unequivocally for the gold standard" (*Morning Oregonian*, Portland, Mar. 11, 1897) his political career was without special distinction. He was an able lawyer, a shrewd political leader, and strong representative of the business interests of his time.

[Oregon newspapers of the period, the journals of the state legislature, and the *Congressional Record* are the available sources for his official career. Biographical sketches are found in H. W. Scott, *Distinguished Am. Lawyers* (1891); *Portrait and Biog. Record of Western Ore.* (1904); *Biog. Dir. Am. Cong.* (1928).]

R. C. C—k.

DOMBROWSKI, JOSEPH. [See DABROWSKI, JOSEPH, 1842–1903.]

DOMINGUEZ, FRANCISCO ATANASIO. [See ESCALANTE, SILVESTRE VELEZ DE, *c.* 1776.]

DONAHOE, PATRICK (Mar. 17, 1811–Mar. 18, 1901), editor, publisher, philanthropist, was in 1872 "the richest and most influential Catholic in New England" (*Pilot*, Boston, Mar. 23, 1901). He was born in Munnery, parish of Kilmore, County Cavan, Ireland, the son of Terrence and Jane (Christy) Donahoe. His mother died when he was an infant. When he was ten years old he came with his father to Boston, Mass. For one year he attended Adams School where, he said, he was "the only boy of Irish, and perhaps, of alien birth." At fourteen he set out to learn the printing trade in the office of the *Columbian Centinel*, and some time later worked temporarily for the *Boston Transcript* where (he said) he nearly lost his job for "not coming to work on Christmas day." His association with Catholic journalism commenced with *The Jesuit, or Catholic Sentinel*, published after 1829 by George Pepper. When this paper was reorganized (1832), he worked on it with H. L. Devereaux, in company with whom he later began (1836) the publication of the *Pilot*. As owner and editor of the *Pilot*, then perhaps the most influential Catholic weekly newspaper in the United States, as publisher for various Irish-American writers among whom Thomas D'Arcy McGee and Anna H. Dorsey were the best known, and as a merchant and a private banker, he amassed great wealth and influence. Benefactions to the American College in Rome, the Boston Home for Destitute Catholic Children, and the victims of the Irish famine of 1848, together with numerous other gifts to churches and charitable institutions, displayed the readiness with which he placed his means at the service of society. He also supported "Father Mathew" (Rev. Theobald Mathew) in an energetic crusade for temperance reform. The great Boston fire (1872) destroyed his publishing plant and church goods store, plunging him deeply into debt. His bank also failed during the panic that followed. Archbishop Williams purchased the *Pilot*, in 1876, to help pay the bank's depositors, and two years later Donahoe started *Donahoe's Magazine*, a monthly periodical devoted to Catholic and Irish-American interests, which circulated widely and published work by such writers as Ethna Carberry and Louise Imogene Guiney. In 1891, having in the meantime partly restored his banking business, he repurchased the *Pilot*, which he continued to publish until his death. In 1893 the University of Notre Dame conferred on him the Lætare Medal, and in 1894 he was tendered a public banquet by admiring fellow townsfolk. He died in Boston, and his funeral was almost a civic event, the Pope sending his Apostolic Benediction and the Irish, whom he had aided so generously, going in throngs to honor his memory. He was married twice, first, on Nov. 23, 1836, to Kate Griffin, who died in 1852, and second, on Apr. 17, 1853, to Annie E. Davis. As a citizen he was a prominent supporter of the Democratic party; as a patriot, during the Civil War, he was identified with the history of the 9th and 28th Massachusetts regiments, which he helped to organize; as an Irish American, he contributed an incalculable amount to the welfare of his fellow emigrants.

[The chief sources of information regarding Donahoe's personality and career are the *Pilot,* for Mar. 23 and 30, 1901; *Donahoe's Mag.,* Apr. 1901; *Mass. of To-Day* (1892), ed. by Thos. Quinn; and *Catholic Builders of the Nation,* IV (1923), 224. His journalistic and publishing enterprises are dealt with in Paul J. Foik, *Pioneer Efforts of Catholic Journalism in the U. S.* (1912), pp. 174–78, and 261–87; J. M. Finotti, *Bibliographia Catholica Americana* (1872). See also obituary in *Boston Transcript,* Mar. 18, 1901.] G. N. S.

DONAHUE, PETER (Jan. 11, 1822–Nov. 26, 1885), capitalist, founder of the Union Iron Works in San Francisco, was born of Irish parents living in Glasgow. His early life seems to have been one of hardship and little schooling. At the age of nine he was working in a Glasgow factory. When he was eleven his parents emigrated to the United States and settled in Matteawan, N. Y., where he worked first in a factory and then on a farm. About 1837 his parents moved to Paterson, N. J., and there Peter was apprenticed to learn the craft of machinist and millwright. His younger brothers, James and Michael, learned the related trades of boilermaking and molding. Upon returning to New York, in 1845, Peter found employment on the construction of a gunboat for the Peruvian government. He accompanied the completed vessel to Peru as assistant engineer, and remained in that country until 1849, when he embarked for the gold-fields of California. Although detained for some months at Tobago with Isthmus fever, he eventually reached San Francisco on the steamship *Oregon.* En route, the vessel's machinery broke down, but Donahue was able to repair it, and for this service the owners rewarded him with $1,000 and urged him to remain in their employ. At this time the lure of the goldfields still drew him, but after six months in the mines he was back in San Francisco where his two brothers had arrived.

Together they opened a crude blacksmith and boiler-making shop at Montgomery St., near Jackson, the first iron works and machine-shop in California. Later this expanded into the great Union Iron Works, named for the works at Paterson, N. J., where Peter had learned his trade as machinist. The Donahue works, first housed in tents, soon moved to what was then called Happy Valley, between Mission, First, and Frémont Sts. For a furnace they utilized the smokestack of a dismantled steamer, and for a blast used a pair of old-fashioned bellows. Here were made the first castings in the state of California. In a short time they added to their business the repairing of engines, the construction of quartz mills, mining machinery, mining pumps, and the erection of gas-works.

In 1852 and 1856 Michael and James sold their interests to Peter, who carried on the business in his own name for a time, erecting a large brick building on the site of the roofless shop of 1849. In 1860 he obtained a contract for building a steamer for the United States government, the *Saginaw,* and in 1863 turned out the monitor *Comanche.* These were the first government vessels produced on the Pacific Coast. The first printing-press made in California was also manufactured in his foundry. In 1865 the Union Iron Works finished, for the San Francisco & San Jose Railroad, the first locomotive built in the state. By 1863 Donahue had become so involved in other important enterprises that he was unable to exercise personal supervision over the mechanical branch of the business. He therefore formed a new partnership with H. J. Booth and C. S. Higgins, under the firm name of Donahue, Booth & Company. Two years later he sold his interest to H. J. Booth & Company.

Not only was Peter Donahue the pioneer foundryman of California but he was also a pioneer in the public-utility development of that state. In 1852 he organized the first gas company for street lighting in San Francisco; and for twenty years preceding his death he was president of this highly prosperous concern. He organized (1861) the Omnibus Street Railway, the first street-car line in San Francisco, and for many years was president of the company. In 1860 he was made treasurer of the San Francisco & San Jose Railroad, and, with an associate, soon acquired two-thirds of the stock. In November 1870 they sold the road to the Central Pacific for $3,250,000. In 1862 Donahue became one of the charter members of the Union Pacific Railroad. In 1870 he acquired a controling interest in the San Francisco & Humboldt Railroad, out of which he created the San Francisco & North Pacific Railroad and its branches and extensions lying in Marin, Sonoma, and Mendocino counties. The town of Donahue in this region was named after him. He was also a director of the San Francisco & Colorado River Railroad Company. Although active in support of the Union cause at the opening of the Civil War and interested in civic affairs throughout his life, he would never accept public office. By his industry and business thrift he accumulated great wealth. A contemporary described him as "one of the most charitable of givers, kindest of benefactors, and most generous of friends." He was twice married: his first wife was Mary Jane

Maguire, whom he married in 1852 and by whom he had four children. In 1864 he married Annie Downey, sister of Gov. J. G. Downey, who survived her husband eleven years. He died in San Francisco.

[The main facts in Donahue's life may be gathered from H. H. Bancroft, *Chronicles of the Builders of the Commonwealth* (1891), I, 442–45, and VI, 139, 303; and the same author's *Hist. of Cal.* (1890), VII (see index); Z. S. Eldredge, *Hist. of Cal.* (1915), IV, 269; B. E. Lloyd, *Lights and Shades in San Francisco* (1876), pp. 308–17; O. T. Shuck, *Sketches of Leading and Representative Men of San Francisco* (1875), pp. 855–60; A. Phelps, *Contemporary Biog. of California's Representative Men* (1882), pp. 370–74; *San Francisco Chronicle* and *Morning Call* (San Francisco), Nov. 27, 1885.]

P. O. R.

DONCK, ADRIAEN VAN DER [See VAN DER DONCK, ADRIAEN, 1620–1655.]

DONELSON, ANDREW JACKSON (Aug. 25, 1799–June 26, 1871), soldier, lawyer, politician, diplomat, was associated from birth with the man for whom he was named. When James Robertson conducted his little band of pioneers through the wilderness to the Cumberland River in the winter of 1779–80, the families and supplies of the party were conveyed by water under the command of Col. John Donelson. After having taken up considerable land in the neighborhood of Nashville, Donelson was killed in the forest, and left his widow with a family which included their children Rachel and Samuel. When Andrew Jackson [*q.v.*] first went to Nashville in 1788, he secured lodging with the widow Donelson, became associated in business with her son Samuel, and married her daughter Rachel. When Samuel eloped with Mary, only daughter of Gen. Daniel Smith, another prominent pioneer, Jackson assisted the young lovers. It was fitting that their son should be named Andrew Jackson. Young Andrew's father died while he was yet a child, and when his mother married a second time, Jackson took his namesake and his wife's nephew to "The Hermitage" and reared him there. He was first sent to Cumberland College in Nashville, and then to the United States Military Academy. On graduating from West Point, where he completed four years' work in three and ranked second in his class, he was appointed aide-de-camp to Gen. Jackson and served with him during the Seminole campaign. Resigning from the army, he now went to Transylvania University at Lexington, Ky., to take up the study of law. In 1823 he was admitted to the bar and began practise in Nashville. In 1824 he married his first cousin, Emily, daughter of Capt. John Donelson, and grand-daughter of Col. John Donelson, the pioneer.

Jackson's first campaign for the presidency was in progress at that time, and Donelson became his confidential secretary. He now made his home at "Tulip Grove," an estate across the way from "The Hermitage," and became once more, in effect, a member of the General's family. During the campaign of 1828, he again served as secretary, and when Jackson was elected, accompanied him to Washington to officiate as private secretary while Emily was to preside as mistress of the White House. Four of their children were thus born in the presidential mansion. When the Eaton storm came up, Emily, like the cabinet ladies, refused to bow to Jackson's mandate that she receive Peggy O'Neill socially, and for this was sent back to Tennessee. Her husband chose to accompany her and they remained in retirement about six months. The General, however, needed Donelson's assistance in getting his state papers into shape, and the family from "Tulip Grove" were presently recalled and restored to favor. Emily died in 1836, and five years later Donelson married another cousin, Mrs. Elizabeth Martin Randolph.

With the end of Jackson's administration, his private secretary returned to Nashville with the General, refusing to take office under the Van Buren administration. Jackson and his friends were not forgotten in Washington, however, and when the question of the annexation of Texas came to a head, President Tyler, hoping to secure Democratic support, appointed Donelson to carry on negotiations with the new republic (J. S. Bassett, *Life of Andrew Jackson,* 1911, II, 742). When Polk came into office, Donelson retained the post, and completed his task in a thoroughly creditable manner (McCormac, *post,* p. 352). His success in this undertaking, as well as his nearness to Jackson, gave him strong claims upon the new administration. Though he was considered for the cabinet, he did not push his claims, and was accredited minister to the Kingdom of Prussia in 1846. This position he retained until 1849, when the Whigs were in power. In 1850 the noted Southern Convention met in Nashville. Donelson took keen interest in the early stages of this movement, but when the second session fell under the influence of the radical Southern element, he withdrew his support (Sioussat, "Tennessee, the Compromise of 1850, and the Nashville Convention," in *Tennessee Historical Magazine,* 1920, IV, 224, 244). In 1851 he succeeded Ritchie as editor of the *Washington Union,* but, not being able to go along with his party in its drift toward sectionalism, he ceased to cooperate with it, and in 1856 accepted the vice-presidential nomination on the

Fillmore ticket. This incident ended his political career.

When Andrew Jackson died, an impoverished old man, he left to his namesake, who had served him so faithfully, his blessing and the sword which his state had presented him. With it he left the injunction that "he fail not to use it when necessary in support . . . of the constitutional rights of our beloved country, should they be assailed by foreign enemies or domestic traitors" (Parton, *post,* III, 651). When the Civil War was precipitated, Donelson was asked to lend his support to the cause of his section, but answered that he could not draw the sword of Jackson against the old flag. Broken by the calamities of the war which he would have done so much to avert, he died at Memphis in 1871.

[The best biographical notices are in J. T. Moore and A. P. Foster, *Tenn., the Volunteer State* (4 vols., 1923), and W. W. Clayton, *Hist. of Davidson County, Tenn.* (1880). Donelson's career, however, is so closely tied up with that of Jackson, that much material on his life is to be found in Jas. Parton, *Life of Andrew Jackson* (3 vols., 1860), E. I. McCormac, *James K. Polk* (1922), and S. G. Heiskell, *Andrew Jackson and Early Tenn. Hist.* (3 vols., 1920–21). A collection of Donelson Papers has been published in the *Tenn. Hist. Mag.,* 1919, III, 51–73 and 134–62. The date of Donelson's birth is recorded in the Donelson family Bible, in the possession of Mrs. Betty Donelson of Nebraska.] T. P. A.

DONGAN, THOMAS (1634–Dec. 14, 1715), soldier, colonial governor of New York, was born at Castletown, in the county of Kildare, Ireland, being a younger son of Sir John Dongan, Baronet. He adopted the profession of arms and spent some years in France in the service of Louis XIV. He was recalled about 1677 and shortly thereafter received from Charles II an appointment as lieutenant-governor of Tangier, which was then under the English flag. He remained at this post until 1680. His friendship for the Stuarts brought him additional preferment, and by a commission dated Sept. 30, 1682, he was appointed governor of New York by its Roman Catholic proprietor, James, Duke of York. On Aug. 25, 1683, he arrived at his new post.

The territory under his jurisdiction included not only New York itself but also the dependencies of Pemaquid, Martha's Vineyard, and Nantucket. During the five years following his arrival, he governed the province with such ability and energy that he has been referred to by competent authority as "one of the very best of all the colonial governors" (Osgood, *American Colonies in the Seventeenth Century,* II, 131). The Duke's instructions provided for the calling of a representative assembly, and one of the new governor's first acts was to issue writs of election. The body thus chosen met for the first time on Oct. 17, 1683, and its first statute defined more fully the organization and powers of the assembly and came to be known as the "Charter of Liberties." After James's accession to the throne, however, the measure was disallowed, and New York, which had now become a royal province, was again without a representative assembly.

Dongan devoted himself most energetically to the development of the colony. He strengthened the defenses and took steps to determine more definitely the boundaries of the province. He even dreamed of establishing a postal system, to extend from Nova Scotia to the Carolinas, which might serve as a bond of union between the English colonies in America. Though he was himself a Roman Catholic, his administration was marked by a broad tolerance in religious matters. In 1687 he submitted to the home government a report on the state of the province which contains a remarkable description of New York at that time. His greatest service, however, consisted in his early recognition of the growing power of the French to the northward and in his insistence that the home government aid him in checking it. French Jesuits were active among the Iroquois and were using their influence for political ends, while efforts were being made from Quebec to establish something in the nature of a protectorate over those tribes. Dongan protested vigorously to De la Barre, the governor of Canada, and to his successor, the Marquis de Denonville. As early as 1684 he had caused the arms of the Duke of York to be erected in the Iroquois villages, a step which he regarded as equivalent to the establishment of a protectorate. By the winter of 1687–88 an open conflict seemed imminent, and Dongan raised a force for the defense of Albany, superintending the arrangements in person. His vigorous policy, which was undertaken almost solely upon his own responsibility, at length bore fruit when James II rather tardily gave it the sanction of his approval.

In August 1688 Dongan was superseded by Sir Edmund Andros, but instead of returning at once to England, he decided to remain in New York, where he was unfortunate enough to fall a victim to the fanatical anti-Catholic crusade which attended the Revolution of 1689 in the colonies. After some vicissitudes he returned to England in 1691. Upon the death of an elder brother in 1698 he became second Earl of Limerick, a title which he retained until his death. In 1713, twenty-nine years after he had erected the arms of the Duke of York in the Iroquois villages, the French by the Treaty of Utrecht formally recognized the English protectorate over those Indians. By his clearness of vision, no less than by the vigor of his policy, Dongan proved himself one of the race of empire builders.

[Good secondary accounts of Dongan's career as governor are to be found in J. R. Brodhead, *Hist. of the State of N. Y.* (1853–71), vol. II; Francis Parkman, *Count Frontenac and New France Under Louis XIV* (1877); and Herbert Osgood, *The Am. Colonies in the Seventeenth Century* (1904–07), vols. II and III. A wealth of source material is to be found in vols. III and IX of *Docs. Relative to the Colonial Hist. of the State of N. Y.* (1853–87). An interesting sketch is that contained in Franklin M. Danaher, *An Address before the Dongan Club of Albany, N. Y., July 22, 1889* (1889). See also Edward Channing, "Col. Thos. Dongan, Governor of N. Y.," in *Proc. Am. Antiquarian Soc.*, Oct. 16, 1907.]

W. E. S.

DONIPHAN, ALEXANDER WILLIAM (July 9, 1808–Aug. 8, 1887), soldier, statesman, was born near Maysville, Mason County, Ky. His father, Joseph Doniphan of King George County, Va., served in the Revolution and after the war went to Kentucky. He returned to his native state and married Anne Smith of Fauquier County, with her going back to Kentucky in 1790, and settling in Mason County. He died there in March 1813, before his youngest son, Alexander, was five years old. When he was eight, the latter was sent to school at Augusta, Ky., under the tutelage of Richard Keene, and at the age of eighteen he graduated from Augusta College. He studied law in the office of Hon. Martin Marshall, and after two years was admitted to practise in Kentucky and Ohio. Removing to Missouri, on Apr. 19, 1830, he began, at Lexington, a long, brilliant, and successful career in his profession, gaining distinction by his eloquence. Although pitted against many lawyers of ability, his influence over juries was almost infallible, and he was employed in nearly every important case in northwestern Missouri. In one of these he defended the Mormon, Orrin P. Rockwell, who was charged with being party to a conspiracy to murder Gov. McNair. The latter recovered from his wounds, but the excitement incident to the Mormon invasion and the dastardly attack caused the outraged community to demand revenge. Doniphan, however, obtained for his client a sentence of five minutes in jail; virtually an acquittal. In 1833 he moved to Liberty, Mo., which place he thereafter regarded as his home.

His qualities of leadership brought him into prominence in the military movements of his time. He took part in the conflict between the State of Missouri and the Mormons, serving as commander of the 1st Brigade under Gen. Lucas. He refused to shoot down Prophet Smith and several other Mormons after their court-martial, pronouncing the order of Gen. Lucas cold-blood murder. The order was later rescinded. In May 1846, at the request of Gov. Edwards, Doniphan organized the 1st Regiment of Missouri Mounted Volunteers for the Mexican War. This regiment was made up of young men from the best families in the state, and Doniphan, who enlisted as a private, was elected colonel. They marched to the rendezvous at Fort Leavenworth, from there with Kearny's men to Fort Bent, and thence into New Mexico, of which territory Doniphan was placed in command. He was permitted to yield this post to Col. Sterling Price, who came later with a large body of troops. Doniphan then proceeded to the western slope of the Rockies and effected a treaty with the Navajo Indians who had been harassing the whites. Later he went to Chihuahua to form a junction with Gen. Wool, and took possession of the city by right of conquest. On the way, his men defeated the Mexicans in the battles of Brazito and Sacramento. This expedition, which ended by land at Matamoras, is still considered one of the most brilliant long marches ever made; the force, with no quartermaster, paymaster, commissary, uniforms, tents, or even military discipline, covered 3,600 miles by land and 2,000 by water, all in the course of twelve months.

Doniphan's part in civil affairs included election to the legislature in 1836, 1840, and again in 1854. The legislature appointed him delegate to the Peace Conference at Washington in 1861, and after attending the sessions of that body he entertained no hope of avoiding the impending war. During his absence he was elected to the state convention called by the legislature Jan. 21, 1861, to determine whether or not Missouri should secede from the Union. He attended this convention at its sessions in St. Louis, and at the very outset opposed the secession of Missouri. He expressed concern, however, for the rights of the states, believing that the intense feeling of the Union men might lead to the concentration of too much power in the federal government. Doniphan never felt called upon to explain any speech or vote made by him in the convention. He was opposed to invasion by Federal or Confederate forces, favoring neutrality.

In June 1861, Gov. Jackson handed him a commission as major-general in command of the State Guard, which he retained two weeks. His reasons for returning it were the loss of his two sons by accidental death, and the shattered condition of his wife's health. He had married, on Dec. 21, 1837, Elizabeth Jane, daughter of John and Elizabeth (Trigg) Thornton. They had only two children. From 1863 to 1868, Doniphan remained in St. Louis, settling at Richmond, Mo., after quiet was restored. There he stayed nearly twenty-five years, practising law and serving as president of the Ray County Savings Bank. His affection for Clay County, and dislike of being considered a rover, caused him still, however, to claim Liberty as his home, and to look upon Richmond as merely his temporary abiding-place. He died at Richmond, but was buried at Liberty, where a monument marks his grave. The State of Missouri erected a monument to his memory at Richmond in 1918.

[Doniphan letters and autobiography in Mo. Hist. Soc. *Santa Fé Republican*, Sept. 10, 1847; H. L. Conard, *Encyc. of the Hist. of Mo.* (1901), II, 292; W. E. Connelley, *War with Mexico 1846–47* (1907), p. 15; A. J. D. Stewart, *Hist. of the Bench and Bar of Mo.* (1898), 386; W. L. Webb, *Battles and Biog. of Missourians* (1900), pp. 278–80; R. A. Campbell, *Campbell's Gazetteer of Mo.* (Rev. ed., 1875), p. 152; *Hist. of Ray County, Mo.* (1881), p. 498; *Hist. of Caldwell and Livingston Counties, Mo.* (1886), p. 137; *Missouri Republican*, Aug. 9, 1887.] S.M.D.

DONLEVY, HARRIET FARLEY [See FARLEY, HARRIET, 1817–1907.]

DONN-BYRNE, BRIAN OSWALD (Nov. 20, 1889–June 18, 1928), Irish novelist, the son of Tomas Fearghail and Jane D'Arcy (McParlane) Donn-Byrne of Forkhill, County Armagh, Ireland, was born in New York City, whither his father, interested in bridges, had come on business. At the age of several months he was taken back to Ireland where his childhood was spent in Armagh and in the Glens of Antrim at Cushendun. He matriculated at University College, Dublin, where he acquired fluent command of Gaelic and became deeply interested in the Sinn Fein movement. There too he came under the influence of Douglas Hyde and acquired a wide knowledge of Irish history and literature. After graduation he expected a diplomatic career and studied briefly in Paris at the Sorbonne and at the University of Leipzig. He gave up this expectation and returned to New York City in 1911 in order to join an Irish girl whom he had met in Dublin at University College, Dorthea Mary, the daughter of Anthony Cadogan of Waterford; they were married Dec. 2, 1911. He hoped to become an Irish poet, but was forced to accept less congenial employment on the *New Catholic Encyclopedia*, and later on the *New Standard Dictionary*. Various bits of his verse had been published in obscure periodicals; in 1912 "The Piper" appeared in *Harper's Magazine*. Through the late Joyce Kilmer [*q.v.*], his friend and colleague on the *New Standard Dictionary*, he took up writing seriously. He received fifty dollars for his first short story, "Battle," published in *Smart Set* in February 1914. He did various hack-writing and book-reviewing. He later became a member of the *Century Dictionary* staff which he left to join the staff of the New York *Sun*. When he was dismissed from the *Sun* because of his "bad English" he accepted a position with the *Brooklyn Eagle*.

Donn-Byrne's short stories found their audience and his contributions to *Smart Set* and to *Harper's Magazine* were numerous. To the direct simplicity of the traditional Irish story-telling he added color and picturesque detail. Although his first novel, *Stranger's Banquet*, was published in 1919, it was not until the publication of his *Messer Marco Polo* in 1921 that he achieved popularity as a novelist. For this narration of Marco Polo's voyage to China as told by a venerable Ulsterman, the most successful and best-known of his books, he drew inspiration from old Irish chronicles and from Coleridge. His *Blind Raftery* (1924) was based upon the story of Raftery, a Gaelic itinerant poet of Cannaugh in the eighteenth century whose songs had been edited by Douglas Hyde. Despite his large payments from the *Pictorial Review*, in which many of his novels ran serially, and the royalties from his many books, he was impecunious. He sold his house at Riverside, Conn., and returned to Ireland where he purchased Coolmain Castle near Bandon, County Cork. There he lived until his sudden death in an automobile accident during June 1928. Donn-Byrne was a typical, romantic, fighting North Irishman. His writings manifest his deep aversion to "progress," his belief in the futility of politics, his love of sport, and his poetic Scots-Irish mysticism. In his work he tried to capture for an instant "a beauty that was dying slowly, imperceptibly, but would soon be gone." And with his feeling for color and his ear for the music of words he succeeded in imparting a mythical and mystical beauty to the Ireland of his imagination.

[Thurston Macauley's *Donn Byrne; Bard of Armagh* (1929), containing bibliographies, is the most complete and satisfactory of existing accounts. See also A. St. John Adcock, *Gods of Modern Grub Street* (1923); *Times* (London), June 20, 1928; *N. Y. Times*, June 20, 1928; Shane Leslie, "A Literary Beau Sabreur," in London *Outlook*, June 23, 1928; Thurston Macauley, "Passport to Tir Nan Og," in *Bookman*, Apr. 1929; Paul Mellon, *Donn-Byrne—His Place in Literature* (N. Y., 1927); *Outlook*, July 4, 1928; private information from Thurston Macauley.] F.M.

DONNELL, JAMES C. (Apr. 20, 1854–Jan. 10, 1927), producer of crude oil, was born in Ireland. Very little is known about his early life and he seems to have dismissed questions concerning it by declaring that "he was not interested in the past at all" (Smith, *post*, p. 29). His parents, James and Elizabeth (Boyd) Donnell, brought him to the United States as a child of two and at the age of eighteen he was working in the oil-fields of Titusville, Pa., hauling crude oil from field to refinery. Six years later he joined the rush to Bradford Field and took leases in the famous Foster Brook Valley near Red Rock and Derrick City. Here he remained for several years as producer and driller of wells. During this time he also bought land in the Richburg and Allentown Fields of New York state. In 1886 he went to Ohio, attracted by the possibilities of the Lima field, and was one of the few drillers who made a success there. In the following year, when the Standard Oil Company purchased the Ohio Oil Company, he became one of the board of directors and later vice-president. At the same time he served the Standard interests in Indiana where he was in charge of drilling operations. When the Clark County fields were opened in 1905, he took personal charge and, realizing the need for transportation, was instrumental in the building of the Illinois Pipe Line Company. He next spent several months in Roumania representing the Roumanian-American Oil Company and in 1907 he helped form the Standard Oil Company of California. With the dissolution of the Standard Oil Company in 1911, he became the president of the Ohio Oil Company and under his leadership this company enjoyed phenomenal growth, paying entirely out of its earnings for its expansion. This took the form of operations in the new fields of Wyoming and also in Montana, New Mexico, Kansas, Oklahoma, Texas, Arkansas, Kentucky, and Louisiana, as well as in Mexico. In 1916 he made a survey of the Peruvian oil-fields which the Standard interests later took over.

Donnell looked upon his wells as living things, and on oil as something that should be conserved by storage in the ground until needed. During his lifetime he drilled some 42,000 wells, in every oil-producing section of the United States. It has been said that sometimes while inspecting a field, he would take the driller's place so that he could "turn screw" for a while. He was married twice: in 1882 to Sadie Flinn who bore one son, and in 1890 to Elizabeth Meeker. He had banking and railroad interests and served as director of the American Petroleum Institute. During the World War he became a member of the National Petroleum War Service Committee. He did much for his local community and won a popular love greater than that accorded most men.

His death removed the last of the "oil giants" with the exception of the senior Rockefeller, one of his closest friends. He was buried in the Maple Grove Cemetery of Findlay, Ohio. Rockefeller said of him then, "He was a remarkable man and shared our confidence to the fullest extent. He will be greatly missed by a multitude who knew him and who [had] . . . the highest honor and esteem for his noble qualities and charming personality."

[Published accounts are L. E. Smith in *Nat. Petroleum News*, Jan. 12, 1927; portrait and biography in *Oil and Gas Jour.*, Jan. 13, 1927. Special mention must be made of the unique scrap-book patiently compiled by C. L. Fleming, vice-president of the Ohio Oil Co., in Findlay, Ohio,—a photostat copy of which was lent to the writer. This work contains clippings from twenty-two newspapers and magazines.] A. I.

DONNELL, ROBERT (April 1784–May 24, 1855), was the strongest preacher of the Cumberland Presbyterians in their early days. He was born in Guilford County, N. C., the son of William Donnell and Mary Bell, Scotch-Irish Presbyterians. In his childhood his parents moved to Tennessee, where his father died when Robert was fourteen. The boy's education went little beyond reading the Bible and religious books under his mother's teaching. He was a popular youth, known for height and strength, feats of hunting and rail-splitting, and expertness with tools. At a camp-meeting in the Cumberland revival his religious life was deepened, and in 1801 he determined to preach. Unable to leave farming for the sake of education, he began to hold prayer-meetings and to "exhort." Under the direction of the "Council" formed in 1805 by the workers in the revival, he rode in circuit over a large territory between the Ohio and the Cumberland rivers, and later did pioneer preaching in northern Alabama. From the independent Cumberland Presbytery, organized in 1810 in succession to the Council, he received ordination in 1813. In the growth of this presbytery into the Cumberland Presbyterian Church Donnell was prominent. He was one of the framers of the church's confession, adopted in 1814. With Finis Ewing he wrote in 1813 the article on the Cumberland Presbyterians in Woodward's edition of Charles Buck's *Theological Dictionary* (1814) which brought the sect to general notice. Meanwhile he was always traveling and preaching, much sought after and greatly influential; and also always studying. In 1818 he married Ann, daughter of Col. James W. Smith, who brought him considerable property. Moving to Alabama, he soon had a cotton-farm near Athens, his home for most of his life. In 1832 he was married a second time, to Clarissa, daughter of Rev. Jacob Lindley.

From his home Donnell constantly went out to preach, sometimes being absent for months, working in Alabama, Tennessee, Kentucky, North Carolina, and Pennsylvania. During nearly fifty years he attended, on an average, a camp-meeting every month, and at each preached once or twice a day, in many cases oftener. He planted many churches, especially in northern Alabama. He gave particular attention to the establishment of congregations and the erection of buildings in towns, among them Nashville and Memphis. Contemporary testimony as to the extraordinary power of his preaching, from all sorts of people, is convincing. He had an imposing presence and a great, expressive voice. By vivid imagery, emotional appeal, and singing added to speech, he often produced tears and shouting. Yet he did much expounding of the Cumberland theology, and was specially remembered for persuasive reasoning. He left always a deep impression of religious reality.

Donnell was first president of the first missionary board of his church, in 1837 moderator of its General Assembly, and all his life an acknowledged leader in its affairs, with a great name for peacemaking. Deeply interested in education, particularly ministerial, he was foremost in the establishment of Cumberland University, at Lebanon, Tenn. In 1846 he became pastor there, attracted chiefly by the presence of students. The last six years of his life he spent in Athens, Ala. The volume, *Thoughts on Various Theological Subjects,* issued in 1852, was his only publication.

[D. Lowry, *Life and Labors of Rev. Robt. Donnell* (1867), containing portrait and forty pages of extracts from his *Thoughts*; R. Beard, *Brief Biog. Sketches of Some of the Early Ministers of the Cumberland Presbyt. Ch.* (1867); T. C. Anderson, *Life of Rev. Geo. Donnell* (1858); F. R. Cossitt, *Life and Times of Rev. Finis Ewing* (1853); B. W. McDonnold, *Hist. Cumb. Presbyt. Ch.* (1888); *Semicentennial General Assembly Cumb. Presbyt. Ch.* (1880), ed. by J. Frizzel, containing important extracts from ecclesiastical records; *Cumb. Presbyt. Digest* (1899), ed. by J. V. Stephens; Woodward's Buck's *Theological Dict.* (1814).]

R. H. N.

DONNELLY, CHARLES FRANCIS (Oct. 14, 1836–Jan. 31, 1909), lawyer, was born in Athlone, County Roscommon, Ireland, the son of Hugh Donnelly and his wife, Margaret Conway, the latter of Welsh descent. In 1837 the family removed to Canada, settling at St. John, N. B., and Charles Francis's education was received in the private schools and the Presbyterian Academy there, and continued privately in Yarmouth, N. S., where his parents resided for a short time. In 1848 they moved to Providence, R. I., and he commenced a classical course with a view to the priesthood. Later this idea was abandoned and he went to Boston in 1856 where he read law, entering the Harvard Law School in 1858 and graduating in 1859. He was admitted to the Suffolk County bar and practised in Boston for a few months, during which he wrote for the local newspapers chiefly upon educational topics. In 1860 he took up his residence in New York City where he remained for two years engaging in literary and journalistic work both there and in Washington, under the pseudonym "Schuyler Conway." In 1862 he returned to Boston and resumed the practise of law. He was early retained on behalf of the Catholic Church in important litigation and his intimacy with the Canon law, to the study of which his previous classical training had directed him, attracted the attention of Bishop Williams of Boston, whose legal adviser he became. For many years he was practically standing counsel to the Catholic Church in Massachusetts and the neighboring states, not only in actual litigation but in numerous questions of a semi-political character involving her constitutional rights and privileges. His handling of matters of this latter nature was particularly successful. He had been instrumental in founding the Home for Destitute Catholic Children, whose fathers had been killed in the Civil War, and thereafter became closely associated with all charitable projects in Boston, in respect to which his kindness "regarded neither race, nor color, nor creed." In 1875 he was appointed chairman of the State Board of Health, Lunacy, and Charity, serving as such for four years and when the legislature in 1879 reorganized the administration of public charities, giving general supervision of the whole system to the Board, he continued a member, devoting much of his time to its work till his retirement in 1907. He took a leading part in the controversy between the Board and Gov. Benjamin F. Butler in 1883. The publication of the correspondence between Donnelly, representing the Board, and the Governor had a marked influence in procuring the defeat of the latter on his seeking reëlection in November of that year. In 1884 he proposed and drafted a bill subjecting dipsomaniacs to the same restraint and treatment as lunatics. Adopted by the General Court in 1885, this act is said to have been the first legislation of its kind in either Europe or America (Conway and Cameron, *post,* pp. 22–23). In 1888 the General Court was the scene of an attempt to pass legislation adverse to separate schools, and Donnelly was retained to represent the Catholic community in opposition. The contest was bitter and prolonged, but he finally convinced the Committee on Education that the Catholics had a right to maintain their own schools under the Bill of Rights and the Constitution, thus winning a notable victory. He displayed marked ability in his conduct of the case, particularly in his handling of the constitutional arguments. He withdrew from active practise in 1900 owing to failing health. He died in Boston, survived by his widow, Amy Francis, daughter of James Collins of Providence, R. I., whom he had married on Sept. 21, 1893.

Politically a Democrat, Donnelly consistently declined public office. Tall, with an erect carriage, clean-cut features, and dignified demeanor, he was an attractive, impressive speaker; and his conscious earnestness invariably induced respect if not conviction. Professionally he stood in the front rank though his practise was circumscribed by the subjects of child welfare, charity, and the interests of the Catholic Church, which absorbed all his best energies. Shortly after his death a volume of his poems, collected by his widow, was printed for private distribution under the title, *Roma and other Poems* (1909). Although he possessed much literary talent, his published work was small.

[See Conrad Reno, *Memoirs of the Judiciary and the Bar of New England* (1901), II, 659; Appletons' *Ann. Cyc. for 1883,* pp. 517, 519; "Foreword" by Mabel Ward Cameron to *Roma and other Poems*; Katherine E. Conway and Mabel Ward Cameron, *Chas. Francis Donnelly, A Memoir, with an Account of the Hearings on a Bill for the Inspection of Private Schools in Mass. in 1888–89* (1909); obituaries in *Boston Post* and *Boston Herald,* Feb. 1, 1909.] H. W. H. K.

DONNELLY, ELEANOR CECILIA (Sept. 6, 1838–Apr. 30, 1917), author, sixth child of Philip Carroll and Catharine (Gavin) Donnelly, was born in Philadelphia and died in West Chester, Pa. Her father, a physician, died soon after her birth, and her mother found it necessary to earn a livelihood for herself and her children. She personally attended to their education; "with solicitous assiduity she cultivated the talents with which [they] had been so richly endowed" (Walsh, *Records,* September 1917). Besides the training imposed by her mother, Eleanor had the benefit of such counsel in instruction as could be offered by her brother, Ignatius Donnelly [*q.v.*], and by her four sisters, all but one of whom were destined to become school-teachers. It was Ignatius who gave her most encouragement to write poetry. Her first publication, "A Little Girl's Hymn to the Blessed Virgin," appeared when she was nine years old. This was naturally a marvel in her community, and other writings followed. The Catholic clergy in particular valued her art; she was of a nature susceptible to religious influence; and very soon she was helping to edit the *Ave Maria,* an ecclesiastical magazine. She considered becoming a nun, and though she abandoned her inclinations in that direction she always, it seems, looked back upon her decision half regretfully. She was "above and beyond all ... Catholic—ultra Catholic" (*Ibid.*), giving nearly all her interest to the Church and its welfare, writing at one moment odes and sonnets to celebrate its festivals, and at another moment historical essays to interpret its progress. Her first book, *Out of Sweet Solitude* (1873), contains some Civil War verse which evidences a passion for social justice, but most of her subsequent books are limited to the mood dominant even in this—one of pious devotion. It was her practise to turn into verse the life of one saint after another, and as soon, apparently, as there were enough of them to group them together, dedicate them to a revered priest of her acquaintance, and publish them. During her seventy years of literary activity she published around fifty volumes, most of them religious poetry, but among them several biographies, and some fiction, all of which is negligible. One of the five Donnelly sisters married young and died soon afterward, but the other four remained spinsters, and, as they grew older, were more and more inseparable. Eleanor, the others were persuaded, was their unique and precious charge, a genius whom they should protect and cherish, one whose least word was to be treasured. They all died several years before her. Her last years were spent chiefly between two convents—St. Benedict's in Washington and Villa Maria in West Chester.

[Introduction by D. I. McDermott to *Poems, by Eleanor C. Donnelly* (1892); H. Walsh, "Eleanor C. Donnelly" in *America,* May 19, 1917, and in *Records of the Am. Catholic Hist. Soc. of Phila.,* Sept. and Dec. 1917, Mar. 1918; *Cath. World,* Mar. 1897; T. M. Schwertner, "Eleanor Donnelly," in *Cath. World,* June 1917; *Who's Who in America,* 1916–17; *Public Ledger* (Phila.), May 1, 1917; *Evening Star* (Washington), May 2, 1917.] J. D. W.

DONNELLY, IGNATIUS (Nov. 3, 1831–Jan. 1, 1901), politician, reformer, the son of Philip Carroll Donnelly, an Irish physician, and his wife Catharine Frances Gavin, was born in Philadelphia. As a boy he attended the free schools of the Quaker City, and as a young man he read law in the office of Benjamin Harris Brewster, later attorney-general of the United States. A trip to the Northwest in the "boom" period of the fifties, however, led him to abandon his native city and the law to seek wealth through land speculation. With his bride, Katharine McCaffrey, and an abundance of ambition, he removed to Nininger, Minn., fancying himself the founder of a future metropolis (see his *Nininger City,* pamphlet, 1856), but the panic of 1857 killed his town and left him heavily burdened with debts. He turned his lots into wheat-fields, and making his home on the site of his first defeat, he ever thereafter considered himself a farmer. He possessed in exaggerated degree the talent of his race for public speaking, and was thus, inevitably perhaps, drawn into politics during the exciting campaigns that preceded the Civil War. He embraced Republicanism wholeheartedly, spoke effectively for it, and at the age of twenty-eight became lieutenant-governor of his state. It was an easy step to Congress, where he spent three terms, 1863–69, in the lower house. Here he supported the war and reconstruction policies of his party and worked so actively for land grants to railroads in Minnesota and the Northwest that he received a stinging public rebuke from Elihu B. Washburne [*q.v.*], then regarded as the "Watchdog of the Treasury." Donnelly replied in kind, and the quarrel that developed seriously damaged his reputation at home. Local party leaders, already disturbed by Donnelly's ambitions, prevented his return to Congress for a fourth term, and his career as a successful politician ended forever.

His career as a regular Republican also ended. Donnelly now contended that the time had come for men to turn their backs upon the old issues arising out of slavery and the war, in order to face the new issues brought forward by the industrial development of the country. Politics, as he saw it, would in the future be a struggle "between the few who seek to grasp all power and wealth, and the many who seek to preserve their rights as American citizens and freemen." He left the Republican party because it seemed to him eternally wedded to the interests of the few, and in so doing he also abjured its protective tariff and hard-money principles. He became successively Liberal Republican, Granger, and Greenbacker, proclaiming his views not only through his matchless oratory, but also through the columns of the *Anti-Monopolist,* an independent weekly newspaper which he edited from 1874 to 1879. He ran for office repeatedly, and as a member of the state Senate for five consecutive years (1874–78) he worked energetically, although usually unsuccessfully, for reform legislation. As a Greenback-Democrat he was defeated for Congress in 1878 by William D. Washburn [*q.v.*], brother of Elihu B. Washburne, and the contest which he brought before the House after the election was thrown out.

Donnelly now retired to his study to write. He was a great lover of books, had collected an excellent library, and had read more widely than most people would have guessed. In literature as in politics he made it his concern to espouse unusual and unproved theories. His first book, *Atlantis: The Antediluvian World* (1882), purported to demonstrate the truth of Plato's story of an Atlantic island, where, according to Donnelly, original civilization developed and from which it spread to the adjoining continents. His second, *Ragnarok: The Age of Fire and Gravel* (1883), attributed the deposits of clay, gravel, and silt on the earth's surface to contact in some bygone age with a mighty comet. His *magnum opus,* entitled *The Great Cryptogram* (1888), attempted to prove by an ingenious cipher that Francis Bacon wrote the works commonly attributed to Shakespeare. All his books attracted wide attention, and the royalties from the first two—the *Cryptogram* was a financial failure—together with the lecture engagements which, as a noted author, Donnelly was called upon to fill, brought the reformer practically the first comfortable and secure income he had ever known. He made a trip to Europe and came back the better fitted by his observations to play the rôle of "Sage of Nininger," in which his amazed Minnesota friends had decided to cast him. He wrote frequently for such magazines as the *North American Review,* and later he produced several more books, one of which, a novel called *Cæsar's Column; a Story of the Twentieth Century* (1891), invited comparison with Bellamy's *Looking Backward* and was comparable to it also in popularity.

Donnelly never succeeded, however, in retiring from politics for long. He ran for Congress in 1884, and in 1887 he appeared once more in the state legislature, this time as a Farmers' Alliance leader. He soon became president of the state Alliance, and he led it almost to a man into the Populist party, in the formation of which he had an active part. He presided frequently over Populist conventions and assemblies, whose resolutions, also, he was almost invariably called upon to draft. The ringing preamble of the Omaha platform of 1892 was entirely from Donnelly's pen. In this same year he ran for governor of Minnesota on the Populist ticket, but was decisively defeated. In 1896, although he supported Bryan, he was lukewarm as to the wisdom of fusion, and he soon came to regard it as a complete betrayal of the reform movement. Thereafter he figured prominently among the Middle-of-the-Road Populists, whose candidate for vice-president he was in the campaign of 1900, and whose views he proclaimed forcefully in a newspaper, the *Representative,* which he edited in his later years. He also served, less conspicuously than formerly, in the Minnesota state legislature. Survived by his second wife, Marian Hanson, whom he married Feb. 22, 1898, he died on the first day of the twentieth century.

Donnelly was a typical nineteenth-century reformer, advocating always reform only through the ballot-box, and reform measures which a few decades later seemed innocuous enough. In his day, however, these reforms were looked upon as thoroughly radical. He was denounced as a "visionary" and the very "prince of cranks." His disregard of the conventional extended beyond the realm of politics and literature to his personal habits and beliefs. Surrounded by bewhiskered Populists, he was as smooth-shaven as a monk. Born into the Catholic Church, he ever failed to embrace that faith, and in his declining years he lent a receptive ear to spiritualism. Left a widower in his sixties, he took to himself a bride of twenty-one. Nevertheless, in spite of his peculiarities he enjoyed great personal popularity. His unfailing wit and humor made him a favorite as an orator. Let it be noised about that Donnelly was to make a speech in the legislature, and the galleries would be packed. His hospitality was unbounded, and in his well-appointed home at Nininger he was the friendly host of many prominent visitors. He was beloved by his neighbors, and by them he was rarely deserted, even at the polls. As a husband and father he possessed those homely virtues which Americans have ever esteemed highly.

[The Donnelly Papers, including numerous MSS., letter-books, and scrap-books, are in the possession of the Minn. Hist. Soc., and are there available for use. E. W. Fish, *Donnelliana: an Appendix to "Cæsar's Column," Excerpts from the Wit, Wisdom, Poetry and Eloquence of Ignatius Donnelly* (1892), is about what its title would indicate. A preliminary survey of Donnelly's life has been made by J. D. Hicks, "The Political Career of Ignatius Donnelly," in the *Miss. Valley Hist. Rev.*, VIII (1921), 80–132, from which the foregoing summary has been made; this article was reviewed in *Minn. Hist. Bull.*, IV (1922), 157. See also list of biographical sketches in *Minn. Hist. Soc. Colls.*, XIV (1912), 182; R. S. Saby, "R. R. Legislation in Minn.," and H. A. Castle, "Reminiscences of Minn. Politics" in *Minn. Hist. Soc. Colls.*, vol. XV (1915); W. W. Folwell, *A Hist. of Minn.* (4 vols., 1921); obituaries in newspapers of Jan. 2, 1901. The quarrel with Washburne is covered in *Cong. Globe*, 40 Cong., 2 Sess.; pp. 2,355 ff.]

J. D. H.

DONOGHUE, JOHN (1853–July 1, 1903), sculptor, was born in Chicago of parents who had come from western Ireland. As a youth he was clerk in the Recorder's office until a change of administration forced him out. In 1875 he entered the Chicago Academy of Design where he won a scholarship with a bust of a Vestal virgin. After two years he was enabled to go to Paris where he studied under Jouffroy at the École des Beaux-Arts and in 1880 exhibited at the Salon a plaster bust, "Phaedra." The following year he returned to America. He held an exhibition in Horticultural Hall, Boston, and in that city he made his "Boxer," using as a model John L. Sullivan, whom he considerably idealized. After reaching Chicago he gained a certain fame from Oscar Wilde's praises, which were also instrumental in enabling him to return to Paris in 1882 or 1883. This time he was under Falguière. To the Salon of 1884 he sent a bronze bas-relief of a seraph, made in Rome. In Rome, likewise, he modeled his best-known work, "Young Sophokles leading the chorus of victory after the battle of Salamis" (1885), a statue suggested by his reading of Plumptre. Of classical statues produced by Americans, it is perhaps the most freshly inspired and pleasing. It was exhibited in the London Royal Academy in 1890. Shortly after the "Young Sophokles" came the "Hunting Nymph," exhibited at the Salon of 1887. To this time also belong some portraits and a statuette, "Hannibal." He returned to America again and to Boston where he did some portrait work. The public library there preserves two bronze busts by him: "Hugh O'Brien" (1888), and "J. B. O'Reilly" (1897). In the late eighties or early nineties he spent about two years in London, exhibiting at the Royal Academy in 1890, besides the "Young Sophokles," a bust of Mrs. Ronalds. He then again went to Rome where he modeled for the Chicago World's Fair a colossal figure called "The Spirit," inspired by Milton. It was so large that he used as a studio the baths of Diocletian. The statue never reached its destination, however. Half of it reached Brooklyn, when the sculptor's funds gave out; this half was finally destroyed and the part left in Rome disappeared. It is said that the Chicago Exposition officials had refused the statue for fear that winds from Lake Michigan might overturn it. It was one of Donoghue's major attempts and its fate was a grievous disappointment to him. He was, however, represented at the Chicago Exposition by the "Young Sophokles," the "Hunting Nymph," and "Kypris." The last-named had figured in the Salon of 1892. Donoghue worked for a time for New York architects in the ornamentation of buildings. The "St. Paul" of the Library of Congress and the "St. Louis of France" for the Appellate Court Building, New York, are due to him. Another recorded work is called "Egyptian Ibis." A second bitter disappointment came when his design for a McKinley memorial for Philadelphia was refused on account of expense.

As a sculptor Donoghue showed much promise though he never reached the first rank. He is now remembered chiefly for his "Young Sophokles." As a man he was tall and handsome, by nature reticent, generous to the point of frequently impoverishing himself, witty, and most winning of manner. Though naturally unaffected he is said to have developed certain eccentricities after meeting and admiring Wilde. Toward the end of his life he became interested in psychical subjects and even contemplated a book on "The New Religion." Worried and oppressed by disappointment and financial difficulties he shot himself. His body was found on the shores of Lake Whitney near New Haven.

[Letter from Mrs. J. J. Schwab, a personal acquaintance; Chas. de Kay in *Art Rev.*, Feb. 1887; W. Lewis Fraser in *Century Mag.*, Apr. 1894; J. C. McCord in *Brush and Pencil*, Aug. 1903; *Am. Art Annual*, 1903; *Illus. Cat. of the Paris Salon*, 1880, 1884, 1887, 1892; *Die Kunst für Alle*, Dec. 15, 1892; Algernon Graves, *The Royal Acad. of Arts* (1905); Lorado Taft, *The Hist. of Am. Sculpture* (1903); *Art World*, Jan. 1917; U. Thieme and F. Becker, *Allgemeines Lexikon der Bildenden Künstler* (1913); *New Haven Evening Leader*, July 2 and 6, 1903; *N. Y. Herald*, July 6, 1903.]

E. G. N.

D'OOGE, MARTIN LUTHER (July 17, 1839–Sept. 12, 1915), Greek scholar, was born at Zonnemaire in the Netherlands. His father, Leonard D'Ooge, was of Huguenot extraction and his mother, Johanna Quintus D'Ooge, came of a Dutch family whose men had for several generations followed the teaching profession. At an early age he came with his parents to Grand Rapids, Mich., where he prepared for college. After receiving the A.B. degree from the University of Michigan in 1862, he was for two years principal of the Ann Arbor High School, resigning that position in 1865 to enter Union Theological Seminary. While still a student at the seminary he accepted in 1867 a call to the University of Michigan as assistant professor of ancient languages. When Prof. Boise resigned his chair in 1868, D'Ooge was made acting professor, and in 1870 professor of the Greek language and literature. He thereupon obtained a two years' leave of absence for study abroad, especially at Berlin and the University of Leipzig, and received his Ph.D. from the latter in 1872. Except for the year 1886–87, when he was on leave as director of the American School of Classical Studies at Athens, and a semester in 1905, when he attended as delegate the International Archæological Congress which met in Greece, he taught continuously at the University of Michigan until his retirement in 1912. In addition to the heavy teaching schedule which he always carried, he served as dean of the College of Literature, Science, and the Arts from 1889 to 1897. The advanced students, to whom he gave his time freely, found him exacting in his standards; he insisted on wide reading and complete mastery of subject matter. While the orators, Homer, and Sophocles appealed to him most strongly, he was keenly interested in every phase of ancient life and thought. In his classroom his pupils felt the great personal charm, vivacity, and unfailing friendliness which made him a popular and well-loved figure in university life. To them, as to his colleagues, his home was always open in the gracious hospitality with which he and Mrs. D'Ooge (*née* Mary Worcester of Auburndale, Mass., whom he married July 31, 1873) delighted to welcome friends of literary and artistic tastes.

His university duties, to which he devoted himself with energy and enthusiastic zeal, left him little time for writing. Besides contributing occasional articles to the *Nation* and various classical journals, he edited *The Oration of Demosthenes on the Crown* in 1875, and the *Antigone* of Sophocles in 1884. His chief work, however, upon which he spent much study and travel, is the scholarly volume *The Acropolis of Athens* (1908). After his retirement he occupied himself with European travel, which always called him insistently, and the translation of the *Arithmetic* of Nicomachus of Gerasa. This was published by his friends and colleagues, Professors Robbins and Karpinski, in 1926 (*Nicomachus of Gerasa, Introduction to Arithmetic*; translated by M. L. D'Ooge with Studies in Greek Arithmetic, by Frank Egleston Robbins and Louis Charles Karpinski. University of Michigan Studies, Humanistic Series, vol. XVI, 1926).

He had only fine scorn for the type of scholar who seeks publicity and preferment. The presidency of the American Philological Association (1883–84) and the other honors which came to him he received with his usual modesty as tributes to his department rather than to himself. He died in Ann Arbor, survived by Mrs. D'Ooge and by his brother, Prof. Benjamin Leonard D'Ooge, the well-known Latinist.

[B. A. Hinsdale and I. N. Demmon, *Hist. of the Univ. of Mich.* (1906); obituary notice by Campbell Bonner in *Classical Philology*, X (1915), 488; appreciation by F. W. Kelsey in *Nation*, Sept. 30, 1915; *Detroit News* and *Detroit Free Press*, Sept. 13, 1915.]

J. G. W.

DOOLITTLE, AMOS (May 18, 1754–Jan. 30, 1832), engraver, was born in Cheshire, Conn., the son of Ambrose and Martha (Munson) Doolittle, being next to the eldest in a family of thirteen. From a craftsman in his native town he began to learn the trade of silversmith, but for some reason turned his attention to engraving on copper. In this he seems to have been his own instructor. While still a young man he left Cheshire, and made his home in New Haven, where he lived the rest of his life. He was one of a number of citizens who memorialized the General Assembly "to construct them a district military company by the name of the Governor's

Second Company of Guards," and thus he became a charter member of that famous organization which is known to-day as the Governor's Foot Guards. When, in the spring of 1775, news came of the battle of Lexington, Doolittle was one of those who under Capt. Benedict Arnold marched to Cambridge. Their services, however, were not needed there at the moment, and they soon returned to New Haven. Doolittle was a practical patriot, and made the expedition serve him to good purpose, for in December of the same year he was advertising in the *Connecticut Journal* four copper plates depicting "the battle of Lexington, Concord," etc., from paintings made by Ralph Earle [*q.v.*]. As representations of what actually took place they can hardly be regarded as of much value. It has been said of them that they are "not to be held amenable to any canons of art, except those formulated and adopted by the artist of his own sweet will" (Andrews, *post,* p. 13). He was an indefatigable worker, turning out from his little shop on the college square a great variety of plates. He seems not to have depended entirely upon the burin for his livelihood, for advertisements in the local papers inform us that he dealt in varnishing, enameling, etc., and that he made silver and metal eagles, and one of his own prints tells us that he had a rolling press. His work as an engraver shows a wide variety of subjects. He furnished numerous portraits and illustrations for books, engraved music, money, and diplomas, and made a number of bookplates. He is said to have assisted Abel Buell [*q.v.*] in engraving the latter's wall map of the territories of the United States according to the Peace of 1783, and he engraved the two maps included in Jedidiah Morse's *Geography Made Easy* (1784). One of Doolittle's principal works, which has received high commendation (Charles Henry Hart, *Catalogue of the Engraved Portraits of Washington,* Grolier Club Publications No. 42, 1904), is his "Display of the United States of America," in which Washington is the central figure surrounded by the coats of arms of the states. There are several variations of this plate. It was followed by a "New Display," in which John Adams was the central figure, and yet again by another "New Display," which carried the portrait of Jefferson. Doolittle was twice married. Regarding his first wife information is lacking, save that her first name was Sally, and that she died Jan. 29, 1797, in her thirty-eighth year (*Connecticut Journal,* Feb. 1, 1797). His second wife was Phebe Tuttle, whom he married on Nov. 8, 1797, and who died in 1825. He died in New Haven and was buried in Grove Street Cemetery.

[Wm. F. Doolittle, *The Doolittle Family in America,* pt. III (1903), pp. 239 ff.; Wm. A. Beardsley, "An Old New Haven Engraver and his Work," published in *Papers of the New Haven Colony Hist. Soc.,* VIII (1914), 132–51, and separately in pamphlet form, with a list (incomplete) of Doolittle's engravings appended; Wm. L. Andrews, *Fragments of Am. Hist. Illustrated Solely by the Works of Those of our own Engravers who Flourished in the XVIIIth Century* (1898); E. G. Porter, *Four Drawings of the Engagement at Lexington and Concord Reproduced from Doolittle's Original Copperplate Engravings with an Explanatory Text* (1883); *Columbian Weekly Register* (New Haven), Feb. 4, 1832. Date of death from tombstone.] W.A.B.

DOOLITTLE, CHARLES LEANDER (Nov. 12, 1843–Mar. 3, 1919), astronomer, was born in Ontario, Ind., the son of Charles and Celia Doolittle. He received his training in astronomy from Prof. J. C. Watson at the University of Michigan. His college course was delayed by his enlistment during the Civil War and later interrupted by service with the United States Northern Boundary Commission along with Lewis Boss, who was in charge of the astronomical observations. Doolittle graduated, however, with the degree C.E., in 1874. Appointed professor of mathematics and astronomy at Lehigh soon after graduation, he remained there until 1895, when he accepted a similar position at the University of Pennsylvania. In 1896 the departments were separated and he became Flower Professor of Astronomy and first director of the Flower Observatory. Here he remained until his retirement in 1912.

Professionally, Doolittle is known chiefly for his researches on the variation of latitude. His observations were begun, before Chandler's investigations of this phenomenon, with a Zenith Telescope which had been discarded by the United States Coast and Geodetic Survey and purchased by Lehigh University for the instruction of engineering classes. The heavy teaching schedule which he was carrying and the small instrumental equipment of the Sayre Observatory set sharp limits to a research program. Ambition, perseverance, and painstaking care, however, achieved results of permanent scientific value even under these conditions. He concluded from his early observations that he had evidence of a variation of latitude. Later, at the Flower Observatory, he came to the conclusion that such a variation could be isolated from sources of systematic error only by making observations under a variety of instrumental conditions. He procured, therefore, a Reflex Zenith Tube. With this instrument and with the Zenith Telescope he continued for many years to make nearly simultaneous observations. The evidence still persisted and the whole series of observations proved a contribution of the highest value in unraveling the tangled mass of evidence. He was the author of: *A Treatise on Practical Astronomy as Applied to Geodesy and Navigation* (1885); *Results of Observations with the Zenith Telescope of the Sayre Observatory from Jan. 19, 1894, to Aug. 19, 1895* (1901); and "Results of Observations with the Wharton Reflex Zenith Tube and the Zenith Telescope of the Flower Astronomical Observatory," in *Publications of the University of Pennsylvania, Astronomical Series* (vol. III, pt. 1, 1908). He was a member of the American Philosophical Society, a Fellow of the American Association for the Advancement of Science, and from 1899 to 1912 treasurer of the American Astronomical Society.

His first wife, whom he married on Sept. 18, 1866, and who died during his first year at Bethlehem, was Martha Cloyes Farrand, also of Ontario, Ind. On May 5, 1882, he married Helen Eugenia Wolle of Bethlehem. His son Eric [*q.v.*] succeeded him as director of the Flower Observatory.

[Obituary by R. H. Tucker in *Pubs. Astronomical Soc. of the Pacific*, XXXI (1919), 103–04; *Who's Who in America*, 1918–19; *Observatory*, XLII, 219–20; *Nature* (London), CIII (1919), 69; *Phila. Press* and *Public Ledger* (Phila.), Mar. 4, 1919.] R. S. D.

DOOLITTLE, ERIC (July 26, 1869–Sept. 21, 1920), astronomer, was born in Ontario, Ind. Practically his whole life was spent in the atmosphere of an astronomical observatory, for his father, Charles Leander Doolittle [*q.v.*], was appointed director of the Sayre Observatory of Lehigh University in 1875 and Eric became his father's assistant and his successor as director of the Flower Observatory of the University of Pennsylvania. He lost his mother, Martha Cloyes (Farrand) Doolittle, the year the family moved to Bethlehem. He was educated in the public schools of Bethlehem and at the Preparatory School of Lehigh University and graduated from the University in 1891 with the degree of C.E. After spending one year as teacher in the Preparatory School, one as instructor of mathematics in Lehigh University, and two in a similar position in the University of Iowa, he went to the University of Chicago for graduate work in astronomy. He had already advanced himself in mathematics by private study and during his year of graduate work he showed great promise. At the suggestion of his professor, the thesis which he had prepared as a requirement for the master's degree was withheld as sufficiently meritorious for a doctor's thesis. He did not complete the requirements for a doctor's degree, however. Called to the University of Pennsylvania in 1896 as instructor in astronomy, he was placed by his father in charge of the new eighteen-inch telescope, made by Brashear, and especially suitable, by reason of its great focal length, to micrometric work. He at once threw himself into the observation of double stars. After working all night he often caught but a short nap before it was time to start for his classes at the University, five miles away. He never slighted his class work and was an enthusiastic and inspiring teacher. He accumulated and published a great mass of double-star observations (see *Publications of the University of Pennsylvania, Astronomical Series,* vols. I–IV, 1901–23), and his authority in this field was so well recognized that Burnham of Yerkes Observatory turned over to him the manuscript notes for the extension of the *General Catalogue of Double Stars.* Thenceforth Doolittle entered on cards, without any clerical assistance, all published observations of double stars. He also found time to finish an extensive work of computation, *The Secular Variations of the Elements of the Orbits of the Four Inner Planets* (1912), and to write many popular articles on astronomy.

During the World War, seeking for the most useful thing he could do, he spent much time studying to be a wireless operator until he was called upon to organize the United States Shipping Board Navigation School at Philadelphia. In attempting to teach large numbers of men and to attend to all the details of organization and administration, he broke down. Although he later returned to his regular duties, he never fully recovered. With a strong tendency to overwork and with an unusual ability to use his time profitably, it is a pity that he was given so much to do without liberal clerical and financial assistance. His favorite diversion was reading Dickens. He was a man of extreme modesty and self-effacement. He had a great gift for friendship, firmly based on complete unselfishness and consideration. The appreciations published after his death all show how much his friends loved him. In 1902 he married Sara Bitler Halliwell of Bethlehem. She was in full sympathy with his ideals and willingly endured the great sacrifices she had to make.

[R. G. Aitken in *Pubs. Astronomical Soc. of the Pacific,* XXXII (1920), 322–24; T. J. J. See in *Astronomische Nachrichten,* CCXII, 183–84; S. G. Barton, *Popular Astronomy,* Nov. 1920 and *Science,* Oct. 22, 1920; *Monthly Notices of the Royal Astronomical Soc.* (London), LXXXI (1921), 255–56.] R. S. D.

DOOLITTLE, JAMES ROOD (Jan. 3, 1815–July 27, 1897), lawyer, statesman, was born in Hampton Township, Washington County, N. Y., the eldest child of Reuben Doolittle of Colonial and English stock and Sarah (Rood) Doolittle. Reared on a farm in western New York, he obtained his preliminary education in the rural school. He graduated from Geneva (now Hobart) College in 1834. In 1837 he was admitted to the bar in Rochester and the same year he married Mary L. Cutting. He began to practise in Rochester, but four years later settled at Warsaw, N. Y., where from 1847 to 1850 he was district attorney of Wyoming County. He also took a prominent part in politics as a Democrat. In 1844 he campaigned extensively for Polk, and at the New York state convention of 1847 he wrote the "corner-stone resolution" in which "the democracy of New York . . . declare . . . their uncompromising hostility to the extension of slavery into territory now free, or which may be hereafter acquired by any action of the government of the United States." This became the essential plank in the Free-Soil platform of 1848 and, in modified phraseology, in the Republican platform of 1856. Doolittle remained a leader of the Barnburner faction of the Democratic party until 1856, except that he supported Van Buren in 1848. Meanwhile (1851) he settled in Racine, Wis., and two years later was elected judge of the first judicial circuit. In 1856 he identified himself with the Republican party.

He was elected, as a Republican, to the United States Senate in 1857 and served till Mar. 4, 1869. His career in politics divides sharply into two periods—before the death of Lincoln and after that event. Although a "state-rights" Republican, prominent in the movement which resulted in Wisconsin's nullification of the Fugitive-Slave Law, he became as senator one of the stanchest and ablest proponents of the doctrine of no compromise with the slave states. Like Carl Schurz, Byron Paine, and other Wisconsin Republicans, he was determined to carry out the party platform, restricting slavery rigorously within the states where it existed under state law. This he believed to be the constitutional method. He was a close personal friend and adviser of Lincoln. Early in 1864 he addressed at Springfield, Ill., a great mass-meeting called to decide whether or not Lincoln must be superseded. In his first dozen words: "I believe in God Almighty! *Under Him I believe in Abraham Lincoln,*" Doolittle aroused such a demonstration for Lincoln that the President's opponents beat a hasty retreat. Johnson's struggle with Congress over reconstruction brought Doolittle into sharp collision with the radical Republicans, who, as he believed, were violating the Constitution in keeping states out of the Union. He ably supported the President, arguing that Johnson was merely carrying into execution Lincoln's policies. On the impeachment question he voted for acquittal; in the presidential canvass of 1868 he supported Seymour against Grant. The Wisconsin legislature, in 1867, called for Doolittle's resignation, which he refused. In 1869 he retired to make his home in Racine, but opened a law office in Chicago where he practised law extensively almost to the day of his death at the age of eighty-two.

Doolittle was an outstanding personality, physically and mentally. His presence on any platform guaranteed an interested audience. His voice was remarkably fine and so powerful that he could address 20,000 persons with perfect success. He was accounted a great lawyer, was a wide reader and popular lecturer on Bible subjects. He was in great demand for speeches on special occasions and on diverse social, religious, and economic themes. His so-called "betrayal" of the Republican party ended his political career. As a Democrat he was defeated for governor of Wisconsin in 1871, for congressman from his congressional district twice, and once for judge of his judicial circuit. His "Johnsonizing" was bitterly resented, but leading Republicans who had known him long pronounced his motives pure. His nature was strongly emotional and somewhat sentimental. He tended to "fundamentalism" in religion, lecturing on the fulfilment of Bible prophecies. The Constitution he construed with Jeffersonian strictness. In practical politics he was keen, shrewd, masterful, winning the encomium of so skilled a political tactician as E. W. (Boss) Keyes. His personality radiated good will and compelled attention.

[There is a biography in *The Doolittle Family in America,* pt. VII (1908), comp. by Wm. F. Doolittle, pp. 653–710. Collections of pamphlets and clippings; also several hundred letters, manuscript speeches, etc., are in State Hist. Lib., Madison, Wis. See also D. Mowry, "Vice-President Johnson and Senator Doolittle," in *Pubs. Southern Hist. Asso.,* vol. IX, and "Doolittle Correspondence" in the same, vols. IX–XI (1905–07); *Biog. Dir. of the Am. Cong.* (1928); obituary in *Chicago Tribune,* July 28, 1897.]

J. S—r.

DORCHESTER, DANIEL (Mar. 11, 1827–Mar. 13, 1907), Methodist clergyman, superintendent of United States Indian schools, was a writer and preacher of wide influence, an able leader in temperance reform and other movements for social betterment, and the leading religious statistician of his time. He was of pure New England stock, a descendant of Elder Brewster. He was born in Duxbury, Mass., the son of the Rev. Daniel Dorchester, a Methodist clergyman, and his wife Mary Otis. He was educated at Norwich Academy (now the Free Academy) and Wesleyan University, leaving the latter in his junior year, 1847, on account of ill health. Wesleyan granted him the degrees of A.M. in 1856 and D.D. in 1874. After holding various charges in the Providence (now Southern New England) Conference he was in 1855 at the age of twenty-eight elected to the state Senate from Mystic, Conn. Here he served with distinction, being chairman of the Committee on Idiocy, the preparation of its report leading to permanent sociological interest. In 1858 he entered the New England Conference in which he held ten pastorates and served three terms as presiding elder. In 1882 he was elected to the Massachusetts legislature from Natick, where he was chairman of the Constitutional Amendment Committee, at the same time serving as president of the Non-Partisan Temperance League. In 1884 and in 1888 he was a member of the General Conference of the Methodist Church. On Dec. 5, 1889, he was appointed by President Harrison superintendent of Indian Schools of the United States, an office which he held for some four years, traveling over 96,000 miles and visiting 105 reservations. He was instrumental in having government appropriations for sectarian Indian schools withdrawn and increased emphasis placed on industrial education, working in this and other matters in close cooperation with Archbishop Ireland [*q.v.*]. The reports of his superintendency are published in the reports of the Department of the Interior.

While he was an administrator of marked ability and a preacher of great power, it was with his pen that he exerted his greatest influence. His first book, one that revealed his ability to use statistics, was his *Report of the Commissioners on Idiocy* (1856). His *Problem of Religious Progress* (1881) was a helpful and timely book. But probably his best-known and most influential book is his *History of Christianity in the United States* (1888), a work of immense industry, thoroughness, and impartiality. Other works are: *Concessions of Liberalists to Orthodoxy* (1878); *The Liquor Problem in all Ages* (1884); *The Indictment of the Liquor Traffic* (1885); *The Why of Methodism* (1887); *Romanism versus the Public School System* (1888); *Christianity Vindicated by its Enemies* (1896). In addition he published many sermons and addresses and wrote much for the magazines and reviews.

Dorchester was a tall man of imposing presence, with a winning countenance. His voice was distinct and far-reaching and his manner in the conduct of public services was dignified. On Apr. 12, 1850, he married Mary Payson Davis of Dudley, Mass., who died in 1874. Of this marriage there were seven children, five of whom survived their father. On Oct. 12, 1875, he married Merial A. Whipple of North Charlestown, N. H., who died Apr. 1, 1895.

[*Who's Who in America*, 1906–07; *Zion's Herald*, Mar. 20, 1907; *Christian Advocate*, Mar. 21, 1907; *Minutes of the New England Conference*, 1907; *Boston Herald*, Mar. 13, and *Boston Post*, Mar. 14, 1907; information as to certain facts from Dorchester's son.]

F. T. P.

DOREMUS, ROBERT OGDEN (Jan. 11, 1824–Mar. 22, 1906), chemist, inventor, was born in New York City, the son of Thomas Cornelius and Sarah Platt (Haines) Doremus [*q.v.*]. He was educated at Columbia College, where he graduated in 1842, and at the University of the City of New York, where he received the degree of M.D. in 1851. He was the first private pupil of John W. Draper [*q.v.*] and his assistant for seven years, and personally assisted Draper in taking the first photograph ever made of the human face. Before the invention of the dynamo, he perfected for demonstration an arc-light, producing the current for it with a huge battery of Bunsen cells. One unit of these cells is still preserved in the Museum of the Department of Chemistry of the College of the City of New York. In cooperation with Tessie du Motay he perfected the latter's processes for the generation of oxygen and its use in increasing the luminosity of a coal-gas flame. Tradition has it that several blocks of streets in the Twenty-third St. region of New York City were really piped for oxygen transmission and the improved gaslights installed along the lines of the oxygen pipes. In 1848, in association with Charles Townsend Harris [*q.v.*], Doremus organized a laboratory for investigation and instruction in analytical chemistry, where he lectured to the students of the New York College of Pharmacy. He was elected professor of chemistry at this institution in 1849. In the following year he was prominent among the founders of the New York Medical College. At his own expense, he equipped for it one of the first analytical laboratories connected with any medical college in the United States. He organized a similar laboratory for the Long Island Hospital Medical College in 1859.

Elected professor of natural history in the New York Free Academy (subsequently called the College of the City of New York) in 1852, with the exception of a trip abroad in 1862–64, he remained actively connected with that institution as professor of chemistry and physics and vice-president until his retirement as professor emeritus in 1903.

The general laboratories in the old Free Academy building on Twenty-third St. were among the first college laboratories and were excellent in design and equipment. There Doremus, an impressive personality and inspiring lecturer, awakened in his audiences and pupils an interest in science unusual at that time. His lectures were noted for their scope and vivid demonstrations. Though handicapped by physical deformity, he was a skilful manipulator. The apparatus, often designed by himself, which he used in his classroom and public lectures was unique in its nature and size. Pieces of it still retained at the City College are so novel as to be really "Museum" specimens. Many of his experiments remain vivid in the minds of his former pupils; his demonstrations of heat reflection, magnetic attraction, heat of hydration of lime, weight of gases, the then entirely novel electric light, primary batteries, oxidation of iron, and dozens of others, were carried through on so large and vivid a scale that one never forgot the phenomenon. He was a dominating figure on the faculty of the college, and his lectures and other outside activities were instrumental in making the college known and in bringing to the public a knowledge of the influence of science on everyday life. He was a prominent member of the Medical Advisory Commission which established the present New York City Department of Health. He greatly influenced medical jurisprudence with his expert investigations in toxicology, and in 1862 he was appointed professor of chemistry, toxicology, and medical jurisprudence in Bellevue Hospital Medical College. Through his efforts, the famous nerve specialist, Brown-Seqquard, came to America to lecture at that institution.

In 1862 Doremus made an important visit to Paris at the request of Emperor Napoleon III, spending two years there in perfecting and introducing a compressed granulated gunpowder for firearms. The cartridge which he patented dispensed with the serge envelope previously used in muzzle-loading cannon and thus avoided the necessity of sponging after firing. This invention was adopted by the governments of the United States and France, and was employed in the Civil and Franco-Prussian wars, besides being used extensively in blasting. In 1862, also, he prepared apparatus for generating chlorine gas between decks for use on the steamer which arrived in New York in that year with an epidemic of cholera on board. The process was again used against cholera in 1875 in the hospital wards of New York. This was the first use of chlorine as a disinfectant on so large a scale. He patented several methods of extinguishing fires by chemical action which resulted in the establishment of several chemical industries needed to make the materials. Another important contribution was the preservation of "Cleopatra's Needle" through the use of melted paraffin forced into the porous stone.

Doremus was prominent in social circles and an ardent lover of good music. He was one of the founders of the Philharmonic Society and the first amateur to be made its president. This was the only American orchestra of its kind at that time. He was instrumental in bringing Adelina Patti, Christine Nilsson, and Ole Bull to the United States, and in advancing their public and private performances. Ole Bull was a close personal friend of his, and Doremus took great pride in the possession of a fine watch presented to him by the eminent violinist. He was a Fellow of the Academy of Science of New York, and the American Geographical Society. His wife was Estelle E. Skidmore, daughter of Capt. Hubbard Skidmore.

[*Who's Who in America*, 1906–07; *City College Quart.*, Dec. 1906; *College Mercury* (C. C. N. Y.), Apr. 1906; C. F. Chandler in *Science*, Mar. 30, and *Sci. American*, Mar. 31, 1906; *Medico-Legal Jour.*, June 1906; *N. Y. Times*, *N. Y. Tribune*, Mar. 23, 1906.]

H. R. M.

DOREMUS, SARAH PLATT HAINES (Aug. 3, 1802–Jan. 29, 1877), social worker, one of the daughters of Elias and Mary (Ogden) Haines, was born at Whitehall and South Sts., near Battery Park, New York City. She was a descendant of Robert Ogden of New Jersey. Her brother, Daniel Haines, was twice elected governor of New Jersey (1843 and 1847), and served as a judge on the supreme court bench of that state from 1852 to 1866. Her father was a New York merchant. Sarah Platt Haines had the educational advantages open to girls in the families of well-to-do New Yorkers at the beginning of the nineteenth century. At nineteen she was married to Thomas C. Doremus of New York. Early in life she became intensely interested in various forms of religious and humane effort, and even the demands of bringing up her family of nine children could not keep her from devoting a large measure of her time and strength to such causes. At a time when women rarely assumed leadership in public movements, she was active in a group of women who secured aid for the Greek revolutionists. This was only the first of a series of humanitarian services, continuing for half a century. Throughout her long life she was notable for unusual energy and persistence in pursuing her ends, as well as for serenity and cheerfulness in disposition. She was heartily seconded in her efforts by her husband, who gave liberally of his personal means as the state of his fortune permitted. Although a member of the Reformed Church in New York, she was chiefly interested in work conducted under undenominational or interdenominational auspices. In at least one notable instance—the Baptist Mission of Grand Ligne in Canada, under Madame Feller—she took an active part in promoting an enterprise controlled by a religious body with which she was not affiliated. Her interest in that work began as early as 1835 and continued for many years. In the decade of the forties the neglected condition of the inmates of New York City prisons appealed to her with especial force. Beginning with the effort to maintain religious services in the city prisons, with which she coöperated, she was led to see the importance of aiding discharged convicts and, with a number of other New York women, organized a home that offered temporary shelter to discharged women prisoners. This was later developed into the Isaac T. Hopper Home. During the last ten years of her life, Mrs. Doremus was president of the association that conducted this refuge. Among pioneer efforts to help the women among New York's worthy poor were the House and School of Industry (1850) and the Nursery and Child's Hospital (1854); with both of these she was associated from the first. In 1855, when Dr. J. Marion Sims was seeking support for a hospital to treat the maladies peculiar to women, it was Sarah Platt Doremus who brought about the incorporation of the Woman's Hospital in the State of New York by the legislature and solicited the aid of wealthy women in starting the institution. She was president of its women's supervisory board at the time of her death. Throughout the Civil War she ministered to the sick and wounded of both armies as occasion arose. The famine sufferers in Ireland in 1869 also enjoyed her bounty. Long identified with the promotion of American foreign missions, she was one of the founders, in 1860, of the Woman's Union Missionary Society, through which the Protestant women of America sought to elevate the condition of their sisters in non-Christian lands. Judged by twentieth-century standards of resources and budget, perhaps most of the organizations through which she labored were relatively feeble and ill-equipped, but they were persistent and held their ground, almost without exception. The importance of her leadership lay very largely in her successful attempt to enlist other women of like environment in organized philanthropic effort. In the second and third quarters of the nineteenth century her achievement in that line of effort was outstanding, if not unique. She died as the result of a fall in January 1877. Her only son was Robert Ogden Doremus [*q.v.*], the distinguished chemist.

[*The Ogden Family in America*, Elizabethtown Branch (1907), comp. by Wm. Ogden Wheeler; the *Missionary Link*, Mar. 1877; annual reports of the Women's Prison Association and the Woman's Hospital; J. Marion Sims, *The Story of My Life* (1884); *N. Y. Times*, Jan. 30, 1877.] W. B. S.

DORGAN, THOMAS ALOYSIUS (Apr. 29, 1877–May 2, 1929), cartoonist, sports-writer, son of Thomas and Anna (Tobin) Dorgan, was born in the tenement district "south of the slot" in San Francisco, Cal. When he was ten years old his right hand was seriously injured, leaving him only the thumb and first knuckle of his forefinger, unfitting him for manual labor, and permanently affecting his social and psychic attitude. At the age of fourteen he left public school and obtained his first newspaper job in the art department of the San Francisco *Bulletin*. Although untutored in drawing, he soon began to produce stinging cartoons of local events and personalities, which resulted in his employment as the comic artist of the *Bulletin* until 1902. In that year his graphic talents recommended him to William Randolph Hearst who was seeking a political cartoonist of the Nast type to lampoon Tammany Hall in its conduct of New York City politics. Dorgan was called to New York to a place on the staff of the *New York Journal*. In the mayoralty contest of 1905 Hearst ran against George B. McClellan, who was supported by Charles F. Murphy, the Tammany boss. Dorgan's powerful cartoons, depicting Murphy in convict's stripes, nearly swung the election to Hearst, the Tammany candidate finally winning by the narrowest margin in the history of the office.

This was Dorgan's only venture into political cartooning. He turned to sports, became an authority on boxing, and was generally called upon to serve as unofficial referee in no-decision bouts. Thousands of dollars changed hands on his decisions, which were never disputed. Between 1900 and 1920 he was at the ringside of every championship boxing match, and dominated the sporting pages of the country with his syndicated sketches and comments signed "Tad"—the initials of his name. It is said of him that he could sketch from memory any important blow or exchange of blows in the major fights of Corbett, Fitzsimmons, Jeffries, and Johnson. George Bellows once declared that Dorgan was without a rival in reproducing the complex movements of prize-fighters in action.

When Dorgan was thirty years old he took over and developed the comic-strip characters of "Judge Rumhauser" and "Silk Hat Harry."

Dorion

Despite their external resemblance to dogs they were in reality human beings—all too human, in fact, as Tad delineated their mortal frailties. Mild social satire, directed chiefly at lower middle-class pretenders and petty officials in their pitiful attempts to appear greater than they were, formed the basis of the "Judge Rummy" cartoons and the later series entitled "Indoor Sports." With a sardonic flick of his pen Tad could puncture hypocrisy and pretense, but the necessity of tickling a daily audience, without giving offense, hampered the exercise of his rapier gift. Personally, he was of a misanthropic, anti-social cast; had he taken the button off his foil he could have ranked just below Hogarth and Daumier as a graphic satirist.

His chief contribution to American life was his colorful use of slang, a large part of which he coined or put into circulation. "Yes, we have no bananas," "23, skidoo," "Officer, call a cop," and "Let him up, he's all cut," are a few of the meaningless but irresistible phrases of his invention. "The first hundred years are the hardest," has passed into proverbial usage, while dozens of his shorter expressions have become an integral part of common speech. "Apple-sauce" means obvious flattery; "chin-music" is idle chatter. A hat was a "skimmer," shoes were "dogs," and a stingy person a "nickel-nurser"—first to Tad and afterward to millions of his contemporaries. Probably his best-known simile was "As busy as a one-armed paper-hanger with the hives."

For the last ten years of his life a chronically bad heart kept Dorgan a house-ridden invalid. With a tremendous effort of will, yet with no apparent diminution of power, he continued to turn out his daily copy, keeping in touch with the sporting world by means of radio and the visits of faithful friends. He was two weeks ahead of his publication schedule when he died of heart-failure at his home in Great Neck, L. I.

[The files of current newspapers are the chief written sources of information; see especially F. P. Stockbridge in *N. Y. Times,* May 6, 1929; W. S. Farnsworth and Bill Corum in *N. Y. Evening Jour.,* May 3, 1929; Westbrook Pegler in *Chicago Tribune,* May 3, 1929; Damon Runyon in *N. Y. American,* May 3, 1929; Norman Klein in N. Y. *Evening Post,* May 4, 1929; editorials in *N. Y. Times* and N. Y. *Evening Post,* May 3, 1929; *N. Y. Herald-Tribune,* May 3, 1929. O. O. McIntyre published an article in Hearst's *Cosmopolitan Magazine,* Mar. 1927, repr. in *N. Y. Jour.,* May 3, 1929; *New Republic,* May 15, 1929. H. M. Robinson, "Tad For Short," in *Century Quart.,* fall issue, 1929.]

H. M. R.

DORION, MARIE (*c.* 1791–Sept. 3, 1850), wife of Pierre Dorion, the younger, interpreter of the Astoria land expedition (1811–12), was a member of the Iowa tribe. Her name appears in early Oregon and Washington records as Marie Aioe (sometimes L'Aguivoise, probably an early variant of the name Iowa). Her father-in-law, the elder Pierre Dorion, born of a prominent Quebec family before 1750, made his way to Cahokia, Ill., as early as 1780, lived for a time in St. Louis, and within a year or two established his permanent home with the Yanktons and married a woman of the tribe. In 1804, as an interpreter, he accompanied Lewis and Clark from the vicinity of the present Glasgow, Mo., to the James, where he was authorized to gather a delegation of Sioux chiefs and take them on a visit to Washington. The younger Pierre Dorion, a half-breed, for a time kept a trading-post for Pierre Chouteau among the Yanktons. He had a Yankton wife, Holy Rainbow, whom he seems to have abandoned about 1806 for the Iowa girl. In March 1811, he set out for St. Louis with Wilson Price Hunt's Astorians, taking with him his Iowa wife and two infant sons. On that long and terrible journey, much of the time afoot, Marie showed a patience and fortitude in enduring fatigue, hunger, and hardships unsurpassed by any of the men. On Dec. 30, near the present North Powder, Ore., she gave birth to a child, and in the forenoon of the next day overtook the party "looking as unconcerned as if nothing had happened to her" and ready to continue the march. The child, however, lived but eight days.

In the second summer following the arrival at Astoria, she and the two surviving children accompanied her husband with the John Reed hunting party to the Boise River country. About Jan. 10, 1814, the two sections of this party, widely separated, were attacked by Indians, and all the men were killed. Escaping with her children on a horse, she fled toward the Columbia River, and after nine days' travel, suffering intensely from cold and hunger, found refuge in a lonely spot in the Blue Mountains. Here she put up a rough hut of pine branches, killed her horse for food, and remained for fifty-seven days. After fifteen days' further travel, again enduring extreme privations, she and her children reached the friendly Walla Wallas. Later in the spring, on the Columbia, she met the last party of the returning Astorians and told them the tragic fate of her comrades.

She lived for a time at Fort Okanagon. About 1819 she married a trapper named Venier, of whom nothing seems to be known. In 1823 she formed a union with Jean Baptiste Toupin, interpreter for many years at Fort Walla Walla, who in 1841 took up land in the Willamette Valley, near the present Salem, and settled there. On July 19 of that year her union with Toupin was legalized by a Roman Catholic church ceremony; her two children by Toupin were legitimized, and her son Baptiste Dorion and daughter Marguerite Venier were "acknowledged" by Toupin. Through the publication of Irving's *Astoria* she became famous. Dr. Elijah White, who visited her in the winter of 1842–43, found her living in comfort and was "much impressed with her noble, commanding bearing." She died at her home. Her son Baptiste. who was employed as a guide by the naturalist J. K. Townsend in 1835 and as an interpreter by Dr. White in 1842–43, and who in 1848 was appointed a second lieutenant in the 1st Regiment of Oregon Riflemen, died in 1849. The other son is said to have been the Paul Dorion of Parkman's *The California and Oregon Trail,* though the identification is disputed.

[J. Neilson Barry, "Madame Dorion of the Astorians," in *Ore. Hist. Quart.,* Sept. 1929, and "The First Born on the Oregon Trail," *Ibid.,* June 1911; Washington Irving, *Astoria* (1836); Doane Robinson, "Our First Family," *S. Dak. Hist. Colls.,* vol. XIII (1926); A. J. Allen, *Ten Years in Ore.: Travels and Adventures of Dr. E. White and Lady* (1851); correspondence with C. H. Carey, author of *Hist. of Ore.* (1922). The episode of Marie Dorion's escape is related in Gabriel Franchère's *Relation d'un Voyage à la Côte du Nord-Ouest de l'Amérique Septentrionale* (Montreal, 1820; English translation, 1854); Ross Cox's *Adventures on the Columbia River* (1831); and Alexander Ross's *Adventures of the First Settlers on the Oregon or Columbia River* (1849). The narratives of Franchère and Ross are contained in *Early Western Travels,* ed. by R. G. Thwaites, vols. VI and VII (1904).] W. J. G.

DORNIN, THOMAS ALOYSIUS (May 1, 1800–Apr. 22, 1874), naval officer, was the son of Bernard and Eliza Dornin. His father, an associate of the Irish patriots who were banished after the rebellion of 1798, settled for a time in Brooklyn, where he became one of the first booksellers to deal almost exclusively in Catholic publications. He soon, however, moved to Baltimore and continued his work there. Thomas Aloysius, born in Ireland, was educated at St. Mary's College, Baltimore, where he was enrolled in 1811 and later years, probably until his entry into the navy on May 2, 1815. Before he was promoted to lieutenant on Jan. 13, 1825, he had served in the Mediterranean on the *Java, Franklin,* and *Peacock,* and seen service under David Porter in the campaign against the West-Indian pirates. In 1826 he cruised in the Pacific on the *Brandywine* and then came home around the world on the *Vincennes.* In 1831–34 he was again in the Pacific on the *Falmouth.* From 1834 to 1836 he was in command of the receiving ship at Philadelphia and was then made commander of the store-ship *Relief,* which was to sail as a part of the Wilkes South Sea Exploring Expedition. He did not, apparently, sail in her, and the ship herself was soon sent back as unsuitable. In 1837, Dornin married Mrs. James Thorburn (*née* Anne Moore Howison), and he was unemployed most of the time till 1841, when he was promoted to the rank of commander at the same time as was Farragut and sent to the Pacific to command the schooner *Shark.* He returned in charge of the *Dale.* In 1844 he began special work in ordnance while attached to the navy yard in Washington. This tour of duty ended in 1851 after he had served with Farragut for a year and a half on a board detailed to revise the ordnance regulations. In this year he was given command of the *Portsmouth* and sent to the Pacific coast of Mexico, his mission being to keep an eye on William Walker's expedition to Lower California. He hired a passenger steamship, the *Columbus,* and proceeded with it and the slow-sailing *Portsmouth* down the Mexican coast to Ensenada Bay, where Walker [*q.v.*] was encamped with 140 followers. Walker, however, departed with all his unwounded men as soon as Dornin arrived. The latter, before he left the vicinity, rescued some American citizens who had been imprisoned by the Mexicans at Mazatlan on suspicion of their being a reinforcement for Walker. After forcing the Mexican insurgents to allow American ships free access to Acapulco he went to Honolulu, where by his presence he supported the United States consul in blocking British and French moves in the Sandwich Islands. His journals of this cruise mention frequent target practises, an indication that Dornin was ahead of many of his brother officers in foreseeing the value of gunnery. He then returned to the United States (1855), received his promotion to captain's rank, and was put in command of the Norfolk Navy Yard, where he remained till 1859.

In that year he went to the Mediterranean as fleet captain but in 1860 was sent to the coast of Africa in command of the *San Jacinto.* Here during the next year, he seized several slavers, landed the slaves in Liberia, and sent the captured vessels into Norfolk, not knowing that the Civil War had already begun. When he was relieved by Capt. Wilkes in October 1861, he returned to the United States in the *Constellation,* and although retired as a commodore in 1862, commanded the naval station at Baltimore till the end of the war. He spent the next few years in charge of lighthouses in Chesapeake Bay, Pamlico Sound, and on the coast between. He passed the last years of his life in Fredericksburg, Va., and Savannah, Ga. He died in the latter city but was buried in Norfolk. Admiral Ammen (*The Old Navy and the New,* 1891, p.

27), says that in 1837 he "spoke with an Irish brogue, but had a bright, kindly face, and was indeed thoroughly an Irish gentleman."

[Dornin's *Brandywine* and *Portsmouth* journals, and his letters as captain of the *Portsmouth* are in the Navy Dept. Lib. The official record of his naval career can be secured from the Bureau of Navigation, Navy Dept. Most of it, and a fuller sketch of his life, is reprinted in L. R. Hamersly, *Records of Living Officers of the U. S. Navy and Marine Corps*, rev. ed. (1870), p. 65.]

W. B. N.

DORR, JULIA CAROLINE RIPLEY (Feb. 13, 1825–Jan. 18, 1913), author, was born in Charleston, S. C., and died in Rutland, Vt. Her father, William Young Ripley, born in Vermont, was living in Charleston as a merchant when he married Zulma DeLacy Thomas, who, with her parents, natives of France resident in the West Indies, had come to South Carolina to escape negro insurrection. Before Julia, the first child of this marriage, was two years old, her mother's frail health caused her family to remove to Vermont, but the invalid died on the day following her arrival. The child lived with her father here and there in New England and for a while in New York City. Her education was somewhat irregular although she acquired some proficiency in Latin. In 1837, William Ripley took up residence permanently in Rutland, where he operated a lucrative business in marble. There his daughter also spent, but for one interlude, the remainder of her tranquil, comfortable existence. After her marriage in 1847 to Seneca M. Dorr, she lived in Ghent, N. Y., but in 1857 she and her husband went back to Rutland, and her husband became associated in business with her father. From the age of twelve she had written verse, but none of it was made public until her husband soon after their marriage permitted specimens of it without her knowledge to be published in a magazine. Her first three books, *Farmingdale* (1854), *Lanmere* (1856), and *Sybil Huntington* (1869), all novels, were published under the name Caroline Thomas. Among her other novels were, *Expiation* (1873), and *In Kings' Houses* (1898), a story of England under Queen Anne. She wrote also in prose, *Bride and Bridegroom* (1873), a book of sentimental advice to young married couples, and three books of travel, *Bermuda* (1884), *"The Flower of England's Face"* (1895), and *A Cathedral Pilgrimage* (1896). She was most widely known for her verse, however, of which there were published certainly as many as ten volumes, beginning with *Poems* (1872), including *Poems . . . Complete Edition* (1892), and ending with *Last Poems* (1913). As a poet—deliberately shunning, it is said, all expressions which she could not with propriety read to children—she gave utterance in respectable but not highly distinguished or passionate phrases to the conventional wisdom of her time and place. Emerson valued her enough to include a poem by her in his anthology, *Parnassus* (1874), and Oliver Wendell Holmes and E. C. Stedman corresponded with her and counted her as a personal friend. She was devotedly attached to her husband, and his death in December 1884 was perhaps the one event of her life which she was not able to explain to herself in terms of what was normally intended.

[H. W. Ripley, *Geneal. of a Part of the Ripley Family* (1867); Hiram Carleton, *Geneal. and Family Hist. of Vt.*, II (1903), 587; W. H. Crockett, *Vermont the Green Mountain State*, vol. V (1921); J. T. Morse, *Life and Letters of O. W. Holmes* (2 vols., 1896); Laura Stedman and G. M. Gould, *Life and Letters of E. C. Stedman* (1910), II, 268, 346; E. C. Stedman and E. M. Hutchinson, *Lib. of Am. Lit.*, vol. XI (1890); *Who's Who in America*, 1912–13; Henry M. Alden in *Harper's Weekly*, Feb. 1, 1913; *Nation* (N. Y.), Jan. 23, 1913; *Rutland Herald*, and *Burlington Free Press*, Jan. 20, 1913.]

J. D. W.

DORR, THOMAS WILSON (Nov. 5, 1805–Dec. 27, 1854), politician and reformer, was born at Providence, R. I., the son of Sullivan and Lydia (Allen) Dorr. His father was a prosperous manufacturer and the family occupied a good social position. Thomas never married, but two of his sisters married prominent men and the son of one of them married the daughter of John Lothrop Motley. Dorr was therefore no plebeian when he led the cause of the unenfranchised classes. As a boy, he attended Phillips Exeter Academy. He graduated from Harvard in 1823, and then went to New York where he studied law under Chancellor Kent and Vice-Chancellor McCoun. He was admitted to the bar in 1827 and returned to Providence to practise. He began his political career as a representative in the Rhode Island Assembly in 1834.

In the half-century following the American Revolution efforts were made nearly everywhere to reap the fruits of that struggle in a wider extension of the limited franchise. In Rhode Island these attempts, made at intervals from 1797 to 1834, had invariably been met by the government with contemptuous obstruction. In 1834 a convention met at Providence to consider the matter again, and Dorr was a member of the committee which drew up an address to the people. All efforts at reform, however, were once more blocked by the legislature. By 1841 Rhode Island was almost the only state which had not adopted practical manhood suffrage. It was also the only state which had not adopted a written constitution, and the old colonial charter, under which the state was ruled, had been outgrown. Under that instrument the original grantees had had the sole right to decide who should have a voice in the management of public affairs, and they had decreed the possession of a moderate landed estate as a qualification for the franchise. By 1840 this obsolete requirement had disfranchised over half the adult male population, and about nineteen towns, having a total population of only 3,500 voters, returned over half the legislature, so that less than 1,800 voters could control the destinies of a state of 108,000 population. Moreover, no person who did not own real estate could bring suit for recovery of debt or obtain redress for personal injury unless a freeholder indorsed his writ.

The situation had become intolerable, and in 1840 the Rhode Island Suffrage Association was formed, and processions and popular meetings held. Dorr took a leading part in the agitation. The legislature refused to remedy such grievances as were in its power, and the old charter did not provide any means of summoning a constitutional convention. A "People's Party," therefore, was formed, which held a convention, adopted a constitution, and submitted it to a vote of the people. There were approximately 14,000 ballots cast in favor of it, and less than 100 cast against it. Of those in favor, over 4,900 were qualified voters so that the proposed constitution was formally approved not only by the majority of the males over twenty-one but, it was alleged, even by a majority of the legal voters. The constitutional question was a delicate one, but the existing government refused to consider any of these acts as legal. It had become sufficiently frightened, however, to call a constitutional convention itself and in turn submit a constitution to the people, though it is difficult to see how these actions were any more legal than those of the People's Party. The government's constitution was defeated by the narrow margin of 676 votes in 16,702. This was the point at which Dorr and his followers may be considered to have made their mistake. The new constitution, though not giving all they had asked, did give them most of the substance. Had they not defeated it they might have had a practical victory. Feeling, however, had become very bitter, and the Dorrites had already put their constitution into effect by electing an entire state ticket with Dorr as governor. In May 1842 there were two governments both claiming the allegiance of the people. The People's Party did not attempt to seize the state house or machinery of government. Both governors issued proclamations, and Gov. King appealed to Washington for federal aid. Dorr then went to Washington to plead his cause before the President. There he received no encouragement, and he returned to Rhode Island. Meanwhile King had proclaimed martial law, offered $5,000 reward for the capture of Dorr, and made wholesale imprisonments of the latter's followers under the "Algerine Law." Some minor clashes occurred between the Dorrites and the state troops. Many of Dorr's followers deserted him and he voluntarily gave himself up at Providence. King and the old government had lost their heads completely and were ruthless in their revenge. Dorr was tried for treason before the state supreme court and sentenced to solitary confinement at hard labor for life. He was committed June 27, 1844. Public opinion finally made itself felt and in 1845 an Act of General Amnesty was passed and Dorr was released after twelve months of his term. In 1851 he was restored to civil rights, and in January 1854 the legislature passed an act annulling the verdict of the supreme court; but this, of course, the court decided was unconstitutional. Dorr's health had been broken, and after his release he lived in retirement until his death. His work, however, bore fruit, for the old oligarchy had yielded at last, and a third constitution had been drawn up and accepted by the people giving manhood suffrage with trifling qualifications. Dorr, though he showed bad judgment at times, was a genuine reformer and not a self-seeking politician.

[Dan King, *The Life and Times of Thomas Wilson Dorr* (1859), deals almost wholly with the suffrage episode, as does A. M. Mowry, *The Dorr War* (1901). There is much information to be found in "Burke's Report," *House Doc. No. 546*, 28 Cong., 1 Sess. See also *Might and Right by a Rhode Islander* (1844), and Wm. Goodell, *The Rights and Wrongs of R. I.* (1842); sketch by Jos. Palmer, in the *Boston Daily Advertiser*, July 18, 1855, reprinted in Palmer's *Necrology of Alumni of Harvard Coll.* (1864).] J. T. A.

DORRELL, WILLIAM (Mar. 15, 1752–Aug. 28, 1846), founder of the Dorrellites, a fanatical sect which flourished in Franklin County, Mass., and spread over into Vermont, was born in Yorkshire, England. Perhaps owing to the fact that he himself could neither read nor write, his name appears not only as Dorrell, but as Dorrel, Dorril, Dorriel, and Dorral, the last being the spelling in the record of his intended marriage. As a youth he joined the British army, served through three campaigns in Ireland, and came to America with Gen. Burgoyne. After the latter's surrender in 1777, he was one of those who disappeared from the army and made their home in this country. He lived in Petersham, Mass., Warwick, Northfield, and finally in Leyden. In 1779 he married Molla Chase, daughter of Henry and Abigail Chase of Petersham, the marriage intention being filed Nov. 23 (*Vital Records of Petersham, Mass.*, 1904, p. 88).

Although illiterate, he seems to have had an appearance and natural gifts which enabled him to exert a strong influence upon people. He was over six feet tall, of muscular form, and ruddy countenance. He had a vigorous mind; an exceptional memory, being able to quote copiously from the Bible simply from hearing it read by his wife; and fluency of speech. Professing to have received a "revelation," he began to preach, and by 1794 had a number of followers. As time went on these were joined by others, not only from Leyden, but from surrounding towns, many of them people of respectable standing. Originally his principal doctrine was that man should not eat flesh or cause the death of any living creature. Accordingly his followers abandoned the use of leather, wore wooden shoes, and used rope for harnesses and tow for cloth. As other revelations came to him he declared that each generation has its messiah, and that he was the messiah of his; that he might be worshipped as God united to human flesh; that no human arm could harm him; that the only resurrection is that from a state of sin to the spiritual life; and that those who are so raised are no more responsible to civil law, or bound by the covenant of marriage. (Rev. John Taylor of Deerfield in 1798 secured from Dorrell a detailed "confession of faith" which was published in the *Greenfield Gazette,* Aug. 20, 1798, and is given in Theophilus Packard's *A History of the Churches and Ministers . . . in Franklin County, Mass.,* 1854, pp. 252–58.) Disregard of conventional institutions and the disgraceful behavior of the Dorrellites at their gatherings brought them into disrepute. The death-blow was given the sect when a certain Capt. Ezekiel Foster, hearing Dorrell say at a largely attended meeting of his followers that "no arm of flesh can harm me," proceeded to pummel him till he renounced his doctrines. He continued to live in Leyden for nearly fifty years, falling into the habit of intemperance, and becoming a charge upon the town. He finally starved himself to death in his ninety-fifth year, by refusing to eat, declaring that he had lived long enough, and that if he continued to eat he would never die.

[*Mass. Spy* (Worcester), Sept. 12, 1798; Zadock Thompson, *A Gazetteer of the State of Vt.* (1824), see "Guilford"; *Hist. and Proc. Pocumtuck Valley Memorial Asso.,* vol. II (1898); Lucy C. Kellogg, *Hist. of the Town of Bernardston, Franklin County, Mass., 1736–1900* (1902).] H. E. S.

DORSCH, EDUARD (Jan. 10, 1822–Jan. 10, 1887), physician, writer of lyrics in German, was born in Würzburg, Bavaria, the son of Francis L. Dorsch (died in 1825), attaché of the Bavarian court, and his wife, Elizabeth. He received his early education in a Catholic institution, entering the University of Munich in his eighteenth year. Medicine was his principal study, subsidiaries were natural sciences, botany, and philosophy. His early lyrics, "Idle Hours of a Munich student," reveal an independent thinker in the oppressive environment of reaction and fundamentalism. After the completion of his work in 1845 he was sent by the Bavarian State to Austria, to supplement his theoretical knowledge with larger practical experience in the hospitals of Vienna. On his return he soon became involved in the liberal movement that fascinated young thinking minds throughout Germany. He served in the capacity of surgeon in the South German revolution, and his active pen incurred the displeasure of the Bavarian government. Escaping capture, he came to America, reaching Detroit in the autumn of 1849. There he heard from his friend Bruckner of a good opportunity for a physician at Monroe, Mich., whither he went with his bride, Sophia Hartung, born in Ingolstadt, Bavaria. Dorsch lived in Monroe the rest of his life. A year after the death of his first wife, he married, in 1885, Augusta (Korte) Uhl.

Though confining himself closely to his profession, Dorsch could not remain aloof from the anti-slavery movement. He became a stanch adherent of the new Republican party, and was presidential elector from the second Michigan district, supporting Abraham Lincoln. He persistently refused all political offices, except the appointment to the Michigan State Board of Education, 1872–78. In the later sixties he accepted the position of examining surgeon of the Pension Office, which he continued to hold until his death. While acting as pension examiner he prepared a draft showing the course and effects of a bullet in the human body, an investigation which was published as authoritative by the Pension Office.

Three volumes of German lyrics represent Dorsch's poetic work. The first, entitled *Kurze Hirtenbriefe an das deutsche Volk diesseits und jenseits des Ozeans* (1851), are the poems of his youth, revolt, and exile. The second, called *Parabasen* (Milwaukee, 1875), is a collection of satires in verse after the manner of the German poets Platen and Prutz. The last volume, *Aus der alten und neuen Welt* (1884), is a selection of the best of his poems from early youth to the date of publication. He was not a poet of passion and genius, but of calm, penetrating reflection, a clear thinker, whose style was correct, smooth, virile. He looked deeply into human life, knew its joys and illusions, and gave them sincere utterance. He had a rich emotional experience to disclose; a lover of liberty, he was expelled from his dearly beloved native land, because he wanted to rid it of princes, priests, and drones. Seeking the land of the free, he found there a trafficking in human flesh and he joined in the fight for the liberation of humanity. Coming with romantic notions of the splendors of the primeval forest, he found it destructive of human life and cultural ideals. Disillusioned in all of his fondest expectations, the poet yet sought happiness in service of the most unselfish kind, that of the frontier surgeon who labors for the sick and suffering, night and day, with meager financial returns and without the glamour of fame. He felt keen satisfaction in never having lost a maternity case, and gloried in the gratitude of the pioneers.

Intimate friends of Dr. Dorsch described him as a man of retiring disposition, a lover of books and the means of culture. He had a large library in his home, paintings, and works of art. His collections of bugs, butterflies, and botanical specimens knew no end. In his garden there was an immense cage containing wild birds and animals, also a pond with blooming lotus plants that he had imported from Egypt, and a well with marble slab and Greek inscription praising the pure water. He bequeathed his books in part to the University of Michigan and in part to the city in which he lived. His second wife left the Dorsch home to the city of Monroe, founding there the Dorsch Memorial Library.

[A collection of papers and MSS. is in the possession of the Lincoln Club of Chicago. Published sources include: *Hist. of Monroe County, Mich.* (1890); ed. by Talcott E. Wing; John M. Bulkley, *Hist. of Monroe County, Mich.* (2 vols., 1913); J. A. Russell, *The Germanic Influence in the Making of Michigan* (1927); *Deutsch-amerikanisches Conversations-Lexicon* (1869–74), ed. by Alex. J. Schem, vol. III; G. A. Zimmermann, *Deutsch in Amerika* (1894), pp. xxxi–xxxii, 51–56 (biographical and critical sketch, and selections from the poems of Eduard Dorsch).] A. B. F.

DORSEY, ANNA HANSON McKENNEY (Dec. 12, 1815–Dec. 25, 1896), author, daughter of William and Chloe Ann (Lanigan) McKenney, was born in Georgetown, D. C., and died in Washington. Her ancestors had been prominent in Maryland for several generations. Her father's people were Quakers, but he himself, after becoming a sort of unattached Methodist preacher, entered the navy as a chaplain. Educated entirely at home, Anna began while still a girl to write verse which proved acceptable to the magazines. She was married in 1837 to Lorenzo Dorsey of Baltimore. They removed after a few years to Washington, where, till his death in 1861, he was connected with the post-office department of the general government. In 1840 she became a Catholic, as her husband did also at about the same time, both of them influenced by the Catholic revival then current in England. Her first considerable writing, *The Student of Blenheim Forest* (1847), is a novel showing the progress toward Rome of a rich and aristocratic young Virginian who had grown up a Protestant. She was responsible during the next forty years for at least thirty publications, some poetry but mostly prose fiction. Nearly everything she wrote was popular, and all of it—whether like *Woodreve Manor* (1852), touching on slavery and devoted to "the merits and the follies of the times," or, like *Palms* (1887), devoted to the life of ancient Rome—was concerned to display before the world what she held to be the infallible light of her Church. Her hesitancy on moral grounds to depict incidents of unjust suffering (as in *Adrift,* 1887, p. 14) naturally curtailed the power of her work. She shunned personal publicity, and judged herself with modesty—she had not, she said, either "the genius of a Longfellow or the highly attuned talent of a Hemans" (*Flowers of Love and Memory,* 1849, Preface). She was the mother of five children, four of whom lived to maturity—one to be killed in battle during the Civil War. Her patriotic advocacy of the Union cause was expressed in the narrative poem, *"They're Coming, Grandad"* (1865), dedicated to the loyal people of Tennessee. As a widow, she continued to live in Washington, busy with her novels and with her children and grandchildren, comforted from time to time by blessings from the Pope and by praise of her work from the ecclesiastical sources in America.

[Conversation with Miss Ella Loraine Dorsey, Washington, D. C., Jan. 21, 1928; E. C. Donnelly, *Round Table of the Representative Am. Cath. Novelists, with Biog. Sketches* (1897); H. R. Evans, *Geneal. Table . . . Line of Descent . . . from Edward Dorsey* (1898); *Catholic Encyc.,* V (1909); *Ave Maria,* Jan. 16, 1897; *Evening Star* (Washington), Dec. 26, 1896.] J. D. W.

DORSEY, JAMES OWEN (Oct. 31, 1848–Feb. 4, 1895), ethnologist, was a son of Thomas Anderson and Mary Sweetser (Hance) Dorsey of Baltimore, Md. At an early age he showed a tendency toward linguistics, having learned the Hebrew alphabet at six and being able to read the language at ten. His education in the primary schools of Baltimore brought him into the Central High School in 1862. A later period of study in the Protestant Episcopal Theological Seminary at Alexandria, Va., saw him ordained a deacon in 1871. Beginning mission work among the Pawnees of Dakota Territory, he soon acquired ability to speak the language, but, hampered by illness, he returned to Maryland and engaged in parish work in 1880. At this period the newly founded Bureau of American Ethnology under Maj. J. W. Powell [*q.v.*] required his services, and he was sent to study the Omaha Indians, returning later to elaborate his notes. In this way he made a number of trips to the West, collecting linguistic material from various Indian tribes. Brief as was his productive career, he published, besides numerous shorter articles in various publications, a creditable number of major works on a difficult subject. The *Annual Reports of the United States Bureau of American Ethnology* contains most of his larger papers, including: "Omaha Sociology" (*Report* for 1881–82); "Osage Traditions" (*Report* for 1884–85); "A Study of Siouan Cults" (*Report* for 1889–90); "Omaha Dwellings, Furniture and Implements" (*Report* for 1891–92); "Siouan Sociology" (*Report* for 1893–94). In Contributions to North American Ethnology he published *The Cegiha Language* (vol. VI, 1890); and *Dakota Grammar, Texts, and Ethnography by Stephen Return Riggs* (vol. IX, 1893). In various outside media he published: "An Account of the War Customs of the Osages" (*American Naturalist*, vol. XVIII, 1884); and in the same journal: "Mourning and War Customs of the Kansas" (vol. XIX, 1885), and "Migrations of Siouan Tribes" (vol. XX, 1886). One of his early papers was: "Of the Comparative Phonology of Four Siouan Languages" (*Annual Report of the . . . Smithsonian Institution for the Year 1883*). *Omaha and Ponca Letters* appeared in 1891 as Bulletin 11, of the Bureau of American Ethnology, and *A Dictionary of the Biloxi and Ofo Languages*, with J. R. Swanton, as Bulletin 47 in 1912. These studies are of a highly specialized character, requiring trained and expert observation and accurate record. To this work he brought method, rapidity, assiduity, and a keen ear. With these qualifications he accomplished much in a short time. A trained scientist, he bent his energies to recording, holding to facts, and promulgating no theories. On the whole, "in the field of linguistics and sociology Mr. Dorsey collected many facts and much data, which are a permanent addition to our heritage of knowledge" (J. N. B. Hewitt, *American Anthropologist*, April 1895). A delicate constitution, accounting for illnesses which at times slowed up his work, did not prevent Dorsey's being an example of the men whose inner fire drives them on to triumph over adverse circumstances. Always finding time to help others from his store of knowledge, he endeared himself to a large circle of fellow workers. He was honored by various learned societies devoted to ethnology. His active efforts, however, were chiefly devoted to the Anthropological Society of Washington and the American Association for the Advancement of Science, of which he was a Fellow. He gave the impression of distinction, of transparency, and of spirituality. Moving among men as a friend, he was loved and revered by all.

[*American Anthropologist*, Apr. 1895, p. 180; *16th Annual Report of the Bureau of Ethnology, 1894–95* (1897), p. lxxxii; *Evening Star* (Washington), Feb. 5, 1895; personal recollections.] W. H.

DORSEY, JOHN SYNG (Dec. 23, 1783–Nov. 12, 1818), anatomist, surgeon, came of an old English family, the D'Orseys, who had settled in Maryland. His father, Leonard Dorsey, was a merchant in Philadelphia. Dorsey was born in Philadelphia and received his early education at a school conducted by the Society of Friends. Evidently he made an early decision to study medicine, for at the age of fifteen years he entered the office of his uncle, the celebrated Dr. Philip Syng Physick [*q.v.*]. He graduated in medicine at the University of Pennsylvania in 1802 at the age of nineteen years, his dissertation being *An Essay on the Lithonthriptic Virtues of the Gastric Liquor* published the same year. Soon after his graduation there was an epidemic of yellow fever, which had been prevalent in Philadelphia, and he was appointed a resident physician to the yellow-fever hospital and gained considerable credit by his study of the disease. In 1803 he proceeded to London and Paris for further study, a course which was followed at that time by the majority of those who were able to round out their medical studies by a sojourn abroad. In London he was welcomed by Edward Home, afterward Sir Edward, and seems to have devoted himself principally to the study of anatomy. He also attended lectures on chemistry by Humphry Davy. In Paris he continued his anatomical studies but does not seem to have been much impressed by French surgery and makes little or no mention of some of the great men of the day whom he must have seen. In December 1804, he returned to Philadelphia and began the practise of medicine, in a short time receiving appointments on the staffs of several hospitals. While recognition of his ability came quickly in this form, it apparently came slowly in the form of practise, even with the support of Dr. Physick. On Apr. 30, 1807, he was married to Maria Ralston, daughter of Robert Ralston, a Philadelphia merchant. In the same year he was appointed to the dispensary staff of the Pennsylvania Hospital and elected adjunct professor of surgery in the University of Pennsylvania. In 1810 he was elected a surgeon to the Pennsylvania Hospital, where in 1811 he ligated the external iliac artery, apparently the first time that this operation was done successfully in America. In 1813 he published a work on *The Elements of Surgery,* in two octavo volumes, for which many of the illustrations were prepared by himself. This was very successful and was given considerable recognition abroad, especially in Edinburgh. It is supposed to represent to a considerable degree the views and practise of Dr. Physick. Three editions were published, the last appearing after the death of the author. In 1816, Dorsey was elected to the chair of materia medica, to undergo another translation in 1818 to the chair of anatomy, in which he succeeded Dr. Wistar. His introductory lecture, delivered on Nov. 2, 1818, was described in the accounts of the day as being a most eloquent effort, but on the night of that lecture he was attacked by typhus fever, and he died within a fortnight.

The contemporary accounts of his life lay stress on his remarkable qualities, personal, social, professional, and artistic. He was interested in music and played on several instruments. His skill in drawing was put to practical use in the illustration of his work on surgery. His appointment at an early age to the staff of the Pennsylvania Hospital is evidence of his surgical ability. To have attained the positions which he held at the time of his death, at thirty-five, is evidence of talents of no mean order.

[N. Chapman, in *Phila. Jour. Med. and Phys. Sci.,* 1820, I, 198; *Am. Medic. Recorder,* II (1819), 1; *Freeman's Journal for the Country* and *Democratic Press,* both of Phila., Nov. 13, 1818; *General Advertiser* (Phila.), Nov. 14, 1818; H. Shoemaker in *St. Louis Medic. and Surgic. Jour.,* IX (1851), 297–301; J. J. Janeway, *A Brief Memoir of . . . John Syng Dorsey* (1853); S. D. Gross, *Living Eminent Am. Physicians and Surgeons* (1861); Jos. Carson, *A Hist. of the Medic. Dept. of the Univ. of Pa.* (1869); H. A. Kelly and W. L. Burrage, *Am. Medic. Biogs.* (1920).] T.M.

DORSEY, SARAH ANNE ELLIS (Feb. 16, 1829–July 4, 1879), author, daughter of Thomas and Mary (Routh) Ellis, was born on her father's plantation near Natchez, Miss., and died in New Orleans. Her education, capped by a tour of Europe, was based chiefly on languages and the fine arts. She was married in 1853 to Samuel W. Dorsey, originally of Maryland, but at the time of his marriage a planter in Tensas Parish, La. A devout woman given to writing, she soon began publishing her pious reflections in the New York *Churchman.* She taught her husband's slaves how to read and write, introduced them to ecclesiastical ritualism, and composed for their use a series of choral services. Her house was burned during the war, and she was surrounded by armies, but she continued to write for magazines. Removing to Texas for greater tranquillity, she became a nurse in a Confederate hospital. The war injured but did not destroy her husband's considerable property. In 1866 she published her voluble but conscientious *Recollections of Henry Watkins Allen,* Confederate governor of Louisiana. In the preface she stated that if that biography were favorably received she might be encouraged to write others, "to progress still further in this, my labor of love; like Old Mortality, freshening the epitaphs, which are already yielding to the corroding tooth of Time, on the gravestones of Southern Heroes." She progressed instead to fiction, all more or less autobiographical in nature, and written as "Filia"—reminiscent of the name "Filia Ecclesiae" bestowed upon her by the *Churchman.* In *Lucia Dare* (1867), begun as early as 1853—touching, before Hale made him memorable, on the romance of Philip Nolan—she carries the reader from England to Mississippi and through the Civil War. Other novels were: *Agnes Graham* (1869), which appeared first in the *Southern Literary Messenger,* June 1863–March 1864, and *Athalie or a Southern Villeggiatura* (1872), which deals with "country diversions or residence," a kind of belated *Horse-shoe Robinson* of the lower Mississippi. During 1874–75 she prepared a series of papers on philosophy for a learned body in New Orleans, and in 1877 she completed her morbid and sensational *Panola, a Tale of Louisiana.* Her husband died in 1875, and after that time she made her home principally at "Beauvoir," Miss. She had known Mrs. Jefferson Davis since the two were girls, and in the beginning of 1877 Davis himself came to live at her house as a guest. It was her desire to collect and edit his writings and his recollections. She became his amanuensis, and in that capacity—and as his friend—she bent herself to obtain from him the important information which he alone could give. Much of this matter appeared in Davis's *Rise and Fall of the Confederate Government* (1881), but she died before the book was completed. At her death it was disclosed that she had made Davis several valuable bequests, including her home.

[Sources not already mentioned: Varina Howell Davis, *Jefferson Davis* (1890); Dunbar Rowland, *Jefferson Davis* (1923), *Mississippi* (1907); J. W. Davidson, *Living Writers of the South* (1869); I. Raymond, *Southland Writers,* vol. I (1870); M. L. Rutherford, *The South in Hist. and Lit.* (1907); Carl Holliday, *A Hist. of Southern Lit.* (1906); *The South in the Building of the Nation,* vol. XI (1909); *New Orleans Times,* July 5, 1879; *Natchez Democrat,* July 6, 1879; *Vicksburg Commercial,* July 7, 1879.] J.D.W.

DORSEY, STEPHEN WALLACE (Feb. 28, 1842–Mar. 20, 1916), senator, was born at Benson, Vt., son of John W. and Marie Dorsey. He received an academic education and moved to Ohio while still a boy. At the outbreak of the Civil War he volunteered and served in the Army of the Tennessee and the Army of the Potomac, remaining in active service to the end. He rose to the rank of captain in the 1st Ohio Light Artillery. Returning to Ohio he resumed his place as an employee of the Sandusky Tool Company and was soon elected its president. On the same day he was elected president of the Arkansas Central Railway Company. This was one of the many companies organized to defraud the state under guise of giving state aid to railroads. By the close of 1871 he was interested in three railroad projects. The Helena (Ark.) *World* said of him: "He came here to promote his railroad interests. He obtained state, county, and city aid, under the most solemn pledges. By trickery, hocus-pocus and legerdemain the gauge of the road was changed from standard to narrow gauge, as adopted. To-day we have a wheelbarrow road from Helena westward, costing nothing in comparison with the one he promised to come here to construct" (quoted in Herndon, *post*, I, 307). From the state he secured indorsement of his railroad bonds to the extent of $1,350,000. Naturally he entered politics and soon after his arrival he became an influential member of the "machine." Here he could look after his railroad interests. The legislature elected him to the Senate and he took his seat Mar. 4, 1873. In his first session he introduced a bill to establish a "National Railroad Bureau for the General Government of the Railroads," but neither he nor any one else ever pushed this move for government control. For several sessions he introduced bills for the organization of Oklahoma territory. Most of his time seems to have been taken up with relief, pension, railroad, District of Columbia and post-office bills, but he exercised very little influence on legislation.

The Democrats having recaptured the state, he did not return to Arkansas. He served as secretary to the Republican National Committee, of which he was a member, though not a resident of Arkansas, and conducted the campaign for Garfield in 1880. In his first Congress he had manifested an interest in the post-office by introducing six bills and four resolutions relating to it. Later in his career he became interested in the Star Routes, and in 1881, along with T. W. Brady [*q.v.*], second assistant postmaster-general, and others, was indicted for conspiring to defraud the government of nearly half a million dollars. Powerful political and newspaper influences were brought to bear in their behalf, and at the conclusion of the first trial the jury stood ten to two for conviction of Brady and nine to three for conviction of Dorsey, but in the second trial they were both acquitted. M. C. Rerdell, Dorsey's private secretary, pleaded guilty in the second trial. Charges of jury-bribing were brought by both the prosecution and the defense, which led to further indictments and dismissal of officials. Dorsey attributed his prosecution to the hostility of Postmaster-General James, and Attorney-General McVeagh, whose appointment as members of Garfield's cabinet he had opposed. After leaving Washington Dorsey conducted a cattle ranch and was interested in mining in New Mexico until 1892. After that date he devoted his time to mining enterprises and investments. About 1901 he moved to Los Angeles and resided there until his death. He married Helen Mary Wack at Oberlin, Ohio, Nov. 20, 1865. Three children were born of this union. Later he married Laura, daughter of Job B. Bigelow of Washington and London.

[D. T. Herndon, *Centennial Hist. of Ark.* (1922); *Cong. Record*, 1873–79; *Proceedings in the Second Trial of the Case of S. W. Dorsey et al.* (4 vols.), which is indexed so that Dorsey's part can be traced; *Appletons' Ann. Cyc.*, 1882 and 1883; Letter from Dorsey's son, Clayton Chauncey Dorsey, giving family history.]

D. Y. T.

DORSHEIMER, WILLIAM EDWARD (Feb. 5, 1832–Mar. 26, 1888), lawyer, journalist, politician, was the son of Philip and Sarah Dorsheimer. His father came from Germany early in the nineteenth century, settling eventually in Buffalo. William was born at Lyons, Wayne County, N. Y. After preparing at Phillips Andover Academy, he entered Harvard in 1849, but was compelled by ill health to withdraw after two years. Admitted to the bar in 1854, he began practise at Buffalo and soon became active in the Democratic party, although his father was one of the founders of the state Republican party and William Dorsheimer himself supported the Republican ticket in 1856 and 1860. After serving on Frémont's staff in the Missouri campaign of the summer of 1861, he returned to Buffalo and formed a law partnership with Spencer Clifton. President Johnson appointed him federal district attorney for the northern district of New York in 1867. He surrendered this position in 1871 to participate in the movement for the election of Horace Greeley, and was a member of the Liberal Republican convention at Cincinnati in 1872. Returning to the Democratic fold, he was elected lieutenant-governor on the ticket with Samuel J. Tilden in 1874, and reëlected with L. C. Robinson in 1876. That summer he was a member of the Democratic convention at St. Louis which nominated Tilden for the presidency. Dorsheimer reported the platform, which, as a member of the committee on resolutions, he had saved from an "inflationist" plank. During the ensuing campaign he made numerous speeches and wrote for both the newspapers and magazines in behalf of the Democratic ticket. He felt that Tilden, through indifference, prevented his being nominated for governor in 1876, wherefore he supported Kelly, the candidate of the Tammany wing, instead of Robinson, the regular nominee. This division within the Democratic ranks insured the election of Cornell, the Republican candidate. This same year the Democratic delegation in the legislature vainly supported Dorsheimer for United States senator against Roscoe Conkling. In the next year, Dorsheimer was one of the Kelly delegates to the Democratic convention at Cincinnati, but the Tilden wing succeeded in having the whole Tammany delegation excluded. Dorsheimer was elected to Congress in 1882. His most important service was on the judiciary committee. He was also chairman of the House section of the joint committee which arranged the celebration upon the completion of the Washington monument. It is alleged that his fellow townsman, Grover Cleveland, wished Dorsheimer to nominate him at the St. Louis convention in 1884, but Kelly had prevented Dorsheimer's being chosen as a delegate, so he attended only as an alternate. The campaign biography (*Life and Public Services of the Honorable Grover Cleveland,* 1884) was from Dorsheimer's pen. For this and other valuable services in the campaign Dorsheimer was appointed federal district attorney for southern New York in 1885. After about a year he resigned this position to direct the New York *Star* which he had bought and converted into a daily. This venture did not prove financially successful, and the worries incident thereto probably increased the illness which took him to Savannah in the winter of 1887, in the vain quest of health. He died there, Mar. 26, 1888. His wife was Isabella, daughter of A. D. Patchin of Buffalo. It was said of Dorsheimer that he possessed "courage, tact, fascination, audacity, rare skill on the platform, creditable associations and marked literary attainments." In addition to the campaign biography of Cleveland he wrote reviews of Parton's lives of Aaron Burr and Thomas Jefferson, in the *Atlantic Monthly* (March and November 1858); a series of articles in the same periodical for 1862, on "Frémont's Hundred Days in Missouri"; a sketch, "Buffalo During the War of 1812" (1863) in the *Publications of the Buffalo Historical Society* (I, 185). He was one of the founders of the Buffalo Historical Society and the Academy of Fine Arts in the same city.

[Besides the sketches in *Appletons' Ann. Cyc.*, 1888, and the *Encyc. of Contemporary Biog. of N. Y.* (1887), data concerning Dorsheimer may be found in R. B. Smith, *Hist. of the State of N. Y.* (vol. III), D. S. Alexander, *Political Hist. of the State of N. Y.*, vol. III (1909), the *Pubs. Buffalo Hist. Soc.*, vols. V, XII; *Report of the Harvard Class of 1853* (1913); J. N. Larned, *Hist. of Buffalo* (1911), vols. I, II; T. C. White, *Our County and its People, A Descriptive Work on Erie County, N. Y.* (1898), vol. I.] M. L. B., Jr.

DOS PASSOS, JOHN RANDOLPH (July 31, 1844–Jan. 27, 1917), lawyer, was born in Philadelphia, the son of Manoel Joquin Dos Passos, of a Portuguese family, and his wife, Lucinda Anne Cattell. Having received his early education at the public schools in his native city, he commenced the study of law under private tutors, and attended law lectures at the University of Pennsylvania. During the Civil War he enlisted in the Pennsylvania militia, taking part in the battle of Antietam and the later campaigns. At the close of hostilities he resumed his law studies and was admitted to the Philadelphia bar in 1865. He practised there a short time, but removed in 1867 to New York City, where he quickly acquired a reputation through his association with the defense in some spectacular murder trials. Attention was first drawn to him through his defense of Emil André who killed his wife in broad daylight on a public street in New York. Apparently the crime was without any extenuating circumstances, but Dos Passos succeeded in inducing the jury to return a verdict of manslaughter, thus saving André's life. He also assisted in the defense of Edward S. Stokes when charged with the murder of "Jim" Fisk, and, on his client's conviction, though not senior counsel, practically conducted the appeal which resulted, in June 1873, in the verdict being set aside. Criminal practise, however, had no attraction for him, and his natural inclinations led him to the special study of problems of finance and exchange. With this object in view he opened an office in close proximity to the New York Stock Exchange and soon acquired an extensive connection among brokers and operators in the financial market. He gradually became known as an expert on the law of commercial exchange and wrote *A Treatise on the Law of Stockbrokers and Stock Exchanges* (1882), which was an immediate success and for a number of years remained the standard text-book on the subject. Confining himself to corporation and banking law, he acquired a large practise of a very responsible and remunerative nature. Possessed of keen business instincts and a natural capacity for delicate diplomacy, he became the confidential adviser of many Wall St. firms. In 1891 he was employed by H. O. Havemeyer [*q.v.*] in the incorporation of the American Sugar Refining Company—the so-called "Sugar Trust"—the legal fee received on account of this work being the largest on record up to that time. For a number of years thereafter he acted as the company's counsel. He also assisted in the formation of other large aggregations, and was a pioneer in the organization and development of the modern trust company. On the subject of trusts he had strong opinions, recognizing as he did both their beneficial and their potentially evil attributes. He believed that the Sherman Anti-Trust Law was "an unnecessary, anomalous and dangerous piece of legislation," and contributed in the public press and through his own publications many suggestions for remedied legislation. He was exceptionally successful in the reconciliation of apparently conflicting interests and the adjustment of disputes in big business. It was mainly owing to his efforts that the reorganizations of the Texas & Pacific, the Reading, and the Erie Railroads were effected. In his later years he took great interest in law reform, some of his views being entirely original and most of them radical in outlook. Shortly before his death he strongly urged in the public press that in a criminal trial the accused should be compelled to testify. He died in New York City, in his seventy-third year. His wife, whom he married on Dec. 17, 1873, was Mary Dyckman Hays.

Although a forceful and impressive speaker, he was prominently in public affairs upon only one occasion, the presidential contest of 1896, during which he undertook a vigorous campaign through Pennsylvania and Virginia on behalf of McKinley, who was a personal friend of his. He was possessed of great physical energy, and when he could get away from his professional employments, devoted himself to open-air pursuits, being a great pedestrian and lover of the country. He was also fond of the sea, and an enthusiastic yachtsman.

He was a constant writer and published, in addition to his book on the stock exchange: *The Interstate Commerce Act: an Analysis of its Provisions* (1867); *A Defence of the McKinley Administration from Attacks of Mr. Carl Schurz and other Anti-Imperialists* (1900); *Commercial Trusts: the Growth and Rights of Aggregated Capital* (1901); *The Anglo-Saxon Century and the Unification of the English Speaking People* (1903); *The American Lawyer* (1907); and *Commercial Mortmain; A Study of the Trust Problem* (1916). He also contributed a number of articles to periodicals and the public press on matters of current interest.

[A competent review of his career, "John R. Dos Passos," by Henry Wollman in *Case and Comment*, July 1917, and extended obituary notices in the *N. Y. Times* and *N. Y. Herald* of Jan. 28, 1917; family names from a son, Louis Hays Dos Passos.] H. W. H. K.

DOTY, ELIHU (Sept. 20, 1809–Nov. 30, 1864), missionary of the Dutch Reformed Church, was born in Berne, Albany County, N. Y. The son of Stephen Holmes and Phebe (Nelson) Doty, he was a descendant of Edward Doty who came to Plymouth on the *Mayflower*, as a servant to Stephen Hopkins. He graduated from Rutgers College in 1835 and from Rutgers Seminary in 1836, because of his advanced age and mental maturity taking the combined courses in five years. He was ordained at Berne, on May 16, 1836, and on May 30 was commissioned by the American Board of Commissioners for Foreign Missions, with which the Dutch Reformed Church was then affiliated. On June 8 he embarked with Nevius, Youngblood, and Ennis as the first missionary band of the New Brunswick Seminary, and arrived at Batavia, Java, on Sept. 15 (*Centennial of the Theological Seminary of the Reformed Church in America, N. Y.*, 1885, p. 117). There they were delayed and hindered by the jealousy of the Dutch government, but after three years of discouraging labor in Batavia and Singapore, Doty began work on the island of Borneo, in June 1839, devoting himself to the Chinese-speaking portion of the population. While his actual missionary labors were unsuccessful, he made several extensive tours of exploration the valuable results of which are incorporated in his *Narrative of a Tour in Borneo*. The Borneo mission failed and was given up for lack of workers (W. E. Strong, *The Story of the American Board*, 1910), but in 1844 Doty joined the Amoy mission, composed of Dutch Reformed missionaries working under the American Board, and here most of his effective work was accomplished. His connection with the American Board ceased on the final transfer of the Amoy work to the newly organized Dutch Reformed Board, Mar. 23, 1858.

Doty was a member for twenty years of the Amoy mission, where by his character and work he left an enduring impression. He baptized the first Chinese woman to be received into church fellowship, baptized the first children of native Christian parents, and was for a time in charge of the first Chinese day school, in the province (P. W. Pitcher, *In and About Amoy*, 1909). At length he gradually withdrew from the distinctively evangelistic work of the mission and gave himself to literary labors, for which he was well adapted. His principal publications include: *Some Thoughts on the Proper Term for God in the Chinese* (Shanghai, 1850); *Translation of Sacramental and Marriage Forms of the Reformed Protestant Dutch Church into Amoy Colloquial* (1853); *Translation and Revision into the Amoy Dialect of Milner's Thirteen Village Sermons, including Milner's Tract on the Strait Gate* (Amoy, 1854); an Anglo-Chinese *Manual of the Amoy Dialect* (Canton, 1855) which is especially important because it formed the basis of manuals long used by missionaries in this region. Doty was a man of unromantic temperament and not much given to the graces; but he was solid, steadfast, and plodding. He was neither widely read nor a profound scholar, but his accuracy, sound judgment, and freedom from prejudice fitted him admirably for his work. On May 13, 1836, he married Clarissa Dolly Ackley of Washington, Conn., who died at Amoy, Oct. 5, 1845. His second wife, Eleanor Augusta Smith of Parsippany, N. J., whom he married on Feb. 17, 1847, died Feb. 28, 1858, at Amoy.

[Unpublished records of the American Board in Boston; E. T. Corwin, *Manual of the Reformed Church in America* (5th ed. 1922), which contains full bibliography of his works; *Christian Intelligencer*, Mar. 30 and Apr. 6, 1865; J. G. Fagg, *Forty Years in South China* (1894); *Biog. Record Theol. Sem. New Brunswick, 1784–1911* (1912), comp. by J. H. Raven; E. A. Doty, *Doty-Doten Family in America* (1897).]

F. T. P.

DOTY, JAMES DUANE (Nov. 5, 1799–June 13, 1865), politician, speculator, was born in Salem, Washington County, N. Y., of Colonial English stock, the son of Chilius and Sarah (Martin) Doty. He was educated in the common schools of Lewis County, N. Y., and at Lowville Academy, read law, and began practise at Detroit, Michigan Territory, in 1819. He was also clerk of the supreme court of the territory and of the territorial council. Doty accompanied Gen. Lewis Cass [*q.v.*] as secretary on his tour of the lakes and ascent of the Mississippi in 1820. In 1823 he became judge of the judicial district of Northern Michigan which included a vast territory west of Lake Michigan. In the same year (April 14) he married Sarah Collins at Whitestown, N. Y., and settled at Green Bay in Michigan Territory. His judgeship required him to travel extensively through wilderness regions, and brought him in contact with Indians, rivermen, traders, hunters, soldiers, government agents, and French and American pioneer settlers, creating many difficult situations which his courage, keenness, and ingratiating manners uniformly overcame. He had many devoted friends and admirers. There is some reason, however, to believe that he diplomatically allied himself with the powerful trading concerns, which alliance may partially explain his facile progress.

Resigning his judgeship, under compulsion, it was said, in 1832, Doty devoted several years to a personal exploration of the West, especially that portion which later became Wisconsin, mapped it, and published a description of the region. One of his objects was to select sites for towns, mills, wharves, etc., for he was an inveterate speculator who was determined, as soon as the lands of Wisconsin were surveyed, to enter a large number of promising tracts scattered through many counties. He was commissioned in 1832 by the War Department to survey the military roads in Wisconsin; he was a member of the legislative council of Michigan from the region west of the lake; he became, in 1839, Wisconsin's delegate in Congress, was reëlected in 1840 and served till 1841 when he became by appointment of President Tyler, governor of the territory. That post he held till 1844, though with one short break during which N. P. Tallmadge was governor.

Doty was the stormy petrel of early Wisconsin politics. He selected the location of the capital, secured its adoption by the territorial council, speculated in lots and became the commissioner to erect the capitol building. These business complications created interests which as governor he sought to protect, thus precipitating an intense struggle with the territorial legislature. While both sides played politics, it is impossible to acquit Doty of actions and intrigues that look grossly irregular. Questions growing out of his action as building commissioner became the subject of congressional discussion, on resolution of his chief rival, Delegate Henry Dodge. It must be said, however, that most of the acts complained of can be explained on the theory that, as a speculator, he was often hard-pressed financially. No proof has been found to establish the comprehensive allegations of dishonesty so voluminously uttered by his political enemies, though this fact does not acquit him of the charges. That he became more interested in his own personal affairs than in the public welfare can hardly be denied.

Doty was a prominent member of the first constitutional convention of Wisconsin, and after statehood had been attained, was for two terms, 1849–53, a representative in Congress. In early life he trained with the Democrats, but in 1840 became a Whig, and later a Republican. In 1861 he was appointed superintendent of Indian affairs with headquarters at Salt Lake, and in 1863 was made governor of Utah Territory. He died in Salt Lake City.

Doty possessed the type of mind which marks the acute lawyer. He was a man of culture, had a good library, enjoyed home and friends, loved to hum traditional songs, to surround himself with objects of sentimental interest. His native endowment set him apart from common men. He possessed a great fund of information about the West. His private life was exemplary; had he been able to resist the temptations to speculate, his career, honorable and distinguished in some ways, but badly marred in others, might have been one of outstanding brilliance and conspicuous worth.

[The most comprehensive general account is Albert G. Ellis, "Life and Public Services of J. D. Doty" in *Wis. Hist. Colls.*, V (1868), 369–77. Doty's manuscript journal with synopses of cases tried by him as judge is in State Hist. Lib., Madison, Wis., together with a few other papers by him; some of these were published in *Wis. Hist. Colls.*, XIII (1895), 163–246. *Memories of the Island Loggery*, by Mary Doty Fitzgerald, his daughter, is a reminiscent poem containing many hints about Doty's domestic interests. It is in *Wis. Mag. of Hist.*, June 1927. See also E. A. Doty, *The Doty-Doten Family in America* (1897).]

J. S—r.

DOUBLEDAY, ABNER (June 26, 1819–Jan. 26, 1893), Union soldier, also credited with originating baseball, was of Huguenot descent. The name was originally spelled "Dubaldy." His grandfather, Abner Doubleday, was a soldier in the Revolution, serving at Bunker Hill, Stony Point, and elsewhere, and ending his army career as a prisoner on the *Jersey*. Upon his release he took to the sea, and finished the war as an officer of a privateer. His son, Ulysses Freeman Doubleday, removed from the family home in Lebanon, Conn., to the state of New York, was a newspaper editor for many years at Ballston Spa and Auburn, and sat in Congress, as a Democrat, for four years. He married Hester Donnelly. Of their three sons, two became colonels of volunteers in the Civil War; and the other, Abner, rose to higher rank. He was born at Ballston Spa, attended school at Auburn and Cooperstown, and prepared himself for the profession of civil engineering. While at school in Cooperstown, tradition has it, he created the game of baseball out of the chaos of the popular bat-and-ball games—"one old cat" and its variants. To him is ascribed the adoption of the diamond-shaped field, the assignment of definite playing positions (his teams had eleven players, however), and the selection of the name "baseball" for the game. The essential facts seem fairly well established. A high commission of baseball experts made a formal report, in 1907, on the origin of the game, after extensive investigation, and declared Doubleday to be its inventor. The original field at Cooperstown is now a public playground, appropriately called Doubleday Field. Doubleday was appointed a cadet at West Point in 1838, graduated in 1842, and was commissioned in the artillery. He was with Taylor's army in Mexico, being engaged in the battle of Monterey, and served against the Seminoles in the hostilities of 1856–58 in Florida. In 1852–53 he was a member of a commission which investigated certain claims for alleged destruction of mines during the Mexican War and pronounced them fraudulent—the "Gardner mine fraud." The remainder of his service before the Civil War was in garrison at posts on the Atlantic Coast. He was promoted to first lieutenant in 1847 and to captain in 1855. In 1852 he married Mary, daughter of Robert M. Hewitt of Baltimore. He was stationed in Charleston harbor in 1860–61, and aimed the first shot fired from Fort Sumter in reply to the Confederate bombardment. His aim was good, but the shot "bounded off from the sloping roof of the [ironclad] battery opposite without producing any apparent effect." In May 1861, he was appointed major of the newly organized 17th Infantry, and served as such in the lower Shenandoah Valley and the defenses of Washington until appointed brigadier-general of volunteers, Feb. 3, 1862. He was assigned to the command of a brigade in McDowell's corps, and took it into action for the first time in a skirmish on the Rappahannock late in August, followed shortly after by the second battle of Bull Run. At the battle of South Mountain, in September, he succeeded to the command of the division, when its chief was wounded, and in that capacity took part in the battles of Antietam and Fredericksburg. He was appointed major-general of volunteers, Nov. 29, 1862. His division was in reserve at Chancellorsville. The battle of Gettysburg brought Doubleday his greatest distinction and his bitterest disappointment. The first day's fight was waged by such Union troops as were within reach, to hold back the Confederate army until the full Union strength could be brought up to the field. Gen. Reynolds was killed, and Doubleday commanded the corps through a day of desperate fighting against heavy odds. He felt that he had fairly earned the permanent command, and when Newton (his classmate at West Point) was assigned that night to take charge of the corps, and he himself was returned to the command of his division, he was deeply humiliated. His resentment toward Gen. Meade, who had made the assignment without full knowledge of the facts, was never appeased. His division was heavily engaged on the second and third days, and took an important part in the repulse of the final great assault. This was his last field service. For the rest of the war he was on duty in Washington. He was mustered out of the volunteer service, Jan. 15, 1866. He had been promoted to lieutenant-colonel in the regular army, Sept. 20, 1863, and on Sept. 15, 1867, he became colonel. While stationed in San Francisco in 1869–71 he obtained the charter for the first cable street railway. He retired from active service, Dec. 11, 1873, and made his home at Mendham, N. J., where he died. He was buried in Arlington National Cemetery.

Doubleday was tall, distinguished in appearance, dignified and courteous in manner. Quiet and cool in times of stress, methodical and deliberate in his ways—he was nicknamed "Forty-eight Hours"—his temperament resembled that of Gen. Thomas. His staff officers have testified to his retentive memory and his faculty for clear statement in giving orders. They noted, too, that he never used a profane word, and that he indulged in neither liquor nor tobacco. He was a man of wide interests and varied attainments. From youth he took pleasure in French and Spanish literature, and in his old age, Cato-like, he studied Sanskrit. He published, in 1876, *Reminiscences of Forts Sumter and Moultrie in 1860–'61*; and in 1882, *Chancellorsville and Gettysburg.*

[The best source of information on Doubleday is a volume published by the state of New York on the occasion of the dedication of monuments at Gettysburg: *In Memoriam, Abner Doubleday 1819–1893 and John Cleveland Robinson 1817–1897* (1918); addresses by staff officers and friends give not only a detailed account of his military career, but also many facts as to his ancestry, early life, and personal characteristics. G. W. Cullum's *Biog. Reg.* (3rd ed., 1891) outlines his military record, II, 132–34. See also *Official Records (Army)*, ser. I, vols. I, II, XII (pt. 2), XIX (pt. 1), XXI, XXV (pts. 1, 2), XXVII (pt. 1), LI. The first day's fighting at Gettysburg is well described by Gen. H. J. Hunt in *Battles and Leaders of the Civil War* (1887–88), III, 255–84. For his connection with baseball, see A. G. Spaulding, *America's National Game* (1911) and F. C. Richter, *Richter's Hist. and Records of Base Ball* (1914).] T. M. S.

DOUBLEDAY, NELTJE DE GRAFF (Oct. 23, 1865–Feb. 21, 1918), naturalist, was born in Chicago, Ill., the daughter of Liverius and Alice (Fair) De Graff. She was educated at St. John's School, New York City, and at the Misses Masters' School at Dobbs Ferry, N. Y. On June 9, 1886, she married Frank Nelson Doubleday at Plainfield, N. J., by whom she had two sons and a daughter. Her husband was at the time of marriage editor of the *Book Buyer* and was subsequently manager of *Scribner's Magazine* and a member of the Doubleday Publishing Company, so she came into a literary atmosphere, with means of expression ready for her use. But it was not until her youngest child was two years old that she published her first book, *The Piegan Indians* (1894). This was followed by: Bird *Neighbors* (1896), *Birds that Hunt and Are Hunted* (1898), *Nature's Garden* (1900), *How to Attract the Birds* (1902), *Birds that Every Child Should Know* (1907), *The American Flower Garden* (1909), *Birds Worth Knowing* (1917), *Birds* (a selection published posthumously, 1926). It is quite evident from any or all of her work that she became a naturalist because she loved flowers and birds rather than because she loved science. While her writings are always accurate, their charm and the explanation of their popularity lie in the intimate and often homely manner in which she describes the habits and habitats of her subjects. Her volumes—many of them profusely illustrated in colors, and all with topics carefully arranged and classified—are adapted both to interest and to instruct. She also wrote many articles for magazines, especially *Country Life.* Her interests were broad, and her magazine work covered such varied topics as agriculture, antique furniture, and the education of the American Indian, as well as the writing of numerous book reviews. All of her writing was produced under the pen name of Neltje Blanchan. Prominent socially, she yet reserved much of her time and energy for work in charitable organizations. Her vivid personality, quick sympathy, and active temperament admirably fitted her for such work. With these qualifications she had the ability to win easily the confidence of those with whom she came in contact. She was a leading member of the Red Cross Society of Nassau, L. I., and in 1917 was selected by the American Red Cross for a special mission in China. Mr. and Mrs. Doubleday left their home, "Effendi Hill," Oyster Bay, L. I., on Dec. 9, 1917, going first to the Philippines, then to Hong Kong and other Chinese cities, before reaching Canton, from which news of her death was unexpectedly cabled to New York in February.

[*Woman's Who's Who of America,* 1914–15; *Who's Who in America,* 1916–17; *N. Y. Times,* Feb. 23, 1918; personal information from a son, Mr. Nelson Doubleday of New York City.] G. G.

DOUGHTY, THOMAS (July 19, 1793–July 22, 1856), painter, was one of the earliest American landscapists of sufficient merit and originality to attain general recognition. Born in Philadelphia, he began work in the leather business at the age of sixteen, and continued in this occupation for some ten years. Then, at the age of twenty-seven, he resolved to pursue painting as a profession. "My mind," he wrote, "was firmly fixed; I had acquired a love for the art which no circumstance could unsettle." He realized that the financial prospect was anything but bright at the start, but he was buoyed up by the hope that as he acquired skill and knowledge his worldly circumstances would be bettered. He seems to have had little other training than that afforded by a short term of instruction in sepia drawing. Nor was he mistaken in anticipating economic privations. However, his love for the art, which "no circumstance could unsettle," combined with an unquestionable talent and good courage, did at length prevail. His reputation grew, and he was for a time rated as the foremost landscape painter of the famous Hudson River school. This was at the time when the men of 1830 were giving new life to landscape work in France. It is recorded that Doughty worked for a long time in Paris, where he painted some of his best canvases, and he also lived in London for a relatively short period, finding some congenial subjects in the suburbs. The most prosperous years of his career were the early thirties, when, in 1833, in company with Chester Harding, Francis Alexander, and Alvan Fisher, he held an exceptionally successful exhibition in Boston. He had a studio in that city for several years, and was a regular exhibitor in the annual exhibitions of the Athenæum. He also exhibited in the Pennsylvania Academy of the Fine Arts, and National Academy of Design. He produced but few pictures, and these met with ready sale. The British minister to the United States paid him $2,500 for one of his landscapes, a price which was considered notable then. But for some unexplained reason his popularity seems to have waned in his later life, and, toward the end, when he was living in New York, neglect, poverty, and sickness made him very unhappy.

His landscapes are rather small, and are usually in a delicate gray tone, the motives being simple river scenes, with the inevitable woody foreground of the period. The most admirable part of a typical Doughty is the sky, which is more subtly observed and more atmospheric in its values than are those of his American contemporaries. He was felicitous in the rendering of silvery effects of light, somewhat akin to those which are associated with the work of Corot, though far less perfect. He found the majority of his subjects along the banks of the Hudson, the Delaware, the Susquehanna, the Seine, and the Thames, being apparently as devoted to river scenery as was Daubigny. His works are to be seen in the Metropolitan Museum of Art, New York City; the Pennsylvania Academy of the Fine Arts, Philadelphia; the Brooklyn Institute of Arts and Sciences; the Corcoran Gallery of Art, Washington; and in many private collections. The two landscapes belonging to the Pennsylvania Academy were shown in 1915 at the Panama-Pacific Exposition, San Francisco.

[Original sources of information as to Doughty's life are few in number, and particulars are almost wholly lacking. Wm. Dunlap's *Hist. of the Rise and Progress of the Arts of Design in the U. S.* (1834; rev. ed., 1918) devotes a little over a page to Doughty, but gives only an incomplete outline of his life. H. T. Tuckerman's *Book of the Artists* (1867) contains a brief narrative and appreciation. All of the subsequent accounts in books of reference appear to be derived mainly from the foregoing notices. Brief obituaries appeared in the *N. Y. Times*, July 24, and *Boston Transcript*, July 25, 1856, the latter copied from the N. Y. *Evening Post*.]

W. H. D.

DOUGHTY, WILLIAM HENRY (Feb. 5, 1836–Mar. 27, 1905), physician, son of Ebenezer Wesley and Margaret (Crowell) Doughty, was born in Augusta, Ga., where his father was a successful business man. He received his preliminary education at the Richmond County Academy, a typical school of the ante bellum South, and began the study of medicine with Doctors Dugas, Ford, Eve, and Campbell. He was graduated at the Medical College of Georgia (now Medical Department of the University of Georgia) in 1855 and at once began the practise of his profession in Augusta where, with the exception of the Civil War period, he lived until his death. At the outbreak of the Civil War he was commissioned surgeon in the Confederate army, serving as operating surgeon successively at the Macon Hospital, the Walker Division Hospital at Lauderdale Springs, Miss., and finally at the Second Georgia Hospital at Augusta. After the close of the war he was appointed instructor at the University of Georgia, becoming professor of materia medica and therapeutics in 1868, which position he held until 1875. Thereafter he devoted himself to his practise until his death.

He was one of the highly efficient general practitioners of an earlier generation. Resourceful, conscientious, and a deep thinker, he was beloved for personal as well as professional reasons, and, as so often happened with his type, he disregarded his own health and continued to work even when suffering from a lingering illness. He devoted much of his time to his cherished hobby, climatology, and was a pioneer in this country in the study of climate in its relation to medical science. He early pointed out that Arizona and neighboring regions afford a favorable climate for tubercular patients. Though he never saw the Pacific Ocean or took a sea voyage, he was one of the first to understand the rôle played by the Japan Current in the maintenance of the equable climate of California, and by reasoning and correlating the data obtained by others, he determined what he thought must be the course of the northern and North-American portions of the current, opinions which were later proved correct, as was also his estimation of the northernmost course of the Gulf Stream.

In medicine he wrote many clinical articles, chiefly in the fields of obstetrics and gynecology, though as a physician he is probably best remembered for his method of reducing dislocations of the clavicle. His paper on this subject was "True Method of Treating Dislocations Upwards and Backwards, of the Scapular End of the Clavicle, with Report of a Case Illustrating the Practise Employed" (*Richmond and Louisville Medical Journal*, July 1876). Among other medical writings are: "Atmospheric Distention of the Vagina in the Knee-Chest Posture" (*American Journal of Obstetrics*, October 1876); "The Primary Conversion of Occipito-Posterior into Occipito-Anterior Positions of the Vertex, with Cases Illustrating the Practice" (*Ibid.*, April 1878); and "Dislocations, Upwards and Backwards of the Scapular End of the Clavicle" (*Journal of the American Medical Association*, Aug. 8, 1891). Much of his work, including papers on climatology, was published in the *Southern Medical and Surgical Journal* and the *Southern Journal* of Augusta. He was instrumental in forming the board of health of his state and drafted the act of the legislature calling it into being. He was married on Oct. 11, 1855, to Julia Sarah, daughter of Dr. William L. Felder of Sumter, S. C. His son, William Henry Jr., became a physician of note and was dean and professor of surgery at the University of Georgia.

[W. J. Northen, *Men of Mark in Ga.*, vol. IV (1908); *Who's Who in America*, 1906–07; *Augusta Chronicle*, Mar. 28, 1905; personal data from a grandson, Dr. Roger C. Doughty of Columbia, S. C.] E. E. H.

DOUGLAS, AMANDA MINNIE (July 14, 1831–July 18, 1916), author, daughter of John N. and Elizabeth (Horton) Douglas, was born in New York City, and obtained her formal education at the City Institute there. In 1853, her family moved to Newark, N. J., where she was to pass the rest of her life. Having early revealed a precocious talent for narration, shown in the telling of long fascinating stories to other children, she studied English and American literature with a private tutor after leaving school and began desultorily to exercise her own pen. At the age of eighteen, however, she was about to take up designing and engraving when illness in the family forced her to stay at home and led her definitely to the pursuit of letters. Before the publication of her first book she contributed numerous stories to the *New York Ledger*, the *Saturday Evening Post*, the *Lady's Friend*, and had already established herself in a literary milieu. She became an important member of the Ray Palmer club—the oldest women's literary organization in the locality—and of the New Jersey Woman's Press Club. Her first book, *In Trust*, appeared in 1866, and from that date until 1913 when her last work, *Red House Children at Grafton*, was brought out, she published one or more volumes every year. In 1893 her novel *Larry* won the $2,000 prize offered by the *Youth's Companion* for the best piece of fiction for young people. Most of her works belonged to three extensive series, the Kathie Series, the Little Girl Series (*A Little Girl in Old New York*, 1896; *A Little Girl in Old Boston*, 1898; *A Little Girl in Old Philadelphia*, 1899, etc.), and the Helen Grant Series. All these were works of fiction intended for young readers. They were loosely constructed domestic chronicles dealing sympathetically with the joys and sorrows of family life, introducing enough of the darker sides of existence to throw into relief the virtues of patience, faith, and honor. Despite the fact that she never married, love of home and children formed the basic theme of all her work. Home in her books is always the haven where sorrows are healed and happiness is found. While her characters exemplify copy-book manners and their geographically informative travels follow guide-book methods and itineraries, there is an undercurrent of warmth and vitality in the work of Miss Douglas that raises her novels somewhat above the level of mere didactic writing. Her clear and simple style, without being brilliant, was well adapted to her audience and subjects. Although she lacked the breadth of interest and humor of her close friend Louisa M. Alcott, her works never rivaling the latter's in popularity, nevertheless during her long life her books circulated widely and even to-day they are in constant demand in public and Sunday-school libraries.

[C. H. J. Douglas, *A Collection of Family Records* (1879); *Woman's Who's Who of America*, 1914–15; *Who's Who in America*, 1916–17; obituaries in *Newark Evening News*, July 18, 1916, and *N. Y. Times*, July 19, 1916. The year of birth is given as 1837 by *Who's Who in America* but as 1831 by the *News* and the genealogy.] G. G.

DOUGLAS, BENJAMIN (Apr. 3, 1816–June 26, 1894), manufacturer, was born at Northford,

Conn., the eighth and youngest child of Capt. William and Sarah (Kirtland) Douglas. His grandfather, William Douglas [*q.v.*], had been a colonel in the Revolution and his father a captain of militia in the War of 1812. He was reared on his father's farm, and his education was limited to a few months' attendance at the district school during the winter. At the age of sixteen he was apprenticed to a machinist and in 1836 began work in the shop of Guild & Douglas at Middletown, Conn., a firm established by his brother William in 1832. Benjamin and William in 1839 acquired the entire interest in the business and continued it under the name of W. & B. Douglas. For a time they ran an ordinary foundry and machine-shop, but after the brothers in 1842 invented the famous revolving cistern stand pump, the resources of the foundry were chiefly devoted to the manufacture of pumps. This pump gained recognition slowly, but eventually enjoyed a world market and brought a fortune to the inventors. William, who had been the mechanical genius of the firm, died in 1858 and Benjamin reorganized the concern into a corporation of which he remained president until his death. By the late seventies the company operated the largest foundry in Connecticut, manufacturing 1,200 styles and sizes of pumps.

Douglas for many years was prominent in Connecticut politics. He was a member of the state Assembly in 1854, and Republican lieutenant-governor of the state in 1861. An ardent abolitionist, he had been a founder of the Republican party in Connecticut, being one of the delegates who nominated Frémont in 1856 and one of the presidential electors who cast a vote for Lincoln in 1860. He was instrumental in the formation of one of the companies of the 1st Connecticut Artillery that went from Middletown. His part in the life of Middletown was likewise important. In addition to his service as mayor, 1849–55, he was chiefly responsible for the founding of the First National Bank of which he was president for many years. He was also president of the Farmers' & Mechanics' Savings Bank, and a trustee of the Middlesex Banking Company and of the Asylum Line Railroad. He threw himself into philanthropy and reform with the same enthusiasm that he did into business. A deacon of the Congregational church for thirty years, and for a long period superintendent of the Sunday-school, he acted as president of the Middlesex Branch of the Connecticut Bible Society and president of the Connecticut State Temperance Union. He served as trustee of Wesleyan University, 1862–85, and of the Connecticut State Asylum for the Insane. He was married on Apr. 3, 1838, to Mary Adaline Parker, daughter of Elias and Grace (Totten) Parker of Middletown, by whom he had six children.

[W. R. Cutter and others, *Geneal. and Family Hist. of the State of Conn.* (1911), I, 293; *Hist. of Middlesex County, Conn.* (1884), 163–64; *Representatives of New England Manufacturers* (1879), I, 194–96; C. H. J. Douglas, *A Coll. of Family Records* (1879); W. F. Moore, *Representative Men of Conn.* (1894), p. 10; J. L. Bishop, *A Hist. of Am. Manufactures* (1866), III, 366, and the *Middletown Penny Press*, June 27, 1894.]

H. U. F.

DOUGLAS, HENRY KYD (Sept. 29, 1838–Dec. 18, 1903), lawyer, soldier, was born at Shepherdstown, near Harper's Ferry, W. Va. His father, Rev. Robert Douglas, was a native of Scotland, who, emigrating to Pennsylvania, married Mary, daughter of Col. John Robertson, and subsequently settled in the Shenandoah Valley. His early education having been obtained privately, Henry Kyd Douglas attended Franklin and Marshall College where he graduated in 1858. He then attended the law school of Judge Brockenbrough at Lexington, Va., obtaining his diploma in 1860, and being admitted to the bar at Charleston, W. Va. Proceeding west he settled in St. Louis, but on the outbreak of the Civil War returned home and enlisted as a private in Company B of the 2nd Virginia Regiment, which formed part of Stonewall Jackson's brigade. He took part in the battle of Bull Run, and rose by successive steps to the rank of captain. In March 1862 he made a spectacular ride, when, selected to convey the order of Stonewall Jackson, then at Mount Jackson, to Gen. Ewell at Brandy Station, he rode 103 miles, crossing the Blue Ridge in a heavy rain-storm, between five in the evening and sunrise the next morning. On his return to his regiment he was appointed inspector-general and aide-de-camp to Jackson. He accompanied the latter throughout the Shenandoah Valley campaigns, the battles of Gaines's Mill, White Oak Swamp, Malvern Hill, and was present when Jackson was killed at Chancellorsville. Promoted major, he was thereafter continually on staff duty till Gettysburg, where he was severely wounded and taken prisoner. Nine months later he was released from hospital and rejoined the Confederate army. In February 1865 he was given command of the Light Brigade in Gen. John B. Gordon's army corps, and after Petersburg his brigade formed the rear guard during the retreat to Appomattox. In the heavy fighting which ensued he was twice wounded, but continued in active command, his brigade firing the last shot and being the last unit of Lee's army to surrender. On being paroled he retired to Shepherdstown, but was arrested for transgressing military regulations and sentenced to three months' imprisonment. A false accusation of association with John Wilkes Booth caused him later to be taken to Washington, but his innocence of this charge was clearly established.

In September 1865 he opened a law office in Winchester, Va., but in November 1867 removed to Hagerstown, Md., where he thereafter made his home. During the labor disturbances of 1877 he commanded the Maryland forces guarding the Baltimore & Ohio and Chesapeake & Ohio railroads, and for some years was lieutenant-colonel of the 1st Maryland National Guard. E. E. Jackson appointed him associate justice of the fourth circuit on Apr. 8, 1891, but he occupied the bench for only seven months, being defeated in the elections of the following November. In 1892 he was appointed adjutant-general of Maryland by Gov. Brown and as such was in command of the state troops during the coal strike in the George's Creek District. He was unmarried.

His brief term on the Maryland bench afforded no opportunity for display of judicial qualities, but he had the reputation of being a sound lawyer, and his fluency of speech enabled him to achieve a measure of success as an advocate. He contributed the articles "Stonewall Jackson's Intentions at Harper's Ferry," and "Stonewall Jackson in Maryland" to *Battles and Leaders of the Civil War* (vol. II, 1887). Not a success as a politician, as a soldier he was in the front rank. Passing through all the grades, at Appomattox he was the youngest brigade commander in either army. He was wounded nine times. Six feet in height, well proportioned, with handsome features and a military bearing which was maintained even in later life, dignified and kindly, he was an outstanding figure in post-war Maryland circles.

[*Franklin and Marshall Coll. Obit. Record*, vol. II, pt. 4, no. 8 (1904); *Portrait and Biog. Record of the 6th Congressional District, Md.* (1898), p. 205; *Who's Who in America*, 1903–05, p. 409; Chas. King, "Long-Distance Riding" in *Cosmopolitan*, Jan. 1894; obituary notices in *The Sun* (Baltimore) and *Baltimore American*, Dec. 19, 1903.]

H. W. H. K.

DOUGLAS, JAMES (Nov. 4, 1837–June 25, 1918), metallurgist, mining engineer, and industrialist, was called by the *Engineering and Mining Journal* "the dean of the mining and metallurgical professions." Yet he began his career with a theological and medical education and was at one time the manager of an insane asylum. His father was a prominent surgeon in the city of Quebec, whence he had come from England, and was a man of philanthropic and cultivated tastes; he introduced the modern treatment of the insane in Canada when he took charge of the Quebec Lunatic Asylum. The father was also named James Douglas; the mother was Elizabeth (Ferguson) Douglas. The son published in 1910 *The Journals and Reminiscences of James Douglas, M. D.*, in memory of his father. The younger James Douglas was born in Quebec. When he was eighteen he went to the University of Edinburgh for two years' study in theology. In 1858 he received an A.B. degree from Queen's University in Kingston, Canada. He then traveled with his father, visiting Europe and Africa. After more study abroad and at home, including some courses in medicine, he was licensed to preach, but not ordained, and served for a time as assistant minister at St. Andrews Presbyterian Church in Quebec. He was married in 1860 in Frankfort, Germany, to Naomi, daughter of Capt. Walter Douglas of Quebec. On the basis of a rather slight instruction in chemistry while studying medicine, he served for several years as professor of chemistry at Morrin College, Quebec. His father had made an unfortunate investment in the Harvey Hill copper mines in Quebec. With Sterry Hunt the son experimented in the extraction of copper from the ores of these mines, and they invented the ingenious Hunt & Douglas process. In later life he paid a tribute to Hunt's influence upon him by writing *A Memoir of Thomas Sterry Hunt, M.D., LL.D.* (1898). At the age of thirty-eight he came to Phoenixville, Pa., to take charge of the copper-extraction plant of the Chemical Copper Company. The plant was not a financial success and was finally destroyed by fire. These were hard years for Douglas and his family. The turning point in his career did not come until he was nearly fifty, but then fortune smiled upon him generously.

In 1880, at the request of the conservative metal-dealers, Phelps, Dodge & Company of New York, he examined some copper claims at Bisbee, Ariz., and on his recommendation these claims were acquired and became the nucleus of the Copper Queen Consolidated Mining Company of which he became president. After several years of seeking an adequate supply of ore, during which his geological insight was of great value, the company began its successful expansion in mining, smelting, and railroading, which helped materially to develop the Southwest, and led to the building in 1886 of the El Paso & Southwestern Railroad. Douglas combined the direction of metallurgical researches and industrial improvements with humanitarian interests. The town of Douglas, Ariz., a smelting center near the Mexican border, was named after him. His policy of publicity for metallurgical improvements helped to dispel secrecy and suspicion in technology in America—an important reform. In 1906 he was awarded the gold medal of the Institution of Mining and Metallurgy (London), and in 1915 the John Fritz Medal for achievement in mining, metallurgy, education, and industrial welfare. He published not only numerous technical papers but also historical books, such as *Canadian Independence, Annexation and British Imperial Federation* (1894), *Old France in the New World* (1905), *New England and New France* (1913). McGill University conferred upon him the honorary degree of doctor of laws, and he later became chancellor of Queen's University. From 1899 to 1901 he was president of the American Institute of Mining Engineers; this institute awards annually the James Douglas gold medal for distinguished achievement in non-ferrous metallurgy. His numerous philanthropies included bequests to educational, medical, and engineering institutions.

His sons, James Stuart and Walter, became prominent in mining and financial circles. Although he lived at Spuyten Duyvil, New York City, and made frequent trips to the Southwest, he did not become a citizen of the United States. In appearance he was spare, bearded, and Scottish-looking. He was a man sincerely loved by many friends, and his personal influence in the mining and metallurgical professions was productive of much good.

[Obituary articles in the *Engineering & Mining Jour.*, July 6, 1918; R. W. Raymond, in *Bull. Am. Inst. Mining Engineers*, Sept. 1918; New York and Montreal newspapers; also an appreciative article by A. R. Ledoux in the *Bull. Am. Inst. Mining Engineers*, Jan. 1916, at the time of the award of the John Fritz medal.]

P. B. M.

DOUGLAS, STEPHEN ARNOLD (Apr. 23, 1813–June 3, 1861), Democratic leader, United States senator, belonged by birth and ancestry to New England but by all the circumstances of his adult life to Illinois and the Mississippi Valley. He was born in Brandon, Vt., and could trace his ancestry through successive generations to William Douglass, a Scotchman who came to Boston about the middle of the seventeenth century. On his mother's side he was related to the Arnolds of Rhode Island. There was, therefore, a strain of Celtic blood in the son of Dr. Stephen A. Douglass and his wife Sarah Fisk. While he was an infant, his father, a young physician, died, leaving the family dependent upon a brother of Mrs. Douglass. To this bachelor uncle Stephen owed his early schooling. For a time he hoped that he might prepare at Brandon Academy for Middlebury College, but this expectation had to be put aside. Instead he served a short apprenticeship to two cabinetmakers. It was a commonplace boyhood, though it was not without significance for the future politician. Vermont was rich in Revolutionary traditions; it fostered the town-meeting as a democratic institution; and it afforded in its own history a classic example of that popular sovereignty which became a veritable shibboleth in the later speeches of Senator Douglas. On the marriage of his mother to Gehazi Granger and of his sister to Granger's son, he followed them to Ontario County, N. Y., where he entered the Canandaigua Academy and later began the study of law. A certain restlessness took possession of him, however, and in June 1833, against the wishes of his mother, he set out for Cleveland, where he was encouraged to believe that he might be admitted to the bar within a year. He fell ill of typhoid fever, and when he left his bed four months later he was resolved to push farther west. After many wanderings which carried him as far as St. Louis, he finally paused at Jacksonville, Ill., forlorn, weary, and impoverished.

Jacksonville was then little more than a frontier village and just recovering from a scourge of cholera. Opportunities of employment were few, and Douglas was glad enough to move on to Winchester, ten miles away, where he was told a schoolmaster was wanted. There he was encouraged to open a subscription school for three months and eventually enrolled forty pupils. Meantime he boarded with the village storekeeper and read what law he could from borrowed books. In the following spring he returned to Jacksonville, and presented himself before a justice of the supreme court for a license to practise law. He still lacked a month of being twenty-one years of age. Though he opened a law office in the court-house, was elected state's attorney for the first judicial district within a year, and became a judge of the supreme court before he was twenty-eight, there is no reason to suppose that he acquired any profound knowledge of the law; but he was "Judge" Douglas to the end of his days. From the outset law was only the handmaid of his political ambitions. His rise as a politician coincided with that of the Democratic political machine in Illinois, in the making of which, indeed, he had a large part.

With a political wisdom beyond his years he urged upon his Democratic friends the necessity of party discipline if they would win elections. He was a stout champion, in season and out, of the methods he had seen in operation in New York under the Albany Regency. Organization from top to bottom was needed. He was a prime mover in the establishment of county and state nominating conventions, and reaped the reward of his exertions by being nominated and elected as Democratic member of the legislature from Morgan County. The tenth General Assembly which met in December of 1836 contained also Abraham Lincoln as a member of the "Long Nine" from Sangamon County. Soon after the adjournment Douglas accepted the post of register of the land office at Springfield, which this Assembly had decided to make the capital of the state. It was a strategic position and he proceeded to make the most of it. From this time on there was hardly a party maneuver in which he did not have a hand. A congressional district convention at Peoria in 1837 put him in nomination for Congress against the stalwart Maj. John T. Stuart, Whig candidate, much to the amusement of the opposition. It was hard to take this stripling seriously. Yet Douglas took himself seriously enough, campaigned over thirty-four counties, and gave the Whigs a scare that they did not forget for many a day. Douglas lost the election by only thirty-five votes. He now stood high in the party conclaves, and as the presidential election drew near he became the chairman of the Democratic state committee and the virtual manager of the Democratic campaign. It was generally conceded that the victory of the Democratic ticket in Illinois was due in no small measure to his efforts. In the autumn of 1840 Douglas was appointed secretary of state by the Democratic governor whom he had helped to elect. In the following months he took an active part in lobbying for the bill to reorganize the supreme court, and again he had his reward when he was appointed to one of the five new judgeships. While discharging his not very onerous duties Judge Douglas kept in close touch with his Springfield friends, who were bent upon sending him to the United States Senate though he lacked a year of the required age. This time vaulting ambition overleaped itself. He was defeated by five votes. A successful gerrymander by the Democrats, however, had created a promising congressional district which included the most populous counties of his circuit; and on June 5, 1843, a Democratic convention nominated him for Congress. In the exciting contest which followed, he addressed public meetings on forty successive days; and when election day came, he was prostrated by a fever from which he did not recover for months. But he won the election by a majority of 461 votes.

He now entered a larger arena. His personal appearance was not in his favor. An observer wrote of him: "He had a herculean frame, with the exception of his lower limbs, which were short and small, dwarfing what otherwise would have been a conspicuous figure. . . . His large round head surmounted a massive neck, and his features were symmetrical, although his small nose deprived them of dignity." What he lacked in dignity and bearing he made up in self-confidence and audacity. He threw himself into the debate which was raging over the bill to remit the fine imposed upon Gen. Jackson at New Orleans and won not only a hearing—which was as much as he had a right to expect—but enthusiastic applause from the Democratic side of the House. Then he made a plea for the support of Polk as president which delighted the wheelhorses of the party, so that he was asked by the Democratic central committee to take an active part in the campaign in the West. Before the presidential election occurred, he had himself been reëlected by a handsome majority over his Whig opponent.

Douglas was impatient with those who would compromise the claim of the United States to the whole of Oregon, and he was one of that small band of congressmen who shouted for "Fifty-four forty" to the bitter end. It was therefore humiliating to find the new President ready to compromise with Great Britain on the forty-ninth parallel. For a time Douglas sulked in his tent. When the war with Mexico came, however, he sprang to the support of the administration and became one of its most vigorous and successful defenders. A third time he was elected to Congress (1846) by an increased plurality. He seemed likely to be a fixture in the House when the legislature of Illinois elected him to the Senate as the colleague of Sidney Breese. He took his seat in December 1847 and was immediately made chairman of the Committee on Territories. It fell to him, therefore, to deal with the most difficult political problems of the next decade, when the anti-slavery movement reached its greatest momentum. Hitherto he had deplored all agitation against slavery which he regarded solely as a domestic institution wholly within the control of the states which countenanced it. Now he was brought face to face with an active demand on the part of political groups in the Northern states that Congress should exercise its powers at least to prevent the extension of an institution which affronted the moral sense of many citizens. At the same time, he was confronted with an equally insistent demand from Southerners of the Calhoun persuasion that no obstacles should be put in the way of those citizens who desired to take their slaves into territory acquired by their common exertions and now the property of the United States.

At this very time, in his own life, Douglas became acutely conscious of the push and pull of opposing forces. On Apr. 7, 1847, he had married Martha Denny Martin, daughter of Col. Robert Martin, a planter of Rockingham County, N. C., and owner also of a plantation in Mississippi. On the death of her father in the following year, Mrs. Douglas fell heir to his property, including some 150 slaves, which her husband, as a politician with Northern constituents, regarded as a distinct liability. There were always those who persisted—unfairly—in interpreting his subsequent career by this economic interest. Circumstances also drew him in an opposite direction. The center of gravity in Illinois politics was steadily shifting from the southern and central counties, originally settled by people from the Southern states, to the northern counties which were feeling the full force of the "Yankee invasion." In the summer of 1847 Douglas took up his residence in Chicago, invested heavily in real estate, and identified himself with those who had visions of the commercial greatness of the lake city. It was largely through his efforts that the projected Illinois Central Railroad from Galena to Cairo was linked with Chicago at the north and with Mobile at the south, by making common cause with the Mobile and Ohio Company, also a suppliant for congressional aid. Thus amended, the Illinois Central Railroad Bill passed both Houses of Congress just as the last of the compromise measures of 1850 came to a vote.

Meantime Douglas had a not unimportant part in framing two of these compromise measures. The bills providing territorial governments for Utah and New Mexico were drafted by him and Congressman McClernand, after conference with such southern Whigs as Toombs and Stephens, and were eventually adopted in their original form, which left the territorial governments free to enact laws on "all rightful subjects of legislation consistent with the Constitution of the United States" and promised that when the territories should be admitted as states, they should be admitted with or without slavery, as their constitutions should prescribe.

Though Douglas had not voted for the Fugitive-Slave Bill—he was unavoidably absent when the vote was taken—he approved of the Act and at Chicago made one of the best defenses of that much misunderstood measure (Johnson, "The Constitutionality of the Fugitive-Slave Acts," *Yale Law Review,* December 1921). Young men were irresistibly drawn to him by his generosity, his courage, his willingness to assume complete responsibility for his acts even at the cost of popularity. It was this younger element in the party which urged his nomination for president in 1852 and would not be suppressed by their elders, who saw something ridiculous in the pretensions of a man of thirty-five. For a time, as the candidate of "Young America" against "Old Fogyism," he gave the supporters of Cass and Buchanan some concern. By the time the Democratic convention met, however, it was clear that he could not win, though on the thirty-first ballot he received the highest vote of any of the candidates. The success of the Democratic ticket in the election of 1852 assured his reëlection as senator, and he was prepared to assume the leadership of his party in Congress, when the death of his young wife changed the current of his life. When he took his seat in the Senate, his colleagues remarked an unwonted bitterness and acerbity of temper. He grew careless in his personal habits, slovenly in his dress, disregardful of his associates. When Congress adjourned, he sought diversion and rest in travels which took him into Russia and the near East. He returned refreshed in body and mind, if not much wiser by contact with the culture of the Old World.

He now entered upon the most turbulent period of his career. During his absence, events in the Middle West had again brought slavery and the territorial problem to the fore. Nebraska—the great area west of Iowa, Missouri, and Arkansas, which he had repeatedly endeavored to organize as a territory—had become an object of serious concern to Missouri politicians, to settlers lawfully or unlawfully in that region, and to promoters of a Pacific railway. No sooner had Congress met than a bill was introduced by Senator Dodge of Iowa for the organization of the territory, and promptly referred to the Committee on Territories. The chairman was soon made aware of the interests involved. Senator Atchison of Missouri, a friend of Douglas, lost no time in explaining his predicament. Under pressure from Thomas H. Benton, an avowed candidate for his seat, who was advocating the organization of Nebraska and St. Louis as the eastern terminus of a great central railway, he—Atchison—had changed his position and was demanding territorial organization without the slavery restriction (P. O. Ray, *The Repeal of the Missouri Compromise,* 1909, ch. iv). Newspapers in his own state and in the South were suggesting the wisdom of some such settlement as that worked out in the territorial bills of 1850 (*Ibid.,* chs. vi, vii). The urgency of some action was apparent from the presence in the House of two delegates, each claiming to represent a provisional government in Nebraska: one west of Missouri; the other, west of Iowa (*Ibid.*, chs. iii, v). Pacific railway interests also focussed upon the committee room of Senator Douglas. Far-sighted persons in the South, who worked through Secretary of War Davis, had persuaded the administration to open negotiations for a cession of Mexican territory which would make possible a southern route to the Gulf of California. These Southern interests were not averse to dilatory tactics with regard to Nebraska, unless concessions were made to them. All but two Southern senators, it was significant, had opposed the passage of a bill for the organization of Nebraska in the preceding session. Then there were the Chicago constituents of Senator Douglas who had visions of a northern route to the Pacific with the lake city as the eastern terminus. To their representations he could not remain indifferent (F. H. Hodder, *The Genesis of the Kansas-Nebraska Act*, 1913).

Out of the Committee on Territories came finally a new bill with a report, Jan. 4, 1854, which asserted that legal opinion was divided on the constitutionality of the Missouri Compromise, but, avoiding a pronouncement on this legal point, held that the compromise measures of 1850 were designed to establish certain great principles applicable to Nebraska as well as to New Mexico and Utah: to wit, that all questions pertaining to slavery in the territories should be left to the decision of the people residing therein by their appropriate representatives. Cases involving title to slaves were to be referred to the local courts, with right of appeal to the Supreme Court of the United States. An attempt by Southern senators to repeal the Missouri Compromise explicitly by amendment to this bill led to the famous Sunday conference of administration leaders at the White House, on Jan. 22, 1854. Out of this conference emerged the Kansas-Nebraska Bill providing for two territories instead of one and declaring the prohibition of slavery in the Act of 1820 "superseded." A subsequent change, the product of frequent caucuses held by Democratic leaders (Johnson, *Douglas*, pp. 243–45), substituted the phrase "inoperative and void," and added the declaration that the bill did not propose to legislate slavery into or exclude it from any state or territory, but "to leave the people thereof perfectly free to form and regulate their domestic institutions in their own way, subject only to the Constitution of the United States." In the ensuing debates Douglas coined a phrase which became his slogan in after years. This fundamental principle hitherto dubbed "squatter sovereignty" he now dignified with the name "popular sovereignty," a principle, he averred, as old as the Revolution ("The Genesis of Popular Sovereignty" in *The Iowa Journal of History and Politics*, January 1905).

Meantime the Independent Democrats in Congress had published their "Appeal . . . to the People of the United States," arraigning the bill as "a gross violation of a sacred pledge" and "a criminal betrayal of precious rights" for personal advantage in the presidential game. The insinuation was unfair. Douglas had nothing to gain from subserviency to the South. His best chance of national preferment, if indeed that had been in his thoughts, lay in the opposite course (Johnson, *Douglas*, pp. 205–06). This is not to say that he was not an opportunist, for such he was by nature and political habit. Facing a question that threatened to rend his party, he sought to unite it on what he genuinely believed to be a fundamental principle. By an appeal to an instinct so elemental in American nature as a belief in political self-determination, he expected to offset any reluctance to brush aside a mere legislative fiat on the subject of slavery. What he failed to gauge accurately was the attachment of the Northern Democrats to what Chase called "a compact binding in moral force" for more than thirty years. Nor could he weaken this attachment by the truly statesmanlike assertion that climate, and not any human enactment, dedicated the whole Northwest to freedom (*Washington Union*, Feb. 2, 1854; *Globe*, 33 Cong., 1 Sess., pp. 278–79). Climate seemed a frail reliance where human freedom was at stake.

Though Douglas made two memorable speeches during the debate in the Senate, the real contest was waged in the House. Here Richardson, speaker of the House, and that adroit parliamentarian Alexander H. Stephens, finally secured the passage of the bill by a scant majority of thirteen; but the master mind was Douglas. To him fell "the marshaling and directing of men," and to him belonged the glory—or the blame. As he returned to Chicago, traveling by the light of his burning effigies as he afterward said, he might have doubted—if he had been so inclined—whether he had achieved his objective. Had he united his party on a principle which would be accepted North and South? As events proved, so far from consolidating his own party, it drove Democrats of strong anti-slavery sentiments into temporary fusion with anti-slavery Whigs and Free-Soilers. Another consequence was the contest between pro-slavery and free-state settlers for the control of Kansas. By the spring of 1856, Kansas had two rival governments: a territorial legislature in the control of the pro-slavery elements, and a free-state government at Topeka which had drafted a constitution and applied for admission into the Union.

When Douglas made his report on Mar. 12, 1856, for the Committee on Territories, to which all matters relating to Kansas had been referred, he fixed the responsibility for the breakdown of popular sovereignty upon those who through organizations incorporated in distant states had sought to control the domestic institutions of Kansas. He found a vindication of his principle in the peaceful history of Nebraska, "into which the stream of emigration was permitted to flow in its usual and natural channels." He insisted that the legislature of Kansas was a legal body and proposed a bill to authorize it under certain restrictions to call a convention to frame a constitution; but neither this nor the Toombs Bill which his committee subsequently reported with amendments, came to a vote, for the country was on the eve of a presidential election and politicians were sparring for time.

Douglas had already been indorsed as candidate for the Democratic nomination by several state conventions, but even before the convention met at Cincinnati, a well-organized movement was under way to nominate James Buchanan [*q.v.*] of Pennsylvania. After the sixteenth ballot, when Buchanan received 168 votes and Douglas 122, Douglas instructed his friends to withdraw his name and to support that candidate who received a majority. On the next ballot Buchanan was unanimously nominated. It was highly creditable to Douglas, under the circumstances, that he put himself unreservedly at the service of the party in the ensuing campaign, speaking in all the doubtful states and contributing liberally out of his own pocket to the party campaign fund. His real-estate ventures in Chicago had proved highly profitable and he was generous to the point of prodigality with his easily acquired wealth.

Soon after the election (Nov. 20, 1856), Douglas married Adèle Cutts, daughter of J. Madison Cutts of Washington and great-niece of Dolly Madison, whom she is said to have resembled in charm of manner. She was indisputably the belle of Washington, beautiful, warm-hearted, and universally loved and admired. It was always a mystery to Washingtonians that she should have chosen to give herself to this unromantic widower, who preferred the society of men, was none too careful in his dress and personal habits, and was convivial beyond even the custom of the day. Yet it proved to be in every respect a happy marriage. She became the devoted partner of all his toils and an affectionate mother to his two boys. She brought to him also distinguished social alliances, and at their residence in Washington dispensed a lavish hospitality that was long remembered.

When Douglas returned to Washington in the fall of 1857, a convention at Lecompton, under the control of the pro-slavery elements, had adopted a constitution which in effect guaranteed the right of property in slaves now in the territory, though the fictitious choice was given to the people of Kansas of voting for the constitution with slavery or the constitution with no slavery. Meantime the free-state people, who had unfortunately taken no part in the election of delegates to this convention, had secured control of the territorial legislature. There could be no doubt that in any fair test a pro-slavery constitution would be decisively rejected. Douglas was disturbed by rumors that President Buchanan approved of this constitution and would recommend favorable action by Congress. He immediately sought an interview with the President and found his fears confirmed, whereupon he threw down the gauntlet and declared that he would oppose the policy of the administration to the bitter end. On Dec. 9, he took the irrevocable step and in one of the really great efforts of his career denounced the Lecompton constitution as a travesty on popular sovereignty. The speech made a profound impression, not only upon those who heard it, but on the country, for no one could mistake its import. Douglas had broken with the dominant pro-slavery faction of his party. In the weeks that followed, he was made to pay the price of insurgency. The party press was set upon him; his friends were turned out of office; he was subjected to scurrilous abuse. Nor did he receive much aid and comfort from the ranks of the opposition. Republicans were slow to trust the author of the Kansas-Nebraska Act. His motives were impugned. The weathercock, it was said, had found which way the wind was blowing in Illinois: he was a candidate for reelection. Under these assaults his health broke and for a fortnight he was confined to his bed, rising only by sheer force of will to make an impassioned plea on Mar. 22, 1858, for fair dealing in Kansas and a defense of his own course. Again he spoke to crowded galleries, and to anxious colleagues who saw in his defection a menace to the integrity of the Democratic party.

In the following April the Democratic state convention of Illinois closed the door to reconciliation with the administration by giving Douglas an unqualified indorsement. It was the signal for a bitter and determined effort to prevent his reëlection to the Senate. For a moment it seemed as though he might receive some Republican support. Eastern Republicans who felt that he was now fighting their battles against the administration counseled their Illinois friends not to oppose him; but these Illinois Republicans had minds of their own and nominated Abraham Lincoln as their first and only choice for the United States Senate. Aside from the relentless and often insidious opposition of the administration, Douglas seemed to have every advantage in this interesting contest. He was known everywhere; he was always sure of an audience; he enjoyed the favor of the Illinois Central Railroad which put special trains at his service; he drew liberally upon his own pecuniary resources; he was aided by a gerrymander which gave the Democrats an advantage in electing members of the legislature. He forfeited some of these advantages, however, when he accepted Lincoln's proposal of a series of joint debates, for Lincoln had no such following and could command no such public attention. The picturesque features of these joint debates, in which Lincoln appears for the first time as a national figure, have given them perhaps an undue importance. So far as Douglas was concerned, they only widened the breach between him and the dominant faction of his party by forcing him to deny the full force of the Dred Scott decision as interpreted by friends of the administration. Douglas professed to accept the decision as commonly understood and to Lincoln's insistent demand that he explain how the people of a territory, under the vaunted principle of popular sovereignty, could forbid slavery, when the Supreme Court had declared that Congress had not that power under the Constitution, he replied that the decision of the Court was only *obiter dictum* on that point and that, no matter what the Supreme Court might at some future time decide as to the abstract question, slavery could not exist anywhere without police regulations, which could only be established by the local legislature. If this was not good law, it was a truthful statement of the course of American history whenever federal law has run athwart deep-seated local convictions. The vote throughout the state gave the Republicans a popular majority, but only a minority of seats in the next legislature. When the two Houses met in joint session, Jan. 6, 1859, Douglas received fifty-four and Lincoln forty-six votes for the United States Senate.

Douglas had won a great personal triumph, but he had still to discover that his worst foes were those of his own political household. He was deposed from the chairmanship of the Committee on Territories and regarded with hardly disguised hostility by his Democratic colleagues from the South. He smothered his resentment, however, attended the Democratic caucus, and gave his cordial support to Slidell's bill for the purchase of Cuba, determined to prove his orthodoxy on party policies wherever he could. On Feb. 23, he was drawn into a debate in which, hard pressed by Jefferson Davis and other Southern senators, he declared himself utterly opposed to any active intervention by Congress to protect slave property in the territories. Thenceforth he threw restraint to the winds and lost no opportunity to force the fighting. In letters which he allowed to find their way into the newspapers, he denounced any attempt to revive the African slave-trade or to read into the party creed any such new issues as a congressional slave code for the territories. He prepared an elaborate essay, which was published in *Harper's Magazine,* on "The Dividing Line between Federal and Local Authority," in which he attempted to reconcile popular sovereignty with the Dred Scott decision.

When, then, the Democratic convention met at Charleston in the following April, the lines on which it would divide were already drawn. The majority report of the Committee on Resolutions asserted the right of Congress to intervene in a territory to protect slave property; the minority reports upheld the principle of non-intervention. Both factions agreed to frame a platform before naming candidates; but when one of the minority reports was adopted seven of the Southern delegates protested and withdrew. The rest of the delegations then proceeded to ballot. Douglas led on all fifty-seven ballots but could not command the necessary two-thirds; and on the tenth day the convention adjourned to meet two months later in Baltimore. There, on June 23, after the withdrawal of the other Southern delegations, Douglas was nominated by acclamation, upon receiving all but thirteen votes on the second ballot. The bolters nominated John C. Breckinridge as their candidate. The Democratic party was hopelessly rent in twain. The nomination of Abraham Lincoln by the Republican party and of John Bell by the Constitutional Union party further complicated the political situation.

At the outset of the campaign Douglas believed that he would carry most of the Southern states and enough free states to insure his election, or at least to throw the election into the House of Representatives; but as the summer wore on, he became less confident. His active personal campaign was sharply criticized as a regrettable innovation; but his intimates knew that his designs now went far beyond any personal ambition. By mid-summer he admitted frankly that Lincoln would probably be elected; his own efforts were bent upon reorganizing the Democratic party and quashing the disunion movement in the South. The popular vote in the election of 1860 was a personal triumph for Douglas, for he alone of all the candidates drew votes from every section of the country and his total vote fell only 489,495 short of Lincoln's. Compared with the vote for Breckinridge and for Bell in the South, his vote was negligible, but at the North he ran far ahead of both. It is difficult to escape the conclusion of a shrewd observer that popular sovereignty had a strong hold upon the instincts of nine-tenths of the American people (*New York Times,* June 26, 1860).

In the critical last weeks of the Buchanan administration, Douglas put himself unreservedly at the service of those who feared for the integrity of the Union and who still believed in the efficacy of compromise. He served on the Committee of Thirteen and voted for the ill-fated Crittenden resolutions. As hopes of congressional action faded, he urged upon Lincoln the calling of a national convention to amend the Constitution so as explicitly to forbid the federal government from interfering with the domestic institution of slavery in the states. The insistence of Douglas, supported by Seward, probably led Lincoln to modify his inaugural address at this point (Johnson, *Douglas,* pp. 464–65). Nothing that Douglas ever did was more to his credit than his support of the new president in the early days of his administration. It was not a matter of trifling importance that Senator Douglas purposely made himself conspicuous at the inauguration and courteously held the President's hat while he read his address. Nor was it without significance that Senator and Mrs. Douglas were among the first to call at the White House and to rally Washington society to the support of the plain, homespun couple who seemed so out of place in the presidential mansion (*New York Times,* Mar. 8, 10, 1861).

Immediately after the firing on Fort Sumter, Douglas accompanied George Ashmun to the White House, at the latter's suggestion, to assure the President of his support. He was cordially received and heard the President read a draft of the proclamation calling for 75,000 volunteers to suppress rebellion. His only criticism was: "I would make it 200,000!" Otherwise their accord was complete. In the columns of the newspapers next morning Democrats read the President's proclamation and a dispatch (written by Douglas) announcing the determination of Senator Douglas fully to sustain the President in the exercise of all his constitutional functions to preserve the Union. From this time on Douglas was in frequent conference with the President. It was on Lincoln's advice that he left the Capital to rouse the people of the Northwest to the seriousness of the crisis. He spoke twice on the way, both times with obvious emotion, deprecating secession and pleading for the support of the government at Washington. On Apr. 25, he made a remarkable speech to his own people in the Capitol at Springfield. Fifty years later, men who had been his political opponents could not speak of it without emotion. "I do not think it is possible," wrote Horace White, "for a human being to produce a more prodigious effect with spoken words" (Herndon-Weik, *Lincoln,* II, 126–27). His great sonorous voice reverberated through the chamber until it seemed to shake the building, stirring men and women to a frenzy of excitement. In a few weeks that great voice was still. Stricken soon after with typhoid fever, he battled resolutely as ever with this last foe, but succumbed on June 3, 1861, his last words a message to his two boys bidding them to obey the laws and support the Constitution.

[Of the first biographies of Douglas published in 1860 for use in the presidential campaign, only that by James W. Sheahan has historical value, but it is both defective and inaccurate for the early part of Douglas's career. A brief sketch was written by W. G. Brown in 1902 for the Riverside Biographical Series, and a *Life* by William Gardner in 1905. Neither was based on intimate study of sources. In 1908 was published Allen Johnson's *Stephen A. Douglas: a Study in American Politics,* the first attempt to use contemporary newspapers to supplement manuscript sources. The footnotes indicate the sources used for it and for the foregoing article. This study was followed by C. E. Carr's *Stephen A. Douglas His Life Public Services, Speeches and Patriotism* (1909), and H. P. Willis's *Stephen A. Douglas* (1910) in the American Crisis Biographies, which contain little new information. In October 1912 the so-called "Autobiography" was first printed in the *Journal of the Illinois State Historical Society,* but it had long been available in manuscript copies. It was hastily written by Douglas in 1838 and never revised, according to Judge Robert M. Douglas. "The Life of Stephen Arnold Douglas" by F. E. Stevens, published in 1924 in the *Journal of the Illinois State Historical Society* (Vol. XVI) contains some fresh information of a personal nature but in general is uncritical and discursive. *Abraham Lincoln 1808–1858* by Albert J. Beveridge (2 vols., 1928), is the only biography of Lincoln which treats Douglas other than as a foil for the hero.]

A. J.

DOUGLAS, WILLIAM (Jan. 27, 1742/3–May 28, 1777), Connecticut sailor and soldier, was born in Plainfield, Conn., the fourth son of John and Olive (Spaulding) Douglas, of a family long prominent in the eastern part of the colony. In 1759, although only sixteen years of age, he enrolled as a clerk in a regiment led by Eleazer Fitch and Israel Putnam in the campaign against Quebec (*Connecticut Historical Society Collections*, vol. X, 1905, p. 170) and served, it is said, as Putnam's orderly sergeant. In early manhood Douglas removed to New Haven, from which port he engaged successfully in the West-Indian trade, building up thereby a modest fortune. On July 5, 1767, he married Hannah Mansfield of New Haven, who bore him four children. He retired from active commercial enterprise about 1774 and established a new home in Northford, about eight miles from New Haven. From the outbreak of the Revolution he was an active supporter of the colonial cause. In April 1775 the Assembly appointed him a major in the militia, but a month later he accepted a captaincy in David Wooster's regiment, raised for service in the Canadian expedition. With this regiment he took part in Gen. Richard Montgomery's advance along Lake Champlain. Because of his nautical experience, Montgomery assigned Douglas to boat service on the lake. He returned to Connecticut in the early winter with his regiment which did not accompany Montgomery down the St. Lawrence to Quebec. During the first three months of 1776 he served as major in a volunteer regiment commanded by Andrew Ward which assisted in preparing the defenses of New York and Brooklyn. At this time the Continental Congress appointed him commodore of the vessels on Lake Champlain in view of his excellent service during the previous year (*Journal of the Continental Congress*, Mar. 26, 1776; American Archives, 4 ser. V, 389, 437–38, 1,378). Douglas declined this command, however, as he preferred to organize and lead a battalion in Gen. James Wadsworth's brigade of Connecticut troops in the New York campaign. Douglas's men were stationed on the extreme right of the American line at the battle of Brooklyn, and he had the mortification of seeing the British in occupation of Fort Sterling, which he had himself helped to erect "in cold, tedious weather." At Kip's Bay, on the Manhattan side of the East River, he commanded a brigade of Connecticut militia on Sept. 15. Under heavy fire from the British war-ships, his raw troops gave way in confusion in spite of strenuous efforts to rally them by Douglas and later by Washington himself. This retreat enabled the British to land on Manhattan, but the incident increased rather than diminished Douglas's reputation for gallantry and coolness under fire. With his battalion he took an active part in the remainder of the autumn campaign, although the necessary hardships and exposure seriously aggravated in him symptoms of tuberculosis which were already well developed. Upon the expiration of the battalion's term of enlistment in December, Douglas at once set about the raising of a new regiment to serve in the Continental Army for the duration of the war, but he was destined never again to take the field. He was elected to the Connecticut Assembly which met on May 12, 1777, but probably was unable to attend since he died at Northford before the month was out. His loss was unfortunate for the Continental Army; he had been unselfishly devoted to the cause and had displayed soldierly qualities of a high order. His portrait shows him to have been tall and slender with an erect carriage and strong features. An older brother, John Douglas (Apr. 12, 1734–Sept. 22, 1809), also served during the Revolution. As lieutenant-colonel and later colonel of Connecticut troops, he took a not very conspicuous part in the siege of Boston and the campaign around New York. From 1777 until the end of the war he held the rank of brigadier-general of militia, in command of the 5th Brigade, but participated personally only in one minor expedition into Rhode Island in the autumn of 1777.

[Some of William Douglas's letters from the field have been printed in Henry P. Johnston, "The Campaign of 1776 around New York and Brooklyn" in *Memoirs of the Long Island Hist. Soc.*, vol. III (1878), and others in the *N. Y. Hist. Soc. Quart. Bull.*, Jan. 1929–Jan. 1930. Information on the military careers of both brothers is to be found in *The Public Records of the Colony of Conn. 1636–1776* (1850–90); *The Public Records of the State of Conn.* (1894–1922), and *Record of Service of Conn. Men in the Revolution.* Genealogical data, portraits of Wm. Douglas and his wife, and a not entirely reliable sketch of his career, are included in Chas. H. J. Douglas, *A Collection of Family Records, with Biog. Sketches, and Other Memoranda of Various Families and Individuals Bearing the Name Douglas* (1879).] L. W. L.

DOUGLAS, WILLIAM LEWIS (Aug. 22, 1845–Sept. 17, 1924), shoe manufacturer, and governor of Massachusetts, was born at Plymouth, Mass., the son of William and Mary C. (Vaughan) Douglas. His father died when the lad was only five, and the latter's only formal education was secured at brief, irregular intervals in the public schools. In his career he was a fine example of the poor orphan boy made successful and eminent almost entirely by his own industry and enterprise. At the age of seven he was bound out to his uncle, a shoemaker, and set to work pegging shoes when he was so small that he had to stand upon a box to reach the bench. His hours were long, and, besides his routine duties in the shop, he had to gather fuel for two fires. At fifteen he was a full-fledged journeyman shoemaker. He then entered a large cotton-mill at Plymouth, his daily wage being thirty-three cents. During a period when he was on crutches because of a broken leg, he hobbled to school two miles each way. After his recovery, he carried on his trade in Hopkinton, Mass., and later in South Braintree, under Ansel Thayer, a famous bootmaker. At the age of nineteen, he enlisted (Feb. 26, 1864) in Company I, 58th Massachusetts Regiment, but he was wounded in the back at Cold Harbor later in that year and spent many months in army hospitals. Discharged at the close of the war, he went West, settling for a time in Black Hawk, Colo., and later in Golden City in the same state, where he was for a time in the retail shoe trade. He returned East and on Sept. 6, 1868, married N. Augusta Terry, at Plymouth.

From 1870 to 1875 Douglas was a superintendent in the Porter & Southworth factory at North Bridgewater (now Brockton), Mass. In 1876, with a borrowed capital of $875, he began manufacturing for himself in a small room, 30 x 60 feet, with five employees and an output of forty-eight pairs of shoes a day. There were times when Douglas was his own buyer, cutter, and salesman, and even his own expressman, and he often worked eighteen and twenty hours at a stretch. In 1879 he moved into larger quarters, and two years later erected a large three-story factory on Pleasant St. In 1884 he took the unprecedented step of advertising his own shoes; and eventually his own portrait, his first trade-mark, was stamped on the soles of all his products. It was not long before his face, printed constantly in the newspapers to advertise Douglas shoes, became familiar to everybody who had eyes with which to see. In 1892, with the erection of a new and still larger factory at Montello Station, Brockton, the business was incorporated, with a capital of $2,500,000, and was soon employing 4,000 operatives. In 1923, the year before his death, it was manufacturing 17,000 pairs of shoes daily and controlling 117 retail stores scattered throughout the country.

Douglas entered political life in 1884 as a Democratic member of the Massachusetts House of Representatives, and in 1886 he sat for a term in the state Senate. He was a councilman of Brockton, and, in 1890, was chosen mayor of that city. He was a delegate to the National Democratic conventions of 1884, 1892, and 1896, and delegate-at-large in 1904. In the last-named year, he ran for governor, and was elected by a large majority, being, however, the only Democrat on the ticket to be successful. While he was in office (1905–06), the legislature was strongly Republican, and he had little influence on law-making. He declined to run for a second term. As governor, he refused to waste time by attending banquets or public functions not associated with his position, and he enjoyed the respect even of his political opponents.

Douglas was a man of simple and unostentatious tastes, who was never ashamed of his early poverty. He was never talkative, and believed in deeds rather than words. A liberal philanthropist, he gave a complete surgical building to the Brockton Hospital and established the Brockton Day Nursery. As an executive, he was fair and just, and was esteemed highly by labor-unions. His only real recreation was work, though he went South each year for a month in Florida, and he owned a summer home at Monument Beach overlooking Buzzard's Bay. After the death of his first wife, he married on Apr. 10, 1913, Mrs. Alice (Kenniston) Moodie. She and two daughters survived him. He died very suddenly in a hospital after an operation, at the age of eighty, and was buried in the Melrose Cemetery, in Brockton, with many distinguished persons following his body to the grave.

[Much information regarding Douglas may be found in *The Boy Who Pegged Shoes* (n.d.), a little pamphlet published by the W. L. Douglas Shoe Company. See also the *Boston Transcript* for Sept. 17, 1924; *Who's Who in America*, 1922–23.] C. M. F.

DOUGLASS, DAVID BATES (Mar. 21, 1790–Oct. 21, 1849), engineer, soldier, teacher, was born at Pompton, N. J. A son of Nathaniel and Sarah (Bates) Douglass, he was of Scotch and English ancestry, both the Douglass and Bates families having lived in Morris County, N. J., since the early years of the eighteenth century. The iron-mining region in which he grew up was not well provided with schools, but the boy was well instructed and disciplined by his mother, a woman of unusual intellectual gifts. He was prepared for college by the Rev. Samuel Whelpley, and entered the sophomore class at Yale. He was determined to become an engineer, but at Yale he could do little to prepare himself. At the time of his graduation, in 1813, however, the country was in the midst of its second war with Great Britain; engineer officers were in demand, and careers were open even when training had been deferred. Douglass was accepted and commissioned as second lieutenant of engineers and ordered to West Point where he could train. During 1814 he saw active service on the Niagara frontier. For his gallant conduct in the defense of Fort Erie he was commended in official dispatches by Gen. Gaines, was promoted to a first lieutenancy and brevetted captain. On Jan. 1, 1815, he was assigned, as assistant professor of natural philosophy, to the Military Academy which was under reorganization at West Point. In December of that year he married Ann Eliza, daughter of Andrew

Ellicott, professor of mathematics at West Point. Quickly taking his place as one of the most progressive and efficient among the younger instructors at the post, Douglass was transferred successively to the chairs of mathematics and engineering, bettered his professional standing, and in the meantime received important outside assignments from the government. He served with surveys of the defenses of Long Island Sound, as astronomical surveyor with a commission to determine the Canadian boundary from Niagara to Detroit, and in the exploration of Lake Superior region conducted in 1820 by Gen. Cass. Later he was employed, as consulting engineer or in charge of special projects, by canal and railroad corporations, as well as by the State of Pennsylvania. The number of such engagements led him to resign from the army in 1831.

For nearly three years he had been interested in the Morris and Essex Canal of New Jersey, then under construction, and particularly in the substitution of inclined planes with mechanical lifting power for canal locks. After leaving West Point he directed that work. At the same time (1832–33) he held a professorship of natural philosophy in the University of the City of New York, later becoming professor of civil engineering and architecture with few required duties. He designed the University's building in Washington Square. More noteworthy, however, was his relation to the New York City water supply. Acting as engineer for the commissioners in 1834–36, he selected the Croton water-shed in preference to two other possible sources in Westchester County, located the route of the aqueduct, and determined all the essential features of the system, including the crossing of the Harlem River on a high bridge. With later enlargement this system continued to supply New York with water for seventy-five years. Before the actual building of the Croton Aqueduct had been begun Douglass was superseded as chief engineer, but his plans were followed in the construction, with slight changes. It appeared that incompatibility had developed between him and the chairman of the Board of Commissioners (see *A Memoir of the Construction, Cost, and Capacity of the Croton Aqueduct*, 1843, compiled from official documents by Charles King, pp. 140–43). His next important undertaking was the planning and laying out of Greenwood Cemetery in Brooklyn. This work occupied him until 1840, when at the suggestion of his friend and former pastor, Bishop McIlvaine [*q.v.*], he was called to the presidency of Kenyon College, then a feeble and struggling institution under the care of the Protestant Episcopal Diocese of Ohio. The authority committed to Douglass as president was only nominal. The college did not flourish and friction developed with the trustees and with the bishop. Although no charges were preferred against Douglass, in 1844 he was requested by the trustees to resign. On his refusal, he was removed; but the trustees at the same time expressed confidence in him and appreciation of his merits. Returning to his profession, he worked on cemetery projects at Albany, N. Y., and at Quebec for several years, but in 1848 was chosen to the professorship of mathematics and natural philosophy at Geneva (later Hobart) College, Geneva, N. Y. There he died in the following year, as the result of a paralytic stroke.

[C. H. J. Douglas, *Family Records*, etc. (1879); F. B. Dexter, *Biog. Sketches Grads. Yale Coll.*, vol. VI (1912); G. W. Cullum, *Campaigns of the War of 1812–1815 against Great Britain, with Brief Biogs. of the Am. Engineers* (1879), pp. 234–66, and *Biog. Reg. U. S. Mil. Acad.* (3rd ed., 1891); C. B. Stuart, "Maj. David Bates Douglass" in *Van Nostrand's Eclectic Engineering Mag.*, Jan. 1872; N. Cleaveland, *Greenwood Cemetery: a Hist. of the Institution* (1866); *N. Y. Express*, Oct. 25, 1849; *The Kenyon Book* (*c.* 1890). The Kenyon College controversy is outlined in D. B. Douglass's pamphlet, *A Statement of Facts and Circumstances Connected with the Removal of the Author from the Presidency of Kenyon College* (1844), *Reply of the Trustees of Kenyon College, to the Statement of D. B. Douglass* (1844), and *A Further Statement of Facts in Answer to the Reply of the Trustees* (1845), by D. B. Douglass.]

W. B. S.

DOUGLASS, FREDERICK (Feb. 1817?–Feb. 20, 1895), abolitionist, orator, journalist, was named Frederick Augustus Washington Bailey, but assumed the name of Douglass after his escape from slavery. He was born at Tuckahoe near Easton, Talbot County, Md., the son of an unknown white father and Harriet Bailey, a slave who had also some Indian blood. As a child he experienced neglect and cruelty, indulgence and hard work; but particularly the tyranny and circumscription of an ambitious human being who was legally classed as real estate. He turned at last upon his cruelest master, and by fighting back for the first time, realized that resistance paid even in slavery. He was sent to Baltimore as a house servant and learned to read and write with the assistance of his mistress. Soon he conceived the possibility of freedom. The settlement of his dead master's estate sent him back to the country as a field hand. He conspired with a half dozen of his fellows to escape but their plan was betrayed and he was thrown into jail. His master's forbearance secured his return to Baltimore, where he learned the trade of a ship's calker and eventually was permitted to hire his own time. A second attempt to escape, Sept. 3, 1838, was entirely successful. He went to New York City; married Anna Murray, a free colored woman whom he had met in Baltimore, and together they went to New Bedford, where he became a common laborer.

Suddenly a career opened. He had read Garrison's *Liberator,* and in 1841 he attended a convention of the Massachusetts Anti-Slavery Society in Nantucket. An abolitionist who had heard him speak to his colored friends asked him to address the convention. He did so with hesitation and stammering, but with extraordinary effect. Much to his own surprise, he was immediately employed as an agent of the Massachusetts Anti-Slavery Society. He took part in the Rhode Island campaign against the new constitution which proposed the disfranchisement of the blacks; and he became the central figure in the famous "One Hundred Conventions" of the New England Anti-Slavery Society. It was a baptism of fire and brought out the full stature of the man. He was mobbed and mocked, beaten, compelled to ride in "Jim Crow" cars, and refused accommodations; but he carried the programme through to the bitter end.

Physically, Douglass was a commanding person, over six feet in height, with brown skin, frizzly hair, leonine head, strong constitution, and a fine voice. Persons who had heard him on the platform began to doubt his story. They questioned if this man who spoke good English and bore himself with independent self-assertion could ever have been a slave. Thereupon he wrote his *Narrative of the Life of Frederick Douglass* which Wendell Phillips advised him to burn. It was a daring recital of facts and Phillips feared that it might lead to his reënslavement. Douglass published the little book in 1845, however, and then, to avoid possible consequences, visited Great Britain and Ireland. Here he remained two years, meeting nearly all of the English Liberals. For the first time in his life he was treated as a man and an equal. The resultant effect upon his character was tremendous. He began to conceive emancipation not simply as physical freedom; but as social equality and economic and spiritual opportunity.

He returned to the United States in 1847 with money to buy his freedom and to establish a newspaper for his race. Differences immediately arose with his white abolitionist friends. Garrison did not believe such a journal was needed and others, even more radical, thought that the very buying of his freedom was condoning slavery. Differences too arose as to political procedure in the abolition campaign. In all these matters, however, Douglass was eminently practical. With all his intense feeling and his reasons for greater depth of feeling than any white abolitionist, he had a clear head and a steady hand. He allowed his freedom to be bought from his former master; he established the *North Star* and issued it for seventeen years. He lectured, supported woman suffrage, took part in politics, endeavored to help Harriet Beecher Stowe establish an industrial school for colored youth, and counseled with John Brown. When Brown was arrested, the Governor of Virginia tried to apprehend Douglass as a conspirator. Douglass hastily fled to Canada and for six months again lectured in England and Scotland.

With the Civil War came his great opportunity. He thundered against slavery as its real cause; he offered black men as soldiers and pleaded with black men to give their services. He assisted in recruiting the celebrated 54th and 55th Massachusetts colored regiments, giving his own sons as first recruits. Lincoln called him into conference and during Reconstruction, Douglass agitated in support of suffrage and civil rights for the freedmen. His last years were spent in ease and honor. He was successively secretary of the Santo Domingo Commission, marshal and recorder of deeds of the District of Columbia, and finally United States minister to Haiti. His second marriage, in 1884, to Helen Pitts, a white woman, brought a flurry of criticism, but he laughingly remarked that he was quite impartial—his first wife "was the color of my mother, and the second, the color of my father." He was active to the very close of his career, having attended a woman-suffrage convention on the day of his death.

[The chief sources of information about Frederick Douglass are his autobiographies: *The Narrative of the Life of Frederick Douglass, an American Slave* (1845), republished in England and translated into French and German; *My Bondage and My Freedom* (1855); *Life and Times of Frederick Douglass* (1881). The best biographies are: F. M. Holland, *Frederick Douglass, the Colored Orator* (1891); C. W. Chesnutt, *Frederick Douglass* (1899); Booker T. Washington, *Frederick Douglass* (1907). There are numerous references in W. P. and F. J. Garrison, *William Lloyd Garrison 1805–1879* (4 vols., 1885–89), and throughout the literature of the abolition controversy. Many of Douglass's speeches have been published.] W. E. B. D.

DOUGLASS, WILLIAM (*c.* 1691–Oct. 21, 1752), physician of Boston, the second child of George Douglass, "portioner" of Gifford and factor for the Marquis of Tweeddale, was born in the town of Gifford, Haddington County, Scotland. He apparently received a liberal education, for he was familiar with Greek, Latin, Dutch, French, and English, and was known to have studied medicine at Edinburgh, Leyden, and

Paris. He came under the influence of Pitcairn, the leading physician of Scotland in his day, and was at Leyden during the supremacy of Boerhaave. In his writings (*e.g.*, letter to Cadwallader Colden, Feb. 20, 1721, *Massachusetts Historical Society Collections,* 4 ser., II, 164) he refers to himself as a medical graduate, but whether he received his degree from Edinburgh or Leyden is not known. After a trip to the West Indies, he settled in Boston in 1718. He was first heard of in the colony in connection with the inoculation controversy. Early in the summer of 1721 a severe epidemic of smallpox broke out in Boston, and Zabdiel Boylston [*q.v.*] was prevailed upon by Cotton Mather [*q.v.*] to carry out inoculations for smallpox during the epidemic. Douglass disapproved strongly of the practise and was the more concerned since he had, "sometime before the small-pox arrived, lent to a credulous vain Preacher, Mather, Jr., the *Philosophical Transactions* Nos. 339 and 377 which contain Timonius' and Pylermus' account of Inoculation from the Levant" (*Ibid.*). Douglass held that inoculation might spread smallpox, and he accordingly published a series of four controversial "inoculation" pamphlets, three of which were anonymous. In 1751, when he finally became convinced of the value of the procedure, he wrote, "The novel practice of procuring the small-pox by inoculation, is a very considerable and most beneficial improvement in that article of medical Practice" (*A Summary, Historical and Political,* II, 406). His chief claim to recognition as a physician rests on his masterly description of an epidemic of scarlet fever, *The practical History of a New Epidemical Eruptive Miliary Fever . . . in Boston New England in the Years 1735 and 1736* (1736). From his account it is clear that this was a genuine epidemic of scarlet fever, and is indeed the first adequate clinical description of the disease, for it antedates that of John Fothergill by twelve years. Douglass described fully the eruption and desquamation, and spoke of the greater susceptibility of children and young persons. He moreover carried out necropsies on individuals dead of the disease.

Douglass was versatile and a man of wide interests. He possessed a large library, recorded observations upon the weather and the variations of the needle of the compass, collected plants, and in 1743 published an almanac (*Mercurius Nov-Anglicanus* by "William Nadir"). He also wrote, *A Summary, Historical and Political, of the First Planting, Progressive Improvements and Present State of the British Settlements in North America* (vol. I, 1749; vol. II, 1751; reprinted in Boston and also in London, 1755; London, 1760), and a treatise on economics entitled, *A Discourse Concerning the Currencies of the British Plantations in America,* etc. (London, 1739; Boston, 1740). The *Summary,* which was written at odd times stolen from his professional work, was often based upon hearsay and tradition since but few documented sources were available to him, and it is therefore marred by many inaccuracies, but it contains a great mass of information on a variety of subjects and is an important source book of early colonial history (Bullock). In his *Discourse* Douglass showed a sound grasp of the principles of exchange, a clear understanding of Gresham's law, and he stated in no uncertain terms that the colony must adhere to the "universal commercial medium" if it is to have dealings with foreign nations. Douglass was highly esteemed in the colony and had a large medical practise. Being a person of strong prejudices he had enemies, but from the records which have come down to us he appears to have been well regarded by all the better educated people of Boston.

[The most authoritative account of Douglass is that of G. H. Weaver, "Life and Writings of Wm. Douglass, M.D., 1691–1752," *Bull. Soc. Medic. Hist. of Chicago,* II, 229–59 (Apr. 1921); see also C. J. Bullock's notes to his reprint of Douglass's *Discourse Concerning the Currencies* in *Am. Econ. Asso., Economic Studies,* II (1897), 265; J. Thacher, *Am. Medic. Biog.* (1828), I, 255; article by Burrage in H. A. Kelly and W. L. Burrage, *Am. Medic. Biogs.* (1920), which gives further references.] J.F.F.

DOVE, DAVID JAMES (*c.* 1696–April 1769), educator, pamphleteer, the son of David and Mary Dove, was born in Portsmouth, England, where his father was a tailor. His early life is obscure. He was a surety in two marriage cases in 1728 in Chichester, where he taught grammar for sixteen years before coming to America. He arrived with his wife in Philadelphia in 1750 and applied for a position in the newly founded Academy. The trustees appointed him English master for one year, beginning Jan. 7, 1751, at a salary of £150. Franklin quickly recognized his unusual abilities. The English school grew in numbers and he was given two assistants. Encouraged by his success he opened in September 1751 an academy for young ladies. He was the first person in Pennsylvania, and perhaps in the colonies, who attempted to supply higher education for women. The trustees of the Academy, however, thought that these new cares caused him to neglect his work in the English school and in February 1753 they reluctantly accepted his resignation which took effect in July. Richard Peters, once a student of Dove's, said that he was a "sarcastic and ill-tempered doggerelizer, who was but ironically *Dove*; for his temper was that of a hawk, and his pen the beak of a falcon pouncing on innocent prey." In 1757 he published *Labour in Vain; or, An Attempt to Wash a Black-Moor White,* a lengthy caricature of Judge William Moore, then under arrest for having libeled the Assembly. His pen turned easily to Hudibrastic verse and the etchings with which he often adorned his broadsides are, despite his lack of formal training, as free and vigorous as any of Gilray or Rowlandson. On the last day of 1758 he issued a pamphlet entitled, *The Lottery. A Dialogue between Mr Thomas Trueman and Mr Humphrey Dupe* and attacking the lotteries then employed by the Academy and other institutions to raise funds as "manifestly no better than public frauds." At this time he conducted a school for both boys and girls in Videll's Alley (now Ionic St.). It was here that Alexander Graydon [*q.v.*] attended school. In his substitution of disgrace for corporal punishment and in other measures Dove showed himself to be well in advance of the pedagogy of his time.

In February 1761 he was unanimously elected to the English mastership of the new Germantown Union School, founded to compete with the Academy in Philadelphia. His tenure began the middle of June, although the Union School was not opened until August. He lodged and boarded twenty of his students in his small quarters at the Union School. To the townspeople who were thus deprived of a source of income this was a genuine grievance; they petitioned the trustees who remonstrated with Dove. The eccentric English master and the trustees were temperamentally incapable of understanding each other; there was bickering and argument. He was meanwhile building his own school alongside the Union School; and when this was completed in the summer of 1763 he resigned and opened his own academy. Under the pseudonym of Philopatrius he published on Feb. 18, 1764, *The Quaker Unmask'd; or, Plain Truth, Humbly Address'd to the Consideration of all the Freemen of Pennsylvania.* This was a defense of the Paxton Boys; in it he suggested that the Quakers were enamored of both Indian squaws and Indian trade and demanded if a Quaker could consistently be the representative of a people who are constantly called upon to make war in their own defense. Noteworthy among the pamphlets and broadsides attacking him was *The Medley* by Isaac Hunt [*q.v.*]. This broadside, containing an etching of Dove probably by Henry Dawkins, accused him of gross immorality. He replied with *The Counter-Medley, being a Proper Answer to all the Dunces of the Medley and their Abettors.* He continued his school in Germantown until 1768 when he was again in Philadelphia conducting a school on Front St., near Arch. In the spring of the following year he died and on April 4, 1769, was buried in Christ Church burying ground.

[*Hist. of the Germantown Academy* (1910); T. H. Montgomery, *Hist. of the Univ. of Pa.* (1900); Alexander Graydon, *Memoirs of his own Time,* ed. by John S. Littell (1846); broadsides and pamphlets in libraries of the Hist. Soc. of Pa., and the Philadelphia Library Company; information from Ernest Spofford and Bunford Samuel of Philadelphia.] F. M.

DOW, HENRY (1634–May 6, 1707), New Hampshire soldier and statesman, the second son of Joan and Henry Dow, was born at Ormsby in Norfolkshire. His father migrated with his family to Watertown in the colony of Massachusetts Bay in 1637, and was there admitted freeman on May 2, 1638. He removed to Hampton in 1644. Henry Dow, Jr., was without formal education but became an important and financially prosperous figure in the town of Hampton and the province of New Hampshire. He was chosen selectman in 1661 and several times reelected to that office. He served as town clerk from 1681 to 1707 (Joseph Dow, *post,* p. 565). He was admitted and sworn as an attorney in 1686 and thereafter represented the town in litigation. He was ensign of the Hampton militia in 1689, captain in 1692, and took part in the first and second intercolonial wars. Dow was sworn in as deputy marshal of the province of New Hampshire in 1680, and was appointed sole marshal of the province at a salary of £5 on Mar. 10, 1681/2 (*Provincial Papers,* XIX, 661, 663, 684). He was appointed justice of the court for New Hampshire under the governments of Joseph Dudley and Edmund Andros, justice of the inferior court of common pleas of the province of New Hampshire in 1695, and senior justice in 1699. He repeatedly represented the town of Hampton in the lower house of the legislature of New Hampshire, serving as clerk and speaker *pro tempore* in 1701 (*Ibid.,* 736). He was treasurer of the province, 1694–95 (*Ibid.,* III, 267, 268), and a member of the Council from 1702 until his death. He was twice married: on June 17, 1659, to Hannah, the daughter of Robert and Lucy Page, and on Nov. 10, 1704, to Mary, the daughter of Capt. Christopher Hussey and widow of Thomas Page and Henry Green. By his first marriage he had four sons.

[R. P. Dow, *The Book of Dow* (1929); Jos. Dow, *Hist. of the Town of Hampton, N. H.* (1893); *Provincial Papers of N. H.,* esp. vols. II, III, XII, XIX, XXXI.] I. M. C.

DOW, LORENZO (Oct. 16, 1777–Feb. 2, 1834), evangelist, was born in Coventry, Conn., fifth of the six children of Humphrey Dean and Tabitha (Parker) Dow. His parents, natives of Coventry, brought up their children frugally, educating them, as Lorenzo said, "both in religion and common learning" (*Journal,* p. 1). In 1794, he began preaching, making his evangelistic excursions on horseback, and in 1796 he was accepted into a tentative connection with the Methodist ministry—only to be suspended after three months. Then he preached again independently, desperately poor and generally ill, but frequently within one week traveling as much as 150 miles and preaching as often as twenty times. In 1798, readmitted to his former status with the Methodists, he soon afterward, though opposed by his ecclesiastical superiors, set out to carry his gospel into Ireland. After about eighteen turbulent months there, he returned to New York in May 1801, and almost immediately left by sea for Georgia. He preached there for a few months, returned to New York, and in November 1802 again turned southward, this time overland, proclaiming everywhere his threats of hell, and hopes of paradise, bringing in many converts. He visited the Indians, delivered the first Protestant sermon ever listened to in Alabama, talked in Charleston freely enough to be, at a later time, convicted for libel, and turning northward, preached through the Carolinas, Tennessee, and Virginia. Remembering that in Ireland he had seen "the first pair that I thought were happy in marriage" (*Eccentric Preacher,* p. 77), he decided to take a wife, and accordingly on Sept. 3, 1804, in Westernville, N. Y., he was married. The bride, Peggy Holcomb, born in 1780 in Granville, Mass., entered into the union upon the express understanding that she would never hinder him in his roamings. Leaving her the day after the wedding, he began a swing to Mississippi and return, preaching constantly, and jotting down in his diary notes of dreams and of actual occurrences. By April 1805 he was home again; in July he started for the Carolinas; in November, taking Peggy with him, he embarked for England. There Peggy bore a daughter, Letitia, who soon died. They returned to America in June 1807, and together, from Boston to Natchez and Natchez to Boston, they toured the country, he, long-haired and braced in a little leather jacket, calling himself "Cosmopolite," reputedly rich both in money and in the gift of prophecy, and she everywhere and always abetting him. In 1818 he again went to England, but soon after his return in 1820, Peggy died. Three months later he was married to Lucy Dolbeare of Montville, Conn. From then on, he wrote more and preached less, issuing, after his habit instituted in 1804, a chaotic torrent of egoistic pamphlets, and constantly revising his journals. Living on his farm in Connecticut, he accumulated affidavits about his own good character, compounded medicines recommended for biliousness, quarreled acrimoniously, litigated, to his sorrow, with his neighbors about a mill race, and stormed incessantly against Whigs, anti-Masons, Catholics, and finally against Methodists, who, he said, were badly tainted with popery. Death came to him suddenly in Georgetown, Md.

[*The Dealings of God, Man, and the Devil; as Exemplified in the Life, Experience, and Travels of Lorenzo Dow . . . Together with his Polemic and Miscellaneous Writings Complete. To Which is Added The Vicissitudes of Life, by Peggy Dow* (1856); *The Eccentric Preacher; A Sketch of the Life of the Celebrated Lorenzo Dow* (1841); C. C. Sellers, *Lorenzo Dow* (1928); W. J. Townsend, H. B. Workman, G. Eayrs, *A New Hist. of Methodism* (1909); H. Asbury, *A Methodist Saint* (1927).] J. D. W.

DOW, LORENZO (July 10, 1825–Oct. 12, 1899), inventor, business man, was born in Sumner, Me., the eldest child of Huse and Zilpha (Drake) Dow. He was one of many thousand children named for Lorenzo Dow [*q.v.*], the irregular preacher and inventor of camp-meetings. His father was a Methodist minister and one of the first circuit riders, who died at the age of forty years from overwork and privations. Lorenzo Dow received his primary education in Sumner, prepared for college at the typical "academy," and won the scholarship to Wesleyan University awarded to the oldest son of any Methodist minister. Following his graduation in 1849 he taught school in Vermont and New Jersey for a year and then went "around the Horn" to California where he remained from 1850 to 1853. In the latter year he returned to the East and after teaching school for a few months in Alabama he went to New York and began the study of law. In 1854 he went to Topeka, Kan., completed his law studies in 1857, entered politics, and in 1858 was elected a judge of the supreme court under the Leavenworth Constitution. The following year he was elected mayor of Topeka and also served as editor of the *Kansas Tribune.*

With the outbreak of the Civil War, he turned his attention to improvements in ordnance and on Oct. 1, 1861, obtained his first patent for a waterproof cartridge. The waterproofing substance used was collodion. Upon the adoption of this cartridge by the federal government Dow went to New York and became associated with the Remington Arms Company, in whose plant the cartridges were to be made. Here he continued his experiments and was granted four additional patents on waterproofing cartridges and shells. This work continued except for one interruption of a business trip to Europe in 1862–63, until 1866, when Dow went to South America and took up engineering work and business in Colombia. He cleared the old Spanish dike leading from the Magdalena River to Cartagena and established a steamboat service thereupon to the interior. Upon completing this work in 1870, he moved with his family to Port of Spain, Trinidad, and for the next three years engaged in mining in various parts of Venezuela.

In 1873 he returned to the United States and for nine or ten years engaged in mining work in Colorado, after which he took up his residence in New York City, remaining there for the balance of his life. In 1896 he organized in New York the Dow Composing Machine Company of West Virginia to develop and market the type-distributing and type-setting machines invented by his son Alexander Dow, patents for which were granted Nov. 24, 1896, and Nov. 28, 1899, respectively. Dow continued as president of this company until his death. He was twice married: first on Dec. 25, 1853, to Elizabeth Penfield of Middletown, Conn., and after her death to Mrs. Sabrina (Smith) Anderson, on Oct. 2, 1862. He was survived by a son and a daughter of his second marriage.

[R. P. Dow, *The Book of Dow* (1929), pp. 250–51; *Alumni Record of Wesleyan Univ.* (1911); obituaries in *N. Y. Tribune* and *N. Y. Times*, Oct. 14, 1899; Wesleyan University Records; Patent Office Records.]

C. W. M.

DOW, NEAL (Mar. 20, 1804–Oct. 2, 1897), temperance reformer, the "father of the Maine Law," was born in Portland, Me., the only son of Josiah and Dorcas (Allen) Dow, both parents being of English and Quaker descent. He was early trained in those principles of temperance, industry, and thrift for which the Society of Friends has always stood, and to these principles he remained constant throughout his life, although eventually dismissed from the Society because of his changing views on the use of "carnal weapons." This break was inevitable, for Dow was a man of intense convictions with the moral and physical courage to support them. To these characteristics he added from childhood robust health, and, although a man of medium size and weight, marked physical strength and vitality. He was educated in the schools of Portland, and at the Friends' Academy in New Bedford, Mass., and desired to go on to college and enter the law, but to this his parents objected, and, in consequence, he entered his father's tanning business, eventually becoming a partner. His interest in books continued, however, and at his death he possessed one of the largest and finest private libraries in the state.

On Jan. 20, 1830, he married Maria Cornelia Durant Maynard, by whom he had nine children, four of whom died in infancy. In business he was as successful as his ambition demanded. He was active on the directorates of several manufacturing and other corporations, becoming, in fact, one of Portland's leading men of affairs. After 1857, however, his connection with business became little more than nominal, owing to his increasing participation in the temperance crusade.

The intolerable amount of intemperance prevailing in Maine during his youth, together with his Quaker training and the interest of his parents in temperance reform, constitute the general background of Dow's interest in the temperance movement. Later, his own experiences with the drink evil as an employer of labor, as a member of the Portland fire department, and as an overseer of the poor, definitely convinced him of the serious need of reform, and led to his active interest in furthering it. At the age of twenty-four, when clerk of the Deluge Engine-Company, he made his first temperance address, successfully opposing the presence of liquor at a Company dinner, while about the same time he interested himself in the temperance program of the Maine Charitable Mechanics' Association of which he was a member. In 1834, as a delegate of the Portland Young Men's Temperance Society, he attended the first state temperance convention at Augusta where the Maine State Temperance Society was organized to discountenance the use of ardent spirits. Four years later, he withdrew from this last society to organize, with others, the Maine Temperance Union which was pledged to total abstinence and resolved to consider the expediency of petitioning the legislature for prohibitory legislation. Not until 1845, however, could the Union be committed definitely to the cause of legislative prohibition, and then only following an intensive campaign of popular education on the wisdom of so radical a step. In this task of educating public sentiment Dow was an indefatigable worker, speaking wherever opportunity offered throughout the state. That the reformers were making progress became evident in 1846 when a prohibitory measure based largely upon the report of Gen. James Appleton [*q.v.*], which had been tabled by the legislature nine years before, was finally enacted. This law, however, proved to be unsatisfactory in the provisions for its enforcement, and the campaign for a more severe law continued. In 1851 Dow was elected mayor of Portland, and the city council at once made him chairman of a committee to visit the legislature and urge the passage of a law "stringent in its provisions and summary in its processes" which would make it possible to drive the illegal liquor traffic from the city. Dow drew up the bill he desired, and, May 26, 1851, was given a public hearing at Augusta in the House of Representatives. So convinced was the legislature that Dow had the popular sentiment of the state behind him that his bill promptly passed both houses by large majorities, and, June 2, 1851, was signed by Gov. Hubbard. Backed by this legislation, Dow returned to Portland and summarily cleaned up the city, despite some interesting opposition. With the passage of the "Maine Law" his reputation as a temperance reformer became world-wide. Extensive speaking tours throughout the North followed, and in 1853 he served as president of the World's Temperance Convention in New York City.

Again elected mayor of Portland in 1855, he was scarcely in office when there occurred the "June riot," the work of elements within the city hostile to prohibition. In the reaction which followed this unfortunate affair the "Maine Law" was repealed by the legislature, but the popular sentiment of the state was in favor of prohibition and in 1858 it was again enacted. In 1857, at the request of the United Kingdom Alliance, Dow had visited England and lectured widely on prohibition.

On the outbreak of the Civil War, Dow, whose hostility to slavery had been only less than his opposition to the liquor traffic, offered his services to his state, and in the fall of 1861 became colonel of the 13th Regiment of Maine Volunteers. In February 1862, he joined Gen. Butler's command and went to the Gulf Department, where he was commissioned a brigadier-general of volunteers on Apr. 28, 1862. At the battle of Port Hudson he was twice wounded, and while recuperating in a private home within the Union lines was captured by the enemy and spent eight months as a prisoner in Libby prison, Richmond, and at Mobile. Eventually, Mar. 14, 1864, he was exchanged for Gen. Fitzhugh Lee. Temporarily broken in health he returned to Portland, and resigned from the army on Nov. 30, 1864. Following the war, he wrote and spoke extensively in behalf of prohibition, not only traveling throughout the United States but, in 1866–67 and 1873–75, again visiting Great Britain. In 1880 he ran for president of the United States as the candidate of the Prohibition party, receiving 10,305 votes. Four years later the people approved a prohibitory amendment to the state constitution and in the campaign for this amendment he took an active part, although then eighty years of age. He died in Portland, retaining to the end an active and vigorous interest in the cause he had done so much by his zeal and courage to further.

[Dow's autobiography, *The Reminiscences of Neal Dow, Recollections of Eighty Years* (1898); H. S. Clubb, *The Maine Liquor Law, its Origin, History and Results, including a Life of Hon. Neal Dow* (1856); a campaign biography by T. W. Organ, *Biog. Sketch of Gen. Neal Dow* (1880); A. A. Miner, "Neal Dow and his Life Work," *New England Mag.*, June 1894; Intimate pictures of Dow in his later years by Frances E. Willard, "Neal Dow's Ninetieth Birthday" and Mrs. Jos. Cook, "Neal Dow as Guest and Host," *Our Day*, Jan., Feb. and July, Aug. 1894, respectively.] W. R. W.

DOWELL, GREENSVILLE (Sept. 1, 1822–June 9, 1881), surgeon, son of James and Frances (Dalton) Dowell, was born in Albemarle County, Va., his parents' home, where he attended the local schools and pursued private study with more than usual success. He attended medical lectures at the University of Louisville (1845–46) and at Jefferson Medical College, receiving the M.D. degree in 1847. He began the practise of his profession at Como, Miss., where on June 29, 1849, he married his first wife, Sarah Zelinda, daughter of John H. White of that place. He practised successively at Memphis, Tenn., and in Gonzales and Brazoria counties, Tex. (1853). In 1863 he entered the Confederate army and served first as surgeon of Cook's Heavy Artillery and later as surgeon-in-chief of the hospital department. After the war he lived at Galveston, Tex., until the end of his life, and in this city acquired a leading professional position. For two years he was professor of anatomy at the Medical Department of Soulé University and he became lecturer in surgery when that institution became the Texas Medical College. He was in charge of the Galveston Hospital for many years, which under government contract cared for marine patients. Though remote from the larger medical centers he managed to publish many papers of worth, and in 1869 founded the *Galveston Medical Journal.* He had charge of the campaign against yellow fever in Vicksburg, Miss., in 1878, being himself immune to the disease from an early attack. In 1868 he married, as his second wife, Mrs. Laura Baker Hutchinson of Galveston.

He is remembered chiefly for his monograph, *Yellow Fever and Malarial Diseases, embracing a History of the Epidemics of Yellow Fever in Texas* (1876), a text which revealed logical application of epidemiological methods as then known and in addition the all-important suggestion that yellow fever is transmitted by mosquitoes. In 1873 he published a short text, *The Radical Cure of Hernia,* in which he described the operation bearing his name. He designed or adapted several surgical appliances, some of which in more or less modified form are still in use, including: a wire speculum, lithotomy instruments, a retention catheter, instruments for extracting bullets and arrow-heads, and a urethrotome. He was original, bold, and resourceful and with better opportunities he might have been a brilliant surgeon. He was noted as a linguist, having knowledge of seven languages.

[*Trans. Am. Medic. Asso.,* XXXIII (1882), 546; W. B. Atkinson, *Physicians and Surgeons of the U. S.* (1878), 199; John F. Y. Paine in H. A. Kelly and W. L. Burrage, *Am. Medic. Biogs.* (1920), p. 327; *Galveston Daily News,* June 10, 1881.] E. E. H.

DOWIE, JOHN ALEXANDER (May 25, 1847–Mar. 9, 1907), founder of the Christian Catholic Apostolic Church in Zion, was born in Edinburgh. His mother, Ann Macfarlane-McHardie, was illiterate; his putative father, her second husband, John Murray Dowie, was by vocation a tailor, by avocation a preacher. John Alexander's childhood was passed in poverty, sickness, and precocious piety. At the age of six he took the temperance pledge and early developed a fanatical hatred of alcohol, as well as a life-long conviction of being a peculiar object of God's care. In 1860 his parents moved to Adelaide, South Australia, where he went to work first with an uncle and then with a wholesale dry-goods firm of which he later became junior partner. This promising business opportunity he abandoned at the age of twenty in order to study for the ministry. He spent two years at the University of Edinburgh, then returned to Australia, and on May 21, 1870, was ordained pastor of the Congregational Church at Alma. Subsequently he was called to Sydney and then to a larger church in Newton, a suburb of Sydney. In 1878, deciding that it was wrong for a minister to receive a salary, he went into evangelistic work so successfully that in 1882 he was able to build a large independent tabernacle in Melbourne. Hitherto he had devoted himself chiefly to the extermination of liquor and tobacco, defying the laws which prohibited his activities (even serving thirty-four days in jail rather than abandon them); but he now found, or fancied, in himself an ability to heal diseases by means of prayer and such healing was henceforth the major feature of his evangelistic work. During all these years in Australia his sincerity seems to have been unquestioned; his pronounced egotism had not yet passed into megalomania, and his later craving for power, luxury, and notoriety had not yet developed.

He came to San Francisco in June 1888 and remained on the Pacific Coast for two years, meeting, however, with an indifferent response. He then moved to Chicago where for the next six years he carried on services of divine healing with steadily increasing success. In 1895 the clergymen and physicians of Chicago attempted to stop his work through the courts, but although nearly one hundred charges were made against him, Dowie won every case. The ill-advised attempt merely advertised him the more. On Jan. 22, 1896, he called a meeting of those interested in forming a new church under his leadership, and on Feb. 22 the Christian Catholic Church in Zion was definitely organized with Dowie as General Overseer. The church prospered from the outset. Dowie blazed the trail later followed by Billy Sunday: his speeches, adorned with American Billingsgate, vituperative and sensational, easily aroused the passions of his ignorant audiences, while their minds were lulled to sleep by the hypnotic rhythm of his style. His enormous brow, large eyes, and venerable beard gave him an impressive appearance, while his bowlegs were hidden in elaborate flowing robes. His claims to divine inspiration grew ever stronger. In 1899 he identified himself with the Messenger of the Covenant prophesied by Malachi, in 1901 he proclaimed himself to be Elijah the Restorer, and in 1904 he consecrated himself the First Apostle. Meanwhile forty-two miles from Chicago he had built up the most amazing town in America, Zion City, composed of something more than five thousand of his followers exclusively. No theatres, dance halls, secret lodges, drug stores, or physicians' offices were permitted; smoking, drinking, and the eating of pork were penalized; whistles blew for public prayers; while every industry in the town, its bank, and its college were owned and entirely controlled by Dowie. With his accounts unaudited, Dowie's private income became considerable. He now kept two expensive homes, one at Zion City and one near Montague, Mich., and lived with an ostentation unbefitting a second Elijah. His church claimed 50,000 members scattered in various parts of the world; its publications were printed in half a dozen languages; missionaries were beginning to be sent out. In the fall of 1903, however, Dowie met his first check. Having determined upon the conversion of New York City, he and 3,000 followers, on ten special trains, invaded the metropolis, and held meetings during a part of October and November, but without permanent result. New York was at first amused, then disgusted, and finally bored. Insistent upon being a celebrity at all costs, Dowie had given wide publicity to the story that he was really the son of a British nobleman, but even this was of no avail; New York refused to be interested in a problematic scandal fifty years old. The trip had cost $300,000 and there were murmurs in Zion City, but Dowie paid no heed; instead, with a dozen of his officers he went on a "Round the World Visitation." Upon his return, in order to meet the now serious financial situation, he commanded every resident in Zion City, on pain of expulsion, to deposit funds in the Zion City bank; with this accomplished he was off on trips to Mexico in a vain attempt to establish the "Zion Paradise Plantation" there. On Sept. 24, 1905, he suffered a serious paralytic stroke and was taken to Jamaica. As soon as the tyrant was disabled, the slaves rose in revolt. Dowie's most trusted friend, Wilbur Glenn Voliva, to whom he had given full powers of attorney, led a movement which on Apr. 2, 1906, deposed the autocrat, took from him all his Zion City properties, and suspended him from membership in the church on account of "polygamous teaching and other grave charges." Dowie at once returned to Chicago, but broken as he was in health he could not make great headway against the rebellion. Nevertheless he fought on gallantly in the courts until his death less than a year later.

[Rolvix Harlan, *John Alexander Dowie* (1906); *The Personal Letters of John Alexander Dowie,* comp. by Edna Sheldrake (1912); *Zion Banner,* 1901–05; *Leaves of Healing,* I–XX; the *Chicago Tribune,* Mar. 10, 1907.]

E. S. B—s.

DOWNER, ELIPHALET (Apr. 4, 1744–Apr. 3, 1806), "the fighting surgeon of the Revolution," was the ninth child of Joseph and Mary Sawyer Downer. Born in what was then Norwich, but is now Franklin, Conn., he settled in Brookline, Mass., where he married Mary Gardner in 1766 and practised medicine till the Revolution. He was a volunteer fighter against the British on their retreat from Lexington, but later ministered to the wounded Redcoats and even collected wine, linen, and money for their relief. After Lexington he served as surgeon of the 24th Continental Regiment of Foot, and was mentioned by Gen. Heath as active and enterprising.

In May 1776, he sailed as surgeon of the privateer sloop *Yankee.* The ship made several rich captures in June, but in July its crew were overpowered by the prisoners aboard and taken first into Dover and then into London. Downer, in a deposition to Franklin, which was sent to the British ambassador in France as a protest against the harsh treatment accorded American prisoners by the British, and which was later circulated in American newspapers, told how the crew were kept in suffocating quarters and were given little attention when sick. Downer himself was confined in various prison ships at London and Sheerness until gangrene set in in one of his legs and he was moved to Haslar Hospital, Gosport. There he recovered, and then escaped to France at some time not later than March 1777 (Stevens Transcripts, No. 670).

From Apr. 16 of that year to about July 6, he served as surgeon of the Continental sloop *Dolphin,* Capt. Samuel Nicholson (Muster Roll of the *Dolphin,* John Paul Jones Papers, vol. I, Library of Congress), which in company with the *Reprisal* and *Lexington,* circled the British Isles and made nineteen captures (Stevens Transcripts, No. 703). In returning to France, however, the *Dolphin* was chased, sprung a mast, and had to throw overboard her guns to get safely into St. Malo. On Sept. 18, 1777, Downer sailed for the United States as a passenger on the *Lexington,* commanded by his former captain of the *Yankee,* Henry Johnson. The next day, however, off Ushant, the ship was captured after a furious engagement of several hours by the British sloop *Alert,* Capt. Bazely, and carried into Dover (Stevens Transcripts, No. 1695). According to his pension claim, Downer volunteered to fight and was severely wounded in the left arm by grape-shot. After confinement in Forton Prison, Portsmouth, from Oct. 13, 1777, to Sept. 6, 1778, he again made his escape to France, this time with fifty-six other Americans, by tunneling under the wall. Downer is said to have been so corpulent that he stuck in the narrow passage until it was enlarged.

When he finally returned to America he was commissioned surgeon-general of the Penobscot Expedition from July to October 1779, and received fifteen dollars in compensation for instruments lost (*Revolutionary Muster Rolls of Massachusetts,* vol. IV, p. 923). After the Revolution he was given a grant of land in the Marietta Reserve, and acted as an agent for the Ohio Company in the sale of land. He died in Brookline, Mass., and is buried in the Walnut Street Cemetery there.

[The fullest accounts of Downer are in S. A. Drake, *Old Landmarks and Historic Fields of Middlesex* (1888) and in D. R. Downer, *The Downers of America* (1900), but their claim that he served on the *Alliance* or with Paul Jones is contradicted by the dates of his imprisonments and of the Penobscot Expedition. His deposition is found in American newspapers of August 1777, *e.g.,* the *Pa. Evening Post* of Aug. 5; his pension claim is in *American State Papers,* Class IX, Claims, vol. I, p. 151. The best account of the cruise of the *Yankee* is in Force, *American Archives,* ser. V, vol. I, cols. 134, 148, 684, 754–55. See also Washington's Regimental Book, MSS. Div., Lib. of Cong.; *Memoirs of Maj.-Gen. Wm. Heath* (1901), pp. 26–27, 184; *New-Eng. Hist. and Geneal. Reg.*, XXXIII, 37, 41 and LXV, 60–62, 143; *Annual Register*, 1778, p. 200; E. E. Hale and E. E. Hale, Jr., *Franklin in France* (1888), I, 122; *Vital Records of Norwich, Conn.* (1913), I, 135; *Vital Records of Brookline, Mass.* (1929), p. 107; *Vital Records of Roxbury, Mass.* (1926), II, 513; *Boston Independent Chronicle*, Apr. 7, 1806.] W. B. N.

DOWNER, SAMUEL (Mar. 8, 1807–Sept. 20, 1881), manufacturer, was born in Dorchester, Mass., the eldest of the four children of Samuel and Catherine (Ayers) Downer. His grandfather, Eliphalet Downer [*q.v.*], had been a surgeon in the Revolution; his father, Samuel, was a successful merchant and eminent horticulturist who had developed new species of apples, pears, and cherries. The younger Samuel attended the public schools of his native town until the age of fourteen, when he began an apprenticeship with the shipping house of Downer & Baldwin. Upon attaining his majority he joined his father under the firm name of Downer & Son, but after three years associated himself with Silas P. Merriam in the wholesale trade with the West Indies. This partnership was dissolved in 1834, and Samuel joined with his father and Capt. William R. Austin in the manufacture and sale of sperm and whale oils and candles, a business which he directed after the retirement in 1844 of the elder partners.

Downer, like other oil men of his time, was interested in finding a substitute for sperm oil, the only known lubricant for fine machinery, and when his attention was called, about 1854, to hydrocarbon oils, he purchased control of a Waltham concern which had a patent for "Coup oil" and with his assistants, Luther and William Atwood and Joshua Merrill [*q.v.*], commenced a series of experiments which resulted not only in an acceptable hydrocarbon lubricating fluid but in kerosene oil suitable for illumination. Atwood and Merrill, while in Scotland on a commission from Downer, discovered new methods of obtaining oil from coal and of purifying it so that it could be used for lighting. Further experiments upon their return to America led Downer to embark heavily in the manufacture of hydrocarbon illuminating oil distilled from albertite, the bituminous coal obtained from Albert County, New Brunswick. To Downer and his assistants belongs the credit of introducing on a wide scale hydrocarbon lubricating and illuminating oils in America.

The industry was assuming large proportions when it was suddenly disrupted by the discovery of petroleum wells in Pennsylvania. Nothing daunted, Downer founded the Downer Kerosene Oil Company, invested in it most of his fortune, and set out for Pennsylvania to exploit the new discovery. Here he "roughed it" for six years, founded the town of Corry, and established a successful refining business with branches in New York and Boston. Important patents were taken out in the Boston refinery by Merrill, and the products extended to include naphthas, paraffines, and other oil products. It was Downer's technical advisers, the Atwoods and Merrill, who were responsible for the notable improvements in refining processes; his own contribution to the rapid introduction of mineral oil illumination was in the field of promotion and business.

Downer was not only an industrial pioneer but also a political radical. He was an ardent member of the Free-Soil party from its inception and drew up the resolutions at the Dorchester meeting called to choose delegates to the Rochester Convention which nominated Van Buren and Adams. Many years later (Aug. 9, 1877) he held a reunion at his home of some 150 leaders of the 1848 movement, an event which aroused wide interest. Like his father he was interested in horticulture, and developed a beautiful harbor summer resort known as Downer's Landing. He was married, on Oct. 13, 1836, to Nancy Melville, by whom he had eight children.

[D. R. Downer, *The Downers of America* (1900), pp. 83–85; *Biog. Encyc. of Mass. in the Nineteenth Century* (1883), II, 189–96, the best account; J. D. Van Slyck, ed., *New England Manufacturers and Manufactories* (1879), I, 202–04; *Boston Daily Globe*, Aug. 10, 1877, containing an account of the Free-Soil reunion; S. D. Hayes, *On the History and Manufacture of Petroleum Products*, a memoir communicated to the Society of Arts, M. I. T., May 14, 1872; W. D. Orcutt, *Good Old Dorchester* (1893); *Boston Post* and *Boston Transcript*, Sept. 21, 1881.] H. U. F.

DOWNES, JOHN (Dec. 23, 1784–Aug. 11, 1854), naval officer, was born in Canton, Mass., the son of Jesse and Naomi (Taunt) Downes. His grandfather, Edward Downes, was a lieutenant in the Revolutionary War; and his great-grandfather, of the same name, who emigrated to Canton from Ireland, was a seafaring adventurer. Entering the navy as a waiter to his father, who served as a purser's steward on the *Constitution*, John was in September 1800 appointed acting midshipman; and in June 1802, midshipman. During the war with Tripoli he served in the Mediterranean and in 1803 participated in Lieut. David Porter's attack on the Tripolitans, being commended for his gallantry in that fight. In 1807 he was promoted to a lieutenancy and two years later was ordered to the *Essex*, Capt. David Porter [*q.v.*]. As first lieutenant on that ship he sailed on Oct. 28, 1812, from the Delaware Capes on what proved to be the most memorable cruise of the War of 1812. In April 1813, in the boats of the *Essex,* he captured in the Pacific two British vessels, of one of which, the *Georgiana,* he took command after she had been fitted out as a cruiser. In June near James Island he captured the *Hector,* a privateer of eleven guns, and two other ships. In the meantime Porter had taken the *Atlantic,* renamed the *Essex Junior,* and to her Downes transferred his flag, as she was a larger vessel than the *Georgiana.* On her he cruised for several months, either alone or in company with his commodore. At the island of Nukahiva, one of the Marquesas group, where the fleet was refitted, he had two sharp encounters with natives, when ashore in command of landing parties. In one of these, he suffered a broken leg. In the bloody engagement of the *Essex* and the *Essex Junior* with the *Phœbe* and *Cherub,* Downes, although still suffering from his wound, played a gallant part. He was highly commended by the secretary of the navy for his services in the Pacific. In 1813 he was made a master commandant, and four years later, a captain.

In May 1815, Downes sailed for Algiers as commander of the *Epervier,* one of the vessels of Commodore Decatur's squadron. In the capture of the Algerine frigate *Meshuda* he maneuvered his vessel so skilfully that he received the praise of his commodore and was shortly placed in command of the flagship of the squadron. In 1818 he was ordered to the *Macedonian* and cruised for several years in the Pacific. After a tour of duty on the *Java* of the Mediterranean station, 1828–30, he was given command of the frigate *Potomac* and of the Pacific station and was ordered to proceed thither by way of Quallah Battoo, Sumatra, and to obtain satisfaction from the piratical Malays at that place for the outrage they had recently committed on the American vessel *Friendship.* Downes reached Quallah Battoo in February 1832. Landing his sailors and marines, he stormed the town and destroyed the greater part of it. This battle, the first American action in the Orient, lasted two hours and a half and resulted in a loss to the Americans of two killed and eleven wounded, and to the Malays of 150 killed. At home the commodore was criticized by some of the newspapers for his severity, but not by President Jackson, who approved of the chastisement.

The cruise of the *Potomac,* which came to an end in 1834, was Downes's last sea service. The rest of his life he spent in shore duty, with several long intermissions when he was on waiting orders. From 1835 to 1842 and again from 1849 to 1852 he served as commandant of the Boston navy-yard. In 1843–45 he was port captain at Boston and in 1852–53 he was a lighthouse inspector. He died at Charlestown, Mass. On Oct. 30, 1821, he was married to Maria Gertrude Hoffman at Upper Red Hook, N. Y. Their son, John Downes, was an officer in the navy, rising to the rank of commander.

[Record of Officers, 1802–55, Bureau of Navigation; Navy Registers, 1814–54; D. T. V. Huntoon, *Hist. of the Town of Canton, Norfolk County, Mass.* (1893), pp. 450–57; G. W. Allen, *Our Navy and the Barbary Corsairs* (1905); David Porter, *Jour. of a Cruise Made to the Pacific . . . in the U. S. Frigate Essex* (2nd ed., 2 vols., 1822); C. J. Deblois, "Private Jour. kept on board the U. S. Frigate *Macedonian,* 1818–19," in Navy Dept. Lib.; *U. S. Naval Inst. Proc.,* XXXVI (1910), 481–500, 707–716.] C. O. P.

DOWNEY, JOHN (*c.* 1765–July 21, 1826), educator and essayist, was one of five children of Capt. John and Sarah Downey of Germantown, Pa. In this vicinity he spent his early life. His father, who was head of the English School of the Germantown Academy, 1769–74 (Manuscript Minutes, Germantown Union School, Mar. 7, 1774), was killed in 1778 in an engagement near Crooked Billet (*Pennsylvania Packet,* May 4, 1778); but through his mother's efforts the son received a classical education at the celebrated Germantown Academy, where he distinguished himself. About 1795 he removed to Harrisburg, where he opened a school in 1796. There he resided till his death. On June 5, 1798, he married Alice Ann Beatty, daughter of James Beatty, an early settler of Harrisburg. He continued to teach school; served the city in the capacity of justice of the peace, 1807–26; was town clerk for many years; and a member of the legislature, 1817–18. While living at Harrisburg he served about a year as first cashier of the Harrisburg Bank; was active in the incorporation of the Harrisburg & Middletown Turnpike Company; and served as treasurer of the board of directors of the stock company authorized by the legislature in 1812 to build the Harrisburg bridge over the Susquehanna River.

As an educator, Downey is best known for his plan of an educational system, proposed in a letter to Gov. Thomas Mifflin, Feb. 24, 1797 (*Notes and Queries,* II, 223–26). He recommended a state system, comprising: first, two or more elementary schools in each township, supported by a tax on property; second, one school in each township, supported in the same way, in which more advanced studies should be taught; third, one academy in each county, supported by a "very moderate assessment," devoted to "more liberal science." He recommended furthermore that attendance in these schools "for a sufficient time should be strictly enjoined under an adequate penalty," and added the suggestion that it might "not be unworthy the attention of the legislature to raise agriculture from its present servilely imitative practice by encouraging scientific pursuits." That he was not visionary, however, is indicated in the shrewd observation that "perhaps the public mind is not ripe for the reception" of such a plan. Though Downey failed to gain the realization of his project, the system he proposed was later commended by Henry Barnard [*q.v.*] as having unusual merit. Besides this educational scheme, Downey is to be credited with the authorship of numerous humorous sketches, chiefly political, contributed by "Simon the Wagoner," "Simon Slim," and "Simon Easy" to the public press, and a compilation called the *Justice's Assistant*. His skill as a Latinist may be judged from his Latin poem on "A Republican Caucus or Democratic Assembly" (*Notes and Queries*, I, 219 ff.).

[Everett H. Brown and others, *A Hist. of the Germantown Academy* (1910); G. H. Morgan, *Annals of Harrisburg* (1858); Jas. P. Wickersham, *A Hist. of Education in Pa.* (1886); the *Commemorative Biog. Encyc. of Dauphin County, Pa.* (1896); W. H. Egle, *Hist. of the Counties of Dauphin and Lebanon* (1883); *Notes and Queries Hist. and Geneal. Chiefly Relating to Interior Pa.* (ed. by W. H. Egle), I, 218, 518; II, 221–27; and III, 200; and the Minutes of the Union School of Germantown (MS.), 1759–77. *The Oracle of Dauphin*, July 22, 1826, contains a notice of Downey's death.]

T. W.

DOWNING, ANDREW JACKSON (Oct. 30, 1815–July 28, 1852), landscape gardener, architect, horticulturist, was born at Newburgh, N. Y. His father, Samuel Downing, originally a wheelwright, moved from Lexington, Mass., to New York shortly after 1800, and finally settled at Newburgh on the Hudson in 1801. Here he established a nursery, which he continued until his death twenty-one years later. Andrew, born late in the lives of his parents, was delicate in health and led a lonely life as a child, finding solitary enjoyment in the natural beauties that surrounded the Newburgh cottage. As he grew older he attended an academy at Montgomery, where he was later remembered as a quiet reserved boy, but proud in spirit. He completed his formal schooling at the age of sixteen, and refusing to be influenced by his mother, who sought to apprentice him as a dry-goods clerk, indicated his taste by joining his elder brother, Charles [*q.v.*], in operating the nursery. He began to make short excursions to the fine estates on the banks of the Hudson for purposes of observation and to better train himself in landscape design. With the Austrian Baron de Liderer, who had a summer home at Newburgh, he explored the hills and dales of the neighborhood, studying and discussing their mineralogical and botanical aspects. In the home of the Baron and that of his wealthy neighbor, Edward Armstrong, he first came in contact with a refined and polished society, and learned much of value for his self-development. Among the guests who came and went, he was most influenced by Raphael Hoyle, the young English landscape painter and Charles Augustus Murray, the English travel writer. Downing now began to write. His first essay was a description of the Danskamer or Devil's Landing Place, near Newburgh, published in the *New York Mirror*. It was followed by an account of Beacon Hill. He then wrote a discussion of novel-reading and several botanical papers which appeared in a Boston journal. Apparently dissatisfied with these efforts, however, he resolved not to publish again until he could write with authority, in the meantime devoting himself to hard work in the nursery, studying landscape gardening, and reading classical literature.

In his twenty-third year (June 7, 1838) he married Caroline Elizabeth DeWint, a young woman of congenial spirit, refinement, and intelligence, the daughter of John P. DeWint of Fishkill Landing on the Hudson. About this time he bought his brother's interest in the nursery and assumed control himself. Immediately following his marriage, he built a house of his own design upon a six-acre tract at Newburgh, molding into it the thoughts which he had evolved through the preceding years. Elizabethan in style, simple yet distinguished in character, with a landscape in harmony and the garden one of its most attractive features, the place was intended to show the possibilities of adapting European ideas to the needs of the New World. Here for years he played the part of gracious and hospitable host. According to George William Curtis, who met him for the first time in 1846, Downing was a tall, slight, Spanish-looking gentleman with a certain aristocratic hauteur and a constant sense of personal dignity, which comported well with his smile of quiet welcome.

Simultaneously with the establishment of his home, he plunged into the preparation of a work on landscape gardening. Completed and published in 1841 under the title, *A Treatise on the Theory and Practice of Landscape Gardening, Adapted to North America*, the book won immediate popularity, passed rapidly through numerous editions the latest being 1921 and was quickly ranked as a classic. Filled with the sense of beauty which is a notable characteristic of

Downing's writings, interesting in content and genial in style, it made a deep impression upon his contemporaries. Loudon, Lindley, and other foreign writers joined in its praise, and from the date of its publication until his death Downing was recognized as the chief American authority on "rural art." In 1841 also, in conjunction with Asa Gray, he brought out the first American edition of Lindley's *Theory of Horticulture.* In 1842 he published *Cottage Residences,* in which the principles of *Landscape Gardening* were applied to the needs of more humble folk. Following the publication of these works, he was elected an honorary member of most of the horticultural societies in America and a corresponding member of numerous foreign societies, and began an extensive correspondence with Loudon and other foreign notables who eagerly sought his opinions. In 1845, Wiley & Putnam published in New York and London, *The Fruits and Fruit Trees of America,* in the preparation of which Downing had been assisted by his brother Charles. This book, the most complete treatise of its kind up to that time, at once established his reputation as a pomologist, and like his other works, was widely read. Although criticized in some quarters because of minor errors in the first edition, due to the vastness of the subject, it nevertheless went through thirteen printings during the author's lifetime. The same year he also edited the first American publication of Mrs. Loudon's *Gardening for Ladies.* In 1846, at the request of Luther Tucker, Downing accepted the editorship of the *Horticulturist,* a new periodical. He continued in this position until his death, his influence upon his contemporaries becoming even more noticeable. His editorials attracted such attention that an extensive correspondence sprang up between him and his readers, and he was thus enabled to establish a personal relation with hundreds who never saw him. Many of these editorials were republished in a posthumous volume, *Rural Essays* (1853).

Downing's increased interest in architecture is shown in his writings and other activities after 1846. In 1849, he published *Additional Notes and Hints to Persons about Building in this Country,* in connection with a work by George Wightwick. This was followed the next year by Downing's *Architecture of Country Houses, Including Designs for Cottages, Farm Houses and Villas.* In 1850 he took a trip to England and France, a visit to which he had long looked forward, for he was a great admirer of the English rural scene. Here he met the notables of the day and was lionized on all sides, but did not neglect to obtain more information to add to his already large store. While abroad, he made an arrangement with Calvert Vaux, a young English architect, which led to a partnership for the purpose of building homes and preparing landscape gardens in America. The combination proved a happy one, and upon his return, with Vaux he designed and constructed the houses and grounds of a number of estates on Long Island, along the Hudson, and elsewhere. In 1851 he was engaged to lay out the grounds for the Capitol, the White House, and the Smithsonian Institution in Washington. His ideas and plans were carried into effect by his successors, but Downing did not live to complete the work. On July 28, 1852, he embarked from Newburgh for New York on the steamer *Henry Clay,* with members of his family and friends. Opposite Yonkers, the captain engaged in a race with another boat. The *Henry Clay* caught fire, and many of the passengers were burned or drowned. Downing, cool in the face of disaster, gave minute instructions to the frightened people about, calmly gathered chairs and threw them overboard to assist those already struggling in the water, and, himself an excellent swimmer, was attempting to save his friends who could not swim when he was last seen alive. His body was not recovered until the next day.

As the first great American landscape gardener, Downing created a national interest in the improvement of country homes and estates, which, as some one has said, made over the face of rural America in his own day. Although a representative of the English, or natural school, he adapted ideas to the requirements of his own land and succeeded in producing a distinctly American art. His influence upon his pupils and successors was marked. Frederick Law Olmsted, Calvert Vaux, and others, were much indebted to him for their inspiration. Downing's book on landscape gardening has probably been more influential in this country than any other work upon the subject. He is also considered by many the greatest single figure in American horticulture.

[Obituaries and other special notices of Downing, in periodicals and transactions of horticultural societies in 1852, especially the article by Mrs. Monell in the *Knickerbocker Mag.,* Oct. 1852; comments in the *Cultivator,* Sept. 1852, and the *Horticulturist,* Sept., Oct., Nov. 1852; sketch by Marshall P. Wilder in *Proc. Am. Pomological Cong.,* 1852; *N. Y. Times,* July 28, 1852; memorial by Geo. W. Curtis and letter of Frederika Bremer in the posthumous *Rural Essays,* mentioned above. For genus of plants named after him see Downingia.]

H. A. K.

DOWNING, CHARLES (July 9, 1802–Jan. 18, 1885), pomologist, horticulturist, and author, although not as well known to the public as his brother Andrew Jackson Downing [*q.v.*], won a sound reputation for his creative work in pomology. Born in Newburgh, N. Y., his taste for horticultural pursuits was early stimulated by close contact with a nursery owned by his father, Samuel Downing. Even while attending an academy in the neighborhood he worked a portion of the time in this nursery and upon the death of his father in 1822, he succeeded to the entire charge of the establishment. His younger brother, Andrew [*q.v.*], was admitted to a partnership in 1834, an arrangement which lasted until 1839, when Charles sold his interest and embarked in the same business elsewhere. About 1850 he discontinued his commercial nursery and henceforward until the end of his career devoted himself to extensive experiments with varieties of fruits. His research activities had much to do with placing nursery gardening on a scientific basis. The test orchard which he developed contained trees and grafts of 1,800 varieties of apples, 1,000 of pears, and other fruits in like measure. He had assisted his brother in the preparation of *The Fruits and Fruit Trees of America* (1845) and following the death of the latter reissued it in edition after edition, adding new material provided by himself, until the volume was twice as large in content as when it first appeared. Andrew had made the book the best publication of the kind in America; Charles by his additions and revisions made it well known abroad. He also wrote many articles upon horticultural subjects under the initials "C. D." His work throughout was conscientious and accurate, and he was internationally recognized as an authority upon pomology, horticulture, and tree growths. Quiet, modest, and retiring, although an active member of horticultural societies, he would never make a public speech. While in New York City in 1883, he was knocked down and run over by a horse-car and never completely recovered from the injuries which he received at that time. His death two years later, after a lingering illness, was a distinct loss in the horticultural world. His wife was Mary Wait, daughter of Samuel Wait of Montgomery, N. Y.

[For articles and notices of Downing see the *Am. Agriculturist, Cultivator, Country Gentleman, Prairie Farmer, Horticulturist, Am. Gardening,* and other agricultural and horticultural periodicals in his period, also L. H. Bailey, *Cyc. of Am. Horticulture* (1906), II, 1,573; *N. Y. Herald, N. Y. Times, N. Y. Tribune,* Jan. 20, 1885.]

H. A. K.

DOWNING, GEORGE (August 1623–July 1684), baronet, ambassador to the Netherlands from Cromwell and Charles II, member of Parliament, was the second graduate of the first class (1642) at Harvard College. He was born in Dublin, the son of Emmanuel Downing of the Inner Temple and his second wife, Lucy Winthrop, sister of John Winthrop [*q.v.*]. The family emigrated to New England in 1638 and settled at Salem, where young Downing came under the influence of the Rev. Hugh Peters [*q.v.*], from whom it is quite probable that he "sucked in [those] principles that, since, his reason had made him see were erroneous" (Beresford, p. 119). Soon he began to disquiet his mother by his desire to rove and his fondness for field sports. After his graduation from Harvard, on Dec. 27, 1643, he was appointed tutor on a yearly salary of four pounds. Restless and ambitious, he was soon scheming to return to England. In the summer of 1645, apparently as chaplain of a ship, he escaped to the West Indies and thence made his way to London. The rest of his career belongs to English history. Downing Street in London is named for him, and Downing College, Cambridge, owes its foundation to a bequest of his grandson.

[J. L. Sibley, *Biog. Sketches Grads. Harvard Univ.*, I (1873), 28–51, 583; C. H. Firth, article on Downing in the *Dict. of Nat. Biog.*, vol. XV (1888); John Beresford, *The Godfather of Downing Street* (1925).]

G. H. G.

DOWSE, THOMAS (Dec. 28, 1772–Nov. 4, 1856), bibliophile, was born in Charlestown, Mass., the seventh of the eight children of Eleazer and Mehitable (Brentnall) Dowse. His father was a leather-dresser. The family fled from Charlestown on June 17, 1775, when that village, including their house, was burned by the British during the battle of Bunker Hill. Soon afterward they settled in Sherborn, Mass. Thomas was a born reader, and it is said that before he was eighteen years of age he had read all the books he could procure in Sherborn. Doubtless this trait was intensified by his lameness, the result of a fall from an apple tree when he was a young child. Trained in his father's trade, he worked for ten years for a wool-puller and leather-dresser in Roxbury, and then set up for himself in that business in Cambridgeport. He was successful, became prosperous, and remained in business until about seventy-four years of age. His leisure hours, early morning and evening, were devoted to reading and to his garden. By buying good books he gradually acquired a remarkable library that was valued at $40,000. He had a special admiration for Sir Walter Scott, and he used to remark, "Lameness drove us both to books,—him to making them, and me to reading them." The only bust that adorned his library was one of Scott. About 1821, as a result of a lottery, he became the owner of a collection of foreign water-colors and engravings that were much admired in Boston.

In the summer of 1856, a few months before his death, he decided to donate his library to the Massachusetts Historical Society, though he was not a member of that organization. The only condition attached to the gift was that the books should be "preserved forever in a room by themselves, to be used only in said room" (*Proceedings Massachusetts Historical Society,* 1 ser. III, 100–09). The gift was accepted and the Dowse library was incorporated in the building of the Massachusetts Historical Society. Of the great figures in American history, Benjamin Franklin was one of Dowse's favorites. In commemoration of him Dowse erected a monument in Mount Auburn Cemetery, and built a tomb for his own remains on an adjacent piece of ground. Among the beneficiaries of his estate were the Massachusetts General Hospital, the city of Cambridge, and the town of Sherborn. His collection of water-colors was given to the Boston Athenæum. A series of lectures is given annually in Cambridge from a foundation known as the Dowse Institute. Socially Thomas Dowse was a recluse. "He kept no company, he joined no clubs, belonged to no mutual-admiration societies, talked little, wrote less, published nothing." He was unmarried. A portrait of him by M. Wight which hangs in the library of the Massachusetts Historical Society suggests that his countenance was serene, intelligent, and kindly. In stature he was tall—six feet or more—and well proportioned.

[The most detailed account of Dowse's life is Edward Everett's "Eulogy" in *Proc. Mass. Hist. Soc.,* 1 ser. III, 361–98; but see also: Wm. B. H. Dowse, *Lawrence Dowse of Legbourne, England, his Ancestors, Descendants and Connections* (1926); *Catalogue of the Private Library of Thos. Dowse Presented to the Mass. Hist. Soc., 1856* (1870).] L. S. M.

DOYLE, ALEXANDER (Jan. 28, 1857–Dec. 21, 1922), sculptor, son of George and Alice (Butler) Doyle, was born in Steubenville, Ohio, and from earliest childhood was familiar with the practical aspects of monument-making, his father being engaged in an important quarrying business. His great-grandfather, Basil Doyle, was a civil engineer who in Revolutionary days removed from Maryland to Ohio, and became one of the first settlers of Steubenville. In 1869, the boy Alexander was taken by his parents to live in Italy, where he studied music, painting, and sculpture. Returning to the United States after about three years, he graduated from the Louisville High School, and in 1874 went back to Italy. He sometimes acted as organist in Italian churches. His studies in sculpture were pursued in the National Academies at Carrara, Rome, and Florence. His masters were Nicoli, Dupré, Pellicia. Whatever artistic training he received abroad was reinforced by his knowledge of the business side of a sculptor's work, especially as regards marble, granite, and limestone. Settling in New York City in 1878, and taking as partner a talented English sculptor named Moffitt, Doyle soon became widely known as a maker of monuments. His agreeable personality, his father's business connections, and the fact that his partner was a Roman Catholic were helpful in securing commissions. Though an honorary member of the Royal Raphael Academy at Urbino, Italy, he joined no American art societies and sent nothing to American art exhibitions. His works, however, are numerous, and are found in widely separated sections of the country—East, South, and Middle West—state committees rightly having confidence in his ability to complete his contracts. The assertion that "at thirty-three he had done more public monuments than any other sculptor, and was producer of more than a fifth of those standing in the country" (*Muncie Star,* Dec. 22, 1922) would seem to stress quantity rather than quality. In 1880, at Hallowell, Me., he married Fannie, daughter of Mark and Sarah Johnson.

Among his prominent works are the heroic seated bronze statue of Horace Greeley, given to the city of New York in 1890, the Soldiers' Monument in New Haven, Conn., a bronze equestrian statue of Gen. Albert Sidney Johnston, a bronze statue of Gen. Robert E. Lee, and a marble statue of Margaret Haughery [*q.v.*], "The Bread Giver," the last three being in New Orleans, La.; the National Revolutionary Monument at Yorktown, Va.; eight colossal marble figures in the State Capitol, Indianapolis; a bronze statue of Gen. Steedman in Toledo, Ohio, and a marble statue of Gen. Garfield in Cleveland. For Atlanta, Ga., he made the marble statue of Senator Benjamin H. Hill, and the bronze statue and monument to Henry W. Grady. In Statuary Hall of the National Capitol he is represented by statues of Thomas H. Benton and Francis P. Blair, given by Missouri, and by the statue of John E. Kenna of West Virginia. His marble portrait with pedestal at the grave of John Howard Payne and his marble portrait statue of the Rt. Rev. William Pinckney are in Washington, D. C.; his Francis Scott Key monument is in Frederick, Md. On the death of his father, Doyle devoted himself to the management of the Bedford (Ind.) limestone quarries which he had inherited. In 1906, when it was decided to erect in Steubenville a statue of Edwin M. Stanton, secretary of war under Lincoln, he undertook the work gratuitously, Steubenville being Stanton's native town as well as his own. He was engaged on this until his retirement in 1911. From that time until his death, eleven years later, he lived in Dedham, Mass., not wholly unoccupied, as he there completed a heroic statue of Lincoln, "to be erected somewhere in Europe after the close of the World War" (*Boston Transcript*, Feb. 6, 1918). He died in Boston, leaving a wife and a daughter.

[Obituaries were printed in the *Boston Transcript*, N. Y. *World*, *Muncie* (Ind.) *Star*, Dec. 22, 1922, and in other dailies. Chas. E. Fairman, *Art and Artists of the Capitol* (1927) gives a brief list of works and one illustration. The Art Library of the Metropolitan Museum, N. Y., has a more nearly complete list published in a folder issued by Doyle himself. See also Jos. B. Doyle, *20th Century Hist. of Steubenville and Jefferson County, Ohio* (1910); Thieme-Becker, *Allgemeines Lexikon der Bildenden Künstler*, IX, 531; *Am. Art Annual*, 1923.]

A. A.

DOYLE, ALEXANDER PATRICK (Feb. 28, 1857–Aug. 9, 1912), Catholic missionary and editor, was one of a family of six children—two of whom became nuns—born to Richard and Matilda (Shea) Doyle of San Francisco. Educated at first in the public schools and later under the auspices of the Jesuits and Christian Brothers, Alexander was graduated from St. Mary's College, San Francisco, in 1875, and received his master's degree a year later. Aroused by a Paulist mission, he entered the Congregation of St. Paul in 1875 and on completion of his theological studies was ordained, May 22, 1880—the first native Californian raised to the priesthood. For twelve years he served on the mission band, giving lectures on Catholic dogma and practises to non-Catholics and retreats for preachers throughout the United States and even in Canada and Mexico. Although without special natural endowment for public speaking, he developed into a winning preacher and a popular confessor. As editor of *Temperance Truth* (1892–1903), founder and a director of the Temperance Publication Bureau, which distributed over a million tracts, and general secretary of the Catholic Total Abstinence Union of America (1894–1904), he contributed largely to the total abstinence movement. He was manager of the Paulist Press, and editor of the *Catholic World* (1893–1904), the leading Catholic magazine, for which he wrote reviews, editorials, and an occasional article; and he founded the Catholic Book Exchange for the dissemination of tractarian literature. As founder (1896) and secretary-treasurer of the Catholic Missionary Union, he collected money for the training of priests for domestic missions. With Father Walter Elliott [*q.v.*] he established in 1902 the Apostolic Mission House as an allied school of the Catholic University (Washington, D. C.) for the normal training of missionaries. As rector of this institution he taught homiletics and pastoral theology, and for the last fifteen years of his life (from 1896) he edited *The Missionary* which he himself had founded. He was superior of Catholic chaplains in the army and navy, and President Taft found him "most careful, conscientious, and candid in his recommendations." Chaplains learned that they could rely on his pastoral counsel.

Always active, seeking no rest save in rotation of labors, he finally suffered a breakdown in health, and he died in his native San Francisco. A devout priest, a liberal man, a friend of civic reform, and an ardent Republican, Father Doyle was widely acquainted among churchmen and political leaders. Archbishop Ireland saw him as a true disciple of Father Hecker's, a patriot and an apostle who was "priestly in every stepping." On his death Theodore Roosevelt who had known him for years wrote (*Catholic World*, September 1912): "It was with Father Doyle that I first discussed the question of my taking some public stand on the matter of race suicide, it having been developed in one of our talks that we felt equally strong on the matter. I have never known any man work more unweariedly for the social betterment of the man, woman, or child whose chance of happiness is least in our modern life. . . . Again and again in speeches which I made I drew largely on the great fund of his accumulated experience."

[*Who's Who in America*, 1912–13; *The Am. Cath. Who's Who*, 1911; *Outlook*, Aug. 31, 1912; *Cath. World*, Sept. 1912, Sept. 1913; *The Missionary*, Sept. 1912, Aug. 1913; *San Francisco Chronicle*, Aug. 10, 1912.]

R. J. P.

DOYLE, JOHN THOMAS (Nov. 26, 1819–Dec. 23, 1906), lawyer, was of Irish descent. His family having been actively implicated in the Irish Rebellion of '98, John Doyle came to the United States in 1815, married Frances Glinden, and settled in New York City, where their son, John Thomas Doyle, was born. He obtained his early education at Columbia College Grammar School, proceeding thence to Georgetown College, D. C., where he graduated in 1838. He then studied law in New York City, and after his call to the bar in May 1842, practised his profession there for nine years. In 1851, when on a vacation in Central America, he met Commodore Vanderbilt and at the latter's instigation, abandoned practise and became general agent of the American Atlantic & Pacific Canal Company

Doyle

in Nicaragua. The company was engaged on Vanderbilt's project of constructing an inter-oceanic canal across Nicaragua, and Doyle remained there two years, assisting in the building of the transit road to the Pacific. During this period he commenced an investigation of Spanish colonial policy, particularly in its relations with the Catholic Church, in the course of which he unearthed much valuable information on the subject of the religious endowments under royal rule. In 1853 it became evident that the canal project would not be brought to a successful issue, and he resigned his position, proceeded to California, and opened a law office in San Francisco. At this time there were many important questions arising out of the former Spanish occupancy remaining to be settled, particularly relative to the property of the Catholic missions and the rights of the Church after the cession. He was retained by Archbishop Alemany [*q.v.*] of San Francisco in this connection, and succeeded in obtaining from the government a ratification of the original title of the Church and the Missions to much of the land which they had enjoyed under Spanish rule. His previous excursions into Spanish colonial history had apprised him of the existence of "The Pious Fund of the Californias," and under instruction from Archbishop Alemany, he made exhaustive researches which disclosed the origin and history of the Fund. In 1697 individual members of the Jesuit order had received royal authorization to undertake the conversion of California, and a fund contributed by private donors was established, the income from which formed a permanent endowment of the missionary church. This fund attained great magnitude and was administered by the Jesuits. In 1772 the missions of Upper California were confided to the Franciscans, and the income of half the fund was appropriated to them. The fund itself had been taken out of the control of the Jesuits and held by the Spanish Crown as a trust estate. On the declaration of Mexican independence, Mexico succeeded the Crown as trustee, and in 1842 by a decree of Santa Anna the trust properties were sold and the proceeds paid into the public treasury, the Mexican government recognizing an obligation to pay six per cent interest annually to the ecclesiastical authorities in order to implement the trust. Since that time nothing had been done and no payments whatever had been made. In 1857, on these facts, Doyle was retained by Archbishop Alemany and Bishop Thadeus Amat of Monterey to act on behalf of the Church. Ultimately he presented the claim before the mixed American and Mexican Commission at Washington in 1870. The commission's jurisdiction was limited by the Treaty of Guadalupe Hidalgo to matters since Feb. 2, 1848. So conclusive was Doyle's presentation that the umpire awarded the Church of Upper California twenty-one years' income from that date, *i.e.*, $904,-700.79, calculated at half the total interest on the sum received by Santa Anna's government, which Mexico paid (*Thadeus Amat et al.* vs. *Mexico*, No. 493 Am. Docket, *United States and Mexican Claims Commission, 1869–1876*). In further proceedings before the Permanent Court of Arbitration at The Hague in October 1902, the Church was awarded $1,426,000 for subsequent interest and it was decreed that Mexico should thereafter pay on this account $43,050 per annum.

Doyle had no taste for public life, and consistently declined to be a candidate for office, but, being keenly interested in transportation problems, accepted a position on the State Board of Commissioners on Transportation in 1878, serving one term. He was opposed to arbitrary regulation of freights by the state, and held that railways are public highways and should be open to all upon equal terms. He led the opposition to the refunding of the debt of the Central Pacific Railway Company, publishing open letters on the subject, which attracted wide attention. In 1888 he retired from general practise, residing much of his time at Menlo Park, San Mateo, Cal., where he died. He was married in 1863 to Antonia Pons of Lyons, France. As a lawyer his chief claim to recognition rests on his remarkable work in connection with the "Pious Fund." He was a great student and reader, a good classical scholar, and had an intimate acquaintance with the Spanish and French languages. Devoting much of his time to a study of Shakespeare, he wrote an article on the trial scene in the *Merchant of Venice* which Furness designated as extremely valuable and the substance of which he included in his Variorum edition of Shakespeare. Doyle also wrote a history of the "Pious Fund" of California (printed in *Papers of the California Historical Society*, vol. I, 1887), and contributed articles on various subjects to local periodicals.

[See *Hist. of the Bench and Bar of Cal.* (1901), ed. by O. T. Shuck, p. 518. This work contains, p. 81, an article, "Recovery of the Pious Fund," written by Doyle. The litigation with Mexico over the Catholic Church claims is exhaustively dealt with in John Bassett Moore, *Hist. and Digest of the International Arbitrations to which the U. S. has been a Party* (1898), II, 1348–52; and *Papers Relating to the Foreign Relations of the U. S.*, 1902, pp. 738–86 and Appendix II thereto. An obituary appeared in the *San Francisco Chronicle*, Dec. 24, 1906.]

H. W. H. K.

DOYLE, SARAH ELIZABETH (Mar. 23, 1830–Dec. 21, 1922), teacher of girls and a leader in behalf of higher education for women, was one of the seven children of Thomas and Martha Dorrance (Jones) Doyle. She was born and spent the whole of her long life in Providence, R. I., of which city a brother, Thomas Arthur, was for sixteen years the mayor. After graduating from the high school she taught in a private school for girls. In 1856 she was appointed teacher in the girls' department of the high school, and in 1878, became its principal. With forty-six years' service as a teacher to her credit, she retired in 1892, and in 1894 Brown University conferred upon her the honorary degree of Master of Arts.

She was not only a gifted teacher, she was also fitted physically and mentally for leadership. Her keen eye betokened an alert brain, and her vigorous frame, unbounded energy. She was a woman of liberal and progressive views, a Unitarian theologically, and was accustomed to express her convictions frankly and firmly. People stood a little in awe of her, but recognized back of her strength and aggressiveness a generous and kindly personality. She was the first woman to preside over a session of the National Education Association, an event which occurred at the meeting in Madison, Wis., in 1884. In 1898 she was named by Mayor Baker of Providence one of a committee of five to investigate the management of the public schools, and served as its secretary. While her major concern was that of furthering the interests of women, she was active in promoting education in general. She was among those who took the lead in establishing the Rhode Island School of Design, which has become one of the principal educational institutions of the state; was a charter member of the corporation; and from 1877 to 1899 its secretary. In 1876 with three or four other women she called a meeting which resulted in the formation of the Rhode Island Woman's Club, and was its first president, continuing in office until 1884. She also took part in the founding of the Rhode Island State Federation of Women's Clubs in 1895. A delegate to the meeting held in New York Mar. 20, 1889, she was appointed on the committee to draft a constitution for the General Federation of Women's Clubs. She was a pioneer worker in behalf of woman's suffrage, believing that the suffrage would react beneficially upon women themselves; and a reason why she was so ardent an advocate of higher education for girls was her conviction that it would make them more eager to grasp civic responsibility. One of her most notable services was in connection with the establishment of a college for women in Rhode Island. Their admission to Brown University had been agitated for some years, but there was strong opposition to coeducation. In 1892, however, women were allowed to become candidates for degrees, and were permitted to take the examinations required of men, though, except as graduate students, they were not admitted to the classrooms. Encouraged by President E. Benjamin Andrews [*q.v.*], in 1895 Miss Doyle headed a committee to secure money to erect a college building for women. The following year this committee was incorporated as the Rhode Island Society for the Collegiate Education of Women, with Miss Doyle as president. Funds for the building were secured and the corporation of Brown then voted to establish a department to be known as the Women's College in Brown University. At her death, which occurred in her ninety-third year, she was honored as one of the leading citizens of the state.

[*Providence Jour.*, Dec. 22, 1922; *Who's Who in America*, 1922–23; Jane C. Croly, *The Hist. of the Woman's Club Movement in America* (1898); Mary I. Wood, *The Hist. of the Gen. Fed. of Women's Clubs* (1912); Walter C. Bronson, *The Hist. of Brown Univ.* (1914); Thos. Woody, *A Hist. of Women's Education in the U. S.* (1929).] H. E. S.

DRAKE, ALEXANDER WILSON (1843–Feb. 4, 1916), art director of the *Century Magazine*, "was the foremost figure in the development of American illustrative art, and was so regarded by his contemporaries" (Johnson, *Remembered Yesterdays*, p. 99). The son of Isaac and Charlotte (Osborn) Drake, he was born in Westfield, N. J., and as a youth took up the study of wood-engraving. Being a good draftsman, he subsequently drew upon the wood blocks for engravers, and studied painting in oils and in water-colors. In 1865 he established himself as a wood-engraver in New York City. Five years later he joined, as head of the art department, the organization which was about to issue *Scribner's Monthly Magazine*. When the ownership and name of the publication were changed, in 1881, Drake's title became that of art director of the *Century Magazine* and of *St. Nicholas*. With the support of the publishers, Charles Scribner and Roswell Smith [*qq.v.*], and the collaboration of the managing editor, Richard Watson Gilder [*q.v.*], through the pages of the *Century* Drake led American illustration into a new era. Himself an artist with a thirsty love of beauty in any form, he had also the technical training of a wood-engraver and the discernment, optimism, and friendly sympathy of a born teacher. These qualities fitted him to recognize ability and, by unsparing criticism, to develop it in a great number of young artists. Under his guidance a new school of wood-engraving grew up, the aim of which was "the truer and more exact reproduction of the work of the artist" rather than its "translation" into other terms (Drake, "A Great Artist in Wood," in *American Magazine,* August 1915). Owing to his initiative, in 1881 and 1882 the *Century* held competitions for wood-engravers which were active in stimulating interest in magazine art. As photographic reproduction was introduced he was quick to study and make use of the new methods. In all of his striving for improvement he was aided by the understanding and hearty cooperation of Theodore L. De Vinne [*q.v.*], the printer, whose mastery of his craft made possible the realization of Drake's ideals. The opportunities afforded illustrators by the type of work which the *Century* demanded were in no small measure responsible for the number of Americans who attained eminence in the field of illustration in the last quarter of the nineteenth century.

Drake was well-known as a collector in several fields. "All beauty was his heritage," said one of his colleagues, "and to him collecting was not, as to many, a fad: it was a quiet, perpetual, glorified enthusiasm that enriched immeasurably his own life and thousands of other lives" (Clarke, *post,* p. 106). His collections included not only bottles and brasses, but ship-models—now in India House, New York—old fashioned bandboxes, chosen for the beauty of the paper with which they were covered, and bird-cages. This last collection is now in the Cooper Institute, where Drake studied drawing and later for a time was a teacher. During the early nineties he yielded to a literary inclination and wrote three short stories which were published in the *Century.* After his death these were gathered into a little volume, *Three Midnight Stories* (1916), containing also tributes from some of his associates. Those who knew him seemed to be unanimous in their affectionate recollection of his "genius for friendship," his "quiet effectiveness," his kindly, lovable spirit. He was married three times: to Hilah Lloyd; after her death, to her cousin, Anne Lloyd; and in 1901, to Edith True. He retired from active work in 1913, and died, three years later, in New York City.

[In addition to references above, see: *Who's Who in America,* 1914–15; articles by C. C. Buel and W. F. Clarke in the *Century Mag.,* May 1916, reprinted, with "A Memory," by A. B. Paine and "A Word of Tribute," by R. U. Johnson, in *Three Midnight Stories;* R. U. Johnson, *Remembered Yesterdays* (1923) and letter in *N. Y. Herald,* Feb. 5, 1916; H. F. Leighton, "The Home of a Veteran Collector," *Am. Homes and Gardens,* Feb. 1913; *Outlook,* Feb. 16, 1916; *N. Y. Times,* Feb. 5, 1916. Joseph Pennell, who felt that American illustration owed much to Drake, commented on him in many places, notably *Modern Illustration* (1895); *Pen Drawing and Pen Draughtsmen* (1920); *The Graphic Arts* (1921); and *Adventures of an Illustrator* (1925).]

J.J.

DRAKE, BENJAMIN (1795–Apr. 1, 1841), lawyer, editor, and biographer, was a younger brother of Daniel Drake [*q.v.*]. He was born in Mays Lick, Ky., his father being Isaac Drake and his mother Elizabeth Shotwell, both of whom had migrated to Kentucky from near Plainfield, N. J., in 1788. Although Benjamin had only rudimentary schooling, yet by hard work and by virtue of the natural strength and honesty of his mind he acquired a style of writing remarkable for its grace, clarity, and accuracy. While still a youth he went to Cincinnati from his father's farm to be clerk in the drug store of his brother Daniel and later a partner in the general merchandise store financed by Daniel Drake and conducted as Isaac Drake & Company. After the failure of this enterprise Benjamin studied law, 1825–26, and practised this profession with great success until compelled to retire by ill health. He contributed special articles, editorials, and stories to the newspapers,—in 1825 to the *Literary Gazette,* published by John P. Foote and after the suspension of this journal to various others. He established with others the *Cincinnati Chronicle* of which he was editor from 1826 to 1834, being succeeded by E. D. Mansfield. In 1827, in conjunction with Mansfield, he published a statistical account of Cincinnati under the name *Cincinnati in 1826.* This was republished in London and Germany for the information of intending immigrants and probably played a considerable part in determining the immigration from those places toward the rapidly developing city and the valley of the Ohio. This book contained an account not only of Cincinnati but also of the agriculture and commerce of the valley at that time. It is a valuable source of historical information. Drake contributed articles also to the *Western Monthly Magazine* and the *Southern Literary Messenger.* His fictitious stories of life in Cincinnati were collected and published under the name of *Tales and Sketches from the Queen City* (1838). His most serious literary works are: *The Life and Adventures of Black Hawk, with Sketches of Keokuk, the Sac and Fox Indians, and the Late Black Hawk War* (1838), *Sketches of the Civil and Military Services of William Henry Harrison* (1840), with C. S. Todd; and *Life of Tecumseh and his Brother, the Prophet, with an Historical Sketch of the Shawanoe Indians* (1841). These are written clearly, plainly, and concisely. The facts he collected with great care as to their accuracy, and these lives remain important sources of historical information of this most interesting and rapidly changing period of our history. *The Life of Tecumseh* was passing through the press at the time of the author's death, in April 1841. According to contemporaries Drake was a man of strict integrity and unusually sound mind, seeking always accuracy of statement. He had polished and courteous manners, was kindly, fond of society, and well liked.

[See E. D. Mansfield, *Memoirs of the Life and Services of Daniel Drake* (1855); obituary by Mansfield in *Cincinnati Chronicle*, Apr. 2, 1841; article by Jas. Hall in the same journal, Apr. 7, 1841; *Cincinnati Gazette*, Apr. 2, 1841; L. A. Leonard, *Greater Cincinnati and Its People, A History* (1927), vol. II. The date given above for Drake's birth follows Mansfield. It is sometimes given as Nov. 28, 1794.] A. P. M.

DRAKE, CHARLES DANIEL (Apr. 11, 1811–Apr. 1, 1892), lawyer, jurist, United States senator, was the son of Dr. Daniel Drake [*q.v.*] and Harriet Sisson. The boy received cultural and literary training in his home, supplemented by academic instruction in Kentucky and Cincinnati schools. In 1827 he entered the naval academy at Annapolis where he remained for three years, resigning because of his sudden decision to study law. Arriving at St. Louis in 1834, he entered the practise of law, but was not a recognized leader of the local bar. Following a brief residence in Cincinnati, he returned in 1850 to St. Louis and shortly became active in politics. In the confused and chaotic political situation of the fifties he appeared, successively, as a Whig, a Know-Nothing, and a Democrat. He was elected as a Democrat to fill a vacancy in the legislature in 1859 and served out the term. In the critical campaign of 1860, Drake supported Douglas for president and the proslavery candidate, C. F. Jackson, for governor. He opposed secession but was not active in the spectacular events of the spring and summer of 1861 which culminated in the military defeat and political elimination of the disloyalists and assured the ultimate success of the Unionist cause. Early in the war, however, he became a leader in the attack on slavery as a legalized institution, an issue which to most Missouri leaders had been distinctly secondary to the preservation of the Union. Drake energetically led the radical or "charcoal" wing of the Unionist party, but from 1861 to 1863 was unsuccessful in his demand for immediate and uncompensated emancipation; the conservatives, led by Gov. Gamble and supported by Lincoln, maintaining control of the situation. By 1863 the radical faction had become a distinct group, well organized under Drake and with a definite program, including immediate emancipation, a new constitution, and a system of drastic disfranchisement (*Proceedings of the Missouri State Convention Held in Jefferson City, June, 1863*). The Radicals increased in strength and were successful in securing the authorization of a constitutional convention. In this body Drake, the vice-president, was easily the most active and conspicuous member. He was the directing force in the formation of the new constitution and the author of the sections dealing with the elective franchise (*Journal of the Missouri State Convention, Held at the City of St. Louis, Jan. 6–Apr. 10, 1865*). He was peculiarly adapted to this position, for, as Carl Schurz wrote, "in politics he was inexorable . . . most of the members of his party, especially in the country districts, stood much in awe of him" (*Reminiscences*, vol. III, 1908, p. 294). So pervasive and masterful was his influence that the adopted constitution became known as the "Drake constitution." The Radicals maintained absolute control of the state from 1865 to 1871, with Drake as their leader.

Never personally popular, he was elected to the United States Senate in 1867 as a recognition and reward for his services to his party. He took his stand with Morton, Wilson, and other extreme Radicals, in enthusiastic support of the Reconstruction measures, which permitted him to give full play to his dogmatism and intolerance. He regarded the wide-spread political and social disorder in the South as a sinister expression of the rebellious spirit in the whites and of a fixed purpose to prevent by violence the operation of the Republican party in the reconstructed states. He acted in accordance with the view that he was "a representative of radical radicalism"; and supported with obvious enthusiasm the Reconstruction legislation of 1867–70 (*Congressional Globe*, 40 Cong., 1 Sess., pp. 41, 99, 109, 356). He regarded the Civil War as a social conflict, the South as a conquered province, and introduced proposals so radical that even his Republican colleagues refused to support them (*Ibid.*, pp. 2,600, 3,920). In the trial of Johnson and in the consideration of the Fifteenth Amendment, Drake took an active part. In the meantime, his dictatorship of the Radical party in Missouri had been questioned, then successfully challenged, by the election of Carl Schurz [*q.v.*] to the Senate in 1869, despite Drake's bitter opposition. The factional division thus created between radicals and liberals came to a decisive test in the state campaign of 1870, where a combination of bolting liberals and Democrats triumphantly carried the state, and so amended the constitution as to end the various discriminations. With the passing of his leadership and almost of his party, Drake's position became precarious. He was unwilling and unable to adjust himself to the changed conditions, and realized that the Democrats would shortly regain control of Missouri. He accepted, therefore, from Grant in December 1870 the appointment as chief justice of the United States Court of Claims, and announced his definite withdrawal from politics. He served with distinction until his retirement in 1885. During his latter years Drake abandoned many of his former extreme views.

[Drake's Autobiography, MS., is useful for his early life, but disappointing for his political career. His views on the issues of the Civil War are in *Union and Anti-Slavery Speeches* (1864). His rise as a leader of the Missouri radicals is traced in the *Missouri Democrat*, 1863–71. A comprehensive account of that period is T. S. Barclay, *Liberal Republican Movement in Mo., 1865–1871* (1926).] T. S. B.

DRAKE, DANIEL (Oct. 20, 1785–Nov. 6, 1852), scientist and physician, was born on the farm of his grandfather, Nathaniel Drake, near Plainfield, N. J., the oldest child of Isaac Drake and Elizabeth Shotwell. His mother was a member of the Society of Friends. His parents were poor, and in April 1788 they migrated with some relatives and friends to Kentucky, landing at Limestone, now called Maysville, on the Ohio River, on June 10. The party bought a piece of forest at Mays Lick, a few miles from Maysville, and here Daniel's boyhood was spent in the hardships of the frontier, helping his father clear the land and farm and his mother with the spinning and dyeing of their clothing. His character of industry, honesty, temperance, accurate observation, and ambition, combined with a deeply poetical love of the beauties of nature, was formed under these influences. His parents early decided to make him a physician, and he was given all the schooling the wilderness afforded. At the age of fifteen, in 1800, he was sent to Cincinnati, or Fort Washington as it was then called, to enter the office of Dr. William Goforth, a leading physician of that small village, where he remained four years studying medicine and Latin. He then became a partner of Dr. Goforth. Feeling the need of more instruction, he went in 1805 for a term to the Medical College of the University of Pennsylvania where he heard Dr. Rush and others. He returned to practise medicine at first in Mays Lick, but in 1807 went back to Cincinnati and became again the partner of Dr. Goforth. In that year he married Harriet Sisson. The greater part of his life was spent at Cincinnati in the practise of medicine, with interludes of a few years during which he lived in Lexington, Ky., and Louisville. He was, by general consent, the leading practitioner in Cincinnati during his residence there.

In 1810, he published a small book entitled *Notices Concerning Cincinnati, its Topography, Climate and Diseases,* which was the germ of his great work on the diseases of the "Interior Valley of North America," published much later, and of the widely known account published in 1815 and called *Natural and Statistical View, or Picture of Cincinnati and the Miami Country, Illustrated by Maps, with an Appendix Containing Observations on the late Earth Quakes, the Aurora Borealis and Southwest Winds.* This small book of two hundred and fifty pages, more commonly known by its abbreviated title, *Picture of Cincinnati in 1815,* contains a careful account of the prehistoric mounds formerly existing on the present site of the city and is their principal record. It contains a great variety of other observations of all kinds, including those on medicinal plants, characteristics of the forest, meteorological data, and so on, and a brief historical account of the settlement of the city. It was widely circulated, and was translated abroad. About this time Drake entered commercial life, first as a proprietor of a drug store and later of a general store which was conducted by his father and brother Benjamin, under the title of Isaac Drake & Company. These ventures were not successful financially.

It was Daniel Drake's great ambition to be a teacher of medicine, and in order to equip himself he returned with Mrs. Drake in 1815 to Philadelphia and took a second course of lectures at the Medical School of the University of Pennsylvania, receiving the degree of M.D. from that institution. He resumed his practise in 1816, and from 1817 to 1818 taught materia medica in the medical department of Transylvania University, Lexington, Ky. His ideals of medical education, which were far ahead of his time, were published in a series of essays in the *Western Medical and Physical Journal* of which he was founder and editor, and were later gathered into a small volume under the title of *Practical Essays on Medical Education and the Medical Profession in the United States* (1832). In the hope of making Cincinnati a great medical center, in 1819 Drake obtained a charter and founded the Ohio Medical College (now the Medical College of the University of Cincinnati), in which he was president and professor of medicine. His efforts, however, were frustrated by the jealousy of some of his colleagues. He was expelled from the presidency by the faculty, on Mar. 6, 1822, was reinstated a week later upon the insistence of the people of Cincinnati, but promptly resigned and left the college. He returned to Transylvania University in 1823, after the failure of his

Drake

plans in Cincinnati, and was dean of the school from 1825 to 1827 and professor for four years. During this period his wife died. After a brief period in Cincinnati, in 1828 he became a member of the faculty of Jefferson Medical College in Philadelphia, returning the following year to Cincinnati and taking with him various colleagues to found a new medical school, to be a department of Miami University. This school, however, existed for but a year, when Drake again became connected with the Ohio Medical College for one year. Once more bickerings led to his withdrawal. He afterward established the medical department of Cincinnati College, which collapsed in 1839. From 1840 to 1849 he resided in Louisville and was a professor at the Louisville Medical Institute, during which period he prepared his great work on the diseases of the Interior Valley. In 1849, the Ohio Medical College being in a critical state, he returned to take charge of it for one year but resigned again, disgusted with the wrangling, and returned to Louisville. In 1852 he returned for the last time to Cincinnati and took charge of the Ohio College, but he died shortly after its opening.

The work upon which Drake's reputation chiefly depends is, *A Systematic Treatise, Historical, Etiological and Practical, on the Principal Diseases of the Interior Valley of North America, as they Appear in the Caucasian, African, Indian and Eskimoux Varieties of its Population.* The first volume, about 900 pages in length, was published in 1850, and the second, of approximately the same length, in 1854, two years after the author's death. It is a mine of information on the topography, meteorology, character of population, customs and diseases, of the interior of North America. It is characterized by the most painstaking accuracy of statement, a graceful and clear style, a most unprejudiced and scientific weighing of evidence, and great caution in inferences. In the spring before he died, he delivered two addresses before the Cincinnati Medical Library Association, "Medical Journals and Libraries" and "Early Medical Times in Cincinnati," which are an accurate picture of early medical history in the United States. He was an honorary member of the Philadelphia Academy of Natural Sciences, the American Philosophical Society, the Wernerian Academy of Natural Sciences of Edinburgh, Scotland, and of the Medical Societies of Massachusetts and Rhode Island. In addition to his activities as a physician and a teacher, he was actively engaged in all public-spirited enterprises of Cincinnati, originating and having a share in the establishment of the Commercial Hospital and Lunatic Asylum, the eye infirmary, the circulating library, the Teacher's College, as well as planning the scheme of canals of Ohio and promoting railway connection with the South, which afterward resulted in that most successful municipal enterprise, the Cincinnati Southern Railway. He was an active advocate of temperance and his private character was above reproach.

[Autobiographical material appears in Daniel Drake, *Pioneer Life in Ky.; A Series of Reminiscential Letters,* etc. (1870), ed. by his son, Chas. D. Drake. The principal biographies are: E. D. Mansfield, *Memoirs of the Life and Services of Daniel Drake* (1855), and O. Juettner, *Daniel Drake and his Followers* (1909). Contemporary accounts include: S. D. Gross, *A Discourse on the Life, Character, and Services of Daniel Drake* (1853), and a sketch in *Trans. Coll. of Phys. of Phila.,* n.s., vol. II (1853), by a personal friend, C. D. Meigs.]

A. P. M.

DRAKE, EDWIN LAURENTINE (Mar. 29, 1819–Nov. 8, 1880), railroad conductor, pioneer petroleum industrialist, was born on his father's farm at Greenville, Greene County, N. Y. He lived there for about eight years, and then his parents moved to Vermont, near Castleton. Here Drake obtained a common-school education and helped on the farm until he was nineteen, when he left home to go to an uncle in Michigan. He was seven months on the way, most of the time working as night clerk on a steamboat plying between Buffalo and Detroit. Always an exceedingly sociable fellow, after a lonely year on his uncle's farm, he sought work in town and became a hotel clerk in Tecumseh, Mich. After two years in this position he went East for a visit to his home and shortly thereafter became a clerk in a dry-goods store in which occupation he continued for four years, first in New Haven, Conn., and later in New York City. About 1845 he moved to Springfield, Mass., where for five years he acted as express agent for the Boston & Albany Railroad, resigning to take a conductor's position on the newly opened New York & New Haven Railroad and moving to New Haven. He continued in this capacity for almost eight years, when ill health required his resignation.

Several years before, he had bought a little stock in the Pennsylvania Rock Oil Company and about the time he gave up his railroad position the oil company engaged him to visit its property on Oil Creek, near Titusville, Pa., and to obtain some corrections in legal papers. His letter of introduction from the company referred to him as "Colonel," simply for the sake of the impression such a title might make. The trip was made by Drake in December 1857, and on the way he studied salt-well drilling operations near Syracuse and Pittsburgh as the original promoter of the oil company, George H. Bissell, had suggested that oil might best be secured by such method. On his return to New Haven within a few weeks Drake's enthusiasm to engage immediately in drilling for oil resulted in the Pennsylvania Rock Oil Company's executing a lease of their lands for this purpose to Drake and another stockholder, the terms of which were a royalty of twelve cents on each gallon of oil produced. Drake, as president of the new company (the Seneca Oil Company), although only a minor stockholder, was immediately employed to proceed with drilling operations, and after many difficulties had been overcome during the succeeding nineteen months he finally struck oil at a depth of sixty-nine feet on Aug. 27, 1859. This was the first time that petroleum was tapped at its source and the first proof of the occurrence of oil reservoirs within the earth's surface. Besides his faith and persistence in the undertaking Drake's foremost contribution was the use of pipe driven to bed-rock to prevent the overburden of clay and quicksand from filling in the drill hole. He failed, however, to patent the idea. Disregarding, too, the advice of friends, he was content for the succeeding four years to be an oil commission merchant and justice of the peace in Titusville. He saved about $16,000 and with it went to New York in 1863, lost almost every penny in oil speculations, broke down again physically, and retired to Vermont. His life from this time on was a search for relief from pain and a losing effort to keep his family from starving. The terrible conditions under which they were living in Long Branch, N. J., was discovered about 1870 and some measure of relief was afforded them through contributions of Titusville citizens. Three years later this help was augmented by a grant of $1,500 annually, made by the Pennsylvania legislature. In 1870 Drake and his family moved to Bethlehem, Pa., where a decade later Drake died and was buried.

Subsequently his remains were removed to Titusville, where a monument was erected to Drake and his wife by that city. He was married first about 1845 to a young woman of Springfield, Mass., who died in 1854. In 1857 he married Laura Dow of New Haven who, with four children, survived him.

[C. A. Babcock, *Venango County, Pa., her Pioneers and People*, vol. II (1919); J. H. Newton, *Hist. of Venango County, Pa.* (1879); Ida M. Tarbell, *Hist. of the Standard Oil Co.*, vol. I (1904); J. McLaurin, *Sketches in Crude Oil* (1896); obituary in *N. Y. Tribune*, Nov. 10, 1880; U. S. Nat. Museum correspondence.]

C. W. M.

DRAKE, FRANCES ANN DENNY (Nov. 6, 1797–Sept. 1, 1875), actress, although a native of New York State, having been born in Schenectady and brought up in Albany, was always regarded as a Western product, and was in fact sometimes called the "Star of the West." Of her family little is known except that the name was Denny and that it appears to have been in comfortable circumstances. She was educated in the Albany schools, but adopted the stage as a profession at the early age of seventeen when she joined the little band of actors, principally members of his own family, shepherded by Samuel Drake through the wilds to entertain the legislators of Kentucky. According to Noah M. Ludlow, at that time likewise a novice but later one of the theatre magnates of the West, she made her début as Julia in *The Midnight Hour*, in the small town of Cherry Valley, N. Y., one of the first halting-places of the troupe. It was not long before the young girl was demonstrating that she was endowed with far greater histrionic gifts than any of her associates, talented as several of them were, and, after two or three years in Kentucky and neighboring states, she returned to the East, going first to Canada and reaching New York in 1820. There she appeared on Apr. 17 at the Park Theatre, playing Helen Worret in *Man and Wife*. After a year or more in the East, she rejoined her former company, and in 1822 or 1823, according to Ludlow, was married to Alexander Drake, the second son of "Old Sam" and a comedian of unusual talent. Her reputation now grew rapidly, and in 1824 she returned to New York as a star. Although she continued to appear in comedy rôles, it was as a tragic actress that her fame was made, and for several years prior to the rise of Charlotte Cushman she was, despite the doubtless greater gifts of Mrs. Duff, generally regarded as the "tragedy queen" of the American stage. For a short time, she and her husband managed a theatre in Cincinnati, but this project was ended by his death in 1830, and she devoted the remainder of her professional life to starring. Although by 1836 her powers had begun to fail, she remained on the stage for a number of years. She was married a second time, to G. W. Cutter, but they were not happy together and separated shortly, the actress resuming the name of Drake. For a time, she lived at Covington, Ky., but died, at an advanced age, on the family farm near Louisville. She left three children, Col. A. E. Drake, U. S. A., Samuel Drake, and Mrs. Harry Chapman; a third son, Richard, was killed in the Mexican War. Mrs. Drake was undoubtedly an actress of great power and one who worked zealously to make the most of her gifts. Her figure and bearing were impressive and she acquired a

Drake

very grand manner which proved exceedingly effective in the popular tragedies and melodramas. Yet she had her lighter side, and has been described as a "most joyous, affable creature, full of conundrums and good nature."

[Reliable first-hand information concerning Mrs. Drake is difficult to discover. Probably the best biographical sketch available is to be found in N. M. Ludlow's *Dramatic Life as I Found It* (1880). There is also material in: J. N. Ireland, *Records of the N. Y. Stage* (1866); Geo. C. D. Odell, *Annals of the N. Y. Stage* (1927–28); *The Autobiog. of Jos. Jefferson* (1889); Joe Cowell, *Thirty Years Passed among the Players in England and America* (1844); Mrs. Frances Trollope, *Domestic Manners of the Americans* (1832), and other works dealing with the early history of the American stage. An obituary published in the *Louisville Courier-Jour.* of Sept. 4, 1875, contains a number of serious errors.]

W. G. B. C.

DRAKE, FRANCIS MARION (Dec. 30, 1830–Nov. 20, 1903), railroad builder, philanthropist, governor of Iowa, the son of Judge John Adams and Harriet Jane (O'Neal) Drake, was born in Rushville, Schuyler County, Ill. His parents were North Carolinians and claimed descent from a brother of Sir Francis Drake. In 1837 the family moved to Fort Madison, Iowa, where Francis received a common-school education. From 1846 to 1852 he lived in Drakeville, Davis County, where he worked as a clerk in his father's store. The excitement following the gold discoveries in California induced him to organize two overland expeditions to Sacramento which he personally conducted with notable success in 1852 and 1854. On his return to Iowa he became a partner in his father's business and continued therein until the Civil War. He was married on Dec. 24, 1855, to Mary Jane Lord. In June 1861 he enlisted and became a captain in the "Appanoose Guards," later included in the Southern Iowa Brigade, with which he saw service in the region of St. Joseph, Mo. In 1862 he enlisted in the 36th Iowa Volunteer Infantry, being commissioned major, and saw service immediately in Kentucky and Tennessee. In January of the following year, his regiment went into winter quarters at Helena, Ark. He was advanced to the rank of lieutenant-colonel, took part in the Yazoo Pass expeditions, and on Apr. 4, 1863, commanded one wing in the battle of Shell Mound. He was absent for some weeks on sick leave but returned to take part in the battles about Little Rock in September. On Mar. 23, 1864, he left on the Camden expedition, a flanking movement to aid the Banks Red River expedition. He participated in the battles of Elkins's Ford, Prairie D'Ane, Camden, Marks's Mills, and Jenkins's Ferry. Of his work at Elkins's Ford on Apr. 4, his commanding officer reported: "Too much praise cannot be awarded to Lt.-Col. Drake for his distinguished gallantry and determined courage." On the 25th, at Marks's Mills, his troop was overwhelmed; he was shot; and the regiment captured. Gen. Sterling Price deemed Drake mortally wounded and authorized his return North. After months in the hospital, however, he recovered and returned to his command. For his notable services he was given, on Feb. 22, 1865, the brevet rank of brigadier-general.

As soon as he was mustered out he returned to Iowa and entered upon the study of law, being admitted to practise in 1866. He had been attracted, by public interest, to the building of railroads, and almost immediately took an active part in their promotion, construction, and operation. In the year of his admission to the bar he became president of the Iowa Southern Railway, running from Alexandria, Mo., to Bloomfield, Iowa. That road, in 1870, was taken over by the Missouri, Iowa & Nebraska Railway, Drake continuing as president, and the line extending west to Van Wert. In 1880 he constructed the Centralia, Moravia & Albia road, which also was absorbed by the Missouri, Iowa & Nebraska. These roads in 1886 became known as the Keokuk & Western Railroad. Drake had all of the dramatic and strenuous experiences of a pioneer railroad builder in the West. His constant and energetic rival was the Chicago, Burlington & Quincy Railroad, and the clashes and competition were often intense. In 1882 he sold his railroad holdings in Iowa and from that year to 1898 was president of the Indiana, Illinois & Iowa Railroad (now a part of the Chicago & Alton), which he began constructing in 1881. His son-in-law, Theodore P. Shonts [*q.v.*], who later achieved distinction in railroad circles, was closely associated with him.

In 1881, the faculty and trustees of Oskaloosa College, of which Drake's brother-in-law, George T. Carpenter, was president, decided to move to Iowa's capital, Des Moines. Local opposition and court proceedings prevented the conversion and removal of capital funds. Carpenter appealed to Drake for aid, and the latter telegraphed a subscription of $20,000. As a result, Drake University was incorporated in May 1881 and opened its doors to students in September following. The institution slowly but steadily grew in stature and strength. Drake served until his death as president of the board of trustees. While not a lavish giver, he was generous of his time, energies, and funds; his gifts of money, all told, amounted to $225,000. In his attitude toward academic programs and instruction he was liberal, tolerant, and sympathetic.

About 1890 he sought the political arena, Congress being his objective, but conditions did not favor him. In 1893 his name was mentioned for the Republican nomination for governor of Iowa. Again others had the inside track. Undiscouraged, however, he began an energetic and systematic canvass for the nomination in 1895 and in what the *Des Moines Leader* characterized as "the most adroitly managed campaign" the state ever had, he entered the state convention at Des Moines, July 10, 1895, as the leading candidate. He was nominated on the sixth ballot, over six ardent and ambitious competitors, and was elected by a substantial plurality. In his inaugural address, Jan. 16, 1896, he pronounced himself in favor of the policy of "local option" which the General Assembly had recently adopted in opposition to the radical advocates of Prohibition, his stand in this matter alienating many of his supporters among churchmen. His administration was signalized chiefly, however, by his call of an extra session of the General Assembly for the revision of the Code of Iowa, in 1897. The legislature heeded his caution not to include educational institutions in the proposed drastic reforms to centralize the control of charitable and penal institutions. A serious illness that aggravated his old army wounds caused him to decline to run for another term, in the forepart of 1897, and on Jan. 11, 1898, he retired to private life. He died at Centerville, Appanoose County, in his seventy-third year.

[Memoranda supplied by Drake's daughter, Mrs. E. D. Goss of Pasadena, Cal., and by J. C. Barrows, Esq., for thirty-five years editor of *The Iowegian* of Centerville; A. A. Stuart, *Iowa Colonels and Regiments* (1865); Reports of the Adjutant-General of Iowa for 1864 and 1865; *Official Records (Army)*, 1 ser. vol. XXXIV; *Roster and Record of Iowa Soldiers in the War of the Rebellion*, vol. V (1911); *The 19th Ann. Report of the Board of R. R. Commissioners for 1896 . . . State of Iowa* (1897); W. W. Baldwin, *Corporate Hist. of the Chicago, Burlington & Quincy R. R. Co.* (1921); *Annals of Iowa*, 3 ser.; B. F. Gue, *Hist. of Iowa*, vol. IV (1903); *Who's Who in America*, 1901–02; *Biog. Dir. Am. Cong.* (1928); *Register and Leader* (Des Moines), Nov. 21, 1903; and the writer's personal recollections.] F. I. H.

DRAKE, FRANCIS SAMUEL (Feb. 22, 1828–Feb. 22, 1885), historian, son of Samuel Gardner [*q.v.*] and Louisa (Elmes) Drake, was born in Northwood, N. H., and died in Washington, D. C. In his earliest memory his family were already living in Boston. His father was the proprietor of the first antiquarian bookstore in Boston, and the prolific editor and author of many works of American history. By 1848, Francis was a lieutenant in the Boston Light Guards, and in that capacity he went to Washington for the ceremonies held in connection with the laying of the corner-stone of the Washington Monument. By 1856, he was married to E. M. Valentine. In 1862 he removed to Kansas. During the Civil War, he served in the army for a brief period in the capacity of adjutant. He was back in Boston by 1871. The next year he published in one bulky volume a *Dictionary of American Biography Containing Nearly Ten Thousand Notices* (1872). In the preface he complains of the difficulty of attaining correct proportions in such a work—there was so much available material about New England and New York, and about politicians, authors, and clergymen, that an editor of his kind was in danger of emphasizing those regions and callings at the expense of others. He had tried, he said, to avoid that error. This book went through subsequent editions in 1874 and 1879. In 1872 he published a *List of Members of the Massachusetts Society of the Cincinnati*, and in 1873, *Memorials of the Society of the Cincinnati of Massachusetts*, and *The Life and Correspondence of Henry Knox*, both objective, dependable, and dry. He was not a member of the Society of the Cincinnati, but was probably "employed" to arrange the *Memorials* in accord with the resolution of the Society (Drake, *Memorials*, iii). His history, *The Town of Roxbury*, was published in 1878. Two years later he contributed to Justin Winsor's *Memorial History of Boston* a series of three articles each on Roxbury and Brighton. He edited Schoolcraft's *Indian Tribes of the United States* in 1884, and in 1885 he published *Indian History for Young Folks*, a book which has since been three times copyrighted—1912, 1919, and 1927. *Tea Leaves, Being a Collection of Letters and Documents Relating to the Shipment of Tea to the American Colonies* appeared in 1884, the editor's introduction comprising half of the entire volume. During the last years of his life he was consistently referred to by the Boston Directories as a "stationer," and one of the newspaper obituaries concerning him said that he was the "proprietor of a large circulating library and periodical store in Boston." At the time of his quite unexpected death, he was in Washington as a representative of the Boston Light Guards at the dedication of the Washington Monument.

[S. G. Drake, *Geneal. and Biog. Account of the Family of Drake* (1845), *Drake of Hampton, N. H.* (1867); *Washington Post*, Feb. 23, 1885.] J. D. W.

DRAKE, JOHN BURROUGHS (Jan. 17, 1826–Nov. 12, 1895), hotel man, was born in Lebanon, Ohio, the son of John Burroughs Drake, a harness-maker from Trenton, N. J., and of Nancy (Hurry) Drake, a Pennsylvanian. He was one of six children. When he was eleven his father died, and the mother's problem of meeting the needs of the family was not easy. John augmented their budget by working in a store, although he somehow obtained what was called a "common school" education. When sixteen he became boy-of-all-work at the Williamson House, the tavern in Lebanon. From this humble beginning in the hotel business he was destined to rise till he became one of the country's foremost landlords. He seems, moreover, to have chosen the vocation deliberately. In 1845 he went to seek his fortune in Cincinnati, seventy-five cents in one pocket and a letter of introduction from Tom Corwin, his fellow townsman, in another. For ten years he was a hotel-clerk, first at the Pearl Street House, then at the Burnett House. He managed to accumulate the capital necessary for his next venture. In 1855 he purchased a quarter interest in the leading hotel in Chicago, the Tremont House. His affairs prospered; in fifteen years he was the sole owner of the hotel. Then came the fire of 1871. The Tremont House was burned, but Drake was still a landlord. While the fire was at its height he made a payment on the Michigan Avenue Hotel at the corner of Michigan Ave. and Congress St. He gambled that it would not burn, although the fire was across the street. It was the only hotel on the South Side to escape the flames. In 1873 he took charge of the Grand Pacific Hotel and here he rose to nation-wide fame as a landlord. He was an ardent Republican and his hotel was the recognized headquarters of that party in the West, but it attracted epicures as well as politicians. As Drake's capital increased he diversified his financial interests. He was one of the organizers of the Union Stock Yards, a director of the Chicago & Alton Railroad, and vice-president of the Illinois Trust & Savings Bank. His foresight is shown in his heavy investments in the Chicago Telephone and the Chicago Edison Electric companies. Altogether, he was one of the aggressive citizens whose energy helped to make Chicago a great city. He was married on Feb. 24, 1863, to Josephine C. Corey, daughter of Francis Edward Corey, a prominent citizen of Chicago. They had five children, three sons and two daughters. The Drake and Blackstone hotels are controlled by their heirs.

[*Encyc. of Biog. of Ill.* (1894), II, 95 ff.; obituary in the *Chicago Daily Tribune*, Nov. 13, 1895.]

W. T. U—r.

DRAKE, JOSEPH RODMAN (Aug. 7, 1795–Sept. 21, 1820), poet, was the son of Jonathan Drake of Pelham Manor, N. Y., seventh in descent from John Drake, who came to Boston and settled in Windsor, Conn., in 1630. This original immigrant was the son of John Drake of Plymouth, England, who, in 1606, was appointed by James I member of a company to attend to the settling of New England. Jonathan Drake married Hannah Lawrence, daughter of Effingham Lawrence of Flushing, L. I. Their son, Joseph, was born in New York City. His early years were saddened by the death of his father and the removal of his three sisters and his mother, after her remarriage, to New Orleans. It was then to near relatives, the Hunts at Hunts Point on East River, and the Rodmans of Rodman's Neck, that he turned for companionship. These associations furnished the background and the immediate inspiration of many of his best poems. In 1813, while he was a student of medicine in a school on Barclay St., New York, through his friend James E. De Kay [*q.v.*], also a medical student, he met Fitz-Greene Halleck [*q.v.*] with whom he was associated in the closest of friendships for the rest of his brief life. In 1816 he received his medical degree—at the head of his class (data from Charles De Kay)—and in October of the same year married Sarah Eckford, daughter of the ship-builder, Henry Eckford [*q.v.*]. Shortly afterward, with her, he visited Europe, travelling in Great Britain and Ireland, France, and Holland. A miniature of Drake, painted by Metcalf about this time, shows golden hair, large, dark-blue eyes, a slender but well-knit figure, and suggests the powers of attraction that charmed his friends. Early in 1819, in partnership with William Langstaff, he opened a drug store. His health began to fail, however, owing, it is said, to overwork in his profession, and in the autumn of the same year he journeyed by coach to New Orleans to visit his mother. When he returned, in the spring of 1820, he was far advanced in consumption, and on Sept. 21, in his twenty-sixth year, he died. He was buried in the private burying ground of the Hunt family at Hunts Point. The spot has been set apart and protected by the City of New York.

The only work of Drake's to be published during his life was the "Croaker Papers," satirical and humorous poems, rich in local allusion, which with Halleck he contributed to the New York *Evening Post*, between Mar. 10 and July 24, 1819. On his death-bed he instructed his wife to destroy his unpublished verse as of no consequence; but his papers were preserved, and much later his daughter, Janet Halleck, who had become the wife of Commodore George Colman De Kay [*q.v.*], published a selection of nineteen poems as *The Culprit Fay and Other Poems* (1835). Of these "The American Flag" and

"The Culprit Fay" are still well known, at least by name; although "Bronx" and "Niagara" deserve attention as nature pieces and the lines "To a Friend" are an interesting statement of his strong preference for indigenous themes in poetry. For several generations American pulses have been quickened by the magniloquent lines of "The American Flag," of which the last quatrain in the published version is by Halleck; and "The Culprit Fay" was long regarded as one of the best American poems. It was written during three days, in August 1816, and was prompted by the challenging remark that American rivers are too poorly furnished with mythological and legendary lore to be subjects for poetry. Its 640 lines display spontaneity and facility rather than mastery or deep originality. Its imperfections are chargeable to the modesty of the author, who thought too highly of poetry to think of himself as a poet and never subjected his powers to the discipline that they merited.

[Information from Drake's grandson, Charles De Kay; J. G. Wilson, *Life and Letters of Fitz-Greene Halleck* (1869), *Bryant and His Friends* (1886), and articles in *Harper's Mag.*, June 1874, and the *Century Mag.*, July 1910; M. A. De Wolfe Howe, *Am. Bookmen* (1898); fresh biographical and critical data, together with an indispensable bibliography by Victor H. Paltsits, in *Trans. Bronx Soc. of Arts and Sci.*, vol. I, pt. IV (1919); obituary in *National Advocate*, Sept. 22, 1820; *The Cambridge Hist. of Am. Lit.* (1917), I, 262, 280–81, 521–22; contemporary appreciation in *Am. Monthly Rev.*, Sept. 1835; comment by N. P. Willis in *Athenæum* (London), Jan. and Feb. 1835; review by E. A. Poe in *Southern Lit. Messenger*, Apr. 1836; other criticism in Burton's *Gentlemen's Mag.*, Jan. 1840, and *Graham's Mag.*, Feb. 1842. Certain fugitive poems not published elsewhere were included in E. A. Duyckinck, *Cyc. of Am. Lit.* (1856).] A. L. B.

DRAKE, SAMUEL (Nov. 15, 1768–Oct. 16, 1854), pioneer actor-manager of the West, was a native of England, where, says Noah M. Ludlow in his *Dramatic Life as I Found It*, he was an actor and theatre manager in the provinces. His name was really Samuel Drake Bryant (statement of his daughter Martha, in 1819, at the time of her second marriage), but he dropped his surname when he went on the stage. In 1810 he came to the United States, bringing with him a large and talented family, composed of his wife (formerly a Miss Fisher), three sons, and two daughters. They landed at Boston, where the parents were during the season of 1810–11 members of the Boston Theatre Company. With it they apparently remained until 1813, when they moved to Albany to join the company of John Bernard, Drake himself becoming stage manager and playing such rôles as Cæsar in *Julius Cæsar*. The next year Mrs. Drake died. About this time, there appeared in Albany a young man named Noble Luke Usher who was endeavoring to collect a band of actors to go to Kentucky, where he had theatres in Louisville, Lexington, and Frankfort. He succeeded in interesting the Drakes, and the following spring (1815) they set out for what was then the Far West. They were joined by two ambitious novices, Ludlow and Frances Ann Denny, a girl of seventeen who later married the manager's second son, Alexander [*v.* Frances Ann Denny Drake], and was for some years the great American "tragedy queen." The journey to Kentucky was a most difficult and dangerous one, as much of the country through which the travelers had to pass was but sparsely inhabited and really wild. The hegira was probably the most heroic in the annals of the American stage. In November, according to Ludlow, the company reached Pittsburgh, where they halted long enough to give a brief season, and then pushed on to their destination. Meeting with success there and completely dispossessing his predecessor, one William Turner, Drake sought to set up his hegemony in neighboring centers, St. Louis, Vincennes, and Cincinnati. In these towns, however, he was not so successful, and during the remainder of his professional career centered his attentions on Kentucky, which state he dominated theatrically for years. After his retirement, he settled on a farm in Oldham County, where he eventually died. While it cannot be said that Drake was the first man to carry the drama into the West, it was unquestionably he who brought the first company of really talented players beyond Pittsburgh and who set the drama on a firm basis in Louisville, Lexington, and Frankfort. Of his five children, all but the youngest son were for a time at least on the stage. Two, Alexander (1798–1830), who was a clever comedian, and Julia (1800–1832), achieved great popularity in the West, and the latter left behind her a daughter who, as Julia Dean [*q.v.*], was a generation later one of the greatest favorites on the American stage.

[N. M. Ludlow, *Dramatic Life as I Found It* (1880), which is the authority (p. 363), for the dates of birth and death; Sol Smith, *Theatrical Management in the West and South for Thirty Years* (1868); W. W. Clapp, Jr., *A Record of the Boston Stage* (1853); "Colley Cibber," *Dramatic Authors of America* (1845); H. P. Phelps, *Players of a Century, a Record of the Albany Stage* (1880); J. S. Johnston, *Memorial Hist. of Louisville* (preface, 1896); W. G. B. Carson, "The Beginnings of the Theatre in St. Louis," *Mo. Hist. Soc. Colls.*, Feb. 1928; C. R. Staples, "The Amusements and Diversions of Early Lexington" (unpublished MS. in the possession of Mr. C. R. Staples, Lexington, Ky.); private information.] W. G. B. C.

DRAKE, SAMUEL ADAMS (Dec. 19, 1833–Dec. 4, 1905), historian, son of Samuel Gardner and Louisa (Elmes) Drake, was born in

Drake

Boston, and died in Kennebunkport, Me. He was educated in the public schools of Boston. On Sept. 14, 1858, he was married in Louisville, Ky., to Isabella G. Mayhew, and at about the same time he went to live in Kansas. There he worked with a newspaper and was correspondent for papers in the East. He was a soldier through most of the Civil War, attaining the rank of brigadier-general in the Kansas militia, and colonel in the Kansas volunteers. His wife died in Cincinnati in 1863, and in 1866 he returned to New England. Soon after returning he married, on Oct. 4, 1866, Olive N. Grant of Kennebunkport, Me. His father and his brother, Francis Samuel Drake [*q.v.*], were both historians, and if his own interests were not already similar to those of his family he was not long in making them so. One of his books, in fact, *The Border Wars of New England* (1897), is the completion of work originally undertaken by his father. Beginning in the early seventies he published books at the rate of about one a year for twenty-five years. Two of these, *Nooks and Corners of the New England Coast* (1875), dedicated to Longfellow, and *The Heart of the White Mountains* (1882), dedicated to Whittier, were little more than sumptuous guide-books. He wrote also a series of semi-popular but dependable histories, dangerously like text-books: *The Making of New England* (1886), *The Making of the Great West* (1887); *The Making of Virginia and the Middle Colonies* (1893); and *The Making of the Ohio Valley States* (1894). But apart from these, the region round Boston was dominant in nearly everything that he wrote, from the *Old Landmarks and Historic Personages of Boston* (1873), *Historic Fields and Mansions of Middlesex* (1874), *Our Colonial Homes* (1894), to his one novel, a boy's book, *The Young Vigilantes, a Story of California Life in the Fifties* (1904). He once referred to a book of his as an "historic-colloquial ramble" (*Old Landmarks of Middlesex,* V), and that characterization—if not too informal for so much imperturbability and so much scrupulous indexing—is fairly apt for most of his work. He was a born antiquarian, and in spite of his occasional respectful comments about the Future, it was the Past only which really interested him. "I think myself," he once wrote, with manifest restraint, "that the New Englander has some good qualities, one among others being his veneration for the things that have a history or embody a sentiment" (*Colonial Homes,* preface).

[S. G. Drake, *Geneal. and Biog. Account of the Family of Drake* (1845), *Drake of Hampton, N. H.* (1867); *Who's Who in America,* 1903–05; *N. Y. Times,* Dec. 5, 1905.]

J. D. W.

DRAKE, SAMUEL GARDNER (Oct. 11, 1798–June 14, 1875), antiquarian, historian, was the son of Simeon and Love Muchmore (Tucke) Drake of Pittsfield, N. H., in which place he was born. He was descended from a line of English ancestors, the first of whom settled in New Hampshire near Exeter about 1640. Samuel submitted to a few years of schooling in New Hampshire villages and at seventeen went to work for an uncle in Boston who removed to Baltimore soon after, taking Samuel and his older brother with him. The anticipated business success was not achieved and after six months Samuel went back to his father and studied for a short time under John Kelly, a lawyer. In 1818 he took charge of the school at Loudon, N. H., at eight dollars a month, and continued to teach, at various places for some years. In 1819–20 he was at Columbia, near Morristown, N. J. Ill health compelled his return home and in 1820–21 he studied medicine under Dr. Thomas Shannon of Pittsfield. He then went back to teaching until 1824, when he decided to become a bookseller. The next year he issued a reprint of Church's *History of King Philip's War* which proved profitable. From 1828 to 1830 he was a book-auctioneer and in 1830 opened a shop in Cornhill, Boston. Two years later he published his *Indian Biography* (1832), which went through several editions under varying titles, being enlarged into the much more important *Book of the Indians,* first published under that title in 1841. In 1836 he published his *Old Indian Chronicle,* and in 1839, *Indian Captivities.* Union College gave him an honorary A.M., in 1843, and soon after he was one of the five founders of the New-England Historic Genealogical Society, serving as its corresponding secretary for twelve years and as president in 1858. He also edited its publication, *The New-England Historical and Genealogical Register,* from its beginning, 1847, until the close of the fifteenth volume. He had long had in mind a history of New England, and, although he never wrote it, he spent the years 1858–60 in Europe, and in England, searching for material. He continued his bookselling business on his return and accumulated a fairly important private library of nearly 12,000 volumes and 50,000 pamphlets, mainly relating to Indians and early colonial history. In addition to many articles and the works already named, he wrote or edited, among others: *Genealogical and Biographical Account of the Family of Drake in America* (privately printed, 1845); *The History and Antiquities of Boston* (1856); Mather's *Indian War of 1675–6* (1862); Mather's *Early History of New England* (1864);

Hubbard's *History of the Indian Wars in New England* (1865); *The Witchcraft Delusion in New England* (3 vols., 1866); *Annals of Witchcraft in New England, and Elsewhere in the United States* (1869); *A Particular History of the Five Years French and Indian War in New England and Parts Adjacent* (1870). He first married on Apr. 12, 1825, Louisa Elmes of Middleborough, Mass., by whom he had five children, among them being Francis Samuel and Samuel Adams Drake [*qq.v.*]. After Mrs. Drake's death, when he was past middle life, he was married again, to a relative, Sarah Jane Drake.

[Rather oddly, the New-Eng. Hist. Geneal. Soc. published no memoir after his death, though they did issue one twelve years before that event (*New-Eng. Hist. and Geneal. Reg.*, vol. XVII, 1863, pp. 197–211), which is naturally incomplete. There is an account by Wm. B. Trask in *Potter's Am. Monthly*, Oct. 1875. See also Drake's own *Genealogical . . . Account.*] J. T. A.

DRAPER, ANDREW SLOAN (June 21, 1848–Apr. 27, 1913), politician, educator, was born at Westford, N. Y., the son of Sylvester Bigelow and Jane (Sloan) Draper. His father was descended from James Draper, a Puritan who settled at Roxbury, Mass., about 1649, and his mother from a Scotch-Irish family which came to the United States from the north of Ireland in 1812. Andrew was educated in the Albany public schools, was graduated from the Albany Academy in 1866, and from the Albany Law School in 1871. From 1866 to 1870, while he was reading and studying law, he taught at the Albany Academy and at a private school at Westford, and was the principal of a grade school at East Worcester. In 1871 he was admitted to the bar, and in the following year married Abbie Louise Lyon of New Britain, Conn. Until 1887 he practised law in Albany in the firm of Draper & Chester. He was a member of the board of education of Albany from 1879 to 1881; in the latter year he became a member of the state legislature, and from then on he was active in New York Republican circles. In 1884 President Arthur appointed him a member of the court of commissioners on the *Alabama* claims.

From 1882 to 1886 he had been a member of the board of the New York State Normal School. In the latter year he was elected state superintendent of public instruction, in spite of opposition by the educational leaders of the state. The latter felt, and had no hesitation in declaring, that he was primarily a politician and only secondarily an educator. His new office was one given by a partisan legislature to one of its partisans, and in 1892 when the legislature became Democratic he lost it. In those six years, however, the educator in him conquered the politician. His skill as the latter enabling him to get bills through the legislature, he obtained for education increased appropriations, more equitable distribution of the school taxes, a first progressive step for more security and regularity foi teachers in their contracts and salaries, licenses for teachers issued by the state on the basis of uniform examinations, and the removal—to a considerable extent—of the appointments of teachers from politics.

His former opponents supported him for reëlection as superintendent in 1892, but to no avail. He announced the resumption of his law practise, but so well known had he become as a school administrator that he was called to Cleveland, Ohio, as superintendent of schools. For two years he remained there and put new life into the school system of that city. In 1894 he accepted the presidency of the University of Illinois. The skill which he had acquired in Albany in handling legislators came to his assistance so that appropriations scarcely to be hoped for were forthcoming for buildings and educational improvements. In 1904 the double-headed system of education in New York State was so consolidated as to put the whole educational system of the state under the Board of Regents. To the new office of commissioner of education the legislature elected him, and after six years—in 1910—the Regents continued him in office during good behavior. Upon bases which he laid, the present organization of the New York State Department of Education is largely founded.

He was given the silver medal of the Paris Exposition in 1900 for his monograph, *Educational Organization and Administration in the United States* (1900), and received several medals and awards at the St. Louis International Exposition in 1904 for his writings and conspicuous services in the field of education. President Roosevelt appointed him a member of the United States Board of Indian Commissioners in 1902, and he later became its chairman. His educational writings are mainly in the form of magazine articles and addresses. These were collected in five volumes, published between 1904 and 1912. He published a book on the Spanish-American War entitled *The Rescue of Cuba* (1899), and another entitled *American Education* (1909), comprising his more notable addresses. He was editor of the department of education in the *Encyclopedia Americana*, of the volume, *Selections from Lincoln* (1911), in the Gateway Series; and editor-in-chief of a ten-volume work entitled *Self Culture for Young People* (1906–07). In manner, Draper was inclined to be somewhat brusque and severe. In his public addresses he gradually became a very forceful speaker. He was deliberate in arriving at his conclusions, but when he had reached them he seldom surrendered to opposition.

[The best estimates of Draper and his work are an article by C. W. Bardeen in *The School Bulletin*, XXXIX, 197 ff.; a memorial address by his former law partner, Judge Alden C. Chester, in *Proc. Fifty-Third Convocation Univ. of the State of N. Y.* (1917); Thos. E. Finegan, *Life and Public Services of Andrew S. Draper* (1914); and a memorial brochure *Andrew Sloan Draper, Commissioner of Education* (1913), issued by the Board of Regents, containing selections from its minutes. See also *Who's Who in America*, 1912–13; *N. Y. Times*, *N. Y. Tribune*, Apr. 28, 1913; and Allan Nevins, *Illinois* (1917).]

J. S—n.

DRAPER, EBEN SUMNER (June 17, 1858–Apr. 9, 1914), manufacturer and politician, was born in that part of Milford, Mass., which is now Hopedale, the youngest son of George and Hannah (Thwing) Draper. His father, and his uncle, Ebenezer D. Draper, had been among the leading members of the famous Hopedale Community and their withdrawal in 1856, while it brought an end to that experiment, opened the way for the rapid expansion in the manufacturing enterprises of Milford and a rapid rise in the fortunes of the Drapers. The chief concern of that region became the factories for the manufacture of cotton machinery operating under the name of E. D. & G. Draper, which in 1868 was changed to George Draper & Son upon the retirement of Ebenezer and the addition of William Franklin Draper [*q.v.*], and again in 1877 to George Draper & Sons upon the admission of George A., George Draper's second son. Into this concern Eben was admitted as a junior partner after study at the Massachusetts Institute of Technology and a short period of training in the machine-shops of Hopedale and the cotton-mills at Lowell and other textile centers. As this concern prospered under the able management of the Drapers, the business interests of the partners widened. Eben became a director in many companies manufacturing cotton machinery and cotton goods and in Milford and Boston banks. In 1907, upon the retirement of his brother, William Franklin, as senior partner, he assumed the management of the Draper mills.

For some twenty years Eben S. Draper divided his time between his business interests and a political career. He became in 1892 a member of the Republican state committee and soon after, its chairman; and as chairman of the Massachusetts delegation to the Republican convention at St. Louis in 1896 he wielded his influence in favor of the gold plank. A presidential elector in 1900, he was elected lieutenant-governor for the three terms 1906–08, and governor for two terms, 1909 and 1910, but was defeated at the hands of Eugene M. Foss in the latter year in the nation-wide reaction against the conservative Taft administration. As governor, Draper gave the state an efficient and businesslike administration which included work for forest conservation and harbor improvement. His economic views were conservative; he twice vetoed a bill providing for stricter enforcement of an eight-hour law for public employees, which action, combined with the fact that he employed only non-union labor on a ten-hour schedule in his own mills, won for him throughout his administration the active opposition of organized labor.

The town of Hopedale was separated from Milford largely through the efforts of the Drapers, and the family gave frequently to the community. Eben S. Draper and his brother built the Unitarian church, and he and his wife presented a hospital to the town. Draper was also responsible for a model-cottage colony for his workers. In spite of these benefits, the Draper mills were the scene, in April 1913, of an exceedingly bitter strike, in which the workmen, mostly immigrant, were led by I. W. W. leaders in demands for a fifty-hour week and higher pay. Draper claimed that conditions in his mills were as good as any in the state, was uncompromising in his refusal to deal with the strike leaders, and eventually broke the strike.

In addition to his local charities, Draper was favorably known throughout the state for his work as president of the Massachusetts Volunteer Aid Association, which raised $400,000 for soldiers' relief during the Spanish-American War, and as head of the Massachusetts committee which raised $1,000,000 for San Francisco fire relief. He was at one time vice-president of the American Unitarian Association and a member of the corporation of the Massachusetts Institute of Technology. He married, on Nov. 21, 1883, Nannie Bristow, a daughter of Gen. Benjamin H. Bristow [*q.v.*] of Kentucky, and by her had three children. Death came to him at Greenville, S. C., as the result of a paralytic stroke.

[See T. W. Draper, *The Drapers in America* (1892), p. 114; Adin Ballou, *Hist. of the Town of Milford* (1882); S. A. Eliot (ed.), *Biog. Hist. of Mass.* (1917), vol. VII. The Boston papers for April 1913 contain the story of the strike and those for Apr. 10, 1914, have long obituaries.]

H. U. F.

DRAPER, HENRY (Mar. 7, 1837–Nov. 20, 1882), astronomer, pioneer in astronomical photography, was reared in an atmosphere of culture and scientific thought. His father was John William Draper [*q.v.*], from 1838 to 1882 professor of chemistry in the University of the City of

New York, and an early investigator of photography; and his mother was Antonia Coetana de Paiva Pereira Gardner, daughter of the court physician of Emperor Dom Pedro I of Brazil. Born in Prince Edward County, Va., where his father was teaching natural philosophy in Hampden-Sidney College, he was taken as an infant to New York City, which was his home for the rest of his life. After transferring, during his sophomore year, from the classical course in the University of the City of New York, he went on to a degree in medicine, completing the course in 1857 but not receiving his diploma until 1858, when he had attained his majority. His thesis, "On the Changes of Blood Cells in the Spleen" (*New York Journal of Medicine,* 1858), was illustrated with photomicrographs. He had spent the year 1857–58 in Europe with an older brother. After receiving his degree of M.D. he served for eighteen months on the medical staff of Bellevue Hospital but in 1860 he left Bellevue to become professor of natural science at his alma mater.

His active interest in astronomy began, apparently, during his year abroad, when he visited Parsonstown to see the great telescope constructed by the Earl of Rosse. On his return from Europe he cast a 15½ inch speculum and constructed a grinding and polishing machine. This was the start of many years of painstaking and ingenious work on the making of reflecting telescopes. In 1860 he built an observatory on his father's estate at Hastings-on-Hudson, where his investigations during the summer months were henceforth carried on. The first instrument placed here was a 15½-inch silver-on-glass reflector, on an alt-azimuth mounting, ingeniously fitted for photography. The plate-holder was at first driven by a sand-clock—the weight of the clock resting on a column of sand which ran out through a hole of variable size. Later, a clepsydra was substituted. Large numbers of photographs of the sun and moon were taken. At the invitation of Joseph Henry, Draper wrote a paper, "On the Construction of a Silvered Glass Telescope 15½ inches in Aperture, and its Use in Celestial Photography," which was published in the *Smithsonian Contributions to Knowledge, No. 180,* July 1864. In 1867 he began work on a 28-inch mirror. This took much of his spare time to 1869 when the telescope was mounted in a new dome. The defining power not proving entirely satisfactory, the mirror was repolished, and it was not until 1872 that the driving clock and accessories were completed. Later he built six other driving clocks before he had one that functioned to suit him.

It was largely with this instrument that Draper did his great work in stellar spectroscopy. In May 1872 he secured his first spectrum of a star —that of Vega. This work involved the design and construction of many spectrographs and the careful investigation of the entire subject of securing stellar spectra. He also photographed the spectra of the moon, Jupiter, and Venus. In his laboratory over the stable behind his New York City house, he accomplished the photographic reproduction of the spectrum of the sun, undertaken for the purpose of securing standards from which the wave-lengths in the stellar spectra could be determined. Here also he made the investigations leading to his interesting conclusion that oxygen made known its presence in the sun by bright lines, and started an animated discussion as to whether the solar spectrum was made up of dark lines on a continuous background or of dark and bright lines. The investigation of the spectra of the elements led to many new difficulties to be overcome. In the use of a carbon disulphide prism he adopted Rutherturd's suggestion of a stirrer to do away with striæ and constructed an even-temperature box which did away with the shifting of the spectrum lines.

In 1874 Draper was chosen, because of his experience, to organize the photographic work of the government expedition to observe the transit of Venus. He worked so devotedly for three months, devising methods, testing instruments and materials, and training observers, that Congress ordered a special gold medal struck in his honor. In 1878 he organized an expedition to observe the total solar eclipse in Wyoming.

Though Draper's most notable work was in astronomy, he was active in other fields. During the Civil War, in 1862, he served three months as surgeon of the 12th Regiment, New York State Militia. From 1866 to 1873 he was professor of physiology in the medical school, University of the City of New York; dean of the faculty, and from 1870 professor of analytical chemistry. He was a member of the National Academy ot Sciences, and of the American Philosophical Society. In 1874, on the death of his father-in-law, Courtlandt Palmer of New York, whose daughter, Mary Anna, he had married in 1867, he was left managing trustee of Palmer's large estate, and proved equal to the task. He was an enthusiastic sportsman, and it was his yearly custom to join his friends Generals Marcy and Whipple for a few weeks' hunting in the Rocky Mountains.

In January 1882 his father died, and until the end of the academic year Draper succeeded him in the chair of chemistry, but he himself died less than eleven months later. His widow, interested in the successful attempts at the Harvard College Observatory to photograph the spectra of many stars simultaneously, placed Draper's eleven-inch telescope at the disposal of that institution, and provided them with generous funds to carry out a great program of securing, for purposes of classification, the spectra of all the brighter stars. Many volumes of "The Henry Draper Memorial" have appeared, containing the positions, magnitudes, and spectra of 225,300 stars, and the survey is now being pushed to still fainter limits.

[G. F. Barker, "Memoir of Henry Draper," in *Biog. Memoirs Nat. Acad. Sci.*, III (1895), 83; "Prof. Henry Draper," in *N. Y. Tribune*, reprinted in *The Sidereal Messenger*, Jan. 1883; W. H. M. C., "Prof. Henry Draper, M.D.," in *The Observatory*, Jan. 1883; Thos. Waln-Morgan Draper, *The Drapers in America* (1892).]

R. S. D.

DRAPER, IRA (Dec. 24, 1764–Jan. 22, 1848), textile-machinery inventor and manufacturer, was born at Dedham, Mass., the son of Abijah and Alice (Eaton) Draper. Abijah, descendant of James ("the Puritan") Draper, who settled at Roxbury, Mass., about 1649, was a farmer and a soldier. He had held every office in the militia up to that of major, in which capacity he commanded Minute Men under Washington at Roxbury. Abijah Draper was very well-to-do for the period, and afforded Ira a good education, though it was mostly in the nature of personal instruction from the family and employed tutors. Ira remained at Green Lodge, Dedham, the family home, helping his father in the management of the estate. In his twenty-second year, on May 31, 1786, he married Lydia Richards of Dedham, and at his father's death he inherited Green Lodge. He began to dabble with mechanical improvement along with his farming, and in this connection constructed a threshing machine and a road scraper. The threshing machine, though one of the first in the country and apparently practicable, did not contribute to later development of the machine. Finding invention more interesting than farming, Draper turned to textile-manufacturing machinery as a field affording considerable opportunity for improvement. He made several minor improvements on looms, among them a "fly shuttle" attachment and a jaw temple. He then conceived and constructed the first rotary temple, the invention which has made his name remembered. The loom temple is a device for keeping cloth spread to its proper width, with the warp threads taut and parallel, to minimize the chafing of the selvage. The old form was a telescoping stick with points at the ends to catch the selvage at either side. It had to be adjusted in length for the width of cloth and the weaver had, from time to time, to move it forward as the cloth was woven. The rotary temple patented by Ira Draper in 1816 was the first practical self-acting temple. In this the cloth was held by a horizontal wheel having a row of teeth set obliquely to its axis. This had the effect of doubling the capacity of the operative by allowing one weaver to attend two looms. The device was improved by a spring mounting in 1829, and in 1840 George Draper, the son of Ira, added another row of teeth to prevent it from marking the cloth. The rotary temple was immediately and almost universally adopted and formed the basis of a profitable and lasting business. By continually improving their temple and purchasing the rights of other inventors the successive Draper descendants built up the Draper Company into the largest temple manufacturer of the world. In 1907 they supplied practically all of the loom temples used in the United States. Ira Draper continued his connection with the business until he was well along in years, when he turned it over to his sons. In 1811 his first wife died and on Mar. 9, 1812, he married her sister Abigail ("Nabby") Richards. He had, by both wives, sixteen children. He died at Saugus, Mass.

[E. H. Knight, *Knight's American Mechanical Dictionary*, 3 vols. (1874–76); T. W. Draper, *The Drapers in America* (1892); T. M. Young, *Am. Cotton Industry* (1903); Patent Office records.]

F. A. T.

DRAPER, JOHN (Oct. 29, 1702–Nov. 29, 1762), journalist, was the seventh child of Richard and Sarah (Kilby) Draper. The *Boston News-Letter* of Jan. 4, 1733, contained this notice: "Mr. Bartholomew Green . . . being dead, . . . it will be carried on . . . by John Draper, (Son-in-law to the said Mr. Green) who has been an Assistant with him in the said News-Letter, . . . And all the Rev. Ministers, or other Gentlemen, both of Town and Country, who may at any time receive any thing worthy of publishing, are desired to send it to the said Draper, . . . And it will yet be endeavoured to render This Weekly Paper as informing and entertaining as possibly can be, to the Satisfaction of all who do or may encourage it." In this fashion did Draper announce that he had become the third publisher of the oldest and one of the best of colonial newspapers. With it, and the attendant printing business, his whole public life was concerned. He held no offices and evidently took no part in town affairs beyond that of the ordinary good citizen. The facts of his domestic life are equally simple. His father was a shopkeeper, selectman, and deacon. John married Deborah (or Dorathy) Green on May 24, 1726, and their one child, Richard, was born on Feb. 24, 1727. The mother died on Dec. 9, 1736, aged thirty-nine years, and the widower took Elizabeth Avery of Truro, as his second wife in October 1737. She survived him many years.

Draper served his apprenticeship under Green, but seems to have done some independent work before his father-in-law's death, since he printed the first forty-seven numbers of Jeremiah Gridley's *Weekly Rehersal,* a political paper which appeared in September 1731. Draper succeeded Green as printer for the governor and Council and passed the position on to his son; for about thirty years his imprint appeared on law and other official publications, as well as upon numerous broadsides and some more permanent output, such as *Ames Almanac.* He subscribed for six copies of Prince's *Chronology.* Under his control the *News-Letter* kept step with colonial progress. Interest in colonial news as well as in European; the growth of information from other colonies; new features, such as "letters to the publisher," clippings, some verse; and a steady enlargement of the space devoted to advertisements: these, and an increase in size, are features of the development. Under him, as under Green, the paper had a distinctly religious tone. When he died his son said of him: "By his Industry, Fidelity, and Prudence in his Business he rendered himself very agreeable to the Public—His Charity and Benevolence; his pleasant and sociable Turn of Mind . . . has made his Death as sensibly felt by his Friends and Relations, as his Life is worthy Imitation" (*News-Letter,* Dec. 2, 1762). Richard Draper [*q.v.*] continued the paper, and on his death his wife, Margaret (Green) Draper [*q.v.*], took charge; but the outbreak of the Revolution was fatal to it.

[Aside from the local records for family facts, the only source on Draper is the newspaper itself, of which complete files are available in photostat. J. T. Buckingham, *Specimens of Newspaper Literature: with Personal Memoirs, Anecdotes, and Reminiscences* (1850), I, 27–29, contains some notes and extracts. See also Mary F. Ayer, "Checklist of Boston Newspapers, 1704–1780," *Colonial Soc. Mass. Pubs.,* vol. IX (1907); and C. S. Brigham, "Bibliography of Am. Newspapers," in *Proc. Am. Antiquarian Soc.,* vol. XXV (Apr. 1915).]

D. M. M.

DRAPER, JOHN WILLIAM (May 5, 1811–Jan. 4, 1882), chemist, historian, was born at St. Helen's near Liverpool, England, the son of the Rev. John Christopher Draper, superintendent of the Wesleyan Methodist Society of the Sheerness Circuit. The latter came of an influential Roman Catholic family, but, attending one of John Wesley's revival meetings, was so effectively converted that he joined the Methodists, was disowned by his people, and spent the rest of his life as a Wesleyan minister. His real name remains unrecorded, that of John Christopher Draper being an assumed one. He was interested in scientific subjects, particularly in chemistry and astronomy, and owned a telescope with which he frequently made observations. He married Sarah Ripley, and John William was the third of their four children. At Woodhouse Grove, an institution supported by the Wesleyans, John William received sound training in mathematics and the classics. Next he went to London University in 1829, where he majored in chemistry under Prof. Edward Turner with whom he maintained a life-long friendship. He also continued his studies in the humanities at London University which was at that time the only institution of its kind in England open to non-conformists. While still a student he married Antonia Coetana de Paiva Pereira Gardner whose family had been attached to the court of Emperor Dom Pedro I of Brazil, her English father being court physician. She was descended from two of Vasco da Gama's captains, Paiva and Pereira, each of whom furnished a vessel of the fleet which first rounded the Cape of Good Hope. The death of John Christopher Draper induced the family, consisting of Mrs. Draper, her daughters, and her son and his wife, to emigrate to the United States where Ripley relatives had been established in Virginia since before the Revolution. They settled in Christiansville, Mecklenburg County. John William Draper had expected to secure a post as instructor in natural history at a local Methodist college, but arrived too late to obtain the appointment. Before leaving England he and an associate had published three papers on geological subjects, and shortly after his arrival in Christiansville he set up his own modest laboratory and proceeded independently with scientific work. His first record from this laboratory appeared in the *Journal of the Franklin Institute* for September 1834 under the title: "Some Experimental Researches to determine the Nature of Capillary Attraction." This was prophetic rather than conclusive, but it set forth the author's belief in the existence of theretofore unrecognized fields of force which have since been made the subject of illuminating study by physical chemists who succeeded him, and it was later to form the basis of his first important book, *A Treatise on the Forces which Produce the Organization of Plants* (1844). Other contributions followed, on such subjects as galvanic batteries, the alleged magnetic attraction of light, analyses of certain minerals.

From an early age Draper had resolved on a scientific career, and his sister Dorothy saw to it that nothing should stand in the way of his fulfilment of this ambition. She had talent as an artist, and by giving lessons in drawing and painting, she had laid aside by 1835 some $4,000, which she advanced to her brother to enable him to continue his studies at the University of Pennsylvania. Here he worked under Robert Hare in chemistry and physics, besides taking the course in medicine, in which he graduated in 1836. His thesis was entitled "Glandular Action." In the work leading to it he engaged in ingenious experimentation in the field of osmosis. He observed the passage of gases through soap bubbles, and applied the principles of osmosis in physiology. His purpose was to ascertain what goes on in the cells of the lungs, how oxygen is introduced into the blood stream, and in what way carbon dioxide escapes from it. These experiments are said to have disclosed "a cardinal fact in modern physiology." Nearly a century later they formed the basis for the study and exposition of the physiological phenomenon called "acapnia," which describes a condition of diminished carbon dioxide content of the blood.

In the fall of 1836 Draper accepted the chair of chemistry and natural philosophy at Hampden-Sidney College, Virginia, which enabled him to "convert experimental investigation, thus far only an amusement, into the appropriate occupation of his life" (Barker, *post,* p. 354). In 1838 he became professor of chemistry in the undergraduate department of the University of the City of New York, where his scholarship, his inquiring mind, and his administrative ability were immediately recognized. The following year he participated actively in the organization of the school of medicine of the university, taking over its chairs of chemistry and physiology. The chancellor, Theodore Frelinghuysen, was on terms of close friendship with this young professor who took an active part in planning and operating the medical courses. In 1839–40 the medical school had from forty to fifty students in attendance; by the following year the number had grown to 239. In 1850 Draper became president of the medical school, continuing to lecture both there and in the undergraduate department. He was unmindful of taking credit to himself, but was ambitious to bring the work of the medical school and of the city of New York as a medical center, to the attention of the public and of physicians. To this end he collaborated with his friend James Gordon Bennett the elder, whom he induced to devote whole pages of occasional numbers of the *New York Herald* to reports of medical lectures and clinics at the university, and to publish a journal, the *Lancet,* to keep physicians informed of the activities of the school and of the progress of research. In 1865 the building of the school of medicine on Fourteenth St. was destroyed by fire, in which Draper lost his library, materials, apparatus, and notes—a catastrophe which, however, did not cause him to omit a single lecture to his classes.

As a man of science Draper is best known by his work on radiant energy. In 1843 he presented a paper "On the Decomposition of Carbonic-Acid and the Alkaline Carbonates by the Light of the Sun," and in 1847 one on "The Production of Light by Heat" which indicated the essential principle of the modern incandescent lamp. Following these came noteworthy contributions on the production of light by chemical action. In 1857 he made the observation that "the occurrence of lines in the spectrum, whether light or dark, is connected with the nature of the substances producing the flame," and that "if we are ever able to acquire certain knowledge respecting the physical state of the sun and other stars, it will be by the examination of the light they emit." Here we find spectrum analysis clearly outlined, and indeed this leadership was acknowledged by Bunsen and Kirchoff, who figured in its later development. Draper was probably the first in America to use a diffraction grating, one being made for him in 1843 by Joseph Saxton of the United States Mint.

He was also a pioneer in photography. In 1839 Daguerre achieved the first practical photography, but the time of exposure required was so long that he and his associates despaired of ever making portraits. Even after the ordeal of posing, the sitter's eyes were never more than blurs in the picture. Samuel F. B. Morse [*q.v.*], a portrait painter, at that time was professor of fine arts at the university, and he went over to Paris to study the technique of making daguerreotypes. He imparted this information to his colleague, Draper, with whom he was on terms of close friendship, and the latter immediately set himself to work on its problems. He subjected the iodine-treated silver plates of Daguerre to the fumes of bromine, and found that this mixture of silver iodide and bromide was especially sensitive to blue light. This early use of silver bromide is especially noteworthy as cutting down the time of exposure. On the roof of his house on Fourth St., adjoining the university, Draper built a glass tank, filled it with a solution of ammonia and copper sulphate, and waited for a bright sunny day. Then, with sunlight projected through his blue tank, he photographed his sister Dorothy, making the first complete portrait of a person ever recorded by the sun. He clamped the sitter's head gently in a vise which later became the head-rest of the professional photographer. The portrait, including the eyes, was very good. After considerable experiment Draper discovered the uselessness of the filter tank, and made his portraits without it, in still shorter time. He sent his original first portrait to his friend Sir John Herschel, the astronomer, who was also an important contributor to the art of photography. It still remains in possession of the Herschel family, and it was lent for exhibition at the World's Fair in Chicago in 1893. Draper forthwith published his findings in the *Philosophical Magazine* of June and September 1840, and this was the beginning of photographic portraiture. In addition to this he instructed men and women in the art on one or two evenings a week for a considerable time, thus giving us the first photographers in America.

Another important contribution was in connection with the electric telegraph. Following the work of Joseph Henry in this country, and of Michael Faraday in London, Morse developed his alphabet, and was able to send messages over short distances. It was generally held, however, that long-distance telegraphy was an impossibility, on the ground that the current would dwindle to insignificance before it had traveled very far. Draper made exhaustive experiments along these lines, and soon was able to demonstrate, by stretching wires on the grounds of a rope-walk, that the resistance of the wires to currents became markedly less as a certain distance was reached; that the initial resistance of the wire was far greater than that of its longer extension. This proved that long-distance telegraphy was feasible, and a great advance in the art was initiated.

Notwithstanding these and other scientific achievements, Draper was more widely known as an author than as a man of research. In 1856 his book, *Human Physiology, Statical and Dynamical,* was published. It presented entirely new and illuminating views of the subject and was speedily translated into many languages. The author held fast to the attitude that we can advance in understanding only by the close study of life-processes in their mechanical and physicochemical reactions, and that, irrespective of prevailing opinions, we should not hesitate to seek the truth. This was the leading text-book on physiology of its period. It contained the first photomicrographs ever published, and it expounded his researches on the relation of carbon dioxide to the portal blood which he likened to the flow of sap in trees. In 1878 he brought out his *Scientific Memoirs,* a collection of papers on radiant energy. But his writings were not confined to scientific matters. In 1860 he delivered a lecture at the meeting of the British Association for the Advancement of Science at Oxford, in which he applied the principles enunciated in his *Human Physiology* to the development of society, and which gave opportunity to Huxley and the Bishop of Oxford for their famous tilt. So profound was the impression made by this address that he was encouraged to set it forth in book form. It resulted in the publication, delayed by the Civil War until 1863, of his *History of the Intellectual Development of Europe,* his *magnum opus.* It remains to-day, after sixty-seven years, a work of prime importance. Draper was an evolutionist according to the type of his fellow leaders in the thought of his day, following the Lamarckian theory of the inheritance of acquired characteristics as this idea prevailed before the advent of Weismann. In regard to the effects of climate he was singularly observant, and he blazed the trail for modern views in regard to its influence on social organization. In historical research he was indefatigable, both at home and abroad, yet he reached his conclusions independently. His ideas have provided the basis for many popular books which have appeared since his time. His style is at once engaging and scholarly. The work ran rapidly through many editions, and was translated into nearly every known langauge. A contemporary review said of this work, "What Comte showed might and ought to be done for the whole world of men, what Buckle commenced for England, Scotland, France, and Spain, Draper has effected for the whole of Europe." The work had a profound influence on nineteenth-century thought.

In 1865 Draper published *Thoughts on the Future Civil Policy of America,* which elaborated his very modern views on geography, his observations on the effects of climate on man, the effects of immigration, the political force of ideas, and the prospective course of national development as he saw it. In 1867–70 there followed his authoritative *History of the American Civil War* in three volumes, for which all documents available in Washington were placed at his disposal by Secretary Stanton. Gen. William T. Sherman personally edited much of the manuscript at Draper's home at Hastings. Draper's *History of the Conflict between Religion and Science* was published in 1874, ran through numerous editions, and was translated into French,

Dutch, German, Spanish, Portuguese, Russian, Polish, Serbian, and Japanese. It has been called a rationalistic classic, and, in common with the *Intellectual Development of Europe,* was placed on the Index Expurgatorius at Rome. Not recognizing the claims of revelation, inspiration, or ecclesiastical authority, Draper was wholly at variance with the upholders of these. He was, however, somewhat of an eighteenth-century deist who sensed divinity in the general order of the universe. He was on terms of amity with liberal clergymen of all denominations except the Roman Catholic, and one of his grandchildren who knew him in his later years declares that, without identifying himself with any sect or order or congregation, he was "a thorough-going Unitarian." Influenced profoundly by the writings of the medieval Arabs, Draper could also be called an Averroist. His family life was happy. The household consisted of three sons and two daughters besides his wife and his sister Dorothy. For several years the Fourth St. house near the university was their home, but in 1840 he bought an estate at Hastings-on-Hudson where he passed the rest of his life.

His wife was a woman of fine mind and an enduring piety. Brought up in the Roman Catholic faith, she became after marriage a liberal Anglican and was in hearty sympathy with her husband in his work. As her health was always frail, the professor's sister, Dorothy Catherine Draper, a beloved member of the household, aided in bringing up the children. Dr. Maximilian Toch, who was Draper's last student, writes of him, "He was a short man, not over five feet two, and in my time he wore a close-cropped beard which was quite white. He spoke with a distinct North of England accent, which at times had a faint burr of the Scotch. He was by no means talkative, but his interest in the intellectual development of Europe and in the conflict between religion and science was so great that even in his chemical lectures he would occasionally bring in expository references to these subjects. While never irreverent toward religion, now that I have a good perspective of him, I realize what a doughty fight he would have waged against the fundamentalists, were he living to-day! His son Henry was very like him, and it was characteristic of both father and son that their lectures were delivered entirely without notes." Of Draper's children, John Christopher taught chemistry and physiology; Henry [*q.v.*] was not only a noted astronomer, but, during the lifetime of his father, was professor of analytical chemistry at the University of the City of New York, and, later on, head of the department up to the time of his death. He married a daughter of Courtlandt Palmer, and their house on Madison Ave., and country home at Dobb's Ferry were distinguished for the important social and scientific meetings held there. The third son, Daniel, was for many years director of the Meteorological Observatory in Central Park, New York. Of the two daughters, Virginia became Mrs. Mytton Maury, and Antonia, Mrs. Edward H. Dixon. The American Scenic and Historic Society recently received from Mrs. Dixon as a gift nine acres of her father's estate at Hastings, together with the Draper Observatory, which is maintained by the Society as a memorial to him.

[Memorial address by Geo. F. Barker, followed by bibliography of Draper's writings, published in *Nat. Acad. Sci. Biog. Memoirs,* vol. II (1886); obituary in *Proc. Am. Phil. Soc.,* Jan.–June 1882; Thos. Waln-Morgan Draper, *The Drapers in America* (1892); personal information from Dr. Maximilian Toch, and from Draper's grandson, Dr. John W. Draper of New York.]

E. H.

DRAPER, LYMAN COPELAND (Sept. 4, 1815–Aug. 26, 1891), historian, collector, librarian, was a native of New York State, and a son of Luke Draper, of colonial English stock, who fought in the War of 1812 as his sire fought in the Revolution. The home atmosphere was redolent of Revolutionary and frontier lore, including that of the Indian fighting of the period 1740–1815. In Lockport, N. Y., Lyman Draper attended the village school, worked in stores, and performed heavy manual labor. He spent a winter in Mobile, Ala., at the home of Peter A. Remsen, who had married his cousin, and then passed two years in college studies at Granville, Ohio. A short course at Hudson River Seminary completed his formal training. His private reading, mainly historical, included all the books he could find which bore on the history of the frontier. Noting the deficiencies both in the quality and quantity of this literature he resolved, at the age of twenty-three, to devote his life to the writing of biographies of Western heroes and to seek from their living contemporaries and descendants the data needed to make his narrative complete and accurate. "This," said Reuben Gold Thwaites (*post,* p. xii), "at once became his controlling thought, and he entered upon its execution with enthusiasm which never lagged through a half century spent in the assiduous collection of material for what he always deemed the mission of his life." With the sympathy and patronage of Remsen who gave him a home at several different periods, he journeyed over the Allegheny frontier area from western New York south to Alabama and Mississippi, seeking out the pioneer survivors, usually very aged men, and taking down from their own lips the stories of perilous adventure and daring they had to tell. For a few months he was joint owner and editor of an unsuccessful weekly in northern Mississippi; for a season he planted sweet potatoes—unsuccessfully, in the same region; for a year or two he held a clerkship under a relative who was superintendent of the Erie Canal at Buffalo. Always, however, his major interest was the collection of material for frontier history. His interviewing was a process of gentle but unrelenting cross-questioning which sifted truth from error as far as that is possible. The reminiscences of the pioneers, carefully recorded, together with supplementary and corrective material gathered from court records, from contemporaneous or later newspaper narratives, from account books, letters, diaries, title deeds, etc., came to fill a long series of volumes. In addition to these notes, Draper also received from many custodians of old papers, original manuscripts which were believed to have an important relation to his quest. In 1852, at the suggestion of his classmate, Charles H. Larrabee [*q.v.*], who had also been his partner in the potato-growing venture, he moved to Madison, Wis., where in 1854 he became secretary of the Wisconsin State Historical Society. In 1858 and 1859 he served as state superintendent of public instruction, and in this capacity obtained the passage by the legislature of a bill providing for township libraries—the funds for which were diverted to meet the exigencies of the Civil War—and attempted to lay the foundation for a library for the state university.

Draper supplied many short biographies to Appletons' *Cyclopædia,* and he published a monumental work on King's Mountain (*King's Mountain and its Heroes,* 1881), but the extended biographies he contemplated were never produced. " 'I have wasted my life in puttering,' he once lamented, 'but I see no help for it; I can write nothing so long as I fear there is a fact, no matter how small, as yet ungarnered' " (Thwaites, p. xvii). His greatest service to history was through his collections. He was a self-trained historian, but in his special field—the dramatic phases of Western history—his critical command of the facts and sources went unchallenged. His interests as a document collector and a writer were restricted to the dramatic; he had no *flair* for political, economic, or social history. As secretary of the Wisconsin State Historical Society, 1854–86, however, he included all aspects of history, and laid broadly the foundations of one of the great historical libraries. He built up a manuscript collection relating to the early fur-trading period in Wisconsin and the Northwest; he took advantage of the opportunity to gather in files of early newspapers; and he began the publication of the *Wisconsin Historical Collections,* now (1930) numbering thirty volumes, of which he edited ten. His editorial notes are of permanent historical value. At his death he bequeathed to the Wisconsin State Historical Society his own invaluable collection, which contains many volumes of Kentucky Papers, Tennessee Papers, Preston and Virginia Papers, Daniel Boone Papers, George Rogers Clark Papers, King's Mountain Papers, Sumter Papers, etc., in addition to Draper's notes.

In person he was diminutive—less than five feet in height and slender, but sturdy and with a marvelous power of endurance. His countenance was benevolent and his general attitude retiring and scholarly, but he was cleverly persistent in any quest he happened to be pursuing. He combined restless activity with painstaking scholarship and a diplomatic tactfulness which rarely failed of its object. Hundreds of the Western pioneers became his devoted helpers in collecting. Draper was married in 1853 to his cousin, the widow of his patron Remsen. After years of invalidism, she died in May 1888, and in October 1889, at Cheyenne, Wyo., he married Mrs. Catherine T. Hoyt, who survived him.

[*Descriptive List of Manuscript Collections, Wis. Hist. Soc.* (1906); *Pubs. State Hist. Soc. of Wis., Calendar Ser.*, vols. I, II and III (1915, 1925, 1930); R. G. Thwaites, "Lyman Copeland Draper: A Memoir," in *Wis. Hist. Colls.*, vol. I (reprint, 1903); Louise Phelps Kellogg, "The Services and Collections of Lyman Copeland Draper," in *Wis. Mag. of Hist.*, Mar. 1922; Jos. Schafer, "The Draper Collection of MSS.," *Pubs. State Hist. Soc. of Wis., Proceedings*, 1922; *Madison Democrat*, Aug. 27, 1891.]
J. S—r.

DRAPER, MARGARET GREEN (fl. 1750–1807), was the wife of Richard Draper [*q.v.*], Boston publisher and printer, whom she married on May 30, 1750. The printers of Boston offer a curious example of a trade carried on by what may be considered as almost a trade-clan owing to constant inter-marriages for several generations. Margaret may have been Richard Draper's cousin and the grand-daughter of Bartholomew Green, another publisher. On the death of her husband, June 5, 1774, she continued to publish *The Massachusetts Gazette and Weekly News-Letter* with her late husband's partner, John Boyle, but they separated before the beginning of the Revolution. She was strongly Loyalist and continued her husband's journalistic policy. After managing the paper alone for several months she formed a partnership with John Howe, and together they published it until Boston was evacuated by the British when it was suspended (Feb. 22, 1776) after a life of seventy-two years, during which time it had often changed its name. All the other papers had had to be published elsewhere after the siege of Boston began, so that the *Gazette,* which had been the first paper to be started in Boston, was the last to be published there before the Declaration of Independence. Margaret Draper left with the British, going first to Halifax and thence to England, where she lived until her death in London, where her will was proved Feb. 12, 1807. Her property in Boston, including land and several buildings, was confiscated by the Americans and sold on Feb. 7, 1783 (*Proceedings of the Massachusetts Historical Society,* 2 ser., X, 107), but she received a pension from the British government.

[Isaiah Thomas, *The Hist. of Printing in America* (1810); J. H. Stark, *The Loyalists of Mass.* (1910); L. Sabine, *Biog. Sketches of Loyalists of the Am. Revolution* (2 vols., 1864); "Checklist of Boston Newspapers, 1704–1780," *Colonial Soc. Mass. Pubs.*, vol. IX (1907).] J. T. A.

DRAPER, RICHARD (Feb. 24, 1726/7–June 5, 1774), Boston printer, was the grandson of Richard Draper who emigrated from England to Boston in 1680, and the son of John Draper [*q.v.*] who married Deborah, the daughter of Bartholomew Green, the publisher of the *Boston News-Letter.* John Draper continued the publication after the death of his father-in-law in 1732, taking into silent partnership his son Richard, who had been brought up to the printing trade. On the death of John in 1762, Richard in turn continued the paper, now called *The Boston Weekly News-Letter and New England Chronicle.* On April 7, 1763, the title was suddenly changed to *The Massachusetts Gazette and Boston News-Letter.* He took a kinsman, Samuel Draper, into partnership in the paper but not in the printing business, the connection lasting several years until the death of Samuel. A little more than a month before his own death, Richard took John Boyle as a partner. Draper's own firm did very little book printing but he was concerned with Edes & Gill, and the Fleets, and in that way was interested in book publishing. On Dec. 2, 1762, he was appointed printer to the Governor and Council in place of his late father. From 1763 to 1766, Richard and Samuel, and from 1767 to 1770, Richard, printed the theses for Harvard, calling himself "Academiæ Typographus." This last position, to his no small mortification, was taken from him and given to Isaiah Thomas in 1771. His main interest, however, appears to have been in journalism and he continued the publication of his paper until his death, changing the name several times (*Publications Colonial Society of Massachusetts,* IX, 431). In May 1768 he entered into a singular arrangement with Green and Russell who published the *Boston Post-Boy.* Each continued to publish his own paper, the *Post-Boy* appearing on Mondays and the *News-Letter* on Thursdays, but a combined paper, the *Massachusetts Gazette,* appeared in two instalments, one-half with each of the other two. This "Adam and Eve" journal ceased in September 1769 and Draper continued the *Massachusetts Gazette and Weekly News-Letter* by himself. Draper acquired a competency and built a substantial brick house on what is now Washington St., Boston. He suffered from constant ill health but was of cheerful disposition and is said to have been "remarkable for the amiable delicacy of his mind, and gentleness of his manners." He was strongly in favor of the British government whose cause was espoused in his paper. On May 30, 1750, he married Margaret Green [*v.* Margaret Green Draper], but they had no children.

[Isaiah Thomas, *The Hist. of Printing in America* (1810); T. W. Draper, *The Drapers in America* (1892); J. H. Stark, *The Loyalists of Massachusetts* (1910); "Checklist of Boston Newspapers, 1704–1780," *Colonial Soc. of Mass. Pubs.*, IX (1907), and "The Printer of the Harvard Theses of 1771," *Ibid.*, XXVI (1927), 1–15.] J. T. A.

DRAPER, WILLIAM FRANKLIN (Apr. 9, 1842–Jan. 28, 1910), soldier, manufacturer, diplomat, was born in Lowell, Mass., a grandson of Ira Draper [*q.v.*] and the eldest son of George and Hannah (Thwing) Draper. His boyhood was spent at Woonsocket, R. I., Ware, Mass., and finally Milford, Mass., where the family moved in 1853 when his father joined the Hopedale Community. Here his father and his uncle Ebenezer started the manufacture of cotton machinery, an enterprise which expanded rapidly after the break-up of the Hopedale Community. At Hopedale, William attended the Community school until the age of sixteen, after which he worked for three years in various New England mills, thoroughly acquainting himself with the process and machinery of cotton manufacture. Enlisting in 1861 in a Milford company which later became Company B of the 25th Massachusetts Regiment, he was elected second lieutenant and began a war experience which extended over nearly four years of active campaigning. He was on Burnside's staff at Roanoke Island, New Bern, and Fort Macon; was commissioned (Aug. 12, 1862) captain in the 36th Massachusetts with which he went through the Antietam campaign and the battle of Fredericksburg; was sent west with the IX Corps in 1863, participating in the capture of Vicksburg and the fighting around Jackson. As a major, he spent the winter of 1863 with his corps in East Tennessee, where they engaged in the siege of Knoxville, and joined Grant in the Virginia campaign in 1864. Promoted to a lieutenant-colonelcy, Draper commanded a regiment in the Wilderness, where he was seriously wounded by a bullet in the shoulder. He recovered sufficiently, however, to join the army before Petersburg, and commanded a brigade at the Weldon Railroad engagement. Troubled by a second wound received at Pegram Farm, he left the service on Oct. 12, 1864, later receiving, before his twenty-third birthday, the brevet ranks of colonel and brigadier-general "for gallant and meritorious services in the field during the war."

Upon his return from active service he entered the employ of the firm of his father and father's brother, E. D. & G. Draper, into which he was taken as partner three years later when his uncle sold out his interest to the young man. William remained as junior partner in the new firm, now known as George Draper & Son, until the death of his father in 1887, when he assumed the leadership. His brothers, George A. and Eben Sumner [*q.v.*], and his two eldest sons in due time became partners, but William F. Draper dominated the business until his resignation as president in 1907. George Draper & Sons (so-called after the admission of George A. Draper in 1877) was in reality a firm which acted as selling agent for other concerns which it controled, and which manufactured cotton machinery. It prospered enormously in the seventies and thereafter by the production of the Sawyer and Rabbeth spindles and many other improvements in spinning and weaving machinery. William F. Draper was well fitted to head such an enterprise, for he inherited to a full degree the inventive and mechanical genius of his father and grandfather, who had both been inventors of textile machinery. He personally patented more than fifty inventions in textile machinery, and these with other improvements promoted and controled by him are believed to have doubled the speed of spinning yarn and to have cut the cost in half (*Representative Men*, pp. 22–26; *Boston Herald*, Jan. 29, 1910). During his later years he turned his attention to weaving in the hopes of achieving similar results. He was counted by many "the leading expert in spinning machinery in this country" (*The Drapers in America*, p. 113) and testified frequently in important patent suits relating to such machinery. In 1891 he made an important contribution to the technical history of cotton spinning in a paper, "The History of Spindles," read before the New England Cotton Manufacturers' Association.

Until 1892 Draper never held any elective office except that of member of the town school committee, although he was a member of the convention which nominated Hayes and an elector-at-large for Harrison. He had been given a large vote in 1889 in the Republican state convention for governor but two years later when the nomination was assured him he declined to be a candidate. In 1892, however, being particularly interested in the tariff he was persuaded to run for Congress, and he served the 11th Massachusetts District in that body until his appointment as ambassador at Rome on Apr. 5, 1897. His attitude on public business was, in general, conservative. He opposed the Wilson tariff, the withdrawal of the Hawaiian annexation treaty, the intervention in Cuba, and was one of a half-dozen Republicans in the House to oppose the censure of Bayard. In spite of his stand on Hawaii he declared strongly some years later against the annexation of the Philippines.

He was ambassador to Italy (1897–1900) during the period of the Spanish-American War and filled the post with satisfaction to both governments. Pressure of private business, however, forced his resignation and brought an end to his public service. He was twice married: first, on Sept. 15, 1862, to Lydia Joy, adopted daughter of David Joy of Nantucket; second, on May 22, 1890, to Susan Preston, daughter of Gen. William Preston of Kentucky. There were five children by the first marriage, and one by the second. Draper's last years were spent in travel and recreation. In 1908 he published a volume of memoirs, *Recollections of a Varied Career*. He died in Washington, where it had been his habit to pass the winter. After his death his widow presented a memorial park to the town of Milford, and in 1912 an equestrian statue of him designed by Daniel Chester French.

[In addition to Draper's *Recollections*, see T. W. Draper, *The Drapers in America* (1892), pp. 112–13; Adin Ballou, *Hist. of Milford* (1882), pp. 719 ff.; *Representative Men of Mass. 1890–1900* (1898); obituaries in Boston papers, Jan. 29, 1910. "History of Spindles" was published in *Proc. Twenty-Sixth Annual Meeting New England Cotton Mfrs.' Asso.* (Apr. 29, 1891), pp. 13–47.] H.U.F.

DRAYTON, JOHN (June 22, 1766–Nov. 27, 1822), governor of South Carolina, jurist, author, was born at "Drayton Hall," near Charleston, the eldest child of William Henry Drayton [*q.v.*] and Dorothy Golightly. Generally with his distinguished father until the last year of the latter's life, he was then placed in the Nassau Grammar School, Princeton, N. J., and in September 1779 entered the freshman class of the College of New Jersey. He did not graduate from the College, but was sent to England to complete his education, probably at the Inner Temple. Returning to South Carolina, he began the practise of law in Charleston and was married, Oct. 6, 1794, to Hester Rose, the daughter of Philip and Hester Rose Tidyman, who before her death in 1816 bore him six children.

In accordance with the family tradition, he entered public life at an early age, serving as a member of the state House of Representatives during most of the years from 1792 to 1798, when he was elected lieutenant-governor. Following the death of Gov. Edward Rutledge [*q.v.*] on Jan. 23, 1800, he was in charge of the executive department, though not officially recognized as governor until his election in his own right, Dec. 4, 1800, for a term of two years. He is said to have been the first governor to pass over the whole upper country and review the militia (O'Neall, *post,* I, 428). Both as lieutenant-governor and governor he urged the establishment of a central institution of higher learning in order to further the political unification of the state and promote public intelligence. Following his recommendation to the General Assembly, Nov. 23, 1801, an act providing for the establishment of the South Carolina College (now University of South Carolina) at Columbia was passed, and approved by him on Dec. 19. The first meetings of the trustees were held at his home in Charleston, and he himself served as president of the Board until December 1802 (Green, *post,* pp. 10–15; Schaper, *post,* pp. 403–06). The college, which was opened Jan. 10, 1805, proved to be a potent factor in drawing together the sections of the state. Very appropriately, it conferred on John Drayton the degree of LL.D., at its first Commencement exercises, Dec. 7, 1807. This same year, he was among the eminent counsel who appeared before the Supreme Court of the United States in the important case, *Rose* vs. *Himely* (4 *Cranch,* 241). He served in the state Senate from 1805 to 1808, when increased representation was given the up-country and he was again elected governor for two years. Appointed in 1812 judge of the United States court for the District of South Carolina, by President Madison, he held this post until his death in Charleston.

Early in his career Drayton published *Letters written during a Tour through the Northern and Eastern States of America* (1794), containing a contrast between the schools of Boston and those of South Carolina which was most unfavorable to his native state. During his first term as governor he published *A View of South Carolina, as Respects her Natural and Civil Concerns* (1802), a valuable descriptive work which was probably inspired by Jefferson's *Notes on Virginia.* Late in his life appeared his *Memoirs of the American Revolution, from its Commencement to the Year 1776, Inclusive; as Relating to the State of South-Carolina and Occasionally Refering* (sic) *to the States of North-Carolina and Georgia* (2 vols., 1821). This useful work was based on manuscripts left by his father, but was given its form by the pen of John Drayton, who, not without vanity, allowed only his own name to appear on the title-page.

[Emily H. Drayton Taylor, "The Draytons of S. C. and Philadelphia," *Pubs. Geneal. Soc. Pa.,* VIII (1923), 21–22; Princeton Commencement Program, 1779, in *Archives of the State of N. J.,* 2 ser., III (1906), 669–71; J. B. O'Neall, *Biog. Sketches of the Bench and Bar of S. C.,* vol. I (1859); Wm. A. Schaper, "Sectionalism and Representation in S. C.," in *Ann. Report Am. Hist. Asso., 1900,* vol. I (1901); E. L. Green, *A Hist. of the Univ. of S. C.* (1916); Manuscript Jours. Senate and House of Representatives of S. C., Columbia; Charleston *City Gazette and Commercial Daily Advertiser,* Nov. 1822; *Charleston Courier,* Nov. 29, 1822.]

J. H. E—y.
D. M.

DRAYTON, PERCIVAL (Aug. 25, 1812–Aug. 4, 1865), naval officer, son of the younger William Drayton [*q.v.*] and his first wife, Ann Gadsden, was born in South Carolina of an aristocratic and distinguished family. Appointed midshipman on Dec. 1, 1827, he was initiated into the theory of his profession at the New York Naval School, and into its practise on the frigate *Hudson* of the Brazil Squadron. He was advanced to the rank of passed midshipman in 1833, and to that of lieutenant in 1838. While in the latter grade he served successively in the Brazil, Pacific, and Mediterranean squadrons, and at the New York navy-yard on ordnance duty. In 1855 he was made commander and three years later was appointed aide to Commodore Shubrick [*q.v.*] in command of the Brazil Squadron and the Paraguay expedition. The outbreak of the Civil War found Drayton on ordnance duty at the navy-yard in Philadelphia, a city which had been his home for upwards of thirty years. Sympathizing with the North in the approaching conflict, he requested on Feb. 25, 1861, that his name be entered in the naval register as a citizen of Philadelphia. In October of that year, he was appointed to the command of the *Pocahontas* and participated in Du Pont's expedition against Port Royal, S. C., fighting against his brother, Gen. Thomas F. Drayton [*q.v.*], and other relatives who had cast in their lot with the Confederacy. Ardent in his devotion to the Union, he wrote that rather than interfere with the success of the war he was ready to sacrifice every relative that he had, painful as it would be. The South Carolina legislature proscribed him and declared him infamous (*National Republican,* Aug. 5, 1865).

Drayton was of great service to Du Pont while that officer was in command of the South Atlantic blockading squadron. He made reconnoissances of St. Helena Sound and adjacent waters and was present at the capture of Fernandina and St. Mary's and at the occupation of Stono River. Made a captain, taking rank from July 16, 1862, he was placed in command of the monitor *Passaic,* the second ship of her class. In this ironclad he bombarded Fort McAllister and took part in Du Pont's attack on Fort Sumter. In letters to the secretary of the navy he was highly commended by his commodore. In December 1863, he was appointed fleet captain of the West Gulf blockading squadron, then commanded by Farragut. On board the *Hartford* he participated in the operations in Mobile Bay, where his services were exceedingly valuable. Farragut warmly expressed his appreciation of them in a letter to Secretary Welles. He was now regarded as one of the ablest officers in the navy and was especially expert as an organizer and administrator. In April 1865, these qualities were recognized by his appointment to the office of chief of the Bureau of Navigation, the leading naval bureau. While holding this position he died in Washington after a few days of illness. He was unmarried. Tall and commanding in appearance, Drayton was the "beau ideal" of a naval officer. Endowed with exceptional mental powers, he ranked high as a naval scholar, reading and speaking several foreign languages. He left to the Naval Academy his coins, shells, and foreign arms, and a letter of Admiral Nelson's. The torpedo boat *Drayton* was named for him.

[Record of Officers, Bureau of Navigation, 1827–65; Navy Registers, 1827–65; *Official Records (Navy),* 1 ser., vols. XIII, XIV, XXI; *Army and Navy Jour.,* Aug. 12, Dec. 16, 1865; *Naval Letters from Capt. Percival Drayton, 1861–1865* (1906); Emily H. Drayton Taylor, "The Draytons of S. C. and Philadelphia," *Pubs. Geneal. Soc. Pa.,* VIII (1923), p. 21.] C. O. P.

DRAYTON, THOMAS FENWICK (Aug. 24, 1808–Feb. 18, 1891), planter, railroad president, Confederate soldier, son of the younger William Drayton [*q.v.*] and his first wife, Ann Gadsden, was born in South Carolina, most probably at Charleston. In 1828 he was graduated from the United States Military Academy and commissioned in the 6th Infantry. One of his classmates was Jefferson Davis, with whom he formed a lasting friendship and to whom he wrote in later life letters which now constitute the chief source of information about him. After serving in garrisons at Jefferson Barracks, Mo., and Newport, Ky., he was assigned (1832) to topographical duty. He participated in the unsuccessful project to build a Charleston, Louisville & Cincinnati Railroad; first as assistant surveyor and subsequently, following his resignation from the army (Aug. 15, 1836), as resident engineer. In 1838 he acquired a plantation in St. Luke's Parish, S. C., which he cultivated until the beginning of the Civil War. Though planting was his chief interest in this period, he occupied from time to time positions of a public, or semi-public, character. From 1842 to 1847 he was captain of a company of South Carolina militia, and from 1851 to 1852 a member of the state board of ordnance. For the next three years (1853–56) he represented his parish in the upper house of the General Assembly. In 1853 he was elected president of the Charleston and Savannah Railroad, which was constructed (see *First Report of the President of the Charleston and Savannah Railroad,* 1855) and successfully operated under his direction until 1861. He regarded the railroad as the most effective means of unifying the South, and he labored with this end in view (letter to Davis, Apr. 9, 1858, Rowland, *post,* III, 216–17). At about the time of his retirement from the army he was married to Catherine Pope. She bore him eight children.

Drayton was commissioned brigadier-general in the Provisional Army of the Confederate States on Sept. 25, 1861. As commander of the military district about Port Royal, S. C., he directed its defense during the successful Federal assaults of Nov. 4–7, 1861 (*Official Records, Army,* 1 ser., VI, 6–14). On this occasion his brother, Capt. Percival Drayton [*q.v.*], led one of the attacking vessels. In July 1862 he was sent to Virginia in command of a brigade which, soon after its arrival, was attached to Longstreet's corps. He took part in the engagements at Thoroughfare Gap, Second Manassas, South Mountain, and Sharpsburg but did not acquit himself creditably. In fact as early as the battle of Port Royal there are to be found in the reports of his superiors (*e.g.,* Brig.-Gen. R. S. Ripley, *Official Records, Army,* 1 ser., VI, 13–14; and Maj.-Gen. J. C. Pemberton, *Ibid.,* p. 110) hints of Drayton's inefficiency as a commanding officer. Hints in South Carolina were followed by positive accusations in Virginia (*e.g.,* Maj.-Gen. D. R. Jones, *Ibid.,* 1 ser., XII, pt. 2, p. 579). "He is a gentleman and a soldier in his own person," Lee wrote Davis, "but seems to lack the capacity to command" (*Ibid.,* 1 ser., XXI, 1,030). In consequence his brigade was broken up, and Drayton himself was detailed as a member of a military court. In August 1863 he resumed field duty but not on the active front. For a time he commanded a brigade in the District of Arkansas and later was in charge of a sub-district in Texas. His last service in the Confederate army was as president of a court of inquiry which investigated Price's Missouri expedition.

His plantation having been damaged by Union soldiers and in part confiscated by the Federal government, Drayton removed at the close of the war to Dooly County, Ga., where he undertook to develop a farm. Though assisted in this enterprise by a bequest of $27,000 from his brother Percival, his efforts were unsuccessful; and in 1871 he accepted a position as agent of the Southern Life Insurance Company, going shortly afterward to Charlotte, N. C. In 1878 he was appointed president of the South Carolina Immigrant Society. His death occurred in 1891 at Florence, S. C.

[*Confed. Mil. Hist.*, V (1899), 387–89; Emily H. Drayton Taylor, "The Draytons of S. C. and Phila.," in *Pubs. Geneal. Soc. Pa.*, VIII (1923), 23; G. W. Cullum, *Biog. Reg.* (3rd ed., 1891); *Official Records (Army)*, 1 ser., esp. vol. VI; Dunbar Rowland, *Jefferson Davis, Constitutionalist, His Letters and Speeches* (1923), vols. III, VII, IX, and X, containing several illuminating letters from Drayton to Davis ranging over the period from 1858 to 1889.] J. H. E—y.

DRAYTON, WILLIAM (Mar. 21, 1732–May 18, 1790), jurist, was the great-grandson of Thomas Drayton, who came to South Carolina from Barbados in 1679 and became the founder of a prominent family. William's father, Thomas, the third of the name in South Carolina, served on the Council, was a justice of the province, and a member of the Commons House of Assembly. He married, on Dec. 26, 1730, Elizabeth, daughter of William Bull [*q.v.*], lieutenant-governor of South Carolina, 1738–55. William, their second son and eldest surviving child, was born at "Magnolia," a plantation on the Ashley River which was acquired by his grandfather, added to by his father, at length (1774) sold by him to his uncle, John, and which, as "Magnolia Gardens," has long been noted for its gorgeous vegetation. On Oct. 6, 1750, he was admitted to the Middle Temple and on June 13, 1755, called to the English bar (Jones, *post*, p. 64). By 1756 he had returned home, begun the practise of law, and become a justice of the peace for Berkeley County. Removing to East Florida after 1763, he was appointed chief justice of the province (warrant dated Feb. 10, 1767) and became *ex officio* a member of the Council. Personal differences between him and John Moultrie, also a South Carolinian, who became lieutenant-governor in 1771, assumed a political character when he advocated the extension of local self-government. In this he had the support of his friend, Dr. Andrew Turnbull, founder of a colony of Greeks, Italians, and Minorcans at New Smyrna (Doggett, *post*, pp. 87–90). In the course of the dispute, Drayton was suspended from the Council, though he was present at its first meeting after Gov. Patrick Tonyn arrived in March 1774 (Siebert, *post*, I, 4). On Feb. 13, 1776, Drayton was suspended from the office of chief justice, the charges against him being: association with the attempt of Jonathan Bryan to make a "fraudulent purchase" of Indian lands; disloyal correspondence with his cousin, William Henry Drayton [*q.v.*], a South Carolina Patriot; and a sympathetic attitude toward the grand jury when critical of the administration (*Ibid.*, p. 34). Meanwhile, Turnbull and Drayton, whom Gov. Tonyn termed "Patriots for the cause of America," went without leave of absence to England to plead their cause, bearing with them resolutions of loyalty signed by many citizens. As a result of their representations, the reinstatement of Drayton without loss of salary was ordered. On Sept. 4, 1776, the governor swallowed the bitter pill and restored the chief justice. He and Turnbull returned to the province the following year to find that the latter's colony was largely broken up, by Tonyn's recruiting activities, they claimed. The chief justice continued to speak freely against Tonyn's measures and "blunders," and advocated capitulation to an invading army of Patriots under Col. Samuel Elbert [*q.v.*] in order that the province might gain freedom from molestation, which he felt the governor's policy would never secure. Though he gave evidences of zeal, his suspension was again voted by the Council on Dec. 16, 1777 (*Ibid.*, p. 64). In the following March he sold his property in East Florida, and on Apr. 1 was suspended as "the head of a faction against administration," which he undoubtedly was. He went to England, where his wife died and he failed to gain reinstatement. He continued to assert his loyalty to the British Empire, but felt that the revolt of the colonies was in no small part due to the conduct of their governors.

Before May 13, 1780, when Turnbull joined him, Drayton was again in South Carolina. Charleston was not evacuated for more than two years, so he could have done little there for the Patriot cause. Thanks to family connections, however, he was soon in good standing in the state. He became judge of the admiralty court. associate justice of the supreme court, and in the autumn of 1789 was appointed first judge of the United States court for the District of South Carolina. He served as such until his death about six months later. His first wife, Mary, daughter of Jacob and Elizabeth (Martin) Motte, bore him nine children, one of whom, William [*q.v.*], attained distinction. His second wife, Mary Gates, to whom he was married about 1780, bore him one child.

[Wm. Drayton, "An Inquiry into the present State, and Administration of Affairs in the Province of E. Fla., with some Observations on the Case of the late Ch. Justice There" (1778), MS. in Lib. of Cong.; warrant in Pub. Record Office, C. O. class 324, 51, p. 307, Lib. of Cong. Transcripts; Carita Doggett, *Dr. Andrew Turnbull and the New Smyrna Colony of Fla.* (1919); W. H. Siebert, *Loyalists in E. Fla., 1774 to 1785* (2 vols. 1929); E. A. Jones, *Am. Members of the Inns of Court* (1924); Emily H. Drayton Taylor, "The Draytons of S. C. and Philadelphia," *Pubs. Geneal. Soc. Pa.*, vol. VIII (1923).]

J. H. E—y.
D. M.

DRAYTON, WILLIAM (Dec. 30, 1776–May 24, 1846), lawyer, soldier, congressman, was born at St. Augustine, East Florida, the youngest child of William Drayton [*q.v.*], chief justice of the province, and his first wife, Mary Motte. When, in the spring of 1778, his parents went to England, where his mother died, the infant was left in the care of Dr. Andrew Turnbull and his Greek wife. He was taken by them to Charleston when they joined his father there in May 1780. Sent to school in England, the boy was called home by the death of his father in 1790, at which date his formal education ended. He became assistant in the clerk's office of the court of general sessions under his brother Jacob, studied law, was admitted to the bar, and before 1812 had attained the first rank in his profession. Mild and courteous in manner, he was a persuasive speaker, renowned for choice diction and precision of language. His practise is said to have brought him an annual income of from $15,000 to $18,000 a year, which enabled him to invest extensively in commercial enterprises (O'Neall, *post*, I, 306–07). A Federalist in politics, he regarded the War of 1812 as unnecessary and deplorable, but offered his own services to the government. He had been associated earlier with the Ancient Battalion of Artillery as an officer, and became lieutenant-colonel of infantry, Mar. 12, 1812, and colonel on July 6 of that year. By this title he was commonly known in later life. On Aug. 1, 1814, he became inspector general (F. B. Heitman, *Historical Register and Dictionary of the United States Army*, 1903). His acquaintance with military affairs was sufficient to cause Andrew Jackson to recommend to Monroe in 1816 his appointment as secretary of war and himself to offer him the same post in 1829 (J. S. Bassett, *The Life of Andrew Jackson*, 1911, I, 339; II, 537).

In 1819 he became recorder and judge of the city court of Charleston, a position which he filled with distinction until 1823. Elected as a Union Democrat to fill the vacancy created by the resignation of Joel R. Poinsett from Congress, he served continuously in that body from Dec. 15, 1825, to Mar. 3, 1833. Both in Washington and South Carolina, he was a vigorous opponent of the tariff, though not averse to compromise, and a strict constructionist of the Constitution, though an implacable foe of nullification. Opposing among others his foster-brother, Robert J. Turnbull [*q.v.*], he was one of the chief organizers of the Anti-Convention or Union party in South Carolina. His oration delivered on July 4, 1831, in Charleston, which contained a severe attack upon the Exposition, was widely circulated, and served as the platform of the Union party (Boucher, *post*, pp. 139–43). After the triumph of the nullifiers in the state, Drayton, though not disposed to yield to their threat of force, tried in Congress to further a compromise on the tariff. His support of the Union gained him wide acclaim in the North and severe criticism at home, where, however, his personal qualities continued to be held in high esteem.

Leaving Charleston in the summer of 1833, he settled in Philadelphia, where until his death he was chiefly engaged in the duties of private life. Succeeding Thomas Dunlap as president of the Bank of the United States in 1841, he closed out the affairs of that institution (Philadelphia *North American*, Apr. 12, 1841; *United States Gazette*, Jan. 4, Feb. 22, 1842). He was twice married: first, to Ann, daughter of Thomas and Martha (Fenwick) Gadsden, who bore him four children, among them Thomas Fenwick and Percival Drayton [*qq.v.*]; second, to Maria Miles, daughter of William and Hannah (Shubrick) Heyward, who bore him five children, two of them attaining maturity. He was buried at Laurel Hill, Philadelphia.

[Wm. Drayton, *An Oration Delivered in the First Presbyt. Ch., Charleston, on Monday, July 4, 1831* (1831); *Address to the People of the Cong. Dist. of Charleston* (1832); J. B. O'Neall, *Biog. Sketches of the Bench and Bar of S. C.* (1859), I, 305–23; C. S. Boucher, *The Nullification Controversy in S. C.* (1916); Carita Doggett, *Dr. Andrew Turnbull and the New Smyrna Colony of Fla.* (1919); Emily H. D. Taylor, "The Draytons of S. C. and Philadelphia," *Pubs. Geneal. Soc. Pa.*, vol. VIII (1923); obituaries in the *Pennsylvanian* (Phila.), May 26, 1846; and *Charleston Courier*, May 28, 1846.]

J. H. E—y.
D. M.

DRAYTON, WILLIAM HENRY (September 1742–Sept. 3, 1779), Revolutionary leader, the son of John and Charlotte (Bull) Drayton, was born near Charleston, S. C. He was a double first cousin of Chief Justice William Drayton [*q.v.*]. Having completed his education in England, at Westminster School and Oxford, he returned to South Carolina, where he married on Mar. 29, 1764, Dorothy Golightly, an heiress, and became a planter. The son of two prominent families, young Drayton naturally turned his attention to politics. Entering the Assembly in 1765, he found himself out of accord with the rising opposition to British administration. In 1769 he contributed a number of able articles to the press, denouncing the non-importation movement, and defending the right of the individual to ignore rules set up without legal authority. Unable to check the popular movement, and having become personally unpopular, Drayton then went to England, where he was received at Court as a promising champion of British rights.

Drayton returned to Carolina to sit with his father and his uncle Thomas on the Council of the province (1772–75), and to serve as assistant judge. Appointed to the latter office by his uncle, Lieutenant-Governor William Bull, the young Carolinian soon realized that, according to custom, he would be superseded by a stranger from abroad. He indignantly denounced this practise in a charge to the grand jury which Lord North brought to the attention of Parliament. He also published *A Letter from "Freeman" of South Carolina to the Deputies of North America* (1774), in which he denied the right of Parliament to legislate for America, and proposed the establishment of a federal system. He suggested that an assembly for North America be empowered to tax the colonies for the Crown and pass general legislation, each province being left to regulate its own internal affairs.

Suspended from the Council (Mar. 1, 1775), Drayton embraced the American cause with zeal. A member of all the important revolutionary bodies in the province, and chairman of several, he performed valuable service in the spring of 1775 in preparing for armed resistance. In the summer he made a tour of the back country, trying to win the inhabitants to the American cause. His mission, however, was largely a failure, as this section felt itself more oppressed by the low country than by England. On his return to Charleston, Drayton was elected president of the provincial Congress, Nov. 1, 1775. He assumed the leadership of the progressives, and with great boldness and energy proceeded to involve the province in war. In the revolutionary councils he always urged the most aggressive measures upon his more conservative associates.

Having been elected chief justice under the state constitution of March 1776, Drayton delivered a series of charges to the grand juries which set Carolinians to thinking of independence, rather than of reconciliation with England. His zeal sometimes misled him, as when he attempted to persuade the Georgians to agree to a union with South Carolina. He desired a military commission, but conservative leaders preferred to make use of him as a commissioner to treat with neighboring states and the Indians, or to answer British offers of peace. Although a man of action rather than a deep political thinker, Drayton's speech in the Assembly on Jan. 20, 1778, shows that he foresaw the operation of sectional forces in the United States, and wished to safeguard the interests of the South. A radical in his opposition to Great Britain and the Loyalists, Drayton was not a social radical, although he promoted the adoption of the state constitution of 1778, which involved the disestablishment of the Church. Still chief justice of South Carolina, he represented the state in the Continental Congress from Mar. 30, 1778, until his death from typhus fever, in September 1779. With the exception of Gouverneur Morris, Drayton was a member of more committees during this period than any other man. His reply to the British peace commission of 1778 was widely read.

[*Memoirs of the Am. Revolution*, vol. I (1821), by Drayton's son, John Drayton [*q.v.*], contains a sketch with portrait. The narrative, based on materials collected by William Henry Drayton, goes down to June 1776. See also: *The Speech of the Hon. Wm. Henry Drayton . . . Delivered on the Twentieth Jan., 1778 . . . upon the Articles of the Confed. of the U. S. of America* (1778); reprints of speeches and articles in Peter Force, *Am. Archives*, 4 ser. vol. IV, V (1843–44), and Hezekiah Niles, *Principles and Acts of the Revolution in America* (1822); MSS. in possession of the Hist. Commission of S. C., *Jours. of the Continental Congress, 1774–89*, vols. X–XV (1908–09); Edw. McCrady, *The Hist. of S. C. in the Revolution 1775–80* (1901); *Pennsylvania Gazette and Weekly Advertiser*, Sept. 15, 1779.] M. D.

DRESEL, OTTO (*c.* 1826–July 26, 1890), concert-pianist and composer, was born in Geisenheim-on-the-Rhine, the son of Johann Dietrich Dresel and Luise Ephardt. He grew up in a progressive, intellectual home, his father being a sympathizer with the German liberal movement of 1848. After he had studied piano and composition with Hiller in Cologne and Mendelssohn in Leipzig, Dresel came to the United States in 1848. He settled in New York, as a concert-pianist and teacher in that middle period when "French, Italian, and English opera companies boarded the swifter and safer steamers for experiments in the American marketplace, and singers and instrumentalists from Germany in particular surged in to exploit the concert and teaching field" (Charles A. and Mary Beard, *The Rise of American Civilization*, I, 798). Dresel, when he returned to America in 1852 after a visit to Germany, made Boston his permanent home, perhaps because in New York, as in New Orleans, the opera with its social corollaries was more esteemed than concert music, and he felt his talent would more quickly win recognition in a more conservative city. Nor was he mistaken in his choice; his merit was soon recognized, and for more than fifteen years he held his place as Boston's foremost resident pianist, whose interpretation of the masterpieces of the classic piano repertoire gave evidence of his taste and technique. His influence was all the more valuable because, as a concert pianist, he avoided the facile brilliancies of such Europeans as Henri Herz, who had toured the United States and Mexico immediately before Dresel established himself in Boston; and Sigismund Thalberg, who played in Boston during his tour of the country in 1856. These virtuosos, like their American contemporary, Louis Moreau Gottschalk, inculcated a worship of mere bravura which Dresel consistently opposed by a conscientious cult of what was qualitatively highest in the literature of his instrument. His exceptional culture, incidentally, prevented his confining his influence to the piano recital. He was instrumental in introducing to the American public the most classic German music. He had collaborated with Robert Franz in supplying accompaniments for the vocal scores of Bach and Handel, and he took special pains to make the Franz songs known. His original compositions include piano pieces, songs, chamber music, an "Army Hymn" for solo, chorus, and orchestra (Boston, Jan. 1, 1863), and a setting of Longfellow's "In Memoriam," soprano and orchestra, to commemorate the fiftieth birthday of Louis Agassiz.

[*Dwight's Jour. of Music* (esp. issues of June 4, 1859, Apr. 28, 1860, Dec. 22, 1861) affords a survey of Dresel's activities in his field. The *Folio,* Boston, Sept. 1890, contains an obituary; and Sebastian Schlesinger has contributed an appreciation of the artist in letter form to the *Am. Art Jour.,* Sept. 6, 1890. See also H. C. Lahee, *Famous Pianists of Today and Yesterday* (1900); obituaries in *Boston Advertiser,* July 29, 1890, and other Boston papers. Dresel's daughter supplied the names of her father's parents and information regarding his birthplace and early life.] F. H. M.

DREW, DANIEL (July 29, 1797–Sept. 18, 1879), capitalist, speculator, son of Gilbert and Catherine (Muckelworth) Drew, was born at Carmel, N. Y., and spent his boyhood on his father's hundred-acre stock-farm with meager schooling. At fifteen he was left by his father's death to make his way, and, in order to earn the hundred dollars paid for substitutes, enlisted in the War of 1812, spending three months at Fort Gansevoort near Paulus Hook, N. J. After a brief service with the Nathaniel Howe menagerie, he found work suited to his temperament as cattle drover and horse trader, collecting live stock in the Hudson and Mohawk valleys and driving it to New York City. His training made him sharp-witted, grasping, and unscrupulous, though his trickiness was combined with a sanctimonious devotion to Methodism. By shrewdness and enterprise he soon became preëminent as a cattle buyer, and with the help of capital supplied by Henry Astor he extended his operations westward, being the first to drive cattle from Ohio, Kentucky, and Illinois across the Alleghanies. In 1829 he took up a permanent residence in New York, making his Bull's Head Tavern at Third Ave. and Twenty-fourth St., with yards for 1,500 cattle, the principal headquarters and exchange for drovers. During 1834 he went into the steamboat business in competition with Cornelius Vanderbilt [*q.v.*], running "anti-monopoly" boats first to Peekskill and then between Albany and New York. Beginning with the steamboats *Westchester* and *Emerald,* he reduced the Albany fare from three dollars to one, added to his fleet a series of well-known vessels, the *Knickerbocker, Oregon, Isaac Newton* (the first 300-foot boat on the Hudson), and *New World,* carried passengers for as little as a shilling, and by adroit management overcame Vanderbilt's opposition. When the Hudson River Railroad opened in 1852 he held undaunted to his line; for twenty-two years he also controlled the Stonington Line in Long Island Sound; and he established a profitable steamboat service on Lake Champlain. Having accumulated capital, he entered Wall St. in 1844, forming the house of Drew, Robinson & Company, which for ten years did a large stock-broking and banking business; and when the death of his partners dissolved the firm he became one of the boldest and craftiest of independent operators. "I had been wonderfully blessed in money-making," he said late in life. "I got to be a millionaire afore I know'd it, hardly" (*New York Tribune,* Sept. 19, 1879, p. 5). His connection with the Erie Railroad began in 1853, and in 1857, assisted by the panic, he forced his election as director. This fiduciary position enabled him to manipulate the Erie stock, and he did so shamelessly, becoming the first notorious type of speculative director. But in the famous Harlem Railroad corner which Cornelius Vanderbilt and John Tobin planned in 1864, he was outwitted, went short on large commitments as the stock rose in five months from 90 to 285, and lost a half million dollars, an episode which left him eager for revenge.

Drew's greatest business battle, affording numerous illustrations of the outrageous business practises permitted just after the Civil War, was the "Erie War" with Vanderbilt in 1866–68. As treasurer of the hard-pressed line, Drew, in the spring of 1866, advanced it $3,500,000, taking 28,000 shares of unissued stock and bonds for $3,000,000 convertible into stock. He simultaneously went short of Erie on a rising market, suddenly unloaded 58,000 shares on the bulls, and as the stock sank from 95 to 50 made enormous profits (C. F. and Henry Adams, *post*, pp. 6–7). Vanderbilt, determined to control the line, made an alliance with Boston speculators who held stock, threatened court proceedings, and frightened Drew and his allies, Jay Gould and James Fisk [*qq.v.*], into a treaty of peace—to which Drew shortly proved treacherous. The crisis came when, in 1868, Vanderbilt, with the aid of court injunctions to stop the Erie printing-presses, tried to corner Drew. But Drew, Gould, and Fisk succeeded, despite the courts, in dumping 50,000 shares of newly printed stock in the market, depressed the price from 83 to 71, and sheared Vanderbilt of millions. Judge Barnard ordered their arrest, and the trio retreated with $6,000,000 in greenbacks to Taylor's hotel in Jersey City, which they fortified. The combat was then transferred from the courts to the legislature at Albany. Gould bought the passage of a bill legalizing the stock issue, and Vanderbilt consented to a peace by which the plundered wreck of the Erie was handed over to Gould and Fisk. While the nation was still gasping at the depths of business dishonesty and political corruption revealed by the Erie War, Drew, Gould, and Fisk used their gains and the proceeds of fresh stock-water for an assault (October 1868) upon bank credit, stock prices, and foreign exchange which ruined thousands. Drew was at the height of his fortunes, but the press voiced general opinion in calling upon every one to treat him and his associates as infamous.

In 1870 Drew's luck failed him, and he was the victim of a combination managed by his former associates, Gould and Fisk, who sold enough Erie stock in England to produce an unexpected rise, cornered him, and were credited with mulcting him of a million and a half. His descent thereafter was rapid. Further stock losses were followed by ruin in the panic of 1873 and the resulting failure of Kenyon, Cox & Company, a firm in which he was largely interested. After many struggles, he filed a schedule in bankruptcy in March 1876, his liabilities exceeding one million and his assets being negligible. In his twenty-fifth year he had married Roxana Mead. Now a broken, illiterate, despised old man, he spent his last years dependent upon his son, William H. Drew, and living at 3 East Forty-second St. In his days of wealth he had built Methodist churches at Carmel and Brewster, N. Y., and had spent roughly $250,000 on the Drew Theological Seminary at Madison, N. J., and a somewhat smaller sum for the Drew Seminary for Young Ladies at Carmel; but his pledges for an endowment for the Drew Theological Seminary and for Wesleyan University at Middletown, Conn., were involved in his bankruptcy. Throughout life he had the tastes and habits of a drover, and he was survived by many stories of his ignorance, naïveté, parsimony, and mixture of piety and rascality.

[Bouck White, *The Book of Daniel Drew* (1910), an incisive semi-fictional study; Robt. H. Fuller, *Jubilee Jim; The Life of Col. Jas. Fisk, Jr.* (1928); C. F. and Henry Adams, *Chapters of Erie* (1871); E. H. Mott, *Between the Ocean and the Lakes; The Story of Erie* (1899); E. P. Oberholtzer, *Hist. of the U. S. Since the Civil War*, II (1922), 560 ff.; Allan Nevins, *The Emergence of Modern America* (1927), 194 ff.; Gustavus Myers, *Hist. of the Great Am. Fortunes*, II (1910), 155 ff.; John Bigelow, ed., *Letters and Literary Memorials of Samuel J. Tilden*, I (1908), 299 ff.; and the press of the day.] A. N.

DREW, GEORGIANA EMMA [See Barrymore, Georgiana Emma Drew, 1856–1893.]

DREW, JOHN (Sept. 3, 1827–May 21, 1862), actor, was born in Dublin, Ireland. His father, an artisan, emigrated to Buffalo, N. Y., and young Drew went to sea. He left his ship in Liverpool, however, and sought employment on the stage. His first American appearance seems to have been at the Richmond Hill Theatre, New York, in 1842. In 1845 he played O'Toole in *The Irish Tutor* at the Bowery Theatre, and there began his career as an actor of Irish rôles. The following year he went to the Chestnut Street Theatre, Philadelphia, and in 1853, with William Wheatley, he leased the Arch Street Theatre in that city. In the company with him here was his brother Frank, and they used to play the two Dromios, made up so exactly alike that the audience would frequently lay bets on which was which, and even the other actors could not tell them apart. Two years later he visited England, and on his return toured America with his wife, Mrs. John Drew [*v.* Louisa Lane Drew]. In 1859 he made a tour to Australia, returning through England, and going back to Philadelphia where his wife was wrestling with the financial problems of the Arch Street Theatre, of which she had assumed the sole management. His popularity as an actor was of much assistance, though for but a brief season. On May 9, 1862, he made his last appearance, in New York. He died in Philadelphia. He married Louisa Lane (Mrs. Mossop) in 1850, and they had three children, John, Georgiana [*qq.v.*], and Louisa (Mrs. Charles Mendum). John Drew was a man of short, rather slender figure, with a plain but jovial face, and he early in life became noted for his impersonations in the Irish plays which were extremely popular in America during the middle and latter half of the nineteenth century, as well as for comedy parts in such plays as *The Road to Ruin* and *London Assurance.* His plain-spoken wife, in her autobiography, says, "Had he lived to be forty-five, he would have been a great actor, but too early a success was his ruin.... Why should he study when he was assured on all sides (except my own) that he was as near perfection as was possible for man to be?" Opposed to this is the testimony of Joseph Jefferson (*Autobiography,* pp. 412–14) who found in his Irish Emigrant "a sincerity ... artistic treatment that wins for it a lasting remembrance in the minds of those who have witnessed it." Jefferson's description—and Jefferson had a keen and critical eye for acting—plainly indicates that Drew possessed no little power to suggest pathos, and that his art, even if natural and unstudied, was admired by other players. Perhaps his wife alone realized how much better it could have been with more work and study. Drew played Sir Lucius with Jefferson, and the latter watched him in other rôles, and says, "I think it has been generally conceded that since Tyrone Power there has been no Irish comedian equal to John Drew." He was, at any rate, the father of one of the most noted stage families of the United States, and as such, if for no other reason, is entitled to a niche in the American theatrical hall of fame.

[*Autobiog. Sketch of Mrs. John Drew* (1899); *Autobiography of Joseph Jefferson* (1890); John Drew, *My Years on the Stage* (1921); T. A. Brown, *Hist. of the Am. Stage* (1870); M. J. Moses, *Famous Actor-Families in America* (1906).]

W. P. E.

DREW, JOHN (Nov. 13, 1853–July 9, 1927), actor, was born in Philadelphia, Pa., the son of John Drew, Sr. [*q.v.*], at the time actor-manager of the Arch Street Theatre, and Louisa (Lane) Drew [*q.v.*], then and later a famous actress. His maternal grandparents had also been players. Young John was sent to boarding schools in or near Philadelphia, and was graduated from the old Episcopal Academy. Although his mother had been on the stage since childhood, and had been manager of the Arch Street Theatre since 1861, John did not show any juvenile interest in acting, and did not appear on the stage till his twentieth year. In 1873 he acted in a farce, *Cool as a Cucumber,* for the benefit of his sister, Georgie (later Mrs. Maurice Barrymore). He considered his début something of a joke, and wasn't even nervous, so that his mother, he says, "was greatly annoyed that I took the thing so lightly." She very soon showed him that acting is not as easy as all that, for he appeared in her company all the next season, acting with a young newcomer of sixteen, Miss Ada Rehan. In 1875, having proved his family aptitude for the stage, and disclosed something of the easy charm of manner, the man-of-the-world poise, which distinguished him in later life, he was offered a position in Augustin Daly's company in New York. His first New York appearance, at the Fifth Avenue Theatre, was as Bob Ruggles in *The Big Bonanza.* The *New York Times* commented on his "agreeable freedom from affectation," and his "frank and welcome heartiness of style." This "agreeable freedom from affectation," or naturalness of acting, characterized Drew's art consistently, and though it was a conscious process, deliberately followed, it caused many people to say that he "always played himself." Later the same year he was one of the company supporting Booth. He played Rosencrantz in *Hamlet,* and other minor rôles. He then supported Adelaide Neilson in *Twelfth Night* and *Cymbeline* (playing Cloten in the latter). The Daly venture having failed, he joined his mother's old friend, Joseph Jefferson, and doubled as the innkeeper and Henrick Vedder in *Rip Van Winkle.* An engagement as Charles Surface at his mother's theatre followed, and then he went on a barnstorming tour with his brother-in-law, the brilliant Maurice Barrymore [*q.v.*], Oxford graduate and noted wit, in a version of *Diplomacy.* There was more adventure than profit in the tour; Barrymore was wounded in a fight in Texas, and another member of the company was killed. In 1879 Daly began again, in the theatre which so long bore his name at Broadway and Twenty-ninth St., and John Drew once more joined his company. For the next fourteen years he acted only with this famous troupe, and soon became one of the "Big Four" of the company—the others being Ada Rehan, Mrs. Gilbert, and James Lewis—who shared in the profits at the end of each season. In spite of many tours through the country, and later, trips to England and even Germany and France, the Daly company was essentially a New York institution, and all its members were closely identified with the life of that city, and known to all the inhabitants. John Drew was both a popular actor in New York, and a figure in the social life. He was an adept in sports, a delightful companion, a sartorial model, and a punctilious gentleman. As an artist, he played in the entire round of

Daly dramas, which included numerous sentimental light comedies and farces adapted from the German, many of the standard old comedies in English, and several of Shakespeare's plays. In all these pieces, of course, he played opposite Miss Rehan, so that their styles became adapted one to the other like hand and glove, and their scenes together were often close to the perfection of comic art. Probably the most famous of their impersonations were those of Katherine and Petruchio. Daly produced *The Taming of the Shrew* in 1887, restoring the induction, and Miss Rehan's regal Kate, a superb creature, mettle for any man's taming, has never been forgotten by those who saw it. Drew's Petruchio was of less heroic proportions, but it was so full of crackling humor that the play became at once, and remained, the high point of the Daly productions. In 1888 Daly took his company to London, and this play was acted by them in the Memorial Theatre at Stratford. In 1888, also, Drew was one of the group of men, headed by Edwin Booth who founded the Players Club in New York.

On Oct. 3, 1892, Drew appeared for the first time as a star, under the management of Charles Frohman, at Palmer's Theatre (later Wallack's), on Broadway at Thirtieth St., New York. The play was *The Masked Ball,* adapted from the French by Clyde Fitch, and the leading woman was a slip of a girl named Maude Adams. In his autobiography (*My Years on the Stage*) Drew gives no reason for leaving Daly's company except the natural desire for a larger salary. The desire to be a star, of course, may naturally be inferred. But it is also true that theatrical styles and methods were changing. Daly's plays were becoming old fashioned and stock companies were giving way to touring companies, organized season by season. Frohman, Fitch, and Miss Adams were all young. They represented the new generation in the theatre, and Drew's own methods of acting and point of view were young, also. By leaving Daly's he aligned himself with the modern movement in the theatre, and for the next two decades his productions, under the Frohman management, always made at the Empire Theatre, New York, about Labor Day, marked, as it were, the official opening of the season, and usually disclosed the newest sample of contemporary polite comedy, staged and acted to the contemporary taste. Drew, during all this period, was the touchstone and standard of high comedy acting in America, and played an important part in the growth of our modern theatre.

After *The Masked Ball,* he produced *Butterflies* by Henry Guy Carleton, Henry Arthur Jones's *The Bauble Shop, Christopher Jr.,* by Madeline Ryley, another French adaptation, and then *Rosemary* by Louis N. Parker and Murray Carson (Sept. 14, 1896). This play was a huge success. Miss Adams was so popular in it that Mr. Frohman made her a star the following year. In it, too, Drew's niece, Miss Ethel Barrymore, appeared as a maid, for her New York début. Drew's next success, and a landmark of the new drama, was Henry Arthur Jones's comedy, *The Liars,* in 1898. He next produced C. Haddon Chambers's delightful comedy, *The Tyranny of Tears,* which he revived many years later, adding, at that time, Barrie's *The Will* as an afterpiece. An attempt to act a stage version of Richard Carvel was a failure; he was by now too closely identified with contemporary rôles. He had great success, however, with two plays by Captain Marshall, *The Second in Command,* and *The Duke of Killicrankie,* and also in *The Mummy and the Humming Bird,* when his nephew, Lionel Barrymore, supported him. He was also the producer of two plays by Somerset Maugham, *Smith* and *Jack Straw,* and of a translation, called *Inconstant George,* from the French play *L'Ane de Burridan.* His one attempt at Shakespeare after leaving Daly was *Much Ado,* in which Laura Hope Crews played Beatrice to his Benedict. It was not a succcess. "I had been away from this style of comedy too long," he says (*My Years on the Stage*), "more than twenty years." He also produced a serious Pinero drama, *His House in Order,* in which Margaret Illington made a name for herself.

Drew's relations with Charles Frohman were close. After the first year, there was only a verbal contract between them, and as Drew was his first star, the little manager had a sentimental interest in his success. Frohman went down on the *Lusitania,* leaving not only Drew but other of his actors at loose ends. Miss Maude Adams never acted again. Drew, now sixty-four years old, and beginning to suffer from failing eyesight, felt keenly the loss of his friend and manager. He attempted a dramatization of *Pendennis,* playing the Major, and revived *The Gay Lord Quex.* In 1921–23 he played the old man's part in Somerset Maugham's play *The Circle*—incidentally disclosing to a wider audience than saw him in *The Will* a capacity for character acting. He also appeared as Sir Peter in a Spring revival, made by the Players Club, of *The School for Scandal* (1923). In 1926 he joined an all star company in a revival of Pinero's *Trelawney of the Wells,* playing of course the part of Sir William. The company did an enormous business

Drew

everywhere, and frequently three or four matinées had to be played a week. But John Drew made no complaints, and was the rock around which the company was built. Peggy Wood, in her little book, *A Splendid Gypsy,* describes the road tour of this company vividly, and gives a touching account of Drew's last days, when he struggled bravely to play, though suffering great pain. His last appearance was in Vancouver, in May 1927, when he got through on sheer grit, and was rushed to San Francisco for the extraction of teeth supposed to be poisoning him. He died in that city on July 9, 1927. How much the "all star" company had been John Drew was proved by the fact that it had to disband after his loss. It had been Drew the public really flocked to see.

John Drew was married in 1880 to Josephine Baker, daughter of Mrs. Alexina Baker, an actress and friend of his mother's. Mrs. Drew died in 1918. They had one child, a daughter, Louisa (Mrs. John Devereaux). Their home was at East Hampton, Long Island, and Drew's social position is further indicated by the fact that he was a member of the Brook and Racquet Clubs as well as being the third president of the Players, succeeding Edwin Booth and Joseph Jefferson. He was a man of medium height, athletic figure, and strong features—the most pronounced being his long nose, inherited from his mother. Early in life he lost the sight of one eye, which resulted in partial blindness during his last years, but his easy bearing, his skilled technique, his charm of character, overcame any handicaps. His artistic method was that of Charles Mathews, his predecessor in England; he sought for matter-of-fact naturalness in stage deportment, even a sort of casual nonchalance, but combined with it, cleverly disguised, the most careful enunciation and the most artful "pointing" of any speech or situation. Though in his younger days he acted many romantic and classic rôles, he is best remembered for his later work in polite contemporary comedy, where his acting method exactly fitted the material, and his ease, naturalness and polish could serve as a direct inspiration to the younger players of the modern stage. He may justly be said to have bridged the gap between the older acting and the new, carrying on the standards of technical proficiency and upholding the dignity of the actor's position, while at the same time adapting his technique to a more realistic theatre and creating, for the new generation, a more satisfactory illusion.

[John Drew, autobiography, *My Years on the Stage* (1923); Peggy Wood, *A Splendid Gypsy: John Drew* (1927); Walter Prichard Eaton, *At the New Theatre* (1912), pp. 103 ff.; Edward A. Ditmar, *John Drew* (1900); M. J. Moses, *Famous Actor-Families in America* (1906); *N. Y. Times,* July 10, 1927.] W. P. E.

DREW, LOUISA LANE (Jan. 10, 1820–Aug. 31, 1897), actress, theatrical manager, was born in London. Her parents were actors, and she was carried on the stage at the age of twelve months. Her widowed mother (later Mrs. Kinloch) brought her to America in 1827, and she appeared at the Walnut Street Theatre, Philadelphia, as the Duke of York to the elder Booth's Richard III. She was a clever mimic and "quick study," and became famous as an "infant phenomenon" over the country, which she toured with her mother. She acted Little Pickle in *The Spoiled Child,* and a protean sketch in which she took five parts. In 1831 she and her mother were shipwrecked off Santo Domingo on the way to Jamaica. Returning to the United States, she joined the Ravel family for a tour. In 1836 she married Henry B. Hunt, an English tenor and actor, and soon after reached a greater maturity of parts, supporting Edwin Forrest and other leading players. When she and her mother had appeared in Boston, their joint salary was $16 a week, but in 1839–40 she alone received $20! For a time she was with Macready, and like most actresses of that period she played a great variety of parts. In 1847, at the Park Theatre, New York, she tore a leaf out of Charlotte Cushman's book, by acting Romeo, and then outdid her by acting Antony. In 1848, she was married a second time, to George Mossop, an Irish singing player. He lived but a year, and in 1850 she married, for a third husband, John Drew [*q.v.*], and bore him three children, John, Georgiana [*qq.v.*], and Louisa, all destined to carry on the stage tradition. After her marriage to Drew, she concentrated more on comedy rôles, for which she was best fitted, playing among many others Peg Woffington, Lydia Languish, Hypolita in *She Would and She Wouldn't,* Lady Teazle, and later her most famous part, Mrs. Malaprop. In 1853 Drew had become part proprietor of the Arch Street Theatre in Philadelphia where his wife had a glimpse of the trials of management, and was forced to take a hand in them. Later they toured together, and separately, and in 1861, while Drew was abroad, she alone assumed once more the management of the Arch Street house, attacking the job with the great resolution characteristic of her, and in the first season herself acting forty-two different rôles. A typical day in that busy theatre is described in their son John's memoirs (*My Years on the Stage*). Her husband died in 1862, and she continued for more than thirty-one years to conduct the Arch Street Theatre, making it one of the best-known stock houses in the country, and herself one of the best-known managers. She was not the first woman in America to manage a theatre and direct an acting company, but she was the first to do so on a considerable scale, and over a term of years. She had a working agreement with Lester Wallack in New York for the exchange of plays, and many visiting stars acted with her company. In this house her children made their débuts, and when she finally retired from the management, she had become the *grande dame* of the American theatre. Thereafter, in her last years, she most delighted to act Mrs. Malaprop, and it is said she would cheerfully journey a thousand miles for a chance to play it. In 1896, she acted in the famous all-star cast of *The Rivals* which Joseph Jefferson had assembled. Her last appearance was in *The Sporting Duchess.* Later she died, in Larchmont, N. Y., having already seen her son John take his place as star and her grand-daughter, Ethel Barrymore, make her début.

Mrs. Drew was not beautiful; quite the opposite. But her long life on the stage had given her a thorough command of her art, and she had a vivid sense of humor and a blunt, honest, energetic, and engaging personality. She was both loved and respected. William Winter called her Malaprop "incomparable." Henry Irving said to Ethel Barrymore, at the time of Mrs. Drew's death, "She was, in her line, the finest actress I have ever seen." Joseph Jefferson (*Autobiography,* p. 401) described how she invented the business of first handing Captain Absolute, by mistake, her own letter from Sir Lucius, and when the mistake was discovered simpered and blushed. "Her manner during this situation was the perfection of comedy," he adds. Her wit, her innate dignity, and her off-stage bluntness and simplicity of manner are described by Francis Wilson, in his *Life of Jefferson.* Perhaps the best testimony to her qualities, however, is found in her son's memoirs, for he tells how she deliberately deflated his pride at his first performance, to make him realize the need of humility and hard work, and how during all his years at Daly's Theatre he consulted with her about his rôles, in the older comedies especially, and how she knew all the traditional "business" of the parts and could tell him what was, and what was not, effective. She was a woman whose entire life and education had been the theatre; she understood it, respected it, gave it fresh dignity, and sent her children into it to carry on its best traditions. Her sharp-edged and racy gifts as a comic actress, combined with her keen mentality and her downright personality and worth as a woman, made her for a generation "the grand old lady" of the American stage.

[*Autobiog. Sketch of Mrs. John Drew* (1899); John Drew, *My Years on the Stage* (1921); *The Autobiography of Joseph Jefferson* (1890); Francis Wilson, *The Life of Joseph Jefferson* (1906); Montrose J. Moses, *Famous Actor-Families in America* (1906); *N. Y. Times,* Sept. 1, 1897.]

W. P. E.

DREXEL, ANTHONY JOSEPH (Sept. 13, 1826–June 30, 1893), philanthropist, banker, the son of Francis Martin Drexel [*q.v.*] and Catherine (Hookey) Drexel, was born in Philadelphia. When he was thirteen years old, and his father's brokerage office had been in existence only two years, he was taken into the office, and his education was confined almost entirely to this office and his home. His cultural education as well as his business training was under the direct supervision of his father, and consisted largely of music and languages. His father was rigorous in his discipline and at the same time liberal in bestowing responsibility, as when he sent the boy by stage-coach to New Orleans for the transfer of a large deposit of gold. He made Anthony Joseph a member of the firm of Drexel & Company in 1847, when the house was ten years old and the new member twenty-one. The latter married Ellen Rozet, daughter of a Philadelphia merchant of French descent.

The death in 1863 of Francis Martin Drexel, founder of the firm, coincided roughly with the close of an era in the financial history alike of the country and of the house of Drexel. The organization of the national banking system, the increase of public debts, and the vast expansion of industrial securities following the war affected the operations of the Drexels both qualitatively and quantitatively. Connections were established with banking houses of San Francisco, New York, London, and Paris. The handling of the flood of investment securities connected with national and local public debts, the building of railways, the development of mining, the growth of the factory system, and the improvement of urban real estate led to the transformation of the firm into essentially a house of investment brokers. During this period of expansion of the firm when its distinctive characteristics and functions were being developed, Anthony J. Drexel was the directing genius. Having lived intimately in contact with the business from the age of thirteen, his native abilities found natural, spontaneous expression in a quick, decisive, and penetrating judgment concerning the feasibility of financing the most intricate of undertakings. His conservatism of judgment and desire to maintain financial stability as against speculative expansion found expression frequently, as in his opposition to the excessively rapid railway development following the Civil War. Although his influence had already been predominant, the death in 1885 of his older brother, Francis, left to him the entire direction of affairs. A magnificent new bank and office building was erected, in wholesome contrast with the prevailing tendency toward ugly and sprawling business architecture. The closing years of his life saw a new era of expansion corresponding to the internationalizing of American trade.

In addition to his banking interests, Drexel engaged in extensive real-estate operations in Philadelphia and its vicinity, adding vastly to his fortune and attempting with some success to improve housing conditions among the working classes. He was also connected with the publishing business, as part owner of the *Public Ledger* in association with his life-long friend, the noted journalist and publisher George W. Childs [*q.v.*]. As a philanthropist he was noted no less than as a banker. He made extensive donations of the conventional kinds, to hospitals, to charitable institutions, and to churches of various denominations. He was associated with Childs in the founding of the Childs-Drexel Home for Aged Printers at Colorado Springs, Colo. His particular interest, however, was in promoting industrial education. His various ideas and projects at length converged in the founding of Drexel Institute at Philadelphia, opened to students in February 1892. His gifts to the Institute totaled about $3,000,000. Distinctive features included an emphasis on technology, free scholarships, and low tuition, night classes, public lectures and concerts, and an unrestricted admissions policy in respect to religion, race, sex, and social class. Drexel was an influential member of the Union League, and of a small group of business men who exercised the controling influence in the régime of President Grant. Like most of the members of the group, he abstained from public office. He died while in quest of health at Carlsbad, Germany.

[*A New Home for an Old House* (Phila., 1927) contains an account of the company and its founders and some excellent illustrations. There are brief sketches in W. W. Spooner, *Historic Families of America* n.d.), and in E. P. Oberholtzer, *Philadelphia: A Hist. of the City and its People* (n.d.), vol. II. A laudatory article by Geo. W. Childs was published in *Harper's Weekly*, July 15, 1893, and reprinted in the *Public Ledger Almanac* for 1894. There is a brief biography in manuscript by J. P. Ryder in the library of Drexel Institute.]

W. B.

DREXEL, FRANCIS MARTIN (Apr. 7, 1792–June 5, 1863), banker, was born at Dornbirn in the Austrian Tyrol, near the Lake of Constance. His father, Franz Joseph Drexel, was a well-to-do merchant of Dornbirn, and his mother, Magdalen Willhelm Drexel, seems to have been a native of the same town. For the son of a merchant, Francis Martin was given somewhat unusual opportunities for study by being sent to Milan at the age of eleven. Here he studied Italian and other languages and began his career as an artist. This was the period of the Napoleonic Wars, and the boy's studies were interrupted by his father's financial difficulties and by efforts to avoid conscription in the armies raised to fight against Napoleon. For several years he continued his studies intermittently in different parts of Europe, painting portraits whenever opportunity afforded, and returning to Austria in 1815. Unsettled conditions in Austria, combined with his roving disposition, sent him once more to various countries of Europe, and in 1817 he set saii from Amsterdam for Philadelphia.

He remained in Philadelphia for nearly ten years, painting portraits, giving lessons in drawing, and establishing promising connections. In 1821 he married Catherine Hookey of Philadelphia. His progress as an artist was interrupted by a quarrel with his brother-in-law and by a return of his *wanderlust,* which took him in 1826 on the first of his South American adventures. Here he remained four years, traveling extensively, making numerous acquaintances among the notables of the Latin-American countries, painting portraits, collecting curios, and accumulating considerable wealth by trafficking in currency as well as by practising his profession. He later made another trip to South America and also visited Mexico. His travels in Europe and America during periods of political disturbance and violent fluctuations taught him the nature and importance of banking and exchange and enabled him to profit handsomely in the incidental buying and selling of notes and currency.

It was the influence of these experiences, combined, perhaps, with a realization that his artistic ability was not of the highest order, that led him to abandon the profession of art and to open a brokerage office, in Louisville, Ky., in 1837. In January of the next year, at 34 South Third St., Philadelphia, he established the brokerage office, for dealing particularly in "uncurrent money," which ultimately grew into the world-famous house of Drexel & Company. For the kind of business for which he was particularly equipped, conditions were propitious. The charter of the Bank of the United States expired in 1836, and securities, whether public or private, as well as ordinary currency, were in a chaotic condition. Drexel's experience and judgment enabled him to develop a prosperous business, and his wealth was further increased by a successful venture in far-western banking during the mid-century gold rush. In his seventy-second year he was struck by a railroad train and killed. The business which he founded was developed by his sons into a position of importance in the rapidly expanding economic life of the country.

[Drexel left a brief autobiography, "Life and Travels of Francis M. Drexel," written in later life for his children and as yet unpublished. Copies of this and of his "Journal of a Trip to South America" are in the archives of the company at Philadelphia. The best brief sketch is in *A New Home for an Old House* (Philadelphia, 1927), pp. 36–41. The frontispiece is an excellent portrait of the founder of the house. See also W. W. Spooner, *Historic Families of America* (n. d.), p. 190.]

W. B.

DREXEL, JOSEPH WILLIAM (Jan. 24, 1833–Mar. 25, 1888), banker, philanthropist, was born in Philadelphia, the third son of Francis Martin Drexel [*q.v.*] and Catherine (Hookey) Drexel. He attended high school in Philadelphia but was largely indebted to his father for his extensive knowledge of languages, art, and music, as well as for his training in banking. On Apr. 18, 1865, he married Lucy Wharton of Philadelphia. Before his business career began, he traveled in the Mediterranean countries, and soon after he became connected with his father's business he represented the firm in Germany. In 1861 he engaged in banking at Chicago, but two years later, upon the death of the elder Drexel, he returned to Philadelphia. As in the case of his father, his knowledge of foreign languages and countries proved to be an important factor in his success as a banker. In 1867 he became one of the partners of the firm of Drexel, Harjes & Company of Paris, and four years later he became associated with J. Pierpont Morgan in the firm of Drexel, Morgan & Company. Thereafter his principal activities were in New York. He was connected with a large number of other financial institutions, being director of eleven banks, including the Garfield National Bank of which he was one of the founders. As a business man his chief significance lay in his serving as a connecting link between the larger banking and brokerage institutions of Philadelphia and New York and between these and European investment bankers. He lived during a period of exceedingly rapid industrial expansion, and vastly increased his inherited fortune by the conservative promotion of the more stable industrial enterprises as well as by handling great quantities of securities issued by national and local governments.

In 1876 he withdrew from active direction of his business interests in order to devote his time to philanthropic, public, and artistic enterprises. He collected an extensive library of music, including noted manuscripts and autographs, and was also interested in etchings. Important collections were bequeathed to the Lenox Library and to the Metropolitan Museum. He was president of the Philharmonic Society of New York and director of the Metropolitan Museum. His interest in public health found expression in his study and promotion of sanitation and in his serving as treasurer of the New York Cancer Hospital. He was deeply interested in the condition of the poor, the unemployed, and the dependent classes. He investigated the conditions of the families of large numbers of prisoners, and spent considerable sums for their relief. In addition to conventional methods of relieving the poor, as by maintaining soup houses, he undertook remedial measures of a distinctive kind. Among his various projects was a "back to the land" movement. He proposed to purchase large tracts, divide them up into small farms, build five-room houses, and sell them at cost on easy terms to worthy but indigent people of the city. Naturally the results, except in cases of occasional individual relief, were insignificant, and there is little indication that Drexel gave serious thought to the underlying causes of the conditions he sought to relieve. He died at the relatively early age of fifty-five as a result of a complication of a disease of the heart and Bright's disease.

[For bibliographical data, see notes following the sketches of his father, Francis Martin Drexel, and his brother, Anthony Joseph Drexel. For his marriage, see A. W. Wharton, *Geneal. of the Wharton Family* (1880), p. 49. The principal obituaries were published in the *N. Y. Times* and the Philadelphia *Public Ledger* of March 26, 1888. Concerning his musical interests, see *Catalogue of Jos. W. Drexel's Musical Library* (1869).]

W. B.

DRINKER, CATHARINE ANN [See JANVIER, CATHARINE ANN, 1841–1922.]

DRINKWATER, JENNIE MARIA (Apr. 12, 1841–Apr. 28, 1900), writer of juvenile fiction and originator of the Shut-in-Society, was born in Yarmouth, Me., the daughter of Capt. Levi P. and Mary Jane (Angus) Drinkwater. She was educated in the public schools and at Greenleaf's Institute, Brooklyn, N. Y. On Mar. 17, 1880, she married Nathaniel Conklin, a Presbyterian minister of New Vernon, N. J., who died in 1892. Beginning to write for the religious press when she was young, she later became widely known through her novels for young people, especially for girls, published under her maiden name. Between 1880 and 1900 more than thirty of these came from her pen. They were written to further the moral and spiritual welfare of their readers, and were pre-eminently suitable for Sunday-school libraries. Young people of their day found them interesting, however, and some of them went through several editions of 30,000 each. Among them are: *Tessa Wadsworth's Discipline* (1879); *Electa* (1881); *Bek's First Corner* (1883); *The Fairfax Girls* (1886); *From Flax to Linen* (1888); *Marigold* (1889); *Second Best* (1891); *Looking Seaward* (1893); *Goldenrod Farm* (1897); *Shar Burbank* (1898). In 1874 she conceived the idea of sympathy, encouragement, and comfort for invalids through correspondence. This resulted in the Shut-in-Society, which grew rapidly and in 1885 was incorporated under the laws of the State of New York. Mrs. Conklin was its first president, and its honorary president at her death.

[Frederick Orr, "Jennie M. Drinkwater," *The Writer*, Aug. 1891; *The Open Window*, June and July 1900; *Who's Who in America*, 1899–1900; *N. Y. Times*, Apr. 30, 1900; and information furnished by Dr. E. D. G. Conkling of Newark, N. J.] H. E. S.

DRIPPS, ISAAC L. (Apr. 14, 1810–Dec. 28, 1892), inventor, engineer, was born in Belfast, Ireland, of Scotch and Irish parents who emigrated to Philadelphia, Pa., with him when he was an infant. He attended the city public schools, completing the curriculum at the age of sixteen, and then was apprenticed to Thomas Holloway, at that time the largest builder of steamboat machinery in Philadelphia. Here he remained for a little over five years, rising rapidly until he was given full charge of fitting and erecting all machinery built by the company. The best customer that Holloway had was the Union Line operating steamboats on the Delaware River. In 1830 this company organized a subsidiary to operate a steam railroad between Camden and Amboy, N. J., and ordered an English locomotive. When the "John Bull," as it was named, arrived in Philadelphia in August 1831, Dripps, then a little over twenty-one, was induced to join the railroad company and was given the task of transporting the knocked-down locomotive from Philadelphia to Bordentown, N. J., and of erecting it there. He had never seen a locomotive before, but with the aid of meager drawings accomplished the job, constructing at the same time a tender and subsequently a cow-catcher for it, and finally served as engineer on its trial trip Nov. 12, 1831. For the succeeding twenty-two years he continued with the Camden & Amboy Railroad. At first he was in charge of locomotive construction in the company's shops at Hoboken. He then was made superintendent of machinery with the additional duty of maintenance of all steamboats operated by the company, and toward the end of his service was superintendent of motive power and machinery. In 1853 he became a partner in the Trenton Locomotive & Machine Works at Trenton, N. J. Before the company dissolved five years later, on account of financial difficulties, he had designed and built a wide tread wheel locomotive for running on two different gaged tracks, and an iron freight-car truck, the first of the well-known diamond-framed pattern. In 1859 he accepted the position of superintendent of motive power and machinery of the Pittsburgh, Fort Wayne & Chicago Railroad and moved with his family to Fort Wayne, Ind. During the succeeding ten years he completely rebuilt the mechanical department. Not only the shops but also much of the machinery and tools were designed by him and, when completed, the establishment was looked upon as the model shop of the country, far superior to anything then extant in the United States. Because of the record he achieved at Fort Wayne, Dripps was made superintendent of motive power and machinery of the Pennsylvania Railroad on Apr. 1, 1870, with headquarters at Altoona, Pa. Here he undertook the construction of the most extensive railroad-shops in the country, when his health failed and he was compelled to resign on Mar. 31, 1872. He served in the company, however, for the succeeding six years as a special agent, devoting most of his time to experimental work, particularly on the determination of the frictional resistance of various classes of locomotives. His health failing to improve, he gave up his work entirely in 1878 and retired to his son's home in Philadelphia. In the course of his career he devised innumerable mechanisms, tools, and the like for use in the construction of locomotives, freight and passenger cars, and steamboat machinery, but never patented any of them. He designed for one of the early steamboats of the Union Line a unique type of screw propeller, and also for the first time on any vessel installed the rudder aft of the propeller. He was married shortly after 1830 at Bordentown, N. J., and was survived by his son William.

[Angus Sinclair, *Development of the Locomotive Engine* (1907); *Locomotive Engineering*, Jan. 1892; *Report of the Proc. . . . of the Am. Ry. Master Mechanics Asso.*, 1893; U. S. Museum records; U. S. Museum correspondence with Pennsylvania R. R. Date of birth from Wm. Dripps, Esq.] C. W. M.

DRISLER, HENRY (Dec. 27, 1818–Nov. 30, 1897), educator, was born on Staten Island, N.

Y., and had his early schooling there. He entered Columbia College in 1835, and remained in close connection with that institution for the rest of a long life. Upon graduation in 1839, he became a classical master in the Columbia Grammar School, and four years later was made a tutor in Greek and Latin in the college; in 1845 he became adjunct-professor of Latin, and in 1857 he succeeded to the first professorship established at Columbia in Latin as a separate field. Ten years later he followed Charles Anthon [*q.v.*] as Jay Professor of Greek. At many times during his distinguished career as scholar and teacher he was called upon to serve the college in other capacities. Thus he was acting president during President Barnard's absence for the year 1878, and again in the interim, 1888–90, between the death of Barnard and the inauguration of Seth Low. At the latter date he became the first occupant of the newly created office of Dean of the College. In 1894, on his retirement as emeritus professor of the Greek language and literature after fifty years of service, he was the recipient of distinguished academic honors. A public reception was tendered by the Columbia alumni, a gold medal was struck in his honor, and a volume of essays on classical subjects was dedicated to him by his former students; the Henry Drisler Fellowship in Classical Philology was founded, and a sum of money was donated as the Henry Drisler Classical Fund for the purchase of books, casts, and other materials of classical study. His interest in the college remained warm and effective after his formal retirement and found expression particularly in generous gifts of valuable books to the library.

His varied activity was not confined to academic halls. As a young student he had felt the need of a public library in New York City, and his continuing interest in this project led to his selection as trustee of the Astor Library and of the New York Public Library. He was also a trustee of the American School of Classical Studies in Athens, and devoted considerable time to its concerns, especially during a year spent mainly in Greece in 1891. He was president of the association of Columbia alumni for eight years from 1872, and vice-president of the Archæological Institute of America for three years following 1886. Deeply religious in nature and always a strong churchman, he served also as trustee of the Trinity School, of the General Theological Seminary, and of the Leake and Watts Orphan Asylum; as a member of the standing committee for his diocese, and as vice-president of the Society for Promoting Religion and Learning. He was the founder of a Greek Club which gathered about him fortnightly for forty years in tribute to the power of his personality and the ardor of his scholarship. Although he was given to certain crotchety conservatisms, as in his bitter enmity to walking-sticks and to tobacco, he brought to his varied activities a rugged strength of character and a broad humanity which made him greatly revered.

He was a profound and exact scholar. Rigorous instruction under Anthon trained his native genius for taking pains to an admirable fitness for linguistic work, especially in lexicography. At a time when a decline in classical scholarship in the United States had almost extinguished original production, he was one of the first Americans to recognize the achievement of the German school which was inaugurating a second renaissance in classical study; and the influence of the distinguished scholars whom he visited in Berlin at a period when Americans were rarely seen there combined effectively with the vital spirit of Anthon in all his maturer work. In collaboration with Anthon he published a number of text-books, and edited Riddle and Arnold's *Copious and Critical English-Latin Lexicon* (1849); and he assisted Anthon in the preparation of several editions of Smith's *Classical Dictionary.* In 1854 his name appeared as joint-editor of Liddell and Scott's recension of Franz Passow's *Greek-English Lexicon,* in acknowledgment of the copious aid unofficially given to the editors. He published a greatly enlarged edition of Charles D. Yonge's *English-Greek Lexicon* (1870), was associate editor of *Johnson's New Universal Cyclopædia* (1875–78), and in addition to many other labors, was general editor of Harper's series of classical texts.

[Articles on Drisler in *Harper's Weekly,* June 9, 1894, and Jan. 1898, both by Harry Thurston Peck; in *Harper's Weekly,* Dec. 11, 1897, by J. Howard Van Amringe; and in the *Columbia Spectator,* Nov. 30, 1897, by Edward Delavan Perry. Further material may be found in the archives of Columbia Univ.; in "Univ. of the State of N. Y. 112th Annual Report of the Regents," *Docs. of the Senate of the State of N. Y., 1899, No. 55*; and in the *Athenæum* (London), Dec. 18, 1897.] E. H. W.

DROPSIE, MOSES AARON (Mar. 9, 1821–July 8, 1905), lawyer, was born in Philadelphia of parents who came from Amsterdam and settled in the United States in 1819. His father, Aaron Moses Dropsie, was a Jew and his mother a Christian, and there had been an agreement that the children were to be allowed to choose their own religion. Three of them chose the Jewish religion, Moses undertaking his obligations at the age of fourteen. He attended a private academy in Philadelphia in charge of Rev. William Mann and received his Jewish training from Isaac Leeser, minister of the Portuguese Congregation in Philadelphia, of whom he wrote a "Panegyric" after the latter's death in 1868. In 1837, he was apprenticed to a watchmaker, and after the expiration of the indenture, which was for a period of two years, he continued in the jewelry business until 1848. At the age of twenty-seven, he decided to study law and entered the office of Benjamin Harris Brewster [*q.v.*], later attorney-general of the United States. He was admitted to practise on Jan. 11, 1851, and rapidly secured an important place at the bar of Philadelphia. He had a commanding personality and a direct and convincing way of presenting an argument, which carried conviction to both judge and jury.

He collected an excellent law library and had a passion for original prints and editions, not for their sale value but because he thought first editions valuable as source books. He was not only a practitioner of the law, but interested in its history. He rendered into English and supplied with notes the *Hand Book of Roman Law* by Dr. Ferdinand Mackeldey, which was published in 1883, and passed through several editions. In 1892, he published a work entitled *The Roman Law of Testaments, Codicils and Gifts in the Event of Death (Mortis Causa Donationes)* based on the Corpus Juris Civilis, and he likewise published a pamphlet, *The Life of Jesus from and Including the Accusation until the Alleged Resurrection* (1890), in which he treated of the trial of Jesus from a lawyer's point of view.

He early evinced public spirit and an interest in the city of Philadelphia. He was one of the pioneers who aided in the establishment of street railways and was elected president of the Lombard and South Streets Railway in 1862, holding that office for twenty years. He was president of the commission in charge of the building of the bridge across the Schuylkill River at South St. (1870), and in 1888 became president of another railway, the Green and Coates Streets Passenger Railroad Company. He was an ardent Whig, a strong supporter of the anti-slavery movement, and in 1856 one of the organizers of the Republican party in the state of Pennsylvania. In 1852, two years prior to the consolidation of the City of Philadelphia under a single mayor, he was a candidate for mayor of the Northern Liberties, but failed of election.

He was an ardent adherent of the Synagogue and joined in much of its charitable work, but principally in work that had to do with religious education. He was secretary and president of the Hebrew Education Society of Philadelphia from 1848 to 1892. He aided the Russian Jews in their difficulties from 1881 on; was president of the board of trustees of the first Jewish College in America, the Maimonides College of Philadelphia, which, however, existed only seven years (1867–73). In 1893, he became president of the board of trustees of Gratz College which was the first Jewish teachers college in America, and he gave the final exhibition of his interest in Jewish learning in his will, by which he bequeathed his entire estate for the foundation of a college in the city of Philadelphia "for the promotion of and instruction in the Hebrew and Cognate languages, and their respective literatures and in the Rabbinical learning and literature," providing further that in the admission of students there should be no distinction on account of creed, color, or sex. Although his will contained no direction as to the name of the College, the Governors decided to call it the "Dropsie College for Hebrew and Cognate Learning." Dropsie was unmarried and during the last fifteen years of his life was blind. He had great vigor and independence of thought and character, and in the years of his blindness refused a companion, which his means would have allowed, going abroad by himself and continuing to take part in the work of the world about him.

[Henry S. Morais, *The Jews of Phila.* (1894); David Sulzberger, in *Pubs. Am. Jewish Hist. Soc. No. 16* (1907) and in *Jewish Encyc.*, vol. V; *Jewish Exponent* (Phila.), *Am. Hebrew* (N. Y.), and *Jewish Comment* (Baltimore), all for July 14 and 21, 1905; family papers and private information.] C. A.

DROWN, THOMAS MESSINGER (Mar. 19, 1842–Nov. 16, 1904), chemist, educator, was the youngest of the three children of William Appleton and Mary (Peirce) Drown of Philadelphia. He attended the public schools of that city and was graduated from the Philadelphia High School in 1859. A keen interest in chemical science led him to establish in his home a laboratory which soon made the rest of the occupants of the house so uncomfortable that his understanding father caused the laboratory to be removed to a small out-building constructed for the purpose. Drown's pronounced liking for chemistry led directly to his study of medicine at the University of Pennsylvania, since at that time chemistry had scarcely begun to maintain an independent existence. He received the doctorate in medicine in 1862, his thesis, "An Essay on Urological Chemistry," being the subject of high commendation. He immediately obtained a coveted opportunity to serve as surgeon on a packet steamer plying between Philadelphia and an English port, but a single round-trip constituted his entire formal career as a medical practitioner, as he determined that happiness for him would be found in the fields of chemistry or metallurgy rather than medicine. He, therefore, devoted the next three years to study, first at the Sheffield Scientific School at Yale, where life-long friendships with Professors Brush and Johnson were begun, and later, at the Lawrence Scientific School, Harvard. His work there with Prof. Wolcott Gibbs had a profound influence upon his later career as a teacher. Gibbs referred to him as "a dexterous worker, attractive in personality, and a gentleman by nature."

Beginning in 1865, Drown spent three and a half years in Europe, studying first at the School of Mines, Freiberg, Saxony, in metallurgical chemistry, and later becoming a pupil of Bunsen at Heidelberg University, a teacher to whom he always paid a high tribute of gratitude for his influence. He married Helen Leighton, at her home in England, shortly before his return to America in 1868. At the age of twenty-seven he had acquired a "thorough theoretical and technical training in chemistry and metallurgy which was almost unique at that time and would be unusual now" (Raymond, *post*). After a brief instructorship at the Lawrence Scientific School, he opened, in 1870, a private analytical and consulting practise in Philadelphia. In 1874, however, he began his fruitful career as a teacher and administrator in the educational field, by accepting a professorship of chemistry at Lafayette College, Easton, Pa. Meanwhile, in 1871, the American Institute of Mining Engineers had been organized at Wilkes-Barre, Pa., and he was elected one of the managers at the first meeting. He resigned this managership in 1873 to accept the much more important secretaryship, with which were combined the duties of editor of the *Transactions,* an office which, while onerous, was congenial to him. He retained this position for ten years and during that time placed the secretarial office on a firm and lasting footing, and brought the *Transactions* to a degree of excellence which was widely acknowledged. Simultaneously with his work for the institute he was establishing a sound system of instruction in chemistry at Lafayette College, based upon a maximum of personal contact between student and teacher and the fundamental thesis that it is the student and not the subject which it is most essential to teach. At the same time he contributed much of value in the development of exact and yet rapid analytical processes for commercial use, which were much needed at that stage of metallurgical developments. A number of his papers were published in the *Transactions* of the institute.

In 1881 he was obliged to sacrifice temporarily his professional plans to meet complications in family affairs, consequent upon the death of his father. He resigned his professorship in 1881 and the secretaryship of the institute in 1883. Throwing himself completely into the new problem, sparing neither strength nor his own funds, and with mature judgment and a high integrity, he brought matters to such an issue that in 1885 he was able to accept a call to the Massachusetts Institute of Technology in Boston, at first as professor of analytical chemistry, and later (1888) as professor in charge of the chemistry department. Still later (1893) the department of chemical engineering was placed in his care. Here, as at Lafayette, he came into close and inspiring contact with his pupils and his previous years of critical survey of analytical work in metallurgical fields while editor served him in good stead. In 1887 he also assumed control of the analytical laboratories established by the Commonwealth of Massachusetts, as a part of a comprehensive plan to examine and protect the water supplies of the state, and also served in an advisory capacity with respect to the plan as a whole, a relationship which continued until his death. No such comprehensive undertaking had previously been attempted, and the pioneer work done in this field under Drown's direction has everywhere been recognized as classic, and has been the foundation for all later work of an allied nature. The results were nearly all published in the annual reports of the State Board of Health.

In 1895, yielding to the appeals of many of his friends and former associates, he accepted the presidency of Lehigh University. He entered upon the duties of the presidential office with exceptional qualifications, having already been successful in both teaching and administration, and possessing a gracious and sympathetic nature, a genial bearing, and a ripe culture. Notwithstanding that his sudden death, after nine years of service, occurred at a time when many of his plans for the university were just coming to fruition, he guided it through a difficult era and secured for it financial support which assured its continued success. His presidential reports, addresses, and other papers on educational topics were constructive and influential. In 1897 he was president of the American Institute of Mining Engineers.

[R. W. Raymond, in *Engineering and Mining Jour.,*

Nov. 24, 1904, and in *Trans. Am. Inst. Mining Engineers,* vol. XXXVI (1906); H. P. Talbot, in *Technology Rev.,* Apr. 1905 and in *Proc. Am. Chemical Soc.,* 1905; Persifor Frazer, in *Jour. Franklin Inst.,* Dec. 1904; J. L. Stewart, in *Alumni Reg.* (Phila.), Jan. 1905; "Thirty-Sixth Ann. Report of the State Board of Health of Mass.," *Public Docs. of Mass. No. 34* (1904); *The Brown and White* (South Bethlehem, Pa.), special edition, Nov. 16, 1904; personal recollections of the writer, covering nineteen years of intimate acquaintance.]

H. P. T.

DRUILLETTES, GABRIEL (Sept. 29, 1610–Apr. 8, 1681), Jesuit missionary, envoy to New England, emigrated from France to Canada in 1643. During the ensuing eight years he endured the hardships of life among the wandering savages north of the St. Lawrence River. At one time he became totally blind because of smoke in the wigwam and sun on the snow. "Filth was my cook and constant companion," he complained. Nevertheless, he accomplished his duties, said mass each day, baptized many savages, and in 1648, was sent to establish a mission on the Kennebec River for the Abnakis. There he became a friend of the Plymouth agent, John Winslow. In 1648 he visited Boston, partly in answer to Winthrop's proposal of 1647 for intercolonial trade, chiefly to obtain help from New England to subdue the Iroquois Indians, whose hostilities were ruining the colony on the St. Lawrence. Received with cordiality by the Massachusetts and Plymouth authorities, he returned to Canada to obtain official authorization for his mission. In September 1651, with Sieur Jean Paul Godefroy, he journeyed to New Haven to appear at a meeting of the commissioners of the New England Confederation. There he plead his cause before the representatives of the four New England colonies. "M. Gabriel Drwellets," writes the chronicler, "Improved his abilities to the utmost to perswade the Commissioners that the English collonies might Joyne in the warr against the Mohauks," but after weighty consideration the Confederation denied his plea. This instance of intercolonial comity, however, throws a pleasing light on the character and manners of the French missionary.

After returning to Quebec in April 1652, he was on service in the neighboring missions until 1656 when he started for the West with the Ottawa Indians, but was driven back and his companion killed by Iroquois. In 1660 Father Dablon [*q.v.*] took Druillettes with him on an extended trip to the North by way of the Saguenay and Lake St. John. Ten years later Druillettes again essayed the voyage to the Northwest, this time successfully, and passed several years in charge of the mission at Sault Ste. Marie. There he was very popular with both white and red men, was present at the pageant of possession in 1671, and retired to Quebec (where he died) only when age rendered him unfit for life in the wilderness. He had a reputation for great sanctity, he was a remarkable linguist, and a man of deep charity and self-sacrifice. He was for a short time the teacher of Marquette [*q.v.*], and whether on the Kennebec, the Saguenay, or the St. Mary's, was beloved both by the Indians and by his fellow missionaries.

[An account by Druillettes of his first visit to New England is in R. G. Thwaites, *The Jesuit Relations* (1896–1903), XXXVI, 83–111. His visit to New Haven is described in *Records of the Colony of New Plymouth,* IX (1859), 199–203. The sketch in *Jesuit Relations,* XXIII, 327, is incomplete. T. J. Campbell, *Pioneer Priests of North America* (1911), III, 70–109, gives an excellent account of the events of his life.]

L. P. K.

DRUMGOOLE, JOHN CHRISTOPHER (Aug. 15, 1816–Mar. 28, 1888), Catholic priest, was born near Granard, County Longford, Ireland, and died in New York City. When he was eight years old, his widowed mother, who had preceded him to America, sent for him to join her in New York. There he took up the trade of a cobbler. Of a devout nature even in childhood, he attracted the notice of his priests and was after a while made teacher in a kind of mission Sunday-school. In 1844, on the invitation of one of his clerical friends, he became a sexton. For a short period around 1850, in addition to his work as sexton, he helped run a small bookstore near his church. This was the only break in the routine of his life till 1863 when he began a course of study preparatory to entering the ministry—first at St. Francis Xavier College in New York, next at St. John's College in Fordham, and finally, in 1865, at the Seminary of Our Lady of Angels, near Niagara Falls. He was ordained in May 1869 and sent as a priest to the church where he had formerly been sexton. His passion to be useful had long since put him in contact with the victims of squalor and wretchedness, and in the late sixties he considered devoting his life to mission work among the freedmen. In 1871, however, he found in New York a type of work for which he was superbly fitted. A lodging house for waifs and newsboys, inaugurated about a year before under Catholic auspices, was failing to accomplish what had been expected. The new priest volunteered to try his hand at making it justify itself. Before he assumed control in the fall of 1871 the number of lodgers had fallen to fifteen, but by the end of 1873 it was necessary to increase the original quarters three times. The value of his work was widely recognized, and in November 1875 his hold on the public confidence was attested by the fact that he raised nearly

$15,000. After this, money came so freely at his call that by the time of his death he had spent on his charitable enterprises about a million dollars, and was caring for from sixteen hundred to two thousand children. His most notable monument is the Mission of the Immaculate Virgin, built in 1881. It was his theory that no youngsters are incorrigible provided they have properly displayed before them as a model the life of one who is "poor, honest, industrious, hard-working and virtuous" (Dougherty, p. 327). "From my experience," he said, "I find that with proper care boys can all be reclaimed" (Dougherty, p. 327). His entire career derived its character and strength from his deep piety and expansive human sympathy.

[J. E. Dougherty, "John Christopher Drumgoole," in *The Charities Rev.*, Sept. 1898; *Cath. Encyc.* (1909); *N. Y. Herald*, Mar. 29, 1888.] J. D. W.

DRURY, JOHN BENJAMIN (Aug. 15, 1838–Mar. 21, 1909), Reformed (Dutch) clergyman, editor, was born in Rhinebeck, N. Y., the son of Alfred and Maria Ann (Schultz) Drury. He graduated from Rutgers College in 1858 and from the New Brunswick Theological Seminary in 1861, was licensed to preach by the Classis of Poughkeepsie, and gained his first ministerial experience in home mission work in Davenport, Ia. In 1864 he returned to his native region as pastor of the First Reformed (Dutch) Church at Ghent, Columbia County, N. Y. On Sept. 2, 1869, he married Henrietta Wynkoop Keese, who outlived him. While attending year in and year out to the duties of a rural minister, he found time for study and reflection and grew steadily too in the esteem of his colleagues. In 1883 he was the Vedder lecturer at the College and Seminary in New Brunswick; in 1885 he taught in the summer school of the American Institute of Christian Philosophy; and in 1886 he was president of the General Synod of the Dutch Reformed Church. He had risen to a position of influence rather through his common sense and trustworthiness, his courtesy and friendly, helpful disposition, than through any showier gifts, for he was not a notably good speaker and had written but little. In 1884 he had published a small book on *Truths and Untruths of Evolution*, which was regarded as somewhat liberal in tendency, and which had shown many a Reformed clergyman that religion was not served by vilifying Charles Darwin and attempting to impugn solidly established facts. Two parish histories and a few articles had also come from his pen, but writing was for him arduous labor. To the end of his life he composed with difficulty, and his articles were characterized more by an obvious effort to be clear and accurate than by any grace of style. His chief work, nevertheless, was to be in religious journalism. In 1887 he resigned his charge and, with the issue of Dec. 7, assumed the editorship of the *Christian Intelligencer*. The *Intelligencer* had recently passed through bankruptcy and, confronted by the growing competition of secular newspapers and magazines, faced a severe struggle for survival. Its continuance seemed essential to the welfare of the Reformed Church. Drury undertook to keep the paper alive. For a long time he had a deficit to deal with at the end of each year, but he persisted in spite of discouragements and ultimately made the paper self-supporting. On the literary side the *Intelligencer* maintained a high standard among religious journals. Drury was a delegate to the Council of Reformed Churches holding the Presbyterian System at London in 1888, at Toronto in 1892, at Washington in 1899, and at Liverpool in 1904. He died after a short illness at his home in New Brunswick, N. J.

[E. T. Corwin, *Manual of the Reformed Church in America* (4th ed., 1902); *Who's Who in America, 1908–09*; J. H. Raven, ed., *Biog. Record Theol. Sem. New Brunswick 1784–1911* (1912); *Cat. of the Officers and Alumni of Rutgers Coll. 1766–1909* (1909); *Christian Intelligencer*, Mar. 17, 24, 31, Apr. 7, 14, 21, 28, 1909.] G. H. G.

DRYDEN, JOHN FAIRFIELD (Aug. 7, 1839–Nov. 24, 1911), senator, pioneer of industrial insurance in America, was born on a farm, at Temple Mills, near Farmington, Me., the son of John and Elizabeth (Butterfield) Dryden. His paternal ancestors came to New England from Northamptonshire, England, in the seventeenth century. He entered Yale College in 1861, but his health broke down during the closing year of his course and he was compelled to abandon his studies. In recognition of his subsequent achievements the university conferred on him the degree of M.A. and entered his name as one of the graduates of the class of 1865. Possibly his ill health may have influenced the choice of his life-work, for soon after leaving Yale he became interested in life insurance in particular relation to the practical solution of the economic problems of the poor. He made a careful study of the methods of the Prudential Assurance Company of London, which had met with considerable success in writing industrial insurance. He himself defined industrial insurance as "life insurance for small amounts, chiefly on the lives of wage-earners and members of their immediate families, with premiums payable weekly and collected from the houses of the insured" (*Addresses and Papers*, p. 85). In 1873 he settled in

Newark, N. J., secured the cooperation of a small group of able men, including Leslie D. Ward, a young physician, and Noah F. Blanchard, a leading leather manufacturer, and wrote the first policy of the Prudential Friendly Society on Nov. 10, 1875. No time could have been less propitious for the launching of a new project, for it was the beginning of an era of depression in industry and commerce, and the discouragements that attended the opening years of this pioneer company would have been fatal to a man less sure of himself or less resolute of purpose than was Dryden. From an insignificant beginning in the basement of the State Bank Building on Broad St., Dryden lived to see The Prudential Insurance Company (so named in 1878) advance under his leadership to a foremost place among the life-insurance companies of the world. The secret of his success was his clear grasp of fundamental principles, combined with indefatigable industry and a remarkable capacity for details. He believed in the practical utility of his plans to provide for the American working people a better and more secure form of thrift than prevailed in 1875 and insurance history has proved the wisdom of his policy.

A Republican all his life, he took an active interest in public affairs. On Jan. 29, 1902, he was elected to the United States Senate, following the death of Senator Sewell. He was opposed by several of the strongest men of the Republican party in New Jersey and the contest resulting in his election was one of the most memorable in the political history of the state. He made a notable record in the Senate as a member of the Committee on the Isthmian Canal, and his speech of June 14, 1906, was a decisive factor in securing the adoption of the lock-canal plan. His expression in 1902 of his views on Chinese exclusion, and his bill providing for federal regulation of insurance were other outstanding evidences of his ability. In 1907, as a candidate for reëlection, he was the choice of the voters in the primary but his opponents were strong enough to produce a deadlock in the joint meeting of the legislature which continued for two weeks. Then, his health breaking down, Dryden yielded to the advice of his physicians and family and withdrew from the contest. In 1909 a collection of his writings was published, under the title, *Addresses and Papers on Life Insurance and Other Subjects.*

He was married on Apr. 7, 1864, to Cynthia Jennings Fairchild, and they were the parents of two children. In personal appearance he was tall, erect, and of distinguished bearing, with clear-cut, high-bred face, in his later years accentuated by silvery beard and moustache, and head crowned with snow-white hair.

[*Statement Addressed to the Republican Members of the Legislature of N. J.—Feb. 4, 1907* (Newark, 1907), by Senator J. F. Dryden; F. L. Hoffman, *Hist. of the Prudential Insurance Co. of America* (1900); W. S. Myers, *Fifty Years of the Prudential* (1927); *John Fairfield Dryden* (1912), pub. by The Prudential Co.; *Proc. N. J. Hist. Soc.*, 3 ser., IX (1914), 118–20; W. E. Sackett, *Modern Battles of Trenton* (1914), vol. II; *Obit. Record Grads. Yale Univ.* (1912); obituary notices in *N. Y. Herald, N. Y. Tribune*, and *N. Y. Times*, Nov. 25, 1911.]

C.R.E., Jr.

DUANE, ALEXANDER (Sept. 1, 1858–June 10, 1926), ophthalmologist, was born in Malone, N. Y., the son of Gen. James Chatham Duane [*q.v.*], military engineer, by his wife Harriet, daughter of Gen. Henry Brewerton of West Point. Because of the uncertain life of an army officer, Alexander Duane was tutored at home, being guided in literature by his mother, a woman of taste and wide reading, and in mathematics by his father. He attended the high school at Portland, Me., while his father was stationed there, and later went to St. Mark's School from which, at the age of fifteen, he entered Union College. He was graduated in 1878 with highest honors, including election to the Phi Beta Kappa society. During his academic years he laid an excellent foundation in languages, especially in German and Latin, and to the end of his life he was able to read and write Latin with ease and pleasure. His son, while at college, often received from him letters in that tongue. He spent a year at the Albany Medical College but transferred to the College of Physicians and Surgeons of New York, where he received his medical degree in 1881. After a year as interne at the New York Hospital, during which he utilized his odd moments by writing medical terms for *Webster's Dictionary*, he began to practise in New York as assistant first to a Dr. Ranney and later to Dr. George Stevens. After a sojourn in Norfolk, Va., in 1888, he worked with Dr. Hermann Knapp [*q.v.*] of New York for two and a half years. Duane's thorough academic training in mathematics and the languages made it possible for him to render peculiar and valuable services to the science of ophthalmology. His mathematics fitted him for dealing with abstruse problems in physiological optics, refraction, and muscular weakness, and to all these subjects he made notable contributions (see especially: "Some New Tests for Insufficiencies of the Ocular Muscles," *New York Medical Journal*, August 1889; *A New Classification of Motor Anomalies of the Eye* (1897); "Paralysis of the Superior Rectus and its Bearing on the Theory of Muscular Insufficiency," *Ar-*

chives of Ophthalmology, 1884, XXIII, 61–84). He also contributed to G. E. de Schweinitz and B. A. Randall's *An American Text-Book of Diseases of the Eye, Ear, Nose and Throat* (1899) and to W. C. Posey and W. G. Spiller's *Eye and Nervous System* (1906), and to J. E. Weeks's *A Treatise on Diseases of the Eye* (1910). As a linguist his greatest service was the translation of the eight successive editions of Ernest Fuchs's *Textbook of Ophthalmology,* the first American edition appearing in 1892 and the eighth and last in 1924. He contributed medical terms to successive editions of *Webster's International Dictionary,* to Foster's *Encyclopedic Dictionary of Medicine,* and to Murray's *New English Dictionary* (Oxford). During the Spanish-American War he served in the navy as lieutenant (junior grade), and during the World War he was acting signal officer of the U. S. S. *Granite State.*

He was a quiet, retiring, and somewhat sensitive personality, much given to hard and persistent work but taking pleasure in the indulgence of his wide literary tastes and in his love of history, astronomy, botany, and music. His photographs show a clear-eyed, simple, kindly face. On July 14, 1891, Duane married Susan Williams Galt of Norfolk, Va., by whom he had three children. His oldest son was killed in action in the World War.

[Two excellent biographies of Duane appeared shortly after his death: J. W. White and others, *Arch. Ophthal.,* 1927, LVI, 66–73; C. Berens, *Am. Jour. Ophthal.,* 1926, 3 ser., IX, 917–22; see also *Who's Who in America,* 1924–25; *N. Y. Times, N. Y. Herald Tribune,* June 12, 1926.] J. F. F.

DUANE, JAMES (Feb. 6, 1733–Feb. 1, 1797), jurist, was born in New York City, probably at the corner of the then King and Queen Sts. He was the son of Anthony Duane (1682–1747), a prosperous New York merchant of Irish birth who came to New York soon after 1700, and of Althea Kettletas, his second wife, daughter of Abraham Kettletas, of Dutch descent, also a well-to-do merchant. James Duane probably received his early education from the Rev. Richard Charlton, a classical tutor, catechist of Trinity Church and later rector of St. Andrews, Staten Island. Without college or university training, he studied law in the office of James Alexander [*q.v.*], presumably from 1747 till his admission to the bar, in August 1754. His private practise grew with astonishing rapidity and embraced a wide variety of cases in all the courts of the province. In the famous case of *Forsey* vs. *Cunningham* (1763), originally an assault and battery case with the enormous damages of £1,500, he successfully maintained that no appeal from the provincial supreme court, in civil cases, lay to the governor in council—long a moot question. This was a defeat for Lieut.-Gov. Colden, whom, however, Duane defended successfully some seven years later in an extraordinary case when the Crown, in the person of Lord Dunmore, sued Colden in chancery for half a year's fees while Colden had been acting in Lord Dunmore's stead. The latter, as chancellor, presided over the trial when he was himself the plaintiff. It was regarded as an extremely courageous act on Duane's part to undertake the defense, several other well-known lawyers having refused the case.

Prerevolutionary activities in New York found Duane definitely on the conservative side. He was one of the prominent citizens who went about among the people attempting to quell the Stamp Act mob in November 1765. In November 1766 he was "busily employed in a new remonstrance to the Parliament respecting our trade" (Duane to R. Livingston, Jr., Nov. 15, 1766, Redmond private collection of Livingston papers). In 1768 he successfully defended the Tory candidate for the Assembly, James Jauncey, from accusations of corruption brought by his radical rival, John Morin Scott. On May 16, 1774, he was appointed to the Committee of Correspondence (Committee of Fifty-one), which on July 4 nominated him one of five delegates to the forthcoming Continental Congress, to which he was subsequently elected after much radical opposition. At the Congress he was a member of the committee which drew up the statement of the rights of the colonists, being largely responsible for the mildness of its tone, and on Sept. 28 he seconded Galloway's plan of union, defending his reactionary stand by stating his belief that the right of regulating trade lay with Parliament because of the "local circumstances of the colonies, and their disconnection with each other" (*The Works of John Adams,* 1850, II, 389). He did, however, sign the "Association" or non-importation agreement on Oct. 20, 1774, though he considered that it went too far. He sat in the New York Provincial Convention and was by it elected to the Second Continental Congress; was a member of the New York Committee of Sixty to carry out the "Association" and of the subsequent Committee of One Hundred. He sat in the Continental Congress almost continuously till 1783, serving on a large number and great variety of committees. His chief services were in connection with financial and Indian affairs and he assisted in making the final draft of the Articles of Confederation. During May and June 1781, violent attacks on his patriotism and accusations of loyalism appeared in the Philadelphia *Freeman's Journal,* but after statements were offered on his behalf by several of his colleagues, including John Jay, Alexander McDougall, William Floyd, and Philip Livingston, the New York Assembly (June 25) and Senate (June 27) passed votes of confidence in him. He entered New York City on its evacuation by the British, Nov. 25, 1783, with Washington and Gov. Clinton, as a member of the Council of the latter. On Feb. 4, 1784, he was appointed mayor of New York, serving till September 1789, during which time his chief duties, both as mayor and as *ex officio* presiding officer of the mayor's court, were in connection with the rehabilitation of the city after the ravages of the British. Washington appointed him the first federal judge of the district of New York in September 1789, which position he held till his permanent retirement from public life on account of ill health in March 1794. He served in the Poughkeepsie Convention of 1788, where he was an ardent advocate of ratification of the Constitution, and sat in the New York Senate almost continuously from 1782 till his resignation, Jan. 27, 1790, to become a federal judge. One of his most intensive interests throughout a long period was in connection with the Vermont-New Hampshire boundary difficulties, in the course of which he represented the "Yorkers" in many private suits, and was their constant advocate before Congress. At one time a reward of £15 was offered by the "Vermonters" for his capture (*Connecticut Courant,* Feb. 5, 1772).

Perhaps his greatest non-professional interest was in land development. Having inherited a large tract of land from his father in the present Schenectady County, he continued to purchase in that immediate neighborhood and elsewhere in the Mohawk Valley till late in life. He was also deeply interested in the Vermont lands and was a heavy loser in the final settlement of that controversy. He was unremitting and in the main successful in his efforts to colonize his Mohawk Valley lands, selling and renting farms on easy terms. He had already begun development before 1765 when he imported a group of Germans from Pennsylvania. The township of Duanesburg (created Mar. 13, 1765) was almost entirely owned by him (portions of it are still in possession of his descendants), but that town did not cover all his holdings.

During his entire life he was vitally interested in Trinity Church, New York, and in King's (later Columbia) College. His domestic life was peculiarly happy. He married, Oct. 21, 1759, Mary, daughter of Robert Livingston, Jr., "third lord" of Livingston manor, by whom he had ten children. Five of these grew to maturity and survived him. Retiring to Schenectady to live in 1795, Duane died there, very suddenly, on the morning of Feb. 1, 1797, and is buried beneath the church at Duanesburg.

[A memoir by Samuel W. Jones appeared in *Doc. Hist. of the State of N. Y., IV* (1851), 1,061. A few copies of this, privately printed (1852), are extant. Some Duane letters were published in *Southern Hist. Asso. Pubs.,* 1903–06, and some of his reports in regard to the boundary controversy in *N. Y. Hist. Soc. Colls.,* vols. II, III (1870–71). The mass of material concerning him is in manuscript form in the possession of the N. Y. Hist. Soc. Diaries, account books, ledgers, etc., privately owned by Mr. Wilmot Townsend Cox, Mr. Geo. Wm. Featherstonhaugh, and Mr. Wm. North Duane have also been consulted, and together with the MSS. in the N. Y. Hist. Soc., form the basis of this sketch.]
S. H. J. S.

DUANE, JAMES CHATHAM (June 30, 1824–Nov. 8, 1897), military and civil engineer, son of James and Harriet (Constable) Duane, was born at Schenectady, N. Y. His grandfather, James Duane [*q.v.*], was a member of the Continental Congress, first mayor of New York after the Revolution, member of the convention that adopted the Constitution, and judge of the United States district court at New York. James C. Duane graduated from Union College in 1844 and from the United States Military Academy in 1848. He served until the Civil War as a subaltern in the Corps of Engineers, United States Army, taking part in the famous Utah expedition under Gen. Albert Sidney Johnston in 1858. When McClellan was placed in command of the armies of the United States and began the organization of the Army of the Potomac, he assigned to Capt. Duane the organization of its engineer and bridge equipage. To this work Duane devoted himself in the winter of 1861–62 and designed the various types of ponton trains and the engineer equipment for the construction of fixed bridges, siege and field works which were so successfully operated during the war. He also organized the battalion of engineers authorized by Congress. With his battalion and equipment he took part in the Peninsular campaign and demonstrated its efficiency at the siege of Yorktown and in the subsequent operations.

When McClellan reorganized his army for the Antietam campaign, Duane was assigned as chief engineer of the army and remained with it until McClellan was relieved. In 1863 he was chief engineer of the Department of the South, until recalled in July again to become chief engineer of the Army of the Potomac, which position he held until the close of the war, taking part in all its operations from the Potomac to

Appomattox. He had never sought a commission in the volunteers and was therefore only a major in 1865, although he received the brevets of lieutenant-colonel, colonel, and brigadier-general in the regular army for distinguished professional services, especially in the siege of Petersburg.

After the war he was engaged in the construction of many of the more important works of the Corps of Engineers—fortifications, lighthouses, and river and harbor improvements, and was a member of the Board of Engineers for Fortifications and River and Harbor Improvements and of the Light House Board. In 1886 he was promoted to brigadier-general and chief of engineers, United States Army. After two years of service in this capacity he retired, June 30, 1888. Shortly thereafter he was appointed a member of the Croton Aqueduct Commission by the mayor of New York, and served as president of the commission until his death. In 1850 he married Harriet Whitehorn Brewerton, daughter of Gen. Henry Brewerton, then superintendent of the United States Military Academy. They had three sons. A distinguished fellow officer (Gen. Cyrus B. Comstock) who served with him during and after the war said: "General Duane possessed that sound good sense which can look at all sides of a question without prepossessions, and which can see the great features of it, without giving details too much importance, gifts that are rare. Of unchanging and inevitable modesty, he accepted the duty that was assigned to him and did it faithfully, instead of pushing his own merits on his superiors or on the public. One needed to know him well to know his full value, and then one classed him among the just, faithful, able men whom to know strengthens one's faith in mankind."

[Cyrus B. Comstock, in *Twenty-ninth Am. Reunion Asso. Grads. U. S. Mil. Acad.* (1898); G. W. Cullum, *Biog. Reg.* (3rd ed., 1891); *Official Records (Army)*.]

G. J. F.

DUANE, WILLIAM (May 17, 1760–Nov. 24, 1835), journalist and politician, was born near Lake Champlain, N. Y., of Irish parentage, his mother being a Sarsfield, descendant of the Irish patriot. On his father's death in 1765, he was taken by his mother to Ireland where, disinherited by her, a Catholic, because of his marriage to Catharine Corcoran, a Protestant, he learned the printer's trade. Going to India in 1787, he established the *Indian World* at Calcutta, which brought him both prestige and fortune. Because of his denunciations of the methods of the East India Company, and his espousal of grievances of army officers, he was arrested without a charge, deported without trial, and his property was confiscated. Returning to London where he served as parliamentary reporter for the *General Advertiser*, later merged with the *Times*, he vainly sought the restitution of his property through Parliament and the courts. Finally despairing of justice, he left England in disgust, and took up his residence in Philadelphia, where he became associated with Benjamin Franklin Bache [*q.v.*] in editing the *Aurora*. In September 1798 Bache died; Duane succeeded him in the editorship and immediately made the *Aurora* the most powerful organ of the Jeffersonians. His genius in controversy and management, his courage and audacity, the sincerity and intensity of his convictions, and his virile style of writing, made him the most effective journalist of his time. Adams and Pickering, wincing under his lash, exchanged views on the possibility of his deportation under the Alien Law. In the spring of 1799 he was arrested on the charge of creating a seditious riot by offering for signatures, petitions for the repeal of the Alien Law, but he was promptly acquitted in the state courts. Because of his exposure of the brutality of the undisciplined and idle volunteer soldiery mobilized for the war with France, projected by the Hamiltonian wing of the Federalists, he was murderously assailed by armed men, and his property saved from destruction only by the timely arrival of a group of Democrats. In the fall of 1799 he was indicted under the Sedition Law, but the trial was postponed until the following June, and then again postponed, and the charge dismissed when Jefferson acceded to the presidency. All these desperate attempts at intimidation failed of their purpose, for he continued in his course with unabated energy. Perhaps his most important service to the nation was his exposure of the secret plan of the Federalists to prevent the election of Jefferson through the notorious Ross Election Bill. Copies of this measure, then pending in the Senate behind closed doors, were sent him under cover, and its publication with vigorous comments so aroused the public wrath that it was defeated. No single person did more to discredit the projected war with France over the X. Y. Z. incident, to make the Alien and Sedition Laws abhorrent, to arouse and munition the masses, and make the triumph of Jefferson in 1800 inevitable.

With Jefferson's election, the career of Duane moved toward an anti-climax. The removal of the capital to Washington deprived his paper of its advantage. The editor, encouraged by Jefferson and Gallatin, opened a store in Washington in expectation of the government contract for printing and stationery, but the plans miscarried, and Duane never forgave the slighting of his claims. He soon broke with Gallatin, and ultimately turned on Madison and Monroe. In local politics, where he remained a power, he led the radical or anti-judiciary faction against Gov. Thomas McKean [*q.v.*], whom he had earlier supported. To Jefferson, however, he remained a faithful follower and devoted friend. His idol sought in numerous ways to serve him, appointing him lieutenant-colonel of rifles in July 1808, and soliciting subscriptions to relieve him of financial embarrassment in 1811. Duane served as adjutant-general through the War of 1812, and continued in the editorship of the *Aurora* until 1822, when he retired to travel in South America. The result was a volume, *A Visit to Colombia in the Years 1822 & 1823* (1826). On his return, he was made prothonotary of the supreme court of Pennsylvania, for the eastern district, and he held this position until his death. In his last years he made an unsuccessful attempt to revive the *Aurora* to fight the National Bank. He wrote several books of indifferent merit on military science, including *Military Dictionary* (1810), *An Epitome of Arts and Science* (1811), *Handbook for Riflemen* (1813), *Handbook for Infantry* (1813). Jefferson, whose friendship he retained through the vagaries of his later years, described him with fidelity in a letter to William Wirt: "I believe Duane to be a very honest man, and sincerely republican; but his passions are stronger than his prudence, and his personal as well as general antipathies render him very intolerant" ("The Letters of William Duane," *post,* p. 259). His first wife died in 1798, a few months before the death of Bache, and in 1800 Duane married Margaret (Markoe) Bache, widow of his colleague and owner of the *Aurora.* By her he had five children.

[There are numerous references to Duane in Frederic Hudson, *Journalism in the U. S.* (1873); G. H. Payne, *Hist. of Journalism in the U. S.* (1920); *Writings of Thomas Jefferson* (1903), vols. XII and XIII; *Works of John Adams,* vols. IX and X (1856); C. G. Bowers, *Jefferson and Hamilton* (1925). Francis Wharton, *State Trials of the U. S.* (1849), pp. 345–91, gives an illuminating report on his trial for creating a riot. "The Letters of Wm. Duane," *Proc. Mass. Hist. Soc.,* 2 ser. XX, 257–394, and Allen C. Clark, "Wm. Duane" in *Records of the Columbia Hist. Soc.,* IX (1906), 14–62, throw an interesting light on his later career.]

C. G. B.

DUANE, WILLIAM JOHN (May 9, 1780–Sept. 26, 1865), lawyer, was born at Clonmel, County Tipperary, Ireland, the son of William Duane [*q.v.*] and his wife, Catharine Corcoran. His early youth was passed in London where his father was employed as a printer, but in 1787 the latter went out to Calcutta to engage in newspaper work, and William John with his mother returned to Clonmel. There he attended a private school for fifteen months—the only schooling he ever received, his mother having been his first teacher. When his father returned from India to become a Parliamentary reporter in London, the family was reunited there, and the boy frequently visited the gallery of the House of Commons to listen to the debates. When in 1796 William Duane moved his family to Philadelphia and assumed editorial charge of the *True American,* William John entered its composing room. Two years later, when the elder Duane became editor of the *Aurora,* he joined the staff of that newspaper, and commenced actively to interest himself in public affairs. In 1806 he relinquished newspaper work, and became the partner of William Levis, a paper merchant. He soon came to the front in local politics and in 1809 was elected to the Pennsylvania House of Representatives on the Republican—later Democratic—ticket. In the same year he wrote, *The Law of Nations, Investigated in a Popular Manner: Addressed to the Farmers of the United States.* In the legislature he was a prominent figure, being chairman of the Committee on Roads and Inland Navigation, and the committee to consider the case of Gideon Olmstead, but on seeking reëlection in 1810 he was defeated owing to party dissensions. In the following year he published, *Letters, Addressed to the People of Pennsylvania Respecting the Internal Improvement of the Commonwealth by means of Roads and Canals,* which had appeared in the columns of the *Aurora.* In 1812 he retired from business to take up the study of law in Philadelphia, and was again elected to the legislature, where he resumed the chairmanship of the Committee on Roads and Canals. He was admitted to the bar June 13, 1815, and through his political associations and diverse public interests, soon acquired an extensive legal connection. He was a candidate for Congress in 1816 and for the state legislature in 1817, but the division in the Democratic party still continued and he was defeated on each occasion. In 1819, however, amity was again obtained and he was elected to the State House of Representatives where he became chairman of the Committee on Banks. He had in the previous year published, *Observations on the Importance of Improving the Navigation of the River Schuylkill for the Purpose of Connecting it with the Susquehanna,* and in the legislature he was indefatigable in promoting improvement of internal means of transportation and communication, becoming chairman of the select committee relating to domestic economy and general stagnation of business. In 1820 he was appointed prosecuting attorney for the mayor's court, a position which he retained for three years, his only fault, it was said, being his leniency to petty offenders. In 1824 he refused a nomination for Congress but later resumed his political activities, becoming a member of the Democratic Committee of Correspondence for Philadelphia in 1828. In 1829 he was chosen a member of the Select Council of Philadelphia. His standing in the party was now high, and in 1831 President Jackson nominated him one of the commissioners under the treaty with Denmark. In May 1833 he accepted the office of secretary of the treasury in Jackson's cabinet and entered upon his duties June 1. Some time previous the President had determined that the government deposits should be withdrawn from the United States Bank and placed with the state banks. This could only be effected by the secretary of the treasury for the time being; the previous incumbent, having declined to accede to Jackson's request, had been transferred to the State Department, and the vacant office conferred upon Duane in the hope that he would be more amenable. He refused, however, to make the transfer prior to the meeting of Congress, and was accordingly dismissed by the President, Sept. 23, having held office less than four months. Duane in 1834 vindicated his conduct in a pamphlet addressed to the people of the United States and subsequently published a well-documented statement of the history of his appointment, tenure of office, and the circumstances of his dismissal entitled, *Narrative and Correspondence Concerning the Removal of the Deposites* [*sic*] *and Occurrences Connected Therewith* (1838). He returned to Philadelphia and practically withdrew from public life but did not resume active practise, only occasionally accepting retainers in the orphan's court from old clients. He was an intimate friend of Stephen Girard [*q.v.*], acted as solicitor for him, drafted his will, in which he was nominated an executor, and after Girard's death in 1831 was actively engaged in the settlement of the estate. The last public office which he held was that of director of Girard College.

As a lawyer his skill in draftsmanship was demonstrated in the course of the contest anent Girard's will, and the trust he inspired was exemplified in the large testamentary and other administrations which he handled in his later days. He was resolutely opposed to litigation, invariably striving to compromise disputes, and only occasionally appeared in court. Despite his desultory education he possessed a broad, though not profound, culture and a wide acquaintance with current thought. His wife was Deborah, daughter of Richard Bache [*q.v.*] of Philadelphia and grand-daughter of Franklin.

[*Biog. Memoir of Wm. J. Duane* (1868); *Biog. Encyc. of Pa. of the Nineteenth Century* (1874), p. 54; J. T. Scharf and T. Westcott, *Hist. of Phila.* (1884), II, 1,137; *Pa. Mag. of Hist. and Biog.*, Jan. 1930.]

H. W. H. K.

DUBBS, JOSEPH HENRY (Oct. 5, 1838–Apr. 1, 1910), clergyman of the Reformed Church (German), college professor, church historian, was a son of Rev. Joseph S. Dubbs and his second wife, Eleanor. His paternal grandfather and his great-grandfather were gunsmiths. The latter, of German stock, is said to have come to America from Switzerland in 1732, settling in Lower Milford Township, Lehigh County, Pa. Joseph Henry Dubbs was born in a rural parsonage, in North Whitehall Township, Lehigh County, about seven miles north of what is now the city of Allentown, his father being a minister of the Reformed Church of that place. Dubbs spoke both English and German from childhood. The reader of his autobiography receives the impression that his boyhood life was somewhat abnormal and lonely. At fifteen he was a sophomore in Franklin and Marshall College, Lancaster, Pa., where he graduated in 1856. In 1859 he graduated from the Theological Seminary of the Reformed Church, situated at that time in Mercersburg, Pa. When about twenty-one years of age he became assistant to his father in the pastorate and one year later the sole pastor of Zion's Reformed Church, Allentown. On Sept. 22, 1863, he married Mary Louisa Wilson of Allentown, daughter of Thomas and Elizabeth (Martin) Wilson. From 1863 to 1871 he was pastor of Trinity Reformed Church, Pottstown, Pa., and from 1871 to 1875, of Christ Reformed Church, Philadelphia. In the latter year he was elected to the professorship of history and archeology in Franklin and Marshall College, which position he held up to the time of his death. Here he was active for about thirty-five years as a teacher and research student, especially along the lines of denominational ecclesiastical history and of local history. His publications, both numerous and valuable, include: *Historic Manual of the Reformed Church in the United States* (1888); *Home Ballads and Metrical Versions* (1888); *Why Am I Reformed?* (1889); *History of the Reformed Church, German* (1895), in American Church History Series; *Leaders of the Reformation* (1898); *The Reformed Church in Pennsylvania* (1902); *History of Franklin and Marshall College* (1903); "Reformed Church in the United States," in

Hastings' Encyclopedia of Religion and Ethics, vol. X (1919), and fragments of autobiography, published in the *College Student* of Franklin and Marshall College (vol. XXVII, 1907, pp. 166–71; vol. XXVIII, 1908, pp. 149–62; vol. XXX, 1909, pp. 87–97). It was said of him at the time of his death that in his field of historical study he had few equals and no superiors, and it is to be added that he is still unexcelled.

Dubbs had a wide range of interests far beyond his specialty. His enthusiasm was unbounded and transmissive; his memory was remarkable for its retentiveness; and he worked with an industry that was sustained and unwearied almost to the close of his life. He had at ready command a rich and varied fund of witty and humorous stories which he could relate as few can. In his nature there was a marked poetic strain; his personality was attractive and winsome. His students admired him because of his enthusiasm and the wide range of his scholarship, and loved him because of his genial spirit and the personal interest he took in them, but they also at times took reprehensible advantage of his leniency.

[Obituary in the *Daily New Era* (Lancaster, Pa.), Apr. 1, 1910, containing the most complete list of his writings ever published; *Reformed Church Messenger,* Apr. 7, 1910; *Who's Who in America,* 1910–11; *Almanac for the Reformed Church in the United States,* 1911; "In Memoriam," by John S. Stahr, president of Franklin and Marshall College, in the *Reformed Church Rev.,* Oct. 1910; biographical sketch by G. T. Ettinger in the *Pennsylvania-German Soc. Proc. and Addresses,* XX (1911), 48–50.] I. H. DeL.

DUBOIS, AUGUSTUS JAY (Apr. 25, 1849–Oct. 19, 1915), civil engineer, was born at Newton Falls, Ohio, the son of Henry Augustus and Catherine Helena (Jay) Dubois. Both his mother and father were of French Huguenot descent. His father was a physician, holding his degree in medicine from Columbia College, while his mother was the grand-daughter of Chief Justice John Jay. After attending the Hopkins Grammar School at New Haven, Conn., Augustus Dubois studied civil engineering in the Sheffield Scientific School at Yale, from which he was graduated in 1869. He continued his studies at Yale for four more years, securing his degree of C.E. in 1870 and that of Ph.D. in 1873. Eighteen months of advanced study at the Royal Mining Academy in Freiberg, Saxony, followed. From 1875 until his death in 1915 he was a teacher of engineering subjects. For two years he was professor of civil and mechanical engineering at Lehigh University. In 1877 he went to Sheffield Scientific School as a teacher of mechanical engineering but in 1884 he was appointed professor of civil engineering there, a position which he filled until his death. He contributed to both the theory and literature of engineering. While doing graduate work at Yale, and later at Freiberg, he made a special study of graphical statics, a science which was new at that time. His *Elements of Graphical Statics and Their Application to Framed Structures* (2 vols., 1875) was the first comprehensive work on this subject to appear in the United States. It was followed by his translation of sections of Weisbach's famous *Mechanics of Engineering,* and of translations from both Weyrauch and Roentgen, in an effort to fill the gap in engineering literature which was being felt in American technical schools at that time. In 1883 his *Stresses in Framed Structures,* giving methods of computing stresses by analytic and graphic processes, was published. *Elementary Principles of Mechanics* (3 vols., 1894–95) followed. These both came into wide use as text-books in engineering schools, and many editions were published. He contributed papers on roof trusses, steam-engines, etc., to various technical publications.

The *Century Magazine* published, between 1889 and 1894, a series of six papers originally prepared as lectures, in which Dubois attempted to establish moral truths on the same fundamental principles which underlie mechanics. Shortly before his death he summarized the conclusions of these lectures in a paper which is to be found in the *Yale Review* for July 1913. The series shows his originality of thought, his conciseness of expression, and clear logic. As a man, he has been described by a colleague, Prof. John C. Tracy, who succeeded him at Sheffield, as having "a sympathetic interest, a ready wit," and added, "Breadth of culture and an unusual power of expression made him a brilliant and inspiring conversationalist. Underneath a quiet and undemonstrative exterior, there was a man chivalrous, sympathetic, always thoughtful of others, loyal and wholly lovable." On June 23, 1883, he was married to Adeline Blakesley, daughter of Arthur Blakesley of New Haven, Conn.

[Mansfield Merriam in *Trans. Am. Soc. Civil Engineers,* LXXXI (1917), 1,699–1,701; obituaries in *Trans. Am. Soc. Mechanical Engineers,* XXXVII (1915), 1,505–06; *Engineering News,* Oct. 28, 1915; *Obit. Record Grads. Yale Univ.,* 1915–16.] K. W. C.

DUBOIS, JOHN (Aug. 24, 1764–Dec. 20, 1842), Roman Catholic prelate, third bishop of New York, was born in Paris. His early education was received at home, whence he passed to the Collège Louis-le-Grand. On the completion of his secular studies he entered the Seminary of St. Magloire, conducted by the Fathers of the Oratory of St. Philip Neri, and was ordained priest on Sept. 22, 1787. He served on the staff of the Church of St. Sulpice in Paris and also acted as chaplain to a community of nuns; but these activities were cut short in less than four years by the French Revolution, and in the spring of 1791 he was obliged to make his escape from France. In August of that year he landed at Norfolk, Va., and through letters of introduction from Lafayette he soon became acquainted with some of the most prominent men in the United States, such as Patrick Henry and James Monroe. The former taught him English; the latter received him into his house in New York; while it was doubtless owing to the influence of Lafayette that Dubois was permitted to celebrate Mass in the State Capitol at Richmond, a courtesy the more remarkable because of the state of feeling toward Catholics in the Virginia of that day. At the earliest opportunity he became an American citizen.

For a while he supported himself by teaching French; then, as soon as he was fitted for active work in his adopted country, he was sent by Bishop Carroll to parochial work in Virginia, first at Norfolk and then at Richmond. In 1794 he was transferred to Frederick, Md., where he built the first Catholic church in western Maryland and ministered to the Catholics of that section and much of the region now comprising West Virginia. During most of this time he was the only priest between Baltimore and St. Louis, and his labors were such as would have broken a man not endowed with splendid health and vigor. In 1807 he withdrew to devote himself to a work that had always attracted him, the education of aspirants to the priesthood, and established a preparatory seminary at Emmitsburg, Md. The following year he joined the Society of St. Sulpice, a community of secular priests whose purpose was to conduct ecclesiastical seminaries, some members of which had left France during the Revolution and founded St. Mary's Seminary in Baltimore.

The curriculum at Emmitsburg was altered in a short time so as to include instruction for laymen as well as for clerics. By 1821, accommodations more substantial than the log structures which had housed the institution became necessary, and Dubois began the erection of a new stone building, but when on the point of completion it was destroyed by fire. Immediately he recommenced, and in a few years a better building rose on the ruins. His labors in this undertaking were prodigious; he was simultaneously president, treasurer and professor; and in addition to these cares he had to meet the opposition of some among Catholics who sought to have him discontinue the courses in theology and thus give up the training of priests. The result of this attempt was that he severed his connection with the Sulpicians (1826) and was busy with plans for the reorganization of Mount St. Mary's at Emmitsburg when he was appointed to the diocese of New York to succeed Bishop John Connolly [*q.v.*].

He was chosen by Propaganda on Apr. 24, 1826, and the choice was confirmed by Pope Leo XII the following Apr. 30; he was consecrated by Archbishop Maréchal in the Cathedral of Baltimore on Oct. 29, 1826, Charles Carroll of Carrollton presenting the ring and the pectoral cross. In his new post he was faced with trying difficulties. The diocese was much larger than it is now; the system of lay trustees, under which church finances were administered by laymen, had given rise to dissensions; and the spirit of nationalism threatened to disrupt the Catholic body. So antagonistic to the new bishop were some of the elements among the New York Catholics that one of his first acts on reaching his see was perforce the issuance of a pastoral letter refuting the charge that his appointment had been brought about by undue French influence.

To meet the urgent need for priests he went to Paris and Rome in 1829 and secured financial assistance from the Society for the Propagation of the Faith and the Congregation of Propaganda. On his return he took up the task of building another seminary, but in New York he had not the success that had been his in Maryland. He completed a seminary at Nyack, N. Y., that was burned down before it could be occupied; the project of one in Brooklyn was never realized; and the one he opened in La Fargeville, N. Y., had to be given up because of its remoteness. Then he had to encounter the problem of trusteeism. At one time the trustees of his own cathedral withheld his salary and appointed in charge of the school attached to the cathedral a priest whom he had suspended; and it was on this occasion that he uttered the words so often quoted: "I am an old man and do not need much. I can live in a basement or in a garret. But whether I come up from the basement or down from the garret, if I have to preach from the top of a barrel on the street corner, I am still your bishop." Amid this distressing situation he struggled bravely and successfully, but the labor wore him down and in 1837 he accepted as coadjutor John Hughes [*q.v.*], a former pupil under him at Mount St. Mary's and later fourth bishop and first archbishop of New York. Two years later he retired from active government, leaving the diocese in the hands of Bishop Hughes, and spent the remaining years of his life in private devotion. He died on Dec. 20, 1842, and was buried in the crypt of St. Patrick's Church (the "Old Cathedral"), New York, where his body now lies.

[F. X. Reuss, *Biog. Cyc. of the Cath. Hierarchy of the U. S.* (1898); John T. Smith, *The Cath. Church in N. Y., A Hist. of the N. Y. Diocese* (1905); M. M. Meline and E. F. X. McSweeny, *The Story of the Mountain* (Emmitsburg, Md., 1911), vol. I, *passim*; *Cath. World* (N. Y.), Jan. 1882; Célestin Moreau, *Les prêtres français émigrés aux États-Unis* (Paris, 1856); J. G. Shea, *A Hist. of the Cath. Church within . . . the U. S.* (1890), vol. III; *N. Y. Daily Express*, Dec. 21, 1842.] E.R.

DU BOIS, WILLIAM EWING (Dec. 15, 1810–July 14, 1881), numismatist, fifth of the eight children of Uriah and Martha (Patterson) Du Bois, was born in Doylestown and died in Philadelphia, Pa. His father, a Presbyterian minister, was descended from the Huguenot Louis Du Bois, who settled on the Hudson River about 1660. His mother was the daughter of Robert Patterson, professor in the University of Pennsylvania and from 1805 to 1824 director of the United States Mint. William was a precocious child; at six he studied the classics, at sixteen he published essays in the weekly papers, and in his early twenties he became a lawyer. An affection of the voice made it impossible for him to talk a great deal, and even caused him to write instead of speak the answers to many of the questions addressed to him. In 1883 this disability made him give up law to become director's clerk in the mint. Two years later he went into the assay department under the direction of Jacob R. Eckfeldt. In 1841 he married Eckfeldt's sister, Susanna, and on Eckfeldt's death in 1872 he succeeded him as assayer. As long as both lived they were intimate friends and faithful collaborators. Eckfeldt, it is said, was mainly concerned with the scientific exactitude of their operations, but it was Du Bois who emphasized also the desirability of giving their findings a permanent record. In 1842 they published their *Manual of Gold and Silver Coins of All Nations*, and in 1850, *New Varieties of Gold and Silver Coins*, both intelligent, exhaustive works showing wide reading and original observations. In the years following, Du Bois published a number of other essays on coinage and related subjects—among them, *On the Natural Dissemination of Gold* (1861), and *Propositions for a Revised System of Weights* (1869). He published several volumes dealing with the genealogy of his own family—Pattersons on the one hand (1847), and Du Boises on the other (1860 and 1876). In this connection he was at pains to declare that an interest in one's ancestors does not of necessity imply vanity. He was writing, he said, only for those directly concerned; on the cover of the Du Bois record of 1860 one is requested, "Please not to leave this exposed to general perusal." In 1872 he published, *A Brief Sketch of Jacob R. Eckfeldt*. He was a member of various learned societies, and he corresponded with many celebrated people in Europe as well as in America. He was earnest and gentle, and among his intimate friends, humorous.

[P. Du Bois, *In Memoriam, Wm. E. Du Bois* (1881); Robt. Patterson in *Proc. Am. Phil. Soc.*, vol. XX (1882–83); *Press* (Phila.), July 16, 1881; *Phila. Record*, July 18, 1881.] J.D.W.

DuBOSE, WILLIAM PORCHER (Apr. 11, 1836–Aug. 18, 1918), theologian, was born near Winnsboro, S. C., at his father's plantation, the son of Theodore Marion and Jane (Porcher) DuBose, of Huguenot descent on both sides, his own being the sixth generation in this country. His grandfather was Samuel DuBose, adjutant on the staff of his uncle, Gen. Francis Marion, in the Revolutionary War. His education was begun at Mt. Sion Institute at Winnsboro, S. C. From there he was sent to the Military College of South Carolina, known as the "Citadel," graduating in 1855 with first honors. Here he received his grounding in mathematics which showed itself later in the accuracy of thought in his teaching and writings. From the "Citadel" he went to the University of Virginia where he received the degree of master of arts, after which he entered the theological seminary of the diocese of South Carolina at Camden, which he left in 1861 to enter the military service of the Confederacy. During the Civil War he served first as adjutant in the "Holcombe Legion" on the staff of his former commandant at the "Citadel" and later as chaplain after being exchanged as prisoner from Fort Delaware. He was wounded several times but never bore arms except on one occasion, a scouting party. After the war he was ordained priest in the Protestant Episcopal Church in 1865 by Bishop Davis of South Carolina and served in the parochial ministry of that diocese at his birthplace, Winnsboro, and then at Abbeville, S. C., until 1871, when he was elected chaplain and professor of ethics and Christian apologetics in the University of the South at Sewanee, Tenn., where he lived and taught until his death in 1918. He was elected dean in 1894 of the theological department of the University, which department he had founded and in which he held the chair of New Testament exegesis. He resigned active teaching and administration in 1908 and was made dean and professor emeritus. DuBose was small in stature, not over five feet eight inches in height, with massive forehead and deep-set gray eyes which betokened the thinker. He wore a full beard and was meticulously careful but simple in his dress, believing that clothes are an index to character. He was gentle, but had the strength of gentleness. His students felt that they were in the presence of a great and good man, but they could not stand in awe of him for he was as approachable as a friendly child and had a keen enjoyment of humor. His lectures were difficult for those who were not philosophically minded but even these never went empty away, for they were enriched by the man's spirit even though they did not grasp his subtleties of thought. His personality was impressive but never overpowering and he encouraged his students to think for themselves. He was affectionately known among them as "The Doctor." He lectured five times a week to the whole body of theological students and each lecture was prepared afresh. He had been teaching twenty years before his first book was published in 1892; as a result he never found it necessary to revise an edition, notwithstanding hostile reviews from the more conventionally minded critics. His positions had been taken after mature thought. In his own field, that of the philosophy of the Christian religion, he was the foremost thinker in the Episcopal Church in America, and, in the opinion of the late Prof. William Sanday of Oxford University, "the wisest Anglican writer . . . on both sides of the Atlantic" (*The Life of Christ in Recent Research,* 1907, chs. x and xi). He was twice married: first, in 1863, to Anne Barnwell Peronneau of South Carolina, who died in 1873, and after her death, to Louisa Yerger of Jackson and Washington County, Miss., in 1878.

Besides *Turning Points in My Life* (1912), a short autobiography consisting of addresses read at a reunion of his old students in his honor at Sewanee in 1911, and numerous essays in the *Constructive Quarterly,* he was the author of six works on philosophical theology. *The Soteriology of the New Testament* (1892) is an exegesis of the New Testament containing his philosophy of salvation; *The Ecumenical Councils* (1897) is a philosophical interpretation of Christian doctrine as set forth by the councils of the early church; *The Gospel in the Gospels* (1906) contains his theology in a systematic but original form. *The Gospel According to St. Paul* (1907) is a theological interpretation of the Pauline teaching, while *The Reason of Life* (1911) is his philosophy of Christianity based upon the Gospels and the Epistles of St. John. *High Priesthood and Sacrifice* (1908) is a philosophical appreciation of the Epistle to the Hebrews. With the exception of the Book of Revelation and one or two minor Epistles his writings cover the whole of the New Testament. He was asked on one occasion to explain the meaning of the Book of Revelation and he replied that he wished he knew. He was born a Platonist and spoke the language of Aristotle. His affiliations were with St. John, but St. Paul has had no more loyal interpreter and defender.

[DuBose's autobiography, *Turning Points in My Life*; family records furnished by his son and two daughters, including an account of his family; G. R. Fairbanks, *Hist. of the Univ. of the South* (1905); *Who's Who in America,* 1918–19; memoir by the Rt. Rev. Wm. A. Guerry, in the *Churchman* (N. Y.), Aug. 31, 1918; editorials, *Ibid.,* Sept. 7, 1918, and in the *Southern Churchman* (Richmond), Aug. 31, 1918; John O. F. Murray, "DuBose and the Problems of Today," in the *Constructive Quart.,* Dec. 1921, and *DuBose as a Prophet of Unity* (1924); personal acquaintance.]

G. B. M.

DU BOURG, LOUIS GUILLAUME VALENTIN (Feb. 13, 1766–Dec. 12, 1833), Roman Catholic prelate, was born at Cap Français, Santo Domingo, the son of Chevalier Pierre Du Bourg de la Loubère et St. Christaut, Sieur de Rochemont, and his wife, Marguerite Armand de Vogluzan. At the age of two he was placed in the care of his grandparents at Bordeaux, France. After completing his classical studies in the Collège de Guyenne, in 1784 he commenced to study theology at the "Petite Communauté des Robertins," an annex to the Seminary of St. Sulpice, Paris, whence, on Oct. 12, 1786, he entered the Seminary proper. He was ordained, probably about the end of 1788, and in the fall of that year he was sent to Issy, near Paris, as rector of a preparatory school. Forced by events of the French Revolution to send home his charges and seek refuge in Paris, in September 1792, he fled to Orense, in Spain, and later sailed for America. Landing at Baltimore on Dec. 14, 1794, he entered at once into relations with the Sulpicians of St. Mary's, petitioned admittance into their Society, and was received on Mar. 9, 1795. Records of the time relate that in Baltimore he gave Sunday religious instruction to the negroes of both sexes. On Sept. 20, 1796, Bishop John Carroll [*q.v*] appointed him to the presidency of the newly founded Georgetown College, an office which he resigned at the end of 1798. On Jan. 24, 1799, he sailed for Cuba to assist in the direction of the Sulpician college lately founded there. When opposition brought about the closing of the institution, he returned to Baltimore, accompanied by a number of his pupils. An academy for West Indian boys, in charge of Du Bourg, was opened at St. Mary's with the sanction of Bishop Carroll; in 1803 this institution was succeeded by St. Mary's College for American boys, Du Bourg remaining its head until 1812. In 1806 he helped to raise funds with which to build the Baltimore cathedral and was instrumental in securing its location on its present commanding site. About this time he became acquainted in New York with Mrs. Elizabeth Ann Seton [*q.v.*], foundress of the Sisters of Charity, prevailed upon her to move to Baltimore, and fostered her incipient Community.

In 1812 he was nominated to the bishopric of New Orleans, but because of the captivity of Pius VII, the Pontifical Bulls were never issued. Accordingly, Archbishop Carroll appointed Du Bourg Administrator Apostolic of that diocese. The task confronting him was exceptionally difficult: for fifty thousand souls he had only fourteen priests, half a dozen of them crippled by old age, and others, led by the Capuchin friar, Anthony de Sedella [Père Antoine, *q.v.*], in open opposition to the new order of things created by the Louisiana Purchase. Later, these difficulties were increased when in January 1815 a British army stood at the gates of New Orleans. Du Bourg at once gauged the situation, and impressed upon all the patriotic duty of supporting the American general. He was tireless in his efforts to assist the people of the threatened city, animating them by his eloquence, giving them material aid, and making the Ursuline Convent a place of refuge. After the battle, in the public celebration of the victory, it is said that Du Bourg, assisted by a college of priests, received Gen. Jackson at the cathedral door and placed a crown of laurel on his head. By this time he had won the affection of many of the citizens but the local clergy continued to oppose him, and in the spring of 1815 he journeyed to Rome to plead for help for his distracted diocese. As a result, the Lazarists were prevailed upon to go to Louisiana; three priests and one lay brother were at once enlisted for the expedition; some secular priests and ecclesiastical students joined them, and other recruits were promised for future needs. On these assurances the Administrator consented to receive Episcopal consecration in the church of S. Luigi de' Francesi on Sept. 24, 1815. Early in 1816, he visited northern Italy, France, and Belgium, recruiting for his diocese five priests, twenty-six seminarians, nine Ursuline nuns, and a few religious of the Sacred Heart. In Lyons he interested charitable persons in his extensive mission (though he cannot be regarded as founder at Lyons of the Society for the Propagation of the Faith), and even enlisted the aid of the King, Louis XVIII, who gave orders for the transportation of his company on the flute *La Caravane* of the French navy. Meanwhile, at home, Sedella, leader of the opposition, was denying the Bishop's vicar-general access to the cathedral. For the prelate to go to New Orleans in such circumstances was to invite riot; accordingly, after landing at Annapolis, Sept. 4, 1817, he settled, temporarily, at St. Louis. When he left for New Orleans, on Nov. 20, 1820, he had almost completed a large brick church and had founded an academy for boys; the religious of the Sacred Heart, under Mother Duchesne [*q.v.*], were carrying out at Florissant their work of female education; St. Mary's Seminary at "the Barrens" was providing for the training of the future clergy of the diocese; a number of parishes in Upper Louisiana had been supplied with pastors; and ways and means were being devised for sending missionaries to the Indians of Missouri. Du Bourg's arrival in New Orleans opened for a while an era of peace; Sedella himself paid him honor and swore allegiance. The Bishop's first foundations were a college for boys in New Orleans and an academy for girls under the sisters of the Sacred Heart at Grand Côteau (1821). In 1822 he went to Washington to obtain government support for an Indian mission. Again success rewarded his efforts: besides obtaining from Secretary Calhoun encouraging promises, by a remarkable coincidence he rescued from disbandment and transferred to Missouri for the work they had contemplated a colony of Jesuits, one of whom was Pierre-Jean De Smet [*q.v.*], the famous Indian missionary of later years.

For some time Du Bourg had petitioned for a coadjutor, and on July 14, 1823, Joseph Rosati [*q.v.*] was appointed to that office. Previously, however, Du Bourg had recommended the nomination of his whilom arch-opponent Anthony De Sedella; and at another time one Angelo Inglesi, whom through sheer infatuation he had rushed to the priesthood. Rumors of these requests caused disaffection among his clergy, and keenly sensitive of their loss of confidence in him, he tendered his resignation to Leo XII on Feb. 1, 1825. For a time he received no reply, but continued to insist upon his release. After Easter 1826 he returned to Europe, and shortly after landing at Havre (July 3), was advised that his resignation was accepted. A few weeks later he was appointed to the See of Montauban; after seven years he was transferred to the Archdiocese of Besançon; and there he died.

[R. H. Clarke, *Lives of the Deceased Bishops of the Catholic Church in the U. S.* (1872), vol. I; L. Bertrand, *Bibliothèque Sulpicienne, ou Histoire Littèraire de la Compagnie de St. Sulpice* (1900), III, 206–14; C. G. Herbermann, *The Sulpicians in the U. S.* (1916), pp. 94–107 and 170–80; C. L. Souvay in *Cath. Hist. Rev.*, Apr.–July 1917, Apr. 1918, and *St. Louis Cath.*

Hist. Rev., Jan. 1920, Apr.–July 1923; F. G. Holweck in *Pastoral Blatt* (St. Louis), Feb. 1918, and *St. Louis Cath. Hist. Rev.*, Jan. 1923; G. J. Garraghan, *Cath. Hist. Rev.*, Jan. 1919; certain information as to family and early life from Trist Wood, Esq., of New Orleans.]

C. L. S.

DUBUQUE, JULIEN (Jan. 10, 1762–Mar. 24, 1810), first white settler of Iowa, was born of Norman parents, Noël Augustin Dubuque and his wife, Marie Mailhot, in the village of St. Pierre les Brecquets, county of Nicolet, in the province of Quebec. He received a good education in the parish schools of his native village and at Sorel, became polished in manner, and was able to express himself well both in speech and writing. Seeking fortune and adventure, he set out for the West, and as early as 1785 was located at Prairie du Chien, Wisconsin. Learning that a band of Fox Indians who had their village on Catfish Creek across the Mississippi in the Iowa country controlled the output of rich lodes of lead, he sought to win their favor. He made numerous presents to them, learned their language, flattered their vanity, and in due time secured permission to work the lead mines. He himself, it is said, drew up the document which Kettle Chief and his associates signed at Prairie du Chien on Sept. 22, 1788, giving "la petite nuit," as he was called, sole permission to work the mines on the Iowa side of the Mississippi (57 *U. S.*, 222–23). Thus secured in his occupancy, he opened new mines, built cabins for his French-Canadian helpers, erected a smelting furnace, and opened a store for trade with the Indians. He used his French-Canadian helpers as overseers, smelters, and rivermen. The actual labor of mining was performed by the squaws and old men of the tribe. Dubuque inaugurated the plan of smelting the lead into pigs for convenience in loading and carrying the metal to St. Louis. In the hope of making himself more secure in the possession of his property, he named his possessions "The Mines of Spain," and humbly petitioned Baron Carondelet, governor of Louisiana, for title to a tract of land seven leagues in length up and down the west bank of the Mississippi and extending three leagues into the interior. With the assent of Andrew Todd, to whom sole permission had been given by Spanish authorities to carry on trade with the Indians in what is now Iowa, the petition was granted (*Ibid.*, pp. 224–26).

Dubuque now redoubled his activities. Twice a year his boats, laden with furs and lead, made the trip to St. Louis where the cargo was exchanged for goods to be used in the Indian trade. His arrival at St. Louis was a welcome event for he was a favorite both with the merchants and the ladies. A man of a little below the usual stature, with black hair and eyes, wiry and well-built, he had all the politeness and grace of a cultured Frenchman.

Despite his monopoly of the trade in fur and lead of the eastern Iowa country, he was a poor manager and fell heavily in debt to Auguste Chouteau [*q.v.*], the merchant prince of St. Louis. In October 1804, Dubuque assigned to his creditor seven-sixteenths of his domain, and agreed that the remainder of his land at his death should go to Chouteau or his heirs. Out of this agreement grew a long controversy that was finally settled by the Supreme Court of the United States, which in 1853 held that Dubuque did not have actual title to the land, merely permission to work the mines (*Chouteau* vs. *Molony*, 57 *U. S.*, 226–42).

When Dubuque died, at the age of forty-eight, the Indians, whose confidence he retained to the last, buried him with all the honors due to a chief. In excavating for the monument to his memory in 1897, workmen discovered his bones and those of an Indian chief who was buried near-by. The bones of Dubuque were placed in a coffin of native walnut and sealed in a sarcophagus at the base of the tower.

[Moses M. Ham, "The First White Man in Iowa," was published in *Annals of Iowa*, 3 ser., II (1896), 329–44. In 57 *U. S.*, 203–42, the decision of the Supreme Court of the United States in the case of *Chouteau* vs. *Molony* reviews the history of Dubuque's career in Iowa. See also Richard Herrmann, *Julien Dubuque, His Life and Adventures* (1922).] B. E. M.

DU CHAILLU, PAUL BELLONI (July 31, 1835–Apr. 30, 1903), African explorer, is sometimes said to have been born in New Orleans, but his own statements indicate that the United States was his country only by adoption and that France was his native land. His father was the agent for Messrs. Oppenheim of Paris at the Gaboon on the west coast of Africa. There Paul spent his early years and received his education in a Jesuit Mission school. He showed a great fondness for natural history and early became acquainted with the native languages and customs. In 1852 he came to the United States and while here secured the support of the Philadelphia Academy of Natural Sciences for an exploring expedition into Central Africa. This trip which he undertook in 1856 lasted nearly four years, and in that time he traveled about 8,000 miles through tropical Africa. He collected many specimens of rare birds and animals and brought back to America the first gorillas ever seen here. He also determined that the Muni, Munda, and tributaries of the estuary of the Gaboon were mere coast rivers but that the St. Nazareth, Mexias, and Fernando Vaz were deltaic arms of the Ogowe, a vast river rising in the interior. Another important contribution was the discovery of the Fan tribe of cannibals. In 1861, two years after his return, he published an account of his journey under the title, *Explorations and Adventures in Equatorial Africa.* This was at first received with ridicule and distrust and led to many a bitter controversy among scientists. One by one, however, Du Chaillu's discoveries were confirmed by later travelers, and his reputation was established. But Du Chaillu was not satisfied with this vindication, and in 1863 he returned to Africa to prove some of his previous statements by scientific observations. His experiences of this two-year trip, including the story of his discovery of the pygmies of the Black Forest, are told in *A Journey to Ashango Land,* brought out in 1867. For the next few years he made his home in New York and devoted himself to lecturing and writing upon equatorial Africa. Chief among the books of this period are: *Stories of the Gorilla Country* (1868), *Wild Life Under the Equator* (1869), *Lost in the Jungle* (1869), *My Apingi Kingdom* (1870), and *The Country of the Dwarfs* (1871). All of these works are very readable and contain interesting, lively descriptions which indicate a keen sense of observation on the part of the author.

In 1871, he went to Sweden and Norway, where, after studying the people and their institutions for more than five years, he began writing *The Land of the Midnight Sun,* published in 1881. This was followed in 1889 by *The Viking Age,* his most ambitious work. His later years were spent quietly in writing and study; but in 1901 he again felt the wanderlust and journeyed to Russia to make a survey similar to the one that he had conducted in Scandinavia thirty years before. It was while on this trip that his death occurred at St. Petersburg.

[The chief sources of information concerning Du Chaillu are sketches of his life in the following magazines: *Bull. Am. Geog. Soc.*, vol. XXXV (1903), no. 2, p. 230; *Nat. Geog. Mag.*, July 1903; *Geog. Jour.*, June 1903; *Scientific American*, May 9, 1903; *Harper's Weekly*, May 16, 1903; and *Independent*, May 14, 1903. Obituaries appeared in the *Sun* (N. Y.), *N. Y. Times*, and *N. Y. Tribune* for May 1, 1903, and in *Novoe Vremya* (St. Petersburg, Russia), Apr. 18–May 1, 1903. See also Du Chaillu, "Last Letters from Russia," in *Lamp*, June 1903.] G. H. B.

DUCHÉ, JACOB (Jan. 31, 1737/38–Jan. 3, 1798), Anglican clergyman, Loyalist, was the son of Col. Jacob Duché, a prosperous Philadelphian, at one time mayor of the city, and his wife Mary Spence. He was graduated with the first class of the College of Philadelphia, in 1757. After a year at Cambridge University, he returned to Philadelphia in 1759 with deacon's orders, and became teacher of oratory at the college and assistant rector of the united parishes of Christ Church and St. Peter's. On June 19, 1759, he was married to Elizabeth Hopkinson, the sister of his friend and classmate, Francis Hopkinson [*q.v.*]. In 1762 he went to England for ordination, and in 1775 he succeeded the Rev. Richard Peters as rector of the united churches. He soon became one of the most popular preachers in the city, but two of his early sermons, *The Life and Death of the Righteous,* and *Human Life, a Pilgrimage,* published in 1763 and 1771 respectively, suggest that his reputation owed more to fervor of delivery than to depth or originality of thought. He early displayed literary ambitions. As an undergraduate he wrote some verse, the most ambitious example of which is *Pennsylvania, a Poem,* published by Franklin Hall in 1756. In 1762 there was published *An Exercise* on the accession of George III, which he and Hopkinson had written for the college commencement of that year. Beginning in March 1772, he published in the *Pennsylvania Packet* a series of twenty letters over the signature "Tamoc Caspipina," a pseudonym derived from the initial letters of the words "the assistant minister of Christ Church and St. Peter's in Philadelphia in North America." Though trite and commonplace, these letters evidently found readers, for in 1774 he republished them in a volume entitled *Observations on a Variety of Subjects, Literary, Moral and Religious.* Later they were reprinted in Philadelphia, Bath, London, Dublin, and Leipzig, sometimes under the original title, sometimes as *Caspipina's Letters.* With some of the later editions was included another work, "The Life and Character of William Penn."

At the beginning of the Revolution, Duché showed such zeal for liberty that he was made chaplain of the Continental Congress. In 1775 he published two patriotic sermons, *The Duty of Standing Fast in Our Spiritual and Temporal Liberties,* and *The American Vine,* the former of which was dedicated to Washington. After the Declaration of Independence, however, he began to lose his enthusiasm, and when Howe took Philadelphia and put him in jail, he experienced a complete change of heart. On Oct. 8, 1777, he wrote Washington a letter in which he severely criticized the Americans and predicted their defeat. He advised the General to urge Congress to recall the Declaration of Independence, and if they should refuse, to negotiate for peace at the head of his army. Washington turned this letter over to Congress, and the members of that body soon disseminated the news of their chaplain's treachery throughout the thirteen colonies

(*Letters of John Adams to His Wife*, p. 320). Those whose hearts had thrilled to Duché's eloquence now cursed him as a traitor, and even Hopkinson wrote him a burning letter of protest. Finding life in Philadelphia unendurable, Duché sailed for England in December 1777. The following year the Pennsylvania Assembly proscribed him and confiscated his property, but allowed his family enough money to enable them to join him in England. There he was rewarded for his recantation by being made secretary and chaplain of an orphan asylum at St. George's Fields, Lambeth Parish, but he never ceased to pine for America. He wrote to Washington and to many prominent Philadelphians, begging for permission to return, but it was not until May 1792 that the exiles at last came home. Although Duché had suffered a stroke of paralysis before leaving England, he lived until Jan. 3, 1798. His wife died as the result of an accident, on May 22, 1797.

Duché's later publications were: *Discourses on Various Subjects* (2 vols., London, 1779); *Sermons Preached in America* (Philadelphia, 1788); and *A Sermon—for the Benefit of the Humane Society* (London, 1791). In his later days he became a convert to the teachings of Swedenborg. This second change of principles and certain eccentricities that he manifested as he grew older caused some of his acquaintances to question his sanity, and hence to judge him more leniently than they once had done. A portrait of Duché and his wife (now in the Hopkins Collection, Historical Society of Pennsylvania), painted by their son, Thomas Spence, gives one a very favorable impression of their appearance. Both had regular and handsome features, expressing kindliness and intelligence, and both had an unmistakable air of culture and refinement.

[See E. D. Neill, "Jacob Duché" in the *Pa. Mag. of Hist. and Biog.*, II (1878), 58–73; Geo. E. Hastings, *The Life and Works of Francis Hopkinson* (1926), esp. pp. 111–13 and 268–75; C. P. Keith, *The Provincial Councillors of Pa.* (1883); Lorenzo Sabine, *Biog. Sketches of Loyalists of the Am. Rev.* (1864); Benjamin Dorr, *A Hist. Account of Christ Church, Phila.* (1859); C. R. Hildeburn, *The Inscriptions in St. Peter's Church Yard* (1874); T. H. Montgomery, *A Hist. of the Univ. of Pa.* (1900); *The Washington-Duché Letters* (1890), ed. by Worthington C. Ford; M. C. Tyler, *The Lit. Hist. of the Am. Rev.* (1897); Francis Hopkinson, *Miscellaneous Essays* (1792), III, ii, 83–88. Tyler and Hastings both give bibliographies. The full titles of Duché's works published in America may be found in Chas. Evans, *Am. Bibliography*, vols. III–VII (1905–12). The most valuable collections of his letters are those of Edward Hopkinson, Esq., of Philadelphia, and Mrs. Francis Tazewell Redwood of Baltimore; others are owned by the Harvard Univ. Lib., the Hist. Soc. of Pa., the Am. Philosophical Soc., the Library Company, Phila., and the Lib. of Cong.]

G. E. H.

DUCHESNE, ROSE PHILIPPINE (Aug 29, 1769–Nov. 18, 1852), religious, teacher, pioneer, was born in Grenoble, Dauphiné, France, the daughter of Pierre François Duchesne and Rose Euphrosyne Périer. From her earliest years she showed the characteristics that had won for her father's family prominence in commerce, law and politics, and that had made the Périers eminent in French finance. These characteristics: an indomitable will, a restless energy, and generous, ardent zeal, were her natural endowment for her work as a pioneer in the missions. Her education, begun at home, was continued in the Convent of the Visitation of St. Mary on the Alpine spur, Chalmont, overlooking Grenoble. On her return home she shared the studies of four of her boy cousins under a tutor, thus strengthening the sturdy qualities already remarkable in her character. Having become a novice in the Convent of St. Mary, Grenoble, she was there when the French Revolution began. The monastery was taken over by the government to be used as a prison for non-juring priests and for Royalists, and the religious whose home it had been were dispersed. During the Reign of Terror, Philippine Duchesne showed herself an angel of pity to its victims in Grenoble. At the close of the Revolution she hoped to rehabilitate the religious of the Visitation in the ruined old monastery, but this proving impossible, she offered herself and the house to the newly founded Society of the Sacred Heart. It was as a professed of that Order that she was sent to America in 1818 by the foundress, Mother Madeleine Sophie Barat.

Such a mission had been Philippine Duchesne's ambition since as a child she had heard a missionary speak of the New World and of the pagan Indians. The two months' voyage from Bordeaux to New Orleans was followed by another no less hazardous, that up the Mississippi to St. Louis, where the travelers were welcomed by Bishop DuBourg [*q.v.*]. In St. Charles, a village some seventeen miles from St. Louis, the religious of the Sacred Heart opened a boarding-school for the daughters of the pioneers of Missouri, and at the same time founded the first free school west of the Mississippi. Later on, at Florissant, Mo., they added to these two works the foundation of a school for Indian girls, the first of its kind to be established under Catholic auspices in the United States. The sisters suffered from hunger, illness, and cold, from opposition, misunderstanding, and failure; yet when her brother offered to send her passage back to France, Mother Duchesne replied: "Use that sum of money to pay the way of two more nuns coming from France to America."

In spite of privations, the pioneers and their wives were glad to confide their children to her and the school records bear well-known names, such as Chouteau, Mullanphy, Pratte.

In 1821 another convent was founded at Grand Côteau, La., and there, as at St. Michael's, La., founded four years later, the religious conducted a boarding-school for the daughters of the planters, a day school for the white children of the parish, and, in addition to these institutions, classes for the instruction of the negroes. Mother Duchesne when stationed in Missouri made two long voyages to Louisiana to visit these schools, and on one of the return journeys contracted yellow fever and was put ashore where she nearly died of exposure and neglect. In founding a convent in St. Louis, she fulfilled an ardent desire of the foundress of her Order, Mother Barat, and by opening a mission school among the Indians of Kansas she realized her own long-cherished hope. At that time she was over seventy and broken in health, but with spirit undaunted she had pleaded to be sent to the red men, and in 1841 she made the perilous voyage up the river to Westport, Kan. Her work among the Potawatomi at Sugar Creek was confined to example and prayer, so that the Indians picturesquely designated her as "the woman who always prays." She had hoped to be left at that post to the end of her life, but was recalled to St. Charles where she remained in humble hidden labor, in suffering and prayer, until her death in November 1852. The members of the Historical Society of Missouri, after discussing what their state owes to its pioneer women, in 1918 voted Mother Philippine Duchesne as the greatest benefactress. They put an account of her life and work into their archives and had her name inscribed on a bronze tablet, placed in the Jefferson Memorial Building, St. Louis.

[*Mother Philippine Duchesne* (1879), by Abbé Louis Baunard, translated from the French by Lady Georgiana Fullerton; M. T. Kelly, *A Life's Ambition* (1910); G. E. McGloin, *Venerable Philippine Duchesne* (1914); *A Grain of Wheat* (1918); Marjory Erskine, *Mother Philippine Duchesne* (1926); unpublished letters and journals.] M.E.

DUDLEY, BENJAMIN WINSLOW (Apr. 12, 1785–Jan. 20, 1870), surgeon, one of the fourteen children of Ambrose Dudley, a captain in the Revolutionary army and later a well-known Baptist preacher, was born in Spotsylvania County, Va. When one year of age he was taken to Kentucky by his parents and grew up near Lexington. His somewhat meager early education was acquired at the Lexington schools and there he began the study of medicine under the direction of Dr. Frederick Ridgely, of whom he always spoke in terms of warmest praise. In 1804 he entered the University of Pennsylvania and there received the degree of M.D. (1806). He returned home and began practise, at the same time, in order to acquire funds for further study, engaging in trade. In 1810 he went to New Orleans on a flatboat and buying a shipload of flour sailed for Europe. In Gibraltar and Lisbon he sold his cargo and made his way through Spain to Paris. Here and in London he spent four years of study under such masters as Larrey, Cooper, and Abernethy. Returning, a member of the Royal College of Surgeons, to Lexington (1814) he began a long career of professional toil, taking no vacations and rarely leaving the city. At the founding of the medical department of Transylvania University (1817) he became professor of anatomy and surgery, his former fellow students, Daniel Drake [*q.v.*] and Richardson, also accepting chairs. Misunderstandings characterized the opening of the new school, followed by pamphleteering, and culminating in a duel in which Dudley wounded Richardson in the thigh and then saved his life by promptly (and with Richardson's permission) stopping the blood flow with his thumb. In 1836 he successfully removed a cataract and gave sight to a man who had been blind since birth, the first operation of its kind in what was then called the West. Lexington having proved too small to support a medical school, in 1837 an attempt was made to transfer the institution to Louisville, but Dudley declined to leave, and followed the waning fortunes of the school until it closed, his last lecture being delivered in 1850. He retired from practise in 1853 except for an occasional consultation. His last years were spent in comfort at "Fairlawn," his country place near Lexington, and there he died.

In many respects Dudley was in advance of his time. He condemned blood letting, saying that a man's life is shortened a year for each bleeding. He had great faith in the value of boiled water in surgery and used quantities of it at the time of his operations and in the after care of his cases. His technique was characterized by absolute cleanliness in every detail for, though bacteriology was an undreamed-of science, he realized that filth, dirt, and impure water in some way contain the seeds of disease. His fear of impure water was particularly valuable during the cholera epidemic in Lexington (1832) when those who followed his advice escaped. He was original in the use of the trephine in traumatic epilepsy and in the treatment (by gradual pressure) of fungus cerebri, and was particularly skilful in the use of the bandage in medical as well as surgical conditions. On the other hand his treatment of tuberculous diseases by wasting diet is hard to reconcile with his otherwise sound views. His chief claim to fame as a surgeon must rest on his operation for bladder stone, in which he was more successful than any surgeon up to that time. During his life he operated in 225 such cases with a loss of only three. His work was all done without anesthesia but the patients' suffering did not destroy his calm self-possession. His surgery was always conservative. He was a pioneer in the preparative treatment of patients requiring operation and not only attempted to return the body as nearly as possible to normal before operation, but also required of his assistants a minute examination of every organ—a forerunner of the medical surveys of the hospital of to-day. He had little taste for writing and had been a successful teacher for years before he published anything. Indeed it is not unlikely that the appearance of the *Transylvania University Journal of Medicine and the Associate Sciences* (1828), edited by his brother-in-law, Dr. Charles W. Short, which required something from his pen, was his only incentive, and apparently all his writings were published in this journal. In the first issue he described the technique of his trephining operation for traumatic epilepsy and in subsequent numbers his operations for fungus cerebri, hydrocele, fractures, calculus, ligation of the perineal artery, the use of the bandage, etc. Gross credits him with being the first in the West to ligate the subclavian artery (1825). He married, in 1821, Anna Maria, daughter of Maj. Peyton Short, who died in early life, leaving three children.

[L. P. Yandell, "A Memoir of the Life and Writings of Dr. Benj. W. Dudley," *Am. Practitioner,* Mar. 1870; Bedford Brown, "Personal Recollections of the late Dr. Benj. W. Dudley," *Trans. Southern Surgic. & Gynecol. Asso.,* 1892; Lewis and R. H. Collins, *Hist. of Ky.* (1874), I, 51, and II, 218; Robt. Peter, *The Hist. of the Medic. Dept. of Transylvania Univ.* (1905), being Filson Club Pubs. No. 20; Sketch by B. W. Dudley in H. A. Kelly and W. L. Burrage, *Am. Medic. Biogs.* (1920); Archibald H. Barkley, *Kentucky's Pioneer Lithotomists* (1913); obituary note in *N. Y. Tribune,* Jan. 25, 1870.]
E. E. H.

DUDLEY, CHARLES BENJAMIN (July 14, 1842–Dec. 21, 1909), railroad chemist, was born at Oxford, Chenango County, N. Y., the son of Daniel and Miranda (Bemis) Dudley. His youth was given over to rugged labor in field and shop with such educational opportunities as the country school and local academy afforded. On Aug. 6, 1862, he responded to Lincoln's call, enlisting in Company A, 114th Regiment, New York Volunteers and serving until he was severely wounded, Sept. 19, 1864, at the battle of Opequon Creek, near Winchester, Va., and invalided home. Longing for a college education, he carried text-books into camp and conned them as he could. He entered Yale College in 1867. Obliged to work his way through, he engaged largely in newspaper work, becoming managing editor of the *Yale Courant* and, later, night editor of the *New Haven Palladium,* but he maintained so high a standard of scholarship in college as to win an oration at Commencement and election to the Phi Beta Kappa. He achieved his Ph.D. at the Sheffield Scientific School in 1874, majoring in chemistry.

On Nov. 10, 1875, he was appointed chemist to the Pennsylvania Railroad Company, and he died in service. Although railroad officials had occasionally, and casually, had analyses, or tests, made by consulting chemists, Dudley was the first person appointed as chemist to a railroad corporation to give his full time to applying his knowledge to the solution of the problems of such an organization. His appointment to this position was made at a time when much skepticism prevailed as to the value of the services of a university-trained scientific man in the practical affiairs of life. Dudley was burly in form, rugged of countenance, had a luxuriant growth of somewhat rebellious hair and beard, which early became grizzled. He chose durable garments of a grayish nature. Limping from the effects of his wound, which necessitated the constant use of a cane, he was a most wintrish looking man. But the crinkles about his eyes revealed his well developed sense of humor and his philanthropic disposition, which was confirmed by the kindliness and warmth of his greeting. Accustomed to mingling with all sorts and conditions of men and having diligently made himself master of his subject, he listened sympathetically to the points of view of those with whom he dealt and discussed the problem tactfully but with definiteness and determination. Entering on his duties at Altoona with enthusiasm, he soon disclosed a multitude of opportunities for the application of chemistry and physics in increasing the economy, efficiency and safety of railroad maintenance and operations. His first publication from this study, "The Chemical Composition and Physical Properties of Steel Rails" (*Transactions American Institute of Mining Engineers,* Vol. VII, 1878, pp. 172–201), created great excitement among steel manufacturers, who viewed with trepidation chemical and physical supervision of their products, and antagonized many metallurgists, but Dudley continued to publish comparisons of laboratory findings with results from practise and his fundamental ideas eventually prevailed.

A series of articles on "Chemistry Applied to Railroads," by Dudley, and his associate chemist, F. N. Pease (*American Engineering and Railroad Journal,* 1889–1902), made widely known the essential value of the chemist in this field. He early stressed purchase according to specifications and was the first to write into specifications descriptions of the tests to be applied. It was through his efforts that the Bureau for the Safe Transportation of Explosives and Other Dangerous Articles, of the American Railway Association, was created, and that Congress was led to enact legislation conferring regulatory powers on the Interstate Commerce Commission. He was twice president of the American Chemical Society; was president, 1902–09, of the American Society for Testing Materials; president of the International Association for Testing Materials; chairman of the National Advisory Board on Fuels and Structural Materials, and head of many other organizations. He was most active in the service of Altoona and the state of Pennsylvania. He married Mary Virginia Crawford, Apr. 17, 1906, but died without issue.

[*Memorial Volume Commemorative of the Life and Life-Work of Charles Benjamin Dudley* (n.d.), pub. by the Am. Soc. for Testing Materials; *Who's Who in America,* 1906–07; *Am. Men of Science* (1906); *Public Ledger* (Phila.), Dec. 22, 1909; personal knowledge.]
C. E. M.

DUDLEY, CHARLES EDWARD (May 23, 1780–Jan. 23, 1841), politician, was born in England during the American Revolution, the son of Loyalist parents. His father, Charles Dudley, an Englishman, was Collector of the King's Customs at Newport, R. I., where he married Catherine Cooke, of a Rhode Island colonial family. In November 1775, he abandoned his office at Newport and sought refuge on board a British ship of war. In the following year he took up his residence in England, where his wife joined him, and in 1780 at Johnson Hall, Stafford, their son, Charles Edward, was born. Ten years later the father died and in 1795 the mother returned to her native town, bringing with her the fifteen-year-old lad, whose schooling was obtained at Newport. Near the opening of the nineteenth century, young Dudley was making voyages from New York to the East Indies as supercargo. During the War of 1812, and probably several years earlier, he was living at Albany, N. Y., where he married Blandina Bleecker, a member of a substantial Albany family. He entered public life in his late thirties. Known as a successful and generous man of affairs and an affable gentleman, he was repeatedly chosen by the Common Council as mayor of Albany and sat in the state Senate from 1820 to 1825.

As a stepping-stone to a place of power in New York State politics, his membership in the "Albany Regency," headed by Martin Van Buren, was more important than any state or local office within his grasp. Like the other members of the Regency, he was a man of personal integrity and, unlike some of the most eminent among them, he had skill and address in dealing with individuals. The details of troublesome patronage problems might safely be left to him, while Van Buren, Marcy, Wright, and other leaders were busied with the big question of public policy. Accordingly, Dudley became and long remained a useful member of the conclave. While he had a seat in the state Senate the Regency had to face the most critical situation in its career—the fight with DeWitt Clinton [*q.v.*]. Dudley, and his fellow senator, Silas Wright, voted for the expulsion of Clinton from the Canal Board, and they also voted to postpone the provision for popular choice of presidential electors. Through their votes the Regency declared itself. Meanwhile, Dudley kept Van Buren, now a Senator at Washington, informed as to Albany developments.

When Van Buren resigned his United States senatorship to become governor of New York, Dudley, having been defeated for a seat in the House of Representatives, was sent to Washington in his place. He was an early example of the business man in the Senate, where he played an inconspicuous rôle, but loyally supported the Jackson administration by his votes. He retired at the end of his term and passed the rest of his life at Albany, retaining his interest in Democratic politics. He received no public recognition from Van Buren as President. In 1856, fifteen years after his death, his widow provided funds for an astronomical observatory at Albany which received her husband's name. She was actuated in this generous act partly by the interest in astronomy that Dudley had manifested during his lifetime.

[Dean Dudley, *Hist. of the Dudley Family* (1886–94), pp. 10 and 203–04 (data supplied by Dudley's widow); Lorenzo Sabine, *Biog. Sketches of Loyalists of the Am. Rev.* (1864), I, 394; Cuyler Reynolds, *Albany Chronicles* (1906); Joel Munsell, *Annals of Albany* (1850–59) and *Colls. on the Hist. of Albany,* vol. II (1867); eulogy by Gov. Washington Hunt, *Inauguration of the Dudley Observatory at Albany* (1856); *Biog. Dir. Am. Cong.* (1928); *Albany Argus,* Jan. 25, 1841.]
W. B. S.

DUDLEY, EDWARD BISHOP (Dec. 15, 1789–Oct. 30, 1855), congressman from North Carolina, governor, railroad president, was born in Onslow County, N. C., where his father, Christopher, was prominent in farming, business, and politics as other Dudleys had been for generations (*Onslow County Record,* Dec. 1, 1827, Jan. 5, 1828). Though his early education was defective, Onslow sent him to the House of Commons (1811, 1812), and the state Senate (1814) where he displayed interest in military affairs. During the War of 1812 he went to Wilmington second in command of the Onslow regiment, and there settled. Big and handsome, genial and generous, the young officer was soon in the House of Commons from Wilmington and manifesting intelligent interest in navigation companies and state banking enterprises. Soon he married Eliza Haywood, of the Raleigh banker-politician family, who eventually bore him five children. When the state board of internal improvements was reorganized in 1824, he became one of its three members. Five years later the death of his father put large financial resources under his control (letter of John Sprunt Hill). Early in 1824 he became the Jackson representative on the anti-Crawford electoral ticket which later cast the state's vote for Jackson; and in late 1829 he became a Jacksonian congressman. His independent spirit, however, soon made him violently anti-Jackson. He was now ready for his big rôle. Returning to the House of Commons from the Wilmington borough, he supported the West in its fight against the Democratic East for constitutional reform and, in turn, secured important legislation, notably for the building of the Wilmington & Raleigh Railroad with state aid. In 1836 he was nominated for governor on the Whig ticket by a series of county conventions, which emphasized national issues (as did his own brief letter of acceptance) but were obviously influenced also by considerations of business and personal liking (*Raleigh Register,* January-March 1836). The West elected him in August (though in November the state went for Van Buren), and two years later reëlected him by a large majority. The years of his governorship (1837–40) marked the beginning of "a new period of economic and social development" (Boyd, *post,* p. 229). To him as chairman of the Internal Improvement and Literary Fund Boards fell primarily the investing of large funds which distribution of the federal surplus brought so as to further banking, railroads and drainage and lay the fiscal foundation for public education; and, despite some complaint of preference to Whigs in the matter, the task was well performed. On the basis of an able report which he procured, he recommended a cautious beginning of state public schools. Keenly sensitive to the economic backwardness of North Carolina —"our Rip Van Winkle"—and captivated by the possibilities in railroad development, he sought to commit the state to a vast scheme of internal improvements financed by a huge state bank (Message, 1838; letters to Swain, March, August 1839); but the legislature would not then follow him. His greatest achievement, however, was the Wilmington & Raleigh Railroad, later (1855) the Wilmington & Weldon, the longest in the world for several years. He secured its charter, led in subscribing its capital, served as its president (1836–37, 1841–47), saved it by his personal credit from bankruptcy, secured its first feeder (the Wilmington & Manchester), and mapped out extensions which, as the Atlantic Coast Line, it later followed "precisely" (Sprunt, *post,* p. 137). He held no public office after 1840. Wealthy and exceedingly hospitable—Webster found his Madeira excellent—he gave little attention to business after 1847. His health becoming poor, he turned toward religion and ultimately joined St. James's Church (letter of Manly to Swain, Nov. 5, 1855), from which he was buried with military honors. The state at large and Wilmington in particular pronounced him among the foremost of benefactors.

[J. H. Wheeler, *Reminiscences and Memoirs of N. C. and Eminent North Carolinians* (1884); J. G. deR. Hamilton, *Party Politics in N. C. 1835–60* (1916); and Jas. Sprunt, *Chronicles of the Cape Fear River* (1914), are most valuable for personal information. W. K. Boyd, *Hist. of N. C.* (1919), and S. A. Ashe, *Hist. of N. C.,* vol. II (1925), supply background and some detail. The *Wilmington Jour.,* Nov. 2, 5, 12, and the *Raleigh Reg.,* Nov. 5, 1855, contain complimentary obituaries. C. L. Coon, *The Beginnings of Public Educ. in N. C.* (1908), vol. II, contains many documents. Some personal letters are in the Swain Papers in possession of the N. C. Hist. Commission. See also Wm. H. Hoyt, *The Papers of Archibald D. Murphey* (1914), esp. I, 291; and, for his activities in the legislature, *Jours. of the Senate and House of . . . Commons of N. C.,* 1816, 1817, and 1834, esp. pp. 219–22.] C. C. P.

DUDLEY, JOSEPH (Sept. 23, 1647–Apr. 2, 1720), colonial governor, born at Roxbury, Mass., was the seventh child of a father already seventy years old, Thomas Dudley [*q.v.*], the second governor of the colony, and his second wife, Catherine (Dighton) Hackburn. The redoubtable Thomas died when Joseph was only five; and the child's mother marrying again, he was brought up by his step-father, the Rev. John Allin (or Allyn), minister of the church at Dedham. Dudley graduated from Harvard in 1665 with the intention of becoming a clergyman but soon turned to politics. The marriages of his sisters, one of them to Simon Bradstreet [*q.v.*], the last governor under the charter, helped Dudley politically and he himself in 1668 married Rebecca (born July 13, 1651), daughter of Edward Tyng, who was an Assistant for thirteen years and afterward a member of the Council. By his wife, who died Sept. 21, 1722, Dudley had thirteen children. He became a freeman in 1672 and was a member of the General Court as representative from Roxbury, 1673–76. He took part in King Philip's War and was then elected to the upper house of the legislature every year, except 1684, until the revocation of the old charter. He frequently served on important committees and from 1677 to 1681 was one of the commissioners of the United Colonies. He also gained much skill and reputation as a negotiator with the Indians.

In 1682 he was chosen to go to England as one of two agents sent to avert the threatened *quo warranto* proceedings and the loss of the charter. The charter was practically lost, however, before he sailed from Boston on May 31. He himself, indeed, was not wholly opposed to an alteration in the form of the colonial government which would bring it more within the control of the imperial authorities. He had wider views than had most of "the faction" at home and, whether from ambition or a genuine belief that he could harmonize the relations between the mother country and the recalcitrant colony, he adopted a line that many of the "die-hard" party in the colony regarded as treasonable. On Oct. 23, 1684, the charter was declared vacated, and when a temporary government was erected Dudley was made president of the Council and governor of Massachusetts, New Hampshire, and the King's Province. The new government assumed office May 17, 1686, the members of the General Court protesting against its legality. It was avowedly of a temporary nature and after seven months gave way to the more comprehensive scheme of unification under Sir Edmund Andros [*q.v.*]. It was fortunate for Massachusetts that Dudley should have bridged over the transition from the old charter government rather than such a man as was first proposed by the English government, but radical Massachusetts felt that she had been betrayed by one of her own household.

His administration ended when Andros arrived at Boston, Dec. 19, 1686, but although superseded as governor he became the most prominent member of Andros's Council and held many offices. He was placed on important committees, made censor of the press, chief justice of the superior court, and had a hand in forcing obedience to the hated laws passed during the Andros régime. In consequence of the feeling against him, it was necessary for his own safety to place him in jail when the Andros government was overthrown in 1689, and he remained confined for ten months until the king ordered him released and taken to England. There, 119 charges, mainly of illegal acts in the administration of justice, were preferred against him by a committee composed of seven of the leading colonists. Dudley made a dignified defense and in the end was properly acquitted of any wrongdoing. Although he apparently had acted in strict conformity with law in carrying out the new royal policy, he had nevertheless made himself the most hated man in New England, a title for which at that time, there was no slight competition.

Although exonerated, Dudley was in an unhappy position. He was distrusted in the land of his birth, which he loved, and the king whom he had served had been replaced by William III. He still had some friends in England, however, notably William Blathwayt, and through their influence was appointed chief of the Council of New York. He yet looked toward New England and an ultimate return there but did able and useful work in his new post. Always a strong "prerogative man," he became unpopular in his new province for much the same reasons that he had gained disfavor in his native one. He was chief justice during the Leisler troubles and took a leading part in Leisler's trial. Although his course was entirely legal it was vastly unpopular and still further damaged his American reputation. In 1692, he resigned office, returned to Massachusetts and settled once more at Roxbury. There he regained the trust of some of his former friends but by February 1693 he was again in England. In London he found old, and made some important new, acquaintances, notably Lord Cutts, who was soon appointed governor of the Isle of Wight and made Dudley his deputy. About this time the latter conformed to the Church of England. He had now become an English official in the homeland, had a recognized position in English society, corresponded with eminent men, among them Sir Richard Steele, and led a very different life from that of his compatriots in Massachusetts.

He still had his property in New England, his expenses were more than his income warranted, and he seemed always to retain a love for his native colony if not for all of its institutions. On Apr. 1, 1702, he received the long-coveted commission as governor of Massachusetts and sailed for Boston on the 13th. The day he landed he met the General Court and began the struggle which was to be continuous for the rest of his public life. With regard to his personal salary, always one of the bones of contention, Dudley compromised, but in all other matters during his administration he exhibited little of the compromising spirit and insisted on upholding the prerogative at the expense of personal popularity. He was more than once threatened with personal violence and on one occasion had to defend himself in England against accusations of serious wrong-doing. He came out of this successfully and, in reality, under the new conditions, had rendered considerable service to the colony. Perhaps his qualities appeared to the best advantage in the military expeditions against Canada. The colonial opposition, however, became too strong and in 1715 he was replaced by Gov. Shute. In the four years of private life still left to him he regained some of his early popularity.

Dudley was unmitigatedly damned by the earlier American historians. He thought in terms of empire rather than of his own province. By the standards of eighteenth-century political life he ranks high in personal integrity. In the broader views taken to-day of the colonial problems, his political ideals need not be harshly condemned. His character, however, remains an unsympathetic one. He was ambitious, self-seeking, cold, and ungrateful to his friends. He loved power for the influence which it gave, and was ambitious to be an English gentleman. The colony, whether from pride or relief, gave him one of the most ostentatious funerals of that funereal age.

[Although limiting itself closely to the aspect indicated in its title, *The Public Life of Joseph Dudley* (1911), by Everett Kimball, is a most excellent and scholarly biography. The bibliography at the end covers all the important source material relating to Dudley. For genealogy see also Geo. Adlard, *The Sutton-Dudleys of England and the Dudleys of Mass.* (1862) and Dean Dudley, *Hist. of the Dudley Family* (1886–94).]

J.T.A.

DUDLEY, PAUL (Sept. 3, 1675–Jan. 25, 1751), jurist, was born at Roxbury, Mass., with which place both his grandfather, Gov. Thomas Dudley, and his father, Gov. Joseph Dudley [*qq.v.*], were intimately associated. The latter married Rebecca, daughter of Judge Edward Tyng, and Paul was their fourth and eldest surviving son. He entered Harvard College in 1686 and graduated in 1690. After reading law for a short time in Boston, he went to England, became a student at the Middle Temple, Nov. 10, 1697, and was called to the bar Nov. 22, 1700. In 1702, having received a commission from Queen Anne as attorney-general of the province of Massachusetts Bay and advocate in the vice-admiralty court at Boston, he returned to America. On his arrival he was appointed attorney-general by the Governor and Council, it being considered expedient not to use the Royal commission in view of a sharp disagreement between the Council and Assembly as to the right to appoint. For some years his position in Boston was difficult, partly because of his zeal in championing the claims of the Crown to interfere in the administration of provincial affairs, but chiefly by reason of the unpopularity of his father and the bitter animosity of the Mather faction. He fulfilled his duties, however, with much tact, and his absolute integrity and sincere patriotism became gradually recognized. One of his first official acts was to take proceedings against and arrest a body of pirates who were infesting the coasts, some of whom were subsequently executed in Boston (*Rex* vs. *Quelch et al.*, 5 *American State Trials*, 330). He was later elected a member of the legislature and the Executive Council, and in that capacity introduced reforms which materially improved the machinery of justice. In 1718 he was appointed a judge of the superior court of judicature, and contemporaries without exception testify that on the bench he displayed great ability. A sound lawyer, energetic, industrious, and attentive to the dispatch of business, he acquired the confidence and respect of the public, and his appointment as chief justice of Massachusetts in 1745 met with unanimous approval. He retained this position till his death, which occurred at Roxbury, Jan. 25, 1751. In 1703 he had married Lucy, daughter of Col. John Wainwright of Ipswich.

He was an accomplished naturalist, deeply interested in the local antiquities, and wrote a number of pamphlets dealing chiefly with natural history, also contributing papers to the Royal Society, which were published in *Philosophical Transactions,* vols. XXXI, XXXII, XXXIII, XXXIV, and XXXIX. He was one of the few Americans to be elected members of that body. In his later years he became a pronounced Puritan in religious matters, and wrote *An Essay on the Merchandize of Slaves and Souls of Men* (1731) and a number of theological tracts. In his will he left a bequest to Harvard College for the purpose of providing an annual lecture or sermon dealing with one of four designated theological subjects. Generous, hospitable, and charitable, "he was apt to be a little antiquated and out of fashion in his dress. . . . When off the Bench he would often be seen conversing familiarly with the commonest people, having his hands upon their shoulders" (Dean Dudley, *post,* p. 526). He could, however, be imperious and even dictatorial, if he considered the occasion demanded it.

[A detailed account of Dudley's ancestry will be found in Dean Dudley, *Hist. of the Dudley Family* (1894), I, 16 ff., which also contains original material for his life and career. See also F. S. Drake, *The Town* of *Roxbury* (1878); Emory Washburn, *Sketches of the Judicial Hist. of Mass.* (1840); Edward Alfred Jones, *Am. Members of the Inns of Court* (1924), p. 65; *Calendar of State Papers, Colonial Ser. 1706–08* (1916).]

H. W. H. K.

DUDLEY, THOMAS (1576–July 31, 1653), governor of the colony of Massachusetts Bay, was the only son of a certain Captain Roger Dudley of whom we know nothing save that he was "slain in the wars," leaving Thomas and his sister orphans at a very early age. Thomas, who was born at Northampton, England, and is said to have inherited £500, was befriended by one "Mrs. Puefroy" during his earlier childhood and sent by her to a Latin school (Adlard, *post*, p. 24). He later became page in the household of the Earl of Northampton, where he was trained in the manners of a nobleman's family. When a young man he was taken as a clerk by a kinsman on his mother's side, Judge Nichols, and became acquainted with legal practise. A little later England went to the support of Henry IV of France, and many young men from Northampton went to the front, Dudley going with them as captain. Although he got as far as Amiens he saw no fighting, and after peace was declared returned to England and settled again in the neighborhood of Northampton. There he met and married, Apr. 25, 1603, Dorothy Yorke (*Colonial Society Massachusetts Publications*, vol. XXV, 1922, p. 18), a lady whom Mather described as "a gentlewoman both of good estate and good extraction" (Adlard, *post*, p. 26). By her he had five children.

About the time of his marriage he became more deeply religious and, probably under the influence of the Puritan clergy of his neighborhood, avowed himself what Mather calls a "judicious Dissenter." In some way he came under the observation of Lord Saye and Sele and certain other noblemen; they recommended him as steward to the young Earl of Lincoln who had just inherited his title and property. The estate was in a very confused condition and encumbered with debts which proved to amount to almost £20,000. In the nine years during which he served the young earl, Dudley not only succeeded in paying off the debts, reducing the estate to order, and increasing the income, but also in arranging a marriage between him and the daughter of Lord Saye and Sele. Apparently Dudley himself, either through his marriage or his own savings, had become well-to-do; retiring from Lincoln's service, he moved to Boston in Lincolnshire where he took a house and became a member of the congregation of the Rev. John Cotton. However, he had proved so useful to the earl that he was requested to return to his service and did so, remaining until he emigrated to New England.

He had been interested in the formation of the Massachusetts Bay Company and had been in close touch with the leaders of that enterprise from at least 1629. In 1630 he sailed on the *Arbella* with Winthrop, Saltonstall, and others of the chief men. They arrived at Salem June 12 and at first settled at Newtown. Before leaving England, Winthrop had been elected governor and Dudley deputy-governor. A somewhat violent disagreement between the two men, the first of many owing to Dudley's touchy and over-bearing temper, occurred when Winthrop abandoned the chosen settlement and moved to Boston. Dudley subsequently moved to Ipswich but after a short time, in order to be nearer the seat of government, definitely settled at Roxbury. Although Dudley was fifty-four years of age when he landed in New England he had still a long public career ahead of him. Throughout the rest of his life he was almost constantly in public office. He was elected governor in 1634, 1640, 1645, and 1650. He was thirteen times made deputy-governor and when not occupying either of these offices was usually to be found in the House as an Assistant. When the Standing Council was inaugurated with the idea of forming a body of members for life, Dudley was one of the three first chosen. When the New England Confederation was formed in 1643 Dudley was one of the two commissioners chosen by Massachusetts to confer with those of the other colonies. He was one of the founders of the First Church at Charlestown, July 30, 1630. He was one of the committee appointed in 1637 to consider the establishment of a college at Cambridge; he was one of the first Overseers of Harvard, and in 1650, as governor, signed the charter for that institution. In fact, there is hardly an event in the life of the colony during his own in which he did not act a part. He was evidently as strong in body as he was unyielding in temper and unbreakable in will. His first wife died, aged sixty-one, at Roxbury on Dec. 27, 1643. On Apr. 14 of the following year he married Mrs. Catherine (Dighton) Hackburn, the widow of Samuel Hackburn of Roxbury. She survived him and took a third husband in the Rev. John Allin (or Allyn) of Dedham. By her, Dudley had three children, the most noted, Joseph [*q.v.*], being Dudley's seventh child, born when the old man was seventy years of age.

Dudley was an able man with marked executive and business ability. His integrity was unimpeachable. His eye, though somewhat religiously jaundiced, was single to the public interest as he saw it. He was something of a scholar and wrote poetry, read in his day though unreadable in ours. In him New England Puritanism took on some of its harshest and least pleasant aspects. He often won approval but never affection. He was positive, dogmatic, austere, prejudiced, unlovable. He dominated by sheer strength of will as a leader in his community. Like many of the others he was no friend to popular government and a strong believer in autocracy. Opposed to the clergy in one respect, he believed that the state should control even the church and enforce conformity as the superior, and not the handmaid, of the ecclesiastical organization. In a poem of his own, found in his pocket after his death, we have his last message. It was, "hate heresy" and

> "Let men of God in courts and churches watch
> O'er such as do a *toleration* hatch."

[There are several volumes on the genealogy of the Dudley family: Geo. Adlard, *The Sutton-Dudleys of England and the Dudleys of Mass.* (1862); Dean Dudley, *Hist. of the Dudley Family* (1886–94); and *The Dudley Genealogies and Family Records* (1848). Cotton Mather has a brief sketch in *Magnalia Christi Americana* (edition of 1853), I, 131–35. He also wrote a longer account which, long thought to be lost, was found and printed by Adlard.] J. T. A.

DUDLEY, WILLIAM RUSSEL (Mar. 1, 1849–June 4, 1911), botanist, the son of Samuel William and Lucy (Chittenden) Dudley, was born at Guilford, Conn., where his ancestor, William Dudley, had settled about 1637. In early youth he became interested in the out-of-doors, especially in plants and birds, and when it came time to go to college he decided to be a botanist and chose Cornell, because at that time this newly founded university offered better facilities in science than did Yale. A letter of introduction brought him in contact with David Starr Jordan, who, although still an undergraduate, was instructor in botany in charge of the laboratory work. Dudley became the collector of plants for Jordan's class, and the two together, as Dr. Jordan says in his *Days of a Man* (I, 55), "roamed over all the hills and to all the waterfalls within thirty miles of Ithaca." On these tramps they began a catalogue of the Cayuga Lake region, which was later completed and published by Dudley. In his junior year he was given the instructorship in botany, which had been left vacant by the graduation of Jordan. In 1874 he was granted the degree of B.S. and two years later that of M.S. In the same year, 1876, he was promoted to assistant professor, a position he held until 1892 when he was called to Stanford University as professor of systematic botany. While at Cornell he was granted a year's leave of absence in 1880 to become acting professor of biology at the University of Indiana, a chair held by Jordan, who was away on leave. Again in 1887 he was granted leave to study abroad at the universities of Berlin and Strassburg.

Stanford University was beginning its second year when Dudley became a member of the faculty, and he entered with enthusiasm into building up his department and especially the botanical collections in the new institution. As a student of trees he became interested in the conservation of the forests and was frequently called upon by the United States forester, Gifford Pinchot, for botanical information and advice in the early development of the national forests in California. He was an active and influential member of the Sempervirens Club, the pioneer organization interested in the preservation of the redwood (*Sequoia sempervirens*), and was instrumental in the establishment of the California Redwood Park, the first public preserve of the redwood. He was appointed on the park commission by the governor of California, and served as secretary of the commission for several years. He was a born teacher of rare quality; his quiet, dignified, courteous manner, his thoroughness and enthusiasm in his work, formed lasting impressions upon his students. Although Dudley was a diligent and thorough student, he wrote comparatively little. Of the approximately forty scientific papers which he published, the more important are: *The Cayuga Flora* (1886); *A Catalogue of the Flowering Plants and Vascular Cryptogams found in and near Lackawanna and Wyoming Valleys* (1892), with Clarence O. Thurston; *The Genus Phyllospadix* (1893); and "The Vitality of Sequoia Gigantea" read in 1905 and published in the *Dudley Memorial Volume.*

Undoubtedly Dudley's most important contribution to science was the collection of the extensive herbarium to which he devoted so much time, labor, and money. All these collections were presented by him to Stanford and form the nucleus of the university's botanical collections, which have been named the Dudley Herbarium, a lasting and growing monument in his honor.

[*Who's Who in America,* 1910–11; *Dudley Memorial Volume* (Stanford Univ., 1911); D. S. Jordan, *Days of a Man* (2 vols., 1922); Dean Dudley, *Hist. of the Dudley Family,* nos. 1 and 4 (1886, 1890).] L. R. A.

DUER, JOHN (Oct. 7, 1782–Aug. 8, 1858), jurist, the second son of William Duer [*q.v.*] and his wife, Catherine Alexander, was born at Albany, N. Y. His education was intermittent and scanty. His father's financial troubles undoubtedly reacted unfavorably on his prospects and in 1798 he enlisted in the United States army. Two years later he obtained his discharge and commenced the study of law in the office of Alexander Hamilton, who had been his father's friend, at the same time taking steps to remedy the deficiencies of his early education by self-instruction. He was admitted as an attorney in 1806, and started practise in Orange County, N. Y., where he soon acquired a good connection, becoming known as a careful adviser and successful advocate. In 1821 he was a delegate from Orange County to the state constitutional convention of that year, and took a distinguished part in its proceedings, being a member of the committee on the judiciary department and exhibiting a grasp of public law, fertility of resource, and capacity for argument which gave him a state-wide reputation. In 1825 he was appointed to fill the vacancy on the commission to revise the New York statutes, caused by the resignation of Chancellor Kent. His fellow commissioners were Benjamin F. Butler and later John C. Spencer, and by a "kind of inspiration . . . the idea came to them of replacing the mass of disconnected statutes by a new and complete system of original laws systematically and scientifically arranged" (Butler, *post*). A large and important section of this work was performed by Duer. (See *The Revised Statutes of the State of New York, 1827–28,* 3 vols., 1829, *1828–35,* 3 vols., *1835–36,* edited by J. Duer, B. F. Butler and J. C. Spencer.) He was actively engaged in the revision till 1827, when he withdrew on his appointment as United States district attorney for southern New York. This latter position he held till the change of administration in 1829, when he resumed practise in New York City. Devoting his attention particularly to commercial and insurance law, he was recognized as an expert in the latter subject. In 1844 he published, *A Lecture on the Law of Representations in Marine Insurance* which attracted wide attention. This was followed by *A Treatise on the Law and Practise of Marine Insurance* (vols. I and II, 1845, 1846), a monumental and exhaustive work, the plan of which contemplated a third volume, which, however, was never completed. He also published a *Discourse on the Life, Character and Public Services of James Kent* (1848). In 1849 he was elected a judge of the superior court of the City of New York, becoming chief justice, May 10, 1857. On the bench he was notable for his personal charm of manner and unvarying dignity, but his inclination occasionally prompted him to merge the judge in the advocate, and he was apt to be somewhat discursive (Butler, *post*). He was the author of six volumes of *Reports of Cases Argued and Determined in the Superior Court of the City of New York* (1–6 *Duer,* 1852–57). His standing as a lawyer was high; Judge Silliman spoke of him as "the very lofty, learned and accomplished John Duer," and Charles O'Conor regarded him as the ablest jurist of his time in America. His opinions carried great weight and were always expressed in a form and language which rendered them models of their kind. He died on Staten Island, in his seventy-sixth year. His wife was Anna Bedford Bunner, daughter of George Bunner.

[The best appreciation of Duer's life and character appeared in Wm. Allen Butler, *The Revision of the Statutes of the State of N. Y., and the Revisers* (1889); see also D. McAdam, *Hist. of the Bench and Bar of N. Y.* (1897), I, 314; "The Duers," N. Y. *Evening Post,* Apr. 27, 1901; *Green Bag,* Sept. 1892; "In Memoriam," 6 *Duer,* preface and p. vi.] H. W. H. K.

DUER, WILLIAM (Mar. 18, 1747–May 7, 1799), merchant and financier, was born in Devonshire, England. His father, John Duer, who was wealthy, owning large plantations in Antigua and Dominica, married Frances Frye, and William was their third son. He was educated at Eton, obtained a commission as ensign in the British army, received an appointment as aide-de-camp to Lord Clive and accompanied the latter when he returned to India as Governor of Bengal in 1764. He was unable to withstand the climate, however, and returned to England. Shortly afterward, on his father's death, he inherited a share in the paternal plantations and went to the West Indies. In 1768, having obtained a contract to supply masts and spars for the British navy, he visited New York for the purpose of purchasing timber. There he met Philip Schuyler of Albany under whose advice he purchased an extensive tract of timber-land on the Hudson River above Saratoga, N. Y., and established large sawmills. He also made other investments. In 1773 he went to England, settled his affairs in that country, and on his return made the province of New York his permanent home. From his first arrival in New York he had associated with the leaders in its public life, and his liberal sentiments induced him to identify himself with the rapidly growing opposition to the home government. In 1775 he was a delegate to the Provincial Congress, being also appointed deputy adjutant-general of the New York troops, with the rank of colonel. In June 1776, he was a delegate to the New York constitutional convention and acted on the committee appointed to draft a constitution for the new state, his agile mind, fertility of expedients, and quick perception showing to advantage. In the same year he acted on the Committee of Public Safety, being designated at this period "as great a rebel as ever had an existence" (*post*). In March 1777, he was chosen as delegate from New York to the Continental Congress, where he was distinguished by his eloquence and extreme activity, serving on seven committees. He was on May 8 appointed first judge of common pleas of Charlotte (now Washington) County, N. Y., a position which he is credited with holding till 1786, *sed quaere*. In addition, he was a member of the Board of War, and a signer of the Articles of Confederation. His strong patriotism was signally displayed on the occasion of the Conway Cabal, when New York was temporarily deprived of its vote because of Duer's serious illness. This gave Washington's opponents in Congress a majority, and they planned to nominate a committee to remove the General from his command at Valley Forge. Word was sent to Duer, and despite his physician's warning that he could only be taken to Congress at the imminent risk of his life, he ordered his litter to be prepared and was about to make the journey, when the faction, hearing of his intent, abandoned the project (Dunlap, *post,* II, 133–34). He resigned from Congress in January 1779, in order to attend to his private affairs, but in July of the following year was appointed commissioner for conspiracies. He became immersed in many and varied commercial and financial projects, was engaged in furnishing supplies to the army, holding some of the largest contracts, and at the close of the war was in all probability a rich man. It was largely due to his efforts that in 1784 the Bank of New York was founded. In March 1786, he was appointed secretary to the Board of the Treasury, and established his residence permanently in New York City, becoming in the same year a member of the New York Assembly. In 1787 he was the prime mover in the Scioto speculation, he and his associates securing a right to purchase from the United States a huge tract of western lands, which they in turn designed to sell chiefly to capitalists abroad, particularly in France and Holland. He was also interested in an attempt to establish an international banking house which should supplant the great Dutch firms in the handling of loans and commercial business generally. In September 1789, the Treasury Department was organized, and Duer was appointed assistant secretary under his friend Alexander Hamilton, but resigned six months later, thus terminating his long connection with public life. Thenceforth he was continuously engaged in speculation on a large scale, involving purchases of lands in Massachusetts, Maine, and Vermont, contracts for army supplies during the Indian troubles of 1791, a project for a national manufacturing society in New Jersey, and large dealings in stocks. He became seriously involved, and when suit was brought against him by the government, regarding two unbalanced charges when he was secretary of the Treasury Board, a catastrophe was precipitated. Hopelessly insolvent, he was arrested for debt on Mar. 23, 1792, and sent to prison. This circumstance caused the first financial panic in the history of New York. Despite strenuous efforts to extricate himself, except for a short period in 1797 when he was released at Alexander Hamilton's intercession, he remained in prison till his death on May 7, 1799.

In 1779 he married Catherine, commonly called "Lady Kitty," daughter of Maj.-Gen. William Alexander [*q.v.*], also known as Lord Stirling, Washington giving the bride away. Of their children, William Alexander Duer [*q.v.*] became chief justice of the superior court of the City of New York. Of tireless energy, persuasive eloquence, and far-sighted, he was a natural leader in his various spheres of activity. He possessed capacity for business, and his operations were always planned with skill and daring, but almost all his promotions failed. His powers of execution were not equal to his conceptions. He undertook too much to give efficient attention to details. The manner of his operations had been much criticized and questions raised as to how far, if at all, he used his official position to advance his private concerns. It is perhaps safe to state that, though many of his acts were ill-advised and lent themselves to misconstruction, there is no evidence to show that they transgressed the law or exceeded the limits set by the standard of the commercial morality of the times. His opinions and sympathies were democratic, and his devotion to the cause of the Revolution was sincere, but in his mode of living he was very much the aristocrat. A contemporary (Manasseh Cutler, *post*), describing a dinner at his house in his prosperous days, says: "Colonel Duer . . . lives in the style of a nobleman. I presume he had not less than fifteen different sorts of wine at dinner and after the cloth was removed."

[Two original authorities for the details of Duer's life are Thomas Jones, *Hist. of N. Y. During the Revolutionary War* (1879), ed. by E. F. De Lancey (1879), II, 587; and an anonymous article in *The Knickerbocker or New York Monthly Mag.*, Aug. 1852, said to be based on the Duer papers in the N. Y. Hist. Soc., but apparently untrustworthy in places. See also J. S. Davis, *Essays in the Earlier Hist. of Am. Corporations* (1917), containing copious references; Wm. Dunlap, *Hist. of the New Netherlands* (2 vols., 1839); *Minutes of the Commissioners for Detecting and Defeating Conspiracies in the State of N. Y. 1778–81* (1909); *Life, Jours. and Correspondence of Rev. Manasseh Cutler* (1888), I, 240–41; T. T. Belote, *The Scioto Speculation and the French Settlement at Gallipolis* (1907); and "The Duers," in N. Y. *Evening Post,* Apr. 27, 1901.]

H. W. H. K.

DUER, WILLIAM ALEXANDER (Sept. 8, 1780–May 30, 1858), jurist, educator, was born at Rhinebeck, N. Y., the son of William Duer [*q.v.*], a member of the Continental Congress, of the Revolutionary Committee of Safety, and of the committee that drafted the first constitution of the state of New York. His mother was Catherine Alexander, daughter of Gen. William Alexander [*q.v.*], claimant to the Scottish earldom of Stirling. As a very young child, Duer went with his parents to live in New York City, where they first rented the Philipse house at the corner of Pine and William Sts., and afterward settled permanently in a residence at "the upper extremity of Broadway," opposite St. Paul's Church. They were fain to content themselves "with this remote residence," Duer explained later, owing to the scarcity of houses. At the age of eleven he was sent to England to be educated, under the care of his maternal aunts, but in a few years he returned and enrolled at Erasmus Hall, in Flatbush, under Dr. Peter Wilson.

On leaving school he entered the law office of Pierre Étienne Du Ponceau [*q.v.*] of Philadelphia, and later that of Nathaniel Pendleton in New York. After interrupting his legal studies to enlist as midshipman against France, serving on the same ship with Decatur and in the same rank, he returned to the law and was admitted to the bar in 1802. He began practise in conjunction with Edward Livingston [*q.v.*], then United States district attorney and mayor of New York, but a little later he formed a partnership with his brother-in-law, Beverley Robinson. At this time he was a contributor to the *Corrector,* a newspaper edited by Dr. Peter Irving in support of Aaron Burr. His former partner Livingston having meanwhile opened a law office in New Orleans, Duer joined him there in a thriving practise in which he devoted himself to the study of Spanish civil law. But the climate disagreed with him and he returned to New York after his marriage, on Sept. 11, 1806, to Hannah Maria Denning, daughter of William Denning, a prominent New York Whig. His friend Irving was now editing the *Morning Chronicle,* and Duer contributed occasional literary articles to this newspaper.

After opening a law office at Rhinebeck, he was elected to the state Assembly in 1814 and served till 1820. As chairman of the Committee on Colleges and Academies he secured the passage of a bill which furnished the basis for ensuing laws on common-school income. He was also chairman of the committee that drafted the law investing Livingston and Fulton with navigation rights in the Hudson River, and in the controversy over this he published two pamphlets (1817, 1819) addressed to Fulton's biographer, Cadwallader D. Colden [*q.v.*]. He aided in legislation concerning the canal system and the abuses of the lottery system. In 1822 he was made a judge of the supreme court of the state, and remained on the bench until 1829, when he resigned to accept the presidency of Columbia College. He held this office until failing health forced him to retire in 1842. His attention was given particularly to certain curricular changes, notably the establishment of scientific courses in which Latin should not be required and the furthering of studies in the modern languages and in Hebrew. He secured the foundation of a number of scholarships and increased the enrollment of the college. Taking personal charge of the freshman course in composition, he also gave to the seniors a course of lectures on constitutional jurisprudence, later published as *A Course of Lectures on the Constitutional Jurisprudence of the United States* (1843). His wise and efficient administration won the admiring affection of his college associates and his eloquence in numerous addresses, largely of political concern, gave him a leading place in the community.

After retiring, Duer lived at Morristown, N. J., where he wrote a biography of his grandfather in *The Life of William Alexander, Earl of Stirling,* published in 1847 by the New Jersey Historical Society. He continued to make frequent public addresses, notably one on education delivered at Columbia College, and one on his early recollections of New York, with reminiscences of Washington's inauguration, before the St. Nicholas Society. These were published as: *The Duties and Responsibilities of the Rising Generation* (1848), and *New York as it Was, During the Latter Part of the Last Century* (1849). His *Reminiscences of an Old Yorker* (1867) was published posthumously.

[The best account of Duer is an article by Wm. A. Duer in the *Columbia Univ. Quart.,* Mar. 1902. See also D. McAdam and others, *Hist. of the Bench and Bar of N. Y.* (1897), vol. I; "The Duers," *Evening Post* (N. Y.), Apr. 27, 1901.] E. H. W.

DUFF, MARY ANN DYKE (1794–Sept. 5, 1857), actress, was born in London, England, the daughter of an Englishman, about whom little is known, except that he died in the service of the East India Company and left his wife and three daughters with small means of support. The girls began their preparation for the stage under the tutelage of D'Egville, then ballet master in the King's Theatre in London. In 1809 they made their first public appearance as dancers in the Dublin Theatre, in Dublin. At a benefit performance at Kilkenny, during the same year, Mary Ann met Tom Moore, the Irish poet, and he fell deeply in love with her. She was said to have been the inspiration of many of his love poems, among which is "Mary, I believed thee true," but she did not return his affections and he married her sister, Elizabeth Dyke. Mary Ann married a young actor, John Duff, whom she had met during her engagement at Dublin Theatre, and with him sailed for America immediately after their marriage, in 1810. On Dec. 31 of that year she made her début in Boston at the Old Federal Street Theatre in the rôle of Shakespeare's Juliet. Her beauty attracted much attention. During the following eight years she studied her art diligently and in February 1818 she appeared again as Juliet and was then acclaimed a great tragic actress. On Dec. 4, 1827, she returned to London, where she played with some success at the Drury Lane Theatre. She remained in England only a short time, however, and on May 20, 1828, she was again back in America. On Apr. 28, 1831, John Duff died. The following year Mrs. Duff continued to play, but with little success. The death of her husband had left her in a state of melancholy and the weight of new responsibilities hindered her work on the stage. During this period she married a man by the name of Charles Young; the marriage, however, was never acknowledged by Mrs. Duff, and was legally dissolved soon after. Mrs. Duff continued to act in Philadelphia, Baltimore, and Washington, playing with her daughter, Mary Duff. She made her last appearance in New York, on Nov. 30, 1835, and shortly after returned to her home in Philadelphia. In this year she married a man by the name of Seaver, a young lawyer of Philadelphia. After a brief engagement in Washington, and her farewell benefit, she went with her husband to New Orleans where they lived for nearly twenty years, and where Seaver's law practise became very prosperous. Mrs. Seaver continued her work on the stage, appearing under her former name, Mrs. Duff, and playing throughout the South with great success. After her retirement from the stage, she was active in religious work. Although she had been brought up in the Catholic faith, she renounced Roman Catholicism for Methodism. After the death of her husband she went to live with her daughter in New York City. The rest of her life was spent in strict seclusion, and she was known only as a kind old lady devoted to her religion. At the age of sixty-three she died of cancer, at her daughter's home in New York. She was the mother of ten children; seven of these, four sons and three daughters, reached maturity. With this load of domestic responsibility she, nevertheless, was acclaimed one of the greatest tragic actresses of her time. Joseph Ireland said of her, "She was endowed by nature with every mental faculty and physical requisite for pure tragedy."

[Jos. N. Ireland's biography, *Mrs. Duff* (1882), written for the American Actor Series; W. W. Clapp, Jr., *A Record of the Boston Stage* (1853); W. D. Adams, *A Dictionary of the Drama*, I (1904), 433.] M. S.

DUFFIELD, GEORGE (Oct. 7, 1732–Feb. 2, 1790), Presbyterian clergyman, prominent in Pennsylvania both in the affairs of his denomination and as an ardent supporter of the American Revolution, was of French Huguenot descent, the family name having been originally Du Fielde. He was the son of George and Margaret Duffield, who, migrating from the north of Ireland some time between 1725 and 1730, settled in Lancaster County, Pa. Here in the township of Pequea he was born. He prepared for college at the Academy of Newark, graduated from the College of New Jersey in 1752, and subsequently studied theology in Pequea under Rev. Robert Smith [*q.v.*]. From 1754 to 1756 he was tutor at the College of New Jersey, being licensed to preach in the latter year, Mar. 11, by the Presbytery of New Castle. Three days earlier he had married Elizabeth, daughter of Rev. Samuel Blair [*q.v.*], who died the following year, and on Mar. 5, 1759, he married Margaret Armstrong, a sister of Gen. John Armstrong [1717–1795, *q.v.*]. In 1757 he was called to the church of Big Spring in conjunction with a recently formed church at Carlisle. His connection with the latter continued until 1772, but his relationship with the former was dissolved in 1769 and he assumed charge of the congregation at Monaghan. He was a man of vigorous personality and aggressive courage. An ardent temperament and facility in extemporaneous speaking made him a popular preacher. His career fell in troublous times. Old Side and New Side Presbyterians were in acrimonious conflict. Duffield, sympathetic toward Whitefield's followers, was emphatically New Side, and his ordination and installation at Carlisle were delayed until September 1759, because of a long-drawn-out controversy with Rev. John Steel, who came to the Old Side church already existing there. The communities to which he ministered were at this period in constant danger of attacks by Indians, and both he and his rival, Steel, captained their parishioners in one or two expeditions against them. The turbulence preceding the Revolution was rising, and Duffield identified himself with the boldest advocates of independence. Having declined two calls to the Second Presbyterian Church, Philadelphia, because it was felt that he was more needed at Carlisle, in 1772 he accepted the pastorate of the newly formed Third, or Pine Street, Church, of that city.

His ministry here had a stormy opening. Both Old Side sentiment and Tory sentiment were against him. The First Church, which had had a hand in establishing the Third, opposed his settlement. The church edifice was once closed against him, and when it was opened by his supporters and he persisted in conducting service after the King's Magistrate had ordered the people to disperse and had been thrown out as a disturber of public worship, he was arrested for aiding and abetting a riot. He had many zealous adherents, however, and came to exert much influence in the city. During the sessions of the Continental Congress John Adams and other delegates sat regularly under his patriotic preaching. Referring to the pastor of the First Church, Mr. Adams wrote "Mr. Sproat is totally destitute of the genius and eloquence of Duffield." After the declaration of independence he was commissioned chaplain of the Pennsylvania militia, and rendered such service that the British offered fifty pounds for his capture. He also served with Rev. William White [*q.v.*] as chaplain to the Continental Congress. Subsequent to the War he served the Third Church as pastor until his death in his fifty-eighth year. He was trustee of the College of New Jersey from 1777 to 1790, active in the organization of the Presbyterian Church after the Revolution, and the first stated clerk of the General Assembly. An account of a two months' missionary tour to frontier inhabitants and the Indians which he made with Rev. Charles C. Beatty [*q.v.*] in 1766, was published by the latter in 1768. Duffield's thanksgiving discourse for the restoration of peace, *A Sermon Preached in the Third Presbyterian Church in the City of Philadelphia on Thursday, Dec. 11, 1783,* was published in 1784.

[*Gen. Cat. of Princeton Univ. 1746–1906* (1908); W. B. Sprague, *Annals Am. Pulpit*, vol. III (1858); Alfred Nevin, *Centennial Biog. Men of Mark of Cumberland Valley, Pa. 1776–1876* (1876); *The Centennial Memorial of the Presbytery of Carlisle* (1889); *Jour. Presbyt. Hist. Soc.*, June 1905; J. T. Headley, *The Chaplains and Clergy of the Revolution* (1864); Ashbel Green, *A Sermon Preached at the Funeral of Rev. George Duffield, D.D., of Philadelphia* (1790); Hughes O. Gibbons, *A Hist. of Old Pine Street Church* (1905).]

H. E. S.

DUFFIELD, GEORGE (July 4, 1794–June 26, 1868), Presbyterian clergyman, grandson of Rev. George Duffield [*q.v.*], and son of George and Faithful (Slaymaker) Duffield, was born in Strasburg, Lancaster County, Pa. His father was for many years comptroller of the state. In the strict Presbyterian circle in which the younger George grew up he was considered "wayward" but outside that circle he probably would not have been regarded as displaying any particularly wicked tendencies. He was precocious enough to graduate from the University of Pennsylvania in his seventeenth year, and, having been converted from his waywardness, to be licensed to preach by the Presbytery of Philadelphia before he was twenty-one, Apr. 20, 1815, after four years' study of theology with Dr. John Mitchell Mason [*q.v.*]. Almost a year and a half later, Sept. 25, 1816, he was ordained and installed pastor of the Presbyterian church, Carlisle, Pa., in which town his grandfather had been a pioneer minister. Like the latter he was a man of strong convictions, outspoken and fearless, making stanch friends and some enemies. His piety and zeal in his calling were never questioned. A strict disciplinarian, he insisted on daily worship and religious instruction in the home, established a Sunday-school for those who did not receive such instruction there, and required all communicants to renounce attendance at dances and theatres, and to abjure worldly amusements in general. In 1832, as the conflict which in 1837–38 split the church was beginning, he became a theological storm center through the publication of *Spiritual Life: or, Regeneration,* in which, it was alleged, he departed from the doctrinal standards of the church. The language of the book is obscure and confusing. Dr. Alexander McClelland is reported to have said of Duffield that "he knew no man so effective and mighty in presenting the practical side of religion, but that when he turned, as he sometimes did, to metaphysics, he got so deep down in the mud that he did not know where he was, nor did anyone else." Charges were brought against him. The Presbytery of Carlisle condemned the book, but since he declared that it was misunderstood and that in reality he had not repudiated the established doctrines, the Presbytery did not discipline the author. The Synod of Philadelphia took exception to this action. Duffield appealed to the General Assembly, but the appeal was not prosecuted. *The Principles of Presbyterian Discipline, Unfolded and Illustrated in the Protests and Appeals of George Duffield, Entered during the Process of the Presbytery of Carlisle, against him April, 1833, in which his Strict Adherence to the Confession of Faith and the Standards of the Church is Shown,* was published in 1835.

The controversy had divided his church, however, and on Mar. 23, 1835, he was dismissed. After brief pastorates at the Fifth Presbyterian

Church, Philadelphia, and at Broadway Tabernacle, New York, on Oct. 1, 1838, he was installed pastor of the First Presbyterian, then known as the Protestant Church, Detroit. Here for thirty years he had a notable ministry; his interest in the cause of education, temperance, and good morals making him prominent in both city and state. He was active in the New School branch of the church, and at the request of its committee on publication prepared a statement of the New School theology. It was not acceptable to a majority of the committee, but was printed in the *Bibliotheca Sacra* in July 1863 under the title "Doctrines of the New School Presbyterian Church." He was also an early and consistent advocate of reunion. Among his numerous published sermons and books are: *The Immorality of the Traffic in Ardent Spirits* (1834); *Discourses on the Sabbath* (1836), in collaboration with Albert Barnes; *A Sermon on American Slavery: Its Nature and the Duties of Christians in Relation to it* (1840); *The Death of Gen. William Henry Harrison . . . or, The Divine Rebuke* (1841); *Dissertations on the Prophecies Relative to the Second Coming of Jesus Christ* (1842); *Millenarianism Defended: A Reply to Professor Stuart's "Strictures on the Rev. G. Duffield's Recent Book on the Second Coming of Christ"* (1843); *The Claims of "Episcopal Bishops," Examined in a Series of Letters Addressed to the Rev. S. A. McCoskry, D.D., Bishop of the Protestant Episcopal Church of Michigan* (1842); *The Bible Rule of Temperance: Total Abstinence from all Intoxicating Drink* (1868). A detailed account of a trip abroad made in 1852 appeared in a series of articles in the *Magazine of Travel.* This periodical, which ran for only a year, was published in book form under the title, *Travels in Two Hemispheres* (1858). While delivering an address before the International Convention of the Young Men's Christian Association at Detroit, June 24, 1868, he suddenly collapsed and died two days later. His wife was Isabella Graham Bethune, grand-daughter of Isabella Graham [*q.v.*], and sister of George Washington Bethune [*q.v.*].

[*The Centennial Memorial of the Presbytery of Carlisle* (1889); *Presbyt. Reunion: A Memorial Volume* (1870); Samuel J. Baird, *A Hist. of the New School and of the Questions Involved in the Disruption of the Presbyt. Ch. in 1838* (1868); *Detroit Free Press,* June 25, 27, 29, 1868.]

H. E. S.

DUFFIELD, SAMUEL AUGUSTUS WILLOUGHBY (Sept. 24, 1843–May 12, 1887), Presbyterian clergyman, hymnologist, was fourth in descent from Rev. George Duffield (1732–1790), grandson of Rev. George Duffield (1794–1868), and the son of Rev. George Duffield (1818–1888) and Anna Augusta Willoughby. His father was a Presbyterian clergyman and writer of hymns, some of which are now widely used in public worship. Samuel was born in Brooklyn, N. Y., fitted for college with William FewSmith at Philadelphia, and graduated from Yale in the class of 1863. The following winter he was in charge of the Adrian, Mich., high school. He then studied theology under his father and grandfather, and was licensed to preach by the Knox Presbytery of Illinois in April 1866. After being in charge of the Mosely Mission, Chicago, for six months, and preaching and studying for a period in New York and Philadelphia, he was called to the latter city and ordained and installed pastor of the Kenderton Presbyterian Church on Nov. 12, 1867. The following year, Oct. 1, in Adrian, Mich., he was married to Hattie S., daughter of Isaac Haywood. He had a brief pastorate in Jersey City in 1870, and was subsequently pastor of the First Presbyterian Church, Ann Arbor, Mich. (1871–74), of the Eighth Presbyterian Church, Chicago (1874–76); acting pastor of the Central Presbyterian Church, Auburn, N. Y. (1876–78); pastor of the Second Presbyterian Church, Altoona, Pa. (1878–81); and thereafter pastor of the Westminster Presbyterian Church, Bloomfield, N. J., relinquishing active work in 1886 because of a heart affection from which he died less than two years later.

He was a man of literary tastes and poetic gifts. A volume of his poems, *Warp and Woof,* was issued in 1870. He had previously published, *The Heavenly Land* (1867), a translation in English verse of *De Contemptu Mundi* by Bernard of Cluny. Five of his hymns, four of them translations, appeared in Charles Seymour Robinson's *Laudes Domini* (1884). His greatest contribution to hymnology, however, is his elaborate work, *English Hymns: Their Authors and History* (1886). At the time of his death he was engaged on a similar work, *The Latin Hymn Writers and Their Hymns* (1889), which was completed and edited by Robert E. Thompson. In collaboration with his father he also prepared and published, *The Burial of the Dead* (1882).

[See *Triennial Meeting and Biog. Record of the Class of Sixty-Three, in Yale College* (1869); *Presbyterian,* May 21, 1887; *Obit. Record Grads. Yale Univ., 1880–90* (1890); John Julian, *A Dict. of Hymnology* (1915). Thompson's preface to Duffield's *The Latin Hymn Writers* contains biographical sketch.]

H. E. S.

DUFOUR, JOHN JAMES (*c.* 1763–Feb. 9, 1827), pioneer viticulturist and founder of the Swiss vineyards in America, eldest child of Jean Jacques Dufour, a Swiss vinedresser, was born in the commune of Chatelard, district of Vevay, Canton de Vaud, Switzerland. He came to America in 1796 with the definite purpose of founding a grape colony to cultivate the grape, for wine. After an extensive search for a suitable situation for the vineyard, he arrived at Lexington, Ky., on Aug. 28, 1798, where he organized a vineyard association. A tract of 630 acres, called the First Vineyard, was purchased on the Kentucky River about twenty-five miles from Lexington. After the vineyard was well started, Dufour sent for his brothers and sisters in Switzerland. They, with relatives and friends, a little band of seventeen, arrived at the First Vineyard in the summer of 1801. They were full of hope but their efforts were doomed to failure, as a fatal disease soon attacked the vines. Some members of the colony then started the Second Vineyard, down the Ohio River at a place now called Vevay, Ind. The subscribers to the Vineyard Association having become disheartened, the association was dissolved and the full burden of carrying on the vineyards rested on the Swiss colony. In 1806 Dufour was obliged to return to Europe. He left the vineyards in the hands of his younger brothers. The second war with England broke out in his absence and he was delayed in returning until 1816. In the meantime his brothers abandoned the First Vineyard and joined the other colonists at Vevay. Here Dufour joined them on his return to America and here he wrote his book, *The American Vine Dresser's Guide* (Cincinnati, S. J. Browne, 1826). He died at Vevay at the age of sixty-four, a few months after his book was published. He was a man of unusual intelligence, forethought, and perseverance. While his grape colony experiments ended in failure, he contributed an important chapter to the history of grape growing in America.

[L. H. Bailey, *Sketch of the Evolution of our Native Fruits* (1898), pp. 21–40; Perret Dufour, "The Swiss Settlement of Switzerland County, Ind.," *Ind. Hist. Colls.*, vol. XIII (1925); *Ind. Horticultural Soc. Ann. Report*, 1872, pp. 128–29.] C. R. B.

DUGANNE, AUGUSTINE JOSEPH HICKEY (1823–Oct. 20, 1884), poet, miscellaneous writer, was born in Boston and first came to public notice through patriotic poems which he contributed to newspapers. After the appearance of *Massachusetts* (1843) and *Home Poems* (1844) he migrated to Philadelphia and set up as an author. His income, which in a few years was sufficient for him to marry and to live with apparent happiness in marriage, came chiefly, it is probable, from his stories of adventure, which he produced in quantity lots for several publishers, including Erastus Beadle. He also compiled books on philosophy, economics, and government and ventured into tragedy with *The Lydian Queen,* which was produced at the Walnut Street Theatre in 1848. His address in 1849 (*McElroy's Philadelphia Directory*) was the southeast corner of Fourth and Walnut Sts. He moved to New York sometime around 1850. There he continued to concoct paper-backed novels; wrote book reviews that kindled the enthusiasm of Thomas Holley Chivers (information from Dr. Lewis Chase) for John Sartain's *Union Magazine* and other periodicals; lampooned his contemporaries in *Parnassus in Pillory* (1851); advanced the cause of Americanism in literature with *A Sound Literature the Safeguard of our National Institutions* (1853), and *Art's True Mission in America* (1853); won a hundred-dollar prize in 1854 with a turgid "Ode to Powers' Greek Slave"; agitated in prose and verse for free land in the West; declaimed, also in both prose and verse, before meetings of fraternal orders and workingmen's organizations; and between 1847 and 1854 brought out seven volumes of his poems. While he was seriously ill in 1855, a Philadelphia friend, James Lesley, Jr., edited a sumptuous volume of his *Poetical Works* (2nd ed., 1856; autograph ed., 1865), with a portrait engraved by Sartain. The head, with its broad, unfurrowed brow, full beard, and flowing hair, bears a simultaneous resemblance to Alfred Tennyson and E. Z. C. Judson. In the prefatory matter the poet alludes to recent bereavements. In the autumn of 1855 the success of the Know-Nothing party landed him in the Assembly as the member for the sixth district of New York, but his career as a statesman lasted for only one term. In the autumn of 1862 Duganne helped to raise the 176th New York Volunteers and was commissioned immediately as its lieutenant-colonel. The regiment was sent to Louisiana. Through no fault of his he and his command were compelled to surrender to a superior force at Brashear (now Morgan) City, La., June 23, 1863, and the rest of his military life was spent ingloriously in prison camps near Hempstead and Tyler, Tex. His *Camps and Prisons: Twenty Months in the Department of the Gulf* (1865), largely autobiographical, is honest, vivid, and packed with detail. Its account of life in Texas during the war is of historical value. Duganne was paroled July 24, 1864, and, having suffered much during his captivity, was mustered out for disability, Sept. 10. At the close of the war, Gov. R. E. Fenton appointed him chief of the bureau of military statistics, and thereafter he was connected with the *New York Tribune,* and the *Sunday Dispatch,* a Masonic sheet of sensational proclivities. *Utterances* (1865) and *Ballads of the War* (complete ed., 1865) contain his martial verse. *Fighting Quakers* (1866), *Governments of the World* (1882), and *Injuresoul* (1884), a dull satire addressed to both Ingersoll and Beecher, are among his last books. Duganne was affable, kindly, and of studious habits. During his last years he was afflicted with tuberculosis. He died at his home in New York of a complication of diseases and was buried in Cypress Hills Cemetery.

[*N. Y. Times* and *N. Y. Tribune,* Oct. 22, 1884; *N. Y. Dispatch,* Oct. 26, 1884; F. B. Hough, *N. Y. Civil List 1777–1863* (Albany, 1863); *Ann. Report Adj.-Gen. State of N. Y.,* 1905; private information.] G. H. G.

DUGDALE, RICHARD LOUIS (1841–July 23, 1883), social economist, was born in Paris of English parents, Richard John Dugdale and his wife, Anna, a descendant of Sir Thomas Cuddon of Shaddingfield Hall, Suffolk. When the boy was seven years old his father, who had been both a manufacturer and a journalist, suffered business reverses. The family returned to England, and Richard was sent for three years to the Somerset School. He came to New York City with his parents in 1851, and attended the public schools until, at the age of fourteen, showing ability in drawing, he was for a time employed by a sculptor. He already had symptoms of heart trouble, and at seventeen went to live with his parents on an Indiana farm. Being unequal to manual labor he learned shorthand, and when the family returned to New York in 1860 he was employed as a stenographer. He attended night classes at Cooper Union, being particularly active in the debating clubs. He had a consuming interest in sociological subjects and resolved to be a social investigator, but since it was before the day of research foundations and he lacked the formal equipment necessary for an academic position, he decided to enter business in order later to accumulate enough to indulge his curiosity. Dugdale lived successively in several houses in Greenwich Village, and in 1871 moved to No. 4 Morton St., which he made a rendezvous for many social reformers. In 1868 he became a member of the executive committee of the Prison Association of New York, to which he gave his hardest work. In 1874 he was appointed a committee of one to inspect thirteen county jails. Struck with the consanguinity of many of the criminals, he used private funds to make a detailed study of one large family connection and in 1875, in a report of the Prison Association, he published "The Jukes, a Study in Crime, Pauperism, Disease and Heredity." This, together with his *Further Studies of Criminals,* was republished in 1877. He found that of 709 persons —540 of "Juke" blood and 169 of other strains connected with the family by marriage or cohabitation—180 had been in the poorhouse or received outdoor relief for a total of 800 years, 140 had been convicted of criminal offenses, 60 were habitual thieves, 7 were murdered, 50 were common prostitutes, 40 women venereally diseased had infected at least 440 persons, and there had been 30 prosecutions in bastardy. These people had cost the State at least $1,308,000. Dugdale's findings created a sensation. He believed that inheritance was of more importance as a limiting factor in determining character than environment, but he tried to give full weight to the latter. In 1880 he became the first secretary of the Society for Political Education, which sought to inform the electorate on social questions. He was an active member of a large number of sociological and civic organizations, and wrote for the reviews and spoke before scientific bodies, particularly on criminology. He was a thin, fair-haired, diffident man, of almost no presence, but had a devoted circle of intimates. He died of his heart trouble, after a long illness. His work has been followed by other similar studies, particularly that of Arthur H. Estabrook, *The Jukes in 1915* (1916), made possible by the finding, in 1911, of Dugdale's manuscript.

[E. M. Shepard, *The Work of a Social Teacher* (1884), being No. VII of the Economic Tracts of the Soc. for Pol. Educ.; historical note in Estabrook, *op. cit.*; G. H. Putnam, *Memories of a Publisher, 1865–1915* (1915); *N. Y. Times,* July 24, 1883.]
B. M—l.

DUGUÉ, CHARLES OSCAR (May 1, 1821–Aug. 29, 1872), Creole poet, was born in New Orleans of French ancestry, the son of François Dugué, a wealthy planter, and Jeanne Marie (Pligne). He was educated in France, principally at the Collège St. Louis in Paris, and perfected his English at Transylvania College in Kentucky. Attracted to the fields of journalism, literature, and law, he wrote for the New Orleans papers, *L'Abeille, La Lorgnette, Le Propagateur catholique,* became editor in chief of *L'Orléanais,* and served for some time as judge of the district court for the parishes of St. Bernard, Jefferson, and Plaquemines. During the years 1847–52, which marked the height of his literary powers, he published: *Philosophie morale* (1847), a volume of miscellany; *Essais poétiques* (1847), a collection of verse; *Mila ou là mort de La Salle* (1852), a romantic drama whose chief figure is La Salle; and *Le Cygne ou Mingo* (1852), a drama in which Tecumseh plays a part. Turning to teaching, he became an assistant superintendent of schools in New Orleans and later president of Jefferson College in St. James Parish. When the doors of the college were closed on account of the Civil War, Dugué was broken in health. He met disaster with fortitude, however; worked on a poem to be entitled *"Homo,"* which he believed was to be his masterpiece, and taught in the New Orleans Normal School. In quest of a publisher and in the vain hope of regaining his lost health he went to Paris, where he died, survived by his wife, Elodie Augustine de Livaudais. His body was brought to New Orleans to rest in the family tomb in St. Louis Cemetery No. 2. In the year of his death, 1872, his last work, *Homo,* was published in Paris by his brother. It is a didactic poem in the form of a dialogue wherein God and Man discourse on the fatality of destiny and the freedom of the will. The book presents philosophical ideas that seek to obtain harmony and conciliation by persuasion.

Dugué is chiefly interesting because of his poetry. He himself believed in the sacredness of his mission and his youthful efforts attracted the attention of Châteaubriand. In his verses written under the influence of both Musset and Vigny at times he reached lyrical heights, especially when melancholy turned his thoughts to his native land. His poetical powers were not sustained, however; he preached the utility of the poet as a benefactor of society, and in later years his poetry assumed a didactic tone which deprived it of spontaneity and lyrical qualities. As a dramatist he was a follower of the so-called *"École de bon sens"* whose chief exponent was Ponsard.

[Chas. Testut in *Portraits littéraires* (1850) penned an interesting study of Dugué. Adrien Rouquette wrote a preface to *Les Essais poétiques* which contains important data. E. Fortier gave a synopsis of *Mila* in *Mémoires du Premier Congrès de la langue français au Canada, Quebec 1915*. The play itself was reprinted by L'Athénée Louisianais in its *Comptes Rendus* (Oct. 1907, Jan. 1908). Dugué's daughter, Sophie Elisabeth (Mrs. John Bendernagel) has furnished some information. See also Grace King, *Creole Families of New Orleans* (1921); E. A. and G. L. Duyckinck, *Cyc. of Am. Lit.* (1856); J. W. Davidson, *Living Writers of the South* (1869); *Lib. of Southern Lit.*, XV (1909), 130; Ruby Caulfeild, *The French Lit. of Louisiana* (1929); brief obituary in *L'Abeille,* Sept. 19, 1872.] L. C. D.

DUHRING, LOUIS ADOLPHUS (Dec. 23, 1845–May 8, 1913), dermatologist, was the son of Henry Duhring of Mecklenburg, Germany, and Caroline (Oberteuffer) Duhring of St. Gall, Switzerland, who migrated to the United States in 1818. They were thrifty, and educated, and the father, who had been moderately successful at home, became a prominent merchant in Philadelphia and gained considerable wealth. The family was particularly interested in music and devoted many of its evenings to concerts at home with friends. Louis was studious, quiet, and retiring in manner and had considerable taste and talent for music. A sister, Julia Duhring, to whom he was devoted, developed talent as a writer. The boy's early education was obtained in Philadelphia private schools; in 1861 he entered the freshman class of the college department of the University of Pennsylvania. At the end of his third year he enlisted, in July 1863, in the 32nd Regiment, Pennsylvania Volunteers; after serving for three months he was honorably discharged, and entered the medical department of the University of Pennsylvania, where he graduated after three years. He then became an interne in the Philadelphia Hospital (Blockley) where he remained fifteen months.

In the summer of 1868 he went for further instruction to Vienna, where he studied under the brilliant Ferdinand Hebra, who was developing dermatology as a special branch of medicine. There were no such specialists in Philadelphia at the time and indeed but few in the United States. After two years, Duhring returned to Philadelphia and began practise as a dermatologist. He immediately organized and opened the "Dispensary for Skin Diseases," with the eminent surgeon, Prof. Samuel D. Gross [*q.v.*], as president of the board of trustees. With this institution Duhring retained connection until 1890, being a consultant after 1880. In 1871 he was made lecturer on skin diseases in the University of Pennsylvania. At this time he was twenty-six years old. In 1876 he published the first part of his *Atlas of Skin Diseases,* a water-color portrayal of diseases with descriptive text. This was the first effort of the kind in the United States and gained for its author considerable distinction. Since the work was not of a remunerative character, Duhring was obliged to draw upon his own purse to finance the venture. In the same year he became visiting dermatologist to the newly opened department of skin diseases at the Philadelphia Hospital (Blockley), continuing in this capacity until 1887. In 1877, he published a *Practical Treatise on Diseases of the Skin.* This was the first American text-book on the subject and served to establish its writer as the leader of his specialty in America. The excellence of the work led to second and third editions within a few years, and the book was later translated into French, Italian, and Russian. After years of experience as a dermatologist he published *Cutaneous Medicine* (part I, 1895; part II, 1898). He was a frequent contributor to medical journals and his articles disclosed a keen insight into the subjects with which he dealt. His most important articles were on what he called "dermatitis herpetiformis," which was closely related to an extremely fatal dermatosis known as pemphigus. Although the great Viennese dermatologist Kaposi and others took opposite sides of the controversy, Duhring successfully maintained his position and trenchantly established dermatitis herpetiformis as a separate clinical entity. Throughout the world this is known to-day as Duhring's Disease, and sufferers from this disease have a far better chance of recovery than from the fatal pemphigus.

Throughout his student days Duhring was conspicuously well dressed and gentlemanly in bearing and exhibited a fondness for music, theatrical performances, public and private, and cotillion dances. About the time of his graduation, however, a shadow was cast upon his lighter nature by the death of a young lady who was looked upon as his fiancée. This caused him to withdraw from social contacts and become increasingly absorbed in his professional labors. The deaths of his two brothers and more particularly that of his beloved sister, in 1892, further saddened his life, and he became more and more an isolated recluse. He lived alone in his domicile and, although many could claim acquaintance with him, no one had the privilege of his intimacy or friendship. As a result, he developed certain eccentricities of manner. He was diffident, retiring, and secretive in conversation, very parsimonious, and expended little upon himself. As a result of judicious investments he acquired for his time considerable wealth. His estate which was largely bequeathed to the University of Pennsylvania and the College of Physicians of Philadelphia, amounted to more than a million and a quarter dollars.

[H. W. Stelwagon, "Memoir of Louis A. Duhring," in *Trans. Coll. Phys. of Phila.* (1914); J. L. Chamberlain, *Universities and Their Sons, Univ. of Pa., 1740–1900* (1901); *Public Ledger* (Phila.), May 9, 1913.]

J. F. S.

DUKE, BASIL WILSON (May 28, 1838–Sept. 16, 1916), Confederate soldier, was born in Scott County, Ky., the son of Nathaniel Wilson and Mary (Currie) Duke. Nathaniel Duke was a naval officer, descended from a Maryland family which established itself in Kentucky in the eighteenth century. His son was educated at Georgetown (Ky.), and Centre College, and at the law school of Transylvania University at Lexington. Admitted to the bar in 1858, he began the practise of law in St. Louis. An enthusiastic state-rights man, he took a very active part in the secessionist movement in Missouri, and engaged in secret operations which exposed him to danger from friends as well as enemies. On one occasion he narrowly escaped summary execution at the hands of a secessionist vigilance committee, by whom he was "suspected of being a suspicious character." Later, his arrest within the Union lines was prevented only by the intervention of his old friend, John M. Harlan, then in the Union army and later a justice of the Supreme Court, who was convinced that Duke was not there in the capacity of a spy,—as, indeed, he was not on this particular occasion, for he was merely taking a short cut to Lexington to pay a visit to his wife. He had married, in June 1861, Henrietta Hunt Morgan, the sister of John Hunt Morgan [*q.v.*], who was soon to distinguish himself as a cavalry leader.

The secessionist movement in Missouri having been checked, Duke enlisted as a private in his brother-in-law's "Lexington Rifles," and was elected first lieutenant. When the Lexington Rifles became a part of the 2nd Kentucky Cavalry, Duke was appointed lieutenant-colonel of the regiment and later became its colonel. He took a conspicuous part in all the operations of Morgan's cavalry command, was wounded at Shiloh, was captured along with the rest of Morgan's men in his spectacular raid through Ohio in 1863, and for a year remained a prisoner of war. Exchanged and rejoining his regiment, Duke was appointed a brigadier-general in September 1864, and commanded a cavalry brigade in eastern Kentucky and western Virginia until Lee's surrender. The infantry in the little army was then disbanded, the guns were spiked, and the wagon train was abandoned; the cavalry, mostly mounted on the draft mules of the train, endeavored to join Johnston in North Carolina. Reaching Charlotte, it was assigned as escort to Jefferson Davis and the fugitive Confederate government. Its general officers, Duke among them, shared in Davis's last council of war, and unanimously declared that further resistance was hopeless. After the party broke up, Duke, with a small force, tried to lead the pursuit away from the direction in which Davis had fled, and then surrendered and was paroled. He eventually settled in Louisville, and resumed law practise. A member of the Kentucky House of Representatives in 1869, he served as commonwealth attorney of the fifth judicial district, 1875–80. For more than twenty years he was a member of the legal staff of the Louisville & Nashville Railroad. His interest in Civil War history was keen, and he wrote extensively on such parts of it as came within his own experiences. His *History of Morgan's Cavalry*, first published in 1867, was reprinted in 1906 with a briefer title. He was a frequent contributor to the *Southern Bivouac,* a magazine the editorship of which he shared for two years (1885–87). He later edited (1893–94) the *Mid-Continent Magazine* and the *Southern Magazine.* The *Reminiscences of General Basil W. Duke, C. S. A.,* appeared in book form in 1911, after having previously been published as separate magazine articles. He also wrote a *History of the Bank of Kentucky* (1895). From 1895 until his death he was a commissioner of Shiloh National Park.

Duke was small in stature and slight of frame. His face was distinguished by the mustache and goatee of the traditional Kentucky gentleman, and by a humorous eye. His cheerfulness was unquenchable. The *Reminiscences,* written in his old age, are full of boyish enthusiasm and enjoyment, as well as shrewd comemnt on political and military measures. He was boyish, too, in his frank hero-worship of Morgan. Strong in his conviction of the justice of the Confederate cause, he could yet clearly appreciate the point of view of his opponents; and four years of war roused in him feelings of warm friendship, rather than of hatred, toward those against whom he fought. Southerners would have described him as chivalrous, and in this instance that much-abused word is appropriate. As a soldier, he was not of the first rank, though an able cavalry commander; but his personality makes him one of the most attractive figures of his time.

[His books, mentioned above, and several papers published in *The Century* (1884–87) and reprinted in *Battles and Leaders of the Civil War* (1887–88) give the best account of his military career. There is a good brief sketch of his life in *Confed. Mil. Hist.* (1899), vol. IX, Ky., pp. 234–36. See also *Official Records (Army),* 1 ser., vols. XVI (pts. 1, 2), XX (pt. 1), XXIII (pt. 1), XXXIX (pts. 1, 3), XLV (pts. 1, 2), XLIX (pts. 1, 2); 2 ser., vol. VI; H. Levin, ed., *Lawyers and Lawmakers of Ky.* (1897).] T. M. S.

DUKE, BENJAMIN NEWTON (Apr. 27, 1855–Jan. 8, 1929), industrialist, philanthropist, was born on the farm of his father, Washington Duke, four miles north of Durham, N. C. Washington Duke, the son of Taylor and Dicie (Jones) Duke, was of English, Scotch-Irish, and Welsh descent. He married in 1852 his second wife, Artelia, daughter of John and Mary Roney of Alamance County. She died in 1858, when Benjamin, her elder son, was three years old. When they became rich, Benjamin and James B. Duke [*q.v.*] gave a science building to Elon College, N. C., in honor of their mother. The boys, with their sister, were cared for until 1863 by aunts who came into Washington Duke's home after his wife's death. In that year their father, though a Unionist, went into the Confederate army, and the children went to live with their grandparents in Alamance. Ben went to neighborhood schools at Harden's and Pisgah Church, and was a playful, sturdy youngster, busy after school with chores about the farm. After the war, when not working at growing and manufacturing tobacco, he was a pupil in the academy of Dr. Morgan Closs in Durham, and later was sent to the Quakers' school at New Garden (now Guilford College).

The Dukes built a factory in Durham in 1874, and in 1878 formed the firm of W. Duke Sons & Company. The firm was one of the first to introduce cigarette machines; it boldly cut the price on their product and extended its market throughout the world. Branch factories having been established in New York in 1884, the Dukes entered the "cigarette war" which ended in a combination, the American Tobacco Company, formed in 1890. Benjamin N. Duke was one of the directors, while his brother James was president. Then followed a series of mergers which gave this corporation control of the industry in America, the Duke brothers being the dominant factors in the whole. On the dissolution of the combination by order of the Supreme Court in 1911, Benjamin Duke diverted his capital to a variety of other undertakings. Already in 1906 he had become president of the Citizens National Bank in Durham, and had reorganized a local railroad, the Cape Fear & Northern, extended its tracks to reach Durham, and changed its name to the Durham & Southern. He became heavily interested in hydro-electric power development in the South, in cotton manufacturing, and in real estate. He was a leader in the South's economic revival. His fortune at one time was estimated at $60,000,000. At the time of his death he had withdrawn from active management of most of these enterprises, his only business positions being those of director in the Southern Power Company, and director of the Durham Realty Corporation, the latter owning hotels and apartment houses in New York and New Jersey. Benjamin N. Duke was not so gifted as his brother James in business organization, but he earlier manifested an interest in educational and charitable work, and influenced members of his family in this direction. He relinquished his design of building an orphanage at Durham when it was suggested to him that Trinity College might be removed from the country to the location he had selected, and he forwarded plans which brought this about in 1892. Between 1898 and 1925 his gifts to the college grew progressively, totaling in excess of $2,000,000. It was undoubtedly Benjamin's example that induced James to make this school the chief object of his benefactions, which resulted in very large gifts by him in 1924 and 1925, and a change of name to Duke University. Benjamin gave to churches, to a negro hospital in Durham, and to many other institutions associated with his young manhood. He married in 1877 Sarah Pearson Angier of Durham, and had two sons and a daughter. He was modest, avoided publicity, and sought to keep his gifts secret. He died at his home in New York, after being confined to the house for months. His body lay in state at Duke University and was buried in Durham.

[See John W. Jenkins, *James B. Duke, Master Builder* (1927); Wm. K. Boyd, *The Story of Durham, City of the New South* (1925); *Who's Who in America*, 1928–29; *N. Y. Times*, and Raleigh (N. C.) *News and Observer*, Jan. 9, 1929.] B. M—l.

DUKE, JAMES BUCHANAN (Dec. 23, 1856–Oct. 10, 1925), industrialist, was the youngest child of Washington Duke and Artelia (Roney) Duke, his mother dying when he was an infant. He and his brother Benjamin Newton [*q.v.*] were born on his father's small farm near Durham, N. C., and soon were plunged into the poverty brought by the Civil War. James attended school in a log house at Harden's and later at Pisgah Church. When the father returned on foot from the Confederate army with a single half-dollar and two blind mules, life was resumed on the home farm, which had been swept clean by the invading army. Luckily, however, a quantity of leaf tobacco had been overlooked, and this was seized upon as the one hope. James and Benjamin helped their father pound it out with hickory sticks in a small log barn on the place, and the tobacco was put in packages labeled "Pro Bono Publico." Hitching their blind mules and supplied with rations, they struck out with their product to the southern part of North Carolina where tobacco was scarce. Meeting with ready sales, they purchased more leaf tobacco, built a larger log house for the manufacture, and found themselves prospering in their venture. They sold 125,000 pounds in 1872, and were as substantial as any in the local industry. James for a time attended the academy in Durham taught by Dr. Morgan Closs, proving quick with figures; he was then sent to a boarding school in Guilford County, but longed for the activity of farm and factory, and went home before the first term was over. Later he completed the course at the Eastman Business College, Poughkeepsie, N. Y., in record time. He was manager of the colored boys in the tobacco factory at the age of fourteen, and at eighteen became a member of the firm of W. Duke & Sons, and gained experience in all branches of the business.

In 1881 the Dukes began manufacturing cigarettes, for which the local "bright" tobacco was particularly adapted, and James soon displaced the hand workers by the new Bonsack machines, which with the aid of William T. O'Brien he perfected. When the law was passed reducing the government tax on cigarettes by two-thirds, Duke immediately reduced the price of his product from ten to five cents a package, two months in advance of the operation of the act. This bold stroke, coupled with world advertising, gave the Duke firm a lead. A new period in his career and in the American tobacco business began when he left Durham and set up a branch factory in New York City in 1884. His firm now invaded the Northern and Western markets, and largely through the pouring out of hundreds of thousands of dollars a year in advertising of every form, by 1889 came to furnish half the country's total production of cigarettes. Soon the five principal cigarette manufacturers were engaged in the celebrated "tobacco war," in which competitive advertising and price concessions ruined profits. The older companies finally offered to buy Duke out, but this was his signal to force the fighting, and in 1890 all were joined in the American Tobacco Company, with $25,000,000 capital and Duke as president. In 1895 the combination began aggressively to absorb companies making other tobacco products, such as all-tobacco cigarettes, chewing tobacco, and snuff. An attempt of capitalists to gain control of enough stock to oust Duke from the headship failed. In 1898 a combination of plug manufacturers was formed, the Continental Tobacco Company, with $75,000,000 capital issued, Duke being president. The two combinations were controlled by the same interests. Duke was voracious for further mergers. Having drawn about him a remarkable group of capitalists, manufacturers, and merchants, including Oliver H. Payne, P. A. B. Widener, Grant B. Schley, William C. Whitney, R. J. Reynolds, and Thomas F. Ryan, he was enabled to form the American Snuff Company in 1900, the American Cigar Company the next year, then the American Stogie Company, and entered the retail field with the United Cigar Stores Company. In 1901 the Consolidated Tobacco Company was formed as a holding company to concentrate control of the American & Continental. After the decision of the Supreme Court in the Northern Securities case, the holding company was discontinued and the three were merged under the original name of the American

Tobacco Company. Duke next began manufacture in England by acquiring Ogden's at Liverpool. Led by W. D. and H. O. Wills, British manufacturers formed the Imperial Tobacco Company to fight the invader. A new tobacco war ensued, marked by Duke's offer to distribute to dealers who bought his product in disregard of the attempted boycott, the entire profits of Ogden's and £200,000 a year for four years. The Imperial threatened to build a factory in America. The result was an agreement by which the Imperial restricted its sales to Great Britain, the Consolidated confined itself to America, and the trade of the rest of the world was the province of the British-American Company, the Duke interests owning two-thirds of its stock and the English one-third. Duke's combinations now controlled 150 factories with a capitalization of $502,000,000. In 1911, after almost five years of litigation, the Supreme Court ordered the American Tobacco Company dissolved as a combination in restraint of trade. Duke bore chief responsibility in the difficult task of setting up the constituent elements in the merger as competitors once more. In 1904 Duke began developing the water powers of the Southern Piedmont. The next year the Southern Power Company was formed, which in twenty years came to supply power to over 300 cotton-mills, to other factories, electric lines, and cities. Duke in 1924 created a trust fund, composed principally of his holdings in the Southern Power Company, which, it is estimated, will eventually amount to $100,000,000; the fund to be used principally in creating Duke University in North Carolina and for hospitalization in the two Carolinas, with as subordinate objects the relief of Methodist churches and ministers, and the care of orphans. Duke was forceful in appearance and manner, full of self-confidence. At the age of forty-eight he married Mrs. William D. McCready of New York. The next year he obtained a divorce, and in 1907 married Mrs. Nanaline Inman of Atlanta. They had one daughter.

[John W. Jenkins, *Jas. B. Duke, Master Builder* (1927); Meyer Jacobstein, *The Tobacco Industry in the U. S.* (1907); Wm. K. Boyd, *The Story of Durham, City of the New South* (1925); *N. Y. Times*, *N. Y. Herald Tribune*, Oct. 11, 1925.]

B. M—l.

DULANY, DANIEL (1685–Dec. 5, 1753), lawyer, descended from a medieval Irish family, the O'Dulaneys, was born in Queen's County, Ireland, in the year 1685. His father was Thomas Delaney. His mother, of whom not so much as her maiden name is known, died before his emigration with two brothers, William and Joseph, to Port Tobacco, Md., where he arrived, a well-educated but penniless youth, about the year 1703. He received financial aid from George Plater, a former attorney-general of the province, studied law under his direction, and was admitted to the bar of Charles County in 1709. The following year he was admitted to plead before the provincial court, and in 1716 was enroled as a student of Gray's Inn, London. Prosperous in his profession, he acquired several thousand acres of wheat land in the valley of the Monocacy, and by encouraging German Palatines to settle there he promoted an industrial revolution in a province that had been producing little except tobacco.

In 1721 Dulany removed permanently to Annapolis and in the following year was chosen a representative of that city in the popular branch of the Maryland Legislative Assembly. He was at once appointed a member of the most important committee of that body, the Committee on Laws, and, holding also the office of attorney-general, he rapidly assumed the leadership of those in opposition to the measures of the proprietor, governor, and council. The chief controversy for ten years immediately following his entrance into the Assembly was regarding the extension of English statutes to Maryland. The proprietor, in 1722, vetoed a bill which he thought seemed by implication to introduce all the English statutes into the province, and he indicated his view that none should be introduced without his consent. Dulany contended that the people of Maryland could not without the English statutes enjoy the privileges which were guaranteed by the Maryland charter. In 1728 he published his arguments on this subject in a small pamphlet entitled, *The Rights of the Inhabitants of Maryland to the Benefit of the English Laws.* Four years later he offered a compromise which was accepted by the proprietor and regarded as favorable to the popular cause. With a view to winning Dulany from the leadership of the opposition, the proprietor, in 1733, appointed him his agent and receiver general, and the same year he and Benjamin Tasker were appointed jointly to the remunerative office of commissary general. In 1734 he was appointed judge of the admiralty, and, in 1736, he was made sole commissary general but was succeeded by Benjamin Tasker in the office of agent and receiver general. Having served for twenty years in the popular branch of the Legislative Assembly, he was sworn into the Governor's Council, Sept. 25, 1742, and was a member of that body until his death in Annapolis eleven years later. In 1743 he drafted an able address to the proprietor on the need of regulating the tobacco industry, and he successfully advocated the enactment of the inspection law of 1747 which improved the quality of Maryland tobacco and resulted in the floating of a stable paper currency. He was married three times: first, to Charity, daughter of Col. John Courts of Charles County; second, to Rebecca, daughter of Col. Walter Smith of Calvert County, and mother of his son, Daniel Dulany [*q.v.*]; and third, to Henrietta Maria, daughter of Philemon Lloyd of Talbot County, and widow of Samuel Chew.

[Nearly all that is known of Dulany is contained in the *Archives of Md.*, and the *Md. Hist. Mag.*, *passim*. Consult also B. L. Dulaney, *Something about the Dulaney (Dulany) Family* (1921), and St. George L. Sioussat, "Economics and Politics in Maryland, 1720–1750, and the Public Services of Daniel Dulany, the Elder," in Vol. XXI of *Johns Hopkins Univ. Studies in Hist. and Pol. Sci.* (1903).] N. D. M.

DULANY, DANIEL (June 28, 1722–Mar. 17, 1797), lawyer, was born in Annapolis, Md., the son of Daniel Dulany [*q.v.*], an able lawyer and political leader, and his wife Rebecca (1696–1737), a daughter of Walter Smith of Calvert County, Md. The younger Daniel was educated in England at Eton College and at Clare Hall, Cambridge University, studied law at the Middle Temple, and was admitted to the bar in Maryland in 1747. Two years later he married Rebecca Tasker, daughter of Benjamin Tasker, who was a member of the Governor's Council and the proprietor's agent and receiver general. In 1751 Frederick County elected Dulany one of its representatives in the popular branch of the Maryland Legislative Assembly. He served there for three years, defending the measures of the government and opposing the violence of the popular faction. In return for this service the governor urged his appointment to the Council. The proprietor preferred to have him continue in the House. He decided not to be a candidate for reelection in 1755, but was returned from Annapolis the following year. In 1757 he was appointed to the Council, where, continuing to serve until the overthrow of the proprietary government, he became, with the exception of the governor, the most influential of the proprietor's officers, several of whom were related to him by the ties of kinship. He was also commissary general from 1759 to 1761 and secretary of the province from 1761 to 1774.

When urging Dulany's appointment to the Council, the governor wrote that he was recognized as a gentleman of the best natural and acquired abilities of any in the province. A few years later Charles Carroll wrote his son that Dulany was a man of great parts and, though not overscrupulous, "indisputably the best lawyer on this continent." His opinions on points of law came to have much the same weight as court decisions. Though largely endowed, he suffered from ill health and haughtiness. His relations with the governor were not cordial.

Within eight months of the passage by the British Parliament of the famous act imposing a stamp tax on the colonies, Dulany produced a pamphlet entitled, *Considerations on the Propriety of Imposing Taxes in the British Colonies, for the Purpose of raising a Revenue, by Act of Parliament* (1765). In this essay he contended that the colonies were not represented in Parliament, could not be effectually represented in that body, and that taxation without representation was a violation of the common law of England. He maintained that the colonists by manufacturing for themselves would remove the danger of being oppressed and teach the mother country to regard her colonies as a part of herself and not merely as her possessions. His forceful arguments ranked foremost among the political writings of the period and were freely drawn upon by William Pitt when speaking for repeal. Another significant pamphlet from his pen, in the form of a letter dated Dec. 30, 1765, was published under the title: *The Right to the Tonnage, the Duty of Twelve Pence per Hogshead on all exported Tobacco, and the Fines and Forfeitures in the Province of Maryland* (1766). The popularity in Maryland which Dulany won by his *Considerations* was lost in 1773 in a controversy with Charles Carroll [*q.v.*] of Carrollton, conducted in the columns of the *Maryland Gazette*, Dulany, writing as "Antilon," defending a proclamation by the governor fixing the amounts of officers' fees, and Carroll, as "First Citizen," contending that as the fees were in effect the same as taxes their amounts should be fixed only by an act of the Legislative Assembly. Dulany was one of the protesters against a resolution passed at a meeting in Annapolis to the effect that Maryland lawyers should bring no suit for the recovery of any debt due from an inhabitant of Maryland to an inhabitant of Great Britain until the Boston Port Bill had been repealed. Having opposed radical factions from the beginning of his public career, he manifested no sympathy for the Revolution and at its outbreak retired to Hunting Ridge, near Baltimore. He resided there as a Loyalist, except during a brief visit to England, until 1781, when nearly all of his property was confiscated and he moved to Baltimore, where he died.

[The chief sources of information about Dulany are the *Md. Archives*; *Md. Hist. Mag.*, esp. vol. XIII (1918), p. 143; and the *Md. Gazette*. An obituary note appeared in the *Federal Gazette and Baltimore Daily*

Advertiser, Mar. 23, 1797. The Md. Hist. Soc. has a small collection of his private papers. Several of his opinions on points of law are published in Volume I of Thomas Harris's and John M'Henry's *Md. Reports* (1809). His controversy with Carroll, edited by Elihu S. Riley, was published as *Correspondence of "First Citizen" Charles Carroll of Carrollton, and "Antilon" Daniel Dulany, Jr.* (1902).] N.D.M.

DULUTH, DANIEL GREYSOLON, Sieur (1636–Feb. 25, 1710), French explorer, wrote his own name "Dulhut." He was born of noble parents at St. Germain-en-Laye near Paris, and because of his rank was early enroled in the company of the King's guard. He and his younger brother, Claude Greysolon, Sieur de la Tourette, were residents of Lyons, since they are called Lyonnais; they were also cousins of the Italian officer, Henry de Tonty [*q.v.*]. An uncle named Patron had gone to Canada and become prosperous, so the brothers Greysolon followed him to Montreal, and Daniel was probably there when Joliet [*q.v.*] in 1674 returned from his epoch-making voyage of the discovery of the Mississippi. The same year Duluth was summoned to France to resume military service, and in the battle of Seneffe was squire for the Marquis de Lassay who was thrice wounded. Duluth escaped unhurt and was soon in Montreal once more, where he bought a house in which he and his brother dwelt.

Duluth had long desired to explore the West and in 1678 set out, probably with secret instructions from the Count de Frontenac, governor of Canada, to explore Lake Superior and the routes from there westward. First it was necessary to make peace between two warring tribes of Indians, who had for several years closed Lake Superior to white men's enterprise. Having made friends with the more eastern tribe of the Chippewa, Duluth and his intrepid band of followers set out in the spring of 1679 on the hazardous mission to reconcile these tribesmen with their hereditary enemies, the Sioux. Nothing more dangerous could be conceived. Duluth, however, wrote to Frontenac that he "feared not death, only cowardice or dishonor." He was successful in his undertaking, meeting the Sioux chiefs somewhere near the site of the city that now bears his name, and forming a peace between them and the Chippewa. Then the Sioux bore him in triumph through the maze of portages and waterways that led to their great village on Lake Mille Lac in northern Minnesota. There Duluth made an alliance between the Siouan Confederacy and France and took possession of their territory for Louis XIV. In token of this ceremony he fastened the arms of France to a great oak tree (see picture of this tree on Hennepin's map of 1683). While among the Sioux, the explorer heard of salt water to the westward, probably an Indian account of Great Salt Lake; this he thought was the western ocean, and he planned to explore in that direction. First, however, he had to return to Lake Superior, where on its northwest shore he counseled with the Assiniboin, and where he passed the winter, probably building a fort in their territory.

Early in the spring of 1680 he advanced by the Brule-St. Croix route to the Mississippi, where he learned that the Sioux had broken the treaty he had made with them and were holding three Frenchmen prisoners. Hastening to his compatriots' aid, he rescued them from the Sioux, bitterly reproaching the latter for their faithlessness. One of the rescued captives proved to be Father Louis Hennepin [*q.v.*], also a veteran of the battle-field of Seneffe. Together the Frenchmen went eastward, Duluth abandoning his plans for further exploration. At Mackinac he learned that his enemies were charging him with illegal trading, a charge he indignantly repudiated. He was never a *coureur de bois,* or one who traded without a license, although he has been frequently accused of so being. Frontenac, however, defended Duluth and sent him to France where he obtained a royal commission.

The next decade Duluth spent in futile efforts to explore westward from Lake Superior, being called into service twice (1684 and 1687) to lead contingents in the armies that invaded the Iroquois territory. In 1686 he was in command of a fort on St. Clair River, and at one time brought to justice the Indian murderers of some Frenchmen in Lake Superior and made exploration safe for years thereafter (*Wisconsin Historical Collections,* XVI, 114–25). Wherever he went he was popular with his colleagues, and the loyalty of the Indians to his wishes was exceptional. He settled disputes in Wisconsin and in the Sioux country; no one did more to establish the empire of France in the Northwest.

In 1690 he was promoted to a captaincy and while in command at Fort Frontenac had the pleasure of receiving his brother La Tourette, laden with furs from a post on Lake Nipigon, where he had diverted trade from the English at Hudson Bay. About 1695 Duluth was forced to retire because of lameness brought on by exposure. His last years were spent quietly at Montreal, where (as his will shows) he lived the life of a gentleman of quality, with good books, fine clothing, faithful service, and, it may be believed, many friends. Among the great French explorers of the seventeenth century he deserves a high place. Since he was singularly modest and silent concerning his exploits, his fame has been somewhat obscured. His contemporaries considered him of great worth, reporting that he was a "highly honorable man, a brave and experienced officer, active in business matters, of high repute and devoted to the service." He gave his time for his king and country not from sordid motives of gain, but from a scientific desire to expand the boundaries of geographical knowledge, and from a patriotic hope to cross the continent for France.

[Because of his partiality for La Salle, Parkman belittled Duluth. Several of the latter's letters are extant, and are published in Pierre Margry, *Découvertes et Établissements des Français dans l'Amérique Septentrionale* (Paris, 1880–82), vol. VI; for a translation of one see L. P. Kellogg, *Early Narratives of the Northwest* (1917), pp. 325–34; see also by same author, *The French Régime in Wisconsin and the Northwest* (1925), *passim*. Two excellent articles are by Wm. McLean, "A Gentleman of the Royal Guard" in *Harper's Mag.*, Sept. 1893; "The Death of Dulhut" in *Proc. and Trans. Royal Soc. of Canada*, 2 ser., IX (1903), 39–47. L. P. K.

DUMMER, JEREMIAH (Sept. 14, 1645–May 25, 1718), silversmith, engraver, portrait-painter, magistrate, was born at Newbury, Mass., the son of Richard Dummer and his wife, Frances, widow of Rev. Jonathan Burr. Richard Dummer, said to have been a native of Bishopstoke, England, settled at Newbury and later at Boston, and in 1635–36 was one of the Governor's Assistants. He had dealings with John Hull, mint master (*Suffolk Deeds,* VI, 235), in whose shop he placed Jeremiah as apprentice. Hull wrote in his diary (Hull, *post,* p. 150), "1st of 5th [1659] I received into my house Jeremie Dummer and Samuel Paddy, to serve me as apprentices eight years. The Lord make me faithful in discharge of this new trust committed to me." Having learned his trade, Dummer set up his own shop and, tall, erect, thin-visaged, a typical Puritan of aristocratic bearing, he entered upon his career as a useful and high-minded citizen of Boston. He was married in 1672 to Anna, daughter of Joshua Atwater, merchant, later prominent at New Haven, Conn. He joined in 1671 the Artillery Company, in which he held offices, but in 1686 when the Massachusetts militia was reorganized he was one of four captains who were not reappointed. His civic services began when he was made constable in 1675. He was a member of the Council of Safety, 1689, and with others signed two petitions addressed to Gov. Andros (Massachusetts Archives, CXXVI, 63, 200). Dummer was a selectman of Boston, 1691–92; justice of the peace, 1693–1718; treasurer of Suffolk County, 1701; overseer of the poor, 1702. He was of the commission appointed in 1700 by the Earl of Bellomont [*q.v.*] to visit Gardiner's Island in search of treasure supposed to have been hidden there by Capt. William Kidd.

Dummer saw his second son, Jeremiah, Jr. [*q.v.*], started in an honorable legal career in England, and he sat a proud man in his pew on Sept. 27, 1716 (as recorded by his first cousin Samuel Sewall) while Mr. Pemberton preached a sermon congratulating another son, William Dummer, upon becoming lieutenant-governor and acting governor of the province. In his social and business relationships he seems to have been fortunate. He died after a long illness. The *Boston News-Letter* of June 2, 1718, commended him as "having served his country faithfully in several public stations, and obtained of all that knew him the character of a just, virtuous, and pious man."

Appreciation of Dummer's exquisite workmanship in silver has been revived in this century by successive exhibitions of colonial silver at the Boston Museum of Fine Arts and the Metropolitan Museum, New York, in whose permanent collections he is well represented. His shop produced some of the finest ecclesiastical and convivial pieces of the period. He also engraved money for Connecticut. In 1921 Frank W. Bayley discovered inscriptions in Dummer's handwriting on portraits of himself and his wife, which suggest that he may have been the earliest native portrait-painter of the English colonies. These likenesses, owned during several generations by descendants of Samuel Dummer of Wilmington, Mass., Jeremiah's eldest son, had previously been attributed to Sir Godfrey Kneller. The backs of the canvases, however, bear these inscriptions in a hand tallying with many Jeremiah Dummer signatures preserved at the Massachusetts Historical Society:

> Jeremiah Dum̄er pinx
> Dei in Anno 1691
> Mei Effigies, Ætat 46

and

> Effigies Anna Dum̄er Ætat 39
> Depicta a Jeremiah Dum̄er
> Anno Dom. 1691

Although no autobiographical or contemporary reference to Dummer's practise of the limner's profession has to date (1930) been found it is plausible and even probable that so clever a craftsman, perhaps having seen some itinerant painter at work, learned to do passable likenesses, such as these are. Likenesses of John Coney [*q.v.*], silversmith, and his wife, who was Mrs.

Dummer's sister, were discovered in 1929 to bear Dummer's signature, and several unsigned portraits in New England may well have come from his hand.

[F. H. Bigelow, *Historic Silver of the Colonies and its Makers* (1917); F. W. Bayley, "An Early New England Limner," in *Old-Time New England,* July 1922; E. E. Salisbury, *Family Memorials* (1885); O. A. Roberts, *Hist. of the . . . Ancient and Honorable Artillery Company of Boston,* vol. I (1895); "Diary of Samuel Sewall" and "Letter Book of Samuel Sewall," in *Mass. Hist. Soc. Colls.,* 5 ser., vols. V–VII (1878–82) and 6 ser., vols. I, II (1886–88), respectively; "The Diaries of John Hull," in *Trans. and Colls. Am. Antiq. Soc.,* III, 110–316 (1857); *New-England Hist. and Geneal. Reg.,* July, October 1881.] F.W.C.

DUMMER, JEREMIAH (*c.* 1679–May 19, 1739), colonial agent, author, who also signed his name Jeremy, was born in Boston, the son of Jeremiah Dummer [*q.v.*], by his wife, Anna Atwater. Jeremiah second was the younger brother of William, lieutenant-governor of Massachusetts 1716–30, who married a daughter of Gov. Dudley. He attended Harvard, graduating in 1699, and then went to Utrecht where he received the degree of Doctor of Philosophy in 1703 (*Colonial Society of Massachusetts Publications,* vol. XVIII, 1917, p. 210). He returned to Massachusetts and took part in the Harvard Commencement of 1704 where he is said to have spoken fluently in Latin (*Ibid.,* p. 376n). After considering the ministry as a career, he decided to enter business, and finding no opening in Boston, went to England and never returned. In England, he made prominent friends and was employed by Lord Bolingbroke in secret negotiations. He received assurances of promotion to an office of honor and profit, but the death of Queen Anne in 1714 ruined that hope. Meanwhile, he had done well and had become a prominent lawyer and a man of fashion (*Ibid.,* vol. XII, 1911, p. 127). In 1710, Sir Henry Ashurst, the Massachusetts colonial agent, died, and his brother declined to accept the proffered post. He recommended that the General Court choose Dummer who, in spite of Gov. Dudley's opposition, received the appointment. Dummer was genuinely interested in New England and in 1711 wrote to the Rev. Mr. Pierpont of Connecticut that a Mr. Yale, formerly governor of Fort George in India, had returned with a prodigious estate and the idea of bestowing some of it on a college at Oxford, as he had no son. Dummer added that he was trying to get him to give some of it to a college in New England and that he would "take care to press it home." (F. B. Dexter, *Biographical Sketches of the Graduates of Yale College, With Annals of the College History,* I, 1885, p. 101.) He succeeded, and Yale's benefactions to the college now bearing his name began. Dummer's interest continued and in 1714 he sent over some seven hundred or a thousand books he had collected for the new institution. Indeed, it was said that he tried, later, to divert some of Thomas Hollis's interest in Harvard College to its Connecticut rival. Meanwhile, in 1712, he had been appointed colonial agent for Connecticut. In that year, he published in London, *A Letter to a Noble Lord, concerning the Late Expedition to Canada,* in which he set forth the efforts made by Massachusetts in the unfortunate Canadian expedition, to counterbalance the charges made by its incompetent commander, Sir Hovenden Walker, who claimed that its failure was due to the lack of cooperation by the colonies. Dummer is said to have unsuccessfully solicited for himself the post of judge-advocate on the expedition (J. G. Palfrey, *A Compendious History of New England,* 1873, IV, 277n). Although he did not return to New England, he appears to have still had property there, as in 1713 he was one of the absentee proprietors of the town of Leicester, Mass. (Emory Wasburn, *Historical Sketches of the Town of Leicester,* 1860, p. 9).

In 1715, when an attack was being made in Parliament on the colonial charters, Dummer wrote his *Defence of the New England Charters* (printed in 1721; reprinted 1745 and 1765). He claimed that these charters had a higher validity than those of corporations in England, as they had been granted in consideration of services to be performed; and that the colonial governments had never forfeited them by any misdoing; also that if there were any ground for forfeiture it would not be to the interest of the crown to resume them; and any legal action should be taken by the lower courts and not by Parliament. Dummer was much opposed to the appointment of Elizeus Burges as governor of Massachusetts, and was mainly instrumental in having him replaced by Shute (*Colonial Society of Massachusetts, Publications,* vol. XIV, 1913, pp. 362 ff.). When Shute returned to England and presented his *Memorial* of grievances, the Massachusetts Assembly forced the appointment of Elisha Cooke as temporary agent to join Dummer in England in refuting the charges. Dummer felt that the Massachusetts government was going too far for its own good in the countercharges made against Shute and that, as a result, it would appear in England as though in reality Massachusetts wanted no English governor at all. He did not hesitate to tell the Assembly so and, as a consequence, in 1721 that body, against the protest of the Council, dismissed him from his agency. In 1730 he was similarly and very curtly dismissed by Connecticut. He died unmarried, at Plaistow, England, and was buried at West Ham, Essex. His services to New England were of high value, but the colonies were rarely grateful to their agents, and Dummer, in addition, seems never to have been wholly trusted. He is said to have had a "vollible tongue," was a skeptic in religion, and not always in sympathy with the extreme radicalism of the colonial Assemblies.

[The facts of Dummer's life must be found in scattered sources. Some of his manuscript letters are in the State Archives of Mass. and in the Mass. Hist. Soc. A few, not important, have been printed in *Mass. Hist. Soc. Colls.*, 1 ser., VI (1800), 78–79 and 3 ser., I (1825), 139–46. His will is printed in the article by J. L. Chester on "The Family of Dummer" in *New-Eng. Hist. and Geneal. Reg.*, XXXV (1881), 254–71 and 321–31, at p. 268.] J. T. A.

DUN, ROBERT GRAHAM (Aug. 7, 1826–Nov. 10, 1900), head of a mercantile agency, was born in Chillicothe, Ohio. His parents were Robert Dun, the son of a clergyman of Glasgow, and Lucy Worthum Angus, whom he had married in Virginia. Robert Graham Dun received his schooling at the local academy at Chillicothe. He was early employed in a store, and shortly after reaching his majority became the proprietor of a small local business. In 1850, Benjamin Douglass, who had married Dun's sister Elizabeth, gave the young man an opportunity to join the organization of Tappan & Douglass, "The Mercantile Agency," in New York City. This business, the first of its kind, had been originated by Lewis Tappan [*q.v.*] after the panic of 1837. At first its service consisted in supplying facts relating to the credit standing of country storekeepers to a few wholesale firms in New York, which paid annual subscriptions to cover the cost of obtaining such information. Under the management of Douglass the scope of its service was being expanded. Dun's first marked success was achieved in dealing with the personnel of the central office. He quickly won the interest and loyalty of his colleagues, which in the later development of the business was an important factor. In 1854 the firm was reorganized as B. Douglass & Company, with Dun as a partner. On the withdrawal of Douglass in 1859, Dun succeeded to his interest, becoming the sole owner, although the profits were shared with various associates who were known to the public as partners in the enterprise; the New York office operated for a time as Dun, Boyd & Company and later as Dun, Barlow & Company. At the outbreak of the Civil War in 1861, R. G. Dun & Company had branches in the principal cities of the country, including several in the South. Like many other enterprises of national scope, "The Mercantile Agency" could do little more than mark time during the war, but the remaining years of the century were signalized by unexampled growth and adaptation to rapid changes in business methods. In that period of transformation, Dun's managerial abilities were severely tested. He had a special gift for associating with him in close sympathy and cooperation men of ability, and this group which shaped the company's policies quietly proceeded to fit them to the changing demands of the business world, taking advantage at the same time of every new device in the mechanism of trade that seemed to promise increased efficiency in the service that they were rendering to the business community. The problem of reaching distant states promptly and receiving needed information from them in time to be of service was vastly greater than in the early days. Speed was entering into every form of business activity. The new conditions called for new methods. The offices of R. G. Dun & Company were among the first to make large use of the typewriter for communications with subscribers. The publishing activities of the house were developed with the expansion of its interests. As early as 1859, the year of Dun's accession to ownership, the first of the series of reference books appeared. The printing required by the efforts to keep up with the clients' requests for information in time attained so great a volume that the company had to install its own plant, employing several hundred persons. On Aug. 5, 1893, *Dun's Review*, containing a weekly report of business conditions, was inaugurated. Dun's researches went everywhere, even beyond continental bounds. Offices were opened in Paris, in Germany—finally, in Australia and South Africa. Personally a retiring man, with domestic tastes, he avoided publicity. He was married twice: first, to Elizabeth Douglass, sister of Benjamin Douglass, and second, to Mary D. Bradford of Milwaukee.

[*Who's Who in America*, 1899–1900; *N. Y. Times*, *N. Y. Tribune*, Nov. 11, 1900; E. N. Vose, *Seventy-Five Years of the Mercantile Agency, R. G. Dun & Co., 1841–1916* (1916); oral statement by R. D. Douglass, of R. G. Dun & Co.] W. B. S.

DUNBAR, CHARLES FRANKLIN (July 28, 1830–Jan. 29, 1900), editor, economist, was born in Abington, Mass., the youngest son of Asaph Dunbar (1779–1867) and Nancy Ford. The father made boots and shoes. Charles was educated at Phillips Exeter Academy and Harvard College, receiving the degree of A.B. in 1851. For a brief period he engaged in his fa ther's and older brothers' business in New Orleans, New York, and Boston. Owing to ill health he bought a farm in Lexington where he remained for a short time, until fully recovered. In 1857 he entered the Harvard Law School and was admitted to the bar in the following year. During 1856, however, he had contributed articles to the *Boston Daily Advertiser,* and in 1859 an opportunity arose whereby he became part owner and associate editor of that journal. This relationship continued for ten years, during the latter half of which he was sole editor. His editorials were vigorous and commanded wide recognition. His support of President Lincoln's administration during the war was whole-hearted, but free from extravagant eulogy of his own party, or rancorous criticism of opponents. In 1869 owing to a return of poor health he sold his interest in the *Advertiser* and resigned his position as editor. Within a few months he was invited by President Eliot of Harvard University at the very beginning of his administration, to become the first professor of political economy at that institution. He hesitated, not only because of poor health, but also on the ground of inadequate preparation. Finally he accepted, after two years of travel in Europe. His scholarly instincts and thorough knowledge of current economic problems quickly proved the wisdom of the choice. For thirty years he was the head of the department; as such he gathered about him a staff of younger scholars which brought prestige to the university. He did much to awaken interest in economics as a science, and to develop sound reasoning. He was especially acquainted with economics of the seventeenth and eighteenth centuries and with Ricardo's school. Although his special interest was in practical problems of banking and finance, he avoided propaganda in the interest of any particular group. He took an active part in the general administration of the university, serving as dean of the college faculty, 1876–82; and upon a subsequent administrative reorganization, as the first dean of the faculty of arts and sciences, 1890–95. In 1886 he assumed the editorship of the *Quarterly Journal of Economics,* the first periodical exclusively devoted to economic science to be established in the United States. To this, until 1896, he gave much time. In addition to these responsibilities, he was a member of the Board of Trustees of Exeter Academy, 1885–98, and for the last five years, president of the board.

Owing to his numerous administrative duties, coupled with frail health, Dunbar did not leave a large legacy of written work. In 1891 he published a compilation, *Laws of the United States, relating to Currency, Finance and Banking from 1789 to 1891,* which served as a most useful compendium for students in banking and finance. In the same year he also published *Chapters on the Theory and History of Banking* (1891). Though a slender volume, this is generally recognized as a classic in economic literature, especially in the treatment of deposit currency and banking reserves. In 1904 appeared *Economic Essays,* edited by Prof. O. M. W. Sprague, which brought together twenty of Dunbar's articles, for the most part previously published in the *Quarterly Journal of Economics* and *North American Review,* together with five that the author left in manuscript form. Four of these essays dealt with the history and methods of economic science; two with taxation; eleven with monetary and banking history, and two with commercial crises. They reveal the careful and patient scholarship of the author; they are free from controversial dogma, and have a permanent place in the historical literature of finance and banking. Notable among them are "Economic Science in America, 1776–1876" (pp. 1–29); "Some Precedents followed by Alexander Hamilton" (pp. 71–93); and "The Bank of Venice" (pp. 143–67).

In appearance Dunbar was of sandy complexion and of good height; his constitution was frail and delicate. He was reserved in conversation and cautious in his judgments. His religious affiliation was with the Unitarian Church. Soon after graduation he married Julia Ruggles Copeland of Roxbury, Mass.; three sons and one daughter survived him. In 1893 he served as the second president of the American Economic Association. He was also a member of the Massachusetts Historical Society and a Fellow of the American Academy of Arts and Sciences.

[Brief memoirs of Dunbar may be found as follows: Remarks by S. A. Green and Chas. W. Eliot, *Proc. Mass. Hist. Soc.,* 2 ser., XIII (1900), 425–28; Memoir by E. H. Hall, *Ibid.,* XIV (1901), 218–28; F. W. Taussig, in *Proc. Am. Acad. Arts and Sci.,* vol. XXXVI (1900–01), and in Dunbar's *Economic Essays* (1904), introduction, pp. vii–xvii; the remarks by President Eliot are reprinted in the *Harvard Grads.' Mag.,* June 1900.]

D. R. D.

DUNBAR, MOSES (June 14, 1746–Mar. 19, 1777), the only person ever executed in Connecticut for treason, was born in Wallingford, Conn., the second of the family of sixteen children of John Dunbar and his wife, Temperance Hall. The father was a Congregationalist; and Moses wrote that "my joining myself to the church [of England] caused a sorrowful breach between my Father and myself." About 1760 the family removed to what was then a part of

Waterbury, Conn., now Plymouth. In 1764 Moses married Phebe Jerome (or Jearom) who lived in that part of Farmington, Conn., which is now within the city of Bristol; and they established there their marital home. In the same year, "upon what we thought sufficient and rational motives," he and his wife left the Congregational Church, in which both had been brought up, and declared themselves of the Church of England. In Connecticut at that time the little Episcopal churches, served by missionaries sent from England and feeling themselves oppressed by the dominant Congregational authorities of the state, were practically unanimous in opposing the movement for American independence, and in supporting the cause of the King. The record book of the early Episcopal Church, which is preserved in the Bristol Public Library, bears on its title-page the significant text: "Fear God; Honor the King." This church Moses and Phebe Dunbar attended, and in this book are recorded the baptisms of their children. On May 20, 1776, Phebe died, having borne seven children of whom four survived. Soon after, Moses married Esther Adams.

The Revolutionary War was now in full progress, and Dunbar was already an object of suspicion. "Having spoken somewhat freely on the subject," he says, "I was attacked by a mob of about forty men, very much abused, my life threatened and nearly taken away, by which mob I was obliged to sign a paper containing many falsehoods." Soon after he says that he was taken before a committee of the Sons of Liberty "and by them ordered to suffer imprisonment during their pleasure, not exceeding five months." When he was released he fled to Long Island where Lord Howe was in command of the royal army, enlisted in the King's service, and received a commission as captain. He was given the dangerous errand of persuading other young men to enlist for the King. He procured the enlistment of a youth bearing the patriotic name of John Adams, but was betrayed to the officers of the state of Connecticut, was committed to jail at Hartford, and was tried in January 1777, for treason. He was convicted and sentenced to be hanged, and the sentence was carried out, Mar. 19, 1777, on a hilltop near Hartford, where the buildings of Trinity College now stand.

After his death his wife with her step-children, and one child of her own, left Connecticut and went to Nova Scotia, as did many of the Loyalists of New England. More than a century after his death, an old house in Harwinton was pulled down, and in the débris of the garret were found two papers, copies of letters written by Dunbar in the Hartford jail on the night before his execution. One was a letter, of an intimate and tender character, to his children; the other was a longer document, and contained an account of his life and a defense of his religious and political faith. Both are heroic in temper and strongly charged with religious feeling.

[This article is condensed from an extended monograph by Epaphroditus Peck, published in the *Conn. Mag.*, VIII (1904), 129, 297. Jos. Anderson, *The Town and City of Waterbury, Conn.* (1896), I, 434–36, gives the full text of Dunbar's letters mentioned above.]

E. P—k.

DUNBAR, PAUL LAURENCE (June 27, 1872–Feb. 9, 1906), poet, was born in Dayton, Ohio. His father, Joshua Dunbar, was born a slave on a plantation in Kentucky, but before the Civil War escaped and made his way to Canada, where he learned to read. He returned to the United States to enroll in the 55th Massachusetts Infantry. After the war he worked in Dayton, Ohio, as a plasterer, and in 1871 married a young widow, Matilda Murphy, who also had been a slave in Kentucky. Of this union Paul Laurence was the only child. Joshua Dunbar died when his son was twelve years of age. Paul was educated in the public schools of Dayton. At the Steele High School he was the only negro student in his class. His gentle, modest demeanor as well as his talent made him popular with his associates; he served as president of the literary society and as editor of the monthly publication of the students; and he composed the song when his class was graduated in 1891. For a while he cherished the thought of being a lawyer; but the best immediate employment that he could find was that of running an elevator in Dayton at four dollars a week. Poems that he wrote appeared from time to time in newspapers issued in or near Dayton, and just before Christmas, 1893, a booklet, *Oak and Ivy*, was printed at the publishing house of the United Brethren at a cost of $125. It was some time before the small edition was exhausted, but at the close of two weeks, by the personal sale of copies on his elevator at a dollar each, Dunbar was able to pay the amount of his bill. In the following year he was employed by Frederick Douglass in the Haiti Building at the World's Columbian Exposition in Chicago. Returning after some months to Dayton, he faced one of the most discouraging periods of his life; but he was befriended and encouraged by Charles Thatcher, a lawyer of Toledo, and Dr. Henry A. Tobey, superintendent of the Ohio State Hospital at Toledo; and these two men assisted toward the printing of a second book of poems, *Majors and*

Minors. This appeared in 1895 and showed great progress, especially more originality in the handling of negro themes. Of the very popular piece, "When Malindy Sings," the poet's mother had been the inspiration. Dr. Tobey, who had bought and distributed a number of copies of *Oak and Ivy,* suggested that James A. Herne, who was appearing in the city in "Shore Acres," be given a copy of the new book. Herne passed this on to William Dean Howells, and the result was an enthusiastic full-page review in *Harper's Weekly* for June 27, 1896. Requests for copies of *Majors and Minors* now poured in; Howells brought Dunbar to the attention of Maj. J. B. Pond, the head of a lecture bureau; and in the same year (1896) Dodd, Mead & Company formally published *Lyrics of Lowly Life,* the author's best-known collection. It was in the introduction to this book that Howells spoke of Dunbar as the first man of African descent and American training who had felt the life of his people esthetically and expressed it lyrically. Within the next few years the poet's success was so great as to be a vogue; in rapid succession he brought out volumes of fiction as well as verse, and he was in great demand as a reader of his poems. His experience with the lecture bureau was not happy, but it took him to England for a memorable visit early in 1897. While there he wrote *The Uncalled* (1898), which reflects his thought of being a minister. On his return to the United States, through the assistance of Col. Robert G. Ingersoll, he was given a place as an assistant in the Library of Congress, where he served at an annual salary of $720 from Oct. 1, 1897, to Dec. 31, 1898. On Mar. 6, 1898, in New York, he married Alice Ruth Moore, a native of New Orleans, a teacher, and an author in her own right. Meanwhile the numerous public readings, the late hours of composition at fever heat, and the confining work at the library told on his strength; and he spent the winter of 1899–1900 in Colorado in a vain search for health. His last years were a record of intense application, of sincere friendships, and a losing fight against disease. He died in Dayton.

Dunbar was singularly beloved by his people; and the story of his life, with its yearning and striving, its love of song, and its irony, has never ceased to appeal to them. He wrote the school song for Tuskegee Institute. Numerous societies were named for him, and in Washington the Dunbar High School. In eminent degree he represented the lyric genius of his race; but, while his most distinctive work was that in dialect, he regretted that the public preferred "a jingle in a broken tongue." His work looked both backward and forward. On one hand it reflected the humor and the pathos of those who lived on old plantations in the South; on the other it struck the key-note of the restlessness of an age that was yet to be. In addition to his poems, collected in one volume, *Complete Poems* (1913), he wrote four novels, *The Uncalled* (1896), *The Love of Landry* (1900), *The Fanatics* (1901), *The Sport of the Gods* (1902), stories and sketches, and in 1900, *Uncle Eph's Christmas,* a one-act musical sketch.

[The *Cambridge Hist. of Am. Lit.,* II (1918), 614, contains a list of Dunbar's volumes, with the exception of *Oak and Ivy* and *Majors and Minors* which were privately printed. The most detailed biography is that by Lida Keck Wiggins in *The Life and Works of Paul Laurence Dunbar* (1907). See also the chapters in Benjamin Brawley, *The Negro in Literature and Art* (1918, 1921, 1929); J. W. Cromwell, *The Negro in Am. Hist.* (1914). Much of the most valuable information about Dunbar, however, was that appearing in newspapers and magazines about the time of his great success in 1896 and at his death in 1906. The writer of this article is indebted to a sketch written with painstaking effort by Prof. P. M. Pearson of Northwestern Univ., and appearing in the *Chicago Times-Herald* of Oct. 14, 1900.]

B. B.

DUNBAR, ROBERT (Dec. 13, 1812–Sept. 18, 1890), engineer, inventor, was born in Carnbee, a short distance inland from the coast of Fifeshire, Scotland. About the beginning of the nineteenth century his grandfather, also Robert Dunbar, emigrated from Scotland and settled in Pickering Township, about twenty miles east of Toronto, Canada, where he purchased a farm and built up around it a warehouse, tannery, wagon shop and blacksmith shop. Around this little group of industries there grew the village of Dunbarton. When young Dunbar was twelve years old his father, William, a mechanical engineer, left Scotland with his family to join his father in Dunbarton. Here Robert prepared for college and was educated as a mechanical engineer. He completed his course at the age of twenty and had the immediate opportunity of demonstrating his engineering skill in designing and building the mechanical equipment for a new shipyard dock at Niagara, Ont. Shortly after the successful completion of this task, he decided to branch out for himself and in 1834, when just twenty-two years old, he went to Buffalo, N. Y. His first jobs here were rebuilding old flour-mills, incorporating in them his ideas for improvements, especially in mechanical handling. From this he progressed until he effected a partnership with C. W. Evans to engage in the design and erection of grain elevators and warehouses. Little is known of the extent of the activities of this partnership during the approximate fifteen years of its existence. Upon its dissolution in 1853, however, Dunbar immediately, with a group of friends, organized the Eagle Iron Works Company in Buffalo to conduct a similar business. In the course of the succeeding fifteen years practically all of the grain elevators in the vicinity of Buffalo were either newly designed by Dunbar or improved by him in the name of the company. During the period of the financial panic of the early seventies the Eagle Iron Works was dissolved, but Dunbar and another partner bought out the establishment and carried on as Dunbar & Howell for a few years. With Howell's retirement the business was conducted as R. Dunbar & Son. During his sixty years' continuous connection with the grain-handling business, Dunbar built up a world-wide reputation as an expert in the design and construction of elevators. Through the almost exclusive employment of his services, Buffalo gained the position of one of the largest grain markets in the United States. Elevators of his design were also constructed by him in Liverpool and Hull, England, as well as in Odessa, Russia. He apparently did not attempt to patent any of his ideas until toward the close of his career, when in the early eighties four patents were granted him for both fixed and portable elevators and conveyors, as well as the operating machinery for them. Dunbar married Sarah M. Howell of Buffalo on Aug. 26, 1840; she with a son and daughter survived him at the time of his death in Buffalo.

[Henry Hall, *America's Successful Men of Affairs*, vol. II (1896); obituaries in *Buffalo Commercial*, Sept. 19, and *Buffalo Express*, Sept. 20, 1890; Patent Office Records; correspondence with N. Y. State Lib.]

C. W. M.

DUNBAR, WILLIAM (1749–October 1810), planter, scientist, the youngest son of Sir Archibald Dunbar, holder of an ancient Scottish earldom, was born in the manor house of Thunderton, near Elgin in Morayshire, Scotland. It is said that he finally inherited, but did not assume, his father's title and estate in Scotland. He is known, however, in the history of Mississippi, his adopted state, as Sir William Dunbar. He received the greater part of his education at Glasgow and then went to London for advanced study in mathematics and astronomy. Here his health failed, and he decided to seek health and fortune in the New World. In 1771 he arrived at Fort Pitt (Pittsburgh), with a supply of goods to the value of £1,000 which he had purchased in London for trade with the Indians. Two years later, he formed a partnership with John Ross, a prominent Scotch merchant of Philadelphia, and established a plantation in the British province of West Florida near Baton Rouge. In Jamaica he purchased a large number of African slaves for use on his plantation. The unsettled condition of the times later resulted in a series of misfortunes which swept away his accumulations; in 1775 some of his most valuable slaves were lost to him through an insurrection; three years later his plantation was thoroughly plundered by Continental soldiers under Capt. Willing; and a short time afterward he was again raided by Spanish soldiers under Galvez. In 1792, with Ross, he opened another plantation called "The Forest," nine miles south of Natchez and four miles east of the Mississippi. Applying his knowledge of chemistry and mechanics to farming, he made his plows and harrows on scientific principles, improved the cotton-gin, first suggested the manufacture of cottonseed-oil, and improved the method of packing cotton by introducing the square bale, utilizing a screw press he invented for that purpose. A few years of prosperity enabled him to purchase his partner's interest in the plantation, and further success enabled him to devote much of his time to scientific investigation.

In 1798, he was appointed surveyor general of the District of Natchez, and served also as a representative of the Spanish government in defining the boundary between the United States and the Spanish possessions east of the Mississippi. Upon the completion of this survey he took the oath of allegiance to the United States and became a warm supporter of its government. During 1799, he made the first meteorological observations in the Mississippi Valley. His interest in science attracted the attention of Thomas Jefferson, to whom in 1799, Daniel Clarke wrote that "for Science, Probity, & general information [Dunbar] is the first Character in this part of the World." At Jefferson's solicitation they entered upon an active correspondence, and on Jefferson's recommendation Dunbar was elected to membership in the American Philosophical Society. In 1804, the President appointed Dunbar and George Hunter to explore the Ouachita River country, and as a result the former became the first man to give a scientific account of the Hot Springs and an analysis of their waters. His manuscript journal of the exploration came into the possession of the American Philosophical Society in 1817, and at the time of the centennial of the Louisiana Purchase was published in *Documents Relating to the Purchase and Exploration of Louisiana* (1904). In 1805 he was appointed to explore the region bordering on the Red River. Among his many contributions to the *Transactions of the American Philosophical Society* are reports on his explorations, on the delta of the Mississippi, and on the sign language by which distant tribes of Indians communicate with each other. He wrote about the animal and plant life that he saw, and he solved the problem of finding the longitude by a single observer without any knowledge of the precise time. He also wrote articles on the fossil bones of a mammoth that he found in Louisiana, and propounded the theory that a profound calm exists inside the vortex of a cyclone. From his own observatory, fitted with elaborate foreign instruments, he observed lunar rainbows and other astronomical phenomena. He was the first man to observe an elliptical rainbow and to make a suitable explanation thereof. His interest in science gained him a reputation as the foremost scientist of the Southwest. He corresponded with, and held as his close friends, Sir William Herschel, Bartram, Hunter, Rittenhouse, and Rush. Even though he was indifferent to politics he was at one time chief justice of the court of quarter sessions, and later a member of the territorial legislature of Mississippi. He died at his home, "The Forest," in October 1810, leaving a widow and several children, each of whom was rendered independent by his large estate. His widow continued on the plantation until her death in November 1821.

[See J. F. H. Claiborne, *Miss. as a Province, Territory, and State* (1880), I, 200–01; *Pubs. Miss. Hist. Soc.*, II, 85–111, 182–83, V, 222; Dunbar Rowland, *Mississippi* (1907), I, 663–65; *Biog. and Hist. Memoirs of Miss.* (1891), I, 1020–21; *Quart. of the Texas State Hist. Asso.*, Apr. 1904, p. 311. For Dunbar's Report to the Spanish Govt. on Boundary Survey, see *Pubs. Miss. Hist. Soc.*, III (1902), 185–205. Fifteen letters from Dunbar to Jefferson will be found in the Jefferson MSS., Lib. of Cong.] F. L. R.

DUNCAN, ISADORA (May 27, 1878–Sept. 14, 1927), dancer, was the first in modern times to raise her profession to the level of a creative art, making it a medium of expression for such varied and profound experiences as had hitherto found utterance in music and literature. Her father, Joseph Charles Duncan, was something of a poet; her mother, Dora Gray, was a skilled musician; the three older children, Raymond, Augustine, and Elizabeth, were all creatively interested in the dance and drama. Shortly after Isadora's birth, in San Francisco, Mrs. Duncan divorced her husband, and the family fell into poverty, so that the child early became familiar with the ugliness of shabby lodgings, cheap meals, and the hard-faced creditor. Equally early she came to know what was always to be to her the more real world of ideal beauty, centered at first in her mother's music. At the age of six she danced and taught dancing, having a little school formed of the children of the neighborhood. In comparison, the drab courses of the public school were exceedingly distasteful to her, particularly as she was much too original and sincere to be understood by the ordinary teacher. Thus, when ten, she decided that she could waste no more time in school but must be about her own work—dancing.

She and her sister, Elizabeth, now for some years taught what they called a "new system," based on improvised movements interpretive of poetry, music, and the rhythms of nature, which gradually brought them a considerable vogue in the drawing-rooms of San Francisco. Then, at the age of seventeen, Isadora decided to follow her star in the East. She and her mother journeyed, with the slenderest resources, first to Chicago, where Isadora, ever scornful of the accepted ballet, had scant success, and then on to New York City, where she obtained an engagement in Augustin Daly's company. Daly, then at the height of his ephemeral fame, had no comprehension of her genius, and after two years she resigned, permanently disillusioned with the popular stage. Joined by Elizabeth and Raymond, she and her mother then traveled on a cattle boat to London. There the whole family spent their days studying Greek art in the British Museum—a study which had an abiding influence on Isadora's dancing—until they were on the verge of starvation. From this they were saved by a chance acquaintance with Mrs. Patrick Campbell, who came upon them dancing in a public park, and who introduced Isadora to an intellectual circle capable of appreciating art inspired by Walt Whitman, Nietzsche, and the Greeks. Applauded private performances in London were succeeded by similar performances in Paris, and the young American, accepted by those who counted, became the artistic sensation of the season. Rejecting lucrative offers from music-halls, she joined the company of Loie Fuller [*q.v.*] for a trip through Germany and then went on alone to a triumphant progress through Budapest, Vienna, Munich, and Berlin, where she aroused the wildest enthusiasm, the students night after night drawing her carriage through the streets to her hotel. In recognition of the communal, almost religious, emotions expressed in her dancing, she was called in Germany, "die göttliche, heilige Isadora."

Suddenly, Isadora fled with her family to study for a year in Athens. There they bought the hill of Kopanos outside the city and attempted to build a temple of dancing on an elaborate scale. The scheme devoured all of Isadora's earnings, and the next year she returned to the stage. In 1904, with the assistance of Elizabeth, she opened a school of the dance for forty children at Grünewald in the outskirts of Berlin. But while she was the energizing spirit of the school, the routine of instruction always bored her and it was no part of her theory of education that the teacher should sink his own life in that of the pupils. In 1905 her daughter, Deirdre, was born, the child of Edward Gordon Craig, and grandchild of Ellen Terry. Essentially pagan, believing in free love and detesting marriage, Isadora disdained to accommodate her life to the demands of conventional morality. In 1906, after a successful American tournée, she met in Paris a generous and art-loving millionaire whom she called "Lohengrin," who was the father of her son, Patrick, born in 1908. Time and again in subsequent years "Lohengrin" came to her assistance in financial difficulties.

In 1913, at the summit of her career, her unusually beautiful and talented children, with their English nurse, were drowned in a closed automobile which rolled into the Seine. She tried to ease her sorrow, first by assisting Raymond in relief work in Albania, then by feverish journeyings in Italy until brought to Viareggio and nursed back to sanity by her friend Eleonora Duse, and, finally, by having another child, unfortunately still-born, whose father was an Italian sculptor. Resolved at last to forget herself in her work, she returned to her school, for which "Lohengrin" now bought the great hotel at Bellevue near Paris, but all her plans were interrupted by the outbreak of the World War. Henceforth, like a broken spar, she was to be tossed from shore to shore at the mercy of political tempests.

The children of the school were first sent to America where Isadora joined them in 1915, only to take them back to Europe almost immediately when she became disgusted with American indifference to the Allied cause. There followed unsuccessful tournées, in South America in 1916 and in the United States in 1917. Finally in 1920 she made another effort to establish her school permanently, this time in Athens at the invitation of Venizelos, but the overthrow of the latter led her to return to Paris where her far-wandering school at last broke up. But she was not yet through. In the summer of 1921 she received an invitation from the Soviet Government to open a school in Moscow, an invitation which she promptly accepted. After vexatious delays, she was given an empty palace in the heart of the city where she gathered about her fifty pupils. This, her last school, was destined to endure, though not under her own management. In May 1922 she was married—the Russian marriage laws being sufficiently liberal to meet her approval—to the half-mad "poet laureate of the revolution," Sergei Yessenin, seventeen years her junior. The education of this handsome peasant-genius now became more important to her than the fortunes of her school. She at once took her young husband to Germany and Belgium and then, in an unlucky hour, decided to bring him to America. Arriving at the height of the panic over "Red" propaganda, they were everywhere suspected of being Bolshevist emissaries and subjected to petty persecution by officious officials. The trip was an utter failure. Isadora's last words to her fellow countrymen were: "You know nothing of Love, Food, or Art. . . . So goodbye America. I shall never see you again."

She and Yessenin returned penniless to Paris where they lived for a time by selling the furniture, article by article, in Isadora's house, after which they made their way with difficulty back to Russia. Meanwhile the unfortunate poet's attacks of madness had become more frequent and violent; soon after their arrival in Moscow he deserted Isadora, sank into the lowest debauchery, and finally took his own life in December 1925. The posthumous sale of his poems brought large royalties which Isadora declined to accept, returning the money to his family. She was beset by poverty, but she had not lost her pride. After her final departure from Russia in September 1924, in western Europe she met with unwonted coldness, owing partly to political prejudice and partly to a very real decline in her own powers. The once taut, exquisite dancer became indolent and flabby with only occasional returns of fiery energy. One more artistic creation remained for her, however: the writing in 1926–27 of her autobiography, *My Life,* in which she achieved a masterpiece of courage and sincerity. More clouded days in Paris and Nice followed and then, none too soon, the end, which came at Nice, in a fittingly individual fashion. Entering an automobile which she was planning to purchase, she cried to her friends, "Je vais à la gloire," and a minute later she was dead, her neck broken by her long scarf which caught in the first revolution of the wheels. Her body was taken to Paris and buried in Père la Chaise.

The special creations of Isadora Duncan's flaming personality such as her renditions of the "Marseillaise," Tschaikowsky's "Marche Slave," and Chopin's "Marche Funèbre" all perished with her, but none the less the influence of her teachings and example have permanently enriched the art of the dance, even the ballet, in every western land.

[Isadora Duncan, *My Life* (1927), and *The Art of the Dance* (1928), ed. with introduction by Sheldon Cheney; Irma Duncan and Allan Ross Macdougall, *Isadora Duncan's Russian Days and Her Last Years in France*

(1929); Mary Desti, *The Untold Story; The Life of Isadora Duncan 1921–1927* (1929); Constantin Stanislawsky, *My Life in Art* (1924), tr. from the Russian by J. J. Robbins; Walter A. Propert, *The Russian Ballet in Western Europe 1909–1920* (1921); Wm. Bolitho, *Twelve Against the Gods* (1929), pp. 305–27; *N. Y. Times*, Sept. 15, 1927.] E. S. B—s.

DUNCAN, JAMES (May 5, 1857–Sept. 14, 1928), labor leader, played a prominent part in the American Federation of Labor during its formative period of uncertainty and its struggle toward a permanent place in the industrial world. He was born in Kincardine County, Scotland, the son of David and Mary (Forbes) Duncan. After serving an apprenticeship as a granite cutter, he came to the United States at the age of twenty-three years. Almost immediately he became interested in the labor movement. In July 1881 he joined the New York local of the Granite Cutters' National Union, now called the Granite Cutters' International Association. Later he moved to Baltimore and was elected secretary of the Baltimore local in 1885. The following year he attended the convention at Columbus, Ohio, at which the Federation of Organized Trades and Labor Unions in the United States and Canada (1881–86) was dissolved and the American Federation of Labor formed. For half a century he was a friend and associate of Samuel Gompers and of others who were active in building up the type of unionism which the American Federation of Labor represents. In 1894, he was elected second vice-president of the American Federation of Labor. Six years later, he became the first vice-president, which office he held until the time of his death. He attended every convention of the Federation from 1886 to 1927, in the latter year, being unable to attend the Annual Convention because of illness.

He also represented labor in several important private and official missions. He was a delegate to the British Trade Union Conference in 1898; in 1911 he represented the American Federation of Labor at the International Secretariat in Budapest; in 1913, he was a member of a United States Commission to study workman's compensation; in 1917, envoy extraordinary of the United States Government on the diplomatic mission to Russia, known as the Root Mission; and, in 1919, a member of the American Labor Mission to the Peace Conference in Paris.

Like many other labor leaders of his generation, Duncan seems to have received very little formal education; but he possessed the excellent qualities of courage, persistency, and love for fellow workers. President William Green, of the American Federation of Labor, said in his address delivered at the funeral service: "I know of no man who possessed a more indomitable will, a higher conception of truth, righteousness and justice, and it was because he possessed those qualities to such an unusual degree that he made such a great success in the organized labor movement." For more than a year preceding his death, he was ill and inactive, having failed to regain strength after a serious operation. In January 1887, he had married Lillian M. Holman of Baltimore. His home for many years had been in Quincy, Mass., where the Granite Cutters' Association has its executive office.

[Obituary statements may be found in the Boston papers, Sept. 15, 1928; *Granite Cutters' Jour.*, Oct. 1928, pp. 1, 3 ff.; *Am. Fed. of Labor Weekly News Service*, Sept. 22, 1928; *International Molders Jour.*, Oct. 1928, p. 597; and in other labor papers. The *Am. Federationist*, Nov. 1928, contains an editorial note. See also *Who's Who in America*, 1928–29.] F. T. C.

DUNCAN, JOSEPH (Feb. 22, 1794–Jan. 15, 1844), frontier politician, governor of Illinois, was born at Paris, Ky. He was the son of Maj. Joseph Duncan, of the United States army, and Anna Maria (McLaughlin) Duncan, both of whom had removed to Kentucky from Virginia. He had little formal schooling and this lack may have been responsible for the keen interest he later displayed in the cause of popular education. Upon the outbreak of the War of 1812, he secured an ensign's commission and was assigned to the 17th United States Infantry. He saw service in the frontier campaigns of the war and participated in the defense of Fort Stephenson on Aug. 2, 1813. In 1818, he removed from Kentucky to Illinois. In the course of time he acquired tracts of land in various parts of the state. His main interest was agriculture before he entered politics, and he considered himself a farmer by occupation. As early as 1823, however, he was commissioned major-general of Illinois militia, and later, during the Black Hawk War, served for a time as brigadier-general of the state volunteer forces. In 1824 he was elected to the state Senate from Jackson County. His notable service in the Senate was his active support of a bill for the establishment of a free public-school system, which became a law in 1825. In state politics he was allied with the faction opposed to Ninian Edwards [*q.v.*]. In 1826, he was elected congressman from Illinois, and served from March 1827 until 1834. As a member of Congress he had the social and political outlook of the frontiersman. He was keenly interested in frontier defense; he advocated the immediate survey and sale of public lands in Illinois and the region to the northward, and favored the distribution among the states of the proceeds of public land sales, the money to be used for internal improvements and education. As time went on, he found himself in marked opposition to President Jackson on various issues, including the bank, internal improvements, and appointments to office. Lack of sympathy with the Jackson administration may have been in part responsible for his decision to return to the field of state politics. In his successful campaign for the governorship in 1834, he was supported by most of the Whigs, though party lines were not yet clearly drawn and his position was still a trifle ambiguous. He was governor of Illinois from 1834 to 1838, and strongly supported the construction of the Illinois and Michigan canal, though he ultimately assumed the position that, in general, internal improvements within the state should be left to private initiative. In 1842, four years after his retirement, he ran for governor a second time, being nominated by the Whigs, but was decisively defeated, and his public career was ended. On May 13, 1828, he had been married to Elizabeth Caldwell Smith of New York City. His residence after 1830 was at Jacksonville, Ill., where he died.

[Elizabeth Duncan Putnam, "The Life and Services of Jos. Duncan, Gov. of Ill., 1834–38," in *Trans. Ill. State Hist. Soc.*, 1919, pp. 107–87, in which a diary covering a part of Duncan's congressional career is printed as an appendix; *Biog. Sketch of Jos. Duncan* (1888), by his daughter, Julia Duncan Kirby, published as Fergus' Hist. Series No. 29 by the Fergus Printing Co., Chicago; E. W. Blatchford, *Biog. Sketch of Hon. Jos. Duncan* (n.d.), read in 1905 before the Chicago Hist. Soc.; obituary in the *Illinoisan* (Jacksonville), Jan. 19, 1844.] W. E. S.

DUNCAN, ROBERT KENNEDY (Nov. 1, 1868–Feb. 18, 1914), chemist, was the son of Robert Augustus Kennedy Duncan, an Irishman who had settled at Brantford, Ontario, and of Susan Hawley, a Canadian. He became interested in science in his preparatory-school days, and later at the University of Toronto specialized in physics and chemistry. Following his graduation from Toronto, in 1892, with the degree of B.A., he secured a fellowship in Clark University, where he remained a year. He was then appointed instructor in physics and chemistry in the Academic High School at Auburn, N. Y. In 1895 he resigned to accept a better opportunity in Dr. Julius Sachs's Collegiate Institute, New York City, where he took advantage of his location to pursue supplemental graduate work in chemistry at Columbia College in 1897–98. He was an instructor at the Hill School of Pottstown, Pa., in 1898; married Charlotte M. Foster of Brantford, Dec. 27, 1899; studied abroad in 1900–01; and was appointed professor of chemistry in Washington and Jefferson College, Washington, Pa., in 1901. He occupied this chair until 1906, continuing his European studies at intervals during this period. His preparatory-school experience and his general educational observations had made clear to him that there existed a great need for writings on chemistry and other sciences that would acquaint the lay public with notable discoveries through plain, easily understood translations of technical papers. He gave special attention to this useful literary work and about 1900 became a contributor to several New York periodicals. In the summer of 1901, after his articles had commanded favor, he was sent abroad by *McClure's Magazine,* to study radioactivity, particularly in the laboratory of Pierre and Marie Curie, in Paris. Two years later A. S. Barnes & Co. assigned him to collect in Europe material that would be suitable for use in preparing the manuscript of a book on new scientific knowledge, and in 1905 and 1906 he made for *Harper's Magazine* a comprehensive study of the relations of modern chemistry to industry in various European countries. Through this literary work he became widely known to the public at large as an interpreter of science. His books, *The New Knowledge* (1905), *The Chemistry of Commerce* (1907), and *Some Chemical Problems of Today* (1911), were of the highest scientific accuracy, but were so composed as to hold the lay reader's attention. Through his studies abroad Duncan became aware of the relative inferiority of the American chemical industry in the utilization of scientific research, and in 1906 he decided to devote the rest of his life to the creation of a system of industrial fellowships. The first fellowship of the kind was established in January 1907 in the University of Kansas, where Duncan had become professor of industrial chemistry on his return from Europe in 1906. By 1910, his great work at Kansas created a demand for his services in Pittsburgh, which, as a large industrial center, offered him special opportunities. He therefore accepted an invitation from Dr. Samuel Black McCormick, then chancellor of the University of Pittsburgh, to inaugurate his system in this institution in a department of industrial research, and the operation of the fellowships was begun in a temporary building on Mar. 1, 1911. Duncan served the University of Pittsburgh as professor of industrial chemistry as well as director of industrial research from the fall of 1910 until his death. He was also director of industrial research at the University of Kansas, 1907–12, and visiting lecturer at Clark University, 1911–14. Andrew W. Mellon and Richard B. Mellon, citizens of Pittsburgh and sons of Judge Thomas Mellon of the class of 1837 at the University of Pittsburgh, noted the practical success of Duncan's educational experiment and saw in his system an apparently sound method of benefiting American industry by the study of manufacturing problems under suitable conditions and by training young men for technical service. In consequence of this interest, in March 1913, they founded Mellon Institute of Industrial Research at the University of Pittsburgh, and later placed the industrial fellowship system on a permanent basis, as a memorial to their father (1813–1908) and also to Duncan. The present home of the institute, which is adjacent to the central group of the University of Pittsburgh, was occupied in February 1915, a year after Duncan's death, by the twenty-three fellowships then in operation. The institute was incorporated in 1927, and its affairs are managed by its own board of trustees. At present (1930) the building is filled to approximate capacity with sixty fellowships. The industrial research is organized on a contract basis, the problem being set by a person, firm, or association interested in its solution, the scientific worker being found and engaged by the institute, and an industrial fellowship being assigned for a period of at least one year. Each holder (fellow) of an industrial fellowship is given for the time being the broadest facilities for accomplishing a defined piece of research, and all results obtained by him belong exclusively to the founder (donor) of the fellowship. Only one investigation is carried out on a particular subject at any one time, and hence there is no duplication of the research activities of the fellowships in operation. By the application of the industrial fellowship system, the institute has been successful in demonstrating to American manufacturers, irrespective of size, that industrial research, properly conducted, is profitable to them.

[Raymond G. Bacon, sketch in *Science*, Apr. 3, 1914; H. J. Haskell, sketch in *Am. Mag.*, Feb. 1911; *Harper's Weekly*, July 27, 1912; *Who's Who in America*, 1912–13; information in the archives of Mellon Institute; biographic notes made by Miss Lois Whittle, Duncan's secretary, 1910–14, who is now secretary to Dr. E. R. Weidlein, director of Mellon Institute since 1921.]

W. A. H.

DUNGLISON, ROBLEY (Jan. 4, 1798–Apr. 1, 1869), medical writer and teacher, was born at Keswick, Cumberland, England, the son of William and Elizabeth Dunglison. He received his early education at Brisco Hill in Cumberland and at Green Row Academy. He was apprenticed to an apothecary, but by the attendance on lectures in Edinburgh, Paris, and London he gained the doctor's degree in 1818 at the Royal College of Surgeons in the last-named city. He later received a diploma from the Society of Apothecaries and became a "surgeon-apothecary." Later, he studied at Erlangen and in 1823 he obtained the M.D. degree from that university. On Oct. 5 of the following year, in London, he married Harriette Leadham. His earliest publication was an extensive compilation of existing views regarding children's diseases, entitled *Commentaries on the Diseases of the Stomach and Bowels of Children* (1824). This book attracted wide attention and resulted in the appointment of its author, on the invitation of Thomas Jefferson, as professor of medicine at the University of Virginia, a position which he held from 1825 to 1833. He was then called to the University of Maryland where for three years he lectured on a variety of medical subjects. It was with the Jefferson Medical College of Philadelphia, however, that he was mainly identified, serving there as professor of the institutes of medicine, 1836–68, and for some years as dean of the faculty. He was in many ways a remarkable man and he undoubtedly exercised a great influence on medical education in the United States. According to Gross (*Memoir*, p. 313), he was a pioneer in the systematic teaching of physiology. He was not, however, a profound thinker, and his knowledge of disease came mainly from reading the work of others rather than from personal observation or research. His wide acquaintance with books and his exceptional industry combined with a certain degree of practical sagacity and attractive methods of presentation gave him an outstanding position as a lecturer and writer. In his day, in America, creative scholarship or productive work based on research and critical observation was not common in medicine, and the ability to express forcefully and clearly the thoughts of others constituted the main ground upon which the reputation of a medical writer or teacher rested. From such a view-point, Dunglison was a great teacher. He was a voluminous writer on many subjects, not medicine alone, and he translated and edited many foreign works. He was looked upon as a close student of philology and general literature. His most noteworthy medical books were: *Human Physiology* (1832); *A New Dictionary of Medical Science and Literature* (1833); *Elements of Hygiene* (1835); *General Therapeutics, or Principles of Medical Practice; with Tables of the Chief Remedial Agents, etc.* (1836); *New Remedies; the Method of Preparing and Administering Them* (1839); *The Practise of Medicine* (1842). The *Dictionary* was extensively used for many years, and in 1874 was revised by his son, Richard J. Dunglison, M.D., and published under the title *Medical Lexicon: A Dictionary of Medical Science*. Most of his books passed through many editions and were widely used. He was active in promoting the printing of books with raised letters for the use of the blind and with William Chaplin prepared *A Dictionary of the English Language for the Use of the Blind* (1860). In many ways he exerted an influence helpful to the community in which he lived. He was a member of a number of medical and other societies, and vice-president for some years of the American Philosophical Society. In 1825 Yale College conferred on him the honorary degree of Doctor of Medicine.

[R. J. Dunglison, *Memoir of Dr. Robley Dunglison* (1870); S. D. Gross, "Memoir of Robley Dunglison," *Trans. Coll. of Physicians of Phila.*, vol. IV, No. 6 (1869), pp. 294–313; *Autobiog. of Samuel D. Gross . . . With Sketches of his Contemporaries* (1887); Franklin Peale, *Memorial of the Late Robley Dunglison* (1869); S. H. Dickson, in *Am. Jour. Medic. Sci.*, July 1869; J. E. Mears, in the *Western Jour. of Medicine* (Indianapolis), Aug. 1869; F. P. Henry, *Hist. of the Medic. Profession in Phila.* (1897).] R. H. C.

DUNHAM, HENRY MORTON (July 27, 1853–May 4, 1929), composer, organist, educator, was the oldest of the three sons of Isaac A. and Augusta L. (Packard) Dunham of North Bridgewater (now Brockton), Mass., a younger brother, also a professional musician, being William H. Dunham, baritone, long of the faculty of the New England Conservatory of Music. Henry at an early age showed musical aptitude which was encouraged by his parents who sent him in 1872 to the New England Conservatory, then recently established in Boston by Dr. Eben Tourjée. Registered as an organ student of George E. Whiting, Dunham became one of a group of young men in the school who were known as "the Doctor's boys," special protégés of Dr. Tourjée, who exerted himself for their rapid advancement. Of these students, nearly all of whom became distinguished musicians, Dunham retained the closest connection with his Alma Mater, from which he was graduated in 1873 and of whose faculty he was a member continuously from 1875 to 1929. His musical education, nevertheless, was not confined to this school, for in 1876 he was graduated from the Boston University College of Music which at that time was closely affiliated with the New England Conservatory. While still an advanced student Dunham gave recitals on the great organ in the Music Hall, playing all the major works of Bach and Thiele. In 1875 he became organist at the Porter Congregational Church, Brockton. He later served at the Cathedral of the Holy Cross and the Church of the Immaculate Conception, Boston. In 1883 began his connection with the Ruggles Street Baptist Church whose musical programs he made famous. He had been reared in the tradition of the English organ school, typified by the works of William T. Best, but during his many years of church playing he kept abreast of all developments in organ construction and composition. His programs in the eighties emphasized Rheinberger, Merkel, and other German composers; later, he became a skilled interpreter of the French masters such as César Franck, Guilmant and Widor. From Ruggles Street he went in 1896 to the Shawmut Congregational Church, Boston. Ten years afterward he became organist of the Harvard Congregational Church, Brookline, at which he served until waning strength compelled him to give up all but his teaching engagements. He had married, June 28, 1887, Helen Hammond of New London, Conn. Their home was at Brookline.

Dunham's sound attainments as organist made it natural that he should compose chiefly for the organ. His sonatas, based on profound contrapuntal knowledge, are known to all serious organists. His *Organ School*, a text-book, published by the New England Conservatory in 1893, has had wide distribution, as has his later *Manual and Pedal Technique* (1914). Becoming interested in his last years in the combination of organ and orchestra, in which some of the greatest composers have not achieved success, he composed several very effective pieces in this form. Notable among them was "Aurora," which depicts the gradual coming of dawn; it was first performed in Symphony Hall, Boston, thereafter at the Hollywood Bowl, and by several leading symphony orchestras. He was a friendly, lovable man, a patient teacher who endeared himself to his many pupils. He was long the oldest instructor, in years of service, at the New England Conservatory, but until his latest year he kept his youthful appearance and enthusiasm. At the Conservatory Commencement of 1925 the fiftieth anniversary of his teaching was celebrated by performance of several of his works, his former pupil Wallace Goodrich, dean of the faculty, conducting the orchestra.

[The *Am. Organist*, in Dec. 1929, commenced the publication of Dunham's memoirs, under the title, "The Life of a Musician." Supplementing a long obituary in *New England Conservatory of Music Bull.*, June 1929, Geo. W. Chadwick, director of the Conservatory, and life-long friend of Dunham's, contributed an appreciation to the *Bulletin*, July 1929. See also Arthur Foote in *Am. Organist*, Nov. 1929; brief sketches may be found in *A Hundred Years of Music in America* (1889), ed. by W. S. B. Matthews; and in Louis C. Elson, *The Hist. of Am. Music* (1904). The obituaries in Boston newspapers of May 5 and 6, 1929, contain inaccuracies.] F. W. C.

DUNIWAY, ABIGAIL JANE SCOTT (Oct. 22, 1834–Oct. 11, 1915), leader of the woman suffrage movement in the Pacific Northwest, was born on a farm near Groveland, Tazewell County, Ill. Her parents, born in Kentucky, were of mixed nationality; the father, John Tucker Scott, Scotch-Irish and English; the mother, Ann Roelofson, German, French, and English. In 1852 the Scott family, father, mother, and ten children, including Abigail and her fourteen-year-old brother, Harvey W. Scott [*q.v.*], set out in ox-team wagons for the Oregon country. The mother and a brother died on this long journey. The others arrived at Lafayette, Ore., in the fall, and Abigail taught a district school throughout the following winter. In the next August, with Benjamin Charles Duniway, she began married life on a "backwoods" farm. After nine years of farm life, an accident to her husband threw upon her the support of her family, increased by six children. After running a boarding-school at Lafayette for three years, she moved her family to Albany where she taught a private school for one year and then launched into trade with a millinery and notions store. Her experience as a business woman in an occupation that brought her into intimate contact with other women brought to her attention the legal inequalities imposed upon her sex and led her to devote her life to the cause of equal rights for women. In 1870 she helped to organize an "Equal Rights Society" at Albany and the next year, selling her store, she moved to Portland. There with the aid of her sons, ranging in years from ten to sixteen, she launched on May 5, 1871, a newspaper, *The New Northwest,* through the columns of which she unceasingly championed the equal rights of women. For sixteen years she continued this paper and at the same time was active in lecturing, and organizing societies throughout the Northwest. She endured many bitter personal attacks and even mob violence before securing a hearing for herself and her cause. Through her efforts, however, in 1873 the Oregon Woman Suffrage Association was organized, and county and local associations throughout the state were founded in the years that followed. During these years petitions were presented to each session of the state legislature. In 1882 that body for the second time enacted a resolution submitting to vote of the people a constitutional amendment which should give the vote to women. The amendment was defeated at the election of 1884 but the agitation continued. In 1883 the legislature of Washington Territory passed a measure, drafted by Mrs. Duniway, that gave the vote to women. From 1887 until 1895 she resided in Idaho, and she won another victory when woman suffrage was adopted there in 1896. She returned to Oregon and revived the movement in that state, but success did not come until the election of 1912, when the suffrage amendment was carried by a vote of 61,265 to 57,104. Mrs. Duniway drew up with her own hand the proclamation signed by the governor of Oregon that announced the final triumph of her long years of devotion to a single cause. Two years later she published *Path Breaking: An Autobiographical History of the Equal Suffrage Movement in Pacific Coast States* (1914), somewhat inaccurate in details. She had previously published two novels: *Captain Gray's Company: or, Crossing the Plains and Living in Oregon* (1859), and, nearly half a century later, *From the West to the West* (1905). In 1876 she published *David and Anna Matson,* in verse.

[R. C. Clark, *Hist. of the Willamette Valley, Ore.* (1927), I, 702–24; Harvey W. Scott, *Hist. of the Oregon Country* (1924); John W. Leonard, ed., *Woman's Who's Who of America* (1914–15); *Morning Oregonian* (Portland), Oct. 12, 1915.] R. C. C—k.

DUNLAP, JOHN (1747–Nov. 27, 1812), printer, was born in Strabane, County Tyrone, Ireland. At about ten years of age he was sent to Pennsylvania to be trained by his uncle, William Dunlap, a printer, who had just married a relation of Mrs. Benjamin Franklin and through this influence had been appointed postmaster of Philadelphia. William Dunlap, who had learned his trade as apprentice to William Bradford, had been engaged as printer in Lancaster, Pa., but in 1757 moved to Philadelphia, where he opened a shop as printer and bookseller. At this juncture it seems probable that he sent to Ireland for his young nephew, who was immediately apprenticed to him to learn the trade of typography. William Dunlap felt he had a call to the ministry, and accordingly, in the year 1766, sold his stock as bookseller, leaving the printing business in charge of John, whose apprenticeship was near its close, while he went to England to receive ordination. Two years later, in 1768, he was given a charge in the parish of Stratton, in King and Queen County, Va., and sold his shop and equipment to his nephew. At this time the business consisted mainly in the printing of books, but in November 1771 John Dunlap began the publication of a weekly newspaper, *The Pennsylvania Packet, or The General Advertiser.* From September 1777 to July 1778, during the British occupation of Philadelphia, he printed his paper in Lancaster, Pa. When he returned to Philadelphia, he changed the period of issue to three times a week, and on Sept. 21, 1784, he began its publication as a daily—the first daily newspaper in the United States. Through numerous changes of ownership and name its tradition has been continued, its present successor being the *Public Ledger* of Philadelphia, by which it was absorbed in 1924. The Declaration of Independence was printed in Dunlap's office from Jefferson's manuscript, and this broadside, signed by Hancock and the Secretary of Congress, was the form in which the Declaration was sent to the various colonial Assemblies and to Europe. From 1778 until the federal government was founded and the capital removed to New York, Dunlap was printer to Congress. Soon after he returned from Lancaster he took David C. Claypoole, who had been his apprentice, into partnership. The Constitution of the United States was printed in the office of Dunlap & Claypoole and was first published in their *Pennsylvania Packet and Daily Advertiser.* The senior partner retired from business in 1795. In the words of a fellow printer: "Dunlap executed his printing in a neat and correct manner. It is said that, whilst he conducted a newspaper, he never inserted a paragraph which would wound the feelings of an individual!" (Thomas, *post,* I, 259). "The amiableness of disposition which might be implied from that sentence was not, perhaps, his talent. However, *de mortuis nil* . . . Dunlap possessed till his death, a handsome fortune (McColloch, *post,* p. 197). In 1780, he was one of ninety-two subscribers to the National Bank for the United States, formed for the purpose of supplying provisions to the army. His subscription was for £4,000. He was also active in military affairs, was one of the original founders of the 1st Troop of Philadelphia City Cavalry, in 1774, and as cornet accompanied the command in the campaign of 1776–77, taking part in the actions at Princeton and Trenton. In 1781, he was elected first lieutenant, and in 1794, captain of this ancient military company. During the Whiskey Insurrection, in 1794, he served as major commanding all the cavalry during the campaign. From 1789 to 1792 he was a member of the Common Council of Philadelphia. He died of apoplexy on Nov. 27, 1812, and was buried with military honors in the burial ground of Christ Church, Philadelphia. He was married, Feb. 4, 1773, to Mrs. Elizabeth Ellison, *née* Hayes of Liverpool.

[Isaiah Thomas, *The Hist. of Printing in America,* repub. in *Trans. and Colls. Am. Antiquarian Soc.,* vols. V and VI (1874); and Wm. McColloch, "Additions to Thomas's Hist.," *Proc. Am. Antiquarian Soc.,* n.s., vol. XXXI, pt. I (1921); *Hist. of the First Troop Phila. City Cavalry* (1875); MS. Records of Christ Church, Phila.; J. H. Campbell, *Hist. of the Friendly Sons of St. Patrick* (1892), p. 109; Henry Simpson, *Lives of Eminent Philadelphians* (1859), p. 325; James Cheetham, *Life of Thomas Paine* (1809), pp. 72 ff.] J. J.

DUNLAP, ROBERT PINCKNEY (Aug. 17, 1794–Oct. 20, 1859), governor of Maine, was born at Brunswick, Me. His grandfather, Robert Dunlap, a native of Barilla, County Antrim, Ireland, was a Presbyterian minister and master of arts of the University of Edinburgh, who settled at Brunswick in 1747. Capt. John Dunlap, son of Rev. Robert, married as his second wife Mary Tappan of Newburyport, Mass., and by traffic in furs and pelts, by shipbuilding and overseas trading, became one of the richest men in the District of Maine. Robert, third son of John and Mary Dunlap, graduated from Bowdoin College in 1815, and was admitted to the bar in 1818. Wealthy, personable, well-liked, he forsook the law and Federalist tradition for a life-long political career as a Jacksonian Democrat. At twenty-six he was in the Maine legislature, serving as representative during the years 1821 and 1822, and as senator during 1824–28 and 1831–33. He presided over the Senate for four years with an unruffled fairness and tact that won commendation from all parties. He was for a time a member of the Executive Council. From 1834 to 1838 he was governor of Maine, having defeated his Federalist-Whig opponents on the Jacksonian platform of the Union with state's rights, opposition to the protective tariff and the banking interests, and persistent championship of the laboring and agricultural classes. He was instrumental in obtaining prison reforms, the first insane asylum in Maine, the first geological survey of the state, and—by the sale of state lands—Revolutionary pensions and a school fund. In June 1837, during Dunlap's term, a Maine census agent was arrested by the governor of New Brunswick in that northeastern territory which had been in dispute since the Treaty of Paris of 1783. Dunlap proclaimed the soil of Maine invaded, called out the militia, entered into correspondence with John Forsyth, secretary of state, and by his vigor and tact brought and kept the critical situation before the eyes of the national government, at the same time holding the long-standing boundary controversy in abeyance throughout his term. In August of the same year (1837) he also commanded national attention when, although a Democrat and sympathetic with the grievances of the South, he refused to extradite to Georgia the master and mate of a schooner on which a slave had stowed away. He served on the Board of Overseers of Bowdoin College, 1821–59, and was president of the Board from 1843 until his death. His advocacy of Freemasonry in the period of the powerful Anti-Masonic party and general disapprobation is significant of his character. In 1825 he married

Lydia Chapman of Beverly, Mass., who bore him three sons and one daughter. He served two terms in Congress, 1843–47; was collector of the port of Portland, 1848; and from 1853 to 1857 was postmaster at Brunswick. He was not prominent in national politics but his friendship and advice were esteemed by his colleagues. Throughout his public life he received an unusual share of respect and popularity. Tall, impressive, with a calm but commanding countenance, he united suavity of manners with an expert knowledge of parliamentary rules and dignified impartiality. He remained a loyal Democrat despite the disruptive slavery issue.

[J. S. C. Abbott, *The Hist. of Maine* (1875; rev. by E. H. Elwell, 1892), pp. 429–31; L. C. Hatch, ed., *Maine, a Hist.* (1919), I, 214 ff.; G. A. and H. W. Wheeler, *Hist. of Brunswick, Topsham, and Harpswell, Me.* (1878), pp. 209, 501, 730–33. Geo. E. Adams, in *Me. Hist. Soc. Colls.*, vol. VII (1876); *Me. Hist. Memoirs* (1922); E. Hamlin, *Life and Times of Hannibal Hamlin* (1899), pp. 61, 102, 110, 304. H. S. Burrage, *Maine in the Northeastern Boundary Controversy* (1919); *Eastern Argus* (Portland, Me.), Oct. 21, 1859; *Am. Freemason* (N. Y.), IV (1859), 478–81; *Freemasons' Monthly Mag.* (Boston), XIX (1859), 24.]

B. M—o.

DUNLAP, WILLIAM (Feb. 19, 1766–Sept. 28, 1839), playwright, theatrical manager, painter, historian, was the son of Samuel Dunlap, a young Irishman who was color-bearer in the regiment known as "Wolfe's Own" on the Plains of Abraham. At the close of the war the regiment was stationed at Perth Amboy, N. J., where Dunlap withdrew from the army, began keeping store, and married Margaret Sargeant. William, their only child, was born at Perth Amboy, where he was reared and educated during his first eleven years. In 1777 the father's Loyalist sympathies made it expedient for the family to take up residence in New York, the British headquarters. A year later, while playing war with other boys, William sustained an injury which completely destroyed the sight of his right eye. The accident brought his formal schooling to an end, but he now resolved to develop a talent for drawing that he had already shown. A local artist was engaged to give him a few lessons, and by the age of sixteen the boy had set up as a professional portraitist. Among his early sitters were George and Martha Washington, whose likenesses he made in pastel while he was visiting friends at Rocky Hill, N. J., near the General's headquarters. In May 1784, the elder Dunlap, now a prospering china importer, sent his son to London to study painting under Benjamin West. During a foreign residence of over three years William applied himself to almost everything except his studies. He took particular delight in the theatre and saw all the leading actors, including Mrs. Siddons in her prime. Naturally he returned to New York scantily prepared to take up his profession. His success was commensurate with his preparation.

It was not long before the studio was deserted for a new interest—the stage. Fired by the recent success of Royall Tyler's *The Contrast,* the first American play to achieve anything like a run, Dunlap wrote a five-act comedy, which he submitted to the managers, but which perished in the greenroom. His second comedy, *The Father; or, American Shandyism,* brought out in 1789 and later reprinted as *The Father of an Only Child,* met with sufficient applause to focus his ambition upon the theatre, and new plays from his pen began to appear on the New York stage at the rate of about one a year. During this period he also ventured into the field of poetry by writing two narrative poems of some length, both of which were included in two contemporary collections of American verse. But such occupations were inadequate for the support of a family (Dunlap had married Elizabeth Woolsey, Feb. 10, 1789); consequently his father made him a partner in his business.

In the spring of 1796 Dunlap took the crucial step of his career when he purchased a one-quarter interest in the Old American Company, New York's sole theatrical concern. He thus entered into partnership with Lewis Hallam and John Hodgkinson, rival actors and sworn enemies of each other. Dunlap's duties as acting manager, treasurer, and bookkeeper of the company were rendered so distasteful by the hostility of his associates that he soon deeply regretted his venture. The second season brought a realignment of interests by Hallam's withdrawal from the firm. The improvement was imperceptible. A more exasperating business associate than the irresponsible Hodgkinson it would stretch the imagination to conceive. The business was being conducted at a steady loss, but when, in January 1798, the managers transferred their company from the old John Street house to the new Park Theatre, they hoped for a reversal of fortune. They hoped in vain. By spring Hodgkinson had decided that Boston offered a more lucrative field, and, disposing of his concerns to his partner, he left Dunlap sole director and manager of the New York theatre. Having discovered that his own plays were but a feeble stimulant to box-office receipts, Dunlap now began to translate French and German successes, particularly those of the then famous Kotzebue. This German dramatist so effectually caught the taste of the town that during the next few years no less than twenty of his pieces were produced, the majority of them translated or adapted by the manager. By the increased support thus gained he contrived to hold his excellent company together. But it was a losing struggle. Grasping associates, a fickle public, yellow fever, ill health, and his own lack of business foresight conspired against his prosperity. In February 1805, Dunlap declared himself a bankrupt and forfeited his entire property.

As a means of supporting his family he now turned to his long-neglected brushes. Miniature portraits being much in demand, he essayed this form of art, although knowing but little of its technique. The season of 1805–06 was spent as an itinerant miniaturist, and, if his returns were small, at least he picked up some knowledge of his craft. In the spring of 1806, T. A. Cooper, formerly a leading actor in Dunlap's company and now manager at the Park, offered his old employer a position as his general assistant at a fair salary. The arrangement continued for over five years. One consequence of this office was a close acquaintance with the distinguished English actor, George Frederick Cooke, whom Cooper brought to America late in 1810 for a tour of the principal cities. During a part of this tour the dissipated player was entrusted to the guardianship of the abstemious Dunlap, who, shortly after the death of the former, turned this contact to good account by writing the *Memoirs of George Fred. Cooke, Esq., Late of the Theatre Royal, Covent Garden* (1813). Upon quitting the theatre for the second time, about the end of 1811, Dunlap again turned to painting. When his custom was interrupted by the War of 1812, he undertook the founding of a magazine, but the *Monthly Recorder* (1813) died with the fifth issue, leaving its editor poorer than before. Fortunately he was appointed assistant paymaster-general to the state militia in 1814, and the problem of how to go on living was temporarily solved. While holding this appointment, he completed a *Life of Charles Brockden Brown* (1815). His governmental employment came to an end late in 1816, and for the last time Dunlap returned to portrait painting. New York was still his headquarters, but he was often forced to turn itinerant and to visit Norfolk, Montreal, Vermont, and various other places in his search for patrons. He now worked chiefly in oil with only an occasional miniature. In 1821 he began a series of large show pictures, a popular form of art of the time. His subjects were usually drawn from the Bible and were often deeply indebted to Benjamin West's canvases of a similar kind. By sending these paintings on tour, the artist somewhat increased his meager earnings and probably did something to educate artistic taste, especially in the rural districts, where they were frequently exhibited. When an insurrection broke out in New York against the reactionary American Academy of the Fine Arts, Dunlap, although a member of that organization, joined forces with the progressives and in 1826 helped to found the National Academy of Design. From its inception he was very active in the affairs of the new society; he was a regular contributor to its annual exhibitions, he held the professorship of historical painting for several years, and served as vice-president from 1831 to 1838.

His last years were marked by continued poverty and much illness. In this condition he was helped and heartened by two successful benefits, one theatrical and one artistic, held for him at New York in 1833 and 1838 respectively. He did comparatively little painting during this final period, but in spite of weakened vitality his pen was never more active. His *History of the American Theatre* was published in 1832, and his two-volume *History of the Rise and Progress of the Arts of Design in the United States* in 1834. Two years later a temperance novel, *Thirty Years Ago; or, the Memoirs of a Water Drinker,* was brought out. His last energy was given to research in the history of New York. A preliminary study, *A History of New York, for Schools,* appeared in 1837. The first volume of the completed *History of the New Netherlands, Province of New York, and State of New York, to the Adoption of the Federal Constitution,* was published in 1839, and the second volume, posthumously, in 1840. Dunlap died, after a stroke of paralysis, in New York and was buried in Perth Amboy. He was survived by his wife and his son John Alexander Dunlap. A daughter, Margaret Ann, had died in 1837.

Dunlap was a man of only moderate talent but of unusual versatility, and he touched the cultural life of his day at many points. As a playwright he was without original ideas, but his craftsmanship was competent, and by employing ideas current on the English stage he was able to manufacture plays that were theatrically interesting and that contributed toward fashioning the tastes of the public and the practise of other writers. For instance, he experimented with the comedy of manners of the sentimental type, then popular abroad, but before Dunlap, except for Tyler's *Contrast,* unattempted in America. In serious drama Dunlap made two important innovations: he was the first in this country to write Gothic or terroristic plays, a species well illustrated by his *Fontainville Abbey* (acted 1795) and *Ribbemont; or, the Feudal Baron* (acted 1796); and he broke away from the formal pseudo-classic manner of the typical eighteenth-century tragedy, to which his American predecessors had adhered. In the two plays just mentioned and also in *Leicester* (acted 1794) he created a definitely romantic atmosphere for tragedy and tragicomedy. It is worthy of note that in these three particulars Dunlap's efforts were quickly followed by a succession of American plays of similar type. If he did not, in all such cases, provide the model for his fellow playwrights, at least he was in the forefront of those who took the unaccustomed path. As a translator he reworked numerous Continental successes both French and German, often with considerable skill. His knowledge of stage technique and his facile, colloquial style sometimes created an adaptation more effective than the original. By bringing these European plays, ephemeral though they were, before the audiences of provincial America, he helped in some measure to give the United States a more cosmopolitan view of contemporary culture. With occasional dramatic work as late as 1828, Dunlap wrote in all approximately thirty original plays and made about the same number of translations. In quality his achievement was far superior to the average of his time. *The Father of an Only Child, The Italian Father* (acted 1799), *Leicester,* and *André* (acted 1798), the last two written in smooth and forceful blank verse, are probably the four most actable American plays of the eighteenth century, and they are interesting reading even to-day. In quantity of output he immensely outranked all predecessors. He was the first man of his country to make a serious business of writing for the stage. Perhaps, then, the title of the father of American drama, which has been applied to him, is no misnomer.

In his office as theatrical manager Dunlap aspired to establish a truly moral and cultural theatre, but popular taste did not support his efforts and he was compelled to compromise. He at least succeeded in offering more encouragement to American playwrights than they had formerly received, and he gave Continental drama its first real hearing in the United States, as well as featuring most of the current British plays. As a painter he must be regarded as a minor figure in an age that produced several great artists. Both his miniatures and his oils commonly show some stiffness and flatness—perhaps because he saw with only one eye. At the same time his subjects look like actual men and women with definite personalities, and in an occasional portrait he displays a power that commands admiration. Of more lasting influence than his plays and paintings are, *A History of the American Theatre* and the *Arts of Design.* In spite of inaccuracies both are still regarded as indispensable authorities, for they contain a fund of first-hand information that could have been provided by no other writer, and in both, the personal side of the actors or artists is so stressed as to produce a readability seldom found in works of this nature.

Dunlap was a man who pursued many interests and championed many causes, and always with large energy and enthusiasm. In the midst of his busy managerial days he found time for effective work in behalf of the abolition of slavery, having already demonstrated the sincerity of his pretension by manumitting the family slaves. He was an ardent American and never lost a chance to defend republican institutions. One result of his numerous activities was that he enjoyed close association with some of the leading men of his day, among them Irving, Bryant, Cooper, Samuel F. B. Morse, Gilbert Stuart, James Kent, and in particular Charles Brockden Brown. He could be a good hater, but his generosity, his love of good-fellowship, and his varied intellectual interests gained him a multitude of friends. Despite many hardships he faced life with cheerful fortitude. Even the strain of his often acute poverty he bore philosophically, conscious that he had forsaken his father's profitable business for the harder service of arts that his age scantily rewarded, but that he honestly loved.

[Certain autobiographical writings of Dunlap's provide the chief source of information about his life. For many years he kept a diary, of which four volumes are extant in the N. Y. Hist. Soc. Lib., and six in the Yale lib.; they cover about ten years between 1786 and 1834. In addition autobiographical sketches are included in *A Hist. of the Am. Theatre* and the *Arts of Design.* A detailed treatment of Dunlap will be found in O. S. Coad, *Wm. Dunlap, a Study of his Life and Works and of his Place in Contemporary Culture* (1917). Special phases of his work are discussed by T. S. Woolsey in "Wm. Dunlap, Painter and Critic, or the Am. Vasari," *Yale Rev.*, July 1914; and by O. S. Coad, in "The Dunlap Diaries at Yale," *Studies in Philology*, July 1927. See also A. H. Quinn, *Hist. of the Am. Drama from the Beginning to the Civil War* (1923), ch. iv; M. J. Moses, *The Am. Dramatist* (1925), ch. iv; G. C. D. Odell, *Annals of the N. Y. Stage*, vols. I and II (1927); and Oscar Wegelin, *A Bibliographical Checklist of the Plays and Misc. Writings of Wm. Dunlap* (1916).]

O. S. C.

DUNLOP, JAMES (1795–Apr. 9, 1856), lawyer, author, was the great-grandson of William Dunlop of County Armagh, Ireland, who in 1738 acquired land grants at Shippensburg and Falling Springs, Pa., and whose descendants continued to be associated with that neighborhood. His father, Andrew Dunlop, a lawyer of Lancaster and Chambersburg, married Sarah Bella Chambers, grand-daughter of the founder of the latter town, on Nov. 13, 1790, and James was born at Chambersburg. The family was well-to-do, and he received a good private education after which he proceeded to Dickinson College, Carlisle, where he graduated in 1812. He then studied law with his father, and after his admission to the Franklin County bar in 1817, commenced practise in Chambersburg. His family connections and natural ability procured for him a flourishing practise, in addition to which he engaged in industrial business, becoming senior partner in the firm of Dunlop & Madeira, owners of the Lemnos Factory at Chambersburg, and manufacturers of edge tools and cutlery. He also took an active interest in local politics, identifying himself with the Jackson Democrats, and was elected to the state Senate for Franklin County in 1824, serving till December 1827. During this period he prepared, "A Memoir on the Controversy between William Penn and Lord Baltimore Respecting the Boundaries of Pennsylvania and Maryland," which was read before the Historical Society of Pennsylvania on Nov. 10, 1825, and published in its *Memoirs,* vol. I (1826). In 1831 he was elected to the state House of Representatives for Franklin County and served one term, but in 1833 the action of President Jackson in withdrawing the government deposits from the United States Bank caused him to dissociate himself from the Democratic party, and he thenceforth practically withdrew from political life. In 1837 he represented the District of Franklin, Cumberland, and Adams counties in the state convention which met at Harrisburg, taking a prominent part in the debates. Though he was a good lawyer and a successful advocate, his business interests had interfered seriously with his legal practise, and in 1838, when industrial conditions became stagnant, he removed to Pittsburgh and commenced practise anew in that city. In 1843 he published Part 1 of a *Treatise on the Duties of County and Township Officers of Pennsylvania,* which dealt with the county commissioners and the assessing and collecting of taxes; but the plan, which contemplated a subsequent volume, was never completed. He also prepared, *The General Laws of Pennsylvania, 1700–1846, Chronologically Arranged with Notes and References to all the Decisions of the Supreme Court of Pennsylvania, Giving Construction to Such Laws* (1847). This work met with immediate favor, and two subsequent editions were called for, the last of which, issued in 1858 after his death, included the state laws up to 1853. He built up a substantial practise in Pittsburgh but considerations of health induced him in 1855 to retire, and he then took up his residence in Philadelphia where he published his *Digest of the General Laws of the United States with References and Notes of Decisions* (1856). A great student, he enjoyed a high reputation as an accomplished lawyer and advocate, though no details of his professional achievements have survived apart from his own legal writings. In person Dunlop was over medium height and somewhat spare in build. Gifted with a brilliant wit and caustic tongue, he was "red headed and humorous, and would rather have lost a fee than have missed a chance to relate an amusing anecdote" (Cooper, *post*). He died when on a visit to Baltimore, Md. His wife was Maria Madeira of Chambersburg.

[Particulars of Dunlop's ancestry will be found in W. M. Mervine, *Harris, Dunlop, Valentine and Allied Families* (1920), and the *Kittochtinny Mag.*, July, Oct. 1905, which latter also contains details of his life. See also John M. Cooper, *Recollections of Chambersburg, Pa.* (1900).]
H. W. H. K.

DUNMORE, JOHN MURRAY, Earl of (1732–Mar. 5, 1809), colonial governor, who held also the titles of Viscount Fincastle, Baron of Blair, of Moulin, and of Tillymont, was the eldest son of William Murray, third earl of Dunmore, and his wife Catherine Nairne, daughter of William, Lord Nairne. The Murrays were descended in the female line from the house of Stuart; and in 1745 the third earl took part in the uprising of the Young Pretender in Scotland. Later he was pardoned for his share in the rebellion, and at his death in 1756 his son John succeeded to the title and estate. Reared in the ancestral home in Scotland, the young earl was a sturdy youth, accustomed to life in the open, but not without knowledge of the amenities of good living, nor without a wide acquaintance with the men of his day. In 1759 he won the hand of Lady Charlotte Stewart, daughter of the Earl of Galloway; and in 1761 was elected one of the sixteen representative peers of Scotland to sit in the British Parliament. The next nine years were passed for the most part at London, in the society of statesmen and eminent men. In 1766, for instance, Dunmore dined with Earl Shelburne when David Hume and a noted poet were the other guests (Lord Edmond Fitzmaurice, *Life of William, Earl of Shelburne,* I, 1875, p. 270); such facts disprove the rumor that the earl was uncultivated and rude in manners and appearance. In 1768 he was again chosen a Scottish peer for Parliament and in 1770 he was appointed by the Earl of Hillsborough governor of the royal colony of New York, an appointment which promised to afford both honor and profit, since it was provided that the governor's salary should not be dependent upon the whims of the colonial legislature, but should be paid from the revenue arising from the duty on tea (*Documents Relative to the Colonial History of the State of New York,* VIII, 1857, p. 223). The earl and his family reached the port of New York on Oct. 19, 1770, and were quartered at the castle, part of the Battery fortifications. The new governor entertained lavishly and was popular with the élite of the city.

After about eleven months, promotion came to Dunmore in his appointment as governor of Virginia. At first he was very popular and the recipient of many courtesies there; his charming wife and children were much admired; a newborn daughter, named Virginia, was adopted by the colony; and the governor's name was given (February 1772) to the new counties of Dunmore and Fincastle. In the Governor's Palace at Williamsburg the colonial gentry dined, among them Washington and other leaders of the patriot party. Dunmore's first clash with this party occurred in 1773 when he dissolved the House of Burgesses for proposing a committee of correspondence on colonial grievances; the next year he again dissolved the House when the burgesses appointed a day of fasting and mourning over the Boston Port Bill. In the midst of these disagreements the Governor issued a call for the colony's militia to put down hostile Indians upon the frontier. He was later accused of inciting this Indian war to divert the minds of the Virginians from their grievances; there is evidence, however, that the Governor was sincere in his desire to protect the outlying settlements from hostile raids. He had in 1773 visited the colony's northwestern frontier, had built Fort Dunmore at the forks of the Ohio, and was preparing to have surveys made and claims entered when the Shawnee Indians became hostile. Determining to subdue them, he summoned the militia of the southwestern counties to collect under Col. Andrew Lewis [*q.v.*] and advance down the Kanawha River while he in person led his contingent west from Fort Dunmore (or Pittsburgh). Lewis's division was surprised on Oct. 10, 1774, at Point Pleasant, and after hard fighting repulsed the Shawnee under their chief, Cornstalk. Thus Dunmore found them humbled and subdued, and on the plains of the Scioto made peace with them. In after years the American soldiers asserted that Dunmore had treacherously attempted to lead the militia into a trap; there is, however, no proof of such a purpose. At the close of the campaign the officers expressed their appreciation of Lord Dunmore's conduct, and the legislature offered him thanks for his defense of the frontier (P. Force, *American Archives,* 4 ser., I, 1837, pp. 962–63). Nevertheless most of the Virginians in his troops were soon in the army of the American Revolution, and the battle of Point Pleasant has been called its first engagement. Meanwhile, as the revolutionary movement gathered force, Dunmore was soon opposed by almost the entire colony. He first removed colonial powder to a ship-of-war, then the patriots gathered and compelled him to pay for it. Threats were openly made that the Governor should be hung, whereupon on June 1, 1775, he retired with his family to the warship *Fowey,* and continued to oppose the colonials. In November he declared martial law and incited the slaves to desert, actions which caused him to be execrated by the whole colony. The troops gathered for a pitched battle at Great Bridge, on Dec. 9, 1775, when the Governor's forces were defeated and he again fled to the ships. On Jan. 1, 1776, he bombarded and fired Norfolk. The last conflict in July was at Gwynne's Island, after which Dunmore finally left Virginia and returned to England, where once more he was one of the Scottish peers sent to Parliament. Several years later he was governor of the Bahamas (1787–96). His death occured at Ramsgate, England.

Dunmore was not fitted for times of revolution; a forthright man with a single-track mind, he had no vision of the colonists' cause, and met the emergency by force rather than by finesse. Had he lived in quiet times, he might have been one of Virginia's popular and successful governors. Personally brave, he showed weakness in the crises, and by rash measures brought about his own downfall.

[R. G. Thwaites and L. P. Kellogg, *Doc. Hist. of Dunmore's War* (1905) gives a sketch of Dunmore as well as of the operations on the frontier. H. J. Eckenrode, *The Revolution in Va.* (1916), is prejudiced and presents the Governor's activities as they appeared to his enemies. See also Jas. M. Rigg, in *Dict. Nat. Biog.,* XIII, 1,285, which gives month of death as May; and Jas. B. Paul, *The Scots Peerage,* vol. III (1906), which gives date of death as Feb. 25, 1809. The Draper MSS., Wis. Hist. Lib., contain some of Dunmore's letters, and correspondence of L. C. Draper with Dunmore's grandsons. One of the latter, Charles Augustus Murray, is authority for the statement that Dunmore died Mar. 5, 1809.]

L. P. K.

DUNN, CHARLES (Dec. 28, 1799–Apr. 7, 1872), lawyer and jurist, was the son of John and Amy (Burks) Dunn. His father was a native of Dublin, Ireland, and his mother was from Virginia. He was born at Bullitt's Old Lick, Bullitt County, Ky., where he spent his early life. He attended schools in Louisville for several years, and had business experience before studying law. He read law under the direction of two prominent lawyers of Louisville and Frankfort. Removing to Illinois in 1819, he completed his law studies and was admitted to the bar in 1820.

He then entered practise at Jonesboro, Ill., where in 1821 he was married to Mary E. Schrader, a daughter of Judge Otto Schrader. In 1829 Dunn was appointed acting commissioner of the Illinois and Michigan Canal, and with his associates surveyed and platted the first town of Chicago. During the Black Hawk War he served as captain of an Illinois company which he had raised. Resuming practise after the war at Golconda, Ill., he was elected in 1835 to the House of Representatives of the Illinois legislature.

In the spring of 1836, he was appointed by President Jackson chief justice of the newly created territory of Wisconsin. This position he held for twelve years, until Wisconsin became a state in 1848, when a state elective judiciary was organized. His office as territorial chief justice was no sinecure. Not only did he preside over the appellate court of three judges, but he served as well as *nisi prius* judge of one of the three districts into which the territory was divided. He was a member of the constitutional convention of 1847–48 which framed the constitution of Wisconsin, serving as chairman of the judiciary committee. The power reserved to the legislature to alter or repeal the charter of any corporation created by it was his work. After retiring from the bench, he served as a senator in the state legislatures of 1853–56. He was a Democratic candidate for Congress in 1858 and for justice of the supreme court in 1860, but as the candidate of the minority party without hope of election. On moving to Wisconsin, Dunn had made his home at Belmont, LaFayette County, for a short period the capital of the territory. In this hamlet in southwestern Wisconsin he lived the remainder of his life. After retiring from the bench he resumed the active practise of law. He died and was buried at Mineral Point, Wis.

In the opinion of his contemporaries, Dunn ranked high, both as a trial, and as an appellate, judge, and during his long practise of law after his retirement from the bench, he was regarded by all members of the Wisconsin bar who knew him as "a great man in a private station." His chief services were in giving to the highest court of a young midwestern state the high character which it has never lost.

[See J. R. Berryman, *Hist. of the Bench and Bar of Wis.* (1898), I, 68–77; *Green Bag*, Jan. 1897; H. A. Tenney and David Atwood, *Memorial Record of the Fathers of Wis.* (1880), pp. 203–11; J. B. Winslow, *The Story of a Great Court* (1912), pp. 33–36; *Report of the State Bar Asso. of Wis. for the Years 1878, 1881 and 1885* (1905), pp. 105–06; 30 *Wis.*, 21–40, and 35 *Wis.*, 21–26. Dunn's opinions as chief justice may be found in Vols. I and II of Pinney's *Wisconsin Reports* (1872–74).]

W. M. S.

DUNN, WILLIAM McKEE (Dec. 12, 1814–July 24, 1887), congressman, judge-advocate general of the United States army, was the son of Williamson Dunn [*q.v.*] and Miriam (Wilson) Dunn. His parents, both of whom were of Scotch-Irish descent, moved from Kentucky to Indiana Territory in 1809, settling on the site of the future town of Hanover, and there their fifth child, William, was born. When he was eleven years old, William rode on horseback behind his father to Bloomington and entered the State Seminary, later Indiana University. He graduated in 1832 and became principal of the preparatory department of the newly organized Hanover College. Elected professor two years later, he went to Yale in order better to fit himself for his new work. In 1837, after a year more of teaching, he resigned his professorship, studied law in the office of an attorney at Madison, and was admitted to the bar. He began practise in New Albany; but, having married Elizabeth Francis Lanier, eldest daughter of James F. D. Lanier [*q.v.*], a wealthy and influential citizen of Madison, he moved to that town, where he formed a partnership with Stephen C. Stevens, a former judge of the Indiana supreme court, and practised until the Civil War.

In 1848 he was elected to the lower house of the Indiana legislature and played an active part in the passage of an act levying a state tax for the support of public schools. His career in the legislature led, in 1849, to his nomination for Congress by the Whigs, but in the election he was beaten by his Democratic antagonist. He was, however, chosen a delegate to the convention that formulated the Indiana Constitution of 1851 and played an active part in the work of that body, especially in matters concerning education and banking. Though a resident of southern Indiana, where Southern influence was strong, he opposed the extension of slavery, and when the Kansas-Nebraska Act led to the formation of the Republican party, he joined it. In 1858 and again in 1860 he was elected by that party to Congress, where his course was marked by energy and decision. During 1861–63 he was a member of the important committee on military affairs of the House. Upon the slavery question and most other issues his opinions were in close harmony with those of President Lincoln. He enlisted in the Indiana Infantry in 1861, and from June to August of that year served as aide-de-camp to McClellan. Having been defeated for reëlection to Congress in 1862, he was after the expiration of his term, appointed judge-advocate for the Department of Missouri, and ultimately rose, in 1875, to be judge-advocate general of the army, retiring in 1881. He died at his summer home, "Maplewood," in Fairfax County, Va.

[W. W. Woollen, *William McKee Dunn: A Memoir* (n.d.), printed for private distribution soon after Dunn's death; *Ind. Univ. Bull. Reg. of Grads. 1830–1916* (1917); T. A. Wylie, *Ind. Univ., Its Hist. from 1820 when Founded to 1890* (1890); *Complete List of the Members of the Senate and House of Representatives of Ind., 1816–1903* (1903); F. B. Heitman, *Hist. Reg. and Dict. U. S. Army* (1903); *Biog. Dir. Am. Cong.* (1928); *Washington Post* and *Evening Star* (Washington), July 25, 1887.] P. L. H.

DUNN, WILLIAMSON (Dec. 25, 1781–Nov. 11, 1854), Indiana pioneer, was born near Crow's Station, not far from Danville, Ky. His parents were Samuel Dunn, a soldier in Dunmore's War and in the Revolution, and Eleanor Brewster. In September 1806, Williamson Dunn married Miriam Wilson, and three years later the pair, with two young children, moved to southern Indiana and built the first house where the town of Hanover now stands. With him Dunn took three negro slaves whom he had inherited and whom he now freed. In 1811 he was made by Gov. Harrison justice of the peace and judge of the court of common pleas of Jefferson County. Soon after the outbreak of the War of 1812, President Madison commissioned him a captain of rangers, and the next year he participated in raids upon hostile Indian towns along the White and Wabash rivers. Later that year he took command of Fort Harrison near Terre Haute. Retiring from the army before the end of the war, he served for a time as associate judge of the circuit court of Jefferson County. Upon the admission of Indiana to statehood in 1816, he was elected a member of the state House of Representatives and was thrice returned to that body. In the third and fourth legislatures he was speaker of the House. In 1820 he was commissioned register of the land office for the Terre Haute district and three years later removed to Crawfordsville, which town he helped to lay out. He held the office until 1829, when he returned to Hanover. In 1837 he was chosen on the Whig ticket to fill a vacancy in the state Senate, and in 1846 was elected probate judge of Jefferson County and was subsequently reëlected.

Throughout his career he took a strong interest in the advancement of education. He donated fifty acres of land to help establish the academy which became Hanover College, and, later, he gave the ground at Crawfordsville on which Wabash College was erected. He was widely esteemed for his ability, probity, and public spirit. One of his sons, William McKee Dunn [*q.v.*], became judge-advocate general of the United States army. Of his family a writer on the early history of Indiana says that no other "equalled the Dunns in bravery and soldierly qualities." They were often called "the fighting Dunns," and were well worthy of the name. Williamson Dunn suffered a sunstroke in September 1854, and died from its effects some weeks later.

[T. M. Hopkins, *Reminiscences of Col. John Ketcham, of Monroe County, Ind.* (1866), pp. 18–22; Wm. W. Woollen, *Biog. and Hist. Sketches of Early Ind.* (1883); W. M. Dunn, *Early Hist. of Hanover Coll.* (1883); A. Y. Moore, *Hist. of Hanover Coll.* (1900); R. T. Burrell, *Complete List of the Members of the Senate and House of Representatives of Ind.* (1903); *Presbyterian Herald* (Louisville), Dec. 7, 1854; *Madison Daily Banner* (Madison, Ind.), Nov. 13, 1854.] P. L. H.

DUNNING, ALBERT ELIJAH (Jan. 5, 1844–Nov. 14, 1923), clergyman, editor, was the only son of Elijah Starr Dunning, a farmer of Brookfield, Conn., and his wife, Abigail Emily Beach. When he was six years old, the family moved to the neighboring town of Bridgewater, where Albert's boyhood was spent in farm work and at the district school. He spent a year at the Institute at Fort Edward, N. Y., and graduated at Bryant & Stratton's Business College at Albany in 1862. He prepared himself for Yale and entered the class of 1867 in the spring of its freshman year. Graduating with high academic and social honors, he proceeded to Andover Seminary where he graduated in 1870. His only pastorate was that of the Highland Congregational Church in the Roxbury district of Boston, where he was ordained and installed Sept. 29, 1870. He was secretary of the Congregational Sunday School and Publishing Society from 1881 to 1889, and editor of *The Congregationalist* from 1889 to 1911. He received the degree of D.D. from Beloit College in 1889.

Dunning's remarkable aptitude as an interpreter of the Bible began to show itself during his pastorate, especially in connection with the Sunday-school, and his important work with men's Bible classes, begun then, continued in various connections throughout his life. As secretary of the Congregational Sunday School and Publishing Society he was active in Sunday-school promotion in various parts of the country, especially in frontier work in the West and in the Southern mountains. He was a member of the International Sunday School Committee from 1884 to 1891 and was for several years in charge of the Sunday-school normal work at Chautauqua. Through his varied activities in this department, his contribution toward bringing the instruction in the Sunday-schools of the country into line with modern biblical study was important.

The earlier years of Dunning's editorship of

The Congregationalist were a period of theological transition. The Congregational churches were passing from the older orthodoxy of the New England theology to a larger way of looking at the Bible and religious truth; and his true liberality, coupled with his rare tact and wisdom, did much toward bringing his denomination through this critical period without disruption. He was the author of the following books: *The Sunday School Library* (1883); *Bible Studies* (1886); *Congregationalists in America* (1894); and *The Making of the Bible* (1911). After the close of his editorship, he engaged in varied professional and literary labor till a few months before his death which occurred at his home in Brookline, Mass. During his latter years he served for several periods as acting pastor of the Congregational Church at Bowdon, Cheshire, England, performing an especially valuable wartime service there in 1916. He traveled extensively, making a trip around the world in 1911–12. He was endowed with the social graces, had a keen sense of humor, and his circle of friends was international. On Dec. 27, 1870, he married Harriet Westbrook of Kingston, N. Y., who survived him with their three sons and one daughter.

[In 1927, Mrs. Dunning issued *Albert Elijah Dunning: A Book of Remembrance,* containing biographical chapters by herself and contributions from many friends, as well as a number of portraits. There are also accounts of Dunning's life in the *Congreg. Year Book,* 1923, and in *Report of the Trigintennial Meeting . . . of the Class of 1867, Yale* (1897); *Supplementary Record of the Class of 1867 in Yale Coll.* (1914); *The Congregationalist* (Boston), June 17, 1911, Nov. 22, 29, Dec. 6, 1923; *Yale Univ. Obit. Record,* 1924.]

F. T. P.

DUNNING, WILLIAM ARCHIBALD (May 12, 1857–Aug. 25, 1922), historian, teacher, was born in Plainfield, N. J. His father, John H. Dunning, was a manufacturer, a man of wide and eager intellectual interests, a close student, and an artist of some talent. His mother was Catherine D. Trelease. Dunning entered Dartmouth in 1877, but remaining there only a year he went to Columbia, where he was graduated in 1881, receiving the degree of A.M. in 1884 and that of Ph.D. in 1885. He was also for a time a student at the University of Berlin. On Apr. 18, 1888, he married Charlotte E. Loomis of Brooklyn, N. Y., who died June 13, 1917. At Columbia he was in succession fellow, lecturer, instructor, adjunct professor, and professor. In 1904 he became the first Lieber Professor of History and Political Philosophy.

His reputation rests upon the twofold basis of his own work as an investigator and writer, and his genius as a teacher. Deeply interested in scholarship and in scholars, he was one of the founders of the American Historical Association, a regular attendant upon its meetings, long a member of its council, and its president in 1913. He was the president of the American Political Science Association at the time of his death. He was a member of the Massachusetts Historical Society and the New York Historical Society. The list of his writings is extensive. It includes: *Essays on the Civil War and Reconstruction* (1898); *Reconstruction, Political and Economic, 1865–1877* (1907); *A History of Political Theories: Ancient and Mediæval* (1902); *From Luther to Montesquieu* (1905); *From Rousseau to Spencer* (1920); with Frederick Bancroft, "A Sketch of Carl Schurz's Political Career" in *The Reminiscences of Carl Schurz,* vol. III (1908); *The British Empire and the United States* (1914); and many articles and reviews published chiefly in the *American Historical Review* and in the *Political Science Quarterly,* of which he was managing editor from 1894 to 1903. He was the first to make scientific and scholarly investigation of the period of Reconstruction, and no one did more than he to rewrite the history of the generation following the Civil War, his own writings being supplemented by the results of investigations in the same field made by his many students. His study of Anglo-American relations is a brilliant piece of writing and an admirable analysis of the subject. His *History of Political Theories* deals with the development of systematic political thought from the classical period to modern times. In it, excluding primitive political theory and limiting the scope of the work to the philosophy of the European Aryan peoples, "he indicated the relation of political philosophy to ethical and juristic concepts and also to the general history of ideas. Nor was he unmindful of the relation between political philosophy and the current institutional development" (Merriam, *post*).

Dunning wrote with great precision and restraint. Highly critical of his own work, he set a lofty standard with respect both to form and content. His ideal was "to remain detached in interest and objective in method. He seemed to fear nothing so much as to be considered prejudiced, unbalanced, immature in judgment, reckless in conclusion" (*Ibid.*). This restraint was, however, much more noticeable in his books than in his short articles and reviews where he allowed his sprightly wit and his human quality free rein. As a lecturer, both to graduate and undergraduate students, he was interesting and stimulating. He never nursed his students; his method was rather that of throwing them overboard to swim for themselves. When once they had shown ability and self-reliance, however, he was the most helpful of critical guides. With them, the "Old Chief," as they affectionately called him, established a relationship of personal friendship which became to many of them a decisive influence in their lives. In 1914, in honor of his presidency of the American Historical Association, sixteen former students published *Studies in Southern History and Politics*, and in 1924 another group celebrated his presidency of the American Political Science Association with *A History of Political Theories, Recent Times*. Dunning had a charming personality, full of enthusiasm and human sympathy, with "a unique quality of princely fellowship and Shakespearian wit." He was a notable figure in any group.

[Chas. E. Merriam, in H. W. Odum, ed., *Am. Masters of Social Science* (1927), also in *Social Forces*, Sept. 1926; *Who's Who in America*, 1922–23; *N. Y. Times*, Aug. 26, 1922; *Springfield Sunday Republican*, Aug. 27, 1922; *The Independent* (N. Y.), Sept. 30, 1922; *Am. Hist. Rev.*, Oct. 1922; personal association over many years.] J. G. de R. H.

DUNSTER, HENRY (1609–Feb. 27, 1658/-59?), first president of Harvard College, was the son of Henry Dunster of the parish of Bury, Lancashire, England, where the younger Henry was baptized Nov. 26, 1609. The family were apparently yeomen or small copy-holders of Balehoult, in the parish of Bury, but the son received a university education at Magdalene College, Cambridge, where he was granted the degrees of B.A. (1630/31) and M.A. (1634). After graduation he taught school and became curate of Bury but, probably on account of non-conformity, emigrated to Massachusetts where he arrived in 1640. His reputation for learning, particularly in the Oriental languages, had preceded him and almost as soon as he arrived he was made president of Harvard, Aug. 27, 1640. The institution which had been but a struggling school soon became a college under his administration. Rules of admission and the principles according to which degrees should be granted were laid down, and scholastic forms established similar to those of the English universities. The establishing act of the General Court in 1642 was probably, and the charter of 1650 avowedly, obtained on Dunster's petition. He was indefatigable in his services, and, although a poor man, gave the college 100 acres of land at a crisis in its affairs. The first president's house and college hall practically owed their existence to him (*Publications of the Colonial Society of Massachusetts*, III, 420), and through the Commissioners of the United Colonies he tried to interest all of the colonies in support of the institution. It may be noted that he had to call the attention of the General Court to the need for influencing graduates to remain in America, as of the twenty who graduated prior to 1646 eleven emigrated to England and remained there permanently. The first printing-press within the present limits of the United States was established in 1639 and two years later transferred to Dunster's own house and placed under his direction. Although he had no means of his own, the colony made no provision for paying him a salary as president other than by the allotment to him of certain taxes, leaving him to do the work of collecting them, which not only threw a large burden upon him but caused him heavy loss. After his resignation there was about £40 still due him which the college asked the General Court to pay him in view of his invaluable services but the Court refused, although after his death it compromised by paying half the sum due to his widow. In 1653 Dunster adopted some of the principles of the Baptists and was forced to resign his presidency, Oct. 24, 1654. After petitioning twice he was allowed to remain in the house built largely by himself until March 1655. In April he was indicted by the grand jury for disturbing the ordinance of infant baptism, convicted, sentenced to public admonition, and put under bonds for good behavior. Either immediately or within a few months he moved to Scituate where he acted as minister for some years, dying there, probably, in 1658/59. He married first, June 22, 1641, Elizabeth (Harris) Glover who died Aug. 23, 1643; and second, in 1644, Elizabeth (Atkinson?) who died Sept. 12, 1690.

[Jeremiah Chaplin, *Life of Henry Dunster* (1872); Samuel Dunster, *Henry Dunster and his Descendants* (1876); Josiah Quincy, *Hist. of Harvard Univ.* (2 vols., 1840); *New Eng. Hist. and Geneal. Reg.*, Apr. 1907, p. 188, Jan. 1926, pp. 86–95; *Pubs. Col. Soc. Mass.*, vols. III (1900), XV (1925), *loc. cit.*] J. T. A.

DUNWOODY, WILLIAM HOOD (Mar. 14, 1841–Feb. 8, 1914), merchant miller, financier, was born in Westtown, Chester County, Pa., of Scotch ancestry, the son of James and Hannah (Hood) Dunwoody. His father as well as three generations before him had been farmers in this county. William attended the country schools until he was fourteen, when he was sent to an academy in Philadelphia for four years. At the conclusion of his course there, he entered the office of his uncle, Ezekiel Dunwoody, who was in the grain and feed business in that city. This association continued for five years, when Dunwoody, at the age of twenty-three, set out for himself and became the senior member of the firm of Dunwoody & Robertson, flour merchants in Philadelphia. Aware of the growing flour industry of Minneapolis, Dunwoody went there in 1869 to purchase flour for eastern firms. Presumably he was very favorably impressed with Minneapolis, for two years later he moved there, making it his permanent home. It had always been his ambition to own and operate a flour-mill, and, immediately upon establishing his residence in Minneapolis, he became a partner in two milling firms in that city. In 1875 he helped to organize the Minneapolis Millers' Association for the purpose of buying wheat for local mills and acted as its general agent, but the association was rather short-lived, because of the ultimate establishment of elevators covering the wheat-growing territory. The experience derived from the association, however, suggested the application of a similar institution to the selling of flour to Europe. The plan was not favored by most of the association, so Cadwallader C. Washburn, the largest individual miller in Minneapolis and the governor of Wisconsin, decided to carry it out alone, and selected young Dunwoody as his foreign representative. Dunwoody spent the year of 1877 in England and Scotland and after many discouragements succeeded in founding a permanent trade between the Old and New Worlds on a very thorough basis. It is generally recognized that the vast volume of the flour business of today is the result of Dunwoody's efforts. Upon his return to Minneapolis in 1878, he devoted his attention to his own flour interests and in 1879 became a partner with Washburn, John Crosby, and Charles J. Martin in the firm of Washburn, Crosby & Company. From that time on he was continuously identified with the establishment. He had other large interests as well, chief of which were the director-presidency of the Northwestern National Bank of Minneapolis for thirty-eight years, followed by the chairmanship of the board from 1911 until his death. He was a director of the Great Northern Railway for twenty-five years, and until he retired from active business; president of the St. Anthony & Dakota Elevator Company and the Barnum Grain Company; and vice-president of the Minneapolis Trust Company. He was a member of the Committee of One Hundred to meet Prince Henry of Prussia in 1902, and of the Chamber of Commerce of Minneapolis and of New York. His philanthropies were many, the most important being the Dunwoody Industrial Institute at Minneapolis, with its endowment of $5,000,000; a million-dollar endowment to the Minneapolis Institute of Arts; and the gift, with an endowment of a million dollars, of his old home near Philadelphia as a home for convalescents. Dunwoody married Katie L. Patten of Philadelphia in 1864, who survived him.

[*Who's Who in America*, 1912–13; Wm. C. Edgar, *The Medal of Gold* (1925); C. B. Kuhlmann, *The Development of the Flour-Milling Industry in the U. S.* (1929); *Minn. Hist. Soc. Colls.*, XIV (1912), 192; obituary notice in *Minneapolis Tribune*, Feb. 9, 1914; U. S. Museum correspondence with the Washburn-Crosby Company.]

C. W. M.

DU PONCEAU, PIERRE ÉTIENNE (June 3, 1760–Apr. 1, 1844), lawyer and author, known in America as Peter Stephen Du Ponceau, was born at St.-Martin, Île de Ré, France. His father was of ancient lineage and held a command in the army at St.-Martin. His early education was obtained at the grammar school there, supplemented by private tuition, and he acquired a thorough knowledge of English and Italian from soldiers of those countries quartered in the town. It had been intended that he should undertake a military career but this had to be relinquished because of his weak eyesight, and in 1773 he entered a college of Benedictine monks at St. Jean Angely with a view to a classical education, but returned to the Île de Ré the next year on the death of his father. His family was Catholic and now desired him to become a priest. So he "took the tonsure" and became a regent in the Episcopal college at Bressuire in Poitou. At the end of 1775, however, he abandoned the idea of entering the Church. Going to Paris, he at first earned his living expenses by translating and teaching, and then became secretary to the philologist, Court de Gébelin. Shortly afterward he was introduced to Baron Steuben who needed a secretary familiar with the English language to accompany him on his approaching journey to America, and who, on learning of Du Ponceau's qualifications, at once engaged him. Embarking from Marseilles, they landed at Portsmouth, N. H., Dec. 1, 1777. Du Ponceau was appointed captain in the Continental Army Feb. 18, 1778, and on Baron Steuben's being appointed major-general and inspector general by Washington at Valley Forge a few days later, he became Steuben's aide-de-camp. Though ill qualified for military life through his near-sightedness, he remained in active service for two years, but in the fall of 1779 he was compelled by an affection of the lungs to retire to Philadelphia on sick leave. Later he recovered sufficiently to join General Greene, but had a relapse which necessitated his leaving the army.

He became a citizen of Pennsylvania, July 25, 1781. Recommended to Robert R. Livingston, secretary for foreign affairs, by Judge Peters, he became Livingston's under-secretary, Oct. 22, 1781, continuing as such till June 4, 1783, and fulfilling his duties with great ability. He had prior to the close of the war determined to enter the legal profession, and after two years of study was admitted an attorney of the court of common pleas at Philadelphia on June 24, 1785, becoming an attorney of the supreme court in the following year. He commenced practise in Philadelphia, the international situation at that period and his own unusual attainments combining to bring him to the front at the bar in a very short time. The United States was neutral in the European conflict, and complicated questions of the conflicting rights of neutrals and belligerents arose continually, which the local practitioners were generally incompetent to handle, whereas Du Ponceau's acquaintance with civil and foreign law and languages caused him to be frequently retained in matters involving international law and practise. He became recognized as a leading authority in this country on that subject and as such appeared constantly before the supreme courts of Pennsylvania and the United States. Much French and other foreign business came to him, and he had among his clients the diplomatic and consular agents of France in the United States. Later in life he was frequently consulted on questions of constitutional law. He never evinced any interest in politics, local or national, and passed a somewhat sequestered life, engrossed in his professional engagements and finding his only recreation in literature and linguistic studies, in which latter field he acquired wide fame. His publications on legal subjects included: a translation from the original Latin of Bynkershoek entitled, *A Treatise on the Law of War . . . Being the First Book of his Quaestiones Juris Publici* (1810) with notes; *A Dissertation on the Nature and Extent of the Jurisdiction of the Courts of the United States* (1824); and *A Brief View of the Constitution of the United States* (1834), the last-named being also translated into French. His contributions to historical and linguistic literature were numerous, particularly on philological subjects, his studies in the languages of the North American Indian being particularly original and suggestive. He was the author of: *English Phonology* (1817), and *A Discourse on the Early History of Pennsylvania* (1821); and also published, *Histoire, mœurs et coutumes des nations indiennes qui habitaient autrefois la Pensylvanie et les États Voisins* (Paris 1822), translated from the English of John Heckewelder; a "Notes and Observations on Eliot's Indian Grammar" (in *Collections of the Massachusetts Historical Society*, 2 ser. IX, 1822); *A Short Description of the Province of New Sweden: Now Called, by the English, Pennsylvania, in America* (1834), translated from the Swedish of Thomas Campanius Holm; *Mémoire sur le système grammatical des langues de quelques nations indiennes de L'Amérique du Nord* (Paris 1838), which procured for him the award of the Volney prize of $2,000 from the French Institute; and *Dissertation on the Nature and Character of the Chinese System of Writing* (1838). His correspondence with John Heckewelder on the languages of the American Indian was published in the *American Philosophical Society, Transactions of the Historical and Literary Committee* (vol. I, 1819, pp. 351–448). His contributions to philology brought him international recognition. In addition, a number of his addresses to the Law Academy of Philadelphia, which he founded in 1821, and contributions to the *Proceedings* of the American Philosophical Society, of which latter body he was elected president in 1828, were republished in pamphlet form. In his later years he became almost blind, and an increasing deafness was an additional obstacle to the prosecution of his investigations. His mental faculties, however, remained unimpaired to the last, and he only relinquished study a few weeks prior to his death. On May 21, 1788, he was married to Anne Perry.

[Four of Du Ponceau's letters, published in the *Pa. Mag. of Hist. and Biog.*, Apr. 1916, give details of his experiences in the Revolutionary period. *A Public Discourse in Commemoration of Peter S. Du Ponceau*, by Robley Dunglison, delivered before the Am. Phil. Soc., Oct. 25, 1844, and republished in *Am. Law Mag.*, Apr. 1845, is comprehensive and eulogistic. An excellent review of his career appeared in 7 *Law Rep.*, 62. See also *Jour. Am. Oriental Soc.*, I (1849), 161; *Western Law Jour.*, May 1844; W. W. Story, *Life and Letters of Jos. Story* (1851); J. B. Linn, *Record of Pa. Marriages Prior to 1810* (1890), II, 584.] H. W. H. K.

DU PONT, ELEUTHÈRE IRÉNÉE (June 24, 1771–Oct. 31, 1834), manufacturer, was born in Paris, the younger son of Pierre Samuel du Pont de Nemours, celebrated member of the physiocratic school of economists and active participant in French public affairs. Turgot was Irénée's godfather, and gave him his baptismal names. His mother was Nicole Charlotte Marie Louise Le Dée. The boy was brought up on his father's estate, "Bois des Fossés," adjacent to the village of Egreville, not far from Nemours. He was an indifferent student under private tutors, though his father's reproaches were probably due less to the boy's neglect than to the parent's solicitude. He early proved to be manly, fond of the out-of-doors, energetic, and capable of making up his own mind. Early in 1788

Lavoisier, his father's close friend, whom Turgot had appointed chief of the royal powder works, took Irénée into the laboratory at Essonne, promising that the boy should have his own post some day. In 1791, when earning only 1,260 francs, he wished to marry Sophie Madelaine Dalmas, daughter of a family beneath his own in station. His father violently opposed the match on every ground, but the young man was determined, fought two duels with another suitor, and was married (Nov. 26), he being twenty and the bride sixteen. About the same time Lavoisier lost his direction of the powder works because of the Revolution. His protégé left Essonne also, assuming active charge of his father's large printing-house in Paris, established earlier in the year to bolster the conservative cause. Father and son suffered several imprisonments, and were in especially grave danger on Aug. 10, 1792, when they went to the Tuileries to defend the king.

In 1797 the Jacobins suppressed the publishing business of the Du Ponts, and the father decided the fortunes of the family should be cast in America, where he had acquaintance with important statesmen, and whither his elder son Victor [*q.v.*] had gone a decade before. Du Pont de Nemours organized a company which was to exploit land in the valley of the James River in western Virginia, and with Irénée, his wife and three children, and other close relatives, took ship in the *American Eagle* in September 1799, arriving at Newport, R. I., the first day of the new year. They moved on to New York, where they received a letter from Thomas Jefferson advising that investment in land be delayed. A part of the company's capital was used to establish a commission business in New York, but this venture was never profitable. Irénée hit upon a project which offered much more. He chanced to go hunting with a Col. Toussard; shooting away all their powder, they bought more to finish out the day. Irénée was impressed with its bad quality and high price, and with Toussard's help made a study of the manufacture of powder in America. He concluded that an expertly conducted establishment, even though small (one stamping mill and one wheel mill) would give a profit of $10,000 a year. Irénée du Pont returned to France for three months at the beginning of 1801 to secure machinery and designs for the manufacture of powder, and received every assistance from the government works at Essonne. Two-thirds of the necessary capital was subscribed by his father's company. Jefferson had urged that the plant be placed near Washington, but Irénée after investigation decided "the country, the people, the location are all worthless." He tried without success to buy the powder works of William Lane at Frankford, near Philadelphia, and finally purchased the farm of Jacob Broom, on the Brandywine River four miles from Wilmington, Del., where there had formerly been a cotton-mill operated by the water power. Alexander Hamilton sought to be of assistance in the founding of the business by securing favor for it from the Delaware legislature.

Irénée du Pont and his family in July 1802 settled in a little log house on the property, and he pushed forward the construction of the mills in spite of many discouragements, particularly in the want of capital. In the spring of 1804 powder was ready for sale, and Jefferson, then president, promised orders from the government. Sales in this year amounted to $10,000, the next year to $33,000, and by 1807 were $43,000. For the first six years the profits, in spite of a bad explosion, averaged about $7,000 a year. In 1811 the profits were more than $40,000, and Irénée du Pont and Peter Bauduy, his active associate, invested in a woolen-mill near the powder works, to be conducted by Victor du Pont. The war between the United States and England put the powder business in an assured position. Du Pont became the principal manufacturer of powder for the government, and supplied large quantities to the American Fur Company and to South American countries. He was made a director of the Bank of the United States, to represent the government, and was widely consulted on problems of industry and agriculture. He continued in the New World his father's interest in farming, an avocation which his descendants have maintained. He was active in the American Colonization Society. He proved his loyalty to the government by refusing to sell 125,000 pounds of powder to the South Carolina Nullifiers in 1833 for $24,000 cash. He insisted, in opposition to Bauduy's wish, that the business should be known by his name, E. I. du Pont de Nemours & Company, which it has continued to this day. His establishment, like some others in America at the period, was semi-feudal in the relations between master and workmen, the latter being housed on the property and fed from the farm. Irénée du Pont, himself sensitive and taking responsibility seriously, was surrounded by persons nervous and high-strung; he lived, in France and America, under circumstances of care and stress; these things made him often abrupt or downcast, but his extraordinary affection for those near to him comes out in all his letters. He died in Philadelphia of cholera, after a brief illness.

[See Bessie G. du Pont, *Life of Eleuthère Irénée du Pont* (12 vols., 1923–26); this is mainly his correspondence, but there are illuminating introductory and connecting notes by the editor. The same author's *E. I. du Pont de Nemours and Co., a History, 1802–1902* (1920) gives more compactly the essential facts concerning the founder. See also Dumas Malone, ed., *The Correspondence between Thos. Jefferson and Pierre Samuel du Pont de Nemours, 1798–1817* (1930); *Del. State Jour. and Statesman* (Wilmington), Nov. 4, 1834; and *Del. Gazette and Am. Watchman* (Wilmington), Nov. 4, 1834.] B. M—l.

DU PONT, HENRY (Aug. 8, 1812–Aug. 8, 1889), manufacturer, was born at Eleutherian Mills, Wilmington, Del., the second son of Eleuthère Irénée du Pont [*q.v.*] and Sophie Madelaine Dalmas. He was a student at Mount Airy Military School, Germantown, Pa., from 1823 to 1829, when he entered the United States Military Academy at West Point. He graduated in 1833, and was made second lieutenant in the 4th Artillery at Fort Monroe, Va. Shortly afterward he served in the Creek country of Alabama, but in June 1834 resigned his commission to join his father in the manufacture of gunpowder. He married Louisa Gerhard in 1837. He had served in the mills sixteen years when, in July 1850, he became head of the firm of E. I. du Pont de Nemours & Company, his partners being his brother Alexis and their nephew, Irénée du Pont. Profits flowing to the company as a result of the Crimean War in 1854 helped Henry du Pont in his policy of progressive management. His older brother Alfred, head of the firm before him, had maintained the tradition of the founder, but when Henry assumed charge a new economic era was dawning. The new farms, mining operations, and railroads needed power. In 1857 Lamont du Pont was granted a patent which enabled the firm to use nitrate of soda from Peru, and much cheaper than the Indian saltpetre, in the manufacture of blasting powder. In 1859 the company bought mills on Big Wapwallopen Creek, Luzerne County, Pa., near the anthracite coalfields, for the manufacture of this blasting powder, thus partially solving an old problem of transportation. This same year Henry du Pont had experiments conducted in the making of hexagonal cakes of powder of large grain for big guns, but this work was interrupted by the Civil War and was not resumed for fifteen years, when it was notably successful. The firm refused to furnish powder to Virginia while the state's loyalty to the Union was in doubt. In 1861 Du Pont was appointed major-general of the Delaware forces, and put down disaffection which, in a state containing the country's largest powder mills, promised to be dangerous. The supply of saltpetre failing, the firm was made the agent of the government in purchasing enormous supplies in England, but the prospect of war demand for powder did not deceive Du Pont, who declared that "the extra demand for powder for war purposes will not equal the regular demand which would have existed had peace continued." The company lost its trade in the South, and, on account of possible capture of cargoes and use by the Confederacy, was prohibited from shipping powder from New York and Philadelphia, which meant that the West Indies, Mexico, and, for a time, California, went unsupplied. Independent mills were established in California in 1861 to meet the needs of the miners. Du Pont supplied army and navy with powder at low prices despite cash payments in the manufacture, high taxes, and very slow remittance on the part of the government.

The intense competition which led up to the panic of 1873 and the stagnation which followed the crisis brought on consolidation in the powder business. The Du Pont firm bought a controlling interest in the Hazard Powder Company in 1876 and in the California Powder Works the same year. Du Pont as he grew older became more cautious. He discountenanced the experiments in "high explosives" which were increasingly successful after 1865, and not until 1876 did his firm begin the manufacture of Hercules powder. He gave his attention principally to the finances of the company, and conducted an enormous correspondence with 500 agents and a half-dozen associated companies, refusing to have a stenographer, and writing by hand 6,000 letters a year. At first a Whig, he became a Republican, and was prominent in Delaware politics. He was of autocratic manner with strangers, but his workmen were nevertheless on easy terms with him. He died following an illness of some months, after fifty-five years in the manufacture of explosives.

[G. W. Cullum, *Biog. Reg.* (3rd ed., 1891); B. G. du Pont, *E. I. du Pont de Nemours and Co., a History, 1802–1902* (1920), and *Life of Eleuthère Irénée du Pont*, vols. 9–11 (1925–26); *Every Evening and Wilmington Daily Commercial*, Aug. 8, 1889; Wilmington *Daily Republican*, Aug. 9, 1889.] B. M—l.

DU PONT, HENRY ALGERNON (July 30, 1838–Dec. 31, 1926), soldier, industrialist, United States senator, was born near Wilmington, Del., the elder son of Henry du Pont [*q.v.*] and his wife Louisa Gerhard. After preparatory training at Dr. Lyons's school near Philadelphia, and one year at the University of Pennsylvania, he entered the United States Military Academy at West Point, graduating at the head of his class in

1861. In the several ranks up to that of major he was engaged in a large number of battles and skirmishes of the Civil War, usually in command of artillery, in northern Virginia and the Valley. The chief of these were the engagements at New Market, Halltown, Winchester, Fisher's Hill and Cedar Creek, all in 1864. He was under fire for the first time at the battle of New Market, when twenty-six years old. As captain of Battery B, 5th Artillery, he did spectacular work in covering the Union retreat. Du Pont retired by echelon of platoons, maintaining such a spirited fire that pursuing Confederates believed the enemy had rallied, and consequently, in drawing up to resist, permitted Gen. Sigel's men to make their escape. Du Pont accomplished this maneuver on his own initiative, other officers having left the field. He was brevetted major for gallant services at Opequon and Fisher's Hill, and received the rank of lieutenant-colonel (Oct. 19, 1864), and the Congressional Medal of Honor for distinguished services and extraordinary gallantry at Cedar Creek. After the war he commanded light artillery and was ranking officer in various army posts in Virginia, the District of Columbia, and Rhode Island. He was a member of the board of officers which assimilated the tactics for the three arms of the service.

His father, head of the firm of E. I. du Pont de Nemours & Company, had long urged him to resign his army commission and join other members of the family in management of the powder manufactory. He was reluctant to leave military life, but did so in 1875; in 1878, at the time of the readjustment following the death of the second E. I. du Pont, he became a member of the firm. His duties were in the office at first, assisting his father in the correspondence, but he was soon placed in charge of negotiations with the officials of other companies (this being the period in which the Du Pont firm was acquiring shares in other powder mills) and he made all arrangements touching the railway transportation of the products. Out of this last connection grew his election (May 1879) to the presidency of the Wilmington and Northern Railroad. After the death of his father in 1889, Du Pont had charge of the settlement of his estate, and this experience led him to urge that the partnership be changed to a corporation; after much discussion and the instituting of compromise to overcome opposition, a charter was taken out under the laws of Delaware in October 1899 and he became one of three vice-presidents. In 1902, following the death of Eugene du Pont, the president, he was asked to assume the presidency, but declined it and retired from the business because his personal affairs required all his time. He helped, nevertheless, to formulate the plan whereby the direction remained in the hands of the family, T. Coleman du Pont, Alfred I. du Pont, and Pierre S. du Pont purchasing the old company for $12,000,000.

His election by the Delaware legislature in 1895 to the United States Senate having been contested on a technical point, the Senate committee recommended that he be seated, but he lost in the general vote; he did not receive the unanimous support of his own party, it was believed, because of his espousal of the gold standard. He served in the Senate, however, from 1906 to 1917, and was chairman of the military affairs committee from 1911 to 1913. Du Pont was distinguished for gracious, courtly manners. In his last years he gave much attention to farming, a traditional interest in his family, and to literary work. Of chief importance among his books are, *The Early Generations of the Du Pont and Allied Families* (1923), *and Rear-Admiral Samuel Francis Du Pont, a Biography* (1926). He also wrote military reminiscences. He was married to Mary Foster.

[H. A. du Pont's *Campaign of 1864 in the Valley of Virginia* (1925) contains much autobiographical matter. See also *Official Records (Army)*, 1 ser., vols. XXXIII, XXXVII, XLIII, XLVI; B. G. du Pont, *E. I. du Pont de Nemours and Company, a History, 1802–1902* (1920); Wilmington *Evening Jour.*, Dec. 31, 1926; *Wilmington Morning News*, Jan. 1, 1927.] B. M—l.

DU PONT, SAMUEL FRANCIS (Sept. 27, 1803–June 23, 1865), naval officer, was born at Bergen Point, N. J., the temporary home of his father, Victor Marie du Pont [*q.v.*], head of the importing house of V. du Pont de Nemours & Company of New York. His paternal grandfather was the distinguished French statesman and author, Du Pont de Nemours. His mother was Gabrielle Joséphine de la Fite de Pelleport, a French woman of unusual mental and literary ability, and the youngest daughter of the Marquis de Pelleport. On the failure of his father's firm in 1805, Samuel Francis was taken by his parents to Angelica, Genesee County, N. Y., where he remained until 1809 when he accompanied them to Delaware, of which state he was thereafter a citizen. From the age of nine to fourteen he attended a boarding school at Mount Airy, Pa., near Germantown.

In December 1815, Du Pont de Nemours, having emigrated to America on Napoleon's return from Elba, wrote to Thomas Jefferson requesting an appointment of midshipman for his grandson. Jefferson replied that he had written to Madison on the subject, and that he hoped that the grandson would in time become "one of our high admirals." On Dec. 19 Madison appointed young Du Pont a midshipman, on waiting orders, and accompanied the appointment with another to the Military Academy at West Point. The son was permitted by his parents to choose between the two services. Influenced, doubtless, by the popularity of the navy, following the War of 1812, the youth chose that service, notwithstanding the fact that his maternal ancestors had been soldiers for generations. Du Pont's first sea service was in 1817 on the *Franklin,* 74, Commodore Charles Stewart, under orders to proceed to the Mediterranean. As there was no naval academy at this time, young midshipmen were instructed in navigation and mathematics by naval schoolmasters on shipboard, and probably Du Pont was so instructed on his first cruise. A portrait of him painted at this time depicts him as a tall and strikingly handsome youth. At maturity his height was six feet, one inch. In 1820 he returned home on the *Erie.* In the following year he was again in the Mediterranean, this time on the *Constitution.* After serving in the West Indies and on the coast of Brazil, he was in 1824 for the third time sent to the Mediterranean where he served as sailing-master on the *North Carolina.* In 1826 at the age of twenty-two years and seven months he was promoted to a lieutenancy. From 1829 to 1832 he was employed on the *Ontario,* cruising in European waters. After his return home he was, on June 27, 1833, married to his first cousin, Sophie Madeleine du Pont, youngest daughter of Eleuthère Irénée du Pont de Nemours [*q.v.*], founder of the powder works. Of great strength of character and of deep sympathies, she was a worthy companion of her husband, whom she long survived, guarding to the end his professional reputation.

During the decade previous to the Mexican War, Du Pont was employed first in the Gulf of Mexico, part of the time in command, successively, of the *Grampus* and the *Warren,* and later in European waters on the *Ohio,* the flagship of Commodore Hull. Promoted commander on Jan. 10, 1843, taking rank from Oct. 28, 1842, he was assigned to the command of the brig *Perry,* which that year sailed for China. Stricken with illness, he was invalided home from Rio de Janeiro. After serving as a member of Secretary Bancroft's board on the organization of the naval school at Annapolis, he sailed from Norfolk in October 1845 as commander of the frigate *Congress,* flagship of Commodore Stockton, with the American commissioner and the consul-general to Hawaii on board. He arrived at San Francisco, by way of Honolulu, about July 1, 1846. The Mexican War was in progress, and Stockton proceeded to Monterey where he took charge of the naval forces in the Pacific and placed Du Pont in command of the sloop-of-war *Cyane.* Taking on board John C. Frémont's battalion, Du Pont disembarked it three days later at San Diego. Proceeding thence down the coast, he reached San Blas, where a landing party spiked the guns of the Mexicans. Entering the Gulf of California, he seized La Paz and at Guaymas burned, or caused the Mexicans to burn, the small fleet there. Within a few months he cleared the Gulf of hostile ships, destroying or capturing thirty of them. On Nov. 11, 1847, he aided Commodore Shubrick, who had succeeded Stockton, in the occupation of Mazatlan. When later the enemy attempted to recover Lower California, Shubrick ordered Du Pont to proceed at once to the Gulf. At San Jose, on learning that a party of Americans were besieged in a mission house three miles inland, he organized a detachment of two provisional companies, led it against the besiegers, and rescued his fellow countrymen. Subsequently he organized several similar expeditions and succeeded in clearing the country of hostile troops. On his arrival at Norfolk in October 1848, the secretary of the navy congratulated him on his "safe return after a long cruise, in which the services of the officers and crew of the *Cyane* were so highly distinguished for gallantry, efficiency, and skill" (H. A. du Pont, *post,* p. 56).

Du Pont now began a tour of shore duty which lasted upward of ten years and which was concerned with some of the most important improvements in naval and marine affairs made in the two decades preceding the Civil War. In 1849 he served as a member of a board appointed by the secretary of the navy to consider a course of study appropriate to a naval academy and to prepare proper regulations for the government of the same. The report of this board, which went into effect on July 1, 1850, provided for a "Naval Academy" comparable to the Military Academy at West Point. Du Pont was appointed superintendent, but after a month the appointment was revoked. His lively interest in naval education led, however, to his frequent selection as a member of the examining board at Annapolis. In 1853 he was one of three naval officers chosen to represent the government at the World's Fair in New York.

In 1851 Du Pont made a valuable report to the secretary of war on the national defenses, in which he discussed the effect on them of the "new element," steam. This was highly commended by Sir Howard Douglas the British expert on naval gunnery. In the same year he was chosen by the secretary of the treasury as one of the members of a board provided for by Congress to inquire into the light-house establishment. The elaborate report of this board laid the basis of a new establishment, in which Du Pont played an important part during the years 1852–57 when he served as a member of the Light-House Board. At different periods he served on boards authorized to revise the rules and regulations of the navy, and he was frequently employed on courts martial and courts of enquiry. He was a member of the famous naval efficiency board of 1855, composed of fifteen naval officers and authorized to examine into the efficiency of all officers above the rank of midshipman. After deliberating for several weeks it reported that 201 officers were incompetent or incapacitated. Its report, which was approved by the secretary of the navy and the president, created a profound sensation. The cause of the affected officers was taken up by their friends both in and outside of Congress, by the public press, and by several state legislatures. The brunt of the criticism fell upon Du Pont. His zeal for naval reform, the excellence of his professional reputation, and his long and efficient service in the navy made him a shining mark for attack. Senator Houston of Texas championed the cause of the affected officers and assailed Du Pont in the Senate. The two Delaware senators, Clayton and Bayard, ably defended him. In the end the affected officers obtained a modification of the act creating the board and its objects were only partly attained.

On Sept. 14, 1855, Du Pont was promoted captain. In 1857 he was ordered to command the new frigate *Minnesota,* one of the largest vessels in the navy, and to proceed to China with William B. Reed, recently appointed American minister to that country. The *Minnesota* was at the mouth of the Peiho River when the combined English and French fleets attacked and captured the Chinese forts there, giving Du Pont an opportunity to acquire information that was to prove useful in similar undertakings of his own during the Civil War. After visiting China, Japan, India, and Arabia, he sailed homeward, reaching Boston in May 1859. In December 1860, he was made commandant of the Philadelphia navy-yard, a post that he held at the outbreak of the Civil War.

Du Pont's first service in the war was performed in Washington as the senior member of the Commission of Conference, appointed by the secretary of the navy to prepare plans for naval operations, to devise methods for rendering the blockade effective, and to collect useful information. Meeting at various times during June–September 1861, it submitted several reports, then strictly confidential, embodying much information and many suggestions, and recommending the establishment of a large naval base on the Carolina or Florida coast, where naval supplies could be stored and warships could safely ride at anchor. Of the several locations that were suggested, Du Pont favored Port Royal, S. C. On Sept. 18 he was relieved from duty at the Philadelphia navy-yard and assigned to the command of the South Atlantic blockading squadron, at the time the most important post in the gift of the Navy Department. He was to have control of all naval operations on the Atlantic coast south of the boundary between the Carolinas. His official designation was "Flag Officer," and his courtesy title, "Commodore." The rendezvous of the squadron was Hampton Roads, where by the end of October a fleet of seventy-five vessels was assembled—the largest up to this time ever commanded by an officer of the navy. Du Pont's flagship was the steam frigate *Wabash,* Commander C. R. P. Rodgers [*q.v.*]; and his chief of staff Commander C. H. Davis [*q.v.*]. A combined naval and military movement against Port Royal was decided upon. The military force, consisting of 14,000 troops, was commanded by Brigadier-General Thomas W. Sherman [*q.v.*]. On Oct. 29 the expedition sailed from Hampton Roads, and, after suffering considerable loss from a gale off Hatteras, reached its destination. By Nov. 7 it was ready for battle. The defenses of the Confederates consisted of two forts, Walker and Beauregard, on opposite sides of the entrance to Port Royal, and of a small flotilla of schooners. Du Pont steamed up the channel in two columns. The main column, consisting of the ten larger vessels and led by the flagship, attacked the forts; the smaller one, consisting of five gunboats, engaged the flotilla. The battle lasted upward of five hours and ended with the abandonment of the forts by the Confederates and their occupation by the Federal troops. The loss of the Union forces was thirty-one; of the Confederates, sixty-three. Since forts have but seldom surrendered to ships, the capture of Port Royal is justly celebrated in the annals of naval warfare. It greatly encouraged the North, depressed by the misfortunes of the army. On Feb. 22, 1862, on the recommendation of President Lincoln, Congress passed a resolution thanking Du Pont for his victory, and on July 30 he was made a rear admiral, taking rank from July 16.

Following the success at Port Royal, Du Pont occupied Beaufort, S. C.; and later captured Tybee Island, thus giving the army a base, from which, with the aid of the navy, in April 1862, it reduced Fort Pulaski. In March of that year, Cumberland Island, Amelia Island, St. Marys, Ga., Fernandina, Fla., and Fort Clinch were captured, the last named being the first fort upon which the flag of the Union was restored. All the sounds of Georgia were occupied, and Jacksonville and St. Augustine were taken. On Feb. 28, 1863, one of the vessels of the squadron destroyed the privateer *Nashville,* a highly creditable performance. Du Pont, who was an excellent organizer, established fourteen blockading stations, on thirteen of which the blockade was effective. On the fourteenth, the Charleston station, however, the Confederates frequently at night eluded the Union vessels.

In the meantime an event had taken place which was destined to influence subsequent naval operations in the war, as well as to affect the rest of Du Pont's naval career. By the success of the *Monitor* over the *Merrimac* in Hampton Roads on Mar. 9, 1862, public attention was directed to the ironclad vessel, and many persons, including the secretary and the assistant secretary of the navy, were led to exaggerate its offensive powers. The capture of Charleston, strongly defended by Fort Sumter, now appeared feasible, and a fleet of monitors was assembled under Du Pont with a view to taking that city. With less faith than the Navy Department in the new vessels, Du Pont tested them in an engagement with Fort McAllister and reported that they were deficient in "aggression or destructiveness as against forts" and that in order to secure success in such operations troops were necessary. He and his officers, however, were of the opinion that Fort Sumter could be reduced (Du Pont, *post,* p. 223; Ammen, *post,* pp. 102–03). On Apr. 7, 1863, he attacked the defenses of Charleston. The battle fleet consisted of seven monitors, the ironclad *New Ironsides* (the flagship), and an armored gunboat. It advanced into action led by the *Weehawken,* Capt. John Rodgers [*q.v.*]. The battle began at 2:50 p. m. and ended at 4:30 p. m., when Du Pont signaled his ships to withdraw from action, intending to resume the attack the following morning. He had suffered a severe reverse, the worst naval defeat of the Civil War. The armored gunboat was so damaged that she sank the next day. Five of the monitors were temporarily put out of action. The fleet fired 139 projectiles and was hit 411 times, being struck almost three times for each round that it discharged (Wilson, *post,* I, 26). The loss of the fleet was about fifty; of the forts fourteen. When in the evening Du Pont learned from his captains the extent of the damage suffered by their ships, he decided not to renew the attack, since it would be futile, a conclusion concurred in by all his leading officers.

The failure of Du Pont was a great disappointment to the North, which had entertained hopes of a brilliant success. On Apr. 13, and again on the following day, the President ordered him to hold his position off Charleston. Rendered unduly sensitive by his defeat and fancying that the President's order implied a censure, he wrote to the secretary of the navy requesting the department not to hesitate to relieve him by an officer who in its opinion was more able to execute the service in which he had failed, the capture of Charleston. While the department was choosing a relieving officer, Du Pont kept his station, and on June 17 two of his ships, the *Weehawken* and the *Nahant,* captured the ironclad *Atlanta,* one of the chief naval prizes of the war. On July 6, on the arrival of the new commander-in-chief, Rear Admiral John A. Dahlgren [*q.v.*], Du Pont hauled down his flag and with this act terminated not only his active service during the war but also the active part of his naval career. In taking official leave of him, Secretary Welles, after referring in complimentary terms to the capture of the *Atlanta,* added, "You may well regard this, and we may with pleasure look upon it, as a brilliant termination of a command gallantly commenced and conducted for two years with industry, energy, and ability" (Ammen, *post,* p. 121).

Meanwhile an acrimonious correspondence had been begun by Du Pont with the Secretary. He believed that Welles was trying to shift to the commander of the fleet the blame that should fall upon the Department. Later, Congress made an investigation. Neither the correspondence nor the investigation sheds much light. Naval officers hold, although not unanimously, that their colleague was badly treated. It would appear that the responsibility for the battle should be shared by Du Pont and the Navy Department, and that any other commander might have failed in the hazardous enterprise. The chances of success, however, would have been considerably increased with Farragut in command.

On leaving the squadron, Du Pont retired to his home at Louviers, on the Brandywine River, near Wilmington, Del. In March 1865, he was in Washington as a member of a naval board charged with recommending for advanced rank those officers who had distinguished themselves in the war. This was his last professional employment. His long service in the hot malarial climate off the Southern coast had impaired his health. His death occurred in Philadelphia, after a brief illness. Deeply religious, Du Pont was an active worker in the Protestant Episcopal Church. He was distinguished in appearance and polished in manners, a dignified gentleman and officer.

In 1882 Congress provided that the circle at the intersection of Massachusetts and Connecticut Avenues in Washington should be called Du Pont Circle and that a statue of the admiral should be erected thereon. Two years later a memorial statue, the work of Launt Thompson, was unveiled in the presence of the secretary of the navy, a committee of naval officers, and members of the Du Pont family. In 1921 this memorial was removed and an artistic fountain, executed by Daniel Chester French, was erected in its place.

[H. A. du Pont, *Rear-Admiral Samuel Francis du Pont* (1926); *Sketch of the Public Services of Rear Admiral S. F. du Pont* (1865); *Official Despatches and Letters of Rear Admiral du Pont* (1883); *Official Records (Navy)*, 1 ser., vols. XII–XIV; "Confidential Correspondence of Gustavus Vasa Fox," ed. by R. M. Thompson and R. Wainwright in *Pubs. Naval Hist. Soc.*, vol. IX (1918); Record of Officers, Bureau of Navigation, 1815–61; Navy Registers 1820–65; *Report of Secretary of the Navy*, 1861–63; Daniel Ammen, *The Atlantic Coast* (The Navy in the Civil War, vol. II, 1883); *U. S. Naval Inst. Proc.*, XXXIII (1907), 1468–73, XXXVIII (1912), 1323–24; G. E. Belknap, "Reminiscent of the Siege of Charleston," *Papers Mil. Hist. Soc. of Mass.*, XII (1902), 155–207; J. G. Nicolay and John Hay, *Abraham Lincoln*, VII (1890), 58–86; H. W. Wilson, *Battleships in Action*, I (1926), 23–27; *Diary of Gideon Welles* (1911), vols. I, II.] C. O. P.

DU PONT, VICTOR MARIE (Oct. 1, 1767–Jan. 30, 1827), diplomat, manufacturer, was born in Paris, the elder son of Pierre Samuel du Pont de Nemours and Nicole Charlotte Marie Louise Le Dée. He was educated under private tutors at his father's country place, "Bois des Fossés," Chevannes, and at sixteen entered the bureau of commerce over which his father presided, his work of collecting trade statistics taking him over all parts of France. He was for a time attached to the bureau of agriculture, but abandoned the line of promotion at home in 1787 to become attaché to the first French legation in the United States. He returned to France two years later to become aide-de-camp to Lafayette when the general was commanding the national guard. In 1791 he was back in the United States as second secretary of legation, but the following year was ordered to France to obtain fuller instructions from the Committee of Public Safety. Genêt had been dispatched to this country as minister by the time Du Pont arrived in France, and the latter was without an appointment. To escape being drafted for the army, which would have been distasteful to a conservative, he joined the constabulary as a gendarme, but pretended illness and was allowed to resign. He was married "before the municipality" to Gabrielle Joséphine de la Fite de Pelleport at Chevannes, Apr. 9, 1794. He was over six feet three inches, handsome, and of charming manners. In 1795 he came to America for the third time, now as first secretary of legation. In July 1796 he was stationed at Charleston as acting French consul for the Carolinas and Georgia, and in 1797 became consul. His work in this post received official commendation, so that his father was able, when the whole legation was recalled incident to the inauguration of the Directory (1798), to have Victor appointed consul-general in the United States. On reaching Philadelphia, however, Du Pont discovered that President Adams would not grant him an *exequatur* because of current controversy with France. Relinquishing his office, Du Pont, his wife, and two children hastily took ship for Bordeaux, where he found his father, his brother Irénée [*q.v.*], and others in the family connection planning to sail for America to make a new start after the disasters of the Revolution. Victor allowed himself to be persuaded to return to the United States with them, especially since his father had committed him to becoming a director in the land and trading company which was projected to rebuild the family fortunes in the new world.

After a delayed start, and a long and trying voyage, all the Du Ponts arrived at Newport, R. I., Jan. 1, 1800. While they were getting their bearings, they took up residence in a pleasant house at Bergen Point, N. J., opposite Staten Island. The firm of Du Pont de Nemours, Père et Fils et Cie remained without definite plans for almost a year, during which time the capital was being spent for maintenance of the family. Victor, in order to be naturalized and thus escape the higher import duties charged on goods consigned to aliens, bought a house and shop in Alexandria, Va. In 1801 he went to France and vainly tried to persuade the government to establish, with the Du Pont firm as agent, a packet line to the United States. Shortly after his return to America his father sailed for Europe, chiefly for business reasons. Victor formed a new firm, V. du Pont de Nemours & Company, of New York, nominally independent of the parent enterprise, which was to remain under the father with headquarters in Paris. Victor believed he might become financial agent of the French government in the United States if he could succeed with a commission business, and in the first year he did well despite inadequacy of capital. He sent cargoes to France and did a good business with the French West Indies, but in August

1805 he failed, largely because the French government refused to honor Santo Domingo drafts on the paymaster of the navy to the amount of 560,000 francs. In 1806 he joined Philip Church in a land development project at Angelica, Genesee County, N. Y., paying $3,000 from his wife's little fortune for 500 acres. This venture was not successful, and when Victor left Genesee three years later the land was assigned to his creditors. He joined his brother Irénée at the powder works of the latter on the Brandywine River near Wilmington, Del., where he became active manager of woolen-mills erected by his brother and Bauduy, the latter's partner. This undertaking was not more successful than others of Victor's; but, gentle and easily influenced, he enjoyed and needed association with his more vigorous brother. He received recognition as a director of the Bank of the United States and a member of the Delaware legislature. He died of heart failure in Philadelphia.

[See Gabrielle Joséphine du Pont de Nemours, *Souvenirs de Madame V. M. du Pont de Nemours* (1908); B. G. du Pont, *E. I. du Pont de Nemours & Co.* (1920), and *Life of Eleuthère Irénée du Pont* (12 vols., 1923–26); *Wilmingtonian and Del. Advertiser*, Feb. 1, 1827; *Am. Watchman and Del. Advertiser* (Wilmington), Feb. 2, 1827.] B. M—l.

DUPRATZ, ANTOINE SIMON LE PAGE (fl. 1718–1758), pioneer, historian, is remembered for his account of Louisiana, which is almost the only source of information about him. The date of his birth is given variously by secondary authorities as 1689 or 1690; and the place, as Holland, the Low Countries, and Belgium. He is said to have seen military service in Germany (Eyries, *post*). His own narrative begins with 1718, in which year he obtained a concession and came to Louisiana to seek his fortune. He reached New Orleans when it had but one cabin. He settled first on Bayou St. John, but dampness and the likelihood of floods led him to take up his abode near Fort Rosalie among the Natchez. Later he was granted a duchy in the Arkansas region. He explored the interior of Louisiana, going as far as the "South Sea." In 1726 he became overseer of a plantation near New Orleans, belonging to the Company of the Indies. This tract, which soon passed into the king's hands, Dupratz managed to the best of his ability, but the venture proved too costly and the post was abolished. He refused Bienville's invitation to remain in Louisiana, and in 1734 returned to La Rochelle whence he had sailed sixteen years before. In 1758 he published in Paris a three-volume work: *Histoire de la Louisiane. Contenant la dècouverte de ce vaste pays, sa description géographique: un voyage dans les terres, l'Histoire naturelle, les mœurs, coutumes, et religion des Naturels avec leur origine; deux voyages dans le Nord du Nouveau Mexique dont un jusqu'a la Mer du Sud*, illustrated with two maps and forty copper-plate engravings. The author used the accounts of Louisiana by Carlevoix and Dumont to check his own. Certain aspects of the man himself appear in his writing. Devoted to his Church, he refused an opportunity to marry an Indian princess and urged the baptism of all slaves. He was apparently kind to his negroes and was highly esteemed by the Indians. He was ever loyal to his superiors, and had a genuine interest in Louisiana. He knew something of astronomy and engineering, and his account includes a consideration of the hydraulic problem at the mouth of the Mississippi.

As a historian, he told the story of the relations between French and Indians, depicted Bienville smoking the calumet with the Tchitimachas, described the massacre at Fort Rosalie, and recorded precious material on pioneer life. He had vision, and saw even at that early date the possibilities latent in the vast territory of Louisiana. As a geographer, he noted the prodigious fertility of the soil, the favorable climate, the abundant streams, the fur-bearing animals, the plant life, the salt mines. He studied the natives, their tribal organization, languages, religion, manners, customs, ceremonies, history. Although discursive in manner, the book is written in a pleasing style and abounds in personal anecdotes which hold the interest of the reader. Little is known of Dupratz after the publication of this volume. It is stated by Eyries (*post*) that his death occurred in 1775.

[The *Histoire de la Louisiane* was translated into English (London, 1763). The anonymous translator claimed to have improved the text, but in the main he followed Dupratz, except where British interests were concerned, especially the tobacco trade and boundaries. The *Gentleman's Magazine*, June 1763, contains a summary of this translation. Both the translator's preface and that of Dupratz repay reading. This work was used as a basis for a compilation entitled, *An Account of La., Exhibiting a Compendious Sketch of its Pol. and Natural Hist. and Topography* . . . (Newbern, 1804). There is a sketch of Dupratz by J. B. Eyries, the noted French geographer, in Michaud's *Biographie Universelle* (1842–65).] L. C. D.

DUPUY, ELIZA ANN (1814–Jan. 15, 1881), novelist, was born in Petersburg, Va., the daughter of a merchant and ship-owner of that place and Norfolk. She was, on her father's side, of French ancestry, and was proud of being a descendant of the Colonel Dupuy who received a land grant on the James River from James II for the little band of Huguenot exiles whom Dupuy led to America. Her maternal grandfather was Capt. Joel Sturdevant, commander of a company in the American Revolution, but she was, as contemporary biographers are careful to state, only "distantly connected with that old pirate known as Commodore Sturdevant." Her early childhood was spent in Norfolk, but while still in her teens she removed with her father to Kentucky. Heavy financial losses at this time made it necessary for her to contribute to the family income, and for this reason she turned to writing. Her first novel, "Merton, a Tale of the Revolution," was at once accepted for publication. Her education had been extremely sketchy, and while in Kentucky she deliberately set about to educate herself in order to take up teaching. On the death of her father she accepted the post of governess with the family of Thomas G. Ellis in Natchez, Miss., and it was here that her first popular novel was written, "The Conspirator," based upon the character and career of Aaron Burr. This appeared in the *New World* when she was only twenty-two years old. Some ten years later Appletons published the novel in book form, when it sold to the extent of 24,000 copies. Her entire life was spent in the South, where she continued to teach and to write voluminously —novels and articles and short stories. Many of the latter were published in the *New York Ledger* under the pen name of Annie Young. Ardent, almost fiery in her Southern sympathies, she was yet able to place her writings in Northern journals even during the Civil War. All her novels are extremely melodramatic, the sensational promise of the titles being more than fulfilled both in plot and in style. She was a systematic worker, doing her writing in the morning and devoting the afternoon to revision. The critics of her own day varied widely in their estimate of her ability. At the one extreme her work was considered "full of scenes of most absorbing interest, while it exhibits the elegance of style and purity of diction which are among Miss Dupuy's characteristics" (Freeman, *post*, p. 377). At the other extreme she was dismissed as lurid and "Miss Braddonish." Her historical novels are the best: *The Conspirator* (1850), *The Huguenot Exiles* (1856), and *All for Love* (1873), although none of them escapes the blight of overemotionalism. Some of her most popular novels were frankly thrillers: *The Cancelled Will* (1872); *The Clandestine Marriage* (1875); *The Discarded Wife* (1875). She died in New Orleans at the age of sixty-seven.

[J. W. Davidson, *The Living Writers of the South* (1869); *The South in the Building of the Nation* (Southern Hist. Pub. Soc., 1909), vol. XI; Ida Raymond (Mrs. Mary I. Tardy), *Southland Writers* (1870), vol. I, and *The Living Female Writers of the South* (1872); Mary Forrest (Julia Deane Freeman), *Women of the South Distinguished in Literature* (1860); B. H. Dupuy, *The Huguenot Bartholomew Dupuy and his Descendants* (1908).]

G. G.

DURAND, ASHER BROWN (Aug. 21, 1796–Sept. 17, 1886), engraver and painter, was of French Huguenot ancestry. His great-grandfather, Jean Durand, fled from Toulouse to England in 1684, thence emigrated to America, and in 1705 was living at Derby, Conn. He had eight children; one of them, Samuel, moved from Connecticut to New Jersey, about 1740, and settled in Newark, where he married, and had six children. His second child, John, born in 1745, on reaching manhood, established himself at Jefferson Village, six miles from Newark; bought land, built a house, married Rachel (Meyer) Post, a young widow, and had eleven children. The eighth child was Asher Brown Durand. His father was a watchmaker, silversmith, farmer, and a "universal mechanic," so versatile that he could turn his hand to almost anything requiring mechanical skill. Asher was a delicate boy, but at the age of seven he was sent to the village school, where he was instructed in "reading, writing, and arithmetic, a little geography, and the whole of the Westminster Catechism (*Life and Times*, p. 20). At vacation time he busied himself with sundry operations in his father's work-shop, making metal trinkets and engraving designs on copper plates. Evidently he inherited some of his father's mechanical ingenuity, for he invented and made his own tools for these purposes. Sagaciously foreseeing the lad's manifest destiny, his father apprenticed him to Peter Maverick, a steel-engraver, in 1812. For five years he served diligently as apprentice in Maverick's shop, his principal employment being to make copies of the illustrations in English books for the use of American publishers. At this time he became acquainted with Samuel Waldo, the portrait painter, and, having received from him advice and instruction in regard to portrait work, he made his first crude essays in that line. When he became of age in 1817 his term of apprenticeship expired; thereupon he was taken into partnership by Maverick. One of the most important jobs given to the firm was the engraving of John Trumbull's historical painting, "The Signing of the Declaration of Independence," now in the rotunda of the Capitol at Washington—the picture alluded to as "the shin piece" by Randolph of Roanoke. Trumbull, judging that the erstwhile pupil now surpassed the master, insisted that this important commission should be executed by Durand, a stipulation which aroused the ire of

Maverick. This partiality brought about strained relations and eventually led to the dissolution of the partnership in 1820. Durand continued work on Trumbull's composition for about three years. When completed, 1823, it was received with general acclaim. It served to establish the reputation of the young engraver.

Encouraged by this success, Durand, never lacking self-confidence, produced an original drawing of a nude female figure in rustic surroundings, and proceeded to make an engraving of it, which he called "Musidora." The subject was suggested by lines from Thomson's *Seasons.* The print met with fair success, and does not appear to have caused any serious disturbance of the peace. A more successful effort in the same line, a reproduction of a nude piece by John Vanderlyn, "Ariadne," was engraved by Durand at a later period, and made a decided stir in artistic circles. It is still considered something of a landmark in the history of steel engraving in America. The plate is now preserved in the National Museum, Washington; the original painting by Vanderlyn, which was made in Paris, belongs to the permanent collection of the Pennsylvania Academy of the Fine Arts, Philadelphia; and Durand's reduced-size copy in oils hangs in the Metropolitan Museum of Art, New York, to which it was given by Samuel P. Avery.

Stimulated by the wide interest manifested in his plate after Trumbull's "Declaration of Independence," Durand now began the production of a long series of engraved portraits of eminent personages in the life of the time. The full list of these portraits, which in perfection of craftsmanship unquestionably excelled any previous work of the kind in America, includes thirty-two clergymen, twenty-three statesmen and publicists, ten popular actors, and seven noted physicians. Dunlap quotes from a letter written by Horatio Greenough, the sculptor, in respect to Durand's engraving after Chester Harding's portrait of Charles Carroll of Carrollton, which had been exhibited in Florence, that it "quite astonished the Italians; they would hardly believe that it was executed by an American." Not only were Durand's portrait plates excellent in point of workmanship, exactitude of likeness, and fidelity to the original paintings, they were and are rarely interesting by reason of the historical consequence of his subjects.

Incessantly active and resourceful, Durand, in the intervals of his more pressing labors, contributed generously to the Annuals, or gift-books, dear to the ladies of the time. In *The Token, The Gift, The Talisman, The Magnolia, The Atlantic Souvenir,* the outstanding features were the illustrations, reproductions of the genre pictures of Leslie, Ingham, Newton, Inman, Chapman, who were as romantic and sentimental as the authors of the tales illustrated. In *The Magnolia* for 1836, for example, two of the best pictures were engraved by Durand—"The Bride of Lammermoor" and "The White Plume." Commercial work of various kinds, especially banknote engraving, in which he engaged with his brother Cyrus [*q.v.*], also engrossed a share of his attention. To his burin are doubtless due many of those pretty vignettes of half-draped figures symbolizing liberty, justice, commerce, agriculture, art, and transportation, which then adorned and to some extent still adorn the paper currency of the nation. Much of the work done in the Bureau of Engraving and Printing since that time owes not a little of its character to the tradition established by Durand. The process does not lend itself to freedom or spontaneity; its limitations are recognized, but so far as its application to financial purposes is concerned, its stiffness, exactitude, and mechanical quality are more or less negligible, since its chief end and aim is to provide protection against the wiles of the counterfeiter. Samuel Isham has very justly pointed out that Durand was a thoroughly competent engraver; he had mastered a variety of technique from the cross-hatching of the school of Raphael Morghen to the stipple of Bartolozzi; his drawing was good, his line clear and strong, and he faithfully reproduced his models.

In 1830, he interested himself in an enterprise called *The American Landscape,* a serial publication of engravings after views of places by native painters, with descriptive text by William Cullen Bryant; but only one number was issued. It contained six plates, all by Durand. He was a member of a club called The Lunch, founded by James Fenimore Cooper and including Bryant, Hillhouse, Halleck, Sands, Vanderlyn, Morse, Jarvis, and Dunlap. He was also a member of a sketch club organized by the art students of New York. The evening meetings of this club were not wholly given over to serious sketching, evidently, for on one occasion we hear of Mr. Bryant frivolously maintaining that "the perfection of bathing is to jump headforemost into a snowbank," while at another conclave we find Mr. G. C. Verplanck throwing new light on the precise form and capacity of antediluvian butter-churns. The Century Club and the National Academy of Design both owed their establishment to the same men who formed the sketch club. Durand was a charter member of the Academy, which opened its first exhibition in 1826, and his first *envoi* was a picture of "Mary Magdalen at the Sepulchre." He continued to exhibit regularly for many years. In 1845 he was elected president of the Academy, and he served until 1861, during which period, a period of considerable difficulties and vicissitudes, he gave much of his time and energy to the duties of the office, and showed wisdom and shrewdness in his administration.

From 1836 he abandoned engraving for the painter's profession and devoted the rest of his long life to work in color. He soon became as successful and famous in this work as he had been in his former specialty. The earliest pictures were mainly portraits and figure pieces; of the latter class were illustrations of episodes in the Bible and several scenes from the pseudo-historical tales of Irving and Cooper, which were highly esteemed. These include "The Wrath of Peter Stuyvesant" (New York Historical Society), painted to order for Luman Reed, his first patron and firm friend; also, "Rip Van Winkle introduced to the Crew of Hendrik Hudson in the Catskill Mountains"; and an interesting incident in *The Spy* by Cooper, the "Last Interview between Harvey Birch and Washington." Of the Old Testament subjects, perhaps the most important was "God's Judgment upon Gog" (1852), now in the permanent collection of the Metropolitan Museum of Art, New York.

After this he did not attempt to paint any more *"machines,"* as the French artists call that kind of pictures, or, as Thackeray denominates them, "thundering big first raters"; he was content now to turn to nature. He traveled to the banks of the Hudson, the Catskills, Lake George, the Adirondacks, Vermont, the White Mountains, the Berkshires, and the valley of the Connecticut, and found ample scope for the exercise of his fine perceptive faculty and the expression of his love for the country. He was shortly entitled to share with Thomas Cole the renown of being the founder of the American school of landscape. The typical Durand landscape is a view of far-reaching fields, meadows, and valleys, with fine trees in the foreground drawn with conscientious care and fidelity in every detail; distant hills enveloped in a summer haze; and a sky which suggests real air and light. In spite of a certain conventionality in the design, the sentiment is genuine, and the work is not without a vein of lyricism. An example is "Summer Woods," engraved in steel by James Smillie and published in the excellent anthology edited by Charles A. Dana, the *Household Book of Poetry* (1875), evidently an illustration to a poem by Mary Howitt. Nothing could more exactly denote the taste of the period in landscape. It is a panoramic view from a hillside overlooking a wide vale through which a stream meanders nearly to the horizon of gently undulating heights. The peaceful pastoral feeling of the scene is very nicely suggested; and not the least engaging part of it is the hint of sunlight on the gilded lower edges of the cirrus clouds floating lazily in the placid summer sky. No wonder that such canvases found favor with the collectors of the day. An idea of the importance attributed to his work by the critics of mid-nineteenth century is to be derived from the ten pages of almost rhapsodic eulogy in Henry T. Tuckerman's *Book of the Artists*. His landscapes are described as grand, true, tender, faultless, "the mirror of reality," and, in one instance, "perfectly Titian-like." Particular praise was due to his wood interiors, which are, indeed, among his most felicitous canvases, though to more modern eyes a thought too literal and niggling. Sound drawing is, however, never to be rated as less than a high merit. In a memorial address to the members of the National Academy, shortly after Durand's death, Daniel Huntington dwelt eloquently on his rendering of the "subtle and infinitely varying effects of atmosphere, of fleeting clouds, mist, sunshine, twilight obscurity, and the thousand wondrous phenomena which form the peculiar glory of landscape."

An interlude in Durand's busy life was his tour of Europe in 1840–41 in company with his friends Casilear and Rossiter. In London he met Wilkie and Leslie, saw Turner and his pictures, visited the current exhibitions, and incidentally attended a masquerade ball, which in his diary he calls a "licensed scene of folly and depravity." After seven weeks in England, he spent a fortnight in Paris, and a shorter time in Antwerp, where he witnessed the inauguration of the statue of Rubens in the Place Verte. Thence he proceeded to Italy and passed the winter in Rome, returning home in June 1841. On Apr. 2, 1821, he was married to Lucy, daughter of Isaac Baldwin of Bloomfield, N. J. She died in 1830, and in 1834 he married Mary Frank of New York, a daughter of Jacob Frank.

Living in New York for a period of fifty-four years, where he was closely identified with every organized movement to foster the arts, greatly loved and admired by a host of friends and colleagues, the intellectual and artistic élite of the city, at a peculiarly interesting stage of the development of native art, officially active for a long term of years as the president of the National Academy, and thriving steadily as one of the most popular landscape painters of his generation, his life was full of the wholesome satisfactions of creative work and friendly associations, and he played an important and honorable part in the arena of American art. His last years were spent in retirement, though they were not by any means inactive. He moved from New York in 1869 to a quiet country home in his birthplace, Jefferson Village, N. J., where he died in 1886, and was buried in Greenwood Cemetery, Brooklyn.

[The standard work on Durand is his own son's biography, *The Life and Times of Asher Brown Durand* (1894), by John Durand, a thorough and readable record, with fifteen illustrations. Other sources include Daniel Huntington, *Asher B. Durand* (1887); Wm. Dunlap, *Hist. of the Rise and Progress of the Arts of Design in the U. S.* (ed. by F. W. Bayley and C. E. Goodspeed, 3 vols., 1918); H. T. Tuckerman, *Book of the Artists* (1867); G. W. Sheldon, *Am. Painters* (1879); J. J. Jarves, *The Art Idea* (1864); Samuel Isham, *Hist. of Am. Painting* (1905); *Biog. and Geneal. Hist. of the City of Newark and Essex County, N. J.* (1898). The Grolier Club of New York has published a check-list of Durand's engraved work.] W. H. D.

DURAND, CYRUS (Feb. 27, 1787–Sept. 18, 1868), engraver, inventor, was born at Jefferson Village, near Newark, N. J., the second child of John and Rachel (Meyer) Post Durand. His father was a watchmaker and silversmith possessing mechanical talent of great versatility, and was engaged in the manufacture of various metal and other trinkets, such as sleeve buttons, arrowheads, powder horns, and engraved copper plates. It was in this environment that Cyrus grew to manhood, his whole education being obtained in the village public school. As a young man he was accumstomed to help in his father's shop, one of his particular duties being the engraving of monograms or other devices on the various articles manufactured. Some of his time, too, was occupied in the design and construction of unusual machinery. At the age of thirty-one he secured a patent for what he called a "grammatical mirror." This machine rendered the abstract rules of grammar and the definitions of the parts of speech intelligible by objective means through a combination of mirrors, slides, wheels, and other mechanical equipment. Four years before this, following the accidental death of his father, Durand had established himself as a silversmith in Newark and had served for a few months in the army during the War of 1812–14. In 1815 he was employed for about a year in Rahway, N. J., to construct machines for carding and weaving hair to be used in the manufacture of carpets. Following this period he continued in his own establishment in Newark, and on Sept. 22, 1818, obtained another patent for a machine to ornament columns. He continued in Newark for about six years after this, when at the suggestion of Peter Maverick, tutor of his younger brother Asher [*q.v.*] in engraving, the brothers established the A. B. & C. Durand Company in New York City, to engage in bank-note engraving. Asher made the designs and Cyrus executed them with machines of his own invention, which included one for ruling straight and wave lines, another for drawing water lines, and a third for making plain ovals. These machines are regarded as the beginning of geometrical lathes by which machine work on bank-notes is universally executed. The company continued as a partnership until 1832, when Asher retired to devote his life to art. Cyrus continued alone, constantly devising new appliances, not only for bank-note engraving but also for engine turning and transfer printing-press work. While it is not definitely known just when, Durand gave up his engraving business in New York and went to Washington, D. C., as an engraver in the Treasury Department. It is presumed that he continued to serve in this capacity after the establishment of the Bureau of Engraving and Printing in 1862 but no record is to be found in that department except a notice of his death in Irvington, N. J. Durand married Mrs. Phœbe Woodruff of Newark.

[John Durand, *The Life and Times of Asher Brown Durand* (1894); *Twentieth Century Biog. Dict. of Notable Americans* (1904), vol. III; records of U. S. Patent Office and Treasury Dept.; *N. Y. Times*, Sept. 21, 1868.] C. W. M.

DURAND, ÉLIE MAGLOIRE (Jan. 25, 1794–Aug. 14, 1873), pharmacist, botanist, usually known in America as Elias Durand, was born at Mayenne, France, the youngest of the fourteen children of André Durand, the local recorder of deeds. At school he developed an aptitude for chemistry; and in October 1808 he was apprenticed to a M. Chevallier, a distinguished chemist and pharmacist of the city, who won his pupil's enduring gratitude by giving him thorough, systematic instruction in laboratory technique and in the elements of the physical and biological sciences. Twenty years later Durand repaid his master in the only way possible, by giving the same excellent instruction to his own apprentices in Philadelphia. After completing his scientific training by a year's study in Paris, he was commissioned as pharmacist in the French army, Feb. 2, 1813, and was assigned to the 3rd Division of the V Corps. He was present at the battles of Möckern, Lützen, Bautzen, Hanau, the Katzbach and Leipzig. He was captured at Hanau but was released almost immediately by a Prussian officer aghast at the losses sustained by his enemy. Durand resigned his commission on Apr. 3, 1814, and secured congenial employment at Nantes, returned to the army for the "Hundred Days," and went back to Nantes after Waterloo. Because of his Napoleonic sympathies, however, he was kept under surveillance and required to report himself every morning to the police. Unable to brook such restraint any longer, he determined to emigrate. He sailed from Nantes on Apr. 16, 1816, in the brig *La Nymphe* and landed at New York the first of July.

For the next few years his life was somewhat nomadic. In Boston he was kindly received by his distant relative, Bishop John Lefebre de Cheverus [*q.v.*], was introduced to various men of science, and was employed by a druggist named Perkins to manufacture Rochelle salt, tartar emetic, ether, and other drugs according to French methods. In Philadelphia he worked for a German, Wesener, who was making chromates and mercurial salts, but the salts affected his health, and he was compelled to quit. During a three months' stay at Bel Air, Md., he studied English assiduously. For one winter he lived with Gerard Troost [*q.v.*] at Cape Sable, Md. Troost, all alone except for his negro laborers, was engaged in manufacturing copperas and was starved for civilized company. Although he had no employment to offer him, he insisted vehemently that Durand stay with him anyway. Finally, in Baltimore in 1817, Durand entered into partnership with his compatriot and fellow pharmacist, Edme Ducatel. In Baltimore, during these years, he began his study of American flora.

Withdrawing from the partnership in 1824, he went to France to purchase apparatus and supplies and in 1825 opened a drug store at the corner of Sixth and Chestnut Sts., in Philadelphia. Resplendent with huge French bottles and other heavy glassware, porcelain jars, mahogany drawers, and marble counters, the shop instantly became fashionable. There was more to it, however, than glitter. Its proprietor, possessing skill and knowledge of a high order, regarded pharmacy as no mere trade but as a learned profession and a public trust. He collected a valuable professional library and took in a number of foreign scientific journals. He introduced to the medical men of the city a long list of foreign medicines, previously unused in the United States, and originated a number of others. Some of these medicines were suggested first by Dr. Samuel Jackson [*q.v.*]. By putting up some of the prescriptions as proprietary remedies with Jackson's name on the labels Durand unintentionally involved his friend in a question of professional ethics. He was also the first to bottle mineral water in this country and invented a machine for bottling it under pressure. Attracted by his social qualities, the physicians of Philadelphia used Durand's Drug Store as an informal club-house. Ultimately Durand's example affected the drug business of the entire country.

Botanists as well as physicians were attracted to his store. He advanced money to many a botanical traveler and often accepted their collections in payment. It was in this way that he acquired Thomas Nuttall's herbarium. Constantine Samuel Rafinesque's he discovered, somewhat the worse for rats, in an old loft and bought it for a small sum. He himself explored the Dismal Swamp of Virginia in 1837 and the mountains of Pennsylvania in 1862 and made numerous shorter excursions with Joseph Bonaparte, then living at Bordentown, N. J., and with other scientific friends. He was elected to the Philadelphia Academy of Natural Sciences (1825), the College of Pharmacy (1825, vice-president 1844), and the American Philosophical Society (1854).

On Nov. 20, 1820, he married Polymnia Rose Ducatel, the daughter of his Baltimore friend. She died Feb. 18, 1822. On Oct. 25, 1825, about the time when he established himself in Philadelphia, he married Marie Antoinette Berauld, whose father, a merchant of Norfolk, Va., was one of the French refugees from the Santo Domingo Insurrection. Her death in 1851 led Durand, in the following year, to make his business over to his son and to give the rest of his life to botanical studies. He was a good Latin scholar. His English was always French in accent and occasionally in idiom, but he wrote the language fluently and well. He was noted for his charities and for his helpful kindness to younger scientists. In 1860 he went to France for a second time and also visited England. In 1868 he took to Paris his own herbarium, containing over 10,000 species and over 100,000 specimens, and presented it to the museum of the Jardin des Plantes, where it was housed in a special gallery as the Herbier Durand. During his retirement he also rearranged and from his own collections supplemented the herbarium of the Philadelphia Academy of Natural Sciences. He gave his botanical library to the Academy and his chemical and pharmaceutical works, together with a herbarium of medical plants, to the Philadelphia College of Pharmacy. He had previously given the College a general herbarium of 12,000 specimens. He died, loved and venerated, in his eightieth year.

His first publication, in collaboration with Joseph Togno, M.D., was a translation with additions of H. M. Edwards and P. Vavasseur's *Manual of Materia Medica and Pharmacy* (1829). His articles on chemical and botanical subjects are listed in the *Catalogue of Scientific Papers Compiled by the Royal Society of London,* vols. II (1868), VII (1877), and IX (1891). He also wrote memoirs of François André Michaux [*q.v.*] and Thomas Nuttall [*q.v.*].

[W. Procter, Jr., memoir in *Am. Jour. of Pharmacy,* XLV (1873), 508–17; T. Meehan, "Obituary Notice of Elias Durand," in *Proc. Acad. Nat. Sci. of Phila.,* 1873, pp. 355–59; C. Des Moulins, *Notice Nécrologique sur M. Élie Durand (Extrait des Actes de la Société Linnéenne de Bordeaux,* t. XXIX, 2e liv., 1873); J. W. England, ed., *The First Century of the Phila. Coll. of Pharmacy 1821–1921* (1922); portrait in J. W. Harshberger, *The Botanists of Phila.* (privately printed, 1899), op. p. 176.] G. H. G.

DURANT, CHARLES FERSON (Sept. 19, 1805–Mar. 2, 1873), aeronaut, scientist, was born in New York City, son of William and Elizabeth (Woodruff) Durant. When he was eighteen, he went to Paris with Eugene Robertson, a French aeronaut, who on July 9, 1825, made an ascension at Castle Garden in honor of the Marquis de Lafayette. With Robertson, Durant made two ascensions in Paris in the summer of 1829, then returned to America and tried to arouse interest in ballooning as a means of transportation. He can be regarded as the first citizen of the United States to make a profession of aeronautics. He was the first native-born American to make a balloon flight in this country. As early as Jan. 9, 1793, Blanchard (a Frenchman) had ascended in a balloon at Philadelphia before President Washington and a large crowd of people, but Durant's flight which took place at Castle Garden, Sept. 9, 1830, was the first in which home-made materials were used and which was performed without assistance from foreign aeronauts. This first balloon was made at the Durant home in Jersey City. Other ascensions at Castle Garden occurred on Sept. 22, 1830; Aug. 24, Sept. 7, 1831; May 29 and June 14, 1833. Durant later made ascensions at Albany, Baltimore, and Boston, all carefully planned and successfully carried out. In Chesapeake Bay he landed on the deck of the steamship *Independence.* He made one ascent in Albany and three from Boston Common. On the last of these (Sept. 13, 1834) he went out beyond the harbor in one air current and returned in another, and after passing the city continued to the west-northwest, landing at Lincoln. He had been in the air about two hours and had reached a height of 8,000 feet. This ascension gave the first direct evidence of the shallow character of the sea-breeze.

In all, Durant made thirteen ascensions but seems to have made nore after his marriage to Elizabeth Hamilton Freeland, Nov. 14, 1837. He was engaged for many years in the business of printing and lithographing and took an active interest in political matters, especially in Jersey City. He spent much time collecting and classifying sea-weed, doubtless because of a business connection with the fish and oyster trade of New York City. He prepared a book on "Algae and Corallines of the Bay and Harbor of New York," and made about thirty copies, each illustrated with actual specimens of sea-weed and other marine flora. One copy was put up for sale at the New York Sanitary Fair and was sold for $150. A copy is in existence in the Jersey City Public Library, and another in the Cryptogamic Herbarium of Harvard University. The American Institute gave him six or more gold medals, one in 1836 for the first silk known to be made in the United States, others for the best specimens of cocoons, raw and sewing silk, and for the successful propagation of silk worms and the utilization of their products. He imported the worms from China. Durant also devised a portable barometer.

He published in 1837 a book entitled *Exposition, or a New Theory of Animal Magnetism, with a Key to the Mysteries,* which attempted to expose the methods employed by the Fox sisters [*q.v.*], then attracting much attention by their so-called spiritualistic exhibitions. He also published a "physical astronomy" but for some reason bought up the entire edition and destroyed all but one copy. His balloon flights were described in the newspapers of New York, Boston, Philadelphia, and also in London and Paris papers.

[A scrap-book of clippings concerning Durant in the New York Public Library; E. A. Dime, "America's First Aeronaut," *Air Travel,* Jan. 1918; Jersey City *Journal,* June 21, 1927; and personal memoranda from Miss Emma Durant.] A. M.

DURANT, HENRY (June 18, 1802–Jan. 22, 1875), Congregational clergyman, first president of the University of California, was born at Acton, Mass., the son of Henry and Lucy (Hunt) Durant. He prepared for college at Phillips Academy, Andover, Mass., and graduated from Yale in 1827, in a class numbering among its members Horace Bushnell and Nathaniel Parker Willis. Following graduation, Durant took charge of the Garrison Forest Academy, Baltimore County, Md. He gave up this position at the end of two years in order to accept a Yale tutorship which he held for four years (1829–33), meanwhile completing the course in the Yale Theological Seminary. On Dec. 10, 1833, he was married to Mary E. Buffett, daughter of the Rev. Platt Buffett of Stanwich, Conn. Later in the same month he was ordained pastor of the Congregational church in Byfield, Mass., and continued in this work until 1849, when he became head of the Dummer Academy in Byfield. This was at the time of the California gold rush. Among the many who were drawn to the West were a few earnest men who went in the interest of the welfare of their fellows. Henry Durant was one of this number. Awake to the possibilities of aiding in the educational development of the new state, he left his position in the East, and arrived in California on May 1, 1853.

At a joint meeting of the Presbytery of San Francisco and the Congregational Association of California held in Nevada City, Cal., on May 10, a plan was formulated to establish an Academy in Oakland (then known as Contra Costa) under the direction of Durant. A month later the Contra Costa Academy opened, with three pupils, in a former fandango house rented by Durant for $150 per month, payable in gold coin in advance. Durant, however, had come to California with "college on the brain," and never for a moment forgot his supreme aim and desire. Consequently it was upon the petition of the Board of Directors of his Academy that the State Board of Education granted a charter to the College of California, Apr. 13, 1855. By the year 1860 an entering class had been prepared, and the College of California began its first session in July with a freshman class of nine and a faculty of two: Henry Durant and Martin Kellogg [*q.v.*]. In 1868 the legislature of California provided for the establishment and support of the state University of California, and in the next year all assets of the College of California were turned over to the University. On Aug. 16, 1870, Henry Durant, now sixty-eight years old, was elected the first president, but he was forced to resign at the end of two years, owing to ill health. Following his recovery, he was twice elected mayor of Oakland and was occupying this office at the time of his death.

Durant was essentially a teacher and an organizer. He left practically nothing in the way of writings. He made no original contribution to literature, to science, or to any other branch of human knowledge. His great contribution to the culture of the West was the part he played in the founding, first, of the College of California, and then later, of the University of California.

[John B. Felton, "A Memorial Address," *Bull. of the Univ. of Cal.*, no. 10, Mar. 1875; W. W. Ferrier, *Coll. and Univ.: The Story of the Coll. of Cal. and its Relation to the Univ. of Cal.* (1921); W. C. Jones, *Illustrated Hist. of the Univ. of Cal.* (1901); *Overland Monthly*, Mar. 1875; S. H. Willey, *Hist. of the Coll. of Cal.* (1887); *Obit. Record of Grads. of Yale Coll.* (1875).]
F. H. S.

DURANT, HENRY FOWLE (Feb. 20, 1822–Oct. 3, 1881), lawyer, evangelist, philanthropist, was descended from Edward Durant, an early settler of Newton, Mass. He was born in Hanover, N. H., to William and Harriet (Fowle) Smith, who christened him Henry Welles, but in 1851, owing to the fact that eleven Boston lawyers bore the name Smith, he adopted that of Durant. In his childhood the family moved to Lowell, where the father practised law for many years. Henry was sent to the Rev. and Mrs. Samuel Ripley of Waltham to be prepared for Harvard, which he entered in 1837. The learning, versatility, and character of Mrs. Ripley seem to have made upon him a more lasting impression than any of the influences of an undistinguished college career. Upon receiving his degree in 1842, he began the study of law with his father, and at the age of twenty-one, was admitted to the bar. After five years' practise in Lowell, he moved to Boston, and here for seventeen years, with a success that was the wonder and the envy of his fellow lawyers, he pleaded cases at the Suffolk Bar. His rapid rise is attributed not only to his merciless cross-examination, his dramatic ability and skill in presentation, but also to his unsparing attention to detail. His defense in the "Eliot School Case," which concerned the reading of the Bible in the public school, is one of his best-known arguments.

On May 23, 1854, he married his cousin, Pauline Adeline Fowle, and to them were born Henry Fowle, Jr., and Pauline Cazenove. The daughter lived but two months, the son to the age of eight. The loss of this child in 1863 brought about a great change in Mr. Durant's activities and purposes. Abruptly abandoning the law, he turned to the service of Christianity, and for some years conducted revival meetings in churches of eastern Massachusetts. Meanwhile, he and his wife had become interested in Mount Holyoke, of which he became a trustee in 1867. After much consideration they determined to devote their country home in Wellesley and the considerable fortune accumulated from his profession and from successful business ventures, to the education of young women. From the time of obtaining the charter of Wellesley (1870) until his death, Mr. Durant's history is identified with that of the college. In name, he was the treasurer; in fact, the physical plant, the faculty, the curriculum, and the health and conduct of the students, were the intimate concern of the founder, who brought to the college the same zest and emotional intensity which he had given to the law. To him higher education and the forming of Christian character were synonymous, but this did not lessen his appreciation of the necessity for laboratories and first-hand materials for scholarly work.

Durant's appearance was striking. His features were clear-cut, his eyes dark and brilliant, and his hair, black in his youth, was always worn longer than the mode. In character he was a perplexing combination of dreamer and master of of practical detail, of fanatic and man of affairs. His wit was keen, his courage undaunted, his love of beauty unfailing.

[Florence Morse Kingsley, *The Life of Henry Fowle Durant* (1924), written in a tone of extreme adulation; Charlotte Conant, *Address Delivered in Memory of Henry Fowle Durant in Wellesley Chapel, Feb. 18, 1906* (1906); Florence Converse, *The Story of Wellesley* (1915); Wm. T. Davis, *Bench and Bar of the Commonwealth of Mass.* (1895), I, 498–99; the *Congregationalist*, Oct. 12, 1881; G. W. Smalley's "Anglo-American Memories," *N. Y. Tribune*, Mar. 28, 1909.] E. D.

DURANT, THOMAS CLARK (Feb. 6, 1820–Oct. 5, 1885), builder of the Union Pacific Railroad, son of Thomas and Sybil (Wright) Durant, was born at Lee, Mass., of colonial and Revolutionary ancestry. He graduated from the Albany Medical College in 1840, but soon joined his uncle in the firm of Durant, Lathrop & Company, exporters of flour and grain. Given charge of the New York office, he expanded the business and also became known as a daring and successful speculator in stocks. Becoming interested in the West, Durant in 1851 joined Henry Farnam [*q.v.*] in constructing the Michigan Southern Railroad; they later contracted to build the Chicago & Rock Island, and then the Mississippi & Missouri. The question of a railroad to the Pacific was in the air, and Farnam and Durant sent Peter A. Dey and Grenville M. Dodge to make surveys. In 1863, Durant alone sent out three parties, including a geologist to report on coal and iron, and claimed to have influenced President Lincoln to choose Omaha as the beginning point of the road. The Pacific Railway Act of 1862 fixed the capital of the Union Pacific at one hundred millions, but permitted organization when two millions had been subscribed and ten per cent of this amount paid. Capital was timid, and only $2,180,000 had been subscribed on Oct. 30, 1863, when Gen. John A. Dix was elected president and Durant vice-president of the company. Durant declared afterward that he had provided or guaranteed the instalments on three-fourths of the subscription (*House Report No. 78*, 42 Cong., 3 Sess., p. 515).

From this time until the completion of the road Durant was the chief figure in the management of the Union Pacific. He was influential in securing the amended act of 1864, which doubled the land grant and permitted the company to issue bonds equal in amount to the United States bonds lent and to make them a prior lien on the road. In securing these and other favorable amendments much money was used, but no actual proof of bribery or of misappropriation was ever adduced. These expenditures were long carried in the famous "suspense account," which was the occasion of much controversy, but Durant's accounts were approved by Presidents Dix and Oliver Ames, and by Treasurer Cisco. During 1863–64, Durant built a few miles of road with the cash in hand and made advances from his personal funds. When H. M. Hoxie, who had contracted to build 100 miles, later extended to 247 miles, was unable to continue, Durant and several associates took over his contract and subscribed $1,600,000, one-fourth in cash, as a building fund. The associates became frightened and refused to pay further instalments. Evidently New York capitalists would not build the road, the failure of which was generally regarded as certain. Meanwhile Durant had secured the charter of the Crédit Mobilier of which he became the largest stockholder and the president. This corporation took over the Hoxie contract, agreeing to take the securities of the road as issued in payment. The Ames brothers, Oakes and Oliver [*qq.v.*], and other New England capitalists came into Crédit Mobilier, thereby becoming stockholders in the road, and secured representation in its directorate in 1866. For the next three years the Durant and Ames factions, or the "New York crowd" and the "Boston crowd," contended for control of the Union Pacific. Durant refused to give the Crédit Mobilier a second contract, and a period of wrangling between the factions ensued. He was ousted from the directorate of the Crédit Mobilier in May 1867, but the effort to drop him from the direction of the road in October failed. Meanwhile (Aug. 16, 1867), Oakes Ames had offered to build 667 miles, and Durant agreed, provided the consent of every stockholder of the road be secured. Later he became one of the seven trustees under the tripartite agreement which assigned the profits of the contract to the Crédit Mobilier. With large funds at his disposal and fortified by a resolution of the executive committee of the Union Pacific (July 3, 1868) which made him practically dictator, Durant drove the work furiously under this contract, and the later Davis contract, regardless of difficulties or cost. Speed had become an obsession. He spent most of his time on the line and said that sometimes he did not remove his clothes for a week. This haste probably doubled the cost of construction. Durant knew that the "Boston crowd" would finally accomplish his downfall, and wished to complete the road first. He joined with President Leland Stanford of the Central Pacific in driving the "last spike," May 10, 1869, but on May 25 was dropped from the directorate.

Broken in health, Durant spent most of his later years in the Adirondacks, where he owned much land. Though crippled financially by the panic of 1873, he promoted a grandiose scheme to develop the iron and timber resources of the Adirondacks, including a railroad from Saratoga across the St. Lawrence into Canada. He had married in 1847 an Englishwoman, Héloise Hannah Timbrel, who with a daughter and a son survived him. He died at North Creek, Warren County, N. Y. Durant was an unusual combination of dreamer and forceful executive. Reticent and quiet in manner, he was able to excite his subordinates to extraordinary exertion. In his associates he aroused deep antagonism or warm admiration.

[An appreciative sketch is in the *N. Y. Tribune,* May 29, 1869, and one, evidently from material furnished by himself, is in *Representative Men of New York* (1872). A sketch by L. O. Leonard, inaccurate in some particulars, is in the *Rock Island Magazine,* Oct. 1926. Information has also been furnished by his daughter and son, who have permitted limited access to his papers. See also *N. Y. Tribune,* Oct. 6, 1885, and references in sketch of Oakes Ames.] H. T.

DURANT, THOMAS JEFFERSON (Aug. 8, 1817–Feb. 3, 1882), lawyer, politician, the son of John Waldo and Sarah (Heyliger) Durant, was born in Philadelphia, where he obtained his early education in the common schools. In 1830 he entered the University of Pennsylvania, but before completing his course, removed in 1834 to New Orleans, where for a short time he held a position in the post-office. He then studied law, was admitted to the Louisiana bar, and opened an office in New Orleans. He rapidly achieved distinction and acquired a lucrative practise, at the same time identifying himself with the Democratic party and becoming active in state politics. He was not a rabid partisan and opposed the annexation of Texas on constitutional grounds, but this did not prevent him from becoming an influential member of the state committee which in 1844 managed the Louisiana campaign of Polk for the presidency. Elected as a Democrat, he served in the state Senate in 1846. Later, President Polk appointed him United States district attorney. He was now recognized as an outstanding figure in local legal and political circles. His practise had brought him wealth, he was a slave-owner, and his reputation for integrity had gained for him the respect of the community, but the outbreak of the Civil War found him aligned against the preponderant sentiment of his fellow citizens. A conscientious and consistent Unionist, he supported Lincoln in the campaign of 1860. He fought strenuously against secession, and when that became a reality he remained in New Orleans, but during the Confederate régime abstained from all political activities. When the Federal forces under Butler occupied the city in 1862 he headed the movement to organize Louisiana as a free state and was offered the position of governor, which he declined. In 1863, however, after Banks had superseded Butler as commander of the Department of the Gulf, Durant became president of the Free State General Committee which was formed to procure the election of a convention to frame a new constitution, and the military governor, G. F. Shepley, appointed him attorney-general and commissioner for the purpose of carrying out the registration of loyal citizens entitled to vote. The constitutional convention of 1864 revised and amended the state constitution of 1852 and abolished slavery, and its work was approved by the president and ratified by the people. Durant, however, held the view that secession had abrogated the constitution of 1852 and that the work of the convention, most of which was not in harmony with his views, was invalid, and from thenceforth he was involved in a bitter controversy with Banks and a powerful section of the Northern sympathizers led by A. P. Dostie. The merits of the dispute, if any, are obscured by the intemperate pamphlet warfare which broke out. Durant evidenced his bitter disapproval of the course of events by removing to Washington, D. C., where he henceforth devoted himself to his profession. The resumption, after 1865, of litigation, suspended throughout the South during the war, had its effect upon the Supreme Court docket, and an abnormal number of appeals from Louisiana came before that Court, a majority involving novel points of constitutional law and military authority. Durant was retained in practically all of these and soon established himself as one of the leading members of the Washington bar. To a thorough theoretical and practical knowledge of the civil law he added a persuasive logic, a facility of language, and a dignity of manner which always assured him an attentive hearing, and he enjoyed a larger practise before the Supreme Court and the Court of Claims than any contemporary, appearing as counsel in no less than 154 reported cases. His sphere of action was narrow, confined almost entirely to civil and constitutional law, bankruptcy, and admiralty, but within these limits he had in his time no superior. His most conspicuous success was obtained in the Slaughterhouse Cases

(16 *Wallace*, 36), where his elaborate argument as leading counsel for the defendants in error was upheld by the Supreme Court. Among his other outstanding cases were: *Coppell* vs. *Hall* (7 *Wallace*, 173), holding that a contract of the British consul at New Orleans to protect cotton of the insurgents was void; *Handlin* vs. *Wickliffe* (12 *Wallace*, 173), deciding that the authority of a judge appointed by a military governor ceases of necessity after the civil constitution of a state functions independent of military control; *Holdane* vs. *Sumner* (15 *Wallace*, 600), where it was held that all statutes of prescription and limitation were suspended in the federal courts during the period of the Civil War; and the Confiscation Cases (7 *Wallace*, 454). In 1881 he was retained as counsel for the United States before the Spanish and American Claims Commission. He died in Washington in the following year. His wife was Mary Elizabeth Harper, a daughter of Robert Withers Harper of Marlboro, Md.

Durant was recognized as a man of great innate ability and the highest character and culture. In 1869, when the number of the Supreme Court judges was increased, and again in 1872, when a vacancy in the Court occurred through the resignation of Judge Nelson, the claims of "the sad-faced and thin featured New Orleans Unionist" (*Boston Daily Advertiser*, Apr. 27, 1867) were urged in many quarters, on the ground that a Southerner was greatly needed to strengthen the Supreme Bench.

[See *Am. Ann. Cyc. and Reg.*, 1863, 1864; John Rose Ficklen, *Hist. of Reconstruction in La.* (1910), *passim*; Charles Warren, *The Supreme Court in U. S. Hist.* (1922); *Letter of Thos. J. Durant to the Hon. Henry Winter Davis, 27 Oct. 1864* (New Orleans, 1864); *Evening Star* (Washington, D. C.), Feb. 4, 1882. For an unfavorable view of Durant's reconstruction activities see A. P. Dostie, *The Political Position of Thos. J. Durant* (New Orleans, 1865), being a reprint of a letter to the chairman of the Committee on Elections, House of Representatives, Dec. 29, 1864. Emily Hagen Reed, *Life of A. P. Dostie* (1868), also gives a bitter partisan picture of Durant.] H. W. H. K.

DURBIN, JOHN PRICE (Oct. 10, 1800–Oct. 19, 1876), Methodist Episcopal clergyman, began his public career at the age of eighteen with no more preparation than a bit of frontier schooling and acquiring the trade of cabinetmaker could give. He was a Kentuckian, born in Bourbon County near Paris, the son of Hozier and Elizabeth (Nunn) Durbin, both children of some of the first settlers in that region. Left in his thirteenth year by his father's death to the care of his mother and the clemency of the world, the eldest of five sons, he was shortly apprenticed; but an urge to the ministry and a display of native talent led to his being licensed as a preacher, Nov. 19, 1818. He began his itinerary on the Limestone Circuit of the Kentucky Conference, and during the next seven years held various charges in Indiana and Ohio, being ordained deacon in 1822, and elder in 1824. Conscious of his deficiencies he spent every minute available in the study of English, oratory, theology and the classics, managing, without interrupting his duties, to do work at Miami University, and at Cincinnati College, which in 1825 granted him a degree. Immediately he was appointed professor of languages at Augusta College, Ky., one of the earliest Methodist experiments in education. On Sept. 6, 1827, he married Frances B. Cook, the daughter of Alexander Cook of Philadelphia, her younger sister subsequently becoming his second wife. Excursions in behalf of the college brought him to notice in the East, and, having now taken up the study of the natural sciences, in 1831 he was appointed professor of these at Wesleyan University, Conn., an office he did not fill because of his election to the chaplaincy of the United States Senate. This same year he edited Thomas Wood's *Mosaic History of the Creation of the World*. He was now launched on a career of national prominence which included the editorship of the *Christian Advocate and Journal* (1832–34); the successful steering of Dickinson College through the opening years of its Methodist history (1834–45); pastorates and presiding eldership in Philadelphia (1845–50); and finally his most distinguished service to American Methodism, secretaryship of the Missionary Society (1850–72). A trip abroad in 1842 resulted in *Observations in Europe* (1844) and *Observations in the East* (1845), well-written books that went through numerous editions.

It was said of him that he lived two lives each so eminent that his fame in the one dimmed that of the other. In spite of physical limitations, for he was small of stature, unprepossessing in appearance, with a voice inclined to be thin and high-pitched, he early came to be regarded as one of the greatest preachers of his day. At his death, however, he was remembered chiefly for his wisdom and generalship in the councils of the church, and for his administrative genius. He was a member of seven General Conferences, covering twenty-eight years. At the first of these, 1844, in the case of Bishop Andrew [*q.v.*], which led to the disruption of the church, he made a long-remembered stand against the Southern delegation, supporting the resolution advising the Bishop to desist from the exercise of his office while connected with slaveholding; yet he was not a radical abolitionist, for he opposed the expulsion of slaveholders from the church (see his article in *Christian Advocate,* New York, July 26, 1855) and indorsed the Colonization Society (see *Addresses Delivered in the Hall of the House of Representatives, Harrisburg, Pa.,* 1852). He was also an early advocate of theological schools and lay representation. His administration of the Missionary Society was one of the great epochs in its expansion. His death from cerebral hemorrhage occurred in New York, and he is buried in Laurel Hill Cemetery, Philadelphia.

[John A. Roche, article in *Meth. Review,* May 1887, and *Life of John Price Durbin* (1889); Abel Stevens, editorial in *Nat. Mag.,* Feb. 1855, and *Hist. of M. E. Church,* vol. IV (1867); *Minutes of Phila. Conference* (1877); *Christian Advocate* (N. Y.), Oct. 26, 1876; *Harper's Weekly,* Nov. 11, 1876; *N. Y. Times* and *N. Y. Tribune,* Oct. 20, 1876, are authority for date of death given above.] H. E. S.

DURELL, EDWARD HENRY (July 14, 1810–Mar. 29, 1887), jurist, traced his descent from Norman Huguenot ancestors whose domicile was in the Channel Islands. His father, Daniel Meserve Durell, a prominent New Hampshire lawyer and chief justice of the court of common pleas, married on June 1, 1800, Elizabeth Wentworth, a descendant of Elder William Wentworth, and Edward Durell was their third son. Born in the "Governor Wentworth house" at Portsmouth, N. H., he attended Phillips Exeter Academy and proceeded in 1827 to Harvard College. Graduating in 1831, he read law in his father's office at Dover, N. H., and was admitted to the bar in 1834. For a short time thereafter he practised law at Pittsburg (Grenada), Miss., but finally settled at New Orleans, Mar. 27, 1837. Combining a sound knowledge of law and a rare gift of incisive speech, he quickly acquired a prominent position at the local bar and influenced the adoption of much-needed reforms in domestic legislation. His outstanding achievement in this line was the statute whereby the Louisiana law that on the death of a father, mother, husband, or wife, the children immediately obtained possession of one-half of the acquits and gains of the matrimonial partnership, was changed so as to give the surviving parent, etc., the usufruct of such half. Elected a member of the New Orleans common council in 1854, he drafted the city charter which became law in 1856. He was a pronounced Unionist, strenuously opposed the ordinance of secession, and on its adoption in 1860 retired for a time from public life. However, when the Federal troops took possession of New Orleans in 1862, at the request of the military governor he drafted the bureau system of municipal government which was then inaugurated, and he was appointed president of the bureau of finance. In 1863 he became mayor of the city by military appointment and the same year was appointed by President Lincoln United States judge of the eastern district of Louisiana, his jurisdiction being extended in 1866 to cover the entire state. He was president of the State Constitutional Convention of 1864, being in that year also a delegate to the Republican National Convention at Baltimore. In 1867 he was instrumental in procuring the abandonment of the confiscation policy as far as it applied to Louisiana. While at Washington on this mission he was offered by Seward and declined the post of minister to Austria as he had two years previously similarly declined an appointment to the Supreme Court of the United States tendered to him by Lincoln. He contemplated retiring from the bench in 1871, but a "respectful remonstrance" of the Louisiana bar, wherein he was referred to as "a tried, faithful, able, learned and incorruptible judge," induced him to reconsider his decision. He had, throughout the embittered reconstruction conflict, avoided open participation or partisanship up to 1872, but the incidents of the state election of that year procured for him an unenviable notoriety. Following the voting a serious situation had arisen owing to the fact that three distinct election boards claimed the right to canvass the returns. Since it appeared that the Governor's board, which in a sense represented the Democratic interests, had completed its canvass and would function prior to its opponents, Durell, out of court at his house on Dec. 5, at nine o'clock at night, issued an unsealed order to the United States marshal to take possession of the statehouse and to give entrance only to certain authorized persons. This "midnight order" was, with the aid of Federal troops, immediately carried into effect. On the following day in court Durell declared the Democratic board illegal and ordered the returns delivered to the "legal" board, thus enabling the Republicans to obtain control of the legislature and state government. To what extent, if any, he acted with the connivance or tacit approval of the Federal administration is not known, but the matter was taken up in Congress, and the proceedings were investigated by the Senate Committee on Privileges and Elections, whose reports condemned his action unreservedly, characterizing the interference of a Federal judge in a state election as "without parallel in judicial proceedings" (see *House Executive Document No. 91,* 42 Cong., 3 Sess.; *Senate Report No. 457,* 42 Cong., 3 Sess.). A move to institute impeachment proceedings against him was terminated by his resignation in 1874 (*Congressional Record,* 43 Cong., 2 Sess., 319–24). Taking up his residence at Newburgh, N. Y., he married, June 8, 1875, Mary Seitz Gebhart of Schoharie, N. Y., to which latter place he subsequently removed and lived until his death. His later years were passed in literary pursuits, including the preparation of a "History of Seventeen Years; from 1860 to the Retiring of the Federal Army from Louisiana and South Carolina," which he did not complete.

[An extended review of his career appeared in the *Granite Monthly,* April 1888. See also J. R. Ficklen, *Hist. of Reconstruction in La.* (1910); E. Lonn, *Reconstruction in La. after 1868* (1918); *Am. Annual Cyc. and Register,* 1872 and 1873, and obituary notice in *Albany Evening Jour.,* Mar. 30, 1887.] H. W. H. K.

DURFEE, JOB (Sept. 20, 1790–July 26, 1847), jurist, author, descended from Thomas Durfee who came to New England in 1660 and settled at Portsmouth, R. I., was born in Tiverton in that state. His parents were Thomas Durfee of Tiverton, at one time chief justice of the court of common pleas of Newport County, and his wife Mary, daughter of Richard Lowden of Newport. His primary education was received at home and in the public schools at Tiverton and Bristol. Entering Brown University in 1809, he graduated with high honors in 1813. He then commenced the study of law with his father, at the same time becoming actively interested in state politics. As a Republican (Jeffersonian), he was elected to represent Tiverton in the General Assembly in the spring of 1816, while yet a law student, and retained the seat for four years, being called to the bar at Newport on Mar. 4, 1817. In 1820 he was elected a member of the federal House of Representatives and remained in Congress till 1825. In 1826 he was again returned to the state legislature, and the following year was speaker of the House, which position he retained till 1829. In 1832 he published *Whatcheer: or Roger Williams in Banishment,* a long poem, which, though favorably noticed in England, did not attract any considerable attention at home. In 1833 he was elected an associate justice of the supreme court of Rhode Island, and two years later, became chief justice, holding the office till his death in 1847. As chief justice he was distinguished for his dignity and courtesy of manner, and though not a great lawyer, his strong common sense, industry, and absolute impartiality commanded the confidence of the bar and the public. His firm stand during the stormy period of the Dorr Rebellion, his early declaration that the movement was illegal, without law and against law, and his subsequent charge to the grand jury on the subject of treason, had great influence in crystallizing public opinion. When open insurrection broke out, he offered his services with the military forces of the state. He was a delegate to the convention called by the legislature to frame a new constitution, and a powerful factor in the solution of its problems. He presided at the trial of Dorr. Inclined to corpulence, he was "physically indolent almost to a proverb" (Thomas Durfee, *post*). Simple and unpretending in manners and conduct, he was taciturn in social circles, for which he had no taste and in which he did not shine. His wife was Judith, daughter of Simeon Borden.

He was the author of *The Panidèa, or An Omnipresent Reason Considered as the Creative and Sustaining Logos by Theoptes* (1846), a somewhat pretentious philosophical work which nobody read. In addition he contributed addresses to various societies on: *Aboriginal History* (1838), *The Idea of the Supernatural among the Indians* (1839), *The Influence of Scientific Discovery and Invention on Social and Political Progress* (1843), *The Progress of Ideas* (1843), and *The Rhode Island Idea of Government* (1846). After his death, *The Complete Works of the Hon. Job Durfee, LL.D., Late Chief Justice of Rhode Island* (1849), edited by his son Thomas [*q.v.*], was published under the auspices of the Rhode Island Historical Society.

[Details of Durfee's ancestry are contained in W. F. Reed, *The Descendants of Thos. Durfee of Portsmouth, R. I.* (2 vols., 1902–05). The chief authority for his life and career is the Memoir by Thos. Durfee, prefixed to the complete edition of his works. See also R. G. Hazard, *A Discourse . . . on the Character and Writings of C. J. Durfee* (1848); Conrad Reno, *Memoirs of the Judiciary and Bar of New England for the 19th Century,* vol. II (1901), pt. 2, p. 2, and *Memorial Biogs. of the New-England Historic Geneal. Soc.,* vol. I (1880), p. 37.] H. W. H. K.

DURFEE, THOMAS (Feb. 6, 1826–June 6, 1901), jurist, was the elder son of Chief Justice Job Durfee [*q.v.*] and Judith (Borden) Durfee. He was born at Tiverton, R. I., and obtained his early education at home. In 1842, having previously received two years' private tuition at East Greenwich, R. I., he entered Brown University, where he graduated in 1846. He then studied law at Tiverton and later at Providence where he was admitted to the Rhode Island bar in 1848. Commencing practise at Providence, he was in 1849 appointed reporter to the supreme court and in that capacity compiled and published *Reports of Cases Argued and Determined in the Supreme Court of Rhode Island,* vol. II (1854). He resigned in 1854 when he was elected by the General Assembly a member of the court of magistrates for the City of Providence. This position he retained by successive reëlections for six years, being presiding magistrate during his last five terms. In 1857 he completed and published *A Treatise on the Law of Highways,* which had been partially written by J. K. Angell [*q.v.*] prior to his death. For many years this remained the standard work on the subject. He retired from the magistracy in 1860 in order to devote himself to private practise, and on the outbreak of the Civil War came to the fore as a strong supporter of the war measures of the administration. In 1863 he was induced to return to public life, entering the General Assembly as representative for Providence. Although he had had no legislative experience he was elected speaker, continuing to act as such till the expiration of his term. In 1864 he headed the Rhode Island delegation to the Republican National Convention at Cincinnati, when Lincoln was nominated for a second term. In 1865 he was elected to the state Senate, but in June of the same year was chosen an associate justice of the supreme court of Rhode Island. He became chief justice on Jan. 28, 1875, and continued to occupy that position till his retirement, Mar. 4, 1891, having completed over twenty-five years of judicial service. An accomplished lawyer, he was, as a judge, inclined to be conservative, and his opinions, never brilliant but eminently sane, commanded respect in professional circles beyond the confines of his state.

Though in 1897 he acted as chairman of the commission to revise the state constitution, he passed the remainder of his life in comparative retirement, dying at Providence in his seventy-sixth year. His wife, whom he married on Oct. 29, 1857, was Sarah, daughter of John Slater.

Durfee's active interests were not confined to the law. He was throughout his life a devoted supporter of Brown University, and rendered notable service to that institution, of which he was successively trustee, chancellor, and fellow. In his leisure he was constantly drawn to literary work of a varied nature, in all of which he displayed fine qualities of scholarship. At the request of the Rhode Island Historical Society he edited, *The Complete Works of the Hon. Job Durfee, LL.D., Late Chief Justice of Rhode Island* (1849), prefixing a memoir of the latter's life. He was the author of *The Village Picnic and Other Poems* (1872), *Gleanings from the Judicial History of Rhode Island* (1883), and a number of occasional addresses on historical subjects which were published in pamphlet form.

[W. F. Reed, *The Descendants of Thos. Durfee of Portsmouth, R. I.,* II (1905), 282; Conrad Reno, *Memoirs of the Judiciary and the Bar of New England,* vol. II (1901); *Representative Men and Old Families of Rhode Island* (1908), p. 1289; *Hist. Cat. Brown Univ., 1764–1914* (1915).] H. W. H. K.

DURFEE, WILLIAM FRANKLIN (Nov. 15, 1833–Nov. 14, 1899), engineer and inventor, was born in New Bedford, Mass., the son of William and Alice Sherman (Talbot) Durfee. His father, a carpenter by trade, acquired a wide reputation for his ability in erecting buildings of large dimensions. A steel furnace, erected for Anderson & Woods in Pittsburgh, in 1868, was one of his achievements. The son, William, received a practical mechanical training under the tutelage of his father and then took a course of special study in the Lawrence Scientific School at Harvard. At the age of twenty he established himself as an engineer and architect in New Bedford, and soon received an appointment as city surveyor. In 1861 he served in the state legislature. As secretary of the military committee, he was active in forwarding legislation for the equipment of troops at the beginning of the Civil War. While holding this office he introduced a resolution requesting Congress to repeal "all laws which deprive any class of loyal subjects of the Government from bearing arms for the common defense" (Reed, *post,* pp. 206 f.). This is said to have been the first definite proposal for the arming of colored troops. In 1862, at the invitation of his cousin, Z. S. Durfee [*q.v.*] and the latter's partner, Capt. E. B. Ward, he went to the Lake Superior district to undertake to test the suitability of certain ores of that district for the manufacture of steel by the process invented by William Kelly [*q.v.*], and almost identical with the Bessemer process. He designed the machinery and apparatus necessary to test the merits of the Kelly process on a large scale, and superintended the construction of a plant at Wyandotte, Mich., ten miles from Detroit, which was opened in the fall of 1864. Here, in September of that year, he supervised the making of the first Bessemer steel produced in America. From this steel, on May 25, 1865, the first American steel rails were rolled. Durfee also established in connection with the plant at Wyandotte a steelworks analytical laboratory, the first ever built in the United States. This achievement alone would have made him a memorable figure in American industrial progress.

Upon leaving the Wyandotte works, he built the Bayview Merchant Mill at Milwaukee. Later he became connected with the Wheeler & Wilson Company at Bridgeport, building for them at Ansonia, Conn., the first furnace for refining copper by the use of gaseous fuel ever constructed in the United States. While he was at Bridgeport he became general manager of a company that controlled patents for the production of castings in wrought iron, and he helped to develop a machine for the production of horseshoe nails. He had a gift for machinery design which he could readily turn to practical advantage, and he found a place for it continually in the various later connections of his life, such as the Pennsylvania Drill Company at Birdsboro, Pa., and the C. W. Hunt Company on Staten Island for which he acted as shop superintendent.

Although an intensely practical man in the industrial world, Durfee was of a studious, scholarly disposition. He had an almost encyclopedic knowledge of the history and past achievements of engineering and combined a talent for research work with his more practical ability. This rare combination of talents made him valuable, in later life, as an expert witness at court in patent cases. Technical papers which he found time to write were published in the proceedings and publications of the societies to which he belonged, such as the Iron & Steel Institute, the Franklin Institute of Philadelphia, and the American Society of Mechanical Engineers. To this latter organization he bequeathed his extensive library, rich in mechanical antiquities collected throughout a lifetime, and it may now be found as a part of the Engineering Societies Library in New York City. He was married in 1880 to Annie Swift of Boston.

[*Jour. Iron and Steel Inst.*, vol. LVI (1899), pt. 2, p. 292; *Trans. Am. Inst. Mining Engineers*, vol. XXX (1901); *Trans. Am. Soc. Mech. Engineers*, XXI (1900), 1161; *Railroad Gazette*, XXXI, 799, 818; and W. F. Reed, *Descendants of Thomas Durfee* (2 vols., 1902–05), I, 528, II, 206.] E. Y.

DURFEE, ZOHETH SHERMAN (Apr. 22, 1831–June 8, 1880), inventor and manufacturer, was born at New Bedford, Mass. His parents, Thomas and Delight (Sherman) Durfee, were members of the Free Will Baptist Church and had resided in Fall River, Mass., before moving to New Bedford in the early part of 1831. He was educated at Friends' Academy, New Bedford. In early youth he learned the blacksmith's trade and later was associated with his father and uncle in that business. Becoming interested in the process of manufacturing steel directly from pig iron, the invention of Joseph Dixon [*q.v.*], Durfee, sponsored by New Bedford capitalists, undertook investigations of the various processes for the manufacturing of iron and steel which led him to believe that William Kelly [*q.v.*] of Eddyville, Ky., was the real inventor of the "Bessemer process" instead of Henry Bessemer of England who had claimed the invention. On the basis of this belief, Durfee, in partnership with Capt. E. B. Ward of Detroit, Mich., obtained control of Kelly's patents in 1861. The same year he went to Europe to study the Bessemer process and to purchase, if possible, Bessemer's rights in the United States. He failed to accomplish the latter object, and on his return home organized a company to protect the use of the Kelly patents. Ward and Durfee, in 1862, invited William F. Durfee [*q.v.*], a cousin of Z. S. Durfee, to assist in erecting an experimental plant at Wyandotte, Wayne County, Mich., for the manufacturing of pneumatic steel; and in May 1863 they and their partners organized the Kelly Pneumatic Process Company, Kelly retaining an interest in any profits the company might make.

During his first visit to England (1861), Durfee had become familiar with the invention of Robert Mushet for using spiegeleisen as a recarburizing agent (patent granted in England, 1856; United States, 1857) and was convinced that it was essential to the "successful conduct of the Kelly and Bessemer processes." In 1863 he was sent to England to secure control of Mushet's patent in the United States, and procured an assignment on Oct. 24, 1864. While Durfee was in England, the experimental works at Wyandotte made its first blow, in September 1864, under the supervision of William F. Durfee—the first Bessemer steel made in the United States. In 1865 a plant at Troy, N. Y., built by Alexander L. Holley [*q.v.*], began to manufacture steel under Bessemer's patents, and the following year the two interests were combined in the Pneumatic Steel Association, a joint stock company organized under the laws of the State of New York, in which was vested the ownership of the patents of both Kelly and Bessemer. Of this company Durfee was made secretary and treasurer, and he held the office until his death in 1880. He is said to have been, also, for a time "previous to 1868, superintendent of the steel works of Winslow & Griswold" located at Troy, N. Y. Throughout his life he was interested in the manufacture of steel. He originated the idea of using the cupola instead of a reverberatory furnace for melting the pig iron for the converter charge, a practise which has become universal. He guarded Kelly's business interests and did more, perhaps, than any other person to get the rights of Kelly recognized in the United States. He was always held in the highest esteem by Kelly. He obtained numerous patents for steel manufacture and iron and steel products, sixteen of which are recorded in *The Official Gazette of the United States Patent Office* between 1862 and 1876. His work was prematurely ended in his fiftieth year, when he died of paralysis at the Butler Hospital, Providence, R. I.

[*Report of the Commissioner of Patents*, 1871; *Official Gazette of the U. S. Patent Office*, vols. I, II (1872), V, VI (1874), VII, VIII (1875), IX, X (1876); J. M. Swank, *Hist. of the Manufacture of Iron in all Ages* (2nd ed., 1892); J. N. Boucher, *Wm. Kelly: A True Hist. of the Bessemer Process* (1924); W. F. Reed, *The Descendants of Thos. Durfee of Portsmouth, R. I.*, vol. I (1902), which is the authority for date of Durfee's birth; Records of Deaths in the City of Providence, R. I., Book 15, p. 30, which gives his age at death as 48 years, 1 mo., and 16 days; information from J. G. Kelly of Braddock, Pa., a son of Wm. Kelly.]

C. M. J.

DURHAM, CALEB WHEELER (Feb. 6, 1848–Mar. 28, 1910), engineer, inventor, was born at Tunkhannock, Pa., the son of Alpha Durham and his third wife, Elizabeth B. Riggs. His father was a Presbyterian minister who, two years after Caleb's birth, went alone to California to seek his fortune in the gold rush, was unsuccessful, and returned in 1852. He contracted fever at Panama on the way and died shortly thereafter in New York City. Subsequently Mrs. Durham moved with her children to Reading, Pa., where Caleb received his early education. The Civil War interrupted his high-school work and he enlisted as a private, first, in Company C, 42nd Pennsylvania Militia, serving in the reserves at Gettysburg, and, second, in Company B, 195th Pennsylvania Volunteers, seeing active service in Maryland and Virginia. Discharged at the expiration of his two years' enlistment in 1864, he went home and entered the employ of the Philadelphia & Reading Railroad Company. In 1866, with the intention of preparing for college, he attended Williston Academy, Easthampton, Mass., and in 1867 entered the University of Michigan at Ann Arbor, to study civil engineering. Two years later he became engaged to marry, gave up his college work, and entered the engineering department of the New York Central Railroad. From 1869 to 1873 he continued in railroad work for several companies in the Middle West and Southwest, but after his marriage, on May 28, 1873, to Clarissa Safford Welles of Ann Arbor, he established himself in Chicago as a civil engineer specializing in sanitation. About 1875 he devised an improved hot-air heater and undertook its manufacture and sale. It proved too costly, however, for general use, and the business was abandoned. Durham meanwhile had turned his attention to house drainage and after much experimentation invented in 1880 what is still known as the Durham System. This consists in the use of a wrought-iron or steel screw-jointed pipe, the specially threaded fittings being designed in such a way as to provide the inclinations necessary in house drainage as well as tight joints and a smooth inner channel. The whole installation, too, is sufficiently rigid to be self-supporting. After obtaining patents, Durham organized the Durham House Drainage Company and carried on business in Chicago for several years. One of his largest contracts at this time was the entire house drainage system for the new city of Pullman, Ill. In 1883 he moved with his family to New York, reorganized his company, and carried on the business there for the remainder of his life. Among the most important installations of his system were those in Carnegie Hall and the Hotel Majestic in New York and the National Capitol at Washington. The last fifteen years of his life were fraught with difficulties induced both by the panic of 1893 and by the failure of the courts to sustain his original patent against various infringers. He was a member of the Civil Engineers' Club of the Northwest, Chicago, and the Engineers' Club, New York. He died at his home in Peekskill, N. Y., survived by four sons.

[*Engineering News*, Apr. 7, 1910; *Univ. of Mich. Cat. of Grads.*, etc. (1923); Alumni records, Univ. of Mich.; Patent Office records; family records and correspondence.]

C. W. M.

DURIVAGE, FRANCIS ALEXANDER (1814–Feb. 1, 1881), author, journalist, and playwright, was through a long period of years a voluminous contributor of poems, humorous articles, short stories, sketches, and miscellaneous material to many newspapers and magazines. The son of Francis and Lucy (Everett) Durivage and a nephew of Edward Everett [*q.v.*], he was born in Boston, but passed a considerable portion of his life in New York and Paris, in which latter city he served as a foreign correspondent of American newspapers. While there he became interested in the Delsarte system of stage procedure and calisthenics, and meeting Steele MacKaye [*q.v.*], who was then conducting a class at Delsarte's house, joined forces with him in disseminating Delsarte's doctrines. When Durivage returned to America he became an active member of a little group of Delsartean enthusiasts who helped to spread the gospel of their master. He signed an article on Delsarte in the *Atlantic Monthly* for May 1871 which he wrote in collaboration with MacKaye. Durivage was the author of several plays, none of which was successful, not even *Monaldi*, another of his collaborations with MacKaye. It was produced at the St. James Theatre in New York on Jan. 8, 1872, with MacKaye himself acting the principal character, its chief object being to exemplify the practical stage theories of the Delsarte system. His literary work was varied and versatile, but without any enduring quality. At one time he was a co-editor of *Ballou's Pictorial.* Among his books were a translation of *Lamartine's History of the Revolution of 1848* (1849), and in collaboration with George P. Burnham, *Stray Subjects Arrested and Bound Over, being the Fugitive Offspring of the Old Un and the Young Un that have been Lying Around Loose, and are now tied up for Fast Keeping* (1848). He also compiled a *Popular Cyclopedia of History* (1845) and *Life Scenes from the World Around Us* (1853). He is referred to by William Winter as one of those of his "early friends in the literary vocation among whom the custom of perfectly candid criticism prevailed." He was a man of many friendships and activities, but the memorials of his personality and the records of his work are widely scattered through many obscure and well-nigh forgotten sources. Durivage was married to Almira Alderworth. His death was due to paralysis.

[Percy MacKaye, *Epoch, the Life of Steele MacKaye* (1927); Wm. Winter, *Old Friends* (1909); O. F. Adams, *Dict. of Am. Authors* (1901); W. R. Alger, *Life of Edwin Forrest* (1877); T. A. Brown, *Hist. of the N. Y. Stage*, vol. III (1903); *New-Eng. Hist. and Geneal. Reg.*, July 1860, p. 219; *N. Y. Herald*, Feb. 3, 4, 1881.] E. F. E.

DURKEE, JOHN (Dec. 11, 1728–May 29, 1782), Revolutionary soldier, colonizer, was born at Windham, Conn., the son of William Durkee and Susannah Sabin. Not long after attaining his majority, he removed to Norwich, making his home on Bean Hill. At various times he was an innkeeper, a justice of the peace, and a member of the General Assembly. On Jan. 3, 1753, he married Martha Wood of Norwich. He served during the French and Indian War, rising from the rank of second lieutenant to that of major of militia. At the time of the Stamp Act he became an ardent Son of Liberty. Heading a body of several hundred armed men, he dramatically forced the Connecticut stamp agent, Jared Ingersoll, to resign at Wethersfield, Sept. 19, 1765; and at a meeting of the Sons of Liberty at Hartford, Mar. 25, 1766, was appointed, together with Israel Putnam, member of a committee to arrange a system of correspondence between the Connecticut Sons of Liberty and those of other colonies. At a town meeting in Norwich in December 1767, he was chosen member of a committee which recommended that in conformity with the example of Boston the inhabitants refrain from the importation of certain articles of British manufacture.

In the spring of 1769, under the auspices of the Susquehanna Company, in which he had acquired an interest, he conducted from Norwich a band of over one hundred emigrants to Wyoming Valley and laid out a settlement surrounded by a stockade which was called Fort Durkee. Later he named the settlement Wilkes-Barré in honor of John Wilkes and Col. Isaac Barré, steadfast champions of colonial rights. He was for a time president of the governing committee. In 1769 and again in 1770 he was captured and taken prisoner to Philadelphia by agents of the proprietary government of Pennsylvania, which claimed the Wyoming Valley as against Connecticut. In 1772 he returned to Norwich but was back again in Wyoming for certain periods in 1773 and 1774, at which date his connection with the settlement ceased.

Word having reached Norwich that the British forces had attacked the people of Boston, he set out on Sept. 4, 1774, with four hundred and sixty-four men, armed and mounted, but returned on learning that the rumor was false. In May 1775, he helped to raise in Norwich a company of one hundred men, including his two sons, which was mustered into the 3rd Connecticut Regiment commanded by Israel Putnam. Despite a frail constitution, he saw extensive service during the war, being present at the battle of Bunker Hill, and in the campaigns conducted by Washington in the middle colonies. His right hand was rendered useless by a wound received at the battle of Monmouth. He served successively as major and lieutenant-colonel of the 3rd Connecticut Regiment; as lieutenant-colonel and colonel of the 20th Regiment, Continental Foot; as colonel of the 4th and 1st Connecticut Line. He died at Norwich "from exhaustion induced by the service" (H. P. Johnston, *Record of Service of Connecticut Men during the Revolution*, p. 315). Fearlessness and decision were his salient characteristics as attested by his popular designation as the "bold man of Bean Hill."

[Besides the work noted above, the chief sources are: F. M. Gaulkins, *Hist. of Norwich* (1866); E. D. Larned, *Hist. of Windham County, Conn.* (2 vols., 1874–80); O. J. Harvey, *Hist. of Wilkes-Barre* (2 vols., 1909); A. A. Browning, "A Forgotten Son of Liberty," in *New London County Hist. Soc. Recs.*, vol. III, pt. II (1912).] E. E. C.

DURRETT, REUBEN THOMAS (Jan. 22, 1824–Sept. 16, 1913), lawyer, historian, was descended from the French family, Duret, which was induced by the excesses of St. Bartholomew's to transfer its domicile to England and there altered the spelling and modified the pronunciation of the name (*Library of Southern Literature*, IV, 1457). From England a branch of the family migrated to Spottsylvania County, Va., and thence their descendants went to Henry County, Ky. Reuben Thomas, son of William and Elizabeth (Rawlings) Durrett, grew up on his father's farm, spent two years, 1844–46, at Georgetown College, Ky., and in 1849 acquired the degree of A.B. from Brown University. The following year, spent in the law school of the University of Louisville, brought him a degree and a sufficient knowledge of law to serve as the basis of a successful, though not uninterrupted, practise for thirty years. In 1852 he was married to Elizabeth H. Bates of Cincinnati; the following year he served as a member of the city council of Louisville; from 1857 to 1859 he was editor and half-owner of the Louisville *Courier,* exchanging expletives and pistol-shots with the redoubtable George D. Prentice, editor of the rival *Journal*; and in 1861 he spent a few weeks in military prison because of his outspoken approval of secession. In these formative years he found time to acquire a reputation as a writer of blank verse and a wider reputation as an orator.

Many of these things, however, appear in perspective as merely the excesses of youth. Durrett's greatest usefulness came after he gave up his practise in 1880. An extensive law business combined with fortunate investments in natural gas had by this time brought him a large fortune, so that thereafter he was able to give liberal indulgence to his tastes. Always a book lover, he now turned his energies to building up his library with the ambition of securing a copy of every book written by a Kentuckian or about Kentucky. His ambition gradually widened to include the entire Ohio Valley with the result that by the time of his death he had acquired what was probably the most valuable private library in the West. Counting some fifty thousand volumes, chiefly on western history, with unique collections of manuscripts and files of old newspapers, the Durrett library became a Mecca for workers in the field of western history. Durrett's reputation was chiefly made by his library but did not altogether depend on it. Utilizing the material he had himself collected, he began to write history, his first work appearing in the *Southern Bivouac* and his later works as publications of the Filson Club which he founded in 1884 and of which he was president until his death. His best-known books are, *John Filson, the First Historian of Kentucky* (1884) and *Traditions of the Earliest Visits of Foreigners to North America* (1908). He was painstaking in his writing and based his historical work on careful research. But his importance lay less in his own writings than in the encouragement he gave to others. For thirty years he was a Mæcenas to all history workers in the West. His library was always open to the student, and his influence on historical work in Kentucky can hardly be overestimated. His interest in books was evidenced not only by his own collection but also by the fact that he established the Louisville Public Library and for many years directed its growth.

In July 1912 Durrett suffered a stroke of paralysis from which he never recovered. He lived for a year unable to talk and with the right side of his face paralyzed. Upon his death in 1913, his library, which he had offered to give to the city of Louisville provided it would build a fireproof building for the storing of it, was sold to the University of Chicago and was removed thither.

[Sketches more or less extensive are in the *Lib. of South. Literature,* vol. IV (1907); *Louisville Evening Post,* Sept. 16, 1913; Louisville *Courier-Journal,* Sept. 17, 1913; *Who's Who in America,* 1912–13; and in M. Joblin & Co., *Louisville, Past and Present* (1875), pp. 254–68. The last named is very full in regard to Durrett's legal qualifications and also gives specimens of his poetry and oratory. The best account of his library is E. A. Henry, "The Durrett Collection, now in the Lib. of the Univ. of Chicago," in *Bibliographical Soc. of America Papers,* VIII (1914), 57.] R. S. C.

DURRIE, DANIEL STEELE (Jan. 2, 1819–Aug. 31, 1892), librarian, was born at Albany, N. Y., the son of Horace and Johannah (Steele) Durrie. He was a descendant of John Steele, first secretary of Connecticut Colony, and William Bradford, first governor of Plymouth Colony. His father died when Durrie was a boy of seven. His formal education was received in a select school at South Hadley, Mass., and at the Albany Academy. As a young man he entered the store of a maternal uncle at Albany and learned the bookselling trade, succeeding to the business in 1844. At Albany, on Oct. 15 of that year, he was married to Ann Holt; to them were born six children. Durrie's business and all his other property were swept away in the great Albany fire of 1848. Unable to resume business, he removed in 1850 to Madison, Wis., in which place he resided thenceforward. At Madison, then a small western town with a population of about 2,000, he resumed for a few years the occupation of a bookseller.

Durrie early made the acquaintance of Lyman C. Draper [*q.v.*], the virtual founder and for over thirty years, from 1854 to 1886, the secretary of the State Historical Society of Wisconsin. Draper interested Durrie in this pioneer work and, in 1856, the latter was elected librarian, a position which he held until his death. With small resources and against great obstacles, these two men devoted the remainder of their lives to the upbuilding of an organization which, finally adopted by the state, became ultimately one of Wisconsin's most highly valued institutions. While primarily occupied with the development and active management of its library, Durrie was interested as well in the other activities of the State Historical Society. He found time to prepare many papers dealing with Wisconsin and Midwestern history. His largest work was *A History of Madison, the Capital of Wisconsin, Including the Four Lake Country,* published in 1874. In the field of genealogy, his most important work was his very useful *Bibliographia Genealogica Americana; an Alphabetical Index to American Genealogies and Pedigrees, Contained in State, County, and Town Histories, Printed Genealogies, and Kindred Works,* the long title suggesting its exhaustiveness. This pioneer bibliographical tool in its field, first published in 1868, passed through several revised and enlarged editions. He also published a genealogy of his mother's family under the title, *Steele Family: A Genealogical History of John and George Steele and Their Descendants* (1857). In manner Durrie was somewhat reserved and retiring, yet he was interested in public matters and always anxious to be of service. In 1858 and 1859, while Draper was superintendent of public instruction of Wisconsin, Durrie was his assistant. Throughout his life he was a devoted and active member of the Presbyterian church. His greatest service was, in collaboration with Draper, the building up, in the pioneer period of a Midwestern state, of a great collection of its fundamental historical material, and in developing in a new commonwealth a vital consciousness of its history.

[J. D. Butler, "Daniel Steele Durrie," in *Proc. State Hist. Soc. of Wis., 1892* (1893), pp. 73–81; obituary notices in *Madison Democrat, Madison Times,* and *Wisconsin State Journal,* Sept. 1, 1892.] W. M. S.

DURYEA, HARMANUS BARKULO (Dec. 13, 1863–Jan. 25, 1916), sportsman, was born in Brooklyn, N. Y., the son of Harmanus Barkulo and Mary (Peters) Duryea. He was a descendant in the sixth generation of Joost Durie, who emigrated with his wife from Mannheim, in the Rhine Palatinate, about 1675 and settled first at New Utrecht and later at Bushwick, Long Island, N. Y. His father was a lawyer, corporation counsel of Brooklyn, member of the Board of Education, Republican assemblyman from Kings County, and major-general in the New York National Guard. The younger Duryea was married in April 1895, in St. George's Chapel, London, to Ellen Winchester, widow of William Weld of Boston, who survived him. He never engaged in business but, enjoying an ample fortune, gave his whole life to sport. As a young man he was interested chiefly in yachting; in later years he devoted almost his entire time to the breeding and management of race horses. In both fields he achieved genuine distinction due not merely to his money but to his personal qualities.

In his youth, during summers spent on the family estate near Red Bank, N. J., he acquired the rudiments of his yachtsmanship in races on the Shrewsbury River. With W. Butler Duncan he originated one-design boat races in the United States, using twenty-one footers built by the Herreshoffs. He also raced several forty-foot yachts. In 1891 he was elected to the New York Yacht Club. For two seasons (1895–96) he sailed a "two and a half rater" at Cowes in some fifty races each season and made the best record for those seasons in his class. For a number of seasons he also had the best record at Newport, R. I. He and Harry Payne Whitney built the seventy-foot sloop *Yankee,* which won many races with Duryea as her pilot. In 1895 the Earl of Dunraven selected Duryea to represent him in the *America's* Cup races of that year. As an amateur pilot he was highly esteemed. During these years he usually passed the winters in shooting on his estate at Hickory Valley, Tenn. He was a president of the United States Field Trial Club and for several years was the leading winner in field trials. Much of his work with horses was done in partnership with Harry Payne Whitney, who for some time after the death of his father, William C. Whitney, ran his horses under the Duryea colors. Duryea and Harry Payne Whitney owned Irish Lad, who won the Brooklyn Handicap in 1903 and the Metropolitan Handicap a year later. When Gov. Charles Evans Hughes of New York secured the enactment of his anti-betting measures, Duryea, seeing no future for racing in the United States, in 1910 took his horses to France. He maintained a breeding farm in Normandy and a racing stable at Chantilly. He won a number of important English and French races, notably the 10,000 Guinea Race in England with Sweeper II in 1912 and in 1914 the Derby, the Biennial of 25,000 francs, and the Prix Noarelles of 30,000 francs—all with his most famous horse, Durbar II. During the racing season it was Duryea's habit to be with his horses every morning soon after daylight and personally direct their training and care. A week before the 1914 Derby, Durbar II was sent by special train to Calais and was met at Dover by another special that made the run to Epsom in record time. All the water and forage for the stay in England were taken along. Duryea went over the Epsom course with his jockey, McGee, giving him detailed instructions for the race. In all he won about $250,000 on this race, which was his last. Early in the autumn, in London, he suffered a severe attack of the grippe; in November he returned to his Tennessee estate, where he grew steadily worse. He died at Saranac Lake, N. Y., and was buried in the family mausoleum at Santa Barbara, Cal.

[Letter to author from Benjamin R. Kittredge, Esq., of Carmel, N. Y., and Strawberry, S. C., Sept. 8, 1928; obituaries in the *N. Y. Times*, *N. Y. Herald*, and *N. Y. Tribune*, Jan. 26, 1916; T. G. Bergen, "Contribs. to the Hist. of the Early Settlers of Kings County, N. Y.," in *N. Y. Geneal. and Biog. Record,* XI (1880), 62–70; editorial in *N. Y. Herald-Tribune,* July 12, 1926.] G. H. G.

DURYÉE, ABRAM (Apr. 29, 1815–Sept. 27, 1890), merchant, soldier, was of warlike Huguenot ancestry, his grandfather, Abraham Durea, having fought in the Revolution, his father and two uncles in the War of 1812. Born in New York City, the son of Jacob and Eliza Duryée, he was educated at the Crosby Street school and the grammar school of Columbia College. Choosing a mercantile career, he made a fortune in mahogany. At the age of eighteen he enlisted in the 142nd Regiment of militia; the next year he was appointed sergeant, and two years thereafter, sergeant-major. In 1838 he married Caroline E. Allen who bore him a son and three daughters. That same year he enlisted in the 27th—later the 7th—Regiment. Soon promoted sergeant, his rise was rapid: captain in 1843, major in September 1845, lieutenant-colonel in November, colonel in 1849. After ten years' devoted service he resigned in 1859 and resisted all efforts to make him reconsider. He was twice wounded while in command of his regiment during the Astor Place riots of 1849, and helped suppress other insurrections. In April 1861 he raised a regiment of volunteers which became the 5th New York, or Duryée's Zouaves. This regiment saw service at Big Bethel, June 10. Shortly afterward Col. Duryée became acting brigadier-general in place of Gen. E. M. Pierce. His command was ordered back to the vicinity of Washington. In command of his old regiment, he fortified Federal Hill, at Baltimore. The President appointed him a brigadier-general in August and he was given charge of the instruction of fifteen regiments. In response to his plea for active service he was transferred to Alexandria in March 1862, and in August commanded a brigade in Ricketts's division in the Valley of Virginia. Duryée's brigade gave good account of itself at Cedar Mountain, Rappahannock Station, Thoroughfare Gap, Groveton. Second Bull Run—where Duryée was twice wounded—Chantilly, and South Mountain. During the Antietam campaign he received three wounds while in command of Ricketts's division. After a furlough of thirty days, he found (November 1862) that a junior officer had been promoted over his head. Unable to secure redress, he resigned in January 1863. After the war he was made brevet major-general of volunteers. Generals Ricketts, MacDowell, Pope, and Meade all commended him in their official reports. Mayor Havemeyer appointed Duryée police commissioner of New York, in 1873, a position which he filled with ability and fidelity. He became dockmaster in 1884 and rendered able service here also. He died of cerebral hemorrhage in his seventy-sixth year, survived by his three daughters.

[For Duryée's career consult F. B. Hough, *Hist. of Duryée's Brigade* (1864); *Official Records (Army)*; Frederick Phisterer, *N. Y. in the War of the Rebellion* (3rd ed., 1912), vols. I, II; Emmons Clark, *Hist. of the Seventh Regt. of N. Y. 1806–89* (1890); Wm. Swinton, *Hist. of the Seventh Regt., Nat. Guard, State of N. Y.* (1870); W. L. Stone, *Hist. of N. Y. City* (1872); Appletons' *Ann. Cyc.*, 1888; C. E. Fitch, *Encyc. of Biog. of N. Y.* (1916); F. B. Heitman, *Hist. Reg. and Dict. U. S. Army* (1903); *N. Y. Tribune,* Sept. 28, 1890.] M. L. B., Jr.

DU SIMITIÈRE, PIERRE EUGÈNE (*c.* 1736–October 1784), artist, antiquary, naturalist, was, according to his own statement, a native of Geneva, Switzerland (*Pennsylvania Archives,* 2 ser., III, 121). Of his life before he came to America in 1765, little is known excepting that he spent about ten years traveling and collecting natural history specimens in the West Indies, subsisting by painting portraits and cutting silhouettes. He landed in New York but soon made his way to Burlington, N. J., where he remained for a short time, and then, in 1766, went to Philadelphia. His first stay in that city seems to have been comparatively short, for he was in Boston in 1767–68 and on May 20, 1769, was back in New York, where he became a naturalized citizen (*Journals of the Legislative Council of New York,* 1861, p. 1708). Some years later, however, in 1777, when he was drafted into the Pennsylvania militia, he presented a petition to the Supreme Council claiming immunity because he was a foreigner, in the course of which memorial he said of himself: "Your memorialist is in no public way of business whatever, nor settled in any part of the Continent. . . . That he has resided for some time past in this city (Philadelphia) it has been entirely owing to the critical situation of public affairs. . . . That his long continuance here has also been extremely detrimental to his general pursuit of natural knowledge, the only object of his travel" (*Pennsylvania Archives,* 2 ser., III, 121). The greater part of his life in America was spent in Philadelphia. He was elected a member of the American Philosophical Society, and for about five years, 1776–81, was one of its curators. He designed the vignette for the title-page of the *Pennsylvania Magazine,* published in 1775–76 by Robert Aitken [*q.v.*], and the frontispiece for the *United States Magazine,* 1779. He submitted to the Continental Congress, at its request, designs for a medal to commemorate the Declaration of Independence and for a Great Seal for the United States, but neither of his designs was adopted. Du Simitière was one of the first good portrait-painters to come to America. He drew a portrait of Washington from a sitting in the year 1779, which was used in the design of the so-called Washington Cent of 1791. He drew a series of thirteen portraits of men prominent in the American Revolution, which were engraved and published in London in 1783. Among them were Washington, Steuben, Deane, Laurens, and Benedict Arnold. John Adams, writing to his wife in 1776, said of Du Simitière: "This M. Du Simitière is a very curious man. He has begun a collection of materials for a history of this revolution. He begins with the first advices of the tea ships. He cuts out of the newspapers every scrap of intelligence, and every piece of speculation, and pastes it upon clean paper, arranging them under the head of that State to which they belong, and intends to bind them in volumes" (*Letters of John Adams,* vol. I, 1841, p. 151). This collection was purchased by the Library Company of Philadelphia after Du Simitière's death. It includes an "almost unique collection of newspapers and rare pamphlets" (Potts, *post,* p. 351). A desire to form a museum appears to have been the chief aim in the artist's life, and in 1782 he advertised his collections of curiosities, under the title of "American Museum," as on view at his residence in Philadelphia. He may thus be considered the founder of the first museum in the United States, probably antedating Peale's Museum by two or three years. He was among the first to realize the importance of gathering collections illustrative of the life and customs of the American Indian, whom he regarded as doomed to extinction by the inroads of Europeans. Whether as antiquary, artist, or naturalist, he was thorough, energetic, intelligent, and talented. The exact date of his death is unknown, but he was buried on Oct. 22, 1784, in St. Peter's burial ground, Philadelphia. His grave is unmarked.

[The main source is a fairly exhaustive sketch of Du Simitière by W. J. Potts, in the *Pa. Mag. of Hist. and Biog.,* Oct. 1889. The date of burial is given from the manuscript Records of Christ Church, Phila., in the Hist. Soc. of Pa. See also Wm. Dunlap, *A Hist. of the Rise and Progress of the Arts of Design in the U. S.* (rev. ed., 1918), III, 297; *Early Proc. Am. Phil. Soc., 1744–1838* (1884).]

J. J

DUSTIN, HANNAH (b. Dec. 23, 1657), pioneer, is said to have been the daughter of Michael and Hannah (Webster) Emerson of Haverhill, Mass. On Dec. 3, 1677, she was married to Thomas Dustin of that place, whose name was variously spelled as Duston and Durston. She bore him thirteen children before 1699, eight of whom were living at the time of the Indian raid on Mar. 15, 1697. Although the date of her death is unknown, she is supposed to have survived her husband, who was still living in 1729. The details of her noted exploit vary much in the forms in which it has been handed down but the main story is clear enough. Apparently Hannah was lying in the house with her week-old baby and the nurse, Mary Neff, while her husband and the other seven children were working and playing at some distance outside when the Indians swept down on the village. They entered the house and captured the three occupants in view of the husband. He rescued the seven children outside, carrying them off to safety but had to abandon his baby and wife, some accounts relating that he did so at her earnest entreaty to save the others. The next day, after killing or capturing forty of the inhabitants of the town, the Indians started their march northward carrying their captives with them. Hannah saw her house in flames as she left and one of the Indians took her infant and brained it by knocking it against a tree. After tramping for some days through the snow and without shoes, the party reached a small settlement of Indians living on an island (now called "Dustin's") at the confluence of the Contoocook and Merrimac rivers a few miles above Concord. There captors and captives halted for a few days before proceeding to the home of the chief, a long distance northward, where the victims were told they would be stripped and forced to run the gauntlet.

On the island was a young English boy who had been captured a year before and with him and Mary Neff, Hannah planned an escape. While the Indians were asleep Hannah and the lad killed ten of them, only a squaw and a small Indian boy escaping. Hannah, the English boy (Samuel Lennardson), and the nurse then started for the settlements but to have proof of the exploit Hannah returned and herself scalped the ten savages, of whom she had killed nine and the boy one. They finally made their way back to Haverhill to find the rest of the Dustin family safe. Hannah and her husband then went to

Boston, where they arrived on Apr. 21, and presented a petition to the General Court explaining the loss of all their property and Hannah's exploit. The Court awarded Hannah £25, and half of that sum each to Mary Neff and Samuel Lennardson. The family has many descendants.

[The best account is by G. W. Chase, *The Hist. of Haverhill* (1861), who reprints the account given by C. Mather, *Magnalia Christi Americana* (1702), who had the story from Hannah herself. R. B. Caverly, *Heroism of Hannah Duston* (1874), is a romantic account. The name Samuel Lennardson is so given on the tablet in Haverhill; in Caverly it appears as Leonardson.]

J. T. A.

DUTTON, CLARENCE EDWARD (May 15, 1841–Jan. 4, 1912), soldier, geologist, son of Samuel and Emily (Curtis) Dutton, was born at Wallingford, Conn. He received his elementary education at Ellington, Conn., entered Yale College in June 1856, and graduated with the degree of A.B. in 1860, at the age of nineteen. In September 1862 he was appointed adjutant of the 21st Connecticut Volunteers. On Mar. 1 of the following year he was promoted to a captaincy and in 1864 transferred to the Ordnance Corps of the regular army, in which he served through the remainder of the war. He was assigned in 1865 for duty at the Watervliet Arsenal, five years later was transferred to the Frankford Arsenal at Philadelphia, and later yet, to Washington, D. C. Here he became associated with Joseph Henry, S. F. Baird, J. W. Powell, and other scientific men of the period through whose influence he was induced to consent to a detail with the United States Geological and Geographical Survey. In this service he made his reputation as a geologist. In 1890 he returned to military duty but resigned his commission in February 1901 to reside for the remainder of his life at Englewood, N. J.

Beginning his geological career with service under Powell in 1875, he devoted the next ten years to a study of the plateau region of the western United States in Utah and Arizona. The results of this work are given in his *Report on the Geology of the High Plateau of Utah* (1879–80), a volume of 307 pages with atlas; his *Tertiary History of the Grand Canyon District* (1882); a quarto volume of 264 pages with a magnificent atlas of 23 plates from drawings by W. H. Holmes; and one on *Mount Taylor and the Zuñi Plateau* (1886), together with several important papers in the annual reports of the survey. In all these he dwelt with particular emphasis upon the physical problems of which the area afforded unusual examples, and became a leading advocate of the then little understood doctrine of isostasy. In the subjects of vulcanism and earthquakes Dutton had been interested from a very early period, and in 1882 he paid a visit to the Hawaiian Islands to study the first-named phenomenon close at hand. Ever receptive of new ideas, he soon became an advocate of the possibilities of radioactivity in promoting vulcanism. His earthquake studies were given fresh impulse by the earthquake of Charleston, S. C., in 1886, of which he made an exhaustive study, subsequently setting forth his views on the general subject in an octavo volume of 314 pages entitled *Earthquakes in the Light of the New Seismology* (1904).

As a geologist he may be said to have inclined to speculation and philosophy. As a scientific writer he was one of the clearest, most impressive and entertaining America has produced. Of military bearing, he was companionable, a good speaker and raconteur and fond of alliterative expressions, as when in one of his public lectures on his return from his Hawaiian trip, he spoke of the native female portion of the population as comparing more than favorably with her "pale pious and pulmonary sisters of the effete east." It is stated that in writing his reports he made little use of notes, holding his subject wholly in mind until his problems were solved and his results fully attained. "When ready, he penned all his own manuscripts rapidly under stimulus of an enthusiasm begotten by a consciousness of his comprehensive and complete knowledge of the subject" (Diller, *post*). He was a member of the Philosophical Society of Washington, the American Academy of Political and Social Science, the Geological and Seismological Societies of America, and the National Academy of Sciences. He was married on Apr. 18, 1864, to Emeline C. Babcock of New Haven. He died of arteriosclerosis at the home of his son in Englewood, N. J.

[Memoir by Jos. S. Diller, with a bibliography of Dutton's most important geological publications, in *Bull. Geol. Soc. of America*, Mar. 1913; *Yale Coll. . . . Biog. Record Class of Sixty, 1860–1906* (1906); *Obit. Record Grads. Yale Univ.*, 1912; personal recollections.]

G. P. M.

DUTTON, HENRY (Feb. 12, 1796–Apr. 12, 1869), jurist, was born in Watertown, Litchfield County, Conn., the son of Thomas and Tenty (Punderson) Dutton. His father, a farmer in a small way, moved when Henry was a child to Northfield, where the boy attended the district school but more often assisted in the farm work. In 1812 he engaged in teaching, at the same time continuing his studies in order to enter Yale College, which he accomplished in 1816, graduating with honors in 1818. He was in debt when he left college, but proceeding to Fairfield, he became principal of the academy there and in two years had paid off all his liabilities. Concurrently with his scholastic work he read law. In 1821 he became a tutor at Yale, continuing his legal studies in his spare time, and was admitted to the Connecticut bar in 1823. In the same year he was married to Elizabeth Elliott Joy. He opened his law office at Newtown, Fairfield County, also undertaking private tuition of Yale students. He represented his district in the General Assembly for two terms, but in 1837 removed to Bridgeport. Here he quickly came to the fore, became state's attorney for Fairfield County, and represented Bridgeport in the legislature during two terms. In 1847 he was appointed Kent Professor of Law at Yale, and removed accordingly to New Haven, where he continued also to practise. In the same year he was appointed one of the commissioners to revise the state statutes, an undertaking which entailed great care and application since there had been no revision for twenty-five years. The task, however, was completed within a year. In 1849 he was elected to the state Senate, serving one term, at the conclusion of which he was elected representative for New Haven in the lower house. In 1852 he became judge of the New Haven County court, remaining such for one year. In 1854 the legislature appointed him governor of the state, the electorate having failed to make a choice at the preceding election, and he held the position for a full term. He had no interests other than the law and its amendment and thus by severe concentration was able to perform competently an enormous amount of work. In 1861 he was chosen judge of the supreme court of errors and of the superior court of Connecticut, to fill a vacancy, and continued to occupy a seat on the bench until Feb. 12, 1866, when, having reached the statutory age of seventy years, he retired. During his tenure of judicial office he had maintained his association with the Yale Law School and on his retirement from the bench devoted his energies chiefly to its affairs. He died at New Haven.

Dutton was not a learned lawyer but possessed an extensive and accurate knowledge of "case law," which he applied with remarkable facility. He was quick to grasp a point, fertile of resource, and at the bar, on the bench, and in the lecture room was adequate for any emergency. As an advocate his strength lay in his ability to present facts forcibly and lucidly to a jury from the practical commonplace standpoint, and as a judge he was expeditious, courteous, and eminently receptive. Somewhat advanced in his ideas on law reform, while he was a member of the legislature he procured the passage of a statute permitting in civil cases parties in interest to testify. He was also sponsor of a bill giving the superior court sole jurisdiction in divorce. He was author of *The Connecticut Digest* (1833), and *A Revision of Swift's Digest of the Laws of Connecticut* (2 vols., 1848–53), in which he was assisted by N. A. Cowdrey.

[Louis H. Bristol, in 37 *Conn. Reports*, 620; John Livingston, *Portraits of Eminent Americans Now Living*, vol. II (1853); *Obit. Record Grads. Yale Coll.*, 1869; Gilbert Cope, *Geneal. of the Dutton Family of Pa. . . . With . . . a Short Account of the Duttons of* Conn. (1871).] H.W.H.K.

DUTTON, SAMUEL TRAIN (Oct. 16, 1849–Mar. 28, 1919), educator and peace advocate, was the eldest child of Jeremiah Dutton, farmer in the town of Hillsboro, N. H., and his wife Rebecca Hammond Train, daughter of a farmer in the same town. On both sides were ancestors in early colonial Massachusetts. Jeremiah Dutton was a stony, strictly orthodox, severely moral, unsocial, intolerant Puritan, respected and shunned by his neighbors. His wife was equally religious, but in her the hardness of Puritanism was absent. She had physical beauty and social charm. She freely gave and freely received sympathy, kindliness, and forbearance, and she had visions that transcended the Dutton farm. Samuel was like his mother, and it was with her encouragement that after completing the studies of the district school he went for a winter to the Francestown Academy and in the fall of 1867 entered the Literary and Scientific Institute at New London to prepare for Dartmouth. Two years later, in the midst of plans for going to Dartmouth, it occurred to him that a country boy ought to attend college in a city. He therefore chose Yale, and graduated in 1873. He expected eventually to enter the Christian ministry, but his funds were low. A part of the cost of his education had been met with borrowed money. The rest had been earned. In need of income he assumed charge of the schools in South Norwalk, Conn., in the fall of 1873. A year later he married Cornelia C. North of New Haven. Some wavering in the choice of a profession followed; for a time he turned to the study of law. The schools under his direction improved so rapidly, however, that he could not escape the consequences, and in 1877 he was elected principal of the Eaton Grammar School in New Haven. From 1882 to 1890 he was superintendent of the New Haven schools, and at the end of this period a national figure in education. Ten fruitful years as superintendent of schools at Brookline, Mass., followed, with numerous outside calls upon his services. He was lecturer on pedagogy at Harvard, 1895–97, at the University of Chicago, 1897–98, and at Boston

University, 1898. In 1900 he became superintendent of the Horace Mann Schools and professor of school administration in Teachers College, Columbia University. Here an interest in the peace movement began and grew to be his ruling passion. He was secretary of the New York Peace Society, chairman of the executive committee of the National Arbitration and Peace Congress, general secretary of the World's Court League, trustee of the World Peace Foundation, and member of the international commission on the Balkan War. He was also a trustee of the College for Women in Constantinople and of the Christian College in Canton, China. He retired from Teachers College in 1915 with the rank of professor emeritus, not to rest, but to work more effectively in the various organizations with which he was still connected.

Dutton was a pioneer in socializing the schools. Wherever he went he sought, and in a unique degree secured, cooperation between parents and teachers, not only for the training of children but for the improvement of the community, including parents. He had a profound interest in his fellow mortals and a genius for approaching all kinds of people and enlisting their support in any cause near his heart. He was also a pioneer in professionalizing the office of superintendent of schools. His views on public education are set forth in his annual reports as superintendent at New Haven and Brookline, and in various educational journals. His views on peace found frequent expression in periodicals, chiefly in *Christian Work,* the *Peace Forum* (later the *World Court*) and the *League of Nations Magazine.* He edited several school text-books and was author of, *Social Phases of Education in the School and Home* (1899); *School Management* (1903); and, in collaboration with David Snedden, *Administration of Public Education in the United States* (1908).

[C. H. Levermore, *Samuel Train Dutton, A Biography* (1922), contains numerous extracts from Dutton's correspondence and other writings, and a bibliography. See also *Obit. Record Yale Graduates,* 1918–19; *N. Y. Times,* Mar. 29, 1919.] H. J.

DUVAL, WILLIAM POPE (1784–Mar. 19, 1854), lawyer, congressman, governor of Florida, was born near Richmond, Va., the son of William and Ann (Pope) Duval. His father was well-to-do and attempted to give his children a good education. William, however, did not complete his schooling, as he left his home at the age of fifteen or sixteen, and went to Kentucky alone. He spent the next two or three years on the frontier. When eighteen, he went to Bardstown to begin the study of law. In 1804 he married Nancy, a daughter of William Hynes, and began practising his profession. Later he served as a Republican in the Thirteenth Congress (1813–15).

A new period in his life began in 1821 when he was appointed by President Monroe as the first judge of the superior court of East Florida. Early in the following year he was made the first civil governor of the territory. His early life among frontiersmen, his legal studies and his experience as a lawmaker were valuable assets in the new position, and his temperament made him a fit leader in a pioneer community. He was courageous and determined, but also democratic and full of humor. Although only five feet seven inches in height, his cheerful and energetic personality nevertheless dominated in the presence of others. Duval took the lead in grappling with the numerous problems that faced the new government. In 1823 he appointed two commissioners to select a site for the future capital, which was finally located at Tallahassee. Duval then began the work which is probably his outstanding achievement, the peaceable removal of the Seminole Indians to South Florida. He was admirably successful, so that there was no serious outbreak by the natives while he was in office. While engaged in his pacification of the Indians, he visited almost every part of northern Florida, and in February 1826 made a long trip overland to Tampa Bay. He often urged the necessity of establishing schools, although the results were disappointingly meager. The chief enactment was the creation in 1831 of the first board of education for Florida. Due to his insistence, the territorial laws were compiled in 1828; and not satisfied with this, he urged in 1833 and 1834 another compilation which was eventually published in 1839. His interest in the conduct of elections was particularly keen so that many of the basic features of Florida's present electoral machinery were adopted during his administrations.

At first Duval was popular, but after some years the increasing electorate began to regard him as the irresponsible representative of the Federal Government. This feeling of discontent was augmented by his strong insistence on his executive prerogatives and his lukewarmness toward the chartering of state banks. Prior to 1833, he vetoed all bills incorporating banks, although many were passed over his veto. The disagreement of the executive and the legislature apparently reached its height in 1833 when he vetoed about one-fifth of the bills passed. Under such conditions it is not surprising that Jackson replaced him in 1834 by John Eaton. Continuing to reside in Florida, he was elected one of Calhoun County's representatives to the Constitutional Convention that assembled in St. Joseph in December 1838. He was defeated for the presidency of the body by one vote, but was chosen chairman of the committee on the executive department. When the legislature of Florida was made bicameral in 1839, he was elected a senator from the Middle District, a position which he held until 1842. He was president of the upper house in 1840. His last public office was that of commissioner in 1845 to settle the disputed northern boundary of the state. He was the unsuccessful Democratic nominee for Congress in 1848.

Duval's wife died of yellow fever on July 14, 1841, at St. Joseph. In May 1843 he took up his residence in St. Augustine, and in 1849 he followed his children to Texas, of which state he was a citizen at the time of his death. He died in Washington, D. C.

[Information about Duval's life before 1804 is derived chiefly from Washington Irving, *The Early Experiences of Ralph Ringwood in Wolfert's Roost* (1865). For his activities in Florida, see chiefly *Am. State Papers, Indian Affairs*, II (1834); *Acts of the Legislative Council of Territory of Fla.* (1831); *Jour. of the Proceedings of a Convention of Delegates to form a Constitution for the People of Fla.* (1838); *Jour. of the Proceedings of the Senate of the Territory of Fla.* (1840–42); John T. Sprague, *The Origin, Progress, and Conclusion of the Fla. War* (1847); and general histories of Florida. Some of his messages before 1832 may be found in the newspapers and, in part, in *Niles' Reg.* For a good description see *The Fla. Jour.* (Apalachicola), Mar. 17, 1841; for obituaries, *Nat. Intelligencer*, Mar. 25, 1854; *Tallahassee Floridian and Jour.*, Mar. 25, Apr. 1, 1854.] J. O. K.

DUVENECK, FRANK (Oct. 9, 1848–Jan. 3, 1919), painter, etcher, sculptor, teacher, was an outstanding figure in the art of his time, and a leader of remarkable influence, numbering many gifted painters among his disciples. His parents were Germans. His father was Bernard Decker; and his mother's maiden name was Katherine Seimers. They came to America from a small town not far from Vechta, in Oldenburg, and settled in Covington, Ky., where, in 1849, Decker died while his son Frank was an infant in arms. The widow subsequently married Squire Duveneck, and her son took the name of his stepfather, being known as Frank Duveneck. In Covington, his birthplace, he left school at an early age to begin work on the interior decorations of Catholic churches; he was employed in the modeling, carving, painting, and gilding of altarpieces and the like, and the unusual merit of his work soon led to his regular employment by a successful ecclesiastical decorator in Cincinnati. As a method of training in craftsmanship this kind of practical experience had undeniable advantages, not the least of which was the remarkable facility that it developed. It goes far to explain much of the character of Duveneck's later accomplishments, more especially the skill and freedom of his manipulation of various mediums. He continued this apprenticeship for several years, constantly gaining in technical knowledge and power.

At the age of twenty-two, when he went to Munich and became a student of the Royal Academy, he was already so well equipped as a painter that, after three months of study in the antique class, he was promoted to Wilhelm Dietz's painting class, where he distinguished himself by taking several prizes. In 1872 he won the composition prize, entitling him to the use of a studio of his own. To this period belongs one of his best-known canvases, the "Whistling Boy," also several other notable pieces of precocious brilliancy and breadth. "It was with the naturalists that he instantly aligned himself," writes his biographer, Norbert Heerman; "theirs was the spirit in which Duveneck approached his work." He approached it with superb confidence and ardor. Nothing is more apparent in his paintings than the hearty gusto with which they were made.

Returning to America in 1873, Duveneck busied himself at once with a church decoration in Chicago and some portrait commissions in Cincinnati, where he held a modest exhibition of a few portraits painted in Munich. The "Young Man with Ruff" was painted at that time; the portrait of Mr. William Adams followed in 1874. The year 1875 was signalized by a Duveneck exhibition in Boston, which proved to be a triumph for the young artist, owing to the vitality and spontaneity of his style. The five canvases shown at the Boston Art Club created a sensation; they were all sold; and the painter was urged to leave Cincinnati and come to Boston, where a dozen commissions for portraits were promised him. Much of this success was to be attributed to the influence of William Morris Hunt. Duveneck, however, was not yet inclined to forsake the training and surroundings of Europe; he went back to Munich, where he worked for two years, until 1877. Then he went to Venice, and a year later we find him again in Munich. The principal pictures of this time were the "Woman with Forget-me-nots," distinctly reminiscent of Rubens and not without a distant echo of Rembrandt; the "Red-haired Man with Ruff," the "Man in Spanish Coat," "Beeches of Polling," and the monochrome self-portrait of 1877.

His "Turkish Page" (1876), first shown at the National Academy, New York, 1877, and now belonging to the Pennsylvania Academy of the Fine Arts, Philadelphia, may be considered one of his most important early compositions. It is rich in color and textures, and the still life is rendered with marked ability. So striking, indeed, was the virtuosity of this and the succeeding works, that Duveneck ran some danger of establishing a reputation for science and manual skill, connoting superficiality and a lack of emotion, but if this be in a measure true of certain *tours de force* of the early days, it is far from being so in the typical examples of the maturer period, which owe much of their enduring worth and charm to their genuine human feeling and sympathetic quality.

To such personal characteristics as these, quite as much as to his knowledge and talent, Duveneck owed his notable success as an inspiring and beloved teacher. His own school of painting, which was started at Munich in 1878, became famous at once; some sixty students, of different nationalities, the majority of them Americans, were enrolled, and the enthusiasm, devotion, industry, and ambition which he knew how to evoke from these young followers proved that he had not mistaken his vocation. The names of a few of his pupils—John W. Alexander, William M. Chase, Frederick P. Vinton, Joseph R. De Camp, John Twachtman, Julius Rolshoven, Oliver D. Grover, Otto Bacher, Robert Blum, Theodore Wendel—are sufficient to show that he was fortunate in his pupils, and that, by the surprising diversity of their styles as well as by the general excellence of their achievements, they bore witness to the breadth and wholesomeness of his personal influence rather than the soundness of his methods of painting. All that he cared about, as Mr. Cortissoz has pointed out, was to see that they got hold of the root of the matter, to foster in them a love of the art of painting for its own sake. He instilled in his boys "a sense of the thrilling excitement, the joy and the dignity, to be got out of the reverent exercise of a painter's instruments." Almost all of them, however, wisely turned away from the fascinating but treacherous bitumen of the Munich school, and several, notably Twachtman, became brilliant exponents of high-keyed luminous impressionism in landscape art.

When Duveneck moved from Munich to Florence, toward the end of 1879, about half of his pupils accompanied him. They remained in Italy about two years, passing the winters in Florence and the summers in Venice, working and enjoying life as only care-free art students may. An interesting glimpse of their boyish ways is given in William D. Howells's *Indian Summer* (1886), wherein the badinage, mockery, and jollity of the Bohemian party as seen in a trattoria are picturesquely described. What they thought about Botticelli and Michelangelo; of old Piloty's things at Munich; of the dishes they had served to them; of the quality of the Chianti; of the respective merits of German and Italian tobacco; of the "over-rated coloring of some of those Venetian fellows"; of the delicacy of Mino da Fiesole; and of many other matters—such were some of the themes of discussion overheard by the hero of the story. In his reminiscences of those student days in Italy, Oliver Dennett Grover has added his testimony to that of others of the group respecting the obligations they were under to the "Old Man." Those days were all too short, he says, but while they lasted they were more significant than a similar period in the lives of most students, because more intensified, more concentrated. It is necessary thus to emphasize Duveneck's influence as a teacher if we would rightly understand the important part he played in the development of art in America. Admirable as are his works in painting, etching, and sculpture, it may well be that in the final appraisal of his achievements his most valuable contribution to the cause of art will be found in his personal influence as a leader of his "boys." Their doings have become a legend and a tradition, not to be omitted in any history of American art.

It was in 1879 that Duveneck painted the portrait of John W. Alexander, the "Woman in Black Scarf," and "The Blacksmith"; but during the two ensuing years he was too much occupied with his school work to find much time for painting. He began to etch in 1880, at Venice, experimenting at first with some very small plates. Most of the dated prints, almost all of Venetian motives, were made in 1883, 1884, and 1885. Characteristic examples, of the highest order of excellence, are the two versions of the "Riva degli Schiavoni," the "Grand Canal," the "Palazzo Ca d'Oro," and "The Rialto." The first-named plates were shown at the first exhibition of the New Society of Painter-Etchers, in London, in the spring of 1881. Apparently, certain members of this society, including Seymour Haden and Alphonse Legros, suspected for a moment that these etchings were the work of Whistler, and that Whistler was trying to play a practical joke on the society. The particulars of this esthetic tempest in a teapot may be found in Whistler's *Gentle Art of Making Enemies* (1890) and in the biography of Whistler by E. R. and J. Pennell. As a matter of fact, Duveneck's etchings of the Riva degli Schiavoni were finished before Whistler made his plates of the same subject. Never did Duveneck succeed in bettering these beautiful plates, which remain his most artistic etchings. The later Venetian compositions, though interesting as fine drawings of architecture, are somewhat too much elaborated as to detail, and lack the stenographic suggestiveness that is proper to the process.

In 1886 Duveneck was married in Paris. His wife, Elizabeth Boott, had been a pupil of Thomas Couture and of William Morris Hunt and was a painter of distinct merit. She was a daughter of Francis Boott, of Boston and Cambridge; her mother was a Miss Lyman, of one of the old families of Massachusetts. Elizabeth Boott had lived and studied in Paris, Florence, and Boston. In 1879 she became a pupil of Duveneck in Munich. Their engagement followed, but the marriage did not take place until nearly seven years later. Two years after that time Mrs. Duveneck died. She was buried in the Allori Cemetery in Florence, where the noble memorial figure in bronze created by her husband marks her grave. This is a recumbent effigy in the mode of the Italian Renaissance, modernized, intimate, and imbued with the deepest personal sentiment. The original model belongs to the Cincinnati Museum. A marble version is in the Museum of Fine Arts, Boston. In the museums of Philadelphia, Chicago, and San Francisco are copies of the Boston marble. Copies from the original model are in the Metropolitan Museum of Art, New York, and in the John Herron Art Institute, Indianapolis. The only other sculptures of consequence made by Duveneck are the seated portrait statue of Ralph Waldo Emerson, now in Emerson Hall, Harvard University—a work in which Clement J. Barnhorn collaborated—and the bust portrait of Charles William Eliot. The superior quality of these few works, more particularly his *magnum opus,* the monument to his wife, gives rise to regret that Duveneck should not have elected to specialize in sculpture.

After his wife's death in 1888, he returned to his old home, Cincinnati, where he remained for the rest of his life. There his time and energy were mainly devoted to teaching, though he did some painting, and acted as adviser in artistic matters in connection with the Cincinnati Museum. He was never without a devoted following, and his influence as instructor during his last years did but continue and extend the extraordinary personal leadership that had been so conspicuous in Munich and Florence and Venice. Thus his last twenty-five years, spent in the Cincinnati Museum and the Cincinnati Art Academy, of which he was the dean of the faculty, were fruitful and busy years. It was his loyalty to the Museum and his many pupils that led him to make the very unusual disposition of his work. He made over to the Museum by gift the great collection of paintings, etchings, sketches, etc., which he considered fit material for continuing to students such help as his own life-work had afforded. The value of such a gift, after a lifetime of useful personal achievement, may be realized only by a pilgrimage to Cincinnati.

The most complete exhibition of Duveneck's works ever made outside of Cincinnati was that at the Panama-Pacific exposition, San Francisco, in 1915. This collection contained thirty oil paintings, thirteen etchings, and a replica of the monument to his wife. A special gallery was set aside for the Duveneck exhibit. Prominent examples among the paintings were the "Whistling Boy," the "Woman with Forget-me-nots," the "Turkish Page," the portraits of William Adams, J. Frank Currier, Professor Loeffts, John W. Alexander, and Mrs. Francis Hinkle. The exhibit as a whole was so impressive that the occasion constituted a veritable apotheosis for the artist. In the words of Christian Brinton, it "served to rehabilitate his name and insure for him that position in the development of American painting which he so rightfully merits" (*Impressions of the Art at the Panama-Pacific Exposition,* 1916, p. 96). The foreign members of the international jury of awards unanimously recommended that in recognition of his distinguished contribution to American art a special medal of honor should be struck and awarded to him. This handsome proposal was promptly indorsed by the entire jury. The significance of the rare honor thus conferred on Duveneck only four years before his death lies not only in the fact that it gave expression to the deliberate opinion of experts, but also that it originated with foreign experts, who presumably could have no personal bias in the matter and were therefore able to take a purely detached view-point.

Duveneck died in the Good Samaritan Hospital, Cincinnati, on Jan. 3, 1919. In the tribute of the Cincinnati Art Club we find these words: "A father to all interested in art . . . He knew hard work in his early days, and it did not narrow him; he knew sorrow, but it did not embitter him. . . . His judgment was always of the best; he was gifted with wonderful vision. He had marvelous power." Temperament counts for so much more than schooling in Duveneck's paintings that it is safe to say he would have gone as far, done as well, and developed as richly, had he obtained his training elsewhere than in Munich. In other words, the Munich methods and the Munich palette formed no essential part of his artistic assets. He outgrew them, and eventually they were abandoned in favor of better methods. His debt was great to Rembrandt, Hals, and Rubens; and he learned more precious things in the Old Pinakothek than in Prof. Dietz's classroom. Naturally a rapid and skilful executant, with a hearty relish for the most rebellious of all mediums, oil paints, it would be little less than astounding that he did not fall a victim to his own wonderful facility, degenerating into a mere star performer of technical prodigies, were it not for the repeated proofs in his pictures of his fine moral qualities—his quick sympathy and the breadth and depth of his interest in human nature. He joined craftsmanship with a kindly disposition; virtuosity with magnanimity; knowledge with modesty. When John S. Sargent said of him that he was the greatest talent of the brush in this generation, he spoke truth, but "talent of the brush" tells only half the story. What makes Duveneck the honored figure that he is in American art is the richness and warmth of his temperament, the generosity of his nature; without these qualities, easily to be discerned in his best works, he would have made no original contribution of enduring value to the sum total of modern art.

[The chief source is Norbert Heermann's *Frank Duveneck* (1918), an excellent biography, containing twenty-two illustrations. The frontispiece is a print after Jos. R. De Camp's portrait of the artist in the Cincinnati Museum. A small anonymous book entitled *Frank Duveneck, 1848–1919*, was issued by the Cincinnati Museum Association at the time of the artist's death. Other references include "Frank Duveneck and His Munich Tradition," by Royal Cortissoz, in *Scribner's Mag.*, Feb. 1927; "Frank Duveneck: Artist and Teacher," by Anna Seaton-Schmidt, in *Art and Progress*, Sept. 1915; "Frank Duveneck," by D. Croal Thomson, in *Connoisseur*, Sept. 1921; "Blakelock and Duveneck," by E. V. Lucas, in *Ladies' Home Jour.*, Feb. 1927; *What Pictures to See in America*, by Lorinda M. Bryant (1915); *Biog. Sketches of Am. Artists* (Lansing, 1924); Samuel Isham, *Hist. of Am. Painting* (1905); *Am. Art Rev.*, Nov. 1880; *Arts and Decoration*, July 1911; *Scribner's Mag.*, Nov. 1915.]

W. H. D.

DUYCKINCK, EVERT AUGUSTUS (Nov. 23, 1816–Aug. 13, 1878), editor, biographer, descended in the seventh generation from Evert Duycking (*sic*) who came to New Amsterdam in 1638, was a son of Evert and Harriet June Duyckinck and a brother of George L. Duyckinck [*q.v.*]. His father was for about forty years a respected publisher of standard literature in New York. In this environment Evert Augustus naturally imbibed a love for good books. He graduated from Columbia College in 1835, where his studious habits, classical attainments, and taste for elegant literature were distinguished (*New York Tribune*, Aug. 15, 1878). He then studied law with John Anthon and was admitted to the bar (1837), but did not practise. For a year (1838–39) he traveled in Europe. Returning home, he took up literature as a definite profession, toward which he had already contributed articles in the *New York Review* on George Crabbe, George Herbert, and Oliver Goldsmith. In April 1840 he married Margaret Wolfe Panton. They soon took up their life-long residence at 20 Clinton Place, which became the resort of the most eminent literary men of the country. Three sons were born, but all died young and without issue. In December 1840, Duyckinck began in company with Cornelius Mathews the editorship of *Arcturus, a Journal of Books and Opinion*, a monthly discontinued after May 1842. Five years later he edited for Osgood & Company, publishers of New York, their new periodical, the *Literary World, a Journal of American and Foreign Literature, Science, and Art.* He edited twelve numbers (Feb. 6–Apr. 24, 1847), then retired. No. 13 was issued by the publishers and Nos. 14–87 (May 8, 1847–Sept. 30, 1848) were edited by Charles Fenno Hoffman [*q.v.*]. The Duyckinck brothers, Evert and George, then bought the periodical, and edited it jointly from No. 88 (Oct. 7, 1848) to No. 361 (Dec. 31, 1853), completing the thirteenth volume. It was the best American literary weekly of its time, but financially unremunerative. The brothers then turned their attention to research and the editing of a *Cyclopædia of American Literature* (2 vols., 1855), which Evert, after George's death, revised and enlarged (2 vols. and supplement, 1866), and which was brought out in a final edition, edited by M. L. Simons, in fifty-two parts (1873–74). It was during this period that Evert Duyckinck edited for Wiley & Putnam a Library of Choice Reading. He also edited the first edition in book form of Thackeray's *Confessions of Fitz-Boodle* (1852), the first American edition of Thackeray's *Yellowplush Papers* (1852), Sydney Smith's *Wit and Wisdom* (1856), and an edition of Willmott's *Poets of the Nineteenth Century* (1857). In 1859 he compiled *Irvingiana*, anecdotes and traits of Washington Irving. Later he edited the *Salmagundi Papers* (1860); Philip Freneau's *Poems Relating to the American Revolution* (1865); Alexander Anderson's *Illustrations to Mother Goose* (1873), and a collection of Anderson's engravings (1873). He wrote the text for the following subscription works, which had a large sale: *National Portrait Gallery of Eminent Americans* (2 vols., 1861–62); *National History of the War for the Union* (3 vols., 1861–65); *Lives and Portraits of the Presidents of the United States* (1865); *History of the World*

(1869–71), largely compiled by his son George (1846–1873), and *Portrait Gallery of Eminent Men and Women of Europe and America* (2 vols., copyright 1873). He wrote memorials of John Allan (1864), Francis L. Hawks (1871), Henry T. Tuckerman (1872), and Fitz-Greene Halleck (1877). At the time of his death he was associated with William Cullen Bryant in editing Shakespeare (3 vols., 1886–88). He was domestic corresponding secretary of the New York Historical Society, and a trustee of Columbia College and the New York Society Library. Lowell (*Fable for Critics,* 1848) referred to him as a ripe scholar and a neat critic, with the soul of a gentleman. Those who knew him best declared with unanimity that he was "singularly free from blemish or blame, and equally exempt from enmity or detraction" (Butler, *post*). In disposition he was retiring, gentle, meditative, hesitant in debate but genial and interesting as a companion. His library of American and English literature and works on art, about 17,000 titles, exclusive of manuscripts, was given to the Lenox Library in two consignments, in 1878 and after his wife's death.

[The N. Y. Public Lib. has a copy of W. C. and C. J. Duyckinck, *The Duyckinck and Allied Families* (1908), with manuscript additions. Also in the N. Y. Pub. Lib. are the extensive Duyckinck Papers which include the correspondence of the brothers, their writings, notebooks, legal papers, and accounts. Diaries of Evert Duyckinck cover 1836–39, 1842–61. The literary letters are from most of the men and women writers of the United States from about 1840 to the close of the Civil War. See also Wm. Allen Butler, *Memorial Sketch* (read before the N. Y. Hist. Soc., Jan. 7, 1879, and reprinted); Samuel Osgood, memoir in *New Eng. Hist. and Geneal. Reg.,* April 1879 (also reprinted); *N. Y. Times, N. Y. Tribune,* and *World,* all for Aug. 15, 1878.] V. H. P.

DUYCKINCK, GEORGE LONG (Oct. 17, 1823–Mar. 30, 1863), editor, biographer, younger brother of Evert Augustus Duyckinck [*q.v.*], attended Geneva (now Hobart College), and then the University of the City of New York, graduating in 1843. He studied law and was admitted to the bar, but never practised. "His organization, both bodily and mental, was of that delicate and sensitive order which finds nothing congenial in the conflicts and sharp issues of the busy world" (Morgan, *post*). He traveled in Europe in 1847–48 and 1857. His life was devoted to religion, literature, and art. He was associated with his brother Evert in editing the *Literary World, a Journal of American and Foreign Literature, Science, and Art* (Oct. 7, 1848–Dec. 31, 1853) and the *Cyclopædia of American Literature* (2 vols., 1855). In 1855 he was elected to the executive committee of the General Protestant Episcopal Sunday School Union and Church Book Society, and in 1857 became its treasurer, devoting himself to wholesome literature for the children of his denomination. For this society he wrote biographies of George Herbert (1858), Thomas Ken (1859), Jeremy Taylor (1860), and Hugh Latimer (1861). He edited an American edition of Shakespeare, based upon J. Payne Collier's, with variorum notes (8 vols., 1853).

[Wm. F. Morgan, *Obituary Notice of the Late Geo. L. Duyckinck* (1863); *N. Y. Times,* Mar. 31, 1863; *N. Y. Tribune,* Apr. 1, 1863; references in bibliography of sketch of Evert Duyckinck.] V. H. P.

DWENGER, JOSEPH (Sept. 7, 1837–Jan. 22, 1893), Roman Catholic prelate, was born in or near Stallotown (now Minster), Ohio, the son of Gerhard Henry Dwenger and Maria Catherina Wirdt. On his father's death in 1840, his mother moved to Cincinnati, where Joseph had his early schooling. Through the death of his mother he became an orphan at the age of twelve. Father Kunkler, a priest of the Community of the Most Precious Blood, who waited on Mrs. Dwenger in her last illness, took Joseph in charge, acted as a sort of guardian to him, and assisted him to pursue his studies for the priesthood. After some time as a student at Mount St. Mary's of the West, Cincinnati, Dwenger was ordained a priest by Archbishop Purcell on Sept. 4, 1859, as a member of the Congregation of the Precious Blood, of whose seminary at Carthagena, Ohio, he was later the founder and first president, and in which he taught as professor. In 1867 he became secretary of the religious congregation to which he belonged, and from that time until 1872 he also filled the rôle of missionary. His services were engaged by many priests, because he was a powerful and very effective pulpit orator. In the year 1872 Pius IX appointed him bishop of Fort Wayne to succeed Bishop John Henry Luers, the first incumbent of this See. Having experienced what it means to be deprived of both father and mother in early childhood, Bishop Dwenger soon became known as the "Orphans' Friend." He built an Orphan Asylum for boys at Lafayette, Ind. (1875), and another for girls at Fort Wayne (1886), both of which are still in use, accommodating some three hundred children. During his administration the diocese of Fort Wayne became renowned throughout the United States for its excellent and well-regulated parochial school system. Every parish of fifty families and upwards had its own school, examined twice a year by one of ten members of a school board, who exercised a very wholesome influence over the schools, contributing much toward their efficiency and progress.

Dwight

Bishop Dwenger was director of the first official American pilgrimage to Lourdes and Rome, in 1874, leaving at the Shrine a bright American flag, which still ornaments a wall of the basilica. Following the Council of Baltimore, held in 1884, he was one of the three prelates designated to carry the report to Rome and to speak for the Church's approbation of the various decrees which this Council enacted. He died in his fifty-sixth year, and was buried in a crypt or mausoleum under the sanctuary of the Cathedral. Archbishop Elder of Cincinnati officiated at the obsequies. The funeral sermon was preached by Bishop Rademacher of Nashville, who became his successor in the See of Fort Wayne in the following year.

[Baptismal Record of St. Augustine's Parish, Minster (then Stallotown), Ohio; H. J. Alerding, *Hist. of the Diocese of Fort Wayne* (1907); *Cath. Hist. Rev.*, Oct. 1916; John H. Lamott, *Hist. of the Archdiocese of Cincinnati* (1921); *The Cath. Church in the U. S. A.* (1912), vol. I; Chas. Blanchard, *Hist. of the Cath. Church in Ind.* (1898), vol. I; *Sadlier's Cath. Directory*, 1893; *Cath. Encyc.*, VI, 150, and VII, 741; *Indianapolis Jour.*, Jan. 23, 1893.] J.F.N.

DWIGHT, BENJAMIN WOODBRIDGE (Apr. 5, 1816–Sept. 18, 1889), educator, author, clergyman, the eldest son of Benjamin Woolsey Dwight and Sophia Woodbridge (Strong) and a brother of Theodore William Dwight [*q.v.*], was born in New Haven, Conn. A year later the family moved to Catskill, N. Y., where his father conducted a hardware business until 1831, when he moved to Clinton, N. Y., and set up as a gentleman farmer. He was elected treasurer of Hamilton College, from which Benjamin was graduated in 1835. After completing his course at the Yale Divinity School in 1838, he taught at Hamilton College for three years; in 1844 founded the First Congregational (now the Central Presbyterian) Church of Joliet, Ill., where he was ordained by the Presbytery of Chicago in 1845; and in 1846 established a commercial and classical school for boys, Dwight's High School, in Brooklyn, N. Y. He continued this school with success until 1858, when he founded a boarding-school in Clinton, maintained until 1863. In his own writings he hinted somewhat mysteriously that external forces caused him to close this institution. For the four years following he conducted a like school in New York City. He inherited the Dwight teaching ability, so prominent in his grandfather, President Timothy Dwight [*q.v.*] of Yale, and made innovations in the curriculum of his schools. He believed his school the first in the country to include German (1846); and he developed a method of encouraging and promoting the brighter pupils without discouraging the duller. In the Clinton School, he included girls among the day students. He educated in all some 2,000 students. In 1854 he founded The Rural Art Association in Clinton, which did much to stimulate intellectual life and to beautify the town. In 1867 he gave up his New York school, retired from teaching, returned to Clinton, and for the rest of his life followed literary pursuits and supplied various pulpits. For a short time he was editor and owner of *The Interior,* a Presbyterian religious weekly in Chicago, Ill. His literary endeavors were in several fields. He published: *Higher Christian Education* (1859); *Modern Philology, First and Second Series* (1864); *History of the Descendants of Elder John Strong of Northampton, Mass.* (2 vols., 1871); *The History of the Descendants of John Dwight of Dedham, Mass.* (2 vols., 1874), a mine of information; *Higher Culture of Woman* (1887); *True Doctrine of Divine Providence* (1887).

Dwight was twice married: first, in 1846, to Wealthy Jane Dewey, daughter of Harvey and Betsey Maria (Harrison) Dewey, by whom he had three daughters and one son; and after her death in 1864, to Charlotte Sophia Parish, by whom he had one daughter. He was of smaller stature than many of the Dwights, but his engraved portrait shows that he had the comeliness characteristic of the family.

[Autobiographical sketches in Dwight's own genealogies of the Dwight and Strong families; W. W. Spooner, *Historic Families of America* (n.d.); *Eighth Gen. Cat. of the Yale Divinity School* (1922); *N. Y. Tribune*, June 13, 1846.] E.W.F.

DWIGHT, EDMUND (Nov. 28, 1780–Apr. 1, 1849), merchant, manufacturer, philanthropist, descended from John Dwight who settled at Dedham, Mass., in 1635, was the seventh of eight children born to Jonathan and Margaret (Ashley) Dwight of Springfield, Mass. His father had been sent without patrimony at the age of ten to Springfield where he had become a leading citizen and merchant in that rising frontier community. Although the family was prosperous, Edmund was brought up to work on the farm and in the store. After a thorough preparation he entered Yale College, from which he graduated in 1799. He read law for some time in the office of Fisher Ames at Dedham, but upon the completion of his studies, decided on a more active career in business. His association with Ames, however, introduced him to the best society of Boston and brought him into contact with many of the keenest minds of eastern Massachusetts, an experience valuable in his education and helpful later in his business. Anxious to travel in Europe before settling down, he proposed to his father that his share of the inheritance be given to him at once. His father's willingness enabled the young man to spend the years 1802–04 abroad.

Returning to America, he associated himself with his father and his brothers, whose business interests now included banking enterprises and branch stores in several towns. In spite of the expanding activities of the Dwight family, Edmund Dwight found time to represent the town of Springfield in the General Court, 1810–13, and 1815, and his interest in politics continued throughout his life. His business during these Springfield years took him frequently to Boston and there he married, Apr. 19, 1809, Mary Harrison Eliot (May 15, 1788–Oct. 12, 1846), daughter of Samuel Eliot, a prominent merchant of that city. This marriage gave Dwight further contacts with the most distinguished merchant families of the seacoast, and in 1816 he removed to Boston.

Establishing a partnership with James K. Mills, he was soon placed by his energy and foresight among the foremost of the entrepreneurs who laid the foundations for New England manufacturing. His was the directing hand in the establishment of three manufacturing centers, Chicopee Falls, Chicopee, and Holyoke, all situated in the Connecticut Valley where he had lived for many years. In 1822 he and his brother Jonathan purchased most of the land later occupied by the village of Chicopee Falls, built a dam to harness the power, and by 1831 had erected four cotton-mills operating first under the name of the Boston & Springfield Manufacturing Company and then of the Chicopee Manufacturing Company. The first-named company in 1825 bought the water rights and land later covered by the city of Chicopee. These water rights were distributed by the Springfield Canal Company, organized in 1831, and along the canal operated by this corporation Dwight built huge mills himself and induced other manufacturers to establish themselves. It was also the Dwight concern which eventually, through the Hadley Falls Company, secured the water rights and built the dam and canals upon which the manufacturing of Holyoke is based. By 1841 his company had the principal direction of cotton-mills, machine-shops, and calico printing works, employing about 3,000 persons. Outside of manufacturing, Dwight's chief business interest was in the promotion of the Western Railroad from Worcester to Albany. He was a member of the first board of directors (1836–39), was elected by the legislature a director on the part of the state in 1842, and until his death continued on the board as a representative either of the state or of the stockholders. He was president of the road in 1843 and during his entire service used his influence for the most durable and scientific construction.

Less spectacular than his business ventures was his notable contribution to the development of public education. Becoming keenly interested in that subject after reading a translation of Cousin's *Report of the State of Public Instruction in Prussia,* he was the center of a group who devised the School Law of 1837 passed under the governorship of Edward Everett [*q.v.*], and became a member of the board of education established by it. This law gave the board large powers to collect information and distribute school funds. To make the board an effective instrument it was necessary to have a secretary of the highest talent, and Dwight made this possible by paying for sixteen years part of the salary of Horace Mann [*q.v.*]. When the board decided that a system of normal schools should be established, he contributed $10,000 on condition that the state appropriate a similar amount, and later offered to raise $5,000 if the state would duplicate it. His generosity also allowed Horace Mann to make his first experiments with teachers' institutes. After Dwight's death, the *Thirteenth Annual Report of the Board of Education* in 1849 asserted that "it was through his exertions, perhaps, more than any other individual, that this Board was established, and through his liberality, more than that of all others, that it was enabled to prosecute the system of measures which has resulted in whatever of success it has achieved."

[B. W. Dwight, *The Hist. of the Descendants of John Dwight of Dedham, Mass.* (1874), II, 894–98; Francis Bowen, "Memoir of Edmund Dwight," in *Barnard's Am. Jour. of Educ.,* Sept. 1857; L. H. Everts, *Hist. of the Conn. Valley* (1879), II, 917, 971–73; L. L. Johnson, *Chicopee Illustrated* (1896); F. B. Dexter, *Biog. Sketches Grads. Yale Coll.,* vol. V (1911); *Boston Atlas,* Apr. 2, 1849.] H. U. F.

DWIGHT, FRANCIS (Mar. 14, 1808–Dec. 15, 1845), lawyer, educator, was born in Springfield, Mass., the sixth in descent from John Dwight, who settled at Dedham, Mass., in 1635, and the eighth of the twelve children of James Scutt and Mary (Sanford) Dwight. His father, a wealthy, enterprising, benevolently inclined merchant, owned a large wholesale and retail emporium in Springfield and six branch stores in as many near-by villages. He imported his wares direct from Europe, his own sloops and schooners conveying them from New York to Hartford, where river boats, also of his ownership, carried them on to Springfield. Francis entered Phillips Exeter Academy in 1822 and Harvard College in 1824, graduated in 1827, and studied law for two years in the school at Northampton. When his brilliant young teacher, John Hooker Ashmun, was appointed to a professorship in the newly organized Harvard Law School, Dwight followed him to Cambridge for his final year (September 1829–July 1830) of study. Subsequently he spent a year or more in travel in England, France, and Germany, partly for the sake of his health, which had been weakened by too close application to his books. In 1834 he was admitted to the Massachusetts bar. On July 4 of that year he married Catharine Van Rensselaer Schermerhorn of Geneva, N. Y. She died on Aug. 20, 1840, and on Apr. 20, 1843, he married Catharine Waters Yates of Albany, N. Y., who outlived him. Although definite information is lacking, Dwight does not appear to have succeeded well with the law, in spite of the good opinion that Justice Joseph Story had formed of him at Cambridge, and probably lost interest in his profession. After a year's practise in Massachusetts he moved out to Michigan Territory, but in 1838 he returned East and settled at Geneva, N. Y., the home of his father-in-law. Meanwhile he had been interesting himself in the Lyceum movement and in popular education. With the encouragement of John Canfield Spencer, then secretary of state of New York and superintendent of common schools, he published in March 1840 the first number of the *District School Journal of the State of New York*, and soon after changed his headquarters to Albany. The paper gained official support and became the organ of the state common-school system. Dwight, by his enthusiasm and wide knowledge, was able to keep his little monthly on a high plane and so to make it of real service to the state. Not long after he was appointed superintendent of the schools of the city and county of Albany, was made a member of the board of directors of the Albany Normal School, and was looked upon as a leader in education. He was but entering on what should have been his real career when "inflammation of the bowels"—not then recognized as appendicitis—cut him short. He had already won the esteem, however, of educators throughout the eastern United States and had done notable work for the public schools of New York.

[B. W. Dwight, *The Hist. of the Descendants of John Dwight* (1874); article in *Barnard's Am. Jour. of Ed.*, Dec. 1858; *Quinquennial Cat., Harvard Univ., 1636–1915* (1915); *Dist. School Jour. of the State of N. Y.*, Jan. 1846.]

G. H. G.

DWIGHT, HARRISON GRAY OTIS (Nov. 22, 1803–Jan. 25, 1862), missionary, the son of Seth and Hannah (Strong) Dwight, and a descendant of John Dwight who settled at Dedham, Mass., in 1635, was born at Conway, Mass. Soon after his birth the family moved to Utica, N. Y., in the schools of which town he secured his early education. In his fifteenth year, he was "hopefully converted" in a religious revival at Utica, and became a member of the local Presbyterian church. He attended the academies in Fairfield and Utica in preparation for college, and in 1821 entered Hamilton College, graduating in the spring of 1825. In the fall of the same year he entered Andover Theological Seminary, Mass., where he took the full three years' course in preparation for foreign missionary service. Graduating in 1828, he secured appointment under the American Board of Commissioners for Foreign Missions and spent the ensuing fifteen months as agent of the Board traveling among the churches. On July 15, 1829, at Great Barrington, Mass., he was ordained to the ministry. On Jan. 4 following, he was married to Elizabeth, daughter of Joshua and Ruth Barker of North Andover, Mass., and on Jan. 21, with her, set sail from Boston on their journey eastward to Turkey. They arrived at Malta on Feb. 27, and leaving his wife there for a time, on Mar. 17 Dwight took ship for Smyrna in company with Dr. Eli Smith, an American Board missionary, to gather information about the Armenians in the interior of Asia Minor with a view to the opening of mission stations. Traveling on horseback, in Turkish costumes, they made a memorable journey of 2,400 miles, going as far as the Caucasus and northwestern Persia. They returned by way of Constantinople, arriving at Malta on July 2, 1831. The results of this important venture in missionary exploration were published by the two authors in 1833 in two volumes entitled *Researches of Rev. Eli Smith and Rev. H. G. O. Dwight in Armenia.*

In May of the following year (1834), Dwight with his wife and an infant son left Malta to take up permanent residence in Constantinople, at first in a suburb and then in Stamboul, the Turkish city proper. For nearly thirty years his special office was that of "missionary to the Armenians," of whom there were about a hundred thousand in Constantinople. He did much literary work, being one of the first American students of the Armenian language. He wrote a geography with special reference to Turkey, several tracts, and many articles in the *Avedaper* (Messenger), which he edited after 1854; and worked on various translations. In English, in addition to his share in the *Researches,* he wrote *Memoir of Elizabeth R. Dwight* (1840), *Christianity Revived in the East* (1850, reissued in

London in 1854 under the title *Christianity in Turkey*), and prepared a catalogue of Armenian literature for the *Journal of the American Oriental Society* (vol. III, 1853).

He sought and held interviews with inquirers, gave lectures on theology, preached frequently, helped in the organization of schools and churches, and was the chief founder of the Armenian Evangelical Church in Turkey. He made several tours of preliminary investigation for his mission, and many tours of inspection. In the summer of 1833 he sailed around the Sea of Marmora, and in the summer of 1834 journeyed into European Turkey. He visited Nicomedia often and aided in the work there. In 1837 Mrs. Dwight and John, one of their four sons, succumbed to plague. Dwight returned the following year to America. During his stay in Washington, D. C., he met Mary Lane of Sturbridge, Mass., who became his bride on Apr. 16, 1839, and who returned with him to Constantinople in the autumn of the same year. Five children, one of whom was Henry Otis Dwight [*q.v.*], were born of this union; four of them survived the death of their mother on Nov. 16, 1860. During the first nine months of 1861 Dwight made a tour of all the stations which had been established by the Board in Turkish and Persian areas, and then returned to America, where he journeyed among the churches on behalf of the Turkish Mission. His death occurred in a railroad accident near Bennington, Vt., and he was buried at Utica, N. Y.

[Many of Dwight's letters recounting his experiences were published in the *Missionary Herald* between 1830 and 1862. See also *Memoirs of Am. Missionaries* (1833); H. C. Haydn, *Am. Heroes on Mission Fields* (Am. Tract Soc., 1890); B. W. Dwight, *The Hist. of the Descendants of John Dwight* (1874); Julius Richter, *Hist. of Protestant Missions in the Near East* (1910); E. M. Bliss, *The Encyc. of Missions* (1891), I, 345; W. E. Strong, *The Story of the Am. Board* (1910); *Gen. Cat. Theol. Sem., Andover, Mass. 1808–1908*; *Essex Register* (Salem, Mass.), Jan. 4, 1830; obituary notice in the *Missionary Herald*, Mar. 1862; information from H. G. Dwight, Esq., and from Miss Cornelia P. Dwight.] J. C. A.

DWIGHT, HENRY OTIS (June 3, 1843–June 20, 1917), missionary, editor, the son of Harrison G. Otis Dwight [*q.v.*] and Mary Lane, his second wife, was born in Constantinople. His entire early education, including the equivalent of high school training, was obtained in Constantinople, for the most part in his own home. When he was ready for college, he came to America and entered Ohio Wesleyan University. He was there only a year, for in September 1861 he enlisted as a private in the 20th Ohio Infantry. He was promoted successively sergeant, second lieutenant, first lieutenant, and brevetted captain. At the close of the war he declined an appointment in the regular army. He served as *aide* on the staff of Maj.-Gen. M. F. Force of the 1st Division, XVII Army Corps, Army of the Tennessee, and was mustered out in July 1865. During 1866–67 he was treasurer of the Northampton, Mass., Street Railway Company. He had "dabbled in engineering" while in the army, and assisted in laying out the city's railway system.

In March 1867 he was married to Mary Bliss, daughter of the Rev. Elisha E. Bliss [*q.v.*], of the Western Turkey Mission, with whom he sailed on Nov. 23, 1867, for Constantinople, to serve under the American Board of Commissioners for Foreign Missions in connection with the mission's business department. He was "Secular Agent" until 1874, and from 1875 to 1899 was general editor of the Turkish publications of the mission. In the latter capacity he performed the great scholarly work of his life, the editing of the *Turkish and English Lexicon* (1890) of Sir James Redhouse.

From 1875 to 1892 he acted as special correspondent of the *New York Tribune*, supplying his paper with valuable news of events from the outset of the reign of Abdul Hamid II. Some of his letters to the *Tribune* formed the basis of a volume, *Turkish Life in War Time*, published in 1881. He also contributed articles on Turkey to magazines in the United States, often writing under an assumed name in order to avoid difficulties with the Turkish censorship. Throughout this period, his intimate understanding of affairs in Turkey made his letters to the United States minister on behalf of the mission useful to the State Department in shaping its policy in the Near East. In 1893 he published *Treaty Rights of American Missionaries in Turkey*. At one time he was mentioned for the post of United States minister at Constantinople, but he felt that he could be of greater use in a humbler but more permanent position. In 1899 he gave up his editorial connection with the mission and returned to America.

He was editor, in 1900, of the *Report* of the Ecumenical Missionary Conference held that year in New York City. In 1901 he resigned from the mission altogether, continuing the general editorial work upon which he had been engaged and devoting his time more fully to authorship. He published *Constantinople and its Problems* (1901); was editor in chief of the *Encyclopædia of Missions* in 1904; was the author of the *Blue Book of Missions*, issued in 1905 and 1907, and of *A Muslim Sir Galahad* (1913). From March 1904 he acted as secretary of the Bureau of Missions, in New York City, and from

Jan. 1, 1907, as recording secretary of the American Bible Society. As historian of this Society he published in 1916 their *Centennial History*.

Although he never held a pastorate, while in America on a furlough in 1880 he was ordained to the ministry by the Council of the Lamoille County (Vt.) Congregational Association. He was married four times. His first wife, Mary Bliss, died at Constantinople on Nov. 15, 1872, at the age of twenty-eight. On Apr. 18, 1874, he married Ardelle Maria Griswold, of the Turkey Mission, who had gone out to Cæsarea in 1869. She died at Constantinople on Dec. 28, 1884, in her thirty-seventh year. In 1887 he married Belle S. Bliss, who died in 1894, in her thirty-sixth year. On Dec. 26, 1900, he married Mrs. Frances Warner Mulford of Roselle, N. J. He died at Roselle shortly after his seventy-fourth birthday.

[*Who's Who in America*, 1916–17; B. W. Dwight, *The Hist. of the Descendants of John Dwight of Dedham, Mass.* (1874), vol. II; *Congreg. Year Book*, 1917; *Missionary Review of the World*, July 1917; *Missionary Herald*, Aug. 1917, and frequent mention, 1867–1901; *N. Y. Tribune*, June 20, 1917; *N. Y. Times*, June 21, 1917; *Foreign Relations of the U. S.*, esp. 1890–1900; information from a son, H. G. Dwight, Esq.] J. C. A.

DWIGHT, JOHN SULLIVAN (May 13, 1813–Sept. 5, 1893), music critic, editor, was born at Boston, Mass., eldest of the four children of Dr. John and Mary (Corey) Dwight. His father, who had studied for the ministry and then become a physician, was a radical freethinker. The boy, a sensitive, affectionate, gentle lad, early gave evidence of literary ability, and before he was sixteen, of an absorbing love of music. Prepared at the Boston Latin School, he entered Harvard College in 1829, maintained a "respectable standing" in his class, and was happily associated with the musical club, the Pierian Sodality. After graduation in 1832, when he delivered the class poem, he became a student in the Harvard Divinity School, where he formed lasting friendships with Theodore Parker and Christopher Pearse Cranch [*qq.v.*]. He completed his course in August 1836, giving a dissertation upon "The Proper Character of Poetry and Music for Public Worship" (*Christian Examiner*, November 1836), and entered upon a period of supplying various pulpits, writing literary reviews for periodicals, and studying and translating German poetry. In 1837 he was one of the leaders in the formation of the General Association of the Members of the Pierian Sodality, later the Harvard Musical Association. He was responsible for most of the translation and all of the notes in *Select Minor Poems translated from the German of Goethe and Schiller* (1839). In 1840 he was called to the pastorate of the Unitarian church at Northampton. On May 20 he was ordained and installed, George Ripley [*q.v.*] preaching the sermon and William Ellery Channing delivering the charge. During the year that followed, two of his sermons, "The Religion of Beauty" and "Ideals of Every Day Life," were published in the first volume of the *Dial*. Although esteemed by his parishioners for his amiability and purity of soul, he did not have the power of disciplined thought which the Northampton congregation required of its preacher. Accordingly, after about a year he resigned, and before long "quietly dropped out of a profession which he felt was no longer congenial."

He had been a member of the Transcendental Club from its beginning and in November 1841 joined Ripley at Brook Farm, where he became one of the leaders. Here he was teacher of music and Latin, and in the former field he found his calling. Instilling in the children and awakening in the adults an appreciation of music and a conception of its power in the enlargement of the spiritual life, he organized Mass Clubs both at West Roxbury and in Boston to sing the great compositions of Mozart, Bach, and Beethoven, and made the *Harbinger*, the organ of Brook Farm and later of the American Union of Associationists, "one of the best musical journals the country has ever possessed" (Cooke, *Dwight*, p. 108). He was a constant contributor to the *Harbinger*, of articles on "Association," literary reviews, and poems, as well as musical criticism; for a while, with Ripley, he edited it, and after its removal to New York upon the break-up of the Brook Farm community in October 1847 he was one of its editorial contributors. During the next four years, residing in Boston, he directed the choir of W. H. Channing's Religious Union of Associationists; lectured on musical subjects; wrote reviews and musical criticisms for Boston and New York journals; contributed a series of monthly articles to *Sartain's Magazine* (1851–52); for a few months conducted in the Boston *Daily Chronotype* a department devoted to Association; and for the first six months of 1851 was musical editor of the *Boston Commonwealth*. On Feb. 12, 1851, he was married to Mary Bullard, a member of his choir.

In the next year, aided by the Harvard Musical Association, he issued the first number of *Dwight's Journal of Music: A Paper of Literature and Art*, of which he was publisher as well as editor and chief contributor until Oliver Ditson & Company took over the publishing in 1858. In the columns of his *Journal* he "translated music into literary form, showed the public what to find in it and how to discover its profound spiritual charm and power" (*Ibid.*, p. 236), and for nearly thirty years exerted an unparalleled influence on the formation of musical taste in America. At the end of that time its purpose had been to some extent accomplished; new schools of music, with whom the editor could not wholly sympathize, were coming into prominence; and the issue of Sept. 3, 1881, was the last.

Although the *Journal* absorbed most of his energy, Dwight found time to translate a number of lyrics and several works on music from the German, to lecture frequently, and to contribute to other periodicals. The *Atlantic Monthly* for September and November 1870 contained two parts of a notable lecture delivered earlier in that year: "Music a Means of Culture" and "The Intellectual Influence of Music." He wrote the chapter on music for Justin Winsor's *Memorial History of Boston* (1881); completed Vol. I (1883) of *The History of the Händel and Haydn Society of Boston, Mass.*, begun by Charles C. Perkins; from 1885 to 1890 assisted in the revision of musical definitions for *Webster's International Dictionary*; and in 1890, for six months, substituted for W. F. Apthorp as musical editor of the *Boston Transcript*. An essay, "Common Sense," in which he discussed philosophy, religion, and politics, written in 1885, appeared in the *Unitarian Review*, May 1890.

Dwight was for eighteen years a trustee of the Perkins Institution for the Blind, and gave to it enthusiastic service. He was one of the earliest members of the Saturday Club, and from 1877 had a large share in the handling of the Club's affairs. He was vice-president of the Harvard Musical Association from 1855 to 1873 and president and librarian from 1873 until his death. In 1865 he was instrumental in the formation among its members of the Philharmonic Society; in 1876 with the establishment of a professorship of music at Harvard he saw the accomplishment of the Association's stated object. After the death of his wife, in 1860, while he was in Europe on his only trip abroad, he made his home for a time with his mother and sister, then in an apartment near the *Journal* office, and after 1873, in the rooms of the Harvard Musical Association. Here he died, in his eighty-first year. Unpractical, gentle, visionary, Dwight "lived sunnily in life-long poverty, loved his friends, loved flowers and music," and by "his rare gift of appreciation and enthusiasm diffused a sense of beauty throughout a whole community" (Perry, *post*).

[Geo. Willis Cooke, *John Sullivan Dwight, Brook-Farmer, Editor, and Critic of Music* (1898) and *Early Letters of Geo. Wm. Curtis to John S. Dwight* (1898); W. S. B. Mathews, in *Music* (Chicago), Sept. 1893; Wm. F. Apthorp, *Ibid.*, Oct. 1893, reprinted from the *Boston Transcript*, Sept. 5, 1893; Bliss Perry, in E. W. Emerson, *The Early Years of the Saturday Club, 1855–1870* (1918); B. W. Dwight, *Hist. of the Descendants of John Dwight, of Dedham, Mass.* (1874); *Boston Evening Jour.* and *Boston Advertiser*, Sept. 6, 1893.]

E. R. D.

DWIGHT, NATHANIEL (Jan. 31, 1770–June 11, 1831), physician, educator, tenth of the thirteen children of Maj. Timothy and Mary (Edwards) Dwight and seventh of their nine sons, was born in Northampton, Mass. His early education was probably in charge of his mother, the gifted daughter of Jonathan Edwards, who conducted a regular school for her children, and whose rare teaching ability was inherited by many of her descendants. He may also have attended the school at Greenfield Hill kept by his brother Timothy [*q.v.*], later president of Yale. Apparently he did not go to college, but he later said himself (Preface to *Geography*) that he was employed "several years in school-keeping." He studied medicine under an eminent Hartford physician, Dr. Mason F. Cogswell; practised in Hartford, and served for a time as assistant surgeon in the army at Governors Island. Resigning from the army, he practised in Westfield, Mass., and New London and Wethersfield, Conn. In 1812 he entered the ministry and settled in Westchester, Conn., returning, however, to medical practise in 1820, in Providence, R. I., and Norwich, Conn. Apparently not financially successful, Dwight was nevertheless accounted a good medical practitioner, "kind and generous to a fault," and a faithful and earnest preacher. Like his brothers, he was tall and well built, though not as fine-looking as most of them. He was married on June 24, 1798, to Rebecca Robbins of Wethersfield, Conn., the daughter of Appleton Robbins and Mary Stillman. Four of their eight children died in infancy.

In 1795 he published *A Short but Comprehensive System of the Geography of the World: by Way of Question and Answer*, which went through numerous editions over a period of years. This effort was enthusiastically received as "better calculated to impress the facts which it contains on the minds of children than any heretofore published," but it was not, as has often been stated, the first school geography issued in the United States, *The American Geography* (1789), by Jedidiah Morse having preceded it. Dwight wrote another schoolbook, *Sketches of the Lives of the Signers of the Declaration of Independence*, first published in 1830, which continued to appear with slightly varying title in subsequent editions up to 1895. His chief addi-

Dwight

tional contribution seems to have been a constructive suggestion for improving the condition of the insane. "As early as 1812, Dr. Nathaniel Dwight of Colchester sent to the convention of the [Connecticut Medical] Society a communication upon the subject of a hospital for lunatics in this State, and a committee was appointed to collect proper information and report" (Speech by Dr. Gurdon W. Russell, Jan. 7, 1873, at the semi-centennial celebration of the Hartford Asylum, *Hartford Daily Courant*, Jan. 8, 1873). He died at Oswego, N. Y., while on a visit.

[B. W. Dwight, *The Hist. of the Descendants of John Dwight of Dedham, Mass.* (2 vols., 1874); Preface to Dwight's *Geography*.]

E. W. F.

DWIGHT, SERENO EDWARDS (May 18, 1786–Nov. 30, 1850), educator, clergyman, fifth of the eight sons of the elder Timothy Dwight [*q.v.*] and his wife, Mary Woolsey, was born at Greenfield Hill in Fairfield, Conn. His early education was conducted at home and in his father's school. From 1796 to 1799 he attended the Hopkins Grammar School in New Haven; in 1803, at the age of seventeen, he graduated from Yale, of which his father was then president, and began his teaching career at Litchfield, Conn. The following year he returned to New Haven as his father's amanuensis, acting at the same time as assistant to Benjamin Silliman [*q.v.*], professor of chemistry. After another year, spent in general study, he was a tutor at Yale, 1806–10, in sole charge of half a class in mathematics, rhetoric, and the classics, and simultaneously studied law, which he practised in New Haven from 1810 to 1816. He was over six feet tall, erect and dignified in his carriage, meticulous in details of dress, handsome and intellectual in countenance and altogether of commanding and striking presence. On Aug. 28, 1811, he was married to Susan Edwards Daggett, daughter of David Daggett [*q.v.*] and Wealthy Ann Munson.

In 1812 he fell victim to a severe lung fever, the mercury treatment for which produced a painful eruption which was to torture him for the rest of his days. Though successful in his law practise, in 1815 he decided to enter the ministry and on Oct. 8, 1816, was licensed to preach by the West Association of Ministers of New Haven County. Shortly afterward he was appointed chaplain of the United States Senate, in which his father-in-law was representing Connecticut, and served during the session 1816–17. The following summer he accepted a call to the famous Park Street Church in Boston, being ordained and installed on Sept. 3, 1817. He remained there until 1826, except for the year 1824–25, which he spent in European travel and a vain search for medical help.

Forced by vocal trouble and ill health to resign his pastorate, he returned to New Haven, and in 1828, in partnership with his youngest brother, Henry, opened a boarding-school for boys, the New Haven Gymnasium, modeled on the German plan. This project was highly successful, but neither brother had sufficient strength to keep it up, and in 1831 it was discontinued. In 1833 he was called to the presidency of Hamilton College, of which his brother Benjamin Woolsey Dwight was then treasurer. As president of Hamilton he raised a $50,000 fund, and also taught metaphysics, moral philosophy, and natural theology. He resigned on Sept. 2, 1835, because of disagreement with the trustees (see *Documentary History of Hamilton College*, 1922), and he never accepted another office, except that of agent for the Pennsylvania Colonization Society which he held from 1835 to 1838. His wife died in 1839; deprived of her mental and spiritual companionship, he survived her in loneliness and suffering for eleven years, living chiefly in New York and engaged largely in reading. In 1850 he went to Philadelphia, hoping to benefit from hydropathic treatments; but he died there in November of that year. He was buried in New Haven.

Soon after his marriage, Dwight wrote his first book, *The Hebrew Wife*, published in New York many years later (1836), and republished in Glasgow (1837). In 1818 he prefaced a five-volume edition of Timothy Dwight's *Theology, Explained and Defended* (1818–19) with a memoir of his father. Assisted by his wife, he worked for many years editing the complete writings of his great-grandfather, Jonathan Edwards; Edwards's *Memoirs of the Rev. David Brainerd* was published in 1822, and ten subsequent volumes, one a memoir of the great divine, were published in 1830 as *The Works of President Edwards: with a Memoir of his Life*. Various sermons and addresses of his own were published, mostly in pamphlet form, during his lifetime, and after his death appeared a volume, *Select Discourses of S. E. Dwight, D.D.* (1851), with a memoir by his younger brother, Rev. William T. Dwight.

[B. W. Dwight, *Hist. of the Descendants of John Dwight of Dedham, Mass.* (2 vols., 1874); memoir by W. T. Dwight, in *Select Discourses*, mentioned above; *Park Street Church Centennial* (1909), ed. by A. Z. Conrad; Wm. B. Sprague, *Annals Am. Pulpit*, vol. II (1857); F. B. Dexter, *Biog. Sketches Grads. Yale Coll.*, vol. V (1911).]

E. W. F.

DWIGHT, THEODORE (Dec. 15, 1764–June 12, 1846), lawyer, author, editor, was born in Northampton, Mass., seventh of the thirteen children of Maj. Timothy and Mary (Edwards) Dwight, whose first-born was Timothy Dwight [*q.v.*]. His father was a well-to-do merchant, landowner, and local office-holder; his mother, a daughter of Jonathan Edwards [*q.v.*], was a woman of remarkable strength of character. Maj. Timothy Dwight died when Theodore was in his thirteenth year, and the boy was brought up by his mother on the farm in Northampton. When he was about twenty, an injury obliged him to give up farming. He studied law with his uncle, Pierpont Edwards [*q.v.*], of New Haven, was admitted to the bar in 1787, and began practise at Haddam, Conn. In 1791 he moved to Hartford and practised there until 1815. He is reported to have been at one time in the early period of his practise on the point of forming a partnership with his cousin, Aaron Burr, the agreement falling through because of a political dispute. He was married on Sept. 9, 1792, to Abigail, daughter of Richard and Mary (Wright) Alsop of Middletown, Conn., and sister of Richard Alsop [*q.v.*], the poet. Dwight soon acquired a reputation as a competent lawyer, an able writer, and an eloquent speaker. A number of his speeches on various occasions during his years at Hartford have survived. One of the most interesting was delivered May 8, 1794, before the Connecticut Society for the Promotion of Freedom, and is noteworthy as an early arraignment of slavery; it contains passages which resemble utterances of Garrison and Phillips. His political addresses show that he shared with most of his contemporaries the enthusiasm for the French Revolution which later turned to fear and aversion. It was during this same period that he became identified with the group of writers known as the "Connecticut Wits." He was himself the author of much verse, but his poetical effusions are of antiquarian rather than literary interest (Parrington, *post*). Some of the New Year addresses, however, contributed to the *Connecticut Courant* and *Connecticut Mirror* are clever imitations of Hudibras and have been frequently quoted by historians.

He was ultra-Federalist in politics, and his views of the opposing party and its doctrines are to be found in his published addresses and in frequent editorial contributions, essays, and verses in the *Connecticut Courant* and *Connecticut Mirror*. His journalistic writings are characterized by the scurrility and personal abuse which were so common in American newspapers of the period. In 1806–07 he served for a single session in Congress, in place of John Cotton Smith, resigned; and from 1809 to 1815 was a member of the Council. He was less prominent as an office-holder, however, than as a party worker, pamphleteer, and editor. He was well known throughout New England, his writings were widely quoted, and he corresponded with leading Federalists in other states. In Connecticut he fought all the reforms proposed by the Republicans prior to the War of 1812, and was earnestly opposed to the latter contest. At the same time he had numerous business interests, maintained a law practise, and was active in various local societies. In 1814 he acted as secretary of the Hartford Convention and in 1833 published the journal of that ill-starred gathering together with a review of the steps leading up to the War of 1812. It is an able defense of the Federalist party, although somewhat too polemical for good historical writing, as is also *The Character of Thomas Jefferson as Exhibited in his own Writings* (1839). In 1815 he moved to Albany, N. Y., where he founded the *Daily Advertiser*; but he remained there less than two years. In 1817 he founded the *New York Daily Advertiser,* and continued in New York City in active management of the paper until 1836, when he returned to Hartford to spend his declining years. His death took place in New York, however, as had that of his wife less than three months earlier.

[W. W. Spooner, *Historic Families of America* (n.d.), p. 110; Dwight Loomis and J. G. Calhoun, *Judicial and Civil Hist. of Conn.* (1895), p. 236; B. W. Dwight, *Hist. of the Descendants of John Dwight* (1874), I, 227–31; V. L. Parrington, in *The Conn. Wits* (1926), pp. xxxiii–xxxv, giving a list of Dwight's principal writings; S. G. Goodrich, *Recollections of a Lifetime* (1856), II, 123; R. J. Purcell, *Conn. in Transition, 1775–1818* (1918), giving an excellent historical setting for Dwight's earlier career; obituary in *N. Y. Tribune,* June 13, 1846.]

W. A. R.

DWIGHT, THEODORE (Mar. 3, 1796–Oct. 16, 1866), author, educator, was born in Hartford, Conn., the son of Theodore [*q.v.*] and Abigail (Alsop) Dwight. His father was the secretary of the Hartford Convention; his mother was a sister of Richard Alsop [*q.v.*]. With such parents it was natural that Theodore should be fed from early childhood on unadulterated Federalism and Calvinism and that the diet should be topped off with a four-year course at Yale, where he graduated in 1814, under his uncle Timothy [*q.v.*], whose memory he revered and whose classroom utterances, taken down in shorthand, he published as *President Dwight's Decisions of Questions Discussed by the Senior Class in Yale College in 1813 and 1814* (1833). He had intended to study theology under his uncle, but an attack of scarlet fever followed by a hemorrhage of the lungs made him relinquish his plans and turn to less strenuous employment. He traveled abroad for his health in 1818–19 and in October 1820 went again to England and France for a longer stay. In Paris he engaged with the Rev. Francis Leo in distributing free copies of De Sacy's French New Testament and was arrested for collecting an unlawful number of persons on the streets. He spoke French, Spanish, and Italian well and had a fair command of German, Portuguese, and modern Greek. At home in New York and in Brooklyn, where he lived from 1833 till his death, he taught school, worked on his father's paper, the *New York Daily Advertiser,* busied himself as author, editor, and translator of English books into Spanish, and engaged in various philanthropic, religious, and educational enterprises. At one time or another he worked for the *Protestant Vindicator,* the *Family Visitor,* the *Christian Alliance and Family Visitor,* the *New York Presbyterian,* and the *Youth's Penny Paper.* A venture of his own was *Dwight's American Magazine and Family Newspaper,* 1845–52. On Apr. 24, 1827, he married Eleanor Boyd of New York. He has the distinction of having introduced vocal music into the New York public schools. From 1854 to 1858 he worked with George Walter to send Free-Soil settlers to Kansas; together they persuaded about 3,000 persons to emigrate to the new territory. His knowledge of the Romance languages, his republicanism, and his desire to protestantize Catholic countries led him to entertain many political exiles from the Latin countries of Europe and the Americas. Of these guests the most famous was Garibaldi, who intrusted to him his autobiography for publication in the United States. Dwight's more important books are: *A Journal of a Tour in Italy in the Year 1821* (1824); *The Northern Traveller, containing the Routes to Niagara, Quebec, and the Springs* (1825; 6th ed., 1841); *Sketches of Scenery and Manners in the United States* (1829); *A New Gazetteer of the United States of America* (1833, with William Darby [*q.v.*], Dwight being responsible for New York, New Jersey, and New England); *Lessons in Greek* (1833, an interesting attempt at a rational method of instruction); *The Father's Book, or Suggestions for the Government and Instruction of Young Children on Principles Appropriate to a Christian Country* (1834, also published in London), of considerable interest; *The School-Master's Friend, with the Committee-Man's Guide: Containing Suggestions on Education, Modes of Teaching and Governing, . . . Plans of School-Houses, Furniture, Apparatus, Practical Hints, and Anecdotes on Different Systems* (1835); *Open Covenants, or Nunneries and Popish Seminaries Dangerous to the Morals and Degrading to the Character of a Republican Community* (1836); *Dictionary of Roots and Derivations* (1837); *The History of Connecticut* (1840); *Summer Tours, or Notes of a Traveler through some of the Middle and Northern States* (1847, originally published in 1834 as *Things as They Are*; republished in Glasgow in 1848 as *Travels in America*); *The Roman Republic of 1849* (1851); an edition with much new material of Maria Monk's *Awful Disclosures* (1855); *Life of General Garibaldi, Translated from his Private Papers with the History of his Splendid Exploits in Rome, Lombardy, Sicily, and Naples to the Present Time* (1861). Dwight's admiration for Garibaldi, it may be added, was unbounded. During his last years he worked in the New York Customs House. He died from shock and injuries received in jumping from a moving train in Jersey City.

[B. W. Dwight, *The Hist. of the Descendants of John Dwight of Dedham, Mass.* (1874); F. B. Dexter, *Biog. Sketches Grads. Yale Coll.,* vol. VI (1912).]

G. H. G.

DWIGHT, THEODORE WILLIAM (July 18, 1822–June 29, 1892), lawyer, educator, grandson of Timothy Dwight [*q.v.*], was born at Catskill, N. Y., the second son of Dr. Benjamin Woolsey Dwight and his wife, Sophia Woodbridge Strong, sister of Theodore Strong, the eminent mathematician. Benjamin Woodbridge Dwight [*q.v.*] was his elder brother. The family moved to Clinton, N. Y., in 1831. As a boy Theodore William was an omnivorous reader and possessed an exceptionally retentive memory. In 1837 he entered Hamilton College, graduating with honors in 1840. He then studied physics in New York City for a short time, later becoming instructor in classics at Utica Academy. He had discovered, however, that "as all roads lead to Rome, so all intellectual aspiration may lead to law," and in 1841 he entered the Yale Law School. He did not complete his course, being in 1842 appointed tutor in Hamilton College, a position which he held for four years, at the same time initiating and conducting an informal class for instruction in law. In 1845 he was admitted to the New York bar. In 1846 he was appointed to the Maynard Professorship of Law, History, Civil Polity, and Political Economy at Hamilton, and during his twelve years' tenure of this chair, laid the foundations for the work with which his name will always be associated. The instruction in law at Hamilton had been perfunctory and did not contemplate any graduate study, but he systematized and extended the course, obtained recognition of a regular department of law in 1853, and laid down the principles upon which it was to be conducted: "The great object aimed at is to store the mind of the student with the fundamental principles of law." His method involved an extensive use of authoritative text-books from which the student obtained a grasp of the principles, and then was taught how to apply them. Cases were only used as illustrations of the propositions formulated in the books. In 1855 the Hamilton Law School was incorporated and he became its head, continuing to hold the Maynard Professorship. Up to this time there had been no law school in New York City, and, in order to supply the want, the trustees of Columbia College in 1858 established the Columbia Law School, offering Dwight the professorship of municipal law in connection therewith. He accepted and in November of that year commenced his initial course of lectures, which were an immediate success, and students enrolled in large numbers. For fourteen years he continued unassisted to lecture on all the topics embraced in private law, justifying the comment that "he was himself the Columbia Law School," and though there was no progress during the Civil War, on its termination the classes became crowded. In addition to his heavy duties at Columbia, he lectured on constitutional law at Cornell, 1869–71, and at Amherst College, 1870–72. In 1873 he was assisted by George Chase [*q.v.*], who was that year appointed instructor, becoming assistant professor of municipal law in 1875. The reputation of the school had now spread far and wide, and the increase of students was such that five professorships were created in 1878, Dwight continuing as warden to direct the policy and superintend the teaching, in addition to lecturing. His method was always the same, and it was, to use his own term, "Socratic, illustrative and expository" (Strong, p. 259). He remained head of the school till June 1891. In that year the trustees of Columbia University determined upon a revolutionary change of policy, involving the adoption of the system, then in vogue at Harvard Law School, of studying law by considering principles as evolved from decided cases, *i. e.,* the "case system." This was the antipodes of the method which he had successfully pursued for thirty-three years, and he accordingly resigned, being, however, appointed professor emeritus. The tradition of his teaching was perpetuated in the establishment of the New York Law School under the auspices of former pupils, with his colleague, George Chase, as dean.

His interests had not been confined to the Columbia Law School, and for years he was an active figure in state matters. In 1866 he and E C. Wines were appointed a committee to examine the prison systems of the state of New York and the following year they published a *Report on the Prisons and Reformatories of the United States and Canada,* which was replete with valuable suggestions. In 1867 he was a delegate to the state constitutional convention and served upon its judiciary committee. He took a prominent part in the municipal reform movement in New York City consequent upon the operations of the Tweed Ring, and in 1873 was chairman of the legislative committee of the Committee of Seventy. In the same year he was appointed by Gov. Dix a member of the commission of appeals, which assisted the New York court of appeals in disposing of its badly congested cause list, and in this capacity his all-round legal learning showed to great advantage. Maintaining his interest in prison reform and social well-being, he became vice-president of the state board of public charities and president of the state Prison Association, and in 1878 was state commissioner to the International Prison Congress at Stockholm. In his early days at Columbia he had been associated as referee or counsel with important testamentary litigation, particularly the Rose and Hoyt Will Cases. In 1886 he was retained as counsel for five professors at Andover Theological Seminary against whom complaints of heterodoxy had been made, and the display of learning, historical and legal, in his argument on their behalf was impressive. His appearances as counsel were rare, however, and only in exceptional cases. There was a theoretical cast to his mind and an absence of the practical which would have been a serious obstacle to successful practise (Strong, *post*). In addition to a number of academic addresses which were later issued in pamphlet form, he published: *Cases Extracted from the Reports of the Commissioners of Charities, in England, and from the Calendars in Chancery* (1863); *James Harrington and his Influence upon American Political Institutions and Political Thought* (1887); and an Introduction to Maine's *Ancient Law,* prefixed to the first American edition of that work (1864). For a number of years he was associate editor of the *American Law Register,* and he was legal editor of *Johnson's Cyclopædia of Literature and Science,* contributing many articles thereto.

Of large build, five feet ten inches in height, with broad shoulders and florid complexion, he was dignified but not distant in manner. Sympathetic, courteous, and always accessible, he possessed a singularly attractive personality, and his influence over his pupils, during their aca demic careers and in after life, was extraordinary. He was married, on Aug. 24, 1847, to Mary Bond, daughter of Asa Olmstead of Clinton, N. Y. His death occurred in Clinton.

[*N. Y. Geneal. and Biog. Record*, Jan. 1886; W. W. Spooner, *Historic Families of America* (n.d.); B. W. Dwight, *The Hist. of the Descendants of John Dwight of Dedham, Mass.* (1874), I, 189; Theron G. Strong, *Landmarks of a Lawyer's Lifetime* (1914), p. 259; *In Memoriam Theodore William Dwight* (n.d.); *Case and Comment*, Apr. 1900; *N. Y. Times*, *N. Y. Tribune*, June 30, 1892.] H. W. H. K.

DWIGHT, THOMAS (Oct. 13, 1843–Sept. 9, 1911), anatomist of Boston, son of Thomas Dwight by his wife, Mary Collins Warren, daughter of —— John Collins Warren, *primus* [*q.v.*], was born in Boston. As a child he was taken abroad and attended school in Paris until about the age of twelve when he returned to complete his education in Boston. He entered Harvard College with the class of 1866, but after two years transferred to the Harvard Medical School where he obtained his degree of M.D. in 1867; he did not take his A.B. degree until 1872 when it was received as of the class of 1866. After completing his work at the medical school he again spent some time abroad, studying natural history and anatomy, and while in the laboratory of Rüdinger of Munich he learned the technique of examining frozen microscopical sections, which he introduced into the United States on his return. Between 1872 and 1877 he held instructorships in comparative anatomy and in histology at the Harvard Medical School, and a professorship of anatomy at Bowdoin from 1873 to 1876; he also served during the years 1873–78 as editor of the *Boston Medical and Surgical Journal*. In 1880 he again accepted an anatomical instructorship at Harvard, and three years later succeeded to the Parkman Professorship of Anatomy in the place of Oliver Wendell Holmes [*q.v.*], retaining this position until his death in 1911. He was president of the Association of American Anatomists in 1894, and was a member of the editorial board of the *American Journal of Anatomy* from its founding. For a number of years he practised surgery in Boston, being surgeon to out-patients at the Boston City Hospital (1877–80), visiting surgeon of the Carney Hospital (1876–83) and president of the staff of the Carney Hospital (1883–98). In 1900 he retired from active surgical work in order to devote his entire time to anatomical research and teaching.

Dwight was deeply interested in the minutiæ of human anatomy, and his chief contributions related to his meticulous studies of the anatomical variations of the skeleton and joints. He collected a notable series of specimens showing the chief variations of certain of the bones of the feet and hands (carpus, tarsus, and cuboid) and described a new element in the foot, the intercuneiform bone. Through his activity many additions were made to the Warren Pathological Museum of the Harvard Medical School. As a teacher he was forceful and eventually popular, though at first the task of filling the chair vacated by Holmes proved difficult. Throughout his life Dwight was an ardent follower of the Roman Catholic faith and supported actively such societies as the St. Thomas Aquinas Academy of Philosophy and Medicine of Rome and the Society of St. Vincent de Paul, of which he was vice-president in 1884 and president in 1887. His study of the variations of the human skeleton had led him to consider the problem of heredity, and he attempted, just before his death, to harmonize the theories of evolution and heredity with the teachings of the Church of Rome. His book, *Thoughts of a Catholic Anatomist*, the proof-sheets of which he corrected during his last illness, was published in 1911, just before his death. His devotion and loyalty to his creed were outstanding in his life and influenced his point of view and his scientific opinions. A list of his numerous anatomical papers is to be found in the *Index Catalogue* of the Surgeon General's Library. His most important contributions were: his Boylston Prize Essay, *The Intracranial Circulation* (1867); *The Structure and Action of Striated Muscle Fibers* (1873); *The Anatomy of the Head, with . . . Plates Representing Frozen Sections* (1876); *Frozen Sections of a Child* (1881); *Description of the Human Spine Showing Numerical Variations* (1901); *Notes on the Dissection and Brain of the Chimpanzee "Gumbo"* (1895); and his chapters in G. A. Piersol's *Anatomy* (1911) on bones and joints, and on the gastro-pulmonary system and accessory organs of nutrition.

[Articles by John Warren in *Anatomical Record*, Nov. 1911, and *Boston Medic. and Surgic. Jour.*, Aug. 14, 1919, the first including a bibliography of Dwight's publications, the second reprinted in H. A. Kelly and W. L. Burrage, *Am. Medic. Biogs.* (1920); *Boston Medic. and Surgic. Jour.*, Sept. 21, 1911; *Jour. Am. Medic. Asso.*, Sept. 23, 1911; T. F. Harrington, *The Harvard Medic. School* (1905), III, 1415.] J. F. F.

DWIGHT, TIMOTHY (May 14, 1752–Jan. 11, 1817), Congregational divine, author, president of Yale College from 1795 to 1817, and throughout these years the dominant figure in the established order of Connecticut, was born in Northampton, Mass., a descendant of John Dwight who came from Dedham, England, in

1635 and settled in Dedham, Mass. His father, Major Timothy, was a successful merchant and the proprietor of a considerable estate. Some light is thrown on his character by the fact that although a graduate of Yale and destined for the law, he "had such extreme sensibility to the beauty and sweetness of always doing right, . . . and regarded the legal profession as so full of temptations to doing wrong, in great degrees or small," that he preferred not to be a lawyer (Benjamin W. Dwight, *History of the Descendants of John Dwight of Dedham, Mass.*, 1874, I, 130). His conscientiousness was indirectly the cause of his death. As judge of probate he had sworn fealty to the Crown, and therefore felt himself debarred from taking any part in the Revolution. To escape the situation to which his scruples gave rise, he bought part of a Crown grant to his deceased brother-in-law, Phineas Lyman, in West Florida, and, with the latter's widow and children and two of his own sons, in 1776 he went to take possession of it. In this unhealthful region he died June 10, 1777, although news of the fact did not reach his family in Northampton until a year later. Six feet and four inches tall and well proportioned, he was by actual test as strong as an ox. In contrast, his wife, Mary, daughter of Jonathan Edwards, was so petite that, according to tradition, he could hold her at arm's length on the palm of his hand. She bore him thirteen children, of whom Timothy was the first-born.

Mary Edwards Dwight was a woman of remarkable character and mental ability. At her death Timothy said that he owed all that he was to her, although in this statement he was not quite fair to his father to whom some of his spiritual traits, as well as his physical stature, may certainly be attributed. She was but seventeen years old at his birth, but almost from the cradle she proceeded to educate him according to ideas of her own. He early displayed a tenacious memory, acquisitiveness, and determination. He learned the alphabet in one lesson, and by the time he was four he was reading the Bible with ease and correctness. When he was six years old he was sent to grammar school, where, contrary to the wishes of his father, who thought him too young, and without the knowledge of his master, he acquired familiarity with Latin by studying the books of the other boys while they were at play. Had the school not been discontinued, he would have been ready for college at the age of eight. His mother continued his instruction, which was supplemented by a short period of schooling under Rev. Enoch Huntington of Middletown, Conn., and at thirteen he entered Yale, having already done much of the work of the first two college years. He graduated in 1769, sharing highest honors with Nathan Strong, and at once became principal of the Hopkins Grammar School, New Haven, returning to Yale in 1771 to remain six years as tutor.

During the first half of his college course he seems to have been guilty of some of the ordinary frailties of humanity, card playing especially, but having reached the mature age of fifteen, he was converted to a more serious view of life, and his native ambition to make a conquest of all knowledge took full possession of him. A resolve to devote fourteen hours a day to study was rigorously kept, and although the college schedule began at 5:30 winters, and at 4:30 summers, he was up an hour earlier reading by candle light. He thus laid the foundation for an affection of the eyes, which subjected him to suffering and limitation for the remainder of his life. While a tutor, in order not to have to take time for exercise, he reduced his eating until his dinners consisted of twelve mouthfuls, asceticism which resulted in a physical breakdown. He recuperated by walking upward of 2,000 miles and riding on horseback 3,000 more, thus beginning the peregrinations and observations, the fruits of which appeared later in records of much value. In 1774 he united with the college church, and soon gave up his original intention to become a lawyer, and turned to theology. The conventional subjects of the day were not his only interest, however. He made a study of sacred music and wrote several anthems. With his fellow tutors, Joseph Howe and John Trumbull, he developed an interest in literature, composition, and oratory at Yale, and sought to broaden its curriculum. Upon receiving his master's degree in 1772 he delivered *A Dissertation on the History, Eloquence, and Poetry of the Bible* which was published that same year. To this literary interest at Yale may be traced the origin of the school known as the "Connecticut" or "Hartford Wits," of which Dwight was one of the most prolific members—a school devoted to the cultivation of belles-lettres, and ambitious to give to America a worthy body of poetry. As a tutor he was noted for his skill as an administrator and was extraordinarily popular. When in 1777 Naphtali Daggett resigned as president *pro tem.*, the students wanted Dwight appointed president. That others also had him in mind is revealed by the appointee, Dr. Stiles, who records: "I have heard of but one Gentleman that disapproves the Choice . . . and he is Hon. Col. Davenport of Stanford a Gent. of Learning & great Merit. He says the Corpora have done wrong in electing me; they should have chosen Mr. Tutor Dwight" (F. B. Dexter, *The Literary Diary of Ezra Stiles,* 1901, II, 231). Before leaving Yale Dwight broke an old tradition by marrying while a tutor, taking for his wife, Mar. 3, 1777, Mary, daughter of Benjamin Woolsey.

His resignation, September 1777, was due to the war. The preceding June he had been licensed to preach by a committee of the Northern Association of Massachusetts, and on Oct. 6, Congress appointed him chaplain of Gen. S. H. Parson's Connecticut Continental Brigade, and he soon joined the army at West Point. He threw himself into the work of instructing and inspiring the soldiery with his characteristic vigor, and according to tradition with notable practical results. He also wrote patriotic songs which became popular in the army, among them "Columbia, Columbia, to glory arise."

The death of his father and the necessity of taking charge of the family affairs in Northampton, compelled him to resign, Jan. 28, 1779 (F. B. Heitman, *Historical Register of Officers of the Continental Army,* 1914). The next five years spent in this Massachusetts town were full of strenuous and varied labors. He ran two large farms, constantly supplied churches, and established a school for both sexes which attracted so many students that he had to employ two assistants. He also became prominent in political affairs, representing his town in county conventions and in 1781 and 1782 in the state legislature, where his activities won him such favor that his friends wished to nominate him for the Continental Congress. Had he been willing to abandon the ministry for public life, he would undoubtedly have risen high. Calls came to him to settle over churches in the vicinity of Boston, which he declined. Connecticut attracted him more, and on July 20, 1783, he accepted an invitation to the pastorate of the Congregational church at Greenfield Hill, where on Nov. 5, he was ordained.

During his twelve years here his fame as an educator, preacher, author, and man of affairs spread. Again he established a school for both sexes to which, in addition to many other enterprises, he gave six hours a day. It became widely and justly celebrated, drawing its students from the Middle and Southern states as well as from New England. Approximately a thousand pupils were educated by him, many of them in all the studies of the college curriculum. Among the clergy his learning and force of character speedily gave him leadership. In 1785 *The Conquest of Canaan,* written several years before, was published, the first epic poem, according to the author, to appear in America. It consists of eleven books in rhymed pentameters, and was an audacious attempt to give the New World an epic such as the *Iliad* was to Greece, and the *Æneid,* to Rome. The Bible story is told with such changes as suited the writer's purpose, and interjected are allusions to contemporary characters and events. It is unbearably tedious to the modern reader, but increased Dwight's prestige, was republished in England in 1788, and was charitably reviewed by Cowper in the *Analytical Review* (III, 1789, 531). A second ambitious work, *Greenfield Hill,* appeared in 1794. In form imitative of eighteenth-century English poets, it describes the scenery, history, and social conditions of the country, and has the patriotic purpose of contributing to the moral improvement of the author's countrymen and of demonstrating to Europeans that America offers the makings for a native poetry of interest and excellence. A rigid Calvinist and a stanch Federalist, Dwight exerted all his personal influence, intellectual equipment, and literary ability against the rising tide of democracy and infidelity, the two being in his mind synonymous; a warfare which he was to continue with a stubborn closed-mindedness for the remainder of his life. He took up the weapon of satire and published, *The Triumph of Infidelity, a Poem* (1788), dedicated to "Mons. de Voltaire," in which he uncorks vials of abuse. Satire was not one of Dwight's gifts. "Probably there can now be left for us on this planet few spectacles more provocative of the melancholy and pallid form of mirth, than that presented by those laborious efforts of the Reverend Timothy Dwight to be facetious at the expense of David Hume, or to slay the dreadful Monsieur de Voltaire in a duel of irony" (Moses Coit Tyler, *Three Men of Letters,* 1895, p. 92). His own religious, social, and political views are set forth in sermons and addresses, among which are: *A Discourse on the Genuineness, and Authenticity of the New Testament* (1794); *The True Means of Establishing Public Happiness* (n.d.), delivered July 7, 1795; *The Nature, and Danger, of Infidel Philosophy* (1798); *The Duty of Americans, at the Present Crisis* (1798), and in Fast Day discourses delivered in 1812. At the request of the citizens of New Haven, on Feb. 22, 1800, he gave an address on Washington, with whom he had personal acquaintance, which was published that same year under the title: *Discourse . . . on the Character of George Washington, Esq.* After the duel between his cousin, Aaron Burr, and Hamilton he preached a sermon on the *Folly, Guilt, and Mischiefs of Duelling* (1805).

The height of his ambition was perhaps achieved when on June 25, 1795, a few weeks after the sudden death of Ezra Stiles, Dwight, having just declined a call to the presidency of Union College, was elected president of Yale. That he was ambitious for position and power he himself confessed shortly before his death. "Particularly," he says, "I have coveted reputation, and influence, to a degree which I am unable to justify." (Sereno E. Dwight's Memoir prefixed to T. Dwight's *Theology,* p. xliii). President Stiles, who had an extreme dislike for Dwight, accusing him of decoying students from Yale for his schools, and suspecting him of trying to undermine him in his own position, also states: "He meditates great Things & nothing but great things will serve him—& every Thing that comes in the Way of his preferment must fall before him. Aut Cæsar, aut nullus" (Dexter, *ante,* II, 531). For more than twenty-one years he administered the college with great ability, exerted an influence over the students such as few presidents achieve, instructed the senior class in rhetoric, logic, metaphysics, and ethics, acted as professor of theology, supplied the college pulpit, gave counsel of weight in the affairs of state, and was altogether the most conspicuous figure in New England. The unregenerate dubbed him "Pope Dwight," while the children of the elect were taught to regard him as second only to St. Paul.

His real greatness has been questioned. Even some of his contemporaries had difficulty in accounting for the exalted place he held in public regard. An admirer, S. G. Goodrich, admits that his greatness was not that of genius and that he was only a man of large common sense and a large heart, inspired by high moral principles, a "Yankee, Christian gentleman—nothing more—nothing less" (*Recollections of a Lifetime,* 1856, I, 355). Unquestionably he had serious limitations. His outlook was narrow; his views of life, his political and social doctrines, all his judgments and all that he wrote, were determined or colored by his theological system. He had a little of the bigotry and uncharitableness of Puritanism at its worst. His literary work was without originality, and of all his poetry, so laboriously constructed, the only bit now generally known is the hymn, "I love thy Kingdom, Lord." Theologically he belonged to the school of his grandfather, Jonathan Edwards, but here he displayed some independence. His views are set forth in a series of sermons, repeated every four years at Yale, that all the students might hear them, and published after his death, *Theology, Explained and Defended* (5 vols., 1818–19), popular in America and abroad. (For analysis of his system, see Williston Walker, *A History of the Congregational Churches in the United States,* 1894, pp. 301–03). His one work which is likely to survive is *Travels in New England and New York* (1821–22), in four sizable volumes, written to record how "New England appeared, or to my own eye would have appeared, eighty or a hundred years before," and to refute foreign misrepresentations of America. It is an astonishingly varied collection of descriptions of natural scenery, agricultural, political, religious, and social conditions, including historical, biographical, and statistical information, and is interlarded with shrewd practical comments.

"On account of his noble person," Goodrich was persuaded, "the perfection of the visible man —he exercised a power in his day and generation somewhat beyond the natural scope of his mental endowments" (*ante,* I, 353). In appearance "he was about six feet in height, and of a full, round, manly form. His head was modeled rather for beauty than craniological display. . . . Dr. Dwight had, in fact, no bumps: I have never seen a smoother, rounder pate than his, which being slightly bald and close shorn, was easily examined. He had, however, a noble aspect—a full forehead and piercing black eyes though partly covered up with large spectacles in a tortoise-shell frame. . . . His voice was one of the finest I have ever heard from the pulpit—clear, hearty, sympathetic—and entering into the soul like the middle notes of an organ" (*Ibid.,* I, 348–49). Dwight's reputation and influence, however, were not due to his looks and manner alone. They are to be attributed in part to his mental equipment. He had a tenacious memory, a wide range of interests, and capacity for keen and minute observation. His mind was stored with a wealth of information on the most diverse subjects. He could talk intelligently with men in almost every walk of life, and frequently demonstrated that he knew how to do a job better than those whose business it was. Forced, because of the condition of his eyes, to depend upon amanuenses, such was his power of concentration that he could dictate to several at one time, turning from one to the other and unaided beginning where he had stopped. With all else he also had sound judgment and common sense. In certain aspects of character, moreover, he was great. However open to criticism his social and political views, he displayed a noble devotion to his country's interests, and no one ever doubted his religious integrity. He had disciplined himself to inflexible conformity to duty, and his industry, perseverance, and self-command came well up to the height of human possibilities. Any one who could accomplish what he did, so handicapped as to be unable to use his eyes for close work for but a short time each day, forced often to get up in the night and walk miles to gain relief from intense pain, compelled to compose both prose and poetry through dictation, and finally keep on his way with fortitude through slow death from cancer, had in him the stuff that compels admiration. By all, too, he was conceded to have been a great teacher. He probably came nearer to exemplifying what the name Mark Hopkins symbolizes than did Hopkins himself. He not only inspired the interest of his students in the studies he taught, but he made his class-work a means of enriching them out of his own great stock of general knowledge, so that to be under him alone was a liberal education. As a college president he had qualities which would have given him high rank in any generation, and from his administration Yale dates her modern era. He made the faculty in cooperation with the president a part of the college government; abolished obsolete customs and methods of discipline; gathered about him able instructors; encouraged the teaching of science; established a medical department, and contemplated the establishment of theological and law departments. His interest in the extension of education and religion led him to give much thought and labor to the founding of institutions which have had permanence and wide influence. He was one of the projectors of Andover Theological Seminary; of the Misssionary Society of Connecticut; and of the American Board of Commissioners for Foreign Missions. His whole life in fact was devoted to great interests, and if he was the personification of the "venerable *status quo*," an exemplifier of Connecticut Puritanism, he was also the personification of all that was finest in it.

[F. B. Dexter, *Biog. Sketches Grads. Yale Coll.*, vol. III (1903) gives list of publications and a copious bibliography. See also Dexter, *Sketch of the Hist. of Yale Univ.* (1887), and "Student Life at Yale under the first President Dwight" in *Proc. Am. Antiquarian Soc.*, Oct. 1917; W. B. Sprague, "Life of Timothy Dwight" in Jared Sparks, *The Lib. of Am. Biog.*, 2 ser., IV (1845), 225–364; Henry A. Beers, *The Conn. Wits and Other Essays* (1920); Vernon L. Parrington, *The Conn. Wits* (1926), and *Main Currents in Am. Thought: The Colonial Mind* (1927); *Cambridge Hist. of Am. Lit.*, vols. I and II (1917–18); M. A. DeWolfe Howe, *Classic Shades* (1928); R. J. Purcell, *Conn. in Transition* (1918); Frank H. Foster, *A Genetic Hist. of the New Eng. Theology* (1907); A. P. Stokes, *Memorials of Eminent Yale Men* (1914), esp. vol. I; J. B. Reynolds, S. H. Fisher, H. B. Wright, *Two Centuries of Christian Activity at Yale* (1901).] H. E. S.

DWIGHT, TIMOTHY (Nov. 16, 1828–May 26, 1916), Congregational clergyman, educator, president of Yale University, was born in Norwich, Conn., of a family noted for its achievements in literary and academic fields. His grandfather, Timothy [*q.v.*], one of the "Hartford Wits," and himself president of Yale for twenty-two years, was a grandson of Jonathan Edwards. The younger Timothy's father, James Dwight, although a successful business man, had the family taste for study. To his mother, however, Susan Breed, a woman of unusual intellectual power, Timothy felt himself above all indebted. "I owed more to her," he says, "in the matter of the awakening of my mental enthusiasm than to any or all the teachers of my childhood and youth" ("How I was Educated," *Forum,* November 1886, p. 251). She was a descendant of Allen Breed, who came to this country and settled at Lynn, Mass., about 1630, and the daughter of John McLaren and Rebecca (Walker) Breed, the former a lawyer, mayor of Norwich, and noted for enterprise, benevolence, and public spirit. Because his mother believed in home education, Timothy did not attend school until he was eleven years old, when he entered the academy in Norwich conducted by Calvin Tracy. He finished his preparation for college at the Hopkins Grammar School, New Haven, where his mother had gone that she might be with her sons during their period of study; entered Yale at the age of seventeen, although he was sufficiently prepared a year earlier; and graduated in 1849.

From boyhood he had looked forward to the life of a Congregational minister, and he was licensed to preach, May 22, 1855, and ordained, Sept. 15, 1861. It was to be his fortune, however, to spend his days in academic surroundings. His sermons were chiefly occasional. A volume of these, most of them preached to Yale students, was published in 1899, under the title, *Thoughts of and for the Inner Life*. From 1849 to 1851, having won the Clark Scholarship for the student who passed the best examination on the studies of the college course, he did graduate work at Yale. He then filled the office of tutor for four years, his fair-mindedness, tact, and humor making him extraordinarily popular. For the first two years of this period he was also enrolled in the Divinity School, where, after study at Bonn and Berlin (1856–58), he was appointed assistant professor of sacred literature, becoming full professor in 1861. On Dec. 31, 1866, he married Jane Wakeman Skinner of New Haven. He was an excellent New Testament scholar according to the standards of the time, and his accuracy and good sense were of much service to the American committee on the revision of the Bible, of which he was a member from 1873 to 1885. He also edited (1884–87) several volumes of the English translation of H. A. W. Meyer's commentaries on the books of the New Testament, and published in 1886 a translation with additional notes of Godet's *Commentary on the Gospel of John.* During his professorship the Divinity School was practically refounded. It was a task requiring great faith, wisdom, courage, and hard work. To all these Dwight contributed more perhaps than any one else.

In 1886 he succeeded Noah Porter as president of the college. From 1866 he had been one of the editors of the *New Englander,* and in 1870–71 had published in it a series of five articles on "Yale College—Some Thoughts Respecting its Future." The recommendations he had there made, he now proceeded to put into execution. An act was secured from the legislature authorizing the title "University"; the various schools were reconstructed and coördinated; and the college became a university in fact. The institution needed more money and buildings. The president did not personally solicit funds, but made clear the opportunity that was offered. He himself turned back his salary into the treasury, and from his inherited fortune contributed more, until the total amounted to over $100,000. He also undertook the duties of treasurer for a period, and supplied the college pulpit. The needed funds came, and the University had great expansion. At the age of seventy he resigned with the remark that he "proposed to do so while he still knew enough to know that he ought to." He was a genial, lovable, modest man, thoroughly human, capable of delightful flashes of humor, intensely practical, and displaying throughout his career indomitable faith and devotion to duty. Besides a number of addresses he published *Memories of Yale Life and Men, 1845–1899* (1903), which contains much autobiographical material.

[Autobiographical articles may be found in the *Forum,* Nov. 1886 and Jan. 1891. See also B. W. Dwight, *The Hist. of the Descendants of John Dwight of Dedham, Mass.* (1874), vol. I; *Timothy Dwight, President of Yale Univ. 1886–99, Memorial Addresses* (1917); *Who's Who in America,* 1916–17; *Record of the Graduated Members of the Class of 1849 of Yale Coll., Prepared for the Quarter Century Meeting . . . 1874* (1875); *Obit. Record, Grads. Yale Univ.,* 1916; *Congregational Year-Book* (1916); *Outlook,* June 7, 1916.]

H. E. S.

DWIGHT, WILLIAM (July 14, 1831–Apr. 21, 1888), manufacturer, soldier, a descendant of John Dwight who helped to settle Dedham, Mass., in 1635, was born at Springfield, Mass., the son of William Dwight and Elizabeth Amelia, daughter of Daniel Appleton White. Three of his brothers became soldiers and two, railroad executives. He went from a private military school to West Point in 1849, but resigned in 1853 before graduation. He engaged in manufacturing, probably of cotton, first at Boston, then at Philadelphia. On Jan. 1, 1856, he married Anna Robeson. Upon the outbreak of the Civil War he entered the military service and was commissioned captain in the 13th United States Infantry in May 1861. The next month he was appointed lieutenant-colonel of the 70th New York Volunteers, of which D. E. Sickles was colonel. Upon the promotion of Sickles, Dwight became colonel in July 1861. At the battle of Williamsburg, May 5, 1862, he was wounded three times and left for dead upon the field. After a short sojourn in a Confederate prison hospital he was exchanged and commissioned brigadier-general, for gallantry at Williamsburg. Dwight's brigade was the first of Grover's division of Banks's army. He led it creditably in the campaigns about Baton Rouge, Bayou Têche, and Irish Bend in the spring of 1863, and through the siege of Port Hudson. It participated in the first assault upon the Confederate works, May 24, and led the attack upon one wing in the final attempt, June 14, to carry Port Hudson by storm. Dwight was a member of the commission which arranged for the surrender of Port Hudson, July 8. After the Texas expedition in the autumn of 1863, he was appointed chief of staff to Banks for the Red River expedition of the following year. In July 1864 he was transferred to the command of the 1st Division of the XIX Corps of Sheridan's army in Virginia. This division was described as "capable and well-disciplined." Winchester, Fisher's Hill, and Cedar Mountain were the chief engagements in which it participated. Dwight remained in the army until January 1866, when he removed to Cincinnati and associated himself with his brothers Daniel and Charles in the management of the White Water Valley Railroad. His death occurred in Boston.

[B. W. Dwight, *The Hist. of the Descendants of John Dwight of Dedham, Mass.* (1874); *Appletons' Ann. Cyc.,* 1888; *Official Records (Army),* ser. 1 and 2; F. Phisterer, *N. Y. in the War of the Rebellion* (3rd ed., 1912); Edward Bacon, *Among the Cotton Thieves* (1867); M. L. Bonham, Jr., "Man & Nature at Port Hudson, 1863, 1917" in *Military Historian and Economist,* Oct. 1917, Jan. 1918.]

M. L. B., Jr.

DYAR, HARRISON GRAY (Feb. 14, 1866–Jan. 21, 1929), entomologist, was born in New York City, the son of Harrison Gray Dyar and Eleonora Rosella Hannum. Both parents were of colonial descent, the American advent of the families dating from 1632 on the father's side and from 1677 on the mother's. He attended the Roxbury Latin School, and in 1889 took his bachelor's degree at the Massachusetts Institute of

Technology. He had been interested in general biology and especially in the study of insects from the age of nineteen; in 1892 he returned to Boston and took the last year of the biology course of the Massachusetts Institute under William T. Sedgwick and spent the summer at the Woods Hole Laboratory of Marine Biology. He then went to Columbia University, where he received his master's degree in 1894. His thesis, published in the *Annals of the New York Academy of Sciences* of May 1894, was an important paper on the classification of Lepidopterous larvæ which, from its originality and scope, established his reputation as an entomologist. His doctoral thesis, published in the same *Annals* for November 1895, was based upon bacteriological work and was entitled "On Certain Bacteria from the Air of New York City." This work was largely done under Dr. T. Mitchell Prudden, whom he assisted in the bacteriological laboratory of the College of Physicians and Surgeons. His main interest, however, continued to be in entomology, and in 1897 he was invited to Washington to fill an honorary position in the United States National Museum. This invitation he accepted, and became custodian of the Lepidoptera, a position he held until his death. After the death of William H. Ashmead [*q.v.*] in 1908, Dyar was placed in charge of the whole of the insect collections of the Museum, but held this position for a comparatively short period. He presented his very large private collection to the Museum, and continued his interest in the Lepidoptera for the rest of his life.

His main work, and the one in which he built up a lasting reputation, was with the mosquitoes. In 1901 he became interested in mosquito larvæ and later was associated with the late Frederick Knab and L. O. Howard in the preparation of a four-volume monograph, *The Mosquitoes of North and Central America and the West Indies.* The work on this monograph was supported by the Carnegie Institution of Washington for the years 1903 to 1906, and after that time the authors relied on help from various other sources. Dyar himself was financially independent and was able to make at his own expense many expeditions into out-of-the-way regions. The monograph was finally completed, the first volume being published in 1912 and the last in 1917, and for many years it has been constantly consulted by the entomologists and medical men of many nations. It was published by the Carnegie Institution of Washington. In 1927, the same institution having approved a plan for the preparation and publication of a single additional volume of taxonomic range only, Dyar with tireless energy prepared a monograph, *The Mosquitoes of the Americas,* including the South-American fauna. This volume was published in 1928, shortly before his death.

Dyar was an indefatigable worker, and published during the last thirty years of his life a constant stream of shorter papers, largely of a taxonomic character. In 1913 he started at his own expense a monthly journal which he called *Insecutor Inscitiae Menstruus,* of which fourteen volumes were issued, which was devoted largely to shorter entomological papers, for the most part taxonomic. He was editor of the *Journal of the New York Entomological Society* from 1904 to 1907 and of the *Proceedings of the Entomological Society of Washington* from 1909 to 1912. In 1924 he was commissioned captain in the Sanitary Department of the Officers' Reserve Corps of the army. He was twice married: on Oct. 14, 1889, to Zella Peabody, and on Apr. 26, 1921, to Wellesca Pollock Allen. He died in Washington, D. C.

[Biog. sketch by L. O. Howard, in *Science,* Feb. 8, 1929, repr. in *Technology Rev.,* July 1929; J. M. Cattell, *Am. Men of Science* (4th ed., 1927); *Who's Who in America,* 1928–29.]

L.O.H.

DYE, WILLIAM McENTYRE (February 1831–Nov. 13, 1899), soldier, staff officer of the Egyptian army, military adviser to Korea, was born in Pennsylvania. On July 1, 1853, he was graduated from the United States Military Academy as brevet lieutenant with a standing above the middle of his class. He had been appointed to West Point from Mansfield, Ohio, where his guardian was a John McCullough. Before the Civil War he served both on garrison duty and on the frontier, with regular promotions. In August 1862 he went to the front as colonel of the 20th Iowa Volunteers, and in the campaigns of the next year served in Missouri and Arkansas. For bravery at Vicksburg he was made brevet major in the regular army, and for gallantry and skill in handling a brigade in the Red River campaign of 1864 he was brevetted lieutenant-colonel. In September 1864 he commanded a brigade during the campaign against Mobile, and later served as assistant provost-marshal-general of Kansas, Nebraska, Colorado, and Dakota. On Mar. 13, 1865, he received the brevets of colonel in the regular army and brigadier-general in the volunteer army for gallant and meritorious service throughout the war. On July 8, 1865, he was mustered out of the volunteers, and on Jan. 14, 1866, was promoted to major and assigned to the 4th Infantry. The quiet life of an officer in time of peace was not to his taste, however, and he was honorably discharged from the army at his own request, Sept. 30, 1870.

On Feb. 18, 1864, he had married Ellen A. Rucker, the daughter of a Chicago judge, and after his resignation from the army he took his family to Marion, Ia., where he engaged in farming. He had one son and two daughters. Though he had a great fondness for agriculture as a hobby, it did not possess the romance of adventure, and when the opportunity came, in 1873, he went to Egypt with other American officers to join the staff of the Egyptian army. Later in 1875 he became assistant to the chief of staff, Gen. C. P. Stone, in the army of Khedive Ismail Pasha in the campaign against Abyssinia, where he was wounded. He returned to New York in June 1878. Two years later he published an account of his adventures under the title of *Moslem Egypt and Christian Abyssinia, or Military Service Under the Khedive* (1880).

After his return to the United States, he served for several years as chief of police of Washington, D. C.; but in 1888 adventure called again and he made haste to answer. Korea had been open to Americans since 1883, and the king of that country had urged the American government to send military advisers to organize his army on modern lines. Since Congress failed to pass legislation for the appointment of officers from the regular army, on the recommendation of Gen. Sheridan, Dye went to Korea in 1888 to become chief military adviser to the Korean government. His duties consisted chiefly in conducting a military academy for the training of Korean officers. He made a careful study of military systems, evolved a series of maneuvers best suited to Korean conditions and to command in a foreign tongue, and later published in the Korean language a small treatise on military tactics. His troops were so well trained as to arouse the commendation of visiting American naval officers, but he was immeasurably handicapped by the failure of Korean officials to cooperate with him and by the impossibility of holding Korean noblemen to strict military discipline. His influence extended only to a small portion of the army, while the rest of it was subject to numerous conflicting influences, both native and foreign. After the beginning of the Sino-Japanese war his men and their arms were tampered with, and when certain Japanese and Koreans murdered the Queen of Korea on Oct. 8, 1895, very few of Dye's men stayed to give their lives for their queen. Until the coming of Russian influence in the spring of 1896, the Korean king retained Dye as a sort of personal body guard. After the Russians came into power they took charge of the army and the general was appointed by His Majesty to supervise the government experiment farm, where he had an opportunity to put his hobby into practical effect. From 1895 to 1898 he wrote a series of six articles on agricultural subjects for the *Korean Repository*. His last relations with the Korean government were marred by controversies over salary. On May 5, 1899, he left Seoul for Muskegon, Mich., where he was confined to his bed until his death in November. He had suffered severely with dysentery for many years.

[Documents concerning Dye's life in Korea may be found in the archives of the Dept. of State and in the archives of the former American legation in Seoul, Korea. There is a biographical sketch in *Thirty-first Ann. Reunion, Asso. Grads. U. S. Mil. Acad.* (1900). See also G. W. Cullum, *Biog. Reg.* (3rd ed., 1891); F. B. Heitman, *Hist. Reg. and Dict. U. S. Army* (1903); Edythe J. R. Whitley, *Hist. of the Rucker Family and Their Descendants* (1927); *Evening Star* (Washington), Nov. 14, 1899.] H. J. N.

DYER, ALEXANDER BRYDIE (Jan. 10, 1815–May 20, 1874), soldier, was born in Richmond, Va., the son of William Hay and Margaret (Brydie) Dyer. Graduated from the United States Military Academy at West Point, July 1, 1837, and promoted to second lieutenant, 3rd Artillery, he was assigned to duty at Fort Monroe, Va., and served in the Florida War of 1837–38. Upon the enlargement of the Ordnance Corps he was transferred to that body in 1838, and served in various ordnance establishments until the outbreak of the Mexican War, when he was assigned to duty as chief of ordnance of the army invading New Mexico. In this campaign he was brevetted a captain "for gallant and meritorious conduct." He was engaged in the actions of Canada, Pueblo de Taos, and Santa Cruz de Rosales, and was wounded on Feb. 4, 1847. He was promoted captain in the Ordnance Corps, Mar. 3, 1853, after fourteen years' continuous service. At the outbreak of the Civil War, though he was a native Virginian, he remained loyal to the Union. On Aug. 21, 1861, he was assigned to the command of the National Armory, at Springfield, Mass., not without opposition, however, as some entertained misgivings of his loyalty. Later when Congress met, the question was raised of the advisability of permitting a Southerner to hold a position of such responsibility, involving, perhaps, the fate of the nation. All suspicions were soon dispelled, however, by the evidence of his tireless industry, and the efficiency with which he administered his new command. He entered at once upon his difficult task with systematic energy and excellent judgment. Workshops were reorganized, grounds enlarged, and buildings erected, thousands of mechanics were employed, and the production of the National Armory was increased to 1,000 rifles a day.

On Mar. 3, 1863, Dyer was promoted major, Ordnance Corps, and the following year, Sept. 12, 1864, was appointed chief of ordnance, United States army, with the rank of brigadier-general. Before he left Springfield to assume his duties at Washington, 3,000 employees of the armory presented him with an address offering him their congratulations for "the well deserved mark of public confidence" just bestowed upon him by his promotion to the head of his department, and assuring him that the termination of his late command was "a source of deep personal grief, and the end of official relations characterized by uninterrupted harmony and kindly feelings." The tremendous task, which the necessities of the nation imposed upon him as chief of ordnance, that of providing the Union armies with munitions of war, required his most watchful care and greatest efforts. His administration of the Ordnance Department won for him the admiration and respect of his fellow officers. He had, however, difficulties with inventors and dishonest contractors, who, failing to gain their ends, were embittered against him and his department, and finally carried their grievances to Congress. He asked for a court martial, which was refused, and then asked for a court of inquiry, which was granted. The inquiry, which was long and thorough, not only exonerated him but held him up as an example worthy of the imitation of all army officers. He was brevetted major-general, United States army, Mar. 13, 1865, for "faithful, meritorious, and distinguished services in the Ordnance Department during the Rebellion." Dyer invented a projectile for cannon which he offered to and which was accepted by the government. He was offered a large royalty on this projectile but refused it, preferring to give his invention to the country. He was married to Elizabeth Allen, on Feb. 6, 1840, and had six children. He was a man of generous and genial temper, of unaffected simplicity, candor, and dignity, and above all of uncompromising integrity. He retained the office of chief of ordnance until his death.

[G. W. Cullum, *Biog. Reg.* (3rd ed., 1891); *Jour. of the Mil. Service Institution,* Sept. 1894; T. H. Price, *The Dyer Family* (1906); *Evening Star* (Washington), May 22, 1874; records in the Adjutant-General's Office, Washington, D. C.]

C. F. C—y.

DYER, ELIPHALET (Sept. 14, 1721–May 13, 1807), jurist, was descended from Thomas Dyer, a cloth manufacturer of Shepton Mallet, Somersetshire, England, who in 1632 arrived in Boston and settled in Weymouth, Mass., where he was prominent in public life. His grandson, Col. Thomas Dyer of Windham, Conn., married Lydia, daughter of John Backus, and their son, Eliphalet, was born at Windham. He graduated at Yale College in 1740, then studied law, and having been admitted to practise before the Connecticut courts in 1746, opened an office in Windham, which remained his home during the whole of his life. Taking a lively interest in public affairs, he was in 1747 elected to represent his district in the General Assembly of which he remained a member by repeated reëlections for fifteen years. Becoming known as a capable and industrious lawyer he soon acquired a good practise, though he devoted much of his time to other interests. In 1753 he was prominent in the organization of the Susquehannah Company, the object of which was to found a Connecticut settlement in the Wyoming Valley, west of the province of New York; and he was a member of the committee which purchased the necessary lands from the Six Nations in 1754. Further progress was blocked by the outbreak of war between England and France and in August 1755 he was appointed lieutenant-colonel of a Connecticut regiment, taking part in the Crown Point operations. In 1758 he commanded a regiment in the expedition which was directed against Canada in that year. In 1762 he was elected a member of the governor's council, a position which he retained for twenty-two years. In 1763 the Wyoming land scheme again came to the front, settlers having commenced to take possession and the proprietaries of Pennsylvania having put forward an adverse claim under a previous Crown grant to William Penn of the area involved. In consequence of this Dyer was sent to England as agent of the Susquehannah Company to procure a confirmation of the title acquired from the Indians, but he was unsuccessful. After his return, he took a prominent part in the rising opposition to the colonial policy of the British government and was a Connecticut delegate to the Stamp Act Congress of 1765. In 1766 he was elected an associate judge of the superior court of Connecticut, continuing, after his elevation to the bench, in close association with the leaders of the colonial cause. In the meantime, efforts were made to settle the Wyoming controversy, and he visited Philadelphia twice with this object in view, going in June 1769 as agent of the Susquehannah Company and in October 1773 as one of three commissioners appointed in that behalf by the Connecticut legislature, but nothing was effected. In 1774 he was appointed delegate from Connecticut to the First Continental

Congress, and in 1775 was a member of the first Connecticut Committee of Safety. Throughout the Revolutionary period he rendered valuable services, acting as a member of Congress and attending the Hartford Convention in 1780 as one of the Connecticut commissioners. He had in 1776 declined an appointment as brigadier-general in the Continental Army, considering that he could serve the cause more effectually in Congress than in the field. In 1781 the dispute as to the Wyoming land title finally came before Congress, and a board of commissioners was appointed to settle the question of jurisdiction as between Pennsylvania and Connecticut. At its session, which was held at Trenton, N. J., Nov. 12, 1782, Dyer appeared as counsel for Connecticut, and after a hearing extending to forty-one judicial days, a unanimous decision was rendered adverse to Connecticut. In 1789 he became chief justice of Connecticut and held that office till 1793. On leaving the bench he retired into private life, residing at Windham till his death. He married Huldah, daughter of Col. Jabez Bowen of Providence, R. I.

John Adams said of him: "Dyer is long winded and roundabout, obscure and cloudy, very talkative and very tedious, yet an honest worthy man, means and judges well." Another side of his character is exhibited in the record of expenses incurred by him as congressman in 1777 as rendered to and paid by Connecticut (*The Connecticut Magazine,* Jan.–Mar. 1906), which shows that he did not despise the good things of life.

[W. L. Weaver, *Hist. of Ancient Windham* (1864), p. 61; Cornelia C. Joy-Dyer, *Some Records of the Dyer Family* (1884); G. H. Hollister, *Hist. of Conn.* (1857), esp. p. 632; J. W. Barker, *Conn. Hist. Colls.* (1856), p. 447; F. B. Dexter, *Biog. Sketches Grads. Yale Coll.,* vol. I (1885).] H. W. H. K.

DYER, ISADORE (Nov. 2, 1865–Oct. 12, 1920), physician, was born in Galveston, Tex., the son of Isadore Dyer, a native of Dessau, Germany, and his wife, Amelia Ann Lewis. After graduation at the Sheffield Scientific School of Yale (Ph.B., 1887), he began the study of medicine at the University of Virginia, but after a year there matriculated at Tulane University where he received his M.D. in 1889. His interneship was at the New York Skin and Cancer Hospital (1890–92) and in 1891 he was, in addition, lecturer at the Post Graduate Medical School. A part of 1892 was spent in graduate study in Paris and London. He became associate professor of dermatology at the Tulane University of Louisiana in 1905, was promoted to professor in 1908, and in that year was made dean: positions which he occupied until his death. From 1892 until its absorption by Tulane, he was also professor of diseases of the skin at the New Orleans Polyclinic. At the outset of his practise in New Orleans he began his life-long interest in leprosy, and not only accomplished much in the treatment of the disease, but also in the proper protection and care of its victims. In 1894 he founded and became president of the first board of control of the Louisiana Leper Home, later to become the National Leprosarium. In 1905 he married Mercedes Louise Percival of Havana, Cuba. His interest in the military service began in 1908 when he was commissioned first lieutenant in the newly organized Medical Reserve Corps of the army. He served on various examining boards from time to time and three days after the entrance of the United States into the World War was made a major. For a time he was inspector and later on duty in the Surgeon-General's Office, War Department. In 1919 he was commissioned colonel in the Reserve. He was a successful dermatologist and one of the foremost leprologists of his time, his contributions to the literature on this malady being very extensive. He was the author of more than a hundred papers on diseases of the skin, medical biography, and essays, some of which were collected in *The Art of Medicine and Other Addresses, Papers, etc.* (1913). He was editor of the *New Orleans Medical and Surgical Journal* from 1896 until his death and co-editor of the *American Journal of Tropical Diseases and Preventive Medicine* (1914–16). He was a man of great native ability and of diversified talents and culture, being internationally recognized not only as a specialist in his chosen field but also as an educator, an executive, and a philanthropist. He was a leader of medical thought and successful as an organizer of scientific and civic bodies. He was a charter member of the National Board of Medical Examiners, a body in which he took great interest as a pioneer in the standardization of medical education. He was a delegate to the International Leprosy Conference in Berlin (1897) and the Brussels Conference on Prophylaxis of Venereal Diseases (1899).

[*Southern Medic. Jour.,* XVIII (1925), 15; *Who's Who in America,* 1920–21; *Medic. Record,* XCVIII (1920), 740; *New Orleans Medic. and Surgic. Jour.,* LXXIII (1920–21), 157–59; *Am. Jour. Trop. Med.,* II (1922), 173; *Yale Univ. Obit. Record,* 1921; New Orleans *Times-Picayune,* Oct. 13, 1920; Records of the Dean's Office, Tulane Univ.] E. E. H.

DYER, LOUIS (Sept. 30, 1851–July 20, 1908), classical scholar, writer, and lecturer, was born in Chicago, Ill., the son of Charles Volney Dyer, M.D., and Louisa Maria (Gifford) Dyer. His father was descended from William and Mary

Dyer [*q.v.*], who came from Somersetshire to Boston in 1635, became adherents of Mrs. Hutchinson, and were driven from Massachusetts Bay to Rhode Island, where they joined the Society of Friends. Charles Dyer practised medicine in Newark, N. J., in New York, and in Chicago, and was prominent in the anti-slavery movement and active in the work of the "Underground Railroad." In 1862 President Lincoln appointed him judge for the United States in the Anglo-American Mixed Court at Sierra Leone. Louis Dyer's independent habit of thinking, his quiet and efficient friendliness, and his interest in social problems, undoubtedly derived from these antecedents. Educated by private tutors in Geneva and near Lyons, he entered first the University of Chicago (1867), then the University of Munich, and finally the sophomore class at Harvard (September 1871). Older than most undergraduates, and matured by extensive travel, he was none the less liked by his classmates, and interested himself in many college activities. At graduation (June 1874) he obtained highest honors in classics. Entering Balliol College, Oxford, in the autumn of 1874, he won the Taylorian Scholarship for proficiency in Italian, and studied there until February 1877, when the illness of his father required his return to Chicago. He became tutor in Greek at Harvard, and in 1881 assistant professor of Greek, a post which he held until June 1887. During this period he published: *A Consideration of the Use of Form in Teaching* (1881); *The Greek Question and Answer* (1884); and an excellent edition of Plato's *Apology and Crito* (1886). After 1887 his life was spent mostly in Oxford, where he had been given the B.A. degree in 1878. In December 1889, he returned to Boston to deliver eight lectures in the Lowell Institute course, later published under the title *Studies of the Gods in Greece at Certain Sanctuaries Recently Excavated* (1891).

In 1893 he was made master of arts at Oxford, and appointed lecturer in German and French at Balliol; he was examiner of schools for the Oxford and Cambridge Schools Examination Committee. In 1893 he published *An Introduction to the Study of Political Economy,* translated from the Italian of Luigi Cossa. During the year 1895–96 he was acting professor of Greek at Cornell University, and in 1899 he delivered three lectures on Machiavelli before the Royal Institution of Great Britain, later published as *Machiavelli and the Modern State* (1904). In 1899 also he contributed to *Notes and Queries for Somerset and Dorset* a series of notes on the career of his ancestor, under the title, "William Dyer, a Somerset Royalist in New England." Returning to the United States, he delivered in 1900 the Hearst Lectures on Greek art in the University of California, visiting, in the next year, many of the American universities, where he lectured on Mycenæ and Cnossus. *Oxford as it is,* published in 1902, was a small but useful volume for the guidance of Rhodes scholars. In 1904 he became a member of a committee of the Oxford Congregation interested in the maintenance of Greek as a compulsory requirement in the university. At the same time he engaged in the work of promoting the Egypt Exploration Fund, which was to yield papyri of inestimable worth, and he was also a prominent member of the council of the Hellenic Society. In all these enterprises his activities were untiring and fruitful. He married, in London (Nov. 23, 1889), Margaret Anne Macmillan, daughter of the publisher, Alexander Macmillan. In June 1890, he purchased Sunbury Lodge, which thereafter became known in Oxford as a center from which radiated kindness, hospitality, and helpfulness, "one of the first places to which cultivated American visitors in England turned, and where they met sympathetic Oxford colleagues." There he was the recognized intermediary between the university and the young American students who began to flock to Oxford under the Rhodes Foundation.

As a classical scholar, Dyer had read widely and with fine appreciation the literatures of Greece and Rome, and his exposition of them was enriched by illustrations from many modern writers of different tongues. His work as a teacher was sound and enduring. He contributed many reviews, letters, and articles to the *Nation* (N. Y.), *Athenæum, Classical Review, Journal of Hellenic Studies,* and *Harvard Studies in Classical Philology*; he preferred, however, to sacrifice further achievement as a scholar to the making of human contacts at Oxford, and his diversity of interests, the warmth of his enthusiasm for the young student's development, his devotion to social work connected with his church or with the succor of neglected children, drew friends to him wherever he went. Domestic affliction, which would have distracted lesser men, never closed his door to the service of others. Gifted with a wide knowledge of men and things, with a joyous wit and humor, and sweetness of disposition, he possessed a charm that few or none could resist.

[*Ninth Report of the Class Secretary of the Class of 1874,* Harvard Univ. (1909), pp. 34–37; *Harvard Coll. Class of 1874, Fiftieth Anniversary, Eleventh Report* (1924), pp. 91–95; *Educational Rev.,* Sept. 1908; *Na-*

tion (N. Y.), July 23, Oct. 15, 1908; London *Times,* July 21, 1908.] C. B. G.

DYER, MARY (d. June 1, 1660), Quaker martyr, was the wife of William Dyer of Somersetshire, England, with whom she came to Massachusetts probably in 1635. According to Gov. Winthrop, Mrs. Dyer was "a very proper and fair woman" (*post,* I, 266), and both she and her husband were well educated and apparently of good family. On Dec. 13, 1635, they became members of Mr. Wilson's church in Boston. During the Antinomian controversy their open sympathy with Mrs. Anne Hutchinson and the Rev. John Wheelwright [*qq.v.*] alienated them from their orthodox neighbors. In November 1637 Dyer was disenfranchised and subsequently disarmed because of his support of Wheelwright, and later, when Mrs. Hutchinson was expelled from the church, Mary Dyer accompanied her as she withdrew from the assemblage. Rumors set afloat following this act, to the effect that Mary's still-born child of which she had been delivered the previous October was "a monster," subjected her to painful notoriety as an object of divine displeasure. From the hostile atmosphere of Boston the Dyers moved to Rhode Island, where in March 1638 William Dyer was among the founders of Portsmouth and where he became a man of consequence. Mary Dyer went to England in 1650 and was joined there the following year by her husband, sent on Colony business. He returned to Newport leaving her in England where she remained until 1657, meantime becoming a Quaker. Passing through Boston on her return to Rhode Island, she was arrested and imprisoned but released upon her husband's entreaty. In 1658 she was expelled from New Haven for preaching Quakerism. The next year, when certain Quakers were imprisoned in Boston, she went to visit them and to "bear witness to her faith," and was again imprisoned. Banished on Sept. 12, 1659, she returned to Rhode Island, but in the next month went back to visit other imprisoned Quakers at Boston, was seized by the authorities, and on Oct. 27 was condemned to be hanged. At the last moment, on petition of her son William, captain of a coasting vessel, she was reprieved and sent back to Rhode Island (Louis Dyer in *Notes and Queries,* December 1899). She again returned to Boston on the 21st of the following May, was again imprisoned and condemned to death, and finally, in spite of the supplications of her husband, she was hanged on the first day of June. When offered her life if she would leave Massachusetts and return no more she said: "Nay, I cannot; for in obedience to the will of the Lord God I came, and in His will I abide faithful to the death." A number of distinguished American families trace their descent to her through one or another of her seven children.

[Horatio Rogers, *Mary Dyer . . . the Quaker Martyr* (1896); C. C. Joy-Dyer, *Some Records of the Dyer Family* (1884); R. M. Jones, *The Quakers in the Am. Colonies* (1911); Geo. Bishop, *New England Judged not by Man's, but by the Spirit of the Lord* (1661, 1667); John Whiting, *A Call from Death to Life* (1660) and *Truth and Innocency Defended* (1702); Jos. Besse, *A Collection of the Sufferings of the People called Quakers* (2 vols., 1753); *Winthrop's Jour.* (2 vols., 1908), ed. by J. K. Hosmer; *Records of the Governor and Company of the Mass. Bay in New England* (1853–54), vol. IV, pt. 1; Louis Dyer, "Wm. Dyer, A Somerset Royalist in New England," in *Notes and Queries for Somerset and Dorset,* June, Sept., Dec. 1899.] J. T. A.

DYER, NEHEMIAH MAYO (Feb. 19, 1839–Jan. 27, 1910), naval officer, was born at Provincetown, Mass., to Henry and Sally (Mayo) Dyer. He was educated in the local public schools, but being a true product of a seafaring town, soon turned to a nautical life. At the age of fifteen he entered the merchant marine. In 1861 he enlisted in the 13th Massachusetts Volunteers but on Apr. 4, 1862, he transferred to the volunteer navy as acting master's mate. About a year later (May 18, 1863) he was made an acting ensign and appointed to command the *Eugénie,* used for blockade work off Mobile. On Jan. 12, 1864, he was promoted to acting master and later this same year was assigned to the *Metacomet,* in which he participated in the battle of Mobile Bay, receiving in person the surrender of the Confederate ship *Selma.* After serving on the *Hartford,* Farragut's flagship, he was ordered North to command the *Rodolph.* After the close of the Civil War, he was one of the few volunteer officers to be retained. He was commissioned lieutenant on Mar. 12, 1868, and ordered to the *Dacotah* of the South Pacific Squadron. On Dec. 18, 1868, he was advanced to the grade of lieutenant-commander and ordered to command the *Cyane,* which was due to proceed to Alaska. In 1870, while on the *Ossippee,* he saved a sailor from drowning and for this act was given a medal and publicly thanked by his commanding officer. For several years thereafter, he performed the various duties to which a line officer is subject, including work at the Torpedo School at Newport in 1873 and lighthouse inspection in 1883. Dyer was advanced to the full grade of commander on Apr. 23, 1883, and after being lighthouse inspector for four years, he was ordered to command the *Marion* at an Asiatic station until 1890. He took the course at the Naval War College in 1894. On July 13, 1897, he was given his captaincy, and in October of the same year was placed in command of the *Baltimore*. After the outbreak of the Spanish-American War, he and his ship were in Dewey's squadron in the Philippines and participated in the battle of Manila Bay, May 1, 1898. For his conduct in this battle, he was advanced seven numbers in rank. His official report to Admiral Dewey shows some of the difficulties under which he worked (*House Document No. 3,* 55 Cong., 3 Sess., pp. 78–79). The citizens of Baltimore presented him with a magnificent gold sword as a token of their esteem. He served throughout the war, and in 1900 was ordered to the Navy Yard at Boston. On Feb. 19, 1901, he was retired with the rank of rear-admiral. His services were duly recognized by the United States nearly twenty years later when on Apr. 13, 1918, the torpedo-boat destroyer *Dyer* was launched. After his retirement he took up his residence at Melrose, Mass. He kept up his interest in naval matters in his connection with the Massachusetts Nautical Training School, and in 1903 and 1904, he was chairman of the board of commissioners of this famous school. Perhaps he took this opportunity of passing on to posterity the love of the sea that he had developed, for he never married and had no sons to follow in their father's footsteps.

[*Who's Who in America,* 1908–09; Navy Register, 1863–97; L. R. Hamersly, *The Records of Living Officers of the U. S. Navy and Marine Corps* (7th ed., 1902); *U. S. Army and Navy Jour.*, Feb. 5, 1910; *Official Records (Navy)*, 1 ser., vols. XVII, XX, XXI, XXII; R. W. Neeser, *Ship Names of the U. S. Navy* (1921), p. 71; *Boston Post* and *Boston Jour.*, Jan. 28, 1910.] A. R. B.

DYLANDER, JOHN (*c.* 1709–Nov. 2, 1741), Lutheran clergyman, was assistant pastor at Börstil, Sweden, in 1737 when he was appointed by Archbishop Steuchius and the Consistory of Upsala to succeed Gabriel Falck as pastor of the Swedish Lutheran congregation at Wicacoa, Pa. (now Southwark, Philadelphia). Accompanied by William Malander of Rosland, a student of theology, he sailed from Stockholm on July 13 and landed at Philadelphia on Nov. 2. Four days later he was installed by his compatriot, the Rev. Peter Tranberg, as pastor of Gloria Dei Church. His ministry, though of only four years' duration, left a deep impression not only on his own people but on his English and German neighbors. Whereas most of the Swedish pastors regarded themselves as merely sojourning in America, Dylander identified himself with the country by marrying a daughter of the merchant, Peter Koch (Kock, Cook). He restored the discipline and finances of his congregation, catalogued the church library, which consisted of thirteen folio and thirty-three quarto volume of substantial Lutheran theology and church history, and established a fund for the relief of the poor. Holding that his duty extended to all whom he had strength to serve, he ministered in their own language to the Germans at Philadelphia, Germantown, and Lancaster, and with astonishing rapidity learned to preach acceptably in English. He often delivered as many as sixteen sermons a week. In his own church, for more than a year, it was his practise to have a service at 8 a. m. in German, the main service in Swedish, and vespers in English. It was the fashion for couples to come to Gloria Dei Church to be married by him; one English clergyman, alarmed by the inroads thus made in his perquisites, complained vainly to the governor to have the practise stopped. Peter Kalm, the famous Swedish naturalist, records that he found Dylander everywhere beloved. In 1741 Benjamin Franklin published a tract for him entitled *Free Grace in Truth: The XXIVth Meditation of Dr. John Gerhard Translated from Latin into English, with Notes for the Better Understanding of the Author's Meaning.* On the authorization of the Upsala Consistory he and Tranberg arranged to ordain Malander on Nov. 2, 1741, but on that very day Dylander died. He was buried under the chancel of his church.

[Pehr Kalm, *En Resa til Norra America* (Stockholm, 1756), translated by J. R. Forster as *Travels into North America* (2nd ed., London, 1772); Israel Acrelius, *Beskrifning om de Swenska Församlingars* (Stockholm, 1759), translated by W. M. Reynolds as *Hist. of New Sweden* (Phila., 1874); C. R. Hildeburn, *A Century of Printing: Issues of the Press in Pa. 1685–1784* (1885), Item 700; A. L. Gräbner, *Geschichte der Lutherischen Kirche in America* (St. Louis, 1892).] G. H. G.

DYMOND, JOHN (May 3, 1836–Mar. 5, 1922), Louisiana sugar-planter, inventor, editor, was born in Canada, a son of Richard and Anne (Hawkens) Dymond, Cornish emigrants. Richard Dymond was for a time a Methodist preacher and later a merchant. In John's childhood the family moved to Zanesville, Ohio. He was educated in the public schools, Zanesville Academy, and Bartlett's College, Cincinnati, worked for a time in his father's store, dabbled in cotton manufacturing, and in the spring of 1860 went to New York, where he at once secured a position as a traveling salesman. In 1862 he was married to Nancy Elizabeth Cassidy of Zanesville. In 1863 he became a broker in New York, in the firm of Dymond & Lally, which three years later opened a branch house in New Orleans and did a tremendous business in Louisiana sugar and molasses as well as in imported sugar and coffee. In the autumn of 1868 the firm purchased the "Belair" and "Fairview" sugar plantations on the Mississippi River, thirty miles below New Orleans, and Dymond began his career as a planter, gradually withdrawing from his city business. In the autumn of 1877 he led the movement resulting in the creation of the Louisiana Sugar Planter's Association, and from 1887 to 1897 was its president. He was one of the leaders in urging the expediency of research work in the culture and manufacture of sugar. This agitation culminated in the organization of the Louisiana Scientific Agricultural Association, of which he was president until his death, and in the establishment of the Audubon Sugar Experiment Station. When in 1888 the sugar-planters of New Orleans, in an endeavor to save the sugar industry from many preventable losses, formed a corporation to publish *The Louisiana Planter and Sugar Manufacturer,* Dymond was chosen as managing editor as well as general manager and president, and served for thirty-four years. He was quick to grasp new ideas in labor-saving devices and in processes, and to aid in their development. The only time in his life that he visited a moving-picture show was when he went to see the interesting picture of a new machine for harvesting sugar-cane. Conspicuous among the devices he helped introduce were the Mallon stubble digger and the McDonald hydraulics; and among the processes, double and triple milling in grinding the cane, the redivivus or multiple effect evaporation, and the so-called dry-vacuum in vacuum boiling. He installed the first nine-roller mill ever erected in Louisiana; patented a sulphur machine, the shelf or cascade machine, which is now in use everywhere; was the first man in the sugar world to weigh sugar-cane received at the mill as the basis for a comprehensive system of cost determination; and was also the first to purchase cane at the mill by weight. With the Hon. Henry McCall he was placed in charge of the experiments in diffusion conducted in the later eighties at Gov. Warmoth's Magnolia Plantation by Norman J. Colman [*q.v.*], then United States commissioner of agriculture. Inventors of new appliances of every sort for use in the sugar factory or in the field always received from him cordial interest and an opportunity to make at "Belair" such trials and experiments as they might wish to conduct. Louisiana then led the sugar world in industrial progress, and many distinguished men from distant lands came there to investigate and study. No visitor to the state ever went away without seeing Dymond at "Belair."

In 1888 he was a delegate to the National Democratic Convention and a member of the platform committee, where he energetically opposed extreme free-trade ideas. When, in September 1894, at a meeting of sugar-planters in New Orleans, the Lily White movement was inaugurated in protest against the Wilson-Gorman tariff act and the planters voted to go into a White Republican party, Dymond, as a protectionist and old-fashioned Democrat, cast the only dissenting vote. He was also involved in local politics, serving as president to the police jury of Plaquemines Parish and as chief executive on Levee Boards. In 1890 he became seriously interested in the anti-lottery movement and was the business manager of the party organ, the *New Delta.* He carried his parish against the lottery, and as president of its police jury declined the proffered gift of $3,000 of lottery money for the maintenance of the public levees during the high-water season of 1891. He was active in the campaign that led to the election of the anti-lottery candidates, Edward D. White and Murphy J. Foster, as United States senator and governor of Louisiana, respectively. In 1892 he sat in the legislature as representative from his parish, which had been under negro control since the Civil War. In 1896 the parish still had a negro sheriff and a negro clerk of the court, but under Dymond's lead white men were elected to all the parish offices, and he himself was reëlected to the legislature. He represented his parish in the state constitutional convention of 1898 and in the state Democratic convention of 1899, and was four times elected state senator, declining reëlection in 1920 on account of failing health.

After the burning of his "Belair" sugar house in 1907 and the sale of two of his large plantations, he gradually turned his attention to other industries. In New Orleans, where he resided most of the time, he edited the *Southern Farmer* and the *Trade Index of New Orleans,* and published *The Louisiana Planter and Sugar Manufacturer, El Mundo Azucarero,* and the *Lower Coast Gazette.* He was a member of the Unitarian church from boyhood, and was honorary president of the First Unitarian Church of New Orleans at the time of his death. He was buried in New Orleans.

[A brief biography, presumably contributed by Dymond, in Alceé Fortier, *Louisiana* (1914), III, 139–43; files of the *Proc. La. Sugar Planter's Asso.,* and the annual *La. Sugar Report,* both ed. by A. Bouchereau; files of *La. Planter and Sugar Manufacturer* and obituary in the issue of Mar. 11, 1922; annual *Reports* of the U. S. Commissioner of Agriculture, especially those for the years 1885–89; obituary and editorial estimate in the New Orleans *Times-Picayune,* Mar. 6 and 7, 1922.]

W. P.

DYOTT, THOMAS W. (1771–Jan. 17, 1861), patent medicine king, glass manufacturer, welfare worker, temperance advocate, came to Philadelphia from England in the nineties with a few shillings in his pocket. He was of Scotch-English parentage, and had been a druggist's apprentice and clerk in London. Renting a small room and basement in Philadelphia, he commenced polishing boots in the day time, and making liquid shoe-blacking at night and was soon selling all of the blacking that he could produce. Saving his earnings, he opened a drug-store and prospered. He soon became the largest maker and dealer in patent medicines in the country, advertising these nostrums and establishing agencies for the wares in remote frontier settlements. He used quantities of glass containers of various sizes and shapes for his drugs and medicines and eventually became an agent for several Pennsylvania and New Jersey glass houses making bottles, window-glass, chemical and "philosophical" apparatus, which he retailed at his drug-store. In 1833 Dyott purchased the Kensington Glass Works, established in 1771 by Robert Towars and James Leacock, buying it from the sons of James Rowland, and also took over an adjacent plant near Gunner's Run, the two properties covering between 300 and 400 acres along the Delaware River. He expanded the factories and was soon making five grades of glass in five separate furnaces. Nearly 450 hands, including 100 apprentices, were employed at the glass works. There were fifty different factory buildings on the premises, besides wharves, docks and farm buildings. Dyott improved the grade of bottle-glass, undersold importations, employed expert mold designers and chippers, and impressed more of his containers with his name, or that of the factory, than any other American glass manufacturer. Many sizes and shapes of bottles were manufactured, the fame of the Kensington output resting, from the glass collector's standpoint, on the fanciful and historical flasks decorated with ships, locomotives, trees, flags, various agricultural and symbolical devices, or with the likenesses of celebrities, including Dyott himself.

At this period of his life, success went to the head of "Dr." Dyott (he had appropriated the title "M.D." as was a custom of patent-medicine men of that era). He adopted an extravagant manner of living and a fantastic form of dress, and considered himself quite a personage. A unique community life was established at the glass works, which was called "Dyottville" and "Temperanceville," and no liquor was allowed upon the premises, although his patent nostrums contained a large percentage of alcohol. The man aimed at combining "mental and moral with manual labor." A twelve-month operating schedule was inaugurated for the first time in the United States, and Dyottville became largely self-supporting, with artisans and farmers, a medical department containing a sick-room, a library, a singing-school, concerts, games, and recreational sports. Life was regulated with precision—a rising bell at daylight, stated hours for baths, crackers and biscuits served during working intermission, supper followed by an hour of leisure, night-school, and prayers. The younger folk were in bed by 8:30 p. m., and at 9:30 p. m. the gates of Dyottville were shut. Discipline, although strict, was nevertheless kindly, and the moral tone of the community high.

The versatile Dyott published *The Democratic Herald* for a time and issued a monthly advertising sheet. He was the author of a treatise called *An Exposition of the System of Moral and Mental Labor Established at the Glass Factory of Dyottville* (1833), and he opened "The Manual Labor Bank," an unchartered institution, maintained entirely upon his personal credit. His philanthropic ideas, however, were his undoing. In 1836 the Schuylkill Bank became financially involved and closed its doors; Dyott could then obtain no specie with which to pay his notes, and after his personal resources became completely exhausted, he failed, and the works were closed. He was indicted for fraudulent insolvency, found guilty, and sentenced to the Eastern State Penitentiary in 1837, but was pardoned before the expiration of his term. After release from prison, he went back to his drug-store, and again acquired considerable wealth. His death occurred in his ninetieth year.

[Jos. D. Weeks, "Reports on the Manufacture of Glass" (1874), in *House Misc. Doc. No. 42, pt. 2*, 47 Cong., 2 Sess.; Carmita de Solms Jones, in *Bull. Pa. Museum*, vol. XXII (1926); Charles Messer Stow, "Dr. Thos. W. Dyott—Welfare Worker in the Glass Industry," in *Boston Transcript*, July 23, 1927; Rhea Mansfield Knittle, *Early Am. Glass* (1927), ch. xviii; *Press* (Phila.), Jan. 19, 1861.] R. M. K.

EADS, JAMES BUCHANAN (May 23, 1820–Mar. 8, 1887), engineer, inventor, was born in Lawrenceburg, Ind., the son of Thomas C. and Ann (Buchanan) Eads. His forebears were English and Irish gentlefolk, the Eads having settled first in Maryland, while his mother's people hailed from Ireland. Thomas Eads was a merchant but never a very prosperous one, and in the hope of bettering his condition periodically moved from one town to another. When James was three years old the family moved to Cincinnati; when he was nine, to Louisville; and when he was thirteen, finally settled in St. Louis, Mo. His schooling ceased here because of the immediate necessity of helping to support the family. He first peddled apples on the street, but in a short time entered the dry-goods store of Williams & Durings as clerk, and through the kindness of Mr. Williams spent most of his spare time in the latter's library. Five years later, in 1838, he became a purser on a Mississippi River steamboat. In this work he had the opportunity to satisfy somewhat his boyish interest in machinery and also to recognize the economic importance of reducing the heavy losses in boats and cargoes. For three years, therefore, while steaming up and down between St. Louis and New Orleans, he concentrated his attention on the invention of a diving bell. He patented it, and in 1842 gave up his purser's job and formed a partnership to engage in steamboat salvaging. The business was successful from the start. Eads personally supervised every job and was as often on the river bottom within his diving bell as on the bell tender. He continued in this work for three years and then sold his interest, married, and organized a glass manufactory in St. Louis, the first west of the Ohio River. This venture proved to be a failure, and Eads found himself in 1848 in debt to the amount of $25,000. With $1,500 advanced by his creditors, he then returned to the wrecking business and by 1857 had not only paid off his indebtedness but also had amassed a fortune which enabled him to give up an occupation requiring almost continual absence from home. During his twelve years on the river he had become more and more interested in the study of the laws which governed its flow and determined its deposits, and had become thoroughly satisfied in his own mind as to the proper manner of combating the destructive action not only of the Mississippi but of all rivers. As early as 1856 he proposed to Congress to remove all snags and wrecks from the Mississippi, Missouri, Arkansas, and Ohio rivers and to keep their channels open for a term of years, but the bill authorizing such action died in the Senate.

From 1857 to 1861 Eads lived in semi-retirement in the happy environment of his family, even indulging in a trip to Europe. In the latter year, however, he was summoned to Washington by President Lincoln to advise with him upon the best methods of utilizing the western rivers for attack and defense. He proposed a fleet of armor-plated, steam-propelled gunboats, of special construction to ward off shell fire, and when the government advertised for bids he submitted one in which he contracted to construct seven of these vessels of 600 tons each, ready for armament in sixty-five days. It was the contract of a bold and self-reliant man and seemingly impossible of execution in view of the existing chaotic industrial conditions; but within two weeks, over four thousand men, scattered all over the country, were engaged in various details of construction, and in forty-five days the first of the seven gunboats, the *St. Louis,* with her boilers and engines aboard, was launched. The other six followed in quick succession, while an eighth—one of Ead's wrecking boats—was rebuilt to incorporate his steam-operated gun mounting. In the course of the war he constructed fourteen armored gunboats, incorporating several new ordnance inventions which he patented; converted seven transports into what were called "tin-clads"; and built four heavy mortar boats, all of which were in active service. His was a most heroic undertaking, and before it was completed his health became seriously impaired, but his indomitable spirit pulled him through, and by 1865 he was again physically fit.

In that year a bill was introduced into Congress authorizing the construction of a bridge across the Mississippi at St. Louis. When the bill was passed it was amended so as to call for a 500-foot centre span and fifty feet of clearance. The project was thought to be impracticable and was so pronounced by a group of twenty-seven of the leading civil engineers in the country. Eads, however, who had been selected by one of the construction companies as its engineer, thought otherwise; and when his plan was finally approved in 1867 he proceeded with the construction of the bridge and successfully completed it in 1874. It is of steel and masonry construction and its center span is 520 feet long. The base of one pier is 136 feet below high water and was sunk through ninety feet of sand and gravel to bedrock. The conditions encountered during the construction were so extraordinary in many respects that only an inventive genius such as Eads possessed could provide the many appliances needed for the subaqueous work and for the superstructure. Known to-day as "Eads Bridge," it is still greatly admired.

Hardly had this work been completed when, in February 1874, Eads made a formal proposition to Congress to open one of the mouths of the Mississippi River into the Gulf and maintain the channel, agreeing to do it at the sole risk of himself and his associates. The proposition was attacked chiefly by army engineers, but after a considerable fight the proposal was accepted, Eads's work to be confined, however, to the small South Pass. Here he had his most desired opportunity to apply his knowledge of the river's currents, and by a system of jetties so arranged that the river deposited its sediments where he wanted them, he successfully accomplished the task four years later, in 1879. This achievement placed him in the foremost rank of hydraulic engineers as his great bridge had placed him in the first rank of bridge engineers. His papers, addresses, and communications to Congress and to the technical magazines, newspapers, and societies during his work at the South Pass are probably unsurpassed in value as engineering expositions on controlling the flow of water, the movements and dispositions of sediment, and the correct methods of river improvement.

The year this work was finished the first meeting of the Panama Canal Congress was held. Eads was opposed to a canal and conceived the idea of a ship railway. He selected the shortest possible route between the two oceans, by way of the Tehuantepec Isthmus, two thousand miles shorter than the Panama route, and from 1880 until his death he worked energetically for such a project. He appeared in Congress and replied to Count De Lesseps who advocated the canal. He obtained a valuable concession from the Mexican government for building the railway and proposed to Congress to build it at his own expense, provided the government would guarantee a dividend of six per cent for fifteen years when it had been proven practical. A bill embodying his suggestion passed the House but failed in the Senate. In 1885 he introduced a new bill in Congress, modified as a result of additional concessions granted by Mexico, and he spent considerable time in Washington for the next two years doing what he could to bring about passage of the bill. His health was far from good, however, and on the advice of physicians, in January 1887 he went to Nassau, Bahama Islands, where he died three months later.

Eads was an engineer of international reputation; his advice was sought not only by many municipalities in the United States but by foreign governments as well. He made plans for the improvement of the harbor of Toronto; advised on improvements for the harbors of Vera Cruz and Tampico; served in an advisory capacity to the Mersey Docks and Harbor Board of Liverpool, and many others. In 1877 the University of Missouri conferred upon him the honorary degree of LL.D., and in 1884 the British Society for the Encouragement of Art, Manufacture, and Commerce awarded him the Albert Medal "as a token of their appreciation of the services you have rendered to the science of engineering." He was the only American up to that time who had received this award. He was a member of the American Society of Civil Engineers, and vice-president in 1882; a fellow of the American Association for the Advancement of Science; a member of the British Institution of Civil Engineers, and of the British Association. Some of his writings, edited by Estill McHenry, were published in 1884 under the title, *Addresses and Papers of James B. Eads*. He was twice married, first to Martha Dillon of St. Louis, who died in 1855 leaving him with two daughters, and two years after her death, to Eunice Eads, the widow of his cousin Elijah, who had three daughters.

[Wm. Sellers, in *Nat. Acad. Sci. Biog. Memoirs,* vol. III (1895); Louis How, *Jas. B. Eads* (1900); sketch by Estill McHenry in *Addresses and Papers,* mentioned above; *Scientific American,* Apr. 23, 1887; *Washington Post, Evening Star* (Washington, D. C.), Mar. 11, 1887; Patent Office records; correspondence with Eads's descendants.]

C. W. M.

EAGELS, JEANNE (June 26, 1894–Oct. 3, 1929), actress, daughter of Edward Eagels, a carpenter, and Julia (Sullivan) Eagels, is said to have been born in Boston and to have moved at the age of two to Kansas City, Mo., but according to her own account (*Who's Who in America,* 1928–29) she was born in Kansas City. Her birth-date has also been given as 1890 (Edward Doherty). At an early age she commenced a stage career, appearing with O. D. Woodward's stock company as Puck in *A Midsummer Night's Dream.* The next eight years she spent touring through small towns of Kansas, Nebraska, and Oklahoma, principally with the Michelson and Levinsky tent company, and playing a wide variety of rôles in such plays as, *For Home and Honor, The Octoroon, Uncle Tom's Cabin,* and *Little Lord Fauntleroy.* Mrs. Eagels, a former school-teacher, accompanied and tutored her daughter, whose public school education had ended abruptly after her first stage appearance. Jeanne's experiences were colorful and exciting during this apprenticeship of barnstorming in cabooses.

Her facility at impersonating famous actresses of the day, a talent she always feared, brought her to the attention of Anna Held, who was greatly impressed by the slight, gawky girl, with her long yellow hair and gray eyes. In 1911 she came to New York and in a few weeks was engaged for a small part in *Jumping Jupiter,* a musical show. Her second part was Olga Cook in *The "Mind-the-Paint" Girl,* at the Lyceum in 1912. Her beauty caused Florenz Ziegfeld to offer her a place in the chorus of the *Follies* at $150 a week, but although she was receiving only $35 she declined, saying, "I am a dramatic actress." John Emerson, then in the Frohman offices, gave her the assignment in her second Broadway play, impressed by what she herself termed her "tremendous nerve." The first important part she played was in the Elsie Ferguson rôle of *The Outcast,* when that play went on tour in the season of

1915-16. After this she appeared as George Arliss's leading lady in three plays, and in David Belasco's success, *Daddies.* In 1922 began her four years' engagement, under the management of Sam H. Harris, as Sadie Thompson in *Rain,* one of the outstanding characterizations of the decade. She played her last legitimate stage rôle for Gilbert Miller in *Her Cardboard Lover,* the engagement ending in her suspension for eighteen months by the Actor's Equity Association, in April 1928, because of her failure to appear in the play in Milwaukee and St. Louis. When her tour thus came to a sudden close, she turned over her home at Ossining to her supporting English cast.

She was married to Edward Harris Coy, a former captain of the Yale football team, in August 1925 at the home of Fay Bainter in Stamford, Conn. Their marriage proved happy for a time, but in June 1928 she instituted divorce proceedings in Chicago, charging cruelty. The charges not being contested, she was granted a divorce on July 14. Her frail physique and an extremely nervous condition, which caused her to be treated by a nerve specialist for nine years before her death, were probably responsible for many of the scenes she created. In the summer of 1924, she had hysterics at Southampton when English customs inspectors questioned her. She twice interrupted performances in *Her Cardboard Lover,* once to have a stage door closed, the second time to have a drink of water. Her suspension by Equity and fine of two weeks' salary ($3,600), caused her to enter vaudeville for a time, and then motion pictures. She was the star of *Man, Woman and Sin,* directed by Monta Bell for Metro-Goldwyn Mayer, and of *The Letter* and *Jealousy* for Paramount. She was under contract to the latter company for another dialogue picture when she died at the Park Avenue Hospital, New York City. Her death was ascribed by her personal physician to "a nervous toxic disorder."

George Arliss said of her acting, "She has the vital sense of time." Ambitious and industrious, she told friends when she was being featured by Belasco, "I'm just beginning and this is not enough." During the sensational run of *Rain* for nearly 1,500 performances, she missed but eighteen. It has been said that off the stage she was, "if possible, more consummately the actress than on it" (Brock, *post*). She had a host of friends in the theatrical profession who mourned her death at the height of her career.

[J. B. Kennedy, "Jeanne Eagels," *Collier's Weekly,* Oct. 1, 1927; H. I. Brock, "Her Road from Yesterday," *Personality Mag.,* Mar. 1928; press books of George C. Tyler, David Belasco, Sam H. Harris, and Paramount; Jeanne Eagels, "The Actor is More Important Than the Play," *Theater Mag.,* Jan. 1928; obituaries in *N. Y. Times* and *Chicago Tribune,* Oct. 4, 1929, and in *N. Y. Herald-Tribune,* Oct. 4, 5, 1929; information secured through the courtesy of Edward Doherty, who at the time this biography was written was preparing a series of articles for publication.]

H. B.

EAKINS, THOMAS (July 25, 1844–June 25, 1916), painter, sculptor, teacher, was born in Philadelphia, where his entire professional life was passed. His paternal grandfather was from the North of Ireland. His father, Benjamin Eakins, was a writing-master, a methodical and deliberate man, whose work as an expert engrosser of manuscripts was in constant demand. A portrait of him by his son, called "The Writing Master," shows him engaged in this kind of work, and is noteworthy for the admirable drawing of the hands, the form and action of which serve to reveal his character. Eakins's mother was Caroline Cowperthwait Eakins. On this side of the family the descent was from English and Dutch stock. As a lad in the Philadelphia high school, Eakins had the reputation of being independent but unobtrusive. An early likeness shows him to have been of a vigorous, determined character, and a portrait taken in middle life further emphasizes these personal traits. On graduation from the high school, he enrolled himself as a student in the Pennsylvania Academy of the Fine Arts, where he obtained a good groundwork for his training as a painter. Then, in 1866, at the age of twenty-two, he sought more advanced instruction in Paris. In the École des Beaux-Arts he came under three instructors, J. L. Gérôme, Léon Bonnat, and the sculptor A. A. Dumont. Spending three years there in arduous study, he became a favorite pupil of that efficient master Gérôme, for whom he had the greatest respect. It was characteristic of him that he should take his work in the school seriously; in fact, so severely did he apply himself that, late in 1869, his health was menaced, and he betook himself to Spain for a rest.

During the seven months that he remained in Spain he painted only two or three pictures and made a few studies. But the most important result of his sojourn was the impression made upon his mind by the great Spanish realists whose works he saw in Madrid, notably Velasquez, Ribera, Goya, and Herrera. There can be no doubt as to the confirmation given by these uncompromising masters to a latent tendency present in the temperament of the young man. He returned to his home in Philadelphia in 1870, the year of the outbreak of the Franco-Prussian War, and there he lived for the rest of his life, busily teaching, lecturing, painting, and making a few pieces of sculpture. Immediately upon his return he began the study of anatomy at the

Jefferson Medical College. This specialty always interested him, and he mastered it with the thoroughness that marked everything to which he directed his attention. It was his knowledge of anatomy that brought him his opportunity to teach in the schools of the Pennsylvania Academy of the Fine Arts in 1873. He became the dean of the faculty of that famous institution, the oldest art school in America, and for many years he was the principal instructor there. When a group of students founded the Art Students' League, they gladly accepted his offer to furnish instruction there also. He was as strong in drawing and perspective as in construction, and he had the happy faculty of making these difficult subjects vitally interesting to his pupils. He worked unsparingly, and in addition to his classes in anatomy, he lectured, painted many portraits, and presently busied himself with certain more elaborate compositions, including two unusually large pictures of surgical clinics,—the "Clinic of Dr. Gross" and the "Clinic of Dr. Agnew."

The first-named work, measuring 96x78 inches, was completed in 1875, and now belongs to the Jefferson Medical College. It was exhibited in Chicago, St. Louis, and Buffalo, and is generally regarded as his masterpiece. Both choice of subject and manner of treatment are indicative of the essentially scientific bent of Eakins's mind. The structure of the body was his lifelong hobby; the strength and the weakness of his art alike arise from this preoccupation. Nothing interested him more than a surgical operation or an autopsy, unless it were a boat-race or a boxing-match. He looked upon the clinic of Dr. Gross with precisely the same professional calm as that of the surgeon, the assistants, and the medical students in the background. The absence of all tension and all dramatic feeling is an unqualified merit, because it is true to the atmosphere of the occasion, and because it corresponds to Eakins's own mental habit. He was always deeply serious, but it would not have been possible for him to be sensational. To his interest in physiology is mainly due his masterly drawing of the human figure in repose or in action, and this is his chief title to distinction.

In the work in question the expression of character is typical of his best efforts. Dr. Gross, occupying the center of the composition, is explaining to the class each successive step in the operation, which is being performed by his colleague, Dr. White. The surgeon, the anesthetician, the nurses, and the students are intent, absorbed, business-like. The light is concentrated on the operating table, the white cloths, the flesh, the instruments, the wound and blood. One feels the momentous nature of the event—what issues of life and death are involved; yet one feels also the impressive atmosphere of expert knowledge, experience, and skill, pervading the scene. Two centuries and a half had passed since Rembrandt, then a young man, painted his "Anatomy Lesson," with much of the same detachment. His work was not more serious than that of Eakins; and it is probably true, as Charles H. Caffin has pointed out, that there is no other painter in America, and few elsewhere, who could have treated the "Clinic of Dr. Gross" at once so realistically and so pictorially. Yet the work was not received with approval; there was no order for it; and it is said that it brought Eakins only $300.

Among the many other pictures by Eakins, which sufficiently illustrate his choice of motives, may be mentioned the huge "Clinic of Dr. Agnew," belonging to the University of Pennsylvania; "Between Rounds" and "Salutat," scenes from the world of Fistiana; the "Pair-Oared Shell" and the "Biglen Brothers Turning the Stakeboat," depicting professional oarsmen in action on the Schuylkill River; and a long series of fishing subjects. In addition to painting, he made a certain number of pieces of sculpture. Two of the reliefs on the battle monument in Trenton, N. J., are from his hand. He modeled the horses ridden by Lincoln and Grant which form a part of the soldiers and sailors monument in Brooklyn, N. Y. He also collaborated with his pupil Samuel Murray in the making of the colossal figures of the prophets which adorn the Witherspoon Building in Philadelphia.

He was a slow, methodical workman, but he was indefatigable. Notwithstanding his intense devotion to work, he maintained his health by systematic outdoor exercise, hunting, fishing, boating, and riding, for he was an ardent sportsman. "He enjoyed the wild rush of his bronco across country, near his haunts in the Welsh Mountains of Pennsylvania," says Harrison S. Morris, "and I recollect one such episode when I found myself astride of a pony which in spite of me followed at a gallop the mad pace which Eakins set on his western nag." And Alan Burroughs recalls that in 1887, when Eakins took a few months' trip in the West, he engaged in a strenuous outdoor existence with ease, and rode horseback all the first day without showing a sign that he had not ridden for years.

To the Centennial Exposition of 1876 Eakins sent the "Chess Players," "Whistling for Plover," several portraits, and a water-color entitled "Baseball." The "Chess Players," which was subsequently acquired by the Metropolitan Museum of Art, New York, exemplifies his power of expression, and might be called a tangible embodiment of cogitation. His portraits are somewhat unprepossessing, certainly not flattering to the sitters, but they have the virtue of honesty, and some of them are memorable American types. Such beauty as they have is that of candid veracity. Some of his own remarks are illuminating: "That's the way it looked to me." "You can copy a thing to a certain limit, then you must use intellect." "Respectability in art is appalling."

In 1881 Eakins was married to Susan H. Macdowell, who had been an art student at the Academy. They had no children. They lived in a modest by-street, Mount Vernon St., and the studio was a plain and dusty third-floor back room, overflowing with pictures and studies. Eakins had another studio, in Chestnut St., below Broad St., at the top of an office building. In his dining-room he had installed a blackboard, so that he might elucidate his ideas at any time by a diagram or an outline. Modest, reticent, though not without consciousness of his own power, his manner of speech was slow and blunt. He was a man of unusual education, and could speak four or five languages. His "quiet but earnest spirit looked out at you from a face that was almost heavy with thought and invention." Toward the end of his life he lost his good health, took on weight, and appeared lethargic in contrast to the energy of his earlier years. He did scarcely any work in his studio during the last six years. His death occurred in 1916, when he was seventy-two. A few medals and a "small flurry of appreciation" were all the symbols of fame that had come to him.

The virility of his nature is evident from his selection of subjects; and his strength of characterization is proved by the truth of expression which makes of each portrait not only an individual personality but a racial type. An outstanding example of this is "The Thinker," a full-length standing figure painted in 1900, which is the most penetrating study of a native type produced by the painter. It is a type as purely American as Abraham Lincoln. Underneath the reserve and sobriety of the style are understanding and feeling. The dry manner of statement is in itself excellent, for it fits the man. It is unique in its plainness. This stark sort of realism, which preserves for us a certain something in America not recorded by any other painter, constitutes Eakins's authentic contribution to American art. It strikes a new note, not melodious, but memorable. It is the work of an unbiased historian who takes things as he finds them and refrains from comment, letting facts speak for themselves, with a Spartan objectivity that in the last analysis becomes not only significant but in some way noble and universal. If the artist had no imagination, he knew how to stir the imagination of his audience. His negative merits are scorn for all that is adventitious, trivial, sensuously charming: the rejection of conventional beauty. In his work there are analogies to that of Walt Whitman and Winslow Homer, possibly to Emerson, too, in his homely moods. The underlying dignity and worth of common things and people are suggested, but without *parti pris.* The clear, cool light in which Eakins envisages the American scene is fatal to all glamour, almost cruel in its crudity, but his work is unique for its fidelity, and has a distinct historical value. In 1930 a collection of thirty-six of his paintings was given to the Pennsylvania Museum, in Philadelphia, by Mrs. Eakins and Miss Mary A. Williams.

[J. McLure Hamilton and H. S. Morris, "Thomas Eakins: Two Appreciations," in the *Bull.* of the Metropolitan Museum of Art, N. Y., Nov. 1917; Alan Burroughs, "Thomas Eakins, the Man," in *The Arts,* Dec. 1923; Alan Burroughs, "Catalogue of Work by Thomas Eakins, 1869–1916," in *The Arts,* June 1924; G. S. Parker, Introduction to the catalogue of the memorial exhibition at the Pa. Acad. of the Fine Arts, Phila., 1917; Henry McBride, "Modern Art," in the *Dial,* Jan. 1926; Louis Kalonyme, "New York Exhibitions from a Personal Angle," in *Arts and Decoration,* Jan. 1926; C. H. Caffin, "Some Am. Portrait Painters," in the *Critic,* Jan. 1904; Royal Cortissoz, "Thomas Eakins," in *Am. Artists* (1923), pp. 77–82; G. W. Eggers, *Bull.* of the Worcester Art Museum, Jan. 1930; F. J. Mather, *International Studio,* Jan. 1930; Bryson Burroughs, Introduction to the catalogue of the loan exhibition of works by Eakins at the Metropolitan Museum of Art, N. Y., 1917; Samuel Isham, *Hist. of Am. Painting* (1905), p. 525; articles by Bryson Burroughs, Robert Henri, and Joseph Brummer, in the catalogue of an exhibition held at Brummer's Galleries, N. Y., 1923; *Public Ledger* (Phila.), June 26, 1916. W. H. D.

EAMES, CHARLES (Mar. 20, 1812–Mar. 16, 1867), lawyer, diplomat, was born at New Braintree, Worcester County, Mass. His mother was a descendant of Ebenezer Tidd, who emigrated from Lexington to New Braintree in 1768. After preparation at Leicester Academy, he entered Harvard from which he was graduated in 1831, the first in a class which included Wendell Phillips and Motley the historian, with both of whom he maintained a friendship until his death. Eames spent one year in the Harvard Law School and then studied law with John Duer in New York City, but whether or not he was admitted to the bar, he abandoned the profession in 1845 to accept a prominent position in the Navy Department at Washington under Secretary George Bancroft. A few months later he engaged in newspaper work and as associate editor of the Washington *Union* acquired a high reputation for his political writings. On Jan. 12, 1849, he was appointed by President Polk as commissioner to Hawaii, succeeding Anthony Ten Eyck. A letter from Secretary of State Buchanan, Feb. 16, 1849, authorized him "to conclude a Treaty with the Hawaiian Government similar in all respects to their Treaties with Great Britain and France" (*Works of James Buchanan,* VIII, 333). Accordingly, he met the Hawaiian plenipotentiary, Gerrit Parmele Judd [*q.v.*], in San Francisco, and there concluded a treaty with him—an accomplishment which had baffled his two predecessors. His work completed, he resigned on Oct. 22, 1849, and returned to newspaper work, first as editor of the *Nashville Union* for six months and then as editor of the Washington *Union* until sent by President Pierce in 1854 as minister resident to Venezuela to succeed Isaac Nevett Steele. A change in administration brought about his resignation and his return to Washington, where he devoted himself to the practise of international law. During the Civil War, Eames was counsel for the Navy Department and the captors in all the prize cases and for the Treasury Department in all the cotton cases. While arguing before the United States Supreme Court the great prize case of the *Sir William Peel,* in which William M. Evarts was the opposing counsel, he was stricken down with the disease that terminated fatally two months later. He rallied sufficiently in a month to appear again in the prize case of the *Grey Jacket,* involving a million dollars, which he won for the government. This was his last professional appearance before his death. During the last five years of his life "his management of prize cases showed him to be one of the best admiralty lawyers of this country, while his great knowledge of international law, supported by a remarkable memory and most acute and indefatigable intellect, won for him at the same time well-deserved distinction and respect" (*National Intelligencer,* Mar. 19, 1867). A fine linguist and a brilliant conversationalist, he made his home a great center for the celebrities of his day in politics, jurisprudence, letters, art, and society. Gov. Andrew, in a glowing obituary notice in a Boston newspaper (Hurd, p. 685), mentioned the home of Mr. and Mrs. Eames as the "most hospitable, agreeable and attractive house in Washington."

[D. Hamilton Hurd, *Hist. of Worcester County, Mass.* (1899), vol. I; Wm. T. Davis, *Bench and Bar of the Commonwealth of Mass.,* II (1895), 397; *Nat. Intelligencer* (Washington), Mar. 19, 1867; *Boston Advertiser,* Mar. 18, 1867.] H. F. W.

EARLE, ALICE MORSE (Apr. 27, 1853–Feb. 16, 1911), author and antiquarian, was born in Worcester, Mass., the daughter of Edwin and Abigail (Clary) Morse, and the granddaughter of Benjamin and Elizabeth (Hoar) Morse. She was very proud of her ancestry, which later gave her membership in the Colonial Dames of America. She was educated at the Worcester High School and at Dr. Gannett's boarding-school in Boston. In 1874 she married Henry Earle, of Brooklyn, N. Y., and the remainder of her life was spent largely in that city and, during the summer, at her father's home in Worcester. After her husband's death, she traveled extensively in Europe with her sister, and was a passenger on the *Republic* when it was rammed in 1908 by the *Florida,* on which occasion she fell into the water accidentally from the life-boat and narrowly escaped drowning. She had four children, three of whom survived her. She died at Hempstead, L. I., N. Y., at the age of fifty-eight, and was buried at her early home in Worcester.

The author's life is mainly the story of the preparation and publication of book after book dealing with the colonial history of America, a subject of which she was an indefatigable student. Her first published writing was an article for the *Youth's Companion* upon some old Sabbath customs which had been related to her by her grandfather. The article in an enlarged form was accepted by the *Atlantic Monthly,* and, in the following year (1891) her book, *The Sabbath in Puritan New England,* was published by Scribners. This was the beginning of a long series of similar treatises: *China Collecting in America* (1892), *Customs and Fashions in Old New England* (1893), *The Diary of a Boston School Girl* (1894), *The Costume of Colonial Times* (1894), *The Life of Margaret Winthrop* (1895), *Colonial Dames and Goodwives* (1895), *In Old Narragansett* (1896), *Colonial Days in Old New York* (1896), *Curious Punishments of Bygone Days* (1896), *Home Life in Colonial Days* (1898), *Child Life in Colonial Days* (1899), *Stage-Coach and Tavern Days* (1900), *Old-Time Gardens* (1901), *Sun Dials and Roses of Yesterday* (1902), and *Two Centuries of Costume* (1903), a work in two volumes which she considered to be her most significant and valuable production. In addition, she assisted in the compilation of *Early Prose and Verse* (1893), and was a contributor to *Historic New York* (1897), and *Chap-Book Essays* (1897). Her articles frequently appeared in magazines, and she also lectured on her favorite topics.

Mrs. Earle owes her place in literature to the fact that she devoted herself to one phase of American history until she had mastered all the available material. Her books fostered the renewed interest in our colonial past which developed toward the close of the nineteenth century, and because she wrote in entertaining fashion, without pedantry or too obtrusive scholarship, her volumes had a considerable sale. It cannot be said that she added much new information to our knowledge of colonial times.

[*Who's Who in America,* 1910–11; the *Writer,* Apr. 1911, p. 48; *N. Y. Times, N. Y. Tribune,* Feb. 18, 1911; certain information supplied by members of the family.] C. M. F.

EARLE, JAMES (May 1, 1761–Aug. 18, 1796), painter, son of Ralph and Phebe (Whittemore) Earle, was born in that part of Leicester now known as Paxton, Mass. He went to England as a young man, probably with his brother Ralph [*q.v.*], and after a period of study attained distinction as a portrait-painter. About 1789 he married, in London, Caroline Georgiana Pilkington Smyth, widow of Joseph Brewer Palmer Smyth of New Jersey, a Loyalist who returned to England during the Revolution. Earle's professional life was spent in London, England, and Charleston, S. C. In London he exhibited sixteen portraits at the Royal Academy of Art, during a period of nine years. In Charleston he painted many portraits, including those of General Charles Cotesworth Pinckney, Edward Rutledge, Mrs. Nellie Custis (Mrs. Lawrence Lewis), Lawrence Lewis, and the Right Reverend Robert Smith. Seven years after his marriage, he returned to America for a visit and concluded to make it his permanent home. He took passage to England to bring his family back, but the vessel first stopped at Charleston, S. C., and there he succumbed to an attack of yellow fever and died. It is unfortunate that Earle's death, in the prime of his life, prevented a wider knowledge of his work in his own country. His brush stroke conveyed a happy combination of grace and distinction of line. A contemporary appreciation ranked him with Copley, Savage, Trumbull, and West, and referred to his unusual ability in giving life to the eye and characteristic expression to every feature.

[W. Dunlap, *Hist. of the Rise and Progress of the Arts of Design in the U. S.* (new ed. 1918), II, 115; Pliny Earle, *The Earle Family* (1888), pp. 90–91; U. Thieme and F. Becker, *Allgemeines Lexikon der Bildenden Künstler,* X (1914), 281; Frick Art Reference Library portrait file; *S. C. State-Gazette and Timothy and Mason's Daily Advertiser,* Aug. 20, 1796.] J. M. H.

EARLE, MORTIMER LAMSON (Oct. 14, 1864–Sept. 26, 1905), educator, was born in New York City, the son of Mortimer Lent and Josephine (Allen) Earle. He was educated at the Ashland Public School in East Orange, N. J., and at Columbia College, where he graduated with high honors in 1886. From the beginning of his college studies he showed a marked proficiency in languages and literature, and a scholarly precision that distinguished all his later work. His principal devotion was to the Greek and Latin tongues, though he gave considerable attention also to French, German, Italian, and Sanskrit. At graduation he was awarded a fellowship in letters for three years. The first and third of these were employed in teaching and research at Columbia; the intervening year, 1887–88, was spent at the American School in Athens. While in Greece, he took part in excavations near Marathon and directed those at Sicyon, on the Gulf of Corinth, where he discovered an interesting theatre containing a statue of Dionysus which now belongs to the Museum at Athens. At the same time his incidental interests led him to an unusual proficiency in several dialects of modern Greek.

Proceeding to the doctorate at Columbia in 1889, Earle was given charge of the instruction in Greek in Barnard College, founded in that year. His sound scholarship at once placed the classical curriculum of the new college on a firm basis. With the exception of three years as associate professor at Bryn Mawr, from 1895 to 1898, he remained at Barnard continuously; and when the latter institution was united with Columbia in 1899 he succeeded to a professorship of classical philology, dividing his time between undergraduate teaching in Barnard and the direction of graduate students in the university. In both schools he showed distinguished gifts for teaching and administration as well as for scholarly production. He was rapidly coming to occupy an almost unique position among American classicists, with discoveries of importance already to his credit, with a paleographical and bibliographical knowledge hardly rivaled in the country, and with an unusual faculty for the interpretation of Roman and Hellenic life and art, when he met an untimely death from a virulent typhoid contracted during a scholarly expedition in Italy. He was survived by his wife, Ethel D. Woodward, whom he had married on June 4, 1892.

In addition to numerous important contributions to classical journals in America and Europe, he published an edition of the *Alcestis* of Euripides (1894), one of the *Œdipus Tyrannus* of Sophocles (1901), and one of the *Medea* of Euripides (1904). At the time of his death he was engaged upon a study of Thucydides, which appeared in the *American Journal of Philology* (October–December, 1905). A posthumous volume of studies was published in 1912 as *The Classical Papers of Mortimer Lamson Earle,* with a memoir by Sidney G. Ashmore.

[Ashmore's memoir; E. D. Perry, "Mortimer Lamson Earle," in the *Columbia Univ. Quart.,* Dec. 1905; *N. Y. Times,* Sept. 27, 1905; archives of Columbia Univ.] E. H. W.

EARLE, PLINY (Dec. 17, 1762–Nov. 29, 1832), inventor, cotton-machinery manufacturer, the son of Robert and Sarah (Hunt) Earle, was born in Leicester, Worcester County, Mass. He traced his descent from Ralph Earle, a resident of Newport, R. I., who was one of the original twenty-nine who there organized themselves "into a civil body politicke" in April 1639. Brought up on his father's farm, he assisted in the farm work as well as the supplemental work which his father had undertaken, that of currying and washing leather. About 1785 Edmund Snow began the manufacture of cotton and wool hand cards in Leicester, and the following year young Earle, then twenty-four years old, started a similar manufactory in the same town. His inherent mechanical ingenuity presumably stood him in good stead for he successfully competed from the beginning with other manufacturers. In 1789 Almy & Brown, machinists of Providence, R. I., engaged him to cover a carding machine for them. This was opportune, for in a few months Samuel Slater became associated with that firm in the manufacture of cotton-spinning machinery, and Earle made for them the cards by which the first cotton was wrought which was spun by machinery in America. In 1791 Earle formed a partnership with two of his brothers to engage in manufacture of machine card clothing. The business became one of the most extensive of its kind in the United States and continued to be for more than twenty-five years. Earle's difficulties in furnishing cards for Slater's machinery directed his attention to the invention of a machine with which to prick the leather for cards, which theretofore had been done by hand. The device was in use in the late nineties, although the patent was not issued until Dec. 6, 1803. This formed the basis of all machines for pricking twilled cards until it was supplemented by the machine which not only pricked the leather but cut and set the teeth in one process. By 1802 the Pliny Earle & Brothers Company was considerably enlarged to include the building of machines for both wool and cotton cards, and by 1804 it had placed wool-carding machines for the accommodation of local farmers upon some stream in each of the several towns of Worcester County and one in Rhode Island. The business flourished during the War of 1812 despite the extremely high prices which had to be paid for raw materials. The sudden termination of the war, however, found the company with a very large stock of expensive raw materials on hand but with no orders for cards. This embarrassed the organization financially to such an extent that it was dissolved. Earle retained what was left of the business and continued it until his death. In addition to his other activities, he was quite an agriculturist. As early as 1820 he engaged in sheep raising and in the cultivation of mulberry trees for the production of silk. He soon found, however, that the cost of culture was too great for the prices which could be secured on manufactured silk. On June 6, 1793, Earle married Patience, daughter of William and Lydia (Arnold) Buffum, in Smithfield, R. I., and was survived by five sons and four daughters.

[Pliny Earle, *The Earle Family* (1888); J. D. Van Slyke, *Representatives of New England Manufacturers* (1879); J. N. Arnold, *Vital Record of R. I.,* vol. VII (1895); Emory Washburn, *Hist. Sketches of the Town of Leicester, Mass.* (1860); *The Mass. Spy* (Worcester), Dec. 5, 1832.] C. W. M.

EARLE, PLINY (Dec. 31, 1809–May 17, 1892), physician and psychiatrist, was born at Leicester, Mass., the brother of Thomas Earle [*q.v.*], and the son of Pliny Earle [*q.v.*] and Patience (Buffum) Earle. He studied at the Leicester Academy and later at the Friends' School, Providence, R. I., from which he graduated in 1828. He taught in this institution until 1835 when he was made principal, but in the meantime began the study of medicine under Dr. Usher Parsons and took his medical degree at the University of Pennsylvania in 1837. He then devoted a year to walking the general hospitals of Paris and a second year to a tour of inspection of European insane asylums from England to Turkey. Returning to the United States, he was made superintendent of the Friends' Hospital for the Insane at Frankford, Pa., in 1840. In 1841 he published a series of articles in the *American Journal of the Medical Sciences* which was reprinted with the title *A Visit to Thirteen Asylums for the Insane in Europe,* and in the same year also published a volume, *Marathon and Other Poems,* contributed originally to various newspapers. Three years later he left Frankford to become superintendent of the Bloomingdale Asylum, New York City, and in 1848 published his *History, Description and Statistics of the Bloomingdale Asylum for the Insane.* He resigned his position in 1845 to make a second tour of Europe and in 1853 there appeared his *Institutions for the Insane in Prussia, Austria and Germany.* On his return he settled in New York as a psychiatrist, was appointed visiting physician to the New York City Insane Asylum,

Blackwell's Island, and lectured on mental diseases at the College of Physicians and Surgeons. Owing to a breakdown in health, however, he retired from active practise in 1855 and for some years lived quietly at Leicester. After the outbreak of the Civil War he gave his services (1862–64) to the Government Hospital for the Insane at Washington, where insane soldiers were interned, and during 1863 also taught materia medica and therapeutics at the Berkshire Medical Institution. In 1864 he was made superintendent of the State Lunatic Hospital, Northampton, Mass., where he remained until his death, although he resigned from active service in 1885. After this period he made, despite his age, a third journey to Europe in the interest of psychiatry. In addition to writings already enumerated he published the following small volumes: *An Examination of the Practice of Bloodletting in Mental Disorders* (1854); *The Curability of Insanity* (1877); and *Popular Fallacies Concerning the Insane* (1890), as well as numerous minor contributions to periodical medical literature. His lifelong hobby was genealogy, and in 1888 he published *The Earle Family: Ralph Earle and His Descendants,* representing fifty years of research. He was a co-founder of the American Medical Association and the American Medico-Psychological Association, of which he was president in 1884. He was also the first president of the New York Psychological Association. A man of much originality and initiative, he led all his colleagues in familiarity with psychiatric institutions, and in the treatment of the insane he was ahead of his age. Incidentally, he delivered lecture courses on various subjects to his interned patients. Among the legal cases in which he was called upon for professional testimony was the trial of Guiteau for the assassination of President Garfield.

[F. B. Sanborn, *Memoirs of Pliny Earle with Extracts from His Diary and Letters, 1830–1892* (1898); *Medic. Record,* July–Dec. 1892; *Medico-Legal Jour.,* 1886, vol. IV, p. 189; H. A. Kelly and W. L. Burrage, *Am. Medic. Biogs.* (1920).] E. P—e.

EARLE, RALPH (May 11, 1751–Aug. 16, 1801), painter, was the son of Ralph and Phebe (Whittemore) Earle, the brother of James Earle [*q.v.*], and the fifth in descent from Ralph Earle, the emigrant ancestor of the family who settled in Newport, R. I. He was born in Shrewsbury, Mass., and probably spent his boyhood in that vicinity. By 1774 he was in New Haven, painting portraits. In the autumn of that year he was again in Massachusetts, where he married his cousin, Sarah Gates, in Leicester. He then returned, unaccompanied, to the itinerancy for which his nature seems to have destined him. In 1775 he is reported to have visited Lexington and Concord, and to have made four paintings of the battles and scenery there. These were engraved by his companion and friend, Amos Doolittle [*q.v.*], who later advertised them for sale in New Haven. As works of art they deserve faint praise, but they have been celebrated as among the first historical paintings to be produced in this country.

From November 1776 until May of the following year, when their second child was born, Ralph and Sarah Earle kept house together in New Haven. Whether his roving nature led him to desert his wife, or whether, as has been written, "he was a Tory, and skedaddled, leaving her behind" (Gates, *post*), he was, at all events, painting portraits in England as early as 1779. There he became an artist of recognized standing. He studied under West, was made a member of the Royal Academy, painted the king and other personages, and, incidentally, married again. His second wife was Anne Whitesides (or Wheelock) by whom he had two more children. He seems to have deserted her on his return to America in the late eighties. Here, again, he busied himself painting portraits in New York, Connecticut, and Massachusetts, though his habits of intemperance and procrastination kept him from realizing his potentialities. Once, when he was imprisoned for debt in New York, Alexander Hamilton induced his wife and other women to sit to him in his cell in order that he might secure his release.

Earle was the best portrait-painter in Connecticut, and most of his subjects were well-known contemporaries. Although his work is uneven, varying both in style and technical perfection, it is almost invariably interesting. Some of his portraits are wooden; others, notably that of Mrs. Charles Jeffery Smith, show considerable vitality and a capacity for acute character portrayal. In his decorative use of flat surfaces, as in the canvases of William and Mary Carpenter (Worcester Art Museum), he suggests the schools of simplification of the early twentieth century. More often, however, he places his subjects in the conventional eighteenth-century setting, making use of draperies and minute cluttered landscapes as background.

Earle died, in 1801, a victim of his own indulgences. His son by his second marriage, Ralph E. W. Earle, was also an artist. After marrying a niece of Mrs. Andrew Jackson, he became, on her death, a protégé of her husband, and in the capacity of friend and portraitist, lived in the White House during the whole of Jackson's administration.

[Much confusion and error exist regarding the life of Ralph Earle, partly because the Earle brothers studied contemporaneously in England, married and had children there, were the fathers of artist sons (James was the father of Augustus Earle), and both died in the United States. The most reliable account of the subject of this sketch is to be found in the *Bull. of the Worcester Art Museum* for July 1916. See also *Ibid.*, Jan. 1917; Wm. Dunlap, *Hist. of the Rise and Progress of the Arts of Design in the U. S.* (1918); H. T. Tuckerman, *Book of the Artists* (1867), p. 54; Samuel Isham and Royal Cortissoz, *Hist. of Am. Painting* (1927), p. 76; Michael Bryan, *Dict. of Painters and Engravers*, I (1886), 451; Pliny Earle, *The Earle Family* (1888), pp. 87–88; C. O. Gates, *Stephen Gates . . . and his Descendants* (1898), p. 44; J. W. Barber, *Hist. and Antiquities of New Haven, Conn.* (1856), p. 157; Emory Washburn, *Hist. Sketches of the Town of Leicester, Mass.* (1860), pp. 207–09. There is a pen-sketch of Earle in Dunlap, I, 260.] M. B. P.

EARLE, THOMAS (Apr. 21, 1796–July 14, 1849), lawyer, was the son of Pliny Earle [*q.v.*], a manufacturer of wool-carding machinery, and Patience (Buffum) Earle, who resided at Leicester, Mass. After attending the common schools and Leicester Academy, he passed several years in his father's employ, but as business was not prosperous he went to Worcester, Mass., in 1816, where he became a clerk in a store. In 1817 he removed to Philadelphia, and engaged in the commission business there for six years. He had no liking or capacity for a mercantile career, however, and in 1824 commenced the study of law. Meantime, in July 1820, he had married Mary Hussey of Nantucket, Mass. On his being admitted as an attorney, Apr. 2, 1825, he opened a law office in Philadelphia, at the same time engaging in literary and political work. His journalistic abilities were quickly recognized and he became editor successively of the *Columbian Observer* and *The Standard*. In the course of his legal studies he discovered that the Constitution of Pennsylvania was extremely defective and needed amendment. This he urged in the local newspapers, but it was not until he had acquired a proprietary interest in *The Mechanics' Free Press and Reform Advocate* and devoted its columns to the subject, that the public became aroused. His continued agitation at length procured the calling of the constitutional convention of 1837, to which he was a delegate. He took a leading part in its deliberations and many of the amendments which he advocated were accepted and embodied in the new constitution. Two reforms, however, which he ardently advocated, the democratization of the judiciary, and the extension of the suffrage to colored people, were rejected after long and acrimonious debate. His views on the franchise procured for him the lasting displeasure of a large section of the Democratic party, thereby destroying all chances of future political preferment. In 1840 at a convention of "Friends of Immediate Emancipation" held at Albany, N. Y., he was selected as candidate of the Liberty party for vice-president of the United States with James G. Birney [*q.v.*] for president, but he was repudiated by the abolitionists in whose name the Liberty party had made the nomination, and his name did not appear upon the ticket. He had been all his life an avowed opponent of slavery, and for a time was editor of *The Pennsylvanian*, the anti-slavery newspaper in the state. Henceforth, he took no active part in public affairs, but devoted himself to literary pursuits. He had in his earlier days published an *Essay on Penal Law in Pennsylvania* (1827) and a pamphlet, *The Right of States to Alter or Annul Charters* (1823). These were followed by his *Treatise on Railroads and Internal Communications* (1830), the first book written in the United States on this subject. His last completed work was *The Life, Travels and Opinions of Benjamin Lundy* (1847). He was an excellent linguist, well acquainted with French, German, Italian, and Spanish, and during his later years was engaged on the compilation of a "Grammatical Dictionary of the French and the English Languages" and a translation of Sismondi's *Italian Republics*, both of which were unfinished at his death.

[Pliny Earle, *The Earle Family* (1888); J. T. Scharf and T. Westcott, *Hist. of Phila. 1609–1884* (1884); *North Am. and U. S. Gazette* (Phila.), July 16, 1849; *Am. Courier* (Phila.), July 21, 1849.] H. W. H. K.

EARLY, JOHN (Jan. 1, 1786–Nov. 5, 1873), Methodist bishop, was born in Bedford County, Va., the thirteenth child of Joshua and Mary (Leftwich) Early. The ancestors of both his father and mother came to Virginia from England about the middle of the seventeenth century. He had little formal education. His parents were Baptists, but in 1804 he joined the Methodist Church. After two or three years he was licensed to preach; in 1813 he became a presiding elder; and in 1832—but for his owning slaves—he would most likely have been made a bishop. The welfare of negroes was one of his chief interests throughout his life. His first work as a minister was among the slaves of Thomas Jefferson, and in 1825 he became president of the Colonization Society which existed in his home, Lynchburg, for the purpose of transporting negroes back to Africa. He was a pioneer advocate of free public education and of railways. He was repeatedly nominated for Congress, was offered the governorship of the territories of Illinois and of Arkansas, and was invited by John Tyler to be his comptroller of the treasury. But he kept himself to his ministry. At one camp-meeting which he conducted a thousand people were converted within a week, and it was "generally conceded that he traveled more, had more souls converted under his ministry, and received more persons into the church than any of his contemporaries" (Flood-Hamilton, p. 553). His primacy in these matters was not based on laxness of method. He refused even to pray for a penitent who would not first go down into the dust, literally, to show his anxiety for salvation (Flood-Hamilton, p. 550). It is probable that he more than any one else should be considered the founder of the Methodist Randolph-Macon College. He was a member of its first board of trustees (1830), and afterward president of the board for about forty years. In 1844 he took an active part in the General Conference of the Methodist Church which resulted in the formation of the Methodist Episcopal Church, South. He was for a while president of the first conference of this new organization, and became one of its first book agents. In 1854 he was made a bishop, but was superannuated in 1866, having suffered a railway accident which permanently injured his health. He died in Lynchburg after a long illness. Early was married twice: first, to Anne Jones, and again in 1822 to Elizabeth Browne Rives, daughter of Anthony Rives.

[A. Stevens, *Compendious Hist. of Am. Methodism* (1868); A. H. Redford, *Hist. of the Organization of the M. E. Ch., South* (1871); T. L. Flood and J. W. Hamilton, *Lives of Meth. Bishops* (1882); R. Irby, *Hist. Randolph-Macon Coll.* (1898); R. H. Early, *Family of Early* (1920); *Richmond Enquirer*, Nov. 6, 1873.]

J. D. W.

EARLY, JUBAL ANDERSON (Nov. 3, 1816–Mar. 2, 1894), Confederate soldier, was born in Franklin County, Va., the son of Joab and Ruth (Hairston) Early. He graduated at West Point in 1837, was commissioned in the 3rd Artillery, and served in Florida against the Seminoles. He was promoted to first lieutenant, July 7, 1838, but resigned, July 31, 1838, studied law, and was admitted to the bar in 1840. With occasional interruptions he practised at Rocky Mount, Va., until the Civil War. He was elected to the legislature as a Whig and served 1841–42, being the youngest member of the house. Volunteering in the Mexican War, he was appointed major of the 1st Virginia Regiment, Jan. 7, 1847, and went with it to northern Mexico. Taylor's campaign being already ended, the regiment saw no fighting but remained in garrison at Monterey. Early returned home on sick leave at one time, escaped uninjured when the steamboat on which he was traveling blew up, and returned to duty in Mexico. Mustered out of the army in April 1848, he resumed his law practise. He was an unsuccessful candidate for election to the state constitutional convention in 1850, and to the legislature in 1853. He opposed secession in 1861, and as a delegate to the state convention voted against it, but immediately entered the Confederate army and fought at Bull Run as colonel of the 24th Virginia Infantry. He was then appointed brigadier-general, and for the next three years served constantly with the Army of Northern Virginia, advancing to the command of a division in 1862 and of a corps in 1864. He was appointed major-general in January 1863 and lieutenant-general in May 1864.

In June 1864 his corps was ordered into the Shenandoah Valley, and for the remainder of the war he was in independent command. In detaching so large a portion of his army Lee hoped that its operations would cause the withdrawal of a still larger force from the Army of the Potomac, now pressing him hard before Richmond. After driving the Union troops, greatly outnumbered, westward into the mountains, Early came down the Shenandoah, crossed the Potomac, levying heavy contributions in supplies and money, and marched on Washington. Though well fortified, the city was garrisoned by a force too small to man the works and consisting largely of recruits and convalescents. On the Monocacy River, Early encountered Lew Wallace, who brought up a small field force to certain defeat, but saved Washington by delaying the Confederate march several hours. As Early's advance came in sight of the fortifications, two army corps, which Grant had sent to the rescue, were landing at the city wharves. After some sharp skirmishing (July 11, 12), Early, recognizing that an assault was now hopeless, withdrew during the second night. Remaining in the lower Shenandoah Valley, he raided far and wide, obstructed communication between Washington and the West, and threatened Maryland and Pennsylvania. The burning of Chambersburg by his orders was an act which contrasts unpleasantly with Lee's conduct when operating over the same ground the year before. To dispose of Early and clear the valley, an army of over forty thousand men was assembled under Sheridan. Early was defeated at Winchester, and Fisher's Hill, but nevertheless assumed the offensive, attacking the Union army at Cedar Creek on Oct. 19, in Sheridan's absence, and for a time driving all before him. But Sheridan arrived on the field after his famous ride "from Winchester, twenty miles away," and the day ended with a Confederate defeat. Early retired up the valley and remained unmolested until March 1865, when his force was almost completely destroyed at Waynesboro. Feeling in the

South was bitter toward him. His disasters were contrasted with Jackson's earlier brilliant successes in the valley, without consideration of the fact that Early was fighting against greatly superior forces commanded by one of the most enterprising of the Union generals. Though Lee's belief in Early's ability was unshaken, he relieved him from duty, realizing that Early could no longer inspire confidence in his own troops. Undismayed by Lee's surrender a few days later, Early started west in disguise, meaning to join Kirby Smith beyond the Mississippi and keep up the struggle. But Smith had also surrendered, and Early continued on into Mexico and thence took ship for Canada, intending to quit the United States permanently. He abandoned a project to lead a Confederate exodus to New Zealand, for none would follow him, and eventually returned home, resuming law practise at Lynchburg in 1869. Later, he was employed by the Louisiana lottery at a large salary, but in the latter part of his life again resided at Lynchburg.

While in Canada, he published *A Memoir of the Last Year of the War for Independence in the Confederate States of America* (1866), useful as the narrative of a leading actor, but marred by the violence of its tone and its tendency to minimize the numbers under his command. Later in life he may have reconsidered his predictions that the negro race would meet a deplorable fate when deprived of the blessings of slavery, but his bitterness against the Federal government did not abate. Events of the war with Spain caused one Confederate veteran to remark that what he anticipated with greatest interest in the next world, was hearing "what Jubal Early would say when he met Fitz Lee wearing a Yankee uniform" (*The Reminiscences of General Basil W. Duke, C. S. A.*, 1911, p. 477). He remained "unreconstructed." Partly, no doubt, for that reason, partly because of his deep interest in the history of the Confederate States, manifested in his presidency of the Southern Historical Society, the disfavor with which he was regarded at the end of the war gave place to admiration, and even adulation, in the South. Personally, however, he was never popular. He consoled himself by the reflection that those who knew him best, liked him best (*Autobiographical Sketch*, p. xxv). A patriarchal beard gave distinction to his appearance, in spite of a stoop due to rheumatism acquired in the Mexican War. Though cold and unprepossessing in manner, he was highly charitable, in the financial sense, and gave liberally to the poor.

[*Lieut.-Gen. Jubal Anderson Early, C. S. A., Autobiographical Sketch and Narrative of the War between the States* (1912); "Gen. Jubal A. Early. Memorial Address by Hon. John W. Daniel," in *Southern Hist. Soc. Papers*, vol. XXII (1894); C. A. Evans, ed., *Confed. Mil. Hist.*, I (1899), 686–88; *Personal Memoirs of P. H. Sheridan* (2 vols., 1888); *Battles and Leaders of the Civil War* (1887), vol. IV; *Official Records (Army)*, 1 ser., vols. XXXVII, XLIII; J. G. Barnard, *A Report of the Defenses of Washington* (1871), being no. 20 of the Professional Papers of the Corps of Engineers U. S. Army; *Norfolk* (Va.) *Landmark*, Mar. 3, 1894.]

T.M.S.

EARLY, PETER (June 20, 1773–Aug. 15, 1817), politician, judge, belonged to that generation of Virginians who migrated to the frontier state of Georgia late in the eighteenth and early in the nineteenth century and left a deep impress on the young commonwealth. He was born in Madison County, Va., was graduated from Princeton in 1792, studied law in Philadelphia, and went with his father, Joel Early, to Greene County, Georgia, in 1795. As a young lawyer at a bar noted for its ability, he soon made a reputation by virtue of his native talent and unusual preparation. He entered politics in 1802, upon his election to Congress, and was a member of the House Committee appointed to conduct proceedings against Samuel Chase, the Federalist Supreme Court judge, whose impeachment he ardently favored. The only other matter of importance with which his name was associated seems to have been the bill to outlaw the African slave-trade, a measure which he supported. He was reëlected to the Eighth and Ninth Congresses and served until 1807. On the expiration of his third term he did not seek reelection, but returned to Greensboro where he was appointed first judge of the Ocmulgee Circuit, just then created. This position he held from 1807 to 1813. He was a model judge, unbending, inflexible, upright, always turning a deaf ear to demagogic appeals.

Elected governor in 1813 for a two-year term, Early was confronted with the problem of seeing that Georgia did her part in the war with Great Britain. He cordially supported the American cause and took great interest in various campaigns against the Indians on the frontier, who, under British instigation, harried the settlements. His administration was signalized by his courageous act in vetoing a stay-law for the relief of debtors. This law had already been in force six years and when the legislature sought to renew it, Early greeted the bill with a stinging veto. He opposed it not only as an unwise and inexpedient measure, but as an unconstitutional impairment of the validity of contracts. He called attention to the fact that the war demand had enabled the people to dispose of their products at good prices and that all who were so minded had been able to pay their debts; dishonest people were taking advantage of the law to defraud their creditors. The law "accustoms men to consider their contracts as imposing no moral obligations, and, by making fraud familiar, destroys the pride of honesty."

In 1815 Early was elected to the state Senate, serving until his death which occurred in Greensboro. In 1793 he had married Anne Adams Smith, daughter of Francis Smith, and sister of Gen. Thomas A. Smith. Two contemporaries, both of whom were friends of the governor, wrote in the same strain about him. He was described as devoid of wit, humor, and "what is called address." One of his friends said, "I never saw him smile . . . his lips were forever compressed and firm . . . his mind was in perfect correspondence with his body; and it never hesitated or faltered."

[The most comprehensive and apparently reliable account of Early's career is that by Joel Crawford in S. F. Miller's *Bench and Bar of Ga.* (1858), I, 345, although there is an error of five years in the date of his death. Later accounts, also erroneous in some respects, are found in W. J. Northen, *Men of Mark in Ga.* (1910), II, 358, and L. L. Knight, *Standard Hist. of Ga. and Georgians* (1917), I, 466, 471, IV, 2166. See also *Biog. Dir. Am. Cong.* (1928), and *Gen. Cat. Princeton Univ., 1746–1906.*] R. P. B.

EASTMAN, ARTHUR MacARTHUR (June 8, 1810–Sept. 3, 1877), firearms manufacturer, promoter of a direct Atlantic cable, was born at Gilmanton, N. H., the son of Ebenezer and Deborah (Greeley) Eastman. His ancestry was distinguished: his grandfather, Ebenezer, served conspicuously as a lieutenant in Stark's brigade at the battle of Bunker Hill; his grandmother, Mary Butler Eastman, was the heroine of B. F. Taylor's poem, "Mary Butler's Ride," which describes one of the romantic episodes of the Revolution; his father was a major of militia. Educated at Gilmanton Academy, he began his business career as a clerk in the country store of Stephen L. Greeley and later opened a store on his own account at Gilmanton. In 1837 or shortly thereafter he moved to Boston, where he engaged with but indifferent success in the wholesale iron trade, and later in company with his brother did a large wholesale grocery business. In 1844 he commenced the manufacture of woolen underwear at Roxbury, Mass., and while engaged in this business acquired interest in a patent spinning-jenny which he took to England in 1849 and disposed of for a handsome sum to English manufacturers. With the outbreak of the Crimean War, Eastman turned his attention to the manufacture of munitions. Securing the patent for an improved breech-loading cannon, he sold it at a large profit to the British government. Foreseeing that the American Civil War would be a long one and learning that the country was especially deficient in cavalry equipment, Eastman bought up large quantities of old arms and made them over into carbines, which, with the expansion of the cavalry force, found a ready market at remunerative prices. In addition to the carbines he furnished other arms to the Federal government, and at the conclusion of the conflict continued to manufacture largely for foreign nations, contracting, in particular, with the French government for carbines.

About 1869 Eastman planned the enterprise which was to be the great work of his life, the laying of a direct ocean cable between Europe and the United States. The difficulties in his way were great. Not only was it necessary to raise $6,500,000 in gold, but also to overcome at every step the powerful opposition of the Anglo-American, the Western Union and the French companies. Securing a charter from New Hampshire and permission from the federal government, Eastman went to Europe, where he was well and favorably known, and there, after five years of tireless effort, he obtained the necessary funds. The American end of the new cable was laid at Rye Beach, N. H., in July 1874 with elaborate ceremonies, and it was in full working order in the next year. It provided the first competition from this country with the Anglo-American Telegraph Company (Bright, *post*, pp. 213–14). Overwork in connection with the cable project undoubtedly hastened Eastman's death, which followed a three weeks' illness. He has been described as a man of great judgment and tact "whose appearance at once arrested attention" (Manchester *Daily Mirror and American*, Sept. 3, 1877). Late in life he became interested in politics, serving as colonel on the staff of Gov. Weston in 1872 and as a member of the New Hampshire constitutional convention of 1876. In the late fifties he laid out a beautiful estate known as "Riverside" on the Merrimac River near Manchester. He married in 1836 Elizabeth H. Moulton of Gilmanton, who with two daughters survived him.

[G. S. Rix, *Hist. and Geneal. of the Eastman Family* (1901), pp. 106, 212; Chas. Bright, *The Story of the Atlantic Cable* (1903), pp. 213–14; *Appletons' Ann. Cyc. 1877* (1878), p. 579; Manchester *Daily Union*, Sept. 3, 1877.] H. U. F.

EASTMAN, CHARLES GAMAGE (June 1, 1816–Sept. 16, 1860), journalist, politician, poet, was born in Fryeburg, Me., the son of Benjamin Clement and Mary Rebecca (Gamage) Eastman, and as a child was taken by his parents to Barnard, Vt. His father was a watchmaker who through accident or temperament never settled in a town large enough to give him steady work. Finally he heard a clear call to preach the gospel. His eleven year old son, deeming even watch-making more comfortable for the family than the Methodist itinerancy, undertook to expostulate with him and was righteously thrashed for his presumption. Charles then left home and thereafter, as he phrased it, "cut his own fodder." He got a little schooling at Windsor, Vt., when he was thirteen, taught school himself for a while, attended the academy at Meriden, N. H., and then went to the diminutive University of Vermont, where he founded the Lambda Iota literary society. To support himself he wrote for the *Burlington Sentinel;* soon journalism engrossed his entire time, and his formal education broke off. His first independent venture, the *Lamoille River Express* (1838), at Johnson in Lamoille County, brought him commendation but no money, and did not last long. At Woodstock in 1840 he started the *Spirit of the Age* as an organ of Jacksonian Democracy. Its editor was young, handsome, and likable, and his terse, racy editorials got themselves read. In 1845 he sold out at an advantage and on Jan. 1, 1846, became editor and part-proprietor of the Montpelier *Vermont Patriot,* a four-page weekly that under his management became the leading Democratic paper in the state. In that same year he married Mrs. Susan S. Havens, a widow, daughter of Dr. John D. Powers of Woodstock. In 1851 he became sole owner of the *Patriot,* which he continued to edit until his death. In 1848 he published a volume of *Poems,* of which 2,000 copies were sold or at any rate distributed, and which brought him many favorable notices and a local reputation as a bard. A volume of selected *Poems* was published, long after his death, in 1880. His verse exhibits respectable metrical skill and at times a pleasing, songlike quality. Generous praise may be given quite honestly to the tense, restrained lines of the "Dirge" and to several others. He was also successful with humorous verses. Eastman was elected a state senator from Washington County in 1852 and again in 1853, was several times an unsuccessful candidate for Congress, and, on President Pierce's appointment, was for six years postmaster at Montpelier. He attended the national Democratic conventions regularly from 1844 on, and was in his later years a member of the Democratic National Committee. Stricken by a fatal disease in the spring of 1860, he nevertheless journeyed to the Democratic conventions at Charleston and Baltimore, took his part in the work, and, in line with his Jacksonian principles, supported Stephen A. Douglas, himself a native Vermonter, against Abolitionists on the one side and Secessionists on the other. He died peacefully at home in the midst of the campaign.

[*Vt. Patriot,* Sept. 22 (by F. A. Eastman), Sept. 29 (collection of obituaries), Oct. 13, Dec. 22, 1860; A. M. Hemenway, ed., *Vt. Hist. Gazetteer,* vol. IV (1882); G. S. Rix, *Hist. and Geneal. of the Eastman Family* (1901); *Gen. Cat. Univ. Vt. 1791–1900* (1901).]

G. H. G.

EASTMAN, ENOCH WORTHEN (Apr. 15, 1810–Jan. 9, 1885), lieutenant-governor of Iowa, state senator, was born at Deerfield, Rockingham County, N. H., the third of the seven children of John and Mary (James) Eastman. His grandfather, Ephraim Eastman, fought at Bunker Hill, and his father was a lieutenant in the War of 1812. As a boy, Enoch worked on his father's farm, was employed in a sawmill, and attended district school. Earning his own way by teaching, he later attended Pembrook and Pittsfield academies. In 1835 he began the study of law in the office of Moses Norris at Pittsfield, and in 1840 was admitted to the bar at Concord. Recognizing the opportunities to be found in the Middle West, Eastman moved to Burlington, Ia., in 1844, and started to practise his profession. Within a few months he was attracting attention throughout the territory by his speeches opposing the boundaries for Iowa as proposed by Congress. The constitutional convention of 1844 had selected the Missouri River as the western border for the new state, but when the constitution came before Congress for approval, the boundary was changed to a line which cut off about one-third of the present state. Together with Fred D. Mills, Theodore S. Parvin, and others, Eastman stumped the territory making vigorous speeches. Largely through their efforts the constitution was rejected, and in no small measure was the acceptance of the Missouri River as the western boundary of Iowa due to Eastman's labors.

On Jan. 8, 1845, he married Sarah C. Greenough of Canterbury, N. H. They lived successively at Burlington, Oskaloosa, and Eldora, Ia. Four years after the death, in 1861, of his first wife, he married Amanda Hall. At Eldora Eastman became a prominent attorney. He was counsel for the city in a successful county-seat contest with Point Pleasant, and participated in many important cases. He was a strong supporter of the Democratic party until the election of President Buchanan, with whose doctrines he did not agree. Thereafter he affiliated with the Republican party, and in 1863 was nominated for the office of lieutenant-governor of Iowa. He was elected, with the largest majority which up to that time had been given to a candidate for this office in the state. His loyalty to his state and to the principles of his party found expression in the motto which he wrote for the Iowa stone in the Washington Monument: "Iowa, Her affections, like the rivers of her borders, flow to an inseparable Union." In 1883 he was elected to the Senate from Hardin County and served one term. This was his last political office.

["Enoch Worthen Eastman," by his friend, T. S. Parvin, was published in the *Iowa Hist. Record,* I, 49–57. Another biographical sketch, by a fellow townsman, W. J. Moir, appeared in the *Annals of Iowa,* 3 ser. VI, 416–24. A discussion of the origin of the inscription on the Washington Monument is found in the *Annals of Iowa,* 3 ser. I, 661–63.] B. E. M.

EASTMAN, HARVEY GRIDLEY (Oct. 16, 1832–July 13, 1878), business man, politician, educator, was born near Waterville, Oneida County, N. Y., the son of Horace and Mary (Gridley) Eastman. His father was a farmer. Eastman began his career by teaching in a business college conducted at Rochester by his uncle, George Washington Eastman. He started a similar school of his own in Oswego in December 1855, married Minerva Clark of Canastota in 1857, and in the spring of 1858 moved his business college to St. Louis. There a bid for publicity turned swiftly into a boomerang. Uninformed of local sentiment, he guilelessly imported some noted Eastern abolitionists—Joshua Giddings, Gerrit Smith, Elihu Burritt, Charles Sumner—to lecture to his young Missourians. Amid the ensuing uproar he decided to try his luck elsewhere and conferred himself, apparently at random, on Poughkeepsie, N. Y., preceding his arrival with a generous quantity of advertising. On Nov. 3, 1859, in a room rented for seventy-five cents a week, with no equipment worth mentioning, he opened Eastman's National Business College to three enrolled students. As more pupils trickled in, their fees were invested in publicity. Eastman gave Horace Greeley $1,500 per insertion for a full page of the *Weekly Tribune,* and Greeley obligingly came up to Poughkeepsie to address the students on the subject of "The Self-Made Man." In one year Eastman spent $60,000 for advertising in five New York newspapers; he shipped catalogues, circulars, and prospectuses by the ton to all parts of the country and even abroad. At home he organized his students into a monster brass band, and celebrated —at suspiciously frequent intervals—the "anniversary" of the college with a huge banquet, music, and speeches. And it paid to advertise. He had 500 students in 1861, 1,200 in 1863, 1,700 in 1864–65. The town swarmed with young men seeking a commercial education and also board, lodging, and sundries. Poughkeepsie prospered; Eastman grew rich. His college, known from the Atlantic seaboard to the Rockies, did its work well, for Eastman taught banking and commercial practise by a laboratory method as effective as it was then novel. Genial, dependable, sanguine, possessed of a magnetic personality and a torrential energy, he became the great man of the town. His castellated residence stood in a park of twenty-seven acres, which was generously thrown open to the public. He had his thumb in every local pie: the Poughkeepsie Ice Club, the First National Bank, a horse-racing association, the Poughkeepsie & Eastern R. R., and in several of them he lost a great deal of money. He built a row of pretentious houses on Eastman Terrace and finally disposed of them at a loss of $60,000. As mayor of the city 1871–74 and from 1877 till his death, he spent the taxpayers' money lavishly for improvements, was sharply criticized, but defended himself successfully. In 1872 and again in 1874 he sat as a Republican in the state Assembly, being sent there by his constituents in order to secure enabling legislation for a projected cantilever bridge across the Hudson. The bridge, it was believed, would put Poughkeepsie on a trunk-line railway between Pennsylvania and New England and would make the city rich. Eastman was vice-president of the company that proposed to build it. He won the needed legislation, but engineering difficulties, lack of money, and the opposition of railway and steamboat companies delayed the completion of the bridge until ten years after his death, which took place in Denver, Colo., where he had gone for his health. A lone, broken bridge pier in the Hudson was known locally for years as "Eastman's monument."

[E. Platt, *The Eagle's Hist. of Poughkeepsie* (1905); *Commemorative Biog. Record of Dutchess County, N. Y.* (1897); J. H. Smith, *Hist. of Dutchess County, N. Y.* (1882); G. S. Rix, *Hist. & Geneal. of the Eastman Family* (1901), II, 802; obituary in *N. Y. Tribune,* July 15, 1878.] G. H. G.

EASTMAN, JOHN ROBIE (July 29, 1836–Sept. 26, 1913), astronomer, was born in Andover, N. H. He was the son of Royal F. Eastman and Sophronia Mayo, descendants of Roger Eastman, who came to Salem in 1638, and of John Mayo, the first pastor of North Church in Boston. Soon after his graduation from Dartmouth, with the M.S. degree, in 1862, he obtained a position as assistant astronomer at the Naval Observatory. Three years later he was promoted to the rank of professor of mathematics. He remained there until his retirement in 1898. Some years later he was given the rank of rear admiral. He was one of that distinguished group of astronomers which included Newcomb and Hall and which gave substantial reputation to the Naval Observatory. From 1872 to 1882 Eastman edited the publications of the Observatory, but the greater part of his life-work in astronomy is represented by a single volume, called the *Second Washington Catalogue of Stars,* published in 1898. It is a peculiarity of this type of research that observations with a meridian circle, continued for many years, furnish material for very laborious and time-consuming computation but for only a thin volume of results. The few figures printed in each line of the catalogue represent many hours of work the value of which to astronomers and laymen is permanent and cumulative.

In 1869 Eastman went to Iowa to observe a total eclipse of the sun. A year later he went on a similar expedition to Sicily, and again, in 1878, to Colorado. The observations were made visually, and each observer recorded or sketched his impressions as best he could. In 1882 the government sent out eight expeditions to different parts of the world to observe the transit of Venus, an event which gave promise of yielding an accurate value for the distance of the sun. Eastman, in charge of one of the parties, was sent to Florida. He also took part in the determination of the longitudes of certain places in the United States. At various times Eastman was president of the Philosophical Society of Washington, president of the Washington Academy of Sciences, general secretary and vice-president of the American Association for the Advancement of Science. In addition to his scientific studies he published a *History of the Town of Andover, N.H., 1851–1906* (1910), containing genealogical as well as historical data. He was married, on Dec. 25, 1866, to Mary J. Ambrose, of Boscawen, N. H.

[R. H. Tucker, "John Robie Eastman," in the *Pubs. of the Astronomical Soc. of the Pacific,* Feb. 1914, pp. 41–42; an obituary in the *Jour. of the British Astronomical Asso.,* Nov. 1913; *Who's Who in America,* 1912–13; Eastman's history of Andover.] R. S. D.

EASTMAN, TIMOTHY CORSER (May 30, 1821–Oct. 11, 1893), cattle merchant, meat packer, was born in Croydon, N. H., the son of Joseph Eastman, a carpenter, and his wife Lucy Powers. He had to begin work at an early age and therefore had little formal instruction. His mother, however, taught a family fireside school in the long winter evenings so that he received an average elementary school education. His father taught him the carpenter's trade at which he worked until he had enough money to carry him through the high school at Meriden, N. H. He then taught school for a time and at the age of twenty-one was able to buy a farm. Imbued with the western fever, he went to Wisconsin for a time, but returned, and in 1849 moved to Ohio. He settled near Cleveland, where he began operating a dairy farm. He was very successful, and in buying and selling cattle for his milk business he laid the foundation for the work which occupied the last forty years of his life. He developed a marvelous gift for judging cattle, and it was not long until he began bringing live stock from Ohio and Kentucky to the East, making his headquarters at Albany, N. Y. In 1859 his business had grown to such proportions that it was necessary to move to New York City. It was at this time that he made the acquaintance of Commodore Vanderbilt and was put in charge of all the cattle business handled by the New York Central Railroad. Soon after settling in New York he began shipping cattle and other live stock out of the country and revolutionized the methods of supplying England and Scotland, in particular, with American beef. He not only shipped thousands of live cattle but was the pioneer in the shipping of dressed meat in quantity as a commercial article in the refrigeration chambers of steamships. His first shipment of this nature was made on Oct. 1, 1875. Some of that beef was sent to Queen Victoria at Windsor Castle for which transaction Eastman's Ltd., his English agency, received the Royal Seal. For some time he was the only one shipping dressed meat in this manner, his weekly exports in 1877 averaging four thousand quarters of beef in addition to one thousand live cattle. In 1889 he promoted retail meat stores in all parts of the United Kingdom and in the same year incorporated The Eastman's Company to carry on his business in the United States and abroad. He served as the president of this concern until his death. He was also a director in the West Side Bank of New York and a member of the New York Produce Exchange. He married Lucy Putnam in 1845 by whom he had one son and one daughter. He died in Tarrytown, N. Y., after a brief illness.

Eastman was a man who started with nothing but who, through native ability in the judging and handling of live stock and through the possession of courage to undertake new things, rose to the leadership of the business in which he was engaged. When he died he was reputed to be one of the wealthiest men in New Hampshire.

[G. S. Rix, *Hist. and Geneal. of the Eastman Family* (1901), pp. 461–62; Edmund Wheeler, *Croydon, N. H., 1866* (1867), p. 99; R. A. Clemen, *Am. Livestock and Meat Industry* (1923), pp. 272, 276–79, 325–26; J. T. Critchell and Joseph Raymond, *Hist. of the Frozen Meat Trade* (1912), p. 190. Obituaries appeared in the

N. Y. Times, Oct. 13, 1893, and the *Independent Statesman* (Concord, N. H.), Nov. 2, 1893.] J. H. F.

EASTMAN, WILLIAM REED (Oct. 19, 1835–Mar. 25, 1925), engineer, clergyman, librarian, was born in New York City, the son of the Rev. Ornan Eastman and Mary Reed. He was graduated from Yale (A.B.) in 1854 with high honors, the youngest member of his class, and at his death was its sole surviving graduate member. He received the degree of A.M. from Yale in 1857. From 1854 to 1859 he was a civil engineer, working on the enlargement of the Erie Canal, the construction of the Michigan Southern and Northern Indiana Railroad, and on the survey of the first railroad from Vera Cruz to Mexico City. In 1859 he entered Union Theological Seminary and at graduation in 1862 was ordained a Presbyterian minister. From July 1862 to July 1864 he was in turn first sergeant of Company H, 22nd Regiment New York State Militia, chaplain of the 165th New York Volunteers, and from Jan. 1, 1863, chaplain of the 72nd New York Volunteers. From 1864 to 1888 he served continuously as pastor of Congregational churches in Grantsville, Mass., Plantsville and Suffield, Conn., and South Framingham, Mass. He was financial secretary for Howard University, 1888–90, living at Wellesley, Mass. In 1890 he executed a complete and rather surprising right-about face. Caught in the rapidly rising tide of the modern library movement and genuinely attracted by its opportunities, he embarked at the age of fifty-five upon a career in a new profession with all the enthusiasm and devotion of youth. More remarkable still, he won a national reputation in the field. He would accept nothing less than the best preparation, and so with the zest of a schoolboy he entered in 1890 the New York State Library School at Albany, completing the course in 1892 with the degree of B.L.S. Immediately appointed to the work of library inspection, supervision, and extension in New York State, for twenty years, in various capacities, as a veritable "library bishop" he shepherded the public libraries of his "diocese" with rare energy and judgment. His genial presence, his tolerance, quick sympathy, and ripe experience with men and affairs, contributed greatly to his success. After his retirement in 1913 he lived in New Haven, and continued to lecture on library subjects, especially to library schools. In 1907 he received the degree of M.L.S. from the New York State Library School.

Eastman came to be perhaps the first authority in his profession on library buildings and equipment. His principal publications (aside from numerous reports, journal articles, and addresses) are in this special field. His lectures in the various library schools, on the economic and efficient construction of library buildings and furniture, were widely influential. He was secretary of the New York Library Association, 1893–99, and its president, 1904–05. He married on Nov. 20, 1867, Laura Elizabeth Barnes, who survived him.

[A sketch in the *Lib. Jour.,* Jan. 1913, is reprinted in *N. Y. Libraries,* Feb. 1913. See also *Yale Univ. Obit. Record* (1925), and *Yale Alumni Weekly,* Apr. 17, 1925.] J. I. W.

EASTON, JOHN (*c.* 1625–Dec. 12, 1705), governor of Rhode Island, was the son of Nicholas Easton [*q.v.*] and as a boy emigrated with him from Wales to Massachusetts. In 1680 he described himself as "aged fifty-five or thereabouts" (*Early Records,* VI, 10). Both father and son were Quakers. They were among the first settlers of Newport and became prominent in the colony of Rhode Island. John Easton frequently represented Newport in meetings of the General Assembly of the colony. In 1653 he was elected attorney-general and was repeatedly reelected to that office. He served as Assistant under the charter of 1663 and in 1674 was elected deputy-governor, his brother Peter being elected to the combined offices of attorney-general and treasurer. John served as deputy-governor from May 1674 until April 1676, and as governor from 1690 to 1695. In 1694 he refused as governor to issue commissions to privateersmen, who, in many cases, were mere pirates, but the deputy-governor did so and involved the colony in difficulty with the home government by his action.

Easton wrote a *Narrative of the Causes which led to Philip's Indian War,* beginning with the death of Sassamon, which was not published until 1858, when F. B. Hough edited and printed it. Although Increase Mather expressed a contemptuous opinion of it (probably because it emanated from Rhode Island), it is now considered valuable evidence, and was again printed in 1913 (*Narratives of the Indian Wars,* C. H. Lincoln, ed.). Easton became an extensive landowner in the colony. He married Mehitable Gant on Jan. 4, 1660, who was the mother of five children. She died Nov. 11, 1673, and he married Alice ——, who died March 24, 1689 (*Vital Record of Rhode Island,* VII, 15, 99). Easton died Dec. 12, 1705, and was buried in the Coddington burial-place, Newport.

[*Early Records of the Town of Providence* (21 vols., 1892–1915); *Records of the Colony of R. I. and Providence Plantations, 1636–1706* (1856–58); *R. I. Court Records* (2 vols., 1920–22); *New-England Hist. and Geneal. Reg.,* XV (1861), 151 n.; S. G. Arnold, *Hist. of the State of R. I.,* vol. I (1859).] J. T. A.

EASTON, NICHOLAS (1593–Aug. 15, 1675), governor of Rhode Island, was a tanner by trade who emigrated from Wales to Massachusetts in 1634, bringing his two sons with him on the *Mary and John.* He first settled at Ipswich, being admitted a freeman Sept. 3. The following year (1635) he was elected representative to the General Court but was dismissed as unduly chosen. In the same year he removed to Newbury. He was an adherent of Wheelright in the Antinomian controversy and was among those disarmed by order of the Court in 1637. With a few others he began a settlement at what is now Hampton, N. H., but was warned off and in 1638 settled at Pocasset (Portsmouth) in Rhode Island. He was almost at once elected one of the "Elders" who were to assist the "Judge" in governing the community, but, disputes having arisen, he joined the Coddington group in secession, and moved to what is now Newport. He built the first house there in April 1639, which two years later was burned by the Indians, probably by accident. He was always prominent in the life of the colony. In 1639 he was one of the two men instructed by the Coddington group to petition Henry Vane to use his influence in procuring for them a patent for the island. He was chosen an Assistant in 1640, was several times reëlected to that office, and served frequently as moderator at meetings of the General Assembly. He was one of the three men chosen in 1653 to see that the "State's [England's] part of all prizes be secured and accompt given." This gave him some trouble five years later in making a proper accounting. Under the first patent, the administrative head of the Colony was designated "president," and Easton held that office from May 1650 to August 1651 and again from May 1654 to Sept. 12, 1654. The charter of 1663 provided for a governor and deputy-governor. Easton held the latter office from 1666 to 1669, again from 1670 to 1671, and was governor from May 1672 to May 1674.

Apparently his first wife (unknown) had died before he left Wales. In 1638 he married Christian, widow of Thomas Beecher, who was probably the mother of seven of his nine children. She lived until Feb. 20, 1665. On Mar. 2, 1671, he was married to Ann Clayton, who survived him. Easton died Aug. 15, 1675, and was buried in the Coddington graveyard, Newport. In his will he named his son John residuary legatee.

[Jas. Savage, *Geneal. Dict. of the First Settlers of New England,* vol. II (1860); H. M. Chapin, *Documentary Hist. of R. I.* (2 vols., 1916–19); *Records of the Colony of R. I. and Providence Plantations, 1636–1677* (1856–57); S. G. Arnold, *Hist. of the State of R. I.* (2 vols., 1859–60); J. Callender, *Hist. Discourse* (1838); *R. I. Court Records* (2 vols., 1920–22.] J. T. A.

EATON, AMOS (May 17, 1776–May 10, 1842), scientist and educator, son of Capt. Abel and Azuba (Hurd) Eaton, was born in Chatham, Columbia County, N. Y. His father was a farmer and descendant of John Eaton who came from Dover, England, about 1635 and settled in Dedham, Mass. Amos was graduated from Williams College in 1799 and fitted himself for the legal profession, but through association in New York with Dr. Samuel L. Mitchill and Dr. David Hosack [*qq.v.*] he became interested in the natural sciences, particularly in botany. After his admission to the bar in 1802 he settled in Catskill as a lawyer and land agent, though continuing his studies of the sciences. As early as 1810 he began a course of popular lectures in botany and published a small text-book on the subject. This was followed in 1817 by *A Manual of Botany for the Northern States,* which met with great popular favor and passed with much revision and many changes of title through eight editions, the last appearing in 1840. He abandoned his law practise altogether about 1815, "owing to a concurrence of circumstances, which our limits will not allow us to explain" (Durfee, *post,* p. 363), and placed himself under the tutelage of Professors Ives and Silliman of Yale College, where he is reported to have been a diligent student.

Having, as he felt, become sufficiently grounded in botany and geology, he moved to Williamstown, Mass., in 1817 where he began giving public lectures which aroused much popular interest and led to similar lectures in Amherst, Northampton, Middlebury, and other towns in New England and along the Hudson. In 1818 he was asked by Gov. Clinton to deliver a course of lectures before the members of the New York legislature. This was undoubtedly the beginning of the work which resulted in 1836 in the establishment of a State Geological Survey. In 1820 Eaton was appointed professor of natural history in the Medical School at Castleton, Vt., and in 1820 and 1821, under the patronage of Stephen Van Rensselaer, he made a geological and agricultural survey of Albany and Rensselaer counties, following it up in 1824, also at Van Rensselaer's instance, with a survey of the district along the Erie Canal. In the same year he was designated senior professor in the Rensselaer School (now Rensselaer Polytechnic Institute) at Troy, N. Y., a position which he retained until his death.

Eaton was a man of indefatigable industry and had to a remarkable degree the gift of arousing interest and enthusiasm in others. He was a vigorous thinker, writer, and compiler, issuing five works on botany, two on chemistry, six on geology, exclusive of a score or more brief notes, and others on educational subjects. Owing to the condition of science at the time much of his work was necessarily faulty in many respects. He failed often to realize possibilities beyond his own immediate observation and deductive reasoning. His successive geological writings became filled with bombastic repetitions of unfounded and erroneous statements, defects that sadly diminished his usefulness in later years. Nevertheless, through his enthusiasm he did more perhaps than any one man of his time in arousing a popular interest in science. He is described as a man of striking personality, of a large frame, portly, and dignified. His face was highly intellectual. "He had an easy flow of language, a popular address and a generous enthusiasm in matters of science which easily communicated itself to his pupils" (Ballard). He was four times married: first, on Oct. 16, 1799, to Polly Thomas, by whom he had one son; second, on Sept. 16, 1803, to Sally Cady, by whom he had five sons; third, on Oct. 20, 1816, to Anne Bradley, by whom he had three children; and fourth, on Aug. 5, 1827, to Alice Johnson, by whom he had one child, a son.

[See H. H. Ballard, "Amos Eaton," in *Colls. Berkshire Hist. and Sci. Soc.* (1897); Calvin Durfee, *Hist. of Williams Coll.* (1860); P. C. Ricketts, *Hist. of the Rensselaer Polytechnic Inst.* (1895); W. J. Youmans, *Pioneers of Science in America* (1896), pp. 112–13. A bibliography of Eaton's geological writings is given by John M. Nickles, *Geol. Lit. on North America, 1785–1918* (1923), in Bull. 746, U. S. Geol. Survey.]

G. P. M.

EATON, BENJAMIN HARRISON (Dec. 15, 1833–Oct. 29, 1904), agriculturist and pioneer in irrigation, was born on a farm near Zanesville, Ohio, where his parents, Levi and Hannah (Smith) Eaton, led uneventful lives. After receiving an elementary education he alternately taught school and farmed in Ohio and Iowa, until the even current of his life was disturbed by the news of the gold discoveries at Pike's Peak. Eaton joined the crowd of adventurers who flocked to the Rockies in 1859, but was, like most of them, unsuccessful as a miner. Leaving Colorado, he went to New Mexico, started farming on the Maxwell Land Grant, and there built his first irrigation ditch. He returned to Colorado in 1864, purchased a farm near the present town of Windsor, and remained in that vicinity for the rest of his life. Northern Colorado was in 1864 an unpromising region for agriculture. Here and there along the river bottoms were small farms; beyond these there stretched the prairie with its cactus and prairie-dog towns. But the young farmer saw promise in the land. Building an irrigation ditch, the first of its kind in the district, he brought water to his land and began to cultivate it. Thereafter his life was spent in acquiring more land and in developing it. He was always land-poor, but continued buying. At his death he held about fourteen thousand five hundred acres of cultivated land, and nearly seven thousand acres not under the plow. After some years of farming, he leased the greater part of his estate and lived in Greeley, the home of the Union Colony. As his holdings increased he constructed more reservoirs and ditches. Six reservoirs held water for his land; one of these, the Windsor Reservoir, was the largest at that time in the state. He built ditches everywhere. As contractor he built the Larimer and Weld Canal which was over sixty miles in length, Canal No. 2 of the Union Colony, the important High Line Ditch near Denver, and others. It was said of him in 1884 that he had "had more to do with the construction of irrigating canals in Colorado than perhaps any other five men in the State" (*Denver Tribune-Republican,* Sept. 15, 1884).

Though Eaton built the town of Eaton which was incorporated in 1888, owned a mill and a business house there, and raised some cattle, he was essentially a leader in agricultural development. Politics formed only an interlude in a busy life. A stanch Republican, he served in the territorial house in 1872, in the council in 1876, and as governor of the state in 1885–86. As legislator and governor he showed a great interest in agricultural matters. He was twice married. His first wife, Delilah Wolf, whom he married in Ohio on May 1, 1856, died in 1857. In 1864 he married Rebecca J. Hill, daughter of Abraham Hill, in Louisa County, Iowa.

[There is no extensive biography of Eaton. Brief accounts are to be found in W. F. Stone, *Hist. of Colo.,* III (1918), 22–25; *Portrait and Biog. Record of the State of Colo.* (1899), pp. 417–18; *Denver Times,* Oct. 31, 1904; *Denver Tribune-Republican,* Oct. 30, 1904. An article in the same paper for Sept. 15, 1884 (erroneously dated Sept. 14 on the first page), is a reprint from the *North British Agriculturalist* for Aug. 27, 1884.]

J. F. W.

EATON, DANIEL CADY (Sept. 12, 1834–June 29, 1895), botanist, was born at Fort Gratiot, Mich., the son of Gen. Amos B. Eaton and Elizabeth Selden. His grandfather, Amos Eaton [*q.v.*], author of botanical text-books, had been an inspiring and influential teacher of botany in America during the first half of the century; his father, though lacking a special scientific education, was keenly interested in natural history. Thus, during his undergraduate years at Yale, Eaton's ambition centered in fitting himself for a professorship of botany in that institution, in which his grandfather had studied. He corresponded freely with such authorities as Torrey, Gray, and Sullivant, and laid the foundation of the large and important herbarium which to-day bears his name. Cryptogamous plants claimed his special attention, and even in his junior year at college he described several new ferns from California in classical Latin form. Following his graduation from Yale in 1857, Eaton spent three successive years at Harvard College, carrying on his botanical studies under Asa Gray, especially in the ferns. During this time he contributed the fern text to Chapman's historic *Flora of the Southern United States* (1860), and published several papers dealing with fern collections from Cuba, Venezuela, Japan, and the Mexican boundary region. Then, with the outbreak of the Civil War, he served with the army commissary department in New York City. In 1864 he was elected to the newly founded professorship of botany in Yale College, and to the end of his active life continued his botanical studies and instruction there. He married, on Feb. 13, 1866, Caroline Ketcham of New York City.

Eaton is best known as a discriminating student of ferns. He not only contributed the fern text to several voluminous botanical reports of the transcontinental railroad survey expeditions, but also published numerous short papers. His most important publication, *The Ferns of North America* (1877–80), is a beautifully illustrated work in two volumes describing in detail the ferns then known from the area north of Mexico. In later years his attention was given mainly to mosses and hepatics. Other activities included the preparation of botanical definitions for *Webster's International Dictionary,* numerous reviews of botanical works for both technical and general periodicals, and genealogical studies for publication. Naturally conservative, his efforts were invariably characterized by precision, thoroughness, and keen insight. Above all, he was no "closet naturalist," but an excellent field student, a lover of outdoor sports, and a devotee of fishing and hunting. A man of simple tastes, his high ideals, culture, and wide technical knowledge combined to make him an inspiring instructor and helpful friend.

[*Bull. of the Torrey Botanical Club,* Aug. 31, 1895; *Botanical Gazette,* Aug. 1895; *Fern Bull.,* July 1890; *Science,* July 19, 1895; *Obit. Record of Grads. of Yale Univ., 1890–1900* (1900); *New Haven Evening Reg.,* June 29, 1895.] W.R.M.

EATON, DORMAN BRIDGMAN (June 27, 1823–Dec. 23, 1899), lawyer, civil-service reformer, was born at Hardwick, Vt., the son of the Hon. Nathaniel and Ruth (Bridgman) Eaton, and educated at the University of Vermont, from which he was graduated in 1848. Thereafter he entered the Harvard Law School, receiving the degree of LL.B. in 1850. A prize essay which Eaton wrote at the time of his graduation from the law school attracted the attention of Judge William Kent who was engaged in preparing a new edition of his famous father's *Commentaries.* Judge Kent invited the young lawyer to become his assistant in the work of editing and several years were devoted to this task, the assistant editor displaying such painstaking care and good legal judgment that Judge Kent took him into partnership. Meanwhile, in 1856 he had married Annie S. Foster of New York City and had been admitted to the New York bar. In active practise Eaton made rapid progress by reason of his ability, courage, and perseverance. He was appointed counsel for the Erie Railroad and became engaged in important legal controversies which grew so bitter that on one occasion he was set upon and severely injured by persons whose identity was never discovered. These injuries kept him from work for a time; but on recovery he plunged once more into active practise and became deeply interested in the movement for civil-service reform, of which he was one of the earliest American advocates. Indeed, he is entitled to share with George W. Curtis and Carl Schurz [*qq.v.*] the honor of having gained for the merit system its first real recognition in the national administration.

From 1870, when he gave up his law practise, to the end of his life in 1899, Eaton was a courageous and persistent fighter in two causes which he had much at heart, the abolition of the spoils system and the reform of city government. In 1873 President Grant appointed him chairman of the national Civil Service Commission, succeeding George W. Curtis, who had resigned; but in 1875 Congress cut off the appropriations for the Commission and caused its work to be suspended. President Hayes, in his inaugural (1877), urged Congress to renew the appropriation and meanwhile invited Eaton to make a study of the civil-service system in Great Britain. This necessitated an extended visit to Europe and resulted in the publication of his well-known volume, *The Civil Service in Great Britain: A History of Abuses and Reforms and their Bearing Upon American Politics,* which appeared in 1880. This book interested a wide circle of readers and proved to be of great value to the movement for civil-service reform in America. It enhanced the author's reputation so notably that he was called upon to draft the bill which became the Pendleton Act of 1883. This statute remains the basis of the federal civil-service system at the present day. Immediately after its enactment President Arthur placed Eaton once more at the head of the national Civil Service Commission, and President Cleveland reappointed him in 1885. On his return to New York City after the conclusion of his service on the Commission, Eaton threw his energies into successive campaigns for the reform of municipal government in the metropolis. He was particularly interested in the reform of the police judiciary and the improvement of public-health administration. He also made a study of city administration in general and finally embodied his program of civic improvement in a volume on *The Government of Municipalities* (1899), which appeared from the press a few months before his death. In its day this book was a notable contribution to the then scanty literature of municipal reform.

Throughout his public career, Eaton was a crusader by instinct, fearless and relentless in the battle for civic righteousness, a citizen with the spirit of a Roman consul. As an educator of public opinion he was determined that his work should not come to an end with his death, and in his will he provided for the establishment of professorships in two American universities, the Eaton Professorship of the Science of Government at Harvard, and the Eaton Professorship of Municipal Science at Columbia, both of which chairs have had distinguished occupants.

[A small memorial volume, *Dorman B. Eaton, 1823–1899*, containing a brief sketch of his life, with eulogies by Carl Schurz and others, was published in 1900. In addition to the books mentioned above, he was the author of various articles in magazines. Incidental data relating to his activities may be found in the various works relating to civil-service reform and to the municipal government of New York City during the last three decades of the nineteenth century. See also N. Z. R. Molyneux, *Hist. Geneal. and Biog. of the Eaton Families* (1911).] W.B.M.

EATON, HOMER (Nov. 16, 1834–Feb. 9, 1913), clergyman of the Methodist Episcopal Church, for twenty-four years agent of its Book Concern, and long prominent among the leaders of his denomination, was born in Enosburg, Vt. His father, Rev. Bennett Eaton, a Methodist preacher, was a descendant of Francis Eaton, who came to America in the *Mayflower*; and his mother, Betsey Maria, daughter of Joel and Hannah (Billings) Webster, was a descendant of John Webster, one of the original proprietors of Hartford, Conn., and a colonial governor. He was educated at Bakersfield Academy, Vermont, and at the Methodist General Biblical Institute, Concord, N. H. In 1857 he joined the Troy Conference, of which he remained a member until his death, and the following year, Apr. 28, he married Hannah, daughter of Jacob and Rowena Saxe of Sheldon, Vt. From 1857 to 1889 he was pastor of eleven churches, and served as presiding elder. In 1889 he was made an agent of the Methodist Book Concern in New York, and in 1912, when a new constitution for the Concern was adopted, he was elected general agent, with duties covering the entire field in this country.

Eaton was a rugged Vermonter of massive frame, with a noble head and clean-cut profile, always dignified in his bearing, and possessing a powerful voice. He had a statesmanlike mind, a large fund of native humor, and though not accustomed to indulge in prolonged debate, he had great capacity for bringing men into line with his purposes. He managed the enormous business of the Book Concern with notable sagacity. The extent to which his abilities were valued by his denomination is shown by the fact that he was a member of ten General Conferences, being first elected in 1872, and then continuously from 1880 to 1912. In 1881 and in 1901 he was delegate to the Ecumenical Methodist Conference in London, and in 1874, fraternal delegate to the General Conference of the Methodist Church in Canada. In addition to his other duties he was for seventeen years (1896–1913) treasurer of the Board of Foreign Missions. He was also a trustee of Syracuse University and of Drew Theological Seminary. His death occurred at his home in Madison, N. J., while his wife was reading to him from one of the denominational papers, and he was buried in the Albany (N. Y.) Rural Cemetery.

[*Christian Advocate* (N. Y.), Feb. 13 and 20, 1913; *Minutes of the Troy Annual Conference of the M. E. Ch.* (1913); Henry C. Jennings, *The Meth. Book Concern* (1924); *Who's Who in America*, 1912–13.] H. E. S.

EATON, JOHN (Dec. 5, 1829–Feb. 9, 1906), educator, was born at Sutton, N. H., the son of John and Janet (Andrew) Eaton. He was reared on his father's farm, supplemented his scanty schooling by home reading, and taught school until he was sent to the Thetford Academy in Vermont. He then worked his way through Dartmouth, graduating in 1854, and went to Cleveland, Ohio, as principal of the Ward School. In 1856 he became superintendent of schools at Toledo, where he had opportunities to develop his marked administrative ability, and took a special interest in the compilation of educational statistics. He continued his earlier purpose of entering the ministry, however, and in 1859 resigned to attend Andover Theological Seminary. Ordained in 1861, he entered the army as chaplain of the 27th Ohio Volunteers, which served first in Missouri and then in Tennessee. In November 1862 Grant selected the young chaplain for the difficult task of caring for the negroes who flocked into the army camps. Under Grant's orders Eaton organized the freedmen into camps where provision was made for their physical needs and their education, and they were set to work picking cotton on abandoned plantations and cutting wood for the river steamboats. Eaton's jurisdiction as superintendent of freedmen was extended over the whole department of the Tennessee, including Arkansas. He was given suitable military rank as colonel of a negro regiment in October 1863, and in March 1865 he was brevetted brigadier-general. When the Freedmen's Bureau, for which Eaton's successful organization was an important precedent, was organized in the same month, he was appointed an assistant commissioner in charge of the District of Columbia, Maryland, and parts of Virginia. He resigned in December and was mustered out. On Sept. 29, 1864, he had married Alice Eugenia Shirley, the daughter of a Vicksburg Unionist.

Aside from his personal interest in the South, Eaton felt the need for a Unionist newspaper at Memphis, his old headquarters, and in 1866–67 he edited the *Memphis Post,* which supported Grant for the presidency and showed its editor's interest in education by advocating a system of free public schools. Under the school law of 1867 he was elected state superintendent for two years. "Eaton's system," however, was opposed by many who objected to spending money for this purpose, and it fell to the ground. Meanwhile he had been active in politics as an editor and as a member of the Republican state committee. Grant accordingly appointed him in 1869 to the board of visitors at West Point, and in 1870 made him Commissioner of Education.

The Bureau of Education, then three years old, was in danger of extinction from congressional neglect. It was Eaton's task to build up the organization and to demonstrate its usefulness. Fortunately, in addition to administrative talent, he had tact and a *flair* for the kind of publicity needed to convince the public and Congress that his bureau was worth while. Moreover, he had the president's cordial support. Eaton thought it the main duty of the bureau to collect educational information and to disseminate it as widely as possible. He stood for no particular educational dogma, but tried to familiarize educators with the best practises here and abroad. Believing in federal appropriations to aid the states in developing school systems, he supported Senator Blair's bill for federal aid. In 1886 he resigned because of his health. Almost immediately he began another phase of his career, as a college president, at Marietta College (1886–91), and then at Sheldon Jackson College at Salt Lake City (1895–99). In 1899 he was asked to organize a public-school system in Porto Rico during the military occupation, and served until May 1, 1900, when he resigned because of serious ill health. He was prominent in various learned societies and other organizations in which he was interested.

[John Eaton, in collaboration with Ethel Osgood Mason, *Grant, Lincoln, and the Freedmen* (1907), gives an autobiographical account of his Civil War experiences, and a biographical sketch by Miss Mason which is the best available. See also Paul S. Peirce, *The Freedmen's Bureau* (1904); the U. S. Bureau of Education *Circulars of Information* and the *Report of the Commissioner of Education,* 1870–86; *Report of the Commissioner of Education* for 1899–1900, I, 221–73, II, 1650; *Who's Who in America,* 1906–07.]

D. L. M.

EATON, JOHN HENRY (June 18, 1790–Nov. 17, 1856), lawyer, politician, was the son of John and Elizabeth Eaton. His father, a maker of chaises who resided at Halifax, N. C., during the Revolutionary period, was coroner of his county and a representative in the Assembly (*State Records of North Carolina,* XI, 1895, p. 712; XVII, 1899, pp. 407, 878; XX, 1902, p. 100). In 1796, as executor for Maj. Pinketham Eaton of the Continental Line, who had been killed in action, he acquired an estate of 4,800 acres of land in what came to be Williamson County, Tenn. (Tennessee Land Office Records, North Carolina Military Warrants, Book D, No. 4, p. 22). At the age of sixteen John Henry attended the University of North Carolina for a time. He afterward studied law and in 1808 or 1809 migrated to Tennessee, taking up his residence in Franklin, the seat of justice for Williamson County. During the War of 1812 he served a brief tour of duty as a private soldier (War Department Records). Just before this, his father died (Records of Halifax County, N. C., Wills, vol. III, p. 526), and his mother removed to Tennessee. Eaton purchased for her a home in Franklin which she occupied until her death in 1843. The family owned slaves and appear to have lived in comfort.

Young Eaton married Myra, daughter of one William Terrell Lewis, who had possessed much land. Another daughter of his married Maj. William B. Lewis. The two Lewises were not related, but both young women were wards of Gen. Andrew Jackson (Parton, *post,* II, 652–53; W. W. Clayton, *History of Davidson County, Tenn.,* 1880, pp. 72–73), a fact of far-reaching significance in the career of Eaton, for in making this marriage he also made his fortune. In 1816 a Nashville newspaper announced that the biography of Andrew Jackson which had been begun by John Reid would be completed by J. H. Eaton. Since the young author was not well known to the people of the community, the editor took occasion to call him to their favorable attention (*Nashville Whig*, June 4, 1816). Published in 1817, *The Life of Andrew Jackson, Major General in the Service of the United States* proved to be a dull, uncritical attempt to lionize the Hero of New Orleans, though it went through at least three English and two German editions. In 1817 Eaton became a speculator in Pensacola lands as a result, it appears, of a tip from Jackson (Parton, II, 407), and in 1818 he was appointed to the United States Senate to complete an unexpired term. In 1819 he became the defender of Jackson on the committee which was appointed to investigate the Seminole affair. The legislature presently elected him to fill the seat which he had originally acquired by appointment, and he held the office until his resignation in 1829.

When Jackson became a candidate for the presidency, Eaton and William B. Lewis were two of the principal members of a little group which formed in Nashville to promote his interests. As a senator in Washington, Eaton was the most influential of this clique and he served as its diplomatic representative to stir up favorable sentiment in various parts of the country. When Jackson's election had been accomplished, it was determined that the secretaryship of war should go to a Tennessean, either to Eaton or Hugh Lawson White. Eaton wrote to White explaining that they were being considered, that Jackson had discussed the matter with him, and that he would withdraw if White wished the place. White made no claim, and Eaton received the appointment. The dissolution of the cabinet, which was brought about partly through the refusal of Washington society to accept Eaton's second wife, Peggy O'Neill (see O'Neill, Margaret L.), served to draw Jackson and Eaton closer together. When Eaton helped to pave the way for the reorganization of the cabinet by resigning his office in 1831, it was Jackson's intention to give the secretaryship of war to H. L. White, and to secure the election of Eaton to the place which would thus be vacated by White in the Senate. But White, having been passed over once, was not now amenable and the plans for Eaton went awry. In 1833 a senatorial vacancy occurred and the president used his influence with the Tennessee legislature to have Eaton elected. But, ironically enough, it was his chief's championship which caused Eaton's defeat (T. P. Abernethy, "The Origin of the Whig Party in Tennessee," in *Mississippi Valley Historical Review,* March 1926, pp. 507–08). Thwarted in this plan for his favorite, Jackson in 1834 made him governor of Florida. In 1836 he was appointed minister to Spain, where he remained for four years. At the time of his return to the United States, Martin Van Buren had just been elected president. Eaton, who had been ready to oppose Van Buren's pretensions to the vice-presidency in 1832 (Parton, III, 421), maintained the antagonism in 1840, thereby causing a break with Jackson and terminating his own political career. He continued to live in Washington until his death in 1856.

[The best of the fragmentary notices of John H. Eaton are to be found in John H. Wheeler, *Reminiscences and Memoirs of N. C.* (1884); James Parton, *Life of Andrew Jackson* (1887); and J. W. Caldwell, *Sketches of the Bench and Bar of Tenn.* (1898). See also Wm. Terrell Lewis, *Geneal. of the Lewis Family* (1893); *Biog. Dir. Am. Cong.* (1928). The date of Eaton's birth is taken from the inscription on his tombstone in Oak Hill Cemetery, Washington, D. C.]

T. P. A.

EATON, JOSEPH ORIEL (Feb. 8, 1829–Feb. 7, 1875), painter, was born at Newark, Licking County, Ohio, the son of William and Margaret (Adams) Eaton. Following his early years in the West, he went to New York City to secure his art education and in time attained distinction. He was a genre and portrait-painter in oil and water-colors and was particularly successful in his portraits of children. He had a fine and sensitive appreciation of nature and quick comprehension of personal characteristics shown in facial expression. It was doubtless this faculty that made him a master in portraying the elusive charms of childhood. The titles of his paintings suggest his versatility and range of interests. However, portraits remained the most important part of his work. His best paintings include: "Landscape,—View on the Hudson" (1868), "Moral Instruction" (1869), "Dawning Maternity" (1871), "Greek Water Carrier" (1872), "Lady Godiva" (1874), and portraits of R. S. Gifford (1869), E. J. Kuntze, and Rev. George H. Hepworth (1870). His own portrait (belonging to the National Academy of Design), and "Looking Through the Kaleidoscope" were exhibited after his death. He was elected an Associate National Academician and became a member of various other organizations.

In 1855 Eaton married Emma Jane Goodman of Cincinnati. He died at his home in Yonkers, N. Y., at the age of forty-six.

[N. Z. R. Molyneux, *Hist. Geneal. and Biog. of the Eaton Families* (1911), p. 759; F. A. Virkus, *Abridged Compendium of Am. Genealogy,* I (1925), 73; C. E.

Clement and L. Hutton, *Artists of the Nineteenth Century*, I (1879), 233; *N. Y. Times*, N. Y. *Evening Post*, Feb. 8, 1875; J. D. Champlin, Jr., *Cyc. of Painters and Painting*, II (1886), 2.]
J. M. H.

EATON, MARGARET L. O'NEILL [See O'NEILL, MARGARET L., 1796–1879.]

EATON, NATHANIEL (*c.* 1609–1674), first head of Harvard College, was a disreputable member of a reputable family. He was a son of the Rev. Richard Eaton, a clergyman of Coventry, England, who had a large family of children including Samuel and Theophilus [*qq.v.*], who were prominent in the settling of New Haven. Nathaniel matriculated at Trinity College, Cambridge, in 1629, but did not take a degree. Three years later he received a license to go to Leyden, and in the following year was studying under Dr. William Ames at Franeker. He emigrated to Massachusetts with his two brothers in 1637. Although they soon went to New Haven, Nathaniel remained in Boston. He was welcomed for his learning and was made head of the infant Harvard College, though he did not have the title of president. On June 6, 1639, the General Court granted him 500 acres of land on condition that he would continue there and teach during the remainder of his life. He was soon in trouble, however, and charged with avarice in withholding food he was supposed to provide for the students. He was also haled into court for having beaten his usher with a heavy club while two servants held the unfortunate man by the arms and legs. Eaton was removed from office, forbidden to teach in Massachusetts again, fined 100 marks and ordered to pay the usher £30, both fine and payment being lowered later to £20 each. Soon after he was tried by the church and excommunicated. Instead of making the payments ordered by the court, he fled to Piscataqua, where he was followed and captured. After giving his word that he would go back peaceably to Boston, he made an escape by force onto a vessel bound for Virginia, leaving his wife and children and £1,000 of debts in Boston. He had gained credit by fraudulently drawing drafts on his brother Theophilus. In Virginia he secured a position as assistant rector in an Anglican church on the Eastern Shore and became a drunkard. He sent for his wife and children to follow him. Against the advice of her friends she did so, taking all but one of the children with her. They were lost at sea on the voyage. Eaton then married again, his second wife being the only surviving child of Thomas Graves of Virginia, formerly of Dorchester, Mass. He is supposed to have deserted her and returned to England. In 1647 he received the degrees of Ph.D. and M.D. from the University of Padua (Venn, *post*). After the Restoration he conformed, was vicar of Bishop's Castle, Shropshire, in 1661, and in 1668, despite his continued bad habits, was made rector of Bideford, Devonshire. He died, a prisoner for debt, in King's Bench prison, Southwark, in 1674.

[D. C. Eaton, "The Family of Nathaniel Eaton," in *Papers of the New Haven Colony Hist. Soc.*, IV (1888), 185–92; John Winthrop, *Journal*, I (1908), 310–15; Thos. Hutchinson, *Hist. of the Colony of Mass. Bay*, I (1764), 90–91; *New-Eng. Hist. and Geneal. Reg.*, XL (1886), 295; J. and J. A. Venn, *Alumni Cantabrigienses*, II (1922), 83. Eaton is mentioned in the histories of Harvard, and an account, with additional references, is in the *Dict. Nat. Biog.*]
J. T. A.

EATON, SAMUEL (1596?–Jan. 9, 1665), clergyman, was the third son of the Rev. Richard Eaton, vicar of Great Budworth, Cheshire. He was born in the hamlet of Crowley in that parish. The father became minister of the church at Coventry and it was there that Samuel's eldest brother, Theophilus [*q.v.*], later governor of New Haven, became acquainted with John Davenport. It is not known where Samuel went to school but he attended Magdalene College, Cambridge, where he received the degree of B.A. in 1624–25 and M.A. in 1628. He entered the church and took orders, but found himself unable to conform under Archbishop Laud, and in 1637 emigrated with his brother to New Haven, where he became the colleague of John Davenport. He seems to have been more liberal-minded than either Davenport or his brother, the chief leaders of the colony, for at a meeting held in June 1639 he objected to the article in the New Haven laws which prohibited all except church members from either voting or holding offices. The other two refused to consider any change, so he withdrew his objections. In 1640 he received from the colony a grant of the territory known as Totoket, now Branford, where he proposed to establish a new settlement under the jurisdiction of New Haven. He determined to go back to England to raise a new company of settlers of his own. On the way he stopped for some time in Boston where he declined an offer to remain permanently. When he reached England he found conditions improved and decided to give up all idea of returning to America. His subsequent life belongs to English biography. He continued as a clergyman and wrote a half-dozen small books on religious topics. During his brief sojourn in America he left no permanent mark, save, perhaps, his protest against the strictness of the theocratic government, and his work in establishing the church with Davenport. He died Jan. 9, 1664/5 without issue.

[There is an account in the *Dict. Nat. Biog.* which contains a bibliography of Eaton's writings. Further references are found in the general works dealing with the early ecclesiastical and political history of New Haven.] J. T. A.

EATON, THEOPHILUS (1590–Jan. 7, 1658), merchant, colonizer, was born at Stony Stratford, England, and was one of the nine children of the Rev. Richard Eaton, later rector of a church at Coventry. There the young Theophilus went to school as a classmate of John Davenport, who was to be his life-long friend. His father wished him to be a clergyman, but since his own taste was for trade he went to London where he was apprenticed to a merchant. He finished his term and became a freeman of the city and a merchant on his own account, trading largely with the Baltic countries. So conspicuously successful did he become that he was elected deputy-governor of the great East-Land Company, visited the northern countries in order to enlarge its business, and according to Mather (*Magnalia,* I, 151) was also appointed agent of Charles I at the Court of Denmark. He resided for a time at Copenhagen and then returned to London. There he married his first wife, to whom he had been engaged for three years but whose name is unknown. After her death a few years later he was married to Ann, the daughter of George Lloyd, bishop of Chester, and widow of Thomas Yale.

Eaton took great interest in the plans for colonizing New England. He had become a strong Puritan and it may be that his interest in the new company was partly commercial and partly religious. In any event, he was one of the original patentees of the Massachusetts Company, and when it was determined to place the management of the company in the hands of ten men, five in New and five in Old England, he was chosen as one of the English five. Within a few years the colony became firmly established. It is not known what finally determined Eaton, then a rich and prosperous merchant in London, to transfer himself and his fortune to America, but he with some others, including John Davenport, emigrated in a body in 1637, forming the wealthiest and, commercially, the ablest group which had yet gone to the New World. They landed at Boston in June. Great efforts were made to keep so valuable an addition within the limits of Massachusetts, and they were offered various sites both there and in Plymouth, but they preferred to establish their own independent colony. Eaton, having heard of the special advantages of the territory about Quinnipiack, explored the country in the autumn, and there the company decided to settle. Accordingly, late in March 1638, they sailed from Boston and arrived, some two weeks later, at what is now New Haven. Thereafter, Eaton's life was bound up with that of the New Haven colony, he and his boyhood friend, John Davenport, being "the Moses and Aaron" of the community (Mather, *Magnalia,* I, 152). At a town meeting held June 4, 1639, the fundamental laws for the new colony were agreed upon, limiting the franchise and office holding to church members. The only dissenting voice was that of Eaton's brother Samuel, who was promptly overridden. From that time on there was no opposition in New Haven to the rule of Theophilus and John. On August 22 those two with five others were chosen to constitute "the church" and they proceeded to admit other members according to their own judgment. Eaton was elected civil governor of the colony and continued to be reëlected annually until his death. In 1643 he was one of the first body of commissioners of the United Colonies of New England. Two years later occurred the celebrated trial of his wife for lying as a result of which she was condemned by the church and excommunicated. His relations with her had not been happy before that time and were less so afterward. In 1655, the colony, having discovered the inadequacy of the laws of Moses, by which they had hitherto governed themselves, appointed Eaton to draw up a new code. This he did with Davenport's help. It was accepted and sent to London where it was printed in 1656.

Eaton had evidently expected to establish himself as a merchant and had entered upon various trading schemes. One of these, an attempt which he and his associates made to establish a fur trading post on the Delaware, brought on long and complicated troubles with the Dutch. As a result, the New Haven men finally had to abandon the enterprise, with the loss of £1,000. Constant diplomatic conflicts with New Amsterdam marked the whole of Eaton's service as governor. In 1646 another effort was made to establish the colony on a mercantile basis. A 150-ton ship was built, freighted, and dispatched to Europe, but was lost and never heard from. Some of the leading men then deserted the colony and returned to England, but Eaton remained, devoting himself thereafter to agriculture. He died suddenly in 1658, having governed the colony for nineteen years in a course marked by wisdom, justice, firmness, and prudence.

[Mather has an account of Eaton in his *Magnalia Christi Americana,* I (1853), 149–55. The Memoir by J. B. Moore in the *Colls. of the N. Y. Hist. Soc.,* 2 ser., vol. II (1849), 467–93, is excellent except for certain genealogical errors. Mrs. Eaton's trial is recorded in the article by Newman Smyth in the *Papers of the New Haven Colony Hist. Soc.*, V (1894), 133–48; her genealogy is given correctly in the *Col. Soc. Mass. Pubs.*, XXV (1924), 417–19. See also Leonard Bacon, *Thirteen Hist. Discourses* (1839); S. E. Morison, "New England and the Western Fur Trade, 1629–1675," in *Col. Soc. Mass. Pubs.*, XVIII (1917), 160–92.]

J.T.A.

EATON, WILLIAM (Feb. 23, 1764–June 1, 1811), army officer, diplomat, was born at Woodstock, Conn., the son of Nathan and Sarah (Johnson) Eaton. After a runaway enlistment in the army at sixteen, he underwent a series of hardships. He managed, however, to prepare himself for Dartmouth, and by alternately teaching and studying, succeeded in graduating in 1790. He then went to teach in Windsor, Vt., and, while holding this position, secured, through the influence of Senator Bradley from that state, the appointment of captain in the United States army. This was in March 1792. On Aug. 22, 1792, he married Eliza Sykes, the widow of Gen. Timothy Danielson, and in the fall of the same year was ordered to the Army of the West, on the Ohio. He was sent to Georgia in 1795, and while there made an enemy of his commandant and was court-martialed. The young officer plead his own cause to the secretary of state, Timothy Pickering, to such effect that he was ordered to Philadelphia without loss of rank. In July 1797, having been charged with a secret mission relating to the William Blount conspiracy, he returned in two days with prisoner and papers. By this time he had progressed so far in the esteem of the secretary of state that he was appointed consul to Tunis, and left for his post in December 1798, accompanied by the special diplomatic agent, James L. Cathcart [*q.v.*]. The government had made, through a French agent, Joseph E. Famin, a treaty with the piratical Bey of that North African country, which was unsatisfactory to the Senate. Eaton and Cathcart succeeded in rearranging this agreement and Cathcart proceeded to Tripoli, which country, in 1801, declared war on the United States. The situation there was unique; the reigning Pasha had usurped his brother's throne. Cathcart had formerly suggested that an attempt be made to effect a peace with the country by reinstating the exiled Hamet Karamanli. The proposition was placed before Congress by Eaton himself in the early part of 1804, some favorable attention was given to his scheme, and in September of the same year, with the title of "Navy Agent to the Barbary States," he returned to the Mediterranean to pursue his venture. On his arrival, he discovered that the exiled Pasha had fled to Upper Egypt. Undaunted, he sought out his charge and brought him to Alexandria. From there began a spectacular march through the Libyan Desert with a motley army of Greeks, Italians, and Arabs, collected along the way. After many seemingly unsurmountable difficulties this strange army arrived at Derne, a Tripolitan seaport. Eaton, with the aid of American gunboats, occupied the town. Victory seemed sure. Suddenly he was ordered to leave Tripoli and instructed that a treaty was being negotiated which would secure the illegal ruler on the Tripolitan throne and provide for the payment of ransom for imprisoned American officers.

Eaton was incensed and humiliated. He returned immediately to America, where his brilliant services had given him great prestige, but the warmth with which he defended himself after the government had supported the treaty-makers made him many political enemies. His feat was mentioned by the president in his annual message, but Eaton's complaints kept him from receiving a medal from the House of Representatives. The remainder of his life was none too happy. In 1807 he was summoned to witness in the Aaron Burr trial; he had been closely associated with Burr, but was able to clear himself before the court. In December of that year he took a seat in the Massachusetts legislature, but because of his too ready utterance of his opinions he was not reëlected. He retired to Brimfield, Mass., where he spent his last years. The fatigues of his active life, the disappointments in his cherished schemes, and his excesses had undermined his health, and he died at forty-seven years of age.

[Charles Prentiss, *Life of the Late Gen. William Eaton* (1813); C. C. Felton, *Life of William Eaton* (1838) in Sparks's Lib. of Am. Biog.; *Hist. Celebration of the Town of Brimfield . . . 1876* (1879); Gardner W. Allen, *Our Navy and the Barbary Corsairs* (1905); *Am. State Papers, Foreign Relations*, II (1832), 281, 702–25; Preble Papers, Lib. of Cong.; C. W. Goldsborough, *The U. S. Naval Chronicle* (1824), pp. 254–56, 272–78; Commanders' Letters, Nos. 1 to 26, and Miscellaneous Letters, III, Nos. 36, 38, 48 (Navy Dept.); *Nat. Intelligencer*, Nov. 20, 1805. There is a popularly written sketch of Eaton in Meade Minnigerode's *Lives and Times* (1925).]

R.B.B.

EATON, WYATT (May 6, 1849–June 7, 1896), painter, was born at Philipsburg, province of Quebec, Canada. He was the son of Jonathan Wyatt and Mary (Smith) Eaton, the former a lumber and shipping merchant and native of New Hampshire. When about eighteen years old, he became a student at the National Academy of Design under Samuel Colman, Daniel Huntington, Leutze, and others, and painted in the studio of Joseph Oriel Eaton [*q.v.*], who became both instructor and friend. In 1872 he took a European trip which widened his horizon considerably. In London he became acquainted with Whistler, then, journeying to the continent, he sought the studio of Gérôme at the École des Beaux-Arts in Paris. Here valuable contacts with Munkácsy, Bastien-Lepage, Dagnan-Bouveret, and others stimulated him in his work in Paris and at Barbizon in the Forest of Fontainebleau, but of all his friendships, that with Millet was of most vital and lasting worth to him. The older artist cast a noticeable influence on the younger, and in his family, Eaton was treated as a son. In addition to required academic work, Eaton painted portraits, figures, and landscapes. At the Salon of 1874 his "Reverie" was exhibited and in 1876 his "Harvesters at Rest." Both were shown at the Universal Exposition of 1878. Later he exhibited a portrait of Mrs. Hawkins, said to be one of the finest canvases in the Salon that year. After returning to America in 1877, Eaton, with Augustus Saint-Gaudens, Walter Shirlaw, and others, founded the Society of American Artists, was its first secretary, and later its president. He was then a teacher at Cooper Institute, New York.

His portraits of the poets Emerson, Whittier, Longfellow, Bryant, Holmes, and Dr. Holland, engraved by T. Cole for the *Century Magazine*, were considered an innovation in magazine work. In 1884 and 1885, while in Europe, he painted a few peasant subjects but eventually became absorbed in portraiture. Notable examples of Eaton's work are his portraits of Bishop Horatio Potter, Roswell Smith, President Garfield (after his death), for the Union League Club of New York, John Burroughs, Senator Franklin Murphy of Newark, and Mrs. R. W. Gilder. The last has won a place among the best pictures produced in this country. During a trip to Canada, in 1892–93, Eaton painted some of the benefactors of McGill University, as well as Sir William Dawson of Montreal and other prominent people. His work there was so successful that other important commissions followed and he spent the remainder of his life chiefly in Canada. Among the best-known of his Canadian portraits are those of Sir William and Lady Van Horne, Sir Donald and Lady Smith, Mr. Angus, and Lady Marjorie and the Hon. Archie Gordon. Eaton's deft use of the brush gave his paintings an unusual delicacy and grace, while his portraiture reveals a rare skill in transcending the limitations of photographic likeness.

Being unequal to an anticipated summer trip abroad in 1896, Eaton went to Newport, R. I., instead, where he died of consumption. His first wife, whom he married on Sept. 24, 1874, was Laura Constance Papelard, born in Château-Thierry, France. After her death, on Feb. 7. 1886, he married, July 23, 1887, Charlotte Amelia Collins.

[N. Z. R. Molyneux, *Hist. Geneal. and Biog. of the Eaton Families* (1911), p. 760; F. F. Sherman, *Am. Painters of Yesterday and Today* (1919), pp. 39–44; G. W. Sheldon, *Am. Painters* (enlarged ed., 1881), pp. 169–74; *Century Mag.*, Oct. 1902; certain information from the New England Hist. Geneal. Soc.] J. M. H.

EBERLE, EDWARD WALTER (Aug. 17, 1864–July 6, 1929), naval officer, was born at Denton, Texas, the son of Joseph Eberle, who came as a youth from Switzerland and was a major in the Confederate army, and Mary Stemler of Georgia. He later settled at Fort Smith, Ark., whither his parents had moved in 1865. In his eighteenth year he entered the United States Naval Academy, graduating about the middle of his class in 1885. Of his sea duty in the decade following, the most profitable, as a rigorous training in old-style seafaring, was three years of charting and survey work in the Fish Commission steamer *Albatross*, off Cape Horn, Alaska, and the west coast of the United States. After duty at the Naval Academy and promotion in 1896 to lieutenant (junior grade), he served three years in the *Oregon*, making the famous cruise around the Horn in the Spanish-American War and commanding her forward turret at Santiago (see Eberle, "The *Oregon* at Santiago," *Century Magazine*, May 1899). Later, at Manila, when Capt. Barker of the *Oregon* succeeded Dewey in command of the Asiatic Squadron during the Philippine Insurrection, he made Eberle his flag lieutenant and acting chief of staff (see Eberle, "The Navy's Cooperation in the Zapote River Campaign," *Proceedings of the United States Naval Institute*, March 1900). A specialist in ordnance, Eberle, then aide to the superintendent at the Naval Academy, wrote the first modern manual of *Gun and Torpedo Drills for the United States Navy*, and in 1901–02 was gunnery officer of the *Indiana*. Again flag lieutenant for Admiral Barker, in the Atlantic Fleet (1903–05), he drew up the first instructions and code for wireless on naval vessels. After study at the War College in 1905, and two years' service as recorder of the Board of Inspection and Survey, he accompanied the world cruise of 1907–08 as executive of the *Louisiana* as far as San Francisco, where he became commandant of the Training Station, 1908–10. During the next two years he commanded the *Wheeling* on a voyage around the world via Alaska, Japan, and the Mediterranean. Captain's rank came to him in 1912 while he was commanding the Atlantic Torpedo Fleet, in which he developed the use of smoke screens and the employment of aircraft against submarines. In the summer of 1914 he was senior officer at Santo Domingo during revolutionary disturbances, in which the navy was engaged in protecting property and arranging a settlement.

As superintendent he administered the Naval Academy, September 1915–January 1919, with marked success through the period of wartime expansion, when classes were tremendously increased, courses compressed, and many reserve officers were in training. At the close of the war he was awarded the Distinguished Service Medal, in February 1918 was made temporary rear-admiral, and on July 1, 1919, was given the permanent rank. In 1919–21 he commanded divisions of the Atlantic Fleet, and from June 1921 to June 1923, the Pacific Fleet, known after reorganization in December 1922, as the Battle Fleet. After this second highest sea command, his general popularity and a belief in his sound judgment and tact in dealing with political leaders prompted his promotion to the highest shore office, that of chief of naval operations, which he held from July 1923 to November 1927, a period when special problems were raised by the expeditionary forces in China and Nicaragua. Following a year on the Navy General Board he retired, Aug. 17, 1928. His death, at the Naval Hospital, Washington, came from an infection above the ear, the result of an injury years before. He was survived by his wife, Tazie, daughter of Randolph Harrison of Virginia, whom he married in San Francisco on Oct. 24, 1889, and by a son, Edward Randolph. Not a bookish man or a great reader, Eberle was successful chiefly because of his remarkable grasp of his profession in its every detail, combined with ability to win the trust and devotion of his subordinates. His whole life was in his work, and to his high rank he brought a frank manliness and a poise of manner which made him esteemed both within and without the service.

[*Everyday Life in the Navy: Autobiography of Rear Admiral Albert S. Barker* (1928); obituaries in the *N. Y. Times*, July 7, 1929; *Army and Navy Jour.*, July 13, 1929; *U. S. Bureau of Navigation (Navy Dept.) Bull. 108*, July 13, 1929.] A.W.

EBERLE, JOHN (Dec. 10, 1787–Feb. 2, 1838), physician, was born probably at Hagerstown, Md., and taken by his parents at an early age to Lancaster, Pa., though it has been stated that he was born at the latter place. His father, a blacksmith, and his mother were both simple farmer folk of German birth or descent. John was twelve years of age before he could speak English. He had no early educational advantages, but, being a constant reader, he acquired sufficient knowledge to enable him to begin the study of medicine with Abraham Carpenter of Lancaster, and enter the University of Pennsylvania in 1806, where three years later he graduated, his thesis being on *Animal Life*. He returned to his home and began to practise medicine. During this period he was drawn into political writing and became the editor of a newspaper. Toward the end of the War of 1812 he was appointed surgeon of the Lancaster militia and served at the battle of Baltimore (1814). Removing to Philadelphia, he helped to found, and for some two years devoted practically his whole time to editing, the *American Medical Recorder*, a quarterly journal first issued in 1818. The *Recorder* was well received in America and Europe and its editor received considerable recognition, for example, election to the German Academy of the Natural Sciences. In 1818 also, he published *Botanical Terminology*, a pocket "companion" for students of botany. His success as a writer encouraged him to publish his *Treatise of the Materia Medica and Therapeutics* (1823) which became a standard text-book and went through five editions. Through the meetings of the Philadelphia Medical Society he was brought in contact with an enthusiastic group of students and teachers, and together with Dr. George M'Clellan gave regular lectures at the Appollodorian Gallery. In 1824, with Dr. Joseph Klapp and Dr. Jacob Green, he proposed to the trustees of Jefferson College at Canonsburg, Pa., to establish a medical department of that college in Philadelphia. This proposal was accepted, and the Jefferson Medical College opened (1825) with Eberle as professor of materia medica, and afterward of the theory and practise of medicine (1825–31). He soon issued a small volume called "Eberle's Notes," a kind of *vade mecum* for the student. The work was sufficiently popular to justify a second edition (1832) and from this grew his *Notes of Lectures on the Theory and Practice of Medicine* (2nd ed., 1834, with four subsequent editions), a text characterized by original thought and not, as were many of that day, a mere compilation of foreign opinions. From 1824 to 1826 he was editor of the *American Medical Review*. Within a few years much litigation and controversy arose at the Jefferson Medical College, and, finances running low, Eberle became discouraged and in 1830 accepted the offer of Daniel Drake [*q.v.*] to organize the faculty for the medical department of Miami University, designed as a competitor of the Medical College of Ohio. Eberle arrived in Cincinnati in 1831 and learned that the old school and its would-be rival had consolidated so that he and

Eberle

his colleagues found themselves members of the conjoint faculty. In 1832 they founded the *Western Medical Gazette*. Shortly thereafter Eberle published his *Treatise on the Diseases and Physical Education of Children* (1833). On the outbreak of cholera in Cincinnati, Eberle and T. D. Mitchell were appointed special health officers. Their report was published in the *Cincinnati Daily Gazette*, June 26, 1832. In 1837 Eberle accepted the chair of the theory and practise of medicine at the reorganized medical department of Transylvania University in Lexington, Ky., where he became one of the editors of the *Transylvania Journal of Medicine*. His health was now beginning to decline so that he was able to do but little teaching. He resigned before completing a full school term, and died in Lexington after less than a year's residence.

He was a brilliant teacher and writer and successful in the debates with other medical men so characteristic of the period. He was a champion of the theory of physiological drug action as opposed to "solidism" as taught by Harrison and others. At the three medical schools at which he was professor he was always popular with the students, who liked his simplicity of manner while admiring his learning. He was an idealist and inclined to be a dreamer, but an incessant worker. Besides the works above mentioned, he was the author of numerous short articles. His *Treatise on the Practice of Medicine*, in two volumes, first appearing in 1830, was published with subsequent revisions, the last being in 1849 with additions by George M'Clellan. His *Treatise on the Diseases . . . of Children* was revised and republished in 1850 by his former colleague, Thomas D. Mitchell. These republications of his works long after his death are sufficient proofs of their popularity.

[Sketch from memory, by T. D. Mitchell, in *Lives of Eminent Am. Physicians* (1861), ed. by S. D. Gross; Robt. Peter, The *Hist. of the Medic. Dept. of Transylvania Univ.* (1905), being Filson Club Pub. No. 20; Otto Juettner, *Daniel Drake and his Followers* (1909); *Autobiog. of Samuel D. Gross* (2 vols., 1887); E. G. Eberle, "John Eberle, 1787–1838" (1924), MS. in Army Medical Lib.; Alexander Harris, *Harris' Biog. Hist. of Lancaster, Pa.* (1872); *Kentucky Gazette* (Lexington), Feb. 8, 1838.]

E. F. H.

VOLUME III, PART 2

ECHOLS - FRASER

(*VOLUME VI OF THE ORIGINAL EDITION*)

CROSS REFERENCES FROM THIS VOLUME ARE MADE TO THE VOLUME NUMBERS OF THE ORIGINAL EDITION.

CONTRIBUTORS
VOLUME III, PART 2

Thomas P. Abernethy	T. P. A.
Adeline Adams	A. A.
James Truslow Adams	J. T. A.
Robert Greenhalgh Albion	R. G. A.
Edmund Kimball Alden	E. K. A.
Edward E. Allen	E. E. A.
William H. Allison	W. H. A.
Katharine H. Amend	K. H. A.
John Clark Archer	J. C. A.
Edward C. Armstrong	E. C. A.
Benjamin Wisner Bacon	B. W. B.
Ray Palmer Baker	R. P. B—r.
Thomas S. Barclay	T. S. B.
Claribel R. Barnett	C. R. B.
Harold K. Barrows	H. K. B.
J. Henry Bartlett	J. H. B.
Ernest Sutherland Bates	E. S. B—s.
William James Battle	W. J. B.
Carl L. Becker	C. L. B.
Elbert J. Benton	E. J. B.
Percy W. Bidwell	P. W. B.
Theodore C. Blegen	T. C. B.
Arthur R. Blessing	A. R. B.
George Blumer	G. B.
Ernest F. Boddington	E. F. B.
Sarah G. Bowerman	S. G. B.
William K. Boyd	W. K. B.
Benjamin Brawley	B. B.
Robert Preston Brooks	R. P. B—s.
Everett S. Brown	E. S. B—n.
L. Parmly Brown	L. P. B.
Frank J. Bruno	F. J. B.
Solon J. Buck	S. J. B.
Guy H. Burnham	G. H. B.
William B. Cairns	W. B. C.
Isabel M. Calder	I. M. C.
Robert G. Caldwell	R. G. C.
James M. Callahan	J. M. C.
Robert C. Canby	R. C. C.
Charles F. Carey	C. F. C.
Richard S. Cartwright	R. S. C—t.
Henry S. Chapman	H. S. C.
Arney R. Childs	A. R. C.
Francis A. Christie	F. A. C.
Dora Mae Clark	D. M. C.
Hubert Lyman Clark	H. L. C.
Oral Sumner Coad	O. S. C.
Frederick W. Coburn	F. W. C.
Fannie L. Gwinner Cole	F. L. G. C.
Edward S. Corwin	E. S. C.
Robert Spencer Cotterill	R. S. C—l.
E. Merton Coulter	E. M. C.
Dorothy P. Cutler	D. P. C.
Chalmers G. Davidson	C. G. D.
Clive Day	C. D.
Roy Day	R. D.
Roy Floyd Dibble	R. F. D.
Gilbert H. Doane	G. H. D.
Eleanor Robinette Dobson	E. R. D.
Dorothy Anne Dondore	D. A. D.
Elizabeth Donnan	E. D.
Edward A. Duddy	E. A. D.
Raymond S. Dugan	R. S. D.
William B. Dunning	W. B. D.
William Frederick Durand	W. F. D.
Lionel C. Durel	L. C. D.
Harrison Griswold Dwight	H. G. D.
Edward Dwight Eaton	E. D. E.
Walter Prichard Eaton	W. P. E.
Edwin Francis Edgett	E. F. E.
Milton Ellis	M. E.
Arthur Elson	A. E.
Ephraim Emerton	E. E.
Charles R. Erdman, Jr.	C. R. E., Jr.
Paul D. Evans	P. D. E.
William Purviance Fenn	W. P. F.
Alexander Clarence Flick	A. C. F.
Percy Scott Flippin	P. S. F.
George T. Flom	G. T. F.
Blanton Fortson	B. F.
Louis H. Fox	L. H. F.
Kuno Francke	K. F.
John H. Frederick	J. H. F.
Claude M. Fuess	C. M. F.
Joseph V. Fuller	J. V. F.
John F. Fulton	J. F. F.
Herbert P. Gambrell	H. P. G.
George Harvey Genzmer	G. H. G.
Virginia Gerson	V. G.
W. J. Ghent	W. J. G.
Lawrence H. Gipson	L. H. G.
Harold C. Goddard	H. C. G.
Armistead Churchill Gordon, Jr.	A. C. G., Jr.
Henry Solon Graves	H. S. G.
Charles W. Hackett	C. W. H.
Percival Hall	P. H.
Philip M. Hamer	P. M. H.
J. G. deR. Hamilton	J. G. deR. H
Talbot Faulkner Hamlin	T. F. H.
Alvin F. Harlow	A. F. H.
Ralph V. Harlow	R. V. H.

Contributors

Fairfax Harrison	F. H.
Mary Bronson Hartt	M. B. H.
George E. Hastings	G. E. H.
Paul L. Haworth	P. L. H.
Fred E. Haynes	F. E. H.
Marshall DeLancey Haywood	M. DeL. H.
Atcheson L. Hench	A. L. H.
Emily Hickman	E. H—n.
Frederick C. Hicks	F. C. H.
John Donald Hicks	J. D. H.
Charles E. Hill	C. E. H.
Homer Carey Hockett	H. C. H.
Frank H. Hodder	F. H. H.
Jean MacKinnon Holt	J. M. H.
Walter Hough	W. H.
Leland Ossian Howard	L. O. H.
Clifford Chesley Hubbard	C. C. H.
Theodora Kimball Hubbard	T. K. H.
William Jackson Humphreys	W. J. H.
Albert Hyma	A. H.
Asher Isaacs	A. I.
Joseph Jackson	J. J.
Edward H. Jenkins	E. H. J.
Allen Johnson	A. J.
James R. Joy	J. R. J.
Louise Phelps Kellogg	L. P. K.
Rayner W. Kelsey	R. W. K.
Allen Marshall Kline	A. M. K.
H. W. Howard Knott	H. W. H. K.
Harry Lyman Koopman	H. L. K.
Edwin W. Kopf	E. W. K.
Leonard W. Labaree	L. W. L.
William Coolidge Lane	W. C. L.
John W. Lang	J. W. L.
George M. Lewis	G. M. L.
Lawrence T. Lowrey	L. T. L.
Robert Luce	R. L.
Clarence H. McClure	C. H. M.
Thomas Denton McCormick	T. D. M.
Philip B. McDonald	P. B. M.
Reginald C. McGrane	R. C. M.
Eva Anne Madden	E. A. M.
William Francis Magie	W. F. M.
H. A. Marmer	H. A. M.
Howard R. Marraro	H. R. M.
Frederick H. Martens	F. H. M.
Asa Earl Martin	A. E. M.
Albert P. Mathews	A. P. M.
David M. Matteson	D. M. M
Lawrence S. Mayo	L. S. M.
Edmond S. Meany	E. S. M.
Leila Mechlin	L. M.
Newton D. Mereness	N. D. M.
George P. Merrill	G. P. M.
Herman H. B. Meyer	H. H. B. M.
Douglass W. Miller	D. W. M.
Edwin Mims, Jr.	E. M., Jr.
Broadus Mitchell	B. M.
Carl W. Mitman	C. W. M.
Frank Monaghan	F. M—n.
Thomas L. Montgomery	T. L. M.
Fulmer Mood	F. M—d.
Albert B. Moore	A. B. M.
George T. Moore	G. T. M.
Harrison S. Morris	H. S. M.
Richard B. Morris	R. B. M.
Jarvis M. Morse	J. M. M.
George S. Myers	G. S. M.
Allan Nevins	A. N.
Charles L. Nichols	C. L. N.
Robert Hastings Nichols	R. H. N.
Roy F. Nichols	R. F. N.
Harold J. Noble	H. J. N.
John S. Nollen	J. S. N.
Walter B. Norris	W. B. N.
David Edward Owen	D. E. O.
Catherine W. Palmer	C. W. P.
Victor H. Paltsits	V. H. P.
Scott H. Paradise	S. H. P.
John I. Parcel	J. I. P.
Stanley M. Pargellis	S. M. P.
Julius H. Parmelee	J. H. P.
Merrill R. Patterson	M. R. P.
Charles O. Paullin	C. O. P.
Frederic Logan Paxson	F. L. P—n.
Henry G. Pearson	H. G. P.
Theodore C. Pease	T. C. P.
Donald Culross Peattie	D. C. P.
Edgar Legare Pennington	E. L. P.
Ralph Barton Perry	R. B. P.
Frederick T. Persons	F. T. P.
A. Everett Peterson	A. E. P.
James M. Phalen	J. M. P.
Paul Chrisler Phillips	P. C. P.
Deets Pickett	D. P.
David deSola Pool	D. deS. P.
Julius W. Pratt	J. W. P.
Edward Preble	E. P.
Frederick Clarke Prescott	F. C. P.
Herbert I. Priestley	H. I. P.
Richard J. Purcell	R. J. P.
Lawson Purdy	L. P.
Belle Rankin	B. R.
Charles Dudley Rhodes	C. D. R.
Irving B. Richman	I. B. R.
Doane Robinson	D. R.
William A. Robinson	W. A. R.
Miriam Theresa Rooney	M. T. R.
Frank Edward Ross	F. E. R.
Ralph L. Rusk	R. L. R.
Carlton Savage	C. S.
Joseph Schafer	J. S.
Carl F. Schreiber	C. F. S.
Montgomery Schuyler	M. Sc—r.
Kenneth Scott	K. S.

Contributors

Muriel Shaver . . . . . . M. Sh—r.
William Bristol Shaw . . . W. B. S—w.
Cornelius Lott Shear . . . C. L. Sh—r.
George N. Shuster . . . . . G. N. S.
Constance Lindsay Skinner C. L. Sk—r.
Alice R. Huger Smith . . . A. R. H. S.
David Eugene Smith . . . . D. E. S.
William Smith . . . . W. S—h.
Thomas M. Spaulding . . . T. M. S.
Samuel Peter Spreng . . . S. P. S.
Harris Elwood Starr . . . H. E. S.
George M. Stephenson . . G. M. S.
Walter B. Stevens . . . . . W. B. S—s.
Wayne E. Stevens . . . . . W. E. S.
Witmer Stone . . . . W. S—e.
Charles S. Sydnor . . . . . C. S. S.
Edwin P. Tanner . . . . . . E. P. T.
David Y. Thomas . . . . . . D. Y. T.
Holland Thompson . . . . . H. T.
Irving L. Thomson . . . . . I. L. T.
Leah Townsend . . . . . . L. T.
William T. Utter . . . . . W. T. U.
Mark Van Doren . . . . . M. V-D.
Henry R. Viets . . . . H. R. V.
Eugene M. Violette . . . . E. M. V.
John D. Wade . . . . J. D. W.
Theodore B. Wagner . . . . T. B. W.
William Cushing Wait . . . W. C. W.
James Elliott Walmsley . . J. E. W.
James J. Walsh . . . . J. J. W.
Langdon Warner . . . . . . L. W.
W. Randall Waterman . . . W. R. W.
Elizabeth Howard West . . E. H. W.
Allan Westcott . . . . A. W.
Arthur P. Whitaker . . . . A. P. W.
Charles Adams White . . . C. A. W.
Horatio S. White . . . . . H. S. W.
Melvin J. White . . . . . . M. J. W.
Walter Lincoln Whittlesey W. L. W—y.
James F. Willard . . . . . J. F. W.
George Edward Woodbine . G. E. W.
Herbert F. Wright . . . . H. F. W.
Walter L. Wright, Jr. . . . W. L. W—t., Jr.
James Ingersoll Wyer . . . J. I. W.
Edna Yost . . . . E. Y.
John Zeleny . . . . J. Z.

DICTIONARY OF

AMERICAN BIOGRAPHY

Echols — Fraser

ECHOLS, JOHN (Mar. 20, 1823–May 24, 1896), lawyer, Confederate soldier, railroad president, was born in Lynchburg, Va., the son of Joseph and Elizabeth F. (Lambeth) Echols. He graduated with honor from Washington College (now Washington and Lee University), did post-graduate work at the Virginia Military Institute, and studied law at Harvard. Returning to Virginia in 1842, he taught in Harrisonburg, and was admitted to the bar of Rockbridge County in November 1843. After practising at Staunton for a short time, he made his home in Monroe County (now W. Va.) till 1861.

He was elected commonwealth's attorney and later a member of the General Assembly, and was one of the two delegates from Monroe County to the convention of 1861. While the convention was in session, but after the adoption of the ordinance of secession, he resigned as a member and on the following day was nominated a colonel of volunteers. Before this nomination was confirmed on Dec. 6, 1861, he had returned to his county and organized a company which was assigned to the 27th Regiment. He commanded this regiment at the first battle of Manassas and afterward until he was severely wounded at Kernstown, Mar. 23, 1862. Returning to the army after his recovery, he was commissioned a brigadier-general and served in the Kanawha Valley for a time under Gen. Loring, whom he afterward succeeded as commander of the Department of Southwestern Virginia. In the summer of 1863 he served, with Howell Cobb and Robert Ransome, on the court of inquiry held at Richmond to determine the cause of the fall of Vicksburg. In 1864 he took his brigade to the Valley under Gen. John C. Breckinridge and played a conspicuous part in the battle of New Market. After fighting with the Army of Northern Virginia from Hanover Junction to Cold Harbor, he went with Gen. Early on his campaign into Maryland, and in the fall of 1864 resumed command of the Department of Southwestern Virginia. After the surrender at Appomattox he led the remnant of his command into North Carolina, escorted President Davis from Greensboro to Charlotte, returned to Greensboro, and was paroled with Johnston's army. He had been commissioned major-general in the last days of the war but the commission failed to reach him.

Identified in sympathies with the older part of the state, he removed soon after the war from Monroe County to Staunton, became the senior member of the law firm of Echols, Bell, and Catlett, and represented Augusta County in the General Assembly. His business abilities were so well recognized that when the National Valley Bank of Staunton was organized he was elected president, continuing in that office after the bank was consolidated with the First National Bank of Staunton. About the same time, with Col. John B. Baldwin and others, he undertook the reorganization of the Virginia Central Railroad, later known as the Chesapeake & Ohio & Southwestern. He served as receiver and general manager, and, after its reorganization as the Chesapeake & Ohio Railway, he secured its extension through Kentucky, and for twenty years was a director and played a large part in determining its policy. His duties as an officer of the Chesapeake & Ohio and its associated roads compelled his residence in Louisville, Ky., for the last ten years of his life, but he remained a citizen of Virginia, returning to cast his vote in elections and keeping in close touch with the state's problems. He was an active member of the board of visitors of the Virginia Military Institute and of Washington and Lee University. In a memorial minute of the board after his death it was said that "he rarely made an enemy and never lost a friend."

Echols was a man of commanding presence, six feet four inches high, weighing two hundred and sixty pounds, with a massive rugged face, a sonorous voice, and the confident manner of an executive. He was twice married: first, to Mary Jane Caperton, sister of his colleague in the convention of 1861; second, to Mrs. Mary Cochran Reid of New York City. He died in his seventy-fourth year at the home of his son in Staunton.

[There is a short sketch of Echols, inaccurate in some details, in *Confed. Mil. Hist.*, III (1899), 591–93, and a longer and better sketch by A. C. Gordon, in *Men of Mark in Va.*, V (1909), 124–29. See also *Report of Brig.-Gen. Echols of the Battle of Droop Mt.* (1864); *Official Records (Army)*; *Battles and Leaders of the Civil War*, vol. IV (1884). Brief biographies and editorials published in newspapers at the time of his death are in the possession of his son's widow in Staunton, Va.] J.E.W.

ECKART, WILLIAM ROBERTS (June 17, 1841–Dec. 8, 1914), engineer, was born in Chillicothe, Ohio, the son of William Roberts and Eleanor (Carlisle) Eckart. In 1842 his parents moved to Cleveland where his father had shipping interests on the Great Lakes. The boy's education, begun in private schools, was continued in the public schools of Cleveland and at St. Clair Academy in that city, where he followed special studies with a view to becoming a civil engineer. In the early fifties his father took his family to Zanesville, Ohio, where he had a managing interest in the Putnam Flouring Mills, the power for which was derived from water-wheels. William's work as an assistant to the millwright in the installation of improved wheels led to an apprenticeship in the shop of Griffith, Ebert & Wedge, and later to an association with the partner Wedge, an engineer trained in the precision methods of the famous Whitworth shops of London. To the high ideals insisted on in all of the work of Griffith, Ebert & Wedge, Eckart attributed much of his success in later years. Contact with the marine work of the shop strengthened his taste for naval service, already formed by travel on the Ohio and Mississippi rivers, and in 1861, after the outbreak of the Civil War, he passed with high honor the examination for naval engineer, was appointed, and ordered to join the fleet on the Pacific Coast. Here he met B. F. Isherwood [*q.v.*], chief engineer of the navy, and was brought into intimate contact with the problems of marine engineering practise. In 1864, because of ill health, he resigned from the navy and took up his residence in San Francisco. In California and in adjacent states he spent the remainder of his life. As a chief draftsman in 1865, he prepared the designs for the first steam locomotive built in California. As superintendent of steam machinery at the United States Navy Yard, Mare Island, he designed and prepared the equipment for a notable research on marine propellers, and served as Isherwood's associate in carrying out this work, the results of which have now become classic in the literature of marine engineering. Later, as partner in an engineering firm at Marysville, Cal., he constructed a small steamer to be used on Lake Tahoe; it had a guaranteed speed of twenty-one miles per hour and was perhaps the fastest boat of its size known at that date. In connection with the great mining boom at Virginia City, Nev., and elsewhere, 1870–80, he encountered, as consulting engineer, the difficult problem of handling enormous quantities of scalding-hot water under pressures represented by thousands of feet of head, a combination of conditions perhaps unprecedented up to that time. Under his direction and guidance, however, mining was successfully carried on to the exhaustion of the ore bodies. With the decline of deep mining in 1880 he again took up his residence in San Francisco. Here as consulting engineer he became responsible for the design of the machinery for the Anaconda Copper Company, with the new and difficult problems which this work presented, and later, as consultant for the Union Iron Works in all matters relating to naval construction, was associated with the pioneer work of building the new steel navy. Finally, to round out the scope and variety of his professional experience, in 1899 he became, as consulting engineer for the Standard Electric Company, responsible for the design and construction of the hydraulic work connected with their first hydroelectric power plant, taking water at a 9,000-foot level and under 1,400 feet head generating 15,000 horse-power—perhaps the pioneer among high head long distance transmission power plants. This work was brought to a successful completion in 1903.

Eckart was always on the firing line of progress and delighted in nothing more than in dealing with new and difficult problems. He was eminently a student in his manner of handling them, and spared no pains in insuring a sound foundation for his proposed solution or mode of treatment. He was notable as a collector of books and professional literature and of fine precision apparatus used in engineering measurements; was a member of many engineering societies and technical organizations, and occasionally contributed papers of value to their transactions. In 1872 he married Harriet Louise Gorham; to them were born three sons and one daughter. After a long period of failing health, during which he retained his keen interest in engineering, he died in Palo Alto, Cal., at the home of his eldest son.

[*Trans. Am. Soc. Mech. Engineers,* XXXVI (1915), 1090; *Builders of San Francisco* (1912); *San Francisco Chronicle, San Francisco Examiner,* Dec. 9, 1914; statement by living sons; personal acquaintance.]

W. F. D.

ECKELS, JAMES HERRON (Nov. 22, 1858–Apr. 14, 1907), lawyer, comptroller of the currency, financier, traced his paternal ancestry to an emigrant from Belfast, Ireland. Both his parents were natives of Cumberland County, Pa. His father, James Starr Eckels, after graduating at the Albany Law School in 1857, took his wife, Margaret Herron Eckels, whom he had married in 1854, to the little town of Princeton, Ill., where his son was born. James Eckels achieved success as an attorney. His son, choosing to follow in his father's footsteps, also attended the Albany Law School, from which he graduated in 1883. While at Albany he made the acquaintance of Gov. Grover Cleveland, a momentous event in young Eckels's career. Establishing himself at Ottawa, Ill., he gained ground rapidly both as a lawyer and as a Democratic politician. He campaigned for his friend Cleveland in 1884 and was consulted in regard to the distribution of patronage in his congressional district. In the campaign of 1892 he made speeches against the tariff and for Cleveland. He rejoiced in the Democratic victory and had hopes of receiving the appointment as United States attorney for Illinois. The country was surprised, as was Eckels, when Cleveland proposed that the thirty-five-year-old attorney should become comptroller of the currency. He took over the duties of that office Apr. 26, 1893.

Within a month after Eckels entered upon his new work the panic of 1893 broke. Bankers who had had misgivings at his appointment now prophesied disaster. That Eckels stood the test of this crisis and came to have the respect of the financiers is the best evidence of his ability. His most important work in this period was the handling of the tangled affairs of national banks which were forced to suspend payment. During the period from 1865 to 1898, 369 national banks were forced into receiverships. Of this number, 181 met disaster in the four years and eight months during which Eckels was comptroller. The energy and efficiency which he demonstrated in meeting the problems of his office showed that Cleveland's confidence in him had not been misplaced. His annual reports contained a number of constructive suggestions for the improvement of the national currency system. He advised, in order to give the currency greater elasticity, that an asset security be devised to take the place of bonds as the basis of the issue of national banknotes. He made a suggestion, later adopted, that a non-partisan commission be appointed to study exhaustively the needs of the nation's monetary system.

In 1896 he was a leader among the Gold Democrats. He was continued in his office by McKinley, but he resigned it on Dec. 31, 1897, to become president of the Commercial National Bank of Chicago. He was one of the leading financiers of that city when heart trouble caused his sudden death on Apr. 14, 1907. He was small in stature. One of his admirers said that "there was not much to Eckels, but what little there was was three-quarters brains." He married Fannie Lisette Reed of Ottawa, Ill., Dec. 15, 1887. A daughter was born to them.

[Thos. P. Kane, *The Romance and Tragedy of Banking,* I (1922), 187–214, is an excellent study of Eckels's service as comptroller by his secretary in that period. See also John G. Heinberg, *The Office of the Comptroller of the Currency* (1926); Francis M. Huston, *Financing an Empire: Hist. of Banking in Ill.,* IV (1926), 156 ff.; *The Ann. Report of the Comptroller of the Currency,* 1893–98; *Chicago Daily Tribune, Chicago Daily News,* Apr. 15, 1907.]

W. T. U.

ECKERT, THOMAS THOMPSON (Apr. 23, 1825–Oct. 20, 1910), telegrapher, was born at St. Clairsville, Ohio, and spent his boyhood on his father's farm, at the same time receiving a common-school education. Catching the enthusiasm for the telegraph at an early age, he went to Wheeling, W. Va., hoping to enter a newly opened telegraph office there. Failing in this he went to New York, after many difficulties, and learned telegraphy in the office of the Morse Telegraph Company. He was next employed by the Wade Telegraph Company on their line between Pittsburgh and Chicago. In 1849 he was appointed postmaster at Wooster, Ohio, but still retained his position with the telegraph company. In 1852 he was made superintendent of the Pittsburgh and Chicago branch line of the Union Telegraph Company, which position he held, with extended jurisdiction, when the line became part of the Western Union Telegraph Company in 1856. In 1859 he resigned to become superintendent of a gold-mining company in Montgomery County, N. C., where he stayed until the outbreak of the Civil War. He went to Cincinnati, Ohio, as head of the United States military telegraph at that place, but in 1862 was called to Washington, D. C., as superintendent of military telegraph, Department of the Potomac, and, with the rank of captain and assistant quartermaster, accompanied Maj.-Gen. McClellan to the Peninsula. In September of the same year he was appointed general superintendent of military telegraph, with the rank of major, and established headquarters in the War Department. In 1864 he was breveted lieutenant-colonel, then colonel, and lastly (Mar. 13, 1865), brigadier-general of volunteers, "for meritorious and distinguished services." On July 27, 1866, Eckert was made assistant secretary of war, resigning Feb. 28, 1867. He had a distinguished war record, always commanded the full confidence of President Lincoln and Secretary Stanton, and was intrusted with military and state secrets. On several occasions he was charged with special commissions of the utmost importance.

Upon resigning from the government service he accepted the position as general superintendent of the eastern division of the Western Union Telegraph Company, which he held until 1875. His strong personality and diplomacy were shown by the manner in which he handled, in 1870, the threatened universal strike of the telegraphers' Protective League, which would have tied up the railways and paralyzed business in general. In 1875 Jay Gould and his associates gained control of the Atlantic & Pacific Telegraph Company and began to compete with the Western Union. Eckert was appointed president of the Atlantic & Pacific and remained as such until 1881, when the company was sold to the Western Union. Gould, however, soon organized another competing company, the American Union Telegraph, and retained Eckert's services as president. This position he held until Gould ended the rivalry by purchasing control of the Western Union. Eckert was vice-president and general manager of the Western Union until 1893, when he was elected president, retained this position until 1900 when he was made chairman of the board of directors, and served in the latter capacity almost until his death. He was also a director in several other corporations. He died at his summer home in Long Branch, N. J., after a long illness. He was survived by two sons; his wife, Emma D. Whitney of Wooster, Ohio, had died in 1868.

Eckert was a pioneer on the administrative side of the telegraph to almost as great an extent as was Morse on the inventive side. A man of great aggressiveness and vigor and a born leader, he organized the government telegraph during the Civil War so that it was of real use, and built up a staff of associates, many of whom stayed with him in later activities. Jay Gould recognized him as a force he needed and shifted him from company to company according to the exigencies of the situation. This made him a leading figure in the struggle between ambitious companies for the telegraphic control of the country. As a man, he had qualities which endeared him to his friends and subordinates.

[*Official Records (Army)*, 1, 2, 3, ser.; D. H. Bates, *Lincoln in the Telegraph Office: Recollections of the U. S. Mil. Telegraph Corps during the Civil War* (1907); *Who's Who in America*, 1910–11; *Electrical Rev. and Western Electrician*, Oct. 29, 1910; *Jour. of the Telegraph*, Nov. 20, 1910.] J.H.F.

ECKFORD, HENRY (Mar. 12, 1775–Nov. 12, 1832), marine architect, and shipbuilder, was born at Irvine, Scotland, the son of John and Janet (Black) Eckford. At the age of sixteen he went to Quebec, Canada, and began studying the principles of ship designing in the yards of his uncle, John Black. After five years of such schooling he settled in New York City, where he soon began shipbuilding on his own account. At the opening of the nineteenth century his yards were on the Long Island side of the East River, near the Brooklyn Navy Yard. Because of the abundance and accessibility of timber, American ships could be built for $35 a ton, as against $50 in England, and $60 in France. Even without the aid of the discriminating laws enacted by Congress, American shipbuilders had a clear advantage. Eckford's ships came to be known for their qualities of strength and speed. The most noticeable change that he brought about in designing was the reduction in the size of the stern frames, but there were also many alterations in the details of the rigging. It was his custom to question the captains of his ships on their return from voyages, learning thus what the behavior of the vessels had been in various circumstances and taking advantage of the knowledge so obtained in planning his next ship. His business was prospering when the War of 1812 came on. After the United States navy decided to build war vessels on Lake Ontario, Eckford supervised the work. The sloop-of-war *Madison*, 24 guns, was constructed by him within forty days from the cutting of the timber in the forests. After the war he returned to New York. During the Monroe administration he was appointed naval constructor at the Brooklyn Navy Yard, and held this office for three years, 1817–20, the *Ohio* and five other line-of-battle ships being constructed on his models. There is no doubt that J. Fenimore Cooper in paying tribute to Eckford's genius and resourcefulness as a naval constructor (see *History of the Navy of the United States of America*, 1839, II, 449) voiced a prevalent opinion. He resigned because of differences among some of the Navy Department officials. Resuming work in his own yards, he built the *Robert Fulton,* which made the first successful voyage by steam from New York to New Orleans and Havana (1822) and after conversion into a sailing vessel made the swiftest sloop-of-war in the Brazilian navy; and frigates for Brazil, Colombia, Peru, and Chile. During the Jackson administration he submitted, at the request of the president, a plan for the reorganization of the navy.

In the twenties Eckford became keenly interested in New York Democratic politics. He invested money in the *National Advocate* and in the campaign of Crawford for the presidency (1824) he controlled that journal, in association with Matthew L. Davis and Jacob Barker (see *Statement of Facts Relative to the Conduct of Henry Eckford, Esq., as Connected with the National Advocate,* by Mordecai M. Noah, New York, 1824). On Apr. 13, 1799, Eckford was married to Marion, daughter of Joseph and Miriam (Dorlon) Bedell. He bought a country estate on Manhattan Island (between Sixth and Eighth Avenues, 21st and 24th Sts., New York City), and there entertained among others, James E. De Kay, Fitz-Greene Halleck, Joseph Rodman Drake [*qq.v*], and kindred spirits. One of his daughters was married to Drake and another to De Kay.

In Eckford's later years the failure of an insurance company in which he was interested took away a large part of his fortune. The last ship that he built was a corvette for the Sultan of Turkey. Aboard this ship, commanded by Commodore George Colman De Kay [*q.v.*], Eckford sailed to Turkey, where he was placed in charge of naval construction, and there, while organizing a navy yard, he died.

[G. W. Sheldon, "Old Shipbuilders of N. Y.," in *Harper's Mag.,* July 1882; and S. G. W. Benjamin, "The Evolution of the American Yacht," in the *Century Mag.,* July 1882; Jas. G. Wilson, *The Life and Letters of Fitz-Greene Halleck* (1869); J. H. Morrison, *Hist. of N. Y. Ship Yards* (1909); Frederick Hudson, *Journalism in the U. S., 1680–1872* (1873); T. H. S. Hamersley, *Gen. Reg. U. S. Navy 1782–1882* (1882); J. E. De Kay, "The Book of the Children of De Kay" (1838), MS. in Lib. of Cong. For additional information see I. C. Pray, *Memoirs of Jas. Gordon Bennett and his Times* (1855). A portrait of Eckford is owned by the Long Island Hist. Soc.]

W. B. S—w.

ECKSTEIN, JOHN (*c.* 1750–*c.* 1817), painter, sculptor, and engraver, was born in Germany, probably in Mecklenburg, about the middle of the eighteenth century, and was active in Potsdam after about 1772. In 1786 he made a death-mask and a plaster bust of Frederick the Great, and in the exhibitions of the Berlin Academy of that year, of 1788, and of 1791, was represented by an equestrian statue of Frederick, in imperial Roman costume. About the year 1794 he settled in Philadelphia, where he resided until 1817. He described himself variously in the city directories as "limner," "engraver," and "merchant," and the directory for 1797 lists John Eckstein & Son as "statuaries." Eckstein was one of the original members of the Columbian Society of Artists, at whose exhibitions he showed examples of modeling, and was also an associate of the Pennsylvania Academy of the Fine Arts. While in Philadelphia, he engraved in stipple several portraits and a design for a "Monument of General Washington" which he proposed for erection—one of the first public suggestions for such a memorial of the first president of the United States. In his "Proposals" for publishing this design (*Poulson's American Daily Advertiser,* Philadelphia, Feb. 19, 21, and 24, 1806), the artist referred to himself as "formerly historical painter and statuary to the King of Prussia." For the third edition of Freneau's *Poems* (Philadelphia, 1809), he engraved frontispieces for the two volumes. They are decidedly of the mixed style, but are full of artistic feeling. In 1812 he exhibited at the Academy Exhibition, in Philadelphia, a model for an equestrian statue of Washington, and in 1813, a "model in burnt clay," entitled "Genius of America." Thomas Sully wrote of Eckstein that he "was a thoroughgoing drudge in the arts. He could do you a picture in still life—history—landscape—portrait—he could model—cut a head in marble—or anything you please. . . . I found him when I removed to Philadelphia [1800] an old man, and he has been dead many years" (Dunlap, *post,* edition of 1918, p. 292). Eckstein's name was apparently dropped from the city directories after 1817 and the exhibition catalogues of the Pennsylvania Academy of the Fine Arts state that he died in that year, although according to Stauffer (*post*) he "was painting and engraving as late as 1822."

[Wm. Dunlap, *A Hist. of the Rise and Progress of the Arts of Design in the U. S.* (1834; rev. ed., 1918); D. M. Stauffer, *American Engravers upon Copper and Steel* (1907); Michael Bryan, *Dict. of Painters and Engravers, Biographical and Critical* (1902); Ulrich Thieme and Felix Becker, *Allgemeines Lexikon der Bildenden Künstler,* X (1914), 331–32.]

J. J.

EDDIS, WILLIAM (fl. 1769–1777), Maryland Loyalist, emerged from years of obscurity during which he had a passion for the drama and experienced certain disappointments, to find in Robert Eden [*q.v.*], governor of Maryland, a patron and benefactor. After a stormy voyage from an English port, he arrived at Annapolis on Sept. 3, 1769, and immediately assumed the duties of secretary to the governor. The following June he was joined by his wife and young son, Eden Eddis. As secretary he acquired an intimate knowledge of the province and as a deeply interested spectator he watched closely the progress of events leading to the Revolution and through its early stages. He traveled on the Eastern Shore and to the back woods of the Western Shore. With the governor he visited many of the leading families. He had an artistic temperament and a fluent pen. From what he saw and heard he wrote letters to friends in England, which were published in London in 1792 under the title *Letters from America, Historical and Descriptive; Comprising Occurrences from 1769, to 1777 Inclusive.* They cover a wide range of subjects, including the personality of the governor, his daily custom, the political disposition of the people, sumptuous fare, rude construction of houses in the back country, the elegance and culture of many of the women, marriage ceremonies, social events, the theatre, horse-racing, servants and the conditions under which they lived, industrial resources and progress, waste of timber, prices, and conditions retarding the growth of towns. In 1772 Eddis was appointed a commissioner of the loan office. He also held the office of surveyor of the customs at Annapolis.

Prospering under the governor's favor, he was anxious for the entire repeal of the Townshend revenue acts in order that cordial relations between the colonists and the mother country might be restored. He did not deny that the grievances of the colonists were genuine but contended that the measures adopted to obtain redress were not justified on "principles of reason or sound policy." He made an appeal for "common sense and common equity" in a communication to the *Maryland Gazette* (Annapolis) which was published Feb. 16, 1775, over the signature, "A Friend to Amity," and reprinted in other colonies. On the departure of his wife and son for England, in September 1775, Eddis became one of the family of Gov. Eden, who advised him to remain as long as the proprietary government was in any degree acknowledged and continued. When summoned before the committee of observation, in June 1776, to give security for his behavior or leave the province, he declared that such security was incompatible with his oath of office. The committee proposed to give him only a few weeks to remain, but the adjustment of accounts and closing out of his business with the loan office occupied him until the last day of May 1777. License for his departure was granted by the Council of the State of Maryland, June 3, 1777. With his arrival in London, Dec. 27, the record of his career is lost, although his grandson, Eden Upton Eddis, was a distinguished portrait-painter.

[Nearly all that is known of Eddis is contained in his *Letters from America*, etc. (1792).] N.D.M.

EDDY, DANIEL CLARKE (May 21, 1823–July 26, 1896), Baptist clergyman, author, was born in Salem, Mass., the younger of the two sons of Daniel and Martha (Honeycomb) Eddy. In 1842, on his reception into the Baptist church, he decided to become a minister. After attending the New Hampshire Theological Institution for several years, he was installed, Jan. 2, 1846, as pastor of the First Baptist Church of Lowell, Mass., which flourished under his vigorous, youthful leadership. On Apr. 9, 1846, he married Elizabeth Stone of Salem, who with two of their four children survived him. In 1850, to recover from an illness, he visited Europe. Years later he made two other excursions to Europe, North Africa, and Palestine. In 1849–50 he published a hortatory volume entitled *The Young Man's Friend.* It sold well, establishing Eddy's reputation in evangelical circles as a sage adviser of the young, and thereafter he gave much of his time to authorship, producing a number of devotional, missionary, ethical, and travel books. In substance his books are thin and commonplace, but he wrote pleasantly, and for many years he was one of the most popular authors in his denomination. Eddy was the sort of man to whom the Know-Nothing party made an irresistible appeal. He preached its principles in church and out, was deep in its conclaves, and when the Know-Nothings carried the Massachusetts election of 1854 he was one of the horde of cracker-box politicians who were swept into the General Court. In the confusion he was elected speaker of the House. In his speech of acceptance he acknowledged that he was ignorant of parliamentary law and usage, and throughout the session the fact was painfully evident. The next election retired him to private life. In 1856 he left Lowell to become pastor of the Harvard Street Baptist Church in Boston. Later he ministered to Baptist congregations in Philadelphia (Tabernacle Church), Boston, Fall River, Boston again, and Hyde Park. In 1876 he was candidate for lieutenant-governor on the Prohibition ticket. In 1881 he was called to the First Baptist Church of Brooklyn, N. Y., where he remained for the rest of his life. He was moderator for four successive terms of the Long Island Baptist Association and served as a president of the Church Extension Society. As pastor and preacher he was much esteemed. Intellectually, however, he did not rise much above his class. He was a friend of the negro and of temperance, but he denounced the novels of Charles Dickens as "tending to badness" and was vociferously intolerant of Catholics, Unitarians, and "higher critics." He died at Cottage City on Martha's Vineyard after an illness of a year.

[*The Eddy Family* (2nd ed., 1884); *Vital Records of Salem, Mass., to 1850,* vols. I and III (1916–24); *Boston Transcript* and *Brooklyn Daily Eagle,* July 27, 1896; *Salem Daily Gazette,* July 29, 1896; *The Examiner,* July 30, 1896; G. H. Haynes, "A Know-Nothing Legislature," *Ann. Report Am. Hist. Asso., 1896* (1897), I, 175–87.] G. H. G.

EDDY, HENRY TURNER (June 9, 1844–Dec. 11, 1921), mathematician, physicist, was born at Stoughton, Mass., the eldest son of Henry Eddy, a Congregational minister, physician, farmer, and inventor, and of Sarah (Torrey) Eddy, a graduate of Mount Holyoke Seminary (now College) where she taught mathematics for three years. In his boyhood Henry Turner Eddy excelled in mental arithmetic, constructed a mechanical model illustrating a cubic algebraic equation, and was interested in birds. He was earnestly religious and prayerful, and lived a sheltered life on the farm where industry was insisted upon and where sports met with no encouragement. While a student at Yale College, from which he was graduated in 1867, he was interested in music and was a member of a church choir, the chapel choir, and the Yale Glee Club. As an undergraduate he received three first prizes and a gold medal in mathematics, a first prize in astronomy, and was elected to Phi Beta Kappa.

After graduation he studied civil engineering in the Sheffield Scientific School and then, since he was not attracted by other professions and his associations were all educational, turned naturally to teaching. After serving one year at the University of Tennessee, he became in 1869 assistant professor of mathematics and civil engineering in Cornell University, acted for a time as head of the department, and received there the degrees of C. E. and Ph.D. In 1873 he went to Princeton as adjunct professor of mathematics and the following year joined the faculty of the University of Cincinnati where he remained for sixteen years as professor of mathematics, astronomy, and civil engineering, being dean of the academic faculty from 1874 to 1877 and also from 1884 to 1889. The year 1879–80 was spent abroad in study. In 1890 he was the acting president and president-elect of the University. From 1891 to 1894 he was president of the Rose Polytechnic Institute. He then went to the University of Minnesota as professor of engineering and mechanics, became dean of the graduate school in 1906 and also, in 1907, head of the department of mathematics and mechanics in the college of engineering. After retirement in 1912 he spent several years on a study of the properties and stresses in reinforced concrete floor slabs. He contributed most by his discerning application of the methods of mathematical physics to the solution of engineering problems. His published writings include: *A Treatise on the Principles and Applications of Analytic Geometry* (1874), *New Constructions in Graphical Statics* (1877), *Thermodynamics* (1879), *Neue Konstructionen aus der graphischen Statik* (1880), *Maximum Stresses under Concentrated Loads* (1890), *The Theory of the Flexure and Strength of Rectangular Flat Plates applied to Reinforced Concrete Floor Slabs* (1913), and numerous papers in scientific journals.

Eddy was married on Jan. 4, 1870, to Sebella Elizabeth Taylor of New Haven, Conn., who died Sept. 3, 1921. They had one son and four daughters. He was a man of quiet scholarly tastes and regularly worked late into the night over abstruse problems in mathematical physics. He had a splendid physique, was courtly in bearing, genial in his intercourse, firm in his convictions, and always an inspiration to his associates who constantly sought his counsel because of his wide, accurate knowledge and sound judgment. He helped many young men in special courses outside the class room and for years was an indefatigable leader of a group of faculty members engaged in regular advanced study. He was a member of the leading scientific and education societies of the country and from time to time held chief offices in several of them. He was a deacon of the First Congregational Church in Minneapolis, a director of St. Anthony Falls Bank, the Pillsbury House Settlement, and the Barnard-Cope Manufacturing Company.

[*Yale Univ. Obit. Record,* 1921–22; *Minneapolis Journal,* Dec. 12, 1921; *Report of the Trigintennial Meeting . . . Class of 1867, Yale* (1897); *Supplementary Record of the Class of 1867 in Yale Coll.* (1912); a copy of a biographical article by Eddy's colleague Prof. A. E. Haynes in the *Minn. Engineer,* Mar. 1912 with margin notes made by Eddy himself; letters from his brother Willard Eddy and his daughter Ruth Eddy Keyes; personal acquaintance.] J. Z.

EDDY, MARY MORSE BAKER (July 16, 1821–Dec. 3, 1910), founder of the Christian Science Church, was a product of New England. She was born on a hillside farm in New Hampshire; she traced her descent from English settlers in Massachusetts in the seventeenth century; and she found her inspiration and her first followers among people who sprang from the same racial stock as herself. She was the youngest of six children born to Mark Baker and his wife Abigail Barnard Ambrose, daughter of Nathaniel Ambrose of Pembroke, all belonging to plain yeoman stock. According to tradition, Mark Baker was a shrewd, hard-working farmer, somewhat self-assertive, but honest and pious. The farm which he cultivated and on which Mary was born, lay in the village of Bow; but he gave up the attempt to make his hillside acres productive when Mary was fifteen, and moved to Sanbornton Bridge (now Tilton). She is described as a delicate child, dainty and rather fragile in appearance, and subject to hysterical seizures (Georgine Milmine in *McClure's Magazine*, January 1907). Just what pathological conditions may have caused this hysteria can now only be conjectured. That the child suffered from some nervous ailment seems clear; but that she made the most of it when her will was crossed seems equally clear. At her best she was bright and winsome; and as the youngest member of the family she was treated with indulgence. Inevitably she became an object of interest to herself and to village folk. She gave herself little airs as one to whom consideration was due; and she rather enjoyed the distinction which delicate health gave. She was described by elderly folk who remembered her as fair of face, with wavy brown hair (*Ibid.*). Her expressive eyes, shaded by long lashes, reflected her moods and remained indeed throughout her life her greatest charm.

Mary's education was desultory. She said in later years that her father kept her out of school a great deal, believing her brain too large for her body. She read much, however, and even, according to her own statement, studied Hebrew, Greek and Latin under the tutelage of her brother Albert (*Retrospection and Introspection*, p. 10, edition of 1898). There is nothing in her writings to suggest that she progressed far in the study of languages, ancient or modern; and despite her statement that she was familiar with Murray's *Grammar* at the age of ten, she exhibited little regard for syntax to the end of her days. Her early letters reveal a characteristic that persisted throughout life—a disposition to see things through the prism of her emotions and to embroider the humdrum facts of everyday life. In a God-fearing household like that of Mark Baker, religious training was as much a part of the daily regimen as eating and drinking. Mary's experience differed in no wise from that of the average New England girl of the time. She was received into membership in the Tilton Congregational Church at the age of seventeen, after some doubts had been expressed of her soundness on doctrinal points. In New England at this time there were currents of thought that must have impinged upon her mind directly or indirectly. The transcendental movement was in full swing as she grew to womanhood. Within a few miles of her home were colonies of Shakers whose strange ideas and practises were matter of common talk. Believers in Spiritualism were numerous in these frontier areas of New England. Mesmerism too was much discussed. The family physician of the Bakers dabbled in mesmerism and even tried the effect of mental suggestion upon Mary Baker for the relief of her hysteria (*McClure's Magazine*, January 1907). A sensitive girl might well have fancied that she heard mysterious voices (*Retrospection and Introspection*, pp. 7–9) and felt herself surrounded by occult forces which she could not define or understand.

In December 1843 Mary Baker married George Washington Glover, a friend of her elder brother, who had removed to Charleston, S. C., and there become a contractor and builder. After a few brief months of married life he fell a victim to "bilious fever" and died in Wilmington, N. C. (*Wilmington Chronicle*, July 3, 1844), leaving her dependent upon the charity of the local lodge of Masons. With their aid she returned to her old home, where she gave birth, in September 1844, to her only son George. Unhappy years followed. Ill-health, slender means, and a sense of humiliating dependence upon relatives, left her in no enviable position. For a time she taught school, with indifferent success. She had indeed no training for self-support, and more and more she gave way to hopeless inertia, living sometimes with her married sister Abigail and sometimes in her father's house. She soon became a chronic invalid, suffering—so her official biographer states—from "a spinal weakness which caused spasmodic seizures, followed by prostration which amounted to a complete nervous collapse" (Sibyl Wilbur, *The Life of Mary Baker Eddy*, edition of 1929, p. 54). At such times her father would take her in his arms and rock her to sleep like a tired child. The practical Abigail had a huge cradle made, which the man-of-all-work or some village boy would keep in gentle motion. In 1849 Mary lost her mother and a year later saw the vacant place occupied by a step-mother. Then her four-year old son was sent away to live with her former nurse who had married and moved to North Groton, N. H., and the young widow was left to her own devices.

Release from this unhappy period of widowhood came in 1853 when she married a relative of the second Mrs. Baker, Dr. Daniel Patterson, an itinerant dentist and homeopathist. They first took up their abode in Franklin, but soon moved to North Groton and finally to Rumney—little New Hampshire villages, where for nine years

Eddy

they almost disappear from view. That they lived in indigent circumstances is clear. Patterson was frequently absent, leaving his wife to a lonely and cheerless existence. In these long years she was often ill; and when in 1862 Patterson injudiciously visited the battlefield of Bull Run, fell into the hands of the Confederates, and was sent to Libby Prison, she returned to her sister's home in Sanbornton Bridge, a helpless invalid. Two or three months in a sanitorium did little for her, and she determined to carry out an earlier purpose and consult Dr. Phineas Parkhurst Quimby [*q.v.*] of Portland, Me., who had acquired a more than local fame by his cures. In October 1862 she presented herself at his office, a rather pitiful figure. Three weeks later, in a letter published in the *Portland Courier,* Nov. 7, 1862, she declared that by virtue of the great principle discovered by Dr. Quimby, who "speaks as never man spoke and heals as never man healed since Christ," she was on the highway to complete health. She returned to her sister's an ardent disciple of Quimby (letters to Quimby, printed in Horatio W. Dresser's *The Quimby Manuscripts,* edition of 1921, pp. 146–59). Several times during the following year, she wrote to him and received absent treatment for various small ills. The death of Quimby in 1866 caused her deep distress and evoked an affectionate tribute in verse, which was printed in a Lynn newspaper (*Ibid.,* pp. 163–64).

Meantime her husband had reappeared and she joined him in Lynn, Mass., where he opened a dentist's office; but they separated in the summer of 1866, and seven years later Mrs. Patterson secured a divorce on the ground of desertion, with permission to resume her former name, Mary M. Glover. She was now (in 1866) forty-five years of age. She was in destitute circumstances; she had lost her father; she was estranged from her sister; she had not seen her son for many years; she was not in good health; she had no certain means of earning a livelihood; and she had no friends to whom she could turn for help. Referring to these years in after life, she wrote: "I then withdrew from society about three years,—to ponder my mission, to search the Scriptures, to find the Science of Mind" (*Retrospection and Introspection,* p. 29). Glimpses here and there behind the curtain which she let fall over these years reveal that she resided in at least five different towns in eastern Massachusetts and found domicile in seven families in turn (affidavits and depositions printed in *McClure's Magazine,* April 1907). From time to time she sought a livelihood by teaching and practising what she called a new system of healing. Her pupils and patients seem to have been chiefly among Spiritualists. Four of the seven households in which she lived professed Spiritualism and one of her first advertisements appeared in a Spiritualist publication (the *Banner of Light,* July 4, 1868). She was still loyal to Quimby and professed no higher purpose than to disseminate his teachings, making use of copies of one of his manuscripts which she called "The Science of Man" (for the origin of these copies see statement of George Quimby in H. W. Dresser's *The Quimby Manuscripts,* pp. 437–38). She was wont to impress people by intimating that she was writing a book; and as early as 1866 she endeavored to find a publisher for a manuscript which may have been a first draft of *Science and Health* (*McClure's Magazine,* April 1907).

On her return to Lynn in 1870, she took into partnership an engaging young man by the name of Richard Kennedy. They rented an apartment of five rooms which served for offices and lodgings, and he hung out his shingle as Dr. Kennedy. Despite his youth—he was barely of age—and want of credentials, he soon enjoyed a thriving practise, while his partner devoted herself to teaching and writing. It was a profitable alliance while it lasted. When they separated two years later, Mrs. Glover had accumulated enough capital to buy the two-and-a-half story house at 8 Broad Street which later became a veritable shrine for her followers. Her first students paid a hundred dollars for their lessons. Subsequently the tuition for twelve lessons was raised to three hundred dollars. This fee, she afterward said, greatly troubled her; but "a strange providence" finally led her to accept it (*Retrospection and Introspection,* p. 61).

Gradually Mrs. Glover lost her sense of dependence upon Quimby and his teachings. The manuscripts which she put into the hands of her students no longer bore his name but contained matter of her own composition (*McClure's Magazine,* May 1907). Little by little, with infinite effort, in her third-floor study under the roof, she was trying to give coherent expression to the "metaphysical" system which she believed would mark an epoch in religious thought and practise. Except for her indomitable will, the task would have been beyond her powers, for she was essentially an ignorant woman—ignorant not only of the very metaphysical terms which she employed, but of some of the elementary facts of human anatomy and physiology and of the requirements of correct usage in composition. Yet few manuscripts have had a more remarkable influence upon American religious history than that which finally found its way into print in

1875 under the title *Science and Health.* Only a thousand copies were printed and these were paid for in advance by two of the author's students (*Ibid.*). Eternal Mind, she wrote in her first chapter, is the source of all being. There is no matter. The dualism of mind and matter is an error. What the five senses report are only beliefs of mortal mind. "Disease is caused by mind alone" (p. 334). Science is the wisdom of the Eternal Mind revealed through Jesus Christ, who taught the power of Mind (*i.e.* Truth, God, Spirit) to overcome the illusions of sin, sickness, and death. Hence the appropriateness of calling metaphysical science "Christian Science." The mission of the metaphysical healer is to put an end to the illusory conflict of mind and body by dispelling the belief in disease and so bringing the patient into harmony with Truth. "The basis of all disease is error or belief; destroy the belief and the sick will recover" (p. 418). "You can prevent or cure scrofula, hereditary disease, etc., in just the ratio you expel from mind a belief in the transmission of disease, and destroy its mental images" (p. 398). Moreover, "Healing the sick through mind instead of matter, enables us to heal the absent as well as the present" (p. 348). In subsequent editions, this doctrine is given more pointed application. "We must understand that the cause and cure of all disease rest with the mind, and address ourselves to the task of preventing the images of disease taking form in thought and effacing the forms of disease in the mind" (edition of 1883, p. 139). "If the auditory nerve is destroyed and the optic nerve paralyzed, that need not occasion deafness and blindness, for mortal mind must say, I am deaf and blind, and believe it, to make it so" (p. 159). "Recollect it is not the body, but mortal mind, that says food is undigested, that the gastric juices, the nervous tissues, and mucous membrane are diseased" (p. 202). "Mind constructs the body, and with its own materials instead of matter; hence no broken bones or dislocations can occur" (p. 220).

Here is the essence of the gospel of Mary Baker Glover and the key to her system of therapeutics. That she owed much to Quimby cannot now be doubted, in the light of his published manuscripts (H. W. Dresser, *The Quimby Manuscripts,* edition of 1921). It is highly probable, however, that she owed much also to the writings of Warren Felt Evans [*q.v.*], who had been a pupil of Quimby and who had published *The Mental-Cure* as early as 1869. It remains true, nevertheless, that in spite of her literary helplessness, her tiresome reiterations, and her faulty logic, she gave a certain propulsive force to her thought which both Quimby and Evans lacked. The glowing assurance that mind working in harmony with the Eternal could triumph over bodily infirmities often brought comfort and faith where mere logic would not convince. In later years, she and her followers laid emphasis on the essential unreality of evil, holding that even sin was primarily wrong thinking (article on "Christian Science" by C. B. Smith in *The Encyclopedia Americana,* VI, 613). Christian Science thus appeared as a spiritually educative force, "interpreting and demonstrating the divine Principle and rule of universal harmony" (Mrs. Eddy, *Rudimental Divine Science*). In this aspect it made a strong appeal to those who felt the need of a sustaining faith in eternal goodness.

It is significant of her compelling personality that Mrs. Glover could always find men and women to become willing servitors in her little court, yet no queen could have been more arbitrary or more difficult to serve. She soon found a substitute for Kennedy in Daniel H. Spofford, who became her ardent admirer and devoted disciple and her first sales-manager. On New Year's Day 1877, Mrs. Glover startled Spofford and her other followers by marrying a new recruit, Asa Gilbert Eddy. She was then in her fifty-sixth year. Eddy was a simple soul of humble origin, capable of a sort of animal-like devotion, but possessed of limited intelligence. Even his bride wrote of his "latent" noble qualities of mind and heart (*McClure's Magazine,* July 1907). Within a year Spofford went into exile in disgrace, for the Christian Scientists' Association notified him that he had been expelled for "immorality." What Mrs. Eddy meant by immorality is best explained by a passage in the second edition (1878) of *Science and Health.* This rare "Noah's Ark" edition, of which only two hundred copies were hastily printed, consisted of two chapters from the first edition and of three new chapters, of which that on mesmerism is most significant. In it the author gave public utterance for the first time to that belief in mental malpractise which offers such a strange contrast to her fundamental tenets. She had come firmly to believe in malicious animal magnetism ("M.A.M."), a mental influence which evil-minded persons could exert, to produce disease or misfortune in others. The doctrine had particular application to Spofford and Kennedy, who, she believed, possessed the power to do her and her cause irreparable harm. Kennedy became in her overwrought imagination a "mental assassin" capable of the darkest crimes. Her prose style never rose to greater heights than in the chapter on "Demonology," in the third edition (1881) of *Science and Health,* when she denounced "this Nero of today." To counteract this baleful influence she devised a method of treatment which became a regular routine for her household in later years. Singly or in groups the inmates would set their minds upon warding off the evil that she vaguely apprehended or specifically mentioned. (These "watches" are described in minute detail by Adam H. Dickey in his *Memoirs of Mary Baker Eddy,* 1927, pp. 45, 107, 123–24.)

The years of Mrs. Eddy's married life with her third husband can hardly be described as happy, nor her mental outlook as generous and charitable. Between 1877 and 1879 she was involved in several litigations both as plaintiff and defendant. Three times in 1878 she brought suit to recover funds which she alleged had been wrongfully withheld. Two of these were decided against her. She was sued by a former student and compelled to pay the referee's award for secretarial and other services rendered by this student. She countenanced at least the strange suit brought by another student against Spofford for injuries sustained from Spofford's practise of malicious magnetism. This suit never came to trial (*McClure's Magazine,* May, July 1907). When Asa Eddy's health began to fail, his wife was certain that he was also a victim of malicious animal magnetism. His condition became so serious after their removal to Boston, however, that, not trusting to her own therapy, she called in a physician, who reported the patient as suffering from an organic disease of the heart. On June 3, 1882, Asa Eddy died of this malady, according to an autopsy performed by this same physician, at Mrs. Eddy's request. In an interview published in the *Boston Post,* June 5, 1882, however, she declared that her husband had died of "mesmeric poisoning" mentally administered by one of her former students, "a malpractitioner" who had been heard to say that "he would follow us to the grave." Had she herself treated her husband in time, she averred, she could have saved his life; but "after a certain amount of the mesmeric poison has been administered it cannot be averted." This malpractitioner was probably Edward J. Arens, whom Asa Eddy had denounced in a preface to the third edition of *Science and Health* as "a certain man" who was publishing parts of the book in a pamphlet of his own. In 1883 Mrs. Eddy brought action against Arens for infringing her copyright, and won her case.

Though Mrs. Eddy did not at first desire an organization to support the new faith (*Science and Health,* 1875, pp. 166–67), she yielded to practical exigencies. The informal group of students who called themselves Christian Scientists in 1875 formed "The Christian Scientists' Association" in 1876; and with her active support they sought and secured a charter as "The Church of Christ, Scientist," Aug. 23, 1879. For many years the membership was small, so small that the Lynn meetings were held in private houses, and it was weakened in October 1881 by the withdrawal of eight prominent leaders who stated that they could no longer follow Mrs. Eddy, because of her "frequent ebullitions of temper, love of money, and the appearance of hypocrisy" (*McClure's Magazine,* August 1907). Two others withdrew because they "could no longer entertain the subject of mesmerism," which seemed to form the main theme of Mrs. Eddy's Sunday talks. Though the faithful remnant indignantly repudiated these charges, Mrs. Eddy found herself a prophet without honor in Lynn and determined to take up her residence in Boston. She had already (1881) secured a charter for another organization, the Massachusetts Metaphysical College, which was to be the training school for practitioners. When she and her husband took up their abode at 569 Columbus Avenue, in the spring of 1882, the college moved with them. In the nine years of its existence, it had no other regular instructor but Mrs. Eddy, and for a short time, her adopted son.

On Apr. 14, 1883, appeared the first number of the *Journal of Christian Science,* a small eight-page publication, with Mary B. Glover Eddy as editor. It not only gave her desire to write free rein, but it carried her influence beyond the confines of New England. It reveals many facets of her interesting personality, for it printed not only her editorials, sermons, and Bible lessons, but her verses, her answers to questions, her acknowledgments of personal gifts, and her caustic replies to critics. But she found the burden heavier than she anticipated, and after a year shifted the responsibility to a succession of unhappy editors, while never allowing control to pass out of her hands. She continued to contribute to its columns and many of her contributions were afterward printed with substantial changes in her *Miscellaneous Writings* (1896). These were not always original productions. She took freely from printed sources without acknowledgment whatever she needed to give pith and point to her thought (*The Christian Science Watchman,* vol. V, 1929. See also Appendix B in E. F. Dakin, *Mrs. Eddy,* ed. of 1930). The "Healing Department" of the *Journal* with its reports of alleged cures undoubtedly won many recruits. Institutes and academies sprang up which became feeders for the Metaphysical College; and every graduate with a diploma became in turn a practitioner and a missionary. In January 1886 the National Christian Science Association was formed and in February a general convention was held in New York.

In this same year appeared a new edition of *Science and Health.* Never content with her handiwork Mrs. Eddy published edition after edition, with various and sundry alterations. This sixteenth edition differed from preceding revisions, however, not merely in general outward form—it was printed in one volume instead of two—but in literary style and content. It had been prepared by Rev. James Henry Wiggin, formerly a Unitarian minister and then employed as literary adviser and editor by the University Press at Cambridge. After her contacts with people of cultivation, Mrs. Eddy had become somewhat conscious of her literary deficiencies; and she never exhibited greater shrewdness than when she brought her manuscript to Wiggin for final revision (Livingston Wright, *How Rev. Wiggin Rewrote Mrs. Eddy's Book,* n.d., reprinted from the New York *World,* Nov. 4, 1906). What Wiggin did was not merely "to defend my grammatical construction," as Mrs. Eddy afterward alleged (*New York American,* Nov. 22, 1906), but to rewrite large portions of the book as only a skilful literary editor could, giving clarity to the thought so far as it could be understood, excising irrelevant matter, and reducing vague forms of expression to simple, idiomatic language. Yet Mrs. Eddy continued to make changes from time to time, and the changes were always a source of profit, for the faithful were always warned to use the latest edition. Her yearly royalties, never less than a dollar a volume, amounted to nearly $19,000 in 1895 (*McClure's Magazine,* April 1908), and could not have fallen short of $50,000 by 1900. In January 1888, the *Journal* announced that Mrs. Eddy had moved into her new house at 385 Commonwealth Avenue, which had been purchased for $40,000.

Already letters printed in the *Journal* and unsigned editorials were suggesting that Mrs. Eddy was "God-sent to the world as much as any character of Sacred Writ" and that perhaps it was left to her to supplement the New Testament and explain the miracles of Jesus. "We are witnessing," said one enthusiastic follower, "the transfer of the Gospel from male to female trust" (sermon reprinted in the *Journal,* April 1889). When Mrs. Eddy appeared in person to address the delegates at the third annual convention of the national association at Chicago June 13, 1888, the entire audience rose to greet her; and after she had finished, scores of believers who had been cured of disease or hoped to be, pressed forward so that they might perchance touch the hem of her garment (letter to the *Boston Traveller,* printed in *McClure's Magazine,* February 1908). She might well have believed that her apotheosis had come.

Signs of dissent in the Boston organization, however, were not wanting. Julius A. Dresser, who had also sat at the feet of Quimby, now pointed out with damaging particularity the indebtedness of Mrs. Eddy to the doctor (*The True History of Mental Science,* 1887). Then a Christian Science practitioner who had attended her own daughter in child-birth was prosecuted for the death of the mother and child; and Mrs. Eddy, thoroughly alarmed, tried to clear her skirts by having the "Committee on Publication" state in a public letter (*Boston Herald,* Apr. 29, 1888), that while the woman had attended her course in obstetrics at the Metaphysical College for a term, she was not fitted to be an *accoucheur* (*sic*). The Christian Science Association, however, came to the defense of the unhappy woman and she was acquitted. These and other incidents shook the faith of some of the Boston Scientists and thirty-six dissenters withdrew from the organization.

Soon after the death of Asa Eddy, there entered into the employ of his widow, Calvin A. Frye, a young machinist from Lawrence, Mass., who had become a Christian Scientist. Of all her many followers he is in many ways the most remarkable. From 1882 until her death, he served her as steward, secretary, bookkeeper, and footman. In July 1888, another individual entered her household who was regarded with some jealousy by the faithful Frye. This was Dr. Ebenezer Johnson Foster, a homeopathic physician of Waterbury, Vt., who had been a student in the Metaphysical College. In November, though he was forty-one years of age, he was formally adopted as a son, taking the name of Ebenezer J. Foster Eddy. "Mother Eddy" was now sixty-eight and in sore need of the sustaining strength of youth. She was tired of students, tired of turmoil, tired of the endless struggle against malicious animal magnetism. In the following spring she transferred her residence to Concord, N. H. "Our dear Mother in God," announced the *Journal* (May 1889), "withdraws herself from our midst and goes up into the Mount for higher communings"; and Mother Eddy further fortified her retreat by issuing Seven Fixed Rules, forbidding the faithful to consult her "verbally or through letters" on matters public or private.

A rude awakening, however, awaited those who fancied that she had withdrawn from active control of the church. It was in these years of retirement that she built the church organization which, next to *Science and Health,* is her most enduring monument.

By a much-criticized financial transaction in 1888, Mrs. Eddy had secured ownership of the lot on Falmouth Street, Boston, which had been acquired as a site for the church by individual gifts (*McClure's Magazine,* March 1908). On September 1, 1892, she conveyed this lot to four trustees, constituting them a perpetual body to be known as the Christian Science Board of Directors, with power to fill vacancies (Deed of Trust, *Church Manual,* 1895). Within five years this board was to build a church edifice costing not less than $50,000 and to maintain regular Christian Science services therein. If the board failed to carry out the terms of the deed, title was to revert to Mary Baker G. Eddy, her heirs and assigns. On Sept. 23, 1892, twelve loyal followers whom she had selected established The First Church of Christ, Scientist, by adopting the rules and by-laws which, she declared, were "impelled by a power not one's own." These twelve with subsequent additions were known as "First Members" and passed upon all candidates for admission. Membership in branch churches did not confer *ipso facto* membership in The Mother Church, nor for that matter did previous membership in the Boston church. There was only one Mother Church. It was officially "The" Mother Church. Branch churches might take the title of First Church of Christ, Scientist, or Second Church of Christ, Scientist, but might not use the article "The" (Art. 12 of By-laws, *Church Manual,* 1895). Here, then, was a national organization made to hand, deriving its powers, its body of doctrine, and its property from a single source.

Mrs. Eddy masked her autocratic authority under the gentle title "Pastor Emeritus"; but she could no more refrain from consolidating her authority by changes in the *Church Manual* than she could desist from revising *Science and Health.* The subsequent history of the Mother Church in her lifetime is written in the steadily expanding by-laws which she dictated. Two other institutions attest her business sagacity: the board of lectureship and the committee on publication. Members of the first were charged with the duty of defending Christian Science against critics and of bearing testimony to the facts pertaining to the life of the Pastor Emeritus. The committee on publication, consisting of one man responsible to the Board of Directors and through it to Mrs. Eddy, was to correct false newspaper articles, and, if need be, bring pressure to bear upon editors who did not yield readily to suggestion. Such a "committee" was to be named in every state of the Union (Dakin's *Mrs. Eddy,* 1929, pp. 259–72, 392–95, contains an excellent account of these institutions).

Whatever may have been Mrs. Eddy's motives for retiring to Concord, it proved to be one of the most sagacious moves in her career. In these long years of absence from the Mother Church—she visited Boston only four times in nineteen years—she escaped the daily contacts with her followers which often brought a degree of disillusionment to them. In retirement she acquired a reputation for saintliness which added immeasurably to her influence. To those who saw her daily, however, she was no saint, but a frail elderly woman pursued by delusions of persecution, forever talking about malicious animal magnetism, and beset by strange superstitions. She was indeed a curiously complex personality, capable of moments of religious exaltation, but capable also of conduct that was unlovely and ruthless, when her will-to-power was crossed. Though she could be gentle and gracious, she cannot fairly be described as unselfish or generous. She often berated Frye like a common scold (E. F. Dakin, *Mrs. Eddy,* ed. of 1930, Appendix A). She evinced no real affection for her son, though she kept up an irregular correspondence with him, had his children vaccinated at her expense, and loaned him considerable sums of money. His illiteracy worried her. "I am even yet too proud to have you come among my society," she wrote in 1898 (N. Y. *World,* Mar. 11, 1907). She crushed possible rivals ruthlessly; and in the case of Mrs. Josephine Woodbury she had to meet a libel suit for a scorching message to the Church on "the Babylonish woman." Only one witness would testify, however, that this outburst was directed specifically against Mrs. Woodbury, who lost her case (see Dakin, *Mrs. Eddy,* Ch. XXII).

Her nocturnal paroxysms, as Foster Eddy called her strange seizures, increased in frequency. At such times either Frye or Foster Eddy would administer a morphine tablet or a physician would be called in to administer a hypodermic (Frye diary, May 3, 4, 1903). From these attacks, nevertheless, she would rise with amazing energy, her mind never more on the alert. Her intimates remarked that some of her most important *coups* followed these seizures. It was out of this tragic experience that another "revelation" came. In the edition of *Science and Health* published in 1905 appeared for the first time the significant statement (p. 464), that, whenever pain too violent for mental treatment occurs, a Scientist may call a surgeon to administer a hypodermic injection. When the pain has ceased, he should "handle his own case mentally." In 1896, after Foster Eddy had been dismissed, Frye became her main support, not only ministering to her personal needs, but acting as confidential secretary, steward, and financial agent. As she grew more feeble with advancing years and a serious disease, she became almost a mythical figure, so that even her directors rarely saw her. Rumors spread that she was in the power of Frye and designing men who were diverting her income to their own use. It was even said that she was dead and that another woman rode behind the drawn curtains of her carriage.

It was these rumors that moved the New York *World* and other newspapers to ascertain the true state of things at Pleasant View. With amazing courage Mrs. Eddy yielded to their importunities, granted an interview, and faced nine reporters on Oct. 30, 1906—a shrinking, pathetic figure. Not satisfied with this achievement, the *World* set on foot the inquiries which eventuated in the suit brought by the "Next Friends"—her son and his daughter and a nephew—to secure the appointment of a receiver of her properties, alleging that she was mentally incapable of managing her affairs and that she was under the control of designing men, naming the chief officials of the church. Thereupon Gen. Frank S. Streeter, counsel for Mrs. Eddy, advised her to execute a deed of trust, placing all her assets in the hands of three trustees. At once Senator William E. Chandler, counsel for the plaintiffs, challenged the competence of Mrs. Eddy to create such a trusteeship. Three masters appointed by the court then examined her to test her sanity, but there the prosecution halted and the defendants settled out of court by liberal financial provisions for the heirs, including Foster Eddy.

These sensational news items appeared in the press just at a time when *McClure's Magazine* was publishing the biography by Georgine Milmine. Greatly perturbed, Mrs. Eddy determined that the church should have a trustworthy newspaper of its own; and eventually she gave her approval of an official biography. The founding of *The Christian Science Monitor* and the publication of Mrs. Sibyl Wilbur O'Brien's *Life of Mary Baker Eddy* followed. One other decision she made: she would leave the place where she had been humiliated and where "M.A.M." was so actively at work. On Sunday, Jan. 28, 1908, preceded by a pilot locomotive for safety's sake, and accompanied by a physician, she took train for Chestnut Hill, where a spacious mansion had been prepared for her. From her carriage she was carried, a mere shadow of her former self, in the arms of a stalwart coachman to an upstairs room in her last domicile (private information).

Her days were now numbered and she knew it (MS. letter to Archibald McLelland, Aug. 18, 1908). For some years she had suffered intensely from a fatal disease, probably gall-stones, and she had sought relief from several Concord physicians at various times (printed statement of A. A. Beauchamp and J. V. Dittemore, Oct. 9, 1928; Frye diary, May 3, 1903). As the disease progressed, only hypodermic injections of morphine would relieve her agony. At Chestnut Hill several Christian Scientists were instructed how to give hypodermics (E. F. Dakin, *Mrs. Eddy*, ed. of 1930, p. 514 note), and she frequently had the services of a regular physician (Frye diary, Aug. 3, 1909). There were times when the pain became unbearable and the Chestnut Hill mansion little better than a "mad-house" (Dickey, *Memoirs, passim;* Frye's diary; the testimony of inmates). In her rational moments Mrs. Eddy was harassed by fears of the growing prestige of Mrs. Augusta Stetson [*q.v.*] in New York. Not less concerned were the directors of the Mother Church to know who would succeed the Pastor Emeritus whose consent was still necessary to every by-law. Mrs. Stetson finally went the way of every rival. At a word from Mrs. Eddy she was expelled from the Mother Church. But the question of succession remained unanswered, when a year later the body of the Pastor Emeritus was borne to its last resting place at Mount Auburn. Three notable achievements survived her: a religious organization with nearly one hundred thousand members, a book of which about four hundred thousand copies had been sold, and an estate appraised at more than two and a half million dollars.

[The most useful source of information in print is still the series of articles by Georgine Milmine in *McClure's Magazine*, 1907–08: "Mary Baker G. Eddy: the Story of her Life and the History of Christian Science." Though sharply critical of Mrs. Eddy, they contain invaluable documentary material. The papers of William E. Chandler in the custody of the New Hampshire Historical Society yield interesting information about the origin and course of the Next Friends' suit. The writer has also been allowed to examine the unique collection of Mr. John V. Dittemore, which contains many unpublished letters of Mrs. Eddy and large portions of the diary of Calvin Frye for the last few years of her life. Her own reminiscences and her official biography have little historical value except as they reveal the impression which Mrs. Eddy desired to make upon her readers. The most impartial and scholarly biography is Edwin F. Dakin's *Mrs. Eddy* (1929), which contains a bibliography of her writings and of the controversial literature about her and her work. A new edition (1930) has additional footnotes and two valuable appendices, one of which contains extracts from the Frye diary.] A. J.

EDDY, THOMAS (Sept. 5, 1758–Sept. 16, 1827), reformer, was the son of James and Mary (Darragh) Eddy of Ireland, who had been Presbyterians in early life, but had joined the Society of Friends before removing to Philadelphia. In this city Thomas Eddy was born. He was apparently influenced even in early youth to serious ideas and unselfish purposes by the religious atmosphere of his home and especially by his association with William Savery, who later became a famous Quaker preacher. His family was of Tory sympathies and Eddy felt the "bitter spirit of persecution" shown by the "Whigs" in Philadelphia after the war. On Mar. 20, 1782, he married Hannah Hartshorne. After experiencing business reverses in various localities he settled in New York City and became successful as an insurance broker. "About 1792," he writes, "the public debt of the United States was funded; this afforded an opportunity for people to speculate in the public funds. In this business I made a good deal of money." He was also successful as an insurance underwriter, and was soon free to devote himself largely to philanthropic activities.

His greatest work as a humanitarian was in the field of prison reform. He became imbued with the progressive ideas of Beccaria, Montesquieu, William Penn, and John Howard. In 1796 he and Gen. Philip John Schuyler journeyed to Philadelphia and examined carefully the penitentiary there (the Walnut Street jail), which then embodied advanced ideas. Eddy and his friends persuaded the New York legislature to authorize two similar penitentiaries in New York. Only one was built at the time, the so-called "Newgate Prison," in Greenwich Village. Thomas Eddy helped superintend the building operations and then acted for several years as inspector and agent of the penitentiary. This prison had no single cells, however, and Eddy soon became convinced that the single-cell system, especially for hardened criminals, was desirable. It had been tried in a small way in England, and in Philadelphia, and Thomas Eddy, by his ardent advocacy of it, aided in its further extension. For more than twenty-five years he devoted himself unsparingly to the reform of prisons and of the penal code in New York. His *Account of the State Prison or Penitentiary House in the City of New York* (1801) is an important document in the history of prison reform. His last great service in this field was to defend and justify the main features of his penitentiary system in 1825 when it was being sharply criticized because of lax administration.

Eddy was apparently interested in or actively associated with most of the progressive movements of his day. He helped DeWitt Clinton initiate and carry through the project of the Erie Canal, and was active in the New York Corresponding Association for the Promotion of Internal Improvement. In 1810 he published "Observations on Canal Navigation" in the *American Medical and Philosophical Register* (N. Y.). He was an active supporter of the New York Hospital and helped to found the Bloomingdale Asylum for the Insane, and wrote *Hints for Introducing an Improved Method of Treating the Insane in the Asylum,* published in 1815. He opposed imprisonment for debt. In 1805 he helped establish a free school for poor children in New York City, which was one of the important steps toward a public school system. He helped found the House of Refuge, the New York Savings Bank, and the New York Bible Society. He was an anti-slavery advocate, and he served on Quaker committees to visit and aid the American Indians. Yet prison reform was his great life-work, and because of his labors in that movement he was sometimes called by his contemporaries, "The John Howard of America."

[S. L. Knapp, *The Life of Thomas Eddy* (1834), an unorganized collection of narrative and eulogy by the author and others, and reprints of the autobiography, correspondence, and reform writings of Eddy; H. E. Barnes, *The Repression of Crime* (1926); W. W. Campbell, *Life and Writings of DeWitt Clinton* (1849); Letter of John W. Francis (on Eddy) in N. Y. Pub. Lib.; brief biographical sketches in the *N. Y. Mirror,* Mar. 8, 1834; Freeman Hunt, *Lives of American Merchants* (1858), I, 329–43.] R. W. K.

EDEBOHLS, GEORGE MICHAEL (May 8, 1853–Aug. 8, 1908), surgeon, was the son of German immigrants, Henry and Catherine (Brull) Edebohls, who came to the United States about 1843. His father, a Hanoverian, was a dairyman in that part of Manhattan known as "Little Germany." As a boy Edebohls attended De La Salle Institute and St. Francis Xavier's College, from which he went to St. John's College, Fordham, N. Y., graduating B.A. in 1871. He then studied medicine at the College of Physicians and Surgeons of Columbia College (M.D. 1875), and for nearly five years thereafter served as a house officer in St. Francis' Hospital, New York City, where he received a wide training and came into close contact with the poor of the East Side. In 1880 he went to Europe intending to study diseases of the eye and ear. He evidently abandoned this idea and occupied his time by filling in the gaps in his theoretical knowledge. On his return he engaged in general practise, but with only moderate success. He then turned his attention to gynecology and in 1887 was appointed gynecologist to St. Francis' Hospital. Possessing a cool head, dextrous fingers and an excellent knowledge of anatomy, he soon earned a reputation as a gynecologist of sound judgment. His minor contributions to medicine were technical. He invented an operating table, a speculum, leg holders, needle holders and other devices. His name will go down to posterity, however, as the originator of Edebohls's operation for Bright's disease, which consisted in exposing the diseased kidneys and stripping off their fibrous coverings or capsules. Though the practise received much unfavorable comment at the time and is now seldom used, the idea underlying it was original and theoretically plausible.

Edebohls's contemporaries held him in high esteem both as a surgeon and as a man. He was tall and erect, grave, dignified and polite, withal somewhat retiring and excessively modest. He disliked controversy, feeling that whatever he contributed to the advance of the medicine of his day should stand or fall on its merits. He was an excellent teacher, presenting his subject clearly and simply. He also wrote well, and in addition to his *Surgical Treatment of Bright's Disease* (1904) contributed freely to the medical literature of his day. On Sept. 19, 1882, he married Barbara Leyendecker, by whom he had several children. While visiting his married daughter in Mexico in 1907 he, with his wife and two sons, contracted typhus fever, of which his eldest son died. The disease is said to have left him in a weakened condition. He died in 1908 of Hodgkin's disease, and was buried at Blauvelt, N. Y., where his father had owned a farm when he was a boy.

[*Who's Who in America*, 1908–09; H. A. Kelly and W. L. Burrage, *Dict. of Am. Medic. Biog.* (1928); *Am. Jour. of Obstetrics*, May 1909; *Deutsche Medizinische Wochenschrift*, vol. XXXIV, 1908, p. 1860.] G. B.

EDEN, CHARLES (1673–Mar. 26, 1722), governor of North Carolina under the Lords Proprietors, 1714–22, used the armorial bearings of the family of Eden of the county palatine of Durham in the North of England. Of the same connection was Sir Robert Eden [*q.v.*], last Royal governor of Maryland. Charles Eden's appointment to the governorship received the approval of Queen Anne at a meeting of the Royal Council on May 18, 1713. It was a year, however, before he came to America, where he was sworn in before the North Carolina Provincial Council "holden at ye house of Capt. John Hecklefield in Little River on ffriday the 28th day of May, Ano. Dom. 1714." Gov. Eden was deeply interested in the religious development of the province, and on Jan. 3, 1715, was chosen a vestryman of "the Eastern Parish of Chowan Precinct" (still existing under the name of St. Paul's Parish) on Queen Anne's Creek. Under the constitution or "Grand Model" framed for the government of Carolina by John Locke, several grades of society were created, the highest title of nobility being "Landgrave." At a meeting of the Lords Proprietors held at St. James's Palace on Feb. 19, 1718, Eden was made a landgrave, being the last person ever to receive that title. His reputation suffered somewhat at one time during his administration from his reported leniency toward the ex-pirate Edward Teach, commonly known as "Black Beard," who had accepted the King's pardon in 1717, but had not, it was believed, entirely discontinued his lawless practises. Enemies of the governor even hinted that he had shared in some of the pirate's questionably gotten gains. Eden, however, presented before the Council a complete story of his dealings with Teach, and ultimately received their approbation. He married Mrs. Penelope Golland, a widow, but left no children. In the eighth year of his governorship he died and was buried at Eden House, his seat in Bertie County. Shortly after his death the name of the town of Queen Anne's Creek was changed to Edenton in his honor. In 1889 his remains, those of "Penelope Eden, his virtuous Consort," and the original monument over them both were removed to the burial ground of St. Paul's Church in that place. His original epitaph, which is in a fine state of preservation, declares that he "governed the province eight years to ye greatest satisfaction of ye Lords Proprietors & ye ease & happyness of ye people. He brought ye country into a flourishing Condition & died much lamented march ye 26, 1722, ætatis 49."

[*Colonial Records of N. C.*, vol. II, pp. 129, 150, 207–08, and 256; Edward McCrady, *The Hist. of S. C. Under the Proprietary Govt., 1670–1719* (1897), p. 718; sketches by M. DeL. Haywood in S. A. Ashe, *Biog. Hist. of N. C.*, vol. I (1905), and in *N. C. Booklet*, Dec. 1903 (repr. in R. A. Eden, *Hist. Notes of the Eden Family*, London, 1907); F. X. Martin, *Hist. of N. C. from the Earliest Period* (1829), vol. I; Hugh Williamson, *Hist. of N. C.* (1812), vol. II; J. H. Wheeler, *Hist. Sketches of N. C. from 1584 to 1851* (1851).] M. DeL. H.

EDEN, ROBERT (Sept. 14, 1741–Sept. 2, 1784), colonial governor, was descended from a prominent family of northern England, the head of which for three generations had borne the title of baronet. His father, Robert, and his grandfather, John, sat in Parliament for Durham. His father married Mary, daughter of William Davison, and to them were born eight sons and three daughters. Four of the sons had notable careers. Robert, the second son, was born in

Durham. Nothing is known of his school days except that he became proficient in Latin and learned to write fluently. His father died when the boy was not quite fourteen years of age and less than two years later he was commissioned as lieutenant fireworker in the Royal Regiment of Artillery. He served two years in Germany during the Seven Years' War, first as ensign and later as lieutenant and captain, in the Coldstream Guards. He married, in 1765, Caroline Calvert, who was a sister of Lord Baltimore, proprietor of Maryland, and in 1768 he was commissioned governor of that province.

With his wife and two infant sons, Eden arrived at Annapolis on June 5, 1769. His first important act as governor was to prorogue the General Assembly to prevent it from voicing a protest against the passage by Parliament of the Townshend revenue acts. In his first address to the Assembly he recommended more adequate provision for education, but during his entire administration he was engaged chiefly as a diplomatist, in the dispute between the two houses of the Assembly over the right to regulate the fees of officers, and in dealing with relations between the colonies and with the mother country during the outbreak of the Revolution. For the difficult situation which confronted him he was admirably qualified by integrity, prudence, affability, and large capacity for making friends among the gentry, enhanced by his fondness for horses and racing. Fees were regulated by his proclamation until the proprietary government ceased to function. In his letters to England he was an apologist for the people of the province. He manifested sympathy with their point of view but deprecated their militant methods and intemperate zeal. "It has ever been my endeavor," he wrote Lord Dartmouth, "by the most soothing measures I could safely use, and yielding to storm, when I could not resist it, to preserve some hold of the helm of government, that I might steer as long as should be possible, clear of those shoals which all here must, sooner or later, I fear, get shipwrecked upon." In April 1776, an intercepted letter from Lord George Germain gave rise to suspicion that Eden was an enemy of the colonists. It was sent through irregular and improper channels to the Continental Congress and that body passed a resolution requesting the Maryland Council of Safety to arrest the governor. Because the suspicion was considered groundless the Council did not do so, but in the following month, on account of orders he had received requiring him to give facility and assistance to British armament, Eden was requested to quit the province. He accordingly left Annapolis, June 26, 1776, on a British warship and after a delay of some weeks in the Chesapeake Bay returned to England aboard another vessel. His conduct in Maryland and the judicious manner of his leaving were highly commended and he was created a baronet, Sept. 10, 1776, as a reward for faithful service. Immediately after the close of the war he returned to Maryland to recover some property and died at Annapolis, in 1784.

[For source of material relative to Eden's administration see *Archives of Md.*, and Wm. Eddis, *Letters from America* (1792). The only important secondary source is B. C. Steiner, "Life and Administration of Sir Robert Eden," *Johns Hopkins Univ. Studies in Hist. and Pol. Science,* 16 ser., nos. 7–9 (1898).] N. D. M.

EDES, BENJAMIN (Oct. 14, 1732–Dec. 11, 1803), journalist, was one of the most influential and active newspaper editors and political writers of the Revolutionary period. He was born in Charlestown, Mass., the son of Peter and Esther (Hall) Edes. His great-grandfather, John Edes, came over from England about 1674. After receiving a meager education in the schools of Charlestown or Boston, he founded, on Apr. 7, 1755, in partnership with John Gill, the *Boston Gazette and Country Journal,* the third paper of its name in that city. Both Edes and Gill were described as "men of bold and fearless hearts." Their paper became the organ of the Patriots, who gave it their undivided support and encouragement. Unwavering in its opposition to the British policy, it fought the political battles of the day continuously in its columns, especially those against the Stamp Act, the tea tax, and the Boston Port Bill. Its office became the resort of the leading opponents of King George III, many of whom contributed to its pages. Report says that the members of the Boston Tea Party assembled at Edes's house on the afternoon of Dec. 16, 1773, later using the *Gazette* office at the corner of Court St. and Franklin Ave. to assume their Indian disguise. The temper and spirit of the time, largely voiced through Edes's own writings, are revealed during a long period of years in the files of the *Gazette.* It was described by Lieut.-Gov. Andrew Oliver in a letter from England as "that infamous paper," and the arrest of both Edes and Gill as instigators of sedition was advised by Sir Francis Bernard, the governor of the colony. During the siege of Boston, Edes secretly conveyed his press and types into the suburbs of Boston and set up his printing office in Watertown.

After the dissolution of his partnership with Gill in 1775, Edes and his two sons, Benjamin and Peter, continued the paper until 1794, when the father took over the business alone. The popularity of the *Gazette* waned during the years following the Revolution, its patriotic mission being apparently completed and all of Edes's efforts to obtain the financial aid of his friends proved unavailing. Its publication was discontinued on Sept. 17, 1798, after a remarkably long and notable career of over forty-three years. He continued his printing business for a short time thereafter, but with little success. Largely because of the depreciation of paper currency, he lost the competency he had acquired before the Revolution, his last years being marked by ill health and poverty. His wife was Martha Starr, to whom he was married about 1754.

[Jos. T. Buckingham, *Specimens of Newspaper Literature, with Personal Memoirs, Anecdotes, and Reminiscences* (1850), vol. I; Frederic Hudson, *Journalism in the U. S. from 1690 to 1872* (1873); Justin Winsor, ed., *The Memorial Hist. of Boston, 1630–1880*, vols. II, III (1881–82); Jas. M. Lee, *Hist. of Am. Journalism* (1923); *New-Eng. Hist. and Geneal. Reg.*, vol. XVI (1862), 16.]
E. F. E.

EDES, ROBERT THAXTER (Sept. 23, 1838–Jan. 12, 1923), physician, author, was born at Eastport, Me., the son of Richard Sullivan Edes, a Unitarian clergyman, and Mary (Cushing) Edes. He came of English ancestors, being descended from John Edes who settled in Massachusetts about 1674. He graduated from Harvard College in 1858 and from the Harvard Medical School in 1861. After a short period of hospital service, he was appointed an acting assistant surgeon in the United States navy, Sept. 30, 1861. He resigned May 31, 1865, after serving as medical officer on a mortar flotilla on the Mississippi River below New Orleans and in Pensacola Bay, in addition to doing duty in various hospital posts. Twice promoted, he finally attained the rank of passed assistant surgeon at the age of twenty-seven.

Returning to Boston, he began to practise medicine and to teach in the Harvard Medical School and at the Boston City Hospital. His first publication was a prize essay on *The Part Taken by Nature and Time in the Cure of Disease* (1868). In 1871 he was appointed assistant professor, and in 1875 professor, of materia medica, and in 1884 Jackson Professor of Clinical Medicine, in the Harvard Medical School. He is said to have been a scholarly and erudite instructor, his differential diagnoses being models of accuracy and thoroughness. In 1885 he founded, with Delafield, Osler, Pepper, and others, the Association of American Physicians. A year later he resigned from the Harvard Medical School because of illness in his family, and went to Washington, D. C., where he remained for five years; during this period he wrote his *Text-Book of Therapeutics and Materia Medica* (1887), in addition to lecturing at Columbian and Georgetown universities. He then became superintendent of the Adams Nervine Asylum in Boston, a position which he held for six years. Here he wrote *The Story of Rodman Heath; or, Mugwumps by one of them* (1894), an anonymous novel, based partly on his Civil War experiences. The next year he delivered the Shattuck lecture before the Massachusetts Medical Society on "The New England Invalid," a lecture which reviewed his experiences at the Adams Nervine Asylum and "foreshadowed with extraordinary perspicacity the modern trend in the treatment of the psychoneuroses" (Taylor, *post*). After an unsuccessful attempt to establish a small private sanatorium for patients with nervous diseases, Edes retired from practise. The death of his son at the age of thirty-two, in 1901, a young man of exceptional promise in medicine, was a blow from which Edes never recovered. He continued to write, however, for the daily papers of Springfield, Mass. His last publication, *Parson Gay's Three Sermons; or Saint Sacrement* (1908), appearing a few years after he retired, was a novel of the Indian Wars of 1757–58. He died at Springfield in his eighty-fifth year, after a long period of semi-invalidism.

Diseases of the nervous system always interested Edes, and he wrote many medical papers on brain tumors, anemia, and allied subjects. "He was always in the forefront of progress and often distinctly ahead of the thought of his time" (Taylor, *post*). Many societies honored him, including the Philosophical Society of Washington, the American Academy of Arts and Sciences, the American Neurological Association, and the Military Order of the Loyal Legion. He was twice married: first, in 1867, to Elizabeth T. Clarke of Boston, by whom he had three daughters and a son; second, in 1881, to Anna C. Richardson, of Dorchester, Mass. She died in 1921.

[E. W. Taylor in *Archives of Neurology and Psychiatry*, IX (1923), 506–09; *Boston Medic. and Surgic. Jour.*, CLXXXVIII (1923), 117; *Jour. Am. Medic. Asso.*, LXXX (1923), 418; *Who's Who in America*, 1922–23; *Boston Evening Transcript*, Jan. 13, 1923.]
H. R. V.

EDGAR, CHARLES (Apr. 9, 1862–Feb. 15, 1922), lumberman, inventor, was born in Metuchen, N. J., the son of Benjamin Winant and Phebe (Dunham) Edgar. Until he was eighteen years old, he attended the public schools of his native town and upon graduation from high school in 1880, went to Chicago, Ill. He found employment with the lumber interests of Chicago, his first job being with the Shepard Lumber

Company. After four or five years of service, during which time the first real steps were being taken in the development of the lumber industry of Wisconsin and Michigan, Edgar moved with his family to Wausau, Wis. Here he entered the employ of the Jacob Mortensen Lumber Company of which he soon became general manager. He continued with this company for four or five years and then formed, with Walter Alexander, the Alexander-Edgar Lumber Company. Edgar was then but twenty-eight years old and had had approximately ten years' experience in the lumber business. In spite of his youth he possessed unusual business ability, and in the succeeding twelve years under his leadership his company played a prominent part not only in the development of the northern lumber areas of Michigan, Wisconsin, and Minnesota, but also of the southern pine districts as well. Throughout this period Edgar maintained a close contact with all branches of the lumbering industry and even found time to perfect certain improvements in saw-mill machinery. As the band saw was originally applied to cutting logs, the backward movement of the log carriage would, if there were any slivers on the cut face of the log, be liable to force those slivers against the smooth edge of the band saw and either distort or break it. To obviate this danger, there was developed a lateral adjustment on the back movement of the carriage called an "off-set," so that the log returned for a new cut out of contact with the saw. Edgar first made an improvement on the "off-set," and then designed a band saw with teeth on both its edges so that the saw cut in both directions and thus eliminated the off-setting mechanism. He patented this device in 1894 and 1895, and subsequently sold the rights to a manufactory in Milwaukee. The process has been in general use by lumber manufacturers for sawing certain classes of small timber ever since. On account of ill health Edgar was compelled to retire from active business about 1902, and for the next ten years lived on his farm near Charlottesville, Va. In 1914, however, because of the death of one of his associates, he was again obliged to take up active work as president and general director of the Wisconsin & Arkansas Lumber Company of Malvern, Ark., and he continued in that capacity until his death. During the World War he was identified with the Southern Pine Emergency Bureau, later was a member of the Lumber Committee of the Council of National Defence, and finally was lumber director of the War Industries Board, in which capacity he served until the end of the war. A distinguished service medal was awarded to him on Apr. 7, 1922, after his death. On Dec. 18, 1884, Edgar was married in Chicago, to Gertrude Pomeroy of Pottsville, Pa., daughter of George W. Pomeroy. At the time of his sudden death in Miami, Fla., he was survived by his wife, three sons, and a daughter. He was buried at Essex Fells, N. J., where he had resided for a number of years.

[*Lumber World Rev.*, Feb. 25, 1922; *Am. Lumberman*, Feb. 18 and Feb. 25, 1922; E. W. Byrn, *The Progress of Invention in the Nineteenth Century* (1900); A. A. Pomeroy, *Hist. and Geneal. of the Pomeroy Family* (1912); *Newark Evening News*, Feb. 16, 1922; Patent Office Records; U. S. Nat. Museum correspondence.]
C. W. M.

EDGERTON, ALFRED PECK (Jan. 11, 1813–May 14, 1897), politician, was born at Plattsburg, Clinton County, N. Y., the son of Bela and Phebe (Ketchum) Edgerton. He was educated at the Plattsburg Academy and after graduation was for a short period editor of a newspaper in that town. In 1833 he removed to New York, where he was a clerk in a mercantile house. Four years later he became the agent of the American Land Company, and of the Messrs. Hicks, and settled at Hicksville, Ohio. He was married, Feb. 9, 1841, to Charlotte, daughter of Charles Dixon, of Portland, Conn. In 1845 he was elected as a Democrat to the Ohio Senate where his ability as a debater made him a prominent leader in his party. After serving in this body 1845–46 and 1846–47, he was elected to Congress from the Toledo district, and served 1851–55. Always a strong opponent of slavery on constitutional grounds, in Congress he vigorously opposed the rescinding of the Missouri Compromise and the Kansas-Nebraska Act. He was chosen financial agent of the state by the Board of Fund Commissioners of Ohio, and in this capacity resided in New York City from 1853 to 1856. The following year he removed to Fort Wayne, Ind., but remained a citizen of Ohio until 1862. In 1859, in association with Hugh McCulloch and Pliny Hoagland, he leased the Wabash & Erie Canal, of which he was the general manager for nine years. In 1868 he was the Democratic candidate for lieutenant-governor of Indiana but was defeated. As a Democrat, he refused to support Horace Greeley in 1872 and came within six votes of being nominated for the vice-presidency on the O'Conor ticket, over John Quincy Adams, second. He was then nominated by the O'Conor Democrats—the "Bourbon" or "Straightout" Democrats—for governor of Indiana, but declined. After many years of retirement from active public service, early in November 1885, he was appointed by President Cleveland a United States Civil Service Commissioner, succeeding Dorman B. Eaton [*q.v.*] as president of the Commission. His appointment was sharply criticized on account of his advanced age and a fear that he was not in sympathy with civil-service reform. President Cleveland grew dissatisfied with his work on the Commission and summarily removed him, Feb. 10, 1889. Edgerton published a letter declaring his dismissal was due to the fact that the President was a "mugwump—a mugwump of mugwumps," which, he defiantly announced, "I am not." For many years Edgerton was president of the board of education of Fort Wayne, Ind., where he resided for two decades, but he died at his country home at Hicksville, Ohio.

[For biographical sketches see Henry Howe, *Hist. Colls. of Ohio* (1896); B. J. Griswold, *The Pictorial Hist. of Fort Wayne* (1917); *Biog. Hist. of Eminent and Self-Made Men of the State of Ind.* (1880), 12th Dist., p. 44; *Ohio Statesmen and Hundred Year Book 1788–1892* (1892); *Biog. Dir. Am. Cong.* (1928); obituary in *N. Y. Times,* May 16, 1897. See also E. J. Benton, "The Wabash Trade Route in the Development of the Old Northwest," in *Johns Hopkins Univ. Studies,* Jan.–Feb. 1903; and for the controversy over his appointment and dismissal as Civil Service Commissioner, see *N. Y. Tribune,* Nov. 5, 1885, Feb. 19, 1889; *Cincinnati Enquirer,* Nov. 5, 1885, and *Nation* (N. Y.), Nov. 12, 1885.] R. C. M.

EDGERTON, SIDNEY (Aug. 17, 1818–July 19, 1900), Abolitionist, congressman, first territorial governor of Montana, was born in New York of old New England ancestry. His parents were Amos and Zerviah (Graham) Edgerton. His father died while Sidney was an infant, and the boy had to educate himself. He studied and taught and in 1844 went to Akron, Ohio, where he again taught school and studied law. In 1846 he graduated from the Cincinnati Law School. Beginning his public life as an Abolitionist, he was a delegate to the Free-Soil Convention of 1848, and continued his fight on slavery during the years following. In 1856 he was delegate to the first Republican National Convention. Elected to Congress in 1858, he served two terms. His efforts were directed toward the abolition of slavery in the territories, in the District of Columbia, and on the public property of the United States. As a Union man he felt the need of holding the West to the East. He was an ardent advocate of a transcontinental railroad and voted for every measure which he thought would promote its construction.

When the territory of Idaho was organized, Mar. 3, 1863, President Lincoln offered the position of chief justice to Edgerton. He took office at Bannack in eastern Idaho (now in Montana) and there remained in charge of the eastern judicial district of the territory. This assignment was distasteful to him for he felt that as chief justice he should have a district nearer the capital. The court had no marshal and no power to enforce its decisions. With bands of road agents infesting the country, Edgerton gave his approval of the vigilantes who were trying to exterminate them. The counties east of the Bitter Root Mountains, dissatisfied with their connection with Idaho, sent Edgerton to Washington to work for a separate territory. He was well acquainted with James M. Ashley, chairman of the House committee on territories, with other congressmen, and with Lincoln. Following the approval of the act forming Montana (May 26, 1864), Lincoln appointed Edgerton governor, legal provision for a temporary government being made May 27. His territory had been overrun by bandits and the majority of its population were opposed to the Union. It was his work to organize government among a hostile people and establish obedience to law. With firmness and tact he undertook the task and during the year of his administration made progress. He foresaw in Montana a great commonwealth and he urged the building of roads and the founding of schools. He was unable to conclude his program, since the succession of Johnson to the presidency led to his resignation.

Edgerton was a man of unusual intellect, pleasing personality, and notable oratorical ability. He had great courage and frankness. He was an Abolitionist when abolition was unpopular, and an agnostic among a people thoroughly devoted to Christianity. He married Mary Wright in 1849 and to them were born eight children. After 1865 he devoted himself to the practise of law, but he did not lose interest in public affairs. When Mark Hanna invited him as a member of the first Republican Convention to sit in the one of 1900, Edgerton declined, stating that there was little in common between the principles held by him and the "fore ordained work" of the latter convention (*Great Falls News,* July 5, 1900).

[Wilbur F. Sanders, "Life of Gov. Sidney Edgerton," in *Rocky Mountain Mag.,* Feb. 1901, and Martha Edgerton Plassmann, "Biog. Sketch of Sidney Edgerton, in *Contributions to the Hist. Soc. of Mont.* III (1900), are sympathetic but fair. See also *Biog. Directory of the Am. Cong., 1774–1927* (1928).] P. C. P.

EDGREN, AUGUST HJALMAR (Oct. 18, 1840–Dec. 9, 1903), soldier and scholar, was born in Vermland, Sweden, the son of Axel and Mathilda Edgren. He was graduated from the Lyceum of Stockholm in 1858, and from the Swedish Royal Military Academy in 1860. His interest in the issues of the American Civil War led him to emigrate to the United States and enlist in the 99th Regiment, New York Infantry, which was incorporated in the Army of the Potomac. He participated in many battles and was promoted to a first lieutenancy for "bravery in action" in 1863; he was then detailed as staff engineer in charge of the construction of fortifications at Yorktown. He returned to his native land in 1863, and remained a lieutenant in the Swedish army until 1870.

By this time the life of the soldier had begun to pall upon him. He had been enabled to follow his scholarly bent during a leave of absence in 1867–68, which he spent studying in France and Germany, and teaching English and German at the Lycée Saint Quentin in Paris. On his return home in 1869 he was promoted first adjutant, but the experience of the two previous years had so whetted his natural appetite for study that he resigned his commission in 1870, returned to the United States, and entered Cornell University, where he received the bachelor's degree in 1871. After a year on the staff of the Riverview-on-the-Hudson Military Academy at Poughkeepsie, he entered Yale College from which he received the degree of Ph.D. in 1874. He had meanwhile become instructor in the Sheffield Scientific School in 1873, and continued there until 1880, when he returned to Sweden to become privat-docent in Sanskrit in the University of Lund. In 1880 he married Marianne Steendorff of Copenhagen, Denmark. In 1881 he spent the summer in further study at the University of Berlin, and was awarded the Norberg Prize of the University of Lund for his work in linguistics.

From 1885 to 1891 he was again in the United States, as professor of modern languages at the University of Nebraska. After an interval of two years (1891–93) at the University of Gotenburg, Sweden, as professor of Germanic languages and rector, he returned to Nebraska, first as professor of Romance languages, later as professor of linguistic science and Sanskrit. To his teaching duties were added, in 1896, the functions of dean of the Graduate School. In 1900 he was recalled to Sweden to represent the United States as a member of the Nobel Institute at Stockholm, at which place he died in December 1903.

Edgren was a linguist and philologist of extraordinarily wide range. He published a long series of monographs and articles on Sanskrit philology and literature, Germanic and Romance languages, and comparative philology, written in Swedish, German, French, and Latin; he edited German, French, and Italian dictionaries, German, French, Spanish, Italian, and Sanskrit grammars, and French school texts. Through translation and criticism he did much to introduce Sanskrit masterpieces and English and American literature to the Swedish people, and to interpret to them American life and educational institutions. He also published two volumes of his own poems. He was a member of many learned societies in both Europe and America, and in 1893 was president of the Royal Society for Science and Literature in Gotenburg. Among his many published works are the following: *A Compendious German and English, English and German Dictionary* (with W. D. Whitney, 1877); "On the Verbal Roots of the Sanskrit Language and of the Sanskrit Grammarians" (*Journal of the American Oriental Society*, 1878); *A Compendious Sanskrit Grammar* (Trübner, London, 1885); *A Compendious French Grammar* (1890); *Kalidasa Shakuntala* (1894), translated from the Sanskrit; "The Kindred Germanic Words of German and English, Exhibited with Reference to their Consonantal Relations" (*Transactions of the American Philological Association*, 1880, vol. XI); "American Graduate Schools" (*Educational Review*, 1898); "En serie af resebref och skildringer fran Amerika" (*Goteborgs Handelstidning*, 1871–73); *Sommarferier i Montezumas land* (Stockholm, 1898); *Dikter i orignal och öfversättning* (Lund, 1884); *Blåklint: Ny Diktsamling* (Stockholm, 1894); *A French and English Dictionary* (1901), with Percy B. Burnet; *An Italian and English Dictionary* (1901), with Giuseppe Bico.

[Data from a son, Arthur Edgren, Esq., Lincoln, Nebr.; *Who's Who in America*, 1901–02; *Obituary Record Grads. Yale Univ.*, 5 ser. (1910); *Nordisk Familjebok* (Stockholm, 1927), VI, 303; *Salmonsens Konversations Leksikon* (Kbønhavn, 1917), VI, 716; *Lincoln The Capital City and Lancaster County, Nebr.* (1916), II, 793; *N. Y. Times*, Dec. 11, 1903.] J. S. N.

EDMANDS, JOHN (Feb. 1, 1820–Oct. 17, 1915), librarian, a descendant of Walter Edmands who emigrated from England and settled in Concord, Mass., in 1639, was the son of Jonathan and Lucy (Nourse) Edmands and was born in Framingham, Mass. He lived and worked on a farm, attending the district school for about three months each summer and winter, until about 1836, when he was apprenticed to a carpenter and house-builder. He was graduated from Phillips Academy, Andover, in 1843, and entered Yale College. During the latter part of his college course he became librarian of the Brothers in Unity, a society in Yale College, and he then prepared a booklet of eight pages, indicating material of assistance to the students in writing or speaking, which was printed in January 1847 under the title, *Subjects for Debate, with References to Authorities*. This was the beginning from which developed the *Index to Periodical Literature compiled by W. F. Poole* [*q.v.*], who followed Edmands as librarian of the Brothers in Unity. After his graduation in 1847, Edmands spent a year in teaching school in Rocky Mount, N. C. He then entered the Yale Divinity School, was licensed to preach by the New Haven West Association of Ministers in 1850, and graduated in 1851. In that year he became assistant in the Yale College Library, serving until 1856, when he went to Philadelphia, to become librarian of the Mercantile Library. With this institution he was connected for fifty-nine years. Doubtless it is due to the fact that he was a retiring, modest person that he has never been given full credit for his pioneer work. He was a much better practical librarian than was Poole, who had a wide interest in books but contributed very little to practical librarianship. Edmands devised a system of classification and put it into operation about the same time that Melvil Dewey began work on his decimal classification. (See Edmands's *Explanation of the New System of Classification Devised for the Mercantile Library of Philadelphia,* 1883.) Although the use of decimals in the Dewey system proved rather more practical in the expansion of the different classes, and won a wider popularity, which it has maintained to the present, Edmands's classification has proved satisfactory wherever it has been employed. He prepared for publication book lists that were of great interest, placing under the titles of important additions to the Library criticisms and discussions of the views of the authors. His list of historical novels, *Finding List for Novels in the Mercantile Library of Philadelphia* (1878), was one of the first efforts in that direction. He was a careful bibliographer, as is proven in his bibliographies of the Latin hymn *Dies Irae* (*Bulletin of the Mercantile Library of Philadelphia,* Oct. 1, 1884, Jan. 1, 1885) and the Junius Letters (*Ibid.,* July 1, 1890–Jan. 1, 1892). He also published a *Catalogue of the Mercantile Library of Philadelphia* (1870), *Reading Notes on Luther* (1883), and *Reading Notes on Wycliffe* (1884). He was one of the original members of the American Library Association, founded in Philadelphia in 1876, and the first president of the Pennsylvania Library Club, founded in 1890. From time to time he contributed to the *Library Journal* practical notes collected during his long service. He was a founder of the Central Congregational Church in Philadelphia, in 1864, and was the clerk and one of the deacons from its organization. He was married three times: first, on Aug. 1, 1854, to Abigail Jane Lloyd, who died in January 1883; second, on June 17, 1889, to Ellen Elizabeth Metcalf, who died in July 1892; and third, on Aug. 23, 1893, to Clarinda Augusta Roberts. Edmands was physically well adapted to his profession; of slight build, with white hair and ruddy cheeks, he moved nimbly but silently in his domain and he had a low voice with clear enunciation. He was ninety-five years of age when he died, and had maintained his mental alertness and interest in current affairs until the last. He left in trust for publication the manuscript of a book which was issued posthumously under the title, *The Evolution of Congregationalism* (1916).

[*Who's Who in America,* 1915–16; *Yale Univ. Obit. Record,* 1915–16; *Hist. Sketch of the Mercantile Lib. of Phila. and the Ninety-third Ann. Report,* 1915; *Library Jour.,* Nov. 1915; *Pub. Libraries,* Nov. 1915; *Evening Bull.* (Phila.), Oct. 18, 1915; *Phila. Inquirer* and *Pub. Ledger* (Phila.), Oct. 19, 1915.] T. L. M.

EDMONDS, FRANCIS WILLIAM (Nov. 22, 1806–Feb. 7, 1863), genre painter, was born in Hudson, Columbia County, N. Y., son of Samuel and Lydia (Worth) Edmonds, and brother of John Worth Edmonds [*q.v.*]. Francis gave early promise of artistic talent, but financial necessity turned his attention from art to an immediate source of income. The youngest of a numerous family, he could not enjoy the educational opportunities afforded his elder brother. When he was sixteen he was offered a position in the Tradesmen's Bank in New York by his uncle, Gorham A. Worth, then its president, and he remained there until 1830 when he returned to Hudson to become cashier of the Hudson River Bank in his native town. He was later cashier in New York City, first in the Leather Manufacturers' Bank, 1832, and later in the Mechanics' Bank, 1839. He assisted in establishing the New York Clearing House in 1853 and the same year helped to organize the Bank Note Engraving Company, later called the American Bank Note Company. He was at one time city chamberlain of New York, and was closely identified with the New York Gallery of Fine Arts, the Sketch Club, Century Association, New York Society Library, and New York Historical Society. In 1855 he retired from business and settled in a country home, "Crow's Nest" on the Bronx River.

Although he lacked conventional art education, throughout his business career he pursued his art in his leisure time with perseverance and devotion to his ideals. Soon after 1826 he became a student at the National Academy of Design, was made an associate in 1837, and National Academician in 1840. He was recording secretary of the institution for a while and became one of its trustees. He first exhibited at the Academy in 1836, under the assumed name F. Williams, the painting "Sammy the Tailor." He gained much through a visit to Europe in 1840, and his study of the art of the Old World, especially in Italy. In the early fifties he made several drawings for notes produced by the American Bank Note Company, among them being "Sewing-Girl," "Grinding the Scythe," "Barn-yard," and "Mechanic." Other notable works are: "Scene from Butler's Hudibras" (1827); "Dominie Sampson" (1837); "The Epicure" (1838); "The Penny Paper" (1839); "Sparkling" (1840, engraved by the Art Union); "The Bashful Cousin" (1842); "Boy Stealing Milk" (1843); "Vesuvius and Florence" (1844); "The Image Peddler" (1844); "The New Scholar" (1845); "Facing the Enemy" (1845; engraved, a popular illustration of temperance reform); "The Sleepy Student" (1846); "Bargaining" (1858); and "Gil Blas and the Archbishop."

Edmonds was twice married: first, while he was cashier of the bank at Hudson, to Martha Norman; and second, on Nov. 4, 1841, to Dorothea Lord. He died at "Crow's Nest" in his fifty-seventh year.

[C. E. Clement and Laurence Hutton, *Artists of the Nineteenth Century* (1879), I, 235; H. T. Tuckerman, *Book of the Artists* (1867); J. D. Champlin, Jr., *Cyc. of Painters and Paintings* (1886), II, 9; Ulrich Thieme and Felix Becker, *Allgemeines Lexikon der Bildenden Künstler*, X (1914), 345; *N. Y. Times*, N. Y. *Evening Post*, Feb. 9, 1863.]

J. M. H.

EDMONDS, JOHN WORTH (Mar. 13, 1799–Apr. 5, 1874), jurist, was the son of Samuel Edmonds, a native of New York City, who, after the Revolution, settled at Claverack Landing (Hudson), N. Y., became prominent in public life, and married Lydia, daughter of Thomas Worth, one of the first settlers of Hudson. He was born at Hudson, and received his early education in the public schools and the Academy there. In 1814 he entered Williams College, Williamstown, Mass., transferring, in 1815, to Union College, Schenectady, N. Y., where he graduated in 1816. He then began to read law at Cooperstown, N. Y., six months later entering the office of Martin Van Buren at Hudson, and completing his studies at the latter's Albany office. On his admission to the Columbia County bar in 1819, he commenced practise at Hudson, at the same time interesting himself in local politics on the Democratic side, and becoming editor of the *Hudson Gazette*, the party organ, at a salary of three dollars a week. In 1827 he was appointed city recorder, which office he retained till his election in 1830 to the state Assembly. In 1831 he was elected to the state Senate, in which body he became prominent, being a member of the judiciary committee and chairman of the bank committee. At this period the resistance of South Carolina to the tariff laws had raised the subject of nullification, and he was a member of the joint committee of the two houses of the legislature which considered and reported on the matter. His able justification of the committee's report procured its adoption in the face of prolonged opposition. He was also chairman of the joint committee which considered the subject of the United States Bank. He did not complete his term, however, resigning in 1836 on his appointment by President Jackson as commissioner to procure the carrying out of the provisions of the treaty between the United States and the Ottawa and Chippewa Indians bordering on Lakes Huron and Superior—his duties therein requiring him to spend some months at Michilimackinac. On his return from the West in 1837, he moved to New York City, where he engaged in practise and obtained a large connection in mercantile circles. In April 1843, Gov. Bouck appointed him inspector of state prisons, in which capacity he effected great and lasting reforms at Sing Sing. The prisons at that time were in bad condition, with little discipline and a large yearly deficit, and the only punishment administered to refractory prisoners was whipping. Prior to his resignation in 1845 he had established order, systematized administration, practically eliminated the deficit, and humanized punishments. In addition he inaugurated a system of rewards for good conduct, and founded a society to aid discharged convicts to earn an honest living. He was appointed judge of the first New York circuit, Feb. 18, 1845. In 1847 he was elected a justice of the state supreme court. Shortly afterward the state justiciary was reorganized under the new state constitution, and, though he had rendered some unpopular decisions, he was nominated for justice of the new supreme court by Tammany and indorsed by the bar. In 1852 he became a judge of the New York court of appeals, but resigned from the bench in 1853 and resumed practise in New York City. He had for some years conducted investigations in the subject of spiritualism. In 1853, becoming convinced that the living could communicate with the dead, he openly announced his belief, and, in collaboration with Dr. Dexter, published *Spiritualism,* a work which provoked much comment, though the honesty of his convictions was never impugned. In 1863 he published *Statutes at Large of the State of New York* (5 vols.), containing the Revised Statutes and General Statutes up to 1863, with elaborate notes and references. The labor involved in this compilation was immense, but so accurate was his work that it was at once accepted by the profession as the standard authority, superseding all former editions. He subsequently prepared two supplemental volumes and an index. In 1868 he compiled *Reports of Select Cases decided in the*

Courts of New York, consisting of cases heard before him on circuit. Several of his occasional addresses were published in pamphlet form and he was a frequent contributor to the *Albany Law Journal.* He died in New York City.

[An excellent contemporary appreciation of Edmonds appeared in Wm. Raymond, *Sketches of the Distinguished Men of Columbia County* (1851), p. 79. His career is also detailed in P. F. Miller, *A Group of Great Lawyers of Columbia County, N. Y.* (1904), p. 172. See, in addition, D. McAdam and others, *Hist. of the Bench and Bar of N. Y.* (1897), I, 317; 1 *Central Law Jour.,* 163; 9 *Albany Law Jour.,* 244; 4 *U. S. Monthly Law Mag.,* ed. by John Livingston, 335; *N. Y. Times, N. Y. Tribune,* Apr. 6, 1874.] H.W.H.K.

EDMUNDS, GEORGE FRANKLIN (Feb. 1, 1828–Feb. 27, 1919), lawyer, senator, was born and spent his childhood on a farm near Richmond, Vt. His parents, Ebenezer and Naomi (Briggs) Edmunds, were both of Rhode Island Quaker origin. His education, conducted in various schools and by private teachers, was frequently interrupted by illness, and poor health eventually forced him to give up the college course for which he had planned. In later years, however, he received numerous honorary degrees. Whatever he may have lacked in formal education seems to have been more than outweighed by an early acquired taste and capacity for individual study. When about seventeen he began the study of law in the office of his brother-in-law, but the threat of tuberculosis obliged him to spend the winter of 1845–46 in the milder climate of Washington, D. C. The opportunity to use the great law libraries of the capital and to hear the leading lawyers of the day in proceedings before the United States Supreme Court constituted what he always considered one of his most valuable educational experiences. He continued study after returning to Vermont and was admitted to the bar in 1849.

He began practise in Richmond but in less than two years moved to Burlington, where professional opportunities were better. In 1852 he married Susan Marsh, daughter of Wyllys Lyman and niece of George P. Marsh, then minister to Turkey. Their married life lasted until her death in 1916 and she was generally considered to have been an influential factor in his professional and political career. Success at the bar came early and throughout the rest of the decade his name appears with increasing frequency in the Vermont Reports. Later, after entering the United States Senate, he devoted himself largely to federal practise and handled many important cases before the United States circuit courts in various parts of the country as well as before the Supreme Court in Washington. There was at that time no legal or ethical objection to a senator's engaging in such work. While Edmunds had much of the conservatism of the legal profession, he showed, both in practise and in his work as a legislator, a clear realization that the changing economic and social needs of the nineteenth century were rendering many common-law concepts inadequate and that these obsolete principles should not be permitted to protect abuses. He continued active work after leaving the Senate, accumulated a comfortable estate, and finally retired about 1897. One of his greatest legal successes came in 1895, when he argued successfully against the constitutionality of the income tax in the famous case of *Pollock* vs. *The Farmers' Loan and Trust Company* (157 *United States,* 429; Edmunds's argument, pp. 482–99). His standing as a legal authority is also shown by the fact that in 1885 he was invited to testify, on a technical matter involving the marriage laws of New York in 1770, before the Committee of Privileges of the British House of Lords.

Important as was Edmunds's professional career, it was overshadowed by his public services. Like many other New Englanders he first attracted the attention of his fellow citizens in town meeting. Then followed a period of service as representative in the legislature 1854–59, the last three years as speaker. In 1861–62 he was a member of the Vermont Senate and president *pro tempore.* His first distinctly national service came in 1864, when he was appointed special counsel by Secretary Seward in an unsuccessful effort to secure the extradition of the St. Albans raiders. He had been, naturally, a supporter of the anti-slavery movement, and became an active Republican. The death of Senator Solomon Foot of Vermont, Mar. 28, 1866, came at a time when the Republican party needed every possible vote for the contest with President Johnson. On April 3, Gov. Paul Dillingham appointed Edmunds to the vacant place. He left promptly for the capital, was sworn in on April 5, and on the following day supplied the one vote necessary to carry the Civil Rights Bill over the President's veto. His career in the Senate, thus begun, covered the next twenty-five years and made him an active and influential participant in most of the important constitutional, legislative, and political developments of the period. Although he was interested in some aspects of foreign policy, especially in the extension of American interests in the Caribbean and in transisthmian canal problems, his most important contributions were in the field of domestic legislation, the ensuing decades offering unusual opportunities to a legislator of his ability and constructive temperament.

Edmunds, for the most part, supported the Rad-

Edmunds

ical policies throughout Reconstruction. When he opposed them, it was usually much to the credit of his sense of honor and decency. Within a few weeks after entering the Senate he had attracted public attention and drawn special commendation from Sumner by a speech against the admission of Colorado with a "white" suffrage qualification in its constitution (*Congressional Globe,* 39 Cong., 1 Sess., p. 2176). His rapid advance to a position of power and importance was seen a year later when he was made chairman of the committee to arrange rules of procedure for the trial of President Johnson. He was prominent in the proceedings preliminary to the trial, voted for conviction, and filed a lengthy and closely reasoned opinion on the President's alleged offenses (Supplement, *Congressional Globe,* 40 Cong., 2 Sess., pp. 424–28). He had been active in securing adoption of the Tenure of Office Act of 1867, and opposed its total repeal in 1869 when it was urged that to President Grant should be restored the entire power so long exercised by his predecessors in office. Almost twenty years later he had a notable clash with the Cleveland administration and a Senate majority when the obnoxious restrictions were finally removed by the act of Mar. 3, 1887. On Dec. 14, 1886, he delivered one of his most notable constitutional arguments (*Congressional Record,* 49 Cong., 2 Sess., pp. 136–40), dealing at considerable length with the removal power and declaring that the existing statutes constituted "a wholesome restraint upon the temptations to abuse in executive power," and that they were necessary for the security of public offices which could not, without them, carry any assurance of "honorable and responsible employments of the Government for fixed terms."

With the passing of Fessenden he was generally considered the ablest constitutional lawyer in Congress, and it must have been a painful experience for him to see many of the principles for which he had contended and which he had succeeded in having embodied in legislation, such as the Ku Klux Act of 1872 or the second Civil Rights Act of 1875, the latter largely his personal handiwork, rejected by the Supreme Court. He became chairman of the committee on the judiciary in 1872 and held this important post until his retirement in 1891, with the exception of the two years of Democratic control, 1879–81. Perhaps his best-known achievement was the act of Jan. 29, 1877, providing for the appointment of the electoral commission, "to regulate the counting of the votes for President and Vice-President and the decision of questions arising thereon," in the disputed election of 1876. Posterity has not agreed as to the equities involved in the original controversy, and the act itself has been criticized as unfair and legalistic, but Edmunds unquestionably made a great contribution toward the settlement of a dangerous crisis, and by securing the adoption of the Electoral Count Act of 1887 rendered less probable its recurrence in the future (see *Century Magazine,* May, June 1913, for interesting interchanges between Edmunds and Henry Watterson on the disputed election of 1876 and the electoral commission). One of his notable legislative successes was the Thurman Act of 1878, framed in collaboration with Senator Thurman of Ohio, also a member of the judiciary committee, and pushed through Congress by their joint efforts in the face of a most determined opposition. By this measure the Central and Union Pacific railroads were compelled to fund their debts to the government and make adequate provision for a sinking fund. The act was intrinsically an important measure and is also a notable step in the development of governmental control of the railroad business.

The act of Mar. 22, 1882, adopted for the purpose of suppressing polygamy in the territories, especially Utah, is the only enactment of his long career which was known by his name. Polygamy he declared to be "an inherent and controlling force in the most intense and anti-republican hierarchy, theocracy, as an organized and systematic government that, so far as my small reading has gone, has ever existed on the face of the earth" (*Congressional Record,* 47 Cong., 1 Sess., p. 1213). The statute itself, although unsatisfactory in its operation until strengthened by the supplementary enactment of 1887, eventually broke the Mormon power and resulted in important changes in the polity of the organization. One of the objects, he stated, was "to take the political power in that Territory out of the hands of this body of tyrants," and the administrative clauses were such as to guarantee adequate enforcement by responsible and independent officers and juries. He was the author of the greater part of the Sherman Anti-Trust Act of 1890, a fact not generally known until many years later. In 1911, in a magazine article of extraordinary interest and historical value, he explained the objectives of the men who drafted the law. It was directed against the "unnatural and unequal distribution of wealth and power," he said, and intended to apply to combinations of labor and capital alike. He pointed out that it was impossible to frame specific definitions for the various offenses at which it was directed, and that literal construction, till then attempted by the courts, had not been intended by the original framers (*North*

American Review, December 1911, p. 801).

Throughout the long financial contest which covered his entire period of service he fought against all forms of public debt repudiation, was a powerful influence in securing the passage of the Specie Resumption Act of 1875, opposed remonetization of silver, and denounced those members of the Republican party who went over to the free silver heresy. In 1897 he was appointed chairman of the monetary commission authorized by the Indianapolis conference, and the reports of this organization exerted great influence on subsequent banking and currency legislation. His support of civil-service reform was consistent and courageous, beginning with his appointment on a retrenchment committee soon after entering the Senate. In 1871 he introduced a bill "to regulate the Civil Service of the United States and promote the efficiency thereof" which in many respects anticipated the Pendleton Act of 1883 to which he gave generous support. In tariff matters he had the views of the orthodox Republican of his time.

He was on confidential terms with Presidents Grant, Hayes, and Arthur, and is reported to have been called into frequent consultation on public business. He declined several important appointments in both the executive and judicial services. Following the death of President Garfield he was elected president *pro tempore* of the Senate, an action which was generally regarded as a special tribute, inasmuch as it made him, under the existing law, next in succession to the presidency of the United States. Edmunds received some support for the presidential nomination in 1880, and four years later a similar movement had a great, if not decisive, influence on the result of the election. He was strongly backed in 1884 by the reform element of the party, including such men as George W. Curtis, John D. Long, who placed his name before the convention in an admirable address, Henry Cabot Lodge, Theodore Roosevelt, Andrew D. White, George F. Hoar, and others. He received a maximum of ninety-three votes. Blaine, the nominee, failed to hold the support of a considerable number of the independents who had backed Edmunds and lost the election as a result. Edmunds himself, while not anxious for the office, had a profound distrust for the Republican candidate and refused to campaign in his behalf, a defection which attracted popular attention and caused considerable dismay in party circles.

During the greater part of his career in the Senate political morality was far from high, but Edmunds came through unsmirched. He had a profound contempt for hypocrisy and humbug and a tongue which on occasion could blister opponents like sulphuric acid. He was never popular with a majority of his colleagues and was often feared. One of them once remarked that if led blindfold into the Senate chamber, he could tell at once, from the nature of the business under discussion, whether or not Edmunds was in his seat. When he was absent, the members usually tried to rush through the petty jobbery which they were reluctant to submit to his keen scrutiny and merciless sarcasm (quoted by F. E. Leupp, in "The Father of the Anti-trust Law," *Outlook,* Sept. 20, 1911, p. 271). It was said of Edmunds, when at the height of his powers, that "his bald head and flowing white beard gave him a resemblance to the classic portrait of St. Jerome, but, unlike that portrait, his head is dome shaped, symmetrical, while his temples are wide apart and full between. He debates a question in a clear, half-conversational manner, occasionally indulging in a dash of sarcasm which makes those Senators who are the objects of it wince. What he says goes into the *Congressional Record* without revision or correction" (Poore, *post,* II, 208). He had few intimates, but his friendship with Thurman, a Democrat, became one of the traditions of the Senate. His lack of amiability and his contentious nature are attested by many of his contemporaries. Senator G. F. Hoar tells how, after making some disparaging remarks about the attractiveness of the presidency, "he smiled and his countenance beamed all over with satisfaction," when reminded of the pleasant possibilities inherent in the veto power.

His resignation in 1891 caused wide-spread comment inasmuch as his hold on Vermont was such as to have insured an indefinite tenure. He gave the illness of his only daughter as the chief reason, though a fellow senator adds that Edmunds believed the Senate was deteriorating and that service therein was losing its attractions (Cullom, *post,* p. 208). In retirement he never lost touch with public affairs, and from time to time, in letters, published articles, or interviews, he expressed opinions with all his old cogency and force. He remained a strong partisan to the end but showed his characteristic independence by occasional criticism of Republican policies, notably the "imperialism" resulting from the war with Spain. For some years after retirement from the Senate he lived in Philadelphia, but his last years were spent in Pasadena, Cal. There his death occurred on Feb. 27, 1919, but his remains were interred at Burlington, Vt. For many years he had occupied the position of an elder statesman, and there had been ample opportunity to weigh his merits and defects. The editorial comment of the *New York Times,* Mar. 1, 1919, can be generally accepted: "He had the dry wit, as he had the twang and the fine, solid, simple, rugged characteristics of his native state. . . . He was . . . one of the most thoughtful, most patriotic, most useful, and most independent of American Statesmen."

[The importance of Edmunds's position in the Senate gave him prominent mention in the memoirs of the period, such as: S. M. Cullom, *Fifty Years of Public Service* (1911); J. B. Foraker, *Notes of a Busy Life* (1916); S. S. Cox, *Three Decades of Federal Legislation* (1886); G. F. Hoar, *Autobiography of Seventy Years* (1903); Ben P. Poore, *Perley's Reminiscences of Sixty Years in the National Metropolis* (1886); *John Sherman's Recollections of Forty Years in the House, Senate, and Cabinet* (1895); J. G. Blaine, *Twenty Years of Congress* (1884–86); A. W. Dunn, *From Harrison to Harding* (1922). *The Nation* and *Harper's Weekly* contain frequent references and editorial comments. Walter H. Crockett has a brief memorial sketch, privately reprinted from *The Vermonter* of August 1919. See also the same author's *Vermont, The Green Mountain State* (1923), IV, 13 ff., V, 271–72; *Geo. F. Edmunds Centenary Exercises, 1828–1928* (1928); and Burlington (Vt.) *Free Press,* Feb. 29, 1928.]
W. A. R.

EDWARDS, BELA BATES (July 4, 1802–Apr. 20, 1852), clergyman, editor, was born in Southampton, Mass., the son of Elisha and Anne (Bates) Edwards. He was a second cousin of Justin Edwards [*q.v.*], and was descended from Alexander Edwards who came to America from Wales, about 1640, and settled in Springfield, Mass. He attended Williams College for one year (1820–21) and then entered Amherst, graduating in 1824. After a year at Andover Theological Seminary, he returned to Amherst as a tutor (1826–28), but then reëntered Andover, taking his degree with the class of 1830. While still in the Seminary he became assistant secretary of the American Education Society, and after his graduation he spent five years (1830–35) in the Boston office, beginning there his long career as editor of educational and religious publications. For nearly sixteen years (1827–43) he was in charge of the *American Quarterly Register,* in which he garnered facts which are of much value to the historian of that period. He founded the *American Quarterly Observer* in 1833 and continued to direct the magazine when it was merged in 1835 with the *American Biblical Repository.*

In 1837, Edwards accepted an appointment as professor of the Hebrew language and literature in Andover Theological Seminary and was ordained to the ministry on Oct. 3, 1837, at Methuen, Mass. In 1842 he and Prof. Edwards A. Park established the *Bibliotheca Sacra,* which he edited during the years 1844–52. Superseding the *Repository* and published in Andover, this quickly became the most scholarly and authoritative of American religious periodicals. He was appointed in 1848 professor of Biblical literature at Andover. During this period he declined the presidency of both Amherst and Dartmouth, as well as the secretaryship of the Board of Commissioners for Foreign Missions. He was a trustee of Amherst College and of Abbot Academy. When, because of his arduous labors, his health broke down in 1845, he made a visit to Florida, followed by a year of travel in Europe. He died at Athens, Ga., of malarial fever, when he was just under fifty years of age. He had married, Nov. 3, 1831, Jerusha Williams Billings, daughter of Col. Charles E. Billings of Conway, Mass., who survived her husband forty-four years. Of their three children, only one daughter was living at the time of his death.

Besides the numerous criticisms and special articles which he printed from time to time in his magazines, Edwards published several books, including *Biography of Self-Taught Men* (1832), *The Missionary Gazetteer* (1832 and 1833), *Memoir of Elias Cornelius* (1833), *Selections from German Literature* (1839), in collaboration with Prof. Park, and a translation of Raphael Kühner's *Grammar of the Greek Language* (1844), in collaboration with Principal Samuel H. Taylor. A selection of his sermons and addresses, edited, with a memoir, by Prof. Park, was published posthumously as *Writings of Professor B. B. Edwards* (2 vols., 1853). Edwards was a remarkably energetic and persistent man, whose restless energy drove him into many projects and eventually wore him out. He was a sound scholar, an excellent linguist, and a fascinating lecturer. A born philanthropist, he was interested in missionary enterprises and social reforms, including temperance and anti-slavery.

[Edwards A. Park, "Life and Services of Prof. B. B. Edwards," in *Bibliotheca Sacra,* Oct. 1852, and memoir in Edwards's *Writings* (1853); W. L. Montague, ed., *Biog. Record of the Alumni of Amherst Coll., 1821–71* (1883); W. B. Sprague, *Annals Am. Pulpit,* vol. II (1857); *Gen. Cat. Theol. Sem., Andover, Mass., 1808–1908* (n.d.).]
C. M. F.

EDWARDS, CHARLES (Mar. 17, 1797–May 30, 1868), lawyer, author, was born at Norwich, England, and educated at Cambridge University, emigrating later to New York, where he studied law and was admitted to the bar. Shortly after commencing practise he became standing counsel to the British consulate general in New York City, a position which he occupied for twenty-five years, and through this connection attracted a select and influential but never extensive clientele. Thorough and reliable, but not brilliant, his untiring zeal, sound judgment, and wide acquaintance with the principles of municipal and international law enabled him to appear to signal advantage in a number of leading cases in the United States courts. He was counsel for the British government and for the owners of the *Crenshaw* and *Hiawatha* in the *Prize Cases* (1862; 2 *Black,* 635–99)—involving the status of the seceding states and perhaps the most momentous in its consequences of all the decisions of the Supreme Court of the United States during the Civil War—where the President's right *jure belli* to institute a blockade of ports in possession of insurgent states which neutrals are bound to regard was established. He also represented the British Government in *in re Thomas Kaine* (1852; 14 *Howard,* 103), where vital matters of jurisdiction in extradition proceedings were argued before the Supreme Court *in banc.* Following the sensational trial of Mrs. Cunningham in 1857 for the murder of Dr. Burdell, he successfully contested on behalf of the heirs and next of kin her claim to the murdered man's estate (see *Cunningham* vs. *Burdell,* 4 *Bradford,* 343).

He was a prolific writer on a variety of subjects and his books had considerable vogue in their day. Among his legal works were: *The Juryman's Guide Throughout the State of New York* (1831); *A Practical Treatise on Parties to Bills and Other Pleadings in Chancery* (1832); *On Receivers in Chancery* (1839); *On Receivers in Equity and under the New York Code of Procedure* (2nd ed., 1857); *The Law and Practise of Referees under the New York Code and Statutes* (1860). These, though favorably received by the profession, were by the nature of their subject ephemeral, but he made a permanent contribution to the legal literature of the State of New York by his *Reports of Chancery Cases Decided in the First Circuit of the State of New York by the Hon. William J. M'Coun* (4 vols., 1833–51), known as "Edwards' Chancery Reports," containing the decisions of Vice Chancellor McCoun from 1831 to 1846. "The reports are well drawn and are often cited, although the tribunal was not of leading authority" (Abbott, *post*). Of his miscellaneous works, the more prominent were *Feathers from my own Wings* (1832), a miscellany of prose and verse; *The History and Poetry of Finger-Rings* (1855), a work of much erudition, containing a large amount of curious out-of-the-way information, conveyed in somewhat turgid language; and *Pleasantries about Courts and Lawyers of New York* (1867).

[Apart from his professional record, source material dealing with Edwards's life and career is scanty. Joseph Sabin states (*Dict. of Books Relating to America,* vol. VI, 1873, p. 97) that he changed his name from Charles Edward Ellis to Charles Edwards in order to inherit some property, but cites no authority in support of his assertion. See D. McAdam, *Hist. of the Bench and Bar of N. Y.* (1897), I, 318; B. V. Abbott and Austin Abbott, *A Digest of N. Y. Statutes and Reports,* I (1860), xvi; H. L. Clinton, *Celebrated Trials* (1897), pp. 84 ff.; obituary in N. Y. *World,* June 1, 1868.]

H. W. H. K.

EDWARDS, HENRY WAGGAMAN (October 1779–July 22, 1847), lawyer, congressman, governor of Connecticut, was born in New Haven. His grandfather was the famous New England divine, Jonathan Edwards [*q.v.*]; his father, Pierpont [*q.v.*], was a lawyer of repute, a member of the Continental Congress, and federal judge for the district of Connecticut; his mother, Frances Ogden, was a New Jersey woman. He was graduated from Princeton with the class of 1797 and, after attending the Litchfield Law School in Connecticut, was admitted to the bar and began practise in New Haven. Shortly after 1800 he became active in the Republican party. He was associated with the local section known as Tolerationists, whose primary purpose was to secure a new state constitution. In 1819 he was elected to Congress on the Republican ticket. He remained in the House until 1823, when he was appointed by Gov. Wolcott to the Senate, to fill the vacancy caused by the death of Elijah Boardman. At the next regular election Edwards was chosen to the Senate in his own right, remaining in office until 1827.

Upon his return to Connecticut, he was for two years a member of the state Senate, and in 1830 was speaker of the House of Representatives. He was first chosen governor in 1833. During that year President Jackson visited the state, and was enthusiastically received by Edwards and the Connecticut Democrats. In the election of 1834 Edwards was defeated by Samuel A. Foot, but the following year he was successful, being then reëlected regularly until 1838. His latter period of office coincided with that era in the development of the state marked by great progress in the construction of railroads. In his messages to the Assembly, he advocated the abolition of property qualifications for voting (*Connecticut Courant,* May 11, 1835), the districting of the state for the choice of national representatives (*Ibid.,* May 14, 1833), increased governmental control of large business interests, and stricter legislation regarding joint-stock companies (*Ibid.,* May 9, 1836). The Hinsdale Act of 1837 was in line with the governor's desires. Edwards advocated the granting of financial aid to railroads, but he was not able to effect any immediate change in the conservative policy of the state (*Ibid.,* May 6, 1837). Finally, he favored the making of a geological survey, as a means of developing the natural resources of the state. Little is known about his family life. His wife was Lydia Miller (Moffatt, *post,* p. 56). A son, Henry P. Edwards, took up the legal profession and became a judge of the supreme court of New York State. In character, Edwards was determined and straightforward. Although a member of a distinguished family, he was hardly a man of brilliance. As a politician, he did not rise above the level of other men of his day.

[The best sketch is contained in *The Governors of Conn.* (1905), by F. C. Norton. Scant information can be gleaned from Wm. H. Edwards, *Timothy and Rhoda Ogden Edwards of Stockbridge, Mass., and Their Descendants* (1903); and R. B. Moffatt, *Pierrepont Genealogies from Norman Times to 1913* (1913). An obituary notice is in the *New Haven Evening Register,* July 23, 1847. Letters in the Conn. Hist. Soc., written by Edwards from Washington to Gideon Tomlinson, are the personal property of the librarian, Mr. A. C. Bates.]

J. M. M.

EDWARDS, JOHN (*c.* 1671–Apr. 8, 1746), silversmith, was born, and probably served his apprenticeship, in Limehouse, London, England, from which place he migrated to Boston. His father, John Edwards, a "chirurgeon," was mentioned in the diary of Samuel Sewall in 1689. According to the records, the younger Edwards was a faithful citizen. He served as tithing-man in 1701, 1708, 1711; as a sergeant of the Boston Artillery Company in 1704; as a constable in 1715; as an assessor from 1720 to 1727; and he was an attendant of the Brattle Street Church. He produced a great deal of silverwork of fine quality, marked with crude capitals in plain quatrefoil, or in quatrefoil with four projections; or Roman capitals in two semicircles with two projections; or crude capitals crowned, fleur-de-lys below in shield (Hollis French, *A List of Early American Silversmiths and their Marks,* 1917). His first wife was Sybil Newmann, the granddaughter of the second John Endecott; his second wife was Abigail Fowle, the widow of William Smith, whose grand-daughter, Abigail Smith, became the wife of John Adams, the second president of the United States. His sons Thomas, Samuel, Joseph, and his grandson Joseph, followed his trade. His sister was the wife of the silversmith, John Allen, who was related by marriage to Jeremiah Dummer, another worker in precious metal. These interrelationships among the craftsmen were the natural result of the apprenticeship system. Prosperous in his business, at his death he left an estate of £4,840, a fairly large sum for his day. In the Supplement to the Boston *Evening-Post* of Apr. 14, 1746, appeared this notice: "Tuesday last died, and Friday was decently interred, Mr. John Edwards, Goldsmith, in the 75th Year of his Age; a Gentleman of a very fair Character, and well respected by all that knew him."

[Stephen Ensko, *Am. Silversmiths and their Marks* (1927); F. H. Bigelow, *Historic Silver of the Colonies and its Makers* (1917); S. G. Drake, *The Hist. and Antiquities of Boston* (1856); C. L. Avery and R. T. H. Halsey, *Am. Silver of the XVII and XVIII Centuries* (1920); *Records of the Church in Brattle Square* (1902).]

K. H. A.

EDWARDS, JOHN (1748–1837), planter, senator, was born in Stafford County, Va., a son of Hayden and Penelope (Sanford) Edwards. He moved in 1780 to that part of Virginia which later became the state of Kentucky, where he speculated in land and got title to about 23,000 acres. This competency made him a leader in a region where the people were soon intent upon gaining statehood. The district of Kentucky was at this time divided into three counties, Jefferson, Fayette, and Lincoln. Edwards settled in Lincoln County, and the year following his arrival he was elected to represent it in the Virginia House of Delegates. He continued to act as a representative in 1782, 1783, 1785, and 1786. In 1783 he became a justice of the peace, which position automatically made him a member of the county court. In 1785 Bourbon County was cut out of Fayette. Edwards took up his residence in this new county, and the next year he became the clerk of the first court to be held there.

In the meantime this western part of Virginia had begun its long and tortuous course toward statehood. Edwards was a member of the two preliminary conventions held in Danville in 1785, and after the formation of Bourbon County he represented that division continuously until statehood was secured. The sinister Spanish activities in connection with the proceedings of 1787 and 1788 did not directly implicate him as they did certain other Kentuckians. In fact Edwards assumed the leadership of the opponents of the Spanish conspiracy. In the convention of November 1788, he reported and read the petition to Virginia for the independence of Kentucky, but he opposed the doctrine that Kentucky would thereby become sovereign and might enter the Union or not as she pleased. He also took part in framing the constitution of 1792.

He first served the new state by acting as one of the electors provided for by the constitution to choose the state senators. Then, in June 1792, he was appointed on a commission to choose a permanent state capital, but was not present when the decision was made giving the honor to Frankfort. As a fitting reward for his service to the district and state, he was unanimously elected one of the two first United States senators to represent Kentucky, but took no very prominent part in the deliberations of the Senate. He returned to Kentucky in 1795 never to leave the state again in an official capacity. He was immediately elected to represent Bourbon County in the state House of Representatives and thereafter, from 1796 to 1800, he was a member of the state Senate. At the latter date he retired to private life on his Bourbon plantation where he died thirty-seven years later. Ninian Edwards [*q.v.*], chief justice of Kentucky in 1808 and later governor of Illinois Territory, was his nephew.

[Lewis and R. H. Collins, *Hist. of Ky.* (1882), I, 23, 351, 354–56, II, 71, 771; Georgie Hortense Edwards, *Hist. Sketches of the Edwards and Todd Families* (1894); *Biog. Dir. Am. Cong.* (1928); *The South in the Building of the Nation* (1909), XI, 313–14; T. M. Green, *The Spanish Conspiracy* (1891), pp. 197, 221–28; Wm. Littell, *Pol. Trans. in and Concerning Ky.* (1806), reprinted as *Filson Club Pub. No. 31* (1926); Breckenridge MSS. (1794), in Lib. of Cong.]

E. M. C.

EDWARDS, JONATHAN (Oct. 5, 1703–Mar. 22, 1758), Congregational clergyman, theologian, philosopher, was the son of Rev. Timothy Edwards of East Windsor, Conn. He was descended from Rev. Richard Edwards, a London clergyman in the age of Elizabeth, whose widow with her second husband, James Coles, and her son William Edwards came to New England about 1640. William and his son Richard were merchants in Hartford, Conn. Timothy, oldest son of Richard, was born in 1669, graduated from Harvard College 1691, and became pastor of East Windsor, May 1694, serving the parish until his death, January 1758. By his marriage with Esther, daughter of Rev. Solomon Stoddard of Northampton, he had eleven children, Jonathan being the fifth child and only son. For lack of schools, the son was taught with other pupils at home, developing precociously under a learned father and a mother of uncommon intellectual power. In September 1716, not yet thirteen, he entered Yale College, which after an initial period of scattered groups of students was now, by vote of the trustees, to open in New Haven. One tutor, however, Rev. Samuel Smith, and his students, refused to come from Wethersfield; and discontent with another tutor, Rev. Samuel Johnson, led the New Haven students, including Edwards, to join the Wethersfield group until, in the summer of 1719, under Timothy Cutler as Rector, the college was finally established in New Haven. Since, after some months, Johnson resigned his tutorship, Edwards cannot have been much affected by this eminent thinker, later a Berkeleian philosopher and president of King's College; but the revolutionary effect already made on Johnson's mind by Newtonian science, emancipating him from the old scholasticism, was paralleled by the formative action of Newton and Locke on Edwards, who at the age of fourteen read Locke's Essay with more delight "than the most greedy miser finds when gathering up handfuls of silver and gold, from some newly discovered treasure" (*Works,* Dwight edition, I, 30). In these college years, as if planning a *Summa* of human knowledge, the youth began to record his reflections on the nature of the human mind and on natural science (*Ibid.,* vol. I, Appendix H, I, pp. 664–771), as well as "Notes on the Scriptures" and "Miscellanies," which he continued in later life (*Ibid.,* vols. VII, VIII, IX). Even at the age of twelve he had shown close and delicate scientific observation in an account of phenomena relating to "flying spiders" (*Ibid.,* I, 23–28), and in college he added a power of theoretic reasoning in terms of Newtonian science. Before him opened a world ranging from the indiscernible atoms of which all bodies are composed to the enormously distant stars that, by his reasoning, must be blazing suns attended like our own by encircling planets. It was a world of natural laws, yet not a mechanism of bodies acting purely by themselves, for body is only intelligible as a resistance of divine power exercised at points of space. Our idea of space is only colored space, and if color be taken away, gone is all space, extension, motion, figure. Color, however, is only in the mind. "The secret lies here: That which truly is the substance of all Bodies, is the infinitely exact, and precise, and perfectly stable Idea, in God's mind, together with his stable Will, that the same shall gradually be communicated to us, and to other minds, according to certain fixed and exact established Methods and Laws" (*Ibid.,* I, 674). This was a boy's venture in Berkeleian Idealism without knowledge of Berkeley.

Even more remarkably the youth divined another aspect of reality than that of orderly related fact, and a mode of apprehension other than that of the logical understanding. In his notes on "Mind" he said: "There has nothing been more without a definition than Excellency; although it be what we are more concerned with than anything else whatsoever: yea, we are concerned with nothing else" (*Ibid.,* I, 693). In this beginning of a study of value, or perfection in any degree, lurks the master idea of his whole career. He discovers a functioning of consciousness independent of intellectual reason without, however, distinguishing the esthetic and the purely religious. Excellency, he finds, consists in greatness—degree of being—and beauty, which is consent or love of being to being. Divine majesty is more, then, than the infinitude of being and power from which the Calvinistic inferences had been chiefly made. It is an infinitude of beauty which is God's love of himself, or, since all things are communications of himself, a love of all things made manifest in the tranquillity and peace that overspreads the world. Later he was to argue that the *due* apprehension, the direct sense of the sweetness of beauty in the divine being, was God's redemptive disclosure of himself to the privileged elect.

Graduating from Yale in September 1720, Edwards spent two years in theological study in New Haven, and in August 1722 began a ministry to a Presbyterian church in New York, from which, owing to meager support, he withdrew in the following May. On May 21, 1724, he was elected to the office of tutor at Yale, though his services were not needed until June. His teaching was interrupted in September 1725 by a long illness, and a year later he resigned to become the colleague of his grandfather, Solomon Stoddard, in Northampton, Mass. The incongruity of his spiritual history with the tradition of this parish was destined to end in painful conflict.

An exquisite charm belongs to Edwards's own narration of his religious development, written about 1740 (*Ibid.,* I, 58–67). Even at the tender age of seven or eight the boy shared in the awakened fervor of the village church, and in a secluded woodland spot led other children in moments of prayer. Absorbing college study checked these susceptibilities, but at the end of that period distress of soul made seeking salvation the main business of his life. Early in 1721 thought and emotion culminated in an experience which was evidence of a heart visited by regenerating grace. Holiness was revealed to him as a divine beauty, in comparison with whose ravishing loveliness everything else was mire and defilement. Rapt by such majesty of worth, his heart panted "to lie low before God, as in the dust; that I might be nothing, and that God might be all, that I might become as a little child." This experience brought with it an acquiescence in the central Calvinist doctrine of absolute divine sovereignty. God's arbitrary apportioning by his sheer pleasure of eternal happiness or everlasting torment in hell had from childhood been a repellent idea. "It used to appear like a horrible doctrine to me." Now objections began to fade. The overwhelming sense of divine infinitude of will pulsing in every object of the vast cosmos and the rapturous experience of supreme beauty and worth in that infinitude convinced him that sheer sovereignty in the bestowal of salvation is the essential glory of divine majesty. This is the view offered in his sermons on divine sovereignty (*Ibid.,* VI, 293; VIII, 105). It is clear that election and reprobation are implicit in the identification of saving grace with an esthetic intuition too intense for all men to share. The notes on "Mind" and his diary (*Ibid.,* I, 76–106; Dec. 18, 1722, May 25 and Aug. 12, 1723) show that Edwards was aware of some divergence here from older divines. It was in any case discrepant with the religiosity typical of the Northampton parish, and the contrast was even more marked by the emotional fervor of his wife, Sarah Pierpont of New Haven, whom he married in July 1727. Four years earlier Edwards had recorded reports of her privileged communion with God when a child of thirteen. She was "always full of joy and pleasure and no one knows for what." In solitude, which she loved to keep, she seemed "to have some one invisible always conversing with her" (*Ibid.,* I, 114). Twenty years later she herself recorded her maturer experiences of divine presence in extreme emotional form and Edwards seems to have valued them as a standard for judging the experiences of others (*Ibid.,* I, ch. XIV). In that household divine grace and human faith had intensities of manifestation rare in the lives of others.

Originally the Congregational churches were formed of those only who by a profession of an experience of saving grace could be accepted as visible saints, but, owing to the great decline of such professions, the Massachusetts Synod of 1662 sanctioned an additional "covenant membership" of such as could offer an intellectual faith and a desire to assume the obligations of the Christian life. In the Northampton neighborhood Edwards's grandfather had brought about another relaxation by admitting all the parish to the Lord's Supper, viewing the sacrament as a possible means of grace for the unregenerate. Membership tended thus to rest on "moral sincerity." Such changes diminished the difference of a Congregational church from the Church of England parish, which embraced all the baptized. Another dangerous possibility opened. The alarming defection of Samuel Johnson, Timothy Cutler, Rector of Yale, and one of the Yale tutors, to the Church of England in 1722 meant an adoption also of the Arminian theology prevalent in the English Church, a theology which rested salvation on human moral effort as well as divine grace. Attention to the Arminian Episcopalian propaganda in Connecticut was stirred the more, in 1729, when Daniel Dwight, born in Northampton and related to the distinguished Partridge family in Hatfield, abandoned Congregationalism for the English Church. From this time, also, Edwards feared an Arminian tendency in neighbors who failed to support his psychology of saving grace. These were his own relatives of the dominant Williams family of Hatfield, and especially his imperious and worldly cousin, Israel Williams, who, graduating from Harvard in 1729, began the prominent career of landholding and public office which won him the style of "Lord of the Valley." Their real opposition was to Edwards's insistence on the "sensible perceiving of the immediate power and operation of the Spirit of God." With them in mind Edwards later defined the controversy (*A Treatise Concerning Religious Affections,* 1746; *Works,* Dwight edition, V, 45): "They say, the manner of the Spirit of God, is to cooperate in a silent, secret, and undiscernible way with the use of means, and our own endeavors; so that there is no distinguishing by sense, between the influences of the Spirit of God and the natural operations of our own minds." From his view of divine immanence Edwards agreed to an undistinguished mingling of the human and divine in the action of the moral conscience; but the vision of divine beauty, which for him meant salvation, came only by supernatural illumination and was sensibly perceived as such. The Rev. Solomon Williams, brother of Israel, held that assurance of saving faith was a man's inference from his moral improvement and the sincerity of his obedience, and "that there is not any spiritual and gracious discovery made to the soul of the infinite beauty and amiableness of God, but as he is in Christ" (*A Vindication of the Gospel Doctrine of Justifying Faith,* 1746, pp. 41, 46).

In his parish, with meager aid from books and limited bodily energy, Edwards lived the life which before the age of twenty he had vowed in his seventy "Resolutions" (*Works,* Dwight edition, I, 67 f.), a life of stern discipline over the springs of impulse and of intense mental application; rising at 4:00 A. M., devoting thirteen hours of the day to study, finding recreation in solitary woodland rambles, during which he jotted down memoranda of his thoughts for later elaboration. After Stoddard's death, Feb. 11, 1729, his own distinctive thought began to find recognition and effect. His discourse in Boston, *God Glorified in the Work of Redemption by the Greatness of Man's Dependence upon Him in the Whole of it* (1731; *Works,* Dwight edition, vol. VII), was published at the request of the Boston ministers. It was a protest against reliance on moral effort, and viewed redemption as known by the spiritual joy attending an effusion of God's beauty on the soul. At home, the younger people became increasingly responsive, and by the autumn of 1734 formed neighborhood meetings of their own for prayer. The parish, too, procured the publication of another sermon typical in title and content: *A Devine and Supernatural Light, Immediately Imparted to the Soul by the Spirit of God, Shown to be both a Scriptural, and Rational Doctrine* (1734; *Works,* Dwight edition, vol. VI). Here again, moral discernments and repentant misery lie only in the sphere of God's common grace, his universal causative action in the limitations of natural law, while saving grace is enacted from God's transcendent freedom. This is a supernatural illumination of the mind, by which the loveliness of God's holiness is seen, and the mind acts here not with ratiocination but with direct intuitive awareness and self-evident certainty. "Reason's work is to perceive truth, and not excellency." As other sermons argued, the natural man has a sottish and brutish blindness even when he repents and prays. Though he had the mental faculties for it, he is ignorant of the excellency of God's nature as one born blind is of colors (*Discourses on Various Important Subjects,* 1738; *Works,* Dwight edition, vol. V)

Objections began from those who were accustomed to milder tests of election, but in spite even of an arrogant categorical veto from Israel Williams of Hatfield, Edwards continued the theme in sermons on Justification by Faith (*Ibid.*) He exhibited faith as a divinely wrought union with Christ by which Christ's righteousness is imputed to the elect without the condition of any qualifying excellence in the recipient. Though openly abused for this, Edwards felt himself divinely vindicated by the striking revival that ensued, the only movement of extent and power since the passing enthusiasm attending the early preaching of John Cotton a century before. In December 1734 there were six sudden conversions and in the following spring they were counted as thirty a week. Since visitors from other towns flocked to Northampton, the revival spread throughout the county and many places in Connecticut. Religious themes absorbed the thought and talk of the whole population of Northampton, even at weddings. Children formed their own religious meetings. One notable conversion was that of Phœbe Bartlett, a child of four, though the majority of conversions counted as indubitable by the critical and cautious Edwards were of people over forty years of age. The revival was skilfully guided by a pastor unsparing in the logic of Calvinism and, like Ignatius of Loyola, a psychological expert in the *exercitia spiritualia.* At the outset the hearer must know his guilt as an actual hater of God: "You object against your having a mortal

Edwards

hatred against God; that you never felt any desire to kill him. But one reason has been, that it has always been conceived so impossible by you, and you have been so sensible how much desires would be in vain, that it has kept down such a desire. But if the life of God were within your reach, and you knew it, it would not be safe one hour." ("Men Naturally God's Enemies," *Works,* Austin edition, VII, 180.) "When you come to be a firebrand of hell . . . you will appear as you are, a viper indeed. . . . Then will you as a serpent spit poison at God and vent your rage and malice in fearful blasphemies." (*Ibid.,* VII, 198; Dwight edition, VII, 58.) Creatures of such iniquity were useful only in their destruction. "The devil is waiting for them, hell is gaping for them, the flames gather and flash about them, and would fain lay hold on them and swallow them up. . . . All that preserves them every moment is the mere arbitrary will and uncovenanted, unobliged forbearance of an incensed God." (*Works,* Dwight edition, VII, 168.) "Though he will know that you cannot bear the weight of omnipotence . . . he will crush you under his feet without mercy; he will crush out your blood, and make it fly, and it shall be sprinkled on his garments, so as to stain all his raiment." (*Ibid.,* VII, 173.) With a change of imagery the preacher pictured the vast liquid mountains of fire and brimstone flowing without rest, giving no rest day or night to all eternity.

Brought thus to the anguished conviction that God was absolutely just in their condemnation and made completely submissive to divine sovereignty, the hearers passed from depth of terror to a calm acquiescence, with a bare hope of possible divine mercy. Regeneration was a third stage of experience in which the submissive heart felt a disinterested joyful adoration in contemplation of the unmerited mercy that would elect any of a race so fallen and corrupt to eternal felicity. Often Edwards had to persuade the penitents that this admiring awe was in fact the impartation of a supernatural light and evidence of a new heart. They did not easily distinguish the divine from the human in this frame of soul. In May the high tension began to subside, partly because despairing seekers now had morbid impulses to commit suicide. Edwards inferred that Satan had regained control.

For some years quieter conditions prevailed and the preaching of Edwards dealt more with Christian love as manifested in the heart and life. This is the theme of *Charity and its Fruits,* a series of sermons preached in 1738, first published by Tryon Edwards in 1851. Edwards was not alone, however, in expecting repetitions of revival fervor, and his communications, private and public, contributed to this result. *A Faithful Narrative of the Surprising Work of God in the Conversion of Many Hundred Souls in Northampton, and the Neighboring Towns and Villages,* published in Boston and London in 1737 (*Works,* Dwight edition, vol. IV), is linked with intenser interests in Scotch churches, and prepared the great social response to the evangelistic tour of George Whitefield in 1740–42. That "Great Awakening," however, evoked divisive tendencies in New England life. Whitefield's denunciations of ministers as devoid of grace, and the fanatic extravagances of unlearned lay itinerants who intruded in the parishes, brought protests against disorderly excitements and convulsive physical effects. Edwards himself offered judicious criticisms in *The Distinguishing Marks of a Work of the Spirit of God* (1741; *Works,* Dwight edition, vol. IV). In 1742, also, partly in answer to Charles Chauncy of Boston, he published *Some Thoughts Concerning the Present Revival of Religion in New England* (*Ibid.,* vol. IV). Here he defends the awakening of 1740 by its moral results, but frankly admits remedial faults incidental to it. His sense of living in a momentous time appears in his argument that Scripture prophecies of the Latter-Day outpouring of the Spirit apply to America as the scene of a prelude to that great manifestation. This was no momentary thought. When not yet twenty he had been eager to see in contemporary events foregleams of some great Advent, and from now on apocalyptic expectancy and calculations were a powerful interest. The theme has place in his correspondence with the Scotch clergyman, William McCulloch (*Ibid.,* I, 196 f., 261 f.), and in the sermons of 1739 which John Erskine of Edinburgh made into *A History of the Work of Redemption* (Edinburgh, 1774); and it dominates *An Humble Attempt to Promote Visible Union of God's People in Extraordinary Prayer for the Revival of Religion* (1747; *Works,* Dwight edition, vol. III). It is obvious that the revival was supported by the conviction of a crisis in human history. Since, however, in Connecticut and central Massachusetts, revivals resulted in social cleavage and church divisions with partisan conflict between exponents of religion as violent emotion and those who regarded it as rectitude of conduct, Edwards needed to intervene further by a series of sermons in 1742–43 which became *A Treatise Concerning Religious Affections,* published in 1746 (*Ibid.,* vol. V). This is the supreme expression of Edwards's psychology of religion. The mind has two activities: understanding, and inclination or will, the latter having inseparable aspects of affections and choice, since man wills what he loves. True religion involves both activities. While in great part it consists in holy affections, there must also be light to the understanding implied in all reasonable affections. At great length he cautions against reliance on mere intensity of feeling, on its effect on the body, on fervor of speech, or on a confidence in righteousness which may be only exalted natural feeling. The conversion of a child of Satan to a child of God lies in the birth of a love of God originating in the disclosure to the soul of God's moral perfections: "A true love to God must begin with a delight in his holiness, and not with a delight in any other attribute; for no other attribute is truly lovely without this." (*Ibid.*, V, 143). This is no gift of new doctrinal information, no initiation into mystical meanings of Scripture. It is a new discernment of the truth already furnished. It is a direct, intuitive vision of the beauty that is in God and Christ, which by its perfect joy convinces the soul of the reality and certainty of divine things. The soul's nature is changed. It shares in the divine light, shares in the character of Christ. Now the affections are brought into beautiful harmony, and new conduct manifests the divinity of the principle from which it flows, a union of Christ with the faculties of the soul. To this analysis of piety Edwards soon added a study of an illustrious example of divine movements in the heart of one who sounded the depths of sorrow and joy. This was *An Account of the Life of the Late Reverend Mr. David Brainerd* (1749), compiled from his diary and papers. (*Ibid.*, vol. X.)

Republications of the *Treatise Concerning Religious Affections* in England and Scotland led to more extensive correspondence with Scotch divines, who initiated a Concert of United Prayer for the Coming of Christ's Kingdom. To the Rev. John Erskine (1747) he announced his intention of writing a systematic attack on Arminianism, beginning with the topic of the Will and moral agency, and from Erskine he received a number of Arminian works of use for this purpose. The project, however, had to be postponed, for in the meantime Edwards was involved in serious difficulty with his parish. He had already in preaching on Religious Affections made known his disapproval of the long standing Stoddardean practise of admitting to full membership without satisfactory evidence of a regenerated heart. Examination of Scripture and the older divines convinced him of the error in this practise. Originally, a Congregational church consisted of visible saints, known as such by a recital of experiences accepted as evidence of a renewal by divine grace. Stoddard, often inconsistent in expression, could be quoted as saying that moral sincerity in professing faith and repentance made a man a visible saint in the sense of the New Testament, and "moral sincerity" had become the catchword of some of his Williams descendants. Edwards could find moral sincerity only in the regenerate, and he would limit membership to those at least who humbly trusted that their heart was now capable of a true Christian life. Gossip exaggerated the rigor of the tests that he would demand. He was in any case placing himself in opposition to the settled usage of all but two churches in the county, and to his socially and politically eminent relatives unfriendly to revivals and revival tests. Israel Williams, now in high military station in the first French and Indian war, fomented discontent in Northampton. No test came until December 1748, when an applicant refused to accept the terms of a profession of Godliness offered by Edwards. Unfortunately, by his own maladroitness in a very different matter, Edwards had alienated many parishioners. In 1744 on hearing of the circulation of books provocative of indecent speech among the young, he had the church appoint a committee of inquiry, and at once from the pulpit read a list of names of those who were to meet the committee. Nearly all the important families found themselves compromised by the publication of the long list in which there was no distinction of witnesses and accused. Their indignation stopped the investigation.

After the difficulty concerning admission to the church in December 1748, Edwards asked the Standing Committee of the church to consent to an exposition of his views in the form of sermons, but the committee preferred an explanation in print. Well aware that dismission from the pastorate would be the probable result, but conscientiously unwilling to admit applicants without the public profession, Edwards offered on Apr. 13, 1749, to resign his charge if, after reading his projected book, the members, with the approval of a mutual council, should so vote. This was the beginning of a long and complicated series of negotiations involving disputed rights of the precinct (the civil community supporting the church) to direct the action of the church organization, the right of Edwards to be heard from the pulpit in defense of his position, his right to secure churches from outside the county (then comprising the three present counties of Franklin, Hampshire, and Hampden) to represent him in the council, as well as the definition of the council's functions when formed. Edwards has left an accurate, detailed record of every incident in the controversy in an unimpassioned, scrupulous journal, which is a monument to his intellectual integrity (*Works,* Dwight edition, I, 313–99). The church finally conceded to him the calling of a mutual council of ten churches, two of the five selected by himself to be drawn from outside the county, and the council to be free to proffer any advice. It met June 19, 1750, but it was incomplete; one church called by Edwards failed to send delegates. Nevertheless, the majority refused to postpone action until the disparity could be remedied. After vain attempts to bring church and pastor to agreement, it voted by its partisan majority of one that the pastoral relation ought to be at once dissolved if the church persisted in that desire. Thereupon more than 200 of the 230 voting (that is, male) members of the church voted for his dismission, and the council on June 22, again by a majority of one, so gave final judgment. The minority united in a published protest. On July 1 Edwards preached his farewell sermon (1750; *Works,* Dwight edition, I, 626), a discourse of the highest dignity and restrained intensity, marked by a strong sense of ministerial authority. His conception of the cause of all the trouble is shown by his warning to watch against the encroachments of Arminianism: "If these principles should greatly prevail in this town, . . . it will threaten the spiritual and eternal ruin of this people, in the present and future generations."

"I am now," he wrote to Erskine, July 5, 1750, "thrown upon the wide ocean of the world, and know not what will become of me, and my numerous and chargeable family" (*Ibid.,* I, 411). Erskine already had offered aid in procuring a call to some Scotch parish, but Edwards, while ready enough to accept the Presbyterian polity, shrank from the uncertainties involved. The Northampton people, long unable to secure another pastor, asked occasional preaching from him, but in November determined opponents got the town to end such service. A friendly minority proposed to join with him in forming a new church, but he refused from an unwillingness to divide the parish. He did, on further solicitation, invite a council of ministers to advise in the matter (May 15, 1751), but in view of an abusive remonstrance addressed to the council, he welcomed the advice of that body that he should accept another charge already offered him. He had been called to be missionary to the Indians in Stockbridge and pastor of the church formed by the Indians and a few white settlers. After two visits of investigation, he settled in Stockbridge, Aug. 8, 1751. A meager church support was to be supplemented by mission funds from the provincial legislature and the London Society for the Propagation of the Gospel in New England.

Until his Northampton house could be sold he struggled with adversity, being heavily in debt for land and house in the new field and for the marriages of two daughters. Wife and children eked out the family living by selling in the Boston market their handwork of lace, embroideries, and painted fans.

More painful still was the necessity of conflict with the greed and intrigues of a resident merchant, Ephraim Williams, a relative of the family which in large part had brought about the catastrophe in Northampton. Education of Indian boys was supported by a grant from the King, by the London Society, and by individual philanthropists in London; and now another English benefactor proposed a school for girls. To remedy previous mismanagement, Edwards secured from the legislature the appointment of three trustees for all the funds. Two of his Williams kinsmen, however, got from London appointment on the Boston board of commissioners of the Society, and brought about the nomination of a woman relative as mistress of the girls' school. Furthermore, one of the new trustees, marrying into the Williams family, came to Stockbridge to assume control. Under this régime, on request from the Boston commissioners Edwards could only report lax arrangements profitable to private pockets; whereupon the Williams group tried to have him and Gideon Hawley [*q.v.*], teacher of the boys' school, removed, and to buy out the lands of settlers who supported them. Owing to the courage and skill of Edwards, however, these intriguers found themselves thwarted and repudiated by settlers, Indians, commissioners, and the legislature. During this time there occurred another skirmish growing out of the Northampton controversy. In August 1749 Edwards had defended himself by publishing *An Humble Inquiry into the Rules of the Word of God, Concerning the Qualifications Requisite to a Complete Standing and Full Communion with the Visible Christian Church* (*Works,* Dwight edition, vol. IV). Though alienated parishioners refused to read it, Elisha Williams [*q.v.*], former Rector of Yale, began a work in reply, but on going to England gave the material to his half-brother, Rev. Solomon Williams of Lebanon, who in 1751 produced a work: *The True State of the Question Concerning the Qualifications Necessary to Lawful Communion in the Christian Sacraments.* In Stockbridge Edwards found time to answer with *Misrepresentations Corrected, and Truth Vindicated* (1752;

Works, Dwight edition, vol. IV), a wearisome masterpiece of controversial subtlety. Done now with these personal battles, he resumed the plan of a general campaign against Arminian theology. Before his early death in his fifty-fifth year he had completed four notable works and had others in prospect.

The youthful notes on "Mind," which evince a philosophic talent of the highest promise, were unknown to his contemporaries. His fame was that of preacher and revivalist. But the publication in 1754 of *A Careful and Strict Enquiry into the Modern Prevailing Notions of that Freedom of Will which is Supposed to be Essential to Moral Agency, Vertue and Vice, Reward and Punishment, Praise and Blame* (*Works,* Dwight edition, vol. II), revealed him as the first great philosophic intelligence in American history. The work shows his debt to Locke but also a profound originality, logical acumen, and critical discrimination in the use of terms. Its purpose was to maintain the dogmas of absolute divine sovereignty and unconditional predestination against Arminian objections found especially in Whitby's *Six Discourses* (1710). There is freedom, for the mind can freely act out its choice. The origination of the choice is nevertheless absolutely determined. It is determined by the motive—that which has the greatest tendency to excite volition by being seen as the greatest apparent good. Man has the natural power to serve God, if he is so inclined; but he will not be so inclined unless God reveals himself as the man's highest good—a revelation which is not for all. Moral responsibility lies in the choice, whatever be its origin, not in the cause of the choice. Necessitation cancels no liberty or moral responsibility. Liberty means only that man can do what he wills, but, as appears from the fact of divine foreknowledge, volitions are determined. God's foreknowledge, which is evidenced by the fulfilment of prophecies, means the certainty of events, and only the will of God establishes their certainty. Adam's fall was a choice caused by motives. In the last analysis the motives were due to God. God wills the system under which sin infallibly comes to pass. The system is God's. The sin is man's.

What then is man's inclination? In 1758 Edwards published his work *The Great Christian Doctrine of Original Sin Defended* (*Ibid.,* vol. II), chiefly in reply to works of John Taylor of Norwich, England, which were widely circulated in New England in the propaganda of Episcopalian churches. Taylor regarded all human propensities as in themselves good, since they act as incentive to the development of controlling reason and virtue. Edwards determines the human tendency by abstracting all restraining divine action—all that insures moral behavior. Man is born depraved and in conditions that infallibly lead to sin. The sin is infinite, for it is sin against infinite being. We were depraved when Adam was depraved. We committed Adam's sin. For what is personal identity? It is a sameness of consciousness explicable only as due to continuity of divine action. Our identity is a constituted identity. God constitutes us one person with Adam. This ingenious novelty was a mode of escape from Taylor's plea that God cannot hold us guilty for the sin of one who represents us without our knowledge or consent.

Between the last two works Edwards had written two others which he then laid aside. One is an essay, "The Nature of True Virtue," a study of the genuine Christian character (first published in *Two Dissertations,* 1765; *Works,* Dwight edition, vol. III). Possibly the formulation may owe something to his disciple Hopkins. Certainly Hopkins and Bellamy, theologically trained in Edwards's home, effectively carried on the formulation here found. Nevertheless, it is an elaboration of what belonged to the notes on "Mind." Virtue, it is argued, is a kind of beauty—that moral beauty which is the form of love, the beauty of a disposition of good will to being in general. "If every intelligent being is in some way related to being in general, and is a part of the universal system of existence; and so stands in connection with the whole; what can its general and true beauty be, but its union and consent with the great whole" (*Works,* Dwight edition, III, 95). This propensity seeks the highest good of being in general. The object that has most of being draws the greatest share of the heart's benevolence. God, then, is the supreme object of virtuous propensity. The ethical thus merges in the religious attitude. All men, to be sure, have "natural conscience." They approve justice and benevolence, they even perceive its beauty, but to love, to taste its primary and essential beauty, belongs only to him whose conscience is enlightened by saving grace. The natural virtues are spurious; they rest on self-love. Disinterested love belongs to God and the redeemed.

Apparently Edwards left this aside for some revision. Did he find that the development of this thought was somewhat incongruous with his Calvinism? The surmise has been made also with reference to the other unpublished work of 1755, "Concerning the End for which God Created the World" (*Ibid.*). This is a high flight in the pantheistic mysticism of his boyhood, and an elaboration of reflections recorded in his "Miscellanies" without use in his sermons. Why a world? An ultimate question. The briefest expression of this hovering contemplation is "that a disposition in God, as an original property of his nature, to an emanation of his own infinite fullness, was what excited him to create the world; and so that the emanation itself was aimed at by him as a last end of the creation." The universe, then, is an exfoliation of God, an emanation, not a creation out of nothing. Nothing has real existence save as it partakes of God. His final end in the great manifestation is Himself. The world exists for His glory. He, the supreme and only excellence, necessarily loves Himself. If God has pleasure in the creature, it is because the creature is His emanation, has the divine essence in him. It is difficult to see how in this view the human self has any distinctive reality, and the surmise again is offered that speculative thought has become independent of the theological system.

Obviously this stern logician had a singular capacity for esthetic joy. The exquisite narrative of his religious experience, almost a poem, exhibits a rare delight in the beauty of nature. His answer to the question, "Why a world?" is that God is the supreme artist who gives Himself expression in infinitely varied perfections. Edwards the theologian could not be content with a rational ethical relation to God. The soul's real response must be the delight of the lover of beauty.

His end was not in Stockbridge. His third daughter, Esther, was married June 29, 1752, to Rev. Aaron Burr, president since 1748 of the College of New Jersey, which in 1756 removed from Newark to Princeton. Two days after Burr's death on Sept. 24, 1757, Edwards was chosen as his successor. On Oct. 19, Edwards wrote in doubt of his fitness for the office, stressing the lack of physical vigor with its check on social responsiveness, as well as his reluctance to abandon further literary projects. He sought counsel of a group of ministers, however, who urged that acceptance was a duty. Given leave to resign his missionary office, he went early in January to Princeton. There he preached regularly and conducted what would now be called a seminar course in theology for seniors. On Mar. 22, 1758, he died of fever following inoculation against smallpox. He was buried in Princeton.

Edwards was tall of stature, slender in form, obviously of delicate constitution. His somewhat feminine visage had comely features and piercing eyes, and his quiet voice, toned with a certain pathos, had penetrating effect by its perfect distinctness and its modulated expression. Venerated for the saintliness of his disciplined character, he was bitterly hated because of a pitiless logical consistency that trammeled life. He created the first great religious revival of modern times; intensified the power of Calvinism to stem the tide of the world's new thought; fused the iron logic of that system with a rapture of mystic communion; and initiated a New England Theology as a new chapter in the history of doctrine.

[A bibliography by John J. Coss of Edwards's published writings and works relating to him appears in the *Cambridge Hist. of Am. Lit.*, I (1917), 426–38, and a bibliography of his publications, in F. B. Dexter, *Biog. Sketches Grads. Yale Coll.*, vol. I (1885). Edwards's *Works* have been twice edited, by Sereno Dwight (10 vols., 1829, vol. I containing Dwight's life of Edwards), and by S. Austin (8 vols., Worcester, 1808–09, repub. in 4 vols., 1843, and several times since). The youthful writings are more exactly reproduced by Egbert C. Smyth in *Andover Rev.*, Jan., Mar. 1890, and in *Proc. Am. Antiquarian Soc.*, n.s., X, 212–47 (Oct. 1895). Additional selections from the "Miscellanies" were printed by A. B. Grosart in *Selections from the Unpublished Writings of Jonathan Edwards* (Edinburgh, 1865), and by E. C. Smyth in *Exercises Commemorating the Two-Hundredth Anniversary of the Birth of Jonathan Edwards held at Andover Theol. Sem. Oct. 4 and 5, 1903* (1904). Other publications from the MSS. are by Tryon Edwards, *Charity and its Fruits* (copyright 1851); E. C. Smyth, *Observations Concerning the Scripture Œconomy of the Trinity* (1880); G. P. Fisher, *An Unpublished Essay of Edwards on the Trinity* (1903). Concerning the MSS. see F. B. Dexter in *Proc. Mass. Hist. Soc.*, 2 ser., XV, 2–16 (Mar. 1901). For Edwards's theology and philosophy see A. V. G. Allen, *Jonathan Edwards* (1890); F. H. Foster, *A Genetic Hist. of the New Eng. Theology* (1907); Jan Ridderbos, *De Theologie van Jonathan Edwards* (1907); G. P. Fisher, *Hist. of Christian Doctrine* (1896); Frank Sanborn, in *Jour. of Speculative Philosophy*, Oct. 1883. Adam Leroy Jones, *Early Am. Philosophers* (Columbia Univ. Press, 1898); E. C. Smyth, *Am. Jour. of Theology*, Oct. 1897; H. N. Gardiner, *Philosophical Rev.*, Nov. 1900; J. H. MacCracken, *Philosophical Rev.*, Jan. 1902; F. J. E. Woodbridge, *Philosophical Rev.*, July 1904; Woodbridge Riley, *Am. Philosophy; The Early Schools* (1907); *Am. Thought* (1915); Mattoon M. Curtis, "Kantian Elements in Edwards" in *Festschrift für Heinze* (Berlin, 1916); Vernon L. Parrington, *Main Currents of Am. Thought*, vol. I (1927); Erich Voegelin, *Uber die Form des Amerikanischen Geistes* (1928).]

F.A.C.

EDWARDS, JONATHAN (May 26, 1745–Aug. 1, 1801), theologian, the second son of his more celebrated father of the same name, was born in Northampton, Mass. At the age of six he went with his father to Stockbridge and lived there among the Mohican Indians, to whom his father was missionary, and learned their language. In January 1758, his father moved with his family to Princeton, N. J., to become president of the College of New Jersey, but died in the following March, his wife, the noted Sarah (Pierpont) Edwards, dying in October of the same year. Thus orphaned, the son was enabled by friends to prepare for the college at Princeton, from which he graduated in 1765. During his course he had a deep religious experience, and made profession of his faith. For a year after graduation he studied theology with his father's friend, Joseph Bellamy [*q.v.*], at Bethlehem, Conn., and for another year preached here and there. He then accepted a tutorship at Princeton. After two years of teaching he became, in January 1769, pastor of the White Haven Church of New Haven, Conn. The year after his settlement he married Mary Porter, who was drowned in 1782. In December 1783, he married Mercy Sabin.

"In person," says his grandson, "Dr. Edwards was slender, erect, and somewhat above the ordinary stature. His complexion was dark; his features bold and prominent; his hair raven black; his eye keen, piercing and intelligent to a remarkable degree." The portrait prefixed to his *Works* indicates that his features and expression were harsh and severe; yet he was a man of tender feelings, generous to the poor, with a special interest in the negroes and a hatred of slavery and the slave-trade. His experience in his first pastorate was not unlike that of his father, for he was unable to heal the divisions that existed at the time of his coming, and two years later the church split on the same issue of the Half-Way Covenant which had made trouble for his father at Northampton. The particular point in question was whether the children of those who were not members of the church should be baptized, a practise to which both the Edwards were opposed. The larger part of his church remained under his pastorate for a number of years, but there came a new access of dissatisfaction owing to the Revolution and to the growth of liberal opinions among his people, and the church dwindled, so that in January 1795 he was dismissed from his charge, on the ground that the church was no longer able to maintain a pastor, though it bore witness to his high character and ability. A year later he became pastor at Colebrook, Conn., where he was able to give time to literary work. After some three years at Colebrook, he accepted the presidency of Union College, Schenectady, N. Y., but, as in his father's case at Princeton, his presidency was short; for he died only two years after taking up the work. Like his father he preached on the first Sunday of the year of his death from the text, "This year thou shalt die."

The similarity of his career to that of his father corresponds to a similarity in their mental qualities. Both were silent and reserved men, somewhat morbidly religious, and devoted to the development of doctrine by the keenest and most uncompromising logic, though not without personal tenderness of feeling. Yet their doctrine, for all its severity, had in it an important progressive element, not generally appreciated as such, which later contributed largely to the more humane teachings known as "progressive orthodoxy." The father took a great step forward by maintaining, in opposition to the older Calvinism, that men could repent if they would, though the will itself was determined from above. The particular contribution of the son to the "improvements" on the older Calvinism was the "governmental" theory of the atonement, as opposed to the previous "satisfaction" theory. This newer theory was not entirely original with him, but gained acceptance mainly through his presentation of it. It declared that the sacrificial sufferings of Christ were not to be understood either as the payment of a debt due to God, or as the infliction on Christ of precisely those sufferings which would otherwise have been endured by those who were forgiven for his sake; they were rather the demonstration, by means of a willing victim, of the moral government of the world, whereby God could without inconsistency forgive freely such as repented and put their trust in Christ. This theory was based on a conception of God as a benevolent moral governor, rather than as an arbitrary sovereign, developed by the elder Edwards. Two important consequences were drawn by the son and his fellow-workers from these conclusions: first, that Christ died for all men and not simply for the elect; second, that neither the sin of Adam nor the righteousness of Christ were imputed to men, moral qualities not being thus transferable. These points, along with the declaration of the ability of men to repent, formed the distinctive characteristics of the New England Theology over against the older "Triangle" of inability, imputation, and limited atonement.

In addition to his discussion of the atonement, Edwards published a defense of eternal punishment and also a defense of his father's theory of the will, a treatise on the Mohican language, and a number of short theological articles. He also edited a number of his father's manuscripts for publication. He lacked the imagination and originality of the elder Edwards, but he had a powerful mind, and gave a great impulse to the development of a more progressive type of thought in theology.

[The chief sources of information are the memoir by his grandson, Tryon Edwards, in *The Works of Jonathan Edwards, D.D., Late President of Union College, with a Memoir of his Life* (2 vols., 1842); and the funeral sermon in the collected edition of his *Works* (2 vols., 1850). For a discussion of his theological thought, see F. H. Foster, *A Genetic Hist. of the New England Theology* (1907). See also Wm. B. Sprague, *Annals Am. Pulpit*, vol. I (1857), p. 653.] B. W. B.

EDWARDS, JULIAN (Dec. 11, 1855–Sept. 5, 1910), stage composer, was born at Manchester, England, where he received his early schooling. He soon showed an aptitude for music, and was placed under Sir Herbert Oakley and Sir George Macfarren for studies in theory and composition, then became "Maestro al piano" with Carl Rosa, and conductor of the Royal English Opera Company. In 1888 he came to America to become leader of the J. C. Duff Opera Company, settled at Yonkers, and was soon identified with the New York musical colony. He married Philippine Siedle, sister of the technical manager of the Metropolitan Opera House. His best-known work in serious vein was the opera *King René's Daughter* (1893), based on the one-act play of Henrik Hertz, and intended for a Sonzogno competition. In this, Iolanthe, the daughter, who has lost her sight through fright at a fire occurring during her childhood, is shown living in a secret vale, surrounded by loving care, and brought up not to know what sight is. A parental marriage contract makes Tristan, Count of the rival Vermandois, her future spouse; but he has never seen her. Entering the vale by chance, he finds her sleeping, awakens her by taking as keepsake a magic amulet by which her physician, Ebn Jahia, kept her at rest, and is completely charmed by her courtesy. Not knowing who she is, he attempts to repudiate his betrothal to the king's daughter. He leaves, but returns with his retainers, to find that his unknown adored and the king's daughter are the same person. This crisis, with her physician's care, restores her sight. Another short opera by Edwards was *The Patriot* (1907), in which Washington, alone, takes refuge from a storm in the house of a Tory who, with a spy, has been plotting the commander's death. The daughter of the house, sympathizing with the Colonials, recoils at having to betray her father, and instead, stays in the room Washington was supposed to occupy and takes the stab intended for him. Other serious operas by Edwards were *Corinne, Elfinella,* and *Victorian,* the last a setting of Longfellow's "Spanish Student," produced by the Royal English Opera Company at Covent Garden in 1883. It was as a creator of light opera of a high standard, however, that he became best known. He could write good concerted music and strong finales, which accounted for his success. His *Brian Boru* (1896) became especially popular and caused its composer to be compared with Balfe. Its plot, which might well serve for serious opera, shows Brian defeating Briton invaders, but coming under the spell of their princess, Elfrida, who uses her power over him to get him taken prisoner by a band of her soldiers. After a rescue he defeats the invaders again, and this time proceeds to his coronation without being bewitched by any foreign siren. The story is strongly dramatic, but fairies, magic fiddles, and comic love scenes, as well as verbal dialogue, give the work a rather light effect. Other notable light operas were: *Jupiter* (1892), *Friend Fritz* (1893), *Dolly Varden* (1901), *The Goddess of Truth* (1896), *The Princess Chic* (1899), *The Jolly Musketeer* (1898), *The Wedding Day* (1897), *The Girl and the Governor* (1907), *The Motor Girl* (1909), *The Maid of Plymouth,* and *The Belle of London Town. When Johnny Comes Marching Home* had a long summer run at McVicker's in 1902. It contained the effective song "My Own United States" which was published separately, with new verses, at the request of the National Song Society. Naturally vigorous and rhythmic, this song is especially noteworthy for its use of the official title of the country instead of the more common but less accurate "America." The composer's more serious style was illustrated by several cantatas, including "Lazarus" (1907), which, led by him in a Sunday concert at the Metropolitan, won much appreciation for its classical learning and oratorio effects of strength; "The Redeemer" (1907), "Mary Magdalen," and "Lord of Life and Love" (1909). His secular works in this form included "The Mermaid" (1907) and "De Montfort's Daughter" (1899), the latter for treble voices. His incidental music to *Quo Vadis* deserves mention, also several song collections, of which *Sunlight and Shadow* was the most successful.

[*Boston Transcript*, Jan. 7, 1897, and Sept. 7, 1910; *Musical Courier*, Sept. 7, 1910; *Musical America*, Sept. 10, 1910; Janet M. Green, "Musical Biographies," being vol. I of the *Am. Hist. and Encyc. of Music* (1908), ed. by W. L. Hubbard; W. J. Baltzell, *Baltzell's Dict. of Musicians* (1911); *Who's Who in America*, 1910–11.]

A. E.

EDWARDS, JUSTIN (Apr. 25, 1787–July 23, 1853), Congregational clergyman, writer of tracts, was born in Westhampton, Mass., the third child of Justin and Elizabeth (Clark) Edwards, and a direct descendant of Alexander Edwards, who came to America from Wales in 1640 and settled in Springfield, Mass. He was a second cousin of Bela Bates Edwards [*q.v.*]. The elder Justin Edwards was a farmer, who allowed his son to go to Williams College, where he graduated in 1810 as valedictorian of his class. To save money, he often walked from his home to college, a distance of forty miles, and he spent his winter vacations in teaching. After some experience as a teacher in Athens, N. Y., he entered Andover Theological Seminary, at Andover, Mass., then a center of orthodox Calvinism, in March 1811. Before he could complete his course, he was elected pastor of the South Church, in Andover, being ordained on Dec. 2, 1812. On Sept. 17, 1817, he was married to Lydia, daughter of Asa Bigelow, of Colchester, Conn., by whom he had six children. His service continued until 1827, when he resigned to accept the agency of the American Temperance Society. On Jan. 1, 1828, he was installed as pastor of the Salem Street Church, in Boston, but his health broke down and he was soon obliged to abandon his clerical duties.

While in Andover, Edwards helped to start some significant social and religious movements. In 1814 he aided in organizing the New England Tract Society, and he was early enlisted in the temperance cause. In 1829 he took a position as corresponding secretary of the American Temperance Society, in which capacity he traveled over a large section of the United States and published a series of pamphlets called the Permanent Temperance Documents which had a large circulation. He maintained his permanent residence in Andover, however, and, on Sept. 7, 1836, was inaugurated as president of Andover Theological Seminary, his salary for five years having been guaranteed by the philanthropist, William Bartlet. On Apr. 19, 1842, when funds for the position were no longer forthcoming, he resigned. For thirty-three years after 1820 he was a trustee of Andover Theological Seminary, being president of the Board from 1850 to 1853. At the formation of the American and Foreign Sabbath Union in 1842, he was chosen secretary, and, during the next seven years, covered more than 48,000 miles and prepared the Permanent Sabbath Documents, of which more than 600,000 copies were printed. He was the author of several widely popular tracts, including: *A Well Conditioned Farm, A Sermon on the Way to be Saved* (1826), *On the Traffic in Ardent Spirit,* and *A Sermon on the Unction from the Holy One* (1830), and many of his sermons were published as pamphlets. The American Temperance Society circulated more pamphlets from his pen than from that of any other man. From 1849 until his death he was employed by the American Tract Society in preparing a brief commentary on the Bible, of which he actually completed the New Testament and as far as the Ninetieth Psalm in the Old Testament. Taken ill in April 1852, he never fully recovered, and in the following year he died at Bath Alum Springs, Va., where he had gone for his health. He was buried in the Chapel Cemetery at Andover. He was tall and erect, with a reserved and stately bearing which often wrongly seemed to be austerity. He was rather awkward in manner, with few oratorical graces, but his homely sincerity impressed his congregations. His speech in the pulpit was direct and practical, and he was an uncompromising Calvinist in his theology.

[Wm. A. Hallock, *A Sketch of the Life . . . of the Rev. Justin Edwards* (Am. Tract Soc., 1855) is somewhat verbose and effusive; an excellent brief account may be found in *Hist. Manual of the South Church in Andover, Mass.* (1859). See also W. B. Sprague, *Annals Am. Pulpit,* vol. II (1859); S. L. Bailey, *Hist. Sketches of Andover* (1880).] C.M.F.

EDWARDS, MORGAN (May 9, 1722 o.s.–Jan. 28, 1795), Baptist clergyman, church historian, was born of Welsh stock in Trevethin Parish, Monmouthshire, England. His first religious training came from the Anglican church, for which he ever retained high respect, but in 1738 he passed over to Baptist views. After attending a village school near his home, he entered the Baptist college at Bristol. At sixteen he had begun to preach and for seven years, while continuing his theological studies, he supplied a small church at Boston, Lincolnshire. Acquiring a smattering of Hebrew and becoming somewhat proficient in New Testament Greek, he later ranked among Baptist ministers in America as a classical scholar. Herein lay the elements of intellectual attainment which impressed his contemporaries. Though his ordination did not occur till June 1, 1757, for nine years, 1750–59, he was pastor at Cork, Ireland. It was here that he married his first wife, Mary, daughter of Joshua Nun of Cork, by whom he had eight children. After preaching for a year at Rye, Sussex, he was proposed by Dr. John Gill to the Baptist church in Philadelphia, Pa., which had written to London for aid in securing a pastor. Arriving in America in May 1761, he began on July 1 his pastorate of ten years. Within this relatively short period falls what may most distinctively be considered his public career.

Although tradition ranks Edwards among the greater ministers of this noted Philadelphia church, there is little specific record of his contribution to the development of the local field. That there was some growth of the church is evidenced by the number of baptisms, by the erection, after about a year, of a larger edifice, and by the appointment of an assistant. His relations with the church were marked by frankness on his part and by liberality on the part of both. For fifteen years Edwards had an obsession that he would die in 1770, and on Jan. 1 of that year he preached a sermon setting forth this idea, using as text, "This year thou shalt die." This event had been erroneously represented as the preaching of his own funeral sermon. It doubtless impaired his reputation and the next year he retired from the pastorate. A recurring habit of intoxication leading much later to his exclusion for several years from membership in the church, was a more important cause of the severance of the pastoral tie. In the broader relations of the denomination, Edwards, from his arrival, occupied an eminent place and became a constructive force. It has been asserted that he took the initiative in the founding of Rhode Island College. He certainly showed zeal in the enterprise, was a prime mover in securing a charter for the college, and in 1767 and 1768 undertook a fairly successful mission in Great Britain, raising funds especially for the president's salary.

At the close of his services with the Philadelphia church, he removed to Newark, Del. He never again entered the pastorate, but traveled widely and gave addresses on religious subjects. On his many journeys he was assiduous in gathering information on Baptist history and developments, preserving it usually in manuscripts arranged according to the states to which the data belonged. This collection, together with his influence upon the preservation of ecclesiastical records, was his chief contribution to church history and the basis of his popular reputation in that field. Of a twelve-volume work which he planned, four parts of *Materials Toward A History of the American Baptists* have been printed, bearing respectively upon Pennsylvania (1770), New Jersey (1792), Rhode Island (in *Collections of the Rhode Island Historical Society*, vol. VI, 1867), Delaware (1885, printed earlier in the *Pennsylvania Magazine of History and Biography*, April, July 1885). Brief manuscript volumes, dealing with Delaware, Virginia, North Carolina, South Carolina, and Georgia are at Crozer Theological Seminary.

Morgan Edwards is frequently referred to as the only Baptist minister in America who supported the British cause in the Revolution. This is an exaggeration, although he is correctly placed among the Loyalists. He was among those Baptists, including James Manning and Isaac Backus [*qq.v.*], who were at the conference at Carpenter's Hall, when in 1774 the attempt was made to win over the Massachusetts delegates to the Continental Congress to the principle of separation of church and state. The next year, before the Committee of Safety, he made a recantation of some indiscreet utterances. He died at Pencader, Del. A second wife of his later years, a Mrs. Singleton of Delaware, had predeceased him.

[A. D. Gillette, ed., *Minutes of the Phila. Bapt. Asso.* (1851); Wm. Rogers, memorial discourse preached in Phila., Feb. 22, 1795, printed in John Rippon, *Baptist Ann. Reg.* (London, 1796) and in David Benedict, *A Gen. Hist. of the Baptist Denomination in America* (1813), II, 294–301; W. W. Keen, *The Bi-Centennial Celebration of the Founding of the First Bapt. Church of the City of Phila.* (1899); Wm. B. Sprague, *Annals Am. Pulpit*, vol. VI (1860); R. A. Guild, *Early Hist. of Brown Univ.* (1897).]

W. H. A.

EDWARDS, NINIAN (Mar. 17, 1775–July 20, 1833), governor of Illinois, senator, was born in Montgomery County, Md., the son of Benjamin and Margaret (Beall) Edwards. His father, a native of Stafford County, Va., and a brother of John Edwards [*q.v.*], United States senator from Kentucky, was a member of the Maryland convention which ratified the Federal Constitution and a representative in the Third Congress. Ninian Edwards was instructed by private tutors and later attended Dickinson College, Carlisle, Pa. After leaving college he entered upon the study of law. In 1795 he removed to Kentucky, where he took up a tract of land on behalf of his father. Within a short time he began the practise of law and almost immediately entered state politics, being elected to the legislature before he was of age. In 1803 he was appointed to the bench and at the age of thirty-two became chief justice of the Kentucky court of appeals.

A decisive event in his early life was his appointment as governor of Illinois Territory by President Madison in 1809, a post which he held until 1818, when the territory became a state. He also became *ex officio* superintendent of Indian affairs, and during the period of his governorship occupied much of his time in maintaining the authority of the United States among the Indians upon the frontier. During the War of 1812 he was active in the defense of the Illinois border, and in the first year of the war organized and led an expedition to Peoria. By the time of the admission of Illinois in 1818, there had emerged from the chaos of territorial politics two factions, an Edwards and an anti-Edwards group, an alignment which persisted through the early years of statehood. At the first state election, Edwards was chosen United States senator for the short term, and was reëlected for the full term in 1819. His career in the Senate was scarcely a brilliant one. He was a strong advocate of legislation which would grant land to settlers on easier terms, and he favored the admission of Missouri as a slave state. He seems to have played little part in the famous convention struggle in Illinois, culminating in 1824, which turned largely on the issue of slavery. In 1824, he resigned from the Senate to accept an appointment by President Monroe as minister to Mexico. Before taking his post, however, he was obliged to resign this office in turn, owing to his having made certain reckless charges against William H. Crawford, secretary of the treasury, which he was unable to substantiate. He sought to rehabilitate and vindicate himself by turning to state politics, and in 1826 was elected governor of Illinois by a narrow margin. Though his power had begun to wane, he was still the main center around which Illinois factional politics revolved. Both before and after his election, he carried on a bitter attack against those who had been responsible for the administration of the state bank at Edwardsville, which added nothing to his popularity. As governor, he urged the removal of the Indians from the state (Washburne, *post,* pp. 306 ff.). He also continued to insist upon the right of the state to that part of the public domain lying within its borders.

He did not seek reëlection in 1830, but two years later he was defeated in an attempt to win a seat in Congress. His political prestige, which had at one time been considerable, was a thing of the past. His decline in power may be explained partly on the basis of certain political shortcomings, partly on the ground of instability of temperament and character. Edwards was not a man of strong political convictions and was inclined to hesitate at critical times. On the other hand, he occasionally acted rashly, with little appreciation of probable consequences. Perhaps the worst that can be said of him is that he was lacking in judgment (Pease, *post,* p. 93). In 1803 he was married to Elvira Lane, and his son, Ninian Wirt Edwards [*q.v.*], later attained to some prominence in the state. He died of cholera at Belleville, Ill.

[Many of the Edwards papers now preserved in the Chicago Hist. Soc. are published in the following: Ninian W. Edwards, *Hist. of Ill. from 1778 to 1833, and Life and Times of Ninian Edwards* (1870); "The Edwards Papers," in *Chicago Hist. Soc. Colls.*, vol. III (1884), ed. by Elihu B. Washburne; "Executive Letter-Book of Ninian Edwards, 1826–1830," in *Colls. Ill. State Hist. Lib.*, vol. IV (1909), ed. by E. B. Greene and C. W. Alvord. For the background of Edwards's career, see S. J. Buck, *Ill. in 1818* (1917); C. W. Alvord, *The Ill. Country, 1673–1818* (1920); and T. C. Pease, *The Frontier State, 1818–1848* (1919). See also Thos. Ford, *A Hist. of Ill. from its Commencement as a State in 1818 to 1847* (1854); John Moses, *Ill. Hist. and Statistical* (1898); *Biog. Dir. Am. Cong.* (1928); and Georgie Hortense Edwards, *Hist. Sketches of the Edwards and Todd Families,* etc. (1894); John Reynolds, *My Own Times, Embracing also the Hist. of My Life* (1855).] W. E. S.

EDWARDS, NINIAN WIRT (Apr. 15, 1809–Sept. 2, 1889), first superintendent of public instruction of Illinois, was born at Frankfort, Ky., the son of Ninian Edwards [*q.v.*], later governor of Illinois Territory, and his wife, Elvira Lane. While attending Transylvania University, from the law department of which he graduated in 1833, young Edwards married, Feb. 16, 1832, Elizabeth P. Todd, elder sister of the future wife of Abraham Lincoln. He was appointed attorney-general of Illinois by Gov. John Reynolds in 1834, but resigned in 1835 and established himself as a merchant at Springfield, Ill. He served in the state legislature as a representative, 1836–40, 1848–51, and as a state senator 1844–48. He was a member of the constitutional convention of 1847. Edwards has been described as proud of his family and name, aloof, one of the most eminent figures in Springfield society (Beveridge, *post,* p. 178). He was, however, a close friend of Abraham Lincoln, being associated with him as a member of the "Long Nine" delegation from Sangamon County. It was at Edwards's house, where she had come on a visit in 1839, that Lincoln first met Mary Todd; it was with Edwards's encouragement that their stormy courtship was begun; and it was in his home that their marriage took place.

In 1852 Edwards deserted the ranks of the Whigs and became a Democrat. Standing for reëlection to the Assembly, he was defeated, and in 1854 he was appointed by Gov. Matteson, under the authority of a law establishing the office, to be superintendent of public instruction. His duties included lecturing in every county in the state and endeavoring to secure uniformity of text-books. He proceeded to perform them earnestly in the face of active hostility to and passive contempt for improvement of the state's educational system. A visit to the East sent him back an advocate of a state normal school, later established near Bloomington (*Urbana Union,* Oct. 22, 1857), which he hoped to support by a share of the publishers' profits from text-books adopted (*Prairie Farmer,* January 1855; *Illinois State Journal,* Dec. 28, 1854; *Ottawa Weekly Republican,* Oct. 7, 1854). His lectures were often treated with contempt, as at Ottawa where nine persons turned out to hear him. He secured, however, from the Illinois legislature of 1855 the passage of a school law, which, though it fell far short of his wishes, laid the foundation of the state's school system (*Report of the State Superintendent of Common Schools . . . of the State of Illinois, Dec. 10, 1854; Laws of the State of Illinois,* 1855, pp. 51–91). His term ended in 1857. Between 1862 and 1865 he held by Lincoln's appointment the place of captain commissary of supplies. In 1870 he published the *History of Illinois from 1778 to 1833 and Life and Times of Ninian Edwards.* The sole value of this work lies in the fact that it contains, very ill-arranged, a large body of his father's papers and letters.

[In addition to references above, see: *Biennial Reports of the Supt. of Public Instruction of the State of Ill.*, 1884–86, p. cxc, 1888–90, p. cxii; Arthur C. Cole, *Era of the Civil War, 1848–70* (1919); Albert J. Beveridge, *Abraham Lincoln, 1809–1858* (1928); *Chicago Tribune*, Sept. 1, 3, 1889; *Daily Inter Ocean* (Chicago), Sept. 3, 1889.] T. C. P.

EDWARDS, OLIVER (Jan. 30, 1835–Apr. 28, 1904), Union soldier, inventor, was born in Springfield, Mass., the son of Elisha and Eunice (Lombard) Edwards. He attended public and high schools in Springfield, graduating from the latter in 1852. In 1856 he went West and built a foundry at Warsaw, Ill., becoming a partner in Neberling, Edwards & Company. Here he remained until the outbreak of the Civil War, when he returned to Massachusetts and entered military service. He raised a company to be part of the Hampden County Regiment, but his men were taken for the 10th Massachusetts Volunteers, then being organized, of which he was appointed first lieutenant and adjutant June 21, 1861. He was selected as senior aide-de-camp, and served as such on the staff of Gen. Couch until Aug. 9, 1862, when he was commissioned major, 37th Massachusetts Volunteers, and directed to organize this regiment, of which he was later made colonel. He served through the Peninsular campaign of 1862, also in the battles of Fredericksburg and Gettysburg, after which he was ordered to New York City, in command of a special brigade, to quell the draft riots of July 1863. On the completion of this duty he returned with his regiment to the Army of the Potomac, and took part in the battle of Rappahannock Station. During the second day of the battle of the Wilderness, when in command of a brigade, he made a charge at the head of the 37th Regiment and succeeded in breaking through the Confederate lines. His service was most conspicuous at the battle of Spotsylvania, where on the second day he held the "bloody angle" for eleven hours with his own brigade, and at the head of twenty-one regiments for thirteen hours thereafter, making twenty-four hours of continuous fighting. He subsequently participated in the battles of the overland campaign and in the defense of Washington, was with Sheridan in his campaign in the Shenandoah Valley, and took part in the battle of Winchester, of which town he was placed in command by that officer. He was offered the provost-marshal generalship of the middle military division, but declined, preferring to command combat troops. In the final assault on Petersburg, his brigade captured many guns and prisoners, and he received the surrender of the city from the mayor, Apr. 3, 1865. At the battle of Sailor's Creek, Edwards with his brigade captured Lieut.-Gen. Early and his staff, Maj.-Gen. Custis Lee with his staff and an entire brigade, and many other prisoners. He received the brevets of brigadier-general, United States Volunteers, Oct. 19, 1864, for gallant and distinguished services at the battle of Spotsylvania Court House, Va., and for meritorious conduct at the battle of Winchester, Va., and major-general, United States Volunteers, for conspicuous gallantry at the battle of Sailor's Creek, Va. He was appointed brigadier-general, United States Volunteers, May 19, 1865, and mustered out of the service, Jan. 15, 1866. On Sept. 3, 1863, he married Ann Eliza Johnson. After the war he was for a year and a half postmaster at Warsaw, Ill., resigning to become general agent of the Florence Machine Company, Northampton, Mass., of which he later became superintendent. While there he patented several improvements on the sewing machine, and invented the Florence spring skate and the Florence oil stove. After being with the Florence Machine Company seven years, he resigned and returned to Warsaw. In 1882 he went to England, where for two or three years he was general superintendent of the Gardner Machine and Gun Company. Returning to Illinois, he served three terms as mayor of Warsaw.

[*Official Records (Army)*; Jas. L. Bowen, *Hist. of the Thirty-Seventh Regiment, Mass. Vols.* (1884) and in *Battles and Leaders of the Civil War*, IV (1888), 177; Alfred S. Roe, *The Tenth Regiment, Mass. Vol. Infantry* (1909); Chas. W. Chapin, *Sketches of the Old Inhabitants and Other Citizens of Old Springfield*, etc. (1893); *Portr. and Biog. Record of Hancock, McDonough and Henderson Counties, Ill.* (1894); *Biog. Rev. of Hancock County, Ill.* (1907); *Ann. Report of the Commissioner of Patents*, pp. 1869 ff.] C. F. C.

EDWARDS, PIERPONT (Apr. 8, 1750–Apr. 5, 1826), lawyer, politician, jurist, was the eleventh and youngest child of the Rev. Jonathan Edwards [*q.v.*] and Sarah (Pierpont) Edwards. He was born in Northampton, Mass., but spent most of his childhood in Stockbridge, where his father served as missionary after dismissal from his Northampton pastorate. He graduated at the College of New Jersey in 1768, studied law, and began practise at New Haven, Conn., in 1771. In May 1769 he married Frances, daughter of Moses Ogden of Elizabethtown, N. J., and after her death, which occurred on July 7, 1800, he married Mary Tucker of Bridgeport, Conn. He spent the greater part of his life in New Haven, although he removed, later on, to Bridgeport. He supported the Revolutionary movement and performed military service during the campaigns in Connecticut. He was elected to the lower house of the legislature in 1777, 1784–85, and 1787–90. He served as speaker for three sessions during the last period. In 1787–88 he was a delegate to the Continental Congress. He supported the Federal Constitution and was a member of the Connecticut ratifying convention.

As a lawyer he was successful and prosperous. He had liberal views in both politics and religion, and if he is not belied, in morals as well. During his political career his character was savagely attacked. Whether he was an ordinary example of the alleged delinquent "minister's sons," a pathological result of too much Calvinism in early youth, or merely the victim of Federalist propaganda, is of no great importance in view of his willingness to assume the defense of minority causes, champion liberalism and religious freedom, and conduct a long and discouraging contest with the dominant elements in Connecticut affairs. In 1800 he took an active part in organizing the Jeffersonian Republicans and for some years thereafter was the recognized leader of the party in the state, serving as chairman of the general committee. He led the movement for a new state constitution and in 1804 defended before the legislature the justices whose commissions had been revoked for participation in the Republican convention of that year. He was especially interested in securing the disestablishment of the Congregational Church and was the object of considerable clerical abuse as a result. A few letters exchanged with President Jefferson show that he was trusted to a large degree with the distribution of federal patronage within the state, and fully realized its importance in establishing an efficient organization.

In 1806 he was appointed judge of the district court of Connecticut by President Jefferson. In this court he served throughout the remainder of his life. Shortly after his appointment, while presiding in the circuit court, he charged the grand jury that it was their duty to consider the authors and publishers of libels against the government, and "diligently enquire after all breaches of law," inasmuch as "such publications, if the authors of them may not be restrained . . . will more effectually undermine and sap the foundations of our Constitution and Government, than any kind of treason that can be named" (*Litchfield Witness,* Apr. 30, 1806). For a Republican, with recollections of the Sedition Law fresh in mind, this was astonishing doctrine. Furthermore it involved, in effect, the principle that the United States courts had jurisdiction at common law, no statutory authority for libel prosecutions having been conferred. In response to Judge Edwards's charge, the grand jury indicted several clergymen and editors, although there was manifest reluctance to push the cases. When, however, the publishers of the *Connecticut Courant* were prosecuted for a libel on President Jefferson and Congress, the federal Supreme Court demolished the doctrine of common-law jurisdiction by declaring that "the legislative authority of the Union must first make an act a crime, affix a punishment to it, and declare the Court that shall have jurisdiction of the offence" (*United States* vs. *Hudson & Goodwin, 7 Cranch,* 34, February term, 1812). The Connecticut libel prosecutions received wide-spread publicity in connection with the newspaper warfare then in progress throughout New England, but can hardly be held to redound to the credit of Judge Edwards.

In 1818 he was a member of the famous Connecticut constitutional convention, serving as chairman of the committee which drafted and presented the new instrument of government. This constitution established most of the reforms which Republicans had demanded for almost twenty years. The calling of the convention was preceded by involved political maneuvers, and Edwards took an important part in developing the strategy by which the various elements opposing Federalist rule were consolidated into a powerful and victorious majority. The adoption of the constitution of 1818, the triumph of "toleration" which he had so long advocated, marks the high point of his career and constitutes his greatest service to the state and indirectly to the country at large.

[The best account of Pierpont Edwards is contained in E. E. Atwater, *Hist. of the City of New Haven* (1887). A very brief sketch can be found in D. Loomis and J. G. Calhoun, *The Judicial and Civil Hist. of Conn.* (1895). See also W. H. Edwards, *The Memorial Volume of the Edwards Family Meeting* (1871) and *Timothy and Rhoda Ogden Edwards . . . and Their Descendants* (1903); and R. B. Moffat, *Pierrepont Genealogies* (1913). Edwards's activities as a politician are referred to in B. C. Steiner, "Connecticut's Ratification of the Federal Constitution" in *Proc. Am. Antiquarian Soc.*, n.s., vol. XXV (1915); and in R. J. Purcell, *Conn. in Transition* (1918). An obituary notice is contained in the *Columbian Register* (New Haven), Apr. 8, 1826.]

W. A. R.

EDWARDS, TALMADGE (1747–June 4, 1821), glove manufacturer, was born of English ancestry in England near the Scottish border. Here he was educated and learned the trade of leather dresser while still in his teens. A younger son, and therefore ineligible, by English law, to inherit the family estate, he emigrated to America about 1770, going first to Rhode Island but later to Beekman's Precinct in Dutchess County, N. Y., where he found employment at his trade.

Edwards

During the Revolution he sided with the colonists, serving in the 6th Regiment of militia of his county. After the war, in 1783, he moved with his family to the more virgin portion of New York in the vicinity of Johnstown, Fulton County, where trading-posts had been established and Indians as well as early settlers brought in skins and furs for trade. Here he started a tannery of his own. In 1784 he bought land within the present city limits of Johnstown, continuing to ply his trade and also opening a general store. Some years earlier, a group of glove-makers, members of the glove guild of Scotland, had settled at Kingsboro, a short distance north of Johnstown. They lived a hand-to-mouth existence, making gloves and mittens for the surrounding settlers. Their process of dressing leather was unsatisfactory, however, and in 1809, having heard of Edwards's success with the "ring-tail" process, William Mills and James Burr induced him to go to Kingsboro to teach his method of leather-tanning to the glove-makers. Edwards, who was in reduced circumstances, thus became directly interested in glove manufacture. Being able to dress leather in quantities and feeling that there should be a larger market for gloves and mittens than existed locally at the time, Edwards secured country girls to come to his tannery in Johnstown to cut out gloves, which were then sent to the farmers' wives to be sewed together. This marked the beginning of the glove and mitten industry in the United States. The first sales of gloves in "wholesale lots" occurred in 1810 when Edwards took a few dozen pairs with him on a horseback trip to Albany to purchase a new stock of merchandise for his store, which he was still operating. On the way, and after he had reached Albany, he sold his pack in dozen and portion-of-dozen lots. In addition to his innovation in organizing the manufacture of gloves, he improved the process of tanning glove leather. He originated the "oil-tan" method for preparing buckskin, a process still in use. About 1780 he had married Mary, daughter of Ezekiel and Mary (Knowles) Sherman, of Exeter, R. I. They had eight children, the eldest of whom, John, represented the 15th Congressional District of New York in the Twenty-fifth Congress, 1837–39. Both Edwards and his wife are buried in the colonial cemetery in Johnstown.

[David H. Sherman, *Records of the Sherman Family* (1887); *Calendar of Hist. MSS. Relating to the War of the Revolution in the Office of the Sec. of State, Albany, N. Y.* (1868), I, 73; Chas. E. Fitch, *Encyc. of Biog. of N. Y.* (1916), vol. IV; correspondence with the Johnstown Public Library.] C. W. M.

EDWARDS, WELDON NATHANIEL (Jan. 25, 1788–Dec. 18, 1873), planter, legislator, president of the North Carolina secession convention, was a native of Northampton County, N. C., the son of Benjamin Edwards. After attending the Warrenton Academy, he read law and began practise at Warrenton, but his professional career was soon terminated, for he entered public life and developed an absorbing interest in agriculture. "Poplar Mount," his plantation near Ridgeway, became under his management almost a model of scientific agriculture. He soon abandoned cotton planting and, centering his attention on grain, hay, fruit, tobacco, and the breeding of improved stock, amassed a large fortune. His game chickens were his particular pride and delight. Genuinely hospitable and fond of society, he kept his home constantly full of guests. He loved children and had them always about him.

A protégé of Nathaniel Macon, he was in politics completely in sympathy with him. He represented Warren County in the House of Commons in 1814 and 1815, and, also in 1815, succeeded Macon in the lower house of Congress, being sworn in with Daniel Webster and serving until 1827, when he declined a reëlection. In Congress he was, like Macon, an advocate of economy. He voted against the tariff of 1826 and the later protective measures, fought the Missouri Compromise, and consistently opposed internal improvements by the federal government, though he championed them by state action. He favored censure of Jackson for the invasion of Florida in 1819, but he later belonged to the Jackson group which opposed the Adams administration. He seldom made a speech and held few committee assignments. From 1833 to 1846 and from 1850 to 1854 he was state senator, and was speaker during the latter period. In 1835 he was a delegate to the constitutional convention, where he was active in the movement to remove Catholic disabilities, and offered an amendment providing for complete religious toleration. Liberal as he was in this particular, he was politically a conservative and voted against the democratic changes in the constitution. In the same spirit, as state senator in 1852, he opposed and thereby defeated the amendment abolishing a freehold qualification of fifty acres of land for voting for state senator, which was his party's chief pledge. His action infuriated his party, but the proposition was hateful to him as depriving property of protection and as a sure sign that "the idea of the Republican system is fast becoming obsolete and that we are rapidly drifting into a pure democracy." In 1857 Edwards was made a commissioner of the sinking fund and served until Congressional Reconstruction abolished the commission and destroyed the sinking fund.

He was a stanch believer in the right of secession and, while he shrank from its exercise, he felt that the election of Lincoln justified it. He became the leader of the secession party organized in North Carolina early in 1861, and presided over its first state meeting held in Goldsboro in March. He was a delegate to the secession convention and was chosen president by the secessionist group. After the first adjournment of the convention in 1862, he occupied himself in retirement by writing his *Memoir of Nathaniel Macon of North Carolina* (1862). Despite the destruction wrought by the Civil War, his last years were spent in comfortable circumstances. In 1823 he had married Lucy Norfleet of Halifax County, who survived him.

[S. A. Ashe, *Biog. Hist. of N. C.*, I (1905), 265; *Jours. of the Senate and House of Commons . . . of N. C.*, 1833–46, 1850–54; J. G. de R. Hamilton, ed., *The Papers of Thomas Ruffin* (1918–20); "Poplar Mount," in Raleigh *Daily Standard*, Aug. 30, 1871.]

J. G. de R. H.

EDWARDS, WILLIAM (Nov. 11, 1770–Dec. 29, 1851), tanner, inventor, was born in Elizabethtown, N. J., the sixth child of Timothy and Rhoda (Ogden) Edwards. His father was the oldest son of Rev. Jonathan Edwards [*q.v.*] and a brother of Jonathan and Pierpont Edwards [*qq.v.*]. When William was a year old, Timothy Edwards removed to Stockbridge, Mass., where he engaged in trade and prospered, only to lose almost everything but his farm during the Revolution. William attended school until he was twelve and then assisted on his father's farm until he was fourteen. In that year he returned to Elizabethtown to learn the tanning trade with his uncle who was conducting the business established by William's maternal grandfather. The work affected his health, and after a year he went back to Stockbridge and remained on the farm until 1787 when he again returned to Elizabethtown, finishing his apprenticeship in 1789. After serving about a year at his trade in East Haddam, Conn., he went to Northampton, Mass., and with the aid of friends built a tannery there. In this plant he incorporated improvements in arrangement, partially reducing the manual labor involved in the process. When the plant burned down in 1799, a new one was immediately built in which he added still other improvements, chiefly through the use of water power and in heating the leaching liquors. During the succeeding fifteen years this business grew rapidly and a company was organized and incorporated, and one by one five tanneries were put in operation about Northampton. As each was built the newest inventions of Edwards were installed. These included rollers for preparing leather and a hide mill for softening dry leather, patented Oct. 19 and Dec. 30, 1812, respectively, and an improved sole leather tanning process, patented on the latter date. The industrial collapse following the War of 1812, coupled with financial manipulations by Edwards's backers, brought about his complete bankruptcy in 1815. Two years later, however, with the assistance of his sons and New York friends in the leather business, he began anew at Hunter, Greene County, N. Y., and built what was for years the largest tannery in the United States. This was burned down in 1830 but was immediately rebuilt, and four years later Edwards retired and removed to Brooklyn, N. Y. The importance of his improvements can probably be gauged best from the fact that with them the cost of tanning sole leather was reduced from twelve cents to four cents a pound. He is to-day recognized as the founder of the hide and leather industry in the United States. In addition to his business, he found time for military service and politics as well. He served in a Berkshire regiment in 1786 during the Shays Rebellion; joined a grenadier militia company while in Elizabethtown; was captain in 1800 and later was colonel in the regular Massachusetts militia, and commanded a regiment of artillery at Boston in 1813. He also repeatedly represented Northampton in the General Court. On his twenty-third birthday he married Rebecca Tappan of Northampton, daughter of Benjamin and Sarah (Holmes) Tappan. They had eleven children, ten of whom as well as his widow, survived him when he died in his eighty-second year in Brooklyn, N. Y.

[*One Hundred Years of American Commerce* (1895), ed. by C. M. Depew; *Memoirs of Col. Wm. Edwards*, written by himself with notes by son and grandson, printed in 1897; Wm. H. Edwards, *Timothy and Rhoda Ogden Edwards of Stockbridge, Mass. and Their Descendants* (1903); Patent Office Records; *N. Y. Tribune*, Dec. 31, 1851.]

C. W. M.

EDWARDS, WILLIAM HENRY (Mar. 15, 1822–Apr. 4, 1909), entomologist, was born at Hunter, Greene County, N. Y., the son of William W. Edwards and Helen Ann Mann. His father, a tanner by trade, was a son of William Edwards [*q.v.*], whose grandfather was Jonathan Edwards [*q.v.*], the great divine. William H. Edwards, born and brought up in the Catskill Mountains, undoubtedly gained his love of nature during his early days. He entered Williams College, and graduated with the class of 1842, then studied law in New York City. In 1846 he made a journey to South America, in the course of which he collected many birds and butterflies, and as a result of which he wrote *Voyage up the*

River Amazon, a delightful book with vivid descriptions of the tropical vegetation and the strange creatures of the Amazon forests. It was published by the Murrays of London in 1847, and in 1909 (according to Bethune, *post*), there was still a steady sale. Alfred Russel Wallace, in his story of his life (*My Life,* 1905, I, 264–65), states that it was the reading of Edwards's book with its graphic descriptions of the flora and fauna and its pleasing accounts of the people that determined Henry W. Bates and himself to undertake their memorable expedition to the Amazon Valley.

Returning to the United States, Edwards was admitted to the New York bar in 1847, and settled at Newburgh on the Hudson. On May 29, 1851, he was married to Catherine Colt Tappan, at Belleville, N. J. Some years later, having become interested in West Virginia coal fields, he removed to Coalburg in that state, where he was the president of the Ohio & Kanawha Coal Company. He owned much land, built railroads and opened coal-mines, and led a very busy life. He always found time, however, to study butterflies and to prepare articles about them for publication. He sent his first contribution to the *Canadian Entomologist* in October 1868, and later published many papers in that periodical, in the *Transactions of the American Entomological Society,* and in the journal called *Papilio.* His main plan throughout his study was to issue in parts a complete and beautiful work on the butterflies of North America. The first part was issued in 1868. It was a quarto pamphlet of beautiful appearance, with plates that were a revelation. The first volume was completed in July 1872, with fifty plates. The second volume was completed in November 1884. The first part of the third volume was issued in December 1886, and the eighteenth and last in 1897. Edwards paid the greatest attention to the life histories of the insects treated, every stage being described and figured. Important discoveries in the way of seasonal dimorphism and trimorphism of certain species were discussed. Nearly all the plates were drawn by Mrs. Mary Peart, and the coloring was done by Mrs. Lydia Bowen. *The Butterflies of North America* received the enthusiastic praise of European biologists, and ranks as one of the finest contributions to the biology of insects that have come from the United States.

At the age of seventy-five, Edwards gave up his studies of butterflies and spent his remaining years in the production of two books of entirely different character. The first of these was a remarkable volume entitled *Shaksper not Shakespeare,* published in 1900, in which he took up with great vigor the question of the authorship of the Shakespearian plays. It shows a wealth of reading and a remarkable combination of the trained legal mind with the trained scientific mind. It is an aggressive book, and insistent upon the thesis that Shaksper, the actor, could not have written the plays attributed to Shakespeare. The second work was *Timothy and Rhoda Ogden Edwards of Stockbridge, Mass., and their Descendants* (1903), a genealogy of the Edwards family.

[C. J. S. Bethune, in *Canadian Entomologist,* Aug. 1909; Henry Skinner, in *Entomological News,* May 1909; F. A. Dixey, in *Proc. Entomological Soc. of London,* 1909, p. lxxxix; J. W. Tutt in *Entomologists' Record and Journal of Variation* (London), Jan.–Dec. 1909, pp. 193–94; *The Entomologists Monthly Mag.* (London), Aug. 1909; *Gen. Cat. . . . Williams Coll.* (1920); *Wheeling Intelligencer,* Apr. 5, 1909.]

L. O. H.

EDWIN, DAVID (December 1776–Feb. 22, 1841), stipple engraver, was a son of the popular English comedian, John Edwin the elder, and a Mrs. Walmsley, described as "a reputable milliner" of Bath (Thomas Gilliland, *The Dramatic Mirror,* 1808, p. 742). He was born in Bath, England, and was articled to Christian Jossi, a Dutch engraver who studied the art of stipple engraving in England and in 1796 returned to Amsterdam, taking with him his apprentice. Disagreements arising, young Edwin left his preceptor before he had completed his apprenticeship and worked his passage across the Atlantic as a foremast hand, landing in Philadelphia in December 1797, when he was barely twenty-one. Without friends or money, he introduced himself to his fellow countryman, T. B. Freeman, a Philadelphia publisher, who welcomed him and gave him employment. Engravers' supplies were not readily available in Philadelphia, and he found it necessary to manufacture his own tools. His first work, "Infancy of the Scottish Muse," after a painting by Cosway, was a title-page for a collection of Scotch airs selected by Benjamin Carr [*q.v.*]. In 1798 he engraved several portraits of actors for a series published by Freeman.

For a time he was associated with Edward Savage [*q.v.*], portrait-painter and engraver, and, according to Dunlap (*post,* II, 202), accompanied that artist to New York. Probably most of his work was done in Philadelphia, however, where most of his engravings were published, although his name did not appear in the Philadelphia Directory until 1806. His skill was immediately recognized, and he had abundant commissions. About 1801 he engraved Gilbert Stuart's portrait of Dr. William Smith, provost of the University of Pennsylvania. He and Stuart became friends, and Edwin thereafter engraved many of Stuart's portraits. For the *Mirror of Taste and Dramatic Censor* (Philadelphia, 1810–11), he engraved portraits which ornamented each monthly number of the magazine. For the other magazines published in Philadelphia, the *Port Folio,* the *Analectic,* and later the *Casket,* he was called upon to furnish many of the portraits and titles which formed the most notable feature of those publications. In addition he produced a large number of separate plates, among them several portraits of Washington after Stuart, Peale, and Birch, and one of Jefferson. During the War of 1812 his talents were in great demand, and he told Dunlap (*post,* II, 203), "that there was no town of any consequence, from Maine to Louisiana, . . . whose citizens were not in his debt for work done." His close application to business, and severe financial losses which he sustained brought on an illness which for a time led him to abandon his profession. He sought a position as clerk in the auction house of his former employer, Freeman, and for a time, engraved only occasionally. He "opened a grocery store . . . but it was closed through bad debts" (Sartain, *post,* p. 194). Between the years 1818 and 1822 inclusive, he was described in the Philadelphia Directories as "grocer and engraver." His last piece of work was a portrait of Gilbert Stuart by John Neagle. According to Simpson (*post,* p. 348), the finishing touches had to be made by Thomas Kelly, much to the humiliation of Edwin.

In 1831 he lost his position with Freeman and could not induce any publisher to entrust him with a plate (Dunlap, II, 204). In the fall of the same year his eyesight failed him as the result of an attack of influenza. For a time he was engaged as a clerk by William Warren [*q.v.*], manager of the Chestnut Street Theatre, Philadelphia (Sartain, p. 54). Mrs. William Francis, a retired actress, who died in 1834, bequeathed Edwin "a dwelling house and some money invested in stocks" (Simpson, *post,* p. 349). When the Artist's Fund Society of Philadelphia was formed in 1835 he became its treasurer and served in that capacity until his death. He died on Feb. 22, 1841, in Philadelphia and was buried in Ronaldson's Cemetery in that city. Dunlap called him "the first good engraver of the human countenance that appeared in this country" (*post,* II, 199) and it is said of him (Simpson, p. 349) that "no engraver in this country ever imparted to his prints more faithfully the peculiarities of manner belonging to the artist whose pictures he copied."

[The principal authority for Edwin's career is the article in Dunlap's *Hist. of the Arts of Design* (1834, rev. ed., 1918), which was mainly founded on the engraver's own letters. See also John Sartain, *The Reminiscences of a Very Old Man* (1899) and Henry Simpson, *The Lives of Eminent Philadelphians now Deceased* (1859). For lists of his works consult Mantle Fielding's *Catalogue of the Engraved Works of David Edwin* (1905); and David McN. Stauffer's *American Engravers upon Copper and Steel* (2 vols., 1907).] J. J.

EELLS, DAN PARMELEE (Apr. 16, 1825–Aug. 23, 1903), banker, capitalist, descended through a line of New England ministers from Samuel Eells of Barnstable, England, who became in 1661 an inhabitant of Milford, Conn., was born in Westmoreland, Oneida County, N. Y. His father was the Rev. James Eells, and his mother, Mehitable Parmelee, daughter of Deacon Dan Parmelee of Durham, Conn. When he was eleven the family moved to Amherst, Lorain County, Ohio, whence in 1839 he was sent to Elyria, and in 1841 to Oberlin to prepare for college, working his way by doing chores and later by being clerk in a store. In 1843, he entered Oberlin College, and in 1844, Hamilton College. After two years he was obliged to leave college to seek means of self-support. He taught the district school in Amherst in the winter of 1846–47, then worked as a bookkeeper in a Cleveland commission house until 1849. He managed to continue his college studies, however, and is listed among the graduates of Hamilton as of the class of 1848 (*General Roll of Hamilton College, 1812–1908*). Later, he was awarded the degree of master of arts, and in 1890 was made an honorary member of the Phi Beta Kappa Society. In 1850 he entered the Commercial Branch of the State Bank of Ohio in Cleveland and continued in its service through successive stages as bookkeeper, teller, and cashier until the expiration of the charter of the bank in 1865. The Commercial National Bank of Cleveland succeeded to the business of the Branch bank. Of this Eells was vice-president. In 1868 he was elected president and continued in that office until his retirement in 1897, a banking career of fifty years. His command of capital enabled him to take an active part in the development of transportation and manufacturing during the last quarter of the nineteenth century. He was one of the promoters of the Lake Erie & Western, of the New York, Chicago & St. Louis, and of the Ohio Central railways. He was one of the founders and first president of the Ohio Central Coal Company, active in the management of the United States Express Company, and of the Otis Iron and Steel Company. His autobiography lists thirty-two companies in which he was a director, in fifteen of which he held an executive office. His industrial interests included oil refining, cement manufacture, iron and steel in all phases, smelting, coal, coke and gas works, electric and steam railway operation. Those in Cleveland who knew him intimately also remember him for his part in many religious, educational, and charitable enterprises. He was a member of the Board of Education of Cleveland (1865–68), a trustee of Lane Theological Seminary, of Lake Erie, Oberlin, and Hamilton colleges. He was described in a memorial address as "a gentleman of the old school,—courtly gracious, genial, affectionate, kind" (Rev. Paul F. Sutphen, May 15, 1904, *Memorial Sermon*). In appearance he was tall, slender, full bearded (portrait in *World's History of Cleveland,* 1896, p. 300).

Eells was twice married. His first wife was Mary M. Howard, daughter of Col. George A. Howard of Orwell, Ashtabula County, Ohio. She died in 1859. In 1861, he married Mary Witt, daughter of Stillman Witt of Cleveland.

[Eells's unpublished autobiography is in Western Reserve Historical Society and is important for an account of his early life. Rev. Paul F. Sutphen's *Memorial Sermon,* May 15, 1904, was printed (15 pp.); copy also in Western Reserve Historical Society Colls.]

E. J. B.

EGAN, MAURICE FRANCIS (May 24, 1852–Jan. 15, 1924), author, diplomat, was born and grew up in Philadelphia. His mother, Margaret MacMullen, of a Scotch-Irish family long settled in Philadelphia, was a constant reader and in later years a devout Catholic. Under her strict discipline, Egan and his sister spent a pleasant, yet rather bookish and secluded childhood. He inherited his mother's religious feeling and love of literature, both of which were dominant influences in his life. From his father, Maurice Florent Egan, a handsome Irishman of good family who landed in Philadelphia in 1825 and made his own way, came a democratic spirit, humor, and irrepressible geniality, which found him ever a host of friends. In the son, democracy mingled happily with love of good wine and good food, of both of which he was a connoisseur, and with fondness for good music and good society. "I was always," he writes half-jokingly, "devoted to all kinds of ceremonials." In this and more important ways, he was admirably fitted for diplomacy. At St. Philip's Parochial School and at La Salle College, where he graduated B.A. in 1873, he enjoyed classical studies, but he profited most from wide independent reading. At seventeen he had an essay, "On Roses," in *Appletons' Journal,* and was soon writing regularly for Philadelphia papers. For three years, 1875–78, he taught and studied philosophy at Georgetown University, also seeing much of social and diplomatic life in Washington. Always a facile writer, he was again busy in newspaper work toward the close of this period, turned out two or three novels, and published sonnets of distinction in *Scribner's.* After desultory study of law and a journey to Texas, he went to New York in the spring of 1878, settling definitely on a journalistic career. He was first sub-editor of *Magee's Weekly,* then, after 1881, associate editor of the *Freeman's Journal,* and in 1888 editor and part-proprietor. Meanwhile, for newspapers and magazines of more general circulation he wrote "ten to fifteen thousand words a week," consisting of book reviews, miscellaneous articles, and verse. Welcomed into the *Century Magazine* circle, he numbered the Gilders, Robert Underwood Johnson, James Huneker, and Augustin Daly among his closer friends. After his marriage, in September 1880, to Katharine Mullin of Philadelphia, he lived in Brooklyn, where his three children were born.

Partly on account of the children, partly because of the desire for quiet and study, Egan accepted in 1888 a professorship of English literature at Notre Dame University, South Bend, Ind. Here he found change, if not rest. A delightful lecturer, entering heartily into town and college life, he exerted a strong liberalizing influence upon faculty and students. A transfer in 1896 to the Catholic University in Washington brought him again fortunately into touch with the political and social world. Prominent among liberal Catholics and familiar with European conditions, he became, in Roosevelt's phrase, "unofficial diplomatic adviser" of three presidents. To both McKinley and Roosevelt he was of service in adjusting the problem of the friars' lands in the Philippines. With Roosevelt an old friendship was renewed at frequent White House luncheons (see Egan, "Theodore Roosevelt in Retrospect," *Atlantic Monthly,* May 1919), and it was Roosevelt who in 1907 appointed Egan minister to Denmark. He was to work for the purchase of the Danish West Indies, and from Copenhagen, "the whispering gallery of Europe," keep the administration in touch with European affairs. Largely through Egan's persistence, the first aim was accomplished in 1916. At Copenhagen his social gifts, political shrewdness, and ardent patriotism found full play. Declining from both Taft and Wilson an ambassadorship at Vienna, he became in 1916 senior diplomat at Copenhagen, and administered his post with great success until the close of the World War. "He was not only the Dean of the Diplomatic Corps," writes Henry Van Dyke, "he was its Prince Charming, the one to whom all turned for help in difficulties" (Introduction to Egan's

Recollections). The story of his service, *Ten Years Near the German Frontier* (1919), was an immediate success. This was followed by *Confessions of a Book Lover* (1922). Reviews, familiar essays, stories, and verse, marked by increasing mellowness and charm, continued to appear until Egan's death, from kidney trouble, at his daughter's home in Brooklyn. In the long list of his writings, including literary criticisms, school text-books, juvenile novels, verse, and translations, *Everybody's St. Francis* (1912) and the stories centering around his Irish-American character, Sexton Maginnis (1902–05), are outstanding. Best of his books is his *Recollections of a Happy Life* (1924), for it most closely reflects the man, and with Egan interest must center, not in his writings primarily, but in the charm of his personality and in his career of varied service.

[Egan's *Recollections of a Happy Life*, itself invaluable, contains also a biographical sketch by T. F. Meehan, and a full list of his writings, pp. 373–74. The Am. Acad. of Arts and Letters published a commemorative tribute by David Jayne Hill, 1924.]

A. W.

EGAN, MICHAEL (1761–July 22, 1814), first bishop of Philadelphia, was in all probability born in Ireland. Historical societies have vainly endeavored to determine the exact place of his birth; inquiries prosecuted through the houses of his Order have resulted only in the information that when as a young man he filled the office of Guardian of St. Isadore's, the house of the Irish Franciscans at Rome, it was generally believed that he was born in Galway—a belief that the archives of that diocese fail to confirm. He was about thirty years old when he returned to Ireland as a missionary priest. Ten years later, he came to America and succeeded Father Antoine Garnier as assistant priest at Lancaster, Pa. In April 1803, he was appointed one of the pastors of St. Mary's Church in Philadelphia. The new See of Philadelphia was erected by Pius VII on Apr. 8, 1808, but owing to the struggle between the Pope and Napoleon, the bulls did not reach America until more than two years later. On Oct. 28, 1810, Bishop Egan was consecrated by Archbishop Carroll in St. Peter's Church, Baltimore.

When Carroll had been asked earlier for his opinion of the several candidates who were being considered, he had written concerning Egan: "He is truly learned, remarkable for his humility, but deficient, perhaps, in firmness and without great experience in the direction of affairs" (Shea, *post*). Every event in the short episcopal career of the mild Franciscan shows that the portrait was limned with insight. That the first bishop of Philadelphia was a man of more than ordinary learning is evident from the fact that he preached in English and German with equal facility and more than average felicity and read and spoke French with ease and fluency. That he was humble is apparent in much of his correspondence with Carroll and others. But his lack of firmness was at times coupled with that obstinacy in matters of small consequence which in some natures, otherwise unassertive, is the substitute for consistent stability.

In response to a letter which the then bishop of Baltimore had written to the trustees of St. Mary's, Holy Trinity, and St. Augustine's, the three existing Philadelphia parishes, it had been agreed that certain sums should be paid by each of these congregations to the new bishop as rector of the cathedral church of St. Mary's and additional proportionate amounts for his fitting maintenance as head of the diocese. The trustees, however, reserved the exclusive rights to the pew rents. It was perhaps inopportune that with the assumption of these obligations, the trustees should almost immediately have planned the enlargement of the cathedral church, for it was not long before they were engaged in a bitter quarrel with the ordinary over financial matters. It is possible that the difficulties might have been composed, but for the dictatorial methods adopted by two priests, Father James Harold and his nephew, William Vincent Harold. The two clerics induced Bishop Egan to sign an address to the congregation which that prelate later assured Archbishop Carroll was "never approved of by me," but signed through "a pliability of disposition" (Griffin, *post*, p. 69). But if the demands of the bishop and his assistants were more definite than diplomatic, the language and the tactics of certain of the laity were neither Christian nor honorable. To make matters worse, the two clergymen who had helped to precipitate the deplorable controversy became as insubordinate as any members of the flock and it was with difficulty that the bishop rid himself of these enemies of his own household. So devastating were the results of the quarrel between clergy and laity, that Archbishop Maréchal, writing to Propaganda some years later, declared that "religion had been almost overthrown in Philadelphia" (Guilday, *post*). Worn out by incessant strife, Bishop Egan developed pulmonary difficulties, and, following an attack of nervous prostration, died on July 22, 1814, three years and nine months after his consecration.

[Martin I. J. Griffin, *Hist. of Rt. Rev. Bishop Egan* (1893); J. D. G. Shea, *Hist. of the Cath. Ch. in the U. S.* (4 vols., 1886–92); Peter Guilday, *Life and Times of John England* (2 vols., 1927); *Am. Cath. Hist. Researches* (see Index); *Cath. Encycl.* (1913).] E. F. B.

EGAN, PATRICK (Aug. 13, 1841–Sept. 30, 1919), politician, diplomat, was born at Ballymahon, County Longford, Ireland, the son of Francis Egan, a civil engineer. Moving with the family in his boyhood to Dublin, at fourteen Patrick entered the employ of the North Dublin City Milling Company, but for several years he studied in the evenings under private tutors. Before he was twenty, he had become head bookkeeper and chief confidential man, and when in 1872 the owners died, he was made responsible for reorganizing the firm into a joint stock company, said to be the largest in Ireland in that day, and was elected managing director. He also founded a successful bakery business in 1868 in partnership with James Rourke.

A man of quick and generous sympathies, intense patriotism, with a joyous Gaelic love for a fight—later in life he confessed that one did him "more good than medicine"—he was stirred by the pitiful condition of the Irish peasants under the grinding system of absentee landlordism, and soon became deeply interested in the land movement. The same qualities of personal integrity, executive ability, and rare judgment of men which brought him early success in business, combined with an irrepressible energy and a charm of personality that won the admiration of even his enemies, made him a dominating figure in Irish politics while yet a young man. He became a member of St. Patrick's Brotherhood in 1860; was one of the founders of the Amnesty Association, whose purpose was to obtain the release of Irish political prisoners; and was said to have originated the Martin election contest of 1869, out of which grew the Home Rule League, organized by him, Archie Butt, John Martin, Professor Galbraith, A. M. Sullivan, and others. He was mainly instrumental in Parnell's first successful campaign, in County Meath, in 1874. The following year he presided over the Supreme Council of the Fenian Brotherhood in Dublin. When the Irish National Land League was organized in October 1879, Charles S. Parnell, Thomas Brennan, and Patrick Egan were named its Executive Council, with Egan as treasurer, and in December of that year he left his business to his partners in order to devote full time to the League. He subsequently handled enormous sums for the League without audit. In December 1880 and January 1881, he was one of the thirteen defendants in the famous State trials, whom the jury acquitted by a vote of ten to two. The Government then suspended the *habeas corpus* so that the suspected Leaguers could be imprisoned without trial, and to prevent the confiscation of the Land League funds, Egan moved the treasury to Paris. Until the close of 1882 he skilfully directed activities for the whole movement, while the other leaders were confined in an Irish prison. He was several times urged to run for Parliament, and was twice unanimously elected, once from Queen's County and once from County Meath, but declined rather than take the oath of allegiance to Great Britain. In December 1882 he resigned as treasurer and returned to his business in Ireland. Shortly afterward he learned of Government plans to arrest him, and in February sailed for Holland, and thence for New York. Soon afterward he settled with his family in Lincoln, Nebr., having sold his share in the Dublin bakery firm to Rourke.

At Lincoln he again entered the grain and milling business, establishing a chain of elevators; and also interested himself in real estate and woolen mills. He took an enthusiastic part in the development of Lincoln during the boom days. He applied for his citizenship papers in 1883 and received them in 1888. He was one of the three who called the great Irish convention of April 1883 at Philadelphia, at which the Land League was dissolved and the Irish National League of America was organized. At the Boston convention a year later, he was elected president of the League, an office which he held two years. In 1888–89, when the Parnell Commission made its sensational inquiry into the truth of the London *Times* articles charging Parnell and Egan with complicity in the Phœnix Park murders, Egan sent evidence from America which proved the letters on which the charges were based to be forgeries.

He threw himself just as vigorously into American politics. Having observed the effect of free trade upon Ireland, he joined the Republican party. He became a close friend of Blaine, and supported him in the campaign of 1884. He was elected delegate-at-large to the Republican National Convention in 1888 by a vote of 594 to 67, and declined the chairmanship of the convention in favor of John M. Thurston. Again he supported Blaine for president, and later swung a large Irish vote to Harrison. Harrison was elected, and Blaine became secretary of state. Egan was thereupon appointed minister to Chile, and served to the end of the administration. All through his term of service, and long afterward, his appointment was bitterly attacked by political opponents, who asserted that here was a flagrant example of the spoils system. Nevertheless, it is certain that Secretary Blaine considered Egan well fitted to carry out his policy of discouraging British influence in South America. Events justified Egan's appointment. At Santiago he quickly established cordial relations with President Balmaceda. In 1890, however, the Balmaceda Government was overthrown by a revolution, and for some time conditions were very unsettled. The position of the American minister through this period was a peculiarly difficult one, and Egan maintained it with suitable dignity, and with his characteristic energy. The chief incidents in his term were his granting of asylum in the American legation to political refugees; the serious *Baltimore* affair, in which about 120 sailors from the U. S. S. *Baltimore* were attacked by mobs while on shore leave at Valparaiso, two being killed and several wounded; and a treaty submitting to arbitration the claims of Chilean and United States citizens, negotiated and signed by Egan. He threw himself wholeheartedly into the work of promoting better diplomatic and commercial relations between the two countries. Although he was unfavorably criticized in a number of historical writings published during the two decades following his term of service, in the words of a recent diplomatic historian "He demonstrated unusual ability. He was singularly upright. Moreover, he was tactful, discreet, and courageous." A survey of his diplomatic correspondence confirms this judgment.

On his return to the United States, Egan settled in New York City, where he engaged in various business enterprises and renewed his activities in Irish and American politics. He supported Bryan in his free-silver campaign. He again became an active leader of the Irish Home Rule sympathizers in America, and vigorously opposed the forces in the United States who supported the move for Irish independence. At the outbreak of the World War he defended John E. Redmond against those who attacked him for holding Ireland loyal to the British Empire. He visited Ireland again only once, in 1914. On Sept. 30, 1919, after an illness of several months, he died at the home of his daughter in New York City.

[Principal sources of information concerning Egan's earlier career are T. P. O'Connor and Robert McWade, *Gladstone-Parnell, and the Great Irish Struggle* (1886), pp. 737–42; Wm. O'Brien, *Recollections* (1905), pp. 135–36; F. Hugh O'Donnell, *A Hist. of the Irish Parliamentary Party* (1910), I, 452, II, 268–73; A. B. Hayes and S. D. Cox, *Hist. of the City of Lincoln, Nebr.* (1899), pp. 309–12. Source material for his work as minister to Chile is found in the U. S. Dept. of State Diplomatic Correspondence, Chile, vols. XXXVII–XLII; *Foreign Relations of the U. S.*, 1891, 1892, 1893; "Message of the President of the U. S. Respecting the Relations with Chile," *House Ex. Doc. No. 91*, 52 Cong., 1 Sess. (1892). His work as minister is described in Osgood Hardy, "Was Patrick Egan a Blundering Minister?" in the *Hispanic Am. Hist. Rev.*, Feb. 1928, pp. 65–81; Jos. B. Lockey, "James Gillespie Blaine," in *The Am. Secretaries of State and Their Diplomacy*, ed. by Samuel F. Bemis, VIII (1928), 155–63. Obituaries appear in *N. Y. Times*, Oct. 1, 1919; London *Times*, Oct. 2, 1919; *Nebr. State Jour.*, Oct. 1, 1919.]

I. L. T.

EGGLESTON, EDWARD (Dec. 10, 1837–Sept. 2, 1902), novelist, historian, was born at Vevay, Ind. His father, Joseph Cary Eggleston, lawyer and politician, was a graduate of the College of William and Mary and belonged to a family of some importance in Virginia from colonial times; his mother, Mary Jane Craig, was the daughter of Capt. George Craig, Western frontiersman and Indian fighter. Before his father's death, in 1846, the family spent much time at the Craig farm, several miles from Vevay, so that the future author of *The Hoosier Schoolmaster* early attended a country school. Some three years in Vevay followed, and then young Eggleston was sent for a long visit in Decatur County, where he enriched his knowledge of uncouth Hoosier dialect and backwoods manners. Meantime, on Dec. 25, 1850, his mother had married Williamson Terrell, a Methodist preacher, and Eggleston returned home in March 1851, not to Vevay, but to New Albany. There the family remained a half year, then spent some two years at Madison, then returned to Vevay, in 1853. Here Eggleston liked the high school and flourished under the special favor of the locally famed Mrs. Julia Dumont, who pleased him with the assurance that he was destined to be an author. In June 1854, he was off for thirteen months in Virginia, spent partly with relatives and partly at the Amelia Academy where his accidental discovery of *The Sketch Book* began the slow process of liberation from his almost fanatical devotion to a narrow religious creed (*Forum*, August 1887). Meantime his growing hatred of slavery caused him to refuse the offer of a course at the University of Virginia; indeed, ill health prevented his attending any college, and his formal schooling was now at an end.

After his return to Indiana he was employed for some time as a Bible agent; but his health, always precarious, was soon completely broken. Fearing death from consumption, he set out westward, but suddenly changed his course for Minnesota, where during the summer of 1856 he restored his health by vigorous labor in the open air; then, after an abortive attempt to reach Kansas and aid the anti-slavery cause, he returned home. Some six months (November 1856–April 1857) on a Methodist circuit in southeastern Indiana wrought, however, new disaster to his health, and he was back in Minnesota the following spring, this time for nine years: he was Bible-agent (1858–59); he was pastor of small churches at Traverse and St. Peter (1857–58), St. Paul (1859–60 and 1862–63), Stillwater (1860–61), and Winona (1864–66); and he tried a variety of other occupations, always frequently interrupted by ill health (*Forty-third Annual Report of the American Bible Society*, 1859; *Minutes of the Annual Conferences of the Methodist Episcopal Church*, 1857–66; and Eggleston Papers). Early in 1866 he gave up the ministry for journalism and removed to Evanston, Ill. He was associate editor (June 1866–February 1867—but much of the time only nominally) of the *Little Corporal* of Chicago. In February 1867, he became editor of the *Sunday School Teacher*, soon renamed the *National Sunday School Teacher;* and even after he had left the West he continued as its corresponding editor, until December 1873. Meantime, as early as 1868, he was announced as "a contributor to all the leading juvenile periodicals in the United States" (*Sunday School Teacher*, vol. III, no. 12); and *Mr. Blake's Walking-stick* (1870) was the first of several small volumes of fantastic fairy lore or moral tales of too sentimental children.

Migrating eastward, Eggleston began in May 1870 a period of about fourteen or fifteen months on the *Independent* (New York), of which he had for some time been Western correspondent (*Independent*, May 12, 19, 1870; and *Scribner's Monthly*, September 1873). His editorial connection, from August 1871, with the then moribund *Hearth and Home* (III, 622) seems to have lasted only a year, but served both to revive the magazine and to start Eggleston on his career as a popular novelist destined to have an important influence in turning American literature toward realism. His first novel, "The Hoosier Schoolmaster" (*Hearth and Home*, Sept. 30–Dec. 30, 1871), was already marked by the sentimental quality as well as by the realism of his later writings. Little read in fiction, he may not have been aware of Bret Harte's recent experiments in local color; at all events H. A. Taine's *Art in the Netherlands* (English translation, 1871) was the conscious influence in this direction. The Ohio River country is the setting of "The End of the World" (*Hearth and Home*, Apr. 20–Sept. 7, 1872), a story of religious fanaticism and racial prejudice. In "The Mystery of Metropolisville" (*Hearth and Home*, Dec. 7, 1872–Apr. 26, 1873) he turned to the Minnesota frontier and made, apparently, some use of Dickens's method in his humorous character portrayals. "The Circuit Rider" (*Christian Union*, Nov. 12, 1873–Mar. 18, 1874), with its setting in southern Ohio at the beginning of Madison's administration, pictures the devoted members of a religious fraternity of which Eggleston himself was once a member. Of the later novels, "Roxy" (*Scribner's Monthly*, November 1877–October 1878) dealt with unusual frankness, for the period, with the problem of marital infidelity against a background of old Vevay life; "The Hoosier Schoolboy" (*St. Nicholas*, December 1881–April 1882) preached a sentimental sermon against the harshness of rural schools; and "The Graysons" (*Century*, November 1887–August 1888) made an incident of Lincoln's law practise in Illinois the climax of a story of love rivalry and crime. *The Graysons* (1888), which deserves to share with *Roxy* (1878) the honor of being Eggleston's best fiction, was the last of his series on Western life. His only other novel, "The Faith Doctor" (*Century*, February–October, 1891), was a satire on the enthusiasm for Christian Science among the socially ambitious of New York. In the meantime he had published numerous stories in *Scribner's Monthly*, from December 1870, and *St. Nicholas*, from January 1876, and had continued his series of volumes of collected stories which was to come to an end with *Duffels* (1893).

Eggleston's religious enthusiasm, long since waning, finally spent itself entirely during his pastorate (1874–79) of the non-sectarian Church of Christian Endeavor, in Brooklyn (*New York Tribune*, Dec. 27, 1877; *New York Times*, Dec. 27, 1879). At the same time with the end of his religious zeal came also the change of his main literary interest from fiction to history. He had, indeed, early come to look upon the novel as a means of making "a contribution to the history of civilization in America" (*The Mystery of Metropolisville*, Preface of 1873); and now he simply adopted a more direct method of achieving the same purpose. His eight historical lectures at Columbia College (*Fourth Annual Report of President Low*, 1893, p. 42), his thirteen historical articles in the *Century* (from November 1882), and his school histories and other minor historical and biographical publications were merely by-products of his work on an ambitious plan for a history of life in the United States, only two volumes of which he lived to complete—*The Beginners of a Nation* (1896) and *The Transit of Civilization* (1901). Both in his prefaces and in his inaugural address as president of the American Historical Association (*Annual Report* for 1900, I, 37–47) he set forth his conception of the ideal history as primarily a record of the culture of a people, not merely or even chiefly a record of politics and war; and no doubt his two memorable volumes, imperfect and fragmentary as they were, had an important part in advancing this view of the historian's function, which is only now becoming orthodox in America.

From 1870 until his first voyage to Europe, late in 1879, Eggleston's home was in Brooklyn; from 1881 until his death he lived at Joshua's Rock, on Lake George, but usually spent his winters in New York or other cities and delivered many lectures. His first wife, Lizzie Snider, whom he had married at St. Peter, Minn., Mar. 18, 1858, died in 1889 (Eggleston Papers), and on Sept. 14, 1891, he married Frances Goode, of Madison, Ind. (*New York Times,* Sept. 15, 1891). His last years, like his earlier life, were troubled with serious illness. Some three years before his death he suffered a stroke of apoplexy from which he never really recovered. Another stroke in August 1902 was followed by his death on Sept. 2 of that year.

[The voluminous Eggleston Papers are in the possession of members of the family at Joshua's Rock, Lake George, and of Frances Eggleston, at Madison, Ind. Citations from these papers have been supplied by Mr. Harlan Logan, of the University of Oxford, who is preparing a full-length biographical and critical study. The chief published sources are Frances Eggleston's pamphlet, *Edward Eggleston* (n.d., 1895), and Geo. C. Eggleston's *The First of the Hoosiers: Reminiscences of Edward Eggleston* (n.d., 1903), a somewhat lengthy but by no means adequate record of Eggleston's life by his brother. Other brief accounts of importance are Washington Gladden's "Edward Eggleston," *Scribner's Monthly,* Sept. 1873; Eggleston's own articles, "Books that have Helped me" and "Formative Influences," *Forum,* Aug. 1887 and Nov. 1890; the anonymous "Edward Eggleston: an Interview," *Outlook,* Feb. 6, 1897. See also sketch in *Who's Who in America,* 1901–02; and obituary in *N. Y. Tribune,* Sept. 4, 1902. Eggleston's books are listed in *Cambridge Hist. Am. Literature* (1917–21), II, 634, IV, 661, 737.] R. L. R.

EGGLESTON, GEORGE CARY (Nov. 26, 1839–Apr. 14, 1911), journalist, novelist, was born at Vevay, Ind., the son of Joseph Cary Eggleston and Mary Jane Craig. After an early youth of play and reading guided by his mother, and a later youth restricted by Methodism, he went to school at Madison and was for something over a year at Indiana Asbury (now De Pauw) University. Straitened circumstances, however, forced him when only sixteen to teach school at Riker's Ridge and to meet those amusing and trying experiences that inspired *The Hoosier Schoolmaster,* of his brother Edward [*q.v.*]. When seventeen, having inherited his family's plantation in Amelia County, Va., he was whisked into an aristocratic, genial, and leisurely life that astonished and charmed him. He then studied law at Richmond College and made friends with the Richmond literary group, especially with John Esten Cooke. In 1861, with many other gentlemen horsemen he saw service in northern Virginia in the 1st Virginia Cavalry, first under Col. J. E. B. Stuart and later under Gen. Fitzhugh Lee. In the autumn he transferred to the field artillery on the South Carolina coast, but in 1863 he was back north in Longstreet's artillery. That winter, as sergeant-major of his battery, doing provost guard duty under Gen. Lindsay Walker, he was detailed because of his legal training to defend the worst offenders before courts martial. In 1864 his battery served as sharpshooters through the bloody siege of Petersburg; and Eggleston, with his brother Joseph as second in command, was in charge of a mortar fort.

Immediately after the war he went to Cairo, Ill., to take a position with a banking and steamboating firm; and there on Sept. 9, 1868, he married Marion Craggs. Later he practised law in Mississippi. The work in both places, however, was uncongenial; accordingly, in 1870, with his wife and one child, he went to New York. Here he began a newspaper and editorial career that lasted, except for short intervals, for twenty years. After a year first as a reporter and later as an editorial writer on the *Brooklyn Daily Union* under the guidance of Theodore Tilton, and after a brief period of free-lance writing, he joined his brother Edward in securing good writers for the *Hearth and Home,* bringing among others Frank R. Stockton to the staff. He was editor-in-chief in 1874 when the magazine was sold. A free-lance again, he wrote for the *Atlantic Monthly, Galaxy, Appletons' Journal,* and other periodicals. In 1875 he became a member of the editorial staff of the New York *Evening Post,* and a chat with William Cullen Bryant soon thereafter brought him the *Post's* literary editorship. Here he stated his views forcibly, candidly, and independently, except when constrained by Bryant's gentleness, and often with excellent humor. He yearned for America to produce its own literature without dependence upon British books and criticism. In 1889, after eight years in which he had been literary adviser to Harper & Brothers, and literary editor and later editor-in-chief of the *Commercial Advertiser,* he was called to the editorial staff of the New York *World* and there for eleven years he wrote under Joseph Pulitzer's inspiring guidance, being his mouthpiece in many of the *World's* political campaigns.

In the quieter periods of his New York life, Eggleston had written excellent non-moralizing boys' stories with his own boys as critics, among others The Big Brother Series (1875–82), and *Strange Stories from History* (1886); he had published the autobiographical *A Rebel's Recollections* (1874), and the novels, *A Man of Honor* (1873) and, with Dolores Marbourg, *Juggernaut* (1891); and he had done much magazine writing and miscellaneous book-making. Now, refusing to yield further to the "call of the wild," as he termed the lure of journalism, and retiring to his Lake George home every summer, he zestfully wrote a score or more of works: boys' stories, history, biography, autobiography, and especially novels. Some of the latter he based upon experiences in Indiana, on the Mississippi, and in South Carolina. His most glamorous memories, however, were of pre-war Virginia. With unbounded affection he wrote *Dorothy South* (1902), *The Master of Warlock* (1903), *Evelyn Byrd* (1904), and seven other novels, many of them containing autobiographical details. The characters in these books are too perfect to seem real, but Eggleston always denied having idealized them. "The greatest joy I have known in life has come," he said, "from my efforts to depict it [ante bellum Virginia life] in romances that are only a veiled record of the facts." His leisurely autobiography, *Recollections of a Varied Life* (1910), describes many newspaper and literary friendships; and *The First of the Hoosiers: Reminiscences of Edward Eggleston* (1903) pictures incidentally and with much charm his own early life. Upon *The History of the Confederate War* (2 vols., 1910), a clear and remarkably fair work, rests his reputation as a historian.

[*Lib. of Southern Literature* (1909), IV, 1525–32 (memoir by J. C. Metcalf) and XVI, p. 14 of bibliog.; Allan Nevins, *The Evening Post: A Century of Journalism* (1922); *Who's Who in America*, 1910–11; *Outlook*, Apr. 29, 1911; *Bookman*, May 1912; N. Y. *Evening Post*, Apr. 15, 1911.] A. L. H.

EGLE, WILLIAM HENRY (Sept. 17, 1830–Feb. 19, 1901), Pennsylvania historian, was the son of John Egle and Elizabeth von Treupel. His father was fourth in descent from Marcus Egle, who in 1743 came to Cocalico Township, Lancaster County, Pa., from the canton of Zurich, Switzerland; his mother was the daughter of John von Treupel, who in 1805 emigrated to Pennsylvania from Nassau, Germany. Left fatherless at the age of four, and motherless at the age of eleven, William Henry found a home with his paternal grandmother, who was to the lad, as he himself declared, "more than a mother." Her stories of frontier scenes and Revolutionary days, drawn from her own experience, probably aroused in him an early interest in history. He received his formal education in private and public schools in Harrisburg, and at the Harrisburg Military Institute. He first earned his living through the printer's trade. After three years in the office of the *Pennsylvania Telegraph*, Harrisburg, he took charge of state printing. In 1853, as editor of the *Literary Companion* and the Harrisburg *Daily Times*, he gained valuable literary experience.

In 1854 he began his study of medicine in the office of a local physician, supporting himself by teaching in a boys' school and working as clerk in the post office. Three years later he entered the medical department of the University of Pennsylvania, graduating in 1859. He settled down to practise his profession in Harrisburg, and on July 24, 1860, was married to Eliza White Beatty. Within three years he was called to Washington to take care of the sick and wounded of the northern armies engaged in the Civil War. During the war he served as surgeon or chief medical officer with several different regiments. At the close of the war he resumed practise in Harrisburg, and in 1870 he became surgeon-in-chief of the National Guard of Pennsylvania, with which organization he maintained his connection until 1899.

Scholars remember Egle gratefully for his contributions to American history. In 1887, upon appointment to the office of state librarian, he began the important work of developing the library as a center of historical research. His own publications include: *An Illustrated History of the Commonwealth of Pennsylvania, Civil, Political and Military* (1876); several county histories, numerous biographies, and genealogical writings. Among the latter may be mentioned his valuable *Pennsylvania Genealogies: Scotch-Irish and German*, and his *Genealogical Record of the Families of Beatty, Egle, Müller, Murray, Orth, and Thomas*, both published in 1886. He corresponded with historical societies, contributed to their magazines, and assisted other scholars in their research. For many years he edited annually: *Notes and Queries, Historical, Biographical, and Genealogical, Relating Chiefly to Interior Pennsylvania.* Perhaps most important of all his historical work was his editing of the *Pennsylvania Archives.* He collaborated with John Blair Linn in the second series, Volumes I–XII, but was sole editor of Volumes XIII–XIX in the same series, and also sole editor of the third series. He was one of the founders, and the first president, of the Pennsylvania German Society. Although he was more widely known for his editorial ability, friends and acquaintances remembered him for his geniality and kindliness. He died of pneumonia, in his seventy-first year.

[*Geneal. Record,* mentioned above; Geo. H. Halberstadt, in the *Jour. Assoc. Mil. Surgeons of the U. S.* (Carlisle, Pa.), Aug. 1901; H. M. M. Richards, in *Pa. German Soc. Proc. and Addresses,* vol. XI (1902); H. E. Hayden, in *Proc. and Colls. of the Wyoming Hist. and Geol. Soc.,* vol. VI (1901); *Notes and Queries . . . Annual Vol., 1900* (1901); *Alumni Reg.* (Phila.), Mar. 1901; *Pa. Mag. of Hist. and Biog.,* Apr. 1901; Theo. B. Klein, in *Trans. Hist. Soc. Dauphin County, Pa.,* vol. I (1903); *Papers Read before the Lancaster County Hist. Soc. Mar. 1, 1901* (1901); *Harrisburg Patriot,* Feb. 20, 1901.] D. M. C.

EGLESTON, THOMAS (Dec. 9, 1832–Jan. 15, 1900), mineralogist, founder of the School of Mines of Columbia College, was the son of Thomas and Sarah (Stebbins) Egleston of New York City. His father came from New England, where his forebears had first settled in 1635. As a boy Thomas was interested in minerals and rocks, making his first collection at the age of thirteen. During his course at Yale, where he graduated in 1854, he took special work in chemistry. In Paris, through his laboratory work in the geology and chemistry departments of the Jardin des Plantes, he attracted the attention of some of the members of the faculty of the École des Mines and they offered him the facilities of their larger institution. He became so interested in his studies in the paleontological laboratory that he decided to take the whole course, which he completed in 1860. Upon his return to America in 1861 he was called to Washington to take care of the sorting and arranging of the geological specimens which had accumulated at the Smithsonian Institution. This work helped him to realize both the need and opportunity for an institution which should occupy in this country such a place as the École des Mines in France. The schools of science existing in the United States at the time were either too general or too special to include distinct and adequate training in mining and metallurgy. In March 1863, therefore, Egleston published a *Proposed Plan for a School of Mines and Metallurgy in New York City,* which he submitted to the trustees of Columbia College, who gave their consent to the experiment, although it was a new departure in American education. Accordingly, the department was opened on Nov. 15, 1864. It was a success from its beginning. In the early years of the institution Egleston was its central and leading spirit but as the work grew by leaps and bounds he limited his attention to his own special departments of mineralogy and metallurgy. His first love was for mineralogy and his work in building up the great mineralogical collection of the School was a remarkable achievement. Shortly after his death the trustees of the university paid him fitting tribute when they attached to the collection the name Egleston Mineralogical Museum as a permanent memorial to its founder.

Egleston was a prolific writer. Nearly a hundred books, pamphlets, and articles on metallurgy and mining engineering in its varied phases give evidence of his literary activity. His most ambitious work was *The Metallurgy of Silver, Gold and Mercury in the United States,* published in two large volumes in 1887 and 1890. His services to New York City were almost as memorable as his contributions to science. Through his efforts a monument was erected to mark the resting place of Audubon, the artist ornithologist. It was, however, in saving Washington Square (facing which he lived for many happy years with his wife, Augusta McVickar) that he won the city's deepest gratitude. Under the notorious "Boss" Tweed, a bill had all but passed which would have given this recreation spot to a group of schemers; but Egleston discovered the purpose of the bill, aroused public opinion, helped to organize the Public Parks Protective Association, with himself as secretary and John Jay as president, and not only stirred the legislators to the point of refusing to pass the bill but put through a resolution providing that Washington Square should be "Kept *forever* as a park for purposes of public health and recreation."

[G. F. Kunz, in *Trans. Am. Inst. Mining Engineers,* vol. XXXI (1902); A. J. Moses, in *The School of Mines Quart.,* Apr. 1900; D. S. Martin, in *Popular Sci. Monthly,* June 1899; *Record and Statistics . . . Class of Fifty-four, Yale Univ.* (1896); *N. Y. Times,* Jan. 16, 1900.] E.Y.

EHNINGER, JOHN WHETTEN (July 22, 1827–Jan. 22, 1889), painter and illustrator, was born in New York City, the son of George and Eliza (Whetten) Ehninger. He graduated B.A. from Columbia College in 1847. Immediately after taking his degree, he was sent to Europe to study painting, spending his earlier years at Düsseldorf, with Leutze. On his second visit to Europe he worked in the Paris studio of Thomas Couture, an eminent historical painter who carried on the traditions of Gros and Paul Delaroche. He visited the principal European art galleries and in 1850 attained his first popular success with "Peter Stuyvesant," illustrating an incident in Washington Irving's *History of New York,* which was engraved for the American Art Union. He made many trips to Europe, the last one of which occurred a year before his death. While abroad he made illustrations for the *Illustrated Times* and the *Illustrated News.* He also drew designs for gift editions of Longfellow's *Courtship of Miles Standish,* Hood's

Bridge of Sighs, and *Ye Legende of St. Gwendoline,* founded upon one of Tennyson's Idylls. The latter illustrations were reproduced by photographs. Ehninger was also a frequent contributor to the exhibitions of the National Academy of Design, New York, and was elected an academician in 1860. His paintings, which usually were in oils, were devoted to genre subjects. In the words of a contemporary critic, "Not only has he proved a faithful student of the elements of his art, but he has attained a degree of practical skill and manifested an individuality rarely achieved in so brief a period" (Tuckerman, *post,* p. 462). According to the same authority he was regarded as "one of the most accomplished draughtsmen among American artists of his period." He died suddenly of apoplexy at Saratoga Springs, N. Y., where for years he had made his home. Some ten years before his death he had married a Miss Beach.

[Henry T. Tuckerman, *Book of the Artists* (1867); *N. Y. Geneal. and Biog. Record,* Apr. 1889; *N. Y. Tribune,* Jan. 23, 1889; *Appletons' Ann. Cyc.,* 1889, p. 629.]

J. J.

EHRLICH, ARNOLD BOGUMIL (Jan. 15, 1848–Nov. 5, 1919), Bible exegete, was born in Wlodawa, Polish Russia, the posthumous and only child of Mordecai and Zelda Biederman Ehrlich. He emerged from the playless childhood of the scholastic Ghetto to marry at the age of fourteen. Three years later, still a Talmud student, he crossed the border into Germany, and there he laid the foundations of his secular learning. Later he settled in Leipzig, where for several years he worked with Germany's most gifted Christian Biblical scholar, Franz Delitzsch. The masterly touch of Ehrlich's unrivaled instinct for Hebrew usage has been traced in Delitzsch's classical Hebrew translation of the New Testament. After a short stay in England, Ehrlich came to America in 1878, armed with a literary knowledge of a large number of languages, an expert knowledge of classical Arabic, and a unique knowledge of the Hebrew Bible. Here all doors were closed to his learning. Christian institutions had no place for this Polish Jew, while Jews suspected his long contact with Delitzsch, the head of the missionary Institutum Judaicum in Leipzig. The first work he obtained in New York was that of rolling barrels. Later he secured an instructorship in the Emanu-El Preparatory School for the Hebrew Union College. When that school closed he supported himself first as a social worker, then as a business man, and finally, as a private Hebrew teacher, the precarious income from which was augmented by the dressmaking skill of his second wife, Pauline Offner.

Ehrlich received scant notice during his life, despite the fact that he had a veritable genius for Biblical interpretation. In the three volumes of his *Mikra ki-Pheschuto* (Berlin, 1899–1901); in his edition of *Die Psalmen* (Berlin, 1905); and in the seven volumes of his *Randglossen zur hebräischen Bibel* (Leipzig, 1908–14), he concentrated a wealth of masterly exegesis, marked by brilliant, if erratic, originality. These volumes are the most comprehensive and valuable contribution to Old Testament scholarship made in America. Ehrlich regarded Biblical higher criticism as premature and unreliable because based on an insufficiently understood text. With extraordinary tenacity and single-mindedness he set himself to establish what he believed to be the true reading and true meaning of the text. To this life task, he brought intuitive verbal and literary keenness. He would say of himself, "I am like a tea taster. I put the word on my tongue, and I know whether it is good or bad." Acute in his understanding of the fine points of Hebrew idiom and syntax, he was contemptuously impatient of sciolists and plodding pedants, declaring that a poet could grasp the real meaning of the Biblical word better than an unimaginative professor relying on lexicon and grammar. Ehrlich's contributions to Biblical exegesis and Hebrew lexicography and grammar are replete with illuminating suggestion, but his excessive quest of originality, the audacity of many of his later suggestions, his contempt for the mistakes of others, and the current preoccupation with the higher rather than the lower criticism of the Bible, have militated against a due recognition of his work. In scholarship as in life he fell between two stools. His treatment of the Biblical text was regarded by many Christian scholars as too Jewish, and by many Jewish scholars as too little Jewish. However, productive Old Testament study of the future must follow Ehrlich in combining the linguistic methods of Christian commentators with Jewish mastery of the Hebrew text and its collateral Hebrew literature.

[Ehrlich published his childhood recollections anonymously in *Saat auf Hoffnung,* XXV (1888), 15–20, XXVI (1889), 18–34, 72–86. His contribution to Biblical scholarship has been appraised in reviews of his works, and more especially by Israel Friedlaender in the *Nation,* Jan. 10, 1920; Joshua Bloch in *Hachme Yisrael B'America* (1915); and by Benzion Halper in *Miqlat,* II (1920), 417–26. See also the *Jewish Encyc.* (1925); *N. Y. Times,* Nov. 6, *N. Y. Tribune,* Nov. 7, 1919.]

D. deS. P.

EICHBERG, JULIUS (June 13, 1824–Jan. 18, 1893), violinist, teacher, composer, was born at Düsseldorf, of a musical family. He was taught at first by his father, and could play the violin acceptably when he was seven years old. Among his other teachers were Eichler of Mainz, Frölich of Würzburg, and, more important, Rietz, who introduced his pupil to Mendelssohn. The latter wrote, as testimonial, "At so early an age, young Eichberg joins to a remarkable firmness and certainty in bowing, and use of his left hand, a great deal of true expression, which will lead him, I doubt not, to become a great artist." In 1842 Eichberg entered the Brussels Conservatory, then headed by Fétis, and studied with Meerts and De Beriot, graduating in 1845 with first prizes in violin and composition. After a brief stay in Frankfurt, he went to Geneva as conductor of an opera troupe, and was retained there for eleven years as conservatory professor and church music leader. In 1857 he migrated to New York; but after two years of desultory teaching and playing, he moved to Boston and made it his permanent home. For seven years he was musical leader at the Boston Museum. In 1867 he established the Boston Conservatory of Music, which flourished for years and of which he was director, 1870–72. At one time he was supervisor of music in the public schools; and he published many singing-books and musical collections for school use. He also founded the Eichberg Violin School. He composed much for his instrument, including graceful solos and valuable studies as well as various ensemble numbers. Among the latter were an Ave Maria and Reverie for violin, 'cello, piano, and organ, given in the old Music Hall, and a Concertino for four violins, performed for the Harvard Musical Association; also several string trios and quartets. Among his piano works is a charming set entitled "Lebensfrühling." For voices he wrote the patriotic quartet "To Thee, O Country Great and Free" (1872), and many songs of real artistic merit, including several settings of Celia Thaxter's words, such as "Sunset," and "O swallow sailing lightly." Most successful, however, and giving the composer most prominence, were his various operettas, or light operas. The first of these, *The Doctor of Alcantara* (1862), had a plot worthy of the palmy days of Italian comedy. Doctor Paracelsus and his somewhat shrewish wife Lucrezia have a daughter, Isabella, who is told that she must marry a certain young man. But before learning his identity, she is charmed by the serenade of Carlos, and asserts her preference for him. Carlos smuggles himself into the house in a basket sent to Inez, Isabella's companion. Left alone a moment, he emerges and hides. Lucrezia forces Inez and the Doctor to throw the basket in the river; and when Inez explains its supposed contents, the latter considers himseif a murderer. The night watch, under the Alguazil Pomposo, harrow him still further with their suspicions. Even when Carlos himself appears, he is taken for a police spy, but he finally dispels the Doctor's anxiety. Entering the house, they drink a toast; but Carlos is given one of the Doctor's decoctions, by mistake, and falls insensible. Again thinking himself a murderer, the Doctor hides the body under a sofa. Balthaser, father of Carlos, enters, and will not move from the sofa, despite his host's schemes; so he is left to sleep there. In the dark, Carlos recovers from the drug (an opiate), and has an unexpected clash with his father, which arouses the household. All ends happily, for it turns out that Carlos is the one for whom Isabella's hand has been asked. Other operettas by Eichberg, also well received, were *The Rose of Tyrol* (1865), *The Two Cadis* (1868), and *A Night in Rome* (1874).

[*Boston Sunday Herald,* June 18, 1887; *Boston Jour.,* Jan. 20, 1893; L. C. Elson, *The Hist. of Am. Music* (rev. ed., 1925); *Grove's Dict. of Music and Musicians* (3rd ed., 1927); *The Art of Music,* vols. IV (1915); XI (1917).] A. E.

EICHHOLTZ, JACOB (Nov. 2, 1776–May 11, 1842), painter, was born in Lancaster, Pa., son of Leonard and Catharine Eichholtz. His grandfather, John Jacob Eichholtz, a native of Bischoffsheim, Bavaria, was one of the earliest settlers of Lancaster, where he was assistant burgess in 1750–52. His wife, Anna Catharine Reichert, established the Bull's Head Tavern in Lancaster in 1765. She was succeeded in the proprietorship by her eldest son, Leonard, father of Jacob. Like his brothers and sisters, the latter received a plain English education. His father did not welcome his early evidence of artistic talent; nevertheless, a friendly sign-painter was engaged to teach the lad rudimentary drawing. His teacher's untimely death brought about Jacob's apprenticeship to a coppersmith, but did not end his dreams of painting. With a bootjack for a palette and any available substitute for a brush he continued his rude efforts. After completing his apprenticeship, he assumed family responsibilities by his marriage to Catharine, daughter of John Hatz, a widow with two children by whom he had four of his own. He divided his time between art and coppersmithing until his portraits assured him a reasonable living. Having acquired a local reputation, upon the suggestion of his friend, Mr. Barton, Eichholtz visited in Boston the celebrated Gilbert Stuart, who welcomed, advised, and encouraged him. He thereupon sought wider opportunity in Philadelphia and, after ten strenuous years in that city, gained sufficient recognition to return to his native town with a fair income. In Philadelphia he had as neighbor and warm personal friend the famous John Sartain, who engraved many of his portraits. Most of Eichholtz's painting was done in Philadelphia, but he did some in Baltimore, during several sojourns of a few weeks at a time, and some in Lancaster. In 1817 his first wife died, and a few years later he married again.

Following the style of Sully and Stuart, between 1810 and 1842 he painted over two hundred and fifty portraits, a few landscapes, and some historical groups. His reading and classical study inspired his decoration for the hose carriage of the Union Fire Company of Lancaster, an allegorical representation of water. In 1818 he painted the portraits of George Graeff and his wife, and about 1822 a portrait of their daughter, Maria, a bit of romance in this connection being that he did it gratuitously because she favorably influenced his suit with Catharine Trissler, who became his second wife and eventually bore him nine children. Other notable portraits are those of Chief Justice John Bannister Gibson, considered an example of the artist's best portraiture, now in the possession of the Law Association of Philadelphia; Col. James Gibson, painted in 1829 for the State House at Dover, at the request of the Delaware legislature; Nicholas Biddle; James Buchanan (now in the Smithsonian Institution); Mrs. Catharine Long (1838, in the Long Asylum for Women); Chief Justice John Marshall (in the Historical Society of Pennsylvania); Admiral David D. Porter; Bishop Ravenscroft (painted for Edward Rutledge); Gov. J. Andrew Shulze (in the Historical Society of Pennsylvania); Thaddeus Stevens (1830), and five self-portraits.

[Wm. Dunlap, *A Hist. of the Rise and Progress of the Arts of Design in the U. S.* (rev. ed., 1918), II, 384–85; Wm. U. Hensel, "Jacob Eichholtz, Painter," an address, published as supplement to *Hist. Papers and Addresses of the Lancaster County Hist. Soc.*, vol. XVI (1912) and abridged in *Pa. Mag. of Hist. and Biog.*, Jan. 1913, pp. 48–75; information from Mrs. D. B. Landis, cor. sec. of the Lancaster County Hist. Soc.]

J. M. H.

EICKEMEYER, RUDOLF (Oct. 31, 1831–Jan. 23, 1895), inventor, manufacturer, was born in Altenbamberg, Bavaria, Germany, the son of Christian and Katherine (Bréhm) Eickemeyer. He was educated in his village schools, the Realschule at Kaiserlautern, and the Polytechnic Institute at Darmstadt, where he completed his studies at the age of seventeen. Immediately thereafter, with his friend and future partner, George Osterheld, he joined the insurgents in the Revolution of 1848. After its collapse the two left Germany for New York, arriving Nov. 20, 1850. In the United States they found employment, first in the building of the Erie Railroad, later with the Buffalo Steam Engine Works, and finally, in 1854, settled at Yonkers, N. Y., where they opened a small machine repair shop. Hat-making was then the chief industry of Yonkers; and through their repair work the partners became familiar with the art, and Eickemeyer began to give serious attention to the improvement of its crude mechanical appliances. He first patented machines to fold the edges of leather hat bands and to sew them into the hat, devising the first "whip-stitch," still used. These were followed by other important inventions such as the first hat-blocking machine, patented in 1865 by the partners; the first successful hat-stretching machines; and a machine to pounce hats in 1869. In this way Eickemeyer, through his products, gradually revolutionized the hat-making industry throughout the world. Following the Civil War, during which he converted his plant into a revolver factory and also served a thirty-day enlistment, he perfected and patented in 1870 a differential gear for a mowing and reaping machine which was profitably sold to a Canadian manufactory. He continued, too, to improve his hatting machinery and to devise additional equipment, including a shaving machine and one to make blocks and flanges. Being a most intelligent man, he had all along followed the progress of scientific thought, especially in electricity, and in the seventies when this science came to the foreground, he began some experimental work in telephony, taking out a number of patents. This experimentation was followed by work on armatures and armature windings which resulted in the perfecting and patenting of the first symmetrical drum armature and the iron-clad dynamo. So superior were they to existing equipment that the demand for them was immediate—armatures for motor manufacturers and iron-clad motors for elevators—and by 1884 the hat machinery factory had been largely converted into a prosperous electric plant and laboratory. Eickemeyer continued with experimental work and soon electric-lighting and railway generators and motors were produced. He and Stephen D. Field [*q.v.*] together developed the first direct-connected railway motor, designing it for use on the New York Elevated Railroad. In addition he made many investigations on hysteresis, high potential phenomena, and alternating-current machinery, devising special instruments for the purpose. In 1892 his business was consolidated with the General Electric Company, but he continued his electrical investigations until his death. He was the discoverer and first employer of the illustrious electrical engineer, Charles P. Steinmetz [*q.v.*]. All told, Eickemeyer secured about a hundred and fifty patents in the United States and abroad. He was active in civic affairs in Yonkers: a fireman in his youth; a militiaman for fourteen years; a water commissioner for twenty-two years; and vice-president of the school board, of which he was a trustee for twenty-three years. He married Mary True Tarbell of Dover, Me., in July 1856, who with six children survived him.

[Theodor Lemke, *Geschichte des Deutschthums von N. Y.* (1893); *Electrical World,* Mar. 16, 1895; *Hatters' Gazette,* Mar. 1, 1895; *Yonkers Gazette,* Feb. 2, 1895; *Electrical Age,* Feb. 2, 1895; *Electrical Rev.,* Jan. 30, 1895; *Evening Star* (Washington, D. C.), Jan. 24, 1895; Patent Office Records; U. S. Nat. Museum correspondence.] C.W.M.

EIDLITZ, CYRUS LAZELLE WARNER (July 27, 1853–Oct. 5, 1921), architect, was the son of Leopold Eidlitz [*q.v.*] and Harriet Amanda Warner Eidlitz, daughter of an architect and of Massachusetts colonial stock. He was born in the house at the foot of West Eighty-sixth St., New York City, which his father had built several years before. Almost from his birth the son was destined for the profession of architecture and at the age of twelve was sent abroad for his education. After three years of school in Geneva, he entered the Royal Polytechnic School in Stuttgart, and in 1871 returned to New York and entered his father's office as a draftsman. On May 23, 1877, he married Jennie Turner Dudley, a descendant of Gov. Thomas Dudley of Massachusetts. His first independent work was the rebuilding in 1878 of St. Peter's Church in Westchester, a church originally built by the elder Eidlitz, which had been badly damaged by fire. This was followed by a railway station in Detroit, and this in turn by the important Dearborn Station in Chicago, completed in 1885. In 1884 Cyrus Eidlitz was successful in a competition for the building of the Buffalo Library, which when completed at once gave him rank as one of the leading American architects. The plan was complicated by the fact that it was necessary to accommodate a library, an art gallery, and the collections of a historical society on a site which was of extreme irregularity, forming a right-angled triangle truncated at the apex which was also the most conspicuous part. The building, of a more or less orthodox German Romanesque, is a splendid solution of unpromising conditions of site and use. Of about the same date were the Telephone buildings in Cortlandt and Broad Streets; followed by the Western Electric Building in Greenwich St., the Fidelity and Casualty Building in Cedar, the Racquet Club in Forty-third St., the Bank for Savings on Fourth Ave. at Twenty-second, and the building for the Bar Association in Forty-fourth running to Forty-third St., all in New York City. The Western Electric Building was an example of a factory and showed that such a structure might be ornamental as well as useful. The Fidelity Building, which reached upward to the extent of ten full stories, was the first "skyscraper" which Eidlitz was called upon to design, his previous efforts having been confined to constructions of less elevation. The pioneers in this class of building had established as an axiom that the edifice must have a powerful base, a plain shaft and a rich crown. This principle was followed by Eidlitz in the design for the Townsend Building at the northwest corner of Broadway and Twenty-sixth Sts. Each of his new designs showed advancement in his art over those preceding. The group of three which comprised the Racquet Club, the Bank for Savings, and the Bar Association were the most important and interesting of his career up to the time of their construction. In the case of the Racquet Club the conditions gave a frontage of 142 feet and that the playing courts at the top of the building should be bounded by solid walls without windows on the front. The design centered in an arcade of five openings running through the second and third stories and dominating the whole front, with great depth to the piers of the arcade, leaving an impression of nobility and power. The Bank for Savings is one of the solidest as well as one of the most dignified in New York, and at the time of its erection was spoken of as one of the most "popular" buildings of the time and is still one of the most classical buildings to be found in New York.

The most noteworthy structure designed by Eidlitz was the *New York Times* Building, constructed in the narrow triangle between Broadway and Seventh Ave., and Forty-second and Forty-third Sts., in New York City. There the manifold requirements of a structure heavy enough for the great presses, and providing sufficient office space for rental in addition to what was needed for the editorial and mechanical staffs of the great newspaper, were complicated by the many additional stories of the tower dominating Broadway and adding so greatly to the advertising value of the site for its purpose. This rich and stately building was eminently successful and still stands a monument to the professional skill of the architect who designed it.

[Montgomery Schuyler, "Cyrus L. W. Eidlitz," *Architectural Record,* Apr. 1906; *N. Y. Times,* Oct. 6, 1921; personal acquaintance.] M. Sc—r.

EIDLITZ, LEOPOLD (Mar. 29, 1823–Mar. 22, 1908), architect, son of Adolph and Julia Eidlitz, was born in Prague, Bohemia. After his school years in that city, he entered the Polytechnic at Vienna in order to train himself for the profession of land-steward, and it was, apparently, while studying the construction of buildings for estates, that he began to take interest in the wider field of architecture. Early in 1843 he came to New York and almost immediately entered the office of Richard Upjohn, the leading exponent at the time of the "Gothic revival" in American architecture, who was then working on the present building of Trinity Church, New York. Eidlitz left Upjohn before long, however, and with a young Bavarian formed the firm of Blesch & Eidlitz, to draw the plans of a new edifice for St. George's Episcopal Church. Blesch seems to have fallen ill soon after the preparation of the drawings, and the work was executed entirely by Eidlitz, who had also drawn the plans for the interior. The partnership lasted only a short while, but it gave Eidlitz an association with a "Grand Prix" of Munich, who had the regular architectural training which he himself lacked. The construction of St. George's Church with its successful German Gothic design and two open spires of carved stone, later taken down as the result of a fire which compelled the reconstruction of the interior, started young Eidlitz upon a successful career as a Gothic practitioner, which at that time meant a church architect. Much of his best earlier work, therefore, was in church design. "Gothic," said Eidlitz, however, "is adequate to every expression," and during his earlier period he designed a number of houses, of which there are examples at Englewood, N. J., and Springfield, Mass., and the Hamilton Ferry House in Brooklyn, an interesting example of carpentry, with bold timber hoods projecting over the slips. Among his churches, St. Peter's, Westchester, N. Y., the Church of the Holy Trinity at Madison Avenue and Forty-second St., New York City, completed in 1853, and the Congregational Church in Greenwich, Conn., show his skill; but his most successful church is considered to be Christ Church, St. Louis, afterward and for many years the Episcopal cathedral of that city. Charles Kingsley found it the "most churchly" church in the United States. Perhaps the most original ecclesiastical building which Eidlitz planned was the synagogue "Emanu-El" at Fifth Avenue and Forty-third St., New York. Erected in 1868 and demolished to make way for a business skyscraper in 1928, it was an extraordinarily successful combination of Gothic structure with Saracenic decoration, including carved and molded as well as colored ornament. The critics of the time attacked the incongruity of a cruciform interior for a Jewish temple. In secular construction, Eidlitz adorned New York with many notable buildings. Among them were the Continental Bank (1856); the American Exchange Bank (1857), the first fireproof commercial building in the city; the old Produce Exchange (1860); the Brooklyn Academy of Music, of the same year; and the Dry Dock Savings Bank (1875). In these, as in other work, he kept reverting to his favorite German Gothic style with marked success.

The most spectacular example of his work was the redesigning of the State Capitol at Albany. When in 1875 Tilden succeeded Dix as governor of New York, a commission was appointed to investigate the partly finished new Capitol. Its scope was extended to include the architecture itself, and as a result, an advisory board was formed with Eidlitz, H. H. Richardson, and F. L. Olmsted as members. The commission's report was strongly against continuing with the commonplace Romanesque design of the previous architect. As a result the changing of the design and plans was entrusted to the three commissioners, who formed the firm of Eidlitz, Richardson & Company to complete the work. His work on this and on the New York Court House was Eidlitz's last significant undertaking.

He wrote a number of professional articles and two volumes: *Nature and Function of Art* (1881) and *Big Wages and How to Earn Them* (1887), the latter a criticism of trades unions which was published anonymously. He was elected to the Century Club in 1859 and an honorary corresponding member of the Royal Institute of British Architects in 1897. Eidlitz had a gift of witty expression; one of the acid sayings much quoted by his friends was: "American architecture is the art of covering one thing with another thing to imitate a third thing which, if genuine, would not be desirable." He was married in 1846 to Harriet Amanda Warner, daughter of Cyrus Lazelle Warner, an architect with whom he was professionally associated soon after coming to the United States. Three of his wife's brothers were architects, and his son, Cyrus Lazelle Warner Eidlitz [*q.v.*], also entered the profession of his father and uncles.

[Montgomery Schuyler, "A Great Am. Architect: Leopold Eidlitz," in the *Architectural Record,* Sept. 1908, and "The Work of Leopold Eidlitz" in the same journal, Oct. and Nov. 1908; *Jour. Royal Inst. of British Architects,* Oct. 17, 1908; *N. Y. Times,* Mar. 23, 1908; personal acquaintance.] M. Sc—r.

EIELSEN, ELLING (Sept. 19, 1804–Jan. 10, 1883), noted lay preacher and founder of the

Norwegian Evangelical Lutheran Church of North America (also called The Ellingian brotherhood, Elling Eielsen's Synod, or simply The Ellingians), was born on the farm Sunve, at Vossestranden, in the district of Voss, Western Norway. His parents were Eiel Ingebrigtsen and Anna Ellingsen Sunve. His father, a farmer and schoolmaster, was for a time influenced by the pietistic movement known as Haugeanism (from Hans Nielsen Hauge, 1771–1824), and it is not unlikely that the boy Elling imbibed something of the devout religious spirit of the Haugeans. As a child he was sociable but of a headstrong nature, and later was subject to moods of melancholy. He showed a religious bent from the age of eight, but then apparently changed and in the years of his youth lived a somewhat wild and uncontrolled life in his home community. In his twenty-second year he experienced a religious awakening; there followed three years of religious depression that once almost drove him to suicide. He looked upon his life as one of sin and degradation, though there appears to be no evidence from those years that he had committed excesses of any kind. He continued to live in Voss until he was twenty-five, then in 1829, went to Bergen, learned there the carpenter's trade, and secured a position. His chief reason for moving to Bergen was that he might be among Haugean friends, and they received him with their characteristic kindly Christian spirit. He remained in Bergen until 1831. There had developed at this time in his mental make-up a strong anti-clerical feeling. The ordained clergy of the State Church were, in his opinion, worldly-minded and negligent of their duty as ministers. Feeling that in his own case he had received no help from the clergy, he came to look upon them as an official class serving the State, an aristocracy, who held themselves aloof from the masses, and made no effort to instruct their humbler charges in morality and right living. The theologically trained clergy were "High Church," and antipathy to everything for which this term stood was a dominant principle with him throughout most of his later life. In Bergen he was permitted to preach to the soldiers and his sermons found so much favor that the captain of the company urged him to enter upon preaching as his life-work. During a long illness at this time he had an experience that he interpreted as a divine call to go out and preach. Accordingly, in 1831 he set out, going to the northern provinces, Trondhjem, Nordland, Tromsö, Finmarken, traveling as an itinerant missionary here and among the Lapps of the extreme North, walking on foot in summer and in the cold of winter, often suffering untold hardships. Thus began a career that lasted for nearly fifty years. During the first eight years he visited all parts of Norway, as well as Sweden and Denmark, usually walking, and preaching two or three times a day, but in 1839 he emigrated to America. At Chicago, in October of that year, he preached in a log cabin the first Norwegian sermon delivered on American soil. The Fox River Settlement, La Salle County, Ill., became his home. Here he at once built himself a house, the second story of which was fitted out as a "meeting-house," where for years he preached regularly, except when he was visiting and preaching in the new settlements that were springing up in Illinois, Wisconsin, and other parts of the northern Middle West. In 1859 he visited settlements recently formed in Texas, and did missionary work among the Potawatomi Indians of Missouri. Yielding to the wishes of his people at Fox River he was ordained, Oct. 3, 1843; less than three years later, Apr. 13–14, 1846, he organized the Evangelical Lutheran Church of America, the largest organization of Norwegian Lutherans in the New World. During the church controversies of the next two decades he sometimes alienated co-religionists by his dictatorial methods and intolerance of opposition; ground that had been gained for his church he sometimes lost again, for he did not have the capacity for cooperation and the talent for organization required of the true leader. Yet he achieved results that were of outstanding significance; and in the pioneer period of Norwegian-American history no one, perhaps, had a greater religious influence among Norwegians that Elling Eielsen. He had married Sigrid Nilson Tufte, in Muskego, Wis., on July 3, 1843. After 1873 the family lived in Chicago, where he died.

[J. Magnus Rohne, *Norwegian American Lutheranism up to 1872* (1926); C. O. Brohaugh og J. Eisteinsen, *Kortfattet Beretning om Elling Eielsens Liv og Virksomhed* (1883); E. O. Mørstad, *Elling Eielsen og den Evangelisklutherske Kirke* (1917); R. B. Anderson, *First Chapter of Norwegian Immigration* (1895); Geo. T. Flom, *A Hist. of Norwegian Immigration to the U. S.* (1909); Th. Bothne, *Kort Udsigt over det Lutherske Kirkearbeide blandt Nordmaendene i Amerika* (1898); *Who's Who Among Pastors in all the Norwegian Synods of America 1843–1927* (1928).]

G. T. F.

EIGENMANN, CARL H. (Mar. 9, 1863–Apr. 24, 1927), zoölogist, educator, was born to parents of moderate means—Philip and Margaretha (Lieb) Eigenmann—in Flehingen, Germany. Sent to the United States in 1877, he grew up in the care of an uncle in Rockport, Ind. In 1882 he entered the state university at Bloomington, where he soon came under the influence of the progressive professor of zoölogy, David Starr

Jordan. Three years later (1885) Eigenmann published his first ichthyological paper, a review of the *Diodontidae* of North America. In 1886, the year he received his bachelor's degree, he made a trip to California, and at San Diego met Rosa Smith, already becoming known by her papers on West Coast fishes. They were married on Aug. 20, 1887, and immediately proceeded to Harvard University to study the immense collections of South American fishes made by Louis Agassiz in 1865. They worked there until December 1888, completing, besides several smaller papers, a monumental review of the catfishes of South America. In 1887 Eigenmann was granted his master's degree by Indiana University, and in 1889, the doctorate. Returning to California, he established a small biological station at San Diego where he and Mrs. Eigenmann studied the fishes of the region.

He was called in 1891 to Indiana University as professor of zoölogy and rendered that institution valuable service during the rest of his life. In 1895 he founded the university's Biological Station at Turkey (now Winona) Lake, remaining its director until 1920. In 1908 he organized the Graduate School, and he was its dean until his death. The following year he went to the Northwest, to collect fishes for the British Museum, and with Mrs. Eigenmann reported the collections before shipping them to London. He then turned his attention toward studies of variation and of the origin and differentiation of the sex cells in certain of his Pacific Coast fish material. This latter work contributed greatly to his reputation. He next undertook a study of the degenerate eyes of the blind creatures inhabiting the caves of Southern Indiana and Kentucky and of the underlying evolutionary causes of this degeneration. The culmination of his studies was the publication, in 1909, by the Carnegie Institution of Washington, of *Cave Vertebrates of America, a Study in Degenerative Evolution,* a magnificent volume and the best known of Eigenmann's many works.

The loan of materials from the Agassiz collection allowed him to begin what he intended to be his greatest work, a monograph of the Characins, the largest family of South American river fishes. Financed in part by the Carnegie Museum of Pittsburgh, in which he was curator of fishes, 1909–18, in 1908 he made a trip to British Guiana which resulted in a ponderous volume, *The Fresh-water Fishes of British Guiana,* published in 1912. The results of other expeditions were embodied in a report entitled *The Fresh-water Fishes of Northwestern South America* (1922), issued by the Carnegie Museum. In 1918 he went again to South America, this time to the high Andes of Peru and along the coast through Chile; the principal result of this trip, *The Fresh-water Fishes of Chile,* was published by the National Academy of Sciences in 1927. On this expedition the strain of the great altitudes broke his strength, previously weakened by fever in Colombia, and from this time his health gradually declined. In 1926 he was taken to his old haunts in Southern California, where after a long illness he died, the great Characin monograph being but a third completed. He was recognized as one of the foremost ichthyologists of the country and, indeed, may be considered one of the four greatest of his time. He was also a teacher of great influence. A kindly man with a heart of gold, and a will of iron, sympathetic, jolly, yet stubborn in carrying out that on which he had set his mind, no professor was ever more beloved by students and colleagues alike, and few will be so kindly remembered.

[Eigenmann's middle initial did not stand for a name. For biographical sketches see *Who's Who in America,* 1926–27; A. W. Henn, in *Annals of the Carnegie Museum,* June 1927; G. S. Myers, in *Natural History,* Jan., Feb. 1928; Eigenmann's scientific papers, totaling upward of 200, are listed in Bashford Dean, *A Bibliography of Fishes* (1916–23), vol. I and supplements.]

G. S. M.

EILERS, FREDERIC ANTON (Jan. 14, 1839–Apr. 22, 1917), metallurgist, was born at Laufenselden, Nassau, Germany, the son of E. J. A. Frederic and Elizabeth Eilers. His father was chief forester of Nassau. Following the gymnasium, Eilers attended the mining school at Clausthal and the University of Göttingen. He came to America in 1859, his first engagement being with Adelberg & Raymond, a firm of mining engineers. From 1866 to 1869 he operated a copper smelter in Carroll County, Va. In 1869 he was appointed a federal deputy commissioner of mining statistics, which position he occupied for seven years, making extensive journeys of investigation throughout the Rocky Mountain and Pacific Slope region in collaboration with the commissioner, Rossiter W. Raymond [*q.v.*]. In those days of inadequate transportation facilities and unsettled condition of the country, such journeys demanded the greatest resourcefulness and involved no little personal danger. At the conclusion of this engagement, Eilers chose the Salt Lake Valley, Utah, as his field of activity, and acquired a part ownership in the Germania Smelter.

From the very first he had recognized the necessity of a more adequate system of metallurgical accounting, that metal losses and operating costs be more accurately known. The metallurgical management of the Germania enabled him to put into practise such systematic accounting and chemical control of furnace operation as he had already warmly advocated in his writing. He was a leader among those who "changed lead smelting from a rule-of-thumb affair to an exact science by working out the theory and practise of slag formation on an accurate chemical basis" (*Engineering and Mining Journal*, Apr. 28, 1917). The present-day practise, however, with so largely pretreated charge, precludes such meticulous regulation. He moved to Leadville, Colo., in 1879, with Gustav Billing building what is now the Arkansas Valley plant, and in 1883 made another move, building at Pueblo, Colo., the Eilers Smelter, which became a veritable metallurgical training school and produced a number of the best-known metallurgists of the United States. Eilers was unquestionably the dean of American lead-silver smelting, the recognized leader in metallurgical theory of that group of well-known pioneers who, throughout Nevada, Utah, and Colorado, developed American lead, silver, and copper smelting so effectively. He also showed ability as a mechanical engineer, devising improvements in furnace and smelter design and construction. With the purchase of the Eilers plant by the American Smelting & Refining Company, he became metallurgical head of that organization, which post he retained until his retirement from active work.

In 1863, four years after arriving in America, he had married Elizabeth Emrich; one son, Karl Eilers, became distinguished as a metallurgist. Notwithstanding his undoubted Americanism, Anton Eilers constantly gave evidence of devotion to his native land, by the practise, for example, of using German at table in the smelter mess at his Colorado plant, and of having served a menu reminiscent of the Fatherland. The many friendships which he made throughout his eventful career were shared by his wife and children and his home was one of greatest charm. His own death was the first break in his large and notably happy family.

[*Who's Who in America*, 1916–17; *Metallurgical and Chemical Engineering*, May 1, 1917; *N. Y. Times*, Apr. 23, 1917; private memoir in possession of the family.]

R. C. C.

EIMBECK, WILLIAM (Jan. 29, 1841–Mar. 27, 1909), geodetic engineer, was born in Brunswick, Germany, the third son of Frederick and Henrietta Eimbeck. He attended public and private schools in his native city and later the Polytechnical and Agricultural College, but considered himself as largely self-educated. In 1857 he came to the United States. Landing in New Orleans, and proceeding to St. Louis, he became a draftsman with Palm & Roberson, locomotive builders. In 1860 he took up civil engineering and for the next nine years he assisted in various municipal and county engineering projects in and about St. Louis. For the last two years of this period he also served as professor of engineering and practical astronomy at Washington University.

In 1869 he assisted, as one of a group of voluntary observers organized by the Coast and Geodetic Survey, in observing the solar eclipse of August of that year. His work in this connection led to his selection as an observer in the party which the superintendent of the Coast Survey took to southern Europe to observe the total solar eclipse of December 1870. The following year he was appointed to the engineering force of the Coast Survey; and here for thirty-five years he was engaged in various phases of geodetic field work, but principally in triangulation, in which branch he made his principal contributions. After various assignments which took him into a number of different eastern and western states, and during which he secured a thorough command of geodetic operations, he was assigned, in 1878, to begin the eastward extension of the primary scheme of triangulation which was to follow approximately the 39th parallel of latitude. Beginning in Nevada he carried this work forward for eighteen years to a connection with another party on the Continental Divide. The region traversed necessitated the carrying of supplies and instruments over hundreds of miles of desert and waste, and included observations on mountain peaks up to 14,000 feet in elevation. On one occasion a remarkably long line of triangulation was observed, a distance between two mountains of 183 miles. The successful execution of this work called for high qualities of leadership and resourcefulness, in addition to the technical qualifications of the geodetic engineer. In 1885, while engaged on the triangulation of the 39th parallel, Eimbeck submitted to the superintendent of the Coast Survey plans and specifications for a new type of base-measuring apparatus. This was later constructed and became known as the duplex base apparatus; and in 1896, along the eastern shore of Great Salt Lake, Eimbeck measured a base of about seven miles in length with this apparatus, the probable error of which was derived as one part in 1,600,000. A description of the duplex base apparatus and the report on the measurement of the Salt Lake base line are given in the *Report* of the superintendent of the Coast and Geodetic Survey for 1897.

A bachelor all his life, Eimbeck was a member

of a number of scientific societies and one of the founders of the Cosmos Club in Washington. A fine figure and of robust health for the greater part of his active life, the onset of Bright's disease compelled him to resign from the Survey in 1906. Three years later he died, in Washington, from a stroke of paralysis and was buried at New Haven, Mo., where members of his family lived.

[*Who's Who in America*, 1901–02; *Science*, July 9, 1909; *Jour. Asso. of Engineering Soc.*, July 1909; Coast and Geodetic Survey records.] H. A. M.

EINHORN, DAVID (Nov. 10, 1809–Nov. 2, 1879), rabbi, son of Maier and Karoline Einhorn, was born in Dispeck, Bavaria. He received a traditionally intensive Jewish education in the school of the village of his birth and in the Talmudic Academy of Fürth. After an abrupt plunge from this circumscribed, compact, and medieval scholastic world into the comparative liberalism of the Universities of Erlangen, Würzburg, and Munich, he emerged a religious radical. For ten years his frankly avowed views debarred him from an appointment as rabbi in Germany. When he was appointed rabbi in 1842, he found himself in constant opposition to the opinions and practises of the orthodox majority of his flock. This led in 1851 to his leaving Germany for Pesth, Hungary. There a reactionary government, confusing religious with political liberalism, closed his temple two months after he had taken office.

There being little prospect in Europe for a rabbi of his radical religious ideas, he turned his eyes to the United States. After four years of waiting, during which he published his system of Jewish theology, *Das Prinzip des Mosaismus und dessen Verhaeltnis zum Heidenthum und Rabbinischen Judenthum* (Leipzig, 1854), he sailed for America in 1855, to become the religious leader of the Har Sinai Synagogue in Baltimore. There his unwavering moral courage and loyalty to the truth as he saw it were notably shown in his attacks on slavery. Though these were launched in German, a language which he regarded as the official tongue of reform Judaism in America, they drew down on him the angry resentment of some of his fellow citizens, and a few nights after Apr. 19, 1861, the night of the Baltimore riot, he had to flee the city under guard to avoid attack from the mob. His congregation would have welcomed him back on condition that he did not refer in the pulpit to the subject of slavery, but he refused all compromise and settled in Philadelphia, where he was soon elected rabbi of Keneseth Israel Congregation. His stand against slavery led to his election as an honorary member of the Union League Club of Philadelphia. In 1866 he was called to New York, as minister of Congregation Adath Jeshurun, merged in 1874 with an orthodox congregation under the new name of Congregation Beth El, where he officiated until he retired from active service in July 1879. Four months later he died.

His literary output in America was considerable. In 1856 he founded *Sinai*, a monthly German magazine devoted to reform Judaism. He issued this for seven years until, as he wrote, "it died in the battle against slavery." Through this organ he waged vigorous controversy with some of his colleagues, both orthodox and reform. In 1856 he published *Olath Tamid*, a reform modification of the traditional Jewish prayer book, with a German translation. This subsequently became the basis of the *Union Prayer Book*, the official liturgy of reform Judaism in America. Ten years later, in Philadelphia, he published *Ner Tamid, Die Lehre des Judenthums dargestellt für Schule und Haus*. A collected volume of his sermons was published in 1880 by his son-in-law, Rabbi Kaufmann Kohler. (In 1844 Einhorn married Julie Henrietta Ochs, of a prominent family in Kreuznach.) He was a leading figure at the Philadelphia Conference of Reform Rabbis in 1869 and at several Jewish Reform conferences in Germany.

As his writings consistently show, he was essentially a theologian, forthright and unyielding in the opinions which he expressed with ardent eloquence. His appreciation of Judaism was rationalizing rather than romantic, universal rather than national. As with most of the other early leaders of reform Judaism in America, who were born and trained in Germany, his religious revolt reflected the liberal politico-cultural ideology current in the newly awakening Germany of the early nineteenth century. By his forceful application of this ideology in the domain of Judaism, David Einhorn became the leading theologian of the reform Judaism of his generation in the United States.

[Besides Einhorn's own works mentioned above, see *David Einhorn Memorial Volume* (1911), by Kaufmann Kohler, containing a biography by Kohler, reprinted from the *Year Book of the Central Conference of Am. Rabbis*, XIX (1909), 215–70, and a memorial oration by Emil G. Hirsch; *Pubs. of the Am. Jewish Hist. Soc.*, No. 5 (1897), 147–52; Adolf Brüll, *Dr. David Einhorn und seine Bedeutung für das Judentum* (Frankfurt, 1882); David Philipson, *The Reform Movement in Judaism* (1907); Jacob Voorsanger, *The Chronicles of Emanu-El* (1900); Jos. Leiser, *Am. Judaism* (1925); F. de Sola Mendes, "America, Judaism" in *Jewish Encyc.* (1901), vol. I.] D. de S. P.

ELBERT, SAMUEL (1740–Nov. 1, 1788), Revolutionary soldier, governor of Georgia, was born in Prince William Parish, S. C., the son of a Baptist clergyman. Deprived of both parents in his early youth, he emigrated to Georgia, prospered exceedingly as a merchant and Indian trader, and attained position and influence in Savannah. At the outbreak of the Revolution he was among the Sons of Liberty and a member of the first Georgia Council of Safety (June 1775). A delegate to the Provincial Congress that met at Savannah in July, he was elected by that body to the Council of Safety, which had charge of public affairs, and was a member of the committee on militia and of the committee appointed to supply the province with arms and ammunition. He then entered the Continental service as lieutenant-colonel (January 1776) and a few months later was promoted to colonel. In the spring of 1777 he commanded the Continental troops in the abortive expedition against East Florida planned by Button Gwinnett [*q.v.*], president and commander-in-chief of Georgia. Elbert landed on Amelia Island, but finding the enemy prepared and a surprise attack impossible, the heat intense, and his stock of provisions low, he made no attempt to conquer the mainland. His presence, however, so frightened Patrick Tonyn, Royal Governor of East Florida, that he summoned the Creeks and sought to dispatch Cherokees into South Carolina or Georgia. Returning to Savannah, Elbert succeeded to the command of the Continental forces in Georgia after the departure of Brig.-Gen. Lachlan McIntosh [*q.v.*] for Washington's headquarters. Threatened with an invasion of Georgia by Brig.-Gen. Augustin Prevost, Maj.-Gen. Robert Howe [*q.v.*] moved southward, intending to strike a blow against East Florida. At Frederica (Apr. 19, 1778), with 300 men and three galleys, Elbert captured the brigantine *Hinchenbrooke,* the sloop *Rebecca,* and a prize brig. While the Howe expedition failed, it had the merit of retarding Prevost's efforts. In the fall of 1778 Col. Archibald Campbell arrived from New York intending to attack Savannah while Prevost marched northward from Florida to join him. Realizing that Girardeau's Bluff (now Brewton Hill) was the key to Savannah, Elbert urged that it be occupied in force. Howe's refusal was followed by the disastrous battle of Dec. 29, 1778. Sunbury having fallen and southern Georgia being occupied by the British, Elbert was unable to assemble sufficient troops to offer effective resistance to Campbell's march upon Augusta. Joining Brig.-Gen. John Ashe [*q.v.*], he commanded the left wing in the battle at Briar Creek, Mar. 3, 1779. The militia fled, but Elbert and his Continental troops fought so bravely that Lieut.-Col. J. M. Prevost was compelled to order up reserves. He then captured Elbert and his remaining troops. Elbert was exchanged in June 1781, commanded a brigade during the siege of Yorktown, and was brevetted brigadier-general (1783). He was one of the commissioners elected (Jan. 22, 1783) to negotiate with the Creeks and Cherokees and later declined an election to the Continental Congress (1784). Elected governor of Georgia in July 1785, he at once took firm measures to put down the band of freebooters inhabiting the district between the St. Mary and Satilla rivers and sought to pacify the Indians on the northern frontier, who were being stirred up by "disaffected and mercenary persons." He was afterward sheriff of Chatham County, vice-president of the Society of the Cincinnati, and Grand Master of the Masonic order in Georgia. He died at Savannah survived by his wife, Elizabeth (Rae) Elbert, and six children.

[Elbert's Order Book, 1776–78, and Letter-Book, 1785, printed in *Colls. of the Ga. Hist. Soc.*, vol. V (1901–02); Jos. Johnson, *Traditions and Reminiscences, Chiefly of the Am. Revolution in the South* (Charleston, 1851) and in the *Hist. Mag.*, Jan. 1868; Chas. C. Jones, Jr., *Life and Service of the Hon. Maj.-Gen. Samuel Elbert of Ga.* (1887) reprinted in *Mag. of Hist. Extra No. 13* (1911); *Revolutionary Records of the State of Ga.* (1908); Lewis W. G. Butler, *Annals of the King's Royal Rifle Corps,* vol. I (London, 1913); F. B. Heitman, *Hist. Reg. of Officers of the Continental Army* (1893); Wm. H. Siebert, *Loyalists in East Fla.* (Pubs. of the Fla. State Hist. Soc. No. 9, 1929); Mrs. Peter W. Meldrim, *Some Early Epitaphs in Ga.* (1924); *Georgia Gazette* (Savannah), Nov. 6, 1788; *Georgia State Gazette* (Augusta), Nov. 8, 1788.]

F. E. R.

ELDER, SAMUEL JAMES (Jan. 4, 1850–Jan. 22, 1918), lawyer, was born in Hope, R. I., the son of James Elder, a sea-captain of Baltimore who was killed when his only child was nine months old. The mother, Deborah Dunbar Keen of Camden, Me., went to Lawrence, Mass., where she opened a boarding house. Samuel's early education was in the schools of Lawrence. He graduated from Yale in 1873 and began reading law in the office of Morse & Hardy, Boston, attending some lectures at the Boston Law School. Admitted to the Massachusetts bar in June 1875, he at once opened his own office. He married, May 10, 1876, Lilla Thomas of Hastings-on-Hudson. Early struggle deepened his native instinct for stern effort, yet he was essentially Latin in temperament, buoyantly tolerant, gifted in friendship.

Success in the law came rapidly. He became a national authority in copyright law and was active in the campaign for international copyright, drafting part of the Act of 1891. He wrote a widely read monograph, *Our Archaic Copyright Laws* (1903), and contributed substantially to the revision of domestic copyright laws in 1909. His great ability lay in the trial of jury cases. He had a rare gift for eliciting information from friendly or reluctant witnesses, perceiving the drift of a jury's mind, revealing the drama of fact. He became a partner with John H. Hardy, later a judge of the superior court of Massachusetts, and Thomas W. Proctor, as Hardy, Elder & Proctor, and in the nineties he formed the firm of Elder, Wait & Whitman. In 1901 he defended Charles R. Eastman, Harvard instructor accused of murder. Acquittal was won in the face of the State's damaging evidence and determination to convict. Not a Christian Scientist, he conducted important litigation for Mary Baker Eddy, advising her in copyright matters and successfully defending her in the Woodbury libel suit. He assisted in sustaining the trust fund created for the church in her will against the attack of her son. In *People* vs. *Cole,* a test case brought by the New York Medical Society against a Christian Science practitioner, he made an argument before the New York court of appeals which reversed the conviction sustained by two courts below.

In 1910 Elder appeared at The Hague with Elihu Root and others as counsel for the United States in the North Atlantic Fisheries Arbitration with Great Britain. He argued three of seven questions, winning a decision in all three. When Taft proposed his Arbitration Treaties, Elder threw his energies into the movement for arbitration. In May 1914, he was elected president of the Massachusetts Peace Society and in 1915, member of the Executive Committee of the League to Enforce Peace. Always a Republican, he served one term in the Massachusetts House, was elected Taft delegate to Chicago in 1908, campaigned for Taft in 1912, and was presiding officer at the Taft banquet in New York after Wilson's election. Effective as a public speaker in important causes, "Sam Elder" was also sought as master raconteur of dialect stories, famous for his wit, contagious laughter, and spontaneous impersonations. His hobbies were the sea and college sports. In his profession he was recognized as a national authority on copyright and as a leader of the Massachusetts bar; as a man he was gifted with the rare power to raise all about him to their highest level of charm and achievement.

[*Proceedings of the Bar of the City of Boston and the Supreme Judicial Court of the Commonwealth of Mass., Feb. 8, 1919; The Life of Samuel J. Elder* (1925), by Margaret M. Elder with chapters by Edmund A. Whitman and Wm. Cushing Wait; *Boston Transcript,* Jan. 22, 1918.]

W. C. W.

ELDER, SUSAN BLANCHARD (Apr. 19, 1835–Nov. 3, 1923), author, daughter of Albert Gallatin and Susan (Thompson) Blanchard, was born at Fort Jessup, Sabine Parish, La. Her father, a graduate of West Point and a captain in the United States army, was stationed at Fort Jessup, a frontier post against the Indians on the Texas border. He later served through the Mexican War, and in the Civil War became a brigadier-general in the Confederate army. Her mother, a native of Massachusetts, died when the daughter was very young. After spending several years in the North with relatives, Susan Blanchard returned to Louisiana and attended the Girls' High School of New Orleans and St. Michael's Convent of the Sacred Heart, St. James Parish. At sixteen she was writing, under the name "Hermine," stories and poems for newspapers. In 1855 she married Charles D. Elder of Baltimore, a brother of Rev. William H. Elder [*q.v.*], Archbishop of Cincinnati. A few years later the Civil War broke, and upon the capture of New Orleans, the Elders took refuge in Selma, Ala., where they turned their home into a Confederate hospital. After Lee's surrender they returned to New Orleans and Susan Elder became a teacher of natural science and mathematics at the Picard Institute and the New Orleans High School. She was on the editorial staff of the *Morning Star* and contributed to various Roman Catholic journals. Her writings include historical and literary criticisms, biographies, stories, poems, and dramas written especially for presentation in Roman Catholic colleges. Her chief published volumes are *James the Second* (1874); *Savonarola* (1875); *Ellen Fitzgerald* (1876), a novel; *The Leos of the Papacy* (1879); *Elder Flowers* (1912), a collection of poems; *Character Glimpses of the Most Reverend William Henry Elder, D.D.* (1911), anonymous; *The Life of Abbé Adrien Rouquette* (1913), a biography of the poet, priest, and missionary of the Louisiana Choctaw Indians; and *A Mosaic in Blue and Gray* (1914). The two predominant motives in the author's life, aside from her domestic affections, were her devotion to the cause of the South and her devotion to the Roman Catholic Church, to which she was a convert early in life. Her prose works show careful study and, in the case of the biographies of her brother-in-law and the Abbé Rouquette, the use of original material. Her one novel was little read outside the South. Her verse, which includes domestic, religious, and patriotic subjects, has deep, usually melancholy, feeling, but little originality, and the expression is often stilted. Noteworthy personal poems are "My Bridal Veil," "The Mother's Round," and "Home," which celebrates her fiftieth wedding anniversary. "Ash Wednesday" and "Palm Sunday" are religious poems of some merit. Probably her best poems are those which reflect the life and emotions of the old South, such as "Mammy's Grieving" and "The Passing of Mammy." Susan Elder was a serious woman to whom life seemed full of struggle and sorrow. Her rather square face, with strong chin, high forehead, and deep-set thoughtful eyes, was sad, but neither severe nor bitter. Upon the death of her husband in 1890, she long continued to live in New Orleans, but in her last years made her home with her only surviving child, a daughter, at whose home in Cincinnati she died.

[*Who's Who in America,* 1906–07; *Woman's Who's Who of America,* 1914–15; J. W. Davidson, *The Living Writers of the South* (1869); Mary T. Tardy, ed., *The Living Female Writers of the South* (1872); *Cincinnati Enquirer,* Nov. 4, 1923.] S. G. B.

ELDER, WILLIAM (July 23, 1806–Apr. 5, 1885), physician and writer, was born in Somerset, Pa., the son of William Gore and Magdalen (Armstrong) Elder. He spent his boyhood in Somerset and on his father's farm and attended the country schools. When he was about twenty he began the study of medicine under Dr. Deane of Chambersburg, Pa., and later became assistant to Dr. Whiteside in Juniata County. He attended lectures at Jefferson Medical College, Philadelphia, and in 1833 established himself in practise at Oakland Mills in Juniata County. On Dec. 24 of that year he married Sara Maclean. He acquired a local reputation as a speaker on anti-Masonry and Colonization and on subjects in the field of "mental and moral philosophy." In 1838 he settled in Pittsburgh and the following year was elected recorder of deeds of Allegheny County on the Whig–Anti-Masonic ticket. He studied law, was admitted to the bar at Bedford, Pa., on Aug. 24, 1842, and in the same year commenced a legal practise in Pittsburgh, in partnership with John F. Beaver. After the Pittsburgh fire of 1845 he moved to Philadelphia, where for a number of years he was occupied with lecturing and writing, first on abolition, then on questions of finance, commerce, taxation, and public wealth. He was in charge of the *Liberty Herald* in 1847 and in 1848 wrote much for *The Republic,* a Free-Soil campaign paper. During this period he also contributed papers, signed "Senior," on political science and finance, to the *National Era* of Washington, and a series, "Familiar Life in Pennsylvania," to the Philadelphia *Press.* His first books were *Periscopics* (1854)—a volume of familiar essays, sometimes not more than a paragraph in length, dealing in an intimate way with matters of religion, politics, economics, philosophy, and literature, gathered from the periodicals for which he had been writing for several years past—and *The Enchanted Beauty* (1855), chiefly a reprint of *Periscopics.* In response to the request of the family of the explorer, he brought out a laudatory but somewhat lifeless *Biography of Elisha Kent Kane* in 1857. Henceforth his work was confined to questions of economic interest. From 1861 to 1866 he was a statistician in the Treasury Department at Washington. In 1863 his *Debts and Resources of the United States* was distributed as one of the pamphlet publications of the Union League of Philadelphia; in 1865 his paper, *How our National Debt can be Paid,* was issued by Jay Cooke as part of his campaign to sell government securities. After the war Elder returned to Philadelphia, where he resided from 1866 to 1873. His most important work, *Questions of the Day: Economic and Social* (Philadelphia, 1871), was intended as "political economy for popular perusal." From it extracts were republished the same year, as *A Short History of a Long Fight: Free Trade and Protection.* The burden of the work is to disprove the tenets of the classical economists of rent, international trade, and population. He was a faithful disciple of Henry C. Carey, as well as a devoted personal friend. In 1880 he read before the Historical Society of Pennsylvania a *Memoir of Henry Carey,* which not only sketched the facts of Carey's life, but surveyed economic writing to that time, in order to determine Carey's place in the hierarchy of economists. Elder was thoroughly imbued with the protectionist doctrines prevalent in Pennsylvania at the time and his later pamphlets practically all relate to that subject. The last twelve years of his life were spent in Washington, as a clerk in the Comptroller's Office in the Treasury Department, where he worked until a short time before his death. The Philadelphia *Public Ledger* (Apr. 6, 1885) contained the following characterization: "A man of brilliant talents, which were veiled from the public eye in his later days by his employment as a statistician in the Treasury Department at Washington, . . . he flourished in the days of the antislavery agitation, being a fervid friend of free soil, free speech, and free men." There might well have been added, "but not of free trade."

[See J. W. Forney in *Progress* (Phila.), Jan. 25, 1879; *Bull. Am. Iron and Steel Asso.* (Phila.), May 15, 1898, repr. from *Home Market Bull.* (Boston), May 1, 1898; obituary in *Evening Critic* (Washington, D. C.), Apr. 7, 1885. The *Hist. Soc. of Pa.* possesses several letters. in MS., and a portrait. Certain information has been supplied by Elder's grand-daughter, Miss Katharine H. Ringwalt of Phila., through the courtesy of Mrs. Fayette B. Dow.] E. D.

ELDER, WILLIAM HENRY (Mar. 22, 1819–Oct. 31, 1904), Roman Catholic prelate, was born in Baltimore, Md., the ninth child of Basil Spalding and Elizabeth Miles (Snowden) Elder. He received his early education in a Catholic private school in Baltimore and in 1831 entered Mount St. Mary's College, Emmitsburg, Md., then presided over by Rev. John Baptist Purcell whom he afterward succeeded as archbishop of Cincinnati. In 1837 he graduated from this institution and in the fall of the same year entered Mount St. Mary's Theological Seminary. In 1842 he was sent to Rome to complete his theological training in the College of the Propaganda, where he received his degree of doctor of divinity. On Mar. 29, 1846, he was ordained priest in the chapel of that institution, the officiating prelate being Msgr. Brunelli. Elder then returned to his alma mater as professor of theology and remained there for eleven years.

On Mar. 3, 1857, he was consecrated bishop of Natchez by Archbishop Kenrick. For twenty-three years he remained in charge of that see, endearing himself to the people of Mississippi by his deep devotion, his dauntless courage, and his manifold acts of charity, which were frequently performed at great personal risk. During the Civil War he visited the camps and battlefields, rendering spiritual and material aid alike to friend and foe. In 1864 the Federal post commandant at Natchez directed him to use a form of prayer for the president of the United States in the churches of his diocese. Deeming this an infringement of religious liberty and refusing to allow any but his ecclesiastical superiors to dictate his episcopal functions, he declined to obey. He was arrested, tried, and convicted; but the decision of the military court was overruled in Washington. In 1878 his diocese was swept by yellow fever, and his acts of mercy during the epidemic won for him universal commendation.

On Jan. 30, 1880, he was transferred to the titular See of Avara and made coadjutor with the right of succession to Archbishop Purcell of Cincinnati, whom he succeeded July 4, 1883. He assumed his episcopal duties when the financial affairs of the diocese were in a chaotic condition. By his prudence and wisdom order was restored; the diocese was built up, much property and several churches were added; new seminaries were founded and old ones were reopened; charitable institutions were placed upon a sound footing; and the number of the faithful increased. He was devotedly attached to his parishioners. "I want to be near my children always," he said when refusing the offers of more comfortable quarters (*Cincinnati Times Star,* Nov. 2, 1904). His personal modesty, his universal charity, his great piety and his sincere catholicity gained him the love and respect of all creeds and denominations.

[J. G. Shea, *Hist. of the Cath. Church in the U. S.* (1892); J. H. Lamott, *Hist. of the Archdiocese of Cincinnati* (1921); *Cath. Encyc.*, V, 373; *Character-Glimpses of Most Rev. Wm. Henry Elder, D.D.* (1911); *Cincinnati Enquirer,* Nov. 1, 1904; and *Cath. Telegraph,* Nov. 3, 1904.]

R. C. M.

ELDRIDGE, SHALOR WINCHELL (Aug. 29, 1816–Jan. 16, 1899), Kansas leader and business man, was born at West Springfield, Mass., the son of Lyman Eldridge, a mechanic, and his wife, Phœbe Winchell. He engaged in business, chiefly as a railroad contractor, at Southampton, Mass., where in 1839 he married Mary Norton. In 1855 he undertook the management of the Gillis House in Kansas City, Mo., which the New England Emigrant Aid Company had bought as headquarters for their emigrants to Kansas Territory. On account of violent opposition to the Aid Company, Eldridge bought the hotel, and for a time he was able to maintain friendly relations with the local public. While in Kansas City he aided the Free-State party in Lawrence in many ways. Early in 1856 he leased the Free State Hotel, built by the Emigrant Aid Company in Lawrence, and also established the first stage lines from Kansas City to Lawrence and Topeka and from Kansas City to Leavenworth and other points. Later in that year the pro-slavery interests secured an indictment under the federal judge against the hotel and two anti-slavery newspapers, recommending their abatement as nuisances, and on May 21 the hotel, the offices of the *Kansas Free State* and the *Herald of Freedom,* and the home of Gov. Robinson were destroyed by a mob. Eldridge was sent to Washington by a committee of citizens to protest to President Pierce against these outrages and he rendered notable service in securing the appointment of John W. Geary as territorial governor of Kansas. Although heretofore a Democrat, he now joined the Kansas delegation at the Republican National Convention in Philadelphia.

On July 9, 1856, he attended the National Convention of the Friends of Kansas in Buffalo, and was appointed the Kansas member of the National Committee, known as the Hyatt Committee. James H. Lane [*q.v.*] had been visiting Northern cities enlisting recruits for the Free-State party in Kansas. As Free-State men had been stopped in Missouri, these recruits were sent across Iowa. Starting without adequate equipment, they became disorganized and were stranded on the way. Eldridge was sent by the National Committee to take charge of them and succeeded in leading them to their destination in safety. Later, with Robert Morrow, he was sent to Chicago to bring back another party of 250 recruits. Upon their arrival in Kansas they were disarmed by Gov. Geary, who by this time had established order in the territory. When the Free-State party captured the territorial legislature, Eldridge induced Gov. Stanton to call a special session, which undoubtedly averted a renewal of hostilities. The legislature submitted the entire Lecompton constitution to popular vote, took control of the militia, gave the command to Lane, and made Eldridge quartermaster-general.

When the Emigrant Aid Company decided not to rebuild the Free State Hotel, Eldridge bought the site and built the Eldridge House. At the outbreak of the Civil War, he enlisted in the 2nd Kansas, was made quartermaster, and served in the Missouri campaign until the regiment was mustered out five months later. In 1863 he was made an army paymaster and served until his resignation a year later. While he was absent in this service, his hotel was destroyed in the sack of Lawrence by Quantrill, Aug. 21, 1863. After the Civil War he became a building contractor, rebuilt the Eldridge House in Lawrence, which he sold soon afterward, built hotels in other cities, and Fraser Hall at the State University. When the crisis of 1873 brought building to a halt, he engaged in mining in Colorado and Arkansas. In these operations he made a fortune which he later lost. His first wife died on Mar. 5, 1869, and in 1871 he married Caroline Tobey of Dundee, N. Y., who survived him. His declining years were spent in retirement at his home in Lawrence. Toward their close, in collaboration with R. G. Elliott, former editor of the *Kansas Free State,* he wrote his "Recollections of Early Days in Kansas."

[Eldridge's "Recollections" in *Kans. State Hist. Soc. Pubs.*, vol. II (1920); F. B. Heitman, *Hist. Reg. and Dict. U. S. Army* (1903); *Kansas City Star*, Jan. 16, 1899.]

F. H. H.

ELIOT, CHARLES (Nov. 1, 1859–Mar. 25, 1897), landscape architect, author, son of Charles William Eliot [*q.v.*], president of Harvard University, and Ellen Derby (Peabody) Eliot, was born in Cambridge, Mass. His early education was received at home and in Europe, where the family spent nearly three of his first ten years. Later he attended school in Cambridge. Among his ancestors were men and women of education, wealth, and position, able to give their children every advantage. Charles early developed a talent for sketching, a sense of locality, a fondness for maps, and an appreciation of scenery—all of which later combined to determine his career. He entered Harvard University in 1878, spending vacations in yachting and camping, and deriving especial benefit from the Champlain Society, a club-camp, which he organized for scientific study on Mt. Desert Island, Me. This experience, which helped him to overcome some of his natural diffidence, brought out his qualities of leadership, organizing power, and persistence, which were notable throughout his professional work. On receiving his B.A. degree from Harvard in 1882, he sought a field in which his natural tastes would find scope and was drawn to landscape architecture, then known in Boston largely through the work of Frederick Law Olmsted [*q.v.*]. Although no school in the country then offered preparation for this profession, several fundamental subjects were taught at the Bussey Institution, a branch of Harvard. There Eliot studied until, in April 1883, he was given the opportunity of an apprenticeship in Olmsted's office, just established in Brookline.

In November 1885, Eliot sailed for a year's study in Europe, visiting England, France, Italy, Germany, Holland, Denmark, Sweden, and Russia. He kept a record of his observations on gardens, parks, and scenery, which forms the beginning of the series of professional writings preserved in *Charles Eliot, Landscape Architect* (*post*). On his return to Boston, he set up in independent practise as a landscape architect (December 1886), and met with increasing recognition and success. Some examples of his early work are the Longfellow Memorial and subdivision of the Norton estate in Cambridge, and White Park, Concord, N. H.

On Nov. 28, 1888, he married Mary Yale Pitkin of Philadelphia. They lived first in Cambridge with President Eliot, then later moved to Brookline. Their family life, although abbreviated by Eliot's untimely death, was an exceptionally happy background for the brilliant professional contribution which he made in scarcely over a decade of practise.

Although he had a substantial amount and variety of work for private individuals and institutions, his main service was directly to the public through his writings for the press, and more especially through his conception and realization of a system of metropolitan park reservations for Greater Boston. He understood and voiced the need for the public acquisition of scenic regions, and his endeavors led to the incorporation in Massachusetts of the Trustees of Public Reservations, composed of certain leading members of the Appalachian Mountain Club and other public-spirited citizens, who proceeded to acquire several threatened areas. Backed by this new organization, Eliot succeeded in securing state legislation establishing the Metropolitan Park Commission (1892), to which he became professional adviser, and in connection with the selection and development of its holdings, formulated principles of park and reservation planning which have exerted a profound influence throughout the country.

In March 1893, at Olmsted's urgent invitation, he joined the Olmsted firm (which then became Olmsted, Olmsted & Eliot), and for four years was concerned with large public and private enterprises in many parts of the United States, still keeping his major interest in the development of the Boston metropolitan parks. Returning from the Hartford parks early in 1897, he died suddenly of cerebro-spinal meningitis, thus cutting off a future of almost unlimited promise. His kindly, earnest uprightness, his family and social connections, his persuasiveness as a public speaker, and his literary and artistic abilities, had placed him in the forefront of a young profession, which he joined with his master, Olmsted, in defining and establishing. The course in landscape architecture at Harvard University, founded in 1900, preserves fitting memorials to him in the Charles Eliot Professorship, the Charles Eliot Travelling Fellowship, and the Charles Eliot collection of books.

[Eliot's principal writings, originally contained in *Garden and Forest,* of the Arnold Arboretum, and his official reports, together with his journals and letters to clients, were collected and edited by President Eliot as a part of the biographical work *Charles Eliot, Landscape Architect* (1902). See also *Class of 1882, Harvard Coll.,* 1882–1907; *Boston Herald,* Mar. 26, 1897.]

T. K. H.

ELIOT, CHARLES WILLIAM (Mar. 20, 1834–Aug. 22, 1926), president of Harvard, and in his day the most influential leader in the educational activities of the country, was the only son of Samuel Atkins [*q.v.*] and Mary (Lyman) Eliot. Through his father he was descended from Andrew Eliot who came from Somersetshire, England, to Beverly, Mass., about 1668. His Eliot ancestors were prominently identified with the cultural, political, and educational development of New England, and were closely associated with Harvard. The father, Samuel A. Eliot, was a graduate of the College and of the Divinity School, and afterwards treasurer and historian of the College. He was prominent in the civic affairs of Boston, became mayor of the city in 1837, was a member of both branches of the state legislature, and was elected to Congress in 1850. Mary Lyman, wife of Samuel A. Eliot, came of similar stock, her father being a leading merchant of Boston, her brother, Theodore Lyman, Jr. [*q.v.*], a well-known philanthropist, and mayor of Boston.

Charles William Eliot was born in Boston, and received his secondary education under the rigorous, coercive methods then employed at the Boston Latin School. His early religious influences, on the other hand, were of the more emancipating sort then emanating from King's Chapel, of which his father was warden and choir-master, and where, at the beginning of the century James Freeman had launched the liberal movement which afterwards developed into Unitarianism. The young Charles entered Harvard in 1849, at the age of fifteen, when the college under the presidencies of Jared Sparks and James Walker was entering upon a period of reaction against the relatively progressive policies of Josiah Quincy. Eliot interested himself in English, and especially in mathematics and science; profiting by the stimulating atmosphere created by Benjaman Peirce, Louis Agassiz, Asa Gray, Joseph Lovering, Jeffries Wyman, and Josiah Parsons Cooke, and having under Cooke the then unique experience for an undergraduate of laboratory and field work in chemistry and mineralogy.

Graduating in 1853 second in his class of eighty-eight, he became tutor in mathematics at Harvard in 1854, and four years later assistant professor of mathematics and chemistry. His teaching brought him into contact with the Medical and Lawrence Scientific schools as well as the college; and gave him the opportunity of introducing the first written examination at Harvard, of emphasizing laboratory exercises, and of offering on a small scale elective as well as compulsory instruction. In 1858 he married Ellen Derby Peabody, daughter of the Rev. Ephraim Peabody, minister of King's Chapel. Failing to secure promotion upon the expiration in 1863 of his five years' term as assistant professor, he severed his connection with Harvard and even considered the abandonment of the teaching profession. Gov. Andrew offered him an appointment as lieutenant-colonel of cavalry in the forces which Massachusetts was mobilizing for the armies of the North; but in the previous year his father had died after suffering severe financial reverses, and the ensuing family responsibilities together with his defective eye-sight compelled him to decline. He sailed for Europe to pursue his studies, and while abroad was appointed to a professorship of chemistry at the Massachusetts Institute of Technology where he resumed his teaching in September 1865.

During these years of sojourn abroad, and

during a second similar trip taken in 1867, Eliot embraced the opportunity of making a first-hand study of European education. These observations, together with his own personal and professional experiences, inspired two articles on "The New Education: Its Organization," which appeared in the *Atlantic Monthly* early in 1869 and attracted wide attention. His broad grasp of contemporary educational problems commended their author to the Harvard Corporation, who were called upon at this time to select a successor to President Thomas Hill. Eliot's election, on Mar. 12, 1869, was first disapproved by the Board of Overseers, and afterwards, on May 19, confirmed by a divided vote. He was inaugurated on Oct. 19, 1869.

Eliot's Harvard presidency marked a new era and not merely a new administration. The country at large was entering upon the period of enterprise and expansion which followed the conclusion of the Civil War. A more liberal and progressive spirit had already begun to appear at Harvard in Hill's administration, and many members of the faculties and governing boards were ready and eager for change. There was a wide-spread feeling that reforms were needed, and Eliot was elected with the full consciousness that he would bring them to pass. This promise of innovation was the principal cause both of his support and of the resistance which he encountered. Although the twenty-second Harvard president, he was only the third layman elected to that office; he was primarily an administrator, rather than a scholar or teacher; by innate capacity, as well as by circumstance and opportunity, he was marked out for leadership.

When Eliot entered upon his term of office in the autumn of 1869 the University consisted of Harvard College, together with Divinity, Law, Medical, Dental and Scientific Schools, having a total enrolment of approximately 1,000 students and 60 teachers. Forty years later, at the close of his administration, the University contained in addition to the above, Graduate Schools of Arts and Sciences, Applied Science and Business Administration, and had a total enrolment of approximately 4,000 students (exclusive of the Summer School) and 600 teachers. The increased ratio of teachers to students was notable, and was reflected in the immeasurable increase of the volume and diversity of instruction. The income-bearing funds of the University amounted to two and one-quarter millions of dollars in 1868–69, and to over twenty millions in 1908–09. There was a corresponding, if not greater, increase in the value of the plant.

Although the major professional schools had existed for many years, the University as a whole had prior to Eliot lacked coherence, both in educational purpose and in administration. Eliot's policy was to draw the different parts of the University together in order that, having acquired an organic relationship, they might then be given a larger autonomy under their own faculties and deans. His general plan, conceived in the opening years of his administration, pressed persistently, and realized gradually as circumstances permitted, was to embrace all undergraduate studies within Harvard College, and establish about this center a complete group of graduate, research, and professional schools. To carry out this plan it was necessary to incorporate the undergraduate Lawrence Scientific School into Harvard College, a change which was approaching completion in 1909; and to require a bachelor's degree for admission to all other parts of the University. This requirement was adopted in the Divinity School in 1886, in the Graduate School in 1892, in the Law School in 1896 (for candidates for the degree, in 1893), and in the Medical School in 1900. The Schools of Applied Science and Business Administration were graduate schools from their foundation, and into the former were incorporated (in addition to engineering) the instruction in architecture, landscape architecture, and forestry, and the research in applied biology which had been conducted at the Bussey Institution.

The plan was never perfectly realized. The University Observatory and Museums retained a semi-detached existence as institutes of research. Summer courses in chemistry, botany, and geology were given as early as 1875, grew speedily in importance, and eventually came to form the nucleus of a "school" with a somewhat fluctuating and ambiguous relation to Harvard College and the Graduate School. Eliot's readiness to undertake novel and irregular ventures is illustrated by the special summer schools held at Harvard for Cuban teachers in 1900, and for teachers from Porto Rico in 1904. On the subject of the higher education of women Eliot had taken an open-minded and hopeful view in his inaugural address. He cooperated with the efforts of those who, under the lead of Mrs. Elizabeth Cabot Cary Agassiz [*q.v.*], inaugurated in 1879 the teaching of private classes of women by members of the Harvard College faculty. In 1882 this instruction assumed a more organized and formal character under the Society for the Collegiate Instruction of Women (commonly known as the Harvard Annex), and in 1894 the present Radcliffe College came into existence as a distinct corporate entity, with degrees guaranteed and countersigned by Harvard. Eliot's attitude throughout was one of cautious, experimental benevolence. But while he was willing for good reasons to depart from it in special cases, he had none the less a comprehensive plan for Harvard University as a whole.

Among Eliot's policies affecting the University none was more fundamental than his care for the teaching personnel. He regarded the recruiting of the faculties from all parts of the United States, and even from abroad, as his most important duty, and the growing prestige of the University in science and letters was evidence of the vigilance and sound judgment which he exercised. The invention of the "Sabbatical Year," and the establishment in later years of the French and German Exchange Professorships, provided opportunities of European contact and greater leisure for research. In 1904–05 the alumni raised $2,300,000 in response to Eliot's appeal for a general increase of faculty salaries. This step was one of the early examples of the "drives" which afterwards came into vogue, and had an important influence on prevailing standards of remuneration in the teaching profession. Not less important was the establishment in 1899 of a liberal system of teachers' retiring allowances, which was maintained independently by the University until in 1906 provision for this purpose was made by the Carnegie Foundation. Academic freedom was jealously safeguarded, and every effort was made to create an atmosphere favorable to productive scholarship.

In Harvard College, the undergraduate department of the University, the most radical change introduced during Eliot's administration was the development of the so-called "elective system." This reform sprang, so far as Eliot was concerned, from his profoundest educational convictions, as set forth in the Inaugural Address of 1869. He believed in giving the individual student a wide latitude of choice in order that he might acquire self-reliance, discover his own bent, rise to higher stages of attainment in his chosen field, and be governed in his work by interest rather than compulsion. He desired, furthermore, that the course of study should give to modern subjects, such as English, French, German, history, economics, and above all the natural sciences, equal rank with Latin, Greek, and mathematics, so that "liberal education" might be more closely related to contemporary life.

In 1824 students of the junior class in Harvard College had been permitted to substitute some other subject for thirty-eight lessons in Hebrew, and seniors might choose between chemistry and fluxions; otherwise all studies were required. Born in 1825 of the report of a committee of the Board of Overseers headed by Judge Joseph Story, the elective system had maintained during the next forty years a continued but precarious existence. Some presidents, like Quincy, Felton, and Hill had supported it, others, such as Everett and Sparks had been opposed; and the faculty usually had been divided. Over and above the natural tendency to cling to the old curriculum, the small size of the faculty presented a serious practical difficulty. Evidently election of studies could not be significant without a considerable range of choice. Furthermore, elective studies could not reach the same level of advancement as the older required studies unless they were pursued consecutively for several years. Attempts to graft election on compulsion by introducing new studies as additions or as "options" to existing requirements, tended to divide the student's time among many elementary studies with proficiency in none. It became evident that the values of the elective system could be realized only provided there was a considerable offering of graded courses in each subject, with the student free to make his choice in his early years. This was Eliot's program, which, like most of his reforms, was put into effect gradually, beginning at once. With some minor exceptions, requirements for seniors were abolished in 1872, for juniors in 1879, and for sophomores in 1884. In 1885 prescriptions for freshmen were materially reduced, but short courses in physics and chemistry were required until 1894, after which the modern language and English requirements alone persisted.

After some years of discussion, especially in the medical faculty, Eliot introduced in 1890 his plan for the shortening of the college course to three years. Unless some such concession were made, he feared that the lengthening and encroachment of the period of professional studies would destroy the liberal college altogether. A degree granted, as at Harvard in Eliot's time, on the satisfactory completion of a certain number of courses, could be taken in a shorter time by the simple expedient of carrying on more courses simultaneously. This would involve intenser application to studies on the part of undergraduates, which Eliot thought both possible and desirable. At the same time he hoped that an improved system of secondary instruction might deliver a riper product to the college, and that the pressure could be lightened by the anticipation of college studies in school, as well as by the use of the summer vacations. Approved both in the faculty and in the Board of Overseers, the new arrangement went partially into effect, although without any statutory recognition of three years as the normal period for the degree. The disorganization of the senior year, the multiplication of unrelated courses in the student's program, and the sacrifice of intellectual thoroughness to the accumulation of course credits, occasioned much criticism, and left the issue unsettled at the close of Eliot's administration.

Under Eliot the disciplinary regulations of Harvard College were greatly liberalized. In 1886, after a decade of agitation the ancient statute of the university requiring attendance at the college chapel was rescinded and all religious activities were put upon a voluntary basis under an interdenominational Board of Preachers. Throughout his entire administration Eliot took a keen interest in athletic policy. In 1888 he instituted the form of control which has since been very widely adopted, with a general athletic committee including alumni and undergraduates as well as officers of instruction. He took an important part in the introduction of stricter rules of eligibility by agreement among the colleges, and especially between Harvard and Yale. Although himself an oarsman and a friend of sport, he was a formidable and tireless critic of football. He believed not only that its intercollegiate competitions received excessive publicity and overemphasis, but that the game was inherently vicious because it placed a premium on the breaking of unenforceable rules, and because its code was a code of war rather than of sport.

A university president could influence primary and secondary education only indirectly through requirements for admission to college and through the dissemination of his ideas. As to admission requirements, Eliot's policy at Harvard was both to raise and to diversify them. High standards of admission were, he believed, a proper means of exerting pressure upon secondary schools to improve the thoroughness of their work. At the same time his attachment to the principle of election and his desire to maintain Harvard as a national college, led him to advocate considerable liberty of choice among entrance subjects, and the recognition of other subjects than the Latin, Greek, and mathematics which had held the field alone before 1870. Important steps in these directions were taken in 1887, when Greek became optional, and again in 1899. His interest in the relation between secondary and higher education led Eliot to participate actively in the work of the New England Association of Colleges and Preparatory Schools from its foundation in 1885, and in that of the National Education Association, of which he became president in 1903. In 1892 he was made chairman of the latter Association's Committee on Secondary School Studies, commonly known as the "Committee of Ten." The report, prepared by Eliot, embodied the valuable recommendations on the teaching of Latin, mathematics, history, and other subjects, submitted by a group of special conferences; defined the scope and sequence of these subjects; and formulated standard programs for secondary instruction. The committee advocated the downward extension of secondary subjects into the elementary grades, and believed that a standard secondary school should fit all of its graduates for college, so that its pupils should be able to postpone their decision as to entering college until they had had the opportunity of fully testing their ambition and competence. This Eliot held to be an important application of democratic principles. The work of this committee had a far-reaching influence upon the curricula of public schools throughout the country, mainly in the direction of standardization and uniformity. It also paved the way for the organization in 1901 of the Board of College Entrance Examinations, a central agency for the setting and grading of written examinations for admission to college, which had been supported by Eliot as early as 1877, and constantly advocated by him.

Eliot's numerous published articles and addresses before teachers' organizations covered a wide range of subjects, and at the same time exhibited a grasp of detail that made his hearers and readers feel that he understood and shared their problems. He believed that by increased application to studies enough time could be saved, especially in the grades, both to enrich the program of the secondary school and to relieve the colleges of the essentially secondary instruction they were compelled to undertake. He argued for the better training and greater security of teachers and for improved hygienic conditions in the school-room; his faith in the beneficence of freedom disposed him to favor so-called "progressive" schools; and with a growing emphasis in later years he insisted upon the importance of the training of the senses, the body, and the imagination.

While primary and secondary education formed the substructure of the college, graduate and professional education formed its superstructure. Here Eliot's influence was even more strongly felt. In his annual report for the year 1871 he wrote: "At whatever sacrifice, the University means to persevere in the good work of raising the standard of its professional schools." Graduate study in the subjects forming parts of the curriculum of Harvard College grew naturally out of the elective system. In 1872 the degrees of Master of Arts, Doctor of Science, and Doctor of Philosophy were established, and candidates for them were admitted to the undergraduate elective courses, which were becoming more numerous and more specialized. This was six years earlier than the epoch-making movement for graduate study launched at The Johns Hopkins University; but Eliot was much impressed by the steps already taken in this direction at Yale, where the degree of Ph.D. had been established in 1860. After an attempt to set apart a further group of courses which should be open only to graduate students, it was voted in 1882 to open all courses to any students, whether graduates or undergraduates, who were qualified to pursue them. In 1890 the Graduate School, afterwards called the "Graduate School of Arts and Sciences," was organized under the same faculty as that of Harvard College and the Scientific School, thus completing the characteristic Harvard organization. Graduates and undergraduates mingled in their courses, and as every teacher in the Faculty of Arts and Sciences was expected to attract graduate students as well as undergraduates, a higher premium was thus put on their scholarship and distinction.

Under Eliot's liberal policy the Harvard Divinity School became a non-sectarian institution of higher learning, instead of a denominational training school for ministers. The Graduate School of Applied Science was discontinued in 1914, but its underlying idea of placing engineering among the learned professions has endured and spread. The Graduate School of Business Administration was a novel departure, the full significance of which became apparent under the administration of his successor. But Eliot's most notable contributions to professional education were in law and medicine.

Throughout a history of more than a century the Harvard Law School has undergone no changes comparable in importance both for the school itself and for legal education in general with those which occurred within the first few years of Eliot's administration. The school had had a period of fame and rapid growth in Justice Joseph Story's time (1829–45), but had subsequently, in spite of its national reputation, declined in numbers, scholarship, and enterprise. Although housed in a building of its own and having an eminent faculty, its methods and organization were modeled on the lawyer's office. There were no requirements for admission and the quality of the students had deteriorated; there was neither gradation of courses, nor examination for graduation; the library was small and badly administered. This general slackness, which was characteristic of the times, was in part due to inertia and neglect, and in part to a desire to attract students, since the revenue was almost wholly derived from tuition fees. Seeing the need of fresh blood and active leadership, Eliot secured the appointment, as Dane Professor and afterwards as dean, of Christopher Columbus Langdell [*q.v.*], a former graduate of the school who was then practising law in New York City, and whose youthful promise had lingered in Eliot's memory from the time when they had been fellow students twenty years before. The partnership of Eliot and Langdell was instrumental in bringing about a rapid succession of reforms, for which Langdell supplied the expert knowledge and creative ideas, and Eliot the strategy and public support; both being endowed with courage and patience. The changes were of two kinds, those affecting organization and those affecting methods of instruction. To the first category belong the inauguration in 1872 of a two-years' course, with examinations both for promotion and for graduation; the lengthening of the course to three years in 1877–78; and the introduction, in the same year, of an admission examination for all candidates for the degree who were not college graduates. The tuition was raised, the library enlarged and reorganized, and the faculty increased. The appointment in 1873 of J. B. Ames, a recent graduate without legal practise, as assistant professor, was the first recognition of legal teaching as a distinct career requiring special qualifications. The reform in methods of instruction consisted in the famous "case system," introduced into his own classroom by Langdell and afterwards by his colleagues. All of these innovations met with stubborn resistance and harsh criticism, and their first effect was to diminish the number of students. But Eliot and Langdell held on unflinchingly until the tide definitely turned in 1883, the year of the building of Austin Hall. The subsequent history of the Harvard Law School was one of steady growth, in size, in resources, and in prestige. It attracted students in increasing numbers from all parts of the world, and through its graduates who became teachers it powerfully affected the general trend of legal education.

Eliot's interest in medicine was more than an educational interest. Preventive medicine, mental and social hygiene, as well as medicine in the narrower sense, were profoundly in accord with his humanitarian philosophy, as being applications of science to social progress. The changes in the Medical School were in many respects parallel to those in the Law School. Here also the time was ripe for reform. The school had begun in 1783 with high standards of admission and of scientific attainment, but during the nineteenth century there had been a change in the direction of more elementary entrance requirements and a relatively practical and commercial emphasis. The medical degree was based largely upon credit for study under a practising physician, for which a certificate was accepted, this, as in the case of legal education, being a survival of the apprenticeship method. Candidates were also required to "attend" two four-months' courses of lectures, only one of which was necessarily taken at Harvard. The principal requirement in connection with these lectures seems to have been the purchase and presentation of "tickets." There were oral examinations for the degree, to be sure, but nine subjects were covered in an hour and a half, and of these it was necessary to pass only five. There were also theses, but it is recorded that when Louis Agassiz heard the best of them read at the Commencement ceremonies in 1867 his "look of mingled wonder, pain, and disgust at their flimsy badness" was "amusing to observe." The faculty depended for their compensation on the students' fees and attached great importance to the size of the enrolment. In addition to these conditions reflecting the general backwardness of professional education in America, a peculiar difficulty in medical education arose from the need of clinical facilities. As late as 1876 two-thirds of the medical students of the country enjoyed no access to clinical material; while the better schools, in order to obtain such material, were obliged to utilize the services of physicians having hospital appointments even when they were incompetent as teachers. That the Harvard School with all these defects should have been one of the best, indicates the state of medical education in the country as a whole. Reforms had been courageously attempted by the Chicago Medical School (afterwards affiliated with Northwestern University) and by the Humboldt Medical College in St. Louis, but without marked influence on the generally prevailing standards, which were at this time so far below those of Europe that it was customary for ambitious American students to complete their medical education in Berlin, Vienna, Paris, or Edinburgh.

Eliot's humanity was shocked by the menace to the community of an ignorant and incompetent medical profession, and the improvement of medical instruction was one of the purposes nearest his heart. The first step was to link the school more closely to the administration of the University, and Eliot provided the link in his own person. It was at a meeting of the medical faculty early in 1870 that there occurred the famous incident related by Dr. Oliver Wendell Holmes, who then belonged himself to the conservative faction. When asked why, after being let alone for eighty years, the faculty should suddenly have been called upon to change everything, Eliot unblushingly answered, "There is a new President." The first annual report of this new president (issued in January 1871) announced that "the whole system of medical education in this country needs thorough reformation." The reformation began at once, though it was disputed at every step by sincere and able advocates of the old order, who thought the innovators both reckless and doctrinaire. A progressive three-years' course, with laboratory work in the medical sciences, was introduced in the autumn of 1871, together with written examinations for the degree, and the requirement that the students should pass in all subjects. The division of the students into classes, with examinations for promotion and provisions for graduate clinical and laboratory study, were introduced in 1874. After 1877 admission requirements were steadily raised. The curriculum being enriched and elaborated, the four-years' course was introduced on an optional basis in 1879–80, and became obligatory in 1892, credit for study with practising physicians having been abandoned in 1889. There was the expected decline in students and income from fees, but this crisis being safely weathered, there began the period of steady growth in strength and repute which has continued down to the present. In 1883, on the hundredth anniversary of its founding, the school moved from the old quarters on North Grove Street, Boston, to a new building on Boylston Street, with greatly increased laboratory facilities. These quarters being outgrown, the present great plant in Brookline was erected in 1905, at a cost of approximately $5,000,000 for buildings, equipment, and endowment. Meanwhile the development of more intimate relations between the school and the Boston hospitals, new and old, greatly improved the opportunities for clinical instruction and interneships. The advance in medical education since 1870 has been a nation-wide movement. Changes similar to those instituted at Harvard in the early years of Eliot's administration were speedily adopted at other universities, such as Pennsylvania and Michigan. The Medical School of The Johns Hopkins University was opened in 1893, and exercised a powerful influence in the direction of advanced entrance requirements and emphasis on scientific research. But though the reform soon spread and had here and there been anticipated, Eliot appears to have been more responsible than any other single individual for the impulse by which it was effectively launched.

During the long period of his presidency, Eliot's private life was comparatively uneventful. His first wife had died in the very month of his election. In 1877 he married Grace Mellen Hopkinson, who was his constant companion until her death in 1924. Of his two sons, the elder, Charles, whose papers he edited under the title of *Charles Eliot, Landscape Architect* (1902), died in 1897; the younger, Samuel Atkins Eliot, survived him. Being much in demand as a speaker he made frequent and sometimes extensive trips in the United States, and at rare intervals went to Europe or the Bermudas. His resignation in 1909, at the age of seventy-five was due to no disability, and marked a change in the kind rather than in the degree of his labors. Henceforth he divided his residence between Cambridge and Mt. Desert, Me., where he had built a house at Northeast Harbor in 1881. He declined offers from both President Taft and President Wilson to nominate him as ambassador to Great Britain, and devoted himself to writing, speech-making, and correspondence, thus continuing the diversified public service for which he had found time even during the years of his presidency.

His educational activities did not cease. As member of the Board of Overseers from 1910 to 1916, he continued to interest himself in Harvard; and as member of the General Education Board and trustee of the Rockefeller Foundation and Carnegie Foundation for the Advancement of Teaching, he took an influential part in shaping the general policies of these great benevolent organizations. In 1911–12 he made a trip around the world under the auspices of a committee containing the president and two former presidents of the United States. In full vigor up to the last year of his life, he died at Northeast Harbor, Aug. 22, 1926, at the age of ninety-two. His body was brought to Cambridge, and after a funeral in Appleton Chapel, was interred in Mount Auburn Cemetery.

Though Eliot's peculiar competence and influence lay within the field of education, his long experience, his wide range of information and his sagacity and public spirit gave weight to his utterances on all the topics of the day. In politics he was an independent with a leaning towards the Democratic party. During the period of the World War he warmly supported President Wilson, both in his early neutrality and in his later advocacy of the cause of the Allies and of the League of Nations. He interested himself in the social effects of modern industrialism, and in a famous speech before the Boston Economic Club in 1902 boldly attacked the closed shop, limitations of output, the uniform wage, and similar restrictive methods practised by organized labor. Profit-sharing, arbitration, and cooperation were his favorite remedies for industrial difficulties. His opinions on these and other issues, such as immigration, the race problem, and the prevention of war, were dictated by adherence to the same fundamental principle of individual liberty which governed his educational policies. He thought the essence of democracy to consist not in equality of attainment or station, but in a social mobility that enabled each man to discover and realize his own special capacities. The "happy life" and its "durable satisfactions" were to be found in health, in the enjoyment of nature, books, and friends, in the exercise of human faculties, but above all in two things: in that "maximum of effort" which a man attains through the interested exercise of his own aptitudes, and in the love of human kind. This optimistic philanthropy, confirmed by his native health of body and of mind, and warmed by his strong domestic affections, found concrete expression in ways that he believed effective and useful rather than merely pleasing. It was in accord with his Unitarian religious training and was the central core of his faith. The certainty of his moral convictions, and his personal discovery that the way of duty and service was also the way of happiness were the premises of his belief in divine immanence and the spiritual order of the world. His was a religion without authority, mysticism, or other-worldliness, but it contributed effectually to his serenity and steadiness of purpose.

Speaking retrospectively of himself as a youth of fifteen, just entering upon his college career, Eliot once said: "He was reserved, industrious, independent and ambitious; he trod the giddy edge of precipices with a complete unconsciousness of danger." Age and experience supplemented but did not eradicate these essential traits. He was eminently qualified for leadership. It was easy for him to reach definite convictions on matters of policy, and in supporting his convictions he was both bold and persevering. Confident of his judgment once it was formed he did not allow personal feelings or interests to deflect him from his course. Although, especially in his early years, he was lacking in tact, he had a profound respect for constitutional methods, and was content to use persuasion rather than coercion, even when this required the postponement of action. By listening to his opponents he learned from them as well as about them, disarmed them, and often won their loyal cooperation. He was incessantly active, and possessed a patience and endurance proportional to his tenacity of will. Physically, he was always in training. He was prominent as an oarsman when in college, was fond of long walks, horse-back riding, bicycling and yachting, and assiduously cultivated his health by diet, sleep, and regular exercise. His imperfect eyesight compelled him to wear glasses, and he carried a disfiguring facial birthmark. These defects only served, however, to heighten the total impression created by his bodily vigor, tall and erect figure, resonant voice, and strong, clear-cut features. As a public speaker he was distinguished not by any histrionic appeal, but by the majesty of his bearing, his candor and air of conviction, his force of character, and by the lucidity of his thought and diction.

Eliot's published writings are extensive. His annual *Reports of the President of Harvard College,* covering a period of forty years, are documents of first importance in the history of education. The more important of his earlier essays and addresses on educational topics are contained in *Educational Reform* (1898), while those dealing with broader political and social questions appeared in *American Contributions to Civilization* (1897). His moral and religious creed was set forth in *The Religion of the Future* (1909), in *The Durable Satisfactions of Life* (1910), and in two books which he himself thought might have lasting value: *The Happy Life* (1896); and the sympathetic appreciation of his neighbor at Northeast Harbor, *John Gilley, Farmer and Fisherman* (1899). A collection of writings after 1914, is to be found in *A Late Harvest,* edited by M. A. DeWolfe Howe (1924); and a comprehensive collection in *Charles W. Eliot, the Man and his Beliefs,* by W. A. Neilson (1926). In the last year of his presidency, challenged to make good his remark that a man might acquire a liberal education by reading fifteen minutes a day from books that could all find room on a "five-foot shelf," he undertook the editing of the *Harvard Classics,* which had a wide circulation and focussed attention upon the question of adult self-education. The preparation of this series of fifty volumes, embracing several hundred authors, and representing every period of human history, is illustrative of the immense range of Eliot's curiosity and information. There was a quality of aptness and simplicity in his style which gave distinction to the phrases which he applied to recipients of honorary degrees at Harvard Commencements, and brought him many invitations to prepare architectural inscriptions, such as those of the World's Fair in Chicago and the Shaw Monument in Boston. He wrote and spoke as a man of affairs, addressing himself directly to the matter in hand. Although devoted to general purposes and firmly attached to a fundamental moral creed, he was as faithfully attentive to detail in discourse as he was circumspect in the overcoming of practical difficulties.

There have been many eminent university and college presidents in America, and the lives of many of them fell in the second half of the nineteenth century, when education felt the quickened impulse of the life of the united nation. As compared with others of this group, such as Hopkins, McCosh, Gilman, and Angell, Charles William Eliot was distinguished by his universality of interest reflecting a peculiarly rounded and complete personality, and by the fact that his perseverance and length of years enabled him to bring to slowly ripened fruition the remote dreams of his own youth.

[C. W. Eliot, "Contributions to the Hist. of Am. Teaching" (autobiographical), *Educational Rev.,* Nov. 1911; E. H. Cotton, *Life of Chas. W. Eliot* (1926); C. F. Dunbar, "President Eliot's Administration," in *Harvard Grads. Mag.,* June 1894, and other articles in the same publication; *The Centennial Hist. of the Harvard Law School* (1918); T. F. Harrington, *Harvard Medic. School* (1905); *The Ninetieth Birthday of C. W. Eliot* (1925); "Report of the Committee of Ten on Secondary School Studies" in *Report of the Commissioner of Education for the Year 1892–93* (U. S. Bureau of Educ., 1895); F. G. Peabody, *Reminiscences of Present Day Saints* (1927); H. H. Saunderson, *C. W. Eliot, Puritan Liberal* (1928); M. A. DeW. Howe, *Classic Shades* (1928); W. DeW. Hyde, "President Eliot as an Educational Reformer," *Atlantic Monthly,* Mar. 1899; C. F. Thwing, "President Eliot's Twenty-five Years of Service," *Forum,* May 1894; *Boston Transcript,* Aug. 22, 1926.]

R. B. P.

ELIOT, JARED (Nov. 7, 1685–Apr. 22, 1763), Congregational clergyman, physician, the son of Joseph and Mary (Wyllys) Eliot, was born in Guilford, Conn. His grandfather was John Eliot [*q.v.*]. He graduated at Yale College, then called the "Collegiate School" of Connecticut, in 1706, and after teaching for about two years was settled over the church in Killingworth, now Clinton, where he served until his death. For more than forty years he never failed to preach at least once every Sunday, and was highly regarded in the colony as a minister and adviser in church matters. Without neglecting the duties of this office, he pursued his interest in natural science and achieved eminence in widely different fields. Inheriting a taste for the practise of medicine from his grandmother, who had been noted for her skill in medicine and surgery, and from his father, also a physician, he received medical instruction from Rev. Joshua Hobart of Southold, L. I. In time he became the leading physician in the New England colonies, and his service was called for in all parts of the colony, as well as in Newport and Boston. "Of all those who combined the offices of clerygman and physician, not one, from the foundation of the American colonies, attained so high distinction as a physician as Jared Eliot." He was an instructor of physicians also, and his influence on medical practise in the colony was wide and lasting.

As a scientist, Eliot became interested in the black sand which at times covered the sea beach. He carried a quantity of it in his saddle bags, from time to time, to an iron furnace in Killingworth, where it was smelted. It proved to be an iron ore from which he extracted excellent iron. His *Essay on the Invention, or Art of making very good, if not the best Iron, from black Sea Sand,* published in 1762, was awarded a gold medal by the Royal Society of London. He was already a member of the society. He was one of the first to develop the ore beds in northwestern Connecticut, where later iron works supplied munitions for the Continental Army, and thus established Connecticut as the "munition state" of the country. During his thirty years as a physician, Eliot had visited all parts of the colony, had met the men of influence, and had become acquainted with the condition of farming throughout Connecticut. This wide observation led him to study possible improvements in farm practise. He bought considerable tracts of land, experimented wisely in their improvement, and embodied his results in an *Essay on Field Husbandry in New England,* published in six parts at intervals in the years from 1748 to 1759. These for a long time were the most widely read and prized agricultural essays in America. With President Ezra Stiles of Yale College, he introduced silk culture into the colony.

Eliot lived at a time when general poverty, the absence of outside intellectual stimulus, and the rudimentary means of communication hindered progress in the sciences in America. In a later century he would have been a specialist; in his own time he was a typical pioneer of applied science. In 1710 he married Hannah Smithson. Of their eleven children, nine grew to maturity. Two became physicians; four were farmers. In all they represented their respective towns in twenty-three sessions of the General Assembly. Eliot was a man of iron constitution, capable of enduring all the rigors of a newly settled country, and tireless in his various activities. "In his house he was liberal, courteous and generous in a gentleman-like hospitality." He made the earliest bequest for the permanent endowment of the Yale Library, the income from which has been used for the purchase of books for one hundred and sixty years. The college trained him for "employment in church and civil state" and he filled his seventy-eight years with useful service to both.

[F. B. Dexter, *Biog. Sketches of the Grads. of Yale Coll. 1701–1745* (1885); *Geneal. of the Descendants of John Eliot, 1598–1905* (ed. 1905); *Two Hundredth Anniversary of the Clinton Congreg. Ch.* (1868); W. B. Sprague, *Annals of the Am. Pulpit,* I (1857), 270.]

E. H. J.

ELIOT, JOHN (1604–May 21, 1690), missionary to the Indians, was baptized in the parish church of St. John Baptist, Widford, Hertfordshire, England, Aug. 5, 1604 and presumably was born a few days earlier. He was the son of Bennett and Lettice or Letteye (Aggar) Eliot. Little is known of his parents although a Norman pedigree has been made out for them. His father owned land in several parishes in Essex and had considerable property. John was the third of seven children, of whom the three youngest were baptized at Nazeing, Essex. John matriculated at Jesus College, Cambridge, Mar. 20, 1619, and received the B.A. degree in 1622, pursuing his studies with an excellent reputation for scholarship, especially in the classics. He taught for a time in the grammar school at Little Baddow, Essex, where he came under the influence of Thomas Hooker. It was there, he afterwards said, that his religious life began, and he determined to become a preacher. Some time later a number of his Puritan friends, about to emigrate to New England, asked him to go with them as their minister. He sailed from England in the ship *Lyon,* with some of the Winthrop family, and reached Boston Nov. 3, 1631. There he was at once employed as substitute for Mr. John Wilson, temporarily in England, and was asked to remain as teacher with him on his return. Before he emigrated he had been engaged to marry Ann (or Hannah) Mumford, who followed him about a year later. They were married in Boston in October 1632. Meanwhile his Essex friends had emigrated to Massachusetts and settled at Roxbury. Declining the Boston offer he settled among them as teacher of their church, a connection which lasted for sixty years. For over forty years he was sole pastor. There he came into close contact with the Indians and with the help of a quick-witted young Long Island native who had been taken prisoner, undertook to learn their language. Eliot was devoted to the study of Hebrew, was a good grammarian, and ready at learning languages. His first preaching to the Indians, however, in 1646, was in English. It was at the Indian settlement at Dorchester Mills. His next effort was at Nonantum, and there he continued to preach and catechize every fortnight through the winter, apparently making some genuine converts. By the summer of 1647 he was preaching to them in their own language. Moreover the work had so far advanced that it was thought best to organize a society in England to help forward it. A number of accounts of the work were published, such as *The Day Breaking* (1647), and in 1649 "The President and Society for Propagation of the Gospel in New-England" was incorporated, which sent over several thousand pounds. Meanwhile, Eliot had been engaged in translating the Bible into the Indian language. The New Testament was published in 1661 and the Old Testament in 1663 —the first Bible to be printed in North America. Its cost, about £1,000, was met in large part by funds from the English society. Other books were also printed in the Indian tongue, and a small Indian college was established at Cambridge. Eliot hoped in time to Christianize and civilize all the tribes in New England, but recognized their distaste for living too near the English. For that reason he made plans for the establishment of an Indian town in the wilderness, and decided on locating it at Natick. In 1651, after a grant was received from the General Court, the town was laid out and several families of "praying Indians" were settled there. Eliot organized what was practically a self-governing Indian community, in which the Indians were left free to manage their local affairs in their own way although they were under the jurisdiction of the general laws of Massachusetts. He continued to organize similar communities, and by 1674 there were fourteen of them, with about 1,100 Christian natives (Byington, *post,* p. 130). Believing that the Indians themselves would make in time the best missionaries to their own people, he carefully taught a number of them to serve as preachers, twenty-four of them being actively engaged in the work at the time of his death. He himself traveled largely over New England among the various tribes, meeting with much opposition from the sachems of some of them, such as the Narragansetts. It is possible that in spite of his saintliness and zeal, he was not wise in the method of segregation which he adopted. In any case the outbreak of King Philip's War scattered the "praying Indians" and to a great extent ruined the work. Although these Indians were loyal to the English, the settlers were in a panic and their treatment of their native wards was unreasoning and cruel. Eliot himself did not escape suspicion and contumely in his efforts to protect them. He and Major Gookin did all they could, at the expense of their popularity, and not wholly without danger from the whites, to mitigate the condition of the Christian natives. After the war was over, Eliot continued his labors, but the faith of the Indians in the good intentions of the Puritans had received a severe shock. The number of villages of "praying Indians" had been reduced from fourteen to four, and they gradually dwindled away.

Besides his work as pastor and missionary, Eliot wrote prolifically. In addition to his translation of the Bible, he published, among other English and Indian works, *A Primer or Catechism, in the Massachusetts Indian Language* (1654); *The Christian Commonwealth* (1659); *Up-Bookum Psalmes* (1663); *Communion of Churches* (1665); *The Indian Primer* (1669); and *The Harmony of the Gospels* (1678). After the Restoration, the Massachusetts government, fearing that the republican sentiments in Eliot's *Christian Commonwealth* might get them into trouble with the home government, condemned and suppressed the book (May 1661), and Eliot had to make a public retraction (*Publications of the Colonial Society of Massachusetts,* vol. XX, 1920, p. 95). He had six children, two of whom, with his wife, survived him. He was one of the most remarkable men of the seventeenth century in New England, and had the rare virtue of thinking of other souls besides his own.

[Mather not only gave an account of Eliot in his *Magnalia Christi Americana* (ed. 1853), I, 526–83, but also wrote *The Triumphs of the Reformed Religion, in America. The Life of the Renowned John Eliot* (1691). The best account is that by E. H. Byington, "John Eliot, the Puritan Missionary to the Indians," in *Papers Am. Soc. Ch. Hist.,* VIII (1897), 109–45. See also Convers Francis, *Life of John Eliot* (1836), in Sparks's *Lib. of Am. Biog.; R. I. Hist. Soc. Pubs.,* n.s. VI (1898), 112–17; *Proc. Mass. Hist. Soc.,* 2 ser. II (1886), 44–50; *Ibid.,* 2 ser. VI (1891), 392–95; Wilberforce Eames, *Bibliographic Notes on Eliot's Indian Bible and on his Other Translations and Works in the Indian Language of Mass.* (1890); *Geneal. of the Descendants of John Eliot* (1905).]

J. T. A.

ELIOT, SAMUEL (Dec. 22, 1821–Sept. 14, 1898), historian, educator, philanthropist, was born in Boston, the son of William Havard and Margaret Boies (Bradford) Eliot. His father, a brother of Samuel Atkins Eliot [*q.v.*], built the Tremont House, interested himself in the musical life of the city, and died suddenly in 1831 while a candidate for mayor. His mother was a daughter of Alden Bradford [*q.v.*]. Eliot graduated first in the class of 1839 at Harvard and after two uncongenial years in Robert Gould Shaw's counting room went to Madeira and thence to Italy to recruit his health. While in Rome he conceived the idea of a history of liberty, to be complete in six parts of two volumes each. In undertaking such a work he mistook literary ambition for capacity, and abandoned the project after some preliminary studies and four volumes of the history had been published. On June 7, 1853, he married Emily Marshall Otis, daughter of William Foster and Emily (Marshall) Otis of Boston, moved to Brookline, and began teaching a few pupils and giving free instruction to the children of workingmen. A devout Episcopalian, he had formed a warm admiration for Thomas Arnold and consciously modeled his career upon Arnold's. Through his ecclesiastical connections he became professor of history in Trinity College, Hartford, Conn., 1856–60, and president of the college, 1860–64. He then returned to Boston and devoted his life to an amazingly large number of educational, religious, and eleemosynary institutions. Among the more important of these were the Massachusetts General Hospital, the Perkins Institute for the Blind, the Massachusetts School for Feeble Minded Youth, Harvard University, St. Paul's School, the Boston Museum of Fine Arts, and the Boston Athenæum. The state had few more useful citizens than this quasi-professional trustee and chairman of boards. His high regard for public education led him to serve as headmaster, 1872–76, of the Girls' High and Normal School. In 1878 he was appointed superintendent of the city schools. He set to work with his customary energy and enthusiasm to enrich the curriculum and to improve the mode of instruction, but the state of his health compelled him to resign two years later and to make his third sojourn in Europe. His manners were those of a Boston gentleman of the old school. Perhaps his most pervasive trait was his religious faith, which expressed itself equally in his simple fervid adherence to the dogmas of his church and in his selfless devotion to the needy, the suffering, and the oppressed of all creeds. He died of heart trouble at Beverly Farms, Mass., and was buried in Mount Auburn Cemetery.

Besides a number of papers, lectures, and addresses, Eliot published a small, privately printed volume of translations from the Spanish poet, José Zorilla (1846); *Passages from the History of Liberty* (1847); *The Liberty of Rome* (2 vols., 1849), which was revised to form Part I of the *History of Liberty: Part I, The Ancient Romans; Part II, The Early Christians* (4 vols., 1853); and a *Manual of United States History* (1856; 4th ed., rev., 1874). He edited *Selections from American Authors* (1879) and *Poetry for Children* (1879), refusing characteristically to accept compensation for his editorial work.

[G. M. Fessenden, "A Geneal. of the Bradford Family," in *New-England Hist. and Geneal. Reg.*, IV (1850), 39–50, 233–45; W. H. Whitmore, *Ibid.*, XXIII (1869), 346–40; W. G. Eliot, *A Sketch of the Eliot Family* (1887); *Harvard Quinquennial Cat. 1636–1915* (1915); *Proc. Mass. Hist. Soc.*, 2 ser. vol. XII (1889); H. W. Haynes, memoir, *Ibid.*, 2 ser. XIV (1901), 105–26; Barrett Wendell, memoir in *Proc. Am. Acad. Arts and Sci.*, XXXIV (1899), 646–51; *Boston Transcript*, Sept. 15, 17, 1898.]

G. H. G.

ELIOT, SAMUEL ATKINS (Mar. 5, 1798–Jan. 29, 1862), statesman and man of letters, was born in Boston, Mass., the third son of Samuel and Catherine (Atkins) Eliot, and a direct descendant of Andrew Eliot, who came to America from Somersetshire about 1668. He graduated from Harvard in the class of 1817 and from the Harvard Divinity School in 1820, but he was never ordained to the ministry. At the death of his father in the latter year, Eliot was left with a considerable fortune. He spent some time in study and then went abroad from 1823 to 1826, traveling extensively in Europe. On June 13, 1826, he married Mary Lyman, daughter of the Boston merchant, Theodore Lyman, by whom he had four daughters and one son, Charles William Eliot [*q.v.*], later president of Harvard. One of Eliot's sisters married Professor Andrews Norton and another George Ticknor, and he was closely connected by blood or marriage with many members of the inner circle of Boston society.

Eliot now entered upon a career of uninterrupted and varied usefulness as a servant of the public. He sat for several terms in the Massachusetts General Court and was an alderman during the mayoralty of his brother-in-law, Theodore Lyman, Jr. [*q.v.*]. Keenly interested in the fine arts, he became the first president of the Academy of Music and delivered an address at the opening of the famous Odeon, Aug. 5, 1835. He was chiefly responsible for the first American performances, in Boston, of Beethoven's symphonies. As a member of the Boston School Committee, he introduced music into the public schools of his city. He himself translated Schiller's "The Song of the Bell," which, set to music by Romberg, was sung at the Academy of Music. Again in political life, he was elected for three consecutive terms (1837–39) as mayor of Boston. When a riot was caused by a collision between a volunteer fire company and an Irish funeral procession, Eliot courageously marched down Broad St. at the head of one hundred militiamen. Later, after an investigation, he disbanded all the volunteer engine companies and established a paid fire department. He also insisted on the formation of a competent police force in the municipality. In 1823, Eliot gave to Harvard Warden's extensive collection of books on American history. From 1842 to 1853 he was treasurer of Harvard College, and, while holding this position, published his *Sketch of the History of Harvard College and of its Present State* (1848).

Although Eliot was strongly opposed to slavery, he believed in the Compromise of 1850. When Robert C. Winthrop was appointed to the United States Senate in 1850 as Webster's successor, Eliot took Winthrop's seat in Congress, serving from Aug. 22, 1850, to Mar. 3, 1851. Webster looked upon the election as indicating approval of his own conduct and said of it, "From the commencement of the government, no such consequences have attended any single election, as those that flowed from Mr. Eliot's election" (*Writings and Speeches of Daniel Webster,* vol. XVIII, 1903, p. 387). While in the House of Representatives, Eliot voted for the compromise measures, including the Fugitive-Slave Law, and was therefore severely denounced by Abolitionists. He defended himself ably in a letter to the *Advertiser,* Oct. 29, 1850. Four years later, though he had declined reëlection to Congress, he presided over a meeting held at Faneuil Hall, Feb. 23, 1854, and again made public his convictions in a vigorous protest against the repeal of the Missouri Compromise. In 1857, a business house in which Eliot had been a silent partner failed, and he and his wife insisted upon turning over their property to pay the debts. He spent his declining years in "honorable poverty" in Cambridge, where he died in his sixty-fourth year, a poor and disappointed man.

As treasurer of the Prison Discipline Society, Eliot was assailed in 1847 by Charles Sumner (E. L. Pierce, *Memoir and Letters of Charles Sumner,* vol. III, 1893, p. 79), but seems to have had the better of the dispute. He was the first president of Boston Provident Association and a warden of King's Chapel. He published *Observations on the Bible, for the Use of Young Persons* (1842), *The Life of Josiah Henson, Formerly a Slave* (1843), and edited selections from the sermons of Francis W. P. Greenwood, with a memoir (1844). He also contributed articles to the *North American Review* and the *Christian Examiner.* He was a high-minded and public-spirited aristocrat, whom even his enemies described as sincere. Sumner said of him (Sept. 2, 1850) that he was "an honest and obstinate man," but a more favorable verdict is that of Webster, who wrote of Eliot (Sept. 12, 1850), "he is considered the impersonation of Boston; ever-intelligent, ever-patriotic, ever-glorious Boston."

[W. G. Eliot, *Sketch of the Eliot Family* (1887); A. P. Peabody, *Harvard Grads. Whom I Have Known* (1890), pp. 149–68; *Boston Transcript,* Jan. 31, 1862.]

C. M. F.

ELIOT, WILLIAM GREENLEAF (Aug. 5, 1811–Jan. 23, 1887), founder of Washington University, St. Louis, was born in New Bedford, Mass., the son of William Greenleaf and Margaret (Dawes) Eliot. After the War of 1812 his parents moved to Washington, D. C., where he went to school. He graduated from Columbian College in 1829, and from Harvard Divinity School, Cambridge, Mass., in 1834. He was ordained in the following August. Wishing to identify himself with the West, he accepted an invitation from St. Louis to go there for the purpose of establishing a church. He organized the First Congregational Society within two months after his arrival in January 1835, and by October 1836 the first building had been erected. During the next fifteen years his church outgrew its equipment, and a second building, The Church of the Messiah, was dedicated in December 1851. During these years he traveled extensively for his church, in accordance with the terms of his ordination, stimulating the erection of church edifices and persuading promising ministers to accept their pulpits. In 1853 Eliot Seminary (later Washington University) was created by a state charter, and the corporation was organized on Feb. 22, 1854. Within another year two further projects were launched: O'Fallon Polytechnic Institute, turned over to the city in 1868, and Smith Academy, which in 1857 was absorbed by the newly created Washington University. Mary Institute, now a flourishing secondary school for girls still connected with the University, was established in 1859. Eliot remained president of the board until 1870, when he became acting chancellor on the death of President Chauvenet. Two years later he was made chancellor. He resigned his position as pastor of his church in 1870, and was given the title of pastor emeritus.

Eliot was a political and philosophical liberal. He was in favor of the gradual emancipation of slaves as early as 1834. He promoted this cause in many ways until its realization and then turned his energies toward the establishment of a workable status for the freedmen. After the Civil War these interests led him into other fields. He advocated temperance reform, woman suffrage, and in his last years he struggled successfully to prevent the establishment of legalized prostitution in St. Louis. He labored to keep Missouri in the Union, working intimately with the local loyalist government, the federal forces, and the Washington government. He secured an order from Gen. Frémont in September 1861, for the creation of the Western Sanitary Commission, which attended the armies west of the Alleghanies. He and four others served without pay in its administration until its dissolution in 1871.

In 1848 he was elected president of the St. Louis school board, whose finances had made free educational work impossible, and by June 1849—the most disastrous year the city had known—he had conceived, and had secured the enactment into state law of a provision for a mill tax for educational purposes which permanently established the financial foundation of the public school system of St. Louis. In addition to his other interests, Eliot was a philanthropist. He was the founder of the Mission Free School in 1856, president of the State Institute for the Blind in 1853, and director in many charitable agencies. He raised sums of money which were immense for his day. The Western Sanitary Commission and Washington University each required millions, and his church assumed heavy charitable and missionary obligations.

Eliot married Abby A. Cranch, daughter of William Cranch [*q.v.*], in 1837. He was a frail man and of small stature. "The contrast was almost pathetic between the smallness of his physical resources and the magnitude of [his] enterprises." He often needed to take extended periods for travel and rest and it was on one of these enforced vacations that he died at Pass Christian. His writings were almost all incidental. He did, however, dramatize the tragedy of slavery in his "Story of Archer Alexander" (1885).

[Eliot's daughter, Charlotte C. Eliot, published *William Greenleaf Eliot, Minister, Educator, Philanthropist*, in 1904. See also Walter G. Eliot, *Sketch of the Eliot Family* (1887); J. G. Forman, *The Western Sanitary Commission* (1864); W. Hyde and H. L. Conard, *Encyc. of Hist. of St. Louis* (1899), II, 674; J. T. Scharf, *Hist. of St. Louis City and County* (2 vols., 1883); J. H. Heywood, "W. G. Eliot," *Unitarian Rev.*, Mar. 1887; *Mo. Republican*, Jan. 24, 1887.] F. J. B.

ELKINS, STEPHEN BENTON (Sept. 26, 1841–Jan. 4, 1911), secretary of war, United States senator, captain of industry, was a son of Col. Philip Duncan and Sarah Pickett (Withers) Elkins, both of whom were Virginians. His father was born in Fauquier County on July 4, 1809, and his mother, whom his father married in Nov. 9, 1840, was born in Culpeper County. His paternal grandfather was a slaveholder of considerable wealth, but, favoring emancipation, he removed to Ohio in 1821 when his son Philip was twelve years of age, settled in Perry County, and bought considerable land in the southern part of the state, including about 3,000 acres in the coal region of the Hocking Valley, which was later sold by Philip for little or nothing.

Young Stephen was a son of the Middle West. He was born on a farm near New Lexington, Perry County, Ohio, and sometime between 1842 and 1847 was taken to the historic big bend of the Missouri River at Westport, Mo., by his parents, who settled there on a farm which furnished him opportunity for useful muscular exercise both before and after he began his preparation for college in a neighboring town. Without fortune and without friends, he entered the University of Missouri at Columbia, from which by diligent study he graduated at the head of his class in 1860 with the B.A. degree, and which later (in 1868) granted him the M.A. degree. He was especially well trained in mathematics, Greek, and Latin. For a year he taught a country school in Cass County, Mo., numbering among his students the later notorious Cole ("Bud") Younger, who during the Civil War saved his life by aiding his escape from the Quantrill guerrillas. At the opening of the Civil War he enlisted in the Union army as a captain of militia in the 77th Missouri Infantry. In so doing, influenced by his knowledge of the Lincoln-Douglas debates and possibly also by his knowledge of incidents on the neighboring Kansas border, he acted against the advice of Gov. Sterling Price to his graduating class of 1860, against the decision of all other members of his class except one, and against his own father and brother, who joined the Confederates.

In spite of financial reverses to his family, which threw him upon his own resources but strengthened his spirit of self-reliance, he entered law school, and in 1864 he gained admission to the Missouri bar. Soon thereafter (1864), in a prairie schooner, he crossed the plains to New Mexico, where he began practise at Messilia and applied himself to the study of the Spanish language in order to aid his transaction of legal business. Within a year after his arrival he was elected to the territorial legislature and in 1865 was reëlected. He was appointed territorial district attorney in 1866 and served until Jan. 14, 1867. On June 10, 1866, he was married to Sarah Jacobs of Wellington, Mo., by whom he had two daughters.

Later he served as attorney-general of the territory (January–March 1867) and as United States district attorney (1867–70). In 1872 he was elected as a Republican to serve as territorial delegate to the Forty-third Congress, defeating a native New Mexican by a majority of 4,000; and in 1874, on his return from Europe, he discovered that he had been reëlected to Congress, where he served until Mar. 3, 1877. He was untiring in efforts to secure the administration of New Mexico to statehood, and made a speech which attracted wide attention, but his bill of Jan.

12, 1876, failed. While residing in New Mexico he became a large landowner and an extensive owner of mines in Colorado.

His later life was influenced by his second marriage, on Apr. 14, 1875, at Baltimore, Md., to Hallie, daughter of United States Senator Henry G. Davis [*q.v.*]. By her he had five children, one of whom, Davis, became a United States senator. For a time after 1876 he devoted his attention to legal practise and the presidency of the Santa Fé First National Bank, which he had founded. He also had a business office and a winter home in New York in connection with certain land, coal, and railroad interests. About 1890, he removed to a new, palatial residence which he built at Elkins, W. Va., a town founded by him in connection with the development of financial and railroad interests in association with his father-in-law and other prominent men. He actively aided the construction of the West Virginia Central & Pittsburgh Railroad (Western Maryland) of which he was vice-president. After 1890 he became interested in options on large tracts of coal lands on the Monongahela near Morgantown. In 1902 he purchased the Morgantown & Kingwood Railroad and by 1907 had completed it eastward to connect with the Baltimore & Ohio at Rowlesburg and made it a valuable factor in the industrial development of the region. He also had an interest with Henry G. Davis in the Coal & Coke Railway.

In national politics Elkins became prominent in 1884, as adviser and political lieutenant of James G. Blaine, the Republican candidate for president. For three successive presidential campaigns he was a member of the Republican National Committee. In 1888 he extended his reputation in West Virginia by speeches on the tariff and by a forcible, practical address on American civilization before the literary societies of West Virginia University. In December 1891 he was appointed secretary of war and served until the close of Harrison's administration. In February 1895 he was elected to the United States Senate, defeating J. N. Camden, the Democrat candidate. Reëlected in 1901 and again in 1907, he served until his death. In the Senate he carefully studied the larger legislative questions, and by his commanding personality combined with genial good nature, courtesy, and optimism he won a leadership especially in commercial and business affairs. As head of the committee on interstate commerce he had charge of measures designed to remove the railroads from politics, to reform and punish abuses in transportation, and to secure larger public control of the great corporations. He was the author and creator of the anti-rebate act of 1903, and joint author of the Mann-Elkins Act of 1910. His strength in debate was due to his common sense and practical experience, his lucidity, and a happy combination of firmness and gentleness. He was a past-master of the art of conciliation and of compromise in harmonizing conflicting interests.

Elkins was an adventurous pioneer of industry, a fearless explorer of undeveloped fields of wealth which he tapped for use. His faith in the industrial opportunities in West Virginia, and his courage, energy, and judgment in undertaking new enterprises of development in an unexplored wilderness, made him a captain of industry and a power in business, a builder of railroads, an operator of mines, and a creator of towns which justified his faith and judgment and won for him a larger influence in the councils of the state and nation. He became preëminently the business man in politics. In physique he was the personification of energetic health, six feet tall, with broad shoulders, muscular limbs, broad and open brow, kindly blue eyes, and a strong jaw. He was gentle and cheerful in manner, and was simple, domestic, and strongly American in tastes and habits, untempted by the ostentations of wealth. He had literary tastes and was a great reader.

[Geo. W. Atkinson and A. F. Gibbens, *Prominent Men of W. Va.* (1890); Chas. M. Pepper, *Life and Times of Henry Gassaway Davis* (1920); J. M. Callahan, *Hist. of W. Va., Old and New* (1923); *Memorial Addresses on the Life and Character of Stephen Benton Elkins* (1912); *Biog. Dir. Am. Cong.* (1928); *Evening Star* (Washington, D. C.), Jan. 5, 1911.]

J. M. C.

ELKINS, WILLIAM LUKENS (May 2, 1832–Nov. 7, 1903), capitalist, was born near Wheeling, W. Va., the seventh and youngest child of George Elkins, a pioneer paper manufacturer in the United States, and his wife Susanna Howell. He received his education in the public schools of Philadelphia, whither the family had moved in 1840. In 1847, however, he left school and started to work as clerk in a grocery store. In 1852 he went to New York City for a year where he engaged in the produce business. Returning to Philadelphia, he formed a partnership with Peter Sayboldt under the firm name of Sayboldt & Elkins in the same line of business. As the firm prospered it soon became necessary to keep perishable fruit for long periods. To do this Elkins built the first large refrigerator in Philadelphia. In 1860 he bought out his partner and continued the business under his own name until other activities forced him to abandon it. Shortly after the discovery of petroleum in western Pennsylvania he made a thorough survey of the oil region, organized many oil companies between 1861 and 1880, and operated extensively in the industry. In 1875 he became a partner in the Standard Oil Company but disposed of this interest in 1880. After spending some time in the oil-fields he concluded that the refining of the oil for illuminating purposes offered tremendous opportunities for profit if it could be conducted on a sufficiently large scale. He therefore established a small refinery in Philadelphia and as opportunities arose acquired or built others until he controlled the oil-refining business in that city. The first gasoline made was the product of one of his refineries. In 1873, in addition to his other enterprises, he became engaged in the manufacture of illuminating gas. He secured an interest in a number of gas works throughout the United States, and was one of the organizers of the United Gas & Improvement Company. In the same year he also became interested in street railways as an investment and was one of the organizers of the Philadelphia Traction Company, later the Philadelphia Rapid Transit Company. In the course of a few years he was connected with similar companies in New York City, Chicago, Pittsburgh and Baltimore. His investments in street railways in Philadelphia led him to engage in developing the outlying parts of that city. With P. A. B. Widener he purchased large tracts of land in the northwest section, erecting thereon some three thousand homes.

Despite his varied business interests he found time to promote the development of art in the United States. Besides accumulating a very valuable art collection he established a prize of $5,000 for the most meritorious painting exhibited by an American artist at the Pennsylvania Academy of the Fine Arts. He also took a keen interest in civic affairs and served one term in City Council in 1876. In 1873 he was a commissioner to the Vienna Exposition and in 1900 went in a similar capacity to the Paris Exposition. He also served as an aide-de-camp with the rank of colonel on the staff of Gov. J. F. Hartranft of Pennsylvania (1874–79). He might have held other offices but cared more for his home and his business.

On Jan. 21, 1857, he married Maria Louise Broomall of Chester County, Pa., by whom he had two sons and two daughters. He died in Philadelphia of heart-failure resulting from arterio-sclerosis. At the time of his death he was a director in twenty-four corporations and left a fortune estimated at $25,000,000. He was considered one of the most successful and sagacious capitalists of Philadelphia and the varied character of his activities bears witness to his remarkable executive ability. He possessed a sturdy physique, and was affable and hearty in manner.

[J. G. Leach, *Geneal. and Biog. Memorials of the Reading, Howell, Yerkes, Watts, Latham and Elkins Families* (1898), pp. 255–58; *Who's Who in America*, 1903–05; *Phila. Inquirer*, Phila. *Pub. Ledger*, Nov. 8, 1903.]

J. H. F.

ELLERY, FRANK (July 23, 1794–Mar. 24, 1871), grandson of William Ellery [*q.v.*], signer of the Declaration of Independence, was born at Newport, R. I., the son of Christopher Ellery and his wife, Clarissa Bird. His father was the first Jeffersonian senator from Rhode Island and died as collector of the port of Newport. On Feb. 19, 1812, Frank Ellery entered the navy as a midshipman. He fought in the first engagement of the War of 1812, the chase of the *Belvidera* by the *President*, and was wounded when the latter's main deck bow gun burst on the fifth shot of the war. Two years later he carried to Macdonough on Lake Champlain a letter of introduction from Oliver H. Perry, and for his services under Macdonough received a sword from Congress and $1,427.13 prize money. Again luck favored him when in 1815 he sailed against the Algerian pirates on the *Constellation*, which participated in the capture of the Algerian flagship *Mashouda*. He cruised with Kearney on the *Enterprise* off the coast of Florida, and in particular assisted in capturing a privateer and slaver off the bar of Amelia Island. He was promoted lieutenant on Mar. 28, 1820, and his claim to have been the first midshipman to be promoted after a regular examination seems to be valid. In 1825 he became associated with Capt. Jesse D. Elliott [*q.v.*] and served the rest of his active career at sea under him, first on the Brazil station on the *Cyane*, and later in the West Indies on the *Erie* and the *Shark*, 1831–32. On Aug. 4, 1835, he married Elizabeth, daughter of Edward Martin of Newport.

In 1839, still a lieutenant, he was given command of the *Enterprise*, was ordered to Brazil, became oppressed with homesickness and anxiety for his family, and sent in his resignation. Though he came to his senses as soon as he returned to the United States and managed to have the resignation cancelled, he was placed on waiting orders for twenty years. By 1856 he was the navy's most ancient lieutenant. He did not help his case in 1858 by a pathetic appeal to President Buchanan, in which he attributed his resigning to temporary aberration of mind.

Most of this period was spent among the green hills of Castleton, Vt., in comparative poverty.

At the beginning of the Civil War, however, though he was sixty-seven years old and had probably never trod the deck of a steam warship, he was called from the farm and put in command of a naval rendezvous, first at Philadelphia and then at Boston, to fit out vessels for the blockade. In 1867 he was placed upon the retired list of commodores as No. 13, no worse place than he would probably have secured if he had served on the sea all his days. He died four years later at Castleton.

[Ellery's memorial to Buchanan is in the Manuscript Division of the Navy Dept. Lib. See also Russell Jarvis, *Biog. Notice of Com. Jesse D. Elliott* (1835), esp. pp. 232 ff., 347. The muster rolls of Lake Champlain are in the Navy Dept. Lib. but do not contain Ellery's name; the pay rolls, also there, do contain it under No. 394. See also Navy Registers; Harrison Ellery, *Pedigree of Ellery of the U. S. A.* (1881); *Army and Navy Jour.*, Mar. 25, 1871.]

W. B. N.

ELLERY, WILLIAM (Dec. 22, 1727–Feb. 15, 1820), signer of the Declaration of Independence, the son of William and Elizabeth (Almy) Ellery, was born in Newport, R. I. His great-grandfather, William, came to Gloucester, Mass., in the late seventeenth century, but his grandfather, Benjamin, moved to Bristol, R. I., and afterward to Newport. His father was a Harvard graduate and held several public offices. Graduating from Harvard in 1747, Ellery spent the next twenty-eight years at Newport engaging in various undertakings. He tried his hand as a merchant, served for a time as a naval officer of the colony, put in two terms as clerk of the General Assembly, and finally, twenty-three years after graduating from college, took up the practise of law. At this he seems to have had considerable success, developing some practise even outside of the colony.

The war with the Mother Country gave Ellery his great opportunity in life. A sincere patriot from the beginning, he had already served on some local committees when he was elected to Congress by the General Assembly, taking his seat May 14, 1776. When the next year the election of delegates was given by the General Assembly to the people, Ellery was again a candidate, as he continued to be every year until 1786. He failed of election only twice, in 1780 and 1782. Even in 1780 he was appointed to office by Congress and thus continued to serve at the seat of government. Ellery's distinctive service was as a committeeman, principally on matters having to do with commerce and the navy. His letters to officials in Rhode Island are evidence of his ability in the handling of details. In 1777 and 1778 he was serving on no less than fourteen committees, including the standing committees on marine, on appeals in prize cases, and on commerce. In 1779 he was appointed as one of the congressional members of the newly created board of admiralty. The next year, upon his failure of reëlection, Congress appointed him one of the non-congressional members of this board.

When hostilities ceased, Ellery became sympathetic with the state-rights movement, which was so strong in Rhode Island. In 1785 he was elected chief justice of the superior court of the state but he never took his seat, urging the necessity of his staying in Congress. At this time he was a particularly valuable member of that body because so many of the older members had withdrawn since the war. After retiring from Congress, Ellery was appointed commissioner of the Continental Loan Office for Rhode Island, which position he held from Apr. 18, 1786, to Jan. 1, 1790. In 1790 he was appointed by Washington collector of the customs for the district of Newport. This position he held for thirty years until his death, being one of the few Federalists who were retained by Jefferson and his successors, apparently because of his Revolutionary record.

When the British occupied Newport during the Revolution they burned Ellery's property in revenge for his activities. It was therefore to discouraging conditions that Ellery returned after the war. In the long years which followed, however, he seems to have rebuilt his fortunes, if we may judge by the list of property advertised by his executors after his death. Ellery's nature was genial and kindly. He had wide knowledge of literature, English, French, and Latin. What proved to be his last morning was spent reading Cicero. He was a prolific letter writer both on public affairs and private, and hundreds of his letters are still preserved. He was twice married: first, in 1750, to Ann Remington of Cambridge, who died in 1764; second, in 1767, to Abigail Cary, his second cousin. Two of his grandsons were Richard Henry Dana and William Ellery Channing.

There is a story, often repeated, to the effect that at the signing of the Declaration of Independence Ellery took his position near the secretary in order to watch the expressions on the faces of the delegates as they affixed their signatures to what might easily prove to be their death warrant, and was able to report that all displayed only "undaunted resolution."

[E. T. Channing, "Life of Wm. Ellery," in Jared

Sparks, *Lib. of Am. Biog.* (1836), is interspersed with long homilies, some of which purport to represent Ellery's thoughts but which probably represent those of the author. Ellery's congressional service is summarized in W. R. Staples, *R. I. in the Continental Congress* (1870), which contains in the appendix 106 letters between him and officials in R. I. Thos. W. Higginson, in *Travellers and Outlaws: Episodes in Am. Hist.* (dated 1889, actually issued late in 1888), published an essay, "A Revolutionary Congressman on Horseback," based on one of the diaries which Ellery kept on trips between his home and the seat of government. Parts of these diaries appear in *Penn. Mag. of Hist and Biog.*, Oct. 1887, Jan. and July 1888. See also Harrison Ellery, *Pedigree of Ellery* (1881); H. R. Palmer, "Wm. Ellery," in *The R. I. Signers of the Declaration of Independence* (1913); *Harvard Univ. Quinquennial Cat., 1636–1925*. There are letters and other MSS. in Lib. of Cong., R. I. Hist. Soc., Mass. Hist. Soc., and elsewhere.]

C. C. H.

ELLET, CHARLES (Jan. 1, 1810–June 21, 1862), civil engineer, who was known throughout his life as Charles Ellet, Jr., was born at Penn's Manor, Bucks County, Pa., sixth of the fourteen children of Charles Ellet, a Quaker farmer, and Mary, daughter of Israel Israel, high sheriff of Philadelphia. Israel, who had grown wealthy in Barbados before 1776, was of Swedish or Dutch descent, and a Universalist. During his youth Ellet met, as he said, "many impediments and disappointments." He had no sympathetic guidance from his eccentric, litigious father, who opposed the boy's determination to become an engineer; but he was devoted to his mother. At seventeen he left home, working as rodman on the Susquehanna survey, then (1828) entering the service of the Chesapeake & Ohio Canal in Maryland as unpaid assistant in field and office and finally becoming assistant engineer at $800 a year. Natural aptitude enabled him to acquire some proficiency in mathematics and language with little formal instruction. In March 1830, with his mother's financial assistance, he went to France to attend the École Polytechnique. He witnessed the July revolution, was received by Lafayette, and traveling by foot inspected European and English engineering works.

By 1834 he had proposed a suspension bridge over the Potomac, surveyed for the Utica & Schenectady railroad, and located the western line of the New York & Erie. After a year as assistant, in 1836 he became chief engineer of the James River & Kanawha Canal, a work intended to connect Virginia tidewater with the Ohio, and completed as far as Lynchburg when Ellet retired (1839). In 1842 he built, at a cost of $35,000, the first important suspension bridge in the United States, over the Schuylkill at Fairmount. Having surveyed the city and county of Philadelphia (1841), he became associated with the Schuylkill Navigation Company, reconstructing that important carrier of anthracite coal, personally negotiating loans at home and abroad, and sustaining a notable controversy with the Reading Railroad, the competing line. In 1847 he left the presidency of the navigation company to build suspension bridges of his own design over the Niagara—a spectacular achievement—and over the Ohio at Wheeling. After he had erected a temporary bridge, the Niagara project was interrupted by litigation and he relinquished that work; but in 1849 he completed his Wheeling bridge, 1,010 feet long, then the world's longest span. Although suit in the Supreme Court, instituted in the name of the State of Pennsylvania by Edwin M. Stanton [*q.v.*] in behalf of Pittsburghers, resulted in a decree of abatement, Ellet saved his bridge by inducing Congress to declare it a post-route—only to witness its destruction by storm in 1854.

For twenty-five years he urged the improvement of Western rivers. The Smithsonian Institution published his *Physical Geography of the Mississippi Valley* (1849); and investigations undertaken for the War Department in 1850 resulted in several reports and his *magnum opus,* published in 1853, *The Mississippi and Ohio Rivers.* His plan for controlling floods and improving navigation by impounding surplus waters in upland reservoirs, was Ellet's great work; but vigorous efforts failed to secure the legislation to effect it. (His reports were reissued in 1927–28 for the Flood Control Committee of the Seventieth Congress.)

He was engineer for the Hempfield Railroad in 1851–55, the Virginia Central in 1853–57—for which in 1854 he built across the Blue Ridge a track of unprecedented curvature and grade—and the Kanawha improvement, in 1858. His knowledge of Virginia topography and resources enabled him to suggest plans for crushing the Confederacy in 1861.

Visiting Europe during the Crimean War, Ellet urged Russia to employ "ram-boats" in the relief of Sebastopol, a bold innovation in naval warfare; and later offered counter-plans to the allies. Returned home, he persistently urged his ram-boat scheme on successive secretaries of the navy, and widely circulated his *Coast and Harbour Defences* (1855). From 1857 he lived in Washington, devoting himself after 1860 to study and exposition of the military situation. Repeated offers of his services to the national and state governments were disregarded until 1862, when the *Merrimac* demonstrated the efficacy of the ram. Two weeks later Ellet was preparing a ram-fleet to clear the Mississippi. Stanton commissioned him a colonel, and made him subject only to the secretary of war. Hastily remodeling nine river boats on the Ohio, Ellet, with a volunteer crew, passed Fort Pillow and, on June 6, after sinking four Confederate boats before Memphis, received the surrender of that city. Ellet—the only Union man injured—died as his boat touched shore at Cairo, June 21, and was buried from Independence Hall, Philadelphia. His wife, Elvira, daughter of Judge William Daniel of Lynchburg, whom he had married in 1837, survived him only eight days. Their son, Charles Rivers Ellet (1843–1863), became a colonel, and a brother, Lieut.-Col. (later Brig.-Gen.) Alfred Washington Ellet (1820–1895), succeeded to the command of the fleet of rams.

Ellet was a prolific writer. Forty-six published works, as well as numerous technical and popular articles, attest his trenchant style in scientific and controversial writing. His *Essay on the Laws of Trade* (1839), a recondite treatise on rate-making, was followed by several pioneer contributions to transportation economics. After 1860 articles for American and English periodicals reveal his grasp of war-time problems; and scathing criticism of McClellan's competency, and the strategy of various Union generals made him a conspicuous, though not always popular, figure. In 1861 he published *The Army of the Potomac and Its Mismanagement,* and the following year, *Military Incapacity and What it Costs the Country.*

Recognized at home and abroad as one of the great engineers of his epoch, Ellet was called the "Brunel of America." Six feet two and slender, he presented a commanding appearance. After 1840 his health, never robust, was precarious, but his restless energy was unabated. Although he was the soul of courtesy, his austere integrity, his dislike for society, and his uncanny skill in controversy repelled intimacy, and perhaps account for his almost incredible activity.

[Notices of Ellet appear in C. B. Stuart, *Lives and Works of Civil and Military Engineers of America* (1871), pp. 257–85; J. T. Headley, *Farragut and Our Naval Commanders* (1867), pp. 209–23; W. D. Crandall and I. D. Newell, *Hist. of the Ram Fleet . . . The Ellets and Their Men* (1907); *Battles and Leaders of the Civil War* (1887), I, 430–59, 611–31; J. S. C. Abbott, "Charles Ellet and His Naval Steam Rams," *Harper's*, Feb. 1866; obituary notice from the *North American* (Phila.), June 22, 1862, in Littell's *Living Age,* Aug. 1862; obituary in *Evening Star* (Washington), June 23, 1862. "Three Letters on the Revolution of 1830" written by Ellet (edited with a biographical note by H. P. Gambrell), *Jour. of Modern Hist.*, Dec. 1929, are of interest. The above sketch, and the writer's forthcoming biography of Ellet, are based on the rich collection of Ellet MSS. preserved by his daughter, Mrs. William D. Cabell of Chicago.]

H. P. G.

ELLET, ELIZABETH FRIES LUMMIS (October 1818–June 3, 1877), author, was born at Sodus Point, Lake Ontario, N. Y., the daughter of Dr. William Nixion Lummis and his second wife, Sarah (Maxwell) Lummis. Dr. Lummis belonged to a New Jersey family and practised medicine in Philadelphia but, purchasing the Pulteney estate at Sodus Point, removed there and became a pioneer in developing western New York. Elizabeth was educated at the Female Seminary, Aurora, N. Y. She began to write when she was fifteen and seems always to have been happiest when she was studying and writing. Her first published work was a translation of Silvio Pellico's tragedy, *Euphemio of Messina* (1834). A volume of original poems and a tragedy based on Venetian history, *Teresa Contarini,* appeared in 1835. In that year or shortly afterward she married Dr. William H. Ellet, professor of chemistry at Columbia College, New York City. He soon became a professor at South Carolina College, Columbia, S. C., where they lived until 1849, when they returned to New York. Two kinds of studies interested Elizabeth Ellet: foreign history and literature, and American history. She was proficient in French, German, and Italian; translated and adapted legends from those languages, and wrote criticism of foreign works. Her books of this type include *The Characters of Schiller* (1839), with a critical essay on Schiller's genius; *Scenes in the Life of Joanna of Sicily* (1840), partly historical, partly imaginary; *Evenings at Woodlawn* (1849), a species of *Arabian Nights,* consisting of adaptations of German legends never before presented in English; *Novelettes of the Musicians* (1852), blendings of fact and fiction of German origin; *Women Artists in all Ages and Countries* (1859). Her books based on American history include: *Women of the American Revolution* (1848); *Domestic History of the American Revolution* (1850); *Pioneer Women of the West* (1852); *Queens of American Society* (1867); *Court Circles of the Republic* (1869). She wrote several miscellaneous books, *Rambles about the Country* (1840), *Family Pictures from the Bible* (1849); *Watching Spirits* (1851); *Summer Rambles in the West* (1853); edited *The New Cyclopædia of Domestic Economy and Practical Housekeeper* (1872); and contributed articles to many magazines, including the *American Quarterly Review,* the *North American Review,* and the *Southern Quarterly*

Ellicott

Review. In 1859 her husband died. She continued to live in New York City, and died there at her home on Twelfth St. During most of her life she was an Episcopalian but in her later years became a Roman Catholic. Though most of her time was absorbed by writing, she gave much attention to her home and was actively helpful in various charities for women and children. Her historical and critical writings show a great amount of careful work and, in spite of a vivid imagination, she was apparently scrupulous not to mix fact and fiction without giving notice in her prefaces. She was intensely patriotic and deeply interested in the contributions of women to American history. Her style in her prose works is gossipy and superficially interesting. Her poetry is neither original nor musical; its best quality is its expression of the love of nature and especially of favorite places, as in "Lake Ontario," "Sodus Bay," and "Susquehannah."

[E. A. and G. L. Duyckinck, *Cyc. of Am. Lit.* (1856); R. W. Griswold, *The Female Poets of America* (1849); Introduction by Anne Hollingsworth Wharton to Mrs. Ellet's *Women of the Am. Revolution* (ed. of 1900); obituaries in the *N. Y. Tribune* and *N. Y. Times*, both June 4, 1877.] S. G. B.

ELLICOTT, ANDREW (Jan. 24, 1754–Aug. 28, 1820), surveyor and mathematician, came of Dutch and English Quaker stock. The eldest son of Joseph and Judith (Bleaker) Ellicott and brother of Joseph Ellicott [*q.v.*], he was born in Solebury township, Bucks County, Pa., picked up the scanty schooling of his day in Solebury and Philadelphia, at twenty-one married Sarah Brown of Newton and took her to the new home of his patriarchal clan in Maryland. His father and uncles, prosperous millers with a turn for mechanics, were the founders (1775) of Ellicott City. The young Andrew shared the family bent, and at the age of fifteen helped his father in the manufacture of a masterpiece among grandfather's clocks, but later his ingenuity turned to the making of transits. His taste for mathematics and the tendencies of his times spoiled him for the career of miller or clockmaker—as they drew him out of the Society of Friends. Soon after his marriage he joined the Maryland militia. At the end of the Revolutionary War, during which he rose to the rank of major, he returned to "Fountainvale," the tribal homestead at Ellicott's Upper Mills. In these years he published a series of almanacs, *The United States Almanack*, of which the earliest known copy is dated 1782.

As a pupil of Robert Patterson in Philadelphia, he had been immensely impressed by the two "mathematicians" sent from England to draw that long-disputed boundary between Pennsylvania and Maryland which no local surveyor was competent to find. It must therefore have given Ellicott a thrill in 1784 to be appointed member for Virginia of the group of surveyors that continued the Mason and Dixon Line from the point where the two Englishmen dropped it in 1767. Moving to Baltimore in 1785, he taught mathematics in the Academy of that town, and in 1786 he served a term in the Maryland legislature. At the same time, however, he was a member of the Pennsylvania commissions for running the western (1785) and northern (1786) boundaries of that state and for surveying the islands in the Ohio and Allegheny rivers (1788). In 1789, when he moved to Philadelphia, he enlisted Franklin's aid in getting himself appointed by the new federal government to fix the southwestern boundary of New York. The site of the present Erie was then in dispute between New York and Pennsylvania and one of the determining points of the controversy lay within the Canadian frontier. As the American surveyors arrived at Fort Niagara before the British commandant's instructions, there was a delay by which Ellicott profited to make the earliest topographical study of the Niagara River. His letter to Benjamin Rush describing the falls, and another to Washington relating his encounter with the British commandant (*Buffalo Historical Society Publications*, XV, 384, XXVI, 22), are among the most readable of his writings. In general, it must be owned, he had a happier hand with the theodolite than with the pen. Only to his adored Sally could he be counted on to write with a touch of life.

Ellicott's work in New York, which established his reputation, brought him a less arduous but more vexatious engagement. In February 1791 he began at Alexandria the survey of the ten-mile square ceded by Maryland and Virginia for the "permanent seat" of the government. This kept him busy until 1793, when he published the first map of the "Territory" of Columbia. He had nothing to do with designing the "Federal City." That was L'Enfant's creation. Ellicott, however, did much of the incidental surveying and marking out of the plan on the ground, and after L'Enfant's dismissal by Jefferson he redrew the plan for the engraver, introducing such alterations as Jefferson instructed him to make. On this account, and because his name appeared on it, whereas L'Enfant's did not, the revised version issued in 1792 became known as the Ellicott plan. His account of the methods employed in surveying the city of Washington is in the *Transactions of the American Philosophical Society*, vol. IV (1799). As a reward for his services in facilitating the publication and execution of the plan, the Commissioners of Washington presented Ellicott with a pair of silver cups. Within a few months, however, relations between recipient and donors grew so strained that Ellicott found his position untenable; and after the final break, at the end of 1793, the Commissioners did their utmost to discredit him (*e.g.,* their letter to Washington of Mar. 23, 1794).

Nevertheless, Ellicott continued to receive public appointments. In 1794 Gov. Mifflin appointed him one of three commissioners to lay out the town of Presqu'Isle (Erie), and he spent the next two years in plotting out a road through the wildest part of Pennsylvania, from Reading to that town. In 1796 he was commissioned to survey the frontier between the United States and Florida. He submitted his report in 1800 and published it at Philadelphia in 1803, with maps and observations (*The Journal of Andrew Ellicott, Late Commissioner on Behalf of the United States . . . 1796 . . . 1800*). For a few years he held the post of secretary to the Pennsylvania Land Office. In 1811 Georgia invited him to run the line between that state and South Carolina—but refused to pay him more than his expenses, because his line ran eighteen miles south of Georgia's hopes. In 1813 he went to West Point as professor of mathematics; and there ended his days in peace, with Sally (mother of nine) still at his side.

[There are four memoirs of Ellicott: C. W. Evans, *Biog. and Hist. Account of the Fox, Ellicott, and Evans Families* (1882), Catharine Van Cortlandt Mathews, *Andrew Ellicott, His Life and Letters* (1908), G. Hunter Bartlett, "Andrew and Joseph Ellicott" in *Buffalo Hist. Soc. Pubs.,* vol. XXVI, and Sally K. Alexander (Ellicott's great-grand-daughter), "A Sketch of the Life of Maj. Andrew Ellicott" in *Records of the Columbia Hist. Soc.* (Washington, D.C.), vol. II (1899). There are also useful references in W. B. Bryan's *Hist. of the National Capital* (1914–16); *Am. State Papers: For. Rel.*. vol. II (1832); and Jas. Wilkinson, *Memoirs of My Own Times* (1816). More valuable for the Washington period is the manuscript material in the Washington, Jefferson, and Digges-Morgan-L'Enfant Papers, in Dist. of Col., Letters and Papers (all at the Lib. of Congress), and in the records of the original Commissioners (among the archives of the Commission on Public Buildings and Grounds, now housed in the Navy Department). A miniature of Ellicott, painted at New Orleans in 1799, is owned by Mr. I. D. Curtis of Litchfield, Conn.]

H. G. D.

ELLICOTT, JOSEPH (Nov. 1, 1760–Aug. 19, 1826), engineer, land agent, was born in Bucks County, Pa., the third son of Joseph and Judith (Bleaker) Ellicott, and brother of Andrew Ellicott [*q.v.*]. His mother was of Dutch stock, his father English. Like his father and brothers he early showed a marked aptitude for science and mechanics. His formal education was limited to the common school of a backwoods county; his native talent was developed in congenial surroundings in Maryland whither his family moved in December 1774. Near Baltimore his father and uncles erected flour mills where new and ingenious mechanical devices were introduced. Here Joseph remained until 1780. After teaching for a time, in 1785 he joined his brother Andrew, from whom he learned surveying, in locating the western boundary of Pennsylvania. During the next fifteen years he took part in one survey after another, first as assistant to his brother in locating the southwestern boundary of New York State (1789) and in the survey of Washington City, later working independently. In 1791 he was employed by the federal government to run the line between Georgia and the territory of the Creek Indians.

The turning point in his career came in 1794 with his entry into the service of the Holland Land Company, a group of Dutch bankers who had invested largely in wild lands in Pennsylvania and New York. Employed at first as an explorer in northern Pennsylvania, he began in the fall of 1797 the survey of the Holland Purchase, a tract of over three million acres in western New York. This survey, which necessitated the subdivision of the lands into townships six miles square, grouped in a series of ranges, required two years for completion. When in the autumn of 1800 the Holland Company was ready to open its lands for settlement, Ellicott was appointed agent under the supervision of the Company's general agent in Philadelphia. For twenty-one years he was the "patroon" of western New York. From his office at Batavia he directed the multifarious details incident to a great land agency. He arranged for the opening of roads through the new country, for internal surveys of the townships into small lots, for the making of contracts for land sales, for the collection of instalments, and for the granting of deeds and mortgages. The leniency of the Holland Company toward its indebted settlers was in large part the result of Ellicott's advice. He founded the city of Buffalo. From the first he appreciated the importance of its site and was responsible for preventing its inclusion within the Indian reservation nearby. In 1803 he had the village laid out on plans similar to those used for the city of Washington. He was a strong advocate of the Erie Canal, a project which promised great benefits to the Holland Company and to Ellicott himself, who had become a large landholder in western

New York. Though he held the position of canal commissioner for a time and directed some of the preliminary surveys, his duties as land agent forced his resignation before the work was well begun.

Ellicott was an impressive person physically, over six feet tall and powerfully built, with a tendency in later life to corpulence. There was something paradoxical in his character. Raised in a Quaker family, he was by nature a fighter; hot-tempered and domineering, he was extremely lenient with the debtors under his control; a wealthy man and something of an aristocrat in his backwoods community, in politics he was a Democrat; no public speaker and in later life averse to all social intercourse, yet for a score of years he was the "boss" of his party in western New York, controlling nominations and appointments. His enemies declared, but quite erroneously, that he used his position as land agent to build up his political power. He never married. At his home in Batavia he surrounded himself with relatives to whom he showed much generosity. About 1818 he fell victim to melancholia and became almost a recluse. This condition and increasing opposition to him because of his political activities unfitted him for his duties as land agent. He resigned by request in 1821 and devoted himself to his private business until his disease forced him into an asylum. He died in 1826.

[Ellicott Evans, "Reminiscences of Jos. Ellicott," *Buffalo Hist. Soc. Pubs.*, vol. II (1880); G. H. Bartlett, "Andrew and Joseph Ellicott," *Ibid.*, vol. XXVI (1922); P. D. Evans, "The Holland Land Co.," *Ibid.*, vol. XXVIII (1924); C. W. Evans, *Biog. and Hist. Accounts of the Fox, Ellicott, and Evans Families* (1882); C. V. Mathews, *Andrew Ellicott* (1908); O. Turner, *Pioneer Hist. of the Holland Purchase of Western N. Y.* (1849).] P. D. E.

ELLIOT, DANIEL GIRAUD (Mar. 7, 1835–Dec. 22, 1915), zoölogist, was born in New York City, the fourth son of George T. and Rebecca Giraud (Foster) Elliot. His father's ancestors were early settlers of New London, Conn.; his mother's were of French origin, settling at New Rochelle, N. Y. Delicate health prevented his entering college, and instead he traveled extensively in Europe, Egypt, Turkey, the West Indies, and Brazil, gaining a wide knowledge of the birds, a subject in which he had always been interested. An artist of no mean attainments, his ambitions led him to the publication of large folios, like those of John Gould, monographing various families of birds with life-size illustrations from his own brush, and from those of Wolf and Keulemans. These included birds of paradise, pheasants, ant thrushes, horn bills, and other species. His own collection of birds, consisting of some one thousand specimens, and covering most of the described species in North America, was the best private collection extant, and was secured by the American Museum of Natural History in 1869. In that same year Elliot removed to London where he remained for some ten years, taking an active part in the affairs of the British Ornithologists' Union and the Zoological Society, and associating intimately with the notable coterie of ornithologists then at the height of their fame—Sclater, Salvin, Seebohm, Newton. During his years abroad he also bought specimens for the American Museum and on his return brought with him a large collection of humming birds, which at that time was probably the most complete in the world. He became one of the founders of the American Ornithologists' Union, and was its second president (1890–91).

In 1894 Elliot left New York to become curator of zoölogy at the recently established Field Museum of Natural History in Chicago, a post which he held for the next twelve years. He turned his attention mainly to the mammals, and published several monographic volumes on the mammals of North and Middle America and the West Indies. Finally, at the age of sixty-one, he personally headed an expedition to Africa for the purpose of enriching the remarkable collection of mammals which he had already brought together at the museum. Returning to New York, he established himself at the American Museum, to the development of which he had given much time and thought. Here, with untiring energy, he began the preparation of his *Review of the Primates* (3 vols., 1912), which involved an immense amount of research, and which took him to all of the principal zoölogical museums of the world.

Personally, Elliot was a notable figure of a man. He was tall and dignified, with full beard, piercing eyes, and a refined modulated voice. He possessed a remarkable memory and a splendid command of language, and his memorial addresses on Coues and Sclater were striking examples of oratory. He was the recipient of many foreign orders and medals given in recognition of his beautiful monographs. After his death the Elliot Medal was established in his honor by the National Academy of Science, for meritorious publications in zoölogy. His long career of activity linked, as it were, the ornithologies of Wilson and Audubon, with their large folio plates, with the meticulous handbooks and synopses of later days, and the transition is clearly seen in his own publications.

In 1858 Elliot married Anne Eliza Henderson, by whom he had two daughters.

[*Who's Who in America,* 1914–15; *The Auk,* Jan. 1917; *Science,* Feb. 4, 1916; *Am. Museum Jour.,* Mar. 1915; personal acquaintance.] W. S—e.

ELLIOT, JAMES (Aug. 18, 1775–Nov. 10, 1839), politician, was born in Gloucester, Mass., the son of James and Martha (Day) Elliot. His father, a sailor, enlisted in the Revolution and died at sea of smallpox, leaving his family destitute. His mother moved to New Salem, in the Berkshires, where as a seamstress, with some aid from relatives, she was able to support her three boys. At the age of seven he went to work for a Captain Sanderson, a farmer and storekeeper of Petersham, who used him kindly. His mother taught him to read the Bible devotedly and also put him through *The Pilgrim's Progress, Dilworth's Speller,* and the *Catechism.* Later a tattered volume of *Josephus* and Rollin's *Ancient History* made him ambitious of an education and of military experience. In 1790 he moved to Guilford, Vt., where he enjoyed the friendship of Royall Tyler [*q.v.*]. On July 12, 1793, he enlisted as the first non-commissioned officer in a company of the second United States Sub-Legion commanded by Capt. Cornelius Lyman, saw service in the Whiskey Insurrection and in the Indian warfare waged in the Northwest Territory, and was discharged at Fort St. Clair on July 1, 1796. Extracts from his journal kept during this period are the most interesting part of *The Poetical and Miscellaneous Works of James Elliot, Citizen of Guilford, Vermont, and late a Non-commissioned Officer in the Legion of the United States* (1798), which was printed for the author in an edition of 300 copies by Thomas Dickman in Greenfield, Mass. This book was his only venture into literature. It attests a culture that, however imitative and undiscriminating, was remarkable in a self-taught, poverty-pinched young soldier and law student. It also exhibits winning qualities of mind: the author's patriotism is noble and generous, he is just and rational in his observations on the Indians, he pleads for the better education of women. In 1803 Elliot was admitted to the bar, began practise in Brattleboro, and in the same year was elected to Congress. He served from Mar. 4, 1803, till Mar. 3, 1809, as a member of the House of Representatives in the Eighth, Ninth, and Tenth Congresses. Officially he was a Federalist, which is the one mystery in his life. He was a democrat in his principles, used "citizen" as a title of address, revered Samuel Adams, George Clinton, Thomas Jefferson, and James Madison, and named his first-born after Madison. For a while he edited the *Freeman's Journal* in Philadelphia, served as captain for a short time in the War of 1812, and then returned to Brattleboro. He was representative in the state legislature for Newfane 1818–19 and 1837–38, was clerk of Windham County 1819 and 1820 and continuously from 1826 to 1836, was register of the probate court Dec. 26, 1822–Nov. 30, 1834, was state attorney of the county 1837–38, was a justice of the peace for twenty-one years, and was always a respected and useful citizen. His wife, Lucy Dow, survived him for thirty years. His brother Samuel was also a distinguished citizen of Vermont.

[*Biog. Directory of the Am. Cong.* (1928); W. G. Eliot, *A Sketch of the Eliot Family* (1887); M. R. Cabot, ed., *Annals of Brattleboro* (2 vols., 1921–22); T. H. Benton, *Abridgment of the Debates of Cong. 1789–1856* (1857–61), vol. III.] G. H. G.

ELLIOT, JONATHAN (1784–Mar. 12, 1846), editor and publicist, was born near Carlisle, England. Coming to New York City at the age of eighteen, he began work as a printer. In 1810 he went to South America, to serve as a volunteer in the revolutionary army under Bolivar; after suffering the hardships of a wound and imprisonment, he returned to the United States in 1813. He is supposed to have served in the American army during the War of 1812, but between the date of his return to this country, and the commencement of his newspaper work, there was little time for fighting, except possibly in the latter part of 1814. His real career began that year. In December 1813, he entered a partnership with two associates, to produce the first daily evening newspaper ever published in Washington, the *Washington City Gazette;* the first number appeared in January 1814. Elliot was the printer. Soon after the capture of Washington, in the following summer, the paper suspended publication. In November 1815 it was revived, as the *Washington City Weekly Gazette,* with Elliot as publisher and editor. In 1817 the journal, now *City of Washington Gazette,* became a daily; this evidence of increasing prosperity may have been due to increased patronage, or—more probably—to lucrative public printing contracts received from the secretary of the treasury, William H. Crawford. In 1826 Elliot sold the *Gazette* and abandoned the newspaper field, except for a brief return in 1828. In that year some of Jackson's opponents started a campaign paper, *We the People,* with Elliot as editor.

As a newspaper man, he took an active part in national politics. In 1816 he advocated the nomination of William H. Crawford, Monroe's chief rival; the rewards for this support have already been mentioned. In 1822 he was still supporting Crawford, although at the same time he made overtures to John Quincy Adams, offering his services in return for a consideration. It seems that Adams, as secretary of state, had formerly given Elliot considerable printing in connection with the census, but Elliot's charges for the work were so extortionate that Adams gave him no more. Thereupon Elliot hinted that he had already ruined Calhoun's chances of getting the presidency, and he threatened to ruin Adams's, too. When Adams remained unmoved by these advances, Elliot redoubled his efforts in behalf of Crawford. Adams's opinion of Elliot was not high; he described him as "an Englishman, having no character of his own—penurious and venal—metal to receive any stamp" (*Memoirs,* VI, 47).

After withdrawing from the newspaper field, Elliot began the work for which he is still well known to-day, the publication of historical material. In 1827 he published the first volume of *Debates, Resolutions, and Other Proceedings in Convention on the Adoption of the Federal Constitution.* This, as he intimated in the preface, was something of a gamble; "the pecuniary risk" was so heavy, he wrote, that he felt impelled to ask for the help of Congress and of the bar. If the venture should prove profitable, other volumes would follow. His wishes were gratified, and between 1827 and 1830 he published three more volumes. The extensive demand for the work warranted a second edition, "much enlarged and improved," published in 1836. Nine years later he added a fifth volume, including Madison's notes of debates in the Federal Convention. Described by Justice Story as "an invaluable repository of facts and arguments," the *Debates* still stand as one of the most valuable collections relating to the Constitution.

In 1827 Elliot also published the first edition of another compilation known as the *Diplomatic Code of the United States of America.* This included the treaties and conventions between the United States and foreign governments, together with abstracts of judicial decisions bearing upon foreign affairs, and a summary of the principles of international law. In a second edition, published in 1834, *The American Diplomatic Code,* the collection was brought down to that date. In the Jackson administration, Secretary of State McLane adopted the "code" for the use of his department. Although the collection of treaties has been superseded by later collections, Elliot's summaries of judicial decisions are still valuable. In 1830 he published a large volume, compiled by J. A. Brereton, entitled *Florae Columbianae,* and in the same year a much better known work of his own: *Historical Sketches of the Ten Miles Square Forming the District of Columbia.* This is the source from which numerous guide books have been drawn. His last work, published in 1845, was the *Funding System of the United States and of Great Britain,* including a mass of statistical extracts from treasury reports, and other material dealing with the public debt.

Though Elliot's *Debates* are known to every student of American history, Elliot himself, the man, is something of a phantom, a mere bibliographical abstraction. One journalist wrote that in "private life he was frank, generous, warm-hearted, an affectionate father, and a kind husband." He was twice married and left four children, one son being Jonathan, Jr., and another, Henry, a member of the bar of New Orleans.

[Obituaries in the Washington *Daily National Intelligencer,* Mar. 13, 1846, and *Daily Union,* Mar. 14, 1846. There are cursory notices of him in the *Memoirs of John Quincy Adams* (1874–77); in W. B. Bryan, *A Hist. of the National Capital* (1914–16); and in a paper by A. R. Spofford, "Washington in Literature," in the *Records of the Columbia Hist. Soc.,* VI (1903), 53–55.] R. V. H.

ELLIOTT, AARON MARSHALL (Jan. 24, 1844–Nov. 9, 1910), philologist, son of Aaron and Rhoda (Mendenhall) Elliott, was born in Wilmington, N. C., and received there his early schooling. Sent in 1862 by his Quaker parents past the military lines to co-religionists in the North, he was graduated from Haverford College in 1866 and again from Harvard in 1868. He then spent eight years in Europe, following Oriental and Indo-European philological courses in the great university centers, studying at first hand the languages and the peoples of France, Germany, Italy, Spain, and Portugal, and supporting himself the while by tutoring and writing travel sketches. After his return he still spent his summers in study abroad, and in addition to his command of the languages of western Europe, he learned Roumanian, Arabic, Russian and modern Greek, as well as Canadian French. In 1876 Elliott was appointed associate in languages in the first faculty of the Johns Hopkins, and in 1892 professor of the Romance languages. He was the American pioneer in organizing the scientific study of the modern languages and literatures. In 1883 he brought about the establishment of the Modern Language Association, was for nine years its secretary and the editor of its publications, and was in 1894 its president. In 1886 he founded the first American technical journal in his field, *Modern Language Notes,* with at the beginning but one subscriber; he employed his own typesetter and during the first seventeen years issued this periodical from his own small press. Contributions from his pen to the literature of his subject appeared in numerous journals and ranged from the most general themes to the most technical.

It was, however, as a trainer of scholars and teachers that Elliott made his deepest impression. The graduate school of Romance languages, which he built up at Johns Hopkins' sent out the majority of the leaders in that domain for a generation, and in addition he frequently, through correspondence, guided for years the studies of promising men whom he had not so much as seen. As a token of the appreciation in which he was held by his fellows, several of his friends published a two-volume memorial, which appeared shortly after his death under the title, *Studies in Honor of A. Marshall Elliott.* His was a moral as well as an intellectual leadership. To a wide range of knowledge and a keen appreciation of scholarship and of the severe discipline which underlies it, he combined inexhaustible patience and geniality. These qualities, along with his sympathetic understanding, faith in men, tenacity in building with the material at hand, and his enduring optimism, secured for him the unquestioned leadership throughout the country in the development not alone of the Romance languages, but of all modern-language work, and he fortunately lived long enough to see this discipline assume in some measure the place he firmly believed that it merited in the intellectual activities of the nation. He married, on June 14, 1905, Lily Tyson Manly, daughter of James E. Tyson of Ellicott City, Md.

[*Modern Language Notes,* Dec. 1910; *Pubs. of the Modern Language Asso.,* Mar. 1911; *Johns Hopkins Univ. Circular,* Jan. 1911; *Harvard Grads. Mag.,* Mar. 1911; *Romanic Rev.,* vol. VIII, July–Sept., 1917, pp. 328–40; E. C. Armstrong, *A. Marshall Elliott: A Retrospect* (1923), Elliott Monographs, no. 15; George C. Keidel, *The Early Life of Professor Elliott* (1917); the *Sun* (Baltimore), Nov. 10, 1910.] E. C. A.

ELLIOTT, BENJAMIN (March 1787–September 1836), lawyer, author, was born in Charleston, S. C., with which city he was closely associated throughout his life. His father was Thomas Odingsell Elliott who married Mary, sister of Charles Pinckney [*q.v.*], and through both parents he traced his ancestry to prominent South Carolina families. The exact date of his birth is not known, but he was baptized Mar. 25, 1787. His primary education was obtained at home and in the public schools, whence he proceeded to the College of New Jersey (Princeton), graduating in 1806, with high honors. Distinguished throughout his academic course for intense application and capacity for research, he carried these characteristics into his law studies which he prosecuted in the office of Thomas Parker of Charleston. On his admission to the bar in 1810 he became a partner of Robert Y. Hayne [*q.v.*], with whom he remained associated till the latter abandoned law for politics. He was early drawn into the nullification controversy, and though as a member of the state legislature for several terms he was not prominent in its proceedings, his profound and exact learning was placed unreservedly at the service of the state-rights party, whose actions received his unqualified support throughout the controversy with the federal government. In his pioneer pamphlet *A Refutation of the Calumnies circulated against the Southern and Western States, respecting the Institution and Existence of Slavery,* published in 1822—the first of its kind—he made one of the ablest expositions and defenses of the attitude of the South in regard to the peculiar institution. In the force of his logic and wealth of constitutional doctrine and illustration he was not surpassed in polemical vigor and learning by any subsequent writer on the subject. He was for some years a member of the Charleston City Council, but his character, training, and inclinations did not contribute to make him successful in public life; he was happiest when immersed in literary composition or research. His work as commissioner in equity and subsequently as master in the equity court of Charleston County, which later position he held at the time of his death, was competently performed, but did not offer any special opportunity for the exercise of his intellectual powers. In addition to the pamphlet before mentioned, he was the author of an *Oration on the Inauguration of the Federal Constitution* (1813); *A Sketch of the Means and Benefits of prosecuting this war against Britain* (1814), a vitriolic pamphlet in support of the war policy of the federal government; and an *Oration delivered in St. Philip's Church, Charleston, S. C., 4 July 1817* (1817)—eloquent but turgid in style. He also made a digest of the acts of Congress and the state referring to the militia, which was published under the title *The Militia System of South Carolina* (1835), and compiled the proceedings in South Carolina preceding the adoption of the Federal Constitution. Elliott died in September 1836, and was buried on the twelfth. His wife was Catharine O. Savage.

[J. B. O'Neall, *Biog. Sketches of the Bench and Bar of S. C.* (1859), II, 402; *Cyc. of Eminent and Representative Men of the Carolinas of the Nineteenth Century* (1892), I, 183; *The South in the Building of the Nation* (1909), XI, 317; *Charleston Courier*, Sept. 12, 1836; certain information supplied by Mabel L. Webber of the S. C. Hist. Soc.]
H. W. H. K.

ELLIOTT, CHARLES (May 16, 1792–Jan. 8, 1869), Methodist clergyman, editor, historian, was born in County Donegal, Ireland, and died in Mt. Pleasant, Iowa. He came to America in 1814, with two years' experience as a preacher, soon afterwards affiliated with the Ohio Methodist Conference, and in 1819 was appointed to the Zanesville circuit. In 1822 he was made a missionary to the Wyandot Indians, and with his wife proceeded into their reservations, under the patronage of a Christianized chief named Between-the-Logs. His experience during this time taught him, he said, that Christianity was "suited to every nation of every description, whether barbarous or civil" (*Reminiscences*, p. 186), and convinced him that it was wise to convert first and civilize later. After his assignment as a missionary he was made presiding elder of the Ohio District, 1824–25, and later, 1833–34, of the Pittsburgh District. From 1827 to 1831 he taught languages in Madison College, operated under Methodist control at Uniontown, Pa., and toward the beginning of 1834 he was made editor of the Pittsburgh Conference *Journal*. In 1836 he was appointed editor of the *Western Christian Advocate*, but returned to the ministry in 1849 and in 1850–51 was presiding elder of the Dayton District. During the long debate within his church as to whether or not slavery was scripturally defensible, he was an ardent contender for the negative, and in 1848 he was appointed by the General Conference of the Northern group of Methodists to write a history of their organization since the withdrawal of the Southern group four years earlier. This appointment resulted in the publication of three works: *The Sinfulness of American Slavery, Proved from its Evil Sources, its Injustice, its Wrongs; . . . Together with Observations on Emancipation and the Duties of American Citizens in Regard to Slavery* (1850); *A History of the Great Secession from the Methodist Episcopal Church in the Year 1845, Eventuating in the Organization of the New Church Entitled the "Methodist Episcopal Church, South"* (1885); *The Bible and Slavery: in which the Abrahamic and Mosaic Discipline is Considered in Connection with the Most Ancient Forms of Slavery, and the Pauline Code on Slavery as Related to Roman Slavery and the Discipline of the Apostolic Churches* (1857). His *Indian Missionary Reminiscences . . . in which is Exhibited the Efficacy of the Gospel in Elevating Ignorant and Savage Men* (1850) is a work calculated not so much for secular inquiries as for theologians. The *Delineation of Roman Catholicism* (1841) sets forth in two volumes what he believed to be the iniquitousness of Rome. He yearned to go to Italy as a missionary, and he is indeed, it is said, more than anyone else, responsible for the Methodist activities inaugurated in Rome shortly after his death. In 1852 he again became editor of the *Western Christian Advocate*. Five years later he was made president of Iowa Wesleyan University, and remained in that position until 1861. There, in 1859, by countenancing the graduation of a woman, he opened the way for coeducation. In 1860 he was requisitioned from Iowa by the Methodist Conference to displace the editor of the *Central Christian Advocate* in St. Louis, who in his pronouncements at that moment was not quite definitely enough anti-southern. There was no trouble on that score with Elliott, but when in 1863 he was summoned back to his college he determined to go. He was president there again 1863–66. He has been spoken of as "a man of genial character and tireless energy" (Barker, *Ohio Methodism*, p. 160), but in much of his writing he appears to be the fanatic rather than the philosopher.

[J. M. Barker, *Hist. of Ohio Methodism* (1898); *Hist. Sketch and Alumni Record of Iowa Wesleyan* (1917); W. W. Sweet, *M. E. Ch. and Civil War* (1912); J. D. Wade, *Augustus Baldwin Longstreet* (1924); J. P. Wickenden, *Hist. of Education in Pa.* (1886); *Christian Advocate* (N. Y.), Jan. 14, 1869; H. C. Jennings, *The Meth. Book Concern* (1924); *Minutes of Ann. Conferences of the M. E. Ch.*, 1819–69.]
J. D. W.

ELLIOTT, CHARLES LORING (Oct. 12, 1812–Aug. 25, 1868), painter, was the son of Daniel and Mehitable (Booth) Elliott. He was born at Scipio, Cayuga County, N. Y., and about 1827 moved with his parents to Syracuse, Onondaga County. His father, an architect, did not encourage the boy's artistic ambitions and placed him as a clerk in a store, but in 1834 yielded to his son's desires and permitted him to go to New York City to study painting. Young Elliott had done some successful architectural drawing for his father and was urged by John Trumbull, in whose studio he worked for a time, to give up all thought of an artist's career and devote himself to architecture. The youth persisted, however, studying under John Quidor and by himself, and at length won even Trumbull's commendation by an illustration from Irving's *Knickerbocker* and a scene from Paulding's *Dutchman's Fireside*. After a decade as an itinerant portrait-painter in central and western New York, during which he painted the portraits of the faculty of Hamilton College, he opened a studio in New York City, which became his permanent home. In 1845 his portrait of Ericsson excited general admiration, being called the best American portrait since the time of Stuart. In this year Elliott was elected an associate of the National Academy and soon afterward he was made an Academician. In 1846 a number of his portraits were sent to the Academy exhibit, including those of Horatio Stone, the sculptor; T. B. Thorpe; Lewis Gaylord Clark; and Sanford Thayer. These were regarded by the ablest judges as the finest work he had yet done; his reputation was established, and thenceforth he was one of the most popular portrait-painters of his time.

His well-known work includes: portraits of Fitz-Greene Halleck; James E. Freeman (belonging to the National Academy); Matthew Vassar (in Vassar College); W. W. Corcoran; James Fenimore Cooper; Governors Bouck, Seymour, and Hunt (in the New York City Hall); Erastus Corning (in the State Library, Albany, N. Y.); and the two artists, Church and Durand. Among his ideal works exhibited at the National Academy in 1866 were "Don Quixote" and "Falstaff." His portrait of Fletcher Harper was considered a masterpiece and was unanimously chosen for the Paris Exhibition as a typical American portrait. He is said to have painted only one landscape, "The Head of Skaneateles Lake." His painting shows an even excellence and a fixed method. He used a brush dipped in freely flowing paint and did not work over any of his detail. He had a delicate sense of art in the management of drapery and in the delineation of a tender expression of the mouth, and a freedom and originality in painting hair. Firm drawing, clean, clear color, and a natural likeness were the characteristics of his portraits, of which he is said to have painted seven hundred. While he did not have the opportunity of study abroad, his work reflects the qualities usually resulting from foreign contacts. Inman warmly praised it for its fidelity, genial quality of expression, and rich, harmonious tones.

Elliott was married to Mary Elizabeth Shire (or Stine), by whom he had one son. His sunny nature and kindliness won him many friends. His only serious fault seems to have been a habit of intemperance, which he eventually overcame by taking a formal pledge witnessed by a friend and signed on the bar after his last drink. He died in Albany, N. Y., in his fifty-sixth year and was buried in Greenwood Cemetery, Brooklyn.

[Samuel Isham, *Hist. of Am. Painting* (1927), pp. 272–76, 529; *N. Y. Evening Post*, Sept. 30, Oct. 1, 1868; Mich. State Lib., *Biog. Sketches of Am. Artists* 5th ed., rev. and enl., 1924), pp. 106–07; L. G. Clarke in *Lippincott's Mag.*, Dec. 1868; C. E. Lester in *Harper's Monthly*, Dec. 1868; C. H. Caffin, *The Story of Am. Painting* (1907), pp. 83, 93–95; H. T. Tuckerman, *Book of the Artists* (1867); Ulrich Thieme and Felix Becker, *Allgemeines Lexikon der Bildenden Künstler*, vol. X (1914); family data.] J. M. H.

ELLIOTT, JESSE DUNCAN (July 14, 1782–Dec. 10, 1845), naval officer, was born in Hagerstown, Md., the son of Robert and Ann Elliott, who were Pennsylvanians. The father, who was descended from the Elliotts of Fincastle, County Donegal, Ireland, was killed in 1794 by the Indians, while serving as a commissary in Gen. Wayne's army. The early schooling of the son was received at Carlisle, Pa., from which place in 1804 he was appointed by President Jefferson a midshipman in the navy. His first cruise was in the Mediterranean on the *Essex* under Commodore James Barron [*q.v.*], and he was with that unfortunate officer when he surrendered the *Chesapeake*. Made a lieutenant in 1810, he was sent to London as a bearer of dispatches to the American minister there. In that city he was "insulted" by an Englishman, who however declined to receive his overtures for a duel. On Apr. 7, 1812, he was married in Norfolk, Va., to Frances C. Vaughan and established an additional bond of sympathy with the South. Early in the War of 1812, accepting a command on the Lakes, he, aided by Capt. Nathan Towson [*q.v.*] of the army, surprised and captured on Lake Erie the two vessels *Detroit* and *Caledonia*. For this well conceived and gallant exploit he was voted a sword by Congress and was, July 1813, promoted master commandant over thirty lieutenants. Twenty years after the war, Towson, then a general, entered into a correspondence with Elliott, claiming that the official report of the capture of the two vessels did not do justice to the army's share therein, but he failed in his object, the provoking of Elliott to a duel.

Placed in command of the naval forces on Lake Erie, Elliott, in the fall of 1812, collected a small fleet of vessels and began the construction of the brigs *Lawrence* and *Niagara*. In the spring he was succeeded by Commodore O. H. Perry [*q.v.*]. After a brief tour of duty on

Lake Ontario, he returned to Lake Erie in August and took command of the *Niagara* as the ranking officer under Perry, and in this capacity had an important part in the battle of Lake Erie, Sept. 10, 1813. Soon thereafter Elliott's precise conduct during the battle was disputed and a controversy arose which raged in and out of the navy for more than thirty years and is without a parallel in American naval history. For upwards of three hours during the battle the *Niagara* was not brought into close action. She rendered Perry relatively little assistance while his flagship was being shot to pieces and made to suffer more than two-thirds of the entire American loss. Elliott's defenders were under the necessity of explaining and justifying his lack of action. Congress did not hesitate to award equal honor to the first and second in command, matching the gold medal given to Perry with a similar one presented to Elliott. The state legislature of Pennsylvania voted Elliott a medal for his gallantry. In 1818 the controversy resulted in Elliott's challenging Perry to a duel and in Perry's preferring charges against Elliott, requesting that he be court-martialed. These were pigeon-holed by President Monroe. On the publication in 1839 of James Fenimore Cooper's *History of the Navy* containing an account of the battle of Lake Erie which was regarded as favorable to Elliott by Perry's friends, the controversy broke out anew and each side presented its case in books, pamphlets, and newspapers. In 1843 Cooper published a reply to Perry's protagonists, which is quite the ablest defence of Elliott, who, greatly pleased, caused a silver medal, bearing an image of his defender, to be made and widely distributed. The Rhode Island Historical Society declined to receive one of the medals and the Rhode Island legislature also showed its partiality for Perry, a native of that state. With the death of the chief participants in the battle the controversy subsided—an appeal was taken to history. Admiral Mahan, who considered the circumstances of the battle at length, reached conclusions favorable to Perry, holding that when that officer brought his ship into close action "he was entitled to expect prompt imitation by the *Niagara*" (*post,* p. 98).

In 1815–16 Elliott commanded the sloop *Ontario* and participated in the war with Algiers. In 1818 he was promoted to a captaincy and from that year until 1822 was a member of a commission appointed to select permanent sites for navy-yards and fortifications. While on the coast of Brazil in command of the *Cyane,* 1825–27, he was offered the post of admiral in the Brazilian navy. From 1829 to 1832 he commanded the West-Indian Squadron. He assisted in suppressing the slave insurrection in Southampton County, Va., and represented the navy at Charleston, S. C., during the nullification troubles in that state. From 1833 to 1835 he was commandant of the Boston navy-yard. His last cruise, made in 1835–38 as commander-in-chief of the Mediterranean Squadron, was marked by many exhibitions of good will to the numerous potentates whom he visited in Europe, Asia, and Africa. Within the squadron, however, there was much discord and he arrived home with several disgruntled subalterns. They preferred charges against him—thirteen in all—some of which now seem ludicrous. Jackson's administration had been succeeded by one much less friendly to the commodore and he was found guilty and sentenced to suspension from the navy for four years, two of which were to be without pay. President Van Buren remitted the penalty respecting pay. In the meantime he had been challenged to a duel by Commodore David Porter, but some of his friends prevailed upon him to settle his differences peacefully. During his suspension he engaged in farming and the raising of fine sheep and hogs, but continued to fight his enemies. A change in the federal administration placed his friends once more in power and on Oct. 19, 1843, President Tyler remitted the remaining period of his suspension. In December 1844 he was given command of the Philadelphia navy-yard and a year later he died.

[Record of Officers, Bureau of Navigation, 1804–45; A. T. Mahan, *Sea Power in Its Relations to the War of 1812* (1919), II, 76–99; *Port Folio,* Dec. 1814, pp. 529–39; C. O. Paullin, *The Battle of Lake Erie* (1918), see pp. 27 and 206–10 for the literature of the Perry-Elliott controversy; *Speech of Com. Jesse Duncan Elliott, U. S. N., Delivered in Hagerstown, Md., on 14th Nov., 1843* (1844); "Commodore Jesse D. Elliott: A Stormy Petrel of the Navy," in *U. S. Naval Inst. Proc.,* Sept. 1928, pp. 773–78.] C. O. P.

ELLIOTT, JOHN (Apr. 22, 1858–May 26, 1925), Scotch painter, was born in Lincolnshire, England, of a noted Border family with which Robert Louis Stevenson was connected. He gave early promise of artistic talent. After drawing from marbles at the British Museum he did cast drawing at the Beaux Arts in Paris. Then at Julien's Academy he spent a profitable year with Carolus Duran, followed by further study in Rome at the San Lucca Academy and in the studio of Don José di Villegas, whom he greatly admired. The Italian atmosphere inspired "The Vintage," one of Elliott's most beautiful works, exuberant with the spirit of youth, brilliant and richly decorative. This mural, ordered by Mrs. Potter Palmer for the dining-room at her home on Lake Shore Drive, in Chicago, was the forerunner of other examples of Elliott's work prized in some of the best houses there. Chief among Elliott's portraits are those of Victor Chapman, Rose Farwell, and one of His Royal Highness, the Duke of Cambridge. Others of note include Lord Ava, son of Lord Dufferin, Marquis of Winchester; General Wauchope; Lady Katherine Thynne, afterwards Lady Cromer; Samuel Ward; Samuel Gridley Howe; and Julia Ward Howe. His so-called "War Portraits," of which there are sixteen, are red chalk drawings of the members of the Lafayette Escadrille and other young Americans killed in the World War. They are preserved at the National Museum in Washington. The silver point drawing of the late King Humbert was treasured by Queen Margaret as the king's best likeness. This process, in which Elliott showed a fine technique, is one dear to the old Italian painters but few modern artists have the skill and patience to employ it.

In 1894 Elliott returned to Rome, commissioned to execute a mural, "The Triumph of Time," to be placed in the Boston Public Library. His "Diana of the Tides," which ranks among the unusual murals chosen for monumental buildings in the United States, was undertaken by Elliott for the National Museum at the request of Mr. and Mrs. Larz Anderson as a tribute to the city of Washington. It is notable as the first gift, by private citizens, of mural art for a public building in the nation's capital. A modernist's conception of the scientific spirit of the age, it expresses in harmonious imagery the heritage of classic times, and portrays with much imaginative treatment natural forces, emotions, and primal passions as conceived by the ancients.

On Feb. 7, 1887, John Elliott married Maud Howe, daughter of the distinguished Julia Ward Howe and Samuel Gridley Howe. They resided for many years in Boston, then moved to Newport, R. I., where Elliott became one of the founders of the Newport Art Association. Declining health, in the months previous to his death, took him, with his wife, to Charleston, S. C., where he died May 26, 1925. He was buried in Mount Auburn Cemetery, Cambridge, Mass.

[*Who's Who in America*, 1924–25; *Art and Progress*, May 1910; *Am. Mag. of Art*, Jan. 1926; *New England Mag.*, 1913–14, pp. 26–34; *N. Y. Times*, May 27 and 28, 1925; information as to certain facts from members of the family.] J. M. H.

ELLIOTT, SARAH BARNWELL (1848–Aug. 30, 1928), author, playwright, suffragist leader, had the Book of Common Prayer bred in her bones. Grand-daughter of Stephen Elliott [*q.v.*], she was the daughter of Stephen Elliott, first Protestant Episcopal bishop of Georgia, sister of Robert W. B. Elliott, first Protestant Episcopal bishop of Western Texas, and had for mother Charlotte Bull Barnwell of a Beaufort (S. C.) family that has given an unending line of bishops and ministers to the Episcopal Church. In the early seventies her father, one of the founders of the University of the South, removed his family from Georgia, where Sarah was born, to Sewanee, Tenn., site of that institution. There on the Cumberland Plateau, except for a year abroad and seven in New York, she lived and died. To home education were added lessons from Sewanee professors and a course, in 1886, at Johns Hopkins.

Her first novel, *The Felmeres,* a protest against a narrow conception of God, was published in 1879. It took its inspiration from the church life into which she was born, as did *A Simple Heart* (1889), and *John Paget* (1893). Fame, however, was to come from other sources, the life of the Tennessee soil. In 1890–91, her "Jerry," a serial in *Scribner's Magazine,* was a literary sensation. The story of a Tennessee Mountain boy, it proceeds toward its end with the inevitability of tragedy. Published in England and Australia, translated into German, not only did it make the fame of its author, but, with the novels of Charles Egbert Craddock, it turned the eyes of America toward the Southern mountaineers, the ultimate outcome being the mountain schools and industries of to-day. It led the Southern novel away from ante-bellum sentimentality. From her log-cabin study among the trees behind her house short stories, later collected in *An Incident and other Happenings* (1899), went to leading magazines. Two novels, *The Durket Sperret* (1898) and *The Making of Jane* (1901), followed, but did not rival "Jerry," on which rests her fame. She wrote also a biography, *Sam Houston* (1900).

From residence in New York (1895–1902) she returned to Sewanee a member of the Woman's Political League and an ardent suffragist. She became president of the Tennessee State Equal Suffrage Association, vice-president of the Southern States Woman Suffrage Conference and of the Civic League of Sewanee. By ancestry she was a Colonial Dame, a Daughter of the Confederacy, and a member of the Historical Society of South Carolina. She was also vice-president of the Association of Southern Writers. It is said of her that everybody liked her. To a gracious personality were added charm, good looks, devotion to all things of good report. Small in stature, attractive in face, she was at her best in evening dress because of the remarkable beauty of her neck and arms. In her last years, with white hair bobbed, she suggested rather a beautiful little boy than a septuagenarian. In her early years she assisted at her mother's "Sundays," when, in high-backed chair and Victorian cap, the Bishop's widow received Sewanee. Her own "Mondays" became famous throughout the state and, according to the *Sewanee Purple,* as a hostess, dispensing hospitality seasoned with humor, wit, and charm, she was an influence "in developing the Sewanee gentleman . . . that cannot be overestimated."

[See *Lib. of Southern Lit.,* vol. IV (1909); *Who's Who in America,* 1914–15; *N. Y. Times,* Aug. 31, 1928; *Sewanee Purple,* Oct. 21, 1928. Information has been received from Miss Louise Finley, librarian, Univ. of the South; Mrs. Margaret Elliott Morris, and Miss Norah Barnwell, and from family records. Rt. Rev. F. F. Reese and Rev. R. Maynard Marshall have made fruitless search in Georgia and South Carolina for a record of Sarah Barnwell Elliott's birth or baptism.]

E. A. M.

ELLIOTT, STEPHEN (Nov. 11, 1771–Mar. 28, 1830), botanist, was born in Beaufort, S. C., the third son of William and Mary (Barnwell) Elliott. He was educated at home until his sixteenth year, then sent to New Haven, where he entered Yale College in February 1788. After his graduation in 1791 he returned to Beaufort and engaged in farming and other pursuits. In 1796 he married Esther Habersham of Georgia. Two years earlier he had been sent from the parish of St. Helena to the State House, where he served for several terms. In 1808 he was elected to the Senate and remained an influential member of that body through the sessions of 1812. His name appears on almost every page of the journals in committee assignments and as the author of bills, two of which were the free school act of 1811 and the bill in 1812 establishing the Bank of the State of South Carolina. He was elected the first president of this bank and served in that capacity until his death. That he was an able executive is indicated by the assertion that "the state bank of South Carolina, owned entirely by the state, was one of the few that made a satisfactory showing during this period" (Hepburn, *post,* p. 103). When Elliott moved to Charleston in 1812 to assume his bank duties he also became identified with the literary life of the city. He was one of the founders of the Literary and Philosophical Society of South Carolina, and served as its president from 1814 to 1830. In 1815 the society received from the Charleston Library Society its scientific collections, which became the nucleus of the Charleston Museum. The latter was further indebted to Elliott for personal collections and for advice and assistance in the arrangement of specimens. In 1816 he was made president of the Library Society and compiled a catalogue of the books belonging to the society. In 1820 he was elected to the presidency of the South Carolina College, but resigned before taking office. He was, however, influential in the establishment of the Medical College of South Carolina, and in April 1824 was elected its first professor of botany and natural history. With Hugh Swinton Legaré he began in 1828 the publication of the *Southern Review,* a quarterly copied after the English reviews of the day. In the next two years he contributed many articles to its pages, all of which are remarkable for their variety of subject matter, their clear, easy style, and their fine discrimination.

Elliott is now known not as a banker, statesman, editor, or planter, but rather as a naturalist. Between 1800 and 1808 he lived in comparative retirement on his plantation at Beaufort, and during this period collected, examined, and prepared the material for his *Sketch of the Botany of South Carolina and Georgia* (2 vols., 1821–24). It is said to have contained 180 genera and 1,000 species more than the *Flora Caroliniana* (1788) of Thomas Walter. His article in the *Southern Review* for November 1829 giving a historical summary of the study of botany showed his familiarity with the work of French, German, and Spanish botanists. Elliott died of apoplexy in 1830. A man of varied talents and extensive information, he was mild and unassuming in character and deportment.

[James Moultrie, *Eulogium on Stephen Elliott* (1830); F. B. Dexter, *Biog. Sketches of the Grads. of Yale Coll.,* IV (1907), 704–07; Wilson Gee, *S. C. Botanists: Biog. and Bibliog.,* Bull. of the Univ. of S. C., no. 72, Sept. 1918; J. G. B. Bulloch, *Hist. and Geneal. of the Habersham Family* (1901); W. A. Clark, *The Hist. of the Banking Institutions Organized in S. C. Prior to 1860* (1922); A. B. Hepburn, *Hist. of Currency in the U. S.* (1915); J. L. E. W. Shecut, *Shecut's Medic. and Philos. Essays* (1819), p. 49; W. G. Mazÿck, *Charleston Museum* (1908).]

A. R. C.

ELLIOTT, WALTER HACKETT ROBERT (Jan 6, 1842–Apr. 18, 1928), Catholic priest, missionary, author, the seventh son of Judge Robert T. Elliott and Frances O'Shea, was born in Detroit, Mich. He was educated in the Catholic schools of that city, and at the age of twelve entered the College of Notre Dame, in Indiana. He did not graduate but went to Cincinnati to take up the study of law in the office of United States District Attorney Warner M. Bateman and was admitted to the bar in 1861. When the Civil War broke out, he enlisted, though under age, in the 5th Ohio Volunteers, at Cincinnati, and served until the close of the war. In 1867 he attended a lecture for non-Catholics given by Rev. Isaac Hecker, one of the five founders of the Missionary Society of Saint Paul the Apostle, more commonly known as the Paulist Fathers. This lecture was the turning point in his life. He went to New York, called on Father Hecker, and was accepted as a postulant for the Paulist Community. On May 25, 1872, he was ordained to the priesthood, together with Adrian Aloysius Rosecrans, son of General Rosecrans, and Thomas Verney Robinson, a Confederate soldier, whose battery had actually fired on Elliott's position at Chancellorsville. His missionary career began a few months after his ordination and covered a period of twenty-seven years. In 1896 he founded *The Missionary,* the official organ of the Catholic Missionary Union. In 1902, in collaboration with Rev. Alexander P. Doyle [*q.v.*], he founded the Apostolic Mission House, at the Catholic University of America, Washington, D. C., for the training of diocesan priests as missionaries. He served the Apostolic Mission House as rector, professor, and rector emeritus until his death there, at the age of eighty-six. He was a man of prayer, austere in his own life, but his austerity was tempered by sympathy, and directed by understanding. He has been called "the Grand Old Man of the American Missions," and a "cornerstone of contemporary Catholic history." Probably no priest has wielded a more far-reaching influence in the United States.

His *Life of Father Hecker,* published in 1891, was followed in 1903 by his *Life of Jesus Christ,* a catena of the four gospels. Other works were: *Jesus Crucified* (1906); *The Sermons and Conferences of John Tauler* (1910); *Parish Sermons* (1913); *The Spiritual Life* (1914); *Manual for Missions* (1922); *Retreat for Priests* (1924); *Retreat for Nuns* (1925); and *Mission Sermons* (1926), this last being a collection of his sermons.

[Archives of the Paulist Fathers; "In Memoriam, Rev. Walter Elliott, Paulist," *The Catholic World,* May 1928, p. 222; Joseph McSorley, C. S. P., "Father Elliott, C. S. P.," *The Catholic World,* June 1928, pp. 296–305; *The Missionary,* June 1928; *N. Y. Times, Evening Star* (Washington, D. C.), Apr. 19, 1928.]

R. S. C—t.

ELLIOTT, WASHINGTON LAFAYETTE (Mar. 31, 1825–June 29, 1888), soldier, was born at Carlisle, Cumberland County, Pa., the son of Jesse Duncan [*q.v.*] and Frances C. (Vaughn) Elliott. His grandfather fought in the Revolution and his father won distinction in the navy in the War of 1812. Elliott accompanied his father on a cruise to the West Indies (1831–32), and on a second cruise (1835) to France on board the frigate *Constitution.* After his return to the United States he entered the preparatory school of Dickinson College, and subsequently the college, leaving the sophomore class to enter the United States Military Academy, July 1, 1841. He resigned from the academy in 1844, and began the study of medicine, but owing to the death of his father, was unable to continue his medical education, and he entered the army as a second lieutenant in the regiment of Mounted Riflemen, May 1846. In December of the same year he was ordered to Mexico with his regiment and took part in the siege of Vera Cruz. During the operations he was taken ill, and shortly after the surrender of the city was returned to the United States and assigned to recruiting duty. He was promoted first lieutenant in 1847, captain in 1854, and served on frontier duty in Dakota, Texas, and New Mexico until the beginning of the Civil War. At the call of the president for volunteers in 1861 he was ordered to Elmira, N. Y., as mustering officer, after which he was assigned to duty in the West and was engaged in the actions at Springfield and Wilson's Creek, Mo. He was commissioned colonel, 2nd Iowa Cavalry, in September 1861, and promoted major in the regular army in November of the same year. He was assigned to General Pope's command, Army of the Tennessee, and participated in the operations at New Madrid, Island No. 10 on the Mississippi, and in the siege of Corinth, where he commanded a cavalry brigade. He executed the raid on the Mobile & Ohio Railroad for which he received the brevet of colonel, United States Army. This was the first cavalry raid of the war, and he was soon after promoted brigadier-general, United States Volunteers (1862), and transferred to the Army of Virginia, in which he was appointed chief of cavalry. He was wounded in the second battle of Bull Run. From November to February 1863 he was in command of the Department of the Northwest, and from February to October commanded the 3rd Division, III Corps, Army of the Potomac. General Rosecrans in asking for the assignment of a cavalry general to his command said: "General Elliott would add 2,000 to our cavalry force. I once more beg he will be sent to me. Honor to him and benefit to the service will result" (*Official Records* (*Army*), 1 ser., XXIII, pt. II, p. 288). He was transferred to the Army of the Cumberland where he commanded the first cavalry division and engaged in reinforcing General Burnside in East Tennessee. He commanded the troops in the brilliant action of Mossy Creek, Tenn., in which he defeated the Confederate General Martin, was appointed chief of cavalry, Army of the Cumberland, engaged in the Atlanta campaign and in the pursuit of the Confederate General Hood. In December 1864, he was assigned to the command of the 2nd Division, IV Corps, and participated in the battles around Nashville. He was in command of the District of Kansas from August 1865 to Mar. 1, 1866, when he was mustered out of the volunteer service. He was promoted lieutenant-colonel, 1st Cavalry, Aug. 31, 1866; colonel 3rd Cavalry, Apr. 4, 1878; and retired from active service Mar. 20, 1879. During the war, General Elliott won five brevets for distinguished conduct, the last of which was major-general, United States Army. After his retirement from the army he became vice-president of the California Safe Deposit & Trust Company, and while attending to his duties in the offices of the company, was suddenly stricken with heart disease, from which he died. He was a soldier of ability, affable, respected and esteemed by his associates, and very popular with his men. He gave much of his time to helping others, and was a director of a number of charitable institutions in San Francisco.

[*Official Register of the Officers and Cadets of the U. S. Mil. Acad.*, June 1843; G. V. Henry, *Mil. Record of Civilian Appointments in the U. S. Army*, vol. I (1869); F. B. Heitman, *Hist. Reg. and Dict. of the U. S. Army*, vol. I (1903); A. A. Stuart, *Iowa Colonels and Regiments* (1865); *Biog. Album of Prominent Pennsylvanians*, vol. I (1888); *Official Records (Army)*, 2 ser. vols. I, VIII, X; *San Francisco Chronicle*, June 30, 1888.] C. F. C.

ELLIOTT, WILLIAM (Apr. 27, 1788–Feb. 3, 1863), writer on sports, the son of William and Phœbe (Waight) Elliott, was born in Beaufort and died in Charleston, S. C. He grew up in surroundings of social and intellectual distinction, mostly in Beaufort, around which lay the vast plantations of his family. From 1806 to 1809 he was at Harvard, in bad health for the most part, but well enough to be considerably above the average in scholarship, and to graduate in the normal time. Returning home, he occupied himself with all that went to make up the life of a gentleman farmer, and in 1817 he was married to Anne Hutchinson Smith. For a number of years he was in politics, a member successively of both branches of the state legislature, but in 1832 he resigned from the Senate rather than carry out the wishes of his constituents to vote for nullification. Scorning "policy," he stood by his convictions, and capped his immolation by administering a formal if somewhat patronizing rebuke to all who disagreed with him (Address to the People of St. Helena Parish, 1832). This rather definitely put an end to his official public career, but he continued by means of open letters and pamphlets to express himself from time to time on questions of general moment. He was particularly interested in the large social and economic implications of farming, and conducted over many years a campaign to show the evils of one-crop system. In June 1851 he published in a newspaper a series of letters which were in 1852 collected into a pamphlet called *The Letters of Agricola.* Agricola was in the main an orthodox Southerner—about slavery and about Northern meddling he was quite clear. Slavery, he declared, was "sanctioned by religion, conducive to good morals, and useful, nay indispensable"; Northern interference was "wicked, unprovoked, and fanatical" (*Ibid.*, p. 7); but for all his orthodoxy he believed it essential that the South introduce manufactures and steer as far away as possible from the folly of secession. In 1846 he published in book form, under his own name, some sketches which had already appeared serially in a Charleston newspaper under the names Piscator and Venator. This book, *Carolina Sports by Land and Water* (republished in South Carolina 1859, 1918, and in England 1867) is dedicated to the principle that man without recreation is like a bow kept always taut. It defends in passing even dancing and the theatre, and with autobiographical verve praises as almost beyond comparison, the delights of fishing and gaming. Altogether, Poeta was a rôle to which this patrician was as much entitled as he was to those of Agricola, Piscator, and Venator; for upon occasion, when mood demanded, he knew how to turn out his verses, and even, in 1850, it is said, published in Charleston a complete tragical drama, *Fiesco.*

[*Southern Quart. Rev.*, July 1847, pp. 67–90; G. A. Wauchope, "William Elliott" in *Lib. of Southern Lit.*, vol. IV (1907); letter, Emma Elliott Johnstone, Apr. 30, 1928; *Harvard Univ. Quin. Cat.* (1910); *Charleston Courier*, Feb. 4, 1863.] J. D. W.

ELLIS, CALVIN (Aug. 15, 1826–Dec. 14, 1883), physician, was born in Boston, the son of Luther Ellis, a prominent iron merchant, who married his cousin, Betsey Ellis. The Ellis family of which he was a member originally came from Essex, England, and settled in Dedham, Mass., in 1634. Calvin Ellis was brought up in an atmosphere of liberality and independence of thought; his family were cultured and well-to-do.

While at Harvard College, he became interested in rowing and was a member of the first Harvard Boat Club. Graduating from college in 1846, he entered the Harvard Medical School and, after a term as resident pupil in the Massachusetts General Hospital, he received his M.D. degree in 1849. He then traveled in Europe for two years, working especially in French and German hospitals on anatomy and pathology. When he returned to Boston, he became assistant in pathology at the Harvard Medical School to Dr. J. B. S. Jackson, an eminent pathologist of that day, and at the same time held the position of admitting physician and pathologist to the Massachusetts General Hospital. In 1863 he was appointed assistant professor of medicine and in 1867, full professor, at the Harvard Medical School, holding the latter position until his death. He was appointed dean in 1869, at the beginning of the reformation period inaugurated by the newly elected president of the university, Charles W. Eliot [*q.v.*], whose ideas he proceeded to carry out in the face of strong opposition on the part of other members of the Medical School faculty. In addition, he was one of the most valuable teachers of his day in the School. His clinical medicine had a sound basis in his long study of pathology; he taught men how to diagnose disease scientifically. Diagnosis by elimination was his method, a procedure which gave to the Harvard Medical School a distinctive stamp. He wrote forty or more medical articles on a variety of subjects, the most important of which was his Boylston prize essay, in 1860, on "Tubercle," which was considered one of the best papers on that subject prior to Koch's discovery of the bacillus. Ellis was a member of many medical and scientific societies, including the American Academy of Arts and Sciences (1859).

He was of a cheerful, sunny disposition, unassuming in manner, scholarly, and with a certain slowness and deliberation about coming to a decision. Once the decision was made, however, and he felt that a certain course of action was the best, no opposition could turn him. His practise was large. His lifelong friend, Bartol, wrote, at the time of his death, "No man living in this community has ever better answered to the image of a true and good physician. . . . He was constitutionally sincere, and had the truth in his race and blood." In his report for the year 1883–84 President Eliot characterized Ellis as, "cautious, exact, conscientious, earnest and cheerful . . . one of the best teachers of medicine the University has ever had."

During the Civil War he was twice sent by the governor of Massachusetts on special commissions to the battle-front. On both occasions he became ill with fever and had to return to Boston. Some nine years before his death he began to have severe stomach symptoms caused by an ulcer, a disease which after long suffering resulted in his death. In the latter days of his life he worked upon the manuscript of a book to be entitled "Symptomatology." This was to have been an encyclopedia of all known symptoms which have been actually proved to occur in connection with various diseases, arranged alphabetically—a colossal work which Ellis was well qualified to write. He died before its completion, however, and the book was never published. Ellis gave freely of his time and money to help educational undertakings and at his death left $150,000 to the Harvard Medical School (*Boston Medical & Surgical Journal,* CX, 1884, p. 186). He never married.

[Henry I. Bowditch in *Proc. Am. Acad. Arts and Sciences,* n.s. XI (1884), 492–501 (with bibliography); T. F. Harrington, *The Harvard Medical School* (3 vols., 1905), II, 902–10; C. A. Bartol, *The Beloved Physician: A Sermon in West Church after the Decease of Dr. Calvin Ellis* (1884); Geo. B. Shattuck, H. I. Bowditch, C. D. Homans, Oliver Wendell Holmes, and others, in the *Boston Medic. & Surgic. Jour.,* CX (1884), 151–56, 166.]

H. R. V.

ELLIS, EDWARD SYLVESTER (Apr. 11, 1840–June 20, 1916), author, son of Sylvester and Mary (Alberty) Ellis, was born in Geneva, Ohio. He was educated at the state normal school of New Jersey, and while little more than a boy he began teaching. At nineteen he was already a writer, at twenty-two he was married, in his early thirties he was superintendent of the Trenton public schools, and after thirty-six he devoted himself exclusively to writing. His first notable book, *Seth Jones, or the Captive of the Frontier* (1860), probably as successful as any of the fiction which he wrote later (around 600,000 copies were sold), was among the earliest of the "dime novels" which glutted America in the second half of the nineteenth century. In Ellis's own case as an author, it was the beginning of a torrent of similar works. Till the middle eighties he held chiefly to fiction, but afterward turned in general in the direction of history, writing books beyond any patient counting. Where his next work would come from, whom it would proclaim as its author, or what it would discuss, remained always a mystery; he had at least eight publishers, in St. Paul, Akron, and Cincinnati, as well as in more customary centers, and he wrote under at least six names other than his own. His themes were developed most often as adventure and hero stories for boys, for whom he wrote also much inspirational biography, and much history. He penned versions of Plutarch and even Thomas à Kempis ,not to mention text-books in grammar, arithmetic, physiology, and mythology. During 1891 in New York he edited *Holiday,* an illustrated juvenile weekly. He wrote for adults a great deal of American history and a number of extended statements about whatever was at the moment uppermost in the public mind, as for instance, *Great Leaders and National issues of 1896* (1896) ; *The Story of South Africa* (1899) ; and *Voters' Guide for the Campaign of 1900.* In his histories, he was extremely fair in his judgments on disagreements actually within the nation, but internationally he adhered to the doctrine of American preëminence. "The record of no people," he said, "can approach it in magnificence of achievement as regards art, science, education, literature, invention, and all that makes for true progress" (*From Tent to White House,* 1899, p. 7). He believed that the normal expectancy of human life is a hundred years, that a teacher should excel in athletic prowess any of his students, and that "the vices of cigarette smoking, of tobacco chewing, of beer and alcoholic drinking, threaten the very existence of the rising generation" (*Continental Primary Physiology,* 1885, p. 9). He was married twice: first in 1862 to Annie M. Deane, and in 1900 to Clara Spalding Brown of Los Angeles. His home was at Upper Montclair, N. J., but he died at Cliff Island, Me.

[*Who's Who in America,* 1916–17; C. M. Harvey, "The Dime Novel in Am. Life," *Atlantic Monthly,* July 1907; *N. Y. Times,* June 22, 1916.] J. D. W.

ELLIS, GEORGE EDWARD (Aug. 8, 1814–Dec. 20, 1894), Unitarian clergyman, historian, was born in Boston, Mass., the fourth son of David and Sarah (Rogers) Ellis. His father was a prosperous merchant and his mother a daughter of a Loyalist exile. Ellis attended several preparatory schools, including the Boston Latin School and the Round Hill School at Northampton, and graduated from Harvard in 1833. He then went to the Divinity School, and after graduation in 1836 remained in Boston for two years, sailing on May 8, 1838, for an extended European trip from which he returned in the following year. On Mar. 11, 1840, he was ordained and became pastor of the Harvard Unitarian Church in Charlestown, where he remained for twenty-nine years. On Apr. 15, 1840, he married Elizabeth Bruce Eager, daughter of William Eager of Boston. She bore him one son and died in 1842. From September 1842 to February 1845 Ellis was co-editor of the *Christian Register,* with Rev. Samuel K. Lothrop, and from 1849 to 1855 he was an editor of the *Christian Examiner,* at first with Rev. George Putnam and subsequently alone. To this latter periodical he was a constant contributor, writing most of the book reviews. His connection with Harvard College was always close. From 1850 to 1879 he was an Overseer and in 1853–54 he was secretary of the Overseers. He was the first to hold the new chair of systematic theology in the Divinity School, delivering his inaugural address July 14, 1857, and serving until 1863. In 1869 he resigned his pastorate and moved from Charlestown to Boston, where he lived a quiet, bookish life until his death. On Oct. 22, 1859, he married, as his second wife, Lucretia Goddard Gould, who died July 6, 1869.

Ellis was always an omnivorous reader and engaged in incessant intellectual work. He compiled a hymn-book in 1845, and in 1844, 1845, and 1847 respectively, he wrote the lives of John Mason, Anne Hutchinson, and William Penn for Sparks's *Library of American Biography.* In 1857 he published *A Half Century of the Unitarian Controversy* and in 1864 delivered a course of lectures on "The Evidences of Christianity" at the Lowell Institute. In January 1869 he delivered two lectures before the Lowell Institute subsequently published under the title: *I. The Aims and Purposes of the Founders of Massachusetts. II. Their Treatment of Intruders and Dissentients* (1869). In these lectures he upheld the Puritans in their intolerance. His interest in history increased; his Lowell Lectures for 1871 were on the provincial history of Massachusetts, and those for 1879 on "The Red Man and the White Man in North America." This last series appeared in book form in 1882. In 1888 he published *The Puritan Age and Rule in the Colony of the Massachusetts Bay, 1629–1685.* He contributed several chapters to Winsor's *Memorial History of Boston* (1880–01) and to the *Narrative and Critical History of America* (1884–89); and several articles to the ninth edition of the *Encyclopædia Britannica;* wrote a *History of the Massachusetts General Hospital* (1872), continuing the work of Nathaniel Ingersoll Bowditch; the *History of the Battle of Bunker's Hill* (1875); memoirs, among others, of Luther V. Bell, Jared Sparks, Jacob Bigelow, and Nathaniel Thayer. He was a constant contributor to the *New York Review,* the *North American Review,* and the *Atlantic Monthly,* in the last of which he published (October 1894) his "Retrospect of an Octogenarian." Perhaps the main interest of his somewhat secluded life was the Massachusetts Historical Society, of which he was vice-president from 1877 to 1885 and president from that date until his death. In his will he left his house and $30,000 to the Society and $10,000 to the American Antiquarian Society.

As an historian of New England he belonged to the old filio-pietistic school and his writings, redeemed by no charm of style, are now out of date and negligible.

[Memoir by O. B. Frothingham in *Proc. Mass. Hist. Soc.*, 2 ser. X (1896), 207–55; *Proc. Am. Antiquarian Soc.*, n.s. IX (1895), 461–69; Waldo Higginson, *Memorials of the Class of 1833 of Harvard Coll.* (1883); A. B. Ellis, "Geo. Edward Ellis," *New Eng. Mag.*, May 1896; *Hist. of the Harvard Church in Charlestown, 1815–79* (1879), pp. 208–35, with bibliography of his publications to 1879; *Christian Reg.*, Dec. 27, 1894.]

J. T. A.

ELLIS, GEORGE WASHINGTON (May 4, 1875–Nov. 26, 1919), colored lawyer, sociologist, and author, the son of George and Amanda Jane (Drace) Ellis, was born in Weston, Platte County, Mo. His early education was received in the public schools at Weston, after which he attended the high school at Atchison, Kan. He then studied for two years in the law department of the University of Kansas, graduating LL.B. in 1893, and was admitted to the Kansas bar. The next four years he spent in the collegiate department of the university, at the same time practising law in Lawrence, Kan., in order to defray his expenses. In 1897 he proceeded to New York City, where he took a two years' course in the Gunton Institute of Economics and Sociology. In 1899 he passed the examination of the United States Census Board, following which he received an appointment in the census division of the Department of the Interior at Washington, D. C., where he remained two years. Here his spare moments were spent in postgraduate work in philosophy and psychology at Howard University. In the routine of his departmental duties he attracted the attention of President Roosevelt, upon whose nomination, confirmed by the Senate, he was in 1902 appointed secretary of the United States legation to the Republic of Liberia. He was induced to accept this position chiefly because of the opportunity it afforded him of studying the social conditions of the colored race in its native habitat, a subject in which he had become intensely interested. The next eight years he spent in Liberia, with Monrovia as his headquarters, but under instructions from Washington he undertook numerous expeditions into the hinterland for the purpose of investigating and reporting upon the various tribes of the interior. He studied the West African from every angle—ethnological, linguistic, sociological, and economic—and made an extensive collection of West-African ethnological specimens illustrating all phases of social life and industrial art, which on his return he lent to the National Museum, Washington, for exhibition. He resigned in 1910 and on his return to the United States opened a law office in Chicago, where he quickly acquired a large and lucrative general practise. He was a good lawyer and excellent speaker, and held briefs not only in all the Illinois courts but also in the Supreme Court of the United States. In 1917 he was elected assistant corporation counsel to the City of Chicago, a position which he held until his death. A strong Republican, a good campaign speaker, with a thorough knowledge of political issues both national and state, he was frequently heard on the public platform, and wielded much influence in the party counsels. In spite of his legal and political activities he continued to maintain his interest in sociological work, and in a series of books, pamphlets, and articles which attracted wide attention he gave to the world the results of his West-African studies. His earliest—and perhaps most scholarly work—was *Negro Culture in West Africa* (1914), a social study of a negro group, selected as typical of the African Black Belt. It received high praise from competent critics for its original research and keen insight. Then followed *The Leopard's Claw* (1917), a novel of adventure in the West-African jungle, and *Negro Achievements in Social Progress* (1915). He was a prolific contributor to scientific and literary periodicals, his articles dealing mainly with social institutions and economic problems of the West-African negro. He was a contributing editor of *The Journal of Race Development*, Clark University, Worcester, Mass., in which publication some of his best studies appeared.

On the nomination of Sir Harry H. Johnston and Dr. J. Scott Keltie he was elected a Fellow of the Royal Geographical Society of Great Britain. He was also the recipient of honors from many other learned societies in Great Britain and the United States. He married, Jan. 27, 1906, Clavender L. Sherman, daughter of Robert Sherman, a member of the Liberian government.

[*Who's Who in America*, 1918-19; *Chicago Tribune*, *N. Y. Times*, Nov. 28, 1919. The article in *The Nat. Cyc. of the Colored Race* (1919), I, 144, is unpretentious and uncritical.]

H. W. H. K.

ELLIS, HENRY (Aug. 29, 1721–Jan. 21, 1806), hydrographer, colonial governor, was the son of Francis Ellis, of County Monaghan, and his wife Joan Maxwell. He studied law in the Temple, but later devoted attention to scientific and geographical research. In 1746 he was appointed by Parliament to search for a northwest passage to the Pacific. Although he failed in this attempt, his *Voyage to Hudson's-Bay, . . . for Discovering a North West Passage* (1748), published in four languages, was well received and resulted in his election as a fellow of the Royal

Ellis

Society. Within a few years he was appointed governor of Georgia. He assumed his duties Feb. 16, 1757, and was cordially received officially and by the colonists in general. With five hundred muskets from the home government, and presents for the Indians, he entered upon his administration with the confidence and support of the colonists assured, despite the fact that upon his arrival he had found "an almost universal discontent arising from the late proceedings and persons in power" (first letter to the Board of Trade). From the beginning of his administration his relations with the Council and with the Assembly were usually harmonious. He showed tact in dealing with the Assembly, especially in the delicate matter of restoring to the governor and Council the right of issuing money and of auditing the accounts. To the bill limiting the duration of the Assembly to three years, and the bill for issuing paper money, however, he refused to give his assent, but referred them to the British government. He convinced the home government that the irregular and unusual proceedings of the courts of the colony made necessary the appointment of the chief justice. He saw the need of guaranteeing the titles to land and provided for this by law, and it was during his administration that the long-standing claim of Thomas Bosomworth and his wife was adjusted. He aided in the establishment of the Episcopal Church in the colony, supporting the law which provided for the division of the districts of the province into parishes and empowering church officials to assess rates for parochial activities. He also made earnest efforts to conciliate the Indians and was especially successful with the Creeks. The difficulties of his administration were increased by the French and Indian War, especially since the colony was not financially able to prepare adequately for defense. Ellis assumed responsibility for the support of some of the militia, and on his own initiative fitted out an armed vessel to protect the colony from French and Spanish attacks along the coast.

There were expressions of general regret when, on account of ill health, Ellis left Georgia on Nov. 2, 1760. Soon after his return to England, he was appointed governor of Nova Scotia, but remained in England for the two and a half years (1761–63) during which his deputy personally performed the duties of the office. He then went to Naples, Italy, where he was interested in maritime researches, and died there.

[A. D. Candler, ed., *Colonial Records of Ga.* (26 vols., 1904–16), vols. VII, VIII, XIII, XVI, XVIII; Colonial Records of Ga. in the Dept. of Archives and Hist., State Capitol, Atlanta, vols. XXVII, pt. 1, XXVIII, pt. 1, XXXIV, XXXIX; P. S. Flippin, "The Royal Government in Ga., 1752–1776," in *Ga. Hist Quart.*, Mar. 1924; W. B. Stevens, *Hist. of Ga.* (1847), I, 427–59; C. C. Jones, *Hist. of Ga.* (1883), I, 515–44; manuscript material in the Lib. of Cong.] P. S. F.

ELLIS, JOB BICKNELL (Jan. 21, 1829–Dec. 30, 1905), botanist, mycologist, was born on a farm near Potsdam, N. Y., the son of Freeman and Sarah Ellis. The duties of a farm lad in the early part of the nineteenth century did not leave much leisure for study, but young Ellis attended the schools which were available when he could be spared from the farm and neglected no opportunity to read such books as were accessible to him. He apparently inherited an unusual interest in nature and her secrets, which was perhaps encouraged rather than discouraged by his parents and teachers. That he succeeded in his efforts to acquire an education is shown by the fact that at the age of sixteen he taught a country school at Stockholm, N. Y. His salary was ten dollars a month, half of which was paid in cash and the balance in grain. Having worked his way through the local academy, he entered Union College at Schenectady at the age of twenty. In spite of having to teach school one winter in order to pay his expenses, he received the B.A. degree in June 1851. He took the courses in botany given at the college, and continued the study and collection of plants while teaching in Germantown, Pa., and at Albany, N. Y. Here he met George H. Cook, later state geologist of New Jersey, who stimulated his interest in science. He already had an interest in fungi, but had been unable to make much progress in their study for want of books. In 1857 he chanced to see a notice of H. W. Ravenel's *Fungi Caroliniani Exsiccati* and immediately began a correspondence with the author, who exchanged specimens with him and assisted him in his study. He continued teaching, but devoted all his spare time to the fungi. In 1856, after an unpleasant teaching experience in the South, due to antipathy to Northerners, he returned to his old home in New York and on April 19 married Arvilla J. Bacon, who proved a valuable assistant in his mycological work. In 1864 he left his teaching to enter the navy, and remained in the service until 1865. He then moved from Potsdam to Newfield, N. J., where he purchased a small place and spent the remainder of his life. Here he devoted more of his time to the collection and study of fungi, corresponding and exchanging specimens with M. C. Cooke, C. H. Peck, W. G. Farlow, and other leading mycologists of the day.

In 1878 he began the preparation and distribution of sets of North-American fungi and from that time until his death devoted all his time to the collection and description of fungi. With the assistance of his wife he named, prepared, and distributed over two hundred thousand specimens. Hundreds of new species were described, and numerous papers written. In 1892 he published his *magnum opus, The North American Pyrenomycetes,* prepared with the assistance of B. M. Everhart. He accumulated one of the largest collections of fungi ever made in North America, now in the herbarium of the New York Botanical Garden, and did more than any other botanist during the period of his activity toward making known the fungi of this country. No student or collector ever appealed to him in vain for assistance or advice. Botanists throughout the world recognized the value of his contributions to mycology, and he was elected to membership in many scientific societies in this and other countries. He was modest and retiring, and imbued with the humility characteristic of the true scientist.

[*Who's Who in America,* 1906–07; *Jour. of Mycology,* Mar. 1906; *Botanical Gazette,* Nov. 1890.]

C. L. Sh—r.

ELLIS, JOHN WASHINGTON (July 15, 1817–Dec. 28, 1910), banker, was born in Williamsburg, Clermont County, Ohio, the son of Benjamin and Sallie (Tweed) Ellis. His paternal ancestors emigrated from Sandwich, England, to Sandwich, Mass., and then removed to what is now a part of Maine, where his father was born. In 1810 Benjamin Ellis started West, settling first in Williamsburg and later in Cincinnati. The son received his early education in Ohio and in New York City where his father resided from 1831 to 1835. For a year and a half he attended Kenyon College at Gambier, Ohio. On Mar. 1, 1835, he left New York for Cincinnati and for two years worked as an office boy. In 1837 he returned to New York, remained there three years, and in March 1840 again left for Cincinnati, where he resided for the next thirty years. On his return to Cincinnati Ellis engaged in trade with the frontiersmen and once accompanied his merchandise as far north as Prairie-du-Chien. After disposing of his wares, he floated down the Mississippi with a cargo of lead from Galena, Ill., destined for New York by way of New Orleans. At New Orleans he visited the slave market and the scenes he witnessed there made him a strong anti-slavery man. He was one of the founders of the Young Men's Mercantile Library Association of Cincinnati and in 1843 was chosen its president. Four years later he organized the wholesale dry-goods firm of Ellis & McAlpin which for many years was one of the leading mercantile houses of Cincinnati. At one time he served as president of the Cincinnati, Hamilton & Dayton Railroad. His opposition to slavery led him to join the Republican party and during the Civil War he was a loyal supporter of Lincoln's administration. Early in 1863 Ellis with eight or ten prominent business men petitioned for a charter for the First National Bank of Cincinnati. In May 1863 the bank was chartered with a capital of one million dollars, which was larger than that of any other national bank in the country with the exception of the First National Bank of Baltimore. From 1863 to 1869 Ellis served as president of this institution. He was frequently consulted by the government on financial problems during the war, and took an active part in the sale of government bonds. Soon after the war Jay Cooke offered him an equal share in his firm but Ellis refused because he did not approve of its methods. From 1870 to 1883 he was the head of Winslow, Lanier & Company of New York, and in that position organized many syndicates for the purchase and sale of bonds for the building and extension of the great transcontinental lines and other railroads. Probably his most significant work was his negotiation in 1881 of a loan of $40,000,000 for the Northern Pacific Railroad, which he sold mostly in London. He also negotiated the operating agreement between the Erie, with Gould and Fisk, and the Atlantic & Great Western Railroad; and was instrumental in purchasing for the Panama Canal Company under the control of De Lesseps the Panama Railroad. For many years he was a member of the American committee of this company in the United States. In 1876 Ellis was president of the Third National Bank of New York City in which Samuel J. Tilden was a large depositor and director. He was called before the congressional committees investigating election returns of that year concerning Tilden's expenditures. He retired from active business in 1883 and continued to reside in New York until his death. In 1845 he married Caroline Satterlee Lindley.

[Correspondence, Letter-Books, and Reminiscences of John Washington Ellis, a manuscript collection belonging to Ralph N. Ellis of New York City; E. R. Ellis, *Biog. Sketches of Richard Ellis . . . and his Descendants* (1888); E. V. Smalley, *Hist. of the Northern Pacific Railroad* (1853), pp. 231–34; *N. Y. Herald,* Dec. 29, 1910.]

R. C. M.

ELLIS, JOHN WILLIS (Nov. 23, 1820–July 7, 1861), governor of North Carolina, was born in the "Jersey Settlement" of Rowan County, N. C., being the eldest son of Anderson and Judith (Bailey) Ellis. The Ellis and Willis families are of Welsh origin. Members were in Massachusetts in the seventeenth century and one

John Ellis married Joanna Willis, of Dorchester. Both families also appear in colonial Virginia, and the local records of Rowan County in 1750 and afterward disclose nine men named Ellis. One of these was Willis Ellis, the grandfather of the later governor, who was a justice of the peace and a colonel of militia in the French and Indian War. Judith Bailey Ellis belonged to one of the wealthiest families of the county. After preliminary schooling under a tutor at the home of a kinsman, Robert Allison, and some months at Randolph-Macon College, Va., John Willis entered the University of North Carolina in 1837 and graduated in 1841. He then read law under Richmond Pearson, preëminent legal instructor of ante bellum North Carolina, was admitted to the bar in 1842, and began the practise of his profession at Salisbury.

He early turned his mind to the public service and in 1843 was a member of the state Democratic convention. In 1844, 1846, and 1848 he represented Rowan County in the North Carolina House of Commons and in the latter year was the legislative leader of the Democratic program for railway construction without aid from the state, which, however, was defeated. In 1848, he was elected a judge of the superior court by the legislature. For service on the bench he had a certain natural fitness, and he received commendation from the Whig as well as Democratic press for the discharge of his duties. Ten years later (1858) he was nominated for the governorship over William W. Holden [*q.v.*], Ellis having the support of the slaveholders and gentry in the party, Holden that of the non-slaveholders and yeomanry. His only opponent in the campaign was Duncan K. McRae [*q.v.*], also a Democrat, who raised the issue of distribution of the proceeds of public land sales among the states as a means of financing internal improvements. Ellis's majority was more than sixteen thousand. As governor, Ellis urged the construction of canals and railroads, and through his effort the various railways of the state arranged a better interchange of freight, each road agreeing to haul the cars of the others. In 1860 he was renominated for office. It was a critical year politically, not only because of the issue in the national election but also because of a demand in the state for the taxation of slaves as property rather than as polls, an attack on the privilege of the slaveholders in the revenue system. The question was raised in the legislature in 1858 by Moses A. Bledsoe, a Democrat of Wake County, but was rejected by the party leaders. The Whigs proved receptive, however, and in 1860 adopted a platform committed to the ad valorem taxation of all kinds of property. The ensuing campaign was the most warmly contested in a decade. The result of the election, held in August 1860, was a Democratic victory, but with a majority approximately ten thousand less than in 1858.

The outstanding problem of Ellis's second administration was the course to be pursued as a result of the election of a Republican president. As early as 1854 Ellis was convinced that slavery interests were doomed so far as federal politics were concerned. In his first inaugural he intimated that the day might come when the South could not enjoy full constitutional rights in the Union, and in 1859, after the John Brown raid, he sought to increase the arms in the arsenal at Fayetteville. After Lincoln's election he approved the course of South Carolina and believed that a Southern Confederacy should be immediately organized. There was strong Union sentiment in North Carolina, however, and the state moved laggardly toward secession. In his message to the legislature in December 1860, Ellis declared that the South would not submit to the principles of the Republican party and recommended that North Carolina call a conference of the neighboring states, to be followed by a convention of the people of North Carolina. He also advised that the militia be reorganized and that a corps of 10,000 volunteers be raised. The suggestion of such measures made clear the existence of three political groups: the Whigs, who opposed them entirely; the radical Democrats, who supported Ellis; and the conservative Democrats, who were willing to have a conference but who opposed a state convention. In the legislature a coalition of Whigs and conservative Democrats delayed action regarding a convention until February 1861, when the matter was submitted to the people and was rejected by a majority of 651. In the meantime, early in January, the legislature appropriated $300,000 for arms and munitions.

Though favoring secession, Ellis's legal mind and temperament made him oppose violent action. Thus when secession sympathizers seized Forts Johnston and Caswell on the lower Cape Fear, he immediately caused their evacuation. The course of events showed, however, that he had been only a step in advance of the state's ultimate action. The firing on Fort Sumter was followed by the call of the Lincoln administration for two regiments of North Carolina militia. This Ellis denounced as a violation of the Constitution and a usurpation of power. He called for 30,000 volunteers to resist invasion, and convened the legislature in extra session. The legislature provided for a state convention, which adopted an ordinance of secession on May 20, 1861. Ellis died, seven weeks later, in the midst of the war activities. He was twice married: first, on Aug. 25, 1844, to Mary, daughter of Philo White, sometime editor of the *North Carolina Star* and minister to Ecuador; second, to Mary Daves of New Bern. All his descendants come from the second marriage.

["John Willis Ellis" in S. A. Ashe and S. B. Weeks, *Biog. Hist. of N. C.*, vol. VII (1908); Anne Garrard, "John Willis Ellis," manuscript thesis, Duke Univ. Lib.]
W. K. B.

ELLIS, POWHATAN (Jan. 17, 1790–Mar. 18, 1863), jurist, senator, diplomat, was born at "Red Hill," Amherst County, Va., the youngest son of Maj. Josiah and Jane (Shelton) Ellis, and was named for the father of Pocahontas, from whom he claimed descent. He was a student in Washington College (now Washington and Lee University) for three years, and graduated from Dickinson College, Pa., in 1810. Three years later he graduated in law from the College of William and Mary, and was admitted to the Virginia bar, practising for a short time in Lynchburg. During the War of 1812, he became lieutenant in a company of Virginia riflemen but saw no actual fighting. In 1815 he met Gen. Andrew Jackson, and a personal friendship grew up between them. A year later the General gave Ellis letters of introduction to some of his friends in the Southwest, including David Holmes, governor of Mississippi Territory. Accompanied by several young men, including two sons of Patrick Henry, his distant cousins, Ellis set out in April 1816 for Mississippi. He stopped for a time at Natchez, but soon removed to Winchester. Under the tutelage of Gen. James Patton, he entered upon his public career just as the territory of Mississippi was emerging into statehood (*Mississippi Historical Society Publications,* vol. VI, 1902, p. 271). In 1818 he was elevated to the supreme bench of the state. Some of his biographers say that Ellis was "extremely indolent," but the fact that he wrote the opinions in approximately two-thirds of the cases decided by the Mississippi supreme court from 1819 to 1824 seems to disprove the accuracy of the accusation. After seven years in this position he received from Gov. Leake an *ad interim* appointment to the seat in the United States Senate made vacant by the resignation of David Holmes. In the Mississippi legislature he was defeated for the honor of filling out the unexpired term, but a year later was elected senator for the full period of six years. Perhaps his most conspicuous action in the Senate was his vote against ratification of the treaty of 1828 with Mexico, which would have restricted the spread of slavery beyond the Mississippi River. He resigned in 1832 to become federal judge of the Mississippi district, upon appointment of President Jackson.

Four years later the President requested him to become United States chargé d'affaires in Mexico City. Edward Livingston pronounced this mission to Mexico the most important of all missions of the United States at that day. Ellis filled his position well throughout most of the year 1836. Within less than a week after the inauguration of President Van Buren, Ellis was appointed envoy extraordinary and minister plenipotentiary to Mexico, but he did not proceed to his post until March 1839, remaining in Mexico for three years after that date. Despite the difficulties of his position, he strove successfully in Mexico to secure the good will of that country, as well as to deserve the approval of his own. When his career as a diplomat closed he returned to Mississippi. In 1847 he was chosen a delegate from Adams County to the state Democratic convention, over which in June he was elected to preside. Here he "especially defended the administration in regard to the war forced upon us by Mexico" (*Mississippi Free Trader,* Natchez, June 23, 1847). Late in life he left Mississippi and returned to Virginia, where he hoped to purchase the old family homestead. This pleasure was denied him. He was married on Feb. 28, 1831, to Eliza Rebecca Winn of Washington, D. C., the beautiful daughter of Timothy Winn, a naval officer (*Daily National Intelligencer,* Mar. 2, 1831). They had two children, a son and a daughter. Ellis spent his last days in Richmond, Va. He was not brilliant, but was a man of unusual tact, dignity, uprightness, and common sense. Ellisville, Miss., is named for him.

[Article, dated Mar. 25, 1863, in *Sou. Lit. Messenger,* April 1863; Thos. H. Ellis, "A Memorandum of the Ellis Family," prepared in 1849, typewritten copy in Lib. of Cong.; J. F. H. Claiborne, *Mississippi, as a Province, Territory and State* (1880), pp. 358, 426; J. D. Lynch, *Bench and Bar of Miss.* (1881), pp. 87–88; Dunbar Rowland, *Mississippi* (1907), vol. I, and *Mississippi the Heart of the South* (1925); *Biog. and Hist. Memoirs of Miss.* (1891); *Daily Richmond Enquirer,* Mar. 19, 1863; Richmond *Daily Dispatch,* Mar. 20, 1863.]
L. T. L.

ELLIS, SETH HOCKETT (Jan. 3, 1830–June 23, 1904), Ohio granger, politician, was born at Martinsville, Ohio. He was the son of Robert and Anna Hockett (Moon) Ellis and was educated in the common schools of Clinton and Warren counties. He was married to Rebecca J. Tressler near Springboro, Aug. 21, 1851. From 1864 to 1872 there developed in the central and northwestern states a great number of farmers' clubs and various organizations known as the "Patrons of Husbandry," or more popuearly as "granges." Ellis became interested in the movement in September 1872, when with fifty of his acquaintances he organized the first grange in the state. He has himself described the early history of the grange in the *Ohio Farmer,* published at Cleveland. His articles, printed from 1900 to 1904, made use of the published proceedings and of other documentary material. He was master of the state grange from its organization, on Apr. 9, 1873, to 1879, again from 1888 to 1892, and from 1896 to 1900. During the intervals when he was not master he was chairman of the executive committee, holding this position from 1879 to 1888, from 1892 to 1896, and from 1900 to the time of his death in 1904. He was chaplain of the national grange for four years and member of the executive committee of the national organization for two years. Besides his activity in the granger movement he was a trustee of Ohio State University from 1879 to 1887, when he was transferred to the board of control of the Ohio Agricultural Experiment Station at Wooster.

Ellis was also the candidate of the Union Reform party for governor of Ohio in 1899. The platform made the initiative and referendum the only plank. Samuel M. Jones was elected mayor of Toledo on the Republican ticket in 1897, but was rejected by his own party in the spring of 1899. He then ran as an independent candidate and received an overwhelming vote. It was understood that he would be a candidate for governor and it was planned for the Union Reform convention to leave the head of that ticket blank that members of the party might vote for Jones. When Ellis was nominated for governor, Jones published a manifesto announcing himself a candidate on a platform declaring for the right of self-government by means of direct nomination of candidates and direct making of laws by the people. Jones received 106,721 votes and Ellis 7,799 out of a total of 908,159. In January 1900, the national committee of the Union Reform party sent out ballots to members of the party for votes for candidates for president and vice-president. The balloting continued through February and March. In April it was announced that Ellis and Samuel T. Richardson of Pennsylvania had been nominated. The platform favored "direct legislation under the system known as the initiative and referendum." It declared that there was "no need or benefit from party except to secure direct legislation." Ellis has been described as the "first candidate ever placed in nomination for president by direct vote of [the] people" (*Who's Who in America,* 1903–05).

Soon after his marriage he settled on a farm near Springboro, living here until 1899 when he moved into Waynesville, where he died five years later as the result of a fall. He was a Quaker, an active church worker, and a leader in the prohibition movement. He was a ready and effective public speaker and had a remarkable memory for names, faces, and the personal interests of others. His large farm was well kept up, with a commodious brick house and good out-buildings. While not a wealthy man, he gave freely of his time, and often of his means, to the improvement of agriculture.

[L. H. Bailey, *Cyc. of Am. Agric.,* IV (1909), 568–69; *Appletons' Ann. Cyc.* (1899), p. 680, (1900), p. 710; Solon J. Buck, "The Granger Movement," *Harvard Hist. Studies,* XIX (1913), 54, 340; J. D. McCabe, *Hist. of the Grange Movement* (1873), pp. 537–38; *Twenty-Third Annual Report of Ohio Agric. Experiment Station* (1904), containing obituary with portrait; S. H. Ellis, "The Union Reform Party," the *Independent,* Oct. 11, 1900; *Cincinnati Enquirer,* June 24, 1904.]

F. E. H.

ELLSWORTH, ELMER EPHRAIM (Apr. 11, 1837–May 24, 1861), soldier, was born at Malta, N. Y., the son of Ephraim D. and Phœbe (Denton) Ellsworth. He attended the public schools at Mechanicsville, N. Y., hoping to enter West Point and follow a military career, but Mechanicsville was a small town and offered no educational advantages by which he could be prepared for the West Point examination, and the family could not afford to send him to a private academy. After leaving school he was employed as a dry-goods clerk. Later he went to New York and from there to Chicago where he was employed as a lawyer's clerk, studied law, and soon became a partner in a patent-soliciting business. Deeply interested in military matters, he secured command of a volunteer military company of cadets which was about to disband through lack of interest, and neglect, introduced the "Zouave" drill, and through his enthusiasm and energy brought the company to a high state of discipline and efficiency. The company was known as the "National Guard Cadets" of Chicago, later the "U. S. Zouave Cadets," and the members were bound to abstain from liquor, tobacco, profanity, and all excesses. The picturesque uniforms and excellent performances of the company soon attracted attention in Chicago, and immense crowds came to their drills. Ellsworth made a tour of the East with his company, giving exhibition drills which were largely attended, and the Zouaves and their commander became well known. He was appointed a major on the staff of Gen. Swift of the Illinois National Guard, and later colonel and assistant-general, and his company was appointed the governor's guards. Returning to Illinois from a tour of the East in

1860, he entered the law office of Abraham Lincoln in Springfield, as a law student, but devoted himself principally to the presidential campaign of that year. After the election, Ellsworth accompanied the President-Elect to Washington, and proposed the formation of a militia bureau, with himself as its chief. While he was awaiting the outcome of his proposals the Civil War broke out, and he hastened to New York and there recruited a regiment from the New York volunteer firemen, dressed them after the fashion of the French Zouaves, and drilled them in the manual of his original Zouave company. The regiment came to Washington, was mustered into the United States service, and was one of the first "three years" regiments of the war. On the occupation of Alexandria, May 24, 1861, Ellsworth saw the Confederate flag flying over the Marshall House and determined to remove it. Going to the roof, he tore down the flag with his own hands. As he descended the stairs with the flag in his arms, he was shot dead by the proprietor of the hotel, one James W. Jackson, who was in turn immediately shot by one of Ellsworth's escort. Ellsworth was young, handsome, and well-known, and his death, being the first of note to occur in the war, produced a profound sensation throughout the country. His body lay in state in the White House, was taken to New York City by special train, and from there escorted to Albany and Mechanicsville, where he was buried.

[See Chas. A. Ingraham, *Elmer E. Ellsworth and the Zouaves of '61* (1925); J. G. Nicolay, *The Outbreak of Rebellion* (1881); John Hay, in *Sunday Morning Chronicle* (Washington, D. C.), May 26, 1861, in the *Atlantic Monthly*, July 1861, and in *McClure's Mag.*, Mar. 1896; *N. Y. Herald*, May 25, 26, 27, 1861; *N. Y. Daily Tribune*, May 25, 26, 1861; N. Y. *World*, May 25, 27, 1861; H. H. Miller, *Reminiscences of Chicago During the Civil War* (1914). Ellsworth's name frequently appears as Ephraim Elmer, but is given as Elmer Ephraim in a manuscript account by his mother, in the N. Y. State Lib., Albany.] C. F. C.

ELLSWORTH, HENRY LEAVITT (Nov. 10, 1791–Dec. 27, 1858), agriculturist, first United States commissioner of patents, was born in Windsor, Conn., son of Chief Justice Oliver Ellsworth [*q.v.*] and Abigail (Wolcott) Ellsworth. He was a twin brother of William Wolcott Ellsworth [*q.v.*], later governor of Connecticut. After graduation from Yale in 1810 he studied law at the Litchfield Law School. In 1813 he married Nancy Allen Goodrich, daughter of Elizur Goodrich [*q.v.*] of New Haven, and settled in Windsor. He practised law and engaged also in agriculture, in which he early showed a special interest, serving as secretary of the Hartford County Agricultural Society in 1818. He moved to Hartford in June 1819, and from August 1819 to March 1821 was president of the Ætna Insurance Company. He became prominent in business and civic affairs, and in the improvement of real estate did much for the prosperity of Hartford. In 1832 he was appointed by President Jackson as commissioner to superintend the settlement of the Indian tribes transplanted to the south and west of Arkansas (for this report, see *House Report No. 474*, 23 Cong., 1 Sess., May 1834, pp. 78–103). On his way West in the same year he accidentally met Washington Irving, Charles Joseph Latrobe, and Count Pourtales, who were traveling together. All three decided to accompany Commissioner Ellsworth. It was thus that Irving obtained his material for *A Tour on the Prairies* (1835). The impressions of Latrobe are recorded in *The Rambler in North America* (1835), and those of Ellsworth in a manuscript letter to his wife, containing 116 pages, which letter is now in Yale University Library.

In April 1835 he was elected mayor of Hartford. He resigned, however, on June 15, having been appointed by President Jackson as United States commissioner of patents. He developed the business of the office in a remarkable manner. From the first he took a special interest in agriculture, and, largely through his influence, Congress was induced in 1839 to make an appropriation for the purpose of collecting and distributing seeds, prosecuting agricultural investigations, and procuring agricultural statistics. This was the first government appropriation for agriculture. Similar appropriations were made in 1842 and subsequent years. Since the Commissioner's annual reports were filled with information for the farmers of the country, the Patent Office by 1845 had assumed in many respects the function of an agricultural bureau, and Ellsworth is now frequently referred to as the "father of the Department of Agriculture." While serving as commissioner of patents he aided his friend Samuel F. B. Morse [*q.v.*] in obtaining the congressional appropriation of $30,000 to test the practicability of the telegraph. On Apr. 30, 1845, he resigned from the Patent Office, and subsequently established himself in Lafayette, Ind., as an agent for the purchase and settlement of public lands, becoming one of the largest landowners in the West. He was one of the earliest to foretell the value of the prairie lands and gave a great impulse to the agricultural operation of that region. (See his "Letter on the Cultivation of the Prairies, Jan. 1, 1837," appended to *Illinois in 1837*, 1837.) He also advocated the use of machinery in agriculture—an idea at that time considered chimerical. He probably used the first mowing-machine ever introduced upon the prairies. His principal writings were his official publications as commissioner of patents, particularly his annual reports, 1837–44, and *A Digest of Patents issued by the United States, 1790–1841* (2 vols., 1840–42).

His health failing, he returned to Connecticut in April 1858, and settled in Fair Haven, where he died a few months later. Of his three children by his first wife, the eldest was Henry William Ellsworth [*q.v.*]. Mrs. Ellsworth died, Jan. 14, 1847, and Ellsworth was married a second time, to Marietta Mariana Bartlett, who died Apr. 17, 1856. He next married Catherine Smith, who survived him. By his will his residuary estate in western lands was bequeathed to Yale University. He was a genial and affable man, of fine character, great public spirit, and vision, and with a deep love for humanity.

[F. B. Dexter, *Biog. Sketches Grads. Yale Coll.*, vol. VI (1912); H. R. Stiles, *The History and Genealogies of Ancient Windsor* (2nd ed., 2 vols., 1891–92), II, 219, 225; J. H. Trumbull, *The Memorial Hist. of Hartford County* (1886), I, 128, 385, 661–62; J. M. Swank, *The Dept. of Agric., its Hist. and Objects* (1872); U. S. Dept. of Agric., *Monthly Reports* for 1871, pp. 267–68; H. B. Learned, *The President's Cabinet* (1912), pp. 309–12, 316; Elmore Barce, *Annals of Benton County* (1925), I, 44–73; Ind. State Board of Agric., *Ann. Report*, 1852, pp. 218–20.] C. R. B.

ELLSWORTH, HENRY WILLIAM (Apr. 7, 1814–Aug. 14, 1864), lawyer, diplomat, was a grandson of Chief Justice Oliver Ellsworth [*q.v.*], and a son of Henry Leavitt Ellsworth [*q.v.*] and his wife, Nancy Allen Goodrich. Born at Windsor, Conn., where his father was practising law, he received his early education at the Ellington School at Windsor and at Hartford, Conn. In 1830 he proceeded to Yale, where he graduated in 1834, subsequently studying for a short time in the law school there. In 1836 he went to Lafayette, Tippecanoe County, Ind., in which neighborhood his father had acquired large tracts of land from the government. Opening a law office in Lafayette, the younger Ellsworth also became a member of the firm of Curtiss & Ellsworth, general land agents, specializing in Wabash and Maumee Valley lands, and, on his father's removal to Washington, D. C., to become commissioner of patents, assumed charge of the latter's extensive Western interests. In 1838 he published *Valley of the Upper Wabash, Indiana, with Hints on its Agricultural Advantages*, etc., embodying much information obtained from his father's papers, and this work, combined with his influential Eastern connections, helped to stimulate active interest in northwestern lands on the part of both speculators and bona fide settlers. He also wrote *The American Swine Breeder, a Practical Treatise on the Selection, Rearing and Fattening of Swine* (1840), and was an occasional contributor to the *Knickerbocker Magazine*. At the same time he participated in the political struggles of the time, was prominent among the supporters of Polk in the election campaign of 1844, and was a presidential elector in that year. On Apr. 19, 1845, he was appointed by President Polk chargé d'affaires to Sweden and Norway. The duties of this position he performed with ability for over four years, but his diplomatic career was brought to a close by an episode the implications of which are even to-day doubtful. Early in 1849 charges were made in the European and home press that in December 1848 Ellsworth had connived at an attempt to smuggle British goods into Sweden, and the facts disclosed in an *ex parte* investigation *prima facie* supported the allegation. In consequence Secretary of State Clayton recalled him as of Apr. 23, 1849, the "President believing that the public service requires a change in the Swedish mission." Ellsworth protested and vigorously defended himself, and a rather pathetic appeal was made to President Taylor by influential public men on his behalf, but in vain; and following a stern letter from Clayton his appointment was terminated July 25, 1849. On returning to the United States he resumed law practise at Lafayette and later at Indianapolis. A large circle of acquaintances evinced their unimpaired belief in his integrity, and he was retained by his father's intimate friend, S. F. B. Morse [*q.v.*], in the actions which Morse took to protect his patent rights. His health, never good, broke down, and he was compelled to relinquish his practise, retiring to New Haven, Conn., where he died at the early age of fifty. He was married, on Jan. 11, 1844, to Mary E. West of Salem, Mass.

[H. R. Stiles, *History and Genealogies of Ancient Windsor*, II (1892), 208, 225, 229; *Hist. of the Class of 1834 in Yale Coll., with Biog. Sketches* (1875), p. 54, unreliable in some particulars; Files and Records, Dept. of State, Washington, D. C.; *Morning Jour. and Courier* (New Haven, Conn.), Aug. 15, 1864.] H. W. H. K.

ELLSWORTH, OLIVER (Apr. 29, 1745–Nov. 26, 1807), statesman, chief justice, the second son of Capt. David and Jemima (Leavitt) Ellsworth, was born in Windsor, Conn., to which town his great-grandfather Josiah Ellsworth had come from Yorkshire, England, about the middle of the seventeenth century. Of his childhood practically nothing of certainty is known. His father, who had set his heart upon Oliver's becoming a minister, gave him the best that the time had to offer in the way of an education. Prepared for college by the Rev. Joseph Bellamy of Bethlehem, he entered Yale in 1762, only to leave that institution for Princeton at the end of his sophomore year. Tradition has perpetuated many stories to account for his leaving Yale, some of which would indicate that his departure was not altogether voluntary; the one sure bit of information concerning it is found in President Clap's journal (July 27, 1764), "Oliver Ellsworth and Waightstill Avery, at the desire of their respective parents, were dismissed from being members of this college" (Brown, *post,* p. 16). Whatever the cause of the episode, it apparently produced no permanent ill-feeling. All of Ellsworth's sons who grew up were graduated from Yale, he himself was afterwards a fellow of the corporation, and in 1790 the college conferred upon him the degree of LL.D.—as did Princeton and Dartmouth in 1797. After two years at Princeton, Oliver, now a B.A., returned home and took up the study of theology with the Rev. John Smalley of New Britain. This study did not long continue, however, for within a year he turned to law. For the next four years he studied that subject, doing some teaching in the interval, and being admitted to the bar in 1771. The following year he married Abigail Wolcott of East Windsor.

Legal business came to him so slowly at first that he found it necessary to support himself by farming and even wood-chopping, financial aid from his father apparently having ceased when he definitely gave up fitting himself for the ministry. Too poor to keep a horse, on days when the court was sitting he was forced to walk from his farm to Hartford and back, a round trip of twenty miles. During the first three years of his practise the returns from his profession, by his own admission, amounted to only three pounds Connecticut currency per annum (Henry Flanders, *The Lives and Times of the Chief Justices,* 1858, 2 ser., p. 62). In 1775, after having already represented Windsor in the General Assembly, he removed to Hartford. From this time his rise at the bar was exceptionally rapid. Noah Webster, who in 1779 came to Ellsworth's office to study law, said that he then had usually from one thousand to fifteen hundred cases on his list, and that there was hardly a case tried in which Ellsworth did not represent one side or the other. This large practise, coupled with the general success of his advocacy, brought him recognition as one of the leaders of the Connecticut bar, and enabled him to lay the foundation of what, by shrewd and careful management, became a large fortune. His position made it inevitable that he should be connected with the courts of his state in ways other than merely as a lawyer. He was appointed state's attorney for Hartford County in 1777, and three years later became a member of the Governor's Council. In 1784 this Council was constituted a supreme court of errors of which Ellsworth, by virtue of his office, became one of the judges. Shortly thereafter he was made a judge of the superior court, in which position he continued to serve for the next four years, his resignation from the Council and the office of state's attorney taking place in 1785. It is indicative of the high regard in which he continued to hold the judicial offices of his native state, that after his return from France, he should have been willing again to accept a place on the Governor's Council, and that in the last year of his life, after having already been chief justice of the United States, he should have consented to act as the first chief justice of the new state supreme court of appeals—a consent which ill health forced him to withdraw before he had ever actually entered upon the duties of the office.

Ellsworth was connected with the revolutionary activities of his state almost from the beginning. Shortly after the outbreak of open hostilities in Massachusetts, Connecticut had instituted her Committee of the Pay Table, a commission of five to supervise the expenditures rendered necessary by the state's war measures. Ellsworth was one of the five. Early in 1776 he was sent to Gen. Washington at Cambridge to seek repayment of the money Connecticut had advanced to her men in the Continental Army; later in the same year he was intrusted with a similar mission to Gen. Schuyler in an attempt to recover other moneys which the state had paid to troops employed in Canada. In 1779 he was chosen a member of the important Council of Safety which, with the governor, was in practical control of all military measures. As early as 1777 the General Assembly had appointed him one of the delegates to represent the state in the Continental Congress; chosen annually, he continued to serve in that capacity for six years, declining a further appointment in 1783. Long before he had even started for Philadelphia, Congress had made him one of a committee of five to investigate the failure of the Rhode Island expedition. The day after he took his seat in Congress (Oct. 8, 1778) he was named a member of the committee on marine affairs. Hardly more than two weeks later he was appointed to the committee on appeals, which listened to appeals brought from the Admiralty courts of the various states, and which "was always composed of the ablest lawyers in the House" (Van Santvoord, *post,* p. 202). Ellsworth became a member of the committee just in time to sit upon the hearing of the appeal in the noted case of Gideon Olmstead and the British sloop *Active*. Details of his activity in the Congress are obscure. In a general way we know that he was a hard worker, able and conscientious, and that he continued to serve on one committee or another as long as his term lasted. Thus in 1780 he was on the committee appointed to consider the best method of carrying out Washington's plan of supplying the army by requisitions of specific articles laid on the different states. With Hamilton and Madison for colleagues he served on two committees, one of which was concerned with the matter of neutrality agreements, and the other of which was so broad in its scope that its work practically amounted to a consideration of a permanent system of administration. Towards the end of his last term, when the unpaid and mutinous soldiers surrounded the building in which the Congress was sitting, he served with Hamilton and Peters on the committee sent by that body to urge upon the executive council of Pennsylvania the calling out of the state militia.

When Connecticut finally decided to send delegates to the Constitutional Convention, Ellsworth, Roger Sherman, and William S. Johnson were selected to represent the state. The part played by this delegation as a whole in the business of the Convention, especially in the matter of the so-called "Connecticut compromise," is clear enough; the exact influence and importance of the individual members is not so clear. By one writer or another each of the three delegates has been given the credit for having brought about the compromise. Ellsworth's motion that "the rule of suffrage in the 2nd branch be the same with that established by the articles of confederation" (Farrand, *post,* I, 468), undoubtedly started the discussion that preceded the compromise, and during the debate he seems to have borne the brunt of the attack of the large-state men; but the accuracy of the statement that "to the resulute efforts and persevering energy of Oliver Ellsworth, more than to any other man in the Convention, is the country indebted for the final compromise of the Constitution which gave to each state an equality of representation in the Senate" (Van Santvoord, *post,* pp. 226–27), may well be questioned. Though it is extremely difficult to gauge the influence of Ellsworth or of any other one man in the Convention, he unquestionably took an active part. His amendment to substitute the words "United States" for the word "national" in a certain resolution then under consideration (G. Hunt and J. B. Scott, *The Debates in the Federal Convention of 1787,* 1920, 131–32) seems to have fixed the title which was thereafter used in the Convention to designate the government. He objected to the payment of representatives out of the federal treasury and proposed payment by the states. He favored the three-fifths ratio in counting slaves as a basis of both taxation and representation; strangely enough, also, he stood out against the abolition of the foreign slave-trade. He was one of the committee of five, of which Rutledge was the chairman, which prepared for the Convention the first official draft of a constitution. His work for the new Constitution did not end at Philadelphia. In the convention which met at Hartford in January 1788 to consider its acceptance or rejection by Connecticut, he spared no effort in explaining it and urging its adoption. His "Letters of a Landholder," printed in the *Connecticut Courant* and the *American Mercury* (November 1787–March 1788) and widely circulated, were written with the same object of ratification in view.

Chosen by Connecticut as one of its first two senators under the Constitution, he represented his state in the United States Senate for a period of seven years, resigning from that body in the spring of 1796 after he had been appointed chief justice. It was in the Senate that the capabilities of Ellsworth appeared to their best advantage. For the work of organization and of practical detail made necessary by the newness of the government, he seems to have been peculiarly fitted. There can be no question as to the predominant position he enjoyed in the Senate; meager as the details are, they are sufficient to show him as an outstanding figure. A hundred years later the memory of his prestige was still alive in Senate traditions—"If we may trust the traditions that have come down from the time of the Administrations of Washington and Adams, when the Senate sat with closed doors, none of them [Webster, Clay, Calhoun] ever acquired the authority wielded by the profound sagacity of Ellsworth" (G. F. Hoar, *Autobiography of Seventy Years,* 1903, vol. II, p. 45). Among other things he reported the first set of Senate rules and considered a plan for printing the journals; he reported back from conference the first twelve amendments to the Constitution which Congress submitted to the states; he framed the measure which admitted North Carolina, and devised the non-intercourse act that forced Rhode Island into the Union; he reported a bill for the government of the territory of the United States south of the Ohio; he drew up the first bill regulating the consular service; he was on the committees to which were referred Hamilton's plans for funding the national debt and for the incorporation of a bank of the United States, both of which he vigorously seconded. Undoubtedly his most important single piece of work was done in connection with his chairmanship of the committee appointed to bring in a bill organizing the federal judiciary. "That the Judiciary Bill which came from this Committee was, to a large extent, drafted by Ellsworth is now well established" (Warren, *post,* p. 59). Sections 10 to 23 of the original draft bill are in his handwriting; Maclay of Pennsylvania, himself one of the committee, records that "this vile bill is a child of his, and he defends it with the care of a parent" (E. S. Maclay, *The Journal of William Maclay,* 1890, pp. 91–92); Madison also, in two different letters, assigns it to Ellsworth (*Letters and Other Writings of James Madison,* vol. IV, 1865, pp. 220–21, 428). All in all, his work in the Senate made him, as John Adams later said, "the firmest pillar of his [Washington's] whole administration" (C. F. Adams, *The Works of John Adams,* vol. X, 1856, p. 112).

Ellsworth was commissioned chief justice of the United States (Mar. 4, 1796) after the Senate had refused to confirm the previous appointment of Rutledge, and after Cushing, the senior associate judge, had declined the honor. For about three years and a half he was actively engaged in the duties of his office, which at that time included the arduous task of riding the federal circuits. His short term of office, coupled with the fact that he was immediately followed by the great Marshall, has been advanced by some of his biographers as the reason for his failure to take a higher rank among the chief justices. The real reason would seem to lie elsewhere. Our available sources of information unite in presenting him as a great lawyer; but neither his reported opinions nor the weight of other evidence justify us in calling him a great judge. His decisions, neither many nor long as they have come down to us, are marked by strong common sense, but hardly by great legal learning. He himself seems to have been conscious of his lack of this latter quality, as also of the inadequacy of his previous training and preparation for his new position, and "he accordingly took a severe course of study and reading" (Brown, *post,* p. 242). He was primarily the advocate rather than the jurist, a champion of the cause he happened to be supporting. This characteristic, which undoubtedly contributed much to his success at the bar, and which showed to very great advantage in his work in the Congress, in the Convention, and in the Senate, could hardly be brought to bear in purely judicial business.

The last notable public service that Ellsworth performed was as commissioner to France in 1799–1800. The mission began inauspiciously, and resulted in no more than partial success. There was decided opposition to it at home because of the harsh treatment which France had recently accorded Pinckney and his associates. Ellsworth, even if he did not share the popular resentment, at least manifested no enthusiasm towards President Adams's new attempt to come to an understanding with France. Reluctantly, and merely "from the necessity of preventing a greater evil," he accepted his commission (February 1799); yet he dreaded the mission and did what he could to postpone it. Consequently it was not until Nov. 3 that he and his colleague William R. Davie [*q.v.*] left Newport on the frigate *United States,* to join William Vans Murray [*q.v.*] in France. After a boisterous passage of more than three weeks they put into Lisbon, rested there a fortnight, and then again set sail, only to be driven off their course by storms and obliged to land near Corunna in Spain. Thence they proceeded overland to Paris, which they did not reach until Mar. 2, 1800. The hardships suffered by Ellsworth during these four months permanently affected his health (Geo. Gibbs, *Memoirs of the Administrations of Washington and John Adams,* 1846, II, 434). It was thought by some of his friends in America that his mind also had been impaired by his physical breakdown, and that this was the reason why no better terms were secured in the French convention (*Ibid.,* pp. 460, 461, 463). After protracted negotiations with Napoleon which lasted into October, the American ministers were obliged to accept an agreement which conformed to neither their earlier hopes nor their instructions. Ellsworth himself was far from satisfied with it, though he regarded it as sufficient in that it kept the United States out of a not improbable war with France (*Ibid.,* p. 463). When Davie and Oliver Ellsworth, Jr., who had been his father's secretary at Paris, and who now bore the latter's resignation of his office of chief justice, left England for America toward the end of October, Ellsworth himself was unable to accompany them. Through the winter he remained in England, traveling by easy stages from place to place, and making an ineffectual effort to regain his health. He left England in March, landed at Boston, where he rested for a few days, and then proceeded to his home in Windsor and, as far as national affairs were concerned, into retirement.

Timothy Dwight describes Ellsworth as "tall, dignified, and commanding" (*Travels; in New-England and New York,* vol. I, 1821, p. 302). "He was particular as to his personal appearance, and never hurried at his toilet" (H. R. Stiles, *History and Genealogies of Ancient Windsor,* vol.

II, 1892, p. 217). By the judgment of his fellows he was a good, and at times a brilliant, conversationalist; yet unlike almost all of his contemporaries in similar stations he was not given to voluminous correspondence. He had an insistent habit of talking to himself, even in the presence of others. His one vice was the taking of snuff, a practise to which he was greatly addicted. It is related by his daughter that "when he was more than ordinarily engaged in thinking, or in writing, he would take out his box at frequent intervals and go through the form of taking a pinch, and would then drop most of the snuff in little piles on the carpet near him. His family sometimes judged of the intensity and depth of his meditations by the number of these piles of snuff around his chair" (*Ibid.*, p. 218). Naturally moderate and conservative, he nevertheless at times manifested a tenacity of purpose that bordered on obstinacy. Aaron Burr said of him, "If Ellsworth had happened to spell the name of the Deity with two d's, it would have taken the Senate three weeks to expunge the superfluous letter" (Brown, *post*, p. 225). Deeply religious, he was throughout his life not only active in the work of his own (Congregational) church, but he also kept up a lively intellectual interest in religious and theological questions, to the study of which he turned more and more after his retirement. He had always been free from the bigotry of Puritan New England; his sufferings and illness did not make him an ascetic. In his very last years, after he had "begun to die" as he wrote one of his friends, agriculture as well as theology occupied his mind, and he published regularly in the *Connecticut Courant* the "Farmer's Repository," a very practical column on agricultural topics. He was a politician as well as a statesman, and at times was not averse to using the methods of politicians to accomplish his purposes. It is on this basis that his seeming connection with an alleged plot to break up the Union can be explained (G. Hunt, *Disunion Sentiment in Congress in 1794*, 1905; Brown, *post*, pp. 228–30).

[In addition to the works already named, see Wm. G. Brown, *The Life of Oliver Ellsworth* (1905); G. Van Santvoord, *Sketches of the Lives and Judicial Services of the Chief-Justices* (1845); Max Farrand, ed., *The Records of the Federal Convention of 1787* (3 vols., 1911); Charles Warren, "New Light on the History of the Federal Judiciary Act of 1789," in *Harvard Law Rev.*, Nov. 1923. In the letters, diaries, autobiographies and other writings of many of the contemporary statesmen there is much scattered material on Ellsworth. A number of his own unpublished letters and papers are in existence, some in the N. Y. Pub. Lib., and others in the possession of several of his descendants. A list of these descendants with their addresses will be found in *A Memorial of the Opening of the Ellsworth Homestead*, a booklet issued by the Connecticut D. A. R. in 1907. The printed decisions of Ellsworth are in Kirby, *Conn. Reports*, and in Dallas, *U. S. Reports*.] G. E. W.

ELLSWORTH, WILLIAM WOLCOTT (Nov. 10, 1791–Jan. 15, 1868), lawyer, congressman, governor, was the son of Oliver Ellsworth [*q.v.*], the second chief justice of the United States, and the twin brother of Henry Leavitt Ellsworth [*q.v.*]. He attended Yale College, graduating with honors in 1810. He then entered the Litchfield Law School conducted by Judges Reeve and Gould. Completing his studies there, he moved to Hartford, where he entered the law office of Judge Thomas Scott Williams. He applied himself industriously to his work, and is reported to have kept himself well informed on the most recent decisions of American and English law. In 1813 he was admitted to the Hartford bar. Four years later, when Judge Williams was sent to Congress, Ellsworth was given charge of his superior's law office. From 1829 to 1834 Ellsworth himself was a member of Congress from Connecticut. He might have enjoyed a longer term in Washington, but he resigned the legislative position of his own accord, it is said, in order to return to law practise. While in Congress he served on the judiciary committee, and as a member of that body was active in preparing measures to carry into effect Jackson's plan for resisting South Carolina nullification. In political sentiments, Ellsworth was an enthusiastic Whig. He favored a protective tariff, and government aid for internal improvements. Reëntering active politics as governor of Connecticut in 1838, he served four successive years. His administration coincided with the beginning of railroad transportation in the state, and in his messages to the legislature, he strove to encourage the further development of railroads and manufactures. He also favored the extension of banks, and state aid for the improvement of schools. Although advocating numerous progressive measures, he was essentially a conservative politician. "The time has come," he declared in 1838, "when experiments upon our dearest interests are no longer to be tolerated; and when experience, that great and unerring teacher in human affairs, is to resume her influence, and put to silence visionary politicians" (*Hartford Courant*, May 5, 1838). After his period of service as governor, Ellsworth again resumed his law practise. In 1847 he was made an associate judge of the state supreme court, which position he held until obliged, because of old age, to retire in 1861. In personal appearance Ellsworth was tall and graceful, and dignified in manner. His portrait, in the state library at Hartford, suggests to the observer an embodiment of a typical

Connecticut Yankee, equally able to trade horses, make a political speech, and offer prayer. Throughout his public career, Ellsworth was in much demand as a speaker. To innumerable political rallies in the forties he poured forth that type of blustering oratory so dear to middle nineteenth-century audiences. He was for forty-seven years deacon in the Hartford Centre Church, and an intimate friend of the popular preacher of the time, Joel Hawes. He was also active in aiding philanthropic institutions, especially the American Asylum for the Deaf and Dumb, and the Hartford Retreat for the Insane. By no means a great man, Ellsworth was successful in a moderate way. He always enjoyed general confidence and respect. He was married on Sept. 14, 1813, to Emily, eldest daughter of the lexicographer Noah Webster.

[F. B. Dexter, *Biog. Sketches of the Grads. of Yale Coll., 1805–1815,* VI (1912), 312–15; F. C. Norton, *The Governors of Conn.* (1905); Dwight Loomis and J. G. Calhoun, *Judicial and Civil Hist. of Conn.* (1895); J. H. Trumbull, ed., *Memorial Hist. of Hartford County, Conn.* (1886), vol. II; 34 *Conn.*, App. (1868).]

J. M. M.

ELMER, EBENEZER (Aug. 23, 1752–Oct. 18, 1843), doctor, soldier, legislator, younger brother of Jonathan [*q.v.*] and father of Lucius Quintius Cincinnatus Elmer [*q.v.*], was the fifth son of Daniel and Abigail (Lawrence) Elmer, of Cedarville, Cumberland County, N. J. His Puritan ancestor, Edward Elmer, came to Cambridge, Mass., in 1632, with Rev. Thomas Hooker's party, and moved in 1636 to Hartford, Conn. There his grandson was born, the Rev. Daniel Elmer, who with his son Daniel came to New Jersey in 1727. After his father's death, Ebenezer helped his mother on the farm, worked aboard shallops in the river trade, had a quarter's schooling in arithmetic under the celebrated teacher, Norbury, and studied seamanship with John Westcott at "Bridge-Town." When he was twenty-one his brother Jonathan began tutoring him in medicine. In two years he had gone through "all the branches usually taught at any medical school" (Elmer, *post,* p. 49). Meanwhile he gave medical aid during the smallpox and dysentery epidemics of 1775. On Feb. 8, 1776, as ensign under Capt. Joseph Bloomfield [*q.v.*], 3rd New Jersey Regiment, he helped recruit the company, and went with the expedition to salvage the attack on Canada. The diary which he kept from Mar. 22, 1776, to May 25, 1777, and thereafter at intervals through the Revolution, gives evidence of his endurance, devotion to duty, shrewd observation, and sincere religious feeling. He was promoted lieutenant Apr. 9, 1776; surgeon's mate Apr. 1, 1777; and surgeon of the 2nd New Jersey Regiment July 5, 1778, acting as such to Nov. 3, 1783. He served at Chadd's Ford, Germantown, Valley Forge, Monmouth, on Sullivan's Indian expedition, at Morristown, Peekskill, and Yorktown. He was one of the founders of the Society of the Cincinnati, and for many years the president of the New Jersey organization.

In 1784 he married Hannah Seeley, a younger sister of his brother Jonathan's wife, and settled down to the practise of medicine at Bridgeton. He was a member of the New Jersey Assembly during the years of 1789–91, 1793–95, 1817 and 1819, serving as speaker in 1791, 1795, and 1817. In the interval between his earlier and later services he sat in the House of Representatives, from 1801 to 1807, as a Jefferson man. His *Address to the Citizens of New Jersey* (1807) is an interesting summary of current politics.

He was a member and vice-president of the state Council in 1807; collector of the port at Bridgeton 1808–17, 1822–32; and in 1814 commanded the brigade stationed at Billingsport to defend the Philadelphia district. Though he did not join the Presbyterian Church until 1825, he founded the first local Sunday-school and was for many years president of the Bible society. He lost his sight about 1840, and died of old age some three years later.

[L. Q. C. Elmer, *Geneal. and Biog. of the Elmer Family* (1860); J. W. Barber and H. Howe, *Hist. Colls. of N. J.* (1868); R. S. Field, *Provincial Courts of N. J.* (N. J. Hist. Soc., 1849); F. B. Lee, *N. J. as a Colony and as a State,* vols. II and III (1902); S. Wickes, *Hist. of Medicine in N. J.* (1879); L. Q. C. Elmer, *The Constitution and Government of the Province and State of N. J., with . . . Reminiscences of the Bench and Bar* (N. J. Hist. Soc., 1872); *Chronicle* (Bridgeton, N. J.), Oct. 21, 1843.]

W. L. W—y.

ELMER, JONATHAN (Nov. 29, 1745–Sept. 3, 1817), physician, legislator, jurist, was the elder brother of Ebenezer Elmer [*q.v.*], and third son of Daniel and Abigail (Lawrence) Elmer of Cedarville, N. J. Because of his frail constitution, his parents decided to give him a good education. He was privately taught, learned Latin and French, and by 1766 began studying medicine at the University of Pennsylvania. He received his Bachelor of Medicine degree in 1768 on a printed thesis "De sitis in Febribus, Causis et Remediis," dedicated to the two Franklins. This, with papers on the theory of the eye, the motion of the heart, and the relations of the air to disease, brought him membership in the American Philosophical Society by 1772. Dr. Benjamin Rush is quoted as saying that in medical knowledge he was exceeded by no physician in the United States (Trenton *Federalist,* Sept. 1817). He was a member of the New Jersey

Medical Society in 1772, and president in 1787. He practised in Roadstown, then at Bridgeton, but preferring "political and judicial business," he became sheriff of Cumberland County in 1772. Two years later he was a member of a local vigilance committee when his brother Ebenezer and others were held for having burned tea taken from the brig *Greyhound.* He drew a Whig grand jury, in May 1775, with their elder brother Daniel Elmer as foreman, and the case was dropped.

He attended the Provincial Congress of New Jersey in the sessions from May to October 1775, and was succeeded by his uncle Theophilus. He was actively interested in organizing local militia and in December 1775, became the head of a Bridgeton association which published a patriotic news-letter, the *Plain Dealer,* of which eight numbers are preserved. Incidentally, he was successively captain and major of a light-infantry company, but was not in active service. He was clerk of Cumberland County for the years 1776–79, 1781, and 1786–89. Appointed a delegate to the Continental Congress on Nov. 30, 1776, he attended the sessions in Baltimore, Philadelphia, Lancaster, and York. He was a member of the Board of Treasury and of the medical committee, and in the latter capacity inspected hospitals in New Jersey and Pennsylvania. His patriotic speeches were widely circulated. He was reappointed to Congress, but complained that the delegates could not exist on their pay. Resigning in September 1778, he returned to his family affairs. He resumed public office, however, serving in the New Jersey council in 1780, in the Congress of the Confederation from 1781 to 1784, and again in the council in 1784. He was surrogate of Cumberland County from 1784 to 1802. As a member of the Congress of the Confederation in 1787–88 he worked zealously for the federal Constitution. He was a warm supporter of Washington and Federalism, and on his election to the first Congress under the Constitution, voted steadily for Hamilton's financial measures. As a representative of the State of New Jersey, he supported the interests of the smaller states under federal union. Maclay wrote, Sept. 3, 1789, "I know not in the Senate a man, if I were to choose a friend, on whom I would cast the eye of confidence as soon as on this little doctor" (*Journal, post,* p. 144). Later, on differing with him as to the location of the capital he amended his former impression with the entry, "I had a good opinion of Elmer once, it is with pain I retract it" (*Ibid.,* p. 389). By voting for the measure to establish the capital on the Potomac, Elmer lost the support of his constituents, and in 1791 was succeeded by John Rutherford; he had drawn a two-year term. In addition to his other activities, he mastered real estate law and prepared himself to revise the New Jersey statutes, a work done by William Paterson [*q.v.*]. He was a member of the 1812 convention which nominated DeWitt Clinton against Madison, and opposed war with Great Britain. Reëlected surrogate in the Federalist revival of 1813 he bade farewell to the court in February 1814, after forty-two years' participation in public life. He held a seat in the Presbyterian church from the time of his marriage to Mary Seeley in 1769, became a member in 1798, served as ruling elder, and finally as delegate to the Presbytery and to the General Assembly. As a student Elmer was diligent and laborious; in person he was formal and stately. He accumulated a very handsome fortune.

[L. Q. C. Elmer, *Geneal. and Biog. of the Elmer Family* (1860); Stephen Wickes, *Hist. of Medicine in N. J.* (1879); F. B. Lee, *N. J. as a Colony and as a State,* III (1902), 52; *Jour. of William Maclay* (1927); *N. J. Medic. Reporter,* I (1884), 133–36; *Gen. Cat. of the Univ. of Pa.* (1922); *Poulson's Am. Daily Advertiser,* Sept. 12, 1817.]

W. L. W—y.

ELMER, LUCIUS QUINTIUS CINCINNATUS (Feb. 3, 1793–Mar. 11, 1883), jurist and legislator, was the only son of Ebenezer [*q.v.*] and Hannah (Seeley) Elmer. After "a good academic education" and one term at the University of Pennsylvania, he studied law for five years with his cousin, Daniel Elmer. He was licensed as an attorney in 1815 and as counsellor in 1818. He married on Oct. 6, 1818, Catharine Hay of Philadelphia. Elected to the Assembly as an independent Democrat in 1820, he served four sessions, was speaker in 1823, and acted also as chairman of the commission delegated to locate a route, and estimate costs and revenues for the Delaware-Raritan canal project. Their report, written by him, favored either state construction or participation, but the project was privately carried out later by Commodore R. F. Stockton [*q.v.*]. In 1824 President Monroe appointed him United States District Attorney for New Jersey. He served with great credit and won the especial confidence of Judge Bushrod Washington [*q.v.*]. As an Adams Democrat, he was superseded in 1829 by Garret Dorset Wall, whose life he later sketched. Simultaneously, from 1824 to 1834, he was prosecutor of the pleas for Cape May and Cumberland counties, and served on the two commissions, in 1824 and 1833, which ended the Hudson River boundary dispute with New York state.

Maintaining his private practise, he published in 1838 a digest of state laws, with notes of related judicial decisions, followed the next year by a volume of legal forms. In the latter year he also served on the joint legislative committee which studied the care of idiotic and insane persons and recommended the asylum system in which New Jersey has since been a leading state (Lee, *post*, III, 292–93). As Democratic congressional candidate in 1842 he upset a previous Whig majority of 1,200 in his district. In the House he became chairman of the committee on elections and submitted their report regarding members elected by general district (see *Congressional Globe*, 28 Cong., 1 Sess., App., pp. 126–30). He also took a stand against the Dorr constitution in Rhode Island (*Ibid.*, 28 Cong., 2 Sess., App., pp. 260–63) which was later advocated by Webster and sustained by the Supreme Court in *Luther* vs. *Borden* (7 *Howard*, 1). On the tariff question he yielded, against his own belief, to the convictions of his constituents and helped defeat the amendments proposed in 1844. Failing of reëlection, he declined to take further part in politics. He served as attorney-general of New Jersey, 1850–52, resigning to become justice of the state supreme court. In this capacity he served for two seven-year periods, 1852–59 and 1862–69, with an *ad interim* appointment in 1861. He then retired from public office—save for his membership on the local board of education—having served almost continuously for forty years.

Elmer was a member of various societies and made numerous addresses before educational and other bodies. He was tireless in charitable, temperance, and church matters, though never able to accept Presbyterian standards in their entirety. He kept abreast of his times in history, government, theology, and science, and was deeply learned in the origins and principles of the law, especially as to land tenures. His opinions were models of terse, vigorous reasoning, strictly limited to the case in hand. His writings include a genealogy of the Elmer family, a history of Cumberland County, N. J., and his *magnum opus, The Constitution and Government of the Province and State of New Jersey, with Biographical Sketches of the Governors . . . and Reminiscences of the Bench and Bar,* published by the New Jersey Historical Society in 1872. Elmer was a calm, dignified man, sometimes cold and severe, but always admired for his integrity. He was happy alike in his family life, his public service, and the mastery of his profession.

[L. Q. C. Elmer, *Geneal. and Biog. of the Elmer Family* (1860); *Proc. N. J. Hist. Soc.*, 2 ser., VIII (1885), 25–45; F. B. Lee, *N. J. as a Colony and as a State,* III (1902).]

W. L. W—y.

ELMORE, FRANKLIN HARPER (Oct. 15, 1799–May 29, 1850), banker, senator, was born in Laurens District, S. C. His father was John Archer Elmore, a native of Virginia, who came to South Carolina in General Greene's army and remained there. His mother was Sarah Saxon. Franklin entered South Carolina College in 1817, and was graduated in 1819. Studying law under Andrew P. Butler, he was admitted to the bar in 1821 and began practise at Walterboro. Becoming solicitor the following year, he served until 1836. During this period he was a member of the governor's staff, a colonel of militia, and a trustee of South Carolina College. While not particularly active in the nullification controversy, he was a supporter of the movement and was a member of the nullification convention, being then and thereafter a devoted disciple of Calhoun. In 1836 he was elected to Congress to succeed James H. Hammond who had resigned. He took his seat December 19, and served to Mar. 4, 1839. In the House he was a consistent defender of slavery and during the time of his service, as a representative of the South Carolina delegation, he wrote to James G. Birney a series of letters of inquiry concerning the abolition movement which with Birney's replies were published in 1838 in *The Anti-Slavery Examiner* (No. 8). He favored the annexation of Texas and advocated federal aid to Southern railroads, in the development of which he was greatly interested.

In 1839 he was elected president of the bank of the state and thereafter made his home in Charleston. Under his management the bank was greatly strengthened and enlarged, and Elmore's skilful defense of it both in his personal contacts and in a series of letters addressed to the people of the state probably saved it from destruction by the group of its opponents led by C. G. Memminger. In his appeal to the people appears his deep interest in the development of the state through the building of railroads, the improvement of agriculture, and the establishment of industries. He himself was not only active in the construction of railroads, but he also developed the iron mines at Cherokee Ford and Limestone Springs.

He never lost interest in politics. In 1844 he was elected a delegate to the Baltimore convention of the Democratic party as a supporter of Calhoun, but discovering the hopelessness of his cause, did not take his seat. He supported Polk, however, who had been a close personal and political friend since their service in the House together, and was by him offered the post of minister to Great Britain which he declined. In 1850 he was appointed to the United States Senate to succeed Calhoun. He took his seat and made one brief speech, but died twenty-eight days from his admission. He is buried in Columbia, S. C.

Elmore was successful as a lawyer, in politics, and in business. He was a good judge of men, and a tactful and adroit manager of them. He loved politics but cared nothing for public office, finding his pleasure in playing and influencing the course of the game. He married Harriet Chesnut, the daughter of Gov. John Taylor of South Carolina.

[Elmore Papers in Lib. of Cong.; J. B. O'Neall, *Biog. Sketches of the Bench and Bar of S. C.* (1859), vol. II; *Diary of James K. Polk* (3 vols., 1910); *Memoirs of John Quincy Adams* (1874–77).] J. G. de R. H.

ELSBERG, LOUIS (Apr. 2, 1836–Feb. 19, 1885), laryngologist, was born at Iserlohn, Prussia, the son of Nathan and Adelaide Elsberg. Brought to Philadelphia by his parents in 1849, he graduated with honor at the high school in 1852; and after two years' experience as teacher in an academy at Winchester, Va., began the study of medicine at Jefferson Medical College, from which he received his degree in 1857. Moving to New York City, he held for a time the position of resident physician at the Mt. Sinai Hospital, in 1859 was one of the editors of the *North American Medical Reporter,* and then went to Europe for postgraduate study. He was fortunate in being a member of the first instruction class of Professor Czermak of Vienna in the then new art of laryngoscopy upon which is based the practise of laryngology. His fellow members, Störck, Türck, Lewin, and Semeleder, all, like himself, became eminent as pioneers. Upon his return to the United States he settled in New York and joined the faculty of the Medical Department of the University of the City of New York, holding the first course of lectures on diseases of the throat in 1861 and conducting the first public clinic for the same in the year following. In 1865 his essay, *Laryngoscopal Surgery Illustrated in the Treatment of Morbid Growths within the Larynx,* published the following year, was awarded a gold medal by the American Medical Association as an epoch-making contribution to a new subject. His other writings include two booklets and numerous reprints of magazine contributions. The first-named are: *Laryngoscopical Medication,* etc. (1864); and *The Throat and Its Functions,* etc. (1880; 2nd ed., 1882). Of reprinted articles the most compendious are: *Neuroses of Sensation,* etc. (1882); *Structure of Hyaline Cartilage* (1881–82); *On Angioma of the Larynx* (1884); *Pneumatometry,* etc. (1875); *Connection of Throat with Other Diseases* (1870). His most important contribution to general science was *Regeneration, or the Preservation of the Organic Molecules,* etc. (1874, reprinted from the *Proceedings of the American Association for the Advancement of Science, 23rd Meeting,* 1874, pt. B, pp. 88–103). His death prevented the completion of a textbook on laryngology.

Elsberg's technical knowledge of music naturally made him the pioneer medical attendant and consultant of opera singers and other high-salaried voice-users; thus he developed a specialty within a specialty. He was equally prominent as a teacher and inspirer of laryngologists. His avocations were biology and microscopy and he read several papers before general scientific bodies; even late in his career he found time to work enthusiastically in the elder Heitzmann's pathological laboratory collaborating in the composition of the latter's *Microscopical Morphology in Health and Disease.* In June 1878 he founded the American Laryngological Association and was elected its first president, but in the following year, as the result of his first breakdown in health, was obliged to forward his presidential address from Aix-la-Chapelle. In 1880 he founded a quarterly, the *Archives of Laryngology,* which he conducted during 1880–82. He applied himself so unremittingly to his manifold activities that his health again suffered, and, although for a time he continued to work on, he succumbed to pneumonia in the forty-ninth year of his age. His wife, whom he married in 1876, was Mary Van Hagen Scoville.

[M. H. Henry, *Life of Louis Elsberg* (1890), written and circulated for the N. Y. Academy of Medicine; obituary notices in *Boston Medic. and Surgic. Jour.,* Feb. 26, 1885; *N. Y. Medic. Jour.,* Feb. 28, 1885; *New Eng. Medic. Monthly,* V (1885–86), 150; *Trans. Medic. Soc. State of N. Y.* (1886), pp. 601–08; *N. Y. Times, N. Y. Tribune,* Feb. 20, 1885.] E. P.

ELSON, LOUIS CHARLES (Apr. 17, 1848–Feb. 14, 1920), music critic, lecturer, author, and teacher, was born in Boston, the son of Julius and Rosalie (Schnell) Elson. He was educated in the public schools of Boston and received his first lessons (in piano) from his mother, studying later with August Kreissmann and Carl Gloggner-Castelli of Leipzig. His first professional activity was in the field of music criticism. Beginning with the editorship of *Vox Humana,* then writing as music critic on the *Boston Courier,* he joined the staff of the *Boston Advertiser* in 1886, retaining that position until his death. In this field he led the way to a more detailed and thorough estimate of musical works and performances than had been customary in the United States, and incidentally treated all artists under his review with courtesy, even when adverse comment proved necessary. His many lectures on music helped to make him known throughout the United States and Canada. These were principally devoted to the various national schools of music and folk-songs, and partly to analyses of works given at symphonic and other concerts. His Boston municipal lectures deserve more than passing mention for their value in educating the musical taste of the public. These were given at public halls and school-houses in connection with concerts by a small but excellent orchestra and occasional soloists. No admission was charged, so large audiences attended, and showed marked attention and desire to learn. The programs, arranged in part by the lecturer, began with the simpler and more melodious classics of Mozart, Schubert, and others which were duly analyzed before the performance, and progressed through the music of Beethoven, the romanticists, the operatic composers, the Liszt-Wagner period, to some modernists.

As a teacher Elson joined the New England Conservatory of Music in 1880. There he soon took charge of the Theory Department, which he developed from meager dimensions to a full and thorough course, equal to that given by the best European conservatories. It included a careful study of musical form and analysis which opened up to the students a wider view in the wonderland of musical appreciation and understanding, supplemented by two sets of lectures, one treating the orchestral instruments and their use and the other dealing with musical history and the lives of great composers. This course, given for forty years, made Elson known and appreciated by thousands of students in all parts of the country, who have carried on his educational work in this field and aimed for his high standard. His popularity as a lecturer was due to his genial personality, commanding presence, ingratiating voice and style of delivery, added to his thorough mastery of the subject in hand. He was able to hold the close attention of his audience, occasionally relieving the serious side of his lecture by a touch of humor or light, appropriate comment or anecdote. As an after-dinner speaker he was noted for his wit and felicity of expression. In addition to his educational works he wrote some music and libretti for operettas and a number of poems of no mean order.

His many books are a notable testimony to his scholarly erudition. They include: *Curiosities of Music* (1880), an earlier work, of popular interest; *German Songs and Song Writers* (1882); *The Theory of Music* (1890), a concise textbook; *The Realm of Music* (1894), a series of essays; *Great Composers and Their Work* (1898), a volume of general appeal; *The National Music of America* (1899), a valuable and original work which treats its subject in detailed and authoritative fashion; *Shakespeare in Music* (1901), explaining the playwright's many musical allusions, some of which had puzzled commentators hitherto; *History of German Song* (1903); *Elson's Music Dictionary* (1905); *Mistakes and Disputed Points in Music and Music Teaching* (1910); *Women in Music* (1918); and *Children in Music* (1918). Perhaps the most generally valuable of all his volumes is *The History of American Music* (1904), which gives a thorough view of the earlier phases as well as the present status of its subject, treating of the interesting debates and acts of the Pilgrims and Puritans with reference to the art; the early composers; the national folk and war songs; the rise of choral and orchestral societies; and the advent of native American musicians in the last few generations. He also edited and contributed to large musical publications such as the *University Musical Encyclopedia* (1912), *The Musician's Guide* (1913), and a supplementary volume to *Famous Composers and Their Works* (1902). In addition to his objective writings in the field of music, he published in 1891, *European Reminiscences Musical and Otherwise,* an account of foreign vacations, written with the delightful humor and geniality that were characteristic of the author. In 1873 he married Bertha Lissner, who survived him with their son, Arthur Elson. A memorial tablet was placed in the New England Conservatory of Music, where he served so long and faithfully, teaching up to the very day of his death.

[Information from Mr. Arthur Elson, and from the Antiquarian Soc., Worcester, Mass.; brief sketch by Arthur Elson on pp. 325–26 of *The Hist. of Am. Music* (rev. ed., 1925); W. S. B. Mathews, *A Hundred Years of Music in America* (1889); *Who's Who in America,* 1920–21; and Elson's catalogued works in the Boston Pub. Lib.] C. A. W.

ELWELL, FRANK EDWIN (June 15, 1858–Jan. 23, 1922), sculptor, son of John Wesley and Clara (Farrar) Elwell, was born at Concord, Mass., and when growing up, had the cultural advantage of contact with many of the fine minds of that town. Left an orphan at four years, he was placed in the care of his grandfather, Elisha Farrar, the village blacksmith, a poor man but a "great character" and a friend of Thoreau. The boy often accompanied these two men in their Sunday morning rambles. He revered Emerson; he was befriended by the Alcotts. Poverty was his lot. At eight years of age he rose early to do the chores for neighboring farmers, in order to help pay for his clothes. Saturdays, he worked with his grandfather at the forge. His forebears on both sides were fighters. His great-grandfather Farrar fought at Concord Bridge, his great-uncle Col. Timothy Bruce at Bunker Hill. Members of the Elwell family served in the Mexican War, and in the Civil War. The sculptor himself belonged for years to the Massachusetts militia; during the Spanish-American War he joined the Engineer Corps as volunteer, but was not actively engaged.

When he was scarcely through high school, his grandfather died. Louisa Alcott continued to prove herself a true friend; May Alcott, noting the boy's talent and love of beauty, had already taught him something of line drawing and later gave him hints as to the modeling of form. His experience at the forge was of value; through an aunt, Miss Louisa Brooks, he found employment with Messrs. Codman and Shurtleff, a Boston firm of instrument-makers. "Whatever executive ability I have," said Elwell, "I owe to Mr. Shurtleff." Even after deciding to become a sculptor, the young man gave much time to the perfecting of surgical instruments, work which trained both eye and hand, and enabled him to note operations in hospitals. Taking a studio in Boston, he showed, among various early attempts, a bust of the painter Gaugengigl, which attracted much attention on account of the lifelike effect of the eyes. Study abroad became his immediate ambition. Aided by loans from Louisa Alcott and from his fellow townsman, the young sculptor Daniel C. French, whose advice and experience were for years of great value to him, he went to Paris in 1878, and entered the Beaux-Arts, later becoming a private pupil of Falguière. In 1881, he exhibited in the Paris Salon a portrait of the Belgian sculptor, Hippolyte le Roy, and in 1883, the realistic bronze figure, "Aqua Viva," a work shown also in Brussels and in London, and now owned by the Metropolitan Museum, New York. In the following year, he broadened his studies by a period at the Royal School of Arts, Ghent, Belgium, there receiving a silver medal for his progress in architecture. He married Molina Mary Hildreth, daughter of a prosperous and cultivated Massachusetts family, and on their return to the United States in 1885 they made their home in New York City. For a time Elwell taught in the National Academy School, and in the Art Students' League. His first commission was for a monument to be placed in Edam, Holland, to commemorate F. H. Pont. He selected an imaginative rather than a realistic treatment, taking as his theme, "The Death of Strength." The group, an angel with a branch of laurel standing over a prostrate lion, is said to be the first ever modeled in the United States to be set up abroad. His next work of importance was the immensely popular "Dickens and Little Nell," given a place of honor at the Columbian Exposition of 1893, and now in Clarence H. Clark Park, West Philadelphia. The group is heroic in size, but hardly monumental in conception; it charms the public through its sympathetic and picturesque qualities. Together with the "Diana and the Lion," now in the Art Institute, Chicago, this work won for the sculptor a gold medal.

Elwell had long felt a deep love for Egyptian art, and he labored for years on his seated statue of "Egypt Awaking," shown in the Salon of 1896, and promptly bought by a French gentleman, M. Gabriel Goupillat. From the knees down, the figure is treated in the hieratic Egyptian manner; above, it gradually emerges into a vivid life finding ultimate expression in the uplifted arms and animated countenance:—a difficult sculptural problem skilfully solved. The striking variety of gifts shown in these and other works denote Elwell's versatility. His equestrian group of Gen. Winfield Scott Hancock at Gettysburg, Pa. (1896), has the necessary monumental qualities, while his "Orchid Dancer" of two years later is all lightness and elegance. The "New Life," a large memorial relief of a draped female figure (placed in the cemetery at Lowell, Mass., in 1899), shows the sculptor in a deeply religious, even mystical mood. Again, his novel and imposing decorative fountain for the Pan-American Exposition, with its crowning figures of "Kronos" and "Ceres," designed somewhat in the Egyptian spirit, revealed his unfettered imagination, and won for him the silver medal (1901). "One was conscious," wrote Taft (*post*, p. 417), "of a strong artistic personality behind prodigious apparitions."

Elwell himself placed a high value on the "artistic personality" and artistic integrity, stressing them in his writings and lectures on art. In 1903, he became curator of statuary in the Metropolitan Museum of Art, New York City. He was admirably energetic and resourceful in this office though nervous instability occasionally obscured his judgment and he was at times over-earnest, even quarrelsome. After two years he returned to his studio-work in Weehawken, giving himself entirely to creative endeavor. His "Dispatch Rider of the Revolution," erected in 1907 at Orange, N. J., is a virile bronze of heroic size, representing a booted and spurred horseman, who has evidently just dismounted; his cloak is still outspread, and gives a good silhouette. Among his other works are figures of

"Greece" and "Rome," New York Custom House; "Admiral Davis," "Gen. Frederick Steele," "The Flag," at Vicksburg, Miss.; "Lincoln Monument," Orange, N. J.; "Amzi Dodd Memorial," Newark, N. J.; "Edwin Booth Memorial," Mount Auburn Cemetery, Cambridge, Mass., and portrait busts of Sir Peter Esselmont (Aberdeen, Scotland); Henry D. Thoreau (Public Library, Concord, Mass.); Levi P. Morton and Garret A. Hobart (United States Capitol, Washington). The Fogg Museum at Harvard University has the bronze statuette "Kronos," presented by the sculptor's son, Bruce Elwell. In his art, he was a lover of nature, a thinker, a worker, a fighter. Whatever he did was done thoroughly, and in a workmanlike way. After many years, Elwell's first marriage was ended by a divorce, and he was married again, to Annie Marion Benjamin. He died suddenly at Darien, Conn., leaving two sons by his first marriage, and one by his second.

[Lorado Taft, *The Hist. of Am. Sculpture* (rev. ed., 1924); C. H. Caffin, *Am. Masters of Sculpture* (1903); *Arena*, Nov. 1905 and Mar. 1908; *Rev. of Revs.* (N.Y.), Feb. 1901; *Overland Monthly*, Aug. 1898; U. Thieme and F. Becker, *Allgemeines Lexikon der Bildenden Künstler*, vol. X (1914); *Who's Who in America*, 1899–1917; obituaries in *N. Y. Times* and *N. Y. Tribune*, Jan. 24, 1922; information from Mr. Daniel C. French.]

A. A.

ELWELL, JOHN JOHNSON (June 22, 1820–Mar. 13, 1900), physician, lawyer, authority in medical jurisprudence, editor, was born near Warren, Ohio. His boyhood was spent on a farm and after a common-school education he entered Western Reserve College and later its medical department, the Cleveland Medical College, from which he received his medical degree in 1846. After practising medicine for several years he studied law, was admitted to the bar in 1854, and began legal practise, particularly in the medico-legal field. He lectured on medical jurisprudence in Ohio University (Athens), the Union Law College, and the medical department of Western Reserve. He was a member of the Ohio legislature from Ashtabula County in 1853–54, and in 1859 wrote *A Medico-Legal Treatise on Malpractice and Medical Evidence, Comprising the Elements of Medical Jurisprudence*, published in 1860. Previous to the issue of this book there had been no treatise on the subject of malpractise, a matter at that time of great importance to the medical profession, for whom any such suit whether lost or won was disastrous and expensive. The book was accurate, concise, and timely, and went through four editions, being the standard work in the United States, Canada, and Great Britain on the part of the field of medical jurisprudence which it covered. In 1857 Elwell established the *Western Law Monthly* and was for years its editor. After the outbreak of the Civil War, on Aug. 3, 1861, he entered the army as captain and assistant quartermaster, and eventually became chief quartermaster of the X Army Corps. After the war he was mustered out of the service with the brevet rank of brigadier-general of volunteers, returned to Cleveland, and continued the practise of law till his death. He wrote for various journals—among other articles one upon the sanity of Guiteau, the assassin of President Garfield—and he was a contributor to and editor of John Bouvier's *Law Dictionary*.

In person he was tall and vigorous, his manners were courtly, his cheeks ruddy, he wore his hair rather long, and he was fond of children. His wife, Nancy Chittenden, bore him four children, none of whom survived him, and on her death he adopted the children of his brother, leaving them his fortune.

[Sketch written by Thomas Hall Shastid from private and other sources and published in H. A. Kelly and W. L. Burrage, *Am. Medic. Biogs.* (1920), and also in *Am. Medicine* (Burlington, Vt.), Feb. 1909, n.s. IV, pp. 94–96, where his portrait is reproduced; J. H. Kennedy and W. M. Day, *Bench and Bar of Cleveland* (1889), p. 256; *Mil. Order of the Loyal Legion, Commandery of Ohio*, Circular No. 13, ser. of 1900; *Ohio in the War* (1868), ed. by Whitelaw Reid; *Hist. of the Cuyahoga County Soldiers' and Sailors' Monument* (1894); catalogues of Western Reserve College, 1846 and following years; *Cleveland Plain Dealer*, Mar. 15, 1900.] A. P. M.

ELWYN, ALFRED LANGDON (July 9, 1804–Mar. 15, 1884), physician by training, but never a practitioner, who made literary and philanthropic pursuits his chief occupation, was born in Portsmouth, N. H., and died in Philadelphia. He was the son of Thomas and Elizabeth (Langdon) Elwyn. His maternal grandfather was John Langdon, governor of New Hampshire and presiding officer of the first United States Senate. Alfred grew up amid surroundings of wealth and social distinction, attended Phillips Exeter Academy (1816), and afterward went to Harvard, from which in 1823—calling himself Langdon-Elwyn—he was graduated. After this, he spent several years in Europe attending the lectures of celebrated physicians, but returned to America in time to be graduated in medicine from the University of Pennsylvania in 1831. He was married in 1832 to Mary Middleton Mease, by whom he had two children, one becoming a clergyman and another the wife of S. Weir Mitchell [*q.v.*]. He did not actively engage in his profession, but having means for the indulgence of his whims delved into various topics, especially history, philology, and botany. He acquired a valuable library of sources for American history, and from it made repeated gifts to historical societies in New England. He was president of the Pennsylvania Institute for the Blind, the School for Feeble Minded Children, the Society for the Prevention of Cruelty to Animals, and the state agricultural society. His *Papers Relating to Public Events in Massachusetts Preceding the American Revolution*, a series of original documents which he had collected, appeared in 1856. In 1859 he published *A Glossary of Supposed Americanisms*. Convinced that New England was almost purely English in origin, in this work he chides British critics of America for their failure to recognize in American speech a language often more historically correct than their own. The chief cause of provincialisms on the western side of the Atlantic, he said, is the lack of a standard. "The people of England have Parliament filled with men of the best education to be their standard; the people of this Country will hardly look to their National Legislature for an example in the use of language or of national refinement" (*Glossary*, p. 11). He wrote, for private circulation among his friends, a religious poem said to give a vivid impression of his faith and piety. Two volumes sometimes ascribed to him, *Letters by Washington, Adams, Jefferson, and Others, Written During and After the Revolution, to John Langdon, New Hampshire* (1880), and *Letters by Josiah Bartlett, William Whipple, and Others, Written Before and During the Revolution* (1889), were in fact compiled by his son, of the same name (letter to this effect written by the son to the Librarian of Congress, July 21, 1916).

[*Phillips Exeter Acad. Catalogue, 1783–1903* (1903); H. G. Ashmead, *Hist. of Delaware County, Pa.* (1884); *Harvard Univ. Quin. Cat. 1635–1915* (1915); *Univ. of Pa. General Alumni Cat.* (1917); *New-England Hist. and Geneal. Reg.* 1884; *Proc. Mass. Hist. Soc.*, 1884–85; letter from T. L. Montgomery, June 11, 1928; *The Record* (Phila.), Mar. 18, 1884.] J. D. W.

ELZEY, ARNOLD (Dec. 18, 1816–Feb. 21, 1871), Confederate soldier, was a member of one of the older families of Maryland. His father, Arnold Elzey Jones, had twice represented Somerset County in the Maryland legislature. His mother, Anne Wilson (Jackson), was of a wealthy and prominent family. Their son, born at "Elmwood," the residence of his parents on the Manokin River in Somerset County, was educated for a military career. He graduated from West Point in 1837 in his twentieth year, and was commissioned as second-lieutenant of artillery. At this time he dropped his last name, Jones, and adopted his second Christian name, the more distinctive Elzey, which was that of his paternal grandmother. He served with credit as lieutenant in the Seminole War, and at the opening of the Mexican War was in command of a battery of artillery at Brownsville on the Texas frontier. He had the honor of firing the first gun in that war, through which he served with distinction, and was twice brevetted for gallant conduct in the battles of Contreras and Churubusco. In 1861 he was serving as captain of artillery with a small number of men in command of the United States arsenal at Augusta, Ga. He surrendered this post to superior forces of the Confederate States immediately after the fall of Fort Sumter, and brought his command back to Washington. He resigned his commission, made his way back to Richmond, and was commissioned lieutenant-colonel in the Confederate army, in command of the 1st Maryland Infantry then in process of organization. At the first battle of Manassas he was ranking as senior colonel—in Gen. Kirby Smith's brigade, and after Kirby Smith was wounded and borne from the field he led the successful charge on the afternoon of that day which turned the tide of battle and routed the almost successful army of McDowell. For this he was complimented by Gen. Beauregard, who called him the "Blucher of the Field," and was promoted brigadier-general on the field of battle by President Davis.

Early in the war his brigade was attached to Stonewall Jackson's forces, and he fought with this division through the Valley campaign and up to the Seven Days' fighting around Richmond. At the battle of Port Republic he had a horse shot under him and was slightly wounded, and at Cold Harbor he was desperately wounded by a ball through his face and head. This wound prevented further active command, but after his recovery he was promoted major-general and placed in command of the Department of Richmond, where he continued till the fall of 1864. While in this position he organized the "Local Defence Brigade" composed of government clerks and workmen. This force did service in the capture of Dahlgren, the repulse of Stoneman's, Kilpatrick's, and Sheridan's attempts on Richmond, and won the praise of Gen. Lee for its fine appearance and quick movements. After a brief service in organization at Staunton he joined Gen. Hood as chief of artillery in the Army of Tennessee, and took part in the operations against Sherman's lines of communications. After the dissolution of Hood's army, he remained in Georgia without definite command till the capture of Jefferson Davis, when he was allowed to return to Maryland. He then retired to a small farm in Anne Arundel County, where he lived for five years with his only son and his wife, Ellen Irwin of Baltimore, to whom he was married in 1845. He died of pneumonia, while on a visit to Dr. Frank Donaldson of Baltimore. Elzey was of modest unassuming manners, known for his intrepid courage, genuinely loved by friends, and thoroughly respected by his fellow officers in both the Federal and Confederate armies.

[Published sources include: *Confed. Mil. Hist.*, vol. II (1899); E. A. Pollard, *Lee and his Lieutenants* (1867); E. Boyle, *Distinguished Marylanders* (1877), pp. 309–18; G. W. Cullum, *Biog. Reg.* (3rd ed., 1891). There is a manuscript sketch written by Levin L. Waters, Elzey's brother-in-law, and now in the possession of his nephew, A. Elzey Waters of Baltimore; and there are some biographical notes in the library of R. D. Steuart, of the *Baltimore News;* F. Moore's *Rebellion Record* contains reports of Elzey's activities at Manassas, Cold Harbor, and in the bread riot in Richmond. An obituary appeared in the *Baltimore Am. and Commercial Advertiser,* Feb. 23, 1871.] J. E. W.

EMBREE, ELIHU (Nov. 11, 1782–Dec. 4, 1820), Abolitionist, was the son of Thomas and Esther Embree, who removed from Pennsylvania about 1790 to Washington County in the territory that soon became the state of Tennessee. He and his brother, Elijah, were among the earliest iron-manufacturers of this region, but unlike his brother, Elihu achieved no notable success in the business world. There was much of the idealist in him, and he became one of the early leaders of the anti-slavery movement. In eastern Tennessee, where he lived, as well as in neighboring communities of the southern Appalachian region, hostility to the institution of slavery was strong. Thomas Embree, a Quaker minister, had addressed the people of Tennessee as early as 1797 in advocacy of gradual Abolition (*Knoxville Gazette,* Jan. 23, 1797). In 1815, under the leadership of Charles Osborn and John Rankin, the Manumission Society of Tennessee was organized. A short time before this, Elihu Embree, who for some years had been a deist and a slave-owner, had embraced the Christian religion, freed his slaves, and joined the Society of Friends. He became a member of this Manumission Society. When Osborn and Rankin with other anti-slavery men left the slave-states, Embree regretted their going and the consequent "loss of so much virtue from these slave states, which held too little before." He determined to carry on the work in Tennessee and he succeeded to their leadership. In March 1819 he began the publication at Jonesboro of the *Manumission Intelligencer.* This weekly paper, a complete file of which seems not to be in existence, was probably the first periodical in the United States devoted wholly to the anti-slavery cause. In April 1820, Embree changed his publication to a monthly and its name to the *Emancipator.* Within a few months it had a subscription list of about two thousand; it was being "extensively circulated in the United States"; and its first two issues had to be reprinted for late subscribers (*Knoxville Register,* Nov. 28, 1820). In its columns Embree took the position "that freedom is the inalienable right of *all men.*" He replied to those who feared that racial equality would follow Abolition that he had "never been able to discover that the author of nature intended that one complexion of the human skin should stand higher in the scale of being, than another." In vigorous terms he condemned slavery and the slave-owner. He called upon the enlightened master voluntarily to set free his slaves. He memorialized the Tennessee legislature to abolish the institution of slavery, "a shame to any people." He denounced those states that sought to exclude free negroes from within their boundaries. When Missouri sought admission into the Union as a slave-state, "Not another foot of slave territory," was his reply. Although the *Emancipator* died with its young and militant editor, Benjamin Lundy's *Genius of Universal Emancipation* was in a sense its successor, and hostility to slavery continued in eastern Tennessee.

[The quotations above, except as otherwise indicated, are from the *Emancipator* as given in E. E. Hoss, "Elihu Embree, Abolitionist," in *Am. Hist. Mag.* (Nashville), Jan. 1897, and also in *Vanderbilt Southern Hist. Soc. Pubs.*, no. 2 (1897). See, in addition, Asa E. Martin's "The Anti-Slavery Societies of Tenn.," in *Tenn. Hist. Mag.*, Dec. 1915, and his "Pioneer Anti-Slavery Press," in *Miss. Valley Hist. Rev.*, Mar. 1916; Caleb P. Patterson, *The Negro in Tenn., 1790–1865* (Univ. of Texas Bull., no. 2205, 1922), *passim;* and obituary in *Knoxville Register,* Dec. 12, 1820. A silhouette of Embree is in the Univ. of Tenn. Lib.] P. M. H.

EMBURY, EMMA CATHERINE (*c.* 1806–Feb. 10, 1863), author, was born in New York, the eldest of the three children of Dr. James R. and Elizabeth (Post) Manley. The family was of English stock, with an admixture of Dutch. Her father, who attended Thomas Paine in his last illness, was a graduate in arts and medicine of Columbia College. From him Emma acquired her powers as a conversationalist and her enthusiasm for books. In conformity with the genteel tradition of the time, she covered reams with her juvenile verse and stories, and when the *New York Mirror* was established she soon became one of its valued, but unremunerated, contributors. Her literary reputation was already in bud when, on May 10, 1828, she married Daniel Embury, president of the Atlantic Bank of Brooklyn, a man of courtly manners and cultivated tastes. They were both fond of hospitality, and Mrs. Embury became the leader of a salon. Though she never claimed authorship as her profession, she produced a large quantity of poems, tales, and essays and was sought by editors as a contributor to their magazines. Several periodicals printed her name in the mast as a member of the editorial staff, although her actual connection appears to have been only that of a well-wisher. Her books include *Guido, a Tale; Sketches from History, and Other Poems* (1828); *Constance Latimer, or The Blind Girl, with Other Tales* (1838); *Pictures of Early Life, or Sketches of Youth* (1830); *American Wild Flowers in their Native Haunts* (1845); *Love's Token Flowers* (1845); *Glimpses of Home Life, or Causes and Consequences* (1848); and *The Waldorf Family, or Grandfather's Legend* (1848). Since her death *The Poems of Emma C. Embury* (1869) and *Selected Prose Writings of Mrs. Emma C. Embury* (1893) have been published, and an address on "Female Education," delivered before the Brooklyn Collegiate Institute for Young Ladies, was included in Anna C. Brackett's *Woman and Higher Education* (1893). Book reviewers habitually confused Mrs. Embury's literary achievements with her virtues as a wife and mother and her charm as a hostess. Even Edgar Allan Poe, whose Southern chivalry was the weak spot in his critical armor, capitulated to her. In her verse, which has the vagueness of imagery, conventionality of theme, and unimpassioned fluency of all bad verse, he managed to detect "poetic capacity of no common order." With better judgment, perhaps, he praised her tales for their freshness and style. "I make a point of *reading* all tales to which I see the name of Mrs. Embury appended. . . . She is not so vigorous as Mrs. Stephens, nor so vivacious as Miss Chubbuck, nor so caustic as Miss Leslie, nor so dignified as Miss Sedgwick, nor so graceful, fanciful, and *spirituelle* as Mrs. Osgood, but is *deficient* in none of the qualities for which these ladies are noted, and in certain particulars surpasses them all." Mrs. Embury is indeed an almost perfect representative of the golden age of the American "female poet." In 1848 a serious illness ended her career as an author and friend of authors. She lived almost fifteen years longer and for the last two years of her life was a complete invalid.

[E. A. Poe, article in *Godey's Mag. and Lady's Book*, Aug. 1846, 76–77; R. W. Griswold, *The Female Poets of America* (1848, 6th ed., 1874); Caroline May, *Female Poets* (1848); T. B. Read, *Female Poets of America* (1848, 7th ed., 1857); E. A. and G. L. Duyckinck, *Cyc. of Am. Lit.* (rev. ed., 1875); *Appletons' Ann. Cyc.* 1863; death notice in *N. Y. Times*, Feb. 14, 1863; C. S. J. Goodrich, "Biog. Sketch of Dr. Jas. R. Manley," *Trans. Medic. Soc. of the State of N. Y.* (Albany, 1852).]

G. H. G.

EMBURY, PHILIP (1728–1773), reputed to have been the first Methodist preacher in America, a descendant of German Protestants who fled from the Palatinate under the persecutions of Louis XIV, was probably born in Ballingrane, County of Limerick, Ireland. The date of his birth is approximately fixed by a family record which states that he was baptized on Sept. 29, 1728 (Crook, *post*, p. 79). He received some education under Philip Guier, the German village schoolmaster of Ballingrane, and in an English school, possibly at Rathkeale. Later he was apprenticed to a carpenter. Methodist preaching began in Limerick in 1749, and received a warm response from the Palatines. On Christmas 1752, Embury states, "the Lord shone into my soul by a glimpse of his redeeming love, being an earnest of my redemption in Christ Jesus" (*Ibid.;* Wakeley, *post*, p. 33). Soon he became a class leader and local preacher. He was recommended for the itinerancy at the conference in Limerick in 1758, and put on Wesley's reserve list. On Nov. 27, 1758, he was married in Rathkeale church to Margaret Switzer of Court Matrix, where the first Methodist church among the Palatines had been erected in part through his exertions. In June 1760 he joined a party of emigrants who sailed from Limerick on the ship *Perry* and arrived in New York on Aug. 11.

Embury worked at his trade and also apparently taught school, for an announcement in Weyman's *New York Gazette* in March and April 1761 states that "Phil. Embury, School Master gives notice that on the first day of May next he intends to teach Reading, Writing, and Arithmetic, in English, in the New School House now building in Little Queen Street, next door to the Lutheran Minister's," etc. (Atkinson, *post*, p. 224). He joined the Lutheran Church but seems not to have been active in religious matters for some years. A card game and the righteous wrath of a woman awakened Embury and started the Methodist movement in America. Mrs. Barbara Heck [*q.v.*], in 1766, burst in upon a card party of her countrymen, broke up the game, and then went to Embury's home and said: "Philip, you must preach to us, or we shall all go to Hell, and God will require our blood at your hands." He preached his first sermon in New York in his own house to a company of five. The congregation grew, and as a result, Wesley Chapel, the first John Street Church, was built in 1768, Embury working on it as a carpenter, and preaching the dedicatory sermon. In 1770 he migrated to what is now Washington County, N. Y., then a part of Albany County, where some of his countrymen from New York City had preceded him.

Here he lived on the farm of his brother-in-law, Peter Switzer, near East Salem, working at his trade, preaching, and acting as civil magistrate. At Ashgrove he established a Methodist society, the first north of New York City. His death is said to have been caused by over-exertion while mowing under a burning sun. A memorandum by Samuel Embury states, "My father, Philip Embury, died in August 1773, aged forty-five years" (*Ibid.*, p. 449). He was buried on a near-by farm, but in 1832 his remains were removed to the cemetery at Ashgrove, and in 1866 to Woodland Cemetery, Cambridge, N. Y., where a monument has been erected.

[See J. B. Wakeley, *Lost Chapters Recovered from the Early Hist. of Am. Methodism* (1858); Wm. Crook, *Ireland and the Centenary of Am. Methodism* (1866); Samuel A. Seaman, *Annals of N. Y. Methodism* (1892); John Atkinson, *Hist. of the Origin of the Wesleyan Movement in America* (1896); Jas. M. Buckley, *A Hist. of Methodism in the U. S.* (1897); and other denominational histories. *Memorial of Philip Embury* (1888) contains a eulogy delivered on the occasion of the removal of his remains to Ashgrove, and others delivered at the unveiling of the monument at Cambridge.]

H. E. S.

EMERSON, EDWARD WALDO (July 10, 1844–Jan. 27, 1930), author, the fourth and youngest child of Ralph Waldo Emerson and his second wife, Lydia Jackson, was born, lived, and died in Concord, Mass. In boyhood he accompanied Henry Thoreau on many an excursion and learned to observe nature with something of his friend's exactness, though never with his passionate absorption. Frail health and an undersized body prevented him from enlisting in the Union army. After his graduation from Harvard College in 1866 and from the Medical School in 1874, he married Annie Shepard Keyes of Concord, Sept. 19, 1874, and began the practise of medicine. Even in his young manhood he was persuaded that his was the generation of the Epigoni, and after his father's death in 1882 he gave up his work as a country doctor and turned to literary pursuits, chiefly of a family and commemorative nature. Gentleness, his major trait, carries over into his writing and constitutes his charm, and perhaps occasionally his defect, as a memoirist. *Emerson in Concord* (1889; first printed in *Memoirs of the Members of the Social Circle in Concord,* 2 ser., 1888), was his first book and is the most delightful and the most intimate of all books on Emerson. He edited the *Correspondence between John Sterling and Ralph Waldo Emerson* (1897), the definitive, well annotated Centenary Edition of his father's writings (1903–04), and, with Waldo Emerson Forbes, the *Journals of Ralph Waldo Emerson* (1909–14), from which, with characteristic self-effacement, he excised all reference to himself. These laborious tasks he performed with admirable fidelity and tact. He published several poems privately, did some magazine work, and issued the *Life and Letters of Charles Russell Lowell* (1907) and, in collaboration with Moorfield Storey, *Ebenezer Rockwood Hoar* (1911). Two memorable volumes, *Henry Thoreau as Remembered by a Young Friend* (1917) and the *Early Years of the Saturday Club* (1918), brought his literary career to a close. He was a member of the Massachusetts Historical Society and a fellow of the American Academy of Arts and Sciences. He also enjoyed local fame as a painter and for several years was an instructor at the Boston Museum of Fine Arts. He was fond of horses and frequently depicted them. By 1919 he began to be troubled by lapses of memory, and his last years were clouded, as his father's had been, by the slow decline of body and mind together. His wife predeceased him by two years; and of their six children only a son, Raymond, outlived him.

[B. K. Emerson, *The Ipswich Emersons, A. D. 1636–1900* (privately printed, 1900); *The Writings of Henry David Thoreau* (MS. ed., 1906); *Who's Who in America, 1928–29*; *Boston Transcript*, Jan. 27, 29, Feb. 1 (article signed "A.F."), 1930; funeral address by Bliss Perry in *Concord Journal*, Feb. 6, 1930; information from Raymond Emerson and M. A. DeWolfe Howe.]

G. H. G.

EMERSON, ELLEN RUSSELL (Jan. 16, 1837–June 12, 1907), ethnologist, author, received her early education in the schools of the period at her birthplace, New Sharon, Me. In due time her parents, Dr. Leonard White and Fanny (Fisk) Russell, sent her to Mount Vernon Seminary at Boston, Mass., where she received the especial instruction of the president, Dr. Robert Cushman. In 1862 she married Edwin R. Emerson. Becoming interested in the subject of the ethnology of the American Indians and seeking to broaden her field, she traveled extensively during four years' stay in Europe, from 1886 to 1889. At this time exploration in Egypt was being actively prosecuted, and she engaged in the study of Egyptology at Paris with the distinguished professor, M. Gaston Maspero. Her first work, *Indian Myths; or Legends, Traditions, and Symbols of the Aborigines of America Compared with Those of Other Countries, including Hindostan, Egypt, Persia, Assyria and China* (1884), is not merely a compilation, but a rational arrangement for which she supplied the ideas and often brilliant deductions. She did not seek to prove too much or wander into impossible situations, propensities too common in writers on the subject. This first work, of 700 pages, represents a great labor and remains valuable to the students of folk-lore, but like all such assemblages of material, is to be read with proper discrimination. After a number of years of study and collection of material, Mrs. Emerson produced *Masks, Heads, and Faces with Some Considerations Respecting the Rise and Development of Art* (1891), which was conceived and executed in the true scientific spirit. The author's indefatigable pursuit of information from the most difficult sources, the arrangement of the abundant data, and the sane presentation in excellent English show her to have been a student of exceptional ability. Incidentally, the preface is a model of clear thinking and felicitous expression. The magnitude of the subject and the preparation required to obtain results is explanation of the fact that Mrs. Emerson published only a few books in her lifetime. *Nature and Human Nature* (1902) completes the list of her larger works. During her long stay in Europe she was made an honorary member of the Société Américaine of Paris, and for her assistance with the exposition held in Madrid, Spain (1892), in celebration of the four-hundredth anniversary of the discovery of America, she received official recognition.

[*Who's Who in America,* 1906–07; Frances E. Willard and Mary A. Livermore, *A Woman of the Century* (1893); *Boston Transcript,* June 12, 1907.] W. H.

EMERSON, GEORGE BARRELL (Sept. 12, 1797–Mar. 4, 1881), educator, was born in Wells, Me., then a part of Massachusetts, one of the nine children of Samuel and Sarah (Barrell) Emerson. His father—a descendant of Thomas Emerson who settled at Ipswich, Mass., about 1636—graduated at Harvard in 1785, served in the Revolutionary War, and was for sixty years an able and scholarly physician and a zealous and observant student of nature. George attended school in the winter and worked on the farm in summer. He prepared for college partly at the Dummer School in Byfield, Mass., and partly under his father's tuition at home, entered Harvard College, and while an undergraduate gave much attention to mathematics and to rather extensive reading of the Greek authors. His vacations were usually spent in teaching in public schools. After graduating in 1817 he was appointed principal of an excellent private school in Lancaster, Mass. Here he showed great skill and efficiency and a natural talent for giving instruction. His health became impaired, and two years later he resigned to become a tutor in mathematics in Harvard. His special gift as a teacher, however, soon led to a call, in 1821, to be principal of the newly established English Classical School, now called the English High School, of Boston. Though his term of service was short he made a lasting impression on the ideals and policy of this school. In 1823, after repeated solicitation, he opened in Boston a private school for young ladies which had a long record of excellence and popularity. In 1855 he retired and ended this phase of his career.

Throughout his life, however, he was an educational leader. He was instrumental in organizing the Boston Mechanics' Institute for mutual instruction in the sciences connected with industrial arts and delivered an address at its opening. In 1830, largely through his efforts, the American Institute of Instruction was founded to study the conditions of schools and promote their improvement. This led to the appointment of a State Board of Education of which Horace Mann was the secretary and to the establishment of state normal schools in Massachusetts. During and after the Civil War Emerson was prominently engaged in efforts for the education of the freedmen in the South. His important published works include: *Houses for Working Men and Women,* an address delivered at the opening of the Boston Mechanics' Institute, Feb. 7, 1827; *The Massachusetts Common School System* (1841); *A Lecture on the Education of Females* (1831), delivered before the American Institute of Instruction; *Moral Education,* a lecture delivered at New Bedford, Aug. 6, 1842; Part II of *The School and Schoolmaster, a Manual for the Use of Teachers, Employers, Trustees, Inspectors . . . of Common Schools* (1842), a copy of which, by act of the Massachusetts legislature, was placed in every school in the state, similar action being taken by the General Assembly of New York; *History and Design of the American Institution of Instruction* (1849); *Manual of Agriculture for the School, the Farm and the Fireside* (1862), with Chas. L. Flint; *Education in Massachusetts: Early Legislation and History* (1869); *The Study of Latin and English Grammar* (1871), a presidential address at a meeting of the Boston Social Science Association, Feb. 21, 1867; *What we owe to Louis Agassiz as a Teacher* (1874), an address before the Boston Society of Natural History; *Reminiscences of an Old Teacher* (1878).

His interest and influence were not confined to educational matters. In his youth he had been a lover and student of field and forest and while engaged in his work as a teacher he found time for studies in natural history, partly as a change and rest from other work. In 1830 the Boston Society of Natural History was formed and in 1837 he was chosen its president. He held this office for six years, during which time a commission was appointed of which he was chairman, to make a zoölogical and botanical survey of Massachusetts. He chose to make a study of the trees and shrubs and devoted ten or twelve weeks of nine successive summers to an exploration of the state. The result of his work was a *Report on the Trees and Shrubs Growing Naturally in the Forests of Massachusetts* (1846), published by the Commissioners of the Zoölogical and Botanical Survey of the state. The second edition, in two volumes, was printed in 1875, and the fifth and last edition in 1903. Some forty years after he began to teach, Emerson visited England, France, Italy, and Germany, observing plants and trees and in the last named country studying the educational system. In 1870 he made a trip to the Pacific Coast.

On June 11, 1823, he married Olivia Buckminster who died in 1832, leaving two sons and a daughter. On Nov. 12, 1834, he married Mrs. Mary (Rotch) Fleming. He was early elected a member of the American Academy of Arts and Sciences. He was a member of King's Chapel from early manhood and became a vestryman and warden. He died in Newton, Mass., in his eighty-fourth year.

[Robt. C. Waterston, *Memoir of Geo. Barrell Emerson* (1884), reprinted from *Proc. Mass. Hist. Soc.*, vol. XX (1882–83); J. H. Morison, in *Unitarian Review*, July 1881; Thos. T. Bouvé, in *Anniversary Memoirs of the Boston Soc. of Natural Hist.* (1880); Asa Gray, in *Proc. of the Am. Acad. of Arts and Sci.*, n.s. VIII (1880–81); H. K. Oliver and Chas. Northend, in *Lectures and Jour. of Proc. of the Am. Inst. of Instruction, July 5–8, 1881* (1882); *Am. Jour. of Educ.*, Sept. 1858; *Boston Daily Advertiser*, Mar. 5, 1881; *Education* (Boston), Nov. 1881; *Jour. of Educ.* (Boston), Mar. 10, 1881; B. K. Emerson, *The Ipswich Emersons, A. D. 1636–1900* (1900).] E. H. J.

EMERSON, GOUVERNEUR (Aug. 4, 1795–July 2, 1874), physician and agriculturist, was born upon a farm near Dover, Kent County, Del., the eldest of the seven children of Jonathan Emerson and his wife, Ann Beel. The Emersons of Delaware were of English Quaker stock, early settlers in Penn's province. At an early age Gouverneur was sent to Westtown School, in Chester County, Pa., conducted by the Society of Friends. Later he attended a boarding school at Smyrna, Del., and then a classical school at Dover conducted by the Rev. Stephen Sykes. He began the study of medicine at the age of sixteen under Dr. James Sykes, a cousin of his mother, and in 1813 went to Philadelphia, where after three years in the University of Pennsylvania and the presentation of an inaugural thesis on "Hereditary Diseases" he was given his degree of M.D. in 1816. He began practise at Silver Lake, Susquehanna County, Pa., but after two years was appointed surgeon of a merchant ship, the *Superior* of Philadelphia, bound for China. The trip to Canton and return occupied sixteen months; in the Indian Ocean the ship was held up and robbed by pirates. Emerson wrote a detailed account of the voyage.

He settled in Philadelphia for practise in 1820. A yellow-fever epidemic had struck the city and he was appointed attending physician to the city dispensary, a position he held for two years. In 1823 he was elected a member of the Board of Health and at the same time appointed its secretary; in this position he was instrumental in drafting the legislation for the control of smallpox in the city. With Dr. Isaac Hays, he recognized the first case of "spasmodic cholera," which ushered in the cholera epidemic of 1832. During the epidemic, which cost over a thousand lives, Emerson had charge of the Hospital for Orphans. For over thirty-five years he was one of the busiest and most successful Philadelphia physicians. In May 1847 he represented the Philadelphia Medical Society at the convention in that city which resulted in the organization of the American Medical Association. He claimed joint authorship, with Dr. Isaac Hays, of the *Code of Medical Ethics* adopted by that society. He was a member of the American Philosophical Society and contributed many brief communications to its published Proceedings. He was a lecturer at the Franklin Institute of Philadelphia on mineralogy, and he had a working knowledge also of botany, geology, and physics.

His chief interest outside of medicine was agriculture. He possessed several farms, which were the scenes of his numerous experiments, particularly on the comparative value of fertilizers. He edited for the United States, Cuthbert W. Johnson's *Farmers' Encyclopedia and Dictionary of Rural Affairs* (1844) and also wrote a pamphlet on *Cotton in the Middle States* (1862). In 1857 the pressure of other interests, however, caused him to relinquish medical practise. During the Civil War he was prominent in the organization of the Union League Club of Philadelphia and in its subsequent activities. He was always interested in social science, and the last work of his pen was a translation from the French of Le Play's *Organization of Labor.* Emerson was tall and slight, with a handsome aristocratic face. He was dignified and courteous, with a gift for conversation and for public speaking. He remained a bachelor all his life and shared a house for years with a bachelor friend. He died suddenly in his office in Philadelphia near the end of his seventy-ninth year.

[W. S. W. Ruschenberger, "A Sketch of the Life of

Dr. Gouverneur Emerson" containing portrait and bibliography, in *Proc. Am. Phil. Soc.*, vol. XXIX (1891); *Phila. Inquirer*, July 3, 1874.] J. M. P.

EMERSON, JAMES EZEKIEL (Nov. 2, 1823–Feb. 17, 1900), machinist, inventor, was born in Norridgewock, Me., where his great-grandfather had originally settled as a Congregational minister. The fourth child of Ezekiel and Amanda (Leeman) Emerson, he was sixth in descent from Joseph and Elizabeth (Bulkeley) Emerson, and seventh from Thomas Emerson who settled at Ipswich, Mass., about 1636. When he was three years old his parents moved to a farm at Bangor, Me., and here he received such education as the schools afforded and assisted in the farm labors as soon as his strength permitted. In the course of the succeeding years until he came of age, he helped his father and at the same time took up carpentry, in which trade he became most proficient. Then for six years he worked as a journeyman at his trade in many towns in Maine, finally settling with his family in Lewiston in 1850. He moved there primarily to build houses for the Lewiston Falls Water Power Company and constructed in the course of two years the first three blocks of houses in Lewiston Falls. During this time, too, he invented an automatic machine to bore, turn, and cut the heads on wood spools and bobbins and organized a manufactory to make this machine. Shortly thereafter, however, he emigrated to California where he engaged in building and lumbering enterprises around Oroville and Sacramento. It was while thus engaged that he turned his attention to the improvement of power-driven circular saws and invented the removable-tooth saw. This he immediately put into successful operation and after organizing a company to manufacture the saw, engaged for six years in traveling about selling and repairing it. Disposing of all of his interests in California in 1859, he returned to the East, settled in Trenton, N. J., and there organized a company to manufacture edge tools. During the Civil War large quantities of cavalry sabres, officer's swords and bayonets were made by his company for the federal government. After the war he became superintendent of the American Saw Company of Trenton, organized to manufacture his circular saw, in which capacity he served until 1871, when after an extensive European trip he settled in Beaver Falls, Pa., and established the firm of Emerson, Ford & Company to manufacture saws. Six years later the firm name was changed to Emerson, Smith & Company. Emerson continued the direction of this organization until about 1890, when he retired from active business. He spent the balance of his life in travel, maintaining, however, a residence in Columbus, Ohio, where he died. To what extent he was interested in public life is not known other than that he ran for Congress on the "Greenback" ticket while a resident of Beaver Falls. Besides his inserted-tooth saw, Emerson's patents included a steel-making process; a combined anvil, shears, and punching machine; a swage for spreading saw teeth and cutting the edges at a single operation; and a steel scabbard for bayonets. He was married twice: first in 1849 to Mary Patee Shepherd of New London, N. H., and second, in 1878, to Mary Belle Woods of New Brighton, Pa.

[*Hist. of Beaver County* (1888), pub. by A. Warner & Co., Phila.; J. H. Bausman, *Hist. of Beaver County, Pa.*, vol. II (1904); *Biog. Encyc. of Pa.* (1874); B. K. Emerson, *The Ipswich Emersons* (1900); *Who's Who in America*, 1899–1900; Patent Office Records; U. S. Nat. Museum Records; date of death from Dept. of Health, Columbus, Ohio.] C. W. M.

EMERSON, JOSEPH (Oct. 13, 1777–May 14, 1833), clergyman and educator, born in Hollis, N. H., the son of Daniel and Ama (Fletcher) Emerson, was a second cousin of Ralph Waldo Emerson and a descendant of Thomas Emerson, who, coming to America in 1635 and settling in Ipswich, Mass., founded a long line of New England clergymen. Joseph, having been in part prepared for college in New Ipswich, N. H., entered Harvard in 1794. Immediately after his graduation in 1798 he taught for a brief term in Framingham, Mass., then returned to Cambridge to study for the ministry, for which he had been destined from his youth. In 1801 he was licensed to preach and at the same time made a college tutor in mathematics, geography, and natural philosophy. Two years later he was called to the newly organized Congregational Church of Beverly, Mass., where he remained until increasing ill health forced his resignation in 1816. During his pastorate in Beverly he was three times married. His first wife, Nancy Eaton, a pupil of his at the Framingham Academy, lived but a short time after their marriage in October 1803. In July 1805 he married Eleanor Reed, who died in November 1808, and on Jan. 16, 1810, he married Rebecca Hasseltine, sister of Mrs. Judson, the missionary. This wife outlived him and carried on his school for several years after his death. To these unions eleven children were born, six of whom lived to maturity.

As early as 1801, certain comments in Emerson's letters, relative to Hannah More's writings on female education, betrayed an interest in the training of women. In 1816, on his return from a short stay in the South, he followed this early bent by opening a seminary for young women,

This school, first conducted at Byfield, Mass., received fifty pupils immediately. In 1821 it was transferred to Saugus, Mass., where Emerson had charge of a parish also. Three years later it was established at Wethersfield, Conn. Its distinguishing feature was the surprising range of its curriculum in a day when few subjects were thought suitable for the feminine mind.

During the Anti-Masonic agitation, Emerson, who was a Mason, wrote a *Letter to the Members of the Genesee Consociation, N. Y.* (1828), which was published in Rochester, protesting against an Anti-Masonic resolution of that body. Despite ill health, which after 1816 frequently caused him to go South, and the insistent demands of church and school, he found time for much writing in the field of education. Among other works he produced a manual, pronounced one of the best of its day (this was probably the *Prospectus of the Female Seminary at Wethersfield, Ct. Comprising a General Prospectus, Course of Instruction, Maxims of Education and Regulations of the Seminary,* 1826), as well as texts in the subjects of history, literature, and theology, some of which went through many editions. He was a devoted reader of Isaac Watts and revised (1832) Watts's *The Improvement of the Mind* for the edification of young women. He was one of the original members of the American Institute of Instruction, founded in 1830. His most enduring work, however, was accomplished through his teaching, two of his students being Zilpah Grant [*q.v.*], who later founded Ipswich Academy, and Mary Lyon [*q.v.*], the founder of Mount Holyoke Seminary, afterward to become the college of that name. He died in Wethersfield.

[Ralph Emerson, *Life of the Rev. Jos. Emerson* (1834); J. L. Ewell, *The Story of Byfield: a New England Parish* (1904); H. R. Stiles, *The Hist. of Ancient Wethersfield, Conn.* (1904), which contains a list of Emerson's published works; B. K. Emerson, *The Ipswich Emersons* (1900); *Am. Annals of Educ. and Instruction,* Aug. 1834.] E. D.

EMERSON, MARY MOODY (Aug. 25, 1774–May 1, 1863), aunt of Ralph Waldo Emerson, was born in Concord, Mass., the fourth of the five children of the Rev. William and Phebe (Bliss) Emerson. Her father's death in 1776 and her mother's marriage in 1780 to the Rev. Ezra Ripley left her to be reared by an aunt and uncle on a lonely farm in Malden. The old couple were desperately poor, and Mary, with a legacy of ten dollars a year for clothes and charity, grew up in poverty and solitude, nourishing her intellect on the Bible, odd volumes of sermons, and a battered *Paradise Lost,* minus covers and title-page, which she conned for years without discovering its author's name. From childhood she was imbued with the bleak grandeurs of High Calvinism, beside which the Unitarianism, Transcendentalism, and humanitarianism that she encountered in later years seemed stunted and unimaginative. Ultimately she inherited the Malden farm, and the proceeds from its sale enabled her to live in penurious independence. For years she made her home with her sister's family at "Elm Vale" in South Waterford, Me., where the beauties of the countryside were to her a source of continuous delight. She ministered to her relatives in sickness, bereavement, and other distress; declined, probably for religious reasons, an offer of marriage from a man whom she esteemed; met many of the notables of the day; migrated from town to town in search of cheap boarding places; became learned in the poets, the theologians, and the philosophers, reading with sharply critical eyes and an inerrant taste for superior writing; kept a voluminous journal; and supervised with inexorable zeal the education and intellectual growth of her nephews, the sons of her deceased brother William [*q.v.*]. Holding that "they were born to be educated," she saw to it that in spite of every obstacle they were educated. Over Ralph Waldo in particular she exercised an influence that dominated much of his early work and that remained strong until the end. To a great extent he formed his style on hers, copying her unpredictable metaphors, her flinty native words, her soaring eloquence. Her intimate knowledge of family history made her the living bond between him and his ancestors. He begged her to bequeath him her journals; he read and reread her papers as late as 1870; in fitting together his essays he borrowed from her as freely as from Plutarch and Montaigne. His love and veneration for her is recorded in his journals and was never stronger than when she broke with him over his theological radicalism and refused to live in the same town with him. Reconciliation did come eventually, for in secret she was proud of him and his fame. With Henry David Thoreau, who also appreciated her, she enjoyed a notable friendship. Emerson and Thoreau saw that she was a religious genius and reverenced her accordingly. Ordinary folk, however, were appalled by her eccentricities, macabre humors, and brutal, sardonic candor. One of them may speak for all: "She was bookish, rather strong-minded, not nice in her habits; would do for these days better than in the time when women were retired and modest in manners, and had great reverence for the stronger sex" (Mrs. A. E. Porter, *apud* B. K. Emerson, *post,* pp. 173–74). She was four feet three inches tall;

until late in life her complexion remained rosy and unwrinkled. The last four years of her long life were spent in the home of her niece, Hannah Upham Haskins (Mrs. Augustus Parsons), in Williamsburgh, Brooklyn, N. Y., where she died. She was buried in Sleepy Hollow Cemetery in Concord.

[R. W. Emerson, *Journals* (1909–14), with silhouette in Vol. IV opp. p. 480, and "Mary Moody Emerson," *Atlantic Monthly*, Dec. 1883, repub. in *Lectures and Biog. Sketches* (1883); F. B. Sanborn, "A Concord Notebook; The Women of Concord—I," *Critic*, Feb. 1906; H. D. Thoreau, *Journals* (1906); J. E. Cabot, *A Memoir of R. W. Emerson* (1887); E. W. Emerson, *Emerson in Concord* (1889); B. K. Emerson, *The Ipswich Emersons 1636–1900* (1900); *Hist. of Waterford, Oxford County, Me.* (1879), pp. 255–56; *N. Y. Daily Tribune*, May 4, 1863; R. F. Dibble, "She Lived to Give Pain," *Century Mag.*, July 1926; Van Wyck Brooks, "The Cassandra of New England," *Scribner's Mag.*, Feb. 1927.]

G. H. G.

EMERSON, OLIVER FARRAR (May 24, 1860–Mar. 13, 1927), philologist, was born near Wolf Creek (now Traer), Iowa, the son of the Rev. Oliver Emerson and his second wife, Maria Farrar, and the seventh in descent from Thomas Emerson of Bishop's Stortford, Hertfordshire, who settled in Ipswich, Mass., about 1636. His father, a graduate of Waterville (now Colby) College and of Lane Theological Seminary, was for more than forty years a home missionary in Iowa. Emerson graduated in 1882 from Iowa (now Grinnell) College, of which his father was a trustee, was superintendent of schools in Grinnell 1882–84 and in Muscatine 1884–85, and was principal of the academy of Iowa College 1885–88. During these years he read assiduously in the literature of several languages and finally concluded that English philology was to be his work. He experimented with the writing of verse, producing among other things a Latin version of "Onward, Christian Soldiers," and for the year 1887 kept a journal in French. In 1888 he won the Goldwin Smith fellowship in English at Cornell, the renewal of which the next year allowed him to complete his work for the doctor's degree under Hiram Corson and James Morgan Hart. Though burdened with too much detail about the early history of English sounds, his dissertation on *The Ithaca Dialect: A Study of Present English* (1891) remained for forty years the most scientific study of the phonology of an American regional dialect. On Sept. 24, 1891, he married Annie Laurie, daughter of Benjamin and Victoria (Nicholson) Logan, by whom he had a son and a daughter. He taught English at Cornell as an instructor 1889–91 and as an assistant professor 1892–96, when he was called to a full professorship at Western Reserve University, where he remained for the rest of his life. His publications are: a *History of the English Language* (1894), *Brief History of the English Language* (1896), *Middle English Reader* (1905), an *Outline History of the English Language* (1906), and carefully edited editions of Johnson's *Rasselas* (1895), *Memoirs of the Life and Writings of Edward Gibbon* (1898), and *Poems of Chaucer* (1911). His several books on the English language, though marred by some minor inaccuracies resulting from hasty preparation, have been widely used, but his best and most characteristic work appeared in his contributions to philological journals. His bibliography, numbering 156 items, includes enduringly significant articles on the author of the "Pearl," Chaucer, Spenser, Shakespeare, Milton, Dryden, Johnson, Gibbon, and Scott. He was equally devoted to the study of language and the study of literature and knew, as few American scholars do, how each may serve the other. In 1923 he was president of the Modern Language Association. His summers were usually spent in his country home on the shore of Lake Erie; he was fond of gardening, tennis, baseball, and cycling. His sense of humor was exiguous; he did not smoke, drink, or play cards, and had few close friends. During the winter of 1926–27 his health broke down, and on his doctor's advice he repaired to Florida. He appeared to be gaining ground when he died unexpectedly at Ocala, Fla. Among Anglists throughout the world his work was known and respected; in the more restricted circle that knew him personally he was held in both respect and affection.

[The posthumously published *Chaucer Essays and Studies* (Cleveland, 1929), contains a biographical introduction by W. H. Hulme and a bibliography by C. S. Northup. See also *Who's Who in America*, 1901–27, and B. K. Emerson, *The Ipswich Emersons 1636–1900* (1900).]

G. H. G.

EMERSON, RALPH (May 8, 1831–Aug. 19, 1914), inventor, manufacturer, the son of the Rev. Ralph and Eliza (Rockwell) Emerson and a distant cousin of Ralph Waldo Emerson, was born in Andover, Mass., where his father was professor of ecclesiastical history at the Andover Theological Seminary. After going through Phillips Academy at Andover, Emerson began teaching school, first in New England but subsequently in Bloomington, Ill., and Beloit, Wis. He also undertook to study law but soon gave that up upon the advice of Abraham Lincoln with whom he had made a lasting friendship. In 1852, the year he was twenty-one, he went from Beloit to Rockford, Ill., and became a partner in a hardware store. Part of his business was furnishing metal stock and supplies to John H. Manny [*q.v.*], pioneer inventor and manufacturer of a reaper. Payment for the supplies thus furnished was made in shares of stock in Manny's business. In 1854 Emerson and his partner became members of Manny's company, and in 1857, after the death of Manny, Emerson acquired control of the reaper business. He was only twenty-six years old at the time but took hold of the enterprise vigorously and successfully. On May 26, 1857, he obtained a patent for an improvement on the tongue and castor wheel of the reaper, and on Jan. 14, 1862, a second one, relating to the lever board and attachment of guards on the improved machine. The company's business under his direction was gradually enlarged to include the manufacture of mowers, binders, and harvesters, as well as reapers. As early as 1861, twelve hundred binders were manufactured after the Burson patents, and in 1867 the first successful Marsh harvester was built. Furthermore, had twine been cheap enough, Emerson would have introduced the Behel twine binder in 1870. As the business enlarged and other people were taken into the firm, its name was changed to Emerson, Talcott & Company in 1876; Emerson Manufacturing Company in 1895; and the Emerson-Brantingham Company in 1909, when Emerson retired from the presidency, retaining the chairmanship of the board of directors. During this development he found time to engage in other business activities, and built up the great Burson Knitting Company of Rockford, Ill., and other knitting concerns in that city. Through his influence Abraham Lincoln was retained in 1855 to defend Manny & Company in the suit brought by C. H. McCormick [*q.v.*] for alleged infringement of certain reaper patents. Manny & Company won the suit (see A. J. Beveridge, *Abraham Lincoln,* 1928, I, 576–83). Emerson's philanthropies were numerous, the greatest, possibly, being the founding of Emerson Institute for the education of negro children at Mobile, Ala., shortly after the Civil War. On Sept. 7, 1858, he married Adaline Elizabeth Talcott of Rockford. In 1909, with her, he published *Mr. and Mrs. Ralph Emerson's Personal Recollections of Abraham Lincoln.* He died in his eighty-fourth year, survived by his widow and five children.

[Robt. L. Ardrey, *Am. Agric. Implements* (1894); *Farm Implement News* (Chicago), Aug. 27, 1914; *Weekly Implement Trade Jour.* (Kansas City), Aug. 22, 29, 1914; *Farm Machinery* (St. Louis), Aug. 25, 1914; *Implement Age* (Springfield, Ohio), Aug. 29, 1914; *Who's Who in America,* 1914–15; B. K. Emerson, *The Ipswich Emersons, A. D. 1636–1900* (1900); *Mobile Register* and *Rockford Republic,* both Aug. 20, 1914.]

C.W.M.

EMERSON, RALPH WALDO (May 25, 1803–Apr. 27, 1882), essayist, poet, was born in Boston of a line which on his mother's side ran back to the early eighteenth century through mercantile men—coopers, distillers—and holders of real estate, but which on his father's side can be traced through preachers to the first colonial generation. His father, William Emerson [*q.v.*], was descended from the Rev. Peter Bulkeley [*q.v.*], first minister of Concord, Mass., who came from England in 1634. Bulkeley's granddaughter married Joseph Emerson whose father, Thomas, came from England in the ship *Elizabeth Ann* in 1635, and settled at Ipswich, Mass. Edward, son of Joseph and Elizabeth (Bulkeley) Emerson, married Rebecca Waldo, and from this union came the Rev. Joseph Emerson of Malden, an industrious scholar who "prayed every night that none of his descendants might ever be rich." His wife was Mary Moody, daughter of the Rev. Samuel Moody, a man of heroic zeal, who went by the name of Father Moody of Agamenticus (Me.). Their son, the Rev. William Emerson of Concord, was a conspicuous patriot at the outbreak of the Revolution, dying as a chaplain near Rutland, Vt., in 1777; he built the Old Manse at Concord. His son, William Emerson [*q.v.*], father of the poet, preached first at Harvard, Mass., but went to Boston in 1799 as minister of the First Church. He had never been especially moved to preach, being possessed of literary ambitions and a certain "levity" which he said wove itself into the web of his whole life; but his son remembered him as a stern if kindly man, and his sermons seem not to have been especially latitudinarian. He loved letters; he polished his sermons for style; in Boston he edited a literary review of some pretensions and of no little distinction. His wife, the poet's mother, was Ruth Haskins of Boston, daughter of the merchant John Haskins, and a woman of pronounced piety—a trait which expressed itself at the same time in a lovely serenity and in an unrelieved severity.

Emerson in his boyhood was serious and somewhat withdrawn from the world of play. Disliked by many neighbor boys for his "lofty carriage of the head," he found sufficient entertainment in books and in the society of his family, where indeed he was often set down as frivolous. From the time he was eight the household maintained itself with difficulty, for in 1811 his mother was left a widow with six children under ten, and the problem of rearing this brood was one of which both she and they were kept acutely conscious. Emerson was particularly attached to his brothers William, Edward Bliss, and Charles Chauncy, the two latter of whom were considered by relations of the family to be quite his equals in intellectual promise; and all four of them were deeply indebted not only to their mother but to their aunt, Mary Moody Emerson [*q.v.*]. "Aunt Mary," a very frequent visitor at the Emersons', was fanatically devoted to the cause of her nephews' education. They were "born to be educated," she said; and her contribution to this process was one to which Ralph, at least, never tired of paying tribute. She combined with a formidable piety which savored of the old dogmatic days a penetrating critical and skeptical talent; positively overbearing when she expressed an opinion, she yet was eager that her nephews should be scholars, orators, and poets, and she knew how to stimulate their intelligences in those directions. She was a writer whose pungent style Emerson always admired. She was a person almost without a rival in her generation for force and picturesqueness. It is probably not fantastic to say that in her struggles to meet the old thought with the new she prepared her famous nephew for the part he was to play as creator and illuminator of a modern faith.

Emerson's education began before he was three, when he was sent to a dame school or nursery conducted by Mrs. Whitwell. A little later he became a pupil at Lawson Lyon's grammar school, and in 1813 he entered the Boston Latin School under Benjamin Apthorp Gould [*q.v.*], spending a part of each day at a private school where he was taught writing. In 1814, when the family was forced by high prices in Boston to take refuge under Dr. Ezra Ripley's roof in Concord, the boy had a taste of village teaching; but the next year he was taken back to Boston, where he spent two years in preparing himself for college. He entered Harvard in August 1817 as "president's freshman," or messenger, being paid for this service with free lodgings in the president's house. He also waited on table at the Commons and tutored in his spare time, and during the winter vacations acted as usher at his uncle Samuel Ripley's school in Waltham. As a student, during the four years he spent at Cambridge, he was by no means docile or regular. His reading was often independent of the requirements; he made no especial impression upon his contemporaries; and afterwards he was to go on record as believing that college had done little for him on the whole. Yet he did draw a good deal from three of his professors, George Ticknor in modern languages, Edward Everett in Greek, and Edward Tyrrel Channing [*qq.v.*] in English composition. He was an enthusiastic member of a literary society, the Pythologian Club; from the year 1820, his third at Harvard, dates the earliest extant volume of those journals which were to be his constant companions for more than fifty years and into which was to go all the literary material of his lectures, essays, and published books. The *Journals,* his best biography whether at this period or in the period of his prime, show him now as a youth of several minds: still very much under the influence of his Aunt Mary, whose letters he copies carefully as if they contained a kind of gospel, yet excited also by new ideas and phrases met in a wide variety of books, and already mortified by religious doubt. If Harvard did little for Emerson, it was at least there that his mind commenced its characteristic and beautiful activity.

Graduating as class poet in 1821, he saw before him a future of school-teaching and at last, in view of what his ancestors had been, of preaching. But his literary ambitions were very strong; he had been seized with a passion for eloquence, and it seemed to him not impossible that he might one day be a professor of rhetoric and elocution. He began, however, merely as an assistant to his older brother William, who, at his mother's house, conducted a finishing school for the young ladies of Boston. After two years he took sole charge, maintaining the school for another year and a half. It was an unhappy time for him. He did not consider himself a success at teaching, though some of his pupils did; his journals are filled with expressions of discouragement and self-doubt; and he seems already to have had misgivings on the score of his call—whenever it should come—as a leader of the faithful. When his family moved in 1823 to Canterbury, four miles from Boston, he experienced relief in the neighborhood of nature and wrote the poem which begins, "Goodbye, proud world! I'm going home." There in 1825 he closed his school, having earned a considerable sum of money and come to a resolution to attempt the ministry, and went to Cambridge to enter the Divinity School.

He had indulged in enough introspection to know that he would never write "a Butler's 'Analogy' or an 'Essay' of Hume." "My reasoning faculty," he told himself in his journal, "is weak." What he did see in himself was a certain strength of "moral imagination." This, combined with such oratorical powers as he could develop, would make his life, he hoped, an effective instrument. As for the dogmas he would be expected to defend, he had more doubts than ever now, but went ahead—to be an orator if nothing else. It is perhaps significant that his studies at the Divinity School were desultory. He had been there only a month when poor health forced him to leave and do work on a farm in Newton; and during the next year and a half the necessity of teaching school, joined with attacks of rheumatism and lung trouble, prevented him from being more than a listener at the lectures. Nevertheless he was "approbated to preach" by the Middlesex Association of Ministers on Oct. 10, 1826, and delivered his first sermon five days after at Waltham. His health then grew worse again, so that he was forced to spend the ensuing winter in Georgia and Florida. Home in the spring, he settled himself for a year in Divinity Hall, whence he issued occasionally to preach in various churches of Boston and the towns of New England. While so employed at Concord, N. H., in December 1827, he met Ellen Louisa Tucker. She was the daughter of Beza Tucker, a Boston merchant, and seventeen years old; "beautiful by universal consent," Emerson told one of his brothers, but already touched with consumption. A year later he was engaged to marry her.

In March 1829 he was elected by the Second Church of Boston to serve as colleague of the Rev. Henry Ware. Within a few weeks he assumed full charge, and on Sept. 30 he married Ellen Tucker, whose death from consumption seventeen months later (Feb. 8, 1831) closed what had been his tenderest and most loving relationship to date, the relationships with his brothers only excepted. Meanwhile he was making a success of his ministry, so soon nevertheless to end. His sermons were distinguished by the sincerity and directness of their language and by a content, more ethical than theological, which charmed the younger members of the congregation. Many of the ideas which in the *Essays* were destined to stir and shock the world were latent here, though as yet not radically presented. He remained on excellent terms with the church until the summer of 1832, when he broke with it, and with the ministry in general, over the Lord's Supper, which he had decided he could administer only if the bread and wine were left out. When the church could not agree, he retired from Boston to think the matter over, returned to preach a sermon in which he made his position once more clear, and offered his resignation. After much debate and with great reluctance it was accepted; and Emerson was free again to indulge in dreams of literary greatness. As for the ministry, he would undoubtedly have abandoned it before long on general principles, though general principles did not enter into the discussion he had carried on so gently with his church. He had been uncomfortable over prayer; and he had recently remarked in his journals: "I have sometimes thought that in order to be a good minister it was necessary to leave the ministry. The profession is antiquated."

Emerson was now in his thirtieth year, and still far from mature. But the decade which followed saw him come to his full powers and into an appreciable measure of the fame which he was to enjoy in his prime. His first move, and one which was to be of incalculable advantage to his mind, was in the direction of Europe. Later on he was to make a great deal of Concord, insisting that it was a sufficient universe in itself; and indeed much of his force he owes to his proud provincialism; but the taste which he now got of an older continent was always vivid upon his tongue. His health threatening to give way once more, he sailed in December 1832 for the Mediterranean, landing at Malta and making soon for Italy, where at Rome he met a friend of Carlyle and secured a letter of introduction to him. He had recently been struck by some unsigned articles in the British reviews, and had taken the pains to discover the name of their author; the destination of all his wanderings, then, was Scotland, and his fondest hope was that he might have conversation with this new mystic who drew so much wisdom from German sources. In Florence he saw Walter Savage Landor; in London, which he reached through Paris, he saw Coleridge and John Stuart Mill; in Scotland, whither he hurried in the summer of 1833, he found Carlyle at last, and spent an afternoon and night at Craigenputtock. "Next morning," said Carlyle, "I saw him go up the hill; I didn't go with him to see him descend. I preferred to watch him mount and vanish like an angel." Carlyle was neither the first man nor the last to feel something angelic in the nature of Emerson and to hit upon such language for describing him; but he yielded to no one in the quality of his devotion. A correspondence lasting almost forty years sprang out of this encounter between men so different in most respects that they filled hundreds of pages in explaining themselves to each other, yet so much alike in their passionate search for new truths that each could always rest secure in the consciousness of an audience at least of one across the Atlantic. When Emerson returned to Boston after a visit to Wordsworth in the Lake Country he had seen the three persons in Europe he most wanted to see. Through Coleridge, Carlyle, and Wordsworth, and ultimately therefore through German idealism, he had arrived in his reading at the set of ideas he would promulgate if the opportunity ever occurred. Plato, the Neo-Platonists, the Sacred Books of the East, and his own native culture had made their several contributions also; but it was these contemporaries who had awakened him. Now he had seen them with his own eyes, had discovered them to be after all not hopelessly beyond the

Emerson

reach of his emulation, and had gained from them the confidence to go ahead on local ground.

His education was now in one sense complete. He had only to absorb and apply the ideas with which he had become acquainted; he had only to live henceforth in constant companionship with the authors whom he had found to be his affinities. In Goethe and the German idealists, and in the English poets and essayists through whom the transcendental point of view was achieving its expression, Emerson like the rest of his generation discovered a refreshing, an apparently inexhaustible source of ideas stimulating both to the reason and to the imagination. Unitarianism had merely opened the New England mind and removed from it some of its more rigorous dogmas; the republicanism of the last century, stemming from French roots, had merely swept clear the social ground for future speculation and experiment; the line of British philosophers which ran back through Hume, Berkeley, and Locke had merely made skepticism possible. Emerson grew up in the Unitarian fold, breathed republicanism as his native air, and admired both Hume and Berkeley; but an essential thing remained to be done, and that was to affirm in new accents the beauty, the dignity, and the infinite importance of the human soul, to announce under what sign man should conquer the great world that had been emptied for him to enter.

His equipment for this task came to him from his reading and from the relationship he began now quite deliberately to cultivate with nature. He had expressed his indebtedness to many authors, and the *Journals* by themselves attest the breadth of his literary experience; but there were certain books to which he was always to return. Montaigne, whom he read in Cotton's translation, he loved both early and late, valuing him for his candor, his calm, and for that aspect of his skepticism which made him not so much a believer in nothing as a believer in all things—an insatiable seeker after life in each of its innumerable forms. For Emerson too was an eager observer of the world; if he was to deny the ultimate importance of appearances, he was to insist also upon the value of knowing appearances in themselves. Only upon the clear-sighted vision of such a skeptic as Montaigne could any significant idealism be reared. So with Plato, whom Emerson appreciated, as Pater did later, for the accuracy and sanity with which he had described the very world he seemed to deny. The dualism of Plato and the doctrine of ideas exercised of course an incalculable influence on Emerson's idealism; but Emerson put an equal estimate upon Plato's understanding of men, and he never tired of praising his master for the realism of his style, a quality which had also endeared Montaigne to him. A third writer, Swedenborg, he read with a certain caution because of the theology there, but with continued excitement because in Swedenborg he found a vocabulary and a procedure which fitted the direction of his own exploring thought. From Swedenborg he learned to speak naturally of "forms" and "correspondences," to see man always at the center of nature, and to work at the problem of relating man's mind to the bewildering pageant of nature's phenomena. From Swedenborg and others, incidentally, he seems to have got the notion of forms ascending spirally through degrees which some have taken as anticipating the theory of evolution.

His reading of Swedenborg had given him a metaphysical approach to nature. His visit to Wordsworth, whose poetry he had known long before, confirmed him in his feeling that he should establish an original relationship with the visible universe. The bookish mystic who returned from Europe was ever afterward to spend an allotted portion of each day in the woods or along the rivers of his native province; and he was by slow degrees, opening his eyes upon beauties strange and new, to effect a marriage between his thoughts and his sensations, between his reading and his experience, which would issue at last in an exciting doctrine communicable—since the soul is identical in all men—to his contemporaries. In the meantime, however, there was the problem of a profession.

He resumed his preaching for a while. Every Sunday during the next four years he occupied some pulpit or other, and as late as 1847 he still preached occasionally. But now also he commenced his lifework as a lecturer, speaking on natural history before the Mechanics' Institute of Boston, where he proceeded to declare the moral and psychological correspondences between Nature and the mind of man. In 1835 he gave six lectures on biography in Boston, following them up in the winter with a series of ten on English literature. This was the first of five annual series which he delivered in the metropolis before audiences that grew more enthusiastic with every hearing. The next year the subject was "The Philosophy of History"; then "Human Culture"; then "Human Life"; and then "The Present Age." The material for these addresses came out of the *Journals,* which now reach the highest point of their interest; and the addresses in turn furnished the basis for the text of the *Essays,* to be published a few years later. Emerson followed the most capricious side of his genius when he came to the act of composition. The *Journals* would receive his thoughts as they occurred to him; the lectures would consist of these thoughts collected in any order that seemed to him most effective at the moment; the *Essays* were often very little altered from the lectures, though paragraphs and pages might be transferred at will from one context to another. It was never, indeed, the order that counted with his audience. The sentences by themselves were "thunderbolts," each one striking in its proper place as if no other sentence had ever been spoken. Emerson's auditors, like his readers later, grew accustomed to a succession of thrills.

His private life was receiving its permanent outline during these years. The deaths of his brothers Edward and Charles in 1834 and 1836 removed his two most intimate relations; but in 1834 he went with his mother to live in Concord, the seat of his forefathers and thereafter always to be his home; and here in September 1835 he brought a second wife, Lydia Jackson of Plymouth—renamed by him, for purposes of euphony, Lidian Emerson. The house he bought for her on the edge of the village was his until he died; here he quickly settled into the daily routine—writing in the morning, walking alone in the afternoon, and talking with friends or with the family in the evening—which nothing but lecture tours could interrupt. Here he made new friends: Margaret Fuller, Amos Bronson Alcott ("He excites me, and I think freely"), Henry David Thoreau, Jones Very, and Nathaniel Hawthorne. Here Thoreau lived as a kind of housekeeper from 1841 to 1843, and again in 1847 while Emerson traveled in Europe. Here Emerson did the better part of his reading—often a random exercise, "for the lustres" of style and apothegm rather than for systems of thought—and here he learned the secret of his writing: strict attention to every fancy or speculation as it came along, and quick determination to set it down on a page of his journal, where an index would enable him to find it as soon as he needed it. In this house was born in 1836 the first of his four children, Waldo, the beloved boy whose death five years later he was to mourn in one of his best poems, "Threnody." Emerson loved children, as he was loved by them, and gave much time to his own; he recorded their sayings, and he did not at all object to their presence in his study while he worked.

The year 1836 was notable for a number of reasons. In this year Emerson saw Carlyle's *Sartor Resartus* through an American edition and published his own first book, *Nature,* on which he had been at work for at least three years. It was far from a popular success, but it was effective where it should have been, in the minds of those who were beginning to think as Emerson did. It was both welcomed and damned as the first clear blast on New England's Transcendental horn. The time had come, said Emerson, to begin life over. "Why should not we enjoy an original relation to the universe? . . . There are new lands, new men, new thoughts. Let us demand our own works and laws and worship." The soul of man, prime as it is in the universe and possessed of powers through which God may immediately be known, still depends upon nature for its nourishment. Nature, being the dress God wears, or the shadow He casts upon the senses, is indispensable for several reasons: it has commodity, or use; it has beauty, which is the cause of delight and the origin of art; it has language, since facts as symbols speak more eloquently to man than his own words do; and it has discipline, because nature is always moral—and so, in the course of man's efforts to understand and conform, teaches and improves him. All this in explanation of Emerson's preliminary announcement that a new world was possible to man, and of his demand that it be created out of man's awakened instincts. The demand, indeed, had already been made by a group of persons, including Orestes Brownson, Theodore Parker, Bronson Alcott, Margaret Fuller, and James Freeman Clarke, which Emerson had helped to form earlier in 1836, and which continued to meet for discussion until 1843. Its members were called Transcendentalists, and though Emerson never accepted the term as adequately descriptive of himself, he defended those who deserved it and was always ready to associate the word with all that was fruitful and forward in contemporary speculation.

In August of the following year he had an opportunity to apply the ideas of *Nature* in a strategic place. Asked to deliver the Phi Beta Kappa oration at Harvard, he responded with *The American Scholar,* delivered in Cambridge Aug. 31, 1837, which James Russell Lowell considered "an event without any former parallel in our literary annals," and which Oliver Wendell Holmes called "our intellectual Declaration of Independence." It was nothing more than a translation of *Nature* into specific terms; let us, he said, as scholars establish an original relation to the universe of philosophy and the arts; let us have done with Europe and all dead cultures, let us explore the possibilities of our own new world. This closing injunction was preceded by an analysis of the scholar's function. The scholar is Man Thinking; his duty is first to know nature, whence all power and wisdom come, then to make

Emerson

himself one with the mind of the past through books, and at last to express himself in action. He should trust himself, for the world is to be asked to trust him. "He is the world's eye. He is the world's heart." And performing as he does the "highest function of human nature," he is to sustain himself at an altitude, never deferring to "the popular cry" but remaining both an aristocrat of the soul and a servant to good men. Hardly had the stir over this address died down when Emerson delivered a heavier shot in his discourse before the graduating class of Divinity College, Cambridge, July 15, 1838. For now it was as if he had decided to clear his mind once for all of any remaining conviction that the Church as constituted was the place for scholars and prophets. He declared it dead and helpless, and called upon the future ministers who sat before him to consider what kind of awakening they must undergo before they could hope to touch the living world. He granted the supreme importance of the religious sentiment; he even granted the importance of the Church, with its precious institutions of Sabbath and pulpit; and he admitted that among the clergy of the day there were exceptions to the generalization he had been forced to make. But, he said, it remained in general true that modern Christianity, by neglecting the soul, by attempting merely to communicate an old revelation, by refraining from exploration of the spiritual resources now as always existing in the moral constitution of man, had ceased to do its proper work. He counseled the graduating class to seek a new revelation proper to the times, to cultivate solitude and self-reliance, and to understand that only in the soul was redemption ever to be sought. The general ideas which underlay the speech, together with its indictment of the ministerial profession, produced naturally a shock. Emerson was attacked in the press, and though liberal Christians did not definitely attack him they agreed that they could never go with him so far. Emerson, unhappy at being the center of a storm, feared for a time that his career both in the church and in the lyceum was finished. It was not, however, as the attendance at his next series of Boston lectures demonstrated. People came to hear him even when they did not expect to agree. At Harvard, however, he was *persona non grata* for almost thirty years.

The group of thinkers and talkers which Emerson had helped to bring together in 1836 had planned a magazine, to be called, perhaps, *The Transcendentalist*. This plan was never realized; but in July 1840, partly as a result of the first effort, *The Dial* commenced publication with Margaret Fuller as literary editor and Emerson as one of the star contributors. *The Dial* continued for two years to express the "highest" thought of New England, running sometimes into extravagances of utterance which earned the ridicule of those untouched by Transcendentalism and the passion for reform. It was a day of reforms, as Emerson himself has humorously recorded, and *The Dial* was an open forum for their promulgation. Emerson's own interest was in the poetry and metaphysics which found their way into its pages rather than in the "practical" aspects of its program; and when at the end of its second year he somewhat reluctantly assumed the editorship he threw his weight upon the philosophical side of the balance. *The Dial,* however, had only two more years to live. When it died in 1844 it was set down as a failure, if a magnificent one. Emerson was perhaps more intimately concerned with a new group he was organizing at about this time for the purposes of conversation, a group which anticipated the Concord School of Philosophy in its aims and conduct.

Around the year 1840 Emerson was engaged in a struggle to define his position with reference to the reforms which had sprung up on all sides. His instinct was to place himself above them, in a region where the principle of compensation would render all such discussion premature and futile; but in spite of himself he was drawn into the arena from time to time. The largest question, of course, was slavery. At first he reminded his friends that this reform like all others must come from within the individuals affected; the negro must elevate himself, and Emerson doubted his capacity to do so. Before long, however, he was addressing meetings of Abolitionists—not always with enough passion, the zealots said. In 1838 he wrote a letter of protest to President Van Buren on the occasion of the removal of the Cherokee Indians from Georgia. Reforms nearer home he was never quite able to take seriously. He attended meetings at which Margaret Fuller, Bronson Alcott, and others laid the plans for Brook Farm in 1840, but failed to catch fire. So did he keep hands off of "Fruitlands," projected by Alcott and some English friends a little later. He did attempt a few reforms within his own household; he ennobled himself with manual labor for a while; he invited the maids to eat with the family, and was perhaps not sorry when they refused; he took up vegetarianism until he found it of little use. In general it may be said that his attitude towards the schemes so abundant in his day for making over the visible world was the attitude of a poet and philosopher; his game was the intellect, and his goal the triumph of invisible—though none the less potent—ideas.

His fame as a lecturer grew as he widened his operations year by year. This was the only way he could make money, and expenses were always increasing. His trips extended now into the West, and the physical effort of traveling was more and more felt. He complained of the "long, weary absences" from his house, his books, his children. What was worse, he suspected the profession. "I live in a balcony or on the street," he wrote; and there were days when he dismissed the whole business as a form of vulgarization. "Are not lectures a kind of Peter Parley's story of Uncle Plato, and a puppet show of the Eleusinian mysteries?" Yet there were few among his listeners to complain that he talked down to them. The sentences came forth in the same order and with the same emphasis that soon were to distinguish the printed *Essays*. The tall, slender man with the brown hair, the intensely blue eyes, the aquiline, angelic features and the abstracted, impersonal smile stood almost motionless as he spoke; and he spoke a doctrine which, however flattering to mankind, it took the closest attention to understand.

This now familiar doctrine, amplified from *Nature* and applied to the concerns of the individual soul, received its final form in the first volume of *Essays*, published in the spring of 1841. The second volume, appearing three years later, combined with the first to consolidate a reputation which, until then local or personal, soon spread through Europe and America. Matthew Arnold has testified to the effect of the *Essays* at Oxford in the forties; and there is no end of testimony that in mid-century America Emerson was felt to be the bringer of a new religion which somehow squared with the times even while it supplied a method for criticizing them. The young especially were his devoted readers, and from this period on his house in Concord was to be the destination of ardent pilgrims. He himself did not rest. In 1845 he delivered a course of lectures on "Representative Men." In 1846, after persistent requests by his publisher, he issued a volume of *Poems* (published in time for Christmas, but dated 1847), to be followed twenty-one years later by a second volume, *May-Day and Other Pieces*. He had always thought verse to be the most perfect mode of utterance, and he had always referred to himself as a poet. Now he offered evidence whereby he might be judged. The judgment has taken some time to become mature, but it is no longer to be doubted that in a few of his pieces he reached a mark which only Whitman, Poe, and Emily Dickinson reached in America during the nineteenth century. Many of his poems are bad; all but two or three are imperfect; but at his happiest he managed a high, rapturous, piercing, and melodious note the only parallel to which is the note of his best prose. It is intellectual poetry that he writes; he moves most naturally in the gnomic rhythm, being all but unsurpassed in the shining force which he can give to an aphoristic couplet, a prophetic quatrain. At its best, however, it is intellectual poetry burning with what he called "aromatic fire." It is the work of a passionate intellect saturated in Wordsworth, Shakespeare, and the lyric masters of the seventeenth century. "Threnody" is one of the most moving elegies in the English language; "Brahma" is perfect in the metaphysical mode; "The Problem," "The Rhodora," "Woodnotes," "Give All to Love," "Bacchus," "Concord Hymn," "Terminus," and the "mottoes" prefixed to the *Essays* are all in their various ways adequate to express the extraordinary, the demonic energy of the man.

In 1847 he went to lecture in England and found himself famous there. His addresses were particularly successful; but he valued more than this success the opportunity to talk once more with the Carlyles, whom he visited in Chelsea. After a round of social events which made him the acquaintance of Sir William Hamilton, De Quincey, Harriet Martineau, Macaulay, Lyell, Thackeray, Dickens, Clough, Tennyson, Froude, and many other notables, he went on to Paris in 1848, returning thence to America with a better opinion of the French than he had had before but with an especial admiration for most things English. His lectures on England the ensuing season were the basis of *English Traits*, published eight years later (1856). The book is full of praise for an old, a rich, and an essentially liberal, humane people. We could not do without English achievements, says Emerson, in letters, religion, government, and trade. Yet he is not sparing in his criticism of a certain contemporary inertia—something he had learned about from Carlyle—which expressed itself in spiritual sluggishness and in a pervasive materialism. He is subtle, sensitive, and often accurate in his appraisal of the national mind; and always in the book he is easily readable. He now extended the circuit of his lectures as far west as the Mississippi; for twenty years he was to make a western tour every winter, speaking oftentimes for as little as ten dollars an evening, and facing audiences in Illinois, for instance, which walked out of the hall after ten minutes of talk which they did not find funny enough. Humor was everywhere in his discourse, but not in the form of jokes. On the whole he was respected wherever he went, and always there was a devoted band of listeners; but the work was wearing. Even this early he talked of growing old, though the full confession still waited to be made. Meanwhile he was giving lectures, on "The Conduct of Life," which were among the most popular and effective he ever gave, and which when published under the same title in 1860 were declared by Carlyle to be the best of all his works.

In 1849 he reprinted *Nature* together with a collection of *Addresses and Lectures.* In 1850 appeared *Representative Men,* and the next year he made a contribution to some *Memoirs* of Margaret Fuller Ossoli, recently dead by drowning off Fire Island. In 1855 he was sent a copy of *Leaves of Grass,* by Walt Whitman of New York. His letter to Whitman acknowledging the volume and greeting this strange, new poet "at the beginning of a great career" has been cited as proof of his extraordinary receptiveness to talent wherever he found it. Certainly the poems of Whitman were different from his own, and poles away from his chaste if radical temperament; certainly it was a sign of his own genius that he could recognize that of the younger man, and a sign too of his character that he could be so generous. The most interesting thing about the incident, however, is the fact that Whitman sent Emerson the book; it might have been expected that the Homer of Manhattan would look askance at the Plato of Concord. Whitman, as a matter of fact, was one of those numerous men of the mid-century who fell under Emerson's influence and remained under it while they lived. It was through reading the *Essays* that he came into possession of his own secret, that he grew confident of his own powers. Emerson's disciples, Thoreau among them, were like that—not disciples at all. Emerson indeed rejected the word, saying that he would bring men not to him but to themselves.

Society and Solitude, published in 1870, had all been written before 1860, but the chief occupation of Emerson's mind during the fifties was politics. He had protested with other men of Massachusetts against the annexation of Texas and the Fugitive-Slave Law; now his *Journals* were filled with comment upon the great issue which was dividing the country. In 1856 he spoke at Concord concerning Brooks's assault on Sumner in the Senate. As the war in Kansas took on ominous proportions he was one of those who advocated sending arms in support of the anti-slavery faction, and when John Brown arrived at Concord in 1857 Emerson became one of his champions. He made a number of anti-slavery speeches which drew hisses from the crowd, and once he was roared down, but his blood for once was up, and he did not care. When the Civil War began he remarked: "Sometimes gunpowder smells good." When he went to lecture at Washington in 1862 he was pleased to be able to discuss the progress of the war with Lincoln, Seward, and the rest.

In the years immediately preceding the war Emerson had formed about him a new group of men, or rather a group with a new name. The Saturday Club, which grew out of a habit he had of meeting certain friends in Boston for occasional dinners, soon flourished as a literary association; at its monthly gatherings he was to take comfort as he got older in the companionship of Longfellow, Hawthorne, Motley, Dana, Agassiz, Holmes, Lowell, and others. He was also to derive a peculiar pleasure from the Adirondack Club, whose members went on outings with him among the mountains he so loved to praise. The impression would be justified that he was a particularly social man. Such, however, was not the case; or at any rate he was social with a difference. All who knew him agreed that he was charming, but his charm still expressed itself at a certain distance. In his *Journals* are many complaints of his own "coldness." The term seems to have been an exaggeration; yet for him it did well enough as a description of his serenely self-reliant temper, a temper nourished in solitude and disciplined by contemplation. Eager as he was for conversation, he himself often supplied less of it than did his hearers; he talked slowly and sometimes with difficulty, and he disliked to laugh.

In 1866 he read to his son Edward Waldo a poem he had written called "Terminus":

> It is time to be old,
> To take in sail.
> The god of bounds,
> Who sets to seas a shore,
> Came to me in his fatal rounds
> And said: "No more!
> No farther shoot
> Thy broad ambitious branches, and thy root.
> Fancy departs: no more invent;
> Contract thy firmament
> To compass of a tent."

He had become aware that his original effort was over and his instinct, as usual, was right. After 1866 he did nothing that was strictly or even partly new, though he kept on with his lecturing and in some measure with his writing. Harvard at this late date signified her reconciliation with him by giving him the honorary degree of LL.D. (1866); in 1867 he was invited to deliver the Phi Beta Kappa oration there; and in 1870, being asked to offer a course of academic lectures, he

Emerson

eagerly responded with a series on "Natural History of Intellect," a subject which had long interested him and which, since it concerned the problem of connecting thoughts with things, was only another form of the one subject he had dealt with from the beginning.

Tired from this and other exertions, Emerson was taken in 1871 for a six weeks' outing in California, a band of friends ushering him there in a private Pullman. He was delighted and overawed; yet young John Muir the naturalist, living in a cabin in the mountains, saw Emerson and decided that he must be only the ghost of his former self. He was imperturbably silent, and at times seemed scarcely to know where he was. From this time on the decline in his powers was regular if not rapid. Outwardly calm and smiling, inwardly he grew blank; it became more and more difficult for him to find the words he needed; in conversation he would forget the names not only of persons but of things, so that he had to paraphrase and pantomime—a fork would be asked for with a gesture of the hand, and an umbrella would be called "the thing that strangers take away." He still lectured or read from old manuscripts but one of his young worshippers, John Burroughs, going with Walt Whitman to hear the great man speak at Baltimore in 1872, wrote afterwards to a friend: "Nothing can be more irrelevant or pitiful than those lectures he is now delivering." His literary work henceforth was of less than the first importance. In 1870 he had written the introduction for a new edition of Plutarch's *Morals;* in 1874 he published an anthology, called *Parnassus,* of the poems in English to which he was most attached; and in 1876 came out one more collection of essays, *Letters and Social Aims,* but only after James Elliot Cabot had been called in to solve the muddle of the manuscripts.

In July 1872 he suffered a blow in the burning of his house at Concord. James Russell Lowell and other friends contributed $17,000 to a fund that would make good the loss and give the old poet a long-needed vacation from lecturing. He sailed soon for Europe, where now for the last time he saw Carlyle and where he met Hermann Grimm, Taine, Turgenev, Browning, Max Müller, Jowett, and Ruskin. After he had satisfied an old desire to see the Valley of the Nile he returned in 1873 to Concord, where as the bells of the village rang welcome he was met at the station by townspeople and schoolchildren who escorted him under a triumphal arch of flowers to his house; in his absence it had been completely restored. The rest of his life passed tranquilly at home. He read occasional addresses to audiences which remembered the former man rather than attended to this one; with the assistance of Cabot he prepared two further volumes for the press; but in general he slid into a serene and dignified senility. At the grave of Longfellow in March 1882, he could not remember the name of the man who was being buried. A few weeks later he himself was stricken with pneumonia, and when he died in April he was buried near Thoreau, his brilliant and independent pupil, who had preceded him in death by twenty years.

A series of posthumous volumes completed the publication of Emerson's writings. His correspondence with Carlyle was edited a year after his death by Charles Eliot Norton. *Lectures and Biographical Sketches* appeared in 1884, *Miscellanies* in the same year, and *Natural History of Intellect* in 1893. His correspondence with John Sterling, Carlyle's friend, came out in 1897; *Letters from Ralph Waldo Emerson to a Friend* (Samuel Gray Ward), in 1899; *Correspondence between Ralph Waldo Emerson and Hermann Grimm,* in 1903; and *Records of a Lifelong Friendship,* his correspondence with William Henry Furness, in 1910. *The Complete Works of Ralph Waldo Emerson* (Centenary Edition, 1903–04), based upon the Riverside Edition of 1883–93, left nothing to be desired except the *Journals;* these appeared in ten volumes between 1909 and 1914.

Emerson's fame both at home and abroad rests securely upon the fact that he had something of permanent importance to say, and that he said it with a beautiful freshness which does not permit his best pages to grow old. His Transcendental excesses are easily forgotten, but it is not possible to forget his manner of announcing that men are exalted creatures, that instinct is to be obeyed, and that the soul is a sensible reality. Let men but stand erect and "go alone," he said, and they can possess the universe. With all his idealism, he emerges from the cloud of serious thinkers who surrounded him in New England by virtue of a durable style, a gift of observation, and a sense of humor. His style is at its best not alone in the *Essays, Representative Men,* and certain chapters of *Nature;* it rises to perhaps its finest height in the concluding paragraph of the chapter on "Illusions" in *The Conduct of Life,* and it makes its sudden appearance in many other places. His ability to understand and describe people is seen in such pieces of contemporary history as *Historic Notes of Life and Letters in New England,* in *English Traits,* and in the biographical sketches he left of Thoreau and his Aunt Mary. His sense of humor is almost everywhere present, informing, refining, and enlightening his utterance and revealing itself if in no other way through an inspired choice of homely words. He is not accepted as a philosopher by the more rigorous members of the profession; yet no one denies him power and permanence as an author of some sort, though Matthew Arnold, lecturing on him in America after his death, sought to prove that he had missed being among the greatest men of letters. Arnold's strictures passed over the fact of Emerson's peculiar effectiveness in prose; and he did the poems also an injustice. The best of them are among the best, the most electrical, in modern English. It remains to be said that the impact of his shining, energizing personality is still strong. Few Americans have been more picturesque; none holds a solider position in the history of American life.

[*A Bibliography of Ralph Waldo Emerson*, by Geo. Willis Cooke, is comprehensive as far down as it comes (1908); for later publications see the bibliography by H. R. Steeves in the *Cambridge Hist. of Am. Lit.*, vol. I (1917), and the several annual bibliographies of American literature. The fullest and best biography is the *Memoir* in two volumes by Emerson's literary executor, Jas. Elliot Cabot (1887). This should be supplemented by Edward Waldo Emerson's *Emerson in Concord* (1889), the most intimate of all the accounts. Biographies by other contemporaries and acquaintances are: Geo. Willis Cooke, *Ralph Waldo Emerson* (1881); Alexander Ireland, *Ralph Waldo Emerson* (1882), dealing principally with Emerson in England; Moncure D. Conway, *Emerson at Home and Abroad* (1882); Oliver Wendell Holmes, *Ralph Waldo Emerson* (Am. Men of Letters Series, 1884); and *The Genius and Character of Emerson; Lectures at the Concord School of Philosophy* (1885), ed. by F. B. Sanborn. David Greene Haskins, *Ralph Waldo Emerson: His Maternal Ancestors* (1887), throws light upon an often neglected aspect of Emerson's origins. The *Journals* (10 vols., 1909–14) are indispensable as autobiography; the best biography based upon full knowledge of them is by O. W. Firkins (1915). The most adequate treatments by European authors are: M. Dugard, *Ralph Waldo Emerson: Sa Vie et son Œuvre* (Paris, 1907) and Paul Sakmann, *Emerson's Geisteswelt* (Stuttgart, 1927). His books have been translated into French, German, Italian, Spanish, Dutch, Russian, and the Scandinavian languages.]

M. V–D.

EMERSON, WILLIAM (May 6, 1769–May 12, 1811), Unitarian clergyman, father of Ralph Waldo Emerson, was born in Concord, Mass., son of Rev. William and Phebe (Bliss) Emerson. His father, minister of the Concord church, was a zealous patriot and was present at the fight at Concord. The son, thrown early on his own resources by the death of his father and the remarriage of his mother, prepared for college at Concord, was graduated from Harvard in 1789, taught school for two years, and after a brief study of divinity at Cambridge was ordained minister of the Unitarian church at Harvard, Mass. His tastes were social, literary, and musical, and he interested himself in the educational as well as the religious features of his work. On Oct. 25, 1796, he married Ruth Haskins of Boston. To eke out his meager salary he taught school and did manual labor on his farm, while his wife kept boarders. "We are poor and cold," he wrote, "and have little meal, and little wood, and little meat, but, thank God, courage enough." He was already attracting attention as a preacher and in 1799 accepted a call to the First Church of Boston, being chosen as one especially fitted to resist "the alarming attacks on our holy religion, by the Learned, the Witty, and the Wicked."

William Emerson was a man of striking personal appearance, tall, handsome, of fair complexion, with courtly manners and a particularly pleasing voice. He commanded in the pulpit a fluent but slightly formal eloquence, the unimpassioned correctness of which was characteristic of an already dying culture. His views were liberal. Indeed he at one time cherished the hope of planting a church in Washington on strictly congregational principles, with no confession of faith, the communion to be administered freely to all who wished to receive it. In Boston he mingled so much in society as to draw a rebuke from his sister, Mary Moody Emerson [*q.v.*], for his "tributes to fashion and parade" and for finding "the present world" too real. His civic and literary interests were multifarious. He was chaplain of the state Senate, Overseer of Harvard College, active member of the Massachusetts Historical Society, editor of the *Monthly Anthology*, and founder of the Anthology Club from whose collection of books grew the Boston Athenæum Library. He was author of *An Historical Sketch of the First Church in Boston* (1812), edited a volume of psalms and hymns, and published various sermons and orations. When he died, at the age of forty-two, he had left a distinct mark on the literary, charitable, and educational life of Boston.

Of his eight children, Ralph Waldo was the fourth. Like this famous son, who strongly resembled him, William Emerson entered the church in deference to family tradition. The suppression of natural inclination is doubtless responsible for the part that the sense of orderliness played in his life. He was, probably, what Ralph Waldo Emerson would have been, had he remained in the church. Father and son together illustrate almost perfectly the relation of the Unitarian and Transcendental movements in New England. The former was a compromise, the latter a spontaneous outburst.

[J. E. Cabot, *A Memoir of Ralph Waldo Emerson* (1887); E. W. Emerson, *Emerson in Concord* (1889); H. S. Nourse, *Hist. of the Town of Harvard, Mass., 1732–1893* (1894); B. K. Emerson, *The Ipswich Emersons* (1900), in which see especially a memoir of Wm. Emerson read before the Mass. Hist. Soc., p. 177; W.

Emery

B. Sprague, *Annals Am. Pulpit*, vol. VIII (1865); Eliza Buckminster Lee, *Memoirs of Rev. Jos. Buckminster, D.D., and of his son, Rev. Jos. Stevens Buckminster* (1894); Geo. Ticknor in the *Christian Examiner*, Sept. 1849.] H. C. G.

EMERY, ALBERT HAMILTON (June 21, 1834–Dec. 2, 1926), engineer, inventor, was born in Mexico, N. Y., the son of Samuel and Catherine Shepard Emery. He was descended from John Emery who came to Boston from England in 1635. After attending public school he entered Mexico Academy and prepared for Rensselaer Polytechnic Institute at Troy, N. Y. Following his graduation as a civil engineer in 1858 he returned to his home and began applying himself to mechanical invention. Within a year he had obtained two patents, one on a cheese press and another on a window-sash fastener. Three years later he went to New York to engage in similar work, and during the Civil War concentrated on ordnance. Between 1862 and 1865 he invented five improvements in projectiles, cannon founding, and percussion fuses. He remained in New York in his chosen profession for twenty years, perfecting annually from one to ten inventions of various sorts, including a wood distillation process and plant, hydraulic presses for various purposes, a device for towing canal boats, a weighing machine, and occasional ordnance inventions. In 1883 he organized the Emery Scale Company in Stamford, Conn., and assigned to it a group of approximately twenty new patents on weighing machinery, pressure gages, dynamometers, and testing machines. The company did not manufacture these, but sublet the construction to others, while Emery employed four or five men in a small shop to make the delicate parts. Competition was too keen, however, with established manufacturers of weighing machinery, and in a short time the company dropped out of the field. Emery then designed a testing machine for the Watertown Arsenal at Watertown, Mass. It was most ingenious, and did much to establish his reputation. It also opened a field for experimental work which has since led to important developments in the realm of mechanics. Emery thereafter continued as a consultant and designer of testing machinery until his death. Two unusual machines of his design are used at this writing at the United States Bureau of Standards, one of 230,000 pounds capacity for tension and compression, and the other of 1,150,000 pounds capacity for tension and 2,300,000 pounds for compression. Although his consulting work consumed the greater part of his time he still continued his inventive work in many lines, but principally in ordnance and hydraulic pressure measuring devices. Based on an invention of the latter type, a railway track scale for weighing cars in motion, which Emery developed, is performing important service for the major railroads of the country as well as for large industrial organizations. Emery was a fellow of the American Association for the Advancement of Science, a member of the American Society of Mechanical Engineers, and of the American Society for Testing Materials. He married Mrs. Fannie B. Myers of Westmoreland, N. Y., on Mar. 3, 1875, who died thirty years before him. Emery's death occurred at Glenbrook, near Stamford, Conn., where he had resided for forty years. He was survived by his only son and a step-daughter.

[Sources of information are *Who's Who in America*, 1926–27; Rufus Emery, *Geneal. Records of Descendants of John and Anthony Emery* (1890); *Trans. Am. Soc. of Mech. Engineers, 1926* (1927); Patent Office Records; communication with U. S. Bureau of Standards; *N. Y. Times*, Dec. 3, 1926.] C. W. M.

EMERY, CHARLES EDWARD (Mar. 29, 1838–June 1, 1898), engineer, was born at Aurora, N. Y., the son of Moses Little and Minerva (Prentiss) Emery and a descendant of John Emery who landed at Boston with his brother Anthony in 1635 and soon moved to Newbury, Mass. Moses Little Emery, an architect and builder, died when his son Charles was two years old. The boy was educated at Canandaigua Academy, and after some experience as draftsman for railroads and manufactories he decided to study law and become a patent attorney. For two years he pursued these studies, but gave them up at the outbreak of the Civil War in order to organize a company of volunteers. His company was not wanted, however, so he enlisted in the navy and received an appointment as third assistant engineer. At the close of hostilities some suggestions which he made regarding experimental steam apparatus, led the chief engineer of the navy to detail him to take part in steam-expansion experiments in New York. He resigned from the navy in 1868 but served as a consulting engineer and on a special advisory committee for years afterward.

At the Novelty Iron Works in New York City he conducted a series of experiments on stationary engines, the records of which were subsequently published by Prof. W. P. Trowbridge in *Tables and Diagrams Relating to Non-Condensing Engines and Boilers* (1872). In 1869–70, as a member of a joint board of engineers representing the Treasury Department, Emery conducted an extended series of experiments to determine the relative value of compound and non-compound engines, the reports of which were published in scientific literature in the

United States and abroad and were the only reliable data extant.

As consulting engineer to the Coast Survey and Revenue Marine, Emery fitted out nearly twenty revenue cutters, being in some cases responsible for the construction of the hulls as well as of the machinery. In 1874 he made an experiment before a board of engineers, comparing a long-stroke, high-pressure condensing engine, a short-stroke, low-pressure condensing engine; a fore-and-aft compound condensing engine, and a high-pressure condensing engine with the cylinder jacketed. The results of this trial, with Emery's analysis, were published in *Transactions of the American Society of Civil Engineers* (vol. III, 1875) and soon after, the University of the City of New York conferred upon him the degree of Ph.D.

As chief engineer and manager of the New York Steam Company (from 1879) "he performed the most remarkable work of his time in the distribution of heat and power from a central steam plant; and his construction was not only the largest, but almost the only one attempted on a large scale which has proved a successful piece of engineering" (*New York Commandery, Military Order of the Loyal Legion, Circular No. 579,* Aug. 20, 1898). For a paper describing this work, read in 1889, the Institution of Civil Engineers (Great Britain) awarded him a Watt Medal and a Telford Premium.

Through private investigations, Emery became an authority on the isochronism of timepieces. He made successful experiments in electricity and built several dynamos and motors that operated by direct current without the use of a commutator. As consulting engineer for the city of Fall River, Mass., he was instrumental in bringing about a novel compromise between the city and the mills, by which the mills agreed to furnish to the city water-power from the Watuppa ponds in consideration of the abatement of taxes on water-power. He was a member of the commission on the purchase of the Long Island Water Supply Company's plant by the City of Brooklyn, and served as a member of a board of experts appointed to give an opinion as to the best method of increasing the number and size of trains on the New York and Brooklyn bridge by changes in the New York terminal. He acted as judge on engines, pumps, and mechanical appliances at the Centennial Exposition in 1876; served as general superintendent of the Fair of the American Institute in New York City in 1869; and was one of the judges at the World's Fair in Chicago. He was a frequent contributor to the technical press.

Emery was married in 1863 to Susan S. Livingston, a great-grand-daughter of Gen. William Livingston, colonial governor of New Jersey

[Rufus Emery, *Geneal. Records of Descendants of John and Anthony Emery* (1890); *New-England Hist. and Geneal. Reg.*, July 1900; *Trans. Am. Soc. Civil Engineers*, vol. XLII (1899); *Trans. Am. Soc. Mech. Engineers*, vol. XIX (1898); and *Trans. Am. Institute Mining Engineers*, vol. XXIX (1899).] E. Y.

EMERY, HENRY CROSBY (Dec. 21, 1872–Feb. 6, 1924), economist, teacher and business man, was the son of Lucilius Alonzo Emery [*q.v.*], judge and later chief justice of the supreme court of Maine. He was a fortunate youth, and his home life in Ellsworth, a small seaport town, was one of singular beauty, rich in intellectual interests. His mother, Anne Stetson Crosby, combined deep religious feeling with broadly Christian tolerance. This spirit she seems to have transmitted to her son. In his wide range of personal relations, in Europe and in the Orient, as well as in American university and political life, he was ever free from petty jealousies, and was always quick to appreciate in others their special accomplishments and to recognize germinating talents. As a boy his devotion to his family was particularly strong and he charmed everyone with his sunny good-nature. Sailing was his favorite amusement, and all the long holidays of school and college years were spent in his boat on the Maine coast. Entering Bowdoin College at sixteen, he easily mastered studies in which his comrades floundered. Literature, especially poetry, interested him particularly at first; later, ethics and philosophy. After his graduation in 1892 he took up graduate studies in economics, first at Harvard (M.A., 1893), and then at Columbia where he attained his doctorate in 1896. A year of travel and study in Germany followed and then he returned to take up teaching at Bowdoin.

As professor of political economy at Yale in 1900 at the age of twenty-eight, he was probably the youngest teacher holding this rank at any large university. Then, he seemed on the threshold of a brilliant and fruitful career. His doctoral dissertation, *Speculation on the Stock and Produce Exchanges of the United States* (1896, published also in the Columbia *Studies in History, Economics and Public Law*), was recognized as the best American work on the subject. It was also a timely work. Popular discussion of the functions of speculation and of its effects was rife. Under the pressure of Populist propaganda, bills had been introduced into Congress to control exchanges. The book which Emery launched on these troubled waters was characterized by thorough comprehension of the mech-

Emery

anism of speculative dealings and by sound analysis of their economic function. It remains a leading authority. But apart from a few periodical articles and a collection of lectures, *Politician, Party and People* (1913), this was his only publication. As a teacher of economics, Henry Emery could hardly fail of success. His magnetic personality infused every subject with a lively interest. His broad humanity enabled him to set forth impartially the opposing points of view of social classes, while his keen intelligence warned against soft-headed reform schemes. Although conservative, his judgments were not dogmatic. In his advocacy of a mild Protectionism, following the nationalistic doctrines of Alexander Hamilton and Friedrich List, he was at variance with most of his colleagues.

Although he remained a member of the Yale faculty until 1915, Emery's academic career practically came to an end in 1909 when President Taft summoned him to Washington to become chairman of the newly created Tariff Board. This position gave scope to a variety of talents which had been latent in New Haven. Aided by a capable technical staff, he planned and carried through pioneer studies in costs of production of dutiable commodities, particularly those in "Schedule K." He had the confidence not only of his associates but of business men, members of Congress, and of the President. In 1913 the Tariff Board passed out of existence through the failure of Congress to appropriate funds, and Emery returned to Yale. But after four years of contacts with men and affairs, he found it difficult to settle down to the academic routine and in 1915 he resigned his professorship. The remaining nine years of his life were spent principally abroad, in Russia and in China, in the employ of the Guaranty Trust Company. These were years full of colorful and unusual experiences, not devoid of useful work. In St. Petersburg, July 14, 1917, he married Suzanne Cary Allinson. Attempting to escape from Russia after the Bolshevik revolution, he was captured by German forces and taken to a prison camp at Danzig. Later he was removed to Berlin, where he enjoyed considerable freedom and watched with lively interest the collapse of the monarchy, opening the way to his escape.

In China, as manager of the Peking branch of the Asia Banking Corporation, he displayed an intelligent grasp of business problems, and, at a time when our diplomatic relations were particularly complicated, his advice in financial matters was often sought by the American minister. In 1920 and 1921 he served on the United International Famine Relief Committee. Early in 1924, on his way home, he was taken ill on shipboard, died, and was buried at sea.

[*Who's Who in America*, 1922–23; *Gen. Cat. of Bowdoin Coll. 1794–1912* (1912); *N. Y. Times*, Feb. 7 and 8, 1924; personal information.] P.W.B.

EMERY, LUCILIUS ALONZO (July 27, 1840–Aug. 26, 1920), jurist, the only son of James S. and Eliza Ann (Wing) Emery, was born at Carmel, Penobscot County, Me., where his father was a merchant. He attended the academy at Hampden, to which town the family moved in 1850, and then entered Bowdoin College, where he graduated in 1861. He studied law at Bangor, Me., and having been admitted to the Penobscot bar in August 1863, commenced practise at Ellsworth, Hancock County, which was his place of residence for the remainder of his life. Interesting himself actively in local politics, he was in 1866 elected county attorney of Hancock County, and two years later entered into partnership with Eugene Hale, United States senator from Maine. In 1874 he became state senator and in 1876 was elected by the legislature state attorney-general, occupying that position for three years. During his tenure of this office he was in charge of much important litigation and displayed a profound knowledge of constitutional law. He was senior counsel for the state in its action against the Maine Central Railroad Company to recover the amount of the tax imposed on that company in respect of its franchise, and sustained the constitutionality of the legislation involved in the state courts, and in the Supreme Court of the United States. The point was a new one, and the decision was regarded as establishing an important precedent (66 *Maine*, 488; 96 *U. S.*, 499). In 1880 he was for the second time elected to the state Senate and acted as chairman of the joint committee on the judiciary. As a member of this body he was responsible for the introduction and enactment of much legislation of permanent importance, the ultimate object of which was the simplification of the law. His great achievement, however, was the introduction of a coördinated system of equity pleading accompanied by appropriate chancery rules, and the extension to the court of full equity powers. In 1883 he was appointed associate justice of the state supreme court, becoming chief justice Dec. 14, 1906, and retaining that position till his retirement June 28, 1911. On the bench he was competent, prompt, resolute, and always master of his court. His jury charges were notable for their clarity and impartiality, and his decisions were always reached after an exhaustive consideration of the law and the facts. His opinions were distinguished by their brevity, and although he was a strong supporter of the doctrine of *stare decisis,* he abstained as a rule from quoting precedents.

In 1889 he had been elected professor of medical jurisprudence in the Maine Medical School, and on the establishment of a law school at Bangor in 1898 by the University of Maine, he took a strong interest therein and joined its staff of lecturers. For a number of years he delivered lectures on Roman law, dealing principally with legal development, on probate law covering the principles and practise, and on "What to do in court and how," embodying the results of his long experience as counsel and judge. After his retirement from the bench he continued to lecture on Roman law at the law school, and his opinion was constantly sought on constitutional questions by the bar and the state government.

He was all his life an insatiable student on philosophical and historical lines, devoting particular attention to the historical development of law. In daily intercourse he was dignified, and slow to realize the humorous side of life. His opinions on public matters were strong, and often expressed in vigorous language. On the divorce problem he was especially emphatic. He considered divorce no evil, but on the contrary, a remedy for evil, and held remarriage of divorced parties necessary to mitigate the social calamity which would result from the existence of a large number of divorced persons who could never marry again. Emery married Anne Stetson Crosby on Nov. 9, 1864. Henry Crosby Emery [*q.v.*], an economist of distinction, was their son.

[Rufus Emery, *Geneal. Records of Descendants of John and Anthony Emery* (1890); *The Green Bag,* Dec. 1895, and Oct. 1911; *Law Notes,* Mar. 1909; *Report of the Maine State Bar Asso.,* 1920–21; *Who's Who in America,* 1918–19.]
H. W. H. K.

EMERY, STEPHEN ALBERT (Oct. 4, 1841–Apr. 15, 1891), teacher, composer, was the son of the famous lawyer and judge, Stephen Emery, of Paris, Me., and his wife Jennett Loring. As a boy, Emery was gifted with such acute musical understanding that he composed little pieces before being able to read notes; later, with the aid of an elder sister, he learned how to write out his musical thoughts. On finishing the usual school work in his home town, he entered Colby College in 1859, but a year there impaired his sight and left him unwell. After a rest, he turned to music as a career. Following his first instruction under Henry S. Edwards, in Portland, he went abroad in 1862. This gave the young man a chance for more serious study at Leipzig, under Plaidy, Papperitz, Richter, and Hauptmann, supplemented by a season at Dresden, under Spindler. Returning to Maine in 1864, Emery gave lessons at Portland until the "great fire" caused such serious financial damage to his pupils' families that he left for a career of larger usefulness in Boston. There he became professor of harmony and piano at the opening of the New England Conservatory, founded by Eben Tourjée [*q.v.*]. His teaching at that institution made him famous, and he numbered among his pupils many musicians of later prominence. It was in connection with this work that he published his well-known *Elements of Harmony* (1879), and his *Foundation Studies in Pianoforte Playing* (1882), written primarily for his own children. He also began a course in theory, though this subject was treated in a rather elementary fashion at the time, with the emphasis on somewhat simple esthetics instead of the detailed analysis of later days. He introduced also into his teaching the enlivening device of a weekly question-and-answer hour, in which the speaker answered all relevant questions that the students had dropped into the box used for that purpose. He was so well liked personally that when he was ill, no less a man than Chadwick took over his lessons, so that the invalid might lose no salary. Emery also became professor of composition and theory at Boston University, which was one of the earliest colleges to create a music department. As one of the assistant editors of the *Musical Herald,* he wrote many interesting articles. His numerous lectures were another factor in extending his influence. His compositions, of which there were about 150, were sometimes rather simple in style, but very popular in their appeal. They included sonatinas of some merit; string quartets which illustrated the composer's classical learning; smaller piano pictures, such as the "Kinderspiel," and "Die Schwester spielt"; and songs and choruses, both sacred and secular. Emery died in Boston.

[Rufus Emery, *Geneal. Records of Descendants of John and Anthony Emery* (1890); G. L. Howe and W. S. B. Mathews, *A Hundred Years of Music in America* (1889); Louis C. Elson, *The Hist. of Am. Music* (ed. 1925); *Musical Herald,* May and June 1891; *Boston Advertiser, Boston Globe,* Apr. 17, 1891; information as to certain facts from Moritz H. Emery and George W. Chadwick.]
A. E.

EMMET, THOMAS ADDIS (Apr. 24, 1764–Nov. 14, 1827), Irish patriot, lawyer, was born in Cork, Ireland. His parents were Robert Emmet (1729–1802), a physician of Dublin, and Elizabeth Mason. Of their large family, three sons grew to manhood. The eldest, Christopher Temple, died in 1789, and the youngest, Robert, was executed on Sept. 20, 1803, for participating in an uprising in Dublin. Thomas Addis entered Trinity College, Dublin, in 1778, graduating four years later; received the Doctorate of Medicine from the University of Edinburgh in 1784; was resident physician at Guy's Hospital, London; practised medicine in Dublin; and became state physician in conjunction with his father. On the death of his brother Christopher, who was a brilliant young lawyer, he abandoned medicine at the request of his father and turned to the bar. After studying in the Temple, London, he was admitted to the Irish bar in 1790, and began practise in Dublin, where he attained immediate success, especially as an advocate. On Jan. 11, 1791, he married Jane Patten, daughter of the Rev. John Patten, a Presbyterian clergyman.

Emmet's gift for oratory and his nationalist sympathies made him prominent, and brought him cases involving political questions. Having allied himself with the Society of United Irishmen, he became the Irish national idol because of his defense of a member charged with treason for having taken the Society's oath. The defendant having been convicted, Emmet moved in arrest of judgment, made an impassioned address, and ended by himself taking the oath in the presence of the court. The prisoner was punished only by the imposition of a fine. In January 1797, Emmet became a director of the Society, and on Mar. 12, 1798, he was, with others, arrested and imprisoned in Newgate Prison, Dublin. The next year they were removed to Fort George, Scotland, where Emmet's wife and children were eventually allowed to join him. He was released on condition that he leave the Empire, was put on board the ship *Ariadne,* and with his family landed in Holland on July 4, 1802. They spent the winter of 1802–03 in Brussels, and that of 1803–04 in Paris, where he represented the United Irishmen. On Oct. 4, 1804, he and his family sailed from Bordeaux, and landed in New York on Nov. 11. Within three days, he made application for naturalization papers.

At first he thought of returning to the practise of medicine, but persons to whom he had letters of introduction, among them Gov. George Clinton, persuaded him not to forsake the law. When he petitioned for permission to practise, much opposition was shown by Federalist lawyers and judges. Eventually a special act of the legislature, waiving the required three years of study within the state, admitted him to the bar of all state courts. Thereafter he quickly won the respect of his colleagues and drew to himself a clientele, financially very profitable according to the standards of his time. In 1812, he was appointed attorney-general of the state, the only office that he ever held, but resigned within a year to return to private practise. His romantic history, the victory over opposition from the bar, and his brilliant talents, made him observed of all; and, according to Judge Story, he became "the favorite counsellor of New York."

Two incidents well illustrate both his character and his professional career. When, as attorney-general, he was prosecuting a criminal case, the defendant's counsel insinuated that the prosecution was actuated by political motives and that Emmet was paying the price of his appointment by conducting it. Emmet's response was that the accusation was false, as the counsellor well knew. "The office which I have the honor to hold," he said, "is the reward of useful days and sleepless nights, devoted to the acquisition and exercise of my profession, and a life of unspotted integrity—claims and qualifications which that gentleman can never put forth for any office, humble or exalted" (Haines, *post,* pp. 113–14). In the year 1815, he argued four prize cases before the United States Supreme Court. In the first of these, the *Mary,* 9 *Cranch,* 126, he and William Pinkney were on opposite sides. While Emmet was speaking, Pinkney showed great impatience, and at the close of Emmet's address, leaped to his feet and said that on the morrow, on which the case was to be continued, he would show that his predecessor was mistaken in every statement of fact and every conclusion of law which he had enunciated. The next day, after Pinkney had spoken, Emmet, in a voice tense with emotion, said, "Of his success to-day the court alone have a right to judge; but I must be permitted to say that, in my estimation, the manner of announcing his threat of yesterday, and of attempting to fulfill it to-day, was not very courteous to a stranger, an equal, and one who is so truly inclined to honor his talents and learning. It is a manner which I am persuaded he did not learn in the polite circles in Europe, to which he referred, and which I sincerely wish he had forgotten there, wherever he may have learnt it" (*Life, Letters, and Journals of George Ticknor,* 1876, I, 40–41). Pinkney then replied only with a few words of "cold and inefficient explanation" but later in the case of the *Nereide,* 9 *Cranch,* 388, he offered a "gratuitous and cheerful atonement, —cheerful because," he said, "it puts me to rights with myself, and because it is tendered not to ignorance and presumption but to the highest worth in intellect and morals, enhanced by such eloquence as few may hope to equal—to an interesting stranger whom adversity has tried and affliction struck severely to the heart—to an exile whom any country might be proud to receive, and every man of a generous temper would be ashamed to offend" (Henry Wheaton, *Some Account of the Life, Writings, and Speeches of William Pinkney,* 1826, p. 500).

The most famous case in which Emmet appeared was that of *Gibbons* vs. *Ogden,* 9 *Wheaton,* 1, in which he and Thomas J. Oakley were pitted against Daniel Webster and William Wirt. Although Emmet's contentions were not sustained by the court, "not even Pinkney at his best," says Beveridge, "ever was more thorough than was Emmet in his superb argument" in this case (*Life of John Marshall,* IV, 1919, p. 427). Webster said after the trial that the erudition, talents, and eloquence of the Irish bar had made their appearance in America in the person of Emmet. Judge Story described him as a man quick, vigorous, searching, and buoyant, who kindled as he spoke, with a voice toned to suit his meaning, and who while easily moved himself had an instantaneous and sympathetic command over the passions of others. While engaged in the trial of the Sailors' Snug Harbor case, in the United States circuit court, he was stricken with apoplexy, and died a few hours later, in his sixty-third year. He was buried in Saint Paul's churchyard, New York, where his grave is marked by a tall shaft.

[Thos. A. Emmet, *The Emmet Family* (1898) and *Memoir of Thos. Addis and Robt. Emmet* (1915); Wm. J. Macneven, *Pieces of Irish Hist.* (1807); Chas. G. Haines, *Memoir of Thos. Addis Emmet* (1829); R. R. Madden, *The United Irishmen, Their Lives and Times,* 2 Ser., vol. II (London, 1843); S. L. Mitchell, *A Discourse on the Life and Character of Thos. Addis Emmet* (1828); Wm. M. Story, *Life and Letters of Jos. Story* (1851); Wm. Cullen Bryant, in the *N. Y. Evening Post,* Nov. 21, 1827; *N. Y. American,* N. Y. *Commercial Advertiser* and N. Y. *Evening Post,* all Nov. 15, 1827; A. O. Hall, in *Green Bag,* July 1896; N. H. Hagan, in *Case and Comment,* Nov. 1917.] F. C. H.

EMMET, THOMAS ADDIS (May 29, 1828–Mar. 1, 1919), physician, was born near Charlottesville, Va. He was the grandson of Thomas Addis Emmet [*q.v.*], the Irish-American lawyer, and the son of Dr. John Patten Emmet, who was born in Ireland but educated in America, and who was one of Thomas Jefferson's original appointees to a professorship in the University of Virginia. His mother was Mary Byrd Farley Tucker, of an old Bermuda family. His early education was far from formal. His grandmother taught him to read at an early age and he had free range of his father's library which was well stocked, mainly with books of travel, history, or science. Among these books he browsed industriously though probably rather discursively. His father taught him to observe and think from an early age and in his wanderings through the fields and woods he had abundant opportunity to exercise his powers of observation. During this period he saw or came into contact with many national celebrities, including John Marshall and the eccentric John Randolph. During 1845–46 he was a student at the University of Virginia but failed to fit into the academic groove, and after a while he entered Jefferson Medical College, Philadelphia, found medicine to his taste, and graduated in 1850.

He then served several years as visiting physician to the Emigrants' Refuge Hospital on Ward's Island, N. Y. The work was both strenuous and hazardous as virulent typhus fever was common in those days and Emmet contracted it. In this work he gained wide experience both with disease and human nature. In 1855, through a change in New York politics, he lost his position at the Emigrants' Hospital. During the same year he met J. Marion Sims, the pioneer gynecologist, who, recognizing his executive ability, appointed him his assistant at the Woman's Hospital, which position he filled until 1861, when he became surgeon-in-chief, continuing until 1872, when he was made visiting surgeon. During this period he developed into a skilful and original surgeon, devising new operations for the repair of injuries received during childbirth based on his own studies. He was the first to show clearly that what were formerly regarded as ulcerations of the womb were really tears, and he devised an operation for their repair which still bears his name. He contributed freely to literature, and his book, *The Principles and Practise of Gynæcology* (1879), went through three editions, was republished in London, and translated into French and German. He freely and generously demonstrated his methods to visiting physicians from all parts of the world. He was recognized both in the United States and in Europe as an outstanding surgeon and received many professional honors both at home and abroad.

His antiquarian activities are said by him to have dated from a period in his boyhood when he was shown the Declaration of Independence. As a result he became interested in the signers and he secured during his life authentic duplicates of every signature in this historic document. He was also one of the best known and foremost collectors of American prints and autographs and during his lifetime he extra-illustrated 150 books. He was always an ardent advocate of home rule for Ireland, especially after his visit to Ireland in 1871, and espoused it with tongue and pen, writing among other things *Ireland Under English Rule* (2 vols., 1903), a vitriolic work on the blunders of England in handling the Irish situation. He is described by one biographer as "a world figure in the fight for Home Rule." He was president of the Irish National Federation of America as long as it lasted, from 1891 until 1901. He was also honorary president of the Robert Emmet Branch of the Irish National Federation in Ireland in Clondalkin, County Dublin. He was awarded the Laetare Medal by the University of Notre Dame in 1898 and in 1906 was made a Knight Commander of the Order of Gregory the Great by Pope Pius X. On Feb. 14, 1854, he married Catherine R. Duncan of Autauga County, near Montgomery, Ala., who died Nov. 14, 1905. By her he had six children including Dr. Robert and Dr. John Duncan Emmet.

[T. A. Emmet, *Incidents of My Life* (1911); *Birthday Dinner to Thos. Addis Emmet . . . With an Autobiog. Narrative* (1905); A. H. Buckmaster, in *N. Y. Jour. of Gynæcol. and Obstetrics,* May, 1892; J. R. Goffe, in *Am. Jour. of Obstetrics* (N. Y.), Apr. 1919, in *Trans. of the Am. Gynecol. Soc.,* XLIV (1919), and in *Surgery, Gynecol. and Obstetrics* (Chicago), Dec. 1919; John Cavanaugh and E. J. McGuire, in *Jour. of the Am. Irish Hist. Soc.,* XVIII (1919); *Album of the Fellows of the Am. Gynecol. Soc.* (1918); *N. Y. Medic. Jour.,* and *Medic. Rec.* (N. Y.), both Mar. 8, 1919; *N. Y. Times,* Mar. 2, 1919.] G. B.

EMMETT, DANIEL DECATUR (Oct. 29, 1815–June 28, 1904), one of the originators of the "negro minstrel" troupe, author of "Dixie," was of Irish descent. His ancestors, Virginia pioneers, had migrated westward beyond the Blue Ridge, and again beyond the Alleghanies, and finally settled in Ohio. His grandfather fought under Morgan at the Cowpens. During the War of 1812, his father, Abraham Emmett, a blacksmith's apprentice, enlisted in the regiment of Col. Lewis Cass. He aided in the defense of Fort Meigs and was present at Hull's surrender. On his return from the war, he took up his interrupted trade at Mount Vernon, Ohio, and married Sarah Zerick in Clinton, Ohio. Daniel was the first of their four children. He had little schooling and at a very early age went to work in his father's blacksmith shop, but after learning to read and write he was apprenticed to a printer and his real education began. At thirteen he worked in the office of the *Huron Reflector* at Norwalk, Ohio, and later in the office of the *Western Aurora* at Mount Vernon, remaining until he was seventeen, when he became a fifer in the army. His first military service was at Newport, Ky.; later he was stationed at Jefferson Barracks, near St. Louis, where in his leisure moments he studied music. He had learned familiar tunes from his mother, who was very musical, and he had composed "Old Dan Tucker" in 1830 or 1831. Discharged from the army July 8, 1835, "on account of minority," in that year he traveled with a circus troupe. In the winter of 1842–43 he organized the "Virginia Minstrels," and designed their ludicrous costumes (white trousers, striped calico shirt, long blue calico swallow-tail coat). His associates in the first troupe were Brower, Whitlock, and Pelham; their instruments were violin, banjo, bones, and tambourine. They made their first appearance in New York at the Bowery Amphitheatre, Feb. 9, 1843, and between that date and Mar. 1, their last New York appearance for that season, they "firmly fixed themselves as among the inaugurators of a half-century institution" (Odell, *post,* IV, 615). The overwhelming success which their performance attained in New York and other American cities led them to undertake a tour of the British Isles, but they were received with little interest and were obliged to return home. In their absence several other successful companies, notably that organized by E. P. Christy [*q.v.*], had become popular. In 1857 Emmett joined the Bryant Minstrels and began to compose negro melodies. One day in 1859 Bryant requested him to write within two days a "walk-around" or "hooray" song of plantation type, with a tune so catchy as to be sung and whistled on the street. Emmett undertook the task, but at first without success. His wife encouraged him, however, and offered to be audience. He had traveled much in the South and, since the day was dark and chill, as he took up his violin he repeated a popular showman's phrase, "I wish I was in Dixie-land." These words suggested the tune that developed into "Dixie," which at once attained immense popularity. Two years later, after the outbreak of the Civil War, at a spectacular performance in New Orleans "Dixie" was sung as a closing number and so stirred the blood of the Southern audience that it was adopted as the war-song of the Confederacy. Emmett composed other songs during the Civil War period, including "The Road to Richmond," "Walk Along, John," and "Here We Are, or Cross Ober Jordan" (1864). From 1865 to 1878 he traveled with his own company, and until 1888 he made Chicago his home. In that year he returned to a little farm just outside Mount Vernon, where he died. His first wife, Catherine Rives, died May 3, 1875, and in 1879 he married Mary Louise (Brower) Bird, who survived him.

[C. B. Galbreath, *Daniel Decatur Emmett, Author of Dixie* (1904); Lawrence Hutton, "The Negro on the Stage," *Harper's,* June 1889; G. H. Odell, *Annals of the N. Y. Stage,* vol. IV (1929); *Who's Who in America,* 1901–02; *Ohio State Jour.* (Columbus), June 29, 1904; information secured through the courtesy of the Rev. Wm. E. Hull, formerly of Mount Vernon and now at Mechanicsburg, Ohio, who was a close friend of Emmett, was with him in the last years of his life, and read his burial service.] F. L. G. C.

EMMONS, EBENEZER (May 16, 1799–Oct. 1, 1863), geologist, physician, teacher, the son of Ebenezer and Mary (Mack) Emmons, was born and received his rudimentary education in Middlefield, Mass. The family were of English descent, the first American ancestor settling in Haddam, on the Connecticut River. As a boy, Emmons showed a fondness for the natural sciences. He was fitted for college at Plainfield and entered Williams at the age of sixteen, graduating with the class of 1818. Coming under the influence of Amos Eaton, and being already predisposed in that direction, it was natural that he should turn to geology as a career. Unfortunately, though perhaps for financial reasons, he does not seem to have entered upon it with the single-mindedness necessary to success. Moreover, a certain obstinacy and inability to see things as others saw them led to his failure in accomplishing the work he might otherwise have done. Completing his course at Williams College, he entered the Rensselaer Institute at Troy, graduating in 1826. Then, after a course in the Berkshire Medical School, he entered upon the practise of medicine in Chester, Mass., later moving to Williamstown. In 1828 he was appointed lecturer in chemistry at Williams College. In 1830 he was appointed junior professor in the Rensselaer Institute, and became a lecturer in the Medical School at Castleton. In 1838, having received an appointment as geologist on the newly organized survey of New York, and also that of professor of chemistry in the Albany Medical School, he took up his residence in Albany, though continuing his lectures, as needed, at Williamstown, and remaining on the medical faculty as professor of obstetrics till 1852. He continued with the New York survey until 1842, when he was appointed custodian of the state collections at Albany, and became engaged in investigations relating to the agricultural resources of the state in which connection he compiled quarto volumes on horticulture and entomology. In 1851 he was appointed state geologist of North Carolina, shortly after which he moved South, and died at his home in Brunswick County in 1863. In 1818, at the age of nineteen he had married Maria Cone, of Middletown.

As a teacher Emmons is said to have been moderately successful and of a kindly disposition, though stern and forbidding in appearance. As a physician he was considered reliable; as a geologist he was an industrious and faithful worker with a keen eye for stratigraphic problems. Through his discovery and persistent advocacy of a formation, or the presence of a system of formations underlying the Potsdam, which he named Taconic, he stirred up a controversy which lasted all of half a century and which undoubtedly embittered the rest of his days. He compiled a geological map of the state which failed to meet with the approval of James Hall and conveniently disappeared. Emmons claimed that it was destroyed. As early as 1826 he had prepared a *Manual of Mineralogy and Geology* for the use of his classes, and in 1854 began the publication of a more pretentious work: *American Geology* (1854–57) in three volumes. It was subjected to severe, and in many cases just, criticism. Much of his North Carolina work was, however, of a high order and well worthy of commendation.

[Sketch by Jules Marcou in the *Am. Geologist*, Jan. 1891; W. J. Youmans, *Pioneers of Sci. in America* (1890); Calvin Durfee, *Hist. of Williams Coll.* (1860). For full bibliography of Emmons's publications see *Bull. 746, U. S. Geol. Survey*.] G. P. M.

EMMONS, GEORGE FOSTER (Aug. 23, 1811–July 23, 1884), naval officer, the son of Horatio and Abigail (Foster) Emmons, was born at Clarendon, Vt. The Emmons family emigrated from England in 1718 and settled in Connecticut. Horatio served throughout the War of 1812 as an officer in the army. George Foster was appointed a midshipman on Apr. 1, 1828, and learned the rudiments of his profession at the New York Naval School. His second extensive cruise was in the Mediterranean on the frigate *Brandywine* in 1830–33. He was warranted passed midshipman in 1834 and two years later was ordered to the bark *Consort,* a surveying vessel. Joining the Wilkes Exploring Expedition in 1838 as acting lieutenant of the *Peacock,* the second ship of the squadron, he remained with that vessel until it was wrecked at the mouth of the Columbia River. In the fall of 1841 he conducted an exploring party overland from the Columbia to San Francisco, obtaining much scientific information and adding not a few objects to the collection of the expedition. In the same year he was commissioned lieutenant. In 1843–46 Emmons served on the *Boston* of the Brazil Squadron. During the Mexican War he was with the *Ohio* of the Pacific Squadron and was employed on shore expeditions in California, including a journey to the Sierra Nevada Mountains as a bearer of dispatches to Gen. Mason. From 1850 to 1853 he was with the Bureau of Construction and Repair in Washington, and it was during this tour of duty that he compiled an exceedingly useful book, *The Navy of the United States from the Commencement, 1775 to 1853, with a Brief History of Each Vessel's Service* *and Fate* (1853). From 1853 (June) to 1856 he was attached to the *Savannah,* the flagship of the Brazil Squadron, part of the time as commander, a grade that he reached in the last-named year.

In May 1861, Emmons was appointed a member of the Light House Board, but in the fall of that year was sent to the Gulf of Mexico on blockade duty. For about two years he served in the Gulf and on the Mississippi River, commanding the *Hatteras, R. R. Cuyler,* and other vessels, and taking several prizes. In January 1862, he captured Cedar Keys, Fla. In 1863 he was promoted captain, taking rank from February 7. In the fall of that year he was fleet captain under Rear-Admiral Dahlgren of the South Atlantic blockading squadron. A year later he returned to the Gulf where he commanded one of the divisions of the West Gulf blockading squadron, with the *Lackawanna* as his flagship. Off the coast of Texas he captured several Confederate blockade-runners, laden with cotton and other supplies. In 1867 Emmons, while in command of the *Ossipee,* conveyed to Alaska the American and Russian commissioners appointed to consummate the purchase of that country by the United States. Commissioned commodore in 1868, he spent the rest of his active duty at shore stations, chiefly as head of the Hydrographic Office in Washington and as commandant of the Philadelphia navy-yard. On Aug. 23, 1873, he was retired as rear-admiral, a grade to which he had been promoted in the previous November. He long resided at Princeton, N. J., where he died. His wife, Frances Antonia Thornton, of Virginia descent, whom he married on Jan. 10, 1843, was the daughter of a purser in the navy.

[Record of Officers, Bureau of Navigation, 1825–1888; *Official Records* (*Navy*), vols. XVII, XVIII, XXI, XXII; Lewis R. Hamersly, *Records of Living Officers of the U. S. Navy and Marine Corps* (3rd ed., 1878); *Army and Navy Jour.,* July 26, 1884; information furnished by Lieut. G. T. Emmons, Princeton, N. J.] C. O. P.

EMMONS, NATHANAEL (Apr. 20, 1745–o.s.–Sept. 23, 1840), Congregational minister, and theologian, the most entertaining of the teachers of the New England theology, representing the "exercisers" as against the "tasters," like most of his school came from a Connecticut country township. He was the twelfth and youngest child of Deacon Samuel Emmons and his wife Ruth (Cone) Emmons of East Haddam, Conn., both of New England Puritan descent. His father was a miller as well as farmer. Nathanael graduated from Yale in 1767 with little learning, for the college was in an unsettled state and his preparation had been poor. After graduation, he studied for two years with neighboring ministers, though he did not make public profession of his religious faith until near the end of that preparation, indicating that his interest in theology was primarily intellectual, an indication confirmed by his later career. For four years thereafter he preached here and there without obtaining a pastorate, doubtless because of his weak voice and unimposing appearance. At last he was called to the church in what soon became the town of Franklin, Mass., on the border of Rhode Island. After considerable hesitation he accepted, and on Apr. 21, 1773, became its pastor, maintaining that relation until he was eighty-two, and continuing to live in the town till his death some thirteen years later. On Apr. 6, 1775, he was married to Deliverance French who died three years later; on Nov. 4, 1779, he married again, his second wife being Martha Williams, who died (Aug. 2, 1829) after nearly fifty years of married life; and, in his old age, on Sept. 28, 1831, he married Mrs. Abigail (Moore) Mills.

He had surprising success as a preacher because of the pungent quality of his sermons. Students came to him in greater numbers than to any other man of his time for instruction in theology and the art of preaching. The principle of that art he expressed in the words, "Have something to say; say it." He had an analytic and critical mind, and keen mother wit, but little creative ability. The peculiarity of his theology was that mental life is merely a series of "exercises," the result of divine action, a theory which would reduce men to puppets, were it not that Emmons imputed to them freedom and moral responsibility. They act of necessity, not from compunction. Although presenting his own views he insisted that his pupils should think for themselves, and think hard, and placed the writings of his opponents before them, so that their training stood them in good stead, while his doctrinal peculiarities gained no permanent hold. Many of his pupils rose to distinction. In person Emmons was a plump little man, with a squeaky voice and a sharp tongue. He chewed tobacco, a practise more usual when he was young than later. He stuck to the customs of his youth, and in his later years "his old three-cornered hat, and his breeches and all that" did look queer. He was a thorough-going patriot during the Revolution, and an equally zealous Federalist thereafter. At the beginning of Jefferson's administration he preached his noted "Jeroboam" sermon, in which he compared the Democrat now become president to the man "who made Israel to sin." His publications, which consist entirely of sermons or parts of sermons, were collected in *Works of*

Nathanael Emmons, D.D. (6 vols., 1842), and republished, with additions, in 1861–63.

[Autobiog. memoir by Emmons, and memoirs by Jacob Ide and E. A. Park, in *Works of Nathanael Emmons, D.D.* (1842), vol. I; E. A. Park, *Memoir of Nathanael Emmons* (1861), also printed as vol. I (1861) of the revised edition of Emmons's *Works;* Thos. Williams, *The Official Character of the Rev. Nathanael Emmons* (1840); M. Blake, *A Centennial Hist. of the Mendon Asso. of Congreg. Ministers* (1853); Wm. B. Sprague, *Annals Am. Pulpit,* vol. I (1857); F. B. Dexter, *Biog. Sketches Grads. Yale Coll.,* vol. III (1903); A. R. Baker, in *Am. Quart. Reg.,* Nov. 1842; A. Bullard, in *Am. Biblical Repository,* Oct. 1843; E. Smalley, in *Bibliotheca Sacra and Theol. Rev.,* Apr., July 1850; E. T. Fitch, in *New Englander,* Jan. 1843; G. P. Fisher, *Ibid.,* July 1861; J. W. Harding, in *Congreg. Quart.,* July 1861; *Christian Examiner,* Nov. 1842; F. H. Foster, *A Genetic Hist. of the New England Theol.* (1907).]

B. W. B.

EMMONS, SAMUEL FRANKLIN (Mar. 29, 1841–Mar. 28, 1911), geologist, mining engineer, was born in Boston, Mass., the son of Nathaniel H. and Elizabeth (Wales) Emmons. His earliest known ancestor on his father's side was Thomas Emmons, one of the founders of Rhode Island Colony, who later became a resident of Boston. His oldest known ancestor on his mother's side was Nathaniel Wales of Yorkshire, England, who came to Boston in 1635 on the ship *James,* sailing from the port of Bristol. His paternal great-grandfather, Samuel Franklin, for whom he was named, was a cousin of Benjamin Franklin. As a boy, Emmons attended a select private school held in the basement of the old Park Street Church, and in his twelfth year entered the then newly established Dixwell Latin School. He was fitted for Harvard, which he entered in his seventeenth year, and graduated with the degree of B.A. in 1861. It is written of him that he applied himself to his studies with great fidelity and could always be depended upon to be fully prepared. In fact, he was one of the most diligent students of his class, but nevertheless took active part in college affairs and was fond of athletics.

Although at the outbreak of the Civil War Emmons had desired to enlist, he yielded to the wishes of his parents and passed the summer of 1861 in Europe with his invalid mother. In the autumn of this same year, while in Paris, he made the acquaintance of a later well-known mining engineer, Eckley B. Coxe [*q.v.*], through whose influence he was induced to fit himself for a course in the École des Mines. He entered the school in 1862 and remained until the summer of 1864. Though the faculty of the school contained men of the stamp of Élie de Beaumont, and A. Daubrée, Emmons thought it best to pass the last year of study in Germany, and in the fall of 1864 registered in the Bergakademie, at Freiberg, Saxony, where he remained until the summer of 1865. While here he was joined by another American, Arnold Hague [*q.v.*], with whom he formed a lasting friendship and laid the foundation for future collaboration. He returned to America in June 1866. Early in 1867, he found that Hague, who had followed him, had received an appointment on the newly organized geological exploration of the 40th Parallel, and through his influence secured an appointment for himself. The work of this survey involved the exploration of an area extending from the eastern ranges of Colorado to the Sierra Nevada in California, with an average width of about 100 miles. The results, so far as Emmons is concerned, appeared mainly in Volume II of the reports entitled *Descriptive Geology* (1877), with which Hague assisted.

Emmons remained with the 40th Parallel survey until the completion of the work, and on the consolidation of all the existing surveys under the direction of Clarence King [*q.v.*], received an appointment as geologist in charge of the Rocky Mountain Division with headquarters at Denver, Colo. Among his first duties was that of undertaking the collection of statistics of the precious metals in collaboration with G. F. Becker. The results of this work were published as a part of Volume XIII of the reports of the Tenth Census. At the same time, he was engaged in an exhaustive study of the mining district of Leadville, Colo., the results of which appeared in 1886 as the *Geology and Mining Industry of Leadville, Colo.* This was the most pretentious work of his career. "Since its organization probably no single publication of the geological survey has exerted a more beneficial influence and stimulated more discussion" (Hague, *post,* p. 324). His bibliography, aside from the titles mentioned, though not large, contains its full share of valuable material. His interest lay largely in the question of the origin of ore deposits.

Emmons was of a quiet and kindly disposition. He had dark hair and complexion, and wore a full, carefully trimmed beard and moustache. "Tall, erect and slender, his carriage was graceful and unstudied" (*Ibid.,* p. 328). Though he was ever ready to discuss problems of a professional nature, and able to express himself clearly and forcibly, when called upon to speak at social gatherings he was found singularly diffident. He became a member of the Geological Society of London in 1874; of the American Institute of Mining Engineers in 1877; was a founder of the Geological Society of America, and its president in 1903. In 1892 he was elected to membership in the National Academy of Sciences. He was also a member of the American Academy of Arts and Sciences, the American Philosophical Society, the Washington Academy of Sciences, and the Geological Society of Washington, and an honorary member of the Société Helvétique des Sciences Naturelles.

Emmons was married three times: first, on Aug. 5, 1876, to Waltha Anita Steeves of New York (divorced); second, on Feb. 14, 1889, to Sophie Dallas Markoe of Washington, D. C., who died June 19, 1896; and third, on Aug. 4, 1903, to Suzanne Earle Ogden-Jones of Dinard, France. He died unexpectedly on Mar. 28, 1911, leaving no children.

[Arnold Hague, "Samuel Franklin Emmons," in *Nat. Acad. Sci. Biog. Memoirs,* VII (1913), 309–34; George F. Becker, sketch in *Trans. Am. Inst. of Mining Engineers,* XLII (1912), 643–61; *Engineering and Mining Jour.,* XCI (1911), 701; personal knowledge and recollection.] G. P. M.

EMORY, JOHN (Apr. 11, 1789–Dec. 16, 1835), bishop of the Methodist Episcopal Church, was born in Spaniard's Neck, Queen Annes County, Md., the son of Robert Emory, and the grandson of John Register Emory. His mother was Frances, daughter of Tristam and Ann Thomas of Wye Neck, Md. Both his parents were ardent Methodists, and their home was a rendezvous for preachers. Although not a lawyer by profession, Robert Emory was associate to Judge James Tilghman of the county bench, and later judge of the orphans' court. He determined that John should be a lawyer, when the latter was but ten years old, and proceeded to educate him for that calling. The boy received a good classical education chiefly under Robert Elliott of Easton, Md., and later of Strasburg, Pa., whither Emory followed him, and at Washington College, Md. He then studied law in the office of Richard Tilghman Earle of Centerville, Md. An earnest, industrious youth, never relaxing or taking exercise, he undermined his health and thereafter always suffered more or less from physical debility. He was admitted to the bar at the age of nineteen, and opened an office in Centerville. Having been converted, and being of intensely religious nature, he acted as class leader and local preacher. Finally, Oct. 9, 1809, he decided to devote his life to the Christian ministry, a decision which caused an estrangement between himself and his father, not healed till just before the latter's death. He was admitted to the Philadelphia Conference on trial in 1810, and the Conference minutes for 1812 list him as having been received into full connection and ordained deacon within the year; and the minutes of 1814, as among those "elected and ordained elders during this year." After serving on several circuits, he was appointed to Academy charge (Union), Philadelphia. On Oct. 12, 1813, he married Caroline Sellers of Hillsboro, Md., who died in 1815, and on May 12, 1818, Ann Wright of Queen Annes County, Md. He was pastor of important churches in the Philadelphia and Baltimore Conferences until 1824, when he was elected assistant agent of the Methodist Book Concern, and in 1828 he succeeded Nathan Bangs as agent. At the General Conference of 1832 he was elected bishop.

A man of sincere devotion, dignity, and discretion, with a clear, well-trained mind, and superior in scholarship to most Methodist ministers of the day, he soon became a highly respected leader of his denomination. A member of the General Conference of 1816, when he was but twenty-seven years old, he was elected to each succeeding session of that body until he was made a bishop, except that of 1824, and at this he acted as secretary. He was a natural controversialist and skilful debater. In 1817 he championed the doctrines of his church in two pamphlets, *A Reply,* and *A Further Reply,* answering an essay in the *Christian Register* (January 1817) by William White, Episcopal bishop, entitled "Some Objections Against the Position of a Personal Assurance of the Pardon of Sin by a Direct Communication of the Holy Spirit." The next year, articles in the *National Messenger* of Georgetown, D. C., by John Wright, a Unitarian minister, called forth rebuttals from Emory in the same paper, which later appeared in pamphlet form under the title *The Divinity of Christ Vindicated from the Cavils and Objections of Mr. John Wright.* At the General Conference of 1820, he was appointed delegate to the British Conference, to further closer relations between the two bodies, and to adjust difficulties which had arisen in Canada, owing to the existence of both British and American Methodist activities there. He spent some weeks in England and performed his mission with tact and success. In the controversy which led to the establishment of the Methodist Protestant Church, while supporting the election of presiding elders by the annual Conference in preference to their appointment by the bishops, he opposed the "reformers" in their effort to secure lay representation in the Conferences, and published his classic work, a *Defence of "Our Fathers," and of the Original Organization of the Methodist Episcopal Church Against the Rev. Alexander M'Caine and Others* (1827). As agent of the Book Concern he displayed originality and administrative ability. He converted the *Methodist Magazine* into the *Methodist Magazine and Quarterly Re-*

view, and conducted it from 1830 to 1832, writing its principal original articles. He also edited a number of volumes, including the "First American Complete and Standard Edition" of *The Works of the Reverend John Wesley, A.M.* (7 vols, 1833). A stanch advocate of education, he had a hand in the organization of Wesleyan University and New York University, and was for a time president of the trustees of Dickinson College. As bishop he served but three years, his death resulting from a fractured skull, caused by his being thrown from his carriage about two miles from his home near Reisterstown, Md. He was buried by the side of Bishop Asbury under the pulpit of the Eutaw Street Church, Baltimore, both bodies later being removed to Mount Olivet Cemetery. A manuscript left at his death was published by his son, Robert, in 1838 under the title, *The Episcopal Controversy Reviewed.*

[The appendix of Robt. Emory's *Life of the Rev. John Emory, D.D.* (1841), contains a sermon preached before the British Conference, and extracts from Bishop Emory's contributions to the *Meth. Mag. and Quart. Rev.* See also Wm. B. Sprague, *Annals Am. Pulpit*, vol. VII (1859); *Meth. Quart. Rev.*, Jan. 1842; Wm. Larrabee, "John Emory," in T. L. Flood and J. W. Hamilton, *Lives of Methodist Bishops* (1882); and denominational histories.] H. E. S.

EMORY, WILLIAM HEMSLEY (Sept. 7, 1811–Dec. 1, 1887), soldier, was born in Queen Annes County, Md., son of Thomas and Anna Maria (Hemsley) Emory. His grandfather came to this country from England in the eighteenth century, and acquired an estate under a patent from the Lord Proprietor of Maryland. He served in the Revolution and his son served in the War of 1812. The estate was originally called "Brampton," but its owner considered it unpatriotic to retain the English name, and changed it to "Poplar Grove." Emory was graduated from the United States Military Academy in 1831, where he was familiarly known as "Bold Emory," and promoted brevet second lieutenant, 4th Artillery. He resigned from the service in 1836, and two years later, on the reorganization of the army, was commissioned first lieutenant in the Topographical Engineers. He served as principal assistant on the Northeastern boundary survey between the United States and Canada (1844–46), and at the outbreak of the Mexican War was assigned as chief engineer officer and acting assistant adjutant-general, Army of the West, and subsequently as a lieutenant-colonel of volunteers, in Mexico. While with the Army of the West he distinguished himself at the battles of San Pasquale, San Gabriel, and the Plains of Mesa, and won two brevets. After the war he was assigned as chief astronomer for running the boundary line between California and Mexico (1848–53), and in 1854 was appointed by the president, both commissioner and astronomer, with full powers, under the Gadsden Treaty. This work was completed in 1857 and he was brevetted lieutenant-colonel for his services. While on these duties he was promoted captain (1851), and on the reorganization of the army in 1855, was promoted major, 2nd Cavalry, one of the new regiments. During his service in the Topographical Engineers he was very active and conspicuous in making surveys, and in compiling and reducing to form such maps as existed of the country west of the Mississippi River. His works appeared as "Notes of a Military Reconnaissance from Fort Leavenworth in Missouri, to San Diego in California," *Senate Ex. Doc. No. 7,* 30 Cong., 1 Sess.; *Observations, Astronomical, Magnetic, and Meteorological, made at Chagres and Gorgona, Isthmus of Darien and at the City of Panama, New Granada* (1850); and "Report on the United States and Mexican Boundary Survey," *House Ex. Doc. No. 135,* 34 Cong., 1 Sess. In 1861 he was assigned to command the troops in Indian Territory, including Forts Cobb, Smith, Washita, and Arbuckle. Finding the country in a state of insurrection, and convinced that he could not hold the forts, he withdrew to Fort Leavenworth, and was the only officer on the frontier who brought his entire command out of the insurrectionary country without the loss of a man. The troops thus saved from capture were of great importance beyond the consideration of numbers, as their timely arrival restored the confidence of the friends of the government in that section, formed the nucleus of General Lyon's army, and probably prevented the secessionists from forcing Missouri into rebellion. Emory was appointed brigadier-general of volunteers in 1862, and served with distinction as brigade, division, and corps commander. He received four brevets, and was twice thanked on the field by the general commanding for the success of his brilliant operations—at Hanover Court House, where he separated the wings of the Confederate army, capturing many prisoners, and again for destroying the railway bridges between Hanover Junction and the Chickahominy, and driving the enemy out of Ashland. He was commissioned major-general of volunteers in 1865, and commanded the Department of West Virginia until mustered out of the volunteer service in January 1866. He commanded successively the Department of Washington, District of the Republican (1869–71), Department of the Gulf (1871–75), and was retired with the rank of brigadier-general, July 1, 1876, after a period of forty-five years of service. Emory was a talented and skilful soldier, always calm and dignified in bearing, courageous and firm. Though apparently stern in character he was really warm-hearted, sympathetic, and generous. In May 1838 he married Matilda Wilkins Bache, a great-granddaughter of Benjamin Franklin.

[Geo. F. Price, *Across the Continent with the 5th U. S. Cavalry* (1883); Albert Gleaves, *Life of an Am. Sailor* (1922); Geo. W. Cullum, *Biog. Reg., Officers and Grads. of the U. S. Mil. Acad.* (3rd ed., 1891), vol. I; *Battles and Leaders of the Civil War* (1888), vol. III; *Official Records (Army)*, 1 ser. vol. XI; obituary in *Ann. Reunion, Asso. of Grads. of the U. S. Mil. Acad.* (1888).] C. F. C.

EMOTT, JAMES (Mar. 14, 1771–Apr. 7, 1850), jurist, was born at Poughkeepsie, N. Y., a son of William Emott and his wife Celia (or Celiatie) Polmantere. He was a descendant in the fourth degree of James Emmott (*sic*), a grantee under the Nine Partners Patent (Great or Lower), issued May 27, 1697, in respect to a large tract of land in New York, now embraced in Dutchess County. This ancestor was an attorney to the King's Bench, and the family was well-to-do, continuing to hold considerable landed property in and around Poughkeepsie. James never entered college, being largely self-educated. Taking up the study of law, he was admitted to the New York bar and commenced practise at Ballston Center, N. Y. From the first he gave indications of great legal ability, and in 1797 was appointed a member of the board of commissioners to hear and determine the vexatious disputes regarding the title to the military bounty lands, known as the "Military Tract," in the then county of Tryon, N. Y., which had been set aside under resolutions of Congress, Sept. 16, 1776, making provision for granting land to officers and soldiers who enlisted for the Revolutionary War. He took an active part in the prolonged investigation which resulted in the adjustment and quieting of all the titles in question (see *Report of the Commissioners for Settling the Titles to Land in the County of Onondaga,* Feb. 17, 1800). In 1800 he moved his office to Albany, and rapidly acquired a leading position at the bar in that city. He was a member of the state Assembly from Albany County in 1804, and was chosen speaker. From 1809 to 1813, as a Federalist, he was representative of Dutchess County in Congress, and in 1814 was again elected to the New York Assembly, becoming speaker of the House in the same year. He continued in the Assembly until the court of common pleas for Dutchess County was organized, when he was chosen as its first judge, April 8, 1817, with Poughkeepsie as headquarters. On the summoning of the constitutional convention in 1821, he was candidate of the conservative element in Dutchess County, but was defeated after a bitter struggle. He was appointed judge of the 2nd New York Judicial District, Feb. 21, 1827, but only retained the position four years, resigning in 1831. After his retirement from the bench, he resumed practise in Poughkeepsie, and devoted much of his time to commercial and financial business. He was one of the incorporators of the Dutchess Mutual Insurance Company, serving on the first board of directors and becoming president. He was also instrumental in founding the Poughkeepsie Savings Bank. Though in his later years he abstained from active participation in public affairs his advice was constantly sought in matters of importance to the community and even in retirement he continued to exercise a preponderant influence in the councils of his native town. He was married twice: on Sept. 20, 1818, to Malissa White; and on Jan. 27, 1821, to Esther (or Hester) Crary. His son by his second wife, James Emott the younger [*q.v.*], became judge of the New York supreme court, and the court of appeals.

[*The Records of Christ Church, Poughkeepsie, N. Y., 1766–1916* (n.d.), vol. II; D. McAdam and others, *Hist. of the Bench and Bar of N. Y.* (1897), I, 321; P. H. Smith, *Gen. Hist. of Dutchess County* (1877); Edmund Platt, *The Eagle's Hist. of Poughkeepsie* (1905), p. 280; Frank Hasbrouck, *Hist. of Dutchess County, N. Y.* (1909); *Biog. Dir. Am. Cong.* (1928).] H. W. H. K.

EMOTT, JAMES (Apr. 23, 1823–Sept. 11, 1884), jurist, was the son of James Emott [*q.v.*], by his second wife, Esther (or Hester) Crary. He was born at Poughkeepsie, N. Y., received his early education at College Hill School in his native town, proceeding thence to Columbia College, New York City, where he graduated at the head of his class in 1841. He then studied law in his father's office at Poughkeepsie, and was admitted to the bar of the supreme court of New York at Poughkeepsie in 1844, immediately afterward commencing practise in that town. In the early period of his professional career he was undoubtedly assisted by his influential family connections and his father's prominent position, but he possessed great natural ability and in a short period became a leading member of the district bar, acquiring a wide practise in all the courts. In 1849 he was appointed district attorney of Dutchess County. In addition to his legal practise he was interested in much business enterprise, and in 1852 became president of the Merchant's Bank of Poughkeepsie, a position which he held till his death—a period of thirty-two years. In 1854, when Poughkeepsie received its city charter, he was, on the nomination of the

Whig party, elected its first mayor by a substantial majority. The following year the Republican party induced him to become its candidate for the position of justice of the supreme court of the state for the 2nd Judicial District. The district was predominantly Democratic, but on this occasion the Democratic party was badly split, and as a consequence Emott was elected. He remained on the bench from Jan. 1, 1856, to Jan. 1, 1864, becoming presiding judge in 1863, and serving *ex-officio* as a judge of the court of appeals during the last year of his term. On the conclusion of his term of office he did not offer himself for reëlection, his party affiliations precluding any chance of success. He brought to the bench a wide experience in all classes of litigation and a knowledge of business methods and financial affairs, which, combined with a clear intellect, capacity for infinite research, and rigorous logic, gave him an enviable standing as a jurist. His opinions were distinguished by lucidity of expression and felicity of form and have been deemed models of judicial composition. On leaving the bench he resumed his legal practise at Poughkeepsie, but shortly afterward opened an office in New York City, where he was retained in much heavy litigation, especially such as involved the law applicable to corporations. In 1869 he was one of the founders of the Association of the Bar of the City of New York and he acted as chairman of its library committee for twelve years. A fervent adherent of the reform party in municipal affairs, he threw himself with great vigor into the campaign against the "Tweed Ring." Appointed a member of the Committee of Seventy, he was indefatigable in his efforts to bring the guilty parties to justice. Recognized now as one of the leaders of the New York bar, "his tall and slender but commanding figure was one of the most familiar sights in the courts" (*Annual Cyclopædia and Register, 1884,* p. 604), but during the last two years of his life he was prevented by ill health from personally acting as counsel. His opinion was, however, frequently sought and he prepared many admirable briefs. Though for twenty years his professional labors centered in New York City he continued to retain a close connection with Poughkeepsie, where he died. On June 16, 1846, he married Mary Helen Crooke, daughter of Robert and Mary Crooke of Poughkeepsie.

A man of few intimate friendships, his sturdy independence of thought, consistency of conduct, and undeviating integrity procured for him unusual respect and confidence in the community. An incessant reader, and a prominent and influential member of the Protestant Episcopal Church, he steeped himself in ecclesiastical and theological literature and lore, particularly relating to the controversies, doctrine, and ritual of the Christian church. His favorite recreation was playing the organ, of which instrument he became a master and to which he devoted a short time every day for years.

["Memorial of James Emott," in *Asso. of the Bar of the City of N. Y. Report,* 1885, p. 81; D. McAdam and others, *Hist. of the Bench and Bar of N. Y.* (1897); Edmund Platt, *The Eagle's Hist. of Poughkeepsie* (1905); Frank Hasbrouck, *Hist. of Dutchess County, N. Y.* (1909); *The Records of Christ Church, Poughkeepsie, N. Y., 1766–1916* (n.d.), vol. II; *Columbia Coll. Gen. Cat., 1754–1888*; *N. Y. Times,* Sept. 12, 1884.]

H. W. H. K.

ENDECOTT, JOHN (*c.* 1589–Mar. 15, 1665), governor of Massachusetts, was the son of Thomas Endecott of Chagford, Devonshire, and Alice (Westlake?) Endecott, a woman of considerable landed possessions in the parish of Stoke-in-Teignhead. His grandfather, John Endecott, held large tin-mining interests in the county, and was a man of some wealth. He survived his son Thomas, who died in 1621, and on his own death some fourteen years later practically disinherited the younger John, whose religious convictions had doubtless run counter to his own. This may serve to explain the fact that in his records and correspondence, the Governor made almost no references to his connections in England. Little is known of Endecott's youth, though it is fairly certain that at an early age he was brought under the influence of the Puritan divine, Rev. John White of Dorchester, and of the Rev. Samuel Skelton, later pastor of the First Church in Salem. He is said also to have seen service against the Spaniards in the Low Countries; certainly he bore the title of "captain" even after he emigrated to Massachusetts. Before he left England, he married Anne Gower, a cousin of Matthew Cradock, the governor of the Massachusetts Bay Company in England.

As a Puritan, Endecott came into close contact with the group interested in colonizing New England. By 1628 the colony at Plymouth had become well established and there were also scattered settlers about the shores of Massachusetts Bay, including the remnant of a fishing settlement at Cape Ann. On March 19 of that year, Endecott was one of six "religious persons" who bought a patent for territory on the Bay from the Plymouth Council in England, and in the royal charter, granted Mar. 4, 1629, he was named among the incorporators. Meanwhile the associators had determined to proceed to the settlement without delay, and on June 20, 1628, Endecott sailed for Massachusetts in the *Abigail* with a small band of colonists, to prepare the way for the larger numbers to follow. There has been much discussion by antiquarians as to the exact official rôle and title which should be accorded to Endecott during the next two years. It is not a matter of the slightest historical or biographical importance whether we call him "the first governor of Massachusetts," and, technically, the problem is practically insoluble. The pertinent facts are that it was evidently intended that he was to be in charge of the colony until the main company should arrive; that he should do everything needful on the spot to pave the way for them; and that he did so. At a meeting of the company in England, Apr. 30, 1629, it was recorded that Endecott had been chosen governor of the Plantation in Massachusetts for one year, or until another had been selected in his place. On Oct. 20 Winthrop was chosen governor under the charter, though he did not reach Massachusetts until the next year.

Endecott landed with his band on Sept. 6, 1628, and settled at Naumkeag, now Salem. He found he had to clear the ground both literally and metaphorically and proceeded to do both. The remnant of the fishing company was under the "governorship" of Roger Conant [*q.v.*], whose tact mitigated difficulties on that score. More vigorous measures were called for against Thomas Morton and his riotous gang at Merry Mount, whither Endecott soon marched and dramatically cut down their celebrated May-pole, admonishing them that "ther should be better walking" (Bradford, *post,* II, 501). By the end of June 1629, the Rev. Samuel Skelton and Rev. Francis Higginson had arrived. It is impossible to determine exactly what Endecott's ideas of church government and Separatism had been when he left England. After his arrival in America he came into touch with the Pilgrims at Plymouth, and when he and the two clergymen organized a church in July it followed the Plymouth model, and was independent of the church in England (Adams, *post,* p. 130). Two members of the Massachusetts colony, John and Samuel Browne, declined to accept Separatism and were finally deported to England by Endecott who, with a complete absence of humor, described them as "schismatical." Little else is known of his rule at this period. It appears to have been eminently successful and to have given the company in England entire satisfaction, though, *pro forma,* he had to be mildly censured for his handling of the recalcitrant Brownes.

In the early summer of 1630 the great migration set in. About a thousand colonists arrived, including John Winthrop [*q.v.*]. Endecott quietly turned over his authority to the new governor and became an assistant. The remainder of his life, however, was spent in the service of the colony. He was assistant in the years 1630–34, 1636–40, 1645-48; deputy-governor 1641–43, 1650, 1654; and governor 1644, 1649, 1651–53, 1655–64. He also frequently held military office and in 1645 was named sergeant-major-general. His importance in the eyes of the leaders cannot be better shown than by the fact that he was one of the three men chosen to the unconstitutional Council for Life, initiated in 1636. The scheme proved abortive, but it is evident that Endecott's life was interwoven at every point with the public life of the colony.

Although frequently holding military office, he possessed none of the qualifications of a military leader. Following the murder of Oldham [*q.v.*] by the Indians in 1636, Endecott was placed at the head of a punitive expedition of a hundred men, which not only proved a complete failure but in its ill-judged operations did much to bring on the Pequot War. His actions brought well-deserved protests from both Saybrook and Plymouth. In 1643 he opposed the unfortunate and uncalled-for policy toward the French indulged in by Winthrop, for which Winthrop was condemned by the United Colonies, and the following year, when Endecott was governor, he did what he could to settle matters on a better foundation. Much has been made of the episode in which Endecott ordered the cross to be cut out of the English ensign as savoring of popery (1634). He was probably no more narrow-minded than many others, however, and aside from the passing criticism in England, the incident is without importance save as it indicates his lack of judgment. Far more essential for a study of the man's character is the part he played in the persecution of the Quakers a few years before his death. Making all allowance both for the political aspects of the problem as it presented itself to the rulers of the colony, and for the harshness of the times, Endecott showed himself blood-thirsty and brutal in his handling of the Quaker cases. He appeared at his worst in this, in many ways, supreme episode of his life. Although not of scholarly tastes, he took an interest in education in the colony, and in 1641 agitated the question of establishing a free school at Salem. Earlier, in 1637, the General Court had appointed a committee to consider the establishment of a college and apparently the following year Endecott took his place on this committee, filling a vacancy caused by the death of one of its members. By the time of the first Commencement of Harvard he was one of the Overseers.

Endecott's first wife died soon after their arrival in Massachusetts, and on Aug. 18, 1630, he married Elizabeth Gibson, by whom he had two sons. He appears never to have been a wealthy man, although he received his various official salaries and several grants of land, including one of a thousand acres and one of a quarter of Block Island. The inventory of his estate shows a value of only slightly over £224. He was always fond of Salem, which he had hoped might be the capital of the colony, and it was only under official pressure that he was induced to move to Boston about 1655, where he died a decade later. He was a thorough-going Puritan in his religious beliefs and in the social legislation which, according to the times, proceeded from them. He was stern and irascible, a man of iron will and of little human sympathy. He was capable, honest, and devoted to the public good as he saw it, but was incapable of conceiving of any good other than as he saw it. He performed useful service in his first two years, before he was supplanted by the coming of the other leading members of the colony, and his strength was always useful to it, but he never measured up to the stature of several of the colony's other leading men.

[Roper Lethbridge, *The Devonshire Ancestry and the Early Homes of the Family of John Endecott* (n.d.); W. D. Chapple, "The Pub. Service of John Endecott in the Mass. Bay Col.," *Essex Inst. Hist. Colls.*, vol. LXV (1929); "Memoir of Gov. Endecott," *New-Eng. Hist. and Geneal. Reg.*, July 1847; S. Salisbury, "Memorial of Gov. Endecott," *Proc. Am. Antiquarian Soc.*, Oct. 1873; W. H. Whitmore, *The Mass. Civil List* (1870); *The Hutchinson Papers* (2 vols., 1865); J. W. Thornton, *The Landing at Cape Anne* (1854); W. Bradford, *Hist. of Plymouth Plantation* (2 vols., 1912); James Savage, *Geneal. Dict. of the First Settlers of New Eng.*, II (1860), 120–23; J. K. Hosmer, ed., *Winthrop's Jour.* (2 vols., 1908); Alex. Young, *Chronicles of the First Planters . . . of Mass. Bay* (1864); *Records of the Gov. and Co. of the Mass. Bay*, vols. I–IV (1853–54); *Essex Inst. Hist. Colls.* V (1863), 73–84, XXV (1888), 137–48; J. T. Adams, *Founding of New Eng.* (1921).]
J.T.A.

ENDICOTT, CHARLES MOSES (Dec. 6, 1793–Dec. 14, 1863), sea-captain, antiquarian, was born in Danvers, Mass., on land which had originally belonged to Gov. John Endecott, from whom he was directly descended in the eighth generation. He was the son of Moses Endicott and Anna (Towne) Endicott and was christened Moses, but his name was legally changed, Mar. 4, 1829, to Charles Moses. He went to school in Salem and Andover and was preparing to go on to college. His father's unexpected death in 1807, however, left the family poor, and he entered the counting-room of his uncle, Samuel Endicott. He was then only fourteen years old. He later moved to Boston to join the firm of William Ropes, but left there in 1812 to go as a supercargo for Pickering Dodge of Salem, on a long voyage to St. Petersburg. At the close of the War of 1812 he took a similar voyage to the Far East, stopping at Calcutta and Sumatra. He was married, June 18, 1818, to Sarah Rolland Blythe, by whom he had two sons. For fifteen years Endicott traded along the Sumatra coast, being engaged chiefly in the importation of pepper. During the delays incidental to the loading of his vessels, he made a careful and reliable survey of the coast and published *Sailing Directions for the Pepper Ports on the West Coast of Sumatra* (1833), intended to accompany his chart of the coast, which was of great service to American mariners and went through many editions. His books are still preserved at the Essex Institute in Salem. In 1830–31, while he was master of the *Friendship,* with a crew of seventeen men, his vessel was attacked by Malays at Qualah Battoo, on the west coast of Sumatra, and, while he was absent on shore, many of his sailors were brutally massacred and his ship was looted. Endicott managed to escape and reach Muckie, where he found three American vessels. With their aid he was enabled to recapture the *Friendship,* which he eventually piloted back to Salem. An effective punishment for this outrage was administered on Feb. 7, 1832, when the United States frigate *Potomac* bombarded the town of Qualah Battoo.

In 1835 Endicott left the sea and settled down as cashier of the Salem Bank. He became interested in antiquarian research and, under the pen name of "Junius Americanus," contributed many papers to the *New-England Historical and Genealogical Register* and to the *Boston Gazette.* He published genealogies of the Endicott, Peabody, and Jacobs families, *Memoir of John Endecott* (1847), as well as other miscellaneous writings.

Endicott was a courtly but rather fussy and peculiar man who became notorious for his eccentric conduct. He once as cashier refused to accept the deposits of one large firm because the bank-notes presented were dirty, and he did not wish to soil his hands. Eventually his idiosyncracies became so marked that he was placed in an asylum, where he died just after reaching his seventieth year.

[There is an excellent life of Endicott by Eben Putnam in the *Memorial Biogs. of the New-England Hist. and Geneal. Soc.*, vol. V (1894). Ralph D. Paine's *Ships and Sailors of Old Salem* (1909), ch. XXV, deals with the tragedy of the *Friendship.* Endicott's own story is told in the *Essex Inst. Hist. Colls.*, vol. I (1859). See also W. C. Endicott, *Memoir of Samuel Endicott with a Geneal. of his Descendants* (1924).] C.M.F.

ENDICOTT, JOHN [See Endecott, John, *c.* 1589–1665.]

ENDICOTT, MORDECAI THOMAS (Nov. 26, 1844–Mar. 5, 1926), naval engineer, was born at Mays Landing, N. J., the son of Thomas

Doughty and Ann (Pennington) Endicott. He was descended from John Endecott, the first governor of the Massachusetts Bay colony. After an elementary education under Presbyterian auspices in his native town, he entered Rensselaer Polytechnic Institute in February 1865, and was graduated in 1868. For the next few years he worked in Wilkes-Barre, Pa., with a civil and mining engineer; in Middletown, Conn., in building the approaches for a bridge; and in Ohio, on the Zanesville-Dresden railroad extension. On May 29, 1872, he married Elizabeth Adams, daughter of George W. Adams of Dresden.

On Feb. 1, 1872, Endicott was appointed an assistant civil engineer at the new League Island naval station at Philadelphia, but he was transferred to the Philadelphia navy-yard itself before receiving his commission in the navy in 1874 as a civil engineer. For the next few years he was at the New London naval station; then followed two years at Portsmouth, five years at Philadelphia, three years at Norfolk, and one year at New York. In 1890 he was brought to Washington as a consulting engineer and given virtual control of all civil-engineering projects. As it was during this period that the navy-yards were undergoing extensive modernization, he had exceptional opportunities to show his professional skill and insight. Thus he had much to do with the introduction of electrical appliances and the adoption of steel and concrete dry docks instead of the old timbered structures. Immediately before the Spanish-American War, when even more important work was in prospect, President McKinley broke precedents, and on Apr. 7, 1898, appointed Endicott as chief of the Bureau of Yards and Docks, a post always before held by an officer of the line. Later Endicott was given the rank of rear-admiral by virtue of his position, and continued in office till 1907. Though he had been retired in the previous November as a rear-admiral, he remained on duty in various capacities till June 1909. Perhaps his most noteworthy achievement was the completion of the floating dry dock *Dewey,* the largest of its type which had then been built.

Endicott also served on the Nicaragua Canal Commission in 1895, as a member of the Armor Factory Board in 1897, as the navy member of the Panama Canal Commission, 1905–07, and even returned to active duty on various boards during the World War. After 1890 he made his home in Washington, D. C. He was a member of the American Society of Civil Engineers, serving as its president in 1911. While his career had been almost wholly devoted to the navy, he was also interested in collecting paintings and rare books. He died of pneumonia, and was buried at Arlington.

[The best sketch of Endicott's life is the memoir published in the *Trans. Am. Soc. of Civil Engineers,* Dec. 1926. His yearly reports as chief of the Bureau of Yards and Docks are included with the reports of the secretary of the navy. The record of his various duties and promotions is on file in the Bureau of Navigation, Navy Dept. See also *Who's Who in America,* 1926–27; *Biog. Record of the Officers and Grads. of Rensselaer Polytechnic Inst., 1824–1886* (1887); *Evening Star* (Washington), Mar. 6, 1926.] W. B. N.

ENDICOTT, WILLIAM CROWNINSHIELD (Nov. 19, 1826–May 6, 1900), jurist, secretary of war, was born in Salem, Mass., a direct descendant in the eighth generation of Gov. John Endecott, and a grandson of Jacob Crowninshield [*q.v.*], a distinguished member of Congress. Endicott was the eldest of the four children of William Putnam Endicott and his first wife, Mary Crowninshield. He was baptized as William Gardner Endicott, but his name was changed, Apr. 19, 1837, by special act of the legislature. He received his early education at Salem Latin School, going from there to Harvard, where he graduated in the class of 1847. After spending some two years in the office of Nathaniel J. Lord, one of the leading attorneys in Salem, he continued his studies at the Harvard Law School (1849–50), and was admitted to the bar of Essex County in November 1850. Three years later he entered into partnership with Jairus W. Perry, under the firm name of Perry and Endicott. He was chosen a member of the Salem Common Council in 1852, 1853, and 1857, and was made its president during his third term. He became city solicitor in 1858, but retired from this position in 1863. He married, Dec. 13, 1859, Ellen Peabody, daughter of George and Clara (Endicott) Peabody, of Salem. He had two children, William Crowninshield Endicott, Jr., born in 1860, and Mary Crowninshield Endicott, born in 1864, who became the wife of the Right Honorable Joseph Chamberlain, the British statesman, and after his death married William Hartley Carnegie, dean of Westminster and chaplain of the House of Commons.

Endicott had originally been a member of the Whig party, but when it disintegrated in 1856, he, like Rufus Choate and many others, joined the Democrats. In 1866, 1867, and 1868 he was an unsuccessful candidate for the office of attorney-general in Massachusetts on the Democratic ticket, and in 1870 he was defeated for Congress by Benjamin F. Butler. In 1873, when the supreme judicial court was enlarged, Endicott, despite his party affiliations, was appointed to that bench by the Republican governor, William B. Washburn, and was after that known in the state as Judge Endicott. Withdrawing in 1882 because of ill health, he spent eighteen months in Europe. On his return he accepted a nomination for governor, but was defeated in November 1884, by George D. Robinson. In February 1885, Grover Cleveland requested Endicott to meet him at Albany and there offered him a place in his cabinet as secretary of war. In this position, which he retained throughout Cleveland's first administration, Endicott distinguished himself "by strict attention to duty and a keen interest in the army and its requirements" (Elihu Root, May 7, 1900). Congress created, Mar. 3, 1885, a Board on Fortifications and Other Defenses, which came to be known as the Endicott Board of Fortifications. The work of this board in carrying out plans for the defense of cities on the Atlantic seaboard was long and laborious, and aroused very favorable comment. During his incumbency, the Apache Indians under Geronimo surrendered; many public buildings and monuments were erected; and the record and pension division of the surgeon general's office was reorganized. He was severely but unjustly criticised because of his approval, May 26, 1887, of a proposal to return captured Confederate flags to the Southern states to whom they had originally belonged.

Endicott, who had himself inherited money and whose wife had a large fortune, did not practise law after leaving the cabinet in 1889, but settled down in his fine old house on Essex Street, in Salem, where he had lived since 1864. Later he moved to Boston, where he maintained a residence on Marlboro St. He usually spent his summers in travel or on his estate in Danvers. He died in Boston, in his seventy-fifth year, of pneumonia, and was buried in Harmony Grove Cemetery, at Salem. Many honors came to him in the course of his career. He was a loyal friend and supporter of Harvard College, serving as Overseer (1875–85) and fellow of the corporation (1884–95). He was president of the Harvard Alumni Association from 1888 to 1890, president of the Peabody Academy of Science in Salem, as well as trustee of the Peabody Education Fund. He was one of the original trustees of Groton School and was elected, Apr. 4, 1864, as a resident member of the Massachusetts Historical Society. He was a member of the famous Saturday Club, in Boston, and often attended meetings.

A patrician by birth and temperament, Endicott had a contempt for anything mean or degrading. Rhodes has rightly characterized him as "an able, liberal, and high-minded man." He was an eloquent speaker, and delivered a brilliant oration in 1878 on the 250th anniversary of the landing of his ancestor on American soil. In appearance he was tall and striking, and his manners were invariably courtly. As a judge, he was impartial, dignified, and just. He represented in his character and career the best of the old New England traditions.

[The best account of Endicott is the memoir by his son, Wm. C. Endicott, in the *Proc. Mass. Hist. Soc.*, 2 ser. XV (1902), 523–34. See also J. H. Choate, "Memoir of Wm. Crowninshield Endicott, LL.D.," *Pubs. Col. Soc. Mass.*, VII (1906), 30–49; "Wm. Crowninshield Endicott," *Proc. Am. Antiquarian Soc.*, n.s., XIV (1902), 20–23; *Boston Transcript*, May 7, 1900. Certain information has been supplied by members of the family.]

C. M. F.

ENGELMANN, GEORGE (Feb. 2, 1809–Feb. 4, 1884), pioneer meteorologist, physician, botanist, was the eldest of the thirteen children of George Engelmann, a doctor of philosophy from the University of Halle, and Julia May, a teacher who came from an artistic family. He was born at Frankfurt-am-Main, where the Engelmanns had established a school for girls. Here he lived until a scholarship from the "Reformed Congregation" enabled him to enter the University of Heidelberg in 1827, where he was befriended by Alexander Braun and Karl Schimper. His interest in botany cannot be credited to these men, however, for he later wrote, "I began in my fifteenth year to become greatly interested in plants." In the fall of 1828 in consequence of an uprising of students Engelmann was obliged to leave Heidelberg. The affair was harmless, but his "democratic tendencies" made it difficult for him at the University of Berlin where he remained but two years. Consequently he moved to the University of Würzburg from which he received his M.D., July 19, 1831. His inaugural dissertation, "De Antholysi Prodomus," was illustrated by a lithograph drawn by the author, and the original sketches, still in existence, give evidence of his skill with the pencil. In 1832 Engelmann went to Paris where he found congenial friends in Braun, Agassiz, Constadt, and others. In September of the same year he sailed for America, for the purpose of investing in the new country some money which had been entrusted to him by his uncle. He reached St. Louis on Feb. 20, 1833. For the next two years he lived on a farm in Illinois, twenty miles east of St. Louis, where he prospected, botanized, and scoured the country studying its plants, minerals, and rocks. After a journey through the Southwest he returned to St. Louis where he settled down in the practise of medicine in December 1835. He became probably the busiest practitioner in the city, with a host of devoted patients not only among the Germans, but among Americans and French as well. He was the first to use obstetrical forceps in this new region, and was among the very first to use quinine in malaria, especially in giving it in large doses "in the interval." In 1840 he was able to return to Kreuznach, where his parents now lived, and where he married, on June 11, a cousin, Dorothea Horstmann, who had lived in the Engelmann family since she was eleven years old. George J. Engelmann [*q.v.*] was their son.

While in his earlier years Engelmann was forced by necessity to give the major portion of his time to medicine, his herbarium and botanical library always adjoined his office. After a third trip to Europe in 1869, he returned to a new house, in which he had no office, kept no office hours, and saw only a few patients in his study. Thus he was allowed to indulge his various interests. His meteorological observations begun in 1836 were continued till the day before his death. He made studies on *Taenia,* the anatomy of the opossum, melanism in squirrels, and on *Menobranchus.* He also deserves credit for first calling attention to the adaptation of the Pronuba moth for accomplishing pollination of the Yuccas, as well as the valuable discovery of the immunity of the American grape to the *Phylloxera.* The study of plants was his greatest delight, however, and it is upon his monographic work on a series of difficult and little understood genera that his reputation must chiefly rest. In addition to the memorial volume of *Botanical Works of the late George Engelmann Collected for Henry Shaw* (1887), Engelmann left a mass of notes, drawings, and observations on plants of all kinds which constitute some sixty large volumes.

Engelmann organized the St. Louis Academy of Science in 1856—the first of its kind to be established west of the Alleghanies. He was an earnest worker in the organization of a paper, called *The Westland,* the main purpose of which was to unite the pioneer settlers and to give information to those in Germany who contemplated emigrating. When it was discontinued a few years later, Engelmann lent his aid to a German daily. He was a member of thirty-three scientific societies at home and abroad. His long time associate Dr. Parry named a mountain peak for him, and many plant species as well as three plant genera commemorate his name.

["Sketch of the Life and Work of the late George Engelmann," a manuscript translation of an autobiographical account left with Engelmann's son; manuscript copy of an address by Wm. Trelease, Engelmann Centenary, St. Louis Acad. of Sci., Feb. 1, 1909; *Biog. Memoirs Nat. Acad. Sci.,* vol. IV (1902); *Proc. Am. Soc. Arts and Sci.,* XIX (1884), 516; *Trans. Acad. Sci. of St. Louis,* IV (1886), 1; *Berichte der Deutschen Botanischen Gesellschaft,* II (1884), xii; *Science,* Apr. 4, 1884; *Mo. Hist. Rev.,* Jan., Apr. 1929.]

G.T.M.

ENGELMANN, GEORGE JULIUS (July 2, 1847–Nov. 16, 1903), gynecologist, obstetrician, was born in St. Louis, Mo. His father, George Engelmann [*q.v.*], a native of Frankfurt-am-Main, was a botanist of international reputation as well as an accomplished physician. He came to America in 1832, settled in St. Louis for practise, and in 1840 returned to Germany to marry Dorothea Horstmann of Bacharach-am-Rhein. The son received his education from his mother until 1856, when for two years he received instruction in various European cities, where his father was engaged in botanical research. Returning to St. Louis with his parents in 1858, he entered Washington University where he was graduated in 1867. His medical education was received abroad, at the University of Berlin (1867–69), at Tübingen (1869–70), and again at Berlin where he received the degree of M.D. in 1871. In the meantime he had served as a volunteer Red Cross surgeon in the Franco-Prussian War. Following graduation he pursued postgraduate study in gynecology and pathology in Vienna where the university gave him the degree of Master in Obstetrics in 1872. After a winter spent in the clinics of Paris and London, Engelmann returned to St. Louis in the spring of 1873. He was given the position of lecturer on pathologic anatomy in the St. Louis Medical College and shortly afterward organized the St. Louis School for Midwives, and the Maternity Hospital. He was engaged in general practise until 1878, when he suffered from a nearly fatal sepsis. Following his recovery he limited his practise to the diseases of women. He moved to Boston in 1895 and died in that city in 1903.

Engelmann was a keen participant in all medical society affairs. His chief interests were, however, the local and national societies of gynecology and obstetrics. He was a member and one time president of the American Gynecological Society, of the Southern Surgical and Gynecological Society, and honorary president of the International Congress of Gynecology and Obstetrics. He also held membership in a number of foreign medical societies. For years he was professor of diseases of women and operative midwifery at the Missouri Medical College and at the St. Louis Post-Graduate School of Medicine. He was an original investigator along the lines of his specialty. Among the most noteworthy of his writings was *Labor among Primitive Peoples, Ancient and Modern,* published in 1882, which appeared in German in 1884 and in French in 1886. Other notable articles were: *Posture of Women in Labor* (1881), *Early History of Vaginal Hysterectomy* (1895), *Menstrual*

Function as Influenced by Modern Methods of Training, Mental and Physical (1900), and "Age of First Menstruation on the North American Continent" (in *Transactions of the American Gynecological Society,* vol. XXVI, 1901, p. 77).

Archæology was Engelmann's diversion. He made extensive researches of the Indian mounds of southeastern Missouri, and accumulated a private museum of flints and pottery. This collection was later given to the Peabody Museum of Archæology at Cambridge, Mass. He donated his father's botanical library and herbarium of one hundred thousand specimens to the Missouri Botanical Garden. Physically he was tall and powerfully built. He had a round ruddy face, large dark expressive eyes, and a dimpled chin. In later life he was quite bald. He was genial, a good talker, with a gift for deep and lasting friendships. He was married twice. His first wife was Emily Engelmann, whom he married in 1879 and who died after a long illness in 1890. In 1893 he married Mrs. Loula Clark.

[L. S. McMurtry in *Trans. Southern Surgic. and Gynecol. Asso., 1903,* XVI (1904), 473–75; Joseph T. Johnson, in *Trans. Am. Gynecol. Soc.,* XXIX (1904), 485–88; *Annals of Gynecol. and Pædiatry,* XVII (1904), 76–80.] J. M. P.

ENGLAND, JOHN (Sept. 23, 1786–Apr. 11, 1842), Roman Catholic bishop of Charleston, S. C., was one of ten children born to Thomas and Honora (Lordan) England. The former was a refugee hedge-schoolmaster, who prospered as a tobacconist in Cork. John attended (1792–1800) a Church of Ireland institution, where as the only "Papist" he was subjected to insults from master and pupils which made him combative. After reading law with the idea of entering this profession, for which Catholics had become eligible, he studied for the priesthood in the College of St. Patrick, Carlow, the first seminary opened with English approval to replace the Continental colleges closed by the French Revolution. On completion of the theological course, he was ordained by Bishop Moylan in North Chapel, Cork, Oct. 10, 1808.

England was assigned as chaplain to the North Presentation Convent (Cork), and in this capacity aided in building an enlarged school. Recognized as a forceful preacher, he was named lecturer in the cathedral. As chaplain at the Magdalen Asylum and for the prisoners in Cork, he became acquainted with the conditions under which men convicted of political and minor criminal offenses were transported to Australia. Writing impassioned articles for the Irish press, he aided in so arousing public opinion that the government undertook the reform of prison ships and ultimately permitted non-Anglican clergymen in the penal settlements (*Orthodox Journal,* 1819; *Dublin Evening Post,* June 7, 1816). So important was his work that an Australian authority speaks of him as "the founder of the Catholic Church in Australia" (E. M. O'Brien, "John England," *The Australian Catholic Record,* April 1928). England, who was also Inspector of Poor Schools, established *The Religious Repository* (or *Repertory*) and a circulating library. For a time he was president of the new St. Mary's Seminary, where he taught philosophy and probably compiled a nationalist *School Primer of Irish History* (1815). In 1813, he was named a trustee of the *Cork Mercantile Chronicle,* for which he wrote extensively. As the responsible trustee, he was fined £100 for his refusal to name the writer of "Commiseration of a Landlord" (Apr. 1, 1816), but the money was soon subscribed by Daniel O'Connell and his friends. For several years England was outstanding in the patriotic fight against the "Veto," a scheme sanctioned by a number of English and Irish bishops by which the government through a concordat with Rome would have a voice in the selection of bishops. The agitation was successful, but the agitator won the hostility of Dublin Castle without gaining episcopal approbation. Refused an exeat which would enable him to enter the foreign missions, England was transferred to a harmless pastorate in the Protestant village of Bandon (1817). This failed to silence the irreconcilable democrat, whom Archbishop Curtis of Armagh later described as a man of intellect and ability who "lacks sacerdotal meekness, and prudence" and who in political matters "does not act with equanimity and sufficient caution." England was not rendered mute; he even won Protestant respect by infusing spirit into a peasant congregation. In 1820 he received apostolic briefs of his appointment to the newly created diocese of Charleston (Carolinas and Georgia), and on Sept. 21 was consecrated by Bishop Murphy in St. Finnbar's Cathedral, Cork. His elevation was popularly considered the "transportation" of a heroic rebel who protested against aristocratic rule in Church and country.

Bishop England landed at Charleston Dec. 30, 1820. He found that his diocese had only five missionaries, a few wretched churches, a disordered treasury, and about 5,000 known Catholics of whom a fifth were negroes. Immediately he made an extended visitation, appointing priests to established congregations, gathering isolated Catholics into groups, and preaching in town halls and in churches the facilities of which were granted by Presbyterian and Episcopalian divines. He proved an indefatigable preacher with a characteristic vehemence of expression, an ardent democrat, who immediately applied for citizenship, and a man of determined principles. Before the year had passed, he visited his brother bishops in the North and called upon President Monroe and John Quincy Adams. This northern trip resulted in England's well-intentioned attempt to settle the Hogan schism in St. Mary's parish, Philadelphia, which was resented by Bishop Henry Conwell as factious interference on behalf of a worthless priest whose conduct and pamphlets were bringing disgrace upon the Church. England's criticism soon aroused the attack of the Hoganites whom he in turn condemned when reviewing the controversy in his *Miscellany.* While he was preaching at St. Peter's in New York (1822), some Irish malcontents unsuccessfully appealed to him against their bishop. This did not improve his relations with Bishop Connolly of New York nor with Archbishop Maréchal of Baltimore who resented England's peacemaking activity as unwarranted meddling in other dioceses.

Oppressed by these controversies, England instituted a democratic constitution for his own diocese which provided for frequent conventions of priests and lay delegates and defined the status of the Church under such captions as doctrine, government, property, membership, and conventions. The pew system and parochial trusteeism were abolished, and all property was held by a diocesan board incorporated by the legislature. Though this innovation was frowned upon by the other bishops and was discarded by England's successor, it worked well under him. In 1822, he opened The Philosophical and Classical Seminary of Charleston, thus winning Chancellor Kent's encomium as the "restorer of classical learning in South Carolina." This academy proved popular among Protestants until it was realized that the income derived from it financed an ecclesiastical seminary, which incidentally annoyed the Jesuits and Sulpicians because it competed with Georgetown College, and St. Mary's, Baltimore. England was determined to train his own seminarians rather than accept foreign priests or men educated by the Sulpicians, with whose rule he was not in sympathy. Although non-Catholics reopened the College of Charleston, England maintained his schools in a fair way. In 1829 he induced the Sisters of Mercy to establish a girls' academy in Charleston. In 1834 he brought in the Irish Ursulines, silencing nativist opposition by playing on Southern feeling against Massachusetts, where an Ursuline convent at Charlestown had been destroyed by a mob. He welcomed negroes at his weather-boarded Cathedral of Saint Finnbar, where he himself instructed them in religion. He accepted slavery, however, maintaining that slaves were better cared for than Irish peasants. In 1835 he opened a school in Charleston for free negroes, arousing an attack upon church property which was frustrated by the arrival of Irish militiamen. To satisfy public opinion, the school was closed. In 1840 he replied to a speech of Secretary Forsyth in Georgia, in which the latter identified Rome with abolitionism because of Gregory XVI's condemnation of the slave-trade. England declared that the Pope had not condemned slavery as practised in America and that the Church accepted the institution, counselling obedience on the part of slaves while encouraging their just treatment. For practical reasons, England, who could hardly have sympathized with slave-owners, was not fearless in his stand (S. L. Theobald, "Catholic Missionary Work among the Colored People of the United States," *Records of the American Catholic Historical Society of Philadelphia,* December 1924).

He was in demand as a preacher in Irish centers and as a lecturer before Catholic lyceums. Among outstanding lectures were: "Classical Education" (1832); "The Nature of Religious Orders" (1835), at a time when native Americans honestly feared the arrival of religious communities; "The Pleasures of The Scholar" (1840), before Franklin College, Ga.; and "American Citizenship," in the Boston cathedral on the occasion of President Harrison's death. He gloried in being the first priest to address the House of Representatives, as he did on Jan. 8, 1826, in the presence of the president, senators, and a crowded gallery. The foundation of the *United States Catholic Miscellany* (1822–61), the first distinctly Catholic paper, was England's greatest achievement. He hoped to make it a national organ, but was unable to win the support of the hierarchy. England believed that he was thwarted at every turn by French ecclesiastics who distrusted his democratic proclivities and whom he considered a menace to Catholic advance because of their aristocratic leanings. The *Miscellany* challenged national attention, for the bishop was an aggressive controversialist who forced the issue with an antagonist at a time when there were plenty of nativist charges. Catholic happenings were emphasized; the struggle for Catholic emancipation was closely followed; and lengthy articles explained Catholic teachings. Catholic writers appear to accept uncritically the statement that England assured the secretary of the Catholic Association in 1828 that he had personally organized 40,000 men in America under the command of Gen. Montgomery to invade Ireland in case emancipation was denied (W. J. Fitz-Patrick, *The Life, Times, and Correspondence of the Right Rev. Dr. Doyle,* 1880; Guilday, *post,* I, 122; Denis Gwynn, *The Struggle for Catholic Emancipation,* 1928, p. 257). The *Miscellany* made England a national figure, yet hardly "the most striking ecclesiastical personality of his day in the United States," and "the foremost intellectual representative of the Irish element in the American Church" (Guilday, I, 43, 475).

England's prolific pen was never idle, although many of his writings were hastily composed and padded with quotations. He was always forceful and logical, though his essays were marred by bitterness as well as an impatience with the American attitude toward his creed and race and by a touch of Celtic exaggeration. Among the best known of his lengthy brochures are: a reprint of the translated *Roman Missal* as used in Ireland with a prefatory explanation of the Mass compiled from French theologians (1822); an *Explanation of the Construction, Furniture, and Ornaments of a Church,* etc., which was written in Rome and published in three tongues at papal expense (1833), republished in Baltimore (1834); *Explanation of the Ceremonies of Holy Week in the Chapels of the Vatican and of those at Easter Sunday in the Church of St. Peter* (1832); *Letters Concerning the Roman Chancery* (1840); *Letters to the Honorable John Forsyth on the Subject of Domestic Slavery* (1844); and *The Garden of the Soul* (1845). England's works were published by his successor, Ignatius A. Reynolds (5 vols., 1849); in abridged form by H. F. McElrone (2 vols., 1900); and in a critical edition under the direction of Archbishop Sebastian G. Messmer (7 vols., 1908).

The insistence of England at home and at Rome upon a national synod which so annoyed Archbishops Maréchal and Whitfield, had much to do with the calling of the Provincial Councils of Baltimore. This did not increase England's popularity any more than his reiterated advice that native priests be raised to the hierarchy rather than Frenchmen, though his own preferential votes for vacant sees went to priests of Irish birth. Named apostolic delegate to Haiti (1833–37) with instructions to draft a concordat, he failed, even accentuating the Gallican stand of the Haitian government. The agreement which he negotiated was so sweeping in concessions that it was not accepted by Gregory XVI. Meanwhile, his own diocese suffered because of his extended absences. Nevertheless, England was true to his inconspicuous diocese, refusing to allow his name in nomination for an Irish see, even that of the archdiocese of Cashel (1833). Though aided by the Leopoldine Society and the Propagation of the Faith, the bishop was always in debt. As there was no immigration, numbers increased slowly; in 1842, there were in his diocese only about 7,000 Catholics, who because of their scattered location required sixty-five churches and chapels with twenty-one priests, entailing a heavy expense. To-day he is chiefly remembered for his long letter to the Society of the Propagation of the Faith (Lyons, France) in which he estimated Catholic leakage in the United States at 3,250,000 souls on the basis of 8,000,000 immigrants from 1786 to 1836, of whom he guessed one half would be Catholics, when official immigration figures indicate only 750,000 immigrants and their descendants. England's figures, accepted as an accurate statement, were (and are) extensively quoted to the discredit of the Church and to the satisfaction of unfriendly critics (Gerald Shaughnessy, *Has the Immigrant Kept the Faith?* (1925) ch. XIV). Saddened by burdens and fatigued by a European trip followed by extensive preaching in Philadelphia and Baltimore, England took to his bed in the last days of 1841 though he lingered for four months.

[Peter Guilday, *The Life and Times of John England* (2 vols., 1927); *Metropolitan Cath. Almanac* (1844); W. G. Read, *The Religious Cabinet,* May 1842; R. H. Clarke, *Lives of the Deceased Bishops of the Cath. Ch. in the U. S.* (1872), I, 271–309; memoirs in the various editions of England's works; J. J. O'Connell, *Catholicity in the Carolinas and Ga.* (1879), J. G. Shea, *Cath. Church in the U. S.* (vols. III, IV, 1890–92); *Cath. Encyc.;* E. M. O'Brien, *The Dawn of Catholicity in Australia* (2 vols., 1928); Thos. O'Gorman, *A Hist. of the Roman Cath. Church in the U. S.* (1895); T. Corcoran, "John England" in *Studies* (Dublin), Mar. 1928.]

R. J. P.

ENGLIS, JOHN (Nov. 27, 1808–Oct. 25, 1888), ship-builder, was born in New York City, the son of John Englis, who had migrated from Scotland in 1795. His formal schooling must have been slight. At seventeen he was apprenticed to the ship-building firm of Smith & Dimon. In the articles of indenture (as reproduced by Sheldon, *post*) George Bell's name appears as step-father of young Englis. It is not known when John Englis the elder died.

After his term of apprenticeship expired, Englis was made foreman in the shipyard of Bishop & Simonson, where he remained eight years, on duty from sunrise to sunset, summer and winter. In 1832 he married Mary Quackenbush, a member of a colonial Dutch family. His work had been chiefly, if not altogether, on sailing ships turned out from the New York yards; but in 1837, when he made a start for himself as a master ship-builder, he decided to center his efforts on steam vessels. There was a demand for these on the inland waters of the country. Englis went to Buffalo, N. Y., then in the period of its first rapid growth after the completion of the Erie Canal, and there built the *Milwaukie, Red Jacket,* and *Empire City,* for service on the Great Lakes. These steamboats were from 210 to 230 feet in length, with a beam of 38 or 39 feet, and 12 feet depth of hold. For speed and grace of line they were a great advance on any of the earlier lake craft. Their wide repute brought their builder orders from New York. He returned to that city and produced from his yards the most famous of the Hudson River and Long Island Sound steamers of that period—the *Albany, Hendrik Hudson, Troy, Knickerbocker, Charter Oak,* and others. The largest of these was the *Hendrik Hudson,* 300 feet long, built in 1845. In 1853 Englis built at Buffalo the *Western World* (348 feet by 45 feet) and the *Plymouth Rock,* a smaller vessel for Great Lakes traffic. Up to the outbreak of the Civil War he continued to build steamboats for New York and New England waters at his yards, located first at the foot of East Tenth St., New York City, and later removed to Greenpoint, on the Long Island side of the East River. The Hudson River boat *Isaac Newton* (1855) was the largest of the series, being 405 feet in length. In 1857–58 his yards launched three Spanish gunboats for service in Cuban waters. Englis was not merely a builder of vessels; he was a self-taught naval architect and designer. He did not, however, make a practise of designing ships; those built in his yards were usually planned by others. In 1861, when the government at Washington was unable to build at its own navy yards the gunboats needed to maintain the blockade of Southern ports, Englis completed the *Unadilla* and delivered it to the Navy Department within eighty-two days. During the war years (1861–65), he built for the government a revenue cutter and for private corporations a number of vessels to be used in Chinese waters. In 1863 he sent out the largest boat in his Hudson River fleet, the *St. John* (417 feet over all). At the time of its launching, this vessel was described as the longest steamship in the world, with the sole exception of the *Great Eastern.* After the war Englis took into partnership his only son, John Englis, and in 1882 two grandsons, William F. and Charles M. Englis, became members of the firm. They continued the building of a variety of steam craft, including ferryboats. The average burden of their ships was 1500 tons, and, with the exception of a few iron ships, wood was the material used throughout the lifetime of the elder Englis. Steel was introduced later, however, and long after the death of the founder, the Englis yards went forward with the construction of steamers for river and lake navigation. It was the only one of the great New York ship-building firms of the early nineteenth century that kept at work through the first decade of the twentieth.

["The Famous Englis Ship Yard," with tabulation of ships built at the Englis yards, 1837–1911, in *Master, Mate, and Pilot* (N. Y.), July 1911 (data supplied by members of the firm); G. W. Sheldon, "The Old Shipbuilders of New York," *Harper's Monthly,* July 1882; *N. Y. Tribune,* Oct. 26, 1888; letter from John Englis, great-grandson of the ship-builder, dated Jan. 18, 1928.]

W. B. S—w.

ENGLISH, ELBERT HARTWELL (Mar. 6, 1816–Sept. 1, 1884), Arkansas jurist, was born in Madison County, Ala., the son of James and Nancy (McCracken) English. His forebears came from England to Virginia about the middle of the eighteenth century. His father was born in Virginia but was taken to Kentucky in early life and later moved to Alabama, where he engaged in cotton culture in the "flush times." Elbert entered the academy at Athens at the age of fourteen and finished the course as then given. For several years he was undecided about a vocation. He taught, learned to be a silversmith and opened a shop in Athens, began the study of medicine, but finally turned to the law, reading under the direction of George S. Houston, afterwards United States senator and governor of Alabama. English was admitted to the bar at Athens in 1839 and practised there several years. He served two terms in the Alabama legislature. In 1844 he moved to Little Rock, Ark., where two years later he was appointed reporter to the supreme court; elected by the legislature to compile the state laws. In his seven years as reporter he issued eight volumes of reports, and *A Digest of the Statutes of Arkansas* was published in 1848. While engaged in these tasks he continued his practise, traveling extensively over the state to attend the courts. In 1854 he was elected chief justice in the place of Judge Watkins, resigned. He was reëlected in 1860 for a term of eight years and continued to serve until the Confederate state government, with which he had cast his lot, was displaced by the loyal Murphy government under the constitution of 1864. He then resumed the practise of his profession. While not a member of the convention of 1874 he was a constant attendant at the sessions of the committee which drew up the articles dealing with the judiciary. At the election (1874) following the adoption of the constitution, he was chosen chief justice and held the position until his death in 1884. He was considered by his associates and the bar an ultraconservative man. According to his successor, Chief Justice S. R. Cockrill, he never undertook to fashion the law according to what he thought it ought to be, but only to find out what it was and to stand rigidly by it. Technicalities counted much with him, and perhaps this fact explains his concurrence in the decision repudiating the state debt. In twenty-three volumes of State Reports, said Mr. Cockrill, "he has placed the indelible impress of his learning, and has therein builded for himself an honorable monument, more enduring . . . than any we can raise to his memory" (43 *Arkansas,* 14). English was a member of the Methodist church and of the Democratic party. He was a Royal Arch Mason and a Knight Templar, held high office in the order, and his Masonic decisions were translated into several languages. On Sept. 30, 1840, he married Julia Agnes Fisher in Athens, Ala. She died in 1871, and in July of the next year he married Mrs. Susan A. Wheless.

[John Hallum, *Biog. and Pictorial Hist. of Ark.* (1887); *Biog. and Hist. Memoirs of Pulaski, Jefferson . . . and Hot Spring Counties, Ark.* (1889); *Encyc. of the New West* (1881); obituary in *Daily Ark. Gazette* (Little Rock), Sept. 2, 1884; information regarding the family from a grand-daughter, Mrs. Julia English Bennett.] D.Y.T.

ENGLISH, GEORGE BETHUNE (Mar. 7, 1787–Sept. 20, 1828), writer, soldier, and diplomat, was born in Cambridge, Mass., son of Thomas English, an immigrant from England, who married Penelope Bethune of Boston. He graduated from Harvard in 1807, "a smart, active, handsome, young man," known already for his linguistic ability. After studying law for a few months, he vainly applied for a commission in the army. Turning to theology, he acquired an M.A. from the Harvard Divinity School and was licensed to preach. Study of Hebrew, combined perhaps with failure as a minister, convinced him that the New Testament was valueless. His conclusions were published in *The Grounds of Christianity Examined by Comparing the New Testament with the Old* (1813). This brochure created a furore and was condemned by eminent churchmen, notably W. E. Channing and Edward Everett. The latter wrote *A Defense of Christianity against the Work of G. B. English* (1814) which convicts English of wholesale plagiarism. From inhospitable New England he moved to the West, where he was at one time editor of a country newspaper and at another, member of the New Harmony Community. Through the influence of John Quincy Adams, he was appointed lieutenant of marines and went on a cruise to the Mediterranean. Resigning his commission at Alexandria, he embraced Mohammedanism and became an officer in the Egyptian army. After attempting unsuccessfully to revive the use of scythe-bearing chariots, he went in 1820 and 1821 with Ismail, son of Mehemet Ali, the Pasha of Egypt, on an expedition to the eastern Sudan. During a campaign which almost reached Abyssinia, he utilized camels for artillery transport. Expected rewards were not forthcoming, so he left the Egyptian service and returned home. He now published *A Narrative of the Expedition to Dongola and Senaar* (London, 1822; Boston, 1823) which deserves credit as one of the first descriptions of that country by a white man; and a counterblast to Everett entitled *Five Pebbles from the Brook* (1824), written some years earlier. Adams now appointed him secret agent of the United States to sound the Turkish government regarding a commercial treaty and the opening of the Black Sea to American trade. Making his way to Constantinople disguised as a Mohammedan and relying for security on his knowledge of Oriental languages and customs, he spent the winter of 1823–24 conferring secretly with Husrev, the wily Capudan Pasha or Grand Admiral, who had long favored American interests. Persuaded to advise a meeting between this Pasha and the commander of the American Mediterranean Squadron, and suspected of being a Greek spy, he departed hurriedly for Washington. His plan adopted, he went to the Levant again in 1825 as interpreter for Commodore John Rodgers [*q.v.*]. The interview took place in 1826 on one of the Ægean Islands, but was fruitful only of presents to the Turk. Distrusted by Rodgers and the United States consul at Smyrna, he returned to America in 1827. Chronically penniless, he importuned Adams for further employment and was about to receive it, when the discovery of obscure but damning facts precluded further aid to one who had been befriended repeatedly, "notwithstanding his eccentricities, approaching to insanity." Less than two months later he died in Washington. English had marvelous ability as a linguist. He is said to have passed as a native Turk with an ambassador of the Porte and to have amazed a Cherokee delegation in Washington by addressing them in their own tongue. Versatile but erratic, he was intellectually shallow and dishonest.

[Samuel Lorenzo Knapp, a friend of English, included a chapter on him in his *Am. Biog.* (1833). Correspondence from his Turkish mission is found in *House Ex. Doc. No. 250, 22* Cong., 1 Sess., pp. 12–20. See also the *Memoirs of John Quincy Adams,* VIII (1876), 62; H. M. Wriston, *Executive Agents in Am. Foreign Relations* (1929); *Proc. Mass. Hist. Soc.,* vol. VIII (1864–65); *Daily Nat. Intelligencer* (Washington, D. C.), Sept. 22, 1828.] W. L. W—t., Jr.

ENGLISH, JAMES EDWARD (Mar. 13, 1812–Mar. 2, 1890), manufacturer, representative, and senator, governor of Connecticut, was born in New Haven, one of a family of nine children. His father, James English, was a shipowner, and had been a customs officer under President Jefferson. His mother, Nancy Griswold, came of a family prominent in Connecticut local history. At the age of eleven, James Edward was bound out to a farmer in Bethlehem, Conn., where he worked two and a half years. After this experience he was sent for two years to a private school, and then was apprenticed to Atwater Treat, a carpenter in New Haven. Under the latter's guidance, he became a designer and contractor. On reaching the age of twenty-three, with Harmonious M. Welch, he established a lumber company, English & Welch, in New Haven. He proved to be a successful business man and made money rapidly. With his growing capital he bought the Jerome Clock Company, originally of Bristol, Conn. The company was later merged with the New Haven Clock Company. English also became interested in real estate and banking. His affairs prospered so consistently that by middle life he was one of the richest men in the state. On Jan. 25, 1837, he married Caroline Augusta Fowler of New Haven. She died in 1874, and some years later, Oct. 7, 1885, he took as his second wife, Anna R. Morris of New York. He was chosen representative to the Connecticut Assembly in 1855, and state senator in 1856 and 1858. In 1861 he was elected to Congress, where he entered the group of "War Democrats" supporting the Lincoln Administration. He spoke but few times in the House, and his remarks upon those occasions were quite brief. In 1862 he opposed the issue of legal tender notes, preferring to have the government raise money by taxation (*Congressional Globe,* 37 Cong., 2 Sess., p. 887). During 1863 he spoke occasionally on tariff matters, to secure terms favorable to Connecticut brass and clock manufacturing interests (*Ibid.,* 37 Cong., 3 Sess., pp. 1317, 1320). In 1864–65 he was one of the few Democrats to support the passage of the Thirteenth Amendment. He became governor of Connecticut in 1867, was reelected in 1868, and again in 1870. Perhaps his most outstanding policy as governor was a plan for local option, to give individual towns in the state the right to decide the liquor question for themselves. In the National Democratic Convention of 1868 English received some consideration as a candidate for the presidency. In 1875 he was appointed by Gov. Ingersoll to fill a vacancy in the Senate caused by the death of Orris S. Ferry. Though in politics he professed to be a Democrat of the Jeffersonian type, in reality he was an independent, voting as circumstances seemed to direct, and striving neither for office nor private advancement. He was, however, more business man than politician. Leaving the Senate in the spring of 1876, he devoted the latter part of his life to his private business in and about New Haven. He was a large stockholder in several important companies, such as the New Haven Clock Company, and the Bristol Brass Company. He owned several business blocks in New Haven, including the building occupied by the First National Bank. From his large fortune he gave liberally to deserving institutions, donating at one time a large sum for the improvement of East Rock Park. He died in New Haven at the age of seventy-eight, being survived by his widow, and one son, Henry F. English, who in memory of his parents made a gift of a building for the use of the New Haven Colony Historical Society.

[E. E. Atwater, *Hist. of the City of New Haven* (1887); F. C. Norton, *The Governors of Conn.* (1905); *Proc. New Haven Colony Hist. Soc.,* 1893; *Biog. Dir. Am. Cong.* (1928); *Geneal. and Family Hist., State of Conn.* (1911); *New Haven Evening Reg.,* Mar. 3, 1890.]

J. M. M.

ENGLISH, THOMAS DUNN (June 29, 1819–Apr. 1, 1902), editor, politician, playwright, was born in or near Philadelphia, of Quaker stock, descended from an ancestor who settled in New Jersey about 1683. His father was probably Robert English. He attended Wilson's Academy in Philadelphia, the Friends' Academy, Burlington, N. J., and the Medical School of the University of Pennsylvania, where he presented a thesis on phrenology, defending the theories of Gall and Spurzheim, and was granted the degree of M.D. in 1839. During the three years following he read law and in 1842 was admitted to the bar, but, as he wrote later, "I . . . never was lawyer enough to hurt me." His energies were turned more to writing for magazines than to practising his professions. As early as 1839 he had begun to write for *Burton's Gentleman's Magazine,* through which connection he met Edgar Allan Poe, one of the editors, of whom he became an intimate and then an adversary. In 1844, he states in his autobiography, "I was President of a political club, and did a good deal of stumping. I dare say that I was unnecessarily offensive in my remarks at times, and provoked a deal of ill-will." In that year he edited a Tyler daily, the *Aurora,* which failed; and held a political appointment as weigher of the port of New York. About this time he published a poem, "The Gallows-Goers," coarse but vigorous, which was widely circulated in the campaign against capital punishment. In 1845 he tried his hand at editing the *Aristidean, A Maga-*

zine of Reviews, Politics and Light Literature, to which both Poe and Whitman were contributors but which failed after six issues. The following year Poe held English up to ridicule in a sketch in his series, "The Literati," published in *Godey's Magazine* in 1846. English retaliated with a card, reprinted in the *Evening Mirror,* charging Poe with forgery. Poe sued Hiram Fuller [*q.v.*], editor of the *Mirror,* and won, but the stir created by this suit did much to becloud the poet's fame for half a century. During the trial English changed his residence to Washington. In 1848, with George Dexter of New York and George Zieber of Philadelphia, publishers, the illustrator F. O. C. Darley, and G. G. Foster, he undertook to bring out a weekly humorous sheet at Philadelphia, the *John Donkey.* "*John-Donkey* was the best humorous periodical that had yet been attempted, labored though some of its wit appears. . . . Its satire was often scurrilous; it attacked Greeley, Poe, and many others. It is said to have attained a circulation at one time of twelve thousand, but libel suits ruined it after it had brayed valiantly from January to July, 1848" (Mott, *post,* p. 426).

From 1852 to 1856 English practised law and medicine at Lawnsville, Va. (now Logan, W. Va.), of which place he was the first mayor. Returning North he settled in Bergen County, N. J. A "Copperhead" in politics during the Civil War, he was elected to the New Jersey legislature from Bergen County and served 1863–64. In 1870 he bought a political magazine, *The Old Guard* (anti-Lincoln), from Chauncey Burr, who had successfully nursed it through seven years, but like his other ventures, it died on Dr. English's hands after a twelve-month. In 1878 he removed to Newark where he lived until his death. For a time he was on the literary staff of the *Newark Sunday Call.* He was elected to Congress as a Democrat in 1890 and served 1891–95, being defeated for a third term. In his last years he was nearly blind. He had married in 1849 Annie Maxwell Meade of Philadelphia, who died June 17, 1899, survived by four children. English died at his home in Newark in 1902.

During his career he published many books—most of which he did not care to acknowledge—began work on a metrical history of America which was never completed but which may have been drawn upon for *American Ballads* (1880), and the *Boy's Book of Battle Lyrics* (1885), wrote more than twenty plays, and was constantly contributing prose and verse to periodicals. "I write poetry," he said toward the close of his life, "because publishers pay me well; publishers pay me well because the public seems to like my themes . . . and so long as I am paid, and no longer, I shall continue to write." As a poet English belonged to "the gnomes and elves of Parnassus" of whose literary by-products George Edward Woodberry remarked: "No quotation could do sufficient injustice to them—they must be read to be properly damned." As a playwright English was notoriously facile and verbose. For Burton he wrote a play in which journeymen printers figured as the main characters. It was written in forty-eight hours, and took eight hours to rehearse. For Oxley, English said, "I wrote a rhyming extravaganza, in which the actors were all to be gigantic frogs." Of his dramas, however, only one, *The Mormons, or Life at Salt Lake,* produced at Burton's Theatre in 1858, was published.

His only bid for lasting literary fame was made on Sept. 2, 1843, when he published in the *New Mirror,* edited by G. P. Morris and N. P. Willis, the engaging poem "Ben Bolt," addressed to a real person of that name. Its charming simplicity attracted composers: the Library of Congress lists twenty-six different compositions to this song; English himself wrote one "entirely for the black keys." In 1848, Nelson Kneass in Pittsburgh adapted a German air and sang the song in the drama, *The Battle of Buena Vista.* In 1894 Du Maurier introduced it into his popular novel, *Trilby.* It was said that the attention paid to English in the House of Representatives was due as much to his authorship of "Ben Bolt" as to any other cause. His daughter Alice collected all his poems except the *Battle Lyrics* in a volume, *The Select Poems of Dr. Thomas Dunn English* (1894), published by subscription. Three years later, another daughter, Florence English Noll, edited his *Fairy Stories and Wonder Tales* (1897), and in 1904 his son-in-law, Arthur H. Noll, brought out a similar volume, collected from periodicals.

[Autobiographical sketch (MS.), in N. Y. Pub. Lib.; autobiographical material in "Down Among the Dead Men," sketches running in *The Old Guard,* 1869–70; Papers of the Superior Court (1846) in the Hall of Records, N. Y.; "Close-up of Poe" in *Saturday Review of Literature,* Oct. 9, 1926; A. H. Noll, "The Truth About 'Ben Bolt' and its Author" in *Midland Monthly,* Jan. 1897; Mary E. Phillips, *Edgar Allan Poe: The Man* (2 vols., 1926), see Index; Hervey Allen, *Israfel* (2 vols., 1926), see Index; *Alumni Register* (Univ. of Pa.), May 1902; *Biog. Dir. Am. Cong.* (1928); A. H. Smyth, *Phila. Mags. and their Contributors, 1741–1850* (1892); F. L. Mott, *A Hist. of Am. Magazines, 1741–1850* (1930); *N. Y. Times,* Apr. 2, 1902; G. T. Swain, *Hist. of Logan County, W. Va.* (1927); information from the English MSS. in the N. J. Hist. Soc. obtained through the courtesy of William S. Hunt, Esq., of Newark.]

C. F. S.

ENGLISH, WILLIAM HAYDEN (Aug. 27, 1822–Feb. 7, 1896), congressman, Democratic candidate for the vice-presidency, historian, was born at Lexington, Scott County, Ind., the son of Elisha G. and Mahala (Eastin) English. On his mother's side he was descended from Jost Hite, one of the first white settlers of the Shenandoah Valley. His parents removed from Kentucky to Indiana in 1818, and there Elisha English, a Democrat, took a prominent part in politics, being at different times sheriff of Scott County, a representative and also a senator in the Indiana legislature, and United States marshal.

Young English attended Hanover College for three years, studied law, and was admitted to the bar at the early age of eighteen. The same year, 1840, he was a delegate to the Democratic state convention at Indianapolis. When Tyler succeeded to the presidency after the death of Harrison, he appointed the young Democrat postmaster of Lexington. In 1843 English was elected clerk of the Indiana House of Representatives, and a year later he received an appointment in the Treasury Department at Washington, a position he held until shortly before the end of Polk's presidency, becoming, soon after, clerk of the United States Senate committee on claims during the historic session of 1850. He next became secretary of the convention that framed the Indiana constitution of 1851, and as speaker, during part of the session of the next House of Representatives, played a leading part in readjusting the laws and machinery of government to the conditions created by the new constitution.

In 1852 he was elected to represent the second Indiana district in the Thirty-third Congress. As a member of that body he voted for the Kansas-Nebraska Bill and was one of the few Northern Democrats so voting who survived the next congressional election. He was reëlected for a third term in 1856 and again in 1858. In the latter year he stood with Douglas in opposing the effort of Buchanan and the South to bring Kansas into the Union under the Lecompton constitution, which had been ratified in an election in which the voters of the Territory had not been given a fair chance to express their views. A conference committee became necessary, and as a member of this committee English played a leading part in framing the compromise known as the English Bill. This measure, which ultimately became a law, in effect offered the people of Kansas a bribe of public land if they would ratify the pro-slavery constitution, a thing which, as English had foreseen, they refused to do.

In 1860 he declined to stand for reëlection and in March 1861 retired to private life. He opposed secession, and denied that the election of a Republican president justified an attempt to break up the Union. In a speech in the House, he warned his Southern associates that his constituents would only "march under the flag and keep step to the music of the Union." Upon the outbreak of war, Gov. Morton offered him command of a regiment, but he declined it. He supported the Union cause, however, and opposed the Knights of the Golden Circle in Indiana.

In 1863 he removed to Indianapolis, and there helped to organize the First National Bank, of which he became president, holding that position until 1877. He played a prominent part in the business life of the city and ultimately became a millionaire. In 1880 geographical and other reasons led the National Democratic Convention to nominate him for the vice-presidency as the running mate of Gen. Hancock. Throughout his life he was interested in scientific and literary matters. While a congressman he was a regent of the Smithsonian Institution, and in later life he was long president of the Indiana Historical Society. For many years he collected material bearing upon the early history of the old Northwest, and ultimately wrote *Conquest of the Country Northwest of the River Ohio, 1778–1783, and Life of Gen. George Rogers Clark* (2 vols., 1896), a book containing much that had never before been published. In 1847, while a clerk at Washington, English married Emma Mardulia Jackson of Virginia. A son and a daughter were born of this union.

[J. P. Dunn, *Commemorative Biog. Record of Prominent and Representative Men of Indianapolis and Vicinity* (1908), pp. 8–18; *Biog. Hist. of Eminent and Self-Made Men of Ind.* (2 vols., 1880), vol. II, 7th Dist., pp. 209–27; J. W. Forney, *Life and Military Career of Winfield Scott Hancock; Sketch of Hon. Wm. H. English* (1880), a campaign biography; *Biog. Dir. Am. Cong.* (1928); *Indianapolis Sentinel,* Feb. 8, 10, 1896.]

P. L. H.

ENNEKING, JOHN JOSEPH (Oct. 4, 1841–Nov. 17, 1916), painter, was born in Minster, Auglaize County, Ohio, the son of Joseph and Margaretha (Bramlage) Enneking. His father, a farmer of German descent, disapproved of his son's artistic inclinations and once thrashed him for an ambitious sketch on the freshly painted barn of the homestead. Enneking received his early education at Mount St. Mary's College, Cincinnati, and later studied art in New York and Boston. Owing to eye-strain, he abandoned art for a time, securing an interest in a large tinware manufactory, but business reverses eventually induced his return to painting as his career. During the Civil War, it is said, he enlisted with a Western regiment and served for over a year, being wounded several times. On Oct. 14, 1864, he was married to Mary E. Elliott of Corinna,

Me. In 1873 he began three years of European art study, chiefly at Paris, under D'Aubigny and at the school of Maître Bonnât where he mastered the grammar of art. Returning to America, he established his home in Hyde Park, but revisited Europe in 1878 for another year of sketching and study in Paris and Holland. He finally opened a studio in Boston, devoting himself thenceforth, for the rest of his life, to landscape and figure painting. He died from pneumonia, at his home in the Hyde Park district, Boston.

Enneking has been called the interpreter of New England in painting as was Edward MacDowell in music. He was a romanticist, intolerant of academic restrictions, an impressionist, luminist, and tonalist whose work expressed emotional freedom and idealism. Remarkable coordination of light, color, mass, and line produced a harmony of result and an elusive manner of portrayal, suggesting what Coleridge called "something between a thought and a thing." His art, despite its varied range, was never obscure or involved, but charmed by its simple descriptive quality, admirably shown in *The Brook,* and his landscapes reflected nature's own quiet poise and strength. Although most prominent as a landscapist, he could paint a masterly portrait, one of his best examples being that of F. B. Sanborn of Concord. He was a medalist at the Paris Exposition, the exhibit of the Charitable Mechanics' Association, and the Pan-American Exposition.

[*World To-Day,* May 1909; Ralph Davol, in *Am. Mag. of Art,* June 1917; W. B. Closson, in *Internat. Studio,* Oct. 1922; *New Eng. Mag.,* Feb. 1909; Jessie B. Rittenhouse, in *Brush and Pencil,* Sept. 1902; *Who's Who in America,* 1899–1900, 1912–13; *N. Y. Times,* Nov. 18, 1916.]
J.M.H.

ENSLEY, ENOCH (Nov. 8, 1836–Nov. 18, 1891), planter, manufacturer, economist, was born near Nashville, Tenn., the son of Enoch and Mary (Rains) Ensley. His mother was the daughter of Capt. John Rains, prominent in the affairs of middle Tennessee. Ensley was educated at Hardeman's Academy, Williamstown County, and at Cumberland University, Lebanon, and was licensed to practise law, but at the age of twenty he moved to Shelby County and engaged in planting cotton, making his home at first on his plantation, about ten miles south of Memphis, and later in the city of Memphis. In 1872 he became president of the Memphis Gas Light Company, continued as president for fourteen years, and during the same time was one of the organizers of the Union and Planters Bank of which he was a director. He also organized the Tennessee Coal, Iron & Railway Company and was later president of the Lady Ensley Coal, Iron & Railway Company. He was regarded as a pioneer in the industrial development of the South. It is notable that no strike took place in any industrial company of which he was a director.

During his life as a planter, Ensley began thinking deeply on economic questions and formulated ideas of taxation which were far in advance of his time. On Sept. 1, 1873, he published in the form of a letter to the governor of the State of Tennessee a pamphlet entitled *What Should Be Taxed and How it Should Be Taxed.* David A. Wells (*post,* p. 556) says that this pamphlet "set forth certain fundamental propositions in respect to local taxation, and supported them with such homely and clear illustrations as to entitle the essay to a permanent place in economic and legal literature." Ensley commenced by proposing the following rule as the basis for a state, city, or county system of taxation: "Never tax anything that would be of value to your state, that could and would run away, or that could and would come to you." He divided property into two classes, movable and immovable, and he said, "I hold it to be true that immovable property has no value till it is occupied or located upon, or brought to subsist or employ movable property, and, as a rule, the more it employs or subsists, the more valuable it becomes, and the greater the inducements or attractions it offers movable property, the more it will have to locate upon it. . . . To undertake to enforce a very oppressive tax on money is ridiculous nonsense. It is impossible. The Maker of all things has forbidden it, in giving to all things their peculiar nature. He has forbidden an oppressive tax on money, by giving it that easy mobility that it can go in a fortnight from Tennessee almost to the uttermost parts of the world." With the exception of a few advanced thinkers in the State of New York no one in the United States had advocated the exemption of personal property from taxation. That a man not yet forty years of age, who had lived all his life in the country or in what was then a small city, should have had these ideas at all and have presented them so ably indicates a grasp of mind that is rare in any age and in any place.

Ensley was twice married: in 1860 he married Laura Martin, daughter of Judge Abram Martin of Montgomery County, Tenn., who died in 1887, and in 1889 he married Mary Leavenworth Beecher. Two children of his first and two of his second marriage lived to grow up.

[*The Politico-Economic Writings of Enoch Ensley* (1892), printed for private distribution; D. A. Wells,

The Theory and Practice of Taxation (1900); Ensley's letter to the Governor reprinted (1900) in an abridged form, under the title *The Tax Question*, with an introduction by Lawson Purdy; *Memphis Appeal-Avalanche*, *Nashville Daily American*, Nov. 19, 1891; certain information from Mrs. Enoch Ensley.] L. P.

ENTWISTLE, JAMES (July 8, 1837–Mar. 23, 1910), naval engineer, was born in Paterson, N. J., the son of Thomas E. and Fanny (Holt) Entwistle. Educated in the public schools of Paterson and New York City, he joined the 8th New York Regiment in 1861 for three months, but on Oct. 29 entered the navy as a third assistant engineer. He was assigned to the gunboat *Aroostook*, which in May 1862 participated with the *Galena*, *Monitor*, and other vessels in attacking Drewry's Bluff and Fort Darling on the James River, was then sent to the Mobile blockade, where it made several captures of vessels, and later, in 1864, cruised off the Texas coast, shelled Confederate batteries, captured a few prizes, and performed the routine of a blockader. In 1866 Entwistle became a first assistant engineer while on the *Mohongo* of the Pacific Squadron. He was then sent on the trial trips of the *Wampanoag*. performed similar duty on the *Ammonoosuc*, and after a year on the *Nipsic*, was ordered to the Great Lakes to the twenty-five-year-old paddle wheel relic, the *Michigan*. This assignment was followed by duty on the monitor *Canonicus* and by a European cruise under Admiral Worden in the *Franklin*.

In 1877 Entwistle began more important engineering work, acting as assistant inspector of machinery at the Morgan Iron Works, New York, and in a similar capacity at Mare Island. In 1881 he was sent to the Far East and became chief engineering officer of the wooden gunboat *Ashuelot* on the China Station. In 1883 that ship, so rotten from years of service that the naval authorities did not dare to order her across the Pacific for repairs, struck a rock off Lamock Island, between Amoy and Swatow, and sank in twelve minutes. Ten of the crew were lost, and Entwistle, though in no way responsible for the accident, was, with the other engineer officer, suspended for one year for neglect of duty in not seeing his men up from below before leaving the ship.

In July 1887, however, he was promoted to chief engineer and sent to the *Enterprise*, in which he spent a disagreeable two and a half years. The crew was unruly, the ship constantly on the go from one European or African port to another, and the captain—temperamentally unable to cope with the situation—resorted to strait-jackets, irons, and other extreme measures. He also reported several of his officers, among them Entwistle, for disobedience. On the return to New York, the commanding officer was court-martialed and suspended for three years. Entwistle was a witness against him. Following this episode came five years of duty as inspector of machinery, most of it spent at Bath, Me., during the construction of the harbor defense ram *Katahdin* and of the gunboats *Machias* and *Castine*. He then sailed to the Orient on the *Boston*, and on Mar. 24, 1897, reported to Commodore Dewey on the *Olympia* as fleet engineer. In this capacity he served at the battle of Manila Bay, was given the Dewey Medal, and in 1901 advanced two numbers for "eminent and conspicuous conduct in battle." He had already been retired, however, in 1899, and as a participant in the Civil War given promotion of one grade on the retired list. Thus he returned to Paterson with the title, rank, and retired pay of a rear admiral. He had never married, and at his death in Paterson his property was left by will to his sister and cousin but with bequests to his housekeeper, to the Paterson Eye and Ear Infirmary, and to the Memorial Day Nursery.

[Accounts of the wreck of the *Ashuelot* in the *Army and Navy Jour.*, Feb. 28, 1883, and subsequent issues, accounts of the McCalla court martial in the *Journal* of 1890, and obituary, Mar. 26, 1910, in the same publication; *Military Order of the Loyal Legion of the U. S., Commandery of the State of N. Y., Circular No. 27, Series of 1910*; Lewis R. Hamersly, *Records of Living Officers of the U. S. Navy and Marine Corps* (7th ed., 1902), pp. 62–63; *Army and Navy Reg.*, Apr. 2, 1910.] W. B. N.

EPPES, JOHN WAYLES (Apr. 7, 1773–Sept. 15, 1823), congressman and senator from Virginia, was born at "Appomattox Manor," in the present City Point, near Petersburg, Va. His father, Francis Eppes of "Eppington," the son of Richard Eppes of Bermuda Hundred, married Elizabeth Wayles, half-sister of Martha Wayles Jefferson. The early education of "Jack" Eppes was pursued at home under the direction of his father. In 1791 he went to Philadelphia, under the care of his uncle, Thomas Jefferson, to complete his college course, especially in the sciences, and to study law. He was admitted to the bar in 1794 and attained prominence in his profession in Richmond. On Oct. 13, 1797, he married his cousin, Mary or Maria Jefferson. Only one of their three children, Francis, survived infancy. Several years after her untimely death at "Monticello" on Apr. 17, 1804, he married Martha, daughter of Col. Willie Jones, Revolutionary statesman of North Carolina, but maintained friendly personal relations with Jefferson, whom he consistently supported in politics. His second wife, who bore him several children, survived till the second year of the Civil War and was a pronounced opponent of Southern secession.

Elected to the Virginia House of Delegates in 1801, Eppes served in that body until he was elected as a Jeffersonian Republican to the Eighth Congress (1803). He served in four successive congresses to Mar. 3, 1811. The Virginia delegation included Thomas Mann Randolph, Jefferson's other son-in-law, and John Randolph of Roanoke, the only man who ever defeated Eppes for public office. After the opposition to Jefferson's foreign policy became organized around John Randolph and his group of friends, Eppes was one of the stanch defenders of the administration both on this question and on the Yazoo Compromise. He served on the ways and means committee, and in the second session of his first Congress narrowly escaped a duel with Randolph (Bruce, *post,* I, 365). Some time previous to 1811 he left the ancestral home at "Eppington," where he had lived from childhood till the death of his father, and bought an estate at "Saratoga" in Buckingham County. He soon built a home at "Millbrook" a few miles from "Saratoga" and thus domiciled himself in Randolph's district. This was a part of Jefferson's strategy, and, urged by the latter and his friends, Eppes opposed Randolph in 1811, but failed of election to the Twelfth Congress. In 1813 he was elected to the Thirteenth Congress, defeating Randolph on the issue of the war with England, which the latter had violently opposed. In 1815 he was again defeated by Randolph for the House of Representatives but in the next year was elected to the United States Senate. He served in this body from Mar. 4, 1817, till April 1819, when he resigned on account of failing health and was succeeded by James Pleasants. Despite the insistence of his friends and of the *Richmond Enquirer* he refused to return to public life. He spent the remainder of his days in the care of his estate at "Millbrook" in Buckingham County, where he died and was buried in the family cemetery.

Eppes was a man of polished manners, well-read, and pleasing in address, though a scholar rather than an orator. He was a successful farmer on a large scale, an active citizen in his own county, and a man without enemies, except those of the Randolph connection.

[There is a brief sketch in the *Biog. Directory of The American Congress* (1928). Frequent passing references are found in S. N. Randolph, *Domestic Life of Thomas Jefferson* (1871); W. C. Bruce, *John Randolph of Roanoke* (1922), and in the files of the *Richmond Enquirer.* For genealogical details, see *Va. Mag. of Hist. and Biog.,* April 1826, pp. 396–97. The Jefferson Manuscripts in the Lib. of Cong. and other repositories contain many of his letters.]

J. E. W.

ERICSSON, JOHN (July 31, 1803–Mar. 8, 1889), engineer and inventor, was born in the province of Vermland, Sweden, the youngest of the three children of Olof and Brita Sophia (Yngström) Ericsson. His father was a mine-owner and inspector, a graduate of the college in Karlstad, the principal town of the province, and well educated, according to the standards of his times. From his mother, who was of Flemish-Scotch descent, John seems to have derived many of his stronger traits. As a boy he is said to have busied himself day after day with the machinery of the mines, making drawings upon paper with rude instruments or constructing models with bits of cord or wood, and thus endeavoring to work out and understand the principles of their operation. In 1811 war with Russia greatly disturbed business conditions in Sweden, and after various reverses, Olof Ericsson was financially ruined. Soon, however, he secured a position as inspector on the Göta Canal, a project which was then again occupying the serious attention of the government. He was able to obtain for his two sons appointment as cadets in a corps of mechanical engineers to be employed in connection with the plans of the government regarding the canal. During the winter of 1816–17, at the age of thirteen, John received from some of the officers of the corps instruction in algebra, chemistry, field drafting, geometry, and the English language. His previous education seems to have been acquired primarily by means of tutors or home lessons, after the manner of the times, and there is evidence that he had thus received instruction in the usual branches and to some extent in drawing and chemistry. Under the instruction of the officers, his training in drawing seems to have been unusually thorough and this, together with a natural aptitude for such work, laid the foundation for the remarkable skill at the drafting-board which he showed in later years.

He remained in the work of this corps, with duties of a rapidly increasing responsibility and importance, until he was seventeen, when he seems to have become stirred with military ambition. Leaving his engineering appointment with its future prospects, he entered the Swedish army as ensign in a regiment of chasseurs. He was detailed to do topographical surveying on a "piece rate" basis of pay, and so rapid and effective was his work that he was carried on the rolls and paid as two men in order that his remuneration might not seem excessive. Even this activity was not sufficient to exhaust his energy, and he set about the preparation of a book of plates intended to be descriptive of the mining machinery employed in his day. He devised means and engraved a considerable number of large copper plates, but there were various delays, and he abandoned the project when it became apparent that because of the rapid advance in mining methods the work would be out of date before the printing could be completed. About this time he became interested in the "flame engine." He seems to have been strongly attracted by the possibility of developing an engine which would use heat in some more direct form than the steam-engine, and with superior economy. Absorbed in this new idea, which never left him, he ceased to be attracted to military life and in 1826, obtaining leave of absence, he went to London, strong in the belief that his path toward success was straight and sure.

In London his first efforts were directed toward the development and introduction of his new engine, but many unexpected difficulties arose, among others those connected with the use of coal as fuel. Driven to other activities by the need of making a living, he engaged during the twelve years of his life in London in a series of remarkable pieces of engineering work, which covered a wide field of practise, and in which his genius clearly showed itself, either by way of original invention or by timely improvements and adaptations in the practise of the day. Among the more important of these interests were: the transmission of power by compressed air; the use of centrifugal blowers for boiler forced draft; the development of new types of steam boilers and of surface condensers for marine engines; the placing of warship engines below the water line for protection against shell fire; the steam fire-engine; the design and construction of a steam-locomotive, the *Novelty,* entered in the Rainhill contest in 1829 (in which Stephenson's *Rocket* was awarded the prize, though Ericsson, handicapped by lack of time and suitable track on which to adjust and perfect the *Novelty,* seems to have achieved a result in some ways superior to that of the *Rocket*); various designs for rotary engines; an apparatus for making salt from brine; superheated steam, and engines for its use; a deep-sea-sounding apparatus embodying the same principle as that later developed by Lord Kelvin in his well-known type; a machine for cutting files automatically; the "flame" or "caloric" engine; and finally the screw propeller as a means of propulsion for steam vessels. His various undertakings brought Ericsson prominently before the engineering world in England and he became known for his wealth of invention, his versatility, and the daring and originality which characterized all his work. While he was occupied with these many enterprises, his leave from his regiment expired. He seems to have neglected the taking of steps for its renewal and was placed technically in the position of a deserter. Through friendly intervention, however, the matter was adjusted by restoration, followed by a promotion to the grade of captain, after which he resigned, thus leaving his military record clear of reproach.

To an increasing degree, especially during the second half of his stay in London, he became absorbed in his work connected with the screw propeller as a means of marine propulsion. He did not invent the screw propeller. Like most great inventions, it was a matter of slow growth through the years, to which many contributed. As early as the seventeenth century and again during the eighteenth, the possibility of developing a propulsive thrust in a fluid medium from a helicoidal surface suitably mounted on a shaft was more or less clearly realized. During the first third of the nineteenth century, experiments were conducted by Stevens, Ressel, Deslisle, and others, but none of these seems to have had any lasting result. In 1833, the helicoidal screw was certainly known to the engineering profession as a possibility for marine propulsion, but just as certainly the paddle-wheel was the accepted agent for marine propulsion, and a bold vision was needed to bring forward a substitute differing so profoundly in form and character of operation and seeming so inadequate in size. In this later stage of development and application, preëminence must be given to Ericsson. From his studies of the steam-engine, he had come to recognize the fact that the slow revolutions possible with the paddle-wheel did not favor the improvement of the engine along indicated lines of progress. Likewise his interest in the problem of placing the motive machinery of warships below the water line led him to appreciate the difficulty of achieving any such purpose with the paddle-wheel as the means of propulsion. In 1833–34 he was engaged by a company in London to carry on experiments with submerged propellers. This work was followed by further study and trial, and finally, in 1837, the *Francis B. Ogden* was built for the special purpose of putting the screw propeller to the test. About this time or shortly after, Capt. Robert F. Stockton and Francis B. Ogden, American consul at Liverpool, led Ericsson to consider a visit to the United States for the purpose of building, under Stockton's auspices, a vessel for the United States navy. During this period he built and named for Stockton a screw steamer, the trials of which attracted much attention at the time. At the same period, his propeller was also fitted to a canal boat, the *Novelty,* plying between Manchester and London. It is claimed, seemingly with reason, that this was the first application of the screw propeller to a vessel actually employed in commercial service.

At length, on Nov. 1, 1839, in pursuance of his plans with Capt. Stockton, he left England for New York, where he arrived on Nov. 23 after a stormy passage. In this visit to the United States he seems to have had two primary objectives, the introduction of his propeller on the canals and inland waters of the country, and the initiation of work on his "big frigate" for the navy, for which he had prepared extended plans in London. When these ends had been accomplished, he expected to return to England. During the remaining fifty years of his life, however, he lived and wrought in the New World and as a citizen of the United States. In 1840, soon after his arrival, a prize was offered by the Mechanics' Institute of New York for the best design of a steam fire-engine. This competition Ericsson easily won, thanks to his own genius and his previous experience in London. In the introduction of his propellers he made excellent progress, especially for boats on the Great Lakes and inland waters, so that by 1844 there were in use some twenty-five vessels with screw propellers. His plans with Capt. Stockton, after some delay, developed to the point where authority was given to proceed with the construction of a steam frigate of about 1,000 tons. Placed in commission in 1844, the U. S. S. *Princeton,* as the first screw-propelled vessel of war, marked a distinct epoch in marine construction. Her principal armament comprised two twelve-inch wrought-iron guns, one brought by Ericsson from England and one designed and built under the direction of Capt. Stockton. At the trials of the ship in 1844 the latter gun exploded, killing the secretaries of state and the navy and some prominent visitors, and wounding many others. This disaster cast a cloud over the name of the *Princeton* and threw an undeserved stigma on Ericsson and all concerned with the ship. It was not until many years afterward that his name was cleared of any kind of reproach or responsibility for this deplorable accident.

In the meantime he was occupied with many projects, chief among them being his renewed work on some form of "caloric" engine, which in 1851 developed into definite design and plans for the *Ericsson,* a ship to be propelled by hot-air or "caloric" engines, as he chose to call them. The vessel was built, but was not a commercial success. The engines were too large and heavy in proportion to the power developed, and the speed was not up to commercial requirements. He also developed designs for "caloric" engines in small sizes, for ordinary stationary service. During succeeding years several thousand of these were sold for a wide variety of industrial uses.

With the outbreak of the Civil War came the great opportunity of Ericsson's life. In both England and France some beginnings had been made looking toward the development of armored ships. In the South these ideas had perhaps taken stronger hold than in the North. Early in 1861 Stephen R. Mallory, Confederate secretary of the navy, began taking active steps to raise the *Merrimac,* which lay submerged at the Norfolk navy-yard, and convert her into an armorclad. This purpose became known in general terms to Federal authorities and occasioned President Lincoln and his cabinet much anxiety. A board was appointed to examine the situation and to recommend the type of vessel best fitted to meet it. During this period Ericsson had forwarded to the President a memorandum in which he offered to construct for the government a vessel "for the destruction of the Rebel fleet at Norfolk and for scouring the Southern rivers and inlets of all craft protected by Rebel batteries." This communication met with no immediate response, but when the board made its report, Sept. 16, 1861, it recommended the construction of three vessels, among them Ericsson's floating battery. C. S. Bushnell was largely instrumental in bringing Ericsson's plans before the board and later he, with other gentlemen of means, John A. Griswold and John F. Winslow, became associated with Ericsson in this project and supplied the capital needed. The keel was laid on Oct. 25, 1861, and the vessel, named the *Monitor* by Ericsson, was launched on Jan. 30, 1862, and turned over to the government on Feb. 19. The completion of this ship in 100 working days from the date of laying the keel seems now almost an impossible undertaking. It was only by a ceaseless struggle against time and through splendid organization and careful subdivision of the work that any such result was possible. This astonishing speed in design and construction was facilitated, furthermore, by the fact that Ericsson was treading on familiar ground. As early as 1854 he had developed a design for an iron-clad warship which embodied all the essential features of the *Monitor.* This was shown in model to Napoleon III, who was then at war with Russia, the hereditary enemy of the inventor's native Sweden, but it was not adopted. Ericsson therefore needed only to bring to the light again this long-matured plan and to proceed rapidly with the details of its realization.

The battle between the *Monitor* and the *Merrimac,* at Hampton Roads, Va., Mar. 9, 1862, marked a definite epoch not only in the naval operations of the Civil War, but more broadly in the world aspects of warship design and construction. A distinctive feature of the *Monitor* was the circular revolving turret, a heavily armored and protected "gun position." Ericsson made no claim to originality in the concept of an armored revolving turret for his big gun position, but rather claimed, and apparently with justice, that the idea of a revolving armored fort long antedates the nineteenth century. Its possibilities, however, were demonstrated by the victory of the *Monitor,* and the principle of the turret was adopted then by naval designers, and has never been abandoned. In improved form it still appears in the armored and protected big gun position in the battleships and cruisers of modern navies. The *Monitor* was far more than a revolving fort, however. Her guns were few and large instead of numerous and of moderate weight and power; she was built of iron rather than of wood; her freeboard was very low rather than high; she depended solely on steam power for propulsion rather than on sails, or sails with steam auxiliary power; and finally, this power was applied through the screw propeller rather than the paddle-wheel. The break with the past was complete. The warship had been transformed from the traditional ideals as represented by the American frigate *Constitution* or the English *Victory,* into an engineering construction, the forerunner of the great armor-clad battleships of the present day.

The result of the battle brought a significant change in the public standing of Ericsson, whose engineering plans and projects had not always met with a full measure of success, and who was by many considered a dreamer. During the preceding years his relations with the officials of the Navy Department had been often strained, and rarely cordial and satisfactory. The deplorable accident on the *Princeton,* and the commercial failure of the "caloric" engines of the *Ericsson,* had combined with other causes to affect adversely Ericsson's standing before the public and with the government authorities. Now, however, he was hailed on every hand as a public benefactor. He received the thanks of Congress on Mar. 28, 1862, and of the legislature of New York a little later. He was likewise the recipient of numerous testimonials and honors and of such praise as might well have disturbed the equilibrium of a less balanced mind. A considerable fleet of vessels of the *Monitor* type, but larger and with such changes as experience had indicated, was ordered, and during the remainder of the war, Ericsson and his associates were busily engaged in designing and constructing them. Notwithstanding the enormous burden which this work entailed, with one design after another called for in quick succession, Ericsson found time in which to carry on negotiations with other maritime nations regarding the construction for them of war-ships of the *Monitor* type. For some time after the war, these projects occupied much of his attention, but in most cases they did not meet with the degree of success for which he had hoped. The leading maritime nations preferred to apply his ideas in their own way, rather than to order vessels directly from him. In several cases, however, more or less faithful copies of the *Monitor* appeared in foreign navies, particularly in the navy of Sweden. Turning to a somewhat different type, in 1869 Ericsson designed and superintended the construction of a fleet of small gunboats for Spain, to be used in Cuban waters.

He next gave his thought to the development of a system of submarine attack by the use of torpedoes, which had made their appearance in crude form during the Civil War and began in the seventies to command increased attention. This was indeed only a return to an idea which had attracted his notice as early as 1826. In 1878, however, the time seemed ripe for pushing the project, and he applied himself with is accustomed vigor to the development of designs for a torpedo and of a method of discharging it under water from a gun located in the bow and opening so as to permit the discharge of the projectile. This constituted his so-called *Destroyer* system and was embodied in a boat of that name built in company with C. H. Delamater [*q.v.*], with whom he had been associated in many experiments. The idea was in essence that of the modern torpedo boat or "destroyer," though the means employed were different in detail. There was, however, no supreme test of war, to permit of its demonstration under service conditions, and in the end the *Destroyer* was left on her builders' hands.

Ericsson's work as an ordnance engineer was generally in advance of his day. Following his experimentation with the one gun of the *Princeton* which stood all tests, he gave, in connection with all his naval designs, much study to problems relating to heavy guns and their mounting. Thus the friction recoil mechanism of the *Monitor's* guns was daring and original and was a great improvement over other methods then in use. Again in 1863 he designed and built for the acceptance of the government a thirteen-inch wrought-iron gun. The design was a distinct advance on the practise of the day, but it placed demands on the makers of forgings which they were unable successfully to meet, and in test the gun developed some slight cracks. This failure led to a controversy between Ericsson and the naval bureau of ordnance which prevented further consideration of his design.

His interest in an entirely different field of engineering practise, that of the steam-engine and its improvement, was always keen and at times the subject occupied much of his attention and study. He did important and pioneer work in compounding and the use of superheated steam. From the engines of the *Princeton* in 1844, themselves a bold and striking departure from conventional practise, to the *Destroyer* in 1878, there proceeded from his fertile mind a long series of types and forms often widely differing in character, but, in his opinion, each design being that which was best adapted to the requirements of the particular case. This work brought him into competition with other able engineers, especially in the field of naval construction. Perhaps the most notable instance of such competition was that of the design of machinery for the two naval ships *Madawaska* and *Wampanoag*. These were two wooden frigates, the largest of their day, built just at the close of the war. Ericsson was commissioned to design the engines for the former and Benjamin Isherwood [*q.v.*], chief engineer of the navy, for the latter. A battle royal ensued between two engineers, both of remarkable genius and wide experience. The types of engine selected and the modes of application of the power differed widely in the two designs. The result was a definite victory for Isherwood. Though the *Madawaska* with the Ericsson machinery showed, on trial, a speed superior to that of any warship at that time afloat, the *Wampanoag* with Isherwood's engine, tested a little later, gave a result definitely superior in sustained sea speed. Neither design, however, was of an enduring type and neither perceptibly influenced subsequent practise.

Keen as was Ericsson's interest in the steam-engine and its improvement, he never lost his preference for a form of engine using heat in what he regarded as a more direct manner, which he believed should be able to displace the steam-engine by reason of its superior efficiency. During his early professional life in Sweden he began a long series of efforts to develop the "caloric" engine, or some other form of flame, hot-air, or gas engine, and almost to the last days of his life he continued the further improvement of his hot-air engine in small sizes for commercial and industrial uses. In his later years he gave much thought and study to the development of an engine which would utilize directly the heat of the sun instead of that derived from the combustion of coal or other hydro-carbon compounds.

Ericsson

In addition, during these later years, he investigated a number of widely diversified scientific problems, more especially those connected with solar energy, the nature of heat, gravitation, and tides and tidal energy as possible sources of power. With the advent of electricity, he also gave some attention to improvements in high-speed engines for electric-lighting purposes. In marine practise he did important pioneer work in the development of the surface condenser, the distiller or evaporator for fresh water, the use of fans for forced draft and for ventilation, together with a vast number of elements and details worked out in connection with his designs for the *Princeton*, the *Monitor*, and other vessels of war. Although the design of the *Monitor* as a type of warship and the introduction of the screw propeller were the outstanding achievements of his career, he made many other contributions to the art and practise of the engineering of his day. In all, they make up a most impressive total, and from them has come, in more or less direct degree, a large and significant content of present approved practise.

Vigorous in body and mind, Ericsson was capable of prodigious industry and endowed with persistence, courage, capacity for the deepest concentration, and unlimited confidence in himself. He was little disposed to care for the help or to heed the criticism of others, was at no pains to keep himself informed of the work of other engineers, and not infrequently would reject a device or idea which had been in previous use in favor of something different and original, even though it might involve only some trivial detail of his work. He was distinctly a light shining alone. He could not and would not work with others. He must lead, he could not follow. His general strategy of approach to his problems was to disregard the past and all precedent and then, having in view only the laws of mechanics, the materials of construction, and the special conditions to be met, to proceed to evolve, by mental process, a fundamental solution for his problem. With passing years the art and practise of engineering made many advances of which he took little or no heed and of which he might often with advantage have availed himself. He was a designing rather than a construction engineer, and his special genius lay in new combinations of the elements of engineering practise in such manner as to further the ends in view. His work was all done in his office at his house, and his natural mode of expression was by way of the drawing-board. Those who have been associated with him have borne witness to the astonishing speed and skill which he exhibited in work of this character. Furthermore, these drawings, when they left his office, were so minute in detail and so carefully checked and verified in dimension and arrangement that as a rule they needed no further attention or correction. A curious and interesting feature of his character was his lack of interest in the work after the design had once left his hands. It is said that he even declined an invitation of the secretary of the navy to inspect the *Monitor* immediately after her fight in Hampton Roads. With this general make-up of character went naturally a quick, imperious temper and a keen sensitiveness to opposition or criticism. In consequence his relations with government officials, with his business associates, and with his friends were not infrequently strained almost to the point of rupture. He had, however, a deep, innate sense of justice and a kindness of heart which led him to forget a cause of offense as quickly as he showed displeasure on what he deemed just occasion. Notwithstanding these asperities of character, he was the recipient of medals, decorations, and honors, and of recognition by learned and technical societies, by governments and organizations of the most varied character, to a degree perhaps which has fallen to the lot of no other who has wrought in the same field of effort. Toward intimate friends and relatives he was kind and generous. For his means, his private gifts were numerous and large and they were made with a whole-hearted generosity. During his later years, his public benefactions were also notable and amounted to no inconsiderable part of his income. Though prudent and careful in many matters, he had little interest in business as such and no capacity for merely "making money." Once he had acquired, through his inventions and business interests, a modest competence, he devoted himself largely to projects remote from the prospect of immediate financial return and lived comfortably on the savings which his work had provided.

On Oct. 15, 1836, in England, he married Amelia Byam, a young woman of fine blood and breeding, the half-sister of the wife of one of his earliest acquaintances in that country. She did not accompany him to the United States but joined him there soon afterward. She was a woman of grace and beauty and Ericsson was proud of her, as she was of his talents. He was too much absorbed in his work, however, to admit the claims of domestic life, and since his wife disliked New York and tired of the isolation in which she was left, it was agreed that it was best for her to return to her family in England until Ericsson should be able to rejoin her there. In the final event, this opportunity never came and they did not meet again, though he made allowance for her support and continued to correspond with her until her death some years later. Ericsson was active to the last. He died one day before the twenty-seventh anniversary of the naval battle at Hampton Roads, the one event with which in the public mind his name will always be associated. His remains were first interred in New York and then in 1890, following a request of the Swedish government, they were returned with impressive ceremonies to his native land, being conveyed by the U. S. S. *Baltimore,* one of the ships of the new steel navy. Both in the United States and in Sweden the event was marked with every honor and dignity which might serve to indicate the significance and value of his life and services to his adopted land and to the world at large.

[John Ericsson, *Contributions to the Centennial Exhibition* (1876); W. C. Church, *The Life of John Ericsson* (2 vols., 1890); Chas. B. Stuart, *The Naval and Mail Steamers of the U. S.* (1853); John Bourne, *A Treatise on the Screw Propeller, Screw Vessels, and Screw Engines as adapted for purposes of Peace and War* (1867); Geo. H. Preble, *A Chronological Hist. of the Origin and Development of Steam Navigation* (1883); R. H. Thurston, *A Hist. of the Growth of the Steam-Engine* (1896); Frank M. Bennett, *The Steam Navy of the U. S.* (1896); Jas. Nicol, *Who Invented the Screw Propeller?* (1858); *N. Y. Times,* Mar. 9, 1889.]

W. F. D.

ERLANGER, ABRAHAM LINCOLN (May 4, 1860–Mar. 7, 1930), theatrical booking agent, manager, and producer, was born in Buffalo of Jewish parents, Leopold and Regina Erlanger, but most of his early life was spent in Cleveland. With practically no education he began his theatrical apprenticeship as cloak-room attendant and call boy at the Academy of Music, and subsequently rose to a position of some influence in the financial management of the Euclid Opera House. For a number of years after leaving Cleveland he traveled as advance agent, and later as manager, for theatrical companies sent out from New York, and came to realize the inefficiency of the existing system of "booking." In theory, operating managers of local theatres were anxious to keep their "time" filled throughout a season; while producing managers in New York were anxious to "book time" so as to provide an uninterrupted succession of performances for their road companies and reduce to the minimum haulage and traveling expenses. In practise, the machinery required to preserve such a delicate balance was lacking; individual agreements between local theatre owners and New

York managers were arrived at haphazardly, and often broken without compunction. The development of a modern booking system with centralized administration was the work in large part of Erlanger and of his partner, Marc Klaw. These two men, who had been thrown together while serving as advance agents on the road, purchased in 1886 one of the small booking agencies in New York and two years later drew up formal articles of partnership. Although during the next few years they made a number of independent theatrical productions and were busy extending their control over a chain of theatres in the South, they owed their increasingly assured position primarily to their activities as booking agents. In August 1896, in association with four other leading managers, Charles Frohman, A. I. Hayman, S. F. Nixon, and J. F. Zimmerman, they organized the Theatrical Syndicate, professedly to bring about certain sorely needed reforms in the booking of shows. The execution of these reforms was entrusted to the firm of Klaw & Erlanger, which was made the booking agency for all attractions presented in theatres controlled by the syndicate. Erlanger, as the more active executive in the firm, came more and more to exercise almost autocratic prerogatives. His office became the clearinghouse for actor, producer and manager. Relishing the endless details of problems involved in the routing of shows over an entire continent, he worked incessantly. Backed by a monopolistic organization, he brooked no opposition from actors or producers. Moreover it has been stated that he was able to give preferential booking to his own productions even over those of Charles Frohman, who was the syndicate member commonly credited with having final jurisdiction over the mass production of shows for syndicate consumption. Erlanger's power rested on the solid economic basis of mounting financial returns to the syndicate and increased financial security to the various elements in the theatrical profession. The scattered idealists who had denounced the syndicate as a commercial monopoly destructive of the art of the theatre, and its members as "adventurers of inferior origin," tried on various occasions to rally, but with little success. The breakdown of the monopoly, when it finally came, was partly the result of a weakening inside the syndicate caused by its inability to furnish satisfactory attractions in sufficient numbers to meet the demands of such a vast chain of theatres, and more particularly the result of the inroads of the Shuberts, a group of rival theatrical managers formerly associated with the syndicate and operating along somewhat similar lines. In spite of the return to a competitive basis, the firm of Klaw & Erlanger continued for many years to hold a dominating position among New York booking agencies. In addition they made a number of productions of their own, and were for several years successfully engaged in the vaudeville business. After the dissolution of partnership with Klaw in 1920, Erlanger continued, as producer and manager, to be one of the outstanding financial powers in the American theatre. Extensive plans for expanding his activities to keep pace with the new era of the talking pictures were interrupted by his death.

[For biographical details see: *N. Y. Times,* Mar. 8, 1930, and Mar. 16, 1930, sec. IX; *Who's Who in the Theatre* (London, 1930), ed. by John Parker; Wm. Danforth, "Abraham Lincoln Erlanger" in *The Green Book Album,* Mar. 1909, p. 541. For the activities of Erlanger and his associates in connection with the Theatrical Syndicate, see: Wm. Winter, *The Life of David Belasco* (2 vols., 1918), vol. II; "The Great Theatrical Syndicate," in *Leslie's Monthly Mag.,* Oct., Nov., Dec., 1904, Jan. 1905; W. P. Eaton, "The Rise and Fall of the Theatrical Syndicate," in *American Mag.,* Oct. 1910; *N. Y. Dramatic Mirror,* supplements to issues of Dec. 18 and Dec. 25, 1897, and Mar. 26 and Apr. 2, 1898; *Washington Post,* Mar. 4, 1906; and scattered material in the volumes of clippings on Charles Frohman, David Belasco, and Minnie Maddern Fiske, in "The Robinson Locke Collection of Dramatic Scrapbooks" in the New York Pub. Lib.] E. M., Jr.

ERNST, HAROLD CLARENCE (July 31, 1856–Sept. 7, 1922), bacteriologist, was born in Cincinnati, Ohio, the son of Andrew Henry Ernst, a successful business man and one of the founders of the Horticultural Society of Ohio, and Sarah H. Otis, an Abolitionist and a pioneer advocate of woman suffrage. One of his brothers was Maj.-Gen. Oswald H. Ernst [*q.v.*]. The family had originally come from Germany during the Napoleonic wars, Ernst's grandfather having left his home on account of his strong opinions on what he regarded as unjust taxation.

After preliminary education in Boston schools, Harold C. Ernst went to Harvard College, where he was graduated in 1876. While in college he became a noted baseball pitcher, one of the first to use a curve ball. He subsequently went to the Harvard Medical School, graduated in 1880, and began the practise of medicine in Jamaica Plain, Mass. When Koch's discovery of the tubercle bacillus was announced in 1882, Ernst went to study in his laboratory, where he learned the rudiments of bacteriology. When he returned to America, he associated himself with the Boston City Hospital and the Massachusetts General Hospital. As early as 1885 he began to lecture on bacteriology in the Harvard Medical School, giving six talks and demonstrations to fourth-year students as a voluntary course. This was probably the first course of lectures in bacteriology given in a medical school in the United States; his laboratory, at first, consisted of a sort of closet in the medical museum. He met with considerable opposition, but by hard work he convinced his opponents of the value of bacteriology to medicine, surgery, and hygiene. He developed the early sterilizing apparatus at the Massachusetts General Hospital, established an antitoxin laboratory for diphtheria in connection with the city of Boston, and for many years supplied from his own laboratory all the vaccine and antitoxin used by the city, as well as tuberculin for testing cattle.

He took an active part in public affairs, appearing frequently before various committees at the Massachusetts State House in regard to better registration laws for physicians, improved vaccination laws, regulations for the testing of cows and the protection of milk, animal experimentation, and similar public health measures. His commanding presence and obvious knowledge made him an ideal spokesman for the medical profession before the legislators. He served successively as instructor, assistant professor, and professor of bacteriology at the Harvard Medical School, holding the latter appointment from 1895 until his death. He assisted in the planning of the new buildings for the Harvard Medical School, opened in 1900, and wrote a brief history of the School for the dedication exercises. He was one of the founders of the American Association of Pathologists and Bacteriologists, and served it for fifteen years as secretary. He was also a member of the American Academy of Arts and Sciences, the Society of American Naturalists, and many medical associations. He wrote numerous papers and books, especially in relation to his specialty. From its foundation in 1896 he edited the *Journal of the Boston Society of Medical Sciences,* which in 1901 became the *Journal of Medical Research,* Ernst continuing as editor until his death. During the World War he served as head of the Northeastern Division Laboratory, with the rank of major.

Ernst was a tall, large man, with powerful shoulders, of rather stern military appearance and at times distinctly austere. His knowledge, especially of details, made him often impatient, but with it all there was a kindly attitude toward people and life. On Sept. 20, 1883, he married Ellen Lunt Frothingham, a member of a distinguished Boston family. They had no children.

[The best account of Ernst is by Dr. John W. Farlow, in *Proc. Mass. Hist. Soc.,* vol. LVI (1923). See also S. B. Wolbach, in *Proc. Am. Acad. Arts and Sci.,* LX, 1924–25; *Boston Medic. & Surgic. Jour.,* Sept. 14, 1922; T. F. Harrington, *The Harvard Medical School* (1905); *Jour. of Medic. Research,* Sept. 1923; *Harvard College, Class of 1876, Tenth Report* (1926). For the beginnings of the Harvard bacteriological laboratory, see the article by Ernst in *Harvard Grads. Mag.,* Mar. 1895; also J. C. Warren, in *Boston Transcript,* Mar. 13, 1912. A note in regard to his career in baseball will be found in the *Boston Sunday Post,* Sept. 10, 1922.]

H. R. V.

ERNST, OSWALD HERBERT (June 27, 1842–Mar. 21, 1926), soldier, engineer, was the son of Andrew Henry Ernst, who, with his father, John C. Ernst, a government official, emigrated from Hanover, Germany, after the Napoleonic occupation, and settled in Ohio. On a country place near Cincinnati, where his well-to-do father indulged in horticulture, Oswald Herbert was born, his mother being Sarah H. Otis of Boston, whom Andrew Henry married there in 1841. After attending private schools, young Ernst entered Harvard in 1858, and two years later, the United States Military Academy, from which he graduated in 1864 near the head of his class. Commissioned first lieutenant of engineers, he saw immediate service as assistant engineer, Army of the Tennessee, and took part in the battle and siege of Atlanta (July 22), and the battle of Ezra Church (July 28, 1864), receiving the brevet of captain for faithful and meritorious services. He was on fortification duty at San Francisco until 1868, and commanded a company at Willet's Point, N. Y., until 1871. Meanwhile, as an astronomer, he accompanied the scientific expedition of 1870 to Spain, to observe the solar eclipse. From 1871 to 1878 he was an instructor at the Military Academy; from 1878 to 1886 he was in charge of river and harbor improvements in the West; and from 1886 to 1889, he was on similar duty in Texas, where he supervised the important work of digging a deep-sea channel to the harbor of Galveston. He was superintendent of public buildings and grounds at Washington, 1889–93, and superintendent of the Military Academy, 1893–98, having meanwhile reached the grade of lieutenant-colonel of engineers.

In the war with Spain which followed, he was commissioned a brigadier-general of volunteers, commanded a brigade in the Porto Rican campaign, and participated in the engagements at Coamo and Asamante, receiving commendation from his superiors (J. H. Wilson, *Under the Old Flag,* II, 1912, pp. 427–48). Following the cessation of hostilities, he served, 1898–99, as inspector-general in Cuba. He then became a member of the original Isthmian Canal Commission, visiting Europe and Central America in connection with the study of a proposed route; and in 1905–06 was a member of the commission which determined that the Panama Canal should have locks. He was in charge of river and harbor improvements at Baltimore, 1900–01, and on similar duty at Chicago, 1901–05, submitting an important report on a project to connect Lake Michigan with the Mississippi River. He was promoted colonel in 1903 and was retired from active service by operation of law, June 27, 1906, with the rank of brigadier-general. He was subsequently given the rank of major-general, Nov. 2, 1916. Ernst served as president of the Mississippi River Commission, and continued as such after retirement. He also served as a member of the International Waterways Commission, and as a director of the Panama Railroad. He published a *Manual of Practical Military Engineering* (1873), as well as numerous professional reports, among which were: *Report Respecting Tunnels under the Chicago River* (1904), *Report Upon Survey with Plans and Estimates of Cost, for a Navigable Waterway . . . from Lockport, Ill., to St. Louis* (1905), and *The Preservation of Niagara Falls* (1906). His death from a heart-attack took place in Washington, as he was nearing his eighty-fourth birthday. Interment with military honors was at Arlington (*Army & Navy Journal,* Mar. 27, 1926). He was survived by his widow, Mrs. Elizabeth Amory (Lee) Ernst, whom he had married in Boston in 1866, by two daughters, and two grandchildren.

[An excellent biographical sketch will be found in the *Ann. Report, Asso. of Grads., U. S. Mil. Acad.,* 1926. See also G. W. Cullum, *Biog. Reg.,* vol. III (1891), supp. vols. IV (1901), V (1910); *Who's Who in America,* 1928–29.]

C. D. R.

ERRETT, ISAAC (Jan. 2, 1820–Dec. 19, 1888), minister of the Disciples of Christ and for many years editor of one of their leading periodicals, was the son of Henry Errett, a native of Arklow, County Wicklow, Ireland. The latter was a student in the University of Dublin when the assassination of his father, William, a stanch Orangeman in a Roman Catholic stronghold, put an end to his schooling. A few years later he emigrated to New York City where he engaged in business and married Sophia Kemmish. Isaac was the fifth of their seven children. When he was about five years old his father died, and his mother soon married Robert Souter, a parsimonious Scotchman, not inclined to do much for his step-children. In 1832 the family moved westward and settled near Pittsburgh. Isaac's early education was obtained chiefly in a bookstore where he was employed, and in the printing office of A. A. Anderson, Pittsburgh, where he worked as apprentice and journeyman. Here for a time he edited a weekly paper, *The Intelligencer.* His father had been active in the Disciples' movement, and Isaac, having been converted and displaying an aptitude for public speaking, was more and more drawn into preaching. On June 18, 1840, he was formally set apart as an evangelist, and in October took charge of a newly formed church in Pittsburgh. The following year, Oct. 18, he married Harriet, daughter of James and Hannah Reeder. Leaving Pittsburgh in 1844, he was subsequently pastor in three Ohio towns, New Lisbon (1844–49), North Bloomfield (1849–51), and Warren (1851–56). In the latter year he joined a company formed to establish a colony in Michigan, engage in the lumber business, and promote religion in that portion of the frontier. The company founded the town of Muir. Errett ministered here and carried on evangelistic work in the country round about. In 1862 he took charge of a new church enterprise on Jefferson Avenue, Detroit, but after two years returned to Muir. From 1857 to 1860 he was corresponding secretary of the American Christian Missionary Society, his duties necessitating numerous trips through the West and South. In December 1860, as agent for Bethany College, he made a tour with Alexander Campbell [*q.v.*], and in 1861 he became co-editor of the *Millennial Harbinger.* He was an active supporter of the Union during the Civil War, visiting camps, making speeches, and even applying for a colonel's commission that he might raise a regiment. From 1866 to 1867 he served as principal of the department of Biblical literature in the Western Reserve Eclectic Institute (Hiram College) and professor of evangelical and pastoral training.

By this time the qualities he had displayed as preacher, organizer, and writer had given him a position of leadership among the Disciples. Accordingly, when early in 1866 the Christian Publishing Association was formed to issue a weekly paper which should honestly and kindly set forth the views of the Disciples, with James A. Garfield [*q.v.*] heading the Board of Directors, Errett was chosen to be its editor. This paper, *The Christian Standard,* was first published in Cleveland; for a short time in Alliance, Ohio, where Errett was president of Alliance College (1868–69); and thereafter in Cincinnati. Editing it with great ability and wisdom until his death, he did much to give direction to the progressive movement in his Church. In 1874 he aided in the organization of the Christian Woman's Board of Missions; in the following year he was one of the founders of the Foreign Christian Missionary Society, and was its president as long as he lived. He delivered the principal address at the funeral service for President Garfield at Cleveland in September 1881. During 1884–85 he was one of the editors of *The Disciple of Christ,* a monthly "devoted to Christian living, learning and literature." His publications were numerous. Among them are: *A Brief View of Missions: Ancient and Modern* (1857); a sermon, *The Claims of Civil Government* (1863); *Walks About Jerusalem: a Search After the Landmarks of Primitive Christianity* (1871); *Talks to Bereans* (1872); *Letters to a Young Christian* (1877); *Our Position: A Brief Statement of the Distinctive Features of the Plea for Reformation Urged by the People Known as Disciples of Christ* (1872?); *Evenings with the Bible, Old Testament Studies* (3 vols., 1884–89); *Why Am I a Christian?* (1889); *Life and Writings of George Edward Flower* (1885). After his death, *Linsey-Woolsey and Other Addresses* (1893) was issued.

[J. S. Lamar, *Memoirs of Isaac Errett* (2 vols., 1893); John T. Brown, *Churches of Christ* (1904); Wm. T. Moore, *A Comprehensive Hist. of the Disciples of Christ* (1909); Alanson Wilcox, *A Hist. of the Disciples of Christ in Ohio* (1918); obituary notice in the *Cincinnati Enquirer,* Dec. 20, 1888.] H. E. S.

ERSKINE, JOHN (Sept. 13, 1813–Jan. 27, 1895), jurist, was born at Strabane, County Tyrone, Ireland. At an early age he was taken by his parents to St. John, New Brunswick, where his father soon died. The family then moved to New York City and John lived there until he was about fourteen years old, when he returned to Ireland to be educated by relatives. In his eighteenth or nineteenth year he went to sea. He had an inquiring mind and a retentive memory, and from his many voyages he acquired an unusual amount of information concerning the various countries and peoples of the world. This, coupled with extensive reading throughout his life, contributed no doubt to the breadth and tolerance of his character. He loved the sea, but when he was twenty-five lung trouble forced him to abandon so rigorous a life, and, seeking a mild climate, he went to Florida. There he taught school for a number of years and later studied law. He was admitted to the bar at the age of thirty-three, and his success as a lawyer was almost immediate. In 1851 he married Rebecca Smith, a daughter of Gen. Gabriel Smith of Alabama. In 1855 he moved to Georgia where he lived, first in Newnan, then in Atlanta, for the rest of his life.

He strongly opposed secession, but because of his tact and moderation he did not lose the friendship of those about him. To free him of the necessity of engaging in the conflict, Gov. Brown of Georgia gave him a civil appointment under the state government. Immediately after the war President Johnson named him federal judge for the district of Georgia and his appointment was confirmed by the Senate in January 1866. He held this position until 1882 when the state was divided into two federal judicial districts and Erskine was assigned to the southern district. He served there a year when, having reached the age of seventy, he retired.

Erskine served through the Reconstruction period, and in the discharge of his judicial functions he had to declare void the Confederate statutes under which debts due Northern citizens had been confiscated, and to make other unpopular rulings, yet so great was public confidence in his integrity and fairness that he entirely escaped the obloquy then attached to federal office-holding in the South. Moreover, many of his decisions were of practical helpfulness, as, for example, his ruling that the act of Congress forbidding ex-Confederate soldiers to practise law was unconstitutional (*ex parte William Law,* 35 *Ga.,* 286); and he aided in preserving racial purity in the South by upholding the right of the state to forbid miscegenation (Hobbs alias Johnson). None of these decisions of his was reversed. In a case of first impression he decided that the federal legal tender acts were constitutional. The Supreme Court of the United States in another case later held to the contrary (*Hepburn* vs. *Griswold,* 8 *Wallace,* 603), but they finally reached Erskine's conclusion, and reversed themselves (see Legal Tender Cases, *Knox* vs. *Lee* and *Parker* vs. *Davis,* 12 *Wallace,* 457). In 1869 Erskine was urged by the leading members of the bar of Georgia, Alabama, and Florida for appointment to the Supreme Court of the United States to fill the vacancy caused by the death of Justice Wayne. He was a kindly man, with a keen sense of humor, and was widely beloved. There can be little question that because of his fair and sympathetic attitude toward a conquered people he aided in making Reconstruction less irksome in Georgia than it was in some of the other Southern states.

[W. J. Northen, *Men of Mark in Ga.* (1911), III, 169; L. L. Knight, *A Standard Hist. of Ga. and Georgians* (1917), V, 2305; *Memoirs of Ga., Hist. and Biog.* (Southern Hist. Asso., 1895), I, 769 ff.; *Testimonials to the Hon. John Erskine, U. S. Judge for Ga., on his Retirement from the Bench* (1885); "A Beautiful Life," in the *Green Bag,* Apr. 1895, vol. VII. Most of Erskine's decisions were delivered prior to the publication of the *Federal Reporter,* and only four of them are to be found there, IX, 753, 920; X, 451; XII, 207. A number of his opinions are printed as an appendix to vol. XXXV, *Ga. Reports,* pp. 286–365. For obituary, see *Atlanta Constitution,* Jan. 28, 1895.] B. F.

ERSKINE, ROBERT (Sept. 7, 1735–Oct. 2, 1780), geographer, was born in Dunfermline, Scotland, the son of Rev. Ralph and Margaret (Simson) Erskine. He received his elementary education at the Dunfermline Grammar School and was a student at the University of Edinburgh in 1748. Because of the necessity of earning his own living, however, he was soon obliged to interrupt his college course, and it was not until 1752 that his name reappeared on the university rolls. Shortly afterward he left college again and went to London where he engaged in business. Through the treachery of his partner, Erskine became heavily involved financially and was declared insolvent, but because of his excellent character and sincerity of purpose he escaped a jail sentence. Supplementing his meager education by further study, he entered the hydraulic engineering field, invented a centrifugal hydraulic engine and other appliances, and as a result of his success was elected a fellow of the Royal Society on Jan. 31, 1771. Gradually he payed off his indebtedness. In 1770, he was asked to go to America as the representative of a group of British capitalists who had invested money in the American Iron Company, whose extensive mines were located in the region which is now the upper part of Passaic County, N. J. To prepare himself for this mission, he spent several months in making a survey of iron mining and manufacturing operations in Great Britain.

Erskine and his wife Elizabeth, whom he had married during the years of his struggle for success, arrived in New York June 5, 1771. He at once entered upon his duties and proved himself to be a man of excellent capacity and thoroughly devoted to the interests of his employers. As early as 1774, however, he was in active sympathy with the colonists, and in the summer of 1775 organized the men in his employ into a military company. Their services were offered to the Provincial Congress, which commissioned Erskine a captain in the Bergen County militia and exempted his men from compulsory military service in any other company. A little later, when Washington passed through northern New Jersey on his way from the Hudson River, he made the acquaintance of Erskine, and upon learning that the latter was an able civil engineer, well acquainted with the region west of the Hudson, offered him the position of geographer and surveyor-general to the Continental Army. Duly commissioned on July 27, 1777, Erskine began work at once upon a series of maps, depicting the physical features of the country from the Hudson River westerly to Ringwood and from Jersey City to Cornwall. For over three years, Erskine worked zealously for the colonial cause, and his maps, which are still preserved, were important factors in the ultimate victory. His death, which occurred on Oct. 2, 1780, was the result of an illness contracted while in the field.

[Albert H. Heusser, *The Forgotten General* (1928); *Proc. N. J. Hist. Soc.*, 2 ser., vol. I (1869); *N. J. Archives*, 2 ser., vol. I (1901); F. B. Heitman, *Hist. Reg. of the Officers of the Continental Army* (ed., 1914); W. S. Stryker, *Official Reg. of the Officers and Men of N. J. in the Revolutionary War* (1872); Erskine Papers, N. J. Hist. Soc. Numerous references to Erskine and his work are found in the Quartermaster-General's records and also in the pension records on file in the office of the Adjutant-General of N. J.] G. H. B.

ERVING, GEORGE WILLIAM (July 15, 1769–July 22, 1850), diplomat, was born in Boston, Mass., the only child of George and Lucy (Winslow) Erving. When Washington captured Boston, the father, a moderate Loyalist, left with his family for Halifax and later for England. The son was educated at Oriel College, Oxford. At twenty-one he followed his father's injunction and returned to the United States.

Samuel Adams furnished him with a letter of introduction to Thomas Jefferson, whose ardent supporter Erving became. On becoming President, Jefferson offered him the post of chargé d'affaires to Portugal, which Erving declined. Jefferson urged upon him the then rather delicate position of consul at Tunis. Instead, Erving accepted the position of agent in London to look after the claims and appeals of American seamen. In 1804, Jefferson transferred him to the legation at Madrid. In the absence of his cousin, James Bowdoin, the minister, Erving became chargé d'affaires. He learned Spanish. He observed and reported in his dispatches the discord in the royal family, the disgrace of Godoy, the arrival of Murat, the crowning of Joseph Bonaparte and the work of the migratory junta. Under the circumstances he could do little to promote American interests. He left Spain for home on Nov. 1, 1809. He reported to Jefferson at Monticello and brought him samples of merino wool.

Madison appointed Erving a special minister to Copenhagen to adjust claims for spoliations. He succeeded beyond expectations. Madison stated that he had never had a more capable and faithful minister. The critical relations with Spain in regard to Florida, the western boundary of Louisiana, and the claims caused Madison to designate Erving as minister to Madrid in 1814. Nearly two years passed before he was received. He then initiated the negotiations which after various shifts between Madrid and Washington culminated in the Treaty of 1819. Erving did not enjoy fully the confidence of John Quincy Adams as secretary of state, yet Adams might have profited by a closer examination of the vigilant and careful dispatches from Madrid, notably that of Feb. 10, 1818, warning Adams of the Royal grants of land in Florida to the King's favorites. For reasons of health and business Erving resigned from the diplomatic service in 1819.

He became a member of the Massachusetts Historical Society in 1822 and presented to it a cabinet of medals struck in Europe in commemoration of leading men and events in America. He translated from the Spanish a part of a treatise by Juan Bautista de Erro, which, with the title, *The Alphabet of the Primitive Language of Spain and a Philosophical Investigation of the Antiquity and Civilization of the Basque People,* was published in 1829. Erving traveled extensively in Europe. He never married. Under the belief that a holograph, a will written in the testator's own hand and without witnesses, was everywhere valid, he left copies of such a will in various places. He died in New York and his considerable wealth was distributed according to the laws of that state governing the property of those who die intestate.

[J. L. M. Curry, *Diplomatic Services of George William Erving* (1890), with an introduction by Robert C. Winthrop, contains a sketch of his official career and also a letter from Erving telling about his ancestry and boyhood. Walter Lowrie and W. S. Franklin, *American State Papers, Foreign Relations,* especially vol. IV (1834), contains many of his dispatches. Several of his letters are found in the MSS. Division of the Lib. of Cong.] C. E. H.

ESBJÖRN, LARS PAUL (Oct. 16, 1808–July 2, 1870), Swedish Lutheran clergyman and educator, was born in Delsbo, Hälsingland, Sweden, the son of Esbjörn and Karin (Lindström) Paulson. Orphaned at the age of seven, he was taught to read by his foster-mother, who encouraged him to enter a school at Hudiksvall. Here and in the gymnasium at Gävle he eked out a meager living by singing in the homes of farmers, who rewarded him with gifts of money, candles, grain, food, and clothing. On June 11, 1832, he was ordained to the ministry of the Church of Sweden. His work as curate at Östervåla and chaplain on an estate at Oslättfors was marked by a strong strain of pietism and interest in the cause of temperance, which brought him into intimate relations with Sweden's great apostles of temperance and pietism—George Scott, an English Wesleyan missionary stationed at Stockholm, and Peter Wieselgren, a pastor in the State Church—a circumstance that blocked his promotion and gained him enemies who even threatened his life. The spontaneity of Scott's "free church" activity magnified by contrast the formalism and spiritual deadness of the Established Church and caused Esbjörn to long for a field of labor among his countrymen in a land where all creeds had equal opportunity. This longing was finally realized on June 29, 1849, when the *Cobden* put out to sea from Gävle with a party of emigrants, of which Esbjörn was the leader.

Although he left Sweden "on leave" from the Established Church in order to minister to its sons and daughters in the Western Republic, he became the founder of an ecclesiastical organization that bore little resemblance to it except in doctrine. At New York he met Olof Gustaf Hedström, a Swedish Methodist pastor, who urged him to affiliate with his denomination. Esbjörn might have accepted this invitation but for his wife's loyalty to Lutheranism and his own aversion to a church that admitted slaveholders to membership. It was not long after the inception of his work as pastor at Andover, Ill., however, that his experience with Eric-Jansonist, Methodist, Baptist, and Episcopal proselyters hardened him into an uncompromising adherent to the symbolical books of the Lutheran Church.

The Swedish pastor's application for financial assistance from the American Home Missionary Society was granted on condition that the congregations he might organize should affiliate with some American church body. This condition was satisfied when he applied for membership in the Lutheran Synod of Northern Illinois at its first meeting in September 1851, notwithstanding the doctrinal laxity of this organization, which caused him to safeguard his own doctrinal position by a reservation. His untiring missionary zeal, efforts to solicit money, and interest in educating pastors caused his election to the Scandinavian professorship at Illinois State University at Springfield, an institution supported by his synod, in September 1858. Dissatisfaction with the administration of the institution and the doctrinal laxity of the "American" element in the synod led to his "sudden and utterly unlooked for resignation" on Mar. 31, 1860, an act that occasioned the secession of the Scandinavians from the synod and the organization of the independent Augustana Synod at Jefferson Prairie, Wis., on June 5, 1860. Upon the opening of Augustana Seminary at Chicago in the fall, Esbjörn became its first president, a position he held until 1863, when he returned to assume the rectorship of Östervåla parish.

He was thrice married: to Amalia Maria Lovisa Planting-Gyllenbåga, who died in 1852; to Helena Magnusson, who died in 1853; and to Gustafva Magnusson, who survived him. Of a kindly disposition, warm-hearted, generous to a fault, and without ostentation and conceit, Esbjörn was impulsive, given to rash statements, and lacking in sagacity and diplomacy. His pioneer labor, personal influence, and important positions won for him the distinction of being the founder of the Swedish Lutheran Church in the United States.

[Printed and manuscript material in the Augustana College library and in the archives of the Augustana Book Concern at Rock Island, Ill.; Erik Norelius, *De svenska luterska församlingarnas och svenskarnes historia i Amerika* (2 vols., 1890–1916), is a comprehensive history of the Swedish Lutheran Church in America and contains a biographical sketch of the founder. The author was a close friend and admirer of Esbjörn. Both sides of this controversial subject are presented by G. M. Stephenson in *The Founding of the Augustana Synod, 1850–1860* (1927), which cites principal sources, and in "The Founding of the Augustana Synod: Illustrative Documents," *Swedish-Am. Hist. Bull.*, Mar. 1928, pp. 1–52. Important letters from Esbjörn are found in the Wieselgren MSS. in the Gothenburg City Library and in the following periodicals and newspapers: *Helsi* (Söderhamn), Jan. 18, 1850, Oct. 8, 1852; *Missions-tidning* (Stockholm), June 1850; *Lunds Missions-tidning* (Lund), Feb. 1852; and *Bibelwännen* (Lund), Sept. 1852. See also, for a brief sketch, J. L. Jensson, *Am. Lutheran Biogs.* (1890).]

G. M. S.

ESCALANTE, SILVESTRE VELEZ DE (fl. 1768–1779), Spanish Franciscan, is known chiefly as a missionary-explorer in New Mexico and adjoining regions about the beginning of the last quarter of the eighteenth century. Concerning his early life, little information is available. It appears that he was born in Spain and that he left there for New Spain in 1768. In the convent of San Francisco in Mexico City, on Feb. 5, 1769, he professed as a Franciscan. For brief periods he served as a missionary in the province of Sonora and at the pueblo of Laguna, in New Mexico. Later he was in charge of the Mission of Our Lady of Guadalupe at the pueblo of Zuñi, where he came to be greatly respected and venerated by the natives. In 1775 he was requested by the governor of New Mexico to make a report concerning the establishment of communication between New Mexico and the provinces of Sonora and California, a land route to Monterey, and the reduction of the Moqui Indians. Accordingly, in company with Alcalde Mayor Cisneros and seventeen mission Indians, Escalante left Zuñi on June 22, 1775, and was gone thirteen days, eight of which were spent among the seven Moqui pueblos and in trying, vainly, to go beyond to the Grand Canyon of the Colorado. A preliminary report of the expedition was sent by Escalante to the Franciscan Provincial, Fray Ysidro Murillo, on Aug. 18, 1775, and a clearer and more extended one on Apr. 30, 1776. In his reports Escalante gave interesting and valuable data concerning the seven Moqui pueblos. Also he recommended that force be used to subjugate and convert the Moquis and that a presidio and

a mission be established among them. In letters addressed to Fray Murillo on May 6 and July 29, 1776, respectively, Escalante summarized earlier Christian activities among the Moquis and expressed a favorable opinion upon a proposed reconnaissance of the country between New Mexico and California. After his letter of May 6, he was called to Santa Fé by Gov. Mendinueta, and while there he drew a map of his journey to Moqui.

His second expedition of note had as its objectives the opening up of direct communication between Santa Fé and Monterey, California, and a reconnaissance, with an eye to their conversion, of the Indian tribes living north and west of the Colorado River. In company with eight soldiers and his superior, Fray Francisco Atanasio Domínguez, Escalante left Santa Fé on July 29, 1776. The route followed was in a northwesterly direction from Santa Fé to Utah Lake, near the present Provo, thence southwest for some two hundred miles to Black Rock Springs where it was proposed to strike due west to Monterey. A fall of snow on Oct. 5, however, caused the party to abandon plans to cross the sierras and to return by way of the Colorado River, the Moqui pueblos, and Zuñi to Sante Fé, which was reached on Jan. 2, 1777. "The journey," says Bolton, "covered some 2,000 miles, and lasted five months of almost continuous horseback travel. Its memory is one of the historical treasures of four states—New Mexico, Colorado, Utah, and Arizona" (*post*). Also an excellent diary of the expedition was kept by Escalante and was signed jointly by himself and Fray Domínguez. A map of curious interest accompanying the diary was drafted by a member of the expedition, Capt. Bernardo Miera y Pacheco. Two years later, Escalante, in a notable letter addressed to his superior, Fray Agustín Morfi, gave a summary, based upon extracts of documents then in the Santa Fé archives, of the Pueblo Indian rebellion of 1680 and of events prior to the reconquest of the province by Vargas in 1692. Soon after writing this letter, Escalante left New Mexico and went to the Franciscan College at Queretaro, and his career thenceforth is obscure.

[An English translation of Escalante's letter to Father Morfi is published in *The Land of Sunshine*, Mar. and Apr. 1900; other of the above-mentioned writings are printed in P. O. Maas's, *Viajes de Misioneros Franciscanos á la Conquista del Nuevo Mexico* (Sevilla, 1915), pp. 64–90, 98–133, and in *Documentos para la Historia de Mexico*, Segunda Série, vol. I (Mexico, 1854), pp. 375–558. The following works are useful: H. H. Bancroft, *Hist. of Utah, 1540–1887* (1889); H. E. Bolton, "Escalante in Dixie and the Arizona Strip," in *The New Mex. Hist. Rev.*, Jan. 1928, pp. 41–72; C. F. Coan, *A Hist. of New Mex.*, vol. I

(1925); Elliot Coues, *On the Trail of a Spanish Pioneer: the Diary and Itinerary of Francisco Garcés*, vol. II (1900); Francisco Antonio López de Figueroa, "Promptuario General . . . de todos los religiosos que han aviado en esta Sta. Prova. del Sto. Evago." (MS., in García Collection, Univ. of Texas).] C. W. H.

ESHER, JOHN JACOB (Dec. 11, 1823–Apr. 16, 1901), bishop of the Evangelical Church (formerly Evangelical Association), the son of John and Ursula (Schmidt) Esher, was born in the Alsatian village of Baldenheim. The Esher family originally came from Switzerland. In the spring of 1832 John and Ursula Esher emigrated to the United States with their children and settled near Warren, Pa. After a few years they moved to Des Plaines, Ill., a settlement near Chicago, where John Jacob grew to manhood. In his tenth year he experienced conversion, and very early in life felt the call to preach the Gospel. In 1845 he was licensed to preach by the newly organized Illinois Conference of the Evangelical Association at its first session. He served his apprenticeship as circuit rider in the frontier missions of the Church, crossing the Mississippi River and looking up new preaching places, with Dubuque as a center. He was ordained deacon in 1847 and elder in 1849. On Aug. 8 of the last-named year he was married to Barbara Schneider. In 1851 he was elected presiding elder, and served in this capacity amid great hardships and privations, and with undaunted courage until he was chosen financial secretary of the Plainfield College of the Evangelical Association of North America (later North Western College and now North Central College, Naperville, Ill.), founded in 1861 at Plainfield, Ill. From this position he was called to Cleveland in January 1862 to serve as editor of the German literature of the denomination.

The General Conference, at its session in Buffalo, N. Y., in October 1863 elected him bishop, and he was reëlected to this office by every subsequent General Conference during his lifetime. He was the only bishop of the church between the death of Joseph Long in 1869 and the election of Reuben Yeakel in 1871. He was the first bishop to visit the churches in Europe and he organized the first European conference of the denomination in 1865. He was also the first bishop of the Church to visit the mission in Japan. Accompanied by Mrs. Esher he toured around the world in 1884–85 and presided at the sessions of the European conferences on the way home. In 1886 he published the story of this tour in a German volume entitled *Ueber Laender und Meere: Meine Reise um die Welt*. From the beginning of Esher's administration there had been considerable opposition to his principles and policies. During the decade of the eighties this opposition increased, and in 1891 resulted in a division, the anti-Esher minority withdrawing to form three years later the United Evangelical Church—a separation terminated in 1922 when the two bodies merged in the Evangelical Church.

In 1893 Esher again visited Japan, and organized the Japan Annual Conference. During the quadrennium following 1895, at the special request of the General Conference, he wrote his work on systematic theology, entitled *Christliche Theologie* (Evangelical Publishing House, Cleveland, 1898). This task he performed while at the same time attending his quota of Conference sessions and meeting his administrative duties with fidelity despite his advancing years. He was orthodox in his theology and firm in his convictions. His sermons were carefully prepared and fervently delivered, making a remarkable impression upon his audiences. Many hundreds were converted and added to the Church through his ministry. He was a man of unusual executive ability and administrative skill and during his episcopacy stamped his own peculiar genius and personality upon his denomination.

[Sources for Esher's life are: his manuscript Journals; Wm. Horn, *Life and Labors of Bishop Esher* (1907); S. P. Spreng, "Hist. of the Evangelical Asso.," in vol. XII of the Am. Church Hist. Series; R. Yeakel, *Hist. of the Evangelical Asso.* (1895); and files of the denominational periodicals, *Der Christliche Botschafter* and the *Evangelical Messenger*. A. Stapleton, *Annals of the Evangelical Asso. of North America and Hist. of the United Evangelical Church* (1900), gives an account of the schism from the minority's point of view.] S. P. S.

ESPEJO, ANTONIO DE (fl. 1581–1583), Spanish merchant in Mexico, has a place in United States history because of his discoveries in New Mexico. In the forty years following the famous exploration by Francisco Vázquez de Coronado in that region, 1540–42, the mining frontier progressed northward, and in 1581, from the mining center of the San Bartolomé Valley, Friar Agustín Rodríguez, a Franciscan lay brother, went forth to make conversions. He was escorted by Francisco Chamuscado and eight other soldiers; two other Franciscans, Francisco López, and Juan de Santa María, went also. The latter was killed by Tanos Indians while attempting to return alone to the south. When the soldiers returned on Jan. 31, 1582, they left López and Rodríguez at Puaray (in Tiguex) to found a mission. The Franciscan Order, disturbed for the safety of the two zealots, sent a relief expedition to bring them back, and Antonio de Espejo —who was visiting at the time in the Valley of San Bartolomé—turned prospector, invested of his wealth in the investigations, which had been approved by a local alcalde, and became leader of the relief party. With him went Fray Bernardino Beltrán and fifteen soldiers. They left San Bartolomé on Nov. 10, 1582, taking 115 horses and mules. Going down the Conchos River to its affluence with the Rio Grande, Espejo passed through the Jumanos territory into the region of the Pueblo Indians. At Puaray they learned that the friars they had come to rescue had already been killed; hence the leader, with the friar conforming, turned to prospecting. They visited first the buffalo plains to the east, and then several of the pueblos on the Rio Grande and its tributaries. Going then westward to Ácoma and Zuñi, they encountered four Christian Mexican Indians left behind by Coronado. Thence Espejo went westward in quest of a reputed lake of gold, which eluded him, though the Moquis gave him four thousand cotton blankets, and rich ores were found farther west in the vicinity of the present Bill Williams Fork.

In the meantime Beltrán, waiting at Zuñi, decided to return to San Bartolomé while Espejo continued prospecting. The latter visited again to the eastward among the Queres, Ubates, and Tanos, finding ores. From the Tanos he turned homeward down the Pecos, being escorted to the Conchos by Jumanos Indians, and reached San Bartolomé on Sept. 20, 1583. The explorations of Rodríguez and Espejo were actually more important than Coronado's in extending the area of Spain. The reports of mineral wealth in the north brought back by these parties of prospectors fanned frontier interest into excitement, and served as the basis of several attempts at occupation, culminating in the real conquest of New Mexico under Juan de Oñate.

[Accounts by Espejo himself are printed in two places in *Colección de documentos inéditos relativos al descubrimiento, conquista y organización de las antiguas posesiones Españolas de America y Oceania*, XV (Madrid, 1871), 102–26 and 163–89. They were compared and edited, with accompanying letters by Espejo, in an English translation by H. E. Bolton, *Spanish Exploration in the Southwest, 1542–1706* (1916), pp. 161–95; see also Bolton's *Spanish Borderlands* (1921). The exploit was carefully studied in H. H. Bancroft, *Hist. of Arizona and New Mexico* (1889), pp. 80–91, with copious annotation from the sources; there are summaries in G. P. Hammond, *Don Juan de Oñate and the Founding of New Mexico* (1927), and G. P. Hammond and A. Rey, *Expedition into New Mexico made by Antonio de Espejo 1582–83*, etc. (1929). A brief relation of the journeys of Rodríguez and Espejo was printed in Richard Hakluyt, *The Principal Navigations* . . ., III (1600), 383–96, in Spanish and English. See also the MacLehose edition of Hakluyt (1915), IX, 169–204. The only known copy of this voyage in the first edition of 1587 is in the Huntington Library. A verbatim reprint was privately issued with preface by F. W. Hodge, London, 1928.] H. I. P.

ESPY, JAMES POLLARD (May 9, 1785–Jan. 24, 1860), educator and meteorologist, was born in Pennsylvania, the son of Josiah and Elizabeth (Patterson) Espy. Many of his relatives during colonial times and later lived in Bedford. The family was of Huguenot origin and the original spelling of the name was Espie. While James, the youngest son, was still an infant his father moved to the Blue-Grass region of Kentucky, and thence, a few years later, to the Miami Valley, Ohio. James remained with his oldest sister who had married and was living at Mount Sterling, Ky. When about eighteen, he entered Transylvania University at Lexington, Ky., from which he graduated in 1808. He then went to Xenia, Ohio, where he taught school and studied law. During the years 1812–17 he was principal of the Academy at Cumberland, Md. He next taught mathematics and the classics in Philadelphia, part of the time at the Franklin Institute. About 1835 he began to devote his whole time to lecturing on and studying meteorological problems, especially his theory of storms. This theory, erroneous in respect to the mechanism of the storm, is sound in that part which attributes precipitation to the upward movement and consequent expansion and cooling of moist air. It was a great contribution to our knowledge of the physical processes of the atmosphere and deservedly brought much renown, and the pleasing title "Storm King," to its author. In 1836 it won the Magellanic Prize of the American Philosophical Society, and it brought an invitation to explain it in person, which he did in 1840, before the British Association for the Advancement of Science, and the French Academy of Sciences. However, there was stress, too, for it involved him in many discussions, some of which, owing to his positive opinions, were not strictly impersonal. In 1841 he published his *Philosophy of Storms*. In 1842 the United States Congress appointed him meteorologist to the War Department, and later, 1848, also meteorologist to the Navy Department. In this capacity he established a series of daily weather observations, compiled weather maps, traced the progress of storms, and submitted in 1843 the first annual weather report. In 1852 Congress directed him to continue his work in connection with the Smithsonian Institution, which had already undertaken the collection of meteorological data.

Espy's chief contribution to the science of meteorology was his convectional theory of precipitation, and his greatest addition to practical meteorology the institution of telegraphic bulletins giving knowledge at one place of the current state of the weather at various and widely different localities, thus laying the foundation of weather forecasting.

While teaching at Cumberland, Md., he was married in 1812, to Margaret Pollard who shared to the fullest his enthusiasm and encouraged him on all occasions in his scientific work. She was delicate, however, and died in 1850. They had no children. At the time of his marriage he took "Pollard" as his middle name. In his earlier life, Espy was an orthodox Calvinist, but later abandoned the doctrine of eternal punishment as inconsonant with the concept of an infinitely loving and merciful God. Possibly his eminently sociable disposition urged his philosophy to this happier conclusion. He died in Cincinnati, in his seventy-fifth year.

[Mrs. L. M. Morehead, *A Few Incidents in the Life of Prof. James P. Espy* (1888); *Report, Internat. Meteorological Cong.*, 1893, Pt. II, pp. 305–16, printed also in *U. S. Dept. of Agric., Weather Bureau Bull.*, No. 11, p. 305 (1894); *Ann. Report of the Board of Regents of the Smithsonian Institution . . . for the Year 1859* (1860), pp. 108–11; F. M. Espy, *Hist. and Geneal. of the Espy Family in America* (1905).] W. J. H.

ESTABROOK, JOSEPH (Dec. 7, 1793–May 18, 1855), teacher, college president, son of Hobart and Anna (Hyde) Estabrook, was born in Lebanon, N. H., and died in Anderson County, Tenn. He was the grandson of Joseph Estabrook, a Revolutionary soldier, and the great-grandson of Nehemiah Estabrook, who moved to Lebanon from Mansfield, Conn. Destined, he thought, for the ministry, he completed his course at Dartmouth College in 1815 and began the study of theology at Princeton. An affection of the voice caused him to change to pedagogy, and from 1817 to 1824 he lived at Amherst, four years as president of the academy and four years as professor of Latin and Greek in the college. Here in 1823 he was married to Nancy Dickinson. As a teacher he was more successful with young boys than with college students, and when at last he went away he left with the citizens of the little town a memory which, it would seem, made up in color for anything it lacked in probity. He was given to elegant ruffles and fine boots, to the prodigious use of snuff, to shooting even on Fast-day, and, capping all, to dreams which told him faithfully how to win $5,000 by lottery. Probably because of his bronchial trouble, in 1824 he went South. For a while he conducted a school for young ladies in Staunton, Va., and afterward a similar school in Knoxville, Tenn. Then he was president of the school in Knoxville—East Tennessee College, 1834–40, and East Tennessee University, 1840–50—which later became the University of Tennessee. During the period from 1826 to 1857 this school was almost entirely under the direction of New Englanders. Neither its other executives imported from Estabrook's section of the country, however, nor the indigenous ones who were at times wedged into the administration, brought it to the pitch of attainment that—with its all-Dartmouth faculty—it maintained throughout the forties. In spite of this success, for some reason he determined to withdraw from public life, and to retire to a place in Anderson County about twenty-five miles distant from Knoxville. There he set out to produce salt by boring into the earth till he could obtain salt water. All his time and much of the money he had accumulated were devoted to this end and it was generally believed throughout the spring before his death that the undertaking was just short of success.

[W. S. Tyler, *Hist. of Amherst Coll.* (1873); Hamilton Child, *Gazetteer of Grafton County, N. H.* (1886); L. S. Merriam, *Higher Education in Tenn.* (1893); E. T. Sanford, *Blount Coll. and the Univ. of Tenn.* (1894), which refers to Moses White, *Early Hist. of the Univ. of Tenn.* (1879); M. D. Bisbee, *Gen. Cat. of Dartmouth Coll. 1769–1900* (1900); C. A. Downs, *Hist. of Lebanon, N. H.* (1908); Thomas Hills, *Three Ancient Cemeteries in N. H.* (1910).] J. D. W.

ESTAUGH, ELIZABETH HADDON (*c.* 1680–Mar. 30, 1762), founder of Haddonfield, N. J., was the elder of the two daughters of John Haddon, a well-to-do anchorsmith of Southwark, England, and Elizabeth Clark, his wife. Her parents were loyal members of the Society of Friends; her father had more than once been fined for his stubborn persistence in attending meeting. In 1698 John Haddon bought from a Quaker neighbor a tract of 500 acres in western New Jersey, intending to emigrate with his family; but circumstances prevented, and in 1701 Elizabeth herself, then in her twenty-first year, was moved to emigrate, "in order to provide a home in the wilderness for travelling Ministers" (*Journal of the Friends Historical Society of London*, vol. XIII, 1916, p. 46). With sturdy faith in the inner light she set out, accompanied by a housekeeper and several men-servants—all Friends—for "Haddonfield," where the original proprietor, John Willis, had erected one or two simple buildings. During the first winter her house became, as she had purposed, a regular stopping-place for Friends traveling from one meeting to another. Before the commencement of her second winter in America she had married, on "the first of Tenth Month" 1702, John Estaugh of Kelvedon, Essex, a young preacher some four years her senior, who had been in America for two years. "In the forepart of his time," Elizabeth wrote many years later, "he traveled pretty much; but in the latter . . . his Good Master, that requires not Impossibilities of his Servants, favored him with being very easy at home; where, through Mercy, we lived very comfortably; . . . few, if any, in a married state ever lived in sweeter Harmony than we did." While John was traveling in the interest of religion, acting as agent for the Pennsylvania Land Company of London, and caring for the American affairs of his increasingly wealthy father-in-law, Elizabeth managed the plantation, ministered to the sick in the vicinity, and fulfilled her vocation of hospitable hostess. In 1713 she built a new house of native brick, "Haddon Hall of Haddonfield," which stood till 1842. It was furnished with fine pieces sent from London by John Haddon, and stood in a garden which was planted with yew and box, and whose walks were paved with English brick. At Haddonfield a village grew up and a Monthly Meeting was established; Elizabeth served as clerk of the Women's Meeting for over fifty years. In 1742, while making a religious visit to Tortola, John Estaugh died. A blank page between entries in the minute-book of Haddonfield Women's Meeting commemorates the time when Elizabeth received the news of his death. She wrote a "Testimony" to his memory, which appeared in the little volume *A Call to the Unfaithful Professors of Truth: Written by John Estaugh in his Life-time; and now Published for General Service* (1744), printed by Benjamin Franklin in Philadelphia.

For twenty years after her husband's death Elizabeth lived on at Haddonfield. "Her heart and house were open to her friends . . . well knowing the value of friendship, [she] was careful not to wound it herself, nor encourage persons in whispering and publishing the failings, or supposed weaknesses of others" (*Piety Promoted,* IV, 419). She had no children of her own, but had adopted Ebenezer Hopkins, the son of her sister Sarah, and in her old age was surrounded by grandnieces and grandnephews. In 1762, after three months of illness bravely borne, she died "as one falling asleep, full of days, like a shock of corn fully ripe" (Testimony of Haddonfield Monthly Meeting).

[Hannah J. Sturge, *Fragmentary Memorials of John and Elizabeth Estaugh* (1881), contains the Testimony of Haddonfield Meeting, which is also the basis for the sketch in *Piety Promoted . . . A New and Complete Ed.*, vol. IV (1854). See also S. N. Rhoads, in *Bull. Friends' Hist. Soc. of Phila.*, June 1909, and in *Notes on Old Gloucester County, N. J.*, ed. by F. H. Stewart, I (1917), 293; *The Two Hundredth Anniversary of the Settlement of Haddonfield, N. J.* (1913); *Am. Hist. Record* (Phila.), Aug. 1873; *Garden Mag.*, July 1912; *New Era Mag.*, Nov. 1920; *Proc. N. J. Hist. Soc.*, 3 ser., VI (1909–10), 149; VII (1912–13), 103. The basis for the accounts of Elizabeth's early life and courtship given by Mary Agnes Best in her *Rebel Saints* (1925) and by Longfellow in ser. 3 of the "Tales of a Wayside Inn" (*Aftermath,* 1873) is "The Youthful Emigrant," by Lydia Maria Child, in her *Fact and Fiction* (1846); but Mrs. Child's sources for much picturesque detail are unknown.]

E. R. D.

ESTERBROOK, RICHARD (Feb. 21, 1813–Oct. 11, 1895), manufacturer, was born in Liskeard, county of Cornwall, England, of Flemish ancestry, the son of Richard and Anna (Olver) Esterbrook. His father was financially interested in tin-mining. He provided his son with a liberal education and immediately upon the completion of his course launched him in a business career by purchasing a shop in Liskeard where young Richard established a stationery business. The enterprise prospered, and he invested his profits in the local tin-mining industry, which, in turn, in the course of a few years yielded him a considerable fortune. He thereupon gave up the stationery business, purchased a home and two farms in the neighborhood of Liskeard, and for upwards of twenty years lived the life of a gentleman farmer. Meanwhile his son, Richard Esterbrook third, had emigrated to Canada and with an uncle begun the manufacture of steel pens. They were unsuccessful, however, and went to Philadelphia where they undertook the enterprise a second time. Their efforts there were unfruitful also, and in 1858 young Esterbrook prevailed upon his father to come to Philadelphia and invest his fortune with them. Bringing with him a corps of skilled workmen whom he had selected in Birmingham, Esterbrook successfully organized the pen company which now bears his name. A few years after his arrival he bought the old water-pumping plant of the city of Camden and it thereupon became the nucleus of the pen factory which has since grown on this site. In his organization, Esterbrook made the wise selection of his own son for general sales manager, and the latter by his genial personality and extraordinary salesmanship succeeded in establishing with the trade a wide distribution of the pens. As is often the case with infant industries —and especially those without an overabundant supply of capital—Esterbrook's company ran into financial difficulties about 1875. Esterbrook, however, had already gained the reputation of a man who always kept his promises, and his largest creditor, who supplied the steel, volunteered to continue to furnish on credit that much-needed raw material as long as necessary. This offer prevented the complete collapse of the business; Esterbrook secured whatever credit he required; and the Esterbrook factory has continued to grow ever since and is to-day (1930) the largest and most modern establishment in the United States for the manufacture of steel pens. From the day of its founding until his death, Esterbrook continued actively as president of the company. He had the faculty in the selection of his employees that resulted in the creation of an organization in which each individual felt himself part of a large family gathered under one roof. Like all of his ancestors, Esterbrook was an orthodox Friend and was a minister of that society both in Philadelphia and Camden. He married Mary Date of Tavistock, England, in 1835, who with a son and a daughter survived him at the time of his death in Camden.

[Wm. B. Estabrook, *Geneal. of the Estabrook Family . . .* (1891); C. S. Boyer, *The Span of a Century: A Chronological Hist. of the City of Camden 1828–1928* (n.d.); obituary in *Public Ledger* (Phila.), Oct. 12, 1895; U. S. Nat. Museum Records, which include information from Mr. J. H. Longmaid, president of the Esterbrook Steel Pen Mfg. Co., and a grandnephew of Richard Esterbrook.] C. W. M.

ESTERLY, GEORGE (Oct. 17, 1809–June 7, 1893), inventor, manufacturer, was born and brought up on his father's farm in Plattekill, Ulster County, N. Y. He sprang from English and German ancestry and was the son of Peter and Rachel (Griffith) Esterly. After receiving a common-school education in Plattekill, he continued with his father both at his birthplace and at Rochester, N. Y., until 1832. During that year he married and moved to Detroit, Mich., where for five years he was engaged in the dairy and provision business, extending his territory by personal peddling as far as Heart Prairie and Janesville, Wis., and in 1843 settled there and began farming. His first harvest of 200 acres of wheat was without any profit to himself because of the fact that farm help was scarce and all operations had to be executed by hand. This was his stimulant for invention, and after a year of experimentation, on Oct. 2, 1844, he patented a horse-pushed harvester or "header," which proved to be the first successful American harvesting machine. It had a wide reel revolving on a horizontal axis, mounted on a box on wheels, which swept the heads of grain against a knife blade, also placed horizontally. The heads fell into the box back of the knife and just in front of the horses, which were hitched to the rear. At the second annual fair of the Chicago Mechanics Institute, held in 1848, Esterly exhibited this machine, with C. H. McCormick [*q.v.*] as his only competitor, and won a gold medal "for the best harvester." Shortly thereafter he contracted with several manufacturers to make his machine and was thus definitely launched in the agricultural-machinery business. He continued to ply his inventive talents, patenting a mowing machine, a plow, a hand-rake reaper, and the first sulky cultivator between 1854 and 1856; a seeder in 1865; and a self-rake reaper in 1870. In 1858 he erected his own manufacturing plant at Whitewater, Wis., taking in his son as partner in 1872, and incorporating the business in 1884. It continued to thrive, concentrating its effort on twine binders and mowers and building up a large export trade, until in 1892 the plant was moved to Minneapolis, Minn., and the enterprise was ruined in the great panic of that time. Outside of his business Esterly was particularly interested in the national currency question. He published a pamphlet in 1874, entitled *A Consideration of the Currency and Finance Question,* and the following year a second one, *A Plan for Funding the Public Debt, and a Safe Return to Specie Payment.* He was married three times: first, on Mar. 4, 1832, to Jane Lewis, who was the mother of his seven children; second, after her death, to Mrs. Amelia Shaff Hall in March 1855; and third, in May 1884, to Caroline Esterly, who with his son and four daughters survived him. His death occurred at Hot Springs, S. Dak.

[L. H. Bailey, *Cyc. of Am. Agric.* (1909), vol. IV; "Evolution of Reaping Machines," *U. S. Dept. of Agric., Office of Experiment Stations, Bull. No. 103* (1902); Prosper Cravath and Spencer S. Steele, *Early Annals of Whitewater, 1836–1867* (1906); R. L. Ardrey, *Am. Agric. Implements* (1894); Patent Office Records; U. S. Nat. Museum correspondence.] C. W. M.

ESTES, DANA (Mar. 4, 1840–June 16, 1909), publisher and traveler, was the son of Joseph and Maria (Edwards) Estes, and a descendant on the paternal side of one of the early English settlers of Maine. His mother was of Scotch-Irish ancestry. He was born in Gorham, Me. In 1855 he went to Augusta, where he became a clerk in a general wholesale and retail country store. Going to Boston in 1859, and making his home there for the rest of his life, he entered the book business, for which he had had so great a liking since early childhood that he had made it the goal of his ambition, and thenceforward it became his life-work. At the outbreak of the Civil War he enlisted in the 4th Battalion Rifles, which became the nucleus of the 13th Massachusetts Infantry, and during the second battle of Bull Run he was disabled by wounds that incapacitated him for further service. Association with various bookselling and publishing houses in Boston followed his recovery, and in partnership with Charles E. Lauriat he eventually established the firm of Estes & Lauriat, devoting himself to the wholesale and manufacturing part of the business, while Lauriat was in active charge of the retail trade of the firm. Their bookstore stood for many years on Washington St., opposite the Old South Meeting House. They were among the earliest booksellers and publishers in the United States to bring to American readers the works of standard European writers, especially of historians and novelists. Among their other specialties, due largely to Estes's energy, was the publication of travel and adventure stories for young readers, notably the Zigzag Journey Series by Hezekiah Butterworth, the Vassar Girl Series by Elizabeth Williams Champney, and the Knockabout Club Series by C. A. Stephens. While he did practically no writing for publication, he edited a series of volumes entitled *Half-Hour Recreations in Popular Science* (1871–79), and he compiled several volumes of juvenile and standard poetry. He had many diversified interests, being an enthusiastic yachtsman and the owner of both a sailing and a steam vessel. He was also an active member of the Browning Society, and a leader in the movement of international copyright. Some years after the publishing part of the business had been removed to the Estes Press Buildings, erected through his enterprise on Summer Street Extension, the partners separated, and he established the new firm of Dana Estes & Company. His business brought him not only the acquaintance but the personal friendship of many eminent men of letters both in America and in Europe. For years he was a great traveler, making extended tours of Europe, Asia, and Africa, becoming a member of the American Association for the Advancement of Science, and during his tours collecting valuable archeological antiquities, some of which were presented by him to the Peabody Museum at Cambridge and to Bowdoin College. He was first married on Apr. 11, 1867, to Louisa S. Reid, by whom he had three sons, and second, on Nov. 10, 1884, to Grace D. Coues Page.

[Chas. Estes, *Estes Genealogies* (1894); Richard Herndon, *Men of Progress . . . State of Me.* (1897); *Who's Who in America*, 1908–09; *Boston Transcript*, June 16, 1909; personal information from members of the family.] E. F. E.

ESTEY, JACOB (Sept. 30, 1814–Apr. 15, 1890), pioneer American organ manufacturer, was the son of Isaac Estey and Patty Forbes. His father, offspring of an English family which had settled in Sutton, Mass., early in the nineteenth century removed to Hinsdale, N. H., where Jacob was born. He had accumulated money, but soon lost it all as a contractor for public roads. As a result, at the age of four, Jacob was adopted by a neighbor farmer named Shattuck. Frequent beatings and chores so surfeited him that, deaf to the call of the soil, he ran off at the age of thirteen, made his way to Worcester, Mass., and managed to secure a common-school education and two years of study at an academy while learning the plumbing trade. In 1834 he walked (to save coach-hire) from Worcester to Brattleboro, Vt., where he established himself as a plumber and, in 1837, married Desdemona Wood, a farmer's daughter. In 1850, when the excitement incident to the discovery of gold in California swept the country, Estey saw better opportunities at home. He invested his savings in a small melodeon-manufacturing shop in Brattleboro. Thenceforward his story is one of the gradual development of a great American industry through Yankee grit and intelligence. The original American reed-organ, known as the melodeon or melodium, had been a development of the *orgue expressif* invented by the Frenchman Brenié, in 1810; yet by 1850 American makers were already using Debaine's improved *harmonium* (invented 1840) as a "melodeon" model. The melodeon had become a popular family instrument, and with increasing population came an increasing demand for it. Jacob Estey hawked his instruments in person, driving his pedler's wagon loaded with melodeons across the country to New York, as well as through the New England states and over the boundary into Canada. With him went a boy who could play the hymn-tunes whose simple harmonies sold his wares. Since currency was scarce in the country districts through which he passed, he took his payment in kind—cheese, butter, farm produce, cattle, and, in Canada especially, horses.

Undaunted by the burning of his little shop in 1857, he secured capital, took in Levi Knight Fuller as a partner, and resumed melodeon building the following year. In 1860 the new firm took the name of The Estey Organ Company. Estey's organ business grew with great rapidity after 1870, and by 1890 was reputed the largest of its kind in the world, with branch agencies in leading European cities, and in South America, Asia, Australia, and Africa. In 1852 the shop employed six workmen and its total value was estimated at $2,700; before the end of the century the firm's output was 1,800 organs a month, and Estey "Cottage Organs" were exported to every part of the globe. In 1885 the Estey Piano Company was organized; and in 1901, eleven years after the death of its founder, the Estey Organ Company initiated the building of large church pipe-organs, in a special factory with modern equipment.

Jacob Estey, influenced, perhaps, by his own hard struggles in early life, was a kindly, sympathetic employer. He was interested in religious and educational movements, helped found Shaw University (Raleigh, N. C.) for colored students, and gave much money to other philanthropic causes and missionary work. In his own special field he is credited with the invention of the *Vox humana* tremolo stop on the reed-organ, though it seems probable this was an adaptation rather than an invention. More plausible is the contention that he was one of the first to employ the "easy payment" plan to further the sale of his organs.

[Alfred Dolge, *Pianos and Their Makers* (1911), vol. I; Daniel Spillane, *Hist. of the Am. Pianoforte* (1890); M. R. Cabot, *Annals of Brattleboro, 1681–1895* (1922), II, 631–33; H. C. Williams, *Biog. Encyc. of Vt. of the 19th Century* (1885); *N. Y. Tribune* and *Burlington* (Vt.) *Daily Free Press* of Apr. 16, 1890; Freund's *Daily Music and Drama*, Apr. 19, 1890.] F. H. M.

ETTWEIN, JOHN (June 29, 1721–Jan. 2, 1802), Moravian bishop, was born at Freudenstadt in Würtemberg, Germany, of religious refugee stock. His great-grandfather, Jean Edwin, lost both parents in the religious persecutions in Savoy in the seventeenth century and escaped into Würtemberg where he found a home at St. George in the Black Forest, and it was here that the grandfather and father of the future bishop were born. His mother's parents had fled from Carinthia into Würtemberg, and settled at Freudenstadt where many of the persecuted from the Austrian dominions were allowed to establish themselves. His parents were in humble circumstances, and John Ettwein secured only the elements of an education, becoming a shoemaker by trade. He was an attendant at the meetings of the Pietists, and in 1738, having fallen under the influence of Moravian missionaries, left his native town and joined the Moravian group at Marienborn. There he prepared himself for missionary work, and he was subsequently appointed to various offices within the Church in Germany, Holland, and England. In the last-named country, he learned the English language. In 1746 he was married to Johanna Maria Kymbel; that same year saw his ordination as a deacon of a church; and in 1754 he sailed to America with his wife in the company of Bishop Spangenberg [*q.v.*] and some fifty Moravians, under the appointment of spiritual adviser to the children of the members of the Church in North America. He also undertook various missions among the Indians of the middle colonies and even as far south as Georgia. In 1763, he was placed in general charge of the Moravian work in North Carolina; at this period, he conducted preaching tours into South Carolina and Georgia, and was also responsible for the property of the Church in these parts. While engaged in these activities, he made the acquaintance of Henry Laurens [*q.v.*], which developed into a lifelong friendship. In 1766, he was appointed assistant to Bishop Nathanael Seidel [*q.v.*] at Bethlehem, Pa., and, in that capacity, continued his journeyings into the back country; he also traveled into New England. When it was necessary to find a new home for the Christian Indians of the Susquehanna, he led a party of them in 1772 across the Alleghanies to the settlement established by the advance party under David Zeisberger [*q.v.*] in the Tuscarawas Valley in Ohio—a pilgrimage that occupied eight weeks.

At the outbreak of the Revolutionary War, having received only kindness at the hands of the British government and not being able to fathom the justification of the bitter hostility that arose against it, Ettwein was a pronounced Loyalist who did not hesitate to thank God in the public services on the occasion of news of a British victory. As a result, he was arrested by the Revolutionary group of Northampton County and was temporarily imprisoned at Easton. As the struggle between the mother country and the colonies progressed, he finally was able to reconcile himself to accept "the independence of the Colonies as a fact against which the Moravian Church ought not to protest" (De Schweinitz, *post*, p. 258). In the course of the war, he acted as the accredited representative of the Moravians in their negotiations with the Continental Congress and the Pennsylvania Assembly over the issues that arose in connection with their refusal to accept enrolment in the armed forces and to subscribe to the Test Act of the year 1777, as well as the issues arising out of their relations with the Indians and losses sustained by the Church in the progress of the war. Largely through the influence of Henry Laurens, the Moravians were freed from the necessity of taking the Test Oath. When the general hospital for the Continental Army was situated at Bethlehem, in the years 1776–77, Ettwein acted as the chaplain.

In the course of the war, most of the Christian Indians whom he had led into the Ohio country were massacred at Gnadenhütten. It was a terrible blow to the Moravian mission work, but, undaunted, Ettwein prevailed upon Congress in the year 1785 to set aside 12,000 acres in the Tuscarawas Valley as a reservation for converted natives, and in the year 1787, he was instrumental in resuscitating the "Society of the United Brethren for Propagating the Gospel among the Heathen"—which had been organized in 1745—and became its president. He also prevailed upon the Pennsylvania Assembly to grant 5,000 acres for a Christian Indian reservation on Lake Erie. In the year 1784, he was elevated to the episcopacy and from that time until 1801, the year preceding his death, he presided over the destinies of the Moravian Church of North America. He died on Jan. 2, 1802, in Bethlehem, Pa. Bishop Ettwein was a man of great force of character, tremendously devoted to the work of the Moravian ministry, at all times outspoken in his language, but winning the respect of supporters and opponents alike by reason of his genuine qualities of manhood. He may be ranked as one of the greatest of the leaders that the Moravian Church has had in North America.

[Edmund de Schweinitz, "John Ettwein, Bishop of the Brethren's Church," in *Trans. Moravian Hist. Soc.*, vol. II (1886); J. T. Hamilton, *Hist. of the Church known as the Moravian Church or the Unitas Fratrum* (1900), also pub. as *Trans. Moravian Hist. Soc.*, vol. VI (1900); *Records of the Moravians in N. C.* (3 vols., 1922–26), ed. by Adelaide L. Fries, pub. by the N. C. Hist. Commission; "Fragments from the Papers of Bishop John Ettwein," in *Trans. Moravian Hist. Soc.*, vol. IV (1895); Reports of the Proceedings of the General Synods of the Moravian Church, 1746–1836 (MSS.); Original Minutes and Documents of the Provincial Synod of the American Moravian Church, 1748–1898 (MSS.).] L. H. G.

EUSTIS, GEORGE (Oct. 20, 1796–Dec. 22, 1858), jurist, eldest of four children of Jacob and Elizabeth Saunders (Gray) Eustis, was born in Boston, Mass. He was educated in the schools of his native city and at Harvard College, from which he graduated in the class of 1815. Soon after leaving college he went abroad as private secretary to his uncle, William Eustis [*q.v.*], who had just been appointed United States minister at The Hague by President Madison. While here he is said to have begun the study of law. Upon his return he went to Louisiana, settled in the city of New Orleans, and by 1822 had been admitted to the bar. An active interest in local politics resulted in his being several times elected to the lower house of the state legislature. From 1830 to 1832 he was state attorney-general, and in 1832 he was appointed secretary of the state of Louisiana, a position he held until 1834. In 1838 he became a justice of the state supreme court. This court had accumulated a very large docket, partly because of litigation resulting from the panic of 1837, partly because of the partial incapacity of two of the judges, but also because of the dilatory methods of the court itself. In derision it was called a "talking court." As a result of public criticism two members resigned, and Eustis and Pierre A. Rost, active leaders of the bar, were given their places. In their efforts to clear the docket, however, they soon found themselves hampered by the presiding judge. Rost, therefore, resigned in May 1839, and Eustis followed his example the next month (H. P. Dart, "The History of the Supreme Court of Louisiana," in *The Celebration of the Centenary of the Supreme Court of Louisiana*, 1913).

Dissatisfaction with the court, as well as with political matters in general, continued; and in 1845 a convention was called to draw up a new state constitution. This constitution provided for a supreme court composed of a chief justice and three associate justices, who were to be appointed by the governor. The court was organized Mar. 19, 1846, with Eustis as chief justice and with associates who were bent upon putting an end to the costly delays of the old system. They adopted rules and methods to this end and eventually caught up with a congested docket. Before the commission of Chief Justice Eustis expired, a new state constitution brought about a change in the personnel of the court. He retired in 1852, and died at his New Orleans home six years later. He has been described as "a man of extensive and elegant acquirements, a good linguist, and a ripe scholar." As a speaker it is said that he could claim no distinction, being neither fluent nor eloquent. Concerning his judicial opinions, Chief Justice Merrick of Louisiana said, "They were, as it became them, more solid than brilliant, more massive than showy. They are like granite masonry, and will serve as guides and landmarks in years to come" (13 *Louisiana*, vii–viii).

The development of the Louisiana educational system was greatly influenced by George Eustis. In 1834, while secretary of state, he urged the establishment of a medical college, which, largely through his efforts, was chartered in 1835. Again, in 1845, he induced the state constitutional convention, of which he was a member, to make provision for the establishment of a university in the city of New Orleans. Two years later was organized the University of Louisiana, now the Tulane University of Louisiana. In 1825 Eustis was married to Clarisse Allain, who belonged to a prominent Louisiana Creole family. She outlived him eighteen years, and died at Pau, France, in 1876. They had six children.

[H. L. Eustis, *Geneal. of the Eustis Family* (1878) is useful but contains some errors. See also J. S. Whitaker, *Sketches of Life and Character in La., the Portraits Selected Principally from the Bench and Bar* (1847); *Law Reporter*, Mar. 1859; *Law Times*, Aug. 20, 1859; reports of the secretary of state of Louisiana; obituaries in the *Daily Picayune* (New Orleans), and the *New Orleans Crescent*, Dec. 23, 1858.] M. J. W.

EUSTIS, GEORGE (Sept. 29, 1828–Mar. 15, 1872), statesman, diplomat, the eldest son of George [*q.v.*], eminent Louisiana jurist, and Clarisse Allain Eustis, was born in the city of New Orleans. He was educated at Jefferson College, St. James Parish, La., and at Harvard College, where, according to the records of that institution, he attended during the session of

Eustis

1844–45 but took no degree. For a time he followed in his father's footsteps and practised law in his native city, but soon forsook it for a political career. He was elected a representative from Louisiana to the Thirty-fourth Congress, and re-elected to the following Congress. While in the House of Representatives he was a member of the committee on commerce, of which Elihu B. Washburne of Illinois was chairman, and was active in the support of measures for the improvement of the navigation of the Mississippi River and of other Southern waterways. At Washington, D.C., he met and married Louise Corcoran, daughter of W. W. Corcoran [*q.v.*], banker, and founder of the Corcoran Art Gallery of that city. They had three children.

When the Civil War broke out, Eustis entered the Confederate service, and was soon appointed secretary of the Confederate legation at Paris, where he served under John Slidell, Confederate minister to France. He was with Mason and Slidell on the famous voyage of the British mail steamer *Trent,* and with them he was held a prisoner at Fort Warren in Boston harbor, until the seizure was declared illegal and they were permitted to proceed on their way. After the war he remained abroad, spending most of his time with his family at "Villa Louisiana," his home at Cannes, France. Being a man of fine intelligence, great social charm, and thoroughly familiar with the French language, law, and literature, he was exceedingly popular in his adopted country, and on terms of intimacy with many of its most important public men. When the Franco-Prussian War broke out, and United States minister Washburne, overwhelmed by the pressure of work, was finding it almost impossible to get the necessary help in his legation, Eustis generously volunteered his services. His knowledge of the French language, his long acquaintance in Paris, and his familiarity with diplomatic usages, enabled him to render invaluable services to his former chief (E. B. Washburne, *Recollections of a Minister to France,* 1887, I, 112–13). It is said that Washburne also employed him to negotiate a postal treaty with the French government. Eustis was far from being a well man, and his work at the legation probably sapped his vitality and hastened his death. At all events, before the siege of Paris his health failed perceptibly, and he sought rest and recuperation at his Cannes home, where he died about a year later from Bright's disease. Mrs. Eustis had died at the same place three years earlier.

[H. L. Eustis, *Geneal. of the Eustis Family* (1878); *Public Life and Diplomatic Correspondence of James M. Mason* (1903), by his daughter, Virginia Mason; Louis Martin Sears, *John Slidell* (1925); *Biog. Dir. Am. Cong.* (1928). Obituary notices in the *Daily Picayune,* Mar. 17, 1872, and *L'Abeille de la Nouvelle-Orléans,* 16 mars, 1872.] M. J. W.

EUSTIS, HENRY LAWRENCE (Feb. 1, 1819–Jan. 11, 1885), engineer, soldier, college professor, was born at Fort Independence, Boston, Mass., the seventh and youngest son of Brig.-Gen. Abraham Eustis and Rebecca (Sprague) Eustis. His grandfather, also Abraham Eustis, was a brother of William Eustis [*q.v.*]. There was an army tradition in the family, and Henry, after taking a degree from Harvard in 1838, accepted an appointment to the United States Military Academy at West Point, where he graduated in 1842 at the head of his class. Commissioned as second lieutenant and assigned by virtue of his high scholarship to the Engineer Corps, he was stationed for a brief period in Washington as assistant to the chief of engineers of the army. In 1843–45 he was placed in charge of the construction of Fort Warren and the Lovell's Island sea wall in Boston harbor; and he then spent two years in directing engineering operations at Newport. He was made assistant professor of engineering at West Point in 1847, but resigned on Nov. 30, 1849, in order to become professor of engineering at Harvard. There he organized the department of engineering in the Lawrence Scientific School, and was dean of the scientific faculty for 1862–63 and from 1871 until his death.

In 1862, although his health was far from good, Eustis secured leave of absence from Harvard in order to become colonel of the 10th Massachusetts Volunteers, and served with the VI Corps, Army of the Potomac, from August 1862 until June 1864. His regiment saw plenty of vigorous action, and he himself was under fire at Williamsport, Fredericksburg, Marye's Heights, Salem, Gettysburg, Rappahannock Station, Mine Run, the Wilderness, Spotsylvania, Cold Harbor, and other lesser engagements. Writing from the battle-field of the Wilderness on May 5, 1864, Eustis said, "Men fell like leaves in autumn; yet the regiment stood firm, never wavered." He was promoted brigadier-general of volunteers on Sept 12, 1863, but resigned from the army on June 27, 1864, because of impaired health. He returned to his college duties in the following autumn and held his Harvard professorship until the close of his life. During the two years before his death he suffered from a lung malady, and, although he courageously kept on with his work, was obliged slowly to reduce the amount of it which he could perform. His physicians sent him to Fernandina, Fla., but the trip did him no good, and he returned to Cambridge to die.

Eustis

Eustis was an unusual combination of the scholar and the man of action. He published many articles on technical and scientific subjects, and won a well-deserved reputation as an engineering authority. He was a fellow of the American Academy of Arts and Sciences and a member of several other learned societies. His interest in antiquarian researches led to the publication of his *Genealogy of the Eustis Family* (1878). On May 2, 1844, he married Sarah Augusta Eckley, by whom he had four children. She died on Jan. 10, 1853. He later married, July 10, 1856, Caroline Bartlett Hall, who bore him two children, and who survived him at his death.

[H. L. Eustis, *Genealogy* (1878); G. W. Cullum, *Biog. Reg.* (3rd ed., 1891); J. L. Chamberlain, *Harvard Univ.* (1900), in Universities and Their Sons; *Boston Transcript*, Jan. 12, 1885; other Boston newspapers; information from members of the Harvard faculty who knew Eustis personally.]
C. M. F.

EUSTIS, JAMES BIDDLE (Aug. 21, 1834–Sept. 9, 1899), statesman, diplomat, was born in the city of New Orleans. He was the fifth child of Judge George Eustis [*q.v.*] and Clarisse Allain Eustis, and a brother of George Eustis [*q.v.*], secretary to the Confederate legation at Paris during the Civil War. His education was obtained in the schools of his native city and at Harvard College, where the degree of LL.B. was conferred upon him in 1854. Two years later he was admitted to the Louisiana bar, and began practise in New Orleans. On Sept. 3, 1857, he married Ellen Buckner, the daughter of a prominent Louisiana planter. There were seven children by the marriage, five of whom survived infancy.

At the outbreak of the Civil War in 1861, Eustis entered the Confederate service. He first served as judge-advocate on the staff of Gen. Magruder, commander of the Trans-Mississippi Department, but after a year was transferred to the staff of Gen. Joseph E. Johnston, with whom he served to the end of the struggle. The war over, he returned to New Orleans and again practised law, but the chief interest of men of his section, during that transitional period from the old to the new régime in the South, was in state politics, and in these he soon became deeply involved. In 1866 he was elected to the state legislature, and was later appointed one of a commission to go to Washington to confer with President Johnson on conditions in Louisiana. During Reconstruction, he was an outstanding leader of the Louisiana Democrats. In 1872 he was nominated for Congress as a candidate-at-large, but was left off by a fusion of tickets. He was elected in this year, however, to the lower house of the state legislature, and in 1874 to the state Senate. While in the legislature he most vigorously opposed the repudiation of the state debts. In January 1876, the legislature elected him United States senator to fill an unexpired term, but in that day of factions and rival legislatures in Louisiana the election was contested, and it was not until Dec. 10, 1877, that he was declared duly elected and permitted to take his seat. His first term ended in the spring of 1879, but after the interval 1879–84, during which he was professor of civil law and lecturer on the land laws of the United States in the University of Louisiana, now the Tulane University of Louisiana, he was again elected to the Senate, taking his seat at the beginning of the special session, Mar. 4, 1885.

During his second term in the Senate, in opposing many of the official acts of President Cleveland, Eustis followed the example of many Southern Democrats. It is said that he carried his opposition to a point where he incurred the personal resentment of the President. When both were temporarily in political retirement, however, there was a reconciliation; and when Cleveland was again a presidential candidate, in 1892, Eustis gave him strong support in the North and East, where he was in great demand on account of his superior ability as an orator. His reward was an appointment as ambassador to France, where he represented his country with ability and distinction. At the end of his ambassadorship he practised law in New York City. He was a member of Tammany Hall, and, as long as health permitted, was active in the work of that organization. He died at his summer home at Newport, R. I.

[H. L. Eustis, *Geneal. of the Eustis Family* (1878); records of the Tulane University of La.; Alcée Fortier, *A Hist. of La.*, vol. IV (1904), and *Louisiana* (1914), vol. I; *Biog. Dir. Am. Cong.* (1928); obituary notice in the *Times-Democrat* (New Orleans), for Sept. 10, 1899; information from Dr. Allan Eustis of New Orleans.]
M. J. W.

EUSTIS, WILLIAM (June 10, 1753–Feb. 6, 1825), statesman, was born in Cambridge, Mass., the son of Benjamin Eustis, a well-known physician, and Elizabeth (Hill) Eustis. After preparing for college at the Boston Latin School, he entered Harvard, graduating with the class of 1772. He then studied medicine under Dr. Joseph Warren, later helping to care for the wounded after Bunker Hill and serving in the Revolutionary army, first as surgeon to the artillery regiment at Cambridge and finally as hospital surgeon. Following the war he carried on the practise of his profession in Boston, but he abandoned it for a time in order to accompany the expedition against Shays (1786–87) as surgeon. He was gradually drawn into politics as an Anti-Federalist and sat for six years (1788–94) in the Massachusetts General Court.

An early adherent of Jefferson, Eustis ran for Congress in 1800 against the Federalist, Josiah Quincy, and was successful after a hotly contested campaign. Two years later he had as his Federalist opponent the young John Quincy Adams, whom he defeated by 1,899 votes to 1,840. Adams later wrote (*Writings,* ed. by W. C. Ford, III, 1914, p. 10), "I had a majority of votes in Boston; but two or three neighboring towns annexed to the Congressional district and a rainy day lost me the election by forty or fifty votes." In 1804 Quincy was again a candidate, and this time Eustis was beaten. During his two terms in the House of Representatives, Eustis cast his vote consistently for the administration policies. In 1807 he was named by President Jefferson as secretary of war to succeed Gen. Henry Dearborn, and he continued in the same position in President Madison's cabinet. He defended the Embargo and Non-Intercourse Acts, and, with George Blake, took part in a notable debate in a Boston town meeting (Jan. 24, 1808) against Harrison Gray Otis and Samuel Dexter [*qq.v.*]. Eustis was in charge of the military affairs of the United States during the critical period leading up to the War of 1812. The War Department was poorly equipped to meet an emergency, but the secretary and his eight clerks set to work at the task of increasing the army and reorganizing it for active duty. Their efforts accomplished little, however, and as soon as the declaration of war was passed (June 18, 1812), everybody joined in the denunciation of Eustis. Henry Clay, in a letter to James Monroe (Aug. 12, 1812), spoke of Eustis as an official "in whom there exists no sort of confidence." Gallatin stated that Eustis's incompetence was universally admitted. In later years the best that Madison could say of him was that he was "an acceptable member of the cabinet" (*Writings,* ed. by G. Hunt, IX, 1910, p. 279). The situation really demanded a forceful and far-sighted leader, with a talent for organization, and Eustis, who had been described as "an amiable man and an efficient politician" (Edward Channing, *A History of the United States,* IV, 1917, p. 459), was not qualified to conduct military campaigns. When he resigned on Dec. 3, 1812, in the face of criticism, the War Department was taken over temporarily by James Monroe, who was also acting as secretary of state.

In 1814 Eustis was appointed by Madison as minister to Holland. He spent four years abroad, returning in 1818 because of ill health. It was impossible for him to keep out of politics, and, having been elected to Congress to fill a vacancy, he held a seat in that body from 1820 to 1823. For three successive years—1820, 1821, and 1822—he ran for governor of Massachusetts against the Federalist, John Brooks, also a physician and a Revolutionary veteran, and was beaten each time by approximately the same small majority. In 1823, when Brooks declined to be a candidate, Eustis defeated the conservative Harrison Gray Otis by a vote of 34,402 to 30,171, carrying not only all the previously Democratic counties, but also Essex, and Hampden, which had never before been in the Democratic column. Eustis's inaugural address, devoted principally to a denunciation of the Hartford Conventionists, provoked a quarrel between him and Otis, whom Eustis never forgave for some of his remarks (Adams, *Memoirs,* Sept. 22, 1824). In 1824 Eustis ran against Lathrop, defeating him by 38,650 to 34,210, in the last gubernatorial campaign in Massachusetts in which a Federalist was a candidate. During Eustis's administration as governor, he entertained Lafayette on the latter's visit to Boston in August 1824. Early in 1825, not long after his second inauguration, he caught a severe cold, which developed into pneumonia. His heart, which had not been strong for some time, weakened rapidly, and he died in his seventy-third year, in the very midst of the excitement aroused by the presidential election which resulted in the victory of his old rival, John Quincy Adams. His body lay in state in the capitol in Boston, and he was interred in the Granary Burying Ground with full military honors. At his death, Lieut.-Gov. Marcus Morton became acting governor.

Eustis was married, on Sept. 24, 1810, to Caroline Langdon, of Portsmouth, N. H., who survived him until 1865. They had no children. He purchased in 1819 the historic Shirley Mansion, in Roxbury, where he entertained in lavish style. He was vice-president of the Society of the Cincinnati from 1786 to 1810 and again in 1820, and delivered an oration before the order on July 4, 1791. A genial, courteous man, he made friends easily and was versed in all the arts of the politician. He was praised after his death for his "frankness of disposition and decision of character," but it was his urbanity, not his ability, which placed him in positions of authority.

[*Memoirs of John Quincy Adams,* vols. I, IV, V, VI (1874–75); S. E. Morison, *The Life and Letters of Harrison Gray Otis, Federalist, 1765–1848* (1913); Thos. Gray, *A Sermon on the Death of His Excellency,*

Wm. Eustis (1825); Justin Winsor, *The Memorial Hist. of Boston*, vol. III (1881); *Biog. Dir. Am. Cong.* (1928); H. L. Eustis, *Geneal. of the Eustis Family* (1878); *Boston Weekly Messenger*, Feb. 10, 1825; *Columbian Centinel*, Feb. 9, 1825.] C. M. F.

EVANS, ANTHONY WALTON WHYTE (Oct. 31, 1817–Nov. 28, 1886), civil engineer, was the eldest son of Thomas M. Evans of Virginia and his wife Eliza Whyte, daughter of Gen. Anthony Walton White of the Continental Army. Born in New Brunswick, N. J., Evans was educated at the Rensselaer Polytechnic Institute, graduating in 1836. After employment for some years on the enlargement of the Erie Canal, he became an assistant to Allan Campbell in the building of the New York & Harlem Railroad; and when, in 1849, Campbell was called to Chile to act as chief engineer of the Copiapo Railroad (from the Bay of Caldera to Copiapo, fifty miles inland), Evans accompanied him. Here he speedily laid the foundation of his fortune and professional fame. He supervised the completion of the Copiapo Railroad, after Campbell had left to undertake the building of another, and when its successfulness had been established, encouraging other states to venture into railroad building, he constructed the line from the seaport, Arica, to Tacna, the inland capital of the province which for years was in dispute between Peru and Chile.

After a visit to the United States, he took charge of the construction of a continuation of the Valparaiso-Santiago railroad extending from Santiago to the southern provinces of Chile; in this connection he made something of a reputation for the bridges he built across several torrential rivers. Upon the completion of this road Evans returned to the United States, opening an office in New York City as a consulting engineer. In this capacity, for the Peruvian railroads built by Henry Meiggs [*q.v.*], he designed the Varrugas viaduct on the Luna & Oroya Railroad. He also acted as agent for a number of foreign railroad companies operating in Australia and New Zealand as well as Central and South America. He purchased nearly all their rolling stock and other supplies and engaged their engineering staffs, disbursing in all several million dollars for his clients. He believed that American rolling stock was superior to that produced anywhere else, and was responsible for the introduction of American locomotives and cars into many foreign countries. His later work carried him over Europe, New Zealand, and Egypt, and while he was a champion of American ideas in railroad construction always, he did not close his eyes to merit elsewhere. He wrote an appreciative paper on the Abt system of railways for steep inclines and his last literary work, not published until after his death, was a letter comparing English and American railroads, which was included in vol. XV (1886) of the *Transactions of the American Society of Civil Engineers* and reprinted as a supplement to Edward Bates Dorsey's book, *English and American Railroads Compared* (1887). Another subject on which he expressed his views in writing, mainly in papers read before engineering societies, was the question of a route for the projected inter-oceanic canal. His preference was for the San Blas route, and he considered the suggestion of a sea-level canal at Panama "simply ridiculous."

Evans's house at New Rochelle was filled with rare books, pictures, and other works of art picked up on his travels, often as presents for his wife, Anna, who was the daughter of John C. Zimmerman, for many years consul-general of Holland in New York City. At his death, in his sixty-ninth year, Evans was survived only by a daughter.

[*Proc. Am. Soc. Civil Engineers*, vol. XIII (1887); H. B. Nason, *Biog. Record Grads. Rensselaer Polytechnic Inst.* (1887); *N. Y. Herald*, Nov. 29, 30, 1886; *Railroad Gazette*, Dec. 3, 1886.] E.Y.

EVANS, AUGUSTA JANE (May 8, 1835–May 9, 1909), author, was born in Columbus, Ga., the first of the eight children of Matthew Ryan and Sarah Skrine (Howard) Evans. The ancestors of both her father and mother were from South Carolina. She was educated almost entirely at home under the supervision of her mother. In the middle forties she went with her family to Texas, living successively in Galveston, Houston, and San Antonio. In 1849 they all returned East and soon took up residence in Mobile. When she was about fifteen or sixteen, she secretly wrote a novel, "Inez, a Tale of the Alamo," and when Christmas came round she presented the manuscript to her father. It was for the most part a jumble of love, war, and anti-Catholicism, set forth in sentences which sag with their own monstrous length, and teem with erudite mythological allusions and reverberating polysyllables. The book was published by the Harpers in 1855, anonymously, and without attracting wide notice. Her next novel was *Beulah* (1859). Like *Inez*, both pedantic and romantic, it attempted to deal with the problems of religious doubt then held so interesting. In little more than a year it ran through editions of 21,000 copies. During the Civil War, Augusta was fervent in the Southern cause. "The sole enthusiasm of my life," she said later, "was born, lived, and perished in the eventful four years of the Confederacy" (Manly, *post*). Some of this enthusiasm found expression in her *Macaria, or Altars of*

Evans

Sacrifice, published in Richmond in 1864. It was austere and pompous, but it accorded with popular taste in the North as well as in the South, and so disastrous was its effect on the morale of the Federal soldiery that certain officers ordered that copies of it be sought out and burned. Her next novel, *St. Elmo* (1866), does not touch upon the war. It is a story of how a simple maiden, Edna Earl, by force of her wisdom and virtue, reclaims for righteousness a sophisticated and sardonic lover. The parody which it seemed to invite was soon written by William Webb of the *New York Times.* It was called *St. Twel'mo,* and accounts for the turgidness of its original by the theory that Edna had as a child swallowed an unabridged dictionary. Nevertheless, *St. Elmo* achieved and maintained a wide popularity. In December 1868, Augusta Evans married Lorenzo Madison Wilson, a rich business man of Mobile. He was a widower with mature children, living at a pretentious country place several miles from town. Although as mistress of the house she was occupied with her domestic duties and family, she did not give up her writing; *Vashti,* a sad but moral story designed to warn young ladies against the sin of wilfulness, appeared in 1869. In 1875 she published *Infelice,* a chronicle of love in wedlock, and in 1887, *At the Mercy of Tiberius,* a mystery story. Her husband died in 1891, and she soon afterward moved into Mobile to live with her unmarried brother, John Howard Evans. In 1902 she published *A Speckled Bird,* dealing with events immediately following the Civil War. Her last book, *Devota* (1907), records her distrust of various social trends of that time, particularly the disposition of women to take part in public affairs. She died suddenly at her home.

[J. D. Freeman, "Mary Forrest," *Women of the South* (1861); J. W. Davidson, *Living Writers of the South* (1869); I. Raymond, *Southland Writers* (1870); J. C. Derby, *Fifty Years Among Authors* (1884); L. C. Holloway, *The Woman's Story* (1889); T. C. DeLeon, "Biog. Reminiscences of A. E. Wilson" in *Devota* (edition of 1913); L. Manly, "A. E. Wilson" in *Lib. of Southern Lit.,* vol. XIII (1910); T. McA. Owen, *Hist. of Ala. and Dict. of Ala. Biog.* (1921); *Mobile Register,* May 10, 1909.] J. D.W.

EVANS, CLEMENT ANSELM (Feb. 25, 1833–July 2, 1911), Confederate general, and historian, was born in Stewart County, Ga., the son of Anselm Lynch and Sarah Hinton (Bryan) Evans. His father's family was of Welsh origin, established first in Virginia and later removing to Georgia. Members of it served in the two wars with Great Britain and against the Creeks in Georgia. His mother's family was of English descent. His education was obtained in the public schools of Lumpkin, Ga., and at William Tracy Gould's law school in Augusta. Licensed to practise in the superior court at Augusta on Jan. 30, 1852, before he was nineteen, he entered partnership with Bedford S. Worrill and practised at Lumpkin. On Feb. 8, 1854, he married Allie Walton of Stewart County. He became judge of the inferior court of Stewart County in 1855, and was a member of the state Senate in 1859–61. A presidential elector in 1860, he voted for Breckinridge, and immediately after the election, in the expectation of war, helped to organize a local military company. He did not serve in it, however, but enlisted the next spring in the 31st Georgia Infantry, of which he was appointed major, being commissioned Nov. 19, 1861. Practically all of his service during the war was with the Army of Northern Virginia. His regiment, of which he became colonel in April 1862, was at first in Stonewall Jackson's division and then successively under Early and Gordon. Evans led his regiment in the Peninsular campaign, acted as brigade commander at times in 1862, including the latter part of the battle of Fredericksburg, and commanded his regiment at Gettysburg. Appointed brigadier-general in May 1864, he was assigned to the command of Gordon's old brigade, which he led in Early's raid against Washington —he was wounded at the battle of the Monocacy —and in the subsequent campaign in the Shenandoah Valley. In November 1864 he succeeded Gordon in the command of the division. At Appomattox, it is said, his division won the last fight of Lee's army. Notice that negotiations for surrender were in progress had reached neither Evans nor the Union troops opposing him, and Evans had just secured a local success, taking several guns and seventy-eight prisoners, when he received news that the surrender had taken place.

At Fredericksburg, in December 1862, he had been very much impressed and depressed by the carnage and suffering which he saw, and he later said that he made up his mind then that if he were allowed to survive the war he would spend the rest of his life trying to teach men how to live together instead of murdering each other. On his thirtieth birthday, Feb. 25, 1863, he resolved to enter the ministry, and after the war, in December 1865, he applied for admission to the North Georgia Conference of the Methodist Episcopal Church, South. The following year, as a circuit rider on Manassas Circuit, Bartow County, he began a ministry of more than twenty-five years. While a resident of Augusta, Ga., he ventured into business, organizing the Augusta Real Estate & Improvement Company and the Augusta & Summerville Land Company, and was a director of the Augusta Exposition Company. His first wife having died in 1884, on Oct. 14, 1887, he married Mrs. Sarah Avary Howard, of Decatur, Ga., who died in 1902. In 1892 he retired from the ministry, feeling himself unfit for parochial duties because of disability resulting from the five wounds he had received in the war.

All the latter part of his life was spent in Atlanta. Upon the organization of the United Confederate Veterans in 1889, he had been chosen as its "Adjutant General and Chief of Staff," and he continued active in the work of the organization for the rest of his life. For twelve years he was commander of its Georgia division, for three years commander of a department (of seven states), and in 1908 was elected commander-in-chief. He published a *Military History of Georgia* in 1895, and then undertook the editorship of the *Confederate Military History,* a work in twelve volumes which appeared in 1899. It deals chiefly with military operations, as its name promises, but includes several articles on other matters, Evans himself contributing to the first volume an extensive "Civil History of the Confederate States." A notable feature is the series of biographical sketches, usually accompanied by portraits, of all the general officers of the Confederate army. After the completion of this historical work, he interested himself in the movement for the establishment at Richmond of the Confederate Memorial Institute, the museum of history and art popularly known as the "Confederate Battle Abbey." He served as president of the organization until his death. The building was completed and opened some years later. He was co-editor with Allen D. Candler of *Georgia,* a three-volume work in cyclopedic form, published in 1906. Educational matters always interested him. He was trustee of three colleges, and helped in the establishment of a loan fund association which has assisted many young men in securing an education. He was also in charge of the finances of the Preachers Aid Association and held public office once more, as a member of the State Prison Commission.

[*Confed. Mil. Hist.* (1899), VI, 415–17; W. J. Northen, *Men of Mark in Georgia,* III (1911), 442–45; *Official Records (Army)*, 1 ser., vols. XXI, XLII (pt. 3), XLIII (pt. 1), LI (pt. 1); *Christian Advocate* (Nashville), July 7, 1911; *Atlanta Constitution* and *Sun* (Baltimore), July 3, 1911; information as to certain facts from a son, Lawton B. Evans, Esq., of Augusta, Ga.]

T. M. S.

EVANS, EDWARD PAYSON (Dec. 8, 1831–Mar. 6, 1917), man of letters, was born in Remsen, Oneida County, N. Y., the son of Evan and Mary (Williams) Evans. His parents were natives of North Wales; his father was a Presbyterian minister. After his graduation in 1854 from the University of Michigan, Evans acted for one year as principal of an academy at Hernando, Miss., taught languages for another year in Carroll College at Waukesha, Wis., and then went to Europe. For three years he studied at the Universities of Göttingen, Berlin, and Munich, and in Germany he found his second mother country. Returning in 1862 to the United States, he was appointed instructor in modern languages in the University of Michigan and promoted the next year to a professorship. His literary career began inconspicuously with translations of Adolf Stahr's two-volume *Life and Works of Gotthold Ephraim Lessing* (1866) and Athanase Josué Coquerel's *First Historical Transformations of Christianity* (1867), and with two text-books, an *Abriss der Deutschen Literaturgeschichte* (1869) and a *Progressive German Reader* (1869, 1870). On May 23, 1868, he married Elizabeth Edson Gibson (Mar. 8, 1832–Sept. 14, 1911), daughter of Willard Putnam and Lucia Field (Williams) Gibson. She was born in Newport, N. H., and at the time of her marriage was living in Ann Arbor. In 1870 Evans resigned his professorship. A few months later he settled as a private scholar and free-lance journalist in his beloved Munich, and before long his high, broad forehead and flowing beard were a permanent feature of the Royal Library.

He devoted himself at first to the study of Sanskrit, Zend, and modern Persian, published articles on Oriental literature, and was offered in 1873 the professorship of Sanskrit in the University of Lahore. An incessant student, he became learned in a half dozen subjects and more than well informed in a score, but his taste ran to the devious and the abstruse. Few heads in his generation could have held more, or more diverse, information than his; and the yeast of thought kept all his knowledge in a genial ferment. He wrote regularly for several German periodicals, especially for the *Allgemeine Zeitung* of Munich, whose staff he joined in 1884, and with less frequency for English and American magazines, including the *Atlantic Monthly,* the *Unitarian Review,* and the *Popular Science Monthly.* His articles on American subjects were gathered into two volumes of *Beiträge zur Amerikanischen Literatur- und Kulturgeschichte* (Stuttgart, 1898, 1903), but his best and most characteristic work is preserved in three fascinating volumes on *Animal Symbolism in Ecclesiastical Architecture* (1896), *Evolutional Ethics and Animal Psychology* (1897), and *Criminal Prosecution and Capital Punishment of Animals* (1904). The first and third are erudite studies in medieval art and law. The second is one of those freaks of scholarship which brilliant but self-taught men produce from time to time; incredible as zoölogy, its stories of sagacious birds and beasts are delightful as literature. All three are written lucidly and vivaciously and bear the stamp of a highly original mind. Mrs. Evans also engaged in authorship. Besides writing for various English and American magazines she published: *The Abuse of Maternity* (1875), *A History of Religions* (1892), *The Story of Kaspar Hauser* (1892), *The Story of Louis XVII of France* (1893)—in which she argued for the claim of Eleazer Williams—*Ferdinand Lassalle and Helene von Dönniges, a Modern Tragedy* (1897), *The Christ Myth, a Study* (1900), and three ephemeral novels. She possessed real ability, but her work is pale and savourless beside her husband's. In 1906 the Evanses moved to Bad Aibling, in the mountains, some forty miles southeast of Munich. Mrs. Evans died in 1911, and in 1914 the outbreak of the European War compelled the aged and lonely scholar to break his long expatriation and return to the United States. Making Cambridge, Mass., his headquarters, he continued to work on an extensive history of German literature, which he had begun soon after his wife's death. Later he moved to New York City, where, in the anxious month preceding the declaration of war with Germany, he died. He was survived by his nephew and adopted son, Lawrence Boyd Evans [*q.v.*].

[*Who's Who in America*, 1899–1917; *N. Y. Times*, Mar. 8, 1917; B. A. Hinsdale, *Hist. of the Univ. of Mich.* (1906), with portrait.] G. H. G.

EVANS, EVAN (1671–1721), Anglican clergyman, second rector of Christ Church, Philadelphia, and active during the first twenty years of the eighteenth century in building up the Anglican Church in the American colonies, was born in Carnoe, Montgomery County, Wales, son of Evan David Evans (Joseph Foster, *Alumni Oxonienses, Early Series*). His family must have been without property, for he matriculated on Mar. 12, 1692 (N.S.) at St. Alban Hall, Oxford, as a pauper scholar and a batteler, a rank between that of a commoner and a servitor. During his first year at Oxford he was fortunate in securing an Ogle scholarship which gave him some slight financial help. In 1695 he received the degree of B.A. from Brasenose College (*Brasenose College Register*, 1909, vol. I, 260), and he may have been rector of Gwaynysgor, Flints, in 1697 (Joseph Foster, *Alumni Oxonienses, 1500–1714*, 1891). In 1700 the Bishop of London sent him out to the colonies as rector of Christ Church, Philadelphia. For about seventeen years he served that church, receiving only the Royal bounty of £50 and whatever contributions the church members chose to make. At the same time he preached without compensation at Montgomery and Radnor, and introduced services in Chester, Chichester, Concord, Oxford, and Perkiomen. Before 1707, largely as a result of his effort and enthusiasm, churches were built at Oxford, Chester, and Newcastle. He preached so persuasively in his native tongue that he kept many Welsh communities from turning non-conformist; and under his influence large numbers of Quakers forsook their own faith and joined the Anglican Church. His interest extended to the other colonies. He conferred with fellow churchmen in New York, and constantly urged the authorities in England to send a bishop to the colonies. His letters are examples of scholarly English and forceful argument, but he was unable to secure a bishop for the American church.

The Bishop of London recognized Evans's ability as a preacher, and in 1707, when the Rector was in England, recommended him to the Society for the Propagation of the Gospel in Foreign Parts as a missionary to Welshmen in America. At that time Queen Anne presented him with communion plate for his church in Philadelphia. The necessity of enlarging the Philadelphia church in 1711 is another evidence of his success in that community.

On returning to America from his last voyage to England, 1714, Evans accepted appointment from the Society for the Propagation of the Gospel to act as missionary at Radnor and Oxford. According to the vestry minutes of Christ Church, he continued to act as rector in Philadelphia until 1718 when he resigned from all his labors in Pennsylvania and accepted a presentment by the governor of Maryland to the church of Spesutia in St. George's Parish, near the present village of Perryman, Harford County. By his will, dated May 25, 1721, and proved on Nov. 10 of the same year, he left a small personal estate and fifteen hundred acres of land in Philadelphia. He was survived by his wife, Alice, and an only child, a daughter, who had married an English rector by the name of Lloyd.

[Wm. S. Perry, *Hist. Colls. Relating to the Am. Colonial Church*, vols. II (1871) and IV (1878); Wm. B. Sprague, *Annals Am. Pulpit*, vol. V (1859); Benj. Dorr, *A Hist. Account of Christ Church, Phila., from Its Foundation* (1841); L. C. Washburn, *Christ Church, Phila.* (1925).] D. M. C.

EVANS, FREDERICK WILLIAM (June 9, 1808–Mar. 6, 1893), reformer and Shaker elder, was born in Leominster, Worcestershire, England, the son of George and Sarah (White)

Evans. His father was of English middle-class stock and held a commission in the British army; his mother appears to have been of somewhat better family. When Frederick was four years of age his mother died, and the boy was cared for by her relatives who sent him to school at Stourbridge. Here he remained, with apparently little profit to himself, until he was eight years old, when his formal schooling came to an end and he joined his aunts and uncles at Chadwick Hall, a large, well-ordered, and successful farm near Worcester. Life could not have been very stimulating intellectually at Chadwick Hall, but it did develop in young Evans a vigorous and sturdy body, together with an understanding of farm management which he was able to put to use in after years. In 1820 with his father and his brother he sailed for the United States; they settled in Binghamton, N. Y., already the home of two of Frederick's uncles. The rugged, bright, but rather illiterate country boy felt sorely the need of a better education, and eventually removed to Ithaca, where the Episcopal minister became his friend and teacher. From Ithaca he went to Sherburne Four Corners, N. Y., and apprenticed himself to a hatter. Here he had access to more books, and the character of his reading inclined him to materialism. He was, therefore, a ready convert to Owenism, and in his enthusiasm actually walked eight hundred miles to join an Owenite community at Massillon, Ohio. The community failed, however, and in the spring of 1829 Evans went back to England where he remained for nearly a year. Returning to New York City in January 1830, he joined the little group of freethinkers and reformers gathered about Fanny Wright, Robert Dale Owen, Robert L. Jennings, and his brother George Henry Evans [*q.v.*], with whose views he heartily sympathized. Combining his means with those of his brother, he assisted him in editing and publishing successively the *Working Man's Advocate*, the *Daily Sentinel*, and *Young America*, as well as a great variety of other publications including the *Bible of Reason*. All of these publications were devoted to radical reform in one field or another, but the brothers put most emphasis upon labor, educational, and land reform. In the midst of this activity Evans visited the community of the United Society of Believers, the Shaker community, at Mount Lebanon, N. Y. So impressed was he with what he saw and learned of Shaker life and doctrine that, after a lengthy visit, to the utter astonishment of his fellow freethinkers in New York City, he joined the society. His final conversion was due, he says, to the spiritual manifestations made to himself alone during several weeks. There was, in truth, no little of the mystic in Evans's character, and to this the element of spiritualism in Shakerism made a strong appeal. Evans's conversion proved thoroughgoing and permanent. For sixty-three years he remained with the North Family at Mount Lebanon and for fifty-seven years presided over the Family as elder. "A born leader and a natural orator," he became in time one of the most prominent of the Shaker leaders in the country, and, through his preaching and writing, did much to clarify and shape Shaker doctrine and practise. His publications in this field include: *Tests of Divine Inspiration* (1853); *A Short Treatise on the Second Appearing of Christ in and through the Order of the Female* (1853); *Ann Lee, a Biography, etc.* (1858), published later under the title, *Shakers. Compendium of the Origin, History, Principles* [etc.] *of the United Society of Believers; Celibacy from the Shaker Standpoint* (1866); *Shaker Communism* (1871); *The Universal Church* (1872). He also published, in 1869, the *Autobiography of a Shaker, and Revelation of the Apocalypse, With an Appendix*. In 1871 and again in 1887 he visited England in the rôle of Shaker missionary, on the last occasion also visiting Scotland. In person he was tall, strong, and vigorous, with "regular and systematic habits." He was a vegetarian for nearly sixty years. As might be expected from his interest in reform, his was "a nature susceptible to the weal or woe of mankind," while "indomitable will, perseverance, persistency, and a determination to carry out what he believed to be his duty to God and humanity, gave him great force of character and made effective his efforts for good" (*Immortalized*, p. 15). Elder Rayson added, however, in his remarks on the death of Elder Evans: "Though firm and uncompromising when principle was at stake, and firm in his adherence to right, yet he had a tender and loving nature, and his love was reciprocated by those who knew him best" (*Ibid.*, pp. 26–27). Evans died at Mount Lebanon in his eighty-fifth year.

[The principal sources of information are Evans's *Autobiography of a Shaker* and *Immortalized: Elder Frederic W. Evans. Affectionately inscribed to the memory of Elder Frederic W. Evans, by his Loving and Devoted Gospel Friends* (1893). See also *N. Y. Tribune*, *N. Y. Times*, Mar. 7, 1893. His writings not noted above are listed in J. P. MacLean, *Bibliography of Shaker Literature* (1905).] W. R. W.

EVANS, GEORGE (Jan. 12, 1797–Apr. 6, 1867), lawyer, politician, was the son of Daniel and Joanna (Hains) Evans and was born in Hallowell, Me. He graduated from Bowdoin College in 1815, was admitted to the bar three years later, and began practise in Gardiner, where he lived for the greater part of his life. In October 1820 he married Ann Dearborn. In 1825 he was elected to the legislature as a National Republican, serving until 1829, the last year as speaker. In 1829 he began a period of twelve years' service in the national House of Representatives. During his first term he made a notable speech (May 18, 1830) opposing the Georgia land policy and the removal of the Indians, but his chief interests were, from the first, in the field of public finance. He was a strong supporter of the protective tariff, internal improvements, and the United States Bank. Among his great speeches in the House might be mentioned his reply to McDuffie on the tariff, June 11, 1832 (*Register of Debates in Congress,* 22 Cong., 1 Sess., pp. 3421 ff.); on the removal of the deposits from the United States Bank, Feb. 3 and Apr. 21, 1834 (*Ibid.,* 23 Cong., 1 Sess., pp. 2574 ff., and pp. 3715 ff.); and on the fortifications bill of the preceding session, Jan. 28, 1836, in which he had a memorable clash with John Quincy Adams (*Ibid.,* 24 Cong., 1 Sess., pp. 2414 ff.). The latter described him (*Memoirs,* IX, 1876, p. 388) as "one of the ablest men and most eloquent orators in Congress. His powers of reasoning and of pathos, his command of language and his elocution, are not exceeded by any member of this Congress; much superior to the last." Adams, like other contemporaries, also commented on his remarkable knowledge of parliamentary law and his mastery of the rules, precedents, and floor tactics of the House.

In 1841 he entered the Senate, and, regardless of seniority rules, was made chairman of its committee on finance, a tribute to the reputation he had made as a minority member of the ways and means committee of the House. He held this position throughout the Twenty-seventh and Twenty-eighth Congresses and was responsible for much of their revenue legislation. Most of his speeches were on financial topics, and in the course of debate on July 25, 1846, Webster, referring to Evans's approaching retirement from the Senate, declared that his understanding of revenue and financial questions generally was equal to that of Gallatin or Crawford. James G. Blaine also described him as "a man of commanding power" and "entitled to rank next to Mr. Webster" among New England senators (*Twenty Years of Congress,* I, 1884, p. 70).

In 1847 the Maine legislature was Democratic and Evans accordingly was obliged to retire. His support of the Webster-Ashburton Treaty, very unpopular in his own state, is reported to have injured him politically and to have led to certain intrigues in the following year which prevented his appointment to a position in President Taylor's cabinet. It had been hoped by his friends that he would become secretary of the treasury. He served for two years, however, as chairman of the commission on Mexican claims and in 1851, refusing the offer of several other federal posts, returned to Maine. He resumed the practise of law and in 1854 removed from Gardiner to Portland. He served as attorney-general of the state in 1853, 1854, and 1856, but the collapse of the Whig party and sundry personal feuds following the convention of 1852 had apparently left him without party affiliations and his conservative temperament made him suspicious of the new Republican organization. He is said to have voted the Democratic ticket in his later years, but his active political career had ended. His practise was large and he had a number of important business interests, serving for some years as president of the Portland & Kennebec Railroad Company. He was an active member of the Maine Historical Society for the greater part of his life, an Overseer for nineteen and a trustee of Bowdoin College for twenty-two years (1826–67). His career, however, shows how readily, under such conditions as prevailed in the fifties, a leader of first-rate ability may be sidetracked, and fail to attain the enduring fame which apparently he merited. To this failure his own inability to grasp the overwhelming importance of slavery as a moral and political issue undoubtedly contributed.

[Biographical notice by R. H. Gardiner, based in large part on newspaper obituaries, published in *Me. Hist. Soc. Colls.,* VII (1876), 457–71; L. C. Hatch, *Maine* (1919), I, 242; *Am. Review; A Whig Journal,* July 1847; N. Cleaveland and A. S. Packard, *Hist. of Bowdoin Coll. with Biog. Sketches of its Grads.* (1882), pp. 182–84; *Biog. Dir. Am. Cong.* (1928); obituaries in *Bangor Daily Evening Times,* and *Bangor Daily Whig and Courier,* Apr. 9, 1867.] W. A. R.

EVANS, GEORGE ALFRED (Oct. 1, 1850–July 14, 1925), physician, a pioneer in the sanatorium and climatic treatment of pulmonary tuberculosis, was born in Brooklyn. His father, Norris Evans, a carriage manufacturer, was of Welsh, and his mother, Sarah Ann Decker, of Holland-Dutch extraction. He attended the local public schools and in 1866, after a course of study at the Hudson River Institute, Claverack, N. Y., entered the Pennsylvania State Agricultural College, from which he graduated in 1870. During the last two years at this institution he pursued studies which were preparatory to a medical training. In the fall of 1870 he registered as a pupil with Prof. James R. Wood [*q.v.*], a well-known surgeon of New York City and entered Bellevue Hospital Medical College, then a new institution, in 1871. Before his graduation in 1873 he served as interne in the New York City Insane Asylum. He at once opened an office in the family residence in Bedford Ave., Brooklyn, but after a year of practise went to Germany to perfect himself in certain branches of the fundamentals of medicine. He confined his studies to the University of Würzburg, and the names of his teachers suggest that he gave especial attention to histology and pathology and probably also to obstetrics and diseases of women and children. Upon his return in 1875 he reëstablished himself in practise and in 1876 he secured an appointment as visiting physician to the Atlantic Avenue Dispensary. In the same year he read before the Kings County Medical Society his first paper on a medical subject, which dealt with the pathological histology of the heart. In 1878 he married Emma Wilmot of Bridgeport, Conn., and in 1879 he aided in founding the Bushwick and East Brooklyn Hospital and Dispensary of which he became visiting physician. Three years later his wife developed pulmonary consumption and he was obliged to take her to Texas, where for two years he practised medicine at San Antonio and at Boerne. In addition to an active general practise, which kept him much in the saddle, he served as head of an embryo sanitarium. The life was full of excitement through the proximity of hostile Indians and bad white men; and he had charge of the case of one Ben Thompson, known as the "last of the desperadoes." As his wife failed progressively Evans was obliged to return North in 1884, in which year Mrs. Evans died. He reëstablished himself at his former Brooklyn residence where he practised until his retirement in 1907. His attention, as a result of his personal experience, had now become focused on the treatment of pulmonary tuberculosis and he became known preëminently as a specialist in diseases of the chest. In 1887 he married as his second wife Zoa L. Macumber. He began to write articles on the treatment of respiratory diseases. He also went exhaustively into the climatological treatment of consumption and published several writings, during 1888–90, which are said to have created a sensation and to have inaugurated the movement which was to make of the lower Catskill region a climatological resort for consumptives. His principal publication was his *Handbook of Historical and Geographical Phthisiology* (1888). His retirement in 1907 was due to heart disease, to which he finally succumbed at the age of seventy-five. Consumption when Evans began to study it seriously was still regarded as practically incurable, and, although he was not as well known to the public as his contemporary, E. L. Trudeau [*q.v.*], he was, according to his colleagues, a force in showing the possibility of cure.

[Manuscript data supplied by Evans's son, Dr. John Norris Evans of 23 Schermerhorn St., Brooklyn; obituaries in *Jour. Am. Medic. Asso.*, Aug. 1, 1925; *Brooklyn Daily Eagle, N. Y. Times,* July 15, 1925.] E. P.

EVANS, GEORGE HENRY (Mar. 25, 1805–Feb. 2, 1856), land reformer, editor of the first labor papers in America, was born at Bromyard, Herefordshire, England, of a lower middle-class family. His parents were George and Sarah (White) Evans. He came to the United States with his father and brother in 1820 and soon became apprenticed to a printer at Ithaca, N. Y. Together with his brother, Frederick William [*q.v.*], he studied the writings of Thomas Paine and the other atheists of the day, with the result that both became confirmed atheists. His brother, however, after a visit to the Shaker community at Mount Lebanon, N. Y., in 1830, abandoned atheism for the religious communism of the Shakers, and subsequently became the most prominent member of that body in America. George Henry, on the other hand, remained an atheist for the rest of his life. He edited *The Man* at Ithaca about 1822, the *Working Man's Advocate* in New York City at various times from 1829 to 1845, and the *Daily Sentinel* and *Young America* at intervals from 1837 to 1853. After 1837 he spent a good deal of his time on a farm in New Jersey where he formulated his principles of agrarianism. His views were similar to those of Henry George [*q.v.*]. From 1827 to 1837 a series of working men's parties developed in Philadelphia, New York, and New England. The first number of Evans's paper, the *Working Man's Advocate,* contained reports of the working men's meetings in New York City in October 1829, and editorials advocating the working men's ticket. Evans took a leading part in the activities of the working men and described his paper as "designed solely to protect and advance their interests."

In 1840 he published a *History of the Origin and Progress of the Working Men's Party* in New York as a warning against the mistakes of that movement and a preparation for a new agrarianism. His theories were produced in opposition to the doctrines of association, Fourierism, and Owenism which were importations from Europe. His land reform was the direct outgrowth of the individualism of Thomas Paine and Thomas Jefferson. It employed the same theories of natural rights to overthrow the power of landed property that they had employed to bring to an end British rule in America. The line of argument was as follows: man's right to life is the source of all other rights. This implies a right to use the materials of nature such as light, air, water, and soil. All others, such as liberty, labor, capital, and education, are acquired or derived. He therefore advocated the right of every man to an inalienable homestead limited to 160 acres, the abolition of all laws for the collection of debts and of imprisonment for debt, the abolition of chattel slavery and wages slavery, and equal rights for women. He condemned monopolies, among which he classed the United States Bank. For more than a quarter of a century he devoted his energies to agitation for land reform. His program of "free homesteads" influenced the labor movement forty years before Henry George's "single tax." They had a common diagnosis and in general held the same theory of treatment, only differing in the method of applying the cure. Evans died at Granville, N. J., in his fifty-first year.

[John R. Commons, *Hist. of Labour in the U. S.* (1918), I, 5, 234, 237, 242–44, 461, 522–31, 537, 559, and *A Doc. Hist. of Am. Industrial Society* (1910), vols. V, VII, VIII, IX; W. D. P. Bliss, *The New Encyc. of Social Reform* (4th ed., 1908), p. 450; Selig Perlman, *A Theory of the Labor Movement* (1928), pp. 176–89; obituary in *N. Y. Tribune*, Feb. 11, 1856.]

F. E. H.

EVANS, HENRY CLAY (June 18, 1843–Dec. 12, 1921), industrialist, politician, was born in Juniata County, Pa., the son of Col. Jesse B. Evans and his wife, Anna Single, both natives of that state. The colonel, who acquired his title in the state militia, was a pioneer in the manufacture of railway cars. When Henry was three years of age, the family removed to Lafayette County, Wis., and here the boy was reared. His father followed the gold rush to California in 1849 and died in Montana in 1869; but the family did not follow him on his wanderings. Young Henry Clay went to school and worked on the farm, and later was employed as a clerk in the office of an older brother who was register of deeds for the county (Scrap-book, *post*).

In the spring of 1864 he joined the Union army and did some campaigning in the neighborhood of Chattanooga. In September of that year he was honorably discharged from the service and secured clerical work with the quartermaster department at Chattanooga. He remained in this position until 1867 when he was sent to the Mexican border in a similar capacity. Here he worked for two years, and then journeyed to Westfield, N. Y., where on Feb. 18, 1869, he married Adelaide Durand. The following year he returned to Chattanooga where he made his home for the remainder of his life. On taking up his permanent residence, he at once became interested in the manufacture of railway cars and organized the Chattanooga Car & Foundry Company. After having controlled this business for two years, he became an official in the Roane Iron Company. He remained for a decade in this work, rising from the position of superintendent of the plant to that of vice-president and general manager. At the end of that time he went back to the Car Company and retained an important interest in it for many years. He was a leading stockholder in several other important local industries.

In 1872, shortly after coming to Chattanooga, he was made school commissioner for the town and took a leading part in the organization of its educational system. In 1873 he was elected alderman, and he served several years in that capacity. In 1881 and again in 1882 he was elected mayor; and in 1884 he made his first race for Congress. Since he was a Republican and his district was normally Democratic, he was defeated in this contest, but cut down the opposition majority to a fraction of its former strength. In 1888 he ran again and this time was successful. During his term in the House of Representatives, he supported the Lodge "force bill" as a matter of party loyalty and against his private convictions. As a result of this action, he failed of reëlection in 1890 (Moore and Foster, *post*, II, 15). Three years later, he was appointed first assistant postmaster-general by President Harrison. In 1894 he was the nominee of his party for the governorship of Tennessee, Judge Peter Turney, the incumbent, being the Democratic candidate. Evans received a plurality vote, but Turney contested the election and a Democratic legislature decided in favor of the plaintiff (*Contest for Governor: Peter Turney, Contestant, vs. H. Clay Evans, Contestee*, 1895). The decision was thoroughly partisan, and it made a national figure of the defeated candidate. In 1896 he ran next to Hobart in the balloting for the vice-presidential nominee of the Republican party, and the following year he was appointed commissioner of pensions by President McKinley, which position he held until 1902. In that year President Roosevelt sent him to London as consul-general, where he remained until 1905.

At the end of this service, he retired to private life at his home in Chattanooga. Gradually he disposed of his major business interests and began to live less strenuously. Once more, however, he was called upon to assume an active rôle. When Chattanooga adopted the commission form of government in 1911, he was elected, on a non-partisan ticket, commissioner of education and health. In this capacity he served a full term of four years, giving all his time to the work. Thus his political career ended as it had begun—in connection with the school system of the city. When he died suddenly, on Dec. 12, 1921, the mayor closed the municipal offices for half a day to do honor to his memory.

[J. T. Moore and A. P. Foster, *Tennessee, the Volunteer State* (1923); Goodspeed Pub. Co., *Hist. of Tenn., Hamilton County Suppl.* (1887), pp. 938–39; *East Tennessee Hist. and Biog.* (1893), p. 228; Scrap-book, clippings on prominent men of Tennessee, sketch of H. Clay Evans, 1906, in Tenn. State Lib.; *Who's Who in America,* 1920–21; *Chattanooga Daily Times,* Dec. 13 and 14, 1921.]
T. P. A.

EVANS, HUGH DAVEY (Apr. 26, 1792–July 16, 1868), lawyer, lay-theologian, and editor of church periodicals, was born in Baltimore, Md., and there spent practically his entire life. He was the son of Joseph and Elizabeth (Davey) Evans and was named after the latter's father, Hugh Davey, a native of Londonderry, Ireland. His own father, whom he never knew, "a merchant in a small way and unfortunate in business," was of Welsh and English descent, son of George Evans, a Baptist deacon, and Rachel Gilpin, a Quakeress. Hugh was brought up in straitened circumstances by his mother, a communicant of the Episcopal Church, of which he was to become a widely known layman. Largely because of his devotion to her—she lived to be eighty-eight—he never married. His schooling was limited, but being from childhood an omnivorous reader, especially of history, he acquired a large stock of information. Beginning the study of law at eighteen, he was admitted to practise on Apr. 19, 1815. Not being "an adroit man of business" or well versed in human nature, he was not a particularly successful practitioner. Nothing he ever did brought him much financial remuneration and he lived a life of simplicity and self-denial. He had the reputation, however, of being learned in the law and was often special judge for trials of causes. In 1817 he was appointed reading clerk to one of the branches of the city council and in 1825 was employed to revise the city ordinances. He began the publication of legal works in 1827, issuing that year *An Essay on Pleading with a View to an Improved System.* This was followed by *Modern Entries, or Approved Precedents, of Declarations, Pleadings, Entries, and Writs* (2 vols., 1831–32), a revision of Thomas Harris's work; and *Maryland Common Law Practice, a Treatise on the Course of Proceedings in the Common Law Courts of the State of Maryland* (1839), a revised edition of which appeared in 1867. He was also an active member of the Maryland State Colonization Society and prepared the legal code for the Colony of Maryland in Liberia.

As time went on his interest in the history, polity, and doctrines of the Protestant Episcopal Church grew more and more absorbing. He had adopted High Church principles and came to be regarded as an authoritative exponent of them. His first theological article appeared in the *Protestant Episcopalian,* May 1835, and was a discussion of the validity of lay baptism. In 1843 he assumed the editorship of *The True Catholic,* a newly established monthly published under the patronage of Bishop Whittingham [*q.v.*] of Maryland. This paper he conducted with ability, writing a majority of the leading articles himself, until it went out of existence at the close of 1856. He was also a regular contributor to *The Register* (1852–53), a newspaper published in Philadelphia in the interest of the Protestant Episcopal Church; to *The Churchman* (1854–56), and *The American Church Monthly* (1857–58), both issued in New York; and during 1857 and 1858 he was editor of *The Monitor,* a weekly paper published in Baltimore by Joseph Robinson. His writings include: *Essays to Prove the Validity of Anglican Ordinations* (1844); 2nd series, 2 vols. (1851); *Theophilus Americanus; or Instructions for the Young Student Concerning the Church and the American Branch of It. Chiefly from the Fifth Edition of Theophilus Anglicanus. By Chr. Wordsworth, D.D., Canon of Westminster . . .* (1851, 1852, 1870); *An Essay on the Episcopate of the Protestant Episcopal Church in the United States* (1855); and *A Treatise on the Christian Doctrine of Marriage* (1870). He was prominent in the conventions of the Diocese of Maryland, and a deputy to all the General Conventions from 1847 until the outbreak of the Civil War, his Union sympathies preventing his election to the Convention of 1862. From 1852 to 1864 he was lecturer on civil and ecclesiastical law in the College of St. James, Washington County, Md., the title and duties of the office finally being changed so as to include lectures on history. Those he delivered in this field were chiefly on the English Constitution. He died in Baltimore and as stipulated in his will he was buried in his mother's grave in St. Paul's Churchyard.

[Hall Harrison, *Hugh Davey Evans, LL.D., A Memoir Founded Upon Recollections Written by Himself* (1870), contains bibliography which lists over a hundred of his contributions to the *True Catholic* and *The American Church Monthly.* An abridgment of same, with bibliography, is prefixed to Evans's *A Treatise on the Christian Doctrine of Marriage* (1870). See also sketch by Hall Harrison in *Am. Church Review,* Feb. 1884; the *Sun* (Baltimore), July 18, 1868.]
H. E. S.

EVANS, JOHN (fl. 1703–1731), deputy governor of Pennsylvania from 1703 to 1707, was of Welsh descent. His father, Thomas Evans, is said to have been a seafaring man, a friend of William Penn. Before coming to Pennsylvania in 1704, John Evans had apparently traveled; and he had a love of literature which led him to bring some books with him. He had been appointed deputy governor by William Penn the year before his arrival. The proprietor wrote of Evans to James Logan, secretary of the province: "He shows not much, but has a good deal to show, and will gain upon the esteem of the better sort. He has travelled and seen armies, but never been in them. Book learning as to men and government he inclines to . . ." (Neill, *post*). As governor of a sober Quaker colony, however, he was an unfortunate choice. His pleasure-loving disposition shocked the colonists. With his companion, the younger William Penn, he led a gay, and probably wild, life. Pennsylvanians reported stories of their delinquencies: tales of riots in taverns, of hand to hand combats with local authorities—a constable on one occasion, an alderman on another. His love affairs brought him further disrepute, until, 1709, he married Rebecca Moore, daughter of John Moore, advocate of the Admiralty court. Evans was a stanch Anglican, anxious to further the interests of the church in America, as he assured the Society for the Propagation of the Gospel (*Historical Collections Relating to the American Colonial Church,* 1878, II, 25; V, 8). That fact alone would have made him objectionable to the Quakers.

He came to America at a time when the proprietorship was in a precarious state, due to attacks of the Crown, disagreements between Pennsylvania and the Lower Counties, and general dissatisfaction of the inhabitants with the government. With the help of Secretary Logan [*q.v.*], Evans tried to uphold the authority of the absent proprietor against the opposition of David Lloyd [*q.v.*], deputy judge, later chief justice of the province, and his associates. He was handicapped by the fact that his powers were not clearly defined. He aroused the wrath of the Assembly by vetoing several bills, including a provision to establish courts, issuing instead an ordinance for the administration of justice. He prorogued the Assembly in spite of its claim to the privilege of adjournment. The Assembly refused to make the necessary appropriation for defending Pennsylvania in the second colonial war with France; and the colonists criticized Evans for the methods to which he resorted. In the spring of 1706 the Quakers were especially indignant because Evans and his friends circulated a rumor that a French naval force was coming up the bay—a ruse to frighten the Quakers into joining the volunteer militia. The merchants of Pennsylvania protested to the proprietor against the erection of a fort at Newcastle, for the commander of the fort was to charge with tonnage duty in powder all vessels passing up or down the river. Inhabitants of the colony seized the commander, and this project for securing means of defense ended in failure. Evans was now bitterly hated, especially by the Quakers. In 1707 the Pennsylvania Assembly sent to William Penn a list of charges against the governor, and after learning from Logan and others that Evans was unsatisfactory, the proprietor appointed a successor. Little is known of Evans's subsequent career. Upon leaving America he retired to Pentry Manor, Denbigh, Wales, where as late as 1731 he was still living.

[Herbert L. Osgood, *The American Colonies in the Eighteenth Century* (1924), II, 262–79; E. D. Neill, "Memoir of John Evans," in *New-Eng. Hist. and Geneal. Reg.,* Oct. 1872.] D. M. C.

EVANS, JOHN (Mar. 9, 1814–July 3, 1897), physician, founder of universities, and railroad builder, attained to prominence in three states, Indiana, Illinois, and Colorado. His birthplace was Waynesville, Ohio. David and Rachel (Burnet) Evans, his parents, were Quakers; the former a successful farmer and storekeeper in a small town, the latter a very religious woman and for a time a crusader against the liquor traffic. From both John inherited qualities that manifested themselves in later life. After attending the schools of Waynesville, he was sent in succession to the Academy at Richmond, Ind., Gwynedd Boarding School for Boys, in Pennsylvania, and Clermont Academy, near Philadelphia. While at Clermont he decided to become a physician. His parents disapproving, he accepted aid from friends, entered Lynn Medical College, Cincinnati, in 1836, and graduated in 1838. He immediately began the practise of medicine, and in the same year was married.

After a year spent in seeking an abiding place, the young physician settled with his wife, Hannah Canby, in Attica, Ind. The characteristics that were to make him eminent appeared immediately. Successful and prominent in his profession, he was at the same time the builder and owner of a profitable business block. He fell under the spell of Matthew Simpson [*q.v.*], later a bishop of the Methodist Church, and left the church of his fathers to join that of the Methodists. He imbibed from Simpson a zeal for education. At the same time he was an ardent anti-slavery man and a leader in the movement to establish the first hospital for the insane in Indiana. After the legislature had acted favorably on the latter proposal, he was selected as the first superintendent of the new institution and moved to Indianapolis in 1845 to keep in touch with its construction. He resigned this office in 1848 to accept the chair of obstetrics in Rush Medical College in Chicago.

Evans now lived in Chicago and later in its suburb which was named for him, Evanston. Again he quickly gained prominence. Professor in Rush, he was also one of the editors and proprietors of the *Northwestern Medical and Surgical Journal* and one of the promoters of the institution later known as the Mercy Hospital. His interests were always broader than his profession, however. An alderman in the city in 1853 and 1854, he was selected as chairman of the committee on schools; during his term of office the first superintendent of schools was chosen. He took a leading part, with Orrington Lunt [*q.v.*], in the foundation of Northwestern University. The generosity which characterized him whenever church or education was concerned was shown in his endowment of two chairs, those of Latin language and literature, and mental and moral philosophy. Behind these activities and supporting them was the capable man of business. He invested in real estate in Chicago and Evanston, and constructed a business block in the former city. The great railroad builder of Colorado was foreshadowed in the director and part builder of the Fort Wayne & Chicago Railroad. On Aug. 18, 1853, he married his second wife, Margaret Patten Gray.

A highly respected professional and business man, Evans was appointed territorial governor of Colorado on Mar. 26, 1862. Once more he moved westward and took up his residence in Denver. As governor he assembled troops and dealt with the Indians; the demands of wartime left little opportunity for more constructive work. After his resignation in 1865 he was elected United States senator by those who hoped to see Colorado become a state; because of the failure of the statehood plan he never sat in Congress. After 1866 he engaged in what were to him more congenial pursuits. A quiet man and an abhorrer of publicity, the Governor, as he was called, was nevertheless always a leader in Colorado. He had given up his profession in 1859, and now devoted his attention to church, education, and business. Always a strong Methodist and an outstanding figure in the affairs of his church, he was generous to all struggling congregations; it is said that for years he gave one hundred dollars to every church of any denomination started in Colorado. Closely connected with this interest was his foundation of Colorado Seminary, later and better known as the University of Denver. He was its founder, its sound rock in times of financial distress, and the president of its board of trustees from its inception until his death.

Behind his frock-coated exterior, great beard, and quiet face lay the ideals of a philanthropist and the spirit of an adventurer in business. It was this spirit that upheld John Evans, the railroad builder. In the late sixties, when it was certain that Denver was not to be on a transcontinental railroad, he led the movement that resulted in the incorporation of the Denver Pacific Railroad & Telegraph Company, which was to connect Denver with the Union Pacific at Cheyenne. When the contractors failed the company, he assumed the responsibility for completing the road that was to save his city from isolation. On the opening of the line in June 1870, he was the hero of the day. He also promoted the South Park Railroad, which afforded a way to the mining districts across the Continental Divide. His last project, the Denver & New Orleans Railroad, incorporated in 1881, was to give Denver an outlet to the South. While engaged in these activities, he invested in land in and near Denver and built an office building, the Evans Block. In the nineties the Governor withdrew from active life. Fame was already his, and wealth. In 1895, by act of the legislature, the great peak lying to the west of Denver was renamed Mount Evans. The people of Colorado honored his memory at the end of his life with what was virtually a state funeral.

[E. C. McMechen, *Life of Gov. Evans* (1924); H. D. Teetor, in *Mag. of Western Hist.*, Apr. 1889; J. W. Whicker, in *Indiana Mag. of Hist.*, Sept. 1923; F. Hall, *Hist. of the State of Colorado* (1889–95); A. H. Wilde, *Northwestern Univ., A Hist.* (1905); J. P. Dunn, *Indiana and Indianans* (1919); N. Trottman, *Hist. of the Union Pacific* (1923); *Senate Ex. Doc. No. 51, Pt. 4*, 50 Cong., 1 Sess., pp. 1849–62; *Northwestern Christian Advocate* (Chicago), May 19, July 7, 1897; *Denver Republican* and *Rocky Mt. News* (Denver), both July 3–7, 1897.]

J. F. W.

EVANS, LAWRENCE BOYD (Feb. 3, 1870–Oct. 30, 1928), lawyer, born in Radnor, Ohio, was descended from Irish and Welsh ancestors. One reached western Pennsylvania just before the Revolution; another, Rev. Evan Evans, came from Wales in 1828; others were of the pioneers who found new homes beyond the Alleghanies. A year after the birth of Lawrence, his parents moved to Noblesville, Ind., where in due course he graduated from the high school. He took the degree of Ph.B. in 1894, at the University of

Michigan, then, going to the University of Chicago, he was quickly appointed a fellow in political science, and took the degree of Ph.D. in 1898. Next, after getting in Kansas a beginner's experience in teaching, he went East to create and head a department of history and public law in Tufts College, where he served as a professor from 1900 to 1912. In entering thus on the life of the scholar, he had doubtless been stimulated by the example of his uncle Edward Payson Evans [*q.v.*], who adopted him as his son. Naturally the mind of Lawrence Boyd Evans turned in the same direction. While at Tufts he made a start by editing several of the series known as Handbooks of American Government, and later two volumes of the Writings of American Statesmen, devoted to Washington and Hamilton. Concluding that he should better equip himself for work in the field that particularly attracted him, in 1911 he entered the Harvard Law School, where he passed three years. Going into a Boston law office, he took up the task that was to be his chief interest during the rest of his days—the study of public law. In 1916 he published *Leading Cases on American Constitutional Law* and in 1917 *Leading Cases on International Law,* both of which have had second editions. Made a member of the commission to compile information for the state constitutional convention which was about to assemble, he contributed much to the value of its *Bulletins,* which were in the nature of monographs in political science; and to his skill as a legal draftsman was due much of the excellent workmanship to be found in the many amendments that followed.

Incidentally, in 1916, he had written a biography of Gov. Samuel W. McCall. Their friendship led to the appointment of Evans in December 1917 as state librarian of Massachusetts. However agreeable to his bookish tastes, the routine employment of librarian left him no time for following his bent, and so in 1919 he accepted the opportunity to go to Washington as counselor of the Brazilian Embassy, the pleasant duties of which office he performed till his death. As they did not require all his time, he was able also to act as contract expert for the War Department, and then through some years to carry on the delicate task of codifying the navigation laws for the United States Shipping Board. It was while so engaged that he was offered appointment to a judgeship in Egypt as a member of the "Mixed Tribunal," but he preferred to stay in his own country.

Ready to work with others for the advancement of the scholarly interests he had at heart, he became, while professor at Tufts, the president of the New England History Teachers Association, and he was a member of the American History and American Political Science associations, the American Society of International Law, and the International Law Association, as well as the Authors' Clubs of Boston and London. Also he served as a member of the Committee on Copyrights of the Section of Patents, Trade Marks and Copyrights of the American Bar Association. In temperament he was cautious, prudent, careful. Both as a scholar and in personal relations, he was conspicuously conscientious. He took life seriously. His chief satisfaction he found in helping others, and notably in the aid he quietly gave to youths in straitened circumstances who were seeking education. In Washington he made his home at the Cosmos Club, where his kindly qualities won him many friends. He never married.

[*Library Jour.*, Jan. 1918; *Who's Who in America,* 1926–27; *Evening Star* (Washington, D. C.), Oct. 30, 1928; *Washington Post,* Oct. 31, 1928; personal acquaintance and information from a relative.] R. L.

EVANS, LEWIS (*c.* 1700–June 12, 1756), geographer, was born in Pennsylvania and spent a considerable portion of his life there. He was early trained as a surveyor and in the pursuit of this occupation traveled extensively throughout the Middle Colonies. During these travels he made many observations and collected much material for "A Map of Pennsylvania, New-Jersey, New-York, And the Three Delaware Counties" which was published in 1749. This map is especially important because it traced in considerable detail the roads centering in Lancaster, York, and Carlisle, over which the great migrations from Pennsylvania across Virginia to the Carolinas and Tennessee took place. In 1752 he published a revision of this map, incorporating several corrections and additions. His best-known map, however, is "A General Map of the Middle British Colonies in America," which included the country from the Falls of the Ohio to Narragansett Bay and from Virginia to Montreal. This was published in 1755 in connection with a pamphlet of *Geographical, Historical, Political, Philosophical and Mechanical Essays: The First, Containing an Analysis of a General Map of the Middle British Colonies in America . . . Printed by B. Franklin and D. Hall. MDCCLV.* In the "Analysis," Evans pointed out the advantages to the English colonies of the Ohio country and urged a general study of that region and the ways by which it might be reached so that the French might be more easily driven out. This map, which was used by Braddock in his campaign, soon came to be regarded as the best map of the region; and because of the care and accuracy with which it was prepared was generally accepted as the standard authority in settling boundary disputes.

In dedicating his map to Governor Thos. Pownall [*q.v.*] with the encomium that he esteemed him the best judge of it in America, Evans, long the tool of the Pownall faction, aroused bitter feeling among the Shirley adherents who, through a letter published in the *New York Mercury* of Jan. 5, 1756, severely criticized the "Analysis" and its writer. Evans, undaunted, published five days later, *Geographical, Historical, Political, Philosophical and Mechanical Essays. Number II,* in which he replied to his opponents in a vigorous fashion. He contemplated continuing the series, but in the following June he died, in New York City, while under arrest for a slander against Gov. Robert Hunter Morris (Stevens, *post,* 1920, p. 13). Another project which he never carried out was that of publishing maps of the separate colonies in greater detail and upon a larger scale. Evans's influence upon maps of America did not terminate with his death, however, for the London publishers pirated his map as early as 1756 and within the next half century repeatedly reissued it. Some of these editions give credit to Evans, while others do not. Chief among the former is Gov. Pownall's map of 1776 which together with his *Topographical Description of North America* (1776) is practically a new and enlarged edition of both Evans's map and his "Analysis." Although Pownall denounced the pirated editions of Evans's work, others continued to issue from the press, and even as late as 1814 the old copper plate of Kitchin's piracy of 1756, after fifty-eight years of life, was reissued as a new and general map.

[Louis A. Holman, *Old Maps and Their Makers* (1925); three studies by Henry N. Stevens: *Lewis Evans: His Map of the Middle British Colonies in America* (1905), *Ibid.,* Second edition, with numerous corrections and additions, including an account of his earlier map of 1749 (1920), and *Lewis Evans, His Map of 1752 Recently Brought to Light* (1924); John F. Watson, *Annals of Phila.* (1857), II, 561; Justin Winsor, *Narr. and Crit. Hist. of America,* vol. V (1887); *Monthly Review, or Lit. Jour.,* Jan., Sept. 1756.]

G. H. B.

EVANS, NATHAN GEORGE (Feb. 6, 1824–Nov. 30, 1868), Confederate general, was born at Marion, S. C., the third son of Thomas and Jane Beverly (Daniel) Evans, and was educated at Randolph-Macon College, and the United States Military Academy, graduating from the latter in 1848. He served in the West with the 1st and 2nd Dragoons until 1855, when he was appointed first lieutenant in the newly organized 2nd (now 5th) Cavalry. He was promoted captain in 1856. He participated in numerous skirmishes with hostile Indians, in one of which, near Washita village, Indian Territory, Oct. 1, 1858, he killed two Comanches in hand-to-hand fight. In 1860 he was married to Ann Victoria Gary, sister of Gen. Martin W. Gary [*q.v.*]. Resigning his commission, Feb. 27, 1861, he was appointed a major and adjutant-general in the South Carolina army, and in that capacity served in the operations against Fort Sumter. In May he was appointed a captain of cavalry in the regular army of the Confederate States. At Bull Run, he commanded a small brigade, posted on the extreme left of Beauregard's corps, guarding the stone bridge. Here he detected the movement of McDowell's army to turn the Confederate flank, shifted his brigade to meet it, and for some time held back the advance, at first alone, and later in conjunction with Bee's command. Heavily outnumbered, Evans's brigade finally broke up, but its resistance had saved the Confederate army and made its final victory possible. He was given temporary rank as a colonel a few days later. In October 1861, he commanded at the battle of Ball's Bluff, an unimportant affair, but regarded at the time, both North and South, as a great and decisive battle. This brought him a vote of thanks from the Confederate Congress, a gold medal from his state, appointment as a brigadier-general, and assignment to the command of an independent brigade which normally served in the Carolinas but was sent so often to temporary duty elsewhere that it has been called the "tramp brigade." Thus it fought at the second battle of Bull Run, at South Mountain, and at Antietam, attached to the Army of Northern Virginia—Evans being in temporary command of a division at the last two of these battles; and in 1863, during the Vicksburg campaign, it was with Johnston's army in the West. Between these two expeditions, Evans commanded it in the little battle of Kinston, N. C., where he was defeated by Union forces greatly superior in numbers. Hitherto his military reputation had been good, though acquired to some extent by accident, but from early in 1863 he was in frequent difficulties. He was tried on charges of intoxication, and acquitted; and again tried and acquitted, a few months later, for alleged disobedience of orders. He was deprived of command for a long period, for Gen. Beauregard, the department commander, considered him incompetent. An inspector-general reported that the discipline and efficiency of his brigade were not satisfactory, and that its commander had lost the confidence of his men (*Official Records* (*Army*), 1 ser., vol.

XXVIII, pt. 2, pp. 583–90). Soon after his return to duty, in the spring of 1864, he was seriously injured by a fall from his horse, and again relinquished command. He was on duty again during the spring of 1865, and accompanied Jefferson Davis for some time after the Confederate government was driven from Richmond. Following the war, he became principal of a high school at Midway, Bullock County, Ala., where he died. "A good type of the rip-roaring, scorn-all-care element," was Fitzhugh Lee's characterization of him. Personal courage he displayed often, and his action at Bull Run was prompt and soldierly, but otherwise he seems to have shown slight fitness for command.

[*Confed. Mil. Hist.* (1899), V, 392–94; G. W. Cullum, *Biog. Reg.* (3rd ed., 1891), II, 365–66; R. M. Johnston, *Bull Run, Its Strategy and Tactics* (1913); *Official Records (Army)*, 1 ser., vols. II, V, VI, XII (pt. 2), XIV, XVIII, XIX (pts. 1, 2), XXVII (pt. 2), XXXV (pts. 1, 2), LI (pts. 1, 2); J. D. Evans, *Hist. of Nathaniel Evans of Catfish Creek and his Descendants* (1905); unpublished Confederate records in the War Department.] T. M. S.

EVANS, NATHANIEL (June 8, 1742–Oct. 29, 1767), clergyman of the Church of England, but better known for his contribution to the beginnings of lyric poetry in America, was born in Philadelphia. His father, Edward Evans, was a merchant and looked forward to a mercantile career for his son. Wishing him to be well educated, however, he sent him to the Academy, recently established by citizens of Philadelphia under the leadership of Benjamin Franklin, and presided over by Rev. William Smith [*q.v.*]. Here he remained six years, winning the warm affection of its head and becoming imbued with his enthusiasm for literature. He was then put into a counting-house, but having little taste for business, at the expiration of his apprenticeship he returned to the Academy, which in 1754 had become a college with the power to grant degrees. In 1765, because of his exceptional gifts and promise, he was awarded an M.A. by special act of the trustees, although he had not previously received a bachelor's degree. Highly commended by prominent Philadelphians both for his prudence and religious zeal as well as for the "many specimens of genius" which he had shown, he went to England where, sponsored by the Society for the Propagation of the Gospel in Foreign Parts, he was ordained by Dr. Richard Terrick, Bishop of London. After several months abroad, he returned as missionary for Gloucester County, N. J., and chaplain to Lord Viscount Kilmorey of Ireland. In less than two years, however, he died of tuberculosis at his home in Haddonfield, N. J., and "thus hastily," as he had written of his friend, the poet Thomas Godfrey, "was snatch'd off in the prime of manhood this very promising genius, beloved and lamented by all who knew him." His body was taken to Philadelphia and buried in Christ Church.

Evans was one of the Philadelphia group which included, among others, Francis Hopkinson and Thomas Godfrey [*qq.v.*], whose members had high literary ideals and sought to develop literature in America. When but sixteen years old he wrote a *Pastoral Eclogue* in which he asks if other lands shall resound with heavenly lays,

> "And this new world ne'er feel the muse's fire,
> No beauties charm us, or no deeds inspire?"

He was the author of *An Ode on the Late Glorious Successes of His Majesty's Arms, and the Present Greatness of the English Nation*, published in 1762, and in the following year wrote exercises performed at the Commencement of the College of Philadelphia and the college at Princeton. (See *Poems*, etc., and *A Dialogue on Peace, an Entertainment given by the Senior Class ... at Nassau Hall*, 1763.) In 1765 he prepared an edition of Thomas Godfrey's works with a memoir, *Juvenile Poems on Various Subjects, with The Prince of Parthia, a Tragedy*. On his way home from England he had met Elizabeth Graeme, later Mrs. Ferguson [*q.v.*], with whom he carried on a versified correspondence. To her, just before his death, and to his old teacher and friend, Dr. Smith, he committed his papers. From these, in 1772, the latter, having secured 759 subscribers, published *Poems on Several Occasions, with Some Other Compositions*. In his introduction the editor includes what seems to have been intended as a preface, written by Evans, and revealing his high conception of the function of poetry. The volume also contains a sermon on "The Love of the World Incompatible with the Love of God" (published separately, 1766). The poems are the work of a youthful student of the English poets, and are imitative of Milton, Cowley, Prior, Gray, and Collins, but are not without beauty, grace, and spontaneity.

[In addition to Dr. Smith's introduction to Evans's *Poems*, see Ellis P. Oberholtzer, *The Lit. Hist. of Philadelphia* (1906); Horace W. Smith, *Life and Correspondence of the Rev. Wm. Smith, D.D.* (1880), vol. I; *N. J. Archives*, 1 ser. vols. XXV (1903) and XXVII (1905), p. 595, ed. by Wm. Nelson; M. Katherine Jackson, *Outlines of the Lit. Hist. of Colonial Pa.* (1906); and the introduction to Archibald Henderson's edition of Thos. Godfrey's *The Prince of Parthia* (1917).] H. E. S.

EVANS, OLIVER (1755–Apr. 15, 1819), inventor, America's first steam-engine builder, was born in New Castle County, near Newport, Del., where his father, Charles Evans, was a farmer of moderate means and of respectable standing. He was descended from Evan Evans [*q.v.*], second rector of Christ Church, Philadelphia. After attending the country school until he was fourteen, Oliver apprenticed himself to a wagon-maker. In this work his mechanical ingenuity came to light almost immediately, but, in addition, he took every leisure moment to gain information from books, particularly on mathematics and mechanics. He thus learned when about seventeen of the atmospheric steam-engine which with its separate condenser was perfected by James Watt in 1769, and the desire of his life thereafter was to devote himself to the development of the steam-engine and its utilization. Because of financial limitations, however, and public ridicule of his ideas, he was past forty before realizing his ambition.

About the time that he reached his majority he was engaged in making card teeth for carding wool, and two years later he perfected a machine which could turn out 1,500 cards a minute. He also projected about this time a plan for "pricking" leather in cards and at the same time cutting, bending, and setting the teeth. He applied to the Pennsylvania legislature for funds with which to introduce the machinery but the grant was refused. In 1780 he joined his brothers, who were millers in Wilmington, and immediately began work on a series of improvements in flour-mill machinery which he completed and put into successful operation five years later. The machines, operated by water-power, included elevators, conveyors, hopper boy, drill, and descenders. They performed every necessary movement of the grain and meal from one part of the mill to another or from one machine to another without the aid of manual labor. Opposition to the devices was universal on the part of millers, as Evans found subsequently in traveling throughout Pennsylvania, Delaware, and Virginia in a fruitless endeavor to introduce his machines.

During these years he had not forgotten the steam-engine, and in 1786 and 1787 he petitioned the legislatures of Pennsylvania and Maryland, respectively, for the exclusive rights to use his "improvements in flour mills and steam carriages" in those states. Pennsylvania granted the mill improvement part of the petition, while Maryland granted the whole of it on the ground that "it could injure no one." Evans thereupon set about in earnest making experiments in steam. He could do this only in a small way because he could find no one willing to contribute to the expense of his undertakings. After devoting thirteen years in Philadelphia, where he had settled shortly after his marriage, to the development of a steam carriage, he laid it aside to concentrate his attention on a stationary steam-engine in the hope of obtaining additional funds through sales. By 1802 he had an engine running in his mill. It was a high-pressure steam-engine with a cylinder six inches in diameter and a piston of eighteen inches stroke. While its construction had used up all of his money, its success soon became known and the following year Evans started in business as a regular engine builder, specializing in high pressure engines, which were then looked upon as the height of folly. He was probably the first man in the United States to make a specialty of this work. In 1804 he constructed a steam dredge for use in the Schuylkill River and transported the scow, which he humorously named "Orukter Amphibole," and machinery under its own power from his mill to the river. He established the Mars Iron Works in 1807, and by 1819 fifty steam-engines which he had built were in use throughout the states of the Atlantic Coast. His last great work was completed in 1817, two years before his death, when he designed and constructed the engine and boilers for the Fairmount Waterworks in Philadelphia. The engine was of the high pressure type, having a twenty-inch cylinder and piston with a five-foot stroke, while the four boilers yielded steam at 200 pounds pressure.

Evans never built a steam carriage such as he advocated, but there is hardly any doubt that had he received the patronage and pecuniary assistance that others, such as Fulton, received, the steamboat and steam carriage might have been in operation in America much earlier. During the close of his life, when machinery began to come into general use in flour-milling, Evans's patents were brazenly infringed, but he succeeded eventually in having his rights sustained. He was the author of two small books on mechanics, *The Young Mill-Wright & Miller's Guide* (1795) and *The Abortion of the Young Engineer's Guide* (1805). In 1780 he was married to the daughter of John Tomlinson, a farmer of Delaware, who with two daughters survived him. In 1810 his two sons-in-law went into business with him, relieving him of some of his business cares.

[Coleman Sellers, Jr., "Oliver Evans and His Inventions," in *Jour. of the Franklin Inst.*, July 1886; Geo. A. Latimer, "A Sketch of the Life of Oliver Evans," in *Harkness' Mag.* (Wilmington, Del.), Mar. 1873; Henry Howe, *Memoirs of the Most Eminent Am. Mechanics* (1844); W. B. Kaempffert, *Popular Hist. of Am. Invention* (1924); J. T. Scharf and T. Westcott, *Hist. of Phila.* (1884); N. Y. *Evening Post*, Apr. 16, 1819; U. S. Nat. Museum correspondence.]

C. W. M.

EVANS, ROBLEY DUNGLISON (Aug. 18, 1846–Jan. 3, 1912), "Fighting Bob Evans," naval officer, one of the four children of Samuel Andrew Jackson and Sally Ann (Jackson) Evans, was born at Floyd Court House, Va. His father, who was a country physician, died when young Evans was ten years of age, and the next year the boy was sent to live with an uncle in Washington, D. C. He received education in the public schools but was so interested in the sea and shipping that he spent much of his time by the Potomac watching the vessels in the harbor. He had about decided to run away to sea when William H. Hooper, a friend of his uncle and delegate to Congress from Utah, suggested that he establish a residence in Utah and then be appointed to the naval academy from that territory. The trip West to accomplish this legality involved perilous adventures with hostile Indians, and at the age of thirteen the boy was in his first fight and incidentally received his first wound. His career at Annapolis was duly begun but was cut short owing to the outbreak of the Civil War. In October 1863 at the age of seventeen, Evans was commissioned acting ensign in the United States navy in spite of family pressure that sought to have him join the Confederate forces.

In the second attack on Fort Fisher, N. C., in January 1864, Evans was ordered to command a company of marines about to engage in an assault by land. He received four wounds, but while lying wounded he managed to kill off a sniper who was trying to exterminate him. He was invalided out of the service but his fighting qualities were so dominant that he appealed to Congress and gained a reinstatement. In 1876 he perfected a long-distance signal lamp much used in the service. He was made commander on July 12, 1878. He was considered an expert on steel-making, especially steel plates. His influence at Washington was a considerable factor in the decision to build battleships of steel in the future. In 1886–87 he was chief inspector of steel, in which capacity he had charge of determining the quality of material about to be used in constructing the new cruisers.

In August 1891 Evans was placed in command of a steel gunboat, the *Yorktown,* and ordered to Chile, between which country and the United States relations were strained. Here he was called upon to manifest all the tact, diplomacy, and patience that was in him. At the same time, he had to uphold the prestige of his country while defying practically the entire Chilean navy with his little gunboat. The following year, in charge of a flotilla, he proceeded to the Bering Sea to stop abuses in the seal fisheries. Although this assignment was also involved in international complications, it was so well performed that he was especially mentioned by the president in a message to Congress, a rare honor in peace times.

Evans attained his captaincy on June 27, 1893, and in 1895 took the *New York* to the Kiel Canal celebration. In 1898 his ship, the *Iowa,* fired the first gun at Cervera's fleet as it came out of Santiago. On Feb. 11, 1901, he was commissioned rear-admiral, and in 1902 he was made commanding officer of the entire Asiatic fleet. While in the Far East, he greatly improved the subcaliber firing practise, and also invented a new loading machine used in the gunnery work. When, in 1907, President Roosevelt decided to send the fleet around the world, Evans was chosen its commander-in-chief. He conducted it through the Straits of Magellan and as far north as Magdalena Bay. Illness overtook him there, however, and he was obliged to retire. In a personal letter, Roosevelt paid him the compliment of stating that the fleet was in better shape when it reached San Francisco than it was when it left Hampton Roads.

In 1871, Evans had married Charlotte Taylor, a sister of his brother officer, Henry C. Taylor. To them three children were born. In spite of his manifold activities, he found time to write two books: *A Sailor's Log; Recollections of Forty Years of Naval Life* (1901), and *An Admiral's Log; being Continued Recollections of Naval Life* (1910).

[Navy Registers and Navy Department records; "Naval Operations of the War with Spain," *House Doc. No. 3,* 55 Cong., 3 Sess.; L. R. Hamersly, *The Records of Living Officers of the U. S. Navy and Marine Corps* (7th ed., 1902); *Who's Who in America,* 1910–11; *Army and Navy Jour.,* Jan. 6, 1912; W. C. Tyler, in *U. S. Naval Inst. Proc.,* Nov. 1926.] A. R. B.

EVANS, THOMAS (Feb. 23, 1798–May 25, 1868), Quaker minister and editor, was a descendant in the third generation of the Gwynedd group of settlers in Pennsylvania. His parents, Jonathan Evans, Jr., and Hannah (Bacon) Evans were residents of the city of Philadelphia and their seven children, five sons and two daughters, were reared in the best traditions of the Society of Friends. The most substantial education of the city was at this time (1812–16) given in the Academy at Fourth and Chestnut Streets. It was one of the Penn Charter Schools. Solomon Roberts was head master and trained his boys in advanced mathematics as well as in ancient languages, including Hebrew. Under him young Thomas acquired a student habit that was lifelong. At the age of twenty-one he established himself as a druggist. The fifteen years (1820–35) embraced in his young manhood were stir-

Evans

ring times in the Society of Friends. For the first five years of this period, he was occupied with constructive work which included a journey (1821–22) on religious service with an English Friend, George Withy, into Ohio and into some of the Southern states. As a climax, a crowded public meeting of a deeply impressive character was held in the Hall of the House of Representatives in Washington (*Washington Gazette,* Jan. 14, 1822). Thomas Evans made this record in regard to it: "The floor was literally strewed with tears, and it was one of the most remarkable meetings I had ever attended."

In 1827 the schism in the Society of Friends culminated. From that date the two bodies were known as Hicksite and Orthodox. Ostensibly, Socinianism caused the break, but a hundred years after, the breach officially healed, one easily perceives that various unhappy circumstances were also responsible. Thomas Evans was associated with his father as an able defender of the orthodox faith but on reflection in later years he characterized the separation as the "most mournful controversy that ever divided a once united people." Ignorance of Quaker principles and history in Evans's opinion had been largely responsible for the whole sorry business, and he henceforth found his life-work, apart from his service as a minister, in an industrious effort to correct this condition. In 1828 he published *An Exposition of the Faith of the Religious Society of Friends,* quoting 181 Friends of the previous centuries in support of the orthodox position. The *Exposition* was followed many years later by *A Concise Account of the Religious Society of Friends* (1856), which under forty-five headings gives the doctrines and practises of the Society. In 1847 he issued a volume entitled *Examples of Youthful Piety,* to meet the needs of the religious training of children. With his brother William, in 1837 he entered upon the publication of *The Friends' Library* (1837–50). This includes fourteen quarto volumes of about five hundred pages each, containing 105 articles, mostly memoirs and journals but also Penn's well-known "No Cross, No Crown," and "The Institution of the Discipline," carefully edited. In 1854 William and Thomas Evans published four volumes under the title, *Piety Promoted, in a Collection of the Dying Sayings of Many of the People Called Quakers.* All this work was done with meticulous care and in the dignified style of the time. It represents a permanent contribution to the history and professed faith of the followers of George Fox. After 1844 Thomas Evans was widely known as a minister. It was said of him that "while he retained all the simplicity and correctness of an apostle, he was eloquent in a high degree." He married Catharine Wistar of Germantown in 1834. After an accident, in 1847, when he was thrown from his carriage, and injured his spine, his health was precarious. In 1851 upon the advice of physicians he took an ocean voyage, and with his wife visited London and the Isle of Wight. He died in Philadelphia in his seventieth year, four of his five children surviving him.

[*Memorials Concerning Deceased Friends: Being a Selection from the Records of the Yearly Meeting of Pa. 1788–1878* (4th ed., 1879); *North American and United States Gazette* (Phila.), June 22, 1868. *Quaker Biographies,* 2 ser., vol. I (1927).]

J. H. B.

EVANS, THOMAS WILTBERGER (Dec. 23, 1823–Nov. 14, 1897), dentist, and philanthropist, born in Philadelphia, Pa., was the son of William Milnor and Catherine Anne (Wiltberger) Evans and a descendant of a family of Welsh Quakers who had emigrated to Philadelphia in 1682. He received a common-school education and at the age of fourteen he became apprenticed to Joseph Warner, a silversmith of Philadelphia whose business included the manufacture of dental implements. Through this association he acquired an interest in dentistry and, in 1841, became a student of Dr. John De Haven White [*q.v.*] of Philadelphia. During the two years he remained with White he attended lectures at the Jefferson Medical College. Before leaving Philadelphia in 1843 he married Agnes Josephine Doyle. He practised a short time in Baltimore, Md., and then joined Dr. Philip Van Patten in his dental practise in Lancaster, Pa. It was during this period that Evans made a series of gold contour filling operations which, exhibited at the Franklin Institute in 1847, brought him his first public recognition. He soon after accepted an invitation to associate himself with Dr. C. Starr Brewster, an American dentist with a large and successful clientele in Paris; he remained with Brewster until 1850, when he opened his own office at 15 rue de la Paix. A friendship with Napoleon III, begun during professional services and assiduously cultivated, laid the foundations of a large private fortune and the most distinguished dental practise of the nineteenth century. A high degree of professional skill, an attractive personality, and a tactful wife enabled him not only to become the dentist to all the important Royal families of Europe, but also, to many of them, a personal friend. As his success grew, Evans's conceit, ever present, became boundless. He came to consider himself not only a successful dentist, but an author and a diplomat. Of his numerous diplomatic missions, which were usually undertaken on his own initiative, he considered the most brilliant to have been that to President Lincoln during the Civil War. This mission, performed during the fall of 1864 and related at length in his *Memoirs,* came at a time when Napoleon was considering the recognition of the Confederacy and, according to Evans, had begun negotiations to that end with the English government. The report of Evans, predicting victory for the North, decided Napoleon against recognition. However, the only evidence for this mission and its remarkable results is that supplied by Evans, who was ever generous in crediting his own exploits. Of greater authenticity are the important services he rendered the Empress Eugénie in escaping from Paris during the riots that followed the disaster at Sedan at the close of the Franco-Prussian War and in establishing her in the English exile. If Evans was naïve, ambitious, and vain, as his *Memoirs* and contemporary testimony both reveal him, he was also generous and charitable. Through his friendship with Napoleon he learned in advance of the improvements in Paris projected by Baron Haussmann; the resulting sagacious investments in real estate formed the basis of his fortune. During the Crimean and the Franco-Prussian wars he spent large sums providing ambulance corps and other measures of relief for the wounded. During the American Civil War he organized the United States Sanitary Commission at Philadelphia. These services have been fully recorded in three volumes by Evans: *La Commission Sanitaire des États-Unis* (Paris, 1865), *Les Institutions Sanitaires pendant le Conflit Austro-Prussien-Italien* (Paris, 1867), and *History of the American Ambulance established in Paris during the Siege of 1870–71* (London, 1873). His single, and unsuccessful, literary effort was a lengthy introduction to the *Memoirs of Heinrich Heine,* published in London in 1884. Evans established and supported the first American newspaper in Paris, the *American Register,* edited by his colleague, Dr. Edward A. Crane; this ceased publication shortly after his death. He was an infrequent contributor to dental journals, but his few publications demonstrate a fertility of resource and originality of thought. His rôle in the history of American dentistry is considerable. He was one of the first to experiment with vulcanite as a base for artificial dentures and in promoting the use of nitrous oxide as an anesthetic. His services in the improvement and use of dental amalgams were valuable, and he was active in the development of technique and mechanisms for the correction of irregularities of the teeth, now known as orthodontia. His own distinguished reputation established the prestige of American dentistry in Europe. It was appropriate that the bulk of his fortune was used in establishing the Thomas W. Evans Museum and Dental Institute, now the Dental School of the University of Pennsylvania.

[*Memoirs of Dr. Thomas W. Evans: The Second French Empire,* ed. by Edward A. Crane (N. Y., 1905; London, 2 vols., 1905; French translation by E. Philippi, Paris, 1910); *N. Y. Times,* Nov. 16, 24, 1897, and Jan. 23, 1898; *N. Y. Tribune,* Dec. 28, 1890; *Saturday Review* (London), Mar. 24, 1906; *Dental Cosmos,* Jan. 1898; letters and MSS. in T. W. Evans Museum and Dental Institute, Phila.; information from Edward C. Kirk and Henry Rainey of Philadelphia, and from Lester L. and Frank L. Evans of Washington, D. C.; private information.] F. M—n.

EVANS, WALTER (Sept. 18, 1842–Dec. 30, 1923), jurist, congressman, was born in Barren County, Ky., the son of Joseph Warder and Matilda (Ritter) Evans. His only formal education was received in the country schools near his father's farm. At the opening of the Civil War he was working as a deputy in the office of the county clerk at Hopkinsville. He entered the Union army as a second lieutenant in the 25th Kentucky Infantry, saw service at Fort Donelson, and was promoted to a captaincy for his conduct in this battle. In 1863 he resigned his commission when his regiment was consolidated with another. After leaving the army he went back to Hopkinsville to resume his work in the office of the county clerk. Later he worked as a deputy in the office of the circuit clerk at the same place. He studied law at night and was admitted to the bar in 1864, practising for the next ten years in Hopkinsville. An increasing reputation is indicated by his election as a representative from Christian County in the lower house of the legislature, 1871–73, and as state senator for the 6th District, 1873–75 (*Journal of the House of Representatives,* 1871–72, p. 1; *Journal of the Senate,* 1873, p. 42). After two years he abandoned his political career for the time being and removed to Louisville where he resumed the practise of law.

Whatever his ability, there can, at least, be no doubt of his prominence in his party at this time. He was a delegate to the Republican National conventions of 1868, 1872, 1880, and 1884, and was one of the men who in 1880 stood firmly for Grant until the end. He had been the unsuccessful candidate of his party for governor of Kentucky in 1879, but in May 1883 he received the reward for his "Stalwart" activities when Arthur appointed him commissioner of internal revenue. After two years in this office a change in the national administration once more consigned him to private life and he resumed the practise of law in Louisville. In 1894 he was elected to Congress from his district, having the distinction of being the first Republican to represent it. He served two terms in Congress. He was a member of the committee on ways and means and chairman of its sub-committee on internal revenue. His chief activities were in connection with the tariff and the passage of pension bills; he had a prominent part in formulating the Dingley Tariff law.

Retiring from Congress on Mar. 4, 1899, he was appointed the same day as federal judge for the district of Kentucky. The appointment was due more to his warm friendship with McKinley, perhaps, than to his merits or reputation as a jurist, but as a matter of fact in this position Evans showed more ability and won more honor than in any other office he held. As a legislator he had shown himself a strong partisan; as a judge he displayed such independence as to attract wide attention and wide criticism. His most widely discussed decisions were those in regard to the "night riders" in the tobacco disturbances in western Kentucky, and, particularly, his decision that the war-time prohibition act was invalid after the conclusion of the World War. He could not be numbered in the list of great jurists, but he possessed the esteem of his contemporaries, of both parties, while he was on the bench.

Evans was twice married: in 1868 to Louise Gowen, who died in 1905, and in 1915 to Sarah Louise Wood of Worcester, Mass. He had two children by his first marriage, neither of whom survived him.

[*Who's Who in America*, 1922–23; *Biog. Dir. Am. Cong.* (1928); *Proc. Twenty-third Ann. Meeting Ky. State Bar Asso.* (1924); *Boston Transcript*, Nov. 19, 1919; *Courier-Journal* (Louisville), *Louisville Herald*, and *Louisville Post*, Dec. 31, 1923.] R. S. C—l.

EVANS, WARREN FELT (Dec. 23, 1817–Sept. 4, 1889), clergyman, author of books on Mental Cure, was born in Rockingham, Vt., sixth of the seven children of Eli and Sarah (Edson) Evans. He was descended from John Evans, one of the early settlers of Roxbury, Mass. His boyhood was that of a farmer's son, but he aspired to a college education and attended Chester Academy to prepare for Middlebury College, which he entered in 1837. In the following year he entered the sophomore class in Dartmouth College, where he remained until the middle of his junior year, when, eager to enter upon the Methodist ministry—and perhaps to wed—he left without a degree. On June 21, 1840, he married Charlotte Tinker, but he was not admitted to the New Hampshire Conference of the Methodist Church until 1844. He was first assigned to the Goffstown mission. He served in no less than eleven charges until 1864 when he withdrew from the Conference. He had been an assiduous reader of Swedenborg and now with a group of followers united with the New Church. Subsequently he wrote three books on Swedenborgianism, none of which had any enduring significance.

Having developed "a nervous affection that was complicated with a chronic disorder" (Leonard, *post*), he visited Dr. Phineas P. Quimby [*q.v.*] of Portland, Me., for treatment in 1863, and became not merely a patient but a disciple of this well-known healer. This was a turning point in his career. He visited Dr. Quimby a second time and then himself began to practise "mental medicine" at Claremont, N. H. Here he wrote in 1869 *The Mental-Cure, Illustrating the Influence of the Mind on the Body, both in Health and Disease, and the Psychological Method of Treatment.* This was followed by *Mental Medicine: a Theoretical and Practical Treatise on Medical Psychology* (1872) and *Soul and Body; or the Spiritual Science of Health and Disease* (1876). These three volumes contain the essential features of his philosophy and therapy. A fourth volume, *The Divine Law of Cure* (1884), was the culmination, the author assures the reader, of a life-long study to which the previous volumes were introductory. His system of therapy is frankly derived from Quimby (*Mental Medicine*, p. 210) whose success was due, Evans believed, to the recognition of the power of suggestion—to reliance upon psychical remedies instead of drugs. "Disease," wrote Evans, "is not so much a mere physical derangement . . . as it is an abnormal mental condition . . . a wrong belief, a falsity" (*Ibid.*, p. 209). "If by any therapeutic device you remove the morbid idea . . . you cure the malady" (*The Divine Law*, p. 9). This, he believed, was the explanation of the cures wrought by Christ. The theoretical basis for mental cure he found in the idealistic philosophy of Berkeley and the German thinkers from Fichte to Hegel, and in the spiritual philosophy of Swedenborg. He has thus many points of contact with the New England Transcendentalists; and he anticipated by some years the doctrine laid down by Mary Morse Baker Eddy [*q.v.*] in *Science and Health.*

Sometime in the year 1870 Evans established a sort of sanitorium—the Evans Home—in Salisbury, Mass., where he is said to have effected all manner of cures by mental treatment and to have taught others to practise mental medicine. His fame was more than local, and, in order to reach those who could not come under his immediate instruction, he published *The Primitive Mind Cure* (1885) and *Esoteric Christianity and Mental Therapeutics* (1886). Those publications had a wide sale, but Evans was never interested in financial profit (Leonard, *post*). He seems to have been a kindly man with "calm and reassuring eyes," "a firm, clear, sweetly modulated voice," and "a character of purity." He is said to have cured his own chronic disorder and he lived until his seventy-second year. He died in 1889, leaving a widow and three children.

[L. S. Hayes, *Hist. of the Town of Rockingham, Vt.* (1907), contains items of genealogical interest. O. Cole and O. S. Baketel, editors, *Hist. of the N. H. Conf. of the Meth. Episc. Church* (1929), give information about Evans's charges. His only biographer is W. J. Leonard, who printed in 1903 a small pamphlet with the title *The Pioneer Apostle of Mental Science: A Sketch of the Life and Work of the Reverend W. F. Evans, M.D.* This undated pamphlet is, however, rather an appreciation than a narrative. The inner life of Evans is best traced in his writings.] A. J.

EVANS, WILLIAM THOMAS (Nov. 13, 1843–Nov. 25, 1918), patron of American art, was born at Clough-Jordan, Ireland, and, as an infant, was brought to the United States by his parents William and Maria Jane (Williams) Evans, both descendants of Welsh officers in Cromwell's army. He was educated in the public schools of New York City, and because of excellent standing in his studies, was permitted to enter the College of the City of New York (then the New York Free Academy) before attaining the age commonly required. After two years at college he entered an architect's office where he studied for a year; and after a third year in college, accepted a position in the counting house of E. S. Jaffray & Company. This led him into a business career, for when two senior clerks, Philo L. Mills and John Gibb, left Jaffray's to form the firm of Mills & Gibb, wholesale dry-goods merchants, he went with them, first as an employee, later, and practically until his death, as a member of the firm.

Undoubtedly his study of architecture turned his attention to art but he himself dated his definite interest in American painting to a book, G. W. Sheldon's *American Painters,* which his wife (Mary Jane Hinman of New York, whom he had married in 1867) gave him on his birthday in 1879. They were living at that time in a house on Van Vorst Square, Jersey City, and there Evans began collecting paintings. So rapidly did acquisitions accumulate that he added a picture gallery to this house. When in 1890 this home was given up Evans sold all the paintings by foreign artists which he owned, retaining only those which were by American painters. In 1892 the family took possession of a new house at 5 West Seventy-sixth St., New York, to which a new gallery had been added, and therein were hung the American pictures. From that time on Evans bought only works by Americans. A large part of the collection which hung in the New York house was sent abroad, by invitation, for display in Austria and Bavaria. This was one of the first exhibitions of American paintings shown abroad, and the Bavarian government decorated Evans with the Order of St. Michael.

Evans, inherently a lover of art, was also a man of business acumen, essentially a friend of American artists, and one of the first to regard the works of American painters as profitable investment. In 1900, when he moved to a new house in Montclair, N. J., which had no picture gallery, Evans sold his entire collection of 270 American paintings, which he had bought in most instances, directly from the painters (see *Catalogue of American Paintings Belonging to W. T. Evans to be sold . . . Jan. 31 and Feb. 1 and 2 . . . on Exhibit at the American Art Galleries,* 1900), and by this sale, which brought him the sum of $159,340, established for the first time market values for the works of American artists. No sooner was this collection sold than he started another. In a comparatively short time the new purchases filled his house in Montclair to overflowing, and even the loft of his stable was turned into a gallery. In March 1907 he offered to the National Gallery of Art (lately legalized by a decree of the Supreme Court of the District of Columbia), a collection of paintings by contemporary American artists, and promptly upon acceptance turned over to the nation forty-three works, including masterpieces by Winslow Homer, LaFarge, Inness, and Wyant withdrawn from his private collection. They were temporarily installed as a loan in the Corcoran Gallery of Art, Washington. To this collection Evans made numerous additions until finally the gift comprised 150 paintings, a bust, and 115 examples of the work of the foremost American wood-engravers.

Through his purchases, made chiefly in the studios, Evans formed many close friendships among the artists. Especially significant was his friendship with Henry W. Ranger, who influenced Evans not only in his selections but in his gift to the National Gallery which, in turn, almost certainly led to the establishment of the Ranger Fund, providing for the yearly addition of works by American painters to the National collection. In Montclair he was active in creating interest in art. He became president of the Municipal Art Commission and by offering to present to Montclair a collection of thirty paintings by American artists of high standing, induced the establishment in 1909 of the Montclair Art Gallery and Museum. He held a third sale of paintings in 1913 and a fourth in May 1916, when the firm of Mills & Gibb went into receivership. This sale was for the benefit of the firm's creditors.

William T. Evans did more perhaps than any other collector to promote interest in American art, and to his liberal patronage many living American artists owe their first step toward success. It is a distressing fact that after giving so generously, his business failed, through no fault of his own, and when he died he was no longer a rich man. He had five daughters and two sons.

[A portrait of W. T. Evans, painted by Jongers and engraved on wood by Henry Wolf, is included in the Evans National Gallery collection. In addition to references above see obituaries in *N. Y. Times, N. Y. Herald,* Nov. 26, 1918. Information supplied by a daughter, Mrs. Luther E. Price, has been supplemented by personal recollections of the writer.] L. M.

EVARTS, JEREMIAH (Feb. 3, 1781–May 10, 1831), lawyer, philanthropist, was born at Sunderland, Vt., being the eldest son of James Evarts who married Sarah, daughter of Timothy Todd, of Guilford, Conn., of which latter place the Evarts family had been residents since 1650. His father moved to Georgia Township in 1787 and his early education was received at the country school there, but in January 1798 he went to East Guilford, Conn., where he was prepared for college by Rev. John Elliott. Entering Yale College in September of that year, he graduated in 1802 (M.A. 1805), and in April 1803 became principal of the Caledonia County Grammar School at Peacham, Vt., remaining there for a year. Deciding however to enter the legal profession he commenced the study of law in Judge Charles Chauncey's office at New Haven, and was admitted to the Connecticut bar in July 1806. He practised in New Haven for over three years but did not meet with success. He had early evinced that somewhat stern puritanical spirit which made him a deeply religious man throughout his life, and a contemporary alleged that he "ever had too much unbending integrity to be a popular lawyer." In January 1810 he was induced to assume the editorship of the *Panoplist,* an organ of the orthodox Congregationalists, published at Boston, and moved to Charlestown, Mass., where he made his permanent home. Abandoning the law, he devoted himself entirely to his editorial duties and missionary enterprise. As an editor, his articles, distinguished for their forcible though simple style, exhibited great powers of analysis, wide knowledge, and critical acumen. He did not confine himself to religious subjects but also discussed the various phases of social, civil, and political relations. Among other matters of general interest which he advocated were the discontinuance of Sunday mails and legislation to cope with intemperance. He was one of the founders of the American Board of Commissioners for Foreign Missions, becoming its treasurer in 1811, a member of its prudential committee in 1812, and corresponding secretary and treasurer in 1821. He also became a manager of the American Bible Society and vice-president of the American Education Society. In 1821 his missionary and other work of a religious and philanthropic nature absorbed so much of his time that the *Panoplist* discontinued publication, though he continued as editor of the *Missionary Herald,* the organ of the A. B. C. F. M. On several occasions when he visited the Southern states, he investigated the condition of the Indian tribes east of the Mississippi, particularly the Cherokees, and as a result strongly opposed the policy of transferring them to Western reservations. His *Essays on the Present Crisis in the Condition of the American Indians* (1829), first published in the *National Intelligencer* under the pseudonym William Penn, presented a powerful indictment of the state and federal governments for their treatment of the aborigines. His attack and charges were reinforced by articles in the *New York Observer* and the *North American Review,* and by the publication of a volume of speeches on the Indian Bill.

Evarts married Mrs. Mehitabel Barnes, daughter of Roger Sherman, in September 1804. Their son was the nationally known lawyer, William Maxwell Evarts [*q.v.*]. He died of consumption at Charleston, S. C., on his way home from Cuba where he had gone in quest of health.

[E. C. Tracy, *Memoir of the Life of Jeremiah Evarts* (1845), has an appendix containing a list of all the papers relative to the Indian question prepared by Evarts for publication; see also G. Spring, *A Tribute to the Memory of the Late Jeremiah Evarts* (1831); F. B. Dexter, *Biog. Sketches Grads. Yale Coll.,* Vol. V (1911), with bibliography; *Boston Recorder,* June 1, 1831, quoting *Charleston* (S. C.) *Observer,* May 14, 1831.] H. W. H. K.

EVARTS, WILLIAM MAXWELL (Feb. 6, 1818–Feb. 28, 1901), lawyer, and statesman, was the son of Jeremiah [*q.v.*] and Mehitabel (Sherman) Barnes Evarts, who were married in 1804. His father was a graduate of Yale College, a lawyer, and editor of the *Panoplist,* an orthodox Congregational magazine. His mother was the daughter of Roger Sherman [*q.v.*], statesman of the American Revolution. Born at 22 Pinckney St., Boston, Evarts was prepared for college at the Boston Latin School, and entered Yale College in 1833. He was one of the founders of the *Yale Literary Magazine,* and was graduated with honors in the "famous class" of 1837, along with Edwards Pierrepont, Samuel J. Tilden, and Morrison R. Waite. The following winter he read law in the office of Horace Everett, at Windsor, Vt., and then attended the Dane Law School of Harvard College. In the autumn of 1839 he entered the office of Daniel Lord, of New York City, as a law student and remained there until his admission to the bar of New York on July 16, 1841. On Aug. 30, 1843, he married Helen Minerva Wardner in Windsor, Vt. By her he had twelve children, nine of whom were living at his death.

For about one year from October 1841, he maintained his own law office at 60 Wall St., and then formed a partnership with Charles E. Butler, the beginning of a great law firm with which he was associated for sixty years, with Charles F. Southmayd, Joseph H. Choate, and Charles C. Beaman [*qq.v.*] as colleagues. In 1842, at the age of twenty-four, he was junior counsel under John J. Crittenden and Thomas F. Marshall in the defense in the New York courts of Monroe Edwards, a notorious Kentucky forger. He spoke an hour and a half in his opening for the defense and, although Edwards was convicted, Evarts's effort drew from Senator Crittenden the prediction that the highest honors of the profession were within his grasp. Political articles in *The New World* by Evarts, during this same period, caused Prof. Felton to describe his political pen as one of the most powerful in the country. His talents were publicly recognized by his appointment in 1849 to be assistant United States attorney for the southern district of New York, an office which he held until 1853. Two incidents led up to the turning point in his career. In 1850 he made a speech in Castle Garden which later was brought forward as evidence of a supposed deplorable leaning in favor of slavery. His speech was in support of the constitutionality of the Fugitive-Slave Law, and dealt with the dilemma presented by abhorrence of slavery and the constitutional recognition of it as an institution. Though called a "Hunker Whig," he nevertheless in 1855 gave $1,000, one-fourth of his whole fortune, to aid the Abolition cause through the Emigrant Aid Company. The opportunity had arrived, he said, "to contend successfully against slavery without violating the laws or sacrificing the Constitution and the Union." His position became clear to the public when, in January 1860, he was engaged to represent the State of New York in the Lemmon Slave Case (20 *N. Y.*, 562), in opposition to Charles O'Conor for the State of Virginia. He successfully maintained the principle that under the United States Constitution, a slave brought from a slave state (Virginia) into a non-slave state (New York) by sea, and there landed with the intention of embarking upon a new voyage to another slave state (Texas) was thereby made free.

The two careers of Evarts, professional and public, thus intertwined at their beginning, remained so until his retirement. His legal skill led him into cases of great public import, and many of his public employments were legal in their requirements. His public and political career, begun as assistant United States attorney, was continued when in May 1860 he went, in the interest of Seward, as chairman of the New York delegation to the Republican National Convention which nominated Lincoln. On the appointment of Seward as secretary of state in March 1861, Evarts was put before the New York legislature as a candidate for the United States Senate, but Ira Harris was elected. On the outbreak of the war he took part in the formation in New York of the Union Defense Committee, of which he was secretary. In April 1863, he was sent on a government mission to England to put an end, if possible, to the building and equipment of vessels for the Confederate navy. He returned to the United States in July, and went again on a similar errand in December, remaining in Europe this time until June 1864. In 1867 he was a delegate to the New York State constitutional convention, in which he served as a member of the judiciary committee. From July 15, 1868, to March 1869, he was attorney-general in President Johnson's cabinet. As president of the Association of the Bar of the City of New York at its organization in 1870, and for ten successive years thereafter, he led movements for law reform and against the political corruption of the "Tweed Ring," which made this private office a quasi-public one. Had it not been for the aggressive opposition of Senator Roscoe Conkling, he would probably have been appointed chief justice of the United States by President Grant on the death of Chief Justice Chase in 1873. His college classmate and colleague at the Geneva Arbitration, Morrison R. Waite, was appointed. This was the second time that the chief justiceship had been almost within his grasp, for, on the death of Taney, his appointment to that office had been strongly urged upon President Lincoln. Evarts was secretary of state for the whole period of President Hayes's term of office, 1877–81; and immediately thereafter he went as delegate of the United States to the Paris Monetary Conference. The New York legislature elected him United States senator on Jan. 20, 1885, for the term beginning in March.

Evarts's legal career ran parallel to and was interspersed between the events of his career as a statesman. In 1857 he won the case of *People* vs. *Draper* (15 *N. Y.*, 532), which sustained the right of the legislature to create a new metropolitan police district including three counties. In 1861 he was of government counsel in the case of the Savannah privateers, charged with piracy; in February 1863, he made the chief argument for the government in a prize case (2 *Black*, 635) which originated in New York; and in 1867 he was employed by the government in the prosecution of Jefferson Davis for treason. In 1866, 1868, and 1870, he argued in the United States Supreme Court the Bank Tax Case (3 *Wallace*, 573), the Legal Tender Case (8 *Wallace*, 603) and the Cotton Tax Case (not reported). An argument of Evarts's that has received the highest praise was that before the Mixed Commission on British and American Claims, in August 1873, for the British claimants in the Springbok Case (J. B. Moore, *A Digest of International Law*, VII, 1906, pp. 728–29) involving the difficult questions of continuous voyage and ultimate destination of ships and cargoes in time of war. Wharton described it as one of the ablest expositions of international law which has ever appeared, and John Bassett Moore said that "no one but a great lawyer with a profound apprehension of the principles of international law could have made such an argument." It is a far cry from such an effort to the case of *Theodore Tilton* vs. *Henry Ward Beecher*, in which, in May 1875, Evarts made the chief summation for the defense. His address required eight court days. A case of great importance was that of *Story* vs. *the New York Elevated Railroad Company* (90 *N. Y.*, 122) in which Evarts in 1882 successfully maintained the position that the owners of property abutting on streets through which elevated roads were built, could compel remuneration for the injury to their property caused by those structures. In 1885, in the *Matter of Jacobs* (98 *N. Y.*, 98), Evarts successfully attacked the constitutional validity of the Tenement House Cigar Law. His last appearance in court was in June 1889, in the case of *Post* vs. *Weil* (115 *N. Y.*, 361). In spite of failing eyesight, he wrote with his own hand a brief of eighty-two pages on the abstruse questions of real property involved, and won the case.

To the above record must now be added the fact that, to use the phrase of the late Frederic R. Coudert, Evarts was "the hero of the three great cases of our generation—the Johnson impeachment, the Tilden election case of 1876, the Geneva arbitration case." On Feb. 24, 1868, President Johnson was impeached by the House of Representatives for high crimes and misdemeanors. Eleven articles of impeachment were presented at the bar of the Senate on Mar. 4, and the trial by Chief Justice Chase and the Senate, which began on Mar. 30, lasted until May 26. The leader of counsel for the managers was Benjamin F. Butler. Evarts was most active for the defense, owing to the illness of Attorney-General Stanbery during the trial. He also made the chief closing argument, beginning on Apr. 28 and ending on May 1, an address of one hundred eighty pages. "His eloquent and solemn appeal," says Sherman Evarts, "lifted the whole proceeding from the murky atmosphere in which it had had its origin, to a region of lofty and patriotic wisdom . . . it arrayed with great force and learning the arguments upon the only serious question of law in the case—that arising from the tenure of office act" (Lewis, *post*, VII, 229). Largely through the efforts of Evarts, the two-thirds vote required by the Constitution for conviction was not obtained.

Evarts's participation in the case of the Savannah privateers and in the prize cases, and his two missions to England during the Civil War, together with his other wide experience in public and professional life, perfectly equipped him for service as counsel in the Geneva Arbitration of 1871–72. Under the Treaty of Washington, May 8, 1871, all claims against Great Britain by citizens of the United States who during the Civil War had suffered loss through activities of Confederate cruisers built, equipped, or manned in England, were referred to arbitration. The United States was represented by Charles Francis Adams (arbitrator), J. C. Bancroft Davis (agent), and Caleb Cushing, Morrison R. Waite, and William M. Evarts (counsel). The last made a notable oral argument, Aug. 5, 6, 1872, on the question of "due diligence," in reply to the printed argument of Sir Roundell Palmer (Lord Selborne). The latter had already formed a favorable opinion of Evarts as a result of an acquaintanceship begun in 1863; and in his memoirs he speaks of him in the highest terms, emphasizing his courtesy and conciliatory attitude. Evarts's name, he says, "was appended to the Case and other documents, of which we so much disliked the tone; but it did not stand alone; it was preceded by that of Mr. Cushing, and followed by that of Mr. Waite" (*Personal Memorials*, vol. I, 1898, p. 248). The meaning of this statement is brought out by a couplet in Selborne's alphabetical verses descriptive of the chief actors at Geneva, which reads:

"E, keen but high-minded, would courteous have been,
If his name were not written two others between"
(*Ibid.*, I, 277).

In the third of the great triad of cases,

the Hayes-Tilden presidential election dispute, Evarts was chief counsel for the Republican party. In the presidential canvass of 1876, both parties made claim to the electoral vote in whole or in part in four states. There being no constitutional or legislative provision for such an emergency, Congress created a commission of fifteen to decide the questions in dispute. Arguments of counsel were made before this commission in February 1877, and Evarts made oral arguments on the Florida, Louisiana, and Oregon cases. Having been criticized for accepting employment in what was considered to be wholly a partisan cause, he took the high ground that it was his duty as a citizen to do so, and that, whatever the consequences, the decision must be in accordance with the Constitution, which gave to the states the exclusive power to regulate the casting and counting of votes and to declare the result of the canvass, leaving to the electoral college the power only of counting the electoral votes certified by the states. His view prevailed, and Hayes was declared elected.

As a statesman, Evarts was adequate to every test that was offered, but no large achievement can be placed to his credit. He came into the Senate when he was sixty-six years of age. If his health had held good, he could, with his long training and experience in affairs of public interest, have made for himself a distinguished place in that body. Soon after he took office, his sight began to be impaired. In 1889 he went to Karlsbad to consult a specialist, but no help was found, and his infirmity increased until he was totally blind. Thereafter he lived in retirement. On Aug. 30, 1893, he and his wife celebrated their golden wedding. In 1897 he suffered an attack of grippe, which left him so weakened that thereafter he was confined to his house; and on Feb. 28, 1901, at the age of eighty-three, he died at his home in New York City.

In personal appearance, Evarts somewhat resembled Rufus Choate. He was extremely spare, and "thin as a lath," but erect and dignified in bearing. He appeared to be exceedingly frail, but had great powers of endurance, as shown by his performance in the Tilton-Beecher trial from which he was not absent once during its course of nearly six months. In one of his pictures he looks like Lincoln. His prominent forehead and nose gave to his face the appearance of massive strength. His eyes were penetrating and severe at times, but his expressive mouth made his countenance refined. He should be likened to an eagle rather than to a hawk. Like Charles O'Conor he habitually wore a frock coat and a high hat tilted a little backward on his head. He was noted as an orator, and could adapt his style to all occasions. His son compiled an impressive collection of his professional arguments, political and patriotic speeches, commemorative addresses, and after-dinner speeches. In the latter, Evarts showed a merry and spontaneous humor, debonair yet dry, and genial yet subtle. His speaking in this vein "rose to the level of the fine arts." He had the "dangerous gift of facility in speech," but his exalted character, both personal and professional, and his earnestness in dealing with serious matters, made him master of a solemn and forceful eloquence suggestive of the best efforts of Daniel Webster. His set speeches and professional arguments possessed one characteristic which is still a tradition. He clothed his thought "with sentences as long as the English language can supply," and with great involution and circumlocution of oratorical style drove on "a whole flock of several clauses, before he came to the close of a sentence." Withal, he was noted for remarkable clearness of statement. Choate said of him that he was the quickest witted man that he had ever met on either side of the water, and Southmayd, another law partner, emphasized his powers of apprehension, "which would mentally anticipate and complete the situation before the narration of facts was finished."

[*Arguments and Speeches of Wm. Maxwell Evarts* (3 vols., 1919), ed., with an introduction, by his son, Sherman Evarts; article by Sherman Evarts in Wm. D. Lewis, *Great American Lawyers,* VII (1909), 203–44; memorials in the *Report of the Twenty-Fourth Annual Meeting of the Am. Bar Asso.* (1901), pp. 624–28, and by Jas. C. Carter in *Annual Reports . . . of the Asso. of the Bar of the City of N. Y.*, 1902, pp. 101–02; Theron G. Strong, *Landmarks of a Lawyer's Lifetime* (1914), ch. 8; *Obit. Record Grads. Yale Univ. . . . 1900–10* (1910), p. 19; *N. Y. Times* and *N. Y. Daily Tribune,* Mar. 1, 1901.]

F. C. H.

EVE, JOSEPH (May 24, 1760–Nov. 14, 1835), inventor, scientist, and poet, youngest child of Oswald (or Oswell) Eve, merchant and sea-captain, and his wife Anne (Moore) Eve, was born in Philadelphia, where his father, originally from the low country of South Carolina, was engaged in the shipping trade. For business and perhaps for political reasons, his family removed to the West Indies and finally settled in the Bahamas about 1774. In his twenties, Eve invented a "machine for the separating of seed from cotton," which as early as 1787 was in use in the islands. Since many applications for the gin were coming from the Southern States, Senator Butler of South Carolina about 1794 presented to Congress a petition for a patent. About 1800 Eve came to live in Charleston County, S. C., at which time his gin was described as working "with two pair of rollers" and requiring "two young men or lads to supply the machine with cotton, as it feeds itself, and will gin out thirty-five pounds of cotton to the hour." It was adapted to animal or water-power. Together with such modifications as the Pottle, Birnie, Simpson, Nicholson, Whitmore, Farris, and Logan gins, it sometimes sold for as much as $250. In 1810 Eve removed to Richmond County, Ga., where he continued to manufacture gins. He built "The Cottage" near Augusta, and here he engaged in such diverse occupations as manufacturing gunpowder, experimenting with steam, and writing poetry. The American army is said to have used some of his gunpowder in 1812, and he obtained patents for a cottonseed huller (1803), metallic bands for power transmission (1828), and two steam-engines (1818 and 1826). The British government failed to adopt for its navy the steam-engine which Eve brought before it in 1826.

From 1820 to 1824 he contributed to Augusta newspapers several short poems and numerous excerpts of two long poems, "Better to Be" and "Projector." After two prospectuses, *Better to Be* appeared in 1823 in book form. It is an answer in couplets to Hamlet's question, and is in six parts of three hundred to five hundred lines each. The work is thoughtful and earnest but not searching or brilliant. Eve's rueful postscript states that "none but himself and the Printer has expressed a wish that it should emanate from the press," his friends having "uniformly employed the refrigerating system" toward a poem with so unpopular a theme as "Let us all be unhappy together." A friend of Benjamin Franklin and Dr. Benjamin Rush, "he was a man of broad culture, untiring energy and kindly, benevolent heart." Shortly before his death, he summarized in an epitaph his own impression of his life:

> "Here rests one fortune never favored,
> He grew no wiser from the past;
> But e'er with perseverance labored
> And still contended to the last."

Eve was married about 1800 to Hannah Singeltary of Charleston County, S. C., who was buried near him at "The Cottage." Joseph Adams Eve, his son, and Paul Fitzsimons Eve [*q.v.*], his nephew, were distinguished physicians of the next generation.

[Sources include: "Extracts from the Journal of Miss Sarah Eve," in *Pa. Mag. of Hist. and Biog.*, V (1881), 19, 191; W. A. Clark, "An Unremembered Poem," with material from Eve's letters, poems, epitaph, etc., in *Augusta Chronicle,* July 14, 1912; a letter from Joseph Eve to Dr. Benjamin Rush, dated Bahama Islands, Nassau, Nov. 24, 1794 (original among the Rush papers, Ridgway Lib., Phila.), printed in C. C. Jones, Jr., *Memorial Hist. of Augusta, Ga.* (1890); a notice in the *City Gazette and Daily Advertiser* (Charleston, S. C.), July 3, 1800; and Samuel DuBose, *Address Delivered at the 17th Anniversary of the Black Oak Agric. Soc., Apr. 27, 1858* (1858), repr. in *A Contribution to the Hist. of the Huguenots of S. C.* (1887), have some account of the Eve gin. See also A. S. Salley, Jr., *Register of St. Philip's Parish, Charles Town, S. C., 1720–58* (1904), *1754–1810* (1927); *Penna. Gazette,* Nov. 1, 1764; *A List of Patents Granted by the U. S., 1790–1836* (1872); *Augusta Herald,* July 4, Nov. 10, 1820, Feb. 6, 1821; *Augusta Chronicle,* Apr. 14, May 29, July 3, 17, 1824; *Charleston Courier,* Nov. 23, 1835.]
L. T.

EVE, PAUL FITZSIMONS (June 27, 1806–Nov. 3, 1877), surgeon, was born at Forest Hall on the Savannah River near Augusta, Ga. His parents, Capt. Oswell and Aphra Anna (Pritchard) Eve, were of Anglo-Irish descent, his father a brother of Joseph Eve [*q.v.*]. He attended Franklin College (now the University of Georgia) at Athens, where he was given the degree of B.A. in 1826. Following graduation he went to Philadelphia, entering the office of Dr. Charles D. Meigs to study medicine and at the same time matriculating at the University of Pennsylvania. Here he obtained his degree of M.D. in 1828, then returned to Augusta, where he spent a year in practise. The next two years he spent in the clinics of the most famous surgeons of London and Paris. In the latter city, he "participated professionally" in the revolution of July 1831. Later, when the Russian army was reported marching upon Warsaw, he offered his services to the Polish government and served in a Warsaw hospital, and later with the Polish forces in the field. Following the fall of Warsaw he returned to Paris, and later in the same year to the United States. He settled for practise in Augusta, where, in 1832, he participated in the organization of the Medical College of Georgia. On the faculty of this school he was professor of surgery until 1850, when he resigned to take the same chair at the University of Louisville, made vacant by the resignation of Samuel D. Gross [*q.v.*]. He remained at the Louisville school through but one course, resigning on account of the illness of his wife. In 1851 he was appointed professor of surgery in the University of Nashville, a position he held for ten years. At the outbreak of the Civil War, he was appointed surgeon-general of Tennessee, later was chief surgeon of Gen. Joseph E. Johnston's army, and still later surgeon in the Gate City Hospital, in Atlanta. After the close of the war, he resumed the teaching of surgery, first at Missouri Medical College, St. Louis, later at the University of Nashville, and finally in 1877, at the newly organized Nashville Medical College. Shortly after this last change he died suddenly while calling upon a patient.

In the forty-five years of his active career, Eve became the leading surgeon and the leading teacher of surgery of the South. He perfected an operation for vesical calculus which was highly successful. His experience with this operation was reported in "A Synopsis and Analysis of One Hundred Cases of Lithotomy" (*Transactions of the American Medical Association,* vol. XXII, 1871). He is credited with being the first American surgeon to perform the operation of hysterectomy. In addition to the teaching positions that he occupied, he was compelled to decline many flattering offers of similar positions. He was for a time co-editor of the *Southern Medical and Surgical Journal* and assistant editor of the *Nashville Journal of Medicine and Surgery.* He contributed nearly six hundred articles to periodical literature. His most notable writings were: *A Collection of Remarkable Cases in Surgery* (1857) and "A Contribution to the History of the Hip-joint Operations Performed during the Late Civil War" (1867), included in the *Medical and Surgical History of the War.* He was president of the American Medical Association in 1857–58. Eve had an unusual experience in military surgery. In addition to his service with the Polish army and in the Civil War, during his professorship at the Medical College of Georgia he served in the Mexican War and he was present as an observer at the battles of Magenta and Solferino in Italy in 1859.

Myopic from childhood and afflicted with tone deafness, he overcame these handicaps by methodical industry. He used neither alcohol nor tobacco at a time when their use was general. His portrait, taken in middle life, shows a serious face with full beard, large nose, and prominent eyes, looking out through thick lenses. He married Sarah Louisa Twiggs, grand-daughter of Gen. Twiggs of the Revolutionary War. She died in 1851, and in the following year he married Sarah Ann Duncan, daughter of a South Carolina clergyman. To this marriage, two sons and a daughter were born, the two sons taking up the profession of their father.

[See *Biog. of Eminent Am. Physicians and Surgeons* (1894), ed. by R. French Stone; D. J. Roberts in *Trans. Med. Soc. State of Tenn.,* 1878; R. Douglas in *Trans. Southern Surgic. and Gynecol. Asso.,* vol. IX (1897); T. C. Dow in *Trans. Am. Medic. Asso.,* vol. XXIX, 1878; sketch of Eve's son in *Southern Practitioner* (Nashville), XXXVII, 26 (1915); *Daily American* (Nashville), Nov. 4, 1877; additional references listed in *Index-Catalogue* of the Surgeon-General's Library. Eve's middle name is variously spelled. The spelling given above was adopted on the authority of a grandson, Duncan Eve, Jr., M.D., of Nashville.] J. M. P.

EVERENDON, WALTER (d. 1725), colonial gunpowder manufacturer, when he first appeared on the stage of American colonial history was described as "a Kentish man." On Aug. 22, 1673, the Rev. John Oxenbridge, the Rev. James Allen, and three laymen formed a partnership to build a powder-mill at Neponset in the township of Milton, across the river from Dorchester, Mass. They soon took in two more partners, and in 1675 appointed Everendon, who had manufactured powder in England, to be the overseer of the mill, which within three months after he took charge was running at full capacity in order to supply the settlers with powder for the prosecution of King Philip's War. The Massachusetts General Court considered the mill of so great importance as a source of supply that they arranged for guarding it and allowed the owners to impress men to build a watch-tower on the other side of the river. Everendon's sole claim to fame is having thus accidentally been instrumental in supplying the colonial forces with much-needed ammunition against the Indians. He was, however, the first man to make powder in America. It has been said that the Dorchester powder was of better quality than that which had been made previously, but the importance of the mill was due to the size of its output at a critical time, for which credit would seem to be due to the capitalists as much as to Everendon. In 1701 the latter bought out one of the partners and gradually acquired the interests of all but one of the others. In 1724 he sold out to his son, and died the following year. The family, which also spelled their name Everden and Everton, continued to manufacture powder until after the Revolution, although by 1775 they appear to have fallen into poverty.

[*Records of the Gov. and Co. of the Mass. Bay,* vol. V (1854); D. T. V. Huntoon, "The Powder Mill in Canton," *New-Eng. Hist. and Geneal. Reg.,* July 1877, and *Hist. of the Town of Canton, Mass.* (1893); A. P. Van Gelder and H. Schlatter, *Hist. of the Explosives Industry in America* (1927), pp. 32–36; A. K. Teele, *The Hist. of Milton, Mass.* (1887), pp. 368–70.] J. T. A.

EVERETT, ALEXANDER HILL (Mar. 19, 1790–June 29, 1847), editor, diplomat, son of the Rev. Oliver and Lucy (Hill) Everett and brother of Edward Everett [*q.v.*], was born in Boston, Mass., where his father was minister of the New South Church. After graduating from Harvard in 1806, being the youngest member of his class and also the one in highest standing, he taught for a time at Phillips Exeter Academy and studied law in the office of John Quincy Adams. He was a member of the Anthology Club, and during the last months of its existence, one of the editors of the *Monthly Anthology* (Mott, *post,* pp. 253 ff.). In 1809, when John Quincy Adams was appointed minister to Russia, Everett accompanied him as private secretary, remaining there for two years. In 1815–16 he was secretary of the American legation at The Hague; in September of the latter year he was married to Lucretia Orne Peabody. Returning to The Hague in 1818 as chargé d'affaires, he served there until 1824. When Adams became president in 1825, Everett was appointed minister to Spain, and held that position for four years. His instructions from Henry Clay, secretary of state, required him to urge upon the Spanish government the importance of recognizing the independence of her revolted colonies in the New World (*American State Papers, Foreign Relations,* V, 866 ff.); and he prepared an elaborate memorandum for this purpose, dated Jan. 20, 1826 (*Ibid.,* VI, 1006–14). The question of whether Spain would be able to hold Cuba and Porto Rico was one of considerable concern at that time. In a confidential communication to President Adams, Nov. 30, 1825, Everett proposed that the United States lend Spain a large sum of money, taking Cuba as security (*Cuba: The Everett Letters on Cuba,* 1897). Everett's extensive diplomatic experience bore fruit in two volumes: *Europe* (1822), and *America* (1827). Each is a general survey of the principal powers of the several continents, "with conjectures on their future prospects." They attracted considerable attention and were translated into several languages. During this period he also published *New Ideas on Population, with Remarks on the Theories of Malthus and Godwin* (1823).

Upon his return to America, he acquired (1830) a controlling interest in the *North American Review,* and succeeded Jared Sparks as its editor. During the five years in which he had charge of it he did much in improving its quality, but it was not a financial success, and at the end of this time he found himself heavily embarrassed. His standing in the community suffered further from the fact that, although he had served in the state legislature for several terms as a Whig, he left that party and joined the Democrats; and his activity in the state elections in 1839 was believed to have contributed to his brother's failure to be reëlected governor (P. R. Frothingham, *Life of Edward Everett,* 1925, pp. 154–55). From this time on, his ties with Massachusetts were severed. For a brief period he served as a confidential agent of the government in Cuba. Later he was president of Jefferson College, in Louisiana, but soon resigned on account of ill health. In 1845, at the beginning of Polk's administration, he was appointed commissioner to China, the first representative of the United States to be designated under the treaty with China which had just been negotiated by Caleb Cushing [*q.v.*]. Forced by illness to turn back from his journey thither, he started again as soon as he felt that his health permitted, but died in Canton not long after his arrival (*Chinese Repository,* July 1847).

Everett was a man of ability and industry, but unstable. The financial and political embarrassment that he caused his popular brother brought him disesteem in Massachusetts that has tended to obscure his creditable earlier career as a diplomat and an editor. His articles for the *North American Review* and other publications, collected in two volumes of *Critical and Miscellaneous Essays* (1845–46), treat of literary, philosophical, and political topics after the manner of the British quarterlies of the period. The *Poems* (1845) are almost entirely imitations and translations.

[In addition to references cited above see E. F. Everett, *Descendants of Richard Everett of Dedham, Mass.* (1902); E. E. Hale, *Sketches of the Lives of the Brothers Everett* (1878), and obituary of A. H. Everett in *Christian Examiner,* Jan. 1848; J. S. Loring, *The Hundred Boston Orators,* etc. (1852); "Letters of J. Q. Adams to A. H. Everett, 1817–37" in *Am. Hist. Rev.,* Oct. 1905–Jan. 1906; F. L. Mott, *A Hist. of Am. Magazines, 1741–1850* (1930). Everett's official correspondence as chargé d'affaires at The Hague and as minister to Spain, together with his private correspondence, 1809–34, is in the possession of the Mass. Hist. Soc. A portrait by Alexander, done while he was at The Hague, belongs to Arthur Hale of Washington, D. C.; and a miniature of about the same date to Philip L. Hale, of Dedham, Mass.] H. G. P.

EVERETT, CHARLES CARROLL (June 19, 1829–Oct. 16, 1900), theologian, was the son of Ebenezer Everett, a lawyer and a first cousin of Edward Everett [*q.v.*], and his wife, Joanna Bachelder Prince. On both sides he came of the purest New England stock. He was born in the family home in Brunswick, Me., there spent his youth, and was graduated at Bowdoin in 1850 at the head of his class. He spent a number of terms at the Bowdoin Medical College, and studied in Europe during the year 1851–52. From 1853 to 1857 he taught modern languages at Bowdoin; for three of these years he acted also as librarian of the college. He was elected to a full professorship by the trustees but the appointment was vetoed by the Overseers on the ground that he was a Unitarian. In 1857 he entered the Harvard Divinity School, graduating in 1859. He had a notable pastorate at the Independent Congregational (Unitarian) Church in Bangor, Me., from 1859 to 1869. During these years he wrote *The Science of Thought,* a treatise on the principles of human knowledge, published in 1869. The book attracted the attention of the Harvard Corporation, who that year called him to the Bussey Professorship of Theology. He became dean of the Divinity School in 1878, and held that office as well as his professorship for the remainder of his life. His was one of the earliest of the important appointments of President Charles W. Eliot [*q.v.*]. The Divinity School was unorganized and there was a wide divergence of opinion as to its status and function. When Everett joined it, the faculty numbered three. At his death the number had grown to nine, the school had become closely coördinated with the university, and its material equipment had been much increased. All this was in no small degree due to the wisdom and practical management of the dean. As early as 1872 he began his course in East Asiatic Religions, perhaps the first course in comparative religions to be given in the United States. He gave both this and the general course in theology as long as he lived.

Although he had studied medicine and had taught modern languages, philosophy, as the vehicle for the study of theology, became his major interest. He solved the problem of the undenominational divinity school by confining his teaching to the realm that lies beneath all the divergent creeds. He taught the possibility of a faith that rested on no creed, and his teaching, although presenting no system of theology, lighted up the whole realm of religion, with Christianity in the supreme place. Men of all faiths were among his pupils, yet he antagonized none and was broad enough to sympathize with all. He was a consummate teacher and many thoughtful ministers of different denominations have looked back to him as the greatest intellectual and spiritual inspiration of their lives.

He was one of the founders of the *New World*—a quarterly review of religion and theology—a constant contributor to its pages, and its senior editor at the time of his death. He also contributed a great number of articles to magazines and reviews. Among his more important volumes were: *The Science of Thought,* previously mentioned; *Religions before Christianity* (1883), which was translated into Dutch for use in the schools of Holland; *Fichte's Science of Knowledge* (1884); *Essays on Poetry, Comedy and Duty* (1888); *Ethics for Young People* (1891); *The Gospel of Paul* (1893). As a writer he had a clear and beautifully simple style. As a preacher he presented wide and deep thought in simple language and with apt illustration. He was modest and unconventional, but dignified, inspiring others with a sense of his reserved power. One writer said: "That which made him great among his fellows was the elevation of his own thought, the purity of his sentiment, and his freedom from artificial limitations, . . . combined with a rare insight into the thoughts of other men, and into the meaning of creeds alien or inferior to his own" (*Christian Register,* Oct. 25, 1900). A good description of his personality is given by his colleague, Professor Emerton: "He moved among us, frail, delicate, feeble of sight and hearing, shy, reticent, never putting himself forward into any place he thought another could fill, yet with such reserves of courage, of strength, of eloquent speech, of fervid enthusiasm, that no person and no righteous cause ever appealed to him in vain for counsel or for help" (*Obituary Record of the Graduates of Bowdoin College, 1900–09,* 1911, p. 75). In August 1859, he married Sarah Octavia Dwinel of Lisbon, Me., who died on Feb. 16, 1895.

[In addition to sources cited above, see S. A. Eliot, *Heralds of a Liberal Faith,* vol. III (1910); E. F. Everett, *Descendants of Richard Everett of Dedham, Mass.* (1902); *New World,* Dec. 1900; *Boston Transcript,* Oct. 17, 1900; *Harvard Grads. Mag.,* Dec. 1900.]

F. T. P.

EVERETT, DAVID (Mar. 29, 1770–Dec. 21, 1813), lawyer, journalist, author, a second cousin of Edward Everett, was born at Princeton, Mass., the son of David Everett, who fought at Bunker Hill, and Susannah (Rolfe) Everett. After attending the academy at New Ipswich, N. H., he taught in the grammar school of that town and wrote for a seven-year-old pupil the famous lines:

> "You'd scarce expect one of my age
> To speak in public on the stage . . ."

Thereafter he entered Dartmouth and graduated in 1795, valedictorian of his class. He next read law with John M. Forbes, and after his admission to the bar, with Thomas O. Selfridge opened an office in Boston. Early becoming interested in politics, he wrote for the *Boston Gazette* over the signature "Junius Americanus" (Loring, *post,* p. 339). He practised from about 1802 to 1807 at Amherst, N. H., and then returned to Boston. In 1809 he founded a newspaper, the *Boston Patriot,* devoted to the Democratic party. Two years later he was made register of probate for Suffolk County, Mass., but a change of administration soon deprived him of this office. During Elbridge Gerry's governorship (1810–12), Everett was clerk of the Massachusetts House of Representatives. In 1812 he became editor of the *Pilot,* but the next year, the serious state of his health requiring a change of residence, he removed to Marietta, Ohio, where he established the *American Friend.* Eight months later he died of tuberculosis. He was survived by his wife, Dorothy Appleton, whom he had married on Dec. 29, 1799.

Everett first gained some prominence as a writer by a series of articles on economic and ethical subjects somewhat in the Poor Richard style, which appeared in the *Farmer's Museum* between May 17 and Dec. 26, 1797, under the title

"Common Sense in Dishabille." A five-act play which he wrote, *Daranzel; or, the Persian Patriot* (printed in 1800), was given a single performance at the Haymarket Theatre, Boston, Apr. 16, 1798, and was revived for two performances, perhaps with the recent death of Washington in mind, at the Federal Street Theatre, Jan. 29 and Feb. 5, 1800. This drama, written in fairly successful blank verse, presents a hero who opposes a tyrant and wins. The prologue exhibits the author's devotion to his country by stressing the absence of tyrants in America; while Daranzel's final speech counsels against factions, with their disregard for law and justice. Something of the same note was struck in Everett's introductory address to an oration delivered by William Charles White at Boston, July 4, 1809. He here inveighed against party rancor and insisted that harmony of sentiment was essential to the nation's welfare. Against the treatment of the United States merchant marine by the British navy Everett wrote a dignified protest, *An Essay on the Rights and Duties of Nations, Relative to Fugitives from Justice, Considered with Reference to the Affair of the Chesapeake* (1807). The outrages committed by the North African pirates called out *Slaves in Barbary,* a two-act play, published in *The Columbian Orator* (1810 and later editions). *The Columbian Orator* also contains a number of poems and dialogues by Everett, several of which reiterate his love of freedom and justice.

[E. F. Everett, *Descendants of Richard Everett of Dedham, Mass.* (1902); I. A. Jewett, *Memorial of Samuel Appleton of Ipswich, Mass.* (1850); J. S. Loring, *The Hundred Boston Orators* (1852); G. T. Chapman, *Sketches of the Alumni of Dartmouth Coll.* (1867); *Proc. Am. Antiquarian Soc.,* n.s., vol. VI (1890); contemporary Boston newspapers.] O. S. C.

EVERETT, EDWARD (Apr. 11, 1794–Jan. 15, 1865), Unitarian clergyman, teacher, statesman, and one of the most famous of American orators, was born in Dorchester, Mass. His parents were the Rev. Oliver and Lucy (Hill) Everett; he was the fourth child in a family of eight, one of his elder brothers being Alexander Hill Everett [*q.v.*]. After graduating from Harvard in 1811, with the highest honors although he was the youngest member of his class, he pursued studies in divinity, and in 1814 received the degree of M.A. His brilliant powers as a speaker promised a notable career. Invited almost immediately to become the minister of the Brattle Street Church (Unitarian), he was installed as pastor of the largest and most fashionable congregation in Boston on Feb. 9, 1814, before he was twenty years old. After a little over a year of service in this position, he accepted an invitation to occupy the recently established chair of Greek literature at Harvard. In 1815 he sailed for Europe to enter upon what proved to be a four-years' period of preparation for his new duties. The degree of Ph.D. which was awarded him at Göttingen in 1817 was the first to be given to an American (*Harvard Graduates' Magazine,* September 1897, p. 14). After two years spent in travel, he began his work at Harvard in 1819. In addition to his academic duties, he was editor of the *North American Review.* In 1822 he joined himself even more closely with the socially élite by his marriage with Charlotte Gray Brooks, a daughter of Peter C. Brooks [*q.v.*], one of the leading business men of Boston, another daughter of whom became the wife of Charles Francis Adams. To Everett and his wife six children were born.

Everett's success as a teacher, bringing the fruits of German scholarship to American undergraduates, is attested by the eloquent words of Ralph Waldo Emerson, who was one of his pupils (*Complete Works,* X, 330–35). Everett was already noted as an orator and for "his radiant beauty of person, of a classic style." His brilliant Phi Beta Kappa oration at Harvard in August 1824 gave impetus to the career in national politics for which he had cherished an ambition. On the occasion of this address Lafayette was present; and the closing words of the speech, directed to the aged hero, were delivered with such fervor that for some moments the audience sat spellbound, and then burst into a tumult of applause. By virtue of Everett's intuitive dramatic sense, the grace of his language, the music of his voice, and above all the magnetism of his presence, he created an unforgettable impression. The oration had the immediate result of bringing him the nomination, made by a convention of independent voters, for representative to Congress for the Middlesex district. He was elected in November.

During his five terms in Congress, from 1825 to 1835, he represented the dominant conservatism of his state, showing great deference to Southern feeling on the slavery question (*Register of Debates,* 19 Cong., 1 Sess., Mar. 9, 1826, p. 1579), supporting the Bank of the United States, and opposing what he termed the "Levellers" (Darling, *post,* p. 132). His declination to run again in 1834 was due to no lack of political ambition. A year earlier his name had been cautiously advanced for the governorship of Massachusetts by his brother, Alexander H. Everett. Hoping to be nominated by a union of the National Republican and Anti-Masonic parties, he declared against Freemasonry, but finding he had offended the Masonic element in the former group, declined to be considered (Darling, *post,* pp. 106–10). In 1835, however, he was elected governor by a combination of Whigs and Anti-Masons, effected in large part by Caleb Cushing [*q.v.*], to whom Everett revealed his ambitions in many letters (Fuess, *post,* I, 162–68). He served four terms as governor, from 1836 to 1839, inclusive, being at length defeated for reëlection by Marcus Morton [*q.v.*], who won by a single vote. The chief constructive measures of his administration were the creation of a state board of education and a system of normal schools, and the grant of a million dollars by the state to aid in the construction of a railroad to the Hudson River.

During a period of rest and travel which followed, he was appointed minister to the Court of St. James's, where he remained from November 1841 until August 1845. On account of his standing in the world of scholarship and letters, his social grace, and his charm as an orator, he was to the British a novel type of American, and their appreciation of him was constantly made manifest. Between the two countries at this time there were differences on such important matters as the settlement of the northeastern boundary and the suppression of the slave-trade on the coast of Africa; but these were adjusted in Washington by Lord Ashburton and Daniel Webster, secretary of state. He had been criticized by some of the Whigs, as by Emerson, who said he was "attracted by the vulgar prizes of politics" (*Journals, 1841–44,* VI, 255), for retaining his post after the accession of Tyler, and he shared the embarrassments of the conservative Whigs incident to the war with Mexico, so his election as president of Harvard in 1846 provided an opportune withdrawal from politics. Finding the duties of the position, disciplinary and otherwise, little to his liking, however, he resigned in 1849.

On two occasions it was his fortune to make a contribution of some importance in the field of the foreign relations of the United States. In 1850, at the request of Webster, he drafted a letter defending the action of President Taylor in sending a special agent to report on the revolution in Hungary. Addressed to Hülsemann, the Austrian chargé d'affaires in Washington, this letter, the ultra-patriotic tone of which was accentuated by alterations made by Webster, upheld the right of the United States to extend sympathy to another nation struggling to achieve popular government. It was meant for popular consumption at home, and as such was highly successful. In December 1852, while Everett himself was secretary of state, he prepared a reply to the proposal of France and England that the United States should unite with them in a tripartite convention guaranteeing to Spain the possession of Cuba and promising to abstain from attempts to acquire it. In rejecting the proposal, Everett argued, in clear-cut and vigorous language, that the United States had a special interest in Cuba on account of its proximity, that she had already purchased Louisiana and Florida, and that it was not "within the competence of the treaty-making power in 1852 effectually to bind the government in all its branches; and, for all coming time, not to make a similar purchase of Cuba." Similar in tone to the Hülsemann letter, the note drew sharp contrasts between the institutions and prosperity of the United States and the state of things in Europe. "What would have been her condition in these trying years but for the outlet we have furnished for her starving millions?" (*The Everett Letters on Cuba,* 1897). The letter received general commendation in the United States, both as a logical application of the Monroe Doctrine and on account of its effective form and popular appeal.

Everett's service of four months as secretary of state terminated with the close of Fillmore's administration in March 1853; but he at once entered the Senate, having been elected for a six-year term by the Massachusetts legislature. His political career, now at its height, was, however, to end ignominiously within fifteen months. Ambition had led him to a field of conflict upon which, because of the strain of timidity in his character, he was unfitted to play the fighting part that the times demanded. The struggle over the question of slavery, allayed somewhat by the compromise of 1850, broke out with fresh and alarming violence over the Kansas-Nebraska Bill. Everett, opposed to slavery, had uniformly deprecated agitation of the question of its abolition, fearing that such agitation would threaten the stability of the Union. Now that Webster was dead, Everett, his ardent disciple and intimate friend, was looked upon as his natural successor. By temperament and by social ties he was affiliated with the Boston Whigs, but their moderate and "Union-saving" attitude placed them at a constantly increasing disadvantage as the tide of anti-slavery sentiment rose in Massachusetts and throughout the North. Everett spoke earnestly against the Nebraska bill, though not with the denunciatory ardor of his colleague, Charles Sumner; unfortunately, however, when the final vote was taken he was absent from the Senate on account of illness. Though his stand was well known, his anti-slavery opponents made much of this "defection," and he became so uncomfortable that he resigned before the end of the session. The remark of his brother-in-law, Charles Francis Adams, that Everett was "stuff not good enough to wear in rainy weather, though bright enough in sunshine" (E. L. Pierce, *Memoir and Letters of Charles Sumner,* III, 1893, pp. 369–70), suggests the trait in his character which made him out of place in political life when the period of compromise was yielding to one of conflict. Perhaps a truer judgment is that his passion for the Union as the greatest experiment of humanity in the art of government was so intense that he would make almost any concession rather than take a stand which might help to bring about its dissolution. As he himself said later in his Gettysburg address: "A sad foreboding of what would ensue, if war should break out between North and South, has haunted me through life, and led me, perhaps too long, to tread in the path of hopeless compromise, in the fond endeavor to conciliate those who were predetermined not to be conciliated" (*Orations and Speeches,* IV, 652). No longer holding office, Everett found opportunity to be of public service in many ways, but in particular by delivering a lecture on the character of Washington, the proceeds of which he contributed to the undertaking recently inaugurated by Ann Pamela Cunningham [*q.v.*] for the purchase and preservation of Mount Vernon as a national monument. A willing traveler, he journeyed the length and breadth of the country, addressing large audiences everywhere, and ultimately turned over to the Mount Vernon Ladies' Association of the Union a total of $69,064. Emphasizing Washington's transcendent accomplishment in establishing the Union, he had opportunity also to turn the thoughts of his listeners to the necessity of preserving it. In the pursuance of this patriotic task he continued till the very outbreak of the Civil War, delivering the lecture no less than 129 times.

In the campaign of 1860 Everett accepted the nomination as vice-president on the ticket of the Constitutional Union party, the candidate for president being John Bell of Tennessee [*q.v.*]. This party, the remnant of the old-line Whigs, deplored the sectional division which had resulted from the agitation of the question of slavery, and in its platform affirmed as the paramount issues of the day "the Constitution of the country, the Union of the States, and the enforcement of the laws." Everett had little wish for a place on the ticket, certainly not for second place; he accepted the nomination half-heartedly and was not surprised at the result of the election. The candidates of the Constitutional Union party

took the third place in the electoral vote; in the popular vote Bell and Everett stood at the bottom of the list.

With the formation of the Southern Confederacy following the election of Lincoln, Everett's course on the path of compromise was nearly ended; and when Sumter was fired upon and he saw his beloved Union attacked, he had no question as to his course. Without delay he gave his whole-hearted support to the government. Though he was sixty-seven years old, his powers as an orator had in no wise failed and his name could draw large audiences. He made it his war service to travel everywhere in the North, describing the issues of the conflict and exhorting his hearers to give their support to a cause in the righteousness of which he believed heart and soul. Hitherto his orations had been eloquent and finished lectures. Now they became calls to action in the presence of danger, all the stronger in their appeal because of his mastery of his art. In the first year of the war, for a period of several months, he spoke twice a week or oftener; as the contest wore on he was always ready to give of his best.

Of these addresses in war time—twenty-three in number, some of them frequently repeated—the best known, by name at least, is the oration delivered at the dedication of the national cemetery at Gettysburg on Nov. 19, 1863. The occasion furnished opportunity for a public address unequaled in American history. Part of Everett's duty was to depict, for the thousands who had thronged the little town, the course of the three days' battle which had made its name famous. He had studied thoroughly the official reports of the commanders, and had familiarized himself with the topography of the field. As he called the roll of its landmarks, Seminary Ridge, the Peach-Orchard, Cemetery Hill, Culp's Hill, and Wolf Hill, Round Top, Little Round Top, he could exclaim, "humble names, henceforward dear and famous!" Less commented on at the time, but more significant as a revelation of Everett's nationalism, was his prophecy of the day of reconciliation that would follow a restored Union. "The bonds that unite us as one People,—a substantial community of origin, language, belief, and law (the four great ties that hold the societies of men together); common national and political interests; a common history; a common pride in a glorious ancestry; a common interest in this great heritage of blessings; the very geographical features of the country; . . . these bonds of union are of perennial force and energy, while the causes of alienation are imaginary, factitious, and transient" (*Orations and Speeches,*

IV, 657). Everett's own effort did not blind him to the unexpected masterpiece of oratory that fell from Lincoln's lips when he himself had finished. "I should be glad," he wrote the President the next day, "if I could flatter myself that I came as near the central idea of the occasion in two hours as you did in two minutes" (Frothingham, *post,* p. 458). Lincoln, in reply, expressing his pleasure in knowing that the little he "did say was not entirely a failure," gave discriminating praise to Everett's performance.

The earnest, sustained, and brilliant contribution made by Everett to the Union cause naturally involved a break with friends and associates of a lifetime. When he consented to become the president of the newly formed Union Club of Boston, he was warned that it was an "Abolition concern" and a "Jacobin Association." On the other hand, he was drawn into fellowship with the "human rights statesmen," and their approbation has contributed in no small measure to his fame. The uncompromising Charles Francis Adams, who had complained that his brother-in-law's timidity was "almost like that of a woman," paid ungrudging tribute to the achievement of these years. "The progress of events had brought him to a point where his fears no longer checked him, for his interests . . . ran on all fours with his convictions. As a consequence he spoke forth at last with all his power what he really felt. To me his four last years appear worth more than all the rest of his life, including the whole series of his rhetorical triumphs" (C. F. Adams, *Dana,* II, 280).

Popular recognition of his war service reached a climax at the end of the presidential campaign of 1864, in which, though in failing health, he had urged the reëlection of Lincoln and the vigorous prosecution of the war. Summoned to Faneuil Hall on the evening of election day, he was greeted with enthusiasm tumultuous and prolonged. Used as he was to applause, the scene was such as he had never witnessed before, and he was "quite overcome." The tribute was not to his oratory, for he "attempted to utter only a few congratulatory sentences"; it was to the patriot and the man (Frothingham, *post,* p. 464). In his last speech, delivered at Faneuil Hall on behalf of the sufferers at Savannah, which had recently been occupied by Sherman's forces, he again sounded the note of reconciliation. "Savannah wants our pork and beef and flour; and I say, in Heaven's name, let us send it to them without money and without price. . . . Let us offer it to them freely, not in the spirit of almsgiving, but as a pledge of fraternal feeling, and an earnest of our disposition to resume all the kind offices of fellow-citizenship with our returning brethren" (*Orations and Speeches,* IV, 755–56). The return itself he did not live to see. The fatigues of the day on which he spoke these words brought on an illness from which he died on Jan. 15, 1865.

Everett's *Orations and Speeches on Various Occasions* (4 vols., 1853–68), which exclude addresses on political topics except for the period of the Civil War, show his scholarly mind and his ardent Americanism. Though carefully finished, they are not excessively artificial, as has sometimes been charged; on occasion, notably in the eulogy on Thomas Dowse delivered before the Massachusetts Historical Society, they reveal a warm and rich humanity. Covering a wide range of subjects, these addresses, though they have no originality of thought, show Everett as a disseminator of enlightening information, and as a master in the art of investing it with the magic of literary form.

[P. R. Frothingham, *Edward Everett, Orator and Statesman* (1925), is sympathetic and judicial in tone. For characterizations of Everett by his contemporaries, see E. W. Emerson and W. E. Forbes, *Jours. of Ralph Waldo Emerson,* VI (1911), 255 ff., VII (1912), 166–70; "Historic Notes of Life and Letters in New Eng.," in *The Complete Works of Ralph Waldo Emerson,* X (1904), 325–70; C. F. Adams, *Richard Henry Dana, A Biography,* II (1890), 279–80; and R. H. Dana, *An Address upon the Life and Services of Edward Everett* (1865). For an admirable later estimate, see Barrett Wendell, *A Lit. Hist. of America* (1901), pp. 253–57. Letters between Everett and John McLean are in *Proc. Mass. Hist. Soc.,* 3 ser. I (1908), 359–93. The Everett papers, a large collection, are deposited with this society. See also Henry Wilson, *Hist. of the Rise and Fall of the Slave Power in America,* vol. I (1875); C. M. Fuess, *The Life of Caleb Cushing* (2 vols., 1923); Arthur B. Darling, *Political Changes in Mass., 1824–48* (1925); *Boston Daily Advertiser* and *N. Y. Daily News,* Jan. 16, 1865.] H. G. P.

EVERETT, ROBERT (Jan. 2, 1791–Feb. 25, 1875), Congregational clergyman and publisher, was born at Gronant, North Wales, the oldest son of Lewis and Jane Everett. He was of mingled Welsh, Scotch, and English blood. His father supported the large family of eleven children by serving as manager of a lead mine; by preference, however, and on occasion, he preached for the Congregationalists. Raised in a strongly Calvinistic atmosphere, Robert early decided to enter the ministry. Soon after graduating from Wrexham Seminary in 1815 he became pastor of the large Congregational church at Denbigh. Though lacking the eloquence of some of his more famous contemporaries in the Welsh pulpit, he possessed such earnestness and learning that he soon gained great influence even outside his own denomination. For some years he was the assistant editor of the *Dysgedydd* (Inquirer), a Congregational periodical. In 1822 he published a catechism which ran through many editions in both Wales and America. Having accepted a call to the Welsh Congregational Church of Utica, N. Y., he emigrated in 1823. For the next forty-five years he held this charge or others in Oneida County. For a time he preached in English, but in 1838 he moved to the township of Steuben where he served two Welsh churches until a few years before his death.

Meanwhile the Welsh Congregationalists had decided to establish a periodical to serve their members. Everett was chosen one of the three editors, and in January 1840 they published the first issue of *Y Cenhadwr Americanaidd* (The American Messenger), a monthly religious review destined during the sixty-one years of its life to hold the foremost place among Welsh-American publications and to exert its influence in Wales itself. Everett assumed active charge as editor at the beginning and in 1842 became its proprietor and sole editor. Until that time the *Cenhadwr* had been printed in Utica but, the frequent trips on horseback to that town proving too burdensome to a clergyman in active service, Everett set up a press first in Remsen, then in his parsonage on his hill farm in Steuben. Here his sons printed the review, the other members of his family assisting in typesetting, proofreading, and sewing of the sheets within the covers.

Everett was a zealous reformer though not an extreme radical. He had welcomed anti-slavery speakers to his pulpit at an early date and himself had long preached the virtue of total abstinence from alcoholic liquors. He now made the *Cenhadwr* the champion among the Welsh-Americans of Abolition and prohibition. Constantly he denounced the interstate slave-trade, the Fugitive-Slave Law, and slavery in the districts under federal control. Elimination of these abuses, he believed, would doom slavery in the South. At first he met stubborn resistance among the Welsh who, though nominally opponents of slavery, refused to abandon the Democratic and Whig ranks for the Liberty Party and who were scandalized by Everett's action in bringing politics into the pulpit and into a religious review. His opponents almost succeeded in ousting him from his pastorates. Fearing that desertion of disgruntled subscribers both North and South might force a suspension of the *Cenhadwr,* Everett in 1843 published most of his abolitionist articles in a new monthly called *Y Dyngarwr* (The Philanthropist). This he distributed free of charge to Welsh preachers whose aid was vital to the "cause." After its suspension at the end of one year he continued his propaganda in the *Cenhadwr.* His campaign in favor of Birney in 1844 showed slight results among the Welsh, though Everett himself had a souvenir of the bitter contest in his carriage horse, "Bobtail Birney," whose tail and mane had been mutilated by his opponents. Slowly however his supporters increased. The *Cenhadwr* gained in quality and in prestige. When it advocated the moderate program of the Free-Soilers, it won many converts; after the Kansas-Nebraska Act it gained far more. Most of the Welsh went with Everett into the young Republican party where they have remained to this day. Though *Cenhadwr* may never have reached a circulation of 2,500, its influence was out of all proportion to its size. In 1853 Everett published in book form a Welsh translation of *Uncle Tom's Cabin.* He was also publisher of a popular Welsh hymnal and for two years, 1850–52, of a small literary monthly called *Y Detholydd* (The Eclectic). He received the degree of D.D. from Hamilton College in 1861. Before leaving Wales he had married (1816) Elizabeth Roberts by whom he had eleven children. Their daughter Mary was one of the earliest woman physicians in America.

[D. Davies, *Cofiant y diweddar Barch. Robt. Everett* (Utica, 1879), is a careful biography in Welsh. The most important source for Everett's life is the file of the *Cenhadwr* included in the Robert Everett collection of Welsh-American periodicals in the library of Harvard Univ. See also Samuel W. Durant, *Hist. of Oneida County, N. Y.* (1878).] P. D. E.

EWBANK, THOMAS (Mar. 11, 1792–Sept. 16, 1870), inventor, manufacturer, author, was born of humble parents in Durham, England. He attended school until he was thirteen years old, and then was apprenticed to the trade of sheet-metal working. He served an indenture of seven years as a tin- and coppersmith, shaped-iron and wire worker, plumber, brass founder, and shot caster. In 1812 he went to London and for seven years more was employed as a tinsmith. With the money he could save he bought books and utilized his leisure in study and reading. He was gradually led to the belief that monarchical institutions limit one's capabilities, and as a result of his conviction emigrated to the United States in 1819 and settled in New York. Shortly after his arrival he began the manufacture of copper, lead, and tin tubing, and for sixteen years continued in this business with marked success. He secured also his first patents, two in 1823 and one in 1832, for improved methods of tinning lead, both sheet and pipe, and two in 1830 and one in 1831 for improved steam safety valves. By 1836, since his business had yielded him a modest competency, he sold it to devote his whole time to study, travel, and writing. His first book, *A Descriptive Account of Hydraulic and other Machines for Raising Water, Ancient and Mod-*

ern, was published in 1842. This was the result of an exhaustive study of devices used for raising water, was profusely illustrated, and was one of the standard works on the subject. The sixteenth edition was published in 1870. From 1845 to 1848 he traveled in South America, studying both the natural phenomena and the industrial arts. Shortly after his return he was appointed commissioner of patents by President Taylor, which office he assumed May 4, 1849, and directed until 1852. His long study and interest in invention, particularly its historical aspects, is reflected in his annual reports which contain enthusiastic and delightful essays upon his favorite theme, and were prepared primarily to arouse popular interest in the industrial application of physical and chemical sciences. Ewbank did not entirely escape Congressional criticism while commissioner. He was accused of discriminating against some would-be patentees, a charge which was never proved, and for publishing his essays in the Patent Office reports. Senator Foote of Mississippi was especially opposed to the essays, which he described as being "more poetically grand, more brilliant, more fanciful, more Byronic than any of the most fanciful poems that Lord Byron ever produced." On the other hand, during his administration Ewbank succeeded in doubling the examining force and laid the foundation for the present rules of practise which greatly expedite the handling of claims. Upon his return to private life he again took up his writing in New York. *The World a Workshop; or, the Physical Relation of Man to the Earth* appeared in 1855; *Life in Brazil,* one of his most entertaining books, in 1856; *Thoughts on Matter and Force* in 1858; and *Reminiscences of the Patent Office* in 1859. Interspersed with these were many pamphlets on as many different subjects, such as "Inorganic Forces Ordained to Supersede Human Slavery," an essay read in 1860 before the American Ethnological Society of which he was one of the founders; and *North American Rock-Writing,* published in 1866. As a member of the commission to examine into the strength of the marble offered for the extension of the Capitol at Washington, Ewbank rendered valuable services by the determination of a method to increase the pressure resistance of building stones. He died, unmarried, in New York.

[*Sci. Am.,* Oct. 1, 1870; *Jour. of Patent Office Soc.,* Sept. 1919; Patent Office reports; *N. Y. Tribune,* Sept. 17, 1870.] C. W. M.

EWELL, BENJAMIN STODDERT (June 10, 1810–June 19, 1894), Confederate soldier, educator, was born in Georgetown, D. C., son of Dr. Thomas Ewell [*q.v.*], of the United States navy, a1.d Elizabeth Stoddert, daughter of the first secretary of the navy. After attending the preparatory department of Georgetown College, he entered the United States Military Academy from Virginia and graduated third in the class of 1832. He was commissioned second lieutenant in the 4th Artillery and detailed as assistant professor at West Point, where for three years he taught mathematics and for another year natural philosophy. He resigned from the army, Sept. 30, 1836, to become principal assistant engineer of the Baltimore & Susquehanna Railroad. Upon its completion in 1839, he accepted the professorship of mathematics and natural philosophy at Hampden-Sidney College, Va., and remained there seven years. During 1846–48 he was the first incumbent of the Cincinnati professorship of mathematics and military science in Washington College (now Washington and Lee University), Va. In 1848 he was elected professor of mathematics and acting president of William and Mary College, and in 1854 became the institution's sixteenth president.

In May 1861, the college suspended activities. Nearly all of the professors and students entered the Confederate army. Ewell, himself a strong Unionist, was convinced that secession was unwise and unconstitutional. Nevertheless he invested practically his entire fortune in Confederate bonds and, although beyond the age for active service, organized the 32nd Virginia Infantry and was appointed its colonel. After helping General Magruder to fortify the Virginia peninsula, he was made assistant adjutant-general to Joseph E. Johnston and served with ability as his chief-of-staff and closest friend, personal and official, until Mar. 20, 1865, when he resigned.

After the war, declining more lucrative professorships at Hampden-Sidney and Washington College, he returned to the presidency of William and Mary. He successfully opposed the projected removal of the institution to Richmond, restored the buildings which Federal troops had burned in 1862 (the main building had been burned in 1859 and rebuilt under Ewell's guidance), organized a faculty, and in 1869 reopened the college. During the next few years, supported by strong statements from Generals Grant and Meade, he sought governmental reimbursement for the restoration of the burned buildings, and, although he was not immediately successful, the Fifty-second Congress indemnified the college for its losses. Meanwhile the cost of repairs and increased operating expenses had diminished the endowment fund, efforts to raise money by subscription had failed, and in 1881 the college was again compelled to close. For seven years Colonel Ewell, unaided, husbanded its scanty revenues. He spent on the college thousands of dollars of his own money, only a pittance of which was ever repaid, kept up inclosures and buildings as best he could, and guarded the institution's charter by driving in from his farm at stated intervals to ring the bell which announced that the college still lived. In 1888 the board of visitors requested the state legislature to combine the college with the educational system of the commonwealth—an idea which Ewell favored—and the application was successful. Ewell now declined any further active connection with the college, but was named president emeritus and held this office until his death.

He was principally responsible for the *Historical Catalogue* (1859) of the college, perhaps the first of its kind in this country. He was a distinguished figure, admired alike for his mental gifts and brilliant address and for his qualities of courage, truth, fidelity, perseverance. His broad-mindedness is revealed in his efforts, after Appomattox, to foster harmony between North and South. His students, who affectionately termed him "Old Buck," loved him for what were perhaps his most noticeable characteristics: his love of his fellow man, his consideration for others, and his faculty of bringing out the best in those with whom he came in contact.

[G. W. Cullum, *Biog. Reg. of the Officers and Grads. of the U. S. Mil. Acad.* (1879), no. 664; Report of the *Twenty-Sixth Ann. Reunion of the Asso. of Grads. of the U. S. Mil. Acad.* (1895), pp. 11–14; obituaries in local newspapers and periodicals, especially the notice in the *Richmond Dispatch*, June 21, 1894; data in Col. Ewell's family Bible and other notes or letters in the possession of his grand-daughter, Mrs. Richard H. Crawford of Norfolk, Va. Col. Ewell's papers and many of his letters are now in the Lib. of the Coll. of William and Mary, Williamsburg, Va.] A. C. G., Jr.

EWELL, JAMES (Feb. 16, 1773–Nov. 2, 1832), physician, was the third son of Col. Jesse Ewell, who married his cousin, Charlotte Ewell. His father came of an old Virginia family, and he was born on the family estate "Bel Air," near Dumfries, Prince William County, Va. He studied medicine with his uncle, James Craik [*q.v.*] of Alexandria, the friend and physician of Washington, and with Dr. Stevenson of Baltimore. After his marriage, Dec. 2, 1794, to Margaret Robertson, daughter of a Virginia physician, he practised for seven years in Lancaster County and at Dumfries, and then, aided by his father's friend President Jefferson, established himself in Savannah, Ga. Here he introduced vaccination, and wrote *The Planter's and Mariner's Medical Companion,* dedicated to Jefferson. Published in Philadelphia, 1807, this was sold widely in the South and West, and ran to ten editions. With its pleasant mingling of poetical quotations, anecdotes, sentiment, and sound practical counsel, it was a valued possession on isolated plantations of the time. After 1809 Ewell lived in Washington, where he became a leading physician. His home was opposite the Capitol and when the British occupied Washington in 1814, his house was made their headquarters. Ewell remained, assuming care of wounded British soldiers, and exercising his influence to protect private property. Criticized later for his friendliness with British officers, he published in the third edition of the *Companion* (1816) an account of the invasion, justifying his conduct and presenting a valuable record of events. Characteristically, this was inserted in the midst of his discussion of fevers, and gave opportunity for a clever satire, *Eulogium on the Capture of Washington, or Bilious Fever,* by "Julius Scaliger" (Baltimore, 1816), which poked fun at the whole book in mock panegyric. About 1830, with a view to better supervision of book sales and to special study of diseases in warm climates, he moved to New Orleans, where he established a successful practise. He died of cholera at Covington, on Lake Pontchartrain. He was of medium height, stout and florid. Of genial, benevolent nature, fond of the best society, he was improvident and easy-going in practical affairs.

[A portrait and biographical sketch of Ewell appear in the tenth edition of his *Medical Companion* (1847). *The Invasion of Washington* is reprinted in the *Records of the Columbia Hist. Soc.*, vol. I, Dec. 1895.] A. W.

EWELL, RICHARD STODDERT (Feb. 8, 1817–Jan. 25, 1872), soldier, was born of Virginian stock in Georgetown, D. C., son of Dr. Thomas and Elizabeth (Stoddert) Ewell, and brother of Benjamin S. Ewell [*q.v.*]. Graduated from West Point in 1840, he was commissioned lieutenant of dragoons and assigned to frontier service. After fighting through the Mexican War and being brevetted for gallantry at Contreras and Churubusco, he resumed his duties on the frontier, was made captain in 1849, and won further distinction against the Apaches in New Mexico in 1857. Although a strong Union man, he resigned, May 7, 1861, to tender his sword to Virginia.

He was appointed colonel in the Confederate army and given charge of the camp of cavalry instruction at Ashland; on June 17 he was promoted brigadier-general. At first Manassas he commanded the 2nd Brigade of Beauregard's army, but had no part in the fighting. In October he was made major-general; led a division under "Stonewall" Jackson in the Shenandoah

Valley campaign, defeating Banks at Winchester and Frémont at Cross Keys; and was prominent in the Seven Days' battles before Richmond, at Cedar Mountain, and in the operations about Manassas Junction. He lost a leg at Groveton, but returned to duty, May 1863, with the rank of lieutenant-general, although to ride he had to be lifted into the saddle and strapped there. Upon the reorganization of the Confederate army into three corps, after Chancellorsville, at Jackson's request Ewell succeeded to the command of the II Corps. He was ordered to clear the Valley of Federals, and effected his purpose brilliantly, his victory at Brandy Station and his rout of Milroy at Winchester leading the newspapers to term him "a re-animate Jackson." He then led the Confederate advance into Pennsylvania, reaching Carlisle before being called back toward Gettysburg. He arrived there soon after the battle commenced, took his position on the Confederate left, and by nightfall occupied the town. He was afterwards criticized for failing to press on and storm Cemetery Hill that evening, but it is now conceded that he acted wisely under Lee's discretionary orders (A. Doubleday, *Chancellorsville and Gettysburg,* 1882, p. 153; Comte de Paris, *The Battle of Gettysburg,* 1886, 1907, pp. 124–26; H. J. Hunt, "The First Day at Gettysburg," in *Battles and Leaders of the Civil War,* 1888, vol. III, p. 284; J. B. Young, *The Battle of Gettysburg,* 1913, pp. 203–07). The second day he launched a spirited attack upon Culp's Hill, and renewed the fighting on July 3. Injured again in his defeat at Kelley's Ford, he resumed his command in time to confront Grant successfully in the first Wilderness engagement. His corps participated in the heavy fighting at or about Spotsylvania Court House, bore the brunt of conflict at the "Bloody Angle," and on May 19 effectively delayed the Federal turning movement. During this action, Ewell's horse was shot under him and he received a fall which incapacitated him for further field service. He was given command of the Department of Henrico, and subsequently of the entire defenses of Richmond. After the evacuation of the city, which he has been wrongfully blamed for firing unnecessarily (*Official Records (Army),* 1 ser., vol. XLVI, 1894, pt. 1; E. A. Pollard, *Secret History of the Confederacy,* 1869, pp. 494–95), Ewell, with a decimated corps, was surrounded and captured at Sailor's Creek, and imprisoned for almost four months at Fort Warren. On his release, he removed to his farm near Spring Hill, Maury County, Tenn., where he died of pneumonia in 1872. He had married, about the close of the war, his cousin and childhood playmate, then a widow, Leczinska Campbell Brown, daughter of Judge Campbell of Tennessee, one time minister to Russia.

Ewell was an able, enterprising, and energetic officer, given to fighting upon the smallest provocation—it was said that to him war meant fight and fight meant kill—and akin to Jackson in the quickness and ardor of his strokes. His tenderness and humanity were, to those who knew him, no less marked; and his many eccentricities of speech or conduct, his temper, his nervousness and absentmindedness but endeared him the more to his men, who knew at first hand his valor, gentle bearing, and high sense of honor. "Bright, prominent eyes, a bomb-shaped, bald head, and a nose like that of Francis of Valois gave him a striking resemblance to a woodcock" (Taylor, *post,* p. 37), which was increased by his habit of putting his head on one side before lisping his occasionally droll and witty, occasionally intolerant and profane, speeches. Under Jackson's influence, it is said, however, he changed remarkably the habits which he had acquired on the plains, and before the war ended revealed a spirit of genuine piety and religious devotion.

[W. P. Snow, *Southern Generals, Their Lives and Campaigns* (1866), and E. A. Pollard, *The Early Life, Campaigns and Public Services of Robert E. Lee with a Record of the Campaigns . . . of his Companions in Arms* (1870), each contains a chapter devoted to Ewell. There are sketches or references of value in C. A. Evans, ed., *Confed. Mil. Hist.,* esp. vol. III (1899); G. W. Cullum's *Biog. Reg. . . . of the U. S. Mil. Acad.* (3rd ed., 1891); *Battles and Leaders of the Civil War* (4 vols., copyright 1884, 1888); and in various biographies of Southern leaders, particularly Longstreet's and Early's. See also F. Marshall's *The Battle of Gettysburg* (1914); and J. B. Young, *Battle of Gettysburg* (1913), ch. 15; *Southern Hist. Soc. Papers,* X (1882), 255–61, 289–302. In *Personal Memoirs of U. S. Grant,* II (1886), 477–78, is related how a remark made by Ewell to a relative and transmitted to Grant first gave him the idea of demanding Lee's surrender. R. Taylor's *Destruction and Reconstruction* (1879) contains anecdotes illustrative of Ewell's character and individuality. His correspondence and papers are in the possession of the William and Mary College Library, Va.]

A. C. G., Jr.

EWELL, THOMAS (May 22, 1785–May 1, 1826), physician, brother of James Ewell [*q.v.*], was born on his father's estate near Dumfries, Va. He studied medicine under Dr. George Graham at Dumfries, Dr. John Weems in Washington, and Dr. Rush at the University of Pennsylvania, publishing at graduation a thesis entitled *Notes on the Stomach and Secretion* (Philadelphia, 1805). Through President Jefferson, his father's friend and classmate at William and Mary, he entered the naval hospital in New York, and from Jan. 16, 1808, to May 5, 1813, was a naval surgeon, assigned to duty in Washington. He was one of four surgeons who reported on the reorganization of the navy medical service

(*American State Papers, Naval Affairs,* vol. 1, 1834, pp. 270–73). On Mar. 3, 1807, he married Elizabeth, daughter of Benjamin Stoddert, first secretary of the navy. Until 1819 he lived in the Stoddert home in Georgetown; later he built a house at 14 Jackson Place, Lafayette Square, in Washington. His resignation from the navy occurred soon after his father-in-law's death, and subsequently he administered the Stoddert property, which included the upper bridge across the Anacostia River, destroyed during the British invasion, and a gunpowder mill at Bladensburg. Ewell is said to have invented and used here a method of making gunpowder by rolling, instead of by the less safe method of pounding. As a writer, he edited the first American edition of Hume's *Essays* (1817), and published several medical works: *Plain Discourses on Modern Chemistry* (1806), used as a text-book at William and Mary; *Letters to Ladies* (1817), which included a project for establishing a large lying-in hospital in Washington by nation-wide subscription; *Statements of Improvements . . . in Medicine* (1819), a collection of various papers, dedicated to Jefferson; and *The American Family Physician* (1824), a well-written popular guide. Ewell was a man of distinguished professional attainments and marked talent for research and invention, with a turn for ridicule, however, and convivial habits which weakened his health. On this account he moved shortly before his death to his country property "Belleville," Prince William County, Va., and afterward to Centerville, Va., where he died. He had four daughters and five sons, two of whom, Benjamin Stoddert [*q.v.*], and Richard Stoddert [*q.v.*], were West Point graduates distinguished in the Civil War.

[H. E. Hayden, *Va. Geneal.* (1891); W. B. Bryan, *Hist. of the Nat. Capital* (1916); *Digested Summary and Alphabetical List of Private Claims . . . Presented to the House of Representatives . . .*, I (1853), 602; other material from family records, partly at the Coll. of William and Mary.] A. W.

EWER, FERDINAND CARTWRIGHT (May 22, 1826–Oct. 10, 1883), Episcopal clergyman, was the son of a well-to-do Nantucket Island ship-owner, Peter Folger Ewer, by his second wife, Mary Cartwright. When he was three years old the family moved to Providence, R. I., and in 1834 to New York. At the age of ten he was sent to the school of Charles G. Green at Jamaica Plain, Mass., and two years later, to one conducted by James B. Thompson in Nantucket. Here he remained, except for a winter in Providence, until he entered Harvard in 1844. From his earliest days the subject of religion was uppermost in his mind. His parents were Unitarian Quakers, but as a child the ritual of the Episcopal Church appealed to him, and convinced of the validity of that church's claims by a precocious study of theological literature, he became a communicant shortly before he entered college. There, however, his reading of German authors and the Unitarian influences of Boston destroyed his faith in the plenary inspiration of the Bible, and he became an infidel. In the meantime financial reverses had befallen his father, and to gain a livelihood Ferdinand took up civil engineering. He joined the California gold rush of 1849, not, he says, because he had the fever for gold, but because he desired not to starve. Finding little to do as an engineer, he drifted into journalism, and for ten years he was prominent as a pioneer editor, vigilante, member of the San Francisco board of education, and finally as a clergyman. For a short time he edited the *Pacific News,* said to have been the first Democratic newspaper on the coast, but he soon became part proprietor and editor of the Sacramento *Transcript,* the first tri-weekly in the interior. This failed because of a strike of the printers, who started a rival publication, and returning to San Francisco, he established a weekly paper, *The Sunday Dispatch,* which also failed. An appointment in 1853 as warehouse clerk in the custom-house, together with reportorial work, insured him a comfortable living, and in 1854, with William H. Brooks, he founded *The Pioneer,* the earliest California literary magazine, which he edited during its short lifetime. On Dec. 9, 1854, he was married to Sophia Mandell Congdon, daughter of Benjamin Congdon of New Bedford. He was among the first writers to recognize the ability and promise of Edwin Booth, then having indifferent success in California, an assistance which the latter in after years gratefully acknowledged. In 1854 he published in *The Pioneer,* "The Eventful Nights of August 20th and 21st," professing to be an account of the death of one John F. Lane, and of certain spiritual communications received from him by the writer. Although intended merely as a piece of imaginative literature, it turned out to be a grand hoax, since spiritualists all over the country, including Judge J. W. Edmonds [*q.v.*] of New York, accepted it as true and made much of it (see F. C. Ewer, *The Eventful Nights of August 20th and 21st; and how Judge Edmonds was Hocussed; or Fallibility of Spiritualism Exposed,* 1855).

Throughout this period his interest in the subject of religion continued, and though at first aggressively infidel, the reading of Cousin's *Psychology* finally started him on a course of thought which resulted in his reconversion to Christianity. On Jan. 17, 1858, he was ordained priest and became rector of Grace Church, San Francisco. Returning East because of ill health in 1860, he was assistant to Dr. Gallaudet at St. Ann's Church for deaf mutes, New York, until 1862, when he became rector of Christ Church. His oratorical powers at once drew large congregations; his varied experiences gave him ability to deal with all classes; and his engaging personal qualities made him widely popular. He was zealously Anglo-Catholic, and wrote much in support of Anglo-Catholicism. A series of sermons preached in 1868 and published the following year under the title of *Sermons on the Failure of Protestantism and on Catholicity,* attracted much attention and aroused hostility. By "Protestantism" he meant the repudiation of the historic Church, the rejection of the divine polity and apostolic ministry, the substitution of the Bible as an authority, and the assertion of the unlimited right of private interpretation and judgment. The overthrow of Protestantism within the Episcopal Church and without he regarded as the great need of the hour, and he hoped for the ultimate reunion of the Roman, Greek, and Episcopal Churches, each purged of its errors. The *Sermons,* together with his introduction of certain ritualistic practises, made trouble for him in his church, and he resigned in 1871. Sympathizers then organized the Church of St. Ignatius of which he was rector until his death. In 1878 he delivered a series of discourses in Newark, N. J., in which his ability as a theologian and controversialist are well illustrated. They appeared in printed form the same year, *Catholicity in Its Relationship to Protestantism and Romanism.* In them he attempted to show the skeptic why he should be a Christian rather than an infidel or Unitarian; a Catholic rather than a Protestant; and an Anglo-Catholic rather than a Roman Catholic. In 1880 he published *The Operation of the Holy Spirit, Four Conferences Delivered at Newark, N. J.,* and *A Grammar of Theology;* in 1883, *What is the Anglican Church?* Ardently devoted to his work, he took little part in public affairs. While preaching in the Church of St. John the Evangelist, Montreal, Oct. 7, 1883, he suffered a cerebral hemorrhage from which he died a few days later.

[A bibliography of his numerous writings is appended to a Memoir by Chas. T. Congdon in a selection from Ewer's sermons, *Sanctity and Other Sermons* (1884). See also Ella S. Cummins, *The Story of the Files: a Review of California Writers and Literature* (1893); *A Hist. of Calif. Newspapers* (1927), repr. from the *Sacramento Daily Union,* Dec. 25, 1858; "The Rector of St. Ignatius's Church," *Frank Leslie's Sunday Magazine,* Oct. 1883; Morgan Dix, "Ferdinand C. Ewer, Priest and Doctor," *Am. Ch. Rev.,* Dec. 1883; *N. Y. Tribune* and *N. Y. Times,* Oct. 11, 1883.] H. E. S.

EWING, CHARLES (June 8, 1780–Aug. 5, 1832), jurist, was a grandson of Thomas Ewing of Londonderry, Ireland, who, emigrating to Southampton, L. I., moved in 1718 to the province of West Jersey and settled at Greenwich in what is now Cumberland County. His youngest child, James Ewing, an active participant in the Revolutionary War and member of the Jersey militia, married Martha Boyd, who was also of Irish extraction, and their only son, Charles, was born at Bridgeton, now in Cumberland County. In 1784 they moved to Trenton, and Charles's early education was obtained at the academy in that town. After spending a year in Philadelphia, where he made a particular study of the French language, he entered the College of New Jersey, at Princeton, in 1796, graduating there in 1798 with high honors, specially distinguishing himself in mathematics. He then studied law in the office of Samuel Leake at Trenton, was licensed to practise as an attorney in November 1802, admitted as a councillor in 1805, and seven years later called to the degree of sergeant-at-law. He married Eleanor Graeme Armstrong, daughter of the Rev. James F. Armstrong of Trenton. Ewing's father had attained a prominent position in Trenton, being mayor and holding other public offices, and no doubt materially assisted his son when the latter commenced practise in that town in 1802. He was for several years recorder of the City of Trenton, and in 1815, against his better judgment, he was Federalist candidate for the state legislature. In 1819 he was appointed commissioner to revise the laws of New Jersey. He enjoyed a wide practise in chancery matters, and for some years was a master and examiner in chancery, acting often in injunction matters for the chancellor in the latter's absence. In October 1824 he was appointed by the legislature chief justice of the supreme court, an office which he only reluctantly accepted, as it involved his relinquishing a lucrative practise. On the bench he quickly displayed remarkable aptitude for judicial work. He exercised extreme care in hearing cases, examining every argument of counsel and meticulously weighing evidence, and yet succeeded in being expeditious in his disposal of the dockets. Establishing himself in the confidence of the bar and the public, he was at the close of his term in 1831 reëlected by a legislature opposed to him in politics. The following year he was called upon to preside at the trial of a chancery suit which attracted wide-spread interest owing to its unusual character. The Society of Friends in 1827 had been split through differences of doctrine into two sections, the Orthodox, and the Hicksite, the latter being in a majority, and the question arose as to which had a right to the endowments of the Quaker school at Crosswicks in Burlington County. The opinion of the chief justice, in favor of the Orthodox adherents, is a masterpiece of close reasoning and cold analysis and so convincing in its logic that the controversy, which in its various aspects might easily have led to prolonged litigation, was forthwith terminated (see 1 *N. J. Equity Reports,* 577 at pp. 594–635).

By instinct a lawyer, he was also a profound student of original sources and the learning of the black-letter era. Conservative by nature and perhaps also by reason of his research work, he disliked innovation in any sphere of life and was a consistent supporter of the common law, legislative changes in which he could never be induced to support. This trait did not, however, obtrude in his judicial work, which in the opinion of contemporaries, concurred in by later authorities, placed him in the front rank of New Jersey jurists. As an advocate he was distinguished by his fair and open attitude, and on the bench he carried this frankness to an extreme, never hesitating to tell a jury exactly what opinion he had formed on the case before them.

[W. W. Spooner, *Historic Families of America* (1908), III, 309–11; E. F. Cooley, *Geneal. of Early Settlers in Trenton and Ewing, "Old Hunterton County," N. J.* (1883), p. 64; S. L. Southard, *An Eulogium upon the Hon. Chas. Ewing, late Chief Justice of N. J.* (1832); E. Q. Keasbey, *The Courts and Lawyers of N. J.* (1912), II, 694; *Green Bag,* Sept. 1891; *Newark Daily Advertiser,* Aug. 6, 1832.] H. W. H. K.

EWING, FINIS (July 10, 1773–July 4, 1841), chief founder of the Cumberland Presbyterian Church, received his unusual name because he was the last of the twelve children of Robert and Mary (Baker) Ewing. He was born in Bedford County, Va., whither his father had come from Ireland. From boyhood he lived on the frontier near Nashville, Tenn., becoming tall and hardy, a leader in sports and Indian warfare. He obtained some advanced schooling, and profited by the debates of a "literary society." In 1793 he married Peggy, daughter of Gen. William David son, and the next year settled in Kentucky, near Russellville, where he soon was a prosperous and influential farmer. Out of a formal religion, the preaching of James McGready [*q.v.*] brought Ewing to a vital Christian experience, and he showed gifts for the ministry. In the great Cumberland revival of 1800 the presbyteries of Transylvania and Cumberland, unable to answer the calls for preachers, licensed and ordained some men, Ewing among them, who did not satisfy Presbyterian educational requirements; they also adopted the Westminster Confession, making exceptions concerning predestinarianism, which did not suit revival work. Because of disapproval of this action by the Kentucky Synod and finally by the General Assembly, in 1810 Ewing and two other ministers formed an independent body, the Presbytery of Cumberland. He then was conspicuous for the power of his ministry. For nine years he had traveled and preached indefatigably in Kentucky and Tennessee, building up congregations in regions religiously destitute, holding camp-meetings, winning everywhere enthusiastic, grateful response. For his ministry he never received money, supporting his growing family by farming.

Courageous, resolute, ardent, in 1810 Ewing was the leader of what was practically a new church. He was principal author of the *Circular Letter* issued by Cumberland Presbytery to justify its founders. In three years the presbytery, because of its evangelistic zeal, grew to a synod. Ewing was one of the framers of a revised Westminster Confession, the adoption of which by the synod in 1814 marked the separate life of Cumberland Presbyterian Church. This revision sought a middle way between Calvinism and Arminianism. Ewing presided over many of the church's meetings, championed its doctrines in controversy, and fostered all its concerns. From about 1812 he was pastor on half-time of Lebanon Church in Christian County, Ky., working also in many other places. With Robert Donnell [*q.v.*] he wrote an account of the Cumberland Presbyterian Church for Woodward's edition of Charles Buck's *Theological Dictionary* (1814), which brought the sect to general notice. In 1820 he removed to central Missouri, following many Kentuckians. At New Lebanon in that state he soon formed a strong church, besides ministering generally to a wide-reaching frontier. In his own house he maintained a training-school for ministers. Of his teaching, his *Lectures on Theological Subjects* (1872), widely circulated among Cumberland Presbyterians, were the outcome. Long a slaveholder, now, in a slaveholding country, he agitated against slavery. He was a pioneer leader of the temperance movement in Missouri. After four years in a church near Lexington, Mo., in 1836 he became pastor in that town. There he was register of the Land Office, supporting himself thus while incessantly active in the ministry. He built up the Cumberland Church to much strength in Missouri. By correspondence and visits he maintained an influential connection with the church in the East. So long as he lived he was its revered "Father Ewing."

[See F. R. Cossitt, *Life and Times of Rev. Finis*

Ewing (1853), with portrait; Richard Beard, *Biog. Sketches of Some of the Early Ministers of the Cumberland Presbyt. Ch.* (1867); E. B. Crisman, *Origin and Doctrines of the Cumb. Presbyt. Ch.* (1856); Robt. Davidson, *Hist. Presbyt. Ch. in Ky.* (1847); his unfavorable view of the founding of the Cumb. Presbyt. Ch. is answered at length by Cossitt, *op. cit*; B. W. McDonnold, *Hist. Cumb. Presbyt.* (4th ed., 1899); E. H. Gillett, *Hist. Presbyt. Ch. U. S. A.* (1864); *Semicentennial General Assembly Cumb. Presbyt. Ch.* (1880), ed. by J. Frizell, containing important extracts from ecclesiastical records; *The Cumb. Presbyt. Digest* (1899), ed. by J. V. Stephens; *Extracts from the Minutes Gen. Assembly Presbyt. Ch. U. S. A.*, 1807–09. Philip Schaff, *Creeds of Christendom*, vol. III (1877), contains the Cumb. Presbyt. revision of the Westminster Confession.] R. H. N.

EWING, HUGH BOYLE (Oct. 31, 1826–June 30, 1905), soldier, author, was born in Lancaster, Ohio, the fourth child of Thomas [*q.v.*] and Maria Wills (Boyle) Ewing. He received his education under private tutors and later at the United States Military Academy, from which, however, he did not graduate. In 1849 he was caught by the gold fever and made the journey to California by way of New Orleans and Texas, thence across Mexico to Mazatlan on the Pacific Coast, and across the Cordilleras on muleback. While in California he was ordered to join an expedition sent out by his father, then secretary of the interior, to rescue immigrants who were trapped in the high sierras by the heavy snows. In 1852 he returned by way of Panama to Washington as the bearer of government dispatches. He then completed his law studies and began to practise his profession in St. Louis, Mo. From 1854 to 1856 he resided in that city, and then removed to Leavenworth, Kan., where he was associated with his younger brother, Thomas, his foster-brother, W. T. Sherman [*qq.v.*], and Dan McCook, in the law firm of Ewing, Sherman & McCook. In 1858 he returned to Ohio in order to take charge of his father's salt works and lands in Athens County. On May 6, 1861, Gov. Dennison appointed him brigade-inspector of Ohio Volunteers and a month later he joined the forces under Gen. McClellan. He served under McClellan and Rosecrans in their West Virginia campaigns and in August 1861 was appointed colonel of the 30th Ohio Infantry. At the battle of South Mountain, Sept. 14, 1862, he led the charge which dislodged the enemy from the summit; and at midnight of that day he received an order assigning him to the command of a brigade. In the battle of Antietam his brigade was stationed upon the extreme left of the army where, according to Gen. Burnside's report, "by a change of front and rear on his right flank, [he] saved the left from being completely driven in" (Randall and Ryan, *post*, VI, 18). After this battle Ewing was favorably mentioned in Col. E. P. Scammon's report "for energy and skilful bravery" (*Official Records* (*Army*), 1 ser., XIX, pt. 1); and on Nov. 29, 1862, he was promoted to the rank of brigadier-general. He commanded a brigade under Sherman during the Vicksburg campaign; and while his troops lay before that city seized and burned the disloyal papers which were sent to his camp; confiscated and arrested the dealers selling "bad whisky" to the soldiers; broke up the vending of cigars and groceries by the soldiers "which he considered a demoralizing custom"; but "acknowledged his inability to check the vice of gambling" (Reid, *post*, I, 854). He led the assaults made by Gen. Sherman on the enemy's works and upon the fall of Vicksburg was placed in command of a division. At Chickamauga his division formed the advance of Sherman's army and suffered great losses in carrying Missionary Ridge. In February 1865 he was ordered to North Carolina and was planning an expedition up the Roanoke River when the war came to an end. On Mar. 13, 1865, he was brevetted major-general "for meritorious services during the war" (*Ibid.*, I, 856) and a year later was mustered out of the service. President Johnson appointed him minister to Holland, in which capacity he served from 1866 to 1870. Upon his return from Europe he practised law in Washington, D. C., until 1874, when he returned to Ohio, buying a small estate near his birthplace where he resided until his death. Ewing traveled extensively in America and abroad and was the author of *A Castle in the Air* (1888); *The Black List; a Tale of Early California* (1893); and a number of magazine articles. In 1858 he married Henrietta Young, the daughter of George W. Young of the District of Columbia. As a soldier Ewing was capable, courageous, and efficient, though a severe disciplinarian. As a man he was respected for his literary attainments, honorable character, and genial disposition.

[E. O. Randall and D. J. Ryan, *Hist. of Ohio* (1912), esp. VI, 17–19; Whitelaw Reid, *Ohio in the War* (1868), I, 853–56, *Official Records* (*Army*), esp. 1 ser., V, XIX, XXIV, XXXI; *Who's Who in America*, 1903–05; E. W. R. Ewing, *Clan Ewing of Scotland* (1922); P. K. and M. E. (Williams) Ewing, *The Ewing Geneal. with Cognate Branches* (1919).] R. C. M.

EWING, JAMES (Aug. 3, 1736–Mar. 1, 1806), Revolutionary soldier, was of Scotch-Irish descent, the son of Thomas Ewing, a member of the Pennsylvania Assembly in 1738–39, and his wife Susanna Howard, widow of James Patterson, the Indian trader. James Ewing was born in Lancaster County, Pa., and married Patience Wright. He served as a lieutenant in the French and Indian War in 1758, and sat in the Pennsylvania General Assembly 1771–75. He was a member of the local committee of safety, and on July 4, 1776, was chosen brigadier-general of Pennsylvania militia, in command of the 2nd Brigade. He had a place in Washington's plan for the attack on Trenton in the winter of 1776–77, being ordered to cross at Trenton Ferry, with the "Flying Camp" and New Jersey militia. Ice and high winds prevented the passage by his detachment, however, and he did not share in the victory. The records are meager regarding his military services, in spite of the high position which he held from the beginning. Even his name is frequently misspelled, appearing as Eving, Erwing, Irwin, Irvin, and Irvine, the last version leading occasionally to his being confused with the contemporary Gen. William Irvine [*q.v.*]. After the war Ewing was vice-president of Pennsylvania 1782–84, a member of the Assembly, and in 1795–99 a member of the state Senate. He was one of the early trustees of Dickinson College at Carlisle, serving from 1783 until his death. He died at Hellam, York County, Pa.

[Samuel Evans, "The Ewing Family of Lancaster and York," *Hist. Reg.* (Harrisburg), Sept. 1844, and an article in *Notes and Queries* (Harrisburg), 3 ser. vol. II (1896); E. H. Bell and M. H. Colwell, *Jas. Patterson of Conestoga Manor and His Descendants* (Lancaster, 1925); Wm. S. Stryker, *The Battles of Trenton and Princeton* (1898); Jared Sparks, ed., *The Writings of Geo. Washington*, IV (1834), 247–49; *Poulson's Am. Daily Advertiser* (Phila.), Mar. 14, 1806.] E. K. A.

EWING, JAMES CARUTHERS RHEA (June 23, 1854–Aug. 20, 1925), Presbyterian missionary, the son of James Henry and Eleanor (Rhea) Ewing, was born in the prosperous and enlightened community of Rural Valley, Armstrong County, Pa. He was of Scotch-Irish stock, and one of a large family of children, of whom seven sons and one daughter reached maturity. In the spring of 1860 the family moved to a farm in the vicinity of Saltsburg, Pa., where Ewing attended the public school. He joined the Presbyterian Church in 1865. He graduated in 1869 from the Saltsburg Academy, and passed his examination for teaching. After three years spent in teaching in the common schools of Indiana and Armstrong counties, he entered in March 1873 the freshman class of Washington and Jefferson College, from which he received the B.A. degree in 1876, graduating with Phi Beta Kappa honors. His next three years were spent in Western Theological Seminary, from which he graduated in 1879. He was married, on June 24 of that year, at Prosperity, Pa., to Jane Sherrard, daughter of the Rev. J. H. Sherrard, and on Sept. 5, at Saltsburg, he was ordained to the Christian ministry. Having applied during his senior year in the seminary for missionary appointment, he received a commission under the Presbyterian Board of Foreign Missions for service in India. With Mrs. Ewing, he sailed from Philadelphia on Oct. 2, 1879, and arrived at Bombay, Dec. 1. They proceeded thence to the United Provinces, first to Mainpuri and soon thereafter to Fategarh. He learned the Urdu language quickly. During 1882–84 he was principal of the Jumna High School in Allahabad, was in charge of the asylum for lepers and the blind, and editor of the mission paper, *Makhzan i Masihi*. He spent the next three years in Saharanpur at the newly established Theological Seminary for the North India Presbyterian Mission. There he published various books, including a Greek-Hindustani dictionary of the New Testament and a Hindustani hymnal. In 1887–88 he and his family visited the United States on furlough but they returned in October 1888, and Ewing was then assigned to the Ludhiana Mission with a view to his working in Forman Christian College, Lahore. From 1888 to 1918 he was principal (president) of Forman College, during which time the institution attained front rank and he himself became one of the best-known and most trusted foreigners in the Panjab. The India government gave aid in the building of the first unit of the college in 1889. During that year Ewing was appointed to several offices in the Panjab University, namely, examiner in English, member of the Syndicate, fellow, and secretary of the faculty of arts. From 1890 to 1907 he was dean of the faculty of arts, and from 1910 to 1917, was vice-chancellor of the university. During the Second Decennial Missionary Conference at Bombay, December 1892 and January 1893, he was a conspicuous and influential figure. His health suffered from his many arduous activities.

During his second furlough, in 1897–98, he was offered the presidencies of Wooster College (Ohio) and Centre College (Ky.), but preferred to continue his service in India. In 1901 he was sent on a special mission to the Philippine Islands to aid in the inauguration of Presbyterian work there. For the part he took in the Panjab earthquake relief work in the fall of 1905, on Jan. 1, 1906, he was awarded by the British Crown the Kaisar-i-Hind Gold Medal, first class. In 1912 he paid a visit to England as a representative of the Panjab University in the Congress of Universities of the British Empire. The directorship of the American Board of Missionary Preparation was offered to him in 1914, but this he also declined. In 1915 the Government of India made him an honorary Commander of the Indian Empire—and later an honorary Knight Commander—and in 1917 on the eve of his retirement and return to America the Panjab University conferred upon him the honorary Litt.D. Having retired from the headship of Forman Christian College and having severed various other connections with India, he spent a year in America. During this time he published his only original volume, *A Prince of the Church in India, being a Record of the Life of the Rev. Kali Charan Chatterjee, D.D.* (1918). He found himself able to return to the East in October 1918 to take up the secretaryship of the Council of Presbyterian Missions in India, and to be the India representative of the Inter-Church World Movement. In January 1920 he suffered a stroke of paralysis, but improved sufficiently thereafter to be able to draft a plan of administration of the joint work of his India mission, and to act as chairman of the standing committee on Christian Education of the National Missionary Council of India.

In 1922 at the age of sixty-eight and after forty-three years of service in India, Ewing retired on a pension from his Board and returned to America where he took up residence in Princeton, N. J., and became a lecturer in the Princeton Theological Seminary. On June 4, 1923, he was elected a member of the Presbyterian Board of Foreign Missions. He died at Princeton two years later, and was buried in the family lot at Saltsburg, Pa.

[R. E. Speer, *Sir James Ewing* (1928); *89th Ann. Report Board of Foreign Missions of the Presbyt. Ch. in the U. S. A.* (1926); P. K. and M. E. (Williams) Ewing, *The Ewing Geneal. with Cognate Branches* (1919); *Who's Who in America, 1924–25*; *State Gazette* (Trenton, N. J.), *N. Y. Times*, Aug. 22, 1925.]

J. C. A.

EWING, JOHN (July 22, 1732–Sept. 8, 1802), Presbyterian clergyman, provost of the University of Pennsylvania, was born in East Nottingham, Cecil County, Md. He was a younger son of Alexander Ewing, one of several sons of that Capt. Ewing who received a sword from William of Orange for his services at the battle of the Boyne. These Scotch-Irish brothers came to America from Londonderry, Ireland, early in the eighteenth century. Alexander Ewing provided his sons with a good education, but since the eldest son inherited the family property, in later life John had to rely upon his own resources. He early displayed an aptitude for learning, which took him from the rural school of his neighborhood to the school kept by Dr. Francis Alison [*q.v.*] at New London Cross Road, Pa. For the privilege of borrowing a book upon mathematics or natural philosophy John Ewing would ride, so it is said, thirty or forty miles. After completing his course and acting as tutor for three years in Dr. Alison's school, in 1754 he entered the senior class of the College of New Jersey, then situated at Newark, and graduated in the same year. He accepted appointment as tutor, serving 1756–58, during which time the college moved to Princeton, and then he returned to Dr. Alison, under whom he studied for the ministry.

Before accepting a pastorate, he filled a temporary post in philosophy, 1758–59, at the College of Philadelphia. About this time he married Hannah Sergeant of Newark, Del. In 1759 he became pastor of the First Presbyterian Church of Philadelphia, which he served for the rest of his life. His interest in education continued; and from 1773 to 1775 he was in England soliciting funds for an academy in Delaware. He corresponded with the Astronomer Royal of Greenwich, England, in an attempt to obtain an observatory for Philadelphia. The Boston Tea Party had prejudiced Englishmen against the colonies, and both of Ewing's endeavors were unsuccessful. While in England he met Dr. Robertson, the great Dr. Johnson, and Lord North, with whom he discussed colonial problems. The University of Edinburgh conferred upon him the degree of D.D. in recognition of his scholarship; and several Scottish towns presented him with their freedom.

In 1779 he was appointed provost of the University of the State of Pennsylvania, chartered in that year by the legislature. From that time until his death his busy career included lecturing in addition to preaching and his other church work. Besides being provost, he was professor of natural philosophy, and it was said of him that in the absence of any other professor, "the Provost could take his place, at an hour's warning, and conduct the instruction appropriate to that Professorship with more skill, taste, and advantage than the incumbent of the chair himself" (Miller, *post*, p. 218). In 1791 the University and the old College of Philadelphia were combined to form the University of Pennsylvania, Ewing continuing as provost. He served with David Rittenhouse [*q.v.*], on several boundary commissions (see, in this connection, his "Memorandum Book," 1784, in *Pennsylvania Archives*, 6 ser. XIV, 1–20). He was a vice-president of the American Philosophical Society, and contributed several articles on astronomy to its publications as well as to Thomas Dobson's *Encyclopædia* (1798), the third, and first American, edition of the *Encyclopædia Britannica.* His university lectures on natural philosophy and a collection of his sermons were published after his death under the titles: *A Plain Elementary and Practical System of Natural Experimental Philosophy* (1809), edited by Robert Patterson, and *Sermons by the*

Rev. John Ewing, D.D. (1812), edited by James P. Wilson. In 1796 Ewing had suffered from a severe illness and he never completely recovered, although he continued his work. He died at the home of his son in Norristown, Montgomery County, Pa.

Ewing was fortunate in possessing both scholarship and an unusual personality. He knew several languages, including Hebrew; and in scientific fields he was an original and critical thinker. In the pulpit or on the lecture platform he needed and used no flourishes of rhetoric; his tall, handsome figure, powdered hair brushed back from a high forehead, and keen eyes made a striking and impressive appearance. In private life he was a genial host and an easy conversationalist; but he was a poor judge of human nature, and suffered financial loss because of over-confidence in his acquaintances.

[Biographical sketch by Robt. Patterson in Ewing's *A Plain Elementary and Practical System of Natural Experimental Philosophy* (1809); Lucy E. L. Ewing, *Dr. John Ewing and Some of his Noted Connections* (1924); J. L. Chamberlain, *Universities and their Sons: Univ. of Pa.* (1901); *Gen. Cat. Princeton Univ.* (1908); John Blair Linn, *A Discourse Occasioned by the Death of the Rev. John Ewing* (1802); *Port Folio* (Phila.), Mar. 1813; Samuel Miller in W. B. Sprague, *Annals Am. Pulpit*, III (1858), 216–19; obituary in *Poulson's Am. Daily Advertiser* (Phila.), Sept. 13, 1802.]

D. M. C.

EWING, THOMAS (Dec. 28, 1789–Oct. 26, 1871), senator from Ohio, cabinet officer, was the second son of George and Rachel (Harris) Ewing. In his "Autobiography" he states that he attached "little importance to remote ancestry"; yet he could trace his lineage back to a Capt. Ewing of lower Loch Lomond, Scotland, who, serving under William of Orange at the battle of the Boyne (1690), was presented with a sword by his sovereign in recognition of conspicuous bravery. Thomas Ewing, a son of this ancestor, came to America from Londonderry, Ireland, and settled in Greenwich, N. J., about 1718. At the beginning of the Revolution, George Ewing enlisted in the 2nd New Jersey Regiment, in which he held the rank of first lieutenant. During the course of the war, he suffered financial reverses and at the termination of hostilities decided to migrate westward. His son Thomas was born near West Liberty, Ohio County, Va. About 1793 the Ewings moved to Waterford on the Muskingum and in the spring of 1798 removed to what is now Ames Township, Athens County, Ohio. Here, on the outskirts of civilization, young Thomas spent his boyhood. He was taught to read by an elder sister and by his own extraordinary efforts acquired a fair elementary education. Books were his delight, and, encouraged by his parents, the boy eagerly read everything he could lay his hands upon. Before he was eight years old he had read the entire Bible and in his autobiography he says that he once walked twenty miles to borrow a translation of Virgil's *Æneid.* The establishment of a circulating library in Ames Township stimulated his insatiable craving for knowledge, while his tenacious and ready memory enabled him to retain the information he acquired. In order to secure funds for a college education, he sought employment in the Kanawha salt works. In the course of two or three years he saved enough from his scanty earnings to free his father's farm of debt, and with the meager surplus enrolled in Ohio University at Athens. His funds were soon exhausted and he was compelled to return to the salt works. Once more he saved his earnings, returned to resume his studies at Ohio University, and in 1815 he and his classmate John Hunter, received the first B.A. degrees ever granted by that institution.

After graduation he studied law in the office of Gen. Philemon Beecher at Lancaster, Ohio, and in August 1816 was admitted to the bar. He rapidly acquired a reputation as one of the best equipped and most successful lawyers in the West. For several years he served as prosecuting attorney of Fairfield County and in that capacity was instrumental in freeing the district of counterfeiters. In 1823 he was defeated for the state legislature but in 1830 was elected to the United States Senate where his keen intellect earned for him the sobriquet of "Logician of the West" (Randall & Ryan, *post,* VI, 8). As a Whig senator he vigorously assailed the Democratic administration, supported the protective tariff policy of Clay, advocated the re-charter of the United States Bank, denounced President Jackson's removal of deposits and his "Specie Circular," opposed the confirmation of Martin Van Buren as minister to England, but voted for the revenue collection bill known as the "Force Bill." He also advocated reduced postal rates, brought about a revision of the land laws, a reorganization of the Post-Office Department, and a bill for the settlement of the Ohio-Michigan boundary. In January 1836 he was defeated for reëlection by William Allen and resumed his practise at Lancaster.

He was appointed secretary of the treasury by President Harrison in 1841, retained this office after the death of Harrison and the succession of Tyler, and as secretary of the treasury helped to draft bills for the re-charter of a national bank. After President Tyler had twice vetoed such measures, Ewing resigned along with the other members of the cabinet. He returned to the practise of law; and it was following his resignation that his reputation as a lawyer was established. Among his more elaborate written professional arguments were those in the case of *Oliver* vs. *Pratt et al.*, involving the title to half the land now occupied by the municipality of Toledo, Ohio; the Methodist Episcopal Church division case; the *McIntire Poor School* vs. *Zanesville;* and the McMicken Will Case, which involved large bequests for education (12 *Wallace,* viii).

On the inauguration of Zachary Taylor as president, Ewing was appointed secretary of the recently created Department of the Interior, which was still unorganized. In his first report, he recommended the erection of a mint near the California gold mines and the building of a railroad to the Pacific. On the death of President Taylor, July 9, 1850, and the accession of Millard Fillmore, a division in the Whig party caused a change in the cabinet. Thomas Corwin was appointed secretary of the treasury and Ewing was appointed to complete the unexpired term of Corwin in the Senate. During this term in the Senate Ewing differed with Clay in his proposals to solve the problems arising as a result of the Mexican War. He opposed the Fugitive-Slave Law and was in favor of the unconditional admission of California as a state. In 1851 he retired from public life, although he never completely lost interest in public affairs.

In 1861 he was appointed a delegate to the Peace Convention and throughout the Civil War he rendered loyal assistance to Lincoln's administration. At the time of the *Trent* affair he wrote President Lincoln: "There is no such thing as contraband of war between neutral ports" and urged the release of Mason and Slidell. His conservatism caused him to oppose the reconstruction policy of Congress, and during his last years he acted with the Democratic party. He gave President Johnson much good advice and cautioned him against removing Stanton as secretary of war. When Stanton was removed in 1868, President Johnson submitted Ewing's name for the vacancy; but the Senate never acted upon the recommendation (J. F. Rhodes, *History of the United States,* vol. VI, 1928, pp. 210–22).

Ewing was a man of great physical strength, over six feet in height, with broad shoulders, a massive frame, and a head of unusual size. His keen, logical mind, his incisive style both in speaking and in writing, his wide range of reading, and his wealth of information made him a lawyer of the first rank and a forceful leader in his day. In public and private life he was a man of strong convictions and an inflexible will, powerful as a friend or as an antagonist, dignified yet sociable in his relations with men, and a stanch believer in the "good old days." In September 1871 Archbishop Purcell of Cincinnati received him into the Catholic Church. On Jan. 7, 1820, Ewing married Maria Wills Boyle by whom he had six children, among them Hugh Boyle Ewing and Thomas Ewing, Jr. [*qq.v.*]. He also adopted, in 1829, William T. Sherman [*q.v.*], the son of his friend, Judge Charles Sherman, and appointed him to West Point in 1836.

[See "The Autobiography of Thomas Ewing," ed. by C. L. Martzolff, in *Ohio Archæol. and Hist. Pubs.,* XXII (1913), 126 ff.; "Diary of Thomas Ewing, Aug. and Sept., 1841," in *Am. Hist. Rev.,* Oct. 1912; Ellen Ewing Sherman, *Memorial of Thos. Ewing of Ohio* (1873); P. K. and M. E. (Williams) Ewing, *The Ewing Geneal. with Cognate Branches* (1919); E. W. R. Ewing, *Clan Ewing of Scotland* (1922); *Biog. Dir. Am. Cong.* (1928); G. I. Reed, *Bench and Bar of Ohio,* I (1897), 75 ff.; E. O. Randall and D. J. Ryan, *Hist. of Ohio* (1912), vols. III–V; *Cincinnati Enquirer,* Oct. 26, 27, 1871; *Cincinnati Commercial, Cincinnati Daily Times and Chronicle,* Oct. 27, 1871. At Ewing's death the U. S. Supreme Court paid him the unusual honor of publishing in their reports an account of his life (12 *Wallace,* vii–ix).]

R. C. M.

EWING, THOMAS (Aug. 7, 1829–Jan. 21, 1896), soldier, lawyer, congressman from Ohio, the fifth child of Thomas [*q.v.*] and Maria Wills (Boyle) Ewing, was born in Lancaster, Ohio. He received his early education in Ohio and at the age of nineteen became one of the private secretaries of President Taylor in whose cabinet his father was secretary of the interior. After a year spent in this position and two more as a claims clerk in Washington, he entered Brown University. In 1855 he attended the Cincinnati Law School and, after admission to the bar, began practising in that city. On Jan. 8, 1856, he married Ellen Ewing Cox, the daughter of Rev. William Cox, of Piqua, Ohio, and during the same year he and his wife moved to Leavenworth, Kan., where he became a member of the firm of Ewing, Sherman & McCook.

As an ardent anti-slavery man, Ewing was largely instrumental in revealing the fraudulent voting for state officers at the election held on Jan. 4, 1858, under the Lecompton constitution. The public indignation aroused by these disclosures prevented the admission of Kansas as a slave-state. (Ewing later wrote an article, "The Struggle for Freedom in Kansas," published in the *Cosmopolitan Magazine,* May 1894.) In 1861 he represented Kansas in the Peace Convention and in January of the same year was chosen the first chief justice of the supreme court of the new state. He resigned his judicial office in September 1862 and recruited the 11th Kansas Volunteers, of which he was appointed colonel. After participating in several severe engagements in Arkansas he was promoted brigadier-general in March 1863. From June 1863 to February 1864 he was in command of the "District of the Border," which comprised Kansas and the western tier of counties in Missouri. In his efforts to exterminate the guerrilla bands which infested this area, Ewing issued his famous Order No. 11, depopulating the counties of Missouri. In March 1864 he was assigned to the command of the St. Louis District. When Gen. Sterling Price invaded Missouri the following September, Ewing was ordered to check and delay the progress of the Confederate forces in their march on St. Louis. He encountered their advance columns in a narrow defile and, disputing every inch of ground, slowly retired to Fort Davidson, a small earthwork adjacent to Pilot Knob. On Sept. 27 Price attacked him but was repulsed with great losses. Ewing soon found his position untenable, however, because the enemy placed batteries on the mountain sides and began to shell the fort. Under cover of darkness Ewing spiked all his guns but two, blew up the magazine and his valuable stores, and started to retreat toward St. Louis. During the next thirty-nine hours his forces marched sixty-six miles, hotly pursued by the foe. At Harrison he entrenched behind railroad ties and for three days held the enemy at bay until relieved by reinforcements from Rolla. "Thus closed a campaign of a week of stubborn fighting, on a comparatively small scale, but still rarely excelled during the war" (Reid, *post,* I, 835). In February 1865 Ewing resigned his commission and soon afterward was brevetted major-general for his services at Pilot Knob. During the next few years he resided in Washington, D. C., where he practised law. President Johnson offered him the positions of secretary of war and attorney-general but Ewing declined both.

In 1870 he returned to Lancaster, Ohio, and during the next twelve years was a conspicuous leader of the Greenback wing of the Democratic party. From 1877 to 1881 he represented the Lancaster district in Congress and as a member of that body was the leader in the movement for preservation of the Greenback currency; advocated the remonetization of the currency; and took a prominent part in the support of legislation to stop the employment of federal troops and supervisors at state elections. His candidacy for the governorship in 1879 on the Democratic ticket was the last of the Greenback movement in Ohio, and, although he was defeated, his brilliant campaign attracted the attention of the country. In 1881 he retired from Congress and politics and removed to New York City where he practised law during the remainder of his life. He was one of the founders of the Ohio Society of New York and was its first president. As a soldier he displayed marked military judgment, courage, and gallantry. His easy and gracious manner made a deep impression on every one he met; while his lofty ideals, his sincerity, his integrity, and his eloquence made him an effective popular leader.

[E. O. Randall and D. J. Ryan, *Hist. of Ohio* (1912), vol. IV; *Official Records (Army)*, 1 ser. XXXII, XXXIV, XLI, XLVIII; *Biog. Dir. Am. Cong.* (1928); G. I. Reed, *Bench and Bar of Ohio* (1897), I, 114 ff.; Whitelaw Reid, *Ohio in the War* (1868), I, 834 ff.; P. K. and M. E. (Williams) Ewing, *The Ewing Geneal. with Cognate Branches* (1919); E. W. R. Ewing, *Clan Ewing of Scotland* (1922); John Sherman, *Recollections of Forty Years* (2 vols., 1895); *Cincinnati Times-Star*, Jan. 21, *Cincinnati Enquirer*, Jan. 22, 1896.]

R. C. M.

EYTINGE, ROSE (Nov. 21, 1835–Dec. 20, 1911), actress, author, teacher, was born in Philadelphia. Evidence points to David Eytinge, professor of languages, and his wife Rebecca, as her parents. Educated at home, she early became an eager student of plays and players. In 1853, following amateur success, she went to Syracuse as juvenile leading lady in Geary Hough's stock company, making her début as Melanie in *The Old Guard* at a salary of seven dollars a week. Her second engagement was at the Green Street Theatre in Albany where she made her first appearance Sept. 10, 1855. This association resulted in her marriage to David Barnes, manager of the theatre. After the birth of a daughter she was divorced from him, some time before 1862. Then came several seasons in New York stock companies during which she supported Booth, as Fiordelisa in *The Fool's Revenge* at Niblo's Garden, and later, notably as Julie in *Richelieu,* at the Winter Garden. In August 1864 she joined the famous Davenport-Wallack combination, with whom one of her pronounced successes was Nancy Sykes in *Oliver Twist,* a part she played with convincing realism. Between seasons, 1866–67, she played Kate Peyton in Daly's dramatization of *Griffith Gaunt* and created for Daly the part of Laura Courtland in *Under the Gaslight.* In 1868 she left Wallack and Davenport for the place of leading lady in Lester Wallack's theatre. Her second marriage probably took place about this time, for in the fall of 1869 she went abroad as the wife of Col. George H. Butler, consul-general to Egypt, and lived for several years in the East. According to Trumble, Butler's violences and dissipations finally forced his wife, by whom he had two sons, to divorce him. She returned to the stage, joining in 1873–74 the brilliant company at Union Square Theatre, where she played Gabrielle in

The Geneva Cross and created the part of Armande in *Led Astray* and the title rôle of *Rose Michel.* With the latter play she began in 1876 a successful starring tour, thereafter appearing in the principal American cities at the head of her own company, supported by her third husband, the English actor, Cyril Searle.

Her most brilliant success as a star seems to have been in *Antony and Cleopatra,* which she produced in New York in 1877. She had studied atmosphere and setting in Egypt whence she brought rich costumes and properties. In temperament and physique, Rose was the passionate and beguiling Queen to the life. "A handsome brunette with brilliant dark eyes, an ample figure, a strong, melodious voice," Winter describes her, adding that no other actress in his remembrance gave a more acceptable performance of Cleopatra than she. She was one of the most temperamental and unmanageable of artists—wayward, capricious, defiant, prone to quarrel with managers and stars, and given to mischievous by-play on the stage which sometimes caused the untimely descent of the curtain. Her character, Winter says, was "formidable."

In 1880 she appeared successfully in London where she was lionized by literary and political notables, among them Dickens, Wilkie Collins, Gladstone, Lord Roseberry, and Charles Reade. After 1884 she rarely appeared, giving much time to training pupils for the stage. She established a school of acting in New York in 1890, and another, later, in Portland, Ore. She dramatized several novels, wrote a play, *Golden Chains,* and a romance, *It Happened This Way* (1890), as well as the racy *Memories of Rose Eytinge* (1905) wherein she describes her stage life, her years in Egypt, and her encounters with celebrities. When she retired from the stage in 1908 a benefit performance was given for her in Portland. She died at Brunswick Home, Amityville, L. I., in the care of the Actors' Fund.

[The *Memories of Rose Eytinge* omits mention of her marriages or parentage and gives almost no dates. See also Arthur Trumble, *Great Artists of the Am. Stage* (1882); Wm. Winter, *Shakespeare on the Stage,* 1, 2, 3 ser. (1911–16); J. B. Clapp and E. F. Edgett, *Players of the Present* (1899), pt. I, p. 96; *N. Y. Dramatic Mirror,* Dec. 27, 1911; *N. Y. Times, Boston Transcript,* Dec. 21, 1911. Most accounts give 1835 as the year of birth, but *Who's Who in America,* 1899–1909, states that she was born in 1838.] M. B. H.

EZEKIEL, MOSES JACOB (Oct. 28, 1844–Mar. 27, 1917), sculptor, known as Sir Moses Ezekiel after receiving knighthood honors from Emperor William I of Germany and King Humbert I and King Victor Emmanuel II of Italy, was born in Richmond, Va. He was the son of Jacob and Catherine (de Castro) Ezekiel, and grandson of Jacob and Rebecca (Israel) Ezekiel, a couple who came from Amsterdam, Holland, and settled in Philadelphia, Pa., in 1808. As a child, his artistic nature showed itself; he wrote poetry, drew, painted; at ten, "he cut figures for little shadow pictures." Leaving school at fourteen, he attempted business life, but, dissatisfied with it, entered the Virginia Military Institute in 1861. After the burning of its buildings by Gen. Hunter's men, he joined the Confederate army with the other cadets, and fought in the battle of New Market. Returning to "V. M. I." after the war, he was graduated with honors in 1866. Again essaying business and again finding it unsatisfactory, he turned toward painting. At the Military Institute he had been a protégé of Gen. Robert E. Lee and his wife, to whose home in the neighborhood he was made welcome, and one of his early pictures is "The Prisoner's Wife," painted for Mrs. Lee. Then sculpture drew him; he made a bust of his father, and an ideal group, "Cain." He studied anatomy and dissections at the Virginia Medical College. After a brief period in Cincinnati, where he attended the Art School, worked in a sculptor's studio, and made a statuette called "Industry," he went to Berlin in 1869, and entered the Royal Art Academy. To eke out his scanty resources, he served for a time as war correspondent in the Franco-Prussian War. On the strength of a colossal bust of Washington, a copy of which is owned by the Cincinnati Museum of Fine Arts, he was admitted into the Society of Artists, Berlin. After three years' study at the Academy under Prof. Albert Wolff, he won the Michael-Beer Prize, never before given to a foreigner; this award ended his anxious poverty and granted him two care-free years of study in Rome. That city was thereafter to be his home, although he made many visits to the United States and at times kept a studio in Paris.

His course at the Virginia Military Institute, with its interlude of actual combat, his prestige from the Roman Prize, his genial nature, and his gift for forming desirable acquaintances, prepared the ground for a career remarkably successful from many points of view, yet lacking the highest artistic values. Partly for economy, partly with an eye to the picturesque, he set up a studio in the Baths of Diocletian (1874). By degrees he beautified it with antiquities and other objects of art. Here for more than thirty years he lived and worked, producing busts and other sculptures of European interest, and sending home many monuments, particularly to the South, proud of her gifted son. Gaining Italian facility without losing German thoroughness, he was a skilful and prolific executant. His studio, with its romantic aspects and its practical products, became something halfway between a salon and a show-place. Concerts of a high order were given there, and in the season it was a weekly rendezvous for the cosmopolitan society of Rome, gentle and simple being received with equal courtesy. Among the sculptor's friends were Cardinal von Hohenlohe and Franz Liszt. Ezekiel made a portrait of the Cardinal and one of the composer, and the Grand-Duke of Saxe-Meiningen ordered a copy of each. Hence from Germany he received the Cross of Merit in Art. His bust of Prof. Alfonso Sella for the University of Rome and that of the Dowager Queen Margherita, together with such works as his "Neptune" fountain at Nettuno, Italy, and his figure of "Faith" in a Roman cemetery, won him Italian fame.

Beginning with his marble group, "Religious Liberty," much applauded at the Columbian Exposition (1893), and ending with his seated statue of Poe erected in Baltimore (1917), the list of his works in the United States is extensive. For the Virginia Military Institute at Lexington, Va., he made a colossal bronze group, "Virginia Mourning her Dead"; for the Confederate Cemetery, Johnson's Island, Ohio, a memorial bronze figure, "The Outlook"; for Charleston, West Va., a bronze statue of Stonewall Jackson; for the court house, Louisville, Ky., a bronze monument to Thomas Jefferson, perhaps his outstanding work, a replica of which belongs to the University of Virginia, Charlottesville. His monument to the Confederate dead was unveiled in Arlington National Cemetery in 1913, President Wilson making the chief address. Numerous other sculptures by Ezekiel are in American public buildings and in private ownership. He has a work in Westminster Abbey, and one in a Paris chapel.

After thirty years of residence in the Piazza delle Terme, he was naturally dismayed when the Italian government took over his quarters at the Baths of Diocletian as an adjunct to its National Museum there. Still active in his art, he took a studio not far from the Piazza del Popolo. As a residence he found a romantic haven in the Tower of Belisarius, given to him by the municipal authorities. There he died, beloved and mourned by many in Rome. He was the last of the American artist-expatriates of his generation; his art forms a link between mid-Victorian smugness and twentieth-century searching. America bore him, Germany trained him, Italy inspired him: all three countries had his love and possess his works.

[A sympathetic account of Ezekiel by a fellow sculptor is given in the address by H. K. Bush-Brown at the Memorial Service, Scottish Rite Temple, Washington, D. C., Mar. 30, 1921, published, with illustrations, in *Art and Archæology*, June 1921. There is a brief biography in *Fairmount Park Art Asso., an Account of its Origin and Activities . . . Issued on the Occasion of its Fiftieth Anniversary, 1921* (1922); other sources are: Lorado Taft, *Hist. of Am. Sculpture* (1903; rev. ed., 1924); a well-illustrated article in *World's Work*, Nov. 1909; *Art and Archæology*, May 1917; *Who's Who in Art*, 1912; obituaries in *N. Y. Times* and *N. Y. Tribune*, Mar. 28, 1917, in other American papers, and in Roman papers. U. Thieme and F. Becker, *Allgemeines Lexikon der Bildenden Künstler*, vol. XI (1915), give additional references.]

A. A.

FABER, JOHN EBERHARD (Dec. 6, 1822–Mar. 2, 1879), pencil manufacturer, was born at Stein, near Nürnberg, Bavaria, the youngest son of George Leonard and Albertina Frederika (Kupfer) Faber. His family for three generations had been makers of writing pencils at Stein, the industry having been started by his great-grandfather, Caspar Faber, in 1761. George Faber was well-to-do and did not at first expect his youngest son to go into the pencil business. He intended him for the profession of law. With that in view young Eberhard, after completing his studies at the Gymnasium of Nürnberg, took lectures in jurisprudence at the Universities of Erlangen and Heidelberg. The subject did not appeal to him, however; he was far more interested in ancient history and literature. In those fields he read widely and became a cultivated scholar. That was hardly the conventional background for a commercial career, yet this young man, on his own initiative, extended his ancestral business over another continent and eventually made the family name as well known in the New World as in the Old. Migrating to America shortly after the Revolution of 1848, young Faber started himself in business in New York City, acting as agent in the United States for the pencil factory at Stein, which was then managed by his oldest brother, J. Lothar Faber. At the same time Eberhard Faber sold on commission various articles of stationery manufactured in Germany and England. In due time he became an American citizen and acquired control of large tracts of cedar-forest land in Florida. He began by exporting cedar wood in logs to pencil factories in Europe and later built a sawmill at Cedar Keys on the Gulf coast of Florida, which cut the cedar logs into slats suitable to be worked up into pencils, and shipped the wood in that form to the European factories. Meanwhile his pencil trade, which had grown from small beginnings, was dependent on the Bavarian factory for its finished product, although a good part of the raw material originated in America. There was also a tariff handicap. Faber believed that he could manufacture pencils advantageously in

New York, provided machinery could be made to offset the difference in labor costs between Europe and the United States. He was nearer the source of cedar-wood supply, but farther from the graphite mines. He was not ready to open his factory until 1861, the first year of the Civil War. This was an unfavorable time for launching such an industry, especially since cedar in quantity could be obtained only from Confederate territory. However, starting on a comparatively small scale, he was able to maintain an output which met the demands of the time. After the war the industry grew rapidly and became firmly established. The graphite was obtained mainly from Austrian mines while the clay, to be used with the graphite, came from Bohemia. When his New York factory on the East River was bnrned in 1872, a larger plant was set up in the Greenpoint section of Brooklyn, where the business went forward at an enhanced pace. Faber was the first pencil manufacturer to attach rubber tips and metallic point protectors to his pencils. He employed the nickel-plating process extensively and operated a factory at Newark, N. J., for the making of rubber bands and erasers. He also produced penholders.

Faber was married, in 1854, to Jenny, daughter of Ludwig Haag of Munich. He left two sons, who succeeded him in his business. For ten years before his death, in 1879, he lived at Port Richmond, Staten Island.

[*N. Y. Times*, Mar. 4, 1879; *The Story of the Oldest Pencil Factory in America* (1924); information as to certain facts supplied by Mr. Eberhard Faber.]

W. B. S—w.

FACKLER, DAVID PARKS (Apr. 4, 1841–Oct. 30, 1924), actuary, was born at Kempsville, Va., the son of David Morris Fackler and Susan Stith (Satchell) Fackler, and a great-grandson of an officer of the Continental Army. He was graduated B.A. in 1859 by the College of the City of New York, taking the gold medal in mathematics. Shortly after his graduation from college he entered the actuarial department of the Mutual Life Insurance Company of New York. In 1862, when only 21 years of age, he suggested the contribution plan for apportioning surplus to life insurance policyholders which in principle is in general use by life insurance companies today. He aided Sheppard Homans, then actuary of the company, in the application of the plan. Resigning in 1865 to become a consulting actuary, he continued as such until his death. In 1871 Fackler took an active part in the deliberations of the first meeting of the National Insurance Convention, having been appointed representative of the State of Tennessee. His chief contribution was his vigorous support of conservative valuation standards in the life insurance business. With Alexander Delmar and others, he opposed the views of a strong inflationist party in the convention. If the attitude of the more optimistic members had prevailed, the difficulties which life insurance companies actually encountered in the deflation period from 1873 to 1896 would have been aggravated. In the sixties and seventies, he was one of the outstanding supporters favoring the enactment of non-forfeiture laws affecting life insurance. In 1877, he was appointed actuary of a committee of policy-holders who were examining the affairs of one of the large life insurance companies. Throughout the eighties he distinguished himself in the fight against tontine life insurance.

Fackler was the guiding spirit in the organization of the Actuarial Society of America in 1889 and was its second president (1891–93). In 1891 he offered prizes for the best essays on the subject "Legislative Interference with Impaired Companies." After the grade of associate had been established by the Actuarial Society, he offered prizes for competitive essays by associates in the years 1900, 1904, and 1908. In 1892 he pointed out, in an address before the National Convention of Insurance Commissioners, the problems growing out of the then unrestrained competition between life insurance companies for new business, and predicted the upheaval in public opinion which gave rise in 1905 to the appointment of the Life Insurance Investigating Committee, by the New York legislature, known as the Armstrong Committee. In 1906 he served as consulting actuary to the New Jersey Senate committee investigating life insurance in that state. In 1900 he was employed by the Post Office Department of the United States government to analyze the affairs of certain "debenture companies," with the result that these companies were put out of business. He was consulted by many of the largest fraternal orders during the nineties, but the conventions of the fraternal orders did not put into effect the sound advice he gave them. About 1900 he was called in by the Knights of Columbus to recommend an adequate rating system. His recommendations were adopted and are still in successful effect. He was actuary of a joint committee of Congress in 1909–11. As late as 1923, he took an active part in the campaign to exempt life insurance premiums from income tax.

On Nov. 17, 1875, he married Elizabeth Leverett Davenport of Hartford, Conn., who died in 1918, leaving three children. He died in Richmond, Va., Oct. 30, 1924.

[*Trans. Actuarial Soc. of America*, vol. XXV, pt. 2 (1924), 371–72; *Hayden's Ann. Cyc. of Insurance, 1900–01* (1901); *Who's Who in America*, 1922–23; *Insurance Monitor*, Jan. 1870; *Proc. Nat. Convention of Insurance Commissioners* for the years 1871 to 1924; the *Spectator*, Nov. 6, 1924; *N. Y. Times*, Nov. 1, 1924. A manuscript bibliography of Fackler's writings, compiled by Edward Bathurst Fackler, Edwin W. Kopf, and Alice W. Smith, has been deposited in the Lib. of Cong., Washington, D. C. This list covers several hundred articles written for the most part during a critical period in life insurance history.] E. W. K.

FAESCH, JOHN JACOB (1729–May 26, 1799), ironmaster, government contractor, was born in the canton of Basle, Switzerland. He came from Hesse-Cassel to New Jersey in 1764 under a seven-years' contract by which the London company was to pay him "2500 guilders per annum Rhenish," as well as all travel expenses, furnish a house and meadow and put him in charge of all their forges, mines, and ironworks. Succeeding "Baron" Hasenclever [*q.v.*] at Ringwood, Charlotteburg and Long Pond, "the smart little Dutchman" was superseded in 1771 by Robert Erskine [*q.v.*], later Washington's surveyor-general, who sued him for unlawfully retaining company property (Erskine papers). It is thought that Faesch had planned to take the property at Mt. Hope. In 1772 with D. Wrisberg he leased a house and an extensive acreage there. He also bought several tracts of land. These and other similar transactions gave rise later to much litigation. He built the famous Mt. Hope furnace, enlarged his charcoal lands to over 10,000 acres, established a high repute for ability and integrity, became a leading citizen and the wealthiest ironmaster in Morris County. He was naturalized in June 1766 by a special legislative act, and on Mar. 24, 1773, he was commissioned one of the county judges. He held the honor during life, and became an ardent Whig.

With the outbreak of the Revolution, Faesch remained loyal, entered the war with zeal, and "cast a large amount of shot and shell for the Government." To carry on his enterprise he had been furnished with about three hundred war prisoners, mostly Hessians, nearly all of whom afterward remained in New Jersey, and an army guard to foil robbers. Occasionally he was honored by visits from Washington. In the post-war slump he moved to Morristown, thence to Old Boonton where he built a house now ninety feet under water in the Parsippany reservoir. He served as a delegate to the New Jersey convention in December 1787 and signed the ratification of the federal Constitution. He subscribed heavily to church and school enterprises, set up a ponderous coach known for long waits at the tavern, and died of dropsy. His business disintegrated in his sons' hands. He was a "generous and large-hearted man, but very aristocratic in his ideas." He married Elizabeth Brinckerhoff of Parsippany by whom he had two sons and two daughters. His second wife, Susan Lawrence Leonard, sister-in-law of Capt. Lawrence of the *Chesapeake*, had no children.

[*Hist. of Morris County, N. J.* (1882), pp. 53–55; A. H. Heusser, *The Forgotten General, Robert Erskine* (1928); *Archives of the State of N. J.*, 2 ser., vol. II (1903), p. 429, vol. III (1906), pp. 460, 479, vol. V (1917), p. 299; Erskine Papers in N. J. Hist. Soc., Newark.] W. L. W—y.

FAGAN, JAMES FLEMING (Mar. 1, 1828–Sept. 1, 1893), planter, soldier, public official, was born in Clark County, Ky., the son of Steven and Kittie (Stevens) Fagan. The first member of the family in America was James Fagan, who came from Ireland and settled in Virginia about the middle of the eighteenth century. The father of the subject of this sketch moved to Arkansas in 1838 and became one of the contractors on the new state capitol. He died two years later, leaving James, then twelve, the chief support of his mother and a younger brother. Under such circumstances his educational opportunities were very meager. His mother married Samuel Adams, former state treasurer and for a time acting governor, but he soon died and again James became the main support of the family. While engaged in farming on the family plantation on the Saline River he was elected to the legislature as a Whig, but served only one term. On the outbreak of the war with Mexico he volunteered, serving in Gen. Archibald Yell's regiment and returning with the rank of lieutenant. In 1856 he was appointed receiver for the State Bank and served two years trying to straighten out that wretched financial muddle. When Arkansas seceded he was among the first to raise military companies and became colonel of the 1st Arkansas Infantry. He was a man of quick and vigorous action. He sent out the call for volunteers before the state had actually seceded (May 6, 1861) and in twenty days after secession had his regiment, 900 strong, in Lynchburg, Va. But Fagan did not remain in the East. He distinguished himself at the battle of Shiloh and was made brigadier-general in September 1862. He was transferred to the Trans-Mississippi Department in time to take part in the battle of Prairie Grove and in 1863 was assigned to raise troops for the defense of Arkansas. He took a prominent part in the repulse of Steele's Camden Expedition, after which, on the recommendation of E. Kirby Smith, he was raised to the rank of major-general. He took part in the last Missouri Expedition of Gen. Sterling Price, from whom he won high praise. Even after the surrender of Gen. Lee he declined Gen. J. J. Reynolds's invitation to surrender on the same terms. He was somewhat defiant about surrendering to "an invisible foe," but finally gave up on June 14 (Thomas, *post*, pp. 304–05, 315–16). After the war his time was divided between planting and politics. His first reappearance in the latter was in the so-called Brooks-Baxter war when he commanded the infantry for Brooks while another former Confederate, Gen. C. P. Newton, commanded for Baxter. He accepted office under President Grant, who appointed him in 1875 United States marshal for the western district at Fort Smith. Two years later he became receiver for the Land Office at Little Rock. These affiliations probably caused his defeat in 1890 when he was a candidate for railroad commissioner. Gen. Fagan was reputed to be a very handsome man and was listed among the figures to be carved on Stone Mountain. He was twice married, first to Mura Ellisiff Beal, sister of Gen. W. N. R. Beal, who bore him three daughters; and second to Lizzie Rapley, who bore him five children.

[*Official Records (Army)*, 1 ser., vols. XIII, XXII, XXXIV, XLI; *Confed. Mil. Hist.*, X (1899), 399, inaccurate in some details; *Reg. of Officers and Agents . . . in the Service of the U. S.*, 1875, 1877; D. Y. Thomas, *Ark. in War and Reconstruction, 1861–74* (1926); *Ark. Gazette*, Sept. 2, and *Southern Standard* (Arkadelphia), Sept. 8, 1893. Family history was furnished by Miss Beatrice Fagan Cockle, Fagan's grand-daughter.] D. Y. T.

FAGES, PEDRO (fl. 1767–1796), first *commandante* of Alta California and later governor, was a Catalan. He came to Mexico in 1767 as lieutenant, 1st battalion, 2nd regiment, Catalonia Volunteers. While fighting Sonora Indians he was ordered to lead twenty-five of his men under Gaspar de Portolá on the "Holy Expedition" the occupation of Alta California, and sailed from La Paz for San Diego on the *San Cárlos*, arriving after a terrible voyage of 110 days. He accompanied Portolá when the latter founded the mission and presidio at Monterey on June 3, 1770, and remained in command after Portolá returned to Mexico. In November 1770 he explored the east shore of San Francisco Bay northward to San Leandro, and in March 1772, again traversed the same region as far as Antioch. His party had been the first to sight the Golden Gate, and his discoveries determined the ultimate location of San Francisco. Strong-willed and practical, the most notable of the early governors, he clashed with Father Serra over the founding of the missions and over the control of the soldiers, whose low morals corrupted the Indian women. There were also squabbles over his alleged opening of the missionaries' mail. Serra went to Mexico in 1773 and procured Fages's recall, on May 4, 1774. For a time the deposed officer served with his regiment at Pachuca, Mexico. In 1781 and 1782 he made two land journeys to the Colorado River to punish Indians who had destroyed two defenseless missions newly established near the present Yuma as way stations between Sonora and Alta California. Then, having recently been made lieutenant colonel (captain on May 4, 1771), he was appointed governor, and marched to San Diego and Monterey, arriving in November 1782.

Fages liked California and served it loyally. He saved it from famine in 1772 by hunting bears for meat near the present San Luis Obispo. The missionaries spoke kindly of him. He encouraged the fur-trade, urged erection of missions and presidios, and favored the importation of artisans to teach the Indians. He began grants of land, chose several mission sites, and bestowed numerous surviving place names. He got on with Father Lasuen even after disagreement over solitary mission service for the friars, and he was complimented as a worthy soldier by Lapérouse and George Vancouver. He became a colonel in 1789. But his wife, Eulalia Callis, whom he brought to Monterey in 1782, hated California and had a mind to leave it. Finally, in 1790, after he had been nagged for years, Fages asked to be relieved. His wife, taking the son Pedro and the daughter, sailed away that fall, and he followed a year later. His life at Monterey had been brightened by his pride in his orchard of six hundred fruit trees, shrubs, and vines.

[H. E. Bolton, ed., "Expedition to San Francisco Bay in 1770: Diary of Pedro Fages," *Acad. Pacific Coast Hist.*, July 1911; H. I. Priestley, ed., "The Colorado River Campaign, 1781–82; Diary of Pedro Fages," *Ibid.*, May 1913, and "An Hist., Pol. and Natural Description of Cal. by Don Pedro Fages," *Cath. Hist. Rev.*, Jan. and Apr. 1919 (the first white man's description of the Indians and their country between San Diego and San Francisco); I. B. Richman, *Cal. under Spain and Mexico* (1911); C. E. Chapman, *A Hist. of Cal.; The Spanish Period* (1921); Z. S. Eldredge, *The Beginnings of San Francisco* (1912). Various letters of Fages, as well as an unpublished diary, are preserved in the Bancroft Lib., Berkeley, Cal.] H. I. P.

FAGET, JEAN CHARLES (June 26, 1818–Dec. 7, 1884), physician, came of a family of French extraction which went to Cuba from Santo Domingo after the negro revolution in the latter place, and from Cuba moved to New Orleans in 1809. Here Jean Charles was born, the only child of Jean Babtiste Faget and his wife, a Miss Le Mormand. After a preliminary education under the Jesuit Fathers of his native city, he was sent to Paris, where from 1830 to 1837 he attended the Collège Rolin. Following seven years of externe and interne service in Paris hospitals, he was given the degree of M.D. by the Faculté de Paris, in December 1844. His graduation thesis was a discourse on sub-pubic cystotomy in young children. He returned to New Orleans in 1845, and became a protagonist of the infectious theory of disease as opposed to the contagionist school. The medical profession of the city included a group of able men, mostly graduates of the Faculté de Paris. The proceedings of the city medical society, reported in *La Gazette Médicale,* show the bitter feud between the medical factions, in language always polite, even though charged with biting sarcasm. It was to this not altogether friendly audience that Faget announced, in 1859, his observation of a pathognomonic sign of yellow fever, by which it could be definitely differentiated from the pernicious malarial fevers which so closely simulated it. He noted that coincident with the rise of the patients' temperature, there was a fall in the pulse-rate, a phenomenon unusual in any fever and always absent in malarial attacks. Though the value of "Faget's sign" was at first disputed, it soon became the conclusive proof of yellow fever. Following the publication of *Mémoires et Lettres sur la Fièvre Jaune et la Fièvre Paludéenne,* in 1864 he was created Chevalier of the Legion of Honor by the French government. In 1856 he published *Études sur les Bases de la Science Médicale,* for which he received a gold medal from the Academy of Caen. He contributed numerous articles in English to the *New Orleans Medical Journal.* He was appointed to the Louisiana State Board of Health, and in 1864 was made a member of the sanitary commission appointed by the Federal Gen. Banks. In March 1865 he went to Paris, remaining two years. Returning to New Orleans, he resided there until his death in 1884. He was married in Paris to Glady Ligeret de Chazet, daughter of Dr. Ligeret de Chazet, and left a large family.

Tall and spare with a clean-cut face, a slightly hooked nose, a high receding forehead and long wavy hair, brushed straight back, Faget was a man of striking appearance. He was deeply religious and affected the dress and bearing of a priest, wearing the silk hat of low crown and broad brim in the winter, black straw hat in the summer, and in cold weather a long black coat fastened with a silver chain and hook. A soft, gentle voice added to the resemblance. He had a large practise among the French and particularly the Creole population of the city, a class he so honorably represented. He gave little thought to the business side of his profession, was a poor charger and a worse collector. He died poor.

[Edmond Souchon, "Original Contributions of Louisiana to Medical Sciences," *La. Hist. Soc. Pubs. for 1914–15,* VIII (1916), 66–88; *New Orleans Medical and Surgical Jour.,* 1884; W. B. Atkinson, *The Physicians and Surgeons of the United States* (1878); L. G. Le Boeuf in H. A. Kelly and W. L. Burrage, *Am. Medic. Biogs.* (1920); *New Orleans Annual,* 1846; *Times-Democrat* (New Orleans), Dec. 8, 1884; information from a grandson, Dr. Edward B. Faget of New Orleans.]

J. M. P.

FAHNESTOCK, HARRIS CHARLES (Feb. 27, 1835–June 4, 1914), banker, philanthropist, came of German ancestry. His family had lived at Ephrata and Harrisburg, Pa., since the middle of the eighteenth century. He was born at Harrisburg, the son of Adam K. and Sybil (Holbrook) Fahnestock. At an early age he left school for a business career, being at first employed in a Harrisburg bank controlled by an uncle. In 1856 he married Margaret McKinley. At the beginning of the Civil War his ability and energy in pushing the sale of the Pennsylvania $3,000,000 bond issue attracted the attention of Jay Cooke [*q.v.*], the Philadelphia banker, and so favorably impressed him that he offered young Fahnestock an interest in the branch of his banking house which he was about to open in Washington. Without contributing capital, Fahnestock was given a one-sixth share and his expenses were guaranteed, and he and Henry D. Cooke [*q.v.*], Jay Cooke's brother, took charge of the Washington office. As the war wore on and brought increasing financial perplexities to the Lincoln administration, the firm, because of its relations with the Treasury Department, came to be regarded as one of the sheet anchors of the government. When Secretary Chase was unable to dispose of the 7.30 war bonds through the usual government agencies, he turned the business over to Jay Cooke & Company, paying a commission of 3/8 of one per cent. on sales, and thus the entire issue was disposed of. For Fahnestock, still in his twenties, such an experience—unparalleled up to that time in this country—was doubtless more valuable than a lifetime of ordinary banking routine. Ability to form independent judgments and to act on them was encouraged and developed in those years.

After the war it was decided to open a New York branch of Jay Cooke & Company, and the burden of this undertaking fell largely on Fahnestock. His interest was 14 per cent., and he retained a like share in the Philadelphia and Washington offices. His chief responsibility had to do with the handling of bonds. The New York business was successful from the start. The branch was opened on Mar. 1, 1866, and in the remaining ten months of that calendar year Fahnestock's share of the profits was $63,000. During the ensuing seven years—an era of post-war speculation and inflation—the Cooke banks generally prospered. The head of the firm became intensely interested in the building of the Northern Pacific Railroad and took over the bonds of that enterprise. The road was projected through a region for the most part then unpeopled and could not hope, even when completed, to receive adequate local support. It became impossible to find a market for the bonds. For a long period the Philadelphia house of Cooke & Company drew on the New York branch for railroad funds until finally resources were exhausted and on Sept. 18, 1873, Fahnestock was compelled to close the doors of the New York office (interview in *New York Herald,* Sept. 19, 1873). He had personally opposed the part taken by the firm in the Northern Pacific bond deals (Oberholtzer, *post,* II, 150, 223, 380 ff., 397, 423). The assets of Cooke & Company, however, amounted to more than twice the liabilities, and within seven years the entire indebtedness was paid off, but the New York office never resumed business.

Fahnestock had not yet reached middle age and he began to build up a second fortune. In the organization of the First National Bank of New York, of which he became a vice-president, he quickly found a post where his abilities could be utilized and rewarded. In the forty years of life that remained to him he accumulated wealth, held directorates in various financial institutions, made large gifts for religious and charitable objects, and in his will disposed of more than $500,000 for public causes. The Charity Organization Society, the Association for Improving the Condition of the Poor, and three New York hospitals —the Presbyterian, St. Luke's, and the Post-Graduate—each received $100,000.

[A. K. and W. F. Fahnestock, *Family Memorial of the Fahnestocks in the U. S.* (1879); E. P. Oberholtzer, *Jay Cooke, Financier of the Civil War* (2 vols., 1907); *N. Y. Times,* June 5 and 14, 1914.] W. B. S—w.

FAIR, JAMES GRAHAM (Dec. 3, 1831–Dec. 28, 1894), forty-niner and financier, derived a fortune from the output of the Comstock lode, and became one of the more prominent of the bonanza senators of the eighties. He was born near Belfast in Ireland, the son of James Fair, who was himself an Irishman of Scotch descent. His mother, a Scot, was named Graham. Brought to Illinois at the age of twelve, he there acquired a respectable education, and at the age of eighteen he joined the great procession to California. Canny and acquisitive, he bothered little with the placer gold, but searched always for the quartz from which it came. Before he was thirty he had a mill on the Washoe in Nevada, and thereafter as he grew in financial stature he was identified with Nevada and California. The vast deposits of auriferous quartz known as the Comstock lode had been discovered before Fair reached Nevada, and for nearly fifteen years it yielded pocket after pocket, the grand but uncertain contents of which kept hysterical speculation alive. This was a sort of mining in which the individual miner, without capital or machinery, had no chance, whereas the mining company and the banking interests behind it might profit from both the output of ore and the greed of a speculative public. The San Francisco bankers controlled Nevada development until Fair and his associates (among whom John W. Mackay was most prominent) captured a group of their holdings, organized them around their own new Bank of Nevada, and stumbled upon the silver and gold pocket of the Consolidated Virginia Mine. This has been thought to be the most valuable single ore pocket ever found. It was Fair's persistent pursuit of a thin meandering vein which led to its discovery in a rock chamber of vast dimension. In March 1873 its yield began to unsettle the market for both metals, and it released so much silver bullion as to induce a great political controversy over the monetary use of that metal. In the next six years the owners took more than one hundred million dollars out of the mine before it was exhausted. Fair held on to most of his share, and converted it not only into luxurious living but into land, buildings, railroads, and other steady sources of income. Several of the Comstock millionaires (Jones, Sharon, Stewart) found their way to the United States Senate, and Fair's turn came when in 1881 a Democratic Nevada legislature elected him for a six-year term. He made no impression on the Senate save to advertise it as a haunt of millionaires, and he rarely took part in its debates. But the gaudiness and irregularity of his life and the social ambitions of his family, to which his wealth allowed full gratification, attracted much attention for two decades.

Fair was married in 1861, at Carson City, to Theresa Rooney, and they had four children before he was divorced by her in 1883. Of these the wife retained the custody of the girls, Theresa Alice and Virginia, while Fair himself retained his sons, James and Charles Lewis. He was ignored when in 1890 the older daughter was married to Hermann Oelrichs of New York, at a ceremony graced by high magnates of the Catholic church and advertised as one of San Francisco's most splendid social displays (*San Francisco Chronicle,* June 4, 1890). Virginia, after his death, married William K. Vanderbilt, Jr. (*San Francisco Chronicle*, Apr. 5, 1899). His sons, like his marriage, gave him no permanent happiness. James committed suicide, and Charles Lewis made a youthful marriage which enraged the father (*New York Herald*, Oct. 24, 1893), and which ended in the death of both husband and wife in a motor accident near Paris (Aug. 14, 1902). Fair disinherited Charles, although he apparently relented shortly afterward.

In his last years, living alone in the Lick House, San Francisco, Fair sought what consolations he could find. His business affairs demanded attention, and in 1887 he was forced to take active charge of the Nevada Bank which had come close to shipwreck. He made several wills, some of which he destroyed. He had apprehensions concerning claimants upon his estate, having before him the litigation over the Sharon estate. He wrote into his will a denial that he was married, or that he had other heirs than the three surviving children by Theresa Rooney, but he left fifty dollars each to any widows or children who might after his death be successful in establishing a right. He died in 1894. The courts broke up the trust in which he had tried to vest his property, and for seven years his estate was involved in contest, litigation, and compromise (*New York Tribune*, Mar. 23, 1902).

[H. H. Bancroft has given Fair considerable desultory space in *Chronicles of the Builders of the Commonwealth*, IV (1892), 188–236; he is included in Henry Hall, *America's Successful Men of Affairs* (1896), II, 293–94; and there is an elaborate local obituary in the *San Francisco Chronicle*, Dec. 29, 1894.]

F. L. P—n.

FAIRBANK, CALVIN (Nov. 3, 1816–Oct. 12, 1898), Methodist clergyman, Abolitionist, the fourth of the ten children of Chester and Betsey (Abbott) Fairbank, was born in Pike Township, Allegany County (now Eagle Township, Wyoming County), N. Y., whither his parents had migrated in 1815 from Vermont. From his mother, a zealous Methodist, he early became imbued with backwoods Methodism; and from a pair of escaped slaves, to whose cabin he was assigned during a quarterly meeting, he learned to abhor slavery. His emotionalism unchecked by education or good judgment, he developed into a militant Abolitionist, eager to distinguish himself, and was one of the few who engaged in the actual abduction of slaves. He began this work in April 1837 while steering a lumber raft down the Ohio River; a negro on the Virginia bank, after a little coaxing, confessed a longing for freedom, was promptly taken aboard the raft, ferried to the Ohio side, and turned loose. Thereafter, as chance offered, Fairbank acted as passenger agent for the underground railway, smuggling runaway negroes from Virginia and Kentucky into Ohio, where he delivered them to Levi Coffin and other Abolitionists for transportation to Canada or to safer parts of the United States. At one time, with money supplied by Salmon P. Chase and others, he bought a young woman who otherwise would have been sold to a New Orleans procurer. He became an adept at disguising and concealing his charges in transit and was entirely without fear. Once he ventured as far as Little Rock, Ark., to find a young negro who had been deprived illegally of his freedom and conducted him safely from there to free soil. In all he effected the liberation of forty-seven slaves. In 1842 he was ordained as a Methodist elder. Gravitating to Oberlin, he enrolled in the preparatory department of the Collegiate Institute, but before the end of the year he was arrested in Lexington, Ky., for his part in the escape of Lewis Hayden and his family. He pleaded his own case, was convicted and sentenced to fifteen years in the Frankfort penitentiary, and served from Feb. 18, 1845, until Aug. 23, 1849, when he was pardoned by Gov. John J. Crittenden. Meanwhile his father had died of cholera at Lexington while working to secure his son's release. Fairbank soon resumed his operations along the Ohio. He was kidnapped at Jeffersonville, Ind., Nov. 4, 1851, spirited into Kentucky, and again sent to the penitentiary on a fifteen-year sentence. This time he was systematically overworked, kept in a filthy cell, and frequently and mercilessly flogged. He was incarcerated until Apr. 15, 1864, when he was pardoned by Lieut.-Gov. Richard T. Jacob. On June 9, 1864, at Oxford, Ohio, he married Mandana Tileston of Williamsburg, Mass., to whom he had been engaged for twelve years. She died Sept 29, 1876, in Williamsburg; and on June 5, 1879, Fairbank married Adeline Winegar. For some ten years he was an employee of missionary and benevolent societies in New York. Later he was superintendent and general agent of the Moore Street Industrial Institute of Richmond, Va. He lectured or preached from time to time, the cruelty and immorality of slaveholders and his own exploits being the staple of his discourses. In his old age he wrote an incoherent and untrustworthy but revealing autobiography. His last days were spent, close to poverty, in Angelica, Allegany County, N. Y.

[*Rev. Calvin Fairbank during Slavery Times: How He "Fought the Good Fight" to Prepare "The Way"* (Chicago, 1890); L. S. Fairbanks, *Geneal. of the Fairbanks Family* (privately printed, 1897); *Gen. Cat. of Oberlin Coll. 1833–1908* (1909); Laura S. Haviland, *A Woman's Life-Work* (Cincinnati, 1881), chap. vi; *Christian Advocate* (N. Y.), May 12, Nov. 3, 1898.]

G. H. G.

FAIRBANKS, CHARLES WARREN (May 11, 1852–June 4, 1918), senator, vice-president, and one of the last of America's "log cabin statesmen," was born in a single-room log farmhouse near Unionville Center, Union County, Ohio. His father, Loriston Monroe Fairbanks, a pioneer from New England, was of Puritan stock, tracing his ancestry directly to a certain Jonathan Fayerbanke (variously spelled), who had emigrated from England to Massachusetts in 1633. Charles's mother, Mary Adelaide (Smith) Fairbanks, was of a family of New Yorkers. Both parents were Methodists and Abolitionists—in its day a potent combination—who reared their numerous brood of children after the fashion of pioneers. Years later as a candidate for office, Charles Warren Fairbanks found it no disadvantage to have been born in a log cabin, to have worked barefoot in the fields, to have walked a mile and a half to the district school, to have observed his parents giving aid and comfort to runaway slaves. A strong taste for books and learning led young Charles in spite of his poverty to enter the Ohio Wesleyan University at Delaware, Ohio, where he "worked his way through" to graduation in 1872. Here he met his future wife, Cornelia Cole, the daughter of Judge P. B. Cole of Marysville, Ohio. Their marriage occurred in 1874. For his alma mater Fairbanks always retained a feeling of interest and affection. After he had achieved prominence he served for years as a member of its board of trustees, and he sent to it the eldest of his four sons and his only daughter.

Young Fairbanks aspired to be a lawyer, and after graduation he found work with the Associated Press, first at Pittsburgh and later at Cleveland, that would leave him free to attend law school at night. In 1874 he was admitted to the bar by the supreme court of Ohio, but, learning of an opening in Indianapolis, he removed thither to begin his practise. Railway litigation was just then beginning to offer an opportunity for the skilful lawyer, and it was as a railway attorney that Fairbanks made his mark. In his first case he was called upon to straighten out the legal affairs of a bankrupt road, and at this task he acquitted himself so creditably that, according to one admirer, "no railroad enterprise of any account has been undertaken in Indiana since then without his having a share in it" (*Independent,* July 7, 1904). Certain it is that clients came to him who could afford to pay well for his services, and in a comparatively short time he had achieved both wealth and fame. For twenty-three years continuously he maintained his Indianapolis office, but his practise extended not only throughout Indiana but also into the neighboring states of Ohio and Illinois.

In Indiana even more than elsewhere law and politics are apt to go hand in hand. Fairbanks was naturally a Republican, and he early began to take part in local political affairs. In 1888, when he was only thirty-six years old, he managed the unsuccessful campaign of Walter Q. Gresham for the Republican presidential nomination, and afterwards supported actively Gresham's rival, Benjamin Harrison. In the campaign of 1896 Fairbanks, who had long advocated the single gold standard, achieved national eminence as temporary chairman and "key-note" speaker of the convention that nominated McKinley. Thereafter the astute Indiana lawyer soon consolidated his control of the Republican party in his state, winning for himself at the same time a place in the national Republican organization hardly less important than that occupied by the celebrated Marcus A. Hanna.

Until he had acquired a satisfactory competence, Fairbanks did not choose to run for office. In 1897, however, he obtained the caucus nomination of the Republican majority in the Indiana legislature for United States senator, and was promptly elected. His wealth made it possible for him, on taking his seat, to leave off the practise of law altogether, and he is said never again to have accepted a retainer. In the Senate he became at once an influential member. He was the close friend and admirer of President McKinley, for whom he was soon recognized as the responsible spokesman in the Senate. He supported the President faithfully in his policies before and during the Spanish-American War; he served creditably on important committees, including ultimately the committee on foreign relations; he advocated persistently the adoption of comprehensive plans for internal improvements, especially waterways; and he was appointed American chairman of the Joint High Commission of 1898, which tried to adjust all outstanding differences between the United States and Canada, but failed because of the acuteness of the Alaskan boundary dispute (W. F. Johnson, *America's Foreign Relations,* 1916, vol. II, pp. 105–06). As the sole or the senior Republican senator from Indiana, he had the chief disposal of patronage in that state, and, when the Republicans captured the legislature in 1902, his reëlection the next year to the Senate followed as a matter of course.

A conservative and a representative of the doubtful state of Indiana, "the home of vice-presidents," Fairbanks was chosen to balance the ticket which Roosevelt headed in 1904. The vice-presidential candidate, who had long since stumped every county in Indiana, now extended his activities to the nation at large, making speeches in thirty-three states and traveling no less than twenty-five thousand miles in the course of the campaign. He was elected, and served four years under Roosevelt. During this time the president and the vice-president, although representing opposite wings of the party, maintained cordial relations. On occasion Fairbanks even found it possible to speak well of the president in public.

After Mar. 4, 1909, Fairbanks did not again hold public office. He maintained his great influence in Indiana politics, however, and in 1916 was again nominated for the vice-presidency, only to lose to another Indianan, Thomas R. Marshall. In the years 1909 and 1910, when Roosevelt was in Africa, Fairbanks toured the world, gaining considerable notoriety from the fact that, when he proposed to address students of the Methodist schools at the American Church in Rome, he was denied an audience by the Pope (*Outlook*, Feb. 19, 1910). In 1912 Fairbanks was chairman of the platform committee in the convention that nominated Taft over Roosevelt, and with his customary regularity, when the split came, he supported the Republican ticket. Both in 1908 and in 1916 he was the "favorite son" candidate of his state for the presidential nomination.

To those who knew Fairbanks only from his public appearances, he seemed a cold and forbidding figure; but to his friends he seemed warm-hearted and genial. He was never known to lose his composure; he worked quietly to accomplish his purposes; and he took himself and his duties with extreme seriousness. As an orator he was content to state his case without rhetorical flights. Tall and slender to a marked degree, he was in no wise ungainly, but rather the suave and polished gentleman. While he was senator, and later also while he was vice-president, he and his wife entered freely into the social life of the Capital; and at one time Mrs. Fairbanks was President-General of the Daughters of the American Revolution. Her death preceded that of her husband by five years.

[F. E. Leupp, "Charles Warren Fairbanks," *Independent*, July 7, 1904; E. I. Lewis, "Senator Fairbanks—The Boy and Man," *Ibid.*, July 21, 1904; John W. Foster, "The Candidate of Indiana for the Presidency," *Ibid.*, Mar. 12, 1908; Thomas R. Shipp, "Charles Warren Fairbanks, Republican Candidate for Vice-President," *Rev. of Revs.* (N. Y.), August 1904; and Addison C. Harris, "Charles Warren Fairbanks," *North Am. Rev.*, May 1908. See also Fairbanks's article, "American Missionaries Abroad," *Outlook*, July 16, 1910.]

J. D. H.

FAIRBANKS, ERASTUS (Oct. 28, 1792–Nov. 20, 1864), governor of Vermont, was born at Brimfield, Mass. He was the eldest of the three sons of Maj. Joseph Fairbanks and Phebe (Paddock) Fairbanks, and was of the seventh generation of the descendants of Jonathan Fairebanke (variously spelled), who migrated from Yorkshire to Massachusetts in 1633 and settled in Dedham in 1636. In 1815 his father moved to St. Johnsbury, Vt., where he built a saw and grist mill. The three sons, Erastus, Thaddeus [*q.v.*], and Joseph, who were all of a practical and mechanical turn of mind, extended the business by developing a foundry and wheelwright shop which prospered and grew into a small manufactory of stoves, plows and agricultural implements. The firm also began to build some of the machinery required in connection with the hemp industry. The need of some method of weighing the wagon loads of the raw material brought into town led Thaddeus Fairbanks to devise a crude apparatus by which grappling chains suspended from a steelyard could lift a wagon from the ground and the approximate weight of the load be thus determined. Although this simple device was an improvement upon existing methods, its inventor was not satisfied with approximate accuracy and continued to study the problem. Later in the same year, 1830, he worked out the basic principle of the improved platform scale and was awarded a patent. In 1834 the brothers founded the firm of E. & T. Fairbanks & Company and devoted their energies chiefly to the manufacture of the new platform scale for which there was a wide-spread and growing demand. Erastus, the oldest of the three brothers, was the head of the firm and its chief executive. Under his energetic and capable management the business expanded rapidly and its products won world-wide renown. The business of the firm doubled in volume every three years from 1842 to 1857, when its growth was temporarily halted by the industrial depression prevailing throughout the country at that time, but it recovered and grew rapidly during the Civil War period and later. The firm continued as a family partnership till 1874 when it was incorporated as the Fairbanks Scale Company.

Despite his business interests, Fairbanks took an active interest in politics and public affairs. In 1836 he was elected as the representative of the town of St. Johnsbury in the lower house of the legislature. He was a presidential elector on the Whig ticket in 1844 and in 1848. In 1852 he was elected by the Whigs as governor of the state. His chief concern as governor was the promotion of education and social welfare. During his administration the legislature passed a state prohibition law, and Gov. Fairbanks, always a strong advocate of the cause of temperance, gave it his cordial approval. This act arrayed a powerful vested interest against his administration, and partially accounts for his failure to secure a reëlection. Although he received a plurality of the popular vote, he did not have a majority, and the election was thrown into the legislature, where his opponent was finally elected by a majority of one on the twenty-sixth ballot. In 1856 he affiliated himself with the rising Republican party and in 1860 was again elected to the office of governor on the Republican ticket, receiving about three times as many votes as his Democratic opponent. His election in this critical year places him in the ranks of the "war governors" of the North. On the same day that Lincoln issued his call for 75,000 volunteers to suppress the insurrection, Fairbanks issued a proclamation convening the legislature in special session "for the purpose of adopting measures for organizing, arming and equipping the Militia of the State, and for cooperating with the General Government in suppressing insurrection and executing the laws." In order that there might be no delay in the preparations for supporting the Union, he authorized the quartermaster-general to pledge the credit of E. & T. Fairbanks & Company for purchasing necessary equipment. When the legislature convened, it passed the necessary legislation for putting the state on a war basis, and in addition voted to place the sum of one million dollars in the hands of the governor to use according to his judgment and discretion. During his entire administration Fairbanks was untiring in his labors, and it is believed that he shortened his life by the intensity of his devotion. He never drew his salary as governor. At the end of his term he retired to private life and died shortly after. He was married on May 3, 1815, to Lois C. Crossman by whom he had eight children. In his private life as well as in business, Erastus Fairbanks was a fine example of the old-fashioned American virtues. He was deeply religious and was an active member of the Congregational Church. With other members of the family he made liberal benefactions to the town of St. Johnsbury.

[*The Vermonter,* June 1896; E. T. Fairbanks, *The Town of St. Johnsbury, Vt.* (1914); C. L. Goodell in *Congreg. Quart.*, Jan. 1867; L. S. Fairbanks, *Geneal. of the Fairbanks Family in America* (1897). Information as to certain facts from Mrs. Henry Fairbanks.]

A. M. K.

FAIRBANKS, HENRY (May 6, 1830–July 7, 1918), clergyman, inventor, manufacturer, was the son of Thaddeus [*q.v.*] and Lucy Peck (Barker) Fairbanks and was born in St. Johnsbury, Vt., where his father was engaged in the iron-foundry business and later in the manufacture of weighing-scales. Young Fairbanks inherited a frail physical constitution which prevented his enjoyment of the life of a normal youth and as a result, he was taught at home until he was ten years old. He spent his tenth year at Lyndon Academy, near his home, and the following year at Pinkerton Academy at Derry, N. H. When he was twelve his father established the St. Johnsbury Academy which young Fairbanks immediately entered and there prepared for college. In spite of his studious habits he had inherited the family interest in mechanics and by reason of his father's business had many opportunities for satisfying this bent. After six years in St. Johnsbury Academy and a year spent in travel in Europe seeking health, Fairbanks entered Dartmouth College in 1850 and graduated in 1853. Immediately thereafter he entered Andover Theological Seminary, but three years later the precarious state of his health again necessitated a European sojourn. After his return he completed his work at the seminary and graduated with the class of 1857. From 1857 to 1860 Fairbanks served in several Congregational pastorates in Vermont and did much missionary work in reviving many of the smaller churches which were dying out. Finding, however, that this work was entirely too strenuous he accepted the chair of natural philosophy and subsequently that of natural history in Dartmouth College where he continued teaching until 1869. In that year, upon the death of his mother, he removed with his family to St. Johnsbury and became associated with his father and uncle in the E. & T. Fairbanks Company. In 1868, while still on the faculty of Dartmouth, Fairbanks secured his first patent, jointly with his father, for scales which automatically weighed grain as it was charged into a hopper. After his connection with his father's company he continued to apply his inventive skill in the weighing field and obtained many patents, particularly for registering and printing scales. He was also interested in the local paper-pulp business and obtained a number of patents on pulp-manufacturing machines and other apparatus of value to this industry. In 1897 he patented still another interesting and valuable invention: namely, an alternating current electric generator. At the time of his death he was vice-president of the E. & T. Fairbanks Company; from 1870 to 1905 he was a trustee of Dartmouth College; and for many years he was president of the board of trustees of St. Johnsbury Academy. Fairbanks was twice married; first, in Hanover,

N. H., on Apr. 30, 1862, to Annie S. Noyes; and second, to Ruthy Page of Newport, Vt., on May 5, 1874. He was survived by his widow and six children.

[L. S. Fairbanks, *Geneal. of the Fairbanks Family in America* (1897); *Who's Who in America*, 1918–19; J. M. Cattell, *Am. Men of Sci.* (2nd ed., 1910); *Proc. Vt. Hist. Soc., 1919–20* (1921); M. T. Runnels, *Memorial Sketches and Hist. of the Class of 1853, Dartmouth Coll.* (1895); Patent Office Records.] C. W. M.

FAIRBANKS, THADDEUS (Jan. 17, 1796–Apr. 12, 1886), inventor, was born on his father's farm in Brimfield, Mass., the son of Joseph and Phebe (Paddock) Fairbanks, and brother of Erastus Fairbanks [*q.v.*]. Though he lived to be ninety years old, Fairbanks was never really well, and as a child was extremely delicate. For this reason most of his early education was obtained at home under the tutelage of his mother. As he grew older and when crops were good, he had the opportunity of augmenting this home study with attendance in the established public schools. It would seem that at an early age he gave evidence of having inherited the characteristic Fairbanks aptitude for mechanics, which he applied in various ways as a youth. When his father moved to Vermont in 1815 and undertook mill construction, Thaddeus assisted him. As a side line they also undertook wagon construction. In 1823, in partnership with his brother Erastus, Thaddeus established a small iron-foundry in St. Johnsbury, Vt., operating it under the name of E. & T. Fairbanks. For the succeeding seven years a variety of small foundry jobs were undertaken, with Thaddeus showing particular interest in the improvement of commodities adapted to manufacture in the foundry. Thus on Apr. 19, 1826, he secured a United States patent for a plow equipped with a cast-iron mold board which, as soon as it was produced by the brothers, met with wide demand. Shortly thereafter he devised a parlor stove as well as a cook stove, both of which were made in the foundry. Besides his inventive work and that of operating the foundry, Thaddeus was employed as manager in one of the hemp mills in St. Johnsbury, and for this enterprise he patented in 1830 a flax and hemp dressing machine. About this time, too, the existing crude method of weighing the hemp purchased from the growers, by suspending the cart and load from one end of a huge wooden steelyard, attracted Fairbanks's attention. For some time he had had in mind the adaptation of a platform upon which a cart with its load of hemp could be rolled and weighed. Accordingly he developed the idea and early in 1831 applied for a patent for a platform scale which was granted on June 13, 1831. This was the first scale of this sort, which has since come into worldwide use and has been adapted in hundreds of forms. Thereafter the main business of the company was the manufacture of scales. Fairbanks continued to make improvements on the existing equipment and also to devise new applications of his basic patent, extending all the way from small apothecary to railroad scales. He also continued his early interest in improvements in heating apparatus and among his later inventions in this field were a draft mechanism for furnaces in 1843, a hot-water heater in 1881, and finally, a feed-water heater. For scales alone, Fairbanks obtained thirty-two patents. In addition to these and his miscellaneous inventions he devised many ingenious machines for facilitating the manufacture of scales. He always felt keenly his early lack of education and in his business career gave financial aid to deserving students. Also, with his brothers Erastus and Joseph, he established St. Johnsbury Academy in 1842, and for twenty years thereafter was its sole support, at his death bequeathing to it a large endowment fund. For his inventions he received many honors, both at home and abroad: the Knightly Cross of the Order of St. Joseph from the Emperor of Austria; the Golden Medal of Siam from the King of Siam; and the token of Commander of the Order of Iftikar from the Bey of Tunis. Scientific study of astronomy and heat constituted his major avocation. He was married on Jan. 17, 1820, to Lucy Peck Barker, a native of St. Johnsbury, and of this union two children were born, his son Henry [*q.v.*] alone surviving him at the time of his death in St. Johnsbury.

[L. S. Fairbanks, *Geneal. of the Fairbanks Family in America* (1897); E. T. Fairbanks, *The Town of St. Johnsbury, Vt.* (1914); J. G. Ullery, *Men of Vt.* (1894); Patent Office Records; obituaries in *Burlington Free Press* and *Boston Transcript*, Apr. 14, 1886.] C. W. M.

FAIRCHILD, CHARLES STEBBINS (Apr. 30, 1842–Nov. 24, 1924), financier and secretary of the treasury, was born in Cazenovia, Madison County, N. Y. His parents, Sidney Thompson and Helen (Childs) Fairchild, had come to Cazenovia from Stratford, Conn., and were both descended from English families that had been domiciled in New England since about 1660. Charles was educated at a local seminary, and at Harvard College, graduating from the latter in 1863. Two years later he graduated from the Harvard Law School and entered the Albany firm of his father, where much of the local business of the New York Central Railroad was transacted. He was married in 1871 to Helen Lincklaen, a distant relative and childhood friend, who was a relative of that Lincklaen who was an associate of Theophilus Cazenove, agent for the

Holland Land Company. Lincklaen had founded Cazenovia on one of the purchases of that company about 1793.

Sidney Thompson Fairchild, father of Charles, was an aggressive Democrat and his son inherited his point of view. "My first speech," the latter once declared, "was a eulogy upon that great Democrat, William L. Marcy. My teachings in Democracy were from the earliest childhood at the knee of Seymour, and later at the side of Tilden. The warmest friendship of my manhood was with Manning" (Cooper Union speech, in opposition to David B. Hill, *New York Tribune,* Feb. 12, 1892). When Samuel J. Tilden took office as governor of New York in 1875 he found Fairchild acting as a deputy attorney-general, and accredited with conscience and ability shown in securing the conviction of the New York police commissioners Charlick and Gardner. Under Governor Tilden's direction, Fairchild conducted the prosecutions in the canal ring frauds, and he was pushed by the Governor into the nomination for attorney-general at the Syracuse convention of the Democratic party in 1875 (*New York Herald,* Sept. 17, 1875). He was elected in November; but two years later Tilden was no longer governor, the canal ring was in a position of influence, and Tammany was in complete control (*New York Herald,* Oct. 4, 1877). Fairchild failed to get a renomination, retired in due time to private life, and returned to his practise of law. President Cleveland in 1885 selected Daniel Manning as secretary of the treasury, and Fairchild as assistant secretary; and when midway in the term Manning's health forced him to retire, Fairchild became secretary on Apr. 1, 1887. He remained in this post until the end of the administration, struggling to put the treasury surplus to use, and to maintain the standard of the currency. Out of office in 1889, he became a banker in New York City, and a philanthropist, with a large influence in the affairs of the Charity Organization Society. He emerged from private life in 1892 to fight Hill's "snap" convention (DeAlva Stanwood Alexander, *Four Famous New Yorkers,* 1923, p. 167); and in 1896 to oppose the Bryan ticket. He was permanent chairman of the Syracuse convention that chose a gold Democratic delegation to go to Indianapolis (*Rochester Herald,* Sept. 1, 1896), and a member of the monetary commission. In his old age he appeared at loyalty meetings; and he sought in 1920 to induce the Supreme Court to intervene to prevent the operation of the woman suffrage amendment to the Constitution. He and his wife, who survived him, continued association wtih "Lorenzo," the old home at Cazenovia, and here he died.

[C. C. Jackson and A. S. Pier, "Chas. Stebbins Fairchild," in the *Harvard Grads.' Mag.,* June 1925, is the best sketch of Fairchild's life.] F. L. P—n.

FAIRCHILD, GEORGE THOMPSON (Oct. 6, 1838–Mar. 16, 1901), educator, college president, was born at Brownhelm, Ohio, the youngest child of Grandison and Nancy (Harris) Fairchild, who with their older children had moved thither from Stockbridge, Mass., two decades earlier. George Fairchild was sent to Oberlin College where he graduated in arts in 1862 and in theology in 1865. On Nov. 25, 1863, he married Charlotte Pearl Halsted, also a graduate of Oberlin. Thenceforth the greater part of his life was devoted to the advancement of education in connection with agricultural institutions. In 1865 he was appointed professor of English literature in the Michigan Agricultural College, but he immediately took upon himself various other duties in order to advance the value and influence of that then rather feeble institution. Thus he was the teacher of moral philosophy and French, had charge of the student rhetoricals and arrangement of the curriculum, and was also active in building up the college library. After fourteen years of service here he was called to the presidency of the Kansas Agricultural College where he spent eighteen years in its development; his wide experience had made him a councilor in matters of vocational education. He was at the same time a member of the State Board of Education. Early in his career he had become a member of the National Teachers Association, and in 1888 was president of the section of industrial education. Later he was one of the advisory committee of the Agricultural Congress at the World's Columbian Exposition. He was also at one time the president of the Association of American Agricultural Colleges and Experiment Stations, and made notable addresses on the proper scope and methods of agricultural education. In 1897, because the faculty did not agree with the ideas of the Populist party, then in control of the state, the Board of Regents severed the connection with the college of every one of the faculty. President Fairchild resigned. He then devoted a year to the preparation of his work, *Rural Wealth and Welfare,* published in 1900. In 1898 he undertook the work of organizing the industrial and agricultural departments in Berea College, having the title of vice-president. A few years later he died, in Columbus, Ohio. He was of a family of educators. His brother James Harris [*q.v.*] was for many years president of

Oberlin, his brother Edward Henry (1815–1889) served for twenty years as president of Berea (*Oberlin Review,* Oct. 15, 1889), and he himself was a man of wide knowledge in educational matters which he untiringly devoted to public service.

[W. J. Beal, *Hist. of the Mich. Agric. Coll.* (1915); L. H. Bailey, *Cyc. of Am. Agric.*, vol. IV (1909); *Who's Who in America*, 1901–02; *Congreg. Year-Book*, 1902; *Nat. Educ. Asso. Jour. of Proc. and Addresses*, 1901.]
E. H. J.

FAIRCHILD, JAMES HARRIS (Nov. 25, 1817–Mar. 19, 1902), educator, president of Oberlin College, with which he was intimately associated for sixty-eight years, was born in Stockbridge, Mass., a son of Grandison and Nancy (Harris) Fairchild. In his own words, he was "born a Yankee of the Yankees." Both of his grandfathers were farmers and Congregational deacons. His father, also a farmer, had been a teacher, as was his mother. When James was about a year old the family emigrated to the Western Reserve of northern Ohio. There was one log house in the forest township where they settled. James remembered running barefoot in the snow to school, and being carried home on the back of a larger boy. At twelve he began Latin in an academy which was opened near his home. At fourteen he went to the new high school in Elyria.

In 1833 Oberlin was founded and in 1834 Fairchild at the age of seventeen entered the first freshman class, supporting himself, at first working four hours a day in a sawmill at five cents an hour. He graduated from the college in 1838 and from the theological department in 1841. During his theological course he served as college tutor in the classics and on graduation was given the entire responsibility of the department of languages. In 1841 he made a journey of nearly 3,000 miles, chiefly by river steamboats and on horseback, to Minden in northwestern Louisiana, to claim in marriage Mary Fletcher Kellogg, who had in 1835 persuaded her father to bring her from their home in Jamestown, N. Y., two hundred miles through the woods in a one-horse wagon to Oberlin, because it was the only school in the country where a woman could study Greek.

In 1847 Fairchild was transferred to the professorship of mathematics, meeting a larger number of students and rapidly growing in influence. In 1849 he was given a few months for visiting eastern institutions; this was his only graduate study outside of Oberlin. In 1858 he was appointed associate professor of moral philosophy and began teaching theology in the seminary. He also served as faculty chairman for administration. In 1866 he was elected president. Identified with Oberlin from its foundation, in close touch with its various departments, a teacher of strength, simplicity, and sympathy, already widely honored and beloved, Fairchild gave service of highest value for twenty-three years, as a president dignified, benign, sagacious, and democratic. Especially distinctive was his influence in effecting the transition from the early to the modern Oberlin, and in dissipating the prejudice against the institution as reputed to be unbalanced and innovative. This admirably poised, serene personality, the embodiment of common sense in thought and action, this mind always expecting and welcoming new aspects of truth, yet singularly sane and conservative, this chivalrous friend and courteous gentleman won all hearts, inspired universal confidence, and set Oberlin upon a great career.

In 1871 President Fairchild traveled in Europe, Egypt, and Palestine. In 1884 he visited the West and Hawaii. In 1889 he insisted upon laying down the presidency, but retained his professorship nine years longer and then continued on the board of trustees the remaining four years of his life. Mrs. Fairchild, the mother of their six daughters and two sons, died in 1890.

President Fairchild published, in 1869, *Moral Philosophy or the Science of Obligation;* in 1883, *Oberlin, the Colony and the College;* in 1892, *Elements of Theology, Natural and Revealed;* and some fifty historical and religious monographs, sermons, and reviews either separately or in various periodicals. In ethics he held that obligation is an ultimate idea, and intuitive perception, grounded in the worth of sentient being. He emphasized the moral and religious unity of the universe, holding that the law of benevolence extends to God as well as to his creatures. His theological teaching was a well-balanced presentation of the New England or governmental system. Although regarding theology as a progressive science, he made little use of contemporary thought in other fields as affecting theological conceptions. A discriminating and vigorous rather than an original or a brilliant thinker, he exercised a vital and abiding influence upon his students.

[A. T. Swing, *James Harris Fairchild* (1907); C. F. Thwing, *Guides, Philosophers and Friends* (1927); autobiographical outline in D. L. Leonard, *Story of Oberlin* (1898), pp. 289–94; brief discussion of his theology in F. H. Foster, *A Genetic Hist. of the New England Theology* (1907), pp. 469–70.] E. D. E.

FAIRCHILD, LUCIUS (Dec. 27, 1831–May 23, 1896), Union soldier, governor, diplomat, was throughout his life identified with the public affairs of the state of Wisconsin. Before the capital of the territory, Madison, had been incorporated as a city he was brought there by his parents, Jairus Cassius and Sally Blair Fairchild. They had come out of New York and New England by way of Ohio, where he was born, in Portage County, and in their mansion on Lake Monona the eastern influence remained strong for eighty years. Jairus was the first treasurer of Wisconsin, and the first mayor of Madison. He sent Lucius for a short time to Carroll College at Waukesha, but the gold fever caught the lad and drew him across the plains to California, where he remained six years with moderate success (*The California Letters of Lucius Fairchild,* edited by Joseph Schafer, now in press). By 1858 Lucius was home again. He was this year elected clerk of the circuit court of Dane County as a Democrat but the war made him a Republican, and he advanced rapidly in his party, helped by his reputation as a soldier. In 1861 he entered the service in the 1st Wisconsin Volunteer Regiment; he was transferred to the 2nd Wisconsin which he commanded as lieutenant-colonel at the second battle of Bull Run. Here its performance was so good that he was made colonel, dating from Aug. 30, 1862. His regiment was one of the five in the "Iron Brigade" (with the 6th and 7th Wisconsin, the 19th Indiana, and the 24th Michigan). He fought with his brigade in Reynolds's corps at Gettysburg, where on the first day his left arm was shattered by a musket ball and he was taken prisoner by the Confederates. This was the end of his active service. He was made a brigadier-general of volunteers, but his health was weakened and the Republican party had nominated him as secretary of state. Mustered out in October 1863, he took up his political duties at Madison the following winter. He was married, Apr. 27, 1864, to Frances Bull, who survived him until 1925, and was herself survived by two of their three daughters. Her social charm, coupled with his political prominence and military bearing, gave them great distinction in the life of their community (F. C. Dexheimer, *Sketches of Pioneer Women of Wisconsin,* 1925, p. 52).

In 1866 General Fairchild became governor of Wisconsin, holding the post through three terms until January 1872. At the expiration of this service President Grant sent him abroad as consul to Liverpool. In 1878 President Hayes transferred him, as consul-general, to Paris; and in 1880 when James Russell Lowell was shifted to London, Fairchild succeeded him as minister to Spain. Ten years of foreign residence was enough. He resigned his post in 1882, and on Mar. 2 of that year was formally welcomed home at a notable reception in the state capitol. He expected to be welcomed to high office as well, but the decade which had elapsed had brought into the control of Wisconsin affairs Senator Philetus Sawyer of Oshkosh, and a group of railroad, land, and timber politicians skilfully managed by Henry C. Payne of Milwaukee and John C. Spooner of Hudson. Fairchild found himself on the outside, a sort of "Rip Van Winkle in politics" (*Madison Democrat,* Jan. 7, 1885). He received kind words and non-political distinctions, but no office. He was mentioned as a favorite son for the Republican presidential nomination in 1884 (F. B. Wilkie, *Chicago Tribune,* May 3, 1884). In January 1885 he was a serious and unsuccessful candidate for the United States senatorship against Spooner, who won the election.

His friends among the veterans were kinder to him. He became state commander of the Grand Army of the Republic, and in August 1886 the national encampment of that society, at San Francisco, made him national commander-in-chief. In this capacity his vigorous patriotism and sharp partisanship made him speak more violently than perhaps he meant when, before a Harlem, N. Y., meeting of the G. A. R., he denounced President Cleveland's order for the return of the Confederate battle flags: "May God palsy the hand that wrote that order. May God palsy the brain that conceived it, and may God palsy the tongue that dictated it" (*New York Herald,* June 16, 1887). Under President Harrison he became one of the federal commissioners to settle the affairs of the Cherokee Indians in Oklahoma. Later he rose to be commander-in-chief of the Military Order of the Loyal Legion. Always possessed of ample means, he lived with dignity in the mansion his father had built, and here he died in 1896.

[Fairchild's papers, letters, and voluminous scrapbooks are in the museums of the Wis. State Hist. Soc. The best sketch of his life, by Louise P. Kellogg, is in the *Wis. Mag. of Hist.,* Mar. 1927. There is a useful memoir in *Circular No. 271,* May 23, 1896, of the Wis. Commandery, Mil. Order of the Loyal Legion.]

F. L. P—n.

FAIRCHILD, MARY SALOME CUTLER (June 21, 1855–Dec. 20, 1921), librarian, was the daughter of Artemus Hubbard Cutler and Lydia Wakefield, and the wife of Edwin Milton Fairchild, whom she married July 1, 1897, at Troy, N. Y. She was born in Dalton, Mass. She seems to have sought the best education then offered to women. In 1875 she was graduated from Mount Holyoke Seminary, where she also taught until 1878. Just why she left teaching seems not to be recorded. but in 1884 she began work in the Columbia College Library at the moment that plans were being developed for the first library school. The school opened Jan. 5, 1887, and Miss Cutler, her interest challenged and her ambition stirred by the new project, was made instructor in cataloguing. In 1889, when the school was moved to the New York State Library in Albany she became its vice-director, and was not only its chief executive but its guiding spirit. For sixteen years she was truly a pioneer. From this parent school she sent out disciples trained in her own habits of accuracy, thoroughness, and broad thinking, who, filled with her ideals, carried into libraries and library schools the purposes and methods of the Albany school. In this way she did much to set the standards of a new calling, for the best years of her life were given to the new public-library movement and to training carefully chosen recruits for its service. The philosophy which her mind constantly sought for this social adjunct found expression in her "Function of the Library" (*Public Libraries,* November 1901). Her interest was particularly enlisted in book selection and evaluation, and in the origins, history, and development of American libraries (*Library Journal,* February 1908). These subjects she deemed fundamental, and to them she gave her best thought and work, developing a substance and a methodology which made them a permanent part of the equipment of the well-trained librarian. In 1889 she was induced to take over the librarianship for the blind in the New York State Library and to that work she applied herself with her usual thoroughness.

Her active and useful career was cut short in 1905 by an illness from which she never fully recovered. This prevented the perfection of her work, and the publication of the substantial results of it. In her retirement she lectured occasionally and indeed for four months in 1909–10 was in charge of the library school of Drexel Institute, but her work was done. She was chairman of the committee in charge of the library exhibit at the Columbian Exposition which assembled a model library of five thousand volumes with a model printed catalogue. Twice a vice-president of the American Library Association, a member of its council 1892–98 and 1909–14, its delegate to the British International Conference in 1903, she abundantly fulfilled her broader professional obligations.

[*Mt. Holyoke Alumnae Quart.,* Apr. 1922; N. Y. State Lib. School *Alumni News Letter,* Mar. 1922; *Who's Who in America,* 1920–21; *Library Jour.,* Oct. 15, 1921, Jan. 1, 1922.] J. I. W.

FAIRFAX, DONALD McNEILL (Mar. 10, 1821–Jan. 10, 1894), rear-admiral, was born in Virginia, the son of George William and Isabella (McNeill) Fairfax. His great-grandfather, the Rev. Bryan Fairfax, though he never assumed the title, was by regular inheritance the eighth baron of Cameron. Donald McNeill was appointed a midshipman from North Carolina in 1837 and promoted to passed midshipman in 1843. Soon afterward he was on the *Missouri* when it was destroyed by fire in Gibraltar harbor, and on the *Princeton* when at Washington in 1844 one of its guns burst and killed several notables. He took part in the capture of Lower California during the Mexican War, and in February 1851 was made lieutenant. In November 1861, as executive officer of the *San Jacinto,* under Capt. Charles Wilkes, he had personal charge of the capture of the Confederate agents, Mason and Slidell, from the English vessel *Trent.* Doubtful of the expediency of this seizure, he executed it—by design—with such artful tact as to prevent the captain of the *Trent* from turning the entire vessel over to him as a prize. During 1862, he commanded the *Cayuga* under Farragut at New Orleans, and during 1863, the *Nantucket* and the *Montauk* off Charleston. He was commandant of midshipmen at Annapolis 1864–65, and he had charge of the *Susquehanna* when it was attacked by a disastrous yellow-fever epidemic in 1867. Promoted to commodore in 1873, he was for five years thereafter commandant of the naval station at New London, and for the two years following governor of the Naval Asylum. He was made a rear-admiral in 1880, and was retired in 1881. He died at his home in Hagerstown, Md. He was married to Josephine, daughter of rear-admiral Andrew Hull Foote.

[D. McN. Fairfax, "Capt. Wilkes's Seizure of Mason and Slidell" in *Battles and Leaders of the Civil War,* II (1887), 135–42; J. A. Woodburn, *The Trent Affair* (1896); T. H. S. Hamersley, *Gen. Reg. U. S. Navy and Marine Corps* (1882); E. W. Callahan, *List of Officers of the Navy of the U. S. and of the Marine Corps* (1901); F. L. Brockett, *The Lodge of Washington* (1876), p. 119; E. D. Neill, *Descendants of Hon. Wm. Fairfax* (1868); Nathaniel Foote, *The Foote Family* (1849); Hagerstown directories; *Army and Navy Jour.,* Jan. 13, 1894; *N. Y. Tribune,* Jan. 11, 1894.] J. D. W.

FAIRFAX, THOMAS (Oct. 22, 1693–Dec. 9, 1781), sixth Lord Fairfax of Cameron and proprietor of the Northern Neck of Virginia, was born at Leeds Castle, County Kent, the eldest son and namesake of his predecessor in the peerage. His mother, Catherine, was the heiress of that Lord Culpeper who was sometime governor-general of Virginia under a patent of Charles II; and he was himself in physique and character a Culpeper, a true representative of the ancient Kentish family which had actively participated in the colonization of Virginia for four generations before Fairfax himself came to play a part on the American scene.

In January 1709/10, Fairfax succeeded to his peerage and began a three-year residence at Oriel College, Oxford (Shadwell, *Registrum Orielense,* II, 25). So far as the evidence goes, his university career was uneventful; even the pleasant tradition of his contribution of a paper to *The Spectator* at this time must be abandoned. After the death of his mother in 1719, he secured a commission in the Horse Guards Blue (Dalton, *George I's Army,* II, 196) and commenced courtier also; holding for a time the post of Treasurer of the Household under the Lord Chamberlain (*Calendar Treasury Papers, 1720–28,* p. 78). His ambition apparently was to arrange a marriage which might have untangled the complications in which an inherited litigation had involved his Fairfax estates in Yorkshire; but failing in that he abandoned a career, and with a quixotic gesture withdrew from the great world to Leeds Castle, there to practise hound-breeding and fox-hunting, as an anodyne to disappointment.

In such seclusion he lived until 1733, when he was roused by a formidable political attack upon the Northern Neck proprietary, launched at the moment when the western movement of the colonial frontier was beginning to give significance to an hitherto unremunerative property right. This vast wilderness manor, ultimately adjudged to include all the territory between the rivers Potomac and Rappahannock and so to make up an area of more than five million acres, had been created in 1649 by Charles II as an intended refuge for a little band of Cavaliers who had forfeited their English estates by support of his father. One of the patentees was Fairfax's great-grandfather Culpeper, whose son, the Virginia governor, later acquired by purchase the shares of the other original proprietors. Culpeper's resident representatives had, however, succeeded in generating such local jealousy and resentment in Virginia that several efforts were made by the colony to persuade the Crown to resume the grant; but Culpeper maintained his claims so stoutly that after his death Virginia's effort was to confine the proprietary boundaries to the straitest limits (H. R. McIlwaine, editor, *Journals of the House of Burgesses of Virginia, 1727–40,* p. 92).

To protect his inheritance from the last such attack, Fairfax first went out to Virginia in May 1735, and there remained until September 1737. His diplomacy was successful for he negotiated a treaty with the Assembly (Hening, *Statutes at Large,* IV, 1814, p. 514) and arranged for such a survey of the territory in dispute as might narrow the issues for consideration by the Privy Council. It was not, however, until 1745 that his cause was finally determined; but then, at long last, Fairfax's extreme claims were justified (*Acts Privy Council,* Colonial, III, 385 ff.; Hening, VI, 1819, p. 198).

Fairfax had never modified his purpose of retirement from the world, and he now decided to live out his life on his American estate. He emigrated definitely in 1747; and, after a sojourn on the Potomac for several years, during which he met and held out a friendly hand to the young George Washington, he established (in 1752) his final residence in the Shenandoah Valley, at a hunting lodge to which he gave the name of a Culpeper manor in Kent,—"Greenway Court." There he took up the traditional English duty of local magistracy. He was commissioned a justice of the peace in all the counties of the Northern Neck and, at Gov. Dinwiddie's request, assumed (in 1754) the active duty of county lieutenant, as commandant of the frontier militia.

Looking back at him across the gulf of the American Revolution, there has been an effort to see in Fairfax the arch Tory, the personification of what came to be the locally hated English government. There is no justification for this in anything he himself did or said, and it is significant that throughout the Revolution the Assembly treated him with marked consideration. The only resident peer in America, he was accorded all the privileges of a Virginia citizen and was never molested, even by the mob. This could only be because it was recognized that his political sentiments were practically inoffensive to the Revolution. Indeed, Fairfax had never been a Tory. On the contrary, he had grown up in the principles of the revolution of 1688, in which his father actively participated.

Fairfax lived in the utmost simplicity. His personal bearing was what would now be called democratic, though he never had the remotest appreciation of what that term has come to mean. The color of the picture painted in *Burke's Peerage,* of his "baronial hospitality," is mere mythology. There was many a contemporary tide-water planter who would have been ashamed of the rude plenty of his table, bereft of luxuries; at which, indeed, his younger brother sneered in 1768. He had no such cellar of Madeira wine as was in his time to be found in most, even moderately well-to-do, Virginia plantation houses. He had, indeed, sent him out every year new clothes of the latest fashion, but, unlike George Washington, he did not wear them. His plate was like his library, sufficient for decent comfort but inadequate for show; such as are used to-day in

East Africa by Englishmen, who, like Fairfax, have sought in the open a surcease of the pains engendered by civilization.

He died at "Greenway Court," Dec. 9, 1781, in his eighty-ninth year, and was buried under the altar of the Frederick parish church. His relics now rest in a crypt beneath the local Christ Church, Winchester. There survives a pleasant portrait of Fairfax, painted before he left England in 1747.

[The available material for the Culpepers and the Fairfaxes and for the development and liquidation of the Northern Neck proprietary, has been collected and critically examined in two privately printed books, *Virginia Land Grants* (1925) and *The Proprietors of the Northern Neck* (1926), which have been closely followed in this sketch.]

F. H.

FAIRFIELD, EDMUND BURKE (Aug. 7, 1821–Nov. 17, 1904), educator, was born at Parkersburg, Va. (now W. Va.). His father, the Rev. Micaiah Fairfield, was graduated at Middlebury College and Andover Theological Seminary. He went to Virginia and there married Mrs. Hannah (Wynn) Neale, daughter of Capt. Minor Wynn. Their son Edmund studied at Denison, Marietta, and Oberlin colleges, receiving his Baccalaureate degree at the last-named in 1842. He continued his study at the Oberlin Theological Seminary and graduated there in 1845. After a short pastorate (1847) in Boston, he became, in 1849, president of Free Baptist College, at Spring Harbor, Mich. In 1853 this school was moved to Hillsdale, Mich., and became Hillsdale College. Fairfield retained the presidency until 1869, but during that period also served as state senator (1857) and lieutenant-governor of Michigan (1859). About this time he altered his views on baptism, left the Baptist fold and became the pastor of the First Congregational Church at Mansfield, Ohio. Some years later (1875) he was appointed president of the normal school, at Indiana, Pa. In 1876 he was elected the second chancellor of the University of Nebraska, then in the eighth year of its existence. Here he remained six years, the last portion of his administration being one of the most tempestuous periods in the entire history of the institution. He was a Fundamentalist, vigorously opposed to the teaching of Darwin, which was permeating even the then remote Middle West. On his faculty were three young instructors, George Edward Woodberry, Harrington Emerson, and George E. Church, all intellectually keen and imbued with the newer thought. As a result of their attempt to introduce the modernism of the day into the young university, all of the professors, as well as the chancellor, resigned from the faculty in 1882. Fairfield accepted the pastorate of the Congregational Church at Manistee, Mich., which he held until 1889 when he was appointed United States consul at Lyons, France, where he remained four years. He returned to settle at Grand Rapids, Mich., but in 1896 he resumed his former charge at Mansfield, Ohio. In 1900 he retired from active public life, and went to Oberlin, Ohio, where he died. He wrote extensively for educational and theological reviews and published separately three addresses: *True National Greatness* (1853), *Liberty and Slavery* (1856), *Christian Patriotism* (1863); and *Wickedness in High Places: A review of Henry Ward Beecher's Case* (1874). A Republican in politics, he took an active part in the political campaigns between 1855 and 1865. He was married three times: first, in 1845, to Lucia A. Denison; second, in 1859, to Mary A. Baldwin; and third, in 1883, to Mary A. Tibbets, who survived him. He was the father of eleven children.

[Albert Watkins, *Hist. of Nebr.* (1905–13), III, 701–02; Nebr. Univ., *Semi-Centennial Anniversary Book* (1919), pp. 120–21; files of Lincoln and Omaha newspapers of the period of Fairfield's administration at the Univ. of Neb.; obituary in *Omaha World-Herald*, Nov. 19, 1904.]

G. H. D.

FAIRFIELD, JOHN (Jan. 20, 1797–Dec. 24, 1847), lawyer, politician, the son of Ichabod and Sarah (Nason) Scamman Fairfield, was born at Saco, Me. Little is known of his early life except that he served on a privateer during the War of 1812 and attended Thornton and Limerick Academies. He engaged in business, unsuccessfully it appears, studied law in a local office, and was admitted to the bar in 1826. He had on Sept. 25, 1825, married Anna Paine Thornton. Soon after his admission to the bar he formed a partnership with George Thacher and the firm soon acquired a considerable practise. Fairfield, being especially successful in jury cases, gave most of his time to court-room work. He had also been appointed reporter of supreme court decisions in 1832 and continued this work until 1835, when he entered the Twenty-fourth Congress as a Democrat. He was reëlected to the Twenty-fifth Congress, but resigned before the completion of his term to accept the governorship of Maine. He made a favorable impression in the House, although he was active in the attempt to force an investigation of the circumstances attending the death of his colleague, Jonathan Cilley, in the famous duel with Graves of Kentucky. On Mar. 8, 1838, he made a notable speech on the Northeastern boundary question (*Congressional Globe*, 25 Cong., 2 Sess., App., pp. 196–203), which undoubtedly contributed greatly to his election as governor in that year.

The boundary dispute was becoming acute

when he took office. On Jan. 23, 1839, he asked the legislature to authorize the land-agent to expel trespassers from New Brunswick and put a stop to illegal timber cutting. This resulted in a clash with the British authorities and a flare of excitement all along the northern frontiers. War was expected on both sides of the line. Governor Fairfield, backed by the legislature and the public opinion of the state, acted vigorously and ordered the militia to occupy the disputed territory. The trouble soon blew over; on Mar. 25 the Governor accepted the *modus vivendi* arranged by General Scott and Governor Harvey of New Brunswick, and the troops were recalled. His promptness and vigor, his readiness to challenge the power of Great Britain, contrasting with the somewhat complacent attitude of the Van Buren administration, had made him a national figure. He was returned to office in the same year. With the Whig landslide of 1840, however, he was defeated for the governorship, but was reëlected in 1841 and 1842, resigning in 1843 to enter the United States Senate for the unexpired term of Ruel Williams. He thus saw the close of the boundary trouble in the Webster-Ashburton Treaty, and shared in the wide-spread dissatisfaction which resulted. In his messages he had insisted that the British claims were flimsy in character and had demanded recognition of the rights of Maine. While in the Senate, in reply to Webster's assertion that the people of Maine were satisfied, he reviewed the whole transaction at great length, pointing out the disregard of Maine rights and interests, but declaring that the people of the state were willing to make the best of the treaty as a matter of necessity (*Globe,* 25 Cong., 1 Sess., pp. 251–53). In 1845 he was reëlected for the full term of six years.

Due to the fact that Fairfield received strong support for the vice-presidency at the Democratic convention of 1844, there was considerable criticism at Polk's failure to give him a cabinet place. Apparently the Southern wing of the party had some doubts as to his orthodoxy on the slavery question. That he was decidedly conservative in his views, however, is shown by his letters, in which he expressed an unwillingness to do anything prejudicial to the institution in the states, and a dislike for the agitation conducted in the House by John Quincy Adams. He also supported the expansion policy of the Polk administration and was a vigorous proponent of a large navy. His sudden death following an operation on his knees, and due apparently to the bungling or quackery of the surgeon, caused great regret and apparently unanimous expressions of opinion that he had been on the way toward unusual distinction in national affairs. His letters, which bespeak a keen analytic mind and a sense of humor, constitute a distinct contribution to our knowledge of Washington life in the days of Van Buren and Polk.

[Arthur G. Staples, ed., *The Letters of John Fairfield* (1922); H. F. Hamilton, "Gov. John Fairfield," *Me. Hist. and Geneal. Recorder,* Jan. 1887; L. C. Hatch, *Maine: A History* (1919); C. E. Hamlin, *The Life and Times of Hannibal Hamlin* (1899); *Daily Eastern Argus* (Portland), Dec. 29, 1847.]

W. A. R.

FAIRFIELD, SUMNER LINCOLN (June 25, 1803–Mar. 6, 1844), poet, was born at Warwick, Mass., the son of Dr. Abner Fairfield and Lucy Lincoln. Upon the death of his father, Sumner went to live with his grandfather, Seth Lincoln, Jr., in Western (now Warren), Mass. Lincoln, who had opposed his daughter's marriage, subjected the sensitive boy to many indignities. Consequently, his mother left her paternal home, and placed Sumner in the grammar school at Hadley, Mass. During 1818–20 he was a student at Brown University, but left because he lacked money, and taught in Georgia (1821) and in South Carolina (1822). In December 1825 he sailed for Europe. After four months there, he returned to America and in September of that year, 1826, married Jane Frazee at New Brunswick, N. J. He proceeded with his bride to Elizabethtown, where all their household effects were seized for debt. Stalked by misfortune, he moved to New York, then to Boston, where he acted in Home's tragedy *Douglas.* Again lacking money, the poet in 1827 was forced to act on the New York stage, but soon secured a teaching position near Charlestown, Va. Dissatisfied with that he returned to Philadelphia for the years 1828–29, became head master at Newton Academy near Philadelphia, but left because of a tragic occurrence. He could never face disagreeable situations. In 1830 he was teaching in New York.

Fairfield finished his masterpiece, *The Last Night of Pompeii,* in 1831, and had it printed in New York in 1832, two years before Bulwer-Lytton's *The Last Days of Pompeii.* He claimed that he had sent Bulwer a copy of the poem which was never acknowledged, and when the novel appeared, charged him with plagiarism. Fairfield's assertions are partly true. Doubtless Bulwer made use of the poem, but merely as a "source." In November 1832, Fairfield began to publish in Philadelphia the *North American Magazine.* He continued to edit it until 1838, save for the suspension of publication in 1837 because of his failing health. Since he was unable to work after the sale of the magazine, his wife did everything possible to support the family, and in 1841 brought out the first volume of his collected works. The second never appeared. In the fall of 1843, attended only by his mother, the poet left Philadelphia for New Orleans, La., where he died the following spring.

Fairfield was a Puritan poet in the Miltonic tradition. He believed that poetry should be written always with the *grand* and *ideal* in mind, but his verses are filled with his own bitterness and morbidity. He and his children all suffered from periodic attacks of insanity. His editorial policy was truth, no matter whom it affected. He had few friends, and his poetry, which strikes at times a high note in early American literature, is now little known. His published works include: *The Siege of Constantinople* (1822); *Poems* (1823); *Lays of Melpomene* (1824); *Mina* (1825); *The Passage of the Sea* (1826); *The Cities of the Plain* (1827); *The Heir of the World* (1829); *Abaddon* (1830); *The Last Night of Pompeii* (1832); and *The Poems and Prose Writings of Sumner Lincoln Fairfield* (1841).

[M. R. Patterson, "Sumner Lincoln Fairfield: His Life and Charge of Plagiarism Against Bulwer-Lytton," 1930, a manuscript thesis in the Brown Univ. Lib.; Jane Fairfield, *The Life of Sumner Lincoln Fairfield* (1874), and *The Autobiog. of Jane Fairfield* (1860). A complete set of the *North Am. Mag.*, containing most of Fairfield's prose and many of his poems, is in the N. Y. State Lib., Albany, N. Y. The Harris Coll. of Am. Poetry, Brown Univ., contains the most nearly complete collection of his poems.]

M. R. P.

FAIRLAMB, JAMES REMINGTON (Jan. 23, 1838–Apr. 16, 1908), composer, and organist, was born in Philadelphia, Pa., the son of Col. Jonas Preston Fairlamb and his wife, Hannah Kennedy. He was playing in church at the age of fourteen, and before he was twenty had held the position of organist and choirmaster in several Philadelphia churches. In 1858 he went to Europe, where, at the Paris Conservatory, he studied piano with Prudent and Marmontel, and voice with Masset. From Paris he passed to Florence and thence to Zürich with President Lincoln's appointment as United States consul to Switzerland. While in Stuttgart, King Karl of Würtemberg awarded him the "Gold Medal for Arts and Sciences" in recognition of his *Te Deum* for double chorus and orchestra, dedicated to that monarch. In 1865 Fairlamb returned to the United States, and established himself in Washington, D. C., where he was active until 1872, as teacher and composer, and with an amateur opera company he himself had organized, produced his grand opera *Valérie*. From 1872 to 1898, he held positions as organist in Philadelphia, Elizabeth, N. J., Jersey City, and New York; and in 1898 became instructor of music in DeWitt Clinton High School in the last-named city. He was twice married: first, in 1866 to Marian Kerr Higgins, daughter of Judge David Higgins of Ohio, and second, to Melusina Therese, daughter of George F. Muller of Pittsburgh. He died at his home in Ingleside, L. I.

A prolific composer, Fairlamb published in all some two hundred compositions, including more than fifty choral works, sacred and secular, and over a hundred songs. Rupert Hughes has conveniently classified him among "The Colonists," *i.e.*, the musical writers belonging to the specific city ganglia or colonies which he regards as a vital phase of American musical development. Associated with the great advance in every phase of musical activity which the United States experienced in the period after the Civil War, Fairlamb cannot be reckoned with those composers who, like Gottschalk and Stephen Foster (the first consciously, the second following the line of least resistence), undertook to develop "nationalist," *i.e.*, folk-music elements in his original work. He was, however, an excellent example of the talented, foreign-trained American musician whose effort aided in establishing higher standards of taste and appreciation in his native land. There can be no question that his work as a composer was qualitative, and that many of his songs, in particular, have spontaneity and charm. He was one of the founders of the American Guild of Organists, and was identified with the first American productions of Sir Arthur Sullivan's *Pinafore* and *The Sorcerer*. Like so many composers, Fairlamb was not particularly successful in the field wherein he was most ambitious to gather laurels. Neither his lighter scores, *Love's Stratagem, Treasured Tokens*, and *The Interrupted Marriage*, nor his posthumous five-act grand opera *Leonello*, achieved public production.

[Rupert Hughes and Arthur Elson, *Am. Composers* (rev. ed., 1914); *Who's Who in America*, 1903–05; *The Art of Music . . . A Dictionary Index of Musicians*, vol. XI (1917); Janet M. Green, "Musical Biographies" (1908), in *The Am. Hist. & Encyc. of Music*, ed. by W. L. Hubbard; Ralph Dunstan, *A Cyclopædic Dictionary of Music* (1925); *Musical Courier*, Apr. 22, 1908; *N. Y. Tribune, N. Y. Times*, Apr. 18, 1908.]

F. H. M.

FALCKNER, DANIEL (Nov. 25, 1666–*c.* 1741), Lutheran clergyman, was born in Langen-Reinsdorf, Saxony, the second son of the Lutheran pastor, Daniel Falckner. While a licentiate in theology at Erfurt, he was associated with Philip Jacob Spener and August Hermann Francke, the leaders of the Pietist movement. In 1693 he joined a group of eccentric millenarians who proposed to retire to the wilderness of Pennsylvania and there await the coming of the Lord.

Led by Henrich Bernhard Köster, Johannes Kelpius, and Johann Gottfried Seelig, the millenarians disembarked at Bohemia Landing, Md., June 19, 1694, and took up their quarters along Wissahickon Creek, near Germantown, Pa., where their society was soon known as *Das Weib in der Wüste*. Falckner was distinguished among them by a slight but unique aptitude for mundane affairs and so became the business head of the society. In 1698 or 1699 he went back to Germany to recruit their ranks up to the mystic number forty and to report on their activities. In answer to a series of questions put to him by Francke, he wrote an account of conditions in Pennsylvania, which was published as *Curieuse Nachricht von Pensylvania in Norden-America* (Frankfort and Leipzig, 1702). This book undoubtedly helped to stimulate German emigration to the colony.

On his return in 1700 he brought with him his brother Justus Falckner [*q.v.*] and a commission empowering Kelpius, Johann Jawert, and himself, acting jointly, to succeed Francis Daniel Pastorius [*q.v.*] as agents for the Frankfort Land Company, who were the proprietors of Germantown. Kelpius, disdaining the affairs of the world, declined to serve, leaving Falckner and Jawert to carry on, with doubtful legality, alone. Of the 25,000 acres that William Penn had promised the Company, only 2,975 had actually been deeded to it; Falckner obtained the remaining 22,025 acres, a tract of meadow land on the Manatawny River in New Hanover Township, Montgomery County. This region became known as Falckner's Swamp. There he organized the first German Lutheran congregation in the province, built a log church, and served as its minister. In 1701 he was elected bailiff of Germantown, but the next year he was turned out. His vigorous conduct of the Company's affairs ended, however, in disaster, the exact nature of which cannot be deduced from the fragmentary and ambiguous evidence now at hand. According to Pastorius, Falckner was a sot, a waster, and a rogue, and, acting in collusion with John Henry Sprögel, swindled the Frankfort Company out of its land. In this instance, however, Pastorius is not an unimpeachable witness; wherever Falckner emerges clearly from the obscure past he is a man of probity. Sprögel, with all four members of the Philadelphia bar in his pay, put Falckner in jail before he secured a deed to the Manatawny tract; on the whole it seems likely that instead of being in collusion with him Falckner was the most miserable of all Sprögel's victims. At any rate, Sprögel got the Manatawny land, and Falckner, impoverished and disgraced, left Pennsylvania in 1709 and never returned.

For the rest of his life he served as a minister to the scattered Lutherans of the Raritan Valley in New Jersey, to whom he had been recommended by his brother Justus. He had a high sense of the duties of his office, as is shown by his refusal to ordain John Bernhard van Dieren and John Caspar Stoever [*q.v.*]. For a time after his brother's death he visited all the Dutch Lutheran congregations between Staten Island and Albany. He and Wilhelm Christoph Berkenmeyer [*q.v.*] worked together cordially, and the only but sufficient evidence for Falckner's ordination is that the truculently orthodox Berkenmeyer accepted him as a colleague. Failing memory—he complained that his head was no better than a pumpkin—finally compelled him to retire. He lived his last days in the home of one of his daughters and amused himself by gathering medicinal plants in the woods.

[J. F. Sachse, *The German Pietists of Provincial Pa.* (1895), *Justus Falckner* (1903), *Falckner's Curieuse Nachricht von Pa.* (1905), "Missives to Rev. A. H. Francke from D. Falckner and J. Falckner," *Pa. German Soc. Proc. and Addresses,* vol. XVIII (1909); A. L. Gräbner, *Geschichte der Lutherischen Kirche in America* (1892); T. E. Schmauk, *Hist. of the Luth. Church in Pa.* (1903); Oswald Seidensticker, *Bilder aus der Deutsch-pennsylvanischen Geschichte* (1885); H. S. Dotterer, *Falkner Swamp* (Schwenksville, Pa., 1879) and *The Perkiomen Region,* I (1895), 5–6, 121–23; S. W. Pennypacker, *Pa. Colonial Cases* (1892) and *The Settlement of Germantown, Pa.* (1899); M. D. Learned, *The Life of F. D. Pastorius* (1908).] G. H. G.

FALCKNER, JUSTUS (Nov. 22, 1672–1723), Lutheran clergyman, was born in Saxony at Langen-Reinsdorf near Crimmitschau, the youngest of the four sons of the local pastor, Daniel Falckner. His father's library was sufficiently rich and extensive to gain a provincial reputation. Both his grandfathers had been Lutheran ministers. Falckner matriculated on Jan. 20, 1693, at the University of Halle, whither he seems to have followed his teacher, Christian Thomasius, from Leipzig. In Halle he came under the influence of August Hermann Francke and composed several hymns imbued with the spirit of Pietism, including the once well-known *"Auf! Ihr Christen, Christi Glieder"* ("Rise, ye children of Salvation") and *"O Herr der Herrlichkeit."* He resided in Rostock and Lübeck for the greater part of the next few years and accompanied his brother Daniel [*q.v.*] to Pennsylvania in 1700. During this period he was probably engaged in tutoring while awaiting a pastoral call; the story, first printed in Tobias E. Biörck's *Dissertatio Gradualis de Plantatione Ecclesiae Svecanae in America* (Upsala, 1731), that he fled to America to avoid the ministry is doubtless a pious legend. Far too much, also, has been made of his connection with the band of mystics on Wissahickon

Creek; he lived with them for only a few months and appears not to have shared in their fantastic beliefs. He was elected a burgess of Germantown in the autumn of 1700 and aided his brother in managing the affairs of Benjamin Furly and the Frankfort Land Company, but his chief concern was for the spiritual welfare of the German Lutheran settlers. A letter of his on this subject was published in Germany as an *Abdruck eines Schreibens an Tit. Herrn D. Henr. Muhlen . . . den Zustand der Kirchen in America betreffend* (1702). At the earnest insistence of the Swedish pastor, Andreas Rudman, he agreed to accept a call to the Dutch Lutheran congregations of New York and the Hudson Valley; and Rudman, Andreas Sandel, and Erick Tobias Biörck accordingly ordained him Nov. 24, 1703, in Gloria Dei Church at Wicacoa in Philadelphia, the Swedish church authorities having previously given them the proper authority. A full record of this ordination, one of the earliest on American soil, has been preserved. Eight days later Falckner began his work in New York and served his vast parish faithfully until his death twenty years later. In his ministrations he traversed the whole Hudson Valley as far North as Albany, going wherever there were German or Dutch Lutherans in need of him. East Jersey and the western end of Long Island also came within the sphere of his activities. He is known to have baptized at least one Indian and to have had several negro parishioners. The records of his ministerial acts are perhaps the best revelation of Falckner's character. After the entry of a baptism or other ceremony, at the close of the year, and on other occasions it was his custom to write a brief prayer, often in true collect form. The simplicity, tenderness, and devotion of these prayers has impressed probably every one who has seen them. To strengthen his people against the proselytizing of the Reformed he wrote his *Grondlycke Onderricht van Sekere Voorname Hoofd-stucken der Waren, Loutern, Saligmakenden Christelycken Leere* (N. Y., Wm. Bradford, 1708). On Rogate Sunday in 1717 he was married by the Rev. William Vesey to Gerritge Hardick of Albany, by whom he had two daughters and a son. After the death in 1719 of Josua von Kocherthal [*q.v.*] he assumed the additional burden of caring for Kocherthal's congregations. During his last years he made his headquarters at Claverack. His last recorded act was a baptism performed at Philipsburgh (Yonkers), Sept. 4, 1723. The day of his death and his place of burial are unknown. He was succeeded by the Rev. Wilhelm Christoph Berkenmeyer [*q.v.*]. Falckner is one of the most winsome figures in the whole history of the Lutheran Church in America.

[B. M. Schmucker, "The Luth. Ch. in the City of N. Y. during the First Century of its Hist," in *Luth. Ch. Rev.*, III, 204–22 (1884); A. L. Gräbner, *Geschichte der Lutherischen Kirche in America* (St. Louis, 1892); J. F. Sachse, *The German Pietists of Provincial Pa.* (privately printed, 1895) and *Justus Falckner, Mystic and Scholar* (privately printed, 1903); H. E. Jacobs, "Justus Falckner" in *Luth. Ch. Rev.*, XXIII, 159–78 (1904); M. G. G. Scherer, "Ordination Certificate of Justus Falckner" in *Luth. World Almanac*, 1924–26, pp. 44–46.]

G. H. G.

FALLOWS, SAMUEL (Dec. 13, 1835–Sept. 5, 1922), bishop of the Reformed Episcopal Church, and nationally known as a religious and civic leader, was born in Pendleton, Lancashire, England, the tenth child of Thomas and Anne (Ashworth) Fallows. His father was a cotton-mill operator, and Samuel's early years were spent in Pendleton, Warrington, and Manchester. Financial disaster in 1848 drove the family to America, and the lure of cheap land and golden opportunities took them to the wilds of Wisconsin, where they settled near Bird's Ruins, later the town of Marshall. Here Thomas, a weaver but no farmer, forced to borrow money at usury, was beaten from the start; but the family struggled along. Samuel adapted himself happily to pioneer conditions, and tree-felling, root-digging, and rail-splitting fostered a naturally strong constitution which sustained a strenuous life of nearly eighty-seven years. In England he had had good schooling, but good schooling was not to be had at Bird's Ruins, nor money to send him elsewhere. Determined and persistent, he secured an education, nevertheless, studying by himself, attending school here and there, paying his way by storekeeping, farm labor, and teaching, and finally graduating from the University of Wisconsin in 1859.

He had already decided to enter the Methodist ministry, and in 1858 had been received into the West Wisconsin Conference on trial. From 1859 to 1861, however, he was vice-president and principal of the so-called Galesville University. In the fall of the latter year, accompanied by his wife, Lucy, daughter of William P. and Lucy (Edwards) Huntington, whom he had married Apr. 9, 1860, he went up into the lumber region to take charge of a church at Oshkosh; but the Civil War soon took him away and made him known throughout the state. On Sept. 25, 1862, he was appointed chaplain of the 32nd Wisconsin Infantry, which office he resigned in June 1863. The following year he helped recruit the 40th Wisconsin Infantry, and became its lieutenant-colonel. On Jan. 28, 1865, he was appointed colonel of the 49th Wisconsin Infantry, and on Oct.

24, was brevetted brigadier-general for meritorious service. He had proved himself a natural leader, and his enthusiastic devotion to public welfare and human interests was generally recognized.

The next ten years he was engaged in pastoral and educational work chiefly in Wisconsin. He served two Methodist churches in Milwaukee (1865–70); was a regent of the University of Wisconsin (1866–74); and from 1870 to 1874, state superintendent of public instruction. In this last capacity his great aim was "a college education, tuition free, for every Wisconsin boy or girl who wanted it," and he succeeded in bringing the university "into practical and vital relations with the public schools" (Fallows, *post*), as a step toward an organized educational system. For a brief period (1874–75) he was president of Illinois Wesleyan University, Bloomington, leaving it to enter the Reformed Episcopal Church, partly because he was naturally inclined to authority and ritual, and also because he believed this new church was peculiarly adapted to meet the needs of the growing West. In July 1875 he became rector of St. Paul's Church, Chicago, and on July 17 of the following year was elected bishop.

For the remainder of his long career, except for a brief residence in Brooklyn in 1878, he was identified with the rapidly expanding life of Chicago. His varied activities, however, took him all over the country. Presidents and convicts were his friends. His interests ranged from prison-reform to simplified spelling. Almost every major humanitarian movement drew from his seemingly inexhaustible vitality. From 1877 to 1879 he carried on a crusade in the interests of his church, traveling twenty-seven thousand miles, and visiting England and Bermuda. Except for this period he retained the rectorship of St. Paul's until his death. For several years he edited *The Appeal,* the official organ of the Reformed Episcopal Church. He early associated himself with the temperance movement, and in 1895 established the "Home Salon" in Chicago, modeled on the typical saloon, but serving drinks of low alcoholic strength, an experiment that had wide notoriety. He founded the People's Institute on the West Side, Chicago; was for twenty-one years president of the board of managers of the Illinois State Reformatory; had a hand, as the friend of labor, in settling serious industrial disputes; was active in the Grand Army of the Republic and all patriotic enterprises, founding in 1890 the American Society of Patriotic Knowledge. In 1908 he inaugurated in Chicago a religious-healing movement. His views on this subject had been expressed in *Science and Health from the Viewpoint of the Newest Christian Thought* (1903). Some sixteen other books were issued by him, including dictionaries and compilations. He was also editor in chief of the *Human Interest Library* (1914–15). When he was seventy-eight years old he visited China, Japan, and the Philippines, with the indorsement of President Taft, to study sociological conditions there. The World War found him as eager to serve as had the Civil War. In the last years of his life he was chairman of the Commission for the Grant Memorial, Washington, and presided at its dedication Apr. 27, 1922. The following June he spoke on "The Value of Science," at the University of Wisconsin Commencement. His career ended in Chicago a few months later, and he was buried in the Forest Home Cemetery.

[Alice K. Fallows, *Everybody's Bishop* (1927); *The Univ. of Wis.* (1900), ed. by R. G. Thwaites; *Chicago Daily Tribune*, Sept. 6, 1922.] H. E. S.

FANEUIL, PETER (June 20, 1700–Mar. 3, 1743), merchant, was the eldest of the eleven children of Anne (Bureau) and Benjamin Faneuil. The father was one of three brothers who came to America by way of Holland after the revocation of the Edict of Nantes. They were admitted members of the Massachusetts colony Feb. 1, 1691, and were among the small number of French Huguenot refugees who were able to bring considerable property with them to this country. One brother, Andrew, settled in Boston, but Benjamin went to New Rochelle, N. Y., where Peter was born. His father died when he was eighteen. Soon after, Peter went to Boston, where his uncle Andrew had become a prosperous merchant and had risen to considerable wealth by fortunate investments in Boston real estate. Peter engaged in business and is said to have acquired some property himself and, what was more important, had become a favorite with his widowed and childless uncle. The older man had lost his wife some years before and seems to have determined that none of his numerous nephews should marry. He first selected Benjamin, the second oldest, as his heir, but on his marriage transferred his affections and changed his will in favor of Peter, who was, and always continued to be, a bachelor. During the elder Faneuil's final illness, which lasted eighteen months, Peter managed his business as well as his own. When he died in February 1738 Peter became executor and residuary legatee. Benjamin was cut off with five shillings, whereas Peter inherited one of the largest fortunes of the day, though he always proved generous to his plentiful collateral relatives. He continued as a prosperous merchant, rolled up money, and named one of his best ships the *Jolly Bachelor*. His main claim to fame, however, is derived from his gift to the town of the building ever since known as Faneuil Hall. He had long been interested in a public market place but for some reason the people were divided in their opinion as to its necessity. He finally offered to donate one, and even on those easy terms, the town was hesitant. When on July 14, 1740, a vote was taken as to its acceptance there were only 367 ayes against 360 noes. Almost before the building was completed, Peter died, and at the first annual town meeting held in it the chief business was a eulogy on the deceased donor. John Smibert was the architect, and it was he who planned the hall to be built over the arched market. The building, which alone has perpetuated Faneuil's name and which has been so noted in the history of the nation, was almost wholly destroyed by fire in 1761. It was then rebuilt and subsequently enlarged.

[There are accounts of Faneuil and his hall in Justin Winsor's *Memorial Hist. of Boston*, II (1882), 259–67, and other town histories, but the best for both is A. E. Brown, *Faneuil Hall and Faneuil Hall Market* (1900).]

J. T. A.

FANNIN, JAMES WALKER (*c.* Jan. 1, 1804–Mar. 27, 1836), colonel in the Texas revolutionary army and leader of the ill-fated expedition to Goliad, was probably born on Jan. 1, 1804. His father was Dr. Isham Fannin, a Georgia planter. The boy, under the shadow of illegitimacy, was adopted by his maternal grandfather, James W. Walker, and was brought up on a plantation near Marion, Ga. On July 1, 1819, at the age of fourteen years and six months, and under the name of James F. Walker, he was admitted to West Point. His cousin, Martha Fort, whom he visited in Philadelphia, described him as a gallant, handsome, sensitive lad. He was evidently not especially devoted to his books, for when, as the result of an unfortunate quarrel with a fellow student, he ran away from West Point in November 1821, he stood sixtieth in a class of eighty-six. Some years after his return to Georgia, he was married to Minerva Fort, by whom he had two daughters. In the autumn of 1834, when his children were two and four years old, and with the assistance of funds supplied by his friends, Fannin removed to Texas, where he settled at Velasco on the Brazos River

From hints in his own letters and from the charges of his enemies, it appears that Fannin was interested in the slave-trade in Cuba. He had made at least one trip to the island, of which he said: "My last voyage from the island of Cuba (with 153) succeeded admirably." At the outbreak of the Revolution his property, which he offered to devote to the cause, consisted of thirty-six negro slaves, whose "native lingo," according to an unfriendly critic, yet betrayed their recent importation (quoted by Smith, *post*, p. 81). He had time for other things, however. As early as the winter of 1834–35, he was back in Mobile, trying to persuade an old army friend to aid the expected revolution. He was evidently a man of influence among his neighbors, and during the next summer he was active in the work of revolutionary committees. On Oct. 2, 1835, at Gonzales, he participated in the first skirmish of the war, and on Oct. 28, at the mission of Concepción, he distinguished himself in a brilliant engagement. On Dec. 10, he was appointed to secure supplies and volunteers in the region west of the Trinity River, a mission which he performed with energy and skill.

During the lull which followed the capture of San Antonio, Fannin became one of the eager advocates of a plan to carry the war into the enemy's country by seizing the Mexican port of Matamoras. The idea was bitterly opposed by Gov. Smith and Gen. Sam Houston; but the Council on Jan. 7, 1836, appointed Fannin their agent, with dictatorial powers, to organize such an expedition. Smith, proving obdurate, was removed, and Houston withdrew for the time on a mission to the Indians, thus leaving Texas for several critical weeks without a responsible government. The chief reason for the calamities that followed, however, was the entirely unexpected energy of Santa Anna. On Feb. 8, Fannin had established himself with 420 American volunteers at Goliad, a strong defensive position on the south bank of the San Antonio River. Nine days later, while Fannin was writing eager letters for reinforcements and for definite orders, Urrea had secured Matamoras and was already marching north. When Fannin commenced his retreat on Mar. 19, he was already too late. In the afternoon, at an unfavorable place in the open prairie, Fannin's immediate force of 200 men was overtaken by Urrea's advance. The next day, after fighting in which twenty-seven Americans were killed and many, including the commander, were severely wounded, Fannin surrendered.

The terms of surrender contained the equivocal phrase: "All the detachment shall be treated as prisoners of war and placed at the disposal of the supreme government." Urrea probably intended to interpret the phrase humanely, but by direct orders from Santa Anna, on the morning of Mar. 27, 1836, the prisoners who had been gathered together at Goliad were led out and shot. Three hundred and thirty were thus killed. Eighty-eight were spared for various reasons, and twenty-seven escaped. Fannin was the last to be executed. He had made serious mistakes as a commander, but in a grave emergency he had proved himself a brave and generous man. Fannin's wife survived him only one year. One of his daughters lived until 1847. The other died insane in 1893.

[For the early life of Fannin, see K. H. Fort, *Memoirs of the Fort and Fannin Families* (1903), pp. 26 and 206; W. F. Brooks, *Hist. of the Fanning Family* (1905), II, 806–07; Elizabeth Brooks, *Prominent Women of Texas* (1896), p. 24; and especially a letter of Fannin's in *Southwestern Hist. Quart.* (*Quart. Texas State Hist. Asso.*), VII, 318 (pr. 1904). The West Point record of James F. Walker has been examined for this sketch by Capt. H. C. Holdridge. For his career in Texas, see Ruby Cumby Smith, "James W. Fannin, Jr., in the Texas Revolution" in *Southwestern Hist. Quart.*, XXIII, 79–90, 171–203, 271–83 (Oct. 1919, Jan., Apr. 1920); H. S. Foote, *Texas and the Texans* (1841), II, 201–18, 224–60; and the letters of one of Fannin's officers in *Southwestern Hist. Quart.*, IX, 157–209 (Jan. 1906). Jose Urrea's account in his *Diario de las Operaciones Militares* (1838), translated by Carlos E. Castañeda in *The Mexican Side of the Texan Question* (1928), is, on the whole, reliable.]

R. G. C.

FANNING, ALEXANDER CAMPBELL WILDER (1788–Aug. 18, 1846), soldier, the son of Barclay and Caroline Henson Orne Fanning, and a descendant of Edmund Fanning who settled at Pequot (New London), Conn., in 1653, was born in Boston, Mass. He entered the Military Academy at West Point on Apr. 14, 1809, as a cadet from that state. He graduated fifteenth in his class on Mar. 12, 1812, and was commissioned first lieutenant, 3rd Artillery. Promoted to captain Mar. 13, 1813, he was severely wounded at the capture of York, Upper Canada, Apr. 27, 1813, and distinguished himself in the repulse of the British naval forces on the St. Lawrence, Nov. 2, 1813. For his gallant defense of Fort Erie he was appointed brevet major Aug. 15, 1814. Serving with Jackson in the Seminole campaign of 1818, he acted for a time as deputy quartermaster-general and made an important reconnaissance to establish contact with the naval force in the Gulf. With a detachment of 200 men he occupied the Spanish post of St. Mark's. He was a member of the court martial which tried Robert Ambrister and Alexander Arbuthnot, and on Apr. 29, 1818, acted as provost-marshal at their execution. While commanding at St. Mark's in November 1818, he gave information about the continuance of Spanish intrigues among the hostile Indians. This information was later used by Jackson in reply to criticisms of his order to Gaines. From St. Mark's he was transferred to Ft. Gadsden, and then served successively at various Northern posts (Detroit, 1822–23; Mackinaw, 1823; Columbus, 1824), and at the artillery school at Fortress Monroe, Va. He was appointed brevet lieutenant-colonel Aug. 15, 1824, and was commissioned major of the 4th Artillery Nov. 3, 1832.

Fanning took an active part in the Seminole War in Florida. His gallant conduct in a battle with the Indians at the Withlacoochee on Dec. 31, 1835, led to his appointment as brevet colonel. His most notable service was the defense of Camp Monroe, later Ft. Mellon, on Lake Monroe, in the heart of the hostile Indian country, against a surprise attack by the Seminoles (Feb. 8, 1837). Though creditable to Fanning and his troops, this affair convinced the commanding general, T. S. Jesup, that the whole plan of campaign in Florida was defective. After further service in rounding up the Seminoles for deportation, Fanning was first transferred to the Canadian frontier, 1840–41, and then detached on recruiting service in the Western Department. He died at Cincinnati, Ohio, Aug. 18, 1846. His wife, a Miss Fowler, died shortly after their marriage.

[W. F. Brooks, *Hist. of the Fanning Family* (1905), I, 248, 354; *Am. State Papers, Mil. Affairs*, III (1860), 96, VII (1861), 800, 832, 870; *Annals of Cong.*, 15 Cong., 2 Sess., pt. II, pp. 2176, 2180, 2198, 2242, 2277, 2302–06, 2326; F. B. Heitman, *Hist. Reg. of the U. S. Army*, I (1903), 412–13; J. T. Sprague, *The Origin, Progress, and Conclusion of the Fla. War . . .* (1848), 168–70, 223–24, 255; G. R. Fairbanks, *Hist. of Fla.* (1871), pp. 294, 305; *Cincinnati Enquirer*, Aug. 20, 1846.]

A. P. W.

FANNING, DAVID (*c.* 1755–Mar. 14, 1825), North Carolina Loyalist, was born at Beech Swamp, Amelia County, Va., the son of David Fanning. Other details regarding his origin are obscure, and the date of his birth is uncertain. His tombstone states that he died at the age of seventy (1825), but he himself stated that he was in his nineteenth year when he went to war in 1775. He was apprenticed to a Mr. Bryan whose harsh treatment induced him to run away, and little further is known of his early days. He is said to have been a carpenter, but in the years immediately preceding the Revolution he was trading with the Catawba Indians, and claimed to own 1,100 acres of land in Virginia (Amelia County) and two slaves. He received his training in cruelty and courage under "Bloody Bill" Cunningham, and not, as has usually been stated, under McGirth. In the dispute with England he at first took the American side, but having been robbed in his Indian trade of a considerable quantity of goods by a gang who called themselves Whigs, he went over to the British in 1775, and began his notorious career.

He signed a paper in favor of the King in May of that year and at once engaged in marauding expeditions against the Whigs. According to his own account he was several times taken prisoner in the course of the next few years, managing always, in one way or another, to be released or to escape. Once, in June 1776, taking advantage of a proclamation of amnesty, he returned to his home, but was soon off again. Captures and escapes continued, if we can believe him, and on July 5, 1781, he was commissioned as a militia colonel by Major Craig of the British forces. According to his own statement, in April 1782 when he was on one of his expeditions, he was married to a girl at Deep River, N. C. Various exploits are attributed to him, such as his sudden descent on Pittsboro when a judicial court or court martial (accounts differ) was sitting, and his capture of all the officials of the court, July 18, 1781. A few weeks later he is said to have taken Col. Alston and thirty men in Alston's own house, and on Sept. 13, 1781, he captured Gov. Burke with his whole suite at Hillsboro. He finally retreated across South Carolina to Charleston and then to Florida, and at the end of the war was one of three who were excluded from pardon in the general amnesty act passed by the State, together with persons guilty of murder, robbery, and rape. In his *Narrative,* written in 1790 (though it was not published until 1861), he denied that he had ever committed rape or any crime not specified by himself. His extreme cruelty may in part be accounted for by a serious physical defect. He had a scalled head, which was so offensive that, as a youth, he was not permitted to eat with other people and when he grew up he wore a silk cap, his most intimate friends never being allowed to see his head uncovered. After the war he moved to New Brunswick, where he became a member of the provincial Parliament, serving from 1791 until January 1801 when he was expelled for an unknown crime for which he was later sentenced to death. He was pardoned, however, and moved to Digby, Nova Scotia, where for a time he was a colonel of militia.

[L. Sabine, *Loyalists of the Am. Revolution* (1864); *Papers of Archibald D. Murphey* (1914), vols. I, II; S. A. Ashe in *Biog. Hist. of N. C.*, V (1906), 90–97; *The Narrative of Col. David Fanning . . . 1775–1783* (by himself) was printed with an Introduction by J. H. Wheeler (Richmond, 1861), reprinted by J. Sabin (New York, 1865); in *The State Records of N. C.*, XXII (1907), 180–239; and by A. W. Savary (Toronto, 1908).]

J. T. A.

FANNING, EDMUND (Apr. 24, 1739–Feb. 28, 1818), North Carolina Loyalist, great-grandson of Edmund Fanning who settled at New London in 1653 and grandson of Thomas Fanning of Groton, Conn., was the son of Capt. James and Hannah (Smith) Fanning of Riverhead, Long Island, N. Y. He was born in Suffolk County, Long Island, graduated from Yale in 1757 and won a Berkeley Scholarship; moved to Hillsboro, Orange County, N. C., where he studied law and in 1762 was admitted to the bar. He at once made his way and within three years was holding such offices as colonel of the militia and register of deeds. He was a cultivated man and soon became a prime favorite with Gov. Tryon who was appointed in 1765, though Fanning did not become, as has often been stated, his son-in-law. In 1766 he was elected to the Assembly and appointed judge of the superior court for the Salisbury district, serving in both capacities for five years. His career, though notable, was a stormy one and his alleged extortions as register have been given as one of the causes of the Regulator movement in the colony. Some of the charges of extortion made against him break down completely on examination and it is not unlikely that they were used to cloak the real objections to him, which were his relations with the governor and his immoral private life. It is difficult to sift and appraise all the evidence but several facts emerge. One was that he was thoroughly hated by the common people and had an extremely bad reputation. On the other hand evidence against him at least partially breaks down on investigation, and after the war his career was distinguished and he received many honors not only from English but from American institutions of learning.

In connection with the Regulator insurrection, his house was fired into by the mob, in April 1768, and he lost the next election, but Tryon at once gave Hillsboro the right of representation and Fanning regained his seat in the Assembly. In September 1770 the Regulators broke up the session of the superior court at Hillsboro, physically maltreated Fanning, and burned his home with all its contents. Without the support of the Governor he would have been helpless, and when Tryon was transferred to the governorship of New York, Fanning went with him as private secretary. He appealed to the legislature of North Carolina for compensation for his losses but without success. He soon received, however, lucrative offices in his new colony. Among these may be mentioned that of surrogate of the City of New York, which he held from 1771, and that of surveyor-general of the Province, to which he was appointed in 1774. With the outbreak of hostilities he became an ardent Loyalist and raised and commanded a corps of troops known as the Associated Refugees or the King's American Regiment of Foot, which acquired a bad reputation for cruelty. He was in active service throughout the war and was twice wounded. In 1779 North Carolina confiscated all his property in that state and shortly before peace was declared he moved to Nova Scotia where in September 1783 he was made councillor and lieutenant-governor. In 1786 he became lieutenant-governor of Prince Edward Island, where charges of tyranny were preferred against him by the people. These were investigated by the Privy Council in England and dismissed in August 1792. At Point Pleasant, near Halifax, Nov. 30, 1785, he married Phoebe Maria Burns, a woman much younger than himself, by whom he had a son and three daughters. He appears to have always had strong influence in England and in December 1782 was made colonel in the British army, becoming major-general in October 1793, lieutenant-general in June 1799, and general in April 1808. In May 1804 he resigned his post of lieutenant-governor, his resignation becoming effective in July 1805, and in 1813 he moved to England, to spend his last years in London, where he died.

[*The Colonial Records of North Carolina*, esp. vols. VII and VIII (1890); M. D. Haywood, *Gov. William Tryon* (1903); Lorenzo Sabine, *Loyalists of the Am. Revolution* (1864); F. B. Dexter, *Biog. Sketches Grads. Yale Coll.*, vol. II (1896); A. B. Warburton, *A Hist. of Prince Edward Island* (1923); W. F. Brooks, *Hist. of the Fanning Family* (2 vols., 1905); British Army List, 1810.]
J. T. A.

FANNING, EDMUND (July 16, 1769–Apr. 23, 1841), sea-captain, explorer, promoter, was born at Stonington, Conn., the son of Gilbert and Huldah (Palmer) Fanning and younger brother of Nathaniel Fanning [*q.v.*]. The "Pathfinder of the Pacific" was the nephew and namesake of Gen. Edmund Fanning [*q.v.*] of the British army. After a brief schooling, at the age of fourteen, he shipped as cabin boy on a coaster. He had risen to mate when he married Sarah Sheffield of Stonington on June 14, 1790. His first experience with the South Seas came in 1792 when he was first mate on a sealing voyage to the South Shetlands. In 1793, a cargo of flour which he was taking to France was seized by the English. Later that year, he received his first command, a West Indian brig. As the nephew of a British general, he twice received special favors when overhauled, and he declined the offer of a commission in the British navy. Ten years later, he also declined the proffered command of a new American frigate. Fanning's real prominence dates from the cruise of the 93-ton ship *Betsey* under his command in 1797–98. Setting out from New York with no cargo except a few trinkets for trading he rounded Cape Horn, secured a full load of sealskins near Juan Fernandez, and rescued a missionary in the Marquesas. On June 11, 1798, he discovered the island which still bears his name. During the next four days, he also discovered Washington (New York) and Palmyra islands to the northwest. These three, with others adjacent, have received the general name of Fanning's Islands. They are about 2,000 miles due south of Hawaii, just above the equator, and have importance as cable stations, Great Britain owning Fanning's Island and the United States, Palmyra. Proceeding to Canton, Fanning exchanged his sealskins for a cargo of teas, silks, etc., which sold for $120,467 after he had returned to New York around the Cape of Good Hope. The capital outlay for the voyage had been only $7,867; the owners' net profit was $53,118 and Fanning himself received more than $15,000. This experience convinced him of the possibilities of the South Sea trade, and he devoted the remainder of his life to promoting it. He lived most of the time in New York, occasionally visiting Stonington where he had a shipyard. As agent for a group of New York capitalists, he promoted and acted as agent for more than seventy expeditions to the South Seas, occasionally taking part himself. He saw that valuable China cargoes could be secured in exchange for sealskins, which cost nothing but a few weeks' labor, or for sandalwood, pearls, tortoise shell, bêche-de-mer, etc., which could be secured from the natives of the islands for a few trinkets. His energetic promotion of exploration arose chiefly from the desire for new fields to exploit, since ruthless slaughter quickly cleaned out the seal rookeries. He studied the charts of early Dutch navigators, experimented with new types of naval architecture, and was a persistent propagandist for both private and official exploration. Some of his expeditions included "scientific gentlemen." His main argument was that increased returns in China imports would more than pay for the cost of the expeditions. This was not always the case. A captain and crew sent to the Fiji Islands for sandalwood in 1803 fell victims to the cannibals. In 1804, however, Edmund's brother, Henry Fanning, rediscovered the Crozet Islands with their extensive seal rookeries. A projected exploring expedition in 1812 was abandoned at the declaration of war. Fanning claims that the regular stationing of American warships on the west coast of South America resulted from his protests at his detention in the *Volunteer* by Chilean officials in 1816. He was agent for the ambitious expedition under Pendleton and Palmer in 1829, in the course of which Palmer Land (Palmer Archipelago) south of Cape Horn was discovered, but the owners lost more than $25,000. Fanning unsuccessfully petitioned Congress for reimbursement in 1830 and 1833, arguing that the expedition was for the general good of the nation. The publication of his memoirs, *Voyages Around the World,* etc. (1833), was effective propaganda and doubtless helped to secure the authorization of the official naval South Seas exploration expedition (1838–42) led by Lieut. Charles Wilkes [*q.v.*]. Fanning, doubtless hurt at not having been called upon for advice or participation, petitioned Congress in 1840 for a loan of $150,000 to undertake a private expedition of his own, but nothing came of his petition. He died at New York the following year, of a broken heart, it is said, four days after the death of his wife. He was survived by a son and daughter, one son having died in infancy.

[The principal source is Fanning's autobiographical *Voyages,* etc. (1833). The second edition (1838) and subsequent editions bore the title: *Voyages to the South Seas, Indian and Pacific Oceans,* etc. A somewhat abbreviated edition was published in 1924 by the Marine Research Society with the title *Voyages and Discoveries in the South Seas.* Additional information is given in his three petitions, *House Ex. Doc. 61, 22* Cong., 1 Sess.; *Sen. Doc. 10,* 23 Cong., 1 Sess.; *House Ex. Doc. 57,* 26 Cong., 1 Sess. Genealogical data and a short biography are given in W. F. Brooks, *Hist. of the Fanning Family* (2 vols., 1905), I, 255, II, 739–57. There is a short sketch in D. C. Seitz, *Uncommon Americans* (1925), pp. 221–30, with a small portrait on fly-leaf.]
R. G. A.

FANNING, JOHN THOMAS (Dec. 31, 1837–Feb. 6, 1911), hydraulic engineer, was a direct descendant in the seventh generation of Edmund Fanning who settled at New London, Conn., in 1653, lived for some years on Fisher's Island, and then became one of the original proprietors of Stonington. The son of John Howard Fanning, a skilled mechanic and contractor for buildings, by his first wife, Elizabeth Pridde, John Thomas Fanning was born at Norwich, Conn., and resided in New England until 1886, after which time he made his home in Minneapolis. He studied architecture and engineering and began his practise in Norwich, where he acted for eight years as city engineer, planning the city's water supply and its cemetery. This work was interrupted by the Civil War, during which he served as a member of the 3rd Connecticut Volunteers and later as field officer in the 3rd Regiment, Connecticut Militia. At the close of the war he was retired with the rank of lieutenant-colonel. On June 11, 1865, he married Maria Louise Bensley of Rhode Island. After the war he resumed practise in New England, first at Norwich, and later at Manchester, N. H. He began to specialize in hydraulics and constructed the water-supply system at Manchester. He soon found his services were in demand all over New England and in New York State for the solution of hydraulic and water-supply problems. In 1881 he published a *Report on a Water Supply for New York and Other Cities of the Hudson Valley* (supplemented in 1884). In 1881, also, he made a report on Lake George as a source of water supply for New York City (see *Sanitary Engineer,* Apr. 6, 1882). In 1884 he published a pamphlet on *Homestead and Suburban Sewerage.* His best-known work, however, was *A Practical Treatise on Water Supply Engineering* (1877). This book was of such practical value that, in revised and enlarged form, it had run into sixteen editions by 1906. In 1885 Fanning went to Minneapolis to report on a power development of the St. Anthony Falls, and after that time, with his residence in Minneapolis, he acted as consulting engineer on many large water-power projects in the West, most notable of which were those on the Weenatahee River, the Missouri River at Great Falls, Mont., at Helena, Mont., at Spokane, Wash., and on the Mississippi River at Minneapolis. He continued, however, to go to all parts of the country to solve city water-supply problems. Some of the cities which employed him on the planning and construction of their water supply and purification systems, in addition to Minneapolis, were Des Moines, Omaha, and Birmingham, Ala. He also made a report on an additional water supply for Rockford, Ill.

Fanning had the reputation for being unusually generous with the help and time he was always ready to give to the younger members of his profession. He served for a year as president of the American Waterworks Association shortly after it came into existence, and was consulting engineer for a time for the Great Northern Railroad, the St. Paul, Minneapolis & Manitoba Railroad, and the Minneapolis Union Railways. In addition to his text-book on hydraulic and water-supply engineering, he contributed technical papers on the subject to the *Transactions* of the American Society of Civil Engineers.

[W. F. Brooks, *Hist. of the Fanning Family* (2 vols., 1905); *Encyc. of Biog. of Minn.* (1900), pp. 266–67; *Engineering News,* Feb. 16, Mar. 2, 1911; *Who's Who in America,* 1908–09; Fanning's own writings.] E. Y.

FANNING, NATHANIEL (May 31, 1755–Sept. 30, 1805), privateersman, naval officer, was born in Stonington, Conn., the eldest of the eight sons of Gilbert and Huldah (Palmer) Fanning. He was descended in the fifth generation from Edmund Fanning, of Limerick, Ireland, who came to Pequot (New London) in 1653 after being "transplanted" in the Cromwellian confiscations. Like his seven brothers, including Edmund [*q.v.*], the explorer, Nathaniel went to sea at an early age, "never having had but barely a common education." Most of his life is obscure except for the years 1778–83. He spent those five years in sea fighting, principally in privateering under Franco-American auspices, incidentally serving three terms in British prisons. In 1778, his third privateering voyage, in the *Angelica* of Boston, resulted in capture and thirteen months' detention in Forton Prison near Portsmouth. Finally exchanged, he reached L'Orient, where he accepted a position as midshipman and private secretary to John Paul Jones on the *Bonhomme Richard.* This was a private arrangement rather than a regular naval appointment. Fanning's only claim to fame came as a result of the fight with the *Serapis* on Sept. 22, 1779. He was captain of the maintop, from which one man crawled out on the yard-arm and dropped a well-aimed hand grenade through an open hatch of the enemy frigate. It exploded a large quantity of powder, killed some twenty men, and did much to bring about the American victory. Fanning admits that as he waded around in gore after the battle, he had intimations of immortal fame. His bravery made him a particular favorite with Jones, who recommended him to Congress for promotion. He served under Jones in the *Ariel* until December 1780, then, with most of the other officers, refused to continue under his command. He charges that Jones frequently kicked his officers and cites numerous instances of brutality, unfairness, and immorality. Fanning thereupon drifted into French service. During 1781, he cruised as second in command of a Morlaix privateer, spending six weeks in a British prison. Fanning invested his profits in a cargo for the West Indies but a shipwreck left him penniless. He became a naturalized French citizen and early in 1782 made two trips to London. He claims that on one of these, he was sounding out the sentiment for peace, while on the other, he carried informal peace proposals from the French Court to Shelburne and others. He made several further cruises, commanding French privateers, and on one occasion sailed straight through the British Channel Fleet pursued by a frigate. He was captured twice again by the British but speedily released. He finally accepted a commission as lieutenant in the French navy, but gave it up at the close of the war, when he returned to America. On Nov. 21, 1784, he married Elizabeth, daughter of Col. Oliver Smith. They had six children, all but one of whom died in infancy. During the next twenty years, Fanning seems to have lived part of the time in New York and part in Stonington. His *Narrative* implies that he continued to follow the sea. On Dec. 5, 1804, he accepted a commission as lieutenant in the United States navy (E. W. Callahan, *List of Officers of the Navy of the United States,* 1901, p. 188), and ten months later, he died of yellow fever while in command of the naval station at Charleston, S. C. His *Narrative of the Adventures of an American Naval Officer,* evidently written in 1801, was published anonymously in 1806, probably by his brother Edmund. In an edition of 1808, the title was changed to *Memoirs of the Life of Captain Nathaniel Fanning.* The *Narrative* gives the best first-hand account of the fight with the *Serapis* and also shows how closely French and American interests were mixed in privateering. It reveals Jones in an unfavorable light and the tone is strongly anti-British throughout. Fanning, it is said, would boast of his exploits by the hour whenever he could find an audience. He had the reputation of being a great dandy in his dress. His picture shows a stocky figure with a round face, high cheekbones and a scowling expression.

[The best account of Fanning's fighting career is the *Narrative,* critically edited for the Naval Hist. Soc. (*Pubs.,* vol. II), in 1912 by John S. Barnes, who points out the false quotations in A. C. Buell, *Paul Jones* (2 vols., 1900), I, pp. 218–20, etc. The most complete secondary account of Fanning's life, with genealogical details, is W. F. Brooks, *Hist. of the Fanning Family* (2 vols., 1905), I, 249; II, 715–38, with portrait.]

R. G. A.

FANNING, TOLBERT (May 10, 1810–May 3, 1874), minister of the Disciples of Christ, educator, editor, was born in Cannon County, Tenn., the son of William and Nancy (Bromley) Fanning, Virginians of English descent. When he was about six years old his parents moved to Lauderdale County, Ala., and much of his youth was spent in the cotton fields. His educational advantages were limited, for the family was large and not well-to-do; but he was eager for knowledge and exerted himself in every possible way to obtain it. In 1832 he was able to enter the University of Nashville from which he graduated in 1835. He had begun evangelistic work some six years before, however, and during his summer vacation in 1833 he made an extensive preaching tour with Alexander Campbell [*q.v.*], and another in 1836, during which they visited Ohio, New York, Canada, and New England. On Dec. 25, 1836, he married Charlotte Fall of Nashville, a former wife, Sarah Shreeve of Nicholasville, Ky., having died shortly after their marriage.

The following year, with Mrs. Fanning, who was a teacher, he opened a boarding and day school for girls at Franklin, Tenn., which in January 1840 they moved to "Elm Crag," a farm about five miles from Nashville. Interested in the advancement of agriculture, he imported some of the best breeds of cattle, sheep, hogs, and horses. He was also a prominent promoter of the Tennessee Agricultural Society, and from 1840 to June 1844 was one of the editors of the *Agriculturist and Journal of the State and County Societies,* "Devoted to the Improvement of the Soil and Mind." Due to his own early struggles, the desire to make education easier for impecunious young men became one of the chief motives of his life, and in January 1843 he opened on his own farm an agricultural school, called the first institution of its kind in the country (*Agriculturist,* January 1843) in which practical instruction in agriculture was combined with the regular academic subjects. The school's success exceeded the expectations of its founder and led to the establishment of Franklin College, which, chartered in 1844, was opened in January 1845 under his presidency. Within six months it had over one hundred and fifty students. Manual training and agriculture were given an important place in the curriculum. The students devoted from two to five hours a day to these branches, and the profits accruing went to them. The institution flourished until the Civil War, though after a period the manual training was curtailed because of difficulty in securing instructors. Young men expecting to enter the ministry were charged no tuition, and it became a leading school among the Disciples of the South. The burning of the main building as the College was reopening after the war brought its existence to a close. The Fannings then bought Minerva College, a nearby school for girls, and conducted it under the name of Hope Institute until Tolbert Fanning's death. He was keenly interested in the natural sciences, and was something of a chemist, botanist, geologist, and conchologist. His carefully classified collection of shells was said to be one of the best in the South. During 1846, assisted by the faculty of Franklin College, he published the *Naturalist and Journal of Natural History, Agriculture, Education and Literature.* In 1850, with Charles Foster, he started the *Naturalist,* which the following year was merged with the *Southern Agriculturist.*

In connection with his other activities, he preached regularly and was a successful editor of religious publications. In 1844 he began the *Christian Review* which some years later became the *Christian Magazine.* From 1854 until its suspension prior to the war, and from 1866 to 1868 he was associated with William and then David Lipscomb in the editorship of the *Gospel Advocate,* a widely circulated paper which had much influence among the Disciples. After 1872 he published the *Religious Historian.* With Benjamin Franklin [*q.v.*] he belonged to the conservative group of Disciples who opposed organized cooperation. Some years subsequent to his death, which occurred after a "violent illness" of four days, Mrs. Fanning deeded Hope Institute to trustees who, according to her wish, established the Fanning Orphan School, which has perpetuated her husband's interest in the training of the young down to the present time.

[W. W. Clayton, *Hist. of Davidson County, Tenn.* (1880); W. T. Moore, *The Living Pulpit of the Christian Church* (1869) and *A Comprehensive Hist. of the Disciples of Christ* (1909); John T. Brown, *Churches of Christ* (1904); Jas. E. Scobey, *Franklin College and Its Influence* (1906); Emma Page, *The Life Work of Mrs. Charlotte Fanning* (1907); Patrick H. Mell, "Industrial Education in the South," in *The South in the Building of the Nation,* vol. X (1909); John Wooldridge, *Hist. of Nashville, Tenn,* (1890), ch. xiv, *passim*; *Republican Banner* (Nashville), May 5, 1874; certain information from Miss Charlotte Fanning, Nashville, Tenn.]

H. E. S.

FARABEE, WILLIAM CURTIS (Feb. 2, 1865–June 24, 1925), anthropologist, ethnologist, was born in Washington County, Pa., the son of Samuel H. and Susannah (Henkins) Farabee. He attended the state normal school, graduated from Waynesburg College in 1894, and after a period of teaching, during which (on Mar. 12, 1897) he was married to Sylvia Manilla Holdren of McArthur, Ohio, he entered the graduate school of Harvard University, where he received his doctor's degree from the division of anthropology in 1903. The same year he was appointed an instructor in anthropology at Harvard. Apart from two relatively minor studies undertaken in Coahoma County, Miss. (1901 and 1902), and an expedition to Iceland (1905) his first opportunity for field work came through the DeMilhau expedition organized under the auspices of the Peabody Museum for ethnological exploration in Peru. As the leader of this expedition (1906–09), Farabee worked in Peru east of the Andes and along the Andean plateau, mapping the region, recording and collecting among the Indians, and studying the archeological evidences of culture in the Andes and northwestern Bolivia. In 1913 the University of Pennsylvania appointed him curator of the section of American anthropology in the University Museum, and placed him in charge of an expedition organized to study the Indian tribes of the Amazon Basin. From March 1913 to June 1916, he explored that region. He traversed and mapped previously unknown country in southern British Guiana, and traced from source to mouth the hitherto indeterminate course of the Corentine River, the boundary between the Guianas. He recorded the cultural and somatic character of the Arawak and Carib tribes in northern Brazil, in British Guiana, and by the headwaters and main tributaries of the Amazon. He collected the pottery, basketry, and feather work of thirty tribes, and made unique collections of ancient handiwork in the pottery and burial-urns excavated on Marajo, Fortelaza, Ilho do Paros, and the Comotins River. Two published studies, *The Central Arawaks* (1918) and *The Central Caribs* (1924), and the Amazon exhibits in the University Museum show the skill and thoroughness with which he amassed and analysed this material. His own narrative of a part of the exploration was published under the title, "A Pioneer in Amazonia" in the *Bulletin of the Geographical Society of Philadelphia,* April 1917. In the interval between the Amazon expedition and his final research in South America, he acted as the ethnologist of the American Peace Commission at Versailles and represented the United States at the centennial of Peruvian independence, held in Lima in 1921.

In 1922, he undertook further field work in South America to study the cultures of the Inca and Megalithic empires. The malignant fever of the Amazon had told on his health, however, and after three months of archeologic work in Peru, he became ill with inflammatory dysentery. Despite the nearly continuous need of rest and medical attention, however, he worked for more than a year in South America. He made detailed drawings of Inca and pre-Inca ruins in the Pisco and Ica valleys and at Lake Titicaca; secured magnificent collections of pottery and textiles through excavations in the Nazca Valley, at Sabania, Pisco, and Puntillo; and took notes for a comprehensive study of the Araucanian Indians of central Chile. In the fall of 1923, he returned to Pennsylvania, with pernicious anemia, and after an illness of two years he died.

Of Farabee's many writings, those issued by the University Museum are listed in the *Museum Journal* (June 1925). His other published papers include, *inter alia,* contributions to the *Papers of the Peabody Museum* (vols. III and X, 1905 and 1922); *Science* (January 1903); *Proceedings of the American Philosophical Society* (vol. LVI, 1917); and the *American Journal of Physical Anthropology* (vol. I, 1918). By temperament as well as by training, he was fitted to deal with the delicate human situations involved in experimental ethnology. He possessed the gift of analysis and exact observation, and also a love of music and art; the precise and impulsive elements harmonized in him, forming a buoyant, sensitive, genial, and rigorously upright character which drew and held men everywhere. Through his personal contacts, in Peru and the Amazon country he developed the mutual goodwill of Indian and white man and exerted an influence toward strengthening the confidence between the United States and South American governments. Through writing and pioneer research, he defined the field of South American ethnology and brought new data to bear on the central problems of anthropology.

[*Who's Who in America,* 1924–25; *Museum Jour.* (Phila.), 1925; *Art and Archæology,* July 1925; *Am. Jour. Archæology,* July–Sept. 1925; *Nature,* Sept. 1925; *Geog. Review,* Oct. 1925; *Am. Jour. Phys. Anthropology,* Oct.–Dec. 1925; "The Farabee Expedition," *Bull. Pan Am. Union,* Mar. 1917; "Dr. Farabee's Last Journey," *Museum Jour.,* June 1926; Farabee's own writings, and certain information from Mrs. Farabee.] D. P. C.

FARAN, JAMES JOHN (Dec. 29, 1808–Dec. 12, 1892), politician, editor, was born in Cincinnati, Ohio, the son of Charles P. and Phœbe K. Faran. His early education was acquired in the public schools of his native city and later completed at Miami University. Upon his graduation in 1831 young Faran entered the law office of Judge O. M. Spencer under whose guidance he received his legal training. In 1833 he was admitted to the bar and began to practise law. His deep interest in public affairs soon made him a factor in the political life of his community and state. He was elected as a Democrat to the Ohio House of Representatives in 1835. In 1837 and again in 1838 he was reelected and during the session of 1838 he served as speaker. His dignity, courtesy, and fairness made him an excellent presiding officer and gained for him an enviable reputation. In 1839 he was elected to the Ohio Senate and was reelected in 1841 and 1842. From 1841 to 1843, as speaker, he again demonstrated his parliamentary ability. In 1844 he was elected to represent Hamilton County in Congress and was returned in 1846. While serving in this capacity he voted for the Wilmot Proviso restricting the limits of slavery. At the close of his second term he voluntarily retired from public life and devoted himself to editing the *Cincinnati Enquirer* which he, together with Washington McLean, had purchased in 1844. As early as 1834 Faran began to write editorials for the *Democratic Reporter* which were published during the heated congressional race between Robert T. Lytle and Bellamy Storer. Ten years later he became one of the proprietors of the *Cincinnati Enquirer* and retained his connection until 1881. Under his editorial supervision the paper became a powerful Democratic organ not only in Hamilton County but throughout the state. He was a vigorous and ready writer, and in his editorials he expounded the principles of Jeffersonian Democracy. In 1854 he was appointed by Gov. Medill one of the commissioners to supervise the erection of the present State House. The following year he was the Democratic nominee for mayor of Cincinnati and after one of the most bitter and exciting campaigns ever known in the city he defeated the Know-Nothing candidate, James D. Taylor, proprietor of the *Cincinnati Times*. During the administration of President Buchanan he was appointed postmaster of Cincinnati but was removed before the expiration of his term because he conscientiously sympathized with Stephen A. Douglas on the Kansas-Nebraska question. This brought to a close his public life. Although he was frequently urged by his friends to allow his name to be suggested for the governorship and other high positions, he preferred to remain in retirement. In 1840 he married Angelina Russell, daughter of Robert Russell of Columbus, Ohio. For more than half a century Faran was a conspicuous figure in Ohio politics. His tall, erect form never failed to attract attention, while his integrity, frankness, firm convictions, and facile pen made him a man of influence in the affairs of his city and state.

[Charles T. Greve, *Centennial Hist. of Cincinnati* (1904), II, 291–92; W. A. Taylor, *Ohio in Congress* (1899), pp. 188–89; *Biog. Cyc. and Portrait Gallery of Ohio*, V (1895), 1194; *Cincinnati Enquirer, Cincinnati Commercial Gazette, Cincinnati Times-Star*, Dec. 13, 1892.]

R. C. M.

FARGO, WILLIAM GEORGE (May 20, 1818–Aug. 3, 1881), expressman, was descended from Welsh ancestors who settled in Connecticut between 1670 and 1680, and lived there for five generations. William Fargo, of the fourth generation, fought in the battle of Yorktown. His son, William C., at sixteen (1807), went "west" to Pompey, N. Y., and was wounded at the battle of Queenstown in the war of 1812. He married Tacy Strong, and William George Fargo was the eldest of their twelve children. At thirteen, twice a week he rode a mail route of thirty miles. For the next eleven years he helped in a village inn, worked in a grocery store, failed as a grocery owner himself, and was the first freight agent at Auburn on the newly completed Auburn & Syracuse Railroad. Meantime, in January 1840, he married Anna H. Williams of Pompey. In 1842 he became messenger for Pomeroy & Company, the express firm between Albany and Buffalo, and the next year was their agent in Buffalo. In 1844 he became messenger for Wells & Company, of which he was one of the three owners, the first express concern west of Buffalo.

This western service joined, in 1850, with two firms operating between Albany and Buffalo to form the American Express Company, with Wells as president and Fargo as secretary. The service had already been extended to Chicago, Milwaukee, Cincinnati, St. Louis, Galena, and Dubuque. In 1852, to meet the demand for transportation to and from the gold diggings, Wells, Fargo & Company was organized for express business to California. Through its friendly relations with the American Express Company, the new firm could offer quick transportation to New York and Boston and to Europe. The Adams Company [see Adams, Alvin], which some years earlier had established service between California and the Gulf, succumbed to financial difficulties in 1855 and left Wells, Fargo & Company in control of the field. Their expresses carried gold-dust, mail, packages, and passengers and conducted the necessary banking business for the community.

The profit realized in the express business during the Civil War led to the organization of competing companies, and in the post-war period, several combinations resulted. In the West, in 1866, a general consolidation of mail stages and express companies from the Missouri to the Pacific was effected by the California legislature and incorporated as Wells, Fargo & Company, but the business showed no profits, and with the completion of the Union Pacific Railroad, the stage lines were dropped. In 1869 a merger of Wells, Fargo & Company with the newly organized Pacific Express Company, a relic of the Adams interest in California, led to over-capitalization at $15,000,000, later reduced to $5,000,000. Meanwhile, in the East, the Merchants Union Express Company, one of the new organizations, became so powerful that in 1868 the American Express Company was compelled to incorporate with it on equal terms in the American Merchants Union Express Company of which Fargo became the president. In 1873 the name was changed to the American Express Company again. The task of retrenchment in a period of post-war deflation and comparative stagnation of business was a challenge to Fargo, and its accomplishment was a tribute to his ability.

Fargo had some part in the local politics of Buffalo, which was his residence until his death. He was the Democratic war mayor of his city, serving two terms, 1862–66, but was defeated as candidate for the state Senate in 1871. He seems to have been a man of commanding presence, genial, popular, conciliatory, interested in his employees and evoking devotion from them. Had he lived in England he might well have won a title and a seat in Parliament. Six of his brothers and one brother-in-law were associated with him in the express business. Of the brothers, James Congdell Fargo (1829–1915) and Charles

Fargo (1831–1900) were the most extensively concerned.

[Alexander L. Stimson, *Hist. of the Express Companies* (1858); *Hist. of the Express Business* (1881); Henry Wells, *Sketch of Rise, Progress and Present Condition of the Express System* (1864); J. J. Giblin, *Record of the Fargo Family Compiled for James Francis Fargo* (1907); article on W. G. Fargo by Francis F. Fargo in *Mag. of Western Hist.*, Apr. 1886; *Encyc. of Contemporary Biog. of N. Y.*, vol. IV (1885); Buffalo Directory, 1844; obituaries in *Buffalo Commercial Advertiser* and *Buffalo Morning Express*, both of Aug. 4, 1881.] E. H—n.

FARIBAULT, JEAN BAPTISTE (Oct. 29, 1775–Aug. 20, 1860), pioneer, was a typical son of the Northwest, coming thither from Canada in fur-trading days and living to see the founding of the states of Iowa, Wisconsin, and Minnesota, where at his advent only Indians had roamed. Faribault's father, Barthélemy, was Royal notary during the French régime; after marrying Catherine Amable Véronneau he settled at Berthier, Quebec province, where their son was born. Jean Baptiste had a good education in the village schools, was destined for a mercantile career, and spent several years at Quebec in the store of a prominent merchant. Adventure appealed to the youth and he desired to go to sea; since his family opposed this plan he was apprenticed (1796) to the North West Fur Company and sent out to its posts in Illinois where he first traded with Potawatomi tribesmen. About 1800 Faribault was assigned to a trading-station among the Sioux on the upper Des Moines River where he had numerous adventures and was once almost assassinated by a jealous half-breed. Later his post was at Little Rapids on the Minnesota River; here in 1805 he took as wife Pélagie, a Sioux daughter of Joseph Hanse or Ainse of Mackinac. Their son Alexander was born the next year, and not long afterwards Faribault withdrew from the North West Fur Company and built a home at Prairie du Chien, where he engaged in the lead trade with Julien Dubuque. He also opened a farm near the village. It was claimed that he favored the Americans during the War of 1812; documents prove, however, that he was in the British militia in the attack in 1814 on Prairie du Chien (*Wisconsin Historical Collections,* IX, 1882, p. 262). At the close of the war he prepared to remove to Lord Selkirk's colony on Red River of the North, but finally decided to become a naturalized American. This same year (1817) a priest visited Prairie du Chien and Faribault had his wife and children baptized (St. Gabriel parish register, 1817). Two years later, at the instance of American army officers he took his family to the vicinity of Fort Snelling at the mouth of the Minnesota River. There he opened a farm on an island, which was submerged by a flood in 1822. The same year he entered the Columbia Fur Company and continued to trade with the Sioux, with headquarters at Little Rapids. When he was wounded in 1836 his wife walked from her home at Mendota to the Little Rapids post in order to give him care.

Faribault was a patron of the church and aided Father Galtier, the first priest in Minnesota, to build a mission house. He was popular with all groups of pioneers and influential with the Indians, who called him Cha-pah-sin-tay (Beaver's Tail). By his influence with the Sioux he maintained peace for many years between them and the pioneers. The city of Faribault, Minn., was named for his son Alexander, but a county in the state obtained its name from the elder Faribault. He died at his daughter's home in St. Paul.

[Faribault's biography, written soon after his death by his friend H. H. Sibley and based in part on autobiographical notes left by Faribault, is in *Minn. Hist. Soc. Colls., III* (1880), 168–79. For a brief sketch, see *Ibid.*, XIV (1912), 216. His French biographer is Joseph Tassé, *Les Canadiens de l'Ouest* (1878), I, 308–35. See also, Pierre-Georges Roy, *La Famille Faribault* (1913); W. W. Folwell, *A Hist. of Minn.*, I (1921), 437; *Wis. Hist. Colls.*, IX (1882). Pike met him on the upper Mississippi in 1804, see Elliott Coues, *The Expedition of Zebulon Montgomery Pike* (1895), I, 76.] L. P. K.

FARLEY, HARRIET (Feb. 18, 1817–Nov. 12, 1907), editor, author, for many years prominent in the factory life of Lowell, Mass., was of old New England stock, the daughter of Rev. Stephen and Lucy (Saunders) Farley, and was born in Claremont, N. H., where her father was pastor of the Congregational church. He moved to Atkinson, N. H., when Harriet was six years old, there joining to pastoral labors the principalship of an academy. She was well trained in the common-school subjects, French, drawing, and ornamental needle-work, and early displayed a lively interest in literature and composition. The family was large, one of the children was an epileptic, the mother was afflicted with a disease that affected both body and mind, and Harriet herself suffered severely from asthma and was thought to be consumptive. At the age of fourteen it was necessary for her to help support herself, and she stated later that at one time or another, she had "plaited palm-leaf and straw, bound shoes, taught school and worked at tailoring." The respectable profession of teaching she was expected to follow was repugnant to her, and being of independent, aggressive disposition, she went to Lowell, Mass., and as a mill-hand supported herself and contributed liberally to the needs of her family.

Many of her associates, like herself, were from country homes, ambitious, and eager for cultivation. Improvement Circles for their benefit were organized in the town, and out of one of these, conducted by a Universalist minister, Rev. Abel C. Thomas, came the *Lowell Offering,* a periodical destined to bring her into prominence both in this country and abroad. Its contents consisted exclusively of contributions from girl-workers in the Lowell mills. As a regular monthly it began in 1841 and was issued under the supervision of Mr. Thomas until October 1842, when it was taken over by Harriet Farley and Harriot Curtis. For a year they employed William Schouler to publish it, and then themselves became editors, publishers, and proprietors. It attracted much attention as indicative of the character and possibilities of American mill operatives; interested Harriet Martineau; was reviewed in the London *Athenæum;* and a compilation from its contents, entitled *Mind Amongst the Spindles,* with an introduction by Charles Knight, was published in England in 1844. Miss Farley issued a volume of her own contributions, *Shells from the Strand of the Sea of Genius,* three years later. At the end of 1845 the magazine was discontinued, but in September 1847 Miss Farley revived it under the title, *The New England Offering.* Only one copy was issued until April 1848, after which it appeared regularly until March 1850. In the latter year, remarks reflecting on New England mill conditions by Senator Jeremiah Clemens of Alabama incited her to publish a pamphlet, *Operatives' Reply to Hon. Jere. Clemens, being a Sketch of Factory Life and Factory Enterprise,* etc. She was also the editor of *Discourses and Essays on Theological and Speculative Topics* (1851), by her father, Stephen Farley, and author of *Happy Nights at Hazel Nook* (1852). In 1854 she married John Intaglio Donlevy (d. 1872), an inventor, and resided in New York. She herself lived to be ninety, dying in that city at the Home for Incurables. She is said to have lectured on "The Laws of Life, or Hints for the Determination of Sex," and in 1880 published *Fancy's Frolics; or Christmas Stories Told in a Happy Home (Hazelnook) in New England.*

[Autobiographical editorial appeared in the *Lowell Offering* for July and Aug. 1845; and the article in Sarah J. Hale's *Woman's Record; or, Sketches of all Distinguished Women* (1853) is largely autobiographical. See also Harriet H. Robinson, *Loom and Spindle, or Life Among the Early Mill Girls with a Sketch of "The Lowell Offering" and Some of its Contributors* (1898); F. W. Coburn, *Hist. of Lowell and Its People* (1920), II, ch. xiv; *Athenæum* (London), Aug. 28, 1841, and Aug. 17, 1844; Lucy Larcom, "Among Lowell Mill-Girls," *Atlantic Mo.*, Nov. 1881; Lucy Larcom, *A New Eng. Girlhood* (1889); *Who's Who in America*, 1906–07; *Rev. of Revs.* (N. Y.), Dec. 1907.] H. E. S.

FARLEY, JOHN MURPHY (Apr. 20, 1842–Sept. 17, 1918), Roman Catholic cardinal, archbishop of New York, was born at Newtown-Hamilton, County Armagh, Ireland, of plain, farming people in circumstances to afford their children a good education. He came to America in 1864 and in that year entered St. John's College, Fordham, N. Y., now Fordham University. He proved a brilliant student and after one year entered the theological seminary (Troy, N. Y.) of the Catholic province of New York. Here he so distinguished himself in his studies that at the end of a year he was chosen by Archbishop McCloskey, on the recommendation of the rector of the seminary, to continue his studies in theology and cognate subjects at the American College, Rome. Three years in Rome gave him the opportunity to secure a broad background of culture and knowledge of classical scenes and put him intimately in touch with the Church's relations to the Christian world. He was in Rome during the whole period of the Vatican Council and became familiar with the personalities of the great prelates of the Church. He was ordained priest in Rome, June 11, 1870, and then returned to New York. His first assignment was as assistant to the pastor at New Brighton, Staten Island. This was a quarter of a century before Staten Island was included within the boundaries of Greater New York, so the future cardinal had his opportunity to do country parish work. He came to know most of the parishioners personally, and the people of the town continued to remember him cordially and followed his rise in the ecclesiastical world with close attention and good wishes.

In 1872, when the Rev. Francis McNierney was appointed bishop of Albany, Father Farley succeeded him as secretary to Archbishop McCloskey. For this position he was eminently fitted. The wide acquaintance with the authorities at Rome which his years in the Eternal City had given him, his deep interest in the liturgy of the Church, his special proficiency in canon law, his methodical temperament, and his courteous manner, all proved valuable. Monsignor Lavelle, pastor of St. Patrick's Cathedral, New York, who was in intimate touch with him for nearly fifty years, says that "he won the hearts of the clergy and the people by his affability, sympathy and resource." After twelve years of service, he was made papal chamberlain—an honor which, it was said, would have come to him before but for his own modesty and unwillingness to be distinguished above other priests of the diocese.

In August 1884 he was appointed pastor of St. Gabriel's Church in East Thirty-seventh St., a populous parish of working people, loyally attached to the Church and eager for all the spiritual opportunities offered to them. Here he showed himself to be a very practical parish priest and his parish was a model of administration. He finished the spire and renovated the interior of the church, then proceeded to the building of a parish hall. He felt that it was extremely important to bring about social contacts among Catholic young folk in order that they might learn to know each other and thus marriages within the Church be more likely to occur. The parish hall was designed to furnish a place for such meetings, and where other friendly contacts among his parishioners might be formed.

In 1891 he became vicar-general of the diocese and president of the Catholic School Board, and later was promoted to the position of auxiliary Bishop of New York. After the death of Archbishop McCloskey, he was appointed archbishop of New York in September 1902. Feuds and ill-feeling were rife among the clergy of the archbishopric because of unfortunate differences of opinion on political and economic questions which had culminated in what is known as the McGlynn affair. Archbishop Farley soon appeased the trouble. How successful he was in this achievement may be gathered from Monsignor Lavelle's expression just after his death, "There was not a faction nor a clique in the diocese he left behind." During his term as archbishop he organized a series of celebrations which attracted wide attention and brought the Catholic Church into prominence before the country. The first of these was the centenary of the diocese of New York. There was a touch of internationalism in it because Cardinal Logue, Archbishop of Armagh, in whose archdiocese Cardinal Farley was born, was invited to come to New York to celebrate the Mass and be the honored guest of the occasion. Two years later in 1910, Archbishop Farley planned the celebration of the consecration of his cathedral, and this attracted even more attention than the celebration of the centenary. He was created cardinal in 1911 and the reverence in which he was held by his people was revealed by the enthusiastic celebration in his honor on his return to New York in January 1912.

One of the works in which he was most interested was the *Catholic Encyclopedia*. There had been no little opposition to it because of the feeling that it could not be made a commercial success, and it was not until after the Cardinal had called a meeting in his own house, himself pledged $5,000, and called for further subscriptions that it became clear that the work would surely go on. In spite of his many labors as archbishop he wrote *The History of St. Patrick's Cathedral* (1908) and ten years later, *The Life of John, Cardinal McCloskey* (1918).

Believing that the success of his archdiocese was dependent largely upon the spiritual progress of his priests, he encouraged their annual retreats and instituted monthly recollections at which a spiritual conference was given by someone who could be relied on to lift up the hearts of his hearers. These he always attended himself if he was in New York, and the gatherings proved a close link between the archbishop and his priests. He provided particularly for the spiritual care of the foreigners in the archdiocese. Mass was said in seven different languages—an index of the many rites which had found their way from eastern Europe; pastoral care was given to the various language groups represented in the population of New York; to see that no one should be neglected was no easy task. Throughout his life a man of prayer and of the spirit, his supreme care was to be the pastor of his flock.

[The principal source is the sketch written by Msgr. Michael J. Lavelle in *Eccl. Rev.* (Phila.), Feb. 1919. The article by Rev. Peter Guilday in *Cath. World*, Nov. 1918, comes from one who had been very intimately in touch with the Cardinal for several years. The life in Jas. J. Walsh, *Our Am. Cardinals* (1926), is the fullest biography to date. See also A. J. Shipman, *His Eminence, Cardinal Farley* (1912); John C. Reville in *America*, Sept. 28, 1918; John T. Smith in *Irish World*, Nov. 2, 1918.] J. J. W.

FARLOW, WILLIAM GILSON (Dec. 17, 1844–June 3, 1919), botanist, was born in Boston. His mother was Nancy Wight (Blanchard) Farlow, but it was probably from his father, John Smith Farlow, man of public affairs, and amateur gardener and musician, that he inherited his love of plants and music. Farlow's scholarship won awards in the Boston high schools which he attended, and in 1862 he matriculated at Harvard, graduating in 1866. Here he came at once under the inspiring and kindly influence of Asa Gray, and proved to be a gifted student. Upon Gray's advice he entered the Harvard Medical School in 1867, since botany was still largely impracticable as a sole profession. At the close of his third year he won a coveted appointment as surgical interne at the Massachusetts General Hospital, and so brilliant was his hospital service that in his final examination he was merely asked where he intended to practise.

Freed from the restrictions of medical training, however, he went at once into the service of Asa Gray as assistant, and after two years, during which he made especially fine studies in the marine *Algae* at Woods Hole, he traveled to Europe, there meeting the great botanists and studying algological herbaria. Most of his time was passed in the laboratory of the great cryptogamic botanist, De Bary of Strassburg, whose influence in the direction of physiology and cytology was a counterbalance to the systematic and philosophical training of Asa Gray. When Farlow returned to America in 1874, he had a distinguished reputation, and received the first special provision for instruction in cryptogamic botany ever offered in this country. For some years he was stationed at the Bussey Institute, and there, as Thaxter says, he may be said to have laid the foundation of American phytopathology, publishing papers on destructive parasites and algal water pollution. The carping regulations of Bussey Institute in that day proved too much for his patience, and in 1879 he was transferred to the main stem of Harvard, at Cambridge, where he built up an unrivalled cryptogamic herbarium and library. His *Contributions from the Cryptogamic Laboratory of Harvard University* were instituted as serial publications in 1883. They number forty titles, of important cryptogamic studies by himself and by his students under his direction. The most celebrated of these papers from his pen was his useful "Host Index of American Fungi" (1888), written with the collaboration of A. B. Seymour. Many of the most distinguished living botanists were trained in his laboratory—William Trelease, W. A. Setchell, K. Miyabe, B. D. Halstead, J. E. Humphreys, and others.

Farlow possessed a phenomenal memory; with the literature of his science he kept so completely *au courant* that, it is said, he often neglected the publication of his own works. Witty, even biting in speech, he was an entertaining talker and always esteemed as a delightful companion and a charming host. His well-known pessimism was but an affectation, as were his many pet aversions. As in systematic botany he was markedly of the conservative school, so in personality he was a typical New England gentleman of his generation. In 1900 he was married to Lillian Horsford.

[W. R. Setchell, "Wm. Gilson Farlow," with bibliography, in *Nat. Acad. Sci. Memoirs*, vol. XXI (1926); Roland Thaxter in *Bot. Gaz.*, Jan. 1920, and in *Harvard Grads. Mag.*, Dec. 1919, reprinted in *Am. Jour. Sci.*, Feb. 1920.] D. C. P.

FARMAN, ELBERT ELI (Apr. 23, 1831–Dec. 30, 1911), jurist, diplomat, was born at New Haven, Oswego County, N. Y., the third son of Zadok and Martha (Dix) Farman. On the paternal side, he was a descendant of William Foreman, a planter of Maryland, who came from London to Annapolis in 1675. On his mother's paternal side, he was descended from Leonard Dix, a settler of Wethersfield, Conn., and on the maternal side from Gov. Thomas Welles. He prepared for college at the Genesee Wesleyan Seminary at Lima, N. Y., attended Genesee College and in his junior year entered Amherst, from which he was graduated in 1855. Upon leaving college, he took an active part in politics, especially in support of John C. Frémont in 1856, delivering stump speeches in the presidential campaigns up to 1888 and serving as a delegate to the Republican National Convention in Philadelphia in 1872. Meanwhile he studied law at Warsaw, N. Y., and was admitted to the bar in 1858 and to the United States courts in 1862. Between these two dates he was one of the publishers of the *Western New Yorker*. From 1865 to 1867 he traveled in Europe and studied languages and international law at the Universities of Berlin and Heidelberg. On his return in January 1868 he was appointed by Gov. Fenton as district attorney of Wyoming County, to fill a vacancy, but was elected to two terms thereafter, serving until 1875. In March 1876 President Grant appointed him diplomatic agent and consul-general at Cairo, Egypt, in which position he was continued by President Hayes, who also appointed him (1880) one of the delegates for the United States on the international commission for the revision of the judicial codes to be applied in the international mixed tribunals in Egypt. His success in this work led on July 1, 1881, to his designation by President Garfield, on the recommendation of Secretary Blaine, as one of the judges of the mixed tribunals. His eight years in Egypt were eventful. In January 1878 former President Grant arrived in Egypt on his tour of the world, and it fell to Farman's lot to act as the General's interpreter, to present him to the Khedive, and to accompany him on the famous voyage of the Nile, which Farman described nearly thirty years later in his *Along the Nile with General Grant* (1904). At the same time he presented to the Khedive Henry M. Stanley, the African explorer, who at that time apparently considered himself an American citizen. Farman also witnessed the riots at Alexandria in June and July 1882, and in January 1883 was designated by President Arthur as a member of the international commission organized to determine the damages to be paid by the people of Alexandria as a result of them. The commission sat for eleven months, examined over 10,000 claims and awarded over $20,000,000. During this time, Farman continued to hold his position in the courts, generally sitting one day a week. His record as consul-general is one of many achievements. He sent to the state department voluminous reports on agriculture, commerce, politics, and finance, many of which were published. At his suggestion, he was directed by the department to negotiate a treaty with Egypt concerning the abolition of the slave traffic in that country and its provinces. This he did, and although orally agreed to, the treaty ultimately failed because of a fall of the ministry. Farman was somewhat more successful in his negotiations for an increase in the number of American judges on the mixed tribunals, and also in securing in 1879 as a gift from the Khedive the granite obelisk known as Cleopatra's Needle in Central Park, New York City. He also made extensive collections of ancient coins, scarabs, bronzes, porcelains, and other antiquities, which are now in the Metropolitan Museum of Art. After his return from Egypt, he was engaged principally in the practise of law in Warsaw, and in the management of his own affairs, delivering occasional lectures and political speeches, and writing accounts of his Egyptian experiences. In this connection he spent the winters of 1894–1900, 1904, and 1906 in Europe. Besides the description of the voyage up the Nile, he also wrote: *Egypt and Its Betrayal; an Account of the Country during the Periods of Ismail and Tewfik Pashas and of How England Acquired a New Empire* (1908), and a *Foreman-Farman-Forman Genealogy* (1911). He was married twice: first, on Dec. 24, 1855, to Lois Parker of Madison, Ohio; second, on Oct. 8, 1883, to Sarah Adelaide Frisbie of Galesburg, Ill. He had three children by the second marriage.

[In addition to Farman's works mentioned in the sketch, see *N. Y. Times,* Jan. 1, 1912.] H. F. W.

FARMER, FANNIE MERRITT (Mar. 23, 1857–Jan. 15, 1915), daughter of John Franklin and Mary (Watson) Farmer, was born in Boston, Mass. Her parents planned to send her to college, but a paralytic stroke which she sustained while she was a student at the Medford high school, forced them to abandon the plan. She eventually recovered her health sufficiently to assist in the housekeeping, and developed such an interest in cooking that her family urged her to attend the Boston Cooking School. After her graduation from that institution in 1889, she was asked to return as assistant to the director the next year. Upon the death of the director she was elected to that position (1891). She resigned some eleven years later to open (1902) a school of her own, known as Miss Farmer's School of Cookery. Always shy and reserved, she shunned publicity and was said never to have subscribed to a clipping bureau or preserved a press notice. Nevertheless, her name became known throughout the land, and *The Boston Cooking School Cook Book,* which she edited in 1896, ran into twenty-one editions before her death. She also published: *Chafing Dish Possibilities* (1898), *Food and Cookery for the Sick and Convalescent* (1904), *What to Have for Dinner* (1905), *Catering for Special Occasions, With Menus and Recipes* (1911), and *A New Book of Cookery* (1912).

In the Boston Cooking School the courses were designed for the training of teachers; in her own school the courses were designed for the training of housewives. Her main interest was in practise, not theory. Her school specialized in invalid cookery and supplied lecturers on that subject to training classes for nurses. Miss Farmer herself gave a course on invalid cookery one year at the Harvard Medical School. Her weekly lectures at the cooking school were largely attended and widely reported in the press. She was much in demand for addresses to women's clubs; and for ten years, assisted by her sister, she conducted a popular page on cookery in the *Woman's Home Companion.*

Some years before her death, another stroke deprived her of the use of her limbs, but as soon as she recovered sufficiently, she continued her lecturing, though compelled to speak from a wheeled chair. She followed closely the régime prescribed by her physician and almost by sheer will-power continued her work. Her last lecture was delivered only ten days before her death. It was said that the achievement of which she was most proud was the introduction of accurate measurements in cooking; and she was sometimes called "the mother of level measurements."

[*Woman's Home Companion,* Dec. 1915; *Journal of Home Economics,* May 1915; *Boston Transcript,* Jan. 15, 1915.] B. R.

FARMER, FERDINAND (Oct. 13, 1720–Aug. 17, 1786), Jesuit missionary, was the son of a Swabian family by the name of Steinmeyer. He adopted the name of Farmer after coming to the United States. His family lived in comfortable circumstances, and his studious habits as a boy early marked him for one of the learned professions. His first inclination was toward medicine and he had given three years to courses in the science of healing when, in 1743, the urge to heal souls as well as bodies caused him to enroll himself among the followers of Loyola at Landsberg. He was eager for foreign missionary service and hoped to be sent to China, but need of a German-speaking priest among the widely scattered Catholic settlers of Pennsylvania and New Jersey caused his superiors to send him to America. He arrived at Lancaster, Pa., in 1752 and served the mission there for six years. He was then transferred to the German parish of St. Joseph in

Philadelphia. That his duties were not those of an assistant in the city church of to-day may be comprehended when it is borne in mind that at this time the whole city of New York was part of St. Joseph's parish in Philadelphia.

While first Father Theodore Schneider, the founder of the original German-Catholic congregation in Philadelphia, and later Father Robert Harding attended to the spiritual needs of the Catholics in and near that city, Father Farmer was "on the road" almost continuously. He penetrated nearly every section of New Jersey and made frequent trips to the country around what is now Greenwood Lake, where he made many converts. That he crossed into New York in the early days of the Revolution, thereby risking the death penalty if captured, seems fairly well established, for while he was careful not to implicate others by committing to writing records of his journeys in territory forbidden to priests, he reported the necessity of having often to travel by night and of more than once being compelled to minister to the sick and dying in the attire of a Quaker merchant. He is generally regarded as the organizer, just prior to the Declaration of Independence, of the first Catholic congregation in New York City—a congregation which in time became the parishioners of St. Peter's, but which in 1785, after ten years of existence, was reported to Bishop Carroll as "yet in a poor situation, and under many difficulties," with only some two hundred communicants (Bayley, *post*).

In 1778, after the capture of Philadelphia, an effort was made by the British to create a regiment of Roman-Catholic volunteers, and much was hoped for the project in Philadelphia if Father Farmer could be induced to become the chaplain. He steadily refused to accept the position and in a letter to a priest in London declared that the offer had embarrassed him on account of his age "and for several other reasons." Five years later his name led all those attached to an address presented to Washington by "the Clergy, Gentlemen of the Law and Physicians of the city of Philadelphia."

"He was," says an old pamphlet of the times, "of a slender form, having a countenance mild, gentle and bearing an expression almost seraphic" (*Researches*, July 1890). He seems to have borne the rigors of his missionary journeys extremely well and was seldom sick. He was one of the first trustees of the University of the State of Pennsylvania, when it was chartered in 1779, a member of the American Philosophical Society, and an astronomer and mathematician who made time to correspond with various learned societies in Europe. He was popular with all classes; his funeral was attended by all the Protestant clergymen of Philadelphia as well as by the trustees of the University and delegations from a number of public bodies.

[*Am. Cath. Hist. Researches*, Jan. 1888, Apr. 1889, Jan. 1890, Jan., Apr. 1897, Jan. 1900; *Am. Cath. Hist. Records*, vols. II–VI (1886–95); Peter Guilday, *The Life and Times of John Carroll* (2 vols., 1922); *Cath. Encyc.*; J. R. Bayley, *A Brief Sketch of the Hist. of the Cath. Church on the Island of N. Y.* (1853); obituary in *Pa. Gazette*, Aug. 23, 1786.] E. F. B.

FARMER, HANNAH TOBEY SHAPLEIGH (Mar. 20, 1823–June 27, 1891), philanthropist, wife of Moses Gerrish Farmer, was born in Berwick, Me., the third daughter of Richard and Olive (Tobey) Shapleigh. Her father was primarily a public-school teacher but, while not a lawyer, maintained a law office in association with another. He was a practical and accurate surveyor, justice of the peace, deputy sheriff, and representative for several terms in the General Court at the state capital. In this environment Hannah grew up and earned the reputation in her early girlhood of "a lass with a great deal of pluck." Sadness entered her life at an early age with the death of a little brother, and within a month of each other two sisters near her own age died of tuberculosis. When she was seventeen her father died of the same disease, leaving his family destitute except for a house in Eliot, Me. To this place the widow moved and there Hannah was obliged to assist her mother in maintaining the home. This she did with her needle as a mantua-maker, going from house to house and earning twenty-five cents a day. On Dec. 25, 1844, she married Moses Gerrish Farmer [*q.v.*] who was a preceptor of the Eliot Academy and lodged with her mother. During the earlier years of her married life the family income was severely limited but Mrs. Farmer was in entire sympathy with her husband's electrical experimentation and invention and was of great assistance to him in the development of many of his important discoveries. She, too, apparently acquired the trend of thought of the inventor for she received a patent rather late in life, on Dec. 11, 1883, for a "head protector." As the family means permitted, she became active in charitable and philanthropic work in and about Boston. With the outbreak of the Civil War and throughout that struggle she originated and conducted public benefits for the soldiers by which large sums of money and supplies were realized and distributed especially through the Christian Commission and other benevolent channels of Boston. In 1888 she built in Eliot a large dwelling in memory of her infant son. This she called "Rosemary Cottage," its purpose being to afford shelter and food to weary and needy women and children. Before her death this institution was given over to the care of the City Missionary Society of Boston. Under the pen name of Mabelle, Mrs. Farmer wrote both prose and poetry, contributing it chiefly to the general press, the theme for most of these writings being for the advancement of the various civic betterment movements in which she was interested. She died in Eliot, survived by her husband and daughter.

[Augustin Caldwell, *The Rich Legacy, Memories of Hannah Farmer* (1892); obituary in *Boston Transcript*, June 28, 1891; U. S. Patent Office records.] C. W. M.

FARMER, JOHN (June 12, 1789–Aug. 13, 1838), antiquarian and genealogist, was born at Chelmsford, Mass., the eldest son of John and Lydia (Richardson) Farmer and seventh in descent from John Farmer whose widow Isabella came to New England in 1669. In his native town he attended a private school kept by the Rev. H. Packard. In 1803 his parents moved to Lyndeboro, N. H., and soon afterward John went to work in a store in Amherst, N. H. There he attended school, when business was dull, and also studied medicine with a local physician, but his slender physique discouraged him from entering the profession. In 1810, and for a few years thereafter, he taught school, an employment in which he excelled. His keenest interest, however, was in genealogy and in local history.

In 1813 he published *A Family Register of the Descendants of Edward Farmer of Billerica, in the Youngest Branch of his Family* (Concord, N. H.). In the following year the Massachusetts Historical Society printed "A Sketch of Amherst, N. H." (*Collections*, 2 ser., vol. II) which he had prepared. This was followed by *An Historical Memoir of Billerica, Mass.* (1816), and "Note on the County of Hillsborough, N. H." (*Massachusetts Historical Society Collections*, 2 ser., vol. VII, 1818). These studies won him recognition among scholars, and in 1822 he received an honorary degree of M.A. from Dartmouth College.

In 1821 Farmer moved to Concord, N. H., where he formed a business connection with Dr. Samuel Morril and opened an apothecary store. From this vocation he acquired the title of "Doctor." His hours of leisure were devoted to the study of New Hampshire annals and New England genealogy, and he produced a number of books in rapid succession: *An Ecclesiastical Register of New Hampshire* (1821); *The New Military Guide* (1822); *The New Hampshire Annual Register* (1822–38 inclusive); *A Genealogical Register of the First Settlers of New England* (1829); *A Catechism of the History of New Hampshire* (1829); and a one-volume edition of the first two volumes of Jeremy Belknap's *History of New Hampshire* (1831). In conjunction with Jacob B. Moore he published *A Gazeteer of the State of New Hampshire* (1823), and *Collections, Historical and Miscellaneous* (3 vols., 1822–24). Of all these works the *Genealogical Register* is the most important, and it is significant that James Savage [*q.v.*] used it as the basis for his *Genealogical Dictionary*. In the *American Quarterly Register* Farmer published sketches of early graduates of Dartmouth College, 1771–83; a list of the graduates of all the colleges in New England; and memoirs of the ministers who graduated at Harvard before 1657. In the last year or two of his life he was appointed by the legislature to examine, arrange, and index the state papers at Concord. This difficult task he performed admirably.

Farmer was of average height, erect and extremely thin. In spite of his very uncertain health there was an animated cheerfulness in his whole aspect. He was highly religious and thoroughly orthodox in his belief. The cause of anti-slavery took a deep hold upon him and he was for a number of years corresponding secretary of the New Hampshire Anti-slavery Society. He was deeply interested in the formation of the New Hampshire Historical Society in 1823, and was its corresponding secretary from 1825 until his death in 1838.

[The best memoir of Farmer is that by Jacob B. Moore in *Am. Quart. Reg.*, Feb. 1839. This is preceded by an engraving of a miniature portrait painted in 1824. John Le Bosquet, *A Memorial . . . of John Farmer* (1884), is an intimate biography. The first sketch in the first issue of the *New-Eng. Hist. and Geneal. Reg.*, Jan. 1847, was "Memoir of John Farmer," an abstract of Moore's memoir. An obituary attributed to Joseph Willard is in the Worcester *Aegis*, Aug. 22, 1838.] L. S. M.

FARMER, JOHN (Feb. 9, 1798–Mar. 24, 1859), cartographer, was born in Halfmoon, Saratoga County, N. Y., the son of John and Catharine Jacokes (Stoutenburgh) Farmer. He received his education in schools in and about Albany, N. Y., and for a time taught in a Lancastrian school in Albany. By invitation of Gov. Cass and the trustees of the University of Michigan, Farmer went to Detroit from Albany in 1821 to take charge of one of the university schools; but about two years later he resigned his position and went to Ohio. Returning to Detroit in 1825, he engaged in surveying and map making. His first map was of the United States government road which had recently been built from Detroit to the Maumee River. While employed by a surveyor named Risdon in connection with a map of Michigan, Farmer took out for himself, in August 1825, three copyrights covering maps of Michigan on scales of eight, eighteen, and thirty miles to the inch. The first of these, which was the only one of the group to be published, appeared in 1826 and was followed within the next ten years by several other maps of the territoiy. Of the latter, the map of 1830, which was accompanied by a small gazetteer, was especially notable, while that of 1835 was the first map which Farmer engraved with his own hand. All of these maps had a wide sale throughout the East and were greatly influential in promoting the extensive immigration into Michigan that took place between 1825 and 1840.

In addition to the maps just described Farmer published several editions of a map of Wisconsin and in 1831 drew for Congress a map of Detroit which was later published in the *American State Papers, Public Lands,* Vol. VI, and even to-day is regarded as the only legal authority and guide to surveys in the older portions of the city. In January 1835 he issued the first map of Detroit on which the size and correct outline of the several lots were shown. Shortly after the publication of this last work Farmer sold his copyrights to a New York map house and entered upon a period of public service during which he held the positions of county surveyor and city treasurer as well as numerous minor offices.

In 1844, he again actively engaged in map making, producing a new map of Michigan. This was followed by other maps of this same state, of Wisconsin, Lake Superior, and the Mineral Region, but the crowning achievement of his career was a large map of Michigan and Wisconsin, size 68 x 72 inches, which appeared in 1859. The hard work attendant upon the drawing and engraving of this map brought on a nervous disease from which he never recovered, his death occurring on March 24, 1859. He was survived by his wife, Roxana Hamilton, whom he had married on Apr. 5, 1826, and by three children.

[Biographical sketch by Farmer's son Silas, in the latter's *Hist. of Detroit and Wayne County and Early Mich.* (2nd ed., 1890), II, 1085–86; Wm. L. Jenks, "A Michigan Family of Map Makers," in *Mich. Hist. Mag.*, Apr. 1927; F. B. Streeter, *Mich. Bibliography* (2 vols., 1921).]

G. H. B.

FARMER, MOSES GERRISH (Feb. 9, 1820–May 25, 1893), inventor, pioneer American electrician, was born in Boscawen, N. H., where his father, Col. John Farmer, was a farmer and prosperous lumber merchant. Both his father and mother, who was Sally Gerrish, were descendants of early seventeenth-century English settlers in New England. For the first sixteen years of his life young Farmer attended school spasmodically, studied music—the piano particularly —and as soon as he was old enough assisted his father both on the farm and in the lumber business. After his father's death, in the fall of 1837, he went to Andover, Mass., entered the famous preparatory school there, and two years later was admitted to the freshman class of Dartmouth College. Here he made rapid progress and was a diligent student, and to augment his limited finances did considerable teaching of piano. This crowding of activities was more than his constitution could stand and he became seriously ill with typhoid fever which left him in such a delicate condition that he was compelled to give up his college work before its completion. About the only thing available in the way of work for him, in view of his physical condition, was school-teaching. While waiting for possible positions in this field, he spent part of the year of 1842 in the office of a civil engineer in Portsmouth, N. H., but in the succeeding winter became assistant in a private school in that city. Upon completing the winter term there, he next accepted the preceptorship of Eliot Academy, Eliot, Me., and went there in the spring of 1843. In 1844 he became the principal of the Belknap School for Girls, in Dover, N. H., and later, of another school in the same city. While in Eliot he lived for a time in the home of a Mrs. Shapleigh, who within eighteen months became his mother-in-law through his marriage to her daughter, Hannah Tobey Shapleigh, on Dec. 25, 1844. [See Farmer, Hannah Tobey Shapleigh.]

From the time he left college and started teaching, Farmer had shown in a variety of ways his innate ingenuity and an intense interest in mechanics and natural philosophy. Besides teaching, he tuned pianos, played the church organ, and was deeply interested in mathematics. As a result of his meeting with a window shade manufacturer of Dover, Farmer, presumably to satisfy his own ideas, devised a machine on which to print shades made of paper as a substitute for linen. Since paper shades could be sold at one-fourth the price of linen, this venture was successful, and in 1845 over 40,000 shades were printed and sold. At about this time Morse and Vail were bringing electricity to the attention of the world through the electro-magnetic telegraph. Farmer was one of those especially attracted to the study of the new power; in fact, he became so enthusiastic that both school-teaching and curtain manufacture lost their charm for him. He began delving into the subject in 1845 and undertook as his first experiment nothing less than an electric railroad. With money earned from curtain manufacture and with the help of his brother, John, he constructed a miniature electric train of two cars, on one of which were mounted the motor and wet batteries, the other being the passenger car. The first exhibition of the train was held in the yard of Farmer's home on July 26, 1847, and during the summer and fall of that year Farmer and his brother held exhibitions in the public halls of Dover and other neighboring cities of New Hampshire and Maine, at which children were drawn around in the passenger car. These exhibitions, although a novelty, were not financially profitable to Farmer, but he was now so wholly engrossed in electricity that when, in December 1847, he was offered the position of wire examiner of the new electric telegraph line between Boston and Worcester, he accepted, and moved to Framingham, Mass., in January 1848. During the succeeding six months, in addition to his regular duties he learned telegraphy and later, in July 1848, was appointed operator in the telegraph office at Salem, Mass., and immediately moved his family thither. Shortly thereafter he took charge of the telegraph between Boston and Newburyport, Mass., and undertook to open up telegraph offices along this line, continuing in this service until 1851.

Meanwhile, all of his spare time had been devoted to electrical experimentation at home. As early as 1848 he had invented an electric-striking apparatus for a fire-alarm service which, in association with Dr. William F. Channing [*q.v.*], he had developed to the point that when Channing succeeded in 1851 in inducing the City of Boston to install a fire-alarm system, the Channing and Farmer invention was selected and Farmer gave up his telegraphic work to serve as superintendent of the system. He had not only devised the signalling mechanisms but also perfected a special water motor to drive the electric dynamos. This was the first electric fire-alarm system in the United States. There was no experience or precedent to follow and as a result there were a multitude of conditions encountered which Farmer with his fertile inventive instincts was able to combat. He resigned the superintendency in 1853 and for several years thereafter worked quietly along developing his various electrical ideas. In 1855 he discovered the means for duplex and quadruplex telegraph and in the same year he read a paper before the American Association for the Advancement of Science on the general subject of multiplex telegraphy. In 1856 he succeeded in depositing aluminum electrolytically, and was induced to go into partnership with several men as electrotypers. The business proved prosperous from the very start, but the panic of 1857 completely wiped out the partners' capital. This financial loss materially restricted Farmer's experimentation for the next few years, but in 1861 he became superintendent of a tobacco-extracting manufactory in Somerville, Mass. Here his chemical knowledge was of great value to him and the business gave him a means of livelihood and permitted him to continue his electrical studies and experiments. Shortly after the failure of his electro-plating business, he had experimented with electricity as a source of light, and in 1858–59 invented an incandescent electric lamp. The filament was a platinum wire and the current was supplied by a wet-cell battery. With two of these lamps arranged in multiple, he lighted the parlor of his home for several months of the summer of 1859. He realized, of course, that a galvanic battery as a source of electricity was impracticable and that a substitute was needed, and after a number of years of experimentation, in 1866 he conceived and patented what is now called the "self-exciting" dynamo. With one of these dynamos, in 1868, he lighted a private residence in Cambridge, Mass., with forty of his incandescent lamps arranged in multiple series and with absolute regulation at the dynamo. In 1872 he was selected to fill the office of electrician at the United States Torpedo Station at Newport, R. I., and moved his family to that place from Salem. While it had been intended that his employment should be for a period of six months, his services were so valuable to the federal government that the appointment was continued for a total period of nine years, during which time he greatly advanced the art of torpedo warfare for the United States navy. Ill health necessitated his resignation in 1881. In the years immediately preceding, however, he had concentrated his attention more and more upon electric power generation and distribution and after leaving the Torpedo Station, as far as his health permitted, he acted as consulting electrician for the United States Electric Light Company of New York. After several years he retired with his family to his summer home at Eliot, Me.

Like many other pioneers, Farmer did not profit greatly from his inventive work. He led the way by thirty years in many applications of the electric current and, whenever he arrived at results which settled in his mind the laws of its action, instead of laboring to perfect a marketable invention, he would lay aside what he had done and proceed in search of the unknown. As the late Gov. Claflin of Massachusetts once said of him, "He was deserving of more honor than he ever received." He was always much interested in charitable and philanthropic movements and late in life carried out the wishes of his wife's father and established a public library at Eliot,

Me. He died suddenly in Chicago, whither he had gone, against the advice of his physician, to prepare an exhibit of his inventions for the World's Fair. He was survived by his daughter and was buried in Eliot.

[*Electricity*, Dec. 21, 1892, May 31, 1893, Aug. 4, 1897; Geo. B. Prescott, *Farmer on the Electric Light* (1879); T. C. Martin and S. L. Coles, *The Story of Electricity* (1919), vol. I; *Religio-Philosophical Jour.*, June 3, 1893; *Sci. Am.*, June 3, 1893; U. S. Patent Office Records.]

C. W. M.

FARNAM, HENRY (Nov. 9, 1803–Oct. 4, 1883), railroad builder, and philanthropist, born in Scipio, Cayuga County, N. Y., was the descendant of Connecticut stock. His parents, Jeffrey Amherst Farnam and Mercy Tracy, belonged to families which had left the Thames Valley in the eighteenth century to establish pioneer farms farther west; and on such a farm he was born and brought up. Studying and teaching in the village school, reading—by the light of the winter fire to save the expense of a candle—what text-books in mathematics he could procure, he prepared himself as a surveyor, and was employed in that capacity on the Erie Canal from 1821 to 1824. In 1825 he went to Connecticut to take the post of assistant engineer in the construction of the Farmington Canal, became chief engineer of that undertaking in 1827, and so remained until 1846, when the canal was abandoned and he acted as chief engineer and superintendent of the railroad which took its place. In 1839 he married Ann Sophia Whitman of Farmington.

The canal, completed from New Haven to Farmington in 1828, and later extended to Northampton, never realized the dreams of its projectors. Of small dimensions (taking boats only of twenty to twenty-five tons), cheaply built (two-thirds of the sixty locks were of wood), it counted a year fortunate when it collected, from the scant traffic, tolls sufficient to cover ordinary maintenance. Breaches were frequent, occasioned by freshets and, so it was charged, by malicious injury. The engineer was out day and night, rain or shine (particularly in rain), driving in his buggy from one point to another of the canal. In his later years, after a broken night, he would often say, "I have been spending the whole night repairing a breach in the old canal."

Work on the canal brought Farnam into intimate relations with Joseph E. Sheffield [*q.v.*], a man of property and considerable business connections, a large stockholder in the canal and contributor of most of the capital to the railroad which succeeded it. The two were associated in a plan to build a railroad from New Haven to

New York, obtained a charter in 1844, but found only one other individual willing at that time to subscribe to stock, and had to abandon the enterprise.

In the twenty-five years devoted to the New Haven-Northampton line Farnam gained little but experience. He got that in full measure, and established a reputation for technical competence, business ability, sound judgment, and integrity. In 1850 he was invited to Chicago, a town approaching a population of 30,000 but still lacking railroad connections with the outside world. In the few years following, the firm of Sheffield and Farnam completed the Michigan Southern Railroad from Hillsdale to Chicago, providing an all-rail line to the East (1852), built the Chicago & Rock Island, giving railroad connection with the Mississippi River (1852–54); Farnam designed and built the first railroad bridge crossing the Mississippi River, at Rock Island (1855), and the firm of Farnam & Durant carried the construction of the Mississippi & Missouri Railroad as far as Grinnell, Iowa. Bridging the Mississippi was resented by the river interests and led to many suits. To defend one of these Farnam engaged Abraham Lincoln, whose argument won the famous Rock Island Bridge case. Early reports of the Chicago & Rock Island Railroad show that the contractors were given a right of way and had to provide practically everything else to make a railroad. Not only did they do the grading, build the bridges, import and lay the iron rails; they also built the stations and freight houses, built the machine shops and equipped them with engines, machinery, and tools, and supplied the rolling stock, from locomotives to hand-cars. They were paid mostly in bonds and stock, so that they had to finance as well as build the road. They also organized the operating force, and Farnam shortly assumed the presidency of the Chicago & Rock Island, and held that place until his retirement in 1863, in his sixtieth year. After several years of travel abroad he returned to New Haven, where he made notable gifts to Yale College and many civic causes. Of him Noah Porter said: "His public spirit was a passion." He combined the homely virtue of his Puritan ancestors with the boldness and breadth of view of the modern business leader, and as a pioneer in railroad construction made a permanent contribution to the development of the country.

[Sources are: Henry W. Farnam, *Henry Farnam* (privately printed, New Haven, 1889), a memoir based on family papers and personal recollections; papers and pamphlets relating to the Farmington canal in the Yale Library; early reports of the Chicago & Rock Island R. R.; obituary in *N. Y. Tribune*, Oct. 5, 1883. Chauncey A. Goodrich, *The Excursion* (1854), "a poetical jeu d'esprit," commemorates the excursion in celebration of the opening of the Chicago & Rock Island.] C. D.

FARNHAM, ELIZA WOODSON BURHANS (Nov. 17, 1815–Dec. 15, 1864), philanthropist, author, was born in Rensselaerville, N. Y., the daughter of Cornelius and Mary (Wood) Burhans. Her mother died when Eliza was six years old, and she was sent to live with an aunt and uncle in Maple Springs, N. Y. In this somewhat backwoods section she found little kindness; her aunt was jealous and nagging, her uncle addicted to whiskey, and Eliza became obsessed with the desire to alleviate misery in the world. She was the only child in the neighborhood who was not allowed to attend school and the only one who read books of her own accord. At about sixteen, she left her uncle's home and went to live with another uncle, who had taken her brother and two sisters when her mother died, and was sent to school for a time. In 1835 she moved to Illinois, where in 1836 she married Thomas Jefferson Farnham [*q.v.*], a young lawyer, to whom she bore three sons. After his return from an expedition to California (1839–40), in 1841 the Farnhams moved to New York. In 1844 Mrs. Farnham accepted an appointment as matron of the female department of the state prison at Sing Sing. She determined to prove that prisoners would respond more satisfactorily to kindness than to the harsh treatment accorded them formerly, met with much success in her experiment, and retained her office until 1848. Meanwhile her husband had removed to Illinois and then to San Francisco, where he died in September 1848. After a brief period of employment at the Institution for the Blind in Boston, in 1849 Mrs. Farnham went to California. Prior to her departure she attempted to organize a party of women to emigrate with her, and her project, which did not prove successful, was indorsed by Judge J. W. Edmonds, Horace Greeley, Henry Ward Beecher, Catharine M. Sedgwick, and other notables. The difficulties of her journey and her experiences on the Coast she later described in a book, *California, Indoors and Out* (1856). She returned to New York in 1856, and devoted the next two years to studying medicine. In 1859 in pursuance of the plan conceived a decade earlier, she organized a society in New York City to assist destitute women in finding homes in the West, and she personally conducted several companies of "emigrants" of this class to California. Shortly after the death of her first husband she was married a second time (*Burhans Genealogy*), to William Fitzpatrick, of Ireland. She retained the name Farnham, however. By this marriage she had one daughter, who died in infancy. In addition to the book already mentioned, Mrs. Farnham was the author of *Life in Prairie Land* (1846); *Eliza Woodson, or, The Early Days of One of the World's Workers* (1864, previously issued in a very small edition, 1859); and *The Ideal Attained* (1865). Although the last two are classed as fiction, all three were based to some extent upon her own experiences. Her most significant work was *Woman and Her Era* (1864), published in two volumes. It is an intelligent discussion of woman's capabilities for other vocations than motherhood. She urged women to develop intellectual interests but in doing so not merely to imitate men. She also edited, wrote the preface to, and illustrated an American edition of a treatise, *Rationale of Crime, and its Appropriate Treatment* (1846), by Marmaduke Blake Sampson. She died at Milton-on-the-Hudson, N. Y.

[In addition to Mrs. Farnham's own writings, see Samuel Burhans, Jr., *Burhans Genealogy* (1894), p. 193; obituaries in *N. Y. Tribune*, Dec. 16, and *N. Y. Times*, Dec. 18, 1864.] M. Sh—r.

FARNHAM, RUSSEL (1784–Oct. 23, 1832), fur-trader, was born in Massachusetts, the son of John and Susan (Chapin) Farnham. Little is known of his early life except that he received a fair education. As a clerk he joined the Astoria sea expedition that left New York on the *Tonquin*, Sept. 6, 1810. In the Oregon country he was one of the most active and adventurous of the party and figured in almost all of the exciting incidents that marked the brief history of the enterprise. On the sale of Astoria to the North West Company, Nov. 12, 1813, he was chosen by Hunt to carry to Astor the company records and the net proceeds of the sale, consisting of about $40,000 in sterling bills on London. Embarking on the company's brig *Pedlar*, he sailed, Apr. 3, 1814, and was landed at Kamtchatka, whence he started afoot, carrying a small pack of provisions, across Siberia. This extraordinary exploit, characterized by his friend Darby as a feat that for bravery, danger, and daring was never equaled by any other man, was successfully accomplished. After enduring great sufferings from hunger and exposure, at one time being reduced to the necessity of cutting off and eating the tops of his boots, he reached St. Petersburg, and later Copenhagen. From the latter port, on or about Oct. 16, 1816, he sailed for Baltimore, ultimately delivering the papers consigned to him into Astor's hands.

For the remainder of his life he continued in the employ of Astor. In 1817–19 he was the manager of the American Fur Company's business on the upper Mississippi. For an alleged violation of the trading laws he and his companion, Daniel Darling, were arrested in the fall of 1817, but on a suit brought by the company were awarded a verdict of $5,000. In 1819 he ventured into the Missouri River trade, but from 1821 was again active on the upper Mississippi. In the same year he began to acquire land in the village of Portage des Sioux, in northeastern Missouri, where he established a well-stocked farm and built a beautiful home. On Oct. 27, 1829, at St. Louis, he married Susan, the daughter of Charles Bosseron, a French settler of wealth and position. Early in 1832 he journeyed east. In October, some months after his return, he went to St. Louis, and on his arrival was stricken with cholera, dying within two hours. He was buried in the Catholic cemetery.

Farnham is described by Darby as of ordinary size, with a powerful frame, and his Copenhagen passport, not quite tallying with Darby as to his stature, adds the information that his hair was light and curly and that he had brown eyes. He was companionable and sociable. "The best meaning and one of the most sanguine of men," was the characterization of him given by his friend Ramsay Crooks, who added that he underwent greater privations "than any half dozen of us."

[See John F. Darby, *Personal Recollections* (1880); Louis Houck, *Hist. of Missouri*, vol. III (1908); Bruce E. Mahan, *Old Fort Crawford and the Frontier* (1926); Stella M. Drumm, "More About Astorians," *Ore. Hist. Soc. Quart.* (Dec. 1923). Other material is in Gabriel Franchère's "Narrative" and Alexander Ross's "Adventures of the First Settlers" (pub. in *Early Western Travels*, ed. by R. G. Thwaites, 1904), vols. VI, VII. The account of Farnham's life in Elihu H. Shepard's *Early Hist. of St. Louis and Missouri* (1870) is largely fiction.]

W. J. G.

FARNHAM, THOMAS JEFFERSON (1804–Sept. 13, 1848), lawyer, traveler, writer, is commonly reported to have been born in Vermont, but the obituary printed in a San Francisco newspaper shortly after his death at that place says he was a native of the state of Maine. For some years prior to 1839 he had been living at Peoria, Ill., engaged in the practise of law. During the fall of 1838 Rev. Jason Lee, superintendent of the Oregon Mission of the Methodist Episcopal Church, went East and on his way gave a number of lectures on Oregon. He had with him two Indian boys, one of whom became ill and was left at Peoria where Lee gave a lecture. In consequence of the new personal information about the Far West nineteen young men of that place and its vicinity decided to make a trip across the continent in the spring. Farnham was one of these, and was chosen captain. They outfitted at Independence, Mo., and, on May 13, took the Santa Fé trail up that river to Bent's Fort on the Arkansas. Most of them afterwards crossed over to Fort St. Vrain on the South Platte and wintered with a party of trappers on Green River. Some deserted to Santa Fé. Only four men went with Farnham, who pushed his way across the Colorado Mountains to Fort Hall, thence down the Snake River Valley to the Walla Walla, and Fort Vancouver. He visited the Whitman Mission, also the settlers on the Willamette, for whom he seems to have written a petition directed to the government of the United States requesting that Oregon be taken under its protection. It was signed by the American settlers generally and was carried back to the United States by Farnham who sailed to the Sandwich Islands on one of the Hudson's Bay Company's vessels, thence securing transportation to Monterey in California. He claims to have been instrumental in liberating from prison certain Americans and Englishmen who had been implicated in a local revolution. Dropping down to San Blas in Mexico, he crossed to the Gulf of Mexico and ascended the Mississippi to Peoria during the summer of 1840. For a time thereafter he lived in New York, where he brought out his most important book: *Travels In the Great Western Prairies, the Anahuac and Rocky Mountains and in the Oregon Territory* (Poughkeepsie, 1841; London, 1843). He later settled near Alton, Ill., but finally removed to San Francisco, in 1846 or 1847, where he practised law during the brief remaining period of his life.

Farnham's *Travels in the Great Western Prairies*, which was reprinted by Thwaites in *Early Western Travels*, is valuable for its description but is unreliable so far as the author's expression of personal opinions goes. He was a fluent and entertaining writer and, having accomplished a transcontinental journey by a route which in some portions was new, he made a contribution to Far West geography which is his sole title to recognition. H. H. Bancroft, with some asperity, pronounced his other book on California, *Life and Adventures in California* (1846), "in all those parts resting on his own observations . . . worthless trash, and in all that relates to the California people a tissue of falsehood" (*Works of H. H. Bancroft*, vol. XX, 1885, p. 735). He was a man of vigorous and engaging personality, who made a strong impression on his fellow men. The *Travels* had a rather wide popularity and both of his books went through several editions.

Farnham married in 1836 Eliza Woodson Burhans [see Eliza Woodson Burhans Farnham], who wrote on prison reform, and later on California. She also aided in bringing Eastern girls to the Pacific Coast to become wives of the pioneer settlers. The Farnhams had three children.

[The best account of Farnham's activities is in R. G. Thwaites, *Early Western Travels,* XXVIII (1906), 10–15. The only obituary notice hitherto discovered is in the *Californian* (San Francisco) for Sept. 16, 1848. Joseph Holman, one of the associates of Farnham, who settled in Oregon, left a narrative of the Farnham party which can be found in S. A. Clarke, *Pioneer Days of Oregon Hist.* (1905), and elsewhere.] J. S.

FARNSWORTH, ELON JOHN (July 30, 1837–July 3, 1863), soldier, was born at Green Oak, Mich., where he received his early education. When he was seventeen years old, his father and mother, James Patten and Achsah (Hudson) Farnsworth, moved to Rockton, Ill., where his mother died soon after arrival. In 1855, young Farnsworth entered the University of Michigan, but in the winter of 1857–58 left college to join Gen. A. S. Johnston's Utah Expedition against the Mormons, as a forage-master. In 1861, he hastened home to join the 8th Illinois Cavalry which his uncle, Col. John Franklin Farnsworth [*q.v.*], was organizing. He became first lieutenant and regimental adjutant, and on Christmas Day, 1861, a captain. In the ensuing two years, which covered the Peninsular campaign, it has been said of Farnsworth that he never missed a battle or skirmish, forty-one in all, in which his regiment was engaged (James Barnet, *The Martyrs and Heroes of Illinois in the Great Rebellion,* 1865). In the spring of 1863, he was commended in orders by Gen. Pleasanton for gallant service in the field; and soon after, Pleasanton appointed him aide-de-camp on his staff, after efficient work as acting chief quartermaster of the IV Army Corps. On June 29, 1863, Farnsworth was promoted from captain to brigadier-general, United States Volunteers, in Kilpatrick's cavalry division; and in justification of this promotion Pleasanton wrote: "Nature made him a general" (letter to J. F. Farnsworth, *Farnsworth Memorial,* p. 322).

In the Gettysburg campaign, Farnsworth's brigade was sent in pursuit of Gen. J. E. B. Stuart's raiding force, and later on July 3, 1863, was in position near Little Round Top on the left flank of the Union army. Here, he received peremptory orders from Kilpatrick to charge the right flank of the Confederate lines. The ground was uneven and broken; the enemy was well posted behind fences and stone walls; everything was unfavorable for a charge. Farnsworth entered a dignified protest but was overruled. The cavalry charge which followed was one of the bravest as well as one of the most disastrous of the entire war; and by military writers has been compared to that of the Light Brigade at Balaclava (C. D. Rhodes, *History of the Cavalry of the Army of the Potomac,* 1900, p. 68). Although the gallant movement penetrated the enemy's lines for nearly two miles and resulted in the desired withdrawal from the front lines of several regiments of Confederate infantry, Farnsworth received five mortal wounds and his devoted command lost nearly one-fourth of its numbers (*Battles and Leaders of the Civil War,* 1887, III, 328–29, 376, 393–96). By his contemporaries he was regarded as a hero. Buried not far from where he fell in battle, his remains were disinterred by his uncle, Col. John F. Farnsworth, and transported to Rockton, Ill., for permanent interment. Farnsworth never married.

[Biographical sketch and complete genealogy of Farnsworth's family in Moses F. Farnsworth, *Farnsworth Memorial* (1897), p. 318, in which reference is made to Abner Hard, *Hist. of the Eighth Cavalry Regt., Ill. Volunteers* (1868); information from the Ill. State Hist. Soc.] C. D. R.

FARNSWORTH, JOHN FRANKLIN (Mar. 27, 1820–July 14, 1897), politician and soldier, was born at Eaton, Canada, of New England ancestry, the son of John Farnsworth and his wife, Sally Patten. At an early age he became a resident of Michigan, practising surveying. In 1842 he set up as a lawyer in St. Charles, Ill., and on Oct. 12, 1846, he married Mary A. Clark. He entered politics as a Democrat but after 1846 he espoused the anti-slavery cause as a supporter of Owen Lovejoy. About 1852 he moved to Chicago and in 1856 he was elected to Congress as a Republican from the 2nd or Chicago district, the Democratic *State Register* characterizing him as "a full-blown Lovejoy abolitionist" (Sept. 25, 1856). In 1858 he was reëlected from the same district. He gained the approval of his anti-slavery constituents by a resolution of inquiry into violations of provisions of the Ashburton Treaty with regard to the slave-trade (*Aurora Beacon,* Jan. 6, 1859), and by a resolution satirizing Buchanan's proposal to annex Cuba by the suggestion of annexing British America (*Belleville Advocate,* Feb. 9, 1859). He was defeated for renomination in 1860 by Isaac N. Arnold, and refused to run as an independent.

At the outbreak of the Civil War, Farnsworth raised the 8th Illinois Cavalry, which was attached to the Army of the Potomac. His nephew, Elon J. Farnsworth [*q.v.*], served under him for a time as captain. J. F. Farnsworth was promoted brigadier-general Nov. 29, 1862, but had previously commanded a cavalry brigade. He served in the Peninsular and Antietam campaigns. Disabled by severe injuries at the end of 1862, he resigned his commission and took the seat in Congress to which he had been elected in the fall. He assumed decisive ground in the Illinois campaign of 1863 on behalf of the Emancipation Proclamation. He voted for the Thirteenth Amendment and spoke for the repeal of the Fugitive-Slave Law (*Rockford Register*, July 9, 16, 1864). He was reëlected to Congress in the fall of 1864, and by virtue of successive elections served until Mar. 3, 1873. With regard to Reconstruction, he was at first one of the radicals. He spoke in favor of the Fourteenth Amendment and of the reconstruction acts. He urged the impeachment of Johnson in 1867, and took an active part in the impeachment proceedings of 1868.

The election of 1870 made it evident that Farnsworth had outstripped the sentiment of his district. His former majority of 14,000 in the election of 1870 had sunk to a plurality of 300. He was not renominated in 1872. In 1874 he contested the 4th District against Hurlbut, the Republican candidate, in a hot campaign (*Chicago Tribune*, Oct. 12 and 28, 1874), and in 1880 was mentioned as a possible Democratic candidate for governor (*Illinois State Register*, Jan. 9, 16, 1880). His political career, however, was at an end. In that year he removed to Washington where he practised law until his death, and acquired a considerable fortune in real estate.

[In addition to contemporary newspapers and the *Congressional Globe*, see Moses F. Farnsworth, *Farnsworth Memorial* (1897); *Biog. Dir. Am. Cong.* (1928); Abner Hard, *Hist. of the Eighth Cavalry Regt., Ill. Volunteers* (1868); *Chicago Tribune* and *Evening Star* (Washington), July 15, 1897.] T. C. P.

FARNUM, DUSTIN LANCY (May 27, 1874–July 3, 1929), actor, was born at Hampton Beach, N. H. The theatre was his natural heritage, for his father was Greenleaf Dustin Farnum, actor and theatrical manager, and his mother, Clara Adèle Legros, actress and opera singer. In his early childhood his parents moved to Bucksport, Me., where he attended the public schools and the East Maine Conference Seminary, a Methodist institution. He began his stage career while still at school, appearing in the summer months with Thomas Shea, and with "The Hidden Hand" Company. With these groups he did singing and dancing specialties. His first opportunity to play parts came in 1897 when he toured New England with the Ethel Tucker Repertoire Company. Then followed eighteen months with Margaret Mather, "stock" in Buffalo, two seasons with Chauncey Olcott, and a short engagement with Blanche Walsh in *Marcelle.* When *Arizona*, by Augustus Thomas, was revived with a new cast at the Academy of Music, New York, Aug. 19, 1901, Farnum made a great success in the part of Lieutenant Denton.

Because of his good work in *Arizona*, he was selected to play the title rôle in *The Virginian*, the dramatization of the book of that title. After a road tour, the play opened at the Manhattan Theatre, New York, Jan. 5, 1904, and Farnum rose from comparative obscurity to fame in a night. The production was so successful that it ran for three seasons. He next appeared in *The Ranger* by Augustus Thomas, and afterward in the short-lived *Rector's Garden* by Byron Ongley. In a long road tour in Edwin Milton Royle's *The Squaw Man* which followed, Farnum pleased critics and public alike as Jim Carston, a part previously created and played with much success by William Faversham. In *Cameo Kirby*, which had been a failure, with Nat Goodwin as star, Farnum won new laurels as a romantic actor. In January 1911, he played in a revival of *The Squaw Man.* Later in the same year he acted with his brother, William, in a Civil War melodrama, *The Littlest Rebel*, by Edward Peple. At the Lyric Theatre, New York, Apr. 28, 1913, he reappeared as Lieutenant Denton in a star revival of *Arizona.*

As public taste changed, the gun-play melodrama went out of favor. Farnum had long considered going into the motion pictures and in the fall of 1913 commenced acting before the camera. He repeated on the screen his success on the speaking stage, playing many of his former parts. Again, as with the speaking stage, the up-to-the-minute public demanded new fare. The brawny, all-virtuous hero gave way to the sophisticated youth of the "flapper" drama. The smaller towns still reveled in melodrama, however, so Farnum continued for some years in his favorite style of acting, retiring from the screen about 1925. He was admirably fitted by natural endowment for playing romantic parts, and according to the majority of his critics, he played them extremely well, excelling especially in the portrayal of Western types. He had a beautiful, "almost a poetic face," according to one critic, with large brown eyes, dark, wavy hair, and a deep resonant voice. It was inevitable that he should become a matinée idol *par excellence.*

Farnum married Agnes Muir Johnston in 1898, and was divorced from her in 1908. On Mar. 23, 1909, he married Mary Elizabeth Conwell, from whom he obtained a divorce on Aug. 18, 1924. That same year he was married to Winifred Kingston, by whom he had a daughter Estelle.

[John Parker, ed., *Who's Who in the Theatre* (1925); Walter Browne and E. De Roy Koch, eds., *Who's Who on the Stage* (1908); T. Allston Brown, *A Hist. of the N. Y. Stage*, vol. III (1903); *N. Y. Times, N. Y. Tribune*, July 5, 1929; *N. Y. Dramatic Mirror*, Jan. 8, 1910; *Variety*, July 10, 1929; clippings on Dustin Farnum in the Robinson Locke Collection in the N. Y. Pub. Lib.] L. H. F.

Farragut

FARRAGUT, DAVID GLASGOW (July 5, 1801–Aug. 14, 1870), naval officer, was the second of the five children of George Farragut [*q.v.*] and Elizabeth (Shine) Farragut and the third member of his family to enter the navy, being preceded by his father and elder brother. He was born at Campbell's Station, a few miles southwest of Knoxville, Tenn., and his name was always borne on the rolls of the navy as from that state. His paternal grandparents were Spanish, and one of his maternal grandparents was Scottish. His mother died when he was seven and he never saw his father after he was nine. The removal of his family to New Orleans in 1807 and the entrance of his father and brother into the navy were important factors in the shaping of his career. It happened that the father of Commander (later Commodore) David Porter was cared for in his last illness by the Farraguts and died at their house. Out of gratitude, Porter, then commander of the New Orleans naval station, adopted young Farragut and promised him a berth in the navy. In 1810, under the protection of his friend and guardian, he was placed in school, first in Washington and later in Chester, Pa., the home of Porter, and on Dec. 17 of that year, at the age of nine and a half, he was appointed midshipman by the secretary of the navy. Until 1814 his name was borne on the rolls of the navy as James Glasgow, and thereafter as David Glasgow, a change doubtless made in honor of his guardian.

In 1811 when Porter was given command of the frigate *Essex,* Farragut sailed with him and saw his first sea service off the coast of the United States. In the War of 1812 when the *Essex* made her memorable cruise in the Pacific Ocean, the young midshipman gave a good account of himself in the various duties that fell to him. He was made a prize master of one of the *Essex's* prizes, the *Alexander Barclay.* "This was an important event in my life," he wrote in his journal, "and when it was decided that I was to take the ship to Valparaiso, I felt no little pride at finding myself in command at twelve years of age." The cruise of the *Essex* came to an end on Mar. 28, 1814, in the harbor of Valparaiso, in her engagement with the *Phoebe* and *Cherub,* the longest and most bloody sea fight of Farragut's career. During the fight he performed the duties of captain's aide, quarter gunner, and powder boy, to the entire satisfaction of Porter, who commended him and would have recommended him for promotion had it not been for his extreme youth.

A prisoner on parole until exchanged in November 1814, Farragut was then ordered to the brig *Spark,* which was fitting for sea at New York, but before she was ready to sail the war came to an end. The years 1815–20 he spent chiefly in the Mediterranean, first on board the *Independence,* then the *Washington,* and finally the *Franklin.* These were all ships of the line and flew the broad pennant of the commander of the squadron. Farragut served as aide, successively, to Commodore Bainbridge, Commodore Chauncey, and Captain Gallagher. Engaged in routine cruising on the station, the American fleet visited the principal Mediterranean ports and gave the young midshipman an opportunity to see many places of historical interest, to enlarge his knowledge of foreign peoples, and to enjoy the social diversions of the squadron. When Charles Folsom, his naval schoolmaster, was appointed American consul to Tunis, Farragut eagerly embraced the opportunity that was happily offered to accompany Folsom to his new post and to pursue there systematically a course of studies under his direction. For nine months Farragut remained ashore, studying the French and Italian languages, English literature, and mathematics. Entering his profession with little schooling, he had to acquire knowledge as best he could. It is rather remarkable that he learned to speak French, Italian, Spanish, and Arabic. In 1826, when living in New Haven, he attended the lectures of the professors at Yale College, and later, when stationed in Washington, those at the Smithsonian Institution, missing but one in eighteen months. His chief schoolroom, however, was the quarterdeck of a ship and his chief schoolmasters were the gallant officers of the old navy, Porter, Bainbridge, and others, for whom he had throughout his life a profound admiration.

Having been made an acting lieutenant of the brig *Spark,* Farragut in 1821 was sent home from the Mediterranean to take an examination preliminary to promotion to a lieutenancy. Ignorant of unimportant naval minutiæ, he failed in the test. In a subsequent examination he passed twenty-second in a class of fifty-three. In 1822 he made a cruise on the *John Adams,* detailed to carry to Vera Cruz Joel R. Poinsett, the American minister to Mexico; and in the two following years he served with the Mosquito fleet under Commodore David Porter, who was entrusted with the difficult task of suppressing piracy in the West Indies. This service while somewhat trivial was at the same time perilous and exhausting. Farragut's first orders were to the *Grey Hound,* commanded by his brother. Later he served as executive officer of the *Sea Gull,* the flagship of the fleet, and for a time he commanded the *Ferret*—his first command of a naval vessel, the obtaining of which he regarded as an important milestone in his career. He participated in several of the encounters with the pirates and acquired a knowledge of the Gulf of Mexico and neighboring waters that was to prove useful in the Civil War.

On Sept. 24, 1823, Farragut married Susan C. Marchant of Norfolk, Va., and henceforth until 1861 made that city his home. A large part of the three decades preceding 1855, when he first became eligible for the highest commands, he spent there, on duty or leave of absence. It was a slack time in the navy and berths at sea were few and hard to obtain. Farragut made numerous requests of the Navy Department for active duty, but these were often refused, for he was not a favorite of the government, with which he had to contend for an equitable share of employment.

In 1840 his wife died after an illness of sixteen years, having been tenderly cared for by her husband, who proved himself a skilful nurse. "When Captain Farragut dies," said a Norfolk woman, who witnessed his devotion, "he should have a monument reaching to the skies made by every wife in the city contributing a stone." On Dec. 26, 1843, he married again and established another tie with Norfolk, for his second wife, Virginia Loyall, was the eldest daughter of William Loyall, a highly esteemed resident of that city and a member of a family with many naval connections.

In 1825 Farragut obtained his lieutenancy and performed his first duty in that grade on the frigate *Brandywine,* then under orders to convey Lafayette to France. In 1829–30 he served on the sloop *Vandalia* off the coast of Brazil, and early in 1833 as the executive officer of the sloop *Natchez,* when she visited Charleston, S. C., to support the federal government in its dispute with the nullifiers. Later in the same year she proceeded to the Brazil Station, where Farragut remained until 1834 when he returned home with the schooner *Boxer.* Four years later he was again at sea, this time as commander of the sloop *Erie,* with orders to proceed to Mexican waters and protect American citizens and property there, endangered by the war between Mexico and France. At Vera Cruz he observed with keen professional interest the attack and capture of the castle of San Juan de Ulloa by the French and formed definite views on the reduction of forts by naval vessels, which were serviceable when he was faced by similar tasks during the Civil War. His last sea duty in the lieutenant's grade was that of executive officer of the ship of the line *Delaware* of the Brazil Station. In 1842, while on this station, he was assigned to the command of the sloop *Decatur,* a position in keeping with the new rank of commander, which he had attained on Sept. 9, 1841.

When in 1845 the government's difficulties with Mexico became acute, Farragut requested the secretary of the navy to assign him to duties in the Gulf, urging as qualifications his long service there and his knowledge of the Spanish language and asking that he might be permitted to participate in the capture of the castle of San Juan de Ulloa, which he thought should be effected by the navy. Not until February 1847, when he was ordered to take command of the sloop *Saratoga,* was his request granted. Before he reached Vera Cruz the castle had surrendered to the army under Gen. Scott, and the officers of the navy, in the words of Farragut, "paid the penalty—not one of them will ever wear an Admiral's flag" (L. Farragut, *post,* p. 158). Acquiring, as Farragut thought, the ill will of his commodore, he was assigned unimportant blockade duties with no chance of distinguishing himself; and he became involved in a dispute with that officer over this assignment. On asking to be relieved, he was ordered home and thus ended what he regarded the most mortifying cruise of his career.

In 1850–52 Farragut was employed in Washington and Norfolk on ordnance duties, and, assisted by other officers, drew up a book of ordnance regulations. Results obtained by him while serving as assistant inspector of ordnance were published in 1854 under the title of *Experiments to ascertain the Strength and Endurance of Navy Guns.* On the outbreak of the Crimean War, he requested that he be sent to the seat of war as an official observer, but he failed to interest the department in his application. In August 1854, he was ordered to proceed to the West Coast and establish a navy-yard at Mare Island, a task of considerable difficulty, and of some privations on account of primitive living conditions. While in California, on Sept. 14, 1855, he was commissioned captain. At the end of four years he returned East by way of the Isthmus of Panama and soon after his arrival was ordered to take command of the sloop *Brooklyn* and proceed to Mexico, then in the throes of one of its periodical revolutions. His chief duty was to carry down and convey from port to port Robert McLane, the new American minister to Mexico. In October 1860 he was relieved of this command.

The winter of 1860–61 Farragut spent at Norfolk on waiting orders. He was in the sixtieth year of his age and he had been in the navy more than forty-nine years. Since 1815 only the Mexican War had offered naval officers an opportunity to win professional distinction and this Farragut had missed. There were officers lower in rank with greater professional reputation. None surpassed him, however, in the painstaking performance of duties, in acute observation of all naval matters, and in ambition for professional success. But these qualities do not always bring advancement in time of peace. Farragut was not a courtier. His independence in thought and act disqualified him as a "climber" either inside or outside of the navy. The Civil War gave him the opportunity he had long desired and for which he was thoroughly prepared.

On Apr. 17, 1861, the Virginia Convention passed an ordinance of secession and it became necessary for Farragut, living in a Virginia city, to choose between the state and the nation. On the morning of the 18th at a common meeting-place where he and his friends were wont to talk over the political news, he expressed his dissatisfaction with the action of the convention and his conviction that Lincoln was justified in calling for troops. One of his friends impatiently informed him that a person of those sentiments "could not live in Norfolk." He calmly replied, "Well, then, I can live somewhere else" (*Ibid.*, p. 204). That evening he left for the North with his family. At the village of Hastings-on-the-Hudson he secured a small cottage, resolved to remain there until called into service. As all officers of Southern descent were under suspicion, he remained unemployed until September when he was made a member of a naval board convened at the New York navy-yard to select incapacitated officers for retirement—a safe and innocuous position.

The most important step toward opening the Mississippi River, one of the major Federal objectives, was the capture of New Orleans. By the fall of 1861 the government had decided upon a naval expedition against this city, and realizing its difficulty and magnitude, sought diligently for an officer equal to the task. Among others, Farragut was considered and his action in leaving Norfolk strongly recommended him, showing, it was thought, "great superiority of character, clear perception of duty, and firm resolution in the performance of it" (Mahan, *post,* p. 123). Proceeding cautiously, the Department ordered Commander D. D. Porter to visit Farragut and sound him out. On receiving a favorable account from its emissary, it ordered him to report in Washington and at a conference held on Dec. 21, at which he showed much enthusiasm for the enterprise and confidence in its success, he was chosen to undertake it. On Jan. 9, he was formally appointed to the command of the West Gulf Blockading Squadron, whose limits were specified as extending from St. Andrew's Bay, Fla., to the Rio Grande and including the coasts of Mexico and Yucatan. His confidential orders, issued on January 20, directed him to "proceed up the Mississippi River and reduce the defenses which guard the approaches to New Orleans, when you will appear off that city and take possession of it under the guns of your squadron" (L. Farragut, *post,* 209).

On Feb. 2, 1862, Farragut sailed from Hampton Roads in the steam sloop *Hartford,* his flagship, a new vessel and one of the finest in the navy, and eighteen days later arrived at Ship Island, the naval rendezvous, about one hundred miles north-northeast of the mouth of the Mississippi. Two months elapsed before his fleet, consisting of seventeen vessels and a mortar flotilla, was ready for operations. The Confederate defenses, forty miles above the Gulf, consisted of Fort Jackson on the west side of the Mississippi, Fort St. Philip a little higher up on the east side, and a flotilla above the forts. The armament of the Unionists was inferior to that of the Confederates (Mahan, *post,* p. 128). The battle began on Apr. 18 with the bombardment of Fort Jackson by the mortar flotilla, commanded by Commander David D. Porter [*q.v.*]. This continued for several days and nights without doing any considerable damage. Farragut now reached the momentous decision to run by the forts before they were reduced—a movement contrary to the orders of the Department and the advice of some of his ablest officers. Before daylight on the 24th, the seventeen ships advanced in a line of three divisions, with Farragut leading the second division. They encountered a terrific fire and the *Hartford* narrowly escaped destruction from a fire-raft, but all but three ships passed the forts. They next engaged the Confederate flotilla and destroyed eleven of its vessels, including the ram *Manassas.* The Union fleet lost 184 men. On the day after the battle it reached New Orleans, which, being defenseless, was taken without bloodshed. On Apr. 28 Forts Jackson and St. Philip surrendered to the mortar flotilla. By his energy, audacity, and application of correct strategic principles, Farragut had won a magnificent victory, the moral effect of which abroad as well as at home was exceedingly great. His achievement made him the leading officer of the navy, a distinction which he held until his death. On July 11, 1862, the President approved a resolution of Congress tendering him and his officers and men the thanks of the nation, and on July 30, he was commissioned a rear-admiral (taking rank from July 16), the first officer in that grade.

Farragut

Had his movements been left to his own discretion, Farragut, after the capture of New Orleans, would have proceeded against the defenses of Mobile. The government at Washington however had given peremptory orders that he should open the Mississippi to the northward and join the fleet of Flag Officer Davis [*q.v.*], which in June captured Memphis. With considerable difficulty he ascended the Mississippi to Vicksburg and on June 28 ran past the defenses there, giving and receiving a heavy fire and losing forty-five men. As Vicksburg was impregnable to a naval attack, about the middle of July he returned to New Orleans. For the rest of 1862 he was chiefly employed in blockade duties. Galveston, Corpus Christi, and Sabine Pass surrendered to his ships, and by December he held the whole of the Gulf coast within the limits of his command, except for Mobile.

The year 1863 opened with several reverses on Farragut's station—the recapture of Galveston and Sabine Pass, the sinking of the *Hatteras* by the *Alabama,* and the escape of the *Florida* from Mobile. These were sore trials to the admiral, whose orders to guard the lower Mississippi held him to that part of his station. He longed for a chance to attack Mobile. "I would have had it long since, or been thrashed out of it," he wrote on Jan. 7. In March he attacked the batteries at Port Hudson and two of his vessels, the flagship and a gunboat, passed them—an achievement he ranked next to the capture of New Orleans. On Aug. 1 he sailed for New York on the *Hartford* for a brief respite from his arduous labors. He and his historic flagship, which had been struck 240 times by shot and shell, were objects of much interest in New York. The Chamber of Commerce adopted and presented to him resolutions of congratulation engrossed on parchment, and the Union League Club gave him a sword, with scabbard of gold and silver and with hilt set in brilliants.

Early in January 1864, Farragut again hoisted his flag on the *Hartford* and sailed from New York for his station in the Gulf, where a new task awaited him, the capture of the Confederate defenses in Mobile Bay. In opening the Mississippi he had shown himself a master of strategy. At Mobile Bay the problem was chiefly one of naval tactics. Would he prove himself equally proficient in this more restricted sphere? Offensive operations had to await the arrival of the necessary ironclads and the movements of the army. The entrance to Mobile Bay, thirty miles from the Gulf, was defended on its east side by Fort Morgan; and nearly three miles distant on its west side by Fort Gaines. Close under Fort Morgan was an open channel used by blockade runners. The rest of the passage was obstructed by a double row of mines, then known as "torpedoes." Farragut's fleet consisted of four ironclads and fourteen wooden ships. Early in the morning of Aug. 5 it steamed down the channel under Fort Morgan, the ironclads leading, followed by the wooden ships lashed in pairs. The *Hartford* was about the middle of the line, carrying the admiral, who had taken an elevated position in the main rigging of his ship, in order to observe the battle from the best vantage-point. At 6.45 A.M. the *Tecumseh* fired the first shot. Soon the forts answered, and then the Confederate flotilla. Off Fort Morgan the *Tecumseh* struck a torpedo and went down, carrying with her nearly all her officers and crew. The other ships fell into confusion. The *Brooklyn* in front of the *Hartford* stopped. Hesitating for a moment at this crisis in the battle, Farragut decided to go on and ordered the *Hartford* to be driven ahead at full speed. A warning cry came from the *Brooklyn,* "Torpedoes ahead!" "Damn the torpedoes!" shouted the admiral, as the *Hartford* took the lead. Her bottom scraped them as she passed over them, but none exploded, although their primers snapped. Soon the whole fleet had safely passed the forts, above which the Confederate flotilla was encountered and dispersed. The loss of the Unionists was 315; of the Confederates 157. On Aug. 7 Fort Gaines surrendered, and on the 23rd, Fort Morgan. The battle of Mobile Bay was the crowning event of Farragut's life. He had reached a position as preëminent in the American navy as that of Nelson had been in the British navy. On Dec. 23 the President approved a bill creating the office of vice-admiral and Farragut was immediately named to fill it. On July 26, 1866, he was commissioned admiral, a grade especially created for him.

Soon after the battle of Mobile Bay the Department chose Farragut to command the naval forces that were to be employed in the reduction of the defenses of Wilmington, N. C. When it learned that his health had been undermined by his long service in Southern waters, it relieved him from the new assignment and gave him a leave of absence. On Dec. 12 he reached New York and was formally received by the city, with many expressions of gratitude and admiration. A few days later some of its leading citizens presented him with a purse of $50,000 in expectation that he would buy a house in the city and reside there, which he did. Late in January 1865, an ominous threat of the Confederate forces on the James River led the Department to send Farragut to meet it. The situation proved not to be serious, and he returned to Washington. This was his last active service in the Civil War.

In April 1867, Farragut was chosen to command the European Squadron and in June he hoisted an admiral's flag on the frigate *Franklin* and sailed for the waters that he had first visited fifty years earlier when a young midshipman. It was a tour of good will. Everywhere he was received with the consideration due to his exalted rank and notable achievements. The cruise came to an end with his arrival in New York on Nov. 10, 1868. In 1869 he visited the Mare Island navy-yard which he had established shortly before the Civil War. On the return trip he suffered at Chicago a severe attack of the heart. Although he rallied, he never completely regained his health. In the summer of 1870 he sailed on the dispatch boat *Tallapoosa* to visit the commandant of the navy-yard at Portsmouth, N. H. He had a premonition that the end was approaching. As he left the ship he was heard to say, "This is the last time I shall ever tread the deck of a man-of-war" (L. Farragut, *post,* p. 541). He died at the house of the commandant in the seventieth year of his age. His body found a temporary resting place at Portsmouth. In September, at the request of the citizens of New York, it was brought to that city, arriving on the 30th, which was observed as a day of mourning. A procession which included President Grant, members of his cabinet, many naval and army officers, and ten thousand soldiers, escorted the body to a train at Forty-seventh St. Thence it was conveyed to Woodlawn Cemetery, Westchester County. Farragut left one child, Loyall Farragut, who died in 1916, leaving no children.

Physically, Farragut was of medium size—his stature about five feet, six and a half inches, and weight not over 150 pounds until late in life when he put on considerable flesh. His complexion was sallow and swarthy, with indications of his Spanish descent. In appearance he was neither handsome nor striking. Owing to much tropical service, he suffered from considerable sickness, including sun-stroke, cholera, and yellow fever. Always alert in body, he delighted in physical exercises, and was a good fencer. His superiority, however, lay chiefly in his mental and moral qualities — courage, initiative, decision, good judgment, and willingness to accept responsibility. He had great aptitude for the naval profession and a strong desire to succeed in it. Secretary Welles said that he would more willingly take risks in order to obtain great results than any other officer of high rank in either the army or the navy, and Lincoln was of the opinion that his appointment was the best made during the war (Welles, *post,* I, 230, 440).

Farragut had two absorbing interests, his profession and his family. His most revealing letters, even upon military matters, are those addressed to his wife or to his son. He was not fond of writing, least of all about his naval successes, and he wrote relatively little. One of his principles of warfare is found in his orders to his captains for passing the batteries at Port Hudson, when he said, "The best protection against the enemy's fire is a well-directed fire from our own guns" (L. Farragut, *post,* p. 316). A few days before the battle of New Orleans he wrote to his wife, "As to being prepared for defeat, I certainly am not. Any man who is prepared for defeat would be half defeated before he commenced. I hope for success; shall do all in my power to secure it, and trust to God for the rest." Before a battle he calculated thus: "I have to take this place. The chances are that I shall lose some of my vessels by torpedoes or the guns of the enemy, but with some of my fleet afloat I shall eventually be successful. I cannot lose all. I will attack regardless of consequences, and never turn back" (L. Farragut, *post,* pp. 218, 316, 544). The letters of Farragut, who late in life joined the Protestant Episcopal Church, contain many expressions of dependence upon a Higher Power. At the critical moment in the battle of Mobile Bay he offered up this prayer: "O God, who created man and gave him reason, direct me what to do. Shall I go on?" "It seemed," the Admiral said, "as if in answer a voice commanded, 'Go on!' " (Mahan, *post,* p. 277).

The most artistic memorial to Farragut is the statue of him by St. Gaudens in Madison Square, New York, given by the Farragut Monument Association and unveiled in 1881. There was also completed that year for the federal government a colossal bronze statue of him, the work of Miss Vinnie Ream, which stands in Farragut Square, Washington. In 1893 Boston erected in Marine Park a statue of him by H. H. Kitson. There is in the Naval Academy Chapel, Annapolis, a memorial window to him, a gift of the graduates of the Academy. Farragut's achievements have been celebrated in verse by Oliver Wendell Holmes, Henry Howard Brownell, and other poets. According to his son, the most satisfactory portraits are those in the Union League Club, and the University Club, New York.

[Record of Officers, Bureau of Navigation, 1810–1870; *Report of Secretary of the Navy,* 1861–65; *Official Records* (*Navy*), 1 ser., vols. XVIII–XXI; L. Farragut, *Life and Letters of David Glasgow Farragut* (1879); A. T. Mahan, *Admiral Farragut* (1892), and *The Gulf and Inland Waters* (1885); R. M. Thompson and R. Wainwright, "Confidential Correspondence of

Gustavus Vasa Fox," *Nav. Hist. Soc. Pubs.*, vol. IX (1918); *U. S. Naval Inst. Proc.*, XLIX (1923), pp. 1961–86; H. W. Wilson, *Battleships in Action* (1926), I, 13–18, 28–31; *Diary of Gideon Welles* (1911), vols. I and II; *Mag. of Hist.* (1922), vol. XXII, extra number, no. 87; J. E. Montgomery, *Our Admiral's Flag Abroad* (1869); *Mil. Order of Loyal Legion, Commandery of D. C., War Papers*, no. 98, Dec. 1916.] C. O. P.

FARRAGUT, GEORGE (Sept. 29, 1755–June 4, 1817), naval and army officer, was born in Ciudadela, the capital of Minorca, when that Spanish island was a British possession. He was the son of Anthony Ferragut and Juana Mesquida, both of Spanish extraction. For more than five centuries members of the Ferragut family had held prominent offices in Minorca in the army, the government, and the church.

George was sent to school at Barcelona but at the age of ten he went to sea and from 1765 to 1772 was employed chiefly in the Mediterranean. Toward the end of this period, while in the Russian service, he aided in the destruction of a Turkish fleet as one of the crew of a fireship that set fire to the fleet. In 1773–75 he was employed in the American seas trading chiefly between Havana and Vera Cruz. In the latter year at New Orleans on hearing of the difficulties between Great Britain and her colonies, he resolved to devote his life and fortune to the service of the Americans. Proceeding to Port-au-Prince he exchanged his cargo for cannon, arms, and ammunition and sailed for Charleston, S. C., where he arrived in 1776. Following a period of service as a lieutenant on a privateer, he was appointed, in 1778, a first lieutenant in the South Carolina navy. After superintending the construction of some of the galleys of that state, he was given the command of one of them and going to sea fought a severe action in the Savannah River.

In 1779 Farragut assisted at the defense of Savannah and in the following year was actively employed at the siege of Charleston, on the fall of which city he was taken prisoner. When exchanged he went to sea on board a privateer and in an engagement had his right arm badly shattered by a musket ball. The use of his arm he never fully recovered. Giving up sea service he made his way to Gen. Marion's headquarters, where he acted as a volunteer. He also served in that capacity at the battle of Cowpens. Then, proceeding to Wilmington, N. C., he was appointed by Gov. Nash of that state to the command of a company of volunteer artillery, which took part in the battle of Beaufort Bridge. When Cornwallis invaded North Carolina, Farragut raised a company of volunteer cavalry with which he harassed the rear of the army of the enemy as it marched into Virginia. The state of North Carolina made him a captain of cavalry and for his military services he received the thanks of Gen. Marion and of the governor of South Carolina.

After the Revolution Farragut earned a livelihood as a mariner until 1792 when Gen. Blount, governor of the Southwest Territory, invited him to take up his residence in Knoxville and appointed him a major of militia. In 1793 he served under Gen. Sevier in an expedition against the Cherokees. Farragut remained in Tennessee until 1807 when President Jefferson made him a sailing master in the navy, and in that year he removed to New Orleans and took command of a naval gunboat. In 1811 he was ordered to the Bay of Pascagoula, Miss., near which he had a large plantation. He was in the navy until discharged, Mar. 25, 1814. His last military service was performed at the battle of New Orleans.

In 1795 Farragut married Elizabeth Shine (1765–1808), who was born in Dobbs County, N. C. Of this union five children were born, the two eldest of whom, William A. C. and David G. Farragut [*q.v.*], were officers in the navy. Farragut died at Point Plaquet, West Pascagoula, Miss. He was a man of courage, a restless adventurer, "by profession a mariner," a fit sire for a great naval officer.

["Memorial of Geo. Farragut to Sec. of the Navy Wm. Jones, May 20, 1814," found in Miscellaneous Letters, vol. IV, no. 57, U. S. Navy Dept.; Loyall Farragut, *Life and Letters of David Glasgow Farragut* (1879), pp. 1–10.] C. O. P.

FARRAR, EDGAR HOWARD (June 20, 1849–Jan. 6, 1922), lawyer, for more than forty years an outstanding figure in the legal and political life of Louisiana, and New Orleans, was born at Concordia, La., the son of Thomas Prince and Anna (Girault) Farrar. He spent his early life in the Mississippi Delta and attended school in Baton Rouge, proceeding thence to the University of Virginia, where he graduated with the degree of M.A. in 1871. He then studied law at the University of Louisiana, was admitted to the bar in 1872, and commenced practise in New Orleans. Giving special attention to municipal and corporation law, he quickly established himself as an authority on those subjects, and in 1878 became assistant city attorney, being appointed city attorney two years later. In 1882, he was appointed by Paul Tulane [*q.v.*] one of the trustees of the fund to establish a university in Louisiana and for years thereafter devoted much of his time to the furtherance of the project. Meanwhile, induced by his experiences as city attorney, he turned his attention to municipal reform. He assisted in the organization and for many years was chairman of the Executive Committee of One Hundred established for the purpose of reforming the city government of New Orleans. He instigated and was one of the most active participants in the movement which resulted in the adoption and installation of an up-to-date sewerage and water system, and revolutionized the health statistics of the city, also drafting the legislation under the provisions of which the new system was constructed and operated. In 1890 during the Mafia agitation he was chairman of the Committee of Safety organized to bring the murderers of Chief-of-Police Hennessy to justice. He was also one of the leaders of the movement which opposed and defeated the proposition to prolong the charter of the Louisiana state lottery. Till within a short time of the campaign preceding the presidential election of 1896, though a strong Democrat, he had not participated to any extent in national politics, but on the nomination of W. J. Bryan he helped to organize the National Democracy or "Gold Democrats," was appointed temporary chairman of the Gold Democratic Convention held at Indianapolis, where he made a speech on the currency question which attracted national attention, and was active in procuring the nomination of John M. Palmer for the presidency. He also participated vigorously in the electoral campaign which followed. In 1906 he was appointed president of the Louisiana Tax Commission, and retained that position for two years. In 1907 he again became a national figure through his celebrated letter to President Roosevelt, drawing attention to the "post roads clause" of the United States Constitution and maintaining that under this clause the federal government had plenary power to enact legislation for the purpose of controlling both interstate and intrastate railroads. His contention was the subject of bitter criticism throughout the country to which he replied in a pamphlet (*The Post Road Power in the Federal Constitution*, 1907) which, in legal circles, was considered a masterly production. In 1910 he was retained as counsel for Edward Hines in the Lorimer Investigation. At the request of Gov. Hall in 1912, he drafted a revision of the state laws affecting corporations, which aroused the vehement opposition of the corporate interests as too radical, and it failed of passage in the legislature. In the following year he prepared the Tax Reform Amendment to the state constitution which has been termed "the greatest practical scheme of taxation and assessment written in America," but his advanced views did not commend themselves to the people and the proposed amendment was decisively defeated. He was associate counsel with S. Untermeyer for the Pujo Congressional Investigating Committee in 1912–13.

Farrar was essentially a corporation lawyer and held a general retainer from some of the largest organizations in the state. Perhaps the outstanding feature of his legal career was the preparation of the ordinances and contracts required in connection with the consolidation of the New Orleans street railways, which he carried to a successful conclusion, contrary to the universal opinion that it was impossible to reconcile the numerous conflicting interests involved. "Practically all of the important bond legislation in the state for a period of forty years was handled by him or through him" (*American Bar Association Journal*, January 1922, p. 12). Despite his corporation connections, however, he had wide sympathies, and consistently supported all measures having for their object the betterment of the people and improvement of the law. Other pamphlet publications of his were: *The Legal Remedy for Plutocracy* (1902), and *State and Federal Quarantine Powers* (1905). He died at Biloxi, Miss. His wife was Lucinda Davis Stamps of New Orleans, whom he married in 1878.

[H. P. Dart, *Edward Howard Farrar* (1922); "The Farrar Familv" in *Va. Mag. of Hist. and Biog.*, vols. VII–X (1899–1903); *La. Bar Asso. Report*, 1922, p. 197; *Lawyer and Banker*, Feb. 1913.] H. W. H. K.

FARRAR, JOHN (July 1, 1779–May 8, 1853), mathematician, physicist, astronomer, was the son of Deacon Samuel and Mary (Hoar) Farrar of Lincoln, Mass., formerly part of Concord. He graduated from Harvard College with the degree of B.A. in 1803, older than most of his classmates. Feeling that he had a call to the ministry, he then proceeded to Andover Theological Seminary, but in 1805 decided to return to Harvard as a tutor in Greek. A year later he received the degree of M.A. and in 1807 he was made Hollis Professor of mathematics and natural philosophy. This position he held until 1836, when he resigned because of ill health. He was elected a fellow of the American Academy of Arts and Sciences in 1808 and was its recording secretary, 1811–23, member of the committee on publications, 1828–29, and vice-president, 1829–31. He was twice married: first, to Lucy Maria Buckminster of Portsmouth, N. H., and second, to Eliza Ware Rotch (1791–1870), writer of numerous books for the young. He received the honorary degree of LL.D. from Brown University in 1833. He died at Cambridge, Mass.

Farrar wrote numerous articles for the *Transactions* of the American Academy of Arts and Sciences, and various monographs of meteorology and astronomy. He did much to make the astronomical and elementary mathematical literature of Europe known in America, translating or adapting the arithmetic of Lacroix (1818), the algebras of Euler (1818) and Lacroix (1825), the spherical trigonometry of Lacroix and Bézout (1820), the geometry of Legendre (2nd ed., 1825), *Elements of Electricity* (1826) and *An Experimental Treatise on Optics* (1826) from the *Précis Élémentaire de Physique* of Biot, the astronomy of Biot (1827), and a tract on comets from Arago (1832). He also wrote *An Elementary Treatise on the Application of Trigonometry to Projection, Mensuration, Navigation, and Surveying* (1822); and *An Elementary Treatise on Mechanics* (1825). He was not a man of much genius, but he had a gift for exposition and a knowledge of French scientific literature that enabled him to be of service to American schools.

[Brief mention in S. A. Eliot, *A Hist. of Cambridge, Mass.* (1913); Josiah Quincy, *Hist. of Harvard Univ.* (1840); *Andover Theol. Sem. Gen. Cat.* (1909); *Hist. Cat. Brown Univ.* (1914); *Quinquennial Cat. of Harvard Univ.* (1925); official letters received in reply to questions.]
D. E. S.

FARRAR, TIMOTHY (Mar. 17, 1788–Oct. 27, 1874), jurist, author, traced his descent from Jacob Farrar, who came from England to America about 1650 and settled at Lancaster, Mass. He was born at New Ipswich, N. H., being the only son of Timothy Farrar, a major in the Revolutionary War, who for more than forty years served in the court of common pleas and the supreme court of New Hampshire. The father settled at New Ipswich in 1770 and on Oct. 14, 1779, married Anna, daughter of Capt. Edmund Bancroft of Pepperell. The younger Timothy was educated at Phillips Academy, Andover, Mass., and at Groton, Mass., entering Dartmouth College in 1803, where he graduated in 1807. He then studied law with Daniel Webster at Portsmouth, N. H., and, on his admission to the Rockingham bar at Exeter in 1810, commenced practise in his home town. In 1813, however, at the solicitation of Webster he became the latter's partner and removed to Portsmouth. When Webster established himself at Boston in 1816, Farrar continued to practise alone at Portsmouth, and in 1817 married Sarah, daughter of William Adams of that town. Five years later he was appointed secretary, treasurer, and librarian at Dartmouth College and took up residence at Hanover, where he also practised his profession. In 1824 he was appointed judge of the New Hampshire court of common pleas, a position which he held until the abolition of the court in 1833. His enforced retirement was a matter of regret to the community since he had exhibited great judicial qualifications, his written decisions being models of logical reasoning, his charges to the jury distinguished for their clarity, and his demeanor on the bench always dignified. On his retirement he resumed practise at Portsmouth, but in 1836 removed to Exeter where he engaged in financial business. In 1844 he took up his residence in Boston, and there passed the remainder of his life, engaging in various business enterprises in addition to an extensive law practise and much literary and historical work. As a legislative draftsman he was considered preëminent. Much of the more intricate legislative work of his period, not only in New Hampshire but in adjoining states, he put into its final form. In 1854 he represented the City of Boston in the General Court. He died at Mount Bowdoin, Boston.

In 1819 Farrar published a *Report of the case of the Trustees of Dartmouth College against William H. Woodward,* which contains the only report of the argument of Jeremiah Mason. He himself was of counsel with Webster in the suit. He compiled a *Memoir of the Farrar Family* (n.d.) for private circulation, and was also the author of a *Review of the Dred Scott Decision* (1857), and a *Manual of the Constitution of the United States* (1867). The latter was a remarkable book considering the advanced age at which he wrote it. He was a frequent contributor to the newspapers and periodicals of his time, particularly the *North American Review,* and *New Englander.* Samuel Lee, who knew him intimately, says that as a scholar he was learned rather than brilliant, and that as a lawyer he was preëminently a safe adviser. However, in his opinions, which he never hesitated to express, he was always positive, not to say aggressive.

[Timothy Farrar, *Memoir of the Farrar Family* (n.d.); Samuel Lee, "Timothy Farrar, LL.D.," in *New-Eng. Hist. and Geneal. Reg.,* July 1875; F. Kidder and A. A. Gould, *Hist. of New Ipswich* (1852), p. 358; C. H. Bell, *The Bench and Bar of N. H.* (1894), p. 356.]
H. W. H. K.

FARRER, HENRY (Mar. 23, 1843–Feb. 24, 1903), etcher, landscape-painter, was born in London, England, the son of a miniaturist, Thomas Farrer. He came to America in 1863. Little is known of his youth, though he was probably in moderate circumstances, since he was mainly self-taught. Upon reaching this country, he established his studio in New York City and painted in both oil and water-color. He made his home in Brooklyn, where he lived until his death. He did some landscapes, chiefly of scenes near the coast, but eventually became most widely known as an etcher, being one of the first and most prolific in America. He exhibited in London, Paris, and New York, and took an active interest in various art organizations. He was a member of the Artists' Fund Society, secretary of the American Water Color Society in 1879 and president of the New York Etching Club in 1881. In the following year he was elected fellow of the Royal Society of Painter-Etchers, London, and in 1885 was made honorary member of the Philadelphia Society of Painter-Etchers. If any question exists regarding the validity of his claim to being an American artist, it may be emphasized that his art follows closely that of his adopted country.

Farrer's work offers an interesting study of his development in technique. His early work was rather detailed and elaborate, but later gained a simplicity and freedom which indicated far greater power. His first serious attempts at etching were made about 1868, with a press and tools which he himself had made. He was obliged, however, to follow more lucrative pursuits until 1877, the year of the formation of the etching club. "The Old Tree," etched in 1872, retouched in 1877, indicates his early tendency to over-elaboration, and reflects, in general, his pre-Raphaelite sympathies. The work of 1877 shows greater skill, but the same deliberate and methodical characteristics. Two beautiful examples of this period and style are "A Cloudy Day" and "A November Day." "Chickens" (1877) and "The Washerwoman" (1877) mark a growing freedom and generous use of the dry-point. "Winter in the Woods," (1878) in which his representation of light and air is excellent, and "December," (1877) which is the largest etching in this class, are both noteworthy in the further development of his style. After this he gradually diminished the use of artificial printing and the dry-point, and placed more emphasis on the etched line. Some of his later etchings are exquisite and masterful. They are not only examples of a fine technique, but display rare individuality and charm.

Farrer's works in other mediums are also worthy of mention. His oil-paintings include: "A Quiet Pool" (1878); "Sunset—Gowanus Bay"; "Road to the Landing" (1881); "Winter," "Autumn" (1882); "Now Came Still Evening On" (1883); and "Sweet Restful Eve" (1884). Two of his best water-colors are "Sunset," and "When the Silver Habit of Clouds Comes Down upon the Autumn Sun" (1884). He sent "A Windy Day" (belonging to Dr. J. G. Holland) and "The Old House on the Hill" to the American Centennial Exhibition of 1876. In 1878 he exhibited "A Quiet Pool" (belonging to Robert Gordon) at the Paris Exposition and also at the National Academy of Design.

[C. E. C. Waters and L. Hutton, *Artists of the Nineteenth Century and Their Works*, I (1879), 247; J. D. Champlin, Jr., *Cyc. of Painters and Paintings*, II (1886), 42; *Am. Art. Ann.*, 1903, p. 140; *Who's Who in America*, 1901–02; *N. Y. Evening Mail*, Feb. 14, 1872; *N. Y. Tribune*, Apr. 19, 1878; *Am. Art Rev.*, Dec. 1879; *Mich. State Lib. Biog. Sketches of Am. Artists* (5th ed., 1924).] J. M. H.

FARWELL, CHARLES BENJAMIN (July 1, 1823–Sept. 23, 1903), man of business, and politician, was born at Mead Creek, near Painted Post, Steuben County, N. Y. Descended from Henry Farwell who was made a freeman of Massachusetts Bay, Mar. 14, 1639, he was the second son of Henry and Nancy (Jackson) Farwell, who were married at Westminster, Mass., on Oct. 5, 1819. He received his early education at Elmira Academy. In 1838 his family removed to Illinois, settling in Mount Morris, Ill., the following year. There he worked as farm-hand and surveyor. In 1844 he removed to Chicago, where he found employment as clerk in various mercantile concerns. Successful real-estate speculation laid the foundation of his fortune. He had probably been financially interested in the mercantile transactions of his brother, John V. Farwell [*q.v.*], for some time before he became a member of the firm of John V. Farwell & Company, dealers in dry-goods, in 1865. To Charles B. Farwell was attributed the completion of the Washington Street tunnel in Chicago.

He had early become interested in politics and served as clerk of Cook County from 1853 to 1861. In 1870, as a Republican, he was elected to Congress over John Wentworth in a closely contested campaign. He was reëlected in 1872, and was unseated in 1876 as a result of a contested election in 1874 (*Chicago Tribune*, May 4, 1876). He was elected once more in 1880 and, on Jan. 19, 1887, was elected to the Senate to fill the vacancy left by the death of John A. Logan but was not returned in 1891 because of the reaction against the McKinley Tariff and the activity of the Farmers' Alliance in Illinois politics. In Congress he played no very active part. The only subjects in which apparently he took any interest were the currency and banking, but his speeches display no particular insight into the question. His rôle was that of a keen politician rather than that of a statesman. In 1870, the *Chicago Tribune* had opposed him as the leader of the "Tammany" of Cook County, alleging corruption against him (Oct. 24, Nov. 1, Nov. 7, 1870). On Feb. 25, 1875, the *Tribune* assailed him for dodging a vote on what it termed a "tax grabbing, whiskey ring measure" in the House. In

1880, as the Blaine leader in the state, he endeavored to manipulate the county and state conventions in such a way as to defeat Logan in the choice of a Grant delegation. He was beaten by Logan in the struggle in the state convention and, apparently, had no decisive part in the later choice of anti-Grant delegates to the national convention (*Chicago Tribune,* May 15, 1880; *Illinois State Register,* May 22, 1880). In the senatorial election of 1885, the Democrats switched their votes to him in a last effort to stave off the election of John A. Logan (*Chicago Tribune,* May 20, 1885). In 1889–90 he quarreled with President Harrison over the patronage.

Farwell was married on Oct. 11, 1852, to Mary Eveline Smith of South Williamstown, Mass. Four of their nine children reached maturity, and their oldest daughter, Anna, married Reginald de Koven [*q.v.*], the composer. After 1870 Farwell's residence was fixed at Lake Forest, Ill., where he was active in the establishment of Lake Forest University and where his death occurred in his eighty-first year.

[A. T. Andreas, *Hist. of Chicago* (3 vols., 1884–86), esp. vols. II, III; *Reminiscences of John V. Farwell, by His Elder Daughter* (2 vols., 1928); Anna F. de Koven, *A Musician and his Wife* (1926); D. P. and F. K. Holton, *Farwell Ancestral Memorial* (1879), corrected and supplemented by *The Farwell Family* (2 vols., 1929); *Biog. Dir. Am. Cong.* (1928); *Congressional Record* and newspapers as cited.] T. C. P.

FARWELL, JOHN VILLIERS (July 29, 1825–Aug. 20, 1908), merchant, the son of Henry and Nancy (Jackson) Farwell, was born in Steuben County, N. Y. Later the family moved to a farm near Big Flats in Chemung County, and when John was thirteen years old, they emigrated in a covered wagon to a squatter's homestead about a hundred miles southwest of Chicago, in Ogle County, Ill. When he was nineteen, after three years of farm work with attendance at Mount Morris Seminary in the winter, young Farwell determined to go to Chicago to follow a commercial life. He worked his way into town on a load of wheat, with $3.45 in his pocket. He had acquired the elements of bookkeeping at the seminary but his first employment was in the office of his uncle, the county clerk. Besides his duties as clerk, for which he received twelve dollars a month, he reported the proceedings of the City Council for a weekly newspaper. These reports seem to have been altogether too literal, with resulting embarrassment to the council. As one chronicler put it, "what was fun to the town was mortification to the Councilmen" (*Biographical Sketches of the Leading Men of Chicago,* 1868, p. 92). He next took employment as salesman and bookkeeper with a dry-goods firm at eight dollars a month, remaining in this position one year, then became a clerk for Hamlin & Day, a similar firm, at $250 a year. After four years without increase of salary, he transferred his services in 1849 to Wadsworth & Phelps, a wholesale dry-goods house, at a yearly stipend of $600. This was the beginning of success; he remained with the firm as salesman and partner until, by a succession of changes in personnel, it became John V. Farwell & Company.

In the spring of 1849 he had married Abigail Gates Taylor, a former schoolmate, who died in May 1851. In that year Farwell was admitted to partnership in the firm, which had become Cooley, Wadsworth & Company, and three years later, in 1854, he married Emeret Cooley, a sister of his partner. Wadsworth retired in 1862 and the firm was reorganized as Cooley, Farwell & Company, the "company" being young Marshall Field [*q.v.*], who had come to Chicago in 1856 and had been employed as a clerk by Cooley, Wadsworth & Company. When Cooley retired in 1864, the name of the organization became Farwell, Field & Company, and Levi Z. Leiter and S. N. Kellogg were admitted to partnership. This arrangement had continued but a single year when opportunity knocked at the door of Field and Leiter in the form of an offer from Potter Palmer to take over his retail dry-goods business in Chicago. With their departure from the firm, Farwell brought in his two brothers W. D. and Charles B. Farwell [*q.v.*], in 1865, to form the firm of John V. Farwell & Company, of which he remained president until his death.

Farwell had foreseen the commercial destiny of Chicago and had boldly expanded his business in anticipation of an enlarged market. In 1851 the firm had sales of $100,000 a year; by 1868 sales were ten millions. The new store was burned in 1870 and no sooner was it rebuilt than it was again destroyed by the Great Fire of 1871, but Farwell rebuilt on a yet larger scale, with unwavering faith in the future growth of the city. This faith was rewarded by the amassing of a very considerable fortune. John V. Farwell & Company remained the leading wholesale dry-goods firm in Chicago until displaced from that position by Marshall Field & Company.

Typical of the pioneer of New England stock, Farwell was enterprising, industrious, and shrewd in business affairs, but dominated in his inner life by a puritanical moral code and a religious fervor. He gave fifty of his first year's earnings of ninety-six dollars to help build the first Methodist church in Chicago. In 1856 he started the Illinois Street Mission to promote the welfare of boys in the city. Having come under the influence of the revivalist, Dwight L. Moody [*q.v.*], he interested himself with Moody in the revival meetings of 1857–58. Through Moody's influence he gave the land for the first Y. M. C. A. building in Chicago, which was also the first of the association's buildings in the country. He also contributed liberally to the Moody Bible Institute. During the Civil War he was president of the Chicago Branch of the United States Christian Commission, organized to promote the spiritual and temporal welfare of the officers and men of the army and navy. In this connection he visited the front, making numerous talks to the soldiers in the camps. So interested was he in Moody's work that he followed him to London in 1867 where Moody was preaching to London's poor. There he met Hogg and Bernardo who were doing rescue work in the slums and also made the acquaintance of George Williams, the father of the Y. M. C. A. Before returning home he visited Glasgow and Edinburgh to see the results of Moody's work. He participated but slightly in the political life of his community. As presidential elector, he cast his vote for Lincoln, and under Grant's administration he served as Indian commissioner. He died in Chicago in his eighty-fourth year.

[*Some Recollections of John V. Farwell* (1911), by his son, John V. Farwell, Jr., and *Reminiscences of John V. Farwell, by His Elder Daughter* (2 vols., 1928), are based on Farwell's unpublished diaries covering the years 1848–51. These diaries are in the library of the Chicago Hist. Soc. Biographical sketches appear in Geo. W. Smith, *Hist. of Ill. and Her People* (1927), IV, 355, and in D. P. and F. K. Holton, *Farwell Ancestral Memorial* (1879), corrected and supplemented by *The Farwell Family* (2 vols., 1929). The *Chicago Daily News* and *Chicago Tribune* of Aug. 21, 1908, have valuable obituaries.] E. A. D.

FASSETT, CORNELIA ADÈLE STRONG (Nov. 9, 1831–Jan. 4, 1898), portrait and figure painter, was born in Owasco, Cayuga County, N. Y., the daughter of Captain Walter and Elizabeth (Gonsales) Strong. On Aug. 26, 1851, at the age of twenty, she married Samuel Montague Fassett, a photographer and artist of Chicago, Ill. She received instruction in water-color painting from J. B. Wandesforde, an English artist, in New York City, then studied crayon drawing and painting in oil under Castiglione, La Tour, and Matthieu during a subsequent three years' sojourn in Paris and Rome. For twenty years she pursued her art career in Chicago, near the end of which time she was elected a member of the Chicago Academy of Design. In 1875 she moved to Washington, D. C., where she was elected to membership in the Washington Art Club and where her studio entertainments became a notable feature of the social life of the city. Her works include numerous portraits in miniature and many in oils. Among the studies painted from life were those of Presidents Grant, Hayes, and Garfield; Vice-President Henry Wilson, said to be one of the most successful for which he ever sat; Charles Foster, then governor of Ohio (now in the State House at Columbus); Dr. Rankin, the president of Howard University, and many other prominent people of Chicago and Washington. Unquestionably, her outstanding work is her representation, in oils, of "The Florida Case before the Electoral Commission" (Feb. 5, 1877), painted from life sittings in the United States Supreme Court-room. It was purchased by Congress and now hangs in the eastern gallery of the Senate wing of the Capitol. It is a large canvas, showing the old Senate-chamber, now the Supreme Court-room, with William M. Evarts the central figure as he addressed the Court in the opening argument. Around him are grouped some two hundred and sixty men and women, well-known figures in the political, social, and journalistic life of Washington at that period. The picture is considered unique because each face is turned in such a way as to present an individual portrait, and the likenesses are so faithful as to be striking in so large a composition. Mrs. Fassett devoted her last years to miniature painting, at which she was very successful. She died suddenly, of heart-failure, in her sixty-eighth year.

[*Am. Art Ann.*, 1898, p. 31; C. E. C. Waters, *Women in the Fine Arts* (1904), p. 121; C. E. C. Waters and Laurence Hutton, *Artists of the Nineteenth Century and Their Works*, I (1879), 248; B. W. Dwight, *Hist. of the Descendants of Elder John Strong* (1871), II, 1484, 1486; *Washington Post*, Jan. 5, 1898.] J. M. H.

FASSETT, JACOB SLOAT (Nov. 13, 1853–Apr. 21, 1924), lawyer, congressman, financier, was born in Elmira, N. Y., the son of Newton Pomeroy Fassett and Martha Ellen (Sloat) Fassett. His mother's father was Jacob Sloat, of Sloatsburg, builder of the first cotton-twine factory in the United States; his father's forebears were originally residents of Vermont. He was educated in the public schools of his native city and in 1871 matriculated at the University of Rochester, from which institution he was graduated four years later with honors. He then took up the study of law in his father's law office in Elmira, and gained admission to the bar as an attorney in 1878 and as a counselor in 1879. After brief service as district attorney for Chemung County, he continued his studies at the University of Heidelberg (1880–81), then returned to the practise of law in Elmira. His interest in politics led to his election, in 1883, to the state Senate, to which he was returned by overwhelming majorities at the three successive elections, serving until 1891. He soon rose to great prominence as chairman of the Senate committees on commerce and navigation and on insurance, and more especially as head of the committee on cities, known at that time as the "Fassett committee" because of its investigation which unearthed notorious evidence of corruption in the departments of New York City (*Testimony, Senate Committee on Cities,* 1890, 2 vols.). In 1891, as a result of the enthusiastic support of the "young Republican" element, he received his party's nomination for governor against the wishes of Platt, who, fearing that Fassett would have to carry the entire weight of his unpopularity, sponsored the candidacy of Andrew D. White (Platt, *post,* p. 216; White, *post,* I, 232–34). He waged an aggressive campaign in which he exposed the corruption under the Hill administration. His defeat at the hands of his Democratic opponent, Roswell P. Flower, by a plurality of about 40,000, was attributed to the opposition of organized labor, to his inability to rid himself entirely of responsibility for allowing the World's Fair to go to Chicago, and to his failure to throw off the stigma of being known as "Platt's man." When refused the nomination in 1894, because of Platt's opposition, he rejected the offer of second place on the state ticket.

Fassett entered national politics in 1880 when he was sent as a delegate to the Republican National Convention at Chicago. From 1888 to 1892 he served as secretary of the Republican National Committee. Appointed by President Harrison to the office of collector of the port of New York, he served for a month and a half in 1891 before entering the gubernatorial campaign. As temporary chairman of the Republican National Convention at Minneapolis in 1892, he sounded the keynote of the campaign. In 1904 he was elected to Congress where he served his district until 1911. Here his characteristic aggressiveness and fearlessness were tempered by party regularity. From 1879 until 1896, as editor and proprietor of the *Elmira Advertiser,* he exhibited in his columns, at least in the later period, symptoms of revolt from the Platt machine in the state.

In later life Fassett devoted himself chiefly to his large business enterprises. As a result of his marriage, Feb. 13, 1879, to Jennie L. Crocker, daughter of Judge E. B. Crocker of Sacramento, Cal., he became extensively interested in Western ranching, mining, and banking. As a banker he was associated with the Second National Bank of Elmira and the Commercial State Bank of Sioux City, Iowa; as a ranch owner he had important interests in New Mexico. He held important mining concessions in Korea and a controlling interest in the exploitation of the hardwood resources of the Philippine Islands. He also had large lumber holdings in Canada, and North Carolina and was financially interested in the manufacture of typewriters and of bottles. He died in Vancouver, B. C., on his return from a business trip to the Orient.

[*Who's Who in America,* 1924–25; C. E. Fitch, *Encyc. of Biog. of N. Y.,* IV (1916), 343–45; *Biog. Directory Am. Cong.,* 1928; De A. S. Alexander, *Four Famous New Yorkers* (1923); T. C. Platt, *The Autobiog. of Thomas Collier Platt* (1910); A. D. White, *The Autobiog. of Andrew Dickson White* (2 vols. 1905); *Sun* (N. Y.), Oct. 8, 9, 22, and Nov. 4, 1891; *N. Y. Times,* Jan. 8, 1904, for Fassett's interests in Korea; N. Y. papers for Apr. 22, 1924.] R. B. M.

FAULK, ANDREW JACKSON (Nov. 26, 1814–Sept. 4, 1898), third governor of Dakota Territory, was born at Milford, Pike County, Pa. In 1815 his parents, John and Margaret (Heiner) Faulk, moved to Kittanning, in Armstrong County, where Andrew received his education in the subscription schools and Kittanning Academy. Later he learned the printing trade, then studied law under Michael Gallagher and Joseph Buffington, though he was not admitted to the bar until 1866. In 1835 he married Charlotte McMath, of Washington County, Pa. Faulk essayed a crusader's rôle in local politics early in life, first through the medium of the *Armstrong County Democrat,* which he edited and published from 1837 to 1841, and then by means of various county offices which he held from 1840 to 1860. He attacked the Pennsylvania law permitting imprisonment for debt and gave active support to Thaddeus Stevens's free-school program. Because of his opposition to the further extension of slavery in the territories, he became an advocate of Col. Samuel Black's anti-slavery resolution in the Democratic state convention at Pittsburgh in 1849, and following its repudiation by the succeeding convention, he shifted from the Democratic to the newly formed Republican party. In 1861 he was appointed by President Lincoln post-trader to the Yankton Indian reservation, on the Missouri River, which at the time was the principal supply base for the military stations and Indian agencies in the upper Missouri country. His work at the post was important, for his tactful and honest policy in dealing with the professedly friendly Yankton Indians did much to prevent their alliance with the hostile Santee Sioux to make war on the whites while the federal troops were occupied in the Civil War. From 1864 to 1866 Faulk was again in Pennsylvania. There he assisted in organizing and superintending the Latonia Coal Company of New York, and promoted the Paxton Oil Company of Pittsburgh.

In 1866 he returned to Dakota as territorial governor and superintendent of Indian affairs, by virtue of President Johnson's appointment. During his two-year term of office he aided the geologist, E. N. Hayden, in calling attention to the mineral resources to be found in the Black Hills by bringing the Black Hills question before the territorial legislature, and by inducing that body to appeal to Congress for help in recovering the region from the Indians. As an advisory member of Gen. Sherman's commission which negotiated the treaty of Fort Laramie, establishing the Indians west of the Missouri River, Faulk aided in opening the Black Hills to white settlers. His policy aimed at peace with the Indians and in achieving that end he showed an unusual knowledge of Indian affairs. After retiring from the governorship he continued to reside at Yankton until his death. He was at various times mayor and alderman of Yankton, United States court commissioner, clerk of the territorial courts for the second judicial district, and for many years president of the Dakota bar association.

[*Press and Dakotan* (Yankton, S. D.), Sept. 8, 1898; (S. D.) *Memorial and Biog. Record* (1897), pp. 223–35; *S. D. Hist. Colls.*, I (1902), 135; *Monthly South Dakotan*, July 1898; *House Jour. . . . of the Legislative Assembly of the Territory of Dakota*, 1866–69, *passim*.] T. D. M.

FAULKNER, CHARLES JAMES (July 6, 1806–Nov. 1, 1884), congressman, diplomat, soldier, was born at Martinsburg, Va. (now W. Va.). His father, Maj. James Faulkner, received the special thanks of the General Assembly of Virginia for his gallant defense of Craney Island, near Norfolk, in the War of 1812. His mother, Sarah Mackey, was the daughter of Capt. William Mackey of the Revolutionary army. Left an orphan at the age of eight years, Faulkner later attributed his success to the discipline of his early struggles. He was graduated in 1822 from Georgetown University, Washington, D. C., attended Chancellor Tucker's law lectures at Winchester, Va., was admitted to the bar in 1829, and soon became a successful practitioner at Martinsburg.

First elected to the House of Delegates in 1829, he served there also in 1831–34. In 1832 he took part in the slavery debate of that period in Virginia, urging the expediency of gradual abolition. In the same year he was appointed by Gov. John Floyd [*q.v.*] as commissioner on the part of Virginia to adjust the boundary dispute between that state and Maryland, and he was largely responsible for the satisfactory solution of the question. In the session of 1833 he made two speeches in the General Assembly, condemning the South Carolina doctrine of nullification but in other respects supporting the state-rights views of Calhoun. In this year he was married to Mary Wagner Boyd, daughter of Gen. Elisha Boyd, and retired to private life, but in 1838 was elected to the state Senate and served till 1842, when he again retired to resume his law practise. In 1843 he was a prominent advocate of the annexation of Texas, and early favored the Mexican War, offering his services to the governor before the declaration of war, and promising that no one who fought in this conflict should want as long as his purse lasted. He stated that if Congress did not offer a bounty he would give every man from Berkeley County who enlisted and won an honorable discharge 150 acres of land in Texas. His speech in 1848 on violations of the federal compact made his name well-known throughout the South. He was a member of the noted Virginia constitutional convention of 1850, and in this same year was elected to Congress, serving in the House of Representatives from 1851 to 1859.

Appointed by President Buchanan minister to France in 1859 he rendered notable service there, securing the recognition by France of the American citizenship of former French citizens. After the beginning of the Lincoln administration Faulkner returned to the United States and was arrested Aug. 12, 1861, on the ground that Virginia was prosecuting a treasonable insurrection and that his sympathies were given to the conspirators. No charges to this effect were ever officially investigated, and in December 1861 he was exchanged for Alfred Ely, a congressman from New York. He then entered the Confederate army and served as assistant adjutant-general on the staff of Stonewall Jackson. In this position he prepared the official battle reports from Jackson's rough notes. After the war, he returned to his home in Berkeley County (now in West Virginia) and resumed his law practise, one of the largest in the South. He was an extensive farmer, president of the Berkeley County Agricultural and Mechanical Association and of the Martinsburg & Potomac Railroad. He was temporary president of the West Virginia constitutional convention of 1872 and was an influential figure in the framing of the constitution of that year. He was elected as a Democrat to the Forty-fourth Congress (1875–77) but declined reëlection. He continued active in the legal profession till his death, at the age of seventy-eight.

[In addition to the brief sketch in the *Biog. Directory Am. Cong.* (1928), there are longer articles in *The South in the Building of the Nation*, XI (1909), and in *Frank Leslie's Illustrated Newspaper*, Feb. 11, 1860. There is a sketch, dealing principally with his imprisonment, in G. W. Atkinson and A. F. Gibbens, *Prominent Men of W. Va.* (1890). The "Case of Charles J. Faulkner," in

Official Records (Army), CXV, gives the correspondence in regard to his arrest; *Official Records (Army)*, LXXI, 367, gives the special order of Maj.-Gen. Hunter to burn Faulkner's dwelling and outbuildings. There are a few letters and copies of speeches in possession of the family of his son, C. J. Faulkner, at Martinsburg, W. Va.]

J. E. W.

FAULKNER, CHARLES JAMES (Sept. 21, 1847–Jan. 13, 1929), United States senator, the second son of Charles James Faulkner [*q.v.*] and Mary Wagner Boyd, born at Martinsburg, Va. (now W. Va.), at "Boydville," the ancestral home which he later inherited by his father's will subject to the life estate of the mother. He had one brother, and six sisters who married into prominent Southern families. In 1860–61, while his father was minister to France, he attended schools in Paris and Switzerland. In 1862 he entered the Virginia Military Institute at Lexington and with other cadets volunteered in the Confederate army. After serving with the cadets in the battle of New Market, he became aide to Gen. John C. Breckinridge and later to Gen. Henry A. Wise, with whom he remained until the surrender at Appomattox.

In October 1866, after a term of study in his father's law office, he entered the department of law of the University of Virginia, from which he graduated with the LL.B. degree in 1868. He was admitted to the bar at Martinsburg in September, and soon attained high rank in the profession. As a Mason he attained distinction in 1879 by his election as Grand Master of the Grand Lodge of West Virginia. In October 1880, he was elected judge of the 13th judicial circuit of West Virginia. His decisions showed impartiality and good judgment. By 1887 he had become prominent in politics. Without being a candidate, he was elected to the United States Senate to succeed J. N. Camden, whose term expired on Mar. 4, and in 1893 was reëlected for a second term. He was chairman of the Democratic state conventions in 1888 and 1892 and of the Democratic congressional committee in 1894, 1896, and 1898. Among the important bills which he framed as senator was that of 1888–89 which became the first general law prohibiting food and drug adulteration. He was also the author of a law for regulation of railways in the District of Columbia. He took a leading part in some of the great contests in the Senate of his period, including that on the Blair Educational Bill which was defeated largely by his activity. He was one of the most active leaders in the defeat of the Force Bill (1890–91). He was appointed a member of a joint commission of the two houses to investigate the cost of railway mail transportation and postal-car service. In 1897–98 he was a member of the joint commission to investigate charities, and reformatory institutions in the District of Columbia. In April 1898 he spoke in favor of the resolutions for intervention in Cuba. In September 1898 he was appointed by the President to membership on the Anglo-American Joint High Commission.

After his retirement from the Senate (1899) he resumed the practise of law with offices in Washington, and Martinsburg, specializing in corporation law and becoming attorney for several railroads. He especially enjoyed his association with the Baltimore & Ohio, for which he had first been employed as counsel in 1868. He was one of the charter members who organized the American Law Institute in May 1923. In May 1918 he closed his Washington office and discontinued his legal work for the combined railroads. Thereafter he resided at Martinsburg until his death. His immediate community treasured him as the finest type of citizen, who was always ready to share actively in common undertakings. His last public appearance was in the sesquicentennial parade of Nov. 12, 1928, in which he rode with an escort of honor. He was first married on Nov. 25, 1869, to Sallie Winn of Charlottesville, Va., by whom he had five children. She died in March 1890. On Jan. 3, 1894, he was married to Virginia Fairfax Whiting of Hampton, Va., by whom he had one son. He died at "Boydville" in the same room in which he had been born over eighty-one years before.

[F. Vernon Aler, *Hist. of Berkeley County* (1888), p. 397; G. W. Atkinson and A. F. Gibbens, *Prominent Men of W. Va.* (1890); Morris P. Shawkey, *W. Va. in Hist.*, vol. IV (1928), pp. 337–38; *Martinsburg Evening Jour.*, Jan. 14, 1929.]

J. M. C.

FAUNCE, WILLIAM HERBERT PERRY (Jan. 15, 1859–Jan. 31, 1930), clergyman, college president, was born in Worcester, Mass., the oldest son of Daniel Worcester Faunce, a Baptist clergyman, and Mary Parkhurst Perry, of Bristol, R. I., a member of Commodore Perry's branch of the family. The first of the Faunce name in America was John, who came to Massachusetts on the ship *Ann* in 1623. Thomas, his son, was the last ruling elder at Plymouth. William was fitted for college in the high schools of Concord, N. H., and Lynn, Mass., and graduated from Brown University in 1880. After graduation he entered the Newton Theological Institution, but spent the year 1881–82 at Brown as an instructor in mathematics. In 1884 he finished his course at Newton, was ordained to the Baptist ministry, became pastor of the State Street Baptist Church, Springfield, Mass., and was married to Sarah Rogers Edson, of Lynn, Mass. In

1889 he was called to the Fifth Avenue Baptist Church, New York City. While on leave of absence in 1895 he was a student at the University of Jena. As a preacher and public speaker, he early won a place among the leaders of his day, not by Demosthenic "action," but by the appeal of his thought and the eloquence of his language. He took a poet's delight in the artistry of words, and his addresses, delivered in a voice flexible and sympathetic, never failed to captivate his audience. His fame brought him appointments as lecturer in the Divinity School of the University of Chicago, 1897–98, and as resident preacher at Harvard, 1898–99. Later he was one of the "Lyman Beecher" lecturers at Yale, delivering a series of addresses, which were published in 1908 under the title, *The Educational Ideal in the Ministry.*

In 1899 he became president of Brown University, succeeding Elisha Benjamin Andrews [*q.v.*]. Upon taking this office he assumed the direction of an inchoate university, which in ten years had more than trebled in numbers. During the three decades of his administration a still greater proportional enlargement occurred; funds increased eight-fold, the greatest building era in the history of the college took place, and with characteristic liberality President Faunce secured the removal of the charter restriction of the presidency to Baptists. His management of the institution won the confidence of men of affairs, and his personal qualities brought him into high favor not only with faculty and students but also with the citizens of Providence, and there was developed a new comity between "town and gown."

In addition to his university work he took an active part in some of the leading religious and educational movements of his time. He was president of the Higher Education Section of the National Educational Association, 1903–04, and of the Religious Education Association, 1906–07. After 1918 he was president of the World Peace Foundation, and was active to the last in its administration and its plans for the future. He was abroad six times. In 1912–13 he made a tour of the world, during which he acquired a deep interest in China, particularly in the part that may be played by American universities in its educational development. One of the results of this journey was his *Social Aspects of Foreign Missions,* published in 1914. Upon entering the ministry the importance of religion overshadowed in his thought every other social interest, but later he became sympathetic with all great social reforms and was active in several.

He was recognized by the Baptists as one of their foremost intellectual leaders and his influence had much to do in holding the denomination to its historic liberalism. Though he described himself rather as a mediator between Modernists and Fundamentalists than as an out-and-out Modernist, a pamphlet was issued by a Fundamentalist in 1922 demanding that the Corporation of Brown University remove him for heresy, and he was denounced in a Fundamentalist mass meeting in New York for an article on "Freedom in School and Church" that he published in the *World's Work* for March 1923. He acknowledged his debt to science for wider horizons, but he appears not to have grasped the unity and the full significance of scientific progress.

In person he was of medium height and sturdy build. His features were rugged. He was selective in his intimacies and naturally reserved. Always a great reader, he had remarkable power for grasping and retaining the contents of a book. He kept up with the affairs of the day and his addresses were pointed with references to matters of current interest. Music played an important part in his life. While a student he had served as a church organist, and in his later life he found in music an inspiration and solace. His summers were spent at Lake Mohonk, and the community there was long virtually his parish. In the seclusion of that mountain park, he did his writing. Among his publications not already mentioned are: *What Does Christianity Mean* (1912), Cole Lectures at Vanderbilt University, in which he discussed the fundamentals of the Christian faith and its place in the modern world; *Religion and War* (1918), Mendenhall Lectures at DePauw University, in which he portrayed the World War as a challenge to the moral leadership of the church and looked forward to an ultimate union of nations to abolish war; *The New Horizon of State and Church* (1918), Bedell Lectures at Kenyon College, in general a study of Christian patriotism and the international mind; *Citations for Honorary Degrees Granted by Brown University, 1900–1924* (1924), which contains his cameo-like characterizations of the recipients; and *Facing Life* (1928), selections from his chapel addresses.

In 1925 he suffered a severe breakdown. He recovered sufficiently to attend to the larger interests of the university until, having reached the age of seventy, he was automatically retired at Commencement, 1929. He had established himself in a new home in Providence with his books around him, and continued to preach and lecture. Less than a year later, however, he died of pneumonia

[*Who's Who in America*, 1928–29; *Hist. Cat. Brown Univ.* (1914); *Newton Theol. Inst. Gen. Cat.* (1899); *Brown Alumni Monthly*, Mar. 1930; *N. Y. Times*, Feb. 1, 1930; Faunce's own manuscript material in the graduate records of Brown University; records of the class of 1880 at Brown; and personal recollections.]

H. L. K.

FAUQUIER, FRANCIS (1704?–Mar. 3, 1768), lieutenant-governor of Virginia, was the eldest son of Dr. John Francis Fauquier, a director of the Bank of England, and Elizabeth Chamberlayne. He himself married Catharine, the daughter of Sir Charles Dalston. He was a director of the South Sea Company in 1751, and was elected on Feb. 15, 1753, a fellow of the Royal Society. In 1756, early in the Seven Years' War, he published *An Essay on Ways and Means of Raising Money for the Support of the Present War without Increasing the Public Debts*, of which there were three editions. In January 1758, he was appointed lieutenant-governor of Virginia. He was in fact governor, as the governor-in-chief (Earl of Loudoun, 1756–63; Sir Jeffrey Amherst, 1763–68) had no share in the administration of the government of the colony.

Fauquier assumed the duties of the governorship of Virginia when the colony was in the midst of the French and Indian War, and worked harmoniously with Washington and the legislature of the colony to bring that conflict to a successful end. He foresaw in the tendencies of his time signs of independence, and warned Pitt in 1760 that if Great Britain should continue her oppressive policy and impose additional taxation, the colonies would certainly offer resistance. From the very beginning of his administration he endeavored to carry out his instructions, in such a way as not to interfere with a practical, peaceful conduct of the affairs of the government. He was explicitly instructed to prevent the speaker of the House of Burgesses from serving any longer as treasurer of the colony. Upon his arrival, instead of attempting to execute this instruction, which would have caused a conflict and which also would have deprived him of a useful and influential man, he frankly agreed with him that they would work together for the best interests of the colony, and so informed the British Board of Trade. His relations with the burgesses were on the whole amicable, for he was clever enough to know when to grant their requests. The House, on the other hand, also desired harmony, and in its relations with the executive, endeavored to accomplish its ends without open conflict. He did not hesitate to exercise his power over that body when he thought that his position demanded it. In 1765, for example, he dissolved the House for passing the resolution against the Stamp Act, introduced by Patrick Henry. This action, even at so critical a period, seemed not to render him especially obnoxious to the colonists. Under his predecessor the House of Burgesses had assumed much power in directing military affairs, yet Fauquier was not interfered with in such matters.

The death of Fauquier on Mar. 3, 1768, at Williamsburg, after ten years of service, deprived the colony of a governor who appreciated conditions there and so administered the government that even during a most critical period the colonists raised no complaint against him but always considered him a friend. A county in Virginia bears his name

[There are many reports and letters in the British Public Record Office sent by Fauquier while in Virginia. A few letters written by him to Colonel Bouquet concerning military forces in Virginia, and one to Sir Henry Moore are in the British Museum. See also *The Speech of the Hon. Francis Fauquier, His Majesty's lieutenant-governor, in the city of Williamsburg, Sept. 14, 1758* (1758); *Dict. of Nat. Biog.*, and P. S. Flippin, "The Royal Government in Va., 1624–1775," Columbia Univ. Studies in Hist., Economics and Public Law, vol. LXXXIV, no. 1 (1919), pp. 133–36.] P. S. F.

FAVILL, HENRY BAIRD (Aug. 14, 1860–Feb. 20, 1916), physician, was born in Madison, Wis., the son of John Favill, a physician of state-wide reputation, and Louise Sophia Baird. He was a descendant in the fourth generation from John Favill who came to America from England before the Revolutionary War, fought in the Continental Army, and later settled in Manheim, Herkimer County, N. Y. On his mother's side he was descended from the Ottawa chief, Kewinoquot. He was educated in the public schools of his native city and in the University of Wisconsin, where he graduated in 1880. Following his graduation from Rush Medical College in Chicago in 1883 and an interneship in the Cook County Hospital, he returned to Madison to practise with his father. From 1890 to 1894 he was a special lecturer on medical jurisprudence at the University of Wisconsin. Relinquishing a large practise, he moved to Chicago in 1894 where he accepted the chair of medicine at the Chicago Policlinic and the adjunct chair of medicine in Rush Medical College. In the latter school he was promoted in 1898 to the Ingalls professorship of preventive medicine and therapeutics and in 1906 to the chair of clinical medicine. With a practise confined to internal medicine he soon built up a large and select clientele, and his reputation became nation-wide. At different times he was on the staffs of the Augustana, Passavant Memorial, and St. Luke's hospitals, and was for many years president of the Chicago Tuberculosis Institute. He was active in the membership of the Chicago Society of Internal Medicine, Chicago Institute of Medicine, and the Physicians' Club. He was also interested in the Association for the Study and Prevention of Tuberculosis, and the National Committee for Mental Hygiene.

Favill's interests were not confined to his profession. He was active in municipal affairs, and fearless in his opposition to corrupt politics. From 1907 to 1910 he was president of the Municipal Voters' League, an organization pledged to good government. He was an ardent advocate of municipal improvement and sanitary progress, acting for many years as trustee of the Chicago Bureau of Public Efficiency and as director of the United Charities. In the later years of his life he became a cattle breeder. He developed a model dairy farm at Lake Mills, Wis., where he spent whatever time he could spare from his professional work. He wrote and lectured upon agricultural and breeding problems and was elected president of the National Dairy Council. It was while attending a meeting of this organization in Springfield, Mass., in February 1916, that he contracted pneumonia and died

Favill will be long remembered in Chicago as a physician of uncommon ability and as a public-spirited citizen. He had a rare gift for public speaking, combining a finely modulated voice with remarkable clarity of expression. He was a model presiding officer. Though so well fitted for medical instruction he displayed no particular interest in his teaching appointments, and made little impress upon his classes. His writings, whether on municipal reform, cattle breeding, or medicine, were characterized by an originality in thought and language. An address entitled "The Public and the Medical Profession, A Square Deal" delivered before the Pennsylvania State Medical Society in 1915 (reprinted in the memorial volume) is an example of his literary skill. Physically he was tall, straight, and powerfully built. Though five generations removed from an Indian maternal ancestor, he had the dark skin, dark mournful eyes, high cheek bones, full lips, and straight hair of the North American Indian. He took no little pride in this aboriginal ancestry. He was married in 1885 to Susan Cleveland Pratt of Brooklyn, N. Y.

[John Favill, compiler, *Henry Baird Favill . . . A Memorial Volume, Life, Tributes, Writings* (1917); *Who's Who in America*, 1914–15.] J. M. P.

FAWCETT, EDGAR (May 26, 1847–May 2, 1904), author, was born in New York, and despite much foreign travel and a residence abroad during his later years, his native city remained throughout his life the principal theme of his literary work. His father, Frederick Fawcett, was an Englishman who became a prosperous merchant in New York; his mother, Sarah Lawrence Fawcett, was of American descent. After obtaining his preliminary education in the public schools of New York, Fawcett entered Columbia College. Here he failed of distinction as a student—his name appeared on the minutes of faculty meetings chiefly as the recipient of admonitions for irregular attendance upon classes—but he gained a campus reputation as a man of letters, and, as a member of the Philolexian literary society, he was prominent in undergraduate literary activities. He graduated in 1867, and three years later Columbia conferred the degree of M.A. upon him. After leaving college, since he was under no necessity of entering a gainful occupation, he devoted himself to literature and "elegant leisure." A prolific writer, he worked in various forms—poetry, the essay, the novel, and the drama. His chief volumes of verse, *Fantasy and Passion* (1878), *Song and Story* (1884), *Romance and Revery* (1886), and *Songs of Doubt and Dream* (1891), reveal but a slender talent. A strained mode of expression and echoes of the major Victorians too often usurped the place of inspiration. In some of the short and simple nature sketches Fawcett is seen at his best. Very characteristic of his cast of mind are several poems which voice his hostility to formal religion and his sympathy with skepticism and science. In *Agnosticism and Other Essays* (1889), which contains an introduction by Robert G. Ingersoll, he again comes to the defense of unbelief, declaring that religion is founded on fear and that miracles are old wives' tales.

It was as a novelist that Fawcett made his bulkiest contribution to the literature of his day. His volumes of fiction number approximately thirty-five, and with wearisome uniformity they reiterate one main theme. With his first novel, *Purple and Fine Linen* (1873), he began an assault on New York's high society, with which he had a first-hand acquaintance, and in book after book—among them *Tinkling Cymbals* (1884), *The Adventures of a Widow* (1884), *An Ambitious Woman* (1884), *Rutherford* (1884), *A Demoralizing Marriage* (1889), and *New York* (1898)—he held up to ridicule the Van Cortlandts, Van Tassels, and other members of a snobbish Knickerbocker aristocracy, as well as the newly rich social climbers, and the "silly striplings" who for the most part made up the masculine element in this exalted set. The picture thus drawn, allowing for the necessary exaggeration of satire, is not unveracious, especially in its presentation of the struggle between the old Dutch patricians and the new plutocrats. At the same time the amateurishness of Fawcett's plots, the woodenness of his characters, the dreary earnestness of his manner, and the monotony of his subjects are sufficient to justify Henry Stoddard's plaint: "Won't somebody please turn this Fawcett off?"

Social satire dominates Fawcett's plays as it does his novels. *A False Friend* (1880), *Our First Families* (1880), *Americans Abroad* (1881), and *Sixes and Sevens* (1881) were all performed in the theatres of New York, and met receptions varying from failure to moderate success. *The Earl* (1887), an imaginative, blank verse drama, was produced at Boston and ran for only a week (*Boston Transcript,* Apr. 12, 1887, and following issues). Contemporary reviews of these unpublished plays suggest that they possessed much the same defects as the novels. His liveliest bit of writing is *The Buntling Ball* (1884), a verse play not intended for the stage. Another satire on New York society, it escapes the charge of monotony by the marked metrical ingenuity it displays, which owes not a little to W. S. Gilbert and takes amusing liberties with Swinburne. *The New King Arthur* (1885), "an opera without music," which makes burlesque of the Arthurian material, evidently for Tennyson's benefit, pleasantly resembles *The Buntling Ball* in its jigging rhymes. Had Fawcett not misunderstood his talent, he would have written more "Buntling Balls" and fewer "Demoralizing Marriages."

Whether from a sense of irritation at the contempt with which certain newspaper critics in New York treated his work, or from some other cause, Fawcett at the age of fifty left America and took up his residence abroad. London was his home during his last years, and here, in bachelor quarters in the Chelsea district, he died after less than a week's illness.

[*Who's Who in America,* 1901–02; A. H. Quinn, *A Hist. of the Am. Drama from the Civil War to the Present Day* (2 vols., 1927); T. Allston Brown, *A Hist. of the N. Y. Stage* (3 vols., 1903); records of Columbia Coll.; N. Y. City Directory; *The Ann. Reg.,* 1904; obituary and other notices in the *N. Y. Times,* Jan. 22, 1880, Oct. 6, 1881, May 3, 1904; the N. Y. *World,* May 3, 1904; the *Times* (London), May 3, 1904.] O. S. C.

FAY, EDWARD ALLEN (Nov. 22, 1843–July 14, 1923), educator of the deaf, was born at Morristown, N. J., the oldest child of Barnabas Maynard Fay and Louise Mills. His descent was from John Fay, who came to America in the *Speedwell* in 1656 and settled in Worcester County, Mass. His father had taught deaf pupils for five years in the New York Institution for the Deaf before settling on the ministry as a profession. When the son was eleven years old his father returned to educational work with the deaf by accepting the principalship of the new state school for the deaf and the blind at Flint, Mich., so young Fay spent a considerable portion of his boyhood in association with deaf young people. He graduated from the University of Michigan in 1862 (M.A. 1865), and in 1863 became an instructor in the New York Institution for the Deaf. Three years later, at the invitation of Edward Miner Gallaudet he joined the faculty of the recently established National Deaf-Mute College, later Gallaudet College, in Washington, D. C. Here he remained as professor and vice-president (1885) until his retirement in 1920, a period of fifty-four years. In 1881 he received the degree of Ph.D. from Johns Hopkins University. From 1870 to 1920, he was also the editor of the *American Annals of the Deaf,* the oldest and best-known magazine dealing with the education of deaf pupils, and the official organ of the Conference of Superintendents and Principals of American Schools for the Deaf, and of the Convention of American Instructors of the Deaf. His contributions to this magazine on various topics number nearly one hundred and fifty. His statistics on methods, pupilage, and the condition of American schools, published yearly in the *Annals,* were so thorough and so accurate that they formed the basis of all statistical statements about American schools for the deaf in all parts of the world.

Fay's teaching was confined largely to the subjects of Latin, French, and German, in which his pupils made amazing progress, but his knowledge of languages was much broader. He became well versed in Greek, Spanish, and Italian. His *Concordance of the Divina Commedia,* begun at the request of the Dante Society of Cambridge, was finished in 1888, and stands as a monument of great scholarly attainment. He edited the *Histories of American Schools for the Deaf,* published in 1893, a valuable collection detailing the work of pioneers in that field of education. Perhaps the greatest work of his life, however, was his *Marriages of the Deaf in America,* completed in 1898. In this study of over thirty thousand marriages he was able to prove that deafness as a rule is not an inherited tendency, despite the fact that consanguineous marriages seem to increase it, and to hold out to deaf people the belief that wisely choosing deaf partners in marriage need not be forbidden.

Fay married Mary Bradshaw in 1871, and

brought up in his home at Kendall Green, which he occupied for half a century, a family of six sons and one daughter.

[*Who's Who in America*, 1922–23; Robert Patterson, "Edward Allen Fay," in the *Am. Annals of the Deaf*, Sept. 1923; *Ibid.*, Sept. 1910, Nov. 1911, and Oct. 1913; information as to certain facts from members of the family, and personal acquaintance.] P. H.

FAY, EDWIN WHITFIELD (Jan. 1, 1865–Feb. 17, 1920), teacher, scholar, author, was born at Minden, La., the fourth of the five children of Edwin Hedge Fay and Sarah Elizabeth Shields. The father was born in the South and was Southern in sympathy though his descent was Puritan and he was a graduate of Harvard. The greater part of his life was spent in teaching. For twelve years he was head of a Presbyterian school for girls, Silliman Institute, at Clinton, La., and for three years state superintendent of public instruction for Louisiana. The mother came of an old Georgia family of culture and distinction. Both parents were intellectual, sincerely religious, and stern in their devotion to duty. Edwin prepared for college in his father's seminary, read widely in his home library, and, unlike most Southern boys, was taught to play the piano. Though he was not particularly athletic he was devoted to tennis and continued to play until his last illness. At nineteen he entered Southwestern Presbyterian University at Clarksville, Tenn., and studied there till he received the degree of M.A. in 1883. Then he taught for a year each in the high schools at Jackson, Miss.; Bonham, and Beaumont, Tex. In 1886 he went to Johns Hopkins, where his major study was Sanskrit, complemented by comparative philology and classics. He received the Ph.D. degree with Phi Beta Kappa honors in 1890, though his dissertation, *The Treatment of Rig-Veda Mantras in the Gṛhya Sūtras*, was not published until 1899. As a student he developed characteristics which he never lost—versatility of intellect, power of concentration, continuous industry, rapidity in work. Besides his major studies he was an enthusiast in modern literature, wrote verse, and taught a Bible class. During the year 1890–91 he was instructor in Sanskrit and classics at the University of Michigan; in 1891–92 he traveled abroad and studied at the University of Leipzig; in 1892–93 he was acting professor of Latin at the University of Texas and for the next six years, 1893–99, he was professor of Latin at Washington and Lee University. In the fall of 1899 he returned to the University of Texas as professor of Latin and held this position till his death, nearly twenty-one years later. He was married Dec. 20, 1904, to Lucy Bell Hemphill, daughter of Charles R. Hemphill, later president of the Presbyterian Theological Seminary at Louisville, Ky.

As a man Fay was not socially inclined. His sensitive and reserved nature would not allow him to make friends casually, but in his close associates he inspired unusual affection. They enjoyed his wit, they respected his attainments, they admired his character. As a teacher he had little patience with idleness, but to serious-minded students he gave, besides a knowledge of the language which he taught, an insight into human values which they did not forget. Not a few count him one of the strongest influences in their lives. As a scholar he won honor by the extent and accuracy of his scholarship and the constant activity of his mind. The items of the bibliography prepared by Morgan Callaway reach a surprising total of one hundred and ninety-three. They include three books: *The History of Education in Louisiana* (1898); *T. Macci Plauti Mostellaria*, with introduction and notes (1902); and his dissertation. The other works were for the most part published in scientific journals; a few appeared in periodicals of a popular character. Although most of the articles were scientific—etymological, semantic, syntactic, textual, or exegetical—some were light, and still others were biographical or historical. Whether scientific or popular, they all showed a keen feeling for style and an individuality which led the editors of the London *Classical Quarterly* to speak of him as one of the "most original-minded of its contributors."

[Morgan Callaway, ed., *In Memoriam Edwin Whitfield Fay, 1865–1920*, in the Univ. of Tex. Bull., no. 2425, July 1, 1924; *Who's Who in America*, 1920–21.] W. J. B.

FAY, JONAS (Jan. 28, 1737 N.S.–Mar. 6, 1818), physician, politician, the son of Stephen and Ruth (Child) Fay, was born at Westborough, Mass. He was fourth in descent from John Fay who came to New England in 1656. In 1756 Jonas Fay served under Col. Samuel Robinson at Fort Edward and Lake George. On May 1, 1760, he married Sarah, daughter of Captain John Fassett, Sr., and about six years later he settled at Bennington, together with his father and brothers. The Fays soon became prominent in the controversy between the governments of New Hampshire and New York over the control of the so-called New Hampshire grants (now the State of Vermont). Consequently, in June 1772, Jonas and his father were appointed the agents of the settlers of the grants to lay their complaint before Gov. Tryon at New York. Two years later he became clerk of a convention held at Manchester to take action in the controversy.

Thence he was, almost without exception, secretary of the various conventions held by the settlers. On May 10, 1775, he was surgeon to the company of Green Mountain Boys which captured Ticonderoga, and, for the remainder of that year, saw active service in the war. In 1776 he was again prominent in the meetings of the settlers. At the Westminster Convention of Jan. 15, 1777, he was appointed a member of the committee to inform the Continental Congress that the settlers of the New Hampshire grants had declared themselves a separate state, independent of New York and New Hampshire, to present a petition asking Congress for recognition as such—a petition ignored by Congress (Doane, *post,* pp. 67–71). Fay continued to represent the new state in the various attempts to win recognition from the Congress. But meanwhile he was a member of the Windsor Convention of July 1777 which drafted the constitution of the state. This convention provided for a temporary government of the state by a Council of Safety, to which Fay was immediately appointed secretary. When the first Assembly met in March 1778, Fay had been elected a member of the Governor's Council, a capacity in which he served until 1785. As a member of that body he must have been cognizant of, if not a party to, the negotiations between Ira Allen [*q.v.*] and Gen. Haldimand, regarding the recognition of Vermont as a British province, although his name is not among those mentioned in Thomas Chittenden's list of those in the secret. On Oct. 29, 1784, he was appointed one of three agents "to transact the necessary business of opening a free trade to foreign powers, through the Province of Quebec" (*Records of the Governor and Council of the State of Vermont,* vol. III, 1875, pp. 397–98). Meanwhile, he was judge of the supreme court of Vermont (1782), and judge of probate (1782–87). He resided at Bennington until 1800, where he quietly practised medicine when not in the state's service. Later he removed to Charlotte and then to Pawlet. He spent his last years at Bennington, however, and died there Mar. 6, 1818. His second wife was Lydia (Warner) Safford whom he married Nov. 20, 1777. He left several children, among them Maj. Heman Allan Fay. Jonas Fay appears to have been a man of some little learning and sagacity, well versed in the political economy of his time. With Ethan Allen [*q.v.*], he was the author of *A Concise Refutation of the Claims of New-Hampshire and Massachusetts-Bay, to the Territory of Vermont,* published in 1780.

[O. P. Fay, *Fay Geneal.* (1898); G. G. Benedict, "The Recovery of the Fay Records," *Proc. Vt. Hist. Soc.,* 1903–04, pp. 49–55; Jonas Fay, *Records of Conventions in the N. H. Grants for the Independence of Vt., 1776–77* (1904); J. E. Goodrich, ed., *Vt. Rolls of the Soldiers in the Revolutionary War, 1775 to 1783* (1904); G. H. Doane, "The Continental Cong. and the N. H. Grants," in the *Vt. Rev.* (Barre, Vt.), Sept.–Oct. 1927; *Vt. Hist. Soc. Colls.,* vol. I (1870), p. 6, II (1871), p. 7; Wm. Slade, *Vt. State Papers* (1823); E. B. O'Callaghan, *Doc. Hist. of the State of N. Y.,* IV (1851), pp. 529–1034; J. B. Wilbur, *Ira Allen, Founder of Vt.* (1928); *Vt. Hist. Gazetteer,* I (1868), 173–74. Date of birth is taken from *Vital Records of Westborough, Mass.* (1903), p. 40.]

G. H. D.

FAY, THEODORE SEDGWICK (Feb. 10, 1807–Nov. 24, 1898), author, diplomat, was born in New York, the eldest child of Joseph Dewey Fay by his first wife, Caroline Broome. His father, a native of Vermont, had studied law in the office of Alexander Hamilton, was a successful practitioner, and gave much time to advocating the abolition of imprisonment for debt. Theodore became a clerk for his father, who died in 1825, and was admitted to the bar in 1828, but in the same year he joined Nathaniel Parker Willis and George Pope Morris as an editor of the *New York Mirror.* He had established his connection with the paper by continuing a series of light essays, entitled "The Little Genius," that had been begun by his father. *Dreams and Reveries of a Quiet Man* (2 vols., 1832) is a collection of his early *Mirror* articles. Though not heavily ballasted intellectually, he was versatile and sprightly, and his work was usually entertaining. In 1833 he married Laura Gardenier of New York and, in Poe's phrase, went "a-Willising in foreign countries" for three years, meanwhile sending home sketches of travel and miscellaneous matter to be published in the *Mirror.* His first novel, the once famous *Norman Leslie, A Tale of the Present Times* (2 vols., 1835) was replete with sentiment, bloodshed, heroics, and moral purpose. Fay's literary friends in New York reviewed it with tremendous enthusiasm, and the book was a best seller until Edgar Allan Poe, beginning his career as a critic, excoriated it in the *Southern Literary Messenger* (December 1835, pp. 54–57). This review proved an even greater sensation than the novel and started a verbal war between Poe and the New York literati. Fay's other novels—*Sydney Clifton* (1839), *The Countess Ida* (1840), *Hoboken, A Romance* (1843)—made pleasant reading for his contemporaries; the first of the three, like *Norman Leslie,* is a tale of "vicissitudes in both hemispheres"; the other two were written to expose the evils of dueling. For the rest of his life Fay lived in Europe. After holding a minor diplomatic post in London, he was appointed secretary of the legation in Berlin by President Van Buren in 1837. He was well liked in Berlin and in 1853 was promoted to be resident minister to Switzerland. On retiring in 1861, he returned to Germany and resided at Blasewitz, near Dresden, and in Berlin, where he died in his ninety-second year. His first wife died while he was minister at Bern; his second wife was of German birth. Until after his eightieth birthday he was active as a writer. *Ulric, or The Voices* (1851) was a narrative poem, somewhat in the manner of Walter Scott, dealing with a German captain of horse who became a disciple of Martin Luther. It reflects Fay's concern for the truths of Christian doctrine, which became stronger as he grew older. He tried his hand at schoolbooks with *A Great Outline of Geography* (2 vols., 1867) and *First Steps in Geography* (1873). *Die Sklavenmacht: Blicke in die Geschichte der Vereinigten Staaten von Amerika* (Berlin, 1865), and *Die Alabama-Frage* (Leipzig, 1872) were replies to hostile propaganda. His most substantial work is a popular political history of Germany, *The Three Germanys* (2 vols., 1889). He also did much writing for magazines. He outlived his friends, whom in later years he saw but seldom, and was almost forgotten by the time of his death.

[O. P. Fay, *Fay Geneal.* (Cleveland, Ohio, 1898); N. Y. *Evening Post,* Nov. 25, 1898; brief notices in E. A. and G. L. Duyckinck, *Cyc. of Am. Lit.* (rev. ed., 1875); R. W. Griswold, *Prose Writers of America,* and *Poets and Poetry of America* (many eds.); T. S. Fay, *Statement* (privately printed, 1845) and *Account of the Death of his Wife, Mrs. Laura Fay, with Observations on Christianity* (Bern, Switzerland, 1856); H. A. Beers, *Nathaniel Parker Willis* (1885); portrait in M. E. Phillips, *Edgar Allan Poe the Man* (1926), p. 523; F. L. Mott, *Hist. of Am. Magazines 1741–1850* (1930).] G. H. G.

FAYERWEATHER, DANIEL BURTON (Mar. 12, 1822–Nov. 15, 1890), leather merchant, philanthropist, was born at Stepney, Fairfield County, Conn., a son of Lucius and Amelia (Beardsley) Fayerweather. His grandfather, Capt. Samuel Fayerweather, was a veteran of the Revolution and the War of 1812. In Daniel's boyhood his father died and he was bound out to a farmer in the neighborhood. The work was hard and the boy had practically no opportunity for schooling. Released from his term of service before its completion, he learned shoemaking and was successful in that trade, but because of uncertain health he was in time forced to look elsewhere for employment. When nothing better offered, he went to Virginia and there engaged in what was called in those days "tin-peddling," or selling wares from door to door through the country. When he could not get cash for his merchandise he took hides in payment and thus made a start in the leather business, from which he was eventually to derive a fortune. So highly did he value education that after he came of age he sought and gained admission to a boys' boarding school in Connecticut, where the pupils were from five to seven years his juniors (letter of John M. Toucey in *Shoe and Leather Reporter,* Dec. 11, 1890).

Having recovered his health in the outdoor life which he led in the South, Fayerweather was ambitious to get into the leather trade, but it was not until 1854, when he was thirty-two years of age, that an opportunity of the kind he had been seeking came to him. He was offered a clerkship in the New York house of Hoyt Brothers which he eagerly accepted, and within one year he was admitted to the firm. From that time on his rise was steady and significant until his death in 1890, when he was senior partner in the house doing the largest leather business in the United States, if not in the world. Fayerweather & Ladew had tanneries in Pennsylvania, Maryland, and West Virginia, as well as in New York. From factories which were operated in New York City an immense output of belting and sole-leather was marketed annually. His success was based on the strictest integrity and the soundest financing. He had few rivals, but continually found and exploited new territory. In the wholesale leather district of New York, near the Manhattan and Brooklyn Bridge, he was known to scores of men as "Dan," and beyond the bounds of that business district his name was rarely heard or printed, even after he had reached the rank of millionaire.

Not one of the men who met Fayerweather from day to day suspected that he was harboring plans of philanthropy on a great scale; most of them underestimated his wealth; and only a few knew of his disposition to give largely of it. He quietly sought the counsel of President Roswell D. Hitchcock of Union Theological Seminary, and from October 1884 to November 1890, only three men knew that on the former date Fayerweather had signed a will giving from $50,000 to $300,000, as well as additional gifts from the residuary estate, to each of a score of American colleges. It was also clear that he had made no provision whatever for having his own name perpetuated as a donor, or for restricting the institutions in the use of the funds bestowed. A codicil made on the day of his death gave full control of the estate to the executors, who, after providing for his widow, Lucy (Joyce) Fayerweather (1824–1892), proceeded to carry out the testator's bequests to the colleges.

[*Commemorative Biog. Record of Fairfield County, Conn.* (1899), p. 987; Samuel Orcutt, *A Hist. of the Old Town of Stratford and the City of Bridgeport, Conn.* (2 vols., 1886); *Shoe and Leather Reporter,* Nov.

20, 1890; *N. Y. Times*, Nov. 17, 1890; *N. Y. Tribune*, *New Haven Evening Reg.*, Dec. 9, 1890.] W. B. S—w.

FAYSSOUX, PETER (1745–Feb. 1, 1795), physician and surgeon, was born probably in Charleston, S. C., whither his mother had emigrated from Southern France, and where in 1746, she married Dr. James Hunter. He served his apprenticeship with his step-father, was sent to Edinburgh University, then the medical center of the world, and graduated in 1769. There also he began his friendship with Benjamin Rush [*q.v.*]. With Alexander Baron, Charles C. Pinckney and Thomas Heyward, Jr., he was elected in 1773 curator of the first museum of natural history in America, at Charleston. At the outbreak of the Revolution, he took a leading part. He served on the committee to collect signatures to the patriots' association in 1775, in 1776 was one of the signers of South Carolina's paper money, and attended the wounded behind the palmetto logs of Fort Moultrie in the first British attack on America. He was also present at the assault on Savannah in 1779 and gave an account of the last hours of Count Pulaski. As senior physician to the South Carolina line he officiated with Moultrie's forces until the surrender of Charleston in 1780. While a prisoner he was arrested with the leading citizens on parole in Charleston and sentenced to exile in St. Augustine, but was released as a surgeon and escaped the fate of the others. He wrote a very graphic letter concerning the British treatment of sick and wounded prisoners during this period, which was widely quoted as evidence of their inhumanity. After his exchange, he joined Greene's army and was appointed, May 15, 1781, chief physician and surgeon of the hospital, Southern Department.

Fayssoux became a charter member of the South Carolina Society of the Cincinnati; served in the legislature of the state and on the privy council of Gov. Moultrie. In 1786 he was one of the incorporators of the Santee Canal Company. He was twice married: first to Sarah Wilson on Jan. 29, 1772, and second, to Ann (Smith) Johnston, in March 1777. He became the father of at least thirteen children from whom all Americans of the name are descended.

It was in the field of his chosen profession that Fayssoux rendered the most conspicuous service to his country. His European education, his alert and open mind, together with his unusual hold on his patients' affections, led David Ramsay [*q.v.*] to accord him first place in his day among the physicians of Charleston. In treating yellow fever, so fatal in coastal Carolina, he was quick to adopt and spread the discoveries of Benjamin Rush, while many of the Northern physicians rejected them. In December 1789 David Ramsay and Alexander Baron met at his house to organize the Medical Society of South Carolina, of which he became the first president, 1790–92. Fayssoux's place in the progress of American civilization rests rather on his position of influence as the leading physician of his section than on any great originality in scientific research. He was quick to recognize truth and to acknowledge it, but he left no published records of his own observations.

[C. G. Davidson's "Surgeon-General Peter Fayssoux" is now in preparation. The sketch in H. A. Kelly and W. L. Burrage, *Am. Medic. Biog.* (1928), is very inaccurate. Best published sources are: J. M. Toner, *The Medic. Men of the Revolution* (1876), and scattered material in the *S. C. Hist. and Geneal. Mag.*] C. G. D.

FEARN, JOHN WALKER (Jan. 13, 1832–Apr. 7, 1899), lawyer, diplomat, was born at Huntsville, Ala., the son of Richard Lee and Mary Jane (Walker) Fearn. His mother was a daughter of John W. Walker, United States senator from Alabama, and a sister of Leroy P. Walker [*q.v.*], Confederate secretary of war. When he was two years old, his father, who was a physician, moved his family to Mobile, and there John Walker Fearn received his early education, in the private academy of Dr. Norman Pinney, an eminent classical scholar. He entered Yale and upon his graduation in 1851 he began the study of law under Judge John A. Campbell. Although Fearn was admitted to the bar in Mobile in 1853, a talent for literature and languages which he had developed at an early age led to his appointment in that year as secretary to the United States minister to Belgium. Three years later he was made secretary of the legation in Mexico, where he served until 1859, when he resigned ostensibly to return to the practise of law at Mobile. These were the days of secession, however, and when the Southern states sent their first commission—William Yancey, Pierre A. Rost, and A. Dudley Mann [*qq.v.*]—to Europe early in 1861 before the outbreak of hostilities, they availed themselves of the experienced services of Fearn. He went to Madrid with Rost early in February 1862, shortly after John Slidell's arrival in Paris, but when Rost resigned because of his cold reception and his poor health, Fearn's position as secretary of legation was vacated by Secretary of State Judah P. Benjamin in a letter to Slidell, dated Sept. 26, 1862. Fearn thereupon returned to America, running the blockade at Charleston, S. C., and after being wrecked under the guns of Fort Moultrie, escaped and secured an appointment on the staff of Gen. Joseph E. Johnston. On Nov. 19, 1862, Benjamin instructed L. Q. C. Lamar to proceed to St. Petersburg to secure the friendly support of the Czar, and Fearn accompanied him as secretary. Russia refused to receive the Confederate commissioner; consequently Fearn returned again and obtained a place on the staff of Gen. William Preston. Early in 1864, when there seemed some hope of recognition of the Confederacy by Mexico, Fearn accompanied Preston [*q.v.*] to Cuba on the way to Mexico, but anticipating a cold reception they returned without reaching the Mexican capital. After 1866 he practised law at New Orleans, La. He was interested in the University of Louisiana and is said to have been appointed to the chair of French, Spanish, and Italian at the Tulane University in 1884. In 1885 President Cleveland appointed him minister resident and consul-general to Greece, Rumania, and Servia. Upon his retirement from this position, about 1887, he established an international law firm with offices in London and New York. On his return to America, he was made chief of the Department of Foreign Affairs of the World's Columbian Exposition at Chicago in 1893. Under Cleveland's second administration Fearn was appointed one of the judges of the International Mixed Tribunal in Egypt and remained a member of that distinguished body until the failure of his health necessitated his resignation. Immediately upon the first attack of rheumatic gout, he set out for home. His friends feared he would die at sea, but he rallied on landing at New York and passed the summer at Newport. On his physician's advice, he moved to Hot Springs, Va., where he died, being survived by his widow, who was Fanny Hewitt, daughter of James Hewitt, a merchant of New Orleans, and by two children, a daughter and a son. The supreme court of Louisiana adjourned at his death as a mark of respect.

[*Obit. Record Grads. Yale Univ., 1890–1900* (1900); *Times-Democrat* (New Orleans), Apr. 9, 1899; Jas. M. Callahan, *The Diplomatic Hist. of the Southern Confederacy* (1901), and Jas. D. Richardson, *A Compilation of the Messages and Papers of the Confederacy,* vol. II (1905).] H. F. W.

FEATHERSTON, WINFIELD SCOTT (Aug. 8, 1819–May 28, 1891), lawyer, congressman, soldier, was born four miles from Murfreesboro, Tenn., the youngest of seven children. His parents, Charles and Lucy (Pitts) Featherston, were recent pioneers from Virginia. Although he became a man of learning, his formal education did not extend beyond the high school, and even this was disturbed in 1836 when he left the studies in which he was engaged at Columbus, Ga., and served as a volunteer in the war against the Creek Indians. After some indecision he chose to study law, and was admitted to the bar in Houston, Miss. His successful legal career, begun in 1840, was interrupted by membership in the Thirtieth and Thirty-first Congresses (1847–1851) to which he was elected on the Democratic ticket over a strong opposition. Though again a candidate in 1850, he shared in the state-wide defeat suffered by the State-rights party. He remained in private life until the beginning of the Civil War. In 1857 he moved to Holly Springs, Miss., and in the following year he married Elizabeth M. McEwen of that city, who lived until the yellow-fever epidemic of 1878. He had lost his first wife, Mary Holt Harris of Columbus, Miss., a few months after their marriage in 1848.

As secession became imminent, Featherston was sent from Mississippi in December 1860 to treat with the Kentucky authorities. Soon after he was elected colonel of the 17th Mississippi Regiment. He was a man of commanding presence, over six feet tall and well proportioned. He served in the Virginia army through the year 1862, taking part in several important battles. In one of these he was wounded, and was promoted to the rank of brigadier-general (Mar. 4, 1862) for skill and gallantry in action. In January 1863 he was sent at his own request to assist in the defense of Vicksburg, but was not captured at the fall of the city. While covering Pemberton's retreat into Vicksburg his brigade was cut off and proceeded to Jackson, Miss., where it joined the army of Gen. Joseph E. Johnston.

At the close of the war, Gen. Featherston returned to Holly Springs, resumed his law practise, and became an important factor in the overthrow of the Ames regimen in Mississippi. He was president of the state tax-payers' convention which met in January 1874 and succeeded himself in the same office a year later. At both times protests were made against the high taxes and needless expenditures of the existing state government. He led the attack on Gov. Ames by introducing in the lower house of the legislature the resolution looking toward the impeachment of the governor, and acted as chairman of the committee which prepared the articles and conducted the prosecution. In addition to his service in the legislature of 1876–78, he was a member of this body in 1880–82, and in the capacity of chairman of the judiciary committee, assisted in the revision of the state code of 1880. In 1882, he became judge of the second judicial circuit of the state. His last public service was in the constitutional convention of 1890, in which he was a member of the judiciary committee. He died at his home in Holly Springs the following year.

[*Jour. of the House of the State of Miss.*, 1876, 1880;

Jour. of the Senate of the State of Miss. Sitting as a Court of Impeachment, 1876; *Memoirs of Miss.* (1891); *Confed. Mil. Hist.*, VII (1899); Dunbar Rowland, *Mississippi* (1907); Reuben Davis, *Recollections of Miss. and Mississippians* (1889); *Memphis Commercial*, May 30, 1891. Featherston's papers, relating chiefly to his military career, are in the possession of his son, D. M. Featherston of Holly Springs, Miss.] C.S.S.

FEBIGER, CHRISTIAN (1746–Sept. 20, 1796), Revolutionary soldier, was born on the island of Fünen, Denmark. He attended a military school and while still a youth joined the staff of his uncle, who was governor of the island of Santa Cruz, in the West Indies. In 1772 he made a tour of the American colonies from Cape Fear to the Penobscot and engaged in the "lumber, fish and horse trade." Lexington found him domiciled in Massachusetts and ten days later he joined Col. Samuel Gerrish's Essex and Middlesex militia regiment. He was promoted adjutant and rendered "valuable service" at the battle of Bunker Hill. He served as Benedict Arnold's brigade-major during the invasion of Canada and was taken prisoner at the assault on Quebec, Dec. 31, 1775. Exchanged in January 1777, he was immediately commissioned lieutenant-colonel of Col. Daniel Morgan's 11th Virginia regiment, Continental line. He was promoted colonel after the battle of Brandywine (September 1777) and took part in the battles of Germantown (October 1777) and Monmouth (June 1778). In July 1779 he was chosen by Washington to command one of the four light infantry regiments organized for the storming of Stony Point. On July 15 Gen. Wayne and Cols. Febiger and Butler made a final reconnaissance and during the night took the fortress by assault. For his share in the triumph Febiger received Wayne's commendation. Gen. Muhlenberg stationed Febiger at Philadelphia in August 1780 with orders to forward arms and clothing to Richmond, where Muhlenberg was hastily assembling troops and equipment for Gen. Gates. In November, Gen. Greene, who had taken over the command in the South, ordered Febiger to remain in Philadelphia as agent for obtaining and forwarding stores to the southern army. In this service "Old Denmark" displayed great talent for procuring supplies from the quartermaster-general and the Board of War. Returning to Virginia, he aided Morgan in suppressing the Loyalist insurrection in Hampshire County (May–June, 1781), served as recruiting officer, and commanded a body of Virginia recruits in Lafayette's army. In the fall of 1781 he wrote to Washington describing himself as "Superintending officer of the Virginia line." At the close of the Revolution he retired from the army and was brevetted brigadier-general by Congress (Sept. 30, 1783). Settling in Philadelphia he was elected treasurer of Pennsylvania (1789–96). He married Elizabeth Carson, daughter of a Philadelphia merchant.

[Henry P. Johnston, memoir in *Mag. of Am. Hist.*, Mar. 1881; and *The Storming of Stony Point on the Hudson* (1900); R. Frothingham, *Hist. of the Siege of Boston* (1849); H. B. Dawson, *The Assault on Stony Point* (1863); Chas. J. Stillé, *Maj.-Gen. Anthony Wayne and the Pa. Line in the Continental Army* (1893); H. A. Muhlenberg, *The Life of Maj.-Gen. Peter Muhlenberg of the Revolutionary Army* (1849); C. Tower, *The Marquis De La Fayette in the Am. Revolution* (1895); *Pa. Mag. of Hist. and Biog.*, Oct. 1903; F. B. Heitman, *Hist. Reg. of Officers of the Continental Army* (1893); Wm. P. Palmer, *Calendar of Va. State Papers*, vols. I, II, III (1875–83).] F. E. R.

FECHTER, CHARLES ALBERT (Oct. 23, 1824–Aug. 5, 1879), actor, was born in London, the twelfth of the thirteen children, of whom eleven died in infancy, of Jean Maria Guillaume and Marie Angélique (Regis) Fechter. His mother, Flemish by birth, Piedmontese by blood, was a maker of artificial flowers and dabbled in verse and fiction. His father, French by birth, German by blood, was a sculptor and designer for jewellers and had in him the makings of a comic actor. Charles spent most of his early years in France. He studied music, painting, and sculpture and was proficient in all three. Acting, however, was to be his career. He joined in 1840 an amateur company playing at the Salle Molière in Paris, suffered the usual vicissitudes of a young player, and by 1848 had attained distinct success. For the next ten years he was the favorite *jeune premier* on the French stage, achieving his greatest triumph as Armand Duval in Dumas's *La Dame aux Camélias* (Vaudeville, Feb. 2, 1852). During these years he was frequently reprimanded by the critics for his bold departures from stage traditions; he manifested on several occasions the temper and obstinacy that marred his otherwise amiable character and finally brought him to catastrophe; and the first signs developed of the disease that cut short his life. In 1857 he became joint manager of the Odéon. When the government forbade him to produce plays that were the exclusive property of the Théâtre Français, he resigned in a huff and determined to try his fortune in London, where he had already acted in French.

His accession to the English stage marked the culmination in London of the vogue of French romantic realism in acting, and inaugurated a revolution in stagecraft. By no means the best actor of the period, Fechter was theatrically the most effective, even when acting in English, which he spoke in the main correctly and fluently but with a French intonation. Before his time no one in England had devoted such attention and resource to the construction and equipment of the stage, the scenery, and other properties, and to costuming. Making his first appearance in the title rôle of Hugo's *Ruy Blas* (Royal Princess's, Oct. 27, 1860) he scored an astounding success. Some months later he invaded the citadel of British theatrical conservatism with his *Hamlet* (Mar. 20, 1861), the merits of which were a subject for lively debate among critics fifty years after its performance. Symbolizing his realism and his break with tradition by wearing a blond wig, he interpreted many passages anew, slurred the famous soliloquies, and portrayed Hamlet as a man of action. His interpretation has been of lasting influence, but the same methods applied to *Othello* (Oct. 23, 1861) resulted in an ignominious failure; in later productions Fechter took the part of Iago and enjoyed his customary success. He became a close friend of Wilkie Collins and Charles Dickens, with whose romanticism in realistic trappings his own art was akin. Fechter was considered the greatest lover ever seen on the English stage, but after a few years his popularity waned. As an actor-manager he became involved in inextricable difficulties, and at the instigation of Dickens, who heralded his appearance with a laudatory article in the *Atlantic Monthly* (August 1869), he turned to America to retrieve himself.

His American career began auspiciously with *Ruy Blas* at Niblo's Garden, New York, Jan. 10, 1870. In Boston, next month, he was received with overwhelming enthusiasm, and in September he returned to that city as manager of the Globe Theatre. A notable company had been assembled, public support was assured, but Fechter quarreled with the younger James W. Wallack and with Mr. and Mrs. Chanfrau, and in January the venture ended dismally. His estrangement from his leading lady, Carlotta Leclercq, and her subsequent marriage in England, threw him into a fit of grief that shook body and mind. After failing as a manager in New York, he returned to England for a few months late in 1872, but the next spring found him acting again in New York. Playgoers in various American cities continued to see him in his repertoire, including Hamlet, Ruy Blas, and Obenreizer in Wilkie Collins's *No Thoroughfare,* but his remaining days were few and evil. His body grew coarse and bloated; sometimes he was too ill to act; at other times he acted though in great distress; his money melted away; and his friends were alienated by his outbursts of temper. Early in 1874 he married Lizzie Price, a handsome and capable Philadelphia actress, who became and remained his devoted slave; but before long it was common knowledge that the marriage was bigamous. He had been married Nov. 29, 1847, to a *pensionnaire* of the Théâtre Français (a Mlle. Rolbert according to the *Dictionary of National Biography,* but the name is in doubt) by whom he had a son and a daughter. He died of cirrhosis of the liver on his farm near Quakertown, Bucks County, Pa. A man of genius, in the estimate of even his severest critics, an eminent actor on the French, the English, and the American stage, he died poor, despised, almost friendless. His monument in Mt. Vernon Cemetery, Philadelphia, bears the inscription, "Genius has taken its flight to God."

[Kate Field, *Charles Albert Fechter* (1882); Joseph Knight, article in *Dict. Nat. Biog.,* XVIII (1889); H. B. Baker, *The London Stage 1576–1888* (1889); Phila. *Times,* Dec. 23, 1878; Phila. *Item,* Aug. 10, 17, 1879; Phila. *Evening Telegraph,* Aug 5, 1879; *Phila. Inquirer,* Aug. 6, 1879; *N. Y. Herald,* Aug. 6, 7, 1879; C. M. Drake, "Report of the Autopsy of Mr. Charles A. Fechter, Tragedian," in *Medic. and Surgic. Reporter,* Aug. 16, 1879; R. G. White, articles in *Nation* (N. Y.), Feb. 24, June 9, 1870; H. A. Clapp, *Reminiscences of a Dramatic Critic* (1902); William Winter, *The Wallet of Time,* I (1913); J. R. Towse, *Sixty Years in the Theatre* (1916); G. C. D. Odell, *Shakespeare from Betterton to Irving* (1919); J. G. Huneker, *Steeplejack* (1920); E. B. Watson, *Sheridan to Robertson* (1926).]

G. H. G.

FEE, JOHN GREGG (Sept. 9, 1816–Jan. 11, 1901), Abolitionist, founder of Berea College, eldest son of John Fee and Elizabeth Gregg, was born in Bracken County, Ky. From his father, a landowner of Scotch and English descent, he received an inflexible will, humanized, however, by his inheritance from a tender Scotch-Irish mother of Quaker stock. Early in life he began to prepare for the ministry, studying first at a subscription school near his home and then at Augusta and Miami Colleges. He graduated from the former. In 1842 he entered Lane Theological Seminary, and after two years consecrated himself to the cause of Abolition. Returning to convert his slaveholding parents, he failed and was disinherited. On Sept. 26, 1844, he married Mathilda Hamilton, also of Bracken County. She was gifted with affection, courage, and endurance, and proved a most sympathetic partner.

Fee established two anti-slavery churches in Lewis and Bracken counties and labored with them for some years, though censured by the Synod for introducing Abolition into Church affairs, and though shot at, clubbed, and stoned. Preaching, speaking at conventions, and the preparation of anti-slavery pamphlets filled his days. In 1853 friends of freedom in Madison County invited him to give a series of sermons. There he established what still stands as Berea Union Church, and in the next year he moved to Berea as its pastor. In 1855 he founded an abolitionist school—now Berea College. About this time he was the victim of a series of mobs. Finally, in 1859, while he was in the East raising money for the college, John Brown's raid occurred. False reports of a speech of his in Henry Ward Beecher's church fanned the flames, and Fee and ten other Bereans were driven from the state. Not until 1863 was he finally able to return to Kentucky to work with the negro soldiers in Camp Nelson. With the close of the war, he returned to Berea to build up both church and college, serving as pastor of the former and trustee of the latter. In 1894 his wife died, and the next year he retired from his pastorate. He remained in Berea, however, preaching and serving the college, until his death.

Fee was a clear thinker and a forceful speaker. He was calm but earnest, and was gifted with an intensity of moral purpose. Considering sects "contrary to the spirit of the Gospel, a hindrance to reform," he established a union church; hating slavery, he fought it in spite of family opposition, ostracism, and violence. He was never influenced by expediency; whatever seemed to him to be right he did without regard for consequences, but with steadfast devotion.

[Nat. Christian Asso., *Autobiog. of John G. Fee* (1891); John A. R. Rogers, *Birth of Berea Coll.* (1903); *Berea Coll., Ky.: An Interesting Hist.*, approved by the Prudential Committee, Cincinnati (1875 and 1883); the *Berea Quart.*, Feb. 1901.] W. P. F.

FEEHAN, PATRICK AUGUSTINE (Aug. 28, 1829–July 12, 1902), Catholic archbishop of Chicago, was born in Killenaule, County Tipperary, Ireland, to Patrick and Judith Cooney Feehan. Despite the penal laws, his father had acquired a sound schooling and speaking knowledge of French. A studious child, Patrick obtained the rudiments of a classical education at home and in a local school, so that at sixteen years of age, he was prepared to enter Castle Knock College. Here he was associated with two boys who were later famed as Lord Russell of Killowen and Archbishop Hale of Tuam. Answering a spiritual call, he entered Maynooth (1847), where he followed the seminary course for five years. In the meantime, his family, selling their dwindling possessions, fled from post-famine Ireland to America. Hence the young deacon gladly embraced the call of Archbishop Peter R. Kenrick of St. Louis, who sent him to his Seminary at Carondelet in final preparation for ordination (Nov. 1, 1852).

Appointed curate of St. John's Church, at St. Louis, Father Feehan proved an earnest preacher rather than an orator. As one who lived through the Irish famine and fever, his heart turned to the poor in the cholera epidemic (1853), when he nursed the sick, attended the dying, and coffined the dead. Assigned to the rectorship of the diocesan seminary at Carondelet, he taught moral theology and sacred scripture for four years when he was placed in charge of St. Michael's Church, St. Louis. A year later he was transferred to the Church of the Immaculate Conception where he won the title of "the priest of the poor." He established a unit of the St. Vincent de Paul Society and made daily visits to the unfortunates in the local jail. During the Civil War, he spent himself administering the sacraments to dying soldiers and in comforting the wounded who crowded the neighboring hospital of the Sisters of Charity. After Shiloh, the wounded were sent to St. Louis in boatloads. No small percentage were Irishmen, but Feehan knew no racial or creedal distinctions in such a crisis. His charity, not his teaching, brought numerous deathbed conversions.

On the resignation of Bishop James Whelan of Nashville, Rome named Father Feehan to that war-torn diocese (1864). Owing to impaired health, he declined, but, on the death of his mother, accepted a second appointment and was consecrated by Archbishop Kenrick (Nov. 1, 1865). The diocese was in chaos: the cathedral and rectory had served as a barracks; every institution was bankrupt; there were only three secular priests in Tennessee. Undaunted, he entered upon the work of reconstruction. While attending the Second Plenary Council of Baltimore (1866) and the Ecumenical Council at Rome (1870), he sought financial aid to rebuild churches and construct chapels and invited priests and religious to enter his mission field. An organizer and a builder, he encouraged the Sisters of Mercy to establish St. Bernard's Academy (1866); he rebuilt St. Cecilia's Dominican Convent and School; he established St. Joseph's Orphanage for the children of dead soldiers; he purchased a cemetery; he erected several parochial schools; and he made trying visitations into inaccessible parts of the diocese. He went through cholera epidemics in 1866, 1873, and the terrible year of 1878, when thousands died, including twelve of his priests who were stricken while attending the dying. The bishop's courageous labors so won the affection of all classes, that sorrow was mingled with satisfaction when, on the death of Bishop Thomas Foley, he was elevated to the newly created archdiocese of Chicago.

Installed as archbishop, Nov. 28, 1880, he was destined to rule the archdiocese for twenty-two years during a time of tremendous municipal and Catholic growth. A remarkable business man, he bought and held property, and, despite criticism, he built in distant suburbs in realization of Chicago's future. Sustained by the courts, he retained riparian rights and reclaimed invaluable lands from the waters of Lake Michigan. During his administration the Catholic population grew from 200,000 to over 800,000, priests increased from 204 to 538, churches and chapels from 194 to 298, colleges and academies from 17 to 28, and seminarians from 34 to 130. In this period of astounding development, he saw his people rise from labor into the professional and financial circles. He witnessed the erection of about 150 parochial schools. He aided in the foundation of the La Salle Institute, Saint Cyril's College, St. Vincent's College, and St. Viateur's College at Bourbonnais. The importance of Feehan's contribution to Catholic education was recognized when the Catholic Educational Exhibit displayed at the Catholic Congress of the United States won general encomiums from the promoters of the World's Fair (1893).

Archbishop Feehan was a social worker in the larger sense. While in Nashville, he had been one of the founders of the Catholic Knights of America (1877), he now supported the Catholic Order of Foresters, and defended the Ancient Order of Hibernians before the Third Council of Baltimore when some of the bishops attacked secret societies. In a quiet way, he was engaged in Americanization. His archdiocese was populated with a large proportion of immigrants of whom great numbers were foreign speaking. Aware of the ravages of drink, he gave full patronage to temperance societies. He walked the streets of Chicago with policemen on their beats in order to learn of social conditions at first hand. He did not hesitate to join civic movements to reform the city and help its submerged and vicious classes. His deepest interest was in Catholic eleemosynary institutions: St. Vincent's Orphan Asylum, his Newsboys' Home, industrial schools and orphanages for girls, the homes of the Good Shepherd, and St. Mary's Training School for boys at Feehanville, where he erected his own summer residence and intimately concerned himself with the work of rehabilitation. Growing old, he sought relief from his burdens and obtained an auxiliary bishop, Peter J. Muldoon (1901). A year later, he was dead. To Catholics of all races and to Chicagoans in general, he had so endeared himself that few would disagree with the eulogy which Archbishop Ryan of Philadelphia delivered over the remains of his lifelong friend. A large, strongly built man, steadfast and frank in his opinions, reserved but kind, and rather unforgiving if deceived, Archbishop Feehan's courage was never broken. He had neither skill nor desire to dabble in secular or ecclesiastical politics. Reputed a good theologian, he wrote practically nothing and left little correspondence. Unswervingly, he confined himself to his official duties, and these he did well.

[C. J. Kirkfleet, Ord. Praem., *The Life of Patrick Augustine Feehan* (1922); *Souvenir of the Silver Jubilee of the Most Rev. P. A. Feehan* (1891); G. J. Garraghan, S. J., *The Cath. Ch. in Chicago* (Chicago, 1921); *Cath. Encyc.*; *Who's Who in America*, 1901–02; *Rev. of Revs.* XXVI, 284; *Chicago American*, July 14, 1902; *Chronicle*, July 15, 1902. *The New World* (a diocesan weekly established by Feehan in 1892), reprinted editorial obituary comments from the secular and Catholic press. *The New World*, Apr. 14, 1900, contained an historical survey of the archdiocese.]

R. J. P.

FEKE, ROBERT (*c.* 1705–*c.* 1750), portrait-painter, styled a "mariner" in Newport records, was born at Oyster Bay, Long Island. The family was not Dutch, as has been stated. Robert Feke, Sr., a Baptist minister, was descended from Robert Feke, or Feake, who settled at Watertown, Mass., and married Elizabeth Fones, widow of Henry Winthrop. The Fekes were of Norfolk, England, a sixteenth-century ancestor being James Feake of Wighton. Little is known of the boyhood of Robert Feke, Jr. His mother was Clemence Ludlam. Several writers repeat the legend that he was disinherited by his Quaker father for adopting the Baptist faith; and that having gone to sea he was taken captive to Spain where he learned to paint. Professor W. C. Poland's researches established that Robert Feke, Sr., was himself a Baptist preacher, so that if the story of the disinheritance has any truth, it applies to the father and not to the artist. Feke's portraiture has no resemblance to Spanish painting of any period; its affinity to the eighteenth-century English school is obvious. It is probable that Feke had seafaring experience and that this brought him to Newport, a prosperous trading town. In 1729 Dean, afterward Bishop, George Berkeley visited Newport; and from internal evidence in Feke's painting some have thought that he either learned to paint from John Smibert, who was of Berkeley's entourage, or that he was influenced at least by Smibert.

On Sept. 23, 1742, Feke married Elinor Cozzens (in several publications styled "Eleanor." See *Newport Hist. Mag.*, I, 204). A tradition records that Mrs. Feke was a Quaker, while her husband remained a Baptist, and that each First-day he escorted her to the door of the Friends' Meeting-House before going to his own church. Feke was thus described by Dr. Alexander Hamilton, a Scottish visitor, in his *Itinerarium:* "This man had exactly the phiz of a painter, having a long pale face, sharp nose, large eyes,—with which he looked upon you steadfastly,—long curled black hair, a delicate white hand, and long fingers." This description agrees with the two Feke self-portraits: one depicting a youth of about twenty; the other, a mature man as he may have looked about 1750. William Dunlap's reference (*History of the Rise and Progress of the Arts of Design in the United States,* 1918, I, 30) to a portrait of a Philadelphia woman, Mrs. Willing, painted in Philadelphia in 1746, has led to discovery of other signed portraits in that city (Hannah R. London, *Portraits of Jews by Gilbert Stuart and other Early American Artists,* 1927, pp. 34, 63, 123). A reference has also been discovered to his painting in Philadelphia in the spring of 1750. Mr. Henry Wilder Foote regards it as certain that in 1741 Feke visited Boston to paint the portrait group of Isaac Royall and family, now belonging to the Harvard Law Library, and again in 1748–49, when he painted more than twenty of his finest pictures, including those of the Bowdoin family. A legendary account which is credible represents Feke as suffering from ill health, a circumstance which led to his going to Bermuda (or possibly Barbados) where he died. He left five children of whom only two daughters had descendants. The widow died in Newport in 1804. Two portraits by Feke, portraying Mary Wanton and Philip Wilkinson, are in the Redwood Library, Newport. The portrait of Rev. John Callender at the Rhode Island Historical Society, in Providence, is now ascribed to Feke, though formerly attributed to Smibert. At Bowdoin College are the very striking likenesses of William and James Bowdoin and their wives. The Cleveland Art Museum has a fine portrait of Charles Apthorp. Of Feke's technique Lawrence Park wrote (*Bulletin of the Cleveland Museum,* July 1919): "The work of his maturity shows Feke to have been a clever draughtsman and although strongly influenced by the conventions of pose which are closely associated with his own and earlier periods, his portraits carry conviction, both as lifelike reproduction of likenesses, and, of the rich, elaborate costumes of velvets, silks and satins which his subjects wore. A pleasing pearliness of tone is found which did not exist when they left the artist's hands."

[See especially *Robert Feke: Colonial Portrait Painter* (to be published in 1930), by Henry Wilder Foote, which gives a full account of what is known of the artist and a descriptive catalogue of about seventy of his works; and *Robert Feke, the Early Newport Portrait Painter,* by Wm. Carey Poland (1907). Besides the authorities cited above there are references to Feke in Wilkins Updike, *A Hist. of the Episcopal Church in Narragansett, R. I.* (2nd ed., 3 vols., 1907); Maude Howe Elliott, "Some Recollections of Newport Artists," in *Newport Hist. Soc. Bull.,* p. 35 (1921). A concise biographical summary prefaces the reproductions with descriptive text of all the portraits attributed to Feke in F. W. Bayley's *Five Colonial Artists of New England* (1929). See also Mary Powell Bunker, *Long Island Genealogies* (1895), pp. 202–3.]

F. W. C.

FELCH, ALPHEUS (Sept. 28, 1804–June 13, 1896), lawyer, senator, governor of Michigan, was born at Limerick, Me., the son of Captain Daniel Felch, a country merchant, and Sally Piper. His grandfather, Abijah Felch, had been a revolutionary soldier and a prominent citizen. When his mother died in 1808, leaving him an orphan, Alpheus lived successively with his grandfathers and with an aunt. He attended the Academy in Limerick, then in 1821 entered Phillips Exeter Academy in New Hampshire. In 1823 he enrolled at Bowdoin College, where he graduated in 1827, and in the same year he took up the study of law. Three years later he was admitted to the bar at Bangor, Me. He began his practise at Houlton, Me., where one of his sisters lived, but on account of his weak lungs, he was advised by a physician to go West. He left in 1833, traveling by stage, steamer, and canal-boat, until he reached Monroe, Mich. From there he planned to go South, but when he arrived in Cincinnati, he contracted cholera. Returning to Monroe, he began to practise law. He married on Sept. 14, 1837, Lucretia W. Lawrence, the daughter of his friend, Judge Wolcott Lawrence. In 1834 he was elected village attorney, and in the next year he became a member of the state legislature. Thereafter he was successively state bank commissioner (1838), auditor-general (1842), justice of the state supreme court (1843), and governor. This last office he filled from Jan. 1, 1846, to Mar. 3, 1847. In 1846 he was elected to the United States Senate, as a Democrat, and served for one term. His career in Washington was not brilliant; his speeches were relatively few and caused no great stir. Nevertheless he won general respect, due to the fact that he never prepared a speech without thorough research. That he was exceedingly painstaking is shown by his speech against the French spoliation claims (*Congressional Globe,* 32 Cong., 1 Sess., app. pp. 564–74), and the speech on land grants to Iowa (*Ibid.,* pp. 145–54). Largely through his efforts a bill was passed by the Senate (*Ibid.,* 32 Cong., 1 Sess., p. 2232; app. pp. 941–64) providing for the construction of a canal at Sault Ste. Marie, which finally was enacted. In 1853, at the conclusion of his senatorial term, he was appointed president of a commission to adjust and settle the Spanish and Mexican land claims under the treaty of Guadalupe-Hidalgo.

In 1856 Felch opened a law office in Ann Arbor, Mich. He had made his home there since 1843. He was greatly interested in the rising university, and upon his death left to it more than 4,000 books and pamphlets. From 1843 to 1847 he was one of the regents and from 1879 to 1883 he was Tappan Professor of Law. He died in Ann Arbor, survived by five children. His written works include a few articles on Michigan history which appeared in the *Michigan Pioneer and Historical Collections.*

[An excellent biography of Felch was published by his friend C. B. Grant in the *Mich. Pioneer and Hist. Colls.*, XXVIII (1900), 94–104. See also G. I. Reed, *Bench and Bar of Mich.* (1897), pp. 161–64; B. A. Hinsdale, *Hist. of the Univ. of Mich.* (1906), pp. 167–68; W. F. Felch, *Memorial Hist. of the Felch Family* (1881), pt. III, p. 58; *Hist. of York County, Me.* (1880), pp. 333–40; the *Ann Arbor Courier*, June 17, 1896; the *Ann Arbor Reg.*, June 18, 1896; and the *Ann Arbor Argus*, June 19, 1896.] A. H.

FELL, JOHN (Feb. 5, 1721–May 15, 1798), merchant, judge, legislator, was born and schooled in New York City. He was a descendant of Symon Felle who subscribed twelve florins for fortifying the town on Oct. 11, 1655 (*Records of New Amsterdam*, 1897, I, 373). As senior partner of John Fell & Company he was a large merchant by 1759, having a fleet of several armed ships. Later he bought 220 acres of land and settled near Paramus, Bergen County, N. J. He was judge of the court of common pleas, 1766–74 and 1776–86 (*New Jersey Archives*, 2 ser., I, 54, 456). A leader in the meeting of 328 citizens of Bergen County who signed patriotic resolutions at the Hackensack Court House on June 25, 1774, he became chairman of the Bergen County committee which made the war locally, chairman of the Standing Committee of Correspondence, and on May 23, 1775, headed the Bergen deputies to the First Provincial Congress at Trenton. His work lay in tightening the grip of the revolutionists on Bergen County and he won fame as "a great Tory Hunter" (Journals of Stephen Kemble, Apr. 23, 1777, *New York Historical Society Collections*, 1883, p. 114). A member of the Provincial Council in 1776, he was taken at his home by Loyalist raiders Apr. 22, 1777, and badly treated in the provost jail in New York City (J. Van Zandt to R. Morris, Nov. 10, 1777), but paroled on Jan. 7, 1778, and released on May 11.

Elected to the Continental Congress, Nov. 6, 1778, he worked with great zeal, being reëlected May 25 and Dec. 25, 1779. Attending steadily from Dec. 5, 1778, to Nov. 28, 1780, he cast 265 votes but put few motions and wrote fewer reports. Though serving on various special committees, his main work was on the standing committee of five "to conduct the commercial affairs of the United States," which met almost daily. He was the New Jersey member on the special foreign affairs committee Jan. 20, 1779, and also on that to estimate state quotas of supplies. He sided frequently with his colleague, W. C. Houston, voting steadily for economy, sound finance, and increase of national authority. Few men have been so solidly useful and so obscure. After serving uneventfully 1782–83 in the New Jersey Council, he sold his Bergen property, moving to New York City and thence to his son Peter's estate at Coldenham, Dutchess County, N. Y., where he died. He was a man of wealth and lived well. He had married Susanna Moskhk, or Marschalk, widow of one McIntosh. His son, Peter Renaudet Fell, was a lieutenant-colonel of Bergen County militia and married Margaret Colden, grand-daughter of Lieut.-Gov. Cadwallader Colden.

[The best accounts are by Wm. Nelson, *N. J. Archives*, 2 ser. I (1901), 456, 54–55n.; *N. J. Hist. Soc. Colls.*, IX (1916), 110–11. Fell's journal of prison days is in *Docs. and Letters to Illustrate the Revolutionary Incidents of Queens County* (1846), ed. by Henry Onderdonk. His list of the prisoners May 11, 1778, is in *N. Y. Geneal. and Biog. Record*, XXIV (1893), 85. Van Zandt's letter as to his hardships is in *Proc. N. J. Hist. Soc.*, n.s., V (1920), 177. Fell also kept a diary while in Congress (MS. in Lib. of Cong., see references "Fell," in E. C. Burnett, *Letters of Members of the Continental Cong.*, III, 1926, 564, IV, 1928, 560); his report on care of war prisoners is in Papers of Cont. Cong., No. 28, Folio 60, MSS. Div., Lib. of Cong.] W. L. W—y.

FELS, JOSEPH (Dec. 16, 1854–Feb. 22, 1914), soap manufacturer, and Single-Tax advocate, was born of German Jewish parents, Lazarus and Susanna (Freiberg) Fels, in Halifax County, Va. His father and mother had come to America under the migratory impulse of 1848. Soon after Joseph's birth they settled in Yanceyville, N. C., where they lived till the end of the Civil War. The boy's schooling was irregular and apparently of slight permanent worth. At Richmond and Baltimore, where the family lived after the war, opportunities were better, but at fifteen Joseph left school for business. For a year he worked with his father, who was engaged in the production of toilet soaps on a small scale. Then for three years father and son represented a Philadelphia soap house in Baltimore, but in 1873 they went to Philadelphia and took a commission with a larger house. Two years later, when he had reached his majority, Joseph went into a partnership with another Philadelphia manufacturer, whom he bought out, after the first year, for the sum of $4,000. This was the beginning of an uninterrupted business success continuing for twenty years. In 1893 he bought an interest in a process of soap-making from naphtha and after experimentation and improvement discontinued the manufacture of toilet soaps and developed the

Fels-Naptha plant, which eventually sent its products to every part of the civilized world.

While in England, planning for the extension of his export trade, Fels formed contacts with leaders of humanitarian effort, notably with George Lansbury, through whom he became interested in the English back-to-the-land movement. At Hollesley Bay Fels bought 1,300 acres of land for the use of the unemployed and later at Maylands, Essex, he devoted 600 acres to the same purpose. He promoted vacant-lot farming in London, as well as in Philadelphia.

It was not until 1905 that Fels became identified with the Single-Tax propaganda, of which he was to become within ten years an outstanding exponent. The humanitarian phase of the movement appealed to him especially. He himself said that a Socialist (Keir Hardie) unwittingly inspired him with zeal for social service that led to his enrolment among the followers of Henry George. Economic theory seems to have had a secondary part in his conversion to the Single Tax; but of the completeness of that conversion no one ever had the slightest doubt. He withdrew from business at a time when continuance seemed to promise great additions to a fortune already large and for the rest of his life devoted his time and his wealth unreservedly to the cause. He announced his decision in a speech to a Chicago audience, in these words: "We cannot get rich under present conditions without robbing somebody, I have done it; you are doing it now, and I am still doing it, but I am proposing to spend the money to wipe out the system by which I made it" (Fels, *post,* p. 159).

This was no empty promise. He was given credit for obtaining the inclusion of the land-tax feature in the British budget of 1909 and the active support of the measure by Lloyd George in a campaign memorable in British politics (Steffens, *post,* p. 746). He devoted not less than $100,000 a year from his private fortune for Single-Tax promotion throughout the world. Of this sum $25,000 annually was spent in England, $5,000 in Denmark, $5,000 in Canada, and considerable amounts in Germany, France, Spain, Italy, and Australasia. One of the Fels enterprises was to procure the translation of Henry George's *Progress and Poverty* into Chinese. Tracts were printed in various languages and widely distributed. To the Fels Fund for Single-Tax promotion he gave $131,000, as against a public subscription of nearly $83,000; but the money represented only a small part of his personal contribution. For years he was in the habit of making platform addresses wherever an audience could be had. A man of small stature, slightly more than five feet in height, and endowed with extraordinary energy and vitality, he was a speaker of force, gifted with persuasive powers of no mean order. He disliked to be known as a philanthropist, but such enterprises as the establishment of health centers in London and the Boys' and Girls' Clubs sponsored by Margaret McMillan had his zealous and practical support. So, too, did the Zionist movement. His wife, Mary Fels, a distant relative, whom he met and married in Keokuk, Iowa, in 1891, was a sharer in his ideals and after his death wrote a sympathetic account of his life and work.

[The chief source of information about Fels is the biography by his wife, *Joseph Fels, His Life Work* (1916). See also an article by Louis F. Post in *The Public* (Chicago), Feb. 27, 1914, and additional material in the same periodical, May 8, 1914; "Joseph Fels, Single Taxer," by F. W. Garrison, in the *Single Tax Review,* Mar.–Apr., 1914; an article by Lincoln Steffens in the *American Mag.,* Oct. 1910; "Fels, a New Type of Philanthropist," by J. D. Miller, in the *New England Mag.,* June 1911; sketch by F. C. Howe in the *Survey,* Mar. 28, 1914, the obituary in the *Public Ledger* (Phila.), Feb. 23, 1914.] W. B. S—w.

FELSENTHAL, BERNHARD (Jan. 2, 1822–Jan. 12, 1908), rabbi, son of Simon and Eva (Gall) Felsenthal, was born at Münchweiler, Bavaria. His was the uneventful life of a quiet scholar. From the age of twenty to thirty-two he taught in a Jewish school in his native village. Then in 1854 he came to the United States, settling as a teacher in Lawrenceburg, Ind., and in 1856 in Madison, Ind. In April 1858, he went to Chicago, where, after three years' service in a bank, he became, in June 1861, the first rabbi of Sinai Congregation, an outgrowth of the Jüdischer Reformverein in which he had been the leading spirit. In 1864, he was elected rabbi of Zion Congregation, Chicago, which he served until he was made Rabbi Emeritus in 1887. His wife, Caroline Levi, died in December 1863, two years after their marriage. A year and a half later he married Henrietta Blumenfeld, who bore him five children, and who died in 1901. He died in his eighty-seventh year.

Such was the unsensational framework within which was lived a singularly unassuming life. Yet, Felsenthal was a leading figure in the development of Reform Judaism in the Middle West, and had a far-flung influence among reform and orthodox Jews alike, due to his fine-fibered personality. When the exigencies of public life called him, he gave himself readily, though primarily as the scholar. In 1879, with Emerson and ten others, he was elected honorary vice-president of the Free Religious Association. He served the Jewish Publication Society of America, and made the first suggestion for the foundation of the American Jewish Historical Society.

The bibliography of his writings lists 315 titles, practically all on Jewish themes. Most of these apply the learning of the past to issues of his day. Two main strands run through them—Reform Judaism and Zionism. His attitude to these movements changed markedly as his knowledge, experience and judgment deepened with advancing years.

As a young man, he pleaded eloquently in his *Kol Kore Bamidbar* (A Voice Crying in the Wilderness, 1859) and other writings and addresses for discarding what he called the outworn elements of Judaism, so that it should appear as the natural religion in the soul of man. He held that "Reform is on the side of life, conservatism on the side of death." Later, he saw with misgivings a generation of Jews growing up, to whom, as he said, "Jewish rites and customs and usages are as unknown as those of the Hindus." When he became convinced that a Reform Judaism which emphasized universalism and negated Jewish national elements, would not fulfil the Jewish mission, but would lead to the absorption of Israel, this conservative Reform Rabbi declared repeatedly, "This extreme Reform we have in America, which knows no limit, will gradually lead to the extinction of Israel and its religion."

Similarly, in his earlier years, he had showed no active sympathy for Jewish Palestinian movements; but when Dr. Herzl organized the Zionist movement in 1897, Felsenthal, in the face of ridicule and derision, was one of the first in America to rally to its support. The septuagenarian and octogenarian Rabbi stood toweringly alone in Reform Judaism as an advocate of Zionism. He taught with tireless vigor, especially in his masterly "Jewish Theses" ("Jüdische Thesen," *Deborah,* September–November 1901; translated in *Menorah Monthly,* November 1901–January 1902), that Judaism was not only a religion, but a national culture, "the sum total of all the manifestations of the distinctively Jewish national spirit." His conviction daily became "more intensified that Zionism alone will be the savior of our nation and its religion, and save it from death and disappearance." Only Zionism, he asserted, could effectively counteract those environmental forces which tend progressively to the assimilation, absorption, and extinction of the Jew. By rising above his contemporaries in the brave expression of his matured evaluation of the two causes to which his life was most fervently given, Reform Judaism and Zionism, the sweet-souled, beloved teacher, Bernhard Felsenthal, attained a permanent and significant place in the history of the ideology of American-Jewish life.

[*Bernhard Felsenthal, Teacher in Israel, Selections from his Writings, with Biographical Sketch and Bibliography* (1924), by his daughter, Emma Felsenthal; *Year Book, Central Conf. of Am. Rabbis,* XVIII (1908), 161–67 and *passim* in earlier volumes; *Pubs. Am. Jewish Hist. Soc. No. 17* (1909), pp. 218–22; *Chicago Hist. Soc. Ann. Report,* 1909; *Reform Advocate* (Chicago), Feb. 8, 1908.]

D. de S. P.

FELT, JOSEPH BARLOW (Dec. 22, 1789–Sept. 8, 1869), antiquarian, was born in Salem, Mass., the son of John and Elizabeth (Curtis) Felt. His father, a shipmaster, died in 1802, and Joseph went to work for a merchant. The reading of biographical works in his leisure hours served as an incentive for a college education. At eighteen he entered the academy at Atkinson, N. H., which was then under the charge of John Vose, a distinguished educator. In 1813 he was graduated from Dartmouth College. After a brief return to mercantile work Felt taught school and studied for the ministry with the Rev. Samuel Worcester of Salem. His first parish, 1821–24, was at Sharon, Mass.; his second and last was at Hamilton. Owing to ill health he retired from pastoral work in 1833, and in the following year removed to Boston. While at Hamilton he acquired a considerable reputation as an antiquarian and local historian. He prepared articles for John Farmer's *Genealogical Register* (1829) and published *The Annals of Salem* (1827, 2nd ed. 2 vols., 1845–59) and a *History of Ipswich, Essex, and Hamilton* (1834). Soon after his removal to Boston he spent three years (1836–39) in classifying and arranging ancient papers in the state archives. In 1830 he was elected a member of the Massachusetts Historical Society, and from 1842 to 1854 he was its librarian. From 1850 to 1853 he was president of the New-England Historic Genealogical Society. Throughout these years he wrote much. His *Historical Account of Massachusetts Currency* (1839) was considered invaluable by numismatologists. In 1847 he finished publishing the *Collections* of the American Statistical Association which contained a large amount of original matter and bore proof of "patient research and thorough work." These were followed by *A Memoir, or Defense of Hugh Peters* (1851), and *The Customs of New England* (1853). His most ambitious work was an *Ecclesiastical History of New England,* the first volume of which appeared in 1851, the second in 1862. Though his zeal for discovering and reading old manuscripts was extraordinary, his literary style was lifeless, and his conclusions were sometimes colored by his own religious sentiments. Consequently, "he will be known and remembered rather as a diligent annalist than as a philosophical historian" (Dexter, *post*). In daily life he was a simple, faithful Christian who occasionally gave offense by his outspoken orthodoxy. On Sept. 18, 1816, Felt married Abigail Adams Shaw, a niece of Mrs. John Adams. After her death in 1859 he married Mrs. Catharine (Bartlett) Meacham, Nov. 16, 1862.

[The best biographical sketch is that by Felt's nephew, J. B. F. Osgood, in the *New-Eng. Hist. and Geneal. Reg.*, Jan. 1870. Henry M. Dexter's memoir in the *Proc. Mass. Hist. Soc.*, XIV (1876), 113–16, appears to have been based on Osgood's sketch, but the closing paragraph is valuable because it gives Dexter's opinion of Felt's historical work.] L. S. M.

FELTON, CORNELIUS CONWAY (Nov. 6, 1807–Feb. 26, 1862), classical scholar, was the son of Cornelius Conway Felton and Anna (Morse) Felton, daughter of David and Abigail (Bayley) Morse of Newbury, Mass. He was a descendant of Lieut. Nathaniel Felton, who came from England to Salem, Mass., in 1633. In 1692 Nathaniel with his wife and two sons signed a protest against the prosecution of a neighbor on the charge of witchcraft. The family continued to be resident in Essex County, and the younger Cornelius Conway was born at Newbury. He began in early childhood to show the ambition for learning which was to mark his career through life. Under the tuition of Simeon Putnam at North Andover he was fitted to enter Harvard College and was graduated there with the class of 1827. His scanty means obliged him, even as an undergraduate, to take precious time for earning money by school-teaching, and after graduation he continued teaching at various "academies." In 1829 he was called to Harvard as tutor in Latin, was made Greek tutor in the following year, promoted to be professor of Greek in 1832, and in 1834 received the Eliot Professorship of Greek Literature which he held until his election as president of the college in 1860. He was married twice: in 1838 to Mary, daughter of Asa Whitney, who died in 1845; and in 1846 to Mary Louisa, daughter of Thomas G. Carey of Boston.

Felton's most prominent quality was the breadth of his intellectual interests. His conception of classical scholarship as set forth in his public utterances was, first, of solid learning grounded in a thorough study of linguistic details and then the widening out of this purely linguistic approach to include the whole life of the people whose language is studied: its geography, its philosophy, its political structure, and every form of its artistic expression. In his inaugural address on assuming the Eliot Professorship he outlined with great force and clearness the course he intended to pursue and throughout his tenure of nearly thirty years he maintained, often in the face of much opposition, the lofty ideal he here laid down.

As an author Felton was active principally as editor of classical texts and selections from Greek writers for academic use. His most popular work consisted of his four courses of lectures before the Lowell Institute in Boston delivered in the years 1852, 1853, 1854, and 1859 and published in two volumes in 1867, five years after his death, under the title: *Greece: Ancient and Modern.* These lectures embodied the results of his long years of study in the records of Greek life and thought, enlivened by his recollections of recent travel in the scenes of ancient culture. Another posthumous volume was *Familiar Letters from Europe* (1866).

He had begun life as a school teacher, and this experience gave him a sympathetic understanding of the needs of elementary and secondary schools. Well informed on the conditions of English and Continental education he maintained that American youth should be trained according to American conditions. He watched with great interest the advancing claims of the natural sciences to a larger place in school programs and favored their recognition, yet always with the reservation that the highest education must be built upon the "humanities" and through the medium of language. For many years he served the public as a member of the School Committee of Cambridge and of the Massachusetts Board of Education, and as one of the Regents of the Smithsonian Institution. He was keenly interested in the detail of academic discipline and in all that concerned the wise regulation of student life. It was in recognition of this quality that in 1849, on the creation of the office of "Regent" under President Sparks, he was chosen as the first incumbent. The purpose of this office, like that of the more recent Dean, was to relieve the president of much of the detail of personal dealing with students, and for eight years he performed its duties with a rare union of strictness and tact. Upon the resignation of President Walker in 1860 the unanimous choice of the governing boards selected Felton as his successor. Although in impaired health he accepted and began his administration with every promise of notable success. Unfortunately, the strain of his new responsibilities proved to be more than he could bear, and after little more than a year, seeking relief in a more genial climate, he died at Chester, Pa.

[Cyrus Felton, *A Geneal. Hist. of the Felton Family* (1886); *Inaugural Address of Cornelius Conway Felton as Eliot Professor of Greek Literature* (Cambridge, 1834); *Addresses at the Inauguration of Cornelius Conway Felton as President of Harvard College, July 19, 1860* (1860); memoir by Henry Barnard, in *Am. Jour. of Educ.*, Mar. 1861; eulogy by Theodore Dwight Woolsey, printed in *Annual Report . . . of the Smithsonian Inst. for the year 1861* (1862); memoir by Geo. S. Hillard in *Proc. Mass. Hist. Soc.*, vol. X (1869); *Proc. Am. Acad. Arts and Sci.*, vol. VI (1866); A. P. Peabody, *Sermon on the Death of Cornelius Conway Felton* (1862); *Boston Daily Advertiser,* Feb. 28, July 16, 1862.] E. E.

FELTON, REBECCA LATIMER (June 10, 1835–Jan. 24, 1930), writer, United States senator, the daughter of Charles and Eleanor (Swift) Latimer, was born near Decatur, DeKalb County, Ga. Her *Country Life in Georgia in the Days of My Youth* (1919) contains reminiscences of her girlhood. After graduation (1852) from the Madison (Ga.) Female College, she was married (1853) to Dr. William Harrell Felton [*q.v.*], who played a noteworthy rôle in Georgia politics. He was an advanced liberal and waged a stubborn fight over many years with the conservative element of his party. In this fight he was ably assisted by his wife. Her ability as a writer and speaker became generally recognized and, though never offering for public office herself, she became a rather important factor in state affairs. For twenty-eight years she was a regular contributor to the tri-weekly edition of the *Atlanta Journal,* and through this medium exercised considerable influence in formulating public opinion in Georgia. As her days lengthened (she died in her ninety-fifth year), her intellect remained undimmed, her interest in public matters persisted, and she was always ready to express in quite positive fashion her views on all sorts of questions, state, national, and international. Among the first to advocate equal political rights for women, an ardent temperance fighter long before prohibition became a national question, a champion of penal reform in Georgia, Mrs. Felton was generally to be found on the side of civic righteousness and progressive legislation. In her well-known book, *My Memoirs of Georgia Politics* (1911), she left unflattering accounts of many important Georgians with whom she and her husband had contended, at the same time paying tribute to those who she felt were on the side of honest government and clean politics.

A member of the board of lady managers of the Chicago Exposition (1893), chairman of the woman's executive board of the Cotton States and International Exposition in Atlanta (1894–95), a juror on the agricultural board of the St. Louis Exposition, and a member of numerous patriotic organizations, she had attained considerable, but chiefly local, prominence before her appointment to the United States Senate made her for the moment a national figure. Following the death of Senator Thomas E. Watson, in September 1922, and before the election of his successor, Walter F. George, in November, Gov. Thomas W. Hardwick made a graceful gesture by giving Mrs. Felton on Oct. 3 an *ad interim* appointment. Taking the oath of office Nov. 21, she attended the session of that day and of Nov. 22, when Senator George was sworn in. Surviving her four sons and her daughter, she lived until Jan. 24, 1930, when she died in an Atlanta hospital. On the afternoon of the following day the Senate adjourned early out of respect for the first and until that time the only woman to become one of its members.

[The *Atlanta Journal,* Jan. 26, 1930, contains many columns devoted to Mrs. Felton's life, including the proceedings in the Senate, and a long editorial tribute. See also *Biog. Directory Am. Cong.* (1928); *Who's Who in the South* (1927). Her papers were left by her will to the Univ. of Ga.] R. P. B—s.

FELTON, SAMUEL MORSE (July 17, 1809–Jan. 24, 1889), civil engineer, was born at Newbury, Mass., the son of Cornelius Conway and Anna Morse Felton, and brother of Cornelius Conway Felton [*q.v.*]. His father, a chaise maker by trade, lost his property during Samuel's youth and moved his family to Saugus where they knew keen poverty. At the age of fourteen the son went into Boston to be clerk and general errand boy at a wholesale grocery store. For four years he earned his living in this way and studied during every spare moment in order to prepare himself for high school. Working as a clerk and bookkeeper, he put himself through the Livingston County high school at Geneseo, N. Y., of which his brother was principal, and saved enough money to enable him to enter Harvard in 1830 where he practically supported himself by teaching. After his graduation in 1834 he spent two years teaching in a private school and then entered upon his engineering career with Loammi Baldwin, Jr., of Boston. Upon Baldwin's death in 1838, Felton succeeded to the business. His first railroad work was in 1841 when he constructed the Fresh Pond Railroad, designed to transport ice into Boston. Two years later he began the construction of the Fitchburg Railroad. From the time he became superintendent of this road in 1845 until his death he was continuously connected with railroad management in this country. In 1851 he removed to Philadelphia to become president of the Philadelphia, Wilmington & Baltimore Railroad. He found the road in a demoralized condition, unsuccessful financially, and badly mismanaged. His efforts to remove the causes for its failure brought down personal abuse on his head, but he was successful, and in a few years the road had become one of the best equipped and most profitably run railroads in the country. During these difficult years he refused the presidency of both the Baltimore & Ohio and the Philadelphia & Reading railroads (the latter at a salary larger than that given to any other railroad official in the country) in order to fulfil what he felt to be his obligations to the stockholders of the Philadelphia, Wilmington & Baltimore.

At the outbreak of the Civil War the Philadelphia, Wilmington & Baltimore became of great strategic importance. It was over this road that Lincoln made his entrance into Washington at the risk of his life. Felton changed the President's advertised route into the capital, arranging for his secret passage from Harrisburg to Washington the night before he was expected, and thus saved him from the Baltimore mob which attacked the train supposed to be carrying him. The service he rendered in the transportation of Union troops during the war can scarcely be overestimated. For his part in getting Gen. Butler's troops to Annapolis and in preparing plans for the cooperation of all railroads centering in Philadelphia, the telegraph lines and Adams Express Company, he received the official thanks of the War Department. But the stinging criticisms he received while performing the almost superhuman duties involved in the task were too much for him and in 1864 a stroke of paralysis forced him to retire from active work. By the following year, however, he had recovered sufficiently to assume the presidency of the Pennsylvania Steel Company engaged in the manufacture of steel rails. Though he devoted much time in the later years of his life to this project, he never gave up his railroad interests. He had retained even during his illness the presidency of the Delaware Railroad, a small road which he had developed in his earlier years with the Philadelphia, Wilmington & Baltimore. From 1873 to 1883 he took an important part in the development of the Pennsylvania Railroad, of which he was a director. He was also one of the organizers and later a director of the Northern Pacific Railroad. In addition to these activities he served as a commissioner of the Hoosac Tunnel from 1862 to 1865 and was for some time managing director of the Lehigh Navigation Company. Felton was twice married: first in 1836 to Eleanor Stetson who died in 1847, and again in 1850 to Maria Low Lippitt.

[Cyrus Felton, *A Geneal. Hist. of the Felton Family* (1886); Thos. Doane and Chas. Harris, "Samuel Morse Felton, A Memoir," in the *Jour. Asso. of Engineering Socs.*, Apr. 1892, abstracted in *Proc. Am. Soc. of Civil Engineers*, Apr. 1893; *Railroad and Engineering Jour.*, Mar. 1889; *Railroad Gazette*, Feb. 1, 1889; *Memorials of the Class of 1834*, Harvard Univ. (1884); *Investigation into the Alleged Misconduct of the Late Superintendent of the Phila., Wilmington and Baltimore Railroad Co.* (2 vols., 1854–55).]

E. Y.

FELTON, WILLIAM HARRELL (June 19, 1823–Sept. 24, 1909), politician, the only child of John and Mary Felton, was born in Oglethorpe County, Ga. His father, who had been a captain in the War of 1812, was a farmer and the boy grew up among rural surroundings. For the purpose of educating their son, his parents moved in 1835 to Athens, seat of Franklin College (as the University of Georgia was then called), from which he was graduated in 1842. Two years later he received his degree from the medical college of the state. Felton's nervous system was such that he was unable to bear the strain of a physician's life. He therefore abandoned it, and took up farming in Bartow County, whither the family moved in 1847. In 1848 he was licensed as a local Methodist preacher and for nearly fifty years filled appointments without remuneration. As a preacher all accounts say that he was extraordinarily effective.

Felton was in early life a Whig and served one term in the legislature (1851) as a member of that party. He volunteered as a surgeon during the Civil War and served in a Macon hospital. After the war he became a Democrat, but in 1874 he entered the race for Congress from the 7th District as an independent candidate. The campaign which followed was among the bitterest and most spectacular in the state's history. Arrayed against Felton were the entire Democratic organization, all the important political leaders, and the press of the district and the state. Single-handed, except for the great assistance of his wife, Felton waged war on the organization and was successful by a small majority. For many years thereafter he was the leader and inspiration of all those elements which disliked ring rule. He became the central figure in Georgia politics. Repeating his success in the two following contests, he served in Congress from 1875 to 1881, and there advocated the remonetization of silver. An organization candidate, Judson C. Clements [*q.v.*], defeated him for reëlection in 1880.

Four years after retiring from Congress Felton was elected to the legislature as representative from Bartow County, and served until 1890. Though now a feeble old man, he was full of fire and an antagonist to be dreaded. In the legislature he championed the re-leasing of the state-owned Western and Atlantic Railroad, the disposition of which constituted the principal issue of the day, but at a much larger rental. He also advocated devoting the rental to elementary education. The bill, practically as he drew it, passed after a strenuous fight lasting through two sessions of the legislature. Felton scathingly denounced the convict leasing system, worked for the establishment of a reformatory for juvenile delinquents, was a champion of higher education and was said to have saved the life of the University, of which he was a trustee, 1879–89. He fought and exposed corruption of all sorts, fearing no man, however powerful or well entrenched in the affections of the people.

Felton's first wife was Anne Carlton of Athens, who died in 1851. In 1853 he married Rebecca Latimer, who was destined to become as well-known as her husband [see Felton, Rebecca Latimer]. In *My Memoirs of Georgia Politics* (1911), Mrs. Felton recounted circumstances very damaging to the reputations of many leading Georgians who had opposed her husband in politics. Felton died at his home in Cartersville, Ga., in 1909, being then in his eighty-seventh year.

[I. W. Avery, *Hist. of the State of Ga. from 1850 to 1881* (1881); L. L. Knight, *A Standard Hist. of Ga. and Georgians* (1917), IV, 2098–2101; sketch by Mrs. Felton in W. J. Northen, *Men of Mark in Ga.* (1908), IV, 103; obituary in *Atlanta Jour.*, Sept. 25, 1909.]

R. P. B—s.

FENDALL, JOSIAS (*c.* 1620–*c.* 1687), colonial governor of Maryland, first attracted attention in 1655. In that year, while William Stone, the proprietary governor of Maryland, was resisting the commissioners of Parliament for the government of that province, Fendall, one of Stone's officers, took a leading part in seizing some arms and ammunition for the governor's force. His services were rewarded by a grant of two thousand acres of land and by appointment, July 10, 1656, as governor. He visited England in 1657 and the following year brought back an agreement under which the government was definitely restored to the proprietor, as well as a new commission curtailing his power as governor. Chafing under criticism of the proprietor for negligence at courts and for contradicting court orders, in March 1659–60, with a number of associates, he suddenly attempted to overthrow the proprietary government and set up in its place a commonwealth in which the supreme power should be vested in a House of Burgesses. Over this body the governor was to preside; but the House, retaining its speaker, was to have the power to adjourn and dissolve. The attempted revolution was easily frustrated. The proprietor asked that Fendall forfeit his life, but the provincial court only issued an order to confiscate his estate and banish him from the province. Subsequently, in response to a petition for mercy, his punishment was reduced to disfranchisement and disqualification for office. He retired to his estate in Charles County where he had a wife, a daughter, a brother, and several servants. In 1678 the freemen of that county were disposed to elect him a delegate to the Assembly, but they were informed by the governor and council that if he were elected his seat would be declared vacant. In April 1679 he was charged with seditious utterances and a warrant was issued for his arrest, but he was not found. About this time he became influential in northern Virginia among the sympathizers of Nathaniel Bacon [*q.v.*] and associated with John Coode [*q.v.*], who a few years later was the principal leader in the overthrow of the proprietary government. Both Fendall and Coode were arrested in 1681 and Fendall, tried in November, was found guilty of atttempting to raise a mutiny in Charles County, fined 40,000 pounds of tobacco, and banished from the province. In 1682 he was resident in Virginia. Two years later (June 1684), it was reported that he was on a London ship in the Potomac River and a warrant was issued for his arrest, but he was not found. Here the record of his career closes. The name of Mary Fendall, his widow and administratrix, appears in court records in 1688.

[The *Archives of Md.*, vols. I, III, V, X, XV, and XLI are the only important primary source of information about Fendall. For secondary sources see B. C. Steiner, "Md. under the Commonwealth," *Johns Hopkins Univ. Studies*, vol. XXIX (1911); W. H. Browne, *Maryland* (1884); J. L. Bozman, *Hist. of Md.* (1837); J. T. Scharf, *Hist. of Md.* (1879); *Md. Hist. Mag.*, Mar. 1906, Sept. 1912.]

N. D. M.

FENGER, CHRISTIAN (Nov. 3, 1840–Mar. 7, 1902), surgeon and pathologist, was born in Breininggaard, Breininge Sogn, Denmark. He was one of twelve children born to Kammerraad Hans Fritz Fenger and Frederikke Mathilde Fjelstrup, both representatives of well-to-do farmer families. He attended Herlufsholm school for eight years, graduating in 1859, followed by a year devoted to engineering in the Polyteknisk Läreanstalt in Copenhagen. In accordance with his father's wishes he turned to the study of medicine, which he pursued at the University of Copenhagen from 1860 to 1865, interrupted by the war with Prussia in which he served as assistant physician. In addition to his service in the Schleswig-Holstein War, he was appointed to an international ambulance during the Franco-Prussian War. After passing the examination for the practise of medicine in 1866–67, he served for three years as assistant in clinical otology to Dr. Vilhelm Meyer. Then followed an interneship of two years in the Royal Frederik's Hospital, and three years as prosector to the Commune hospital. The latter service furnished Fenger a splendid opportunity for investigation in pathology and morbid anatomy. In this period he wrote several noteworthy articles including one on cancer of the stomach which was his thesis for the degree of doctor of medicine conferred in 1874. In the spring of 1875 Fenger went to Alexandria, Egypt, to take over the practise of his brother, who was also a physician, while the latter was away. On his brother's return, he was appointed to the office of *Médecin du Quartier de Kalifa* in Cairo. From 1875 to 1877 he remained here making a special study of the highly prevalent trachoma and bilharziosis, but was compelled, on account of chronic dysentery, to resign and seek a temperate climate. Due to an acquaintance with some American army officers he decided to come to the United States. He arrived in the fall of 1877 and settled in Chicago. Shortly afterward he was married to Caroline Sophie Abildgaard, a native of Denmark.

In Chicago Fenger immediately attracted attention by his profound knowledge of pathology in autopsies performed at the morgue of the Cook County Hospital. He was appointed chief pathologist of that hospital in 1878 and held that position until 1893. During that time he exercised an influence upon scientific medicine in Chicago greater than any other man of his period. It can be truly said that he introduced real pathology to Chicago. He created a following which developed Senn, Murphy, and the Mayos in surgery, and Hektoen, Le Count, and Wells in pathology. Though his name suggests the surgeon, he was never a brilliant operator. He lacked manual dexterity, but this was compensated for by his unequaled diagnostic skill and knowledge of morbid anatomy. He was appointed curator of Rush Medical College Museum in 1880, professor of surgery in the College of Physicians and Surgeons in 1884, professor of surgery at Northwestern University in 1893, and professor of surgery at Rush Medical College in 1899. Though he spoke English poorly and with halting words, he was an able teacher. In his surgical clinics he was wont to forget the patient in the earnestness of his discussion of the pathology involved.

For twenty years after 1880 he was attending and consulting surgeon at Cook County Hospital. It was upon and through the internes of this hospital that he exerted his most profound influence and it was among them that he developed the following which might well have been called the Fenger school. He was in addition surgeon-in-chief of the Passavant Memorial, German, and Lutheran Tabitha hospitals from the time they were organized until his death. At different times he was also attending surgeon at Mercy and Presbyterian hospitals. Stricken with pneumonia in Chicago, his last illness was attended by the élite of the city's profession, all former students of their beloved professor. He was a prolific writer of journal articles on subjects relating to surgery, pathology and diagnosis. These were republished in 1912 under the joint editorship of Ludwig Hektoen and C. G. Buford as the *Collected Works of Christian Fenger.*

[There is a short autobiography of Fenger in the *Collected Works*, vol. I. See also *Surgery, Gynecol. and Obstetrics*, July–Dec. 1922; *Am. Medicine*, July–Dec. 1902; *Bull. Soc. Medic. Hist.*, 1913; *Ibid.*, 1923; *Ill. Medic. Jour.*, 1924.]

J. M. P.

FENNELL, JAMES (Dec. 11, 1766–June 13, 1816), actor, one of the most erratic figures ever connected with the American stage, was born in London of Welsh, Scotch, and Irish ancestry. His father, John Fennell, in the Pay Corps of the navy, who had lived in New York for some years, and his mother, a former Miss Brady, were, according to Fennell's own statement, so indulgent that he early developed the vice of obstinacy. After some preliminary schooling he was sent to Eton at about thirteen, and then to Trinity College, Cambridge, where he enjoyed a frolicsome career—inadequate preparation for the church, for which his parents had destined him. After leaving the university, Fennell undertook to study law in London, but, having contracted heavy gambling debts, he turned to the stage in an effort to recoup his losses. Given his first opportunity by John Jackson, manager of the Theatre Royal, Edinburgh, he made his début in June 1787, as Othello, a character which remained one of his principal rôles. After a short engagement at Edinburgh, Thomas Harris, director of Covent Garden Theatre, London, accepted him for a half dozen performances and then attempted to retain him for the coming season, but, being bound to Jackson, Fennell returned to Scotland for the winter. At the end of this season a quarrel arose between him and Woods, a favorite Scotch actor, over the matter of parts, and Fennell was compelled to leave the Edinburgh stage. After some acting in the provinces, he returned to Covent Garden for a short engagement, but when differences of opinion necessitated his withdrawal, he started a weekly paper, the *Theatrical Guardian,* in which, during its brief existence, he professed to right all stage wrongs. On May 10, 1792, he married Miss B. H. Porter and went to Paris for the honeymoon. Following this sojourn he wrote *A Review of the Proceedings at Paris during the Last Summer* (1792).

In the summer of 1793, having signed a contract with Thomas Wignell, manager of the new

Chestnut Street Theatre in Philadelphia, Fennell arrived in America. At his Philadelphia début, which, because of an epidemic of yellow fever, was delayed until Feb. 19, 1794, he was received with great favor. Accepted with equal cordiality by the social world, he soon found that his expenditures were exceeding his income. To remedy the situation he patented a device for extracting salt from sea-water, induced many influential Philadelphians to invest in the project, and temporarily abandoned the stage. But the enterprise failed and brought ruin upon its originator. Fennell's subsequent career was largely an alternation between the stage, where he always made money, and the salt-works, where he always lost it. With amazing persistence he erected a succession of manufactories along the coast, but disaster invariably befell them, and he was repeatedly jailed—once for sixteen months—for fraudulent practises, although apparently he had no intent to deceive, being always one of the heaviest losers himself. On Sept. 8, 1797, Fennell made his first appearance in New York and won the enthusiastic approval of the audience. Between 1800 and 1806 he played with some regularity at the Park Theatre, New York, but much of his time then, as throughout his whole life, was occupied with assorted and ill-fated projects—salt making, lectures on physics, lectures in defense of the Bible, a school of elocution, a boys' school on the Eton model, a magazine, a Shakespeare concordance, etc. In his later years ill-health and dissipation so weakened his powers that, when he took his farewell of the stage at Philadelphia in 1814 in the rôle of Lear, his decay matched that of the character he was impersonating.

In his prime Fennell was one of the most prominent tragedians in America. Although his gigantic figure lacked grace and his powerful voice lacked flexibility, he possessed histrionic gifts which, if cultivated as assiduously as he cultivated salt, might have placed him at the very top of his profession. As it was, he was sure of an audience whenever he chose to perform. During an engagement at Philadelphia in 1806 he played thirteen nights to receipts of $13,000, at one time said to be the greatest instance of patronage ever given to American drama (Clapp, *post*, p. 89). Among Fennell's writings are a five-act comedy, *Lindor and Clara; or, the British Officer* (1791), and a few other unimportant plays, but his chief work is his *Apology*, an eccentric but fairly reliable record of his life, in which he makes no attempt to conceal his many shortcomings.

[*An Apology for the Life of Jas. Fennell. Written by Himself* (1814); contemporary newspapers; D. E. Baker, and others, *Biographia Dramatica* (1812); William Dunlap, *A Hist. of the Am. Theatre* (1832); W. B. Wood, *Personal Recollections of the Stage* (1855); John Bernard, *Retrospections of America* (1887); G. C. D. Odell, *Annals of the N. Y. Stage*, vols. I and II (1927); John Jackson, *The Hist. of the Scottish Stage* (1793); W. W. Clapp, *A Record of the Boston Stage* (1853).]

O. S. C.

FENNER, ARTHUR (Dec. 10, 1745–Oct. 15, 1805), fourth governor of Rhode Island, was born in Providence, R. I. His great-grandfather, Capt. Arthur Fenner, was born in England in 1622, and emigrated early in life to Providence. His home, which because of its huge chimney was called "the Castle," remained in existence for about one hundred and fifty years. Capt. Fenner's first wife was Mehitable, daughter of Richard Waterman, by whom he had six children. Of these, his son Thomas was the father of Arthur, who served in the British-American army as ensign in one of the companies which took part in the invasion of Canada in 1759, married Mary Olney, and became the father of Arthur Fenner, the governor. Little is known of the youth of the latter, but in December 1774, on recommendation of the Continental Congress he was appointed one of the "Committee of Inspection." He was also for many years clerk of the court of common pleas in Providence. When the question of the ratification of the federal Constitution arose, the contest was especially severe and protracted in Rhode Island. Gov. John Collins had favored calling a convention to decide the matter, and in consequence had become unpopular. Fenner was a member of the party opposed to adoption, and was appealed to by the citizens of Newport and Providence to head a compromise ticket upon which there should be a Federalist for deputy-governor and an equal number of Federalist and Anti-Federalist assistants. He referred the matter to the freemen of the colony; the Anti-Federalists were successful, and on May 5, 1790, the Rhode Island General Assembly declared Arthur Fenner (Anti-Federalist) governor, and Samuel J. Potter (Federalist) deputy-governor. Final action on the Constitution was deferred until the last week in May, when on the twenty-ninth by a count of thirty-four to thirty-two, the Assembly voted for ratification. In the following June, Gov. Fenner convened the General Assembly in special session and all officers took oath to support the Constitution newly adopted. In August 1790 President Washington made a visit to Newport and Providence to welcome Rhode Island into the Union. At the wharf in Providence a throng gathered to greet the President, and the Governor led the largest and most distinguished procession which the town had ever known. In 1791 Fenner was once more elected governor and was successively reëlected until his death at Providence in 1805. His wife was Amey, daughter of Gideon Comstock.

[J. P. Root, *Geneal. of the Fenner Family* (1887), reprinted from *R. I. Hist. Mag.*, Jan. 1887; *Biog. Cyc. of Representative Men of R. I.* (1881); S. G. Arnold, *Hist. of the State of R. I. and Providence Plantations* (2 vols., 1859–60); Edward Field, ed., *State of R. I. and Providence Plantations* (3 vols., 1902).] I. B. R.

FENNER, BURT LESLIE (Sept. 1, 1869–Jan. 24, 1926), architect, the son of Edward B. and Margaret Virginia (Taylor) Fenner was born in Rochester, N. Y. His father's family had come from England two generations before. After graduating from high school he attended the University of Rochester (1888–89), spent the following year in architectural work in Rochester, then studied at the Massachusetts Institute of Technology (1890–91). In the fall of 1891 he entered the office of McKim, Mead & White, then famous not only for its work, but known also as the best place for an ambitious draftsman to learn the essentials of good architecture. His advancement in the office was rapid and on Jan. 1, 1906, he was taken into the firm, remaining with them as a partner for the rest of his life. His duties were chiefly administrative and executive and after the deaths of Stanford White (1906) and Charles F. McKim (1910) he became, in fact, the executive head of the firm.

Fenner was greatly interested in city planning and was instrumental in the preparation of the report of the heights of buildings commission which was issued in 1913 and which was directly responsible for the passage by the New York legislature of the amendment to the New York City charter enabling the board of estimate and apportionment of the city to enact the comprehensive zoning ordinance of 1916. In 1918 he was made general manager of the United States Housing Corporation created under the Department of Labor. Despite labor difficulties, administrative red tape, congestion on the railroads, and scarcity of materials, he succeeded in creating an organization which efficiently produced workmen's villages at strategic points from the Atlantic to the Pacific. The chronic labor difficulties in the building trades in the three or four years following the war impressed upon him the importance of the relation of the architect to the labor unions. In 1922 he was made chairman of the committee appointed jointly by the New York chapter of the American Institute of Architects and the Building Trades Employers Association to inquire into the controversies and scandalous conditions which had produced the famous Brindell investigation. In this position he had not only to fight the mutual suspicions of unions and contractors, but also a considerable hostile opinion among architects and the public. One of the matters at issue was the admission of new members to the unions, and the preservation of high standards of technical skill. The result was the formation of the apprenticeship commission of which Fenner was made president, establishing a basic apprenticeship system supervised and supported by the contractors and the unions, and having the official cooperation of the American Institute of Architects. Fenner became a member of the American Institute of Architects in 1908, a fellow in 1913, its secretary in 1915–16, and for several years was a member of its board of directors. In 1910–11 he was recording secretary of the New York chapter and president in 1919–21. He was married Dec. 9, 1896, to Louise McKittrick of Brooklyn, by whom he had one son. He died suddenly of heart-failure at his home at Croton-on-Hudson, and was buried at Sleepy Hollow.

[*Am. Architect*, Feb. 5, 1926; *Jour. of the Am. Inst. of Architects*, Mar. 1926; *Architectural Record*, Mar. 1926; obituaries in *N. Y. World* and *N. Y. Times*, Jan. 26, 1926; *Who's Who in America*, 1924–25; and information as to certain facts supplied by Fenner's son, Ward W. Fenner.] T. F. H.

FENNER, CHARLES ERASMUS (Feb. 14, 1834–Oct. 24, 1911), soldier, jurist, was a member of a well-known Southern family. His grandfather, Dr. Richard Fenner of North Carolina, fought in the Revolutionary War and was one of the original members of the Society of the Cincinnati. His father, Dr. Erasmus D. Fenner, a distinguished physician, married Annie America Callier, who was of Scotch-Irish descent, settled in New Orleans in 1840, and assisted in the founding of the *New Orleans Medical Journal* in 1844. He himself was born at Jackson, Madison County, Tenn., and received his early education in the New Orleans public schools, proceeding thence to the Western Military Institute of Kentucky. Having completed his academic training at the University of Virginia he studied law in the office of J. P. Benjamin at New Orleans, took a course in the law department of the University of Louisiana, and was admitted to the Louisiana bar in 1855. Commencing practise in partnership with L. E. Simmonds, a leading member of the New Orleans bar, he rapidly came to the front. On the outbreak of the Civil War he entered the Confederate army as first lieutenant in the Louisiana Guards and served in Virginia under Gen. Magruder, being promoted captain. In April 1862, his term of enlistment having expired, he organized Fenner's Louisiana battery of light artillery at Jackson, Miss., and took part in the fighting at Port Hudson, serving later under Gen.

Joseph E. Johnston in the Army of Tennessee. Attached to Gen. J. B. Hood's forces in the Nashville campaign, his battery covered the rear of the Confederate army on the retreat from Nashville. He was with Gen. R. Taylor's detachment when the latter surrendered at Meridian in 1865. He had consistently declined promotion since it would necessitate severing connection with his battery.

On the termination of hostilities he resumed practise in New Orleans and in November 1865 was elected a member of the first post-war Louisiana legislature, serving one term. This was the only occasion upon which he sought political honors, though he took an active interest in public affairs and was conspicuous whenever any matter of vital interest to the city or state was agitated. When the Nicholls and Packard controversy came to a head in 1876 he prepared the resolution which was passed at the mass meeting in Lafayette Square setting forth the inalterable antagonism of the people to the Packard government and announcing that the latter could only be maintained in power by military force. During these years his reputation as a lawyer steadily increased and he achieved an outstanding position at the bar. In 1880 he was appointed by Gov. Wiltz an associate justice of the supreme court of Louisiana, and, being reappointed by Gov. McEnery on the expiration of his term in 1884, retained this position till 1894. As a member of the judiciary his wide experience, firm grasp of legal principles, and eminently sane outlook made him a strong figure and he enjoyed the confidence and respect of the entire community. On leaving the bench he resumed practise, confining himself to consultations, and his services were requisitioned in an advisory capacity in much difficult litigation up to within two years of his death.

Apart from the law, his chief interest lay in educational work. He had at the request of Paul Tulane become first vice-president of the board of administrators of the Tulane Fund, and as such took a prominent part in the organization of the Tulane University of Louisiana, being elected in 1884 professor of civil law—a position which, as a member of the administration, he was unable to accept. In 1892 he became president of the board, continuing in active contact with all phases of the work of the university till his resignation in 1908. He was also a member of the board of trustees of the Peabody Educational Fund. A fluent and impressive speaker, he was much in request on patriotic and anniversary occasions and was the author of a number of legal and historical addresses and papers.

He married, Oct. 16, 1866, Caroline, daughter of Jacob V. Payne, a leading New Orleans merchant of his time.

[See *Who's Who in America*, 1910–11; J. R. Ficklen, *Hist. of Reconstruction in La.* (1910); *Official Records (Army)*; obituary notices in the *Picayune* and *Times-Democrat* (New Orleans), Oct. 25, 1911.] H. W. H. K.

FENNER, JAMES (Jan. 22, 1771–Apr. 17, 1846), governor of Rhode Island, son of Gov. Arthur Fenner [*q.v.*] and Amey Comstock, was born in Providence. He entered Rhode Island College, now Brown University, in 1785, graduating four years later at the head of his class. He began his political career as a member from Providence in the Rhode Island General Assembly. In 1804 he superseded Christopher Ellery as United States senator from Rhode Island, and served until 1807, when he resigned. In that year he was elected governor, which office he held until 1811 and again from 1824 to 1831. In May 1818, he was elected chief justice of the Rhode Island supreme court but declined the office. From 1822 to 1833 he was the first president of the Rhode Island Historical Society. During the enlargement of the suffrage, known as the Dorr Rebellion, Fenner took sides with the so-called Law and Order party, which opposed Dorr. Following the defeat, by a narrow margin, of the first government or "Freemen's" constitution, a convention was held in 1842 which framed and submitted to the people of Rhode Island a constitution designed to replace the royal charter still in force. The constitution was overwhelmingly approved, and under the new government Fenner became the first governor, holding office from 1843 to 1845.

Fenner was a good politician. It was said of him, in view of his responsiveness to popular feeling, that "few public men in Rhode Island history have been more successful in trimming their sails to catch an approaching breeze." In 1827, at the time of a strong temperance movement in Rhode Island, the governor on election day, instead of indulging in the usual convivial practise, donated one hundred dollars to the Newport public-school fund. Later, when the Dorr party appealed for intervention by the federal government he called an extra session of the General Assembly to take action upon what he termed "an unwarrantable interference of the national government with the internal affairs of an individual state." After 1845 Fenner retired to his "What Cheer" estate, and on his death in 1846 was accorded a public funeral. His wife was Sarah, daughter of Sylvanus and Freelove (Whipple) Jenckes of Providence, whom he married in November 1792.

[*The Biog. Cyc. of Representative Men of R. I.*

(1881), p. 197; Edward Field, ed., *State of R. I. and Providence Plantations* . . . (3 vols., 1902); *Proc. R. I. Hist. Soc.*, 1873–74, p. 87; R. I. Legislative Manual; A. M. Mowry, *The Dorr War* (1901).] I. B. R.

FENNO, JOHN (Aug. 12, 1751 o.s.–Sept. 14, 1798), editor, was born in Boston, probably the son of Ephraim Fenno, leather-dresser and alehouse keeper, and Mary Chapman. His first employment, as an usher in Samuel Holbrook's Writing School, indicates that he had received some education. The orderly books which Fenno kept while secretary to Gen. Artemas Ward, covering the period from Apr. 20 to Sept. 16, 1775, are examples of his excellent penmanship and evidence of his war service. He was married to Mary Curtiss on May 8, 1777. Trying his hand at trade, he imported largely and unwisely at the close of the Revolution, eventually compounded with his creditors, and went to New York to retrieve his fortunes in "a printing way" in 1789. He had "in some sort been an adjutant-general to [Benjamin] Russell" of the *Massachusetts Centinel* (*Massachusetts Historical Society Collections,* 5 ser., III, 1877, p. 123), where his literary achievements were so "very handsome" that his plan for a newspaper "for the purpose of disseminating favorable sentiments of the federal Constitution and the Administration" was not ignored by the Federalists (King, *post,* I, 357). Fenno's *Gazette of the United States* was established in New York, Apr. 11, 1789, but was published in Philadelphia beginning Apr. 14, 1790. It was the editor's ardent hope that his little three-column folio, printed on a sheet seventeen by twenty-one inches, would become the dignified journal of a dignified court; but Jefferson and his colleagues, discovering Fenno's attempt "to make way for a king, lords, and Commons" (Ford, *post,* V, 361), matched press with press, and between the *Aurora* of Benjamin F. Bache [*q.v.*] and the *National Gazette* of Philip Freneau [*q.v.*] Hamilton's protégé was forced into undignified controversies. In the one personal encounter between the editors, Bache's use of his cane proved decisive. Yet the tone of the *Gazette of the United States* was somewhat above the average of its contemporaries, and the Federalists were well served through its columns. The circulation never exceeded 1,400, a quarter of which was gratis. The *Gazette* had the aid of prominent Federalists. Alexander Hamilton was especially active, contributing articles under various pseudonyms and rescuing the editor from bankruptcy in 1793 by raising $2,000 to dispose of pressing creditors (King, *post,* I, 501).

Fenno died in Philadelphia during the yellow-fever epidemic of 1798 "with all his blooming virtues thick upon him" (*Russell's Gazette,* Boston, Sept. 24, 1798). His son, John Ward Fenno, carried on the paper until 1800, when he sold it.

[P. L. Ford, ed., *The Writings of Thos. Jefferson* (1892–99), *passim;* MS. papers of Alexander Hamilton in Lib. of Cong.; "Belknap Papers," II, 122–23, 126, 132, in *Mass. Hist. Soc. Colls.,* 5 ser., vol. III (1877); J. T. Scharf and T. Westcott, *Hist. of Philadelphia,* III (1884); W. G. Bleyer, *Main Currents in the Hist. of Am. Journalism* (1927); C. R. King, *Life and Correspondence of Rufus King,* I (1894); S. E. Forman, "The Pol. Activities of Philip Freneau," in *Johns Hopkins Univ. Studies in Hist. and Pol. Science,* 20 ser., nos. 9–10 (1902), an account that is unfriendly to Fenno.] T. D. M.

FENOLLOSA, ERNEST FRANCISCO (Feb. 18, 1853–Sept. 21, 1908), poet, student of Oriental art, was the son of Manuel Francisco Ciriaco Fenollosa, a Spanish musician, who, having as a youth enlisted in the band attached to an American frigate, came to the United States in 1838 and finally settled in Salem, Mass., where he married Mary Silsbee. Their son prepared for college at the Hacker Grammar School and at the Salem High School, and entered Harvard with the class of 1874. He graduated first in his class, was chosen poet, and was awarded a fellowship which he used for further study at Cambridge, first in philosophy and then in the Divinity School. In January 1877, he entered the newly founded school at the Boston Museum of Fine Arts. In 1878 he went to Japan where he taught political economy and philosophy at the Imperial University at Tokio for two years (1878–80); then philosophy and logic for six years (1880–86). When the Tokio Fine Arts Academy and the Imperial Museum were opened in 1888, he was made manager of both institutions. Brought into intimate contact with Japanese artists and men of culture, the sensitive young esthete became a professing Buddhist and was baptized under the name of Tei-Shin. His Japanese name in art was Kano Yeitan Masanobu, showing him to have been an apprentice accepted by the ancient and conservative academy of the Kano. He was decorated by His Imperial Highness, the Emperor of Japan, with the fourth, later with the third, class of the order of the Rising Sun; and with the third class of the Sacred Mirror. In 1890 he returned to the Boston Museum of Fine Arts to become curator of the department of Oriental art. There he remained until 1897 when he again went to Japan to serve as professor of English literature in the Imperial Normal School at Tokio. After three years he returned to the United States to write and lecture on Oriental subjects. In June 1878 he had married Lizzie Goodhue Millett. A son and a daughter were born to them. After their divorce he married, in 1895,

Mary McNeill. He died in London, Sept. 21, 1908.

Estimates of his contributions to the study of Oriental art vary greatly. It has been said by some that he discovered the subject; by others, that he made no important contribution to it. His most significant work *Epochs of Chinese and Japanese Art* (2 vols., 2nd ed., 1912) was compiled after his death by Mary McNeill Fenollosa, from a "rough pencil draught." It is lamentably full of tentative statements and errors, which, had he lived, he would undoubtedly have corrected. Some of the errors have been corrected in bulletins of the Boston Museum of Fine Arts and in the footnotes of a critical Japanese translation. Nevertheless, though Western knowledge of Oriental art has progressed since his death, it has followed the path blazed by him. While his information was derived from his Japanese friends, his conclusions were his own and they were formed at a time when there was no background of Western appreciation. Besides various monographs on phases of Oriental art, he published *The Masters of Ukioye* (1896), an historical description of Japanese paintings and color prints exhibited at the New York Fine Arts Building; and a book of poems, *East and West*; *The Discovery of America and Other Poems* (1893). The poem, "East and West," was delivered before the Phi Beta Kappa society at Cambridge, June 30, 1892. After his death, his literary executor, Ezra Pound, published, in part from his notes and manuscripts, *Cathay* (1915), translations, chiefly from the Chinese; *Certain Noble Plays of Japan* (1916); and *'Noh'; or, Accomplishment, a Study of the Classical Stage of Japan* (1916).

[An account of Fenollosa is contained in the preface, written by Mary McNeill Fenollosa, to his *Epochs of Chinese and Japanese Art*. The report of the fiftieth anniversary of the Class of 1874, Harvard College, contains a sketch. Further information has been derived from *Who's Who in America*, 1908–09, and from his daughter, Mrs. Moncure Biddle.] L. W.

FENTON, REUBEN EATON (July 4, 1819–Aug. 25, 1885), United States senator, governor of New York, banker, was born in Carroll, Chautauqua County, N. Y., the youngest son of George W. and Elsie (Owen) Fenton. Forced to curtail his academic and legal studies at the age of seventeen when his father failed in business, he devoted himself assiduously to lumbering in an effort to retrieve the family losses. For years his life was spent in the logging camps and in piloting his rafts down the Allegheny and Ohio rivers. At length, having paid his father's debts and secured a comfortable competence for himself, he entered upon a crowded political career, partly prefaced by a term of eight years as supervisor of Carroll, beginning in 1843. In 1849 he was elected to the Assembly as a Democrat. He was sent to Congress in 1852 when the controversy arose over the Kansas-Nebraska Bill. His maiden address against this measure (*Congressional Globe*, 33 Cong., 1 Sess., pp. 156 ff.), marked his secession from the Democratic party on the slavery question. He was one of the leaders in the formation, and afterward in the conduct, of the Republican party, serving in 1855 as presiding officer of the first Republican state convention in New York. In 1854 he was defeated for Congress on the Know-Nothing ticket, but in 1856 he was elected as the Republican candidate, serving until 1864, when he resigned to become governor of New York. Nominated to head the state ticket in 1864, he fully appreciated the importance of vindicating the President by bringing about Gov. Seymour's downfall, and was credited with a vigorous campaign. His vote exceeded that of Lincoln and he at once became a figure of national importance. In the campaign of 1866, despite many obstacles, he was reëlected by a majority of over 13,000 (E. A. Werner, *Civil List . . . of the . . . State of New York*, 1888, p. 166).

Fenton's conduct in office gave rise to conflicting estimates of his ability as an executive. He is associated with proposals of reform in the registry law and the prison system, and with numerous educational reforms,—the establishment of Cornell University, of state normal schools, and the abolition of the school rate bills (*Messages from the Governors*, V, 605, 695, 697, 778–81, 850–55). Hence, even the *New York Times* (Feb. 4, 1868) conceded that his "administration of state affairs" had in the main been a success. A contrary impression, however, was created by ugly newspaper allegations. When, in 1868, Fenton signed the bill which legalized the acts of the Erie directorate, charges were made that his signature had been bought (*New York Herald*, Apr. 21–30, 1868; *New York Times*, Apr. 20–May 8, 1868; *Sun*, Apr. 21, 1868; also *New York Commercial Advertiser*, Jan. 2, 1869; the *Nation*, Mar. 18, 1869), although a subsequent investigation did not support them (see *Documents of the Senate of the State of New York*, 1869, no. 52, pp. 146–48, 151–55).

Fenton succeeded in building up one of the most powerful political machines in the history of the state and came to be regarded as its ablest political organizer after Martin Van Buren. This achievement had been effected not without making a powerful group of enemies who eventually brought about his political downfall. In 1869 Fenton engaged in a ruthless campaign against

Edward D. Morgan [*q.v.*] for the senatorial nomination. His success, due to his liberal disposition of choice assignments, aroused much factional feeling (*Harper's Weekly*, June 24, 1871). After his election to the Senate in that year, he made strenuous attempts to keep in the favor of President Grant. When it was obvious that Conkling was to be the distributor of the state patronage, Fenton offered to withdraw his own candidacy for the presidency if the patronage question could be settled satisfactorily (*New York Times*, July 24, 1872). Relations were terminated between him and Conkling. The latter, capitalizing the support of the administration, carried the feud to his own state, and brought about the defeat of Fenton in the state convention of 1871. Finally, the recognition of the Murphy-Arthur organization in New York City was a stunning blow from which Fenton never recovered. In 1872 he supported the candidacy of Horace Greeley for the presidency.

On the expiration of his senatorial term in 1875, he devoted himself principally to his business interests. He served as president of the First National Bank of Jamestown and gained a reputation for his special knowledge of monetary affairs. In 1878 President Hayes sent him abroad as chairman of the United States commission to the International Monetary Conference held in Paris in that year. He died in Jamestown, N. Y. His first wife, Jane, daughter of John Frew of Frewsburg, whom he married in 1838, died two years later. His second wife, Elizabeth, daughter of Joel Scudder, survived him.

[Biographical material is found in Obed Edson and Georgia Drew Merrill, *Hist. of Chautauqua County* (1894); Chauncey M. Depew, *Orations, Addresses, and Speeches* (1910), I, 259 ff.; *A Sketch of the Life of Gov. Fenton* (1866), a political pamphlet; obituary notices of Aug. 26, 1885, in *N. Y. Times* and N. Y. *World*. Fenton's public papers as governor are found in *State of N. Y., Messages from the Governors*, vol. V (1909), ed. by Chas. Z. Lincoln. His political career is treated in Homer A. Stebbins, *A Political Hist. of the State of N. Y., 1865–69* (1913), and De Alva S. Alexander, *A Political Hist. of the State of N. Y.* (1909), vols. II, III.]

R. B. M.

FENWICK, BENEDICT JOSEPH (Sept. 3, 1782–Aug. 11, 1846), Roman Catholic prelate, second bishop of Boston, was born near Leonardtown, St. Marys County, Md., one of the ten children of Col. Richard Fenwick and his wife Dorothy, daughter of Joseph Plowden of "Resurrection Manor." He was a great-grandson of Cuthbert Fenwick, who came to this country with Leonard Calvert [*q.v.*] in 1634. In his eleventh year he entered Georgetown College where he distinguished himself as a student, and, after finishing his course in philosophy, was an instructor. Having resolved to become a priest, in 1805 he took up the study of theology at the Sulpician Seminary, later St. Mary's, Baltimore. When, however, in 1806 the Society of Jesus was reëstablished in the United States and a novitiate was opened at Georgetown College, Fenwick was one of the first to be admitted. On Mar. 12, 1808, he was ordained priest by Bishop Leonard Neale [*q.v.*]. The following year, with Father Anthony Kohlmann, S. J. [*q.v.*], he was sent to New York City where the two took charge of St. Peter's Church. The Diocese of New York had been erected in 1808, but its first bishop, Richard Luke Concanen, died before he could reach America, and his successor, Bishop John Connolly [*q.v.*], did not arrive until Nov. 24, 1815. Father Kohlmann administered the diocese until early in 1815 when he was recalled to Maryland, and thereafter, until Bishop Connolly came, Father Fenwick was in charge. During this critical period these two priests labored devotedly and successfully. They soon opened a school for young men, the New York Literary Institution, which, under the direction of Father Fenwick, came to be held in high regard by Protestants as well as Catholics. In accordance with plans prepared by him, St. Patrick's Cathedral was commenced on a plot of ground between Broadway and Bowery Road. Traveling extensively through the diocese, he reclaimed many wandering Catholics and made some notable converts. In the spring of 1817 he was transferred by his superiors to Georgetown where he served as president of the college and as pastor of Trinity Church. In the fall of 1818, however, at the request of Archbishop Maréchal, who conferred upon him the power of vicar-general, he was sent to Charleston, S. C., where, displaying great tact and administrative ability, he did much to heal long-standing schisms. After the erection of the Diocese of Charleston in 1820, and the coming of Bishop John England [*q.v.*], Father Fenwick was retained for a time as vicar-general, but in May 1822 he was appointed minister of Georgetown College and procurator-general of the Society of Jesus in the United States (Clarke, *post*). He succeeded his brother, Rev. Enoch Fenwick, S. J., as president of the college, serving from September 1822 until 1825 (Shea, *Memorial*), when he was sent to assume spiritual direction of the Carmelite Convent, then located in Charles County, Md. On May 10, 1825, he was made bishop of Boston, and Nov. 1 of that year was consecrated in the Cathedral at Baltimore.

A task of great magnitude confronted him upon his arrival at Boston. His diocese comprised all of New England, and in its whole extent there were only two or three church buildings worthy the name, and but two or three priests. He had also to encounter an intense prejudice against Catholicism on the part of Protestants. With difficulty, since there was a general scarcity of clergy, he managed to secure a few able assistants. In the hope of increasing his staff, he gave instruction personally to candidates for the priesthood, and in 1827 had the satisfaction of ordaining two of his pupils, one of whom, James Fitton [*q.v.*], carried on zealous missionary labors for many years in all parts of New England. From the start he devoted much attention to the education of the young, opening a Sunday-school in the Cathedral, and when the latter was enlarged in 1828, establishing a day school in the basement, which was conducted by his ecclesiastical students. He moved the Ursuline Convent to a more suitable site in Charlestown, where the nuns opened an academy for girls. On Aug. 11, 1834, the convent was destroyed by an anti-Catholic mob. That the truths of the Church might be "explained, and moderately, but firmly defended," he started in Boston *The Jesuit, or Catholic Sentinel,* one of the earliest Catholic papers in the country, the first number of which appeared on Sept. 5, 1829. Its name was several times changed, and it was finally called *The Pilot.* Under his patronage Sisters of Charity came to Boston in 1832, opened a free school for girls, and established St. Vincent's Orphan Asylum. As the exodus from Ireland brought many immigrants to Boston, he urged them to go forth into other sections of New England, and in 1834, having secured a half township of land in Aroostook County, Me., he established there the Catholic colony of Benedicta. In 1842 he received from Father Fitton land in Worcester upon which the latter had erected a school for the higher education of young men. This the Bishop put under the care of the Jesuits and it became the College of the Holy Cross. Such was the energy and success of his administration that at his death the diocese contained some forty churches with attendant priests, and from it had been carved the Diocese of Hartford, which comprised Connecticut and Rhode Island.

He was a man of great personal charm, a brilliant conversationalist, witty and humorous. Firm and uncompromising in his convictions, he was nevertheless humble, tender-hearted, and charitable toward all. He was an accomplished scholar, well informed in widely different fields, but of practical rather than speculative turn of mind. His business ability was of a high order, and he possessed many of the qualities that make an able statesman. The long period of suffering that preceded his death he bore with fortitude and cheerfulness, and not having been able to lie down for weeks, he died sitting in his chair.

[*The Metropolitan Cath. Almanac and Laity's Directory for . . . 1850* (1849); Geo. L. L. Davis, *The Day-Star of Am. Freedom* (1855); Jas. Fitton, *Sketches of the Establishment of the Ch. in New England* (1872); Wm. Byrne and others, *Hist. of the Cath. Ch. in the New England States* (1899), vol. I; Richard H. Clarke, *Lives of the Deceased Bishops of the Cath. Ch. in the U. S.* (rev. ed., 1888), vol. I; John G. Shea, *A Hist. of the Cath. Ch. Within the Limits of the U. S.*, vols. III, IV (1890–92), and *Memorial of the First Centenary of Georgetown College, D. C.* (1891); *Brownson's Quart. Rev.*, Oct. 1846; *The Cath. Encyc.*, II, 705; family history from Mr. A. F. King of Leonardtown, through the courtesy of Mr. R. J. Purcell.] H. E. S.

FENWICK, EDWARD DOMINIC (Aug. 19, 1768–Sept. 26, 1832), first Catholic bishop of Cincinnati, was the fourth of eight children born to Ignatius and Sarah Brooke (Taney) Fenwick, who were both descended from Baltimore's first colonists and occupied ancestral lands in St. Marys County, Md. Like some of his forebears, Ignatius Fenwick was a notable figure: an ardent patriot, a colonel in the Revolution, a member of the Committee of Public Safety, a framer of the state constitution, and a man of affluence who was proud of his aristocratic connections. Edward faced the trials of the war era during which both his mother and father died, the latter in 1784, leaving him dependent on relatives and tutors. Although the penal laws were abolished, there were no Catholic schools, so that the youth, following the old practise, was sent to Europe. He entered Holy Cross College, Bornhem, Belgium (1784), an English Dominican foundation, and probably completed his classical studies at Liège. Joining the Dominicans, he served a severe novitiate before taking the vows of a friar preacher (1790). Continuing his philosophical studies, he was ordained at Ghent (Feb. 23, 1793) somewhat hurriedly because of unsettled political conditions. Escaping with their lives, the Dominicans fled from the French invaders and sought refuge on an estate in Surrey, England, where they founded Carshalton College. As an American citizen, Father Fenwick was left behind as procurator in the hope of saving the community property. This he was unable to do. The college was fired and partially destroyed, and Fenwick was harshly treated. On protestation, he was released from prison and found his way to England. He spent several happy years in teaching at Carshalton, attending a mission at Woburn Lodge, and continuing his theological studies, but he felt that his life's mission was to establish an American province of his order, as the Irish Augustinians had succeeded in doing. After encountering many obstacles and conducting much tedious correspondence, finally, aided by Richard

Luke Concanen, an Irish Dominican in Rome and later Bishop of New York, and encouraged by Bishop Carroll, Father Fenwick obtained the consent of his English provincial and of Pius J. Gaddi, the superior general in Rome. But men were scarce and the order, impoverished by war and confiscations, could not advance the necessary money. Not until September 1804, were Fenwick and his volunteer-companion, Robert Anthony Angier, O. P., ready to sail from London to Norfolk, Va.

After an absence of twenty years, the friar was welcomed by the Fenwicks of Maryland, though in this religious family given to vocations a priest occupied no unique position. Father Fenwick longed to erect a priory in his native state, but Bishop Carroll urged the claims of Kentucky where there were numbers of scattered Catholics who had emigrated from Maryland. Temporarily assigned to the mission at Piscataway, Fenwick visited Kentucky (1805) where at first he was warmly received by Stephen Badin [*q.v.*] who had spent lonely years in the frontier missions. Disposing of his lands in Charles County, Md., Fenwick purchased 500 acres in Washington County near Springfield, Ky., in the heart of the Catholic settlements. Here, assisted by two recently arrived Dominicans (Samuel T. Wilson and William R. Tuite), he transformed the farmhouse into the convent of St. Rose of Lima, the mother-house of the Dominican Order in the United States. The College of St. Thomas Aquinas (1807) was housed in a brick building and St. Rose's Church was erected (1812) from bricks made by the fathers and their parishioners. Relieved by the more erudite Dr. Wilson of his duties as prior and teacher, Fenwick engaged in itinerant missionary work throughout Kentucky and Ohio and into the North. At Cincinnati, on refusal of a site for a chapel, he built a small structure outside the city (1811). Within a few years, as the German and Irish immigrants arrived, he had a respectable frame church (1819). Aided by his nephew, Father N. D. Young, O. P., Fenwick's labors in the wilderness attracted such attention that when Bishop Flaget urged that Cincinnati be constituted the seat of a new diocese, Pius VII named the Dominican as its bishop. It was a proud day at St. Rose's when Dr. Flaget consecrated Fenwick and Bishop David preached the sermon (Jan. 13, 1822). Accompanied by Father Wilson as his vicar-general, Bishop Fenwick traveled through the woodland trail by wagon, actually swimming the Kentucky River.

The following year he paid his visit to Rome, where he attended the coronation of Pope Leo XII who displayed a practical interest in the Cincinnati diocese by presenting books, plate, and an elaborate tabernacle. Traveling in Italy, and France, Fenwick sought volunteer priests and obtained promises of financial aid. As a result of this journey, he induced such famous figures as Martin Kundig, Frederick Rese, Samuel Mazzuchelli, and John M. Henni to cast their lot in the frontier missions of America. Returning to Cincinnati, he continued his missionary work, preaching at court-houses to non-Catholic audiences, making conversions, gathering the isolated Catholics of Ohio into congregations, and gradually building small churches in towns like Lancaster. In 1828, he was further burdened with a life appointment as Dominican provincial. At the First Provincial Council of Baltimore (1829), he could report a prosperous diocese with a rapidly increasing immigrant population. Near his cathedral and diocesan seminary, he erected in 1831 the Athenæum, later St. Francis Xavier College as a school and a lyceum, whose public lectures attracted the élite of Cincinnati. Aware of the value of the press, he founded, in the same year, *The Catholic Telegraph,* which still flourishes as a diocesan weekly paper. While on a laborious visitation, he fell a victim to the cholera and was buried in Wooster before the nearest priest, John M. Henni, arrived. Later his remains were interred in the new cathedral and still later in a large mausoleum in St. Joseph's Cemetery.

[V. F. O'Daniel, *The Right Rev. Edward Dominic Fenwick* (1920), containing full bibliography; R. H. Clarke, *Lives of the Deceased Bishops of the Cath. Ch. in the U. S.* (1872), I, 328–52; J. H. Lamott, *Hist. of the Archdiocese of Cincinnati, 1821–1921* (1921); C. P. Maes, *Life of Rev. Chas. Nerinckx* (1915); M. J. Spalding, *Sketches of the Early Cath. Missions of Ky.* (1844); B. J. Webb, *The Centenary of Catholicity in Ky.* (1884); J. G. Shea, *Hist. of the Cath. Ch. Within the Limits of the U. S.*, vols. II, IV (1890–92); *The Truth Teller* (N. Y.), Jan. 26, 1833.]

R. J. P.

FENWICK, GEORGE (1603–Mar. 15, 1656/7), colonist, was the son of George Fenwick of Brinkburn and his wife Dorothy Forster. On Feb. 11, 1621/2, he was admitted to Gray's Inn (Joseph Foster, *Register of Admissions to Gray's Inn, 1521–1889*). In 1626 he bought the estate of Brinkburn. In 1632 Fenwick was one of the group of lords and gentlemen to whom the Earl of Warwick, president of the Council for New England, granted forty leagues of territory west of the Narragansett River. He is not named in the patent but in 1635 signed the commission of John Winthrop, Jr., sent over as governor, and agreements between the patentees and Winthrop and Lyon Gardiner, who were to oversee the construction of a fort, the laying out of a town, and the building of houses. In 1636 Fenwick visited

Saybrook, the town at the mouth of the Connecticut River begun by Winthrop and Gardiner. He soon returned to England and there married Alice, daughter of Sir Edward Apsley and widow of Sir John Boteler. In the summer of 1639 Fenwick and his wife sailed to New England and took up their residence at Saybrook. They were joined by Fenwick's sisters, Mary and Elizabeth, and three children were born to them. Fenwick expected the other patentees at Saybrook, but with the assembling of the Long Parliament in 1640, they came into power in England and remained there. In December 1644 Fenwick sold the fort at Saybrook to Connecticut and agreed that the territory between the Connecticut and Narragansett rivers should be settled under the jurisdiction of Connecticut if that were possible. On Oct. 22, 1645, he conveyed to the town of Guilford in the New Haven Colony, land to the west of the Connecticut River. From 1643 to 1645 he was one of the commissioners of the New England Confederation. In 1644, 1645, 1647, and 1648 he was elected a magistrate of the Connecticut Colony although at the time of his election in 1647 and 1648 he was in England. Probably in November 1645, Lady Fenwick died and was buried at Saybrook, and Fenwick, with one daughter, returned to England. Early in the following year he wrote to his sister Mary to bring her niece and nephew to England. He was elected to the Long Parliament in 1645 and added to the parliamentary commission for plantations. He was named a member of the High Court of Justice appointed to try Charles I, but did not serve. He was a colonel in the parliamentary army and in 1648 governor of Tynemouth, in 1649 governor of Berwick, and in the following year governor of Edinburgh and Leith. In 1652 he married Katherine, the daughter of Sir Arthur Hesilrige. He was elected from Berwick to the Parliaments of 1654 and 1656 and was one of the members excluded from the latter Parliament by the Council. He died on Mar. 15, 1656/7. His widow married Col. Philip Babington. Although he had instructed his sister in 1646 to bring her nephew to England, his will, dated Mar. 8, 1656/7, makes no mention of a son but names his daughters, Elizabeth and Dorothy, as co-heirs. Elizabeth married Sir Thomas Hesilrige, and Dorothy, Sir Thomas Williamson. Fenwick left his property in America to his sister Elizabeth, who had remained in Connecticut and married Capt. John Cullick.

[*Calendar of State Papers, Domestic Series*; *Conn. Colony Pub. Records*, vol. I (1850); *New Plymouth Colony Records*, vols. IX and X (1859); *Winthrop's Journal* (2 vols., 1908), ed. by J. K. Hosmer; "Winthrop Papers," in *Mass. Hist. Soc. Colls.*, 4 ser. vols. VI, VII (1863–65), 5 ser. vols. I, VIII (1871, 1882); C. H. Firth, and R. S. Rait, *Acts and Ordinances of the Interregnum* (3 vols., 1911); *Hist. Mag.*, Feb. 1871; Northumberland County Hist. Committee, *A Hist. of Northumberland* (12 vols., 1893–1926); Benj. Trumbull, *A Hist. of Conn.* (2 vols., 1818).]

I. M. C.

FENWICK, JOHN (1618–December 1683), colonist, son of Sir William Fenwick, was described as of Bynfield, Berkshire, England. In 1640 he was a law student at Gray's Inn, London; but soon afterward was an officer in Cromwell's horse. Fighting manfully for the Puritan cause, he was commissioned major (Johnson, "Memoir," p. 55). At the execution of Charles I, Major Fenwick, at the head of a squadron of cavalry, was present to preserve order. Originally an Independent in religion, the Cromwellian trooper later joined the Society of Friends. He was one of the group with whom originated the idea of a Quaker colony in America. It was to him, in trust for the Quaker merchant, Edward Byllinge, that, in March 1673/74, Lord John Berkeley made over his half of New Jersey. By arrangement with Sir George Carteret, partner of Berkeley, New Jersey was divided geographically, and the Friends secured the portion lying along the Delaware, henceforth known as West New Jersey. Thither Fenwick sailed in the ship *Griffin* with a party which included his three daughters, Elizabeth, Anna, and Priscilla, two sons-in-law, and five grandchildren. At Salem he planted, in June 1675, the first Quaker settlement on the Delaware. Styling himself "Chief Proprietor," he planned an elaborate development. Though a Friend by conviction, it would seem that the spirit of "the World's People" was not entirely dead in the ex-major for he became involved in contentions with other Friends interested in West Jersey. A misunderstanding with Byllinge was arbitrated by William Penn who, to the chagrin of Fenwick, adjudged one-tenth of the province to him and nine-tenths to Byllinge. A more serious quarrel resulted from the conduct of John Eldridge and Edmund Warner, Friends who had loaned Fenwick money for his colony. Them he accused of trying to defraud him of his rights as proprietor. In 1682 he was finally pacified by an arrangement which confirmed him in the possession of 150,000 acres at Salem, commonly called Fenwick's colony, and made over the other conflicting claims to William Penn. Meanwhile another antagonist had arisen in Sir Edmund Andros, governor of New York, who had ordered Fenwick to desist from exercising authority at Salem. The ex-Cromwellian resisted with spirit and was twice imprisoned by Andros. On one occasion when summoned by the Governor's lieutenant, he bolted himself in his house and refused to go "without he was carried away either dead or alive, and if anyone dare to come to take him it was at their peril, and he would do their business" (*New Jersey Archives,* I, 190). In spite of this un-Quakerlike defiance, he was compelled temporarily to submit. In 1680, however, James, Duke of York, surrendered his claims over West Jersey. In Fenwick's will William Penn was named guardian of his three favorite grandsons. Fenwick was twice married. His first wife, mother of his daughters, was Elizabeth, daughter of Sir Walter Covert. His second wife, Mary Burdett, did not accompany him to America.

[Accounts of Fenwick's career are found in R. G. Johnson, "Memoir of John Fenwicke" in *Proc. N. J. Hist. Soc.,* IV (1850), 53, and in *An Hist. Account of the First Settlement of Salem in West Jersey* (1839), by the same author. Fenwick's activities in West Jersey may be traced in *N. J. Archives,* vol. I (1880). See also Samuel Smith, *Hist. of the Colony of Novo Cæsaria or New Jersey* (Burlington, 1765; Trenton, 1877).]

E. P. T.

FENWICKE, JOHN [See FENWICK, JOHN, 1618–1683].

FERGUSON, ALEXANDER HUGH (Feb. 27, 1853–Oct. 20, 1911), surgeon, was born in Manilla, Victoria County, Ontario, seventh of the nine children of Alexander Ferguson and Annie McFadyen, both natives of Argyleshire, Scotland. His preliminary education was obtained in the common schools of the neighborhood and at Rockwood Academy. The family later moved to Winnipeg and there he attended Manitoba College. He began the study of medicine in Winnipeg under Dr. John H. O'Donnell in 1877 and took his M.D. degree at Trinity Medical College, Toronto, in 1881. He began practise in Buffalo, N. Y., but returned to Winnipeg in 1882 to be near his aged mother. Here he practised his profession for twelve years.

Shortly after his arrival in Winnipeg he was appointed registrar of the College of Physicians and Surgeons of Manitoba. The following year he took the initiative in founding the Manitoba Medical College. In the new faculty he was professor of physiology and histology during the years 1883–86 and professor of surgery from 1886 to 1894. He was surgeon-in-chief of St. Boniface Hospital and a member of the staff of Winnipeg General Hospital. He went to Chicago in 1894 to become professor of surgery at the Chicago Post-Graduate Medical School and Hospital, and in 1900 was appointed, together with Dr. Albert J. Ochsner [*q.v.*], to the chair of surgery in the medical department of the University of Illinois. He was on the surgical staffs of the Post-Graduate Hospital, the Chicago Hospital, and the Cook County Hospital for the Insane.

He was a member of the British Medical Association and was the first president of the Manitoba branch. He was a fellow of the American Surgical Association, of the American Association of Obstetricians and Gynecologists, and of the Southern Surgical and Gynecological Association, in addition to holding membership in local societies. In 1906 the King of Portugal conferred upon him the decoration of Commander of the Order of Christ of Portugal in recognition of his surgical achievements.

His practise in Winnipeg gave him an experience in hydatid disease of the liver such as came to no other man in America and these cases followed him to Chicago. He originated a method of treating hernia and improved the technique of cleft palate operations. He was one of the first to advocate decortication of the kidney for chronic Bright's disease. He contributed more than a hundred articles on surgical subjects to medical periodicals, was the author of a book entitled *The Technic of Modern Operations for Hernia* (1907), and was engaged upon a text-book of surgery at the time of his death which occurred in Chicago, following three months' illness from septicemia due to a carbuncle. He was survived by his wife, Sarah Jane Thomas of Nassagaweya, Ontario, whom he had married in 1882, and by two sons.

Ferguson was an athlete and foot-ball player in his youth and kept his close-knit, powerful figure to the end. Abounding in energy, he was genial and companionable but with an easily aroused pugnacity. Although filling teaching appointments throughout his entire professional career he had but a mediocre gift for instruction, except by the example of his operative skill.

[Of the biographical sketches of Ferguson appearing in periodical literature, those by Dr. A. J. Ochsner in the *Illinois Medic. Jour.,* 1912, and by Dr. C. W. Barrett in the *Am. Jour. of Obstetrics,* June 1913, are noteworthy. A sketch, with portrait, appears also in *Trans. Southern Surgic. and Gynecol. Asso.,* 1912. See also *Who's Who in America,* 1908–09.]

J. M. P.

FERGUSON, ELIZABETH GRAEME (Feb. 3, 1737–Feb. 23, 1801), poet, translator, writer of letters and journals, was the youngest child of Dr. Thomas Graeme and his wife, Ann Diggs (Keith, *post,* pp. 161–64). Dr. Graeme owned an imposing house in Philadelphia and a country estate called Graeme Park. The family were prosperous, and entertained lavishly (*Port Folio*). At the age of seventeen Elizabeth became engaged to William Franklin [*q.v.*], the son of Benjamin Franklin. In the summer of 1757 he went to London, where he found feminine society that overtaxed his constancy. He soon quarreled with his fiancée, and in 1762 he was married in

London to a Miss Elizabeth Downes. Disappointed in love, Elizabeth Graeme turned to poetry for consolation and made a careful translation of Fénelon's *Télémaque*. She still continued to grieve, however, and her health declined until her parents in 1764 sent her to London in hope that change of scene might help her to forget her trouble. Through her father's friend, the Rev. Richard Peters, who was abroad at the same time, she made many interesting acquaintances. She was on intimate terms with the Penn family and their friends; and according to tradition, she met Lawrence Sterne and was treated with special courtesy by the King (*Ibid.*). She had treatment from the famous Dr. John Fothergill and returned home much improved in health, but still sad in spirit because her mother had died during her absence.

Mistress, now, of her father's house, she made it a gathering place for the literary set of Philadelphia. A manuscript journal of her travels and her *Télémaque*, which she revised from time to time, gave her a local reputation as a writer. With Nathaniel Evans [*q.v.*], who had accompanied her and Richard Peters on the voyage from England, she carried on a discreet flirtation in verse. She made a metrical version of the Psalms, celebrated important incidents in verse, and wrote voluminously to her friends. Her writings are not without interest, but they probably would not be remembered to-day had not later events given the author an unhappy notoriety.

On Apr. 21, 1772, she was married to Henry Hugh Ferguson, a Scotchman ten years younger than she. In the autumn of the same year Dr. Graeme died, and she inherited Graeme Park, where she and her husband resided until the outbreak of the Revolution. In the fall of 1775 Ferguson went to England and Scotland on business. Returning two years later, he accompanied Howe's army to Philadelphia in September 1777. In November, after Washington had refused to allow him to go to Graeme Park, he became commissary of prisoners under the British commander. Gen. Washington had so much faith in Mrs. Ferguson's patriotism that he allowed her to visit her husband whenever she wished. She undoubtedly sympathized with her fellow countrymen, but her longing for peace and her devotion to her husband, who was unscrupulous enough to make her a catspaw, soon led her into some questionable enterprises. She was made the bearer of a letter from the Rev. Jacob Duché [*q.v.*] to Washington, urging the American general to surrender, and later she was empowered by Gov. George Johnstone, one of the peace commissioners, to offer Joseph Reed a heavy bribe if he would bring about a settlement satisfactory to the British (see W. B. Reed, *Life and Correspondence of Joseph Reed,* 2 vols., 1847). Both attempts failed, and Mrs. Ferguson soon found herself in trouble. Ferguson was attainted and proscribed, and his personal property was confiscated and sold. Mrs. Ferguson's estate was also confiscated and would have been sold but for her friends among the patriot leaders. In 1781 she received permission to retain Graeme Park during her lifetime, and in 1791 she was allowed to sell it. Her dead sister's son and daughter, whom she had reared, and a friend, Eliza Stedman, were the companions of her last years. She died in comparative poverty and was buried at Christ Church.

Mrs. Ferguson had many admirable qualities—intellectual culture, taste, sincere piety. When her husband was commissary of prisoners, she did much to relieve the sufferings of those unfortunates. Even in adversity she gave freely to charity. She was a dutiful daughter, a loyal friend, and a conscientious foster-mother. These virtues have disposed her biographers to pass lightly over her faults and deal gently with her memory.

[The chief source for the biography of Elizabeth Graeme Ferguson is a sketch and a collection of letters published by the late Simon Gratz in the *Pa. Mag. of Hist. and Biog.*, July–Oct. 1915. Other biographical sketches are found in the *Port Folio,* June 1809; Elizabeth Ellet, *The Women of the Am. Revolution* (1848); R. W. Griswold, *The Female Poets of America* (1853); E. A. and G. L. Duyckinck, *Cyc. of Am. Lit.* (1856); *Memoirs of the Hist. Soc. of Pa.* vol. I (1864); G. P. Keith, *Provincial Councillors of Pa.* (1883); Moses Coit Tyler, *The Lit. Hist. of the Am. Rev.* (1897); M. Katherine Jackson, *Outlines of the Lit. Hist. of Colonial Pa.* (1906); H. M. Ellis, *Joseph Dennie and His Circle* (1915); and Geo. E. Hastings, *The Life and Works of Francis Hopkinson* (1926). The Ridgway Lib. (Phila.), owns the MS. of Mrs. Ferguson's *Télémaque*, the Hist. Soc. of Pa., that of her metrical version of the Psalms. Both possess letters and other biographical material. Her metrical epistles to Nathaniel Evans were published in his *Poems on Several Occasions* (1772) and in Duyckinck's *Cyclopedia;* one of them is quoted by Tyler. Griswold's collection contains selections from *Télémaque.*]

G. E. H.

FERGUSON, THOMAS BARKER (Aug. 8, 1841–Aug 11, 1922), Confederate soldier, scientist, diplomat, was born in Berkeley County, near Charleston, S. C., the son of James and Abby Ann (Barker) Ferguson. His great-grandfather, James Ferguson, came to Charleston from Scotland late in the seventeenth century, and his grandfather, Thomas Ferguson, was prominent in state politics during the Revolution. After attending elementary schools in Charleston, Thomas Barker Ferguson went to the state Military Academy, where he graduated in 1861 and immediately entered the Confederate service as a cadet engineer. With his classmates he helped construct and operate a battery on Morris Island which prevented the U. S. S. *Star of the West* from relieving Fort Sumter in April 1861. Serving throughout the Civil War, he rose to the rank of major before he was twenty-five. While in command of the artillery of Walker's division of Johnston's army at Jackson, Miss., in 1863, he was shot through the lungs, but recovered in time to become before the end of the war commander of the First Military District, which included South Carolina, Georgia, and Florida. In 1867 he moved to Baltimore and married Jane Byrd, daughter of Gov. Thomas Swann of Maryland. He organized the Maryland State Fish Commission in 1870 and long served as a member. After acting as judge of awards for the Centennial Exposition at Philadelphia in 1876, he was sent as assistant commissioner of the United States to the Paris Exposition of 1878. Appointed on his return as assistant commissioner of fish and fisheries of the United States, he served until 1887, inventing meanwhile many improvements in the apparatus used for incubating fish eggs. He published in 1880 a monograph on pisciculture (in Vol. V of the *Reports* of the United States Commission to the Paris Exposition, 1878) which set forth his many discoveries in that field. In February 1894 he was appointed by President Cleveland minister to Sweden and Norway. After spending four uneventful years in Stockholm, he returned to the United States and lived in Washington, D. C. Devoting himself to inventing, he produced an improved coffee pot and the *Cadmus,* both patented in 1903. The latter was a copy book for beginning students in writing and forced the pupil to follow the example instead of copying his own errors. He died while visiting his daughter in Boston, Mass. A prominent clubman with a wide circle of friends, Ferguson performed valuable services through his researches in fish propagation.

[*American Biog. Directories, District of Columbia, 1908–09* (1908); obituaries in *Boston Transcript* and *Boston Post,* Aug. 11, 1922, and *Evening Star* (Washington), Aug. 12, 1922; U. S. Department of State, Records of the Appointment Bureau.]

W. L. W—t., Jr.

FERGUSON, WILLIAM JASON (June 8, 1844–May 4, 1930), actor who saw Lincoln shot, was born in Baltimore, Md., the son of Alexander and Ann (Wilson) Ferguson, both Scottish emigrants. After the death of his father in 1848 and of his grandfather, James Wilson, a few years later, Ferguson, then a boy of nine, was obliged to abandon his schooling and contribute to the support of his family. He was first a newsboy, later a printer's devil on the *Baltimore Clipper,* and at the age of sixteen a train-boy on the Baltimore & Ohio Railroad. His stage career began in 1863 when he was hired as call boy at Ford's Theatre in Washington. There the shooting of Lincoln occurred on Apr. 14, 1865, during the run of *Our American Cousin* with Laura Keene. The construction of the box, which concealed its occupants from the audience, and the disposition of the other actors at the time of the assassination, support the claim that Ferguson was the sole witness. His description has been accepted as the most reliable account of the shooting, and has appeared in the *Saturday Evening Post* (*post*), the *New York Times* (Apr. 18, 1915), and finally in book form as *I Saw Booth Shoot Lincoln* (1930).

Immediately after the assassination Ford's Theatre closed, but Ferguson continued on the stage, serving his apprenticeship in various companies, touring New York and Pennsylvania with Sherry's troupe, later joining the Ravels, Ben de Bar's, the Bidwell company, and Mrs. Conway's stock company. In the fall of 1872 he was engaged to play juveniles at Wallack's Theatre in New York City. Thereafter he remained in New York, establishing himself in a house in Brooklyn, and playing "enough melodrama characters to populate a town" (*New York Times, post*). He appeared with Mr. and Mrs. W. J. Florence in 1875, and with Mantell and Maurice Barrymore in Al Hayman's stock company in 1886. In 1890 he began his association with Richard Mansfield, with whom he played character rôles in *Master and Man* (1890), *Don Juan* (1891), *Ten Thousand a Year* (1892), and *Beau Brummel,* the unusual success of which was attributed to Ferguson's deft characterization of Mortimer (*New York Times, post*). Later he joined the Charles Frohman company, creating in 1895 the part of Stephen Spettigue in *Charley's Aunt.* Until his retirement he was to be found at any time adding to the comic zest of some Broadway performance. After half a century on the legitimate stage, Ferguson added motion-pictures to his routine with the filming of *The Deep Purple* in 1915. He made fourteen in all, many of which were film versions of his earlier stage successes. His mobile face, his sense of timing, and above all his mastery of the art of gesture and pantomime made him especially valuable to motion-pictures. During the filming of *The Yosemite Trail* in 1922, he broke his hip, thereby ending a long and energetic career. His last years were spent with a niece and nephew in Baltimore.

Shortly after leaving Ford's Theatre, Ferguson married Fannie Pierson, an actress, who died within a few years. In 1880 he married Catherine Ferrell, who survived him.

[T. Allston Brown, *A Hist. of the N. Y. Stage*, vol. III (1903); Ada Patterson, "An Eccentric Comedian of the Old School" in *Theatre Mag.*, May 1908; Wm. J. Ferguson, "I Saw Lincoln Shot," and Merle Crowell, "Ferguson—Who saw the Greatest Murder in Modern History," in *Am. Mag.*, Aug. 1920; *Saturday Evening Post*, Feb. 12, 1927; Baltimore *Sun*, May 6, 1930; *Washington Post*, May 8, 1930; *New York Times*, May 8, 1930; *Billboard*, May 17, 1930; information as to certain facts from Mr. W. E. Croggan and Miss Katharine F. Mazan, Ferguson's nephew and grand-daughter.] C. W. P.

FERGUSON, WILLIAM PORTER FRISBEE (Dec. 13, 1861–June 23, 1929), clergyman, reformer, was born in Delhi, N. Y., the son of Phineas Rice and Electa Ann (Frisbee) Ferguson. His mother was a descendant of Edward Frisbee, one of the first settlers of Branford, Conn., who died in 1690. William graduated from Walton Academy, N. Y., in 1884, and from Drew Theological Seminary in 1887. This same year he was admitted to the Troy Conference of the Methodist Episcopal Church, and on Apr. 5, married Lena Grace Hathaway of Sidney Center, N. Y. Transferred to the Mexico Conference, he engaged in missionary work until 1889, when, having become a member of the New York Conference, he was stationed in Bangall, N. Y. In 1888 he received the degree of B.A. from Texas Wesleyan College at Fort Worth. He was principal of the Mohawk Collegiate Preparatory Institute, Utica, N. Y., in 1891, and the following year was principal of Utica Private Academy. In 1893 he was transferred to the Northern New York Conference, but withdrew from the Methodist Church, and until 1896 served as pastor of the Presbyterian church at Whitesboro, N. Y.

He was a militant Prohibitionist, as early as 1880 contributing verses to the *Living Issue*, published in Utica, N. Y., and actively supporting the candidates of the Prohibition party in the presidential campaign of 1884. After 1896 he was engaged chiefly in editorial work, being on the staff of the *Voice*, New York, from 1897 to 1899, and serving as managing editor of the *New Voice*, Chicago, from 1899 to 1902. Once more shifting his denominational allegiance, he became pastor of the Universalist church, Harriman, Tenn., and proprietor and editor of the *Citizen* in 1904–05. In the latter year he took charge of the Third Universalist Church, Brooklyn, N. Y., and assumed proprietorship of the *Defender*, New York. Purchasing the *Home Defender* of Chicago in 1907, and merging his own paper with it, he took over the subscription list of the *New Voice*, previously discontinued, and issued a publication called the *National Prohibitionist*. This was consolidated with the *Vindicator*, Franklin, Pa., in 1911, of which he was in charge until 1916. He also edited the *Venango Daily Herald* of Franklin (1912–19), and later the *News Herald* and the *Citizen-Press*. He was an effective speaker and presented the subject of prohibition from the platform in many different sections of the country. In 1900 he published *The Canteen in the United States Army; a Study of Uncle Sam as a Grog-Shop Keeper*; and in 1902, *Prohibition in the United States*. His popularity was attested by the large vote he received as Prohibition candidate for Congress from the Twenty-eighth District of Pennsylvania in 1914, and as candidate for the state legislature from Venango County in 1918. In the Prohibition Convention of 1916 he had strong support for the presidential nomination, but he transferred it to J. Frank Hanly. During the later years of his life he carried on investigations in Isle Royale, Lake Superior, and published "Michigan's Most Ancient Industry: the Pre-Historic Mines and Miners of Isle Royale" (*Michigan History Magazine*, July–October 1923), and "The Franklin Isle Royale Expedition" (*Ibid.*, October 1924).

[E. S. Frisbee, *The Frisbee-Frisbie Geneal.* (1926); W. P. Tolley, *Alumni Records of Drew Theol. Sem. 1867–1925* (1926); *Minutes N. Y. Conference M. E. Ch.* for 1892 and 1893; *Who's Who in America*, 1928–29; E. H. Cherrington and others, *Standard Encyc. of the Alcohol Problem*, vol. III (1926); *N. Y. Times*, June 25, 1929.] H. E. S.

FERNALD, CHARLES HENRY (Mar. 16, 1838–Feb. 22, 1921), entomologist, teacher, was born at Fernald's Point, Mount Desert Island, Me., the son of Eben and Sophronia (Wasgatt) Fernald. He was a thorough New Englander by ancestry, by training, and in his personality. His father was a ship-owner, and the boy's ambition naturally was to become a ship captain. He spent his summers from the age of fifteen to twenty-one at sea and his winters in teaching and in studying. At twenty-one he entered the Maine Wesleyan Seminary, preparing for entrance to Bowdoin College. The Civil War broke out, and he entered the navy, serving until 1865, when he resigned with the rank of ensign. During his three years of naval duty he studied constantly, completing the Bowdoin College course. In 1871 this college gave him the honorary degree of master of arts. On Aug. 24, 1862, he was married to Maria Elizabeth Smith of Monmouth, Me. On his return from the war, he taught at Litchfield and Houlton Academies, and in 1871 was made professor of natural history in Maine State College. His first interest in natural history had begun in his study of sea forms as a boy. Later he became interested in geology and still later in botany and zoölogy. In his new position he taught all branches of natural history but became more and more interested in insects, publishing papers on a variety of topics. He gradually concentrated on the study of certain comparatively unknown groups of *Microlepidoptera*, especially the *Pyralidae* and the *Tortricidae*. In 1886 he was made professor of zoölogy in the Massachusetts Agricultural College at Amherst, holding the position until his retirement in 1910. During this period he developed admirable postgraduate courses in entomology.

Although he was not a prolific writer, Fernald's work was careful and sound. His reputation as a taxonomist rests principally upon his studies of the *Tortricidae*. In this field he was well-known to European workers and was in constant correspondence with the leading English, French, and German entomologists. He made frequent trips to Europe, and his entomological learning was perhaps especially appreciated by Lord Walsingham who was in his time the world's leading authority on the *Microlepidoptera*. Fernald also gained a high reputation in economic entomology and held at one time the position of state entomologist of Massachusetts and was president of the American Association of Economic Entomologists in 1896. On the appearance of the gipsy moth in New England, he was at once consulted and, down to the time when the federal government entered the field, had virtual charge of scientific aspects of the fight which the state instituted against this pest and later against the brown-tail moth. Mrs. Fernald, who was also an entomologist, was the first person to recognize the gipsy moth in New England in the summer of 1889 while her husband was absent on one of his European trips. Fernald's greatest achievement, however, was that of a teacher of entomology. He was one of the first Americans to teach the subject systematically. He aroused great interest and enthusiasm among his students, and trained many men who are prominent in this work to-day. Through his influence one of the first buildings erected specially in the name of entomology on any college campus was built at Amherst in 1910. This building was named Fernald Hall.

[Excellent biographical accounts of Fernald are those by A. F. Burgess in the *Jour. of Economic Entomology*, Apr. 1921 (with portr.), and Annette F. Braun in *Entomological News*, May 1921. Some accounts of his career will also be found in an "Address at the Dedication of the Entomology and Zoology Building of the Massachusetts Agricultural College," by L. O. Howard (*Science*, Dec. 2, 1910). The fullest account and an excellent portrait will be found in *Entomology and Zoology at the Mass. Agric. Coll.* (1911), a pamphlet published by the college.] L. O. H.

FERNALD, JAMES CHAMPLIN (Aug. 18, 1838–Nov. 10, 1918), Baptist clergyman, author, editor, was born in Portland, Me., the son of Henry Baker and Mabel (Collins) Fernald. He graduated from Harvard College, where he received one of the Bowdoin prizes, in 1860, and from the Newton Theological Institution in 1863. On Apr. 27, 1869, he married Mary Beulah Griggs of Rutland, Vt., one of the early graduates of Vassar College. She died of consumption on June 7, 1870, in her twenty-second year. On June 18, 1873, he married Nettie Barker of McConnelsville, Ohio, who survived him. Until 1889 he remained in the active ministry, holding pastorates at Rutland, Vt., 1862–65; Waterville, Me., 1865–66; Granville, Ohio, 1869–72; McConnelsville, 1876–77; Clyde, 1877–79; Galion, 1879–80; Springfield, 1880–85; and Garretsville, 1885–89. During the Civil War he was in the service of the Massachusetts Soldiers' Aid Society before Fredericksburg, in the Washington hospitals, and at Gettysburg. He traveled in Europe for his health, 1866–67, and when health and voice again failed him became a clerk in the Treasury Department at Washington, 1873–75. He was an ardent Prohibitionist and through his writings and lectures for the cause made the acquaintance of Isaac K. Funk [*q.v.*], who was another. Funk took Fernald with him to New York to help edit the *Homiletic Review* and the *Voice*, which was an organ of the Prohibition movement. Fernald's use of economic as well as moral arguments for teetotalism was then somewhat novel, and his *Economics of Prohibition* (1890) was in its day an influential book. When Funk organized the editorial staff of the *Standard Dictionary* he placed Fernald in charge of synonyms, antonyms, and prepositions. The choice was unusually lucky, for although his scientific knowledge of English was meager Fernald did possess an extraordinary gift for comparing and contrasting words. His work for the *Standard* (1893–94) was revised and extended for the *New Standard* (1913), was used generously in various abridgments of the two large dictionaries, and as a separate publication, *English Synonyms and Antonyms* (1896, revised and enlarged, 1914), has enjoyed a large, and well-earned, popularity. His *Connectives of English Speech* (1904) has also been much used as a work of reference. He was the editor of several abridgments of the *Standard* dictionaries, but the merits of these books were due to his assistants rather than to himself; he lacked the executive capacity, regard for details, and patience indispensable to a lexicographer. He lived in Washington, D. C., as a teacher, 1905–09. He died at his home in Upper Montclair, N. J.

[Letter to author from Dr. Frank H. Vizetelly, Feb. 28, 1928; *Who's Who in America,* 1918–19, which contains a list of Fernald's writings; *Quinquennial Cat. of Harvard Univ. 1636–1915* (1915); *Report of Class of 1860, Harvard Coll., 1860–80* (1880); *Ibid., 1895–1900* (1900); *Gen. Cat. of the Newton Theol. Institution* (1899); *N. Y. Times,* Nov. 11, 1918.] G. H. G.

FERNOW, BERNHARD EDUARD (Jan. 7, 1851–Feb. 6, 1923), forester, author, teacher, was born in Inowrazlaw, Posen, Germany. His father, who held a distinguished position in the service of the Prussian government, was a man of unusual culture both in literature and music and his home was a musical center for some of the most renowned artists of the time. The son received his education at the gymnasium at Bromberg, the University of Königsberg, and the Hanover-Münden Forest Academy. He served as a volunteer in the Franco-Prussian War in 1870. After the war he entered the Prussian forest service, and, before coming to America in 1876, had attained the grade of Forstkandidat. When young Fernow reached the United States, eager to practise his chosen profession, he found that forestry was almost unknown. There had been some legislative effort to encourage the planting of trees on the prairies and elsewhere, but the conception of forestry as applied to the protection and perpetuation of existing forests was new in America. A few far-sighted scientists and others had urged the necessity for a better handling of forest resources, but no steps had been taken to check the forest fires and the wasteful methods of exploitation of timber. Bernhard Fernow found a pioneer field of endeavor. In 1878 he was employed as manager of a large tract of land in Pennsylvania owned by the Cooper-Hewitt mining interests, a post which he held for seven years. He began at once to write articles about forestry. He soon attracted the attention of scientists and others who were interested in the subject, and was called into consultation in connection with various proposals for forest legislation. In 1882 he was instrumental in organizing the American Forestry Congress (later the American Forestry Association), which consistently has been one of the most influential national agencies for the promotion of forestry. He was secretary of that organization for twelve years.

In 1886 he was appointed chief of the Division of Forestry in the United States Department of Agriculture. He at once became the recognized leader of the forestry movement. Under his direction many important investigations were made regarding the American forests, the life characteristics of different important species of trees, the qualities of the wood produced, and the economic consequences of forest destruction. He promoted federal and state legislation for the protection of forests from fire and other adverse agencies. He vigorously attacked the neglect of the forests on the public domain and proposed specific legislative measures for their conservation. It was largely due to Fernow's efforts that legislation was finally enacted for the establishment of the present system of National Forests. Congress authorized the withdrawal of forest lands from the public domain in 1891, but six years more were required to secure the needed legislation making provision for the care of the federal forest reserves. The law as finally passed in 1897 carried the principles that Fernow had outlined in his early proposals.

In 1898 he retired from the government service, to organize at Cornell University the first collegiate school of forestry in the United States. The State of New York acquired a large tract of land in the Adirondack Mountains, as an instructional and demonstration forest for the new school. A conflict of opinion arose in a few years over the methods of handling the tract, and the controversy resulted in the withdrawal in 1903 of the State's support of the project in the Adirondacks and also of the School of Forestry. During the next four years Fernow engaged in a private consulting practise. He advised private timber landowners regarding their special problems; he conducted exploration in the West Indies and Mexico; he gave courses of lectures at the Yale School of Forestry in 1904; and in 1906 inaugurated the work of forestry at the Pennsylvania State College. In 1907 he was called to the University of Toronto to organize and administer a department of forestry. In this position he served with great success and distinction until his retirement from active university work in 1919. As emeritus professor he continued to live in Toronto, in close association with the school which he had founded, until his death in 1923.

Fernow was a vigorous writer and public speaker. His most important books were: *Economics of Forestry* (1902); *A Brief History of Forestry in Europe, the United States, and Other Countries* (1907); and *The Care of Trees, in Lawn, Street and Park* (1910). In addition he prepared or edited over fifty government and other bulletins and circulars and had to his credit over two hundred articles and addresses on subjects relating to forestry. He was responsible for the establishment in 1902 of the *Forestry Quarterly,* the organ of the Society of American

Foresters, and was the editor of that publication and of its successor, the *Journal of Forestry*, until 1922. Fernow was a thorough scholar in science and was widely read in literature and philosophy. He was also an accomplished musician. An enthusiast with deep convictions, and possessed of an argumentative disposition, he was frequently a center of professional controversy. He retained, however, the respect of those who differed with him. He was a great teacher, inspiring his students to a high standard of scholastic endeavor and to the best professional ideals. In 1879 he was married to Olivia Reynolds of Brooklyn, N. Y., who survived him. There were five children of this marriage, four sons and one daughter.

[*Jour. of Forestry*, Apr. 1923; Filibert Roth, "A Great Teacher of Forestry Retires," in *Am. Forestry*, 1910; the *Annual Reports* of the Division of Forestry, U. S. Dept. of Agric., 1887–98; numerous scattered references in the forestry periodicals from 1886 to 1923; obituary in the *Globe* (Toronto), Feb. 7, 1923.]

H. S. G.

FERNOW, BERTHOLD (Nov. 28, 1837–Mar. 3, 1908), historian, archivist, editor, was born in Inowrazlaw, Posen, Germany, the eldest of thirteen children. His father was Edward F. Fernow, a Prussian Landrat, and his mother Bertha von Jachmann, sister of Admiral Jachmann. Prepared by private tutors, he entered the gymnasium at Magdeburg, 1849, from which he transferred to Bromberg in 1856. Enamored of rural life, the young man devoted himself to the study of agriculture from 1858 to 1860. In the latter year he served as a lieutenant in the Reserve of the Prussian army. In 1861, on the advice of his father, he emigrated to the United States, bought a farm in Iowa, and became a naturalized citizen. He espoused the Union cause in the Civil War and in 1862 volunteered as a private in the 4th Missouri Cavalry. In 1863 he was promoted to second lieutenant of the 3rd United States Colored Infantry and served in South Carolina and Florida. He was detailed as topographical engineer in the coast division of Sherman's army in 1864, and mustered out Oct. 31, 1865. For the next ten years he was engaged in commerce in New York City and Berlin as an employee of the Hamburg American Steamship Company and of a Berlin bank. His heart was in America, however, and in 1874 he purchased a farm at Metuchen, N. J., where he cultivated strawberries on a large scale.

In 1875 he met John Bigelow [*q.v.*], secretary of State of New York, by whom he was appointed keeper of historical records, and began to devote himself to scholarly tasks. With enthusiasm and ability, from 1876 to 1883 he added Volumes XII, XIII, and XIV (published 1877–83) to *Documents Relating to the Colonial History of the State of New York*. In 1882 he accepted a position under the Regents of the University of the State of New York, which he held until 1889. Under these new auspices he compiled Volume XV ("New York in the Revolution," published 1887) of the *Documents*. He wrote *Albany and Its Place in the History of the United States* (1886), and prepared articles on "New Netherland" and the "Middle Colonies" for Justin Winsor's *Narrative and Critical History of America* (vol. IV, 1885, and vol. V, 1887). After 1889 he was employed in private compilations and research. In 1890 *The Ohio Valley in Colonial Days* was published at Albany as No. 17 of Munsell's historical series. For the Colonial Dames of New York Fernow prepared the *Calendar of Wills on File and Recorded in the Offices of the Clerk of the Court of Appeals, of the County Clerk at Albany and of the Secretary of State 1628–1836* (1896). *New Amsterdam Family Names and their Origin* appeared in 1898; and *Albany and New York Families*, translated from Dutch Bibles, in 1900. From 1898 to 1902 he was employed by the New Jersey Historical Society to compile a "Calendar of Records in the Office of the Secretary of State 1664–1703," and to make abstracts of wills (1670–1730)—in Volumes XXI and XXIII of the *New Jersey Archives* (1899, 1903). He edited *The Records of New Amsterdam from 1673 to 1674 anno Domini* (7 vols., 1897), published under the authority of the City of New York, and for the Colonial Dames, *The Minutes of the Orphanmasters of New Amsterdam, 1655 to 1663* (2 vols., 1902–07). In 1902 a "Calendar of Council Minutes 1668–1783," originally intended as part of the series of *Documents Relative to . . . Colonial History*, was published by the New York State Library as *Bulletin: History 6*.

Fernow was a man of versatile mind, deep sentiment, and striking personality. Large physically, well-groomed, sociable, an entertaining conversationalist, and a delightful comrade, he was a frequent guest in the best homes of Albany. His mind was orderly and encyclopedic, and his translations and compilations, although not without errors, were done creditably. The last two years of his life were spent in the preparation of "The World's Largest Libraries," which was finished shortly before his death in the National Home for Disabled Volunteer Soldiers at Togus, Me. He was unmarried.

[An account of Fernow's life prepared by Capt. E. B. Van Winkle, Lieut. A. T. Gurlitz, and Gen. J. G. Wilson as a memorial, on Sept. 30, 1908, was printed as *Circu-*

lar No. 29, Ser. of 1908, at New York City by the Military Order of the Loyal Legion. See also *Who's Who in America,* 1908–09; the N. Y. Comptroller's Report, *Assembly Docs.* 1877–85, and *Education Dept. Bull. No. 462* (1910); some unprinted magazine articles and an autobiographical sketch are in the State Lib., Albany, N. Y.] A. C. F.

FERREL, WILLIAM (Jan. 29, 1817–Sept. 18, 1891), meteorologist, was born in Fulton County, Pa. His Scotch-Irish grandfather, William Ferrel, came to America about 1785, and married an English woman by the name of Veach. Their son Benjamin married a Miss Miller, of German origin, and William Ferrel, born in 1817, was the first of their family of six boys and two girls. Although the home was only a log cabin with a mud and stick chimney, William got a little schooling in reading, writing, and arithmetic. In 1829 the family moved to a farm in Berkeley County, Va. (now W. Va.). Here William was kept busy in the fields, but went to school two winters in the usual log cabin of the times with greased paper windows. About this time he happened to see a copy of Park's *Arithmetic,* with a brief discussion of mensuration at the back; the diagrams fascinated him, but he had no money to buy the book. He shortly got work in a neighbor's harvest field, however, and thus earned fifty cents, his very first money. As soon as possible, he went to a town some distance away eager to spend his all for the coveted book. Then came a great shock, the price of the book was sixty-two and a half cents, and quickly a greater joy, for the storekeeper reduced the price to the boy's limit. The book was mastered in short order. In 1834 he obtained a copy of Gummere's *Surveying* that contained a number of miscellaneous problems requiring a knowledge of geometry for their solution. He knew no geometry, but solved them nevertheless, using barn doors for blackboards and pitchforks for chalk and compass. These barn-door diagrams he often went to see in later life. In the spring of 1839 he entered a preparatory school connected with Marshall College, Pa. Here he first saw an algebra. The next winter he taught school, and then returned to Marshall College, where by the fall of 1841 he had completed all the mathematics offered, and the extra work of a volunteer class besides. After teaching for two years, he entered Bethany College from which he graduated on July 4, 1844.

In the fall of this year he went to Liberty, Mo., where he taught about eighteen months, until ill health obliged him to stop. He next taught for seven years in Todd County, Ky. In the spring of 1854 he opened a school in Nashville, Tenn. In 1856 he published his famous "Essay on the Winds and the Currents of the Ocean" in the *Nashville Journal of Medicine and Surgery.* This essay treats, in a non-mathematical manner, of the effect of the rotation of the earth on the courses of winds and currents. It immediately attracted great attention in France, and later equal attention in other countries. In the spring of 1857 he went to Cambridge, Mass., to work on the *American Ephemeris and Nautical Almanac.* He returned in the fall to Nashville, taking work with him, but the following spring gave over his school to a partner and went back to Cambridge. In 1867 he entered the Coast and Geodetic Survey, and there published many important papers, and also devised a tide-predicting machine. From 1882 to October 1886 he had a high position in the Signal Service and published many additional papers on meteorology. In addition to his publications in book form, "Tidal Researches" (*United States Coast and Geodetic Survey Report,* 1874, Appendix), *Meteorological Researches* (1877–82), *Recent Advances in Meteorology* (1886), and *A Popular Treatise on the Winds* (1889), the bibliography of his writings includes about a hundred titles.

After resigning from public service he spent the remaining six years of his life with certain of his brothers and sisters in Kansas, in pleasant ease and comfort until his final dropsical illness. His own problems and a few intellectual friends (he was too diffident to have many) absorbed all his time. Humor, frivolity, and even romance —he never married—were foreign to his nature. In early life he was a Campbellite, but in later years a Unitarian. He was a member of the American Academy of Arts and Sciences and of the National Academy of Sciences, and an honorary member of the Royal Meteorological Society and of others of like character.

[Cleveland Abbe, "Memoir of William Ferrel," in *Nat. Acad. Sci., Biog. Memoirs,* vol. III (1895), with bibliography; autobiographical sketch dated Jan. 1888 printed with the above memoir; Wm. M. Davis, "William Ferrel," in *Proc. Am. Acad. Arts and Sci.,* vol. XXVIII (1893).] W. J. H.

FERRERO, EDWARD (Jan. 18, 1831–Dec. 11, 1899), Union soldier, was born at Granada, in Spain, of Italian parents, who removed to New York a year or two after his birth. The father established a dancing-school which became both successful and fashionable, and the son continued it with equal success, also teaching dancing at West Point. In 1859 he published *The Art of Dancing, Historically Illustrated.* Meanwhile he had entered the militia and by 1861 had worked up to the rank of lieutenant-colonel. He was mustered into the volunteer service as colonel of the 51st New York Infantry, Oct. 14, 1861, and commanded his regiment in the North Carolina expedition of the following winter, fighting at Roanoke Island and New Berne. At the second battle of Bull Run, at Chantilly, South Mountain, Antietam, and Fredericksburg, he commanded a brigade. His appointment as brigadier-general of volunteers, which was delivered to him on the battlefield at Antietam, expired Mar. 4, 1863, when the Senate adjourned without confirming his nomination, but he was reappointed, May 6, 1863. The IX Corps, to which his brigade belonged, joined Grant's army in June, and took part in the close of the Vicksburg campaign. In the defense of Knoxville, late in 1863, Ferrero commanded a division. When the IX Corps returned to the Army of the Potomac, in the spring of 1864, he was transferred to the command of a newly organized colored division, which saw its first serious fighting at the Petersburg crater. Ferrero's division was originally selected by Burnside to lead the assault, as soon as the mine should be exploded, but both Meade and Grant disapproved the choice, believing that such a task should not be given to new and untried troops. In the event, however, the leading division did not advance out of the crater, and it was Ferrero's division, pushing through the disorganized troops in front, that actually delivered the assault on the heights beyond, and was repulsed with heavy loss. The responsibility for the failure was fixed in part upon Ferrero, who exercised little control over his troops and left them to fight practically uncommanded. A similar criticism had been made of his conduct at the siege of Knoxville, where it was said that his division's gallant defense against the Confederate assault of Nov. 28–29, 1863, was made without any orders from him. Apparently a division was a larger body of troops than he was competent to command in action. During the latter part of the war he was stationed in the defenses of Bermuda Hundred. He was mustered out, Aug. 24, 1865. Returning to New York, he leased and managed several large ballrooms in succession, including, for seventeen years, that in Tammany Hall. He was a member of the Tammany Society, though he took no part in politics. He gave up his last holding, the Lenox Lyceum, a few months before his death.

[F. B. Heitman, *Hist. Reg. and Dict. of the U. S. Army* (1903), I, 417; obituary in the *N. Y. Tribune*, Dec. 14, 1899; *Official Records (Army)*, 1 ser., vols. IX, XIX (pt. 1), XXI, XXXI (pt. 1), XL (pts. 1, 2, 3).] T. M. S.

FERRIS, GEORGE WASHINGTON GALE (Feb. 14, 1859–Nov. 22, 1896), civil engineer, inventor of the Ferris Wheel, was the son of George Washington Gale Ferris and Martha (Hyde) Ferris, and was born at Galesburg, Ill., but moved with his parents to Carson City, Nev., in 1864. After graduation from the military academy at Oakland, Cal., he entered the Rensselaer Polytechnic Institute from which he received his engineering degree in 1881. After a few months in the railroad contracting office of Gen. J. H. Ledlie in New York City, he helped to locate seventy-eight miles of the proposed Baltimore, Cincinnati & Western Railroad in West Virginia, and a narrow-gauge road three and a half miles long in Putnam County, N. Y. As engineer, and later general manager for the Queen City (W. Va.) Coal Mining Company (1882) he designed and built a coal trestle in the Kanawha River and located and built three 1,800-foot tunnels. He next became interested in bridge-building, was employed successively by several companies, and achieved something of a reputation for concrete work under heavy pressure in pneumatic caissons.

In 1885 he took charge, for the Kentucky and Indiana Bridge Company of Louisville, of the testing and inspection of steel and iron bought at Pittsburgh. Foreseeing an increase in the use of structural steel, at that time just being introduced in bridge work, he familiarized himself with the processes involved in its manufacture and from the duties and responsibilities of his inspecting position developed a new profession. Eventually he organized the firm of G. W. G. Ferris & Company at Pittsburgh, with a corps of engineers and assistants to conduct mill and shop-work inspection and testing throughout the country. He was connected with this company until within about a week of his death. After the organization was functioning well, however, he turned his personal attention toward the promotion and financing of large engineering projects, and was concerned in the construction of bridges across the Ohio River at Wheeling, Cincinnati, and Pittsburgh.

When Daniel H. Burnham [*q.v.*], chief of construction for the World's Columbian Exposition, challenged the civil engineers of the country to produce something to rival the Eiffel Tower of the Paris Exposition, Ferris's imagination was fired, and in an effort to achieve something entirely new he designed the Ferris Wheel. He undertook its construction against the advice of friends and business associates. In the midst of the severe financial depression which the country was experiencing in 1892, the financing of the proposition was rather a difficult matter; at first the scheme was looked upon as fantastic; not for some months was he granted a concession, and not until after the Fair had opened was the wheel completed. Rising 250 feet above the Midway, carrying thirty-six cars, each with a capacity of some forty passengers, revolving under perfect control, and stable against the strongest winds from Lake Michigan, it excited general attention. The daring and accuracy involved in its design and the precision of machine work involved in its construction won the admiration of engineers. The most spectacular feature of the Exposition, it proved also a profitable investment. Ferris died less than four years later. He was survived by his wife, Margaret Beatty of Canton, Ohio.

[H. B. Nason, *Biog. Record Officers and Grads. Rensselaer Polytechnic Inst.* (1887); Carl Snyder, "Engineer Ferris and his Wheel," *Rev. of Revs.* (N. Y.), Sept. 1893; Wm. H. Searles, "The Ferris Wheel," *Jour. Asso. Engineering Socs.*, Dec. 1893; F. G. Coggin, "The Ferris and Other Big Wheels," *Cassier's Mag.*, July 1894; *Engineering Record*, Nov. 28, 1896; *Pittsburgh Post*, Nov. 23, 1896.] E. Y.

FERRIS, ISAAC (Oct. 9, 1798–June 16, 1873), Reformed Dutch clergyman, university president, was born in New York, the son of John and Sarah (Watkins) Ferris, and was of English descent. His father, a poor man with a large family of children, could do little to educate him, but Isaac traded a pair of skates for a Latin grammar, attended the instruction of a blind classical master named Neilson, and graduated in 1816 at the head of his class in Columbia College. For a short period during the War of 1812 he appears to have been a soldier under his father, who was then a captain and quartermaster in the army. He taught Latin for a year or two at Albany and then began the study of divinity under the Rev. John Mitchell Mason [*q.v.*]. When Mason on account of ill health was compelled to dismiss his pupil, Ferris resorted to the New Brunswick Theological Seminary, where he graduated in 1820. Licensed by the Classis of New Brunswick, he labored as a missionary for five months in the Mohawk Valley, and on Dec. 30, 1820, married Catharine Burchan, who died Sept. 9, 1837. His second wife was Sarah J. Crygier, who died July 2, 1848; his third wife, whom he married Oct. 1, 1850, was Letitia Storm. Among them they bore him twelve children. For thirty-three years Ferris was an active and successful minister, serving the Reformed Church at New Brunswick, N. J., 1821–24, the Second Church at Albany, N. Y., 1824–36, and the Market Street Church in New York, 1836–53. At Albany his unflinching devotion to the sick and dying of all creeds during the cholera epidemic of 1832 was remembered with gratitude forty years after the event. In New York he founded Rutgers Female Seminary. In 1840 he became a member of the American Bible Society and for the last twenty-six years of his life was chairman of its committee on distribution. In 1852 he helped organize the New York Y. M. C. A. On his advice the Reformed Dutch Church in 1858 appointed its own board of foreign missions; as its first corresponding secretary he did much to further its work in India, China, and Japan. Ferris Seminary in Yokohama was named in his honor. His most responsible post was the chancellorship of the University of the City of New York, to which he was elected in 1852. The University at that time was heavily involved in debt, had been without a chancellor for two years, and was moving rapidly toward chaos. Ferris was a good executive, and his majestic presence, confident address, and wholesome courage inspired confidence. By June 14, 1854, he had paid off a debt of $70,250. Acting as secretary of the financial committee of the University Council, he personally audited the accounts and saved the University not a little money. During his administration $215,000 was added to the funds, and the standards of scholarship were raised. While chancellor he was also professor of moral philosophy and of the evidences of revealed religion. In 1870 he retired as chancellor emeritus, built himself a house at Roselle, N. J., and, though still active in behalf of missions and charities, lived his few remaining years in quietness.

[J. L. Chamberlain, ed., *N. Y. Univ.* (1901); C. E. Crowell, *Partial Geneal. of the Ferris Family* (privately printed, 1899); *Cat. of the Officers and Grads. of Columbia Univ.* (16th ed., 1916); J. H. Raven, ed., *Biog. Record Theol. Sem. New Brunswick 1784–1911* (1912); E. T. Corwin, ed., *Manual of the Reformed Ch. in America* (4th ed., 1902), containing list of published sermons, papers, and addresses.] G. H. G.

FERRIS, JEAN LÉON GÉRÔME (Aug. 8, 1863–Mar. 18, 1930), historical painter, born in Philadelphia, derived his name, as well as, in some respects, his manner as an artist, from Jean Léon Gérôme, the celebrated painter of France. His exquisite and delicate art savored of the Gallic master, but with the difference that it was devoted to native American subjects. His mother, Elizabeth Anastasia (Moran) Ferris, was a sister of the Philadelphia artists Edward, Peter, and Thomas Moran [*qq.v.*] His father, Stephen James Ferris, was a painter and etcher of note in old Philadelphia, when Christian Schussele [*q.v.*] was the teacher of painting at the Pennsylvania Academy of the Fine Arts. There he acquired the gift of drawing, of which his son wisely said: "What success I may have had in depicting the human face and expression is owing to his instruction. He knew more about the fundamental principles of their production than any artist I have ever met" (information from

Mrs. Ferris). Gérôme Ferris began his studies in Philadelphia under his father and Schussele. The former was a devotee of Gérôme and Fortuny, and in 1881 he took his son to Spain to pursue the footsteps of the latter artist. The younger Ferris thus began his career in an atmosphere of the finest of the fine arts, where his tradition and inspiration were coupled with vigorous drawing and educated fidelity to fact. In Granada, where his father was painting a portrait of the Marquesa de Heredia, Ferris sold to that lady the first of his pictures. Beginning thus in the land and under the shadow of Fortuny it was natural, as a next step, for him to enter the Académie Julian in Paris in 1884 to study under Bouguereau, and while there to receive from the great artist for whom he was named the "most valuable personal criticism," and the direction to confine his attention to historical painting.

He studied for a time in London and in Madrid, and traveled through France, Spain, and Morocco painting small scenes of the life he saw, making these early efforts in genre in order to acquire from studies of the living model technique later to be used in his interpretation of history. In 1888 he went to England and Belgium to furnish his mind for the delightful and engrossing task he had adopted. He made studies of the seventeenth century, its architecture, customs, dress—always with the idea of a series of paintings of the history of his own country. He made special study of early American vehicles and ordnance, and turned over to the New York Historical Society and the National Museum much of the data he accumulated; models constructed on the basis of his studies are now in Congress Hall Museum, Philadelphia. He had considerable skill in handicraft; and built in miniature the boats, the caravels, and the battleships he painted. The accurate knowledge thus gained imparted a sense of reality to his canvases. The secret of his art was the application of the careful technique caught from France to the things of home.

About 1900 he began the series of some seventy historical paintings which constituted his greatest work. They carry the spectator from the adventures by sea of the early settlement of America, through all the stages of the unfolding drama of the nation's development down to Abraham Lincoln. Two later scenes were added, "A Word to the Kaiser" in 1902, and a marine, "Sunk Without Trace," in 1917. It was the artist's purpose to give consecutively the story of the American people. To effect this object he arranged with the City of Philadelphia that all his work would be shown, appropriately, in that room in Independence Hall where Washington was inaugurated in 1793. The collection now (1930) hangs in a special gallery in Congress Hall as a loan to the city and under agreements that forbid its being scattered.

Ferris was whimsical, genial, and witty. His humor showed itself in his droll smile and in such deft extravaganzas as his volume of silhouettes of the great ladies and gentlemen of the Revolution, many known, not a few invented, and only one genuine. The antique paper used in this book, the insignia and postmarks, all from the hand of the artist, would deceive a connoisseur, if the title of the volume were not given as "Sundri Impostures Innocentes: Pictor J. L. G. Ferris, Philadelphia, MCMXXVIII." He died in Philadelphia, where he had lived most of his fruitful and happy life. On May 17, 1894, he had married Annette S. Ryder of Brewster, N. Y. They had one daughter who died before her father.

[Warren W. Brown, "J. L. G. Ferris, America's Painter-Historian," in *Print Connoisseur,* Apr. 1924; *Who's Who in America,* 1928–29; *Who's Who in Art,* 1912; *Art News,* Apr. 12, 1930; *Public Ledger* (Phila.), Mar. 19, 1930; personal information.]

H. S. M.

FERRIS, WOODBRIDGE NATHAN (Jan. 6, 1853–Mar. 23, 1928), educator, governor, United States senator, son of John Ferris, Jr., and Estelle (Reed) Ferris, was born near Spencer, Tioga County, N. Y. He was educated at the Spencer Union Academy, the Candor Union Academy, the Oswego Academy, and the Oswego Normal and Training School. In 1873 he entered the University of Michigan as a medical student but left after six months of study to become principal of the Free Academy at Spencer, N. Y. In 1875 he organized the Freeport Business College and Academy at Freeport, Ill. The next year he became a member of the faculty of Rock River University at Dixon, Ill. From 1877 to 1879 he was principal of the Dixon Business College and Academy, which he founded, and from 1879 to 1884, superintendent of schools of Pittsfield, Ill. In 1884 he founded the Ferris Institute at Big Rapids, Mich. From a small beginning this institution developed under Ferris's presidency until it had a total yearly enrolment of more than two thousand students. About twenty thousand students were graduated prior to the founder's death.

Ferris's political career began in 1892 when the Democrats of the 11th Michigan District nominated him for representative in Congress. He was defeated, as he was in his race for governor in 1904. He was elected governor in 1912 and was reëlected in 1914. A fourth nomination for governor in 1920 resulted in defeat. Although the Republicans controled both branches of the legislature during his administrations, Ferris got along harmoniously with them. He showed his political courage during the strike in the Upper Peninsula copper mines in 1913 when he mobilized the entire National Guard for the protection of life and property. The affectionate popular appellation of "Good Gray Governor" attests to his success. In the campaign of 1922, he was nominated for the United States Senate and was elected, the first Democratic senator from Michigan since Charles E. Stuart in 1863. In 1924 he was the choice of the Michigan Democrats for the nomination for president and received the vote of the state delegation on the first ballot. An ardent Prohibitionist, he publicly opposed the presidential nomination of Gov. Alfred E. Smith of New York in 1928 (*New York Times,* Mar. 8, 1928). He died in Washington, D. C., after a short illness. He was married in 1874 to Helen F. Gillespie of Fulton, N. Y., and three sons were born to them. After the death of his wife in 1917 he wrote a memoir of her, "Mrs. Nellie G. Ferris," published in the *Michigan History Magazine* (January 1919). In 1921 he was married a second time, to May Ethel McLoud of Indianapolis, Md.

[*Biog. Dir. Am. Cong.* (1928); *Who's Who in America,* 1926–27; *Mich. Biogs.* (1924), I, 288–89; *Mich. Manual* (1913), p. 728; articles on Ferris by J. G. Hayden and John Fitzgibbon in the *Detroit News,* Mar. 23, 1928; memorial addresses in the Senate, May 6, 1928, published separately, *Sen. Doc. No. 100,* 70 Cong., 1 Sess. (1929) and in *Cong. Record,* 70 Cong., 1 Sess., pp. 8241–48, which also includes a completed but undelivered address by Ferris on education; a memorial folder, especially valuable for photographs, issued by the Ferris Inst. (n. d.); *The Crimson and Gold,* 1928, pub. by the students of the Ferris Inst.] E. S. B—n.

FERRY, ELISHA PEYRE (Aug. 9, 1825–Oct. 14, 1895), lawyer, governor of Washington, was the son of Pierre Peyre Ferry, one of Napoleon's colonels of cavalry, who emigrated from France in 1814, settled first near Sandusky, Ohio, and then removed to a village which later became Monroe, in the southeastern corner of Michigan. The veteran's love for the name Peyre was transmitted to his sons and by them, in turn, to all their own children. After finishing in the public schools of his birthplace, Monroe, Mich., Elisha began the study of law, and in 1845 was admitted to the bar. The next year (1846) he moved to Waukegan and began his life-work. In addition to establishing the foundations of an unusual public career in that Illinois town, he began also a beautiful family life, on Feb. 4, 1849, by becoming the husband of Sarah B. Kellogg, daughter of Dr. David Kellogg of Waukegan. Ferry was a successful lawyer from the beginning of his practise and public office came to him early. He became Waukegan's first mayor, was elected a presidential elector in the campaigns of 1852 and 1856, was a member of the Illinois constitutional convention in 1862, and for two years thereafter served as a bank commissioner of Illinois. During the Civil War he also served as assistant adjutant-general, with the rank of colonel, on the staff of Gov. Yates. In this capacity he aided in forwarding many Illinois regiments to the field and in the course of that duty made a friend of Gen. Grant, who, on becoming president in 1869, appointed him surveyor-general of Washington Territory and promoted him to the governorship in 1872. Soon after he assumed that office it was announced that Emperor William I of Germany, as arbitrator, had decided the San Juan case in favor of the United States, and Gov. Ferry promptly transferred the large archipelago to Whatcom County for temporary government. He was reappointed in 1876. At the end of his second term in 1880 he moved to Seattle and resumed his work as a lawyer and a banker with the firm of McNaught, Ferry, McNaught & Mitchell and with the Puget Sound National Bank. When Washington was admitted to statehood, he was elected its first governor. He administered satisfactorily the problems growing out of the transition from territorial to state government. On Feb. 12, 1899, in the fourth year after his death, the legislature named Ferry County in his honor.

[Brief biographies may be found in C. B. Bagley, *Hist. of Seattle* (1916), III, 534–35; H. H. Bancroft, "Washington, Idaho and Montana," *Hist. of the Pacific States,* vol. XXVI, 1890, pp. 279, 282, 314; Georgiana M. Blankenship, *Early Hist. of Thurston County, Wash.* (1914), pp. 65–66; Elwood Evans and others, *Hist. of the Pacific Northwest—Ore. and Wash.* (1889), II, 324; H. K. Hines, *An Illus. Hist. of the State of Wash.* (1893), pp. 644–45; E. S. Meany, *Govs. of Wash.* (1915), pp. 47–49; C. A. Snowden, *Hist. of Wash.: the Rise and Progress of an Am. State* (1909), vol. IV, *passim*; *Seattle Post Intelligencer,* Oct. 14 and 15, 1895.] E. S. M.

FERRY, ORRIS SANFORD (Aug. 15, 1823–Nov. 21, 1875), representative, and senator, was born in Bethel, Conn., the son of Starr and Esther (Blackman) Ferry. A career in the business of his father, a substantial hat-manufacturer, had been contemplated for him, but after he had served a brief apprenticeship, it became apparent that his tastes lay elsewhere. With his father's permission, he withdrew from the business to prepare for college. A graduate of Yale College in the class of 1844, he achieved especial distinction in literary and forensic activities. In the pages of the *Yale Literary Magazine,* which he served as an editor, Ferry was represented by such varied contributions as book reviews, essays on political trends, and a novel of life in colonial New England.

His natural inclinations drew him to the law. His professional training was obtained in the offices of Thomas W. Osborne of Fairfield and of Thomas B. Butler of Norwalk. In 1846 he was admitted to the bar and took up his practise in Norwalk. In the following year he was married to Charlotte Bissell, daughter of Gov. Clarke Bissell. He served his local community as judge of probate (1849–56) and as state's attorney for Fairfield County (1857–59). Meanwhile, he had entered upon his political career. In 1855 and 1856 he was a member of the Connecticut Senate. Although at the time a relatively young man, he was made chairman of the committee on the judiciary. In 1858, after having failed of election to Congress two years previously, he was sent to the House of Representatives, where he served on the committee on Revolutionary claims and on the famous Committee of Thirty-three on "the disturbed condition of the country." In 1860 he lost his seat to a Democrat. Upon the declaration of war, he was made colonel of the 5th Connecticut Volunteers. During the Shenandoah campaign in the spring of 1862 he was promoted brigadier-general. Later he saw service with the Army of the Potomac, in North and South Carolina, and finally with the X Army Corps on the James River. He resigned his commission on June 15, 1865.

His election to the Senate in 1866 was probably the result of a deadlock between the two leading candidates for the nomination, although his enemies were ready to ascribe the victory to chicanery. Hitherto he had been regarded as a radical on Reconstruction, so much so indeed that one hostile paper remarked editorially, "Ferry is as radical a man as can be found in Connecticut" (*New Haven Register,* May 11, 1866). Once in the Senate, however, he pursued a fairly moderate course. Despite the profound abhorrence with which, as a New Englander, he regarded the slave-holding oligarchy, he favored a general policy of conciliation; yet he voted for the conviction of President Johnson and was one of those who filed opinions on the case. When he sought reëlection in 1872, his future was precarious. Both by his manner of obtaining election and by his conduct in the Senate he had alienated the regular Republicans. Fortunately for him, a coalition of Democrats and Liberal Republicans came to his aid. His reëlection was hailed by the Liberal Republicans as a presage of success, but he made haste to dissociate himself from Greeley's candidacy, referring to it as "mere mid-summer madness" (*New York Tribune,* May 25, 1872). During his last term in the Senate he was handicapped by a progressive spinal disease. He died on Nov. 21, 1875, still in the prime of life. Save for a period of youthful skepticism he had been a devout Christian throughout his life. A leading member of the First Congregational Church of Norwalk, once he prepared and delivered a series of lectures on the validity of the Christian revelation.

[The various histories of the Class of 1844, Yale College, contain useful biographical data, as do the *Memorial Addresses on . . . Orris S. Ferry* (1876) published by order of Congress. In the *Diary of Gideon Welles* (1911), II, 505–06, 509, III, 523, and *The Speeches, Correspondence and Political Papers of Carl Schurz* (1913), II, 374, 377, III, 1, V, 35, will be found brief but suggestive comments. See also *Obit. Record Grads. Yale Coll.,* 1876; J. A. Hamilton in *Congreg. Quart.,* Apr. 1877; *Biog. Encyc. of R. I. and Conn.* (1881); W. F. Moore, *Representative Men of Conn.* (1894); *Hartford Courant,* Nov. 22, 1875; the *Congregationalist,* Dec. 9, 1875; files of *New Haven Register* and *Hartford Courant,* especially for the campaigns of 1866 and 1872.]

D. E. O.

FERRY, THOMAS WHITE (June 1, 1827–Oct. 14, 1896), senator from Michigan, was born on Mackinac Island, the son of William Montague Ferry and Amanda White. His father had been brought up on a farm in New England, but later in life had studied in Union College, and in 1822 was ordained in New York to the Presbyterian ministry. In the same year he established a mission on Mackinac Island; the next year he opened a school for Indian children. Thanks largely to the assistance of his wife, his labors began to bear fruit (Williams, *post*). Mrs. Ferry was the eldest daughter of Thomas White, of Ashfield, Mass. She had been well educated and was deeply religious. Her second child, Thomas White, was born in the Mission House, which since 1845 has served as a summer hotel (Wood, *post,* I, 414). In 1834 the Ferry family removed from the island to a tract of wild land near the mouth of the Grand River, where the father founded the town of Grand Haven, and built up a flourishing lumber business (obituary in the *Grand Haven Union,* Feb. 6, 1868). Thomas, after having graduated from the village school, was variously employed until he became a clerk in Elgin, Ill. Two years later he returned and became his father's partner in the lumber business. At the age of twenty-one he was elected member of the board of supervisors of Grand Haven, and in 1850 he entered the state legislature, serving until 1852. From 1857 to 1858 he was a state senator, in 1860 he was a delegate to the Republican National Convention at Chicago, from 1865 to 1867 and from 1869 to 1871, a member of Congress. In the campaign of 1871 he succeeded in obtaining a seat in the Senate at Washington.

He was an expert in finance, and after the financial crisis of 1873, was the first to submit a plan for the remedy of existing evils. On Dec. 2 and 4, 1873, he presented propositions to remove the monopoly feature of the national banking system, to stop the contraction of too much paper currency, and to issue a low-interest convertible bond. His speeches on finance were characterized by concise statements, sound logic, and a lack of oratorical display. On Dec. 21, 1874, he introduced a resolution for revising and reclassifying the rules of the Senate, and two years later his revision was adopted unanimously and without amendment.

On Mar. 9, 1875, he was elected president *pro tempore* of the Senate, and in this capacity he acted at different times thereafter. During the famous Hayes-Tilden electoral count of 1877 he presided over the sixteen joint meetings of Congress which resulted in a decision in favor of Hayes. It was a time of intense excitement, and apparently only the vigor and ability of Ferry, who had no precedent to guide him, prevented a national disaster. His integrity and industry were such that under Hayes he was reëlected president *pro tempore* of the Senate without nomination of an opposing candidate. In 1883 he was defeated for a third term as senator by Thomas W. Palmer of Detroit. The rest of his life was shadowed by this disappointment and by the failure of the lumber business which he and his brother, E. P. Ferry, had organized. He died in Grand Haven, from cerebral apoplexy during the night of Oct. 13–14, 1896. He was never married.

[Sources include an article by Ferry's elder brother, W. M. Ferry, "Ottawa's Old Settlers," in *Mich. Pion. and Hist. Colls.*, XXX (1906), 572–82; M. C. Williams, "The Old Mission Church of Mackinac Island," *Ibid.*, XXVIII (1900), 187–96; L. M. Miller, "Reminiscences of the Mich. Legislature of 1871," *Ibid.*, XXXII (1903), 431–41; E. O. Wood, *Historic Mackinac* (1918); *Biog. Dir. Am. Cong.* (1928); obituaries in *Grand Haven Daily News*, Oct. 14, 1896, *Washington Post* and *Detroit Free Press*, Oct. 15, 1896. In the Pub. Lib. at Grand Haven there is a large scrap-book, containing excerpts from newspapers relative to the early history of Grand Haven and the family of Ferry.] A. H.

FERSEN, HANS AXEL, Count Von (Sept. 4, 1755–June 20, 1810), Swedish soldier, statesman, was born at Stockholm of a family distinguished by long public service. He was the son of Field-Marshal Fredrik Axel and Countess Hedvig Catharina von Fersen, born Countess De la Gardie. At the age of fifteen he was sent abroad to study and spent four years in military schools at Brunswick, Turin, and Strasbourg. After five months in Paris, he then returned to Sweden. He was twenty-three when he again visited Paris. Rich, well-favored, and ambitious, "le beau Fersen," as he was called, soon became a favorite of Queen Marie Antoinette—so much a favorite that he was regarded with some jealousy by other courtiers. Like most young French liberals of the day he was inspired by a passion for liberty and sought a commission in the French expeditionary force which was to go to the aid of the American colonies in their struggle for independence. Through the influence of the Queen, and of Vergennes and Breteuil, old friends of his father, he was made colonel of a French regiment and appointed aide-de-camp to the Count of Rochambeau. In this capacity he rendered distinguished service in America.

Fersen embarked with the expeditionary force at Brest in May 1780 and arrived at Newport, R. I., in the following August. In October, already high in the confidence of his chief, he was sent to meet Gen. Washington at Hartford, whither the Count of Rochambeau was to repair for their first consultation. Thereafter he was a frequent bearer of dispatches between the two commanders. He served gallantly at Yorktown; and after the surrender of Cornwallis, he was sent secretly to hasten the embarkation of the French siege artillery, in order to elude two English frigates which might have barred their way to Baltimore. This mission he successfully accomplished. He returned to France with the French troops in 1783. His letters to his father, frequently printed in French and in English translation, contain shrewd observations on American characteristics, interesting comments on episodes of the Revolution, notably Arnold's treason, and illuminating accounts of the military operations which culminated in the victory at Yorktown.

His later life has no points of contact with America. In Europe, however, he had a distinguished career. He is best remembered for his daring attempt to rescue the royal French family in 1791. It was he who arranged the ill-fated flight to Varennes, himself driving their coach through the streets of Paris. He rendered notable service to his own sovereign King Gustavus III, as statesman and diplomat, suffered a temporary eclipse under the regency, but was made *Riksmarskalk* (imperial marshal) in 1801. He met an undeserved death in 1810 at the hands of a mob, who believed him and his sister implicated in the alleged poisoning of the newly elected King, Prince Christian Augustus.

[R. M. De Klinckowström, *Le Comte de Fersen et La Cour de France* (2 vols., 1877–78); F. F. Flach, *Grefve Hans Axel von Fersen* (1896); L. L. T. Gosselin, *Le Drame de Varennes juin 1791* (1908); O. G. von Heidenstam, *Marie-Antoinette, Fersen et Barnave; leur Correspondance* (1913). F. V. Wrangel, *Lettres d'Axel de Fersen à son Père pendant la Guerre de l'Indépendance d'Amérique* (1929), is the most complete collection of Fersen's American letters. Some of these are translated in Katharine P. Wormeley's *Diary and Correspondence of Count Axel Fersen* (1902). They have also been twice printed in translation in *Mag. of Am. Hist.*, May, June, July 1879 and Jan., Feb. 1891.]

FESSENDEN, FRANCIS (Mar. 18, 1839–Jan. 2, 1906), lawyer, soldier, was the third son of William Pitt and Ellen (Deering) Fessenden of Portland, Me. He attended Portland Academy and Westbrook Seminary, graduated from Bowdoin College in 1858, and studied law at Harvard and in his grandfather's office. He went to New York in 1860 to complete his studies and was traveling in Minnesota when the Civil War began. He at once offered his services and was commissioned captain in the regular army by Secretary Cameron. He was assigned to the 19th Infantry and spent the first part of the war in recruiting, guarding prisoners, and similar routine duties. In March 1862 he was ordered to rejoin his regiment then under General Buell's command in Tennessee. He arrived in time to take part in the battle of Shiloh and was badly wounded in the arm. While recovering he was placed in non-combatant service but in September 1862 was appointed colonel of the 25th Maine Infantry and assigned to the defense of Washington. From March until July 1863, he was stationed at Centerville, Va., where his younger brother, Samuel, had fallen the year before.

When the 25th Maine was mustered out he was placed in command of the 30th Maine Infantry, a carefully selected unit composed almost entirely of veteran soldiers. In January 1864 the regiment was ordered to the Gulf and took part in the exhausting and bloody Red River campaign. On Apr. 23, Colonel Fessenden led a brilliant and successful assault on Monett's Bluff which was reported to have saved the retreating army from disaster. He was wounded a second time and lost his right leg by amputation a few days later. He was immediately recommended for the rank of brigadier-general by Secretary Stanton and the nomination was promptly confirmed by the Senate. In September 1864 he returned to duty in Washington and in the following spring was again assigned to active service. He was engaged in various administrative duties, now that the fighting was over, in Maryland, West Virginia, and the Shenandoah Valley, and also served as a member of the commission which tried and condemned Captain Wirz, former commandant of Andersonville Prison. In November 1865 he was made major-general of volunteers. He was also brevetted major-general in the regular army for gallant and meritorious services during the war, and on the reorganization of that army in 1866 was appointed lieutenant-colonel of the 45th Infantry. He declined the appointment and asked to be brought before a retiring board by which he was placed on the retired list with the rank of brigadier-general.

After the war Fessenden returned to Portland and resumed the practise of law with his brother. He was not especially interested in a political career, serving only for a year as alderman and a single term as mayor (1876), declining renomination in both cases. He was an Overseer of Bowdoin College for many years. He performed a noteworthy service by collecting many of his father's letters and miscellaneous papers, and his *Life and Public Services of William Pitt Fessenden*, published posthumously in 1907, is a creditable biography. He was married, on Aug. 26, 1863, to Ellen W. Fox.

[Francis Fessenden, *Life and Pub. Services of Wm. Pitt Fessenden* (2 vols., 1907); W. E. S. Whitman and Charles H. True, *Maine in the War for the Union* (1865); *Portland Soldiers and Sailors*, compiled by members of the Bosworth Post, G. A. R. (1884); *Boston Transcript*, Jan. 2, 1906; *Biog. Encyc. of Me. of the Nineteenth Century* (1885), pp. 224–29; *Obit. Record of the Grads. of Bowdoin Coll. . . . for the decade ending 1 June 1909* (1911).]

W. A. R.

FESSENDEN, JAMES DEERING (Sept. 28, 1833–Nov. 18, 1882), lawyer, soldier, was the eldest son of William Pitt and Ellen (Deering) Fessenden. He graduated from Bowdoin College in 1852, studied law, was admitted to the bar in 1856 and became a member of his father's law firm. On Nov. 5 of the same year he married Frances C. Greeley. He was active in the large practise carried on by his father's firm and showed great professional promise, but on the outbreak of the Civil War promptly entered military service, receiving a captain's commission. He recruited a company of sharpshooters and spent the first winter of the war in a Virginia camp, engaged in various administrative and training duties. In March 1862 he was transferred to the staff of Gen. Hunter and performed important services in South Carolina. He is reported to have organized and disciplined the first regiment of colored soldiers in the national service although Gen. Hunter's action was afterward disallowed and the regiment disbanded for the time being. He was promoted to the rank of colonel later in the year and took part in operations against Charleston in the spring of 1863. Severely injured by a fall from his horse, he was transferred to mustering and disbursing service during the summer months of 1863, but in September was ordered on active service with Gen.

Hooker who was then transferring two corps to the west for operations on the line between Nashville and Chattanooga. He took part in the heavy fighting at Lookout Mountain and Missionary Ridge, and was officially complimented by Gen. Hooker.

Fessenden was prominent in Sherman's campaign against Atlanta in 1864, and was recommended for the rank of brigadier-general for services at Resaca, Ga., on May 15. He also distinguished himself in the battles of New Hope Church, Kenesaw Mountain and Peach Tree Creek, and was again recommended for promotion by Gen. Hooker. On Aug. 8 he was appointed brigadier-general in recognition of his services in the Atlanta campaign. He was then transferred to Virginia and received a command under Gen. Sheridan. He took part in the battle of Cedar Creek and spent the last winter of the war performing administrative duties at Winchester, Va. After leading a brigade in the Grand Review at Washington, May 23, 1865, he was ordered on special service in Georgia and South Carolina. In recognition of distinguished services he was brevetted major-general of volunteers and mustered out Jan. 15, 1866. He then resumed the practise of law in Portland and in 1868 became register of bankruptcy under the act of Congress, and served in that capacity until the repeal of the law in 1878. He also served three terms in the legislature, 1872–74. He is described as a man of quiet and unassuming manner, efficient and reliable as a soldier and equally so in civil life. His father's letters show that he occupied a special place in the confidence and affection of the distinguished statesman.

[Francis Fessenden, *Life and Pub. Services of Wm. Pitt Fessenden* (2 vols., 1907); W. E. S. Whitman and Charles H. True, *Maine in the War for the Union* (1865); *Biog. Encyc. of Me. in the Nineteenth Century* (1885), pp. 302–07; *Portland Transcript*, Nov. 25, 1882; *Portland Soldiers and Sailors*, compiled by members of the Bosworth Post, G. A. R. (1884); F. B. Heitman, *Hist. Reg. and Dict. of the U. S. Army* (1903), vol. I.]
W. A. R.

FESSENDEN, SAMUEL (July 16, 1784–Mar. 19, 1869), lawyer, Abolitionist, was born at Fryeburg, Me., the son of William and Sarah (Clement) Fessenden. He attended Fryeburg Academy, graduated at Dartmouth in 1806, taught school for a short time, studied law, was admitted to the Maine bar in 1809, and began practise at New Gloucester, where he resided until he moved to Portland in 1822. On Dec. 16, 1813, he married Deborah Chandler who took into their household William Pitt Fessenden [*q.v.*], his illegitimate son. He secured a considerable practise from the start and is reported to have greatly increased his local prestige by thrashing the town bully in front of the court-house. He was well over six feet in height, strikingly handsome, an effective speaker, and usually referred to as "General." He actually held that rank in the militia. While at New Gloucester he was active in politics, as what Democrats loved to denounce—"a high-toned Federalist." From 1813 to 1815 he represented the town in the General Court at Boston, and in 1818–19 served in the Senate. While in the lower house in 1814 he made two notable speeches, one denouncing the national administration for the depressed conditions in Maine and the other, at a later session, supporting the call for the Hartford Convention. These have been frequently quoted by subsequent historians as illustrating the lengths to which prominent Federalists were willing to go in the direction of disunion. Following the separation of Maine from Massachusetts he represented Portland in the legislature, 1825–26.

While he had shown ability as a legislator and politician and for a time seemed destined for active political life, he failed to follow up his early success. This was due, apparently, to two reasons. On moving to Portland he formed a partnership with Thomas A. Deblois which lasted more than thirty years and became increasingly absorbed in professional work. Fessenden was especially interested in the law of real property and handled most of the business in that field while his partner handled commercial cases. Between them, they had probably the largest practise in the state prior to the Civil War, and the senior member was generally accepted as belonging to a select group of two or three outstanding leaders at the bar. Many successful lawyers received their training in this office. A second reason for his withdrawal from politics was his growing interest in the slavery question and dislike of the attitude maintained by both major parties. He became a member of the Anti-Slavery Society, held office, took an active part in its propaganda, and incurred the odium attached to membership in such a radical organization. He was a candidate for Congress and also for the governorship on Liberty party tickets, apparently for the purpose of demonstrating the growing strength of anti-slavery sentiment. He was not, however, as extreme in his doctrines as some of his associates, and believed in the necessity of preserving the union of the states.

In 1861 he retired from active practise and spent his last years in the home of one of his sons. He was blind for some years before his death. His personal qualities were such as to gain him the affection and respect of associates and the public at large. He was equally considerate and generous to younger members of the bar, poor clients, and negro refugees.

[Wm. Willis, *A Hist. of the Law, the Courts, and the Lawyers of Me.* (1863); C. E. Hamlin, *The Life and Times of Hannibal Hamlin* (1899); *New-Eng. Hist. and Geneal. Reg.*, Apr. 1871. See also Francis Fessenden, *Life and Public Services of William Pitt Fessenden* (2 vols., 1907), which contains much valuable material on various members of the family and gives a special sketch of Samuel Fessenden: I, 34–39.] W. A. R.

FESSENDEN, THOMAS GREEN (Apr. 22, 1771–Nov. 11, 1837), poet, journalist, inventor, was the most important American satirist in verse between Trumbull and Lowell. He was born in Walpole, N. H., the eldest son of the Rev. Thomas Fessenden, the liberal pastor of the Walpole church for forty-seven years, himself an author, and his wife Elizabeth, daughter of the Rev. Samuel Kendall of New Salem, Mass. Thomas Green Fessenden was prepared for Dartmouth probably by his Tory grandfather at New Salem, and assisted himself through college by teaching and conducting singing schools. He was graduated valedictorian in 1796, with some literary reputation for pieces of verse, mainly humorous, contributed over the pen-name "Simon Spunkey" to the *Dartmouth Centinel* and to the better known *Farmer's Weekly Museum* at Walpole, then edited by the essayist Joseph Dennie [*q.v.*], with whom he had begun a lasting friendship. His two most popular poems were "The Country Lovers," or "Jonathan's Courtship," first published as a broadside, probably in 1795, and as a pamphlet in 1796, and "The Rutland Ode." The former was the prototype and perhaps the model for Lowell's "The Courtin'." The latter was a Federalist campaign song, first sung, to music set by the author, at the Fourth of July celebration in 1798 at Rutland, Vt., where Fessenden was studying law.

In May 1801 Fessenden abandoned his law practise at Rutland and sailed for England as agent for a local company to secure English patent rights for a recently invented hydraulic device, which upon further testing proved fraudulent. He spent the next two years and his remaining funds in London in attempts to perfect this device and a new type of grain-mill. In February 1803 he rallied to the defense of another Yankee, Elisha Perkins [*q.v.*], whose "metallic tractors," after enjoying an enormous sale, were being attacked by the reputable medical profession. Fessenden, under the alias "Christopher Caustic, M.D., LL.D., A.S.S.," threw together a vigorous Hudibrastic satire, *Terrible Tractoration*, a pretended assault on the tractors, but actually ridiculing the most prominent of the skeptical physicians of England and Scotland. Despite its small merit, the book was surprisingly popular, and well received in the reviews, and was several times reprinted. This was followed by his *Original Poems* (London 1804, Philadelphia 1806), chiefly selections from the Dartmouth and Rutland periods, with some added anti-Jacobin satires and literary parodies.

In July 1804 he returned, hailed as "the American Butler," to Boston, where he wrote and published in 1805, *Democracy Unveiled: or Tyranny Stripped of the Garb of Patriotism*, the most celebrated and virulent assault on Jefferson and the minor Democratic leaders, coarse and libellous to a degree not tolerable to-day. It is a long poem in six loosely constructed cantos, in Hudibrastic couplets grouped in quatrains, with copious footnotes outweighing the pages of text. Second and third editions, greatly enlarged, appeared later in 1805 at Boston, and in 1806 at New York. From Aug. 30, 1806, to Aug. 22, 1807, "Dr. Caustic" edited the *Weekly Inspector*, a Federalist partisan magazine, at New York, where he ran afoul of the youthful Salmagundi group, who ridiculed him as "Dr. Christopher Costive." In 1808 or 1809, after a sojourn with Dennie in Philadelphia, he retired to Brattleboro, Vt., and entered upon a less eventful but more useful period, practising law; editing the *Brattleboro Reporter*, 1815–16, and the *Bellows Falls Advertiser*, 1817–22; and compiling such legal and instructive works as the *Essay on the Law of Patents* (1810), *American Clerk's Companion* (1815), *Miniature Bible* (1816), and *The Ladies' Monitor* (1818). He married, at forty-two, in September 1813, Miss Lydia Tuttle, of Littleton, Mass.

In July 1822 Fessenden removed to Boston to establish the *New England Farmer*, editing it until his death, with the assistance of men like Timothy Pickering, John Lowell, and Daniel Webster as contributors. Simultaneously, he carried on three other periodicals devoted to agricultural interests, encouraged the introduction of silk culture in Massachusetts, and got out third and fourth editions of *Terrible Tractoration* in 1836 and 1837. In 1827 and 1830 he secured patents for two heating devices, the chief being a portable steam and hot-water stove, virtually a single hot-water radiator attached to an upright stove. In 1835 and again in 1836, he was elected by a large majority to the Massachusetts General Court as Whig representative from Boston and was a candidate for reëlection at the time of his death. For about the last two years of Fessenden's life Nathaniel Hawthorne, then editor of the *American Magazine of Useful and Entertaining Knowledge*, at Boston, was a lodger with the

Fessendens, and subsequently he wrote a eulogy which until recently was the best source of information concerning Fessenden (*Works*, 1883, XII, 246–63). It has been said that Fessenden's niece, Catherine Ainsworth, whom Hawthorne met at this time, was the original of Phebe Pyncheon in *The House of the Seven Gables.*

[Porter G. Perrin's *Life and Works of Thomas Green Fessenden* (1925); G. T. Chapman, *Sketches of the Alumni of Dartmouth Coll.* (1867); *Boston Advertiser*, Nov. 13, 1837.] M. E.

FESSENDEN, WILLIAM PITT (Oct. 16, 1806–Sept. 8, 1869), lawyer, politician, financier, was the son of Samuel Fessenden and Ruth Greene, and a descendant of Nicholas Fessenden who came to America in the seventeenth century and settled at Cambridge, Mass. He was born out of wedlock at Boscawen, N. H., and spent his early years in the home of his grandparents at Fryeburg, Me., but when his father married in 1813 he became a member of the new household. He appears to have been a precocious boy and his entrance to college was delayed for some time on account of his extreme youth. He graduated from Bowdoin College, nevertheless, in 1823, although his diploma was withheld for a year on the ground that he had been "repeatedly guilty of profane swearing" and had "indicated a disorganizing spirit" and that "his general character and the bad influence of his example" called for punishment. Fessenden himself denied that he had been guilty of some of the alleged offenses. He was destined to receive the honorary degree of doctor of laws from Bowdoin in 1858 and to be a member of the governing boards of the college for the last twenty-six years of his life.

After graduation he studied law, with some interruptions, and was admitted to the bar in 1827. After two years at Bridgton he moved to Portland and except for a year in Bangor, maintained a residence there for the rest of his life. After his return from Bridgton he made his first appearance in public office when in 1831 he was elected to the legislature on the anti-Jackson ticket. He was engaged to Ellen, sister of Henry Wadsworth Longfellow, and her death before their marriage was a great blow to him. On Apr. 23, 1832, he married Ellen Maria Deering, daughter of James Deering, a prominent Portland merchant. In 1835 he formed a partnership with William Willis which lasted until his election to the United States Senate almost twenty years later. He had by 1835 established a reputation as one of the able lawyers of the state. In a few years he was considered by many the equal of his father, then the leader of the Maine bar, against whom he frequently appeared in important litigation. He was active in the Whig party and in 1837 by special invitation accompanied Daniel Webster on a tour of several months in the western states. He was for many years on cordial terms with the great Whig leader, who had been his godfather in 1806, and with his family, but his letters show that he had some definite reservations as to Webster's political conduct and the chapter closed with Fessenden in opposition to his nomination for the presidency at the Whig convention of 1852.

In 1839 he was elected to another term in the Maine legislature, being a member of the judiciary committee and assisting in a revision of the statutes. The following year he was elected to Congress, where he remained a single term. His two years in the lower house were, naturally enough, without special distinction but some of his remarks in debate seem to have drawn favorable attention. His letters show that this first experience in Washington gave him certain unfavorable impressions of public life and participants in it, which he retained to the end. Unlike his abolitionist father, he was in the beginning conservative on the slavery issue, but a view of the situation at Washington aroused his contempt for "the mean subserviency of these northern hirelings" (Fessenden, *post,* I, 23), and in another letter he expressed admiration of John Quincy Adams for "his indomitable spirit and the uprighteousness of his soul." From that time on his hostility to the institution grew steadily and the following decade saw him among the active organizers of the new Republican party.

For twelve years following his retirement from Congress he held no important public office although he served two terms in the legislature in 1845–46 and 1853–54, was active in Whig party councils, and was several times an unsuccessful candidate for the national Senate and House. The growth of anti-slavery sentiment in Maine was decidedly to his advantage and on Jan. 4, 1854, an anti-slavery combination in the legislature elected him to the United States Senate. He was sworn in on Feb. 23, and on Mar. 3 delivered the first great speech of his senatorial career, in opposition to the Kansas-Nebraska bill (*Congressional Globe,* 33 Cong., 1 Sess., App., pp. 319–24). For the next fifteen years he was one of the dominant figures in national affairs.

In 1857 he was assigned to the finance committee which, under existing rules, then handled both revenue and appropriation bills in the upper house. He had approximately ten years' service in the committee, more than half of this period as chairman, and, due to the responsibilities entailed by the Civil War, earned a permanent place among American public financiers. In 1857, when his most important work began, he suffered a severe loss in the death of his wife and his own health became permanently impaired. He is reported to have been one of the numerous victims of the mysterious epidemic said to have originated in the National Hotel. Thereafter he was inclined to be morose and unsociable in his habits and given to displays of irritability which would have been ruinous to any one but a man of commanding ability and high character. With a few friends, however, he was always on the best of terms and his letters to members of his family are hard to reconcile with his reputation for harshness and austerity. His constant references to his garden in Portland, or to fly-fishing on Maine trout streams, disclose a very different personality from the one appearing in speeches on the Morrill tariff, Reconstruction, and the Fourteenth Amendment.

As a leader of the opposition to the Buchanan administration he advanced steadily in prestige and he was now regarded as one of the greatest debaters who had yet appeared in Congress. Contemporaries sometimes found it hard to realize that a man of his slight physique, poor health, and unobtrusive manners was nevertheless one of the greatest intellectual forces in the government. In 1859 he was elected for a six-year term and was thus assured of a full share in the opportunities and responsibilities of the Civil War. "Let them stand firm like men and not tremble and shake before rebellion," he wrote when the final break impended, and his own conduct justified such advice.

When the Thirty-seventh Congress met in July 1861, he became chairman of the finance committee and carried a tremendous burden of work and responsibility in putting the finances of the country on a war footing. He did a great deal of the preliminary work in preparing bills and was in charge of their passage on the floor of the Senate. His reputation as a debater is seen to be well deserved by an examination of the debates on the great revenue and appropriation measures of the war period. His quick temper is equally apparent and even with the lapse of years the rasp of some of his comments can still be felt. He consistently tried, apparently, to confine expenditures to the legitimate outlays necessitated by the war, to avoid dangerous and wasteful precedents, to follow strictly the regular rules of procedure, and, as far as possible in view of extraordinary needs, to be economical and businesslike. "It is time for us to begin to think a little more about the money" he declared on one occasion early in the war, "the event of this war depends upon whether we can support it or not" (*Congressional Globe,* 37 Cong., 2 Sess., p. 1038). Such a course inevitably meant opposition to a variety of personal and sectional projects and stirred the wrath of the proponents of a swarm of expensive, futile, but popular measures growing out of wartime conditions.

In general Fessenden supported Secretary Chase's financial program and did much to secure its adoption by Congress. In the very important matter of the legal-tender notes, resorted to in 1862, he expressed disapproval and voted for the unsuccessful Collamer amendment striking this feature from the bill. His speech on the evils of irredeemable paper and the dangers of inflation is a classic on the subject (*Ibid.,* pp. 762–67). He admitted, however, that the situation was without a parallel in the history of the United States and afterward stated that the legal tenders were probably the only resource available at the time. Later on, as secretary of the treasury, he stood firm against further inflation, and when the war was over assumed the offensive against greenback heresies. In one matter he had a clearer vision than most of his colleagues or Secretary Chase himself, namely, the need of a drastic taxing program, which was too long delayed by political cowardice and inertia. At the first war session he declared himself in favor of an income tax as best calculated to meet current needs (*Ibid.,* 37 Cong., 1 Sess., p. 255).

On June 29, 1864, Secretary Chase resigned and President Lincoln promptly selected Fessenden as his successor, sending the nomination to the Senate while Fessenden himself was seeking a White House appointment to recommend Hugh McCulloch. He accepted the post reluctantly and with a definite understanding that he would be relieved as soon as the situation permitted. Faced at the beginning with an almost empty treasury, unpaid bills, including the army's pay, maturing loans, inadequate revenue, and countless difficulties in detail, he was able during his brief tenure to meet emergencies and to turn the department over to his successor in relatively sound condition. He raised the interest rate on government bonds and through the sales organization of Jay Cooke marketed another great loan, standing firmly against any further inflation of the currency. He had been reëlected to the Senate for a third term on Jan. 5, 1865, and his resignation as secretary took effect on Mar. 3.

With the prestige of the preceding years behind him Fessenden was certain to take an outstanding part in Reconstruction. As Lincoln had said of him he was "a Radical without the petulant and vicious fretfulness of many Radicals" (J. G. Nicolay and John Hay, *Abraham Lincoln,* 1890, IX, 100). His opposition to some features of the Confiscation Act, his refusal to be stampeded into an attempt to expel Senator Garrett Davis who had written some foolish resolutions which were alleged to be treasonable, and similar incidents, had tended to differentiate his position from that of Sumner, Wade, and other leaders. As a matter of fact, however, in his views as to policy toward the Southern states, he was, as Carl Schurz says, "in point of principle not far apart from Mr. Stevens" (*The Reminiscences of Carl Schurz,* III, 1908, p. 219). On Dec. 21, 1865, he became chairman of the famous joint committee on Reconstruction and its report, largely his personal work, is one of the great state papers in American history. His views of Reconstruction might well be summarized by his statement in reply to President Johnson's attack on the committee. He said the South had been subdued under the laws of war and "there was nothing better established than the principle that the conquerors had the power to change the form of government, to punish, to exact security, and take entire charge of the conquered people" (Fessenden, *post,* II, 9–10). He was equally emphatic that Reconstruction was a function of Congress and not of the President.

Fessenden's feeling toward the latter was made perfectly clear. He had little respect for him as a man and thoroughly disapproved of his policies and official conduct. He believed, however, that the President had not been guilty of any impeachable offenses and that the attempt to apply the remedy of impeachment would permanently lower the standards of American politics and government. He declined to vote on the Tenure of Office Act, but said that he disapproved of it on principle and that it would be productive of great evil. By 1867 he was definitely aligned with the conservatives. When impeachment finally came his position as a majority leader was especially difficult. His own view, stated again and again, was that the impeachment trial was a judicial process, not the summary removal of an unpopular and ill-advised executive. To a relative he wrote, "If he was impeached for general cussedness, there would be no difficulty in the case. That, however, is not the question to be tried" (Fessenden, *post,* II, 184). To Neal Dow, who had written him that Maine expected him to vote for conviction, he replied in terms worthy of Edmund Burke: "I wish you, my dear sir, and all others my friends and constituents, to understand that . . . I, not they, have solemnly sworn to do impartial justice. . . . The opinions and wishes of my party friends ought not to have a feather's weight with me in coming to a conclusion" (*Ibid.,* II, 187–88). The official reasons for his vote of "not guilty" are found in the lengthy opinion which he filed in the official record (*Congressional Globe,* 40 Cong., 2 Sess., pp. 452–57).

Fessenden undoubtedly reached the high point of his career by this vote, but it brought a tremendous storm of partisan denunciation which he faced courageously and in confidence that his course would eventually be justified by events. Throughout his senatorial career he showed himself indifferent to public opposition or acclaim, and he had already taken the unpopular side on many less conspicuous issues. As the excitement of the trial passed away, the country began to appreciate his courage and wisdom and he lived long enough to realize that the tide was turning. Whether he could have secured a reëlection is problematical as his death occurred before the attitude of the majority in the Maine legislature was definitely settled. His ability and strength of character, had he survived and been returned to the Senate for another term, would have been of inestimable value in the following decade. As it was, even if he appears at times to have interpreted America in terms of ledgers, balance sheets, and Supreme Court decisions, and if he lacked the sympathetic understanding of the feelings and motives of the common man which characterized Lincoln, he has a secure place among the great leaders of the Civil War era when courage in governmental circles was not always as much in evidence as on the battlefield.

[*Life and Public Services of William Pitt Fessenden,* by his son Francis Fessenden (2 vols., 1907), is the best source of information. While defective in arrangement and methods of presentation it gives a fair and comprehensive survey of his activities and contains personal correspondence and other material not available in official records. Brief sketches also occur in the following: G. H. Preble, "William Pitt Fessenden," *New-Eng. Hist. and Geneal. Reg.,* Apr. 1871; A. F. Moulton, *Memorials of Maine* (1916); L. C. Hatch, *Maine: A History,* vol. II (1919), and *Hist. of Bowdoin Coll.* (1927).]

W. A. R.

FETTERMAN, WILLIAM JUDD (1833?–Dec. 21, 1866), soldier, was the son of Lieut. George Fetterman, who entered the army from Pennsylvania, served at Fort Trumbull, Conn., from 1829 to 1833, and while stationed there married Anna Marie C. Judd, daughter of Bethel Judd of New London, on Apr. 18, 1831. His mother died in his infancy, and no record of his youth appears to be available. He entered the army, from Delaware, at the outbreak of the Civil War in 1861 and was twice brevetted for gallant and meritorious service, at the battle of Murfreesboro and again at the battle of Jonesboro. After the war he continued in the regular army, was transferred on Sept. 21, 1866, to the 27th Infantry with the rank of captain, and sent out to Fort Phil Kearny, Wyo., to report to Col. Henry B. Carrington, in command at that post. He arrived at his station in November. He was of genial and dashing personality and at once became popular socially and with the subordinate officers and men. He was not familiar with frontier conditions or with Indian warfare and held rather a contemptuous view of the conservatism of his superiors and their manifest belief in the difficulty of the situation. On one occasion he declared that he could ride safely through the Indian country with eighty men (Hebard and Brininstool, *post,* I, 305). Consequently, when upon the morning of Dec. 21, 1866, an Indian alarm was signaled from the outlook, on Sullivan Hill, although Fetterman was the senior captain in the post, Col. Carrington directed Capt. J. W. Powell to take command of a troop of eighty men and go out to relieve the wood train, then upon its last trip for the season, to the forest upon Piney Island seven miles distant. When this order was given to Capt. Powell, Fetterman at once stepped forward and asserted his seniority. Col. Carrington, recognizing his right, with misgivings conceded it, but with distinct orders, several times repeated, under no circumstances to pass beyond the crest of Lodge Trail Ridge. So it was that Fetterman rode away with precisely the number of men that he had boasted would be sufficient to carry him safely through the Indian country. In disobedience to his orders he allowed Red Cloud to entice him beyond Lodge Trail Ridge where an ambush was prepared for him. There, fighting most gallantly, he with his entire command was killed; not a single white man survived. The Fetterman massacre has gone into history as one of the great tragedies of the frontier, only surpassed by the fate of Custer ten years later.

[*Official Records* (*Army*), 1 ser., XX (pt. 1), p. 404, XXII (pt. 3), p. 553, XXVIII (pt. 1), *passim*; F. B. Heitman, *Hist. Reg. and Dict. U. S. Army* (2 vols., 1903); G. R. Hebard and E. A. Brininstool, *The Bozeman Trail* (2 vols., 1922); Margaret I. Carrington, *Ab-sa-ra-ka, Land of Massacre* (1878); C. T. Brady, *Indian Fights and Fighters* (1904).]

D. R.

FEW, IGNATIUS ALPHONSO (Apr. 11, 1789–Nov. 28, 1845), college founder and president, son of Ignatius and Mary (Chandler) Few, was born on a plantation near Augusta, Ga. His grandfather, William Few, a native of Maryland, moved to North Carolina in 1758, and to Georgia soon after 1771. He had three sons, the most notable of whom, William [*q.v.*], after representing Georgia in the Constitutional Convention and in the United States Senate, married in New York City and went there to live. Another of the three sons was Ignatius, a captain in the Revolutionary army, and afterward a successful planter and merchant. When Ignatius, Jr., was about fifteen he was despatched to New York to be educated under the supervision of his uncle William. He entered a school in Bergen, N. J., and later went to Princeton, where he remained for a considerable time without registering in the college. Here he studied privately, music, French, drawing, and fencing. He soon went back to New York where he studied for a while longer before returning to Georgia. In Augusta, he turned his attention to law, but about 1811 he married Selina Carr, and retired to an extensive farm not far distant. In 1815 he went to Savannah as colonel of a regiment intended to save the town from an expected attack by the British, but the enemy did not appear. During the years following he gave himself passionately to general reading, and even to the writing of poetry, in which "he evinced a talent which would have done him honor, had graver pursuits permitted its cultivation" (Sprague, *post*). By 1823 his business had pretty well disintegrated and he went to Augusta to practise law. In the autumn of 1824, it became plain that he had tuberculosis, and from then on, "frequent discharges of arterial blood from his pulmonary vessels, sometimes alarmingly rapid and profuse, continued to appear through the several subsequent years of his life" (Summers, p. 308). For a number of years he had grieved his friends by avowing himself a skeptic, but about this time he became open to religious conviction. In 1826 or 1827 he joined the Methodist Church, in 1828 he became a minister, and in the time before 1835, when he was retired, he preached in Savannah, Columbus, and Macon. As early as 1832 he was convinced that the Methodists of Georgia should conduct a college of their own, and began urging them to such an enterprise. There was little sympathy with his project, and he made a temporary compromise with himself by furthering, under Methodist control, a secondary school in which the students supported themselves by laboring on a farm. In 1837 the college he had advocated was chartered under the name Emory. He was made its president, and it was located near the farm-school already in operation. The first session began in 1838. The president's financial problems were from the first grave, but he would not be bound by anything so inexcusable as lack of funds. He had $100,000 in subscriptions signed by prominent Methodists, and that seemed to him justification for erecting the really necessary buildings and also for aiding the farm-school, which was itself by that time practically defunct. Many of the subscriptions remained unpaid, and things went from bad to worse till the summer of 1839. Then he resigned, his "continued and increasing disease," he said, "having rendered that course indispensable" (*Longstreet, post*). He was a member of the first conference of the Methodist Church, South, which met in Louisville in 1845, and he is reported to have drawn up the official report on the division of the Methodist Church. His health was intermittently wretched till his complete breakdown in March 1845. "He died in Athens, Ga., in perfect tranquillity, sitting in a large arm-chair" (Sprague, *post*).

[T. O. Summers, *Biog. Sketches of Eminent Itinerant Ministers* (1858); W. B. Sprague, *Annals Am. Pulpit*, vol. VII (1859); G. G. Smith, *Hist. of Methodism in Ga. and Fla.* (1877); C. E. Jones, *Education in Ga.* (1889); W. J. Northen, *Men of Mark in Ga.*, vol. II (1910); J. D. Wade, *Augustus Baldwin Longstreet* (1924).] J. D. W.

FEW, WILLIAM (June 8, 1748–July 16, 1828), statesman, soldier, banker, belonged to a Quaker family which emigrated from England in 1682, settling in Pennsylvania. His father, William Few, removed to Maryland and there married Mary Wheeler, a Catholic. Later on he became a Methodist and William, Jr., born near Baltimore, was reared in that faith. Failing as a tobacco planter in Maryland, the elder William Few removed his family in 1758 to North Carolina where his son became inured to the hardships of frontier life and received a meager schooling at the hands of itinerant teachers. He developed an omnivorous appetite for reading and really educated himself. In North Carolina the Few family became involved in the "Regulator" war, and a brother, James, was summarily hanged after the battle of Alamance (1771). A few days later the paternal farm, with cattle and horses, was destroyed by the British. Shortly thereafter, having gone bond for some of the "Regulator" outlaws, the elder William Few found himself involved in legal and financial difficulties and with his family removed to the Quaker settlement in St. Paul's Parish, Ga., near Wrightsboro, leaving the younger William behind to settle his affairs. The latter joined his family in 1776, when the entire connection became ardent Revolutionists. Benjamin Few, an older brother, was a colonel of militia, William Few, Jr., a lieutenant-colonel, and Ignatius Few, the youngest brother, a captain and brevet-major of dragoons.

During the Revolutionary period, in addition to his service in the field, William Few, Jr., was twice a member of the General Assembly of Georgia, and a member of the Executive Council of the state. He served as surveyor-general of Georgia and commissioner to the Indians, and was twice a delegate to the Continental Congress. When the war closed he was again elected (1783) to the General Assembly and was again sent as a delegate to the Continental Congress. In 1787 he was one of the six Georgia delegates to the Philadelphia Convention which drafted the Constitution of the United States; he was one of the two (Abraham Baldwin being the other) who remained throughout the convention and signed the new Constitution, and was a member of the state convention (1788) which ratified it. Few was one of the first United States senators sent from Georgia under the new government. His term expired in 1793. He did not offer for reëlection, but returned to Georgia, served a fourth term in the state Assembly, and shortly thereafter (1796) was appointed judge of the 2nd (federal) judicial circuit of Georgia. This office he held for three years and resigned. In 1799, then in his fifty-second year, he removed to New York City. Almost immediately he assumed a position of importance. For four years he served in the General Assembly; he became inspector of state prisons; and served as an alderman in the city. From 1804 to 1814 he was a director in the Manhattan Bank and he ended his career as president of the City Bank. He died at the home of his son-in-law, Maj. Albert Chrystie, at Fishkill-on-the-Hudson.

Few is described as tall, slender, erect, of grave and dignified demeanor. He was a stanch believer in revealed religion and a liberal giver of his wealth to all good causes. His wife, Catherine, daughter of Commodore James Nicholson, and three daughters survived him.

["Autobiog. of Col. Wm. Few of Ga.," *Mag. of Am. Hist.*, Nov. 1881; *Jours. of Cong.*; *Revolutionary Records of the State of Ga.* (1908); Chas. C. Jones, Jr., *Biog. Sketches of the Delegates from Ga. to the Continental Cong.* (1891); *Biog. Dir. Am. Cong.* (1928); Marion Letcher, in Wm. Northen, *Men of Mark in Ga.*, vol. I (1907); *N. Y. Spectator*, July 25, 1828; *Augusta Chronicle and Ga. Advertiser*, Aug. 2, 1828.] R. P. B—s.

FEWKES, JESSE WALTER (Nov. 14, 1850–May 31, 1930), ethnologist, was born in Newton, Mass., the son of Jesse and Susan Emeline (Jewett) Fewkes. He had the local advantages of schooling and was prepared for Harvard College, where he graduated in 1875 and received the degree Ph.D. in 1877. Working his way through college, he was uncertain as to what line to follow. Leaning for a time toward electricity, he conducted a number of experiments in that field, but finally through the magnetism of Louis Agassiz took up marine zoölogy. Many papers on echinoderms and other forms of sea life at-

Fewkes

test this phase of his work, which was advanced by a course in zoölogy at Leipzig. After his return from Germany he became assistant in the Museum of Comparative Zoölogy at Harvard and secretary of the Boston Society of Natural History. Transferring his interests to anthropology, he took up the work of the Hemenway Southwestern Archeological Expedition lately directed by Frank Hamilton Cushing [*q.v.*], and founded the *Journal of American Ethnology and Archæology* for the publication of the results. This journal, of which five numbers were issued, contains some of Fewkes's best work. In 1895 he became connected with the Bureau of American Ethnology, his first undertaking being the investigation of the classic ancient pueblo of Sikyatki in the Hopi Reserve, northeastern Arizona. The report on this exploration marks the introduction of zoölogical methods to archeology; the analysis of zoömorphic designs led to the connection of current Hopi designs with the ancient ("Archeological Expedition to Arizona in 1895," *17th Annual Report, Bureau of American Ethnology,* 1898, pt. 2, pp. 519–744). This association with the Hopi Indians, whose customs and art evidently relate to ancient predecessors, led Fewkes to the intensive study of their cults. A long list of publications covering their history and religious life ensued, among the more striking being: "The Snake Ceremonials at Walpi" (*Journal of American Ethnology and Archæology,* vol. IV, 1894); "Tuscayan Snake Ceremonies" (*16th Annual Report, Bureau of American Ethnology,* 1897, pp. 267–312); "Hopi Katchinas, drawn by Native Artists," describing the figurines representing the numerous deities of the Hopi pantheon (*21st Annual Report,* 1903, pp. 3–126); "The Tuscayan New Fire Ceremony" (*Proceedings of the Boston Society of Natural History,* vol. XXVI, 1895, pp. 422–58); "The Winter Solstice Ceremony at Walpi" (*American Anthropologist,* March, April 1898); "The New-Fire Ceremony at Walpi" (*Ibid.,* January–March 1900). Intensive work at the Hopi pueblos was followed by archeological researches among the ancient ruins of Arizona, New Mexico, Colorado, and Utah. Typical ruins in all parts of this region were scientifically explored by Fewkes and accounts of the results promptly published. Realizing the heritage that the United States possesses in these ancient remains, he sought whenever possible to clear out rooms and protect broken walls against further injury, leaving the sites for public education. Evidence of this pioneer work is seen in the cliff dwellings and pueblos of the Mesa Verde, at Casa Grande, Ariz., and in other localities. Always adequately presented from a full store of knowledge, his reports on the archeology of the Pueblo region are incomparable. Notable among these are "Two Summers' Work in Pueblo Ruins" (*22nd Annual Report, Bureau of American Ethnology,* 1904, pt. 1, pp. 3–195), the Sikyatki report mentioned, and many others. He discovered a new type of naturalistically and geometrically decorated pottery, in the Mimbres Valley, N. Mex., indicating an extinct tribe of Pueblo relationship (*Smithsonian Miscellaneous Collections,* vol. LXIII, no. 10, 1914, pp. 1–53). In 1926 he explored what was to be his last work in the Southwest, an important ruin called Elden Pueblo, near Flagstaff, Ariz. (*Ibid.,* vol. LXXVIII, no. 7, 1926, pp. 207–32). While his work was principally with the ethnology and archeology of the Southwest, he prosecuted explorations in Porto Rico ("The Aborigines of Porto Rico and Neighboring Islands," *25th Annual Report, Bureau of American Ethnology,* 1907, pp. 3–220), and eastern Mexico ("Certain Antiquities of Eastern Mexico," *Ibid.,* pp. 221–84). Taking up the archeology of the eastern United States in its relation to present tribes, he carried on work in Tennessee, Georgia, and other Southern states. At Weeden Island, near Tampa, Fla., he excavated a large ancient mound (*Smithsonian Miscellaneous Collections,* vol. LXXVI, no. 10, 1924, pp. 88–98) and continued investigations on the keys to the south. In the press of exploration and the preparation of reports he found opportunity to write several papers of general scope: "Sun Worship of the Hopi Indians" (*Annual Report of the Smithsonian Institution,* 1918, 1920, pp. 493–526); "Great Stone Monuments in History and Geography" (*Smithsonian Miscellaneous Collections,* vol. LXI, no. 6, 1913), and "The Sun's Influence on the Hopi Pueblos" (*American Anthropologist,* January–March 1906). After long service in the Smithsonian as ethnologist, in 1918 he was accorded promotion and became chief of the Bureau. Scientific societies at home and abroad honored him; in recognition of his contributions to the exhibits of the Columbian Historical Exposition held in Madrid in 1892 the Queen Regent of Spain made him a Knight of the Order of Isabella the Catholic, and in 1894 he received a gold medal from King Oscar of Sweden. One of his important contributions to anthropological science was the demonstration of the value of the study of living tribes in solving the problems of archeology. In his work among the Hopi he proved by the traditions relating to anciently occupied sites the story of the migrations of the clans that coalesced to form the tribe. The exploration and repair of ruins now customary was begun through his efforts. The first phonographic records of Indian songs were made under his direction. In the intimate study of Indian secret ceremonies begun by A. M. Stephen and Frank Hamilton Cushing he had no equal. Among the Hopi he was initiated into the Snake and Flute fraternities and given the name Naquapi, "Medicine Bowl." To this day his memory is green among these Indians. As a result of his numerous explorations an immense body of artifacts flowed into the collection of the National Museum through the Bureau of American Ethnology. These thousands of specimens form one of the most valuable archives in existence. They are material which students will perennially come to examine.

Around the camp fires in the desert he was a most comradely companion. With Dr. Fewkes and his gentle wife, who always accompanied him, all people coming into contact felt an atmosphere of friendliness. No mask of seriousness blocked the success of this master explorer. Broadly cultivated in the arts and sciences, he was at home among men of his rank and embraced all men by his intensely human qualities. After the death of his first wife, Florence Gorges Eastman, to whom he was married in 1883, he married in 1893 Harriet Olivia Cutler of Cambridge, Mass. He retired from the Bureau in 1928 and died two years later at his home in Forest Glen, Md.

[*Harvard College Class of 1875, Fiftieth Anniversary Report* (1925); *Who's Who in America*, 1928–29; Frances Sellman Nichols, *Biog. and Bibliog. of Jesse Walter Fewkes* (1919); *Evening Star* (Washington), May 31, 1930; *Sunday Star* (Washington), *N. Y. Times*, and *Washington Post*, June 1, 1930; personal information.]
W. H.

FFOULKE, CHARLES MATHER (July 25, 1841–Apr. 14, 1909), collector of and authority on tapestries, was born in Quakertown, Bucks County, Pa., where his family had settled in 1712 on land granted them by John, brother of William Penn. His parents were Benjamin Green Ffoulke and Jane Mather. He was the second son, one of six children. With his brothers and sisters he was educated in the Friends' School at Quakertown and attended regularly the Friends' Meeting. At sixteen he was sent for a year to a boarding school at Gwynedd and later to the Friends' Central High School at Philadelphia. In 1860, when only nineteen years of age, he himself was made principal of the Friends' School in Quakertown.

Being a Quaker, to his bitter disappointment he was not allowed to join the Union army at the time of the Civil War but instead, went into the wool business. As buyer for the firm of Davis & Ffoulke, he traveled extensively in this country, and through exposure on one of these trips, contracted rheumatism with which he battled for the rest of his life. In 1872, on account of ill health, he gave up his business and went to Europe, where he met and, in December of that year, married Sarah Cushing of New York. It was through his wife, who had had training as an artist, that he became interested in art and it was during this first trip to Europe that he acquired something more than a working knowledge of the paintings of the great masters, as well as three foreign languages—French, German, and Italian.

The Ffoulkes returned to America in 1874, settled in Philadelphia, and for another ten years Ffoulke devoted himself exclusively and very successfully to business. By that time he had acquired sufficient means to be able to purchase works of art which, on a previous journey, he had coveted. In 1884 he and his family, consisting of his wife and children (one son and three daughters), went to Europe and took up residence in Nice. The disastrous effects of the earthquake of 1887 caused them to change their residence to Florence, and it was here that Ffoulke took up the study of tapestries, which he pursued with the utmost diligence. A friendship with an Italian painter brought him into contact with a leading Italian collector and authority on textiles, Giuseppe Salvadori, from whom he learned much concerning technique. His first valuable purchase was a set of Flemish tapestries, historically important, rich in gold and silver, which he found and acquired in Munich.

In 1888 his improved health permitted his return to America and he took up his residence then in Washington. The following year, while in Europe, he had the good fortune to be presented by a friend to the Princess Barberini and was given opportunity to examine the great Barberini collection of tapestries, many pieces of which had then been stored for thirty years. This entire collection he later acquired (with the consent of the Italian government) and brought to the United States. The collection included series depicting Dido and Æneas, Judith and Holofernes, and the life of Christ. The collection was too large even for the gallery Ffoulke had prepared for it in Washington, and he therefore disposed of some of the pieces. The largest set, illustrating the life of Christ, was thus obtained for the Cathedral of St. John the Divine in New York.

A confirmed invalid after 1892, for years before his death Ffoulke was unable to walk a step, and from a man of commanding stature became pitiably dwarfed and crippled. Wherever he went he was carried, but so heroically did he disregard his physical disabilities that others forgot them. In 1904, though terribly broken in health, he went abroad with his wife, daughter, and youngest son, and after spending some time in France and Italy, wintered in Egypt, where he made a special study of Egyptian weavings. It was while he was on this trip that the King of Belgium requested and secured the loan of his Flemish tapestries for the Exposition in Brussels in 1905.

Charles M. Ffoulke was essentially public-spirited and a leader. After establishing himself in Washington he helped to secure a charter from Congress for a National Academy of Art (inactive) and was instrumental in organizing the National Society of the Fine Arts (later the Washington Society of the Fine Arts), of which, in 1907, he became president. During his presidency of this society he organized a fine exhibition of tapestries and textiles, which was held in the Corcoran Gallery of Art and for which he wrote a descriptive catalogue. During his last years he frequently discussed with friends the establishment of a national organization to quicken interest in, and appreciation of art in America and to serve as a channel for the expression of public opinion in matters pertaining to art that might call for legislative action. These plans materialized in the organization of the American Federation of Arts, a little more than a month after his death, which occurred in New York, where he had gone for treatment.

[Foreword by Glenn Brown to *Ffoulke Collection of Tapestries* (1913); obituary in *Evening Star* (Washington, D. C.), Apr. 16, 1909; personal recollections.]

L. M.

FFRENCH, CHARLES DOMINIC (1775–Jan. 5, 1851), Catholic priest, son of a Church of Ireland prelate and cousin of Lord Ffrench, was born in Galway, Ireland. On his mother's death, the boy was reared by a religious aunt and tutored by a liberal-minded father and a scholarly parson. Following servants to chapel, he joined the Catholic Church along with a brother, Edmund, who became bishop of Galway (died, 1852). The boys were assailed on all sides; Trinity College was closed to them; in accordance with the penal laws, they were cut off from their inheritance; as sons of a Protestant they could not study for the priesthood in state-aided Maynooth seminary. In despair, they turned to the Dominican priory, where they continued their classical training in preparation for the College of Corpo Santo at Lisbon, where Charles was ordained, Dec. 21, 1799. Two years later, on his way to Ireland, his ship was captured by Spaniards and he was taken to Galicia as a prisoner. Soon released, he made his way via Portugal and England to Ireland where he ministered for eight years. Among his converts was an American merchant who urged his enlistment in the American missions. Armed with letters from his provincial and Archbishop Troy, he went to Lisbon and thence to Canada where he arrived in September 1812. Appointed vicar in Quebec, he made such an appeal to Protestants, that under Anglican pressure his bishop sent him to St. John, New Brunswick (1813), where he built a chapel from which he attended Indian stations over an immense area. He learned the native dialect and was unusually successful until exposure from falling through an ice-hole into a bayou impaired his robust constitution.

In 1817, he joined the diocese of New York and attended missions through New Jersey and New York state. In the course of his duties, he said the first mass at Claremont, N. H., and took part in the conversion of the Rev. Daniel Barber. Racial troubles with certain trustees of St. Peter's Church, New York, as well as charges concerning loans on New Brunswick lands where he had hoped to establish a Dominican priory, caused him considerable annoyance. He set forth for St. John in 1822, but his ship was wrecked. Largely because of his skill and courage, the long boats were lowered and landed at Kingston, R. I., without even the loss of the steerage passengers whom the captain would have abandoned. Continuing his journey, he obtained evidence for *A Short Memoir . . . in Vindication of . . . the Character of Rev. Charles Ffrench* (c. 1826). Apparently this refutation ended the charges of his detractors. In 1826, he joined Bishop Fenwick [*q.v.*] at Boston and was assigned to Eastport, Me., where he built a church and established an Indian mission at Pleasant Point. At intervals he attended Irish camps on canals; in 1827 he took over Dover, N. H., as a station and within a year erected St. Aloysius's Church (*Truth Teller,* New York, July 26, 1828). Assigned to Portland, Me., Father Ffrench, despite nativist threats, built St. Dominic's Church and incidentally converted J. M. Young, later Catholic bishop of Erie, Pa. With noteworthy zeal, he gathered together congregations at Quincy and Newburyport, Mass. (*Catholic Telegraph,* Sept. 7, 1833). In 1839, without leave of absence, he went to Rome in hopes of bringing Dominicans to Portland. On his return, he served as pastor of Greece, N. Y., where he constructed a small church; but with the accession of Bishop Fitzpatrick, he was recalled to the Boston diocese and given charge of Lawrence, Mass. (1846), where he built the church and school of the Immaculate Conception and attended mass-stations at Methuen, Andover, and Haverhill.

A powerful man who carried his 350 pounds without being unwieldy, he finally surrendered to death after a few weeks of inactivity. Of him Bishop Fitzpatrick, who was not uncritical, confided to his notes that he was zealous and regular, buoyant and amicable, and no bearer of ill will even to opponents, whose faults he presented in a favorable light with an effort "as amusing as it was edifying."

[*U. S. Cath. Hist. Soc., Records and Studies*, vol. II, pt. 1 (1900) pp. 40 ff.; *The Cath. Almanac* (1852), p. 243; *Hist. of the Cath. Church in the New England States* (1899), ed. by W. Byrne; *U. S. Cath. Intelligencer*, May 11, 1832; photostat copies in the Dominican House of Studies, Washington, D. C., of Ffrench's account of his life (1840) in archives of San Clemente, Rome, of Bishop Bayley's notes, of broadsides in the trustees' dispute, and of Bishop Fitzpatrick's obituary *Memoranda*, in Vol. IV in the Boston archdiocesan archives.] R. J. P.

FIELD, BENJAMIN HAZARD (May 2, 1814–Mar. 17, 1893), philanthropist, was born at Yorktown, Westchester County, N. Y. A descendant of Robert Field, who came from England about 1630 and migrated to Rhode Island about 1638, he was the son of Hazard and Mary (Bailey) Field and first cousin of Maunsell Bradhurst Field [*q.v.*]. He attended the North Salem (Westchester County) Academy, a well-known school at that time, directed by the Rev. Hiram Jelliff, and as a lad entered the office of his uncle, Hickson W. Field, a commission merchant in New York City. In 1838 he was married to Catherine M. Van Cortlandt de Peyster, a member of an old New York family. In the same year he took charge of his uncle's business, which involved much trading with foreign countries, and conducted it successfully for more than a quarter of a century. Having been joined by his son as a partner, he retired at fifty-one from commercial activities, remaining a silent partner and devoting the rest of his life to philanthropy in various forms, giving his time and thought unreservedly to every public enterprise with which his name was associated.

Within a year he became president of the Home for Incurables, a New York institution that was virtually alone in its field. To this undertaking Field gave his attention continuously until his death—a period of twenty-seven years, during which he was said to have been absent from only seven monthly meetings of the Board of Managers. He gave liberally for specific needs of the Home, and the chapel, built in 1885, was the joint gift of himself and his wife, but far more important was the personal care that he lavished on the institution, differing in no degree from the attention that a sagacious business man would give to a profit-making enterprise. At the same time he was interested in the New York Eye and Ear Infirmary and in like agencies of healing. In 1880 he was one of a small group of public-spirited citizens who founded the New York Free Circulating Library, which twenty years later formed the nucleus of the circulation department of the New York Public Library. At his death, in 1893, he was president of this organization. He worked for it enthusiastically for years, often at the sacrifice of personal comfort, when those who saw the importance of branch libraries on New York's East Side were few and were compelled to get on with scant resources.

Field was a life member, treasurer, and president of the New York Historical Society and also gave support to the American Geographical Society and the American Museum of Natural History. He aided the Society for the Prevention of Cruelty to Children, the Working Women's Protective Union, and the Sheltering Arms. His philanthropies were never showy; he seems to have had nothing to do with any public cause that he had not seriously studied and in every project for which he assumed official responsibility he would not rest until he knew the details of organization more thoroughly than most corporation directors know what is going on in their own companies. In his case the philanthropic motive wholly replaced the motive of personal enrichment. It became a greater joy to him to see good accomplished by his efforts and his money than it had been in his earlier years to accumulate the riches that made his philanthropies possible.

[F. C. Pierce, *Field Geneal.* (2 vols., 1901); J. T. Scharf, *Hist. of Westchester County, N. Y.* (1886), 443–45; *27th Ann. Report Home for Incurables* (1893); Scharf, *Hist. of Westchester County, N. Y.* (1886), *N. Y. Times*, Mar. 18, 1893.] W. B. S—w.

FIELD, CHARLES WILLIAM (Apr. 6, 1828–Apr. 9, 1892), Confederate soldier, engineer, was born at "Airy Mount" in Woodford County, Ky., descended from Henry Field who settled in Virginia in the seventeenth century, and the youngest son of Willis and Isabella Miriam (Buck) Field. He was graduated from the United States Military Academy on July 1, 1849, and assigned to the 2nd Dragoons (present 2nd Cavalry) as brevet second lieutenant. Until 1855, he served on the frontier in New Mexico, Texas, and Kansas. He was promoted first lieutenant on Mar. 3, 1855, and the next year was detailed instructor in cavalry tactics at the Military Academy. He became captain on Jan. 31, 1861, and resigned his commission to enter the Confederate service as captain of cavalry on May

30 of the same year. Appointed colonel of the 6th Virginia Cavalry in September 1861, he organized that regiment at Manassas and served in "Jeb" Stuart's cavalry division until Mar. 9, 1862, when he became brigadier-general and commanded an infantry brigade which participated in the fighting against McDowell's advance on Fredericksburg and opened the Seven Days' battles in the attack on Mechanicsville, June 26, 1862. He was in the battles of Cedar Mountain and Second Bull Run (Manassas). In the latter he received a desperate wound through the hips, from which he never entirely recovered. As a token of the esteem in which he was held by his superiors, he was promoted major-general in February 1864 and given command of that crack fighting unit, Hood's old Texas division (Longstreet's corps), which he led in the vanguard of the troops that checked Grant's flank movement in the Wilderness. One company in his 4th Texas (Gregg's) Brigade lost every officer and man in that fight. Field was with Lee, Longstreet, and Jenkins when Longstreet was seriously wounded and Jenkins killed by fire from Confederate troops, supposed to be Mahone's, who mistook them for Federals. Until the end of the war Field was constantly engaged and he bore a heavy part in the bloody fighting at Cold Harbor, Deep Bottom, and before Petersburg. At Appomattox his division, the only thoroughly organized and effective body of troops in the Army of Northern Virginia, its nearly 5,000 men comprising more than half of the infantry surrendered by General Lee, "with bands silent, and flags nevermore to be unfurled, . . . stacked arms and became again true and orderly citizens of the United States."

After the war Field engaged in business in Baltimore and Georgia until 1875 when he became colonel of engineers of the Egyptian Army and its inspector-general during the Abyssinian War. In recognition of his services he was decorated by the Khedive with the Order of the Medjidie. In 1877 he returned to the United States and on Apr. 18, 1878, became doorkeeper of the House of Representatives of the Forty-sixth Congress. From 1881 to 1885 he was a civil engineer in the service of the United States and from 1885 to 1889 superintendent of the Hot Springs (Ark.) Reservation. In 1857 he married Monimia Mason of Virginia, by whom he had two sons. Of vigorous intellect and indomitable will, of superb physique, Field was the *beau sabreur.* In the words of Gen. Bradley T. Johnson (*post*), "Gentle and tender as a woman, and bold and true as Bayard, no better man ever strode horse or drew blade in peace or war." On the twenty-seventh anniversary of the surrender at Appomattox, he died in Washington, D. C.

[G. W. Cullum, *Biog. Reg. Officers and Grads. U. S. Mil. Acad.* (3rd ed., 1891); Bradley T. Johnson in *Asso. Grads. U. S. Mil. Acad., Ann. Reunion,* 1893, pp. 145–49; F. C. Pierce, *Field Geneal.* (2 vols., 1901).]

J. W. L.

FIELD, CYRUS WEST (Nov. 30, 1819–July 12, 1892), merchant, capitalist, promoter of the first Atlantic cable, sprang from typical New England stock. The founder of the family in America was Zechariah Field, who came from England about 1629; he was the grandson of John Field, astronomer, and was born in the old home at Ardsley, Yorkshire. Capt. Timothy Field, grandfather of Cyrus Field, served in the Continental Army under Washington. His son, David Dudley Field [*q.v.*], was graduated from Yale in 1802, became a Congregational minister, and married Submit Dickinson, daughter of Capt. Noah Dickinson of Somers, Conn. She was known as "The Somers Beauty." Cyrus West Field, their eighth child and seventh son, was born at Stockbridge, Mass. He was named after Cyrus Williams, a bank president, and the predecessor, West, of David Field in the pastorate at Stockbridge. The boy had a careful, Puritanical upbringing. His mind seems to have matured early. At the age of fifteen he abandoned the idea of a college education such as several of his brothers received, and persuaded his father to let him leave home and seek his fortune. With eight dollars in his pocket, he drove fifty miles to the Hudson and sailed down the river. In New York, where an older brother helped him, he became an errand-boy in the well-known dry-goods store of A. T. Stewart & Company on Broadway. For the first year he received $50 in wages, for the second year $100; board and lodging cost him $2 a week. His clothes were home-made from Stockbridge. After three years in New York he resigned at Stewart's and went to Lee, Mass., as assistant to his brother Matthew, a paper-manufacturer, who sent him on occasional trips. In less than two years he started in business for himself as a paper-manufacturer at Westfield, Mass., but shortly afterward was invited to become a partner in the firm of E. Root & Company, wholesale paper dealers, Maiden Lane, New York City. When he was twenty-one years old, he married Mary Bryan Stone of Guilford, Conn., his father performing the ceremony. Now, when everything looked promising, came one of those sudden changes of fortune which were to follow him through life. Six months after his marriage, the firm of E. Root & Company failed (Apr. 2, 1841), and though Field was only a junior partner, upon him fell the burden of the debts. Out of this financial wreck he built up the firm of Cyrus W. Field & Company, his brother-in-law Joseph F. Stone being his partner. Such long hours did Field work to clear off the debts of the old company that his children saw him only on Sundays. In 1849 the family physician advised a trip to Europe because of overwork. Field and his wife visited England and the Continent. At the age of thirty-three he had paid all debts with interest, and was wealthy enough to retire from business, having over $250,000, all of which had been made in less than nine years. With his friend, Frederick E. Church [*q.v.*], the landscape-painter, he then took a trip to South America, crossed the Andes, and brought back an Indian boy and a live jaguar.

In 1854 he met a Canadian engineer, Frederick N. Gisborne, who was promoting a telegraph line across Newfoundland for the purpose of connecting with fast steamers to run between St. John's and Ireland, thus shortening by several days the transmission of important news from one side of the Atlantic to the other. There was talk of using carrier-pigeons between Newfoundland and the mainland of Nova Scotia. While Field studied a globe in his library, the idea of a cable between Newfoundland and Ireland came to him. Next morning he wrote to S. F. B. Morse [*q.v.*] and to M. F. Maury [*q.v.*] of the National Observatory at Washington. Morse and others, both in America and Europe, had had the idea before, but no promoter such as Field had taken it up. The longest submarine cables up to this time were between England and Holland, and Scotland and Ireland, where no great depths complicated the problem. After a favorable governmental charter had been obtained granting a fifty years' monopoly, a company of prominent New Yorkers was formed and $1,500,000 subscribed. The men who joined in this somewhat visionary scheme included Field's neighbors and friends, Peter Cooper, Wilson G. Hunt, Moses Taylor, and Marshall O. Roberts. When Field was fully started in this new enterprise, his partner Stone died, and a little later his only son; other difficulties began to arise, testing the courage and perseverance for which he became justly famous. Two and a half years were consumed in putting a telegraph line across Newfoundland and connecting it by cable with the mainland. A company was organized by Field in England and capital subscribed; Sir Charles T. Bright and John W. Brett cooperated and prominent people like Thackeray and Lady Byron took stock. Soundings were made in the ocean between Newfoundland and Ireland, and a shallow tableland or "telegraph plateau" discovered under Maury's direction. The British government assisted by lending a ship to help lay the cable and by guaranteeing a generous annual sum for official messages. At Washington when similar measures were proposed, opposition arose; but a bill was squeezed through by a narrow margin, and the large frigate *Niagara* was assigned to help the British *Agamemnon*. The laying of the cable was begun in 1857 with very little knowledge of how such things should be done. Several hundred miles had been laid out from Valentia, Ireland, when the cable broke; over $500,000 lost in the depths of the Atlantic! To cap the disappointment to Field, the financial depression of 1857 forced his mercantile firm in New York into bankruptcy and debt. Undeterred, in 1858 he tried the plan of having the two ships meet in mid-ocean, splice their cable ends, and start in opposite directions, one toward Ireland and one toward Newfoundland. On three of these attempts the cable quickly broke, and the ships returned to Ireland. There was talk of abandoning the enterprise. A fourth attempt was made, however, and proved successful; the ships arrived at their separate destinations on the same day, Aug. 5, 1858. A copper wire 1,950 miles long connected Trinity Bay with Valentia, through water over two miles deep. On Aug. 16, after the necessary adjustments had been made, Queen Victoria sent a message to President Buchanan. Hilarious celebrations were held, and Field was toasted by the same wiseacres who a few weeks before had called him a fool. In New York a two-day "cable carnival" was held, in "glorious recognition of the most glorious work of the age." At about the same time the cable stopped working. Several hundred messages had been sent in the three weeks of operation but now only vague signals came over the wire. This was perhaps due to faulty insulation or to using an electric current of too high a potential in the various experiments that had been tried. Among the scientists who advised about the trouble were Sir Charles Wheatstone and Professor William Thomson (afterward Lord Kelvin). The populace which had lauded "gallant" and "bold Cyrus" now began saying that the cable had not worked at all, and that the messages had been faked in order to permit him to sell his stock at a high price. The fact that he had not sold his stock made no difference to the story; nor did the clear evidence that a large sum of money had been saved the British government by the quick transmission of news from England to Canada to the effect that peace had been made with China, so that two regiments of soldiers which had been ordered from Canada to India were called back.

Field's telegraph stock declined sharply in value, and the next year his New York office and warehouse burned with heavy loss.

In 1859 Field was again in London and funds were raised for a new cable and for possible repairs to the old one. His personal business reverses and the Civil War now intervened. During the war Field talked and wrote to influential officials both in the United States and England about the need for a cable. Before the war was over he had engaged the world's largest steamer, the *Great Eastern*, to lay a new cable on condition that if it were not successfully laid no payment would be made, but that £50,000 would be paid in shares of the telegraph company for a successful laying. A heavier and better-insulated cable was started out from Valentia. When more than half of the distance had been covered, the cable parted. Grappling was tried and the cable picked up, but lost each time. Additional funds were raised by a reorganization of the company, and another cable ordered. During the summer of 1866 experience and technical improvements won the long fight; a new cable was successfully laid and the cable of 1865 grappled for and recovered. In 1867 Congress voted Field a gold medal but because of the stupidity of a government clerk several years elapsed before he received it.

Field gave early support to the idea of laying a cable to the Hawaiian Islands, thence to Asia and to Australia, and corresponded with various foreign officials about it. During the controversies between the United States and England following the Civil War, he lent the influence resulting from his acquaintance with such men as Gladstone, John Bright, and the Duke of Argyll toward smoothing over the international difficulties. His already extensive travels were continued by trips to Iceland and around the world. In 1877 he interested himself in the efforts being made to give New York a system of elevated railways. The project was in financial straits. He offered to purchase a majority of the stock and to serve as president without salary if the creditors would accept bonds at sixty cents on the dollar. He contributed largely to make the elevated lines a reality. Other activities included participation with Jay Gould in the development of the Wabash Railroad, and control of a New York newspaper, the *Mail and Express*. In 1881 when President Garfield was shot, Field started the movement to raise a sum of money for the bereaved family; over $362,000 was raised, of which he contributed $5,000. A few years later during the illness of Gen. Grant he was deterred from a similar service by a modest note from Grant. In a few more years Field himself was to be in need of similar help. His investments were depreciating rapidly in value, partly because of operations of men whom he considered as friends. On his seventy-second birthday he found that of the fortunes which he had invested in telegraph and elevated-railway stocks only a few thousand dollars were left. His last years were saddened by financial and domestic troubles. A gleam of happiness, however, came in 1890 when he and his wife celebrated their golden wedding. They had had seven children and many grandchildren. The family had lived at Gramercy Park in New York City but had spent many of their summers in a fine country house at Irvington-on-Hudson. Field's wife died a year after the golden wedding, and Field himself less than a year after his wife. He was buried in Stockbridge.

He was a courageous and spirited man, with strong persuasive powers and a quick, decisive manner. He possibly overestimated the value of his enthusiasm and frankness in overcoming the selfishness and ingratitude of others. When misfortunes overtook him, less brilliant men than he remarked sagely that he was too visionary and chivalrous for a workaday world. Of his brothers, David Dudley [*q.v.*] was an eminent jurist and law reformer, Stephen Johnson [*q.v.*] became a justice of the United States Supreme Court, and Henry Martyn [*q.v.*] attained some distinction as a clergyman and author.

[The best source is *Cyrus W. Field, His Life and Work* (1896), by Isabella Field Judson, his daughter; this includes autobiographical notes and many letters. Other references are *Cyrus W. Field* (n.d.), *History of the Atlantic Telegraph* (1867), and the revised *Story of the Atlantic Telegraph* (1892), all by Henry Martyn Field; *The Story of the Atlantic Cable* (1903), by Chas. Bright; *The Telegraph in America* (1886), by Jas. D. Reid; *The Atlantic Telegraph* (1866), by W. H. Russell; *The Laying of the Telegraphic Cable* (1858), by John Mullaly; *N. Y. Tribune*, July 13, 1892.] P. B. M.

FIELD, DAVID DUDLEY (May 20, 1781–Apr. 15, 1867), Congregational clergyman, local historian, was born at East Guilford (now Madison), Conn. He was the younger son of Capt. Timothy and Anna (Dudley) Field and a descendant of John Field, an English astronomer, whose grandson, Zechariah Field, came to Massachusetts about 1629. He early displayed a taste for the ministry. As a boy he was wont to mount a rock and preach as long as his youthful companions might listen; as he walked on the seashore he shouted texts at the waves. His family encouraged him and he was prepared for college by his pastor, John Elliott. He graduated from Yale with high honors in 1802 and studied divinity with Dr. Charles Backus of Somers. Field had gone to Somers for theological instruction; there he also found a wife, and in October 1803 married Submit, the fourth daughter of Capt. Noah Dickinson. In September 1803 he had been licensed to preach by the Association of New Haven East. After preaching five months as a candidate at Haddam he was made pastor of the Congregational church. He remained in Haddam exactly fourteen years. For five months in 1818 he was on a missionary tour in western New York; on his return he stopped in Stockbridge, Mass., and preached several sermons. After a trial of three months, on Aug. 25, 1819, he was installed as pastor of the Congregational church at Stockbridge at a salary of $600 a year. He returned in 1837 to his old church in Haddam to bring peace and harmony to a divided flock. Seven years he preached in the little church at Haddam and seven years in the near-by village of Higganum. Early in 1851 he was persuaded to retire and moved to Stockbridge, where he remained until his death sixteen years later. There were two daughters and eight sons, of whom four —David Dudley, Cyrus West, Stephen Johnson, and Henry Martyn [*qq.v.*]—achieved distinction in the life of nineteenth-century America.

Field had long been interested in gathering the details of local history and in 1814 he published a small *History of the Towns of Haddam and East-Haddam, Connecticut.* Five years later the Connecticut Academy of Arts and Sciences published his *Statistical Account of the County of Middlesex.* He edited and prepared the *History of the County of Berkshire, Mass.* (1829), and published a *History of the Town of Pittsfield . . . Mass.* (1844). He was appointed historian of his class in 1842 and his *Brief Memoirs* were privately printed in 1863. He published several other local histories and five sermons, including a *Warning against Drunkenness* (1816), delivered at the execution of Peter Lung at Middletown. His historical work was distinguished chiefly by his unwearying labor and practical common-sense.

[F. C. Pierce, *Field Geneal.* (2 vols., 1901); F. B. Dexter, *Biog. Sketches Grads. Yale Coll.*, vol. V (1911); Henry M. Field, *Life of David Dudley Field* (1898) and *Record of the Family of the late Rev. David Dudley Field* (privately printed, 1880); Henry B. Dawson in *Hist. Mag.*, June 1867.] F. M—n.

FIELD, DAVID DUDLEY (Feb. 13, 1805–Apr. 13, 1894), lawyer, law reformer, born at Haddam, Conn., was the eldest son of Rev. David Dudley Field [*q.v.*] and Submit (Dickinson) Field. On his mother's side he was descended from Capt. Noah Dickinson who had served with Gen. Putnam in the French war. He attended the Academy at Stockbridge, Mass., and Williams College, from which he withdrew before the graduation of his class in 1825. He studied law with Harmanus Bleecker in Albany, and with the firm of Henry and Robert Sedgwick in New York. In 1828, he was admitted to the New York bar, and two years later became the partner of Robert Sedgwick on the retirement of Henry. He was married three times: first to Jane Lucinda Hopkins, who died in 1836; second, to Mrs. Harriet Davidson, who died in 1864; and third, to Mrs. Mary E. Carr, who died in 1876. Field attained some prominence in politics although his temperament was not such as to fit him for great success in that field. He was too rigid and unbending, and too likely to form and express opinions without regard to party leadership. He was Democratic nominee for election to the New York Assembly in 1841, but was defeated. Later, he broke vehemently with his party on two important issues,—the annexation of Texas, which he rightly declared meant war with Mexico; and the slavery question. In 1847 he was a delegate to the Democratic convention in Syracuse, where he introduced the "Corner-Stone" resolution, declaring "uncompromising hostility to the extension of slavery into territory now free, or which may be hereafter acquired by any action of the Government of the United States" (H. M. Field, *post,* p. 115). When the Republican party nominated Frémont for president, Field favored his candidacy; and when Lincoln spoke for the first time in New York City, Field was one of his supporters on the platform at Cooper Institute. Although not a delegate to the Chicago convention of 1860, Field attended, and his influence with Horace Greeley and others at the time when they had conceded the nomination to Seward, is thought by many to have been chiefly responsible for Lincoln's nomination. He was chairman of the New York delegation to the Peace Conference in Washington in 1861. After the assassination of Lincoln, he ceased to act with the Republicans. In 1876, at the suggestion of Tilden, he was elected to Congress to fill the two months' unexpired term of Representative Smith Ely, in order that he might participate in the Hayes-Tilden election contest.

Field's political activities, though important in themselves, were in reality mere episodes in a life devoted to law and law reform. He was prominent as a lawyer for sixty years and in the great cases litigated in the ten years following the Civil War was an outstanding figure. Many of these cases involved constitutional questions of the utmost importance, for example, the Milligan case, which was argued in 1867 before the United States Supreme Court on the part of the United

States, by Attorney-General Stanbery and Benjamin F. Butler, and for Milligan by Field, Jeremiah S. Black and James A. Garfield. The decision upheld the contention that, since the civil courts were open, the military commission which had tried and convicted Lamdin P. Milligan was without jurisdiction in the case; and that, the period of suspension of the writ of *habeas corpus* having expired, a writ should be issued and Milligan discharged from custody.

Then followed the Cummings case in which Field and his associates convinced the United States Supreme Court of the invalidity of the Missouri constitutional provision requiring all citizens to take an oath of loyalty declaring that they had not been in armed hostility to the state or given aid and comfort to persons engaged in such hostility. The McCardle case of 1868 involved the constitutionality of the Reconstruction Act of 1867 under which military governments had been set up in states lately in rebellion. McCardle was being held for trial before a military commission in Mississippi on the charge of inciting to insurrection, disorder, and violence. On the hearing in the United States Supreme Court, eminent counsel including Charles O'Conor were associated with Field for McCardle, and the case was argued on its merits. Before a decision was rendered, the act of 1867 was amended, and subsequently McCardle was discharged. A fourth constitutional case argued by Field was the Cruikshank case (1875) in which the constitutionality of the Enforcement Act of 1870 was involved. The decision of the circuit court for Louisiana convicting Cruikshank of conspiring to prevent negroes from exercising their right to vote, was, upon reasoning adduced by Field, reversed by the United States Supreme Court.

A chapter in Field's professional life which was the subject of bitter controversy concerned the Erie Railroad litigation of 1869. Field was counsel for Jay Gould and James Fisk [*qq.v.*] and was charged by Samuel Bowles and others with unprofessional conduct in having, it was alleged, in connection with a stockholders' meeting, engaged in a conspiracy to carry an election for Fisk and Gould by the use and abuse of legal process and proceedings. A large amount of controversial literature was produced, characteristic examples of which were by Charles Francis Adams (*Chapters of Erie,* 1871), by George Ticknor Curtis (*An Inquiry into the Albany and Susquehanna Railroad Litigations of 1869*), by Jeremiah S. Black (*Galaxy,* March 1872), and by Albert Stickney (*North American Review,* April 1871; *Galaxy,* October 1872). Field's conduct was considered by the Committee on Grievances of the Association of the Bar of the City of New York, which presented a report "of such a character that the consequences to Mr. Field, if the recommendations had been adopted, would have been of the most serious character" (Theron G. Strong, *Landmarks of a Lawyer's Lifetime,* 1914, p. 192). No vote was taken on the recommendations. His opponents also put the worst construction on the fact that, from 1873 to 1878, he served as chief counsel for the defendant in the prosecution of "Boss" Tweed, who had become a director, along with Gould and Fisk, of the Erie Railroad.

Field's skill and learning as a lawyer were, however, never questioned. He served with distinction as counsel for Tilden in opposition to William M. Evarts, before the Hayes-Tilden Electoral Commission of 1876. As late as 1882, when he was seventy-seven years old, he argued for the plaintiff the case of *New York* vs. *Louisiana* before the United States Supreme Court. But while he was a leader among practising lawyers, the work in which he made for himself a permanent name was that of law reform, with special reference to codification, both of municipal and international law. He had been at the bar only eleven years when in 1839 he began an agitation from which he did not desist until his death. His purpose was to reduce to written form the whole body of law of New York, both substantive and adjective, and in the latter field to combine in one series of proceedings actions both at law and in equity. It was through his efforts that there were added to the New York State Constitution of 1846 provisions (Article I, Section 7, and Article VI, Section 24) directing the legislature to appoint three commissioners to "reduce into a written and systematic code the whole body of the law of this state, or so much and such parts thereof as to the said Commissioners shall seem practicable and expedient"; and three other commissioners "to revise, reform, simplify and abridge the rules, practice, pleadings, forms and proceedings of the courts of record." The legislature at its next session appointed the required commissions, of which Field became a member. Largely through his personal effort two procedural codes were prepared and reported to the legislature. The first commission to codify the substantive law produced no permanent result, and a new commission with Field as chairman was not appointed until 1857. Between 1860 and 1865, complete political, civil and penal codes were reported, but only one of them, the Penal Code (1881) was adopted by the legislature. The Civil Code was twice rejected by the Assembly and thrice passed by it, on two occasions receiving the assent of the Senate, but failing to obtain the approval of the governor. The concept of these codes was wholly Field's, and the execution of them almost equally so. With him on the commission were William Curtis Noyes and Alexander W. Bradford, but neither of them did any large part of the work of codification, which was done by Field with the assistance of Austin Abbott, Benjamin Vaughan Abbott and Thomas G. Shearman. The struggle for the adoption of the Civil Code was a battle royal between Field, almost single-handed, and the leaders of the New York bar. James C. Carter was appointed by the Association of the Bar of the City of New York to head the opposition, by means of arguments and addresses to the successive legislatures and governors. The struggle was not devoid of personal bitterness. "Few men," says Strong, "have been subjected to greater ridicule and abuse than David Dudley Field," but, he continues, "the Code of Civil Procedure . . . is a monument to his legal capacity, untiring zeal and constructive force that will immortalize his name as the 'Father of the Code'" (*Landmarks of a Lawyer's Life,* p. 420). The Civil Procedure Code has been adopted in whole or in part by twenty-four states, as well as by several foreign nations. Almost equal recognition has been given to the Criminal Procedure Code. The state of California adopted all five of the "Field" codes.

The passion for codification was almost an obsession with Field, and so it came about naturally that while engaged in the struggle for the adoption of his New York Codes, he headed a movement for the codification of the law of nations. The drafting of the New York Codes was completed in 1865. The successful issue, during the next year, of his brother's attempt to lay the Atlantic cable stirred Field's imagination, and caused him to believe that a further bond between nations might be forged by the preparation of an international code. At the Manchester meeting of the British Association for the Promotion of Social Science, in September 1866, he proposed the appointment of a committee to prepare the outline of such a code. The committee was appointed with Field as a member. When the work moved slowly because the widely separated members could not meet for conference, Field essayed the task alone. With the assistance of Austin Abbott, Howard P. Wilds, Charles F. Stone and President F. A. P. Barnard of Columbia College, he prepared, and published in 1872, a *Draft Outline of an International Code,* dealing with the relations between states in time of peace. The second edition, published in 1876, included Part II on War. An Italian translation of the first edition was published in 1874, and a French translation of the second edition, in 1881. From 1866 to his death, Field visited Europe nearly every year to attend conferences devoted to international affairs, before which he read many papers; and he was instrumental in the formation of the Association for the Reform and Codification of the Law of Nations, the first meeting of which was held in Brussels in October 1873.

Both as a lawyer and as a jurist, Field made a deep impression on his generation. His positive achievements were of a high order, such as could come only from a man of great natural ability and of extensive learning. At the same time, he was aggressive and relentless in the prosecution of his designs, strong in his feelings and passions, positive in his opinions, and combative in temperament. One of his maxims was, "The only men who make any lasting impression on the world are fighters." Therefore he made many enemies, and a few stanch friends. All found him stalwart and impressive. Some found him cold and forbidding, while others who professed to know him more intimately found in him a magnetic and sympathetic personality.

[The chief sources of information are Field's own writings contained in *Speeches, Arguments and Miscellaneous Papers* (3 vols., 1884–90), ed. by A. P. Sprague; a *Life* by Henry Martyn Field (1898); Helen K. Hoy's biographical sketch in Lewis's *Great Am. Lawyers* (1908), V, 125–74; and an article by S. Newton Fiero in *N. Y. State Bar Association Proc.*, 1895, XVIII, 177–93; F. C. Pierce, *Field Geneal.* (1901); *Am. Law Rev.*, May–June, 1894; *N. Y. Tribune*, Apr. 14, 1894; *High Finance in the Sixties,* ed. by Frederick C. Hicks (Yale Univ. Press, 1929).] F. C. H.

FIELD, EUGENE (Sept. 2?, 1850–Nov. 4, 1895), author, was the son of Roswell and Frances (Reed) Field. The exact date of Eugene Field's birth is uncertain. He himself gave both Sept. 2 and Sept. 3, preferring Sept. 3 in his later years (*Auto-Analysis,* privately printed, 1894). Family tradition inclines to Sept. 2. His latest biographer (Slason Thompson, *Life of Eugene Field,* 1927) conjectures that he may whimsically have favored the double date in order that friends who forgot Sept. 2 might have a chance "to make amends." His father was a native of Vermont who had removed to St. Louis, Mo., and who was legal counsel for Dred Scott. His mother was also of Vermont ancestry, the daughter of a professional musician. She died in 1856, and her two children, Eugene and Roswell, Jr., were put in the care of a cousin, Miss Mary Field French, of Amherst, Mass. Eugene attended for a time a private school at Monson, Mass., and he spent most of the academic year 1868–69 at Williams College. In the summer of 1869 his father died and in the following autumn he entered Knox College, Galesburg, Ill. Here he completed the year, probably not very profitably. The next year he spent at the University of Missouri, where his brother was a junior. After an unimportant attempt to be an actor, he went abroad in the autumn of 1872, taking with him a college chum. Here he saw something of Great Britain, France, and Italy, and spent all that was available of a considerable inheritance from his father. On his return he married (Oct. 16, 1873) Julia Sutherland Comstock, of St. Joseph, Mo., to whom he had become engaged two years before when she was but fourteen years of age. In spite of the youth of the bride and considerable parental hesitation the marriage proved a happy one. Mrs. Field not only endured, but seems to have enjoyed the eccentricities of her husband; she aided in keeping his business affairs from complete wreck, and she was a devoted mother to her eight children; while Field himself wrote a year before his death, "It is only when I look and see how young and fair and sweet my wife is that I have a good opinion of myself." After spending the little remainder of his patrimony on a wedding trip, he turned to newspaper work, and held successively editorial positions on the *St. Joseph Gazette,* the *St. Louis Journal,* the *Kansas City Times,* and the *Denver Tribune.* In 1883 he joined the staff of the Chicago *Morning News* (renamed the *Record* in 1890) with which he remained till the time of his death. His chief task was the conducting of a column on the editorial page, "Sharps and Flats." In 1889–90 he took an extended trip to Europe, partly for his health, which was precarious during his later years. He continued to be active, however, and wrote his stint of newspaper copy on the day of his death. For some time he lived in Buena Park, a suburb of Chicago, and here not long before he died he acquired a house and grounds of his own which he nicknamed "The Sabine Farm." His experiences in planning and remodeling furnished material for his series of sketches, "The House." In spite of his ancestry and his boyhood in New England Eugene Field always considered himself a thorough Westerner. He declined flattering calls to Eastern newspapers on the ground that he would feel cramped and repressed in the East; and he introduced the word "Western" rather obtrusively into the titles of two of his best-known volumes.

Field possessed a whimsicality which showed itself both in his personal relationships and in his writings. He seems to have fascinated most of those who knew him. The stories of his ingenious, elaborate, and sometimes apparently heartless practical jokes, and of his fertile schemes for inducing friends to buy his meals and pay his bills may impress some readers less favorably than friendly narrators expected. In his writings he was as odd and as irrepressible as in private life. Although his editorial superiors are said to have rejected many of his extreme paragraphs, his column made free with the names of friends, enemies—so far as he had enemies—and strangers; telling imaginary anecdotes, creating imaginary precocious children for childless persons, announcing the engagements of well-known people in the most embarrassing fashion. One of his favorite practises was to attribute to various notables his own verses—not merely burlesques, but some of his better serious poems. The "Wanderer" was published as the work of Madame Modjeska, the actress; and his "Divine Lullaby" and some other bits were ascribed to Judge Cooley, the first head of the Interstate Commerce Commission. The daily contributions to "Sharps and Flats" included not only ephemera, but verse and prose that has become classic of its kind. While in no sense a poet of depth and power, and given to such affectations as the elaborate concoction of verse in real and imaginary dialects—Old English and Dutch particularly—he could cleverly hit the popular taste in both humorous and pathetic bits. His most successful humorous poem, "The Little Peach," written while he was still in Denver, was long recited and sung by many comedians. It is interesting to notice that on this his own comment was "Popular, but rotten" (*Auto-Analysis*). A less boisterous humor is seen in "Just 'fore Christmas." He set most store, however, by his pathetically sentimental poems and his poems for children. Here there is considerable sameness, which he tried to relieve by resorting to his artificial dialects. He dealt many times with the joys of Christmas, and with the death of a child and the toys and tokens left behind. The best treatment of this latter theme is in "Little Boy Blue." The most successful of the lullabies is "Wynken, Blynken, and Nod," which keeps the Dutch imagery, but avoids the dialect. He also wrote a number of short tales, mostly fanciful or sentimental, which have not on the whole lasted so well as the better verse.

Two of Field's chief interests in his later years were Horace and book-collecting, and both were extensively reflected in his column. He made free—and to the devout classicist irreverent—paraphrases of some of Horace's *Odes,* which were first printed in "Sharps and Flats" and were afterward issued, together with others by Roswell Field, as *Echoes from the Sabine Farm* (privately printed 1891, published 1892). His interest in rare and beautiful books led to the creation of the "Saints and Sinners" anecdotes; a group of well-known Chicago bibliophiles, among them three divines, were supposed to meet in a corner of a local book-store and talk of their treasures and of things in general. Later, Field began, and had almost finished at the time of his death, a series of sketches arranged as an imaginary autobiography, "The Love Affairs of a Bibliomaniac."

He was by no means the first American newspaper paragrapher to conduct an individual column, but his practise differed from that of most of his predecessors; and while his audacious indulgence in personalities could not safely be followed, he has had a strong influence on the later development of an interesting feature of American journalism. "Sharps and Flats" had more serious prose and verse than most earlier columns, and of better quality. The humor was whimsical, sometimes subtle, rather than of the slap-dash order. Of especial importance was the introduction of literary and bibliographic material in a journal of the sort for which Field wrote. Almost all of his writings of importance were first published in the newspapers with which he was connected, though not all in his special columns. His first booklet, *The Tribune Primer* (Denver, 1882), compiled from rather cheap humorous bits in the *Denver Tribune,* is now a rare collector's item, as is *Culture's Garland* (Boston, 1887), a collection of satirical skits the nature of which may be inferred from the descriptive sub-title, *Being Memoranda of the Gradual Rise of Literature, Art, Music, and Society in Chicago and other Western Ganglia,* followed by a wreath of sausages as title-vignette. Other works published in his lifetime are *A Little Book of Western Verse* (1889); *A Little Book of Profitable Tales* (privately printed 1889, published 1890); *With Trumpet and Drum* (1892); *Second Book of Verse* (1892); *The Holy Cross and Other Tales* (1893). He also contributed an introduction to Stone's *First Editions of American Authors* (Cambridge, 1893). After his death a collected edition of his works—not including the *Tribune Primer* or *Culture's Garland*—was published in New York (10 vols., 1896), enlarged by the addition of two volumes of *Sharps and Flats* collated by Slason Thompson (1900). There have been various collections of his poems and stories for children, with illustrations and music. Since his death there have been private editions of various selections from his otherwise uncollected writings. (See *Cambridge History of American Literature,* II, 543, IV, 641, for a more inclusive bibliography.)

[Field recounted briefly the facts of his life in a sketch at the time of the publication of *Culture's Garland* (reprinted in *Eugene Field's Creative Years,* pp. 10–11), and at slightly greater length in the opening paragraphs of his *Auto-Analysis.* The many obituary notices consisted mostly of facts from the *Auto-Analysis* supplemented by anecdotes. *Yenowine's Illustrated News* issued a Eugene Field *Supplement* (Milwaukee, Nov. 30, 1895). The most important biographies are Slason Thompson, *Eugene Field, a Study in Heredity and Contradictions* (2 vols., 1901); Chas. H. Dennis, *Eugene Field's Creative Years* (1924); Slason Thompson, *Life of Eugene Field* (1927). Numerous anecdotes and bits of reminiscence have been written by former newspaper associates, actors, literary friends, and others. See for example Francis Wilson, *The Eugene Field I Know* (1898); E. C. Stedman, *Genius and Other Essays* (1911).]

W. B. C.

FIELD, HENRY MARTYN (Apr. 3, 1822–Jan. 26, 1907), clergyman, author, born at Stockbridge, Mass., was a son of David Dudley [*q.v.*] and Submit (Dickinson) Field and a descendant of Zechariah Field who emigrated to Boston about 1629 and later settled in Connecticut. As a youth he was sickly and was given to study. He entered Williams College at the age of twelve and at fourteen delivered a temperance address in the church at Tyringham. He was graduated in 1838 and several months later entered the Theological Seminary at East Windsor, Conn. In 1840 he was licensed to preach and the following year graduated from the Seminary, delivering an oration on "The Ministry favorable to the Highest Development of Mind." When his brother, David Dudley [*q.v.*], offered to advance him money for study in Germany, his father warned him to eschew German rationalism and he went to New Haven for a year. That he was called to St. Louis in 1842 as pastor of the Third Presbyterian Church and thus escaped settling in New England, Field always regarded as a special providence. After five years he resigned and went to Europe. He visited Ireland in the year of the great famine. While living in Paris he witnessed the revolution of 1848. He went to Italy and observed Roman Catholicism; he felt sad to think that it was all a splendid pageant, but no religion (*Good and Bad in the Roman Catholic Church,* 1849, p. 5). Having returned to New York, he sought out the descendants of the Irish patriots living in that city and in 1851 published a popular history, *The Irish Confederates and the Rebellion of 1798.* In May 1851 Field married Laure Desportes who after having been seriously involved in the Choiseul-Praslin tragedy (see London *Times,* Sept. 2–4, 1847) had left Paris and settled in New York. In the same year he became pastor of a Congregational church in West Springfield, Mass. He resigned in 1854, moved to New York, and bought an interest in the *Evangelist,* of which he later became sole owner and editor.

He published in 1867 the *History of the Atlantic Telegraph* of which his brother, Cyrus West [*q.v.*], had been a chief promoter.

In 1875–76 Field made an extended tour of the world seeking to forget the recent death of his wife. He described this tour in two volumes published in 1877: *From the Lakes of Killarney to the Golden Horn* and *From Egypt to Japan.* A journey to the East in 1882 and a tour of the Mediterranean in 1886–87 each resulted in the publication of three volumes. His travel books, written in a discursive and faintly ecstatic style, were the delight of a large public which yearned for amusement and edification. Field was a liberal and progressive influence within the Presbyterian Church. He long advocated a revision of the Westminster Confession of Faith. He was one of the first to make a study of the reconstruction problems of the South for himself. In 1888 he entered a long public discussion with Robert G. Ingersoll [*q.v.*] in an effort to persuade him of the sublimity of the idea of God, but the latter only congratulated him upon having "bidden farewell to the Presbyterian church" (*Field-Ingersoll Discussion,* 1888, pp. 6, 61). Field had sometimes used the *Evangelist* to exploit the distinguished family to which he belonged. In 1880 he issued privately a *Record of the Family of the Late Reverend David Dudley Field.* He wrote biographies of his brothers David Dudley and Cyrus West and had planned a volume on his brother Stephen Johnson, a justice of the United States Supreme Court. When in the evening of his life he contemplated the past, his melancholy was tinged with regret that his brothers had been born to great deeds and he but to celebrate them.

[Autobiographical fragments in Field's own writings; *Boston Transcript,* Jan. 28, 1907; *Who's Who in America,* 1903–05; private information.] F. M—n.

FIELD, HERBERT HAVILAND (Apr. 25, 1868–Apr. 5, 1921), zoölogist and bibliographer, was born of Quaker parents, Aaron and Lydia Seaman (Haviland) Field, in Brooklyn, N. Y. His early education was at the Friends' School and the Brooklyn Polytechnic Institute. He received the B.A. degree from Harvard in 1888, the M.A. in 1890, and the Ph.D. in 1891. His graduate work was in the department of zoölogy but in connection with his own research he became deeply interested in the problem of simplifying and clarifying bibliographical methods. After completing his work at Harvard, he went abroad, continuing his zoölogical studies at Freiburg, Leipzig, and Paris.

During the years 1892–95, he published several important papers upon which his reputation as a zoölogist rests, but his interest centered more and more clearly in bibliography, and primarily in the problem of how to make the essential contents of current zoölogical literature available to the workers in that rapidly expanding field of research. Wherever he went he took occasion to confer with teachers, investigators, and librarians, seeking advice and encouragement in the formation and development of his plans. He recognized in Dewey's decimal system of classification of knowledge for library purposes a most valuable aid and by combining it with a system of index cards, he believed he saw the solution of his problem. By the prompt publication and distribution of such cards, workers in the zoölogical laboratories of the world could be kept continually in touch with the current literature bearing on their particular problems. Obviously a central publication office where the indexing should be done, and the cards printed, and from which they could be distributed, was a prime requisite. After careful consideration, Field selected Zürich, Switzerland, as the most suitable place for such an office and there in 1895, he established the "Concilium Bibliographicum," with which his name has ever since been associated. In 1903 he was married in London to Nina Eschwege and established a home in Zürich. His greatest difficulty was finding the financial support for what was necessarily an expensive undertaking, of interest to a very limited constituency. He gave generously from his own by no means abundant resources, and he received subventions from Switzerland, from Zürich, and from various scientific foundations and organizations. Throughout his whole life, however, his work was hampered by inadequate financial support.

Field was a man of striking appearance and personality, with unusual linguistic ability. He used Latin, Italian, French, German, Dutch, and Russian as well as his native tongue and was therefore a particularly desirable member of international gatherings. He was also gifted with an exceptional memory, manifested not only in an ability to quote freely from literature and conversations but especially in the power of reproducing music to which he had been a listener. He was conspicuous for orderliness and pertinacity, qualities without which he could never have established and maintained the Concilium.

[Field's own accounts of the foundation of the Concilium in *Papers and Proc. 26th Meeting, A. L. A.* (1904) and in *Annotationes Concilii Bibliographici,* Dec. 1907; Henry B. Ward, "Herbert Haviland Field," in *Science,* Nov. 4, 1921; Karl Hescheler, "Dr. Phil. Herbert Haviland Field," in *Nekrologen zu den Verhandlungen der Schweizerischen Naturforschenden Gesellschaft* (Schaffhausen, 1921); *Who's Who in America,* 1920–21; *Nature,* Apr. 21, 1921; *N. Y. Times,* Apr. 7, 1921.] H. L. C.

FIELD, JOSEPH M. (1810–Jan. 28, 1856), actor, playwright, journalist, is said to have descended from the dramatist, Nathaniel Field, Shakespeare's contemporary (Lilian Whiting, *Kate Field,* 1899, p. 4). The family came originally from Warwickshire, but subsequently settled in Ireland, and while some chroniclers state that Field was born in England, his probable birthplace was Dublin, where his father, Matthew, was a prominent Catholic. While Joseph was still an infant the family emigrated to Baltimore and then to New York (*Longworth's New York Directory,* 1817–18, p. 198). His education could not have been extensive, for he appeared at the Tremont Theatre, Boston, as early as 1827 (*Columbian Centinel,* Nov. 28, 1827). Three years later he made his New York début at the Park Theatre, but by 1833 he was playing at New Orleans and soon came to be recognized as one of the leading actors on the southwestern circuit. Under the management of Sol Smith he appeared at Cincinnati, St. Louis, Mobile, and lesser towns. At this time Field regarded himself as a tragedian, but afterward, in the words of N. M. Ludlow (*Dramatic Life as I Found It,* 1880, p. 436), under whose management he also served, he "settled down to what he really was clever in,—eccentric comedy." In 1837 he married Smith's leading actress, the beautiful Eliza Riddle, and thereafter the two frequently played together in the southwestern theatres, the season of 1839–40 being spent at New Orleans. During this period Field contributed scores of poems, signed "Straws," to the New Orleans *Picayune,* most of them commenting humorously on current affairs. In 1840 the *Picayune* sent him to Europe as a correspondent. Five years later, after further experiences in the theatre, including engagements in New York and Philadelphia, he was associated in the founding of the St. Louis *Reveille,* a noted newspaper during the six years of its life (William Hyde and H. L. Conard, *Encyclopedia of the History of St. Louis,* 1899, III, 1638). In May 1852, after having directed the Mobile Theatre for two years, he opened the handsome new Varieties Theatre at St. Louis. Though his company was one of the best that had yet appeared in that city, he found the enterprise so unprofitable that he abandoned it in the fall of 1853 (*Missouri Republican,* Nov. 8, 1853, and following issues). During his last years he confined his efforts chiefly to Mobile, and there he died after a lingering illness. He was survived by his wife and daughter, Mary Katherine Keemle [*q.v.*], who as "Kate Field" became a celebrated lecturer.

Field was a prolific writer of plays, none of which was published. At least one, however, *Job and His Children,* produced at St. Louis, Aug. 25, 1852, exists in manuscript and gives evidence of some command of situation and character. It is known that his *Victoria* (1838) had as main persons the British queen and James Gordon Bennett; that *Family Ties* (1846) won a five hundred dollar prize offered by the actor Danforth Marble and was given at the Park Theatre; that *Oregon, or the Disputed Territory* (1846) dealt with the northwest boundary dispute. His chief published work, *The Drama in Pokerville; The Bench and Bar of Jurytown, and Other Stories* (1847), is a collection of crudely humorous tales. Field was a man of varied abilities, whose very versatility, so his contemporaries thought, was a bar to distinction in any one pursuit.

[Aside from references cited above, see Sol F. Smith, *Theatrical Management in the West and South* (1868), *passim*; J. T. Scharf, *Hist. of St. Louis City and County* (2 vols., 1883); J. N. Ireland, *Records of the N. Y. Stage* (2 vols., 1866–67); A. H. Quinn, *A Hist. of the Am. Drama from the Beginning to the Civil War* (1923). The records of Mount Auburn Cemetery, Cambridge, Mass., have been used to verify dates of birth and death.]

O. S. C.

FIELD, KATE [See FIELD, MARY KATHERINE KEEMLE, 1839–1896].

FIELD, MARSHALL (Aug. 18, 1834–Jan. 16, 1906), merchant, was born near the village of Conway, Mass., the son of John and Fidelia (Nash) Field and a descendant of Zechariah Field who came to Dorchester, Mass., about 1629. He attended the district school and a private school in Conway, but his school life ended by the time he was seventeen, when he left home to become a clerk in the dry-goods store of Deacon Davis at Pittsfield. Here he remained for five years, a quiet, unassuming, but courteous clerk, giving little promise of success. He was offered a partnership in the business, but his interest was in the fast-developing West and, accordingly, he left Pittsfield for Chicago in 1856. Although the city had more than doubled in population in the four years 1852–56, it was still a mud town with wooden sidewalks. Field, having no capital, took employment as a clerk in the wholesale dry-goods firm of Cooley, Wadsworth & Company, the leading wholesale house in the city. His salary was $400 the first year; he slept in the store and saved $200.

He was employed as traveling salesman as well as clerk in the store, and his travels about the country impressed him with the opportunity for business expansion. Courteous and good-looking, he soon built up a following at the store. In January 1861 he became general manager and the next year a partner in the firm which was now Cooley,

Farwell & Company. In 1864 Levi Z. Leiter was admitted to partnership, and the firm became Farwell, Field & Company. Hardly had the firm become established under its new name when Potter Palmer, wishing to retire from the retail and wholesale dry-goods business he had built up, offered it in 1865 to Field and Leiter. Palmer financed the new organization of Field, Palmer & Leiter, retiring himself in 1867. Within eight years Field had risen from the position of clerk at $400 a year to become head of a successful business in which he had an interest of $260,000. He was now thirty years old. When Potter Palmer withdrew from the firm in 1867, Henry Field and later Joseph Field, brothers of Marshall, were taken in. The firm remained Field, Leiter & Company until 1881 when, upon the withdrawal of Leiter, it became Marshall Field & Company, Field owning the principal interest. The business weathered the loss of its store and stock of goods in the Chicago Fire of 1871, and the ensuing panic of 1873. Hardly had this latter trial passed, when the retail store was again burned in 1877. Nothing could prevent the success of the business under Field's management, however. As early as 1868 sales amounted to $12,000,000 a year; by 1881 they were $25,000,000, and before Field's death, had reached $68,000,000.

Field, like A. T. Stewart in New York and Wanamaker in Philadelphia [*qq.v.*], promoted a new type of merchandising. His was a one-price store, with the price plainly marked on the merchandise. Goods were not misrepresented, and a reputation for quality merchandise and for fair and honest dealing was built up. Sales were for cash. When credit was extended, payment was exacted on the date when due. Goods could be bought on approval and exchanged. Courtesy toward customers was an unfailing rule. Stocks of goods were bought at wholesale for cash in anticipation of consumer demand and then a demand for them was created. Thus Field was able to undersell competitors who waited for the demand to appear and then bought on the open market. "His business was his passion," says one of his former partners. His thorough grasp of detail, his ability to select able managers, and a skilful handling of employees all counted in making him one of the most successful merchants of his time. Buying agencies were operated on a world-wide scale, the whole output of manufacturing plants was contracted for. As a final step the company organized its own manufacturing establishments, making a large part of the goods sold in its stores. Field's partners became millionaires, but as they accumulated wealth he bought them out to make room for able younger men in the business.

Field took no active part in politics, or in the social life of the city, and gave little time to charity, education, or public welfare. As one of the organizers of the Commercial Club of Chicago, however, he helped toward the founding of the Chicago Manual Training School. He donated ten acres of ground as a site for the new University of Chicago and later gave $100,000 to that institution. In 1893, his gift of a million dollars made possible the Columbian Museum at the Chicago World's Fair. This later developed into the Field Museum of Natural History. By a provision of his will, a gift of $8,000,000 was made available for the new building for that institution, a splendid marble structure on the lake front in Grant Park. Field seems to have had no scientific interest in the founding of the museum but to have acted solely on the prompting of his friends who were interested in preserving the valuable collection which had been gathered for the Columbian Exposition. The gift which seems to have given him the greatest personal satisfaction was that of a library to the town of Conway near the place where he was born. It was at the dedication of this building that he made his first and only public address. While he was recognized as a power in the financial and business world, he remained through life a quiet, genial man, without the arrogance and air of superiority which sometimes accompany the acquisition of wealth.

Field was first married in January 1863 to Nannie Scott, daughter of Robert Scott of Ironton, Ohio. She died in 1896, and in 1905 he was married to Mrs. Delia Spencer Caton, this second marriage occurring a few months before his death, which came suddenly as a result of pneumonia. It seems to have been his desire to create a great family estate. The bulk of the large fortune which he had accumulated was left in trust for his grandchildren Henry and Marshall Field III, who were not to come into full possession of the estate until thirty-nine years after Field's death. In the event of the death of the heirs, the estate was to go to other members of the Field family to the third generation. It is of interest to note that this type of bequest was held contrary to American standards by the Illinois legislature and an act was passed prohibiting such accumulations in trust beyond the time when the heirs living at the time of the death of the testator shall come of age. The bulk of Field's estate was in real estate in the business district of Chicago.

[Biographical sketch by Thos. W. Goodspeed in *The Univ. of Chicago Biog. Sketches,* I (1922), 1–34; F. C.

Pierce, *Field Geneal.* (2 vols., 1901); Geo. W. Smith, *Hist. of Illinois and Her People* (1927), IV, 354; S. H. Ditchett, *Marshall Field & Company; the Life Story of a Great Concern* (1922); *Chicago Daily Tribune, Chicago Daily News,* and *Chicago Record-Herald,* Jan. 17, 1906.] E. A. D.

FIELD, MARY KATHERINE KEEMLE (Oct. 1, 1838–May 19, 1896), journalist, author, lecturer, actress, was a woman of exceptional though eccentric intellectual gifts, and was continuously in the public eye and mind, mainly as a valiant apostle of reforms, from her youth until her death. She was born in St. Louis, the daughter of Joseph M. Field [*q.v.*], an actor, playwright, and manager, and Eliza (Riddle) Field, a popular actress. Her early schooldays and childhood were passed in St. Louis, and at the age of sixteen she went to Boston to visit relatives and to study at Lasell Seminary for girls. Beginning her frequent travels and sojourns abroad in 1859, she went to Europe with her uncle and aunt, living for varying periods in Paris, Rome, and Florence (where she was joined by her mother in 1860), and forming there enduring friendships with the Brownings, the Trollopes, George Eliot, Charlotte Cushman and other distinguished people. In his *Autobiography* (ch. XVII) Anthony Trollope refers to her as his "most chosen friend," whom not to mention "would amount almost to a falsehood." After returning to America, she lived for a time successively in Boston, Newport, and New York, resuming her studies of art, music, and the drama, writing essays for magazines and doing regular correspondence for daily newspapers. Undaunted by the ill success of her first attempt to become an actress, when on Nov. 14 and 21, 1874, she acted Peg Woffington for only two performances at Booth's Theatre, New York, she appeared afterwards at intervals for several years in that play, in pieces written by herself, and as leading woman with John T. Raymond in *The Gilded Age.* Under the name of Mary Keemle she acted in London in *Extremes Meet,* a comedy of her own writing, and also as Volante in *The Honeymoon.* She gained considerable vogue as a correspondent from London and elsewhere of the *New York Herald,* the *New York Tribune,* and other newspapers. From time to time she engaged in battles for such causes as international copyright, Hawaiian annexation, temperance, prohibition of Mormon polygamy, and in the interests of a futile organization she founded and called the Cooperative Dress Association. As a whole, her activities had little lasting effect, and many of the reforms she sought would have been as easily and as quickly accomplished without her aid. Her manner on the lecture platform was easy and vivacious, her newspaper correspondence and books of travel are graphic, her commentary upon actors is entertaining, although not especially authoritative. In everything she did she was vitally in earnest, and she had multitudes of friends who were attached to her even though they had little sympathy with her self-imposed tasks. During the last five years of her life she edited a paper called *Kate Field's Washington,* which she made a pulpit for the preaching of her social, economic, and political faith. Her religious beliefs were strong, but she was not attached to any sect. She died in Honolulu, whither she had gone on one of her many quixotic jaunts, and as a newspaper correspondent. Her published books are, *Adelaide Ristori* (1867); *Planchette's Diary* (1868); *Mad on Purpose, a Comedy* (1868); *Pen Photographs of Charles Dickens's Readings* (1868); *Hap-Hazard* (1873), travel and character sketches; *Ten Days in Spain* (1875); *History of Bell's Telephone* (1878); and *Charles Albert Fechter* (1882), in the American Actor Series.

[Lilian Whiting, *Kate Field; a Record* (1899); W. J. McGee, "Memorial of Kate Field" in *Columbia Hist. Soc. Records* (Washington, D. C.), vol. I (1897); Anthony Trollope, *An Autobiography* (1883); Michael Sadleir, *Anthony Trollope, a Commentary* (1927); Kate Field's own books and newspaper correspondence; character sketch in *N. Y. Times, Saturday Review of Books and Art,* Sept. 28, 1901; obituary notices in *N. Y. Herald,* May 31, 1896, and *N. Y. Tribune,* May 31, 1896; review of her *Ten Days in Spain* in *N. Y. Times Saturday Review of Books and Art,* May 28, 1898; and numerous other newspaper articles about her.] E. F. E.

FIELD, MAUNSELL BRADHURST (Mar. 26, 1822–Jan. 24, 1875), lawyer, author, traced his descent from Robert Field, a friend of Roger Williams, who, coming from Sowerby, Yorkshire, England, *c.* 1630, settled at Flushing, Long Island, in 1645. His father, Moses Field of New York City, and Peekskill, N. Y., married May 17, 1821, Susan Kittredge Osgood, daughter of Samuel Osgood [*q.v.*], first commissioner of the United States Treasury. Maunsell B. Field received his early education at Peekskill, and in 1837 proceeded to Yale University, graduating in 1841, with the highest honors and delivering the valedictory. Considerations of health delayed his choice of occupation, and in the spring of 1843 he undertook an extensive tour throughout Europe, Asia Minor, and Egypt. On returning to the United States in December 1845, he studied law and was admitted to the New York bar in January 1848. During that year he again visited Europe, and on his return joined John Jay in practise in New York City. The law, however, did not appeal to him, and, being financially independent, he went to Europe again in the autumn of 1854, becoming temporarily secretary of legation to John Y. Mason, the United States minister to France, and visiting Madrid on a special mission to Pierre Soulé, United States minister to Spain. He was nominated commissioner for the State of New York to the Paris Universal Exposition of 1855, and served as president of the board of United States commissioners on that occasion, but declined a permanent appointment as secretary of legation which was offered him by President Pierce.

In 1861 he accepted the position of deputy assistant-treasurer of the United States at New York City, and fulfilled the duties of his office so efficiently that Secretary Chase in September 1863 promoted him to assistant secretary of the treasury at Washington, D. C. On June 1, 1864, the assistant treasurership of the United States at New York City became vacant, and Chase strongly recommended Field's appointment to the office. Field, however, had no political backing in New York and President Lincoln declined to make the appointment, saying he could not afford to quarrel with either of the two factions into which the Republicans of that state were at that time split. This ultimately led to Chase's resignation, and Field remained assistant secretary. The exigencies of the Civil War had made his position exceedingly onerous, and his health had materially suffered, so he resigned July 1, 1865, and President Johnson appointed him collector of internal revenue for the 6th District of New York, a position which he retained till 1869. In 1873 Gov. Dix appointed him judge of the 2nd judicial district court of New York City to fill a vacancy, and he remained on the bench till Jan. 1, 1875.

His legal equipment was mediocre, but as a civil servant he was earnest, efficient, and tireless, and enjoyed the complete confidence of his superiors. He had much literary ability, and was a close friend of G. P. R. James, collaborating with him in writing *Adrian; or, The Clouds of the Mind* (1852). He prepared a French edition of the Annual Report for 1854 of the Bureau of Indian Affairs, entitled *Les hommes rouges de l'Amérique du Nord* (1855), and in 1869 published a small volume of poems. The best known of his works is *Memories of Many Men and of Some Women* (1874), being his own reminiscences written in a vivacious and charming manner. He married, Jan. 7, 1846, Julia, daughter of Daniel Stanton of Stockbridge, Mass.

[F. C. Pierce, *Field Geneal.* (2 vols., 1901), contains details of Field's ancestry and a short sketch of his life; but his *Memories of Many Men and of Some Women* (1874) remains the only authority for many important incidents of his career. See also *Semi-Centennial Hist. and Biog. Record of the Class of 1841 in Yale Univ.* (1892); *Hist. of the Bench and Bar of N. Y.*, I (1897), 326, ed. by D. McAdam and others; De Alva S. Alexander, *A Political Hist. of the State of N. Y.* (1909), III, 95.]

H. W. H. K.

FIELD, RICHARD STOCKTON (Dec. 31, 1803–May 25, 1870), senator, jurist, author, was born in White Hill, Burlington County, N. J., the son of Robert and Abigail (Stockton) Field. His paternal ancestor, Robert Field, emigrated from England about 1630, moving to Rhode Island about 1638. His mother was the daughter of Richard Stockton [*q.v.*], a signer of the Declaration of Independence. Upon the death of his father in 1810 the family moved to Princeton, where Richard S. Field received his education, being graduated from the College of New Jersey at the age of seventeen, with the class of 1821. After studying law with his uncle, Richard Stockton, he was admitted to the bar in 1825 and began his practise in Salem, N. J., where in 1831 he married Mary Ritchie. The next year they moved to Princeton which was their home for the rest of their lives.

Field's political career began with his election to the Assembly in 1833, to which body he was twice reëlected. In 1838 he was appointed attorney-general of New Jersey, serving until 1841, when he resigned to devote himself to the regular practise of his profession in Princeton. His relatives, the Stockton family, were largely interested in the Camden & Amboy Railroad and the Delaware & Raritan Canal Company, and he occupied himself in the professional duties arising in connection with the business of those transportation systems.

When a constitutional convention was called in New Jersey in 1844 Field was one of its prominent members and served on the committee relating to the appointing power. Since the abuses arising from legislative appointment had been one of the chief defects of the first constitution this committee occupied a very important position in the convention and accordingly brought its members special notice. Field also served as chairman of the committee on the common schools and secured the adoption of Section 7 of Article IV of the present constitution which set up the school fund. Inasmuch as his greatest service to his state was his achievement in developing New Jersey's educational system, it is significant to note the stress he laid upon this subject in the State's one and only constitutional convention. When the Law Department of the College of New Jersey was opened in 1847, he became professor of constitutional law and jurisprudence, serving until 1855. For a number of years he advocated the creation of a state normal school and his efforts were finally rewarded by the Act of Feb. 9,

1855, creating such an institution. He was made a member of the board of trustees and was at once elected its president, continuing to act in that capacity until his death. The annual reports of this board to the legislature from 1855 to 1870 were all written by him and bear testimony to his knowledge of and interest in this branch of the educational system of the state.

In November 1862 Gov. Olden appointed Field to fill a vacancy in the United States Senate. This appointment was in recognition of his service in organizing the Union-Republican party in New Jersey in 1862 (Knapp, *post,* p. 1310). Since the Democratic party was in control of the state legislature and supplanted him upon meeting in January, Senator Field occupied his seat but a few weeks. During his short service, however, he gained national prominence by his able argument in support of the power of the president to suspend the writ of *habeas corpus* (*Congressional Globe,* 37 Cong., 3 Sess., pp. 28, 216–20); and in recognition of his effective support of the administration on this occasion and also for that in his state during 1861–62, President Lincoln appointed him in January 1863 judge of the district court of the United States for the district of New Jersey, to fill the vacancy caused by the death of Philemon Dickerson. Field served on the bench until Apr. 19, 1870, when he was stricken with paralysis and fell senseless from his seat. He died five weeks later in Princeton. He was one of the founders of the New Jersey Historical Society in 1845 and was serving as its third president at the time of his death. His most important literary work, "The Provincial Courts of New Jersey" (*New Jersey Historical Society Collections,* vol. III, 1849), was written in connection with the work of the Society.

Among his other writings are: *Trial of Rev. William Tennent* (1851); *The Federal Convention of 1787* (1853); *The Papers of Gov. Lewis Morris* (1852); *The Constitution Not a Compact between Sovereign States* (1861); *Life and Character of Chief Justice Hornblower* (1865); *Life and Character of Hon. James Parker* (1869); and several other addresses.

[A. Q. Keasbey, "Memoir of the Hon. Richard S. Field," *Proc. N. J. Hist. Soc.,* 2 ser., II (1872), 111–132; C. H. Hart, *A Necrological Notice of the Hon. Richard Stockton Field . . . read before the Numismatic and Antiquarian Soc. of Phila.* (1870); F. C. Pierce, *Field Geneal.* (2 vols., 1901); *Biog. Dir. Am. Cong.* (1928); *Gen. Cat. Princeton Univ.* (1908); C. M. Knapp, *N. J. Politics During the Period of the Civil War and Reconstruction* (1924); *Daily State Gazette* (Trenton), May 27, 1870.]

C. R. E., Jr.

FIELD, ROBERT (*c.* 1769–Aug. 9, 1819), painter of portraits in oil, miniaturist, engraver, was a native of Great Britain who practised his profession in the United States and Nova Scotia. According to a Halifax tradition he was born in Gloucestershire, England. This the Thieme and Becker *Allgemeines Lexikon der bildenden Künstler* (vol. XI, 1915) states as a fact, but inquiries directed to Gloucester antiquarians have failed to establish it. Field advertised himself as "late of London," and it is known that in 1790 he joined the engraving class at the Royal Academy School. This date is the basis of the birth date tentatively assigned above. His earliest known work was his mezzotint portrait of Rev. Thomas Warton.

Possibly at the suggestion of Benjamin West, Field left England on Feb. 27, 1794, landing at Baltimore, where he soon gained the friendship and substantial support of Robert Gilmor, a noted connoisseur and collector. Thus began a residence of fourteen years in the United States, during which Field painted at Philadelphia, Baltimore, Washington, and Boston. His engraved portraits of Washington and Hamilton were advertised in the *American Minerva and New York Advertiser* of Apr. 23, 1795 (Piers, p. 12). The former work appeared, but the latter was never issued (Boston Museum of Fine Arts, *A Descriptive Catalogue of an Exhibition of Early Engraving in America,* 1904, p. 34). Field is believed by his biographer, Harry Piers, not to have painted the Washington miniature now owned by the Mount Vernon Ladies' Association and by them attributed to him. In 1801, however, he visited Mount Vernon and painted Mrs. Washington from life. His American paintings in oil were unsigned, and some of the Philadelphia "Stuarts" are suspected of being the work of Robert Field. During several years' residence in the capital he painted many celebrities and won social recognition. In 1805, following the example of Stuart and Malbone, he removed to Boston, then a fast-growing seaport. William Dunlap, author of *A History of the Rise and Progress of the Arts of Design in the United States* (1834), who met Field in Boston, wrote of him: "He was a handsome, stout, gentlemanly man, and a favorite with gentlemen. . . . I remember two very beautiful female heads by him; one of Mrs. Allen, in Boston, and one of Mrs. Thornton, of Washington" (edition of 1918, II, 119). At Boston Field made several engravings and a notable miniature of his fellow artist, Henry Sargent.

The growing tension between the United States and England may have caused Field, who never had been naturalized, to return to British territory. In 1808 (not in 1807 as stated in the Boston Museum's *Descriptive Catalogue*), he set up as a "portrait painter, in oil and water-colours, and in miniature" at Halifax, thus advertising himself in the *Royal Gazette,* May 30, 1808 (Piers, p. 52). Nova Scotia at the time was prosperous because of the American Embargo, and Field found much employment. He was befriended by Sir John Wentworth, royal governor, whose portrait he painted (it is now in Government House). A good singer and conversationalist, he became a social favorite. He was active in Masonry. His portrait of Sir A. Cochrane, painted in 1810, was exhibited at the Royal Academy, London, and of that year was his likeness of the Right Reverend Charles Inglis, bishop of Nova Scotia, now in the British National Portrait Gallery. By 1815 Field's income from portraiture must have fallen off, for he then opened a book-shop in Water St., Halifax. In 1816, evidently seeking new employment, he went to Jamaica where, after presumably indifferent success, he died of yellow fever.

[Harry Piers, *Robert Field, Portrait painter in oils, miniature and water colours and engraver* (1927), and reference in "Artists in Nova Scotia," *N. S. Hist. Soc. Colls.,* XVIII (1914), 112–19; other authorities cited above. The earlier biographical sketches of Field are fragmentary and superficial.] F. W. C.

FIELD, ROSWELL MARTIN (Sept. 1, 1851–Jan. 10, 1919), author, youngest of the six children of Roswell Martin and Frances (Reed) Field, was born in St. Louis and died at his home in Morristown, N. J. His father, descended from Zechariah Field, who came to Massachusetts from England about 1629, went to college and studied law in New England, and in 1839 removed to Missouri. Roswell's mother, though living in St. Louis at the time of her marriage, was also of New England origin. When she died in 1856, the boy and his brother Eugene [*q.v.*], a year older than himself, were sent to live with their father's niece, Miss Mary Field French, in Amherst, Mass., and their grandmother in Newfane, Vt. Roswell was educated at Phillips Exeter Academy and at the University of Missouri; and he studied law in Vermont in the office of his uncle, Charles Kellogg Field. Perhaps the chief hero held up before him in his youth was Oliver Cromwell, and he seems always to have been affected by the Cromwellian seriousness. In 1874 he was still enough stirred by his college fraternity ritual to compose for a grand convention of Phi Kappa Psi a poem celebrating love among the brethren and the grief of all of them upon the death of any. Far later than 1874, he nerved himself, in spite of his devoted love for his brother Eugene, to reprimand him for attempting always to be humorous. On the death of their father in 1869, the two brothers inherited an assured livelihood. Roswell soon put an end to his formal education, and went into journalism. Generally in an editorial capacity, he worked in San Francisco, in St. Louis, and in Kansas City. In Kansas City he was married, in October 1885, to Henrietta Dexter. Later he worked on newspapers in New York and Chicago, and in the latter city for about fourteen years he conducted in the *Post* a column called "Lights and Shadows." He retired six years prior to his death. Beginning in 1891 he published a number of books—first, in collaboration with his brother Eugene, *Echoes from the Sabine Farm,* a series of verse translations from Horace. *In Sunflower Land, Stories of God's Own Country* (1892), is made up of sketches of village and farm life in Missouri and Kansas, mostly sentimental, but with touches of humor and realism. He wrote a memoir of his brother prefixed to *A Little Book of Western Verse,* the first volume of the "Sabine Edition" of Eugene Field's collected works published in 1896. *The Muses Up to Date* (1897) comprises six plays for children written by Roswell Field and his wife. Part rhyme and part prose, they are directed in general, as the authors explain in their preface, toward the goal of "plenty to do and little to say." *The Romance of an Old Fool* (1902) rehearses what came near being a love affair between January and May, but was shifted to a more seemly affair between May and June. *The Bondage of Ballinger* (1903), and *Little Miss Dee* (1904) are conventional novelettes showing how young love and antique virtue go hand in hand, but *Madeline* (1906) is concerned, after the manner of medieval romance, with the affairs of Sir Dives, who finds joy at last as a book collector, and of his poor relation Madeline and his friend Master Pauper, both of whom, after a short moment of matrimony, find joy at last "in the flowering meadow and along the pleasant stream" of Heaven (*Madeline,* p. 104).

[Phillips Exeter Acad. *Catalogue, 1783–1869* (1869); Univ. of Mo. *Catalogue* 1870–71; C. K. Field, *Geneal. Hist. of the Family of the Late Gen. Martin Field* (1877); Slason Thompson, *Life of Eugene Field* (1927); *Who's Who in America,* 1918–19; *N. Y. Times,* Jan. 11, 1919.] J. D. W.

FIELD, STEPHEN DUDLEY (Jan. 31, 1846–May 18, 1913), electrical engineer, inventor, was born in Stockbridge, Berkshire County, Mass., the son of Jonathan Edwards and Mary Ann (Stuart) Field. His education was directed at first toward law, and he attended Williams Academy and then Reid Hoffman's School in Stockbridge. When, however, through the efforts of his uncle, Cyrus West Field [*q.v.*], the first Atlantic cable was successfully laid in 1858, and a telegraph office was opened at Stockbridge in his father's law office, Stephen, then twelve years old, became intensely interested in telegraphy. Completing his schooling at Dutchess County Academy, Poughkeepsie, N. Y., in 1863 he went to California as a telegraph operator for the California State Telegraph Company, and after two years in this service spent three more with the Collins Overland Telegraph in British Columbia. He then was made an inspector with the San Francisco Fire Alarm Telegraph Company in which capacity he served until 1872 when he organized the California Electrical Works to develop his original ideas for electrical improvements. One of his first inventions was a multiple call district telegraph box, and in 1878 he designed, built, and equipped a telephone line sixty miles long with twenty-four stations. The following year he designed and subsequently perfected a dynamo as a substitute for the galvanic battery in the generation of electric current for telegraph apparatus, and after solving the problems of using this equipment in combination with the quadruplex telegraph, he sold the system to the Western Union Telegraph Company. He then turned his attention to the electric railway. He was without capital, however, and returned to Stockbridge in 1879. Shortly thereafter he imported from Germany several Siemens electric motors and built an electric locomotive which he operated on a special track near his home in August 1880. After devoting three years to invention in this field, in cooperation with Edison he built and operated an electric railway at the Chicago Railway Exposition in 1883. Having covered his improvements by patents, Field next turned his attention to the stock ticker. He soon designed one surpassing in speed anything of its kind then in use, which led to the organization of the Commercial Telegram Company. During the three years he devoted to this work, however, other inventors became active in the electric railway field and when it seemed that his own patents would be involved in litigation, Field sold them to a group of large electrical interests. In 1887, with Rudolf Eickemeyer [*q.v.*], he invented and constructed a direct-connected, side-bar electric locomotive which was tried out on the New York Elevated Railroad. He was resident engineer during the construction and equipment of a 150-kilometer electrical railway in Geneva, Switzerland (1897–1900). In 1909 he invented and installed the first submarine quadruplex telegraph between Key West and Havana. Field obtained over one hundred patents covering nearly every branch of electrical engineering. He was a charter member and later fellow of the American Institute of Electrical Engineers and was a manager of the Institute's first board of directors. He married Celestine Butters of San Francisco on Sept. 30, 1871, who with a son and daughter survived him at the time of his death in Stockbridge.

[*Who's Who in America,* 1912–13; *Electrical Review and Western Electrician,* May 24, 1913; *Electrical World,* May 24, 1913; *Proc. Am. Inst. Electrical Engineers,* July 1913; F. C. Pierce, *Field Geneal.* (2 vols., 1901); H. M. Field, *Record of the Family of the Late D. D. Field* (1880); *Boston Transcript,* May 19, 1913.]

C. W. M.

FIELD, STEPHEN JOHNSON (Nov. 4, 1816–Apr. 9, 1899), jurist, United States Supreme Court justice, was born in Haddam, Conn. His father was the Rev. David Dudley Field [*q.v.*], a graduate from Yale College in 1802, and a descendant of Zechariah Field, who emigrated from Yorkshire, England, to Boston about 1629. His mother was Submit Dickinson, daughter of Noah Dickinson of Somers, Conn. Both his grandfathers had been officers in the Revolution. He was one of a family of eight sons and two daughters, among whom were David Dudley, Cyrus W., and Henry M. Field [*qq.v.*], and the future mother of Justice David Josiah Brewer [*q.v.*] of the Supreme Court. In 1829 Stephen accompanied his sister and her husband, the Rev. Josiah Brewer, to the Levant, where he remained for two and a half years, one winter of which was passed in Athens. Besides acquiring considerable fluency in modern Greek, Stephen imbibed a valuable lesson in religious tolerance, conceiving for the religious devotion, sobriety, and honesty of the Turks an especial admiration. He also displayed marked bravery in ministering on one occasion to victims of the plague. Returning to the United States, Stephen in September 1833 entered Williams College, from which he graduated valedictorian of his class in 1837. His instructor in his senior year was Mark Hopkins, president of the college, who gave courses in rhetoric, logic, natural theology, and metaphysics. His training was thus almost exclusively in abstract subjects and governed by the idea that the facts of life are best evaluated in the light of a few established principles. Field had originally thought to become a teacher of languages, but in 1838 he entered upon the study of the law in his brother David Dudley's office in New York City, later completing it in that of John Van Buren, afterward attorney-general of New York, at Albany. Upon admission to the bar in 1841, Stephen became his brother's partner in a firm which lasted till 1848. David Dudley during this period was deep in the agitation which led in 1850 to the submission to the New York legislature of his codes of civil and criminal procedure, an interest which Stephen shared. Returning from a second visit to Europe, Stephen set sail for California by way of Panama on Nov. 13, 1849, arriving at San Francisco Dec. 28 of the same year. Freed at last from the family leading-strings, Field now found himself in an environment which was a stimulus to self-assertion in the highest degree. Besides his legal training he possessed good health, moral and physical courage, and a mind which was healthily responsive to its tangible surroundings. The experiences of this period are recounted in his *Reminiscences of Early Days in California,* which he dictated in 1877. The book evinces devotion to the fact and energy of purpose, as well as some appreciation of humorous situations.

Field landed with ten dollars in his pocket, of which seven were spent in getting his two trunks ashore. The cost of living soon forced him to repair to a settlement on the Sacramento, later named Marysville, which was at the center of the gold-mining region. The day he arrived he purchased—on paper—sixty-five town lots, and a few days later instigated the organization of a local government, he himself being elected alcalde. In this capacity he enforced a stern justice, and order reigned. His fees of office, receipts as attorney, and investments brought him a quick prosperity, which was presently shattered, however, in consequence of his falling out with the newly appointed state judge for the district, one Turner. In the course of this absurd feud Field was disbarred, reinstated, disbarred again, sent to jail for contempt of court, heavily fined, and his life threatened; while on his own part, following the advice of a member of the state supreme court, he purchased a brace of pistols and acquired the subtle art of shooting from the pocket.

In the autumn of 1850 Field was elected to the state legislature. He promptly introduced and procured the passage of an act reorganizing the state judiciary, whereby his enemy Turner was relegated to a desolate region in the northern section of the state. A friend of Turner next challenged Field to a duel, but when Field accepted, backed down and apologized. Later Field became similarly involved with Turner's successor, Barbour. Barbour, too, challenged, was accepted, and withdrew.

Field's chief constructive work in the legislature was the drafting of civil and criminal practise acts for the state. While based in large measure on his brother's codes, they embodied many changes in deference to local conditions and habits, as well as to Spanish legal ideas. One feature of the Civil Practise Act was the famous section 621, which ordered the courts in cases involving mining claims to admit proof of miners' customs. Noteworthy, too, were the provisions in the act for liberal exemptions of debtors' property from forced sale. Field himself owed some eighteen thousand dollars at this time, on which he was paying interest at the rate of ten per cent. per month.

Disappointed in his further political ambitions, Field returned to Marysville and a lucrative practise of the law. On Sept. 2, 1857, he was elected to the state supreme court. The important litigation of the period concerned titles to land and the subjacent minerals. By the treaty of 1848 the United States had confirmed "existing grants." What, however, purported to be existing grants were often forged, while authentic grants frequently overlapped. Proof of authenticity, furthermore, was difficult on account of the chaotic state of the Mexican archives. Nor was it settled to what extent such grants should be construed by common law ideas and to what extent by Spanish-Mexican ideas. Previous to Field's accession the court had won small confidence in its handling of these complex questions. Its membership had fluctuated violently; it had repeatedly overruled itself; and some of the judges had proved corrupt. Field's leadership, both on score of learning and of native ability, was promptly conceded by his colleagues. Of deliberate and announced purpose, he couched his decisions in broad terms in order to head off future litigation. Some of his rulings provoked violent criticism; and that in the so-called "City Slip Cases" (16 *Cal.,* 591), in which he appears to have gone out of his way to upset earlier decisions, became a political issue. In his handling of squatters' rights, on the other hand, of the rights of mortgagors, and of the question of title to minerals, he manifested a healthy pragmatism in discarding common law notions; while in *ex parte Newman* (9 *Cal.,* 502), in dissenting from a decision pronouncing void a Sunday closing act, he asserted broadly the power of the legislature "to legislate for the good order, peace, welfare, and happiness of society," and to adopt special measures for the protection of labor. On the United States Supreme Court his numerous dissents were usually on the other side of such questions.

Upon the outbreak of the Civil War, Field as a Buchanan Democrat instantly aligned himself with the pro-Union party which kept California in the Union. Although the United States Supreme Court was at this time in confessed need of a member acquainted with the land and mining cases coming to it from the Pacific Coast, it was not until Mar. 1, 1863, that Congress finally authorized the new justiceship and attendant circuit judgeship. On the urgent suggestion of the congressional delegations of California and Oregon, Field was promptly nominated to the post, and unanimously confirmed, Mar. 10, 1863. The same summer, while presiding over the new United States circuit court at San Francisco, he delivered, in the case of *United States* vs. *Greathouse* (26 *Fed.*, 18, no. 15,254), a noteworthy charge on the subject of treason under the Constitution. He took his seat in the Supreme Court the first Monday of the ensuing December.

Few more convinced doctrinaires in constitutional exegesis have ever sat on the supreme bench than Field. The practical spirit of accommodation to tangible fact characteristic of many of his opinions as state judge seems to have taken wing. The reason is, no doubt, that when brought into contact with problems of constitutional construction, he was thrown back upon a set of ideas with which his mind had become thoroughly imbued in his early youth. From the point of view thus supplied, the Constitution was the perfect code which took account of all relevant facts from the beginning, and in the interpretation of its lucid phraseology it was impossible for loyal intention and good will to go far astray.

Field's theory of the relation of the national government and the states was the dualistic one of the Jacksonian, ante-bellum court: "a national government for national purposes, local governments for local purposes," and each "sovereign" within its assigned sphere, so that neither was dependent upon or subordinate to the other in any degree, nor, indeed, capable of clashing with it so long as the powers of each were properly defined. To this statement there was one seeming exception, for it was the rôle of the judicial branch of the national government to draw the line between the national and state spheres of action. The exception was, however, only apparent, for the Court acted merely in a *judicial* capacity and was therefore the mere mouthpiece of the Constitution. Confronting his theory of the nature of the federal system was his doctrine of natural rights. This, too, was a boyhood inheritance; but the recrudescence of the doctrine at this period was due partly to the contemporary discussion of freedmen's rights, partly to the individualistic preachments of the then dominant "classical school" of political economy, and partly, in Field's own case, to his Western experience.

The question naturally arises of the entire compatibility of the two outstanding elements of Field's constitutional creed. There was a time when he urged that the national government should be recognized as the guarantor of the sum total of human rights, on the basis of the contention that the term "privileges and immunities of citizens of the United States," as used in section one of the Fourteenth Amendment, comprised the fundamental rights of citizenship in all free governments (16 *Wallace*, 36); and this in the face of Justice Miller's cogent warning that such a construction of the phrase in question would entirely subvert the federal system. A doctrinaire, in other words, is not necessarily a good logician. It should be added that Field's habitually positive manner of expression was very likely to lead him into a statement of principles which conflicted with other principles which he accepted with equal fervor but which were not at the moment relevant to the problem before the Court.

The following cases in which Field spoke for the Court are especially worthy of note: the Test Oath Cases (4 *Wallace*, 277, and 333); *Paul* vs. *Virginia* (8 *Wallace*, 168); *The Daniel Ball* (10 *Wallace*, 557); Tarbles' Case (13 *Wallace*, 397); State Tax on Foreign-held Bonds (15 *Wallace*, 300); *Pennoyer* vs. *Neff* (95 *U. S.*, 714); *Escanaba Bridge & Transportation Company* vs. *Chicago* (107 *U. S.*, 678); *Barbier* vs. *Connelly* (113 *U. S.*, 27); *Gloucester Ferry Company* vs. *Pennsylvania* (114 *U. S.*, 196); and *Chae Chan Ping* vs. *United States* (130 *U. S.*, 600). In the Test Oath Cases he scandalized radical Republican opinion by joining forces with the ante-bellum judges against the other Lincoln appointees. Many of the other cases represent early formulations of important principles later further developed by the Court. In *Chae Chan Ping* vs. *United States* we find him, in contradiction of previously expressed views, invoking in support of the right of the national government to exclude aliens, its prerogative as the government of a sovereign nation. But his most characteristic opinions were dissenting opinions. Those in volume 100 of the *United States Reports* run to over eighty vehement pages and ring the changes on the doctrine of the duality of the federal system. They were ineffectual. His dissents in the Slaughterhouse Cases (16 *Wallace*, 36, 83) and in *Munn* vs. *Illinois* (94 *U. S.*, 113, 136) were, on the contrary, contributions of the utmost importance to the later development of constitutional law. The former elaborates the interpretation of the "privileges and immunities" clause of the Fourteenth Amendment which was mentioned above, and which is to-day, so far as the property and ancillary rights are concerned, incorporated in the Court's version by the "due process of law" clause of the same amendment. The latter offers, in relation to the power of government to regulate prices, a distinction between "property devoted to a public use" and "property merely affected with a public interest," which seems also, recently, to have been ratified by the Court (see *Wolff Packing Company* vs. *Court of Industrial Relations, 262 U. S.,* 522). To the end Field repelled the proposition that Congress could validly give paper money the quality of legal tender (110 *U. S.,* 421, 451), resisted the creation of special administrative agencies for the handling of deportation cases (149 *U. S.,* 698, 744), and joined enthusiastically in tearing down the powers of the original Interstate Commerce Commission. His last considerable opinion was his dissent in *Brown* vs. *Walker* (161 *U. S.,* 591, 628), where he gives the constitutional immunity of witnesses fantastic scope. Meantime, in his concurring opinion in the first Income Tax Case (157 *U. S.,* 429, 586), he had delivered himself of an aggrieved warning against "class legislation." "The present assault on capital," he predicted, was "but the stepping-stone" to "a war of the poor against the rich" (p. 607).

The most dramatic chapter of Field's judicial career is that comprising his work as presiding judge in his home circuit. In the Chinese Immigrant Case (3 *Sawyer,* 144) and the famous Queue Case (5 *Sawyer,* 552), he boldly defied local sentiment on the Chinese question, and in the Sharon will litigation he met fearlessly the threat of assassination. A will filed by one Althea Hill was found to be a forgery. Later Miss Hill's attorney, David S. Terry, who had been an associate of Field's on the California supreme court, married his client. On account of their outrageous conduct in court, Terry and Miss Hill were held for contempt in the term of 1888. Terry, who was already known as the assassin of Senator David S. Broderick [*q.v.*], now proclaimed his intention of shooting Field if the latter returned to California in the summer of 1889. Field returned none the less, although with a guard whose protection he had reluctantly consented to accept. The outcome of the matter was the shooting of Terry himself by this guard in a dining car at Lathrop, Cal., on the morning of Aug. 14, 1889, as Terry approached Field with the apparent intention of assaulting him. The episode, which is related in his *Annoyances of My Judicial Career* (printed and paged with the 1893 edition of his *Reminiscences of Early Days*), led to the celebrated case of *in re Neagle* (135 *U. S.,* 1), the Court's opinion in which, by Justice Miller, marks a wide departure from Field's dualistic theory of the Union.

Field was married June 2, 1859. His bride was Virginia Swearingen of San Francisco; no children were born to them. In 1870 he purchased for his permanent home in Washington, a section of the Old Capitol at the corner of A and First Sts., N. E. Here, in a spacious library, he spent his mornings from seven to eleven-thirty in methodical labor. At eleven-thirty he went to Court. The late afternoon he spent in recreation, and his evenings in society, of which he was extremely fond. One of his closest friends was Justice Miller, who was his antithesis in temperament and his frequent antagonist on the bench. Field was one of the avowedly Democratic members of the Electoral Commission of 1877, and his opinion in the Florida Case is the most effective presentation of the Democratic contention that the Commission was duty-bound to go into the merits of each case on the question of fraud. Partly because of this, his name was occasionally mentioned for the Democratic nomination in 1880, and again in 1884; but the hostility of the Democratic machine of his own state, due to the decisions just mentioned in support of the constitutional rights of Chinese, prevented his candidacy from making much headway. Upon Cleveland's election the latter year Field set about to prevent his enemies from gathering any of the spoils of victory and was successful in this enterprise for some months (Swisher, *post*). Later, however, when Cleveland appointed Fuller to the chief-justiceship, a post to which Field himself aspired, a coolness developed between the President and the Justice. It would seem that Mrs. Field's social ambitions were reflected in her husband's political ambitions (*Ibid.*). In 1890 Field was chosen by his brethren to be the Court's spokesman at the celebration in New York of its first centenary. His address on that occasion is an informing confession of constitutional faith (134 *U. S.,* App.).

To judge from his portraits, Field must have appeared to his contemporaries the very embodiment of judicial dignity. His bald and lofty dome, his broad brow and dark eyes, his long straight nose and flowing beard, endowed him with a truly patriarchal aspect. He was of better than average stature, and of great dignity of carriage, despite a slight lameness from an injury to one of his knees incurred while he was a law student in his brother's office.

Field had the misfortune to tarry on the bench over long. In the 1895 term he spoke for the Court in only four brief opinions and in the 1896 term he delivered no opinions. Eventually Justice Harlan was designated by the other justices to convey a hint to Justice Field that he should resign (C. E. Hughes, *The Supreme Court of the United States,* 1928, 75–76). Field himself had been of a committee which had waited on Justice Grier years earlier on a like errand. In April 1897 he did resign, the resignation to take effect the following Dec. 1, a stipulation which enabled him to exceed Marshall's incumbency by two months! The letter which he sent his associates on the occasion of his retirement (168 *U. S.,* App.) recalls with obvious pride that he was the last of Lincoln's appointees, that as state judge and justice of the Supreme Court he had rounded out forty years of judicial service, and that first and last he had prepared some 1,042 opinions, 620 of them on the Supreme Court. He survived his retirement a little over a year.

[H. M. Field, *Record of the Family of the Late Rev. David Dudley Field* (1880); F. C. Pierce, *Field Geneal.* (1901); S. J. Field's own *Reminiscences; Some Account of the Work of Stephen J. Field* (1881; 1895), ed. by C. F. Black with an introductory sketch by John Norton Pomeroy; J. N. Pomeroy, Jr., and Horace Stern in *Great Am. Lawyers,* vol. VII (1909), ed. by W. D. Lewis; G. C. Gorham, *Biog. Notice of Stephen J. Field* (1892); 8–22 *California Reports*; 68–168 *U. S. Reports*; Carl B. Swisher, *Stephen J. Field, Craftsman of the Law* (in press, 1930); obituaries in *Boston Transcript* and *Washington Post,* Apr. 10, 1899.] E. S. C.

FIELD, THOMAS WARREN (1821–Nov. 25, 1881), author, born in Onondaga Hill near Syracuse, N. Y., was the son of a small tradesman. After a brief education in the elementary schools he became a teacher; in the long career that followed he "was everything by starts, and nothing long." He moved to New York City in 1844, where he became an engineer. After a time in business as a florist he moved to the village of Williamsburgh (now in Brooklyn), N. Y., and did surveying and school-teaching. On May 14, 1849, he was made the principal of Public School No. 18 on Mauger St., Brooklyn. Through fortunate investments in real estate he acquired wealth and considerable property, especially in Bushwick Avenue where he established a nursery which he called "Weirfield" in honor of his first wife, Charlotte E. Weir. His income enabled him to retire and devote himself to fruit culture. He had previously published, in 1848, a thin volume of verse, *The Minstrel Pilgrim,* greatly influenced by Shelley and the romantics. In 1858 he published a manual on *Pear Culture.* Field became a member of the Board of Education in 1854 and served for twenty-one years. From 1865 to 1873 he was an assessor and from 1873 until the time of his death he was superintendent of public instruction in Brooklyn. His avocation was scholarship: in 1865 he edited Alexander Garden's *Anecdotes of the American Revolution* and in 1869 he edited for the Long Island Historical Society a collection of original documents on the battle of Long Island (published as Vol. II of the Society's *Memoirs*), to which he contributed an introduction of more than three hundred pages. Other volumes which he issued were *Historic and Antiquarian Scenes in Brooklyn and its Vicinity* (1868); an edition of the *Relation of Alvar Nuñez Cabeça de Vaca* (1871); and *The Schoolmistress in History, Poetry and Romance* (1874). For many years Field had been collecting books dealing with American Indians. In 1873 he published a catalogue of his library: *An Essay Towards an Indian Bibliography,* which listed 1,708 items and contained critical notes distinguished alike for their delightful spirit and for their erudition. In 1875, because of a decline in real-estate values and because of legal expenses incurred in a scandal that time has effectively obscured, he was forced to sell his library. With the *Essay* as a basis a *Catalogue* was compiled, listing 2,663 items and containing the original notes by Field and many additions by his friend, Joseph Sabin. The sale by auction brought more than $13,500. After the death of his first wife, Field married Helen Tuttle, who was killed in an accident on the Hudson River Railroad on the day of her wedding. His third wife, Emiline Van Siclen, he divorced in 1874 after she had become involved with Thomas Kinsella, the editor of the *Brooklyn Daily Eagle.* Alice E. Martin, whom he married in 1876, survived him.

[*American Bibliopolist,* June 1875; N. Y. *Evening Post,* May 21, 1875; J. G. Shea in *N. Y. Tribune,* May 24 and 26, 1875; *Brooklyn Eagle,* Nov. 25, 1881; *N. Y. Times, N. Y. Sun,* and *N. Y. Tribune,* Nov. 26, 1881; private information.] F. M—n.

FIELD, WALBRIDGE ABNER (Apr. 26, 1833–July 15, 1899), jurist, was a descendant of John Field, an English astronomer, through his great-grandson Thomas Field of Yorkshire, who, *c.* 1667, settled in Providence, R. I. Through his grandmother, Elizabeth Williams, wife of Pardon Field of Chester, Vt., Walbridge A. Field was also a lineal descendant of Roger Williams [*q.v.*]. The eldest child of Abner Field, a merchant and banker of Chester and Springfield, Windsor County, Vt., who married on Feb. 16, 1832, Louisa, daughter of David Griswold, he was born at Springfield, where his youth was spent, his primary education being received in the common schools. Continuing his studies successively at the Perkinsville Academy, the Springfield Wesleyan Seminary, and Kimball Union Academy, Meriden, N. H., in September 1851 he entered Dartmouth College, where "he held through his whole course the standard of absolute perfection, a rank touched by only two other men in the history of the college—Rufus Choate and Professor Putnam" (Noble, *post*, p. 68). After his graduation in 1855 he remained at Dartmouth for two years as tutor in Latin, Greek, and mathematics. He then commenced the study of law in Boston under Harvey Jewell, but returned to Dartmouth in 1859, teaching mathematics for two terms, after which he attended the Harvard Law School, and was admitted to the Suffolk County bar May 12, 1860. Commencing practise in Boston in association with Jewell, he took an active interest in municipal affairs, was a member of the Boston School Board in 1863 and 1864, and served in the Common Council, 1865–67. At the same time his legal ability was recognized and in July 1865 he became assistant United States district attorney for Massachusetts under Richard Henry Dana, an office which he continued to hold until his appointment in 1869 as assistant to E. Rockwell Hoar, the attorney-general of the United States, and consequent removal to Washington, D. C. A year later he resigned, returning to Boston to resume private practise in partnership with Jewell and W. Gaston. The firm enjoyed a high reputation and an influential clientele, which brought them important corporation business and litigation. Field possessed none of the qualifications of a successful jury lawyer, but his infinite capacity for research was utilized in the preparation of trial briefs, and he appeared to great advantage in appellate court work, where his sound knowledge of law, impressive presentation of facts, and a singular clarity of argument always carried weight. In 1876 he was the Republican candidate for the representation of the 3rd Massachusetts district in the Forty-fifth Congress and served till Mar. 28, 1878, when, his election having been contested, the House awarded the seat to his Democratic opponent. In the same year he was elected to the Forty-sixth Congress. He served his full term, but a political career had no attraction for him and he declined a renomination. He was appointed associate judge of the supreme judicial court of Massachusetts by Gov. Long on Feb. 21, 1881. Possessing all the attributes of judicial strength—wide grasp of principles, mastery of procedure, sound common sense, and patience—he commanded the respect of the profession and the confidence of his colleagues, and his promotion to the chief justiceship by Gov. Brackett, Sept, 4, 1890, met with unqualified approval. His tenure of judicial office, extending over eighteen years, was not marked by decisions of outstanding interest and he was not called upon to solve any unusual problems involving important legal principles, but his written opinions—over eight hundred in number and distinguished for their terse language and rare literary excellence—uniformly displayed a complete comprehension of all the relevant facts and legal points involved and an almost mathematical precision of reasoning. Not brilliant, but an eminently sane and accurate thinker, he had no patience with extreme views or eccentric natures. He was twice married: on Oct. 4, 1869, to Eliza Ellen, daughter of William McLoon of Rockland, Me., who died Mar. 8, 1877; and on Oct. 31, 1882, to Frances Eaton, daughter of Nathan Allen Farwell of Rockland.

[F. C. Pierce, *Field Geneal.* (1901), which contains (II, 919) an extended biography; John Noble, "Memoir of Walbridge A. Field" in *Proc. Mass. Hist. Soc.*, 2 ser. XIX (1905), 61 ff.; E. P. Scales, *Class of 1855 of Dartmouth Coll.* (1885), p. 17; *Biog. Dir. Am. Cong.* (1928); Conrad Reno, *Memoirs of the Judiciary and Bar of New England* (1900), p. 5; 174 *Mass. Reports*, 591; *Tributes of the Bar and of the Supreme Judicial Court of the Commonwealth to the Memory of Walbridge Abner Field* (1905), which reprints some of the preceding material; obituary notices in *Boston Sunday Jour.*, July 16, 1899; *Boston Advertiser* and *Boston Transcript*, July 17, 1899.]

H. W. H. K.

FIELDS, ANNIE ADAMS (June 6, 1834–Jan. 5, 1915), author and wife of James T. Fields [*q.v.*], was born in Boston, the daughter of Dr. Zabdiel Boylston Adams, a well-known physician, and Sarah May (Holland) Adams. She was a descendant on her father's side of Henry Adams, of Braintree, who settled in New England in 1633. She was one of a large family, and was educated at home and in the school kept by George B. Emerson [*q.v.*]. In 1854, at the age of twenty, she became the second wife of James T. Fields, the publisher, who was seventeen years older than she. Writing just before the marriage, Fields asked Miss Mitford, "Have you room in your heart for one more American? Her name is Annie Adams, and I have known her from childhood, and have held her on my knee many and many a time." Mrs. Fields spoke of her wedding as sweeping her "suddenly out upon a tide more swift and strong and all-enfolding than her imagination had foretold." It was not long before the "exquisite eager young woman," endowed with most of the social graces, had established a kind of salon in her home at 148 Charles St. Her husband's wide acquaintance with writers brought many distinguished people to his study, where they were held by his wife's beauty and charm. Over a long course of years she formed intimate friendships with Hawthorne, Whittier, Lowell, George William Curtis, Harriet Beecher Stowe, Holmes, Agassiz, Lydia Maria Child, and Henry James, as well as Thackeray, Dickens, and Landor. She traveled extensively with her husband, sometimes abroad and later on his lecture trips through the United States. She was of great assistance to him in his work, relieving him of responsibilities to which he was too busy to attend. After his death, in 1881, the Fields house still continued to be a social center for literary people in Boston. Mrs. Fields herself had unusual literary gifts and was the author of several volumes. *Under the Olive* (1881), her first book, was followed by *How to Help the Poor* (1883). Her *James T. Fields, Biographical Notes and Personal Sketches* (1881), was an interesting tribute to her husband. *Whittier, Notes of His Life and of His Friendships,* appeared in 1893, shortly after that poet's death. Other volumes by her are: *A Shelf of Old Books* (1894); *The Singing Shepherd and Other Poems* (1895); *Authors and Friends* (1896); *The Life and Letters of Harriet Beecher Stowe* (1897); and *Letters of Sarah Orne Jewett* (1911). For many years she kept a diary, begun in 1863 and maintained regularly until 1876, after which date it was written only intermittently. Many magazine articles also appeared from her pen during her lifetime. She died in the midst of the World War, having outlived most of her contemporaries.

[M. A. De W. Howe, *Memories of a Hostess, A Chronicle of Eminent Friendships Drawn Chiefly from the Diaries of Mrs. James T. Fields* (1922); Henry James, *The American Scene* (1907) and "Mr. and Mrs. James T. Fields," *Atlantic Monthly,* July 1915; *Boston Transcript,* Jan. 5, 6, 1915.] C. M. F.

FIELDS, JAMES THOMAS (Dec. 31, 1817–Apr. 24, 1881), author and publisher, was born in Portsmouth, N. H., the son of a shipmaster who died at sea when James was only four years old, leaving a widow and two small sons. The boy, who had bookish tendencies, was educated in the local public schools, but spent much of his time reading in the Portsmouth Athenæum, where he developed a taste for good literature. At the age of fourteen, feeling obliged to help support his family, he went to Boston as clerk in a bookstore, where he soon, according to Mrs. Fields, displayed an uncanny gift of predicting what kind of volume a customer was likely to want. Such was his enterprise that he was made, at twenty-one, a junior partner in the publishing house of Ticknor, Reed & Fields, of which he was later the head, the firm being known, after Reed's retirement in 1854, as Ticknor & Fields. In business Fields was orderly and methodical, and thoroughly understood both the financial and literary sides of his occupation. He had an amazing capacity for making and retaining friends. Reserved and shy at meeting strangers, he was exuberant and jovial with his intimates. His even temper, his hospitality, his chivalry, and his sympathy were his outstanding characteristics. In 1847, 1851, 1859, and 1869 he visited Europe, making the acquaintance of many notable writers, and he was early a member of the famous Saturday Club.

When, in 1859, the *Atlantic Monthly* came into the hands of Ticknor & Fields, Lowell was still the editor, but he resigned in May 1861, and Fields took his place, holding the position until 1870. Because of his extensive literary acquaintance and sound critical acumen, he made an admirable editor, and the periodical flourished under his management. He was able to secure the best contemporary writers as contributors, and it was not long before he was acknowledged as a patron of letters. He was given the degree of LL.D. by Dartmouth in 1867. In 1870 he withdrew from active business with a comfortable fortune. After his retirement, although his health was supposed to be impaired, he became a successful popular lecturer, making frequent tours of the larger cities. Like Dickens, whom he emulated, he had a gift for entertaining audiences, mainly by putting them at once in a personal relationship with himself. At one period he had twenty-seven topics upon which he was prepared to speak.

He was also something of a figure in literature. In his eighteenth year he read the anniversary poem before the Boston Mercantile Library Association, and in 1849 he published a volume of *Poems* (reprinted in 1854), followed by *A Few Verses for a Few Friends* in 1858. His *Yesterdays with Authors* (1872), containing sketches, largely reminiscent, of Thackeray, Hawthorne, Dickens, Wordsworth, and Miss Mitford, ran through many editions and is still sold and read. Other works of his are: *Hawthorne* (1876), *In and Out of Doors with Charles Dickens* (1876), and *Underbrush* (1877), a collection of articles on various subjects. In conjunction with the critic, Edwin P. Whipple, he edited the *Family Library of British Poetry* (1878). In 1881, just before his death, *Ballads and Other Verses,* containing many poems from his earlier volumes, was issued.

As a young man, Fields was betrothed to Mary Willard, eldest daughter of Simon and Mary (Adams) Willard, but she died before they could be married. In 1850 he married her younger sister, Eliza Josephine Willard, but she lived only a short time. Fields then took for his second wife, in 1854, her cousin, Annie Adams, a most attractive woman who became a personage in Boston society [see Annie Adams Fields]. They had no children. He died at his house on Charles

St., Boston, from angina pectoris, after a long period of illness. In reviewing his life, the *Boston Transcript* (Apr. 25, 1881) said of him rightly: "He has been from early manhood an educator of the public, and never stooped to vitiate the popular taste."

[Mrs. Fields's *Jas. T. Fields, Biog. Notes and Personal Sketches* (1881) is rich in material. See also E. P. Whipple, "Recollections of James T. Fields," *Atlantic Monthly*, Aug. 1881; Henry James, "Mr. and Mrs. James T. Fields," *Atlantic Monthly*, July 1915; M. A. de W. Howe, *The Atlantic Monthly and its Makers* (1919), and sketch in E. W. Emerson, *The Early Years of the Saturday Club* (1918). There is an excellent obituary in the *Boston Transcript*, Apr. 25, 1881.] C. M. F.

FILLEBROWN, THOMAS (Jan. 13, 1836–Jan. 22, 1908), dentist, author, educator, a son of James Bowdoin and Almira (Butler) Fillebrown of Winthrop, Me., received his early education in the Winthrop public school, and Towle Academy, and the Maine Wesleyan Seminary, from which he graduated in 1859. After serving a term as a teacher in the public school of his native town, he began the study of dentistry with his father. He became a member of the dental firm of Strout & Fillebrown at Lewiston, Me., but shortly afterward established an independent practise at Portland. When the dental department of the Harvard University Medical School was established in 1867, Fillebrown entered its first class, and received the dental degree of D.M.D., in 1869. He served as one of the instructors of that institution until 1883, and as its professor of operative dentistry and oral surgery for the next twenty-one years. In 1883, he received the degree of M.D., from the medical school of Bowdoin College.

From 1869 until shortly before his death Fillebrown practised dentistry in Boston, and became one of the leading authorities of his day on the use of cohesive gold-foil for filling teeth. He was also known as a skilful oral surgeon. Beginning in 1873, he contributed a number of articles to dental journals on operative dentistry, oral surgery, hypnosis as an anesthetic, and the physiology of vocalism. In 1889 he published *A Text-book of Operative Dentistry*, which was a standard work on the subject for many years. He was a teacher of ability and a fluent public speaker, who took a prominent part in dental association work, and he was an active member of several medical societies, including the American Medical Association. He was instrumental in bringing about the consolidation of the American Dental Association and the Southern Dental Association, which merged in 1897 as the National (later the American) Dental Association, with Fillebrown as its first president. From 1871 to 1874 he was president of the Harvard Dental Alumni Association. He was also a member of the Massachusetts Society of the Sons of the American Revolution. He died in his seventy-third year and was interred at Portland, Me. His life was devoted to his family and his profession, and his influence as a dental teacher and writer was far-reaching. On Sept. 2, 1861, he married Helen Dalton of Kent's Hill, Me. They had three daughters and two sons.

[C. B. Fillebrown, *Geneal. of the Fillebrown Family* (1910); *Dental Cosmos*, Mar. 1908; B. L. Thorpe in the *Hist. of Dental Surgery*, edited by C. R. K. Koch, vol. III (1910); *Index of the Periodical Dental Literature* for 1839–95 (4 vols., 1923–27); *Gen. Cat. of Bowdoin Coll.* (1912); *Boston Transcript*, Mar. 23, 1908.] L. P. B.

FILLMORE, JOHN COMFORT (Feb. 4, 1843–Aug. 14, 1898), musician, theorist, was born on a farm near Franklin, New London County, Conn., the son of John L. and Mary Ann (Palmer) Fillmore. Though there is no record of his early training, it is certain that he entered Oberlin from New Lyme, Ohio, in 1862 and was graduated in 1865. There was as yet no music department at Oberlin College, but music instruction was provided for those desiring it, and Fillmore studied organ, and probably piano, under George W. Steele. He had evidently decided upon a musical career during his college course, for after his graduation he went to Leipzig where he studied under Moritz Hauptmann, Ernst Richter, and Benjamin Papperitz, who were eminent theorists as well as fine organists. During 1867–68 he was instructor in instrumental music at Oberlin. In 1868 he became professor of music at Ripon College, Wisconsin, remaining until 1878, when he accepted a similar position in the Milwaukee College for Women. In 1884 he founded the Milwaukee Music School and was its director until 1895 when he accepted a call to Pomona College, Claremont, Cal. He held this position until his death, which occurred at Taftville, Conn., within six miles of his birthplace. He was survived by his wife, Eliza Hill Fillmore, and two sons.

Fillmore was an important figure in his time, and was keenly interested in placing music in the college curriculum. As early as 1883 he was known as an important theorist. He also became interested in the music of the American Indian and spent much time among various tribes, writing down their tribal calls, ceremonial songs, and weird rhythms. As an authority on Indian music he was closely associated with Alice Fletcher [*q.v.*] and Francis La Flesche and collaborated with them in writing *A Study of Omaha Indian Music* (1893) and several magazine articles.

He was an enthusiastic and an inspiring teacher, whose genial disposition won him many friends, especially in his own profession. His appearance was not prepossessing, partly because of his long reddish beard and florid complexion. He is known as the author of: *Pianoforte Music: Its History, with Biographical Sketches . . . of its Greatest Masters* (1883); *New Lessons in Harmony* (1887); *Lessons in Musical History* (1888); *On the Value of Certain Modern Theories,* of von Ottingen and Riemann (1887); and as the translator of Riemann's *Klavierschule* and *Natur der Harmonik.*

[W. S. B. Mathews, *One Hundred Years of Music in America* (1889); *Oberlin Coll. Hist. Cat. 1833–1908*; Theodore Baker, *Biog. Dict. of Musicians* (1900); newspaper clippings; and information as to certain facts from Fillmore's son, Thomas Fillmore, and Clarence S. Brigham of the American Antiquarian Society.]

F. L. G. C.

FILLMORE, MILLARD (Jan. 7, 1800–Mar. 8, 1874), thirteenth president of the United States, was the oldest son and second child of Nathaniel and Phoebe (Millard) Fillmore, who about 1798 emigrated from Bennington, Vt., to Locke, Cayuga County, N. Y., where Millard was born. The Fillmore family had resided in New England for several generations. John Fillmore (or Phillmore), "mariner," of Ipswich, Mass., who purchased an estate in Beverly, Mass., in 1704, was the first known ancestor in America. The Fillmores had acquired neither prominence nor wealth in their New England residence, and the younger pioneer family in New York suffered the privations and hardships common to the frontier. Equally typical of the frontier of the early nineteenth century were Millard's youthful experiences. He worked on his father's farm, tried his hand as an apprentice at the clothier's trade, and attended school at none too frequent intervals until the age of eighteen, when he began to read law in the office of a Cayuga County judge. When the family moved to East Aurora, near Buffalo, young Fillmore continued his law study, teaching school meanwhile to make ends meet, until in 1823 he was admitted to the bar of Erie County. He opened a law office in East Aurora and remained there till 1830, when he moved his practise to Buffalo, henceforth his home. He had already become active in politics. In 1828 he met Thurlow Weed, with whose support he was elected to the legislature of New York in that year as an Anti-Mason. The close association with Weed endured for twenty years. When Weed, discarding the original principles of the Anti-Masonic party, undertook to lead it into the coalition against Jackson in 1834, Fillmore followed him, thus becoming a Whig (Charles McCarthy, "The Anti-Masonic Party," *Annual Report of the American Historical Association,* 1902, vol. I). Meanwhile he had served three terms in the state legislature and in 1832 had been elected to Congress. He did not stand for reëlection in 1834, but in 1836 was again elected and served thereafter for three consecutive terms, declining renomination in 1842. In Congress he was a Clay Whig, though with a healthy degree of independence, as when he refused to join Clay's fight for the reëstablishment of a national bank. He rose rapidly into prominence in the party, and when the election of 1840 gave the Whigs a majority in the House of Representatives, Fillmore became chairman of the ways and means committee and in that capacity took a leading part in framing the tariff of 1842, which was in harmony with his belief in protection.

Fillmore was put forward by his friends for the vice-presidential nomination in 1844, and when he failed to secure that, was nominated for governor of New York against Silas Wright, the Democratic candidate. His defeat and that of Clay at the head of the national ticket he attributed to "the Abolitionists and foreign Catholics" (Severance, *post,* II, 268). Three years later he was elected comptroller of the State of New York, but after holding that office little over a year (Jan. 1, 1848–Feb. 20, 1849) he resigned in order to take up his duties as vice-president of the United States. He owed his nomination for that office in part to the influence of the Clay following, who, angered at the choice of Zachary Taylor for first place on the ticket, refused to accept Abbot Lawrence, the Massachusetts cotton manufacturer, as the nominee for vice-president, declaring they would not "have cotton at both ends of the ticket" (*Autobiography of Thurlow Weed,* 1883, p. 585). Discovery by Southern Democrats of a letter written ten years before in which Fillmore had expressed mild anti-slavery views gave some embarrassment to his Southern friends but did not prevent the triumphant election of the Whig ticket (Severance, *post,* II, 174, 281–82; U. B. Phillips, "The Correspondence of Robert Toombs, Alexander H. Stephens, and Howell Cobb," *Annual Report of the American Historical Association,* 1911, II, 128).

Shortly after Fillmore's inauguration as vice-president there occurred a break in the cordial relations which he had long maintained with Thurlow Weed and with William H. Seward, now a senator from New York. The loss of these political friends was to some extent compensated for by a reconciliation with Daniel Webster, with whom an unfortunate misunderstanding had arisen several years before (DeA. S. Alexander, *Political History of the State of New York,* II, 1906, 37–38, 79–80; Severance, *post,* II, 274–75). Soon after the election Fillmore had written to a friend: "I regard this election as putting an end to all ideas of disunion. It raises up a national party, occupying a middle ground, and leaves the fanatics and disunionists, North and South, without the hope of destroying the fair fabric of our Constitution" (Severance, *post,* II, 286). How far this estimate was from the truth was revealed when Congress convened in December 1849, and proslavery and anti-slavery men fought bitterly over the various aspects of the slavery question. Over the angry debate in the Senate Fillmore, as vice-president, presided with firmness, fairness, and good humor, but no amount of mere suavity could permanently help the situation. When Clay, in the Senate, proposed his well-known measures of compromise, President Taylor, Louisiana slave-owner though he was, opposed any yielding to the South and in that course had the support of Seward and the more extreme anti-slavery Whigs, while Webster threw his whole influence on the side of Clay and compromise (H. D. Foster, "Webster's Seventh of March Speech and the Secession Movement, 1850," in the *American Historical Review,* January 1922). Fillmore was apparently slow in determining his stand. In April he said in a private letter that he approved the President's plan (*Quarterly Publications of the Historical and Philosophical Society of Ohio,* April-June 1918, p. 43). Early in July, however, according to his own statement, he had a conversation with President Taylor in which he plainly intimated that if he were called upon to give a deciding vote on the bill embodying the various compromise measures, he should vote in favor of it (Severance, *post,* II, 321–24). The sudden death of Taylor, July 9, 1850, called Fillmore to the presidency. Taylor's cabinet resigned, and Fillmore's prompt appointment of Webster as secretary of state and Crittenden of Kentucky as attorney-general demonstrated unmistakably his alliance with the moderate Whigs who favored compromise. In a message to Congress, Aug. 6, 1850, Fillmore urged the propriety and expediency of indemnifying Texas for the surrender of her claim upon New Mexico, adding a plea for the adjustment of all the outstanding controversies. That this message was decisive in persuading Congress to take the first step toward compromise was the opinion of a hostile observer, Salmon P. Chase, who wrote that it won six New England votes in the Senate (*Annual Report of the American Historical Association,* 1902, II, 217). Clay's composite compromise bill—the "omnibus bill"—could not pass Congress as a whole, but it was separated into its component parts, and one by one these passed House and Senate and became law, receiving their most consistent support from Northern Democrats and Southern Whigs. A vital part of the compromise, from the Southern point of view, was the Fugitive-Slave Law, and this too Fillmore signed (Sept. 18, 1850), thereby drawing from the Abolitionists a torrent of abuse such as that which had greeted Webster's "Seventh of March" speech. Unmoved by such criticism, the President spared no effort in enforcing the unpopular law.

The compromise measures of 1850 were the outstanding domestic achievement of Fillmore's administration. Though his part in them damned him with the Abolitionist clique (and hence with historians for the next half-century), it appears now as the work of a cool-headed conservative who, like Lincoln later, placed the preservation of the Union above any specific settlement of the slavery question.

In the contest for the Whig nomination for the presidency in 1852, Fillmore had the cordial support of the Southern Whigs. The New Englanders generally supported Webster, while the Seward Whigs, the extreme anti-slavery group, favored Gen. Winfield Scott. Could the friends of Webster and Fillmore have combined on either, they could have controlled the convention, but when this proved impossible, the nomination went to Scott. The ensuing campaign was the last in which the Whig party took active part. With the rise of the Republican party many conservative Whigs, both North and South, found a temporary abiding place in the American or Know-Nothing party, which, originating as a Protestant-nativist body, now appeared to many a means of uniting North and South on an issue not connected with the slavery question. When Fillmore, in 1856, was tendered the presidential nomination by this party, he accepted it and in his campaign stressed the value of the Union and the dangers of sectionalism. In the election he ran a poor third to Buchanan and Frémont. Always for conciliation rather than coercion, Fillmore opposed the Lincoln administration in its conduct of the Civil War and in the election of 1864 supported McClellan (Severance, *post,* II, 431–35). During Reconstruction his sympathies were with President Johnson (*Ibid.,* II, 106–10).

Fillmore was the first chancellor of the University of Buffalo, one of the founders of the

Buffalo Historical Society and its first president, a founder of the Buffalo General Hospital, and an interested worker in various other civic, educational, and philanthropic enterprises. A proffered degree of D.C.L., from Oxford University he declined in 1855 on the ground that he possessed no literary or scientific attainments to justify his accepting it (*Grosvenor Library Bulletin,* December 1920). While such of Fillmore's letters and speeches as are preserved make him seem singularly colorless, his contemporaries have left testimony to his impressive presence, kindly blue eyes, and gracious manner, all of which seem borne out by his portraits. "He was strictly temperate, industrious, orderly," writes the historian Rhodes, "and his integrity was above reproach." He was twice married: to Abigail Powers of Moravia, N. Y., on Feb. 5, 1826, and after her death in 1853, to Caroline Carmichael McIntosh, a widow of Albany, on Feb. 10, 1858.

[The best existing biography of Fillmore is W. E. Griffis, *Millard Fillmore* (1915). Many of his letters, speeches, and public papers were edited by Frank H. Severance and published under the title "Millard Fillmore Papers," vols. I and II, in the *Buffalo Hist. Soc. Pubs.,* vols. X and XI (1907), and a large collection of manuscript letters received by Fillmore, 1849–53, is in the possession of the Buffalo Hist. Soc. See also *N. Y. Tribune,* Mar. 9, 1874.] J. W. P.

FILSON, JOHN (*c.* 1747–October 1788), explorer, historian, has a unique and permanent place in Kentucky history, because he wrote the first history of Kentucky, made the first map of it, and published (and in all probability wrote) the first account of Daniel Boone. Very little is known of him before he appeared in Kentucky in 1783. The date of his birth is unknown, although the year 1747 seems the most probable conjecture (R. T. Durrett, *post*). He was born on a farm in the township of East Fallowfield in southeastern Pennsylvania. His father was Davison Filson, and his grandfather John Filson, an emigrant from England (Jillson, *post,* p. 139). Nothing is known of his early life in Pennsylvania beyond the fact that he was taught by the Rev. Samuel Finley, later president of the College of New Jersey. No record of Revolutionary service has been found, but his coming to Kentucky was apparently for the purpose of taking up land on certain Virginia military warrants which had come into his possession. He seems to have spent his first year in Kentucky teaching a private school in Lexington (G. W. Ranck, *History of Lexington, Kentucky,* 1872, p. 96). It is evident from his writings that he was much better educated than most Kentuckians of the time. He secured several thousand acres of land in Kentucky, and as a sequel to this achievement wrote his *Discovery, Settlement, and Present State of Kentucke* (1784, 1st ed.), with the purpose, as it appears from internal evidence, of attracting immigrants and thereby increasing the value of land. The descriptive portions of this famous book are vivid and attractive; the historical setting is inadequate, misleading, and often quite inaccurate. An appendix to the book contains "The Adventures of Col. Daniel Boon." The "Boon" is written in the first person but it certainly was not written by Boone himself. There has been much dispute over the authorship but its stilted, pedantic style clearly indicates that it was written by Filson himself. It contains many mistakes of fact as well as continual sins of diction, but it established the reputation of Boone and, more than anything else, was responsible for his place in Western history. The book also contained a map of Kentucky—the first and a remarkably accurate one. The map was published separately, also, and among his contemporaries Filson seems to have been better known for this map than for anything else. There being no printing press in Kentucky at the time, Filson journeyed to Wilmington, Del., and had his book published there in 1784. The map was published at Philadelphia in the same year. The *Discovery* was very popular, running through several editions in London and Paris the next few years (Lewis Collins, *History of Kentucky,* 1874, II, 183).

Filson returned to Kentucky in 1785 and took up his residence at Louisville where he engaged in business as a fur trader. Restlessness and land hunger led him into several trips to the Illinois country in 1785 and 1786. In the latter year he once more visited his home in Pennsylvania, returning to Kentucky in 1787. After this he appears twice in Kentucky affairs: on January 19, 1788, when he published in the new-born *Kentucky Gazette,* at Lexington, a prospectus of a school which he proposed to establish there, and in August of the same year when he published in the same paper a prospectus of a town he and some associates proposed to lay out in Ohio on a tract of land bought from Judge Symmes. This town, first named Losantiville, is the present Cincinnati. While surveying with Symmes up the Little Miami, Filson was killed by an Indian in October 1788 (*The Correspondence of John Cleves Symmes,* 1926, ed. by B. W. Bond, p. 46).

[All that is known of John Filson, or can reasonably be conjectured, is contained in R. T. Durrett, *John Filson, the First Historian of Ky., An Account of his Life and Writings,* Filson Club Pubs., no. 1 (1884). John Wilson Townsend, *Kentuckians in Hist. and Lit.* (1907), has a sketch of him. P. Lee Phillips, *The First*

Map of Ky. (1908), deals with him as a cartographer. W. R. Jillson has published (1929) a facsimile reproduction of the original Wilmington edition of *Filson's Kentucke,* with a sketch of his life and a full bibliography. The Filson Club Pubs., no. 35. Manuscript journals and diaries of his trips to Vincennes are in the Draper Manuscripts of the State Hist. Soc. at Madison, Wis.]

R. S. C—l.

FINCH, FRANCIS MILES (June 9, 1827–July 31, 1907), jurist and poet, was born in Ithaca, N. Y., of New England stock, the son of Miles Finch, a merchant, and his wife, Tryphena Farling. He was educated at Ithaca Academy and at Yale College (A.B., 1849), where he clearly showed literary proclivities, as editor of the *Yale Literary Magazine,* winner of a prize for English composition, and class poet. Both before and after graduation he wrote many college songs which are still sung. Returning to Ithaca he read law, was admitted to the bar, and gained repute as a practising lawyer. On May 25, 1853, he married Elizabeth, daughter of Robert May Brooke of Philadelphia. During Grant's first administration he served as a district collector of internal revenue. He took up the central work of his life in 1880, being twice appointed to fill vacancies and then elected for the full term of fourteen years as associate judge of the New York court of appeals. Sitting regularly until Dec. 31, 1895, he wrote more than 750 opinions, widely known for their knowledge of the law, clear and cogent reasoning, and unusual refinement and grace of style.

A close friend of Ezra Cornell and Andrew D. White [*qq.v.*], he was active in the founding of Cornell University, as a trustee and especially as a legal counselor. After serving as a non-resident lecturer in the Cornell Law School from its foundation in 1887, and as dean from 1892, upon his retirement from the court of appeals he became professor of the history and evolution of law and taught actively until four years before his death. In 1899 he was chosen president of the New York State Bar Association.

Though a successful lawyer and a distinguished judge he is most widely known as a poet. He wrote verses infrequently but continuously from his college days to the end of his life. For the centennial celebration of the Linonian Society of Yale, 1853, he wrote as an "episode" in a longer poem his well-known "Nathan Hale." On hearing that the women of Columbus, Miss., had "strewn flowers alike on the graves of the Confederate and of the National soldiers," he composed his famous poem, "The Blue and the Gray," first published in the *Atlantic Monthly* (September 1867) and soon printed and recited everywhere in both North and South. It is probably not an exaggeration to say "that all the orations and sermons and appeals for the restoration of kindly feeling between the two sections have been exceeded in real effect upon the national heart by this simple poem" (White, *post,* p. vi). Most of his poems were written and printed occasionally; at the end of his life he made a collection, published posthumously as *The Blue and the Gray and Other Verses* (1909), containing a preface in which he refers to his verses as "only incidents along the line of a busy and laborious life." He perhaps accounts for both his small output of verse and its sincerity in his reply on being offered at the opening of Cornell University a professorship of rhetoric and literature: "My whole life as a lawyer has been a battle against literary longings. I have kept the most earnest part of my nature in chains. I fear I have done it so long as to make full liberty dangerous to me" (*Ibid.,* p. vii). Notable among his addresses are: *The Life and Services of Ezra Cornell* (1887) and *Chief Justice John Marshall, Marshall Day Address* (1901).

In his appearance kindliness shone through a look of judicial austerity, and the many tributes paid him at the celebration of his seventy-fifth birthday emphasized not merely his eminence as a judge but his personal charm and genius for friendship. He was perhaps happiest in his large library and in his garden overlooking Cayuga Lake. "So strong was his love of home life that nothing could induce him to visit other lands, or even to travel far in his own" (A. D. White, as cited).

[A. P. Stokes, *Memorials of Eminent Yale Men* (2 vols., 1914); *Yale Univ. Obit. Record,* 5 ser. (1910); *Exercises in Honor of Francis Miles Finch* (Cornell Univ., 1902), in which E. W. Huffcut notes Finch's most important legal opinions; *Cornell Alumni News,* Aug. 1907; E. H. Woodruff, in *Cornell Law Quart.,* vol. IV, nos. 3 and 4; Andrew Dickson White, *Autobiography* (1905) and "Preliminary Word" in *The Blue and the Gray and Other Verses*; *Proc. N. Y. State Bar Asso.,* 1908; obituaries in *Evening Post* (N. Y.), July 31, 1907; *N. Y. Times, N. Y. Tribune,* Aug. 1, 1907.]

F. C. P.

FINCK, HENRY THEOPHILUS (Sept. 22, 1854–Oct. 1, 1926), author and music critic, was one of the most versatile and gifted members of his profession. He was born in Bethel, Shelby County, Mo., the fourth of five children of Henry Conrad Finck and Beatrice (Fink) Finck. Both parents came from towns adjacent to Stuttgart in Würtemberg, but were unrelated and unacquainted until they met in Bethel. The father was an apothecary, which occupation included the duties of a physician, and was also an excellent violinist. He took time to give his children musical instruction in piano and stringed instruments, and when Henry was seven, gave the boy a 'cello. The mother died when Henry was still a child. The father then removed to Oregon where his children would be beyond the turmoil of the Civil War. Instead of taking the route by covered wagon, he chose the long but less tedious route by way of Panama. The family settled at Aurora Mills whither a colony formerly situated at Bethel had removed. There Henry attended the school conducted by Christopher Wolf, an ex-clergyman and graduate of Göttingen. When Wolf found that young Finck had the dream of entering Harvard, and was trying to educate himself in the classics, he offered gratuitous instruction. Wolf's thorough training enabled Finck to read any Greek or Latin writer at sight, which so impressed the Harvard examiners that they admitted him to sophomore standing in the classics. Each year he secured a scholarship of three or four hundred dollars, and was graduated with the highest honors in the class of 1876. Though he majored in philosophy and psychology, he also studied harmony and musical history under J. K. Paine. His skill on the 'cello furnished opportunity for playing with Paine, also for practising in the secret hours of the night on the piano in the basement of University Hall. Though disappointed at his failure to obtain the Parker fellowship, with which he expected to continue his studies in philosophy and psychology in European universities, he decided that he must in some way secure means to go to Bayreuth, to attend the first Wagner Festival. His funds were depleted, but he borrowed five hundred dollars from an uncle, and through his friends John Fiske and W. D. Howells he arranged to write several articles for the New York *World,* and one for the *Atlantic Monthly.* At the close of the festival, he wintered in Munich, hearing much music and eking out an existence by tutoring. Upon his father's earnest solicitations that he begin his life work, he returned to America, but went to Cambridge as a resident graduate in philosophy and won the Harris scholarship of six hundred dollars annually. This gave him three more years in Berlin, Vienna, and Heidelberg (1878–81). He relaxed his efforts for a doctorate, and while he wrote many philosophical articles for the *Nation* and the *World,* he was hearing much music and unconsciously preparing himself for the work of a music critic.

In August 1881 Finck became music critic for the *Nation,* continuing in this capacity until his retirement in May 1924. For forty years, beginning in 1882, he gave annually twenty-four lectures on musical history at Mrs. Thurber's Conservatory. In 1890 he married Abbie Helen Cushman, a pupil of Joseffy, who shared her husband's tastes and assisted him in his writing. So successfully did she adopt his literary style that their best friends could not detect the authorship of her contributions to his works. At the close of his active career he had written seventeen books. During the last two years of his life he wrote his memoirs under the title of *My Adventures in the Golden Age of Music,* the final revision of which was completed almost on the eve of his death. He was authoritative and entertaining, whether he wrote on humorous, musical, or seriously philosophical topics, and he was an equally interesting lecturer. He probably knew intimately a larger number of famous artists than any other critic, even among those of whom he had not written in laudatory terms. He was the champion of Wagner, Chopin, Schumann, Liszt, Grieg, Tschaikovsky, Dvořák and MacDowell, but he had an unmitigated contempt for Brahms. He was in some ways a militant critic, with strong convictions, yet he was open-minded toward the best in the newer music. It is characteristic of the man that, although his real middle name was Gottlob (after his mother's distinguished brother, Prof. Fink of Tübingen University), Finck considered the name too Teutonic, and since there was no exact English equivalent, translated it as faithfully as possible to Theophilus.

His psychological and anthropological works are: *Romantic Love and Personal Beauty* (1887), his first book; *Primitive Love and Love Stories* (1899); *Food and Flavor* (1913); *Girth Control* (1923); and *Gardening with Brains* (1922). His musical works include: *Chopin and Other Musical Essays* (1889); *Wagner and His Works* (2 vols., 1893), translated into German; *Pictorial Wagner* (1899); *Anton Seidl, a Memorial by his Friends* (1899); *Songs and Song-Writers* (1900); *Grieg and his Music* (1909); *Success in Music* (1909); *Massenet and his Operas* (1910); *Richard Strauss* (1917); and the following edited collections: *Fifty Master Songs* (1902); *Fifty Schubert Songs* (1903); *Fifty Grieg Songs* (1909); *One Hundred Songs by Ten Composers* (1917); and *Musical Laughs* (1924). He also wrote three books of travel: *The Pacific Coast Scenic Tour* (1890); *Spain and Morocco* (1891); and *Lotus Time in Japan* (1895).

[*My Adventures in the Golden Age of Music* (1926), which gives family history; Louis C. Elson, *Hist. of Am. Music* (1904); Theodore Baker, *A Biog. Dict. of Musicians* (1900); N. Y. *Evening Post,* May 31, 1924, Oct. 2, 1926; *N. Y. Times,* Oct. 2, 1926; and newspaper clippings.]

F. L. G. C.

FINDLAY, JAMES (Oct. 12, 1770–Dec. 28, 1835), soldier, congressman, was born in Franklin County, Pa., the third son of Samuel and Jane (Smith) Findlay. In 1793 he and his wife, Jane Irwin, removed from Pennsylvania to Virginia, thence to Kentucky, and ultimately settled in Cincinnati, Ohio. In his adopted state Findlay quickly rose to prominence. In 1798 he became a member of the first territorial legislative council and three years later was appointed the first receiver of public moneys in the newly established land office at Cincinnati. The following year he was appointed United States marshal for the District of Ohio, being the first to hold this office. He served two terms as mayor of Cincinnati, in 1805–06, and again in 1810–11. At the time of the Burr conspiracy (1806) he held the rank of brigadier-general in the state militia, and in company with Maj.-Gen. John S. Gano was ordered by Gov. Tiffin to take charge of the military operations at Cincinnati and help in suppressing the proposed expedition from Blennerhasset's Island. At the outbreak of the War of 1812 Gen. Findlay was placed in command of the 2nd Ohio Volunteer Infantry with the rank of colonel in the regular army. He was present in Detroit at the surrender of Gen. William Hull, which he vigorously denounced (J. G. Forbes, *Report of the Trial of Brigadier-Gen. Hull,* 1814, pp. 29, 45, *passim*). In the family correspondence there is a letter which states that Gen. Findlay was urged "to put Hull in irons, but he would not, as he said there is [was] no precedent for it" (Goss, *post,* III, 27). He was commended for his services at Detroit by Gen. Hull and was promoted to the rank of major-general in the state militia in which capacity he served for many years. In June 1812 he began the erection of Fort Findlay, which was named in his honor, and upon the site of this fort the present town of Findlay, in Hancock County, was founded. In 1824 he was elected to Congress as a Jacksonian Democrat from the 1st district, composed of Hamilton and Clermont counties. He continued to represent this district until 1833 when he was succeeded by Robert T. Lytle. The year following his retirement from Congress he was nominated on the Democratic ticket for governor but was defeated by Robert Lucas. A lawyer by profession, an active officer in the state militia, one of the proprietors of the *Liberty Hall and Cincinnati Gazette,* and a partner in the Cincinnati Bell, Brass & Iron Foundry, his interests touched many aspects of the life of his local community. As a stanch supporter of President Jackson's policies, he was an influential Ohio Democrat. His sterling integrity, unquestioned patriotism, and warm hospitality gained for him the respect of his fellow citizens. Although he had a natural reserve in manner which gave strangers the impression of austerity, "he was the soul of kindness and geniality."

[C. F. Goss, *Cincinnati, the Queen City* (4 vols., 1912); E. O. Randall and D. J. Ryan, *Hist. of Ohio,* III (1912); "Ohio in the War of 1812" in the *Ohio Archæol. and Hist. Quart.,* July 1919; "Selections from the Torrence Papers," in the *Quart. Pubs. of the Hist. and Philos. Soc. of Ohio,* July 1906, Jan.–Mar. 1907, July–Sept. 1908, July–Sept. 1909, Apr.–June 1911, July–Sept. 1911; G. A. Worth, "Recollections of Cincinnati, 1817–1821," in the *Quart. Pubs. of the Hist. and Philos. Soc. of Ohio,* Apr.–July 1916; J. Burnet, *Notes on the Early Settlement of the Northwest* (1847); H. Howe, *Hist. Colls. of Ohio* (3 vols., 1891).]
R. C. M.

FINDLEY, WILLIAM (1741–Apr. 5, 1821), congressman, was a descendant of one of the signers of the Solemn League and Covenant in Scotland. His grandparents emigrated to North Ireland during the persecution of the Presbyterians by the last two Stuart kings. In their adopted country, where William Findley was born, the members of the family played a conspicuous part in the thrilling events of the time. While the formal education of William was limited, he had a strong intellect, which he cultivated by reading. He landed in America in 1763 and established himself in a flourishing Scotch-Irish settlement near Waynesboro, in what is now Franklin County, Pa. For several years he worked at the weaver's trade, to which he had been apprenticed in Ireland, and at the same time he taught school for a number of terms. After his marriage in 1769, he purchased a farm and settled thereon. He identified himself with the interests of the colonists in the long controversy with the mother country and vigorously espoused their cause. He became a member of the first committee of observation from his county, and upon the opening of hostilities he entered the army and soon rose to the rank of captain. Near the close of the war he moved beyond the mountains into Westmoreland County to a farm near the present site of Latrobe. He was elected to the council of censors, on which he served from 1783 to 1790, and held various other public offices, among which were those of assemblyman, state supreme executive councilman, and delegate to the state constitutional convention of 1789–90.

Findley displayed early in life that ability for leadership which won for him a long and creditable career in public service. Indeed, he was a consummate politician. Because of his large personal acquaintance and his inherent ability he became a formidable factor in shaping public opinion not only in western Pennsylvania but throughout the state. An Anti-Federalist, he vigorously opposed the ratification of the Federal Constitution and later Hamilton's financial measures. In 1791 he was elected to Congress, where he served continuously until 1817 with the exception of four years, from 1799 to 1803, when he served in the state Senate. Although openly hostile to the Federalist legislative program, he was consulted frequently by Washington and his cabinet concerning frontier problems. Especially significant was Findley's persistent opposition to the early practise of referring practically all questions of importance to the heads of departments for their consideration. It was upon a recommendation made by him that the first standing committee, that of ways and means, was appointed.

Findley was one of the prominent men identified with the Whiskey Insurrection of 1794. Feeling as he did that the tax on whiskey was exorbitant and unjust, he encouraged open resistance to the government at first. Later, however, he counseled moderation and obedience to the law and displayed real statesmanship in working for a compromise. In 1796 he published a *History of the Insurrection in the Four Western Counties of Pennsylvania,* in which he attempted to vindicate his own position as well as to furnish an acceptable apology for those who participated actively in the insurrection. Throughout his public career Findley was a faithful guardian of the interests of the frontiersmen, who were his associates and his friends.

[R. M. Ewing, "Life and Times of Wm. Findley," *Western Pa. Hist. Mag.,* Oct. 1919; G. D. Albert, *Hist. of the County of Westmoreland, Pa.* (1882); J. H. Campbell, *Hist. of the Friendly Sons of St. Patrick and of the Hibernian Soc. 1771–1892* (1892); W. C. Armor, *Scotch-Irish Bibliog. of Pa.* (1906); *Pa. Mag. of Hist. and Biog.,* vol. V (1881); *Democratic Press* (Phila.), Apr. 11, 1821.] A. E. M.

FINE, HENRY BURCHARD (Sept. 14, 1858–Dec. 22, 1928), mathematician, was born at Chambersburg, Pa., the son of Lambert Suydam Fine, a Presbyterian minister, and Mary Ely Burchard. The father died in 1869. His widow, after living for a time at Winona, Minn., removed to Princeton, N. J., in 1875. Her son Henry finished his preparation for college by private study and entered the College of New Jersey (now Princeton University), in 1876. He led his class for four years, and was graduated with first honors in 1880. At first he devoted himself to the study of the classical languages, but before graduation he turned to the study of mathematics. After spending a year as a fellow at Princeton in physics, he was made instructor in mathematics. He served in this capacity until granted leave of absence for study abroad. He spent a year and a half at Leipzig, under Felix Klein, received the doctor's degree from that University in 1885, and on his return to Princeton was made assistant professor of mathematics. In 1891 he was appointed to the Dod Professorship of Mathematics, and from that time on, until his death, he was either the virtual or the titular head of the department of mathematics.

Fine published a few original papers on the general topic of singularities of curves, but his real interest was in the exact logic of mathematics, and its presentation to students. He embodied his views as to how mathematics should be taught in several text-books: *The Number System of Algebra* (1891); a *College Algebra* (1905); *Coördinate Geometry,* with Henry Dallas Thompson (1909), and *Calculus* (1927). He was a member of the American Mathematical Society and served for a term (1911) as its president. He was also a member of the American Philosophical Society and of the Mathematical Association of America. He was an active member of the Princeton faculty and served on various committees. In 1903, when Woodrow Wilson was president of the university, he was appointed dean of the faculty, with oversight of the scholarship and discipline of the students. He introduced the policy of establishing rules laying down standards of scholarship which were reasonable and intelligible, and of enforcing these rules rigorously and almost automatically. This policy was justified by its results. In the controversies which raged during Wilson's administration on various questions of academic policy, he supported the president. After Wilson resigned the presidency in 1910, Fine was practically acting president under the nominal presidency of John A. Stewart, the senior member of the board of trustees, until John Grier Hibben was elected president in 1912. He then resigned his office as dean of the faculty.

In 1909 Fine was appointed dean of the scientific departments. He continued in this office until his death, and contributed greatly to the development of a broad and sound engineering curriculum, and to the strengthening of the scientific departments by the appointment of men of proved ability in research and by the acquisition of a considerable endowment for research. A large part of this endowment was given by his personal friends, as a token of their admiration and affection. His interests and activities were closely bounded by the academic life. When Woodrow Wilson became president of the United States he offered to send Fine as ambassador to Germany, and later offered him a place on the Federal Reserve Board. Both of these offers he declined. He was a member of the Presbyterian Church but took no part in church work. The only public office which he held was a membership on the board of education of Princeton Borough. He was married, Sept. 6, 1888, to Philena Fobes of Syracuse, N. Y., who died in April 1928. His eldest child, Capt. John Fine, died from an illness developed by his service at the front in the World War. An older daughter also died in her youth. A younger daughter survived him. His death resulted from the collision of a motor-car with the bicycle which he was riding.

[The catalogues of Princeton University; the *Princetonian*, and the *Princeton Alumni Weekly*, particularly that of Jan. 11, 1929; R. S. Baker, *Woodrow Wilson, Life and Letters*, vol. II (1927); *N. Y. Times*, Dec. 23 and 24, 1928.] W. F. M.

FINK, ALBERT (Oct. 27, 1827–Apr. 3, 1897), railroad engineer and operator, generally regarded as the father of railway economics and statistics in the United States, was born in Lauterbach, then located in the Grand Duchy of Hesse-Darmstadt, the son of Andres S. and Margaret (Jacob) Fink. He was educated at private and polytechnic schools at Darmstadt, being graduated in engineering and architecture in 1848. Unsympathetic with the forces that triumphed in the German revolution of that year, he emigrated to the United States in 1849, and entered the drafting office of the Baltimore & Ohio Railroad under Benjamin H. Latrobe [*q.v.*], chief engineer. He was soon placed in charge of design and erection of bridges, stations, and shops for the section of the railroad from Grafton to Moundsville, Va. (now W. Va.).

During this period he invented the bridge truss which bears his name, and which was first used in the bridge over the Monongahela at Fairmont, Va. (now W. Va.), in 1852, the three spans of 305 feet each comprising at the time the longest iron railroad bridge in the United States. He became section engineer and later division engineer, but left the Baltimore & Ohio in 1857 to become construction engineer of the Louisville & Nashville Railroad, with headquarters at Louisville, Ky. Here he planned and superintended the erection of a freight and passenger station, then turned his attention to bridging Green River, about seventy-four miles south of Louisville, an achievement that attracted much attention because of its engineering difficulties. The bridge was constructed over a wide gorge, at a considerable distance above water, and at an angle to the main direction of the stream. It was at the time the largest iron bridge on the continent of North America, except for the Victoria Bridge at Montreal.

At this same period Fink designed and constructed a new court-house for the city of Louisville. In 1859 he took charge of the machinery of the Louisville & Nashville Railroad, in addition to buildings and bridges, and in 1860 became chief engineer of that railroad. During the Civil War, much of the property of the Louisville & Nashville was destroyed, and it fell to him to carry out the work of reconstruction. At the end of the war, the railroad was in good physical condition, and found it comparatively easy to settle its accounts with the government, because of the intelligent and complete records which Fink had maintained. In 1865 he was promoted to general superintendent. During the succeeding ten years he rehabilitated the line, built up business-like relations with competing and connecting railroad companies, and as an engineer completed his crowning work, the bridge across the Ohio River at Louisville. The total length of the bridge was one mile, and the principal span of 400 feet over the Indiana channel of the river was the longest truss bridge in the world. Following the death of the president of the railroad in 1869, Fink was given wider powers through appointment as vice-president and general superintendent.

He now began in his annual reports to publish information as to the real cost of transportation. He analyzed and standardized freight rates, establishing them upon an accounting and statistical basis. He raised accounts and statistics to the level of a science—the economics of railway operation. His report of 1874, generally known as "The Fink Report on Cost of Transportation," is regarded as the foundation stone of American railway economics. At the time, this report was called "the fullest investigation into the cost of railroad transportation ever published in our country or language" (*Railway Gazette*, May 30, 1874). In addition, he took an active part in extending the Louisville & Nashville Railroad beyond Nashville as far as Montgomery, Ala., which involved large financing, partly negotiated in England. The wisdom of his financial measures, both in financing and in operation, was thoroughly tested during the panic of 1873, when the Louisville & Nashville was one of the few railroads which continued payment of interest on its funded debt, and escaped bankruptcy.

In 1875 he resigned, his intention being to retire from active life and engage in literary work on various railroad problems. This intention was frustrated by the offer of the executive directorate of the Southern Railway & Steamship Association, then recently formed, with principal offices in Atlanta, Ga. The railroads between 1870 and 1880 were engaged in considerable warfare among themselves, there being no effective regulation of rates or other railway practises, and the wiser heads among railway officials recognized the necessity of appointing a man of known ability and integrity to iron out their difficulties. In his two years as commissioner Fink undertook to eliminate, or at least to smooth down, the many points at which the twenty-five competitive Southern railways found themselves at loggerheads, and to give to the public a stabilized set of freight rates on which they could depend. He was successful in bringing a fair degree of order out of the existing chaos.

In 1877, he again decided to retire, but at the urgent request of the chief executives of the four trunk lines centering in New York City, he organized the Trunk Line Association in an effort to settle the disastrous rate war then in progress. He became its commissioner, with powers and duties similar to those he had held in Atlanta, and met with success summed up by Charles Francis Adams as follows: "It is safe to say that the greatest of all these combinations—that of the Trunk Lines—is held together only by the personal influence and the force of character of one man, its Commissioner" (quoted in *Transactions of the American Society of Civil Engineers,* XLI, 635). The Interstate Commerce Act of 1887, beginning the period of government regulation, made work of his type less vital, and this fact, together with his failing health, led him to retire from active work in 1889. The rest of his life he spent largely in his Kentucky home, devoting himself to study and research. He died at a sanitarium on the Hudson River in his seventieth year. During his young manhood Fink was married in Baltimore and after the death of his first wife he was married a second time, on Apr. 14, 1869, to Sarah Hunt of Louisville.

[Memoir in *Trans. Am. Soc. Civil Engineers,* XLI (1899), 626–38; "Albert Fink . . . A Bibliographical Memoir" (1927), and Chas. K. Needham, "The Life and Achievements of Albert Fink," read before the Filson Club, Louisville, Ky., in 1920, both MSS. in possession of the Bureau of Railway Economics, Washington, D. C.; J. G. Wilkes, "Albert Fink, Pioneer Railroader," *Louisville & Nashville Employees Mag.,* Aug. 1927; obituaries in *Railroad Gazette,* Apr. 9, 1897, and *N. Y. Times,* Apr. 4, 1897.] J. H. P.

FINLAY, CARLOS JUAN (Dec. 3, 1833–Aug. 20, 1915), physician, was born in Camagüey, Cuba, to Dr. Edward Finlay, native of Scotland, and Isabel de Barrés, of French birth. His early education was obtained in France, mainly in the Lycée of Rouen. He graduated in medicine from the Jefferson Medical College, Philadelphia, in 1855 and from the University of Havana in 1857. His first venture in practise was in Lima, Peru, but after a few months he returned to Cuba. He spent the greater part of the years 1860–61 in Paris in postgraduate study. He practised for a time in Matanzas but practically all of his professional career was passed in Havana. Though a general practitioner he specialized to some extent in ophthalmology. In 1865 he presented a paper before the Havana Academy of Science in which he gave the result of seven years of observation upon the influence of atmospheric alkalinity upon the incidence of yellow fever. Then and for many years after he ascribed great etiological importance to the alkalinity of the air. There is no explanation for his reasons for abandoning this theory, but in 1881 before the same society he read a paper entitled *The Mosquito Hypothetically Considered as the Agent of Transmission of Yellow Fever.* This paper was received with utter indifference.

For the following twenty years he held to the advocacy of the mosquito theory, building up a good circumstantial case against the *Stegomyia,* though repeated efforts at producing the disease experimentally were futile. His arguments, together with the work of Ross and the Italians in demonstrating the conveyance of malaria by the mosquito, and the observations of Dr. Henry Rose Carter [*q.v.*] upon what he termed the "extrinsic incubation" of yellow fever, caused the Reed board in 1900 to concentrate on the mosquito theory of causation. At the outbreak of the Spanish-American war Finlay, then 65 years old, went to Washington and offered his services to the American government. He participated in the Santiago campaign and later was on duty in Havana. He was associated with Guiteras, Gorgas, and Albertini on the Army Yellow Fever Commission which passed judgment on the diagnosis of every suspected case of the disease. In 1902 the Cuban government appointed him chief health officer and president of the Superior Board of Health. In 1909 he was retired with a pension and an honorary title. The triumph of his views on yellow fever brought him many honors. In 1908 the French government made him an officer of the Legion of Honor, and in 1911 he was elected a corresponding member of the French Academy of Medicine. The Liverpool School of Tropical Medicine in 1901 granted him the Mary Kingsley medal. The Jefferson Medical College gave him the honorary degree of LL.D., and he was elected a fellow of the College of Physicians of Philadelphia. In 1903 he was elected president of the American Public Health Association, in which capacity he presided over the meeting held at Havana in 1905.

Finlay's character combined a keen mentality and a tireless persistence with the utmost geniality and graciousness of manner. Physically he was rather undersized and of a delicate constitution. An attack of chorea in his childhood left him with an impediment of speech which interfered much with his effectiveness as a public speaker. He was married on Oct. 16, 1865, in Havana to Adela Shine, a native of the Island of Trinidad. A son, Carlos Eduardo, followed his father in the practise of medicine in Havana.

[*Selected Papers of Dr. Carlos J. Finlay* (1912); Aristides Agramonte, "Dr. Carlos J. Finlay—a biographical Sketch," in *New Orleans Medic. and Surgic. Jour.* (July 1916), LXIX, 55–60, reprinted in *Sanidad y Beneficencia*, "Número Extraordinario en homenaje á la memoria del Dr. Carlos J. Finlay" (July–Aug. 1918); obituary notices in *N. Y. Times*, Aug. 21, 1915, *Bull. Pan. Am. Union*, Sept. 1915, *Am. Pub. Health Asso. Jour.*, Nov. 1915.]

J. M. P.

FINLAY, HUGH (*c.* 1731–Dec. 26, 1801), was born in Scotland and emigrated to Quebec shortly after the capitulation of the country to Gen. Amherst in 1760. He entered business as a merchant, and was appointed a justice of the peace, an office of great importance at a time when there was a mere handful of English people in the midst of a large French community. He had the valuable qualification of understanding and speaking the French language. When Benjamin Franklin, deputy of the postmaster-general of England, decided after the Treaty of Paris in 1763 to extend the limits of the Colonial Post-Office to include the newly acquired territory, he came to Quebec, opened post-offices in that town, at Three Rivers, and at Montreal, and placed the Canadian section under Finlay. In 1765 Finlay was appointed to a seat in the Governor's Council, and, being a public-spirited person, fell into the position of "general-utility" man for the government. Among the services which he undertook to manage was the control of the roads and the transportation system. His zeal in the public service having attracted attention, in 1772 he was appointed post-office surveyor or inspector. In this capacity he explored in 1773 the uninhabited country between Quebec and Falmouth, Me., to ascertain the practicability of a post-route between Canada and New England. The expedition was so successful that the governor of New Hampshire was induced to open a road along the Connecticut River, where connection could be made with the country on the watercourse of the St. Francis, which emptied into the St. Lawrence. On Oct. 2, 1773, Finlay set out from Falmouth on a more extended tour, embracing the whole postal system from Maine to Georgia. His report is a valuable survey of the condition of the country on the eve of the Revolution.

On his return to New York, he learned of Franklin's dismissal on Jan. 31, 1774, and of his own appointment on Feb. 25 as joint deputy postmaster-general with Thomas Foxcroft of Philadelphia. The recognition of the independence of the colonies, however, made a readjustment necessary, and in July 1784, Finlay was appointed deputy postmaster-general of Canada. In 1787, by direction of the governor-general, Finlay made a journey to Halifax, Nova Scotia, through a country in large part wilderness, and established a mail-route which passed through the principal settlements in the Maritime Provinces. On his return he was placed in charge of the whole postal service of British North America. In 1792 he concluded a convention with the postmaster-general of the United States, the chief object of which was to provide for the conveyance to and from New York of mails between Canada and Great Britain. In 1799 disaster fell upon him. Owing to defalcations on the part of a postmaster for whom he was responsible, Finlay was dismissed from his office as a defaulter. That he was not regarded as blameworthy by the governor-general or his associates in Quebec is shown by the fact that he retained all his provincial offices, including that of legislative councilor until his death.

[W. M. Smith, *Hist. of the Post Office in British North America, 1639–1870* (1920); F. H. Norton, ed., *Journal Kept by Hugh Finlay, Surveyor of the Post Roads on the Continent of North America, . . .* (1867); Ruth Lapham Butler, *Doctor Franklin, Postmaster General* (1928).]

W. S—h.

FINLEY, JAMES BRADLEY (July 1, 1781–Sept. 6, 1856), Methodist preacher, one of the most distinguished evangelical pioneers of the West, was born in North Carolina, the son of Robert W. and Rebecca (Bradley) Finley. His paternal grandfather was a Scotch settler in Pennsylvania; on his mother's side he was of Welsh and English descent. His father, first a Presbyterian then a Methodist minister, a man of restless, adventuresome spirit, was constantly on the move. Engaged in missionary work in the Carolinas and Georgia when James was born, he soon settled in Virginia, then crossed the mountains and established himself in Ohio, then removed to the cane-brakes of Kentucky, from which, turned out of house and home by land pirates, he migrated to Ohio again, settling near Chillicothe. As a result James grew up to be a typical backwoodsman, a man of stalwart frame, resourceful and courageous, versed in all the lore of the forests, intimately acquainted with the ways of wild beasts and Indians. His education was not neglected, however, for his father, who had conducted a school during his sojourn in Kentucky, gave him a good knowledge of the classics. To please his parents he also applied himself to the study of medicine, and being admitted to practise in 1800, in connection with his preceptor he visited and prescribed for the sick: but all the while his heart was in the forest. He finally decided to adopt a hunter's life, and having on Mar. 3, 1801, married Hannah Strane, chosen in part because he deemed her fitted to share such a career, he built a cabin in the wilderness three miles from any neighbor.

His conversion at the Cane Ridge camp-meeting in August 1801 eventually took him from his dogs and guns, though not altogether from the forest, and sent him in pursuit of souls. In 1810 he entered the Western Conference of the Methodist Church on trial and in 1812 was received in full connection. For seven years he traveled long and difficult circuits, his backwoodsman's training and understanding of the people proving most advantageous; for twenty-one years he was superintendent of extensive districts; for six, missionary among the Indians. In this capacity he shared with John Stewart the distinction of being father of the famous Wyandott Mission, the Indians showing him unusual respect and devotion. For three years he was chaplain to the convicts in the state penitentiary; for six he was pastor of churches; and for one, conference missionary. As an evangelist and organizer he had notable success. He was eight times elected to the General Conference, and at the 1844 session proposed and defended the resolution whereby Bishop Andrew [*q.v.*] was requested to desist from exercising his office, because of his connection with slavery.

His wide experience and observation, together with his habit of journalizing the principal happenings of his life, resulted in a number of publications which throw light on the conditions and events of pioneer days in Ohio. Among them are: *History of the Wyandott Mission at Upper Sandusky, Ohio* (1840); *Autobiography of Rev. James B. Finley; or Pioneer Life in the West* (1853), edited by W. P. Strickland; *Sketches of Western Methodism* (1855), edited by W. P. Strickland; *Life Among the Indians* (1857), edited by D. W. Clark. In his *Memorials of Prison Life* (1850), edited by B. F. Tefft, he describes "what I saw and heard and experienced during my first year as chaplain."

[Consult Finley's published works; also, *Minutes of the Annual Conferences of the M. E. Church for 1857*, p. 441; Abel Stevens, *Hist. of the M. E. Church in the U. S. A.*, vol. IV (1867); Wm. B. Sprague, *Annals Am. Pulpit*, VII (1860), p. 531; J. M. Buckley, *A Hist. of Methodism in the U. S.* (2 vols. 1897). *Selected Chapters from The Hist. of the Wyandott Mission*, ed. by R. T. Stevenson, was published in 1916.] H. E. S.

FINLEY, MARTHA FARQUHARSON (Apr. 26, 1828–Jan. 30, 1909), author, was born in Chillicothe, Ohio, the daughter of Dr. James Brown and Maria Theresa (Brown) Finley, who were first cousins. Both Finleys and Browns were of Scotch-Irish descent, natives of Pennsylvania. Martha Finley's grandfather, Gen. Samuel Finley, was a personal friend of Washington, a major in the Revolutionary army, and a general in the War of 1812, in which his son, her father, also fought. Farquharson, Gaelic for Finley, was sometimes used by Miss Finley as a pen name. She was educated in private schools in Philadelphia and in South Bend, Ind., where her father moved when she was a child. She lived there until she was about twenty-five, then went to New York and Philadelphia. She taught school for a time and in 1853–54 began writing newspaper stories and Sunday-school books, published by the Presbyterian Publication Committee. Soon her juvenile books of this type became so popular that she gave her whole time to writing them. In 1876 she visited Elkton, Md., the home of some of her relatives, and so liked the place that she settled there, in a spacious house with beautiful grounds. Here all of her later work was done and she continued to write almost to the end of her life, in spite of old age and poor health. She was of a social nature and gave much time to her many friends and to the activities of the Presbyterian Church. She died at her home in Elkton. Miss Finley produced altogether about a hundred volumes, nearly all juveniles, many of them in series. Her greatest popular success was the *Elsie* series, but the *Mildred* series, the Do Good Library, the Pewit's Nest Series, and the Finley Series (not juvenile) also had large sales. *Elsie Dinsmore* appeared in 1868. The good little girl there portrayed won such approval from parents and Sunday-school teachers that other *Elsie* books followed rapidly until by 1905 over twenty-five had been written and Elsie had become a grandmother. The *Mildred* series began in 1878 with *Mildred Keith* and extended to seven volumes by 1894. Typical of her Sunday-school books, outside these series, are: *Grandma Foster's Sunbeam, The Little Helper, Loitering Linus, Milly; or the Little Girl who Tried to Help Others and to do them Good* (all 1868), and *Willie Elton, the Little Boy Who Loved Jesus* (1864). She attempted several novels, among them *Wanted—a Pedigree* (1871), *Signing the Contract* (1879), and *The Thorn in the Nest* (1886), but their success was not striking. Miss Finley's books are among those which changing standards have thrown into the discard. Her Elsie and Mildred, once held up as examples by many parents and beloved by most children, are to-day considered abnormally docile and unpleasantly priggish. Their psychology is not that esteemed desirable for children, yet for many years Miss Finley held a leading place among writers of juvenile books.

[Warren S. Ely, *The Finleys of Bucks* (1902); *Who's Who in America*, 1908–09; Frances E. Willard and Mary A. Livermore, *Am. Women* (1897); Mildred Rutherford, *Am. Authors* (1894); Ruth Suckow, "Elsie Dinsmore: A Study in Perfection," *Bookman*, Oct. 1927; obituary in the *Baltimore Sun*, Jan. 31, 1909.]

S. G. B.

FINLEY, ROBERT (Feb. 15, 1772–Oct. 3, 1817), Presbyterian clergyman, educator, organizer of the American Colonization Society, was born in Princeton, N. J. His father, James, was a yarn merchant of Glasgow. With his wife, whose maiden name was Angres, he came to Princeton at the suggestion of his Old-Country friend, John Witherspoon, then president of the College of New Jersey. Here he engaged in weaving, and during the Revolution was a clothier to American troops. Robert, a scholarly, precocious youth, entered the College of New Jersey when he was eleven, graduating in 1787. He then engaged in teaching, first in the grammar school at Princeton, later in an academy at Allentown, N. J., and afterward in Charleston, S. C. In 1792, having decided to enter the ministry, he returned to Princeton, studied theology under Dr. Witherspoon, and also acted as tutor in the college. He was licensed to preach Sept. 16, 1794, and in April of the following year was called to the church at Basking Ridge, where he was ordained June 16, 1795. In May 1798 he married Esther Caldwell, daughter of the "soldier-parson," Rev. James Caldwell [*q.v.*].

For almost twenty-two years he served the church at Basking Ridge with great devotion and success, and in connection with his pastoral work conducted a school for boys which came to have the reputation of being one of the best in the country. For eleven years (1807–17) he was also a trustee of the College of New Jersey. In association with Rev. George S. Woodhull of Cranbury, N. J., he was responsible for the plan of Biblical instruction for the young by means of regular class work which was recommended to the churches by the General Assembly of May 1816. His interest in the welfare of the colored race led him in 1816 to be the prime mover in the organization of the American Colonization Society. The idea of colonization was by no means new and various influences were working toward the result that Finley achieved, but it fell to his lot to be the agency which finally effected it. Not very optimistic but determined, he went to Washington about the first of December 1816, and published a pamphlet *Thoughts on the Colonization of Free Blacks*, which attracted much attention. He called on President Madison, Henry Clay, and other prominent persons who gave him encouragement. His activities resulted in a meeting to consider his project, held Dec. 21, at which Clay presided. It was voted that a society be formed, and at an adjourned meeting, Dec. 28, the organization was formally effected. On Jan. 1, 1817, officers were elected, Hon. Bushrod Washington being chosen president and Finley one of the vice-presidents. He then returned to New Jersey and went to Trenton where after time spent in removing prejudices, he succeeded in having a state society formed auxiliary to the one established in Washington. In April 1817 he resigned his pastorate to become president of the University of Georgia. He removed with his family to Athens, Ga., in May, but during the summer while traveling about the state in the interests of the college he contracted a fever which cut short his career. Several of his sermons were published, one on the Baptism of John (1807), and *A Discourse on the Nature and Design, the Benefits and Proper Subjects of Baptism* (1808); also one on the death of Rev. William Boyd of Lamington (1807), and two in the *New Jersey Preacher* (1813).

[Isaac V. Brown, *Memoirs of the Rev. Robert Finley, D.D.* (1819), 2nd ed. enlarged (1857); Wm. B. Sprague, *Annals Am. Pulpit*, IV (1858); *Memorial of the Semi-Centennial Anniversary of the Am. Colonization Soc.* (1867); A. L. Hull, *A Hist. Sketch of the Univ. of Ga.* (1894); John F. Hageman, *Hist. of Princeton and Its Institutions* (2 vols., 1879); *Proc. N. J. Hist. Soc.*, 4 ser., VII (1922), 326; Archibald Alexander, *A Hist. of Colonization on the Western Coast of Africa* (1846); E. M. Coulter, *College Life in the Old South* (1928).]

H. E. S.

FINLEY, SAMUEL (1715–July 17, 1766), Presbyterian clergyman, president of the College of New Jersey from 1761 to 1766, was a Scotch-Irish immigrant who arrived in Philadelphia, Sept. 28, 1734. Like Gilbert Tennent [*q.v.*] whose friend and fellow worker he became, he was born in the County of Armagh, Ireland. When he arrived in Pennsylvania he had received a good education and was bent upon becoming a minister. He put himself under the care of the New Brunswick, N. J., Presbytery, and was probably a student for some years in William Tennent's Log College. On Aug. 5, 1740, he was licensed to preach, and on Oct. 13, 1742, he was ordained. At the time of his licensure the Great Awakening was under way and Finley followed Whitefield and Gilbert Tennent into New Jersey and carried on a notable evangelistic work in Deerfield, Greenwich, and Cape May. Later he preached for some months in Philadelphia. During this period he exhibited the acrimonious controversial spirit which accompanied the Awakening and joined in the arraignment of the "unconverted ministry." As early as Jan. 20, 1740/41, he delivered in Nottingham, Pa., a discourse of much severity, which was published under the title, *Christ Triumphing, and Satan Raging, a Sermon on Matth. XII. 28,* which was reprinted in Boston and Edinburgh, the latter edition with an indorsement by Whitefield, beginning: "The following sermon was written by a worthy friend of mine abroad." In 1743 in Cape May he had a public disputation of two days' duration with Rev. Abel Morgan on the subject of baptism, and in 1746 he published *A Charitable Plea for the Speechless; or, The Right of Believers' Infants to Baptism Vindicated.* Morgan put forth a rejoinder, and in 1748 Finley replied with *A Vindication of the Charitable Plea for the Speechless.* In 1743 also he published *Satan Stripp'd of His Angelic Robe . . . the Substance of Several Sermons Preach'd . . . January 1742–3, Shewing the Strength, Nature, and Symptoms of Delusion, with an Application to the Moravians*; and *Clear Light Put Out in Obscure Darkness: Being an Examination and Refutation of Mr. Thompson's Sermon, Entitled The Doctrine of Convictions Set in a Clear Light.* In August of this same contentious year, having received a call to Milford, Conn., he was sent thither by his presbytery with permission "to preach for other places thereabouts, when Providence may open a door for him." Invited to preach to the Second Society, New Haven, a "Separatist" congregation without legal standing, he was arrested while on his way to the meeting, and later expelled from the colony as a vagrant.

In June 1744 he became pastor of the church in Nottingham, Pa., often referred to as in Maryland since it was on the boundary line. Here he remained seventeen years, his reputation for ability and scholarship steadily increasing. In connection with his pastoral work, he conducted a school which became widely known, in which were trained such men as Benjamin and Jacob Rush, Ebenezer Hazard, and Col. John Bayard. A tradition that his scholars were systematically birched every Monday morning on general principles of discipline is probably unreliable, for whatever the spirit displayed in his controversial utterances, he was esteemed for his kindness and courtesy. Pupils of his describe him as "a man of small stature and of a round and ruddy countenance": remarkable "for sweetness of temper and politeness of behaviour." He seems to have carried on extensive correspondence with clergymen abroad and in 1763 received the degree of D.D. from the University of Glasgow, on recommendation, it is said, of Dr. Samuel Chandler. On May 31, 1761, he was unanimously elected president of the College of New Jersey, having already been an active trustee for ten years. His administration was a successful one, but was cut short by his early death. Among his published sermons not already mentioned are *The Approved Ministers of God,* ordination sermon of John Rodgers, Mar. 16, 1749; *The Curse of Meroz, or, The Danger of Neutrality in the Cause of God, and Our Country* (1757), preached during the French and Indian War, arraigning pacificism, and displaying the Scotch-Irish attitude in Pennsylvania as contrasted with the Quakers'; *Faithful Ministers, the Fathers of the Church* (1752), on the death of Rev. John Blair; *The Madness of Mankind* (1754); *The Power of Gospel Ministers* (1755); *The Disinterested and Devout Christian,* on the death of President Davies, preached May 28, 1761; and *The Successful Minister of Christ, Distinguished in Glory,* on the death of Gilbert Tennent, preached Sept. 2, 1764.

He was twice married; first to Sarah Hall, and in 1761 to Anne, daughter of Matthew Clarkson of New York. His death occurred in Philadelphia where he had gone for treatment, and he was buried in the Second Presbyterian Church there by the side of Gilbert Tennent, both bodies being later removed to the cemetery of that church.

[A. Alexander, *Biog. Sketches of the Founder and Principal Alumni of the Log College* (1845); Rich. Webster, *A Hist. of the Presbyt. Ch. in America* (1857); Wm. B. Sprague, *Annals of the Am. Pulpit,* vol. III (1858); John Maclean, *Hist. of the Coll. of N. J.* (1877); Thos. Murphey, *The Presbytery of the Log College* (1889); *Memorial Book of the Sesquicentennial Celebration of the Founding of the Coll. of N. J.* (1898).]

H. E. S.

FINN, FRANCIS JAMES (Oct. 4, 1859–Nov. 2, 1928), Jesuit, author, educator, created a Catholic juvenile literature in English. The son of John and Mary (Whyte) Finn, he was born in St. Louis, Mo. In 1876 he entered St. Louis University, and a year later joined the Society of Jesus, though poor health deferred the official date of entry until Mar. 24, 1879. From the Jesuit Novitiate at Florissant, Mo., he went in 1881 to St. Mary's College, Kansas, and thence, two years later, to the Jesuit house of philosophical and theological studies at Woodstock, Md. The continued delicacy of his health necessitated this somewhat irregular course, and delayed the completion of his training until 1894. Meanwhile he had been ordained a priest by Cardinal Gibbons (June 29, 1891), and had taught in St. Xavier's College, Cincinnati, and Marquette College, Milwaukee, Wis. His career is almost an index to the number of Jesuit institutions then existing. St. Mary's College, at that time an obscure and struggling preparatory school, furnished the young Jesuit professor with material which he developed into a series of stories for boys. *Percy Wynn* (1889) and *Tom Playfair* (1892) attained vast and almost immediate popularity, supplying American Catholic counterparts of the Tom Brown books. They blended pranks, fun, shrewd observation, idealism, and deft moral teaching. Though Finn could not keep to the level of these first stories, other books followed in rapid succession: *Harry Dee* (1893); *Claude Lightfoot* (1893); *Mostly Boys* (1897); *New Faces and Old* (1896); *Ada Merton* (1896); *Ethelred Preston* (1896); *That Football Game* (1897); *The Best Foot Forward* (1900); *His First and Last Appearance* (1900); *But Thy Love and Thy Grace* (1901); *The Haunt of the Fairies* (1906), a drama; *The Fairy of the Snows* (1913); *That Office Boy* (1915); *Cupid of Campion* (1916); *Lucky Bob* (1917); *His Luckiest Year* (1918); *Facing Danger* (1919); *Bobby in Movieland* (1921); *On the Run* (1922); *Lord Bountiful* (1923); *The Story of Jesus* (1924); *Sunshine and Freckles* (1925); and *Candles' Beams* (1927). Various Jesuit schools furnished the background for most of these stories, though several of them are not concerned with college life. Finn was appointed professor of literature and the classics in St. Xavier's College, Cincinnati, in 1897. Two years later, primarily because of ill health, he was relieved of teaching and assigned to the staff of St. Xavier's Church, in the same city. His chief duty became the direction of the parish school at 520 Sycamore St. Though he was constantly writing a book and had taken on added literary tasks—editing the *St. Xavier Calendar* and sponsoring the Little Flower Library—he devoted most of his energy to the school. This, frequented by children of twenty-one immigrant nationalities, became the first fee-less Catholic school in the United States, owing largely to the ability of its director in raising an endowment. Father Finn also encouraged frequent social gatherings at which Catholic young men and women might meet—a relatively novel idea in the nineties. He died in Cincinnati, Ohio. If he had lived a few months longer, he would have celebrated his fiftieth year as a Jesuit. His life spanned the period of the development of the Jesuit educational system in the United States, and he may fairly be said to have rendered it an incomparable service by making the boarding school idea appeal to thousands of boys. He is likewise considered an example of the priest in social work, interested less in the solution of a difficult social problem than in meeting an urgent immediate need.

[*Father Finn, S. J., the Story of His Life, Told by Himself* . . . (1929), edited by Daniel A. Lord; Records, Jesuit Novitiate, Florissant, Mo.; *America*, Nov. 17, 1928; the *Dial* (St. Mary's College, Kansas), December 1928; the *Commonweal*, Nov. 28, 1928; *The American Catholic Who's Who* (1911); *Cincinnati Enquirer*, Nov. 2, 1928.]

G. N. S.

FINN, HENRY JAMES WILLIAM (June 17, 1787–Jan. 13, 1840), actor, playwright, the son of George Finn, a retired officer of the British navy, and of his wife Elizabeth, was born at Sydney, Nova Scotia, and was reared in New York City. He was educated at Traphagen's Academy, Hackensack, and Finley's Latin School, Newark. If, as has been stated (Ireland, *post*, I, 332), he later attended Princeton, it is at least certain that he did not graduate. After completing his formal education, he studied law for two or three years in New York and then visited England. There he joined a band of strollers and worked up to the Haymarket Theatre, London, where he played small parts in 1811 and 1812 (John Genest, *Some Account of the English Stage*, 1832, vol. VIII, pp. 243, 316). His first American appearance of which a record is available occurred at Philadelphia in 1817 (Wood, *post*, p. 213). His New York début at the Park Theatre followed, Jan. 16, 1818, and throughout the rest of his life his New York engagements were numerous. In 1818 he was acting successfully in Savannah, Ga. Two years later, with I. K. Tefft, he edited the *Savannah Georgian*. Being both restless and versatile, Finn returned to England in 1821, devoting himself to miniature painting and provincial acting until he obtained a leading position at the Surrey Theatre, London. On Oct. 28, 1822, he became associated with the Federal Street Theatre, Boston (*Columbian Centinel*, Oct. 5 and 26, 1822). Here he at first essayed such parts as Hamlet, Othello, and Richard III, but finding Cooper, Forrest, and Kean in secure possession of the tragic rôles, he turned to eccentric comedy, in which he became one of the distinguished actors of the day. A melodrama by Finn, *Montgomery; or, the Falls of Montmorency* (1825), which was brought out at Boston, Feb. 21, 1825, and repeated four times during the rest of the season (*Boston Patriot and Mercantile Advertiser*, Feb. 21–Apr. 18, 1825), though a wretched piece of playmaking, provided its author with a good vehicle for his peculiar type of comic acting in the Yankee, Welcome Sobersides. At about the same time he became a partner of Thomas Kilner in the management of the Federal Street Theatre. When a rival house, the Tremont, was built in 1827, Finn hastened to England and brought back some excellent recruits. After two years of competition the rivals were forced to combine, but Finn, though withdrawing from management, remained with the company and continued to delight Boston audiences to the end of his life. He also made frequent starring trips through the country, especially the South, where he was an immense favorite. While returning to his home in Newport, R. I., from a Southern tour, he lost his life when the steamboat *Lexington* was burned in Long Island Sound. Theatrical benefits were held at Boston and New York for his family, which consisted of his wife Elizabeth, daughter of Snelling Powell of the Boston theatre, and several children. Aside from *Montgomery,* Finn's plays included *Removing the Deposits* (1835), a satire on President Jackson's financial policy, and *Casper Hauser; or, the Down Easter* (1835), both unpublished. In 1831 he brought out an *American Comic Annual,* in which he gave free rein to his incurable weakness for outrageous puns. His contemporaries were agreed that Finn honored the stage not only as a comic artist, but also as a witty, generous, and courteous gentleman.

[J. N. Ireland, *Records of N. Y. Stage* (2 vols., 1866–67); W. B. Wood, *Personal Recollections of the Stage* (1855); Sol (Solomon Franklin) Smith, *Theatrical Management in the West and South* (1868), pp. 76, 103, 109, 121, 153; N. M. Ludlow, *Dramatic Life as I Found It* (1880), pp. 474 ff.; W. W. Clapp, *A Record of the Boston Stage* (1853), *passim.* The date of Finn's birth and the names of his parents are taken from the records of the parish of St. George, Sydney, N. S.] O.S.C.

FINNEY, CHARLES GRANDISON (Aug. 29, 1792–Aug. 16, 1875), revivalist, educator, intimately associated with the early history of Oberlin College and from 1851 to 1866 its president, was born in Warren, Conn., the son of Sylvester and Rebecca (Rice) Finney. He was of early New England stock, and his father was a soldier in the Revolutionary War. When he was two years old his parents joined the westward migration, settling in Hanover (now Kirkland), Oneida County, N. Y., where among pioneer conditions he grew up. He attended such common schools as existed there, and spent two years at Hamilton Oneida Academy, Clinton, where the principal, Seth Norton, took especial interest in him, training his natural ability for music, and stimulating his desire for a college education. After the removal of his parents to Henderson, on Lake Ontario, he taught a district school for several years, and then went to Warren, Conn., to prepare for Yale. He did not enter, however, being persuaded by his schoolmaster that he could do the work of the college curriculum by himself in two years. Accordingly he went to New Jersey where he taught and studied privately. In 1818 he entered the law office of Benjamin Wright, Adams, N. Y., and later was admitted to the bar.

At this period he was a handsome fellow, six feet two inches tall, erect, alert, full of energy and fond of outdoor sports. Having a musical voice of wide range, he organized the young people of the town into a chorus and trained them; he also took great delight in playing the 'cello. Fond of dancing and attractive personally, he was popular at all social gatherings. He had the moral stamina and religious tendency of his New England ancestry, but as a youth had received little religious training. Not until in his study of the law he came across references to Mosaic institutions, did he own a Bible. What preaching he had heard repelled him. Although at Adams he attended the church services and was a friend of George W. Gale [*q.v.*], its pastor, he was frankly critical of the dogmas taught and the prevailing practises. His own study of the Bible, however, together with his natural religious sensitiveness, finally resulted, after violent struggles, in his conversion. This event and his immediate subsequent experiences were attended by great emotional excitation. He seemed to see the Lord standing before him; he received a "mighty baptism of the Holy Spirit," and wept aloud with joy and love; wave after wave came over him, until he cried, "I shall die if these waves continue to pass over me" (*Memoirs,* p. 20). At another time, he beheld the glory of God about him, and a light ineffable shone into his soul. He saw all nature worshipping God except man, and broke into a flood of tears that mankind did not praise God.

His conversion involved a retainer from the Lord to plead his cause. He thought no more of the law, but straightway applied himself to the conversion of his fellow men. In 1823 he put himself under the care of the St. Lawrence Presbytery as a candidate for the ministry. Some of the members urged him to study theology at Princeton, but he refused on the ground that he did not want to be under such influences as they had been. His pastor, Mr. Gale, and another clergyman were accordingly appointed to superintend his studies. Extremely independent, and aggressively opposed to Gale's views on the atonement, he worked out his theology largely on the basis of his own study of the Scriptures. The Presbytery licensed him, however, in March 1824, and he was ordained in July of the same year. The following October he married Lydia Andrews of Whitestown, Oneida County, N. Y.

For almost a decade he conducted revivals in the Middle and Eastern States with results that attracted attention all over the country. He cast aside the ordinary conventions of the pulpit; used expressive language and homely illustrations; was startlingly direct and even personal in his appeal to men's consciences and in his prayers, so that he was threatened with tar and feathers, and even with death. He portrayed the terrible guilt and awful consequences of disobeying the divine law, and put the fear of God into his hearers. His command over all classes was phenomenal; he broke down contrary wills by his logic and by the superior force of his own will. Violent physical manifestations resulted from his preaching; people burst into tears, shrieked, fainted, and fell into trances. Nevertheless, he produced permanent beneficial results; lives were transformed and whole towns cleansed. His views, methods, and idiosyncrasies subjected him to widespread persecution and misrepresentation, and awakened severe criticism, even in his own denomination. Lyman Beecher and Asahel Nettleton opposed him vigorously. As a result a convention was held at New Lebanon, N. Y., in July 1827, composed of Presbyterian and Congregational ministers, friends and opponents of Finney, to consider the points in controversy. The general effect of this gathering seems to have been in Finney's favor.

In 1832 he became pastor of the Second Free Presbyterian Church, New York, for the use of which Lewis Tappan and others had leased the Chatham Street Theatre. At his installation service he was stricken with the cholera, which was then prevalent in the city. After he recovered, his labors resulted in many converts and the establishment of several other churches. He shortly became dissatisfied with the working of the disciplinary system in Presbyterian churches, and the Broadway Tabernacle was organized for him, its place of worship being constructed in conformity with his desires. He withdrew from the Presbytery in 1836, and the church became Congregational in polity. While in New York he delivered lectures on revivals, which were printed weekly in the *New York Evangelist,* and published in book form in 1835. The work went through many editions and was widely read abroad. He also took a decided stand on the slavery question, but did not, he says, "make it a hobby, or divert the attention of the people from the work of converting souls" (*Memoirs,* p. 324).

While he was in New York, young men asked him to take them as students in theology. Having no time for such work, he proposed as a partial substitute to give a course of theological lectures each year, and a room in the Tabernacle was provided for this purpose. When, however, in 1835, after the students at Lane Seminary had left that institution because of restrictions placed on discussion of the slavery question, he was invited to establish a theological department for them in the newly founded college at Oberlin, Ohio, and Arthur Tappan had guaranteed him financial support, he accepted. He retained his pastorate in New York, giving to it about six months of the year. This dual arrangement was detrimental to his health, and on Apr. 6, 1837, his connection with the church was severed. During the thirty-eight remaining years of his life he was connected with Oberlin College, upon the character of which he exerted a powerful influence. From 1851 to 1866 he was president, although relieved of much administrative detail; and from 1835 to 1872 he was also pastor of the First Congregational Church, Oberlin. He long carried on his evangelistic work during a part of each year, visiting Great Britain in 1849–50 and again in 1859–60, where his preaching had great effect. Through the *Oberlin Evangelist,* established in 1839, to which he contributed regularly, his views on doctrinal and practical matters were disseminated. As his theology developed, certain aspects of it aroused opposition. He was in general a New School Calvinist, but the emphasis that he laid upon the individual's ability to repent was exceptional. He also taught that sin and holiness, which he viewed as attaching only to voluntary actions, cannot coëxist in a person; and that a high plane of experience is possible in the Christian life, in which one becomes superior to one's weakness and enjoys a state of spiritual stability, which he designated as sanctification. This view was attacked as tending to Arminianism and Perfectionism, and "Oberlin theology" was long in ill-repute among more conservative Calvinists. Having this exalted idea of what a Christian should strive to attain, and feeling that a church should always be at a revival pitch, he was averse to popular amusements and other pursuits which might prove a hindrance. He was a strong advocate of temperance and opposed to the use of tobacco, and even tea and coffee. Although made a Mason in his youth he attacked the order later and published in 1869 *The Character, Claims, and Practical Workings of Freemasonry.* His *Lectures on Systematic Theology* were published in two volumes in 1846 and 1847, and after some revision, republished in England in 1851. Among his other works are: *Sermons on Important Subjects* (3rd ed., 1836); *Lectures to Professing Christians* (1837); and *Skeletons of a Course of Theological Lectures* (1840). In the forties he was an editor of the *Oberlin Quarterly Review* and later was a frequent contributor to the *Advance* and the *Independent.* Two volumes of sermons delivered at Oberlin and reported by Prof. Henry Cowles were published posthumously as *Sermons on Gospel Themes* (1876) and *Sermons on the Way of Salvation* (1891). Finney's first wife died in 1847, and he later married Mrs. Elizabeth Ford Atkinson, after whose death in 1863 he married Mrs. Rebecca (Allen) Rayl, an assistant principal of the women's department at Oberlin. He retained his vigor in an unusual degree to the last, delivering his final course of lectures in his eighty-third year. Death came at the end of a quiet Sunday in August, from some affection of the heart.

[*Memoirs of Rev. Charles G. Finney, Written by Himself* (1876), deals chiefly with his evangelistic activities. A more complete account of his life and characteristics, including a lengthy statement of his theology, may be found in G. Frederick Wright's *Charles Grandison Finney* (1891). See also Wm. C. Cochran, *Charles Grandison Finney: Memorial Address* (1908); D. L. Leonard, *The Story of Oberlin* (1898); Nathan Sheppard, *Heroic Stature* (1897); Hiram Mead, "Charles Grandison Finney," *Cong. Quart.*, Jan. 1877; Jas. H. Fairchild, "The Doctrine of Sanctification at Oberlin," *Ibid.*, Apr. 1876; *Reminiscences of Rev. Charles G. Finney* (1876); F. H. Foster, *A Genetic Hist. of the New England Theology* (1907); reviews of Finney's *Lectures on Systematic Theology* by Geo. Duffield in *Biblical Repository*, Apr., July 1848 and by Charles Hodge [*q.v.*] in *Biblical Repertory and Princeton Rev.*, Apr. 1847; G. F. Wright, "Dr. Hodge's Misrepresentations of President Finney's System of Theology," *Bibliotheca Sacra*, Apr. 1876, and "President Finney's System of Theology in its Relation to the So-Called New England Theology," *Ibid.*, Oct. 1877; A. T. Swing, "President Finney and an Oberlin Theology," *Ibid.*, July 1900.] H. E. S.

FINOTTI, JOSEPH MARIA (Sept. 21, 1817–Jan. 10, 1879), Roman Catholic priest, bibliographer, was born at Ferrara, Italy, the son of Francis M. and Rose (Tassinavi) Finotti. His boyhood was made unhappy by his father, a judge, who treated the lad with unfeeling severity. Put to school to the Jesuits, he almost immediately evinced a desire to enter the Order and was received into the Company on Oct. 28, 1833. The reading, when he was twelve years old, of Botta's history of the War for Independence had awakened in him an interest in the United States, and in 1845 he accompanied Fr. James Ryder to America to work in the Maryland Province. He was ordained at Georgetown, D. C., in August 1847 and engaged in the ministry first at Frederick, Md., and later at Alexandria, Va. On Mar. 4, 1852, he left the Jesuits. "I felt as if the people with whom I lived were too hollow, impulsive hearts & idle brains, & made up my mind to come to Boston, where I have friends, slow to be made such, but steady & firm," he wrote later (unpublished letter in archives of the New-England Historic Genealogical Society). He was attached to Bishop Fitzpatrick's cathedral from April 1852 until December 1856, when he was appointed to the charge of the parishes of Brookline and Brighton. Always busy and often ill, he performed his parochial duties with exemplary fidelity and found time to write or translate several pious stories and to act as literary editor of the Boston *Pilot*. He also made a fine collection of coins and medals, which he later disposed of. His principal avocation was the forming of a remarkable, and perhaps unique, collection of American Catholic publications and the compiling of his valuable *Bibliographia Catholica Americana: A List of Works Written by Catholic Authors and Published in the United States: Pt. I, 1784–1820* (1872), which he did not live to complete. "To this work," he wrote in the preface, "I have allotted all *subsecivas horas* for some years, while it has also happened that at times I could not copy one single title for months. Duties too sacred to be neglected kept me busy at something else. The most favorable time for work was when an old-fashioned N. E. rheumatism (envious friends most perversely call it *podagra!*—my physician assures me *on oath* 'tis a slander) would at stated times confine me to an *otium cum dignitate*, days, weeks, and months, on a venerable armchair in my library. Fortunately, whilst the underpins of the animal fabric were all ablaze, the upper story was cool and free, ready to take in storage day and night. In sooth, it has been my harvest time." Of his other works the only one to need mention is the posthumously published *Mystery of the Wizard Clip* (Baltimore, 1879), a curious narrative of miraculous occurrences at Smithfield, W. Va. In 1876 precarious health compelled him to relinquish his work. After sojourns at the Seminary of Mount St. Mary's near Cincinnati, and at Omaha, he joined Bishop Machebœuf at Denver. Reinvigorated by the mountain air, he accepted a pastoral charge at Central City, Colo., and labored with his customary zeal. In December 1878, while returning from a station where he had said mass, he slipped and fell on the ice. He died a few weeks later from the effects of the fall.

[*Cat. of the Library of the late Rev. Joseph M. Finotti* (1879) with biog. preface by John Gilmary Shea; *Cat. of the Balance of* [*his*] *Library* (1880); *New-Eng. Hist. and Geneal. Reg.*, July 1880; *Boston Transcript*, Jan. 22, 1879; article "Finotti" in the *Cath. Encyc.*, vol. VI (1909); notes of his life made by Finotti on the back of an invitation to be present at a reunion of the Philodemic Soc. of Georgetown Coll., July 2, 1867 (in archives of Georgetown Univ.).] G. H. G.

FISCHER, EMIL FRIEDRICH AUGUST (June 13, 1838–Aug. 11, 1914), opera singer, the son of Ignatia Caroline Achten, a concert soprano, and Johann Friedrich Fisher, a well-known court opera singer of Gratz, was born in Brunswick, Germany. He made his début in Gratz, Austria, in 1857, as the Sénéchal in Boieldieu's *Jean de Paris*. After singing in Pressburg, Stettin, and Brunswick, he became director of the Dantzig Opera in 1863, a position he held until the outbreak of the Franco-Prussian War. In 1875 he accepted a position as solo bass at the Royal Opera in Rotterdam, leaving it five years later for a similar one at the Dresden Court Opera. In 1885, with Lilli Lehmann and Anton Seidl, he was engaged as a principal for the second season of German opera at the New York Metropolitan. Thereafter he was more or less intimately associated with the Metropolitan's activities until his final retirement in 1898. Versatile, a good natural actor, he was at home in French and Italian as well as German opera. As Mephistopheles in *Faust* and Ramfis in *Aïda* he was well known, but he was at his best in the Wagnerian rôles of the Landgrave, *Tannhäuser*; King Henry, *Lohengrin*; King Mark, *Tristan*; Wotan, *Walküre*; Hagen, *Siegfried*; and Hans Sachs, *Die Meistersinger*. His interpretation of this last rôle is generally regarded as its superlative American exposition, and his felicitous mingling of bluff good-nature, humanity, and idealism in the characterization of the cobbler-poet is still regarded as a model. He was opposed to singing Wagner in translation, and insisted that in the Wagner operas, "the function of the singer is to explain in words what the orchestra is saying." During the long years of his connection with the Metropolitan Opera House Fischer sang in 101 operas and appeared in America 839 times. Both as a man and as an artist he was very popular. The benefit performance given on Mar. 15, 1907, in honor of the fiftieth anniversary of his appearance on the operatic stage, in which he took part as Hans Sachs in an act from *Die Meistersinger*, yielded nearly $7,000. After his retirement he devoted part of his time to teaching, spending his winters in New York. He died in Hamburg, of cancer of the stomach, on one of his summer trips to Europe.

[H. E. Krehbiel, *Chapters of Opera in New York* (1908); "Old Wagner Singers Greatest," an interview with Fischer, in *Musical America*, May 20, 1911; *Ibid.*, Sept. 12, 1914; *N. Y. Times*, Sept. 4, 1914.] F. H. M.

FISH, HAMILTON (Aug. 3, 1808–Sept. 6, 1893), statesman, the son of Nicholas [*q.v.*] and Elizabeth (Stuyvesant) Fish, was born in New York and received his primary education in the private school of M. Bancel. He graduated with highest honors from Columbia College in 1827 and, after studying law in the office of Peter A. Jay for three years, was admitted to the bar and formed a partnership with William B. Lawrence, editor of Wheaton's *Elements of International Law*. True to the Federalist principles of his father, he adhered to the Whig party and became its candidate for the state assembly in 1834, failing to carry his Democratic district. His next candidacy, for Congress in 1842, was successful, but he was not returned for another term. He was defeated also in 1846 for the lieutenant-governorship of the state by the opposition of the "anti-renters," whose attacks on the patroons' land-leasing system he had denounced. Next year, however, he was chosen for the office in a special election, and in 1848 he was elected governor. His administration was signalized by the passage of acts establishing free schools throughout the state and by extensions of the canal system. His attitude on the main national question of the time, as indicated by the declarations in his annual messages against the opening of California and New Mexico to slavery, was satisfactory enough to permit his selection for the treasury post in a reconstruction of the cabinet planned by President Taylor but cut off by his death (*Autobiography of Thurlow Weed*, 1883, p. 591).

Fish was not renominated for governor, but was supported by the Seward-Weed Whigs for the United States Senate in 1851. A deadlock in the legislature lasting over two months, caused by one Whig senator's dissatisfaction with his refusal to commit himself to the compromise measures of 1850, was only broken in his favor by a vote taken in the absence of two Democrats. In the Senate he achieved no special distinction. He followed his senior colleague, Seward, and his friend, Sumner, in their opposition to the repeal of the Missouri Compromise, though he was not disposed to make slavery a dominant issue in politics. Regretting the demise of the Whig party, he finally joined the Republican as the one according most nearly with his principles, but did not enter very energetically into its earlier activities. After the expiration of his term as senator he took his family to Europe for a stay of two years. By the time he returned his convictions had crystallized sufficiently to warrant him in working for Lincoln's election and in advising the outgoing administration to adopt a firm policy toward South Carolina and the seceding states. He was concerned in the outfitting of the *Star of the West* for supplying Fort Sumter, and expressed to Gen. Scott the opinion that the firing on the ship meant war. During the Civil War he served on the Union defense committee of his state and as a commissioner of the federal government for the relief of prisoners, contributing to the ultimate negotiation of the exchange agreement.

He had no special political or personal claim to a place in Grant's cabinet, although their acquaintanceship had extended to his entertainment of the General in his home. He had no desire for office and was unresponsive to suggestions of a ministerial post. When, after encountering several difficulties in early appointments, the President offered him the post of secretary of state, he promptly declined by telegraph, but followed his refusal by a reluctant acceptance through a personal mission of Gen. Babcock (*New York Tribune*, Jan. 25, 1879). He was commissioned Mar. 11, 1869. Intending to serve only until the administration had become stabilized, he remained in office through both of Grant's terms, despite repeated offers of resignation. He became a pillar of the administration and an influence for moderation in all its policies. In his own department he was an efficient executive, introducing reforms in the organization of personnel and classification of records. He brought to bear upon his duties a calm and orderly legal mind, a generally cautious temperament, and a fund of patience in working toward his ends against discouraging odds.

Fish's conduct of foreign relations in general was greatly affected by the question of annexation of the revolution-torn Dominican Republic. He sanctioned a mission of Gen. Babcock thither which, from an inquiry concerning the acquisition of a naval base at Samana Bay, developed into an irregular agreement with the government in power for annexation. Grant strongly favored the project, and Fish, though doubtful, authorized the negotiation of a formal treaty, concluded Nov. 29, 1869, which failed of ratification by the Senate. Grant's attempt, in 1871, to put the measure through by joint resolution was likewise defeated, despite the removal of Senator Sumner, its powerful opponent, from his position as chairman of the foreign relations committee. The President's need of Fish's support in these efforts and his antipathy toward Sumner, which arose out of their failure, favored the success of the Secretary's policies in other fields, albeit the breach of Fish's friendship with Sumner, which he attempted vainly to avert, was a painful experience.

The most notable achievement of Fish's administration of his office was the settlement of the controversy with Great Britain over damages suffered by Northern commerce during the Civil War through the British government's conduct as a neutral. The central factor in this controversy was the havoc wrought by Confederate cruisers equipped or supplied in British ports; and, commemorating the most famous of these, the American demands became, as stated in the final treaty, "generically known as the '*Alabama* claims.'" But behind these lay a mass of obscure grievances which in some minds extended to holding England's recognition of Confederate belligerency responsible for doubling the length of the war, with resulting liabilities which transcended monetary compensations and could only be extinguished by such a gesture as the cession of Canada. This view of the case was put, in part by implication, by Senator Sumner in the debate which led to rejection, in April 1869, of a convention concluded by the previous administration. Since the President inclined to the same view, Sumner's speech set the tone of Fish's official policy for nearly two years, as expressed in instructions to Motley, the minister in London, and conversations with Thornton, British minister at Washington (*Senate Executive Document 11*, 41 Cong., 3 Sess., pp. 2–5; *Papers Relating to the Foreign Relations of the United States*, III, 1873, 329–36; E. L. Pierce, *Memoir and Letters of Charles Sumner*, 1893, IV, 409–10, 414; Adams, *post*, pp. 156–57, 160). Informally, however, he let it be understood that he was disposed to accept much less drastic terms, and a personal exchange of views to this effect was begun with Sir John Rose, a Canadian commissioner in the confidence of the British government, in July 1869 (J. C. B. Davis, *Mr. Fish and the Alabama Claims*, 1893, pp. 45–46). Not until November 1870, when Sumner's influence was waning through his opposition to the President's Dominican policy, did Fish intimate to the British minister the possibility of a settlement not including territorial compensation (Adams, *post*, p. 162). In January 1871 an understanding was reached through Rose for a joint high commission to arrange a settlement of the *Alabama* claims in connection with various questions regarding Canada at issue between the two governments—boundaries, fishing rights, navigation, and trade (J. B. Moore, *History and Digest of the International Arbitrations to which the United States Has Been a Party*, I, 1898, 523–31). Sumner's now categorically expressed opinion, that a definitive settlement could be based only on "the withdrawal of the British flag . . . from this hemisphere," was brushed aside. His removal from his committee chairmanship took place before the resulting agreement reached the Senate for ratification, but he did not then oppose it.

The commissioners began their work in March and on May 8, 1871, signed the Treaty of Washington, providing for arbitration of the *Alabama* claims under a set of definitions of neutral duties which held a neutral power bound to "use due diligence to prevent the fitting out, arming, or equipping" of belligerent cruisers in its ports. The arbitration conducted at Geneva encountered difficulties owing to the fact that, since the British government refused to admit in advance its neglect of these duties and its consequent liability, the American government refused to limit its claims, but put forward a number of indirect ones in addition to the damage directly inflicted by the Confederate cruisers. These were at last eliminated, in accordance with Fish's design, by the tribunal which, on Sept. 14, 1872, rendered a decision on the direct claims against Great Britain, fixing the amount of damages at $15,500,000. A most disturbing controversy was thus honorably settled. Some of the Canadian questions dealt with in the treaty, such as fishing rights and arrangements regarding trade, dragged on; but the water boundary in the Strait of San Juan de Fuca was adjusted in favor of the United States by an arbitral decision of the German Emperor in October 1872.

A stubborn insurrection in Cuba gave rise to a set of problems which embarrassed Fish throughout his eight years in office, obliging him to press on the Spanish government the claims of Americans for reparation of injuries at the hands of local authorities and to respond to its complaints regarding filibustering activities in the United States. Efforts to persuade Spain to an accommodation with the rebels accompanied his exertions to defeat advocates of recognition of them as belligerents and of intervention in their favor. Fish was personally opposed to such recognition, but he had to keep the possibility of its expediency in mind. The President was disposed to favor recognition of belligerency. On Aug. 19, 1869, during an absence from Washington and while Fish was in the midst of an earnest though futile correspondence with Spain over a plan of pacification based on Cuban independence and the abolition of slavery, he signed a proclamation of neutrality. Fish deferred promulgating this document and later received Grant's acknowledgment that it had been a mistake (Adams, *post,* p. 19). Largely because of Grant's need of his support in the policy of Dominican annexation, Fish persuaded the President to reverse his attitude and declare recognition of belligerency unjustified in his annual message of Dec. 6. The same situation helped him to secure a still stronger special message on June 13, 1870, when the advocates of recognition attempted, unsuccessfully, to push through a joint resolution of Congress in its favor. Meanwhile the American government's efforts with Spain were met with fair promises of reforms and redress of grievances, of which the fulfilment continually fell short. The tension was somewhat relieved, however, by an agreement, reached Feb. 11, 1871, for a joint commission at Washington to decide on American claims for damages.

The situation in Cuba, whicn remained unimproved, continued to present fresh difficulties, and Fish's instructions to Sickles, the minister at Madrid, had been displaying for a year a rising impatience with the Spanish government, when, in November 1873, a crisis arose which threatened to bring on hostilities. The steamer *Virginius,* under American registry and with a mainly American crew, but belonging to the Cuban revolutionary committee in New York and employed in its filibustering enterprises, was captured and taken into a Cuban port, where the Spanish authorities summarily executed the captain and fifty-three of the crew and passengers. In an ultimatum to the Spanish government of Nov. 14, Fish demanded release of the ship and survivors, signal punishment of the culpable officials, and a salute to the American flag within twelve days under threat of a severance of diplomatic relations. Warlike feeling rose in both countries, and Sickles had actually asked for his passports, when, on Nov. 27, Fish reached an understanding with the Spanish minister at Washington to dispense with the salute if his government was able to prove the illegality of the ship's registry. This condition was easily met. The critical phase of the affair lasted only a fortnight, but the questions of indemnities and punishment of the responsible officials dragged on as additions to the already numerous causes of friction with Spain.

A fresh start toward a general settlement was made with the appointment of Caleb Cushing as minister to Spain in February 1874. By holding up recognition of the new government of Alfonso XII until the *Virginius* indemnity claims were met, an award was secured, Mar. 11, 1875 (Department of State, *Instructions, Spain,* XVII, 177; *Papers Relating to the Foreign Relations of the United States,* 1875, vol. II). With this question disposed of, the way was opened for negotiations of a broader scope looking toward the independence or autonomy of Cuba. These were initiated by Fish's instruction to Cushing of Nov. 5, 1875, which was to be read to the minister of foreign affairs. It pointed out the necessity of bringing about the pacification of Cuba if relations between the United States and Spain were to continue "even on their present footing"; otherwise, "it may be the duty of other governments to intervene." Copies of the instruction were sent for communication to the British and the principal Continental governments, inviting them to express similar views to Spain. This diplomatic campaign was upset by the transmission to Cushing, on Nov. 15, of a Spanish note meeting by specific undertakings all the particular points raised in recent correspondence. Fish finally, in an instruction of Mar. 1, 1876, reduced his suggestions regarding Cuban administration to reforms in the direction of self-government and the effective abolition of slavery.

The Spanish government parried these by noncommittal replies while pouring into Cuba reinforcements which practically extinguished the insurrection by the end of the year. With the satisfaction of American claims by awards of the joint commission and the elimination of various other causes of complaint, the discussions over Cuba ended.

In the course of Fish's long tenure of office, many other problems of foreign relations came before the United States. The government assumed the protection of the interests of North German subjects in France during the Franco-Prussian War and vainly offered its good offices for peace and its counsel for a moderate settlement. Fish and the minister at Paris, E. B. Washburne, successfully confronted Bismarck in asserting the right to pass sealed dispatches through the German lines during the siege of the city. Fish's advice contributed to the attainment of an understanding between the belligerents which prevented the extension of hostilities into the Far East. Concerning America's own relations with China, Fish upheld rigidly the special position of American citizens under early treaties, and he pursued a policy of cooperation with the European governments in affirming and extending foreign rights and prestige. An attempt by an armed expedition to extort a convention from Korea on the treatment of shipwrecked sailors was unsuccessful. American interests in the Pacific area were greatly promoted by a treaty of commercial reciprocity with Hawaii in 1875, which virtually incorporated those islands into the economic system of the United States.

Two attempts were made by Fish to secure agreements for the construction of an interoceanic canal. The first was with Colombia for use of the Panama route, but the treaty signed at Bogota on Jan. 26, 1870, was so amended by the Colombian Senate that the strategic value of the enterprise was destroyed and the United States failed to ratify. The second attempt was made in negotiations at Washington with a special envoy of Nicaragua, in February 1877, but no agreement could be reached as to the status of a proposed neutral zone. Among other questions which occupied Fish's attention, but which were marked by no definite developments, were almost incessant troubles on the Mexican border, handled generally with tactful regard for Mexican susceptibilities, and a controversy with Great Britain over the principles of extradition, in which Fish upheld the view that, in the absence of definite provisions to the contrary, embodied in a convention, the charge brought in court need not be identical with that on which surrender was obtained. One of the unpleasant incidents of his official business was the recall at his demand of the Russian minister Catacazy, in 1871, for interference in the *Alabama* claims negotiations and public abuse of the President.

After his retirement from office Fish did not again emerge from the private life of a gentleman of ample means and cultivated tastes. Not least, indeed, among his qualifications for the principal office he held was his eminently respectable personality, combining cordiality with dignity, which gave a tone of culture and refinement to an otherwise rather tawdry administration. He had married, on Dec. 15, 1836, Julia Kean, descendant of William Livingston, first governor of New Jersey. She created for him a charming home life, and her graciousness and tact as a hostess effectively adorned the generous hospitality which made their house the social center of Washington and contributed notably to the smooth conduct of official business. They had eight children, three of them sons. Nicholas, the eldest, was for some years in the diplomatic service, finally resigning the legation in Belgium to devote himself to banking. Hamilton was private secretary to his father as secretary of state, member and speaker of the New York Assembly, assistant treasurer of the United States at New York, and member of the Sixty-first Congress. Stuyvesant [*q.v.*] became a financier and railway executive. Like his father, Fish played a prominent part in non-political civic and social affairs. For long periods of years he served as trustee of Columbia College and as president-general of the Society of the Cincinnati. He was also a president of the Union League Club and of the New York Historical Society, besides taking an active part in other literary and philanthropic organizations and in the affairs of the Episcopal Church.

[C. F. Adams, Jr., *Lee at Appomattox and Other Papers* (1902), contains extracts from diaries and letters. See also A. E. Corning, *Hamilton Fish* (1918); Senator G. F. Edmunds, *Proceedings of the Leg. of the State of N. Y. in Memory of Hon. Hamilton Fish, held . . . Apr. 5, 1894*; J. V. Fuller, in *Am. Secretaries of State and their Diplomacy*, with bibliographical note, vol. VII (1928); DeA. S. Alexander, *A Political Hist. of the State of N. Y.*, II (1906); *N. Y. Tribune*, Jan. 25, 1879, Sept. 8, 1893; *N. Y. Times*, Sept. 8, 1893.] J. V. F.

FISH, NICHOLAS (Aug. 28, 1758–June 20, 1833), Revolutionary officer, prominent citizen, was born in New York City of well-to-do parents, Jonathan and Elizabeth (Sackett) Fish, tracing descent on his father's side from early seventeenth-century colonists of Massachusetts and settlers of Newtown, Long Island. After an attendance, but not graduation, at the College of New Jersey, he entered the New York law office of John Morin Scott. At this time he formed a lifelong friendship with Alexander Hamilton, a student at King's College. They were fellow members of a drill corps and of a group which debated public questions (J. C. Hamilton, *Life of Alexander Hamilton,* 1834, I, 47). In 1775 Fish joined Malcolm's New York regiment, in which he held the ranks of lieutenant and captain before he became Gen. Scott's brigade-major, Aug. 9, 1776. He was present at the inglorious encounter on Long Island and was a chronicler of the flight of the militia after the British crossed the river. He was commissioned by Congress, Nov. 21, 1776, as major in the 2nd New York Regiment of the Continental Army. In the following year he took part in the two actions at Bemis Heights leading up to Burgoyne's surrender. He was appointed a division inspector under Steuben in 1778, and commanded a body of light infantry at the battle of Monmouth. As major in Clinton's brigade he served in Sullivan's expedition against the Indians in 1779. During the next two years he was with Lafayette's force, becoming Col. Hamilton's second-in-command in the Yorktown campaign. He was among the leaders of the American advance party in the assault of the redoubts on Oct. 14, 1781, and organized the defense of the position captured by Hamilton's unit. Recalling Fish's part in this operation, Lafayette gave into his custody a wreath presented at the Yorktown ceremony of Oct. 19, 1824, "as a deposit for which we must account to our comrades" (A. Levasseur, *Lafayette in America in 1824 and 1825,* 1829, I, 184–85). Through the remainder of the war Fish was with Washington's main army and was brevetted lieutenant-colonel at its close.

Following the resignation of his commission in 1784, he was appointed adjutant-general of the state of New York. In 1793 he was made supervisor of the revenue for the district of New York by President Washington. From 1806 to 1817 he held office as alderman, leading the opposition to Tammany and serving on many civic committees, including that of defense in the War of 1812. As Federalist candidate for lieutenant-governor, in 1810, he made a strong but unsuccessful run against DeWitt Clinton. His large and handsome person, and his dashing yet dignified bearing assured him a social popularity which was greatly enhanced by his marriage, on Apr. 30, 1803, to Elizabeth Stuyvesant, a descendant and heiress of the famous Dutch governor. Among the offices which he held in various societies was the presidency of the New York Society of the Cincinnati, and he was for some years chairman of the board of trustees of Columbia College. He was named an executor of Hamilton's will, in tribute to their friendship, and he gave the statesman's name to his eldest son. The family whose fortune and prestige he founded has contributed distinguished names to the nation's political and business life in three succeeding generations.

["Obituary general order of the Society of the Cincinnati," June 20, 1833 (in *N. Y. Evening Courier,* June 21, 1833); M. J. Lamb, *History of the City of N. Y.,* vol. II (1881); DeA. S. Alexander, *A Political Hist. of the State of N. Y.*; Albert Wells, *Am. Family Antiquity,* III (1881), 154.]

J. V. F.

FISH, PRESERVED (July 3, 1766–July 23, 1846), merchant, ship-owner, was born in Portsmouth, R. I., the son of Preserved Fish. There is no foundation for the often-repeated story that his unusual name was bestowed by a New Bedford fisherman who found him as an infant, adrift at sea in an open boat. The name had come down through several generations of descendants of Thomas Fish who was settled at Portsmouth in 1643. As a boy, he worked at first in his father's blacksmith shop and then tried farming. Finally he shipped on a whaler for the Pacific and by twenty-one had risen to captain. Endowed with an unusual amount of Yankee shrewdness and sharpness, Fish realized that more money could be made in selling whale oil than in gathering it. He became a merchant at New Bedford for a few years and then, after a political quarrel, impulsively sold his property for half its value. Like many other New Englanders of that day, he moved to New York with its wider range of business possibilities. In 1817 he was one of the twenty-eight brokers of the New York Exchange Board, the nucleus of the New York Stock Exchange, but he is principally remembered as the founder of an organization which eventually rose to first place in New York mercantile and shipping circles. The firm started in 1815 as Fish & Grinnell, and soon included three New Bedford brothers, Joseph, Henry, and Moses Hicks Grinnell. Originally the partners confined themselves to marketing part of New Bedford's whale-oil output. It was remarked that they "sold two kinds of oil, good and bad." By 1823 they were operating a line of four packets to Liverpool, competing with the Black Ball Line, and were also running a line of packets to New Orleans. Shortly after that, Fish left the firm. His eccentric disposition may account for the several sharp breaks in his business career. By 1832 Robert B. Minturn [*q.v.*] was a partner in the old firm which now became Grinnell, Minturn & Company. Under that name it secured an unquestioned primacy in New York foreign commerce. Fish, in the meantime, had gone to Liverpool where he formed a partnership with Edward

Carnes and Walter Willis. The firm was not successful financially, and broke up in two years. Returning to New York, Fish entered another partnership which lasted barely six months, and then retired from active business for seven years. He returned to it again about 1836, becoming president of the Tradesman's Bank and holding that position until his death. Fish was a Quaker until late in life when he turned Episcopalian. Though he was an active Jacksonian Democrat, he joined the Whigs in 1837 in opposition to Van Buren. He was married three times.

[Most of the material for Fish's life is to be found in the advertisements and notices in contemporary New York newspapers. There are frequent references to him in J. A. Scoville, *The Old Merchants of N. Y. City* (4 vols., 1863–66), but Scoville includes the fisherman story and must always be used with caution. There are genealogical notices in C. S. Brigham, *Early Records of the Town of Portsmouth* (1901), pp. 22, 293, 321, 371. See also Bayard Tuckerman, ed., *The Diary of Philip Hone* (2 vols., 1889), *The Merchants' Mag.*, Dec. 1846; the *Banker's Mag.*, Sept. 1846; *N. Y. Herald* and *N. Y. Tribune*, July 24, 1846.] R. G. A.

FISH, STUYVESANT (June 24, 1851–Apr. 10, 1923), railroad executive and banker, descended from New York colonial families, was one of the sons of Hamilton [*q.v.*] and Julia (Kean) Fish. He was born and grew up in New York City, where as a boy he had the best private school advantages then afforded, entering Columbia College at sixteen. There, in a class of less than fifty, he passed an enjoyable four years, being chosen as a junior chairman of the *Columbiad* Committee, and in senior year holding the office of class president. He was an honor man, with such competitors as Brander Matthews, R. Fulton Cutting, and Oscar S. Straus. His commencement oration was on the then unusual subject of political economy as a study. In 1874 Columbia awarded him the degree of M.A.

Immediately after graduation, in 1871, young Fish acquired clerical experience in the New York offices of the Illinois Central Railroad, but, after having become secretary to the president of the road in 1872, entered an opening which awaited him in the banking business of Morton, Bliss & Company. He remained with that house five years. Wall Street never appealed to him, however; constructive railroading was far more to his liking. In 1877 the young man was made a director of the Illinois Central. After holding various posts of responsibility in the management of that railroad, he became in 1887 president of the company. From Chicago to New Orleans the line had maintained itself by the traffic originating in its own territory. Four-fifths of its freights were the products of farm, forest, and mine. It was Fish's policy from the beginning to extend the facilities of the road in such a way as to create new traffic, thus continually building up an independent, self-sustained system, extending through the Mississippi Valley from the Lakes to the Gulf and fed by various tributary lines. The Illinois Central was almost the only north-and-south road of importance that prospered for a long term of years after the Civil War. In the nineteen years of his presidency, Fish increased the operated mileage of the road and its allied lines by 175 per cent. The gross receipts during that period were increased by 365 per cent., and dividends on the common stock showed an increase of 227 per cent. It was said that no other American railroad had so long a record of continuous dividend payments. A good part of its stock was held by small individual investors along its lines. Fish had installed a system by which the company's employees might purchase stock.

As a railroad administrator Fish succeeded too well for his own personal interest. The Illinois Central was developed into a property that was coveted by other corporations. In the course of the rapid expansion of the Harriman interests in Western and Central railroads it was seen that the president of the Illinois Central would, sooner or later, be forced to fight to retain his control. Before that issue was crystallized, however, Fish had antagonized powerful financiers in New York who were potential allies of Harriman. The antagonism came about through the uncompromising stand taken by Fish as a member of the committee appointed to investigate the charges preferred against officials of the Mutual Life Insurance Company, of which he was a trustee, in 1906. He demanded a thorough "house-cleaning," without fear or favor. In this demand he was not supported by his associates on the committee and he resigned both his committee membership and his trusteeship of the company, giving the facts to the press. The threat was then made in Wall Street that he would be deposed from the presidency of the Illinois Central, and within eight months he was actually ousted from office by the votes of directors who owed their seats in the board to Fish himself, one of those directors being Edward H. Harriman (Affidavit of Fish, printed with brief for the complainants, *George F. Edmunds, et al.* vs. *Illinois Central Railroad Company et al.*, p. 42).

Fish was a member of the Monetary Commission that was the outcome of the Indianapolis Monetary Conference of 1879. He was for many years vice-president and director of the National Park Bank of New York and also served as a trustee of the New York Life Insurance and Trust Company. He was president of the American Railway Association, 1904–06, and chairman of the seventh International Railway Congress, Washington, 1905.

A man of fine physical presence, he delighted in outdoor life on his estate at Garrison, N. Y. Early in life, June 1, 1876, he married Marian Graves Anthon, who became a social leader in New York and Newport. She died in 1915. The characteristic good-nature and air of *camaraderie* that made Fish beloved by hosts of friends may have led some to underestimate his moral sturdiness, but when the time of crisis came and he had made his decision, even the sacrifice of valued friendships could not cause him to waver. Still less could the lure of wealth affect his judgment. He died in his seventy-second year, survived by two sons and a daughter.

[For biographical information see J. R. Totten, "Stuyvesant Fish," in the *N. Y. Geneal. and Biog. Record*, Oct. 1923; *Undergraduate Hist. of the Class of 1871, Columbia College* (1871); *Who's Who in America*, 1922–23; obituary in *N. Y. Times*, Apr. 11, 1923. On Fish as a railroad executive and his deposition from the presidency of the Illinois Central, see the *Railway Age* (Chicago), Oct. 19 and 26 and Nov. 9, 1906; also an editorial in the *World* (N. Y.), Nov. 8, 1906, entitled "The Sandbagging of Stuyvesant Fish." The annual reports of Fish as president of the Illinois Central describe the development of that road from 1887 to 1906; besides these he wrote magazine articles and addresses on the broader aspects of American railroad building and operation.]

W. B. S—w.

FISHBACK, WILLIAM MEADE (Nov. 5, 1831–Feb. 9, 1903), governor of Arkansas, was born in Jeffersonton, Culpeper County, Va., son of Frederick and Sophia Ann (Yates) Fishback. His paternal ancestor, John Fishback, brought a colony from Germany and settled in Virginia about 1714. A descendant named Frederick moved into Maryland and acquired a farm where the town of Frederick, named for him, now stands. The family soon moved back into Virginia, where William was born. He was graduated at the University of Virginia in 1855, taught school for a while, and then studied law in Richmond. In 1857 he moved to Springfield, Ill., where he had business relations with Abraham Lincoln. The next year he moved to Arkansas and settled at Fort Smith, Sebastian County. When secession was being agitated Fishback made strong speeches against it, and was elected to the state convention of 1861 as an opponent of disruption; but after the bombardment of Fort Sumter he introduced a resolution to the effect that any effort to coerce a state should be resisted by Arkansas "to the last extremity," and he voted for secession. In June 1862, he and David Walker, president of the convention, went to Missouri and took the oath of allegiance. Fishback then went on to St. Louis, where he acted for a time as one of the editors of the *St. Louis Democrat*. After the fall of Little Rock (1863), Gen. J. M. Schofield sent him back to Arkansas to raise a regiment of loyal troops, but he failed to accomplish his mission.

When the loyal state government was organized in 1864 under Isaac Murphy [*q.v.*] as governor, Fishback was elected to the United States Senate. He presented his credentials in May 1864; and Senator Lane of Kansas moved that the oath be administered to him. Senator Sumner of Massachusetts, however, made a speech in opposition and the matter was delayed until February 1865, when the House resolved that neither senators nor representatives from the states lately in rebellion should be seated until both Houses had passed on the matter. A motion to admit Fishback was then defeated, 18 to 27. While waiting for this decision he edited for a time the *Unconditional Union* at Little Rock and served as special agent of the Treasury Department. He returned to Sebastian County and was elected as delegate to the constitutional convention of 1874. Though he had been loyal since 1862, he had become disgusted with the Carpet-Bag régime and he took a prominent part in undoing its work. He was a member of the legislatures of 1877 and 1879. In the latter he introduced what came to be known as the "Fishback Amendment" to the constitution, prohibiting the collection of any tax to pay the bonds issued by the Carpet-Baggers in aid of railroads and levees, as well as any new bonds to take up the "Holford" bonds, which were first issued in 1836 to the Real Estate Bank and which were clearly illegal. The amendment failed to receive the necessary majority, but it was resubmitted in 1884 and adopted. At the same election Fishback was again elected to the legislature. In 1892 he was elected by the Democrats as governor and served one term (1893–95). The most important event of his administration was the creation of the St. Francis Levee District covering 1,500 square miles, which resulted in the reclamation of nearly one million acres of valuable farm lands. On Apr. 4, 1867, he married Adelaide Miller, who bore him six children. He died at Fort Smith.

[Besides the *Journals* of the Convention of 1861 and of the state House of Representatives, and the *Official Records (Army)*, see W. M. Kemper, *Geneal. of the Fishback Family in Am.* (1914); *Who's Who in America*, 1901–02; Fay Hempstead, *A Pict. Hist. of Ark.* (1890); John Hallum, *Biog. and Pict. Hist. of Ark.* (1887), I, 468–70; T. S. Staples, *Reconstruction in Ark., 1862–74* (1923); D. Y. Thomas, *Ark. in War and Reconstruction, 1861–74* (1926). Information about family history was obtained from L. F. Fishback.]

D. Y. T.

FISHER, ALVAN (Aug. 9, 1792–Feb. 13, 1863), painter, was born in Needham, Norfolk County, Mass., the son of Aaron and Lucy (Stedman) Fisher and a brother of John Dix Fisher [*q.v.*]. His father and his grandfather, Capt. Ebenezer Fisher, both served in the Revolution. As a lad, Alvan went to Dedham, Mass., where his permanent interests were centered. Until after the age of eighteen he worked in a country store but, finally, against the advice of friends, he decided to be an artist and became a pupil of John R. Penniman, with whom he remained about two years. Penniman was an excellent ornamental painter, but the mechanical method he imparted to his pupil proved a great disadvantage to the latter. It was years before Fisher could break away from the fixed early habits. His life as an artist began in 1814 when, for a year, he undertook to paint portraits at a very cheap rate. He then turned his attention to barnyard scenes, portraits of animals, and pictures of rural life, a field rarely touched at that time, and therefore comparatively profitable. In 1819 he decided to undertake portrait-painting and this finally became his specialty.

Alvan Fisher is said to have been the first landscape-painter who hung out a professional sign in Boston, where he had a studio on Washington Street near Summer (Gerry, *post*). In 1825 he visited England, France (where he spent some time in study), and Italy, and enjoyed a trip through Switzerland on foot. Upon returning to the United States he established himself as a portrait-painter in Boston where he lived many years. On June 3, 1827, he married at Dedham, Mass., Lydia, daughter of Abner and Martha (May) Ellis, by whom he had one son. Fisher died in Dedham at the age of seventy-one.

He had a distinct talent for art, and combined with it the unusual ability to make it pay. At the age of forty-three he invested savings amounting to $13,000 and lost every cent, but immediately set about retrieving his finances and, finally, through more fortunate investments, accumulated a small fortune. An interesting feature of his work was the painting of incidents in his landscapes. He rarely painted from nature but depended upon a good memory and fragmentary notes and sketches. He produced many excellent likenesses, notably that of the phrenologist Spurzheim, done from recollection. Among the works which he himself mentioned in a letter to Dunlap (*post*) are: "The Escape of Sargeant Champ"; "Mr. Dustin Saving Children from the Savages"; "The Freshet"; and "Lost Boy."

[P. A. Fisher, *The Fisher Geneal.* (1898), pp. 177 and 273–74; Wm. Dunlap, *A Hist. of the Rise and Progress of the Arts of Design in the U. S.* (rev. ed., 1918), III, 32–34; H. T. Tuckerman, *Books of the Artists* (1867), p. 67; *An Alphabetical Abstract of the Record of Deaths in the Town of Dedham, Mass., 1844–90* (1895); S. L. Gerry, "The Old Masters of Boston," *New Eng. Mag.*, Feb. 1891.]
J.M.H.

FISHER, CLARA (July 14, 1811–Nov. 12, 1898), actress, singer, was the daughter of Frederick George Fisher, an Irish Shakespearian scholar and a London auctioneer. Earlier he had been librarian in Brighton where he became the intimate of playwrights and actors. Four of his six children made reputations on the stage. Clara was four when he began to teach her to recite. She was six when she made her sensational début at Drury Lane Theatre (Dec. 10, 1817) as Prime Minister of Lilliput, in a children's version of Garrick's *Gulliver,* reciting also excerpts from *Richard III.* The miniature majesty of her Lord Flimnap, the precocious villany of her Richard, made her a child celebrity overnight. After repeating her triumph at Covent Garden, she starred in the United Kingdom for a decade, constantly widening her repertory. Her verbal memory was prodigious, as was her grasp of characters presumably beyond a child's ken. One of her early feats was the impersonation of half-a-dozen widely different parts in a single play. Injudicious managers forced her into a succession of mature male rôles. Before she was twelve she had played Shylock, Sir Peter Teazle, Goldfinch, Dr. Pangloss, Dr. Ollapod, and Young Norval. Ireland declares she could portray the soul of a grown man despite her child's physique; and Hutton records that when cast with actors of regulation size, she threw them out of drawing, dominating the scene. Her Richard was seriously compared with that of Kean.

In 1827, her family having removed to New York, she made her American début at the Park Theatre, her instant success precipitating the "Clara Fisher craze." Box offices were mobbed when she appeared, poems were written to her, fashions, hotels, babies and stage-coaches named after her. At sixteen she is described as bewitching rather than beautiful, daintily petite, her graceful head boyishly "bobbed," her action spirited, her expression artless and gay, full of a captivating archness. Her dramatic singing of Scottish heroic ballads made a hit by virtue of her personality rather than her voice. During her extensive American starring tour which carried her West and South, she seems to have played fewer men's than boys' parts, appearing often in light comedy rôles like Little Pickle in *The Spoiled Child,* or Maria in *Actress of All Work.* Her marriage (Dec. 6, 1834) to the Irish composer, James Gaspard Maeder, marked her decline as a juvenile star. The financial crisis of 1837 swept away her early professional earnings. As leading lady of stock companies supporting most of the great stars, she became, according to Hutton, one of the most finished artists on the American stage. Among her best parts were Ophelia, the Fool in *Lear,* Viola, Clari in the *Maid of Milan,* Lady Teazle, and Lady Gay Spanker. Gradually abandoning her youthful parts, she later played the stage old lady until her retirement in 1889. When she died at Metuchen, N. J., she was the oldest actress in America. Mrs. Maeder had seven children, three of whom identified themselves with the stage: Frederick as actor and dramatist; Mollie as a soubrette; and Frank as theatrical agent and manager. Her autobiography mentions four brothers and sisters who appeared on the American stage: John, Charles who married Joseph Jefferson's daughter, Jane (Mrs. George Vernon), and Amelia.

[*Autobiography of Clara Fisher Maeder* (1897) with portraits and introduction by Douglas Taylor; Laurence Hutton, *Curiosities of the Am. Stage* (1891); sketch by J. N. Ireland in B. Matthews and L. Hutton, *Actors and Actresses of Gt. Brit. and the U. S.* (1886), III, 259–72; C. T. Congdon, *Reminiscences of a Journalist* (1880); *N. Y. Times,* Nov. 13, 1898.] M. B. H.

FISHER, CLARK (May 27, 1837–Dec. 31, 1903), naval engineer, inventor, was the eldest son of Mark and Virtue Gage Fisher, and was born at Levant, Me. He prepared for college in the schools at Newport, Me., and at the Trenton Academy in Trenton, N. J., and he was graduated from the Rensselaer Polytechnic Institute in 1858 with a degree in civil engineering. He entered the United States Navy in May of the following year as a third assistant engineer. He was promoted to second assistant engineer in July 1861, and to first assistant engineer in May 20, 1863. During the Civil War he took part in the engagements at Whitehouse Landing, and at Pocotaligo in 1862. He was with the forces which attacked Morris Island in Charleston Harbor and bombarded Fort Sumter. He participated also in the attack on Fort Wagner and Stone Inlet in 1863; in the advance up the James River; and in the attack on Howlett's, and the Dutch Gap Canal in 1864. In 1862 he was taken a prisoner at Magnolia Station, S. C., but escaped after being confined but one night. His younger brother, Otis, was killed at Fort Fisher. After the war was over, he did some brilliant experimental work for the navy at the Brooklyn Navy Yard which established the value of oil as a fuel. He originated the devices which were used for the economic combustion of this fuel in the experiments. He received his appointment as chief engineer, U. S. N., on Jan. 23, 1871, but resigned the following March on account of the death of his father who had been one of the founders of the Eagle Anvil Works at Trenton, N. J., in the forties and had now left his interest in them to his only surviving son. From 1874 till 1891 scarcely a year elapsed without the issuing of some new patent to Clark Fisher which meant new products for or improvements on old products of the Eagle Works. His first patents were for a railroad spike and a cast-iron anvil. Later patents included rail joints, a hydro-pneumatic engine, combined anvil and vise, a spring motor, lifting jack, and a railroad tie. The Eagle Anvil Works, established by Mark Fisher and developed for thirty years by Clark Fisher, are still doing a business in Trenton. In 1898 Fisher married Harriet White in London. His last years were spent in travel and at his home "Whitehall," at Flushing, Long Island, but he kept an active interest in business until his last illness.

[S. M. Studdiford, *A Memorial of Clark Fisher* (1904); *Trans. Am. Soc. Mech. Engineers,* XXV (1904), 1130–31; E. M. Callahan, *List of Officers of the Navy of the U. S. and of the Marine Corps, from 1775 to 1900* (1901); Geo. A. Wolf, *Industrial Trenton* (1900); H. B. Nason, *Biog. Record Officers and Grads. Rensselaer Polytech. Inst., 1824–86* (1887); private information.] E. Y.

FISHER, DANIEL WEBSTER (Jan. 17, 1838–Jan. 28, 1913), Presbyterian clergyman, for twenty-eight years president of Hanover College, Indiana, was born at a place called Arch Spring, in Sinking Valley, then a part of Huntingdon County, Pa. His father, Daniel, was a well-to-do farmer of German descent who had married a woman of Dutch ancestry, Martha Middleswarth. When he was fourteen years of age young Daniel entered Milnwood Academy, located at Shade Gap, and later finished his preparation for college at Airy View Academy. He graduated from Jefferson College in 1857, and from the Western Theological Seminary three years later. In April 1860, having been accepted by the Presbyterian Board of Foreign Missions for service and appointed to Siam, he was ordained by the Presbytery of Huntingdon. On the 25th of the same month he married Amanda D. Kouns, daughter of Michael Kouns of Ravenswood, Va. (now W. Va.). The illness of his wife as they were about to sail for their foreign station caused them to postpone the journey, and ultimately led him to resign his appointment. In the autumn of 1860 he took charge of the Thalia Street Church, New Orleans, but owing to the outbreak of the Civil War, he returned North in June of the following year. From 1861 to 1876 he was pastor of the First Presbyterian Church, Wheeling, W. Va. A trip abroad followed. Upon his return he supplied various churches, and had been ministering for a year and a half to the

Second Presbyterian Church, Madison, Ind., when on July 8, 1879, he was elected president of Hanover College. The institution was financially embarrassed and its existence in jeopardy, but under his administrative skill it was kept alive through the crisis, and as the years went on it increased in endowment, buildings, and efficiency. During the twenty-eight years of his presidency, he continued active in the affairs of his denomination. In 1866 and in 1874 he had been a member of the General Assembly, and he was again a member in 1889 and in 1900. In the latter year the Assembly appointed a committee to consider changes in the Westminster Confession of Faith, and as one of its members he assisted in shaping the "Brief Statement of the Reformed Faith" which the Assembly adopted in 1902. For many years he was a director of McCormick Theological Seminary. President Harrison in 1889 appointed him one of the commissioners to visit the Mint of the United States. After his resignation as president of Hanover he lived at Washington, D. C., and engaged in writing. In 1909 he published *A Human Life, An Autobiography with Excursuses;* and in 1911, *The Unification of the Churches* and *Calvin Wilson Mateer, Forty-five Years a Missionary in Shantung, China.* His son, Walter L. Fisher, was secretary of the interior under President Taft.

[Wm. A. Millis, *The Hist. of Hanover College from 1827 to 1927* (1927); *Who's Who in America*, 1912–13; Alfred Nevin, *Encyc. of the Presbyt. Ch. in the U. S. A.* (1884); *Evening Star* (Washington), Jan. 28, 1913.]
H. E. S.

FISHER, EBENEZER (Feb. 6, 1815–Feb. 21, 1879), Universalist clergyman, educator, was born on Plantation No. 3, now Charlotte, Washington County, Me., where his father and uncle had established themselves when it was a wilderness. He was a descendant of Anthony Fisher who came to Boston from England in 1637, and settled in Dedham, Mass., and son of Ebenezer and Sally (Johnson) Fisher. He grew up under frontier conditions, a sober-minded boy, early inured to long hours of toil in the open, with limited opportunities for schooling, but an eager reader of whatever books and papers came within his reach. His father was a liberal in religion; his mother, an earnest Baptist; and his mind early turned to questions of theology. When about sixteen he went to Sharon, Mass., and worked in a furniture establishment with his brother-in-law. Returning to his home at nineteen, for the next four years he taught school for a part of each year. In 1840 he was elected representative to the Maine legislature, where despite his youth he was put on one of the most important committees, that of revising the state statutes. He had determined to enter the ministry and in 1839 had for six months supplied for his board the Milltown Universalist Society. Most of the money he received as a state official went into books needful for his theological preparation. He joined the Maine Universalist Convention in 1840, and on Sept. 27, 1841, married Amy W. Leighton of Pembroke, Me. He was pastor of the Universalist church at Addison Point, near his home, from July 1841 to May 1847, when he was installed pastor of the Salem, Mass., Universalist church. In October 1853 a throat affection forced him to resign, but in November of that year he was able to take charge of the South Dedham Universalist church, of which he was pastor until 1858.

During these years in Massachusetts he became known as an able preacher and contributor to denominational periodicals. The most notable achievement of his career, however, was in connection with the theological department of St. Lawrence University, an institution chartered by the State of New York in 1856 for the purpose of "conducting a college in the town of Canton, St. Lawrence County, . . . and to maintain a theological school." Of the latter, the first Universalist theological school in the country, Fisher became the first principal, being installed Apr. 15, 1858, and serving for more than twenty years. Beginning with practically nothing to work with, in the face of many difficulties, especially during the Civil War, he administered its affairs, taught, raised funds, and insured its permanency. In 1869 he was offered a professorship in the new divinity school of Tufts College, which he declined. Death came to him suddenly one morning, ten years later, while he was on his way to the school. He was a man of large frame and noble head, its bald top "shining like a helmet," with a face both stern and kind. He was direct, practical, and unsentimental, terse in verbal expression, without wide range of learning, but sure of what he knew, and thoroughly honest; a person to inspire respect and confidence. The *Universalist Quarterly* from 1849 to 1876 contains numerous articles from his pen, and sermons by him appear in the *Trumpet* from 1849 to 1857. A discussion between him and Rev. J. H. Walden, entitled *The Christian Doctrine of Salvation,* was published in 1869.

[P. A. Fisher, *The Fisher Geneal.* (1898); Geo. H. Emerson, *Memoir of Ebenezer Fisher, D.D.* (1880); *Sixty Years of St. Lawrence* (1916); *Christian Leader*, Feb., Mar., 1879.]
H. E. S.

FISHER, GEORGE JACKSON (Nov. 27, 1825–Feb. 3, 1893), physician, bibliophile, collector, was born at North Castle, Westchester County, N. Y. Of his ancestry little is known except that the family name probably was originally Vischer and that his father was a farmer. When the boy was eleven years old the family moved to the central part of the state, where he became so attuned to rural life that cities never possessed any attractions for him. A *flair* for nature study developed and led him to the study of medicine; and from the first he was a collector. His preceptor was Prof. Nelson Nivison of Mecklenburg and Syracuse University, while his first course of lectures was taken in the medical department of the University of Buffalo and his medical degree was received from the University of New York in 1849. After a short sojourn with his preceptor at Mecklenburg he removed in 1851 to Sing Sing, now Ossining, N. Y., where he continued to practise until his death. He received numerous honors and distinctions: among them an honorary M.A. from Madison University in 1859; the presidency of New York State Medical Society in 1874; and an appointment as delegate to the International Medical Congress, 1876. His library comprised between 4,000 and 5,000 volumes of classics and he was particularly proud of his collections of anatomies and works on monstrosities. His collections of illustrations comprised nearly 500 portraits and 450 medals, the latter representing an investment of $1,000. At his death these collections seem to have been broken up. The portraits found their way to the Johns Hopkins Hospital Library.

He was active not only as surgeon, performing most of the major operations, but as a writer. In 1861 he published *Biographical Sketches of the Deceased Physicians of Westchester County, New York;* a paper "On the Animal Substances employed as Medicines by the Ancients" appeared in the *American Medical Monthly,* January 1862; and "Diploteratology: An Essay on Compound Human Monsters," in *Transactions of the Medical Society of the State of New York,* 1865–68. Twenty short papers written by him on the *Old Masters of Anatomy, Surgery and Medicine* appeared serially in the *Annals of Anatomy and Surgery* (1881–84); he contributed articles on *Teratology* to *Johnson's New Universal Encyclopedia* and also to Wood's *Reference Handbook of the Medical Sciences* (1889); and he wrote *A History of Surgery* for Ashhurst's *International Encyclopædia of Surgery* (1886). He embellished his own copies of S. D. Gross's *Autobiography* and *The Gold-Headed Cane* with many illustrations and autograph letters (the last work was left incomplete). He was a big, bluff and hearty, hospitable man, who never wearied of showing his treasures to the numerous physicians who made the pilgrimage to his home. His death resulted from an infection which he received while he was amputating a limb.

[The most complete record is the biographical sketch by Joseph H. Hunt, M.D., in the *Trans. of the Med. Soc. of N. Y.* (1893). The writer of this article was privileged to meet the doctor and to see his collections in 1885. The facts in the famous suit for slander are stated in *Wm. P. Woodcock, Jr., M.D. (of Sing Sing) against George Jackson Fisher (of Sing Sing). Proceedings at the Trial of Above Entitled Cause. Supreme Court. Westchester Co. White Plains. September 1873.*] E. P.

FISHER, GEORGE PARK (Aug. 10, 1827–Dec. 20, 1909), Congregational clergyman, historian, was the son of Lewis Whiting and Nancy (Fisher) Fisher, and a grandson of Lewis and Luther Fisher, whose descent is traced to the family of Samuel Fisher, the noted Quaker apologist and martyr, contemporary and friend of George Fox. He was born in Wrentham, Mass., where he attended the public schools until he entered Brown University from which he graduated in 1847. For a year after graduation he studied at Yale Divinity School, where Nathaniel W. Taylor was closing his great career as teacher of systematic theology. Thereafter Auburn Theological Seminary claimed him for a time; but he completed his three-years' theological course in 1851 at Andover, Mass., where Prof. Edwards A. Park was the leading influence. He thus secured the best training that the leaders of "New England Theology" could offer. It was then unusual for theological students to engage in graduate study abroad, but Fisher, still unsatisfied, spent the years 1852–54 in Germany, where he became acquainted with the theological celebrities of the time and received thorough training in the methods of historical research.

On his return in 1854 he was called to the Livingston Professorship of Divinity in Yale College, which at that time included the office of regular pastor and preacher of the college church (Congregational). Accepting this invitation he was ordained and installed as pastor of the Church in Yale College Oct. 24, 1854. He continued in this position until 1861, bringing out in 1858 a printed *History of the Church in Yale College.* His printed addresses during this incumbency include two sermons, *National Faults* (1860), and *Thoughts Pertinent to the Present Crisis* (1861), besides obituaries of his former teachers in the Divinity School, Nathaniel W. Taylor and Josiah Willard Gibbs. In April 1860 he married Adeline Louisa Forbes of New Haven, by whom he had two sons and a daughter. In 1861 he resigned the pastorate of the college church to accept a professorship of ecclesiastical history in the

Divinity School, where he taught continuously for forty years, remaining in active service until 1901. From 1895 until 1901 he also served as dean of the school and continued his connection with it as professor emeritus until his death.

Professor Fisher is vividly remembered by his former associates in the teaching of history for both the matter and the manner of his contributions. Of medium height, erect, handsome, and well-built, he had a gracious and genial address and a flow of witty anecdote which made him especially apt as host or as an after-dinner speaker. The combination of these qualities with unusual good sense and sobriety of judgment made him for years a fitting president of the American Society of Church History. It also won for him from a long succession of classes in the Divinity School a preëminent place as teacher, his lectures being not merely lucid and instructive, but thoroughly enjoyable. He himself found equal pleasure both in entertaining at his stately home a succession of distinguished guests and in the social contacts of the Century Club, New York, of which he was long a member. Far-reaching as was his influence at Yale through his effective work in the classroom, it was broadened and intensified in the country at large by the successive volumes that came from his study. Of these the first considerable work was his *Essays on the Supernatural Origin of Christianity* (1865). It was followed in 1866 by his *Life of Benjamin Silliman,* and this, after an interval of seven years, by *The Reformation* (1873), *The Beginnings of Christianity* (1877), *Faith and Rationalism* (1879), *Discussions in History and Theology* (1880), *The Christian Religion* (1882), and *The Grounds of Theistic and Christian Belief* (1883). These, together with his *Manual of Christian Evidences* (1890), attest his interest in apologetics during the conflict of orthodox church historians with the Tübingen school of criticism. Other writings, mostly of the later period, show him no less at home in the field of general history. Among them may be mentioned his *Outlines of Universal History* (1885), *The Colonial Era* (1892), and *A Brief History of the Nations* (1896), besides his *History of the Christian Church* (1887), *History of Christian Doctrine* (1896), and his edition of *An Unpublished Essay of Edwards on the Trinity* (1903). These show that while Fisher was quite ready to take up the cudgels of apologetic polemics when occasion required, he was from the heart both a liberal in sentiment and a true historian in his sincere desire to reach an impartial judgment. This genuinely conservative yet broad-minded disposition made him both a trusted leader in the Congregational fellowship and a judicious guide in the affairs of the Divinity School.

[The best available characterization of man and work is that presented by his successor at Yale, Prof. Williston Walker, in an obituary address printed in the *Yale Divinity Quart.,* Jan. 1910. See also E. P. Parker in *Hartford Daily Courant,* Dec. 22, 1909; *Brown Alumni Monthly,* June 1902, Jan. 1910; *Nation,* Dec. 23, 1909; *Outlook,* Jan. 1, 1910; P. A. Fisher, *The Fisher Geneal.* (1898); *Who's Who in America,* 1908–09.] B. W. B.

FISHER, GEORGE PURNELL (Oct. 13, 1817–Feb. 10, 1899), lawyer, jurist, was descended from John Fisher who came to Pennsylvania with William Penn in 1682. His father, Thomas, was twice high sheriff of Sussex County, Del., and twice high sheriff of Kent County—an unparalleled distinction—and commanded a brigade of Sussex County militia in 1812. He moved to Milford, Kent County, in 1815, where his third wife, Nancy Owens, daughter of Robert and Sallie Owens of Sussex County, gave birth to her only son, George Purnell Fisher. Fisher's early education was received in the county schools. At seventeen he attended St. Mary's College, Baltimore, but the following year transferred to Dickinson College, Carlisle, Pa., from which he was graduated in 1838. He at once entered the law office of John M. Clayton, a family connection, and at the same time tutored the latter's sons. In 1840 he married Eliza, daughter of Truston Polk McColley, a Milford merchant of Scotch ancestry, and after his admission to the bar in 1841, he settled at Dover, winning "marked success from the beginning" (Lore, *post,* p. 7).

It was not long before the young lawyer became enamored of politics, serving his political apprenticeship as clerk of the state Senate (1843), member of the state House of Representatives from Kent County (1844), and secretary of state of Delaware under the Democratic governors Joseph Maull and William Temple (1846–47). When John M. Clayton became secretary of state (1849–50) under President Taylor, Fisher served as his confidential clerk and participated actively in the negotiations which led to the Clayton-Bulwer Treaty. By Taylor's appointment, he adjudicated certain claims of American citizens against Brazil (1850–52), and at Fillmore's request, he acted as his private secretary until Fillmore's son came to Washington. In March 1855 Gov. Causey appointed Fisher attorney-general of Delaware for a term of five years, at the expiration of which he was the candidate of both wings of the People's party for election to the Thirty-seventh Congress, being elected by a majority of 247, although the state was normally Democratic. By 1862, however, when he was renominated by the Republican party, the state had swung back again and he was defeated.

At Washington in 1861, he soon won the high regard of Lincoln, becoming the almoner of federal patronage in his state and helping to prepare a bill to carry out Lincoln's plan of gradual emancipation in Delaware. The project failed, but Fisher's efforts so impressed Lincoln that, on the abolition of the old courts and the creation of a supreme court for the District of Columbia, he appointed Fisher as one of the four justices, on Mar. 11, 1863, eight days after his congressional term had expired. Fisher is said to have displayed great ability on the bench and was praised especially for his conduct, in January 1867, of the first trial of John H. Surratt for participation in Lincoln's assassination. In May 1870 he was appointed by President Grant as United States attorney for the District of Columbia, but five years later he returned to Delaware. He was recalled to public life by President Benjamin Harrison in June 1889 to serve as first auditor of the treasury, a position which he held until the change of administration in 1893. The last years of his life he devoted to reading and literary pursuits, dying after a brief illness at Washington. Three years before his death he wrote to his daughter his reminiscences of houses and people in Dover when he was a lad of seven ("Recollections of Dover in 1824," *Delaware Historical Society Papers,* no. LV, 1896). His biographers describe him as without vindictiveness, a lovable and agreeable gentleman.

[Chas. B. Lore, "The Life and Character of George P. Fisher," *Del. Hist. Soc. Papers,* no. XXXVI (1902); H. C. Conrad, *Hist. of the State of Del.* (3 vols., 1908); Job Barnard, "Early Days of the Supreme Court of the District of Columbia," *Columbia Hist. Soc. Records,* XXII (1919), 1–35; obituaries in *Washington Post* and *Evening Star* (Washington), Feb. 11, 1899.] H. F. W.

FISHER, JOHN DIX (Mar. 27, 1797–Mar. 3, 1850), Boston physician, a pioneer advocate of education for the blind, was born to Aaron and Lucy (Stedman) Fisher at Needham, Mass. He was a younger brother of Alvan Fisher [*q.v.*]. After graduation from Brown University in 1820 and from the Harvard Medical School in 1825, he gave two years to professional study in Europe, chiefly in Paris, paying special attention to auscultation under Laënnec, the author of it, and becoming one of the first in America to utilize this aid to diagnosis. In his own practise he extended the application of it to diseases other than those of the chest, and he published the results of his findings. From investigations made abroad he issued, soon after his return, a book with illustrations, *Description of the Distinct, Confluent, and Inoculated Smallpox,* etc. (1829), which was highly esteemed. He wrote little, however, but served much in other ways. He was a pioneer in the use of etherization in childbirth; in fact, he was always zealous in behalf of the objects of the Boston Society for Medical Improvement. The Massachusetts Medical Society made him a member. Towards the end of his rather short life he was elected an acting physician of the Massachusetts General Hospital.

While a student in Paris he became interested in alleviation of another sort, that of the condition of blind children. Making a careful study of the means and methods used there in the National Institution ior the Youthful Blind, that parent of all such schools, he presented his survey before influential friends in Boston and so aroused their enthusiasm that a meeting was called, a legislative bill prepared and promptly enacted, incorporating the New England Asylum, which later became the Perkins Institution and Massachusetts School for the Blind. This was in 1829. He was its vice-president and physician until his death, and for one year, while its director was abroad, administered it and wrote its annual report; for all which service it seems that he would take no fee.

Fisher introduced into America the movement for educating the blind (Eliot, *post*) and in his friend and fellow physician, Samuel Gridley Howe [*q.v.*], discovered the man to launch it. In token of his service Perkins Institution has named one of its family units Fisher Cottage and has carved the name of Dr. Fisher on its central mural tablet. At his death his many friends met to consider what measures should be taken to express their respect for his memory. The meeting was called to order by Charles Sumner, fitting resolutions were passed, and it was voted to set up a monument to him in Mount Auburn Cemetery, Cambridge, Mass. That monument, which is of white marble, bears this inscription: "Erected to the memory of John Dix Fisher, M.D., by those who loved him for his virtues—The Physician and the friend of the poor—The early and efficient advocate for the education of the blind—The liberal deviseth liberal things, and by liberal things shall he stand."

[Walter Channing, *Sketch of the Life and Character of John D. Fisher, M.D.* (1850); *Medic. Communications Mass. Medic. Soc.,* vol. VIII (1854); H. A. Kelly and W. L. Burrage, *Am. Medic. Biogs.* (1920); Samuel Eliot, "The Perkins Inst. and Mass. School for the Blind," *New Eng. Mag.,* Feb. 1897; M. Anagnos, "Education of the Blind," *Perkins Inst. Ann. Report, 1881* (1882); *Hist. Cat. Brown Univ.* (1914); *Boston Daily Atlas,* Mar. 4, *Boston Daily Bee,* Mar. 5, *Puritan Recorder* (Boston), Mar. 7, 1850.] E. E. A.

FISHER, JOSHUA FRANCIS (Feb. 17, 1807–Jan. 21, 1873), publicist, historical student, humanitarian, was born in Philadelphia, to a position of social and financial security. His father, Joshua Fisher, descended from John Fisher, one of Penn's first company of English Quakers who settled in Pennsylvania about 1682, was the son of a wealthy Quaker merchant. He married Elizabeth Powel Francis, daughter of Tench and Anne (Willing) Francis, but died a few months later, before the birth of his only child. Joshua Francis Fisher was brought up by his mother and her sister and brother-in-law. He had all the school advantages open in his time to wealthy Philadelphians. In 1825, at the age of eighteen, he was graduated from Harvard College and soon began the study of law under Joseph R. Ingersoll. Following his admission in 1829 to the Philadelphia bar, he served for a brief time as attaché to the United States legation in France, while William C. Rives was minister to that country. Having an ample income, he never practised his profession. His interests were largely in American history and his studies in that then neglected field, while limited in scope, were for that day singularly penetrating and definitive. Of his published essays the most noteworthy are: "Some Account of the Early Poets and Poetry of Pennsylvania" (*Pennsylvania Historical Society Memoirs,* vol. II, pt. 2, 1830); "A Discourse . . . on the Private Life and Domestic Habits of William Penn" (*Ibid.,* vol. III, pt. 2, 1836); and the memoir "Andrew Hamilton, Esq., of Pennsylvania" (*Historical Magazine,* Morrisania, N. Y., August 1868). The Penn brochure indicates in particular a valuation of social and economic data in estimating historical characters that was far in advance of the writer's time. Fisher was one of the early members of the Historical Society of Pennsylvania and from 1828 to 1865 was more or less active in its management.

While Fisher was still in his early twenties the care and education of the blind began to appeal strongly to him. With the exception of the Perkins Institution at Boston there were nowhere in the United States schools that provided advanced instruction for that unfortunate group of people. Fisher, commissioned by Roberts Vaux to investigate European methods in their training, returned from abroad with a report which was influential in the founding at Philadelphia of the Pennsylvania Institution for the Instruction of the Blind, the second institution of its kind in the country. He was one of the incorporators and remained a member of the board of managers until his death—a period of forty years of service.

In March 1837 Fisher married Eliza Middleton, the youngest daughter of Gov. Henry Middleton of South Carolina, and thus became allied with a representative family of the "slave-holding aristocracy." As the slavery discussion grew more intense, during the fifties, Fisher became interested in efforts to reconcile the conflicting claims of North and South. He wrote *Concessions and Compromises* (1860), a pamphlet that proposed certain changes in the method of enforcing the provisions of the Constitution touching upon slavery. Although his own political views were conservative and inclined far more toward nationalism than toward sectionalism in any form, his sympathies in the Civil War were with the Confederacy because he felt that the South as a section had been unfairly treated by the North as a section. After the war he gave liberally of his personal wealth to rehabilitate the fortunes of members of his wife's family who had lost all they had in the conflict. In the Reconstruction measures of Congress he saw only injustice.

Long before the war was ended Fisher had turned his attention to evils that he conceived to inhere in the representative system. It is reported that as a young man he had conversed with De Tocqueville on the subject. He was one of the first Americans to become familiar with the writings of Thomas Hare, the English advocate of minority representation. While he recognized the gravity of the evils that Hare attacked, he could not accept his scheme as a practical remedy in America. He thought, however, that the subject should be discussed in the United States and to that end published *The Degradation of our Representative System and its Reform* (1863). In 1866 he brought out a pamphlet on *Reform in Our Municipal Elections,* one of the earliest American discussions in that field.

[*Recollections of Joshua Francis Fisher Written in 1864* (privately printed 1929), ed. by Sophia H. Cadwalader; Anna Wharton Smith, *Geneal. of the Fisher Family, 1682–1896* (1896), pp. 93–95; *Pa. Inst. for the Instruction of the Blind, Annual Report,* 1873; B. F. Perry, *Reminiscences of Public Men* (1883), pp. 277–84; obituary in the *World* (N. Y.), Jan. 24, 1873.]

W. B. S—w.

FISHER, PHILIP [See Copley, Thomas, 1595–*c.* 1652].

FISHER, SIDNEY GEORGE (Mar. 2, 1809–July 25, 1871), lawyer, author, son of James L. and Ann Eliza (George) Fisher, was born in Philadelphia, where he also died. He graduated from Dickinson College in 1827, read law under Joseph Ingersoll in Philadelphia, and was admitted to the bar a few weeks before he was twenty-one. The routine of his law practise seems to have engrossed him for many years. By 1838 he had proceeded far enough in the world to be summoned back to make an address before his alma mater, and in 1851 he was married to Elizabeth Ingersoll. About this time he became interested in farming, and devoting much of his time to Maryland plantations of his in Cecil and Kent counties, he adopted these two names as convenient signatures for his occasional contributions to the newspapers. In 1856 he published a volume of undistinguished verse, *Winter Studies in the Country,* and wrote for the Philadelphia *North American,* "Kanzas and the Constitution," an essay which—endorsing slavery but condemning the political rapaciousness of the South—so recommended itself to a group of Bostonians that they reprinted it as a pamphlet (1856). *Rustic Rhymes,* composed largely of two-and-three-stress lines, and *The Law of the Territories,* urging the retention of the Missouri Compromise, appeared in 1859. The next year, he published *The Laws of Race as Connected with Slavery,* an erudite plea for white supremacy, based to a great degree on his acceptance of slavery and his conviction that only people of "Saxon" derivation have any real desire for political freedom. *The Trial of the Constitution* (1862), his most voluminous work, restates in 390 pages the doctrines he had already promulgated concerning the great national issues of his time. In the *North American Review* for July 1864 he published an article, later issued in a pamphlet, called "A National Currency," upholding in general the policy of the government in issuing legal-tender notes. He made frequent addresses here and there before associations of farmers, advocating diversification of crops whenever he did not consider it more important to praise Daniel Webster, and to declare the idea of Union the one end to which all other political ideas in America should be made subservient. His son, named for him, with whom he has sometimes been confused, spelled his first name not Sidney, but Sydney.

[Dickinson College *Catalogue* (1840); *A Reply to a Pamphlet Recently Published by Sidney George Fisher, Esq., entitled "A National Currency"* (1865); L. D. Avery, *Geneal. of the Ingersoll Family in America* (1926), which, however, gives the name of Fisher's father incorrectly; Townsend Ward, "The Germantown Road and its Associations," *Pa. Mag. of Hist. and Biog.,* V (1881); letter from Sydney George Fisher to Librarian of Congress, Feb. 1903; letter from Registrar Dept. Public Health, Phila., to author, July 5, 1928.]

J. D. W.

FISHER, SYDNEY GEORGE (Sept. 11, 1856–Feb. 22, 1927), lawyer and historian, was the only child of Elizabeth (Ingersoll) and Sidney George Fisher [*q.v.*]. He was descended on his father's side from John Fisher who accompanied William Penn to America on his first voyage, and on his mother's side from Jared Ingersoll, a distinguished lawyer who was judge of vice-admiralty for the middle colonies at the outbreak of the Revolution. His father was a Philadelphia lawyer who gave much of his time and efforts to public affairs and was especially active with his pen during the period of the slavery crisis and the Civil War. Sydney's boyhood was largely spent at his father's country home, now a part of residential Philadelphia near Eighth and Erie avenues; there he acquired along the creek that intense love of nature and outdoor life which remained a passion with him, in spite of his absorption later in literary labors. He was prepared for college at St. Paul's School, Concord, N. H., and entered Trinity College at Hartford, from which he received his B.A. degree in 1879. His literary bent was early manifested; while in college he edited the school magazine. From Trinity College he entered Harvard as a law student and remained there for two years. In 1883 he was admitted to the bar in Pennsylvania and began the practise of law.

He will be remembered chiefly for his historical writings, which began in 1896 with the publication of *The Making of Pennsylvania,* followed the next year by his *Pennsylvania, Colony and Commonwealth* and *The Evolution of the Constitution,* the latter of which went through three editions; in 1898 there appeared his *Men, Women, and Manners in Colonial Times* in two volumes, which also was published in three editions; and in 1899 *The True Benjamin Franklin* which went into seven editions. In 1900 appeared *The True William Penn* that ran into four editions; in 1902, *The American Revolution and the Boer War: An Open Letter to C. F. Adams* which held up to scorn the latter's opposition to a continuance of the struggle on the part of the Boers; also in this year, *The True Story of the American Revolution,* with five editions to its credit. This history of the Revolution, after being reshaped, rewritten, expanded, and very greatly improved, appeared in 1908 in two volumes, under title *The Struggle for American Independence.* In 1909 Fisher wrote an article for the *Nation* entitled "The South and the Negro"; in 1911 he published *The True Daniel Webster*; and in 1912 he wrote "The Legendary and Myth-making Process in Histories of the American Revolution," which was first read before the American Philosophical Society and then published in its *Proceedings* (vol. LI, no. 204, April–June 1912). In 1917 came his *American Education,* and finally in 1919 *The Quaker Colonies. A Chronicle of the Proprietors of the Delaware* (Chronicles of America Series). His *Pennsylvania: Colony and Commonwealth* is sketchy, impressionistic, and not always accurate (*American Historical Review,*

April 1897); but *The Evolution of the Constitution* is a more carefully constructed piece of work, collating for the first time all the provisions of the colonial charters and the early state constitutions relating to the same subjects (*Ibid.*, October 1897). *The True History of the American Revolution* put in high light "certain facts about the Revolution upon which the best historians and teachers of history have been agreed for twenty years" (*Ibid.*, July 1903). It is not a well-balanced account of that epoch but it did have the merit of being the first popular work which challenged the orthodox interpretation. He reached the high point in his rôle of historian in *The Struggle for American Independence*, with his insistence on the thesis that the American design from the beginning of the struggle was independence as the result of certain political ideas and material interests (*Ibid.*, October 1908).

In addition to his activities as a lawyer and historian Fisher was deeply interested in educational questions. His first published work was *Church Colleges; Their History, Position and Importance with Some Account of the Church Schools*, which appeared in 1895 and was concerned with a survey of Episcopalian educational institutions in the United States. For many years previous to his death he served as the president of the board of trustees of his alma mater, Trinity College, and he was also a trustee of the Institution for the Education of the Blind and of the Library Company of Philadelphia. His volume on *American Education* came out of his endeavor to grapple with certain educational problems in connection with his service of these boards. As a lover of the out-of-doors he spent many winters in Florida, much of the time in a shanty-boat on the Kissimmee River; and in Pennsylvania he finally took up his residence at Essington on the Delaware some miles below Philadelphia and close to the Corinthian Yacht Club of which he was an enthusiastic member. It was at Essington that he died in 1927. He was never married; his attachment to his own family, however, led him to retain possession of the ancestral home, Mount Harmon, on the Sassafras River near Chesapeake Bay.

[L. D. Avery, *A Geneal. of the Ingersoll Family in America, 1629–1925* (1926); *N. Y. Times, Public Ledger* (Phila.), Feb. 23, 1927; *Who's Who in America*, 1926–27; memoir prepared by Wm. M. Meigs (MS).]

L. H. G.

FISHER, THEODORE WILLIS (May 29, 1837–Oct. 10, 1914), psychiatrist, was born at Westboro, Mass., the son of Milton Metcalf and Eleanor (Metcalf) Fisher; his family, of English origin, settled in Dedham, Mass., as early as 1638. He was educated at Phillips Academy, Andover, and the Harvard Medical School (M.D. 1861). From 1862 to 1863 he served as surgeon to the 44th Massachusetts Volunteer Militia and at one time was in charge of the Foster General Hospital at New Bern, N. C. Always interested in mental disease, on his return to Boston, he became assistant superintendent of the Boston Lunatic Hospital in 1863, retiring to private practise in 1869. His services, after 1870, were soon in demand and he was made examining physician to the Board of Overseers of Public Institutions in Boston and examiner for the public insane. His reputation as a psychiatrist and alienist grew rapidly and "in the seventies, he was the leading expert in his branch in Boston and was frequently called on to testify as a witness in court" (Channing). In 1872 he published *Plain Talk about Insanity*, which served further to establish his reputation as a psychiatrist; his advice was sought by the state when erecting new hospitals for patients with mental disease. He practised successfully until 1881, when he accepted the position as superintendent of the Boston Lunatic Hospital. Here, until 1895, when he retired on account of his health, he carried out his progressive ideas and established something of a national reputation. During this period he taught in the Harvard Medical School (1884–98). He wrote few, but sound, papers such as *Cerebral Localization* (1889), emphasizing the new field of brain surgery. In 1881 he was called by the defense to testify at the Guiteau trial. Fisher was not allowed to express his full opinion in court; he thought Guiteau insane and therefore irresponsible. After the declaration of sanity, he, as well as other alienists, made a vigorous report on the subject (*Boston Medical and Surgical Journal*, June 29, 1882), criticizing sharply the conduct of the counsel for the defense.

Fisher belonged to many medical societies, including the New England Psychological Society, the Boston Society for Medical Improvement, the Massachusetts Medical Society, and the American Medical Association. He was one of the founders in 1880 of the Boston Society of Psychiatry and Neurology and its president in 1893. He married, in 1858, Maria, daughter of Dr. Artemus Brown of Medway, Mass. After the death of his first wife he married again, in 1873, Ella Richardson of Boston. Four children survived him. Dr. Fisher was an active, energetic man, at times thought brusque by those that did not know him well. As an expert in court he was straightforward, truthful, and was never known to be guilty of trickery or under-handedness. Like most experts of his day, he believed it his duty to be a medical attorney and lay stress on points that would help the side that called him. His chief recreations were fishing and hunting, of which he was very fond. Death came to him after many years of invalidism from a chronic hereditary mental disease long well intrenched in his family. Although he knew the fatal nature of the malady, he bore himself with exceptional bravery, as was consistent with his character.

[W. Channing and others in *Boston Medic. and Surgic. Jour.*, Jan. 21, 1915, CLXXII, 117; *Medic. & Surgic. Hist. of the War of the Rebellion* (1888), pt. III, vol. I, p. 555; *Jour. Am. Medic. Asso.*, Dec. 5, 1914; T. F. Harrington, *The Harvard Medical School* (1905), III, 1503; P. A. Fisher, *The Fisher Genealogy* (1898); *Boston Transcript*, Oct. 12, 1914; letters from intimate friends.]

H. R. V.

FISK, CLINTON BOWEN (Dec. 8, 1828–July 9, 1890), Prohibitionist, was born on that frontier of western New York to which the newly opened Erie Canal had brought opportunity and hope. Benjamin Bigford Fisk, his father, was a descendant in the fifth generation from William Fiske, who came to Salem, Mass., before 1637. Lydia Aldrich Fisk, his mother, was of Welsh extraction. Benjamin Fisk failed to find his opportunity in New York, and moved his family into Michigan Territory while Clinton was still an infant. Here he died, leaving Clinton to educate himself and grow to manhood in almost "pinching poverty" (J. O. Foster, *Our Standard Bearer*, 1888, 7). In Coldwater, a county town on the Michigan Southern Railroad, Clinton played tuba in the village band, married Jeannette Crippen in 1850, and prospered as a small banker, only to be broken by the panic of 1857. The outbreak of the Civil War found him living in St. Louis, Mo., acquainted with both Lincoln and Grant, and ready to turn to arms. He served first in the home guards and took part in the seizure of Camp Jackson (May 9, 1861); the following summer he recruited and became colonel of the 33rd Missouri Volunteers (J. T. Scharf, *History of St. Louis*, 1883, I, 468). His career as a civilian soldier was distinguished. On Nov. 24, 1862, he became a brigadier-general of volunteers, and before he was mustered out he received his brevet major-generalcy. He fought over Arkansas and Missouri, took part in the campaign against Price, and was on the verge of retirement when the murder of President Lincoln postponed his discharge from the service.

Fisk was detailed to the Freedmen's Bureau in 1865 as assistant commissioner of the bureau of refugees, freedmen, and abandoned lands for Kentucky and Tennessee. It is reported that Johnson defended his appointment with the remark: "Fisk aint a fool, he wont hang everybody" (A. A. Hopkins, *Life*, 1910, 94). He found in this office the most distinctive portion of his career (American Unitarian Association, *From Servitude to Service*, 1905, 201). An ardent Methodist, and imbued with the spirit of missionary activity, he saw in the freedmen an opportunity for social and spiritual service. In an abandoned army barrack at Nashville, where he exercised almost dictatorial power for a time, he opened in 1866 a school for the negroes which developed after his discharge, and which was chartered in 1867 as Fisk University (J. Wooldridge, *History of Nashville*, 1890, 422). The American Missionary Association took Fisk University under its charge, and Fisk, who soon appeared as a prosperous banker in New York, continued to support it. As it developed along the lines of the small college and normal school it was one of the earliest approaches to the large problem of negro education. Fisk's interest in this need of the colored race marked him for broader service. In 1874 President Grant placed him on the Board of Indian Commissioners, of which he was president from 1881 until his death (*Report of the Secretary of the Interior*, 1890, II, 780). The Methodist Book Concern owed much to his services on its governing committee after 1876 and he continually attended the national and international conferences of his church.

Fisk appears in his private life to have been both popular and austere. In the army his aversion to drink and profanity was thrown into contrast by the readiness with which his associates took to both. He was an abstainer, with interest in the movement which placed the national Prohibition party in the field in 1872; but he continued to vote the Republican ticket until the campaign of 1884. In this contest the Prohibition nominee, Gov. John P. St. John of Kansas, polled some 150,000 votes, nearly fifteen times as many as a Prohibition candidate had hitherto received. His total was perhaps due to protest votes of Republicans who would not vote for Blaine and could not bring themselves to vote for Cleveland; but to the Prohibitionists it looked like the dawn of a new era. A wave of temperance emotion swept the country, and two years later the party in New Jersey induced Fisk to become a candidate for governor in that state (*New York Tribune*, May 29, 1886). In 1888, with the renomination of Cleveland a foregone conclusion, and with an impressive Blaine boom suggesting that once more Blaine might be the Republican candidate, the Prohibition party met at Indianapolis on May 30. Before the eastern delegates left home it was agreed that Fisk was to be the candidate (D. L. Colvin, *Prohibition in the United States*, 1926, 187). He was nominated without opposition on the second day of the convention, and received almost 250,000 votes in the following November (E. H. Cherrington, *The Evolution of Prohibition in the United States of America,* 1920, 234). He died two years later in New York.

[The best biography of Fisk is Alphonso A. Hopkins, *The Life of Clinton Bowen Fisk* (1910), which first appeared as a campaign biography in 1888. See also F. C. Pierce, *Fiske and Fisk Family* (1896), and the *N. Y. Times,* July 10, 1890.] F. L. P—n.

FISK, JAMES (Oct. 4, 1763–Nov. 17, 1844), lawyer, politician, son of Stephen and Anna (Bradish) Green Fisk, was born at Greenwich, Mass., and traced his descent from Nathan Fiske, who was in Watertown in 1642. His father died when James was two years old. His childhood, as far as is known, was one of privation and limited opportunities. He was self-educated but his speeches show a wide range of information and a thorough command of English. He served over three years in a Massachusetts line regiment of the Revolutionary army and while in Congress once remarked that it had been a valuable experience which he never regretted. After the close of the war he engaged in farming near Greenwich, represented the town for several sessions in the General Court (1791–96), and became a Universalist preacher. On Apr. 27, 1786, he married Priscilla West. In 1798 he moved to Barre, Vt. This region was still in many respects frontier territory and Fisk apparently led the typical life of many of its leaders. He cleared a farm, preached occasional sermons for neighboring congregations, studied law, was admitted to the bar, and soon acquired a position of local influence. As a Jeffersonian Republican he represented Barre in the legislature in 1800–05, 1809–10, and again in 1815. He also served as judge in the Orange County Court for 1802 and 1809.

In 1805 he entered the Ninth Congress and served until the adjournment of the Tenth in 1809. The Federalists of New England still treated Republican representatives with condescension or contempt and Fisk underwent some of these disagreeable experiences. He was a man of real ability, however, and his position as a New England Republican undoubtedly gave him more prominence than he might otherwise have had. One of his early speeches, on Spanish relations (*Annals of Congress,* 9 Cong., 1 Sess., pp. 966–73) is an able production. He followed orthodox Jeffersonian doctrines, favored economy, reduction in army and navy, the gunboat program, strict construction, and the rest. He supported the Embargo and was defeated in 1808 as a result. He was reëlected in 1810, however, and served throughout the Twelfth and Thirteenth Congresses. He gave full support to the Madison administration, voted for war in 1812, denounced Federalist disloyalty, and was one of the most effective leaders of the New England minority, serving on both the ways and means and judiciary committees. He shared the prevalent idea that Canada would be easily conquered and in one of his speeches urged that such a conquest was the safest way to protect commerce. On the other hand, he believed that a navy had proved "the bane of every country which has had anything to do with it" (*Ibid.,* 12 Cong., 1 Sess., pp. 969–70).

In 1812 Fisk declined President Madison's offer of a judgeship in the Indiana Territory, and on his retirement from Congress in 1815 served for a year as member of the supreme court of Vermont. In 1817, he was elected to the United States Senate but served for only a few weeks, resigning Jan. 8, 1818, to accept the post of federal collector of revenues for the district of Vermont, serving until 1826. He moved to Swanton in 1819 and lived there until his death. In his later years he appears to have been regarded as a local Nestor with a great fund of reminiscences about the men and events of the Jeffersonian era. Physically he is said to have borne a strong resemblance to Aaron Burr, and to have had the same flashing, penetrating eye.

[W. H. Crockett, *Vermont,* vol. V (1923); *Records of the Gov. and Council of the State of Vt.,* vol. V (1877), pp. 460–61; *Biog. Directory Am. Cong.* (1928); F. C. Pierce, *Fiske and Fisk Family* (1896), pp. 156–59, 262–64.] W. A. R.

FISK, JAMES (Apr. 1, 1834–Jan. 7, 1872), capitalist, speculator, was the son of James and Love B. (Ryan) Fisk, of Bennington, and later Brattleboro, Vt. After scanty schooling, he was successively waiter in a hotel, ticket-seller for the Van Amberg circus, and salesman with his father's "traveling emporium," which he later purchased and operated himself, graciously admitting his father to his employ. A boastful, flashy, genial youth, with endless impudence and push, he was soon aspiring to larger spheres. He branched from peddling into a jobbing business for Jordan & Marsh of Boston, entered their wholesale department in 1860, and managed large war contracts for them on a commission basis. Later he went South to buy cotton in the occupied districts for a Boston syndicate, handled extensive purchases for Northern ports, and England, and became wealthy enough to launch into business for himself. His Boston establishment as dry-goods jobber was badly hit in 1865 by postwar deflation, and a brokerage office in Broad Street, New York, was a failure. But his conceit, swaggering energy, and taste for speculation were undiminished. He recouped his fortunes by acting as agent in the sale of Daniel Drew's

Stonington steamboats to a Boston group, returned to New York, and with Drew's support founded in 1866 the brokerage house of Fisk & Belden.

Fisk's rise to fortune was thereafter rapid. Drawn into the "Erie War" between Drew and Vanderbilt, he became a director of the Erie, helped Gould and Drew despoil it, and was an able, self-assertive second in all their schemes. During the battle royal of 1868, when Vanderbilt with the aid of Justice Barnard tried to capture the line, it was he who evaded Barnard's injunction against the issue of more stock by seizing 50,000 ready-signed shares, who used them to break Vanderbilt's attempted corner, thus netting millions for the trio, and who led the famous flight with Gould and Drew to Taylor's Hotel in Jersey City. When Drew and Vanderbilt made peace, Fisk and Gould shared control of the half-wrecked Erie Railroad. They at once embarked on a series of bold and unscrupulous ventures. They increased the Erie stock during the summer of 1868 from $34,265,000 to $57,766,000, where it stood on Oct. 24. Part of the proceeds was used for expansion, the two managers—Fisk as comptroller, Gould as president—leasing other railways, building branches, buying steamboats, rolling-mills, and car shops, and adding new equipment; part was used in reckless speculative forays. They launched a campaign with Drew in the fall of 1868 to make credit tight and raise the price of gold which reacted disastrously upon the nation's business and was felt even in Europe, but which netted them large sums. They also carried out a cornering operation which was so outrageous that Erie stock was stricken from the brokers' board; a raid upon the United States Express Company, whose stock they manipulated at will; and a raid upon the Albany & Susquehanna Railroad which resulted in a pitched battle of gangs of employees near Binghamton. These raids, exasperating public sentiment, culminated in the famous Black Friday attempt to corner the gold market (September 1869), when once more hundreds were ruined and all business suffered a profound shock. The coup disastrously failed, and Fisk flatly repudiated contracts of many millions through his responsible partner Belden. American opinion regarded him and Gould as public enemies, but he flippantly told a Congressional committee that the money had "gone where the woodbine twineth."

Meanwhile Fisk, now a fat, jovial, brassy voluptuary, was leading a life of half-barbaric prodigality. Buying Pike's Opera House at Twenty-third St. and Eighth Avenue he fitted up costly offices there, at the same time producing dramas and French opera bouffe; he leased the Academy of Music and put on grand opera till the expense chilled him; swaggered as "admiral" of the Fall River and the Bristol lines of steamboats, which he controlled; placed on the Hudson its largest ferryboat, the *James Fisk*; bought a summer garden for a restaurant; kept a large stable; and diverted the East by his antics as colonel of the 9th Regiment of the New York militia, a post to which he bought his way in May 1870. His visit with this regiment to Boston on Bunker Hill Day in 1871, when he asked permission to celebrate "divine service" on Boston Common, was one of the best-advertised episodes of his career. His end befitted his flashy life. After keeping numerous mistresses he singled out the actress Josie Mansfield as his favorite, quarreled over her and over business transactions with the dissolute Edward Stokes, was fatally shot by the latter in the Grand Central Hotel on Jan. 6, 1872, and died the next day. A spectacular funeral, with every honor from the Tammany administration and a cortège including the 9th Regiment and a band of two hundred pieces, was accompanied by innumerable denunciatory sermons and editorials. He was survived by his wife, Lucy D. Moore, of Springfield, Mass., whom he married in November 1855.

[F. C. Pierce, *Fiske and Fisk Family* (1896); Willoughby Jones, *Jas. Fisk, Jr., The Life of a Green Mountain Boy* (1872); R. H. Fuller, *Jubilee Jim: The Life of Col. Jas. Fisk, Jr.* (1928); Bouck White, *The Book of Daniel Drew* (1910); C. F. and Henry Adams, *Chapters of Erie* (1871); E. H. Mott, *Between the Ocean and the Lakes: The Story of Erie* (1899); *N. Y. Tribune*, Jan. 8, 1872, and other newspapers of the day.] A. N.

FISK, WILBUR (Aug. 31, 1792–Feb. 22, 1839), Methodist clergyman, educator, son of Isaiah and Hannah (Bacon) Fisk, was born in Brattleboro, Vt. To this state his father, a descendant of William Fiske, who came to Salem before 1637, had migrated from Massachusetts, finally settling at Lyndon, Caledonia County. There he achieved little financial success, but proved himself a worthy citizen, frequently representing his town in the legislature, and serving as chief justice of the county court. Resemblances between his career and that of James Fisk (1763–1844) have caused some authors to refer to Wilbur as James's son. From childhood Wilbur was frail, and early became subject to pulmonary hemorrhages from causes which brought his career to an end at the height of his influence. Much farm work and scant schooling characterized his boyhood, but by independent study and some preparation at a school in Peacham, he managed to enter the sophomore class at the University of Vermont in 1812. When its buildings were turned into barracks the following year he entered Brown University, graduating in 1815. Although reared in the fervid atmosphere of early New England Methodism, he was without deep religious feeling and confessedly fond of amusements and ambitious for worldly honors. With the view to becoming a statesman he entered the law office of Isaac Fletcher at Lyndon, soon leaving it because of financial needs to be tutor in the home of a Col. Ridgely, near Baltimore. The religious training of his childhood prevented him from viewing a worldly career with equanimity, however, and he finally surrendered himself to the call of the ministry. He joined the New England Conference on probation in 1818, being received into full connection in 1820, and ordained elder in 1822. On June 9, 1823, he married Ruth Peck of Providence, R. I.

From his appearance in the ministry church historians date a new epoch in New England Methodism. He is said to have been the first college-bred minister of that denomination in the Eastern states, and he did much to lessen the contempt with which it was viewed in that section because of its indifference to learning. Not only did he lead Methodism of the East in educational enterprises, but his influence was felt throughout the whole church, for his abilities and charm made him respected and beloved everywhere. (See Abel Stevens, *History of The Methodist Episcopal Church in the United States,* 1867, IV, 288.) His pastoral work, including three years as presiding elder in the Vermont district, was brief. In 1825 he was elected principal of Wesleyan Academy, Wilbraham, Conn., which he had helped to establish, leaving it in 1830 a thriving institution, to become first president of Wesleyan University, Middletown, Conn., which also he had helped to found, and to the development of which he devoted the remainder of his life, saving it by his wisdom, confidence, and energy from the fate of similar early Methodist institutions. A member of the General Conferences of 1824, 1828, and 1832, he was active in behalf of increased educational facilities, and his advocacy in his own Conference of conference educational societies was the beginning of a movement which culminated in the formation of the Methodist Board of Education. In 1828 he was elected bishop of the Methodist Church in Canada, which office he declined partly because of poor health, but particularly because he was devoted to his work in New England. He was an early advocate of temperance and the formation of temperance societies; a promoter of missions; an opponent of the Abolitionists, though opposed to slavery; an advocate of colonization; and a defender of Methodist doctrines in a number of articles and published sermons. In 1835 Wesleyan sent him to Europe for the benefit of his health and to study educational institutions. While there the General Conference of 1836 elected him bishop, but upon his return he declined this honor. The results of his trip are incorporated in *Travels in Europe* (1838). Upon his return the disease from which he had so long suffered progressed rapidly. Death came to him in his forty-seventh year, and he was buried in the College Cemetery, Middletown.

[F. C. Pierce, *Fiske and Fisk Family* (1896); Jos. Holdich, *The Life of Willbur Fisk* (1856); Geo. Prentice, *Wilbur Fisk* (1890); Wm. B. Sprague, *Annals Am. Pulpit,* vol. VII (1859); Daniel D. Whedon, "Tribute to the Memory of President Fisk," *The Meth. Mag. and Quart. Rev.,* Oct. 1839; B. C. Steiner, *Hist. of Educ. in Conn.* (1893); and standard histories of Methodism.]

H. E. S.

FISKE, AMOS KIDDER (May 12, 1842–Sept. 18, 1921), editor, author, was born in Whitefield, N. H., the son of Henry and Lucinda (Keyes) Fiske. His father's ancestors came to Massachusetts from England about the middle of the seventeenth century. During his childhood, it was necessary for him to work both on his parents' farm and in a cotton-mill in a near-by village. Left an orphan at sixteen, he continued working as a factory hand, but determined to set aside enough money to launch him on his way through school. During 1860–61 he attended the Appleton Academy at New Ipswich, and in 1862, still having to earn his livelihood, he entered Harvard. He was graduated in 1866, with the highest honors. Soon afterward he went to New York. There he taught for a year, and then studied law for a year. One of the lawyers in the office where he studied was George Ticknor Curtis, who was busy at that time writing his life of Daniel Webster. Young Fiske, it seems, had a large hand in the more detailed aspects of that biography but no mention of him occurs in the preface. In 1867, he began his fifteen years' connection with the *Annual Cyclopædia.* In 1870, he was married to Caroline Child of Cambridge, sister of Francis J. Child [*q.v.*] of Harvard. From 1874 to 1877 he was an editor of the *Boston Globe,* but with that exception, he was nearly all of the time from 1869 to 1919 on the editorial staff of various New York newspapers—notably with the *Times,* 1869–71, 1878–97, and with the *Journal of Commerce,* 1902–19. In 1888 when his son, Philip Sidney, was old enough to enter Harvard, his family removed to Cambridge. His two daughters went to Radcliffe. From 1890 to 1914 he published nine books. The first of these, *Midnight Talks at the Club,* is a series of genial, wise essays on topics of contemporary interest. *Beyond the Bourne* (1891) is a spiritualist story. Though he published *The Story of the Philippines* in 1898, and *The West Indies* in 1899, his interest during the last several decades of his life was divided chiefly between economic subjects and subjects having to do with Hebrew folk-lore. In *Jewish Scriptures* (1896), *The Myths of Israel* (1897), and *The Great Epic of Israel* (1911), he assumes that the Old Testament is not the "specially inspired word of God" (*Great Epic*, p. 4), but he exhibits great admiration for it not only as a curious document but as a source of beauty and wisdom; and he is avowedly bent on encouraging in his day an acquaintance with the Bible. *The Modern Bank* (1904) is almost entirely descriptive, but *Honest Business* (1914) is an entertaining, non-technical record of the author's conclusions about the economic structure of society—feelings conservative in general, but controlled always by an instinct for fairness. For the last year and a half of his life he was in delicate health, living in Cambridge at the home of his two daughters.

[F. C. Pierce, *Fiske and Fisk Family* (1896); Harvard Univ. *Quin. Cat.* (1910); *Who's Who in America, 1920–21*; *N. Y. Times*, Sept. 22, 1921; *N. Y. Jour. of Commerce*, Sept. 23, 1921.] J. D. W.

FISKE, DANIEL WILLARD (Nov. 11, 1831–Sept. 17, 1904), editor, librarian, book-collector, born in Ellisburg, N. Y., was the son of Daniel Haven and Caroline (Willard) Fiske, and traced his descent from Nathan Fiske, who was in Watertown, Mass., in 1642. Of his parents he himself wrote in 1857: "My father is from the most undoubted Puritan stock of Massachusetts, and was born there. . . . My mother is from Vermont, and among the hills of this latter state I spent some of the pleasantest hours of my boyhood." He attended Cazenovia Seminary and Hamilton College, but left the latter in his second year to go abroad to study the Scandinavian languages. After two years in Copenhagen and at the University of Upsala, Sweden, he returned to New York in 1852, taking a place in the Astor Library, where he remained until 1859. The following year he was general secretary of the American Geographical Society. Meanwhile from 1857 to 1860, he edited with Paul Morphy the newly founded *American Chess Monthly*. In Copenhagen Fiske had been connected with the United States legation; in 1861 he was appointed attaché to the legation in Vienna. Upon his return to the United States he spent two years (1863–65) with the *Syracuse Daily Journal*, later became a book-dealer in Syracuse, and in 1867 joined the staff of the *Hartford Courant*. While traveling abroad the next year he was called to be librarian and professor of North-European languages at Cornell University. Here his constructive services in the development of the institution were notable. In 1880 he married Jennie McGraw of Ithaca. At her death in 1881 he inherited a large fortune. Two years later he severed his connection with the university and passed the remaining years of his life in Europe. From 1883 to 1886 he rented the Villa Forini in the eastern quarter of Florence, a mansion previously occupied by the American minister, George P. Marsh. In 1892 he purchased and remodeled the Villa Landor, well above Florence, and just under Fiesole. In these attractive and historic villas he dispensed a generous but unassuming hospitality and devoted himself to intellectual pursuits.

The scope of Fiske's interests is suggested by his literary activities and his honorary connections. He was an early member of the National Institute of Arts and Letters, an honorary member of the National Icelandic Literary Society, and corresponding member of the Royal Society of Northern Antiquities, Copenhagen. He was given special distinction in 1892 by King Humbert I of Italy, and in 1902 by Christian IX of Denmark, chiefly in recognition of the wide extent of his literary achievements. He was an assiduous collector of rare and perfect book collections, a romantic crusader for a reformed and modernized Egyptian alphabet, a zealous propagandist for the game of chess, and a lifelong devotee to the advancement of Icelandic civilization. His writings were numerous and varied, including much admirable verse, reprints from which were published in the three volumes of the *Memorials* (*post*). He died in 1904 and was interred by the side of his wife in the memorial chapel which was constructed by the trustees of Cornell in the university grounds. In addition to his valuable book collections which he presented to Cornell, relating to Dante, Petrarch, Icelandic history and literature, and the Rhæto-Romanic language, he gave a fund of more than half a million dollars for the uses and purposes of the library.

[The record of Fiske's life may be found in the two following works by his literary executor, Horatio S. White: *Memorials of Willard Fiske* (3 vols., 1920–22); *Willard Fiske, Life and Correspondence* (1925). See also *Papers of the Bibliog. Soc. of America*, vol. XII, July–Oct. 1918 (Willard Fiske Memorial), which includes a bibliography of Fiske's writings on Iceland, a list of the Cornell University Library publications on Icelandic literature, on the Fiske Foundation, and a record of the catalogues of the various collections given by Fiske to the university library.] H. S. W.

FISKE, FIDELIA (May 1, 1816–July 26, 1864), missionary to the Nestorians, was a descendant of William Fiske who came to Salem, Mass., from the County of Suffolk, England, before 1637, later settling in Wenham; and the daughter of Rufus and Hannah (Woodward) Fiske. She was born on a hill-top farm in Shelburne, Mass., where in 1761 her great-grandfather, Ebenezer Fiske, Jr., had established himself. Her parents were plain, New England country folk, hard-working, intelligent, and religious. From childhood her own religious tendencies were pronounced, and her eagerness to read whatever she could lay her hand on was so keen that by the time she was eight years old she had perused with interest, if not with full understanding, Cotton Mather's *Magnalia,* and had twice read through Timothy Dwight's *Theology.* She attended district school, and at seventeen became a district school teacher, in which occupation she continued for a period of six years, broken by brief terms of study at Franklin Academy, Shelburne Falls, and at a select school in Conway. In 1839 she entered Mount Holyoke Seminary, graduating in 1842, and immediately becoming an instructor in that institution. The intense religious and missionary zeal of the principal, Mary Lyon [*q.v.*], strengthened in Fidelia Fiske an early predilection for Christian service abroad, so that when in 1843 Rev. Justin Perkins [*q.v.*], who had founded a mission among the Nestorians a few years before, came to Mount Holyoke in search of teachers, she promptly volunteered and was accepted.

Under authorization of the American Board of Commissioners for Foreign Missions she sailed from Boston Mar. 1, 1843, and arrived in Oroomiah (Urumiah) in June of that year. Here she commenced a work which is credited with having been a potent factor in improving the condition of women in Persia, and displayed a spirit which has given her a place among those who in missionary annals are held up as ensamples. The story of her service is the story of the first fifteen years of the notable Oroomiah Seminary, a boarding school for girls, of which she was practically the founder. While successful in establishing this institution in the face of much native opposition and endless difficulties, she did much by personal ministrations and evangelistic labors to instruct and uplift women and children wherever she could reach them. She had gone to Persia with the expectation of remaining until death, but ill-health forced her to return in July 1858. Home again, she addressed missionary meetings and was a kind of chaplain to Mount Holyoke Seminary. An invitation to become principal she declined in the hope that she would be able to return to Persia, but her constitution was too seriously impaired, and death came to her at Shelburne in her forty-ninth year. She had been able, however, to prepare, *Memorial, Twenty-fifth Anniversary of Mount Holyoke Female Seminary* (1862), and at the time of her death was at work upon *Recollections of Mary Lyon,* which was published in 1866. She also furnished the material for Thomas Laurie's *Woman and Her Saviour in Persia* (1863), which contains much information about her work.

[D. T. Fiske, *The Cross and the Crown, or Faith Working by Love as Exemplified in the Life of Fidelia Fiske* (1868); Harriet B. Genung, *The Story of Fidelia Fiske* (1907); *Missionary Herald,* Sept., Nov., 1864.]

H. E. S.

FISKE, GEORGE CONVERSE (Feb. 28, 1872–Jan. 8, 1927) classicist, educator, was born at Roxbury Highlands, Mass., the eldest son of George Alfred and Kate (Washburn) Fiske. The greater part of his youth was spent at Ashmont, Dorchester, Mass., and from 1884 to 1890 he prepared for college at the Boston Latin School, of which his father was head master. As a student at Harvard he displayed that ability, energy, and thoroughness which stamped indelibly his professional career, for he worked his way through college and was graduated in 1894 with honors. He continued his training in the Harvard graduate school where he received the degrees of M.A. in 1897 and Ph.D. in 1900. After a summer spent in England and northern Germany he taught Latin and Greek in Belmont and was instructor in Greek at Phillips Andover Academy until Jan. 1, 1901, when he was appointed instructor in Latin at the University of Wisconsin. He became an assistant professor in 1902, associate professor in 1907, and professor in 1924. He was married on Dec. 26, 1908, to Augustine Louise Elleau at Newark, N. J.

His chosen fields of research were ancient religion, satire, and rhetorical theory. His most notable contribution to classical studies was his *Lucilius and Horace,* published by the University of Wisconsin in 1920, which won for him in this country and in Europe recognition as one of the leading authorities on Roman satire. The following articles bear witness to his scholarly investigations: "Notes on the Worship of the Roman Emperors in Spain" (*Harvard Studies in Classical Philology,* vol. XI, 1900, pp. 101–39); "The Politics of the Patrician Claudii" (*Ibid.,* vol. XIII, 1902, pp. 1–59); "Lucilius, the *Ars Poetica* of Horace, and Persius" (*Ibid.,* vol. XXIV, 1913, pp. 1–36); "Cicero's *Orator* and Horace's *Ars Poetica*" (*Ibid.,* vol. XXXV, 1924, pp. 1–74, written in collaboration with Mary A. Grant); "Lucilius and Persius" (*Transactions of the American Philological Association,* vol. XL,

1909, pp. 121–50); "The Plain Style in the Scipionic Circle" (*Classical Studies in Honor of Charles Forster Smith,* 1919, Wisconsin Studies in Language and Literature, No. 3), pp. 62–105; and "Augustus and the Religion of Reconstruction" (*Ibid.,* 2 ser., no. 15, 1922, pp. 111–33). During the World War he acted as secretary of the university committee on war publications, and was the author of a number of articles, among which was one on the "Violation of the Neutrality of Belgium" (reprinted in the *War Book of the University of Wisconsin*). At the time of his death he had just completed an article on "Cicero's *De Oratore* and Horace's *Ars Poetica*" and was engaged in writing a book on Greek and Roman rhetoric for the series Our Debt to Greece and Rome. There was much of the grandeur of the Roman Cato in Fiske's absolute honesty, his uncompromising and lofty ideals, and his courage in the face of misfortune; but above all his friends and acquaintances experienced and appreciated his sympathy and help, ever at their command. As senior editor of the *Classical Bulletin* his editorials were of real service and inspiration to the teachers of Latin in the state of Wisconsin. He was a frequent visitor at the high schools, and he took a keen interest and active part in the classical meetings and in the educational policies of the university, where he was an advocate of high standards and of sound methods of education.

[*Who's Who in America,* 1926–27; *Latin Bull. of the Univ. of Wis.,* Jan. 1927; the *Nation,* Feb. 16, 1927; the *Classical Jour.,* Mar. 1927; *Classical Philol.,* July 1927; the *Harvard Grads.' Mag.,* Mar. 1927; *Harvard Coll. Class of 1894,* 1894–1919.] K. S.

FISKE, HALEY (Mar. 18, 1852–Mar. 3, 1929), insurance official, lawyer, was born at New Brunswick, N. J., a son of William Henry and Sarah Ann (Blakeney) Fiske, and a brother of Stephen Fiske [*q.v.*]. His grandfather, Haley Fiske, had established an iron-foundry at New Brunswick, which was continued by his sons until after the Civil War. Fiske attended a private school, was matriculated at Rutgers College, and graduated B.A. in 1871. He then worked as a reporter on local newspapers, studied law, and within two years became a clerk in the law office of Arnoux, Ritch & Woodford, of New York. The firm was counsel for the Metropolitan Life Insurance Company and after Fiske's admission to the New York bar he was assigned to take charge of that company's litigation. Having shown marked ability as a trial lawyer, he was made a member of the law firm. Meanwhile he acquired, through his contact with the Metropolitan's affairs, so broad a knowledge of the insurance field that in 1891, when John R. Hegeman became president of the company, he brought about the election of Fiske as a vice-president. At that time the Metropolitan was a comparatively small insurance company, with about $258,000,000 of insurance in force and from $10,000,000 to $11,000,000 of annual premium. It was a stock company with a capital of $2,000,000 and dividends limited to 7 per cent. In 1902, largely as the result of Fiske's advocacy, the state legislature enacted a law which placed the actual control of the company in the hands of the policyholders. It was provided that all policyholders whose insurance had been in force for a year or more might vote for directors on condition that two-thirds of the directors elected should collectively own a majority of the capital stock. By 1914 the company's surplus had reached $40,000,000, while the assets totaled $500,000,000. Meanwhile Fiske had popularized and expanded the ordinary life business through the payment of bonuses to the insured. In 1915 the company was completely mutualized. The stockholders having been paid off, the election of officers was conferred on the policyholders alone.

A national health campaign that may fairly be characterized as statesmanlike was initiated by the company in 1909, when Fiske, because of President Hegeman's illness, was virtually the executive head of the organization. The problem was to conserve the health of the workingmen and their families who made up almost 10,000,000 of the policyholders. An army of visiting nurses was mobilized and set to work in the industrial centers of the nation. As a result, within nine years the company's mortality rate was reduced one-fifth. By 1921 more than 2,000,000 individuals had benefited from the nursing in their homes. The death rate from tuberculosis, typhoid, and acute contagious diseases was lowered for Metropolitan policyholders more rapidly than for the population in general. The actual money saving to the company was estimated at $3,500,000 a year. One outcome of Fiske's personal interest in health promotion was the company's investment of $7,500,000 in New York apartment houses to rent at a maximum of nine dollars a room together with loans on housing developments elsewhere (Haley Fiske, "Home—$9 a Room," in *Collier's,* Aug. 14, 1926). On the death of Hegeman, Fiske succeeded to the presidency of the Metropolitan in 1919. The company was already recognized as the largest financial institution in the world. Fiske himself had been identified with the policies which caused its rapid expansion and with others which made it a factor of growing importance in relation to public welfare, especially in American industrial centers.

All those policies were vigorously upheld during the ten years of his presidency. At the time of his sudden death, the company had in force about seventeen and one-half per cent of all life insurance reported, involving more than 42,000,000 policies.

Throughout his life Fiske gave the impression of unusual physical vigor. After he was seventy he occasionally played tennis. He was a leading layman of the Anglo-Catholic wing of the Protestant Episcopal Church, contributed liberally to the various church enterprises, notably the building of the Cathedral of St. John the Divine, and was versed in theology and church history. He was twice married: first, on Jan. 10, 1878, to Mary G. Mulford who died in 1886 and second, on Apr. 27, 1887, to Marione Cowles Cushman, who survived him. He left four daughters and two sons.

[F. C. Pierce, *Fiske and Fisk Family* (1896); *N. Y. Times*, Mar. 4, 1929; *Who's Who in America*, 1928–29; "The Metropolitan as a Public Institution," in the *Eastern Underwriter*, Apr. 8, 1921; and the *Insurance Field* (Louisville, Ky.), Mar. 8, 1929.] W. B. S—w.

FISKE, JOHN (Apr. 11, 1744–Sept. 28, 1797), naval commander, merchant capitalist, militia officer, traced his descent from John Fiske, who was in New England in 1637. Born at Salem, Mass., he was the son of Anna Gerrish Fiske and the Rev. Samuel Fiske, a talented divine whose usefulness was prematurely ended by quarrels with his parishioners. After a common-school education the son went to sea, forged ahead rapidly, and when barely twenty-one he was master of a brigantine voyaging to Spain. At the outbreak of the Revolution, his affairs were prospering, and he was well liked. In 1775 he acted as member of the Salem committee of safety and correspondence. In the next year, after a state navy had been authorized by the Massachusetts General Court, Fiske was commissioned captain of the brigantine *Tyrannicide* (Apr. 20). He was not the first naval officer of the state to receive a commission, despite Bentley's assertion, for that of Capt. Jeremiah O'Brien bore the date of Mar. 15, 1776. Fiske put to sea in July, captured a British prize four days after sailing, and in August he brought in three more. Other cruises followed. From February till October 1777, Fiske commanded the brigantine *Massachusetts*, then in March, by order of the board of war, Captains Fiske, Haraden, and Clouston sailed to harass enemy shipping off the coasts of western Europe. It was a notable cruise in the annals of the state navy. Many prizes fell into their hands some of which escaped, but Fiske took eight vessels. He put in at Marblehead late in July, but was soon at sea again, watching for English ships returning from the West Indies. He captured some prizes and returned to Salem in mid-October. Meantime, his professional honor having been assailed, an investigation of the charges made against him was made and he received a public vindication. In 1778 he was recommended for another command, and was offered the *Hazard*, but he refused it, alleging that it was not formidable enough.

Fiske now set up as a merchant, and his ventures proved fortunate till near the end of his life. He continued to buy ships, and fitted them out for voyages to the Mediterranean and to the East and West Indies. In 1791 he was elected master of the Salem Marine Society and he then urged Congress to establish aids to navigation on the Massachusetts coast (*Laws of the Salem Marine Society*, 60–62, 131). After the war he filled a few minor civic offices acceptably. In 1792 he attained the rank of major-general in the state militia, and during his term of service he greatly strengthened its morale. Capt. Fiske was a bluff, hearty man, vehement but reasonable and honest. He was generous to clerks and captains, and his reputation for hospitality was justly celebrated. In 1766 he married Lydia Phippen and had by her several children. She died in 1782. His second wife, Martha Lee Hibbert, whom he married in 1783, died in 1785 and the following year he married Sarah Wendell Gerry who, with three children by his first wife, survived his death.

[Wm. Bentley, *Funeral Discourse* (1797); *The Diary of Wm. Bentley* (1905–11); *Essex Inst. Hist. Colls.*; C. O. Paullin, *The Navy of the Am. Revolution* (1906); G. W. Allen, *A Naval Hist. of the Am. Revolution* (1913); *Mass. Soldiers and Sailors of the Revolutionary War* (1896–1907); *Vital Records of Salem* (1916–25), which gives Apr. 11, 1744, as date of birth; *Laws of the Salem Marine Soc.* (1914); J. B. Felt, *Annals of Salem* (1827); F. C. Pierce, *Fiske and Fisk Family* (1896).] F. M—d.

FISKE, JOHN (Mar. 30, 1842–July 4, 1901), philosopher, historian, only child of Edmund Brewster and Mary Fisk (Bound) Green, was born at Hartford, Conn., and was baptized Edmund Fisk. His original legal name was thus Edmund Fisk Green, which was changed by act of legislature in 1855 to John Fisk, the final *e* being added five years later without legal action. The Greens were of New Jersey Quaker ancestry. Little is known of them except that the child's grandfather was a substantial merchant in Philadelphia. The Bounds and Fisks were of English Puritan descent, branches of both families, after having been for some generations in Massachusetts, having established themselves in Middletown, Conn. There, subsequent to his graduation from Wesleyan University, Edmund

Green became a lawyer and married Mary Bound, Sept. 15, 1840. Green was in turn a journalist in Hartford, private secretary to Henry Clay in Washington, and owner and editor of a paper in Panama, where he died in 1852. During the later years of the marriage, his wife taught school in New York and Newark, and the child spent most of his time with his grandparents in Middletown. On his mother's second marriage, to Edwin Wallace Stoughton, a well-to-do New York lawyer, later United States minister to Russia, the son elected to remain at the Fisk home in Middletown, and it was then that he took the name of his great-grandfather on his mother's side.

The boy was extremely precocious, and at eight years of age wrote that he had then read about two hundred volumes, mostly on philosophy, chemistry, astronomy, grammar, mathematics, and "miscellaneous things," including some in Spanish. Throughout life the range and variety of his linguistic attainments were extraordinary, and when not yet twenty he could read German, French, Spanish, Italian, Portuguese, Latin, Greek, and Anglo-Saxon, and, less readily, Dutch, Danish, Swedish, Hebrew, Chaldee, and Sanskrit, while he had also "dipped into" Zend, Gothic, Wallachian and Provencal (Clark, *post,* I, 254).

At first he attended private schools in Middletown, and from 1855 to 1857, Betts Academy, Stamford, Conn. Returning to Middletown, he studied for two years under the Rev. H. M. Colton as tutor, preparing for Yale. He preferred Harvard, however, with its more liberal atmosphere, and after a year of study by himself and under a tutor at Cambridge, he entered the sophomore class in 1860. His wide reading in science and philosophy had already led him to heterodox opinions in religion, with the social results inevitable in a small New England town of that period. He did not fare much better at Harvard, where through an accidental discovery in a bookshop, he became an enthusiastic disciple of Herbert Spencer, whose long series of volumes were then in course of publication and to which Fiske at once subscribed. His vast reading—the boy studied from twelve to sixteen hours daily—bore important fruit even before graduation. Two articles, one pointing out fallacies in Buckle's *History of Civilization in England,* published in his senior year in the *North American Review,* clearly aligned him with the most advanced thinkers of the day on evolution. His views brought him into conflict with the Harvard authorities, who warned him of expulsion, should he attempt to spread his opinions. In spite of some difficulties, however, he received his degree of B.A. in 1863.

The Civil War, then raging, had left him utterly cold at first; and although later he became interested, he does not seem to have considered taking a part in the great conflict. Before graduation he had become engaged to Abby Morgan Brooks, daughter of Aaron Brooks, of Petersham, Mass., to whom he was married Sept. 6, 1864. His mother, who was now well-to-do, seems to have been willing to assist him financially; but his marriage made the choice of a career imperative. That choice was between law and teaching, but he found the latter closed to him, at least at Harvard, on account of his open advocacy of the doctrine of evolution. In July 1864 he passed his examination for the bar, without formal study at the law school, and was admitted, taking his degree of LL.B. the following year. Although he started to practise in Boston, he had few clients, and his heart was not in his work. Some months before his marriage he had begun a correspondence with Spencer, and philosophical interests now dominated him. With the support of both his own and his wife's family, he decided to trust solely to writing for his living, taking a house in Cambridge, which was thenceforth to remain his home. The situation at Harvard had now altered. After a conflict between the reactionary and progressive factions, in which Fiske had taken part by articles in the *Atlantic Monthly,* and the *Nation,* Charles W. Eliot had been elected president. As one direct result of this invigorating change, Fiske was asked to deliver a course of lectures in 1869 on "The Positive Philosophy." During the next three years, although still encountering much opposition, he lectured on both philosophy and history, giving public courses in Boston also. In 1872 he was appointed assistant librarian of the college at a salary of $2,500 a year, and soon after published his first important volume, *Myths and Myth-Makers.* The following year, 1873, owing to the generosity of a friend who gave him $1,000 to continue his studies in Europe, and a year's leave granted him by Harvard, he was able to go abroad. In England, where his writings had already made him known, he met Spencer, Darwin, Huxley, Lewes, Clifford, Tyndall, and others, and while in London wrote his two volumes on *The Outlines of Cosmic Philosophy* (1874). After some months on the Continent he returned to Cambridge.

In 1879, having resigned as librarian at Harvard, he delivered a course of lectures on American history at the Old South Church, and, in the autumn of the same year, a similar course in London with great success. He now entered upon a life career as perhaps the most popular lecturer

Fiske

on history America has ever known. For some years, however, his chief interest still centered in science and philosophy, as is evidenced in part by the list of his published volumes: *The Unseen World* (1876), *Darwinism and Other Essays* (1879), *Excursions of an Evolutionist* (1884), *The Destiny of Man Viewed in the Light of his Origin* (1884), *The Idea of God as Affected by Modern Knowledge* (1886).

About this time he turned from philosophy to history as a main preoccupation, due, according to some, to financial need, and, according to others, to his wish to study America from the standpoint of an evolutionist. As early as 1880 he had delivered a course of lectures before the Royal Institution of Great Britain in London, many times repeated in the United States, and in 1885 he published these under the title of *American Political Ideas Viewed from the Standpoint of Universal History.* The following year he became one of the editors of *Appletons' Cyclopædia of American Biography,* wrote six articles for the *Atlantic Monthly,* and lectured extensively. Fiske loved comfort and an ample scale of living, and he had to provide for six children. He undertook much heavy work, therefore, mainly for its financial return. That under the circumstances his books maintained their easy and flowing style is somewhat remarkable. These appeared in rapid succession in his new historical field: *The Critical Period of American History, 1783–89* (1888); *The Beginnings of New England* (1889); *The War of Independence* (1889); *Civil Government in the United States* (1890); *The American Revolution* (2 vols., 1891); *The Discovery of America* (2 vols., 1892); *A History of the United States for Schools* (1894); *Old Virginia and her Neighbors* (2 vols., 1897); *Dutch and Quaker Colonies* (2 vols., 1899). There also appeared in the last years of his life or soon after his death, several volumes dealing with philosophy and history, including: *The Origin of Evil* (1899); *A Century of Science and Other Essays* (1899); *Through Nature to God* (1899); and *Life Everlasting* (1901), in one group; and in the other, *The Mississippi Valley in the Civil War* (1900); *Essays, Historical and Literary* (2 vols., 1902); *New France and New England* (1902); *How the United States became a Nation* (1904). His only biographical work on a large scale was his life of *Edward Livingston Youmans, Interpreter of Science for the People* (1894). Three other titles indicate his varied interests: *Tobacco and Alcohol* (1869), *History of English Literature, abridged from Taine* (1872), and the article on Schubert in the *Cyclopædia of Music.* He was a devoted music lover, an excellent performer, and an occasional composer.

In his later years, Fiske made two more visits to England and traveled extensively through the United States, including Alaska. He had delivered lectures at Washington University, St. Louis, since 1881, and had been professor of American history there since 1884, although he continued to reside at Cambridge. As the years passed he failed to receive the Harvard professorship which would have gratified him. The reason may possibly be found in a shift from the former opposition to Fiske as an evolutionist to a slight mistrust of him as a scholar. In June 1894, however, he received signal honors: the degree of Litt.D., from the University of Pennsylvania, and that of LL.D., from Harvard University. Shortly before his death, Yale University had signified its intention of giving him an LL.D., and he had been asked to represent the New World and to deliver an address at the millennial celebration in honor of King Alfred at Winchester, England, but his death intervened. He had long been forcing himself at a rate of production too great for any man. Constant appearance on the lecture platform, and the traveling this involved, overtaxed him. Never given to sports or exercise, his tendency to corpulency had so grown upon him that he had come to weigh over three hundred pounds. On July 4, 1901, worn by overwork and exhausted by the heat, he died at Gloucester, Mass. He was survived by his widow and five children, and was buried at Petersham, where he had long been in the habit of spending the summer.

It has been said of him that "philosophers were inclined to think of him at his best as an historian, and historians to urge that he was primarily a philosopher" (*Nation,* Jan. 24, 1918). The truth is that he was neither a profound scholar nor an original thinker in either domain. He first came before the public as a lucid, brilliant, and courageous defender of the new doctrine of evolution. Darwin, Spencer, and Huxley all claimed him as no mean ally in the fight for scientific truth. He was the chief exponent of the new ideas in America, and, now that the bitterness of that fight has largely been forgotten, it is easy to belittle the importance of the service he rendered to American thought. Although in science, as in history, he relied upon others and did no original research, the lucidity and charm of his style made him unrivaled as a popularizer. In science he contributed only one original suggestion, that of the importance of the long and helpless childhood of the human infant in influencing the psychological complex of the family as a social unit.

Even in that he was forestalled two thousand years ago by Anaximander, but the idea was a genuine contribution as made by Fiske. In tracing the development of his thought, allowance must be made for the much stronger hold which religious ideas and emotions had upon him than upon the English leaders; the various stages of his writing show the struggle to harmonize these with the scientific doctrines which he also defended. He could never bring himself to abandon what he felt to be man's deepest interests—his religious beliefs and ideals—and much of his popular success was probably due to this very effort to combine two conflicting attitudes, even though this involved, as one critic averred, the use of the "block system" in his mind (W. D. Howells, *post*).

In the historical field, Fiske was solely a popularizer, and in spite of his strong adhesion to evolution his historical writing was not, as has so often been claimed, philosophical. Far from making any original contribution of material or interpretation, he merely narrated conspicuous facts, and he did that not authoritatively, but with a charm of style rare among American historians. He never got below the surface, and his reliance upon secondary works not seldom involved him in errors of fact. In spite of such criticisms, however, Fiske was one of the most important intellectual influences in America in the last quarter of the nineteenth century. He was probably the most admirably fitted among all his contemporaries to lead the fight for evolution among his countrymen; and the charm of his historical writings and lectures not only instilled an interest in the subject into a vast number of people but was the prime cause of not a few of the distinguished scholars of to-day first turning to history as their life-work.

[J. S. Clark, *The Life and Letters of John Fiske* (1917); reviewed in the *Nation*, Jan. 24, 1918; T. S. Perry, *John Fiske* (1906); Josiah Royce, "John Fiske," the *Unpopular Rev.*, July, Sept. 1918; Mrs. S. Van Rensselaer, "Mr. Fiske and the Hist. of N. Y.," *North Am. Rev.*, July 1901; W. D. Howells, "John Fiske," *Harper's Weekly*, July 20, 1901; G. L. Beer, "John Fiske," the *Critic*, Aug. 1901; A. McF. Davis, "John Fiske," *Proc. Am. Acad. of Arts and Sci.*, Aug. 1902; F. C. Pierce, *Fiske and Fisk Family* (1896).]

J. T. A.

FISKE, STEPHEN RYDER (Nov. 22, 1840–Apr. 27, 1916), journalist, theatrical manager, was born at New Brunswick, N. J. He was the son of William Henry and Sarah Ann (Blakeney) Fiske, the brother of Haley Fiske [*q.v.*], and a descendant of William Fiske, who came to Salem, Mass., before 1637. Before he was twelve he was being paid for his newspaper contributions and at fourteen he was editing a small paper. He entered Rutgers College in 1858 but upon the appearance, some two years later, of the opening chapters of a novel satirizing the professors and their methods, he was duly asked to resign. Upon leaving college he went to New York where he became connected with the *New York Herald* which he served as editorial writer, special correspondent, and war correspondent during the Civil War. As the *Herald's* special correspondent, he accompanied the Japanese princes, the Prince of Wales (later King Edward VII), and President Lincoln on tours of the United States. Although many stories are told of the ingenuity exercised by newspapermen in attempting to file dispatches ahead of those of rival correspondents, one of the best of these records how Fiske telegraphed passages from the Bible from Niagara Falls to New York to hold the wires from competitors. He was recalled from the seat of war to become dramatic critic of the *Herald* in 1862. He continued as critic until 1866 when he sailed for England on the yacht *Henrietta* in the first Atlantic yacht race.

Fiske's rapidly moving career next took him to Italy where he was with Garibaldi at Rome during the revolution, and thence to London where he became manager of St. James's Theatre and the Royal English Opera Company, and engaged in several journalistic projects. In 1873 he produced at St. James's a version of Sardou's play, *Rabagas,* written by himself, with Charles Wyndham playing the title-rôle. Upon his return to the United States, he took over the management of the Fifth Avenue Theatre, New York, Oct. 15, 1877, succeeding Augustin Daly. There Mary Anderson and Madame Modjeska made their New York débuts, the former on Nov. 12, 1877. Edwin Booth and Joseph Jefferson played under his management in 1878. Following his retirement as manager of the theatre in January 1879, Fiske founded the *New York Dramatic Mirror* and took an important part in the establishment of the Actors' Fund. After giving up control of the *Mirror,* he devoted several years to the writing of plays. During the last ten years of his life, he was connected with *The Sports of the Times* (originally *The Spirit of the Times*) and was regarded as the dean of active dramatic critics. His better known plays included: *Corporal Cartouche*; *Martin Chuzzlewit* (adapted from Dickens's novel); *My Noble Son-in-law*; and *Robert Rabagas.* He was also a writer of sketches and stories some of which he published, as *English Photographs, by an American* (London, 1869); *Off-hand Portraits of Prominent New Yorkers* (1884); *Holiday Stories* (1891); and *Paddy from Cork, and Other Stories* (1891).

[F. C. Pierce, *Fiske and Fisk Family* (1896); *Who's*

Who in Music and Drama, 1914; *Who's Who in the Theatre*, 1912; *Who's Who in America*, 1914–15; the *N. Y. Times*, Apr. 28, 1916; the *N. Y. Dramatic News*, May 6, 1916.] D. W. M.

FITCH, ASA (Feb. 24, 1809–Apr. 8, 1879), entomologist, the son of Asa Fitch, M.D., and Abigail (Martin) Fitch, was the descendant of a long line of colonial ancestors (on the paternal side from the Brewsters of Plymouth). His father was prominent in the medical profession and in various positions of public trust. The son was born at Fitch's Point, Salem, N. Y., passed his boyhood on a farm, and attended the academy at Salem. He began a diary shortly after the age of twelve, which he continued for the rest of his life. He was attracted first to botany, and collected and drew flowers and plants. In 1826 he entered the Rensselaer School at Troy (later the Rensselaer Polytechnic Institute). Here he followed his natural-history bent and took up zoölogy, quickly concentrating on entomology. After graduation, upon his father's advice, he began the study of medicine, graduating at the Vermont Academy of Medicine at Castleton in 1829, afterwards working at the Rutgers Medical College in New York City, and finally being admitted to practise from the office of Dr. March of Albany. All through his medical studies he continued work in entomology; lacking books, he copied by hand from the various entomological works which he found in libraries in the different towns in which he studied. In 1830 he became assistant professor of natural history in the Rensselaer Institute, and accompanied an expedition from the school to Lake Erie in the same year. He began the practise of medicine in 1831 at Fort Miller, N. Y. On Nov. 15, 1832, he married Elizabeth McNeil of Stillwater, N. Y.

In 1838 he gave up practise and returned to Salem, becoming interested in agriculture. His close connection with agriculture combined with his deep interest in insects made him what would be termed to-day an economic entomologist. He devoted most of his time to the study of the insects of his vicinity, making early studies of various grain insects and beginning to publish in 1845 in the *American Quarterly Journal of Agriculture and Science* and in the *Transactions of the New York State Agricultural Society*. He was then employed to collect and name the insects of the State of New York for the State Cabinet of Natural History. In 1854 he was appointed state entomologist of New York and held this position for seventeen years. During this time he published annual reports which were standard among the entomologists and agriculturists of the United States for many years and are still considered of great value. His work was sound and far-reaching. He observed and recorded a mass of biological facts concerning the principal crop pests of that time, and, with his knowledge of both the biology of the insects and farming practises, he was able to make many valuable recommendations to the farmers of his state. Scientifically, his work was thoroughly sound, and his correspondence with scientific leaders in other parts of the country as well as in Europe was very great.

Fitch's appointment as state entomologist of New York was the first great practical step taken in the United States properly to investigate the problem of insect damage. It is true that T. W. Harris had prepared and the State had ordered published (in 1841) his admirable *Report on the Insects of Massachusetts Injurious to Vegetation*; but applied entomology had hitherto received no such definite official recognition as that implied in Fitch's appointment. In fact, the growth of official economic entomology in America dates from 1854. For a long time he worked virtually alone, and his admirably written and excellently arranged reports, based almost entirely upon his personal investigations, were of very great value to the agriculturists of the whole country and served as models to the state entomologists who began to be appointed years later. His style was simple and straightforward, but by no means devoid of charm; and his studies of the life history of many species were so full and so useful as to be almost beyond criticism.

His health began to fail in the late sixties, and his final report was published in 1870. He lived a quiet life until his death in 1879. C. V. Riley and P. R. Uhler [*qq.v.*], then both young men, visited him in 1870, and seem to have been impressed especially by his careful manuscript notes which at that time numbered 55,000 and were contained in 148 books. Many of these notebooks are now the property of the United States National Museum. Fitch was a deeply religious man and conducted daily family prayers and Bible readings. It is said, however, that on one occasion he interrupted his reading of the scriptures to reach for collecting apparatus with which to capture a rare moth that had alighted on his Bible.

[An appreciative biographical sketch by E. P. Thurston will be found in the *Pop. Sci. Monthly*, Nov. 1879. Another, written by C. V. Riley, is to be found in the *Am. Entomologist*, May 1880. It is in this last account that the story is told of the visit of Riley and Uhler. For ancestry see Emma C. Brewster Jones, *Brewster Geneal.* (1908), I, 209–10.] L. O. H.

FITCH, CLYDE [See FITCH WILLIAM CLYDE, 1865–1909].

FITCH, JOHN (Jan. 21, 1743–July 2, 1798), metal craftsman, inventor, was born on his father's farm in Windsor township, Hartford County, Conn. He was the fifth child of Joseph and Sarah (Shaler) Fitch and was descended from Thomas Fitch of Essex, England, whose five sons emigrated to Connecticut early in the seventeenth century. At the age of four he started attending "a dame school." He was an apt pupil, especially in "figures," but at the age of ten was taken from school and put to work on the farm. For a number of years, however, all of his leisure was spent in reading such books as he could secure, his especial interests being geography, astronomy, and mathematics. His physical weakness and inability to do his share of the farm work created in his father and older brother an antagonistic attitude which made his boyhood most unhappy. When he was fifteen, in an effort to get away from this environment, Fitch prevailed upon his father to hire him out to the local storekeeper. This work was not to his liking, except that it accomplished his deliverance from the farm, and for the succeeding six years he tried his hand at various occupations, all of which had unfortunate endings. He shipped on a coastwise sailing vessel but was mistreated by the mate; he apprenticed himself successively to two clock-makers but was not permitted to study or handle either time-pieces or tools, being kept at simple brass work or farm labor. Through these apprenticeships, however, he did acquire the rudiments of brass working and founding, and on the completion of his second term, on his twenty-first birthday, he set up a brass shop of his own in East Windsor. Doing odds and ends in brass founding, and cleaning or repairing clocks when owners could be induced to trust them in his hands, he paid off in two years the debt incurred when he set up his business, and then saved a bit of money all of which he lost through an unfortunate investment in potash manufacture, of which he knew nothing. Trying to recoup his losses by engaging again in brass work, he made the mistake of designing and equipping a plant of far greater capacity than the locality warranted. This embarrassment, coupled with the experience of an unhappy home life (he had married Lucy Roberts of Simsbury, Conn., on Dec. 29, 1767), was too much for him, and early in 1769 he left his family, business, and state.

Wandering southward, he eventually settled in Trenton, N. J., and in the course of seven years built up a profitable brass and silversmith business, only to have it wiped out in the Revolutionary War. He enlisted in a Trenton company and was made a lieutenant but soon left the army to take charge of the Trenton gun factory. He later gained considerable profit selling tobacco and beer to the Continental Army and made an occasional attempt to resume his silversmith's trade. Investing his money in Virginia land-warrants, he secured a surveyor's commission, spent the whole of 1780 in surveying lands along the Ohio River and locating his own claims, and recorded in his own name 1,600 acres in Kentucky. Early in 1782 he set out on a second expedition but was captured by Indians, turned over to the British, and held prisoner in Canada almost till the close of that year. Upon being exchanged, he settled in Bucks County, Pa., organized a company to acquire and exploit lands of the Northwest Territory, and made several surveying trips thither between 1783 and 1785, but all of his projects came to naught with the establishment of the federal policy of dividing the territory into mile-square sections, irrespective of the quality of the land. After the last of his surveying expeditions he made and engraved a map of the Northwest Territory from Hutchins's and Morrow's maps, with additions.

Back again in Bucks County, Fitch turned his attention to the invention of a steamboat, and from 1785 until his death thirteen years later devoted his whole time to this project. The question of financial assistance was ever his main stumbling-block. After failing to secure subsidies from the Continental Congress and several scientific societies, he turned to the state legislatures, and from New Jersey in 1786 and in 1787 from Pennsylvania, New York, Delaware, and Virginia, he obtained the exclusive privilege, for fourteen years, of building and operating steamboats on all the waters of these several states. Meanwhile he had built a number of rather successful models and with these and his privileges as talking points succeeded in organizing a company of prominent Philadelphians whose money, added to that which he made through the sale of his map of the Northwest Territory, enabled him to start work on a 45-foot boat. He was assisted, especially in the construction of the engine, by Henry Voight, a watchmaker. On the Delaware River at Philadelphia, Aug. 22, 1787, in the presence of the members of the Constitutional Convention then in session, the vessel was successfully launched and operated. It was propelled by a series of twelve paddles—six to a side, arranged like those of an Indian war canoe—and operated by steam power. In 1787–88 the claims of James Rumsey [*q.v.*] to priority in the application of steam to boat propulsion precipitated a controversy which elicited pamphlets from both sides but did not affect Fitch's monopoly, or deter him from proceeding immediately to work on another and larger boat. In July 1788 he launched a 60-foot boat propelled by a steam paddle wheel. With this boat he carried as many as thirty passengers on numerous round-trip voyages between Philadelphia and Burlington, N. J., on one occasion (Oct. 12, 1788) covering the twenty miles up-stream in three hours and ten minutes. Public indifference toward steam navigation still persisted, however, and in an attempt to overcome it Fitch persuaded the members of his company to give him funds to build a third and larger boat in 1790. This vessel was put in regular service on the Delaware River and its schedule of sailings, well maintained, was advertised in the Philadelphia daily papers; but the only encouragement Fitch received from this accomplishment was the grant of a United States patent on Aug. 26, 1791. Later in that same year he obtained French letters patent, and started the construction of a fourth boat appropriately named *Perseverance*. Before completion this was wrecked by a violent storm at Philadelphia and the disaster so discouraged the members of Fitch's company that they declined to advance any more money. In desperation Fitch went to France, but met with no better success there in securing financial aid, even though he possessed a French patent. Working his way back as a common sailor, he returned to Boston in destitute circumstances and ill health and from there was taken by his brother-in-law to his birthplace at East Windsor. Here he remained two years or more but without attempting to see his wife or children. About 1796 he decided to return to Kentucky to claim his lands. On the way he stopped in New York long enough to try once more to arouse interest in his invention, for he still had his monopoly. He converted a ship's yawl into a steamboat capable of carrying four people and operated it on Collect Pond, which once existed just off Broadway near City Hall. This craft was moved by a screw propeller. The demonstration was in vain, however, and, wholly discouraged, he went on to Kentucky and settled at Bardstown, where after two years he died.

While Fitch constructed four successful steamboats, he gave little or no attention to construction and operating costs, failed completely to see the need for demonstrating the economical aspects of steam navigation, and accordingly lost all financial support. For this reason, the steamboat era may be said to begin with Robert Fulton [*q.v.*], who launched his first steamboat after the death of Fitch.

[One volume of Fitch's manuscript autobiography, written during his residence in Bardstown, is now the property of the Phila. Library Company (Ridgway Branch); the other volume is in the possession of the Pa. Hist. Soc. The main body of his papers is in the Lib. of Cong.; there are also diaries in Yale Univ. Lib. Biographies are: Charles Whittlesey, "Life of John Fitch" in Jared Sparks, *Lib. of Am. Biog.*, 2 ser., vol. VI (1845); Henry Howe, *Memoirs of the Most Eminent American Mechanics* (1841); Thompson Westcott, *Life of John Fitch* (1857). See also *Memorial to John Fitch* (Govt. Printing Office, 1915); *John Fitch* (1912), comp. for Admiral Bunce Section, Hartford, Conn., No. 42, Navy League of the U. S.; W. B. Kaempffert, *Popular Hist. of Am. Invention* (2 vols., 1924).] C. W. M.

FITCH, SAMUEL (Jan. 16, 1724–Oct. 4, 1799), lawyer and Loyalist, was born in Lebanon, Conn., the son of Joseph and Anne (Whiting) Fitch, the grandson of Rev. James Fitch, first minister of Norwich, and great-grandson of John Mason of Pequot fame. James Fitch's brother was the great-grandfather of Gov. Thomas Fitch [*q.v.*]. Samuel was graduated from Yale in 1742, received the M.A. degree and was ranked socially sixth in a class of seventeen which included Joseph Hawley, later a prominent Whig of western Massachusetts, and Jared Ingersoll of Stamp Act notoriety. In 1746 he was lieutenant in a regiment raised for the Canadian expedition. Admitted to the bar in Connecticut, he was courting Elizabeth Lloyd of the manor of Queen's Village on Lloyd's Neck, Long Island, when in 1750 at the suggestion of her brother Henry who was a merchant in Boston, he started to practise in that town. The wedding took place in March 1753 at the manor. In 1761 or 1762 he was one of the first group elevated to the begowned and bewigged class of barristers, and in 1766 Harvard gave him the M.A. *ad eundem*. Evidently the law was his chief if not only interest: there is no record of nonprofessional activity except membership in the Fire Club, and an invitation four times repeated to inspect schools, the last betokening prominence in the community. John Adams was an intimate, and at Adams's suggestion in 1768 Fitch was made acting advocate general in the Court of Admiralty, serving until 1776. According to Adams, he never received a royal commission; but in this last statement Adams may have been mistaken, since there is in the Public Record Office a commission dated November 1769. Holding this office probably determined Fitch's political attitude, though his Loyalist brother-in-law, who had married into the Hutchinson family, may have been influential. Fitch was an addresser to Hutchinson on the governor's departure in 1774 and to Gage on his arrival and leaving, was a protester against the Solemn League and Covenant, and remained in Boston during the siege, departing for Halifax at the evacuation. He was proscribed and banished by the Act of September 1778 and his property confiscated the next year, but there is no record of action under the law. His party to Halifax numbered seven, which probably did not include his son William, who became an ensign in the 65th Regiment, then in Boston, on Aug. 16, 1775, and who remained in the army until he was killed by the Maroons in Jamaica on Sept. 12, 1795, as colonel of the 83rd Regiment which he had raised in Dublin in 1793. Fitch had a pension for four children, probably including a daughter who predeceased him in England. He did not remain in Halifax but seems to have been in Ireland in September, and reached London on Dec. 7, 1776. Hutchinson presented him to Lord North on Jan. 23, 1777, and Samuel Quincy speaks of him as being in residence in February. Except for casual mention in the papers of fellow Loyalists, little is known of his last years. He was one of the Loyalist addressers to the King in 1779. He received from the British government a pension of £260, and during the war £550 a year for the loss of his professional income. Before his death he received further compensation to the amount of £5,000. The family was intimate with the Copleys and the artist made a painting of Col. William and his two sisters, probably begun about 1794 but not finished until 1801. The ladies were described as "fond of company and gaiety, but with scanty means of gratifying their taste" (Martha B. Amory, *Domestic and Artistic Life of John Singleton Copley*, 1882, p. 196). Fitch died in London and was buried in the graveyard of St. Mary's Church, Battersea. His wife survived him less than five months.

[Edward Alfred Jones, *The Loyalists of Mass.* (1930), pp. 134–35; Lorenzo Sabine, *Biog. Sketches of Loyalists of the Am. Revolution* (1864), I, 425; F. B. Dexter, *Biog. Sketches Grads. Yale Coll.*, vol. I (1885); the Mason pedigree in *New-Eng. Hist. and Geneal. Reg.*, XV, 121, are the main sources; but *Papers of the Lloyd Family of Lloyd's Neck, L. I.* (2 vols., 1927), in *N. Y. Hist. Soc. Colls.*, adds new material. See also *Jour. and Letters of Samuel Curwen* (1842), *passim*. There is scattered information in the papers of John Adams and of Fitch's fellow Loyalists.]

D. M. M.

FITCH, THOMAS (*c.* 1700–July 18, 1774), lawyer, colonial governor, was a great-grandson of Thomas Fitch, one of the earliest settlers of Norwalk, Conn., and was born in that town, the son of Thomas Fitch, Jr., and his wife Sarah. As a member of the town's wealthiest and most prominent family, he entered readily into the inner political group of the colony of Connecticut and by his own abilities gained a position of leadership. He graduated from Yale College in 1721 and three years later married Hannah Hall of New Haven, who bore him eight children. He began his political career in 1726 as deputy from Norwalk to the General Assembly, serving on four subsequent occasions during the next five years. He was an Assistant in 1734–35 and again during 1740–50, when, upon the death of Gov. Jonathan Law and the advancement of Deputy Gov. Roger Wolcott, he was chosen deputy governor by the Assembly over the heads of the three senior Assistants. He was reëlected by the freemen in each of the three following years. In 1754, when Gov. Wolcott came under popular suspicion in connection with the embezzlement of most of the cargo of a Spanish ship which had put into New London harbor in distress, as a result, Fitch attained the distinction of being the first man to defeat a Connecticut governor for reëlection when the latter was an avowed candidate. Fitch was elected governor and held the office continually thereafter until 1766 when he was defeated because of his attitude in the Stamp Act controversy. Although regularly nominated for the magistracy in each of the remaining years of his life, he was never again elected. He was a deputy from Norwalk in 1772 but never held any royal appointments in Massachusetts as has sometimes been inferred (Gipson, *post*, p. 296, note 2).

Fitch was a lawyer by profession. In this capacity he served the colony on several occasions, including notably the land controversy with the Mohican Indians and the dispute with Massachusetts over the boundary. He was given charge of the revision of the laws of Connecticut, a task which he completed with some assistance in 1749. As deputy governor from 1750 to 1754 he was regularly appointed, as was the custom, chief judge of the superior courts. Many years after Fitch's death President Dwight of Yale referred to him as "probably the most learned lawyer, who had ever been an inhabitant of the Colony" (*Travels*, III, 504). He had various other interests as well. In 1740, together with two associates, he secured from the Assembly a fifteen-year monopoly of the right to make steel within the colony, experiments in which enterprise conducted at Simsbury were reported as successful four years later. As a young man he served as supply for the pulpit of the Norwalk church and in 1765 there appeared a tract, attributed to Fitch, which analyzed the Saybrook Platform of the consociated churches of Connecticut.

It was, however, in his capacity as governor during a term which included the last intercolonial war and the Stamp Act controversy that he was most distinguished. He was an ardent supporter of the British cause during the war and was largely responsible for the fact that the Connecticut Assembly more than once exceeded its quota of troops, although he did not entirely escape the impatient criticism of the British commanders-in-chief. When, after the close of the war, proposals were first made for parliamentary taxation of the colonies, the Assembly requested Fitch and certain others to draw up the objections of the colony to such legislation. The resulting "Book of Reasons," for which the governor was chiefly responsible, was a clear and concise statement of the constitutional, historical, and economic arguments of the colony against the proposed stamp tax (*Reasons why the British Colonies in America, Should not be Charged with Internal Taxes, by Authority of Parliament; Humbly offered for Consideration in Behalf of the Colony of Connecticut*, 1764). Fitch's legalistic mind, which had been most helpful in this work, caused his downfall when the Stamp Act had finally been passed. Although he was unsympathetic to the tax, he believed in submission to parliamentary enactment and considered it his duty to take the oath required of all governors by the act. In defense of his action he published a small tract which contained logical reasoning and sound arguments but which completely ignored the feelings and passions of the colonists (*Some Reasons that Influenced the Governor to Take, and the Councillors to Administer the Oath, Required by the Act of Parliament; commonly called the Stamp-Act. Humbly submitted to the Consideration of the Publick*, 1766). Neither this pamphlet, however, nor the support of the conservatives of the colony, was able to save him in the election of May 1766. Although little is known of his personality, he displayed in all his actions a high sense of duty, courage, and an outlook on politics which extended beyond the confines of his little colony and included the larger world of the British Empire.

[Sources include: *The Public Records of the Colony of Conn.*, vols. VII–XII (1873–81), ed. by C. J. Hoadley; "The Fitch Papers . . . 1754–76," ed. by A. C. Bates with an introduction by Forrest Morgan in *Conn. Hist. Soc. Colls.*, vols. XVII and XVIII (1918–20); "Correspondence of Connecticut with the British Government," in *Conn. Hist. Soc. Colls.*, I (1860) and *Correspondence of Wm. Pitt . . . with Colonial Governors . . . in America* (2 vols., 1906), ed. by G. S. Kimball; Edwin Hall, *The Ancient Hist. Records of Norwalk, Conn.* (1847); Moses Dickinson, *A Sermon, Delivered at the Funeral of the Honorable Thomas Fitch, Esq.* (1774); F. B. Dexter, *Biog. Sketches Grads. Yale Coll.*, vol. I (1885); L. H. Gipson, *Jared Ingersoll* (1920); D. H. Van Hoosear, "A Complete Copy of the Inscriptions . . . in the Oldest Cemetery in Norwalk, Conn.," *Fairfield County Hist. Soc. Reports*, 1893–95. The inclusion of a sketch of Fitch in Lorenzo Sabine, *Am. Loyalists* (1847), is quite misleading in its implications.]

L. W. L.

FITCH, WILLIAM CLYDE (May 2, 1865–Sept. 4, 1909), playwright, was the son of Capt. William Goodwin Fitch of Hartford, Conn. (at the time of his marriage in 1863 a lieutenant in the Union Army), and of Alice Maud (Clark) Fitch of Hagerstown, Md. Born at Elmira, N. Y., his first four years were spent traveling with his parents from army-post to army-post, at the end of which time Capt. Fitch resigned from the service, and the family moved to Schenectady, N. Y., where they settled down for the next ten years. A small and delicate child, Clyde was nevertheless endowed with irrepressible spirits and originality. At nine he was editing "The Rising Sun," a weekly magazine all written out in his own large round hand. Its editorials consisted principally of humorous and precocious observations upon the neighbors; his other contributions were verse and such stories as "The Missing Hand; or Marie Gertrude Antoinette de la Rue—a thrilling tragedy à la Miss Goodrich." He originated The Hookey Club, consisting of himself and "Mollie" Jackson, his favorite playmate; its secret meetings seem to have been held for the sole purpose of deciding which one of them could invent the best excuse for not going to church. At nine or ten, he made his first venture into theatricals. He collected a small group of little girls into a very lively company, and drilled them in melodramas, mostly of his own concoction, made the costumes and the scenery, and acted all the "hero" parts himself. When the performances were over, he would lead the whole company down-town and have tintypes taken of it in the most thrilling scenes. His favorite play was *Blue Beard*.

At thirteen he began to grow restless under his mother's constant watchful care, and begged his father to send him away to some school "where he could be more like other boys." During the next winter—spent with an aunt at Hartford, Conn.—he attended the high school there, and the following year he was sent to the school for boys at Holderness, N. H., to prepare for college. In a letter to his mother at this time he wrote: "I think I ought to have something to say about what college I am to go to, when four years of my life are to be spent there, . . . I am not so delicate, my dear, as you think, and please don't write to any college about my being delicate, or about the climate, boys don't like to be talked about that way, and *I* don't, anyway." Amherst was finally decided upon, and Fitch entered the class of 1886. Prof. John F. Genung later said of him, "Fitch was not by any means my best student, but he was one of my most interesting pupils and I always felt he was a genius." His college activities were principally literary and dramatic. "Billy Fitch," as he was known on the campus, contributed to almost every issue of the *Student* and for a time was its editor. After his freshman year he lived at the Chi Psi Lodge where he decorated the walls of his room with a frieze of apple blossoms, and painted over the fireplace *"O, ye fire and heat, Bless ye the Lord."* In his sophomore year, it was Fitch who "staged" the annual ceremony of burning up the class text-books on Analytical Geometry, which he called "The Funeral of Anna Lit." The *Student* in its next issue described the obsequies, as "having surpassed anything of a like nature ever witnessed at Amherst." "And as a result," writes Prof. Chilton Powell, "the Faculty eliminated future ceremonies of the kind." Fitch was an inveterate theatre-goer. On one vacation he and his chum, Tod Galloway, went to eleven plays in six days. His first essay as a playwright happened in his junior year. The Chi Psi Fraternity was to give an entertainment, and had done what had never been done before—invited the faculty. They had chosen to give a one-act operetta, *Il Jacobi,* only to find on rehearsal that it would not suffice to fill the evening. Walking home from chapel Fitch gloomily discussed with Galloway what was to be done about it. Two hours later he summoned Galloway to his room and read him a second act to *Il Jacobi,* cleverer than the original, which at the performance made the hit of the evening. Fitch belonged to the Junior and Senior Dramatics, and besides designing costumes and scenery, he painted a curtain. He produced Wycherley's *The Country Girl* and acted the rôle of Peggie Thrift. He appeared as Constance in *She Stoops to Conquer,* and as Lydia Languish in *The Rivals.* At his graduation he was chosen Grove Poet.

Capt. Fitch then tried every means of persuasion to induce his son to take up the profession of architecture; the idea of literature as a livelihood seemed to him absurd, and he frowned still more upon the thought of his son's writing for the stage. Fitch, however, had made up his mind. He felt the necessity of independence and was determined to go to New York and make his own way. Arriving at his goal in the autumn, he brought with him several letters of introduction; but before presenting any of them, decided to make a tour of the newspaper offices. He first tried the *World,* where he was told there was nothing for him. It was a hot morning, but unbaffled he went on to the *New York Times.* There they suggested "he might go over and hang around the Hoboken docks and see if anything turned up." But before he reached the street again, he had already made his decision—"If anything *does* turn up at the Hoboken docks, it won't be me!" His next efforts toward making a living were the writing of jokes and verses for *Life* and *Puck,* stories for children, and a novel, "A Wave of Life," published in *Lippincott's Magazine,* 1891. Meanwhile he was tutoring two small children. This trying experience having come to an end, Fitch made his first trip abroad, meeting his mother in Paris. Paris instantly took possession of him—as Italy did afterward; it answered the color and spontaneity in his nature and ignited the creative in him. There he met Massenet, Sybil Sanderson, Bernhard Berenson, and others, and sometimes read his writings to them. One night on a balcony, he read aloud *Frederick Lemaître,* a one-act play he had just finished, and became so impassioned, that a little Marquise, who lived below, sent up a note: "Would the American ladies and gentlemen please make a little less noise." From Paris he went to London, where the Æsthetic Movement, though on the wane, was still prevailing, and he, at twenty-three, felt its sway. He carried about with him a volume of Vernon Lee, and at Walter Pater's little house in Earl's Terrace, he met many of the rising younger writers. Returning to New York, he took rooms in the old Sherwood Studios on West Fifty-seventh St. He was still writing children's stories for the *Churchman,* the *Independent,* and other magazines (collected in book form in 1891 under the title of *The Knighting of the Twins*) and was giving readings from Browning, Praed, and Keats. In spite of short funds, he was never an "attic poet"; on the contrary, with tapestry, books, old furniture (rickety perhaps but beautiful), stuffs and pictures—gleanings from the old Paris shops—he created a charming place where he received his friends at tea, in a blue velvet coat with a pink carnation in his buttonhole—and always there was a manservant at the door to take one's hat.

Among the letters of introduction Fitch had brought with him to New York was one to E. A. Dithmar, dramatic editor of the *New York Times,* who soon began taking him to the opening nights at the theatres. At this time, Richard Mansfield had been hunting in vain for a man who would write a play around the character of Beau Brummell and, in despair, appealed to Dithmar. Without hesitation, Dithmar recommended Clyde Fitch. The actor and the playwright met in Philadelphia and Fitch set to work. It was not all plain sailing, however. The experienced actor made many valuable suggestions; but impatient and temperamental, he nearly drove Fitch into a sanatorium before the play was completed. Mansfield lacked confidence in the piece up to the last dress rehearsal. That morning, striding up and down the stage, he muttered to W. J. Ferguson "We can't do this play tomorrow—it will be a failure. We shall have to put on *A Parisian Ro-*

mance." But Fitch stuck it out; and when the curtain rose on that brilliant opening night, it proved to be the first of his many triumphs.

Fitch's next productions were: *Betty's Finish,* a one-act play of college life (Boston Museum, 1890), *Frederick Lemaître* (Tremont Theatre, Boston, 1890), and *Pamela's Prodigy* a comedy of the period of 1830 (Royal Court Theatre, London, 1891). His first drama of contemporary life, *A Modern Match,* was well constructed, strong and human, and an obvious broadening out of his work. After a successful season, the foreign rights were bought by Mr. and Mrs. Kendal, who appeared in it in London, Dublin, and elsewhere, under the title of *Marriage 1892.* The following six years were filled with hard work and many variations of fortune. During this time Fitch wrote seven original plays and eleven adaptations from foreign sources; two of these, *Gossip* and *A Superfluous Husband* in collaboration with Leo Ditrichstein. *The Masked Ball,* from the French of Bisson and Carré, for John Drew (his first appearance as a star) and Maude Adams, had a long run of popularity. Mrs. Langtry in Fitch's *Gossip,* Otis Skinner in a charming production of Fitch's *His Grace de Grammont,* and Madame Helena Modjeska in the title rôle of Fitch's *Mistress Betty* (revised in 1905 as *The Toast of the Town*), were the high spots of those years. There were failures too, but Fitch met these with his remarkable faculty of working even harder in the face of defeat. Meanwhile he made his annual trips abroad, watching the trend of the Continental theatres.

Fortune smiled upon him in the simultaneous opening in 1898 of *The Moth and the Flame* in Philadelphia, with Effie Shannon and Herbert Kelcey, and *Nathan Hale* in Chicago, with Nat Goodwin and Maxine Elliott. *The Moth* drew capacity audiences at one theatre, while *Nathan Hale* was turning people away at the other. Fitch was dazed. Kelcey, meeting him at the theatre the morning after the opening, found him staring at an open telegram. It was from Nat Goodwin: "Breaking all records line from box-office around the corner. Nat." "Tell me, Kelcey," Fitch gasped, "do you think this is *true,* or is Goodwin joshing me?" Also during the same year Charles Frohman successfully produced Fitch's *Barbara Frietchie,* a drama of the Civil War, with Julia Marlowe in the title rôle. Experience, by now, convinced the managers it was to their own profit to give Fitch free rein in the entire production of his plays—the choice of casts, the rehearsing, and the staging. Actors liked being directed by him; they soon recognized the actor in him, and behind his patience and tact, the driving force of "a man who knows his job." He was often criticized for his insistence upon small details; once a man sitting in front at a scenic rehearsal, exclaimed, as Fitch climbed down from the stage into the orchestra stalls, disgusted because some "property" had not arrived: "Why do you bother so much about such little things?" "Because," answered Fitch, "I think they are *very important*; I believe in watching every bit of scenery, every action, every incidental blessed thing connected with the production. It is the 'little things' that quickest show the lack of study and preparation." To such infinite pains Fitch owed much of his success. No other American dramatist of his day could present the so-called "Society plays" as Fitch did; he knew the chatter of the drawing room as well as its setting, and from the first speech, no aside was needed to reveal to the audience what sort of people it was about to have the pleasure of meeting.

Fitch was now (1901) thirty-six years old, and, in appearance, the unmistakable man of the world. His swinging walk, flowing overcoat, thick stick (a book or a manuscript always under his arm), and his habit of talking to himself as he came along, made him a conspicuous figure. He disliked intensely being pointed out in public places, yet he took a boyish pleasure in seeing his name screamed out in electric lights over the entrance to a theatre. The year 1901 marked for him the beginning of a future of uninterrupted prosperity. Four of his plays—*The Climbers, Captain Jinks* (with Ethel Barrymore), *Barbara Frietchie* (a return engagement), and *Lover's Lane,* were all running in New York at the same time, to packed theatres. Praise from the critics, however, was still given grudgingly, and Fitch was never able to overcome his depression over their continued adverse attitude. Though at the crest of success he never slackened in his work; writing, personally attending to his productions, and rushing off to other cities for the try-out of new plays—besides, of course, being constantly in social demand. In the spring of 1902 the strain of overwork began to tell on him, and on his physician's advice to go to the country for rest he bought a piece of land at Greenwich, Conn., and before sailing again for Europe he started to build "Quiet Corner." While in Europe he was threatened with appendicitis. At Berne, Switzerland, he was advised to go to St. Moritz, where under care he might avoid an operation. At St. Moritz he slowly improved; but in the autumn, without fully regaining his strength, he returned home, bringing back with him two complete new plays, *The Stubbornness of Ger-*

aldine and *The Girl with the Green Eyes.* Between this date and 1907 he produced sixteen plays: ten of them original and six adaptations. On Jan. 7, 1907, he had two plays open on the same night—*The Straight Road,* and *The Truth.* For the latter, in which Clara Bloodgood played the leading rôle, he had high hope, feeling that in it he had achieved his best. The critics gave unstinted praise to *The Straight Road* (a melodrama of the New York slums), while towards *The Truth* they were lukewarm. Fitch's disappointment was bitter. From "Quiet Corner" he wrote, "Of course I am pretty depressed over the abuse I get in the press. . . . A few days will tell the tale. But I have very little hope." A week later the critics had changed their tone. Fitch wrote again: "The *Evening Sun* was fine and *so was Alan Dale today*—very fine—*my best!* But, also, I fear *they come too late!* . . . It will be a dreadful blow to me—as it will convince me that it is impossible for me *to* succeed in New York *with the present press.* Which will mean my laying down my pen." Fitch was right, the damage was done, *The Truth* closed after a few weeks of vain struggle. Three months later, however, the play made an enormous hit in London. At the end of the first performance the brilliant audience rose and cheered and called again and again for the author. The acting of Marie Tempest as Becky was hailed by all the papers as "a triumph." Fitch afterward saw *The Truth* acted in Germany, Italy, Russia, Hungary, and Scandinavia, repeating its London success in each country. In the fall of 1907 Mrs. Bloodgood toured with the play, but after two happy months of success, the tour was brought to a sudden termination by her tragic suicide.

At the end of that season Fitch began fighting a losing battle against failing health, but he would not give up. Forced to spend much of his time in the country, he took his manuscripts and his friends with him. Nothing was too good for the latter. Once, accused of liking too many people, he answered—"*I've* always thought, if you like a lot of other people, you often learn new ways to please the ones you like best." Between 1907 and 1909 he wrote and produced two original plays, *A Happy Marriage* and *The Bachelor,* and adapted a farce from the German, *The Blue Mouse.* While writing on this farce, the idea came to him of a tremendous climax for a new play (*The City*). From then on, this drama possessed him so completely that he could think of nothing else, writing feverishly, at a furious pace, "as though he knew the night was coming." On June 25, 1909, nervously worn out, he boarded the *S. S. Lorraine* for Havre, leaving behind him the finished work. After two weeks in Paris, he crossed to London to see *The Woman in the Case* (first produced in 1905), which was having a sensational success. Happy over its reception, he could not stand the excitement of the demands its popularity made upon him. Very tired, he slipped away, returning to Paris; and started on a lonely tour through the Tyrol. He carried with him the manuscript of a light comedy, writing on the way. Returning by way of Châlons-sur-Marne, he was taken acutely ill there on Aug. 30, and an emergency operation was resorted to that night. On Sept. 4 a brief cable brought the news to New York of his death. Three months later, on the night of Dec. 21, *The City* opened at the Lyric Theatre. Every seat was filled. The feeling was intense. By the end of the second act, the developing horror of impending catastrophe swept the audience into a demonstration seldom witnessed in a New York theatre—a scene of hysterical confusion. Men were shouting, women fainted. The *New York Tribune* (Dec. 22, 1909) said, "The art employed is remarkable; the effect is at moments mighty." Fitch's plays will live in the history of the American drama like Congreve's of the gay Restoration period—as mirrors of their day or, as Mr. John Corbin once said, "They are not only pictures of their time, they are documents of the period."

[Twelve of Fitch's best-known plays were published after his death in *Plays by Clyde Fitch* (4 vols., 1915), memorial edition, ed. by M. J. Moses and Virginia Gerson. The same editors also published *Clyde Fitch and his Letters* (1924). For criticism see W. P. Eaton, *At the New Theatre and Others* (1910); Wm. Lyon Phelps, *Essays on Modern Dramatists* (1921); A. H. Quinn, *A Hist. of the Am. Drama from the Civil War to the Present Day* (1927), I, 265–96. Quinn, *op. cit.*, II, 288–92 and the *Cambridge Hist. of Am. Lit.*, IV (1921), 765–67, give additional references and list Fitch's plays with dates of production.]

V. G.

FITLER, EDWIN HENRY (Dec. 2, 1825–May 31, 1896), manufacturer, was born in Philadelphia, Pa., the son of William and Elizabeth (Wonderly) Fitler. His father was a prosperous leather merchant and tanner. Since his parents were in easy circumstances, young Fitler received an excellent academic education. Planning to adopt the law as a profession, he entered the office of Charles E. Lex, a prominent lawyer of Philadelphia, but after four years of legal study he decided that his natural tastes were for mechanical pursuits. Accordingly, he abandoned law for a more congenial occupation, and obtaining a position in the cordage house of his brother-in-law, George J. Weaver, began to lay the foundation of his life-work. Two years later, at the age of twenty-three, he was admitted to partnership in the firm, known first as George J. Weaver

& Company and later as Weaver, Fitler & Company (Philadelphia Cordage Works). Under his management labor-saving machinery was introduced, much of it being of his own invention. These inventions were not patented but were freely offered to the trade and many were adopted by other cordage manufacturers. By 1870 he had purchased the interests of most of his other partners and the firm name was changed to Edwin H. Fitler & Company (Philadelphia Cordage Works). At the time of his death, the factory, situated in the Bridesburg section of Philadelphia, was one of the largest cordage works in the United States.

Fitler was one of the most successful and best-known business men of his time. He was noted for his keen perceptions and the rapidity and correctness of his decisions. His position in the trade is attested by the fact that he was repeatedly elected president of the American Cordage Manufacturers Association. His relations with his employees were of the most cordial character. It is said that he never had labor troubles in his plant. He was intensely patriotic and at the outbreak of the Civil War threw the whole weight of his influence into the Union cause, and personally outfitted a company from among his employees. He took an active part in the work of projecting and organizing the Centennial Exposition and in 1875–76 was a member of its board of finance. He was also one of the founders of the Philadelphia Art Club.

Until 1887 he successfully avoided public office, but in that year was prevailed upon to run for mayor of the City of Philadelphia and was elected by nearly 30,000 majority. He was the first mayor under the new city charter and during his administration many reforms were instituted and many improvements were made in all branches of the city government. Rigidly adhering to his own ideas and his own policies regardless of political or other pressure, he won the confidence of the whole community. At the Republican National Convention held at Chicago in 1888 he received the vote of the entire Philadelphia delegation, also of several delegates from other parts of Pennsylvania and a few from other states, as their choice for president of the United States. After his retirement from the mayoralty in 1891 he again devoted himself to his business. He was a director of the National Bank of the Northern Liberties and served as both vice-president and president of the Union League. He died, after a long illness, at his country estate near Philadelphia. His wife, whom he married in 1850, was Josephine R. Baker.

[W. W. Fitler, *Geneal. of the Fitler and Allied Families* (1922), pp. 26–29; J. T. Scharf and Thompson Westcott, *Hist. of Phila.* (1884), III, 2311 ff.; obituaries in the *North American*, the *Press*, and the *Public Ledger*, of Phila., June 1, 1896.] J.H.F.

FITTON, JAMES (Apr. 10, 1805–Sept. 15, 1881), Roman Catholic missionary, was born in Boston, Mass. He was of English and Welsh descent, the son of Abraham Fitton, an emigrant from Preston, England, and Sarah Williams. After attending the public schools of Boston, and an academy conducted by Rev. Virgil Horace Barber, S. J., at Claremont, N. H., he prepared for the priesthood under the personal instruction of Bishop Fenwick [*q.v.*] of Boston, and was by him ordained on Dec. 23, 1827. His ministry covered a period of more than fifty years, during the first half of which he traveled in almost every section of New England, a zealous missionary indifferent to hardship and persecution. Churches sprang up everywhere along his path. He was first sent to labor among the Passamaquoddy Indians of Maine. Later he was commissioned to look after the spiritual wants of the faithful scattered over the state of Vermont. In July 1830 he went to Connecticut where he was the second resident priest in what is now the Diocese of Hartford. Here he remained for the next six years, sometimes alone and sometimes with assistants. From Hartford, which was his residence, he went forth "to wherever a child of the faith was to be found." Every county of the state was traversed repeatedly; stations were established in the larger towns, and also in Massachusetts and Rhode Island. In 1836 Worcester became his headquarters, and his field of labor included the eastern part of Connecticut, the central and western parts of Massachusetts, and extended down the Blackstone Valley into Rhode Island. Purchasing some sixty acres of land on a hillside at Worcester, he erected buildings and opened Mount St. James Seminary. This property he deeded to Bishop Fenwick in 1842, and it became the site of the College of the Holy Cross, the first Catholic college in New England. In 1843 Father Fitton was put in charge of the Church of SS. Peter and Paul, Providence, and the following year Bishop Tyler assigned him to duty in Woonsocket, Pawtucket, and Newport. When Newport was made a parish in 1846, he became its pastor. While here he built the beautiful church of Our Lady of the Isle. In compliance with the dying request of his friend, Father William Wiley, he was called from Newport to East Boston in 1855 to complete an edifice for the Church of the Most Holy Redeemer, which the former had begun. He continued as pastor of this church until his death, twenty-six years later.

He published: *The Triumph of Religion* (n.d.); *Sketches of the Establishment of the Church in New England* (1872); and *St. Joseph's Manual: containing a Selection of Prayers for Public and private devotion* (1877).

[Wm. Byrne and others, *Hist. of the Cath. Ch. in the New England States* (1899); John G. Shea, *A Hist. of the Cath. Ch. Within the Limits of the U. S.* (1890); *The Cath. Encyc.* (1909); Wm. Lincoln, *Hist. of Worcester, Mass.* (1837); Chas. Nutt, *Hist. of Worcester and its People*, vol. II (1919); *Boston Marriages, 1752–1809* (1903); *Diary of Christopher Columbus Baldwin* (1901); *N. Y. Freeman's Jour. and Cath. Reg.*, Oct. 1, 1881; Fitton's own *Sketches . . . of the Church in New England.*]
H. E. S.

FITZ, HENRY (Dec. 31, 1808–Nov. 6, 1863), telescope maker, was born in Newburyport, Mass., the son of Henry and Susan Bradley (Page) Fitz. His grandfather, Mark Fitz, was town clerk and a person of consequence in Newburyport. Henry's first occupation was that of printer, but, thinking that printing did not offer scope enough for his inventive faculty, he became a locksmith. At that time the locksmith was a more important man than he has ever been since, and Fitz, whose skill enabled him to do two days' work in one, prospered in his new trade and devoted his surplus energy to experiments with optical glass. About 1835 he constructed his first reflecting telescope. During the winter of 1844 he devised a method of perfecting object-glasses for refracting telescopes. The next autumn, at the Fair of the American Institute, his exhibit of an instrument with a six-inch aperture attracted favorable attention and won him the patronage of several astronomers. Though its lenses were ground from ordinary American flint glass, this telescope was considered an excellent one. Fitz now moved to New York and gave all his time to the manufacture of telescopes, which he carried on with conspicuous success. In time he was a little prior to Alvan Clark [*q.v.*], and had he lived longer he would probably have carried his art as far and become as well-known. His methods were of his own invention and were refined to a point where he could detect the expansion of an object-glass effected by passing a finger over its surface on a frosty night (*New York Tribune, post*). He is said to have made use of local polishing fifteen years before the process was developed in Europe. His instruments were highly prized. He made a large number of six-inch telescopes, including one that Lieut. James M. Gilliss [*q.v.*] took with him on the United States Astronomical Expedition to the Southern Hemisphere and that found a permanent home in the Chilean government's observatory. With another six-inch Robert Van Arsdale of Newark, N. J., was able to discover several comets. Fitz made various eight- and nine-inch telescopes, among them a nine-inch that belonged to the British chargé d'affaires at Montevideo. He made one instrument of ten inches for a Mr. Vickers of Baltimore, two of twelve inches for the University of Michigan and for Vassar College, two of thirteen inches for the Dudley Observatory at Albany, N. Y., and for a group of men in Allegheny, Pa., and at least one of sixteen inches, which was owned by a Mr. Van Duzee of Buffalo. For Lewis Morris Rutherfurd [*q.v.*] he made five telescopes—of four, five and three quarters, six, nine, and eleven and one quarter inches, the last an instrument of remarkable defining power. His ambition in his later years was to build a twenty-four inch telescope. He was about to sail for Europe to select the glass when death overtook him.

[*N. Y. Tribune*, Nov. 7, 1863; James Hill Fitts, *Geneal. of the Fitts or Fitz Family in America* (1869); *Vital Records of Newburyport, Mass., to the End of the year 1849* (1911), I, 138.]
G. H. G.

FITZ, REGINALD HEBER (May 5, 1843–Sept. 30, 1913), Boston pathologist and clinician, the son of Albert Fitz, a government consul, and his wife, Eliza R. Nye, was born at Chelsea, Mass. After attending the Chauncy Hall School he entered Harvard where he received the degrees of B.A. (1864) and M.D. (1868), both with distinction. He began the study of medicine under Jeffries Wyman [*q.v.*], and later came under the influence of H. J. Bigelow, O. W. Holmes, and Edward H. Clarke [*qq.v.*]. During his last year at the medical school he served as house physician to the Boston City Hospital. In 1868 he went to Vienna where he studied pathology for several months under Rokitansky and Skoda, and also had contact with Billroth, the surgeon. At this time, however, the school of pathology at Vienna was in its decline. The Berlin school, on the other hand, was in the ascendant under Rudolf Virchow, who was then making his great contribution to scientific medicine through the application of the microscope to the study of diseased tissue ("cellular pathology"). He taught that disease was not an independent entity, but merely *life* under altered conditions. Fitz spent a year in the stimulating atmosphere of Virchow's laboratory, and laid the foundation for his career as a pathologist. While in Berlin he published an important paper in Virchow's *Archiv für pathologische Anatomie und Physiologie* (vol. LI, 1870, pp. 123–26) on the microscopic changes occurring in a respiratory disease known as bronchiectasis. Much stirred by the methods and teaching of his Berlin master, Fitz returned to America in 1870 and became instructor in pathology at the Harvard Medical School. His academic advancement proved unusually rapid. In 1873 he became assistant professor of pathological anatomy, and full professor in 1878. In 1892 he was transferred to the Hersey Professorship of the Theory and Practice of Physic. From 1887 until 1908 he was visiting physician to the Massachusetts General Hospital. He was also an active member of all local and national medical societies, being president of the Association of American Physicians for the year 1893–94.

Fitz's contributions to medicine were numerous and important. Soon after his return to America he began to write upon a great variety of pathological conditions, notably tuberculosis, ectopic pregnancy, and intestinal obstruction. For many years he interested himself in a group of cases in which the patients had rapidly succumbed after acute attacks of right-sided abdominal pain, and in 1886 published his remarkable paper, "Perforating Inflammation of the Vermiform Appendix; With Special Reference to its Early Diagnosis and Treatment" (*Transactions of the Association of American Physicians,* I, 1886, 107–35) in which he named the disease now known as appendicitis, proved its origin from the appendix, and advocated radical surgical intervention for its cure. He also described the more important features of the clinical diagnosis of the condition. This paper has always been looked upon as one of the three or four classics of modern scientific medicine, being a model of form as well as of substance. The literature of his subject was exhaustively treated, a series of more than 250 carefully recorded cases was painstakingly analyzed, and finally, by a process of shrewd deductive reasoning, he drew a few sweeping conclusions from the facts disclosed. In 1889 he analyzed a second series of seventy-two cases. In the same year he elucidated a rarer abdominal disease known as acute pancreatitis, describing its characteristic pathology and indicating the chief clinical points of distinction between it and other acute abdominal conditions (*Boston Medical and Surgical Journal,* Feb. 21–Mar. 7, 1889). In addition to these two specific contributions, Fitz exerted a wide influence upon scientific pathology, especially in America. Being the earliest of Virchow's students to return to America, he was the first to introduce the microscopic study of diseased tissue. In his constant emphasis upon the need for cooperation between pathology and clinical medicine and surgery, he did much to advance rational therapeusis.

Personally Fitz was conservative and industrious, with unusual gifts as a teacher, and a fondness for administrative duties. He served regularly upon committees at the Harvard Medical School, and secured many reforms in the curriculum of medical study. It is said that before conducting a post-mortem examination he would often ask the physician in charge of a case to express an opinion as to the nature of the pathological process involved. If the findings failed to confirm the prediction Fitz never hesitated to point out the faulty logic or imperfection of the clinical examinations which had led to the diagnostic error. On such occasions he spared himself no more than his fellows, but his rather ruthless verbal dissections often irritated his older colleagues, though they never ceased to delight his students. His lectures were erudite, clear, and incisive. "He had a habit of tilting his head backward, closing his eyes, talking with extreme rapidity and fluency, never missing a word, for 61 minutes in the hour. . . . It was as if he read a carefully prepared lecture from the inside of his eye lids" (Blake, *post*). On his sixty-fifth birthday his former students published a collection of medical papers dedicated to him (*Boston Medical and Surgical Journal,* May 7, 1908). He died in his seventy-first year, following an operation for a long-standing gastric ulcer. In 1879 he married Elizabeth, daughter of Edward H. Clarke, by whom he had two daughters and two sons, one of whom, Reginald, became a physician.

[W. W. Keen and C. W. Eliot, *Memorial Addresses Delivered at the Harvard Medic. School, Nov. 17, 1913* (1914); John B. Blake in the *Harvard Alumni Bull.,* 1914; F. C. Shattuck in the *Harvard Grads.' Mag.,* Dec. 1913; *Boston Medic. and Surgic. Jour.,* Oct. 23, 1913; *Boston Transcript,* Oct. 1, 1913. A list of appreciations and obituaries is to be found in the *Index Cat. of the Lib. of the Surgeon General's Office, U. S. Army,* 3 ser., V (1925), 783. Certain of Fitz's unpublished manuscripts have been deposited in the Boston Medical Library.]

J.F.F.

FITZGERALD, DESMOND (May 20, 1846–Sept. 22, 1926), hydraulic engineer, was born at Nassau, Bahama Islands, the son of Lionel Charles William Henry and Sarah Caroline (Brown) Fitzgerald. His father, a captain in the British army, was born in Turlough Park in northwestern Ireland. His mother, born at Nassau, was a daughter of Patrick Brown, president of His Majesty's Council, and Desmond through her was closely related to one of the best-known families of Rhode Island. The family moved to Providence, R. I., when Desmond was a child, and there he received his early education. At twelve he spent a year in Paris studying art, with the idea of becoming a sculptor. He then entered Phillips Academy at Andover, Mass., graduating in 1864. While still under age he became deputy secretary of Rhode Island and later private secretary to Gen. Burnside, the governor of the state, and during this period he began to study engineering in the office of a firm in Providence. His first engineering work, in the Middle West, led to his appointment some six years later as chief engineer of the Boston & Albany Railroad (1871–73). He had already begun to display the characteristics of energy and thoroughness which marked his entire career. In 1870, he married Elizabeth Parker Clark Salisbury of Brookline, Mass.

In 1873 Fitzgerald began his career as a hydraulic engineer by becoming superintendent of the western division of the Boston water works. Here most of his pioneer work was done in connection with the sanitary protection of water supplies, the improvement of reservoirs, and the study of *algæ* and bacteria in drinking water. He designed and constructed some of the largest and most important storage reservoirs built by the city of Boston during these years. Due largely to his efforts a suit was brought by the city to prevent the pollution of one of the reservoirs, which was won after seven years' litigation in the courts of the state.

He was a pioneer in the study of color in water and of methods of reducing it by swamp drainage, as well as of the effect of sunlight in bleaching stored water. He was the first to establish a biological laboratory in connection with water supply. One of his assistants in this work was George C. Whipple [*q.v.*] who later became prominent as a sanitary engineer. Fitzgerald made a long series of experiments at the Chestnut Hill reservoir upon the subject of evaporation from water area which for the first time afforded a fundamental basis and formula for the study of the subject. His paper on "Evaporation" (*Transactions of the American Society of Civil Engineers,* September 1886), as well as that on "Rainfall, Flow of Streams and Storage" (*Ibid.,* September 1892) received the Norman Medal of the American Society of Civil Engineers, of which he was a member for many years, and president in 1899. When the metropolitan water board absorbed the Boston supply works in 1898, he continued in charge of operation until his resignation in 1903. He later continued for some years in consulting practise, and was connected with many projects of importance, including the Chicago drainage canal, and the water supplies of Washington, San Francisco, and Manila. He was also one of the experts of the Metropolitan Sewerage Commission of New York City.

Fitzgerald was a distinguished lover and patron of art. Soon after his return to Boston in 1871 he became a collector. In 1913 he erected in Brookline his art gallery, an attractive brick building near his house, which became a center of interest in paintings, and Korean and Chinese pottery and porcelains. His gallery was open daily and was a gathering place on Sunday afternoons for his family and friends. Here he will perhaps be best remembered, easy and calm in manner, interesting and illuminating in conversation, and always kindly.

[Desmond Fitzgerald, *Family Notes* (1911); *Who's Who in America,* 1926–27; *New-Eng. Hist. and Geneal. Reg.,* Jan. 1927, pp. 63–72; *Trans. Am. Soc. Civil Engineers,* vol. XCII, 1928, pp. 1656–61.] H. K. B.

FITZGERALD, EDWARD (Oct. 26, 1833–Feb. 21, 1907), Roman Catholic prelate, was born in Limerick, Ireland, of an able family of Celtic and German Palatinate descent. He accompanied his parents to America in 1849 and soon after entered the Lazarist Seminary at the Barrens, Mo., from which he transferred to Mount St. Mary's Seminary, Cincinnati. On the completion of his theological studies at Mount St. Mary's, Emmitsburg, Md., he was ordained by Archbishop Purcell, Aug. 22, 1857, and assigned to St. Patrick's Church, Columbus, which was then under interdict for the insubordination of the trustees. During his pastorate of nine years, he organized a model parish. On June 22, 1866, he was preconized as bishop of Little Rock, Ark. Following his consecration by Archbishop Purcell on Feb. 3, 1867, he set forth for his war-torn, bankrupt diocese which had only five priests, 1,600 scattered communicants, and three charitable institutions under the Sisters of Mercy. He lived the life of an itinerant missionary and was preaching the Gospel on the frontier when he was called to the Vatican Council in Rome. In this assembly, on July 13, 1870, in the preliminary ballot on the doctrine of infallibility, Fitzgerald voted negatively. Unlike fifty-five of his brother bishops in the same group who took occasion to retire from Rome, Fitzgerald remained for the final ballot a few days later when only he and Aloisio Ricci of Cajazzo, Italy, voted *non placet.* However, when the dogma was pronounced, he "testified his acceptance of the decree on the papal primacy and infallibility to the Holy Father himself" (F. J. Zwierlein, *The Life and Letters of Bishop McQuaid,* II, 1926, 60). This determined attitude did not appear to injure Fitzgerald's position, though a leading Catholic editor, James McMaster of the *Freeman's Journal,* never grew tired of repeating that "the Bishop of Little Rock had in vain butted his head against the Big Rock" (United States Catholic Historical Society, *Historical Records and Studies,* March 1921, p. 15). Fitzgerald remained in his obscure diocese, though his name was third on the list of nominees for Purcell's coadjutor, until his resignation and retirement to St. Joseph's Infirmary at Hot Springs about a year before his death.

As ruler of the diocese, Fitzgerald was unusually active and capable. Unable to obtain a sufficient number of secular priests for an impoverished people, he called upon the Benedictines at St. Meinrad, Ind., who established an abbey at Spielerville or Subiaco in Logan County (1876) and founded Subiaco College (1887), and upon the Fathers of the Holy Ghost from Marienstatt, who settled near Morrillton (1879). Around these foundations, thriving German communities developed. The bishop also took great interest in a Polish settlement at Marche, and the Italian communities at Sunnyside, Barton, New Gascony, and Tontitown. In 1883, he represented the province of New Orleans at the conference of American bishops in Rome in preparation for the meeting of the Third Plenary Council of Baltimore (1884). As a member of the latter, he urged prudent caution in imposing compulsory parochial education. This did not imply a lack of interest in Catholic education, however, for during his life he aided in the establishment of eight academies, and built twenty-nine schools in forty-one parishes, as well as two colored industrial schools at Pine Bluff. Above all, he left to his successor a harmonious diocese of 20,000 people under sixty secular and religious priests.

[*The Cath. Encyc.* (1910), vol. IX; J. D. G. Shea, *The Hierarchy of the Cath. Ch. in the U. S.* (1886), pp. 275–76; J. H. Lamott, *Hist. of the Archdiocese of Cincinnati, 1821–1921* (1921), p. 353; *Who's Who in America,* 1906–07; D. T. Herndon, *Centennial Hist. of Ark.* (3 vols., 1922).] R. J. P.

FITZGERALD, EDWIN [See FOY, EDDIE, 1856–1928].

FITZGERALD, OSCAR PENN (Aug. 24, 1829–Aug. 5, 1911), Methodist bishop, author, son of Richard and Martha Jones (Hooper) Fitzgerald, was born in Caswell County, N. C., and died in Monteagle, Tenn. His father and mother were intensely pious. They regularly attended revivals and camp-meetings, and Oscar at the age of four had already seen much of such matters. At that time one of his favorite diversions was to assemble a group of his playmates and preach to them, calling them to repentance after the approved formulas. He attended the schools of the community until he was thirteen, when he went to Lynchburg, Va., to take a position in a newspaper office. Soon after his father enlisted for the Mexican War, and he was obliged to go home and help support his mother. He did this by running a country school. Upon the return of his father he went to Richmond to work for John Moncure Daniel [*q.v.*], then editor of the *Examiner.* There he read widely and attended many lectures—among others, the one given by Poe on the poetic principle. After several years in Richmond, he lived for a brief time in Columbia, S. C., and in Macon, Ga. In Macon, during a protracted illness, he found his thoughts running on religion, and on his recovery he felt a strong religious bent. In 1853 he entered the Methodist ministry and in 1854 was sent to Savannah. He developed into an effective preacher, always somewhat dominated in his method by the far from subtle clerical models he had observed in his childhood. He had the faculty of making the unrighteous doubtful of their final welfare, and when he had been in Savannah about a year his superiors determined to send him to California as a missionary. He set out by way of New Orleans, and at Enon, Ala., on Feb. 16, 1855, he was married to Sarah Banks. In California, after preaching for a while, he became editor of the *Pacific Methodist Advocate* and the *Christian Spectator*; and although he was openly sympathetic with the South in the Civil War, he was from 1867 to 1871 state superintendent of public education. In 1872 he was offered the Democratic nomination for the United States Senate. From 1878 to 1890 he edited the Nashville, Tenn., *Christian Advocate,* and in 1890 he was made a bishop. He continued to reside in Nashville. In 1880 he published *California Sketches,* some notes on his experiences in the West; a "Second Series" followed in 1881. *Glimpses of Truth,* made up of sententious, pious extracts from the *Advocate,* was published in 1883. A small volume of the same general tenor, *The Whetstone,* offering a thought for every day in the year, was published in 1897. *Upper Room Meditations* (1903) is smoother in its approach but essentially the same kind of book. The bishop's most notable writing was a series of biographies of great or near-great Southern religionists —*Dr. Summers* (1884), *John B. McFerrin* (1888), *Judge Longstreet* (1891), some sketches under the title *Centenary Cameos* (1885), and *Eminent Methodists* (1896). These works, while valuable as social history, do not always retain the briskness and charm found in them by a generation familiar with their theme; they are sentimental and discursive, likely at any time to break into apostrophe to some place or person or state of affairs quite irrelevant to the subject in hand. *Sunset Views* (1901) and *Fifty Years* (1903) are primarily autobiographical, but they contain a number of informal essays and the briefs of several lectures and sermons. They seem to vouch so far as concerns the personal qualities of their author for great sweetness and modesty, for a lovable thing almost like shyness. During the last ten years of his life he was infirm in health and unable to carry out the active duties of his office.

[Sources not already named: *Who's Who in America*, 1910–11; the *Independent*, Sept. 20, 1900; *N. Y. Tribune*, Aug. 6, 1911; *Nashville Banner*, Aug. 7, 1911; *Christian Advocate*, Aug. 11, 1911.] J. D. W.

FITZGERALD, THOMAS (Dec. 22, 1819–June 25, 1891), editor, publisher, playwright, was born in New York City, in a building in Franklin Square which stood on the site later occupied by the publishing house of Harper & Brothers. He removed to New Brunswick, N. J., at an early age and became connected with the *Fredonian*, then the only newspaper issued there. Having learned the practical work of journalism, he returned to his native city as a reporter on the New York *Commercial Advertiser*, but while still a youth he went to Tallahassee, Fla., where he was made editor of the *Tallahassean*. In 1847 he left the South and settled in Philadelphia. With George C. Foster, Robert G. Govett, and John F. Carter, he organized a company to publish a weekly newspaper called the *City Item*. This was first issued Sept. 25, 1847, but it did not prosper, and at the end of its second year Fitzgerald had bought the shares of his partners and was issuing the paper himself. In 1850 he purchased the *Pennsylvania Volunteer*, and subsequently the *Fireside Visitor* and the *Bazaar*. These were incorporated with his original paper, which was published under different headings during his ownership, and which, on Sept. 10, 1870, appeared as an afternoon daily entitled the *Evening City Item*. As such it was a pioneer in developing modern methods of distribution for afternoon newspapers, and due to the excellent system which was organized, the paper at one time claimed to have a circulation of 90,000 copies a day.

Through the columns of the *Item*, Fitzgerald advocated many needed and progressive reforms. He urged the construction of street railways, the removal of unsightly market houses which then cluttered some of the main streets of Philadelphia; he called for the uniforming of the police, the establishment of the fire and police telegraph system, and the erection of a public morgue. Having traveled over a considerable part of the United States, he was unfavorably impressed with the characteristic and severe red brick fronts of Philadelphia buildings, and started the movement which resulted in the building of modern stone structures, of more attractive architecture. As a member of the board of controllers of the public schools in the city, he worked for the improvement of school buildings, and for the introduction of music into the schools. His personal interest in music was shown by his early advocacy of the Academy of Music as a suitable home for grand opera in Philadelphia. All of his reforms were realized. When baseball was becoming popular through the organization of professional and semi-professional clubs, Fitzgerald's newspaper was the first, and for a long time the only Philadelphia journal which devoted space to reporting the games. This was due, no doubt, to the fact that for five years, from 1860 to 1865, he was president of the Athletic Base Ball Club, which he had helped to organize.

Not only music but art and the drama attracted Fitzgerald. He assembled a fine gallery of paintings, and for half a dozen or more years, produced a number of dramas which met with success. The first of these was *Light at Last*, first played at the Arch Street Theatre, Philadelphia, Dec. 30, 1867. It was followed by *Patrice, or the White Lady of Wicklow* with Laura Keene in the title-rôle, *Wolves at Bay, Tangled Threads, The Regent, Who Shall Win, Perils of the Night*, and *Bound to the Rock*. For many years the journalist made an annual tour of Europe, and wrote for his newspaper most entertaining and sprightly letters. While on such a trip in 1891, he became ill, and died in London. His remains were brought to Philadelphia where they were buried. His wife was Sarah Levering Liter, daughter of Dr. George W. Liter. Four sons and one daughter survived him.

[*Public Ledger* (Phila.), June 26, 1891, for obituary sketch; and the *Proof-Sheet* (Phila.), Sept. 1870.] J. J.

FITZGIBBON, CATHERINE [See Irene, Sister, 1823–1896].

FITZHUGH, GEORGE (Nov. 4, 1806–July 30, 1881), lawyer, sociologist, was born on what was known as the Brenttown tract, in Prince William County, Va. His father was Dr. George Fitzhugh of "Belmont," King George County, and his mother Lucy Stuart of "Mt. Stuart," of the same county. His paternal grandfather was John Fitzhugh, who married Alice Thornton. George Fitzhugh regarded himself as a descendant of William Fitzhugh, the immigrant, who was military commandant and land agent under Lord Fairfax in Northern Virginia in the seventeenth century, and of a hardly lesser personage, Col. William Fitzhugh, of "Marmion," Stafford, now King George County. Painstaking research, however, has failed to verify the connection. George Fitzhugh's parents, when he was six, moved to the neighborhood of Alexandria, then the center of the aristocratic "Chotank" region, populated by descendants of Cavaliers and Huguenots. Here he lived until he was twenty-three, receiving scant education in a field school, and afterwards reading law. In 1829 he married Mary Brockenbrough, and seems to have moved then to Port Royal, Caroline County, where he was long engaged in law practise, specializing in criminal cases. He had nine children, three of whom died in infancy. In Buchanan's administration, Fitzhugh was employed in the attorney-general's office, in the land claim department, at which time James D. B. De Bow knew him as a convivial soul. About 1856 he went North, and at the house of his relative, Gerrit Smith, the Abolitionist, met Harriet Beecher Stowe. On this trip he lectured in Boston, and returned to the South a stouter defender of negro slavery. He wrote for the New York *Day Book* and *Richmond* (Virginia) *Examiner,* and from 1857 to 1867 contributed regularly to *De Bow's Review,* generally on the subject of the political economy of the South. His best-known formal works were: *Sociology for the South; or, the Failure of Free Society* (1854), and *Cannibals All! or, Slaves without Masters* (1857). Though not the first to set forth the advantages of the Southern slave system, Fitzhugh deserves credit for seeking to convert the debate, on the Southern side, from a mere negative rebuttal into an aggressive doctrine of positive benefits. He believed that free capitalist society, animated by the *laissez faire* doctrines of Adam Smith, was a gross failure. It deserved the denunciation it received at the hands of the Utopian socialists—Owen, Fourier, St. Simon and their American followers, such as Horace Greeley. Exploitation of the working class by capitalist and landlord plunged the real producers into destitution. But Fitzhugh did not follow the socialists in their plans for reform, which he characterized as chimerical. He found that the patronal economy of the slave South answered every constructive purpose. The masses of workers had more real liberty and their only true security when they were the chattels of their employers, who thus had the strongest interest to preserve their health and morale. To the eve of the Civil War, Fitzhugh was hopeful of converting the North to his doctrines, and of eventually seeing the Southern aristocracy, which he regarded as racially superior to the Northern, dominant in the Union. In his advocacy of manufacturing in the South he was evidently influenced by H. C. Carey. He died at Huntsville, Tex.

[*Virginia Mag. of Hist. and Biog.,* from Oct. 1899 to Oct. 1901 for the Fitzhugh genealogy; Fairfax Harrison, *Landmarks of Old Prince William* (1924), I, 186, 194; Fitzhugh's article in *De Bow's Review,* Jan. 1861, and scattered autobiographical references in his books.]

B.M.

FITZHUGH, WILLIAM (1651–October 1701), lawyer, was the son of Henry Fitzhugh of the town of Bedford, England, barrister-at-law. He was born at Bedford and was baptized Jan. 10, 1651, according to parish records, though the exact date of his birth is not known. Indeed, practically nothing is known of his life in England. He undoubtedly received an excellent education, including a thorough training in law, probably in his father's chambers. He emigrated to Virginia about 1670 and established himself on the Potomac in what was then Stafford County, Va. There he purchased a large estate and settled down to the life of a planter and exporter, at the same time practising law. Adapting himself quickly to his new environment, he soon acquired a leading place as a lawyer, and his agricultural and mercantile ventures proved extremely successful. In 1682 and 1683 he came to the fore as counsel for the accused in the celebrated Beverley case. Maj. Robert Beverley, clerk of the House of Burgesses, had declined to supply the governor and council with copies of the legislative journals without permission of the House and thus incurred the enmity of the governor. The latter had him arrested on a variety of charges and an application for a writ of *habeas corpus* was refused. Fresh charges were preferred upon which he was found guilty, though he was finally released after begging pardon on his bended knees. Fitzhugh's letter to Beverley relative to his rights is extant and displays deep knowledge on some extremely intricate legal questions (*Virginia Magazine, post,* October 1893). He was a member of the Virginia House of Burgesses for some years and found himself on two occasions involved in legal entanglements in which he was charged with misrepresenting his claims for emolument, but apparently he was never brought to trial. In 1687 as lieutenant-colonel of the county militia, he commanded the force which was collected to oppose the raids of the Seneca Indians. In 1692 he prepared a digest of the laws of Virginia, with a preface reviewing their development, which he sent to England with a view to publication, but apparently no steps were taken to implement his wishes, and the manuscript has disappeared. Almost all the information we possess as to the details of his life after 1679 is derived from the remarkable series of letters—213 in number—addressed by him to his relatives and intimates in England, as well as to business men there, the originals of which are in the Harvard Library. They cover the period between May 15,

1679, and Apr. 26, 1699, and are extremely valuable from a historical standpoint in that they afford an intimate insight into the business processes of a prominent Virginia capitalist of those times. He died in Stafford County, Va., in October 1701. He married May 1, 1674, Sarah, daughter of John Tucker of Westmoreland County, Va. His grand-daughter, Sarah, became the wife of Edward Barradall [*q.v.*], attorney-general of Virginia.

["The Fitzhugh Family," in the *Va. Mag. of Hist. and Biog.*, Oct. 1899, Jan. 1900; "Letters of Wm. Fitzhugh," *Ibid.*, July 1893 to Oct. 1898 (excepting Apr. 1898); "Will of Wm. Fitzhugh," *Ibid.*, Jan. 1895; P. A. Bruce, *Institutional Hist. of Va. in the Seventeenth Century* (2 vols., 1910); H. R. McIlwaine, ed., *Jours. of the House of Burgesses of Va., 1659/60–1693* (1914).]

H. W. H. K.

FITZPATRICK, BENJAMIN (June 30, 1802–Nov. 21, 1869), governor of Alabama, United States senator, was born in Greene County, Ga., the son of William and Anne (Phillips) Fitzpatrick. His forebears came originally from Virginia. His father served in the Georgia legislature for nineteen years. Bereft of both of his parents at the age of seven, his education was severely limited; in fact, he never attended school more than six months. He removed to Alabama in 1816, while it was yet a part of Mississippi Territory, to assist in the planting interests of his elder brothers whose lands lay on the east side of the Alabama River about six miles above Montgomery. He studied law in the office of Judge N. E. Benson and was admitted to the bar at the age of twenty-one years. Soon afterward he formed a professional partnership with Henry Goldthwaite of Montgomery. His legal success is attested by the fact that he was soon elected solicitor of the Montgomery district, in which position he served for two terms. Ill health led him to retire in 1827 to a plantation which he had acquired in the Alabama Valley about six miles west of Montgomery. For twelve years he engaged exclusively in planting, developing one of the most attractive estates in the region. Here, "surrounded by all the comforts wealth can bring, he dispensed a boundless hospitality" (Brewer, *post*, p. 240).

During the year that Fitzpatrick abandoned law for planting he married Sarah Terry Elmore, a member of one of the most distinguished families of the state, and by his marriage also became the brother-in-law of Dixon H. Lewis [*q.v.*], the state's most powerful state-rights leader and a member of Congress from 1829 until his death in 1848. This union laid the basis of Fitzpatrick's political fortunes. In 1840 he was called out by the Democratic party convention to stump the state for Martin Van Buren, who was being sorely pressed by the Whigs. He showed himself a man of unusual talents in this campaign and was chosen by his party for the governorship before the end of the year. He was elected the following year over James W. McClung, an independent Whig candidate. He was reëlected without opposition for a second term. Fitzpatrick's messages to the legislature were remarkable documents for one who had never had the advantage of schools. His administration is notable for the overthrow of the state banking system which had degenerated into a public evil.

At the end of his second term he repaired again to his plantation, and, his first wife having died in 1837, in 1846 he was married to Aurelia Rachel Blassingame of Marion, Ala. From planting he was called back into politics in 1848 by Gov. Chapman to fill the unexpired term of Dixon H. Lewis, in the United States Senate. In 1853 he was appointed by Gov. Collier to fill the vacancy in the federal Senate caused by the resignation of William R. King who had been elected vice-president of the United States. Two years later he was elected to the Senate for a full term of six years. His high standing in that body is indicated by the fact that he was chosen president *pro tempore* in 1857 and served in that capacity till 1860. The National Democratic Convention, held at Baltimore in 1860, offered him the nomination for vice-president on the Douglas ticket. This he declined, probably because there was no chance for victory, though he himself declared that he could not run with Douglas because he did not approve the "squatter sovereignty" doctrine.

Fitzpatrick was by nature conservative and imperturbable. Though a personal and political friend of Yancey, he opposed the latter's "Alabama Platform" and ranged himself by the side of King, Winston, Collier, Campbell, and Hilliard to prevent Yancey and Samford from taking Alabama out of the Union in 1850. Though an ardent Southerner, he held steadfastly to the view, down to the outbreak of hostilities, that secession was not the proper remedy for the South's grievances, well founded though they were. But when secession came he withdrew from the federal Senate and supported wholeheartedly the Southern cause. When the war was over he undertook to help reconstruct the state in a manner acceptable to President Johnson, but was for a time imprisoned with other prominent leaders. In 1865 he was unanimously elected to preside over the constitutional convention assembled in pursuance of President Johnson's plan of reconstruction. This was his last public function, for soon afterward he was disfranchised. He maintained, however, a lively interest in public questions until his death.

[W. Brewer, *Alabama* (1872); W. G. Brown, *Hist. of Ala.* (1900); J. W. Du Bose, *The Life and Times of Wm. L. Yancey* (1892); Wm. Garrett, *Reminiscences of Public Men in Ala.* (1872); A. B. Moore, *Hist. of Ala.* (1927), vol. I; T. M. Owen, *Hist. of Ala. and Dict. of Ala. Biog.* (1921), vol. III; *Trans. Ala. Hist. Soc.*, vol. IV (1904); B. F. Riley, *Makers and Romance of Ala. Hist.* (n.d.); *Mobile Daily Register*, Nov. 23, 1869.]

A. B. M.

FITZPATRICK, JOHN BERNARD (Nov. 15, 1812–Feb. 13, 1866), third Roman Catholic bishop of Boston, was born in Boston and died there though he had traveled extensively in his lifetime. His parents were Bernard Fitzpatrick and Eleanor Flinn, both natives of Tullamore, Ireland, who settled in Boston in 1805, coming from Baltimore where there had been family connections since colonial days. Through his father he was kinsman of the Fitzpatricks of Upper Ossory whose coat of arms Pope Pius IX combined with that of the See of Boston when appointing him Assistant at the Pontifical Throne (*Ecclesiastical Review*, July 1911, p. 5). His mother was a Daughter of the American Revolution, her father, James Flinn, who lies buried on Boston Common, having served with the Massachusetts militia before his marriage in Baltimore to the beautiful Mary Kinsella, a descendant of William Bard, the founder of Bardstown, Ky.

From his mother, who taught for a time at the Boylston School, he received his early training. Later he attended the Adams School and the Boylston School, under Master Fox, where he was a brilliant student. In September 1826, he entered the famous Boston Latin School from which he was graduated in June 1829. References to his school friendships appear in *Early Memories* (1913, p. 56), by Henry Cabot Lodge, whose uncle, George Cabot, was a classmate, and also in the *Ode on the 250th Anniversary of Boston Latin School* (privately printed, n.d.), by Thomas Parsons [*q.v.*], the Dante scholar and poet, who also graduated at the same time. His course was strictly classical and was guided chiefly by Benjamin Apthorp Gould, Frederick Percival Leverett, and Samuel Parker Parker.

College studies were made at the historic Collège de Montréal which he entered in September 1829. Here, after four years of study under the priests of the Société de Saint-Sulpice, most influential of whom was Rev. John Larkin (United States Catholic Historical Society, *Historical Records and Studies*, vol. IV, pt. 1, 1906, p. 97), John Fitzpatrick sustained so ably his theses in philosophy at a public disputation, August 1833, in competition with J. U. Beaudry, later the Canadian jurist, and Ambrose Manahan, of New York, afterwards a doctor of the Propaganda, Rome, that he was appointed a *Régent* or tutor on the college faculty. Three years more of study in addition to teaching did not satisfy his own high standard of preparation for the priesthood, so that after a brief visit at home in August 1837 he sailed for Paris.

At the Grand Séminaire de Saint-Sulpice, Paris, where M. Antoine Garnier, the great linguist, who had done parish work in Baltimore while his parents were resident there, was Superior, and the brilliant Abbé Le Hir was professor of Hebrew, he made his final studies for the priesthood (L. Bertrand, *Bibliothèque Sulpicienne*, 1900, vol. II). Already tonsured at Boston by his bishop, Benedict Fenwick, S. J., Sept. 8, 1834 (dismissorial letters in Bibliothèque St.-Sulpice, Montreal), he received minor orders Dec. 22, 1838, at the hands of Mgr. de Quélen, Archbishop of Paris; subdiaconate May 28, 1839, and diaconate Dec. 21, 1839, both from Mgr. Blanquart de Bailleul, then Bishop of Versailles; and priesthood June 13, 1840, *sede vacante*, in the Church of St. Sulpice, from the hands of Mgr. Pierre Dominique Marcellin Bonamie, titular Archbishop of Chalcedon and second superior of the Picpussiens (Records of the *Société de Saint-Sulpice*, Paris). His priestly life in Boston, though brief, was of that superior quality which warranted his advancement to the episcopacy. Accordingly, in the new division of New England following the Fifth Provincial Council of Baltimore, he was consecrated Bishop of Callipolis and coadjutor of Boston Mar. 24, 1844, in the Chapel of the Convent of the Visitation at Georgetown, D. C. On Aug. 11, 1846, upon the death of Bishop Fenwick [*q.v.*], he succeeded to the See of Boston.

Fitzpatrick's episcopal career was a series of worrisome problems and of personal triumphs. His chief duty was the organization of the diocese to meet the needs of the great Irish immigration which began almost immediately after he was enthroned. Out of this underlying problem came many others, including the dispute over Bible reading in the public schools (1859), the inspection of the convents (1854), and the opposition to Catholic schools and colleges (1849–65). Had it not been that the Bishop was especially gifted in diplomacy, the course of church and state in Massachusetts might have been much more uneven than it has been. A man of letters himself, his great care was for the higher education of his clergy, and, through them, of the people. To this end he established regular annual collections for the assistance of diocesan theological students; invited priests distinguished for cultural talents to work in the diocese, even temporarily; encouraged the Jesuits, already at Holy Cross College, to rebuild there, to take over St. Mary's parish, Boston, start Boston College, and renew the Abenaquis mission in Maine; invited the Sisters of Notre Dame from Cincinnati to teach in the parochial schools; approved the establishment by diocesan priests of the weekly *Boston Catholic Observer,* 1847–49; and acted as European agent for the foundation of the Provincial Seminary at Troy, N. Y. (Farley, *post;* Gabriels, *post*).

Recognition of his personal talents came largely from the literary world, though he had no time to prepare anything for publication save a few letters and pastorals which, for the most part, are hidden in the files of the *Pilot.* He was invited to be a member of the Thursday Evening Club of congenial Bostonians (Edward Warren, *The Life of John Collins Warren,* 1860, I, 371). Harvard College, which was denied his allegiance in undergraduate days, made him an alumnus in 1861, the only Catholic bishop ever to receive the degree of doctor of sacred theology from that institution. In 1862 he was invited to become a member of the American Academy of Arts and Sciences.

Disinclined to ostentation of any kind, simple and retiring in his tastes, Bishop Fitzpatrick would have been glad to have relinquished the dignity and distinctions which he carried so gracefully had he been allowed to choose his own career in the Church. The exigencies of the period, however, required unremitting service from those most competent, and obedience as well as strong faith was among his virtues. The apostle of temperance, Father Mathew, the Vatican astronomer, Father De Vico, S. J. (A. J. Thébaud, *Three-Quarters of a Century,* 1904, III, 343), the American philosopher, Orestes Brownson (the *Convert,* 1877, p. 280), all received from him a gracious reception and warm encouragement. The members of many old New England families, carried into membership in the Catholic Church on the tide of the Oxford movement, turned to him for sincere sympathy and sound advice and found both. Gov. Andrew and the statesmen of the time relied upon his loyal integrity and judicious influence. Yet, although he was appraised by the first personal representative of the Holy Father to visit America, Cajetan, Cardinal Bedini, as one of the three ablest bishops of the United States at the time (1853), his reputation to-day endures only within the confines of the diocese which he organized in spite of tremendous obstacles, where his personal character forms a great part of the background of the history of the Catholic Church in New England. In appearance he was tall and well-poised, with regular features and high forehead. His figure is close to that of Gov. Andrew in the bas-relief "Departure for the War" on the Soldiers and Sailors Monument on Boston Common. His body rests in the crypt of the Cathedral of the Holy Cross which he had planned but was unable to build because of the financial uncertainties of Civil War times.

[The most authentic account of Fitzpatrick's life is found in the pamphlet, *In Memoriam, John Bernard Fitzpatrick* (1866). Obituaries appeared in *Proc. Am. Acad. Arts and Sci.,* VII, 116 (May 29, 1866); *Sadlier's Cath. Dir.,* 1867; *Boston Daily Advertiser,* Feb. 14, 1866. See also R. H. Clarke, *Lives of the Deceased Bishops* (1872), II, 310; John Murphy Farley, *The Life of John, Cardinal McCloskey* (1918); Henry Gabriels, *Hist. Sketch of St. Joseph's Provincial Seminary, Troy, N. Y.* (1905). The date of Fitzpatrick's birth is usually given as Nov. 1, 1812. That given above, Nov. 15, is based on baptismal records.] M. T. R.

FITZPATRICK, MORGAN CASSIUS (Oct. 29, 1868–June 25, 1908), educator, congressman, was born at Tuscaloosa, Ala., the son of Louisa (Cross) and Joel M. Fitzpatrick who had recently moved from Tennessee and in 1874 returned to that state. Young Fitzpatrick, brought up on a farm in Smith County, was educated in the common schools of his community, at Elmwood Institute in Tennessee, at National Normal University, Lebanon, Ohio, and graduated from the law college of Cumberland University, Tenn., in 1890. Of robust physique, magnetic personality, and considerable mental endowments, he began a varied and promising career. Making his home in Hartsville, in Trousdale County, where in 1894 he married Maggie May De Bow, he taught school, practised law, became county superintendent of education (1893–94), edited the *Hartsville Vidette* (1895–96), and was elected in 1894 as representative from Trousdale, Sumner, and Wilson counties to the lower house of the Tennessee legislature. As a legislator, holding the chairmanship of the committee on education and common schools, he displayed qualities of energy and leadership. He was reelected to the state House of Representatives and in 1897 was chosen to be its speaker. In the following year he became chairman of the Democratic executive committee of the state, a position that he retained for four years. As a Democratic leader in Tennessee he was instrumental in securing the election of his friend, Benton McMillin, as governor, and was rewarded by him with appointment in 1899 to the office of state superintendent of public instruction. During the four years of Gov. McMillin's two administrations Fitzpatrick retained this position and did much to arouse the people of the state, whose more wealthy citizens sent their children to private schools and academies, to a realization of the responsibility of the state for an adequate and well-financed system of public education. As legislator and as superintendent he advocated and was instrumental in securing the enactment of a uniform text-book law, a county high-school law that enabled counties to establish public high schools and thus bridge the gap, particularly in evidence in rural counties, between the elementary schools and the colleges and universities, and a law making school districts and civil districts coextensive. To Peabody Normal College (now George Peabody College for Teachers) and to state and county teachers' institutes he gave support as much needed instruments for improving the qualifications of the state's teachers. He sought in many ways to better the state's educational system but he constantly insisted, with some eventual success, that Tennessee's educational defects resulted not primarily from an inadequate system but from "the lack of funds with which to employ better teachers on better salaries and to double the terms of our schools." In 1902 he was elected to the Fifty-eighth Congress. He did not seek reëlection, however, for his health had become seriously impaired. He moved his residence to Gallatin where he practised law until his death.

[Information from Fitzpatrick's brother, Mr. A. J. Fitzpatrick of Castalian Springs, Tenn., Mrs. Isabel Hayes Williams of Johnson City, Tenn., and others; *Who's Who in America*, 1903–05, which is inaccurate in certain details; *Journals* of the House of Representatives of Tenn.; *Reports* of the Superintendent of Public Instruction of Tenn.; obituary in Knoxville *Journal and Tribune*, June 26, 1908.] P. M. H.

FITZPATRICK, THOMAS (*c.* 1799–Feb. 7, 1854), trapper, guide, Indian agent, was one of the eight children of Mary (Kiernan) Fitzpatrick, and was born in County Cavan, Ireland. Nothing is known of his early years except that he acquired the fundamentals of a good education. Before he was seventeen he came to the United States. He drifted West and in time seems to have become an Indian trader. He first came into notice as one of the company of trappers engaged by Gen. William Ashley [*q.v.*] for his second expedition up the Missouri in 1823. He took part in the two battles with the Arikaras in that year; and late in September, at Fort Kiowa, a trading-post near the present Chamberlain, S. D., was chosen by Ashley as second in command of a small party under Jedediah S. Smith [*q.v.*], directed to penetrate the Wyoming wilderness. Reaching the Bighorn Mountains, the party wintered with the Crows, and in the following March (1824) crossed to the Green River by South Pass, thus making the effective discovery of that afterward famous thoroughfare. As a leader of trapping parties Fitzpatrick remained with Ashley and his successors—Smith, Jackson, and William L. Sublette—until the summer of 1830, when with James Bridger, Milton G. Sublette, and two others he took over the interests of this firm and formed the Rocky Mountain Fur Company. The latter company was dissolved in 1834, Fitzpatrick, Bridger, and M. G. Sublette continuing the business; but the American Fur Company had become dominant in the mountains, and the partners within a year became its employees.

With the decline of the fur-trade Fitzpatrick varied his trapping ventures by serving as a guide. In 1841 he led the first Pacific-bound emigrant train (the Bidwell-Bartleson company), accompanied by Father De Smet's missionary party, as far as Fort Hall, continuing with De Smet to the Flathead country, in what is now northwestern Montana. On his return the following year he met the White-Hastings Oregon party near Fort Laramie and guided it to Fort Hall. In 1843–44 he served as guide to Frémont's second expedition, and in 1845 to Kearny's expedition to South Pass and to Lieut. J. W. Abert's expedition along the Purgatory and the Canadian rivers. In 1846 he guided Kearny's Army of the West to Santa Fé, continuing with Kearny on the march to California until beyond Socorro, N. Mex., when he was sent East with the dispatches brought from the Coast by Kit Carson.

His many encounters, peaceful as well as belligerent, with the Indians had made him widely known and both feared and respected among them. Because of an accident suffered from the bursting of a rifle they called him "Broken Hand," "Bad Hand," or "Three Fingers," and because of the premature graying of his locks through a terrible experience with the Grosventres they called him also "White Hair." On his arrival at Westport in November 1846, he learned that a new agency—that of the Upper Platte and the Arkansas—had been established and that on Aug. 6 he had been appointed agent. His charges were mainly the Cheyennes, the Arapahos, and certain bands of Sioux, and his field was the region between Fort Laramie and Bent's Fort (after 1849 Bent's second fort, farther down the Arkansas). About 1850 he married Margaret, the daughter of an Indian trader, John Poisal, and an Arapaho woman. In the fall of the year, for some unknown reason, he was removed from his post, but on the demand of the Missouri delegation in Congress was reappointed. Mar. 12, 1851.

In cooperation with Col. D. D. Mitchell, superintendent of the Central Agency at St. Louis, he arranged the great Indian council held near Fort Laramie in September 1851, and negotiated the treaties signed there with the plains tribes north of the Arkansas. On July 27, 1853, at the second Fort Atkinson, near the present Dodge City, Kan., he induced the turbulent Comanches, Kiowas, and Kiowa Apaches to sign a treaty which for a time brought peace. Called to Washington for a conference, he arrived in the capital about Jan. 1, 1854. While stopping at Brown's Hotel he was seized with an attack of pneumonia, which proved fatal. His remains rest in an unmarked grave in the Congressional Cemetery.

Of the three outstanding "mountain men" of the trapper and early emigrant periods—Fitzpatrick, Carson, and Bridger—the first-named was esteemed by his contemporaries as the greatest and the most capable. By a capricious turn of history his achievements were forgotten, while his rivals became famous. His letters in the files of the Indian Office reveal a man of keen intelligence and sound judgment, studious, reflective, and informed, and with an exceptional gift of expression. His skill as a guide was highly praised by De Smet, Frémont, Kearny, and Abert, and his efficiency as an Indian agent by virtually all who were acquainted with his work. He treated the Indians with a justice that won their confidence and admiration and caused him to be long remembered by them—in the words of Chief Little Raven, of the Arapahos, in 1865—as "the one fair agent" they had ever had.

[This sketch is based on researches of the writer and of Prof. LeRoy R. Hafen for the forthcoming book, *Broken Hand, the Life-Story of Thomas Fitzpatrick*; and on information from Mrs. M. G. McCarthy, grandniece of Fitzpatrick. Published sources include Frémont's reports, *Sen. Doc. No. 243,* 27 Cong., 3 Sess., and *Sen. Doc. No. 174,* 28 Cong., 2 Sess.; Kearny's and Abert's reports, *Sen. Doc. No. 1, No. 438,* 29 Cong., 1 Sess. References are found in H. M. Chittenden, *The Am. Fur Trade of the Far West* (1902); H. M. Chittenden and A. T. Richardson, *Life, Letters and Travels of Father Pierre-Jean De Smet, S. J.* (1905); E. L. Sabin, *Kit Carson Days* (1914); W. J. Ghent, *The Road to Oregon* (1929); J. C. Alter, *Jas. Bridger* (1925); H. C. Dale, *The Ashley-Smith Explorations* (1918); J. S. Robb, under pseud. of "Solitaire," in the *St. Louis Reveille,* Mar. 1, 1847. An obituary was published in the *Daily Globe* (Washington, D. C.), Feb. 9, 1854.]

W. J. G.

FITZSIMMONS, ROBERT PROMETHEUS (June 4, 1862–Oct. 22, 1917), alias "The Cornishman," "The Antipodean," "Fighting Bob," "Freckled Bob," "Ruby Robert," and "The Village Blacksmith," a pugilist, actor, and gentleman of leisure, was born in Helston, Cornwall, England. When he was only a child, his parents emigrated to Timaru, New Zealand, where his father opened a blacksmith shop in which Robert toughened his muscles for some years. Though reared in a highly devout atmosphere—"My mother," he once said, "believed everything in the Bible, and the old man was worse than mother about religion"—he soon showed a stronger preference for boxing than for theology; and from 1880 to 1890 he acquired an ever-increasing reputation as New Zealand's most promising pugilist. Having come to San Francisco in 1890, he shortly leaped into fame by winning the world's middleweight championship from Jack Dempsey, the "Nonpareil," at New Orleans on Jan. 14, 1891. His most notable victory came on Mar. 17, 1897, when he whipped James J. Corbett at Carson City in a fight that lasted fourteen rounds. Until the last round Corbett seemed to be winning with ease; but in that round Fitzsimmons suddenly drove a terrific left-hand blow to the pit of Corbett's stomach and then smashed the same fist against Corbett's jaw. In less than three seconds Fitzsimmons had accomplished three epochal feats: he had knocked out an Irishman on Saint Patrick's Day, he had won the heavyweight championship of the world, and he had invented the terrible "solar plexus punch" that will always be associated with his name. In an athletic sense, however, Fitzsimmons was already old; and on June 9, 1899, he lost his crown to James J. Jeffries in the eleventh round of a battle at Coney Island. The next year he quickly disposed of those two redoubtable fighters, Tom Sharkey and Gus Ruhlin; but in 1902 Jeffries again laid him low, although Fitzsimmons broke all the knuckles of his right hand against Jeffries's ponderous jaw. "I felt them bust in my glove like a piece of chalk," Fitzsimmons explained. From 1903 to 1914 the aged veteran fought eight times; his last battle was waged in his fifty-second year. Though he engaged in over 360 fights, he died without a scar.

Fitzsimmons has been aptly described as "a cannon-ball on a pair of pipe-stems." His knock-kneed legs were so lean that he wore thick underwear to hide their thinness, and he weighed barely 160 pounds; but he had the shoulders and arms of a giant. In action he preferred to stand still, with his left foot advanced and his body weaving around on his hips; when he did move, he awkwardly shuffled along in a flat-footed fashion. His powerful torso was crowned by a small head scantily covered with ragged wisps of sandy hair, beneath which two quizzical blue eyes blinked innocently amid a mass of freckles. He was easy-going, good-natured, and rather sentimental. He lost most of his money to various fleecers and sharpers; he liked to sing old-fashioned hymns in his high, falsetto voice; and when he defeated Corbett, he wept with such copious joy that his wife compelled him to desist.

He was married four times, though the name of his first wife, by whom he had one son, is unknown. In 1894 he married Rose Julian, an acrobat, who bore him two sons, Robert and Martin, and a daughter, Rosie. Rose died in 1904, and the next year he wedded Julia May Gifford, a singer, who was touring with him in a play called "A Fight for Love." A few months later she left him for another man with whom Fitzsimmons wished to fight a duel; but common sense finally triumphed, and in 1915 he married Temo Ziller, an Italian, with whom he lived until his death from double pneumonia while he was on a vaudeville engagement in Chicago. A little later, his wife was denied a petition that she might exhume his corpse in order to remove the diamonds that studded his teeth.

[Robt. H. Davis, *"Ruby Robert," Alias Bob Fitzsimmons* (1926); *Physical Culture and Self-Defense* (1901), by Robert Fitzsimmons, with introduction by A. J. Drexel Biddle; Henry Sayers, *Fights Forgotten* (n.d.); Jeffery Farnol, *Famous Prize Fights* (1928); various newspaper items, notably *Chicago Tribune*, Oct. 22, 1917, and *N. Y. Times*, Oct. 19, 20, 22, 23, 25, 29, and Dec. 16, 1917.]

R. F. D.

FITZSIMMONS, or FITZSIMONS, THOMAS (1741–Aug. 26, 1811), congressman, was born in Ireland. As a youth he went to Philadelphia, where he embarked on a mercantile career. On Nov. 23, 1761, he married Catharine Meade, daughter of a prosperous and influential merchant, Robert Meade, the great-grandfather of Gen. George G. Meade. A few months later, he formed a partnership with his brother-in-law under the firm-name of George Meade & Company, which carried on an extensive mercantile and commercial business, particularly with the West India Islands. FitzSimons not only warmly espoused the cause of the colonists in the controversy with England but, after the opening of hostilities, raised and commanded a company of militia, which saw service in a number of important campaigns. In addition, he served on the Council of Safety and the Navy Board and took an active part in the construction of fire ships and other military equipment. Near the end of the war, George Meade & Company contributed £5,000 (Flanders, *post*) towards a general subscription for the immediate necessities of the army. FitzSimons was elected in 1782 to the new Congress established under the Articles of Confederation. In the closing months of the war he labored strenuously to induce the government to pay all the arrears due to the soldiers, since he felt that the meeting of this obligation should precede their demobilization. He became a member of the Pennsylvania Board of Censors in 1783; and later he served several terms in the state legislature. As a member of the Convention that framed the Federal Constitution of 1787, he took an active part in the debates, advocating, among other things, the establishment of a strong national government, the placing of rigid restrictions on suffrage and office-holding, the conferring upon Congress of the power to tax imports and exports, and the granting to the House of Representatives and the Senate equal authority in the making of treaties.

In 1789, he was elected to the first national House of Representatives, where he served until 1795. He identified himself immediately with those members who supported Hamilton in his nationalistic measures and he was in accord with practically the entire program of the Federalist party. From the opening of the Federal Convention of 1787 until his retirement from Congress he advocated persistently the making of provisions for the retirement of the debt of the United States and the levying of a protective tariff for the encouragement of manufactures. After his defeat in the election of 1794 by a Democrat, John Swanwick, he retired to private life. With the exception of a position on the commission for the liquidation of the claims of British creditors provided for under the Jay Treaty, he held no political offices. Nevertheless, he continued to manifest intense interest in public questions and was frequently consulted by the federal and the state governments. On a number of occasions, he joined Stephen Girard, Robert Morris, Joseph Ball, Charles Pettit, James Coxe, and others to memorialize Congress on the question of "the spoliations of France on American commerce" and the interference with American trade by British cruisers. FitzSimons was opposed to the establishment of the Embargo on the ground that it was "unjust, impolitic, and oppressive" and that, as a means of coercion, it was "weak, inefficient, and useless." The enforcing law he regarded as an invasion of the principles of civil liberty. In 1810 he served on a committee of Philadelphia business men organized to induce Congress to re-charter the United States Bank.

Although he was conspicuous as a political leader, it was in the establishment of firm foundations in business and commerce that FitzSimons was especially noteworthy. In 1781, he was influential in establishing the first bank of America—the Bank of North America, and became one of its trustees. He was a founder and a director of the Insurance Company of North America and was for many years the president of the

Philadelphia Chamber of Commerce. In 1805, as a result of obligations incurred by Robert Morris and other business associates, he went into bankruptcy. While he recouped his financial losses to a considerable extent, he never regained his former prestige. For many years he was a trustee of the University of Pennsylvania and was interested actively in the advancement of public education in the state. He was a member of the Hibernian Society, was the largest single contributor to the erection of St. Augustine's Church in Philadelphia, and was a participant in many philanthropies. He died in Philadelphia.

[FitzSimons spelled his name thus in signing the Constitution; it has since been variously spelled. Biographical sketches include: Henry Flanders, "Thos. Fitzsimmons," *Pa. Mag. of Hist. and Biog.*, II (1878), 306; J. T. Scharf and T. Westcott, *Hist. of Phila.* (1884), vol. I; Henry Simpson, *Lives of Eminent Philadelphians* (1859); J. H. Campbell, *Hist. of the Friendly Sons of St. Patrick and of the Hibernian Soc. of Phila., 1771–1892* (1892); J. A. Farrell, "Thos. FitzSimons," *Records Am. Cath. Hist. Soc.*, Sept. 1928.] A. E. M.

FLAD, HENRY (July 30, 1824–June 20, 1898), engineer, inventor, was born at the Rennhoff, in the Grand Duchy of Baden, near Heidelberg, Germany, the son of Jacob and Franziska (Brunn) Flad. Less than a year after his birth his father died and his mother moved to Speyer in the Rhine Palatinate, where Flad received his early education. He then took the polytechnic course in the University of Munich and graduated in 1846. After spending two years in the engineering service of the Bavarian government, he took part in the Revolution of 1848 as captain of a company of army engineers. With the collapse of this movement, Flad was forced to flee his native land and sailed for the United States, landing in New York in the autumn of 1849. After serving for a short time as a draftsman in an architect's office there, he secured a position as an engineer in the construction of the New York & Erie Railroad. For the succeeding eleven years he was engaged in railroad construction work both in the East and Middle West. With the outbreak of the Civil War Flad enlisted in the Union army and served admirably in the "Engineer Regiment of the West," maintaining railroad communication and building defensive works, and passing through all the grades from private to colonel. After the war he returned to St. Louis and as assistant engineer to James P. Kirkwood, worked on plans for an improved water supply for St. Louis. Three years later he was made a member of the reorganized board of water commissioners and served continuously for eight years during which time the city's water-works were completed and put into service. Meanwhile he met James B. Eads and when the latter began the construction of the famous "Eads Bridge," Flad joined him as assistant engineer. Some of the boldest features of this enterprise, such as the method of erecting masonry without false work, were due to Flad.

Following several years of consulting engineering practise, Flad was elected first president of the newly constituted Board of Public Improvements of St. Louis in 1877, which office he held continuously for nearly fourteen years. Through his characteristically determined efforts the city's system of public works was taken out of politics and put on a firm engineering and financial basis, in which respect St. Louis became a model city. In 1890 Flad resigned this office to accept an appointment as member of the Mississippi River Commission, a position which he retained until his death. As an engineer, Flad was remarkable for his great fertility of invention. While a water commissioner, he secured patents for filters and water meters; while with Eads, he devised, among other things, a hydrostatic and hydraulic elevator, deep-sea sounding apparatus, pressure gages, and a pile driver; when in public service, he secured patents for methods of preserving timber and sprinkling streets. He was also interested in transportation, and received a number of patents on electro-magnetic and straight air-brakes, systems of rapid transit, and cable railways. Lastly, while on the Mississippi River Commission, he invented a recording velocimeter and a rheobathometer, and obtained a third patent for a device for indicating the velocity of running fluids. He was a member of the American Society of Civil Engineers (president in 1886); founder of the Engineers' Club of St. Louis (president, 1868–80); and a member of the Loyal Legion. He was twice married: first, to Helen Reichard in Germany, in 1848; and second, to Caroline Reichard at Potosi, Mo., on Sept. 12, 1855 (or 1856). At the time of his sudden death in Pittsburgh he was survived by two daughters and a son.

["Memoir of Henry Flad," *Trans. Am. Soc. of Civil Engineers*, Dec. 1899; abstract from application of Henry Flad for membership in the Military Order of the Loyal Legion, Dec. 4, 1889; *Resolution of Miss. River Commission*, Dec. 5, 1898; *Resolutions of the Board of Public Improvement of the City of St. Louis*, dated June 24, 1898; *St. Louis Globe-Democrat*, June 21, 1898; U. S. Patent Office Records; U. S. National Museum correspondence.] C. W. M.

FLAGET, BENEDICT JOSEPH (Nov. 7, 1763–Feb. 11, 1850), first Catholic bishop of Bardstown, Louisville, was a posthumous peasant child born in Contournat, Auvergne, France. As his mother died in his infancy, he was reared and educated by an aunt who sent him to the neighboring college of Billom. At the age of seventeen, he entered the University of Clermont, paying his expenses by tutoring. In 1783 he entered the Sulpician Seminary at Clermont, then went to Issy, near Paris. Ordained in 1786, he taught dogma and moral theology at the Seminary of Nantes and later at the Seminary of Angers where he was associated with John Baptist Mary David [*q.v.*]. When the latter institution was seized by the Revolutionists, Flaget escaped and found refuge with friends in Billom. Then, with the permission of Superior-General Emery, he set sail with Fathers Badin and David for America, where they were welcomed by Bishop Carroll. Flaget was assigned to Vincennes, but was delayed on the way for six months at Pittsburgh because of low water. Here he won the friendship of Gen. Wayne, commandant at the post, to whom he had letters from Carroll. Going down the Ohio on a flatboat, he stopped at the little post of Cincinnati and again at Louisville, a village of a few houses, where his former superior at Issy, Father Richard, was stationed as a missionary. At the falls of the Ohio he met George Rogers Clark, who escorted him to the small French settlement of Vincennes in December 1792. He found affairs there in bad condition, since the Creoles and half-breeds had been long without a priest, but he quickened their religious life, regularized their marriages, and baptized their children. Despite a threatening Indian outbreak, the missionary offered to go on tour among the western tribesmen. He was recalled, however, in 1795, to serve as vice-rector and as a teacher at Georgetown College. There he met President Washington whom he warmly admired. Three years later he was sent to Havana to aid in founding a projected Sulpician Seminary which did not materialize. While in Cuba, he eked out a living by tutoring a wealthy Spanish planter and enjoyed the society of Louis Philippe, an honored exile. He returned to the United States in 1801 bringing a score of Spanish students to St. Mary's in Baltimore, where he taught for eight years. It was at this time that he seriously thought of joining the rigorous Trappist community.

From this quiet retreat he was named by Rome to the newly established See of Bardstown on Bishop Carroll's recommendation and at the suggestion of Father Badin who was still serving the Kentucky missions. Overwhelmed by the appointment, he sought in vain through Carroll and his superior to avoid the honorable burden for which in his humility he felt so unworthy. He went abroad, seeking the advice of Dr. Emery, and was ordered to accept the bishopric with the understanding that he could continue a Sulpician. On his return to Baltimore, he made a retreat for forty days before his consecration by Archbishop Carroll on Nov. 4, 1810, and then journeyed to Bardstown. He found there a primitive missionary diocese with Fathers Nerinckx, Badin, O'Flynn, and four Dominicans serving 1,000 Catholic families and native tribesmen. Flaget entered the work with a will. He did ordinary missionary work, traveling throughout Kentucky, Tennessee, Missouri, the Northwest, and Canada. In 1817, he rode on horseback to St. Louis where he installed Bishop Dubourg. In answer to a petition of Gen. Harrison and the people of Vincennes for a permanent priest, he again visited his old mission. At Detroit he was hospitably received by Gen. Cass whose kindness was frequently noted in various missionary journals. He was always active among the Indians, and in 1818 was a counselor for 10,000 Indians at St. Mary's during a peace conference with federal agents. In 1817, his episcopal labors were somewhat lightened by the appointment of Bishop David as coadjutor. An indication of his growing influence was seen by Rome's request for his advice in the creation of new dioceses, in the Hogan schism, in the controversy between the Sulpicians and the bishop of Quebec, and his frequent services in consecrating newly appointed ecclesiastics.

Resigning in 1832, Flaget was succeeded by Bishop David but when the latter resigned a year later he was again given charge of the diocese with Bishop Chabrat as the new coadjutor. During the cholera year he ministered to the dying until brought to the point of death. Recovering, he spent two years in Europe. He visited all the French dioceses on a papal commission in the interest of the Society for Propagation of the Faith which contributed men and money to the missions of the Middle West. In 1841 the episcopal see was removed to Louisville, necessitating the building of a new cathedral. Nine years later, when Bishop Flaget died, he left to his successor a well-administered diocese, an advanced and preparatory seminary, a high school, four small colleges, eleven academies, a hospital, an orphan asylum, a Good Shepherd home, and the famous monastery of De La Trappe at Gethsemane, Ky.

[*Vie de Mgr. Flaget, Évêque de Bardstown et Louisville, par le Prêtre qui accompagnait . . . pendant les voyages . . . en Europe* (Paris, 1851); R. H. Clarke, *Lives of Deceased Bishops of the Cath. Ch. in the U. S.* (1872), I, 144–63; M. J. Spalding, *Sketches of the Life, Times, and Character of the Rt. Rev. Benedict Jos. Flaget* (1852), and *Sketches of Early Cath. Missions in Ky.* (1844); the *Metropolitan*, IV (1856), 521–30; Cardinal Wiseman, *Essays* (1853), II, 95; B. G. Webb, *The Centenary of Catholicity in Ky.* (1884); J. S. Johnston, *Memorial Hist. of Louisville to 1896* (1896), I, 114 ff.; C. G. Herbermann, *The Sulpicians in the U. S.*

(1916), pp. 143–61; Peter Guilday, *The Life and Times of John England* (1927); Sister Columba Fox, *The Life of the Rt. Rev. John Baptist Mary David* (1925); the *Metropolitan Cath. Almanac for the year . . . 1851.*]

R. J. P.

FLAGG, AZARIAH CUTTING (Nov. 28, 1790–Nov. 24, 1873), editor, politician, traced his ancestry from Thomas Flegg, a member of an old Norfolk family, who, leaving Scratby, England, in 1637, settled at Watertown, Mass., in 1641, and whose descendants apparently about 1700 changed their name to Flagg. His father, Ebenezer Flagg, married Elizabeth Cutting of Shoreham, Vt., and resided at Orwell, Vt., where he was born. When eleven years old he was apprenticed to a cousin of his father's, a printer in Burlington, Vt., with whom he spent five years. In 1806 he entered the employ of a firm of publishers, where he found opportunities to remedy the deficiencies of his early education. In 1811 he moved to Plattsburg, N. Y., and on the outbreak of the War of 1812 was commissioned lieutenant and quartermaster in the 36th Regiment, New York militia. He was engaged in the defense of Plattsburg, being present at a number of engagements, and was rewarded by Congress for gallant service. In 1813 he joined the staff of the *Plattsburg Republican,* became its editor, and continued as such till 1825. Entering with ardor into the political field where DeWitt Clinton and Van Buren were the leading New York figures, he developed a capacity for vigorous writing and trenchant speaking which soon brought him to the front. In 1823 he was elected to represent Clinton County in the New York Assembly and subsequently was admitted to the inner circle of the "Albany regency." In 1826 Gov. DeWitt Clinton appointed him secretary of state, an office which he held for seven years. He was elected by the legislature state comptroller under Gov. Marcy in 1834, serving till 1839. In 1842 he was reëlected and continued in the position until the state constitution of 1846 came into operation. During his nine years' tenure of this office he established himself as "an able, methodical, keen and sagacious financier" (Proctor, *post*), though his views regarding public improvements have been stigmatized as short-sighted. In 1842 the legislature adopted the "stop and tax policy" of suspending all public works and imposing a direct tax, pledging a portion of the Erie Canal revenues to provide a sinking fund for the extinguishment of the public debt. Flagg was not, as has been mistakenly asserted, the originator of the scheme, but he was active in its support. He was a strong opponent of the Bank of the United States.

In 1846 he removed to New York City where he took an active part in the organization of the "Barnburners'" faction of the Democratic party, becoming one of its most prominent leaders. In 1852, after the reunion of the Democratic party, he was elected comptroller of the city of New York, and, being reëlected in 1855, held office till 1859, when he retired from public life. His political career was distinguished for his unassailable integrity, consistent adherence to principles, and an unwavering support of Van Buren throughout all the latter's vicissitudes. A believer in "Free speech, Free labor, and Free men," he vehemently combated the pro-slavery sentiment within his party. For fourteen years prior to his death he was totally blind, but this affliction did not affect his naturally high spirits and he continued to the end to take a keen interest in political events. He was a frequent contributor to newspapers on public questions of the day, and was also the author of "Internal Improvements in the State of New York," a series of articles which appeared in Hunt's *Merchants' Magazine* in 1851, and *A Few Historical Facts Respecting the Establishment . . . of Banks . . . in the State of New York from 1777 to 1864* (1868). He was married to Phœbe Maria Coe on Oct. 20, 1814.

[N. G. and L. C. S. Flagg, *Family Records of the Descendants of Gershom Flagg* (1907), p. 48; *Ann. Reg.,* 1873, p. 291; L. B. Proctor, *The Bench and Bar of N. Y.* (1870), p. 289; P. S. Palmer, *Hist. of Plattsburg, N. Y.* (1877); DeA. S. Alexander, *A Pol. Hist. of the State of N. Y.,* vols. I and II (1906); H. D. A. Donovan, *The Barnburners* (1925); J. D. Hammond, *Life and Times of Silas Wright* (1848); *N. Y. Times,* Nov. 26, 1873; Flagg letters in the Tilden Library, N. Y. Pub. Lib.]

H. W. H. K.

FLAGG, EDMUND (Nov. 24, 1815–Nov. 1, 1890), author, diplomat, was born in Wiscasset, Me., the only son of Edmund and Harriet (Payson) Flagg. His ancestor, Thomas Flagg, came to America and was a resident of Watertown before 1641. Graduated with distinction from Bowdoin College in 1835, Edmund with his widowed mother and his sister went soon afterward to Louisville, Ky. There he worked as a tutor, and in 1836 began with the *Daily Journal* a connection which lasted till 1861. During 1837–38 he read law in St. Louis, and wrote articles for the *Daily Commercial Bulletin.* In 1838 he published in two small volumes *The Far West,* originally a series of sketches done for the Louisville *Journal* to describe a summer spent on the Illinois and Missouri prairies. He returned to Louisville in 1839, and between the poems, romances, and plays which he had already begun disseminating, joined with George D. Prentice in publishing the *Literary News Letter.* After a few months, largely for the sake of his health, he went to Vicksburg to help Sergeant S. Prentiss with his law practise, but, as an occasional contributor to the *Daily Whig*, fell into quarrels with the editor of the *Sentinel* and was wounded in the consequent duel. In 1842 he settled in Marietta, Ohio, and through 1843 edited the *Weekly Gazette*. Then he returned to St. Louis, where he edited the *Evening Gazette*, served as court reporter, wrote a book on *Mutual Insurance* (1846), and many plays elucidating for the Mississippi Valley the legends of *Mary Tudor* (1844), *Ruy Blas* (1845), and *Catherine Howard* (1847). His novel *Edmond Dantes*, derived both as to plot-origin and style from *The Count of Monte Cristo*, and so advertised, was published in St. Louis in 1849 and in Philadelphia in 1884. During 1849, as secretary to the American minister in Berlin, he traveled extensively in Europe, and he had scarcely returned to St. Louis, where he set up as a lawyer, before he was appointed consul to Venice. After about two years at that post he again went to St. Louis, where he edited the *Democratic Times*, and wrote in somewhat lyrical prose his two-volume illustrated book, *Venice, the City of the Sea, 1797–1849* (1853). In 1854 he went to Washington, and until 1870—except for the period 1858–60, when he was again primarily a journalist—worked in the civil service, much of the time as a statistician in the Department of State. There he wrote a number of official reports, most notably the *Report of the Commercial Relations of the United States with all Foreign Nations* (4 vols., 1856–57), and composed articles about the West and a variety of other subjects for whoever, apparently, came asking. On Feb. 18, 1862, he married Kate Adeline Gallaher of West Virginia. After 1871 he lived on a farm called "Highland View," near Falls Church, Va. There he wrote his romance *De Molai* (1888), dealing with the suppression of the Templar Knights by Philip the Fourth of France in the fourteenth century. Crowded with intrigue, hazardous escapes, and spectacular descriptions, it is dedicated to the De Molay Mounted Commandery of Washington and is on the title-page expressly commended for "Templar Knights, the whole Masonic Fraternity, scholars, and the public."

[S. H. Lancey, *Native Poets of Me.* (1854); W. T. Coggeshall, *The Poets and Poetry of the West* (1860); G. B. Griffith, *Poets of Me.* (1888); *Bowdoin Coll.*, "List of the Published Writings of Edmund Flagg" and "Obit. Record of the Grads. of Bowdoin Coll.," in *Lib. Bull., June 1891–June 1895* (1895); N. G. and L. C. S. Flagg, *Family Records of the Descendants of Gershom Flagg* (1907); C. A. Flagg, *Descendants of Josiah Flagg* (1920).]

J. D. W.

FLAGG, GEORGE WHITING (June 26, 1816–Jan. 5, 1897), genre painter, was born in New Haven, Conn., the son of Henry Collins and Martha (Whiting) Flagg. He traced his descent from Thomas Flagg who emigrated to Massachusetts in 1637. His father, a half-brother of Washington Allston, was a native of South Carolina, but long a resident of New Haven where he practised law and took a prominent part in civic affairs. In 1824 the family moved to Charleston, S. C., for a few years. George Flagg began his study of art in the South and came to be known as a child prodigy. Following his instruction there, he spent eighteen months with his uncle, Washington Allston, and Osgood Bowman in Boston. Then Luman Reed, a wealthy patron of artists, became interested in his work and in 1834 sent him to Europe, where he studied in London, Paris, and Italy. On his return he was for a time with his uncle, but finally settled in New York City, where he was elected an honorary member of the National Academy of Design in 1842 and an academician in 1851. He was again in London in 1861, but returned to New York some five years later. After 1867 he exhibited very little, and in 1879 retired to Nantucket. His personality, keen interest in his profession, and conversational gifts made him a welcome figure in social circles, and he counted many friends among noted artists and writers of his day. On Feb. 14, 1849, he was married to Louisa Henriques of New Haven, Conn., who bore him four children.

To some extent, Flagg's work was purely ideal and done without the use of a model. His early works, previous to study abroad, include: "A Young Greek," "Jacob and Rachel at the Well," and "Murder of the Princes in the Tower." His later paintings include: "Laying of the Atlantic Cable," "Landing of the Pilgrims," "Washington Receiving his Mother's Blessing," frequently engraved, "The Good Samaritan," "Haidee," "The Match Girl," "The Scarlet Letter," "Columbus and the Egg," and a portrait of Washington Allston. The first four of these were Flagg's principal historical works, painted in New Haven for the late James Brewster. "Haidee" depicts a single figure, revealing in its treatment the influence upon Flagg of the Italian masters. The "Mouse Boy" is a homely portrayal of a little street vendor displaying for chance pennies some white mice carried in a box strapped to his neck. Flagg visualized him in his native atmosphere, against Italian skies, with the carefree indolence of a Genoese urchin. Several of Flagg's paintings are in the Luman Reed collection at the New York Historical Society. Among them are "The Woodchopper's Boy," "The Match Girl," "Lady and Parrot," and "The Nun." Some of his best work is in the South, including portraits of the wife of Gov. Aiken, Judge King, and United States Minister Gadsden.

[N. G. and L. C. S. Flagg, *Family Records of the Descendants of Gershom Flagg* (1907), p. 125; Ernest Flagg, *Geneal. Notes on the Founding of New England* (1926); C. E. Clement and Lawrence Hutton, *Artists of the Nineteenth Century and Their Works* (1879), I, 255; J. D. Champlin, Jr., *Cyc. of Painters and Paintings*, vol. II (1887); Wm. Dunlap, *Hist. of the Rise and Progress of the Arts of Design in the U. S.* (1834), II, 448; H. T. Tuckerman, *Book of the Artists* (1867), pp. 404–08; H. W. French, *Art and Artists in Conn.* (1879); J. B. Flagg, *The Life and Letters of Washington Allston* (1892); N. Y. *Evening Post*, Jan. 6, 1897.]

J. M. H.

FLAGG, JARED BRADLEY (June 16, 1820–Sept. 25, 1899), painter, clergyman, was born in New Haven, Conn., the son of Henry Collins and Martha (Whiting) Flagg, and brother of George Whiting Flagg [*q.v.*]. He attended a Lancasterian school and later went to Trinity College, Hartford, but did not graduate. At sixteen he began his training in art, receiving instruction from his brother and his uncle, Washington Allston. At this time he painted a portrait of his father which was exhibited at the National Academy and won favorable notice. He settled for a time in Hartford, Conn., where he became prominent as a portrait-painter, but in 1849 he moved to New York. There he studied theology, was ordained a deacon in the Protestant Episcopal Church in 1854, and priest in 1855. He was rector of the church of St. James at Birmingham, Conn. (1854–55), and of Grace Church, Brooklyn Heights, where he remained until 1863. Upon the termination of the latter rectorate he gave up ministerial service. Meanwhile he had continued his painting, having been elected to the National Academy in 1849. On Dec. 30, 1841, Flagg was married, in Hartford, Conn., to Sarah R. Montague of that city. Their son Montague became a well-known genre painter. Mrs. Flagg died Jan. 25, 1844, and on Dec. 1, 1846, he was married to Louisa Hart, daughter of Dr. Samuel Hart of New Britain, Conn. After the death of his second wife, Jan. 18, 1867, he was married, Jan. 19, 1869, to Josephine Bond, daughter of Judge Bond of Cincinnati, Ohio.

Flagg, though perhaps best known as a portraitist, also painted some ideal pictures. His work, characterized by refinement, found contemporary favor with a large circle of people. He was a chosen adviser in the establishment of the Yale Art Library, and to the field of biography he contributed the *Life and Letters of Washington Allston*, published in 1892. His death occurred in New York City. His best-known paintings include: "Angelo and Isabella," from *Measure for Measure* (1849), which won the artist election of the National Academy; "Paul before Felix" (1850); "Poet's Captive" (1877); "Holy Thoughts"; "Grandfather's Pet"; and "Hester Prynne in Prison." Among his portraits are those of Bishop Littlejohn (1880), Chief-Justice Church of New York (1884), Frederick Tappan (1896), John Jay, Reverdy Johnson, Henry Stanbery, Judge Peckham, and several of Commodore Vanderbilt.

[N. G. and L. C. S. Flagg, *Family Records of the Descendants of Gershom Flagg* (1907), pp. 123–26; H. T. Tuckerman, *Book of the Artists* (1867), p. 408; Ernest Flagg, *Geneal. Notes on the Founding of New England* (1926); H. W. French, *Art and Artists of Conn.* (1879); J. D. Champlin, Jr., *Cyc. of Painters and Painting*, vol. II (1887); F. B. Dexter, *A Cat. . . . of the Portraits, Busts, etc., Belonging to Yale Univ.* (1892); the *Hartford Daily Courant* and *N. Y. Times*, Sept. 26, 1899.]

J. M. H.

FLAGG, JOSIAH (May 28, 1737–*c.* 1795), musician, established a liaison in New England between psalmody and the musical forms now called classical. He was born in Woburn, Mass., the son of Martha and Gershom Flagg. On Apr. 7, 1760, in Boston, where he was apparently then residing, he married Elizabeth Hawkes. He has been described as "a man of energy and enthusiasm, and for some time the most important local musician" (W. A. Fisher, *Notes on Music in Old Boston*, 1918, p. 10). His first known musical publication appeared in 1764 as *A Collection of the best Psalm Tunes in two, three and four parts, from the most approv'd Authors, fitted to all Measures, and approv'd by the best Masters, in Boston New England, to which are added some Hymns and Anthems, the Greater part of them never before Printed in America. By Josiah Flagg. Engraved by Paul Revere.* This book introduced the anthem to the English colonies. Its success led Flagg to bring out in 1766 another work bearing on its title page *Sixteen Anthems, Collected from Tans'ur, Williams, Knapp, Ashworth & Stephenson, To which is added, A few Psalm Tunes. Engraved and Printed by Josiah Flagg, and sold by him at his House near the Old-North Meeting-House.* Religious as these pieces were they were regarded as "light music." Flagg was adventuring, however, in the field of secular music. A military band which he founded and drilled gave its first concert June 29, 1769, at Concert Hall, and ended its program with the then popular "British Grenadiers" (*Boston Chronicle*, June 26–29, 1769). A benefit concert advertised for June 7, 1770, was to be adorned by "a duet to be sung by a gentleman who lately read and sung in Concert Hall, and Mr. Flagg," and on May 13, 1771, through a notice in the *Boston Evening Post*, the colonial impresario solicited patronage for a concert on May 17, following, of "vocal and instrumental musick accompanied by French horns, hautboys, etc., by the band of the 64th Regiment." At another benefit concert, Oct. 4, 1771, Flagg introduced, evidently as a novelty, selections from *Acis and Galatea* "lately composed by Mr. Händel." The latest record of his performances was made when he announced, for Oct. 28, 1773, in Faneuil Hall, his "final Grand Concert," to be given by upwards of fifty performers. Leaving Boston, Flagg settled in Providence, where he is recorded as having served as lieutenant-colonel in Elliott's regiment during the Revolution. With him in the same regiment was his son Josiah. Though little is known of the last years of his life, doubtless it was his "Widow Flagg" for whose relief the flutist, Stone, gave a concert in Boston, Jan. 31, 1795, and who was advertised as the mother of the "miscreant son, Josiah Flagg, junr."

[N. G. and L. C. S. Flagg, *Family Records of the Descendants of Gershom Flagg* (1907); O. G. T. Sonneck, *Early Concert Life in America* (1907); Geo. Hood, *A Hist. of Music in New England* (1846); M. D. Gould, *Church Music in America* (1853); F. L. Ritter, *Music in America* (1883); *Records of the State of R. I.*, vols. VIII–X (1863–65), edited by J. R. Bartlett; and Benj. Cowell, *Spirit of '76 in R. I.* . . . (1850), pp. 88–89. Sonneck's conjecture that Flagg was born about Nov. 5, 1738, is in conflict with the date given in the Flagg genealogy, but can be accounted for by the fact that a Josiah Flagg, son of Josiah and Mary Willis Flagg, was born in Boston, Oct. 22, 1738. The dates of birth and marriage for the subject of this sketch have been taken from the published records of Boston and Woburn, Mass.] F.W.C.

FLAGG, JOSIAH FOSTER (Jan. 10, 1788–Dec. 20, 1853), pioneer dentist, anatomical artist, early experimenter in dental porcelain, was born in Boston, the son of Josiah Flagg, Jr., said to be the first native-born American dentist, and grandson of Josiah Flagg [*q.v.*]. His early education was indifferent or less. He was an industrious and ingenious boy who enjoyed labor on the farm or in the workshop, but who, according to a younger brother, "utterly repudiated books." When about sixteen he was apprenticed to learn the trade of cabinetmaker; but shortly after, through "a simple stratagem of his father," he suddenly developed a love of reading, and a desire for study which changed the course of his career. He was sent to an academy at Plainfield, Conn., and in 1811 entered the office of Dr. J. C. Warren as a student in medicine and surgery. While under the latter's tutelage he developed a fine skill in dissecting, and an uncommon mechanical ability in devising and making delicate instruments. Without formal instruction but with a strong native instinct for color and form, he became a considerable artist in painting, designing, and wood-engraving. In 1813 he worked with Dr. Warren in publishing a new edition of Haller's work on the arteries under the title *Anatomical Description of the Arteries of the Human Body*. Flagg reproduced the copper engravings by wood-cuts of his own with such skill that he made a reputation for the book and for himself. Having graduated in 1815 from the Boston Medical College, he began his career as a practising physician and surgeon in Dover, N. H., and at Uxbridge, Mass., then moved to Boston and took up the practise of dentistry. On Oct. 18, 1818, he married Mary Wait. He soon achieved an active dental practise but his interest in general medical problems was never lost. About 1821 he devised for the treatment of long-bone fractures a special apparatus and splints which were used for years in the Massachusetts General and other hospitals, and he was the first dentist to design (1828) a set of extracting forceps to fit the necks of the various forms of human teeth. Flagg's chief contribution to his profession was the making of "mineral teeth," in 1833, after laborious experiments with Dr. N. C. Keep. Prior to this time artificial teeth were carved from hippopotamus teeth or ivory—or human teeth were used—all of which were "corruptible." The story of Flagg's adventures with charlatans in unavailing efforts to purchase mysterious secrets regarding the baking of translucent porcelain, of his own orderly and effective experiments and researches which led to knowledge now fundamental in the manufacture of artificial teeth, is an interesting chapter in the history of dentistry and of porcelain art. He took a prominent part, in 1846, in opposing the granting of a patent on the recently discovered use of sulphuric ether as an anesthetic. He was also one of the early believers in homeopathy, and an ardent teacher of its principles. He founded the School of Design for Women, in Boston, and was interested in a wide range of public activities. Personally he was attractive and approachable, but unhesitating in the expression of opinion. He was uncle to the late Prof. J. F. Flagg of Philadelphia, with whom his name is often confused.

[N. G. and L. C. S. Flagg, *Family Records of the Descendants of Gershom Flagg* (1907); the *Dental News Letter*, July 1854; the *Am. Jour. of Dental Sci.*, July 1854; the *Boston Medic. and Surgic. Jour.*, Jan. 11, 1854; *The Harvard Medic. School* (1905), III, 453. The date of birth is taken from the account of Flagg's life by his brother, John Foster Brewster Flagg, in the *Dental News Letter*. *Index of the Periodical Dental Literature* is unreliable, since it confuses Josiah Foster, John Foster Brewster, and J. Foster Flagg.] W.B.D.

FLAGG, THOMAS WILSON (Nov. 5, 1805–May 6, 1884), naturalist, author, second of the ten children of Isaac and Elizabeth Frances (Wilson) Flagg, was born in Beverly, and died in Cambridge, Mass. His father's ancestor,

Thomas Flagg, came from England to Massachusetts in 1637. Thomas Wilson Flagg—he later dropped the first name—graduated from Phillips Andover Academy in 1821, spent a few months at Harvard, and later studied medicine at the Harvard Medical School, 1824–25, and with a doctor in Beverly. He never practised. He was married in Beverly on Jan. 2, 1840, to Caroline Eveleth. His residence was at different times in Beverly, Boston, and Andover, and after 1866 in Cambridge. In Boston, he was an insurance agent, and around 1844, a clerk at the customs-house. Over a long period he wrote articles for the *Atlantic Monthly* and for various political and horticultural magazines. He wrote also a number of books. In the *Analysis of Female Beauty* (1834) he set forth in little essays of alternate verse and prose, with a fair quota of physiognomical details, the qualities of intellect which he held such details to indicate. Ten years later came *The Tailor's Shop: or, Crowns of Thorns and Coats of Thistles. Designed to Tickle Some and Nettle Others; Intended Chiefly for Politicians. Inscribed to Those Whom They May Fit.* This opus, fathered by Pope and mothered by a somewhat bumptious Americanism, flays many of the wicked, two of whom were "Smirk, the City Editor," and "Puff the Poet." In 1861, he published *Mount Auburn. Its Scenes, Its Beauties, and Its Lessons,* a lugubrious compilation of writings by himself and others, relating specifically to the cemetery near Boston, and generally to all mortuary matters everywhere. The first memorably notable evidence of his interest as a naturalist—an interest which dominated his life—was in 1857, when he published *Studies in the Field and Forest. A Prize Essay on Agricultural Education* appeared in 1858, *The Woods and By-Ways of New England* in 1872, and *The Birds and Seasons of New England* in 1875. The last two volumes, a little bulky for practical purposes, were in 1881 divided into three volumes, with new titles, *Halcyon Days, A Year with the Birds,* and *A Year Among the Trees.* He wrote only about subjects which he could investigate without ranging far from home, and he was certainly not an avid scientist, but he observed carefully and affectionately, and he set down his findings in prose which, if impersonal and unsuggestive, has always the merit of clarity and down-rightness. In the dedication to *Woods and By-Ways,* after recalling Thoreau's opinion that he lacked spirit, he undertook to explain himself. "My life," he wrote, "has been too retired for that sort of personal adventure which inspires enthusiasm. Few men save those who from religious motives have retired from the world have lived so little in communication with it as I have. I am not a member of any society or club, of any church or institution, trade, profession, or organization. I have lived entirely without honors, and have never rejected any. My wife and children have been the only companions of my studies and recreations. But, perhaps from this cause alone, I have been very happy."

[Sources not already named: W. G. Barton, "Thoreau, Flagg and Burroughs" in *Essex Inst. Hist. Colls.,* Jan.–Mar. 1885; N. G. and L. C. S. Flagg, *Family Records of the Descendants of Gershom Flagg* (1907); Phillips Acad. (Andover), *Biog. Cat. 1778–1830* (1903); Beverly, Mass., *Vital Records to the End of 1849* (1907); *Boston Transcript,* May 7, 1884.] J. D. W.

FLAGLER, HENRY MORRISON (Jan. 2, 1830–May 20, 1913), capitalist and promoter, son of Rev. Isaac and Elizabeth (Morrison) Flagler, was born at Hopewell, just outside of Canandaigua, N. Y. His father, a poor Presbyterian minister, was descended from Zachariah Flegler, a German Palatine who reached the United States about 1710. Young Flagler attended the district school until he was fourteen, when he decided to strike out for himself. By way of the Erie Canal and a lake boat he made his way to Sandusky, Ohio. With some difficulty he secured employment in a country store at Republic, Ohio, at five dollars a month and board. He saved money both here and at Fostoria, Ohio, where he worked later, and about 1850 became a grain-commission merchant at Bellevue, Ohio, and was also interested in a distillery. While in Bellevue he met John D. Rockefeller, then engaged in the produce business in Cleveland, and occasionally sold grain through him. When Flagler had accumulated about $50,000 he moved to Saginaw, Mich., to engage in the manufacture of salt, but lost his entire capital and owed almost as much more.

Flagler then removed to Cleveland, set up again as a grain merchant, and renewed his acquaintance with Rockefeller, who was becoming interested in petroleum. The firm of Rockefeller & Andrews, formed in 1865, became Rockefeller, Andrews & Flagler, two years later, and in 1870, the Standard Oil Company was incorporated. It is generally agreed that, next to Rockefeller himself, Flagler was the strongest man in the organization (Ida M. Tarbell, *post,* I, 50). Rockefeller himself says: "For years and years this early partner and I worked shoulder to shoulder; our desks were in the same room. We both lived on Euclid Avenue a few rods apart. We met and walked to the office together, walked home to luncheon, back again after luncheon, and home again at night. On these walks, when we were away from the office interruptions, we did our thinking, talking and planning together" (*Ran-*

dom Reminiscences, 1909, pp. 12–13). Throughout the stormy years of the development of the great organization Flagler was active in its management, and he retained his connection with it until near the end of his life, resigning as vice-president in 1908 and as director in 1911.

In 1883 he visited Florida for the first time and was fascinated by the region, but was annoyed by the poor transportation and hotel facilities. In 1886 he purchased the Jacksonville, St. Augustine & Halifax River Railroad and later some other short lines, which he improved and combined as the Florida East Coast Railway. In 1892 construction was begun southward from Daytona; Palm Beach was reached in 1894, and Miami, then only a clearing, in 1896. Meanwhile he had built a string of palatial hotels along the line; the Ponce de Leon and the Alcazar at St. Augustine, the Ormond at Ormond, the Royal Poinciana and the Breakers at Palm Beach, and the Royal Palm at Miami. In this work of transforming neglected beach and swamp into one of the most luxurious playgrounds in the world he found his second youth. He was also interested in the man of small means who settled along the line, and encouraged agriculture and fruit growing.

Perhaps his greatest achievement was the extension of the railway from Miami to Key West. Much of the fifty miles on the mainland was through the Everglades where it was difficult to make a firm road-bed. Then followed 106 miles over and between the islands. In some cases the shallow water between the keys was filled in with stone. Concrete viaducts were built where this was impossible, or else great drawbridges which permitted shipping to pass. There is one almost continuous bridge seven miles long. All construction was of the most substantial kind. In spite of formidable obstacles, the road was completed in 1912 and formally opened the next year. It materially shortened the line to Cuba. A steamer carries the passengers and ferries take the freight cars, making the journey to Havana in six hours. Meanwhile Flagler had dredged the harbor of Miami, and established a steamship line to Key West and another to Nassau, where he opened the Colonial and Royal Victoria hotels. His total investments in Florida exceeded forty million dollars. While these investments were not unprofitable as a whole, undoubtedly his capital would have brought him greater returns elsewhere.

He married, first, Nov. 9, 1853, Mary Harkness, who had three children, of whom only one, Harry Harkness Flagler, survived his father. On June 6, 1883, he married Ida A. Shourds, who became hopelessly insane. In 1901 the Florida legislature passed a general act making incurable insanity for four years a cause for divorce, and on Aug. 14, 1901, a divorce was granted Flagler. Ten days later, on Aug. 24, he married Mary Lily Kenan of Kenansville, N. C., who survived him, and to whom he left the bulk of his fortune. He died at his home, "Whitehall," at West Palm Beach.

Flagler's career divides naturally into two parts as distinct as if they were separate lives. Brought up in poverty and trained in the stern Rockefeller school, he was a grim, shrewd, rather ruthless man of business, who worked steadily and played little or not at all, until he was fifty-five. In Florida, he continued to work, but also developed a new attitude toward humanity. He thoroughly enjoyed his rôle of builder of a state, and seemed to feel a sense of personal responsibility for every settler on his railroads and for every one of his many employees. They, in turn, repaid him with admiration and loyalty. He built many schools, churches, and hospitals, always insisting that his gifts be anonymous. He read widely, and though sensitive about his increasing deafness, enjoyed conversation with his friends.

[Sources include, *In Memoriam Henry Morrison Flagler* (n.d.), containing the address of Flagler's pastor, Rev. George Morgan Ward, and many newspaper clippings, published in 1915; Ida M. Tarbell, *Hist. of the Standard Oil Co.* (2 vols., 1904) and other accounts of that organization; E. S. Luther, "The Transformation of the Florida East Coast," in *Bankers' Mag.*, Feb. 1909; Edwin Lefèvre, "Flagler and Florida," in *Everybody's Mag.*, Feb. 1910, and other articles, more or less inaccurate, in periodicals; H. G. Cutler, *Hist. of Fla. Past and Present* (1923), I, *passim*; obituaries in *Fla. Times-Union* (Jacksonville), and *N. Y. Times*, May 21, 1913, and *Outlook*, May 31, 1913.] H. T.

FLAGLER, JOHN HALDANE (Sept. 3, 1836–Sept. 8, 1922), manufacturer, capitalist, was born at Cold Spring, Putnam County, N. Y., the son of Harvey K. and Sarah Jane (Haldane) Flagler. He attended the academy at Patterson, Dutchess County, N. Y. (not at Paterson, N. J., as usually given), and, in 1854, entered the iron business with his uncles, John and James Haldane of New York, who operated the Greenwich Iron Works. After a visit to Europe to study methods of making iron tubes, he was given charge of the Boston branch of the business in 1860, and furnished some of the iron used in the construction of the *Monitor,* and other boats of this class. With the increasing demand for tubing for the growing oil industry, Flagler and his brother, Harvey K. Flagler, formed in 1867 the firm of J. H. Flagler & Company which was merged with the National Tube Works Company in 1869, with works in East Boston. It was soon seen that Boston was too far both from raw materials and from the principal market for the product, and in 1872 the branch at McKeesport, Pa., began production. This plant was the first to use gas furnaces under the Siemens patent in the manufacture of iron, and Flagler later obtained seven patents for improvements in the manufacture of pipe. The East Boston plant was discontinued in 1874, and the plant at McKeesport became the largest producer of pipe in the world, employing over 4,500 men when Flagler resigned as general manager in 1888. During his stay in McKeesport, he was active in the affairs of the town and had a large part in its development from an unsightly village to a prosperous manufacturing city. In 1909, when he revisited the scene of his labors, he was given a reception by some forty of his old employees who had worked for the company more than twenty-five years. He continued as director of the National Tube Works Company until 1899, at which time it became the National Tube Company. From this time his interests were diversified—banking, insurance, manufacturing and mining, and he served as officer or director in many corporations, maintaining an office in New York until his death. He was a successful business man, who gained and kept the loyalty of his associates and subordinates, an enthusiastic yachtsman, and a member of various philanthropic, cultural, and scientific organizations, but seems to have avoided publicity. At his death he bequeathed a considerable portion of his fortune to charitable and public use. He was married three times: in 1856 to Anna H. Converse, a daughter of one of his associates; in 1894, to Alice Mandelick who died in 1918; and, in 1921, to Beatrice Wenneker who, with one daughter of his first marriage, survived him. He died of pneumonia at his home at Greenwich, Conn.

[Material on Flagler's life is fragmentary, and many of the published sketches are inaccurate. The account in the *Hist. of Allegheny County, Pa.* (1889), was approved by him. All the New York papers of Sept. 9, 1922, contain obituary notices, and the account of the reception given him at McKeesport in 1909 is contained in a privately printed volume, *Reception to Mr. John H. Flagler, McKeesport, Forty Years After* (1910). Most of the material for this sketch has been furnished by Mr. A. M. Saunders through the Research Department of the National Tube Co.] H. T.

FLANAGAN, WEBSTER (Jan. 9, 1832–May 5, 1924), leader of the Republican party in Texas, was born in Claverport, Ky. His parents, James W. and Polly Miller Flanagan, placed their family and their goods in a flatboat, and by way of the Ohio, the Mississippi, and the Red rivers, removed to Texas where they settled on a plantation near Henderson in the spring of 1844. The elder Flanagan, afterwards United States senator, took an active part in the politics of his day, and was prominent in the ranks of the Whigs. His son, who inherited his friendly manners and his genius for political manipulation, soon followed in his steps. Webster Flanagan was admitted to the bar in 1859, but from the beginning made his legal activities distinctly subordinate to his interests as a village merchant, a breeder of fine cattle, and a political leader. The two, father and son, were ardent supporters of Sam Houston in his bitterly contested campaigns for the governorship, and in 1860 canvassed their section of Texas in behalf of the Bell and Everett ticket. Both were strong Union men and opposed secession. In spite of this position, Webster Flanagan joined the Confederate army in 1862 and served for the remainder of the war. In the summer of 1865, the young soldier wrote a characteristic letter to Johnson's recently appointed reconstruction governor, A. J. Hamilton: "I want an office, and a good one. I think I am entitled to it, and I know you are willing to make an appointment where there is merit. I was one of the few who braved the secession storm in my country . . . I would like to be one of the Assessors or Collectors of Revenue. . . . If not that, anything that will pay" (Hamilton Papers, Austin). This frank appeal bore fruit, and from that time, except in the eight lean years under Cleveland, Flanagan was continually in office until the inauguration of Wilson in 1913. For many years he was collector of internal revenue, first at El Paso and then at Austin. By 1890 he was the recognized leader of his party in the state, and was given the empty honor of a nomination to the governorship in a campaign in which he was, of course, defeated by the redoubtable James S. Hogg. In quiet times he found time to build a local railroad from Henderson to Overton. He was celebrated as a sportsman, and, as an importer of Jersey cattle, he did much to improve the dairy business of his part of the state.

In national Republican conventions, Flanagan was always prominent. In 1880 he won a certain amount of fame as a member of the faithful group known as the "Grant Guard." When a delegate from Massachusetts declared disgustedly that "certain ones had an eye to the offices," the delegate from Texas came into the center of the stage demanding, "What are we here for, except the offices?" Whereupon Godkin remarked in the *Nation* that Webster Flanagan was the honestest man at the convention and deserved the vice-presidential nomination (*Nation,* June 10,.1880) He was twice married and had ten children. His first wife, whom he married Dec. 20, 1853, was Elizabeth Graham. After her death in 1872 he married Sallie P. Ware. He was a man of medium height, well built and vigorous, and has been described as kindly, cheerful, and friendly.

[This sketch is based largely on the personal reminiscences of friends and members of the Flanagan family. See also W. S. Speer and J. H. Brown, *The Encyc. of the New West* (1881), pp. 405–06; C. W. Ramsdell, *Reconstruction in Tex.* (1910), pp. 204–07, 296, 304; *Who's Who in America*, 1914–15; and the files of the *Henderson Times.*] R. G. C.

FLANAGIN, HARRIS (Nov. 3, 1817–Oct. 23, 1874), governor of Arkansas, was born in Roadstown, Cumberland County, N. J., son of James and Mary Flanagin. He received a fairly good education in a Quaker school of New Jersey and then went to Clermont, Pa., to teach in a seminary. Soon after this he moved to Illinois where he again tried teaching and while at this work studied law. In 1837 he moved to Arkansas and opened a law office in Greenville, the county seat of Clark County, but later moved to Arkadelphia, the new county seat. In 1842 he was elected to the legislature, but dropped out of politics and devoted his time to his profession. He was married, on July 3, 1851, to Martha E. Nash. In 1861 he represented his county in the secession convention. When the motion for submitting to the people the question of cooperation or secession came up he voted against it, but in the second session, after the bombardment of Fort Sumter, he voted for withdrawal from the Union. He entered the army as captain of Company E, 2nd Regiment, Arkansas Mounted Rifles, and rose to the rank of colonel. While serving at Knoxville, Tenn., he received notice that the people of Arkansas would decide next day whether he or Henry Rector [*q.v.*] should be governor. This is said to have been the first notice he had had of his candidacy. Owing to the strength of the anti-Rector faction, led by R. H. Johnson, whom Rector had defeated in 1860, Flanagin was elected by a vote of more than two to one. He was inaugurated Nov. 15, 1862. The two great problems before him were to help prosecute the war and to care for the civilian population, who were suffering from the scarcity of clothing, food, and medicine. While the governor cooperated with Kirby Smith in raising troops, the legislature appropriated $1,200,000 for the relief of suffering in the devastated areas, $300,000 to encourage manufacturing of essentials, and even assigned the governor $1,000,000 to carry on manufacturing on the account of the state, but very little came of these efforts, for the treasury was generally empty. Shortly before the cessation of hostilities Flanagin attended a conference of governors at Marshall, Tex., to decide upon what terms they should surrender to the Federal authorities. Returning to Arkansas he requested A. H. Garland [*q.v.*] to open negotiations with Gen. J. J. Reynolds with a view to the cooperation of the Confederate state government with the Unionist government which had been established under Isaac Murphy, for the calling of a state convention and the restoration of a government which Congress would recognize. Reynolds, however, would accord no sort of recognition, and in May 1865 the Confederate state government dissolved. Flanagin was told that he would be allowed to deliver up the archives and would not be molested as long as he remained quiet. He then retired to Arkadelphia and, as soon as conditions permitted, resumed the practise of law. He was elected to the constitutional convention of 1874, but died during the second session.

[*Official Records (Army)*, see Index; manuscript journals of the secession convention of 1861 and the constitutional convention of 1874; *Ark. Hist. Asso. Pubs.*, II (1908), 267, 362–423; *Arkansas State Gazette* (Little Rock, 1861–66), *Arkansas True Democrat* (Little Rock), *Washington* (Ark.) *Telegraph*, incomplete files of which may be found in the Lib. of the Ark. Hist. Commission; Fay Hempstead, *Pictorial Hist. of Ark.* (1890); D. Y. Thomas, *Ark. in War and Reconstruction, 1861–1874* (1926); obituary in *Ark. Gazette* (Little Rock), Oct. 24, 1874.] D. Y. T.

FLANDERS, HENRY (Feb. 13, 1824–Apr. 3, 1911), lawyer, author, was the son of Charles Flanders, one of the leaders of the New Hampshire bar of his time, who married Lucretia Kingsbury, and practised law at Plainfield, Sullivan County, N. H. Born at Plainfield, Henry Flanders was educated at Kimball Academy, N. H., and Newbury Seminary, but did not receive a university training, although in 1856 he was given the honorary degree of M.A. by Dartmouth College. In 1842 he commenced the study of law in his father's office and in 1845 was admitted to the New Hampshire bar. He then spent some time in the South, and married Elizabeth O. Barnwell of South Carolina in 1847. After his return to the North he made his home in Philadelphia, and on being admitted to the Philadelphia bar in 1853, commenced practise in that city. From the outset he devoted especial attention to maritime law, his studies on that subject being prosecuted to such purpose that early in his career he wrote two works, *A Treatise on Maritime Law* (1852) and *A Treatise on the Law of Shipping* (1853), which gave evidence of deep research and unusual ability. Distinguished for lucid exposition and attractive style, these works in a short time became acknowledged authorities upon the subjects with which they dealt. He soon acquired an extensive practise and in course of time attained high rank among the leaders of the Philadelphia bar, being considered one of the ablest admiralty lawyers in the country. He did not, however, confine himself to his professional work, and in 1855, published the first volume of *The Lives and Times of the Chief Justices of the Supreme Court of the United States from Jay to Marshall,* the second volume appearing in 1858. Written in an attractive manner, this work was well received and stamped him as an author of much promise. Then followed (1856) an edition with illustrative notes, of the *Memoirs of Richard Cumberland, Written by Himself,* and *An Exposition of the Constitution of the United States* (1860), which latter work passed through several editions. His last text-book was *A Treatise on the Law of Fire Insurance* (1871), which had all the characteristics of his early works and was for a number of years a standard authority. He also wrote a romance, *The Adventures of a Virginian* (1881), which was published under the pseudonym Oliver Thurston. He was a member of the commission for the collation of the Acts of the Assembly of Pennsylvania, and with James T. Mitchell undertook the arduous and minute research which that task involved, the outcome being the publication of *The Statutes at Large of Pennsylvania from 1682 to 1801, Compiled under the Authority of the Act of May 19, 1887* (16 vols., 1896–1911). In 1904, being then eighty years old, Flanders was elected a member of the auxiliary faculty of the Law School of the University of Pennsylvania and as such lectured on legal biography until shortly before his death, a period of seven years. The subject was unique in the annals of law schools and, despite his advanced age, his treatment of it was completely successful. He discussed the great lawyers and judges of England and the United States not only from the legal standpoint but also in relation to their influence upon public affairs—varying his themes from time to time—and drew large audiences. In addition to the books already mentioned, he wrote a number of addresses on legal and historical subjects delivered before various societies, some of which were subsequently published. He was also the author of two pamphlets, *Must the War Go On?* (1863) and *Observations on Reconstruction* (1866), which attracted national attention and provoked wide discussion. A practitioner of the old school, he retained throughout his long life all the characteristics of a bygone age. Genial yet dignified, noted for his courtesy and consideration, his was a singularly attractive personality.

[See *Univ. of Pa. Law Rev.,* May 1911; *Pa. Bar Asso. Report,* 1911; *Who's Who in America,* 1910–11; *Public Ledger* (Phila.), Apr. 4, 1911. The first of these accounts gives 1824 as the year of Flanders's birth: other accounts, following *Who's Who,* give 1826.]

H. W. H. K.

FLANDRAU, CHARLES EUGENE (July 15, 1828–Sept. 9, 1903), jurist, soldier, author, was born in New York City, the son of Thomas Hunt and Elizabeth (Macomb) Flandrau. His father, who came of Huguenot ancestry, was a law partner of Aaron Burr, and his mother, who was of Irish blood, was a half-sister of Alexander Macomb, the commanding general of the United States army from 1828 to 1841. Flandrau's school days, which were over at thirteen save for a few months in his seventeenth year, were supplemented by practical experience gained through three years at sea and three spent sawing veneers in a New York mahogany mill. In 1851, after having studied law in his father's office at Whitesboro, N. Y., he was admitted to the bar, and for the next two years he practised with his father. In November 1853 he went West with his friend, Horace R. Bigelow, and commenced practise in St. Paul, the capital of Minnesota Territory. The two partners were not deluged with business, and the following year Flandrau settled at Traverse des Sioux, a frontier village on the Minnesota River. Here his ability as a lawyer, coupled with his enterprise, integrity, and geniality, soon won him wide popularity. In 1856 he represented his district in the territorial Council and in the same year he was made agent for the Sioux Indians. In 1857 he was a member of the Minnesota constitutional convention; according to a contemporary, "his hand is visible in nearly every provision" of the resultant state constitution (John B. Sanborn, in *Minnesota Historical Society Collections,* X, 769).

Though Flandrau was only twenty-nine in 1857, that year witnessed his appointment as associate justice of the territorial supreme court, and upon Minnesota's admission to the Union in 1858 his service was continued by popular election. During his seven years on the supreme bench, a foundational period in its history, the court made 495 decisions, of which Flandrau wrote the opinions in 227 cases. When the Sioux outbreak occurred in the summer of 1862, the terrorized settlers of the Minnesota Valley turned to Flandrau for leadership, and the judge—his portrait suggests a frontier military officer rather than a jurist—promptly turned soldier. He commanded the voluntary defenders of New Ulm, and in the campaign that followed he was colonel in charge of the defense of the southern frontier. In 1864 he resigned from the supreme court. After three years in Nevada and Missouri, he returned, in 1867, to Minnesota, to open a law office in Minneapolis with Judge Isaac Atwater. As a Democrat, Flandrau swam against the political current in his state following the Civil

War. He was an unsuccessful candidate for governor in 1867, and two years later he was defeated for the office of chief justice. In 1870 he removed to St. Paul, where he built up a large law practise and lived for the remainder of his life.

Flandrau helped both to make and to write the history of Minnesota. His *History of Minnesota and Tales of the Frontier* (1900) is valuable for its spirited personal reminiscences and vivid recountals of frontier episodes. He also wrote a succinct account of "The Indian War of 1862–1864, and Following Campaigns in Minnesota," in *Minnesota in the Civil and Indian Wars* (vol. I, 1890); a history of Minnesota (pp. 7–117) in *Encyclopedia of Biography of Minnesota* (1900); and several papers published in the *Collections* of the Minnesota Historical Society. He was married in 1859 to Isabella R. Dinsmore of Kentucky, who died in 1867, and in 1871 to Mrs. Rebecca Blair Riddle of Pittsburgh. He had two daughters by his first wife, and two sons by his second.

[*Minn. Hist. Soc. Colls.*, X (1905), 767–830; *Hist. of the Bench and Bar of Minn.* (1904), ed. by H. F. Stevens, II, 1–7; T. M. Newson, *Pen Pictures of St. Paul, Minn.* (1886), pp. 406–08; W. H. C. Folsom, *Fifty Years in the Northwest* (1888), p. 576; *Hist. of Ramsey County and St. Paul* (1881), p. 524; *Progressive Men of Minn.* (1897), ed. by M. D. Shutter and J. S. McLain, p. 121; *St. Paul Globe*, Sept. 10, 1903.] T. C. B.

FLANNERY, JOHN (Nov. 24, 1835–May 9, 1910), banker, cotton-factor, was born in Nenagh, County Tipperary, Ireland, the son of John and Hannah (Hogan) Flannery. The famine and revolutionary period of the middle nineteenth century ruined the elder Flannery; whereupon, in 1851, the father and son emigrated to the United States. The father, however, remained only a short time and died on the vessel that was taking him back to Ireland. The son, after holding minor clerical positions in various places, settled down permanently in Savannah late in 1854. Fond of martial affairs, he joined a noted military organization, the "Irish Jasper Greens," and on the outbreak of the Civil War, went, with the rank of a junior lieutenant, as a volunteer with that company, into the Confederate army. Promoted to a captaincy (October 1862), he served throughout the war, returning in 1865 to Savannah. Resuming his interrupted business at the age of thirty, he occupied for nearly half a century a position of leadership in his community. He became a partner in the cotton-commission firm of L. J. Guilmartin & Company, which after some years was dissolved and reorganized under the title of John Flannery & Company. Twenty-four years after this reorganization he incorporated his concern as the John Flannery Company (1901) for the purpose of admitting into the business a number of the younger men who had served him long and faithfully. This corporation was for years one of the most important cotton-houses in Savannah. Flannery retired from business in 1906.

During his long career he was always among the leaders in enterprises undertaken for the good of Savannah. He was an organizer and director and for twenty-five years the president of the Southern Bank, later the Citizens and Southern Bank, one of the strongest of the Southern financial institutions. He was a member of the committee that erected the Cotton Exchange building and was president of the Exchange; he was for many years chairman of the City Sinking Fund Commission; as an organizer of the Savannah Hotel Company he took part in the construction of the famed De Soto Hotel; and he was a director in many other corporations, railway, utility, and manufacturing. He was active also in the civic, social, religious, and philanthropic life of the community. A devoted Catholic, he established a fund of $50,000 (since grown to $100,-000), the interest of which was to be used to aid Catholic enterprises in Georgia. He was for fifty years an ardent supporter of the Jasper Greens military company; was vice-president of the Hibernian Society, and took a keen interest in the Georgia Historical Society. He was married to Mary Ellen Norton of Taliaferro County, Ga., in 1867, and they had six children. In his personal life Flannery was simple and unostentatious.

[A. D. Candler and C. A. Evans, *Cyc. of Ga.* (1906), vol. II; *Who's Who in America*, 1912–13; long obituary notice and a tribute to Flannery by Bishop Keiley in *Savannah Morning News*, Mar. 9, 1910.] R. P. B—s.

FLATHER, JOHN JOSEPH (June 9, 1862–May 14, 1926), mechanical engineer, university professor, was born at Philadelphia, the son of Henry and Sarah (Hockensmith) Flather. His father was an Englishman, his mother a native Virginian, and the son received his early education in private schools in Scotland, and in the high school at Bridgeport, Conn. He early showed a pronounced mechanical bent and in 1880 entered the mechanical engineering department of the Sheffield Scientific School at Yale, graduating with the degree of Ph.B., in 1885. For several years following his graduation he was engaged in engineering practise, obtaining a thorough and varied knowledge of industrial technology. He served a full machinist's apprenticeship in several New England shops, including Flather & Company, Nashua, N. H., the Howe Sewing Machine Company, of Bridgeport, Conn., and the Armstrong Manufacturing Company. He was later designer and foreman for the Ansonia Electric Company and the Hotchkiss Manufacturing Company of Bridgeport. The intimate knowledge of machine-shop practise and methods which he obtained during these years was markedly in evidence during all of his later professional life. In 1888 he entered upon his teaching career as an instructor in mechanical engineering at Lehigh University. He held this position for three years, at the same time carrying on graduate studies at the Sibley College of Mechanical Engineering, Cornell University, under Prof. Thurston, then at the height of his fame. He received the degree of master of mechanical engineering in 1890.

As the mechanical engineering department at Lehigh University, under the direction of Prof. Klein, was then accounted one of the strongest in the country, Flather's career as a teacher of engineering began under the most favorable conditions. Though only twenty-nine years old at the time, he received a call in 1891 to a professorship in mechanical engineering at Purdue University, one of the largest technical schools in the West. After seven years' service at Purdue, he was called to the University of Minnesota as professor of mechanical engineering and head of the department, which position he held until his death. The department developed under his direction from a small beginning to one of the strongest departments in the Engineering College, and with this development, Flather had a peculiarly intimate connection in that at one period or another he personally taught practically every course in the curriculum. He was an effective and inspiring teacher, and during his nearly thirty years of service at Minnesota, many distinguished engineers and engineering teachers received their training at his hands.

He early became deeply interested in technical research, and the versatility of his intellect is strikingly shown by the scope of his investigations. His earlier work, begun at Lehigh in 1888, was in the field of steam- and gas-engine performance and the transmission and measurement of power, in which latter field he became a national authority. He spent many years in the study of power-plant development, giving especial attention to the movements of gases in chimneys and to tall chimney design. During his later years he was engaged in the investigation of problems in heating and ventilation and refrigeration. He was a frequent contributor to technical journals throughout his professional career, and he also published two monographs, *Dynamometers and the Measurement of Power* (1892) and *Rope-Driving* (1895). He was joint author with Prof. Chas. E. Lucke of Columbia University, of *A Text Book of Engineering Thermodynamics* and *Handbook of Thermodynamic Tables and Diagrams,* both published in 1915.

In addition to his university activities in teaching and research, he carried on a widely diversified practise as a consulting engineer, his work including the design of factories, power-plants and municipal water-works and electric-light plants. In a profession so exacting technically that it all too frequently turns its followers into narrow specialists, he was conspicuous for his broad culture and learning. He had traveled widely at home and abroad, and had made a particular hobby of the history of engineering, upon which he was writing a treatise at the time of his death.

He was married twice: on June 18, 1890, to Harriet Frances Lum, of Stamford, Conn., who died in 1917; and on Feb. 23, 1925, to Florence Evelyn Foster, of Dayton, Ohio. He died suddenly and unexpectedly of heart-failure at the height of his professional career, maintaining his full activity up to the very day of his death.

[*Who's Who in America,* 1926–27; *Trans. Am. Soc. Mech. Engineers,* vol. XLVIII (1927); *Jour. Am. Inst. Electrical Engineers,* vol. XLV (July 1926); *Proc. Soc. for the Promotion of Engineering Education,* vol. XXXIII (1926).]

J. I. P.

FLEEMING, JOHN [See FLEMING, JOHN, fl. 1764–1800].

FLEET, THOMAS (Sept. 8, 1685–July 21, 1758), printer, was born in Shropshire, England. As a youth he took an active part in opposing the high-church party, which eventually brought such rage upon him that he hid himself and took the earliest chance of leaving England for America. Soon after his arrival at Boston, "about the year 1712," he set up a printing-house in Pudding Lane, now Devonshire St. He had learned the printing art at Bristol. He was a good printer and did much work for the booksellers. T. Crump, another printer, was associated with him, 1715–17. From 1729 to 1731, Fleet was printer to the Massachusetts House of Representatives. In 1731 he left Pudding Lane for a house in Cornhill, which he purchased in 1744. It was spacious, served as both his residence and printing-house, and contained a convenient shop. It bore the trade-sign of "Heart and Crown." In a front chamber he conducted evening auctions of books, household goods, and other merchandise (*Boston News-Letter,* Mar. 7, 1731).

On Sept. 27, 1731, J. Draper had printed the first number of the *Weekly Rehearsal,* a half-sheet periodical edited by Jeremiah Gridley [*q.v.*], a young lawyer. It was made up largely of moral, political, and commercial essays. On Aug. 21, 1732, Fleet took over the printing and by Apr. 2, 1733, was its sole owner. It appeared regularly as a weekly morning news-sheet, but was discontinued with number 202 on Aug. 11, 1735. Fleet next began (Aug. 18), an evening paper, numbering it 203, with the *Boston Evening-Post,* as title, but changed the serial numbering to "2" with the next issue. This paper copied the London press and included Fleet's "own humorous paragraphs." It engaged but little in either political or religious controversy; none the less, for a paragraph in the issue of Mar. 8, 1741, Fleet was threatened with prosecution by the government. After his death it was continued as a morning weekly by his sons, Thomas and James, until crushed by the war, on Apr. 24, 1775. He owned several negroes, some of whom worked in the printing-shop. One ingenious slave worked the press, set type, and cut woodblocks for illustrating small books and broadsides. Fleet is credited (by Evans) with more than 250 publications, besides his newspapers, between 1713 and 1758. He printed many works of the Mathers, and tracts relating to the George Whitefield controversy. *The Sovereignty and Goodness of God . . . being a Narrative of the Captivity and Restauration of Mrs. Mary Rowlandson* (1720), John Williams's *The Redeemed Captive* (1720), Samuel Penhallow's *The History of the Wars of New-England with the Eastern Indians* (1726), *The New England Primer Enlarged* (1737–38), *A Brief Narrative of the Case and Tryal of John Peter Zenger* (1738), Joseph Addison's *Cato* (1750), and Michael Wigglesworth's *The Day of Doom* (1751), are a few titles which attest the importance of his imprimatur. In the third decade of the nineteenth century the claim was made that the collection of Mother Goose's nursery rhymes was derived from Fleet's mother-in-law and was first printed by him in 1719. No such publication by him has ever been found. That collection is an English adaptation by Robert Samber from the French tales of Perrault, which in English first saw the light in London about 1750 (*Athenæum,* Jan. 21, 1905).

Fleet died at Boston, after a long illness, July 21, 1758, leaving three sons, two daughters, and his widow, Elizabeth, daughter of Isaac and Elizabeth Vergoose or Goose, whom he had married on June 8, 1715. The tribute of the press was that he "was remarkable for his Understanding and Industry in the Business of his own Profession," as well as for "extensive Knowledge of the World," and of "a friendly and benevolent Disposition."

[The principal sources are Isaiah Thomas's *Hist. of Printing in America* (2nd ed., 1874), I, 98–104, 145, and II, 42–49; Chas. Evans, *Am. Bibliog.*, vols. I–III (1903–05); Clarence S. Brigham, "Bibliog. of Am. Newspapers," *Proc. Am. Antiquarian Soc.*, Apr. 14, 1915–Oct. 20, 1915; W. H. Whitmore, *The Original Mother Goose's Melody . . . with Introductory Notes* (1889); and Boston and New York newspapers for July 1758. The best of the known files of Fleet's newspapers is in the possession of the American Antiquarian Society.]

V. H. P.

FLEISCHMANN, CHARLES LOUIS (Nov. 3, 1834–Dec. 10, 1897), manufacturer, capitalist, was born near Budapest, Hungary, of Jewish stock, the son of Abraham and Babette Fleischmann. His father was a distiller and yeast maker. Charles, the second of seven children, all of whom emigrated to the United States, established himself in New York as a distiller and later in Cincinnati, where he formed a partnership with James W. Gaff. Between 1866 and 1872 he patented a plow, a cotton-gin and its improvements, and several processes and devices used in distilling. In 1870, at the instigation of his partner, he began to make yeast by a Hungarian method with which he had been long familiar. The patent (No. 102,387; Apr. 26, 1870) for making compressed yeast from the froth or scum formed during the manufacture of malt or spiritous liquors was taken out, however, by his brother Henry, who assigned it to Fleischmann & Gaff in return for an annuity. This yeast was slow in finding a market, so that the partners nearly failed. As a last resort they put on a huge exhibit at the Philadelphia Centennial Exposition, at which spectators could see the yeast made, the dough set, and the bread baked, and could then adjourn to a restaurant and eat the bread. The exhibit was popular; the restaurant yielded a cash profit; and the advertising value of the enterprise was enormous. Thereafter there was no trouble in selling Fleischmann's yeast. He devised an elaborate system, perhaps the first of its kind, for delivering his product fresh to the grocers; formerly the dapper Fleischmann yeast cart with its neatly groomed horse was a common sight on American streets. After Gaff's death in 1879, Fleischmann bought his share in the business for $500,000. His wealth grew rapidly. He became a director in some twenty-five Cincinnati enterprises and was president of a cooperage company, a large vinegar works in Illinois, a newspaper company, and the Market National Bank. He took a hand in civic affairs, was fire commissioner in 1890, was elected as a Republican to the state Senate in 1879 and again in 1895, and was a friend and adviser of William McKinley. Fleischmann was a shrewd, far-sighted, masterful business man, but there was nothing stingy or cautious about him. He liked long chances and venturesome risks, and took them frequently. He exercised a paternal watchfulness over his employees, let them know what he thought of them, and pensioned them when they were too old or ill to work. He gave lavishly to local charities and educational institutions, raised the debt on St. Peter's Cathedral, and was reputed to spend one hundred dollars a day on private largesse. His life insurance policy, his $80,000 sea-going yacht *Hiawatha,* and his "Schloss" at Fleischmann's in the Catskills were famous in their time. Characteristic of his generosity, and of his sense of power, was his treatment of the cashier of the Market National Bank, who absconded in 1893 with the bank's reserve of $160,000. Fleischmann, fearing a disastrous run, made up the loss out of his own pocket, accepted a deed for the cashier's house, and kept the whole transaction a secret until after the man's death. Then he deeded the house back to his widow. He stocked his residence at Avondale with costly French oil-paintings and bronzes, installed a Steinway in the conservatory, and for hours at a time would play by ear any music that he had heard, whether grand opera or ragtime, while his guests, according to their own reports, sat spellbound. In 1890 his doctor ordered him to spend as much time as possible outdoors and suggested that a horse would be the thing. Fleischmann thereupon bought a string of expensive blooded horses, established a trotting farm at Millstone, N. J., and made himself one of the foremost patrons of the turf. It was estimated that in six years' time he had spent at least $800,000 on his new hobby. He died at his home of apoplexy. He was survived by his wife, who had been Henrietta Robertson of New York, by one daughter, and by nis two sons, Julius, who became mayor of Cincinnati, and Max, a well-known sportsman.

[*Cincinnati Commercial Tribune, Times-Star,* and *Enquirer,* Dec. 10–15, 1897; W. A. Taylor, *Ohio Statesmen and Annals of Progress 1788–1900* (1899); U. S. Patent Office Records; additional information from Max C. Fleischmann (son) and from Hugo A. Oswald.]

G. H. G.

FLEMING, ARETAS BROOKS (Oct. 15, 1839–Oct. 13, 1923), jurist, governor of West Virginia, coal operator, was born on a farm near Middleton, Va. (now West Virginia), of a prominent family of Scotch-Irish origin. He was the great-grandson of William Fleming, who emigrated to America in 1741 and obtained a patent to land in Pennsylvania, and the youngest son of Benjamin F. and Rhoda (Brooks) Fleming. In 1859, after attending private and select schools, he entered the University of Virginia where he completed the law course under John B. Minor. In 1860 he began the practise of law in Gilmer County and also opened a private school. At the opening of the Civil War he returned to Fairmont, near his birthplace, where he served as prosecuting attorney from 1863 to 1867. After the close of the war, on Sept. 7, 1865, he married Caroline Margaret Watson and entered a law partnership with Judge Alpheus Haymond, who, in 1872, was elected to the state supreme court of appeals. Fleming was elected to the legislature in 1872, was reëlected in 1874 and was an active leader in founding the Fairmont State Normal School. Until 1878 he was attorney for the Baltimore & Ohio Railroad, and for the next ten years he was judge of the circuit court of his district. In 1888 he was the Democratic candidate for governor. After an exciting election before the legislature he was finally elected in February 1890. As governor, through his addresses and published articles, he attracted attention to the undeveloped mineral and timber resources of his state. He had been identified since 1874 with the coal development of the Monongahela Valley in association with his father-in-law, James Otis Watson, the pioneer coal operator of the region. He was also associated with J. N. Camden in the building of the Monongahela River Railroad of which he became a director. In 1901 at the organization of the Fairmont Coal Company (later the Consolidation Coal Company) he became a director, a position which he continued to hold until he retired from active business. He also was actively interested in the building of electric traction lines both local and interurban, and was one of the organizers and a director of the National Bank of Fairmont. He was recognized as a leading corporation lawyer. His natural, dignified simplicity and cordiality won him hosts of friends.

[J. M. Callahan, *Hist. of W. Va., Old and New* (3 vols., 1923); G. W. Atkinson and A. F. Gibbons, *Prominent Men of W. Va.* (1890); G. W. Atkinson, *Bench and Bar of W. Va.* (1919); *N. Y. Times,* Oct. 14, 1923.]

J. M. C.

FLEMING, JOHN (fl. 1764–1800), printer and Loyalist, whose name is often spelled Fleeming, was a Scotsman, of whose early life no records are available. He arrived in Boston in 1764, and was first a partner of William Macalpine and then of John Mein. Thirty-odd publications by him in these connections have been listed (Charles Evans, *American Bibliography,* vol. IV, 1907), mostly religious in character, but including *Fleeming's Register for New England and Nova-Scotia . . . and an Almanack for 1772* (1771), John Dickinson's *Letters from a Farmer* (1768), and William Knox's *The Controversy Between Great Britain and Her Colonies Reviewed* (1769). On Dec. 21, 1767, Mein & Fleeming began to publish the *Boston Chronicle,* patterned after the *London Chronicle* and at first a weekly periodical rather than a newspaper. Mein was the efficient editor, and the paper featured selections from foreign journals and works of popular English authors rather than colonial news. Volume I had an index! The *Chronicle* was well patronized, becoming a semi-weekly in its second year, the first regular one in New England; but with the development of the political controversy it became the chief Tory organ, subsidizing being hinted, and Mein was obliged to leave Boston before the end of 1769. Fleming continued the *Chronicle.* Mein had, independently, a bookshop, and an assignment of English debts for this shop coming into the hands of Boston Radicals, they tried, according to James Murray, to levy on the printing-office as well, in order to put an end to the newspaper. This attack was frustrated by a pledge for the value of Mein's interest, but lack of patronage caused a suspension of the paper with the issue for June 25, 1770. Fleming continued the printing-office during 1770–73, issuing the register and almanac, and a few other works, including the report of the Boston Massacre trial and William Gordon's plan for life insurance. According to Isaiah Thomas [*q.v.*], who was a contemporary Boston printer, Fleming left for England in 1773. If this was the case, he seems to have returned. The name John Fleming appears among the signers of a loyal petition to King George III in July 1776 (see E. A. Jones, *The Loyalists of Massachusetts,* 1930, p. 308). Alice, sister of Dr. Benjamin Church [*q.v.*], married, probably at Portsmouth on Aug. 8, 1770, a John Fleming, variously described as a high Scotch Tory, a printer, and a stationer; and Church's treasonable correspondence was carried on with this "brother," then in besieged Boston. There is little doubt that this Fleming was the earlier printer, who may have returned as a civil official of the army. His name does not appear in the partial list of those who left at the evacuation, or in that of the disaffected who remained. He was proscribed and banished by the Act of September 1778; but no proceedings concerning his estate or application for English pension have been found. Thomas adds that he returned to the United States several times after 1790 as agent of a French commercial house, and that he died in France after 1800.

[Isaiah Thomas, *Hist. of Printing in America* (2nd ed. 1874), I, 151–52, gives the main facts concerning the Boston printer. The deduction of the connection with Church is based on various sources; the correspondence is in *Am. Archives,* 4 ser., III, 1485–86.] D. M. M.

FLEMING, JOHN (Apr. 17, 1807–Oct. 27, 1894), pioneer missionary among the Indians, was born in Mifflin County, Pa., the son of John and Mary (McEwen) Fleming. He attended Mifflin Academy and Jefferson College, Canonsburg, Pa., graduating in 1829. After further study in the Princeton Theological Seminary he was ordained to the Presbyterian ministry, Oct. 24, 1832. Early in the next year he began his missionary work under the American Board of Commissioners for Foreign Missions among the Creek Indians near Fort Gibson, on the Arkansas River, in the territory of the present state of Oklahoma. His wife opened a school and he began preaching through an interpreter, at the time associating intimately with the Indians in order to learn their language. His chief claim to remembrance is that he was the first to reduce to writing the Muskoki or Creek language, which was a task of peculiar difficulty on account of the numerous and puzzling combinations of consonants involved. After about a year he produced an elementary book of some hundred pages on the study of the language, which also contained hymns and portions of the Bible in the native tongue. His next work, *Short Sermon: Also Hymns, in the Muskokee or Creek Language,* was printed in Boston in 1835. In the same year he published through the Cherokee Press his *Istuti in Naktsoky, or The Child's Book,* followed in 1836 by his most important work, *The Maskokee Semahayeta, or Muskokee Teacher.*

The Creek mission proved unsuccessful and was closed by the government. This failure and the state of his wife's health caused Fleming to transfer from the American Board to the Presbyterian Board of Foreign Missions under whose auspices he spent a year among the Wea Indians in Kansas. This mission having been withdrawn on account of denominational competition, he spent the year 1839 on Grand Traverse Bay, Mich., at a mission to the Chippewas and Ottawas. He had made substantial progress in learning the language as well as in religious and educational work, when his wife died, and he was compelled to withdraw from the Board. From 1840 to 1848 he served two four-year pastorates at the Presbyterian churches at Middle Tuscarora, and at Fairfield, Pa. From 1849 to 1875 he was engaged in missionary work in La Salle County, Ill., under the Presbyterian Boards of Missions and of Publication. He then removed to Gilson, Nebr., where he supplied various churches till 1879, and then to Ayr in the same state where he died. He was married to Margaret Longstreth Scudder, Nov. 1, 1832. She died May 21, 1839, and on Apr. 26, 1843, he married Rebecca Clark Patterson, who survived him with one daughter by his first marriage and four sons and two daughters by the second.

[Princeton Theological Seminary, *Necrol. Report*

(1895); *Biog. and Hist. Cat. of Washington and Jefferson Coll.* (1889); Am. Board of Commissioners for Foreign Missions, *Reports,* 1833–37; Board of Foreign Missions, Presbyterian Church, *Ann. Reports,* 1838–39.]
F. T. P.

FLEMING, WILLIAM (Feb. 18, 1729–Aug. 5, 1795), soldier and statesman, was born at Jedburgh, Scotland, son of Leonard and Dorothea Fleming, and allied to several noble families. After studying medicine at the University of Edinburgh, he entered the British navy as a surgeon's mate, and while in this service was captured by the Spaniards. Released after a rigorous imprisonment, he resigned from the navy to try his fortunes in Virginia; landed at Norfolk in August 1755; and proceeded to Williamsburg, where he obtained an ensign's commission in the regiment commanded by Col. George Washington. During the next eight years he was engaged in border warfare, serving as lieutenant and surgeon on Forbes's and Abercromby's campaigns and on the Cherokee Expedition of 1760–61; was with Andrew Lewis at Fort Chiswell; and, as captain in Adam Stephen's regiment, commanded at Vaux's and Stalnaker's frontier forts. Following the peace of 1763 he settled in Staunton, Va., where he resumed the profession of medicine and where he married, Apr. 9, 1763, Anne, daughter of Israel Christian. Five years later he gave up active medical practise to farm his Botetourt (now Montgomery) County estate, "Bellmont," where he passed the rest of his life.

In 1774 he raised the Botetourt Regiment which he commanded, as colonel, at the battle of Point Pleasant. While leading the left column into action, he was twice struck, but continued on the field until compelled by a third, more serious wound to withdraw. As a recompense for his gallant behavior and the injuries which rendered him unable to practise surgery, the Virginia Assembly voted him £500 (*Journal of the House of Burgesses,* session beginning June 1, 1775). His wounds, from which he never entirely recovered, kept him from field service in the Revolution, but he was commissioned county lieutenant of Botetourt by the Committee of Safety, Apr. 1, 1776, and again did valuable work in defending the frontier. From May 1777 through October 1779, he represented the district of Botetourt, Washington, Montgomery, and Kentucky in the Virginia Senate; and in 1780 became a member of the Council. In both bodies he took an active part, especially in Western affairs, warmly supported the conduct of the war, and furthered various domestic reforms. He twice headed commissions to Kentucky, to settle land-titles, 1779, and to investigate public accounts, 1782; served in 1783 as commissary to the troops there; and sat in the Danville Convention (1784), which initiated the steps leading to Kentucky's separate statehood. As a member of the Virginia Council, he was, June 1–12, 1781, in the interim between Governors Jefferson and Thomas Nelson, the acting chief executive of Virginia; and for his acts in this capacity, which included calling out the militia to oppose Cornwallis and taking other defensive measures, was subsequently indemnified by the Assembly (Hening's *Statutes at Large,* X, 567). His last appearance in public life was in 1788, when he represented Botetourt in the state convention which ratified the Federal Constitution: here, under instructions, he voted to ratify, but on the final roll-call abandoned this position and sustained the qualifying amendments which the convention adopted.

In his person, the energetic soldier and practical man of affairs united with the pious and hospitable country gentleman. His large investments in land, increasing in value, made him wealthy. His dignity, courtesy, and engaging address combined with his intellectual attainments to make him a favorite in the social life of his day, which he greatly enjoyed. He was an enthusiastic advocate of popular education, possessed one of the finest libraries in western Virginia, and himself had a talent for naïve yet forceful expression, apparent in his letters, his Orderly Book and Journal indispensable among contemporary documents dealing with Dunmore's War—and his account of his experiences and impressions in Kentucky in 1779.

[Fleming's papers, including his Manuscript Journal in Kentucky, are in the Draper MSS., State Hist. Soc. of Wis. Of the numerous brief notices which have been written of Col. Fleming, practically every one confuses him in one or more respects with his contemporary, Judge William Fleming of Cumberland County, Va.; several confuse him with John Fleming, who migrated from Virginia to Kentucky, and after whom Fleming County, Ky., is named. The best and fullest sketch of him is that by H. B. Grigsby, in "The History of the Virginia Federal Convention of 1788," *Va. Hist. Soc. Colls.,* n.s., X (1891), 40–54 (with other references in vols. IX and XI), but this is not free from errors. See also R. G. Thwaites and L. P. Kellogg, *Doc. Hist. of Dunmore's War* (1905) and *The Revolution on the Upper Ohio* (1908), which contain letters and other writings by him; V. A. Lewis, *Hist. of the Battle of Point Pleasant* (1909); and J. A. Waddell, *Annals of Augusta County* (2nd ed., 1902). T. Roosevelt, *The Winning of the West* (4 vols., 1889–96) has some important references to Fleming, but makes the curious error of naming him president of the Danville Convention which was presided over by Samuel McDowell.]
A. C. G., Jr.

FLEMING, WILLIAM MAYBURY (Sept. 29, 1817–May 7, 1866), actor, manager, soldier, was born at Danbury, Conn. As a young lad he came to New York City and was engaged in the counting-room of the *Commercial Advertiser.* After some little experience as an amateur actor he made his first professional appearance on the stage, Jan. 7, 1839, playing Shylock to the Portia of Charlotte Cushman, who at that period was struggling for recognition, and for whom the occasion was a benefit performance. Fleming was billed as "a young gentleman, his first appearance." After appearing in the same character in Philadelphia on Mar. 31, 1840, at the Walnut Street Theatre, he joined a troupe of players managed by John Oxley and went to Kingston, Jamaica, but the climate did not agree with him and in six months' time he returned to the United States. He was next seen at the Bowery Theatre in 1843, playing the Cloud King in the romantic drama *The Bronze Horse*. Later he appeared at the same house as Lord Cornwallis in a historical play entitled *Putnam, or the Iron Son of '76*. During the season of 1845–46, he acted with the companies managed by Ludlow and Smith, at their New Orleans and Mobile theatres. On June 7, 1847, he assumed the management of the Odeon Theatre, Albany, N. Y., but soon relinquished it. In December of the next year, he was at the St. Charles Theatre, New Orleans, and here he played Hamlet, Othello, Romeo, and Richelieu, as well as Sergeant Austerlitz in *The Maid of Croissey*. In 1852 he married Emily Sophia Chippendale, an actress of the famous English theatrical family of that name.

In 1853 Fleming became the manager of the National Theatre in Boston. In this position he persistently denounced the law then existing throughout Massachusetts prohibiting performances on Saturday nights, and took every possible occasion to speak of it as illiberal and a source of vice and disturbance. On June 30, 1856, he leased for the summer Burton's Chambers Street Theatre, in New York, for the purpose of presenting his wife to the New York public. He then returned to the National in Boston, where he was seen as Richelieu, but he met with little success. On Feb. 5 of this year he produced a new play entitled *Palomba of the Carbonari*, written for him by Col. Spencer Wallace Cone of New York, the father of Kate Claxton. Though it was well received, and Fleming in impersonating the leading character was much commended, the play failed to attract much attention.

At the beginning of the Civil War Fleming relinquished his business interests at great financial loss, and entered the army as paymaster on the staff of Gen. William T. Sherman. He was one of those who participated in the famous march to the sea. He was mustered out of service in March 1866, and died in New York City some two months later. He was buried at Greenwood Cemetery, Brooklyn. While he never attained great fame as either actor or manager, he did achieve conspicuous success in both fields of endeavor, and his efforts were always worthy and dignified.

[T. Allston Brown, *Hist. of the Am. Stage* (1870); H. P. Phelps, *Players of a Century* (1880); N. M. Ludlow, *Dramatic Life as I Found It* (1880); *N. Y. Tribune*, May 8, 1866; certain facts from Maybury Fleming and Maybury William Fleming.] R. D.

FLEMING, WILLIAMINA PATON STEVENS (May 15, 1857–May 21, 1911), astronomer, was the daughter of Robert and Mary (Walker) Stevens. She was born in Dundee, Scotland, and educated in the public schools of that place; for a time she was a teacher there. In 1877 she married James Orr Fleming, and in December of the following year came with him to America and settled in Boston. A position accepted apparently as a means of livelihood led to a distinguished astronomical career. She entered Harvard College Observatory in 1879, as a temporary employee, and two years later was given a permanent position, with duties of copying and ordinary computing.

At this time photography, after years of experimenting, was being adapted as a means of systematic astronomical research. Short-focus cameras, to take a plate covering a large area of the sky, were soon accumulating a permanent record of celestial phenomena; a large prism placed in front of an object glass made it possible to photograph on one plate the spectra of a great number of stars. Mrs. Fleming was put in charge of the ever-growing photographic library, with responsibility for indexing and examining the plates. This was a new field with few precedents. No one could tell her what she would find. Gifted with keenness of vision, a clear and logical mind, courage and independence, she made the most of her opportunity.

Her most important work was done with the objective-prism plates. While the stellar spectra could be classified in a general way in Secchi's four types, it was soon found in the course of this work that many of the spectra have intermediate characteristics and that there is no definite break in the transition from one type to the next. The number of types was very considerably increased. Each spectrum on each plate was examined with a magnifying glass. The resulting classification of 10,351 stars is published in the "Draper Catalogue of Stellar Spectra" (*Annals of the Astronomical Observatory of Harvard College*, vol. XXVII, 1890). Spectra which did not fit into the classification were marked on the plate as "peculiar." Mrs. Fleming was at work on a "Memoir on Peculiar Spectra" when she was stricken with her last illness. Her suspicions aroused by the peculiarities she observed, she discovered ten *novæ* and over two hundred variable stars. She found that stars with banded spectra and bright lines were practically sure to be variables, a generalization which has been amply substantiated. She was not content, however, with discovery alone, but in order to facilitate the determination of the characteristics of their light-variation, she undertook the very laborious work of measuring the positions and magnitudes of sequences of comparison stars for each of 222 of the variable stars she had discovered (*Ibid.*, vol. XLVII, pt. 1, 1907, and pt. 2, 1912).

She was made an honorary member of the Royal Astronomical Society of London and received the Guadalupe Almendaro medal of the Sociedad Astronomica de Mexico. At her death in 1911 she left one son. Dr. Annie J. Cannon, who has taken up and carried on the work of spectral classification, says of her, "Mrs. Fleming was possessed of an extremely magnetic personality and an attractive countenance, enlivened by remarkably bright eyes. . . . Her bright face, her attractive manner, and her cheery greeting with its charming Scotch accent, will long be remembered."

[E. C. Pickering, *In Memoriam Williamina Paton Fleming* (1911); tributes by Annie J. Cannon in *Astrophysical Jour.*, Nov. 1911, *Sci. American*, June 3, 1911, and *Science*, June 30, 1911; H. H. Turner in *Monthly Notices Royal Astron. Soc.*, Feb. 1912; G. A. Thompson, *New Eng. Mag.*, Dec. 1912; *Nature* (London), June 1, 1911; *Das Weltall* (Berlin), July 15, 1911; *Jour. Brit. Astron. Asso.*, May–July 1911; *Who's Who in America*, 1910–11.]

R. S. D.

FLETCHER, ALICE CUNNINGHAM (Mar. 15, 1838–Apr. 6, 1923), ethnologist, and writer on Indian music, was born in Cuba, the daughter of Thomas G. Fletcher and Lucia Adeline Jenks, during a temporary sojourn of her parents on that island. (The year 1845, given as the date of her birth in *Who's Who in America*, is incorrect.) She herself attributed her almost lifelong interest in American Indian ethnology to the early influence of Prof. F. W. Putnam [*q.v.*], of the Peabody Museum of American Archeology at Harvard, whom she often called her "god-father in science." Her development as an ethnologist was furthered by an extensive study of the Plains Indians and her personal interest in their problems. She lived among them for a number of years, and adopted as her son a young Omaha, Francis La Flesche, a brother of Bright Eyes [*q.v.*]. In 1880 she originated the system of lending small sums to the Indians for buying land and building houses. She next was instrumental in securing the allotment of land in severalty for the Indians, and acted as a special agent to carry out the allotment work among the Omaha (1883–84), the Winnebago (1887–89), and the Nez-Percé Indians (1890–93). In 1882 she became interested in the work of the Peabody Museum, in whose list of officers her name appeared as assistant in 1886 and where she held the Thaw fellowship, created for her in 1891. Thereafter, for many years the results of her investigations among the Sioux, Omaha, Winnebago, Pawnee and other Indian tribes were largely published in the *Reports* and *Papers* of that institution. In 1896 she became vice-president of the American Association for the Advancement of Science; in 1903, president of the American Anthropological Society of Washington; and in 1905, president of the American Folk-Lore Society.

She was a pioneer in the field of American Indian music. Her paper on that subject presented at the Chicago Anthropological Congress of 1893 inaugurated work in a field in which, though many others have since shared in its development, she remained until her death the most distinguished figure. In the nineties she recorded the Hako Ceremony of the Pawnee Indians, and secured the first complete record of the ritual and music of a Plains Indian religious ceremony. It was the first time that any white observer had been permitted to step behind the veil of the Red Man's esoteric mysteries, and set down for scientific study religious beliefs and observances hitherto impossible to witness. Her personal influence with the Indians enabled her to add to the archeological treasures of the Peabody Museum, among other objects, the Sacred Tent of War of the Omaha. Of the forty-six monographs which she contributed to American ethnology her chief work is "The Omaha Tribe" (*Twenty-seventh Annual Report of the Bureau of American Ethnology,* 1911), an authoritative, monumental study of its subject, the result of many years of research, and written in collaboration with her adopted son, Francis La Flesche. Of specific musical interest are: "The Study of Indian Music" (*Proceedings of the National Academy of Sciences,* vol. I, 1915, pp. 231–35); "A Study of Omaha Indian Music" (*Archæological and Ethnological Papers of the Peabody Museum,* vol. I, no. 5, June 1903), published "after ten years of study on the subject"; "Love Songs Among the Omaha Indians" (*Memoirs of the International Congress of Anthropology,* Chicago, 1894); and "Indian Songs" (*Century Magazine,* January 1894).

Miss Fletcher was one of the most authoritative interpreters of the North American Indian and his soul-life, his religious and his social concepts. A woman of lovable character, who had proved herself the Indian's friend in practise as well as in theory, by her sympathetic kindness she won the confidence of the chiefs and leading medicine-men of the tribes among whom she worked. As a result she was made free of their most sacred ceremonies; the Indians had no hesitancy in singing for her their sacred tribal songs as well as their play-songs, and she was thus able to record much of that inner life of the American aborigine which as a rule is carefully concealed from the ordinary investigator.

[Chas. C. Willoughby in *Fifty-seventh Report of the Peabody Museum of Am. Arch. and Eth., 1922–23* (1924); Walter Hough in *Am. Anthropologist*, Apr.–June, 1923, with complete bibliography; E. H. Fletcher, *The Descendants of Robt. Fletcher of Concord, Mass.* (1881); *Evening Star* (Washington, D. C.), Apr. 7, 1923.] F. H. M.

FLETCHER, CALVIN (Feb. 4, 1798–May 26, 1866), lawyer, banker, was a descendant of Robert Fletcher who, coming from England in 1630, settled at Concord, Mass. Jesse Fletcher, of the sixth generation, was a resident of Westford, Mass., when he married Lucy Keyes, Aug. 8, 1782. He afterwards engaged in farming at Ludlow, Vt., where his son Calvin was born and spent his youth. The latter's early education was scanty, and he was able to attend school at Randolph and Royalton only intermittently. In April 1817, leaving home he endeavored to ship before the mast at Boston but failed. He thereupon turned westward and made his way principally on foot to Pennsylvania, where he worked as a laborer for a time, and then proceeded to Urbana, Champaign County, northwestern Ohio. There he taught school, and in the autumn of 1817 entered the law office of James Cooley, subsequently United States chargé d'affaires in Peru. In 1819 he went to Richmond, Va., and was licensed to practise law there, but returning to Urbana was admitted to the Ohio bar in 1820, and became Cooley's partner. In 1821, however, he moved to Indianapolis, which had just been made the capital of Indiana, and was the first lawyer to practise there. From thenceforth it was his home. Commencing with no financial resources, he soon acquired a lucrative legal connection. He became prosecuting attorney for Marion County in September 1822, serving as such for a year, and in August 1825 was appointed state's attorney for the 5th judicial district, embracing eight counties. This position he also held for a year, when he was elected to the state Senate, continuing in the legislature till 1832. He enjoyed a large and increasing practise, both on circuit and before the supreme court, and became the acknowledged leader of the district bar. In 1834 the legislature appointed him on a committee to organize a state bank, an undertaking which was successfully accomplished. He was approached in 1836 with a proposal that he become a candidate for Congress but declined, saying that he preferred to adhere to his profession and educate his children. In 1843 he relinquished his law practise on being appointed president of the branch office of the State Bank at Indianapolis, and thereafter confined his attention to banking, becoming the head of the Indianapolis Banking Company when the charter of the State Bank expired. He was largely interested in agriculture, owning and himself working a 1,600 acre farm on the outskirts of the city.

Physically a man of great strength with remarkable powers of endurance, he was always, as his son said, "constitutionally on the drive," incessantly at work. Of simple tastes, he lived unostentatiously and took no pleasure in public life though in private he was extremely sociable. He died in Indianapolis from injuries received through being thrown from his horse. He was twice married: on May 1, 1821, to Sarah Hill of Fleming County, Ky., and on Nov. 5, 1855, to Mrs. Keziah Price Lister, née Backhurst.

[E. H. Fletcher, *The Descendants of Robt. Fletcher of Concord, Mass.* (1881); W. B. Trask, "The Honorable Calvin Fletcher," in *New-Eng. Hist. and Geneal. Reg.*, Oct. 1869, a comprehensive sketch containing obituaries and autobiographical letter.] H. W. H. K.

FLETCHER, HORACE (Aug. 10, 1849–Jan. 13, 1919), writer and lecturer on nutrition, was born in Lawrence, Mass., the youngest of the four children of Isaac and Mary (Blake) Fletcher, and the eighth in descent from Robert Fletcher, an Englishman who settled in Concord, Mass., in 1630. He was an enthusiastic and persistent traveler. At nine he tried to run away to sea; between his school days in New London, N. H., and his single year at Dartmouth College he shipped on a whaling voyage to the Pacific and acquired his lifelong affection for Japan; later he circled the globe four times and penetrated into obscure recesses of Mexico, Central America, Japan, and the Dutch East Indies. Combining salesmanship with travel, he was connected at one time or another with thirty-eight different business houses. In 1881 he married Grace Adelaide Marsh of San Francisco, which was his headquarters for some thirty years. He made a fortune as a manufacturer of printers' ink and importer of silks and other Oriental merchandise, was one of the founders of the Bohemian Club, and was famous locally as a snap shooter and all-round athlete. In 1892 he was manager of the New Orleans Opera House. At another time he was art correspondent of the Paris edition of the

New York Herald. He liked to paint and exhibited his pictures both in the United States and abroad. In 1895, however, a life-insurance company declined to accept him as a risk, and Fletcher realized suddenly that he was fifty pounds overweight, harrowed by indigestion, and subject to frequent illness. He tried several cures without result, consoled himself with the New Thought, and—imbued with the American business man's idea of "service"—wrote two books, *Menticulture, or The A-B-C of True Living* (1895) and *Happiness as found in Forethought minus Fearthought* (1897), to spread his gospel of health and happiness. Traces of the New Thought stuck to his doctrines until the last, but his final recovery of his normal exuberant good health he attributed to the simple procedure of chewing his food thoroughly. Thenceforth he devoted the greater part of his time to popularizing his principles. They were: to eat only when genuinely hungry; to eat whatever appealed to the appetite; to chew each mouthful until it "swallowed itself"; to eat only when free from anxiety, depression, or other preoccupations; and to enjoy one's food. To a nation rather inclined to gulp two of its daily meals and to eat till surfeited at the third Fletcher's teachings could do little harm and might accomplish some good. He himself was one of the best-natured and least fanatical of reformers; he enjoyed the good things of life and was publicly seen taking second helpings of turkey. He lectured and wrote indefatigably, and some of his books (see *Who's Who in America*) were translated into German, Italian, Hungarian, Polish, and Russian. In America "Fletcherism" and "fletcherize" became current words. A chubby little man, nattily dressed, bubbling with good humor, he was a favorite with newspapermen and magazine writers, who helped valiantly to spread his fame and his instruction. He himself made no money by his propaganda: he lectured without charge and subsidized research in nutrition at Yale University and the University of Cambridge. Though his doctrines were not new nor entirely true, his work and influence were on the whole beneficial. During his last years he lived chiefly in Venice. He celebrated his fiftieth birthday by riding almost two hundred miles on a bicycle. During the War of 1914–18 he engaged in welfare work in Belgium, teaching the refugees to make the most of their scant rations. He died of bronchitis in Copenhagen, worn out by his zeal for the welfare of others.

[See E. H. Fletcher, *The Descendants of Robert Fletcher* (privately printed, 1881); *Gen. Cat. Dartmouth College 1769–1910* (1910–11); *Who's Who in America,* 1918–19; H. T. Finck, "Horace Fletcher, Gluttony's Opponent," in N. Y. *Evening Post,* Jan. 14, 1919; editorial in N. Y. *World,* Jan. 15, 1919; obituaries in *N. Y. Times* and *Herald,* Jan. 14, 1919. For articles by and about Fletcher see *Readers' Guide to Periodical Literature,* 1900–14.]

G. H. G.

FLETCHER, JAMES COOLEY (Apr. 15, 1823–Apr. 23, 1901), missionary, the son of Calvin [*q.v.*] and Sarah (Hill) Fletcher, and a brother of William Baldwin Fletcher [*q.v.*], was born in Indianapolis, Ind. He prepared for college at the Indianapolis Seminary, and at Phillips Exeter Academy, Exeter, N. H., and graduated from Brown University in 1846. While in college he became a member of the Richmond Street Congregational Church of Providence, R. I. After one year at home, he entered Princeton Theological Seminary and took the full course there. Toward the close of his senior year, on Apr. 25, 1849, he was licensed to preach by the Presbytery of New Brunswick, N. J. He spent the following year in theological study at Paris, France, and Geneva, Switzerland, and married, on Aug. 28, 1850, in Geneva, Henrietta, daughter of the Rev. Dr. César and Jenny Malan. On his return to America shortly thereafter, he took service for a year with the American and Foreign Christian Union. He was ordained on Feb. 13, 1851, by the Presbytery of Muncie, Ind., and at the close of the same year went to Brazil as missionary of the Christian Union and chaplain of the Seaman's Friend Society. During the year 1852–53 he was first secretary *pro tem.* and then acting secretary of the United States legation at Rio de Janeiro, a position which brought him into intimate relations with the Emperor Dom Pedro II. In 1854, after a visit to Chile, he returned to the United States for several months. During 1855–56 he was agent in Brazil for the American Bible Society, traveling about 3,000 miles in the service, visiting certain German and Swiss colonies south of Rio, and journeying north as far as Pernambuco. On hearing at Pernambuco of the illness of his wife in Europe, whither she had gone from Rio with their daughter, Julia Constance (born in Rio Sept. 24, 1853), he sailed to join her. From 1856 to 1862 he lived in Newburyport, Mass., engaged in writing, preaching, and lecturing. In particular he collaborated with the Rev. D. P. Kidder in the publication in 1857 of their important volume, *Brazil and the Brazilians.*

In 1862–63 he was agent in Brazil of the American Sunday School Union, cooperating with the American Bible Society. He made a journey of 2,000 miles up the Amazon to the borders of Peru, gathering natural history specimens for Prof. Louis Agassiz—a journey which led to an expedition by Agassiz himself in 1865. During 1864–65 he went on a semi-official mission to the

Brazilian government and induced it to join with the United States government in establishing and subsidizing the United States and Brazil Mail S. S. Company. In 1868–69 he was Brazilian agent of the American Tract Society. From 1869 to 1873 he resided in Portugal as United States consul at Oporto for the full period and during the year 1870 acted also as United States chargé d'affaires at Lisbon. On Oct. 22, 1872, he married at the consulate in Oporto his second wife, Frederica Jane Smith. From 1873 to 1890, save for a brief visit to the United States, he resided in Naples, Italy, engaging in voluntary missionary work with the Waldenses and the Free Church of Scotland; and contributing numerous articles to American newspapers and magazines. He prepared an article on Naples for the *Encyclopædia Britannica.* He returned to the United States in 1890 and took up his residence in Los Angeles, Cal., serving as stated supply of the Presbyterian Church at Wilmington, Cal., during 1892, and at La Crescenta, Cal., from 1893 until his death. On Jan. 2, 1897, he married Mrs. Elizabeth (Murton) Curryer of Oakland, Cal. During the last six years of his life he was president of the Los Angeles School of Art and Design. He died and was buried at Los Angeles. He was survived by his third wife and by a son and a daughter of his first marriage.

[In addition to *Brazil and the Brazilians,* see *Am. and Foreign Christian Union* (later *Christian World*), organ of the Am. and Foreign Christian Union, vols. II–VI, 1852–55; *Ann. Reports Am. Bible Soc.,* 1855, 1856, 1863, etc.; *Necrological Report, Princeton Theol. Sem.,* 1902; H. O. Dwight, *Centennial Hist. Am. Bible Soc.* (1916); Robt. Fletcher, *The Descendants of Robert Fletcher of Concord, Mass.* (1881); *Minutes of Gen. Assembly Presbyt. Church,* 1902.] J. C. A.

FLETCHER, RICHARD (Jan. 8, 1788–June 21, 1869), jurist, sixth in line of descent from Robert Fletcher, a Yorkshireman who settled at Concord, Mass., in 1630, was the son of Sarah (Green) and Asaph Fletcher, a physician and prominent local politician of Leicester, Mass., and Cavendish, Vt. He was born at Cavendish, and spent his boyhood there, obtaining his early education at the local schools. Proceeding to Dartmouth College, he graduated in 1806 with the highest honors. He then became principal of the academy at Salisbury, N. H., but in 1809 took up the study of law at Portsmouth with Daniel Webster. On being admitted to the New Hampshire bar in Rockingham County in 1811 he commenced practise at Salisbury, removing later to Portsmouth, where he quickly established a reputation for reliability which combined with a natural instinct for circuit work to attract an ever increasing professional connection. In 1819, seeking a larger sphere he moved to Boston, was admitted to the Suffolk County bar in 1820, and at once took his place with the leading Massachusetts practitioners. Always a student, his wide reading gave him a comprehensive command of the law and his devotion to his clients' interests made him an admirable advisor. Though never erudite in the academic sense his knowledge of mercantile and maritime law was profound. It was as a jury lawyer that he was most successful. Not eloquent, he was master of a straightforward, almost conversational style of speaking which by its very simplicity favorably impressed a jury, and his marshalling of the facts of a case compelled conviction. No advocate of his time was more skilful in the conduct of a trial. His greatest triumph, however, was obtained in the Charles River Bridge Case, in which, against the almost unanimous opinion of the Boston bar, he successfully contested before the Massachusetts supreme court the claim of Harvard University to an exclusive franchise of bridging the Charles River between Charlestown and Boston (*The Proprietors of Charles River Bridge* vs. *The Proprietors of Warren Bridge, et al.,* 6 *Pickering,* 376; 7 *Pickering,* 344; 11 *Peters,* 420). Decided by a bare majority in the Supreme Court of the United States, it was "one of the most noted and historic cases ever argued before that tribunal" (Warren, *post*). In 1836 he was elected to the Twenty-fifth Congress as a Whig representative. At Washington his "enforced contact and daily association with men whose profanity and immorality shocked him beyond measure," was, he said, unbearable (Gordon, *post*), and he declined a renomination. He was appointed a judge of the Massachusetts supreme court, Oct. 24, 1848, but resigned Jan. 18, 1853, giving as his reason that he found his judicial duties so unremitting as to leave no time for reading or thinking on any other subject. He returned to the bar for a short time, but retired from practise in 1858. Throughout his life he was a devout member of the Baptist Church, and an unusually acute sense of religious responsibility pervaded all his social and professional contacts. He never married. Noted in his lifetime for his discriminating benefactions, he by his will bequeathed upward of $100,000 to Dartmouth College, which from 1848 to 1857 he had served as a trustee.

[E. H. Fletcher, *Fletcher Geneal.: An Account of the Descendants of Robt. Fletcher of Concord, Mass.* (1881); *Biog. Dir. Am. Cong.* (1928); Conrad Reno, *Memoirs of the Judiciary and the Bar of New England* (1901), II, 711; *Am. Law Rev.,* Oct. 1869; G. T. Chapman, *Sketches of the Alumni of Dartmouth Coll.* (1867), p. 127; J. K. Lord, *Hist. of Dartmouth Coll., 1815–1909* (1913), pp. 404–05; A. J. Gordon, *The Service of a Good Life* (1869); Charles Warren, "The Charles

River Bridge Case," *Green Bag*, June, July 1908; *Boston Transcript*, June 22, 1869.] H. W. H. K.

FLETCHER, ROBERT (Mar. 6, 1823–Nov. 8, 1912), medical scholar, bibliographer, was born in Bristol, England, the son of Robert Fletcher and Esther Wall. His father was an attorney and accountant. Following his preliminary studies he was taken into his father's office with a view to a career in the law. After two years, however, he decided to take up the study of medicine. He entered the Bristol Medical College in 1839, later transferring to the London Hospital, where he completed his studies. He was made a member of the Royal College of Surgeons and a licentiate of the Society of Apothecaries in 1844. He came to the United States in 1847 and settled in Cincinnati, Ohio, for the practise of his profession. Following the outbreak of the Civil War, he became surgeon of the 1st Regiment of Ohio Volunteers, in which capacity he served for nearly three years in the field. He was then placed in charge of Hospital No. 7, at Nashville, Tenn., and later made chief medical purveyor of the Army of the Cumberland. In the meantime he had been commissioned a surgeon of volunteers, and at the end of the war received the brevets of lieutenant-colonel and colonel, "for faithful and meritorious service." Declining a commission in the regular establishment, he took up his residence in Washington and had an active part in the preparation of two volumes of *Statistics, Medical and Anthropological, of the Provost Marshal General's Bureau* (1875), compiled under the supervision of Col. Jedediah H. Baxter, Medical Corps, United States Army, prefacing this valuable work with a treatise on the science of anthropometry. In 1876 Fletcher became associated with the library of the surgeon-general's office as assistant to Col. John Shaw Billings [*q.v.*], who was then engaged in the preliminary work upon the *Index-Catalogue of the Library of the Surgeon General's Office,* the first volume of which appeared in 1880. Through the first series of this publication Fletcher was chief assistant to Billings in the work of redaction. After the completion of the first series of the *Index-Catalogue* in 1895, Billings retired from the army and the continuation of the work devolved upon Fletcher, who applied himself to it until the beginning of his last illness. In 1879 Billings and Fletcher, as co-editors, put out the *Index Medicus,* as an extra-official publication. It ran through twenty-one volumes (1879–99), was suspended for a time, then began publication again in 1903, being issued by the Carnegie Institution of Washington, with Fletcher as editor-in-chief from 1903 to 1911. Despite thirty-five years of exacting preoccupation on these two bibliographical publications, he found time for numerous contributions to the literature of anthropology and the history of medicine. His monograph *On Prehistoric Trephining and Cranial Amulets* (1881) was the first treatment of the subject in the English language, and covered everything on the subject up to the time of its publication. The paper on "Medical Lore of the Older English Dramatists and Poets" (*Bulletin of The Johns Hopkins Hospital, May–June* 1895), was equally complete and scientific. The "Tragedy of the Great Plague at Milan in 1630" (*Ibid.,* August 1898), was a literary achievement, the story of which was suggested by an old Italian print. Fletcher's interest in the poetry of his native England was given further expression in his essay on "Myths of the Robin Redbreast in Early English Poetry" (*American Anthropologist,* April 1889), and he cherished an unfulfilled ambition to bring out an enlarged paper containing the results of his later investigations of the subject. Perhaps from his early legal studies he took a deep interest in medical jurisprudence, on which subject he was a lecturer at the Columbian (now George Washington) University, Washington, during the years 1884–88 and at The Johns Hopkins Hospital Medical School from 1897 to 1903. He was an active member of The Johns Hopkins Historical Society and contributed many of his historical essays to its publications.

Fletcher was a man of striking personality. "Above the medium height," says Sir William Osler (*post,* p. 293), "always well groomed and with a dignified military bearing, age made him a typical courtly gentleman of the old school. He had a rare gift for friendship. After his jurisprudence lecture . . . many of us would gather, delighted to hear Dr. Fletcher's reminiscences of the profession, which went back to the forties. He had met Sir Astley Cooper and he knew well the famous old men of the Bristol School and could tell tales of the Middle West in the palmy days of Drake and Dudley and Caldwell. It was a rare treat to dine with him quietly in his club in Washington. He knew his Brillat-Savarin well and could order a dinner that would have made the mouth of Cœlius Apicius to water."

In 1910 he received the gold medal of the Royal College of Surgeons, a distinction conferred upon but eleven physicians in ninety years, among them Lord Lister and Sir James Paget. He had an attack of diphtheria in the spring of 1911 which left him enfeebled until his death the following year. He was married in 1843 in his native Bristol to Hannah, daughter of John Howe.

[Sir Wm. Osler, "Robert Fletcher," in *Bristol Medi-*

co-Chirurgical Jour., vol. XXX (1912); F. H. Garrison in H. A. Kelly and W. L. Burrage, *Am. Medic. Biogs.* (1920); *Who's Who in America*, 1912–13; *Evening Star* (Washington, D. C.), Nov. 8, 1912.]

J. M. P.

FLETCHER, THOMAS CLEMENT (Jan. 22, 1827–Mar. 25, 1899), lawyer, soldier, and governor of Missouri, was born at Herculaneum, Mo., the son of Clement B. Fletcher and Margaret (Byrd) Fletcher, emigrants from Maryland to Missouri in 1818, and both descended from early colonial ancestors. He received his education in the subscription school at Herculaneum, where he had for a teacher Willard Frissell, an emigrant from Massachusetts. At the age of seventeen he was given work in the circuit clerk's office and in 1846 was appointed deputy circuit-clerk. Three years later, at the age of twenty-two, he was elected to that office. He was married to Mary Clara Honey in 1851, admitted to the bar in 1856, and appointed land agent for the Southwest Branch of the Pacific Railroad (now the St. Louis & San Francisco), whereupon he moved to St. Louis. Politically, he was a Benton Democrat, and a strong opponent of slavery, although he came of a slave-owning family. After 1856 he became a Republican and, as a delegate to the Chicago convention, was an ardent supporter of Abraham Lincoln for the nomination in 1860.

At the outbreak of the Civil War he was appointed by Gen. Lyons as assistant provost-marshal-general with headquarters at St. Louis. He became colonel of the 31st Missouri in 1862, was wounded and captured at Chickasaw Bayou but exchanged in May 1863, was present at the fall of Vicksburg and the battle of Chattanooga, and commanded a brigade in the Atlanta campaign. Returning home on account of illness in the spring of 1864, he recovered in time to organize the 47th and 50th Missouri regiments and to command the Union army which, at the battle of Pilot Knob, Mo., checked Gen. Price's army and probably saved St. Louis from capture. For this achievement Fletcher was given a vote of thanks by the Missouri legislature and brevetted brigadier-general by President Lincoln. While with Sherman he was nominated by the Republicans for governor over Charles D. Drake. He was elected by a large majority and reëlected in 1866. Thus he served as governor of Missouri from January 1865 to January 1869, during the most trying period of reconstruction.

His administration was confronted with many serious problems; notably: amnesty for those who had fought against the United States; the disposal of the railroads which the state had acquired through the failure of the railroad companies to pay interest on the bonds which the state had guaranteed; and the reorganization of public education. The roads were sold under a guarantee of early completion and the state debt materially reduced; the public-school system was thoroughly reorganized and great progress was made in free education for all children of the state. The governor was unsuccessful, however, in his repeated efforts to obtain a constitutional amendment abolishing the test oaths as a qualification for voting and for engaging in the professions. Subsequent events soon proved the wisdom of his recommendations. He strongly advocated normal schools for training teachers, greater support for the state university, and especial attention to agricultural education. Upon the conclusion of his term as governor, he returned to St. Louis and practised law for a time and then moved to Washington, D. C., where he engaged in the practise of this profession until his death.

[Biography by J. H. Reppy, in *The Messages and Proclamations of the Govs. of the State of Mo.*, vol. IV (1924), ed. by G. G. Avery and F. C. Shoemaker; H. L. Conard, *Encyc. of the Hist. of Mo.*, vol. II (1901); W. B. Stevens, *Centennial Hist. of Mo.* (1921), I, 407; sketch in Boonville *Weekly Advertiser*, Mar. 31, 1899; obituary in *Evening Star* (Washington, D. C.), Mar. 27, 1899; articles in Jefferson City *People's Tribune*, Mar. 27, Apr. 3, June 26, 1867.]

C. H. M.

FLETCHER, WILLIAM ASA (June 26, 1788–Sept. 19, 1852), jurist, traced his descent from Robert Fletcher, who, emigrating from England, established himself at Concord, Mass., in 1630. One of his descendants, Joshua Fletcher, a Congregational minister of Westford, Mass., married Sarah Brown in 1775. He owned a farm at Plymouth, N. H., where their son, the future judge, was born. In 1813 William Asa Fletcher was engaged in business in Salem, Mass., removing later to Esperance, Schoharie County, N. Y., where he studied law. About 1820 he went to Michigan, at that time under territorial government, and in 1821 established himself in a law office at Detroit. Two years later he was appointed chief justice of the county court of Wayne County, holding this position till Nov. 22, 1825, when he became attorney-general of the territory. He then resumed private practise in Detroit and in 1830 became a member of the Territorial Council. In 1833 the Council established a judicial circuit, embracing all the organized counties in the territory, excepting Wayne County, and he was appointed circuit judge. Since this necessitated his residing within his district, he removed to Ann Arbor. His work was onerous owing to the extensive area embraced within the circuit, and his constitution was probably permanently impaired in the performance of his duties.

After Michigan had attained statehood, a supreme court was created of which Fletcher in 1836 became the first chief justice under appointment from Gov. Stevens T. Mason. The following year he was commissioned to revise the statutory law, both state and territorial, and in pursuance thereof prepared and arranged *The Revised Statutes of the State of Michigan,* which were adopted by the legislature in 1837 and published the following year. The revision, though evincing ability and great industry, was performed under stress of heavy judicial work, and proved unsatisfactory. As chief justice, however, Fletcher displayed high qualities, combining a firm grasp of legal principles and an intricate cognizance of the changing conditions of an immature community. His decisions were always adapted to the realities of Western life without sacrificing the spirit of the law, and in conducting the business of his court he was efficient and expeditious. Nevertheless some unfortunate failings, not uncommon among the early settlers in the West, deprived him of the respect which the dignity of his office should have commanded. He resigned from the bench in 1842, returned to practise, and was appointed regent of the University of Michigan, a position which he retained till 1846. His first wife, whom he married before he went West, he divorced in 1843. In 1846 he married Adeline D. Doyle.

[E. H. Fletcher, *Fletcher Geneal.: An Account of the Descendants of Robt. Fletcher of Concord, Mass.* (1881); 4 *Mich. Reports,* 19, and *Mich. Biogs.* (1924), I, 299; *Green Bag,* II, 379; *Proc. Mich. State Bar Asso.,* 1918, p. 191; R. B. Ross and G. B. Catlin, *Landmarks of Wayne County and Detroit* (1898). Much of Fletcher's career still remains obscure. The date of death is taken from the Fletcher genealogy; other sources give 1853.]

H. W. H. K.

FLETCHER, WILLIAM BALDWIN (Aug. 18, 1837–Apr. 25, 1907), physician, a brother of James Cooley Fletcher [*q.v.*], was born on a farm which has since been covered by a thickly populated section of the city of Indianapolis, Ind. His father, Calvin Fletcher [*q.v.*], was a lawyer who came from Vermont to Indiana in 1821. His mother was Sarah Hill, a native of Kentucky. After studying for a time with Louis Agassiz he attended the College of Physicians and Surgeons in New York where he received the degree of M.D., in 1860. He returned to Indianapolis for practise, but his plans were disrupted by the outbreak of the Civil War. After some service incident to the mobilization of Indiana troops at Camp Morton, Indianapolis, he enlisted as a musician and entered the secret service. He was captured and sent to Libby Prison, where he spent nine months caring for the sick in the hospital. Following a bayonet wound received while trying to escape and a stay in hospital, he was exchanged and discharged. In 1862 he again took up his practise in Indianapolis and in 1868 he took part in the organization of the Indiana Medical College. On this faculty he held various chairs for the following six years. In 1875 he went to Europe where he spent two years in the hospitals of London, Paris, Dublin, and Glasgow. Returning home, in 1879, he was given the professorship of nervous diseases in the newly organized Central College of Physicians and Surgeons, Indianapolis. In 1883 he was appointed superintendent of the Indiana Central Hospital for the Insane. During the five years of his incumbency of this position he introduced many reforms, including the abolition of restraint and the employment of women physicians for the women patients. Resuming private practise, he established a sanitarium for the care of nervous and mental diseases.

Though best known as an alienist, Fletcher was also an able anatomist and an accomplished surgeon. In his teaching he combined an unusual command of language with a facility for illustration by rapid drawings. His interests were otherwise varied. In 1883 he was appointed to fill a vacancy and served part of one term in the Indiana state Senate, and some years later he was instrumental in securing the passage (1889) of the law providing for the Board of State Charities. He was an ardent supporter of the temperance movement and advocated the establishment of a state institution for the treatment of alcohol addicts. His contributions to the *Transactions of the Indiana State Medical Society* include: "Human Entozoa" (1866); "Cerebral Circulation in the Insane" (1887); "Purulent Absorption as a Cause of Insanity" (1892); "The Effect of Alcohol upon the Nervous System" (1895); and "A Consideration of the Present Laws for the Commitment of the Insane in Indiana" (1901). He also published *Cholera, its Characteristics, History, Treatment,* etc. (1866), and *Stray Papers on Cerebral Subjects* (1892). Fletcher was a large heavy set man, brusque, and described as being "without fear or reverence." He was married in 1862 to Agnes, daughter of James O'Brien of Indianapolis. They had three sons and four daughters. Failing health compelled him to spend his last days in Florida and he died in Orlando in that state. On Apr. 27, 1907, the day of his funeral in Indianapolis, the *Indianapolis Morning Star* published a commemorative poem, "The Doctor," written by James Whitcomb Riley.

[E. H. Fletcher, *Fletcher Geneal.: An Account of the Descendants of Robt. Fletcher of Concord, Mass.*

(1881); R. H. Ritter, in *Trans. Ind. State Medic. Soc.*, 1907; G. W. H. Kemper, *Medic. Hist. of Ind.* (1911); R. F. Stone, *Biog. of Eminent Am. Physicians and Surgeons* (1894); H. A. Kelly and W. L. Burrage, *Am. Medic. Biogs.* (1920); *Who's Who in America*, 1906–07; *Jour. Am. Medic. Asso.*, May 4, 1907.] J. M. P.

FLICKINGER, DANIEL KUMLER (May 25, 1824–Aug. 29, 1911), clergyman of the United Brethren in Christ, pioneer in the establishment and long a leader in the extension of their missionary work, was the son of Jacob and Hannah (Kumler) Flickinger. He was of Swiss descent, his father's ancestors being Swiss Mennonites, and his mother, the daughter of Bishop Henry Kumler, Sr. His parents migrated from Franklin County, Pa., to Butler County, Ohio, in 1818, and Daniel was born in Sevenmile, the sixth in a family of fourteen children. His father was a prosperous farmer, local preacher, and operator of a distillery. Opposed to higher education, he refused his son's request to be permitted to go to college in lieu of receiving a $5,000 farm when he was twenty-one. As a result, a common-school training was all Daniel received until after he reached his majority, when he attended a seminary for a year with a view to entering college. Poor health, however, thwarted his ambition. On Feb. 25, 1847, he married Mary Linter, and in 1850 joined the Miami Conference of the United Brethren. After a year on a circuit he bought a home in Oxford with the intention of studying at Miami University, but the death of his wife, leaving him with two children, the youngest a week old, again kept him from college. From 1851 to 1855 he preached, traveled in the West with Bishop Jacob Glossbrenner, and was city missionary in Cincinnati. The Conference of 1853 ordained him, and that year, Jan. 9, he married Bishop Glossbrenner's daughter, Catherine, who died in August 1854.

The United Brethren established their Home Frontier and Foreign Missionary Society in 1853, and in January 1855, with D. C. Kumler and W. J. Shuey [*q.v.*], Flickinger sailed for Africa to select a mission site. This enterprise was the beginning of a long career of strenuous missionary activity. After seventeen months he returned, bringing with him his third wife, Susan Woolsey, a mission teacher, whom he married Oct. 30, 1855. In 1857 he made a second visit to Africa, and that year the General Conference elected him secretary of the missionary society. This position he held, except for a short break in 1857–58, until 1885. From 1885 until 1889 he was missionary bishop. After the division in his denomination, which occurred that year, he supplied various churches, some of them Congregational, until 1895 when he withdrew from the liberal and united with the radical wing of the United Brethren, serving as its missionary secretary from 1897 to 1905. Soon after, he returned to the liberal branch, reuniting with the Miami Conference in August 1906. He is described as "a small man, of slight build, never in robust health, but of keen temper and dauntless purpose. He cared nothing for brilliancy or showy methods, but only for results. . . . In his consecration and utter abandonment to his work, he stood out quite alone" (A. W. Drury, *History of the Church of the United Brethren in Christ*, 1924, pp. 493–94). Twelve times he journeyed to Africa, being shipwrecked twice and once nearly dying of fever; and eight times to the missions of Germany; besides making frequent visitations to the conferences and mission fields of the United States. He kept careful diaries, contributed much to church periodicals. edited the *Missionary Visitor* from 1865 to 1885, and wrote books. Among the latter are: *Offhand Sketches of Men and Things in Africa* (1857); *Ethiopia, or Twenty Years of Missionary Life in Western Africa* (1877); *The Church's Marching Orders* (1879); *Our Missionary Work from 1853–89* (1889); and with W. J. Shuey, *Discourses on Doctrinal and Practical Subjects* (1859). In 1907 he published an autobiographical work, *Fifty-five Years of Active Ministerial Life*. He attended the Miami Conference at Dayton, Aug. 23–28, 1911, and died Aug. 29, at Columbus. He was buried at Oxford, Ohio.

[Besides works mentioned above, see Daniel Berger, *Hist. of the Ch. of the United Brethren in Christ* (1897); H. A. Thompson, *Our Bishops* (1889); *Who's Who in America*, 1910–11; R. E. Flickinger, *The Flickinger Family Hist.* (1927).] H. E. S.

FLINT, ALBERT STOWELL (Sept. 12, 1853–Feb. 22, 1923), astronomer, was born in Salem, Mass., the son of Simeon Flint, a business man, and Ellen Rebecca Pollard. Both belonged to old New England families. The only indication in the boy of the future astronomer seems to have been a fondness for learning the constellations. At Harvard, while taking the classical course, he became interested in mathematics. After graduation in 1875, he taught school for a time in California and then returned to Boston to study mechanical engineering in the Massachusetts Institute of Technology. Shortly, however, he recognized his true calling and went to Princeton to study under Charles A. Young. There, early in 1879, he participated in the determination of the latitude of the Princeton Observatory, his contribution being eighty-two observations with the zenith-telescope of twenty-eight pairs of stars on nine nights. He continued his studies with Ormond Stone at Cincinnati (M.A., University of Cincinnati, 1880), and in 1881 went to Washington as computer in the Naval Observatory.

His main contribution to science began with his removal in 1889 to the Washburn Observatory at the University of Wisconsin, where he at first assisted S. J. Brown in the reobservation of the secondary stars in Auwer's catalogue, and later completed the program. In 1893 he began his work with the meridian circle on the parallaxes of stars. Observation of the first series was completed in three years and the parallax determinations for one hundred stars were published in 1902. Although one or more screens were used to cut down the light of the brighter stars, he was able to detect errors and make corrections in his observations in the nature of a magnitude equation. Kapteyn, in his paper on the distances of stars, says, "It was mainly the confidence gained by the practical confirmation of my provisional results by Flint's work which induced me to publish the present paper without further delay" (Stebbins, *post*, p. 371). A definite measure of Kapteyn's opinion is furnished by the fact that he gave Flint's observations two-thirds of the total weight of all other observations.

With a self-recording transit micrometer and a new device for avoiding magnitude equation, another series of parallax observations was begun in 1898, continued for seven years, and reduced in another seven years. These parallaxes were, naturally, superior even to the earlier ones. The observing hours required by his problem were from dusk to about 9:00 P. M. and again from about 3:00 A. M. until dawn—one of the most exacting and confining of observing programs. Nevertheless, Flint found time to act as secretary and editor of the Wisconsin Academy of Sciences and to take an active part in the work of the Unitarian Church. He was fond of music and poetry and his chief recreations were rowing and tramping. He retired in 1920 but continued to work at the observatory. In 1884 he was married to Helen A. Thomas of Washington, D. C., who with a son and two daughters survived him.

[Joel Stebbins in *Pop. Astron.*, June–July 1923; *Pop. Astron.*, Mar. 1923; *Pubs. Astron. Soc. of the Pacific*, Apr. 1923 (XXXV, 129); *Nature* (London), Mar. 31, 1923.]

R. S. D.

FLINT, AUSTIN (Oct. 20, 1812–Mar. 13, 1886), physician, one of the most eminent American practitioners and teachers of his century, the son of Dr. Joseph Henshaw Flint of Northampton, Mass.; grandson and namesake of Austin Flint, a surgeon in the Revolutionary army, and great-grandson of Edward Flint, likewise a medical practitioner, was born in Petersham, Mass. After undergraduate studies at Amherst and Harvard, he received his medical degree from the latter institution in 1833. Although he probably never studied abroad, some of his teachers were in close touch with the brilliant French school of the day and from the first he pursued the statistical method and habit of case recording of the eminent Parisian clinician Louis; and even comparatively early in his career he had accumulated thousands of folios of notes intended to serve as a basis for his major text-books, which, he held, should be written only after ripe experience. Following a short stay in Northampton, he settled in Boston but after a few years' experience moved to Buffalo (1836) as a better field for a young and ambitious man. He was professor of medical theory and practise at Rush Medical College, Chicago, in 1844–45, and in 1845 established the *Buffalo Medical Journal* which he conducted for ten years. In 1847, with F. H. Hamilton and J. P. White, he founded the Buffalo Medical College. While nominally a resident of Buffalo and from 1847 to 1861 titular incumbent of the local chair of medicine, he filled the same chair in the University of Louisville, 1852–56; and in the New Orleans Medical College, 1859–61.

Although his nominal residence was transferred to New York in 1859, he does not seem to have been entirely settled there until 1861. In moving to the metropolis at the age of forty-nine he defied the local tradition that success is possible only to a young man with proper local background and influence. Failure was freely predicted and active opposition encountered; and some of the juniors of Flint's rival consultants seem never to have forgiven his success. He began his metropolitan career by accepting the chair of pathology and practical medicine at Long Island College Hospital in 1861, and in the same year cooperated with others in founding Bellevue Hospital Medical College. He became the first incumbent of the chair of internal medicine in the latter institution. For the next quarter of the century he performed the functions of hospital physician, teacher, text-book author, and consultant. By 1863 he was giving special courses in physical diagnosis. He was president of the New York Academy of Medicine, 1873; delegate to the International Medical Congress at London, 1881; and president of the American Medical Association, 1883–84. But for his sudden death from apoplexy, in 1886 he would have had the distinction of reading a paper by request before the British Medical Association, and in 1887 would have been president of the International Medical Congress at Washington.

His literary activity throughout his entire career was prodigious. At first he wrote chiefly for periodicals. He also wrote a few small monographs on such subjects as fevers and dysentery, and elementary works on diseases of the chest and on physical diagnosis. His earliest volume in the last-named field was published in 1856 under the title, *Physical Exploration and Diagnosis of Diseases Affecting the Respiratory Organs.* Numerous editions and revisions with several changes of title continued to appear until 1920. Thus the volume brought out in 1865 was known as the *Compendium of Percussion and Auscultation,* etc., that of 1880 was entitled *Manual of Auscultation and Percussion,* while the most recent, the so-called eighth edition, appeared in 1920 as *A Manual of Physical Diagnosis.* His classic work, *A Treatise on the Principles and Practice of Medicine,* appeared in 1866. The sixth edition was published the year of his death (with the collaboration of Prof. William H. Welch, who incorporated all of the newer bacteriological teaching), and the seventh in 1894. He published some smaller text-books which were limited to single editions; *Phthisis* (1875), and *Clinical Medicine* (1879) are but examples. The list of his minor writings is a long one. He inculcated the doctrine of self-limitation of acute disease which spares the patient much useless drugging; and his receptivity to new ideas was shown in his prompt acceptance of Koch's microbian theory of the origin of tuberculosis. He contributed greatly to the knowledge of chest pathology and diagnosis, taught early in his career that "pulmonary phthisis" is in reality a form of tuberculosis, and popularized the use of the binaural stethoscope.

He was a man of imposing presence and of an unusually well-balanced character. His domestic relations were most fortunate and he enjoyed in his work the constant cooperation of his wife, Anne Skillings, and his son Austin [*q.v.*], also a physician. Few medical men who have made no revolutionary discoveries have been eulogized as was Flint, both in the United States and abroad.

[*Official Report of the Memorial Meeting of the N. Y. County Medic. Asso. in Honor of the Late Austin Flint, M.D., LL.D.* (1886); H. R. M. Landis, in *Johns Hopkins Hosp. Bull.*, June 1919; *Jour. Am. Medic. Asso.*, Mar. 27, 1886; *Medic. Record*, Apr. 24, 1886; *Trans. Medic. Soc. State of N. Y.* (1887); *Lancet* (London), Mar. 20, 1886; *British Medic. Jour.*, Apr. 17, 1886.] E. P.

FLINT, AUSTIN (Mar. 28, 1836–Sept. 22, 1915), physician, physiologist, and alienist, was born in Northampton, Mass., the son of Austin Flint [*q.v.*] and Anne (Skillings) Flint. He was an undergraduate at Harvard during 1852–53 and left his class to take up engineering, but soon decided to go over to the ancestral profession of medicine and spent the years 1854–56 in study at the University of Louisville, where his father was a member of the faculty. He took his degree in medicine at Jefferson Medical College, Philadelphia, in 1857. At some time during this period he must have been at Buffalo, however, for in October 1855, before graduation, he published in the *Buffalo Medical Journal* an analysis of 106 cases of felon, nearly all from the practise of Prof. F. H. Hamilton of that city. Another undergraduate activity consisted of experiments on the frog which he made at Jefferson Medical College and summed up in a graduation thesis entitled "Phenomena of Capillary Circulation." By coating the frog with collodion he was able to show the effects of asphyxia on the circulation of the web of the foot. His thesis was published in the *American Journal of the Medical Sciences* in July 1857. Immediately upon graduation he was made professor of physiology in the Buffalo Medical College, of which his father had been one of the founders, and at the same time took over the editorship of the *Buffalo Medical Journal.* At this time he had barely attained his majority. Removing with his father to New York, during 1859–60 he was professor of physiology in the New York Medical College, but in 1860–61 he joined his father at New Orleans where he filled the same chair in the local medical school. Here he made experiments on large alligators, studying the heart's action outside the body, respiration, the functions of the liver, the spinal-nerve roots, and so forth. In 1861, again with his father, he was one of the founders of Bellevue Hospital Medical College and its first professor of physiology. This chair he held for thirty years. He seems to have served no period of pupilage in European laboratories, but instead, throughout the entire period of the Civil War he ranked as an assistant surgeon at the New York General Hospital. In 1862 he published a paper on a previously unknown excretory function of the liver, in which he maintained that the cholesterin of the bile is transformed to a substance which he termed stercorin. Six years later, when this paper chanced to obtain a French translation, he was awarded a prize of 1,500 francs from the Institute of France. (Because of a controversy which arose he received only a tardy and imperfect acknowledgment of priority.) During the period 1865–68 he held the chair of physiology in the Long Island College Hospital, while between 1867 and 1869 he spent much time in work on the subject of dietaries for the inmates of state institutions. In 1870 he made a series of studies of muscular power, et cetera, of the pedestrian,

Weston, and in the following year (1871) he published a monograph, *On the Physiological Effects of Severe and Protracted Muscular Exercise.* (More mature observations, "On the Source of Muscular Power," appeared in the *Journal of Anatomy and Physiology* for October 1877.)

In 1867 Flint began to publish his great work entitled *The Physiology of Man.* It filled five volumes, the last of which appeared in 1873. The demand for it was so great that a second edition was issued immediately, bringing the subject up to the last-named date. In addition, the volume on the nervous system was separately published in 1872 (*Physiology of the Nervous System*) and the whole major work was condensed into one volume in *A Textbook of Human Physiology* (1876; 4th ed. 1888). At the International Medical Congress in Philadelphia in 1876 he read a paper which summed up his practical knowledge of physiology.

For many years he was an attending physician at Bellevue and wrote many clinical papers, most of them in special reference to perverted physiology. In 1887 he read a paper on fever before the International Medical Congress. His interest in insanity is said to have been a result of his studies in mental physiology; as early as 1878 he was made a member of the consulting board of the New York Lunatic Asylum. In 1887 he attended the Bellevue lectures of the alienist, Dr. C. F. MacDonald, and not long afterward he extended his interest to criminology, penology, and forensic practise in general. In 1894 he was a member of a commission to investigate the administration of the Elmira Reformatory. Eventually he became one of the most eminent of medical witnesses and figures in many famous cases. His interest in physiology did not flag, however, and from 1898 to 1906 he was professor of that subject in the new medical department of Cornell University. Some of his papers were gathered into two volumes and published in 1903 under the title, *Collected Essays and Articles on Physiology and Medicine.* Some of his work is uncredited; for example his early studies of natural-color photography. Flint was married on Dec. 23, 1862, to Elizabeth B. McMaster of Ballston, N. Y., who survived him; one of their sons (also named Austin) became a physician, the sixth in direct descent to enter the medical profession.

[Flint's *Collected Essays*, etc., covering the period 1855–1903; H. A. Kelly and W. L. Burrage, *Am. Medic. Biogs.* (1920); *Who's Who in America,* 1914–15; *N. Y. Medic. Jour.*, Sept. 25, 1915; *N. Y. Times*, Sept. 23, 1915.] E. P.

FLINT, CHARLES LOUIS (Mar. 8, 1824–Feb. 26, 1889), agriculturist, was born in Middleton, Mass., son of a farmer, Jeremiah Flint, Jr., and his wife Polly Howard. His boyhood was passed on a farm. In 1841 he entered Phillips Andover Academy. He worked his way through Harvard College, graduating in 1849, taught for a short time, and then returned to Cambridge in the fall of 1850 to study law. After two years in the Harvard Law School, he entered a law office in New York City and was admitted to the New York bar. In college he had won the prize offered by the Essex Agricultural Society for the best essay on Indian corn, which was published in the Society's *Transactions* for 1849, and in the *Transactions of the New York State Agricultural Society, 1849* (1850). His agricultural writings attracted the attention of Marshall P. Wilder who recommended him for the position of secretary of the newly organized Board of Agriculture of Massachusetts. Flint was induced to give up his law practise in New York to take up the work of the Board in Boston in 1853, and remained its secretary for twenty-seven years. He initiated and continued a valuable series of reports and did much to encourage and direct the agricultural interests of the state. He made a tour of the rural districts of Europe in 1862 and gave an account of his trip in the *Tenth Annual Report* (1863) of the Massachusetts Board of Agriculture. He was a commissioner from Massachusetts to the International Exhibition at Hamburg in 1863, and before returning, visited agricultural schools in Europe and made a detailed report on them published in the *Eleventh Annual Report* (1864) of the Board.

He was deeply interested in education, had a conspicuous part in the founding of the Massachusetts Institute of Technology, was a member of the Boston School Committee, and took an active interest in the erection of the buildings for the high schools. He was one of the founders of the Massachusetts Agricultural College, chartered in 1862, was elected secretary of its board of trustees in 1863, and held the position twenty-two years. For four years he also gave lectures at the college on dairy farming. On the resignation of President Clark in 1879 Flint was elected president until a permanent president could be found, and served without pay. He resigned Mar. 24, 1880, and in June of the same year he also resigned as secretary of the Board of Agriculture. He had become president of the New England Mortgage Security Company, in which position he continued until shortly before his death. At the time of his death he was president of the Massachusetts Agricultural Club, having succeeded to the office on the death of Marshall P. Wilder. He was a member of the Council of the Boston Society of Natural History and of the New-England Historic Genealogical Society. Besides periodical articles and the valuable series of reports of the Massachusetts Board of Agriculture, which he edited from 1853 to 1880, he wrote several books, among the more important of which were the following: *A Practical Treatise on Grasses and Forage Plants* (1857), published in several subsequent editions under a shorter title; *Milch Cows and Dairy Farming* (1858), also published in several editions from 1858 to 1889; *Manual of Agriculture for the School, the Farm and the Fireside* (1862), published jointly with George Barrell Emerson [*q.v.*]; *How to Make the Farm Pay* (1869), in collaboration with Charles W. Dickerman; "Agriculture in the United States," a chapter in *One Hundred Years' Progress of the United States . . . By Eminent Literary Men* (1870); "A Hundred Years' Progress of American Agriculture" published in the United States Department of Agriculture *Report,* 1872, pp. 274–304, and in the *Twenty-first Annual Report* (1874) of the Massachusetts State Board of Agriculture. Flint married, in 1857, Ellen E. Leland of Grafton, Mass., who died in 1875. He died in Hillman, Ga., where he had gone to benefit his health. He was buried in Grafton, Mass. He left three children, two sons and a daughter.

[*Proc. Boston Soc. Nat. Hist.,* XXIV (1890), 199–200; *Trans. Mass. Horticultural Soc., 1889* (1890), pp. 134–38; L. B. Caswell, *Brief Hist. of the Mass. Agric. Coll.* (1917); *Vital Records of Middleton, Mass.* (1904); *Boston Daily Advertiser,* Feb. 28, 1889.]

C. R. B.

FLINT, TIMOTHY (July 11, 1780–Aug. 16, 1840), missionary, writer, was born near North Reading, Mass., the son of William and Martha (Kimball) Flint. He attended the local grammar school and Phillips Academy at Andover, Mass., and graduated from Harvard in 1800. After teaching at Cohasset for one year, he preached at Marblehead, where he married Abigail Hubbard. In 1802 he accepted a call to the parish of Lunenburg, then a part of Fitchburg, Mass., from which he asked his dismissal in 1814. The next year he spent chiefly on missions in New Hampshire and adjacent states, and in the fall of 1815 he and his family began a journey westward under the auspices of the Missionary Society of Connecticut. A good account of this and of his later experiences is found in his *Recollections of the Last Ten Years, Passed in Occasional Residences and Journeyings in the Valley of the Mississippi* (Boston, 1826). After a winter spent in preaching pilgrimages made from his headquarters at Cincinnati, he asked for a transfer. Then followed a fairly pleasant sojourn in St. Charles, Mo.; a disappointing pilgrimage to Arkansas; a trying voyage back up the Mississippi and Missouri, and subsequent prostration by fever and ague; the determination after a brief experiment in farming to go back to New England by way of New Orleans; preaching and lecturing in that vicinity; and the principalship of the seminary of Rapide at Alexandria.

The personal record closes with a journey back to his native section as a last resort after a long and exhausting illness. Apparently *Francis Berrian; or the Mexican Patriot* (2 vols., Boston, 1826) was started on the return trip, and thereafter Flint's work was chiefly literary. He issued at Cincinnati the *Western Monthly Review* from May 1827 to June 1830 and was for a brief period editor of the *Knickerbocker; or, New-York Monthly Magazine.* In addition to his books he published numerous translations and articles, and in 1831 he edited *The Personal Narrative of James O. Pattie* (reprinted in R. G. Thwaites, *Early Western Travels,* vol. XVIII, 1905). For the last years of his life he traveled widely, north and south, seeking for health which failed to return. He died on a visit to Salem, Mass., Aug. 16, 1840.

A disciple of Châteaubriand, confessedly enthralled by the "notion of new and more beautiful woods and streams," Flint was destined to find that but "a few weeks' familiar acquaintance with the scene dispels the charms and the illusions of the imagination." So, like most romanticists, he continued to seek refuge beyond the horizon. When his many sojourns in the Mississippi Valley proved disappointing, he found consolation in picturing the barbaric magnificence of Mexico and the superb scenery of the Rocky Mountains. From the hum-drum life of every day he sought relief in melodramatic action. His plots themselves are banal and tediously prolonged and improbable. There is significance, however, in the way in which he supplements Cooper's chronicles of warfare between red men and white by a new romance of the border, in his depictions of romantic scenery, and still more in his reflection of his own personality or, to put it broadly, of the typical romantic dreamers of his age. Francis Berrian tells how as a youth he fancied himself situated "in one of the boundless prairies of the West." *The Life and Adventures of Arthur Clenning* (Philadelphia, 1828) reveals the author's delight in an idyllic existence on a tropical island even though his rescued castaways somewhat reluctantly decide that society is best for mankind. In *The Shoshonee Valley* (Cincinnati, 2 vols., 1830) William Weldon and his Mandarin wife Yensi. "alike disgusted with social and civilized life . . . resolved to join the Indians in the interior!" Elder Wood in the latter book and the minister's family in *George Mason, the Young Backwoodsman; or 'Don't Give up the Ship'* (Boston, 1829), reprinted in London in 1833 as *Don't Give up the Ship; or the Good Son,* resemble the Flints in their disappointments and their dreams.

A similar romantic note is struck in his nonfiction. *A Condensed Geography and History of the Western States* (2 vols., Cincinnati, 1828), reprinted with additions as *The History and Geography of the Mississippi Valley* (2 vols., Cincinnati, 1832), contained enough of the glamour of the West to cause one contemporary to complain that it was too interesting for reference. *Indian Wars of the West* (Cincinnati, 1833) uses that old stand-by of the story teller—the border conflicts. *The Biographical Memoir of Daniel Boone, the First Settler of Kentucky* (Cincinnati, 1833), which went through some fourteen editions, deals with one whom Flint designated "the Achilles of the West" and with that paradisical epoch to which, according to him, all true Kentuckians looked back as "the period of romance." The *Recollections,* written at one of the most interesting periods in the Valley's history, is a repository of picturesque and romantic information, a panorama of social and economic evolution, and a valuable record of delicate beings like himself who suffered most in the forward march of civilization.

[J. E. Kirkpatrick, *Timothy Flint, Pioneer, Missionary, Author, Editor, 1780–1840* (1911), gives a full bibliography. Flint's son Micah (1803–1837) was one of the more creditable of the minor Western poets. His *Hunter and Other Poems* was published in Boston in 1826, and the father included many of Micah's pieces in his own volumes.] D. A. D.

FLINT, WESTON (July 4, 1835–Apr. 6, 1906), librarian, government official, born in the township of Pike, Wyoming County, western New York, was the son of Nicholas and Phebe Burt (Willoughby) Flint. His father came of Dutch and English ancestors who settled near Otsego Lake, N. Y. His mother was a descendant of the old English family of Willoughby de Broke and d'Eresby. His maternal grandfather was a soldier in the War of 1812, while his paternal grandfather was in the army at Saratoga when Burgoyne surrendered. In 1852 Weston Flint began teaching, and in 1855 he entered Alfred Academy, at Alfred Center, N. Y., from which he was graduated in 1858. He then proceeded to Union College, Schenectady, where he was graduated in 1860. After teaching in New York, Pennsylvania, and Ohio, he went to St. Louis to assist in caring for the sick and wounded of the Union army. While there he was appointed military agent for Ohio, acting also for Michigan and New York. From 1866 to 1869 he was attorney for claims in St. Louis, and active in Missouri state politics. In 1866 he was one of the organizers and secretary of the Southern Loyalist Convention of Philadelphia, and in 1868 was a delegate to the Republican National Convention at Chicago. He became editor and publisher of the St. Louis *Daily Tribune,* and was also the organizer and secretary of the second board of the Geological Survey of Missouri.

In 1871 he was appointed United States consul at Chin Kiang, China, but returned to the United States in 1874 to engage in literary work and lecturing. In 1877–78 he attended the Law Department of the National University at Washington, D. C., and received the degree of LL.B. The following year he attended the Law School of Columbian University in the same city, and received the degree of LL.M. The degree of Ph.D. was conferred upon him by Alfred University in 1886.

For the ten years 1877–87 he was librarian of the scientific library of the United States Patent Office. Under his direction the library was reorganized and two large catalogues were prepared: *Catalogue of the Library of the United States Patent Office* (1878) and . . . *Additions from 1878 to 1883* (1883). He was prominent in the organization of the United States Civil Service Commission, and for a time was acting chairman, and also one of the examiners. In 1888 he served with the committee of the United States Senate which investigated the operations of the civil service; and in 1889 he was appointed statistician of the United States Bureau of Education, and as such prepared the report on *Statistics of Public Libraries in the United States and Canada,* issued in 1893. On Sept. 29, 1898, he became librarian of the newly organized Washington (D. C.) Free Public Library (later the District of Columbia Public Library) of which he was then a trustee. His wide reading, his great love of books, and his ability as an organizer placed the library on a firm foundation. He retired from active work because of poor health on Aug. 31, 1904, about a year and a half before his death.

Weston Flint was a handsome man of fine presence, dignified and courteous. His interests, mostly of an intellectual character, were quite diverse with a strong bent toward the literary and scientific. He was secretary of the Anthropological Society of Washington, a member of the American Historical Society, of the American Association for the Advancement of Science, of the American Library Association, of the American Folk Lore Society, of the National Geographic Society, and of the Society for University Extension. He was also a member of the Washington Board of Trade and of its committee on libraries. He was a Freemason and a member of the Presbyterian Church. In 1883 he was married to Lucy Romilda Brown of Ohio, by whom he had one son.

[*Who's Who in America*, 1906–07; *Library Jour.*, May 1906; *Alfred Univ. Year Book*, 1905–06; *Evening Star* (Washington, D. C.), Apr. 6, 1906; slight personal knowledge.] H. H. B. M.

FLORENCE, THOMAS BIRCH (Jan. 26, 1812–July 3, 1875), congressman, editor, was born in the Southwark district of Philadelphia, the son of David Florence, a boat-builder. He was placed in public school when six years old but upon the death of his father was apprenticed to a carpenter and later to a hatter. In 1833 he went into the hat business for himself but failed in 1841. Early in life he became interested in politics, and as he was a fluent speaker and writer took an active part in the affairs of the Democratic party. When his business failed he was elected secretary of the board of controllers of the public schools for the City and County of Philadelphia, which position he ably filled until 1849. In 1850 he was appointed one of the board of mercantile appraisers for the City and County of Philadelphia. Before the war with Mexico he was elected colonel of the 5th Regiment of the state militia. Thus, being connected with military affairs, on the opening of the war he requested that a volunteer company, of which he was captain, be accepted for service in Mexico, but the company was not used. After two unsuccessful attempts he was elected as a Democrat to the Thirty-second and to the four succeeding congresses (Mar. 4, 1851–Mar. 3, 1861), where he served as a member of the committee on naval affairs and invalid pensions and during which time he became very popular with his constituents because of his ability to obtain contracts for the Philadelphia Navy Yard. He served as a delegate to the Philadelphia "National Union Convention" of 1866. In 1868 and 1874 he tried for reëlection but was unsuccessful. He owed much of his political popularity to his championship of the temperance cause and to his activities in connection with Philadelphia volunteer fire companies, as well as to his fraternal affiliations. He was one of the founders of a secret organization called "The Brotherhood of the Union." He professed the warmest interest in the poor and laboring classes and was widely known under the cognomen of "the widow's friend." Throughout his life he had a liking for journalism and was connected in one way or another with quite a number of newspapers in Philadelphia; among these were the *Daily Keystone and People's Journal,* which was established in 1844 and lasted three years, and the *National Argus* (Democratic), published from 1853 to 1861. After leaving Congress he resided in Washington, D. C., where he edited and published a Democratic afternoon daily, the *Constitutional Union* (1863–68), and subsequently became the proprietor of the Sunday *Gazette.* He died in Washington in 1875, of gangrene resulting from an accident that occurred during the campaign for reëlection to Congress in the previous year.

[*Biog. Dir. Am. Cong.* (1928); Chas. Lanman, *Biog. Annals of the Civil Govt.* (1876); E. P. Oberholtzer, *Philadelphia: A Hist. of the City and its People* (4 vols., 1912), II, 306–07; *U. S. Mag. and Democratic Rev.*, Feb. 1851; obituary in *Public Ledger* (Phila.), July 5, 1875.] J. H. F.

FLORENCE, WILLIAM JERMYN (July 26, 1831–Nov. 19, 1891), actor, author, was baptized Bernard Conlin, son of Peter (or Michael) and Mary (Flynn) Conlin. He assumed the name Florence for the stage. He was born in Albany, but grew up in New York in the old Thirteenth Ward. Among East Side boys he was famous for his genius for impersonation, his irrepressible humor, and his phenomenal memory. When a call boy at the Old Bowery Theatre he is said to have reproduced for Chanfrau an entire unpublished one-act piece "out of his head." His formal education was cut short by the death of his father, and Bernard, at fifteen, had to help support his mother and her seven younger children. He contrived, while working as a cub reporter and later in a type foundry, to prepare himself for the stage by rehearsing at night with the gifted amateurs of James E. Murdoch's Dramatic Association. His first spoken part was that of Peter in *The Stranger* with the stock company at the Marshall Theatre, Richmond, Va., Dec. 6, 1849.

Florence demonstrated early in his career his ability in Shakespearian rôles, but his first Irish part, that of Hallagan in Brougham's play *Home,* at Niblo's Garden in 1850, determined his bent toward dialect impersonation. In 1851 he scored with Brougham a hit in an eccentric hoax, *A Row at the Lyceum,* which raised him from the first walking-gentleman class. The season of 1852 saw him supporting a succession of stars at the Broadway Theatre, among whom were Mr. and Mrs. Barney Williams. In 1853 he married the latter's sister, Malvina Pray, a popular danseuse, and with her he began a highly successful starring venture in a play of his own, *The Irish Boy and the Yankee Girl.* After an extensive American tour, they played a fifty-night engagement at Drury Lane followed by triumphs in the provinces. From this time until the coalition with Joseph Jefferson in 1889, Florence and his wife enjoyed unbroken success as twin stars. They confined themselves for nearly a decade to Irish-American comedy, varied by burlesque and melodrama. It was not until 1861 that Florence played the first of the great parts which, according to Winter, established his rank among the leading actors of his time.

During almost forty years as a star Florence made not one failure, though his notable triumphs are confined to a few strongly contrasted parts—Captain Cuttle, in *Dombey and Son,* which won Dickens's praise; Bob Brierly, in *The Ticket-of-Leave Man*; Obenreizer, in *No Thoroughfare*; Bardwell Slote, in *The Mighty Dollar,* said by Hutton to be his most enduring character; Sir Lucius O'Trigger, in *The Rivals*; and Zekiel Homespun, in *The Heir-at-Law,* played at the last with Jefferson. Critics agree that his supreme gifts were his talent for impersonation and his skill in drawing vivid and convincing human types. He has been classed among four leading comedians on the American stage, among six on the English-speaking stage, and was one of the few Americans to win the ribbon of the Société Histoire Dramatique of France. His work with Jefferson was an example of the finest type of artistic team-play. When he died in Philadelphia, at the height of his powers, it was said that no other actor save Booth or Jefferson could have been so widely missed.

Florence enriched his personality by travel, study, and by varied human contacts. Wherever he went he gathered about him a brilliant circle of friends of many professions. At sixty he was still "Billy Florence": jaunty, well-set-up, with an air of what Winter calls "affluent health." By his personal life, as well as by his finished artistry, Florence won respect for his profession.

[Brander Matthews and Lawrence Hutton, eds., *Actors and Actresses of Great Britain and the U. S.* (1886), V, 115–30; Wm. Winter, *The Wallet of Time* (1913), I, 233–39; F. E. McKay and C. T. Wingate, eds., *Famous Am. Actors of Today* (1896), chapter by A. E. Berg; the *Public Ledger* and the *Press* (Phila.), Nov. 20, 1891; and the Robinson Locke dramatic collection in the N. Y. Pub. Library.] M. B. H.

FLOWER, BENJAMIN ORANGE (Oct. 19, 1858–Dec. 24, 1918), editor and social reformer, was born in Albion, Ill., founded by his grandfather George Flower [*q.v.*], an Englishman who, having visited the United States in 1816, finally came here to settle in 1818, bringing with him his father, Richard [*q.v.*], his mother, and several brothers and sisters. Benjamin was the son of Rev. Alfred and Elizabeth (Orange) Flower. He was educated in the public schools of Evansville, Ind., to which place the family moved in his boyhood, and at Kentucky University. He had originally intended to follow the example of his father and an older brother, George Edward, and enter the ministry of the Disciples of Christ, but a change in his theological views, which ultimately resulted in his becoming a Unitarian, led him to turn to journalism. His first venture was in connection with the *American Sentinel* of Albion, Ill., a social and literary weekly, which he edited until 1880. He then went to Philadelphia where he was associated in a secretarial capacity with his brother, Dr. Richard C. Flower. On Sept. 10, 1885, he married Hattie Cloud of Evansville, Ind.

Becoming increasingly interested in social reform, he soon left Philadelphia for Boston and began an agitation for betterment in human relations through various publications and other agencies, which he continued until his death. He had a lively sympathy for the poor and oppressed, a passion for what he conceived to be justice, and an enthusiastic belief in a coming reign of human brotherhood with all its attendant blessings. Frequently his motives were more to be praised than his insight and wisdom, and in his later years especially, a fanatical zeal distorted his outlook, and unbalanced his judgment. At Boston he established in 1886 the *American Spectator,* merging it later with the *Arena,* "a liberal in the field of magazines," which he founded in 1889 and edited until December 1896. From June 1897 to March 1898, with Frederick U. Adams [*q.v.*], he edited the *New Time,* Chicago, "a magazine of social progress" formerly known as the *New Occasions.* He was co-editor with Anna C. E. Reifsnider of the *Coming Age,* St. Louis and Boston, until it was merged with the *Arena* in the fall of 1900, after which he was on the editorial staff of the latter and in 1904 again became editor-in-chief. He founded and for two years, October 1909 to November 1911, edited the *Twentieth Century Magazine,* Boston, a forum for the discussion of great social, political, and educational questions, and an advocate of direct legislation through initiative, referendum, and recall, government ownership of public utilities, equal suffrage, and compulsory arbitration. In his later years he became obsessed with the idea that the supreme menace to democracy is "the monarchial and democracy-destroying, upas-like Roman hierarchy, which is in effect a government within our Government, whose theory of rule is in *direct opposition to vital and fundamental principles* of our liberal democracy" (B. O.

Flower, *Righting the People's Wrongs*, 1917, p. 5). As president of the Menace Publishing Company, Aurora, Mo., and editor of the *Menace*, a virulent anti-Catholic publication, he made his last journalistic enterprise an attempt to arouse opposition to this alleged peril.

In addition to his editorial work, he was a frequent contributor to magazines, and the author of a number of books. Among the latter are: *Lessons Learned from Other Lives* (1891); *Civilization's Inferno, or Studies in the Social Cellar* (1893); *The New Time* (1894); *Gerald Massey: Poet, Prophet, and Mystic* (1895); *The Century of Sir Thomas More* (1896); *Whittier: Prophet, Seer, and Man* (1896); *Persons, Places, and Ideas: Miscellaneous Essays* (1896); *How England Averted a Revolution of Force; a Survey of the Social Agitation of the First Ten Years of Queen Victoria's Reign* (1903); *Christian Science, as a Religious Belief and a Therapeutic Agent* (1909), a defense; *Progressive Men, Women, and Movements of the Past Twenty-five Years* (1914); and *The Patriot's Manual* (1915). He was much interested in psychical research, and believed that the reality of the future life would ultimately be demonstrated, and was president of the National League for Medical Freedom, and of the Free Press Defense League. His death occurred in a hospital in Boston.

[Richard Herndon and Edwin M. Bacon, *Men of Progress in the Commonwealth of Mass.* (1896); *Who's Who in America*, 1918–19; Hamlin Garland, "Roadside Meetings of a Literary Nomad," *Bookman*, Jan. 1930; *N. Y. Herald*, Dec. 25, 1918.] H. E. S.

FLOWER, GEORGE (1788–Jan. 15, 1862), Illinois pioneer, was born at Hertford, England, the eldest son of Richard Flower [*q.v.*]. In 1814 he accompanied Morris Birkbeck [*q.v.*] on a three months' tour through France. In 1816 he visited the United States, traveling west to Illinois and south to Tennessee, and spending a good part of the following winter at Monticello with Jefferson, to whom he brought a letter of introduction from Lafayette. He joined Birkbeck at Richmond in the spring and conducted him and his party to Edwards County, Ill. On the way both fell in love with Eliza Julia Andrews, daughter of the Rev. Mordecai Andrews and a friend in England of the Birkbeck family. She declined Birkbeck's proposal and was married to Flower at Vincennes, Ind., with Birkbeck present at the ceremony. The two men decided to colonize a large tract of prairie land in Edwards County, and while Birkbeck remained on the spot Flower went back to England to publish Birkbeck's account of their journey and to raise money and settlers. When he returned in 1818, bringing his parents, brothers, and sisters with him, he found that Birkbeck would have nothing to do with him and that necessary business with him must be carried on through an intermediary. This breach damaged their project hopelessly and produced a luxuriant crop of gossip. At the time of his death in 1825 Birkbeck was probably seeking to effect a reconciliation. Flower never lost an opportunity to speak well of the character and achievements of his former partner. He laid out the village of Albion, imported good breeds of sheep and cattle, and would sell land only to actual settlers. These he also sought to help with pamphlets such as *The Errors of Emigrants* (London, n.d.) and *The Western Shepherd . . . Containing Instructions for the Breeding and the Proper Management of Sheep, and their Pastures* (New Harmony, Ind., 1841). To the *Lowell* (Mass.) *Courier*, he wrote a letter descriptive of the prairies, which was translated into Norwegian and probably did something to encourage Norwegian emigration to the West. At Albion he had to contend with drouth, poor soil, intractable English immigrants, and the rough element on the frontier, to whom his good manners and good education were an inexcusable offense. When he joined the movement to prevent the legalized introduction of slavery into Illinois he was pursued with threats and insults, and finally a ruffian murdered his eldest son, Richard, and was triumphantly acquitted by the jury. In 1849 he crossed the Wabash and settled at New Harmony, Ind. His once considerable fortune was gone; all that he had left was the household furniture and the family plate. His last years were nevertheless serene and not without honor. He lived with his various children, and while residing at Mt. Vernon, Ohio, wrote a history of the English settlement in Edwards County. It and some other papers were presented to the Chicago Historical Society. He and his wife died on the same day at the home of their daughter in Grayville, Ill.

[Flower's *Hist. of the English Settlement in Edwards County, Ill.* (Chicago, 1882), edited by E. B. Washburne, is the ultimate source of most information about him. The Chicago Historical Society has portraits of him and his wife.] G. H. G.

FLOWER, LUCY LOUISA COUES (May 10, 1837–Apr. 27, 1921), philanthropist, was born in Boston, Mass., the daughter of Charlotte H. (Ladd) and Samuel E. Coues. Most of her childhood was spent in Portsmouth, N. H. In 1853 her father received an appointment in the government service and moved to Washington, D. C. Lucy was sent to school at the Packer Collegiate Institute, Brooklyn, N. Y., but was forced to leave before graduating. For a time she worked in the United States Patent Office as a draftsman. In 1859 she accepted a position in the public schools of Madison, Wis., and a year later she was appointed assistant in the Madison High School. In 1862, when the public schools were closed for lack of funds, the building was lent to Miss Coues for the purpose of conducting a private school. In the same year she married James M. Flower, a lawyer of Madison. In 1873 they moved to Chicago. Mrs. Flower devoted her educational interests to various Chicago institutions. She became a member of the board of management of the Half-Orphan Asylum and later a member of the board of the Chicago Home for the Friendless. In 1886 she prepared for the state legislature of Illinois a bill providing for an industrial school for homeless boys. The bill was defeated but it aroused considerable attention and subsequently such a school was started under private management. In 1888 she was influential in organizing the Lake Geneva Fresh Air Association and for three years had complete charge of the selection of children to be sent to the camp. In 1891 she was appointed a member of the Chicago school board—the third woman to hold that position—and served until 1894. She worked to establish industrial training and kindergartens in the public schools. Following this incumbency she became a trustee of the University of Illinois. With the decline of her health, she and her husband moved to Coronado, Cal., where her remaining years were spent in leisure. She died at the age of eighty-four.

[*Woman's Who's Who of America*, 1914–15; *Chicago Tribune* and *Chicago News*, Apr. 28, 1921.] M. Sh—r.

FLOWER, RICHARD (1761–Sept. 2, 1829), Illinois pioneer, was born in England, presumably in Hertfordshire, the son of a tradesman, George Flower. He married a daughter of Edward Fordham of Kelshall near Royston and for more than twenty years was proprietor of a flourishing brewery in Hertford. Like his elder brother, Benjamin Flower [*q.v.* in *Dictionary of National Biography*], he was somewhat of a reformer and took naturally to pamphleteering. When Government paid no heed to his *Observations on Beer and Brewers, in Which the Inequality, Injustice, and Impolicy of the Malt and Beer Tax are Demonstrated* (Cambridge, 1802), he disposed of his business, invested the proceeds in an estate, "Marden," three miles from the town, and devoted his time to agriculture and sheep husbandry. As a dissenter he was galled especially by the tithe and published *Abolition of Tithe Recommended, in an Address to the Agriculturalists of Great Britain* (Harlow, 1809; another edition, 1813). Extortionate taxes, the mounting poor rate, and the low price of farm products made matters still worse for him in the years following the Napoleonic wars, and at the persuasion of his friend, Morris Birkbeck, and of his eldest son, George Flower [*qq.v.*], he sold "Marden" in 1818 for £23,000 and emigrated, with his wife, three sons, and two daughters, to the United States. The next winter he spent in Lexington, Ky., while George Flower was laying out the village of Albion in southeastern Illinois. A heavy loss to him was the death, that winter, of his second son William. *Letters from Lexington and the Illinois* (London, 1819) and *Letters from the Illinois, 1820, 1821* (London, 1822) were answers to the strictures of William Cobbett [*q.v.*]. In the spring of 1819 he moved to Albion and occupied the "Park House," which his son had built for him. There he entertained visitors from all over the United States and England, regaling them with plum pudding and other English dishes. For some years the house was an object of interest because of its plastered and papered walls, its ornamental stone hearth, and elegant furniture. Flower built a two-story brick tavern and several other buildings, founded what was probably the first library in Illinois, and conducted religious services every Sunday. In the fight to check the introduction of negro slavery he took a prominent part. By his American neighbors he was respected rather than liked, for they distrusted his dignity and the freedom with which he expressed his opinions. In 1824 he returned to England as agent for George Rapp [*q.v.*] and negotiated the sale of the village and lands of Harmony, Ind., to Robert Owen. His youngest son, Edward Fordham Flower [*q.v.* in *Dictionary of National Biography*], went over with him and remained in England. Flower died at Albion on Wednesday, Sept. 2, 1829, after a protracted illness.

[Geo. Flower, *Hist. of the English Settlement in Edwards County, Ill.* (Chicago, 1882); Benj. Flower, *Statement of Facts Relative to the Conduct*, etc. (privately printed, Harlow, England, 1808). For correct date of death see the Vandalia *Ill. Intelligencer*, Sept. 12, 1829 (erroneously dated Sept. 13, on the first page). The Illinois pamphlets have been reprinted by R. G. Thwaites, *Early Western Travels, 1748–1846*, X (Cleveland, 1904), 85–169, and by E. E. Sparks, *The English Settlement in the Illinois* (Cedar Rapids, Iowa, 1907).]

G. H. G.

FLOWER, ROSWELL PETTIBONE (Aug. 7, 1835–May 12, 1899), governor of New York, was born in Theresa, Jefferson County, N. Y. His parents, Nathan Monroe and Mary Ann (Boyle) Flower, were well-to-do Americans of English and Scotch-Irish stock, whose ancestors had been in the country since before 1700. Nathan was a wool carder, cloth manufacturer, and farmer, and died while the son was yet a boy. Roswell passed his youth on a large farm, graduated from high school in 1851, and in early manhood entered business as a jeweler in Watertown, the seat of Jefferson County. During 1854–60 he was assistant postmaster of the town. In 1859 he married Sarah M. Woodruff and thereafter his life was directed into a career of banking and politics. He became administrator of the large estate of one of his wife's relatives, Henry Keep, the president of the New York Central Railroad, who died in 1869. This brought about his removal to New York City, although he always maintained a close connection with Watertown and built a Presbyterian church for his birthplace. In 1873 he was admitted to the New York stock exchange, and later in the year he formed a brokerage partnership with F. C. Benedict. Under varying firm names this business continued for the rest of his life, and in his last years he was regarded as a power on the Street, being connected most prominently with Brooklyn Rapid Transit and Federal Steel. "His word," said one of his associates (Russell Sage), "was worth $1,000,000 at any time" (New York *Evening Post,* May 13, 1899).

Having firm Democratic principles and access to considerable means, Flower was a person of importance in the counsels of the Democrats in New York City. The papers of the opposition made much of his wealth. The *World* alleged that Flower "had a barrel and would take out the bung" (Sept. 17, 1891); and an opponent to his advancement denounced him as a "flamboyant millionaire" (D. S. Alexander, *Four Famous New Yorkers,* 1923, p. 153). He received his first political preferment when in 1881 President Garfield sent Levi P. Morton abroad as minister to France, leaving thereby a vacancy in the eleventh New York congressional district (*New York Herald,* Mar. 22, 1881). The Republicans nominated William Waldorf Astor for the vacancy. Flower was put up by the Democrats and was elected. Before this term was out the *Tribune* suspected that there was a "bee in Mr. Flower's bonnet" (May 6, 1882). The elaborate dinners which he was described as serving in Washington were interpreted as symptomatic of larger ambitions. In the New York Democratic convention of 1883 he is stated to have financed John Kelly of Tammany Hall in a vain fight against Daniel Manning, who managed to remain in control of the party. The next year Tammany quite frankly urged him as a presidential candidate in the hope of heading off the Cleveland movement. He was suggested for the nomination as governor in September 1885, but the convention offered him only the post of lieutenant-governor, which he declined to accept (*New York Herald,* Sept. 27, 1885). In 1888 he was returned to Congress from what was by that time the twelfth New York district. He was reëlected in 1890, during which campaign he was for a while chairman of the Democratic congressional committee.

Tammany was again in control in 1891, after a long period of partial eclipse, and Flower was brought forward and nominated for governor. In the ensuing campaign he was elected over Jacob Sloat Fassett, the choice of Platt and the Republicans, and held office from 1892 to 1895. Before his term ended, there was a Republican uprising in both state and city, and the Democratic leaders discarded Flower as a candidate. He accordingly withdrew his name before the Democratic convention met (New York *World,* Sept. 19, 1894), and, for the most part, devoted the rest of his life to his private affairs. In 1896, however, he was aroused by the nomination of Bryan and took a lead among the New York gold Democrats, whose delegation he headed to Indianapolis. As temporary chairman of the convention there he declared: "This gathering is notice to the world that the Democratic party has not yet surrendered to Populism and Anarchy" (*New York Tribune,* Sept. 3, 1896). He also spoke often in the campaign. He died unexpectedly in 1899, at the Long Island Country Club, where he was in the habit of resorting on Fridays for rest and recreation. He was always a sportsman, and in his youth he was a crack shot.

[The best sketch of Flower's life is in the *N. Y. Herald,* Sept. 17, 1891. See also *Biog. Dir. Am. Cong.* (1928).] F. L. P—n.

FLOY, JAMES (Aug. 20, 1806–Oct. 14, 1863), Methodist Episcopal clergyman, noted in his church as an editor, writer, and hymnologist, was born in New York. His father, Michael, was an emigrant from Devonshire, England, by occupation a practical horticulturist, who in 1802 married in New York, Margaret Ferris, a native of that city. James received a good secondary-school training and entered Columbia College, but his father, deeming a practical education of more value, withdrew him, and sent him to England to study and practise horticulture at the Royal Gardens, London. Upon his return he worked for a time with his father, and in 1829 was married to Jane Thacker. His parents were devoted Methodists, and in 1831 when he himself experienced conversion, he was in the employ of Waugh and Mason, the Book Agents of the denomination. He became teacher in an African Sunday-school, and through the gradations of class leader, exhorter, and local preacher, finally stepped into the ministry, being admitted to the New York Conference on trial in May 1835; ordained deacon in 1837; and elder in 1839.

His ecclesiastical career had an unfortunate opening. Having, presumably, pledged himself to refrain from agitating the church by discussing the slavery question, as required of those made deacons, he aided in the preparation of an anti-slavery tract and attended an anti-slavery convention. Accordingly, at the Conference of 1838, with two others, he was charged with contumacy and insubordination, tried, and suspended. Upon his written promise to conform to rule in the future, however, the suspension was lifted. (See J. M. Buckley, *A History of Methodists in the United States,* 1896, p. 390.) Notwithstanding this event he soon rose to prominence in the Conference, and later, when it was divided, in the New York East Conference. He was appointed to important churches, served as presiding elder of the New York district, and was a member of the General Conferences of 1848, 1856, and 1860, at the latter having the gratification of seeing the *Discipline* put on an anti-slavery basis. It was in the literary field, however, that he became most widely known. Upon his motion the General Conference of 1848 appointed a committee which recommended a revision of the church hymnal. The revised version which appeared in 1849 was largely the work of two laymen, R. A. West and David Creamer [*q.v.*], and Floy, and owed much to the latter's knowledge and taste. The General Conference of 1856 elected him corresponding secretary of the Tract Society and editor of the *National Magazine,* which he ably conducted until lack of financial support caused its discontinuance in 1858. Keenly interested in religious education, he prepared *Graduated Sunday School Textbooks,* three volumes (1861–62). For almost a quarter of a century he was one of the foremost contributors to the *Methodist Quarterly Review.* Some of his articles for this periodical may be found in a posthumous edition of his writings, *Literary Remains of Rev. Dr. Floy: Occasional Sermons and Reviews and Essays* (1866). A companion volume, *Old Testament Characters Delineated and Illustrated,* appeared the same year. Death came to him suddenly from a cerebral hemorrhage at his home in New York. His first wife having died about 1859, he later married Emma Yates, whose death occurred a few weeks before his own.

[The edition of his writings mentioned above contains a memoir. See also *Minutes of the N. Y. East Annual Conference* (1864); Daniel Curry, "James Floy, D.D.," *Meth. Quart. Rev.,* Jan. 1864; addresses in *In Memoriam: Memorial Services of the Rev. James Floy, D.D.* (1864); and obituary in *Christian Advocate* (N. Y.), Oct. 22, 1863.]

H. E. S.

FLOYD, JOHN (Apr. 24, 1783–Aug. 16, 1837), surgeon, governor of Virginia, was of Old Dominion ancestry. William Floyd of Accomac County, Va., settled in Amherst County and married Abadiah Davis, said to be a great-granddaughter of Powhatan. John Floyd, the elder, one of twelve children of William, was married to Jane Buchanan, niece and ward of Col. William Preston. The third and youngest child of this marriage, John Floyd, was born at Floyd Station, Ky., two weeks after his father had been killed by Indians. He learned to read and write at his mother's knee and attended school in the neighboring log school-house till he was thirteen years old, when he entered Dickinson College, Carlisle, Pa. A serious illness prevented his graduation. In May 1804, he married Letitia Preston, daughter of his father's friend, Col. William Preston, and then spent two years in the study of medicine in the University of Pennsylvania, graduating at the end of this time. After a brief practise at Lexington, Va., he removed to Christiansburg, and soon became widely known as a successful physician.

He served as a surgeon with the rank of major in the War of 1812 until he was elected as a nationalist to the General Assembly in 1814. Here he voted for all resolutions giving power to the federal government. In 1817 he was elected to Congress from the "Abingdon District" and was continuously reëlected for twelve years. He supported Clay's proposition for sending a minister to Buenos Aires; favored the immediate recognition of Argentina; defended Andrew Jackson's policy in Florida and opposed his censure; and was one of the four Virginia representatives who voted for the Missouri Compromise. He has been given the credit for first proposing in Congress, Jan. 25, 1821, the occupation and territorial organization of the Oregon country. His identification with the interests of the frontier may be attributed to his boyhood life and to his intimate association with William Clark, with Thomas H. Benton, and with George Rogers Clark, for whom both a brother and a son were named in his family. His Oregon Bill was introduced and defeated several times, and when he retired from Congress in 1829 he was best known as its sponsor. He took an active part in the election of Jackson and was disappointed in not being recognized in the cabinet. From 1829 to 1830 he engaged in the practise of his profession and gave much attention to scientific grazing, in anticipation of the future of his section of the state.

On Jan. 9, 1830, he was elected governor of the state by the legislature, as the choice of the state-rights element, and in 1831 was reëlected for a three-year term. Without committing himself on the question of a white or a mixed basis of representation then agitating the state, he accepted heartily the compromise constitution of 1830, and exerted himself to promote the development of transportation facilities for the western part of the state. After the Nat Turner insurrection he was in sympathy with the western members who were working for abolition. Later he accepted the pro-slavery doctrines of Prof. Thomas R. Dew, of the College of William and Mary, and gave himself to the defense of state sovereignty. This resulted in a complicated struggle against Jackson and Ritchie, later against Van Buren, and attempts to unite Clay and Calhoun as leaders of a new party. Floyd himself was supported by South Carolina for the presidency.

Soon after retiring from office in 1834 he suffered a stroke of paralysis and died Aug. 16, 1837. He was the father of nine children, one of whom was John Buchanan Floyd [*q.v.*].

[C. H. Ambler, *The Life and Diary of John Floyd* . . . (1918); N. J. Floyd, *Biog. Geneal. of the Va.-Ky. Floyd Families* (1912), pp. 75–80; *Hist. of Va.* (6 vols., 1924), II, 462–65; sketch by J. E. Walmsley in the *Memorial Volume of Va. Hist. Portraiture* (1930); the Floyd Manuscripts in the Lib. of Cong., and manuscripts in the possession of Robt. M. Hughes of Norfolk, Va., *Richmond Enquirer*, Jan. 12, 1830, Feb. 12, 1831.]

J. E. W.

FLOYD, JOHN BUCHANAN (June 1, 1806–Aug. 26, 1863), governor of Virginia, secretary of war, Confederate general, was the son of Gov. John Floyd [*q.v.*] and Letitia (Preston) Floyd. He was born at Smithfield, the Preston home in Montgomery County, Va. His early life was spent in what was then the frontier of Virginia, and to this circumstance he owed much of his athletic ability and vigorous physique. He was educated under the care of his remarkably intellectual mother and in the well-selected library of his serious-minded father. He was graduated in 1829 from South Carolina College. His record was high and he was a favorite pupil of the famous Dr. Thomas Cooper [*q.v.*]. In 1830 he married his cousin, Sally Buchanan Preston, grand-daughter of Gen. William Campbell, of King's Mountain fame, and sister of William C. Preston [*q.v.*], distinguished orator and senator from South Carolina. He began the practise of law at Wytheville, Va., but was soon led by the Arkansas cotton boom to take up law and cotton-planting on a large scale in that state. He lost forty slaves and had his own constitution shattered by a malignant fever in 1837, and returned to Virginia with an enfeebled frame and a wrecked fortune. He began again the practise of law in Abingdon and met with marked success, being able in a few years to pay off his heavy debts. In 1847 he was elected delegate from his county to the General Assembly and reëlected in the following year. He was a conspicuous leader of the internal improvement party which advocated appropriations for railroads and other public works. While he was still in the House of Burgesses he was elected governor for the three-year term beginning Jan. 1, 1849. In this office he was *ex-officio* chairman of the board of public works of the state; and his messages, reports, and active interest had a marked influence on the industrial fortunes of Virginia. As a representative of the western part of the state he was deeply interested in the constitutional convention of 1850 which first established universal suffrage in Virginia. In politics Floyd was a state-rights Democrat, and after his retirement from the office of governor in 1852, while practising law at Abingdon he was presidential elector of the Democratic party. When the Know-Nothing party seemed likely to carry the state in 1855, he again became a candidate for the General Assembly in opposition to this party and was elected, and thus contributed largely to win back many of the Virginia Whigs from their new allegiance. This was the hardest fought campaign in Virginia previous to the struggle over secession, and Floyd's services were recognized in his selection the next year to deliver a key-note speech for Buchanan in New York at the Merchant's Exchange, Oct. 2, 1856. Though believing in the state-rights policies of Jefferson and Madison, he was a strong opponent of secession until after his retirement from Buchanan's cabinet. As late as Dec. 3, 1860, he wrote a letter to the *Richmond Enquirer* strongly advising against secession.

Floyd was appointed secretary of war by President Buchanan and their relations throughout 1859 were unusually cordial, as shown by their personal correspondence, but several important incidents giving rise to controversy occurred during 1860. One was the appointment of a quartermaster-general. Floyd urged Joseph E. Johnston for the place, while Jefferson Davis favored Albert Sidney Johnston. Floyd's recommendation was adopted, and to this many attribute the animosity of Davis subsequently shown to both Johnston and Floyd. Another incident was the reported sending of arms to the Southern states in excess of their requirements and with a view to approaching war. On Feb. 18, 1861, the military committee of the House of Representatives, of which Benjamin Stanton of Ohio was chairman, reported the facts as they appeared in the records of the Department. The War Department was making the difficult transition from flint-lock muskets to percussion. It appeared that Secretary Floyd, acting in pursuance of the law of Mar. 3, 1825, had sold 31,610 of these flint-lock muskets altered to percussion. Then, failing to consummate a sale of 250,000 others, he transferred in the spring of 1860, 40,000 of these, together with 65,000 percussion muskets and 10,000 rifles, from Northern to Southern arsenals. It is probable that the transfer was designed to make room for newer arms in Northern arsenals. The committee refrained from any comment on the Secretary's action; but the chairman is said to have expressed the opinion (quoted by Jeremiah S. Black, in a letter to Henry Wilson; see Black's *Essays and Speeches,* 1885, pp. 266 ff.), that the charges against Floyd were founded in "rumor, speculation and misapprehension."

The most exciting and controverted incident, however, was Major Anderson's occupation of Fort Sumter and Floyd's resignation. After South Carolina seceded, Dec. 20, 1860, and in fact for some time previous, Anderson's position in Charleston Harbor was much discussed in cabinet. Cass and Black favored reinforcing him; Floyd and Thompson opposed this course on the ground that it would precipitate a collision. On President Buchanan's refusal to order Anderson back to Fort Moultrie, Floyd resigned Dec. 29, and Buchanan accepted his resignation two days later in a friendly letter which expressed appreciation of his willingness to serve until a successor had been selected. In *Mr. Buchanan's Administration on the Eve of the Rebellion* (p. 186) published in 1866, after Floyd's death, Buchanan states that he had requested his resignation on Dec. 23, on account of an apparent defalcation of $870,000 of Indian trust bonds in the interior department, for which acceptances given by Floyd in the War Department to army contractors had been substituted. Yet on Dec. 25 Buchanan referred to Floyd a protest from Pittsburgh citizens against sending heavy cannon to Southern states, signing his letter "Your friend, very respectfully" (*Official Records, Army,* 3 ser. I, 15. Original in possession of Robert M. Hughes, Norfolk, Va.); and Floyd attended cabinet meetings through the 27th of December. On Feb. 12, 1861, a select committee of the House to which was referred "the fraudulent abstraction" of Indian trust funds in the Department of the Interior, made a unanimous report, which, while not holding Floyd responsible in this matter, declared the issue of acceptances "unauthorized by law and deceptive and fraudulent in character" and irreconcilable "with purity of private motives and faithfulness to public trusts" (*House Report No. 78,* 36 Cong., 2 Sess., pp. 19–20). In the opinion of Jeremiah Black, Floyd was not guilty "of anything worse than reckless imprudence" (*Essays and Speeches,* p. 13), and "had no connection whatever in thought, word, or deed, with the abstraction of the Indian trust funds from the Interior Department." Certainly he did not himself profit by the transactions with the army contractors. In 1868 the Supreme Court by a divided bench held the issue of acceptances in violation of the law and of the limitations which it imposed on all officers of the government (*The Floyd Acceptances, 7 Wallace,* 666).

After Virginia seceded he raised a brigade of volunteers and entered the Confederate military service. His brigade was part of Lee's army in West Virginia and was engaged in the small battles of Cross Lanes and Carnifex Ferry; and he was congratulated by President Davis and Secretary Benjamin for his action. Later he was ordered to reinforce Albert Sidney Johnston and was sent by him to Fort Donelson. Before the surrender of that fort he withdrew with his brigade, pursuant to an agreement with Gen. Buckner, to whom he turned over the command. President Davis then removed him from command without a court of inquiry, for failing to ask for reinforcements, for not evacuating sooner, and for abandoning command to Buckner and escaping with his own troops (*Official Records, Army,* 1 ser. VII, 254). Two months later he was made a major-general by the General Assembly of Virginia, but his health broke down from exposure on Big Sandy River, and on Aug. 26, 1863, he died at his adopted daughter's country house near Abingdon.

[A short account of Floyd written by Robert W. Hughes may be found in E. A. Pollard, *Lee and his Lieutenants* (1867), pp. 783–807; another, by John W. Johnston, in *John P. Branch Hist. Papers of Randolph-Macon Coll.,* June 1913, pp. 78–103; and still another in N. J. Floyd, *Biog. Geneal. of the Va.-Ky. Floyd Families* (1912), 81–92. Floyd's administrative career is discussed unfavorably by J. F. Rhodes, *Hist. of the U. S.,* III (1895), 236–41; an opposite view is expressed in B. W. Duke, *Hist. of Morgan's Cavalry* (1867), pp. 115–18. Numerous local references indicate a high opinion in Virginia of Floyd's business ability. For the Sumter crisis, see S. W. Crawford, *The Genesis of the Civil War* (1887). The resignation from the cabinet is discussed by Rhodes (*op. cit.*), who bases his opinion of Floyd's "treachery" chiefly on his Richmond speech of Jan. 11, 1861; but the report in the *N. Y. Herald,* Jan. 17, does not sustain this view. See also an article by Robert M. Hughes in *Harper's Weekly,* May 11, 1912; reprinted in *Tyler's Quar. Hist. and Geneal. Mag.,* Jan. 1921. On military events, besides the *Official Records (Army),* 1 ser., vols. V, VII, see *Battles and Leaders of the Civil War* (1887), I, 126–48, 398–428. These latter accounts should be supplemented by W. P. Johnston, *The Life of Gen. Albert Sidney Johnston* (1878), pp. 433–76, 495–500.]

J. E. W.

FLOYD, WILLIAM (Dec. 17, 1734–Aug. 4, 1821), signer of the Declaration of Independence, congressman, was born at Brookhaven, Long Island, the eldest son of Nicoll and Tabitha (Smith) Floyd, and the great-grandson of Richard Floyd who emigrated from Wales in the seventeenth century and settled on Long Island. Though coming from a wealthy family, he had only a limited academic education, and at eighteen, upon the death of his father, he assumed the rôle of landed proprietor. His important family connections and his bounteous hospitality soon won for him an important place in the civic and military affairs of his community. He was made an officer in the militia of Suffolk County and rose to the rank of major-general. At the outbreak of the War for Independence, he waived personal considerations and aligned himself with the patriotic cause. He served in the Continental Congress from 1774 to 1777 and from 1778 to 1783 (Force, *post,* 4 ser. I, 324). Since his participation was neither aggressive nor brilliant, he played a subsidiary rôle in the New York delegation. Edward Rutledge, writing to John Jay in 1776, placed him in the category of those members who "tho' good men, never quit their chairs" (Bancroft, *post,* I, 105). On the other hand, Floyd was an excellent committeeman, serving on the committee on clothing in 1776, and on the boards of admiralty and the treasury in 1779. His independence of judgment and his sane view-point won him the respect of his colleagues. He and his family suffered severe hardships because of his adherence to the cause of the Revolutionists. When the British made their first descent on Long Island, he headed a body of militia and drove them off; but in 1776 the invading army took possession of his property, and his family was forced to seek refuge in Connecticut. His few absences from Congress were due to his anxiety over his estate, which by the end of the war had been reduced to ruin.

Floyd's career in the Continental Congress was followed by a notable term of service in the Senate of his state, in which he lent his weight to the adoption of a conservative and stable financial policy (Waln, *post,* p. 142). He served an uneventful term in the First Congress, 1789–91, and was an unsuccessful candidate for reëlection to the Second. In 1795 he was a candidate for lieutenant-governor as the opponent of Stephen Van Rensselaer. Though well advanced in years, he continued to serve in a number of official capacities, acting as presidential elector in 1792, 1800, 1804, and as late as 1820, as delegate to the state constitutional convention in 1801, and once more as state senator in 1808. In 1784 he had purchased a tract of land on the headwaters of the Mohawk in what is now Oneida County. As time went on he came to devote more and more attention to the cultivation of this tract, finally removing there in 1803, to assume a pioneer life at the advanced age of sixty-nine. Here he enjoyed uninterrupted health until a short time before his death which occurred at Westernville, N. Y. He was married twice: first to Isabella Jones of Southampton, and second, to Joanna Strong of Setauket. Neither by mentality nor temperament could Floyd lay claim to unusual distinction. He was essentially a practical man whose plans were carried out methodically. Despite his frank and independent manner, and a decorous deportment which discouraged intimacy, he secured constant proofs of popular favor.

[B. F. Thompson, *Hist. of Long Island,* IV (1918), 167–77; John Sanderson and Robert Waln, Jr., eds., *Biog. of the Signers to the Declaration of Independence,* IV (1823), 129–50; *Biog. Dir. Am. Cong.,* 1774–1927; manuscript letters among the Revolutionary Papers of the Bancroft Collection in the N. Y. Pub. Library, and extracts in E. C. Burnett, *Letters of Members of the Continental Cong.* (4 vols., 1921–28); and in Peter Force, *Am. Archives* (9 vols., 1837–53).] R. B. M.

FLÜGEL, EWALD (Aug. 4, 1863–Nov. 14, 1914), philologist, was born in Leipzig, the third son of Karl Alfred Felix and Pauline (Mencken) Flügel. His grandfather, Johann Gottfried Flügel (1788–1855), acquired a thorough knowledge of English during his *Wanderjahre* 1810–19 in America. Home again in Leipzig, he was American consul, representative for northern Europe of the Smithsonian Institution, and author of a *Complete Dictionary of the English and German . . . Languages* (1830). Karl Alfred Felix Flügel (1820–1904) inherited his father's consular, Smithsonian, and lexical activities. He revised the dictionary as a *Practical Dictionary of the English and German Languages* (2 vols., 1847) and, after it had gone through fifteen editions, replaced it with a *Universal English-German and German-English Dictionary* (1891; 1894) in three large volumes. One of Ewald's earliest tasks was to copy slips for this work. Strangely enough, he found it difficult to master English, although in later life he spoke the language with idiomatic vigor and with scarcely a trace of his German origin. He attended the Nikolaischule in Leipzig, studied at the universities of Freiburg and of his native city, and received the doctorate in 1885 for a dissertation on *Thomas Carlyles Religiöse und Sittliche Entwicklung und Weltanschauung* (1887), of which an English translation by Jessica Gilbert Tyler was published in 1891. During these years he was strongly influenced by Rudolf Hildebrand, whose contributions to the Grimm *Wörterbuch* served as models for

Flügel's life-work. In 1888 he married Helene Burckhardt of Magdeburg and became *privat-docent* at the University of Leipzig. In 1889 he and Gustav Schirmer assumed the editorship of *Anglia.* Flügel himself founded the *Beiblatt zur Anglia.* In 1892, against the advice of Moses Coit Tyler and other American friends, he accepted the professorship of English philology in Leland Stanford, Junior, University. Disappointment at the slowness of promotion in Germany, strong American sympathies, and perhaps also a certain restlessness, effected the decision, which was in some ways rash. Of his various publications the most important were an edition of Sir Philip Sidney's *Astrophel and Stella* and *Defence of Poesie* (1 vol., 1889) and "Die Nordamerikanische Literatur" (1907), which was published in R. P. Wülker's *Geschichte der Englischen Literatur* (II, 413–541). Neither these nor any of his other studies was more than a respite from the great task to which with increasing devotion he dedicated his life. This was a Chaucer dictionary, or rather an historical dictionary of the Chaucerian vocabulary, which he undertook at the instigation of Frederick James Furnivall and which had been originally projected as a cooperative enterprise. As Flügel planned it, it would have filled five or six massive volumes and have set a new standard of lexicographical achievement in a limited field. "No mere description can do justice to the dignity and amplitude of this work of scholarship, if it could have been completed and published." [Tatlock and Kennedy, *post,* p. xii.] Flügel expected to finish the work in 1921. He was able to devote three days a week to it—days that began at 5:00 A. M. and closed late in the evening—and through the support of the Carnegie Institution of Washington he had the years 1904–07 entirely free for the lexicon, which, in Carlylean fashion, he alternately called his *Schmerzenskind* and his daily delight. But in Germany, in 1906, he suffered a sunstroke that for a while threatened his life, and heart disease developed soon thereafter. Concealing his condition from everyone except his son Felix, he worked on, hoping to complete the manuscript before the final attack. Repeated entreaties to publish the dictionary in parts were parried, for he knew that time spent on the proofs would be irreparably lost for the manuscript. He died three months after the outbreak of the European War of 1914–18 with his dictionary complete, subject to additions and revision, as far as "hewe." Friends in Europe and America mourned a great scholar and an admirable man. His library of 14,000 volumes now belongs to Stanford University. In 1925 the Flügel family transferred the manuscript of the lexicon and the collection of materials to the Middle English dictionary being edited at Cornell University.

[*Flügel Memorial Volume* (1916); *Addresses in Commemoration of Ewald Flügel* (privately printed, London, 1925); *Ewald Flügel, eine Darstellung seines Lebens und Wirkens* (*Germanische Studien,* XLI, Berlin, 1926)—with bibliographies; R. M. Alden, letter in the *Nation,* Jan. 7, 1915; E. Einenkel, "Ewald Flügel," *Anglia,* XXXIX (1915); *Who's Who in America,* 1914–15; J. S. P. Tatlock and A. G. Kennedy, *Concordance to the Complete Works of Geoffrey Chaucer* (1927), pp. x–xii; *Moses Coit Tyler* (1911), ed. by Jessica Tyler Austen; W. D. Briggs in *Stanford Alumnus,* Nov. 1914; for specimen pages of the Chaucer dictionary see *Anglia,* vols. XXXIV (1911) and XXXVII (1913) and Ewald Flügel, "Benedicitee," in *Matzke Memorial Volume* (1911).]

G. H. G.

FOGG, GEORGE GILMAN (May 26, 1813–Oct. 5, 1881), lawyer, editor, diplomat, the son of David and Hannah Gilman (Vickery) Fogg was born at Meredith Center, N. H. He attended New Hampton Academy, graduated from Dartmouth College in 1839, studied law at Harvard and in the office of Judge Warren Lovell in Meredith Village, and began practise at Gilmanton Iron Works in 1842. After four years he moved to Concord and maintained a residence there for the rest of his life. He never married. He was active in politics, being a pioneer in the Free-Soil movement, and in 1846 was chosen secretary of state for a term of one year. A few years later he took an active part in the organization of the Republican party. He was the founder of the *Independent Democrat* of Concord and from 1846 to 1861 devoted himself largely to journalism. Under his direction the paper became one of the most influential in the state, and his editorial utterances were widely quoted throughout New England. From 1855 to 1859 he was state law reporter and for some years state printer as well. As a delegate to the Republican Convention of 1860, he was a strong supporter of Lincoln and in 1861 was appointed minister to Switzerland, holding the post until Oct. 16, 1865. Switzerland offered few of the problems found at London or Paris where belligerent rights, neutral duties, and the ever present possibility of intervention required so much diplomatic activity. In July 1861, he reported that, "here . . . the rebels have no friends," and on the close of the war, that Lee's surrender caused almost as much rejoicing as though it had been a Swiss victory. The dispatches published in *Papers Relating to Foreign Affairs* show that his work was largely of routine character, but performed to the satisfaction of both countries. In 1864 he represented the United States at the Geneva conference on the amelioration of conditions for the sick and wounded in time of war.

In 1866–67 Fogg served out the unexpired term of Daniel Clark in the United States Senate. He resumed editorial work but was now on bad terms with several of his party leaders, due, in part at least, to his failure to secure another diplomatic post. Although he continued to be active in both journalism and party management for some years longer, his influence seems to have declined. He was interested in the New Hampshire Historical Society and many local organizations in Concord, and was a trustee of Bates College. For several years prior to his death he was broken in health and able to do little work. He was one of the ablest journalists in the history of the state, and it was as a newspaper editor that he made his chief contribution to political history.

[C. H. Bell, *The Bench and Bar of N. H.* (1894); J. O. Lyford, *Hist. of Concord, N. H.* (1903); J. O. Lyford, *Life of Edward H. Rollins* (1906); *Concord Daily Monitor*, Oct. 6, 1881; the *People and N. H. Patriot* (Concord), Oct. 13, 1881.] W. A. R.

FOLGER, CHARLES JAMES (Apr. 16, 1818–Sept. 4, 1884), jurist, secretary of the treasury, son of Thomas Folger, was born on the island of Nantucket, from which, at the age of twelve, he removed with his parents to Geneva, N. Y. His ancestors for generations had been New England whalers, tracing their origin to John Folger who came over from Norfolk, England, in 1635. Folger attended Geneva (now Hobart) College, from which he was graduated with the highest honors of his class in 1836. He took up the study of law at Canandaigua, was admitted to the bar in Albany in 1839, and started practise in Lyons, Wayne County. After a year he returned to Geneva where he maintained his home throughout the remainder of his life. On June 17, 1844, he married Susan Rebecca Worth.

Folger assumed his first important public office at the age of twenty-six, when, in 1844, he was appointed judge of the court of common pleas of Ontario County, and soon after was made master and examiner in chancery. From 1851 to 1855 he served as county judge. While originally a Democrat, Folger passed into the Republican fold over the Free-Soil bridge in 1854. In 1861 he was elected to the state Senate and was reëlected three times, serving until 1869, and acting for four years as president *pro tempore*, and, throughout the period, as chairman of the judiciary committee. In the latter capacity he was noted for his conservative course and his stanch resistance to any modification of the law of marriage and divorce (*Geneva Courier*, Sept. 10, 1884), and to important reforms in criminal procedure (*Autobiography of Andrew Dickson White*, I, 137). Throughout these years Folger was one of the keenest critics of unsound legislation. "Whenever a bill was read a third time he watched it as a cat watches a mouse," wrote a contemporary (*Ibid.*, p. 101). He consistently opposed the "accursed mildew of town bonding" (*Geneva Courier*, Sept. 10, 1884), and was an uncompromising foe to stock-jobbers. He attracted special attention during these years by his hostility to Gov. Reuben E. Fenton of his own party and by his prominence in the legislative contest of 1868 between Vanderbilt and the New York Central and Gould and the Erie.

His most valued service to his state was rendered in the field of constitutional reform and interpretation. In the state convention of 1867 he was chairman of the judiciary committee, and to his efforts are attributed material changes in the judicial system. He was the foremost public sponsor of the proposed constitution, which was rejected by the people in 1869. He was elected an associate judge of the state court of appeals in 1870. The fact that he had been the choice of both the Republican and Democratic tickets in that election led to charges of a corrupt Tammany alliance (*N. Y. Times*, May 17, 18, 1870). On the death of Chief Justice Church in 1880, Folger was designated by Gov. Cornell to fill the unexpired term of that office. In November of that year he was reëlected to the bench of the court of appeals, which he left shortly to take up his duties in the cabinet of President Arthur. In his term on the bench Folger rendered frequent opinions which revealed a valuable grasp of questions of constitutional law (see, for example, *People ex rel. Lee* vs. *Chautauqua County*, 43 *N. Y.*, 10; *People* vs. *Bull*, 46 *N. Y.*, 57).

During this later period of his life Folger assumed a more active rôle in national politics. He was a prominent candidate for the United States senatorial nomination in 1867, but finally withdrew in favor of Conkling. In the following year he was active at the Republican National Convention at Chicago in demonstrating to other state delegations that New York was not solid for Reuben E. Fenton for Vice-President (*N. Y. Times*, May 20, 1868). In 1869 he resigned from the state Senate to accept an appointment from President Grant as United States assistant treasurer in New York City, in which capacity he served for one year. Although he first refused the office of attorney-general in Garfield's cabinet, he finally accepted the treasury portfolio under President Arthur in 1881. Under his administration the public debt was reduced over $300,000,000, the largest reduction which had ever been effected up to his time.

During his administration offices in the Treasury Department were put in the classified service under Civil Service rules. His correspondence with James B. Butler, chief of the appointment division of the Treasury Department, reveals that even before these reforms, Folger attempted to maintain a high standard of personnel.

In 1882, through the joint efforts of President Arthur and Conkling, Folger was given the Republican nomination for governor, despite the stiff fight which Gov. Cornell made for renomination in an administration-packed convention (*N. Y. Times,* Sept. 22, 23, 1882; *Harper's Weekly,* Sept. 30, Oct. 21, 1882). His Democratic opponent was Grover Cleveland, who polled almost 200,000 votes more than Folger, the largest majority which had ever been scored in a contested election. Folger was a man of distinguished personal appearance, gentle in bearing, modest and even diffident, but withal an impressive speaker and conscientious in the execution of his public duties. His correspondence discloses the saving grace of a rich sense of humor.

[Outlines of Folger's career may be found in S. R. Harlow and S. C. Hutchins, *Life Sketches of the State Officers, Senators, and Members of the Assembly of the State of N. Y. in 1868,* pp. 81–84; and in Chas. Andrews, *An Address Commemorative of the Life of the Late Hon. Chas. J. Folger* (1885). See also Homer A. Stebbins, *A Pol. Hist. of the State of N. Y., 1865–69* (1913); Chas. Z. Lincoln, *The Constitutional Hist. of N. Y.,* 5 vols. (1906); and DeA. S. Alexander, *A Pol. Hist. of the State of N. Y.,* vol. III (1909). The N. Y. Pub. Lib. has a collection of the unofficial correspondence of Secretary Folger with James B. Butler, 1881–84. Obituaries in *N. Y. Tribune, N. Y. Times,* and N. Y. *Evening Post,* Sept. 5, 1884; and *Geneva Courier,* Sept. 10, 1884.]

R. B. M.

FOLGER, HENRY CLAY (June 18, 1857–June 11, 1930), lawyer, capitalist, philanthropist, collector of Shakespeariana, was born in New York, the eldest of the eight children of Henry Clay and Eliza Jane (Clark) Folger, and tenth in descent from Peter Folger [*q.v.*]. His father was a dealer in wholesale millinery and later an official in two meter companies. After preparing at Adelphi Academy in Brooklyn, Folger entered Amherst College, where, though obliged to earn part of his expenses, he carried off prizes in English composition and oratory and was elected to Phi Beta Kappa. Through Charles Millard Pratt, his friend since boyhood and his room-mate at Amherst, he secured a clerkship in the firm of Charles Pratt & Company, oil refiners, already a part of the Standard group, and began work July 1, 1879, a few days after his graduation. That autumn, without giving up his position, he began the study of law at Columbia and received his LL.B. degree *cum laude* and was admitted to the New York bar in 1881. On Oct. 6, 1885, he married Emily Clara, daughter of Edward Jordan of Elizabeth, N. J. For a number of years they resided in Elizabeth, later moving to Brooklyn and establishing their summer home at Glen Cove, L. I. Folger's career in the Standard Oil Company covered almost half a century. After serving as officer or director of various subsidiaries, he was advanced Dec. 4, 1911, to the presidency of the Standard Oil Company of New York, resigned Mar. 31, 1923, to assume the chairmanship of the board, and retired five years later to devote all his time to the completion of his Shakespeare Memorial.

Folger had been deeply influenced by the writings of Emerson, and through Emerson, especially through the "Remarks at the Celebration of the Three Hundredth Anniversary of the Birth of Shakespeare," which he read while at Amherst, he learned to revere Shakespeare as the first of poets. A few years later the study of J. O. Halliwell-Phillipps's reduced facsimile of the First Folio acquainted him with the problems of Shakespearian bibliography and criticism and set him to buying Shakespeariana with an ardor and intelligence probably unparalleled in the history of book collecting. In Mrs. Folger, a graduate and master of arts of Vassar College, he had an enthusiastic and highly competent associate, and as their collection grew they discovered that it was in their power to gather a unique Shakespearian library. Folger enjoyed his collection for its own sake, enjoyed the triumphs and hazards of the quest, and, most of all, enjoyed in anticipation the eventual use that he planned to make of his treasures. Since publicity would have been ruinous to his project, he acquired his books as silently as possible and held them rather privately; in the world of Shakespearian scholars the Folger collection was as an invisible planet whose magnitude could be conjectured only by the irresistible force with which it attracted lesser bodies to it. Pending the completion of his plans, he was compelled to store his books in several vaults in New York and Brooklyn and never saw his library assembled. In England, where its extent was more fully known than in the United States, pressure was put on him to give the collection a permanent home at Stratford-on-Avon, but his ambition, as he wrote in a letter of Jan. 19, 1928, was "to help make the United States a center for literary study and progress." Early in 1928 he announced, very briefly and quietly, that he would erect a library in Washington for the promotion and diffusion of knowledge in regard to the history and writings of Shakespeare. The announcement conveyed no intimation of the fact that this was the most munificent gift ever made for the study of literature. The square on East Capitol Street immediately behind the Library of Congress had already been secured as the site, and the collection, the finest in existence, numbered over 70,000 volumes, together with pamphlets, documents, manuscripts, playbills, oil-paintings, water-colors, prints, statues, medals, musical scores, costumes, and other objects. It included many rare or unique volumes of Elizabethan plays and poetry and many association books, and was especially rich in Shakepeare Quartos and Folios. Of the less than two hundred known copies of the First Folio, upwards of eighty, including a number of the best, were in the Folger collection.

In Folger himself the masterful qualities of a great executive were ennobled by a rich humanity. In manner he was unassuming, gentle, at times whimsically humorous. He presided over board meetings with captivating wit and urbanity and had a genius for developing the latent powers of his subordinates and for holding their admiration and affection. His architects, Alexander B. Trowbridge and Paul P. Cret, were of the considered opinion that he was also the one perfect client in the history of architecture. The cornerstone of the Memorial was laid May 28, 1930. Two weeks later Folger died in St. John's Hospital, Brooklyn, after an operation. By his will he left his entire residuary estate, with careful instructions for its administration by the Trustees of Amherst College, to complete and maintain the Folger Shakespeare Memorial.

[J. F. Jameson, *Hist. of the Class of 1879 in Amherst Coll., 1879–1929* (1882–1929); *Amherst Coll. Biog. Record Grads. and Non-Grads.* (1927); *Who's Who in America*, 1928–29; information from Mrs. Henry Clay Folger and from Frederick Wm. Ashley, J. Franklin Jameson, Wm. Adams Slade, and Alexander Buel Trowbridge.] G. H. G.

FOLGER, PETER (1617–1690), Nantucket pioneer, was the son of John Folger of Norwich, England, and his wife, Mirriba Gibs. He emigrated to Massachusetts with his parents about 1635 and probably accompanied Thomas Mayhew, Jr., in 1642 from Watertown to Martha's Vineyard. There he was employed as a schoolmaster and surveyor and helped Mayhew in his missionary work among the Indians. Cotton Mather praised him in the *Magnalia* (Hartford, 1853, II, 429–30) as "an able godly Englishman . . . well learned in the Scripture"; Thomas Prince, in his appendix to Experience Mayhew's *Indian Converts* (London, 1727, p. 291), repeated this commendation word for word. In 1644 Folger married Mary Morrils, an indentured servant, whom he had bought for £20 from the Rev. Hugh Peters. The money was wisely spent; and their youngest child, Abiah, born on Nantucket Aug. 15, 1667, became the mother of Benjamin Franklin. In the summer of 1659 Tristram Coffin and his party stopped at the Vineyard on their way to inspect Nantucket Island, which they proposed to buy from Thomas Mayhew. Folger went with them as surveyor and interpreter in their dealings with the sachems. He was on the Island surveying in 1661 and 1662, and was so useful to the new proprietors that on July 4, 1663, they offered him a half-share of land if he would remove there with his family. Teacher, Indian interpreter, weaver, miller, clerk of the town and court, he was an indispensable citizen. Once he did get into bad odor by joining the "insurrection" of the half-share men, an abortive effort of the proletariat to wrest the political control from the original shareholders. Folger's little part in it was construed as contempt of court, and for want of a bond of £20 he was put in the Nantucket jail—"Where never any English-man was put," he wrote to Gov. Edmund Andros, "and where the Neighbors Hogs had layed but the Night before, and in a bitter cold Frost and deep Snow. They had onely thrown out most of the Durt, Hogs, Dung, and Snow. The Rest the Constable told me I might ly upon if I would . . ." (Starbuck, *post*, p. 54). He survived even this indignity, however, and resumed his old place in the community. He joined the Baptist church at Newport, R. I., in 1675 and later immersed a convert or two in Waiptequage Pond. It is on record that at least one of his Indian friends regarded this new aquatic doctrine as heretical. Folger was the author of *A Looking-Glass for the Times, or The Former Spirit of New England Revived in This Generation* (Boston, John Foster, 1676). "It was written in 1675," said his grandson in the *Autobiography*, "in the homespun verse of that time and people, and addressed to those then concerned in the government there. It was in favor of liberty of conscience, and in behalf of the Baptists, Quakers, and other sectaries that had been under persecution, ascribing the Indian wars and other distresses that had befallen the country, to that persecution, as so many judgments of God to punish so heinous an offense, and exhorting a repeal of those uncharitable laws. The whole appeared to me as written with a good deal of decent plainness and manly freedom." The piece consists of four octosyllabic couplets followed by one hundred and five ballad quatrains. It is a good pamphlet, with decent plainness and manly freedom in abundance, but with no poetry. Folger's courage in publishing it has been slightly overestimated, for at that time Nantucket belonged to the province of New York. As long as he stayed on his sandy, wind-swept isle, the Massachusetts ministers could not lay hands on him.

[A. Starbuck, *The Hist. of Nantucket* (1924); *New-Eng. Hist. and Geneal. Reg.*, vols. VII, XII, XVI; F. B. Hough, *Papers Relating to the Island of Nantucket* (1856); J. W. Jordan, "Franklin as a Genealogist," *Pa. Mag. of Hist. and Biog.*, XXIII (Apr. 1899), 1–22. The *Looking-Glass* is accessible in *R. I. Hist. Tracts No. 16* (Providence, 1883) and in E. A. and G. L. Duyckinck, *Cyc. Am. Lit.* (3rd ed., 1875).] G.H.G.

FOLGER, WALTER (June 12, 1765–Sept. 8, 1849), lawyer, scientist, traced his descent from John Folger who, coming from Norwich, England, in 1635, settled at Watertown, Mass., but moved to Martha's Vineyard in 1642, accompanied by his son, Peter [*q.v.*]. In 1661 the latter went to Nantucket for the purpose of surveying land and ultimately made his permanent home there. Walter Folger of the fourth generation from him, a resident of Nantucket, married Elizabeth, daughter of Thomas Starbuck, and their son Walter was born on the Island, which continued to be his domicile during the whole of his long life. Attending only the elementary schools, he "never went to any institution of learning where anything above the alphabet, spelling, reading in the Bible and surveying were taught" (Lydia E. Hinchman, *post*). On leaving school he settled down to a course of self-tuition, which was as remarkable for its range as for the results achieved. He taught himself the higher branches of mathematics, mastered the principles and practise of mechanics, and though never apprenticed to any craftsman became an expert watch-maker and clock-maker, at which business he made a living for a number of years. On Dec. 29, 1785, he married Anna Ray. In 1788, at the age of twenty-three, he commenced work on the construction of a clock, incorporating features such as had never been attempted prior to that time. Devoting merely his spare time to the task, he completed the undertaking in less than two years, and in 1790 exhibited in perfect working order what has since been known as "Folger's astronomic clock." In addition to the usual functions of marking the passage of time, it designated the year and day of the month. The rising and setting of the sun and moon and their exact paths were indicated by balls which moved in exact astronomic time each day and night, and the chief phenomena resulting from the obliquity of the moon's path to the ecliptic were also displayed. Other extraordinary features exhibited the mechanical genius and delicate workmanship of the designer (*Collections of the Massachusetts Historical Society*, 2 ser., III, 1815). On the completion of this remarkable object he turned to other fields, studying in the first place medicine and science. In the meanwhile he "acted as surveyor of land, repaired watches, clocks and chronometers, made compasses, engraved on copper and other metals, made chemical and other scientific discoveries, calculated eclipses and understood and spoke the French language." Among his discoveries was the process of annealing wire. He made contributions, chiefly mathematical, to scientific periodicals, wrote *A Topographical Description of Nantucket* (dated May 21, 1791, and printed in *Collections of the Massachusetts Historical Society*, vol. III, 1794) and published an almanac in 1790 and 1791.

He then turned his attention to the law, studying by himself as was his wont; was admitted as a counselor-at-law in 1807, and practised for about twenty years. In 1808 he was elected representative of Nantucket in the Massachusetts General Court, becoming in 1809 state senator, which position he held for five years. On the outbreak of the War of 1812 he established a cotton- and woolen-mill on Nantucket and with his family operated it with complete success. In 1816 he was elected representative from the Nantucket district of Massachusetts to the Fifteenth Congress as a Democrat, and, being reëlected served from Mar. 4, 1817, to Mar. 3, 1821. In 1822 he again became state senator for one term. In his law practise he was as successful as in other spheres, becoming in 1828 a judge of the court of common pleas and the court of sessions in Nantucket. He remained on the bench for six years, and it is a striking tribute to his judicial qualities that no appeal was ever taken from any of his decisions. At the time of his death he was engaged upon the compilation of a genealogy of the Nantucket families. He was buried in the Friends Burying Ground.

[Wm. G. Folger, *Memoir of the Late Walter Folger* (1874), reprinted from the Nantucket *Inquirer*, Sept. 21, 1849, and "The Folger Family," in *New-Eng. Hist. and Geneal. Reg.*, July 1862; L. C. Hinchman, *Early Settlers of Nantucket* (2nd ed., 1901); *Proc. of the Nantucket Hist. Asso.* (1920); A. Starbuck, *The Hist. of Nantucket* (1924).] H.W.H.K.

FOLK, JOSEPH WINGATE (Oct. 28, 1869–May 28, 1923), lawyer, prosecutor, governor, was the son of Henry B. Folk, a leading lawyer in Brownsville, Tenn., and Martha Estes, of a pioneer Virginia family. He was educated in the public schools and in the School of Law of Vanderbilt University, graduating in 1890. For four years he practised law in Brownsville with his father before removing to St. Louis, where he entered the lucrative field of corporation law but devoted considerable attention to politics. By tradition a Democrat, Folk soon became active in the Jefferson Club, a local but powerful organization of young Democrats. He held important positions in this body during the campaigns of 1896 and of 1898, and became well-known in party circles. In 1900, he was asked by a committee of Democrats to accept the nomination for circuit attorney, the chief law-enforcing officer of St. Louis. He reluctantly agreed and became the accidental beneficiary of a unique combination, in that his candidacy was supported by the Democratic boss and machine, who believed him to be "safe," and by the reform element. He was elected by a scant plurality.

In 1901–02, he instituted an investigation which led to a series of sensational exposures of the actual government of St. Louis and of the alliance between corrupt business and corrupt politics. Acting quickly on vague and accidental information, Folk secured definite proof of bribery of members of the municipal assembly in the passage of a street-railway franchise, and brought to indictment for bribery and for perjury seven of the principals. He then pressed forward, despite bitter political and financial opposition, to the exposure of three other notorious public utility franchise deals and to the demonstration of civic corruption and the open exploitation of the city by a sinister, bipartisan combination. Thirty-nine indictments, twenty-four for bribery and thirteen for perjury, were secured, including twenty-one members of the municipal assembly, the city boss, Edward Butler, that indispensable negotiator between politics and business, and several of the leading men of wealth. Twelve were sent to the penitentiary, others turned state's evidence or became fugitives from justice (*American State Trials,* vol. IX). He also assisted materially in the investigations of alleged bribery and graft in the Missouri legislature and among certain state administrative officials, with results that shocked the public conscience and made clear the cynical corruption in the process of government. There was about Folk a persistence and rigid honesty, combined with a calm relentlessness, which brought to this quiet, smiling, even-tempered man of thirty-three the support of the better elements of all parties and the bitter and undying opposition of all organization politicians. In 1903, he became an active candidate for governor. Most of the party leaders and committeemen in the cities were hostile and used questionable methods to defeat him, but his supporters in the rural counties were well organized and successful (*St. Louis Globe-Democrat,* March 1904). Through their majority of the credentials committee the Folk forces were able to control the convention; he was nominated on the first ballot, and many of his ideas were written into the platform. The election results were significant: Roosevelt carried the state for president by 25,000; Folk, for governor by 30,000, while every other state officer elected was a Republican in a state since 1868 overwhelmingly Democratic (*Official Manual of the State of Missouri,* 1905–06). The new governor proceeded on the Roosevelt idea, that the executive is the steward of the public welfare, and under his leadership, notable advances were made in the enactment and honest enforcement of statutes of a regulatory character, such as anti-lobby, dram-shop control, and public-utility laws, while in the field of social-welfare legislation important laws were enacted. Two devices intimately associated with the progressive era, the direct primary and direct legislation, were written into the constitution and laws of Missouri. Both measures were forced upon a reluctant state Assembly by Folk. He unwisely became a candidate in 1908 for the nomination as United States senator and was defeated by the incumbent, W. J. Stone, a master of political strategy.

In 1910, chiefly to remove him from Missouri politics, he was endorsed for president, but two years later the organization shelved him and supported Champ Clark. In the first Wilson administration, he served as solicitor for the state department, and later in a more congenial position, that of chief counsel for the Interstate Commerce Commission. He secured the nomination for the Senate in 1918, but was defeated in the election by his Republican opponent. In every campaign for elective office he had the relentless and organized opposition of the urban machines and their leaders. Folk's lack of political acumen and his harshness toward politicians were unfortunate. The years from 1918 to 1923 were spent chiefly in Washington in the successful practise of law, and as counsel for Peru and for the Egyptian National Committee. He suffered a nervous breakdown in 1922 and died suddenly at the home of his sister in New York City the following year. His wife, Gertrude Glass, whom he married on Nov. 10, 1896, survived him.

[Lincoln Steffens, *The Shame of the Cities* (1904) and *The Struggle for Self-government* (1906); Claude Wetmore, *The Battle against Bribery* (1904); J. D. Lawson, *American State Trials,* vol. IX (1918); J. L. Blair, "The St. Louis Disclosures," in *Proc. of the Detroit Conf. for Good City Govt. and . . . of the Nat. Municipal League* (1903); W. A. White in *McClure's Mag.* (Dec. 1905); T. S. Barclay, *A Period of Political Uncertainty* (1928); J. C. Jones, memoir of Folk in *Messages and Proclamations of the Governors of the State of Mo.,* IX (1925); *Who's Who in America,* 1922.

23; *N. Y. Times, Evening Star* (Washington, D. C.), and *St. Louis Globe-Democrat,* all of May 29, 1923.]

T. S. B.

FOLLEN, CHARLES (Sept. 4, 1796–Jan. 13, 1840), German liberal refugee, first professor of German literature at Harvard, Abolitionist, Unitarian preacher, was the son of Christoph Follenius, a prominent judge at Giessen, Hesse-Darmstadt. He entered the university of his native town in the spring of 1813, not yet seventeen years old, devoting himself to the study of law and ethics, but soon, at the rising of the German people against Napoleon, joined a company of volunteers. He as well as two of his brothers served throughout the campaign on French soil. After the conclusion of peace in 1814, resuming his studies at Giessen, he eagerly plunged into the progressive student movement —the so-called *Burschenschaftsbewegung.* A commanding personality, a fiery orator, an inspiring writer of verse, he easily rose to leadership among the radical youths of the Giessen *Burschenschaft,* pledged to republican ideals and the overthrow of the old feudal order. Although he was himself absent in 1817 from the great liberal demonstration on the Wartburg, he was one of its chief promoters and organizers. Even after his appointment, in 1818, to a lectureship at the University of Jena, undismayed by official warnings and censures, he carried on what was in effect revolutionary propaganda, and it is not surprising that, when on Mar. 23, 1819, the reactionary writer Kotzebue was assassinated by Karl Sand, a close student friend of Follen's, the latter should have been arrested and tried as an accomplice. No evidence could be found against him, however, and he was acquitted, but since he was dismissed from the university and placed under strict police surveillance, so that all avenues for a useful public career in Germany seemed closed to him, he decided to leave the country and serve the cause of freedom elsewhere. After a brief stay in Paris early in 1820, where he made the acquaintance of Lafayette, he went to Switzerland, and taught Latin and history for a year in the cantonal school of Chur, until in the autumn of 1821 he was called as lecturer on jurisprudence and metaphysics to the newly reorganized University of Basel. Here he spent three active and highly successful years. In 1824, however, the Prussian government, fearful lest his democratic and cosmopolitan teachings should spread in Germany, not only forbade its subjects to attend the University of Basel, but, supported by the other members of the Holy Alliance, demanded Follen's extradition, on the charge of his subverting the foundation of society. Now America seemed the only asylum left. On Nov. 1, 1824, Follen and his friend Karl Beck sailed from Havre for New York.

Follen's American career also was a tragic mixture of high aspirations and deep disappointments. At first his ideals appeared to be realized in the new country. Through George Ticknor, to whom he was introduced by Lafayette, he received an offer from Harvard College of an instructorship in German, which he accepted with the understanding that he should also have an opportunity to give lectures on law. He entered upon this position in December 1825, and in the next few years displayed a most remarkable versatility. In addition to teaching the German language to college classes and lecturing on jurisprudence before select audiences of Boston lawyers, he gave practical lessons in the new art of gymnastics made popular by "Father" Jahn, wrote linguistic text-books, literary readers, theological and philosophical essays, preached occasionally in Unitarian churches and around Boston, and in 1829 even accepted an additional regular instructorship in ethics and history at the Harvard Divinity School. It is no wonder that a man of such parts should have been gladly received by the intellectual and social élite of New England. In September 1828, he married a woman of aristocratic breeding, Eliza Lee Cabot. In March 1830, he acquired American citizenship; in April of the same year, a son was born to him; in August, he was appointed, for a term of five years, professor of German literature at Harvard College.

Even before the appearance, in January 1831, of Garrison's *Liberator,* Follen had boldly spoken out against slavery in his Boston "Lectures on Moral Philosophy" of 1830, but it was Garrison's and Whittier's example which urged him into action against slavery. In 1834, he joined the New England Anti-Slavery Society, and at its first convention held in Boston, well knowing that he thereby risked his own future, he drafted the "Address to the People of the United States." There seems no doubt that this address was the immediate cause of the severance of Follen's connection with Harvard College. When the tenure of his professorship expired in August 1835, it was not renewed, although his striking success as a teacher had widely and emphatically been recognized. From now on all the more eagerly he devoted himself to upholding his ideals of reform and progress in every sphere of life. At a hearing before a committee of the Massachusetts legislature in January 1836, he protested with vigor and dignity against a proposed attempt to inhibit the publication of Abolitionist writings. In an article in the *Quarter-*

ly Anti-Slavery Magazine, October 1836, he laid bare all the various forms of oppression which seemed to him to endanger true democracy in this country, among them the political and legal inferiority of women, the general subserviency to wealth, the sectarianism of the churches, the formalism and conventionality of academic instruction. In the various positions which he filled during the following three years, as private teacher, lecturer, and Unitarian minister, he never ceased to make the training of original and independent individuals his primary object. His last ministry was at East Lexington, Mass. On the return trip from a course of lectures on German literature before the Merchants' Library Association in New York, he perished with nearly all the passengers and crew of the steamer *Lexington,* which caught fire in Long Island Sound, during the night of Jan. 13–14, 1840.

[*The Works of Chas. Follen, with a Memoir of his Life* (5 vols.), the first volume (1842) of which contains the admirable *Life* by Mrs. Eliza Lee Cabot Follen, herself a gifted writer of stories, essays, and verse; Kuno Francke, "Karl Follen and the German Liberal Movement," in *Papers of the Am. Hist. Asso.,* vol. V (1891), pp. 65–81; Geo. W. Spindler, *Karl Follen; a Biographical Study* (1917), a critical monograph, containing an excellent bibliography.] K.F.

FOLLEN, ELIZA LEE CABOT (Aug. 15, 1787–Jan. 26, 1860), author and prominent member of the Massachusetts anti-slavery group, was born in Boston, the fifth of the thirteen children of Samuel and Sarah (Barrett) Cabot. Her father, a descendant of John Cabot who, coming from the island of Jersey in 1700, settled in Salem, Mass., was engaged in foreign commerce. For a number of years during Eliza's girlhood he was in Europe where he served as secretary of the commission to England under the Jay Treaty to settle the American spoliation claims. Her mother, a woman of strong character and notable mental attainments, was the daughter of Samuel and Mary (Clarke) Barrett, the latter a daughter of Richard Clarke [*q.v.*], and sister of Sussannah Farnum Clarke who married John Singleton Copley [*q.v.*]. Eliza received an excellent education, and became a cultivated woman of marked intellectual ability, deeply interested in religious and social problems, and firm and outspoken in her convictions. After the death of her father in 1819, her mother having died ten years earlier, she and two of her sisters established a home of their own. Her family connections brought her into contact with many of the leading people of Boston; she was prominent in literary and religious circles, and numbered among her friends such personages as William Ellery Channing and Henry Ware [*qq.v.*].

She was one of a little group of men and women who established a Sunday-school in connection with the Federal Street Church, and with other members of the group was accustomed to meet once a week in Dr. Channing's study for the discussion of religious questions. When Charles Follen [*q.v.*] came to Boston and had been introduced to Miss Cabot by Catharine M. Sedgwick [*q.v.*], she took him to these gatherings and an intimate friendship between Follen and Channing ensued. Dr. Follen, in fact, nine years younger than Miss Cabot, became her protégé; she suggested to him that he enter the ministry; and encouraged him to think that, though a foreigner, he would succeed. The woman in Germany to whom he was engaged refusing to leave home and friends for America, on Sept. 15, 1828, he and Miss Cabot were married. Thereafter their fortunes were joined until his tragic death a little more than eleven years later. A son, Charles Christopher, was born to them on Apr. 11, 1830. In 1841–42 she published in five volumes *The Works of Charles Follen, with a Memoir of His Life.*

Mrs. Follen's interest in the education of children and her connection with the Sunday-school movement gave direction to her literary activity. For two years beginning in April 1828, she edited the *Christian Teacher's Manual;* and from 1843 to 1850, the *Child's Friend.* Her books for the young were voluminous, some of them passing through numerous editions. *The Well-Spent Hour* (1827) was especially popular. Writing from Liverpool, Mrs. John T. Kirkland remarked in a letter dated Aug. 23, 1830: "Among the literary productions of America which have found their way across the Atlantic is our cousin Follen's Well-Spent Hour and Christian Teacher's Manual. . . . She seems to be considered one of the lights of the New World, associated with Dr. Channing and Mr. Ware" (*Proceedings of the Massachusetts Historical Society,* 2 ser., vol. XIX, 1906). Mrs. Follen also published *Selections from the Writings of Fenelon,* with a memoir of his life (1829); *The Skeptic* (1835); *Sketches of Married Life* (1838); and *Poems* (1839).

In addition to her writing she undertook the work of preparing her son and other boys for Harvard College; and was active in the support of the anti-slavery movement, furnishing numerous tracts and poems, and serving on the executive committee of the American Anti-Slavery Society. She was also a counselor of the Massachusetts Society, and a member of the Boston Female Anti-Slavery Society. Altogether she was for years one of the notable personages of Boston. Every one respected her, but not every one loved her. J. Peter Lesley [*q.v.*]

wrote to his stepmother, June 21, 1847, "We called together on Mrs. Follen, relict of the lamented Dr. Follen who perished in the Lexington, last evening and found her one of those enthusiastic, partisan souls, who can see no faults in friends, nor virtues in enemies" (Mary Lesley Ames, *Life and Letters of Peter and Susan Lesley,* 1903). In general, however, she was spoken of with great reverence. James Russell Lowell, writing of the women who conducted anti-slavery bazaars in Faneuil Hall, characterized her thus:

"And there, too, was Eliza Follen,
Who scatters fruit-creating pollen
Where'er a blossom she can find
Hardy enough for Truth's north wind,
Each several point of all her face
Tremblingly bright with inward grace,
As if all motion gave it light
Like phosphorescent seas at night."

Her death, occasioned by typhoid fever, was coincident with her "annual festival," the meeting of the American Anti-Slavery Society.

[See L. Vernon Briggs, *Hist. and Geneal. of the Cabot Family* (2 vols., 1927); *Ann. Report Am. Anti-Slavery Soc., 1860* (1861); Mary E. Dewey, *Life and Letters of Catharine M. Sedgwick* (1871); Geo. W. Cooke, *Unitarianism in America* (1902); *Liberator,* Jan., Feb., 1860. Mrs. Follen's biography of her husband contains valuable but meager information about herself. Lowell's lines appeared in the *Pennsylvania Freeman,* Dec. 27, 1846, and are reprinted in W. P. and F. J. Garrison, *Wm. Lloyd Garrison,* III (1889), 179.] H. E. S.

FOLLEN, KARL THEODOR CHRISTIAN [See FOLLEN, CHARLES, 1796–1840].

FOLSOM, CHARLES (Dec. 24, 1794–Nov. 8, 1872), librarian, teacher, editor, was born in Exeter, N. H., the son of James Folsom and Sarah Gilman, and a descendant in the seventh generation of John Foulsham of Hingham in Norfolk, who came to America in 1638. He was fitted for college at Phillips Exeter Academy and graduated from Harvard in 1813. After a year's teaching he began the study of theology, but his health failing, he obtained the post of chaplain and instructor in mathematics on the *Washington,* the flag-ship of the Mediterranean Squadron. One of his pupils at this time was David G. Farragut [*q.v.*], who became his lifelong friend. In the autumn of 1817 Folsom was appointed consul *ad interim* at Tunis where he found many ancient remains to interest him, but in 1819 he rejoined the squadron. He became chaplain on the *Columbus* and private secretary to Commodore Bainbridge, with whom he visited the principal Mediterranean ports. Returning to the United States, he began his connection with Harvard College. From 1821 to 1824 he was tutor in Latin, from 1821 to 1826 he taught Italian. and from 1823 to 1826 he was librarian of the Harvard Library. Here his helpful and generous spirit was reflected in the increasing liberality of the library administration. For some fifteen years beginning in 1824 he was employed at the University Press, where he soon became a partner in the concern and corrector of the press. He rendered signal service to the writers of his day by his varied scholarship and diligent attention to detail, and was often called the Cambridge Aldus, but his "passion for exact and minute accuracy" often interfered with his administrative efficiency. In 1826–27 he collaborated with W. C. Bryant in editing the *United States Review and Literary Gazette* (see P. Godwin, *A Biography of William Cullen Bryant,* 1883, II, 213–28). Some years later, with Andrews Norton, he edited the *Select Journal of Foreign Periodical Literature* (4 vols., 1833–34), the earliest publication of its kind, but neither periodical long endured.

From 1841 to 1845 Folsom conducted a school for young ladies in Temple Place, Boston, and in 1846 he became librarian of the Boston Athenæum. His scholarship, good judgment, dignity, and kindliness endeared him to the frequenters of the library. A letter which he wrote to Samuel A. Eliot, Oct. 27, 1845, contains an admirable statement on the management and aims of a public library (Parsons, *post*). In 1853 he took an active part in the New York conference of librarians, the first gathering of the kind held in the United States (*Norton's Literary and Educational Register for 1854,* pp. 49–94). After retiring from the Athenæum in 1856 he spent the remainder of his days in Cambridge, always ready to devote his time and strength in helpful service to his friends, but leaving little from his own pen in print beyond a few contributions to the *Proceedings* of the Massachusetts Historical Society, the American Antiquarian Society, and the American Academy of Arts and Sciences. He was an excellent Latin scholar and his editions of Cicero and Livy, the former edited while he was still in college, were long used as school texts. He was married, Oct. 19, 1824, to Susanna Sarah McKean, daughter of Prof. Joseph McKean, of Cambridge. In March 1869 he suffered an attack of paralysis from which he partly recovered, but a second stroke was fatal.

[The best account of Folsom is the "Memoir of Chas. Folsom" by Theophilus Parsons in the *Proc. Mass. Hist. Soc.,* XIII (1875), 26–42, also printed separately, supplemented by a long letter from John G. Palfrey, *Ibid.,* XII (1873), 308–13, and a shorter notice in the *Proc. Am. Acad. of Arts and Sci.,* IX (1874), 237–38. See also "The Librarians of Harvard Coll.," in the *Lib. of Harvard Univ. Bibliog. Contributions,* no. 52 (1897), 37–38; A. P. Peabody's *Harvard Reminiscences* (1888), pp. 100–04; Boston Athenæum, *The Athenæum Centenary* (1907), p. 104; Jacob Chapman, *A Geneal. of the*

Folsom Family (1882), p. 121; and an article by Nathaniel S. Folsom and Jacob Chapman in the *New-Eng. Hist. and Geneal. Reg.*, Apr. 1876, reprinted separately. The Boston Public Library has several volumes of Folsom's manuscript correspondence, and the Harvard Library has unpublished lectures and addresses, 1841–52, and memoranda of letters from the University Press, 1840–41.] W. C. L.

FOLSOM, GEORGE (May 23, 1802–Mar. 27, 1869), author, antiquarian, was born in Kennebunk, Me., the son of Thomas and Edna (Ela) Folsom. He was descended from John Foulsham who landed at Hingham, Mass., and in 1638, settled in Exeter, N. H. Gen. Nathaniel Folsom, who distinguished himself in the French and Indian War, and was a member of the Continental Congress, was a less remote ancestor. George's father, a tavern-keeper and also a jeweler moved from Kennebunk to Portland in 1809, so that the boy's early education was in the latter city and at Phillips Academy in Exeter. He was graduated from Harvard in 1822, and then started to study law in the office of Judge Ether Shepley at Saco, Me. In leisure moments, however, he showed a predilection for historical research in writing a *History of Saco and Biddeford* (1830). He practised law first in Framingham, and then in Worcester, Mass., where his keener interest turned to the American Antiquarian Society. The second volume of that society's *Transactions and Collections*, published in 1836, was produced under Folsom's direction. In 1837 he made New York City his home and almost immediately identified himself with the New York Historical Society. He became the society's librarian, editing the *Collections* for the year 1841 in which source materials for Dutch New York were emphasized. Folsom is to be remembered, indeed, for his quiet insistence that source materials demand the attention of those who would seek the truth in history. His linguistic ability as well as the breadth of his interest was shown in his production in 1843 of the *Dispatches of Hernando Cortez*, translated from the original Spanish for the first time. Another volume, *Mexico in 1842 . . . to which is added an account of Texas and Yucatan and of the Santa Fé Expedition*, followed, at a time when popular attention was being drawn to Texas and Mexico.

Folsom had political interests also. Though he was at first a Whig, he was elected in 1844 to the New York state Senate as a "Native American," and his friendship with President Taylor brought to him in 1850 an appointment as chargé d'affaires to the Netherlands. Three years in that office were followed by three years of travel before his return to New York, where, for the year 1858–59 he was editor of the *Historical Magazine*. His preface to volume II, modestly subscribed "G. F.," states that he sought no other reward than "the gratification of an old taste." His selection of a summer home in Brattleboro, Vt., identified him with that state as well as New York during the remainder of his life, and accounts for his active interest in the reorganization of the Vermont Historical Society. He was president of the American Ethnological Society in New York from 1859 until his death and was a member of the American Geographical and Statistical Society, the Deaf and Dumb Society, and the Union League Club. He died in Rome where he had gone for his health. In 1839 he married Margaret Cornelia Winthrop of New York.

[Helen S. Folsom, *In Memoriam* (1871); J. Chapman, *A Geneal. of the Folsom Family* (1882), not wholly reliable; M. R. Cabot, *Annals of Brattleboro*, vol. II (1922), 744–45; *Proc. Am. Antiquarian Soc.*, Apr. 28, 1869; remarks by Robt. C. Winthrop in the *Proc. Mass. Hist. Soc.*, vol. XI (1871); the *Christian Reg.*, July 24, 1869; *New-Eng. Hist. and Geneal. Reg.*, Oct. 1869; obituary in *N. Y. Tribune*, May 4, 1869.] A. E. P.

FOLSOM, NATHANIEL (Sept. 18, 1726–May 26, 1790), soldier, politician, was born at Exeter, N. H., son of Jonathan and Anna (Ladd) Foster. Letters during his official career would indicate, by their grammar and spelling, that he enjoyed few educational advantages. In 1755, during the Crown Point expedition, he gained distinction by skilful handling of a New Hampshire company in the famous fight with the French and Indians under Baron Dieskau near Lake George. He seems to have acquired a permanent interest in military matters, for he held several commands in the militia during succeeding years while engaged in mercantile business at Exeter. In 1774 he attended the First Continental Congress and with his colleague, John Sullivan, signed "the Association." In the following year he was active in revolutionary proceedings in New Hampshire and a member of the Provincial Congress. On the outbreak of hostilities in Massachusetts he was placed in command of three regiments of New Hampshire militia. Detained in the state by administrative duties, however, he did not reach the scene of action until a few days after the battle of Bunker Hill. On June 30 he was placed in command of the entire state militia with the rank of major-general. He remained in the field for some months and his reports show the difficulties encountered in maintaining discipline during the siege of Boston. The doughty warrior, John Stark, proved especially troublesome and probably cost the participants Continental commissions. Folsom finally returned to New Hampshire and performed useful services in equipping, organizing, and training soldiers to meet frequent requisitions throughout the war.

In addition to his military services he was a member of the Council in 1776 and of two constitutional conventions, served repeatedly in the legislature and on the Committee of Safety and was a judge in the court of common pleas. He was a delegate to the Continental Congress in 1777–78 and again for a brief period in 1779–80. In the former term he served on the treasury board and also on a special committee of three to confer with Washington on the condition of the army. A letter to President Meshech Weare of New Hampshire shows that he was dissatisfied with the Articles of Confederation and realized fully the divergent interests of Northern and Southern states due to the existence of slavery. While not one of the outstanding figures of Revolutionary history he ranks high among those who directed New Hampshire affairs in the dangerous transition from colony to state. He was twice married; first to Dorothy Smith and after her death in 1776, to Mrs. Mary (Sprague) Fisher.

[Brief sketches of Folsom are given by Henry M. Baker, "Nathaniel Folsom," in *Poc. N. H. Hist. Soc.*, IV (1906), 253–67; by Cyrus P. Bradley, "Memoir of Nathaniel Folsom," in *N. H. Hist. Soc. Colls.*, V (1837), 216–21; and by C. H. Bell in *Pa. Mag. of Hist. and Biog.*, II (1878), no. 4. See also *New-Eng. Hist. and Geneal. Reg.*, Apr. 1876; J. Chapman, *A Geneal. of the Folsom Family* (1882); and E. C. Burnett, *Letters of Members of the Cont. Cong.*, I–IV (1921–28), *passim.*]
W. A. R.

FOLWELL, SAMUEL (*c.* 1768–Nov. 26, 1813), miniature painter and engraver, spent the greater part of his professional life in Philadelphia. The year of his birth cannot be ascertained with certainty, for the burial records of Philadelphia give his age at death as forty-five years, while a notice of his death in *Poulson's American Daily Advertiser*, Nov. 27, 1813, described him as "a limner, in his forty-ninth year." It is recorded (Dunlap, *post*, III, 300) that he was in New York in 1790, and went to New England two years later, which is probably true, since there are in existence still some book-plates engraved for residents of New Hampshire in 1792. His name first appeared in the Philadelphia directory for 1793, in which he is described as "limner." For the following four years his name is absent from the directories, but in that for 1798 he is set down as "miniature painter and fancy hair worker." From that year until his death he evidently was a resident of Philadelphia, generally engaged in painting miniatures, and making a few engravings. Stauffer asserts that he was also a cutter of silhouettes, and that he conducted a school, which may have been carried on after his demise by his widow. "Very few examples of the engraved work of Folwell have been seen; and his two portraits are executed in a combination of aquatint and stipple which is rather pleasing in effect, though showing an unpractised hand" (Stauffer, *post*, I, 81). Folwell's chief claim to remembrance lies in his silhouette of George Washington, said to have been painted from life. Though executed at an unknown date, it has been several times followed more or less closely by other engravers, and has become a type, probably best seen in the frontispiece to Henry Wansey's *Journal of an Excursion to the United States* (Salisbury, 1796). He also engraved a bust of Washington. The artist died in Philadelphia and was buried in the German Presbyterian burial ground, which was long ago obliterated.

[D. M. Stauffer, *Am. Engravers upon Copper and Steel* (2 vols., 1907); Museum of Fine Arts, Boston, *A Descriptive Cat. of an Exhibition of Early Engraving in Am.* (1904); Wm. Dunlap, *A Hist. of the Rise and Progress of the Arts of Design in the U. S.* (rev. ed. 1918), vol. III; Philadelphia directories. The date of death is taken from *Poulson's Am. Daily Advertiser*, Nov. 27, 1813. The burial records give Nov. 25.] J. J.

FOLWELL, WILLIAM WATTS (Feb. 14, 1833–Sept. 18, 1929), historian, first president of the University of Minnesota, was born on a farm in Romulus, N. Y., the son of Joanna (Bainbridge) and Thomas Jefferson Folwell. His ancestry was preponderantly English, with some admixture from the north of Ireland, tempered by long residence in Pennsylvania or Maryland before the migration to western New York. He found his parents sympathetic to his desire for education, and was prepared for college at academies at Nunda, Geneva, and Ovid, N. Y. His schooling was interrupted by two years of teaching in district schools, and each summer was spent at farm work. In the fall of 1854, he matriculated as a sophomore at Hobart College, Geneva, N. Y. Although he was out of residence a part of his senior year, teaching Greek and Latin at Ovid Academy, he was graduated in June 1857. During the following winter he continued to teach at Ovid, but in 1858 he returned to Hobart as "adjunct professor" of mathematics. He also taught Latin and Greek, and studied law. The next year he decided to abandon law for philology, and it was as a student of philology that he matriculated at the University of Berlin in the fall of 1860. News of the secession of South Carolina terminated his work at Berlin and sent him on a long-projected tour of Europe, which he was disinclined to put off longer, as he expected in the event of war to return to the United States. He reached home in October 1861, and in January 1862 was commissioned first lieutenant in the 50th New York Volunteer Infantry—later the 50th New York Engineers. He served throughout the war in the Army of the Potomac building bridges and fortifications, and at the end of the war he had reached the rank of major—lieutenant-colonel by brevet.

On Mar. 13, 1863, Folwell married Sarah Hubbard Heywood of Buffalo, N. Y., and in 1865 he removed to the small settlement of Venice, Ohio, near Sandusky, to enter the merchant milling business owned by his father-in-law. In 1868 he went to Kenyon College as professor of mathematics and civil engineering, and in 1869 he became president of the incipient University of Minnesota. In this position he proved to be ahead of his times. He advocated and tried to put into practise a junior college system; he initiated the movement for state aid to education in order that high schools might be encouraged to prepare students for the university; he instituted a winter short course of lectures for farmers; and he proposed the removal of the university from its original small urban campus to an ample suburban life. He had difficulties, however, with a board of regents which considered itself charged with the details of university management and looked upon the president as its factotum. After fifteen years of his presidency the friction still remained. Folwell was apparently not sufficiently politic for the position, and he resigned, continuing his librarianship and the congenial professorship of political science, and making way for the coming of Cyrus Northrop as president of the university. It is characteristic of Folwell that he became a sincere friend and admirer of his successor. In 1919 he was given the title of president-emeritus of the university and in 1925 he was honored with the only LL.D. degree ever conferred by that institution. A volume of his *University Addresses* was published at Minneapolis in 1909.

Besides serving the university as president, professor, and librarian, Folwell took the lead in establishing the Minnesota Geological and Natural History Survey in 1872, aided in founding the Minneapolis Society of Fine Arts and served as its president from 1883 to 1888, served on the Minneapolis park commission from 1889 to 1907 and as its president from 1895 to 1903, and was a member of the state board of charities and corrections from 1896 to 1902. He was president of the Minnesota Historical Society from 1924 to 1927, devoting much time and energy to its work despite his advanced age, and retired with the title of president-emeritus. After his retirement from the university in 1907 he set himself to write a comprehensive history of Minnesota. He had prepared for the American Commonwealths Series, *Minnesota, the North Star State* (1908), and while so doing had acquired not only much material unusable in so short a volume but also the desire to continue work in the field. The result was a critical and comprehensive *History of Minnesota* based on extensive research in the original sources. Rejecting a liberal offer from a commercial publisher, Folwell determined to give the work to the people through the Minnesota Historical Society, and it was published by that institution in four volumes from 1921 to 1930. A few weeks before his death he completed a volume of interesting reminiscences.

In his later years, Folwell maintained his eminent position in the community which he had helped to develop. He was friend and counselor to leaders of its civic and economic life, and his influence was sought by proponents of plans for civic advancement. Kindly, urbane, tolerant, and liberal, he brought an enlightened and cultured mind to the consideration of community problems. In person, he was slight of build, with an erect carriage, keen dark eyes, and an old-world courtliness of manner. His greatest charm was his whimsicality, a humorous originality of thought and speech which even in his ninety-sixth year bore witness to his critical faculties and intellectual detachment.

[An extensive collection of Folwell Papers, including correspondence, diaries, notes, and a copy of the reminiscences, is in the possession of the Minnesota Historical Society. An outline of Folwell's career is in *Who's Who in America*, 1928–29.] S. J. B.

FONDA, JOHN H. (*c.* 1797–*c.* 1868), frontiersman, was born in Watervliet, Albany County, N. Y. The only source of information regarding him is the series of his dictated reminiscences, published, with a brief editorial note, in the *Prairie du Chien Courier* in 1858, and republished in the *Collections* of the State Historical Society of Wisconsin. After considerable schooling Fonda was put in a lawyer's office, where he remained two years. The lure of the West claimed him, however, and with a small party he started, probably in the spring of 1819, for Texas. Near the site of Fort Towson, Okla., established five years later, he parted from his companions, and after various activities in that region decided on a journey to Santa Fé. With two other men he set out upon his trek in the spring of 1823. A considerable part of the route was probably then first traversed by American white men (*Southwestern Historical Quarterly,*

July 1919). Arriving in Santa Fé, he went on to Taos, where he wintered.

By October 1824 he had returned from the Southwest and was in St. Louis, where for a year he worked as a mason and bricklayer. In the fall of 1825 he started by steamboat up the Mississippi, but at the mouth of the Illinois debarked and with five companions set out for the little settlement of Chicago at Fort Dearborn. From Chicago he went by boat to Juneau's trading house (Milwaukee) and then to Fort Howard and the Green Bay settlement. In the winter of 1827–28, as a dispatch-bearer, he made the hazardous journey to Fort Dearborn and back in the creditable time of a little more than two months. He might have continued in this service, but preferred to move on. He next appears, in the summer of 1828, at Fort Crawford (Prairie du Chien) where, in the following April, he enlisted as a soldier. Zachary Taylor, who became the commandant in July, seems to have regarded him highly, and he became a corporal and later a quartermaster's sergeant; but he fell ill, and at the end of two years' service obtained his discharge. In the following year he enlisted for the Black Hawk War and was on board the *Warrior* when it aided in the destruction of the Sauk chief's band at the mouth of the Bad Axe.

Fonda must have made journeys not recorded in his reminiscences. He says that he had been "over about every one of the States and Territories." Twelve years of wandering seem to have satisfied him, for he then obtained a land warrant for his services as a volunteer, married Sophia Gallerno (Sept. 4, 1834), and settled down. His subsequent history is that of a respected citizen of Prairie du Chien, successively elected to the offices of constable, coroner, and justice of the peace, and a genial raconteur of interesting narratives. His reminiscences, though sometimes faulty as to fact, are vivaciously and dramatically told.

[John H. Fonda, "Early Reminiscences of Wis.," *Wis. Hist. Colls.*, vol. V (1868); Cardinal Goodwin, "John H. Fonda's Explorations in the Southwest," *Southwestern Hist. Quart.*, July 1919; additional information supplied by W. E. Martner, Prairie du Chien, Wis.]

W. J. G.

FONT, PEDRO (d. Sept. 6, 1781), Franciscan missionary in charge of the Indian mission of San José de los Pimas, Sonora, Mexico, had gained such a reputation as a man of learning and cartographer, by the year 1774, that when Capt. Juan Bautista de Anza [*q.v.*] was sent on a second expedition from his Sonora presidio, San Ignacio de Tubac, in order to establish a mission and presidio on the Bay of San Francisco, he was directed to accompany the expedition "on all the journey, so that as one skilled in these matters, [he] may observe latitudes." On Jan. 4, 1776, the expedition reached San Gabriel (near the present Los Angeles), and on Feb. 21, with Father Font in attendance, set out northward along the California coast. On Mar. 10, the expedition reached Monterey and here, at the mission of San Carlos Borromeo, Father Font was entertained by Fathers Junípero Serra, Francisco Palou and Juan Crespí, in connection with whom he made observation of the sun's elevation. On Mar. 23, 1776, Anza with Father Font and eleven or twelve men left Monterey for San Francisco Bay. At sight of the port of San Francisco, the Father was overjoyed, hailing it as a "wonder of nature." It was the duty of Father Font to keep by graphometer and compass close tabulation of the course of the expedition, and this he did particularly with reference to the Bay of San Francisco. Toward the west he observed the Farallon Islands, the elevation of which he set down. Within the Bay he counted eight islands, four of which he sketched for his diary. He figured the latitude of the point at the entrance to the Bay (Fort Point) as 37° 49′ uncorrected, the actual latitude being about 37°47′. He took with him a record of observations by Father Crespí who had visited the region in 1774. Journals had been kept by both Fathers Crespí and Palou, and of these Father Font made use by studying them on the spot. Of the selection of a site for a presidio he wrote: "The commander decided to erect the holy cross on the extremity of the white cliff at the inner point of the entrance to the port, and we went there at eight o'clock in the morning. We ascended a small low hill, and then entered a table-land, entirely clear, of considerable extent, and flat, with a slight slope towards the port; it must be about half a league in width and a little more in length, and keeps narrowing until it ends in the white cliff. This table-land commands a most wonderful view, as from it a great part of the port is visible, with its islands, the entrance, and the ocean, as far as the eye can reach—even farther than the Farallones. The commander marked this table-land as the site of the new settlement, and the fort which is to be established at this port, for, from its being on a height it is so commanding that the entrance of the mouth of the port can be defended by musket-fire, and at the distance of a musket-shot there is water for the use of the people, that is, the spring or pond where we halted. I again examined the mouth of the port and its configuration with a graphometer, and attempted to survey it; the plan of it is the one I here set down" (Diario del P.

Font. John Nicholas Brown manuscript in the Library of Congress). On Apr. 4, 1776, the Anza expedition began its return south, and by June 2, the return had been accomplished. The diary of Father Font, as signed by him at Tubutama May 11, 1777, contains various carefully drawn maps, and in its completed form is a document of extreme interest and readability. It is perhaps the chief distinction of Father Font to have contributed to American history a graphic account of the expedition which resulted in the selection of what has proved to be the site of the city of San Francisco. The death of Father Font occurred at Pitíque, Sonora, Sept. 6, 1781.

[*The Anza Expedition of 1775–1776*, ed. by F. J. Teggart, in *Pub. of the Acad. of Pacific Coast Hist.*, vol. III, no. 1 (Mar. 1913); I. B. Richman, *San Francisco Bay and California in 1776*, with three maps and outline sketches drawn by Pedro Font (1911); Rev. Fr. Zephyrin Engelhardt, *Missions and Missionaries of Cal.*, vol. II (1912); C. E. Chapman, *The Founding of Spanish Cal.* (1916) and *A Hist. of Cal.—the Spanish Period* (1921); H. H. Bancroft, *Hist. of Cal.*, vol. I (1884).]
I. B. R.

FOOT, SAMUEL AUGUSTUS (Nov. 8, 1780–Sept. 15, 1846), representative, senator, governor of Connecticut, was born in Cheshire, Conn., the seventh child of John and Abigail Hall Foot. His father was a Yale graduate and minister of the Congregational church in Cheshire. Samuel proved to be a rather precocious child. Entering Yale at the age of thirteen, he graduated in 1797. For a few months after graduation, he read law in an office in Washington, Conn., and then attended the noted law school in Litchfield, Conn. Handicapped by a delicate constitution, he was so plagued by headaches that he was unable to continue his studies more than a few months. Abandoning the law, he moved from Litchfield to New Haven, and found employment in the shipping trade that centered around the famous Long Wharf. By 1803 he had built up a business of his own, trading chiefly with the West Indies. To strengthen his none too robust health, he took occasional voyages on his own vessels. When New England shipping was all but ruined by the Embargo and the War of 1812, Foot gave up the New Haven enterprise in 1813, and retired to his father's estate in Cheshire. For the remainder of his life he was a farmer and politician. He took an active part in the movement to secure a new state constitution, becoming one of the Tolerationists, as members of the reforming party were called. In terms of national party politics, Foot was an Anti-Federalist, or Republican. He was elected to the lower house of the state legislature in 1817, and again the following year. For two years thereafter he was a member of Congress from Connecticut. In 1822 and 1823 he was once more in the state Assembly, and then in Congress for another term. Returning to the Connecticut Assembly in 1825, he was chosen speaker. The following year he was elected United States senator, to succeed Henry W. Edwards. He gained unexpected publicity in the Senate by offering a resolution, on Dec. 29, 1829, instructing the committee on public lands to inquire into the expediency of limiting the sales of public lands (*Annals of Congress*, 21 Cong., 1 Sess., p. 3). It was this resolution which led to the famous Webster-Hayne debate. Upon the expiration of his senatorial term in 1833, Foot was elected a member of the House of Representatives, but he resigned his seat in 1834 to become governor of Connecticut. He was not reëlected and retired from politics, save for a single appearance in 1844, when, having changed his former party affiliations, he was a presidential elector on the Henry Clay ticket (*Hartford Daily Courant*, Nov. 4, 1844). He died at his home in Cheshire on Sept. 15, 1846, survived by his widow, Eudocia Hull, daughter of Gen. Andrew Hull of Cheshire, and three sons, one of whom, Andrew Hull Foote [*q.v.*], became a famous naval officer in the Civil War. Because of his shift in party affiliations, just before his death, obituary notices were markedly brief and apologetic. Though Samuel Augustus Foot, his father, and grandfather spelled the name without a final *e* (transcripts of records in the Connecticut State Library), their descendants have adopted the longer form.

[F. B. Dexter, *Biog. Sketches of the Grads. of Yale Coll.*, V (1911), 281–83; F. C. Norton, *The Governors of Conn.* (1905); Nathaniel Goodwin, *The Foote Family* (1849); E. E. Atwater, *Hist. of the City of New Haven* (1887); obituary notice in *New Haven Daily Register*, Sept. 16, 1846.]
J. M. M.

FOOT, SOLOMON (Nov. 19, 1802–Mar. 28, 1866), lawyer, politician, son of Solomon and Betsey (Crossett) Foot, was born at Cornwall, Vt. His father, a physician, died while he was still a child, but in spite of many difficulties and privations he secured an education, graduating at Middlebury College in 1826. For five years following graduation he engaged in teaching, most of the time as principal of Castleton Seminary, interrupted by one year (1827–28) as tutor at the University of Vermont. He studied law in the meantime, was admitted to the bar in 1831, and established himself in practise at Rutland. Though an able lawyer his early and long-continued activity in public affairs prevented his attaining real eminence at the bar. In 1833 he was elected to the legislature as representative of Rutland. He was reëlected in 1835, 1837, 1838, and 1847, and in each of the last three terms served as speaker. In the latter capacity, declared Senator Poland, "he first displayed that almost wonderful aptitude and capacity as the presiding officer of a deliberative assembly, which afterward made him so celebrated throughout the nation" (*Congressional Globe,* 39 Cong., 1 Sess., p. 1908). He was a member of the constitutional convention of 1836 and prosecuting attorney of Rutland County from 1836 to 1842.

He was an active Whig and as such was elected to Congress in 1842, serving two terms until 1847 when he declined a renomination and returned to his legal practise. His service in the House was without special interest or distinction but he was strongly opposed to the Mexican policy of the administration and denounced the war which resulted. In 1850 he was elected to the United States Senate and served until his death sixteen years later, being at that time the senior member in point of continuous service. His opposition to the extension of slavery led him to join the new Republican organization when the Whig party finally disintegrated. During his first term in the Senate he also served for a year (1854–55) as president of the Brunswick & Florida Railroad Company, visiting England in connection with the sale of its securities and the purchase of material.

Foot was not distinguished as an orator and most of his remarks are brief and pointed interjections in the course of debate. His speech of Mar. 20, 1858, on the proposed admission of Kansas under the Lecompton Constitution (*Congressional Globe,* 35 Cong., 1 Sess., App., pp. 153–58) shows, however, that he was capable of sustained argument and close reasoning, had he wished to devote himself to long set addresses. It was as a presiding officer that he appears to have made the deepest impression on his contemporaries. He was president *pro tempore* throughout most of the Thirty-sixth Congress and all of the Thirty-seventh, besides being often called on to preside when the regular incumbents were not available. "He was perhaps more frequently called to the . . . chair than any other Senator," said J. B. Grinnell of Iowa, who also declares that his services had left a permanent impress on the parliamentary decorum and methods of the Senate (*Congressional Globe,* 39 Cong., 1 Sess., p. 1924). In parliamentary law, Charles Sumner testified, "he excelled and was master of us all." Fessenden, Reverdy Johnson, and others paid similar tribute to his fine presence, fairness, courage, and dignity in the chair as well as to the personal qualities which made him one of the most popular members of the upper chamber. When his death was announced, the splenetic Gideon Welles, never given to flattery of his associates, and usually suspicious of senators in particular, wrote in his diary (*Diary of Gideon Welles,* 1911, II, 466) that he had been a firm friend of the Navy Department, was "*pater senatus* and much loved and respected." His most notable committee service was rendered as chairman of the committee on public buildings and grounds, in which capacity he was able, in spite of the stringency of the Civil War, to push forward the completion of the Capitol. Judged by occasional remarks in the course of debate on appropriation bills, he appears to have had certain ideals as to the future development of the government property in Washington not altogether common at that time. He was twice married: July 9, 1839, to Emily Fay; and Apr. 2, 1844, to Mary Ann (Hodges) Dana. He died in Washington, D. C.

[Geo. F. Edmunds, in *Addresses Delivered before the Vt. Hist. Soc., Oct. 16, 1866* (1866); N. Seaver, *A Discourse delivered at the Funeral of Hon. Solomon Foot* (1866); L. Matthews, *Hist. of the Town of Cornwall, Vt.* (1862); N. Goodwin, *The Foote Family* (1849); G. W. Benedict, in *Hours at Home* (N. Y.), July 1866; W. H. Crockett, *Vermont,* V (1923), 368–69; *Proc. Vt. Hist. Soc. for the Years 1919–1920* (1921); *Daily Morning Chronicle* (Washington, D. C.), Mar. 29, 30, Apr. 2, 1866; *Rutland Daily Herald,* Mar. 29–Apr. 2, 1866; *Burlington Times,* Mar. 31, Apr. 7, 1866; *Vt. Watchman & State Jour.* (Montpelier), Apr. 6, 1866.]

W. A. R.

FOOTE, ANDREW HULL (Sept. 12, 1806–June 26, 1863), naval officer, was born in New Haven, Conn., second son of Senator Samuel A. Foot [*q.v.*] and Eudocia Hull Foot. The son departed from family tradition and added an *e* to his name. In 1813 the family moved to Cheshire, Conn., where Andrew attended the Episcopal Academy of Connecticut. After a few months at West Point, June–December 1822, his fixed desire to enter the navy was gratified by his appointment, Dec. 4, as acting midshipman. The boy served first in the West Indies under Porter, then three years in the Pacific. A strong call to religion, during a Caribbean cruise in 1827, marked the beginning of the intense reforming spirit of his later years. After cruises in the Mediterranean and around the globe, 1837–41, and two years at the Philadelphia Naval Asylum, he was again in the Mediterranean as first lieutenant of the *Cumberland.* On this vessel he formed a temperance society, did away with the grog-tub, and made her the first temperance ship in the navy. His example and subsequent exertions were chiefly responsible for abolishment of the spirit ration, finally accomplished in 1862.

in command of the *Perry* on the African coast, 1849–51, he showed not only customary zeal in protecting American vessels against British search, but quite unusual energy against the slave-trade. His captures, and the book he wrote, *Africa and the American Flag* (1854), together with his articles and speeches (one published as *The African Squadron . . .* , 1855), figured considerably in arousing sentiment against the traffic. After five years ashore, including service on the efficiency board of 1855 which cut dead-wood from the service, he was in the Far East, 1856–58, in command of the sloop *Portsmouth.* As senior officer present at Canton, during hostilities between England and China, he commanded a party of 287 American seamen which, in punishment for attacks on our flag, stormed and demolished the four barrier forts below the city, with 176 guns and 5,000 defenders, Nov. 20–22, 1856 (see "Capture of the Barrier Forts," by E. N. McClellan, *Marine Corps Gazette,* September 1920). In charge of the Brooklyn Navy Yard at the outbreak of the Civil War, Foote had a reputation, not for great brilliance, but for rigid standards of duty and extraordinary persistence. These qualities were tried to the utmost during his command, from Aug. 26, 1861, of naval operations on the upper Mississippi. Though officered by the navy, his flotilla was under army control, and Foote, subject to orders, as he said, "from every brigadier," overcame incredible difficulties in getting his mortars and twelve gunboats completed, equipped, and manned. This he considered a greater accomplishment than his subsequent hard-fought battles in cooperation with the army at Fort Henry on the Tennessee River, Feb. 6, 1862, and at Fort Donelson on the Cumberland, Feb. 14, which broke the Confederate line of defense in northern Tennessee. At Fort Henry, with four ironclads and three wooden boats in lines abreast, he poured in a heavy fire at close range which forced surrender before the arrival of the army. It was characteristic of Foote's religious fervor, fondness for public speaking, and the touch of vanity in his nature, that on the Sunday after the battle he preached in a church at Cairo on the text, "Ye believe in God; believe also in me." At Donelson the enemy guns were placed much higher, and his seven vessels had to retire after a heavy bombardment, the fort surrendering to Grant next day. In the pilot-house of the *St. Louis,* the Commodore suffered slight wounds in the arm and foot. During the advance down the Mississippi in the next spring he operated more cautiously, realizing that his flotilla was the chief defense of the upper river. He sanctioned, however, the running of the batteries at Island No. 10 by the *Carondelet,* Apr. 4, and by the *Pittsburg* on the 6th, which hastened the surrender of the position a day later. Broken in health and still on crutches from his wound at Donelson, Foote had to leave the flotilla on May 9, turning it over to his old friend Charles Henry Davis [*q.v.*], though he retained nominal command until June 17. He was promoted rear admiral on July 16, and during the next winter was chief of the bureau of equipment and recruiting. Eager again for duty afloat, and always in high favor with his old schoolmate Secretary Welles, he was appointed, June 4, 1863, to succeed Du Pont in command of the squadron before Charleston. But he was then a sick man, and died of Bright's disease in New York on his way South. Foote was twice married: on June 22, 1828, to Caroline Flagg of Cheshire, who died in 1838, and on Jan. 27, 1842, to his second cousin Caroline Augusta Street of New Haven. A daughter by the first marriage and two sons by the second survived him. He was of medium stature, with keen black eyes and erect carriage. "He was not a man of striking personal appearance," writes his subordinate Walke, "but there was a sailor-like heartiness and frankness about him which made his company very desirable" (*Battles and Leaders of the Civil War,* I, 360). In spite of nervousness and occasional petulance, he had a gentle, lovable nature, and he had also the drive and tenacity essential to successful command. "Foote had more of the bulldog," said Commodore C. R. P. Rodgers (J. M. Hoppin, *Life of Andrew Hull Foote,* 1874, p. 404), "than any man I ever knew."

[*Diary of Gideon Welles,* 3 vols. (1911); R. M. Thompson and R. Wainwright, eds., "Confidential Correspondence of Gustavus Vasa Fox," in *Pubs. of the Naval Hist. Soc.,* X (1919), pp. 3–57; C. H. Davis, *Life of Charles Henry Davis, Rear Admiral, U. S. N.* (1899); Nathaniel Goodwin, *The Foote Family* (1849); Foote Manuscripts, 20 vols. (1822–63), in Lib. of Cong.; *Battles and Leaders of the Civil War,* 4 vols. (1887–88); *Official Records (Navy),* XXII, XXIII, *passim; Hours at Home* (N. Y.), May 1865; *N. Y. Herald,* June 27, 1863.]

A. W.

FOOTE, HENRY STUART (Feb. 28, 1804–May 20, 1880), senator, governor of Mississippi, was born in Fauquier County, Va. His parents, Richard Helm Foote and Jane Stuart, were cousins and of English and Scotch ancestry. After graduating from Washington College, now Washington and Lee University, in 1819, Foote studied law and was admitted to the bar at Richmond in 1823. He soon moved to Tuscumbia, Ala., and then to Mississippi, where he lived at various times in Jackson, Natchez, Vicksburg, and Raymond, practising law and sometimes editing newspapers. As a criminal lawyer he is said to have had no equal in Mississippi ("Proceedings of the Nashville Bar," *Daily American,* May 21, 1880). His first political move was an unsuccessful campaign for membership in the Mississippi constitutional convention of 1832. His reputation was increased by ably defending Jackson on the stump in 1835. In 1839 he resigned the office of United States surveyor-general south of Tennessee and entered the state legislature as representative of Hinds County. His interest in the independence of Texas is shown by a visit to that country in this same year, an interest which eventuated in his first book, *Texas and the Texans* (2 vols., 1841). In 1847 he was elected to the United States Senate, where he ardently supported the compromise measures of 1850. All the other Mississippi congressmen opposed these measures, particularly his colleague in the Senate, Jefferson Davis. Heated words passed, not only over the measures themselves, but over the question of the right of secession and the attitude of their constituents toward these questions (*Congressional Globe,* 31 Cong., 1 Sess.). The antagonism was personal as well as public, for three years earlier Foote and Davis had exchanged blows at their boarding house (Dunbar Rowland, *Jefferson Davis, Constitutionalist,* 1923, VII, 393 ff.). In view of the fact that the Mississippi legislature passed resolutions censuring Foote for advocating the compromise measures, his defeat of Davis for the governorship of that state in 1851 is surprising, and is a monument to his great ability as a stump speaker. His administration, 1853–54, was marked chiefly by the fierce struggle between the Union and state-rights factions, the latter being successful to the chagrin of Foote. Five days before the expiration of his term, Foote resigned the governorship and moved to California. He returned to Mississippi after four years, but his lack of harmony with the people of that section in regard to disunion soon led to his removal to Tennessee.

In view of his opposition to secession, Foote might be accused of inconsistency in entering the lower house of the Confederate Congress, but he was at least consistent in criticizing President Davis and his administration. When Lincoln's peace proposals were not accepted, Foote left Richmond in disgust, sent his resignation to the Confederate Congress, and after a brief incarceration by the Confederate authorities, entered Union territory. When his communications to Seward and Lincoln on the subject of terms of peace were coolly received, Foote departed for Europe. He might well be called the Vallandigham of the South. He attempted to justify his part in the Civil War and its preliminaries in his book, *The War of the Rebellion* (1866). In this work he vigorously opposed the idea that the war was an "Irrepressible Conflict." He also wrote *Casket of Reminiscences* (1874), a valuable and interesting commentary on many of Foote's prominent friends and opponents, and *Bench and Bar of the South and Southwest* (1876).

For a short time before his death, which occurred in Nashville, Tenn., he was superintendent of the United States Mint in New Orleans. He was twice married: first to Elizabeth Winters in Tuscumbia, Ala.; and after her death to Mrs. Rachel D. Smiley of Nashville, Tenn. In person, he was small, with a large, bald head. He was a charming conversationalist and an able public speaker but he too often indulged in personalities, a trait which resulted in four formal duels and other less formal encounters.

[In addition to Foote's writings, particularly his *Casket of Reminiscences,* and the references in the body of this sketch, brief notices of him may be found in Reuben Davis, *Recollections of Miss. and Mississippians* (1889); F. A. Montgomery, *Reminiscences of a Mississippian in Peace and War* (1901); Dunbar Rowland, *Mississippi* (1907); *Appletons' Annual Cyc.* (1880); *Miss. Official and Statistical Reg.* (1908); *Ibid.* (1917). His private letters and papers are apparently lost (*Miss. Hist. Soc. Pubs.,* V, 239), though the writer was permitted to examine a thirty-seven-page manuscript sketch of his life that is in the possession of Mrs. A. L. Bondurant, University, Miss., which was written shortly before his death, and was based on notes furnished by Foote for that purpose.]

C. S. S.

FOOTE, LUCIUS HARWOOD (Apr. 10, 1826–June 4, 1913), lawyer, diplomat, was born at Winfield, N. Y., son of Lucius and Electa (Harwood) Foote. His father, a Congregational minister, held pastorates in New York, Ohio, Illinois, and Wisconsin. Young Lucius attended Knox College and Western Reserve but did not graduate from either. Because of a restless temperament he could not confine himself to the routine of school work. In 1853, the lure of the West led him to join a group of young men who were going overland to California. There he took up the study of law. He was admitted to the bar in 1856, and the same year began a four-year term as municipal judge of Sacramento. From 1861 to 1865 he was collector of the port of Sacramento, and in 1862 he married Rose Frost Carter of San Francisco. He was adjutant-general of California 1872–76 and in the latter year was a delegate to the Republican National Convention. On Mar. 3, 1879, "General" Foote, as he was known after having served as adjutant-general, was commissioned consul at Valparaiso, Chile. The American minister, Kilpatrick, having died Dec. 2, 1881, the son of Secretary of State Blaine was named chargé, but Foote was actually in charge of the legation from Mar. 22

to July 31, 1882. Early in August he returned home on leave. On Feb. 5, 1883, while still in the United States, he was sent to Aspinwall, Colombia, on a special consular mission. While he was on this mission, he was appointed to a more important charge. The treaty just negotiated between the United States and Korea (1882) called for the exchange of diplomatic representatives, and Foote, with the rank of envoy extraordinary and minister plenipotentiary, was commissioned by President Arthur for the post (Feb. 27, 1883). With Mrs. Foote, he arrived in Korea May 13, the first minister from a Western power accredited to that country. The tension between Japan and China over Korea made the mission a difficult one. During the days of bloodshed which followed the *coup d'état* of December 1884, he was zealous in his efforts to protect foreigners. The Japanese government expressed appreciation for his "brave and humane conduct" during the revolt. Foote also received thanks from the Chinese government but there is no record of commendation from his own. He was notified on July 14, 1884, that Congress had reduced the rank of the post in Korea to that of minister resident and consul-general, with no change in salary. He was offered a commission in this capacity but he declined, stating that, "to these people, proud that the United States should have sent to them a Minister of the first rank, it is impossible to explain the reasons for the change without leaving the most unfortunate impressions." In reply the Department of State asked him to take his departure on leave, so that it would be unnecessary to explain. Leaving Chemulpo Jan. 19, 1885, he and Mrs. Foote returned to the United States by way of Tokio, where they were received by the Emperor.

As a result of the strain of these experiences in Korea, Mrs. Foote died soon after their return. Thereafter Foote did not reënter public life. In 1891 he was elected treasurer of the California Academy of Sciences and secretary of its Board of Trustees and to these positions he was reëlected each year until his death. During these years he took an active part in the affairs of the Bohemian Club of San Francisco, of which he was a charter member. He also published two volumes of poems, *On the Heights* (1897) and *The Wooing of the Rose and Other Poems* (1911). His associates remember him as a large man of distinguished bearing with a genial disposition and a pleasing personality.

[There is no biography of Foote. His letters and papers were destroyed in the San Francisco fire of 1906. The material for this sketch is derived from the archives of the Department of State, and from recollections of relatives and associates. See also Nathaniel Goodwin, *The Foote Family* (1849); O. T. Shuck, *Hist. of the Bench and Bar of Cal.* (1901); San Francisco *Call*, and *San Francisco Chronicle*, June 5, 1913. The statement in *Who's Who in America*, 1912–13, is inaccurate in many details.] C. S.

FOOTE, SAMUEL AUGUSTUS [See Foot, Samuel Augustus, 1780–1846].

FORAKER, JOSEPH BENSON (July 5, 1846–May 10, 1917), governor of Ohio, United States senator, was born on a farm near the village of Rainsboro, Highland County, Ohio, the son of Thomas S. and Margaret (Reece) Foraker. On his father's side, Foraker was of English and Scotch-Irish descent, the forefathers of his paternal grandfather, John Fouracre, having emigrated to this country from Devonshire, England, while his paternal grandmother was of Scotch-Irish origin. In 1820 his paternal grandparents left their home on Bombay Hook Island, in Delaware Bay, for a farm near Rainsboro; and early in the same century his mother's family came from Virginia to Ohio and settled at Reece's Mills on the Rocky Fork of Paint Creek. When Foraker was only two years old his father bought a farm near Reece's Mills and at the same time acquired the flour and sawmills which his wife's grandfather had built on the mill-site. The next thirteen years of Foraker's life was spent on the farm at Reece's Mills. He performed the usual tasks that are the lot of a farmer boy; achieved a local reputation as an expert swimmer and good horseman; developed a fondness for fishing which he retained through life; and attended the district school during the winter months, and on Sundays the Methodist Episcopal Church of which his parents were devout and active members. As a boy Foraker displayed a lively interest in politics, a fondness for reading, especially war history, and an aptitude for declamation. When he was fifteen years old he went to Hillsboro to accept a clerical position in the office of his uncle who was auditor of Highland County. He remained there until July 14, 1862, when he enlisted in Company A, 89th Regiment, Ohio Volunteer Infantry. His regiment was assigned to the XIV Corps of the Army of the Cumberland, participated in the Chattanooga and Atlantic campaigns, and accompanied Gen. Sherman on his march to the sea and then through the Carolinas and thence to Washington for the Grand Review. Foraker served with his regiment in all these engagements except the battle of Chickamauga, when he was away on special duty. Enlisting as a private he was promoted on Aug. 26, 1862, to the rank of sergeant; advanced to first lieutenant, Mar. 24, 1864; and was brevetted captain, ranking from Mar. 19, 1865, "for efficient services during the recent campaigns in Georgia and the Carolinas" (Foraker, *Notes of a Busy Life*, I, 71). Following the fall of Atlanta he was detailed for duty in the signal service and later was assigned as a signal officer to the staff of Gen. H. W. Slocum, whose aide-de-camp he had been; and on several occasions was selected for service that required courage and daring. He was highly commended for his bravery in carrying the news of the capture of Savannah to the United States fleet off the coast; and his bold ride as a messenger of Gen. Slocum in need of reinforcements at the battle of Bentonville (Mar. 19, 1865) attracted the attention of Gen. Sherman.

Foraker's war experiences made him appreciate more keenly the importance of an education; and in 1866, after a year at Salem Academy, he enrolled as a student in Ohio Wesleyan University. Two years later he transferred to Cornell and was a member of the first class graduated in 1869 from that institution. While a student at Ohio Wesleyan he began the study of law, and on Oct. 14, 1869, he was admitted to the bar and commenced to practise in Cincinnati. On Oct. 4, 1870, he married Julia Bundy, the daughter of H. S. Bundy of Jackson County, Ohio. His natural inclinations soon led him to enter politics, and from 1879 to 1882 he was judge of the superior court of Cincinnati. In 1883 he was nominated by the Republicans for governor on a platform favoring the taxation and regulation of the liquor traffic, but he was defeated by Judge George Hoadly because many former Republicans, disapproving of sumptuary legislation, deserted the party ranks. Two years later Foraker was elected governor, after a spirited campaign in which he demonstrated his skill as a debater in his discussions with Judge Hoadly, who was again his opponent. Foraker was reëlected in 1887 and nominated a fourth time in 1889, but was defeated. During his two administrations he secured the passage of much-needed legislation and proved himself a forceful executive in rigorously enforcing the law; but he also revealed a penchant for the dramatic and the sensational. He induced the legislature to pass a law taxing liquor which avoided the constitutional objections to previous enactments, secured the establishment of a state board of health, obtained the enactment of statutes providing for the appointment of bipartisan boards of elections and the registration of voters in the large cities, and improved the system of taxation by appointing tax assessors. On several occasions his actions as governor aroused much discussion. When in 1889 an organization of saloon keepers in Cincinnati boldly announced their intention of remaining open on Sundays in defiance of the law, he sent a letter to the mayor, ordering him to "smite every manifestation of such a spirit with a swift and heavy hand" (*Ibid.*, I, 414). Probably his most sensational utterance was in connection with President Cleveland's order of 1887, calling for the return of all captured battle-flags to their respective states. Foraker attracted national attention at this time by declaring: "No rebel flags will be surrendered while I am governor" (*Ibid.*, I, 242). This provoked his enemies to call him "Fire Alarm" and "Bloody Shirt" Foraker; but the popular response only whetted his zeal in appealing to the passions engendered by the war (*Ibid.*, I, 278).

Upon his retirement from the governorship he resumed the practise of law, but in 1896 he was elected senator from Ohio and reëlected in 1902. During his two terms he was recognized as one of the foremost constitutional lawyers in that body and one of the ablest leaders of his party, while his aggressive personal attacks on prominent men kept him constantly before the public. He was an early champion of the Cuban revolt, a strong defender of Admiral Schley in his controversy with Admiral Sampson, a supporter of President McKinley's Philippine policy, and he was primarily responsible for the organization of the civil government of Porto Rico. He consistently opposed President Roosevelt's policies, notably in the case of the admission of Oklahoma, Arizona, and New Mexico, the passage of the Hepburn Rate Bill (see the *Atlantic Monthly*, XCVIII, November 1906, 577–86), and the President's dismissal of an entire company of negro soldiers for alleged participation in a riot at Brownsville, Tex. During the presidential campaign of 1908 William R. Hearst published certain letters written by John D. Archbold, vice-president of the Standard Oil Company, which revealed that Senator Foraker had been in the company's employ while in office and had received $29,500. He maintained that the money was remuneration for his services as legal counsel for the company in Ohio, and denied that it was compensation for preventing pending national legislation deemed "vicious" by the Standard Oil Company. In addition to this $29,500, he accepted a loan of $50,000 from Archbold for the proposed purchase of the *Ohio State Journal*; the loan was repaid after the enterprise had been abandoned. The disclosures compelled him to retire from public life. In 1914 he attempted to return to politics and became a candidate for the Republican senatorial nomination but was defeated in the primaries by Warren G. Harding. This defeat convinced Foraker that his public career was ended and he devoted his remaining years to the writing of his memoirs, in which he stated, looking back over his twelve years of service in the Senate, "I do not find an important vote or speech that I would recall if I had the power to do so" (*Ibid.*, II, 478).

Foraker was a conspicuous figure in every Republican National Convention from 1884 to 1904, and on three occasions he nominated Ohio candidates for the presidency (John Sherman, 1884; William McKinley, 1896 and 1900). Toward the close of his career he was on unfriendly terms with Mark Hanna (H. D. Croly, *Marcus Alonzo Hanna; His Life and Work*, 1912) and after the latter's death, he was the state leader of his party. His great skill as a stump orator made him an effective advocate; his solid legal attainments were generally respected; and while he was frequently engaged in bitter controversy with members of his party and by his opponents was considered a reactionary, none ever questioned his courage or fearlessness.

[Foraker's *Notes of a Busy Life* (2 vols., 1916) is an invaluable source for his career. It is carefully evaluated in the *Am. Hist. Rev.*, XXI (July 1916), 835–37, and in the *Polit. Sci. Quart.*, XXXI (Dec. 1916), 590–603. See also *Memorial to Jos. Benson Foraker* (1917); *Sketch of Jos. Benson Foraker* (1883; 2nd ed., 1885); *Who's Who in America*, 1916–17; *N. Y. Times*, May 11, 1917. For the Archbold-Foraker letters and the ensuing controversy, consult the *Cincinnati Enquirer*, Sept. 17–19, 21, 26, 1908; *Nation* (N. Y.), Sept. 24, Oct. 1, 1908; *Outlook*, Oct. 3, 1908; *World's Work*, Nov. 1908. A sketch of his administrations while governor may be found in E. O. Randall and D. J. Ryan, *Hist. of Ohio*, vol. IV (1912).] R. C. M.

FORBES, EDWIN (1839–Mar. 6, 1895), painter, etcher, writer, was born in New York City, the son of a carpenter, Joseph C. Forbes, and his wife Ann. He began the study of art at the age of eighteen, continuing after 1859 under the tutelage of Arthur F. Tait. At first he concentrated upon animal painting, but later extended his field to genre and landscape. In 1861 he was engaged to accompany the Army of the Potomac as staff artist for *Frank Leslie's Illustrated Newspaper* in which his sketches of camp life and battle-fields appeared throughout the Civil War. The habit of quick and trenchant drawing from life which he developed during his years at the front influenced all his later production, and the sketches themselves were his main stock in trade for the rest of his life. Upon his return to New York in 1865 the best of these, "Lull in the Fight," painted from a drawing of the Battle of the Wilderness, was exhibited at the National Academy in New York and at the Boston Athenæum. In 1876 copperplate etchings from his war sketches were published as *Life Studies of the Great Army*, and received an award at the Centennial Exposition in Philadelphia. The original prints were bought by Gen. William T. Sherman, and were placed in his office in the War Department in Washington. In 1884 a bill was introduced in Congress providing for the purchase and preservation in the government archives of the Forbes Historical Collection, which contained the original drawings made during the war, but the bill was defeated.

Forbes continued to draw upon his war experiences for illustrations for children's histories. He contributed ninety-six etchings to *Gen. William T. Sherman, his Life and Battles, Mostly in One Syllable Words* (1886), written by his wife, Ida B. Forbes; ninety-five to Josephine Pollard's *Our Naval Heroes in Words of Easy Syllables* (1886); and eighty-two to H. W. Pierson's *Life and Battles of Napoleon Bonaparte: In Words of One Syllable* (1887). These were hastily and crudely produced, and of an even merit with the texts which they illustrated. Eventually he wrote his own reminiscences, *Thirty Years After, An Artist's Story of the Great War* (1891), which were chatty and entertaining, but written solely as a vehicle for his remaining sketches.

Forbes was a member of the French Etching Club, and in 1877 was elected honorary member of the London Etching Club. He did not as a rule bite his own plates, and both his etchings and paintings are more interesting for the vigor of their drawing than for the nicety of their execution. A few years before his death he suffered a paralysis of his right side, and thereafter painted and wrote with his left hand. He died at his residence on Lenox Road, Flatbush, New York.

[*Cat. Forbes Hist. Art Coll.* (1881); C. E. Clement and Laurence Hutton, *Artists of the Nineteenth Century and their Works* (1899); H. T. Tuckerman, *Book of the Artists* (1867); James Laver, *A Hist. of British and Am. Etching* (1929); *N. Y. Herald, N. Y. Times, Boston Transcript*, Mar. 7, 1895.] C. W. P.

FORBES, JOHN (1710–Mar. 11, 1759), British officer, was a son of Col. John Forbes of Pittencrieff, Dunfermline, Fifeshire. "Though bred to the profession of physic," he chose in 1735 to purchase a cornetcy in the 2nd Royal North British Dragoons, the Scots Greys. The War of the Austrian Succession brought to his regiment six years of service on the Continent and great honor, and to himself rapid promotion and various staff positions. A lieutenant when the Greys reached Flanders, he became a captain and aide-de-camp to his colonel, Sir James Campbell, a year after Dettingen, and a major and deputy quartermaster-general after Fontenoy. In 1745 he was a lieutenant-colonel in the army, and in 1750 lieutenant-colonel of his regiment. In February 1757 he was given the colonelcy of the 17th Foot, and accompanied his regiment to Halifax. His attachment to the Campbells and his staff experience assured him a place at Loudoun's table, and he served as adjutant-general until March 1758, continually offering valuable suggestions, and keeping the staff in good humor by a blunt and merry wit. The promotions of December 1757 made him a brigadier-general in America only, and Abercromby assigned him, at Pitt's orders, the command of the expedition against Fort Duquesne. His force consisted of Montgomery's Highlanders, a detachment of Royal Americans, and some five thousand provincials from Pennsylvania, Virginia, Maryland, and North Carolina. Forbes contended with the reluctance of the Pennsylvania Assembly and the absolute refusal of the Maryland Assembly to appropriate funds; the delayed arrival of his own train of artillery and his regulars; the "disagreements, constant jarring, and animosity among the troops of the various provinces"; the indifference of the inhabitants along the route, who were not eager to provide transportation; the impatience of his Cherokee allies, who withdrew early in the campaign; the suspicious attitude of the Western Indians; the rivalry of his own officers, among whom Bouquet and Grant were his chief supports; and the continual rainfall which turned a road constructed with much labor into a long morass. But in spite of these and a "thousand little obstacles," the army steadily penetrated into the wilderness, cut through Bedford and Ligonier, over Laurel Hill, the road which later became a highway of Western expansion, and at regular intervals built blockhouses which safeguarded communication with the East, and gave to this advance the character, not of a simple raid, but of a permanent conquest.

Throughout the entire campaign Forbes was troubled by the malady which finally caused his death. From September on he followed his advance parties in a hurdle slung between two horses, in which the least movement brought intense pain. Such suffering often caused explosions in his private letters, but in his actual relations with his army he preserved his plain, democratic manners and his wise discretion, and animated the whole force with his spirit. He fully appreciated the importance of winning the French Indians, and gave his complete approval to the negotiations of Christian Frederick Post. Not even the defeat of Grant's large skirmishing party at Loyalhanna prevented the eventual adherence of the Western Indians to the British. When finally a light column lay within striking distance of Fort Duquesne, the French garrison, deserted by the savages, evacuated the stronghold without firing a shot. On Nov. 25, five months after the expedition started, Forbes raised the British flag over the new "Pittsburgh." He was carried back to Philadelphia a dying man, "a spectacle the most shocking and deplorable," "looking like an emaciated old woman of eighty." His body was buried with military honors in the chancel of Christ Church.

[The best brief accounts of Forbes's life and character are the sketch in the *Dict. Nat. Biog., Supp.*, and the death notice in the *Pa. Gazette*, Mar. 15, 1759. Meager additional information of his European career is found in Edward Almack, *Hist. of the Second Dragoons, "Royal Scots Greys"* (1908); Duncan Warrand, *More Culloden Papers*, III (1927), 208; A. N. Campbell-Maclachlan, *Wm. Augustus, Duke of Cumberland* (1876). For his American career the chief collections are the Bouquet Papers in the British Museum, transcribed for the Canadian Archives; the Chatham Papers and departmental papers in the Public Record Office; the Loudoun and Abercromby Papers in the Henry E. Huntington Library and Art Gallery, San Marino, Cal.; and *The Writings of Geo. Washington*, ed., Ford, II (1889). A bibliography of the expedition is in the *Monthly Bull. of the Carnegie Lib.*, June 1908; and Irene Stewart has compiled in a convenient form the *Letters of Gen. John Forbes relating to the Expedition against Fort Duquesne in 1758* (1927). See also A. B. Hulbert, *Historic Highways of America*, vol. V (1903); and Francis Parkman, *Montcalm and Wolfe* (1884), vol. II.] S. M. P.

FORBES, JOHN (d. Sept. 17, 1783), clergyman and magistrate in East Florida, was a native of Strathdon, Scotland. He was the son of Archibald Forbes of Deskrie (1713–1793), and according to family tradition, was born in 1740. He received his education at King's College in old Aberdeen, where he passed through the ordinary course of Greek, mathematics, and philosophy, and attended lectures in divinity. The University of Aberdeen conferred on him the degree of M.A. in the spring of 1763. He was then recommended to the bishops of the Church of England for ordination to the ministry. Florida having become a British possession, Parliament promptly made provision for four ministers of religion and two schoolmasters. John Forbes was the first clergyman licensed to officiate in East Florida; and on May 5, 1764, he gave the customary bond to be conveyed to his missionary field, St. Augustine, where the larger number of East Florida settlers had gathered. From all accounts he was conscientious in the discharge of his parochial duties; but his field was difficult and the territory quite extensive; besides, he was the only English clergyman in East Florida during most of the British occupation. Once a year he generally visited the most remote parts, "at a considerable expense and great fatigue." Advantageous offers to go elsewhere were refused. During his incumbency, a church was built at St. Augustine. On Feb. 2, 1769, he was married in Milton, Mass., to Dorothy Murray, daughter of James Murray.

As one of the few educated men in the province, Forbes proved an asset to the local government. He was made a member of the colonial Council by Gov. James Grant; and this appointment was confirmed by the Privy Council, June 7, 1771. Subsequently he became sole judge surrogate of the court of vice-admiralty and assistant judge of the courts of common law in the province; and when Chief Justice William Drayton [*q.v.*] was suspended from office by Gov. Patrick Tonyn, Forbes was commissioned (Mar. 30, 1776) to act in his place till His Majesty's pleasure could be known. Drayton carried his appeal to London in person, and succeeded in becoming reinstated. The friction between him and Gov. Tonyn was soon renewed; and in December 1777, Drayton was suspended a second time, and Forbes was again appointed in his place, but his appointment was not confirmed. In the several posts he occupied, he won the commendation of his governors, who wrote letters to the home office regarding his qualifications and integrity. When the growing intensity of the Revolutionary War involved the maintenance of a military force in St. Augustine, a regular army chaplain was assigned to the station; but Forbes officiated as his deputy. So far as his parish work was concerned, he never had a helper or substitute until the Rev. James Seymour, a Tory missionary who had left Augusta, Ga., sought refuge in Florida. In 1783, after nearly twenty years in the province, he returned to England on leave of absence, in bad health. He was the bearer to Lord North of a letter in behalf of the Florida Loyalists. He died in England, Sept. 17, 1783, leaving a widow and three sons: James Grant Forbes (1769–1826), John Murray Forbes (1771–1831) [*q.v.*], and Ralph Bennet Forbes (1773–1824). Among his grandsons were Robert Bennet Forbes (1804–1889) and John Murray Forbes (1813–1898) [*qq.v.*].

[A. Forbes, *Memorials of the Family of Forbes of Forbesville* (1905); S. F. Hughes, ed., *Letters and Recollections of John Murray Forbes* (2 vols., 1899); N. M. Tiffany, ed., *Letters of Jas. Murray, Loyalist* (1901); W. H. Siebert, *Loyalists in East Fla., 1774 to 1785* (2 vols., 1929); *Acts of the Privy Council*, Col. Ser., vol. V (1912); E. L. Pennington, "John Forbes," in *Florida Hist. Quart.*, VIII, 164–68, January 1930. Documents bearing on Forbes's university work are among the MSS. of Fullham Palace, London. Letters from Forbes and correspondence relating to his work are in the Public Record Office: Colonial Office, Class 5, and in the Stevens Transcripts in the Lib. of Cong.]

E. L. P.

FORBES, JOHN (1769–May 13, 1823), merchant, son of James and Sarah (Gordon) Forbes, was born in Scotland, probably in Aberdeenshire. Emigrating to America in his youth, he entered the employ of Panton, Leslie & Company, a trading firm operating on the Spanish-Indian frontier. William Panton, a Scottish Tory from Georgia, had obtained from the Spanish government a monopoly of the Creek trade, which he had built up under English rule, and later also a monopoly of the Cherokee, Chickasaw, and Choctaw trade, the firm being granted special privileges of trade and religious nonconformity. In 1792 Forbes was admitted to partnership, and given charge of the Mobile branch and the Choctaw and Cherokee trade, while Panton had headquarters at Pensacola. In the reorganization of the business following Panton's death Forbes became in 1804 the head of the new firm, John Forbes & Co. Notwithstanding his ability and energy, the fortunes of the house did not prosper. The causes were many: trade demoralization attendant upon the European wars; competition of rival merchants who attacked its monopoly and special privileges; and robberies committed by William Augustus Bowles [*q.v.*] and his Indian followers, all of which combined to cause losses estimated in 1804 at approximately $67,000, and after the War of 1812 at $100,000 more. To recoup these losses, Forbes by diplomacy and persistence secured in 1804 and 1811 large cessions of land from Spain and the Indians, part of which land, on the Appalachicola River, is known as the "Forbes purchase." This tract he sold in 1817 to Colin Mitchel and the title was subsequently confirmed by the United States Supreme Court after the cession of Florida to the United States (*Mitchel et al.* vs. *U. S.*, *9 Peters*, 711).

About 1817 Forbes went to Cuba, and after a short stay in Havana, became a merchant in Matanzas. Panton, in a letter to Carondelet (Oct. 15, 1793), describes Forbes as "a young man of as much real ability and honour as I ever met with." His extant papers and his career show him to have been a man of keen business ability, resourcefulness, persistence, and determination. Besides his trading interests, he owned a sawmill in Alabama and a sugar plantation in Cuba. He left two daughters, born out of wedlock, who inherited the bulk of his $150,000 estate. His will shows that he lived and died a Catholic.

[*Am. State Papers: Indian Affairs*, I, II (1832–34), *Public Lands*, III–VI (1859–60); J. F. H. Claiborne, *Miss. as a Province, Territory and State* (1880); P. J. Hamilton, *Colonial Mobile* (1898); A. J. Pickett, *Hist. of Ala.* (2 vols., 1851); C. M. Brevard, *A Hist. of Fla.* (2 vols., 1924–25); W. H. Siebert, *Loyalists in East Fla.* (2 vols., 1929); R. L. Campbell, *Hist. Sketches of Colonial Fla.* (1892); East Fla. Papers in Lib. of Cong.]

E. H. W.

FORBES, JOHN MURRAY (Aug. 13, 1771–June 14, 1831), lawyer, diplomat, was born at St. Augustine, Fla., the son of Rev. John Forbes [*q.v.*], the rector at that place, and Dorothy (Murray) Forbes of Milton, Mass. In 1773 his mother took him to Massachusetts for his education. After studying under Dr. Samuel Kendall of Weston, he entered Harvard College, where he was a classmate and friend of John Quincy Adams and the youngest member of the class of 1787. In the same year, together with Adams, he took up the study of law at Newburyport. In January 1788 he attended some of the debates of the Massachusetts convention called to ratify the new Federal Constitution, and declared himself a stanch Federalist. He began the practise of law at Boston in 1794, but abandoned it in 1796 and went to Europe. In Paris, he was one of the signers of a testimonial to James Monroe upon the latter's recall. In 1801 he was appointed consul, residing at Hamburg and Copenhagen until about 1819, when he returned to the United States.

His most important public service dates from the following year, when the influence of John Quincy Adams, then secretary of state, obtained for him an appointment in a new field. The agent for the United States in both Chile and Buenos Aires, J. B. Prevost, seemed to Adams excessively sympathetic toward the revolutionists. Unable to discipline him, since he was President Monroe's protégé, Adams procured the appointment of Forbes to whichever of the two posts Prevost should choose to relinquish. Forbes thus went to South America at a critical period in an important capacity, for he was the secretary of state's most trusted agent in southern South America. In his instructions dated July 5, 1820, he was described as agent for commerce and seamen. Finding upon his arrival at Buenos Aires (October 1820) that Prevost had just been ordered out of the city by the revolutionary government, Forbes immediately took up his duties at that place. Throughout his residence he justified Adams's confidence in him, for, while he exhibited a brief enthusiasm for the Argentine statesman, Rivadavia, he showed no excessive partiality for the rest of the Argentinians. Upon the appointment of Caesar Rodney as minister, Forbes was commissioned as secretary of legation (Jan. 27, 1823); and when Rodney died in June 1824, he acted as chargé d'affaires from that time until he received his commission as chargé (dated Mar. 9, 1825). He continued in this capacity until his death. He retained until the end that "uncommon share of wit" and gaiety of temper, which his sober friend Adams deplored. Afflicted with the gout in his declining years, he is said to have chosen for his crest "a gouty foot couchant, crossed by two crutches rampant," with the motto: *"Toujours souffrant, jamais triste."*

His name is associated with some important developments in Hispanic-American relations. In 1821 he obtained an alteration of the policy of Buenos Aires in regard to privateering, and in 1822 a modification of its ordinance of maritime police. In the latter year he informed that government of the decision of the United States to recognize the South American republics. In 1823 he sought to gain its adherence to the principles of the Monroe Doctrine, and in subsequent years he resisted its attempt to interpret the Doctrine to suit its own convenience.

[Wm. R. Manning, *Dip. Corr. of the U. S. Concerning the Independence of the Latin-American Nations* (3 vols., 1925); *Proc. Mass. Hist. Soc.*, 2 ser., XVI (1902), 343, note 2; *Ibid.*, III (1886–87), 208–11; C. F. Adams, ed., *Memoirs of John Quincy Adams* (12 vols., 1874–77); A. K. Teele, *The Hist. of Milton, Mass., 1640 to 1887* (1887), pp. 567–68; F. L. Paxson, *The Independence of the So. Am. Republics* (2nd ed., 1916), 164–72; W. S. Robertson, "South America and the Monroe Doctrine, 1824–1828," in *Pol. Sci. Quart.*, Mar. 1915, 82–105; *Am. State Papers: Foreign Relations*, III (1832), 342–43; *Ibid., Commerce and Navigation*, I (1832), 820; F. J. Urrutia, *Los Estados Unidos de America y las Republicas Hispanoamericanas de 1810–1830* (Bogotá, 1918).]

A. P. W.

FORBES, JOHN MURRAY (Feb. 23, 1813–Oct. 12, 1898), a business man, and also an active participant in public affairs, was born in Bordeaux, France, the son of Ralph Bennet and Margaret Perkins Forbes of Boston, Mass., and grandson of Rev. John Forbes [*q.v.*], rector at St. Augustine in East Florida. At the age of fifteen he entered the counting-house of his uncles in Boston, and presently went to Canton, China, to represent them. During seven years in the Orient he gave evidence of unusual business abilities; and when he returned to America at the age of twenty-four, he had accumulated a fortune sufficient to enable him to take a position of importance in the commercial world. During the next nine years his investments on land and sea prospered, and in 1846 he turned his attention to railroad building and management in the West.

A group of capitalists, of whom he was the prime mover, purchased the unfinished Michigan Central Railroad from the State for $2,000,000, carried it to Lake Michigan, and then to Chicago, at the same time supplying funds for the connecting link between Detroit and Buffalo through Ontario. He next financed and put in operation the roads from Chicago to the Mississippi River and across Iowa, which formed the nucleus of what later became the Chicago, Burlington & Quincy system, and he was also responsible for the building of the Hannibal & St. Joseph Railroad in Missouri. During the period of the Civil War and the years immediately following, his attention was given chiefly to public affairs; but in consequence of the panic of 1873 and of the necessity for effecting a change in the management of the Chicago, Burlington & Quincy, he became again the leading spirit in the direction of its affairs, occupying the position of president for two or three years, ending in 1881. He brought to the problems of railroad-building energy, courage, sound business judgment, integrity, and a broad view of the relation of the railroads to the public interest. Through the force of his personality the roads in which he was interested acquired a character and stability which distinguished them sharply from most of the railroads of that day.

His important public service began at the outset of the Civil War, when he became the most active helper of Gov. John A. Andrew in putting the State of Massachusetts on a war footing. Of his many activities perhaps the most distinctive was the help which he rendered in the organization of its negro regiments. At Washington his knowledge of maritime affairs made him particularly helpful to the Navy Department. In 1863 he was sent unofficially to England to purchase, if possible, the ships known as the Laird rams, which were then being built for the Confederacy; and later he himself, with a few others, built a cruiser, larger than the Confederate *Alabama,* which he intended to sell to the government at cost. He organized the Loyal Publication Society, an effective bureau for propaganda; he was constantly consulted by officials in all branches of the government; he was untiring in giving suggestions and practical help on many matters of moment. His intense desire that the war should be prosecuted vigorously made him chafe at Lincoln's "slowness"; and he often made use of friends who had Lincoln's ear to put before him policies, such as the arming of the blacks, which he believed essential to Northern success. He was known to be disinterested, and his influence and accomplishment were great in proportion; furthermore, he consistently maintained the policy of keeping himself in the background and letting the credit for his actions go to others. After the war he was for some years a member of the national executive committee of the Republican party; but in 1884, as a protest against the nomination of James G. Blaine, he left the party and voted for Cleveland.

On Feb. 8, 1834, Forbes was married to Sarah Hathaway of New Bedford. Of their six children the oldest son, William Hathaway, became president of the Bell Telephone Company. His summer home, from 1857, was the island of Naushon at the entrance of Buzzard's Bay, and he made the place memorable by the simple yet generous hospitality that he exercised and the distinguished men and women who were his guests. It is Forbes's quality as host that is the theme of Ralph Waldo Emerson's well-known characterization of him in *Letters and Social Aims* (Riverside Edition, p. 101). "Never was such force, good meaning, good sense, good action, combined with such domestic lovely behavior, such modesty and persistent preference for others. Wherever he moved he was the benefactor. It is of course that he should ride well, shoot well, sail well, keep house well, administer affairs well; but he was the best talker, also, in the company. . . . Yet I said to myself, How little this man suspects, with his sympathy for men and his respect for lettered and scientific people, that he is not likely, in any company, to meet a man superior to himself. And I think this is a good country that can bear such a creature as he is."

[Sarah Forbes Hughes, *Letters and Recollections of John Murray Forbes* (2 vols., 1899); Henry Greenleaf Pearson, *An American Railroad Builder, John Murray Forbes* (1911). Three volumes of *Letters* and three of *Reminiscences,* privately printed, contain abundant biographical details and reveal Forbes as a remarkably vigorous and racy writer.] H. G. P.

FORBES, ROBERT BENNET (Sept. 18, 1804–Nov. 23, 1889), sea-captain, China merchant, ship-owner, writer, was born in Jamaica Plain near Boston, Mass., the son of Ralph Bennet and Margaret (Perkins) Forbes, and brother of John Murray Forbes (1813–1898) [*q.v.*]. The family was of Scottish descent on both sides. His education included a year in France and three years at Milton Academy. Upon his father's failure in business, he entered the employ of his uncles, James and Thomas H. Perkins, outstanding Boston merchants whose interest in him contributed to his advancement. At thirteen years of age, he sailed before the mast in one of their ships for China. At twenty he received command of another Perkins ship for a three-years' voyage around the world. In 1830, when Perkins & Company, at Canton merged with Russell & Company, to form the most powerful American house in China, Forbes secured their lucrative storeship at Lintin. His New England conscience excused the opium trade as no worse than dealing in ardent spirits. He returned to Boston, married Rose Green Smith on Jan. 20, 1834, and was prospering as consignee of China cargoes for Russell & Company. Then, nearly ruined in the panic of 1837, he went out to Canton again to recoup his fortunes, arriving in time to play a prominent rôle in the outbreak of the Opium War. In March 1839, the Chinese commissioner demanded the destruction of all opium at Canton. Two months later, Forbes became head of Russell & Company, in place of John C. Green who returned home. Determined to boycott the Canton hongs, the British merchants retired to Macao and Hong Kong, urging Forbes to join them. He says that he replied that "I had not come to China for my health or pleasure, and that I should remain at my post as long as I could sell a yard of goods or buy a pound of tea." As a result, the Americans did a rushing business, not only in their own goods but British as well, until their real blockade was clamped down in June 1840. Forbes returned to Boston, having made up all his losses, with a "handsome profit" to boot.

He was in China again as head of Russell & Company from 1849 to 1851, serving also as American and French vice-consul. By that time, he had entered the third state of his career, that of ship-owner. Altogether, he was connected with sixty-eight vessels as part owner or supervisor of construction. He invented the "Forbes rig" for sailing vessels, described as "a pole topmast fiddling abaft," later improved and patented by Howes. He was among the first to have faith in the screw propeller and iron hulls. In 1844–45, he was a principal owner of three-screw, auxiliary steamers, the *Midas* and *Edith,* pioneers in Chinese and Indian waters, and the *Massachusetts,* a transatlantic packet. A tug, named for him, had the first iron hull built in New England. He sent small iron steamers to China, California and South America on the decks of sailing vessels, an idea as ingenious as his earlier sending of ice to the Orient. He was always interested in humanitarian work. In 1847, he commanded the U. S. S. *Jamestown,* loaned to carry contributions from Boston to the Irish famine sufferers. He jumped into the sea to make daring rescues after a collision in 1849. He energetically supported coastal life-saving work, nautical training-ships and sailors' homes. During the Civil War, he organized a short-lived "Coast Guard" unit; supervised the construction of nine gunboats, some of which were with Farragut at New Orleans; assisted his brother in the English mission to check the Laird rams; and lost money building warships for the Union navy on his own account. He was always an enthusiastic sportsman. He was "commodore" of the first informal yacht club in Boston, and at sixty-five he took up fox hunting at Pau. He is said to have had unusual personal charm. His pictures show a man of medium height with a kindly face, less severe in its lines than his brother's. In his youth he was known as "Black Ben," but by thirty he was gray. During his last years, he was deaf and in poor health. He resided in Boston, with a summer home at Milton near-by. Until the end, he was a prolific writer in his many fields of interest. His writings, most of them pamphlets, include: *Remarks on China and the China Trade* (1844); *The Voyage of the Jamestown,* etc. (1874); *An Appeal to Merchants and Ship Owners, on the Subject of Seamen* (1854); *On the Establishment of a Line of Mail Steamers . . . to China* (1855); *Remarks on Ocean Steam Navigation* (1855); *Remarks on Magnetism and Local Attraction* (1875); *The Forbes Rig* (1862); *Means for Making the Highways of the Ocean more Safe* (1867); *Personal Reminiscences* (1876; 3rd ed., 1892); *The Lifeboat and other Life-saving Inventions* (1880); *New Rig for Steamers* (1883); *Notes on Navigation* (1884); *Loss of Life and Property in the Fisheries* (1884); and *Notes on Ships of the Past* (1888).

[The principal source is his own delightful volume of *Personal Reminiscences.* The third edition (1892) contains three portraits. He gives further autobiographical material in his *Notes on Navigation.* There are scattered references in *Letters and Recollections of John Murray Forbes,* ed., Sarah F. Hughes (2 vols., 1899); and memorial remarks in *Proc. Mass. Hist. Soc.,* 2 ser., V (1889–90), 142–44.]

R. G. A.

FORBES, STEPHEN ALFRED (May 29, 1844–Mar. 13, 1930), entomologist, naturalist, was the son of Isaac Sawyer and Agnes (Van Hoesen) Forbes. On his father's side he was of Scotch ancestry, the original American ancestor, Daniel Forbes, marrying Rebecca Perriman at Cambridge, Mass., in 1660. His mother was of Dutch and English origin, and two of her ancestors, John Howland and John Tilley, came over on the *Mayflower.* Stephen Alfred was born at Silver Creek, Ill. His father was a farmer, and died when Stephen was ten years old. An older brother, Henry, then twenty-one years old, had been independent since he was fourteen, working his way toward a college education, but on his father's death he abandoned his career, took the burden of his father's family on his shoulders, and supported and educated the children. He taught Stephen to read French, sent him to Beloit to prepare for college; and when the Civil War came he sold the farm and gave the proceeds (after the mortgage was paid) to his mother and sister for their support. Both brothers then joined the 7th Illinois Cavalry, Henry having retained enough money to buy horses for both. Stephen, enlisting at seventeen, was rapidly promoted, and at twenty became a captain in the regiment of which his brother ultimately became colonel. In 1862, while carrying dispatches, he was captured and held in a Confederate prison for four months. After liberation and three months in the hospital recuperating, he rejoined his regiment and served until the end of the war. He had learned to read Italian and Spanish in addition to French, before the war, and studied Greek while in prison.

He was a born naturalist. His farm life as a boy and his open-air life in the army intensified his interest in nature. After the close of the war, he began at once the study of medicine, entering the Rush Medical College where he nearly completed the course. His biographers have not as yet given the reason for the radical change in his plans which caused him to abandon medicine at this late stage in his education; but the writer has been told by his son, that it was "because of a series of incidents having to do mainly with operations without the use of anesthetics which convinced him that he was not temperamentally adapted to medical practice." His scientific interests, however, had been thoroughly aroused, and for several years while he taught school in southern Illinois, he carried on studies in natural history. In 1872 through the interest and influence of Dr. George Vasey, the well-known botanist, he was made curator of the Museum of State Natural History at Normal, Ill., and three years later was made instructor in zoölogy at the normal school. In 1877 the Illinois State Museum was established at Springfield; and the museum at Normal, becoming the property of the state, was made the Illinois State Laboratory of Natural History. Forbes was made its director. During these years he had been publishing the results of his researches rather extensively, and had gone into a most interesting and important line of investigation, namely the food of birds and fishes. He studied intensively the food of the different species of fish inhabiting Illinois waters and the food of the different birds. This study, of course, kept him close to entomology, and in 1884 he was appointed professor of zoölogy and entomology in the University of Illinois. The State Laboratory of Natural History was transferred to the university and in 1917 was renamed the Illinois Natural History Survey. He retained his position as chief, and held it up to the time of his death. He was appointed state entomologist in 1882 and served until 1917, when the position was merged in the survey. He retired from his teaching position as an emeritus professor in 1921. He served as dean of the College of Science of the university from 1888 to 1905.

All through his career he had been publishing his writings actively. As early as 1895, Samuel Henshaw, in his *Bibliography of the more Important Contributions to American Economic Entomology* (Pt. IV A–K, nos. 661–762), listed 101 titles. It is said that his bibliography runs to more than five hundred titles. And the range of these titles is extraordinary; they include papers on entomology, ornithology, limnology, ichthyology, ecology, and other phases of biology. All of his work was characterized by remarkable originality and depth of thought. He was the first writer and teacher in America to stress the study of ecology, and thus began a movement which has gained great headway. He published eighteen annual entomological reports, all of which have been models. He was the first and leading worker in America on hydrobiology. He studied the fresh-water organisms of the inland waters and was the first scientist to write on the fauna of the Great Lakes. His work on the food of fishes was pioneer work and has been of very great practical value. He was a charter member of the American Association of Economic Entomologists and served twice as its president. He was also a charter member of the Illinois Academy of Science; a member of the National Academy of Sciences and of the American Philosophical Society; and in 1928 was made an honorary member of the Fourth International Congress of Entomology. Indiana University gave him the degree of Ph.D., in 1884, on examination and presentation of a thesis. He married, on Dec. 25, 1873, Clara Shaw Gaston, whose death preceded his by only six months. A son, Dr. Ernest B. Forbes of State College, Pa., and three daughters survived him.

[An article in *Science*, Apr. 11, 1930, by Henry B. Ward; and another in *Jour. of Economic Entomology*, Apr. 1930, by Herbert Osborn. See also an autobiographical letter, written in 1923, printed in *Sci. Monthly* (N. Y.), May 1930; *Who's Who in America*, 1928–29; and F. C. Pierce, *Forbes and Forbush Geneal.* (1892).] L. O. H.

FORBUSH, EDWARD HOWE (Apr. 24, 1858–Mar. 8, 1929), ornithologist, came from a long line of ancestors the earliest of whom emigrated from Scotland to Massachusetts about 1660. His parents, Leander Pomeroy Forbush and Ruth Hudson Carr, resided at the time of his birth in Quincy, Mass., where the father was principal of the Coddington School. From early childhood he had an all-absorbing interest in the great outdoors and spent much of his time watching the birds and quadrupeds, and later in hunting and trapping them. At fourteen he took up taxidermy and was soon skilful in the preparation of specimens. He left school at fifteen, determined to forego a college education, to be independent and self-supporting, and to prepare himself through his own initiative for what he seemed best fitted to do. At first he turned to collecting natural history specimens, visited Florida and British Columbia, and brought back a large assortment of material. With a companion he established a "naturalists' exchange" where specimens and taxidermists' supplies could be procured; later he became curator and president of the Worcester, Mass., Natural History Society, and in this connection established one of the first summer natural history camps for boys. As the years passed he discovered, to use his own words, "that life, not death, would solve our riddles, and that it was more essential to preserve the living than the dead." This indeed became the keynote of his later life.

In 1891 when the imported gipsy-moth became a menace to shade and fruit trees in Massachusetts, a commission was appointed by the governor to effect its control. Forbush was made director of the work, and at once realized the seriousness of the situation and the need for drastic measures. From the beginning, however, his work was handicapped by the short-sighted policy of the legislature in refusing adequate appropriations, and in 1900, seeing nothing but failure ahead, he resigned. He had already accomplished much in keeping the pest in check and his report, *The Gypsy Moth* (1896), became the most important work on the subject.

During this period Forbush had never lost his interest in ornithology. His reports on birds as insect destroyers, published while carrying on the gipsy-moth campaign, attracted much attention and resulted in his appointment as ornithologist to the Board of Agriculture of Massachusetts. In this position he at once set about educating the public to the economic value of birds and the importance of their protection. He traveled and lectured in all parts of the state and published a series of reports which attracted wide attention. Though he also published two more pretentious volumes, *Useful Birds and their Protection* (1907), and *A History of the Game Birds, Wild-Fowl and Shore Birds* (1912), which exerted an influence beyond the borders of Massachusetts, his greatest contribution to ornithological literature was his *Birds of Massachusetts and Other New England States,* the first volume of which appeared in 1925, the second in 1927, while the third was published after his death. This work was in reality an ornithology of northeastern North America embodying the results of his life's studies, as well as quotations from the more important observations of others, while the beautiful illustrations from the brushes of Louis Agassiz Fuertes [*q.v.*], and Allan Brooks added greatly to the value of the work.

Forbush was a fellow of the American Ornithologists' Union and a member of its council, a founder and president of the Massachusetts Audubon Society, president of the Northeastern Bird Banding Association and the Federation of Bird Clubs of New England, and was associated with the work of the National Association of Audubon Societies. He married on June 28, 1882, Etta L. Hill of Upton, Mass.

[F. C. Pierce, *Forbes and Forbush Geneal.* (1892); John B. May, "Edward Howe Forbush: A Biog. Sketch," in *Proc. Boston Soc. of Nat. Hist.*, Apr. 1928; *Boston Transcript*, Mar. 8, 1929; personal acquaintance.]

W. S—e.

FORCE, MANNING FERGUSON (Dec. 17, 1824–May 8, 1899), soldier, jurist, author, was born in Washington, D. C., the son of Peter [*q.v.*] and Hannah (Evans) Force. His father's ancestors were French Huguenots who came to America upon the revocation of the Edict of Nantes; his mother's family was Welsh and emigrated to Pennsylvania. He prepared for West Point at a boarding school in Alexandria, Va., but a change in his plans caused him to go to Harvard, where he entered as a sophomore. In 1845 he received his bachelor's degree and three years later he graduated from law school. In January 1849 he removed to Cincinnati where he spent a year in the office of Walker & Kebler studying law. Upon his admission to the bar in 1850 he became one of the firm of Walker, Kebler & Force.

He practised law until the commencement of the Civil War, when he entered the volunteer service as major of the 20th Ohio Regiment. He was rapidly promoted to lieutenant-colonel and colonel of this regiment; took part in the capture of Fort Donelson and the battle of Pittsburg Landing; and campaigned with Gen. Grant in 1862–63 in southwestern Tennessee and northern Mississippi. When Gen. Sherman marched on Jackson during the siege of Vicksburg, Force was placed in command of the 2nd Brigade and "was employed to guard the road as far back as Clinton." After the siege of Vicksburg he received the XVII Corps gold medal of honor by award of a board of officers; and on Aug. 11, 1863, was appointed brigadier-general. During Gen. Sherman's Meridian and Atlanta campaigns, he commanded a brigade, which on July 21, 1864, attacked and carried a fortified hill in full view of Atlanta. The next day Gen. Hood endeavored to capture this hill and in the terrible battle which ensued, Force was shot through the upper part of his face. For a time it was thought the wound was mortal but on Oct. 22, he was able to report for duty although he carried throughout life the marks of the wound. In recognition of his "especial gallantry before Atlanta," he was brevetted major-general on Mar. 13, 1865. He commanded a division in Gen. Sherman's army during the latter's march from Atlanta to Savannah and across the Carolinas. At the close of the war he was appointed commander of a military district in Mississippi where he remained until mustered out of the volunteer service on Jan. 11, 1866. Although he was tendered a civil office and appointed colonel of the 32nd Regular Infantry, he declined both offers.

He resumed the practise of law in Cincinnati and in 1866 was elected judge of the common pleas court. At the expiration of his term in 1871 he was reëlected. In the fall of 1876 he was nominated by the Republican party for Congress but was defeated. He was elected judge of the superior court of Cincinnati the following year and in 1882 received the nomination of both parties for that office and was unanimously reëlected. In 1887, owing to ill health, he declined a renomination. The following year he was appointed commandant of the Ohio Soldiers' and Sailors' Home of Sandusky, which position he held until his death. On May 13, 1874, he married Frances Dabney Horton, of Pomeroy, Ohio.

From his father Force inherited a fine literary taste and throughout his life he was deeply interested in historical and archeological studies. He was the author of *Pre-Historic Man. Darwinism and the Mound Builders* (1873); *From Fort Henry to Corinth* (1881); *Some Observations on the Letters of Amerigo Vespucci* (1885), and other works. He prepared the eighth edition of Walker's *Introduction to American Law* (1882), the third edition of Harris's *Principles of Criminal Law* (1885), and at the time of his death was engaged upon his *General Sherman,* published in 1899.

[James Landy, *Cincinnati Past and Present* (1872), pp. 309–14; H. Howe, *Hist. Colls. of Ohio,* I (1890), 570; *Memorial of Manning F. Force, Presented to the Literary Club of Cincinnati, May 26, 1899*; *Official Records (Army)*; *Circular No. 32,* series of 1899, Military Order of the Loyal Legion of the U. S., Commandery of the State of Ohio; *Ohio Arch. and Hist. Pubs.,* vol. IV (1896); Cincinnati *Commercial Tribune,* May 9, 1899.]

R. C. M.

FORCE, PETER (Nov. 26, 1790–Jan. 23, 1868), archivist, historian, son of William and Sarah Ferguson Force, was born near Passaic Falls, N. J. His boyhood was spent largely in New York, and in New York City he learned the printer's trade. During the War of 1812 he served in the army, entering as a private and coming out a lieutenant. In 1815 he moved to Washington, D. C., with his employer, to work on government-printing contracts. The Washington printers of his day were almost inevitably drawn into politics; Force was no exception to this rule. In 1822 he was elected to the city council. and later to the board of aldermen, serving for a time as president of each of these bodies. A supporter of John Quincy Adams in the campaign of 1824, he naturally became a Whig when the new party was formed; in 1836 he was elected mayor of Washington, on the Whig ticket. Two years later he was reëlected, without opposition. In 1848 he again became a candidate for the same office, but this time he was badly beaten, standing lowest of the three candidates. In 1823 he established a semi-weekly newspaper, the *National Journal,* devoted to the candidacy of John Quincy Adams. In 1824, the campaign year, the paper became a daily, and continued as such until 1831. Although a Whig, Force seems to have taken his politics decently, as he did everything else, and to have avoided the bitter partisanship of some of his contemporaries. In this respect his political career was typical of his whole life. His relations with his associates were always pleasant. On various occasions he was accorded honors, perhaps not important in themselves, but suggestive of the esteem in which he was held. When he was only twenty-two years old, for example, he was chosen president of the New York Typographical Society. Later, in Washington, he became president of the National Institute for the Promotion of Science, and a member of the board of managers of the Washington National Monument Society. Never a jovial man, but on the contrary rather quiet and reserved, he was possessed of a pleasing geniality that attracted people to him.

Force is best known, however, not as a politician or newspaper man, but as a collector and editor, first of statistical, then of historical material. In 1820, and for the eight years following, he printed a register of the public offices; from 1820 to 1836, with the exception of a three-year interval when he was immersed in politics, he published the *National Calendar,* later *National Calendar and Annals of the United States,* an annual of historical and statistical information. Then he collected and published four volumes entitled: *Tracts and Other Papers, Relating Principally to the Origin, Settlement, and Progress of the Colonies in North America* (Washington, 1836–1846). These are reprints of rare pamphlets bearing on the early history of the colonies. His father, a soldier in the Revolution, seems to have inspired in him a lively interest in the history of that movement. As a result, the son devoted the greater part of his middle and later years to the collection of historical materials dealing with the colonial period and the Revolution. In this connection Force brought out his greatest work, the monumental volumes known as the *American Archives.* As originally planned, the project involved the publication, in twenty or more folio volumes, of important original materials of American history from the seventeenth century through 1789—official documents of various kinds, legislative records, and private correspondence of special significance. The work was begun under contract with the Department of State, under authority of an act of Congress. The six volumes of Series Four were published from 1837 to 1846, and by 1853 three volumes of the Fifth Series had appeared. These nine covered the years 1774–1776. At that point the work suddenly stopped; Secretary of State Marcy refused to approve Force's plans for the completion of the undertaking, and no more volumes appeared.

Marcy's decision was a serious blow to Force, and to the cause of historical study in America. Basing his hope of reimbursement on a definite contract, sanctioned by Congress, Force had gone heavily into debt in order to secure his material. Now, at the age of sixty, he was faced with actual hardship. He might have sought relief through a petition to Congress, or by judicial process, but this he refused to do. Fortunately his situation was not as bad as it had at first seemed. In compiling the *Archives* he had procured an extraordinary mass of historical material, much of it extremely rare. Although he was inspired by the collector's urge to accumulate, he had shown good business judgment in his purchases. He found himself therefore in possession of a large library of considerable commercial value. This he finally sold to the Library of Congress for $100,000.

In addition to his work on the *Archives,* Force made some other contributions to American history. He was the first scholar to discover that the so-called Mecklenburg Declaration of Independence of 1775 was not what it purported to be. Then he published *The Declaration of Independence, or Notes on Lord Mahon's History of the American Declaration of Independence* (London, 1855). Occasionally, too, he printed a paper on a subject not directly related to his field: in 1852, *Grinnell Land: Remarks on the English Maps of Arctic Discoveries, in 1850 and 1851*; and in 1856, a "Record of Auroral Phenomena observed in the Higher Northern Latitudes" (*Smithsonian Contributions to Knowledge,* Vol. VIII). These minor works perhaps are of interest merely to the antiquarian, but the *American Archives* are still indispensable to every student of the American Revolution.

[The best account is the short paper by A. R. Spofford, in the *Records of the Columbia Historical Society,* vol. II (1899), pp. 218–33. See also "Peter Force," in *Am. Hist. Record,* Jan. 1874; and G. W. Greene, "Col. Peter Force—the American Annalist" in *Mag. of Am. Hist.,* Apr. 1878. There are scattered references to him and to his work in W. B. Bryan, *History of the National Capitol* (2 vols., 1914–16) and in the *Memoirs of John Quincy Adams,* vols. VI, VII, and IX. The private papers of Force are in the Lib. of Cong.] R. V. H.

FORD, DANIEL SHARP (Apr. 5, 1822–Dec. 24, 1899), editor, publisher, philanthropist, was born in Cambridge, Mass. His father, Thomas Ford, a native of Coventry, England, came to the United States about 1800. Like his more distinguished son, Thomas Ford was a devout Christian, and a generous helper of the poor and unfortunate. He died when Daniel was only six months old, and the boy grew up in a family which, though never in actual poverty, had continually to contend with narrow circumstances. The son had only a common-school education, but he supplemented that with constant reading and careful practise in writing. He learned the trade of a printer, and was employed first as a compositor and later as a bookkeeper in the office of the *Watchman and Reflector,* a prosperous weekly Baptist journal, published in Boston. Before he was thirty he had, with borrowed capital, bought a share in the firm which published this paper, and in 1857 he and his partner, J. W. Olmstead, bought the *Youth's Companion,* which had been founded thirty years before by Nathaniel Willis. Not long afterward the firm dissolved partnership; Olmstead kept the *Watchman and Reflector,* apparently the more profitable of their publications, and Ford devoted the rest of his life to the editorial and business management of the *Youth's Companion.* Therein he displayed very unusual abilities. He took it, as a small Sunday-school paper for young children, and gradually developed it into the most popular and successful family journal in the country. Its circulation grew from seven thousand in 1857 to more than half a million copies at the time of Ford's death. Carefully avoiding the didactic tone in the stories and articles which he printed, he succeeded in establishing the paper as a powerful influence for high literary and moral standards. Yet so modest and self-effacing was the editor that the paper was published under the assumed firm-name of Perry Mason & Company, and it is said that his own name never appeared in any part of the paper until the article announcing his death was printed early in 1900.

Ford was always deeply interested in religion and was a generous helper of religious enterprises. For many years he supported the Ruggles Street Church, a Baptist missionary institution in the Roxbury district of Boston, and during the later years of his life he often gave, always unostentatiously, as much as $50,000 a year to church and charitable work in Boston. At his death the larger part of his fortune of more than two million dollars was bequeathed to the various missionary and benevolent associations of the Baptist Church in New England. Almost a million dollars went to the Baptist Social Union of Boston, and with that money the Union built Ford Hall, the headquarters of various religious organizations, and the meeting place of the Ford Hall Forum, one of the early institutions for the helpful public discussion of modern social, economic, and religious problems in this country. Ford himself declared in his will that he wished his gift to stimulate the interest of the members of the Social Union "in the welfare of those who are dependent upon the returns from their daily toil for their livelihood," adding that the moment demanded closer personal relations between Christian business men and the American workingmen, because of the workingman's "religious indifference, his feverish unrest and his belief that business men and capital are his enemies. This attitude of mind," he concluded, "forbodes serious perils, and Christianity is the only influence that can change or modify them." Ford's wife was Sarah Upham, of Melrose, Mass.

[Brief biographical sketches of Ford's life appeared in the *Watchman*, Dec. 28, 1899; the *Youth's Companion*, Feb. 1, 1900; and the *Boston Transcript*, Dec. 26, 1899. See also J. L. Harbour, "How Ford Hall Came to be Built" in *Democracy in the Making* (1915), edited by Geo. W. Coleman.] H. S. C.

FORD, GORDON LESTER (Dec. 16, 1823–Nov. 14, 1891), lawyer, bibliophile, tracing his American ancestry from Andrew Ford, an Englishman who emigrated to Weymouth, Mass., in 1654, was the son of Lester and Eliza (Burnham) Ford. He was born at Lebanon, Conn. At the age of eleven he was sent to New York to enter the employ of his mother's brother, Gordon Burnham, a successful merchant. After this time his only schooling consisted of two terms in one of the city's night-schools. Even at that early age, he showed an innate aptitude for business and bookkeeping, and subsequently became accountant for the firm later well known as H. B. Claflin & Company. During these earlier years he lived with the family of the Quaker, John Gray, imbibing from such association many of the traits of that sect which he exhibited throughout his life. When still a young man, he entered the office of the United States marshal, studied law in his leisure moments, and was admitted to the New York County bar in 1850. He never seriously practised his profession, however, but devoted himself to business enterprise, in which he was uniformly successful. In 1852 he became president of the New London, Willimantic & Palmer Railroad, which position he held till 1856, when, soon after his marriage, he retired, and after a year or two in the suburbs of New York, made his home in Brooklyn. He speedily became identified with the leading institutions of that city. One of the earliest advocates of the abolition of slavery, he was largely instrumental in founding the Brooklyn *Union* in 1863. Appointed United States collector of internal revenue for the third collection district in 1869, he was removed in 1872 because he refused to allow political assessments for campaign purposes. Hitherto a stanch Republican, he now associated himself with the Liberal Republicans and was one of the Brooklyn delegates to the Cincinnati convention of May 1873, at which Horace Greeley was nominated for the presidency, though Ford himself actively supported Charles Francis Adams. In 1873 he became business manager of the *New York Tribune,* continuing in that position till 1881. Two years later he was elected president of the Brooklyn, Flatbush & Coney Island Railroad, but held the position for only a few months, retiring in order to devote himself to his private business affairs. He was heavily interested in Brooklyn commercial and financial institutions, particularly in the Peoples, Franklin and Hamilton Trust companies, and had with great prescience invested in real estate prior to the expansion of the city. From the first he associated himself with all movements aiming at the promotion of intellectual and artistic progress of the city. He was one of the founders of the Brooklyn Academy of Music and the Brooklyn Art Association, to both of which he gave much time and service. The Brooklyn Library, the Long Island Historical Society, and the Hamilton Club, organized in 1882 to take the place of the Hamilton Literary Association of Brooklyn, are also institutions with which he was intimately associated.

Throughout his life he was an enthusiastic, yet discriminating collector of books and manuscripts, relating principally to the history of America. His collection became the most valuable private library in America and before his death, the choicest collection of Americana in the world, containing 50,000 volumes, nearly 100,000 manuscripts, and autographic matter valued then at $100,000 (*Bulletin of the New York Public Library,* III, 1899, p. 52). He married Emily Ellsworth, daughter of Prof. William C. Fowler of Amherst, Mass., and grand-daughter of Noah Webster. Eight children were born to them, two of whom, Paul Leicester Ford [*q.v.*] and Worthington Chauncey Ford, inherited their father's literary and historical interests. Gordon Lester Ford's only literary production was a foreword to *Websteriana, a Catalogue of Books by Noah Webster* (1882), though he superintended the publication of a number of volumes of original and previously unpublished material from his collection. In 1899 his entire library was presented to the New York Public Library by his sons in memory of their father.

[Obituary notice in *Brooklyn Daily Eagle,* Nov. 14, 1891; E. R. Ford, *Ford Geneal.* (1916), pp. 12–13; private information.]
H. W. H. K.

FORD, HENRY JONES (Aug. 25, 1851–Aug. 29, 1925), editor, publicist, historian, came of English stock on his father's side and of Welsh stock on his mother's. He was born in Baltimore, Md., the son of Franklin and Anne Elizabeth (Jones) Ford. His father, a wholesale flour merchant, died when he was only nine, leaving the family in straitened circumstances. Henry attended the public schools in Baltimore until the age of seventeen, when he went to work in a wholesale dry-goods store, first as general utility boy, then as assistant bookkeeper. When he was barely twenty-one chance threw in his way a job on the *Baltimore American,* of which he became managing editor six years later. On Feb. 18, 1875, he married Bertha Batory of Howard County, Md. In 1879 he moved to New York to become editorial writer on the *Sun,* then under the management of Charles A. Dana, who exercised a formative influence upon the thought and style of the younger man. In 1883 he became city editor of the Baltimore *Sun,* and then in succession managing editor of the Pittsburgh *Commercial Gazette* (1885–95) and of the *Chronicle-Telegraph* (1895–1901), and finally editor of the *Pittsburgh Gazette* (1901–05).

The first of those writings on political history and government which brought him his reputation was *The Rise and Growth of American Politics; a Sketch of Constitutional Development* (1898), the outcome of reading and reflection "out of hours" through many years. For the first time this volume set forth the reciprocal action of party organization and governmental structure upon each other. As an editor he had come to realize the importance of the control of public expenditures, which involved the fundamental problem of the relation of executive and legislature in a constitutional government. To his mind the course of English constitutional history pointed to the only practical solution of this problem. The function of the executive was to govern; the rôle of the legislative to criticize and control. Yet as early as 1898 he discerned—what has since become manifest—signs of impaired efficiency in the British cabinet system, and he believed the presidency a much securer basis for democratic government if the essential principle of the British system could be recovered.

In 1906 he lectured in Johns Hopkins University and in the University of Pennsylvania. Two years later he was invited by President Woodrow Wilson of Princeton University to become professor of politics, his first academic post. When Wilson became governor of New Jersey he appointed Ford commissioner of banking and insurance (1912); and after he became president he sent him on a confidential mission to the Philippines, presumably to report on governmental conditions in those islands. In February President Wilson appointed him *ad-interim* member of the Interstate Commerce Commission. He served until May 1921 when he was replaced by an appointee named by President Harding. During this interval, in addition to conducting investigations in several important cases, he prepared a noteworthy decision on the subject of the Commission's power, under the Transportation Act of 1920, in relation to intrastate rates (*Rates, Fares, and Charges of New York Central Railroad Company,* 59 *I. C. C.,* 290), holding in effect that such rates were within the mandate to the Commission to prescribe a rate level which would enable the railroads to maintain an adequate and efficient service for the country at large. In 1922 the Supreme Court sustained this view (*Wisconsin Railroad Commission* vs. *Chicago, Burlington & Quincy Railroad Company,* 257 *U. S.,* 563).

During these years he published the following volumes: "The Evolution of Democracy: an Historical Sketch" (in *Problems in Modern Democracy,* 1901); *The Cost of Our National Government; a Study in Political Pathology* (1910), lectures on the Blumenthal Foundation at Columbia University; *The Scotch-Irish in America* (1915); *The Natural History of the State; an Introduction to Political Science* (1915); *Woodrow Wilson, the Man and His Work; a Biographical Study* (1916), primarily a campaign biography; *Washington and His Colleagues* (1918) and *The Cleveland Era* (1919), in The Chronicles of America Series; *Alexander Hamilton* (1920). He was also a frequent contributor to magazines; and some of these articles were published separately, notably "Darwinism in Politics and in Religion," which appeared serially in *The Living Church* (June to September 1909). His last work, *Representative Government,* published in 1924, like all of his writings, bears the stamp of a philosophical mind, richly stored with the harvest of years of reading. His death occurred at Blue Ridge Summit, Pa., after an extended illness. He was survived by his widow and four children.

[*Who's Who in America*, 1922–23; the present writer in the *Am. Pol. Sci. Rev.*, Nov. 1925, XIX, 813–16; data furnished by Mrs. Henry Jones Ford.] E. S. C.

FORD, JACOB (Feb. 10, 1738–Jan. 11, 1777), soldier, powder-maker, was the second son of Jacob and Hannah (Baldwin) Ford, of Morristown, N. J., and a grandson of John Ford who came from Duxbury, Mass., to Woodbridge, N. J., about 1701. His father, tavern-owner and iron-manufacturer, was long a county judge and built the oak-planked, ship-calked house which became Washington's headquarters. After attending the local school, the younger Jacob went into business. On Jan. 27, 1762, he married Theodosia Johnes by whom he had four sons and two daughters. By 1764 he had become the owner of the Middle Forge near Morristown and before 1770 he had bought 2,000 acres north of Denmark, building a forge and a house there, and somewhat later a stone mansion at Mt. Hope. But about 1773 he sold his property to John Jacob Faesch [*q.v.*], and moved to Morristown to look after his father's interests. Under the act passed by the Provincial Congress, June 3, 1775, he became colonel of militia in Morris County, commanding a battalion of over 800 officers and men.

The Fords were among "the first adventurers in blooming iron works," and cast shot and shell for Washington's army. By aid of a loan from the Provincial Congress of £2,000 on good security, without interest, they built early in 1776 their famous powder-mill in the thicket by the Whippanong River near the Morristown-Whippany road, not far from their own home. Col. Benoni Hathaway managed both mill and storage magazine, near the town green. Fieldpieces ambushed in Hathaway's yard commanded the approach. The mill produced "good powder and in useful quantities," one ton per month, at agreed prices, enabling the owners to repay the loan.

Ford did military service at Bergentown, the Helderbergs, and at Albany, earning the commendation of Robert Yates, who wrote on Oct. 28, 1776: "We are all much pleased with your activity and spirit" (Peter Force, *American Archives*, 5 ser., III, 1853, 579). He beat off British raids on Morristown so successfully and captured so much material, that Matthias Williamson wrote to Washington, Dec. 8, 1776, "it is chiefly owing to his zeal in the American cause, as well as his great influence with the people, that the appearance of defence at this post has been kept up" (*Ibid.*, pp. 1120, 1189). While repelling Leslie's brigade at Springfield, Dec. 17, 1776, he caught "mortal cold" in the "Mud Rounds"; and at Morristown, Dec. 31, he fell from his horse on parade to die eleven days later of pneumonia. Washington ordered a military funeral with full honors, an unusual tribute for army contractors. On Dec. 18, 1795, the county court ordered half-pay for his widow from Jan. 10, 1777 (*Proceedings of the New Jersey Historical Society*, April 1917). He is buried beside his father, who died Jan. 19, 1777, in the first Presbyterian churchyard at Morristown, and his monument records an ability, character, and humanity in which those who knew him implicitly trusted.

[The Ford genealogy is in *N. Y. Geneal. and Biog. Record*, Apr. 1922. Local details are given in A. M. Sherman, *Historic Morristown* (1905), and in E. D. Halsey, *Hist. of the Washington Asso. of N. J.* (1891). See also J. M. Swank, *Hist. of the Manufacture of Iron in All Ages* (1892), p. 116: *Proc. N. J. Hist. Soc.*, Jan. 1870; Peter Force, *Am. Archives*, 5 ser., III (1853); and *N. J. Archives, Docs. Relating to Revolutionary Hist. of the State of N. J.*, I, 1776–77 (1901), which ontains extracts from American newspapers.]

W. L. W—y.

FORD, JOHN BAPTISTE (Nov. 17, 1811–May 1, 1903), inventor, river-captain, manufacturer, was born in Danville, Ky., the son of pioneer parents, Jonathan (?) and Margaret (Baptiste) Ford. He learned what he could of reading and writing at home, then became an apprentice to John Jackson, a near-by saddler, but when the latter did not permit him to go to school, he made his way to New Albany, Ind., and thence to Greenville, where he learned the trade. Later he bought his master's shop to which he added a grain, flour, and commission business. At the age of twenty, he married Mary, the daughter of Benjamin Bower, who had assisted him with his education. He then sold his saddle business and opened a general store in Greenville. Prospering in this he began the manufacture of kitchen cabinets and later feed-cutting boxes for farmers. Just prior to the Civil War he set up a foundry and rolling-mill with railroad and commercial iron as his products. While so engaged he saw the possibilities of steamboat building. During the Civil War he and his two sons built and sold river-boats, and operated a line of thirty-eight steamboats and flatboats which they captained. The fleet served both the North and South in a purely commercial way during the war, being always in danger of destruction from one or the other. This dangerous venture, however, proved to be financially successful. At this time he sold his iron business for $150,000 and embarked on the manufacture of plate glass. By his reading he had become interested in the plate-glass industry of Belgium and England. Writing to the *Scientific American*, he raised the question as to the possibility of making plate glass in America.

The answer given him on all sides was discouraging. The cost of labor in the United States was said to be too high and raw materials too hard to secure. Despite this dark outlook, Ford obtained numerous glass formulae, engaged the services of expert workmen, and imported European machinery. Then, with his sons, he worked for ten years in a factory situated in New Albany, just across the river from Louisville, Ky. The depression following the Civil War, with the panic of 1873 as its climax, robbed the seventy-year old man of his fortune and he was forced to finance the undertaking with $30,000 obtained from the sale of an invention of a glass tube to New York interests. This tube was a rough glass sewer pipe which made the detection of stoppage easier. In addition he realized $20,000 as commission for the sale of Gen. Frémont's western holdings.

At the age of seventy-three Ford moved to Creighton, near Pittsburgh, and established the Ford Plate Glass Company. Successful from the beginning, this company soon occupied a number of plants, and Ford City became the "glass city." The industry earned for its owner a second great fortune. Later, when he entered one of the earliest of the great combines, he held with his sons a majority of the stock of the Pittsburgh Plate Glass Company, the Ford company being the largest unit. In this combination he was associated with John Pitcairn of the Pennsylvania Railroad Company who was the president. But in 1893 the Fords disagreed with Pitcairn on a question of policy and decided to sell their holdings. Thereafter, Edward Ford established his own glass-factory in Toledo, Ohio. In addition to his activities as a glass-manufacturer, the elder Ford established a large industry in Wyandotte, Mich., called the Michigan Alkali Company, the first American company to manufacture soda-ash, baking soda, and other important by-products. He also aided in bringing into utilization the gas deposits in the great Pittsburgh industrial district and himself conducted a successful pipe-line company.

Ford was a man of great vision, and was not afraid of change. In his lifetime he turned his hand to numerous enterprises, and was successful in nearly all of them. A friend of religion and learning, he built and equipped Methodist churches at Greenville, Ford City, and Wyandotte, as well as a Presbyterian church at the last-named place. He made liberal donations to Allegheny College, and at Tarentum he built and furnished a Young Men's Christian Association building and supplied it with an endowment. As a citizen he earned the highest regard of his associates. As an employer he enjoyed peaceful relations with his men during his whole career, and on the occasion of his eightieth birthday had the unusual honor of seeing a monument of himself erected by the employees of the Ford City plant. He was also awarded a medal and made an honorary member of the French Academy of Sciences.

[*Pittsburgh Chronicle Telegraph,* Nov. 18, 1901; the *News* (Jefferson, Ind.), Nov. 19, 1891; *Pittsburgh Press, Post,* and *Dispatch,* May 2, 1903; the *Commoner and Glassworker,* May 9, 16, 1903; and *Ford City,* a booklet privately printed by John N. McCue in 1917.]

A. I.

FORD, JOHN THOMSON (Apr. 16, 1829–Mar. 14, 1894), theatre manager, was the son of Elias and Anna (Greanor) Ford and was born in Baltimore. His ancestors were early Maryland settlers and some of them took part in the Revolutionary War. For a few years he attended public school in Baltimore and then became a clerk in his uncle's tobacco factory in Richmond. Not caring for this work, he became a book-seller. He then wrote a farce dealing with local matters, entitled *Richmond As It Is,* which was produced by a minstrel company called The Nightingale Serenaders. This farce met with not a little success; and George Kunkel, the owner and manager of the Serenaders, offered him a position with the organization. He accepted, and for several seasons traveled as business manager of this company throughout the United States and Canada.

In 1854, he assumed control of the Holliday Street Theatre, Baltimore, and this he managed for twenty-five years. In 1871, he built the Grand Opera House in that city; he also built three theatres in the city of Washington. His first theatre in Tenth Street was destroyed by fire and on the same site he built the theatre known as Ford's Theatre. He was the manager of this house at the time of the assassination of President Lincoln. Soon after this national tragedy he, together with his brother Harry Clay Ford, was incarcerated for thirty-nine days in the Old Capitol Prison. Since there was no evidence of their complicity in the crime, the brothers finally were fully exonerated and set free. The theatre was seized by the government and Ford was paid $100,000 for it by Congress. At the same time an order was issued prohibiting forever its use as a place of public amusement. On June 9, 1893, while five hundred government employees were at work, the front part of this building collapsed and twenty-eight persons were killed. It was soon after rebuilt. During his career, Ford also managed theatres in Alexandria, Va., Philadelphia, and Richmond. It was at the Richmond

Theatre, in 1857, that Edwin Booth, then under Ford's management, first met the lovely Mary Devlin whom he later married. Joseph Jefferson was then the stage manager and a member of the company of this theatre. Ford also managed a great number of traveling as well as resident companies which included the greatest stars and actors of his generation. He was honest and honorable in all his numerous business dealings. During the *Pinafore* craze, for example, he was the only American manager who paid Gilbert and Sullivan a royalty on the opera. This action prompted the authors, in presenting their next opera to America, to entrust their business affairs to him; and he leased the Fifth Avenue Theatre, New York, for the production of *The Pirates of Penzance*. For a period of forty years he was an active, prominent, and useful factor in civic life. He was connected with many banking and financial concerns, and his business advice was sought and relied on. He was president of the Union Railroad Company, member of the Board of Directors of the Baltimore & Ohio Railroad, vice-president of the West Baltimore Improvement Association, and trustee of numerous philanthropic institutions. In 1858, while serving as president of the city council, he was by force of circumstances made acting-mayor of the city of Baltimore and this position he filled with marked ability. His winning and gracious personality won him a host of friends. He died suddenly after an attack of the grippe, leaving a widow, Edith Branch Andrew Ford, who was the mother of eleven children.

[William Winter, *Life and Art of Jos. Jefferson* (1894); J. T. Scharf, *Hist. of Baltimore City and County* (1881); *Baltimore: Its Hist. and Its People,* II (1912), 145; Baltimore *Sun* and *N. Y. Tribune,* Mar. 15, 1894; private information.]

R. D.

FORD, PATRICK (Apr. 12, 1835–Sept. 23, 1913), journalist, was born in Galway, Ireland, the son of Edward and Anne (Ford) Ford. His parents died when he was a child, and in 1842 he was brought to America by friends who settled in Boston. There he attended the public schools and the Latin School. He worked as a youngster in the newspaper office of William Lloyd Garrison, began his active career as a journalist in 1855, and in 1859–60 was editor and publisher of the Boston *Sunday Times*. During the Civil War, as a member of the 9th Massachusetts Regiment he took part in the charge at Fredericksburg. He was married in March 1863 to Odele McDonald. From 1844 to 1846 he lived in Charleston, S. C., and edited the *Charleston Gazette,* but in 1870, returning North, to New York, he founded a paper called the *Irish World*. For the rest of his life his chief interest seems to have been championing the cause of Ireland. He conceived that the plight of that land had been brought about almost entirely by English despotism, and as time went on he hated England more and more inexorably. In 1874 he was one of the founders of the Greenback Labor party. In 1880–81 he organized in the United States 2,500 branches of the Irish Land League, and raised and dispatched for its support at home over $300,000—a dole which he eventually doubled. He advocated complete Irish independence: Home Rule never seemed to him any more than a compromise, Gladstone nothing more than an opportunist. He thought that the peasants should for a while refuse to pay their rents, and that at length they should rise in concerted rebellion. In support of these ideas he published in 1881 *A Criminal History of the British Empire*—originally letters addressed to Gladstone in the *Irish World,* and in 1885, *The Irish Question and American Statesmen.* He was a sensational antagonist, whose methods could be justified only by the extreme provocation which in his own mind, at least, was too amply existent. For all his explosiveness, he was in a way effective. He was the means, it is said, of bringing thousands of Democrats in the presidential election of 1884 to desert their party and vote for Blaine, and Gladstone is reported to have said ruefully: "But for the work the *Irish World* is doing and the money it is sending across the ocean, there would be no agitation in Ireland" (Ford, *Criminal History,* Preface, ed. 1915). He continued editing his paper almost till the time of his death. He died at his home in Brooklyn.

[P. H. Bagenal, *The Am. Irish* (1882); *Who's Who in America,* 1912–13; *N. Y. Times,* Sept. 24, 1913. See also Ford, "The Irish Vote in the Pending Presidential Election," in *North Am. Rev.,* Aug. 1888.]

J. D. W.

FORD, PAUL LEICESTER (Mar. 23, 1865–May 8, 1902), historian, novelist, was born in Brooklyn, the son of Gordon Lester Ford [*q.v.*] and Emily Ellsworth (Fowler) Ford, both of New England ancestry. An injury to the spine having dwarfed his growth, he was educated wholly by private tutors and his own omnivorous reading in the Clark Street home, where his father had gratified a scholarly taste by collecting one of the finest private libraries in America (now part of the New York Public Library). His brilliant and versatile mind early developed a love for study, especially in Americana; and with the encouragement of his father and his brother, Worthington C. Ford, he showed a precocious expertness in bibliographical activities.

The gift of a small press enabled him to print at the age of eleven *The Webster Genealogy, Compiled for Presentation only by Noah Webster, New Haven, 1836, with Notes and Corrections by his Great-Grandson, Paul Leicester Ford.* As his physical constitution triumphed over the suffering of his childhood, he largely mastered the treasures—pamphlets, manuscripts, and rare prints as well as books—stored in all parts of the house and especially in a large room more than fifty feet square at the rear. This library, the shelves orderly but the tables filled with "huge masses of books, pamphlets, papers, proof-sheets, and engravings in cataclysmic disorder," was one of the distinctions of Brooklyn, and the house a literary and social center.

From work in bibliographical research and editing rare materials, Ford progressed to more ambitious literary activities. Together with his father and his brother Worthington he formed the Historical Printing Club, which from time to time reprinted rare materials ultimately including fifteen volumes of *Winnowings in American History* (1890–91) edited by the two brothers. Other early productions were *Websteriana* (1882) a catalogue of Noah Webster's books in the Ford collection, and *Bibliotheca Chaunciana: A List of the Writings of Charles Chauncy* (1884). The centenary celebrations of post-revolutionary events helped turn his attention to a larger field, and at twenty-one he produced *Bibliotheca Hamiltoniana: A List of Books Written by or Relating to Alexander Hamilton, 1789–95*; *A List of Treasury Reports and Circulars Issued by Alexander Hamilton, 1789–95,* and *A List of Editions of the Federalist.* Thus fairly launched, he filled the next few years with scholarly publications which either made available material long lost to sight, such as his *Pamphlets on the Constitution of the United States, Published During its Discussion by the People, 1787–88* (1888), or offered a guide through historical thickets, as in his *Franklin Bibliography* and his *Check-List of American Magazines Printed in the Eighteenth Century* (1889). The appeal of all these publications was to learned circles, but he showed a taste for more popular topics in *The Ideals of the Republic: or, Great Words from Great Americans* and in his essay on *Who Was the Mother of Franklin's Son* (1889). His growing reputation as a scholar led the Historical Society of Pennsylvania to invite him to edit the writings of John Dickinson, of which the first volume appeared in 1895. A full list of his productions would be tiresome. The energy which later impressed his friends was now fully evident, but there was no carelessness or haste, his power of sustained effort being matched by his willingness to take minute pains.

Ford's versatility, the fact that fortunate inheritance gave him complete leisure, and a certain restlessness of temper, enabled him at a little past twenty-five to undertake successfully an astonishing number of labors. He launched into fiction in 1894 with *The Honorable Peter Stirling, and What People Thought of Him,* a study of political life based partly on observations made during an unsuccessful attempt to enter politics in the first ward in Brooklyn, and a book which, after failing temporarily to obtain notice, was lifted to best-seller rank by a popular impression that the picture of the hero was drawn from President Cleveland. This Ford denied, saying that the character was suggested by several public men. Though ill-constructed and sentimental, the novel offered truthful glimpses of municipal and state politics. Ford was meanwhile editing his collection of *The Writings of Thomas Jefferson* (10 vols.), of which the first volume appeared in 1892. For this he made extensive studies in the French foreign office, the archives in Washington, collections of state historical societies, and the private papers of many of Jefferson's contemporaries. The edition, with its critical and explanatory notes, still holds its place as the best yet made. He was still reprinting and editing little-known historical materials, such as the *Essays on the Constitution of the United States, Published 1787–88,* and the *Writings of Christopher Columbus Descriptive of the Discovery and Occupation of the New World* (1892). Moreover, he was about to venture into biography. In 1896 appeared the most popular book on Washington since Weems, his *The True George Washington,* a collection of informal essays on various aspects of the man, which succeeded in humanizing Washington without detracting from his greatness or dignity. It was based upon research in various special collections, notably the William F. Havemeyer library and the state department archives, and owed much to Worthington C. Ford, editor of Washington's writings. It soon passed through nearly a score of editions and has probably done more to furnish a correct view of Washington than any other single work.

In the last five years of Ford's life his literary pursuits became even more multifarious, while he successfully combined the rôles of popular novelist, historical scholar, and bibliopole. His *Janice Meredith: A Story of the American Revolution* (1899), an adroit combination of history and romance, owed part of its inspiration to his own study and part to S. Weir Mitchell's earlier success, *Hugh Wynne, Free Quaker*. It has marked faults of construction and lacks distinction of style, but it shows that the author was steeped in the literature of the time. Its portraits of Washington, Hamilton, and others, with their faults as well as virtues, are vividly done; and the wealth of semi-realistic detail makes it an enlightening study of the social life of the time. Ford lacked both the imagination and art to attain a high place as novelist, but even if considered merely as the brilliant diversion of a historian this book has more than ephemeral value. More than 200,000 copies having been sold, *Janice Meredith* was dramatized and staged (1901–02) with Mary Mannering in the chief rôle (T. A. Brown, *History of the New York Stage,* 1903, III, 365). In 1897 he had published *The New England Primer; A History of Its Origin and Development*; and in 1899 he brought out *The Many-Sided Franklin,* a book which essayed the same goal as the previous work on Washington but has since been largely superseded. Among his minor works of fiction were *The Great K. and A. Train-Robbery* (1897); *Wanted: A Match-Maker* (1900); and *Wanted: A Chaperon* (1902). Ford had also served as editor of the *Library Journal* from 1890 to 1893. He married in 1900 Mary Grace Kidder, of a prominent Brooklyn family, and removed to Manhattan, where at 37 East Seventy-seventh St. he had built a house. He was a noted diner-out, a member of various clubs, being especially interested in the Century, the Reform, and Grolier Clubs, and a lover of rural pleasures and exercise. While he was at the height of his activities, Ford's life was tragically terminated by his brother Malcolm W. Ford, once known as the best all-round amateur athlete in the United States, who, being disinherited and in financial difficulties, fatally shot Paul in his home and then killed himself.

[Private information; obituaries in the New York press, especially the *Evening Post* of May 9, 1902; Lindsay Swift, "Paul Leicester Ford at Home," the *Critic,* Nov. 1898; "Two American Writers," the *Outlook,* May 17, 1902; Arthur Bartlett Maurice, "Paul Leicester Ford," the *Bookman,* Feb. 1900.] A. N.

FORD, THOMAS (Dec. 5, 1800–Nov. 3, 1850), governor of Illinois, was born in Fayette County, Pa. His father was Robert Ford, of a Maryland family. His mother, Elizabeth, was the daughter of Hugh Logue and Isabella Delaney, both natives of Ireland. By a former marriage she was the mother of George Forquer, who by the time of his death in 1837 had risen to be the Jackson leader in Illinois. Robert Ford died in 1803, and the next year his widow removed first to St. Louis, then to New Design in the future Monroe County, Ill. Despite the straitened circumstances of the family, Thomas Ford managed to get a common-school education. Later his half-brother helped him to spend a year at Transylvania University; then with the encouragement of Daniel P. Cook he studied law. After a term of practise in Waterloo, Ill., he set up with Forquer in partnership at Edwardsville, 1825–29, and for the following six years, 1829–35, he served as state's attorney at Galena and Quincy, Ill. On Jan. 14, 1835, he was elected circuit judge by the state legislature, serving until Mar. 4, 1837, when he resigned to become judge of the Chicago municipal court. He was again elected circuit judge, Feb. 23, 1839. When the Democratic general assembly reorganized the state supreme court to swamp a Whig majority, he was elected to the court Feb. 15, 1841, and held office till he resigned to run for governor in 1842.

Ford's first recorded participation in politics was with his half-brother as henchman of Gov. Ninian Edwards. When Forquer, as Edwards's nominee, ran against Joseph Duncan for Congress in 1828, Ford contributed newspaper articles attacking Duncan (*Illinois Intelligencer,* July 5, 12, 19, 26, 1828). After the final overthrow of the Edwards faction, Ford apparently took no active part in politics until 1842. In the latter year the Whig and Democratic nominees for governor, Joseph Duncan and Adam W. Snyder, had long and vulnerable records to defend. The Democratic loss was therefore more apparent than real when Snyder died May 14, 1842. The leaders of the party turned to Ford, and after ten days' entreaty he consented to run. With no chance to gather ammunition for the election on Aug. 1, the Whigs lost to Ford by a vote of 39,020 to 46,507 (T. C. Pease, *Illinois Election Returns,* 1923, p. 126). The new governor faced a difficult situation. The state was burdened with a debt on which state taxes could not even pay the interest. In his history of Illinois Ford later stated with probable truth that his influence could have turned his party to the policy of repudiating the state debt (p. 292). Instead he secured the adoption of a scheme suggested by Justin Butterfield of Chicago by which the state was to make clear its willingness to shoulder its financial obligations to the extent of its ability, and foreign bondholders were to advance enough money to complete the Illinois and Michigan Canal, the tolls from which were to be applied to the liquidation of the debt. At the same time Ford interposed his influence to secure the peaceful termination of the state banks, which had fallen into difficulties.

In Ford's administration also a troublesome situation arose regarding the Mormon community. The murder of Joseph and Hyrum Smith at Carthage was the signal for the outbreak of open hostilities between the Mormons and the Gentiles in western Illinois. Ford repeatedly called out the militia to preserve order, and maintained that expediency demanded the withdrawal of the Mormons from the state, though he was criticised for playing for Mormon votes (*Alton Telegraph*, Aug. 21, 1844). But despite any censure which he received, Ford had the right to look back on his term with satisfaction. He had saved the state's credit, and assured its integrity and future prosperity. At the end of his term, though he was asked to run against Douglas for the Senate, he resumed the practise of law at Peoria. Unfortunately he was overtaken by tuberculosis, and at his death in 1850 was virtually dependent on charity. His wife, Frances Hambaugh, whom he had married on June 12, 1828, was worn out by nursing him and died a few weeks before him. He left five children for whose financial benefit he had some time before begun his *History of Illinois from its Commencement as a State in 1818 to 1847*. It was finally published under the auspices of James Shields in 1854. It is an interesting work. It covers essentially the period of Ford's personal observation of Illinois politics, and though the narrative is a good commentary on American democracy, his characterizations of public men are overdrawn and often unfair.

[*The Hist. of Peoria County* (1902), edited by David McCulloch, contains a short autobiography found among Ford's papers after his death. See also "Governors' Letter-Books, 1840–1853," and C. M. Thompson, "A Study of the Administration of Gov. Thos. Ford," in *Ill. State Hist. Lib. Colls.*, VII (1911); Chas. Ballance, *Hist. of Peoria, Ill.* (1870); U. F. Linder, *Reminiscences of the Early Bench and Bar of Ill.* (1879); T. C. Pease, *The Frontier State* (1918); J. F. Snyder, in *Jour. of the Ill. State Hist. Soc.*, July 1910 and Apr. 1911; John Reynolds, eulogy of Ford in *Belleville Advocate*, Nov. 14, 1850.]

T. C. P.

FORDYCE, JOHN ADDISON (Feb. 16, 1858–June 4, 1925), physician, was born in Guernsey County, Ohio, the son of John and Mary (Houseman) Fordyce, of Scotch and German ancestry, respectively. He was educated at Adrian College, Adrian, Mich., where he received the degree of B.A. in 1878. Graduating in medicine from Northwestern University Medical College in 1881, he served as interne for the next two years in the Cook County Hospital. From 1883 to 1886 he practised medicine in Hot Springs, Ark., then gave up his practise and for three years studied in Europe. The major part of his time there was devoted to the study of histo-pathology of the skin, under Kaposi, in Vienna, a part of his training which later profoundly influenced his writings. He was also a pupil of Lassar and of Behrend, and at the St. Louis Hospital, Paris, studied under Besnier, Vidal, and Fournier. In 1888 he received the degree of M.D. from the University of Berlin.

Returning to the United States in the same year Fordyce began the practise of medicine in New York City, specializing in dermatology and genito-urinary diseases. Within a few years his specialty became limited to dermatology and syphilology. From 1889 to 1893 he was instructor and lecturer in the New York Polyclinic Hospital. He was then appointed professor of dermatology in the Bellevue Hospital Medical College, where he remained for the next five years. In 1898, when New York University and Bellevue Hospital Medical College amalgamated, he accepted the position of professor of dermatology and syphilology in that institution. At this time (1898) the question arose whether patients having syphilis should be under the care of genito-urinary surgeons or of the dermatologists. More than to any one man, the credit is due to him for bringing clearly to the fore the advantages of having the treatment of syphilis in the hands of the dermatologist.

In 1912 Fordyce accepted an invitation to become professor of dermatology and syphilology at the College of Physicans and Surgeons of Columbia University and held that position until his death. Other hospital connections included that of visiting genito-urinary surgeon and later visiting dermatologist to the City Hospital from 1893 to 1925, and that of consulting dermatologist to the Presbyterian Hospital, Fifth Avenue Hospital, Woman's Hospital, New York Infirmary for Women and Children, and the Neurological Institute. He was also special consultant to the United States Public Health Service. He contributed well over one hundred authoritative articles to medical literature, and throughout his career was actively associated with American dermatological journals. As early as 1889 he became associated with Dr. P. A. Morrow, as editor of the *Journal of Cutaneous and Genito-urinary Diseases* (later the *Journal of Cutaneous Diseases, Including Syphilis*, and now the *Archives of Dermatology and Syphilology*). In 1892 he became sole editor of the journal, and though he resigned that position five years later, he retained a place on the editorial committee until 1920. In addition to his own research and writings, he did a great deal to stimulate original work by his contemporaries and associates. Probably one of his most important contributions to American medicine was his organization—in spite of numerous difficulties—of one of the best-known and best-equipped teaching centers of dermatology in the United States. Prior to this time, a man wishing to specialize in dermatology was forced to seek the necessary knowledge in clinics abroad. Fordyce was an indefatigable worker, and his tact and forceful personality attracted a group of men who with him constituted a brilliant staff, known throughout the world. He had the quality of leadership and was especially kind and lenient to younger men. Many of his pupils and associates are now prominent and successful specialists. Over one hundred and fifty post-graduate students received their training under his supervision.

On June 29, 1886, Fordyce married Alice Dean Smith. They had two children. He was a member of the American Museum of Natural History, New York Zoölogical Society, New York Academy of Sciences, and the Metropolitan Museum or Art. Of several hobbies, photography, probably, interested him most. With Dr. George M. MacKee, he photographed and arranged one of the most comprehensive collections of pictures of dermatological diseases in existence. His death in 1925 followed an operation for appendicitis.

[George M. MacKee, "John Addison Fordyce, M.D.," in *Archives of Dermatol. and Syphilol.*, Aug. 1925; *Who's Who in America*, 1924–25; H. A. Kelly and W. L. Burrage, *Dict. of Am. Medic. Biog.* (1928); *N. Y. Times*, June 5, 1925.] G. M. L.

FOREPAUGH, ADAM (1831–Jan. 22, 1890), showman, at the age of nine was working in his father's meat-shop in Philadelphia. At twenty, having learned the butchering trade thoroughly, he set out for the West. In time he settled in Cincinnati and in a shop of his own earned the capital to establish a stage-line business in Philadelphia. This in turn he relinquished to deal in horses, which he had learned to judge expertly. He supplied the animals for some of the early horse-car lines of New York and also for a large number of the two hundred or more circuses which were roving over the United States. In 1862 he sold horses to the famous Johnny O'Brien Circus but at the end of the season had to take a share in the business in payment. He and O'Brien divided the show in 1864. O'Brien took the Great National Circus on the road, while Forepaugh remained in Philadelphia with the most famous of American clowns, Dan Rice, who had brought with him his trick horse, Excelsior, and his trained Burmese cattle. This attraction brought him such success that by 1868 he was giving Rice a thousand dollars a week and paying his expenses. He had already bought a very good menagerie belonging to Jerry Mabie, the first of the smaller circusmen whose shows he absorbed. In 1867 he made his first road tour under his own name, and from this beginning made money steadily as he built up his show. In his later years his receipts averaged a quarter of a million dollars a year. In 1868 he tried dividing his show, sending one part East and the other West, but since he was never satisfied to delegate responsibility, he reunited the shows at the end of the season. In the following year he put his circus into two tents, one for the menagerie and one for the performance. This innovation drew in a great many people from the churches, who could look at animals with a free conscience, but who had scruples about watching human performers. By 1877 the circus was so large that he had to give up slow horse transportation and travel on railroads. Barnum's Greatest Show on Earth was now his most formidable rival, but the two showmen came into open conflict only in 1880, when they began to compete with each other in the same towns. The expense of the rivalry was so large that Barnum sued for peace and in 1882 a contract was signed which provided for a division of the routes between them, though the armistice was only temporary.

Forepaugh in his twenty-six years as the owner of a circus had only one partner, O'Brien, from whom he parted at the end of their third year together. During his career he attended to all important matters himself, checking his own payrolls and frequently counting the ticket returns. He bought the food-stuffs in each town and usually appeared in the cook-tent to do the butchering. His show was, distinctly, the show of Adam Forepaugh, and he always sat on the opening day in an open pavilion in front of the big tent, receiving friends and welcoming newcomers. His red face and flying side-whiskers were familiar to all.

[Geo. Conklin, *The Ways of the Circus* (1921); Maria Ward Brown, *Reminiscences of Dan Rice* (1901); Geo. Middleton, *Circus Memoirs* (1913); Wm. Lambert, *Show-life in America* (1925); the *Press* (Phila.), Jan. 24, 1890.] K. H. A.

FORESTER, FRANK [See HERBERT, HENRY WILLIAM, 1807–1858].

FORESTI, ELEUTARIO FELICE (1793–Sept. 14, 1858), United States consul, university professor, was born in Conselice, province of Ferrara, Papal States, in 1793. Little is known of his early years other than that he was a precocious pupil in the local schools. He studied at the University of Bologna, where in 1809 he obtained the degree of *dottore in legge*. Returning to his native town, he received successively the appointments of provisory assistant judge in the court of Ferrara, assistant professor of eloquence and belles-lettres in the lyceum, and justice of the peace, an office which necessitated his removal to Polesine. Later he was made praetor, under the Emperor's warrant, in Crespino, in the Lombardo-Venetian kingdom. About this time he became actively interested in Carbonarism. He was immediately admitted not only to all the grades of the society, but was also made a Guelph cavalier. Shortly afterwards a treacherous colleague revealed to the accredited agents of Austria and of Pope Pius VII the activities of this mysterious revolutionary combination in and around Ferrara, and on Jan. 7, 1819, Foresti and others who had been named as adherents of Carbonarism were arrested and hurried off to the Piombi, a famous prison in Venice. After a trial lasting more than a year, the final decision arrived at Venice in November 1821. Believing his fate sealed, Foresti made an unsuccessful attempt to commit suicide by plunging a penknife into his breast and swallowing fragments of a broken bottle. After two dreary years of imprisonment, aggravated by ingenious moral torture, he was condemned to death, but the sentence was later commuted to twenty years' imprisonment in the dungeons of Spielberg, Moravia, Austria.

In 1835 Ferdinand signalized his accession to the throne by a decree liberating the Italian patriots, but condemning them to exile in America. Foresti and his fellow prisoners arrived in New York on Oct. 20, 1836. Three years later, in 1839, he was appointed professor of Italian language and literature in Columbia College. In 1841, he became an American citizen, and in the following year he was appointed professor of Italian language and literature at New York University (then the University of the City of New York), holding this post as well as that of Columbia until the spring of 1856. In connection with his teaching of Italian, he edited Ollendorff's *New Method of Learning to Read, Write, and Speak the Italian Language* (1846). He also published, in 1846, *Crestomazia Italiana,* containing prose selections from the best Italian writers.

Unlike many of his fellow exiles who took no active part in the political movements in Italy, Foresti soon became interested in the *Giovine Italia*, a liberal organization which Mazzini had established. He entered into extensive correspondence with Mazzini, and finally became his official representative in America. In 1841 Foresti was made president of the Central Association of New York (Congrega Centrale di New York), and in 1850 was appointed delegate of the Triumvirate in America (delegato del Triumvirato), an organization the object of which was to give moral and material support to Mazzini. To further the cause of the latter, Foresti in 1850 founded an Italian review in New York entitled *L'Esule Italiano,* which, however, had a short existence. In May 1853 Franklin Pierce appointed Foresti United States consul to Genoa, but the Sardinian government decided peremptorily not to receive him. Gradually, however, Foresti began to recognize the benefits and advantages of a constitutional monarchy and went over to the side of the Sardinian government. He finally sailed for Italy in 1856, taking up his residence in Piedmont. His friends, including some of the leading citizens of his adopted country, then applied to President Buchanan for his appointment as United States consul at Genoa, to which post he was finally assigned in May 1858. Brief, however, was his enjoyment of the distinction, for he died of dropsy on Sept. 14, 1858.

[For further details on the life of Foresti consult: "Ricordi di Felice Foresti," published in Atto Vannucci's *I Martiri della Libertà Italiana* (Milan, 1878), vol. II; "Political and Personal Reminiscences of Prof. Felice Foresti," *N. Y. Times,* July 7, 1854; American newspapers from 1836 to 1858; H. T. Tuckerman, "E. Felice Foresti," *Atlantic Monthly,* Nov. 1859; Mario Menghini, ed., *Lettere di G. Garibaldi, Q. Filopanti, e A. Lemmi a Felice Foresti, e Lettere di Felice Foresti a G. Lamberti e a G. Mazzini* (Imola, 1909); diplomatic correspondence on Foresti in the archives of the U. S. Department of State, Washington, D. C., 1853, 1854, and 1858; *Scritti editi ed inediti di Giuseppe Mazzini* (Imola, 48 vols., 1906–27).] H.R.M.

FORGAN, JAMES BERWICK (Apr. 11, 1852–Oct. 28, 1924), banker, was born at St. Andrews, Scotland, the son of Robert Forgan and Elizabeth Berwick. His father had established himself in St. Andrews as a manufacturer of golf clubs and golf balls. The son was intended for the law and after his education at Forres Academy of which his uncle was rector, he was apprenticed to a lawyer at St. Andrews. Within a year, however, he took an apprenticeship as clerk in the branch of the Royal Bank of Scotland at St. Andrews. Through a former employee of the bank, he was persuaded to go to Canada as an employee of the Bank of British North America. He arrived in Montreal in 1873 and shortly thereafter was transferred to the Halifax branch, where he remained for a little more than a year. After a brief interim of a year and a half with an insurance company, during which time he married Mary Ellen Murray, daughter of a Halifax merchant, he returned to banking as paying teller for the local branch of the bank of Nova Scotia in 1875. Thereafter his advance was rapid. He was made inspector of branch banks and in 1885 became agent in charge of the branch at Minneapolis, Minn. His qualities as a banker were quickly recognized by Minneapolis business men and he was made cashier of the

Northwestern National Bank of Minneapolis in 1888. Recognizing the opportunities for success in his profession in the rapidly expanding West, Forgan at this time became an American citizen. While in the employ of the Northwestern National he came in contact with Lyman Gage, then president of the First National Bank at Chicago and later secretary of the treasury under McKinley. Through Gage, Forgan in 1892 became a vice-president of the Chicago bank, and remained with it until his death. By 1900 he had become a principal stockholder and the president. Through a series of mergers with smaller Chicago banks, and by radical changes in the internal organization of the bank, he made the First National one of the most powerful institutions of its kind in the West. Perhaps his most important contribution to banking was his work with the Chicago Clearing House Committee with which he was associated for twenty-five years. He was largely responsible for the system set up through this committee in 1906, and now widely imitated, of clearing-house bank examination for member banks. He also took a lively interest in currency reform, and acted as vice-chairman of the currency committee of the Amercan Bankers' Association in its conferences with the National Monetary Commission on Banking reform. After the Federal Reserve system was organized he served for six years as director of the Reserve Bank at Chicago, and as member of the executive committee and president of the Federal Advisory Council of the Reserve System for a like period.

Except for a number of addresses on currency reform and clearing-house bank examination, Forgan left only one publication, *Recollections of a Busy Life,* written when he was seventy-two and published just before his death. In it he gives the key to his dominant interest in life: "My life has been so absorbed in, and my energy so concentrated on, the growth and development of the banks which have commanded my services, that my life story has been practically inseparable from theirs."

[Forgan's autobiography, *Recollections of a Busy Life* (1924); *Chicago News*, and *Chicago Tribune*, Oct. 29, 1924.] E. A. D.

FORMAN, DAVID (Nov. 3, 1745–Sept. 12, 1797), Revolutionary soldier, was born in Monmouth County, N. J., the son of Joseph Forman, a wealthy New York shipping merchant, and Elizabeth (Lee) Forman. He was descended from Robert Forman, a dissenter, who emigrated from Buckinghamshire, England, to Holland and thence to America, where he became one of the eighteen patentees of Flushing, on Long Island (1645), and died at Oyster Bay in 1671. David Forman is said to have attended the College of New Jersey, but did not graduate. On Feb. 28, 1767, he married Ann Marsh, by whom he had eleven children. In June 1776 he was appointed colonel of one of the New Jersey regiments sent to reinforce Washington at New York. Six months later he suppressed a Loyalist uprising in Monmouth County (November 1776) and was chosen by Washington to command one of the new Continental regiments authorized by Congress. He was commissioned brigadier-general by the New Jersey legislature in the spring of 1777 and commanded the Jersey militia at the battle of Germantown (October 1777). Shortly thereafter Washington permitted Forman to withdraw his uneasy militia from the main army, Maj.-Gen. Philemon Dickinson having expressed concern for the safety of the Jerseys. Forman resigned his commission in November 1777 because of differences with the legislature. He was later attached to Maj.-Gen. Charles Lee's staff by Washington's order, presumably because of his knowledge of the region. Lee petulantly refused his aid, and following the battle of Monmouth (June 1778), Forman joined the other officers in testifying against Lee at the court martial. Throughout the remainder of the war he busied himself with the suppression of the pine robbers and armed Loyalist refugees of the Jersey coast. His harsh treatment of the disaffected, characterized by inhumanity, earned for him a reputation for brutality in a vicious partisan warfare. He also kept Washington informed of the movements of British vessels off the adjacent coast (1780–82). In the spring of 1782 the "Honorable Board of Associated Loyalists" in New York sent an expedition against a Continental post on Toms River commanded by Capt. Joshua Huddy. Huddy was captured, taken to New York, and hanged. Forman repaired to Washington's headquarters to demand retaliation. Washington wrote to the British commander-in-chief demanding that those guilty be delivered to the Americans. Sir Henry Clinton ordered a court martial for their trial, but complained of American cruelty in New Jersey, especially in Monmouth County, where Forman, called by the Loyalists "Devil David," had been actively persecuting the King's loyal subjects "with all the vindictiveness of his strong nature." Washington warned Gov. William Livingston (May 6, 1782) that he would yield to the British all Jersey militia committing acts contrary to the laws of war. After the war Forman was judge of the court of common pleas for Monmouth County. In 1794 he moved to Chestertown, Kent County, Md., and later visited Natchez, where he owned a large estate. Attacked by apoplexy while there, he recovered somewhat, and sailed from New Orleans for New York. The vessel was captured by a British privateer in the Gulf and taken to the Bahamas, during which voyage Forman died.

[*Docs. Relating to the Revolutionary Hist. of the State of N. J.*, I (1901), IV (1914); Anne S. Dandridge, *Forman Geneal.* (1903); Jared Sparks, ed., *The Writings of Geo. Washington* (12 vols., 1834–37); *Proc. of a General Court-Martial, Held . . . for the Trial of Maj.-Gen. Lee* (1778); Wm. S. Stryker, *The Battle of Monmouth* (1927); F. Ellis, *Hist. of Monmouth County, N. J.* (1885); *Somerset County Hist. Quart.*, Oct. 1917.]

F. E. R.

FORMAN, JOSHUA (Sept. 6, 1777–Aug. 4, 1848), early advocate of the Erie Canal, author of the New York Safety Fund plan, was born at Pleasant Valley, Dutchess County, N. Y., to which place his parents Joseph and Hannah (Ward) Forman, both natives of New Jersey, had removed from New York City. After graduating from Union College in 1798, he studied law in Poughkeepsie and New York, but in 1800 removed to Onondaga County, then almost a wilderness. He practised law at the village of Onondaga Hollow until 1819, when he removed to the present site of Syracuse, of which he has been officially recognized as the founder. Since land titles at that time were in a state of almost hopeless confusion, and litigation was consequently brisk, lawyers could prosper in apparently insignificant hamlets. In 1813 Forman was appointed the first judge of the court of common pleas in the county and served ten years. He was an able business man, as well as a good citizen, and was interested in many enterprises in the county. He built a tavern and grist-mills, organized a company to work the gypsum deposits near by, and greatly improved the methods of manufacturing salt. He was active in establishing public institutions, and while living in Syracuse procured the passage of an act to lower the level of Lake Onondaga, making it possible to drain the adjacent swamps, and thereby greatly improving health conditions in the vicinity.

Transportation was a vital question in a region where roads were often quagmires, and there was much talk of building canals to connect the various settlements, but no comprehensive plan was proposed. In 1807 Forman, though a Federalist in a Republican county, was elected to the Assembly, and in 1808 introduced and carried a resolution to appoint a joint committee to consider "the propriety of exploring and causing an accurate survey to be made of the most eligible and direct route for a canal, to open a communication between the Tidewaters of the Hudson River and Lake Erie" (*Publications of the Buffalo Historical Society*, II, 28). This was the beginning of legislative action which finally resulted in the construction of the Erie Canal. In his later years Forman was inclined to claim the credit of originating the idea, but it is clear that some months previously Jesse Hawley had published a series of articles advocating the measure in the *Genesee Messenger*. However, Forman constantly advocated building the canal, and in 1825, as president of the village of Syracuse, represented the town and the county at the opening celebration.

He frequently speculated in land, and at one time controlled the heart of the present city of Syracuse, which he laid out into lots. Due to his investments his affairs became involved, and about 1826 he removed to New Brunswick, N. J., to work a copper-mine. He continued to take keen interest in his native state, especially in the banking situation, which was then quite unsatisfactory. On the election of Martin Van Buren to the governorship, Forman offered him a plan to insure the redemption of bank-notes by requiring all banks to contribute to a guarantee fund. He had gained the germ of the idea from reading of a somewhat similar plan of mutual guarantee of indebtedness in practise among the Hong merchants of China. Van Buren, after consultation with his financial advisers, approved, and sent a special message to the legislature enclosing the plan (Jan. 26, 1829), together with a full explanation by Forman. With considerable modification the plan was enacted into law as the Safety Fund Act, and became an important landmark in the financial history of the state (*Journal of the Assembly*, 1829).

The same year Forman, who had previously purchased an immense tract of wild land in North Carolina, removed to the village of Rutherfordton in that state. He spent the remainder of his life there, engaged in disposing of his lands and in various business enterprises until a stroke of paralysis reduced his activities. He was highly esteemed by his neighbors and associates (J. H. Wheeler, *Historical Sketches of North Carolina from 1584 to 1851*, 1851, p. 399). His first wife was Margaret Alexander of Glasgow, Scotland, who died just before his removal to North Carolina. Later he married Sarah Garrett of Warm Springs, Tenn. He was a man of wide information and high character. Though said to be a good lawyer, he was essentially a promoter and builder. His boundless faith in the development of the United States sometimes caused him to be regarded as visionary, but his early advocacy of the Erie Canal, his faith in Syracuse, and the idea of the Safety Fund are solid contributions to the public welfare.

[A sketch by J. V. H. Clark in *Onondaga*, vol. II (1849), was reprinted by Forman's son-in-law, Gen. E. S. Leavenworth, in *Geneal. of the Leavenworth Family* (1873). The latter corrected a common error in the date of Forman's death, but did not mention his second wife, who appears in *The Forman Geneal.* (1903), by Anne S. Dandridge and in a sketch by E. E. Dickinson in the *Mag. of Am. Hist.*, June 1882. His connection with the Erie Canal is discussed at length in *Buffalo Hist. Soc. Pubs.*, vol. II (1880), and in David Hosack's *Memoir of De Witt Clinton* (1829). For his connection with the Safety Fund see John Jay Knox, *A Hist. of Banking in the U. S.* (rev. ed. 1900).] H.T.

FORMAN, JUSTUS MILES (Nov. 1, 1875–May 7, 1915), author, was born in Le Roy, N. Y., the son of Jonathan Miles and Mary (Cole) Foreman. His father, who was born in 1804, had by a former marriage four children, the youngest of whom was born in 1838. Justus was the only child of his mother. The first of the family in America was William Foreman, who came from England to Maryland about 1675. William's grandson, John, while returning from an expedition in one of the British colonial wars, married and settled in New England. Justus spent most of his boyhood in Minnesota, the home of one of his half-brothers. There he attended the Minneapolis schools, and was a student for one year at the state university. He entered Yale in the fall of 1895, was graduated in 1898, and studied art in Paris until 1901. While abroad he began writing the numerous stories which appeared then and later in various American magazines. In 1902 he published a novel, *The Garden of Lies*, the first of a series of romances which appeared at the rate of about one a year for the remaining years of his life. His writings were uniformly tense and full of action, and they dealt in general with European and American characters who were both rich and aristocratic. They were extremely popular in France and England as well as in America, but the interest with which they were received seems likely to become less and less comprehensible.

Forman found great enjoyment in traveling, and was as much in England and France as in New York. Between times he visited Greece, Turkey, Africa, Australia, and the Orient. The East infatuated him, and he adorned his house with mysterious silken hangings and bronze statues of Buddha. As time went on it seemed to him that a divan more effectively than a chair inspired his genius. In 1904–05, a play in which he had collaborated, based on his *Garden of Lies*, was successfully produced in London. His next attempt at drama, *The Hyphen*, written, according to gossip, in nine days, was put on in New York in the spring of 1915. It dealt in a sensational manner with a theme then much in the public mind—that of divided or hyphenated political allegiance, particularly as in the case of German-Americans. In early May he set out for Europe on the *Lusitania* as a war correspondent for the *New York Times*. He was never heard of after the boat was sunk.

[Yale Coll. *Triennial Record of the Class of 1898* (1902), *Class of Ninety-Eight Statistics* (1910); E. E. Farman, *Foreman, Farman, Forman Geneal.* (1911); *Who's Who in America*, 1914–15; *N.Y. Times*, Apr. 25, May 8, 1915.] J.D.W.

FORNEY, JOHN WIEN (Sept. 30, 1817–Dec. 9, 1881), Philadelphia journalist, was born at Lancaster, Pa., of German descent, the son of Peter and Margaret (Wien) Forney. His brief schooling was terminated when at thirteen he went to work in a store. Three years later he became an apprentice in the printing-office of the Lancaster *Journal*. When he was twenty he became editor and part owner of a dying newspaper, the Lancaster *Intelligencer*, and in two years brought it to sufficient prosperity to enable him to unite it with the *Journal* and to marry Elizabeth Mathilda Reitzel in 1840. As a Democratic editor Forney attached himself at the outset of his career to the political fortunes of James Buchanan, whose presidential ambitions he made the means of his own advance locally and nationally. When Buchanan became secretary of state in 1845, President Polk appointed Forney deputy surveyor of the port of Philadelphia. This plum enabled its recipient to sell out at Lancaster and remove to Philadelphia, where in partnership with A. Boyd Hamilton he became editor and proprietor of the *Pennsylvanian*.

After the defeat of the Democrats in 1848, he sought election as clerk of the House of Representatives, but in spite of Buchanan's aid he failed to secure the position until 1851. He rendered active service in the campaign of 1852 and then became an editorial writer for the Washington *Daily Union*, the paper that enjoyed the executive patronage. In 1854 he was admitted to partnership in this paper and aided his partner A. O. P. Nicholson in obtaining the lucrative printing contracts of the House of Representatives. Meantime, he had become involved in a journalistic feud with a Virginia newspaper rival, Beverly Tucker of the Washington *Sentinel*, in which the powerful Virginia Democrats sided with Tucker. Forney resented also what he considered Southern persecution of his friend Gov. Reeder in his Kansas difficulties. Finally, his friendship for Buchanan when Pierce was seeking renomination made his situation more than ever impossible, so in 1856 he relinquished his share in the *Union*, after presiding over the House of Representatives most successfully during the strenuous scenes of the two months' struggle for the speakership in 1855–56. This release left him free to devote himself to his great ambition, Buchanan's nomination and election as president.

Then came the question: what was to be the reward for his twenty years' loyalty? Both Buchanan and Forney agreed that he should have the *Union* with the fortune that came from the congressional printing. But Forney's enemies blocked this move. Then Forney desired to be senator from Pennsylvania; but Cameron defeated him, in spite of the fact that President Buchanan's influence gained the caucus nomination for him. Buchanan then offered him his choice of the Liverpool consulship or the naval office at Philadelphia; but Forney was committed to other men for these posts, and Mrs. Forney, who was in an unfortunate state of health, was bitterly opposed to his accepting either position. The twenty years of loyalty soon melted into distrust and dissatisfaction. Forney decided to go back to Philadelphia journalism, and there established the *Press* ostensibly in support of Buchanan in August 1857. Buchanan, however, could not or would not aid him with public printing. When Walker came back from Kansas and Douglas opened fire upon the Buchanan administration, Forney joined forces with them; by 1860 he had become a Republican and had resumed his old position as clerk of the House; a year later he became secretary of the Senate and continued in that position until 1868.

In 1861 Forney founded the *Sunday Morning Chronicle,* and on Nov. 3, 1862, he began publishing a daily edition (the *Daily Morning Chronicle*), at the suggestion, it was afterward said, of President Lincoln, who feared the influence in the Army of the Potomac of the *New York Tribune,* which was critical of the administration (see *Sunday Chronicle,* Dec. 11, 1881). At all events, with the *Chronicle* and the *Press,* Forney actively supported the Lincoln administration. He also supported President Johnson at first, but when the radicals began their warfare upon the administration Forney followed them and Andrew Johnson had no more virulent critic than Forney's *Chronicle.* During Grant's administration Forney sold out his Washington paper (1870) and went back to Philadelphia. Here he became collector of the port (1871) but retired within a year. The remaining ten years of his life were spent in journalism, travel, and lecturing. In 1878 he founded and edited at Philadelphia a weekly magazine called *Progress.* Once more he changed his political allegiance, becoming a Democrat and writing *The Life and Military Career of Winfield Scott Hancock* (1880) as a campaign biography. He also wrote *Anecdotes of Public Men* (2 vols., 1873–81) and *The New Nobility* (1881). Throughout his life he had proved to be enterprising and energetic but emotional and unstable, sentimental in his loyalties, bitter in his hates. He possessed an unusually accurate instinct for winning causes, but in spite of his ability to support the victors, he generally had enemies sufficiently powerful to prevent his obtaining much profit from his foresight.

[*Forty Years of Am. Journalism: Retirement of Mr. J. W. Forney from the Phila. "Press"* (1877); Alex. Harris, *Biog. Hist. of Lancaster County* (1872); *Phila. Press,* Dec. 10, 12, 13, 1881; *Phila. Record* and Phila. *Public Ledger,* Dec. 10, 1881; Washington *Sunday Chronicle,* Dec. 11, 1881; *Progress* (Phila.) Dec. 17, 1881; *Printers' Circular* (Phila.), Dec. 1881. A large and revealing collection of Forney's letters is to be found in the Jeremiah S. Black Papers, Lib. of Cong., and in the Buchanan Papers, Hist. Soc. of Pa. H. O. Folker, *Sketches of the Forney Family* (1911), gives the name of Forney's mother as Wein, but the cemetery record gives Wien for his middle name.] R. F. N.

FORNEY, MATTHIAS NACE (Mar. 28, 1835–Jan. 14, 1908), engineer, editor, inventor, was born in Hanover, Pa., the son of Matthias Nace and Amanda (Nace) Forney. He was educated in the public schools of Hanover and studied three years in a boys' school in Baltimore. At the age of seventeen he apprenticed himself to Ross Winans, a locomotive builder in Baltimore, and spent three years in the shop and one in the drafting room. He then became a draftsman for the Baltimore & Ohio Railroad in Baltimore and held this position for three years. Feeling that the prospect for advancement was rather slight, he went into business in Baltimore late in 1858, but after three years of indifferent success he returned to his earlier employment, this time as a draftsman for the Illinois Central Railroad in Chicago. In the course of his three years' service here he designed, and in 1866 obtained a patent, for an "improved tank locomotive" which afterwards became known as the Forney engine. It was designed especially for suburban and city train service and was exclusively used on the New York, Brooklyn, and Chicago elevated railroads until superseded by the electric locomotive. About 1865 Forney went to Boston to superintend the building of locomotives then being made for the Illinois Central by the Hinkley & Williams Works, and upon the completion of the work he remained with the company partly as a draftsman and partly as a traveling agent. Late in 1870 he became an associate editor of the *Railroad Gazette,* published in Chicago. The publishing office was transferred to New York after the Chicago Fire of 1871, and in 1872 Forney purchased a half-interest in the journal and served as editor until the end of 1883, when ill health compelled him temporarily to relinquish all active work. As editor of the *Railroad Gazette,* "he fought almost alone at the beginning against the general adoption of the narrow gauge, and was finally successful in turning the tide" (*American Engineering and Railroad Journal,* February 1908). In 1886 he purchased the *American Railroad Journal* and *Van Nostrand's Engineering Magazine* which he consolidated, edited, and published under the name of *Railroad and Engineering Journal* until 1893, and as *American Engineer and Railroad Journal* until he sold it in 1896. In the course of his busy life he obtained thirty-three patents pertaining to the railway industry. Beside his tank locomotive he patented a number of improvements on railway car seats, an interlocking switch and signal apparatus, furnace doors, steam-boilers, feed water-heaters for locomotives, and similar devices. In 1873 he published in the *Railway Gazette* and in 1875 in book form his *Catechism of the Locomotive,* which has been the instruction book of thousands of railroad men and has passed through several editions. He also was the author of the first edition of *The Car-Builders' Dictionary* (1879), of a *Memoir of Horatio Allen* (1890), and of *Political Reform by the Representation of Minorities* (1894). He was a member of the Master Car Builders' Association, and while secretary from 1882 to 1889 he brought about its reorganization so that it would be more in touch with railroad officials and railroad companies. He was elected a life member in 1890. He was active in the American Free Trade League, the American Peace Society of Boston, and the Citizens' Union and Anti-Imperialists' League of New York. He was an honorary member of the American Railway Master Mechanics' Association and was one of the organizers of the American Society of Mechanical Engineers. In 1902 his "Reminiscences of Half a Century" was published in the *Official Proceedings of the New York Railroad Club* (vol. XII, no. 7). He married in 1907, at the age of seventy-two, Mrs. Annie Virginia Spear of Baltimore, and died in New York City survived by his widow.

[*Trans. Am. Soc. of Mech. Engineers,* XXX (1908); Angus Sinclair, *Development of the Locomotive Engine* (1907) and memoirs of Forney in *Report of the Proc. . . . of the Master Car Builders' Asso.* (1908) and in *Report of the Proc. of the Am. Railway Master Mechanics' Asso.* (1908); *Am. Engineer and Railroad Jour.,* Feb. 1908; *Cassier's Mag.,* Mar. 1908; *Railroad Gazette,* Jan. 17, 1908; *Railway Age,* Jan. 24, 1908; H. O. Folker, *Sketches of the Forney Family* (1911); U. S. Patent Office records.] C. W. M.

FORNEY, WILLIAM HENRY (Nov. 9, 1823–Jan. 16, 1894), lawyer, Confederate soldier, congressman, was born at Lincolnton, N. C., the son of Peter and Sabina Swope Hoke Forney. The Forneys were descended from Jacob Forney, whose father, a Huguenot, fled from France after the revocation of the Edict of Nantes, and settled in Alsace. Jacob, left an orphan at the age of fourteen, went to Amsterdam and thence to Pennsylvania. In 1752 he married a Swiss girl, Maria Bergner; and in 1754 they removed to North Carolina. In 1835, his son Peter moved his family to Calhoun County, Ala., and occupied lands in the fertile Coosa Valley. William was graduated from the University of Alabama in 1844, and afterward read law in the office of his brother, Daniel Munroe Forney of Jacksonville, Ala. When the war with Mexico began, he enlisted with the 1st Alabama Volunteers and served as lieutenant in the siege of Vera Cruz. After one year of service he returned to Jacksonville and resumed the study of law. He was admitted to the bar in 1848 and with the exception of the year 1859, when he served in the legislature, he practised law constantly down to 1860. As a lawyer he established a reputation that was "more solid than brilliant." On Oct. 4, 1854, he was married to Mary Eliza Woodward, daughter of a prosperous merchant of Calhoun County.

Forney entered the Confederate ranks as captain of the 10th Alabama Regiment, and served on the Virginia battle-front. He won a reputation as a zealous and fearless leader. He was wounded thirteen times, and at Gettysburg was crippled for life. He was captured at Gettysburg and imprisoned for a year. When released upon exchange he returned to the Army of Northern Virginia, "still a cripple and hobbling on crutches" and was promoted colonel. Shortly before the surrender at Appomattox he was raised to the rank of brigadier-general. He returned to Jacksonville, maimed and broken in health, and resumed his law practise for such business as one who had been so conspicuous in the Confederacy could procure under the régime of Reconstruction. He was elected to the state Senate in 1865 and served until the Reconstruction measures were put into operation. When the Carpet-Bag government was overthrown he was elected to Congress where he served continuously from 1875 to 1893. He became a stalwart political figure in the seventh district. Although he was too conservative for many of the depressed and disgruntled farmers, his integrity and sturdiness and his distinguished war record, the marks of which he bore upon his huge frame, made him an unbeatable candidate for office.

[H. O. Folker, *Sketches of the Forney Family* (1911); W. Brewer, *Alabama: Her Hist., Resources,*

War Record, and Public Men (1872); A. B. Moore, *Hist. of Ala. and Her People* (1927); T. M. Owen, *Hist. of Ala. and Dict. of Ala. Biog.*, vol. III (1921); B. F. Riley, *Makers and Romance of Ala. Hist.* (1915); J. C. Du Bose, *Notable Men of Ala.*, vol. II (1904); *Official Records (Army)*; *Mobile Daily Reg.*, Jan. 18, 1894; *Biog. Dir. Am. Cong.* (1928).] A.B.M.

FORREST, EDWIN (Mar. 9, 1806–Dec. 12, 1872), earliest American-born actor of the first rank, was born in Philadelphia, Pa., the son of William Forrest, a Scotchman by birth, and Rebecca Lauman of German parentage. William Forrest left his large family unprovided for when he died in 1819, and young Edwin left school to run errands in a store, and thereafter was self-educated. His early bent toward the stage was indicated by his juvenile imitations of the family minister, and by his attempts, at the age of eleven, to impersonate a girl on the stage of the South Street Theatre. Persisting in his ambition to act, he made a début at the Walnut Street Theatre, Nov. 27, 1820, as Young Norval, and won sufficient encouragement to take up acting as a profession—not, probably, that the encouragement had to be great. The next few years were spent in the hard school of the frontier theatre. He joined a roving company playing in Pittsburgh and the Ohio River towns, and when that failed found odd jobs to keep alive. Sol Smith records in his *Theatrical Management in the West and South for Thirty Years* (1868) that Forrest played a negro part in Smith's farce, *The Tailor in Distress,* in Cincinnati, in 1823, perhaps the earliest "black face" impersonation in our theatre. Shortly after Smith had to rescue the despondent youth from a circus, which he had joined as a tumbler, and sent him to New Orleans, where a position was open in the company of James H. Caldwell, then theatrical czar of the South. Forrest was a powerful, handsome, wilful, unschooled youth, not yet twenty, when he reached New Orleans, and his character must have been affected by the life into which he was thrown, at once gay, sophisticated, crude, and cruel. Among his admired friends in New Orleans was Col. Bowie, who used to fight duels naked, armed with the famous knife he invented. Passions were violent and uncontrolled, and something of the violence and unrestraint of Forrest's later years may well be attributed to his early days in New Orleans, when he himself challenged Caldwell to a duel over a lady—the older man, however, sensibly refusing to fight.

In the autumn of 1825 Forrest secured an engagement at Albany, at $7.50 a week, where for a time he supported the guest star, Edmund Kean. The great English actor, whose flaming style was to Forrest's taste, took a fancy to the young American, and while Forrest played Yago to his Othello, and other supporting rôles, taught him both by example and friendly precept. Though Forrest's style became distinctly individual, its best features were undoubtedly shaped by his study of Kean, especially his electrifying climaxes of passion. It is recorded that he played Iago as a "gay and dashing" blade, which pleased Kean greatly. As an example of his violent personal characteristics, once at Albany he gambled all night, won all the money, then hurled the cards in the fire, threw the money on the floor, and never gambled again. On June 23, 1826, Forrest made his first appearance in New York, at the Park Theatre, then the leading theatre of America. He boldly chose to play Othello, against the advice of his fellows. The result was a triumph for this stocky, athletic, handsome youth of twenty. He was at once engaged for the new Bowery Theatre, at a salary of $800 a year, and the ensuing season played there with increasing success such parts as Damon, Jaffier (in *Venice Preserved*), William Tell, and Mark Antony. For so young an actor, the popular acclaim was enormous, but even then the patrons of the Bowery Theatre were, as we would say now, "low brow," and Forrest must inevitably have responded to their love for exhibitions of his puissant animal vigor and sonorous utterance. The more critical public supported the Park, and both they and most of the reviewers preferred the acting of Macready, then on a visit to America. A modern biographer might well speculate whether the proud, arrogant young American, aggressively national in feeling, seeing the critical acclaim going to the English visitor, did not even then lay by the zealous passions which were later to result so disastrously. His second year at the Bowery, Forrest received $200 a night, and from then on became one of the most affluent American actors. Three years later he went to the Park Theatre, where he offered prizes for American plays, thus being the first actor definitely to encourage native dramatic authorship. The first prize play was *Metamora,* a drama of Indian life by John H. Stone, produced at the Park Dec. 15, 1829, and the second was Robert M. Bird's tragedy, *The Gladiator,* in which he played Spartacus, produced Sept. 26, 1831. Both dramas, adapted to Forrest's vigorous style and love for characters of rugged, primitive heroism, were long popular in his repertoire. In all, he gave over $20,000 in prizes during the next few years, for nine dramas, but of these, two plays, one called *Jack Cade,* and Bird's *The Broker of Bogota,* were all that succeeded on the stage.

In 1834, having now completely won New

York, and also acquired a small fortune (as well as making his family in Philadelphia comfortable), Forrest retired for a trip to Europe. New York citizens gave him a parting banquet, and a medal, honoring him as the first great American actor. After visiting Europe, he emerged as Spartacus at Drury Lane—our first dramatic challenge to the Old World. His enormous physical vigor, rough realism, heroic voice, and also his flash of tragic dignity, captured the London theatregoers. He was fêted by the great, and also met and loved Catherine Norton Sinclair, daughter of a singer. They were married June 23, 1837, by the Rev. Henry Hart Milman, author of *Fazio*. His return to America was marked by further triumphs. At the Park, in New York, for example, it is recorded that he drew $4,200 in three performances, which was a high record for those days.

In 1845 Forrest and his wife again visited England. Several leading English actors, including Macready, were unemployed, and there seems to have been some resentment in London against the "foreign invasion." At any rate, when Forrest appeared as Macbeth, which was not one of his happy impersonations, three separate claques hissed him. With no actual grounds for the belief, Forrest nursed the idea that Macready was behind this affront to his professional vanity, and when Forrest nursed an idea, it grew stronger with the days. Shortly thereafter, being in Edinburgh when Macready was playing Hamlet there, Forrest sat in a box and hissed loudly at the moment when Macready was mincing and waving a handkerchief to simulate madness. It was, of course, a petty, undignified, and supremely silly thing to do; and it stirred up a hornet's nest of passions, which Forrest did not soothe by a letter to the London *Times* trying to justify his actions. The sequel was tragic, and marks one of the strangest episodes in our theatrical history.

Macready, himself an actor noted for his temper and vanity, made another tour of America in 1848–49. America had already taken sides in the controversy started in England, and the two camps were unfortunately divided to no small extent along social lines. The "highbrows" were for Macready; the galleries, the Bowery boys, the rank and file, saw American "almighty independence" personified in their hero, Forrest. It was democracy versus Anglomania to them. Macready's tour was stormy in many places—except Boston, where he was taken to the bosom of the Back Bay—but nothing fatal occurred until May 1849, when Macready was to make his farewell appearance at the Astor Place Opera House in New York. Forrest was acting at the Broadway Theatre, and many people believed, though none could ever prove, that he had a hand in what followed. Probably he did not, but he seems to have done little to prevent. On May 8 Macready attempted to act Macbeth, and was howled down by a riotous mob of Forrest adherents who packed the playhouse. His friends, and "the better element" in the city, determined that he should be heard, and persuaded him to appear again on May 10, this time seeing to it that the audience was friendly. But they could not control the streets. A great angry mob gathered, and began to stone the theatre. They smashed all the windows, and were actually attempting to wreck the structure and get at Macready when the 7th Regiment was called out. The actor was hustled to safety in disguise, and the mob started fighting the militia, till finally, in desperation, the order was given to fire. Twenty-two persons fell dead, and thirty-six wounded. Then the mob dispersed, leaving a wrecked theatre behind, and a black shadow on the reputation of Edwin Forrest from which he could never quite emerge.

Hard on the heels of this trouble came the domestic difficulties which embittered the rest of his life, cost him many friends, and were a scandal in the nose of the nation for several years. In this same spring of 1849 he had surprised his wife in what he considered too close proximity to the actor, George W. Jamieson, and a violent scene had followed. Mrs. Forrest, however, soothed him, and the matter might have passed, had he not presently discovered in her room a letter from Jamieson to her, which spoke of "being worthy of her love," and of the happiness she had given him. Forrest, in the words of his biographer, Alger, was "struck to the heart with surprise, grief and rage." He got a fixed idea that this letter indicated gross infidelity, not merely indiscretion. Jealousy, wounded vanity, and to do him credit, hurt love, gnawed at him. The couple separated, agreeing to keep their secret. But such a secret Forrest could not keep. Stung by rumors and gossip which said he had mistreated his wife, he entered suit for divorce in Philadelphia. Mrs. Forrest, to protect her reputation, entered a counter suit in New York. The case came to trial in December 1851, lasted six weeks, and probably filled more space in the newspapers of the land than any similar trial before, or perhaps since. The coarseness of speech and irascibility of temper to which Forrest was stung in the trial lost him hundreds of admirers, even friends. He assaulted the Puritan dandy, N. P. Willis, in Central Park because of some caustic comment the latter had made. Willis sued him and collected a dollar. He sued Willis for libel, and collected

$500. Meanwhile the divorce case went against him, and he was assessed alimony and costs. With his fixed idea of his wife's guilt, this seemed to him a bitter injustice, and five times he appealed the case, always losing, the final verdict eighteen years later assessing him $64,000, of which Mrs. Forrest had to pay $59,000 in various expenses!

In January 1852, just as the first trial ended, Forrest defiantly rode the storm and acted for sixty-nine nights at the Broadway Theatre, New York. The publicity of the trial packed the theatre to the roof every night, and Forrest made speeches between acts, vindicating his conduct. His adherents, who had considered the verdict wrong, cheered him to the echo. Money continued to roll into his coffers. But from that time on he alternated acting with long periods of retirement to a large and lonely house he built on North Broad St., Philadelphia, where, according to William Winter, he "brooded upon himself as a great genius misunderstood, and upon the rest of the world as a sort of animated scum." In 1860 he reappeared in New York as Hamlet, to vast audiences, and later packed the huge Boston Theatre. In 1866 he played to $2,500 a night in Chicago, and in thirty-five nights in San Francisco drew as his share $20,000 in gold. In 1865, however, he suffered a partial paralysis of the sciatic nerve, which increasingly hobbled his regal gait and humbled the Herculean, athletic figure which had been his pride, and the public turned to younger players. His last appearance was as a reader in New York in the autumn of 1872. On Dec. 12, 1872, he died alone in his house in Philadelphia. It was found that he had willed nearly his entire estate as a home for aged players, and the Forrest Home in Philadelphia still keeps his memory fresh.

Criticisms of vanished actors are mostly vain things. Alger speaks of "the heroic traits and pomp of Forrest's parts, the impassioned energy and vividness of the delineations, the bell, drum and trumpet qualities of his amazing voice." William Winter describes him as "a vast animal, bewildered by a grain of genius." The facts seem to be that he dominated an audience by his unique animal vigor and his outbursts of impassioned speech, and that he was happiest in rôles which showed strong-willed, elemental characters in revolt, or in later years such characters as Lear, and Coriolanus. He himself was a strong-willed character in perhaps unconscious revolt against the idealized classic drama which was all he knew. In a later age he might possibly have been tamed to a superb John Gabriel Borkman. Personally, he was a victim of uncontrolled, egocentric passions, of vanity and arrogance; yet he was capable of large generosities and true and noble understanding of noble characters—altogether a fascinating and stormy comet that blazed across our early stage.

[W. R. Alger, *Life of Edwin Forrest* (2 vols., 1877), is a partisan biography, dreary with Saharas of moralizing, but gives fairly the essential facts. See also M. J. Moses, *The Fabulous Forrest* (1929); "The Forrest Divorce Case," reported for the *Police Gazette* (N. Y.), 1852; *Account of the Terrific and Fatal Riot at the N. Y. Astor Place Opera House* (1849); Brander Matthews and Laurence Hutton, *Actors and Actresses of Great Britain and the U. S.* (1886), vol. IV, containing a biography by Lawrence Barrett and many excerpts from contemporary criticism; William Winter, *The Wallet of Time* (1913), vol. I; Jos. Jefferson, *Autobiography* (1890), containing amusing records of Forrest's temper.]

W. P. E.

FORREST, FRENCH (Oct. 4, 1796–Nov. 22, 1866), naval officer, was born in St. Marys County, Md., son of Maj. Joseph Forrest and Elizabeth French Dulany. Appointed midshipman June 9, 1811, he was in the *Hornet* in her victory over the *Peacock*, Feb. 24, 1813, and is said to have served under Perry on Lake Erie, though he is not listed among Perry's officers. After years of routine service he was commissioned captain Mar. 30, 1844, and in the Mexican War commanded the *Cumberland* and later the *Raritan*, flagships in the squadron off Vera Cruz, in which as staff officer and division commander he took a distinguished part in operations against Mexican ports. He commanded the second division in the attack on Alvarado, Oct. 16, 1846, and led a landing force of about 200 in operations, Nov. 23–26, against Tabasco. Speaking of his work here, Capt. W. H. Parker says that Forrest "did not know the meaning of the word fear" (*Recollections of a Naval Officer*, 1883, p. 74), but adds that he was very methodical, and describes amusingly his efforts to get his force organized. His company was attacked by superior forces on the 25th but held its ground till the withdrawal of the ships next morning. He was officer in charge of the landing of Scott's army at Vera Cruz, Mar. 9, 1847, in which over 10,000 men were put ashore in five hours, an operation perfectly carried out, though with but slight opposition. From June 1855 to August 1856, he was head of the Washington Navy Yard, and then commanded the Brazil Squadron until May 1859, except when it was enlarged in 1858 for a demonstration against Paraguay, in which he commanded the rear division. In the Civil War he became captain in the Virginia navy, Apr. 12, 1861, and in the Confederate navy, June 10, standing third in seniority. Parker remarks that Forrest had a fine record and with better opportunities would have distinguished himself in the

Confederate service (*Ibid.*, p. 328), but he was piqued at Buchanan's promotion over him (*Official Records, Navy,* 2 ser., vol. II, p. 256). As head of the Norfolk Navy Yard from Apr. 23, 1861, he had general charge of alterations on the *Merrimac,* and at the battle of Hampton Roads steamed boldly out in the little tug *Harmony* to offer assistance when the *Merrimac* ran aground. Delays in repairs to the *Merrimac* caused his transfer, May 24, 1862, to the head of the bureau of orders and detail. From March 1863 to May 1864, during a period of relative inactivity, he commanded the James River Squadron. Commodore Forrest was a strikingly handsome man, with regular features, and in earlier years dark curling hair. He was fond of objects of art, and in his home at Alexandria, Va., collected many curios from foreign voyages. His wife was Emily Douglas, daughter of John D. Simms, chief clerk of the navy department, whom he married in 1830. He died at the home of his brother Bladen in Georgetown, D. C.

[This account is based partly on navy department records and family papers. Many references to Forrest are in the *Official Records* (*Navy*). See also H. E. Hayden's *Va. Geneal.* (1891), p. 343; J. T. Scharf's *Hist. of the Confederate States Navy* (1887); and P. S. P. Conner, *The Home Squadron under Commodore Conner in the War with Mexico* (1896).] A. W.

FORREST, NATHAN BEDFORD (July 13, 1821–Oct. 29, 1877), Confederate general, eldest son of William and Mariam (Beck) Forrest, was born in Bedford County, Tenn. (The boundary drawn at a later date places his birthplace in Marshall County.) His great-grandfather, Shadrach Forrest, who was possibly of English birth, is known to have removed about 1730–40 from Virginia to North Carolina, and there his son and grandson were born. They moved to Tennessee in 1806. William Forrest worked at his trade as a blacksmith there until 1834, when he moved into Mississippi. His death in 1837 threw upon the eldest son, then a boy of sixteen, the responsibility for the support of a large family. At first as a farm laborer, later as a horse and cattle dealer in a small way, and then as a trader in slaves and real estate, Forrest provided for their necessities, and gradually accumulated capital enough to purchase cotton plantations in Mississippi and Arkansas, which made him a rich man. He was married in 1845 to Mary Ann Montgomery. After 1849 he lived in Memphis, and was for some time an alderman. He enlisted in the Confederate army as a private in June 1861, but having raised a battalion for mounted service and equipped it at his own expense, he was appointed lieutenant-colonel in October. He took part in the defense of Fort Donelson, where he vigorously opposed the decision to surrender, declaring that it would be possible for a great part of the force to cut its way out. With the permission of the commanding general, he led his own command through a gap in the encircling line of Union troops, and brought it off in safety. Promoted colonel, he fought at Shiloh and was severely wounded during the retreat. Appointed brigadier-general in July 1862, he began the career of brilliant cavalry raiding which made him famous. From then until the end of the war he was chiefly engaged in bold raids against the Union communications or against posts deep within the Union lines. The wisdom of expending the army's cavalry upon such operations has been questioned, but there is no question of the brilliancy of Forrest's execution of the policy. Fighting generally on foot, and using his horses only as a means of rapid transportation, he covered ground with great speed and delivered surprise attacks against fortified posts, against superior forces in the open field, and even, on occasion, against river gunboats. A Union raid, made quite in Forrest's own style by Col. A. D. Streight in the spring of 1863, was broken up by Forrest's vigorous pursuit, ending in the capture of the whole force near Cedar Bluffs, Ala. Shortly after, Forrest received what was thought to be a fatal wound at the hand of a junior officer, aggrieved at an order of assignment, but Forrest killed his assailant, and recovered from his wound in time to take part in the Chickamauga campaign. Soon after the battle, he had a fierce altercation with Gen. Bragg, whom he accused of jealousy and unfair discrimination. Forrest was violent and insubordinate, while Bragg seems to have shown great forbearance; but Jefferson Davis, apparently feeling that Forrest was not being used to the best advantage, transferred him out of Bragg's command, and appointed him major-general. In the spring of 1864 Forrest raided as far north as Paducah, Ky. The one serious blot on his reputation is the slaughter of the negro soldiers which followed his capture of Fort Pillow, Apr. 12, 1864. No one now supposes him to have ordered a massacre, but his responsibility cannot so easily be put aside. It is inconceivable that he should have been ignorant of the temper of his men; yet he took no precautionary measures, but on the contrary sought to terrify the garrison by a threat of no quarter, as was his custom. If his men this time took him at his word—it is well attested that they entered the fort shouting "Forrest's orders"—it seems clear where the blame should lie. In June he gained one of his most notable victories, defeating a superior force under Gen. Sturgis at Brice's Cross Roads, Miss.

An engagement with Gen. A. J. Smith at Tupelo in July was at best a drawn battle, and is frequently called a Union victory. Here Forrest was wounded again, but retained his command, leading his cavalry in a buggy until he was able to ride once more. He was in chief command of the Confederate cavalry in the Nashville campaign. In February 1865 he was made lieutenant-general, and with the remnants of his cavalry corps opposed Wilson during the spring until his final defeat at Selma early in April. After his surrender, in May, he returned to his cotton plantations. He was involved in the early activities of the Ku Klux Klan, but his connection with the order does not seem to have lasted long. For some years he was president of the Selma, Marion & Memphis Railroad, a new road the construction of which resulted in financial disaster. He died at Memphis.

Forrest was of great height and commanding presence. Habitually he was mild in manner, quiet in speech, exemplary in language, in all respects appearing as the kind-hearted, considerate man that he actually was. He drank little, and used tobacco not at all. In anger or excitement he was transformed into a seeming maniac, terrifying to look upon, savage and profane. The excitement of battle, however, never impaired his observation or his judgment, but rather made them more keen, though his aggressive spirit led him sometimes to ride into the thick of the fight and join in personal combat, like a trooper rather than a general. He was several times wounded, and it has been reckoned up that twenty-nine horses were shot under him. His courage in cold blood was as great as in the heat of battle. Alone, and with no other weapon than a knife, he once overawed and dispersed a mob bent on lynching; and he dared to apologize, knowing himself to be in the wrong, when once challenged to a duel. Though wholly without formal education, he was able to speak and write clear and grammatical English. The tradition that his language was uncouth and that he was practically illiterate is founded on his utter inability to learn to spell and his habitual use of a few quaint dialectal expressions, such as *mout* for *might* and *fit* for *fought.* He had a talent for mathematics which had no opportunity to develop far. The military instinct in the man came near to genius. As he never commanded a considerable force of all arms, it remains a matter of speculation what he might have done in charge of an army, but as a leader of mounted troops he has had few equals.

[There are biographies by John Allan Wyeth, *Life of Gen. Nathan Bedford Forrest* (1899), and J. Harvey Mathes, *Gen. Forrest* (1902), and a brief sketch in *Confed. Mil. Hist.* (1899), I, 699–702. A eulogy by Lord Wolseley, published in the *United Service Mag.* (London), Apr.–May 1892, and reprinted in part in *Southern Hist. Soc. Papers,* XX (1892), 325–35, is often quoted. See also Thomas Jordan and J. P. Pryor, *Campaigns of Lieut.-Gen. N. B. Forrest* (1868); J. W. Morton, *The Artillery of Nathan Bedford Forrest's Cavalry* (1909); articles in *Battles and Leaders of the Civil War* (1887–88), vols. I, III, IV; *Official Records (Army)*, especially 1 ser., vols. VII, XXX (pts. 1, 2), XXXII (pt. 1), XXXIX (pt. 1), XLV (pt. 1); obituary in *Public Ledger* (Memphis), Oct. 30, 1877.] T. M. S.

FORSYTH, JOHN (Oct. 22, 1780–Oct. 21, 1841), statesman, was born at Fredericksburg, Va., the son of Robert and Fanny (Johnson) Houston Forsyth. His father, a descendant of James Forsyth, who came to Virginia from Scotland in 1680, won a major's rank in the Revolution, then served as the first federal marshal of Georgia. The son was educated at Princeton, then after his graduation in 1799 studied law and was admitted to the bar in 1802. Six years later, with his appointment as attorney-general of Georgia, his political career began. As representative, United States senator, governor of Georgia, minister to Spain, and secretary of state, he gave thirty years of his life to the public service. His first years in Congress (1813–18) coincided roughly with Madison's second term, and Forsyth was one of the President's supporters. He was promoted to the Senate late in 1818, but had scarcely taken his seat when he resigned to accept the appointment as minister to Spain (February 1819). The only work of importance which fell to him in this position was to procure the ratification by the King of the treaty of 1819, ceding Florida to the United States. His conduct in these negotiations added nothing to his fame. He had not yet developed the suavity and tact for which he later was known. Disliking the Spanish, he was peremptory and impatient, and was rebuked by the Spanish foreign office for his bad manners (McCormac, *John Forsyth,* p. 303). He succeeded, however, in securing the ratification of the treaty.

While Forsyth was still in Europe, his old constituency in Georgia reëlected him to Congress. This second period of congressional service extended from March 1823 to March 1827. In the latter year he was elected governor of Georgia. After one rather uneventful term he was again elected to the United States Senate and served from Nov. 9, 1829, to June 27, 1834. His second incumbency came during a period of importance in our national history. The country was divided politically by the issues raised during the "reign" of Andrew Jackson. The fight over the protective tariff, culminating in the nullification movement, was perhaps the most interesting episode of Jackson's career. In this and in other bitter controversies with his enemies, a group which included nearly all of the prominent figures of the time, Jackson had the unswerving support of John Forsyth, who was one of his ablest champions. The two factions in Georgia at this time were the State-rights, or Troup party, comprising the planter aristocrats, and the Clark men, who were unionist in feeling. Forsyth had entered Congress in 1823 as an adherent of the State-rights party, and had supported Troup when the latter, as governor, had challenged the federal government in connection with the removal of the Indians. At heart, however, he was a unionist, and though long identified with the Troup faction, he was gradually alienated from his erstwhile State-rights supporters by the trend of events after 1828.

The nullification issue may be said to have begun in 1828 with the passage of the "tariff of abominations." As governor, Forsyth had denounced the measure in a message to the legislature and had referred to the possibility of neutralizing it by state action. In the Senate, with Troup, he voted against the tariff act of July 1832, which gave no relief to the South. Feeling was running high in that quarter. South Carolina, under Calhoun's leadership, was moving towards nullification. In November 1832 a convention met at Milledgeville, the capital, to denounce the tariff and to throw Georgia's support to South Carolina, even to the point of nullification. J. M. Berrien, an enemy of the President, was the leader of the nullifiers; Forsyth led the opposition. He not only regarded nullification as an ineffective constitutional remedy, but, as a strong administration man, felt called upon to support Jackson. On the second day of the convention Forsyth introduced resolutions calling for the appointment of a committee to examine the credentials of the members of the convention. This precipitated an oratorical contest surpassed by few in Georgia history. Berrien, who had been dubbed the "American Cicero," and Forsyth, regarded by contemporaries as the "best off-hand debater in the world," locked horns for three days. Forsyth contended in the debate that the convention was in no wise representative of Georgia sentiment since the members had not been selected in such a manner as to empower them to speak for the state. Many counties were wholly unrepresented. After protracted debate, his proposal was voted down, whereupon he seceded, followed by fifty of his adherents. His withdrawal proved permanent and had the effect of sobering the convention. Some of the newspapers denounced him; others praised him. The legislature left no room for doubt as to its position. Clear-cut resolutions were adopted condemning both nullification and the action of the convention. Meanwhile South Carolina proceeded to nullify the tariff acts of 1828 and 1832, eliciting from President Jackson his December proclamation. In March following, Congress passed the Force Bill. Forsyth cast his vote in favor of the bill, and for this he was severely condemned. In Macon he was burned in effigy. Grand juries elsewhere charged him with apostasy to Georgia and the South, and demanded his resignation.

It would be an exaggeration to affirm that in challenging the authority of the convention to speak for the state, in seceding from the convention, and in vigorously combating the doctrine of nullification Forsyth was responsible for Georgia's final action. Other leading politicians of the state were quite as strongly opposed to radical action. Had he aligned himself with Berrien, however, the two might have committed the state to nullification, and had Georgia supported South Carolina, the movement might have spread to alarming proportions. Certainly he stood out in the anti-nullification fight more distinctly and fearlessly than any other leader.

While Forsyth was still in the Senate Jackson began his fight on the second Bank of the United States. Endorsing the President's attitude toward the bank, the Georgian delivered a striking speech after the Senate had passed the resolutions censuring Jackson for removing the government deposits. He justified the President's conduct, and in his peroration paid him an eloquent tribute for his courageous stand in the nullification crisis. "The cup of bitterness, humiliation, and woe passed untasted from our lips. Would it thus have passed away if that despised, reprobated, vilified, hated, but just and stern, old man had not occupied the House and the hearts of the people?" In recognition of the services of the senator, Jackson in 1834 appointed him secretary of state. Forsyth held the post for the remainder of Jackson's term and through the administration of Van Buren. During these years the most interesting matters which awaited settlement were the disagreeable contest with France over the treaty of 1831 and the question of the admission of Texas into the Union. The quarrel with France concerned the adjustment of our claims for losses to American vessels during the Napoleonic wars. In 1831 Jackson succeeded in negotiating a treaty with France according to which $5,000,000 were to be paid in six annual installments, and the United States was to lower the duties on French wines. Though the American government immediately carried into effect her part of the agreement, internal political conditions in France were such that Louis Philippe was unable to get the Chamber to make the necessary appropriations to pay the annual installments on the American debt. A long, bitter, and irritating contest followed. Jackson, adamant in insisting upon our rights, and supported by Forsyth and Livingston, our ambassador, succeeded in arranging for the payment of the installments (McCormac, *post*, ch. ii). John Fiske well summarized the incident: "The days when foreign powers could safely insult us were evidently gone by."

The Texas question presented a grave problem. A number of negotiators or ministers extraordinary were sent from time to time by Texas after the revolution from Mexico to discuss recognition and annexation with President Jackson and with Secretary Forsyth. The reports of the emissaries to their government showed that they had great difficulty in learning just what the attitude of the administration was. Forsyth seemed generally to be opposed to both recognition and admission, but in the end nothing had been done at the time of his retirement.

By all accounts Forsyth was a man of uncommon personal attractions. His form and features were described as classical, his manners courtly. He was even-tempered and had a rich sense of humor. As an orator he had few equals. His voice was clear, resonant, pleasant to the ear, and well modulated, and his contemporaries appear to have almost unanimously agreed that he was the most powerful debater of his time. He was "acute, witty, full of resources, and ever prompt,—impetuous as Murat in a charge, adroit as Soult when flanked and outnumbered" (Miller, *post*, p. 51). Strongly inclined toward fashionable life and its "heartless formalities," he was not a popular man, for he had little concern for the interests of the masses; his world was that of the diplomat and courtier. In early life he married Clara, the daughter of Josiah Meigs, the first president of Franklin College (later the University of Georgia), and established a home near Augusta, Ga. Of his children the best-known were John, minister to Mexico in 1856; and Julia, wife of Alfred Iverson, United States senator from Georgia.

[Stephen F. Miller, in *The Bench and Bar of Ga.* (1858), vol. II, gives an excellent sketch of Forsyth's career. See also Jennie Forsyth Jeffries, *A Hist. of the Forsyth Family* (1920); W. F. Northen, ed., *Men of Mark in Ga.*, II (1910); E. Merton Coulter, "The Nullification Movement in Ga.," in the *Ga. Hist. Quart.*, Mar. 1921; U. B. Phillips, *Ga. and State Rights* (1902), published as vol. II of the annual reports of the American Historical Association; C. G. Bowers, *The Party Battles of the Jackson Period* (1922); E. I. McCormac in *Am. Secretaries of State and their Diplomacy*, vol. IV (1928)].

R. P. B—s.

FORSYTH, JOHN (Dec. 31, 1810–Oct. 17, 1886), Associate Reformed clergyman, college professor, was born in Newburgh, N. Y., the son of John and Jane (Currie) Forsyth. His father, who emigrated to the United States from Scotland, seems to have been a devout Calvinist, for clergymen of that persuasion, coming to Newburgh to act as examiners in the Associate Reformed Seminary, were regularly entertained in the Forsyth home. From these clerical visitors the boy may have caught his ambition to enter the ministry. Upon his graduation from Rutgers College in 1829 he studied theology at the University of Edinburgh, where he had Thomas Chalmers for a teacher. He was licensed by the Presbytery of Aberdeen in April 1833, was ordained by the Presbytery of New York in July of the following year, and was pastor of the Second Associate Reformed Church in Philadelphia until 1837. In these few years he had gained in his own denomination a reputation for piety and learning sufficient to secure him a call to the seminary in his native town. Since that institution had only two professors, Forsyth had to cover the fields of Hebrew, Greek, and archeology and at the same time act as pastor of the Union Church in Newburgh. In 1845, after eight years of teaching, he resigned from the seminary. He was professor of Latin in the College of New Jersey 1847–53, and then returned to the Newburgh seminary, this time as professor of church history and exegetical theology. As further evidence of his varied interests and his willingness to teach almost any subject, he filled the chair of English literature and rhetoric in Rutgers College 1859–62, lectured on history at the College of New Jersey 1864–72, and then became chaplain and professor of geography, history, and ethics in the United States Military Academy at West Point, serving from July 28, 1871, till Dec. 12, 1881, when he was put on the retired list. During these years Forsyth had written diligently for various church papers, especially for the *Christian Intelligencer*. To the *Biblical Repertory and Princeton Review* he contributed a number of substantial articles. He also published sermons and occasional addresses, translated and annotated several books on theology, and did a good deal of work for the English edition of Lange's *Commentary*. As a man he was greatly esteemed for his learning, piety, kindliness, and courtesy. For many years he was president of the Newburgh board of education. There, in the town of his birth, he lived out his life and was survived by his wife, Ann D. Heyer.

[*Biog. Notices of Grads. of Rutgers Coll. deceased during the Academical Year ending in June 1887* (1887); *Gen. Cat. of Princeton Univ. 1746–1906*

(1908); F. G. Forsyth de Fronsac, *Memorial of the Family of Forsyth de Fronsac* (1903); *A Record of the Inscriptions in the Old Town Burying Ground of Newburgh, N. Y.* (1898); G. W. Cullum, *Biog. Reg. of the . . . U. S. Mil. Acad.*, vol. I (3rd ed., 1891); *N. Y. Daily Tribune*, Oct. 18, 1886; *Christian Intelligencer* (N. Y.), Oct. 20, 1886; E. T. Corwin, *Manual of the Reformed Ch. in America* (4th ed., 1902) contains list of writings.] G. H. G.

FORSYTH, THOMAS (Dec. 5, 1771–Oct. 29, 1833), Indian agent, explorer, lived under two flags. He first rendered allegiance to Great Britain, since he was born at Detroit while it was still an English outpost; later he became an American citizen and actively aided the United States on the frontier. His father, William Forsyth, emigrated about 1750 from the north of Ireland; enlisted in a Royal regiment, and was wounded in 1759 at the battle on the Plains of Abraham. In 1764 at Quebec he married Ann, widow of John Kinzie, then moved to Detroit, where before the birth of his son, he opened a famous inn, close to the fort. Thomas grew up with such education as the frontier town afforded, and after his father's death in 1790 entered the fur-trade, acting as clerk for George Sharp. His first assignment was at Saginaw among the Ottawa Indians. After the Americans in 1796 took possession of Detroit young Forsyth with a partner named Richardson opened a fur-trade post near Quincy, Ill. In 1804 he formed a partnership with his half-brother, John Kinzie, who had just settled at Chicago. Forsyth took station at Peoria Lake, after having married that same year at Detroit Keziah Malotte, who as a child had been captured by Indians during the frontier wars. He lived at Peoria until the hostilities of the War of 1812 began, but during the war removed his family to St. Louis. Before 1812 he had offered his services to the American government and had been appointed Indian sub-agent. He was successful in persuading the powerful tribe of the Potawatomi on the Illinois River to remain neutral during the struggle, although a price was put upon his head by British agents, and he was preserved from assassination or capture only by the good-will of his Indian friends. He protected the exposed frontier of the Americans and ransomed captives taken at Chicago in 1812, notably Lieut. Helm. After the treaty of peace he was employed in negotiations with the Indians of his locality. He also kept his agency at Peoria until 1819, when he was sent on a mission to the Indians of the headwaters of the Mississippi and ascended the stream in a keel-boat, examining the country as he went. Later in the same year he was promoted to a full agency and stationed at Fort Armstrong, near Rock Island, where he cared for the tribes of the Sauk and Foxes, and came to be known to them as Mah-tah-win (The Corn). After his retirement in 1830 he lived at St. Louis, where he engaged himself in writing his experiences and what he knew of Indian languages, manners, and custom. It has been said of him that he had a "well-balanced mind in a sound and athletic body. He was a gifted talker and a most pleasant and entertaining companion. Benevolence and kindness of heart were his predominant traits. . . . His private life was amiable and blameless" (Scharf, *post*, II, 1293–94). His share in opening the West to civilization and in saving the frontier from Indian depredations was considerable.

[Forsyth's manuscripts are in the Mo. Hist. Soc., and in the Wis. Hist. Soc. The latter agency has published his Mississippi journal and a biographical sketch in *Wis. Hist. Colls.*, VI (1872), 188–214; and other papers and letters in *Ibid.*, XI (1888), 316–52. His "Account of the Manners and Customs of the Sauk and Fox Indians" is printed in E. H. Blair, *Indian Tribes of the Upper Miss. Valley and Region of the Great Lakes* (1911), II, 183–245. See also John Reynolds, *Pioneer Hist. of Ill.* (1887), 246–52; E. B. Washburne, *Edwards Papers* (1884), *passim*.] L. P. K.

FORTEN, JAMES (Sept. 2, 1766–Mar. 4, 1842), sail-maker, was descended from people who had lived in Pennsylvania for several generations. His father, Thomas Forten, died when he was but seven years old. James attended in Philadelphia the school of the Quaker Abolitionist, Anthony Benezet, but left in 1775, when he was not more than nine years of age, and went to work to help his mother. At fourteen he entered the service of the colonial navy, in the *Royal Louis*, commanded by Capt. Decatur, and was among those captured by the British ship *Amphion*. It happened, however, that the commander's son was on board, who exacted from his father the promise that James should not be forced to enlist in the English service. This pleased the young negro, for he feared being sold into slavery in the West Indies. In course of time he was transferred to a prison ship lying near New York, and he remained there through a raging pestilence until the prisoners were exchanged. Another voyage then took him to London for a year. On his return to Philadelphia he was apprenticed to Robert Bridges, a sail-maker, and in his twentieth year he became foreman of the working force. He afterwards became owner of the sail-loft, and about this time married the woman who became the mother of his eight children. Prospering in business, he ultimately won a considerable fortune.

In 1814, with Richard Allen and Absalom Jones, Forten secured 2,500 negro volunteers to protect the city of Philadelphia. His establishment was near the water, and at different times not less than seven persons were saved from drowning by his promptness and efficiency. Under date of May 9, 1821, the Humane Society of Philadelphia gave him a formal certificate of appreciation for having rescued four of these persons. In his mature life Forten was keenly interested in the welfare of the negro people, and in 1817 presided over a meeting in Bethel Church called to oppose the designs of the American Colonization Society. In his business he refused to furnish rigging to the owners of slave-vessels. He was also interested in the work of the temperance and the peace societies, and defended woman's rights. His success in business and his philanthropic spirit made him easily one of the foremost negroes in the country in his time. He commanded the highest respect in Philadelphia, and his funeral was attended by a vast throng of people.

[Robt. Purvis, *Remarks on the Life and Character of Jas. Forten* (1842); L. Maria Child, *The Freedmen's Book* (1865); *Wm. Lloyd Garrison: The Story of his Life Told by his Children* (4 vols., 1885–89), *passim*; B. T. Washington, *The Story of the Negro* (1909).]

B. B.

FORTIER, ALCÉE (June 5, 1856–Feb. 14, 1914), educator, author, historian, civic leader, was born in St. James Parish, La., the son of Florent Fortier, of French Breton stock, and Edwige Aime, daughter of a beloved planter. After his early schooling in New Orleans, Fortier went for some time to the University of Virginia, studied law, then left a banking clerkship to enter the teaching profession. After a short experience in the New Orleans Boys' High School, he became principal of the preparatory department of the University of Louisiana (later Tulane University). In 1880 he was given the chair of French in the university, in 1894 he became professor of Romance languages, and in 1913 he was made dean of the graduate department. His devotion to Tulane was unbounded. He studied constantly, specializing in Romance languages under Elliott at Johns Hopkins and in Paris under Passy. His *Sept grands Auteurs du XIXe siècle* (1889), *Histoire de la Littérature française* (1893), and other studies for the classroom show able scholarship. His great interest, however, lay in Creole history and customs, and to this field he contributed *Bits of Louisiana Folklore* (1888); *Louisiana Studies* (1894); *Louisiana Folk Tales* (1895); a *History of Louisiana* (1904), his masterwork; and an *Encyclopedia of Louisiana* (1908). In addition to these works, he published *Le Château de Chambord* (1884); *Central America and Mexico* (1907), written in collaboration with J. R. Ficklen; *Gabriel d'Ennerich* (1886); and *Voyage en Europe* (1895). He also made frequent contributions to the press, to encyclopedias, and to the *Comptes Rendus* of l'Athénée Louisianais.

Fortier was so devoted to his native state that he refused several calls to important universities. He was for twenty-two years president of l'Athénée Louisianais; for eighteen he directed the Louisiana Historical Society; and he was a member of every French and Franco-American organization in Louisiana. He also took part in civic affairs, serving as chairman of the civil service commission, as curator of the Louisiana State Museum, and as a member of the state board of education. Outside of the state he gained a wider recognition of his ability as president of the American Folklore Society, of the Modern Language Association, of the Fédération de l'Alliance Française. A devout Roman Catholic, he was five times president of the Catholic Winter School, an active member of the St. Vincent Society, and a contributor to the *Catholic Encyclopedia.* As a man Fortier was active and energetic; as a writer, straightforward and sincere. Believing that conscious effort was necessary to preserve Creole tradition and culture, by painstaking labor and study he paved the way for the scientific study of Louisiana history. His wife was Marie Lanauze, who with five of their eight children survived him.

[Obituary notices were published in the *Daily States, Daily Item, Picayune, Times-Democrat,* and *l'Abeille* at the time of his death. The *Comptes Rendus* of l'Athénée Louisianais, Apr. 1, 1914, contains a good biographical sketch. See also Grace King, *Creole Families of New Orleans* (1921); the *Times-Democrat,* Mar. 20, 27, 1892; *The South in the Building of the Nation* (1909), vol. XI; *The Lib. of Southern Literature* (1909), vol. IV; *Biog. and Hist. Memoirs of La.* (1892), vol. I.]

L. C. D.

FORWARD, WALTER (Jan. 24, 1786–Nov. 24, 1852), congressman, secretary of the treasury, was born at Old Granby (now East Granby), Conn., the son of Samuel and Susannah Holcombe Forward. When he was fourteen years of age, his parents moved to a farm near Aurora, Ohio. After working with his father for three years, he left home without money, and made his way to Pittsburgh, then a town of fewer than 5,000 inhabitants, to begin the study of law. By the merest accident he secured employment and the opportunity to study in the office of Henry Baldwin [*q.v.*], one of the best-known attorneys in Pennsylvania and subsequently associate justice of the United States Supreme Court. Among his other duties Forward edited for Baldwin for several years the *Tree of Liberty,* a Democratic paper of wide circulation and influence. So rapidly did his legal work progress that he was admitted to the bar in 1806, and soon established an enviable record as a trial lawyer. After a creditable tenure in the state legislature, Forward was chosen at a special election, Dec. 2, 1822, to take the place of Henry Baldwin who had resigned his seat in Congress and he was reëlected to the following Congress, serving until Mar. 4, 1825. Both in the committee on manufactures and on the floor of the House, he advocated the enactment of a high protective tariff, a policy which he vigorously upheld during the remainder of his life. He failed of reëlection to the Nineteenth Congress. In 1824, he attended the congressional caucus (the last of its kind ever held) which nominated William H. Crawford for the presidency; but as a protest against this method of nomination he gave his support to Andrew Jackson in the campaign. Four years later, however, he definitely allied himself with the National Republicans. In 1830, he was a delegate to the general convention of the National Republicans at Baltimore; and in 1834 he played an important part in the formation of the Whig party. He was an outstanding member of the Pennsylvania constitutional convention of 1837–38. Among other things he advocated suitable provisions for the education of the poor at public expense.

Partly as a reward for his services in the campaign of 1840, President Harrison appointed Forward district attorney for the western district of Pennsylvania. Upon declining to accept this position he was named the first comptroller of the currency. Following the death of President Harrison and John Tyler's accession to the presidency, he was appointed secretary of the treasury in the reorganized cabinet. Although embarrassed in many ways by the deflection of the Whig leaders from Tyler and by his own repeated disagreement with the policies of his chief, he continued in office until Feb. 28, 1843, when he resigned to resume the practise of law. With the return of the Whigs to power in 1849 under President Zachary Taylor, he was appointed Nov. 8, 1849, chargé d'affaires to Denmark. After spending two years at Copenhagen, he returned to Pittsburgh to become president judge of the district court of Allegheny County. He was an active member of the Methodist Church, a devoted worker in the cause of temperance, one of the founders of the Pittsburgh Philosophical and Philological Society, and a lifelong advocate of internal improvements. He married Henrietta Barclay of Greensburg, Pa., Jan. 31, 1808.

[The best single account is found in an article by Robert M. Ewing, "Hon. Walter Forward," published in the *Western Pa. Hist. Mag.*, Apr. 1925, with an excellent bibliography. See also J. W. F. White, "The Judiciary of Allegheny County," in *Pa. Mag. of Hist. and Biog.*, July 1883; H. M. Brackenridge, *Recollections of the West* (1868); J. N. Boucher, *A Century and a Half of Pittsburgh and Her People* (1908); *Pittsburgh Gazette*, Nov. 25, 1852.] A. E. M.

FORWOOD, WILLIAM HENRY (Sept. 7, 1838–May 12, 1915), army medical officer, was born at Brandywine Hundred, Del., to Robert and Rachel Way (Larkin) Forwood. He was educated in the local public schools and in Chester Academy at Chester, Pa. He was graduated from the medical department of the University of Pennsylvania in 1861, just as the Civil War was beginning. In August of that year he was appointed assistant surgeon in the army and detailed as executive officer of Seminary Hospital at Georgetown, D. C. After a few months of this service he was sent to field duty as regimental surgeon of the 14th Infantry and later served as acting medical director of Sykes's division in the Army of the Potomac. Following a short tour in the office of the medical director in Washington, he again saw field duty as surgeon of the 6th Cavalry in Stoneman's division. He took part in the battles of Yorktown, Gaines's Mill, Malvern Hill, the second Bull Run, Antietam, Gettysburg, and Brandy Station. In the latter engagement he received a severe gunshot wound through the chest. After his recovery he was assigned as executive officer of Satterlee General Hospital at West Philadelphia and later was placed in command of the medical storeship *Marcy C. Day.* The end of the war found him in command of Whitehall General Hospital near Bristol, Pa., a hospital of two thousand beds, which he had built. Routine post duty in the West and South occupied much of Forwood's next twenty-five years. He had experience with cholera in Kansas and with yellow fever in Texas. During the years from 1879 to 1883 he acted as surgeon and naturalist for the military reconnaissance and exploring expeditions to the northwest which were conducted annually under instructions from Gen. Philip Sheridan. President Arthur and Secretary Robert T. Lincoln accompanied the last of these expeditions. In 1890 Forwood became attending surgeon at the Soldiers' Home at Washington. During part of his service here he occupied the chairs of surgery and surgical pathology (1895–97) and of military surgery (1897–98) in the medical department of the Georgetown University, which conferred upon him the honorary degree of LL.D. When the Army Medical School was organized in 1893 he became professor of military surgery, and with the reorganization of the school in 1901, following the Spanish War, he returned to it as president of the faculty. The flood of sick coming up from Cuba in the summer of 1898 caused the establishment of a great hospital and convalescent camp at Montauk Point, L. I., and of this camp Forwood was made chief medical officer. Later in the year he selected the site and superintended the construction of a general hospital for returning troops at Savannah, Ga. In December he was ordered to San Francisco as chief surgeon of the Department of California, a position of increasing importance on account of probable hostilities in the Philippines. In 1901 he returned to a desk in the office of the surgeon-general in Washington. When Gen. Sternberg retired in June 1902, Forwood had but three months to serve before his own compulsory retirement for age. He was, however, appointed surgeon-general of the army for this brief period, an act which gave great satisfaction to the whole medical service. Retired in September 1902, he lived quietly in Washington until his death.

Forwood's more important contributions to professional literature are his monographs on military surgery in Vol. II of William H. Dennis's *System of Surgery* (1895–96) and in Vol. II of J. C. Warren and A. P. Gould's *International Textbook of Surgery* (1900). From February 1898 to February 1899 he was in charge of "The Military Surgeon," a supplement to the *National Medical Review*. Never a remarkable operator himself, he was a profound student of surgery and was an able instructor. His army career shows him frequently assigned to positions calling for executive skill. He was married on Sept. 28, 1870, to Mary Osbourne, daughter of Antrim Osbourne of Media, Pa. They had no children.

[*Alumni Reg.* (Univ. of Pa.), Nov. 1902; J. E. Pilcher, *The Surgeon Generals of the Army* (1905); *Medic. News* (N. Y.), June 14, 1902; *Mil. Surgeon*, June 1915; *Evening Star* (Washington), May 12, 1915.] J. M. P.

FOSDICK, CHARLES AUSTIN (Sept. 16, 1842–Aug. 22, 1915), author, was known to successive generations of youthful readers only by his pen name of Harry Castlemon. In the forty years beginning with 1864 he published fifty-eight boys' books, some of which ran into as many as thirty editions. Although he had ingratiating rivals in Oliver Optic, Horatio Alger, Edward S. Ellis, and G. A. Henty, he was perhaps the most beloved of them all. His popularity began to decline in the first years of the twentieth century, but even in 1912 publishers found it profitable to keep all his books in print. He was born at Randolph, N. Y., the son of John Spencer Fosdick by his first wife, Eunice Andrews. While he was still a baby the family moved to Buffalo, where his father was principal of a public school. Charles attended the Central High School. One day his composition teacher remarked casually that it was possible that some of the boys in the class might later earn their living by writing. Years afterward Fosdick recalled the incident and believed that his ambition to become a writer had been awakened by it. When the Civil War broke out he went to Cairo, Ill., and enlisted as a landsman in the Mississippi Squadron. He served on gunboats patrolling the great river, saw the bombardment of Vicksburg as well as minor engagements, and was steadily promoted until at last he was made superintendent of coal for the squadron. These years on the Mississippi were his preparation for authorship. Although his later books deal with regions and adventures unknown to him at first-hand, his earlier ones are filled with reminiscences, adaptations, and enlargements of his own experiences. When the war on the river ended and he was once more free, he secured a position as clerk in a store at Villa Ridge, Ill., about ten miles north of Cairo, and in his spare time labored over his writing. When he was twenty-five he married Sarah Stoddard of Villa Ridge. His first book, *Frank, the Young Naturalist* (1864) was so successful that Fosdick proceeded to take his hero, Frank Nelson, through the adventures in which he himself had participated on a gunboat, in the woods, before Vicksburg, on the lower Mississippi, and on the prairie. To a generation of youngsters whose fathers had fought in the Civil War, these books made an irresistible appeal with their brisk, unadorned narrative, their exemplification of manly virtues in place of the namby-pamby of the Rollo books, their air of reality, and their full-blooded Northern patriotism. Fosdick usually wrote his books in series of three or six, each story in itself complete but temptingly baited with allusions to previous and subsequent adventures of its hero and his friends. Among them were a Gunboat, a Rocky Mountain, a Sportsman's Club, a Frank Nelson, a Boy Trapper, a Roughing It, a Rod and Gun, a Go-Ahead, a War, a Houseboat, an Afloat and Ashore, and a Pony Express series—names that suggest Fosdick's relation to Fenimore Cooper, the Davy Crockett legend, and the American cult of the outdoors. Though a diligent and rather careful writer, he made no large profit on his books, which he appears to have sold to his publishers for a lump sum. From 1875 on he lived in Westfield, N. Y. His wife acted as his copyist and proof-reader and helped him in numerous other ways; when she died in 1904 he gave up writing, traveled a little, and spent his last years with his son in Hamburg, N. Y. By the time of his death he had been almost forgotten as a person.

[*Who's Who in America,* 1914–15; *Buffalo Express,* Aug. 23, 1915; N. Y. *Evening Post,* Aug. 28, 1915; L. L. Fosdick, *Fosdick Family* (privately printed, 1891), p. 128; letter to author from Raymond B. Fosdick, his nephew, June 15, 1928.] G.H.G.

FOSDICK, WILLIAM WHITEMAN (Jan. 28, 1825–Mar. 8, 1862), author, was born in Cincinnati, the son of Thomas R. Fosdick, a banker. His mother, Julia (Drake) Fosdick, was an actress, the daughter of Samuel Drake [*q.v.*], and by a later marriage the mother of Julia Dean [*q.v.*]. As a boy he studied at home under a Rev. Samuel Johnson; later he attended the Cincinnati College and the Transylvania University in Kentucky. In the two or three years after he left college, in addition to writing much poetry, he studied law in Louisville, spent a winter in Mobile, then after further roaming settled down as a lawyer in Cincinnati. During 1848–49 he traveled in Texas and Mexico, and in 1851 published in Cincinnati his historical romance, *Malmiztic the Toltec, and the Cavaliers of the Cross.* Its style was ornate and eloquent, but by that, perhaps, he was so much the more definitely recognized as "promising," and in 1852 he changed his residence to New York. He lived there for five or six years, ostensibly a lawyer but in fact somewhat of a litterateur. In 1855 he published *Ariel and Other Poems,* in which he carried the story of the sprite beyond the record in *The Tempest.* He had been attracted to the subject, he said, by the remembrance that it was only in this play that Shakespeare had recognized America. Other themes discussed in the volume were Daniel Boone, William Cullen Bryant, and a New York wedding-feast, handled in parody of the *Ancient Mariner.* During his residence in New York he had two experiences which he specially did not enjoy—the lecture tour which he made through New England in behalf of the Nebraska Emigration Company, and the destruction by fire, in the Harper publishing house, of a manuscript upon which he had put all his hopes of literary distinction. About 1857 he returned to live in Cincinnati and there spent his last years. He was most agreeable personally, and for some time after his death he persisted in local tradition as a "born poet, a true wit, a boon companion of artists and literary men, a courteous gentleman, loved and admired by every man, woman, and child who knew him" (Venable, *post,* p. 114).

[W. T. Coggeshall, *Poets and Poetry of the West* (1860); *Cincinnati Daily Commercial,* Mar. 10, 1862; W. H. Venable, *Beginnings of Literary Culture in the Ohio Valley* (1891).] J.D.W.

FOSS, CYRUS DAVID (Jan. 17, 1834–Jan. 29, 1910), clergyman, educator, bishop of the Methodist Episcopal Church, was born in Kingston, N. Y., the son of Cyrus, also a Methodist minister, and Jane (Campbell) Foss. From boyhood he showed high intellectual ability, and after preparing for college at Amenia Seminary, he entered Wesleyan University, Middletown, Conn., from which he graduated at the head of his class when he was but twenty years old. Returning to Amenia as instructor in mathematics, he remained there until 1857, during the last year of which period he was principal. He then joined the New York Conference of the Methodist Church, and until 1859 was stationed at Chester, N. Y. From that time until he was elected president of Wesleyan University in 1875, his appointments were all to churches in New York and Brooklyn. On Mar. 20, 1856, he was married to Mary E. Bradley of Salisbury, Conn., who died Sept. 7, 1863; and on May 10, 1865, to Amelia Robertson of Peekskill, N. Y.

When he became head of Wesleyan, it was in such financial straits that its existence seemed imperiled, but largely through his wisdom and energy the peril was averted and the institution put on a sound basis. It was not financial success alone that marked his administration, however, and "no president of Wesleyan University," according to its historian, "was ever more respected; none was ever more beloved" (C. T. Winchester, "Historical Sketch of Wesleyan University," in Frank W. Nicolson, *Alumni Record of Wesleyan University,* 1911). The General Conference of 1880 elected him bishop, and he took up his episcopal residence in Minneapolis, changing it to Philadelphia in 1888, where it remained until his death. He was a fraternal delegate to the British Wesleyan Conference, London, in 1886; and officially visited the Methodist missions of Europe that same year. In 1893 he made a similar visitation in Mexico, and in 1897–98 one in India and Malaysia; while in 1906–07 he undertook a missionary tour of observation around the world. From 1888 to 1906 he was president of the Methodist Board of Church Extension. Good judgment and fixity of purpose characterized all his administrative work. He was a stanch believer in Methodism, and gave unwavering acceptance to the ancient doctrines as expressed in the Apostles' Creed. Not only his abilities but his kindness, his unfailing courtesy, and his innate goodness won him esteem and affection. His sermons were direct, forceful, rich in allusions, and fired with enthusiasms for Christian beliefs and institutions. A short collection of them under the title, *Religious Certainties,* was published in 1905. One of the fruits of his missionary tours was *From the Himalayas to the Equator* (1899). The National Temperance Society published his sermon, *Temperance and the Pulpit* (1871), and the periodicals of his day contain numerous contributions from him.

[The *Christian Advocate* (N. Y.), Feb. 3, 1910, contains portrait and sketch of his career. See also a memoir by John G. Oakley, in *Minutes of the ... N. Y. Conf. of the M. E. Ch.* (1910); obituary notices in Phila. *Press* and *Public Ledger,* Jan. 30, 1910; and *Who's Who in America,* 1908–09.] H. E. S.

FOSS, SAM WALTER (June 19, 1858–Feb. 26, 1911), poet, journalist, humorist, librarian, was born at Candia, N. H., the son of Dyer and Polly (Hardy) Foss. He was of Huguenot origin and through his father a descendant of Stephen Bachiler, the ancestor of Webster, Fessenden, Allison, Whittier, and other well-known men. His father was a farmer, and highly esteemed by his fellow townsmen. His mother died when he was four years old. As a boy he worked on the farm and went to school in winter. When he was fourteen his father, having married again, moved to Portsmouth, N. H. The son attended the Portsmouth High School, in which he received literary encouragement, and at graduation in 1877 he was chosen class poet. The following year he spent at the Tilton Seminary. He then entered Brown University and was graduated in 1882. As a student he was poor in purse, and, living at a distance from the college, took little part in student activities. In his vacations he worked on his father's farm. He contributed poems to the *Brunonian,* the college literary fortnightly, of which he became an editor, and was class odist and poet. During the year after graduation he was a book agent in company with his friend William E. Smythe. The two bought the Lynn, Mass., *Union* in 1883, changing its name in the same year to the *Saturday Union.* Foss became proprietor and sole editor in 1884. Having arranged for the supply of a humorous column, he found himself one week without it, and was forced to write the column himself. The compliments on his humor which he received encouraged him to continue to write the column, and in time his work attracted the notice of Wolcott Balestier, the editor of *Tid-Bits,* who sought his contributions. Soon he made connections with *Puck, Judge,* the *Sun,* and other New York publications, as well as with the *Christian Endeavor World* and the *Youth's Companion.* In 1887 he went to Boston to become editor of the *Yankee Blade* and an editorial writer for the *Boston Globe.* He held both positions for seven years. During this period he wrote a poem a week for his own paper, and in 1893 and 1894 a poem a day for a syndicate. In 1898 he became librarian of the Somerville Public Library, and this position he held during the rest of his life. Though he came untrained into librarianship, he was soon regarded as a force in public library activity, and in 1904 he was elected president of the Massachusetts Library Club. His latest literary activity was writing the "Library Alcove" for the *Christian Science Monitor* (Oct. 6, 1909–Mar. 1, 1911). His poetry was collected and published under the titles *Back Country Poems* (1892); *Whiffs from Wild Meadows* (1895); *Dreams in Homespun* (1897); *Songs of War and Peace* (1899); *The Song of the Library Staff* (1906); and *Songs of the Average Man* (1907). His class poem, *The Hesperian,* was printed in the *Brunonian* for June 21, 1882. To his last volume were added in 1911 eight poems, closing with his noble swan-song, *The Trumpets,* written at Christmas time when he was contemplating going to the hospital. In speech Foss was rapid and unstudied. In manner he retained a trace of the farmer boy. The medallion by Recchia in the Somerville Public Library and in replica at Brown University is a marvelously lifelike portrait representing him as a laughing philosopher. He married in 1887 Carrie Maria Conant, daughter of the Rev. Henry W. Conant of Providence, R. I.

Foss won his popularity as a humorous poet chiefly in dialect, the everyday speech of the New Hampshire countryman, but his work is essentially a philosophy of life unfolding itself through humorous examples. He had always a fellow-feeling with those who toil, and a contempt for idlers and self-pitiers. His best-known poem, *The House by the Side of the Road,* goes back to Homer for its inspiration. His *Calf-Path* is a permanent contribution to satire. He was a master of rhythm and rhyme, with an Aristophanian *flair* for word jugglery. His poetry is unfailingly sincere, representing not merely his convictions but also his personal life. Like many another humorist he found himself the prisoner of his popularity, for the public, having come to count on him to raise a laugh, took little interest in most of his serious or purely poetic writings. He had looked forward to retiring with an independence sufficient to permit him to write regardless of money returns, but he died in harness.

[*Who's Who in America,* 1910–11; M. S. Woodman, *Sam Walter Foss, Poet, Librarian and Friend to Man* (1922); H. L. Koopman, in *Brown Alumni Monthly,* Oct. 1908; Peter MacQueen, in the *Nat. Mag.,* May 1909; W. E. Foster, in the *Brown Alumni*

Monthly, Apr. 1911; J. M. Chapple, in the *Boston Globe*, Feb. 27, 1911; W. E. Jillson, in the *Providence Jour.*, June 11, 1922; *Hist. Cat. of Brown Univ., 1864–1914.*] H.L.K.

FOSTER, ABIEL (Aug. 8, 1735–Feb. 6, 1806), clergyman, congressman, was the son of Asa and Elizabeth (Abbott) Foster. He was born at Andover, Mass., graduated at Harvard in 1756, studied theology, and in 1761 was ordained minister at Canterbury, N. H., then a rapidly growing frontier settlement. His father had invested in lands in this district and several of his brothers moved there about the same time. For eighteen years he continued his ministerial duties in this town and its records show that he was also active in various secular affairs. The last years of his pastorate were embittered by a factional quarrel in the church and in 1779 he was formally dismissed. He now abandoned the ministry and henceforth devoted himself to public service. While pastor he had been twice married: on May 15, 1761, to Hannah Badger, daughter of Joseph Badger of Gilmanton (died Jan. 10, 1768); and on Oct. 11, 1769, to Mary Rogers, daughter of Samuel and Hannah (Wise) Rogers of Ipswich, Mass. He was an active supporter of the Revolutionary movement and a member of the Provincial Congress at Exeter in 1775. From 1779 to 1783 he represented Canterbury in the legislature, and was a delegate to Congress from 1783 to 1785. The records of the latter body show that he was faithful in attendance and active in the performance of miscellaneous routine duties. In 1784 he was appointed a judge in the court of common pleas and continued his duties for four years. This court did not as yet require the services of men learned in the law, and justice could be satisfactorily administered by persons of integrity and common sense. Following the adoption of the Constitution he was elected to the First Congress, was defeated for reëlection, and in the interim between March 1791 and his election to the Fourth Congress in 1794, devoted himself to New Hampshire affairs, serving in the Senate 1791–93, one term as president of that body, and also as a member of the important constitutional convention of 1791–92. His second period of service in Congress covered the years from Dec. 7, 1795 to Mar. 4, 1803. His health began to fail during his last term and he retired from active politics in the latter year. He was never active in debate but consistently supported Federalist policies, and he was a dependable member of that party. William Plumer, whose judgments of his contemporaries were inclined to harshness, describes him as "more distinguished for practical than theoretical knowledge" but possessed of honesty and sound judgment. Furthermore, "he never avoided voting upon any question."

[A brief sketch by Wm. Plumer appears in *N. H. State Papers*, XXI (1892), 798; James O. Lyford, *Hist. of the Town of Canterbury, N. H., 1727–1912* (1912); Wm. Patrick, *Hist. Sketches of Canterbury, N. H.* (1834); *New-Eng. Hist. and Geneal. Reg.*, Oct. 1858, Jan. 1859, Jan. 1876.] W.A.R.

FOSTER, ABIGAIL KELLEY (Jan. 15, 1810–Jan. 14, 1887), Abolitionist and woman's rights advocate, was the daughter of Wing and Diana (Daniels) Kelley of Pelham, Mass. She was of Irish-Quaker descent, and James Russell Lowell in the well-known "Letter from Boston" (*Pennsylvania Freeman*, Jan. 1847), in which he describes the Abolitionist leaders, refers to her as "A Judith, there, turned Quakeress." Abby Kelley, as she was usually called by contemporaries and subsequent writers, became a teacher at Worcester, Millbury, and Lynn. While teaching in the Friends School in the last-named town she was impressed by Garrison's attack on slavery and in 1837 abandoned teaching for the lecture platform, giving her services gratuitously to the anti-slavery cause. She conducted a campaign in Massachusetts in company with Angelina Grimké and is reported to be the first Massachusetts woman to have regularly addressed mixed audiences. The latter innovation was the source of much scandal to her contemporaries. She was denounced by the clergy as a menace to public morals, and her meetings were occasionally broken up by mobs. For some years she endured an incredible amount of insult and abuse. (For a typical instance occurring in Connecticut, see L. A. Coolidge, *Orville H. Platt*, 1910, pp. 5–7.) In 1839 the American Anti-Slavery Society indorsed the right of women to speak on its platform, but a year later her appointment to its executive committee caused a serious split in the organization. Her presence as a delegate at the world anti-slavery convention at London in 1840, and its refusal to recognize women delegates, caused an equally serious disturbance.

As a pioneer Abigail Kelley performed important services for her cause. She was a leader in the radical Abolitionist group, and became a well-known figure throughout the North. She was in a favorable position while attacking the evils of slavery to point out the serious legal, economic, and political disabilities of women. After 1850 she was more prominent as an advocate of woman's rights than as an anti-slavery leader; and she took a prominent part, with her husband, Stephen Symonds Foster [*q.v.*], whom she married Dec. 31, 1845, in most of the woman's rights conventions for the next twenty years. Her appearance at the anniversary convention of 1880, together with Lucy Stone, as the only surviving leaders of the famous gathering of thirty years before, attracted great attention. The woman's rights movement had become fairly respectable by 1880, and had attracted many who would have shrunk from the hardships of pioneering. Her remark in the convention of 1851, in reply to some disparagement of the Abolitionists, that "bloody feet have worn smooth the paths by which you came up hither," is both poignant and significant. She was fearless in denouncing the conservatism of the church and clergy, and repeatedly declared that they must shoulder much of the responsibility for the wrongs of women. She was probably somewhat less extreme than her husband in both her religious and political views but was nevertheless a decided radical in both. In addition to her work in the woman's rights cause she was active in support of prohibition and minor humanitarian interests. She is described by those who knew her as an attractive, kindly person with unassuming manners, and a good housekeeper. On the platform she was an effective speaker for many years but her voice finally gave out from overuse. She was an invalid in her last years.

[Harriet H. Robinson, *Mass. in the Woman Suffrage Movement* (1881); *Wm. Lloyd Garrison, 1805–79: The Story of his Life Told by his Children* (1885–89); Elizabeth Cady Stanton, and others, *Hist. of Woman Suffrage* (3 vols., 1881–87); Lillie B. C. Wyman, "Reminiscences of Two Abolitionists," in *New England Mag.*, Jan. 1903; obituary articles in the *Nation* (N. Y.), Jan. 20, 1887, and *Boston Daily Advertiser*, Jan. 15, 1887.] W. A. R.

FOSTER, BENJAMIN (July 31, 1852–Jan. 28, 1926), landscape-painter, art critic, was the son of a Maine lawyer and politician, Paulinus Mayhew Foster, who traced his lineage to old Salem and Martha's Vineyard families, and Lydia (Hutchins) Foster. Ben, as he was always called, was born in North Anson where his father practised for twenty-five years, holding various public posts and serving for two sessions as president of the state Senate. In 1860 the family moved to Richmond, Me., where the following year Paulinus died. He seems to have left his family in straitened circumstances, for Ben, the seventh of ten children, was early thrown on his own resources. At eighteen he went to New York to seek work. A dreamy, sensitive lad, a keen lover and delicate observer of nature, he was destined to spend twelve years in mercantile drudgery in the city. He was thirty before he rebelled and determined to devote himself to painting. He studied first in New York with Abbott Thayer and at the Art Student's League, then went to Paris.' After a year under Olivier Merson and Aimé Morot, he came back to develop his own individual landscape style in oil and water-colors, unhampered by theories or by any consuming desire for popularity. Six months of every year he spent in the romantic hill-country about his farm at Cornwall Hollow, Conn. The quiet, meditative moods of nature appealed to him: mysterious atmospheric effects, dawn, twilight, moonlight, the aspect of night in the hills; and these he rendered with intimate knowledge, a mastery of tone, and "a large feeling for unity," which caused French critics to compare him to Cazin. His landscapes, begun in the open, were worked out from memory in the studio, in order to allow time for the "sublimation of the ideal from the real."

Foster won the first of scores of awards at the Chicago World's Fair, in 1893. In 1900 he exhibited at the Paris Exposition, winning a bronze medal. The following year he was brought into national prominence when the French government purchased for the Luxembourg his picture "Lulled by the Murmuring Stream," a scene in a little New England village at night. He was the first American painter after Winslow Homer to be so honored. His most important success at home was the winning of the Carnegie Prize in 1906 from the National Academy of Design. He received the Webb Prize at the exhibition of the Society of American Artists in New York in 1901; a silver medal at the Pan-American Exposition in 1901; and for his picture "Misty Moonlight" a silver medal and $1,000 at the International Exhibition of the Carnegie Institute, at Pittsburgh in 1900. He was given an award at the St. Louis Exposition in 1904; the Innis gold medal at the exhibition of the National Academy of Design in 1908; a gold medal for "October," at the exhibition of the National Arts Club in 1917, and the Altman Prize of the National Academy of Design in 1917 for his picture "Summer Moonrise." He was elected to membership in the Society of American Artists in 1897, to the National Academy in 1904, to the National Institute of Arts and Letters, and to various water-color societies, local and national. Only a few months before his death he was awarded by popular vote the People's Prize at the annual show of the Newport Art Association for his picture "In Maine." He was for many years art critic of the New York *Evening Post* and a contributor to the *Nation*. A bachelor, he was long resident at the National Arts Club, Gramercy Square, New York City, and was buried from the galleries of the club.

[F. C. Pierce, *Foster Geneal.* (1899), pp. 835–36; *Biog. Sketches of Am. Artists*, Michigan State Library (5th ed., 1924), pp. 117–18; *The Fine Arts Journal*, XXXIV (Apr. 1916), 176–80; A. S. Randall.

"Conn. Artists and Their Work: Ben Foster," in *Conn. Mag.*, IX (1904), 139–43; *N. Y. Times*, Jan. 29, N. Y. *Evening Post*, Jan. 28, the *Art News*, Feb. 6, 1926.] M. B. H.

FOSTER, CHARLES (Apr. 12, 1828–Jan. 9, 1904), dry-goods merchant, congressman, governor of Ohio, secretary of the treasury, was the son of Charles W. Foster, a Massachusetts Scotch-Irishman, who in 1826 followed Laura Crocker to Seneca County, Ohio, and married her that year. He was born within the present limits of Fostoria, a name which commemorates his father. From earliest infancy the boy lived in the atmosphere of his father's business, a general store, kept for some time in one end of the log cabin which was the family dwelling. At the age of fourteen he was withdrawn from an academy at Norwalk after a scanty schooling, because his time was needed in the store, and four years later he became his father's partner. Throughout life he was primarily a business man, expanding his enterprises until they included banking and the gas and oil industry, and amassing a fortune, much of which was lost during the financial stress of the nineties. He was active in recruiting for the Civil War, and expected to become colonel of a regiment, but on his parents' plea remained at home. There his war service took the form of aid to soldiers' families, through credit extended in the neighborhood.

Although an ardent Republican and interested in public affairs, Foster was never a candidate for office until in 1870, when his friends persuaded him that no one else could carry his congressional district for the party. He was successful that year in this normally Democratic district, as well as in 1872, 1874, and 1876. In 1878, however, in consequence of a gerrymander of the district he was defeated. In Congress, as a member of the ways and means committee, he took a prominent part in exposing the frauds practised under the Sanborn contracts and the moiety law. He thus encountered the redoubtable "Ben" Butler, and won a national reputation by crossing swords in debate with this champion of the spoilsmen. As a member of the sub-committee which investigated the Louisiana contested election of 1874, he joined in a report which brought consternation to the radicals by holding against the Republican faction in the state. Later he was one of those who assured the Southern leaders that Hayes (who hailed from the same congressional district), if elected president, would withdraw the federal troops from the South.

In 1879 he was nominated by the Republicans for governor as a sound-money candidate, to oppose Thomas Ewing. He turned his business experience to good account in the contest. He introduced the preëlection poll to forecast the result, sent workers into doubtful districts, and made the first large use of money in Ohio elections. The Democratic papers sought to discredit him as "a man who knew no higher occupation during the war than measuring calico." In ridicule they called him "Calico Charlie." His friends, however, turned the epithet to good account; the women wore calico gowns and the men neckties of the same material during the campaign, and he won the election by a majority of more than 17,000. Two years later he won reëlection by an increased majority. As governor, he continued to apply his ideas of business efficiency. He appointed bipartisan boards for managing public institutions, and advocated mine inspection, forest protection, and careful revision of the tax system. The liquor question, which had seemed too dangerous for any party, he had the courage to face. He sponsored the Pond Law for the taxation of saloons, and in the election of 1883 procured the submission of amendments to enable the voters to indicate their preference for prohibition or a license system. These amendments were rejected, and the entire Republican ticket was defeated, in consequence of which Foster's leadership was for a time discredited.

In 1880 he attended the Republican National Convention as a delegate-at-large, under instructions to support John Sherman for the presidential nomination. It was rumored that he neglected opportunities to promote Sherman's interests, hoping that if Blaine were nominated he himself might be named for the vice-presidency, or that, in case of Garfield's nomination, he might be sent to the latter's vacated seat in the Senate. Sherman, who was losing a cabinet post with the retirement of Hayes, and who felt entitled to the senatorship if he failed of the presidential nomination, believed that on both counts Foster was disloyal to him. Foster explained his course and withdrew from the senatorial race, and the breach between the men was outwardly healed. Though he was talked of for a cabinet position under Garfield, a close friend, Foster was persuaded to retain the governorship. In February 1891, however, Harrison named him for the secretaryship of the treasury. In this position he favored international bimetallism but not domestic free coinage. He believed in the Sherman Silver Purchase Act as a permanent policy, and pledged himself to maintain the parity of gold and silver. Although he was strongly criticized during his incumbency, and possibly unjustly so, it cannot be said that he rendered notable service while in this office.

Upon the expiration of Harrison's term Foster

resumed his private life in Fostoria as a business man, and so continued to the end of his days. In 1853 he had married Ann M. Olmsted, daughter of Judge Jesse Olmsted, who bore him two daughters. He was a man of medium height, compact figure, genial face, and affable manners. Growing up in the "woods" with the "people," he was always "Charlie" to everybody, even when governor.

[F. C. Pierce, *Foster Geneal.* (1899), pp. 854–57; *The Biog. Cyc. . . . with an Hist. Sketch of the State of Ohio,* II (1884), 470–71; E. O. Randall and D. J. Ryan, *Hist. of Ohio* (1912), IV, 342–46; C. R. Williams, *The Life of Rutherford Birchard Hayes* (1914), I, 464–66, 534, II, 66–67, 129, 400; *Diary and Letters of Rutherford B. Hayes,* published by the Ohio State Archaeological and Hist. Soc. (5 vols., 1922–26), III, 259, 274, 575, IV, 46–47; Nevin O. Winter, *A Hist. of Northwest Ohio* (1917), 290–91, 596; John Sherman, *Recollections of Forty Years* (1895), II, 769–91; W. S. Kerr, *John Sherman, His Life and Public Services* (1907), II, 54–95; the *Coshocton Democrat,* Sept. 30, Oct. 7, 1879, containing typical partisan attacks upon Foster as gubernatorial candidate; A. J. Baughman, *Hist. of Seneca County, Ohio* (1911), I, 286–87; the *Ohio State Jour.* (Columbus), Jan. 3, 1882, Jan. 10, 1904; the *Commercial Tribune* (Cincinnati), Jan. 10, 1904.] H. C. H.

FOSTER, CHARLES JAMES (Nov. 24, 1820–Sept. 12, 1883), editor of sporting journals and authority on the history of the turf, was born at Bicester, Oxford, England, the son of Samuel and Elizabeth Foster. His family were tenants of the Earl of Jersey, a famous rider to the hounds and patron of the turf, who bred and trained his own horses on his Oxfordshire estate. One of Charles's earliest recollections was that of standing by his father's knee on frequent occasions, as over their pipes and home-brewed ale the latter discussed racers with Mr. Ransome, Master of the Horse to the Earl. His own uncle, Henry King, was recognized as one of the best judges of horses in England and his cousin William Foster was an active turfman. He received a good education at Northampton, but at the age of eighteen shipped on a merchantman and for a number of years followed the sea. In 1848 he came to Boston, drifted westward to Cincinnati, and finally settled in Columbus. Here he is said to have found a place in a law office, and to have been on terms of more or less intimacy with Clement L. Vallandigham, Salmon P. Chase, and Samuel S. Cox [*qq.v.*]. In 1857 he became associate editor of the *Ohio Statesman.*

Interested chiefly in sports, he now began to contribute to *Porter's Spirit of the Times* articles signed "Privateer," rich in the lore of the English turf, interlarded with interesting anecdotes, and written in a lively style. He also wrote for it "The High-Mettled Racer," the first installment of which appeared Aug. 15, 1857, a story of English country sporting life, which reveals a high degree of literary ability. After the establishment of *Wilkes' Spirit of the Times* in 1859 the "Privateer" articles were continued in that periodical, and when in 1860 George Wilkes went to England to attend the fight between John Heenan and Tom Sayers he asked Foster to come to New York and help run the paper during his absence. This temporary connection was made permanent and for fourteen years much of the journal's success was due to Foster's knowledge, industry, and skill as a writer. In 1875, with J. D. McIntyre and J. Edwards Whitehead, he established the *New York Sportsman,* with which he was connected until his death.

He never married, but lived with two maiden sisters in a cosy country home in Astoria. His knowledge of famous horses and their achievements was extensive and detailed, and he kept his information up to date by inspecting all the great stables of the country before each racing season. He was almost equally conversant with the prize ring, while game cocks, which it is alleged he "bred and occasionally bled in sequestered nooks on Long Island" were one of his minor interests. His writings were accepted as authoritative. To *Wilkes' Spirit of the Times,* he contributed a series of articles, beginning July 21, 1860, on "Lives and Battles of Distinguished Pugilists." A more notable series was "The Derby Winners, Historical Sketches of the Winners of the Derby for Fifty Years," which appeared in the *New York Sportsman* between Dec. 9, 1876, and Nov. 24, 1877. He wrote the article on "Turf" for Appletons' *American Cyclopædia* (1876), and edited Hiram Woodruff's *The Trotting Horse of America* (1868). He also edited Adam H. Bogardus's *Field, Cover, and Trap Shooting* (1874), and to "Sketches of the Actors," begun in the Jan. 11, 1862, number of *Wilkes' Spirit of the Times,* he made several contributions including sketches of Charlotte Cushman, Maggie Mitchell, and James H. Hackett. That of the last-named appears in Hackett's *Notes and Comments upon Certain Plays and Actors of Shakespeare* (1863). A novel, *The White Horse of Wootton,* was published in 1878. He died in Astoria in his sixty-third year and was buried in Columbus.

[Foster's writings contain autobiographical material. See also *N. Y. Tribune* and *N. Y. Herald,* Sept. 13, 1883; *N. Y. Clipper,* Sept. 22, 1883; the *Spirit of the Times,* Sept. 15, 1883; *Wallace's Monthly,* Oct. 1883; and John H. Wallace, *The Horse of America* (1897).] H. E. S.

FOSTER, DAVID SKAATS (Jan. 23, 1852–June 23, 1920), author, was born in Utica, N. Y., the son of Thomas and Eliza Pearson (Skaats) Foster. His ancestor, Reginald Foster, came from England and settled in Ipswich, Mass., in

1638. David attended the public schools at his home and later studied in Germany. Languages, of which he finally mastered five or six, were his chief interest. In 1874 he married Mary C. Williams, daughter of William A. Williams of Little Falls, N. Y. For most of his life he was a coal and iron merchant in Utica, but in the years following 1887 he published about twelve books. The first of these, *The Romance of the Unexpected,* is made up of a number of poems, for the most part narrative, sing-song, and sentimental. It was popular enough to be reissued in the following year, with a few additions and under a new title, *Rebecca the Witch* (1888). With the exception of *The Divided Medal,* a prose mystery story published in 1914, to which some thirty-five pages of verse were appended, these two volumes seem to have ended his career as a poet. The first of his novels, *Casanova the Courier* (1892), a story of Americans in Europe, established the model for most of what he was to write later. It is facile and sentimental, crowded with action and superficial humor. *Elinor Fenton* (1893), dealing with country people in the state of New York, seems to represent a determination of the author to confine himself to a stricter realism, but in *Spanish Castles by the Rhine* (1897), rather a series of stories than a novel, he yielded again to his dominant impulse for the romantic. After the appearance of this book he published nothing until 1910, when with *Flighty Arethusa* he inaugurated a series of novels which were more and more confessedly popular in their appeal, with incident tumbled over incident, mystery hidden behind mystery, and with platitude giving place mainly to dogmatism. Perhaps the most glaring example of this last quality in all his writing is in the war story *Mademoiselle of Cambrai* (1920), in which he indulges himself in the sentiment that a certain city "contained about five thousand human beings and some thirty thousand Germans" (p. 11). His wife died in 1895, and though he continued head of his mercantile firm in Utica, he made his home for the last few years of his life in Syracuse.

[F. C. Pierce, *Foster Geneal.* (1899); *Who's Who in America,* 1920–21; Syracuse and Utica city directories.] J. D. W.

FOSTER, EPHRAIM HUBBARD (Sept. 17, 1794–Sept. 6, 1854), United States senator, was born near Bardstown, Ky., the son of Ann (Hubbard) and Robert Coleman Foster who in 1797 moved to the neighborhood of Nashville, Tenn. At the age of nineteen Foster graduated from Cumberland College (later the University of Nashville). In the Creek War he served as secretary to Andrew Jackson. He studied law in the office of John Dickinson whose wealthy widow, Jane Mebane Lytle, he married in 1817. Virile, quick tempered, deeply affectionate, and strongly partisan, he became one of the most popular members of the Nashville bar. Until his entrance into politics his firm had, perhaps, the most lucrative practise in the state. From 1827 to 1835 he was three times elected to the Tennessee House of Representatives. Twice he was unanimously chosen speaker of the house. In 1833 he opposed John H. Eaton, John Bell, and Felix Grundy in a long and bitter contest for election to the United States Senate. On the fifty-fifth ballot Grundy was chosen. In the presidential campaign of 1836 Foster deserted the leadership of Andrew Jackson and gave his support to Hugh Lawson White. He became one of the most prominent Whig leaders of the state. Upon the resignation of Felix Grundy from the Senate to enter Van Buren's cabinet, he received the executive appointment to the vacancy for the 1838–39 session. For the six-year term, beginning in 1839, he had already defeated William Carroll, but he saw no service under this election. The succeeding Democratic legislature instructed the state's Whig senators to support the measures of the national Democratic administration. Foster resigned immediately (Nov. 15, 1839), and Grundy defeated him for the vacancy thus created. Four years later, however, upon the death of Grundy, he defeated William Carroll for the term ending in 1845. His most notable act in the Senate was to vote against the admission of Texas into the Union, on the specious plea that though he favored admission the resolution under consideration conceded too much to Northern Abolitionists (*Congressional Globe,* 28 Cong., 2 Sess., pp. 359, 362). This vote placed him on the defensive in his gubernatorial campaign of 1845. Chosen by the Whigs after other leaders had declined the nomination, he conducted a vigorous campaign against his Democratic opponent, Aaron V. Brown, but was defeated by less than two thousand votes. This ended his political career.

[Family Bible in the possession of Mrs. Edgar W. Foster of Nashville; Davidson County records; *Jour. of The House of Representatives of the State of Tenn.,* 1827–43; *Nashville Whig,* 1845; J. C. Guild, *Old Times in Tenn.* (Nashville, 1878), pp. 71–77; brief and partly inaccurate sketches in W. W. Clayton, *Hist. of Davidson County, Tenn.* (1880), pp. 113–15, and Joshua W. Caldwell, *Sketches of the Bench and Bar of Tenn.* (1898), pp. 198–201; obituaries in *Nashville Daily Gazette,* Sept. 8, *Nashville Daily Union and American,* and *Republican Banner and Nashville Whig* (daily), Sept. 9, 1854. The Tennessee State Library possesses an oil portrait of Foster by Washington B. Cooper.] P. M. H.

FOSTER, FRANK PIERCE (Nov. 26, 1841–Aug. 13, 1911), physician, immunologist, editor, lexicographer, was born in Concord, N. H., the son of William Parker Foster and Susan Webster Call, a niece of Daniel Webster. At the age of fifteen his life-work was suggested through an operation performed on his right forearm—the extirpation of a large birthmark—by Henry J. Bigelow [*q.v.*]. Not long after this experience he registered as a pupil with Dr. C. P. Gage of Concord, with whom he studied the fundamental subjects of botany, chemistry, and anatomy. In 1859 he attended lectures at the Boston Medical School but took his degree at the College of Physicians and Surgeons, New York, in 1862. He at once began his internate at the New York Hospital where his first distinction was a detail to treat the sick sailors of the friendly Russian squadron, then stationed in the harbor. With the expiration of his internate in 1864 he served as ship's surgeon on a Pacific mail steamer for one voyage. In 1865 he spent six months as acting assistant-surgeon in the United States army. In May 1866 he began his service as house physician of the New York Dispensary where he had a chance to witness the abuses of the then universal practise of arm-to-arm vaccination. He became an earnest propagandist for the use of animal lymph, and at the early age of twenty-five was the pioneer and champion of the cause which forced him into controversy with the leaders of his profession. He established a vaccine farm at Cos Cob, N. Y., and soon the demand for his vaccine quills became so great that he seemed on the highroad to prosperity. In time, however, the manufacture of the virus became general, and the use of animal lymph compulsory. That he attempted to commercialize the production of vaccine is hardly credible in view of his complete lack of interest in money matters.

Foster's battle for the introduction of animal lymph lasted for years, due to the fact that at the outset he was opposed by the medical societies and a majority of the physicians. In 1870 he made a report to the New York Academy of Medicine, which was at the same time a sort of candidate's thesis for membership, and won the latter only after a sharp conflict. In 1872 he was awarded the alumni prize of his alma mater for his essay on animal vaccination and in the following year delivered by request an essay on the same theme before the British Medical Association—an almost undreamed-of honor for a young American physician. During the first years of his medical practise Foster specialized in dermatology, and was one of the founders of the New York Dermatological Society, but about 1870 he became more interested in gynecology and obstetrics. In 1881 he was elected a fellow of the American Gynecological Society and for years held the appointment of surgeon to the Women's Hospital. In 1887 he founded the New York Clinical Society. In time his literary activity seems to have been exerted at the expense of his clinical career. After a term of service under Dr. Shrady of the *Medical Record,* he became connected with the publishing house of D. Appleton, taking over the editorship of the *New York Medical Journal,* which he held from 1880 until his death. He devoted twelve years of his life to the compilation of the *Illustrated Encyclopedic Medical Dictionary,* issued serially in four volumes between 1888 and 1894, and in 1904 brought out a one-volume edition of *Appletons' Medical Dictionary.* He also edited the *Reference Book of Practical Therapeutics* (2 vols., 1896–97), and with the collaboration of Edward Althaus, published the 1902–03 edition of George J. Adler's *German and English Dictionary.* He compiled the medical terms for the *Standard Dictionary* and was chairman of the committee on nomenclature of the American Medical Association. He had an extraordinary gift for making friends and was on terms of intimacy with an unusual number of the leaders of the profession. His wife was Georgiana Molleson, of New York, whom he married on Oct. 18, 1869.

[There is a sketch of Foster written by his son, Hugh Molleson Foster, in *Medical Life,* Aug. 1927. See also H. A. Kelly and Walter L. Burrage, *Dict. of Am. Medic. Biog.* (1928); *N. Y. Medic. Jour.,* Aug. 19, 1911; *Lancet* (London), Sept. 2, 1911; *N. Y. Herald,* Aug. 15, 1911.] E. P.

FOSTER, GEORGE BURMAN (Apr. 2, 1858–Dec. 22, 1918), Baptist clergyman, educator, the son of Oliver Harrison Foster and Helen Louise (Skaggs) Foster, was born in Alderson, W. Va. He obtained his collegiate education at Shelton College, W. Va., 1876–79, and at West Virginia University where he received the degree of B.A. in 1883. Meanwhile, in 1879, he had been ordained to the Baptist ministry, and in 1883–84 he was pastor at Morgantown, Pa. On Aug. 6, 1884, he was married to Mary Lyon, daughter of Prof. Franklin Lyon of West Virginia University. After completing his theological work at Rochester Theological Seminary where he graduated in 1887, he served as pastor at Saratoga Springs, N. Y., 1887–91. Essentially of scholarly rather than of ministerial temperament, he gave up his pastorate in the latter year in order to carry on theological studies in Germany. The year 1891–92 he spent most fruitfully in the Universities of Göttingen and Berlin, and shortly after his return he was granted the degree of Ph.D. by Denison University. The rest of his life was devoted to teaching and writing. He was professor of philosophy at McMaster University, 1892–95; associate professor and professor of systematic theology at the University of Chicago, 1895–1905; and professor of philosophy of religion at the University of Chicago from 1905 until his death at the age of sixty.

Foster was one of the ablest and most influential theological writers of his time in America. Tolerant by nature, well-read in philosophy, thoroughly conversant with European Biblical scholarship, he was a powerful force toward the liberalizing of orthodox Christianity. For this reason he was bitterly attacked in 1909 by the Rev. Johnston Myers, fundamentalist pastor of the Immanuel Baptist Church, Chicago. Delighting in debate, Foster sought rather than shunned controversy. In 1917 and 1918 wide attention was given to his public debates with Clarence Darrow on the subjects, "Is Life Worth Living?" and "Resolved: that the Human Will is Free." Darrow is reported subsequently to have said that Foster was the most intellectual man he ever knew.

Foster warred consistently against authority and tradition, and rejected the rationalistic arguments for religion, but defended eloquently the personal faith of the heart. Religion he regarded as something experimental, growing or declining with the age, but essential to man's nature, and, in form, completely expressed in the life and legend of Christ. The sanctions of religion he considered almost wholly pragmatic. His chief writings were: *The Finality of the Christian Religion* (1906); *The Function of Religion in Man's Struggle for Existence* (1909); *The Function of Death in Human Experience* (1915); "The Contribution of Critical Scholarship to Ministerial Efficiency," in G. B. Smith, *Guide to the Study of the Christian Religion* (1916); *Christianity in its Modern Expression* (1921).

[*Chicago Daily Tribune*, Dec. 23, 1918; John W. Leonard, ed., *Men of America* (1908); *Who's Who in America*, 1918–19.] E. S. B—s.

FOSTER, HANNAH WEBSTER (1759–Apr. 17, 1840), author, was the daughter of Grant Webster, a Boston merchant of standing. Prof. John W. Webster of Harvard College was her nephew. Little is known of her childhood and education but as a girl and young woman she had a local reputation for cleverness as well as beauty. She contributed to newspapers political articles which attracted the notice of Rev. John Foster, a popular clergyman of Brighton, Mass. They were married in April 1785 and she was warmly welcomed into his parish, where she became a leader in social and literary activities. In 1797 she published the book which was the sensation of the time in New England, has since been a puzzle for antiquarians and local historians, and has caused much criticism to be directed against the author's veracity. It appeared as *The Coquette; or, The History of Eliza Wharton . . . By a Lady of Massachusetts* (1797). Purporting to be a novel founded on fact, it tells the story of the love of "Eliza Wharton," a young woman of good Massachusetts family, for Pierpont Edwards [*q.v.*], and recounts the details of her elopement with him, and her death at the Bell Tavern, Danvers, Mass., at the time of the birth of her child. The possibility of a secret marriage is discussed but remains a mystery. The real "Eliza Wharton" was Elizabeth Whitman, who had died less than ten years before the publication of *The Coquette*. Hannah Foster's husband was a cousin of the wife of Deacon John Whitman of Stow, who was himself a cousin of Elizabeth Whitman's father. Through this family connection, Hannah Foster was probably in possession of most of the facts, or rumors, current concerning the Whitman case. She has, however, been censured for serious misstatement and exaggeration. It has been said of her (Dall, *post*) that she had a vivid imagination and made no attempt to adhere to the facts of the story, if she ever knew them, and further (Bolton, *post*) that since Elizabeth Whitman's seducer has never been identified she had no justification for representing him as Pierpont Edwards. From a literary standpoint, *The Coquette* is a prototype of Richardson's *Clarissa Harlowe* and Susanna H. Rowson's *Charlotte Temple*, a moral tale of the unhappy fate of one who strays from the path of virtue. At the time of its publication it was absent from few homes where any reading was done, and many editions have since appeared. In 1798 Mrs. Foster published *The Boarding School; or, Lessons of a Preceptress to her Pupils* in the preface of which the author states that she has "employed a part of her leisure hours in collecting and arranging her ideas on the subject of female deportment." A certain Mrs. Williams, living on the banks of the Merrimac, is the fictional preceptress of a very select boarding-school admitting only seven pupils at a time. Her didactic lectures on reading, dress, politeness, amusements, directions for the government of the temper and manners, and filial and fraternal affection, form the subject matter of the book. After her husband's death, Mrs. Foster resided in Montreal, Canada, the home of her two daughters, both of whom were writers of essays and magazine articles. She died in Montreal, at the home of her daughter Elizabeth L. (Foster)

Cushing, wife of Dr. Frederick Cushing, physician at the Emigrant Hospital.

[F. C. Pierce, *Foster Geneal.* (1899), p. 238; Jane E. Locke, "Hist. Preface, including a Memoir of the Author," in the 1855 edition of *The Coquette*; C. K. Bolton, *The Elizabeth Whitman Mystery*, published by the Peabody, Mass., Hist. Soc. (1912); Caroline H. Dall, *The Romance of the Association; or One Last Glimpse of Charlotte Temple and Eliza Wharton* (1875); J. P. C. Winship, *Hist. Brighton*, vol. I (1899).] S. G. B.

FOSTER, JOHN (1648–Sept. 9, 1681), engraver, printer, was the second son and fourth child of Hopestill and Mary (Bates) Foster. He was born in that part of Dorchester, Mass., which later became South Boston, and was baptized on Dec. 10, 1648, by Richard Mather. His father was a brewer and a member of the General Court. His mother was the daughter of James Bates who came from England in 1635, was several years a selectman of Dorchester, and in 1641 represented Hingham in the General Court. John Foster graduated from Harvard in 1667 and two years later, probably in October, began teaching English, Latin, and writing in his birthplace. As early as 1671 he "took up engraving as an avocation," and became the earliest wood-engraver of English America. A few years later he bought a printing-plant which Marmaduke Johnson [*q.v.*] had fitted out just before his death. Foster took over the establishment and early in 1675, starting business "over against the Sign of the Dove," became the pioneer printer of Boston. He produced his best work after 1678, having in that year acquired a new font of long primer. He had no training in his art, but had picked it up by observation at Samuel Green's shop in Cambridge, and although his career as a printer lasted less than seven years (1675–81), in that time the issues of his press amounted to about fifty pieces. His extant works are very rare, some exist only in one copy, and a few that have vanished are recorded only inferentially. He printed fifteen pieces by Increase Mather; two each by James Allen, John Eliot, William Hubbard, Benjamin Keach, Thomas Thacher, Samuel Willard, and Roger Williams; an edition of the poems of Anne Bradstreet, and some shorter pieces of verse. Eighteen of his publications were sermons, three were historical works, and three broadsides. Of the latter, one on the smallpox and measles was the earliest treatise concerning a medical subject printed in the colonies. He also printed a catechism, a harmony of the gospels, a confession of faith, a church government, and a platform of church discipline. In addition to these works he compiled annual almanacs (1675, 1676, 1678–81) for which he made his own astronomical calculations. He wrote a paper on "Comets, their Motion, Distance and Magnitude," for his almanac of 1681, together with "Observations of a Comet seen this last Winter 1680." He had a smattering knowledge of medicine and in his will left some "Medicinal Books." Chief among some ten wood-cuts attributed to him are a three-quarter length portrait of Rev. Richard Mather which is considered the earliest portrait engraved in the colonies; a "Map of New England" for Hubbard's *Narrative of the Troubles with the Indians* (1677); and a view of Boston and Charlestown taken from Noddles Island. Foster died of tuberculosis at Dorchester in his thirty-third year, and his memory was honored by two printed funeral elegies in verse. His interment was in the Dorchester burying-ground. By his last will, dated July 18, 1681, when his body was "weak & languishing," but his "understanding not distempered or impaired," he ordered his printing-press and appurtenances at Boston to be sold to pay his Boston debts, his funeral expenses, and to provide twenty or thirty shillings "to pay for a pair of handsome Gravestones." His house at Dorchester he left to his widowed mother, who was his sole executrix. At his death the value of his estate amounted only to something over a hundred pounds.

[The chief source concerning Foster and his work is Samuel A. Green's *John Foster: the earliest Am. Engraver and the first Boston Printer* (1909). This final work supersedes Green's earlier contributions in *Proc. Mass. Hist. Soc.*, Oct. 12, 1899, ch. i of his *Ten Facsimile Reproductions relating to various Subjects* (1903), and *Remarks on John Foster* (1905). John L. Sibley's *Harvard Grads.*, II (1881), 222–28, has a good sketch which Green has thoroughly used.] V. H. P.

FOSTER, JOHN GRAY (May 27, 1823–Sept. 2, 1874), army officer, the son of Perley and Mary (Gray) Foster, was born at Whitefield, N. H. His father moved to Nashua in 1833 and John completed his early education in the city schools and at Hancock Academy. In 1842 he received an appointment to the United States Military Academy and graduated fourth in the class of 1846. He was commissioned second lieutenant in the corps of engineers and after a brief term of service in Washington, D. C., was ordered on active service under Gen. Scott in Mexico. He took part in the siege of Vera Cruz and the subsequent advance into the interior, being severely wounded at the battle of Molino del Rey, Sept. 8, 1847. He received two citations for distinguished service in this campaign, but on recovery from his wound, was relegated to the more obscure, though useful, routine duties of an engineer officer in time of peace. Until 1860 he performed miscellaneous services, including a two-year term as assistant professor of engineering (1855–57) at the Military Academy. On July 1, 1860, he was commissioned captain of engineers and when the war began a few months later was engineer in charge of the United States fortifications in Charleston Harbor. He was in Maj. Anderson's command at Fort Sumter and his reports—the laconic, professional observations of the trained soldier—have contributed largely to our historical knowledge of the memorable weeks in the spring of 1861 (see the *Official Records (Army)*, 1 ser., vol. I, which contains many official memoranda and reports, including an interesting "engineer journal" of the bombardment, pp. 16–25).

On Oct. 23, 1861, Foster was appointed brigadier-general of Volunteers and in the following March he was brevetted colonel in the United States army. He took a prominent part in the North Carolina expedition, including the capture of Roanoke Island and New Bern, and on July 1, 1862, was placed in command of the Department of North Carolina. He retained this command for several months, engaging in several local operations of considerable importance in the early part of 1863. Later in the same year he took part in operations for the relief of Gen. Burnside at Knoxville, Tenn., and in December succeeded the latter in command of the Department of the Ohio, although he was soon afterward obliged to ask to be relieved because of accidental injuries. On May 26, 1864, having partially recovered, he was assigned to command the Department of the South, where he later coöperated with Gen. Sherman in the movements against Savannah and Charleston. During the last months of the war he was in command in Florida with headquarters at Tallahassee. He had been made major-general of Volunteers, ranking from July 18, 1862, and on Mar. 13, 1865, was brevetted major-general in the United States army. On Mar. 7, 1867, he was commissioned lieutenant-colonel, corps of engineers.

Foster spent the remainder of his life in routine work. He engaged in survey and construction operations on the New England coast and from 1871 to 1874 was assistant to the chief of Engineers. In 1869 he published *Submarine Blasting in Boston Harbor, Mass.; Removal of Tower and Corwin Rocks,* which was long an authoritative treatise on the general subject. He was considered a dependable, courageous officer who understood both the virtues and defects of the volunteer. He knew how to adapt the raw material of the Civil War levies to the tasks at hand, and was an especially competent administrator. He was married on Jan. 21, 1851, to Mary L. Moale, daughter of Col. Samuel Moale of Baltimore. After her death in 1871 he married, on Jan. 9, 1872, Nannie Davis, daughter of George M. Davis of Washington, D. C.

[Frank G. Noyes, "Biog. Sketch of Maj.-Gen. John G. Foster," *Granite Monthly,* June 1899, written from Foster's personal papers; Clarence E. E. Stout, "John Gray Foster," *Ibid.,* May 1882; F. C. Pierce, *Foster Geneal.* (1899); Otis F. R. Waite, *N. H. in the Great Rebellion* (Claremont, N. H., 1870), pp. 607-08; G. H. Gordon, in *Sixth Ann. Reunion of the Asso. of Grads. of the U. S. Mil. Acad.* (3rd ed. 1891). The N. H. Hist. Soc. has a small collection of Foster's papers, including both military and personal correspondence.] W. A. R.

FOSTER, JOHN PIERREPONT CODRINGTON (Mar. 2, 1847–Apr. 1, 1910), tuberculosis specialist, the son of Eleazer Kingsbury Foster by his wife Mary Codrington, was born in New Haven, Conn., and received his early education at Gen. Russell's Collegiate and Commercial Institute. After graduating from Yale in 1869 he developed pulmonary tuberculosis and passed several years in Florida for his health. There he engaged in sugar planting. He eventually returned to New Haven to enter the Yale Medical School, and received the degree of M.D. in 1875. He began to practise immediately and attended a large number of undergraduates at the university. Through his influence a local infirmary was erected in which members of the university could receive medical treatment. From 1877 till his death he held the position of instructor in anatomy as applied to art under the auspices of the department of fine arts at Yale. In 1879 he became surgeon to the United States Marine Hospital Service, a post which he held until 1910.

Foster's chief contribution to medicine arose from his interest in the problem of tuberculosis. He became convinced very early that rest and fresh air were vital for tuberculosis patients, and he was the first in America to experiment with Koch's tuberculin which he employed on Dec. 3, 1890, in treating a case of pulmonary tuberculosis. It was used in Baltimore a week later by Osler (*Johns Hopkins Hospital Bulletin,* Jan. 1891), but its value as a therapeutic agent is still uncertain. He helped to establish the National Association for the Study and Prevention of Tuberculosis in 1905, and was vice-president of the sixth International Congress of Tuberculosis. He was also largely instrumental in founding the Gaylord Farm Sanatorium near Wallingford, Conn., which was opened in September 1904. Foster's writings were earnest and clear and through them he did much to stimulate interest in the prevention of tuberculosis. He died of pneumonia. He had married on July 1, 1875, Josephine Theresa Bicknell of New York.

[*Proc. Conn. State Medic. Soc.,* 1910, 316–20; *Jour. Am. Medic. Asso.,* Apr. 16, 1910; H. A. Kelly and W. L. Burrage, *Am. Medic. Biogs.* (1920); R. B. Moffat,

Pierrepont Geneal. (1913); *Who's Who in America,* 1910–11; *Seventh Biog. Record of the Class of 'Sixty-Nine, Yale Coll., 1894–1904* (1910); *New Haven Evening Reg.,* Apr. 1, 1910.] J. F. F.

FOSTER, JOHN WATSON (Mar. 2, 1836–Nov. 15, 1917), lawyer, soldier, editor, diplomat, secretary of state, professor, was born in Pike County, Ind., where his father, Matthew Watson Foster, was a successful farmer. His mother, Eleanor Johnson, came of a Virginia family. Foster attended the University of Indiana (B.A. 1855), where through study and in debate he developed the anti-slavery convictions implanted by his father. After a year at the Harvard Law School he spent another year in a law office in Cincinnati before he associated himself in the practise of law at Evansville with Conrad Baker, one of the ablest lawyers of Indiana. In 1859 he married Mary Parke McFerson who received repeatedly in his writings tributes for her counsel, assistance, and affection. When the Civil War broke out Foster's zeal for the anti-slavery cause and for the Union led him to enlist. Gov. Morton sent him a commission as major. For his share in the capture of Fort Donelson he was promoted lieutenant-colonel, and for his meritorious service at Shiloh he was made a colonel. He commanded a brigade of cavalry in Burnside's expedition into East Tennessee and was the first to occupy Knoxville in 1863. He learned to know Grant, Sherman, and Thomas. Foster states in his *Memoirs* that his military life enlarged his knowledge of men and gave him a fuller self-confidence.

After the war Foster became editor of the *Evansville Daily Journal,* the most influential paper in Southern Indiana. In 1872, he served as chairman of the Republican state committee. As such he was instrumental in bringing about the reëlection of Oliver P. Morton to the United States Senate and of Gen. Grant to the presidency. The next year President Grant designated him as minister to Mexico. He served there during the transition from the Lerdo to the Diaz régime and under trying circumstances succeeded in making himself highly agreeable to the Mexican government.

Early in 1880, President Hayes transferred him to St. Petersburg. He remained there a year and had little to do except to attend ceremonies and to plead for leniency in the treatment of American Jews. He returned to Washington and set up in the practise of law. In 1883, President Arthur offered him the appointment as minister to Spain. Foster accepted. He negotiated a reciprocity treaty affecting the trade with Cuba, but the treaty failed to meet the approval of the Senate. During Cleveland's first administration Foster practised law. Harrison appointed him on a special mission to Madrid to negotiate another reciprocity treaty. This treaty became effective and for two years greatly facilitated American trade with Cuba and Porto Rico.

During the latter part of Harrison's administration Foster became the agent for the United States in the Bering Sea or fur-seal arbitration. Two unexpected events weakened the case of the United States. As a part of the transfer of Alaska, Russia had delivered to the Department of State a mass of archives in the Russian language. These were reputed to show—and Foster so believed—that Russia had exercised exclusive territorial jurisdiction over Bering Sea. Foster employed one Ivan Petroff to select the pertinent documents and to translate them. Petroff furnished the translations to support the American contention. Copies of the documents and their translation occupied a prominent place in the case. Several weeks after their submission to counsel for Great Britain a clerk in the Department of State, William C. Mayo, discovered discrepancies. Petroff confronted with the evidence admitted his guilt. Foster promptly informed the British legation in Washington of the circumstances of the case and explained to the British agent how the perfidy had been imposed upon him. The second untoward event occurred during the oral arguments before the tribunal at Paris. Russia had supported the stand taken by the United States for the protection of the fur-seals. On June 21, 1893, Sir Richard Webster asked permission to read a document which had been laid before Parliament. Russia had conceded to Great Britain that seals could be taken anywhere outside a zone of thirty miles around the Russian islands on the Asiatic side of Bering Sea. The United States lost the case on all points with the exception that the tribunal allowed a prohibited zone of sixty miles around the Pribilof Islands.

For about eight months during 1892 and 1893 and partly overlapping the period of the fur-seal arbitration Foster served as secretary of state. As such he negotiated a treaty of annexation with the Republic of Hawaii. This negotiation took place so shortly after the establishment of the republic under the domination of American citizens there and under such questionable circumstances that when Cleveland succeeded to the presidency he withdrew the treaty from the Senate. Another important event in his term was the *Baltimore* incident. Capt. W. S. Schley of the *Baltimore* in Santiago harbor, Chile, had given shore leave to a number of sailors and officers. Whatever the cause may have been, a fight ensued in which two sailors were killed and seventeen wounded. Foster called attention to the fact that reparation was due the injured and the dependents of those who had been killed. Chile proposed arbitration. Foster replied that inasmuch as questions of national honor were involved a frank and friendly offer of voluntary compensation would be accepted as a proof of good-will. Thereupon Chile offered $75,000 in gold which was accepted as satisfactory.

At the close of the Chino-Japanese War, December 1894, the Chinese foreign office invited Foster, then a private citizen, to join the Chinese commissioners in the negotiation of peace with Japan. He accepted, and performed a creditable service in bringing about an agreement between Li Hung Chang and Marquis Ito. Later, in 1907, Foster represented China at the Second Hague Conference. In 1903 Great Britain and the United States agreed to arbitrate their differences about the Alaska-Canadian boundary. The United States designated Foster as agent to take charge of the preparation of the case. Greatly to his credit the tribunal sustained substantially his arguments and conclusions. As a lawyer in Washington Foster represented various governments, notably the Mexican. Probably the most important case concerned the Weil and La Abra claims of over a million dollars, which had been awarded to the United States by a claims commission. Foster found and proved that the awards had been obtained through fraud. Through his efforts Mexico was reimbursed for payments made on these claims.

Foster delivered numerous lectures on various phases of international relations which found their way later into periodicals and pamphlets. He was especially interested in foreign missions and in arbitration. His courses at George Washington University comprised the salient features of American diplomatic history from 1776 to 1876, the rules and procedure of diplomatic intercourse, which developed into the best book of its kind written by an American, and an outline of the relations of the United States with the Orient. Included in his printed works, which are marked by a good perspective, a restrained and apt use of anecdote, optimism, and a clear and readable style, are the following: *A Century of American Diplomacy, 1776–1876* (1900); *American Diplomacy in the Orient* (1903); *Arbitration and the Hague Court* (1904); *The Practise of Diplomacy* (1906); and *War Stories for my Grandchildren* (1918).

[Foster wrote his own biography in *Diplomatic Memoirs* (2 vols., 1909). He describes accurately and with human interest the events in which he took part and the men and women whom he met. The volumes for the appropriate years of the foreign relations of the United States contain a record of his official work as minister to various countries and as secretary of state. See also Wm. R. Castle, Jr., in *Am. Secretaries of State and their Diplomacy*, vol. VIII (1928); José L. Suarez, *Mr. John W. Foster* (Buenos Aires, 1918); *N. Y. Times*, Nov. 16, *Evening Star* (Washington, D. C.), Nov. 15, 1917.]

C. E. H.

FOSTER, JUDITH ELLEN HORTON (Nov. 3, 1840–Aug. 11, 1910), lawyer, temperance reformer, was a daughter of Jotham and Judith (Delano) Horton. She was born at Lowell, Mass., where her father had a charge as a Methodist minister. Her mother died when Judith was five years old and her father died five years later. She then lived with a married sister in Boston and there received some education, particularly in music, which was continued at Wesleyan Seminary, Lima, N. Y. After an unfortunate marriage, which ended in a divorce, she went to Chicago and directed musical instruction in a mission school situated in the Bridgeport district. In 1869 she married a young lawyer, Elijah C. Foster, a native of Canada who was a graduate of the University of Michigan Law School. They made their home in Clinton, Iowa, where he entered the practise of his profession. In spite of family cares and responsibilities, she determined to study law with him, and within three years she was admitted to the bar (1872), becoming one of the first women lawyers engaged in regular practise in the United States.

Among the cases that came to her and her husband were several that involved the aggressions of local liquor dealers and their sympathizers. This litigation seems to have directed her attention especially to the temperance movement. She became interested in the famous "Women's Crusade" that began in Ohio and moved rapidly westward, aiming through moral suasion to put an end to local liquor-selling. Very early in the history of the Woman's Christian Temperance Union she became identified with that organization, falling under the spell of its able and eloquent leader, Frances E. Willard. It was then that Mrs. Foster's abilities as a public speaker were disclosed and utilized. She also came to be counted on as an efficient member of the national staff, serving for many years as the superintendent of the legislative department of the Union.

After she had been engaged for nearly a decade in aggressive reform work, and by her speechmaking had established a reputation in Iowa, a campaign began for the adoption of a prohibitory amendment to the state constitution. Women in Iowa at that time (1882) had no vote, but their influence was admittedly an important factor in securing the passage of the amendment by the legislature, though it was afterward declared void on technical grounds by the supreme court of the state. In this campaign Mrs. Foster, through her platform abilities as well as her organizing skill, rose to a place of leadership. Her appeal to the voters was non-partisan in spirit. She did not believe that the temperance cause could be advanced by using the usual party organizations. In this matter she soon found herself in disagreement with the views of Frances Willard and other officers of the W. C. T. U., who were bent on committing the national body to the indorsement of a third-party movement for prohibition. For four years she combated this effort in national conventions, and finally, in 1888, when further resistance seemed hopeless, she seceded from the Union with her colleagues from Iowa. She then organized the Woman's Republican Association of which she was president until her death. She proposed to continue her labors for temperance reform through a non-partisan W. C. T. U., but this never became a strong or effective organization.

Besides her indefatigable labors in behalf of Republican candidates in successive presidential elections, she inspected mobilization stations during the Spanish-American War, at the request of President McKinley; went to St. Petersburg in 1900 as the representative of the United States at the International Red Cross Conference; made a special report to President Roosevelt in 1906 on the condition of women and children in industry; endeavored to secure state laws for the protection of child workers; and served in 1908 as special agent of the Department of Justice to inspect the condition of federal criminals in federal and state prisons. She achieved notable success as a public speaker at a time when women were only beginning to play a part in politics; and in all her activities she was prompted and governed by a masterly and usually dependable quality of common sense.

[Frances E. Willard, *Woman and Temperance* (1883); E. C. Adams and W. D. Foster, *Heroines of Modern Progress* (1913), pp. 245–79; *The Reg. and Leader* (Des Moines, Ia.), Aug. 12, 1910; *Who's Who in America, 1910–11. The Stand. Encycl. of the Alcohol Problem,* vol. III (1926), ed. by E. H. Cherrington, contains an article on Mrs. Foster and on prohibition in Iowa.]

W. B. S—w.

FOSTER, LAFAYETTE SABINE (Nov. 22, 1806–Sept. 19, 1880), Connecticut editor, judge, United States senator, was the eldest son of Daniel and Welthea Ladd Foster. His father, a descendant of Miles Standish, had been a captain in the Revolutionary War. Lafayette was born in Franklin, near Norwich, Conn. The family had slender means, and when he reached college age he was obliged to support himself. He attended Brown University, graduating with high honors in 1828. The following year he taught in an academy in Queen Annes County, Md., and then began the study of law in the office of Calvin Goddard of Norwich, who had been an active Federalist politician, and member of the Hartford Convention of 1814. In 1831 he was admitted to the New London County bar. Two years later he opened a law office in Hampton, in Windham County, but in 1835 returned to Norwich, which became his home thereafter. In 1835 he became editor of the *Norwich Republican,* a Whig journal (Caulkins, *Norwich,* pp. 582–83). On Oct. 2, 1837, he married Joanna, daughter of James Lanman of Norwich, judge and United States senator. After her death in 1859, he married, Oct. 4, 1860, Martha Lyman of Northampton, Mass. Two daughters and a son were born of the first marriage, but all of them died in childhood. There were no children from the second marriage.

Foster became interested in politics early in his career. He first represented Norwich in the General Assembly in 1839. He was reëlected in 1840, from 1846 to 1849 served three years in succession, and later served two single terms, in 1854 and 1870. Four times he was speaker of the House of Representatives. In the state elections of 1850 and 1851 Foster was the unsuccessful Whig candidate for governor. During 1851 and 1852 he was mayor of Norwich. In 1854 he was chosen United States senator, subsequently holding that position twelve years, from 1855 to 1867. While in the Senate he spoke frequently but his chief distinction was his election as president *pro tempore* of the Senate. In 1866 he failed to receive the Republican caucus nomination for a third senatorial term, presumably because his opinions were too conservative. In 1870 he became a judge of the Connecticut superior court, and served until 1876. He supported Horace Greeley for president in 1872. Later he was nominated for national representative by a combination of Democrats and liberal Republicans, but was not elected. In 1878 he served on a commission studying a simplification of legal procedure in Connecticut, and during 1878–79 he was a member of a commission to settle a boundary dispute with the state of New York. In appearance, Foster was slight and unimpressive, his expression being grave and serious. He possessed, nevertheless, both humor and caustic wit, with which he frequently enlivened the otherwise dull sessions of legislative assemblies wherein he spent so much of his life.

[*Memorial Sketch of Lafayette S. Foster* (privately printed, Boston, 1881); F. C. Pierce, *Foster Geneal.*

(1889); F. M. Caulkins, *Hist. of Norwich, Conn.* (1866); D. Loomis and J. G. Calhoun, *Judic. and Civil Hist. of Conn.* (1895); "Brown Univ. Necrology for 1880–1881," printed in *Providence Daily Jour.*, June 15, 1881; *Hartford Daily Courant*, Sept. 21, 1880.]
J. M. M.

FOSTER, MURPHY JAMES (Jan. 12, 1849–June 12, 1921), lawyer, governor of Louisiana, son of Thomas Jefferson and Martha (Murphy) Foster, was born on a plantation near Franklin, La. On his father's side he was of English, French, and Spanish descent; and on his mother's side, of English and Irish. His paternal grandparents, Levi and Leida (Demaret) Foster, were residents of Louisiana before its purchase in 1803. He was educated at a private school in Franklin, at Washington and Lee University, and at Cumberland University, Lebanon, Tenn., from which he graduated in 1870 (*Who's Who in America*, 1920–21). He was also graduated from the law department of Tulane University in 1871 and engaged immediately in the practise of law in New Orleans. He entered politics early and was elected in 1876 from St. Mary Parish to the state legislature, the so-called McEnery legislature, but was prevented from taking his seat by the Kellogg government. In 1879, following the termination of the Carpet-Bag rule in Louisiana, he was elected to the state Senate from the tenth district and served continuously for three terms of four years each (1880–92). He was elected president of the Senate in 1888 and served in that capacity for two years.

In 1890 the question of renewing the charter of the Louisiana State Lottery Company came up for consideration in the state legislature. This company had been granted a charter by the Carpet-Bag legislature in 1868 for a period of twenty-five years, in consideration of an annual license fee of $40,000. It now offered to pay $1,250,000 a year for twenty-five years if its charter were extended. This proposal of the company thereupon became the dominant issue in the state. Foster was bitterly opposed to the renewing of the charter and led the fight against it in the Senate. He became the candidate of the anti-lottery faction of the Democratic party for governor in the primary election of 1892 and was elected by a majority of over 32,000 in a total vote of over 126,000. The proposal to renew the charter of the Lottery Company was overwhelmingly defeated and the company discontinued business in Louisiana in December 1892 and withdrew to Honduras.

Foster was reëlected governor in 1896 in a campaign marked by great political bitterness between the Democrats and the "Lily White" Republicans—the sugar planters of Louisiana, hitherto Democrats, who felt they were being deprived by the Wilson-Gorman Act of 1893 of the protection they needed against Cuban sugar. This Lily White Republican party was so called because they aimed to keep it a strictly white man's organization. They nominated John Newton Pharr, a former Confederate soldier, for governor and polled such a heavy vote for him that they contested the election in the state legislature. The decision of the legislature was however in Foster's favor, and he served until 1900. As an outcome of this campaign and very largely through the influence of Foster, a new state constitution was adopted in 1898, which made it impossible for any political party to use ignorant colored voters in future elections, by denying the right to vote to those who could not read and write or who did not own property whose assessed valuation was at least $300, and by adopting the famous "grandfather clause."

In 1900 at the expiration of his second term, Foster was elected to the United States Senate by the Louisiana state legislature and was reëlected by the people of the state in 1906, serving for twelve years. On being defeated for reëlection in 1912, he resumed the practise of law at Franklin but was shortly appointed United States collector of customs at New Orleans. He was holding that position at the time of his death. He was married to Rosa Rosetta Ker on Apr. 20, 1881. Nine children survived his death.

[The best account of Foster's part in the Anti-Louisiana Lottery Movement is in B. C. Alwes, *Louisiana Lottery Company*, which was submitted to the history department of the Louisiana State University in 1929 as a thesis for the master's degree. A brief account of Foster's part in the formation and adoption of the constitution of Louisiana in 1898 is to be found in Alcée Fortier, *Louisiana* (1909). See also J. W. Leonard, *Men of America* (1908); *Daily Item*, Feb. 26, 1898; *Times-Democrat* and *Daily Picayune*, Jan.–Mar. 1898; and obituary notices in the New Orleans newspapers of June 13, 1921.]
E. M. V.

FOSTER, RANDOLPH SINKS (Feb. 22, 1820–May 1, 1903), clergyman, bishop of the Methodist Episcopal Church, was the son of Israel and Polly (Kain) Foster. His grandfather, Thomas Foster, had emigrated from England, settled in Berkeley County, Va., and died of wounds inflicted by Indians while he was on an expedition in Kentucky. Randolph was born in the county jail, Williamsburg, Clermont County, Ohio, of which his father was the jailer. Later the family moved to Kentucky where the boy grew up. At an early age he entered Augusta College, Kentucky. While there it was his misfortune to become known as a remarkable "boy preacher," and unwise counselors persuaded him to leave college and enter the ministry when he was but seventeen years old. He regretted this action subsequently, but such were his intellectual gifts and his diligence in study that he not only attained wide eminence as a preacher, but became one of the best-known writers on religious and theological subjects among the Methodists of his day. In 1837 he was admitted to the Ohio Conference on probation, was received into full connection and ordained deacon in 1839 and was made elder in 1841. In July 1840 he married Sarah A. Miley of Cincinnati.

The first thirteen years of his ministry were spent in western Virginia and Ohio. Toward the close of this period he came into prominence as a writer, publishing in 1849 his *Objections to Calvinism As It Is, in a Series of Letters Addressed to Rev. N. L. Rice, D.D.*, a Presbyterian who had assailed the doctrines of Methodism. It is a work marked by intellectual vigor and clear, concise statement, and furnished busy preachers with an arsenal of facts and argument wherewith to defend themselves against the frequent attacks of the Calvinists. In 1850 he was transferred to the New York Conference and stationed at the Mulberry Street Church, New York. All his subsequent pastorates were in or about that city. The following year appeared one of his most widely read books, an extensive, practical discussion of holiness and how it may be attained, entitled *Nature and Blessedness of Christian Purity*. A revised edition was published in 1869 under the title, *Christian Purity or the Heritage of Faith*. In June 1856 he was elected president of Northwestern University, though he did not assume duties until the fall of 1857. The institution was in its infancy and its resources were insufficient. Foster had no taste for drudgery or business, even disliking to manage his own affairs, and in 1860 he returned to the active ministry. In 1868 he became professor of systematic theology at Drew Theological Seminary, and from 1870 to 1872, when he was elected bishop, he filled the office of president. His duties as bishop carried him to all the Conferences in this country and to Mexico, South America, Europe, and the East. In 1902 he went on the non-effective list, and the closing years of his life, spent near Boston, were devoted to work upon his *Studies in Theology*, an attempt at a thorough discussion of fundamental problems. Six volumes were published (1889–99).

He was tall and impressive in appearance, and stalwart in mind and character. His outlook was broad and his interest was in things cosmic. As a bishop he was sometimes criticized for arbitrariness and harshness. He loathed ecclesiastical politics and was honest and plain-spoken, but kind at heart. His preaching had in it both intellectual power and deep emotionality. Much of what he wrote belongs to the past generation, but discloses a mind of the best type. He was indifferent to authority, and "he would have as soon appealed to the Fathers for the truth of the multiplication table as for the truth of anything depending upon reason" (Borden P. Bowne, *Zion's Herald,* May 6, 1903). Among his publications not already mentioned are: *Beyond the Grave* (1879), extensively criticized because of some of its conclusions; *Centenary Thoughts for Pew and Pulpit* (1884); *Philosophy of Christian Experience* (1890); *Union of Episcopal Methodisms* (1892).

[*Minutes of the Ann. Conferences of the M. E. Ch.* (1837); *Thirey & Mitchell's Encyc. Directory and Hist. of Clermont County, Ohio* (1902); M. S. Terry, "Bishop Randolph S. Foster," in *Meth. Rev.*, Jan.–Feb. 1904; *Christian Advocate,* May 7, 1903; Arthur H. Wilde, *Northwestern Univ.: A Hist.* (1905); Estelle F. Ward, *The Story of Northwestern Univ.* (1924); *Boston Transcript* and *Boston Herald,* May 2, 1903.] H. E. S.

FOSTER, ROBERT SANFORD (Jan. 27, 1834–Mar. 3, 1903), Union soldier, was born at Vernon, Jennings County, Ind., the son of Riley S. and Sarah (Wallace) Foster. He attended the local schools, and at the age of sixteen went to Indianapolis, learned the tinner's trade, and later was employed in his uncle's store. He was mustered into the volunteer service, Apr. 22, 1861, as captain of the 11th Indiana Infantry, a three-months "Zouave" regiment of which Lew Wallace was colonel and which met the enemy at Romney in June. Appointed major of the 13th Indiana Infantry, June 19, 1861, he served in Rosecrans's brigade at the battle of Rich Mountain and in the West Virginia campaign of the summer and fall of 1861. He was promoted lieutenant-colonel of his regiment on Oct. 28, 1861, and colonel, Apr. 30, 1862, and commanded it in the Shenandoah Valley campaign against Jackson, in the spring of 1862. Ordered to the Peninsula to join the Army of the Potomac, the regiment arrived at Harrison's Landing July 3, in time to help cover the retreat of the army. Later, it was transferred to Suffolk, Va., whose fortified lines covering Norfolk and Portsmouth against attack from the south withstood a siege by Longstreet in the spring of 1863. Foster was appointed brigadier-general of volunteers, June 12, 1863, and commanded a brigade stationed on Folly Island, Charleston Harbor, during Gillmore's siege operations against the city, in the fall and winter. In the spring of 1864 the brigade was transferred to Florida, but returned to southeastern Virginia before summer. Foster was then on duty for some weeks as chief of staff of the X (Gillmore's) Corps, in Butler's Army of the James. In June, in command of an infantry brigade to which was attached a small force of cavalry, artillery, and engineers, he crossed the James and seized a base at Deep Bottom, near Richmond; and through the summer took part in many demonstrations, under Hancock and Sheridan, against that city. In October he was put in command of a division of the X Corps for the operations around Petersburg; and after the X Corps was merged (December 1864) in the newly organized XXIV Corps, he served at first as its chief of staff and later in command of its 1st Division in the siege of Petersburg. It was Foster's division which assaulted and carried Fort Gregg. It took part in the final pursuit of Lee's army, and was in action at Appomattox up to the last. Foster was a member of the military commission which tried the persons involved in Lincoln's assassination. He resigned from the volunteer army, Sept. 25, 1865, and declining an appointment, offered him in 1866, as lieutenant-colonel in the regular army, he spent the rest of his life in Indianapolis. He was city treasurer, 1867–72, United States marshal for the district of Indiana, 1881–85, and for many years president of the city board of trade. He helped in the establishment of the Grand Army of the Republic. His wife was Margaret R. Foust, whom he married in May 1861; she died thirty years later, on May 7, 1891.

[Chas. W. Smith, "Life and Military Services of . . . Robert S. Foster," in *Ind. Hist. Soc. Pubs.*, vol. V, no. 6 (1915); *Who's Who in America*, 1901–02; *Official Records (Army)*, 1 ser., vols. XII (pt. 1), XVIII, XXVII (pt. 2), XXXVI (pt. 2), XL (pts. 1, 2, 3), XLII (pts. 1, 2, 3), XLVI (pts. 1, 2, 3); obituaries in *Indianapolis Jour.*, and *Indianapolis Sentinel*, Mar. 4, 1903; unpublished documents in the War Dept.] T. M. S.

FOSTER, ROGER SHERMAN BALDWIN (Apr. 21, 1857–Feb. 22, 1924), lawyer, author, was a descendant of Reginald Foster of Little Badow, Essex, England, who emigrated in 1638 and obtained a grant of land in Ipswich, Mass., in 1641. His father, Dwight Foster, associate justice of the supreme judicial court of Massachusetts, married Henrietta Perkins, daughter of Gov. Roger S. Baldwin of New Haven, Conn., Aug. 20, 1850. Roger was born at Worcester, Mass., where his parents resided. Having obtained his early education at the Boston Latin School, he went to Europe, studied at the University of Marburg, 1873–74, and on his return completed his education at Yale University (B.A. 1878). He then entered the Columbia Law School, graduated LL.B. there in 1880, and on his admission to the New York bar, in the same year commenced practise in New York City. From the outset he ear-marked the branches of the law in which he subsequently became a specialist, by publishing a short work on *The Taxation of the Elevated Railways in the City of New York* (1883), and an address in which he discussed *The Constitutional Aspects of the Conflict between the President and the Senate* (1886). Then followed: *The Federal Judiciary Acts of 1875 and 1887* (1887); *A treatise on pleading and practice in Equity in the Courts of the United States* (1890); and *A treatise on Federal practice in civil causes with special reference to patent cases and the foreclosure of railway mortgages* (2 vols., 1892). The material in the two last treatises was subsequently expanded and incorporated in *A treatise on Federal Practice* (4 vols., 4th ed., 1909).

In 1892, serious rioting by strikers occurred in Pennsylvania, resulting in the indictment of the advisory committee of the citizens of Homestead for treason against the state. This action induced Foster, when the question was still *sub judice,* to write an article, "Treason Trials in the United States," which appeared in the *Albany Law Journal,* Oct. 29, 1892, wherein, though expressing no opinion on the pending case, he demonstrated that there was no precedent for a conviction of treason, except where there had been an insurrection of a general nature involving resistance to a general public law or an intention of subverting the government. Such was the cogency of this article that the Homestead proceedings were abandoned. He was appointed by Gov. Flower counsel to the Tenement House Commissioners in 1894 and in that capacity established the constitutionality of the act which declared that tenement houses in New York City previously erected should be furnished by the owners with water when so directed by the board of health, the court holding that it was a proper exercise of the police power of the state (*Health Department of the City of New York* vs. *Rector . . . of Trinity Church,* 145 *N. Y.*, 32). He subsequently drafted the Tenement House Acts of 1895, the first comprehensive legislation on the subject in New York State.

In 1895 he published *Commentaries on the Constitution of the United States,* historical and judicial, a work which displayed great erudition and placed him in the front rank of constitutional lawyers. In the same year, in collaboration with E. V. Abbot, he produced *A treatise on the Federal income tax under the Act of 1894.* In 1896 he was instrumental in procuring the appointment of a receiver for the Bay State Gas Company, this provoking the animosity of Thomas W. Lawson, the Boston financier, who bitterly attacked him in his book, *Frenzied Finance* (1905), though all the charges therein were publicly retracted later. He was retained in January 1900 with Charles J. Faulkner, as counsel for Senator William A. Clark of Montana, in the proceedings before the committee on privileges and elections of the United States Senate, consequent upon the allegation that Clark's election as senator had been procured by gross corruption and bribery. His speech on behalf of Clark was considered a forensic masterpiece (*Senate Report, No. 1052,* 56 Cong., 1 Sess.).

He was a frequent traveler, principally in countries outside the beaten track, and during 1912 spent considerable time in Asia Minor, searching for the sites of the seven churches mentioned in the Book of Revelations. He also subsequently visited Armenia, making an unofficial report on conditions in that country at the request of President Wilson. He lectured from time to time at Columbia, Yale, and other universities, on various phases of American history, and on classical subjects. In addition to the works mentioned he wrote in 1914 *A treatise on the Federal income tax under the Act of 1913,* and in 1922 a small book, *Liberty of contract and labor law,* for the American School of Correspondence. He was also the author of pamphlets on varied topics and contributed to the press articles descriptive of his travels. He married, on Feb. 22, 1921, Laura Pugh Moxley.

[F. C. Pierce, *Foster Geneal.* (1899); *Who's Who in America,* 1924–25; *N. Y. Law Jour.,* Feb. 25, 1924; J. M. Lamberton, ed., *Quarter-Centenary Record of the Class of 1878, Yale Univ.* (1905); *Yale Univ. Obit. Rec. of Grads.* (1924); private information.] H. W. H. K.

FOSTER, STEPHEN COLLINS (July 4, 1826–Jan. 13, 1864), composer, was the son of William Barclay Foster, a merchant of Pittsburgh, Pa., and Eliza Clayland Tomlinson. He was descended on both sides from Scotch-Irish emigrants, the earliest of whom, Alexander Foster, had settled in Lancaster County, Pa., around 1728. His grandfather, James Foster, fought in the Revolution, and his father was quartermaster and commissary of the United States army during the War of 1812. After training in the Allegheny and Athens academies, Foster entered Jefferson College in July 1841; however, his predilection for music and "something perfectly original about him" (letter of Eliza C. Foster in Milligan, *post,* p. 13) rendered formal education distasteful to him, and he left school in August, continuing his education with tutors in Pittsburgh. Although he had already written several pieces, including "The Tioga Waltz" for four flutes, which was performed at the Athens Academy Commencement, and "Open Thy Lattice, Love," published in 1844, a musical career was not considered suitable for him, and in 1846 he was sent to Cincinnati to keep books for his brother, Dunning Foster. Here it became evident through the general popularity of some of his negro ballads, "Louisiana Belle," "O Susanna," "Uncle Ned," and "Away Down South," which led to their publication in *Songs of the Sable Harmonists* (1848), that Foster's talent might prove profitable, and he returned to his parents' home in Allegheny City to devote himself exclusively to music.

At this time the most successful of the music-hall entertainments were the negro minstrels, and in writing songs for them Foster found his happiest medium. In 1849 "Nelly was a Lady," published that year in *Foster's Ethiopian Melodies,* was popularized by the then famous Christy's Minstrels, and in 1850 several of his ballads were taken into the repertories of the Christy, Campbell, and New Orleans Serenaders companies. In 1851 Foster sold to E. P. Christy [*q.v.*] the privilege of singing his songs from manuscript before their formal appearance, reserving to himself all publication rights. This proved to be a successful arrangement for both Christy and Foster. Each contributed to the popularity of the other. In the same year "The Old Folks at Home" was published, and in 1852 "Massa's in the Cold Ground," both of which were among Foster's best songs. The following year saw the publication of "My Old Kentucky Home" and "Old Dog Tray." Of the latter 125,000 copies are said to have been sold within eighteen months of publication (Milligan, *post,* p. 68). With these two songs he deserted the dialect of his earlier works, to return to it only in two minor ballads.

With the exception of a trip to New Orleans in 1852 (probably his only excursion into the South), and a short residence in New York in 1853, Foster remained in Pittsburgh until 1860. For the most part he wrote little and ineffectively, and only in 1860 with the publication of "Old Black Joe" asserted himself with his former power. In July of that year he went to New York where he spent the remainder of his life. He wrote ceaselessly, turning out forty-eight songs in one year, but his music was almost without exception reiterative and commonplace. He spent his last years in poverty and obscurity, drinking heavily, and selling his songs to music stores for small cash sums. He died, after a short illness, in the charity ward of the Bellevue Hospital. He had married Jane Denny McDowell of Pittsburgh in July 1850, from whom he was separated a few years before his death. Foster's music was primitive, limited, and uneven, but his best songs gave permanent expression to one phase of American life—the nostalgic melancholy of the negro—and remain a valuable contribution to the folk-literature of American music.

[The best biography of Foster is H. V. Milligan, *Stephen Collins Foster* (1920). A more reticent treatment is the book by his brother, Morrison Foster, *Biog., Songs, and Musical Compositions of Stephen C. Foster* (1896). Other material appears in W. R. Whittlesey and O. G. Sonneck, *Cat. of the First Editions of Stephen C. Foster* (1915); *Musical America,* July 2, 1921, Apr. 25, 1929; *Musical Courier,* Jan. 11, 1923, Mar. 22, 29, 1930; *Musical Observer,* July 1, 1926; *Atlantic Monthly,* Nov. 1867; *N. Y. Times,* June 13, 1926.] C.W.P.

FOSTER, STEPHEN SYMONDS (Nov. 17, 1809–Sept. 8, 1881), Abolitionist, reformer, son of Asa and Sarah (Morrill) Foster, was born at Canterbury, N. H. His father's family had long been prominent in this vicinity and several of its members had been active in New Hampshire politics. He was the ninth child in a family of thirteen and at an early age became accustomed to hard work on the farm. He then learned the trade of carpenter and builder, but becoming interested in the religious life, decided to prepare himself for the ministry. In his early twenties he entered Dartmouth College and graduated in 1838. While an undergraduate he was attracted by the growing anti-slavery movement, which at that time had many supporters at Dartmouth. Such a crusade had a strong appeal for a man of his humanitarian instincts. He had formulated a creed of his own, based largely on the Sermon on the Mount, and regardless of resultant complications in every-day life, endeavored to govern himself thereby. While at Dartmouth he served a jail sentence rather than perform militia duty, and incidentally, started an agitation which eventually produced drastic reforms in the wretched prison system of rural New England.

On leaving college he entered Union Theological Seminary but his stay at the institution was brief. He had already been assailed by doubts as to whether the churches were genuine upholders of Christian principles, and when the seminary refused accommodations for a meeting protesting against the government's course in the Northeastern Boundary embroglio, he dropped his studies, and soon after severed connections with the church and organized religion in general. For some years he made a precarious living as an anti-slavery lecturer, and one of his associates, Parker Pillsbury [*q.v.*], has left a vivid record of the hardships, discouragements, and persecutions Foster encountered while campaigning in New Hampshire. He was associated with the extremist group, was a close friend of Garrison, and probably second only to the latter in influence and activity in the early years of the agitation. Like Garrison he denounced the Constitution and was ready to dissolve the Union. He accompanied his colleague on several lecture tours and became equally well known as an agitator, not only in New England, but throughout the Northern states. Eventually he settled on a farm near Worcester but continued to appear as a public speaker and lecturer.

Foster grasped one essential principle, namely, that "slavery is an American and not a Southern institution." Business, politics, and religion were, he believed, committed to the maintenance of the *status quo.* He detested the attitude of religious bodies especially and, about 1841, adopted the expedient of visiting various churches, interrupting services with a polite request for a hearing on the slavery issue. He was repeatedly ejected, several times prosecuted, and more than once roughly handled by offended worshipers, but he attracted attention to the cause which could hardly have been gained by more decorous methods. His career as lecturer was exciting, at least in the earlier years. Fearless, resolute, and gifted with an unusual command of denunciatory language, he was repeatedly jeered and pelted by unfriendly audiences. He wrote occasional newspaper articles but only one production of note. This pamphlet, *The Brotherhood of Thieves; or a True Picture of the American Church and Clergy* (1843), one of the most vitriolic works of the anti-slavery era, passed through more than twenty editions and was widely circulated. He remained with the extremists throughout the long contest over slavery but became interested in sundry other reform movements. Besides advocating woman suffrage, he was a temperance worker, an advocate of world peace, and an energetic supporter of the rights of labor. His refusal to pay taxes because women were denied the suffrage more than once forced his friends to bid in his farm at sheriff's sale. On Dec. 31, 1845, he married a kindred spirit, Abigail Kelley [*q.v.*], Abolitionist lecturer and pioneer in the woman's rights movement.

Foster was a successful farmer and his property near Worcester was one of the best managed and most productive in the district. His contemporaries describe him as of rugged features, rather ungainly in general appearance, his hands hard and gnarled with labor, but he possessed a wonderful voice. Despite the vehemence of his platform manners he is said to have been gentle and kindly in his personal relations. He seems to have suffered from an overdeveloped logical sense and a complete lack of humor. Probably Wendell Phillips made as fair an estimate of Foster's work as might be given when at his funeral he declared: "It needed something to shake New

England and stun it into listening. He was the man, and offered himself for the martyrdom."

[J. K. Lord, *Hist. of Dartmouth Coll.* (1909); J. O. Lyford, *Hist. of the Town of Canterbury, N. H.* (1912); Lillie B. C. Wyman, "Reminiscences of Two Abolitionists," *New Eng. Mag.*, Jan. 1903; Parker Pillsbury, *Acts of the Anti-Slavery Apostles* (1883); *Wm. Lloyd Garrison, 1805–79: The Story of his Life Told by his Children* (1885–89); *Hist. of Woman Suffrage*, Elizabeth Cady Stanton, Susan B. Anthony, Matilda J. Gage, eds. (3 vols., 1881–87); Parker Pillsbury, Memoir in the *Granite Monthly*, Aug. 1882; the *Nation*, Sept. 15, 1881; *Boston Daily Advertiser*, Sept. 9, 10, 1881; *Worcester Daily Spy*, Sept. 9, 1881.] W.A.R.

FOSTER, THEODORE (Apr. 29, 1752–Jan. 13, 1828), United States senator, was born in Brookfield, Mass. His father was Jedediah Foster, judge of the superior court of Massachusetts, and his mother Dorothy Dwight of Dedham, a descendant of John Dwight and also of William Pyncheon, an incorporator of the Massachusetts Bay Company, who came to America in the fleet with John Winthrop. Theodore Foster graduated from Rhode Island College, now Brown University, in the class of 1770, the second class which the college sent out. On Oct. 27, 1771, he married Lydia Fenner, daughter of Arthur Fenner, Jr., afterwards governor of Rhode Island, and became the father of three children. He made law his profession and from 1776 to 1782 served as deputy from Providence in the General Assembly. In the year 1781 the town of Foster was created in his honor, and this town he represented in the lower house of the General Assembly from 1812 to 1816. During the years 1776–85, he became the close associate of Gov. Stephen Hopkins, then in retirement. The two men possessed a strong taste for history and collaborated in the collection of historical material. In 1785 Foster was made judge of the Rhode Island court of Admiralty. In 1786 he received the degree of M.A. from Dartmouth College, and in 1794 became a trustee of Brown University, a position which he held until 1822. In 1786 he opposed the paper money delusion then prevailing in Rhode Island. He favored the adoption of the Constitution of the United States, and on the admission of Rhode Island to the Union in May 1790, he and Joseph Stanton, Jr., were elected senators, a loan of one hundred and fifty dollars being made to the two senators to enable them to "take their seats promptly." On Aug. 12, 1790, he brought with him from Philadelphia the President of the United States for a first official visit to Rhode Island. He was an ardent Federalist, supporting the financial policy of Hamilton and Jay's treaty with Great Britain. While in Philadelphia he patronized the bookstores, attended public lectures, and, occasionally, theatres. Part of his time he spent in residence with a French family, for the purpose of perfecting himself in the French language, and in December 1800, he was appointed on a committee to make a translation of so much of the journal of the "late envoys of the United States to the French Republic," as was communicated in French. He supported President John Adams, and in 1800 Aaron Burr against Thomas Jefferson for president. In 1800 his brother, Dwight Foster, became his colleague in the Senate and for nearly three years they sat together. Both retired from office in March 1803. On his retirement he withdrew to the town of Foster and there, in company with his intimate friend, Dr. Solomon Drowne, established himself at Mt. Hygeia where he became, it is said, the most assiduous antiquarian within the limits of the state. He long contemplated writing a history of Rhode Island and grouped his material, but never completed the undertaking. His first wife, Lydia, having died in 1801, on June 18, 1803, he married Esther Millard, daughter of Rev. Noah Millard of Foster, by whom he had five children. His death occurred in Providence, R. I., on Jan. 13, 1828.

[W. E. Foster, *R. I. Hist. Soc. Colls.*, vol. VII (1885); E. Field, *State of R. I. and Providence Plantations at the End of the Century*, vol. I (1902); S. G. Arnold, *Hist. of the State of R. I. and Providence Plantations*, II (1860); *Biog. Cyc. of Representative Men of R. I.* (1881), p. 138; R. M. Bayles, *Hist. of Providence County, R. I.*, II (1891), 629; *Hist. Cat. of Brown Univ., 1764–1904* (1905); *New-Eng. Hist. and Geneal. Reg.*, Oct. 1847; F. C. Pierce, *Foster Geneal.* (1899); *R. I. Am. and Providence Gazette*, Jan. 15, 1828; *Mass. Spy* and *Worcester County Advertiser*, Jan. 23, 1828. The Foster Papers are in the custody of the R. I. Hist. Soc.] I.B.R.

FOULK, GEORGE CLAYTON (Oct. 30, 1856–Aug. 6, 1893), naval officer, diplomat, the third son of Clayton and Caroline (Rudisill) Foulk, was born in Marietta, Pa. His paternal ancestors were largely of English stock, with a mixture of Swedish, and had lived in Delaware since early in the eighteenth century. His mother's family were of German descent. In 1872 Foulk was appointed to the United States Naval Academy, and was graduated in 1876, third in his class. He immediately went on Asiatic station, where he served during two cruises, and attracted the favorable attention of his commanding officers by reason of his studious habits and of his knowledge and execution of his duties. During the summer of 1882 he and two other young naval officers crossed little-known Siberia into Russia, and made a valuable report on that country to their government. On his return to America Foulk received his ensign's commission as of Nov. 25, 1877, and took a post in the naval library.

In May 1883 the first American minister to

Korea, Gen. Lucius H. Foote [*q.v.*], took up his residence in that country. In September the first Korean Mission to a Western nation arrived in Washington. When they returned to Korea on board the *Trenton,* Foulk was detailed as naval attaché to the American legation in Korea, and accompanied the Mission on the voyage. Gen. Foote had created an excellent impression at the Korean Court; the United States was in high favor as being a disinterested, friendly power; and Foulk was well received. The rivalries of Japan, China, Russia, and Great Britain made the American position very difficult. In January 1885 when Gen. Foote left Korea, Foulk was placed in charge of the legation. For the next two years he was faced with problems of extreme delicacy by reason of the conflicting aims of the Powers and of the inability of Korea to protect her own interests. Alone during the two years, unpaid for months at a time, with failing health, with limited advice or attention from Washington, in the midst of intrigue and open hostility, he conducted his office with skill and marked ability, and with credit to his country. At his own request he was relieved in June 1886 by William H. Parker, but was soon recalled. He was finally withdrawn as attaché in June 1887, despite the protests of the Korean King. The action was taken on the demand of the Chinese government and of the Korean foreign office, which was under the latter's influence, because of Foulk's close relations with the King and his refusal to acquiesce in Chinese domination. Previously he had declined the King's invitation to become personal adviser to His Majesty. He was recalled to Washington where he was given commendation and his commission of lieutenant, junior grade (as of May 1, 1884), but his valid claims for back pay were disallowed, and now that his services were no longer a necessity he was discarded by the Department of State.

He had married a Japanese, Kane Murase, whom he had known for many years, during the summer of 1887, and he returned to Japan, where he resigned his commission. For two years he was employed by the American Trading Company of Yokohama, but a business career did not appeal to him, and in 1890 he resigned to take a position as professor of mathematics at Doshisha College, Kyoto. Here he remained until his death, a valued member of the faculty, despite his failing health induced by the severe strain of his work in Korea. He died at the age of thirty-seven years, and was buried in Kyoto.

[Tyler Dennett, "Early Am. Policy in Korea, 1883–87," *Pol. Sci. Quart.*, Mar. 1923; *Army and Nav. Jour.*, Sept. 16, 1893; E. W. Callahan, *List of Officers of the Navy of the U. S. and of the Marine Corps* (1901); U. S. Navy Registers, 1877–89. A collection of Foulk's letters and letter-press copies of his dispatches is deposited in the N. Y. Pub. Lib., and other collections are held privately. The originals of his dispatches are in the archives of the state and navy departments in Washington and of the former American legation in Seul, Korea.] H. J. N.

FOWLE, DANIEL (October 1715–June 8, 1787), printer, author, was born in Charlestown, Mass., where the records of the First Church state that Daniel, son of John and Mary (Barrell) Fowle, was baptized on Oct. 16, 1715. In consequence of the death of both parents in 1734 he was placed under the guardianship of S. Trumbull. At about the same time he was apprenticed to Samuel Kneeland, a printer in Boston, and in 1740 became associated with Gamaliel Rogers in the firm of Rogers & Fowle, a partnership which continued for ten years. The two had a flourishing business, printed much of importance, and because of the quality of their ink, which was of their own manufacture, and the best in the country at the time, they produced imprints comparing favorably with those of to-day. On Mar. 2, 1743, they began the publication of the *Boston Weekly Magazine,* discontinued after the fourth number, but followed in September by the *American Magazine and Historical Chronicle,* a monthly issue which was continued for more than three years. It was the first magazine in the colonies to survive for so long a time. In 1748 they established a weekly newspaper, *The Independent Advertiser,* which attracted notable correspondence and had a good circulation but was discontinued in 1750 when the partnership was dissolved. They are said to have published also a duodecimo edition of the New Testament about 1745, but since no copies have been found to substantiate the contention, the matter remains in doubt. In addition to these undertakings they carried on a regular printing business of books and pamphlets which was exceeded in Boston only by that of their competitors, Kneeland & Green.

After the dissolution of the partnership Fowle carried on the business alone for four years; then the tenor of his life changed. In 1754 the Excise Act passed the General Court causing wide-spread and bitter discussion. A number of anonymous pamphlets was printed among which was an allegory entitled *The Monster of Monsters.* Fowle was brought before the General Court on suspicion of having been the printer of the obnoxious article, and was confined for three days in the common jail. This act of injustice aroused his resentment to such a degree that he wrote and printed in 1755 a pamphlet entitled *A Total Eclipse of Liberty* and during the following year *An Appendix to the Late Total Eclipse of Lib-*

erty. While he was still feeling the unfairness of his treatment he was approached by citizens of Portsmouth, N. H., with a view to his removal there. Promised the position of government printer of that province, he decided to leave Massachusetts Bay, where liberty of the press was threatened, and removed to Portsmouth. He was the first printer in New Hampshire, and on Oct. 7, 1756, issued the first number of the *New Hampshire Gazette.* Though his printing business was not large, the apprentices from his office started other printing centers in the state.

Fowle's labors continued until his death on June 8, 1787. The records of King's Chapel, Boston, show his marriage to Lydia Hall on Apr. 11, 1751. Since his wife's death preceded his own by several years and their union was without issue, in 1784 he transferred his newspaper to John Melcher and George Jerry Osborne, two of his apprentices. When the latter withdrew, he adopted John Melcher as his son, leaving to him all his property and business interests.

[Isaiah Thomas, *The Hist. of Printing in America . . .* (2nd ed., 1874), published by the Am. Antiquarian Soc.; J. T. Buckingham, *Specimens of Newspaper Literature* (2 vols., 1850); T. B. Wyman, *The Geneal. and Estates of Charlestown* (1879), vol. I; Charles Evans, *Am. Bibliog.*, vols. II and III (1904–05); R. H. Peddie, *Printing: A Short Hist. of the Art* (1927).] C. L. N.

FOWLE, WILLIAM BENTLEY (Oct. 17, 1795–Feb. 6, 1865), educator, was the third son of Henry and Elizabeth (Bentley) Fowle, and was born in Boston, Mass. His father was a man of considerable literary attainment, and a Freemason of high rank whom financial troubles had forced to take up the trade of pump and block maker. His mother was the sister of the eminent divine and scholar, William Bentley [*q.v.*], and a woman of rare intellect. William attended his first school at the age of three and there learned the *Assembly's Shorter Catechism* by heart. At six he had memorized Caleb Bingham's *Young Ladies' Accidence,* and at ten he had received the Franklin Medal for proficiency in grammar; but so unconscious was he of the meaning of the words he learned that when he entered the Boston Latin School at thirteen he was unable to give the perfect participle of the verb *to love.* In later life he said, "It is not to be wondered at, therefore, that I hated grammar; had no faith in the utility of teaching it as it was then taught, and determined to reform the method if I ever had a good opportunity."

He was prepared for college at fifteen, but due to his father's financial difficulties he was apprenticed to Caleb Bingham [*q.v.*], whose bookstore at 44 Cornhill, Boston, was the favorite resort of school-teachers. There he found ample opportunity to indulge his taste for reading and to discuss the latest educational theories. In 1821 he was called upon to organize and teach a school of 200 children who were too old for the primary and too ignorant for the grammar schools. By employing the novel monitorial system by which the more advanced pupils aided in teaching the more backward, he gained such success that in a year's time his school won high commendation from Mayor Quincy. In this school Fowle introduced blackboards, map drawing, written spelling lessons, and by an act even more radical, he abolished corporal punishment. In 1823, upon the establishment of the Female Monitorial School, Fowle gave up his book business to take charge of it. This was probably the first school in the country to have scientific apparatus adequate to illustrate the subjects taught, and most of it was constructed under Fowle's supervision. In this school he introduced for the first time such subjects as vocal and instrumental music, calisthenics, and needlework. His leisure he devoted to the compilation of school textbooks, of which he published more than fifty during his life, and to the delivery of scientific lectures to his pupils and their friends. With remarkable versatility he described the mysteries of the atmosphere, the solar system, chemistry, mineralogy, and geology, delivering from fifteen to twenty lectures every season for seventeen years.

In 1842 Fowle undertook the publication of the *Common School Journal,* which Horace Mann had started four years earlier, and from 1848 to 1852 he edited as well as published it. Throughout his friendship with Mann, Fowle rendered invaluable aid in the many sharp collisions which occurred between his superior and the more conservative teachers of the day. He was one of Mann's most able assistants in the Teachers' Institute, conducting over a hundred meetings of the organization in Massachusetts and neighboring states. His last public activity was to open a monitorial school on Washington St., Boston, which he conducted until 1860. He died at his home at Medfield, Mass.

Although Fowle was by nature kindly and tolerant, his opponents in matters of school administration found him a merciless antagonist. He was also consistently bitter in his denunciation of slavery. He was a member of the state legislature in 1843, and a member of several learned organizations. In addition to his fifty published books his written lectures, mostly on scientific subjects, numbered more than sixty, and his newspaper essays more than five hundred. His first wife, whom he married on Sept. 28, 1818, was Antoinette Moulton, daughter of Ebenezer Moulton. On Nov. 26, 1860, he married Mary Baxter Adams, daughter of Hon. Daniel Adams, of Watertown.

[*Am. Jour. of Educ.*, June 1861; *New-Eng. Hist. and Geneal. Reg.*, Apr. 1869; *Boston Daily Advertiser*, Feb. 9, 1865; *Worcester Daily Spy*, Feb. 16, 1865.] S. H. P.

FOWLER, CHARLES HENRY (Aug. 11, 1837–Mar. 20, 1908), bishop of the Methodist Episcopal Church, was born in Burford (now Clarendon), Ontario, Canada. His father, Horatio Fowler, was of Connecticut ancestry. His mother, Harriet Ryan, was the daughter of the Rev. Henry Ryan, a herculean Irishman who was one of the founders of Methodism in Upper Canada. Having lost his property in the Papineau rebellion, Horatio Fowler sought asylum with relatives in western New York, and later settled on a farm near Newark, Ill. Here Charles Henry grew up, and by dint of hard work and plain living was graduated in 1859 from Genesee College, Lima, N. Y., where he majored in mathematics, oratory, and mischief, ranking high in each. After a few months in a Chicago law office, "Whirlwind" Fowler swung off into the Methodist itinerancy. In 1861 he graduated valedictorian from Garrett Biblical Institute, entered Rock River Conference, and was ordained deacon in 1864 and elder in 1865. He had been a pastor eleven years in Chicago when the Great Fire threw its glare upon him. In a country-wide campaign for funds to rebuild the burned churches, thousands of Eastern Methodists heard from the lips of this young Westerner the dramatic story of that devouring flame. His reputation was made. From that hour he was always in the Methodist mind when anything of importance was to be said or done. In 1872 he was in his first General Conference, where he nearly unhorsed the veteran editor of the *Christian Advocate*. The next year he was elected president of Northwestern University, Evanston, Ill., not because of unusual educational equipment, but because there was a big piece of work to be done, and Fowler was the most resourceful man in sight to do it. In four years he expanded its professional schools, laid far-sighted plans for its future, enlisted the support of powerful Chicago business men, and lifted the young institution to an important place among universities of the Middle West. In 1874 he was a fraternal messenger from his church to the Methodist Episcopal Church, South, carrying the first olive branch after thirty years of separation. His friends idolized him and believed that there was nothing beyond his powers. As editor of the *Christian Advocate* (1876–80) he carried the circulation to the highest point in its history. As corresponding secretary of the Missionary Society (1880–84), his ubiquity, business capacity, forceful personality, and inspiring oratory, changed the whole missionary outlook of his church. Every fourth year, in the General Conference, his keen intellect, flashing wit, audacious speech, and strong convictions had full play. In 1884 he was elected bishop. His official residences were San Francisco (1884–92), Minneapolis (1892–96), Buffalo (1896–1904), and New York City (1904–08). In these years he presided over the Methodist Conferences in every part of the United States, and was sent by his colleagues to all the the mission fields, everywhere relieving irritated situations by balm or surgery, and launching advance movements such as the universities of Peking and Nanking in China, and the Methodist church in St. Petersburg. The Nebraska Wesleyan University and the Twentieth Century Forward Movement, which brought $20,000,000 into Methodist treasuries, owe their origin to his vision and constructive genius. His knowledge of the work and personnel of the church enabled him to select with extraordinary skill the right man for important administrative positions. Through these years he was a popular preacher, lecturer and occasional orator. He chose appealing themes, had a powerful voice and impressive bearing, and his diction combined the quaint, the startling, the humorous, and the majestic. His earliest book was *Fallacies of Colenso Reviewed* (1861), followed several years later by *Wines of the Bible* (1878). His collected addresses were published as *Missions and World Movements* (1903); *Missionary Addresses* (1906); *Addresses on Notable Occasions* (1908); and *Patriotic Orations* (1910). Fowler was married in 1868 to Myra A. Hitchcock, daughter of the Rev. Luke Hitchcock, of Chicago, who with a son survived him.

[Files of the *Christian Advocate* (N. Y.) and other Methodist periodicals; obituaries in the *Christian Advocate*, Mar. 28, 1908, *Northwestern Christian Advocate* and *Central Christian Advocate*, Mar. 25, 1908, *Cal. Christian Advocate*, Mar. 26, Apr. 2, 1908, and *Meth. Rev.*, Mar.–Apr. 1911; A. H. Wilde, *Northwestern Univ.* (1905); Memoir by W. F. Anderson in *Minutes . . . of the N. Y. Conference of the M. E. Ch.*, 1908; manuscript fragment of a biographical sketch by Fowler's son, Carl H. Fowler.] J. R. J.

FOWLER, FRANK (July 12, 1852–Aug. 18, 1910), painter, critic, was born in Brooklyn, N. Y., the eighth of ten children of John and Margaret (Westervelt) Fowler. His early education was conducted at the Adelphi Academy in Brooklyn and later continued in Europe where he studied painting, for two years as the pupil of Edwin White in Florence and after 1875 at the École des Beaux-Arts and under Carolus Duran. In 1878 Duran's "Gloria Mariæ Medicis," a fresco for the Luxembourg which he had helped to paint, was exhibited at the Paris Salon. In the same year one of his own portraits was entered in the first exhibition of the Society of American Artists, and his study of "Young Bacchus" was shown at the Paris Exposition. He returned to America in 1880 and established a permanent studio in New York. With the construction of the Waldorf Hotel, which opened in March 1893, he was commissioned to design the ball-room ceiling, a three-paneled fresco representing "Music" and "Dance," done in the lavish manner of the decade. Although with this came his first general recognition, throughout his life it was in portrait-painting that his talents were most evident. As a critic he particularly deplored the dedication of portraiture to human interest, which he contended had "deprived the world of much that is genuinely ornamental" ("Portraits as Decoration," *Scribner's Magazine,* December 1909), a theory which he had generous opportunity to put to proof. His list of subjects was long and distinguished, including among others William Dean Howells, Charles A. Dana, Archbishop Corrigan, and Governors S. J. Tilden and Roswell P. Flower, whose portraits were hung in the executive chamber in Albany. Although his treatment was in the main conventional, it had elements of distinction and decorative effectiveness.

Aside from numerous critical contributions to magazines, Fowler published three books on art technique: *Oil Painting* and *Drawing in Charcoal and Crayon* in 1885, and *Portrait and Figure Painting* in 1894. These were all intended for the instruction of beginners, but with their elementary precepts contained some wholesome advice. He received awards at exhibitions in Paris, 1889, Atlanta, 1895, Buffalo, 1901, Charleston, 1902, and Berlin, 1903. He was a member of the National Academy of Design, and the American Fine Arts Society. He married Mary Berrian Odenheimer, an artist and writer, on Nov. 28, 1878.

[*Who's Who in America,* 1908–09; W. T. Westervelt, *Geneal. of the Westervelt Family* (1905); *Am. Art News,* Sept. 17, 1910; *N. Y. Times, N. Y. Herald,* Aug. 20, 1910; *Am. Art Annual,* 1910–11.] C. W. P.

FOWLER, GEORGE RYERSON (Dec. 25, 1848–Feb. 6, 1906), surgeon, the son of Thomas Wright Fowler, master mechanic, and Sarah Jane Carman, was born in New York City. When the father entered the service of the Long Island Railroad in 1856 the family moved to Jamaica. At the age of thirteen the boy started to master railway operation. He began with telegraphy and other duties of station agents, then served his apprenticeship in the machine-shops. In 1866 he decided to work his way through a medical school and changed from railroading to an occupation better suited to this purpose. For the next five years he was connected with a manufactory in Bridgeport, Conn., and at the end of that time, in 1871, obtained a medical degree from Bellevue Hospital Medical College. He at once settled in Brooklyn, and when the Bushwick and East Brooklyn Dispensary was established in 1878 his reputation as an operator was such that he was given the berth of visiting surgeon. With the establishment of the Methodist Episcopal Hospital in 1887 he became a member of its surgical staff. In 1889 he was similarly associated with St. Mary's Hospital and also became senior surgeon at the German Hospital. In 1895 he became surgeon-in-chief at the Brooklyn Hospital and was one of the professors of surgery in the New York Polyclinic Medical School and Hospital. Seven years later he was made surgeon-general of the New York National Guard. He served in the Spanish-American War as surgeon-major, medical inspector, consulting surgeon, and chief of the operating staff of the VII Corps. When the New York State Board of Medical Examiners was established under the control of the regents of the University of the State of New York, he was made examiner in surgery. It was on the occasion of one of his trips to Albany in this connection that he was stricken with appendicitis and succumbed after an operation. Fowler was a voluminous contributor to periodical medical literature. His literary career, however, culminated in the publication in 1906, after twelve years of effort, of a two-volume work entitled *A Treatise on Surgery.* This work appeared after his death, so that he was denied the opportunity of publishing a revised edition. He was a co-founder of the Anatomical and Surgical Society of Brooklyn in 1878 and was chosen its president in 1880. He was also for several years the associate editor of its official *Annals of Anatomy and Surgery* which was subsequently merged into the *Annals of Surgery.* He was much given to European travel and was a delegate to the international medical congresses at Moscow in 1897 and at Paris in 1900. While on a trip to England in 1884 he conceived the idea of introducing into the United States class instruction in first aid to the injured. The idea was first tried out in the annual encampment of the state militia at Peekskill in 1885, after which the movement spread throughout the country, and the United States government ordered its introduction into all military posts. Presumably as the direct result of this initiative he was elected as the first president of the Red Cross Society of Brooklyn in 1890.

Fowler was best known and performed his greatest service as an abdominal surgeon. In this field he was one of a small group of pioneers which included William T. Bull and Charles McBurney. The publication in 1894 of his *Treatise on Appendicitis* was regarded as a classic on the subject and was followed two years later by a German translation and in 1900 by a revised and enlarged edition. His name has been given to the posture which he devised to secure adequate drainage after abdominal operations, known descriptively as the "elevated drainage position." He was married, on June 10, 1872, to Louise R. Wells of Norristown, Pa. He was the father of four children, of whom two sons entered the medical profession.

[*Brooklyn Medic. Jour.*, Mar., Aug. 1906; *Surgery, Gynecol. and Obstetrics,* Apr. 1924; *Medic. Record,* Feb. 10, 1906; H. A. Kelly and W. L. Burrage, *Am. Medic. Biogs.* (1920); *N. Y. Times, N. Y. Tribune,* Feb. 7, 1906.] E. P.

FOWLER, JOSEPH SMITH (Aug. 31, 1820–Apr. 1, 1902), senator, was born in Steubenville, Ohio, the son of James and Sarah (Atkinson) Fowler, both natives of Maryland. He attended country schools for a time and then began to teach in Shelby County, Ky. Later he returned to Ohio, and in 1843 was graduated from Franklin College at New Athens. At Bowling Green, Ky., he again taught school and at the same time studied law, and in 1845 became professor of mathematics at Franklin College, Davidson County, Tenn., where he remained for four years. On Nov. 12, 1846, he married Maria Louisa Embry of Tennessee. His occupation and whereabouts in the years following 1849 are not known, but in 1856 he was made president of Howard Female Institute at Gallatin, Tenn., and remained there until the outbreak of the Civil War in 1861. He had been opposed to slavery since childhood, and he did not believe in the right of secession, but he had lived long enough in the South to be sympathetic with the Southern people, and would doubtless have remained there if it had not been for Davis's "forty day" proclamation, which caused him to move with his family to Springfield, Ill. In 1862 he returned to Nashville, and Johnson made him state comptroller in the military government. He was an efficient officer, and was prominent in the work of reconstruction, particularly in relation to the abolition of slavery. In May 1865 he was elected United States senator but was denied his seat until July 1866. In Tennessee he had been on intimate terms with Johnson, but he differed with him as to Reconstruction, was one of the signers of the call for the Southern Loyalists' convention in 1866, and attended as a delegate. In the Senate he voted for most of the radical measures, including the reconstruction acts, although he did not approve of the provision for military government. He served faithfully but without any special distinction on many committees, and frequently participated in debate. Judging from the reports, he was an effective speaker. He was of average ability only, but was distinctly level-headed. He was radical, but was inclined to be liberal. When Johnson removed Stanton, Fowler, like Henderson, declined to vote for the resolution declaring the removal an illegal act. He watched the House during the process of impeachment and was horrified at its dangerous passion, which he thought likely to precipitate a revolution. When impeachment had first been attempted, he had thought the President impeachable, but as time passed he had found that opinion "based on falsehood," and that Johnson was being attacked for pursuing Lincoln's policy. He then saw in the impeachment plan a plot contrived by leaders "neither numerous nor marked for their prudence, wisdom, or patriotism, . . . mere politicians, thrown to the surface through the disjointed times," bent on "keeping alive the embers of the departing revolution," and with "more of sectional prejudice . . . than of patriotism" (*Congressional Globe,* 40 Cong., 2 Sess., p. 4508). His attitude was soon made clear to the radicals who attempted to coerce him by threats and slander, but he quietly ignored them and voted "Not Guilty," with the quiet statement, "I acted for my country and posterity in obedience to the will of God." He filed a strong opinion, joined with Henderson and Ross in refusing to vote for the resolution of thanks to Stanton, and in July excoriated B. F. Butler for his report on the charges of corruption. In spite of his radical advocacy of negro suffrage, he voted against the Fifteenth Amendment, believing it wiser to move more slowly, and thinking that female suffrage should be included. He retired from the Senate in 1871 and returned to Tennessee. He supported Grant in 1868, but by 1872 was utterly disgusted with his administration and was an elector at large on the Greeley ticket. After some years he moved to Washington and remained there practising law until his death.

[*Who's Who in America,* 1901–02; *Biog. Dir. Am. Cong.* (1928); *Cong. Globe,* 39–41 Congresses; *Proceedings in the Trial of Andrew Johnson* (1868); E. G. Ross, *Hist. of the Impeachment of Andrew Johnson* (1896); D. M. DeWitt, *The Impeachment and Trial of Andrew Johnson* (1903); *Washington Post* and Washington *Evening Star,* Apr. 2, 1902.] J. G. de R. H.

FOWLER, ORIN (July 29, 1791–Sept. 3, 1852), Congregational clergyman, congressman, was born in Lebanon, Conn., the son of Capt. Amos and Rebecca (Dewey) Fowler. He was the oldest boy and the sixth child in a family of twelve. Prepared for college by his pastor, Rev. William B. Ripley, he entered Williams in 1811, but remained there for only one term. After further study at Bacon Academy, Colchester, Conn., he became a member of the sophomore class at Yale, graduating in 1815. For a short time he was preceptor of the academy in Fairfield, Conn., relinquishing the position in order to devote himself to a course in theology under Rev. Heman Humphrey [*q.v.*] of that town. On Oct. 14, 1817, he was licensed to preach by the Association of the Western District of Fairfield County; and on June 3, 1818, at Farmington, Conn., he was ordained by the North Association of Hartford County with a view to missionary work in the West. After a year spent chiefly in Indiana he returned to Connecticut. To the *Christian Spectator,* August and September 1819, he contributed "Remarks on the State of Indiana." He was installed as pastor of the Congregational church, Plainfield, Conn., on Mar. 1, 1820. The following year, Oct. 16, he married Amaryllis, daughter of John H. Payson of Pomfret, Conn. After a pastorate of nearly eleven years, having incurred the ill will of some of his parishioners who professed to believe reports derogatory to his character, he was dismissed by the Windham Association of Ministers, Jan. 27, 1831, although a public investigation had revealed nothing affecting his standing as a Christian minister. On July 7, 1831, he became pastor of the Congregational church in Fall River, Mass.

Reference to a long-standing dispute over the boundary-line between Massachusetts and Rhode Island in a series of discourses published under the title *An Historical Sketch of Fall River from 1620 to the Present Time* (1841) launched him on a political career. His fellow townsmen made him one of a committee to represent them before boundary commissioners of the two states. Their decision was displeasing to the town, and Fowler defended its position under the pseudonym "Plymouth Colony" in articles appearing in the *Boston Daily Atlas* between Sept. 17 and Oct. 18, 1847. As a result of these, on Oct. 20, 1847, the Whig convention of Bristol County nominated him to the state Senate and he was elected. Here he was influential in causing the commissioners' report to be rejected by Massachusetts. His career in the legislature brought about his election to Congress in 1848 as a Free-Soil Whig, and the following year he took up his residence in Washington, although he was not formally dismissed from his church until May 1850. He was reëlected for a second term, but died in Washington, Sept. 3, 1852. He was an opponent of slavery and an advocate of temperance laws and cheap postage. "His strength in the House consisted not so much in eloquence and readiness of debate as in diligent research and knowledge of facts." Besides several speeches his publications include a sermon preached at the ordination of Israel G. Rose, Mar. 9, 1825, entitled *The Duty of Distinction in Preaching Explained and Enforced* (1825); *The Mode and Subjects of Baptism* (1835), and *A Disquisition on the Evils of Using Tobacco* (1833, 1835, 1842).

[W. B. Sprague, *Annals of the Am. Pulpit,* II (1857); F. B. Dexter, *Biog. Sketches of the Grads. of Yale Coll.,* VI (1912); *Congressional Globe,* 32 Cong., 2 Sess., p. 28].

H. E. S.

FOWLER, ORSON SQUIRE (Oct. 11, 1809–Aug. 18, 1887), phrenologist, son of Horace and Martha (Howe) Fowler, was born at Cohocton, Steuben County, N. Y. He was educated, however, in Massachusetts, under the Rev. Moses Miller (at Heath) and the Rev. Mr. Clark (at Buckland); in the Ashfield Academy; and at Amherst College, where he graduated in 1834. From this training he emerged a characteristic product of the day, with a mass of ill-digested information, many enthusiastic theories, and much reformatory zeal. With his younger brother and disciple, Lorenzo, he at once moved upon New York City. Already extravagantly devoted to the cause of phrenology—his interest in which had been aroused in college by his fellow student Henry Ward Beecher—he plunged into controversy with one "Vindex" (see his *Answer to Vindex, with Other Phrenological Matter,* Baltimore, 1835), and in 1837, with the collaboration of his brother, published *Phrenology Proved, Illustrated, and Applied,* which ran through some thirty editions. In 1840 the two brothers, who had organized the firm of O. S. & L. N. Fowler, began the publication of the *Phrenological Almanac;* in 1842 they assumed the editorship and publication of the *American Phrenological Journal and Miscellany,* founded by Nathan Allen in Philadelphia in 1838; in 1844 S. R. Wells entered into partnership with them and their firm became Fowlers & Wells until 1863 when both the brothers withdrew, Lorenzo to settle in London, Orson to reside in Boston and later in Manchester, Mass. Meanwhile Orson had produced an extraordinary number of semi-scientific and pseudo-philosophical works whose portentous titles indicate their contents. Such were, among many others: *Love and Parentage, applied to the Improvement of Offspring, including Important Directions and Suggestions to Lovers and the Married concerning the Strongest Ties and the Most Momentous Relations of Life,* and its sequel, *Amativeness: or, Evils and Remedies of Excessive and Perverted Sexuality, including Warning and Advice to the Married and Single* (both of which had reached forty editions by 1844).

Fowler's interests were universal and he supposed himself able to solve the problems of every department of knowledge by means of "phrenology and physiology" alone. Without special training in philosophy, science, or medicine, and with only a smattering of physiology itself, he undertook to answer the most difficult questions in these fields. His inordinate conceit, however, saved him from deliberate charlatanry, and, in the sense in which alchemy was the forerunner of chemistry, his emphasis upon hereditary and physiological factors in matrimony may be taken as a wild and crude form of eugenics. He also had interesting though bizarre notions of house-building, set forth in *A Home for all; or, the Gravel Wall, and Octagon Mode of Building* (1849), written in collaboration with his brother. The amazing mélange of scientific facts, popular superstitions, and personal fancy which came from his fluent pen procured him an immense reputation in his own day. Throughout middle life (1850–70), he spent most of his time in extensive and lucrative lecture-trips in the United States and Canada, charming ignorant audiences equally by his assumption of scientific knowledge and by the extreme sentimentality of his fundamental outlook on life. In old age he returned to the writing of books, similar to his earlier ones in both content and title. His interest in matrimony was practical as well as theoretical: he was married three times: on June 10, 1835, to Mrs. Martha Chevalier, daughter of Elias Brevoort of New York City; on Oct. 26, 1865, to Mrs. Mary Poole, daughter of William Aiken of Gloucester, Mass.; on Mar. 21, 1882, to Abbie L. Ayres, daughter of Ebenezer Ayres, Osceola, Wis. He died near Sharon Station, Conn., in his seventy-eighth year.

[Fowler's own writings; *Amherst Coll. Biog. Record Grads. and Non-Grads.* (1927).] E. S. B—s.

FOX, CHARLES KEMBLE (Aug. 15, 1833–Jan. 17, 1875) actor, son of George Howe and Emily (Wyatt) Fox, was born in Boston, Mass. He was the younger brother of George W. L. Fox [*q.v.*]. When six years of age he played the child in *The Carpenter of Rouen* at the old Eagle Theatre in his native city. His father was property man at the Tremont Street Theatre and there Charles also acted on occasions. While still a child he traveled with his family through the New England towns, giving performances wherever possible. After living for a time in Troy, N. Y., the family moved to Providence, R. I., and in that city, from 1846 to 1850, as members of the Howard-Fox Dramatic Company, Charles and his brothers James and George, with their sister Caroline, received their practical stage training.

On Sept. 27, 1852, Charles appeared in the rôles of Phineas Fletcher and Gumption Cute in the George Aiken version of *Uncle Tom's Cabin* at the Museum in Troy. His mother, Emily Fox, took the part of Ophelia in the same production. The play was an immediate success and ran for one hundred nights. In a farce which nightly followed the drama, Charles was featured as Peter Paul Pearlbutton. The following season he made his first New York appearance at the National Theatre as Gumption Cute. Later, on Oct. 28, 1867, he was seen as Snug in the revival of *A Midsummer Night's Dream* at Mrs. John Wood's Olympic (formerly Laura Keene's) Theatre. At the same house he appeared in *Hickory Dickery Dock* and in the burlesque of *Macbeth,* and was also cast as Lawyer Marks in one of the many revivals of *Uncle Tom's Cabin.* For a short period in 1869 he formed a traveling arrangement with Tony Denier and played through the Western states. This enterprise soon proved unsuccessful, however, and in 1870 he returned to the Olympic. During the season of 1873–74, he toured through New England, the West, and the South with the Fox Pantomime Troupe. Then after traveling with his brother's company, he played his last engagement at Fox's Broadway Theatre, May 16, 1874, appearing as Pantaloon in *Humpty Dumpty at Home.* It was in this rôle in the various fantasies concerning "Humpty Dumpty" that he was mainly identified; indeed his miming of the part was the best ever presented before an American audience, but he was a competent actor in any line. Throughout his life his theatrical activities were closely associated with those of his more famous brother George, to whom he was of practical and artistic value, as well as an excellent foil. To his creative genius much of the business employed in the pantomimes must be credited.

Fox died in New York City from typhoid fever which he contracted while playing in Tennessee. He and his brother were so strongly attached to each other that at his death his brother George suffered a great blow. He was married three times. His first wife was Kate Denin, a well-known actress; his second wife was Mary Hewins, who later wrote for the *Dramatic Mirror* under the name of the Giddy Gusher; his last wife was Mrs. Dulaney. He and his brother George were buried at Mount Auburn Cemetery, near Boston.

[T. Allston Brown, *A Hist. of the N. Y. Stage* (3 vols., 1903); *N. Y. Tribune,* Jan. 20, 1875; information as to certain facts from Cordelia Howard Macdonald.]

R. D.

FOX, GEORGE WASHINGTON LAFAYETTE (July 3, 1825–Oct. 24, 1877), actor, manager, son of George Howe and Emily (Wyatt) Fox, and brother of Charles Kemble Fox [*q.v.*], was born in Boston, Mass. At the age of five he made his first appearance on the stage as one of the children in *The Hunter of the Alps,* at the Tremont Street Theatre, Boston, for the benefit of Charles Kean. Later he secured a position as errand boy in a Boston department store but continued to act in various productions in the city. From 1846 to 1850 he was a member of the Howard-Fox dramatic company at Providence, R. I. He first appeared in New York at the National Theatre, Nov. 25, 1850, as Christopher Strap in *A Pleasant Neighbor,* and continued to appear at the same theatre until the summer of 1858. During these years he essayed a variety of rôles, including melodrama, farce, burlesque, and pantomime. He also acted as stage-manager. He was first billed as Lafayette Fox, then L. Fox, then G. W. Fox, and finally as G. L. Fox. On Mar. 31, 1851, when Edwin Booth was seen for the first time in New York as Richard III at the National, Fox played Toby Twinkle in the afterpiece, *All that Glitters is not Gold.* In July 1853, at a time when business was depressed at the theatre, Fox persuaded his manager to produce George Aiken's version of *Uncle Tom's Cabin.* It ran from that date, almost consecutively, until April 1854, and was still later revived.

After leaving the National, Fox decided to become a manager as well as an actor and on Aug. 7, 1858, with James W. Lingard, he leased the Bowery Theatre. The two continued as lessees and managers of the house until Aug. 6, 1859, when they gave it up to open the New Bowery on Sept. 5, 1859. Then came a call for three months' volunteers, and Fox left to serve as lieutenant in the 8th New York Infantry, which took part in the battle of Bull Run. On July 26, 1861, he returned from military to theatrical life and met with a hearty reception. Due to a disagreement with his partner, however, Fox withdrew from the New Bowery and in April 1862 opened the theatre which had been Brougham's Lyceum, Wallacks, and Mary Provost's, calling the house George L. Fox's Olympic. This venture was of short duration. On May 17, 1862, he went back to the old Bowery Theatre as lessee, and here he was seen in many parts, assuming four and five rôles in the course of an evening. Here also he made pantomime—a form of art which he later made famous—a great success. His managerial connection terminated May 11, 1867. He next appeared at Mrs. John Wood's Olympic Theatre (formerly Laura Keene's), Oct. 28, 1867, as Bottom in a gorgeous revival of *A Midsummer Night's Dream.* Theatregoers long remembered his impersonation of this rôle. Then on Mar. 10, 1868, he was seen at this theatre for the first time in a pantomime called *Humpty Dumpty,* in which he won instant and prolonged success and played the part with which he is mainly identified. It has been stated that in the city of New York alone, he appeared in this part 1,268 times (Brown, *post,* III, 116). Still at the Olympic in 1870, he presented his inimitable travesty of *Hamlet* which ran for ten weeks. Edwin Booth greatly enjoyed watching Fox revel in this fun.

On Apr. 6, 1874, Fox assumed managership of the house which had been Daly's Theatre, changing the name to Fox's Broadway Theatre, but in six weeks' time he resolved to retire as a manager. He made his last appearance in *Humpty Dumpty in every Clime* at Booth's Theatre, Nov. 27, 1875. Having shown signs of dementia, he was removed to an insane asylum. He recovered sufficiently to return to his Brooklyn home but soon after he suffered a paralytic stroke and was then taken to the home of his sister, Caroline Fox Howard, in Cambridge, Mass., and there he died. He was married twice. His first wife was Caroline Gould; his second wife was Mattie Temple who acted with him. As a comic actor Fox was exceedingly clever but in the annals of the American stage he stands as the peer of pantomimists.

[T. Allston Brown, *A Hist. of the N. Y. Stage* (3 vols., 1903); *N. Y. Tribune,* Oct. 25, 1877; information as to certain facts from Cordelia Howard Macdonald.]

R. D.

FOX, GILBERT (1776–1807?), engraver, actor, singer, was born in England, and at an early age was apprenticed to Thomas Medland, line-engraver, in London. "It so happened that an American (Edward Trenchard), who practised engraving in Philadelphia without knowledge of the art, went on a voyage of discovery to London and finding young Fox, in the year 1793, bound by an apprentice's articles to Medland, a well-known engraver of that city, conceived the design of purchasing the youth's time if he could induce him to cross the seas to Philadelphia, the place of the adventurer's abode, and teach him what he had learned from Medland. Fox's reward was to be liberty and good wages" (William Dunlap, *History of the Rise and Progress of the Arts of Design in the United States,* 1834, II, 46). Fox came to this country in 1795, and after the completion of his contract with Trenchard, decided to teach drawing in a seminary for young ladies. Marrying one of his pupils, his position as drawing master was declared vacant, and in 1798 he joined the company of the Chestnut Street Theatre in Philadelphia as a singer. For his benefit at the theatre, Apr. 25, 1798, Fox induced Joseph Hopkinson to write the national song, "Hail, Columbia" to the then familiar tune of "The President's March." When it was sung at the production it caused a sensation which lasted for many months (G. H. Preble, *The Flag of the United States,* ed. 1880, p. 715).

Fox was connected with the New York Theatre during the seasons from 1799 to 1802, and at the same time, continued occasionally to engrave plates. Nearly all of his engravings are in line. He etched a view of the Chestnut Street Theatre, Philadelphia, for William Birch, about this time, and three plates for William Mavor's *Voyages,* volumes XV and XVIII (Philadelphia, 1803). He also engraved a portrait of Kotzebue for Dunlap's German theatre. In 1804 he went to Boston, where he was a member of the Boston Theatre company until 1807. He appears to have done some engraving at the same time (*Polyanthos,* May 1807). As a player he is said to have been "a versatile, pleasant actor, good in tragedy, comedy, or comic opera" (W. W. Clapp, Jr., *Record of the Boston Stage,* 1853, p. 82), and though he had an impediment in his speech, stuttering in private conversation, on the stage he lost all self-consciousness and hesitation. After 1807 all trace of Fox seems to be lost, but Dunlap states (*ante,* p. 47), that his father bequeathed him one thousand pounds, which might suggest that he returned to his native land. The same writer quotes a contemporary as remarking that "'he had some excellent qualities, but prudence was not one of them.'"

[In addition to the sources mentioned, see D. McN. Stauffer, *Am. Engravers upon Copper and Steel* (1907), vol. I; John Bernard, *Retrospections of America* (1887), pp. 116, 121, 302; *Polyanthos,* 1806–07; J. N. Ireland, *Records of the N. Y. Stage* (2 vols., 1866–67); Wm. Dunlap, *A Hist. of the Am. Theatre* (1832), p. 191; Boston Museum of Fine Arts, *A Descriptive Cat. of an Exhibition of Early Engraving in America* (1904).] J. J.

FOX, GUSTAVUS VASA (June 13, 1821–Oct. 29, 1883), assistant secretary of the navy, was born in Saugus, Mass., the son of Dr. Jesse and Olivia (Flint) Fox. After spending two years at Phillips Academy, Andover, he received an appointment to the United States Naval Academy at Annapolis, where he graduated in 1841 as a midshipman. For the next fifteen years he had an adventurous life in various governmental assignments, being occupied during the Mexican War in the transportation of troops to Vera Cruz. After having earned his promotion to the rank of lieutenant in 1852, he resigned in 1856, married Virginia Woodbury, a daughter of Judge Levi Woodbury of New Hampshire, and settled down as agent of the Bay State Mills in Lawrence, Mass.

The Civil War offered Fox the great opportunity of his career. In February 1861, when it became obvious that Maj. Anderson and the garrison of Fort Sumter in Charleston Harbor were in grave danger, Montgomery Blair, who had married Mrs. Fox's sister, urged Gen. Winfield Scott to consult Fox. The latter promptly went to Washington and submitted a plan for relieving Anderson, but it was vetoed by the vacillating President Buchanan. When Lincoln was inaugurated on Mar. 4, he at once asked Fox to prepare a scheme for reinforcing Fort Sumter, and sent Fox to Charleston for an interview with Anderson. On Apr. 9, although a volunteer with no regular standing in the navy, Fox set out from New York with a formidable squadron, but, because of unavoidable delays, he did not reach Charleston until Apr. 12, just in season to observe the opening bombardment of the fort. Unable to intervene until the other vessels of his fleet arrived, Fox had no alternative except to take Anderson and his seventy men on board when Sumter was evacuated, and return to New York. For his part in the affair he was given high praise by President Lincoln.

Remaining in Washington, Fox was appointed on May 9, 1861, chief clerk of the Navy Department under the irascible Secretary Gideon Welles, and on Aug. 1 he was made assistant secretary of the navy, the post having been created for him. His knowledge of naval matters was an important element in the success of his department during the war. He was largely responsible for important changes in personnel and procedure; he suggested Admiral Farragut as commander of the New Orleans expedition; he was an early advocate of the "turret vessel," or *Monitor,* invented by John Ericsson, and he persuaded Welles to let it be used in action. His chief thought that Fox was occasionally too officious, but honesty compelled him to admit that his subordinate was indispensable. Although Welles's diary is sometimes critical of Fox's manner, it gives the impression that the secretary relied on him unreservedly. In the judgment of James Ford Rhodes, Fox "joined to probity executive ability of a very high order" (*History of the United States*, 1909, V, 221).

At the close of hostilities, Fox resigned (May 22, 1866), and the unsentimental Welles made this entry in his diary: "His manner and ways have sometimes given offense to others, but he is patriotic and true" (*Diary of Gideon Welles*, II, 512). Meanwhile Fox had been selected by President Johnson as the bearer of a congratulatory resolution passed by Congress, expressing the satisfaction of the American people at the escape of Alexander II, Czar of Russia, from the attack of an assassin; and he went, escorted by a fleet, to Russia, stopping at European ports to display the turreted ironclad, *Miantonomoh*, the first monitor to cross the Atlantic. On his return on Dec. 13, 1866, after a hospitable and elaborate reception by the Czar, Fox became agent of the Middlesex Company, in Lowell, Mass. There, on Dec. 9, 1871, he was paid the honor of a state visit by the Grand Duke Alexis, third son of the Czar. He later resigned to join the firm of Mudge, Sawyer & Co., in Boston, and died shortly afterwards in New York City.

In his prime, Fox was a large, rather corpulent man, with a full beard and a confident bearing. His sanguine temperament and sanity of outlook were refreshing to those who had to meet him officially. He was an affectionate and considerate husband. A narrative of his experiences on the Russian expedition was prepared by his secretary J. F. Loubat, and published in 1873, fully illustrated with engravings of the eminent personages who entertained the American representatives (*Narrative of the Mission to Russia in 1866, of the Hon. Gustavus Vasa Fox, Assistant Secretary of the Navy*). His official papers were bequeathed by his widow to the three sons of Montgomery Blair, by whom they were afterward published (*Confidential Correspondence of Gustavus Vasa Fox, Assistant Secretary of the Navy, 1861–65*, edited by Robert Means Thompson and Richard Wainwright, 2 vols., 1918–19). The documents which they contain are of significance to students of the Civil War period.

[There is an account of Fox's career in the *Proc. Mass. Hist. Soc.*, vol. XX (1884), prepared by Robert G. Winthrop. Another sketch of Fox appeared in the *Phillips Bull.*, published by Phillips Academy, Andover, for July 1927, written by Claude M. Fuess. See also *Official Records (Navy)*, 1 ser., I; *Diary of Gideon Welles* (3 vols., 1911); *Boston Transcript*, Oct. 30, 1883.]

C. M. F.

FOX, HARRY (Sept. 29, 1826–Sept. 4, 1883), contractor, was born in Westfield, Mass., where his father, Hiram Fox, was a poor mechanic. When a youth he showed a marked aptitude for working with machinery. At the age of eighteen he was apprenticed to learn the machinist's trade in his native town. Two years later he was sent out with a steam-excavator, said to have been the first one built, to work on the Northern New Hampshire Railroad. By his success in handling it he soon became the chief operator and thus began a long career of excavation by steam. During the next ten years he was employed by several railroads, including the Grand Trunk Railway in Canada. Fox went to Chicago in 1856 and formed a partnership with John P. Chapin, then mayor of the city. They began to widen and deepen the channel of the Chicago River with a special steam-dredge which Fox had brought with him. Although the contract required the firm to carry the dredged earth out into the lake, Fox quickly saw that this material could be used to raise the grade of the city. This was the beginning of the work of raising the city several feet above the old prairie level and was for many years an important feature of the Chicago improvements. The partnership between Chapin and Fox came to an end in 1860 and Fox, to increase the scope of his activities, formed a new partnership with William B. Howard, a noted bridge-builder. For the next fifteen years the history of the firm of Fox & Howard is the history of the topographical improvement of Chicago. They first opened up and made navigable the north and south branches of the river. Having completed this they deepened the old river channel, straightened the banks, and built more than fifteen miles of dock line along the river. By their dredging and construction of piers they were able to create a satisfactory harbor for Chicago. They built the dozen bridges which spanned the Chicago River. In 1865 they successfully undertook the enlargement of the Illinois and Michigan Canal and in the same year began the work of raising the grade of the city of Cairo. Their steam-dredges made extensive improvements on many Lake Michigan harbors, notably at White River, Pentwater, Pere Marquette, and Manistee. They constructed many railroad bridges in the South and in the Middle West; they built the fourteen-hundred-foot bridge over the Fox River at Green Bay and the bridge across the Illinois River at Pekin. The partnership of Fox & Howard ended in 1875; Fox later became connected with the firm of Fitz-Simons & Connell. Among the numerous works executed by Fox are the Baraboo extension of the Chicago & Northwestern Railway system and the extension of the Atchison, Topeka & Santa Fé up the Grand Cañon of the Arkansas River in Colorado. On Nov. 25, 1852, he married Emeline

Buxton Chamberlain, of Newbury, Vt., by whom he had two children. He died of apoplexy at the Walker House in Salt Lake City while returning from a pleasure trip to the Pacific Coast.

[*Biog. Sketches of the Leading Men of Chicago* (1868); F. P. Wells, *Hist. of Newbury, Vt.* (1902), p. 514; *Chicago Tribune*, Sept. 5, 1883; private information.] F. M—n.

FOX, JOHN WILLIAM (Dec. 16, 1863–July 8, 1919), novelist, son of John William and Minerva Worth (Carr) Fox, was born at Stony Point, Ky., and died at Big Stone Gap, Va. His father was a school-teacher, and John's education until he was fifteen was chiefly at home. Then he attended Transylvania College in Lexington, and from 1880 to 1883, when he was graduated, he was a student at Harvard. His scholastic interest seems to have been confined to literary subjects, but he was a good athlete and an enthusiastic amateur actor, especially of the rôles of women. After leaving Harvard he worked for a brief time with the New York *Sun*, attended the Columbia Law School for two months, returned to newspaper work with the *New York Times*, and in February 1885, his health having failed, went home to Paris, Ky., for a year's rest. Later he joined his father and brother in some mining ventures in the Cumberland Mountains, and actually went into the mountains to live. With him were a number of young men who, like himself, had recently left college and were anxious for excitement. They could not, however, let the new world they had invaded go onward as it would; they organized a volunteer police force among themselves and in a short time made life in the mountains as safe as in a great metropolis. After his business and police activities, Fox turned to teaching, but the mountaineers continued to dominate his mind, and before long he began publishing about them a series of writings which showed a mastery of their dialect, and of their ways and thoughts. He published in all more than a dozen volumes, the best of which depend always for their worth upon this same mastery, and upon the instinct for story-telling which in his case seemed to be infallible. *A Mountain Europa* (1894) was the first of a series of novelettes which later included *A Cumberland Vendetta* (1895), *Hell fer Sartain* (1897), *Christmas Eve on Lonesome* (1904), and *A Knight of the Cumberland* (1906). *The Kentuckians* (1897) is concerned more with the aristocratic lowlands than with the mountains, but in *Blue Grass and Rhododendron* (1901), more essay than fiction, he returned to his old emphasis upon the mountains. During the Spanish-American War, his writing was interrupted by his going to Cuba as a Rough Rider, but he soon left that organization and became a war correspondent for *Harper's Weekly*. In this capacity he witnessed a great deal of actual fighting, much of which he soon used as material in the novel *Crittenden* (1900). He also went as a correspondent for the war between the Japanese and the Russians, but was forced to come home without reaching the front. *Following the Sun Flag* (1905) is a flat, querulous account of this experience. *The Little Shepherd of Kingdom Come* (1903), *The Trail of the Lonesome Pine* (1908), *The Heart of the Hills* (1913), and *Erskine Dale, Pioneer* (1920) are novels dealing with the mountaineers, and at times—most notably in the *Little Shepherd*—with mountaineers in contact with the urbane civilization to the west of them. These books were all romantic in outlook and made little contribution to thought, but they were enormously popular, and the *Little Shepherd*, for all its sentimentality, doubtless furthered a realization throughout this country that the Civil War was evil and for the most part inexcusable. The celebrity of the books kept their author always in the public consciousness, and for years he went about giving dialect readings from his own works. Some of the accounts and photographs of him give the impression that he was a poseur, but the general testimony is that in his personal relations he was affable and humorous. In 1908 he married the comic opera singer, Fritzi Scheff, and took her to live at his home at Big Stone Gap. They were later divorced. His death was from pneumonia.

[E. F. Harkins, *Little Pilgrimages*, Second Series (1903); E. A. Alderman and J. C. Harris, *Lib. of Southern Literature* (1909); W. L. Burrage, ed., *Class of 1883 Harvard Coll., 1883–1913*; J. W. Townsend, *Ky. in Am. Letters* (1913); *Who's Who in America*, 1918–19; *N.Y. Times*, July 9, 13, 1919.] J. D. W.

FOX, MARGARET (Oct. 7, 1833–Mar. 8, 1893), medium, and her younger sister, Kate, were daughters of John D. and Margaret Fox, who had moved from a farm in Canada in 1847 to one near Hydesville, in Wayne County, N. Y. According to an interview given by Margaret (New York *World*, Oct. 21, 1888), the children began the rappings for the excitement of mystifying their superstitious mother, who believed that the creakings and cracklings of the old house were caused by "spirits." The children's pranks only confirmed her delusion. At first the taps were made by the bumping of an apple tied on a string but later, when more secrecy was needed, by movements of the toes. The mother told neighbors of the sounds and soon the countryside was gossiping about them. An elder sister, Mrs. Leah Fish, who lived in Rochester, took Kate and later

Margaret to her home and invited neighbors to come to hear the mysterious sounds which occurred in their presence. Years later Margaret said that this sister was fully aware that the children controlled the rappings and herself tried to imitate them, though unsuccessfully because of the lesser flexibility of her joints. An older brother, David, suggested that the spirits might be able to communicate if the alphabet were spelled out for them. This suggestion was readily acted upon and words were soon tapped out. The fame of the "Rochester Rappings" spread with such rapidity that Leah felt able to take the little girls to New York in the summer of 1850, where they began séances which brought them a hundred dollars and more a night. The newspapers, with the exception of the *New York Tribune* (June 8, 1850), took them lightly; but Horace Greeley was sufficiently interested to make arrangements for Kate's education. The two sisters with their mother then toured the country. Numberless rivals and imitators appeared immediately, among them Victoria Woodhull [*q.v.*] and Ira Erastus Davenport [*q.v.*]. The followers of Andrew Jackson Davis [*q.v.*] recalled that in his rambling revelations he had spoken of communications with the dead, and hailed the rappings as a fulfilment of his prophecy. As the excitement increased, he cautiously agreed. "Spiritualist circles" were formed throughout the country, using his writings as a guide, and some of these in time became "churches."

While in Philadelphia, Margaret had met the Arctic explorer, Dr. Elisha Kent Kane [*q.v.*]. He was a scientist and was antagonistic to the new spiritualism, but he was attracted to the medium. He tried to take her away from her Spiritualist friends and their influence and to have her educated. During his absences, however, she continually slipped back to the excitement of the circles. After his return from the Arctic, he saw her only briefly before he left for the journey on which he died in 1857. She proclaimed that he had acknowledged a common-law marriage with her before her relatives, and, to the distress of his family, assumed his name. In an attempt to obtain a small annuity which he may have intended to give her, she published his letters to her (Margaret Fox, *The Love Life of Dr. Kane,* 1866). The authenticity of sections of these letters has been questioned. For some time she did not return to the circles, but economic necessity drove her at length to a somewhat indifferent participation. The cult had spread to England where Harriet Martineau and Elizabeth Browning were among the interested investigators. Kate was married to H. D. Jencken in 1872; and in 1876 Margaret joined her sister in London. The sisters had openly quarreled with Leah, now Mrs. Underhill, who was most actively promulgating the new religion, insisting that the performances of the sisters were beyond their control. On Oct. 21, 1888, Margaret, now a convert to Roman Catholicism and unhappy in the continual deceit, openly exposed the chicanery of Mrs. Underhill at the Academy of Music in New York. When Margaret explained the methods by which the rappings were obtained, the sensation was tremendous. Spiritualists, however, insisted that the confession was made for money and while Margaret was under the influence of alcohol. Later, indeed, she recanted, when her lecture tour proved a financial failure. She returned to the rappings for a living, resorting to drink frequently till the time of her death in 1893 in Brooklyn.

[*Rochester Knockings* (1851), reprinted from the *Buffalo Medic. Jour.*, Mar. 1851, and D. M. Dewey, *Hist. of the Strange Sounds or Rappings* (1850) are contemporary accounts, to which Mrs. Ann Leah (Fox) Underhill, in *The Missing Link in Modern Spiritualism* (1885), adds little. Harry Houdini based his story, *A Magician Among the Spirits* (1924) on documents which he collected and on interviews with friends of Margaret Fox. For newspaper accounts of the exposure, see N. Y. *World,* Oct. 21–22, 1888; *N. Y. Herald,* May 27, Sept. 24–25, Oct. 22, 1888. Obituaries in *N. Y. Tribune,* Mar. 10, 1893, and *N. Y. Herald,* Mar. 9, 1893.]

K. H. A.

FOX, RICHARD KYLE (Aug. 12, 1846–Nov. 14, 1922), journalist, encourager of sporting contests, was born in Belfast, the son of James and Mary (Kyle) Fox. His mother was a daughter of Henry Kyle, a Presbyterian minister; his father was a carpenter and mason. As a boy Fox was employed in the office of a religious paper, the *Banner of Ulster,* and out of his earnings paid two shillings a week for his schooling. For twelve years he worked on the *Belfast News Letter.* He married Annie Scott of Belfast in 1869; and in 1874, with barely enough money to pay their passage, they emigrated to New York, where Fox began as an advertising solicitor for the *Wall Street Journal.* Within a year he took the business managership of the *National Police Gazette,* whose incompetent owners were heading rapidly toward bankruptcy. In 1877 he relieved them of their accumulated debts and worries and became sole proprietor of the weekly, which he conducted for forty-five years and bequeathed to his sons. During the first years of his ownership it was the most lurid journal ever published in the United States, its sixteen pages being filled with highly spiced accounts of crime and scandal, with illustrations that matched the text. The whole paper was enlivened by a burly gusto; under "Noose Notes," for example, hangings were reported with the vivacity of smart dramatic criticism; and another department, maintained by volunteer contributors throughout the country, was devoted exclusively to "Crimes of the Clergy." From the beginning, however, some space was occupied by sporting news, and Fox gradually transformed his sheet into an intelligent sporting and theatrical paper, retaining only the luscious front-page illustration as a memento of its rowdy youth. Much of the advertising that he printed was open, however, to serious objection. He introduced condensed journalism in the United States and revolutionized the method of reporting sporting news. "Be interesting and be quick about it," was, in effect, his injunction to his reporters. "Tell your story in three paragraphs at most. If you can't tell it in three, tell it in two. And if you can't tell it in two, get out of here." He was one of the first to use pictures lavishly. Beginning in the eighties, he was the first to use tinted paper. He originated the prize contest as a device for increasing circulation and likewise the practise of holding various events under the auspices of a journal. He offered medals and trophies for sculling, football, shooting, running, wrestling, and other contests. To John L. Sullivan [*q.v.*] he gave a $4,000 belt studded with diamonds, emeralds, rubies, and sapphires, and later spent much of his leisure looking for a prize-fighter who could beat him. He backed several of Sullivan's most promising opponents, and is said, in all, to have given $1,000,000 to amateur and professional athletes. He himself played no games and did not know the rules of the commonest sports. His first wife, by whom he had six children, died in New York in 1890, and in 1913 he married Emma Louise (Raven) Robinson, who survived him. He collected costly furniture and rugs, traveled, and had a ranch at Arcadia, Los Angeles County, Cal. In England he was a social favorite. His shrewdness and insouciance are the subject of many picturesque anecdotes. He died at his home in Red Bank, N. J., leaving an estate valued at $3,000,000.

[*N. Y. Times*, Nov. 15, 21, Dec. 22, 1922; *World* and *Morning Telegraph* (N. Y.), Nov. 15, 1922; editorial in *N. Y. Herald*, Nov. 16, 1922; *Nat. Police Gazette*, Dec. 2, 1922; Walter Davenport, articles in *Collier's*, Mar. 10, 24, 1928; H. L. Mencken and G. J. Nathan, article in *Smart Set*, Feb. 1923, pp. 33-35; information from Fox's son, Charles J. Fox.] G. H. G.

FOX, WILLIAMS CARLTON (May 20, 1855–Jan. 20, 1924), diplomat, was born in St. Louis, Mo., the son of Elias Williams and Eusebia (Johnson) Fox. His father was a hardware dealer, originally of Buffalo, N. Y., and his great-grandfather was Capt. Samuel Pratt, a Revolutionary soldier and one of the founders of Buffalo. After attending Washington University in his native city and the Pennsylvania Military College at Chester, Pa., he began the study of law. He abandoned the latter, however, when offered in 1876 the American consulship at Brunswick, Germany, by President Grant, a personal friend of his father. Four years later, on May 1, 1880, he married Louise Ludewig of that place, and continued thereafter to serve as consul until 1888, building up a record which led to his going to Persia in 1891 as vice-consul-general. When the cholera epidemic of 1892 spread over almost all of Asia and Europe, he was in charge of the American legation at Teheran. He organized and financed the American Missionary Hospital and Dispensary, which proved so effective in combating the cholera that he received the thanks of the Shah and the Presbyterian Board of Foreign Missions. Resigning the same year, he was prevailed upon by the American minister to Greece, Rumania, and Servia, Truxtun Beale, to remain in Athens as his secretary until the following year. After his return to the United States, he joined his father who had removed to Washington in 1885 and with others purchased the *National Republican*, in the management of the enterprise, but tiring of this, in 1896 he began publishing in New York and carried on for some time the first strictly diplomatic and consular journal ever attempted in the United States, the *Diplomatic and Consular Review*. This resulted in his being called to the chief clerkship of the International Bureau of the American Republics in 1898. In this capacity he developed much of the detail necessary for the Second and the Third Conferences of American States, and represented the Bureau at both. In the Second Conference, held in Mexico City, 1901–02, he aided in securing recognition of the Bureau as an international American institution with the franking privilege and the obligation of the director to attend all future international American conferences. His efforts were rewarded by his advancement in 1905 to the post of director of what is now called the Pan American Union, and it was in this capacity that he attended the Third Conference at Rio de Janeiro in 1906, one of the results of which was a plan to erect as headquarters a building for the Bureau in the city of Washington. At the suggestion of Elihu Root, Andrew Carnegie was induced to contribute $750,000 for this project to supplement subscriptions which Fox had secured from the American republics themselves. Under his direction arrangements were perfected for the Columbus Memorial Library and for the holding of two international sanitary conferences in Washington in 1903 and 1905. Meanwhile, he had also served as a member of the United States

Government Board of Management of the Pan-American Exposition at Buffalo in 1901, the Louisiana Purchase Exposition at St. Louis in 1904, and the Lewis and Clark Exposition in 1905. Early in 1907 his services were recognized by President Roosevelt by his appointment as minister to Ecuador. Later in the same year he was designated by the President to represent him on the board of arbitration for the settlement of the controversy between the government of Ecuador and the Guayaquil & Quito Railway Company. On Aug. 18, 1911, he resigned his diplomatic post and retired to private life in New York City, devoting some of his time to the writing of articles on international affairs for American and European periodicals. He died at the Lutheran Memorial Hospital in that city after a long illness.

[*Who's Who in America*, 1922–23; *Men and Women of America* (1910); *N. Y. Times*, *N. Y. Herald*, Jan. 21, 1924; *Foreign Relations of the U. S.*, 1892, 1907–10; information as to certain facts from Fox's associates. His achievements for the Pan American Union are recorded in the publications of that institution.] H. F. W.

FOXALL, HENRY (May 24, 1758–Dec. 11, 1823), iron-founder, was born in Monmouthshire, England, the son of an obscure blacksmith. His parents were devout followers of John Wesley and intimate friends of the family of Francis Asbury. He shared the courage and honesty though not the piety of his parents. He worked as an iron-moulder in Birmingham until 1794 when, restless and dissatisfied with his limited opportunities, he went to Ireland. There he became superintendent of important iron-works near Dublin and later at Carrick-on-Shannon. Through the exhortation of an itinerant Methodist preacher and the persuasion of his wife, Ann Haward, he first became conscious of his sinful state and for some months was "weary and heavy-laden and sorrowed after a godly sort." At length he found consolation. He renounced his worldly pleasures, including card-playing to which he had once succumbed, and in the enthusiasm of his conversion began to preach publicly. This function of a lay minister he exercised to the day of his death.

In 1797 he emigrated from Ireland to Philadelphia and formed a partnership with Robert Morris, Jr., the son of the Revolutionary financier, in the Eagle Iron Works. There they did a general foundry and machine business and made cannon for the War Department. Foxall, having severed his connection with Morris, moved to Georgetown, D. C., in 1800 and established the Columbian Foundry. For the next fifteen years he made cannon, cannon-shot, and gun-carriages for the government. The capacity of his foundry was later (1836) estimated to have been 300 heavy guns and 30,000 shot a year. Foxall rendered valuable service to the nation in the War of 1812 when the government, having no foundry of its own, was forced to depend upon a few private establishments. Although he built up a large fortune from his contracts, his dealings with the government were conducted with remarkable honesty and even generosity. When, in 1807, Dearborn, the secretary of war, was considering the establishment of a national foundry, he consulted Foxall whose reply (*American State Papers, Military Affairs*, I, 215–17) revealed his unusual public spirit. In 1815 he sold his foundry to Gen. John Mason and the next year went to England. His wife having died after their arrival in Philadelphia from Ireland, he married a second time, while he was in England. He returned to America and was mayor of Georgetown from 1821 to 1823, but had gone back to England and was living at Handsworth near Birmingham when he died.

His gifts to religious bodies were many. In 1814 he gave the ground and the funds for the building of the Foundry Chapel at 14th and G Streets, Washington. He once replied in a jocular vein to a friend's criticism of this gift: "No doubt you have some reason for thinking I have sinned in turning out these grim instruments of death; but don't you think therefore, that I should do something to save the souls of those who escape?" In person he was small and compactly built. While his ordinary dress was plain and simple, his dress in the pulpit was of great elegance—rich black velvet, white muslin, silk stockings, and shoes with silver buckles. Despite his piety and frequent prayer he was fond of the society of worldly people and is said to have enjoyed the friendship of Jefferson, Madison, Monroe, and Gouverneur Morris.

[Madison Davis, "The Old Cannon Foundry above Georgetown, D. C., and its First Owner, Henry Foxall," in *Records of the Columbia Hist. Soc.*, vol. XI (1908); Jos. Entwisle in *Wesleyan-Methodist Mag.* (London), Jan., Aug. 1824; private information.] F. M—n.

FOY, EDDIE (Mar. 9, 1856–Feb. 16, 1928), comedian, son of Richard and Ellen (Hennessy) Fitzgerald, was born in New York City. He was named Edwin. His father, a tailor, entered the Federal army in 1861 and died of a wound two years later, leaving his family in poverty. To aid his mother and two sisters, Edwin began singing and dancing on the streets at the age of eight, in company with a wandering fiddler. His mother removed to Chicago in 1865, where the boy blacked boots, sold papers, and did odd jobs, meanwhile trying to get into theatrical work. At sixteen he began calling himself Foy and received his first salary for acting when he appeared briefly in a concert hall. In 1878 he formed a partnership with James Thompson, and the two for several years sang and danced in the mining camps and "boom towns" of the West, among them Dodge City, Leadville, Denver, Tombstone, Butte, and San Francisco. They appeared with Emerson's Minstrels in San Francisco in 1882 and with Carncross's Minstrels at Philadelphia in 1884. Foy next played in melodrama and comedy, including *Baron Rudolph* and *Jack-in-the-Box,* and spent two periods in the Alcazar Stock Company in San Francisco. In 1887, while playing with Kate Castleton in *Crazy Patch,* he began using the clownlike facial make-up which became a sort of trade-mark for him. His quizzical countenance, with the small mouth upcurving at the corners, was happily suited to such a character. He had stage mannerisms which were peculiarly his own, and many were the imitations of him in later years. By this time he had made such a reputation as an eccentric farceur that he was engaged by David Henderson of Chicago to play leading comedy parts in his series of gorgeous extravaganzas. The first in which Foy appeared was *The Crystal Slipper,* 1888. This was followed by *Bluebeard, Sindbad,* and *Ali Baba.* Foy left Henderson in 1894 to star in *Off the Earth*; then in *Little Christopher Columbus,* 1895; *Hotel Topsy Turvy,* 1898; *The Strollers,* 1901; and *The Wild Rose,* 1902. In 1903 he was engaged to play the comic Sister Anne in an elaborate fantasy, *Mr. Bluebeard.* While he was appearing in this play in the Iroquois Theatre, Chicago, Dec. 30, 1903, fire broke out, the audience became panic-stricken, and more than six hundred lives were lost. Foy played a hero's part. Sending his little son, who was in the wings, out in care of a stage hand, he ran to the footlights, striving to quiet the audience and to bring down the asbestos curtain. He left only when a shower of blazing fragments fell over him and set his wig afire.

Foy had leading comedy parts in *Piff! Paff! Pouf!,* opening in 1904; *The Earl and the Girl,* 1905; *The Orchid,* 1907; *Mr. Hamlet of Broadway,* 1908; and *Up and Down Broadway,* 1910. *Over the River* (1911 to 1913) was his last musical comedy. He was married in 1878 to Rose Howland, who died in 1884. In 1890 he married Lola Sefton, who died in 1894, leaving a daughter. In 1896 he married Madeline Morando, by whom he had seven children. He went into vaudeville with these children in 1913, and with the exception of a short engagement in motion-pictures, continued in that work for ten years. His third wife died in 1918, and in 1923 he married Marie Combs, who survived him. In 1923 he and his family appeared in a comedy, *That Casey Girl,* after which he retired. In the autumn of 1927, however, he entered vaudeville again in a short play entitled *The Fallen Star,* in which he was appearing when he was stricken suddenly and died at Kansas City.

[Foy's autobiography, *Clowning Through Life* (written in collaboration with Alvin F. Harlow), appeared just before his death in 1928. Obituaries appeared in leading American newspapers on Feb. 16 and 17, 1928.]
A. F. H.

FRALEY, FREDERICK (May 28, 1804–Sept. 23, 1901), merchant, banker, was born in Philadelphia, Pa., the son of John Urban Fraley and Ann Elizabeth Laskey Fraley, both of whom had been born in Philadelphia. He received his preliminary education at a school attached to St. John's Lutheran Church and then attended Thomas Watson's private school which he left in 1817. During the next three years he studied languages and literature under private tutors and also began the study of law. He chose, however, to devote himself to commercial activities. At the age of seventeen he entered the hardware store of Thomas Cooper, and in 1826 went into partnership with the firm of Reeves, Buck & Company, in the wholesale hardware business. He remained with them until 1840, when he became secretary of the American Fire Insurance Company. In 1847 he was made president of the Schuylkill Navigation Company, and continued in that office until 1888. Elected treasurer of the Centennial Board of Finance in 1873, he remained in charge of its affairs until its final dissolution in 1893. In 1858 he was appointed a manager of the Western Saving Fund Society, and twenty years later was elected its president, which office he held until his death. He was one of the founders of the Franklin Institute in 1824, serving for many years as its treasurer, and for a short time as its corresponding secretary. In 1842 he became a member of the American Philosophical Society and successively filled the offices of secretary, vice-president, and president (1880–1901). He was chosen a member of the board of directors of the Girard College for orphans in 1847, was appointed chairman of the committee on instruction, and for a short time served as acting-president of the institution. In 1853 he was elected a trustee of the University of Pennsylvania, and was also a manager, and for some time the treasurer, of the Pennsylvania Institution for the Blind. Upon the organization of the Philadelphia Board of Trade in 1833 he took an active part and was elected one of its first directors. Five years later he was elected secretary of this body; in 1866 he became a member of its executive council; in the following year he was made one of the vice-presidents, and in 1887 he was elected president of the Board, which position he held until his death. He also took part in the organization of the National Board of Trade in 1868 and served as its president from that time until his death.

Fraley always took an interest in public affairs. From 1834 to 1837 he was a member of the Common Council of Philadelphia and from 1837 to 1840 was a member of the Senate of Pennsylvania. In the years 1853 and 1854 he served on the committee of citizens of Philadelphia which devised the scheme for the consolidation of the city, his chief share in that work being the framing of the system of financial administration of the municipal government. He also took an active part in the work of the Sanitary Commission of the city and was a member of the executive committee of the Sanitary Fair of 1864. He seemed to have both a tremendous capacity for work and an accurate memory for facts and details—a trait which seemed to suffer no impairment from advancing years. Until his death he took an active part in the business and cultural life of Philadelphia, and was considered one of the most successful men of his time. In 1832 he married Jane Chapman Cresson. He died of old age in his ninety-eighth year.

[University of Pennsylvania, *Ann. Report of the Provost*, 1901–02; *Who's Who in America*, 1901–02; *Proc. Am. Philos. Soc.*, 1901, pp. i–ix; *Ann. Report of the Philadelphia Board of Trade*, 1902; J. T. Scharf and Thompson Wescott, *Hist. of Philadelphia* (1844), III, pp. 2343–44; *Philadelphia Inquirer, Public Ledger* (Phila.), Sept. 24, 1901.]

J. H. F.

FRANCHÈRE, GABRIEL (Nov. 3, 1786–Apr. 12, 1863), fur-trader, was born in Montreal, the son of Gabriel and Félicité (Marin) Franchère. The Franchère family was of good French stock of the upper middle-class. Jacques, the first of the name in Canada, came as a ship's surgeon to New France early in the eighteenth century, when Montreal was the depot for the vast French fur-trade; and, seeing the possibilities which this new life offered, Jacques abandoned the sea. He prospered moderately. Under the British régime, his son Gabriel had become an established merchant, in good standing, though not wealthy, at the time of the younger Gabriel's birth. Gabriel *fils* was twenty-four years old and was serving as a merchant's apprentice when the fur-traders' realm was startled by the news of John Jacob Astor's plans to secure a monopoly of the Pacific Coast fur-trade. In the hope of making his fortune and with a great curiosity to see new lands, so he tells us, Franchère engaged in Astor's service. He left Montreal in a birch-bark canoe manned by nine voyageurs, who were also new employees of Astor. The party portaged the canoe from the St. Lawrence to the Richelieu River and, again, between Lake Champlain and the Hudson at Lansingburg, from which point they paddled down stream to Long Island, landing at "the village of Brooklyn." On Sept. 6, 1810, Franchère sailed from New York, being one of the "singing, smoking, gossiping, scribbling groups" of whom Capt. Thorn of the *Tonquin* complained so bitterly. Thus Franchère assisted in the founding of Astoria, near the mouth of the Columbia, witnessed the sale of Astor's property to the Canadian North West Fur Company for $40,000, and saw the capture of the fort by the British in 1813. Because of his knowledge of the local Indian tongue the Nor' Westers induced him to remain there in their service for five months. He left on Apr. 4, 1814, with the first overland brigade, arriving in Montreal after his four years of exile in September 1814. Next year he married Sophie Routhier. He was employed as Astor's Montreal agent, and for some years before 1833 by the North West Fur Company. In 1834 he became Astor's agent at Sault Ste. Marie, and remained there until 1838 or 1839. After the liquidation of Astor's American Fur Company Franchère was employed for a time by Pierre Chouteau [*q.v.*] of St. Louis, before establishing his own fur-trading company in New York.

Having written his reminiscences of Astoria for his family and friends, Franchère was urged to prepare them for publication. He sought the aid of Michel Bibaud, a well-known Canadian editor, and in 1820 his *Relation d'un Voyage à la Côté du Nord Ouest de l'Amérique Septentrionale, dans les années 1810, 11, 12, 13, et 14,* was published in Montreal by C. B. Pasteur. The original manuscript is in the Toronto Public Library. The book came into notice in the United States when the Oregon question was stirring Congress. In the Senate, on May 25, 1846, Thomas H. Benton translated passages from it to reinforce his fiery demands for American acquisition of Oregon (*Congressional Globe,* 29 Cong., 1 Sess., pp. 860–61). Franchère, loyal to his adopted country, took a keen interest in the great question. He went to Washington and conferred with Senators Benton, Webster, and Clay. In 1853 he revisited Montreal where he was treated respectfully as a noted author. The French edition of his book was one of the sources of Irving's *Astoria.* The English version by J. V. Huntington of Baltimore, with the title *Narrative of a Voyage to the Northwest Coast of America* and containing some changes and additions, was published by Redfield, New York, in 1854.

In this edition, Franchère corrected Irving's aspersions on the Canadians of Astor's expedition. He died on Apr. 12, 1863, in St. Paul. After the death of his first wife in 1837 he married Mrs. Charlotte (Osborn) Prince.

[Franchère's fellow clerks, Ross Cox and Alexander Ross, also wrote accounts of Astoria: Ross Cox, *Adventures on the Columbia River* (1831) and Alexander Ross, *Adventures of the First Settlers* (1849). There is a reprint of Franchère's *Narrative* in *Early Western Travels*, vol. VI (1904). See also Constance Lindsay Skinner, *Adventurers of Oregon* (1920), in The Chronicles of America Series; Joseph Tasse, *Les Canadiens de l'Ouest* (2 vols., 1878); B. P. Avery, "Death of a Remarkable Man," in *Minn. Hist. Soc. Colls.*, VI (1894), pt. III; *N. Y. Times*, Apr. 15, 1863. Otto Fowle, *Sault Ste. Marie and Its Great Waterway* (1925), contains letters of Franchère as agent of the American Fur Co.] C. L. Sk—r.

FRANCIS, CHARLES SPENCER (June 17, 1853–Dec. 1, 1911), editor, diplomat, born at Troy, N. Y., was the son of Harriet Elizabeth Tucker and John Morgan Francis [*q.v.*]. Unlike his father, he enjoyed the advantages of education and travel made possible by the former's success. Educated at the Troy Academy and at Cornell University, where he was graduated in 1877, he profited from the contacts which he had already made in his travels. His training as a journalist, however, was as soundly practical as his father's, for he learned at first hand the routine of a newspaper office. Indeed, it was largely through his initiative that the *Times*, a small, one-man daily, became a modern city journal hous in a plant provided with the latest mechanical contrivances. In 1881 he became joint proprietor and general manager, and in 1897, on the death of his father, proprietor and editor-in-chief. He himself was succeeded by his son, John Morgan Francis, a graduate of Cornell and an athlete of note.

Charles Spencer Francis was also an ardent Republican, and played an important though obscure rôle in both state and national politics. As with his father, his loyalty was largely personal. In state politics he advanced the fortunes of Gov. Frank S. Black, of Troy, with whom he had been associated in a campaign against municipal corruption. In national politics he was one of the first leaders to advocate the nomination of William McKinley, and he gave to Theodore Roosevelt the undeviating support which he had given to his predecessor. During his father's missions to Athens and Vienna he had acted as his private secretary. As a reward for his services, President McKinley therefore included his name in his list of appointments, nominating him, in 1900, envoy extraordinary and minister plenipotentiary to Greece, Roumania, and Servia, a post which he assumed exactly thirty years after it had been held by his father. Later, under President Roosevelt, he became ambassador to Austria-Hungary. After four years of service he resigned in 1910.

Endowed with a rugged and vigorous physique, Francis delighted in out-of-door activities. At college he won the intercollegiate sculling championship, and in later years he acquired a reputation as an amateur naturalist. His *Sport Among the Rockies* (1889) is the record of an excursion of friendly spirits in the mountains of Montana. Because of this bent, he was strongly attracted by military life, and served for eleven years as captain, major, and colonel on the staff of the 3rd Division, New York State National Guard. He was also aide-de-camp, with the rank of colonel, to Gov. Alonzo B. Cornell. He married, on May 25, 1878, Alice Evans of Ithaca, daughter of Prof. Evan W. Evans.

[*Charles S. Francis: A Personal Tribute* (1901); *Who's Who in N. Y.*, 1911; Rutherford Hayner, *Troy and Rensselaer County, N. Y.* (3 vols., 1925); *Cornell Alumni News*, Dec. 6, 1911; *N. Y. Tribune*, Mar. 20, Apr. 9, 1906; *N. Y. Times*, Dec. 6, 1911.] R. P. B—r.

FRANCIS, CHARLES STEPHEN (Jan. 9, 1805–Dec. 1, 1887), pioneer bookseller, publisher, was born in Boston, the son of David and Mary (Moore) Francis. His father was of the publishing firm of Munroe & Francis, which brought out the first New England edition of Shakespeare. Under the tuition of his father Charles had an exceptional opportunity to learn the art of printing and of selling books. At twenty-one he ventured to New York to launch into business for himself. His first store was in a fortunate location on lower Broadway near the residences of the wealthiest citizens. When the movement uptown started the bookseller went with it, first to 252 Broadway under Peale's Museum, then to 554 Broadway. In 1838 his brother entered into partnership with him, and about 1842 the firm became known as C. S. Francis & Company. Among the many publications which brought the establishment into general recognition was *Francis's New Guide to the Cities of New York and Brooklyn, and The Vicinity*, appearing first in 1853. It was revised and reprinted periodically, with somewhat changed title, during the next dozen years. It carried a notice of the bookshop which advertised that "Strangers, as well as Citizens, will find this a pleasant place of resort at all times of day and evening," which proved indeed to be the case. Because the firm published H. W. Bellows's *Discourse Occasioned by the Death of William Ellery Channing* (1842), Orville Dewey's *Discourse on Slavery and the Annexation of Texas* (1844), William Ware's *Zenobia* (1838), and other works by Unitarian authors, members of that faith found the atmosphere of the store particularly congenial. Bibliophiles from all parts of the country were attracted to the shop by the fine character of the work which Francis did. Due to his enterprise the company had an agency in London and was able to fill orders for foreign publications with commendable promptness. The firm also boasted a circulating library, "the largest in the city," of new publications as well as of periodicals (*Guide,* 1853, p. 136). Children's books were a specialty, including the works of Hans Christian Andersen, and Charles and Mary Lamb. In 1860 the firm dissolved, but Francis continued in the business for a decade more before retiring to Tarrytown, where he passed his last years. His first wife was Catharine Rebecca Jewett, whom he married on Sept. 2, 1830. After her death in 1841, he married Averic Parker Allen, Sept. 29, 1849. He had five children, of whom Harriet Moore, a daughter, married John Rogers [*q.v.*].

[C. E. Francis, *Francis: Descendants of Robt. Francis of Wethersfield, Conn.* (1906); J. C. Derby, *Fifty Years among Authors, Books and Publishers* (1884); W. L. Andrews, *The Old Booksellers of N. Y. and Other Papers* (1895), pp. 45–46; the *Publisher's Weekly,* Dec. 10, 1887; *N. Y. Times, N. Y. Tribune,* Dec. 3, 1887.]
A. E. P.

FRANCIS, CONVERS (Nov. 9, 1795–Apr. 7, 1863), Unitarian clergyman, educator, a descendant of Richard Francis, who settled in Cambridge, Mass., in 1636; grandson of Benjamin Francis, a weaver and soldier of the Revolution, and Lydia Convers; and son of Convers and Susannah (Rand) Francis; was born in Menotomy (West Cambridge), Mass. He was the fifth of six children, the youngest being Lydia Maria, later Mrs. Child [*q.v.*], who attributed to him her early mental stimulus. He grew up in Medford, Mass., to which place his father moved and established a bakery, famous for its "Medford Crackers." Much of his time as a boy was spent in the baker shop, where he became an expert. "I could *break* and *mould* and *flat* and *dock* as well as the best," he says; . . . "and how many hundreds upon hundreds of barrels of crackers did I wipe!" He had a passion for books, however, and his father decided to give him a college education. He prepared at a local academy, graduated from Harvard in 1815, and for the next three years studied divinity there. He was ordained a Unitarian minister on June 23, 1819, and settled over the First Church of Watertown, Mass., where he remained twenty-three years. On May 15, 1822, he married Abby Bradford Allyn of Duxbury, Mass. In 1842 he succeeded Henry Ware, Jr., as professor of pulpit eloquence and pastoral care at the Harvard Divinity School, which office he held until his death some twenty-one years later.

He was of modest, retiring disposition, and scholarly in his tastes. During the period of his active ministry he found much time for research and writing, and he then laid the foundation for the reputation which he later enjoyed of being one of the best-informed scholars on theological subjects in the country. He was one of the first in America to apply himself to a sedulous study of the German language and literature, especially in the religious field, and was a veritable encyclopedia of information regarding them. Interested in history and biography, he was one of the most active members of the Massachusetts Historical Society, and helped in the preparation of its *Collections,* to which he contributed "Memoir of Rev. John Allyn, D.D., of Duxbury" (3 ser. V, 1836), "Memoir of Gamaliel Bradford, M.D." (3 ser. IX, 1846), and "Memoir of Hon. John Davis, LL.D." (3 ser. X, 1849). In 1830 he published *An Historical Sketch of Watertown, in Massachusetts, from the First Settlement of the Town to the Close of Its Second Century.* For Jared Sparks's *Library of American Biography,* he wrote "Life of John Eliot, the Apostle to the Indians" (Vol. V, 1836), and "Life of Sebastian Rale, Missionary to the Indians" (2 ser. VII, 1845). He also published a number of sermons and historical addresses, and was a frequent contributor to the *Christian Disciple,* the *Christian Examiner,* the *American Monthly Review,* the *Unitarian Advocate,* the *Scriptural Interpreter,* and the *Liberal Preacher.*

[Biographical data may be found in *Proc. Mass. Hist. Soc.,* Apr. 9, 1863, and Mar. 9, 1865. The latter contains a list of Francis's publications. Numerous letters to him from his sister are contained in *Letters of Lydia Maria Child* (1883). See also John Weiss, *Discourse Occasioned by the Death of Convers Francis, D.D., delivered before the First Congreg. Soc., Watertown, Apr. 19, 1863* (1863), and obituaries in *Boston Daily Advertiser,* Apr. 9 and July 15, 1863.]
H. E. S.

FRANCIS, DAVID ROWLAND (Oct. 1, 1850–Jan. 15, 1927), merchant, governor of Missouri, secretary of the interior, ambassador to Russia, was born in Richmond, Ky., the son of John Broaddus and Eliza Caldwell (Rowland) Francis. Both parents were of Kentucky pioneer stock, combining English, Scotch, and Welsh strains. His grandfather, Thomas Francis, was a soldier in the War of 1812; his father had been sheriff of Madison County. David was educated in Rev. Robert Breck's academy for girls, the principal desiring to have a comrade for his own son. By the aid of his mother's brother, David Pitt Rowland, the boy was able to enter Washington University in St. Louis, where he took the four years' classical course, graduating in 1870 with the degree of B.A. He had hoped to study law, but the opportunity was lacking and he returned to the Kentucky farm, until this same uncle found a position for him in the commission house of Shryock & Rowland. Here he not only learned the business of commission merchant, but paid off his college debts, and in six years had accumulated enough capital to found his own house, D. R. Francis & Brother, Commission Company, grain merchants.

His engaging personality made him a marked man in the community. In 1884 he was made president of the Merchants' Exchange; and in the same year was sent as delegate-at-large to the National Democratic Convention at Chicago. In 1885 he was elected mayor of St. Louis, defeating by 1,527 votes a Republican who had been elected four years earlier by a majority of 14,000. He gave the city a business administration, fearlessly cutting expenses and defeating corrupt legislation by his vetoes. At the conclusion of his term of office he was elected governor, serving until 1893. He carried to this office the same business principles and secured from the legislature a series of constructive measures. On the resignation of Secretary Hoke Smith in August 1896, Francis was appointed secretary of the interior and served through the rest of President Cleveland's administration. He was an earnest defender of forest reserves and it was on his recommendation that the president set aside by proclamation some 21,000,000 acres, and refused to sign the sundry civil bill which contained a rider that would have given the president authority subsequently to modify or vacate any executive order creating forest reserves (John Ise, *The United States Forest Policy,* 1920, pp. 129–32). His opposition to Bryan and free-silver cost him political prestige in Missouri and for a decade he was out of politics. In the meantime, however, he took an active part in promoting the Louisiana Purchase Exposition, was elected president of the corporation, and in a trip to Europe by personal solicitation secured the participation of foreign governments—an experience which he recounted in *A Tour of Europe in Nineteen Days* (1903). The history of the exposition he narrated in *The Universal Exposition of 1904* (1913).

In 1908, declaring the free-silver issue closed, he sought party harmony by advocating the nomination of Bryan in the Democratic National Convention at Denver, but refused to consider for himself the second place on the ticket. In 1910, he was a candidate for election to the United States Senate, but was defeated in the Democratic primary by James A. Reed. Though he had declined a diplomatic appointment to one of the South American states, he was nominated ambassador to Russia by President Wilson in 1916, and the nomination was confirmed in open session of the Senate without the customary reference to a committee. His service began under the old régime. After the Russian revolution, he supported the Kerensky provisional government; and under the Bolshevik régime he still stayed on, although given permission to return. He moved the embassy from place to place, lived on trains, appealed to the Russians to stand by the allies, warned against German intrigues, and refused to heed threats of personal violence until even his robust health gave way. On Nov. 6, 1918, he was carried on a stretcher to an American warship and taken to a London hospital for an operation, from which he never fully recovered. In 1876 he had married Jane Perry, daughter of John D. Perry, a pioneer railroad builder. Six sons were born to them, three of whom followed their father's business career.

[Walter B. Stevens, *David R. Francis, Ambassador Extraordinary and Plenipotentiary* (n.d.); Harry B. Hawes, "David Rowland Francis," in *Mo. Hist. Soc. Colls.,* Oct. 1927; St. Louis *Globe-Democrat,* Jan. 16, 1927. Information contained in the books by Francis, cited above; and in his *Russia from the Am. Embassy Apr. 1916–Nov. 1918* (1921) and *David R. Francis, His Recollections and Letters* (1928).] W. B. S—s.

FRANCIS, JAMES BICHENO (May 18, 1815–Sept. 18, 1892), hydraulic engineer, was born at Southleigh, Oxfordshire, England, the son of John Francis and Eliza Frith (Bicheno) Francis. His father was superintendent and constructor of one of the early short railroads in the south of Wales and it was quite natural that his son should be trained to follow in his footsteps. Accordingly after a bit of an education at Radleigh Hall and Wantage Academy in Berkshire, young Francis became assistant to his father at the early age of fourteen on the construction of some canal and harbor works connected with the railroad. Here he remained two years and then was employed by the Great Western Canal Company in construction work, particularly in Devonshire and Somersetshire. After two years with this company and in the hope of finding greater opportunities in America, Francis arrived in New York City in the spring of 1833 and almost immediately was employed by Maj. George W. Whistler, a prominent early American engineer, in the construction of the Stonington Railroad (Connecticut). A year later Whistler became chief engineer of a group known as the "Proprietors of the Locks and Canals on the Merrimack River," organized to expand the company's machine-shop business to include locomotive construction. Francis, then eighteen years old, accompanied Whistler to Lowell, Mass., and entered the service of the proprietors as a draftsman. One of his first tasks was that of dismembering, measuring, and making detailed working drawings of a newly imported locomotive built by Stephenson in England and purchased to serve as a model for the engines of the Boston & Lowell Railroad. This was the beginning of locomotive building in New England. In 1837 Whistler resigned and Francis, at the age of twenty-two, was made his successor. In the course of the succeeding three or four years Francis conducted his office most efficiently, and although there was a decline in locomotive construction, the demand for the design and erection of cotton-mills increased. About 1841 the proprietors undertook through a specially appointed commission to determine the quantities of water drawn by the mills along the canal, and Francis was entrusted with the details of securing the needed data. So well did he conduct this work, involving much original experiment, that when in 1845 his employers decided to give up the machine-shop and confine their full attention to the development of water-power facilities at Lowell, Francis was made chief engineer and general manager. From that time on, for more than forty years, he not only looked after the firm's water-power interests, but acted as consulting engineer to all of the factories using the power. It has always been claimed that Francis was in large part responsible for Lowell's rise to industrial importance. In 1846 he began the work of water-power development by the construction of the Northern Canal. In this, as in all of his subsequent work, he made thorough investigations and conducted many experiments before undertaking actual construction. In 1849, on behalf of the manufacturing interests of Lowell, he went to England to study timber-preservation methods. Upon his return he designed and constructed works at Lowell for both kyanizing and burnettizing timber. About this time Francis turned his attention to hydraulic turbines and designed one based on the Howd patent but with the vanes reshaped to bring about a combination of the radial and axial flow turbine. This type, known as the mixed flow or Francis turbine, is to-day the one most generally used for low head installations. Tests of the design, his simultaneous researches on the flow of water through draft tubes, over weirs, and through short canals, as well as the rules for runner and draft tube design which he formulated were published by Francis in 1855 under the title *The Lowell Hydraulic Experiments.* Much of these data is used in engineering practise at the present time. For the associated companies' benefit Francis devised a complete system of water supply for fire protection purposes and had it in operation in the Lowell district many years before anything equally complete was to be found elsewhere. In 1870 he undertook and completed another notable work, namely, the design and construction of hydraulic lifts for the guard gates of the Pawtucket Canal. Again, between 1875 and 1876, he reconstructed the Pawtucket Dam across the Merrimac River. Francis's fundamental practise of holding closely to experiment caused him to become probably the first person in America to conduct actual tests on large cast-iron girders. His habits of thought were unusually methodical and accurate. These qualities, combined with his insistence upon investigating every question put to him, enabled him to supplement the deficiencies of his early education and training so that he became one of the best equipped engineers of his time. While his duties were most arduous, he found time to write over two hundred valuable papers for various learned societies. He was one of the original members and president in 1874 of the Boston Society of Civil Engineers. He joined the American Society of Civil Engineers at its first meeting in 1852 and was its president in 1880. In addition to his regular duties in Lowell, he was consulted in the construction of the Quaker Bridge Dam on the Croton River, N. Y., and the retaining dam at St. Anthony's Falls on the Mississippi River. He was a member of the Massachusetts state legislature for one year; served five years in the Lowell city council; was for twenty years president of the Stonybrook Railroad, and for forty-three years a director of the Lowell Gas Light Company. As an engineer, referee, and expert, Francis was probably called upon to decide more varied questions of importance than usually falls to the lot of one man. This was due to his strength of character, solidity, and strong common sense. He married Sarah Wilbur Brownell of Lowell on July 12, 1837. One of his sons succeeded him upon his retirement from active business in 1885, and at the time of his death in Lowell he was survived by his wife and six children.

[*Jour. Asso. Engineering Socs.*, Jan. 1894; *Proc. Am. Soc. Civil Engineers*, vol. XIX (1893); *Proc. Am. Acad. of Arts and Sci.*, n.s., vol. XX (1893); *Contributions of the Old Residents' Hist. Asso., Lowell, Mass.*, vol. V, pp. 2 (1894); F. W. Coburn, *Hist. of Lowell and Its People* (1920), vol. I; *Boston Transcript*, Sept. 19, 1892.]

C. W. M.

FRANCIS, JOHN BROWN (May 31, 1791–Aug. 9, 1864), governor of Rhode Island, United States senator, was the son of John and Abby (Brown) Francis, and a great-grandson of

Tench Francis [*q.v.*]. He was born in Philadelphia, Pa., but shortly thereafter his father established his residence in Providence, R. I. There the elder Francis soon died and the son went to live with his grandfather, John Brown [*q.v.*], a prominent Providence merchant. Young Francis prepared for college at the university grammar school, then entered Brown University, from which he graduated in 1808. He spent some time in the office of the Providence firm of Brown & Ives, and afterwards entered the Law School at Litchfield, Conn. Upon the death of his grandfather he inherited the estate of the latter and to its management he devoted some years. In 1821 he made his home at Spring Green, Warwick, R. I., the country seat of the Browns. His first wife was a cousin, Anne Carter Brown, only daughter of Nicholas Brown [*q.v.*], whom he married on June 18, 1822. She died in 1828 and on May 22, 1832, he married Elizabeth Willing Francis Harrison, who was also a cousin, the daughter of Thomas Willing Francis of Philadelphia. Francis represented Warwick in the Rhode Island General Assembly as a member of the House of Representatives from 1825 to 1829 and as senator from 1831 to 1832. In January 1831 he was nominated for governor by the National Republican party. He declined the nomination, but was given such a strong endorsement by the National Republican press that when brought forward for governor, nearly two years later, by the Anti-Masons and Democrats, the mouths of the National Republicans were stopped. He retired from the governorship in 1838. On the outbreak of the Dorr Rebellion in 1842 he was appointed by Gov. King one of three commissioners to proceed to Washington to solicit President Tyler's aid in maintaining the state constitutional officers in authority. In the same year he was elected to the state Senate as a representative of the Law and Order party, opposed to Thomas Wilson Dorr. Two years later, upon the resignation of William Sprague, United States senator from Rhode Island, Francis was made his successor. His term expired in March 1845, whereupon he was returned to the Rhode Island Senate, to which body he was reëlected annually until 1856. Francis was a man of genial temperament and was highly esteemed. He was greatly interested in education in Rhode Island and exerted upon it a strong influence. He was a life member of the Rhode Island Society for the Encouragement of Domestic Industry; treasurer of the Rhode Island Historical Society and one of its vice-presidents; from 1828 to 1857 a trustee of Brown University; and from 1841 to 1854 chancellor of the institution. He died at Warwick.

[C. E. Francis, *Francis: Descendants of Robt. Francis of Wethersfield, Conn.* (1906); Edward Field, ed., *State of R. I. and Providence Plantations* (3 vols., 1912); *Proc. R. I. Hist. Soc.*, 1872–73; *The Biog. Cyc. of Representative Men of R. I.* (1881); C. P. Keith, *The Provincial Councillors of Pa.* (1883); C. P. Fuller, *The Hist. of Warwick, R. I.* (1875); *Providence Daily Jour.*, Aug. 10, 1864.]

I. B. R.

FRANCIS, JOHN MORGAN (Mar. 6, 1823–June 18, 1897), editor, publicist, diplomat, was born at Prattsburg, N. Y., the son of Richard and Mary (Stewart) Francis. From his father, a midshipman in the British navy who emigrated to America in 1795, married, and settled in Steuben County, N. Y., he inherited the rugged physique characteristic of the family. Since he was next to the youngest of thirteen children, he received little formal education. His training as a journalist, however, provided him with an excellent background for a successful career. Beginning at fifteen as an apprentice on the *Ontario Messenger*, at Canandaigua, N. Y., he served successively in the editorial departments of the *Wayne Sentinel* and the *Rochester Daily Advertiser*. On Dec. 8, 1846, he married a woman of considerable literary talent, Harriet Elizabeth Tucker, daughter of Pomeroy Tucker, editor of the *Sentinel*, and established himself in Troy as editor-in-chief of the *Northern Budget*. While connected with the *Budget*, a Democratic paper, of which he eventually became joint proprietor, he advocated the claims of the Free-Soil party. In 1849 he sold his interests and removed to New York to engage in business. He soon returned to Troy, however, to take charge of the *Daily Whig*; and in 1851 he founded the *Troy Daily Times*, with R. D. Thompson as partner. When the latter withdrew in 1853, he became the sole owner. Under his hands the *Times* was one of the leading papers of the state. Realizing the importance of local news, he stressed it consistently, and by the consequent popularity of the paper he contributed much to the strength of the Republican party, which he joined on its inception. In his devotion to the Union he never wavered. As a result the building occupied by the *Times* was sacked by a mob during the draft riots of 1863. Publication was suspended, however, for only a day; and the paper continued to gain in influence. When Francis died, he was succeeded by his son, Charles Spencer Francis [*q.v.*].

Although he never swerved from the ideals in which he believed, he was essentially practical in his approach toward public affairs. In New York he was a member of the state constitutional conventions of 1867–68 and 1894, in both of which he played a prominent part. In national politics he was also an influential figure. In 1856 he was a delegate to the first convention of the Republican party, and at the convention of 1880 he was one of the "die-hards" who supported President Grant. In recognition of his Republicanism he had been appointed in 1871 minister to Greece, where he remained for three years. After a tour of the world, he again engaged in politics. In 1881 President Garfield, to whom he had transferred his allegiance, included his name as minister to Belgium in his tentative list of appointments, but did not live to make the nomination. President Arthur, embarrassed by other commitments, named him to the post at Lisbon. In 1884 he was promoted to the mission at Vienna. He resigned the following year.

[C. E. Francis, *Francis: Descendants of Robt. Francis of Wethersfield, Conn.* (1906), p. 194; files of the *Troy Daily Times,* especially the supplement of June 25, 1901, and the anniversary issue of June 25, 1926; a memorial volume published in 1897, containing sketches, appreciations, and reprints of newspaper obituaries; the volumes of reminiscences by his wife, especially *By Land and Sea* (1891); Rutherford Hayner, *Troy and Rensselaer County, N. Y.* (3 vols., 1925); Geo. B. Anderson, *Landmarks of Rensselaer County* (1897); N. B. Sylvester, *Hist. of Rensselaer County, N. Y.* (1880); *N. Y. Times,* June 19, 1897; *Northern Budget,* June 20, 1897.] R. P. B—r.

FRANCIS, JOHN WAKEFIELD (Nov. 17, 1789–Feb. 8, 1861), physician, was born in New York City, the son of Melchior Francis, a German immigrant, whose death made it necessary for the boy to apprentice himself early in life to George Long, a printer. He had a natural bent for study, however, and after expert tutoring by two Irish clergymen he was able to enter Columbia College in 1807, with advanced standing. Upon his graduation in 1809 he at once began the study of medicine under David Hosack [*q.v.*]. Entering the new College of Physicians and Surgeons he became its first graduate (in 1811) and forthwith accepted a partnership with his preceptor, which continued until 1820. Appointed lecturer in medicine and materia medica in the College of Physicians and Surgeons, he voluntarily served without fees. When the school merged with the Medical Department of Columbia, he was given professorships in both subjects and spent the year 1816–17 studying in Europe. Upon his return he was given a third chair, that of forensic medicine, to which was added in 1819 a fourth, obstetrics. Meanwhile, from 1810 to 1814, with Hosack, he edited the *American Medical and Philosophical Register.* On the way to becoming New York's foremost obstetrician, he published in 1821 an edition of Thomas Denman's *Introduction to the Practice of Midwifery.* In 1826, with four others, he entered upon the work of establishing the new Rutgers Medical College, but owing to litigation the venture was short-lived. During the four years of the school's existence, however, he taught obstetrics and forensic medicine. On Nov. 16, 1829, he married Maria Eliza Cutler of Boston. His income had now reached $15,000 annually and probably never fell below that figure. In 1830 he formally retired from teaching and for some years remained devoted to his practise and numerous avocations. He was interested in many different attempts to promote the general welfare; with Drs. Mott and Stearns, he founded the New York Academy of Medicine (1846) and was its second president (1847–48); in the fifties he lent James Marion Sims [*q.v.*] the aid which made it possible to establish the Woman's Hospital; he was largely responsible for the founding of the State Inebriate Asylum at Binghamton; toward the close of his career, shortly before the opening of the Bellevue Hospital Medical College, he gave clinical instruction in the wards of Bellevue Hospital. He was pronounced by Dr. Marshall Hall while on a visit to New York, the most representative physician of his generation.

Outside the field of his profession, his prominence as an officer or honorary member of ethnological, fine arts, historical, typographical, horticultural, and antiquarian societies, and his countless personal charities, made "our learned and jolly Dr. Francis" (*The Diary of Philip Hone,* 1889, II, 210) one of the best-known and best-loved figures in New York. Compared by contemporaries both to Dr. Johnson and to Dr. Franklin, he possessed remarkable powers of observation and memory, was enthusiastically interested in the progress of science, and a devoted lover of letters. Though he had little time for methodical reading, he bought books constantly, delighted in literary conversation, "and seemed to regard attendance, without fee or reward, upon authors, artists, and actors, the highest privilege of his profession" (Tuckerman, *post,* p. xli). His own writings, in addition to several medical papers, consisted largely of biographical sketches and occasional addresses. His anniversary discourse, delivered before the New York Historical Society, Nov. 17, 1857, was published in enlarged form under the title *Old New York; or, Reminiscences of the Past Sixty Years* (1858; 1866). Reflecting as it does his many literary friendships, it is a valuable source for the social and literary history of the city during the period of his lifetime. Samuel Ward Francis [*q.v.*], was his son.

[H. T. Tuckerman, "Biog. Essay," in *Old New York* (ed. 1866); Valentine Mott, *Eulogy on the late John W. Francis* (1861), A. K. Gardner, *Eulogy on John W. Francis* (1861); H. M. Storer, in *Memorial Biogs. of the New-Eng. Hist. Geneal. Soc.,* vol. IV (1885); E. A. Duyckinck in *Hist. Mag.,* Apr. 1861.] E. P.

FRANCIS, JOSEPH (Mar. 12, 1801–May 10, 1893), inventor, manufacturer, was born in Boston, Mass., the son of Thomas and Margaret Francis. Until he was eleven years old Francis enjoyed the normal boy's life, but in 1812 his father died and to help support his widowed mother and six other children Francis became a page in the Massachusetts state Senate, remaining there four years. His particular interest, however, had always been in boats, especially unsinkable ones, and he is said to have built one with cork in its ends when only eleven years old, which with four men aboard could not be sunk. From 1816 to 1819, through the kindness of a near relative who was engaged in the boat-building business, Francis was given a corner of the plant for his experiments and succeeded in building there a fast rowboat with this unsinkable feature in it. He exhibited it at the Mechanics Institute Fair in Boston that year and received "honorable recognition." Hoping to find a market in New York, Francis went there in 1820 but for years was unsuccessful either in obtaining orders for life-boats or in finding any one to stake him in his experimental work. At last, around 1837, he produced a wooden boat which withstood the severest tests ship-owners could devise, and Francis's name was made. Almost immediately orders for boats were received from many European countries and from within the United States. After patenting the idea in 1838 and contracting with the Novelty Iron Works of New York to manufacture the boats, Francis turned to further experimenting. In the years that followed he invented and built many kinds of boats: portable, screw boats, molded boats, "hydrogiene" life-boats, launches, cargo boats, and double or reversed-bottom boats. Within fifteen years practically every craft sailing out of New York harbor swung Francis life-boats from its davits.

As early as 1838 Francis had in mind the invention of a boat adaptable for saving life on wrecked vessels, and about 1840 had constructed a decked-over boat of wood to run back and forth on a hawser between ship and shore. Actual tests, however, indicated that wood was not strong enough to withstand the force of heavy seas and Francis thereupon turned to metal. He found that flat iron plates likewise were unsuitable, but became convinced that these same plates when corrugated would possess ample strength for his purpose. He was then faced with the additional difficulties not only of manufacturing corrugated metal but of shaping the corrugated sheet to the irregular curves of a boat. After four years of tedious, discouraging, and costly work, he solved the problem through the use of cast-iron dies which he himself designed, and was granted a patent Mar. 25, 1845, for the use of corrugated metal in the construction of all boats and vessels. His first successful corrugated iron life-boat made in accordance with his patented process is preserved in the National Museum at Washington. While he was engaged in this work, the International Shipwreck Society for All Nations, under the direct patronage of the King of France, made him a "benefactor," and in 1843 both the French and English sections of the society requested him to form an American section. The result was that through his efforts the American Shipwreck and Humane Society was organized out of which grew the United States Life-saving Service.

Two years after Francis had obtained the patent on his corrugated metal boat, the Novelty Iron Works built what was considered a perfect life-boat. Three years passed, however, before an opportunity came to test it. The boat had been placed at one of the life-saving stations on the New Jersey coast and in January 1850 the British ship *Ayrshire,* with two hundred passengers aboard, was wrecked off Squan Beach. Through the use of Francis's life-boat all but one of the passengers were rescued. Between 1850 and 1855 Francis worked constantly on the application of his corrugated metal patent to a variety of devices including water-tight army wagons for river crossings. Models of these reached various parts of Europe, resulting in orders from Italy, Russia, Brazil, Germany, and England, as well as from the military service of the United States. In 1855 Francis went abroad and remained there approximately eight years. In France, Austria, and Russia he gave exhibits of his life-saving apparatus and military boat-wagons and granted concessions for the manufacture of his inventions in England and Germany. One of his greatest accomplishments while in Europe was the construction of a fleet of light-draft corrugated iron steamers for the Russian government, which unassembled were transported over the Ural Mountains to the Aral Sea in Asia. There they were assembled and successfully put into service. Subsequently Francis established a manufactory for corrugated iron steamers in Russia. Upon his return to the United States in 1863, he continued his researches, extending the application of his corrugated metal patent to floating docks and harbor buoys. He invented among other things a metallic cloth hood for sentinels in a storm, a circular yacht, and a table joist car-lock. For his inventions and services he received numerous medals (now in the National Museum at Washington), gifts, and decorations both at home and abroad, among which were a congressional medal of gold, presented by President Harrison in 1890; the Franklin Institute medal, 1854; a gold medal from King Ferdinand III of Sicily; a gold snuff-box, diamond-studded, from Napoleon III in 1856; and the Royal Order of Knighthood of St. Stanislaus from the Czar of Russia. With increasing age Francis devoted most of his time to travel and philanthropic activities, spending his summers in the Great Lakes region and his winters in New York. He wrote and published in 1885 *A History of Life-Saving Appliances.* His wife was Ellen Creamer of Salem, Mass., and at the time of his death at Cooperstown, N. Y., he was survived by an only son. He was buried in Minneapolis, Minn.

[Jos. Francis, *Hist. of Life-Saving Appliances* (1885); Jas. L. Pond, *Hist. of Life-Saving Appliances . . . Manufactured by Jos. Francis: with Sketches and Incidents of his Business Life . . .* (1885); *Francis' Metallic Life-Boat Co.* (1852, 1853); *Harper's New Monthly Mag.*, July 1851; *Lippincott's Mag.*, Jan. 1885; *Sci. American*, May 20, 1893; *Boston Transcript*, May 11, 1893; National Museum Records; Patent Office Records.] C. W. M.

FRANCIS, SAMUEL WARD (Dec. 26, 1835–Mar. 25, 1886), physician, author, was a son of Maria Eliza Cutler and John W. Francis [*q.v.*] of New York City. His mother was an aunt of Julia Ward Howe [*q.v.*]. For many years the Ward and Francis families lived as one household at the corner of Bond Street and Broadway, New York. Samuel Ward Francis was named for his maternal grandfather, an eminent banker. His own father, a man of German descent, was one of the best-known New York physicians of his day, and had an unusual range of acquaintance with the writers and scientists of the period. The boy grew up in a home which was famed as a meeting-place of authors, artists, and professional folk. Receiving his B.A. degree at Columbia College in 1857, he decided to study medicine and spent three years at the Medical Department of the University of the City of New York, taking the degree of M.D. in 1860. In the preceding year he had married Harriet H. McAllister of California.

Belonging to a family of physicians, with a father and two brothers who were members of that profession, Francis seems to have prepared with zest for a career in medicine and surgery, but that did not by any means absorb his energies or his mental activities. In the year of his graduation from college he took out a patent on a "printing machine" which in several essential points anticipated the typewriter by almost twenty years. The principal feature of this contrivance is said to have consisted in arranging a row of hammers in a circle, so that when put in motion they would strike in the same place. A piano keyboard was connected. "The paper is moved along by means of a spring and catch, so connected with the keys that it shall move the paper a distance of one letter whenever a key is struck. On the face of each hammer a letter is cut in relief, in such a position that its impression on the paper will be parallel with those of the others. At the end of each line the 'car' which carries the paper is drawn back by the hand" (*Report of the Commissioner of Patents*, 1857, II, 437). The machine had a complicated and heavy type-bar action, but it had features which later inventors employed to advantage, such as the principle of a type guide (C. V. Oden, *Evolution of the Typewriter*, 1917, p. 15).

Having inherited his father's facility in writing, Francis early in his career produced several works of interest to his profession. *Biographical Sketches of Distinguished Living New York Surgeons* (1866) and *Biographical Sketches of Distinguished Living New York Physicians* (1867) appeared while the author was in his early thirties. Later he wrote several essays and novels which included: *Inside Out; A Curious Book* (1862); *Life and Death; A Novel* (1871); *Curious Facts, concerning Man and Nature* (1874–75); and *Memoir of the Life and Character of Prof. Valentine Mott* (1865). In 1863 Francis went to Newport, R. I., to live and to practise his profession. He was there for the remaining twenty-three years of his life, with the exception of some time spent in travel. He took an active part in the Sanitary Protection Association founded in 1878, resulting in the creation of the Newport Board of Health. During the twenty-one years, beginning in 1858, he received patents on sixteen inventions, including a machine for canceling postage stamps (1863), a heating and ventilating device for railroad-cars (1868), a sewing-machine (1875), a signal for telephone and telegraph lines (1879), and various lesser contrivances.

[The *Medic. Record*, Apr. 3, 1886; *Trans. R. I. Medic. Soc.*, vol. III, pt. IV (1886); *Am. Phrenological Jour.*, Dec. 1857; *Providence Jour.*, Mar. 26, 27, 1886; annual reports of the commissioner of patents, 1857–79.] W. B. S—w.

FRANCIS, TENCH (d. Aug. 16, 1758), lawyer, was a descendant of Philip Francis, Mayor of Plymouth, England, in 1642, and the son of John Francis, dean of Lismore, Ireland, and rector of St. Mary's Church, Dublin, who married a Miss Tench. His brother, Philip, was the father of Sir Philip Francis, the reputed author of the Junius Letters. Despite the fact that he attained eminence in after life, held high office and became the undisputed leader of the Pennsylvania bar of his time, very little is known of the intimate details of his life (Eastman, *post*). He was born in Ireland, probably in Dublin, but the date is unknown and no details of his childhood are available. He received his education in England, studied law in London, and went to America before 1720 in the capacity of attorney for Lord Baltimore, taking up his residence in Kent County, Md., where he opened a law office. From 1726 to 1734 he was clerk of Talbot County Court, in which latter year he was elected burgess for Talbot County in the Maryland Assembly, continuing a member of the legislature for three years. In 1736 he became deputy commissary-general and registrar of wills of Talbot County, an office which he held till 1738. In the latter year he moved to Philadelphia, and there acquired an extensive practise. He had not only a profound knowledge of law but a natural gift of eloquence as well, which placed him in a class by himself as an advocate. As a consequence, in the brief space of three years he became recognized as the leader of the bar throughout the state. In 1741 he was appointed attorney-general of Pennsylvania. In this position he maintained his high reputation, and during his tenure of office labored unceasingly to maintain the effective and impartial administration of the law within his jurisdiction. He acted as one of the Pennsylvania representatives on the joint commission to adjust the boundaries of that province and Maryland in 1750. In the same year he was appointed recorder of Philadelphia and despite the heavy nature of his responsibilities, continued to perform the duties of both his offices with eminent success for five years. When he retired in 1755 his health had been undermined by his strenuous labors. At the time of his death in Philadelphia, Franklin's *Pennsylvania Gazette* stated that he had served the province "with the highest Reputation." He married Elizabeth, daughter of Foster Turbutt of "Ottwell," Talbot County, Dec. 29, 1724, "under romantic circumstances" (O. Tilghman, *post*). His daughter, Margaret, married Chief Justice Edward Shippen [*q.v.*]; a grandson, Col. Tench Tilghman, was one of Washington's aides, and a great-grandson, John Brown Francis [*q.v.*], was governor of Rhode Island.

[C. E. Francis, *Francis: Descendants of Robt. Francis of Wethersfield, Conn.* (1906); Oswald Tilghman, *Hist. of Talbot County, Md.* (2 vols., 1915); F. M. Eastman, *Courts and Lawyers of Pa.* (1922), I, 253; C. P. Keith, *The Provincial Councillor* (1883); J. H. Martin, *Bench and Bar of Philadelphia* (1883); F. N. Thorpe, *Benj. Franklin and the Univ. of Pa.* (1893); *Pa. Gazette*, Aug. 24, 1758.] H. W. H. K.

FRANCKE, KUNO (Sept. 27, 1855–June 25, 1930), historian, philologist, was born in Kiel, the son of Judge August Wilhelm S. and Katharine Marie (Jensen) Francke. After attending the Gymnasium of his native city he studied from 1873 to 1878 at the Universities of Kiel, Berlin, Jena, and Munich and came under the influence of Friedrich Paulsen, Rudolf Eucken, Michael Bernays, Erwin Rohde, Wilhelm von Giesebrecht, and Heinrich von Brunn. Taking his degree in 1878 at Munich with a dissertation *Zur Geschichte der Lateinischen Schulpoesie des XII. and XIII. Jahrhunderts* (Munich, 1879), he spent a year in Italy as recipient of the König Ludwig Stipendium in history, taught from 1880 to 1882 in the Kiel Gymnasium, publishing a study *De Hymni in Cererem Homerici Compositione, Dictione, Aetate* (Kiel, 1881), and then became an assistant editor, under Georg Waitz, of the *Monumenta Germaniae Historica.* His contribution to that great series is to be found in the first two volumes of the *Libelli de Lite Imperatorum et Pontificum Saeculis XI. et XII.* (1891–92). In 1884, through his friend Ephraim Emerton, he was called to Harvard University as instructor in German and began teaching that autumn, with Bernard Berenson among his first pupils. He was advanced to assistant professor in 1887, to associate professor in 1892, and to professor of the history of German culture in 1896. On June 27, 1889, he married Katharine Gilbert of Gilbertsville, N. Y., who with two of their three children survived him. In 1891 he became an American citizen. In 1896 appeared his most widely read book, *Social Forces in German Literature,* which in 1901 was renamed *History of German Literature as Determined by Social Forces.* His *Kulturwerte der Deutschen Literatur in ihrer Geschichtlichen Entwicklung* (vol. I, Berlin, 1910; vol. II, 1923) covers the same field in greater detail. *Weltbürgertum in der Deutschen Literatur von Herder bis Nietzsche* (Berlin, 1928) was to form part of the third volume, which was left incomplete at the author's death. Francke's scholarship was wide and accurate and illumined by a poetic idealism and a broad humanity, but his originality lies in his grasp of the principle that literary history is inseparable from the general history of culture. His other publications, besides numerous contributions to newspapers, magazines, and scholarly periodicals, include: *Glimpses of Modern German Culture* (1898); *German Ideals of To-day* (1907); *A German-American's Confession of Faith* (1915); *The German Spirit* (1916); *Personality in German Literature before Luther* (1916); *Deutsches Schicksal* (Dresden, 1923)—his only published volume of poetry; *German After-War Problems* (1927); and *Deutsche Ar-*

beit in Amerika (Leipzig, 1930)— an autobiography. He was editor-in-chief of *German Classics of the XIX and XX Centuries* (1913–14). In 1902, with generous support from Adolphus Busch of St. Louis, Hugo Reisinger of New York, and the German Emperor, he founded the Germanic Museum at Harvard, of which he was curator until 1917 and honorary curator thereafter. During the European War (1914–18) he bore himself with perfect dignity and sanity, submitting to vehement denunciation from all sides, to spying and letter-opening, and to ostracism by men who had been his friends for years. It was characteristic of him that he wrote his reminiscences of this period without bitterness and without pride. Retiring from Harvard University in 1917, he withdrew to his country retreat at Gilbertsville, N. Y., and devoted himself to writing the second volume of his *Kulturwerte,* traversing the period from the Reformation to the Enlightenment and accomplishing what he himself regarded as his best work in literary history. A few years later he again enjoyed public regard as the most distinguished Germanist in America. He was also a poet of distinction. He was a close and sympathetic student of American culture, and to the *Dictionary of American Biography,* of which he was a valued friend, he contributed the article on his Harvard predecessor, Charles Follen [*q.v.*]. He died at Cambridge, Mass., after a brief illness and was buried at Gilbertsville.

[Kuno Francke, *Deutsche Arbeit in Amerika* (Leipzig, 1930); Arthur Davison Ficke, "The Recollections of Kuno Francke," *Harvard Grads.' Mag.,* June 1930; S. E. Morison, *Development of Harvard Univ. 1869–1929* (1930), with portrait; *Deutsche Zeitgenossen-Lexikon* (Leipzig, 1905); *Who's Who in America,* 1930–31; *Nation* (N. Y.), July 9, 1930; *Saturday Rev. of Literature,* July 5, 1930; *N. Y. Times,* June 26, 1930.]

G. H. G.

FRANKLAND, LADY AGNES SURRIAGE (1726–Apr. 23, 1783), wife of Sir Charles Henry Frankland, Bart., was born at Marblehead, Mass., the fourth of the eight children of Edward and Mary (Pierce) Surriage, and was baptized Apr. 17, 1726. Her father was a poor fisherman, her mother a grand-daughter of John Brown, an affluent London merchant, who settled at Pemaquid (now Bristol, Me.) in 1625 and bought a tract of land, later known as the Brown Right, from the Indians. Agnes became a maid-of-all-work at the Fountain Inn in Marblehead, where in the summer of 1742 her black ringlets, black eyes, and smooth complexion aroused the interest of Charles Henry Frankland (May 10, 1716–Jan. 11, 1768) who from 1741 to 1757 was collector of the port of Boston. According to family tradition, Agnes was scrubbing the tavern floor when they first saw each other, and Frankland, noting the girl's scanty dress and bare feet, gave her a crown to buy her a pair of shoes. Impressed by her beauty and intelligence, he persuaded her parents to let the girl be educated in Boston at his expense. In 1746, by the death of his uncle, Sir Thomas Frankland, Member of Parliament and a Lord of the Admiralty, he succeeded to the baronetcy of Thirsk in the North Riding of Yorkshire. About this time Agnes Surriage became his mistress. The liaison created scandal; and Frankland, to shield the girl from insult, bought 480 acres at Hopkinton, built a mansion, and lived with her there until 1754, when Frankland returned to England to help settle a family lawsuit. His family did not welcome Miss Surriage. Frankland next took up his residence at Lisbon. On Nov. 1, 1755, the city was destroyed by an earthquake, "on which day," Frankland recorded in his journal, "I was providentially saved. I was buried in ruins. . . . Hope my providential escape will have a lasting good effect upon my mind." He thereupon married Agnes Surriage, who, according to the family story, had effected his rescue. On their return to England she was received cordially by his family and friends. They lived in Massachusetts again from 1756 to 1758, their Boston house being the Clarke mansion on Garden Court Street and Bell Alley, described in Fenimore Cooper's *Lionel Lincoln*; and Lady Frankland became at once one of the leaders of Boston society. She was a woman of great charm and refinement. Not the least of her graces was the unfailing love and kindness that she showed to her family and to the friends of her girlhood. Later they returned to Lisbon, where Frankland served as British consul-general. After her husband's death Lady Frankland came back to the Hopkinton estate, on which she lived until the outbreak of the Revolution forced her to remove to Boston and thence to England. Her estate, in spite of her Loyalist sympathies, was not confiscated. In 1782 she married John Drew, a wealthy banker of Chichester. She died the next year and was buried in St. Pancras' Church in Chichester. Her story has been told by Oliver Wendell Holmes in the ballad of "Agnes" in *Songs in Many Keys* (1861) and by Edwin Lassetter Bynner in a novel, *Agnes Surriage* (1886, 1923).

[Elias Nason, *Sir Chas. Henry Frankland, Baronet* (Albany, N. Y., 1865); N. P. Sanborn, *The Fountain Inn: Agnes Surriage and Sir Harry Frankland* (Marblehead Hist. Soc., 1905); Frankland's Journal is in the library of the Mass. Hist. Soc.]

G. H. G.

FRANKLIN, BENJAMIN (Jan. 17, 1706–Apr. 17, 1790), printer, author, philanthropist, inventor, statesman, diplomat, scientist, was born in Milk Street, Boston. His father, Josiah, came to New England "about 1682" (moving from Banbury to Boston, 1685) from Ecton, Northamptonshire, England, where the parish records of his Protestant ancestors run back to 1555 (Smyth, *The Writings of Benjamin Franklin,* I, 228; III, 453). His mother, second wife of Josiah, was Abiah, the daughter of Peter Folger, a man of liberal views who taught the Indians to read and wrote some doggerel verse (*A Looking Glass for the Times*). Benjamin was the tenth son of Josiah, and the youngest son of the youngest son for five generations. He learned to read at a very early age, probably taught by his father who destined him for the church as "the tithe of his sons," and sent him at eight years to the Boston Grammar School. The expense proving too great, he was transferred within less than a year to George Brownell's school for writing and arithmetic. At the age of ten he was taken into his father's business (tallow chandler and soap boiler). Disliking this, he was apprenticed at twelve years to his half-brother, James, a printer, who later (1721) started the *New England Courant,* the fourth newspaper established in the British colonies. In 1722 James was "taken up, censur'd, and imprisoned for a month." During this time the paper was issued under the management of Benjamin, his status as apprentice being concealed by a "flimsy" (dishonest) device (*Writings,* I, 248). Repeated quarrels with his brother led Benjamin to leave Boston for Philadelphia, where he arrived in October 1723, at the age of seventeen.

At this early age Benjamin was already an expert printer, and had begun that close application to reading, writing, reflection, and self-improvement which, continued through life, was one secret of his intellectual eminence and of his practical success. Besides a few books in his father's house, he had access to the small library of Matthew Adams. Bunyan, Plutarch, Defoe, and Cotton Mather came his way. Tyron's book on "vegetable diet" interested him. Cocker's arithmetic, Seller's work on navigation, and an English grammar (Greenwood?) were studied. Locke's *Essay,* some works of Shaftesbury and Collins, Xenophon's *Memorabilia,* the "Art of Thinking by Messrs. du Port Royal"—all of these were pored over and reflected upon to some purpose. By some happy chance he bought an odd volume of Addison's *Spectator,* which he read "over and over," the style of which he thought "excellent, and wished, if possible, to imitate." Making notes of the ideas in several papers, he laid them by, and after some days "try'd to compleat the papers again. . . . Then I compared my *Spectator* with the original, discovered some of my faults, and corrected them" (*Writings,* I, 241). Thus playing the "sedulous ape," the boy acquired a vocabulary and fashioned his style. One day he composed a labored "essay," signed it Silence Dogood, and secretly slipped it under the door of his brother's shop. To his great delight it was printed. Others followed, fourteen in all—his earliest publications, crude indeed but characteristic.

Franklin arrived in Philadelphia with one Dutch dollar and a copper shilling. Obtaining employment in the print-shop of Samuel Keimer, he soon demonstrated his ability and made a circle of friends. Through his brother-in-law, Robert Holmes, he fell under the notice of the eccentric Gov. Keith, who urged him to set up for himself and sent him off to London to buy equipment, promising him letters of credit for the purpose. In London (1724), no letters of credit being forthcoming, Franklin found employment at Palmer's (later at Watts's) printing-house. At the former he set up William Wollaston's *The Religion of Nature Delineated* (1725) which inspired him to write and print a refutation—*A Dissertation on Liberty and Necessity, Pleasure and Pain* (1725), in which he presented, cleverly for a boy, the current theory of necessity. He returned to Philadelphia in October 1726, with Mr. Denham, a Quaker merchant, in whose shop he served as clerk, learning accounts and becoming "expert in selling." Upon the sudden death of Denham, Franklin was once more employed by Keimer, but in 1728 left him to form a partnership with Hugh Meredith. In 1730 he became sole owner of the business, including *The Pennsylvania Gazette* (founded in 1728 by Keimer) which Franklin and Meredith had purchased in 1729.

Established in business on his own at the age of twenty-four, Franklin settled down. On Sept. 1, 1730, he "took to wife" Deborah Read, the daughter of his first landlady. Since she was already married to a certain Rogers who had deserted her (never afterwards heard of) the marriage was a common-law union. To them two children were born: Francis Folger (1732–1736), and Sarah (1744–1808), later the wife of Richard Bache. Franklin had besides two illegitimate children: William Franklin, later governor of New Jersey and a Loyalist during the Revolution, and a daughter. Franklin's wife was an illiterate person (*Writings,* X, 289; S. G. Fisher, *True Benjamin Franklin,* p. 116), incapable of sharing, or even of understanding, the importance of his intellectual interests. But she was devoted to him, even taking William Franklin to live in the house for a time, and by her industry and thrift contributed to his material comfort and welfare. "She proved a good and faithful helpmate, assisted me much by attending the shop; we throve together, and have ever mutually endeavor'd to make each other happy" (*Writings,* I, 311). Marrying chiefly in order to relieve the strain of youthful passion, Franklin thus makes the best of a bad business.

From 1730 to 1748 Franklin applied himself to business, won a competence, and laid the foundation of his fame at home and abroad. Industry and thrift contributed to the prosperity of his business. "In order to secure my credit and character as a tradesman, I took care not only to be in *reality* industrious and frugal, but to avoid all appearance to the contrary. I drest plainly; I was seen at no places of idle diversion. I never went out a fishing or shooting; a book, indeed, sometimes debauch'd me from my work, but that was seldom, snug, and gave no scandal; and, to show that I was not above my business, I sometimes brought home the paper I purchas'd at the stores thro' the streets on a wheel-barrow" (*Writings,* I, 307–08). But the chief reason for his success was his capacity for making friends, influential and otherwise, his uncanny instinct for advertising himself and his paper, and above all the sense, novelty, and charm of the things he wrote for it. Nothing better exhibits the man, or better illustrates his ingenuity as an advertiser, than *Poor Richard's Almanack* (1732–57). "Richard Saunders," the Philomath of the *Almanack,* was the Sir Roger de Coverley of the masses, pilfering the world's store of aphorisms, and adapting them to the circumstances and the understanding of the poor. "Necessity never made a good bargain." "It is hard for an empty sack to stand upright." "Many dishes make diseases." "The used key is always bright." The *Almanack* was immediately successful, and commonly sold about ten thousand copies. "As poor Richard says" became a current phrase, used to give weight to any counsel of thrift. The work made Franklin's name a household word throughout the colonies, and gave a homespun flavor to American humor. The introduction to the last *Almanack* (Father Abraham's speech at the auction) spread the fame of Poor Richard in Europe. It was printed in broadsides and posted on walls in England, and, in translation, distributed by the French clergy among their parishioners. It has been translated into fifteen languages, and reprinted at least four hundred times.

Although in origin a business venture, Poor Richard was a genuine expression of Franklin's passion for improving himself and others. He was forever laboring consciously to perfect his mind and his character. He taught himself (beginning in 1733) to read French, Spanish, Italian, and Latin. In 1727 he established the "Junto," a debating club devoted to the discussion of morals, politics, and natural philosophy. He was easily the best informed and the most skilled in discussion. At first he was inclined to be argumentative, given to laying traps for his opponents (a trick learned from Socrates), in order to show up their errors or stupidities. Finding this not useful, since it got him disliked and only confirmed his opponents in their opinions, he deliberately adopted the habit of expressing himself "in terms of modest diffidence; never using . . . the words *certainly, undoubtedly,* . . . but rather say, I conceive or apprehend, . . . or, *it is so, if I am not mistaken.* This habit, I believe, has been of great advantage to me when I have had occasion to inculcate my opinions" (*Writings,* I, 244, 338). Thus early in life Franklin trained himself in the fine art of inducing others to appropriate as their own the ideas or the projects which he wished to have prevail.

In the same pragmatic way Franklin set about devising a religion for the practise of the useful virtues. He regretted his youthful essay on *Liberty and Necessity,* suspecting, from sad experience, that a materialistic doctrine, "tho' it might be true, was not very useful." It seemed to him far more useful to believe in God and to infer that "though certain actions might not be bad *because* they were forbidden [by Revelation] . . . yet probably these actions might be forbidden *because* they were bad" (*Writings,* I, 296). At the age of twenty-two he drafted "Articles of Belief and Acts of Religion" (*Ibid.,* II, 91). The substance of the creed which he held throughout his life was that the one God, who made all things and governs the world through his providence, ought to be worshipped by adoration, prayer, and thanksgiving; that the most acceptable service of God is doing good to men; that the soul is immortal, and that God will certainly reward virtue and punish vice, either here or hereafter. Aiming at "moral perfection," he made a list of the useful virtues, which turned out to be thirteen—Temperance, Silence, Order, Resolution, Frugality, Industry, Sincerity, Justice, Moderation, Cleanliness, Tranquillity, Chastity, and Humility. To each of these in turn he gave "a week's strict attention, marking down in a book the measure of daily success achieved in the practice of each." Thus he went through "a course compleat in thirteen weeks, and four courses a year." He was surprised to find himself "so much fuller of faults" than he had imagined, but persisting for some years he had the satisfaction of "seeing them diminish." To propagate these simple doctrines and practises, Franklin designed (1732) to write a book on "The Art of Virtue," and to unite all men of good will in a society for the practise of it (*Writings,* I, 326; IV, 12, 121; 377; J. G. von Herder, *Sämmtliche Werke,* 1830, XVII, 10, 16).

His passion for improvement made him the leader in many movements for the benefit of his community. He initiated projects for establishing a city police, and for the paving and the better cleaning and lighting of city streets. He was largely instrumental in establishing a circulating library in Philadelphia, the first in America, 1731; in founding in 1743 the American Philosophical Society, incorporated 1780; a city hospital, 1751; and an Academy for the Education of Youth, opened in 1751, incorporated, 1753 (the origin of the University of Pennsylvania). Franklin rarely solicited public office; but he was too public-spirited to avoid such honors. In 1729 he supported the popular demand for paper money (*Writings,* I, 306; II, 133). He was clerk of the Pennsylvania Assembly (1736–51); member for Philadelphia (1751–64); deputy postmaster at Philadelphia (1737–53), and, jointly with William Hunter, deputy postmaster-general for the colonies (1753–74). This was one of the few offices he ever solicited (*Ibid.,* X, 173–74). In the latter capacity he made visits of inspection to nearly every colony, and not only increased the frequency and efficiency of the mail deliveries, but made the post-office a financial success as well.

In the intervals of his varied activities as printer, philanthropist, and politician, Franklin found time for the study of science. It was probably in England that his attention was first turned to "Natural Philosophy." There he met Mandeville, and Dr. Pemberton, the secretary of the Royal Society, and was "extremely desirous" of seeing Newton, then at the height of his fame. Returning to America he was soon discussing, in the Junto, such questions as: "Is sound an entity or a body?" "How may the phenomena of vapors be explained?" As early as 1737 he was writing, in the *Gazette,* on earthquakes (*Writings,* I, 54). In the same year, prevented from observing an eclipse of the moon by a "northeaster," he was surprised to learn that the storm struck Philadelphia sooner than it struck Boston; which led him to the discovery that northeast storms on the Atlantic coast move against the wind (*Ibid.,* II, 311; IV, 16). About 1744 he invented the "Pennsylvania Fireplace," a stove with an open fire-box, which heated rooms better with less expense (*Ibid.,* II, 246). He contrived a clock which told the hours, minutes, and seconds with only three wheels and two pinions in the movement (improved by James Ferguson, it was known as Ferguson's clock, *Ibid.,* I, 52). Every sort of natural phenomenon enlisted his interest and called forth some ingenious idea. In one short letter he speaks of linseed oil, hemp land, swamp draining, variations in climate, northeast storms, the cause of springs on mountains, sea-shell rocks, grass seed, taxation, and smuggling (*Ibid.,* II, 310). So fascinating was natural philosophy to Franklin that he determined to make it his vocation. Business was a game which he could play with skill, but he cared little for it, or for the money it brought, except as a guarantee of independence. At the age of forty-two he had won a competence. Besides the income from some real estate, his business was worth perhaps £2,000 a year. In 1748 he therefore entered into a partnership with his foreman, David Hall [*q.v.*], who was to run the business, relieving Franklin "of all care of the printing office" and paying him £1,000 annually, an arrangement which lasted eighteen years. "I flatter'd myself that, by the sufficient tho' modest fortune I had acquir'd, I had secured leisure during the rest of my life for philosophical studies and amusements" (*Ibid.,* I, 373–74). The leisure acquired lasted without serious interruptions for no more than six years; but it was during these years that he made those electrical experiments on which his fame as a scientist chiefly rests.

Franklin became interested in electricity about 1746, when Peter Collinson sent to the Philadelphia Library an "electric tube." With this fascinating toy he spent all of his spare time. "I never was before engaged in any study that so totally engrossed my attention" (*Writings,* II, 302). After four months he sent to Collinson an amazingly precise, clear, and intelligible account of his experiments. He noted "the wonderful effect of pointed bodies, both in *drawing off* and *throwing off,* the electrical fire." He noted that a person "standing on wax" was differently affected by the electrical charge than a person standing on the floor; and from this fact, tested in a variety of ways, "there have arisen," he says, "some new terms among us: we say B (and bodies like circumstanced) is electrised *positively;* A, *negatively.* Or, rather, B is electrised *plus;* A, *minus*" (*Ibid.,* II, 302–10). He was soon experimenting with "Muschenbroek's wonderful bottle" (Leyden jar), and was confirmed in his "single fluid" theory (*Ibid.,* I, 95; II, 325). "The eleven experiments, to each of which a single brief paragraph is given, cover the essential phenomena of the condenser. As statements of fact they will stand almost without revision or amendment to the present day" (E. L. Nichols, in *Record of the Celebration of the Two Hundredth Anniversary of the Birth of Benjamin Franklin,* p. iii; *Writings,* II, 328). Franklin was not the first to suggest the identity of lightning and electricity; but he proposed a method of testing the theory by erecting an iron rod on a high tower or steeple (letter to Collinson, July 29, 1750; *Writings,* II, 426, 437). On May 10, 1752, Mr. Dalibard, who knew of Franklin's proposed method through Collinson's publication of Franklin's letter in 1751, performed the experiment with success at Marley-la-Valle. The experiment was successfully repeated at Paris but failed in England. Franklin, not having the means of testing his own method, devised a simpler one. This was the famous kite experiment, performed by Franklin in the summer of 1752, and described by him in a letter to Collinson, Oct. 19 (*Ibid.,* III, 99). These experiments, together with Collinson's publication of his letters on the subject (*Experiments and Observations on Electricity, Made at Philadelphia in America, by Mr. Benjamin Franklin,* London, 1751, reprinted with additions, 1753, 1760–62. *Ibid.,* I, 15–16), which were immediately translated into French, established Franklin's fame as a scientist. The degree of Master of Arts was conferred on him by Harvard and by Yale (1753), and by William and Mary (1756). His fame pleased as much as it surprised him. More than ever he desired to devote his time to "philosophical studies," which it now seemed might be something more than mere "amusements."

His dream of leisure for philosophical studies was never to be realized. Six years after retiring from private business, public affairs began to claim him in earnest, and during the rest of his life he was chiefly engaged in politics and diplomacy. In 1754 he was sent to represent Pennsylvania at the Albany Congress, called to unite the colonies in the war against the French and Indians. His "Plan of Union" was adopted by the Congress in preference to others; but "its fate was singular: the assemblies did not adopt it, as they all thought there was too much *prerogative* in it, and in England it was judged to have too much of the *democratic*" (*Writings,* I, 388; III, 197). Meantime the war had intensified the old dispute between the Assembly and the proprietors (descendants of William Penn, who lived in England and by the charter were privileged to appoint and instruct the governors of Pennsylvania). The chief grievance was that the proprietors forbade the governor to pass money bills for defense unless the vast proprietary estates were exempt from taxation (report of the Assembly committee, drafted by Franklin, 1757. *Ibid.,* III, 370). The proprietors proving obdurate, the Assembly decided to appeal directly to the British government, and in 1757 Franklin was sent to England to present its case.

The business of his first mission was not settled for nearly three years. In 1760, after two hearings before the Privy Council, a bill of the Assembly taxing the proprietary estates, except unsurveyed waste lands, was allowed by the King. In spite of the long delay, perhaps because of it, Franklin remained in England until 1762. These five years were perhaps the happiest of his life. He resided with Mrs. Margaret Stevenson, at 7 Craven St., where he became at once the beloved and well-cared-for foster father of the family. With Mrs. Stevenson, and especially with her daughter Mary, he formed an enduring friendship. In the Craven Street house he set up an "electrical machine" and carried on experiments. He indulged his humor by composing "The Craven Street Gazette" in which the doings of Her Majesty's Court were related with becoming solemnity. He made journeys—to Holland, to Cambridge, to the ancestral home at Ecton. He became intimate with Collinson, Fothergill, Priestley, Strahan; and corresponded with Lord Kames, David Hume, and Dr. Johnson. He visited the University of Edinburgh, received the degree of LL.D. from St. Andrews (1759), and of D.C.L. from Oxford (1762). He followed the war with interest, opposed the clamor for peace in 1760 by publishing in the *London Chronicle* a satire "On the Meanes of Disposing the Enemie to Peace" (*Writings,* IV, 90); and argued at length the advantages of taking Canada rather than Guadaloupe from France ("The Interest of Great Britain Considered," *Ibid.,* IV, 35). To this pamphlet, which tradition supposes to have had some influence with the government, there was appended a brief paper written in 1751 and first published in 1755 which in some points anticipates the Malthusian theory of population ("Observations on the Increase of Mankind, the peopling of Countries," etc., *Ibid.,* III, 63. See T. R. Malthus, *An Essay on the Principles of Population,* ed., 1803, pp. iv, 2). In these papers he argued: (1) that in America, where land is easily obtained, population doubled every twenty years; (2) that where land is easily obtained manufactures will not develop; (3) that Canada (including the Mississippi Valley) was accordingly more valuable than Guadaloupe since (a) becoming populous it will furnish rich markets for British goods, but (b) remaining indefinitely agricultural it will not compete with British industry.

In 1762 Franklin returned reluctantly to Philadelphia, envying the "petty island" its "sensible, virtuous and elegant Minds" (*Writings,* IV, 194), and flirting with the idea of settling his affairs so that "in two years at farthest . . . I may then remove to England—provided we can persuade the good Woman to cross the seas" (*Ibid.,* IV, 182). Pressure of affairs, or perhaps the "good Woman," persuaded him to conclude that *"old Trees cannot safely be transplanted"* (*Ibid.,* IV, 217); but, new disputes arising with the proprietors, the Assembly once more sent him to England to obtain a recall of the Charter. This object was not attained, was indeed submerged in the greater issue raised by Grenville's proposal to levy a stamp tax in the colonies. In the second interview between Grenville and the colonial agents Franklin was present and protested against the measure, suggesting instead the "usual constitutional method" of raising a revenue. Perceiving that the bill would be enacted, he advised his friends to make the best of it. "We might as well have hindered the sun's setting. . . . But since 'tis down . . . let us make as good a night of it as we can. We may still light candles" (*Ibid.,* IV, 390). When Grenville applied to the colonial agents to recommend Americans for the new office of stamp distributor, Franklin named his friend John Hughes for Philadelphia; and failing to foresee opposition to the act he sent over some stamped papers to be sold by his partner. These acts laid him open to the charge of having urged the law in order to profit by it; his house was menaced, and his wife advised to seek safety (*Writings,* X, 226–27; Bigelow, *Life of Franklin,* I, 460, 467); but his prestige was soon restored by his famous "examination" before the House of Commons. In February 1766, during the debates on the repeal of the Stamp Act, he was called before the House (committee of the whole) and questioned on the subject. Of the 174 questions asked, some were put by opponents, some by friends, of the act (Bigelow, I, 507, note). The replies, brief, lucid, and to the point, aimed to show that the tax was contrary to custom, and administratively impracticable both on account of the circumstances of the country and the settled opposition of the people (*Writings,* IV, 412). Published immediately (Ford, *Franklin Bibliography,* 127) and widely read, the performance greatly increased Franklin's influence in America and his reputation abroad. "The questions . . . are answered with such deep and familiar knowledge of the subject, such precision and perspicuity, such temper and yet such spirit, as do the greatest honor to Dr. Franklin, and justify the general opinion of his character and abilities" (*Gentleman's Magazine,* July 1767, p. 368).

In 1766, after the repeal of the Stamp Act, Franklin requested permission to return to Philadelphia, but the Assembly reappointed him its agent (Bigelow, I, 513, note). He was also named colonial agent of Georgia (1768), New Jersey (1769), and Massachusetts (1770). These appointments, together with his outstanding reputation, made Franklin a kind of ambassador extraordinary from the colonies to Great Britain. During those years he worked persistently for reconciliation: urging his American friends to avoid indiscreet conduct (*Writings,* V, 42, 197, 204, 222); in England defending the colonies in private conversation and by published articles (*Ibid.,* V, 78, 127, 206, 236). Until the passing of the coercive acts (1774) he never quite despaired; but as the years passed he became less hopeful. A more serious note creeps into his correspondence; his sympathies become more American, less British. As early as 1768 he complained that all his efforts were without avail except to make him suspect: "In England, of being too much of an American, and in America, of being too much of an Englishman" (*Ibid.,* V, 182). His close observation of British politics abated both his admiration for the English government and his expectation that conciliatory measures would prevail. In 1768 he wrote, no doubt in an unusually depressed mood: "Some punishment seems preparing for a people, who are ungratefully abusing the best constitution and the best King . . . any nation was ever blessed with, intent on nothing but luxury, licentuousness, power, places, pensions, and plunder" (*Ibid.,* V, 133). He welcomed every prospect of returning to America. He had indeed friends enough in England to live there comfortably the rest of his days, "if it were not for my American connections, & the indelible Affection I retain for that dear Country" (*Ibid.,* V, 382).

As his admiration for England abated and his love of America deepened, his ideas on American rights became more precise and more advanced. In 1765 he did not doubt the right of Parliament to levy the Stamp Act. In 1766 he defended the distinction between internal and external taxes, contenting himself with an ironical and prophetic comment: "Many arguments have lately been made here to shew them [Americans] . . . that if you have no right to tax them internally you have none to tax them externally, or make any other law to bind them. At present they do not reason so; but in time they may possibly be convinced by these arguments" (*Writings,* IV, 446). By 1768 Franklin was himself convinced. In order to resist the Townshend duties (1767), Dickinson and Samuel Adams had devised ingenious arguments designed to admit the right of Parliament to legislate for the colonies while denying the right to tax them (*Ibid.,* I, 97). Franklin caused Dickinson's letters to be published in England, but writing to William Franklin Mar. 13, 1768, he brushed aside these too subtle distinctions. "The more I have thought and read on the subject, the more I find myself confirmed in opinion, that no middle doctrine can be well maintained, I mean not clearly with intelligible arguments. Something might be made of either of the extremes; that Parliament has a power to make *all laws* for us, or that it has a power to make no laws for us; and I think the arguments for the latter more numerous and weighty, than those for the former" (*Ibid.,* V, 115). Two years later he deprecated the use of such phrases as *"supreme authority of Parliament,"* and urged Americans to base their rights on the theory that the colonies and England were united only, "as England and Scotland were before the Union, by having one common Sovereign, the King" (*Ibid.,* V, 260). Thus early did Franklin accept the doctrine later formulated in the Declaration of Independence.

Appointed agent by the Massachusetts House of Representatives, Oct. 24, 1770, Franklin's American sympathies were intensified by the truculent unfriendliness of Hillsborough, who refused to recognize the appointment until approved by Gov. Hutchinson. Too long absent from America to form an independent judgment of the situation in Massachusetts, he was further prejudiced by the colored accounts of it transmitted by Samuel Cooper and Thomas Cushing. Although deprecating violence, and advising the Boston leaders that the government contemplated no new taxes, he agreed with Samuel Adams that good relations could not be established until the British government had repealed the tea duty. He welcomed the establishment of correspondence committees, and suggested, as a means of bringing "the Dispute to a Crisis," that the colonies should "engage . . . with each other . . . never [to] grant Aids to the Crown in any General War, till . . . [their] Rights are recogniz'd by the King and both Houses of Parliament" (1773. *Writings,* VI, 77). He was convinced of Hutchinson's "duplicity," and thought his controversy with the House of Representatives would discredit him in England. While encouraging the anti-British party in Boston, Franklin contrived to exasperate the anti-American party in London. He published two pointed satires, "Edict by the King of Prussia," and "Rules by which a Great Empire may be reduced to a Small one" (*Ibid.,* VI, 118, 127), which did more to aggravate than to compose the quarrel (see Mansfield's opinion, *Ibid.,* VI, 145); and, wittingly or unwittingly, he contributed much to the final breach by his part in the famous affair of the "Hutchinson Letters." In 1772 an unknown member of Parliament showed Franklin certain letters, six of which were written by Gov. Hutchinson in 1768–69, said to have been addressed (the name had been erased) to William Whately, former secretary of Grenville, urging drastic measures on the ground that "there must be an abridgment of what are called English Liberties" (the letters are in J. K. Hosmer, *Life of Hutchinson,* 1896, p. 429). By permission of the possessor, Franklin sent the letters to Thomas Cushing, with the stipulation that they should be returned to him without being either copied or printed (*Writings,* V, 448; VI, 265; X, 260). The letters were shortly printed in Boston and circulated in London, the immediate result of which was a duel between Thomas Whately, executor of the estate of William Whately, and John Temple, whom Whately accused of stealing the letters. To exonerate Temple, Franklin declared that he alone had procured and transmitted the letters, and that neither Thomas Whately nor Temple had ever had possession of them (*Ibid.,* VI, 284). In conservative circles Franklin was at once denounced as an incendiary and a thief; the government dismissed him from his office as deputy postmaster-general (*Ibid.,* VI, 191); and on Jan. 29, 1774, at a hearing before the Privy Council in the Cockpit on a petition of the Massachusetts House to remove Hutchinson, Solicitor General Wedderburn, on the assumption that Franklin had purloined the letters, denounced him in unmeasured terms as a man without honor who would "henceforth esteem it a libel to be called a man of letters: *homo* TRIUM *literarum*" —a man of three letters, *i.e. FUR,* the Latin word for thief (*Ibid.,* X, 269; Bigelow, II, 201. For full account of the episode, see *Writings,* VI, 258–89; X, 258–72; Bigelow, II, 200–38; R. H. Lee, *Life of Arthur Lee,* 1829, I, 266; P. O. Hutchinson, *Diary and Letters of Thomas Hutchinson,* 1883, I, 81; J. K. Hosmer, *Hutchinson,* ch. XII). Supported by his friends, and convinced that the sending of the letters was "one of the best actions of his life" (*Writings,* X, 270), Franklin remained in England, aiding Pitt in his fruitless efforts at conciliation (*Ibid.,* VI, 318–98; X, 272 ff.; Bigelow, II, ch. VII), until Mar. 20, 1775, when he sailed for America.

On May 6, 1775, the day following his return to Philadelphia, Franklin was chosen a member of the second Continental Congress. Conciliation seemed to him now no more than a vain hope. To satisfy the moderates he supported the Petition to the King, giving "Britain . . . one opportunity more of recovering the friendship of the colonies," but "I think she has not sense enough to embrace [it], and so I conclude she has lost them forever" (*Writings,* VI, 408). He sketched a Plan of Union for the colonies; organized the Post-Office, of which he was the first postmaster-general; served on the commissions sent to induce the Canadians to join the colonies, to advise Washington on defense, and to listen to Howe's peace proposals (*Ibid.,* VI, 457 ff.; F. Wharton, *Diplomatic Correspondence of the U. S.,* 1889, II, 139; Bigelow, II, ch. XII); and on the committee to draft the Declaration of Independence (C. L. Becker, *Declaration of Independence,* 1922, ch. IV). As a member of the committee appointed Nov. 29, 1775, to correspond "with friends in Great Britain, Ireland, and other parts of the world" (*Journals of the Continental Congress,* Nov. 29, 1775), he prepared the instructions (Wharton, II, 78) for Silas Deane whom the committee sent to France in 1776, and through Barbeu Dubourg, the translator of his works, did much to facilitate Deane's reception by Vergennes. Encouraged by letters from Deane, Congress decided, Sept. 26, 1776, to send a commission of three to negotiate a treaty with France. Franklin, Deane, and Jefferson were first chosen (*Journals of the Continental Congress,* Sept. 26, 1776). Upon Jefferson's declination, Arthur Lee was appointed in his place. Franklin was then almost seventy years old: "I am but a fag end, and you may have me for what you please" (*Writings,* X, 301). His last act before leaving Philadelphia (Oct. 26) was to lend Congress some three or four thousand pounds. He arrived in France Dec. 4, 1776.

Unwilling as yet to recognize the rebellious colonies, the French government could not openly receive Franklin; but the French people gave him a welcome rarely if ever accorded to any foreigner. He was already well known in France through two previous visits in 1767 and 1769 (E. E. Hale, *Franklin in France,* 1887, I, 2–19), and through the translations of his scientific works, parts of Poor Richard, and the examination in Parliament. To the readers of Plutarch and Rousseau nothing could be more appropriate than that this backwoods sage and philosopher should now come to plead the cause of a young nation claiming its "natural right" to freedom from oppression. And Franklin had only to be himself to play the part allotted to him. His fur cap (very rarely worn indeed), covering unpowdered gray locks; his simple dress and unpretentious manners; his countenance, shrewd, placid, benignant; his wit and wisdom, homely indeed but somehow lifted above the provincial; the flexibility of his unwarped and emancipated intelligence, and the natural courtesy with which the sage from Arcady demeaned himself, without arrogance and without servility, in the most sophisticated society in the world—all this made Franklin more than an ambassador: it made him a symbol, the personification of all the ideas dear to the Age of Enlightment. To the French people Franklin was Socrates born again in the imagined state of nature. At Passy, where M. Ray de Chaumont placed at his disposal part of the Hôtel de Valentinois, he lived for nine years, in comparative seclusion, and yet the object of unmeasured adulation. His sayings were treasured and repeated as *bon mots.* His portrait was to be seen everywhere in shop windows and in many private houses. His image was stamped on innumerable medals, medallions, rings, watches, snuff-boxes, and bracelets. John Adams, who later replaced Silas Deane, contrived, in spite of characteristic exaggeration and a certain irascible jealousy, to describe exactly the impression which Franklin made in France. "His reputation was more universal than that of Leibnitz or Newton, Frederick or Voltaire, and his character more beloved and esteemed than any or all of them. . . . His name was familiar to government and people . . . to such a degree that there was scarcely a peasant or a citizen, a *valet de chambre,* coachman or footman, a lady's chambermaid or a scullion in a kitchen who was not familiar with it, and who did not consider him as a friend to human kind. When they spoke of him, they seemed to think he was to restore the Golden Age" (*Works of John Adams,* 1856, I, 660).

Franklin's popularity contributed much to the success of his diplomatic mission. On Dec. 28, 1776, the Commissioners, secretly received by Vergennes, presented their instructions and requested a treaty of commerce (Wharton, II, 248): and on Feb. 2, they went so far as to promise that if France became involved in war with Great Britain on account of such a treaty, the United States would not "separately conclude a peace, nor aid Great Britain against France or Spain" (*Ibid.,* 260). Vergennes was more than willing to aid in disrupting the British Empire in order to redress the European balance in favor of France; but he could not take the decisive step until the King consented, and wished not to do so without the cooperation of Spain or until it was clear that the colonies would be content with nothing less than independence (E. S. Corwin, *French Policy and the American Alliance of 1778,* 1916, chs. I–VI). Meantime, Franklin had been in communication with British agents through unofficial messengers; and in April 1778 he negotiated directly with Hartley, a member of Parliament, who came over to Paris. These overtures came to nothing, however, because of the British refusal to grant independence to the American colonies as a condition of peace (B. Faÿ, *post,* pp. 431 ff.). Franklin's contribution to the success of Vergennes's policy was indirect, but not unimportant. His mere presence in France, intensifying popular enthusiasm for the Americans and encouraging American privateers to operate from French ports, made it increasingly difficult for the French government to avoid a rupture with Great Britain in any case; while his relations with persons in England gave life to the rumor that the colonies, failing the aid of France, would as a price of independence join Great Britain in the conquest of the French and Spanish West Indies, a rumor which Vergennes, without crediting, made use of to persuade the King (Corwin, ch. VI). In the actual negotiations for an alliance (Dec. 1777–Feb. 1778), which the King authorized after the Battle of Saratoga, Franklin seems to have desired the French government to guarantee the conquest of the Mississippi Valley (where he was personally interested in certain land grants) as a condition of peace, a point which Vergennes, not wishing to alienate Spain, was unwilling to concede (Corwin, 153, referring to B. F. Stevens's *Facsimiles of Manuscripts in European Archives,* vol. XXI, no. 1831). The final treaties (a treaty of commerce, and a treaty of "defensive alliance . . . to maintain effectively the . . . independence absolute and unlimited of the United States") were signed Feb. 6, 1778.

Meantime the relations between the commissioners were anything but cordial. Arthur Lee, an incurably vain, suspicious, and wrong-headed person, charged Beaumarchais and Deane, and by implication Franklin, with incompetence and venality, especially in connection with the supplies furnished the colonies through the dummy company of Beaumarchais, Hortalez et cie (R. H. Lee, *Life of Arthur Lee,* II, 27, 50, 52, 125; Fisher, *True Benjamin Franklin,* pp. 279 ff.). The arrangements between Beaumarchais and Vergennes (L. L. de Loménie, *Beaumarchais and His Times,* 1856, III, 124–30) were made before Franklin arrived in France, and Deane was the American agent in whom Beaumarchais confided. Franklin, leaving the business to Deane whom he trusted, seems not to have informed himself of the exact nature of the understanding (Hale, I, 52–55). The most that can rightly be charged against Franklin is that he appointed as his secretary his grandson, Temple Franklin, an incompetent boy; that his accounts were accordingly in confusion; and that he appointed as naval agent at Nantes his nephew, Jonathan Williams, who proved incompetent if not venal (Fisher, pp. 293 ff.). Franklin made it a rule never to engage in personal controversies; he had learned early in life that "spots of dirt" thrown on one's character were best left alone since "they would all rub off when they were dry." He suffered Lee's "magisterial snubbings and rebukes" with a serene patience that rarely failed (see, however, *Writings,* VII, 129–38); but he had more important tasks than the hopeless one of setting Arthur Lee right. Being the only American with whom Vergennes cared to deal, the chief burden of the negotiations with the French government fell to him. He also served virtually as consul, judge of admiralty, and director of naval affairs. He negotiated for the exchange of prisoners in England (Hale, I, chs. XI, XVIII). He was burdened with innumerable applications, from Americans desiring recommendation in France, from Frenchmen desiring recommendation in America (*Writings,* VII, 30, 36, 38, 43, 58, 77, 80). In addition he found time to publish articles designed to strengthen American credit abroad (*Ibid.,* I, 82, 86). In April 1778, John Adams, replacing Deane, came to Paris, offended de Chaumont by offering to pay rent for Franklin's house at Passy (Bigelow, II, 429–30), helped Franklin to straighten out his account (*Ibid.,* 447), was made "sick to death" by the Lee-Deane controversy, and recommended that the commission be replaced by a single agent. Lee was of the same opinion, suggesting himself as the proper person (R. H. Lee, *Life of Arthur Lee,* II, 127). On Sept. 14, 1778, Congress appointed Franklin sole plenipotentiary (*Journals of the Continental Congress,* Sept. 14, 1778). With his status made definite his life became pleasanter. He found some time to write on scientific subjects (*Writings,* VII, 209; VIII, 9, 115, 189, 244, 246, 285, 309); to carry on a gay and frivolous correspondence with Madame Helvetius and Madame Brillon; and to amuse himself and his friends with satires and bagatelles printed on his excellent Passy press (*Ibid.,* X, ch. XI; Bigelow, II, ch. XVII; J. C. Oswald, *Benjamin Franklin, Printer,* 1917, chs. XIV–XV; L. S. Livingston, *Franklin and his Press at Passy,* 1914). But if his life was pleasanter, his responsibilities were if anything heavier. For three years his chief service was to obtain money; his chief task to persuade Vergennes to overlook irregular methods and to honor debts for which the French government was in no way obligated. Aside from negotiating loans, Franklin was expected to meet the innumerable bills of exchange which were drawn on him, by Congress, by John Adams in Holland, by John Jay in Spain, by ship captains fitting out in any port that was handiest, even by his villifiers, Arthur Lee and Ralph Izard (*Writings,* VII, 382, 405; VIII, 14, 59, 139, 142, 174, 200, 208, 211, 217; X, 337 ff., 374 ff.; Hale, I, ch. XXI; W. C. Bruce, *Benjamin Franklin,* 1917, II, 281 ff.). On Mar. 12, 1781, on the ground that excessive duties were impairing his health, Franklin tendered his resignation to Congress (*Writings,* VIII, 221). He was well aware that the friends of Lee, Izard, and Adams were about to move for his recall (*Ibid.,* VIII, 236, 250; X, 342), and his resignation was probably no more than a shrewd political move designed to defeat the motion. At all events, when Congress voted to continue him, he slyly remarked: "I must . . . buckle again to Business, and thank God my Health & Spirits are of late improved . . . I call this Continuance an Honour . . . greater than my first Appointment, when I consider that all the Interest of my Enemies, united with my own Request, were not sufficient to prevent it" (*Ibid.,* VIII, 294).

On June 8, 1781, Franklin was named one of the commissioners to negotiate peace with Great Britain (*Journals of the Continental Congress,* June 8, 1781). While awaiting the arrival of Jay and Adams he assumed responsibility for the preliminary conversations, of which he wrote a detailed account (*Writings,* VIII, 459 ff.; Wharton, V, 535 ff.). Resisting every suggestion that the colonies should make a separate peace, and keeping Vergennes informed of every step, he proposed as a basis of negotiation: (1) independence; (2) the cession of the Mississippi Valley; (3) fishing rights "on the banks of Newfoundland, and elsewhere." He objected to the British claim for the recovery of debts (later he conceded that just debts should be paid). He took the ground that Congress could not compensate the Loyalists, since the confiscation acts were state laws; but he suggested that Britain might contribute much to *real* conciliation by voluntarily ceding Canada, in which case the Loyalists might possibly be compensated by grants of wild lands in that country (E. Channing, *History of the United States,* 1912, III, 352 ff.). Uncertain of the outcome of the naval war, the British government was apparently ready early in June to make peace on Franklin's terms (Wharton, V, 572; *Writings,* VII, 572). But at this point two circumstances contributed to give a new direction to the negotiations. Jay, arriving June 23, and suspecting the sincerity of the British, delayed matters by insisting that the British commissioners be authorized to treat with the United States as an independent state. Meantime British naval successes, culminating in the relief of Gibraltar, Oct. 10, strengthened the hands of the British commissioners, who now renewed the demand for compensation to the Loyalists, and objected to the American claim (injected into the negotiations by Adams) of a right to dry fish on British coasts. When the conference reached an impasse on these points, Franklin came forward with a proposal which seems to have turned the scale in favor of the Americans. On Nov. 29, according to Adams, Franklin "produced a paper from his pocket, in which he had drawn up a claim, and he said the first principle of the treaty was equality and reciprocity. Now, they demanded of us payment of debts, and . . . compensation to the refugees. . . . Then he stated the carrying off of goods from Boston, Philadelphia, and the Carolinas, . . . and the burning of towns, etc., and demanded that this might be sent with the rest." After further discussion of Franklin's counter demand for compensation, the British commissioners accepted the American "ultimatum respecting the fishery and the loyalists" (Wharton, VI, 87); and on the following day the preliminaries were signed (*Ibid.,* 96).

In negotiating and signing the preliminaries without keeping the French government informed, the commissioners violated not only the instructions of Congress, but Franklin's earlier agreement with Vergennes. The responsibility for this step rests with Jay and Adams, who were convinced: (1) that Franklin was too subservient to French influence; and especially, (2) that France and Spain were secretly working to restrict the boundaries of the United States to the Alleghanies (for the views of Adams and Jay, see Wharton, V, 703, 740, 750, 864; VI, 11–51). The latter was true of Spain; true of France only so far as Vergennes was bound to consider the interest of Spain (Corwin, pp. 331 ff.). Franklin's "subserviency" was only a superior diplomacy; but he yielded to his colleagues in order to maintain harmony. When Adams, shortly after his arrival (Oct. 26), gave Franklin his and Jay's reasons for ignoring Vergennes, "the Doctor," Adams reports, "heard me patiently, but said nothing; but at the next conference with Oswald, he turned to Jay and said: 'I am of your opinion, and will go on with these gentlemen in the business without consulting this court.' He accordingly met with us in most of our conferences, and has gone with us in entire harmony and unanimity throughout" (Wharton, VI, 91). Upon receiving the preliminaries, Vergennes wrote Franklin a sharp formal protest (*Ibid.*, 140). It is possible that Vergennes, hampered by his obligations to Spain, was really pleased with the outcome, and that his protest was merely formal, and so understood by Franklin. It is difficult to suppose that Vergennes was unaware of the separate negotiations. Earlier he had himself said that each country "will make its own Treaty. All that is necessary . . . is, that the Treaties go hand in hand, and are sign'd all on the same day" (*Writings*, VIII, 512). Although the negotiations had not gone "hand in hand," it was stipulated in the preliminaries that the final treaty "is not to be concluded until terms of peace shall be agreed upon between Great Britain and France" (Wharton, VI, 96). There was therefore some basis for Franklin's reply to Vergennes's protest, in which he admitted that the commissioners had been "guilty of neglecting a point of *bienséance*," but contended that in substance there had been no breach of agreement since "no peace is to take place between us and England till you have concluded yours" (*Ibid.*, 144). He added: *"The English, I just now learn, flatter themselves they have already divided us."* Few diplomats, taking Vergennes's protest at its face value, would have ventured to unite with this bland apology a request for twenty million livres, or have contrived so to word it as to have obtained from the irritated minister a grant of six millons. The final peace was signed Sept. 3, 1783. The story that for this occasion (or for the signing of the treaty with France in 1778) Franklin donned the suit of Manchester velvet last worn when Wedderburn denounced him in The Cockpit (*Writings*, X, 271; Bigelow, II, 204) seems to be without adequate evidence to support it (J. B. Moore, *Digest of International Law*, 1906, V, 659–61).

On Dec. 26, 1783, Franklin reminded Congress of its promise to recall him after the peace was made (*Writings*, IX, 141). Not until May 2, 1785, did he receive notice of the desired release. He left Passy, July 12, in one of "the King's Litters, carried by mules" (*Ibid.*, 363), to embark from Havre de Grace. He arrived in Philadelphia Sept. 14, having profitably employed his time on the long voyage in making "Maritime Observations" and writing a detailed account of "The Causes and Cure of Smoky Chimneys" (*Ibid.*, IX, 372–462). He was shortly chosen president of the executive council of Pennsylvania. After serving in this capacity for three years, he was chosen a member of the Constitutional Convention which met in May 1787. Although suffering from the stone he attended the sessions regularly for over four months. Like Jefferson, this master of discussion was no speechmaker; and his few formal discourses were written out and read. The text of the last speech as printed by Smyth, p. 607, is incomplete and incorrect (see the text in Elliot's *Debates*, 1845, V, 554, which follows more nearly the Franklin autograph original in the Cornell University Library). None of his cardinal ideas was adopted. He favored a single chamber, an executive board, and opposed the payment of salaries to executive officials. Yet Franklin contributed not a little to the final result. His immense prestige, and the persuasive effect of his kindly personality and genial humor, were of great value in calming passions and compromising disputes. When the convention was at a dead-lock over the question of representation, Franklin said: "If a property representation takes place, the small states contend that their liberties will be in danger. If an equality of votes is to be put in its place, the large states say their money will be in danger. When a broad table is to be made, and the edges of the planks do not fit, the artist takes a little from both, and makes a good joint" (Elliot's *Debates*, V, 266). Franklin's first proposal for a compromise was not adopted; but he was a member of the committee appointed to adjust the matter, and largely responsible for the compromise actually incorporated in the Constitution (*Ibid.*, 273–74, 487). Although the Constitution was not to his liking, he urged in his inimitable manner that it be unanimously adopted. "I confess that there are several parts of this Constitution which I do not at present approve, but I am not sure I shall never approve them. . . . The older I grow, the more apt I am to doubt my own judgment. . . . Though many . . . persons think . . . highly of their own infallibility . . . few express it so naturally as a certain French lady, who . . . said: 'I don't know how it happens, sister, but I meet with nobody but myself who is always in the right'—*il n'y a que moi qui a toujours raison.* . . . On the whole, sir, I cannot help expressing a wish that every member of the Convention . . . would with me, on this occasion, doubt a little of his own infallibility, and, to make manifest our unanimity, put his name to the instrument" (*Ibid.*, 554–55).

During the last five years of his life Franklin lived in a commodious house near Market Street with his daughter (his wife died in 1774) and his grandchildren. He invented a device for lifting books from high shelves (*Writings,* IX, 483), wrote to his numerous friends at home and abroad, entertained his neighbors and the many strangers come to do him homage, enjoying to the last that ceaseless flow of "agreeable and instructive conversation" of which he was the master and the devotee (see Cutler's description, *Ibid.,* X, 478). His last public act was to sign a memorial to Congress for the abolition of slavery. He died Apr. 17, 1790, at the age of eighty-four years. At his funeral twenty thousand people assembled to do him honor. He was buried in Christ Church Burial Ground under a stone bearing a simple inscription of his own devising: *Benjamin and Deborah Franklin* (*Ibid.,* 489, 508).

Great men are often hampered by some inner discord or want of harmony with the world in which they live. It was Franklin's good fortune to have been endowed with a rare combination of rare qualities, and to have lived at a time when circumstances favored the development of all his powers to their fullest extent. He was a true child of the Enlightenment, not indeed of the school of Rousseau, but of Defoe and Pope and Swift, of Fontenelle and Montesquieu and Voltaire. He spoke their language, although with a homely accent, a tang of the soil, that bears witness to his lowly and provincial origin. His wit and humor, lacking indeed the cool, quivering brilliance of Voltaire or the corrosive bitterness of Pope and Swift, were all the more effective and humane for their dash of genial and kindly cynicism. He accepted without question and expressed without effort all the characteristic ideas and prepossessions of the century—its aversion to "superstition" and "enthusiasms" and mystery; its contempt for hocus-pocus and its dislike of dim perspectives; its healthy, clarifying scepticism; its passion for freedom and its humane sympathies; its preoccupation with the world that is evident to the senses; its profound faith in common sense, in the efficacy of Reason for the solution of human problems and the advancement of human welfare.

For impressing his age with the validity of these ideas, both by precept and example, Franklin's native qualities were admirably suited. His mind, essentially pragmatic and realistic, by preference occupied itself with what was before it, with the present rather than with the past or the future, with the best of possible rather than with the best of conceivable worlds. He accepted men and things, including himself, as they were, with a grain of salt indeed but with insatiable curiosity, with irrepressible zest and good humor. He took life as it came, with the full-blooded heartiness of a man unacquainted with inhibitions and repressions and spiritual *malaise,* as a game to be played, with honesty and sincerity, but with shrewdness and an eye to the main chance, above all without pontifical solemnity, without self-pity, eschewing vain regrets for lost illusions and vain striving for the light that never was. Both his achievements and his limitations spring from this: that he accepted the world as given with imperturbable serenity; without repining identified himself with it; and brought to the understanding and the mastery of it rare common sense, genuine disinterestedness, a fertile and imaginative curiosity, and a cool, flexible intelligence fortified by exact knowledge and chastened and humanized by practical activities.

Not only was Franklin by temperament disposed to take life as it came and to make the most of it; in addition fate provided him with a rich diversity of experience such as has rarely fallen to the lot of any man. Rising from poverty to affluence, from obscurity to fame, he lived on every social level in turn, was equally at ease with rich and poor, the cultivated and the untutored, and spoke with equal facility the language of vagabonds and kings, politicians and philosophers, men of letters, kitchen girls, and *femmes savantes.* Reared in Boston, a citizen of Philadelphia, residing for sixteen years in London and for nine in Paris, he was equally at home in three countries, knew Europe better than any other American, America better than any European, England better than most Frenchmen, France better than most Englishmen, and was acquainted personally or through correspondence with more men of eminence in letters, science, and politics than any other man of his time. Such a variety of experience would have confused and disoriented any man less happily endowed with a capacity for assimilating it. Franklin took it all easily, relishing it, savoring it, without rest and without haste adding to his knowledge, fortifying and tempering his intelligence, broadening his point of view, humanizing and mellowing his tolerant acceptance of men and things—in short chastening and perfecting the qualities that were natively his; so that in the end he emerges the most universal and cosmopolitan spirit of his age. Far more a "good European," a citizen of the world, than Adams or Jefferson, Washington or Hutchinson, he remained to the end more pungently American than any of them. Jefferson said that Franklin was the one exception to the rule that seven years of diplomatic service abroad spoiled an American. Twenty-five years of almost continuous residence abroad did not spoil

Franklin. Acclaimed and decorated as no American had ever been, he returned to Philadelphia and was immediately at home again, easily recognizable by his neighbors as the man they had always known—Ben Franklin, printer.

The secret of Franklin's amazing capacity for assimilating experience without being warped or discolored by it is perhaps to be found in his disposition to take life with infinite zest and yet with humorous detachment. Always immersed in affairs, he seems never completely absorbed by them; mastering easily whatever comes his way, there remain powers in reserve never wholly engaged. It is significant that his activities, with the exception of his researches in science, seem to have been the result, not of any compelling inner impulse or settled purpose, but rather of the pressure of external need or circumstance. He was a business man, and a good one; but having won a competence he retired. He was an inventor and a philanthropist, but not by profession; perceiving the need, he invented a stove or founded a hospital. He was a politician and a diplomat, and none more skilled; but not from choice; for the most part he accepted as a duty the offices that were thrust upon him. He was a writer, a prolific one; yet his writings were nearly all occasional, prompted by the need of the moment. His one book, the *Autobiography,* was begun as something that might be useful to his son; that purpose served, it was never finished. He was a literary artist of rare merit, the master of a style which for clarity, precision, and pliable adhesion to the form and pressure of the idea to be conveyed has rarely been equaled. Yet once having learned the trade he was little preoccupied with the art of writing, content to throw off in passing an acute pragmatic definition: Good writing "ought to have a tendency to benefit the reader. . . . But taking the question otherwise, an ill man may write an ill thing well. . . . In this sense, that is well wrote, which is best adapted for obtaining the end of the writer" (*Writings,* I, 37). It has been said that Franklin was not entrusted with the task of writing the Declaration of Independence for fear he might conceal a joke in the middle of it. The myth holds a profound symbolic truth. In all of Franklin's dealings with men and affairs, genuine, sincere, loyal as he surely was, one feels that he is nevertheless not wholly committed; some thought remains uncommunicated; some penetrating observation is held in reserve. In spite of his ready attention to the business in hand, there is something casual about his efficient dispatch of it; he manages somehow to remain aloof, a spectator still, with amiable curiosity watching himself functioning effectively in the world. After all men were but children needing to be cajoled; affairs a game not to be played without finesse. Was there not then, on that placid countenance, even at the signing of the great Declaration, the bland smile which seems to say: This is an interesting, alas even a necessary, game; and we are playing it well, according to all the rules; but men being what they are it is perhaps best not to inquire too curiously what its ultimate significance may be.

One exception there was—science: one activity which Franklin pursued without outward prompting, from some compelling inner impulse; one activity from which he never wished to retire, to which he would willingly have devoted his life, to which he always gladly turned in every odd day or hour of leisure, even in the midst of the exacting duties and heavy responsibilities of his public career. Science was after all the one mistress to whom he gave himself without reserve and served neither from a sense of duty nor for any practical purpose. Nature alone met him on equal terms, with a disinterestedness matching his own; needing not to be cajoled or managed with finesse, she enlisted in the solution of her problems the full power of his mind. In dealing with nature he could be, as he could not be in dealing with men and affairs, entirely sincere, pacific, objective, rational, could speak his whole thought without reservation, with no suggestion of a stupendous cosmic joke concealed in the premises. Franklin was indeed "many sided." From the varied facets of his powerful mind he threw a brilliant light on all aspects of human life; it is only in his character of natural philosopher that he emits a light quite unclouded. It is in this character therefore that the essential quality of the man appears to best advantage. Sir Humphry Davy has happily noted it for us. "The experiments adduced by Dr. Franklin . . . were most ingeniously contrived and happily executed. A singular felicity of induction guided all his researches, and by very small means he established very grand truths. The style and manner of his publication [on electricity] are almost as worthy of admiration as the doctrine it contains. He has endeavoured to remove all mystery and obscurity from the subject; he has written equally for the uninitiated and for the philosopher; and he has rendered his details amusing as well as perspicuous, elegant as well as simple. Science appears in his language in a dress wonderfully decorous, the best adapted to display her native loveliness. He has in no case exhibited that false dignity, by which philosophy is kept aloof from common applications, and he has sought rather to make her a useful inmate and servant in the common habitations of man, than to preserve her merely as an object of admiration in temples and palaces" (*Collected Works of Sir Humphry Davy,* 1840, VIII, 264–65).

[The Franklin Manuscripts are chiefly in four depositories: the Library of the American Philosophical Society at Philadelphia (76 vols., 13,000 documents in nine languages; see I. M. Hays, *Calendar of the Papers of Benjamin Franklin in the Lib. of the Am. Phil. Soc.,* 1908); the Library of Congress (Stevens Collection, 14 vols., nearly 3,000 documents; see W. C. Ford, *List of the Benjamin Franklin Papers in the Lib. of Cong.,* 1905); the Library of the University of Pennsylvania (800 documents; see "Calendar of the Papers of Benjamin Franklin in the Library of the University of Pennsylvania," published as an appendix of the work of I. M. Hays cited above); the Library of the Historical Society of Pennsylvania (660 documents). The original MS. of the *Autobiography* is in the Huntington Library at San Marino, Cal. For an account of the Franklin MSS., see A. H. Smyth, *Writings of Benjamin Franklin,* I, 1–12; and Bernard Faÿ, *post.*

Of the many collected editions of Franklin's works the chief are: *Memoirs of the Life and Writings of Benjamin Franklin . . .* (6 vols., 1818), by his grandson, Temple Franklin; *The Works of Benjamin Franklin* (10 vols., 1836–40), by Jared Sparks, who "corrected" the text where he thought Franklin guilty of bad taste or vulgarity; *The Complete Works of Benjamin Franklin* (10 vols., 1887–88), by John Bigelow; *The Writings of Benjamin Franklin, Collected and edited with a Life and Introduction* (10 vols., 1905–07), by Albert Henry Smyth. The last-named edition has been used for the present article. The famous *Autobiography* has been issued in innumerable editions and under various titles. For the curious history of the manuscript and the various editions, see P. L. Ford, *Franklin Bibliography,* pp. 179 ff. The best edition is *The Life of Benjamin Franklin Written by Himself* (3 vols., 1874), ed. by John Bigelow, who supplemented the *Autobiography* (which recounted Franklin's life only to 1757) by a judicious selection from his correspondence.

The chief secondary works are: Jas. Parton, *Life and Times of Benjamin Franklin* (2 vols., 1864), anecdotal, interesting, not too critical; J. B. McMaster, *Benjamin Franklin as a Man of Letters* (1887); Edward E. Hale and Edward E. Hale, Jr., *Franklin in France . . .* (2 vols., 1887–88), chiefly valuable for documents printed; J. T. Morse, *Benjamin Franklin* (1889); A. W. Wetzel, "Benjamin Franklin as an Economist," in *Johns Hopkins University Studies,* vol. XIII (1895); Sidney George Fisher, *The True Benjamin Franklin* (1899); Paul Leicester Ford, *The Many Sided Franklin* (1899); Luther S. Livingston, *Franklin and his Press at Passy* (1914); J. C. Oswald, *Benjamin Franklin, Printer* (1917); William Cabell Bruce, *Benjamin Franklin Self-Revealed* (2 vols., 1917); J. M. Stifler, *The Religion of Benjamin Franklin* (1925); Malcom R. Eiselen, *Franklin's Political Theories* (1928); Bernard Faÿ, *Franklin, the Apostle of Modern Times* (1929); J. Henry Smythe, Jr., *The Amazing Benjamin Franklin* (1929). For Franklin bibliography before 1889, see P. L. Ford, *Franklin Bibliography: A List of Books Written by, or Relating to Benjamin Franklin* (1889).] C. L. B.

FRANKLIN, BENJAMIN (Feb. 1, 1812–Oct. 22, 1878), minister of the Disciples of Christ, editor of religious periodicals, was the son of Joseph and Isabella (Devold) Franklin, and a descendant of John Franklin, brother of Benjamin Franklin [*q.v.*]. He was born in what is now Belmont County, Ohio, but his parents soon moved to a part of Morgan County which later became Noble County, and settled on a stream known as Salt Run. Joseph Franklin was a farmer, miller, and cabinetmaker, and as Benjamin grew up he became more or less proficient in all these occupations. In 1832 he went with his uncle, Calvin Franklin, to Henry County, Ind., then practically a wilderness. There he built himself a house, and on Dec. 15, 1833, married Mary Personnett. He supported himself chiefly as a carpenter, but from 1837 to 1840 with his uncle he ran a grist-mill. In the meantime he had been converted under the ministry of Samuel Rogers, one of the pioneer Disciples of that section, and had immediately engaged in evangelistic work. After 1840 as preacher, controversialist, and editor he devoted himself wholly to the interests of religion, becoming one of the most prominent Disciples of the West.

Although he was pastor of a number of churches, he was preëminently an evangelist. He made journeys into Eastern and Western states, and into Canada. More than seven thousand persons, it is estimated, were converted under his preaching. The meagerness of his schooling was something of a handicap, but he knew the Bible thoroughly, understood human nature, and acquired a good practical knowledge of subjects connected with his work. One of the people himself, he spoke and wrote in their language, and had great popularity among them. He became widely known also as a public debater, some of his disputations being published: among them, *An Oral Debate on the Coming of the Son of Man, Endless Punishment, and Universal Salvation* (1848), carried on in Milton, Ind., Oct. 26, 27, 28, 1847, with Erasmus Manford; *Predestination and the Foreknowledge of God, A Discussion Held in Carlyle, Ky.* (1852), with Rev. James Matthews; and *Debate on Some of the Distinctive Differences Between the Reformers and Baptists* (1858), with Elder T. J. Fisher.

It was as an editor and publisher, however, that he exerted his widest influence. In January 1845 he began issuing the *Reformer,* afterward called the *Western Reformer,* published first in Centerville, Ind., and later at Milton, a sixteen-page monthly. Alexander Hall's paper, the *Gospel Proclamation,* Loydsville, Ohio, was consolidated with it in 1850, and it became the *Proclamation and Reformer.* Soon Franklin moved the paper to Hygeia, Ohio, and in partnership with Elder D. S. Burnet edited it and also the *Christian Age,* a weekly. Financial difficulties finally led to the discontinuance of the former, and the *Christian Age* was sold; but in 1856 Franklin started the *American Christian Review,* published in Cincinnati, which he edited until his death. It was long one of the most influential religious periodicals among the Disciples in that part of the country. Although earlier he seems to have been sympathetic toward the formation of the American Christian Missionary Society and other attempts at organized cooperation, he now set himself against everything deemed progressive, and was the leader of the "old fogies" in their conflict with the radicals. His supporters christened his paper "Old Reliable," and his opponents dubbed him "Editorial Pope." He was much broken in health during the last ten years of his life, but persisted in carrying on the warfare. He also published two volumes of his sermons, *The Gospel Preacher* (vol. I, 1869; vol. II, 1877). One of his tracts, *Christian Experience; or, Sincerity Seeking the Way to Heaven*, was popular for more than a quarter of a century; and in the year after his death, selections from his writings, *A Book of Gems*, was issued. He is buried in Anderson, Ind., where after 1864 he made his home.

[Jos. Franklin and J. A. Headington, *The Life and Times of Benj. Franklin* (1879); Wm. T. Moore, *The Living Pulpit of the Christian Ch.* (1869) and *A Comprehensive Hist. of the Disciples of Christ* (1909); John T. Brown, *Churches of Christ* (1904); Alanson Wilcox, *A Hist. of the Disciples of Christ in Ohio* (1918); obituary in *Indianapolis Jour.*, Oct. 24, 1878.] H. E. S.

FRANKLIN, JAMES (Feb. 4, 1696/7–February 1735), printer, was born in Boston, the son of Josiah and Abiah (Folger) Franklin. After learning the printer's trade in England he returned home in March 1717, bringing with him a press, type, and other supplies. Among the sundries, it transpired later, were some brisk new ideas about journalism. At first business was slow, but in December 1719 he was employed by William Brooker to print the *Boston Gazette*. After issuing forty numbers Brooker disposed of the *Gazette* to the new postmaster, Philip Musgrave, who took the printing from Franklin and gave it to Samuel Kneeland. Piqued and out of pocket, Franklin took a risky revenge by launching a third paper in a community that gave but scant support to two. On Monday, Aug. 7, 1721, the *New England Courant* made its first appearance and soon set all Boston by the ears. Increase Mather, after reading a few numbers, publicly stopped his subscription, but Franklin twitted him on sending his grandson in private to buy the paper at the higher price charged for single copies. Cotton Mather was appalled: "A wickedness never parallel'd any where upon the Face of the Earth!" he ejaculated in his diary ("Diary of Cotton Mather, 1707–24," *Collections of the Massachusetts Historical Society*, 7 ser. VIII, 1912, 663). What particularly enraged the Mathers were the jeers of the paper at the experiments in inoculating for the smallpox. Actually the *Courant* was a novelty in that it was literary in tone and inclined to be disrespectful of official dignity, whether civil or ecclesiastical. Having only restricted access to what little news there was, Franklin made his paper a homespun, Yankee imitation of Addison and Steele's *Spectator*, gathered about him a group of young wits, including William Douglass [*q.v.*], as contributors, and gave Boston the liveliest secular reading it had yet perused. Of the contributors the most brilliant was James's brother Benjamin, who has given his account of the enterprise in the *Autobiography*. James himself wrote some prose and doggerel verse for the *Courant*. For a while the paper enjoyed a precarious immunity from interference because of the wrangle for control of the press between Gov. Shute and the Assembly. Trouble was finally precipitated by an oblique reference to official dawdling about the pirates on the coast; James served a month in jail for his contumely in the issue of June 11, 1722. During his brother's absence Benjamin carried on the paper with superior impudence. For rude remarks about church members on Jan. 14, 1723, James was forbidden by the court "to print or publish the *New England Courant*, or any other pamphlet or paper of the like nature except it be first supervised by the Secretary of the Province." Thereafter the *Courant* appeared in Benjamin's name, even though on Sept. 30, 1723, James had to advertise for a "likely lad for an Apprentice"—the best apprentice in the New World having recently absconded. Sometime in 1726 Franklin abandoned his paper and removed to the more congenial climate of Rhode Island. Settling at Newport, he brought with him the first press to be used in that colony, printed a pamphlet there in 1727, an edition of Berkeley's *Alciphron* in 1730, and as public printer, part of an edition of the laws of Rhode Island in 1731. He also printed linens, calicoes, and silks, and in September 1732 started the *Rhode Island Gazette*. His widow, daughters, and son James carried on the business after his death.

[I. Thomas, *Hist. of Printing in America* (1810); *New-Eng. Hist. and Geneal. Reg.*, Jan. 1857, July 1862; C. A. Duniway, *The Development of Freedom of the Press in Mass.* (1906); E. C. Cook, *Literary Influences in Colonial Newspapers 1704–50* (1912); S. G. Arnold, *Hist. of the State of R. I.*, vol. II (1860); W. C. Ford in *Proc. Mass. Hist. Soc.*, LVII (1924), 336–53; W. G. Bleyer, *Main Currents in the Hist. of Am. Journalism* (1927). Files of the *New England Courant* (neither complete) are in the Mass. Hist. Soc. Library and in the Burney Collection of early British newspapers in the British Museum. The Mass. Hist. Soc. has photostat copies of the British Museum numbers that supplement its file.] G. H. G.

FRANKLIN, JESSE (Mar. 24, 1760–Aug. 31, 1823), senator, was born in Orange County, Va., the third son of Bernard and Mary (Cleveland) Franklin. He received scarcely the rudiments of an education, leaving school before he reached the age of twelve, but this deficiency was later to some extent made up by extensive reading. At seventeen he was a Revolutionary soldier, and according to family tradition a lieutenant, but, after the habit of many Revolutionary warriors, he soon returned home. Before 1776 his father had determined to move to North Carolina, and he now sent the youth to spy out the land. After an extended search young Franklin chose a fertile spot in Surry County to which the family presently repaired. The region swarmed with Loyalists, and in a short time Franklin was captain and adjutant in a patriot regiment commanded by Benjamin Cleveland [*q.v.*], his maternal uncle. He distinguished himself at the battle of King's Mountain, and received the sword of Capt. Ryerson who took command of the British when Ferguson fell. Afterwards he continued in service in the partisan warfare of the period, and was intensely hated and feared by the Loyalists who finally captured and hanged him with his own bridle, only to have it break and allow him to escape. He was a volunteer at Guilford Court-House where he again displayed dashing courage. The close of the war found him a major of militia.

The war ended, Franklin moved to Wilkes County and a few years later married Meeky Perkins, the daughter of Hardy Perkins of Rockbridge County, Va., a woman of great beauty, ability, and strong character. In 1784 he was elected to the House of Commons, and by annual election he served until 1787 and again from 1789 to 1791. In 1792 he returned to Surry and represented that county in 1793 and 1794. In the latter year he was elected to Congress and served one term. In the House he was an ally of his colleague, Nathaniel Macon, whose views, particularly in relation to economy in government, coincided with his own. At the close of his term he was elected to the Commons for two successive years, and in 1798 was elected to the United States Senate, serving from 1799 to 1805. During the impeachment trial of Judge Pickering, he was chosen president *pro tempore,* his friend Macon being at the same time speaker of the House. Franklin voted for the conviction of Pickering and also for the conviction of Justice Samuel Chase. As chairman of a special committee he reported adversely to the suspension of the Ordinance of 1787 in order to secure the admission of Cuban refugees with their slaves. He spoke seldom in the Senate, but was active and valuable in committee work, and won nationally the reputation he had at home for hard practical sense, straightforward simplicity, and fine integrity. Defeated for reëlection, his county at once sent him to the state Senate for two terms. In 1806 he was again elected to the United States Senate and served from 1807 to 1813. During this second term he was again prominent in committee work. As chairman of the committee to investigate the connection of Senator Smith of Ohio with the Burr conspiracy, he recommended his expulsion and ably managed the trial which resulted in acquittal followed by Smith's resignation. He was an eager advocate of the War of 1812, but just as it began he was defeated and retired to private life. In 1816 he was appointed by President Madison a commissioner with David Meriwether and Andrew Jackson to treat with the Chickasaws and Cherokees, and in September, at the Chickasaw Council House, he signed treaties with both tribes. He was appointed a commissioner to sell lands acquired from the Cherokees, and was also a member of a commission to determine the boundary line with Georgia. In December 1820 he was elected governor, but declined reëlection the following year on account of bad health. He died of dropsy at his home after an illness of nine months.

[J. T. Alderman, "Jesse Franklin," in *N. C. Booklet,* Jan. 1907; S. A. Ashe, ed., *Biog. Hist. of N. C.,* IV (1906), 133; L. C. Draper, *King's Mountain and its Heroes* (1881); E. W. Caruthers, *Interesting Revolutionary Incidents . . . Chiefly in the "Old North State,"* 2 ser. (1856); North Carolina legislative journals; J. S. Bassett, ed., *Correspondence of Andrew Jackson,* II (1927), 236, *passim.*] J. G. deR. H.

FRANKLIN, WILLIAM (1731–Nov. 16, 1813), last royal governor of New Jersey, was the son of Benjamin Franklin [*q.v.*], and was reared in the household of his father, whose common-law wife, Deborah Read, is alleged to have been William's mother. As a child William showed a fondness for books which was encouraged by his father. Later he felt the urge for military adventure in King George's War and tried to ship on a privateer fitting out at Philadelphia. In this he was balked, but a commission was secured for him in the forces of Pennsylvania. Though still a minor he saw active service against the French on the New York frontier, and acquitting himself well, rose to be a captain. He then returned to Philadelphia and became the close companion of his father, who at this time (1750) wrote of him to his grandmother: "Will is now nineteen years of age, a tall proper Youth, and much of a Beau. He acquired a Habit of Idleness—but begins of late to apply himself to Business, and I hope will become an industrious Man" (Smyth, *post,* III, 4). Under his father the young man became comptroller of the General Post Office (1754–56) and also clerk of the Pennsylvania Provincial Assembly, but in 1757 when Benjamin Franklin went to England as agent for Pennsylvania and New Jersey, William accompanied him. In London he entered the Middle Temple and in due time was called to the bar. On several trips to the Continent he enjoyed the great privilege of being his father's companion and also aided him in scientific investigations. When in 1762 Oxford conferred the degree of D.C.L. upon Benjamin Franklin, William Franklin was honored by that of M.A. It is evident that the handsome and promising young American fitted easily into British society. Becoming acquainted with the Earl of Bute, William Franklin was named through his influence governor of New Jersey in 1763. It is said that the appointment was given without the solicitation of either himself or his father. Probably it was made with a view to attaching Benjamin Franklin more closely to the British interest. The advancement of William Franklin was bemoaned by John Penn (W. A. Duer, "The Life of William Alexander, Earl of Stirling," in the *Collections of the New Jersey Historical Society,* II, 1847, 70) but nevertheless well received in New Jersey. At first Franklin proved tactful and generally successful. He avoided quarrels with the Assembly and showed interest in such practical reforms as the improvement of roads and agriculture and the mitigation of imprisonment for debt. With the outbreak of the controversies leading to the Revolution, however, he found himself in a hard position. Although he realized in some degree the force of the American demands, he did not have the rugged democratic instincts of his father, and accordingly, in strict conformity with his instructions, upheld the principle of authority. The naming by an extra-legal convention at Perth Amboy of delegates to the Stamp Act Congress in October 1765 began the conflict, and from that time on Franklin was in constant controversy with the growing patriot party in New Jersey. His course led eventually to complete estrangement from his father whose arguments were wasted upon him and who characterized his son as "a thorough government man" (Smyth, *post,* VI, 144). Even after the outbreak of hostilities Franklin remained in New Jersey collecting and transmitting to England all the information he could secure regarding the situation. Still endeavoring to exercise his commission he was on June 15, 1776, declared by the Provincial Congress of New Jersey "an enemy to the liberties of this country," and his arrest was ordered. Eventually he was sent to Connecticut where he was quartered at East Windsor at the house of Capt. Ebenezer Grant. After rather severe treatment he was exchanged in 1778 and acted for a time as president of the Board of Associated Loyalists at New York, but he soon returned to England. In 1784 a partial reconciliation took place by letter between himself and his father (Smyth, *post,* IX, 252). For the loss of his estate the commissioners of Loyalist claims in England allowed him £1,800, a figure which shows that he was not rich. For the rest of his life he received a pension of £800 per annum. In person he was tall and handsome, and of a convivial disposition. He was a thorough man of the world, and "not a stranger to galantry." Just before he left England for New Jersey, on Sept. 4, 1762, he married Elizabeth Downes, born in the West Indies. She was greatly respected and admired but died while her husband was a prisoner in Connecticut. During her illness Congress denied William Franklin's prayer to visit her. Whitehead states that Franklin later married as his second wife an Irish woman. He left one natural son, William Temple Franklin, who acted as secretary for Benjamin Franklin while the latter was in Paris, and later edited his works.

[A biographical study by Wm. A. Whitehead is in *Proc. N. J. Hist. Soc.,* III (1849), 137. Notices of his life are also found in Whitehead, *Contributions to the Early Hist. of Perth Amboy* (1856), p. 185; L. Sabine, *The Am. Loyalists* (1847); *Docs. Relating to the Colonial Hist. of the State of N. J.,* IX (1885), 369–643, X (1886). See also A. H. Smyth, *The Writings of Benj. Franklin* . . . (10 vols., 1905–07); Chas. H. Hart, "Who was the Mother of Franklin's Son," in *Pa. Mag. of Hist. and Biog.,* July 1911, and "Letters from Wm. Franklin to Wm. Strahan," in *Ibid.,* Oct. 1911; Jas. M. Stifler, *The Religion of Benj. Franklin* (1925); and Sydney Geo. Fisher, *Benjamin Franklin* (1927); *Gentleman's Mag.* (London), Nov. 1813.] E. P. T.

FRANKLIN, WILLIAM BUEL (Feb. 27, 1823–Mar. 8, 1903), soldier and business executive, was born at York, Pa. His father, Walter S. Franklin, was clerk of the House of Representatives from 1833 to 1838. His mother, Sarah, was a daughter of Dr. William Buel of Litchfield, Conn. Entering West Point along with U. S. Grant in 1839, he graduated in 1843 at the head of the class, and was commissioned in the Topographical Engineers, then a separate corps of the army. His first employment was on the survey of the Great Lakes, and later he was with Kearny's expedition to the South Pass. In the Mexican War he accompanied Gen. Wool's command, and was present at the battle of Buena Vista. On July 7, 1852, he married Annie L. Clark of Washington. He was promoted first lieutenant in 1853 and captain in 1857. For some years preceding the Civil War he was on duty in Washington, where he was superintending engineer in charge of the construction of the dome of the Capitol and of the addition to the Treasury Building. When several new regiments of the regular army were organized, he was appointed (May 14, 1861) colonel of the 12th Infantry, and soon after was made brigadier-general of volunteers. He commanded a brigade at Bull Run—raw regiments, of which one claimed its discharge on the morning of the battle, and some of those that remained were of little more use than the one that left. Franklin did as well with his indifferent material as could be expected, however, and was soon given a division, which he commanded when the Army of the Potomac moved to the Peninsula in 1862. In May he was assigned to the command of the VI Corps, and led it successfully throughout the Peninsular campaign and at Antietam. He was appointed major-general of volunteers, July 4, 1862. In Burnside's reorganization of the army, late in 1862, Franklin was put in command of the "Left Grand Division," consisting of the I and VI corps. After the disastrous battle of Fredericksburg, Burnside requested his removal from the army, holding him partially responsible for the failure, and this opinion was indorsed by the Congressional Joint Committee on the Conduct of the War (*Senate Report No. 108*, 37 Cong., 3 Sess., 1863, pt. 1), which, however, did not have before it the text of Burnside's orders. Franklin published a *Reply* (1863, 2nd ed. 1867; also found in *Official Records, Army,* 1 ser., vol. LI, pt. 1), but he was not restored to the command of which he had been deprived in the Army of the Potomac, and was left for some months unemployed. In the summer of 1863 he was sent to Louisiana and assigned to the command of the XIX Corps, which he reorganized and brought to a high state of discipline. He took part in the expedition to Sabine Pass, Tex., in September 1863, and in the unfortunate Red River expedition next spring. While he was on sick leave, recuperating from a wound received at the battle of Sabine Cross Roads, the train on which he was traveling was intercepted (July 11, 1864) by a detachment from Early's army, then attacking Washington, but he escaped from his captors during the next night. He had no further service in the field. He resigned his major-generalcy of volunteers, Nov. 10, 1865, and his colonelcy in the regular army, Mar. 15, 1866, and became vice-president and general manager of Colt's Fire Arms Manufacturing Company at Hartford, an employment in which he continued until 1888. He was president of the commission in charge of building the new state capitol, 1872–73, consulting engineer, 1873–77, and superintendent, 1877–80. He was a presidential elector, voting for Tilden, in 1876; adjutant-general of the state for two years; chairman of the board of judges of engineering and architecture at the Philadelphia exposition of 1876; and commissioner-general of the United States for the Paris Exposition in 1888. He died at Hartford. Franklin was one of those generals who, rising to conspicuous positions early in the war, thereafter passed into comparative obscurity because of adverse circumstances for which they were in no way to blame. Grant declared, late in the war, that he "would feel strengthened" with Franklin commanding the right wing of his army before Richmond (*Official Records, Army,* 1 ser., vol. XL, pt. 2, p. 559); and suggested putting him in the actual military command of Butler's Army of the James (*Ibid.*, pt. 3, 123), relegating Butler to administrative duties.

[G. W. Cullum, *Biog. Reg.* (3rd ed., 1891), II, 152–54; *Who's Who in America,* 1901–03; *Thirty-fourth Ann. Reunion Asso. Grads., U. S. Mil. Acad.* (1903), pp. 203–20; J. L. Greene, *Gen. Wm. B. Franklin, and the Operations of the Left Wing at the Battle of Fredericksburg* (1900), and *In Memoriam: Wm. Buel Franklin* (1903), by the same author; *Mil. Order of the Loyal Legion of the U. S., Commandery of the State of N. Y., Circular No. 19* (1903); *Official Records (Army),* 1 ser., vols. II, XI (pts. 1, 2), XIX (pt. 1), XXI, XXVI (pt. 1), XXXIV (pts. 1, 2, 3), LI (pt. 1).]

T. M. S.

FRASCH, HERMAN (Dec. 25, 1851?–May 1, 1914), pharmacist, chemical engineer, inventor, was born in Gaildorf, Würtemberg, Germany, of Lutheran parentage. His father, Johannes Frasch, was mayor of the town. Herman Frasch came to America in 1868, took a position in the Philadelphia College of Pharmacy, and through private studies interested himself in chemistry, which he visioned was destined to play an important rôle in the development of his adopted country. Becoming interested in the petroleum industry he removed to Cleveland about 1877, opened a chemical laboratory, and devoted himself principally to the problem of refining petroleum. In this undertaking he obtained his first patent in December 1877. In 1885 he moved to London, Ontario, and organized the Empire Oil Company. At this time he made his most important contributions to the refining of petroleum oils, and devised his efficient and economical method of desulfurizing crude petroleum oils. The value of the highly offensive Canadian and Ohio oils, which hitherto had been used only for fuel purposes, was enhanced to such an extent as to place these refined oils on a parity with standard grades of Pennsylvania illuminating oils. The Frasch process for desulfurizing crude oils is based upon the reaction between a metallic oxide, especially that of copper, and the sulfur compounds contained in crude oils, whereby stable copper sulfides are formed. The method is relatively inexpensive, since it includes the recovery of copper oxide, which may be used repeatedly. Between 1887 and 1894 twenty-one American patents were issued to Frasch dealing with the refining of Canadian and similar petroleum oils. These patents, and the Empire Oil Company as well, were subsequently purchased by the Standard Oil Company, and the firm's refineries throughout the country were promptly equipped and operated under the Frasch method. During these years Frasch secured numerous patents on subjects entirely foreign to the petroleum industry. These included patents on processes for producing white lead directly from galena, for making sodium carbonate from salt by the ammonia process, for making elements for thermal electrical generators, and for manufacturing carbon for electric-light carbons. Although the value of Frasch's method for refining sulfur-bearing crude oils was inestimable, raising the value of such oil from fourteen cents a barrel to one dollar, it was overshadowed by his later inventions bearing upon sulfur mining. In this work his first patent was granted Oct. 20, 1891. The process which he developed involved melting the sulfur in the mine by means of superheated water forced down into the mine through a pipe, allowing for the discharge of the molten sulfur through an inner tube. By this means the sulfur could be poured into huge bins and made ready for shipment. His experiments extended through many years and involved large expenditures of money, but were strikingly successful. Following the invention of the process the Union Sulphur Company was organized of which Frasch became president. This company worked the sulfur deposits in Louisiana and was soon able to wrest the control of the world's supply of sulfur from the Anglo-Sicilian Company which hitherto had enjoyed practically a monopoly of the business. Prior to the development of the Louisiana mines, the United States produced less than five-tenths of one per cent. of the sulfur consumed within its boundaries. After Frasch's process came into use, the United States exported large quantities of sulfur.

Frasch received in 1912 the Perkin gold medal, the coveted prize of American chemists, in recognition of his distinguished services to the chemical industries. At its presentation he was designated "one of our greatest industrial chemists and chemical engineers." His discoveries affected the economics of a nation and to him belongs the undisputed credit of having founded the American sulfur industry. He was a quiet, unassuming man, but by his boldness of conception and courage, and by his energy and perseverance, he brought to realization the daring dreams of his genius. He died in Paris, France, on May 1, 1914, after a long illness. He was married twice. His first wife was Romalda Berks, whose Dutch forebears had settled in Berks County, Pa. After her death in 1869 he was married, several years later, to Elizabeth Blee of Cleveland.

[Frasch's address delivered upon the presentation of the Perkin medal on Jan. 19, 1912, is contained in the *Jour. of the Soc. of Chem. Industry* (London), Feb. 29, 1912, and in the *Jour. of Industrial and Engineering Chemistry*, Feb. 1912. See also *Ibid.*, June 1914; *Zeitschrift für Angewandte Chemie*, May 15, 1914; *Chemiker-Zeitung*, June 6, 1914; *Jour. of the Soc. of Chem. Industry*, May 30, 1914; *World's Work*, July 1914; *N. Y. Times*, May 2, 1914.] T. B. W.

FRASER, CHARLES (Aug. 20, 1782–Oct. 5, 1860), miniature painter, the fourteenth and youngest child of Alexander and Mary (Grimké) Fraser, grew to manhood surrounded by relatives and friends who had taken part in the Revolution. His education began at a classical school and was continued at the College of Charleston, but at an early age he showed an artistic bent which was intensified by his association with Sully, Malbone, and Washington Allston. With these young men, who like himself were destined to stand high among early American artists, he enjoyed a pleasant friendship. Educated by his guardians for the legal profession, he was admitted to the bar in 1807 and continued to practise law until 1818, by which date he had accumulated a competency. This enabled him to pursue professionally the art which had always attracted his taste and ambition, and to the study of which he had given his hours of leisure. Having already developed from his education a strong literary taste, his practise at the bar strengthened his intellectual power and gave him great breadth of outlook. It brought him into contact, too, with a group of distinguished lawyers who maintained "that high character for courtesy, learning, and liberality imparted to the Charleston Bar by eminent men who had studied their profession at the Inns of Court in London."

When Fraser abandoned the law for art he retained many of his former interests. He was often called upon to deliver public addresses, and for many years attended the weekly meetings of the Conversation Club, where he met such leaders of thought as Stephen Elliott, Agassiz, Dickson, Bachman, Gilman, Holbrook, and Ravenel. Among the numerous essays which he read at these meetings were his "Reminiscences of Charleston," an authentic picture of the community, published in 1854. He was a member of the board of trustees of the College of Charleston as early as 1817, and served in that capacity and as treasurer for nearly forty years. A few reasonably creditable verses survive to justify William D. Porter's description of him as "a man of exquisite taste and refinement, artist, scholar, and poet" (*Year Book of the City of Charleston*, 1882, p. 283). It was to his miniatures, however, which he painted in large numbers, and with conspicuous success, that Fraser owed his general recognition. There are listed in the catalogue of works exhibited in 1857 some 313 miniatures and 139 oil-paintings, which probably represented only a fraction of his work. Most of the prominent Carolinians of his day sat to him, and he was chosen by the city of Charleston to paint a miniature of Lafayette at the time of his visit there in 1825. His characterizations were deft, subtle, uncompromising, and withal sympathetic. His early style was strongly influenced by Malbone, but as his art matured, he abandoned Malbone's cross-hatching for stippling, and enlarged the color chart. His best work—in a period of distinguished miniatures—bears comparison with that of any miniature painter of his day.

[Alice R. Huger Smith and D. E. Huger Smith, *Chas. Fraser* (1924), contains fifty reproductions of Fraser's miniatures. See also Chas. Fraser, "Fraser Family Memoranda," in *S. C. Hist. and Geneal. Mag.*, Jan. 1904; H. B. Wehle and Theodore Bolton, *Am. Miniatures, 1830–50, and a Biog. Dict. of the Artists* (1927); Wm. Dunlap, *Hist. of the Rise and Progress of the Arts of Design in the U. S.* (1834), II, 150; A. R. H. Smith in *Art in America*, June 1915; *Charleston Courier*, Oct. 6, 1860.] A. R. H. S.